# The Merriam-Webster Dictionary

*A Merriam-Webster* ®

PUBLISHED BY POCKET BOOKS NEW YORK

# THE
# MERRIAM-WEBSTER
# DICTIONARY

POCKET BOOK edition published August, 1974

12th printing.......................May, 1976

This POCKET BOOK® edition of
THE MERRIAM-WEBSTER DICTIONARY
has been printed from brand-new plates.

POCKET BOOK editions are published by
POCKET BOOKS,
a division of Simon & Schuster, Inc.,
A GULF+WESTERN COMPANY
630 Fifth Avenue,
New York, New York 10020

Trademarks registered in the United States and other countries.

---

ISBN: 0-671-80591-6.

# Preface

THE FIRST Merriam-Webster Pocket Dictionary was published in 1947. It soon won the respect of the dictionary-buying public, and a second edition, called the New Merriam-Webster Pocket Dictionary, was brought out in 1964. With the publication in 1973 of Webster's New Collegiate Dictionary (the eighth in the Merriam-Webster series of Collegiates dating from 1898), a third edition has become necessary if the needs of those who want an up-to-date record of present-day English in compact form are to be met. The Merriam-Webster Dictionary, an enlarged and completely revised work, is designed to meet these needs. Its approximately 57,000 entries constitute the core of the English language, and every definition is based on examples of actual use found among the more than 11,500,000 citations in the Merriam-Webster files.

The heart of The Merriam-Webster Dictionary is the A–Z vocabulary. It is followed by several sections that dictionary users have long found helpful: a list of foreign words and phrases that frequently occur in English texts but that have not become part of the English vocabulary; a list of the nations of the world; a list of places in the United States having 12,000 or more inhabitants, with a summary by states; a similar list of places in Canada, with a summary by provinces and territories; and a section devoted to widely used signs and symbols. The A–Z vocabulary is preceded by a series of Explanatory Notes that should be read carefully by every user of the dictionary. An understanding of the information contained in these notes will add markedly to the satisfaction and pleasure that come with looking into the pages of a dictionary.

The Merriam-Webster Dictionary is the product of a company that has been publishing dictionaries for more than 125 years. It has been edited by an experienced staff of professional lexicographers who believe that the user will find in it "infinite riches in a little room."

**Editor in Chief**
Henry Bosley Woolf

**Senior Editors**
Edward Artin • F. Stuart Crawford
E. Ward Gilman • Mairé Weir Kay
Roger W. Pease, Jr.

**Associate Editors**
Gretchen Brunk • Robert D. Copeland
Grace A. Kellogg • James G. Lowe
George M. Sears

**Assistant Editors**
William Parr Black • Kathleen M. Doherty
Kathryn K. Flynn • Kerry W. Metz
James E. Shea, Jr. • Anne H. Soukhanov
Raymond R. Wilson

**Editorial Consultant**
Philip W. Cummings

## Editorial Staff

**Librarian**
Alan D. Campbell

**Departmental Secretary**
Hazel O. Lord

**Head of Typing Room**
Evelyn G. Summers

**Clerks and Typists**
Maude L. Barnes • Florence Cressotti
Patricia Jensen • Maureen E. McCartney
Mildred M. McWha • Catherine T. Meaney
Frances W. Muldrew • Mildred C. Paquette
Genevieve M. Sherry • Francine A. Socha

**Typographic Designer**
Michael Stancik, Jr.

# Explanatory Notes

## Entries

A boldface letter or a combination of such letters set flush with the left-hand margin of each column of type is a main entry. The main entry may consist of letters set solid, of letters joined by a hyphen, or of letters separated by one or more spaces:

> **hot** ... *adj*
>
> **hot–blood·ed** ... *adj*
>
> **hot dog** ... *n*

The material in lightface type that follows each main entry on the same line and on succeeding indented lines explains and justifies its inclusion in the dictionary.

The main entries follow one another in alphabetical order letter by letter: *bill of exchange* follows *billion; Day of Atonement* follows *daylight saving time*. Those containing an Arabic numeral are alphabetized as if the numeral were spelled out: *4-H* comes between *fourfold* and *Four Hundred; 3-D* comes between *three* and *three-dimensional*. Those derived from proper names beginning with abbreviated forms of *Mac-* are alphabetized as if spelled *mac-*: *McCoy* comes after *macaw* and before *mace*.

A pair of guide words is printed at the top of each page. These indicate that the entries falling alphabetically between the words at the top of the outer column of each page are found on that page.

The guide words are usually the alphabetically first and the alphabetically last entries on the page:

## Afghan hound • agave

Occasionally the last printed entry is not the alphabetically last entry. On page 101, for example, *bruiser* is the last printed entry, but *bruising*, an inflected form at ¹*bruise*, is the alphabetically last entry and is therefore the second guide word. The alphabetically last entry is not used, however, if it follows alphabetically the first guide word on the succeeding page. Thus on page 201 *detector* is not a guide word because it follows alphabetically the second homograph *detective* which is the first guide word on page 202.

Any boldface word—a main entry with definition, a variant, an inflected form, a defined or undefined run-on, an entry in a list of self-explanatory words—may be used as a guide word.

When one main entry has exactly the same written form as another, the two are distinguished by superscript numerals preceding each word:

> ¹egg ... *vb*      ¹rash ... *adj*
>
> ²egg *n*           ²rash *n*

Words precede word elements made up of the same letters; solid compounds precede hyphened compounds; hyphened compounds precede open compounds; and lowercase entries precede those with an initial capital:

> self ... *n*
>
> self- *comb form*
>
> run·down ... *n*
>
> run–down ... *adj*
>
> run down ... *vb*
>
> fed·er·al ... *adj*
>
> Federal *n*

The centered periods within entry words indicate division points at which a hyphen may be put at the end of a line of print or writing. Thus the noun *res·er·va·tion* may be ended on one line and continued on the next in this manner:

> |           | *res-*       |
> | *ervation* | *reser-*    |
> | *vation*   | *reserva-*  |
> | *tion*     |             |

Centered periods are not shown after a single initial letter or before a single terminal letter because printers seldom cut off a single letter:

> evict ... *vb*
>
> mighty ... *adj*
>
> oleo ... *n*

Nor are they usually shown at the second and succeeding homographs of a word:

> ¹pi·lot ... *n*
>
> ²pilot *vb*
>
> ³pilot *adj*

There are acceptable alternative end-of-line divisions just as there are acceptable variant spellings and pronunciations, but no more than one division is shown for any entry in this dictionary.

A double hyphen at the end of a line in this dictionary (as in the definition at **jaguar**) stands for a hyphen that belongs at that point in a hyphened word and that is retained when the word is written as a unit on one line.

When a main entry is followed by the word *or* and another spelling, the two spellings are equal variants. Both are standard, and either one may be used according to personal inclination:

**lou·ver** *or* **lou·vre**

If two variants joined by *or* are out of alphabetical order, they remain equal variants. The one printed first is, however, slightly more common than the second:

**coun·sel·or** *or* **coun·sel·lor**

When another spelling is joined to the main entry by the word *also*, the spelling after *also* is a secondary variant and occurs less frequently than the first:

**fo·gy** *also* **fo·gey**

Secondary variants belong to standard usage and may be used according to personal inclination. If there are two secondary variants, the second is joined to the first by *or*. Once the word *also* is used to signal a secondary variant, all following variants are joined by *or:*

**wool·ly** *also* **wool·ie** *or* **wooly**

Variants whose spelling puts them alphabetically more than a column away from the main entry are entered at their own alphabetical places and usually not at the main entry:

**tsar** . . . *var of* CZAR

Variants having a usage label appear only at their own alphabetical places:

**la·bour** *chiefly Brit var of* LABOR

To show all the stylings that are found for English compounds would require space that can be better used for other information. So this dictionary limits itself to a single styling for a compound:

**book·sell·er**

**yes–man**

**home run**

When a compound is widely used and one styling predominates, that styling is shown. When a compound is uncommon or when the evidence indicates that two or three stylings are approximately equal in frequency, the styling shown is based on the analogy of parallel compounds.

A main entry may be followed by one or more derivatives or by a homograph with a different functional label. These are run-on entries. Each is introduced by a lightface dash and each has a functional label. They are not defined, however, since their meanings are readily derivable from the meaning of the root word:

**healthy** . . . *adj* . . . **— health·i·ly** . . . *adv* **— health·i·ness** . . *n*

**as·sent** . . . *vb* . . . **— assent** *n*

A main entry may be followed by one or more phrases containing the entry word or an inflected form of it. These are also run-on entries. Each is introduced by a lightface dash but there is no functional label. They are, however, defined since their meanings are more than the sum of the meanings of their elements:

¹go . . . *vb* . . — go to bat for : . . .

¹hand . . . *n* . . . — at hand : . . .

Defined phrases of this sort are run on at the entry constituting the first major element in the phrase. When there are variants, however, the run-on appears at the entry constituting the first major invariable element in the phrase:

¹seed . . . *n* . . . — go to seed *or* run to seed : . . .

Boldface words that appear within parentheses (as **co·ca** at **co·caine** and **jet engine** and **jet propulsion** at **jet-propelled**) are run-in entries.

Attention is called to the definition of *vocabulary entry* on page 775. The term *dictionary entry* includes all vocabulary entries as well as all boldface entries in the section headed "Foreign Words and Phrases."

# Pronunciation

The matter between a pair of reversed virgules \        \ following the entry word indicates the pronunciation. The symbols used are explained in the chart printed inside the front and back covers.

A hyphen is used in the pronunciation to show syllabic division. These hyphens sometimes coincide with the centered periods in the entry word that indicate end-of-line division:

**vol·ca·no** \väl-ˈkā-nō\

Sometimes they do not:

**grind·er** \ˈgrīn-dər\

A high-set mark ˈ indicates major (primary) stress or accent; a low-set mark ˌ indicates minor (secondary) stress or accent:

**cat·bird** \ˈkat-ˌbərd\

The stress mark stands at the beginning of the syllable that receives the stress.

A syllable with neither a high-set mark nor a low-set mark is unstressed:

**fig·ment** \ˈfig-mənt\

The presence of variant pronunciations indicates that not all educated speakers pronounce words the same way. A second-place variant is not to be regarded as less acceptable than the pronunciation that is given first. It may, in fact, be used by as many educated speakers as the first variant, but the requirements of the printed page are such that one must precede the other:

**eco·nom·ic** \ˌek-ə-ˈnäm-ik, ˌē-kə-\

**flac·cid** \ˈflak-səd, ˈflas-əd\

Symbols enclosed by parentheses represent elements that are present in the pronunciation of some speakers but are absent from the pronunciation of other speakers, elements that are present in some but absent from other utterances of the same speaker, or elements whose presence or absence is uncertain:

fo·liage \'fō-l(ē-)ij\

duke \'d(y)ük\

Thus, the above parentheses indicate that some people say \'fō-lē-ij\ and others say \'fo-lij\; some \'dük\, others \'dyük\.

When a main entry has less than a full pronunciation, the missing part is to be supplied from a pronunciation in a preceding entry or within the same pair of reversed virgules:

neth·er·most \-,mōst\

pa·la·ver \pə-'lav-ər, -'läv-\

The pronunciation of the first two syllables of *nethermost* is found at the main entry *nether*. The hyphens before and after \'läv\ in the pronunciation of *palaver* indicate that both the first and the last parts of the pronunciation are to be taken from the immediately preceding pronunciation.

In general, no pronunciation is indicated for open compounds consisting of two or more English words that have own-place entry:

motor vehicle n

Only the first entry in a sequence of numbered homographs is given a pronunciation if their pronunciations are the same:

¹mea·sure \'mezh-ər, 'māzh-\ n

²measure vb

The pronunciation of unpronounced derivatives and compounds run on at a main entry is a combination of the pronunciation at the main entry and the pronunciation of the other element as given at its alphabetical place in the vocabulary:

— re·morse·less adj

— at last

Thus, the pronunciation of *remorseless* is the sum of the pronunciations given at *remorse* and *-less;* that of *at last,* the sum of the pronunciations of the two elements that make up the phrase.

Partial pronunciations are usually shown when two or more variants have a part in common:

hos·tile \'häs-t°l, -,tīl\

# Functional Labels

An italic label indicating a part of speech or some other functional classification follows the pronunciation or, if no pronunciation is given, the main entry. The eight traditional parts of speech are indicated as follows:

| | |
|---|---|
| fa·ce·tious . . . *adj* | log·ger·head . . . *n* |
| al·to·geth·er . . . *adv* | in·to . . . *prep* |
| if . . . *conj* | we . . . *pron* |
| amen . . . *interj* | stul·ti·fy . . . *vb* |

Other italicized labels used to indicate functional classifications that are not traditional parts of speech include:

| | |
|---|---|
| blvd *abbr* | -hood . . . *n suffix* |
| self- *comb form* | -fy . . . *vb suffix* |
| super- . . . *prefix* | Na *symbol* |
| -ous . . . *adj suffix* | ought . . . *verbal auxiliary* |
| -al·ly . . . *adv suffix* | |

Functional labels are sometimes combined:

can·ta·bi·le . .    *adv or adj*

## Inflected Forms

### NOUNS

The plurals of nouns are shown in this dictionary when suffixation brings about a change of final -*y* to -*i*-, when the noun ends in a consonant plus -*o* or in -*ey*, when the noun ends in -*oo*, when the noun has an irregular plural or a zero plural or a foreign plural, when the noun is a compound that pluralizes any element but the last, when the noun has variant plurals, and when it is believed that the dictionary user might have reasonable doubts about the spelling of the plural or when the plural is spelled in a way contrary to what is expected:

| | |
|---|---|
| dairy . . . *n, pl* dair·ies | al·ga . . . *n, pl* al·gae |
| po·ta·to . . . *n, pl* -toes | broth·er–in–law . . . *n, pl* brothers–in–law |
| lack·ey . . . *n, pl* lackeys | [1]fish . . . *n, pl* fish *or* fish·es |
| zoo . . . *n, pl* zoos | [1]pi . . . *n, pl* pis |
| tooth . . . *n, pl* teeth | [3]dry . . . *n, pl* drys |
| deer . . . *n, pl* deer | |

Cutback inflected forms are used when the noun has three or more syllables:

atroc·i·ty . . . *n, pl* -ties

The plurals of nouns are usually not shown when the base word is unchanged by suffixation, when the noun is a compound whose second element is readily recognizable as a regular free form entered at its own place, or when the noun is unlikely to occur in the plural:

car·rot . . . *n*

rad·ish . . . *n*

horse·fly . . . *n*

po·lyg·a·my . . . *n*

Nouns that are plural in form and that regularly occur in plural construction are labeled *n pl*:

bifocals . . . *n pl*

Nouns that are plural in form but that are not always construed as plurals are appropriately labeled:

taps . . . *n sing or pl*

## VERBS

The principal parts of verbs are shown in this dictionary when suffixation brings about a doubling of a final consonant or an elision of a final *-e* or a change of final *-y* to *-i-*, when final *-c* changes to *-ck-* in suffixation, when the verb ends in *-ey*, when the inflection is irregular, when there are variant inflected forms, and when it is believed that the dictionary user might have reasonable doubts about the spelling of an inflected form or when the inflected form is spelled in a way contrary to what is expected:

beg . . . *vb* begged; beg·ging

equate . . . *vb* equat·ed; equat·ing

¹fry . . . *vb* fried; fry·ing

²panic *vb* pan·icked . . .; pan·ick·ing

obey . . . *vb* obeyed; obey·ing

¹break . . . *vb* broke . . .; bro·ken . . .; break·ing

¹trav·el . . . *vb* -eled *or* -elled; -el·ing *or* -el·ling

²visa *vb* vi·saed . . .; vi·sa·ing

²chagrin *vb* -grined . . .; -grin·ing

The principal parts of a regularly inflected verb are shown when it is desirable to indicate the pronunciation of one of the inflected forms:

²spell *vb* spelled \'speld, 'spelt\; spel·ling

²season *vb* sea·soned; sea·son·ing \'sēz-(ͤ-)niŋ\

Cutback inflected forms are usually used when the verb has three or more syllables, when it is a disyllable that ends in *-l* and has variant spellings, and when it is a compound whose second element is readily recognized as an irregular verb:

mul·ti·ply . . . *vb* -plied; -ply·ing

cav·il . . . *vb* -iled *or* -illed; -il·ing *or* -il·ling

for·go *or* fore·go . . . *vb* -went . . .; -gone . . .; -go·ing

The principal parts of verbs are usually not shown when the base word is unchanged by suffixation or when the verb is a compound whose second element is readily recognizable as a regular free form entered at its own place:

> ²shield *vb*
>
> ¹out·reach . . . *vb*

## ADJECTIVES & ADVERBS

The comparative and superlative forms of adjectives and adverbs are shown in this dictionary when suffixation brings about a doubling of a final consonant or an elision of a final -*e* or a change of final -*y* to -*i*-, when the word ends in -*ey*, when the inflection is irregular, and when there are variant inflected forms:

> ¹fat . . . *adj* fat·ter; fat·test
>
> ¹sure . . . *adj* sur·er; sur·est
>
> ¹dry . . . *adj* dri·er . . .; dri·est
>
> hors·ey *or* horsy . . . *adj* hors·i·er; -est
>
> bad . . . *adj* worse . . .; worst
>
> ³well *adv* bet·ter . . .; best
>
> sly . . . *adj* sli·er *also* sly·er . . .; sli·est *also* sly·est

The superlative forms of adjectives and adverbs of two or more syllables are usually cut back:

> scanty . . . *adj* scant·i·er; -est
>
> ¹ear·ly . . . *adv* ear·li·er; -est

The comparative and superlative forms of regularly inflected adjectives and adverbs are shown when it is desirable to indicate the pronunciation of the inflected forms:

> strong \'stròŋ\ *adj* stron·ger \'stròŋ-gər\; stron·gest \'stròŋ-gəst\

The inclusion of inflected forms in -*er* and -*est* at adjective and adverb entries means nothing more about the use of *more* and *most* with these adjectives and adverbs than that their comparative and superlative degrees may be expressed in either way: *kindlier or more kindly; kindliest or most kindly.*

At a few adjective entries only the superlative form is shown:

> ²mere *adj* mer·est

The absence of the comparative form indicates that there is no evidence of its use.

The comparative and superlative forms of adjectives and adverbs are usually not shown when the base word is unchanged by suffixation or when the word is a compound whose second element is readily recognizable as a regular free form entered at its own place:

> ²quiet *adj*
>
> un·hap·py . . . *adj*

Inflected forms are not shown at undefined run-ons.

## Capitalization

Most entries in this dictionary begin with a lowercase letter. A few of these have an italicized label *often cap*, which indicates that the word is as likely to be capitalized as not, that it is as acceptable with an uppercase initial as it is with one in lowercase. Some entries begin with an uppercase letter, which indicates that the word is usually capitalized. The absence of an initial capital or of an *often cap* label indicates that the word is not ordinarily capitalized:

> spice . . . *n*
>
> ba·bel . . . *n, often cap*
>
> Quak·er . . . *n*

The capitalization of entries that are open or hyphened compounds is similarly indicated by the form of the entry or by an italicized label:

> living room *n*
>
> in·dia ink . . . *n, often cap 1st I*
>
> all–Amer·i·can . . . *adj*
>
> German shepherd *n*
>
> lazy Su·san . . . *n*
>
> Jack Frost *n*

A word that is capitalized in some senses and lowercase in others shows variations from the form of the main entry by the use of italicized labels at the appropriate senses:

> Apoc·ry·pha . . . *n* 1 *not cap*
>
> ¹Pres·by·te·ri·an . . . *adj* 1 *often not cap*
>
> cath·o·lic . . . *adj* . . . 2 *cap*
>
> east·ern . . . *adj* 1 *often cap* . . . 3 *cap*

## Etymology

This dictionary gives the etymologies for a number of the vocabulary entries. These etymologies are in boldface square brackets preceding the definition. Meanings given in roman type within these brackets are not definitions of the entry, but are meanings of the Middle English, Old English, or non-English words within the brackets.

The etymology gives the language from which words borrowed into English have come. It also gives the form of the word in that language or a representation of the word in our alphabet if the form in that language differs from that in English:

> ae·gis . . . [L, fr. Gk *aigis* goatskin]
>
> ¹sav·age . . . [ME *sauvage*, fr. MF, fr. ML *salvaticus*, fr. L *silvaticus* of the woods, wild . . .]

An etymology beginning with the name of a language (including ME or OE) and not giving the foreign (or Middle English or Old English) form indicates that this form is the same as the form of the entry word:

**ibi·dem** . . . [L]

**na·dir** . . . [ME, fr. MF . . .]

An etymology beginning with the name of a language (including ME or OE) and not giving the foreign (or Middle English or Old English) meaning indicates that this meaning is the same as the meaning expressed in the first definition in the entry:

**tur·quoise** . . . [ME *turkeis, turcas,* fr. MF *turquoyse* . . .]

Small superscript figures following words or syllables in an etymology refer to the tone of the word or syllable they follow. They are, accordingly, used only with forms cited for languages in which tonal variations distinguish words of different meaning that would otherwise sound alike.

**kow·tow** . . . [Chin *k'o¹ t'ou²,* fr. *k'o¹* to bump + *t'ou²* head]

## Usage

Three types of status labels are used in this dictionary—temporal, regional, and stylistic—to signal that a word or a sense of a word is not part of the standard vocabulary of English.

The temporal label *obs* for "obsolete" means that there is no evidence of use since 1755:

**³post** *n* **1** *obs*

The label *obs* is a comment on the word being defined. When a thing, as distinguished from the word used to designate it, is obsolete, appropriate orientation is usually given in the definition:

**far·thin·gale** . . . *n* **:** a support (as of hoops) worn esp. in the 16th century to swell out a skirt

The temporal label *archaic* means that a word or sense once in common use is found today only sporadically or in special contexts:

**com·mon·weal** . . . *n* . . **2** *archaic*

**mar·gent** . . . *n, archaic*

A word or sense limited in use to a specific region of the U.S. has an appropriate label. The adverb *chiefly* precedes a label when the word has some currency outside the specified region, and a double label is used to indicate considerable currency in each of two specific regions:

**low·ery** . . . *adj, NewEng*

**²wash** *n* . . . **6** *West*

**do·gie** . . . *n, chiefly West*

**goo·ber** . . . *n, South & Midland*

Words current in all regions of the U.S. have no label.

A word or sense limited in use to one of the other countries of the English-speaking world has an appropriate regional label:

> **chem·ist** . . . *n* . . . **2** *Brit*
>
> **loch** . . . *n, Scot*
>
> **²wireless** *n* . . . **2** *chiefly Brit*

The label *dial* for "dialect" indicates that the pattern of use of a word or sense is too complex for summary labeling: it usually includes several regional varieties of American English or of American and British English:

> **¹boot** . . . *n, dial*
>
> **cal·a·boose** . . . *n* . . . *dial*

The stylistic label *slang* is used with words or senses that are especially appropriate in contexts of extreme informality:

> **¹rap** . . . *n* . . . **3** *slang*
>
> **tick·er** . . . *n* . . . **3** *slang*

There is no satisfactory objective test for slang, especially with reference to a word out of context. No word, in fact, is invariably slang, and many standard words can be given slang applications.

Definitions are sometimes followed by verbal illustrations that show a typical use of the word in context. These illustrations are enclosed in angle brackets, and the word being illustrated is usually replaced by a lightface swung dash. The swung dash stands for the boldface entry word, and it may be followed by an italicized suffix:

> **¹let·ter** . . . *n* . . . **4** . . . ⟨the ~ of the law⟩
>
> **prac·ti·cal** . . . *adj* . . . **5** . . . ⟨a good ~ mechanic⟩
>
> **depth** . . . *n* . . . **2** . . . ⟨the ~s of the woods⟩
>
> **¹fill** . . . *vb* . . . **6** . . . ⟨laughter ~ed the room⟩

The swung dash is not used when the form of the boldface entry word is changed in suffixation, and it is not used for open compounds:

> **en·gage** . . . *vb* . . . **2** . . . ⟨*engaged* his friend's attention⟩
>
> **drum up** *vb* **1** . . . ⟨*drum up* business⟩

Definitions are sometimes followed by usage notes that give supplementary information about such matters as idiom, syntax, and semantic relationship. A usage note is introduced by a lightface dash:

> **fro** . . . *adv* . . . — used in the phrase *to and fro*
>
> **²gang** *vb* **1** . . . — usu. used with *up*
>
> **¹jaw** . . . *n* **1** . . . — usu. used in pl.
>
> **¹ada·gio** . . . *adv or adj* . . . — used as a direction in music
>
> **blast off** . . . *vb* . . . — used esp. of rocket-propelled devices

Sometimes a usage note is used in place of a definition. Some function words (as conjunctions and prepositions) have chiefly grammatical meaning and little or no lexical meaning; most interjections express feelings but are otherwise untranslatable into lexical meaning;

and some other words (as honorific titles) are more amenable to comment than to definition:

**or** . . . *conj* — used as a function word to indicate an alternative

**¹in** . . . *prep* **1** — used to indicate physical surroundings

**hal·le·lu·jah** . . . *interj* . . . — used to express praise, joy, or thanks

**ex·cel·len·cy** . . . *n* . . . **2** — used as a title of honor

## Sense Division

A boldface colon is used in this dictionary to introduce a definition:

**found·ry** . . . *n* . . . **:** a building or works where metal is cast

It is also used to separate two or more definitions of a single sense:

**³yellow** *n* **1 :** a color between green and orange in the spectrum **:** the color of ripe lemons or sunflowers

Boldface Arabic numerals separate the senses of a word that has more than one sense:

**idol** . . . *n* **1 :** a representation of a deity used as an object of worship **2 :** a false god **3 :** an object of passionate devotion

A particular semantic relationship between senses is sometimes suggested by the use of one of the two italic sense dividers *esp* or *also*. The sense divider *esp* (for *especially*) is used to introduce the most common meaning included in the more general preceding definition:

**no·to·ri·ous** . . . *adj* **:** generally known and talked of; *esp* **:** widely and unfavorably known

The sense divider *also* is used to introduce a meaning related to the preceding sense by an easily understood extension of that sense:

**¹flour** . . . *n* **:** finely ground and sifted meal of a cereal (as wheat); *also* **:** a fine soft powder

The order of senses is historical: the sense known to have been first used in English is entered first. This is not to be taken to mean, however, that each sense of a multisense word developed from the immediately preceding sense. It is altogether possible that sense 1 of a word has given rise to sense 2 and sense 2 to sense 3, but frequently sense 2 and sense 3 may have developed independently of one another from sense 1.

When an italicized label follows a boldface numeral, the label applies only to that specific numbered sense. It does not apply to any other boldface numbered senses:

**craft** . . . *n* . . . **3** *pl usu* **craft**

**¹fa·ther** . . . *n* . . . **2** *cap* . . . **5** *often cap*

**²preview** *n* . . . **2** *also* **pre·vue** \-,vyü\

**pub·li·can** . . . *n* . . . **2** *chiefly Brit*

At *craft* the *pl* label applies to sense **3** but to none of the other numbered senses. At *father* the *cap* label applies only to sense **2** and the *often cap* label only to sense **5**. At *preview* the variant spelling and pronunciation apply only to sense **2**, as does the *chiefly Brit* label at *publican*.

## Cross-Reference

Four different kinds of cross-references are used in this dictionary: directional, synonymous, cognate, and inflectional. In each instance the cross-reference is readily recognized by the lightface small capitals in which it is printed.

A cross-reference following a lightface dash and beginning with *see* is a directional cross-reference. It directs the dictionary user to look elsewhere for further information:

> ¹yen . . . *n* . . . — see MONEY table

A cross-reference following a boldface colon is a synonymous cross-reference. It may stand alone as the only definition for an entry or for a sense of an entry; it may follow an analytical definition; it may be one of two or more synonymous cross-references separated by commas:

> **maize** . . . *n* : INDIAN CORN
>
> **chap·let** . . . *n* . . . **2** : a string of beads : NECKLACE
>
> ²**dress** *n* . . . **2** : FROCK, GOWN
>
> **cheek** . . . *n* . . . **2** : IMPUDENCE, BOLDNESS, AUDACITY

A synonymous cross-reference indicates that a definition at the entry cross-referred to can be substituted as a definition for the entry or the sense in which the cross-reference appears.

A cross-reference following an italic *var of* ("variant of") is a cognate cross-reference:

> **Gipsy** *var of* GYPSY

Occasionally a cognate cross-reference has a limiting label preceding *var of* as an indication that the variant is not standard English:

> **chaunt** . . . *archaic var of* CHANT
>
> **har·bour** *chiefly Brit var of* HARBOR

A cross-reference following an italic label that identifies an entry as an inflected form (as of a noun or verb) is an inflectional cross-reference:

> **feet** *pl of* FOOT
>
> **worn** *past part of* WEAR

Inflectional cross-references appear only when the inflected form falls at least a column away from the entry cross-referred to.

## Synonyms

A boldface **syn** near the end of an entry introduces words that are synonymous with the word being defined:

> ¹**fear** . . . *n* . . . **syn** dread, fright, alarm, panic, terror, trepidation

Synonyms are not definitions although they may often be substituted for each other in context.

## Combining Forms, Prefixes, & Suffixes

An entry that begins or ends with a hyphen is a word element that forms part of an English compound:

> **maxi-** *comb form* **1** . . . ⟨*maxi*-kilt⟩
>
> **ex-** . . . *prefix* . . . ⟨*ex*-president⟩
>
> **-ship** . . . *n suffix* **1** . . . ⟨friend*ship*⟩

Combining forms, prefixes, and suffixes are entered in this dictionary for two reasons: to make understandable the meaning of many undefined run-ons which for reasons of space would be omitted if they had to be given definitions and to make recognizable the meaningful elements of new words that are not well enough established in the language to warrant dictionary entry.

## Lists of Undefined Words

Lists of undefined words occur after the entries *anti-*, *in-*, *non-*, *over-*, *re-*, *self-*, *semi-*, *sub-*, *super-*, and *un-*. These words are not defined because they are self-explanatory: their meanings are simply the sum of a meaning of the prefix or combining form and a meaning of the second element.

## Abbreviations & Symbols

Abbreviations and symbols for chemical elements are included as main entries in the vocabulary:

> **govt** *abbr* government
>
> **Fe** *symbol* . . . iron

Abbreviations have been normalized to one form. In practice, however, there is considerable variation in the use of periods and in capitalization (as *vhf*, *v.h.f.*, *VHF*, and *V.H.F.*), and stylings other than those given in this dictionary are often acceptable.

# A Dictionary of
# the
# English Language

**A**

¹**a** \'ā\ *n, pl* **a's** *or* **as** \'āz\ *often cap* **1** : the 1st letter of the English alphabet **2** : a grade rating a student's work as superior

²**a** \ə, (')ā\ *indefinite article* : ONE, SOME — used to indicate an unspecified or unidentified individual ⟨there's ∼ man outside⟩

³**a** *abbr, often cap* **1** acre **2** alto **3** answer **4** area

**AA** *abbr* **1** Alcoholics Anonymous **2** antiaircraft **3** associate in arts

**AAA** *abbr* American Automobile Association

**A and M** *abbr* agricultural and mechanical

**A and R** *abbr* artists and repertory

**aard·vark** \'ärd-,värk\ *n* [obs. Afrikaans, fr. Afrikaans *aard* earth + *vark* pig] : a large burrowing ant-eating African mammal

**ab** *abbr* about

**AB** *abbr* **1** able-bodied seaman **2** bachelor of arts

**ABA** *abbr* American Bar Association

**aback** \ə-'bak\ *adv* : by surprise ⟨taken ∼⟩

**aba·cus** \'ab-ə-kəs\ *n, pl* **aba·ci** \'ab-ə-,sī, -,kē\ *or* **aba·cus·es** : an instrument for making calculations by sliding counters along rods or grooves

¹**abaft** \ə-'baft\ *adv* : toward or at the stern : AFT

²**abaft** *prep* : to the rear of

**ab·a·lo·ne** \,ab-ə-'lō-nē\ *n* : a large edible sea mollusk with an ear-shaped shell

¹**aban·don** \ə-'ban-dən\ *vb* [ME *abandounen*, fr. MF *abandoner*, fr. *abandon*, n., surrender, fr. *a bandon* in one's power] : to give up : FORSAKE, DESERT — **aban·don·ment** *n*

²**abandon** *n* **1** : a thorough yielding to natural impulses **2** : ENTHUSIASM, EXUBERANCE

**aban·doned** \ə-'ban-dənd\ *adj* : morally unrestrained syn profligate, dissolute

**abase** \ə-'bās\ *vb* **abased; abas·ing** : HUMBLE, DEGRADE — **abase·ment** *n*

**abash** \ə-'bash\ *vb* : to destroy the composure of : EMBARRASS — **abashment** *n*

**abate** \ə-'bāt\ *vb* **abat·ed; abat·ing** **1** : to put an end to ⟨∼ a nuisance⟩ **2** : to decrease in amount, number, or degree

**abate·ment** \ə-'bāt-mənt\ *n* **1** : DECREASE **2** : an amount abated; *esp* : a

deduction from the full amount of a tax

**ab·a·tis** \'ab-ə-,tē, 'ab-ət-əs\ *n, pl* **ab·a·tis** \'ab-ə-,tēz\ *or* **ab·a·tis·es** \-ət-ə-səz\ : a defensive obstacle of felled trees with sharpened branches facing the enemy

**ab·at·toir** \'ab-ə-,twär\ *n* : SLAUGHTERHOUSE

**ab·ba·cy** \'ab-ə-sē\ *n, pl* **-cies** : the office or term of office of an abbot or abbess

**ab·bé** \a-'bā, 'ab-,ā\ *n* : a member of the French secular clergy — used as a title

**ab·bess** \'ab-əs\ *n* : the superior of a convent for nuns

**ab·bey** \'ab-ē\ *n, pl* **abbeys** **1** : MONASTERY, CONVENT **2** : an abbey church

**ab·bot** \'ab-ət\ *n* [ME *abbod*, fr. OE, fr. LL *abbat-, abbas*, fr. LGk *abbas*, fr. Aramaic *abbā* father] : the superior of a monastery for men

**abbr** *abbr* abbreviation

**ab·bre·vi·ate** \ə-'brē-vē-,āt\ *vb* **-at·ed; -at·ing** : SHORTEN, CURTAIL; *esp* : to reduce to an abbreviation

**ab·bre·vi·a·tion** \ə-,brē-vē-'ā-shən\ *n* **1** : the act or result of abbreviating **2** : a shortened form of a word or phrase used for brevity esp. in writing

¹**ABC** \,ā-(,)bē-'sē\ *n, pl* **ABC's** *or* **ABCs** \-'sēz\ **1** : ALPHABET — usu. used in pl. **2** : RUDIMENTS

²**ABC** *abbr* American Broadcasting Company

**ab·di·cate** \'ab-di-,kāt\ *vb* **-cat·ed; -cat·ing** : to give up (as a throne) formally — **ab·di·ca·tion** \,ab-di-'kā-shən\ *n*

**ab·do·men** \'ab-də-mən, ab-'dō-mən\ *n* **1** : the cavity in or area of the body between the chest and the pelvis **2** : the part of the body posterior to the thorax in an arthropod — **ab·dom·i·nal** \ab-'däm-ən-ᵊl\ *adj* — **ab·dom·i·nal·ly** \-ē\ *adv*

**ab·duct** \ab-'dəkt\ *vb* : to take away (a person) by force : KIDNAP — **ab·duc·tion** \-'dək-shən\ *n* — **ab·duc·tor** \-tər\ *n*

**abeam** \ə-'bēm\ *adv or adj* : on a line at right angles to a ship's keel

**abe·ce·dar·i·an** \,ā-bē-sē-'der-ē-ən\ *n* : one learning the rudiments of something

**abed** \ə-'bed\ *adv or adj* : in bed

**ab·er·ra·tion** \,ab-ə-'rā-shən\ *n* **1** : deviation from the normal or usual : DERANGEMENT **2** : failure of a mirror or lens to produce exact point-to-point correspondence between an object and its image — **ab·er·rant** \a-'ber-ənt\ *adj*

**abet** \ə-'bet\ *vb* **abet·ted; abet·ting** [ME *abetten*, fr. MF *abeter*, fr. OF *beter* to bait] **1 :** INCITE, ENCOURAGE **2 :** ASSIST — **abet·tor** *or* **abet·ter** \-ər\ *n*

**abey·ance** \ə-'bā-əns\ *n* **:** a condition of suspended activity

**ab·hor** \əb-'hȯr, ab-\ *vb* **ab·horred; ab·hor·ring :** LOATHE, DETEST — **ab·hor·rence** \-əns\ *n*

**ab·hor·rent** \-ənt\ *adj* **:** LOATHSOME, DETESTABLE

**abide** \ə-'bīd\ *vb* **abode** \-'bōd\ *or* **abid·ed; abid·ing 1 :** DWELL, REMAIN, LAST **2 :** BEAR, ENDURE

**abil·i·ty** \ə-'bil-ət-ē\ *n, pl* **-ties :** the quality of being able **:** POWER, SKILL

**ab·ject** \'ab-,jekt, ab-'jekt\ *adj* **:** low in spirit or hope **:** CRINGING — **ab·jec·tion** \ab-'jek-shən\ *n* — **ab·ject·ly** \'ab-jekt-lē, ab-'jekt-\ *adv* — **ab·ject·ness** *n*

**ab·jure** \ab-'jur\ *vb* **ab·jured; ab·jur·ing 1 :** to renounce solemnly **:** RECANT **2 :** to abstain from — **ab·ju·ra·tion** \,ab-jə-'rā-shən\ *n*

**abl** *abbr* ablative

**ab·la·tion** \a-'blā-shən\ *n* **:** removal by cutting, erosion, melting, or vaporization — **ab·late** \a-'blāt\ *vb*

**ab·la·tive** \'ab-lət-iv\ *adj* **:** of, relating to, or constituting a grammatical case (as in Latin) expressing typically the relation of separation and source — **ablative** *n*

**ablaze** \ə-'blāz\ *adj or adv* **:** being on fire **:** BLAZING

**able** \'ā-bəl\ *adj* **abler** \-b(ə-)lər\; **ablest** \-b(ə-)ləst\ **1 :** having sufficient power, skill, or resources to accomplish an object **2 :** marked by skill or efficiency — **ably** \-blē\ *adv*

**-able** *also* **-ible** \ə-bəl\ *adj suffix* **1 :** capable of, fit for, or worthy of (being so acted upon or toward) ⟨break*able*⟩ ⟨collect*ible*⟩ **2 :** tending, given, or liable to ⟨knowledge*able*⟩ ⟨perish*able*⟩

**able-bod·ied** \,ā-bəl-'bäd-ēd\ *adj* **:** having a sound strong body

**abloom** \ə-'blüm\ *adj* **:** BLOOMING

**ab·lu·tion** \ə-'blü-shən, a-'blü-\ *n* **:** the washing of one's body or part of it

**ABM** \,ā-(,)bē-'em\ *n* **:** ANTIBALLISTIC MISSILE

**Ab·na·ki** \ab-'näk-ē\ *n, pl* **Abnaki** *or* **Abnakis :** a member of an Indian people of Maine and southern Quebec

**ab·ne·gate** \'ab-ni-,gāt\ *vb* **-gat·ed; -gat·ing 1 :** SURRENDER, RELINQUISH **2 :** DENY, RENOUNCE — **ab·ne·ga·tion** \,ab-ni-'gā-shən\ *n*

**ab·nor·mal** \ab-'nȯr-məl\ *adj* **:** deviating from the normal or average — **ab·nor·mal·i·ty** \,ab-nər-'mal-ət-ē, -(,)nȯr-\ *n* — **ab·nor·mal·ly** \ab-'nȯr-mə-lē\ *adv*

**¹aboard** \ə-'bȯrd\ *adv* **1 :** on, onto, or within a car, ship, or aircraft **2 :** ALONGSIDE

**²aboard** *prep* **:** ON, ONTO, WITHIN

**abode** \ə-'bōd\ *n* **1 :** STAY, SOJOURN **2 :** HOME, RESIDENCE

**abol·ish** \ə-'bäl-ish\ *vb* **:** to do away with **:** ANNUL — **ab·o·li·tion** \,ab-ə-'lish-ən\ *n*

**ab·o·li·tion·ism** \,ab-ə-'lish-ə-,niz-əm\ *n* **:** advocacy of the abolition of slavery — **ab·o·li·tion·ist** \-'lish-(ə-)nəst\ *n or adj*

**A-bomb** \'ā-,bäm\ *n* **:** ATOM BOMB — **A-bomb** *vb*

**abom·i·na·ble** \ə-'bäm-(ə-)nə-bəl\ *adj* **:** ODIOUS, LOATHSOME, DETESTABLE

**abominable snow·man** \-'snō-mən, -,man\ *n, often cap A&S* **:** a mysterious animal reported as existing in the high Himalayas and usu. thought to be a bear

**abom·i·nate** \ə-'bäm-ə-,nāt\ *vb* **-nat·ed; -nat·ing** [L *abominari*, lit., to deprecate as an ill omen, fr. *ab-* away + *omen* omen] **:** LOATHE, DETEST

**abom·i·na·tion** \ə-,bäm-ə-'nā-shən\ *n* **1 :** something abominable **2 :** DISGUST, LOATHING

**ab·orig·i·nal** \,ab-ə-'rij-(ə-)nəl\ *adj* **:** ORIGINAL, INDIGENOUS, PRIMITIVE

**ab·orig·i·ne** \,ab-ə-'rij-ə-nē\ *n* **:** a member of the original race of inhabitants of a region **:** NATIVE

**aborn·ing** \ə-'bȯr-niŋ\ *adv* **:** while being born or produced

**¹abort** \ə-'bȯrt\ *vb* **1 :** to cause or undergo abortion **2 :** to terminate prematurely ⟨~ a spaceflight⟩ — **abor·tive** \-'bȯrt-iv\ *adj*

**²abort** *n* **:** the premature termination of a spacecraft's action, procedure, or mission

**abor·tion** \ə-'bȯr-shən\ *n* **:** a premature birth occurring before the fetus can survive; *also* **:** an induced expulsion of a fetus

**abor·tion·ist** \-sh(ə-)nəst\ *n* **:** a producer of abortions

**abound** \ə-'baund\ *vb* **1 :** to be plentiful **:** TEEM **2 :** to be fully supplied

**¹about** \ə-'baut\ *adv* **1 :** on all sides **2 :** AROUND **3 :** NEARBY

**²about** *prep* **1 :** on every side of **2 :** near **to 3 :** on the verge of **:** GOING ⟨he was just ~ to go⟩ **4 :** CONCERNING

**about-face** \-'fās\ *n* **:** a reversal of direction or attitude — **about-face** *vb*

**¹above** \ə-'bəv\ *adv* **1 :** in the sky; *also* **:** in or to heaven **2 :** in or to a higher place; *also* **:** higher on the same page or on a preceding page

**²above** *prep* **1 :** in or to a higher place than **:** OVER ⟨storm clouds ~ the bay⟩ **2 :** superior to ⟨he thought her far ~ him⟩ **3 :** more than **:** EXCEEDING

**above·board** \-,bȯrd\ *adv or adj* **:** without concealment or deception **:** OPENLY

**abp** *abbr* archbishop

**abr** *abbr* abridged; abridgment

**ab·ra·ca·dab·ra** \,ab-rə-kə-'dab-rə\ *n* **1 :** a magical charm or incantation against calamity **2 :** GIBBERISH

**abrade** \ə-'brād\ *vb* **abrad·ed; abrad·ing 1 :** to wear away by rubbing **2 :** to wear down in spirit **:** IRRITATE — **abra·sion** \-'brā-zhən\ *n*

**¹abra·sive** \ə-'brā-siv\ *adj* **:** tending to abrade **:** causing irritation ⟨~ relationships) — **abra·sive·ly** *adv* — **abra-sive·ness** *n*

²**abrasive** *n* : a substance (as emery or pumice) for grinding, smoothing, or polishing

**abreast** \ə-'brest\ *adv or adj* **1** : side by side **2** : up to a standard or level esp. of knowledge

**abridge** \ə-'brij\ *vb* **abridged; abridg·ing** [ME *abregen*, fr. MF *abre-gier*, fr. LL *abbreviare*, fr. L *ad* to + *brevis* short] : to lessen in length or extent : SHORTEN — **abridg·ment** *or* **abridge·ment** *n*

**abroad** \ə-'brȯd\ *adv or adj* **1** : over a wide area **2** : out of doors **3** : outside one's country

**ab·ro·gate** \'ab-rə-ˌgāt\ *vb* **-gat·ed; -gat·ing** : ANNUL, REVOKE — **ab·ro-ga·tion** \ˌab-rə-'gā-shən\ *n*

**abrupt** \ə-'brəpt\ *adj* **1** : broken or as if broken off **2** : SUDDEN, HASTY **3** : so quick as to seem rude **4** : DISCON-NECTED **5** : STEEP — **abrupt·ly** *adv*

**abs** *abbr* absolute

**ab·scess** \'ab-ˌses\ *n* [L *abscessus*, lit., act of going away, fr. *abscedere* to go away, fr. *abs-, ab-* away + *cedere* to go] : a collection of pus surrounded by inflamed tissue — **ab·scessed** \-ˌsest\ *adj*

**ab·scis·sa** \ab-'sis-ə\ *n, pl* **abscissas** *also* **ab·scis·sae** \-'sis-(ˌ)ē\ : the co-ordinate of a point in a plane obtained by measuring parallel to the horizontal axis

**ab·scis·sion** \ab-'sizh-ən\ *n* **1** : the act or process of cutting off **2** : the natural separation of flowers, fruits, or leaves from plants — **ab·scise** \ab-'sīz\ *vb*

**ab·scond** \ab-'skänd\ *vb* : to depart secretly and hide oneself

**ab·sence** \'ab-səns\ *n* **1** : the state or time of being absent **2** : WANT, LACK **3** : INATTENTION

¹**ab·sent** \'ab-sənt\ *adj* **1** : not present **2** : LACKING **3** : INATTENTIVE

²**ab·sent** \ab-'sent\ *vb* : to keep (oneself) away

**ab·sen·tee** \ˌab-sən-'tē\ *n* : one that is absent or absents himself

**absentee ballot** *n* : a ballot submitted (as by mail) in advance of an election by a voter who is unable to be present at the polls

**ab·sen·tee·ism** \ˌab-sən-'tē-ˌiz-əm\ *n* : chronic absence from work

**ab·sent-mind·ed** \ˌab-sənt-'mīn-dəd\ *adj* : unaware of one's surroundings or action : INATTENTIVE — **ab·sent-mind·ed·ly** *adv* — **ab·sent-mind-ed·ness** *n*

**ab·sinthe** *or* **ab·sinth** \'ab-ˌsinth\ : a liqueur flavored esp. with worm-wood and anise

**ab·so·lute** \'ab-sə-ˌlüt, ˌab-sə-'lüt\ *adj* **1** : free from imperfection or mixture **2** : free from control, restriction, or qualification **3** : lacking grammatical connection with any other word in a sentence ⟨~ construction⟩ **4** : POSI-TIVE ⟨~ proof⟩ **5** : relating to the fundamental units of length, mass, and

time **6** : relating to a temperature scale on which the zero point (**absolute zero**) corresponds to complete absence of heat equal to −273.16°C **7** : FUN-DAMENTAL, ULTIMATE — **ab·so·lute·ly** *adv*

**absolute pitch** *n* **1** : the position of a tone in a standard scale independently determined by its rate of vibration **2** : the ability to sing or name a note asked for or heard

**absolute value** *n* : the numerical value of a real number without regard to sign

**ab·so·lu·tion** \ˌab-sə-'lü-shən\ *n* : the act of absolving; *esp* : a remission of sins pronounced by a priest in the sac-rament of penance

**ab·so·lut·ism** \'ab-sə-ˌlüt-ˌiz-əm\ *n* **1** : the theory that a ruler or govern-ment should have unlimited power **2** : government by an absolute ruler or authority

**ab·solve** \əb-'zälv, -'sälv\ *vb* **ab·solved; ab·solv·ing** : to set free from an obligation or the consequences of guilt **syn** pardon, confess, shrive

**ab·sorb** \əb-'sȯrb, -'zȯrb\ *vb* **1** : AS-SIMILATE, INCORPORATE **2** : to suck up or take in in the manner of a sponge **3** : to engage (one's attention) : EN-GROSS **4** : to receive without recoil or echo ⟨a ceiling that ~s sound⟩ — **ab·sorb·ing** *adj* — **ab·sorb·ing·ly** *adv*

**ab·sor·bent** *also* **ab·sor·bant** \əb-'sȯr-bənt, -'zȯr-\ *adj* : able to absorb ⟨~ cotton⟩ — **ab·sor·ben·cy** \-bən-sē\ *n* — **absorbent** *also* **absor·bant** *n*

**ab·sorp·tion** \əb-'sȯrp-shən, -'zȯrp-\ *n* **1** : a process of absorbing or being absorbed **2** : concentration of atten-tion — **ab·sorp·tive** \-tiv\ *adj*

**ab·stain** \əb-'stān\ *vb* : to restrain oneself **syn** refrain, forbear — **ab·stain·er** *n* — **ab·sten·tion** \-'sten-chən\ *n*

**ab·ste·mi·ous** \ab-'stē-mē-əs\ *adj* [L *abstemius*, fr. *abs-* away + *temetum* mead] : sparing in use of food or drink : TEMPERATE — **ab·ste·mi·ous·ly** *adv*

**ab·sti·nence** \'ab-stə-nəns\ *n* : volun-tary refraining esp. from eating certain foods or drinking liquor — **ab·sti·nent** \-nənt\ *adj*

**abstr** *abbr* abstract

¹**ab·stract** \ab-'strakt, 'ab-ˌstrakt\ *adj* **1** : considered apart from a particular instance **2** : expressing a quality apart from an object ⟨*whiteness* is an ~ word⟩ **3** : having only intrinsic form with little or no pictorial representa-tion ⟨~ painting⟩ — **ab·stract·ly** *adv* — **ab·stract·ness** \-'strak(t)-nəs, -ˌstrak(t)-\ *n*

²**ab·stract** \'ab-ˌstrakt; *2 also* ab-'strakt\ *n* **1** : SUMMARY, EPITOME **2** : an abstract thing or state

³**ab·stract** \ab-'strakt, 'ab-ˌstrakt; *2 usu* 'ab-ˌstrakt\ *vb* **1** : REMOVE, SEPARATE **2** : to make an abstract of : SUMMA-RIZE **3** : to draw away the attention of **4** : STEAL — **ab·stract·ed·ly** \ab-'strak-təd-lē, 'ab-ˌstrak-\ *adv*

**abstract expressionism** *n* : art that expresses the artist's attitudes and emotions through abstract forms — **abstract expressionist** *n*

**ab·strac·tion** \ab-'strak-shən\ *n* **1** : the act of abstracting : the state of being abstracted **2** : an abstract idea **3** : an abstract work of art

**ab·struse** \əb-'strüs, ab-\ *adj* : hard to understand : RECONDITE — **ab·struse·ly** *adv* — **ab·struse·ness** *n*

**ab·surd** \əb-'sərd, -'zərd\ *adj* [MF *absurde*, fr. L *absurdus*, fr. *ab-* from + *surdus* deaf, stupid] : RIDICULOUS, UNREASONABLE — **ab·sur·di·ty** \-ət-ē\ *n* — **ab·surd·ly** *adv*

**abun·dant** \ə-'bən-dənt\ *adj* [ME, fr. MF, fr. L *abundant-, abundans*, prp. of *abundare* to abound, fr. *ab-* from + *unda* wave] : more than enough : amply sufficient **syn** copious, plentiful — **abun·dance** \-dəns\ *n* — **abun·dant·ly** *adv*

¹**abuse** \ə-'byüz\ *vb* **abused; abus·ing 1** : to attack in words : REVILE **2** : to put to a wrong use : MISUSE **3** : MISTREAT — **abu·sive** \-'byü-siv\ *adj* — **abu·sive·ly** *adv* — **abu·sive·ness** *n*

²**abuse** \ə-'byüs\ *n* **1** : a corrupt practice **2** : MISUSE **3** : MISTREATMENT **4** : coarse and insulting speech

**abut** \ə-'bət\ *vb* **abut·ted; abut·ting** : to touch along a border : border on

**abut·ment** \ə-'bət-mənt\ *n* : a structure that supports weight or withstands lateral pressure (as at the end of a bridge)

**abut·tals** \ə-'bət-ºlz\ *n pl* : the boundaries of lands with respect to adjacent lands

**abysm** \ə-'biz-əm\ *n* : ABYSS

**abys·mal** \ə-'biz-məl\ *adj* : immeasurably deep : BOTTOMLESS — **abys·mal·ly** *adv*

**abyss** \ə-'bis\ *n* **1** : the bottomless pit in old accounts of the universe **2** : an immeasurable depth

**abys·sal** \ə-'bis-əl\ *adj* : of or relating to the bottom waters of the ocean depths

**ac** *abbr* account

**Ac** *symbol* actinium

**AC** *abbr* **1** alternating current **2** [L *ante Christum*] before Christ **3** [L *ante cibum*] before meals

**aca·cia** \ə-'kā-shə\ *n* : any of numerous leguminous trees or shrubs with round white or yellow flower clusters

**acad** *abbr* academic; academy

**ac·a·deme** \'ak-ə-ˌdēm\ *n* : SCHOOL; *also* : academic environment

**ac·a·dem·ic** \ˌak-ə-'dem-ik\ *also* **ac·a·dem·i·cal** \-i-kəl\ *adj* **1** : of or relating to schools or colleges **2** : literary or general rather than technical **3** : theoretical rather than practical — **ac·a·dem·i·cal·ly** \-i-k(ə-)lē\ *adv*

**ac·a·de·mi·cian** \ˌak-əd-ə-'mish-ən, ə-ˌkad-ə-\ *n* : a member of a society of scholars or artists

**ac·a·dem·i·cism** \ˌak-ə-'dem-ə-ˌsiz-əm\ *also* **acad·e·mism** \ə-'kad-ə-ˌmiz-əm\ *n* : manner, style, or content conforming to the traditions or rules of an academy or movement

**acad·e·my** \ə-'kad-ə-mē\ *n, pl* **-mies** [Gk *Akadēmeia*, school of philosophy founded by Plato, fr. *Akadēmeia*, gymnasium where Plato taught, fr. *Akadēmos* Greek mythological hero] **1** : a school above the elementary level; *esp* : a private high school **2** : a society of scholars or artists

**acan·thus** \ə-'kan-thəs\ *n, pl* **acan·thus·es** *also* **acan·thi** \-'kan-ˌthī\ **1** : any of a genus of prickly herbs of the Mediterranean region **2** : an ornamentation (as on a column) representing the leaves of the acanthus

**a cap·pel·la** *also* **a ca·pel·la** \ˌäk-ə-'pel-ə\ *adv or adj* [It *a cappella* in chapel style] : without instrumental accompaniment ⟨the choir sang *a cappella*⟩

**acc** *abbr* accusative

**ac·cede** \ak-'sēd\ *vb* **ac·ced·ed; ac·ced·ing 1** : to become a party to an agreement **2** : to express approval **3** : to enter upon an office **syn** acquiesce, assent, consent, subscribe

**ac·ce·le·ran·do** \ä-ˌchel-ə-'rän-dō\ *adv or adj* : gradually faster — used as a direction in music

**ac·cel·er·ate** \ik-'sel-ə-ˌrāt, ak-\ *vb* **-at·ed; -at·ing 1** : to bring about earlier **2** : to speed up : QUICKEN — **ac·cel·er·a·tion** \-ˌsel-ə-'rā-shən\ *n*

**ac·cel·er·a·tor** \ik-'sel-ə-ˌrāt-ər, ak-\ *n* **1** : one that accelerates **2** : a foot-operated pedal for controlling the speed of a motor-vehicle engine **3** : an apparatus for imparting high velocities to charged particles

**ac·cel·er·om·e·ter** \ik-ˌsel-ə-'räm-ət-ər, ak-\ *n* : an instrument for measuring acceleration or vibrations

¹**ac·cent** \'ak-ˌsent\ *n* **1** : a distinctive manner of pronunciation ⟨a foreign ∼⟩ **2** : prominence given to one syllable of a word esp. by stress **3** : a mark (as ′, ‵, ˆ) over a vowel in writing or printing used usu. to indicate a difference in pronunciation (as stress) from a vowel not so marked — **ac·cen·tu·al** \ak-'sench-(ə-)wəl\ *adj*

²**ac·cent** \'ak-ˌsent, ak-'sent\ *vb* : STRESS, EMPHASIZE

**ac·cen·tu·ate** \ak-'sen-chə-ˌwāt\ *vb* **-at·ed; -at·ing** : ACCENT — **ac·cen·tu·a·tion** \-ˌsen-chə-'wā-shən\ *n*

**ac·cept** \ik-'sept, ak-\ *vb* **1** : to receive willingly **2** : to agree to **3** : to assume an obligation to pay

**ac·cept·able** \ik-'sep-tə-bəl, ak-\ *adj* : capable or worthy of being accepted — **ac·cept·abil·i·ty** \ik-ˌsep-tə-'bil-ət-ē, ak-\ *n*

**ac·cep·tance** \ik-'sep-təns, ak-\ *n* **1** : the act of accepting **2** : the state of being accepted or acceptable **3** : an accepted bill of exchange

**ac·cep·ta·tion** \ˌak-ˌsep-'tā-shən\ *n* : the generally understood meaning of a word

¹**ac·cess** \'ak-ˌses\ *n* **1** : ATTACK, FIT **2** : capacity to enter or approach **3** : a way of approach : ENTRANCE

²**access** *vb* : to get at : gain access to

**ac·ces·si·ble** \ik-'ses-ə-bəl, ak-\ *adj* : easy to approach —**ac·ces·si·bil·i·ty** \ik-,ses-ə-'bil-ət-ē, ak-\ *n*

**ac·ces·sion** \ik-'sesh-ən, ak-\ *n* **1** : something added **2** : increase by something added **3** : the act of acceding to an office or position

**ac·ces·so·ry** *also* **ac·ces·sa·ry** \ik-'ses-(ə-)rē, ak-\ *n, pl* **-ries 1** : something helpful but not essential **2** : a person who though not present abets or assists in the commission of an offense *syn* appurtenance, adjunct, appendage **accessory** *adj*

**ac·ci·dence** \'ak-səd-əns\ *n* : a part of grammar that deals with inflections

**ac·ci·dent** \'ak-səd-ənt\ *n* **1** : an event occurring by chance or unintentionally **2** : CHANCE ‹met by ~› **3** : a nonessential property

¹**ac·ci·den·tal** \,ak-sə-'dent-ᵊl\ *adj* **1** : happening unexpectedly or by chance **2** : happening without intent or through carelessness *syn* casual, fortuitous, incidental, adventitious — **ac·ci·den·tal·ly** \-'dent-(ᵊ-)lē\ *also* **ac·ci·dent·ly** \-'dent-lē\ *adv*

²**accidental** *n* : a musical note (as a sharp or flat) not belonging to the key indicated by the signature

**ac·claim** \ə-'klām\ *vb* **1** : APPLAUD, PRAISE **2** : to declare by acclamation *syn* extol, laud — **acclaim** *n*

**ac·cla·ma·tion** \,ak-lə-'mā-shən\ *n* **1** : loud eager applause **2** : an overwhelming affirmative vote by shouting or applause rather than by ballot

**ac·cli·mate** \'ak-lə-,māt, ə-'klī-mət\ *vb* **-mat·ed; -mat·ing** : to accustom to a new climate or situation — **ac·cli·ma·tion** \,ak-lə-'mā-shən, ,ak-,lī-\ *n*

**ac·cli·ma·tize** \ə-'klī-mə-,tīz\ *vb* **-tized; -tiz·ing 1** : ACCLIMATE **2** : to become acclimated — **ac·cli·ma·ti·za·tion** \-,klī-mət-ə-'zā-shən\ *n*

**ac·cliv·i·ty** \ə-'kliv-ət-ē\ *n, pl* **-ties** : an ascending slope

**ac·co·lade** \'ak-ə-,lād\ *n* [F, fr. *accoler* to embrace, fr. L *ad-* to + *collum* neck] : a recognition of merit : AWARD

**ac·com·mo·date** \ə-'käm-ə-,dāt\ *vb* **-dat·ed; -dat·ing 1** : to make fit or suitable : ADAPT, ADJUST **2** : HARMONIZE, RECONCILE **3** : to provide with something needed **4** : to hold without crowding

**ac·com·mo·dat·ing** *adj* : OBLIGING

**ac·com·mo·da·tion** \ə-,käm-ə-'dā-shən\ *n* **1** : something supplied to satisfy a need; *esp* : LODGINGS — usu. used in pl. **2** : the act of accommodating : ADJUSTMENT

**ac·com·pa·ni·ment** \ə-'kəmp-(ə-)nē-mənt\ *n* : something that accompanies another; *esp* : subordinate music to support a principal voice or instrument

**ac·com·pa·ny** \ə-'kəmp-(ə-)nē\ *vb* **-nied; -ny·ing 1** : to go or occur with : ATTEND **2** : to play an accompaniment for — **ac·com·pa·nist** \-(ə-)nəst\ *n*

**ac·com·plice** \ə-'käm-pləs, -'kəm-\ *n* : an associate in crime

**ac·com·plish** \ə-'käm-plish, -'kəm-\

*vb* : to bring to completion *syn* achieve, effect, fulfill, discharge, execute, perform - **ac·com·plish·er** *n*

**ac·com·plished** \-'plisht\ *adj* **1** : COMPLETED **2** : EXPERT, SKILLED

**ac·com·plish·ment** \ə-'käm-plish-mənt, -'kəm-\ *n* **1** : COMPLETION **2** : something completed or effected **3** : an acquired excellence or skill

¹**ac·cord** \ə-'kord\ *vb* [ME *accorden*, fr. OF *acorder*, fr. L *ad-* to + *cord-, cor* heart] **1** : GRANT, CONCEDE **2** : AGREE, HARMONIZE — **ac·cor·dant** \-'kord-ᵊnt\ *adj*

²**accord** *n* : AGREEMENT, HARMONY

**ac·cor·dance** \ə-'kord-ᵊns\ *n* **1** : ACCORD **2** : the act of granting

**ac·cord·ing·ly** \ə-'kord-iŋ-lē\ *adv* **1** : in accordance **2** : CONSEQUENTLY, SO

**according to** *prep* **1** : in conformity with ‹paid *according to* ability› **2** : as stated or attested by ‹*according to* her he wasn't home›

¹**ac·cor·di·on** \ə-'kord-ē-ən\ *n* : a portable keyboard instrument with a bellows and reeds

²**accordion** *adj* : folding like the bellows of an accordion ‹~ pleats›

**ac·cost** \ə-'kost\ *vb* : to approach and speak to esp. aggressively

¹**ac·count** \ə-'kaúnt\ *n* **1** : a statement of business transactions **2** : an arrangement with a vendor to supply credit **3** : NARRATIVE, REPORT **4** : WORTH **5** : a sum of money deposited in a bank and subject to withdrawal by the depositor - **on account of** : because of — **on no account** : under no circumstances — **on one's own account** : on one's own behalf

²**account** *vb* **1** : CONSIDER ‹I ~ him lucky› **2** : to give an explanation — used with *for*

**ac·count·able** \ə-'kaúnt-ə-bəl\ *adj* **1** : ANSWERABLE, RESPONSIBLE **2** : EXPLICABLE — **ac·count·abil·i·ty** \-,kaúnt-ə-'bil-ət-ē\ *n*

**ac·coun·tant** \ə-'kaúnt-ᵊnt\ *n* : a person skilled in accounting — **ac·coun·tan·cy** \-ᵊn-sē\ *n*

**account executive** *n* : a business executive (as in an advertising agency) in charge of a client's account

**ac·count·ing** \ə-'kaúnt-iŋ\ *n* **1** : the art or system of keeping and analyzing financial records **2** : an explanation of one's behavior

**ac·cou·tre** *or* **ac·cou·ter** \ə-'küt-ər\ *vb* **-cou·tred** *or* **-cou·tered; -cou·tring** *or* **-cou·ter·ing** \-'küt-ə-riŋ, 'kü-triŋ\ : to equip esp. for military service — **ac·cou·tre·ment** *or* **ac·cou·ter·ment** \ə-'kü-trə-mənt, -'küt-ər-mənt\ *n*

**ac·cred·it** \ə-'kred-ət\ *vb* **1** : to endorse or approve officially **2** : CREDIT — **ac·cred·i·ta·tion** \-,kred-ə-'tā-shən\ *n*

**ac·cre·tion** \ə-'krē-shən\ *n* **1** : growth esp. by addition from without **2** : a product of accretion

**ac·crue** \ə-'krü\ *vb* **ac·crued; ac·cru·ing 1** : to come by way of increase **2** : to be added by periodic growth — **ac·cru·al** \-əl\ n

**acct** abbr account; accountant

**ac·cul·tur·a·tion** \ə-ˌkəl-chə-ˈrā-shən\ n **1** : intercultural borrowing between diverse peoples resulting in new and blended patterns **2** : the process by which one acquires the culture of a society

**ac·cu·mu·late** \ə-ˈkyü-myə-ˌlāt\ vb -lat·ed; -lat·ing [L accumulare, fr. ad- to + cumulare to heap up] : to heap or pile up **syn** amass, gather, collect — **ac·cu·mu·la·tion** \-ˌkyü-myə-ˈlā-shən\ n — **ac·cu·mu·la·tor** \-ˈkyü-myə-ˌlāt-ər\ n

**ac·cu·rate** \ˈak-yə-rət\ adj : free from error **:** EXACT, PRECISE — **ac·cu·ra·cy** \-rə-sē\ n — **ac·cu·rate·ly** adv — **ac·cu·rate·ness** n

**ac·cursed** \ə-ˈkərst, -ˈkər-səd\ or **ac·curst** \ə-ˈkərst\ adj **1** : being under a curse **2** : DAMNABLE, EXECRABLE

**ac·cus·al** \ə-ˈkyü-zəl\ n : ACCUSATION

**ac·cu·sa·tive** \ə-ˈkyü-zət-iv\ adj : of, relating to, or being a grammatical case marking the direct object of a verb or the object of a preposition — **accusative** n

**ac·cuse** \ə-ˈkyüz\ vb **ac·cused; ac·cus·ing** : to charge with an offense **:** BLAME — **ac·cu·sa·tion** \ˌak-yə-ˈzā-shən\ n — **ac·cus·er** n

**ac·cused** \ə-ˈkyüzd\ n, pl **accused** : the defendant in a criminal case

**ac·cus·tom** \ə-ˈkəs-təm\ vb : FAMILIARIZE, HABITUATE

**ac·cus·tomed** \ə-ˈkəs-təmd\ adj : USUAL, CUSTOMARY

¹**ace** \ˈās\ n [ME as a die face marked with one spot, fr. OF, fr. L, unit, a copper coin] **1** : a playing card bearing a single large pip in its center **2** : a point (as in tennis) won by a single stroke **3** : a golf score of one stroke on a hole **4** : an aviator who has brought down five or more enemy planes **5** : one that excels

²**ace** vb **aced; ac·ing** : to score an ace against (an opponent)

³**ace** adj : of first rank or quality

**ac·er·bate** \ˈas-ər-ˌbāt\ vb **-bat·ed; -bat·ing** : IRRITATE, EXASPERATE

**acer·bi·ty** \ə-ˈsər-bət-ē\ n, pl **-ties** : SOURNESS, BITTERNESS — **acerb** \-ˈsərb\ adj

**ac·e·tate** \ˈas-ə-ˌtāt\ n **1** : a salt or ester of acetic acid **2** : a fast-drying fabric made of fiber derived from cellulose and acetic acid; also : a plastic of similar composition used for phonograph records

**ace·tic** \ə-ˈsēt-ik\ adj : of, relating to, or producing acetic acid or vinegar

**acetic acid** n : a colorless pungent liquid acid that is the chief acid of vinegar and is usu. manufactured

**ac·e·tone** \ˈas-ə-ˌtōn\ n : a volatile flammable fragrant liquid used as a solvent

**ace·tyl·cho·line** \ə-ˌsēt-ᵊl-ˈkō-ˌlēn\ n : a compound that is released at some nerve endings and is active in the transmission of nerve impulses

**acet·y·lene** \ə-ˈset-ᵊl-ən, -ᵊl-ˌēn\ n : a colorless flammable gas used as a fuel (as in welding and soldering)

**ace·tyl·sal·i·cyl·ic acid** \ə-ˌsēt-ᵊl-ˌsal-ə-ˌsil-ik-\ n : ASPIRIN 1

**ache** \ˈāk\ vb **ached; ach·ing 1** : to suffer a usu. dull persistent pain **2** : LONG, YEARN — **ache** n

**achieve** \ə-ˈchēv\ vb **achieved; achiev·ing** [ME acheven, fr. MF achever to finish, fr. a- to (fr. L ad-) + chief end, head, fr. L caput] **1** : to gain by work or effort **syn** accomplish, fulfill, effect — **achieve·ment** n — **achiev·er** n

**Achil·les' heel** \ə-ˌkil-ēz-\ n : a vulnerable point

**Achilles tendon** \ə-ˌkil-ēz-\ n : the strong tendon joining the muscles in the calf of the leg to the bone of the heel

**ach·ro·mat·ic** \ˌak-rə-ˈmat-ik\ adj : giving an image almost free from extraneous colors (~ lens) — **ach·ro·mat·i·cal·ly** \-i-k(ə-)lē\ adv

**achy** \ˈā-kē\ adj **ach·i·er; ach·i·est** : afflicted with aches — **ach·i·ness** n

¹**ac·id** \ˈas-əd\ adj **1** : sour or biting to the taste; also : sharp or sour in manner **2** : of or relating to an acid — **acid·i·ty** \ə-ˈsid-ət-ē\ n

²**acid** n **1** : a sour substance **2** : a usu. water-soluble chemical compound that has a sour taste, reacts with a base to form a salt, and reddens litmus **3** : LSD — **acid·ic** \ə-ˈsid-ik\ adj

**ac·id·head** \-ˌhed\ n : an individual who uses LSD

**acid·i·fy** \ə-ˈsid-ə-ˌfī\ vb **-fied; fy·ing 1** : to make or become acid **2** : to change into an acid — **acid·i·fi·ca·tion** \-ˌsid-ə-fə-ˈkā-shən\ n

**ac·i·do·sis** \ˌas-ə-ˈdō-səs\ n : an abnormal state of reduced alkalinity of the blood and body tissues

**acid test** n : a severe or crucial test

**acid·u·late** \ə-ˈsij-ə-ˌlāt\ vb **-lat·ed; -lat·ing** : to make acid or slightly acid — **acid·u·la·tion** \-ˌsij-ə-ˈlā-shən\ n

**acid·u·lous** \ə-ˈsij-ə-ləs\ adj : slightly acid : SOURISH

**ack** abbr acknowledge; acknowledgment

**ack-ack** \ˈak-ˌak\ n [Brit. signalmen's telephone pron. of AA, abbr. of anti-aircraft] : an antiaircraft gun; also : its fire

**ac·knowl·edge** \ik-ˈnäl-ij, ak-\ vb **-edged; -edg·ing 1** : to admit as true **2** : to admit the authority of **3** : to express thanks for; also : to report receipt of **4** : to recognize as valid — **ac·knowl·edg·ment** also **ac·knowl·edge·ment** n

**ac·me** \ˈak-mē\ n : the highest point

**ac·ne** \ˈak-nē\ n : a skin disorder marked by inflammation of skin glands and hair follicles and by pimple formation esp. on the face

**ac·o·lyte** \ˈak-ə-ˌlīt\ n : one who assists the clergyman in a liturgical service

**ac·o·nite** \ˈak-ə-ˌnīt\ n **1** : any of several blue-flowered or purple-flowered poisonous plants related to the buttercups **2** : a drug obtained from a common Old World aconite

**acorn** \'ā-ˌkȯrn, -kərn\ *n* : the nut of the oak

**acorn squash** *n* : an acorn-shaped dark green winter squash with a ridged surface and sweet yellow to orange flesh

**acous-tic** \ə-'kü-stik\ *adj* **1** : of or relating to the sense or organs of hearing, to sound, or to the science of sounds **2** : deadening sound ⟨∼ tile⟩ **3** : operated by or utilizing sound waves — **acous-ti-cal** \-sti-kəl\ *adj* — **acous-ti-cal-ly** \-k(ə-)lē\ *adv*

**acous-tics** \ə-'kü-stiks\ *n sing or pl* **1** : the science dealing with sound **2** : the qualities in a room that make it easy or hard for a person in it to hear distinctly

**ac-quaint** \ə-'kwānt\ *vb* **1** : INFORM, NOTIFY **2** : to make familiar : cause to know

**ac-quain-tance** \ə-'kwānt-ᵊns\ *n* **1** : personal knowledge **2** : a person with whom one is acquainted — **ac-quain-tance-ship** *n*

**ac-qui-esce** \ˌak-wē-'es\ *vb* **-esced; -esc-ing** : to accept or comply without open opposition **syn** consent, agree, assent, accede — **ac-qui-es-cence** \-'es-ᵊns\ *n* — **ac-qui-es-cent** \-ᵊnt\ *adj* — **ac-qui-es-cent-ly** *adv*

**ac-quire** \ə-'kwī(ə)r\ *vb* **ac-quired; ac-quir-ing** : to come into possession of : GET

**ac-quire-ment** \-mənt\ *n* **1** : the act of acquiring **2** : ATTAINMENT, ACCOMPLISHMENT

**ac-qui-si-tion** \ˌak-wə-'zish-ən\ *n* **1** : ACQUIREMENT **2** : something acquired

**ac-quis-i-tive** \ə-'kwiz-ət-iv\ *adj* : eager to acquire : GREEDY — **ac-quis-i-tive-ly** *adv* — **ac-quis-i-tive-ness** *n*

**ac-quit** \ə-'kwit\ *vb* **ac-quit-ted; ac-quit-ting** **1** : to pronounce not guilty **2** : to conduct (oneself) usu. satisfactorily — **ac-quit-tal** \-ᵊl\ *n*

**acre** \'ā-kər\ *n* **1** *pl* : LANDS, ESTATE **2** — see WEIGHT table

**acre-age** \'ā-k(ə-)rij\ *n* : area in acres : ACRES

**ac-rid** \'ak-rəd\ *adj* **1** : sharp and biting in taste or odor **2** : bitterly irritating : CAUSTIC — **acrid-i-ty** \a-'krid-ət-ē, ə\ *n* — **ac-rid-ness** *n*

**ac-ri-mo-ny** \'ak-rə-ˌmō-nē\ *n, pl* **-nies** : harsh or biting sharpness of language or feeling : ASPERITY — **ac-ri-mo-ni-ous** \ˌak-rə-'mō-nē-əs\ *adj*

**ac-ro-bat** \'ak-rə-ˌbat\ *n* [F *acrobate*, fr. Gk *akrobatēs*, fr. *akrobatos* walking up high, fr. *akros* topmost + *bainein* to go] : a performer of gymnastic feats — **ac-ro-bat-ic** \ˌak-rə-'bat-ik\ *adj*

**ac-ro-bat-ics** \ˌak-rə-'bat-iks\ *n sing or pl* : the performance of an acrobat

**ac-ro-nym** \'ak-rə-ˌnim\ *n* : a word (as *radar*) formed from the initial letter or letters of each of the successive parts or major parts of a compound term

**ac-ro-pho-bia** \ˌak-rə-'fō-bē-ə\ *n* : abnormal dread of being at a great height

**acrop-o-lis** \ə-'kräp-ə-ləs\ *n* : the upper fortified part of an ancient Greek city

¹**across** \ə-'krȯs\ *adv* **1** : to or on the opposite side **2** : so as to be understandable or acceptable : OVER ⟨get the point ∼⟩

²**across** *prep* **1** : to or on the opposite side of ⟨ran ∼ the street⟩ ⟨standing ∼ the street⟩ **2** : on at an angle ⟨slapped him ∼ the face⟩; *esp* : on so as to cross a log ⟨∼ the road⟩

**across-the-board** *adj* **1** : placed in combination to win, place, or show ⟨an ∼ bet⟩ **2** : including all classes or categories ⟨an ∼ wage increase⟩

**acros-tic** \ə-'krȯs-tik\ *n* **1** : a composition usu. in verse in which the initial or final letters of the lines taken in order form a word or phrase **2** : a series of words of equal length arranged to read the same horizontally or vertically — **acrostic** *adj* — **acros-ti-cal-ly** \-ti-k(ə-)lē\ *adv*

**acryl-ic** \ə-'kril-ik\ *n* **1** : ACRYLIC RESIN **2** : a paint in which the vehicle is acrylic resin

**acrylic resin** *n* : a glassy thermoplastic used for cast and molded parts or as coatings and adhesives

¹**act** \'akt\ *n* **1** : a thing done : DEED **2** : STATUTE, DECREE **3** : a main division of a play; *also* : an item on a variety program **4** : an instance of insincere behavior : PRETENSE

²**act** *vb* **1** : to perform by action esp. on the stage; *also* : FEIGN, SIMULATE, PRETEND **2** : to conduct oneself : BEHAVE **3** : to perform a specified function **4** : produce an effect

³**act** *abbr* **1** active **2** actual

**ACT** *abbr* Australian Capital Territory

**actg** *abbr* acting

**ACTH** \ˌā-ˌsē-(ˌ)tē-'āch\ *n* : a protein hormone of the pituitary gland that stimulates the adrenal cortex

**act-ing** \'ak-tiŋ\ *adj* : doing duty temporarily or for another ⟨∼ president⟩

**ac-tin-ism** \'ak-tə-ˌniz-əm\ *n* : the property of radiant energy (as light) whereby chemical changes are produced — **ac-tin-ic** \ak-'tin-ik\ *adj* — **ac-tin-i-cal-ly** \-i-k(ə-)lē\ *adv*

**ac-tin-i-um** \ak-'tin-ē-əm\ *n* : a radioactive metallic chemical element

**ac-tion** \'ak-shən\ *n* **1** : a legal proceeding **2** : the manner or method of performing **3** : ACTIVITY **4** : ACT **5** *pl* : CONDUCT **6** : COMBAT, BATTLE **7** : the events of a literary plot **8** : an operating mechanism ⟨the ∼ of a gun⟩; *also* : the way it operates ⟨stiff ∼⟩

**ac-tion-able** \'ak-sh(ə-)nə-bəl\ *adj* : affording ground for an action or suit at law

**action painting** *n* : abstract expressionism marked esp. by the use of spontaneous techniques (as dribbling, splattering, or smearing)

**ac-ti-vate** \'ak-tə-ˌvāt\ *vb* **-vat-ed; -vat-ing** **1** : to spur into action; *also* : to make active, reactive, or radioactive **2 :** to treat (as carbon) so as to improve adsorptive properties **3 :** to aerate (sewage) to favor the growth of organisms that cause decomposition **4 :** to set up (a military unit) formally; *also* **:** to call to active duty — **ac·ti·va·tion** \,ak-tə-'vā-shən\ *n*

**ac·tive** \'ak-tiv\ *adj* **1 :** causing action or change **2 :** asserting that the grammatical subject performs the action represented by the verb (~ voice) **3 :** BRISK, LIVELY **4 :** presently in operation or use **5 :** tending to progress or to cause degeneration (~ tuberculosis) — **active** *n* — **ac·tive·ly** *adv*

**ac·tiv·ism** \'ak-ti-,viz-əm\ *n* **:** a doctrine or practice that emphasizes vigorous action for political ends — **ac·tiv·ist** \-vəst\ *n or adj*

**ac·tiv·i·ty** \ak-'tiv-ət-ē\ *n, pl* **-ties 1 :** the quality or state of being active **2 :** an occupation in which one is engaged

**ac·tor** \'ak-tər\ *n* **:** one that acts in a play or motion picture — **ac·tress** \-trəs\ *n*

**ac·tu·al** \'ak-ch(ə-w)əl\ *adj* **:** really existing **:** REAL — **ac·tu·al·i·ty** \,ak-chə-'wal-ət-ē\ *n* — **ac·tu·al·iza·tion** \,ak-ch(ə-w)ə-lə-'zā-shən\ *n* — **ac·tu·al·ize** \'ak-ch(ə-w)ə-,līz\ *vb* — **ac·tu·al·ly** \'ak-ch(ə-w)ə-lē\ *adv*

**ac·tu·ary** \'ak-chə-,wer-ē\ *n, pl* **-ar·ies :** one who calculates insurance risks and premiums — **ac·tu·ar·i·al** \,ak-chə-'wer-ē-əl\ *adj*

**ac·tu·ate** \'ak-chə-,wāt\ *vb* **-at·ed; -at·ing 1 :** to put into action **2 :** to move to action — **ac·tu·a·tor** \-,wāt-ər\ *n*

**act up** *vb* **1 :** MISBEHAVE **2 :** to function improperly

**acu·ity** \ə-'kyü-ət-ē\ *n, pl* **-ities :** keenness of perception

**acu·men** \ə-'kyü-mən\ *n* **:** mental keenness and penetration **syn** discernment, insight

**acu·punc·ture** \'ak-yü-,pəŋk-chər\ *n* **:** an orig. Chinese practice of puncturing the body (as with needles) to cure disease or relieve pain — **acu·punc·tur·ist** \,ak-yü-'pəŋk-chə-rəst\ *n*

**acute** \ə-'kyüt\ *adj* **acut·er; acut·est** [L *acutus,* pp. of *acuere* to sharpen, fr. *acus* needle] **1 :** SHARP, POINTED **2 :** containing less than 90 degrees (~ angle) **3 :** sharply perceptive; *esp* **:** mentally keen **4 :** SEVERE (~ distress); *also* **:** rising rapidly to a peak and then subsiding (~ inflammation) **5 :** of, marked by, or being an accent mark having the form ´ — **acute·ly** *adv* — **acute·ness** *n*

**ad** \'ad\ *n* **:** ADVERTISEMENT

**AD** *abbr* **1** after date **2** [L *anno Domini*] in the year of our Lord

**ad·age** \'ad-ij\ *n* **:** an old familiar saying **:** PROVERB, MAXIM

**¹ada·gio** \ə-'däj-(ē-,)ō, -'däzh-\ *adv or adj* **:** in slow time — used as a direction in music

**²adagio** *n, pl* **-gios 1 :** an adagio movement **2 :** a ballet duet or trio displaying feats of lifting and balancing

**¹ad·a·mant** \'ad-ə-mənt, -,mant\ *n* [ME, fr. OF, fr. L *adamant-, adamas* hardest metal, diamond, fr. Gk] **:** a stone believed to be impenetrably hard — **ad·a·man·tine** \,ad-ə-'man-,tēn, -,tīn\ *adj*

**²adamant** *adj* **:** INFLEXIBLE, UNYIELDING — **ad·a·mant·ly** *adv*

**Ad·am's apple** \,ad-əmz-\ *n* **:** the projection in front of the neck formed by the largest cartilage of the larynx

**adapt** \ə-'dapt\ *vb* **:** to make suitable or fit (as for a new use or for different conditions) **syn** adjust, accommodate — **adapt·abil·i·ty** \ə-,dap-tə-'bil-ət-ē\ *n* — **adapt·able** *adj* — **ad·ap·ta·tion** \,ad-,ap-'tā-shən, -əp-\ *n* — **adap·tive** \ə-'dap-tiv\ *adj*

**adapt·er** *also* **adap·tor** \ə-'dap-tər\ *n* **1 :** one that adapts **2 :** a device for connecting two dissimilar parts of an apparatus **3 :** an attachment for adapting apparatus for uses not orig. intended

**add** \'ad\ *vb* **1 :** to join to something else so as to increase in number or amount **2 :** to combine (numbers) into one sum

**ad·dend** \'ad-,end\ *n* **:** a number to be added to another

**ad·den·dum** \ə-'den-dəm\ *n, pl* **-da** \-də\ **:** something added; *esp* **:** a supplement to a book

**¹ad·der** \'ad-ər\ *n* **1 :** a poisonous European viper or a related snake **2 :** any of various harmless No. American snakes (as the hognose snake)

**²add·er** \'ad-ər\ *n* **:** one that adds; *esp* **:** a device that performs addition

**¹ad·dict** \ə-'dikt\ *vb* **1 :** to devote or surrender (oneself) to something habitually or excessively **2 :** to cause (a person) to become physiologically dependent upon a drug — **ad·dic·tive** \-'dik-tiv\ *adj*

**²ad·dict** \'ad-(,)ikt\ *n* **:** one who is addicted (as to a drug)

**ad·dic·tion** \ə-'dik-shən\ *n* **:** the quality or state of being addicted; *esp* **:** compulsive need for habit-forming drugs

**ad·di·tion** \ə-'dish-ən\ *n* **1 :** the act or process of adding; *also* **:** something added **2 :** the adding of numbers to obtain their sum **syn** accretion, increment, accession

**ad·di·tion·al** \ə-'dish-(ə-)nəl\ *adj* **:** coming by way of addition **:** ADDED, EXTRA — **ad·di·tion·al·ly** \-ē\ *adv*

**¹ad·di·tive** \'ad-ət-iv\ *adj* **1 :** of, relating to, or characterized by addition **2 :** produced by addition — **ad·di·tiv·i·ty** \,ad-ə-'tiv-ət-ē\ *n*

**²additive** *n* **:** a substance added to another in small quantities to effect a desired change in properties (food ~s)

**ad·dle** \'ad-ᵊl\ *vb* **ad·dled; ad·dling** \'ad-(ə-)liŋ\ **1 :** to throw into confusion **:** MUDDLE **2 :** to become rotten (addled eggs)

**addn** *abbr* addition

**addnl** *abbr* additional

**¹ad·dress** \ə-'dres\ *vb* **1 :** to direct the attention of (oneself) **2 :** to direct one's remarks to **:** deliver an address to

**3 :** to mark directions for delivery on

²**ad·dress** \ə-'dres, 'ad-,res\ n **1 :** skillful management **2 :** a formal speech **:** LECTURE **3 :** the place where a person or organization may be communicated with **4 :** the directions for delivery placed on mail

**ad·dress·ee** \,ad-,res-'ē, ə-,dres-'ē\ n **:** one to whom something is addressed

**ad·duce** \ə-'d(y)üs\ vb **ad·duced; ad·duc·ing :** to offer as argument, reason, or proof **syn** advance, allege, cite

-**ade** \'ād\ n suffix **1 :** act **:** action ⟨block*ade*⟩ **2 :** product; esp **:** sweet drink ⟨lime*ade*⟩

**ad·e·nine** \'ad-²n-,ēn\ n **:** a purine base that codes hereditary information in the genetic code in DNA and RNA

**ad·e·noid** \'ad-(ᵊ-),nòid\ n **:** an enlarged mass of tissue near the opening of the nose into the throat — usu. used in pl. — **ad·e·noi·dal** \,ad-(ᵊ-)'nòid-əl\ adj

**aden·o·sine tri·phos·phate** \ə-'den-ə-,sēn-trī-'fäs-,fāt\ n **:** ATP

¹**ad·ept** \'ad-,ept\ n **:** EXPERT

²**adept** \ə-'dept\ adj **:** highly skilled **:** EXPERT — **adept·ly** adv — **adept·ness** n

**ad·e·quate** \'ad-i-kwət\ adj **:** equal to or sufficient for a specific requirement — **ad·e·qua·cy** \-kwə-sē\ n — **ad·e·quate·ly** adv

**ad·here** \ad-'hiər, əd-\ vb **ad·hered; ad·her·ing 1 :** to give support **:** maintain loyalty **2 :** to stick fast **:** CLING — **ad·her·ence** \-'hir-əns\ n — **ad·her·ent** \-ənt\ adj or n

**ad·he·sion** \ad-'hē-zhən, əd-\ n **1 :** the act or state of adhering **2 :** bodily tissues abnormally grown together after inflammation **3 :** the molecular attraction between the surfaces of bodies in contact

¹**ad·he·sive** \-'hē-siv, -ziv\ adj **1 :** tending to adhere **:** STICKY **2 :** prepared for adhering

²**adhesive** n **:** an adhesive substance

**adhesive tape** n **:** tape coated on one side with an adhesive mixture; esp **:** one used for covering wounds

¹**ad hoc** \'ad-'häk, -'hōk\ adv [L, for this] **:** for the case at hand apart from other applications

²**ad hoc** adj **:** concerned with a particular purpose ⟨an ad hoc committee⟩

**adi·a·bat·ic** \,ad-ē-ə-'bat-ik\ adj **:** occurring without loss or gain of heat — **adi·a·bat·i·cal·ly** \-i-k(ə-)lē\ adv

**adieu** \ə-'d(y)ü\ n, pl **adieus** or **adieux** \ə-'d(y)üz\ **:** FAREWELL — often used interjectionally

**ad in·fi·ni·tum** \,ad-,in-fə-'nīt-əm\ adv or adj **:** without end or limit

**ad in·ter·im** \ad-'in-tə-rəm, -,rim\ **:** for the intervening time — **ad interim** adj

**adi·os** \,ad-ē-'ōs, ,äd-\ interj — used to express farewell

**ad·i·pose** \'ad-ə-,pōs\ adj **:** of or relating to animal fat **:** FATTY

**adj** abbr **1** adjective **2** adjutant

**ad·ja·cent** \ə-'jās-ᵊnt\ adj **:** situated near or next **syn** adjoining, contiguous, abutting, juxtaposed

**ad·jec·tive** \'aj-ik-tiv\ n **:** a word that typically serves as a modifier of a noun — **ad·jec·ti·val** \,aj-ik-'tī-vəl\ adj — **ad·jec·ti·val·ly** \-ē\ adv

**ad·join** \ə-'jòin\ vb **:** to be situated next to

**ad·join·ing** adj **:** touching or bounding at a point or line

**ad·journ** \ə-'jərn\ vb **1 :** to suspend indefinitely or until a stated time **2 :** to transfer to another place — **ad·journ·ment** n

**ad·judge** \ə-'jəj\ vb **ad·judged; ad·judg·ing 1 :** JUDGE, ADJUDICATE **2 :** to hold or pronounce to be **:** DEEM **3 :** to award by judicial decision

**ad·ju·di·cate** \ə-'jüd-i-,kāt\ vb -**cat·ed; -cat·ing :** to settle judicially — **ad·ju·di·ca·tion** \ə-,jüd-i-'kā-shən\ n

**ad·junct** \'aj-,əŋkt\ n **:** something joined or added to another but not essentially a part of it **syn** appendage, appurtenance, accessory

**ad·jure** \ə-'jùr\ vb **ad·jured; ad·jur·ing :** to command solemnly **:** entreat earnestly **syn** beg, beseech, implore — **ad·ju·ra·tion** \,aj-ə-'rā-shən\ n

**ad·just** \ə-'jəst\ vb **1 :** to bring to agreement **:** SETTLE **2 :** to cause to conform **:** ADAPT, FIT **3 :** REGULATE ⟨∼ a watch⟩ — **ad·just·able** adj — **ad·just·er** or **ad·jus·tor** \ə-'jəs-tər\ n — **ad·just·ment** \ə-'jəs(t)-mənt\ n

**ad·ju·tant** \'aj-ət-ənt\ n **:** one who assists; esp **:** an officer who assists a commanding officer by handling correspondence and keeping records

¹**ad·ju·vant** \'aj-ə-vənt\ adj **:** serving to aid or contribute **:** AUXILIARY

²**adjuvant** n **:** something that enhances the effectiveness of medical treatment

¹**ad-lib** \'ad-'lib\ adj **:** spoken, composed, or performed without preparation

²**ad-lib** vb **ad-libbed; ad-lib·bing :** IMPROVISE — **ad-lib** n

**ad lib** \'ad-'lib\ adv [NL ad libitum] **1 :** at one's pleasure **2 :** without limit

**ad li·bi·tum** \ad-'lib-ət-əm\ adj [NL, in accordance with desire] **:** omissible according to a performer's wishes — used as a direction in music

**ad loc** abbr [L ad locum] to or at the place

**adm** abbr administration; administrative

**ADM** abbr admiral

**ad·man** \'ad-,man\ n **:** one who writes, solicits, or places advertisements

**admin** abbr administration

**ad·min·is·ter** \ad-'min-ə-stər\ vb **ad·min·is·tered; ad·min·is·ter·ing** \-st(ə-)riŋ\ **1 :** MANAGE, SUPERINTEND **2 :** to mete out **:** DISPENSE **3 :** to give ritually or remedially ⟨∼ quinine for malaria⟩ **4 :** to perform the office of administrator — **ad·min·is·tra·ble** \-strə-bəl\ adj — **ad·min·is·trant** \-strənt\ n

**ad·min·is·tra·tion** \əd-ˌmin-ə-'strā-shən, (ˌ)ad-\ *n* **1** : the act or process of administering **2** : MANAGEMENT **3** : the body of persons directing the government of a country **4** : the term of office of an administrative officer or body — **ad·min·is·tra·tive** \əd-'min-ə-ˌstrāt-iv\ *adj* — **ad·min·is·tra·tive·ly** *adv*

**ad·min·is·tra·tor** \əd-'min-ə-ˌstrāt-ər\ *n* : one that administers; *esp* : one who settles an intestate estate

**ad·mi·ra·ble** \'ad-m(ə-)rə-bəl\ *adj* : worthy of admiration : EXCELLENT — **ad·mi·ra·bly** \-blē\ *adv*

**ad·mi·ral** \'ad-m(ə-)rəl\ *n* [ME, fr. MF *amiral* admiral & ML *admiralis* emir, *admirallus* admiral, fr. Ar *amīr-al-* commander of the (as in *amīr-al-baḥr* commander of the sea)] : a commissioned officer in the navy ranking next below a fleet admiral

**ad·mi·ral·ty** \'ad-m(ə-)rəl-tē\ *adj* : relating to or having jurisdiction over maritime questions (~ law) (~ court)

**Admiralty** *n* : a former British government department having authority over naval affairs

**ad·mire** \əd-'mī(ə)r\ *vb* **ad·mired**; **ad·mir·ing** [MF *admirer*, fr. L *admirari*, fr. *ad-* to + *mirari* to wonder] : to regard with high esteem — **ad·mi·ra·tion** \ˌad-mə-'rā-shən\ *n* — **ad·mir·er** *n* — **ad·mir·ing·ly** \-'mī-riŋ-lē\ *adv*

**ad·mis·si·ble** \əd-'mis-ə-bəl\ *adj* : that can be or is worthy to be admitted or allowed : ALLOWABLE (~ evidence) — **ad·mis·si·bil·i·ty** \-ˌmis-ə-'bil-ət-ē\ *n* — **ad·mis·si·bly** \-'mis-ə-blē\ *adv*

**ad·mis·sion** \əd-'mish-ən\ *n* **1** : the granting of an argument **2** : the acknowledgment of a fact **3** : the act of admitting **4** : the privilege of being admitted **5** : a fee paid for admission

**ad·mit** \əd-'mit\ *vb* **ad·mit·ted**; **ad·mit·ting 1** : to allow to enter **2** : PERMIT, ALLOW **3** : to recognize as genuine or valid — **ad·mit·ted·ly** *adv*

**ad·mit·tance** \əd-'mit-ᵊns\ *n* : permission to enter

**ad·mix** \ad-'miks\ *vb* : MINGLE, MIX

**ad·mix·ture** \ad-'miks-chər\ *n* **1** : MIXTURE **2** : something added in mixing

**ad·mon·ish** \ad-'män-ish\ *vb* : to warn gently : reprove with a warning **syn** chide, reproach, rebuke, reprimand — **ad·mo·ni·tion** \ˌad-mə-'nish-ən\ *n* — **ad·mon·i·to·ry** \ad-'män-ə-ˌtōr-ē\ *adj*

**ad nau·se·am** \ad-'nȯ-zē-əm\ *adv* : to a sickening degree

**ado** \ə-'dü\ *n* **1** : bustling excitement : FUSS **2** : TROUBLE

**ado·be** \ə-'dō-bē\ *n* [Sp, fr. Ar *aṭ-ṭūb* the brick, fr. Coptic *tōbe* brick] **1** : sun-dried brick; *also* : clay for making such bricks **2** : a structure made of adobe bricks — **adobe** *adj*

**ad·o·les·cence** \ˌad-ᵊl-'es-ᵊns\ *n* : the process or period of growth between childhood and maturity — **ad·o·les·cent** \-ᵊnt\ *adj or n*

**adopt** \ə-'däpt\ *vb* **1** : to take (a child of other parents) as one's own child **2** : to take up and practice as one's own **3** : to accept formally and put into effect — **adop·tion** \ə-'däp-shən\ *n*

**adop·tive** \ə-'däp-tiv\ *adj* : made or acquired by adoption (~ father) — **adop·tive·ly** *adv*

**ador·able** \ə-'dōr-ə-bəl\ *adj* **1** : worthy of adoration **2** : extremely charming - **ador·ably** \-blē\ *adv*

**adore** \ə-'dōr\ *vb* **adored**; **ador·ing** [MF *adorer*, fr. L *adorare*, fr. *ad-* to + *orare* to speak, pray] **1** : WORSHIP **2** : to regard with reverent admiration **3** : to be extremely fond of — **ad·o·ra·tion** \ˌad-ə-'rā-shən\ *n*

**adorn** \ə-'dȯrn\ *vb* : to decorate with ornaments - **adorn·ment** *n*

**ad·re·nal** \ə-'drēn-ᵊl\ *adj* : of, relating to, or being a pair of endocrine organs **(adrenal glands)** located near the kidneys that produce several hormones and esp. epinephrine

**adren·a·line** \ə-'dren-ᵊl-ən\ *n* : EPINEPHRINE

**adrift** \ə-'drift\ *adv or adj* **1** : afloat without motive power or moorings **2** : without guidance or purpose

**adroit** \ə-'drȯit\ *adj* **1** : dexterous with one's hands **2** : SHREWD, RESOURCEFUL **syn** deft, clever, cunning, ingenious - **adroit·ly** *adv* - **adroit·ness** *n*

**ad·sorb** \ad-'sȯrb, -'zȯrb\ *vb* : to take up (as molecules of gases) and hold on the surface of a solid or liquid — **ad·sorp·tion** \-'sȯrp-shən, -'zȯrp-\ *n* — **ad·sorp·tive** \-'sȯrp-tiv, -'zȯrp-\ *adj*

**ad·sor·bate** \ad-'sȯr-bət, -'zȯr-, -ˌbāt\ *n* : an adsorbed substance

**ad·sor·bent** \-bənt\ *adj* : having the capacity to adsorb — **adsorbent** *n*

**ad·u·late** \'aj-ə-ˌlāt\ *vb* **-lat·ed**; **-lat·ing** : to flatter or admire excessively — **ad·u·la·tion** \ˌaj-ə-'lā-shən\ *n*

**¹adult** \ə-'dəlt, 'ad-ˌəlt\ *adj* [L *adultus*, pp. of *adolescere* to grow up, fr. *ad-* to + *-olescere* (fr. *alescere* to grow)] : fully developed and mature — **adult·hood** *n*

**²adult** *n* : one that is adult; *esp* : a human being after an age (as 18) specified by law

**adul·ter·ant** \ə-'dəl-tə-rənt\ *n* : something used to adulterate another

**adul·ter·ate** \ə-'dəl-tə-ˌrāt\ *vb* **-at·ed**; **-at·ing** [L *adulterare*, fr. *ad-* to + *alter* other] : to make impure by mixing in a foreign or inferior substance — **adul·ter·a·tion** \-ˌdəl-tə-'rā-shən\ *n* — **adul·ter·a·tor** \-ˌrāt-ər\ *n*

**adul·tery** \ə-'dəl-t(ə-)rē\ *n, pl* **-ter·ies** : sexual unfaithfulness of a married person — **adul·ter·er** \-tər-ər\ *n* — **adul·ter·ess** \-t(ə-)rəs\ *n* — **adul·ter·ous** \-t(ə-)rəs\ *adj*

**ad·um·brate** \'ad-əm-ˌbrāt\ *vb* **-brat·ed**; **-brat·ing 1** : to foreshadow vaguely : INTIMATE **2** : to suggest or disclose partially **3** : SHADE, OBSCURE — **ad·um·bra·tion** \ˌad-əm-'brā-shən\ *n*

**adv** *abbr* **1** adverb **2** advertisement
**ad val** *abbr* ad valorem
**ad va·lor·em** \,ad-və-'lōr-əm\ *adj*
: imposed at a percentage of the value
⟨an *ad valorem* tax⟩

¹**ad·vance** \əd-'vans\ *vb* **ad·vanced;
ad·vanc·ing 1** : to bring or move
forward **2** : to assist the progress of
**3** : to promote in rank **4** : to make
earlier in time **5** : PROPOSE **6** : to
raise in rate : INCREASE **7** : LEND —
**ad·vance·ment** *n*

²**advance** *n* **1** : a forward movement
**2** : IMPROVEMENT **3** : a rise esp. in
price or value **4** : OFFER — **in ad·
vance** : BEFOREHAND

³**advance** *adj* : made, sent, or furnished
ahead of time

**ad·van·tage** \əd-'vant-ij\ *n* **1** : superiority of position **2** : BENEFIT, GAIN
**3** : the first point won in tennis after
deuce — **ad·van·ta·geous** \,ad-
,van-'tā-jəs, -vən-\ *adj* — **ad·van·ta·
geous·ly** *adv*

**ad·vent** \'ad-,vent\ *n* **1** *cap* : a peni-
tential period beginning five Sundays
before Christmas **2** : ARRIVAL; *esp,
cap* : the coming of Christ

**ad·ven·ti·tious** \,ad-vən-'tish-əs\ *adj*
**1** : ACCIDENTAL, INCIDENTAL **2** : arising or occurring sporadically or in
other than the usual location ⟨~ buds⟩
— **ad·ven·ti·tious·ly** *adv* — **ad·
ven·ti·tious·ness** *n*

¹**ad·ven·ture** \əd-'ven-chər\ *n* **1** : a
risky undertaking **2** : a remarkable
and exciting experience **3** : a business
venture — **ad·ven·tur·ous** \-'vench-
(ə-)rəs\ *adj*

²**adventure** *vb* **-ven·tured; -ven·tur·
ing** \-'vench-(ə-)riŋ\ : RISK, HAZARD

**ad·ven·tur·er** \əd-'vench-(ə-)rər\ *n*
**1** : a person who engages in new and
risky undertakings **2** : a person who
follows a military career for adventure
or profit **3** : a person who tries to gain
wealth by questionable means — **ad·
ven·tur·ess** \-'vench-(ə-)rəs\ *n*

**ad·ven·ture·some** \əd-'ven-chər-
səm\ *adj* : inclined to take risks

**ad·verb** \'ad-,vərb\ *n* : a word that
typically serves as a modifier of a verb,
an adjective, or another adverb — **ad·
ver·bi·al** \ad-'vər-bē-əl\ *adj* — **ad·
ver·bi·al·ly** \-ē\ *adv*

¹**ad·ver·sary** \'ad-və(r)-,ser-ē\ *n, pl
-sar·ies* : FOE

²**adversary** *adj* : involving antagonistic
parties or interests

**ad·ver·sa·tive** \əd-'vər-sət-iv\ *adj*
: expressing opposition or adverse circumstance — **ad·ver·sa·tive·ly** *adv*

**ad·verse** \'ad-'vərs, 'ad-,vərs\ *adj*
**1** : acting against or in a contrary direction **2** : UNFAVORABLE — **ad·verse·ly**
*adv*

**ad·ver·si·ty** \ad-'vər-sət-ē\ *n, pl* **-ties**
: hard times : MISFORTUNE

**ad·vert** \ad-'vərt\ *vb* : REFER

**ad·ver·tise** \'ad-vər-,tīz\ *vb* **-tised;
-tis·ing 1** : INFORM, NOTIFY **2** : to
call public attention to esp. in order to
sell — **ad·ver·tis·er** *n*

**ad·ver·tise·ment** \,ad-vər-'tīz-mənt;

əd-'vərt-əz-mənt\ *n* **1** : the act of advertising **2** : a public notice intended
to advertise something

**ad·ver·tis·ing** \'ad-vər-,tī-ziŋ\ *n* : the
business of preparing advertisements

**ad·vice** \əd-'vīs\ *n* **1** : recommendation with regard to a course of action
: COUNSEL **2** : INFORMATION, REPORT

**ad·vis·able** \əd-'vī-zə-bəl\ *adj* : proper to be done : EXPEDIENT ¬ **ad·vis·
abil·i·ty** \-,vī-zə-'bil-ət-ē\ *n*

**ad·vise** \əd-'vīz\ *vb* **ad·vised; ad·
vis·ing 1** : to give advice to : COUN-
SEL **2** : INFORM, NOTIFY **3** : CONSULT,
CONFER — **ad·vis·er** *or* **ad·vi·sor**
\-'vī-zər\ *n*

**ad·vised** \əd-'vīzd\ *adj* : thought out
: CONSIDERED ⟨well-*advised*⟩ — **ad·vis·
ed·ly** \-'vī-zəd-lē\ *adv*

**ad·vise·ment** \əd-'vīz-mənt\ *n* : careful consideration

**ad·vi·so·ry** \əd-'vīz-(ə-)rē\ *adj* **1**
: having or exercising power to advise
**2** : containing advice

¹**ad·vo·cate** \'ad-və-kət, -,kāt\ *n* **1**
: one who pleads another's cause **2**
: one who argues or pleads for a cause
or proposal — **ad·vo·ca·cy** \-və-
kə-sē\ *n*

²**ad·vo·cate** \-,kāt\ *vb* **-cat·ed; -cat·
ing** : to plead in favor of — **ad·vo·ca·
tion** \,ad-və-'kā-shən\ *n*

**advt** *abbr* advertisement

**adz** *or* **adze** \'adz\ *n* : a cutting tool
that has a curved blade set at right
angles to the handle and is used in
shaping wood

**AEC** *abbr* Atomic Energy Commission

**AEF** *abbr* American Expeditionary Force

**ae·gis** \'ē-jəs\ *n* [L, fr. Gk *aigis* goat-
skin] **1** : SHIELD, PROTECTION **2** : PA-
TRONAGE, SPONSORSHIP

**ae·o·li·an harp** \ē-,ō-lē-ən-\ *n* : a box
having stretched strings that produce
varying musical sounds when the wind
blows on them

**ae·on** \'ē-ən, 'ē-,än\ *n* : an indefinitely
long time : AGE

**aeq** *abbr* [L *aequales*] equal

**aer·ate** \'a-(ə)r-,āt\ *vb* **aer·at·ed;
aer·at·ing 1** : to supply (blood) with
oxygen by respiration **2** : to supply or
impregnate with air **3** : to combine or
charge with gas — **aer·a·tion** \a-(ə)-
'ā-shən\ *n* — **aer·a·tor** \'a-(ə)r-,āt-ər\
*n*

¹**ae·ri·al** \'ar-ē-əl, ā-'ir-ē-əl\ *adj* **1** : inhabiting, occurring in, or done in the
air **2** : AIRY **3** : of or relating to aircraft

²**aer·i·al** \'ar-ē-əl\ *n* : ANTENNA 2

**ae·ri·al·ist** \'ar-ē-ə-ləst, ā-'ir-\ *n* : a
performer of feats above the ground
esp. on a flying trapeze

**ae·rie** \'a(ə)r-ē, 'i(ə)r-ē\ *n* : a highly
placed nest (as of an eagle)

**aero** \'a(ə)r-ō\ *adj* **1** : of or relating to
aircraft **2** : designed for aerial use

**aer·o·bat·ics** \,ar-ə-'bat-iks\ *n sing
or pl* : performance of stunts in an airplane or glider

**aer·o·bic** \a,(-ə)r-'rō-bik\ *adj* : living
or active only in the presence of oxygen
⟨~ bacteria⟩ — **aer·obe** \'a-(ə)r-,ōb\

**aer·o·bi·cal·ly** \-bi-k(ə-)lē\ adv
**aero·drome** \'ar-ə-,drōm\ n, chiefly Brit : AIRFIELD, AIRPORT
**aero·dy·nam·ics** \,ar-ō-dī-'nam-iks\ n : a science that deals with the motion of gaseous fluids and with the forces acting on bodies in such fluids — **aero·dy·nam·ic** \-ik\ or **aero·dy·nam·i·cal** \-i-kəl\ adj — **aero·dy·nam·i·cal·ly** \-i-k(ə-)lē\ adv
**aer·ol·o·gy** \,a(-ə)r-'äl-ə-jē\ n 1 : METEOROLOGY 2 : a branch of meteorology that deals esp. with the air — **aer·o·log·i·cal** \,ar-ə-'läj-i-kəl\ adj — **aer·ol·o·gist** \,a(-ə)r-'äl-ə-jəst\ n
**aero·naut** \'ar-ə-,not\ n : one who operates or travels in an airship
**aero·nau·tics** \,ar-ə-'not-iks\ n : a science dealing with the operation of aircraft or with their design and manufacture — **aero·nau·ti·cal** \-i-kəl\ or **aero·nau·tic** \-ik\ adj — **aero·nau·ti·cal·ly** \-i-k(ə-)lē\ adv
**aero·pause** \'ar-ō-,poz\ n : the level at which the atmosphere becomes ineffective for human and aircraft functions
**aero·plane** \'ar-ə-,plān\ chiefly Brit var of AIRPLANE
**aero·sol** \'ar-ə-,säl, -,sol\ n 1 : a suspension of fine solid or liquid particles in a gas 2 : a substance (as an insecticide or cosmetic) dispensed from a pressurized container as an aerosol
**aero·space** \'ar-ō-,spās\ n : the earth's atmosphere and the space beyond — **aerospace** adj
**aery** \'a(ə)r-ē\ adj **aer·i·er; -est** : having an aerial quality : ETHEREAL
**aes·thete** \'es-,thēt\ n : a person having or affecting sensitivity to beauty esp. in art
**aes·thet·ic** \es-'thet-ik\ adj 1 : of or relating to aesthetics : ARTISTIC 2 : appreciative of the beautiful — **aes·thet·i·cal·ly** \-ik-(ə-)lē\ adv
**aes·thet·ics** \-'thet-iks\ n : a branch of philosophy dealing with beauty and the beautiful
**aes·ti·vate** \'es-tə-,vāt\ vb **-vat·ed; -vat·ing** : to pass the summer in a state of torpor
**aet** or **aetat** abbr [L aetatis] of age; aged
**AF** abbr 1 air force 2 audio frequency
¹**afar** \ə-'fär\ adv : from, at, or to a great distance
²**afar** n : a great distance
**AFB** abbr air force base
**AFC** abbr automatic frequency control
**af·fa·ble** \'af-ə-bəl\ adj : courteous and agreeable in conversation — **af·fa·bil·i·ty** \,af-ə-'bil-ət-ē\ n — **af·fa·bly** \'af-ə-blē\ adv
**af·fair** \ə-'faər\ n [ME affaire, fr. MF, fr. a faire to do] 1 : something that relates to or involves one : CONCERN 2 : a romantic or sexual attachment of limited duration
¹**af·fect** \ə-'fekt, a-\ vb 1 : to be fond of using or wearing 2 : SIMULATE, ASSUME, PRETEND
²**affect** vb : to produce an effect on : INFLUENCE, IMPRESS

**af·fec·ta·tion** \,af-,ek-'tā-shən\ n : an attitude or mode of behavior assumed by a person in an effort to impress others
**af·fect·ed** \ə-'fek-təd, a-\ adj 1 : pretending to some trait which is not natural 2 : artificially assumed to impress others — **af·fect·ed·ly** adv
**af·fect·ing** \ə-'fek-tiŋ, a-\ adj : arousing pity, sympathy, or sorrow ⟨an ~ story⟩ — **af·fect·ing·ly** adv
¹**af·fec·tion** \ə-'fek-shən\ n : tender attachment : LOVE — **af·fec·tion·ate** \-sh(ə-)nət\ adj — **af·fec·tion·ate·ly** adv
²**affection** n : DISEASE, DISORDER ⟨an ~ of the brain⟩
**af·fer·ent** \'af-ə-rənt, -,er-ənt\ adj : bearing or conducting inward toward a more central part ⟨~ nerves⟩
**af·fi·ance** \ə-'fī-əns\ vb **-anced; -anc·ing** : BETROTH, ENGAGE
**af·fi·da·vit** \,af-ə-'dā-vət\ n [ML, he has made an oath] : a sworn statement in writing
¹**af·fil·i·ate** \ə-'fil-ē-,āt\ vb **-at·ed; -at·ing** : to associate as a member or branch — **af·fil·i·a·tion** \-,fil-ē-'ā-shən\ n
²**af·fil·i·ate** \ə-'fil-ē-ət\ n : an affiliated person or organization
**af·fin·i·ty** \ə-'fin-ət-ē\ n, pl **-ties** 1 : KINSHIP, RELATIONSHIP 2 : attractive force : ATTRACTION, SYMPATHY
**af·firm** \ə-'fərm\ vb 1 : CONFIRM, RATIFY 2 : to assert positively syn aver, avow, avouch, declare, assert — **af·fir·ma·tion** \,af-ər-'mā-shən\ n
¹**af·fir·ma·tive** \ə-'fər-mət-iv\ adj : asserting that the fact is so : POSITIVE
²**affirmative** n 1 : an expression of affirmation or assent 2 : the side that upholds the proposition stated in a debate
¹**af·fix** \ə-'fiks\ vb : ATTACH, ADD
²**af·fix** \'af-,iks\ n : one or more sounds or letters attached to the beginning or end of a word and serving to produce a derivative word or an inflectional form
**af·fla·tus** \ə-'flāt-əs\ n : divine inspiration
**af·flict** \ə-'flikt\ vb : to cause pain and distress to syn try, torment, torture — **af·flic·tion** \-'flik-shən\ n
**af·flic·tive** \ə-'flik-tiv\ adj : causing affliction : DISTRESSING — **af·flic·tive·ly** adv
¹**af·flu·ence** \'af-,lü-ən(t)s; a-'flü-, ə-\ n : abundant supply; also : WEALTH, RICHES — **af·flu·ent** \-ənt\ adj
**af·ford** \ə-'fōrd\ vb 1 : to manage to bear or bear the cost of without serious harm or loss 2 : PROVIDE, FURNISH
**af·for·es·ta·tion** \a-,fōr-ə-'stā-shən\ n : the act or process of establishing forest cover
**af·fray** \ə-'frā\ n : FIGHT, FRAY
**af·fright** \ə-'frīt\ vb : FRIGHTEN, ALARM — **affright** n
**af·front** \ə-'frənt\ vb 1 : INSULT 2 : CONFRONT — **affront** n
**afft** abbr affidavit
**af·ghan** \'af-,gan, -gən\ n : a blanket or shawl of colored wool knitted or crocheted in sections

**Afghan hound** n **:** a tall slim swift hunting dog with a coat of silky thick hair and a long silky topknot

**af·ghani** \af-'gan-ē\ n — see MONEY table

**afi·cio·na·do** \ə-,fish(-ē)-ə-'näd-ō, -,fis-ē-\ n, pl **-dos :** DEVOTEE, FAN

**afield** \ə-'fēld\ adv or adj **1 :** to, in, or on the field **2 :** away from home **3 :** out of the way **:** ASTRAY

**afire** \ə-'fī(ə)r\ adj or adv **:** being on fire **:** BURNING

**aflame** \ə-'flām\ adj or adv **:** FLAMING

**AFL–CIO** abbr American Federation of Labor and Congress of Industrial Organizations

**afloat** \ə-'flōt\ adj or adv **1 :** being on board ship **2 :** FLOATING, ADRIFT **3 :** flooded with water

**aflut·ter** \ə-'flət-ər\ adj **1 :** FLUTTERING **2 :** nervously excited

**afoot** \ə-'fut\ adv or adj **1 :** on foot **2 :** in action **:** in progress

**afore·men·tioned** \ə-'fōr-'menchənd\ adj **:** mentioned previously

**afore·said** \-,sed\ adj **:** said or named before

**afore·thought** \-,thȯt\ adj **:** PREMEDITATED ⟨with malice ~⟩

**a for·ti·o·ri** \,ä-,fȯrt-ē-'ȯr-ē\ adv [NL, lit., from the stronger (argument)] **:** with even greater reason

**afoul of** \ə-'faúl-əv\ prep **1 :** in or into collision or entanglement with **2 :** in or into conflict with

**Afr** abbr Africa; African

**afraid** \ə-'frād, South also ə-'fre(ə)d\ adj **:** FRIGHTENED, FEARFUL

**A–frame** \'ā-,frām\ n **:** a building having triangular front and rear walls with the roof reaching to the ground

**afresh** \ə-'fresh\ adv **:** ANEW, AGAIN

**Af·ri·can** \'af-ri-kən\ n **1 :** a native or inhabitant of Africa **2 :** NEGRO — **African** adj

**African violet** n **:** a tropical African plant widely grown indoors for its velvety fleshy leaves and showy purple, pink, or white flowers

**Af·ri·kaans** \,af-ri-'käns\ n **:** a language developed from 17th century Dutch that is one of the official languages of the Republic of So. Africa

**¹Af·ro** \'af-rō\ adj **:** of or relating to African or Afro-American culture

**²Afro** n, pl **Afros :** an Afro hairstyle

**Af·ro–Amer·i·can** \,af-rō-ə-'mer-ə-kən\ adj **:** of or relating to Americans of African and esp. of Negroid descent — **Afro–American** n

**aft** \'aft\ adv **:** near, toward, or in the stern of a ship or the tail of an aircraft

**¹af·ter** \'af-tər\ adv **:** AFTERWARD, SUBSEQUENTLY

**²after** prep **1 :** behind in place **2 :** later than **3 :** intent on the seizure, mastery, or achievement of ⟨he's ~ your job⟩

**³after** conj **:** following the time when

**⁴after** adj **1 :** LATER **2 :** located toward the rear

**af·ter·birth** \'af-tər-,bərth\ n **:** structures and membranes expelled from the uterus after the birth of young

**af·ter·burn·er** \-,bər-nər\ n **1 :** an auxiliary burner attached to the exhaust pipe of a turbojet engine for injecting fuel into the hot exhaust gases to provide extra thrust **2 :** a device for removing unburned carbon compounds from exhaust

**af·ter·care** \-,keər\ n **:** the care, nursing, or treatment of a convalescent patient

**af·ter·deck** \-,dek\ n **:** the rear half of the deck of a ship

**af·ter·ef·fect** \'af-tə-rə-,fekt\ n **1 :** an effect that follows its cause after an interval **2 :** a secondary effect coming on after the first or immediate effect has subsided ⟨~s of a medicine⟩

**af·ter·glow** \'af-tər-,glō\ n **:** a glow remaining where a light has disappeared

**af·ter·im·age** \'af-tə-,rim-ij\ n **:** a usu. visual sensation continuing after the stimulus causing it has ended

**af·ter·life** \'af-tər-,līf\ n **:** an existence after death

**af·ter·math** \-,math\ n **1 :** a second-growth crop esp. of hay **2 :** CONSEQUENCES, EFFECTS **syn** sequel, result, outcome

**af·ter·noon** \,af-tər-'nün\ n **:** the time between noon and evening

**af·ter·shave** \'af-tər-,shāv\ n **:** a usu. scented lotion for use on the face after shaving

**af·ter·taste** \-,tāst\ n **:** a sensation (as of flavor) continuing after the stimulus causing it has ended

**af·ter·tax** \'af-tər-,taks\ adj **:** remaining after payment of taxes and esp. of income tax ⟨an ~ profit⟩

**af·ter·thought** \-,thȯt\ n **:** a later thought; also **:** something thought of later

**af·ter·ward** \'af-tə(r)-wərd\ or **af·ter·wards** \-wərdz\ adv **:** at a later time

**Ag** symbol [L argentum] silver

**AG** abbr **1** adjutant general **2** attorney general

**again** \ə-'gen, -'gin\ adv **1 :** once more **:** ANEW **2 :** on the other hand **3 :** FURTHER, MOREOVER **4 :** in addition

**against** \ə-'genst\ prep **1 :** directly opposite to **:** FACING **2 :** in opposition to **3 :** as defense from **4 :** so as to touch or strike ⟨threw him ~ the wall⟩; also **:** TOUCHING

**¹agape** \ə-'gāp, -'gap\ adj or adv **:** having the mouth open in wonder or surprise **:** GAPING

**²aga·pe** \ä-'gä-pā, 'äg-ə-,pā\ n **:** self-giving loyal concern that freely accepts another and seeks his good

**agar** \'äg-,är\ n **1 :** a gelatinous colloid extracted from a red alga and used esp. as a gelling and stabilizing agent in foods **2 :** a culture medium containing agar

**agar–agar** \,äg-,är-'äg-,är\ n **:** AGAR

**ag·ate** \'ag-ət\ n **1 :** a striped or clouded quartz **2 :** a child's marble of agate or of glass resembling agate

**aga·ve** \ə-'gäv-ē\ n **:** any of several spiny-leaved plants related to the amaryllis

**agcy** *abbr* agency

**¹age** \ˈāj\ *n* **1** : the length of time during which a being or thing has lived or existed **2** : the time of life at which some particular qualification is achieved; *esp* : MAJORITY **3** : the latter part of life **4** : the quality of being old **5** : a long time **6** : a period in history

**²age** *vb* **aged; ag·ing** *or* **age·ing 1** : to grow old or cause to grow old **2** : to become or cause to become mature or mellow

**-age** \ij\ *n suffix* **1** : aggregate : collection ⟨trackage⟩ **2 a** : action : process ⟨haulage⟩ **b** : cumulative result of ⟨breakage⟩ **c** : rate of ⟨dosage⟩ **3** : house or place of ⟨orphanage⟩ **4** : state : rank ⟨vassalage⟩ **5** : fee : charge ⟨postage⟩

**aged** \ˈā-jəd *for 1*; ˈājd *for 2*\ *adj* **1** : of advanced age **2** : having attained a specified age ⟨a man ~ forty years⟩

**age·less** \ˈāj-ləs\ *adj* **1** : not growing old or showing the effects of age **2** : TIMELESS, ETERNAL ⟨an ~ story⟩

**agen·cy** \ˈā-jən-sē\ *n, pl* **-cies 1** : one through which something is accomplished : INSTRUMENTALITY **2** : the office or function of an agent **3** : an establishment doing business for another **4** : an administrative division of a government **syn** means, medium

**agen·da** \ə-ˈjen-də\ *n* : a list of things to be done : PROGRAM

**agent** \ˈā-jənt\ *n* **1** : one that acts **2** : MEANS, INSTRUMENT **3** : a person acting or doing business for another **syn** attorney, deputy, proxy

**agent pro·vo·ca·teur** \ˈäzh-,äⁿ-prō-,väk-ə-ˈtər, ˈā-jənt-\ *n, pl* **agents provocateurs** \ˈäzh-,äⁿ-prō-,väk-ə-ˈtər, ˈā-jən(t)s-prō-\ : a person hired to infiltrate a group and incite its members to illegal action

**age of consent** : the age at which one is legally competent to give consent (as to marriage)

**age-old** \ˈāj-ˈōld\ *adj* : having existed for ages : ANCIENT

**ag·er·a·tum** \,aj-ə-ˈrāt-əm\ *n, pl* **-tums** : any of a genus of tropical American plants that are related to the daisies and have small showy heads of blue or white flowers

**ag·gior·na·men·to** \ə-,jȯr-nə-ˈmen-tō\ *n, pl* **-tos** : a bringing up to date

**¹ag·glom·er·ate** \ə-ˈgläm-ə-,rāt\ *vb* **-at·ed; -at·ing** [L *agglomerare* to heap up, join, fr. *ad-* to + *glomer-, glomus* ball] : to gather into a mass : CLUSTER — **ag·glom·er·a·tion** \-,gläm-ə-ˈrā-shən\ *n*

**²ag·glom·er·ate** \-rət\ *n* : rock composed of volcanic fragments

**ag·glu·ti·nate** \ə-ˈglüt-ᵊn-,āt\ *vb* **-nat·ed; -nat·ing 1** : to cause to adhere : gather into a group or mass **2** : to cause (as red blood cells or bacteria) to collect into clumps — **ag·glu·ti·na·tion** \-,glüt-ᵊn-ˈā-shən\ *n*

**ag·gran·dize** \ə-ˈgran-,dīz, ˈag-rən-\ *vb* **-dized; -diz·ing** : to make great or greater — **ag·gran·dize·ment** \ə-ˈgran-dəz-mənt, -,dīz-; ,ag-rən-ˈdīz-\ *n*

**ag·gra·vate** \ˈag-rə-,vāt\ *vb* **-vat·ed; -vat·ing 1** : to make more severe : INTENSIFY **2** : IRRITATE — **ag·gra·va·tion** \,ag-rə-ˈvā-shən\ *n*

**¹ag·gre·gate** \ˈag-ri-gət\ *adj* : formed by the gathering of units into one mass

**²ag·gre·gate** \-,gāt\ *vb* **-gat·ed; -gat·ing** : to collect into one mass

**³ag·gre·gate** \-gət\ *n* : a mass or body of units or parts somewhat loosely associated with one another; *also* : the whole amount

**ag·gre·ga·tion** \,ag-ri-ˈgā-shən\ *n* **1** : the collecting of units into a mass or whole **2** : a group, body, or mass composed of many distinct parts

**ag·gres·sion** \ə-ˈgresh-ən\ *n* **1** : an unprovoked attack **2** : the practice of making attacks **3** : hostile, injurious, or destructive behavior or outlook esp. when caused by frustration — **ag·gres·sor** \-ˈgres-ər\ *n*

**ag·gres·sive** \ə-ˈgres-iv\ *adj* **1** : tending toward or practicing aggression; *esp* : marked by combative readiness **2** : marked by driving energy or initiative : ENTERPRISING — **ag·gres·sive·ly** *adv* — **ag·gres·sive·ness** *n*

**ag·grieve** \ə-ˈgrēv\ *vb* **ag·grieved; ag·griev·ing 1** : to cause grief to **2** : to inflict injury on : WRONG

**aghast** \ə-ˈgast\ *adj* : struck with amazement or horror

**ag·ile** \aj-əl\ *adj* : able to move quickly and easily — **agil·i·ty** \ə-ˈjil-ət-ē\ *n*

**ag·i·tate** \ˈaj-ə-,tāt\ *vb* **-tat·ed; -tat·ing 1** : to move with an irregular rapid motion **2** : to stir up : EXCITE **3** : to discuss earnestly **4** : to attempt to arouse public feeling — **ag·i·ta·tion** \,aj-ə-ˈtā-shən\ *n* — **ag·i·ta·tor** \ˈaj-ə-,tāt-ər\ *n*

**ag·it·prop** \ˈaj-ət-,präp\ *n* : political propaganda promulgated esp. through the arts

**agleam** \ə-ˈglēm\ *adj* : GLEAMING

**aglit·ter** \ə-ˈglit-ər\ *adj* : GLITTERING

**aglow** \ə-ˈglō\ *adj* : GLOWING

**ag·nos·tic** \ag-ˈnäs-tik, əg-\ *adj* [Gk *agnōstos* unknown, unknowable, fr. *a-* un- + *gnōstos* known, fr. *gignōskein* to know] : of or relating to the belief that the existence of any ultimate reality (as God) is unknown and prob. unknowable — **agnostic** *n* — **ag·nos·ti·cism** \-ˈnäs-tə-,siz-əm\ *n*

**ago** \ə-ˈgō\ *adj or adv* : earlier than the present time

**agog** \ə-ˈgäg\ *adj* [MF *en gogues* in mirth] : full of excitement : EAGER

**¹a-go-go** \ä-ˈgō-,gō\ *n* **1** : DISCOTHEQUE **2** : a usu. small intimate nightclub for dancing to live music

**²a-go-go** *adj* **1** : of, relating to, or being an a-go-go ⟨~ dancers⟩ **2** : being in a whirl of motion or excitement **3** : being in the latest fashion : very up-to-date

**ag·o·nize** \ˈag-ə-,nīz\ *vb* **-nized; -niz·ing** : to suffer or cause to suffer agony — **ag·o·niz·ing·ly** *adv*

**ag·o·ny** \ˈag-ə-nē\ *n, pl* **-nies** [ME *agonie*, fr. L *agonia*, fr. Gk *agōnia* struggle, anguish, fr. *agōn* gathering, contest for a prize] **:** extreme pain of mind or body **syn** suffering, distress

**agony column** *n* **:** a newspaper column of personal advertisements relating esp. to missing relatives or friends

**ago·ra** \ˌäg-ə-ˈrä\ *n*, *pl* **ago·rot** \-ˈrōt\ — see *pound* at MONEY table

**ag·o·ra·pho·bia** \ˌag-ə-rə-ˈfō-bē-ə\ *n* **:** abnormal fear of being in open spaces — **ag·o·ra·pho·bic** \-ˈfō-bik, -ˈfäb-ik\ *adj*

**agr** *or* **agric** *abbr* agricultural; agriculture

**agrar·i·an** \ə-ˈgrer-ē-ən\ *adj* **1 :** of or relating to land or its ownership ⟨~ reforms⟩ **2 :** of or relating to farmers or farming interests — **agrarian** *n* — **agrar·i·an·ism** *n*

**agree** \ə-ˈgrē\ *vb* **agreed; agree·ing 1 :** ADMIT, CONCEDE **2 :** to settle by common consent **3 :** to express agreement or approval **4 :** to be in harmony **5 :** to be similar **:** CORRESPOND **6 :** to be fitting or healthful **:** SUIT

**agree·able** \ə-ˈgrē-ə-bəl\ *adj* **1 :** PLEASING, PLEASANT **2 :** ready to consent **3 :** SUITABLE — **agree·able·ness** *n* — **agree·ably** \-blē\ *adv*

**agree·ment** \ə-ˈgrē-mənt\ *n* **1 :** harmony of opinion or action **2 :** mutual understanding or arrangement; *also* **:** a document containing such an arrangement

**ag·ri·cul·ture** \ˈag-ri-ˌkəl-chər\ *n* **:** FARMING, HUSBANDRY — **ag·ri·cul·tur·al** \ˌag-ri-ˈkəlch-(ə-)rəl\ *adj* — **ag·ri·cul·tur·ist** \-rəst\ *or* **ag·ri·cul·tur·al·ist** \-(ə-)rə-ləst\ *n*

**agron·o·my** \ə-ˈgrän-ə-mē\ *n* **:** a branch of agriculture that deals with the raising of crops and the care of the soil — **ag·ro·nom·ic** \ˌag-rə-ˈnäm-ik\ *adj* — **agron·o·mist** \ə-ˈgrän-ə-məst\ *n*

**aground** \ə-ˈgraůnd\ *adv or adj* **:** on or onto the bottom or shore ⟨ran ~⟩

**agt** *abbr* agent

**ague** \ˈā-gyü\ *n* **:** a fever with recurrent chills and sweating; *esp* **:** MALARIA

**ahead** \ə-ˈhed\ *adv or adj* **1 :** in or toward the front **2 :** into or for the future ⟨plan ~⟩ **3 :** in or toward a more advantageous position

**ahead of** *prep* **1 :** in front or advance of **2 :** in excess of **:** ABOVE

**ahoy** \ə-ˈhȯi\ *interj* — used in hailing ⟨ship ~⟩

**¹aid** \ˈād\ *vb* **:** to provide with what is useful in achieving an end **:** ASSIST

**²aid** *n* **1 :** ASSISTANCE **2 :** ASSISTANT

**AID** *abbr* Agency for International Development

**aide** \ˈād\ *n* **:** a person who acts as an assistant; *esp* **:** a military officer assisting a superior

**aide-de-camp** \ˌād-di-ˈkamp, -ˈkäⁿ\ *n*, *pl* **aides-de-camp** \ˌādz-di-\ **:** AIDE

**aid·man** \ˈād-ˌman\ *n* **:** an army medical corpsman attached to a field unit

**ai·grette** \ā-ˈgret, ˈā-ˌgret\ *n* **:** a plume or decorative tuft for the head

**ail** \ˈāl\ *vb* **1 :** to be the matter with **:** TROUBLE **2 :** to be unwell

**ai·lan·thus** \ā-ˈlan-thəs\ *n* **:** any of a genus of Asiatic trees or shrubs with pinnate leaves and ill-scented greenish flowers

**ai·le·ron** \ˈā-lə-ˌrän\ *n* **:** a movable part of an airplane wing or of an airfoil external to the wing

**ail·ment** \ˈāl-mənt\ *n* **:** a bodily disorder

**¹aim** \ˈām\ *vb* [ME *aimen*, fr. MF *aesmer* & *esmer*; MF *aesmer*, fr. OF, fr. *a-* to (fr. L *ad-*) + *esmer* to estimate, fr. L *aestimare*] **1 :** to point a weapon at an object **2 :** to direct one's efforts **:** ASPIRE **3 :** to direct to or toward a specified object or goal

**²aim** *n* **1 :** the direction of a weapon **2 :** OBJECT, PURPOSE

**aim·less** \-ləs\ *adj* **:** lacking purpose **:** RANDOM — **aim·less·ly** *adv* — **aim·less·ness** *n*

**ain't** \ˈānt\ **1 :** are not **2 :** is not **3 :** am not — though disapproved by many and more common in less educated speech, used orally in most parts of the U.S. by many educated speakers esp. in the phrase *ain't I*

**Ai·nu** \ˈī-nü\ *n*, *pl* **Ainu** *or* **Ainus 1 :** a member of an indigenous Caucasoid people of Japan **2 :** the language of the Ainu people

**¹air** \ˈaər\ *n* **1 :** the gaseous mixture surrounding the earth **2 :** a light breeze **3 :** compressed air ⟨~ sprayer⟩ **4 :** AIRCRAFT ⟨~ patrol⟩ **5 :** AVIATION ⟨~ safety⟩ **6 :** the medium of transmission of radio waves; *also* **:** RADIO, TELEVISION **7 :** the outward appearance of a person or thing **:** MANNER **8 :** an artificial manner **9 :** MELODY, TUNE

**²air** *vb* **1 :** to expose to the air **2 :** to expose to public view

**air bag** *n* **:** a protective impact-triggered inflating bag positioned in front of automobile passengers

**air·borne** \ˈaər-ˌbȯrn\ *adj* **:** supported or transported by air

**air brake** *n* **1 :** a brake operated by a piston driven by compressed air **2 :** a surface (as an aileron) for lowering an airplane's speed

**air·brush** \-ˌbrəsh\ *n* **:** a device for applying a fine spray (as of paint) by compressed air — **airbrush** *vb*

**air cavalry** *n* **:** army troops equipped and trained for transportation by air

**air-con·di·tion** \ˌaər-kən-ˈdish-ən\ *vb* **:** to equip with an apparatus for filtering air and controlling its humidity and temperature — **air con·di·tion·er** \-ˈdish-(ə-)nər\ *n*

**air·craft** \ˈaər-ˌkraft\ *n*, *pl* **aircraft :** a weight-carrying machine (as an airplane, glider, helicopter, or balloon) for navigation of the air

**aircraft carrier** *n* **:** a warship with a deck on which airplanes can be launched and landed

**air·drome** \-ˌdrōm\ *n* **:** AIRPORT

**air·drop** \-ˌdräp\ *n* **:** delivery of cargo or personnel by parachute from an airplane in flight — **air-drop** *vb*

**Aire·dale terrier** \,aər-,dāl-\ *n* : any of a breed of large terriers with a hard wiry coat

**air·field** \'aər-,fēld\ *n* **1** : the landing field of an airport **2** : AIRPORT

**air·flow** \-,flō\ *n* : the motion of air relative to a body in it

**air·foil** \-,fóil\ *n* : an airplane surface (as a wing or rudder) designed to produce reaction from the air

**air force** *n* : the military organization of a nation for air warfare

**air·frame** \-,frām\ *n* : the structure of an airplane or rocket without the power plant

**air·freight** \-'frāt\ *n* : freight transport by air in volume; *also* : the charge for this service

**air gun** *n* **1** : a rifle operated by compressed air **2** : a hand tool that works by compressed air; *esp* : AIRBRUSH

**air lane** *n* : AIRWAY 1

**air·lift** \'aər-,lift\ *n* : a supply line operated by aircraft — **airlift** *vb*

**air·line** \-,līn\ *n* : an air transportation system including equipment, routes, personnel, and management

**air line** *n* : a straight line

**air·lin·er** \-,lī-nər\ *n* : a large passenger airplane operated by an airline

**air lock** *n* **1** : an airtight chamber separating areas of different pressure **2** : a stoppage of flow due to an air bubble

**air·mail** \'aər-'māl, -,māl\ *n* : the system of transporting mail by airplane; *also* : mail so transported — **airmail** *vb*

**air·man** \-mən\ *n* **1** : an enlisted man in the air force in one of the three ranks below sergeant **2** : AVIATOR

**airman basic** *n* : an enlisted man of the lowest rank in the air force

**air mass** *n* : a large horizontally homogeneous body of air

**air mile** *n* : a mile in air navigation equal to a nautical mile

**air-mind·ed** \'aər-'mīn-dəd\ *adj* : interested in aviation or in air travel

**air·mo·bile** \-,mō-bəl, -,bēl\ *adj* : of, relating to, or being a military unit whose members are transported to combat areas usu. by helicopter

**air·plane** \-,plān\ *n* : a fixed-wing aircraft heavier than air that is driven by a propeller or by a rearward jet and supported by the reaction of the air against its wings

**air pocket** *n* : a condition of the atmosphere that causes an airplane to drop suddenly

**air police** *n* : the military police of an air force

**air·port** \'aər-,pōrt\ *n* : a place maintained for the landing and takeoff of airplanes and for receiving and discharging passengers and cargo

**air·post** \-'pōst\ *n* : AIRMAIL

**air raid** *n* : an attack by armed airplanes on a surface target

**air·ship** \-,ship\ *n* : a lighter-than-air aircraft having propulsion and steering systems

**air·sick** \-,sik\ *adj* : affected with motion sickness associated with flying — **air·sick·ness** *n*

**air·space** \-,spās\ *n* : the space lying above a nation and coming under its jurisdiction

**air·speed** \-,spēd\ *n* : the speed (as of an airplane) with relation to the air as distinguished from its speed relative to the earth

**air strike** *n* : an air attack

**air·strip** \-,strip\ *n* : a runway without normal airport facilities

**air·tight** \'aər-'tīt\ *adj* **1** : so tightly sealed that no air can enter or escape **2** : leaving no opening for attack

**air-to-air** *adj* : launched from one airplane in flight at another : involving aircraft in flight

**air·wave** \'aər-,wāv\ *n* : AIR 6 — usu. used in pl.

**air·way** \-,wā\ *n* **1** : a regular route for airplanes **2** : AIRLINE

**air·wor·thy** \-,wor-thē\ *adj* : fit or safe for operation in the air (an ~ plane) — **air·wor·thi·ness** *n*

**airy** \'a(ə)r-ē\ *adj* **air·i·er; -est 1** : LOFTY **2** : lacking in reality : EMPTY **3** : DELICATE **4** : BREEZY

**aisle** \'īl\ *n* [ME *ile*, fr. MF *alle* wing, fr. L *ala*] **1** : the side of a church nave separated by piers from the nave proper **2** : a passage between sections of seats

**ajar** \ə-'jär\ *adj or adv* : partly open

**AK** *abbr* Alaska

**AKA** *abbr* also known as

**AKC** *abbr* American Kennel Club

**akim·bo** \ə-'kim-bō\ *adj or adv* : having the hand on the hip and the elbow turned outward

**akin** \ə-'kin\ *adj* **1** : related by blood **2** : similar in kind

**Al** *symbol* aluminum

**AL** *abbr* Alabama

¹**-al** \əl\ *adj suffix* : of, relating to, or characterized by ⟨directional⟩

²**-al** *n suffix* : action : process ⟨rehearsal⟩

**Ala** *abbr* Alabama

**ALA** *abbr* American Legal Association

**al·a·bas·ter** \'al-ə-,bas-tər\ *n* **1** : a compact fine-textured usu. white and translucent gypsum mineral often carved into objects (as vases) **2** : a hard translucent calcite

**a la carte** \,al-ə-'kärt, ,äl-\ *adv or adj* : with a separate price for each item on the menu

**alac·ri·ty** \ə-'lak-rət-ē\ *n* : cheerful readiness : BRISKNESS

**a la mode** \,al-ə-'mōd, ,äl-\ *adj* [F *à la mode* according to the fashion] **1** : FASHIONABLE, STYLISH **2** : topped with ice cream

¹**alarm** \ə-'lärm\ *also* **ala·rum** \ə-'lär-əm, -'lar-\ *n* [ME *alarme*, fr. MF, fr. It *all'arme*, lit., to the weapon] **1** : a warning signal **2** : the terror caused by sudden danger

²**alarm** *also* **alarum** *vb* **1** : to warn of danger **2** : to arouse to a sense of danger : FRIGHTEN

**alarm·ist** \ə-'lär-məst\ *n* : a person who is given to alarming others esp. needlessly

**al·ba·core** \'al-bə-ˌkōr\ *n, pl* **-core** *or* **-cores :** any of several tunas

**Al·ba·nian** \al-'bā-nē-ən\ *n* **:** a native or inhabitant of Albania

**al·ba·tross** \'al-bə-ˌtrȯs, -ˌträs\ *n, pl* **-tross** *or* **-tross·es :** a large web-footed seabird related to the petrels

**al·be·it** \ȯl-'bē-ət, al-\ *conj* **:** even though **:** ALTHOUGH

**al·bi·no** \al-'bī-nō\ *n, pl* **-nos :** a person or lower animal lacking coloring matter in the skin, hair, and eyes — **al·bi·nism** \'al-bə-ˌniz-əm\ *n*

**al·bum** \'al-bəm\ *n* **1 :** a book with blank pages used for making a collection (as of stamps) **2 :** one or more phonograph records or tape recordings carrying a major musical work or a group of related selections

**al·bu·men** \al-'byü-mən\ *n* **1 :** the white of an egg **2 :** ALBUMIN

**al·bu·min** \al-'byü-mən\ *n* **:** any of various water-soluble proteins of blood, milk, egg white, and plant and animal tissues

**al·bu·min·ous** \al-'byü-mə-nəs\ *adj* **:** containing or resembling albumen or albumin

**alc** *abbr* alcohol

**al·cal·de** \al-'käl-dē\ *n* **:** the chief administrative and judicial officer of a Spanish or Spanish-American town

**al·ca·zar** \al-'käz-ər, -'kaz-\ *n* **:** a Spanish fortress or palace

**al·che·my** \'al-kə-mē\ *n* **:** medieval chemistry chiefly concerned with efforts to turn base metals into gold — **al·chem·ic** \al-'kem-ik\ *or* **al·chem·i·cal** \-i-kəl\ *adj* — **al·che·mist** \'al-kə-məst\ *n*

**al·co·hol** \'al-kə-ˌhȯl\ *n* [NL, fr. ML, powdered antimony, fr. Sp, fr. Ar *al-kuḥul* the powdered antimony] **1 :** the liquid that is the intoxicating element in fermented and distilled liquors **2 :** any of various carbon compounds similar to alcohol **3 :** beverages containing alcohol — **alcoholic** *adj*

**al·co·hol·ic** \ˌal-kə-'hȯl-ik, -'häl-\ *n* **:** a person affected with alcoholism

**al·co·hol·ism** \'al-kə-ˌhȯl-ˌiz-əm\ *n* **:** continued excessive and usu. uncontrollable use of alcoholic drinks; *also* **:** the abnormal state associated with such use

**al·cove** \'al-ˌkōv\ *n* **1 :** a nook or small recess opening off a larger room **2 :** a niche or arched opening (as in a wall)

**ald** *abbr* alderman

**al·der** \'ȯl-dər\ *n* **:** a tree or shrub related to the birches and growing in wet areas

**al·der·man** \'ȯl-dər-mən\ *n* **:** a member of a city legislative body

**ale** \'āl\ *n* **:** an alcoholic beverage brewed from malt and hops that is usu. more bitter than beer

**ale·a·tor·ic** \ˌā-lē-ə-'tȯr-ik\ *adj* **:** improvised or random in character ⟨~ music⟩

**ale·a·to·ry** \'ā-lē-ə-ˌtōr-ē\ *adj* **:** ALEATORIC

**alee** \ə-'lē\ *adv* **:** on or toward the lee

**ale·house** \'āl-ˌhaus\ *n* **:** a place where ale is sold to be drunk on the premises

**alem·bic** \ə-'lem-bik\ *n* **:** an apparatus formerly used in distillation

**¹alert** \ə-'lərt\ *adj* [It *all' erta*, lit., on the ascent] **1 :** watchful against danger **2 :** quick to perceive and act — **alert·ly** *adv* — **alert·ness** *n*

**²alert** *n* **1 :** a signal given to warn of danger **2 :** the period during which an alert is in effect

**³alert** *vb* **:** WARN

**ale·wife** \'āl-ˌwīf\ *n* **:** a food fish of the herring family abundant esp. on the Atlantic coast

**Al·ex·an·dri·an** \ˌal-ig-'zan-drē-ən\ *adj* **1 :** of or relating to Alexander the Great **2 :** HELLENISTIC

**al·ex·an·drine** \-'zan-drən\ *n, often cap* **:** a line of six iambic feet

**al·fal·fa** \al-'fal-fə\ *n* **:** a leguminous plant widely grown for hay and forage

**al·fres·co** \al-'fres-kō\ *adj or adv* **:** taking place in the open air

**alg** *abbr* algebra

**al·ga** \'al-gə\ *n, pl* **al·gae** \'al-(ˌ)jē\ **:** any of a group of lower plants having chlorophyll but no vascular system and including seaweeds and related freshwater plants — **al·gal** \-gəl\ *adj*

**al·ge·bra** \'al-jə-brə\ *n* **:** a branch of mathematics using symbols (as letters) in calculating — **al·ge·bra·ic** \ˌal-jə-'brā-ik\ *adj* — **al·ge·bra·i·cal·ly** \-'brā-ə-k(ə-)lē\ *adv*

**Al·ge·ri·an** \al-'jir-ē-ən\ *n* **:** a native or inhabitant of Algeria

**Al·gon·quin** \al-'gäŋ-kwən\ *n* **:** a member of an Indian people of the Ottawa river valley

**al·go·rithm** \'al-gə-ˌrith-əm\ *n* **:** a rule of procedure for solving a problem (as in mathematics) that frequently involves repetition of an operation

**¹alias** \'ā-lē-əs, 'āl-yəs\ *adv* [L, otherwise, fr. *alius* other] **:** otherwise called

**²alias** *n* **:** an assumed name

**¹al·i·bi** \'al-ə-ˌbī\ *n* [L, elsewhere, fr. *alius* other] **1 :** a plea offered by an accused person of not having been at the scene of commission of an offense **2 :** a plausible excuse (as for failure)

**²alibi** *vb* **-bied; -bi·ing 1 :** to offer an excuse **2 :** to make an excuse for

**¹alien** \'ā-lē-ən, 'āl-yən\ *adj* **:** FOREIGN

**²alien** *n* **:** a foreign-born resident who has not been naturalized

**alien·able** \'āl-yə-nə-bəl, 'ā-lē-ə-nə-\ *adj* **:** transferable to the ownership of another ⟨~ property⟩

**alien·ate** \'ā-lē-ə-ˌnāt, 'āl-yə-\ *vb* **-at·ed; -at·ing 1 :** to transfer (property) to another **2 :** to make hostile where previously friendship has existed **:** ESTRANGE — **alien·ation** \ˌā-lē-ə-'nā-shən, ˌāl-yə-\ *n*

**alien·ist** \-nəst\ *n* **:** PSYCHIATRIST; *esp* **:** one testifying in legal proceedings

**¹alight** \ə-'līt\ *vb* **alight·ed** *also* **alit** \ə-'lit\; **alight·ing 1 :** to get down (as from a vehicle) **2 :** to come to rest from the air **syn** dismount, land, perch

²**alight** *adj* : lighted up

**align** *also* **aline** \ə-'līn\ *vb* **1** : to bring into line **2** : to array on the side of or against a cause — **align·ment** *also* **aline·ment** *n*

¹**alike** \ə-'līk\ *adj* : LIKE **syn** similar, comparable

²**alike** *adv* : EQUALLY

**al·i·ment** \'al-ə-mənt\ *n* : FOOD, NUTRIMENT

**al·i·men·ta·ry** \,al-ə-'men-t(ə-)rē\ *adj* : of, relating to, or functioning in nourishment or nutrition

**alimentary canal** *n* : a tube that extends from the mouth to the anus and functions in the digestion and absorption of food and the elimination of residues

**al·i·mo·ny** \'al-ə-,mō-nē\ *n, pl* **-nies** [L *alimonia* sustenance, fr. *alere* to nourish] : an allowance paid by a man to a woman after her legal separation or divorce from him

**A-line** \'ā-,līn\ *adj* : having a flared bottom and a close-fitting top ⟨an ~ skirt⟩

**alive** \ə-'līv\ *adj* **1** : having life : LIVING **2** : being in force or operation **3** : SENSITIVE **4** : ANIMATED

**aliz·a·rin** \ə-'liz-ə-rən\ *n* : an orange or red crystalline compound made synthetically and used as a red dye

**alk** *abbr* alkaline

**al·ka·li** \'al-kə-,lī\ *n, pl* **-lies** *or* **-lis** **1** : a substance (as carbonate of sodium, carbonate of potassium, or hydroxide of sodium) that has marked basic properties **2** : a mixture of salts in the soil of some dry regions in such amount as to make ordinary farming impossible — **al·ka·line** \-kə-lən, -,līn\ *adj* — **al·ka·lin·i·ty** \,al-kə-'lin-ət-ē\ *n*

**al·ka·lin·ize** \'al-kə-lə-,nīz\ *vb* **-ized; -iz·ing** : to make alkaline

**al·ka·loid** \'al-kə-,lȯid\ *n* : any of various usu. basic and bitter organic compounds found esp. in seed plants

**al·kyd** \'al-kəd\ *n* : any of numerous thermoplastic synthetic resins used for protective coatings

¹**all** \'ȯl\ *adj* **1** : the whole of **2** : the greatest possible **3** : every one of

²**all** *adv* **1** : WHOLLY **2** : so much ⟨~ the better for it⟩ **3** : for each side ⟨the score is two ~⟩

³**all** *pron* **1** : every one : the whole number ⟨~ of you are welcome⟩ **2** : the whole : every bit ⟨~ of the money is gone⟩ **3** : EVERYTHING

**Al·lah** \'al-ə, ä-'lä\ *n* : the supreme being of the Muslims

**all-Amer·i·can** \,ȯl-ə-'mer-ə-kən\ *adj* **1** : composed wholly of American elements **2** : representative of the U.S. as a whole; *esp* : selected as the best in the U.S. — **all-American** *n*

**all-around** \,ȯl-ə-'raùnd\ *adj* : having ability in many fields : VERSATILE

**al·lay** \ə-'lā\ *vb* **1** : to reduce in severity **2** : to put at rest **syn** alleviate, lighten

**all clear** *n* : a signal that a danger has passed

**al·lege** \ə-'lej\ *vb* **al·leged; al·leg·ing** **1** : to state as a fact without proof **2** : to bring forward as a reason or excuse — **al·le·ga·tion** \,al-i-'gā-shən\ *n* — **al·leg·ed·ly** \ə-'lej-əd-lē\ *adv*

**al·le·giance** \ə-'lē-jəns\ *n* **1** : loyalty owed by a citizen to his government **2** : loyalty to a person or cause

**al·le·go·ry** \'al-ə-,gōr-ē\ *n, pl* **-ries** : the expression through symbolic figures and actions of truths or generalizations about human conduct or experience — **al·le·gor·i·cal** \,al-ə-'gōr-i-kəl\ *adj*

¹**al·le·gro** \ə-'leg-rō, -'lā-grō\ *adv or adj* : in a brisk lively tempo — used as a direction in music

²**allegro** *n, pl* **-gros** : an allegro movement

**al·le·lu·ia** \,al-ə-'lü-yə\ *interj* : HALLELUJAH

**al·ler·gen** \'al-ər-jən\ *n* : something that causes allergy — **al·ler·gen·ic** \,al-ər-'jen-ik\ *adj*

**al·ler·gist** \'al-ər-jəst\ *n* : a specialist in allergy

**al·ler·gy** \'al-ər-jē\ *n, pl* **-gies** [G *allergie*, fr. Gk *allos* other + *ergon* work] : exaggerated or abnormal reaction to substances, situations, or physical states harmless to most people **syn** susceptibility — **al·ler·gic** \ə-'lər-jik\ *adj*

**al·le·vi·ate** \ə-'lē-vē-,āt\ *vb* **-at·ed; -at·ing** : to make easier to be endured **syn** lighten, mitigate — **al·le·vi·a·tion** \ə-,lē-vē-'ā-shən\ *n*

**al·ley** \'al-ē\ *n, pl* **alleys** **1** : a narrow passage between buildings **2** : a place for bowling; *esp* : a hardwood lane

**al·ley·way** \'al-ē-,wā\ *n* **1** : a narrow passageway **2** : a narrow street giving access to the rear of buildings

**All·hal·lows** \ȯl-'hal-ōz\ *n, pl* **Allhallows** : ALL SAINTS' DAY

**al·li·ance** \ə-'lī-əns\ *n* : a union to promote common interests **syn** league, coalition, confederacy, federation

**al·lied** \ə-'līd, 'al-,īd\ *adj* : joined in alliance

**al·li·ga·tor** \'al-ə-,gāt-ər\ *n* [Sp *el lagarto* the lizard, fr. L *lacertus* lizard] : a large aquatic reptile related to the crocodiles but having a shorter and broader snout

**alligator pear** *n* : AVOCADO

**al·lit·er·ate** \ə-'lit-ə-,rāt\ *vb* **-at·ed; -at·ing** **1** : to form an alliteration **2** : to arrange so as to make alliteration

**al·lit·er·a·tion** \ə-,lit-ə-'rā-shən\ *n* : the repetition of initial sounds in adjacent words or syllables — **al·lit·er·a·tive** \-'lit-ə-,rāt-iv\ *adj*

**al·lo·cate** \'al-ə-,kāt\ *vb* **-cat·ed; -cat·ing** : ALLOT, ASSIGN — **al·lo·ca·tion** \,al-ə-'kā-shən\ *n*

**al·lot** \ə-'lät\ *vb* **al·lot·ted; al·lot·ting** : to distribute as a share or portion **syn** assign, apportion, allocate — **al·lot·ment** *n*

**all-out** \'ȯl-'aùt\ *adj* : using maximum energy or resources ⟨an ~ offensive⟩

**all over** *adv* : EVERYWHERE

**al·low** \ə-'laů\ *vb* **1** : to assign as a share ⟨~ time for rest⟩ **2** : to reckon as a deduction **3** : ADMIT, CONCEDE **4** : PERMIT **5** : to make allowance ⟨~ for expansion⟩ — **al·low·able** *adj*

**al·low·ance** \-əns\ *n* **1** : an allotted share **2** : money given regularly as a bounty **3** : the taking into account of mitigating circumstances

**al·loy** \'al-,ȯi, ə-'lȯi\ *n* **1** : a substance composed of metals fused together **2** : an admixture of something that debases — **alloy** *vb*

**all right** *adv or adj* **1** : SATISFACTORILY **2** : YES **3** : beyond doubt : CERTAINLY

**All Saints' Day** *n* : a church feast observed November 1 in honor of all the saints

**All Souls' Day** *n* : a day of prayer observed November 2 for the souls of the faithful departed

**all·spice** \'ȯl-,spīs\ *n* : the berry of a West Indian tree of the myrtle family or the mildly pungent and aromatic spice made from it; *also* : the tree

¹**all-star** \,ȯl-,stär\ *adj* : composed wholly or chiefly of star performers

²**all-star** \'ȯl-,stär\ *n* : a member of an all-star team

**all told** *adv* : with everything counted

**al·lude** \ə-'lüd\ *vb* **al·lud·ed; al·lud·ing** : to refer indirectly or by suggestion — **al·lu·sion** \-'lü-zhən\ *n* — **al·lu·sive** \-'lü-siv\ *adj* — **al·lu·sive·ly** *adv* — **al·lu·sive·ness** *n*

**al·lure** \ə-'lůr\ *vb* **al·lured; al·lur·ing** : to entice by charm or attraction allure *n* —**al·lure·ment** *n*

**al·lu·vi·um** \ə-'lü-vē-əm\ *n, pl* **-vi·ums** *or* **-via** \-vē-ə\ : soil material (as clay or gravel) deposited by running water — **al·lu·vi·al** \-vē-əl\ *adj or n*

¹**al·ly** \ə-'lī, 'al-,ī\ *vb* **al·lied; al·ly·ing** : to unite in alliance

²**al·ly** \'al-,ī, ə-'lī\ *n, pl* **allies** : one united with another in an alliance

**-al·ly** \(ə-)lē\ *adv suffix* : ²-LY ⟨terrifically⟩

**al·ma ma·ter** \,al-mə-'mät-ər\ *n* [L, fostering mother] **1** : a school, college, or university that one has attended **2** : the song or hymn of a school, college, or university

**al·ma·nac** \'ȯl-mə-,nak, 'al-\ *n* : a publication containing astronomical and meteorological data and often a miscellany of other information

**al·man·dite** \'al-mən-,dīt\ *n* : a deep red garnet containing iron and aluminum

**al·mighty** \ȯl-'mīt-ē\ *adj* **1** *often cap* : having absolute power over all ⟨*Almighty* God⟩ **2** : relatively unlimited in power

**Almighty** *n* : GOD 1

**al·mond** \'äm-ənd, 'am-; 'al-mənd\ *n* : a small tree related to the peach; *also* : the edible nutlike kernel of its fruit

**al·mo·ner** \'al-mə-nər, 'äm-ə-\ *n* : an officer who distributes alms

**al·most** \'ȯl-,mōst, ȯl-'mōst\ *adv* : only a little less than : NEARLY

**alms** \'ämz, 'älmz\ *n, pl* **alms** [ME almesse, almes, fr. OE ælmesse, ælms, fr. L eleemosyna alms, fr. Gk eleēmosynē pity, alms, fr. eleēmōn merciful, fr. eleos pity] : something given freely to relieve the poor

**alms·house** \-,haůs\ *n, Brit* : a privately financed home for the poor

**al·oe** \'al-ō\ *n* **1** : any of various succulent mostly African plants related to the lilies **2** *pl* : the dried tonic and purgative juice of the leaves of an aloe

**aloft** \ə-'lȯft\ *adv* **1** : high in the air **2** : on or to the higher rigging of a ship

**alo·ha** \ə-'lō-ə, ä-'lō-hä\ *interj* — used to express greeting or farewell

**alone** \ə-'lōn\ *adj* **1** : separated from others **2** : not including anyone or anything else : ONLY **syn** lonely, lonesome, lone, forlone — **alone** *adv*

¹**along** \ə-'lȯŋ\ *prep* **1** : on or near in a lengthwise direction ⟨walk ~ the street⟩ ⟨sail ~ the coast⟩ **2** : at a point on or during ⟨stopped ~ the way⟩

²**along** *adv* **1** : FORWARD, ON **2** : as a companion or associate ⟨bring her ~⟩ **3** : all the time ⟨knew it all ~⟩

**along·shore** \ə-'lȯŋ-'shȯr\ *adv or adj* : along the shore or coast

¹**along·side** \-,sīd\ *adv* : along or by the side

²**alongside** *prep* : side by side with; *specif* : parallel to

**alongside of** *prep* : ALONGSIDE

**aloof** \ə-'lüf\ *adj* : removed or distant in interest or feeling : RESERVED — **aloof·ness** *n*

**al·o·pe·cia** \,al-ə-pē-sh(ē-)ə\ *n* : BALDNESS

**aloud** \ə-'laůd\ *adv* : using the voice so as to be clearly heard

**alp** \'alp\ *n* : a high mountain

**al·paca** \al-'pak-ə\ *n* : a So. American mammal related to the llama; *also* : its wool or cloth made from this

**al·pha·bet** \'al-fə-,bet, -bət\ *n* : the set of letters used in writing a language arranged in a conventional order

**al·pha·bet·ic** \,al-fə-'bet-ik\ *or* **al·pha·bet·i·cal** \-i-kəl\ *adj* **1** : of or employing an alphabet **2** : arranged in the order of the letters of the alphabet — **al·pha·bet·i·cal·ly** \-i-k(ə-)lē\ *adv*

**al·pha·bet·ize** \'al-fə-bə-,tīz\ *vb* **-ized; -iz·ing** : to arrange in alphabetic order — **al·pha·bet·iz·er** *n*

**al·pha·nu·mer·ic** \,al-fə-n(y)ů-'mer-ik\ *adj* **1** : consisting of letters and numbers and often other symbols ⟨an ~ code⟩; *also* : being a character in an alphanumeric system **2** : capable of using alphanumeric characters

**al·pha particle** \,al-fə-\ *n* : a positively charged particle identical with the nucleus of a helium atom that is ejected at high speed in various radioactive transformations

**alpha ray** *n* : a stream of alpha particles

**alpha rhythm** *n* : an electrical rhythm of the brain occurring 8 to 13 cycles per second and often associated with a state of wakeful relaxation

**alpha wave** *n* : ALPHA RHYTHM

**Al·pine** \'al-,pīn\ *adj* **1** : relating to, located in, or resembling the Alps **2** *often not cap* : of, relating to, or growing in the biogeographic zone above timberline

**al·ready** \ol-'red-ē\ *adv* **1** : prior to a specified or implied time : PREVIOUSLY **2** : so soon

**al·right** \ol-'rīt\ *adv* : ALL RIGHT

**al·so** \'ol-sō\ *adv* : in addition : TOO

**al·so-ran** \-,ran\ *n* **1** : a horse or dog that finishes out of the money in a race **2** : a contestant that does not win

**alt** *abbr* **1** alternate **2** altitude

**Alta** *abbr* Alberta

**al·tar** \'ol-tər\ *n* **1** : a structure on which sacrifices are offered or incense is burned in worship **2** : a table used as a center of ritual

**al·tar·piece** \'ol-tər-,pēs\ *n* : a work of art to decorate the space above and behind the altar

¹**al·ter** \'ol-tər\ *vb* **al·tered; al·ter·ing** \-t(ə-)riŋ\ **1** : to make or become different **2** : CASTRATE, SPAY — **al·ter·a·tion** \,ol-tə-'rā-shən\ *n*

²**alter** *abbr* alteration

**al·ter·ca·tion** \,ol-tər-'kā-shən\ *n* : a noisy or angry dispute

**al·ter ego** \,ol-tər-'ē-gō\ *n* : a second self; *esp* : a trusted friend

¹**al·ter·nate** \'ol-tər-nət, 'al-\ *adj* **1** : arranged or succeeding by turns **2** : every other — **al·ter·nate·ly** *adv*

²**al·ter·nate** \-,nāt\ *vb* **-nat·ed; -nat·ing** : to occur or cause to occur by turns — **al·ter·na·tion** \,ol-tər-'nā-shən, ,al-\ *n*

³**al·ter·nate** \-nət\ *n* : SUBSTITUTE

**alternating current** *n* : an electric current that reverses its direction at regular short intervals

**al·ter·na·tive** \ol-'tər-nət-iv, al-\ *adj* : that may be chosen in place of something else — **alternative** *n*

**al·ter·na·tor** \'ol-tər-,nāt-ər, 'al-\ *n* : an electric generator for producing alternating current

**al·though** *also* **al·tho** \ol-'thō\ *conj* : in spite of the fact that : even though

**al·tim·e·ter** \al-'tim-ət-ər, 'al-tə-,mēt-ər\ *n* : an instrument for measuring altitudes

**al·ti·tude** \'al-tə-,t(y)üd\ *n* **1** : vertical elevation : HEIGHT **2** : angular distance above the horizon **3** : the perpendicular distance from a vertex of a geometric figure to the opposite side or from a side or face to a parallel side or face; *esp* : the altitude on a base

**al·to** \'al-tō\ *n*, *pl* **altos** [It, lit., high, fr. L *altus*] : the lowest female voice; *also* : a singer or instrument having the range of such a voice

**al·to·geth·er** \,ol-tə-'geth-ər\ *adv* **1** : WHOLLY **2** : on the whole

**al·tru·ism** \'al-trü-,iz-əm\ *n* : unselfish interest in the welfare of others — **al·tru·ist** \-əst\ *n* — **al·tru·is·tic** \,al-trü-'is-tik\ *adj* — **al·tru·is·ti·cal·ly** \-ti-k(ə-)lē\ *adv*

**al·um** \'al-əm\ *n* **1** : either of two colorless crystalline compounds containing aluminum that have a sweetish sour taste and are used (as to stop bleeding) in medicine **2** : a colorless aluminum salt used in purifying water and in tanning and dyeing

**alu·mi·na** \ə-'lü-mə-nə\ *n* : the oxide of aluminum occurring in nature as corundum and in bauxite

**al·u·min·i·um** \,al-yə-'min-ē-əm\ *n*, *chiefly Brit* : ALUMINUM

**alu·mi·nize** \ə-'lü-mə-,nīz\ *vb* **-nized; -niz·ing** : to treat or coat with aluminum

**alu·mi·num** \ə-'lü-mə-nəm\ *n* : a silver-white malleable ductile light metallic element that is the most abundant metal in the earth's crust

**alum·na** \ə-'ləm-nə\ *n*, *pl* **-nae** \-(,)nē\ : a woman graduate or former student of a college or school

**alum·nus** \ə-'ləm-nəs\ *n*, *pl* **-ni** \-,nī\ [L, foster son, pupil, fr. *alere* to nourish] : a graduate or former student of a college or school

**al·ways** \'ol-wēz, -wəz, -(,)wāz\ *adv* **1** : at all times **2** : FOREVER **3** : without exception

**am** *pres 1st sing of* BE

¹**Am** *abbr* America; American

²**Am** *symbol* americium

**AM** *abbr* **1** amplitude modulation **2** ante meridiem **3** master of arts

**AMA** *abbr* American Medical Association

**amah** \'äm-(,)ä\ *n* : an Oriental female servant; *esp* : a Chinese nurse

**amain** \ə-'mān\ *adv* : with full force or speed

**amal·gam** \ə-'mal-gəm\ *n* **1** : an alloy of mercury with another metal used in making dental cements **2** : a mixture of different elements

**amal·gam·ate** \ə-'mal-gə-,māt\ *vb* **-at·ed; -at·ing** : to unite into one body or organization — **amal·ga·ma·tion** \-,mal-gə-'mā-shən\ *n*

**aman·u·en·sis** \ə-,man-yə-'wen-səs\ *n*, *pl* **-en·ses** \-,sēz\ : one employed to write from dictation or to copy what another has written : SECRETARY

**am·a·ranth** \'am-ə-,ranth\ *n* **1** : an imaginary flower held never to fade **2** : any of various coarse herbs sometimes grown for their showy flowers — **am·a·ran·thine** \,am-ə-'ran-thən, -,thīn\ *adj*

**am·a·ryl·lis** \,am-ə-'ril-əs\ *n* : any of various mostly bulbous herbs with clusters of often bright-colored flowers like lilies

**amass** \ə-'mas\ *vb* : ACCUMULATE

**am·a·teur** \'am-ə-,tər, -ət-ər, -ə-,t(y)ùr, -ə-,chùr, -ə-chər\ *n* [F, fr. L *amator* lover, fr. *amare* to love] **1** : a person who engages in a pursuit for pleasure and not as a profession **2** : a person who is not expert — **amateur** *adj* — **am·a·teur·ish** \,am-ə-'tər-ish, -'t(y)ùr-\ *adj* — **am·a·teur·ism** \'am-ə-,tər-,iz-əm, -ət-ə-,riz-, -ə-,t(y)ùr-,iz-, -,chùr-,iz-, -chə-,riz-\ *n*

**am·a·tive** \'am-ət-iv\ *adj* : disposed or disposing to love : AMOROUS — **am·a·tive·ly** *adv* — **am·a·tive·ness** *n*

**am·a·to·ry** \'am-ə-,tōr-ē\ *adj* : of or expressing sexual love

**amaze** \ə-'māz\ *vb* **amazed; amaz·ing** : to overwhelm with wonder : ASTOUND **syn** astonish, surprise — **amaze·ment** *n* — **amaz·ing·ly** *adv*

**am·a·zon** \'am-ə-,zän, -ə-zən\ *n* **1** *cap* : a member of a race of female warriors repeatedly warring with the ancient Greeks of mythology **2** : a tall strong masculine woman — **am·a·zo·ni·an** \,am-ə-'zō-nē-ən\ *adj, often cap*

**amb** *abbr* ambassador

**am·bas·sa·dor** \am-'bas-əd-ər\ *n* : a person accredited to a foreign government as an official representative of his own government — **am·bas·sa·do·ri·al** \-,bas-ə-'dȯr-ē-əl\ *adj* — **am·bas·sa·dor·ship** *n*

**am·ber** \'am-bər\ *n* : a yellowish fossil resin used esp. for ornamental objects; *also* : the color of this resin

**am·ber·gris** \'am-bər-,gris, -,grēs\ *n* : a waxy substance from the sperm whale used in making perfumes

**am·bi·dex·trous** \,am-bi-'dek-strəs\ *adj* : using both hands with equal ease — **am·bi·dex·trous·ly** *adv*

**am·bi·ence** *or* **am·bi·ance** \'am-bē-əns, äⁿ-byäⁿs\ *n* : a surrounding or pervading atmosphere

**am·bi·ent** \'am-bē-ənt\ *adj* : SURROUNDING

**am·big·u·ous** \am-'big-yə-wəs\ *adj* : capable of being understood in more than one way — **am·bi·gu·i·ty** \,am-bə-'gyü-ət-ē\ *n*

**am·bi·tion** \am-'bish-ən\ *n* [ME, fr. MF or L; MF, fr. L *ambition- ambitio*, lit., going around, fr. *ambitus*, pp. of *ambire*, fr. *ambi-* around + *ire* to go] : eager desire for success, honor, or power

**am·bi·tious** \am-'bish-əs\ *adj* : characterized by ambition — **am·bi·tious·ly** *adv*

**am·biv·a·lence** \am-'biv-ə-ləns\ *n* : simultaneous attraction toward and repulsion from a person, object, or action — **am·biv·a·lent** \-lənt\ *adj*

¹**am·ble** \'am-bəl\ *vb* **am·bled; am·bling** \-b(ə-)liŋ\ : to go at an amble

²**amble** *n* : an easy gait esp. of a horse

**am·bro·sia** \am-'brō-zh(ē-)ə\ *n* : the food of the Greek and Roman gods — **am·bro·sial** \-zh(ē-)əl\ *adj*

**am·bu·lance** \'am-byə-ləns\ *n* : a vehicle equipped for carrying the injured or sick

**am·bu·lant** \'am-byə-lənt\ *adj* : moving about : AMBULATORY

¹**am·bu·la·to·ry** \'am-byə-lə-,tōr-ē\ *adj* **1** : of, relating to, or adapted to walking **2** : able to walk about

²**ambulatory** *n, pl* **-ries** : a sheltered place (as in a cloister) for walking

**am·bus·cade** \'am-bə-,skād\ *n* : AMBUSH

**am·bush** \'am-,bùsh\ *n* : a trap by which concealed persons attack an enemy by surprise — **ambush** *vb*

**amdt** *abbr* amendment

**ameba, amebic, ameboid** *var of* AMOEBA, AMOEBIC, AMOEBOID

**ame·lio·rate** \ə-'mēl-yə-,rāt\ *vb* **-rat·ed; -rat·ing** : to make or grow better : IMPROVE — **ame·lio·ra·tion** \-,mēl-yə-'rā-shən\ *n*

**amen** \(')ā-'men, (')ä-\ *interj* — used esp. at the end of prayers to express solemn ratification or approval

**ame·na·ble** \ə-'mē-nə-bəl, -'men-ə-\ *adj* **1** : ANSWERABLE **2** : easily managed : TRACTABLE

**amend** \ə-'mend\ *vb* **1** : to change for the better : IMPROVE **2** : to alter formally in phraseology

**amend·ment** \ə-'men(d)-mənt\ *n* **1** : correction of faults **2** : the process of amending a parliamentary motion or a constitution; *also* : the alteration so proposed or made

**amends** \ə-'men(d)z\ *n sing or pl* : compensation for injury or loss

**ame·ni·ty** \ə-'men-ət-ē, -'mē-nət-\ *n, pl* **-ties 1** : AGREEABLENESS **2** : something conducing to comfort or convenience **3** *pl* : the conventions observed in social intercourse

**Amer** *abbr* America; American

**amerce** \ə-'mərs\ *vb* **amerced; amerc·ing 1** : to penalize by a fine determined by the court **2** : PUNISH — **amerce·ment** *n*

**Amer·i·can** \ə-'mer-ə-kən\ *n* **1** : a native or inhabitant of No. or So. America **2** : a citizen of the U.S. — **American** *adj* — **Amer·i·can·ism** \-ə-kə-,niz-əm\ *n* — **Amer·i·can·iza·tion** \ə-,mer-ə-kə-nə-'zā-shən\ *n* — **Amer·i·can·ize** \ə-'mer-ə-kə-,nīz\ *vb*

**Amer·i·ca·na** \ə-,mer-ə-'kan-ə, -'kän-\ *n pl* : materials concerning or characteristic of America, its civilization, or its culture; *also* : a collection of these

**American plan** *n* : a hotel plan whereby the daily rates cover the cost of room and meals

**am·er·i·ci·um** \,am-ə-'ris(h)-ē-əm\ *n* : a radioactive metallic chemical element artificially produced from uranium

**Amerind** *abbr* American Indian

**Am·er·in·di·an** \,am-ə-'rin-dē-ən\ *adj* : of or relating to American Indians or their culture

**am·e·thyst** \'am-ə-thəst\ *n* [ME *amatiste*, fr. OF & L; OF, fr. L *amethystus*, fr. Gk *amethystos*, lit., remedy against drunkenness, fr. *a-* not + *methyein* to be drunk, fr. *methy* wine] : a gemstone consisting of clear purple or bluish violet quartz

**ami·a·ble** \'ā-mē-ə-bəl\ *adj* **1** : AGREEABLE **2** : having a friendly and sociable disposition — **ami·a·bil·i·ty** \,ā-mē-ə-'bil-ət-ē\ *n* — **ami·a·bly** \'ā-mē-ə-blē\ *adv*

**am·i·ca·ble** \'am-i-kə-bəl\ *adj* : FRIENDLY, PEACEABLE — **am·i·ca·bly** \-blē\ *adv*

**amid** \ə-'mid\ *or* **amidst** \-'midst\ *prep* : in or into the middle of : AMONG

**amid·ships** \ə-'mid-ˌships\ *adv* **:** in or toward the part of a ship midway between the bow and the stern

**amino acid** \ə-ˌmē-nō-\ *n* **:** any of numerous nitrogen-containing acids that include some which are the building blocks of proteins

**¹amiss** \ə-'mis\ *adv* **1 :** FAULTILY **2 :** IMPROPERLY

**²amiss** *adj* **1 :** WRONG **2 :** out of place

**am·i·ty** \'am-ət-ē\ *n, pl* **-ties :** FRIENDSHIP; *esp* **:** friendly relations between nations

**am·me·ter** \'am-ˌēt-ər\ *n* **:** an instrument for measuring electric current in amperes

**am·mo** \'am-ō\ *n* **:** AMMUNITION

**am·mo·nia** \ə-'mō-nyə\ *n* [NL, fr. L *sal ammoniacus* sal ammoniac, lit., salt of Ammon, fr. Gk *ammōniakos* of Ammon, fr. *Ammōn* Ammon, Amen, an Egyptian god near one of whose temples it was prepared] **1 :** a colorless gaseous compound of nitrogen and hydrogen used in refrigeration and in the making of fertilizers and explosives **2 :** a solution (**ammonia water**) of ammonia in water

**am·mo·ni·um** \ə-'mō-nē-əm\ *n* **:** an ion or radical derived from ammonia by combination with hydrogen and known in compounds (as ammonium chloride)

**ammonium chloride** *n* **:** a white crystalline volatile salt used in batteries and as an expectorant

**am·mu·ni·tion** \ˌam-yə-'nish-ən\ *n* **1 :** projectiles fired from guns **2 :** explosive items used in war **3 :** material for use in attack or defense

**am·ne·sia** \am-'nē-zhə\ *n* **:** abnormal loss of memory — **am·ne·si·ac** \-z(h)ē-ˌak\ *or* **am·ne·sic** \-zik, -sik\ *adj or n*

**am·nes·ty** \'am-nə-stē\ *n, pl* **-ties :** an act granting a pardon to a group of individuals — **amnesty** *vb*

**am·nio·cen·te·sis** \ˌam-nē-ō-ˌsen-'tē-səs\ *n* **:** the surgical insertion of a hollow needle through the abdominal wall and uterus of a pregnant female esp. to obtain fluid for the determination of sex or chromosomal abnormality

**amoe·ba** \ə-'mē-bə\ *n, pl* **-bas** *or* **-bae** \-(ˌ)bē\ **:** any of various tiny one-celled animals that lack permanent cell organs and occur esp. in water and soil — **amoe·bic** \-bik\

**amoe·boid** \-ˌbȯid\ *adj* **:** resembling an amoeba esp. in moving or readily changing shape

**amok** \ə-'mək, -'mäk\ *adv* **:** in a murderously frenzied manner

**among** \ə-'məŋ\ *also* **amongst** \-'məŋst\ *prep* **1 :** in or through the midst of **2 :** in the number or class of **3 :** in shares to each of **4 :** by common action of

**amon·til·la·do** \ə-ˌmän-tə-'läd-ō\ *n, pl* **-dos :** a pale dry sherry

**amor·al** \ā-'mȯr-əl\ *adj* **:** neither moral nor immoral; *esp* **:** being outside the sphere to which moral judgments apply — **amor·al·ly** *adv*

**am·o·rous** \'am-(ə-)rəs\ *adj* **1 :** inclined to love **2 :** being in love — **am·o·rous·ly** *adv* — **am·o·rous·ness** *n*

**amor·phous** \ə-'mȯr-fəs\ *adj* **1 :** SHAPELESS, FORMLESS **2 :** not crystallized

**am·or·tize** \'am-ər-ˌtīz, ə-'mȯr-\ *vb* **-tized; -tiz·ing :** to extinguish (as a mortgage) usu. by payment on the principal at the time of each periodic interest payment — **amor·ti·za·tion** \ˌam-ərt-ə-'zā-shən, ə-ˌmȯrt-\ *n*

**¹amount** \ə-'maȯnt\ *vb* **1 :** to reach as a total **2 :** to be equivalent

**²amount** *n* **1 :** the total number or quantity **2 :** a principal sum plus the interest on it

**amour** \ə-'mȯr, ä-, a-\ *n* **:** a love affair esp. when illicit

**amour pro·pre** \ˌam-ˌūr-'prȯprə, ˌäm-ˌūr-'prȯpr'\ *n* **:** SELF-ESTEEM

**amp** *abbr* ampere

**am·per·age** \'am-p(ə-)rij\ *n* **:** the strength of a current of electricity expressed in amperes

**am·pere** \'am-ˌpiər\ *n* **:** a unit of electric current equivalent to a steady current produced by one volt applied across a resistance of one ohm

**am·per·sand** \'am-pər-ˌsand\ *n* [fr. *and per se and*, spoken form of the phrase *& per se and*, lit., (the character) *&* by itself (stands for the word) *and*] **:** a character & used for the word *and*

**am·phet·amine** \am-'fet-ə-ˌmēn, -mən\ *n* **:** a compound or one of its derivatives used esp. as a stimulant of the nervous system and formerly as a nasal decongestant

**am·phib·i·an** \am-'fib-ē-ən\ *n* **1 :** an amphibious organism; *esp* **:** any of a group of animals (as frogs and newts) intermediate between fishes and reptiles **2 :** a vehicle designed to operate on both land and water

**am·phib·i·ous** \am-'fib-ē-əs\ *adj* [Gk *amphibios*, lit., living a double life, fr. *amphi-* on both sides + *bios* mode of life] **1 :** able to live both on land and in water **2 :** adapted for both land and water **3 :** made by joint action of land, sea, and air forces invading from the sea; *also* **:** trained for such action

**am·phi·bole** \'am-fə-ˌbōl\ *n* **:** any of a group of rock-forming minerals containing calcium, magnesium, iron, aluminum, and sodium combined with silica

**am·phi·the·ater** \'am-fə-ˌthē-ət-ər\ *n* **:** an oval or circular structure with rising tiers of seats around an arena

**am·pho·ra** \'am-fə-rə\ *n, pl* **-rae** \-ˌrē\ *or* **-ras :** an ancient Greek jar or vase with two handles that rise almost to the level of the mouth

**am·ple** \'am-pəl\ *adj* **am·pler** \-plər\; **am·plest** \-pləst\ **1 :** LARGE, CAPACIOUS **2 :** enough to satisfy **:** ABUNDANT — **am·ply** \-plē\ *adv*

**am·pli·fy** \'am-plə-ˌfī\ *vb* **-fied; -fy·ing 1 :** to expand by extended treatment **2 :** to increase (voltage, current, or power) in magnitude or strength

**3 :** to make louder — **am·pli·fi·ca·tion** \,am-plə-fə-'kā-shən\ *n* — **am·pli·fi·er** \'am-plə-,fī(-ə)r\ *n*

**am·pli·tude** \-,t(y)üd\ *n* **1 :** ample extent : FULLNESS **2 :** the extent of a vibratory movement (as of a pendulum) or of an oscillation (as of an alternating current or a radio wave)

**amplitude modulation** *n* **1 :** modulation of the amplitude of a radio carrier wave in accordance with the strength of the signal **2 :** a broadcasting system using amplitude modulation

**am·pul** *or* **am·pule** *or* **am·poule** \'am-,pyül, -pül\ *n* **:** a small sealed bulbous glass vessel used to hold a solution for hypodermic injection

**am·pu·tate** \'am-pyə-,tāt\ *vb* **-tat·ed; -tat·ing :** to cut off (∼ a leg) — **am·pu·ta·tion** \,am-pyə-'tā-shən\ *n*

**am·pu·tee** \,am-pyə-'tē\ *n* **:** one who has had a limb amputated

**amt** *abbr* amount

**amuck** \ə-'mək\ *var of* AMOK

**am·u·let** \'am-yə-lət\ *n* **:** an ornament worn as a charm against evil

**amuse** \ə-'myüz\ *vb* **amused; amus·ing :** to entertain in a light or playful manner : DIVERT — **amuse·ment** *n*

**AMVETS** \'am-,vets\ *abbr* American Veterans (of World War II)

**am·y·lase** \'am-ə-,lās, -,lāz\ *n* **:** any of several enzymes that accelerate the breakdown of starch and glycogen

**an** \ən, (')an\ *indefinite article* **:** A — used before words beginning with a vowel sound

**¹-an** \ən\ *or* **-ian** \(ē-)ən\ *also* **-ean** \(ē-)ən, 'ē-ən\ *n suffix* **1 :** one that belongs to 〈American〉 〈Boston*ian*〉 〈crustac*ean*〉 **2 :** one skilled in or specializing in 〈phonetic*ian*〉

**²-an** *or* **-ian** *also* **-ean** *adj suffix* **1 :** of or belonging to 〈American〉 〈Florid*ian*〉 **2 :** characteristic of : resembling 〈Mozart*ean*〉

**anach·ro·nism** \ə-'nak-rə-,niz-əm\ *n* **1 :** the error of placing a person or thing in a period to which he or it does not belong **2 :** one that is chronologically out of place — **anach·ro·nis·tic** \ə-,nak-rə-'nis-tik\ *adj*

**an·a·con·da** \,an-ə-'kän-də\ *n* **:** a large So. American snake that crushes its prey

**an·a·dem** \'an-ə-,dem\ *n* **:** GARLAND, CHAPLET

**anae·mia, anae·mic** *var of* ANEMIA, ANEMIC

**an·aer·obe** \'an-ə-,rōb\ *n* **:** an anaerobic organism

**an·aer·o·bic** \,an-ə-'rō-bik\ *adj* **:** living, active, or occurring in the absence of free oxygen

**an·aes·the·sia, an·aes·thet·ic** *var of* ANESTHESIA, ANESTHETIC

**ana·gram** \'an-ə-,gram\ *n* **:** a word or phrase made by transposing the letters of another word or phrase

**¹anal** \'ān-ᵊl\ *adj* **1 :** of, relating to, or situated near the anus **2 :** of, relating to, or characterized by the stage of personality development during which

in psychoanalytic theory one is concerned esp. with feces **3 :** of, relating to, or characterized by personality traits (as parsimony and ill humor) considered typical of fixation at the anal stage of development

**²anal** *abbr* **1** analogy **2** analysis; analytic

**an·al·ge·sia** \,an-ᵊl-'jē-zhə\ *n* **:** insensibility to pain — **an·al·ge·sic** \-'jē-zik, -sik\ *adj*

**an·al·ge·sic** \-'jē-zik, -sik\ *n* **:** an agent for producing analgesia

**analog computer** \,an-ᵊl-,ȯg-, -,äg-\ **:** a computer that operates with numbers represented by directly measurable quantities (as voltages)

**anal·o·gous** \ə-'nal-ə-gəs\ *adj* **:** similar in one or more respects but not homologous

**analogue** *or* **an·a·log** \'an-ᵊl-,ȯg, -,äg\ *n* **1 :** something that is analogous or similar to something else **2 :** an organ similar in function to one of another animal or plant but different in structure or origin **3 :** a chemical compound structurally similar to another

**anal·o·gy** \ə-'nal-ə-jē\ *n, pl* **-gies 1 :** inference that if two or more things agree in some respects they will prob. agree in others **2 :** a likeness in one or more ways between things otherwise unlike — **an·a·log·i·cal** \,an-ᵊl-'äj-i-kəl\ *adj* — **an·a·log·i·cal·ly** \-i-k(ə-)lē\ *adv*

**anal·y·sis** \ə-'nal-ə-səs\ *n, pl* **-y·ses** \-,sēz\ [NL, fr. Gk, fr. *analyein* to break up, fr. *ana-* up + *lyein* to loosen] **1 :** separation of a thing into the parts or elements of which it is composed **2 :** an examination of a thing to determine its parts or elements; *also* **:** a statement showing the results of such an examination **3 :** PSYCHOANALYSIS — **an·a·lyst** \'an-ᵊl-əst\ *n* — **an·a·lyt·ic** \,an-ᵊl-'it-ik\ *or* **an·a·lyt·i·cal** \-i-kəl\ *adj*

**an·a·lyze** \'an-ᵊl-,īz\ *vb* **-lyzed; -lyz·ing :** to make an analysis of

**an·a·pest** \'an-ə-,pest\ *n* **:** a metrical foot of two unaccented syllables followed by one accented syllable — **an·a·pes·tic** \,an-ə-'pes-tik\ *adj or n*

**an·ar·chism** \'an-ər-,kiz-əm\ *n* **1 :** the theory that all government is unnecessary and undesirable **2 :** TERRORISM — **an·ar·chist** \-kəst\ *n* — **an·ar·chis·tic** \,an-ər-'kis-tik\ *adj*

**an·ar·chy** \'an-ər-kē\ *n* **1 :** a social structure without government or law and order **2 :** utter confusion — **an·ar·chic** \a-'när-kik\ *also* **an·ar·chi·cal** \-ki-kəl\ *adj*

**anas·to·mo·sis** \ə-,nas-tə-'mō-səs\ *n, pl* **-mo·ses** \-,sēz\ **1 :** the union of parts or branches (as of blood vessels) **2 :** NETWORK

**anat** *abbr* anatomy

**anath·e·ma** \ə-'nath-ə-mə\ *n* **1 :** a solemn curse **2 :** a person or thing accursed; *also* **:** one intensely disliked

**anath·e·ma·tize** \-,tīz\ *vb* **-tized;**

**-tiz·ing :** to pronounce an anathema against : CURSE

**anat·o·mize** \ə-'nat-ə-‚mīz\ *vb* **-mized; -miz·ing :** to dissect so as to examine the structure and parts; *also* : ANALYZE

**anat·o·my** \ə-'nat-ə-mē\ *n, pl* **-mies** [LL *anatomia* dissection, fr. Gk *anatomē*, fr. *anatemnein* to dissect, fr. *ana-* up + *temnein* to cut] **1 :** a branch of science dealing with the structure of organisms **2 :** a separating into parts for detailed study : ANALYSIS, ANATOMIZING — **an·a·tom·ic** \‚an-ə-'täm-ik\ *or* **an·a·tom·i·cal** \-i-kəl\ *adj* — **an·a·tom·i·cal·ly** \-i-k(ə-)lē\ *adv* — **anat·o·mist** \ə-'nat-ə-məst\ *n*

**anc** *abbr* ancient

**-ance** \əns\ *n suffix* **1 :** action or process ⟨furtherance⟩ **:** instance of an action or process ⟨performance⟩ **2 :** quality or state : instance of a quality or state ⟨protuberance⟩ **3 :** amount or degree ⟨conductance⟩

**an·ces·tor** \'an-‚ses-tər\ *n* [ME *ancestre*, fr. OF, fr. L *antecessor* one that goes before, fr. *antecedere* to go before, fr. *ante-* before + *cedere* to go] : one from whom an individual is descended — **an·ces·tress** \-trəs\ *n*

**an·ces·try** \'an-‚ses-trē\ *n* **1 :** line of descent : LINEAGE **2 :** ANCESTORS — **an·ces·tral** \an-'ses-trəl\ *adj*

**¹an·chor** \'aŋ-kər\ *n* **:** a heavy metal device attached to a ship and so made that when thrown overboard it catches hold of the bottom and holds the ship in place

**²anchor** *vb* **an·chored; an·chor·ing** \-k(ə-)riŋ\ **:** to hold or become held in place by or as if by an anchor

**an·chor·age** \'aŋ-k(ə-)rij\ *n* **:** a place suitable for ships to anchor

**an·cho·rite** \'aŋ-kə-‚rīt\ *also* **an·cho·ret** \-‚ret\ *n* **:** one who lives in seclusion esp. for religious reasons — **an·cho·ress** \-k(ə-)rəs\ *n*

**an·chor·man** \'aŋ-kər-‚man\ *n* **1 :** the member of a team who competes last **2 :** a broadcaster who coordinates the activities of other broadcasters

**an·cho·vy** \'an-‚chō-vē, an-'chō-\ *n, pl* **-vies** *or* **-vy :** a small herringlike fish used esp. for sauces and relishes

**¹an·cient** \'ān-shənt\ *adj* **1 :** having existed for many years **2 :** belonging to times long past; *esp* : belonging to the period before the Middle Ages

**²ancient** *n* **1 :** an aged person **2** *pl* **:** the peoples of ancient Greece and Rome

**an·cil·lary** \'an-sə-‚ler-ē\ *adj* **1 :** SUBORDINATE, SUBSIDIARY **2 :** AUXILIARY, SUPPLEMENTARY

**-ancy** \ən-sē\ *n suffix* **:** quality or state ⟨flamboyancy⟩

**and** \ən(d), (')an(d)\ *conj* — used to indicate connection or addition esp. of items within the same class or type or to join words or phrases of the same

grammatical rank or function

**¹an·dan·te** \än-'dän-‚tā, -'dänt-ē\ *adv or adj* [It, lit., going, prp. of *andare* to go] **:** moderately slow — used as a direction in music

**²andante** *n* **:** an andante movement

**and·iron** \'an-‚dī(-ə)rn\ *n* **:** one of a pair of metal supports for firewood in a fireplace

**and/or** \'an-'dor\ *conj* — used to indicate that either *and* or *or* may apply ⟨men ~ women means men *and* women or men *or* women⟩

**an·dro·gen** \'an-drə-jən\ *n* **:** a male sex hormone

**an·droid** \'an-‚droid\ *n* **:** an automaton with human form

**an·ec·dote** \'an-ik-‚dōt\ *n* [F, fr. Gk *anekdota* unpublished items, fr. *a-* not + *ekdidonai* to publish, fr. *ex* out + *didonai* to give] **:** a brief story of an interesting usu. biographical incident — **an·ec·dot·al** \‚an-ik-'dōt-əl\ *adj*

**an·echo·ic** \‚an-i-'kō-ik\ *adj* **:** free from echoes and reverberations

**ane·mia** \ə-'nē-mē-ə\ *n* **1 :** a condition in which blood is deficient in quantity, in red cells, or in hemoglobin and which is marked by pallor, weakness, and irregular heart action **2 :** lack of vitality — **ane·mic** \ə-'nēmik\ *adj*

**an·e·mom·e·ter** \‚an-ə-'mäm-ət-ər\ *n* **:** an instrument for measuring the force or speed of the wind

**anem·o·ne** \ə-'nem-ə-nē\ *n* **:** a small herb related to the buttercups that has showy usu. white flowers

**anent** \ə-'nent\ *prep* **:** ABOUT, CONCERNING

**an·es·the·sia** \‚an-əs-'thē-zhə\ *n* **:** loss of bodily sensation

**an·es·the·si·ol·o·gy** \-‚thē-zē-'äl-ə-jē\ *n* **:** a branch of medical science dealing with anesthesia and anesthetics — **an·es·the·si·ol·o·gist** \-jəst\ *n*

**¹an·es·thet·ic** \‚an-əs-'thet-ik\ *adj* **:** of, relating to, or capable of producing anesthesia

**²anesthetic** *n* **:** an agent (as ether) that produces anesthesia — **anes·the·tist** \ə-'nes-thət-əst\ *n* — **anes·the·tize** \-thə-‚tīz\ *vb*

**anew** \ə-'n(y)ü\ *adv* **:** over again : from a new start

**an·gel** \'ān-jəl\ *n* [ME, fr. OF *angele*, fr. L *angelus*, fr. Gk *angelos*, lit., messenger] **1 :** a spiritual being superior to man **2 :** an attendant spirit ⟨guardian ~⟩ **3 :** a winged figure of human form in art **4 :** MESSENGER, HARBINGER **5 :** a person held to resemble an angel — **an·gel·ic** \an-'jel-ik\ *or* **an·gel·i·cal** \-i-kəl\ *adj* — **an·gel·i·cal·ly** \-i-k(ə-)lē\ *adv*

**an·gel·fish** \'ān-jəl-‚fish\ *n* **:** any of several compressed bright-colored tropical fishes

**an·gel·i·ca** \an-'jel-i-kə\ *n* **:** a biennial herb related to the carrot whose roots and fruit furnish a flavoring oil

**¹an·ger** \'aŋ-gər\ *n* [ME, affliction, anger, fr. ON *angr* grief] **:** a strong feeling of displeasure **syn** wrath, ire, rage, fury, indignation

²**anger** *vb* **an·gered; an·ger·ing**
\-g(ə-)riŋ\ : to make angry

**an·gi·na** \an-'jī-nə\ *n* : a disorder (as
of the heart) marked by attacks of intense pain — **an·gi·nal** \an-'jīn-³l\
*adj*

**angina pec·to·ris** \-'pek-t(ə-)rəs\ *n*
: a disease marked by brief paroxysmal
attacks of chest pain precipitated by
deficient oxygenation of heart muscles

**an·gio·sperm** \'an-jē-ə-,sperm\ *n* : any
of a class of vascular plants (as orchids
or roses) having the seeds in a closed
ovary

¹**an·gle** \'aŋ-gəl\ *n* 1 : the figure
formed by the meeting of two lines in a
point 2 : a sharp projecting corner
3 : a point of view 4 : a special technique or plan : GIMMICK

²**angle** *vb* **an·gled; an·gling** \-g(ə-)liŋ\
: to turn, move, or direct at an angle

³**angle** *vb* **an·gled; an·gling** \-g(ə-)liŋ\
: to fish with a hook and line — **an·
gler** \-glər\ *n* — **an·gling** \-gliŋ\ *n*

**an·gle·worm** \'aŋ-gəl-,wərm\ *n*
: EARTHWORM

**An·gli·can** \'aŋ-gli-kən\ *adj* 1 : of or
relating to the established episcopal
Church of England 2 : of or relating
to England or the English nation —
**Anglican** *n* — **An·gli·can·ism**
\-kə-,niz-əm\ *n*

**an·gli·cize** \'aŋ-glə-,sīz\ *vb* -**cized;**
-**ciz·ing** *often cap* 1 : to make
English (as in habits, speech, character,
or outlook) 2 : to borrow (a foreign
word or phrase) into English without
changing form or spelling and sometimes without changing pronunciation
— **an·gli·ci·za·tion** \,aŋ-glə-sə-'zā-
shən\ *n, often cap*

**An·glo** \'aŋ-glō\ *n, pl* **Anglos** : a non-
Latin Caucasian inhabitant of the U.S.

**an·glo·phile** \'aŋ-glə-,fīl\ *also* **an·
glo·phil** \-,fil\ *n, often cap* : one who
greatly admires England

**an·glo·phobe** \'aŋ-glə-,fōb\ *n, often
cap* : one who is averse to England and
things English

**An·glo-Sax·on** \,aŋ-glō-'sak-sən\ *n*
1 : a member of any of the Germanic
peoples who invaded England in the 5th
century A.D. 2 : a member of the English people 3 : OLD ENGLISH — **Anglo-
Saxon** *adj*

**an·go·ra** \aŋ-'gōr-ə, an-\ *n* 1 *cap* : a
cat, goat, or rabbit with a long silky
coat 2 : yarn or cloth made from the
hair of an Angora goat or rabbit

**an·gry** \'aŋ-grē\ *adj* **an·gri·er; -est**
: feeling or showing anger **syn** enraged, wrathful, irate, indignant —
**an·gri·ly** \-grə-lē\ *adv*

**angst** \'äŋst\ *n* : a feeling of anxiety

**ang·strom** \'aŋ-strəm\ *n* : a unit of
length equal to one ten-billionth of a
meter

**an·guish** \'aŋ-gwish\ *n* : extreme pain
or distress esp. of mind

**an·guished** \-gwisht\ *adj* : full of
anguish : TORMENTED

**an·gu·lar** \'aŋ-gyə-lər\ *adj* 1 : having

one or more angles 2 : sharp-cornered
3 : being thin and bony — **an·gu·lar·
i·ty** \,aŋ-gyə-'lar-ət-ē\ *n*

**An·gus** \'aŋ-gəs\ *n* : any of a breed of
black hornless beef cattle originating in
Scotland

**an·hy·drous** \an-'hī-drəs\ *adj* : free
from water

**an·i·line** \'an-³l-ən\ *n* : an oily poisonous liquid used in making dyes, medicines, and explosives

**an·i·mad·vert** \,an-ə-,mad-'vərt\ *vb*
: to remark critically : express censure
— **an·i·mad·ver·sion** \-'vər-zhən\ *n*

¹**an·i·mal** \'an-ə-məl\ *n* 1 : a living
being capable of feeling and voluntary
motion 2 : a lower animal as distinguished from man; *also* : MAMMAL

²**animal** *adj* 1 : of, relating to, or derived from animals 2 : of or relating to
the physical as distinguished from the
mental or spiritual **syn** carnal

**an·i·mal·cule** \,an-ə-'mal-kyül\ *n*
: a tiny animal usu. invisible to the
naked eye

**an·i·mal·ism** \'an-ə-mə-,liz-əm\ *n*
: SENSUALITY

¹**an·i·mate** \'an-ə-mət\ *adj* : having life

²**an·i·mate** \-,māt\ *vb* -**mat·ed; -mat·
ing** 1 : to impart life to 2 : to give
spirit and vigor to 3 : to make appear
to move ⟨~ a cartoon for motion pic-
tures⟩ — **an·i·mat·ed** *adj*

**an·i·ma·tion** \,an-ə-'mā-shən\ *n* 1
: LIVELINESS, VIVACITY 2 : an animated
cartoon

**an·i·mism** \'an-ə-,miz-əm\ *n* : attribu-
tion of conscious life to nature as a
whole or to inanimate objects — **an·i·
mist** \-məst\ *n* — **an·i·mis·tic** \,an-
ə-'mis-tik\ *adj*

**an·i·mos·i·ty** \,an-ə-'mäs-ət-ē\ *n, pl*
-**ties** : ILL WILL, RESENTMENT

**an·i·mus** \'an-ə-məs\ *n* : deep-seated
resentment and hostility

**an·ion** \'an-,ī-ən, -,ī-,än\ *n* 1 : the ion
in an electrolyte that goes to the anode
2 : a negatively charged ion — **an·
ion·ic** \,an-ī-'än-ik\ *adj* — **an·lon·
i·cal·ly** \-i-k(ə-)lē\ *adv*

**an·ise** \'an-əs\ *n* : an herb related to
the carrot with aromatic seeds (**aniseed** \-ə(s)-,sēd\) used in flavoring

**an·is·ette** \,an-ə-'set, -'zet\ *n* : a usu.
colorless sweet liqueur flavored with
aniseed

**ankh** \'aŋk\ *n* : a cross having a loop
for its upper vertical arm and serving
esp. in ancient Egypt as an emblem of
life

**an·kle** \'aŋ-kəl\ *n* : the joint or region
between the foot and the leg

**an·kle·bone** \,an-kəl-'bōn, 'aŋ-kəl-
,bōn\ *n* : the proximal bone of the
tarsus that bears the weight of the body

**an·klet** \'aŋ-klət\ *n* 1 : something (as
an ornament) worn around the ankle
2 : a short sock reaching slightly above
the ankle

**ann** *abbr* 1 annals 2 annual

**an·nals** \'an-³lz\ *n pl* 1 : a record of
events in chronological order 2 : HIS-
TORY — **an·nal·ist** \-³l-əst\ *n*

**an·neal** \ə-'nēl\ vb : to make (as glass or steel) less brittle by subjecting to heat and then cooling

¹**an·nex** \ə-'neks, 'an-,eks\ vb **1** : to attach as an addition **2** : to incorporate (as a territory) within a political domain — **an·nex·a·tion** \,an-,ek-'sā-shən\ n

²**an·nex** \'an-,eks, -iks\ n : a subsidiary or supplementary structure

**an·ni·hi·late** \ə-'nī-ə-,lāt\ vb -lat·ed; -lat·ing : to destroy completely — **an·ni·hi·la·tion** \-,nī-ə-'lā-shən\ n

**an·ni·ver·sa·ry** \,an-ə-'vərs-(ə-)rē\ n, pl -ries : the annual return of the date of some notable event and esp. a wedding

**an·no Do·mi·ni** \,an-ō-'däm-ə-nē, -'dō-mə-, -,nī\ adv, often cap A [ML, in the year of the Lord] — used to indicate that a time division falls within the Christian era

**an·no·tate** \'an-ə-,tāt\ vb -tat·ed; -tat·ing : to furnish with notes — **an·no·ta·tion** \,an-ə-'tā-shən\ n — **an·no·ta·tor** \'an-ə-,tāt-ər\ n

**an·nounce** \ə-'naůns\ vb -nounced; -nounc·ing **1** : to make known publicly **2** : to give notice of the arrival or presence of — **an·nounce·ment** n

**an·nounc·er** \ə-'naůn-sər\ n : a person who introduces radio or television programs, reads commercials and news summaries, and gives station identification

**an·noy** \ə-'nói\ vb : to disturb or irritate esp. by repeated acts : VEX **syn** irk, bother, pester, tease, harass — **an·noy·ing·ly** \-'nói-iŋ-lē\ adv

**an·noy·ance** \ə-'nói-əns\ n **1** : the act of annoying : the state of being annoyed **2** : NUISANCE

¹**an·nu·al** \'an-yə(-wə)l\ adj **1** : covering the period of a year **2** : occurring once a year : YEARLY **3** : completing the life cycle in one growing season ⟨~ plants⟩ — **an·nu·al·ly** \-ē\ adv

²**annual** n **1** : a publication appearing once a year **2** : an annual plant

**annual ring** n : the layer of wood produced by a single year's growth of a woody plant

**an·nu·i·tant** \ə-'n(y)ü-ət-ənt\ n : a beneficiary of an annuity

**an·nu·i·ty** \ə-'n(y)ü-ət-ē\ n, pl -ities : an amount payable annually; also : the right to receive such a payment

**an·nul** \ə-'nəl\ vb an·nulled; an·nul·ling : to make legally void — **an·nul·ment** n

**an·nu·lar** \'an-yə-lər\ adj : ring-shaped

**annular eclipse** n : an eclipse in which a thin outer ring of the sun's disk is not covered by the moon's disk

**an·nun·ci·ate** \ə-'nən-sē-,āt\ vb -at·ed; -at·ing : ANNOUNCE

**an·nun·ci·a·tion** \ə-,nən-sē-'ā-shən\ n **1** : the act of announcing **2** cap : March 25 observed as church festival commemorating the announcement of the Incarnation

**an·nun·ci·a·tor** \ə-'nən-sē-,āt-ər\ n : one that annunciates; specif : a usu.

electrically controlled signal board or indicator — **an·nun·ci·a·to·ry** \-sē-ə-,tōr-ē\ adj

**an·ode** \'an-,ōd\ n **1** : the positive electrode of an electrolytic cell **2** : the negative terminal of a battery **3** : the electron-collecting electrode of an electron tube — **an·od·ic** \a-'näd-ik\ or **an·od·al** \-'nōd-ºl\ adj — **an·od·i·cal·ly** \-i-k(ə-)lē\ or **an·od·al·ly** \-ºl-ē\ adv

**an·od·ize** \'an-ə-,dīz\ vb -ized; -iz·ing : to subject a metal to electrolytic action as the anode of a cell in order to coat with a protective or decorative film — **an·od·iza·tion** \,an-,ōd-ə-'zā-shən, -əd-\ n

**an·o·dyne** \'an-ə-,dīn\ n : something that relieves pain : a soothing agent

**anoint** \ə-'nóint\ vb **1** : to apply oil to esp. as a sacred rite **2** : CONSECRATE — **anoint·ment** n

**anom·a·lous** \ə-'näm-ə-ləs\ adj : deviating from a general rule : ABNORMAL

**anom·a·ly** \ə-'näm-ə-lē\ n, pl -lies : something anomalous : IRREGULARITY

¹**anon** \ə-'nän\ adv, archaic : SOON

²**anon** abbr anonymous; anonymously

**anon·y·mous** \ə-'nän-ə-məs\ adj : of unknown or undeclared origin or authorship — **an·o·nym·i·ty** \,an-ə-'nim-ət-ē\ n — **anon·y·mous·ly** \ə-'nän-ə-məs-lē\ adv

**anoph·e·les** \ə-'näf-ə-,lēz\ n [NL, genus name, fr. Gk anōphelēs useless, fr. a- not + ophelos advantage, help] : a mosquito that transmits malaria to man

¹**an·oth·er** \ə-'nəth-ər\ adj **1** : any or some other **2** : being one in addition : one more

²**another** pron **1** : an additional one : one more **2** : one that is different from the first or present one

**ans** abbr answer

¹**an·swer** \'an-sər\ n **1** : something spoken or written in return to or satisfying a question **2** : a solution of a problem

²**answer** vb an·swered; an·swer·ing \'ans-(ə-)riŋ\ **1** : to speak or write in reply to **2** : to be responsible **3** : to be adequate — **an·swer·er** n

**an·swer·able** \'ans-(ə-)rə-bəl\ adj **1** : liable to be called to give an explanation or satisfaction : RESPONSIBLE **2** : capable of being refuted

**answering service** n : a commercial service that answers telephone calls for its clients

¹**ant** \'ant\ n : any of various small insects related to the bees and living in communities usu. in earth or wood

²**ant** abbr antonym

**Ant** abbr Antarctica

**ant-** — see ANTI-

¹**-ant** \ənt\ n suffix **1** : one that performs or promotes (a specified action) ⟨coolant⟩ **2** : thing that is acted upon (in a specified manner) ⟨inhalant⟩

²**-ant** adj suffix **1** : performing (a specified action) or being (in a specified condition) ⟨propellant⟩ **2** : promoting (a specified action or process) ⟨expectorant⟩

**ant·ac·id** \ant-'as-əd\ *adj* : counteractive of acidity — **antacid** *n*

**an·tag·o·nism** \an-'tag-ə-‚niz-əm\ *n* **1** : active opposition or hostility **2** : opposition in physiological action — **an·tag·o·nis·tic** \-‚tag-ə-'nis-tik\ *adj*

**an·tag·o·nist** \-nəst\ *n* : ADVERSARY, OPPONENT

**an·tag·o·nize** \an-'tag-ə-‚nīz\ *vb* **-nized; -niz·ing** : to provoke the hostility of

**ant·arc·tic** \ant-'ärk-tik, -'ärt-ik\ *adj, often cap* : of or relating to the south pole or the region near it

**antarctic circle** *n, often cap A&C* : a circle of the earth parallel to its equator approximately 23°27' from the south pole

**ant cow** *n* : an aphid from which ants obtain honeydew

¹**an·te** \'ant-ē\ *n* : a poker stake put up by each player before he sees his hand; *also* : an amount paid : PRICE

²**ante** *vb* **an·ted; an·te·ing** **1** : to put up (an ante) **2** : PAY

**ant·eat·er** \'ant-‚ēt-ər\ *n* : any of several mammals (as an aardvark) that feed on ants

**an·te·bel·lum** \‚ant-i-'bel-əm\ *adj* : existing before a war; *esp* : existing before the U.S. Civil War of 1861–65

**an·te·ced·ent** \‚ant-ə-'sēd-ᵊnt\ *n* **1** : a noun, pronoun, phrase, or clause referred to by a personal or relative pronoun **2** : a preceding event or cause **3** *pl* : the significant conditions of one's earlier life **4** *pl* : ANCESTORS — **antecedent** *adj*

**an·te·cham·ber** \'ant-i-‚chām-bər\ *n* : ANTEROOM

**an·te·choir** \'ant-i-‚kwī(ə)r\ *n* : a space enclosed or reserved for the clergy and choristers at the entrance to a choir

**an·te·date** \'ant-i-‚dāt\ *vb* **1** : to date (a paper) as of an earlier day than that on which the actual writing or signing is done **2** : to precede in time

**an·te·di·lu·vi·an** \‚ant-i-də-'lü-vē-ən, -dī-\ *adj* **1** : of the period before the biblical flood **2** : ANTIQUATED, OBSOLETE

**an·te·lope** \'ant-ᵊl-‚ōp\ *n, pl* **-lope** *or* **-lopes** [ME, fabulous heraldic beast, prob. fr. MF *antelop* savage animal with sawlike horns, fr. ML *anthalopus*, fr. LGk *antholops*] : any of various mammals related to the oxen but with smaller lighter bodies and horns that extend upward and backward

**an·te me·ri·di·em** \'ant-i-mə-'rid-ē-əm\ *adj* : being before noon

**an·ten·na** \an-'ten-ə\ *n, pl* **-nae** \-(‚)ē\ *or* **-nas** [ML, fr. L, sail yard] **1** : one of the long slender paired sensory organs on the head of an arthropod (as an insect or crab) **2** *pl* **-nas** : a metallic device (as a rod or wire) for sending out or receiving radio waves

**an·te·pe·nult** \‚ant-i-'pē-‚nəlt\ *also* **an·te·pen·ul·ti·ma** \-pi-'nəl-tə-mə\ *n* : the 3d syllable of a word counting from the end — **an·te·pen·ul·ti·mate** \-pi-'nəl-tə-mət\ *adj or n*

**an·te·ri·or** \an-'tir-ē-ər\ *adj* : located

before in place or time　**syn** preceding, previous, prior

**an·te·room** \'ant-i-‚rüm, -‚rúm\ *n* : a room forming the entrance to another and often used as a waiting room

**an·them** \'an-thəm\ *n* **1** : a sacred composition usu. sung by a church choir **2** : a song or hymn of praise or gladness

**an·ther** \'an-thər\ *n* : the part of the stamen of a seed plant that contains pollen

**ant·hill** \'ant-‚hil\ *n* : a mound thrown up by ants or termites in digging their nest

**an·thol·o·gy** \an-'thäl-ə-jē\ *n, pl* **-gies** [NL *anthologia* collection of epigrams, fr. MGk, fr. Gk, flower gathering, fr. *anthos* flower + *logia* collecting, fr. *legein* to gather] : a collection of literary selections — **an·thol·o·gist** \-jəst\ *n* — **an·thol·o·gize** \-‚jīz\ *vb*

**an·thra·cite** \'an-thrə-‚sīt\ *n* : a hard glossy coal that burns without much smoke — **an·thra·cit·ic** \‚an-thrə-'sīt-ik\ *adj*

**an·thrax** \'an-‚thraks\ *n* : a destructive bacterial disease of warm-blooded animals (as cattle and sheep)

**anthrop** *abbr* anthropology

**an·thro·po·cen·tric** \‚an-thrə-pə-'sen-trik\ *adj* : interpreting or regarding the world in terms of human values and experiences

¹**an·thro·poid** \'an-thrə-‚póid\ *adj* **1** : resembling man **2** : resembling an ape

²**anthropoid** *n* : any of several large higher apes (as a gorilla)

**an·thro·pol·o·gy** \‚an-thrə-'päl-ə-jē\ *n* : a science dealing with man and esp. his origin, development, and culture — **an·thro·po·log·i·cal** \-pə-'läj-i-kəl\ *adj* — **an·thro·pol·o·gist** \-'päl-ə-jəst\ *n*

**an·thro·po·mor·phism** \‚an-thrə-pə-'mór-‚fiz-əm\ *n* : an interpretation of what is not human or personal in terms of human or personal characteristics : HUMANIZATION — **an·thro·po·mor·phic** \-fik\ *adj*

**an·ti** \'an-‚tī, 'ant-ē\ *n, pl* **antis** : one who is antoned

**anti-** \‚ant-i, -ē; ‚an-‚tī\ *or* **ant-** *or* **anth-** *prefix* **1** : opposite in kind, position, or action **2** : opposing : hostile toward **3** : counteractive **4** : preventive of : curative of

antiaircraft　antifascist
anti-American　anti-imperialism
antibacterial　anti-imperialist
anticapitalist　antilabor
anti-Catholic　antimalarial
anticlerical　antimicrobial
anticolonial　antislavery
anti-Communism　antispasmodic
anti-Communist　antisubmarine
antidemocratic　antitank
antiestablishment　antitrust

**an·ti·bal·lis·tic missile** \‚ant-i-bə-‚lis-tik-, ‚an-‚tī-\ *n* : a missile for intercepting and destroying ballistic missiles

**an·ti·bi·ot·ic** \-bī-'ät-ik, -bē-\ *n* : a substance produced by an organism (as a fungus or bacteria) that in dilute solution inhibits or kills harmful microorganisms — **antibiotic** *adj*

**an·ti·body** \'ant-i-,bäd-ē\ *n* : a bodily substance that specifically counteracts the effects of a foreign substance or organism (as a disease-producing microorganism) introduced into the body

**¹an·tic** \'ant-ik\ *n* : a ludicrous act

**²antic** *adj* [It *antico* ancient, fr. L *antiquus*] **1** *archaic* : GROTESQUE **2** : PLAYFUL

**an·ti·can·cer** \,ant-i-'kan-sər, ,an-,tī-\ *adj* : used or effective against cancer 〈~ drugs〉

**An·ti·christ** \'ant-i-,krīst\ *n* **1** : one who denies or opposes Christ **2** : a false Christ

**an·tic·i·pate** \an-'tis-ə-,pāt\ *vb* **-pat·ed; -pat·ing 1** : to foresee and provide for beforehand **2** : to look forward to — **an·tic·i·pa·tion** \-,tis-ə-'pā-shən\ *n* — **an·tic·i·pa·to·ry** \-'tis-ə-pə-,tōr-ē\ *adj*

**an·ti·cli·max** \,ant-i-'klī-,maks\ *n* : an event or statement esp. closing a series that is strikingly less important than what has preceded it — **an·ti·cli·mac·tic** \-klī-'mak-tik\ *adj*

**an·ti·cline** \'ant-i-,klīn\ *n* : an arch of stratified rock — **an·ti·cli·nal** \-'klīn-°l\ *adj*

**an·ti·co·ag·u·lant** \,ant-i-kō-'ag-yə-lənt\ *n* : a substance that hinders the clotting of blood

**an·ti·cy·clone** \,ant-i-'sī-,klōn\ *n* : a system of winds that rotates about a center of high atmospheric pressure — **an·ti·cy·clon·ic** \-sī-'klän-ik\ *adj*

**an·ti·de·pres·sant** \,ant-i-di-'pres-°nt, ,an-,tī-\ *or* **an·ti·de·pres·sive** \-'pres-iv\ *adj* : used or tending to relieve psychic depression 〈~ drugs〉 — **antidepressant** *n*

**an·ti·dote** \'ant-i-,dōt\ *n* : a remedy to counteract the effects of poison

**an·ti·elec·tron** \,ant-ē-ə-'lek-,trän, ,an-,tī-\ *n* : POSITRON

**an·ti·fer·til·i·ty** \-fər-'til-ət-ē\ *adj* : tending to control excess or unwanted fertility : CONTRACEPTIVE 〈~ agents〉

**an·ti·freeze** \'ant-i-,frēz\ *n* : a substance added to a liquid to prevent its freezing

**an·ti·gen** \'ant-i-jən\ *n* : a usu. protein or carbohydrate substance (as a toxin or an enzyme) that when introduced into the body stimulates the production of an antibody — **an·ti·gen·ic** \,ant-i-'jen-ik\ *adj* — **an·ti·ge·nic·i·ty** \-jə-'nis-ət-ē\ *n*

**an·ti·grav·i·ty** \,ant-i-'grav-ət-ē, ,an-,tī-\ *n* : a hypothetical effect resulting from cancellation or reduction of a gravitational field — **antigravity** *adj*

**an·ti·he·ro** \'ant-i-,hē-rō, 'an-,tī-\ *n* : a protagonist who is notably lacking in heroic qualities (as courage)

**an·ti·his·ta·mine** \,ant-i-'his-tə-,mēn, ,an-,tī-, -mən\ *n* : any of various drugs used in treating allergies and colds

**an·ti·hy·per·ten·sive** \-,hī-pər-'ten-siv\ *n* : a substance that is effective against high blood pressure — **antihypertensive** *adj*

**an·ti·knock** \,ant-i-'näk\ *n* : a substance that when added to the fuel of an internal-combustion engine helps to prevent knocking

**an·ti·log·a·rithm** \,ant-i-'lóg-ə-,rith-əm, ,an-,tī , -'läg-\ *n* : the number corresponding to a given logarithm

**an·ti·ma·cas·sar** \,ant-i-mə-'kas-ər\ *n* : a cover to protect the back or arms of furniture

**an·ti·mag·net·ic** \,ant-i-mag-'net-ik, ,an-,tī-\ *adj* : having a balance unit composed of alloys that will not remain magnetized 〈an ~ watch〉

**an·ti·mat·ter** \'ant-i-,mat-ər\ *n* : matter composed of the counterparts of ordinary matter

**an·ti·mo·ny** \'ant-ə-,mō-nē\ *n* : a brittle silvery white metallic chemical element used in alloys

**an·ti·neo·plas·tic** \,ant-i-,nē-ə-'plas-tik, ,an-,tī-\ *adj* : inhibiting or preventing the growth and spread of neoplasms or malignant cells

**an·ti·neu·tron** \,ant-i-'n(y)ü-,trän\ *n* : the uncharged antiparticle of the neutron

**an·ti·no·mi·an** \,ant-i-'nō-mē-ən\ *n* : one who denies the validity of moral laws

**an·tin·o·my** \an-'tin-ə-mē\ *n, pl* **-mies** : a contradiction between two seemingly true statements

**an·ti·nov·el** \'ant-i-,näv-əl, 'an-,tī-\ *n* : a work of fiction that lacks all or most of the traditional features of the novel

**an·ti·ox·i·dant** \,ant-ē-'äk-səd-ənt, ,an-,tī-\ *n* : a substance that opposes oxidation — **antioxidant** *adj*

**an·ti·par·ti·cle** \'ant-i-,pärt-i-kəl, 'an-,tī-\ *n* : an elementary particle identical to another elementary particle in mass but opposite to it in electric and magnetic properties

**an·ti·pas·to** \,ant-i-'pas-tō, ,änt-i-'päs-\ *n, pl* **-tos** : HORS D'OEUVRE

**an·tip·a·thy** \an-'tip-ə-thē\ *n, pl* **-thies 1** : settled aversion or dislike **2** : an object of aversion — **an·ti·pa·thet·ic** \,ant-i-pə-'thet-ik\ *adj*

**an·ti·per·son·nel** \,ant-i-,pərs-°n-'el, ,an-,tī-\ *adj* : designed for use against military personnel 〈~ mine〉

**an·ti·per·spi·rant** \-'pər-spə-rənt\ *n* : a cosmetic preparation used to check excessive perspiration

**an·tiph·o·nal** \an-'tif-ən-°l\ *adj* : performed by two alternating groups — **an·tiph·o·nal·ly** \-ē\ *adv*

**an·ti·pode** \'ant-ə-,pōd\ *n, pl* **an·tip·o·des** \an-'tip-ə-,dēz\ [ME *antipodes*, pl., persons dwelling at opposite points on the globe, fr. L, fr. Gk, fr. pl. of *antipod-, antipous* with feet opposite, fr. *anti-* against + *pod-, pous* foot] : the parts of the earth diametrically opposite — usu. used in pl. — **an·tip·o·dal** \an-'tip-əd-°l\ *adj* — **an·ti·po·de·an** \(,)an-,tip-ə-'dē-ən\ *adj*

**an·ti·pol·lu·tion** \,ant-i-pə-'lü-shən\ *adj* : designed to prevent, reduce, or eliminate pollution 〈~ laws〉

**an·ti·pope** \'ant-i-,pōp\ *n* : one

elected or claiming to be pope in opposition to the pope canonically chosen

**an·ti·pov·er·ty** \,ant-i-'päv-ərt-ē, ,an-,tī-\ *adj* **:** of or relating to legislation designed to relieve poverty

**an·ti·pro·ton** \-'prō-,tän\ *n* **:** the antiparticle of the proton

**an·ti·quar·i·an** \,ant-ə-'kwer-ē-ən\ *adj* **1 :** of or relating to antiquities **2 :** dealing in old books — **antiquarian** *n* — **an·ti·quar·i·an·ism** *n*

**an·ti·quary** \'ant-ə-,kwer-ē\ *n, pl* **-quar·ies :** a person who collects or studies antiquities

**an·ti·quat·ed** \'ant-ə-,kwāt-əd\ *adj* **:** OUT-OF-DATE, OLD-FASHIONED

**¹an·tique** \an-'tēk\ *adj* **1 :** belonging to antiquity **2 :** OLD-FASHIONED **3 :** of a bygone style or period

**²antique** *n* **:** an object made in a bygone period

**³antique** *vb* **-tiqued; -tiquing :** to finish or refinish in antique style **:** give an appearance of age to

**an·tiq·ui·ty** \an-'tik-wət-ē\ *n, pl* **-ties 1 :** ancient times **2 :** great age **3** *pl* **:** relics of ancient times **4** *pl* **:** matters relating to ancient culture

**an·ti·Sem·i·tism** \,ant-i-'sem-ə-,tiz-əm, ,an-,tī-\ *n* **:** hostility toward Jews as a religious or social minority — **an·ti·Se·mit·ic** \-sə-'mit-ik\ *adj*

**an·ti·sep·tic** \,ant-ə-'sep-tik\ *adj* **:** killing or checking the growth of germs that cause decay or infection — **antiseptic** *n* — **an·ti·sep·ti·cal·ly** \-ti-k(ə-)lē\ *adv*

**an·ti·se·rum** \'ant-i-,sir-əm, 'an-,tī-\ *n* **:** a serum containing antibodies

**an·ti·so·cial** \-'sō-shəl\ *adj* **:** contrary or hostile to the well-being of society ⟨crime is ~⟩ **2 :** disliking the society of others

**an·tith·e·sis** \an-'tith-ə-səs\ *n, pl* **-e·ses** \-,sēz\ **1 :** the opposition or contrast of ideas **2 :** the direct opposite

**an·ti·thet·i·cal** \,ant-ə-'thet-i-kəl\ *or* **an·ti·thet·ic** \-ik\ *adj* **:** constituting or marked by antithesis — **an·ti·thet·i·cal·ly** \-i-k(ə-)lē\ *adv*

**an·ti·tox·in** \,ant-i-'täk-sən\ *n* **:** an antibody that is able to neutralize a particular toxin, is formed when the toxin is introduced into the body, and is produced in lower animals for use in treating human diseases (as diphtheria); *also* **:** a serum containing antitoxin

**an·ti·tu·mor** \,ant-i-'t(y)ü-mər, ,an-,tī-\ *adj* **:** ANTICANCER

**an·ti·ven·in** \-'ven-ən\ *n* **:** an antitoxin to a venom; *also* **:** a serum containing such antitoxin

**ant·ler** \'ant-lər\ *n* [ME *aunteler,* fr. MF *antoillier,* fr. L *anteocularis* located before the eye, fr. *ante-* before + *oculus* eye] **:** the solid usu. branched horn of a deer — **ant·lered** \-lərd\ *adj*

**ant lion** *n* **:** any of various insects having a long-jawed larva that digs a conical pit in which it lies in wait for insects (as ants) on which it feeds

**ant·onym** \'ant-ə-,nim\ *n* **:** a word of opposite meaning

**an·trum** \'an-trəm\ *n, pl* **an·tra** \-trə\ **:** the cavity of a hollow organ or a sinus

**anus** \'ā-nəs\ *n* **:** the posterior opening of the alimentary canal

**an·vil** \'an-vəl\ *n* **1 :** a heavy iron block on which metal is shaped (as by hammering) **2 :** INCUS

**anx·i·ety** \aŋ-'zī-ət-ē\ *n, pl* **-eties 1 :** painful uneasiness of mind usu. over an anticipated ill **2 :** abnormal apprehension and fear often accompanied by physiological signs (as sweating and increased pulse), by doubt about the nature and reality of the threat itself, and by self-doubt

**anx·ious** \'aŋk-shəs\ *adj* **1 :** uneasy in mind **:** WORRIED **2 :** earnestly wishing **:** EAGER — **anx·ious·ly** *adv*

**¹any** \'en-ē\ *adj* **1 :** one chosen at random **2 :** of whatever number or quantity

**²any** *pron* **1 :** any one or ones ⟨take ~ of the books you like⟩ **2 :** any amount ⟨~ of the money not used is to be returned⟩

**³any** *adv* **:** to any extent or degree **:** at all ⟨could not walk ~ farther⟩

**any·body** \-,bäd-ē, -bəd-\ *pron* **:** ANYONE

**any·how** \-,haů\ *adv* **1 :** in any way **2 :** NEVERTHELESS; *also* **:** in any case

**any·more** \,en-ē-'mōr\ *adv* **:** at the present time

**any·one** \-(,)wən\ *pron* **:** any person

**any·place** \-,plās\ *adv* **:** ANYWHERE

**any·thing** \-,thiŋ\ *pron* **:** any thing whatever

**any·time** \'en-ē-,tīm\ *adv* **:** at any time whatever

**any·way** \-,wā\ *adv* **:** ANYHOW

**any·where** \-,hweər\ *adv* **:** in or to any place

**any·wise** \-,wīz\ *adv* **:** in any way whatever

**AO** *abbr* account of

**A–OK** \,ā-ō-'kā\ *adv or adj* **:** very definitely OK

**A1** \'ā-'wən\ *adj* **:** of the finest quality

**aor·ta** \ā-'ȯrt-ə\ *n, pl* **-tas** *or* **-tae** \-ē\ **:** the main artery that carries blood from the heart — **aor·tic** \-'ȯrt-ik\ *adj*

**ap** *abbr* **1** apostle **2** apothecaries'

**AP** *abbr* **1** additional premium **2** Associated Press

**apace** \ə-'pās\ *adv* **:** SWIFTLY

**Apache** \ə-'pach-ē *for 1;* e-'pash *for 2*\ *n, pl* **Apache** *or* **Apach·es** \-'pach-ēz, -'pash-(-əz)\ **1 :** a member of an Indian people of the southwestern U.S.; *also* **:** any of the languages of the Apache people **2** *not cap* **:** a member of a gang of criminals esp. in Paris

**ap·a·nage** *var of* APPANAGE

**apart** \ə-'pärt\ *adv* **1 :** separately in place or time **2 :** ASIDE **3 :** to pieces **:** ASUNDER

**apart·heid** \ə-'pär-,tāt, -,tīt\ *n* **:** a policy of racial segregation practiced in the Republic of So. Africa

**apart·ment** \ə-'pärt-mənt\ *n* **:** a room or set of rooms occupied as a dwelling; *also* **:** a building divided into individual dwelling units

**ap·a·thy** \'ap-ə-thē\ *n* **1** : lack of emotion **2** : lack of interest — INDIFFERENCE — **ap·a·thet·ic** \,ap-ə-'thet-ik\ *adj* — **ap·a·thet·i·cal·ly** \-l-k(ə-)lē\ *adv*

**ap·a·tite** \'ap-ə-,tīt\ *n* : any of a group of minerals that are phosphates of calcium used as a source of phosphorus

**APB** *abbr* all points bulletin

**¹ape** \'āp\ *n* **1** : any of the larger tailless primates (as a baboon or gorilla); *also* : MONKEY **2** : MIMIC, IMITATOR; *also* : a large uncouth person

**²ape** *vb* **aped; ap·ing** : IMITATE, MIMIC

**apeak** \ə-'pēk\ *adj or adv* : being in a vertical position (with oars ~)

**ape–man** \'āp-'man, -,man\ *n* : a primate intermediate in character between true man and the higher apes

**aper·çu** \ȧ-per-süē, ,ap-ər-'sü\ *n, pl* **aperçus** \-süē(z), -'süz\ : an immediate impression; *esp* : INSIGHT

**aper·i·tif** \,äp-,er-ə-'tēf\ *n* : an alcoholic drink taken as an appetizer

**aper·ture** \'ap-ə(r)-,chur, -chər\ *n* : OPENING, HOLE

**apex** \'ā-,peks\ *n, pl* **apex·es** *or* **api·ces** \'ā-pə-,sēz, 'ap-ə-\ : the highest point : PEAK

**aph·a·nite** \'af-ə-,nīt\ *n* : a dark extremely fine-grained rock — **aph·a·nit·ic** \,af-ə-'nit-ik\ *adj*

**apha·sia** \ə-fā-zh(ē-)ə\ *n* : loss of power to use or understand speech — **apha·sic** \-zik\ *adj*

**aph·elion** \a-'fēl-yən\ *n, pl* **-elia** \-yə\ : the point of a planet's or comet's orbit most distant from the sun

**aphid** \'ā-fəd, 'af-əd\ *n* : a small insect that sucks the juices of plants

**aphis** \'ā-fəs, 'af-əs\ *n, pl* **aphi·des** \'ā-fə-,dēz, 'af-ə-\ : APHID

**aph·o·rism** \'af-ə-,riz-əm\ *n* : a short saying stating a general truth : MAXIM — **aph·o·ris·tic** \,af-ə-'ris-tik\ *adj*

**aph·ro·dis·i·ac** \,af-rə-'diz-ē-,ak\ *adj* : exciting sexual desire — **aphro·disiac** *n*

**api·ary** \'ā-pē-,er-ē\ *n, pl* **-ar·ies** : a place where bees are kept — **api·a·rist** \-pē-ə-rəst\ *n*

**api·cal** \'ā-pi-kəl, 'ap-i-\ *adj* : of, relating to, or situated at an apex — **api·cal·ly** \-k(ə-)lē\ *adv*

**apiece** \ə-'pēs\ *adv* : for each one

**aplomb** \ə-'pläm, -'pləm\ *n* [F, lit., perpendicularity, fr. MF, fr. *a plomb*, lit., according to the plummet] : complete composure or self-assurance

**APO** *abbr* army post office

**apoc·a·lypse** \ə-'päk-ə-,lips\ *n* : a writing prophesying a cataclysm in which evil forces are destroyed — **apoc·a·lyp·tic** \-,päk-ə-'lip-tik\ *or* **apoc·a·lyp·ti·cal** \-ti-kəl\ *adj*

**Apoc·ry·pha** \ə-'päk-rə-fə\ *n* **1** *not cap* : writings of dubious authenticity **2** : books included in the Septuagint and Vulgate but excluded from the Jewish and Protestant canons of the Old Testament **3** : early Christian writings not included in the New Testament

**apoc·ry·phal** \-fəl\ *adj* **1** *often cap*

: of or resembling the Apocrypha **2** : not canonical : SPURIOUS — **apoc·ry·phal·ly** \-ē\ *adv*

**apo·cyn·thi·on** \,ap-ə-'sin-thē-ən\ *n* : APOLUNE

**apo·gee** \'ap-ə-(,)jē\ *n* [fr. *apogee* point at which the moon is farthest from the earth, fr. F. *apogée*, fr. NL *apogaeum*, fr. Gk *apogaion*, fr. *apo* away from + *gē*, *gaia* earth] : the point at which an orbiting object is farthest from the body (as the earth or moon) being orbited — **apo·ge·an** \,ap-ə-'jē-ən\ *adj*

**apolit·i·cal** \,ā-pə-'lit-i-kəl\ *adj* **1** : having an aversion for or no interest in political affairs **2** : having no political significance — **apolit·i·cal·ly** \-k(ə-)lē\ *adv*

**apol·o·get·ic** \ə-,päl-ə-'jet-ik\ *adj* : expressing apology — **apol·o·get·i·cal·ly** \-i-k(ə-)lē\ *adv*

**ap·o·lo·gia** \,ap-ə-'lō-j(ē-)ə\ *n* : APOLOGY; *esp* : an argument in support of justification

**apol·o·gize** \ə-'päl-ə-,jīz\ *vb* **-gized; -giz·ing** : to make an apology : express regret — **apol·o·gist** \-jəst\ *n*

**apol·o·gy** \ə-'päl-ə-jē\ *n, pl* **-gies** **1** : a formal justification : DEFENSE **2** : an expression of regret for a discourteous remark or act

**apo·lune** \'ap-ə-,lüin\ *n* : the point in the path of a body orbiting the moon that is farthest from the center of the moon

**ap·o·plexy** \'ap-ə-,plek-sē\ *n* : sudden loss of consciousness caused by rupture or obstruction of an artery of the brain — **ap·o·plec·tic** \,ap-ə-'plek-tik\ *adj*

**aport** \ə-'pōrt\ *adv* : on or toward the left side of a ship

**apos·ta·sy** \ə-'päs-tə-sē\ *n, pl* **-sies** : a renunciation or abandonment of a former loyalty (as to a religion) — **apos·tate** \ə-'päs-,tāt, -tət\ *adj or n*

**a pos·te·ri·o·ri** \,ä-pō-,stir-ē-'ōr-ē\ *adj* [L, lit., from the latter] : characterized by or derived by reasoning from observed facts — **a posteriori** *adv*

**apos·tle** \ə-'päs-əl\ *n* **1** : one of the group composed of Jesus' 12 original disciples and Paul **2** : the first prominent missionary to a region or group **3** : one who initiates or first advocates a great reform — **apos·tle·ship** *n*

**ap·os·tol·ic** \,ap-ə-'stäl-ik\ *adj* **1** : of or relating to an apostle or to the New Testament apostles **2** : of or relating to a succession of spiritual authority from the apostles **3** : PAPAL

**¹apos·tro·phe** \ə-'päs-trə-(,)fē\ *n* : the rhetorical addressing of an absent person as if present or of an abstract idea or inanimate object as if capable of understanding (as in "O grave, where is thy victory?")

**²apostrophe** *n* : a punctuation mark ' used esp. to indicate the possessive case or the omission of a letter or figure

**apos·tro·phize** \ə-'päs-trə-,fīz\ *vb* **-phized; -phiz·ing** : to address as if present or capable of understanding

**apothecaries' weight** *n* : a system of weights used chiefly by pharmacists — see WEIGHT table

**apoth·e·cary** \ə-'päth-ə-ˌker-ē\ *n, pl* **-car·ies** [ME *apothecarie*, fr. ML *apothecarius*, fr. LL, shopkeeper, fr. L *apotheca* storehouse, fr. Gk *apothēkē*, fr. *apotithenai* to put away] : DRUGGIST

**apo·thegm** \'ap-ə-ˌthem\ *n* : APHORISM, MAXIM

**apo·the·o·sis** \ə-ˌpäth-ē-'ō-səs, ˌap-ə-'thē-ə-səs\ *n, pl* **-o·ses** \-ˌsēz\ 1 : DEIFICATION 2 : the perfect example

**app** *abbr* 1 apparatus 2 appendix

**ap·pall** *also* **ap·pal** \ə-'pȯl\ *vb* **ap·palled; ap·pall·ing** 1 : to overcome with horror : DISMAY

**Ap·pa·loo·sa** \ˌap-ə-'lü-sə\ *n* : a rugged saddle horse of a breed developed in western No. America that has a mottled skin, vertically striped hooves, and a blotched or dotted patch of white hair over the rump and loins

**ap·pa·nage** \'ap-ə-nij\ *n* 1 : provision (as a grant of land) made by a sovereign or legislative body for dependent members of the royal family 2 : a rightful adjunct

**ap·pa·ra·tus** \ˌap-ə-'rat-əs,-'rāt-\ *n, pl* **-tus·es** *or* **-tus** 1 : a set of materials or equipment for a particular use 2 : a complex machine or device : MECHANISM 3 : the organization of a political party or underground movement

¹**ap·par·el** \ə-'par-əl\ *vb* **-eled** *or* **-elled; -el·ing** *or* **-el·ling** 1 : CLOTHE, DRESS 2 : ADORN

²**apparel** *n* : CLOTHING, DRESS

**ap·par·ent** \ə-'par-ənt\ *adj* 1 : open to view : VISIBLE 2 : EVIDENT, OBVIOUS 3 : appearing as real or true : SEEMING — **ap·par·ent·ly** *adv*

**ap·pa·ri·tion** \ˌap-ə-'rish-ən\ *n* : a supernatural appearance : GHOST

**ap·peal** \ə-'pēl\ *vb* 1 : to take steps to have (a case) reheard in a higher court 2 : to plead for help, corroboration, or decision 3 : to arouse a sympathetic response — **appeal** *n*

**ap·pear** \ə-'piər\ *vb* 1 : to become visible 2 : to come formally before an authority 3 : SEEM 4 : to become evident 5 : to come before the public

**ap·pear·ance** \ə-'pir-əns\ *n* 1 : the act of appearing 2 : outward aspect : LOOK 3 : PHENOMENON

**ap·pease** \ə-'pēz\ *vb* **ap·peased; ap·peas·ing** 1 : to cause to subside : ALLAY 2 : PACIFY, CONCILIATE; *esp* : to buy off by concessions — **ap·pease·ment** *n*

**ap·pel·lant** \ə-'pel-ənt\ *n* : one who appeals esp. from a judicial decision

**ap·pel·late** \ə-'pel-ət\ *adj* : having power to review decisions of a lower court

**ap·pel·la·tion** \ˌap-ə-'lā-shən\ *n* : NAME, DESIGNATION

**ap·pel·lee** \ˌap-ə-'lē\ *n* : one against whom an appeal is taken

**ap·pend** \ə-'pend\ *vb* : to attach esp. as something additional : AFFIX

**ap·pend·age** \ə-'pen-dij\ *n* 1 : something appended to a principal or greater thing 2 : a subordinate or derivative body part (as a limb) *syn* accessory, adjunct

**ap·pen·dec·to·my** \ˌap-ən-'dek-tə-mē\ *n, pl* **-mies** : surgical removal of the intestinal appendix

**ap·pen·di·ci·tis** \ə-ˌpen-də-'sīt-əs\ *n* : inflammation of the intestinal appendix

**ap·pen·dix** \ə-'pen-diks\ *n, pl* **-dix·es** *or* **-di·ces** \-də-ˌsēz\ 1 : supplementary matter added at the end of a book 2 : a narrow blind tube usu. about three or four inches long that extends from the cecum in the lower right-hand part of the abdomen

**ap·per·tain** \ˌap-ər-'tān\ *vb* : to belong as a rightful part or privilege

**ap·pe·tite** \'ap-ə-ˌtīt\ *n* [ME *apetit*, fr. MF, fr. L *appetitus*, fr. *appetere* to strive after, fr. *ad-* to + *petere* to go for] 1 : natural desire for satisfying some want or need esp. for food 2 : TASTE, PREFERENCE

**ap·pe·tiz·er** \'ap-ə-ˌtī-zər\ *n* : a food or drink taken just before a meal to stimulate the appetite

**ap·pe·tiz·ing** \-ziŋ\ *adj* : tempting to the appetite — **ap·pe·tiz·ing·ly** *adv*

**appl** *abbr* applied

**ap·plaud** \ə-'plȯd\ *vb* : to show approval esp. by clapping

**ap·plause** \ə-'plȯz\ *n* : approval publicly expressed (as by clapping)

**ap·ple** \'ap-əl\ *n* : a rounded fruit with firm white flesh and a seedy core; *also* : a tree related to the roses that bears this fruit

**ap·ple·jack** \-ˌjak\ *n* : a liquor distilled from fermented cider

**ap·pli·ance** \ə-'plī-əns\ *n* 1 : INSTRUMENT, DEVICE 2 : a piece of household equipment (as a stove or toaster) operated by gas or electricity

**ap·pli·ca·ble** \'ap-li-kə-bəl, ə-'plik-ə-\ *adj* : capable of being applied : RELEVANT — **ap·pli·ca·bil·i·ty** \ˌap-li-kə-'bil-ət-ē, ə-ˌplik-ə-\ *n*

**ap·pli·cant** \'ap-li-kənt\ *n* : one who applies — **ap·pli·can·cy** \-kən-sē\ *n*

**ap·pli·ca·tion** \ˌap-lə-'kā-shən\ *n* 1 : the act of applying 2 : assiduous attention 3 : REQUEST; *also* : a form used in making a request 4 : something placed or spread on a surface 5 : capacity for use

**ap·pli·ca·tor** \'ap-lə-ˌkāt-ər\ *n* : one that applies; *esp* : a device for applying a substance (as medicine or polish)

**ap·plied** \ə-'plīd\ *adj* : put to practical use

**ap·pli·qué** \ˌap-lə-'kā\ *n* : a fabric decoration cut out and fastened to a larger piece of material — **appliqué** *vb*

**ap·ply** \ə-'plī\ *vb* **ap·plied; ap·ply·ing** 1 : to place in contact : put or spread on a surface 2 : to put to practical use 3 : to employ with close attention 4 : to submit a request personally or by letter

**ap·point** \ə-'point\ *vb* 1 : to fix or set officially (~ a day for trial) 2 : to name officially 3 : to fit out : EQUIP

**ap·poin·tee** \ə-ˌpȯin-'tē, ˌa-\ *n* : a person appointed

**ap·point·ive** \ə-'pȯint-iv\ *adj* : subject to appointment

**ap·point·ment** \ə-'pȯint-mənt\ *n* 1 : the act of appointing 2 : a nonelective office or position 3 : an arrangement for a meeting 4 *pl* : FURNISHINGS, EQUIPMENT

**ap·por·tion** \ə-'pōr-shən\ *vb* **ap·por·tioned**; **ap·por·tion·ing** \-sh(ə-)niŋ\ : to distribute proportionately : ALLOT — **ap·por·tion·ment** *n*

**ap·po·site** \'ap-ə-zət\ *adj* : APPROPRIATE, RELEVANT — **ap·po·site·ly** *adv* — **ap·po·site·ness** *n*

**ap·po·si·tion** \ˌap-ə-'zish-ən\ *n* : a grammatical construction in which a noun or pronoun is followed by another that explains it (as *the poet* and *Burns* in "a biography of the poet Burns")

**ap·pos·i·tive** \ə-'päz-ət-iv, a-\ *adj* : of, relating to, or standing in grammatical apposition — **appositive** *n*

**ap·praise** \ə-'prāz\ *vb* **ap·praised**; **ap·prais·ing** : to set a value on — **ap·prais·al** \-'prā-zəl\ *n* — **ap·prais·er** *n*

**ap·pre·cia·ble** \ə-'prē-shə-bəl\ *adj* : large enough to be recognized and measured — **ap·pre·cia·bly** \-blē\ *adv*

**ap·pre·ci·ate** \ə-'prē-shē-ˌāt\ *vb* **-at·ed**; **-at·ing** 1 : to value justly 2 : to be aware of 3 : to be grateful for 4 : to increase in value — **ap·pre·ci·a·tion** \-ˌprē-shē-'ā-shən\ *n*

**ap·pre·cia·tive** \ə-'prē-shət-iv, -shē-ˌāt-\ *adj* : having or showing appreciation

**ap·pre·hend** \ˌap-ri-'hend\ *vb* 1 : ARREST 2 : to become aware of 3 : to look forward to with dread 4 : UNDERSTAND — **ap·pre·hen·sion** \-'hen-chən\ *n*

**ap·pre·hen·sive** \-'hen-siv\ *adj* : viewing the future with anxiety — **ap·pre·hen·sive·ly** *adv* — **ap·pre·hen·sive·ness** *n*

¹**ap·pren·tice** \ə-'prent-əs\ *n* 1 : a person learning a craft under a skilled worker 2 : BEGINNER — **ap·pren·tice·ship** *n*

²**apprentice** *vb* **-ticed**; **-tic·ing** : to bind or set at work as an apprentice

**ap·prise** \ə-'prīz\ *vb* **ap·prised**; **ap·pris·ing** : INFORM

**ap·proach** \ə-'prōch\ *vb* 1 : to move nearer to 2 : to take preliminary steps toward — **approach** *n* — **ap·proach·able** *adj*

**ap·pro·ba·tion** \ˌap-rə-'bā-shən\ *n* : APPROVAL

¹**ap·pro·pri·ate** \ə-'prō-prē-ˌāt\ *vb* **-at·ed**; **-at·ing** 1 : to take possession of 2 : to set apart for a particular use

²**ap·pro·pri·ate** \ə-'prō-prē-ət\ *adj* : fitted to a purpose or use : SUITABLE *syn* proper, fit, apt — **ap·pro·pri·ate·ly** *adv* — **ap·pro·pri·ate·ness** *n*

**ap·pro·pri·a·tion** \ə-ˌprō-prē-'ā-shən\ *n* : money set aside by formal action for a specific use

**ap·prov·al** \ə-'prü-vəl\ *n* : an act of approving — **on approval** : subject to a prospective buyer's acceptance or refusal

**ap·prove** \ə-'prüv\ *vb* **ap·proved**; **ap·prov·ing** 1 : to have or express a favorable opinion of 2 : to accept as satisfactory : RATIFY

**approx** *abbr* approximate; approximately

¹**ap·prox·i·mate** \ə-'präk-sə-mət\ *adj* : nearly correct or exact — **ap·prox·i·mate·ly** *adv*

²**ap·prox·i·mate** \-ˌmāt\ *vb* **-mat·ed**; **-mat·ing** : to come near : APPROACH — **ap·prox·i·ma·tion** \ə-ˌpräk-sə-'mā-shən\ *n*

**appt** *abbr* appoint; appointment

**ap·pur·te·nance** \ə-'pərt-(ə)nəns\ *n* : something that belongs to or goes with another thing *syn* accessory, adjunct, appendage — **ap·pur·te·nant** \-(ə)nənt\ *adj*

**Apr** *abbr* April

**apri·cot** \'ap-rə-ˌkät, 'ā-prə-\ *n* : an oval orange-colored fruit resembling the related peach in flavor; *also* : the tree bearing it

**April** \'ā-prəl\ *n* [ME, fr. OF & L; ME, fr. OF *avril*, fr. L *Aprilis*] : the fourth month of the year having 30 days

**a pri·o·ri** \ˌä-prē-'ōr-ē\ *adj* [L, from the former] 1 : characterized by or derived from reasoning from self-evident propositions 2 : independent of experience — **a priori** *adv*

**apron** \'ā-prən, -pərn\ *n* [ME, alter. (resulting fr. incorrect division of *a napron*) of *napron*, fr. MF *naperon*, dim. of *nape* cloth, modif. of L *mappa* napkin] 1 : a garment tied over the front of the body to protect the clothes 2 : a paved area for parking or handling airplanes

¹**ap·ro·pos** \ˌap-rə-'pō, 'ap-rə-ˌpō\ *adv* [F *à propos*, lit., to the purpose] 1 : OPPORTUNELY 2 : SUITABLY

²**apropos** *adj* : being to the point **apropos of** *prep* : with regard to

**apse** \'aps\ *n* : a projecting usu. semicircular and vaulted part of a building (as a church)

¹**apt** \'apt\ *adj* 1 : well adapted : SUITABLE 2 : having an habitual tendency : LIKELY 3 : quick to learn — **apt·ly** *adv* — **apt·ness** \'ap(t)-nəs\ *n*

²**apt** *abbr* apartment

**ap·ti·tude** \'ap-tə-ˌt(y)üd\ *n* 1 : capacity for learning 2 : natural ability : TALENT 3 : APPROPRIATENESS

**aqua** \'ak-wə, 'äk-\ *n, pl* **aquae** \'ak-(ˌ)wē, 'äk-ˌwī\ *or* **aquas** 1 : WATER; *esp* : an aqueous solution 2 : a light greenish blue color

**aqua·cade** \'ak-wə-ˌkād, 'äk-\ *n* : an elaborate water spectacle consisting of exhibitions of swimming, diving, and acrobatics accompanied by music

**aqua·lung·er** \-ˌləŋ-ər\ *n* : an underwater swimmer who uses a breathing device

**aqua·ma·rine** \ˌak-wə-mə-'rēn, ˌäk-\ *n* 1 : a bluish green gem 2 : a pale blue to light greenish blue

**aqua·naut** \'ak-wə-,nȯt, 'äk-\ *n* **:** a scuba diver who lives and operates both inside and outside an underwater shelter for an extended period

**aqua·plane** \-,plān\ *n* **:** a board towed behind a speeding motorboat and ridden by a person standing on it — **aqua·plane** *vb*

**aqua re·gia** \,ak-wə-'rē-j(ē-)ə\ *n* **:** a mixture of nitric and hydrochloric acids that dissolves gold or platinum

**aquar·i·um** \ə-'kwar-ē-əm\ *n, pl* **-i·ums** *or* **-ia** \-ē-ə\ **1 :** a container in which living aquatic animals and plants are kept **2 :** a place where aquatic animals and plants are kept and shown

**aquat·ic** \ə-'kwät-ik, -'kwat-\ *adj* **1 :** growing or living in or frequenting water **2 :** performed in or on water — **aquatic** *n*

**aqua·vit** \'äk-wə-,vēt\ *n* **:** a clear liquor flavored with caraway seeds

**aqua vi·tae** \,ak-wə-'vīt-ē, ,äk-\ *n* [ME, fr. ML, lit., water of life] **1 :** ALCOHOL **2 :** a strong alcoholic drink

**aq·ue·duct** \'ak-wə-,dəkt\ *n* **1 :** a conduit for carrying running water **2 :** a structure carrying a canal over a river or hollow **3 :** a passage in a bodily part

**aquo·ous** \'ā-kwē-əs, 'ak-wē\ *adj* **1 :** WATERY **2 :** made of, by, or with water

**aqueous humor** *n* **:** a limpid fluid occupying the space between the lens and the cornea of the eye

**aqui·cul·ture** *or* **aqua·cul·ture** \'ak-wə-,kəl-chər, 'äk-\ *n* **:** cultivation of the natural produce of water

**aqui·fer** \'ak-wə-fər, 'äk-\ *n* **:** a water-bearing stratum of permeable rock, sand, or gravel

**aq·ui·line** \'ak-wə-,līn, -lən\ *adj* **1 :** of or resembling an eagle **2 :** hooked like an eagle's beak ⟨an ~ nose⟩

**ar** *abbr* arrival; arrive

**¹Ar** *abbr* Arabic

**²Ar** *symbol* argon

**AR** *abbr* Arkansas

**-ar** \ər\ *adj suffix* **:** of or relating to ⟨molecular⟩ **:** being ⟨spectacular⟩ **:** resembling ⟨oracular⟩

**Ar·ab** \'ar-əb\ *n* **1 :** a member of a Semitic people of the Arabian peninsula **2 :** a member of an Arabic-speaking people — **Arab** *adj* — **Ara·bi·an** \ə-'rā-bē-ən\ *adj or n*

**ar·a·besque** \,ar-ə-'besk\ *n* **:** a design of interlacing lines forming figures of flowers, foliage, and sometimes animals

**¹Ar·a·bic** \'ar-ə-bik\ *adj* **:** of or relating to Arabia, the Arabs, or Arabic

**²Arabic** *n* **:** a Semitic language of southwest Asia and north Africa

**Arabic numeral** *n* **:** one of the number symbols 1, 2, 3, 4, 5, 6, 7, 8, 9, and 0

**ar·a·ble** \'ar-ə-bəl\ *adj* **:** fit for or cultivated by plowing **:** suitable for crops

**arach·nid** \ə-'rak-nəd\ *n* **:** any of a class of usu. 8-legged arthropods comprising the spiders, scorpions, mites, and ticks — **arachnid** *adj*

**Arap·a·ho** *or* **Arap·a·hoe** \ə-'rap-ə-,hō\ *n, pl* **Arapaho** *or* **Arapahos** *or*

**Arapahoe** *or* **Arapahoes :** a member of an Indian people of the western U.S.

**ar·ba·lest** *or* **ar·ba·list** \'är-bə-ləst\ *n* **:** a medieval crossbow with a steel bow

**ar·bi·ter** \'är-bət-ər\ *n* **:** one having power to decide **:** JUDGE

**ar·bit·ra·ment** \är-'bit-rə-mənt\ *n* **1 :** the act of deciding a dispute **2 :** the judgment given by an arbitrator

**ar·bi·trary** \'är-bə-,trer-ē\ *adj* **1 :** determined by will or caprice **:** selected at random **2 :** AUTOCRATIC, DESPOTIC — **ar·bi·trari·ly** \,är-bə-'trer-ə-lē\ *adv* — **ar·bi·trari·ness** \'är-bə-,trer-ē-nəs\ *n*

**ar·bi·trate** \'är-bə-,trāt\ *vb* **-trat·ed; -trat·ing** **1 :** to act as arbitrator **2 :** to act on as arbitrator **3 :** to submit for decision to an arbitrator — **ar·bi·tra·tion** \,är-bə-'trā-shən\ *n*

**ar·bi·tra·tor** \'är-bə-,trāt-ər\ *n* **:** one chosen to settle differences between two parties in a controversy

**ar·bor** \'är-bər\ *n* [ME *erber* plot of grass, arbor, fr. OF *herbier* plot of grass, fr. *herbe* herb, grass] **:** a bower formed of or covered with vines or branches

**ar·bo·re·al** \är-'bōr-ē-əl\ *adj* **1 :** of, relating to, or resembling a tree **2 :** living in trees

**ar·bo·re·tum** \,är-bə-'rēt-əm\ *n, pl* **-retums** *or* **-re·ta** \-'rēt-ə\ [L, place grown with trees, fr. *arbor* tree] **:** a place where trees and plants are grown for scientific and educational purposes

**ar·bor·vi·tae** \,är-bər-'vīt-ē\ *n* **:** any of various scale-leaved evergreen trees related to the pines

**ar·bu·tus** \är-'byüt-əs\ *n* **:** TRAILING ARBUTUS

**¹arc** \'ärk\ *n* **1 :** a part of a curved line (as of a circle) **2 :** a sustained luminous discharge of electricity (as between two electrodes)

**²arc** *vb* **:** to form an electric arc

**ARC** *abbr* American Red Cross

**ar·cade** \är-'kād\ *n* **1 :** a row of arches with their supporting columns **2 :** an arched or covered passageway; *esp* **:** one lined with shops

**ar·cane** \är-'kān\ *adj* **:** SECRET, MYSTERIOUS

**¹arch** \'ärch\ *n* **1 :** a curved structure spanning an opening (as a door or window) **2 :** something resembling an arch **3 :** ARCHWAY

**²arch** *vb* **1 :** to cover with an arch **2 :** to form or bend into an arch

**³arch** *adj* **1 :** CHIEF, EMINENT **2 :** ROGUISH, MISCHIEVOUS — **arch·ly** *adv* — **arch·ness** *n*

**⁴arch** *abbr* architect; architecture

**ar·chae·ol·o·gy** *or* **ar·che·ol·o·gy** \,är-kē-'äl-ə-jē\ *n* **:** the study of past human life as revealed by relics left by ancient peoples — **ar·chae·o·log·i·cal** \-kē-ə-'läj-i-kəl\ *adj* — **ar·chae·ol·o·gist** \-kē-'äl-ə-jəst\ *n*

**ar·cha·ic** \är-'kā-ik\ *adj* **1 :** belonging to an earlier time **:** ANTIQUATED **2 :** having the characteristics of the language of the past and surviving chiefly in specialized uses ⟨~ words⟩ —

**ar·cha·i·cal·ly** \-i-k-(ə-)lē\ *adv*

**arch·an·gel** \'ärk-,ān-jəl\ *n* : an angel of high rank

**arch·bish·op** \ärch-'bish-əp\ *n* : a bishop of high rank — **arch·bish·op·ric** \-ə-(,)prik\ *n*

**arch·dea·con** \'dē-kən\ *n* : a clergyman who assists a diocesan bishop in ceremonial or administrative functions

**arch·di·o·cese** \-'dī-ə-səs, -,sēz, -,sēs\ *n* : the diocese of an archbishop

**arch·duke** \-'d(y)ük\ *n* : a prince of the imperial family of Austria

**arch·en·e·my** \'ärch-'en-ə-mē\ *n, pl* **-mies** : a principal enemy

**ar·chery** \'ärch-(ə-)rē\ *n* : the art or practice of shooting with bow and arrows — **ar·cher** \'är-chər\ *n*

**ar·che·type** \'är-ki-,tīp\ *n* : the original pattern or model of all things of the same type

**arch·fiend** \'ärch-'fēnd\ *n* : a chief fiend; *esp* : SATAN

**ar·chi·epis·co·pal** \,är-kē-ə-'pis-kə-pəl\ *adj* : of or relating to an archbishop

**ar·chi·man·drite** \,är-kə-'man-,drīt\ *n* : a dignitary in an Eastern church ranking below a bishop

**ar·chi·pel·a·go** \,är-kə-'pel-ə-,gō, ,är-chə-\ *n, pl* **-goes** *or* **-gos** 1 : a sea dotted with islands 2 : a group of islands

**ar·chi·tect** \'är-kə-,tekt\ *n* : a person who plans buildings and oversees their construction

**ar·chi·tec·ton·ic** \,är-kə-,tek-'tän-ik\ *adj* : of, relating to, or according with the principles of architecture

**ar·chi·tec·ton·ics** \-'tän-iks\ *n sing or pl* : structural design

**ar·chi·tec·ture** \'är-kə-,tek-chər\ *n* 1 : the art or science of planning and building structures 2 : method or style of building — **ar·chi·tec·tur·al** \,är-kə-'tek-chə-rəl, -'tek-shrəl\ *adj* — **ar·chi·tec·tur·al·ly** \-ē\ *adv*

**ar·chi·trave** \'är-kə-,trāv\ *n* : the supporting horizontal member just above the columns in a building in the classical style of architecture

**ar·chive** \'är-,kīv\ *n* : a place for keeping public records; *also* : public records — usu. used in pl.

**ar·chi·vist** \'är-kə-vəst, -,kī-\ *n* : a person in charge of archives

**ar·chon** \'är-,kän, -kən\ *n* : a chief magistrate of ancient Athens

**arch·way** \'ärch-,wā\ *n* : a passageway under an arch; *also* : an arch over a passage

**arc lamp** *n* : a gas-filled electric lamp that produces light when a current arcs between incandescent electrodes

¹**arc·tic** \'ärk-tik, 'ärt-ik\ *adj* [ME *artik,* fr *L articus,* fr. Gk *arktikos,* fr. *arktos* bear, Ursa Major, north] 1 *often cap* : of or relating to the north pole or the region near it 2 : FRIGID

²**arc·tic** \'ärt-ik, 'ärk-tik\ *n* : a rubber overshoe that reaches to the ankle or above

**arctic circle** *n, often cap A&C* : a circle of the earth parallel to its equator

approximately 23°27' from the north pole

**-ard** \ərd\ *also* **-art** \ərt\ *n suffix* : one that is characterized by performing some action, possessing some quality, or being associated with some thing esp. conspicuously or excessively ⟨bragg*art*⟩ ⟨dull*ard*⟩

**ar·dent** \'ärd-ªnt\ *adj* 1 : characterized by warmth of feeling : PASSIONATE 2 : FIERY, HOT 3 : GLOWING — **ar·dent·ly** *adv*

**ar·dor** \'ärd-ər\ *n* 1 : warmth of feeling : ZEAL 2 : burning heat

**ar·du·ous** \'ärj-(ə-)wəs\ *adj* : DIFFICULT, LABORIOUS — **ar·du·ous·ly** *adv* — **ar·du·ous·ness** *n*

¹**are** *pres 2d sing or pres pl of* BE

²**are** \'a(ə)r\ *n* — see METRIC SYSTEM table

**ar·ea** \'ar-ē-ə\ *n* 1 : a flat surface or space 2 : the amount of surface included (as within the lines of a geometric figure) 3 : REGION 4 : range or extent of some thing or concept : FIELD

**area code** *n* : a 3-digit number that identifies each telephone service area in a country (as the U.S. or Canada)

**area·way** \-,wā\ *n* : a sunken space for giving access, air, and light to a basement

**are·na** \ə-'rē-nə\ *n* [L *harena, arena* sand, sandy place] 1 : an enclosed area used for public entertainment 2 : a sphere of activity

**arena theater** *n* : a theater with the stage in the center of the auditorium

**ar·gent** \'är jənt\ *adj* : of or resembling silver : SILVERY

**ar·gen·tine** \'är-jən-,tīn, -,tēn *for 1;* -,tēn *for 2*\ *n* 1 : SILVER 2 *cap* : a native or inhabitant of Argentina

**ar·gen·tite** \'är-jən-,tīt\ *n* : a dark gray mineral that is an important ore of silver

**ar·gil·la·ceous** \,är-jə-'lā-shəs\ *adj* : CLAYEY

**ar·gon** \'är-,gän\ *n* [Gk, neut. of *argos* idle, lazy, fr. *a-* not + *ergon* work; fr. its relative inertness] : a colorless odorless gaseous chemical element found in the air and used for filling electric bulbs

**ar·go·sy** \'är-gə-sē\ *n, pl* **-sies** 1 : a large merchant ship 2 : FLEET

**ar·got** \'är-gət, -,gō\ *n* : the language of a particular group or class esp. of the underworld

**argu·able** \'är-gyə-wə-bəl\ *adj* : open to argument, dispute, or question

**ar·gue** \'är-gyü\ *vb* **ar·gued; ar·gu·ing** 1 : to give reasons for or against something 2 : to contend in words : DISPUTE 3 : DEBATE 4 : to persuade by giving reasons

**ar·gu·ment** \'är-gyə-mənt\ *n* 1 : a reason offered in proof 2 : discourse intended to persuade 3 : QUARREL

**ar·gu·men·ta·tion** \,är-gyə-mən-'tā-shən\ *n* : the art of formal discussion

**ar·gu·men·ta·tive** \,är-gyə-'ment-ət-iv\ *adj* : inclined to argue

**ar·gyle** *also* **ar·gyll** \'är-,gīl\ *n, often cap* : a geometric knitting pattern of varicolored diamonds on a single background color; *also* : a sock knit in this pattern

**aria** \'är-ē-ə\ *n* : an accompanied elaborate vocal solo forming part of a larger work

**ar·id** \'ar-əd\ *adj* **1** : DRY, BARREN **2** : having insufficient rainfall to support agriculture — **arid·i·ty** \ə-'rid-ət-ē\ *n*

**aright** \ə-'rīt\ *adv* : RIGHTLY, CORRECTLY

**arise** \ə-'rīz\ *vb* **arose** \-'rōz\; **aris·en** \-'riz-ᵊn\; **aris·ing** \-'rī-ziŋ\ **1** : to get up **2** : ORIGINATE **3** : ASCEND *syn* rise, mount, spring, issue

**ar·is·toc·ra·cy** \,ar-ə-'stäk-rə-sē\ *n*, *pl* **-cies** **1** : government by a noble or privileged class; *also* : a state so governed **2** : the governing class of an aristocracy **3** : UPPER CLASS — **aris·to·crat** \ə-'ris-tə-,krat\ *n* — **aris·to·crat·ic** \ə-,ris-tə-'krat-ik\ *adj*

**arith** *abbr* arithmetic

**arith·me·tic** \ə-'rith-mə-,tik\ *n* : mathematics that deals with computations with numbers — **ar·ith·met·ic** \,ar-ith-'met-ik\ *or* **ar·ith·met·i·cal** \-i-kəl\ *adj* — **ar·ith·met·i·cal·ly** \-i-k(ə-)lē\ *adv* — **arith·me·ti·cian** \ə-,rith-mə-'tish-ən\ *n*

**Ariz** *abbr* Arizona

**ark** \'ärk\ *n* **1** : a boat held to resemble that of Noah at the time of the Deluge **2** : the sacred chest in which the ancient Hebrews kept the tablets of the Law

**Ark** *abbr* Arkansas

**¹arm** \'ärm\ *n* **1** : a human upper limb **2** : something resembling or corresponding to the human upper limb **3** : POWER, MIGHT ⟨the ~ of the law⟩ — **armed** \'ärmd\ *adj* — **arm·less** *adj*

**²arm** *vb* : to furnish with weapons

**³arm** *n* **1** : WEAPON **2** : a branch of the military forces **3** *pl* : the hereditary heraldic devices of a family

**ar·ma·da** \är-'mäd-ə, -'mād-\ *n* : a fleet of armed ships

**ar·ma·dil·lo** \,är-mə-'dil-ō\ *n*, *pl* **-los** : a small burrowing mammal with head and body protected by an armor of bony plates

**Ar·ma·ged·don** \,är-mə-'ged-ᵊn\ *n* : a final conclusive battle between the forces of good and evil; *also* : the site or time of this

**ar·ma·ment** \'är-mə-mənt\ *n* **1** : military strength **2** : arms and equipment (as of a tank or combat unit) **3** : the process of preparing for war

**ar·ma·ture** \'är-mə-,chur, -chər\ *n* **1** : protective covering **2** : the part including the conductors in an electric generator or motor in which the current is induced; *also* : the movable part in an electromagnetic device (as an electric bell or a loudspeaker)

**arm·chair** \'ärm-,cheər\ *n* : a chair with supports for the arms

**armed forces** *n pl* : the combined military, naval, and air forces of a nation

**arm·ful** \'ärm-,fúl\ *n* : as much as the arm can hold

**arm·hole** \'ärm-,hōl\ *n* : an opening for the arm in a garment

**ar·mi·stice** \'är-mə-stəs\ *n* : temporary suspension of hostilities by mutual agreement : TRUCE

**arm·let** \'ärm-lət\ *n* : a band worn around the upper arm

**ar·mor** \'är-mər\ *n* **1** : protective covering **2** : armored forces and vehicles — **ar·mored** \-mərd\ *adj*

**ar·mor·er** \'är-mər-ər\ *n* **1** : one that makes arms and armor **2** : one that services firearms

**ar·mo·ri·al** \är-'mōr-ē-əl\ *adj* : of or bearing heraldic arms

**ar·mo·ry** \'ärm-(ə-)rē\ *n*, *pl* **ar·mor·ies** **1** : a place where arms are stored **2** : a factory where arms are made

**arm·pit** \'ärm-,pit\ *n* : the hollow under the junction of the arm and shoulder

**arm·rest** \-,rest\ *n* : a support for the arm

**ar·my** \'är-mē\ *n*, *pl* **armies** **1** : a body of men organized for war **2** *often cap* : the complete military organization of a country for land warfare **3** : a great number **4** : a body of persons organized to advance a cause

**army ant** *n* : any of various nomadic social ants

**ar·my·worm** \'är-mē-,wərm\ *n* : any of various moths whose larvae move about destroying crops

**ar·ni·ca** \'är-ni-kə\ *n* **1** : any of several herbs related to the daisies **2** : a soothing preparation of arnica flowers or roots used on bruises and sprains

**aro·ma** \ə-'rō-mə\ *n* : a usu. pleasing odor : FRAGRANCE — **ar·o·mat·ic** \,ar-ə-'mat-ik\ *adj*

**¹around** \ə-'raúnd\ *adv* **1** : in or along a circuit **2** : on all sides **3** : NEARBY **4** : in various places **5** : in an opposite direction ⟨turn ~⟩

**²around** *prep* **1** : ENVELOPING ⟨trees ~ the house⟩ **2** : along the circuit of ⟨go ~ the world⟩ **3** : to or on the other side of ⟨~ the corner⟩ **4** : NEAR ⟨stayed right ~ home⟩

**arouse** \ə-'raúz\ *vb* **aroused**; **arous·ing** **1** : to awaken from sleep **2** : to stir up — **arous·al** \-'raú-zəl\ *n*

**ar·peg·gio** \är-'pej-(ē-,)ō\ *n*, *pl* **-gios** [It. fr. *arpeggiare* to play on the harp, fr. *arpa* harp] : a chord whose notes are performed in succession and not simultaneously

**arr** *abbr* **1** arranged **2** arrival; arrive

**ar·raign** \ə-'rān\ *vb* **1** : to call before a court to answer to an indictment **2** : to accuse of wrong or imperfection — **ar·raign·ment** *n*

**ar·range** \ə-'rānj\ *vb* **ranged**; **-rang·ing** **1** : to put in order **2** : to come to an agreement about : SETTLE **3** : to adapt (a musical composition) to voices or instruments other than those for which it was orig. written — **ar·range·ment** *n* — **ar·rang·er** *n*

**ar·rant** \'ar-ənt\ *adj* **1** : THOROUGHGOING **2** : notoriously bad

**ar·ras** \'ar-əs\ *n*, *pl* **arras** **1** : TAPESTRY **2** : a wall hanging or screen of tapestry

**¹ar·ray** \ə-'rā\ *vb* **1** : to arrange in order **2** : to dress esp. splendidly

²**ar·ray** *n* **1** : a regular arrangement **2** : rich apparel **3** : an imposing group

**ar·rears** \ə-'riərz\ *n pl* **1** : a state of being behind in the discharge of obligations ⟨in ~⟩ **2** : overdue debts

¹**ar·rest** \ə-'rest\ *vb* **1** : STOP, CHECK **2** : to take into legal custody

²**arrest** *n* : the act of taking into custody by legal authority

**ar·ri·ère–pen·sée** \,ar-ē-,er-päⁿ-'sā\ *n* [F, fr. *arrière* in back + *pensée* thought] : a mental reservation

**ar·riv·al** \ə-'rī-vəl\ *n* **1** : the act of arriving **2** : one that arrives

**ar·rive** \ə-'rīv\ *vb* **ar·rived; ar·riv·ing 1** : to reach a destination **2** : to be near or at hand ⟨the time to go finally *arrived*⟩ **3** : to attain success

**ar·ro·gant** \'ar-ə-gənt\ *adj* : offensively exaggerating one's own importance — **ar·ro·gance** \-gəns\ *n* — **ar·ro·gant·ly** *adv*

**ar·ro·gate** \-,gāt\ *vb* **-gat·ed; -gat·ing** : to claim or seize without justification as one's right

**ar·row** \'ar-ō\ *n* **1** : a missile shot from a bow and usu. having a slender shaft, a pointed head, and feathers at the butt **2** : a pointed mark used to indicate direction

**ar·row·head** \'ar-ō-,hed\ *n* : the pointed end of an arrow

**ar·row·root** \-,rüt, -,rüt\ *n* : an edible starch from the roots of a tropical American plant; *also* : a plant yielding arrowroot

**ar·royo** \ə-'rȯi-ə, -ō\ *n, pl* **-royos 1** : WATERCOURSE **2** : a water-carved gully or channel

**ar·se·nal** \'ärs-nəl, -ⁿn-əl\ *n* **1** : a place for making and storing arms and military equipment **2** : STORE, REPERTORY

**ar·se·nic** \'ärs-nik, -ⁿn-ik\ *n* **1** : a solid brittle poisonous chemical element of grayish color and metallic luster whose compounds are used as insecticides and in drug preparations **2** : a very poisonous oxygen compound of arsenic used in making glass and in insecticides — **ar·sen·i·cal** \är-'sen-i-kəl\ *adj or n* — **ar·se·ni·ous** \är-'sē-nē-əs\ *adj*

**ar·son** \'ärs-ⁿn\ *n* : the malicious burning of property

¹**art** \'ärt\ *n* **1** : skill acquired by experience or study : KNACK **2** : a branch of learning; *esp* : one of the humanities **3** : systematic use of knowledge or skill in making or doing things **4** : the use of skill and imagination in the production of things of beauty; *also* : works so produced **5** : ARTFULNESS

²**art** *abbr* **1** article **2** artificial **3** artillery

**-art** — see -ARD

**ar·te·ri·al** \är-'tir-ē-əl\ *n* : a through street or arterial highway

**ar·te·ri·ole** \är-'tir-ē-,ōl\ *n* : one of the small terminal twigs of an artery that ends in capillaries — **ar·te·ri·o·lar** \-,tir-ē-'ō-lər\ *adj*

**ar·te·rio·scle·ro·sis** \är-,tir-ē-ō-sklə-'rō-səs\ *n* : a chronic disease in which arterial walls are abnormally thickened and hardened — **ar·te·rio·scle·rot·ic** \-'rät-ik\ *adj or n*

**ar·tery** \'ärt-ə-rē\ *n, pl* **-ter·ies 1** : one of the tubular vessels that carry the blood from the heart **2** : a main channel of communication; *esp* : a principal road with through-traffic facilities — **ar·te·ri·al** \är-'tir-ē-əl\ *adj*

**ar·te·sian well** \är-,tē-zhən-\ *n* **1** : a bored well gushing water like a fountain **2** : a relatively deep-bored well

**art·ful** \'ärt-fəl\ *adj* **1** : INGENIOUS **2** : CRAFTY — **art·ful·ly** \-ē\ *adv* — **art·ful·ness** *n*

**ar·thri·tis** \är-'thrīt-əs\ *n, pl* **-ti·des** \-'thrīt-ə-,dēz\ : inflammation of the joints — **ar·thrit·ic** \-'thrit-ik\ *adj or n*

**ar·thro·pod** \'är-thrə-,päd\ *n* : any of a major group of invertebrate animals comprising those (as insects, spiders, or crabs) with segmented bodies and jointed limbs — **arthropod** *adj*

**ar·ti·choke** \'ärt-ə-,chōk\ *n* : a tall herb related to the daisies; *also* : its edible flower head

**ar·ti·cle** \'ärt-i-kəl\ *n* [ME, fr. OF, fr. L *articulus* joint, division, dim. of *artus* joint] **1** : a distinct part of a written document **2** : a nonfictional prose composition forming an independent part of a publication **3** : a word (as *an, the*) used with a noun to limit or give definiteness to its application **4** : a member of a class of things; *esp* : COMMODITY

**ar·tic·u·lar** \är-'tik-yə-lər\ *adj* : of or relating to a joint

¹**ar·tic·u·late** \är-'tik-yə-lət\ *adj* **1** : divided into meaningful parts : INTELLIGIBLE **2** : able to speak; *also* : expressing oneself readily and effectively **3** : JOINTED — **ar·tic·u·late·ly** *adv* — **ar·tic·u·late·ness** *n*

²**ar·tic·u·late** \-,lāt\ *vb* **-lat·ed; -lat·ing 1** : to utter distinctly **2** : to unite by joints — **ar·tic·u·la·tion** \-,tik-yə-'lā-shən\ *n*

**ar·ti·fact** \'ärt-ə-,fakt\ *n* : a usu. simple object (as a tool) showing human workmanship or modification

**ar·ti·fice** \'ärt-ə-fəs\ *n* **1** : TRICK; *also* : TRICKERY **2** : an ingenious device; *also* : INGENUITY

**ar·ti·fi·cer** \är-'tif-ə-sər, 'ärt-ə-fə-sər\ *n* : a skilled workman

**ar·ti·fi·cial** \,ärt-ə-'fish-əl\ *adj* **1** : produced by art rather than nature; *also* : made by man to imitate nature **2** : not genuine : FEIGNED — **ar·ti·fi·ci·al·i·ty** \-,fish-ē-'al-ət-ē\ *n* — **ar·ti·fi·cial·ly** \-'fish-(ə-)lē\ *adv* — **ar·ti·fi·cial·ness** \-'fish-əl-nəs\ *n*

**artificial respiration** *n* : the rhythmic forcing of air into and out of the lungs of a person whose breathing has stopped

**ar·til·lery** \är-'til-(ə-)rē\ *n, pl* **-ler·ies 1** : large caliber mounted firearms **2** : a branch of the army armed with artillery — **ar·til·ler·ist** \-'til-ə-rəst\ *n*

**ar·ti·san** \'ärt-ə-zən, -sən\ *n* : a skilled manual workman

**art·ist** \'ärt-əst\ *n* **1** : one who practices an art; *esp* : one who creates objects of beauty **2** : ARTISTE

**ar·tiste** \är-ˈtēst\ *n* : a skilled public performer

**ar·tis·tic** \är-ˈtis-tik\ *adj* : showing taste and skill — **ar·tis·ti·cal·ly** \-ti-k(ə-)lē\ *adv*

**art·ist·ry** \ˈärt-ə-strē\ *n* : artistic quality or ability

**art·less** \ˈärt-ləs\ *adj* **1** : lacking art or skill **2** : free from artificiality : NATURAL **3** : free from guile : SINCERE — **art·less·ly** *adv* — **art·less·ness** *n*

**art nou·veau** \ˌär(t)-nü-ˈvō\ *n, often cap A & N* : a late 19th century decorative style characterized by sinuous lines and leaf-shaped forms

¹**arty** \ˈärt-ē\ *adj* **art·i·er**; **-est 1** : showily imitative of art **2** : pretentiously artistic — **art·i·ly** \ˈärt-ᵊl-ē\ *adv* — **art·i·ness** \-ē-nəs\ *n*

²**arty** *abbr* artillery

**ar·um** \ˈar-əm\ *n* : any of a genus of plants with flowers in a fleshy enclosed spike including many grown for their showy foliage

**ARV** *abbr* American Revised Version

¹**-ary** \ˌer-ē\ *n suffix* : thing or person belonging to or connected with ⟨functionary⟩

²**-ary** *adj suffix* : of, relating to, or connected with ⟨budgetary⟩

**Ary·an** \ˈar-ē-ən, ˈer-; ˈär-yən\ *adj* **1** : INDO-EUROPEAN **2** : NORDIC **3** : GENTILE — **Aryan** *n*

¹**as** \əz, (ˌ)az\ *adv* **1** : to the same degree or amount : EQUALLY ⟨~ green as grass⟩ **2** : for instance ⟨various trees, ~ oak or pine⟩ **3** : when considered in a specified relation ⟨my opinion ~ distinguished from his⟩

²**as** *conj* **1** : in the same amount or degree in which ⟨green ~ grass⟩ **2** : the same way that ⟨farmed ~ his father before him had farmed⟩ **3** : WHILE, WHEN ⟨spoke to me ~ I was leaving⟩ **4** : THOUGH ⟨improbable ~ it seems⟩ **5** : SINCE, BECAUSE ⟨~ I'm not wanted, I'll go⟩ **6** : that the result is ⟨so guilty ~ to leave no doubt⟩

³**as** *pron* **1** : THAT — used after *same or such* ⟨it's the same price ~ before⟩ **2** : a fact that ⟨he's rich, ~ you know⟩

⁴**as** *prep* : in the capacity or character of ⟨this will serve ~ a substitute⟩

**As** *symbol* arsenic

**AS** *abbr* **1** Anglo-Saxon **2** antisubmarine

**asa·fet·i·da** *or* **asa·foe·ti·da** \ˌas-ə-ˈfit-əd-ē, -ˈfet-əd-ə\ *n* : an ill-smelling plant gum formerly used in medicine

**as·bes·tos** *also* **as·bes·tus** \as-ˈbes-təs, az-\ *n* : a nonburning grayish mineral that occurs in fibrous form and is used as a fireproof material

**as·cend** \ə-ˈsend\ *vb* **1** : to move upward : MOUNT, CLIMB **2** : to succeed to : OCCUPY ⟨~ed the throne⟩

**as·cen·dan·cy** *also* **as·cen·den·cy** \ə-ˈsen-dən-sē\ *n* : controlling influence : DOMINATION

¹**as·cen·dant** *also* **as·cen·dent** \ə-ˈsen-dənt\ *n* : a dominant position

²**ascendant** *also* **ascendent** *adj* **1** : moving upward **2** : DOMINANT

**as·cen·sion** \ə-ˈsen-chən\ *n* : the act of ascending

**Ascension Day** *n* : the Thursday 40 days after Easter observed in commemoration of Christ's ascension into heaven

**as·cent** \ə-ˈsent\ *n* **1** : the act of mounting upward : CLIMB **2** : degree of upward slope

**as·cer·tain** \ˌas-ər-ˈtān\ *vb* : to learn by inquiry — **as·cer·tain·able** *adj*

**as·cet·ic** \ə-ˈset-ik\ *adj* : practicing self-denial esp. for religious reasons : AUSTERE — **ascetic** *n* — **as·cet·i·cism** \-ˈset-ə-ˌsiz-əm\ *n*

**ascor·bic acid** \ə-ˌskȯr-bik-\ *n* : VITAMIN C

**as·cot** \ˈas-kət, -ˌkät\ *n* : a broad neck scarf that is looped under the chin and sometimes pinned

**as·cribe** \ə-ˈskrīb\ *vb* **as·cribed**; **as·crib·ing** : to refer to a supposed cause, source, or author : ATTRIBUTE — **as·crib·able** *adj* — **as·crip·tion** \-ˈskrip-shən\ *n*

**asep·tic** \ā-ˈsep-tik\ *adj* : free or freed from disease-causing germs

**asex·u·al** \ˈā-ˈsek-sh(ə-w)əl\ *adj* **1** : lacking sex or functional sex organs **2** : involving no sexual action ⟨an ~ spore⟩

**as for** *prep* : with regard to : CONCERNING ⟨*as for* the others, they were late⟩

¹**ash** \ˈash\ *n* : a tree related to the olives; *also* : its tough elastic wood

²**ash** *n* **1** : the solid matter left when material is burned **2** : fine mineral particles from a volcano **3** *pl* : the remains of the dead human body

**ashamed** \ə-ˈshāmd\ *adj* **1** : feeling shame **2** : restrained by anticipation of shame ⟨~ to say anything⟩ — **asham·ed·ly** \-ˈshā-məd-lē\ *adv*

**ash·en** \ˈash-ən\ *adj* **1** : of or resembling ashes; *esp* : ash-colored **2** : deadly pale

**ash·lar** \ˈash-lər\ *n* : hewn or squared stone; *also* : masonry of such stone

**ashore** \ə-ˈshȯr\ *adv* : on or to the shore

**ash·ram** \ˈäsh-rəm\ *n* : a religious retreat esp. of a Hindu sage

**ash·tray** \ˈash-ˌtrā\ *n* : a receptacle for tobacco ashes

**Ash Wednesday** *n* : the 1st day of Lent

**ashy** \ˈash-ē\ *adj* **ash·i·er**; **-est** : ASHEN

**Asian** \ˈā-zhən, -shən\ *adj* : of, relating to, or characteristic of the continent of Asia or its people — **Asian** *n*

**Asi·at·ic** \ˌā-z(h)ē-ˈat-ik\ *adj* : ASIAN — sometimes taken to be offensive — **Asiatic** *n*

¹**aside** \ə-ˈsīd\ *adv* **1** : to or toward the side **2** : out of the way : AWAY

²**aside** *n* : an actor's words heard by the audience but supposedly not by other characters on stage

**aside from** *prep* **1** : BESIDES ⟨*aside from* being pretty, she's intelligent⟩ **2** : with the exception of ⟨*aside from* one D his grades are excellent⟩

**as if** *conj* **1** : as it would be if ⟨it's *as if*

nothing had changed⟩ **2 :** as one would if ⟨he acts *as if* he'd never been away⟩ **3 :** THAT ⟨it seems *as if* nothing ever happens around here⟩

**as·i·nine** \'as-ᵊn-ˌīn\ *adj* [L *asininus*, fr. *asinus* ass] **:** STUPID, FOOLISH — **as·i·nin·i·ty** \ˌas-ᵊn-ˈin-ət-ē\ *n*

**ask** \'ask\ *vb* **asked** \'as(k)t\; **ask·ing 1 :** to call on for an answer **2** UTTER ⟨~ a question⟩ **3 :** to make a request of ⟨~ him for help⟩ **4 :** to make a request for ⟨~ help of him⟩ **5 :** to set as a price **6 :** INVITE

**askance** \ə-ˈskans\ *adv* **1 :** with a side glance **2 :** with distrust

**askew** \ə-ˈskyü\ *adv or adj* **:** out of line **:** AWRY

¹**aslant** \ə-ˈslant\ *adv or adj* **:** in a slanting direction

²**aslant** *prep* **:** over or across in a slanting direction

**asleep** \ə-ˈslēp\ *adv or adj* **1 :** in or into a state of sleep **2 :** DEAD **3 :** NUMBED **4 :** INACTIVE

**as long as** *conj* **1 :** on condition that ⟨do as you like *as long as* you get home on time⟩ **2 :** inasmuch as **:** SINCE ⟨*as long as* you're up, turn on the light⟩

**as of** *prep* **:** AT, DURING, FROM, ON ⟨takes effect *as of* July 1⟩

**asp** \'asp\ *n* **:** a small poisonous African snake

**as·par·a·gus** \ə-ˈspar-ə-gəs\ *n* **:** a tall perennial herb related to the lilies; *also* **:** its edible young stalks

**as·pect** \'as-ˌpekt\ *n* **1 :** a position facing a particular direction **2 :** APPEARANCE, LOOK **3 :** PHASE

**as·pen** \'as-pən\ *n* **:** any of several poplars with leaves that flutter in the slightest breeze

‖**as·per·i·ty** \a-ˈsper-ət-ē, ə-\ *n, pl* **-ties 1 :** ROUGHNESS **2 :** harshness of temper

**as·per·sion** \ə-ˈspər-zhən\ *n* **:** the act of calumniating; *also* **:** a calumnious remark

**as·phalt** \'as-ˌfȯlt\ *or* **as·phal·tum** \as-ˈfȯl-təm\ *n* **:** a dark solid or somewhat plastic substance that is found in natural beds or obtained as a residue in petroleum refining and is used in paving streets, in roofing houses, and in paints — **as·phal·tic** \as-ˈfȯl-tik\ *adj*

**asphalt jungle** *n* **:** a big city or a specified part of a big city

**as·pho·del** \'as-fə-ˌdel\ *n* **:** any of several Old World herbs related to the lilies and bearing flowers in long erect spikes

**as·phyx·ia** \as-ˈfik-sē-ə\ *n* **:** a lack of oxygen or excess of carbon dioxide in the body usu. caused by interruption of breathing and causing unconsciousness

**as·phyx·i·ate** \-sē-ˌāt\ *vb* **-at·ed; -at·ing :** SUFFOCATE — **as·phyx·i·a·tion** \-ˌfik-sē-ˈā-shən\ *n*

**as·pic** \'as-pik\ *n* [F, lit., asp] **:** a savory meat jelly

**as·pi·rant** \'as-p(ə-)rənt, ə-ˈspī-rənt\ *n* **:** one who aspires **syn** candidate, applicant

**as·pi·rate** \'as-p(ə-)rət\ *n* **1 :** an independent sound \h\ or a character (as the letter *h*) representing it **2 :** a consonant having aspiration as its final component

**as·pi·ra·tion** \ˌas-pə-ˈrā-shən\ *n* **1 :** the pronunciation or addition of an aspirate; *also* **:** the aspirate or its symbol **2 :** a drawing of something in, out, up, or through by or as if by suction **3 :** a strong desire to achieve something noble; *also* **:** an object of this desire

**as·pire** \ə-ˈspī(ə)r\ *vb* **as·pired; as·pir·ing 1 :** to have a noble desire or ambition **2 :** to rise aloft

**as·pi·rin** \'as-p(ə-)rən\ *n, pl* **aspirin** *or* **aspirins 1 :** a white crystalline drug used to relieve pain and fever **2 :** a tablet of aspirin

**as regards** *or* **as respects** *prep* **:** in regard to **:** with respect to

**ass** \'as\ *n* **1 :** a long-eared animal smaller than the related horse **:** DONKEY **2 :** a stupid person

**as·sail** \ə-ˈsāl\ *vb* **:** to attack violently — **as·sail·able** *adj* — **as·sail·ant** *n*

**as·sas·sin** \ə-ˈsas-ᵊn\ *n* **:** a murderer esp. for hire or fanatical reasons

**as·sas·si·nate** \ə-ˈsas-ᵊn-ˌāt\ *vb* **-nat·ed; -nat·ing :** to murder by sudden or secret attack — **as·sas·si·na·tion** \-ˌsas-ᵊn-ˈā-shən\ *n*

**as·sault** \ə-ˈsȯlt\ *n* **1 :** a violent attack **2 :** an unlawful attempt or offer to do hurt to another — **assault** *vb*

¹**as·say** \'as-ˌā, a-ˈsā\ *n* **1 :** a test (as of gold) to determine characteristics (as weight or quality) **2 :** analysis (as of an ore or drug) to determine presence of one or more ingredients

²**as·say** \a-ˈsā, 'as-ˌā\ *vb* **1 :** TRY, ATTEMPT **2 :** to subject (as an ore or drug) to an assay **3 :** to make a critical estimate of **4 :** to prove to be of a particular nature by means of an assay

**as·sem·blage** \ə-ˈsem-blij, 3 & 4 also ˌas-ˌäm-ˈbläzh\ *n* **1 :** a collection of persons or things **:** GATHERING **2 :** the act of assembling **3 :** an artistic composition made from scraps, junk, and odds and ends **4 :** the art of making assemblages

**as·sem·ble** \ə-ˈsem-bəl\ *vb* **as·sem·bled; as·sem·bling** \-b(ə-)liŋ\ **1 :** to collect into one place **:** CONGREGATE **2 :** to fit together the parts of **3 :** to meet together **:** CONVENE

**as·sem·bly** \ə-ˈsem-blē\ *n, pl* **-blies 1 :** a gathering of persons **:** MEETING **2** *cap* **:** a legislative body; *esp* **:** the lower house of a legislature **3 :** a signal for troops to assemble **4 :** the fitting together of parts (as of a machine)

**assembly line** *n* **:** an arrangement of machines, equipment, and workers in which work passes from operation to operation in a direct line

**as·sem·bly·man** \ə-ˈsem-blē-mən\ *n* **:** a member of a legislative assembly — **as·sem·bly·wom·an** \-ˌwùm-ən\ *n*

**as·sent** \ə-ˈsent\ *vb* **1 :** CONSENT **2 :** AGREE, CONCUR — **assent** *n*

**as·sert** \ə-'sərt\ vb **1** : to state positively **2** : to maintain against opposition : DEFEND syn declare, affirm, protest, avow, claim — **as·sert·ive** \-'sərt-iv\ adj — **as·sert·ive·ness** n

**as·ser·tion** \ə-'sər-shən\ n : a positive statement

**as·sess** \ə-'ses\ vb **1** : to fix the rate or amount of **2** : to impose (as a tax) at a specified rate **3** : to evaluate for taxation — **as·sess·ment** n — **as·ses·sor** \-ər\ n

**as·set** \'as-ˌet\ n **1** pl : the entire property of a person or company that may be used to pay debts **2** : ADVANTAGE, RESOURCE

**as·sev·er·ate** \ə-'sev-ə-ˌrāt\ vb **-at·ed; -at·ing** : to assert earnestly — **as·sev·er·a·tion** \-ˌsev-ə-'rā-shən\ n

**as·sid·u·ous** \ə-'sij-(ə-)wəs\ adj : steadily attentive : DILIGENT — **as·si·du·i·ty** \ˌas-ə-'d(y)ü-ət-ē\ n — **as·sid·u·ous·ly** adv — **as·sid·u·ous·ness** n

**as·sign** \ə-'sīn\ vb **1** : to transfer (property) to another **2** : to appoint to a duty **3** : PRESCRIBE ⟨~ a lesson⟩ **4** : FIX, SPECIFY ⟨~ a limit⟩ **5** : ASCRIBE ⟨~ a reason⟩ — **as·sign·able** adj

**as·sig·na·tion** \ˌas-ig-'nā-shən\ n : an appointment for a lovers' meeting; also : the resulting meeting

**assigned risk** n : a poor risk (as an accident-prone motorist) that an insurance company if forced to insure by state law

**as·sign·ment** \ə-'sīn-mənt\ n **1** : the act of assigning **2** : something assigned

**as·sim·i·late** \ə-'sim-ə-ˌlāt\ vb **-lat·ed; -lat·ing** **1** : to take up and absorb as nourishment; also : to absorb into a cultural tradition **2** : COMPREHEND **3** : to make or become similar — **as·sim·i·la·tion** \-ˌsim-ə-'lā-shən\ n

¹**as·sist** \ə-'sist\ vb : HELP, AID — **as·sis·tance** \-'sis-təns\ n

²**assist** n **1** : an act of assistance **2** : the act of a player who enables a teammate to make a putout (as in baseball) or score a goal (as in hockey)

**as·sis·tant** \ə-'sis-tənt\ n : one who assists : HELPER

**as·size** \ə-'sīz\ n **1** : a judicial inquest **2** pl : the regular sessions of the superior courts in English counties

**assn** abbr association

**assoc** also **asso** abbr associate, association

¹**as·so·ci·ate** \ə-'sō-s(h)ē-ˌāt\ vb **-at·ed; -at·ing** **1** : to join in companionship or partnership **2** : to connect in thought

²**as·so·ci·ate** \-s(h)ē-ət, -shət\ n **1** : a fellow worker : PARTNER **2** : COMPANION **3** often cap : a degree conferred esp. by a junior college ⟨~ in arts⟩ — **associate** adj

**as·so·ci·a·tion** \ə-ˌsō-s(h)ē-'ā-shən\ n **1** : the act of associating **2** : an organization of persons : SOCIETY

**as·so·cia·tive** \ə-'sō-s(h)ē-ˌāt-iv, -shət-iv\ adj : of, relating to, or involved in association and esp. mental association

**as·so·nance** \'as-ə-nəns\ n : repetition of vowels esp. as an alternative to rhyme in verse

**as soon as** conj : immediately at or just after the time that ⟨we'll start as soon as he comes⟩

**as·sort** \ə-'sòrt\ vb **1** : to distribute into like groups **2** : HARMONIZE

**as·sort·ed** \-'sòrt-əd\ adj : consisting of various kinds

**as·sort·ment** \-'sòrt-mənt\ n : a collection of assorted things or persons

**ASSR** abbr Autonomous Soviet Socialist Republic

**asst** abbr assistant

**as·suage** \ə-'swāj\ vb **as·suaged; as·suag·ing** **1** : to make (as pain or grief) less : EASE **2** : SATISFY syn alleviate, relieve, lighten

**as·sume** \ə-'süm\ vb **as·sumed; as·sum·ing** **1** : to take upon oneself **2** : to pretend to have **3** : to take as granted though not proved

**as·sump·tion** \ə-'səmp-shən\ n **1** : the taking up of a person into heaven **2** cap : a church festival commemorating the Assumption of Mary and celebrated on August 15 **3** : a taking upon oneself **4** : PRETENSION **5** : SUPPOSITION

**as·sur·ance** \ə-'shùr-əns\ n **1** : PLEDGE **2** : CERTAINTY **3** chiefly Brit : INSURANCE **4** : SELF-CONFIDENCE **5** : AUDACITY

**as·sure** \ə-'shùr\ vb **as·sured; as·sur·ing** **1** : INSURE **2** : to give confidence to **3** : to state confidently to **4** : to make certain the attainment of

**as·sured** \ə-'shùrd\ n, pl **assured** or **assureds** : the beneficiary of an insurance policy

**as·ta·tine** \'as-tə-ˌtēn\ n : an unstable radioactive chemical element

**as·ter** \'as-tər\ n : any of various mostly fall-blooming leafy-stemmed herbs with daisylike purple, white, pink, or yellow flower heads

**as·ter·isk** \'as-tə-ˌrisk\ n [L asteriscus, fr. Gk asteriskos, lit., little star, dim. of astēr] : a character * used as a reference mark or as an indication of the omission of letters or words

**astern** \ə-'stərn\ adv or adj **1** : behind a ship or airplane : in the rear **2** : at or toward the stern of a ship or aircraft **3** : BACKWARD

**as·ter·oid** \'as-tə-ˌrȯid\ n : one of thousands of small planets between Mars and Jupiter with diameters under 500 miles — **aster·oi·dal** \ˌas-tə-'rȯid-ᵊl\ adj

**asth·ma** \'az-mə\ n : an often allergic disorder marked by difficulty in breathing and a cough — **asth·mat·ic** \az-'mat-ik\ adj or n

**as though** conj : as if

**astig·ma·tism** \ə-'stig-mə-ˌtiz-əm\ n : a defect in a lens or an eye causing improper focusing — **as·tig·mat·ic** \ˌas-tig-'mat-ik\ adj

**astir** \ə-'stər\ adj : being in action : MOVING

**as to** prep **1** : ABOUT, CONCERNING ⟨uncertain as to what went on⟩ **2**

: according to ⟨graded *as to* size⟩

**as·ton·ish** \ə-'stän-ish\ *vb* : to strike with sudden wonder — AMAZE — **as·ton·ish·ing·ly** *adv* — **as·ton·ish·ment** *n*

**as·tound** \ə-'staund\ *vb* : to fill with bewildered wonder — **as·tound·ing·ly** *adv*

¹**astrad·dle** \ə-'strad-³l\ *adv* : on or above and extending onto both sides

²**astraddle** *prep* : ASTRIDE

**as·tra·khan** \'as-trə-kən, -,kan\ *n, often cap* : KARAKUL

**as·tral** \'as-trəl\ *adj* : of or relating to the stars

**astray** \ə-'strā\ *adv or adj* **1** : off the right way or route **2** : into error

¹**astride** \ə-'strīd\ *adv* **1** : with one leg on each side **2** : with legs apart

²**astride** *prep* : with one leg on each side of

¹**as·trin·gent** \ə-'strin-jənt\ *adj* : able or tending to shrink body tissues — **as·trin·gen·cy** \-jən-sē\ *n*

²**astringent** *n* : an astringent agent or substance

**astrol** *abbr* astrology

**as·tro·labe** \'as-trə-,lāb\ *n* : an instrument for observing the positions of celestial bodies

**as·trol·o·gy** \ə-'sträl-ə-jē\ *n* : divination based on the supposed influence of the stars upon human events — **as·trol·o·ger** \-ə-jər\ *n* — **as·tro·log·i·cal** \,as-trə-'läj-i-kəl\ *adj*

**astron** *abbr* astronomer; astronomy

**as·tro·naut** \'as-trə-,nòt\ *n* : a traveler in a spacecraft

**as·tro·nau·tics** \,as-trə-'nòt-iks\ *n* : the science of the construction and operation of spacecraft — **as·tro·nau·tic** \-ik\ *or* **as·tro·nau·ti·cal** \-i-kəl\ *adj* — **as·tro·nau·ti·cal·ly** \-i-k(ə-)lē\ *adv*

**as·tro·nom·i·cal** \,as-trə-'näm-i-kəl\ *or* **as·tro·nom·ic** \-ik\ *adj* **1** : of or relating to astronomy **2** : extremely large ⟨an ~ amount of money⟩

**astronomical unit** *n* : a unit of length used in astronomy equal to the mean distance of the earth from the sun or about 93 million miles

**as·tron·o·my** \ə-'strän-ə-mē\ *n, pl* **-mies** : the science of the celestial bodies and of their magnitudes, motions, and constitution — **as·tron·o·mer** \-ə-mər\ *n*

**as·tro·phys·ics** \,as-trə-'fiz-iks\ *n* : astronomy dealing with the physical and chemical constitution of the celestial bodies — **as·tro·phys·i·cal** \-i-kəl\ *adj* — **as·tro·phys·i·cist** \-'fiz-(ə-)səst\ *n*

**as·tute** \ə-'st(y)üt, a-\ *adj* [L *astutus*, fr. *astus* craft] : shrewdly discerning; *also* : WILY — **as·tute·ly** *adv* — **as·tute·ness** *n*

**asun·der** \ə-'sən-dər\ *adv or adj* **1** : into separate pieces **2** : separated in position

**ASV** *abbr* American Standard Version

**asy·lum** \ə-'sī-ləm\ *n* [ME, fr. L, fr. Gk *asylon*, neut. of *asylos* inviolable, fr. *a-* not + *sylon* right of seizure] **1** : a place of refuge **2** : protection given to esp. political fugitives **3** : an institution for the care of the needy or afflicted and esp. of the insane

**asym·met·ric** \,ā-sə-'me-trik\ *or* **asym·met·ri·cal** \-tri-kəl\ *adj* : not symmetrical — **asym·me·try** \(')ā-'sim-ə-trē\ *n*

**as·ymp·tote** \'as-əm(p)-,tōt\ *n* : a straight line that is associated with a curve and tends to approximate it along an infinite branch — **as·ymp·tot·ic** \,as-əm(p)-'tät-ik\ *adj* — **as·ymp·tot·i·cal·ly** \-i-k(ə-)lē\ *adv*

¹**at** \ət, (')at\ *prep* **1** — used to indicate a point in time or space ⟨be here ~ 3 o'clock⟩ ⟨he is ~ the hotel⟩ **2** — used to indicate a goal ⟨swung ~ the ball⟩ ⟨laugh ~ him⟩ **3** — used to indicate position or condition ⟨~ rest⟩ **4** — used to indicate means, cause, or manner ⟨sold ~ auction⟩

²**at** \'ät\ *n, pl* **at** — see *kip* at MONEY table

**At** *symbol* astatine

**at all** \ət-'òl, ə-'tòl, at-'òl\ *adv* **1** : in all ways : without restriction ⟨will go anywhere *at all*⟩ **2** : in any way : in any circumstances ⟨not *at all* likely⟩

**at·a·vism** \'at-ə-,viz-əm\ *n* : appearance in an individual of a remotely ancestral character; *also* : such an individual or character — **at·a·vis·tic** \,at-ə-'vis-tik\ *adj*

**ate** *past of* EAT

¹**-ate** \ət, ,āt\ *n suffix* **1** : one acted upon (in a specified way) ⟨distill*ate*⟩ **2** : chemical compound or element derived from a (specified) compound or element ⟨phenol*ate*⟩; *esp* : salt or ester of an acid with a name ending in *-ic* ⟨acet*ate*⟩

²**-ate** *n suffix* : office : function : rank : group of persons holding a (specified) office or rank ⟨professor*ate*⟩

³**-ate** *adj suffix* **1** : acted on (in a specified way) : brought into or being in a (specified) state ⟨temper*ate*⟩ **2** : marked by having ⟨chord*ate*⟩

⁴**-ate** \,āt\ *vb suffix* : cause to be modified or affected by ⟨camphor*ate*⟩ : cause to become ⟨activ*ate*⟩ : furnish with ⟨aer*ate*⟩

**ate·lier** \,at-³l-'yā\ *n* **1** : an artist's studio **2** : WORKSHOP

**athe·ist** \'ā-thē-əst\ *n* : one who denies the existence of God — **athe·ism** \-,iz-əm\ *n* — **athe·is·tic** \,ā-thē-'is-tik\ *adj*

**ath·e·nae·um** *or* **ath·e·ne·um** \,ath-ə-'nē-əm\ *n* : LIBRARY 1

**ath·ero·scle·ro·sis** \,ath-ə-rō-sklə-'rō-səs\ *n* : arteriosclerosis characterized by the deposition of fatty substances in and the hardening of the inner layer of the arteries — **ath·ero·scle·rot·ic** \-'rät-ik\ *adj*

**athirst** \ə-'thərst\ *adj* **1** : THIRSTY **2** : EAGER, LONGING

**ath·lete** \'ath-,lēt\ *n* [ME, fr. L *athleta*, fr. Gk *athlētēs*, fr. *athlein* to contend for a prize, fr. *athlon* prize, contest] : one trained to compete in athletics

**athlete's foot** n : ringworm of the feet
**ath·let·ic** \ath-'let-ik\ adj 1 : of or relating to athletes or athletics 2 : VIGOROUS, ACTIVE 3 : STURDY, MUSCULAR
**ath·let·ics** \ath-'let-iks\ n sing or pl : exercises and games requiring physical skill, strength, and endurance
¹**athwart** \ə-'thwȯrt\ adv : obliquely across
²**athwart** prep 1 : ACROSS 2 : in opposition to
**atilt** \ə-'tilt\ adv or adj 1 : in a tilted position 2 : with lance in hand
**Atl** abbr Atlantic
**atlas** \'at-ləs\ n : a book of maps
**atm** abbr atmosphere; atmospheric
**at·mo·sphere** \'at-mə-,sfiər\ n 1 : the mass of air surrounding the earth 2 : a surrounding influence 3 : pressure of air at sea level used as a unit in physics 4 : a dominant effect — **at·mo·spher·ic** \,at-mə-'sfiər-ik, -'sfer-\ adj — **at·mo·spher·i·cal·ly** \-i-k-(ə-)lē\ adv
**at·mo·sphe·rics** \,at-mə-'sfiər-iks, -'sfer-\ n pl : disturbances produced in radio receiving apparatus by atmospheric electrical phenomena
**atoll** \'a-,tȯl, -,täl, 'ā-\ n : a ring-shaped coral island surrounding a lagoon
**at·om** \'at-əm\ n [ME, fr. L atomus, fr. Gk atomos, fr. atomos indivisible, fr. a- not + temnein to cut] 1 : a tiny particle : BIT 2 : the smallest particle of a chemical element that can exist alone or in combination
**atom bomb** n : a very destructive bomb utilizing the energy released by splitting the atom
**atom·ic** \ə-'täm-ik\ adj 1 : of or relating to atoms, atomic energy, or atomic bombs 2 : extremely small
**atomic clock** n : a precision clock regulated by the natural vibration of an atomic system
**atomic energy** n : energy that can be liberated by changes (as by fission or fusion) in the nucleus of an atom
**atomic number** n : the number of protons in the nucleus of an element
**atomic pile** n : REACTOR 3
**at·om·ize** \'at-ə-,mīz\ vb **-ized** **-iz·ing** : to reduce to minute particles
**at·om·iz·er** \'at-ə-,mī-zər\ n : a device for reducing a liquid to a very fine spray (as for spraying the throat)
**atom smasher** n : ACCELERATOR 3
**aton·al** \ā-'tōn-ᵊl\ adj : marked by avoidance of traditional musical tonality — **ato·nal·i·ty** \,ā-tō-'nal-ət-ē\ n — **aton·al·ly** \ā-'tōn-ᵊl-ē\ adv
**atone** \ə-'tōn\ vb **atoned**; **aton·ing** 1 : to make amends 2 : EXPIATE
**atone·ment** \ə-'tōn-mənt\ n 1 : the reconciliation of God and man through the death of Jesus Christ 2 : reparation for an offense
**atop** \ə-'täp\ prep : on top of
**ATP** \,ā-,tē-'pē, ā-'tē-,pē\ n [adenosine triphosphate] : an ester that supplies energy for many cellular processes by undergoing enzymatic hydrolysis
**atri·um** \'ā-trē-əm\ n, pl **atria** \-trē-ə\ also **atri·ums** 1 : the central hall of a

Roman house 2 : an anatomical cavity or passage; esp : one of the parts of the heart that receives blood from the veins — **atri·al** \-trē-əl\ adj
**atro·cious** \ə-'trō-shəs\ adj 1 : savagely brutal, cruel, or wicked 2 : very bad : ABOMINABLE — **atro·cious·ly** adv — **atro·cious·ness** n
**atroc·i·ty** \ə-'träs-ət-ē\ n, pl **-ties** 1 : ATROCIOUSNESS 2 : an atrocious act or object
¹**at·ro·phy** \'a-trə-fē\ n, pl **-phies** : decrease in size or wasting away of a bodily part or tissue
²**atrophy** vb **-phied**; **-phy·ing** : to cause or undergo atrophy
**at·ro·pine** \'a-trə-,pēn\ n : a poisonous drug from belladonna and related plants used to relieve spasms and to dilate the pupil of the eye
**att** abbr 1 attached 2 attention 3 attorney
**at·tach** \ə-'tach\ vb 1 : to seize legally in order to force payment of a debt 2 : to bind by personal ties 3 : FASTEN, CONNECT 4 : to be fastened or connected
**at·ta·ché** \,at-ə-'shā, ,a-,ta-, ə-,ta-\ n : a technical expert on the diplomatic staff of an ambassador
**at·ta·ché case** \ə-'tash-ā-, ,at-ə-'shā-\ n : a small suitcase used esp. for carrying papers and documents
**at·tach·ment** \ə-'tach-mənt\ n 1 : legal seizure of property 2 : connection by ties of affection and regard 3 : a device attached to a machine or implement 4 : a connection by which one thing is attached to another
¹**at·tack** \ə-'tak\ vb 1 : to set upon with force or words : ASSAIL, ASSAULT 2 : to set to work on
²**attack** n 1 : an offensive action 2 : a fit of sickness
**at·tain** \ə-'tān\ vb 1 : ACHIEVE, ACCOMPLISH 2 : to arrive at : REACH — **at·tain·abil·i·ty** \ə-,tā-nə-'bil-ət-ē\ n — **at·tain·able** adj
**at·tain·der** \ə-'tān-dər\ n : extinction of the civil rights of a person upon sentence of death or outlawry
**at·tain·ment** \ə-'tān-mənt\ n 1 : the act of attaining 2 : ACCOMPLISHMENT
**at·taint** \ə-'tānt\ vb : to condemn to loss of civil rights
**at·tar** \'at-ər\ n [Per 'atir perfumed, fr. Ar, fr. 'itr perfume] : a fragrant floral oil
**at·tempt** \ə-'tempt\ vb : to make an effort toward : TRY — **attempt** n
**at·tend** \ə-'tend\ vb 1 : to look after : TEND 2 : to be present with : ACCOMPANY 3 : to be present at 4 : to pay attention 5 : to apply oneself 6 : to take charge
**at·ten·dance** \ə-'ten-dəns\ n 1 : the act or fact of attending 2 : the number of persons present
¹**at·ten·dant** \ə-'ten-dənt\ adj : ACCOMPANYING 〈~ circumstances〉
²**attendant** n : one that attends another to render a service
**at·ten·tion** \ə-'ten-chən\ n 1 : the act or state of applying the mind to an ob-

ject **2** : CONSIDERATION **3** : an act of courtesy **4** : a position of readiness for further orders assumed on command by a soldier — **at·ten·tive** \ə-'tent-iv\ *adj* — **at·ten·tive·ly** *adv* — **at·ten·tive·ness** *n*

**at·ten·u·ate** \ə-'ten-yə-ˌwāt\ *vb* -at·ed; -at·ing **1** : to make or become thin **2** : WEAKEN — **at·ten·u·a·tion** \-ˌten-yə-'wā-shən\ *n*

**at·test** \ə-'test\ *vb* **1** : to certify as genuine by signing as a witness **2** : MANIFEST **3** : TESTIFY — **at·tes·ta·tion** \ˌa-ˌtes-'tā-shən\ *n*

**at·tic** \'at-ik\ *n* : the space or room in a building next below the roof

**¹at·tire** \ə-'tī(ə)r\ *vb* -tired; -tir·ing : DRESS, ARRAY

**²attire** *n* : DRESS, CLOTHES

**at·ti·tude** \'at-ə-t(y)üd\ *n* **1** : the arrangement of the parts of a body : POSTURE **2** : a mental position or feeling with regard to an object **3** : the position of something in relation to something else **4** : the position of an aircraft or spacecraft relative to a reference datum (as the horizon or a particular star)

**at·ti·tu·di·nize** \ˌat-ə-'t(y)üd-ⁿn-ˌīz\ *vb* -nized; -niz·ing : to assume an affected mental attitude : POSE

**attn** *abbr* attention

**at·tor·ney** \ə-'tər-nē\ *n, pl* -neys : a legal agent qualified to act for persons in legal proceedings

**attorney general** *n, pl* **attorneys general** *or* **attorney generals** : the chief legal representative and adviser of a nation or state

**at·tract** \ə-'trakt\ *vb* **1** : to draw to or toward oneself : cause to approach **2** : to draw by emotional or aesthetic appeal **syn** charm, fascinate, allure — **at·trac·tive** \-'trak-tiv\ *adj* — **at·trac·tive·ly** *adv* — **at·trac·tive·ness** *n*

**at·trac·tant** \ə-'trak-tənt\ *n* : something that attracts; *esp* : a substance used to attract insects or other animals

**at·trac·tion** \ə-'trak-shən\ *n* **1** : the act or power of attracting; *esp* : personal charm **2** : an attractive quality, object, or feature **3** : a force tending to draw particles together

**attrib** *abbr* attributive

**¹at·tri·bute** \'a-trə-ˌbyüt\ *n* : an inherent characteristic **2** : a word ascribing a quality; *esp* : ADJECTIVE

**²at·trib·ute** \ə-'trib-yət\ *vb* -ut·ed; -ut·ing **1** : to explain as to cause or origin ⟨∼ the illness to fatigue⟩ **2** : to regard as a characteristic **syn** ascribe, credit, charge — **at·trib·ut·able** *adj* — **at·tri·bu·tion** \ˌa-trə-ᵇbyü-shən\ *n*

**at·trib·u·tive** \ə-'trib-yət-iv\ *adj* : joined directly to a modified noun without a copulative verb ⟨red in red hair is an ∼ adjective⟩ — **attributive** *n*

**at·tri·tion** \ə-'trish-ən\ *n* **1** : the act of wearing away as if by rubbing **2** : a reduction (as in personnel) as a result of resignation, retirement, or death

**at·tune** \ə-'t(y)ün\ *vb* : to bring into harmony : TUNE

**atty** *abbr* attorney

**atyp·i·cal** \ā-'tip-i-kəl\ *adj* : not typical : IRREGULAR

**Au** *symbol* [L *aurum*] gold

**au·burn** \'ò-bərn\ *adj* : reddish brown — **auburn** *n*

**au cou·rant** \ˌō-kù-'räⁿ\ *adj* [F, lit., in the current] : UP-TO-DATE

**¹auc·tion** \'òk-shən\ *n* [L *auction-, auctio*, lit., increase, fr. *auctus*, pp. of *augēre* to increase] : public sale of property to the highest bidder

**²auction** *vb* **auc·tioned; auc·tion·ing** \-sh(ə-)niŋ\ : to sell at auction

**auction bridge** *n* : a bridge game in which tricks made in excess of the contract are scored toward game

**auc·tion·eer** \ˌòk-shə-'niⁿr\ *n* : an agent who conducts an auction

**auc·to·ri·al** \òk-'tōr-ē-əl\ *adj* : of or relating to an author

**aud** *abbr* audit; auditor

**au·da·cious** \ò-'dā-shəs\ *adj* **1** : DARING, BOLD **2** : INSOLENT — **au·da·cious·ly** *adv* — **au·da·cious·ness** *n* — **au·dac·i·ty** \ò-'das-ət-ē\ *n*

**¹au·di·ble** \'òd-ə-bəl\ *adj* : capable of being heard — **au·di·bil·i·ty** \ˌòd-ə-'bil-ət-ē\ *n* — **au·di·bly** \'òd-ə-blē\ *adv*

**²audible** *n* : AUTOMATIC 2

**au·di·ence** \'òd-ē-əns\ *n* **1** : a formal interview **2** : an opportunity of being heard **3** : an assembly of listeners or spectators

**¹au·dio** \'òd-ē-ˌō\ *adj* **1** : of or relating to frequencies (as of radio waves) corresponding to those of audible sound waves **2** : of or relating to sound or its reproduction and esp. high-fidelity reproduction **3** : relating to or used in the transmission or reception of sound

**²audio** *n* **1** : the transmission, reception, or reproduction of sound **2** : the section of television equipment that deals with sound

**au·di·ol·o·gy** \ˌòd-ē-'äl-ə-jē\ *n* : a branch of science dealing with hearing — **au·di·o·log·i·cal** \-ē-ə-'läj-i-kəl\ *adj* — **au·di·ol·o·gist** \-ē-'äl-ə-jəst\ *n*

**au·dio·phile** \'òd-ē-ō-ˌfīl\ *n* : one who is enthusiastic about high-fidelity sound reproduction

**au·dio·vi·su·al** \ˌòd-ē-ō'-vizh-(ə-w)əl\ *adj* : of, relating to, or making use of both hearing and sight

**au·dio·vi·su·als** \-wəlz\ *n pl* : audiovisual materials (as filmstrips)

**¹au·dit** \'òd-ət\ *n* : a formal examination and verification of financial accounts

**²audit** *vb* **1** : to make an audit of **2** : to attend (a course) without expecting formal credit

**¹au·di·tion** \ò-'dish-ən\ *n* : HEARING; *esp* : a trial performance to appraise an entertainer's merits

**²audition** *vb* **au·di·tioned; au·di·tion·ing** \-'dish-(ə-)niŋ\ : to give an audition to

**au·di·tor** \'òd-ət-ər\ *n* **1** : LISTENER **2** : a person who audits

**au·di·to·ri·um** \ˌòd-ə-'tōr-ē-əm\ *n* **1** : the part of a public building where an audience sits **2** : a hall or building used for public gatherings

**au·di·to·ry** \'ȯd-ə-‚tȯr-ē\ *adj* **:** of or relating to hearing or the sense of organs of hearing

**auf Wie·der·seh·en** \‚au̇f-'vēd-ər-‚zān\ *interj* — used to express farewell

**Aug** *abbr* August

**au·ger** \'ȯ-gər\ *n* **:** a boring tool

**aught** \'ȯt, 'ät\ *n* **:** ZERO, CIPHER

**aug·ment** \ȯg-'ment\ *vb* **:** ENLARGE, INCREASE — **aug·men·ta·tion** \‚ȯg-mən-'tā-shən\ *n*

**au gra·tin** \ō-'grat-ᵊn, ȯ-, -'grät-\ *adj* [F, lit., with the burnt scrapings from the pan] **:** covered with bread crumbs, butter, and cheese and browned

¹**au·gur** \'ȯ-gər\ *n* **:** DIVINER, SOOTHSAYER

²**augur** *vb* **1 :** to foretell esp. from omens **2 :** to give promise of **:** PRESAGE

**au·gu·ry** \'ȯ-g(y)ə-rē\ *n, pl* **-ries 1 :** divination from omens **2 :** OMEN, PORTENT

**au·gust** \ȯ-'gəst\ *adj* **:** marked by majestic dignity or grandeur — **au·gust·ly** *adv* — **au·gust·ness** *n*

**Au·gust** \'ȯ-gəst\ *n* [ME, fr. OE, fr. L *Augustus*, fr. *Augustus* Caesar] **:** the eighth month of the year having 31 days

**au jus** \ō-'zhü(s), -'jüs; ō-zhᵫ\ *adj* **:** served in the juice obtained from roasting

**auk** \'ȯk\ *n* **:** a stocky black-and-white diving seabird that breeds in arctic regions

**auld** \'ȯl(d), 'äl(d)\ *adj, chiefly Scot* **:** OLD

**aunt** \'ant, 'änt\ *n* **1 :** the sister of one's father or mother **2 :** the wife of one's uncle

**au pair girl** \'ō-‚paər-\ *n* **:** a foreign girl living in England who does domestic work for a family in return for room and board and the opportunity to learn the English language

**au·ra** \'ȯr-ə\ *n* **1 :** a distinctive atmosphere surrounding a given source **2 :** a luminous radiation

**au·ral** \'ȯr-əl\ *adj* **:** of or relating to the ear or to the sense of hearing

**aural** *pl of* EYRIR

**au·re·ate** \'ȯr-ē-ət\ *adj* **1 :** of a golden color or brilliance **2 :** RESPLENDENT, ORNATE

**au·re·ole** \'ȯr-ē-‚ōl\ *or* **au·re·o·la** \ȯ-'rē-ə-lə\ *n* **:** HALO, NIMBUS

**au re·voir** \‚ō-rə-'vwär\ *n* **:** GOOD-BYE

**au·ri·cle** \'ȯr-i-kəl\ *n* **1 :** the external ear **2 :** a chamber of the heart that receives blood from the veins and forces it into a ventricle **3 :** an angular or ear-shaped anatomic part

**au·ric·u·lar** \ȯ-'rik-yə-lər\ *adj* **1 :** AURAL **2 :** told privately **3 :** known by the sense of hearing **4 :** of or relating to an auricle

**au·rif·er·ous** \ȯ-'rif-(ə-)rəs\ *adj* **:** gold-bearing

**au·ro·ra** \ə-'rōr-ə\ *n, pl* **auroras** *or* **au·ro·rae** \-(‚)ē\ **1 :** AURORA BOREALIS **2 :** AURORA AUSTRALIS — **au·ro·ral** \-əl\ *adj*

**aurora aus·tra·lis** \-ȯ-'strā-ləs\ *n* **:** a display of light in the southern hemisphere corresponding to the aurora borealis

**aurora bo·re·al·is** \-‚bȯr-ē-'al-əs\ *n* **:** streamers or arches of light in the night sky that are held to be of electrical origin and appear esp. in the arctic regions

**AUS** *abbr* Army of the United States

**aus·pice** \'ȯ-spəs\ *n, pl* **aus·pic·es** \-spə-səz, -‚sēz\ [L *auspicium*, fr. *auspic-, auspex* diviner by birds, fr. *avis* bird + *specere* to look, look at] **1 :** observation in augury **2 :** a prophetic sign or omen **3** *pl* **:** kindly patronage and protection

**aus·pi·cious** \ȯ-'spish-əs\ *adj* **1 :** affording a favorable auspice **2 :** FORTUNATE, PROSPEROUS — **aus·pi·cious·ly** *adv*

**aus·tere** \ȯ-'stiər\ *adj* **1 :** STERN, SEVERE, STRICT **2 :** ABSTEMIOUS **3 :** UNADORNED ⟨~ style⟩ — **aus·tere·ly** *adv* — **aus·ter·i·ty** \ȯ-'ster-ət-ē\ *n*

**aus·tral** \'ȯs-trəl\ *adj* **:** SOUTHERN

**Aus·tra·lian** \ȯ-'strāl-yən\ *n* **:** a native or inhabitant of Australia — **Australian** *adj*

**Aus·tri·an** \'ȯ-strē-ən\ *n* **:** a native or inhabitant of Austria — **Austrian** *adj*

**Aus·tro·ne·sian** \‚ȯs-tro-'nē-zhən\ *adj* **:** of, relating to, or constituting a family of languages spoken in the area extending from Madagascar eastward through the Malay peninsula to Hawaii and Easter Island

**auth** *abbr* **1** authentic **2** author **3** authorized

**au·then·tic** \ə-'thent-ik, ȯ-\ *adj* **:** GENUINE, REAL — **au·then·ti·cal·ly** \-i-k(ə-)lē\ *adv* — **au·then·tic·i·ty** \‚ȯ-‚then-'tis-ət-ē\ *n*

**au·then·ti·cate** \ə-'thent-i-‚kāt, ȯ-\ *vb* **-cat·ed; -cat·ing :** to prove genuine — **au·then·ti·ca·tion** \-‚thent-i-'kā-shən\ *n*

**au·thor** \'ȯ-thər\ *n* **1 :** one that writes or composes a literary work **2 :** one that originates or creates — **au·thor·ess** \-th(ə-)rəs\ *n*

**au·thor·i·tar·i·an** \ȯ-‚thär-ə-'ter-ē-ən, ə-, -‚thȯr-\ *adj* **1 :** characterized by or favoring the principle of blind obedience to authority **2 :** characterized by or favoring concentration of political power in an authority not responsible to the people

**au·thor·i·ta·tive** \ə-'thär-ə-‚tāt-iv, ȯ-, -'thȯr-\ *adj* **:** supported by, proceeding from, or being an authority **:** TRUSTWORTHY — **au·thor·i·ta·tive·ly** *adv*

**au·thor·i·ty** \ə-'thär-ət-ē, ȯ-, -'thȯr-\ *n, pl* **-ties 1 :** a citation used in support of a statement or in defense of an action; *also* **:** the source of such a citation **2 :** one appealed to as an expert **3 :** power to influence thought or behavior **4 :** freedom granted **:** RIGHT **5 :** persons in command; *esp* **:** GOVERNMENT

**au·tho·rize** \'ȯ-thə-‚rīz\ *vb* **-rized; -riz·ing 1 :** to give legal power to **2 :** SANCTION **3 :** JUSTIFY — **au·tho·ri·za·tion** \‚ȯ-th(ə-)rə-'zā-shən\ *n*

**au·thor·ship** \'ȯ-thər-,ship\ *n* **1** : the state of being an author **2** : the origin of a piece of writing

**au·tism** \'ȯ-,tiz-əm\ *n* : absorption in self-centered subjective mental activity (as daydreaming, fantasies, delusions, and hallucinations) esp. when accompanied by marked withdrawal from reality — **au·tis·tic** \ȯ-'tis-tik\ *adj*

**au·to** \'ȯt-ō\ *n, pl* **autos** : AUTOMOBILE

**au·to·bahn** \'ȯt-ō-,bän, 'aȯt-\ *n* : a German expressway

**au·to·bi·og·ra·phy** \,ȯt-ə-bī-'äg-rə-fē, -bē-\ *n* : the biography of a person narrated by himself — **au·to·bi·og·ra·pher** \-fər\ *n* — **au·to·bi·o·graph·i·cal** \-,bī-ə-'graf-i-kəl\ *adj*

**au·toch·tho·nous** \ȯ-'täk-thə-nəs\ *adj* : INDIGENOUS, NATIVE

**au·toc·ra·cy** \ȯ-'täk-rə-sē\ *n, pl* **-cies** : government by one person having unlimited power — **au·to·crat** \'ȯt-ə-,krat\ *n* — **au·to·crat·ic** \,ȯt-ə-'krat-ik\ *adj* — **au·to·crat·i·cal·ly** \-i-k(ə-)lē\ *adv*

**au·to·gi·ro** *also* **au·to·gy·ro** \,ȯt-ō-'jīr-ō\ *n, pl* **-ros** : a rotary-wing aircraft that employs a propeller for forward motion and a freely rotating rotor for lift

¹**au·to·graph** \'ȯt-ə-,graf\ *n* **1** : an original manuscript **2** : a person's signature written by hand

²**autograph** *vb* : to write one's signature on

**au·to·in·tox·i·ca·tion** \,ȯt-ō-in-,täk-sə-'kā-shən\ *n* : a state of b ng poisoned by substances produced within the body

**au·to·mate** \'ȯt-ə-,māt\ *vb* **-mat·ed; -mat·ing** **1** : to operate by automation **2** : to convert to automatic operation

¹**au·to·mat·ic** \,ȯt-ə-'mat-ik\ *adj* **1** : INVOLUNTARY **2** : made so that certain parts act in a desired manner at the proper time : SELF-ACTING — **au·to·mat·i·cal·ly** \-i-k(ə-)lē\ *adv*

²**automatic** *n* **1** : an automatic device; *esp* : an automatic firearm **2** : a substitute play called by a football quarterback at the line of scrimmage

**au·to·ma·tion** \,ȯt-ə-'mā-shən\ *n* **1** : the technique of making an apparatus, a process, or a system operate automatically **2** : the state of being operated automatically **3** : automatically controlled operation of an apparatus, process, or system by mechanical or electronic devices that take the place of human operators

**au·tom·a·tize** \ȯ-'täm-ə-,tīz\ *vb* **-tized; -tiz·ing** : to make automatic — **au·tom·a·ti·za·tion** \-,täm-ət-ə-'zā-shən\ *n*

**au·tom·a·ton** \ȯ-'täm-ət-ən, -ə-,tän\ *n, pl* **-atons** *or* **-a·ta** \-ət-ə, -ə-,tä\ **1** : an automatic machine; *esp* : ROBOT **2** : a creature who acts mechanically

**au·to·mo·bile** \,ȯt-ə-mō-'bēl, -'mō-,bēl\ *n* : a usu. 4-wheeled self-propelling vehicle for passenger transportation on streets and roadways — **au·to·mo·bil·ist** \-'bē-ləst, -,bē-\ *n*

**au·to·mo·tive** \,ȯt-ə-'mōt-iv\ *adj* **1** : SELF-PROPELLING **2** : of or relating to self-propelling vehicles and esp. automobiles and motorcycles

**au·to·nom·ic nervous system** \,ȯt-ə-'näm-ik-\ *n* : a part of the vertebrate nervous system that governs involuntary actions and that consists of the sympathetic nervous system and the parasympathetic nervous system

**au·ton·o·mous** \ȯ-'tän-ə-məs\ *adj* : having the right or power of self-government — **au·ton·o·mous·ly** *adv* — **au·ton·o·my** \-mē\ *n*

**au·top·sy** \'ȯ-,täp-sē, 'ȯt-əp-\ *n, pl* **-sies** [Gk *autopsia* act of seeing with one's own eyes, fr. *autos* self + *opsis* sight] : examination of a dead body usu. to determine the cause of death — **autopsy** *vb*

**au·to·stra·da** \,aȯt-ō-'sträd-ə, ,ȯt-ō-\ *n* : a high-speed motor road of several lanes first developed in Italy

**au·tumn** \'ȯt-əm\ *n* : the season between summer and winter — **au·tum·nal** \ȯ-'təm-nəl\ *adj*

**aux** *or* **auxil** *abbr* auxiliary

¹**aux·il·ia·ry** \ȯg-'zil-yə-rē, -'zil-(ə-)rē\ *adj* **1** : providing help **2** : functioning in a subsidiary capacity **3** : accompanying a verb form to express person, number, mood, or tense ⟨~ verbs⟩

²**auxiliary** *n, pl* **-ries** **1** : an auxiliary person, group, or device **2** : an auxiliary verb

**aux·in** \'ȯk-sən\ *n* : a plant hormone; *esp* : one stimulating growth in length

**av** *abbr* **1** avenue **2** average **3** avoirdupois

**AV** *abbr* **1** ad valorem **2** audiovisual **3** Authorized Version

¹**avail** \ə-'vāl\ *vb* : to be of use or advantage : HELP, BENEFIT

²**avail** *n* : USE ⟨effort was of no ~⟩

**avail·able** \ə-'vā-lə-bəl\ *adj* **1** : that may be utilized **2** : ACCESSIBLE — **avail·abil·i·ty** \-,vā-lə-'bil-ət-ē\ *n*

**av·a·lanche** \'av-ə-,lanch\ *n* : a mass of snow, ice, earth, or rock sliding down a mountainside

**avant-garde** \,äv-,än(t)-'gärd, -,äⁿ-\ *n* : those esp. in the arts who create or apply new or experimental ideas and techniques — **avant-garde** *adj*

**av·a·rice** \'av-(ə-)rəs\ *n* : excessive desire for wealth : GREED — **av·a·ri·cious** \,av-ə-'rish-əs\ *adj*

**avast** \ə-'vast\ *vb imper* : a nautical command to stop or cease

**av·a·tar** \'av-ə-,tär\ *n* [Skt *avatāra* descent, fr. *avatarati* he descends, fr. *ava-* away + *tarati* he crosses over] : INCARNATION

**avaunt** \ə-'vȯnt\ *adv, archaic* : AWAY, HENCE

**avdp** *abbr* avoirdupois

¹**ave** \'äv-,ā\ *n* : an expression of greeting or parting

²**ave** *abbr* avenue

**Ave Ma·ria** \,äv-,ā-mə-'rē-ə\ *n* : HAIL MARY

**avenge** \ə-'venj\ *vb* **avenged; aveng·ing** : to take vengeance for — **aveng·er** *n*

**av·e·nue** \'av-ə-ˌn(y)ü\ *n* 1 : PASSAGE-WAY 2 : a way of attaining something 3 : a broad street esp. when bordered by trees

**aver** \ə-'vər\ *vb* **averred; aver·ring** : to declare positively

¹**av·er·age** \'av-(ə-)rij\ *n* [modif. of MF *avarie* damage to ship or cargo, fr. It *avaria*, fr. Ar *'awārīyah* damaged merchandise] 1 : ³MEAN 4 2 : a ratio (as a rate per thousand) of successful tries to total tries ⟨batting ~ of .303⟩

²**average** *adj* 1 : equaling or approximating an average 2 : being about midway between extremes 3 : being not out of the ordinary : COMMON

³**average** *vb* **av·er·aged; av·er·ag·ing** 1 : to be at or come to an average 2 : to be usually 3 : to find the average of

**aver·ment** \ə-'vər-mənt\ *n* : AFFIRMATION

**averse** \ə-'vərs\ *adj* : having an active feeling of dislike or reluctance ⟨~ from publicity⟩ ⟨~ to exercise⟩

**aver·sion** \ə-'vər-zhən\ *n* 1 : a feeling of repugnance for something with a desire to avoid it 2 : something decidedly disliked

**avert** \ə-'vərt\ *vb* 1 : to turn aside or away ⟨~ the eyes⟩ 2 : to ward off

**avg** *abbr* average

**av·gas** \'av-ˌgas\ *n* : gasoline for airplanes

**avi·an** \'ā-vē-ən\ *adj* : of, relating to, or derived from birds

**avi·ary** \'ā-vē-ˌer-ē\ *n, pl* -ar·ies : a place where live birds are kept usu. for exhibition

**avi·a·tion** \ˌā-vē-'ā-shən, ˌav-ē-\ *n* 1 : the operation of heavier-than-air airplanes 2 : aircraft manufacture, development, and design — **avi·a·tor** \'ā-vē-ˌāt-ər, 'av-ē-\ *n*

**aviation cadet** *n* : a student officer in the air force

**avi·a·trix** \ˌā-vē-'ā-triks, ˌav-ē-\ *n, pl* -trix·es \-trik-səz\ *or* -tri·ces \-trə-ˌsēz\ : a woman airplane pilot

**av·id** \'av-əd\ *adj* 1 : craving eagerly : GREEDY 2 : enthusiastic in pursuit of an interest — **avid·i·ty** \ə-'vid-ət-ē, a-\ *n* — **av·id·ly** *adv*

**avi·on·ics** \ˌā-vē-'än-iks, ˌav-ē-\ *n pl* : the production of electrical devices for use in aviation, missilery, and astronautics — **avi·on·ic** \-ik\ *adj*

**avi·ta·min·osis** \ˌā-ˌvīt-ə-mə-'nō-səs\ *n* : disease resulting from vitamin deficiency — **avi·ta·min·ot·ic** \-mə-'nät-ik\ *adj*

**avo** \'av-(ˌ)ü\ *n, pl* **avos** — see *pataca* at MONEY table

**avo·ca·do** \ˌav-ə-'käd-ō, ˌäv-\ *n, pl* -dos *also* -does : the soft oily edible fruit of a tropical American tree; *also* : this tree

**avo·ca·tion** \ˌav-ə-'kā-shən\ *n* : a subordinate occupation pursued esp. for pleasure : HOBBY

**av·o·cet** \'av-ə-ˌset\ *n* : any of several long-legged shorebirds with slender upward-curving bills

**avoid** \ə-'vȯid\ *vb* 1 : to keep away

from : SHUN 2 : to prevent the occurrence of 3 : to refrain from — **avoid·able** *adj* — **avoid·ance** \-ᵊns\ *n*

**av·oir·du·pois** \ˌav-ərd-ə-'pȯiz\ *n* [ME *avoir de pois* goods sold by weight, fr. OF, lit., goods of weight] 1 : AVOIRDUPOIS WEIGHT 2 : WEIGHT, HEAVINESS; *esp* : personal weight

**avoirdupois weight** *n* : a system of weights based on the pound of 16 ounces and the ounce of 16 drams

**avouch** \ə-'vaúch\ *vb* 1 : to declare positively : AVER 2 : GUARANTEE

**avow** \ə-'vaú\ *vb* : to declare openly — **avow·al** \-'vaú(-ə)l\ *n*

**avun·cu·lar** \ə-'vən-kyə-lər\ *adj* : of, relating to, or resembling an uncle

**await** \ə-'wāt\ *vb* : to wait for : EXPECT

¹**awake** \ə-'wāk\ *vb* **awoke** \-'wōk\ *also* **awaked** \-'wākt\; **awaked** *also* **awoke** *or* **awo·ken** \-'wō-kən\; **awak·ing** : to bring back to consciousness after sleep : wake up

²**awake** *adj* : not asleep; *also* : ALERT

**awak·en** \ə-'wā-kən\ *vb* **awak·ened; awak·en·ing** \-'wāk-(ə-)niŋ\ : AWAKE

¹**award** \ə-'wȯrd\ *vb* 1 : to give by judicial decision ⟨~ damages⟩ 2 : to give in recognition of merit or achievement ⟨~ a prize⟩

²**award** *n* 1 : a final decision : JUDGMENT 2 : something awarded : PRIZE

**aware** \ə-'waər\ *adj* : having perception or knowledge : CONSCIOUS, INFORMED — **aware·ness** *n*

**awash** \ə-'wȯsh, -'wäsh\ *adv or adj* 1 : washed by waves or tide 2 : AFLOAT 3 : FLOODED

¹**away** \ə-'wā\ *adv* 1 : from this or that place ⟨go ~⟩ 2 : out of the way 3 : in another direction ⟨turn ~⟩ 4 : out of existence ⟨fade ~⟩ 5 : from one's possession ⟨give ~⟩ 6 : without interruption ⟨chatter ~⟩ 7 : without hesitation ⟨fire ~⟩ 8 : at a distance in space or time ⟨far ~⟩ ⟨~ back in 1910⟩

²**away** *adj* 1 : ABSENT 2 : DISTANT ⟨a lake 10 miles ~⟩

¹**awe** \'ȯ\ *n* 1 : profound and reverent dread of the supernatural 2 : respectful fear inspired by authority

²**awe** *vb* **awed; aw·ing** : to inspire with awe

**awea·ry** \ə-'wi(ə)r-ē\ *adj* : WEARIED

**aweigh** \ə-'wā\ *adj* : just clear of the bottom and hanging perpendicular ⟨anchors ~⟩

**awe·some** \'ȯ-səm\ *adj* 1 : expressive of awe 2 : inspiring awe

**awe·struck** \-ˌstrək\ *also* **awe·strick·en** \-ˌstrik-ən\ *adj* : filled with awe

**aw·ful** \'ȯ-fəl\ *adj* 1 : inspiring awe 2 : extremely disagreeable 3 : very great — **aw·ful·ly** \-ē\ *adv*

**awhile** \ə-'hwīl\ *adv* : for a while

**awhirl** \ə-'hwərl\ *adv or adj* : in a whirl : WHIRLING

**awk·ward** \'ȯ-kwərd\ *adj* 1 : CLUMSY 2 : UNGRACEFUL 3 : difficult to explain : EMBARRASSING 4 : difficult to deal with — **awk·ward·ly** *adv* — **awk·ward·ness** *n*

**awl** \'ȯl\ *n* : a pointed instrument for making small holes

**awn** \'òn\ *n* : one of the bristles on a spike of grass — **awned** \'ònd\ *adj*

**aw·ning** \'òn-iŋ\ *n* : a rooflike cover (as of canvas) extended over or in front of a place as a shelter

**AWOL** \'ā-,wòl, ,ā-,dəb-əl-yù-,ō-'el\ *n, often not cap* : a person who is absent without leave — **AWOL** *adv or adj*

**awry** \ə-'rī\ *adv or adj* 1 : ASKEW 2 : out of the right course : AMISS

**ax** *or* **axe** \'aks\ *n* : a chopping or cutting tool with an edged head fitted parallel to a handle

**ax·i·al** \'ak-sē-əl\ *or* **ax·al** \-səl\ *adj* 1 : of, relating to, or functioning as an axis 2 : situated around, in the direction of, on, or along an axis — **ax·i·al·ly** \'ak-sē-ə-lē\ *adv*

**ax·i·om** \'ak-sē-əm\ *n* [L *axioma*, fr. Gk *axioma*, lit., honor, fr. *axioun* to think worthy, fr. *axios* worth, worthy] 1 : a statement generally accepted as true : MAXIM 2 : a proposition regarded as a self-evident truth — **ax·i·om·at·ic** \,ak-sē-ə-'mat-ik\ *adj* — **ax·i·om·at·i·cal·ly** \-i-k(ə-)lē\ *adv*

**ax·is** \'ak-səs\ *n, pl* **ax·es** \-,sēz\ 1 : a real or imaginary straight line passing through a body that actually or supposedly revolves upon it ⟨the earth's ∼⟩ 2 : a lengthwise central line or part (as a plant stem) around which

parts of a body are symmetrically arranged 3 : one of the reference lines of a system of coordinates 4 : an alliance between major powers

**ax·le** \'ak-səl\ *n* : a spindle on which a wheel revolves

**axle·tree** \-(,)trē\ *n* : a fixed bar with bearings at its ends on which wheels (as of a cart) revolve

**ayah** \'ī-ə; 'ä-yə\ *n* [Hindi *āyā*, fr. Port *aia*, fr. L *avia* grandmother] : a native nurse or maid in India

¹**aye** *also* **ay** \'ā\ *adv* : ALWAYS, EVER

²**aye** *also* **ay** \'ī\ *adv* : YES

³**aye** *also* **ay** \'ī\ *n, pl* **ayes** : an affirmative vote

**AZ** *abbr* Arizona

**aza·lea** \ə-'zāl-yə\ *n* : any of various rhododendrons with funnel-shaped blossoms and usu. deciduous leaves

**az·i·muth** \'az-(ə-)məth\ *n* 1 : an arc of the horizon measured between a fixed point and the vertical circle passing through the center of an object 2 : horizontal direction — **az·i·muth·al** \,az-ə-'məth-əl\ *adj*

**Az·tec** \'az-,tek\ *n* : a member of an Indian people that founded the Mexican empire and were conquered by Cortes in 1519 — **Az·tec·an** *adj*

**azure** \'azh-ər\ *n* : the blue of the clear sky — **azure** *adj*

---

**B** ¹**b** \'bē\ *n, pl* **b's** *or* **bs** \'bēz\ *often cap* 1 : the 2d letter of the English alphabet 2 : a grade rating a student's work as good ²**b** *abbr, often cap* 1 bachelor 2 bass 3 bishop 4 book 5 born

**B** *symbol* boron

**Ba** *symbol* barium

**BA** *abbr* bachelor of arts

**bab·bitt metal** \'bab-ət-\ *n* : an alloy used for lining bearings; *esp* : one containing tin, copper, and antimony

**bab·ble** \'bab-əl\ *vb* **bab·bled; bab·bling** \-(ə-)liŋ\ 1 : to utter meaningless sounds 2 : to talk foolishly or excessively — **babble** *n* — **bab·bler** \-(ə-)lər\ *n*

**babe** \'bāb\ *n* 1 : BABY 2 *slang* : GIRL, WOMAN

**ba·bel** \'bā-bəl, 'bab-əl\ *n, often cap* [fr. the Tower of *Babel*, Gen 11:4–9] : a place or scene of noise and confusion; *also* : a confused sound **syn** hubbub, racket, din, uproar

**ba·boon** \ba-'bün\ *n* [ME *babewin*, fr. MF *babouin*, fr. *baboue* grimace] : a large ape of Asia and Africa with a doglike muzzle

**ba·bush·ka** \bə-'büsh-kə, -'bùsh-\ *n* [Russ, grandmother, dim. of *baba* old woman] : a kerchief for the head

¹**ba·by** \'bā-bē\ *n, pl* **babies** 1 : a very young child : INFANT 2 : the youngest or smallest of a group 3 : a childish person — **baby** *adj* — **ba·by·hood** *n* — **ba·by·ish** *adj*

²**baby** *vb* **ba·bied; ba·by·ing** : to tend

or treat often with excessive care

**baby's breath** *n* : any of a genus of herbs that are related to the pinks and have small delicate flowers

**ba·by-sit** \'bā-bē-,sit\ *vb* **-sat** \-,sat\; **-sit·ting** : to care for children usu. during a short absence of the parents — **ba·by-sit·ter** *n*

**bac·ca·lau·re·ate** \,bak-ə-'lòr-ē-ət\ *n* 1 : the degree of bachelor conferred by colleges and universities 2 : a sermon delivered to a graduating class

**bac·ca·rat** \,bäk-ə-'rä, ,bak-\ *n* : a card game played esp. in European casinos

**bac·cha·nal** \'bak-ən-ºl, ,bak-ə-'nal, ,bäk-ə-'näl\ *n* 1 : REVELER 2 : drunken revelry or carousal : BACCHANALIA

**bac·cha·na·lia** \,bak-ə-'nāl-yə\ *n, pl* **bacchanalia** : a drunken orgy — **bac·cha·na·lian** \-'nāl-yən\ *adj or n*

**bach·e·lor** \'bach-(ə-)lər\ *n* 1 : a person who has received the usu. lowest degree conferred by a 4-year college 2 : a man who has not married — **bach·e·lor·hood** *n*

**bachelor's button** *n* : a European plant that is related to the daisies and has blue, pink, or white flower heads

**ba·cil·lus** \bə-'sil-əs\ *n, pl* **-li** \-,ī\ : any of numerous rod-shaped bacteria; *also* : a disease-producing bacterium — **bac·il·lary** \'bas-ə-,ler-ē\ *adj*

¹**back** \'bak\ *n* 1 : the rear or dorsal part of the human body; *also* : the corresponding part of a lower animal 2 : the part or surface opposite the front 3 : a player in the backfield in football — **back·less** \-ləs\ *adj*

²**back** *adv* **1 :** to, toward, or at the rear **2 :** AGO **3 :** so as to be restrained or retarded **4 :** to, toward, or in a former place or state **5 :** in return or reply

³**back** *adj* **1 :** located at or in the back; *also* **:** REMOTE **2 :** OVERDUE **3 :** moving or operating backward **4 :** not current **syn** posterior

⁴**back** *vb* **1 :** SUPPORT, UPHOLD **2 :** to go or cause to go backward or in reverse **3 :** to furnish with a back **:** form the back of

**back·ache** \'bak-,āk\ *n* **:** pain in the back; *esp* **:** a dull persistent pain in the lower back

**back–bench·er** \-'ben-chər\ *n* **:** a rank-and-file member of a British legislature

**back·bite** \-,bīt\ *vb* **-bit** \-'bit\; **-bit·ten** \-'bit-ᵊn\; **-bit·ing** \-'bīt-iṇ\ **:** to say mean or spiteful things about someone who is absent — **back·bit·er** *n*

**back·board** \-,bōrd\ *n* **:** a board or construction placed at the back or serving as a back

**back·bone** \-'bōn, -,bōn\ *n* **1 :** the bony column in the back of a vertebrate that encloses the spinal cord and is the chief support of the trunk **2 :** firm resolute character

**back·drop** \'bak-,dräp\ *n* **:** a painted cloth hung across the rear of a stage

**back·er** \'bak-ər\ *n* **:** one that supports **syn** upholder, champion, sponsor, patron

**back·field** \-,fēld\ *n* **:** the football players whose positions are behind the line

**back·fire** \-,fī(ə)r\ *n* **:** a premature explosion in the cylinder or an explosion in the intake or exhaust passages of an internal-combustion engine — **back·fire** *vb*

**back·gam·mon** \'bak-,gam-ən\ *n* **:** a game played with pieces on a double board in which the moves are determined by throwing dice

**back·ground** \'bak-,graund\ *n* **1 :** the scenery behind something **2 :** the conditions that form the setting within which something is experienced; *also* **:** the sum of a person's experience, training, and understanding

**back·hand** \'bak-,hand\ *n* **:** a stroke (as in tennis) made with the back of the hand turned in the direction in which the hand is moving; *also* **:** the side on which such a stroke is made — **back·hand** *vb*

**back·hand·ed** \'bak-'han-dəd\ *adj* **1 :** using or made with a backhand **2 :** INDIRECT, DEVIOUS; *esp* **:** SARCASTIC

**back·ing** \'bak-iṇ\ *n* **1 :** something forming a back **2 :** SUPPORT, AID; *also* **:** a body of supporters

**back·lash** \'bak-,lash\ *n* **1 :** a sudden violent backward movement or reaction **2 :** a strong adverse reaction — **back·lash·er** *n*

¹**back·log** \-,lóg, -,läg\ *n* **1 :** a large log at the back of a hearth fire **2 :** a reserve esp. of unfilled orders **3 :** an accumulation of unperformed tasks

²**backlog** *vb* **:** to accumulate in reserve

**back of** *prep* **:** BEHIND

¹**back·pack** \'bak-,pak\ *n* **:** a camping pack supported by an aluminum frame and carried on the back

²**backpack** *vb* **:** to hike with a backpack — **back·pack·er** *n*

**back·ped·al** \'bak-,ped-ᵊl\ *vb* **:** RETREAT

**back·rest** \-,rest\ *n* **:** a rest for the back

**back·side** \-'sīd\ *n* **:** BUTTOCKS

**back·slap** \-,slap\ *vb* **:** to display excessive cordiality — **back·slap·per** *n*

**back·slide** \-,slīd\ *vb* **-slid** \-,slid\; **-slid** *or* **-slid·den** \-,slid-ᵊn\; **-slid·ing** \-,slīd-iṇ\ **:** to lapse morally or in religious practice — **back·slid·er** *n*

**back·spin** \-,spin\ *n* **:** a backward rotary motion of a ball

¹**back·stage** \'bak-'stāj\ *adv* **1 :** in or to a backstage area **2 :** SECRETLY

²**back·stage** \'bak-,stāj\ *adj* **1 :** relating to or occurring in the area behind the proscenium and esp. in the dressing rooms **2 :** of or relating to the private lives of theater people **3 :** of or relating to the inner working or operation

**back·stairs** \-,staərz\ *adj* **:** SECRET, FURTIVE; *also* **:** SORDID, SCANDALOUS

¹**back·stop** \-,stäp\ *n* **:** something serving as a stop behind something else; *esp* **:** a screen or fence used in a game (as baseball) to keep a ball from leaving the field of play

²**backstop** *vb* **1 :** to serve as a backstop to **2 :** SUPPORT

**back·stretch** \'bak-'strech\ *n* **:** the side opposite the homestretch on a racecourse

**back·stroke** \-,strōk\ *n* **:** a swimming stroke executed on the back

**back·swept** \-,swept\ *adj* **:** swept or slanting backward

**back talk** *n* **:** an impudent, insolent, or argumentative reply

**back·track** \'bak-,trak\ *vb* **1 :** to retrace one's course **2 :** to reverse a position or stand

**back·up** \-,əp\ *n* **:** one that serves as a substitute or alternative

¹**back·ward** \'bak-wərd\ *or* **back·wards** \-wərdz\ *adv* **1 :** toward the back **2 :** with the back foremost **3 :** in a reverse or contrary direction or way **4 :** toward the past; *also* **:** toward a worse state

²**backward** *adj* **1 :** directed, turned, or done backward **2 :** DIFFIDENT, SHY **3 :** retarded in development — **back·ward·ness** *n*

**back·wash** \'bak-,wȯsh, -,wäsh\ *n* **:** backward movement (as of water or air) produced by a propelling force (as the motion of oars)

**back·wa·ter** \-,wȯt-ər, -,wät-\ *n* **1 :** water held or turned back in its course **2 :** an isolated or backward place or condition

**back·woods** \-'wudz\ *n pl* **1 :** wooded or partly cleared frontier areas **2 :** a remote or isolated place

**ba·con** \'bā-kən\ *n* **:** salted and smoked meat from the sides or back of a pig

**bac·te·ri·cid·al** \bak-,tir-ə-'sīd-°l\ *adj* : destroying bacteria — **bac·te·ri·cide** \-'tir-ə-,sīd\ *n*

**bac·te·ri·ol·o·gy** \bak-,tir-ē-'äl-ə-jē\ *n* **1** : a science dealing with bacteria **2** : bacterial life and phenomena — **bac·te·ri·o·log·ic** \bak-,tir-ē-ə-'läj-ik\ *or* **bac·te·ri·o·log·i·cal** \-'läj-i-kəl\ *adj* — **bac·te·ri·ol·o·gist** \bak-,tir-ē-'äl-ə-jəst\ *n*

**bac·te·rio·phage** \bak-'tir-ē-ə-,fāj\ *n* : any of various specific bacteria-destroying viruses

**bac·te·ri·um** \bak-'tir-ē-əm\ *n, pl* **-ria** \-ē-ə\ [NL, fr. Gk *baktērion* staff] : any of a large group of microscopic plants including some that are disease producers and others valued esp. for their fermentations — **bac·te·ri·al** \-ē-əl\ *adj*

**bad** \'bad\ *adj* **worse** \'wərs\; **worst** \'wərst\ **1** : below standard : POOR; *also* : UNFAVORABLE ⟨a ~ report⟩ **2** : WICKED; *also* : not well-behaved : NAUGHTY **3** : DISAGREEABLE ⟨a ~ taste⟩; *also* : HARMFUL **4** : DEFECTIVE, FAULTY ⟨~ wiring⟩; *also* : not valid ⟨a ~ check⟩ **5** : SPOILED, DECAYED **6** : UNWELL, ILL **7** : SORRY, REGRETFUL **syn** evil, wrong, putrid — **bad·ly** *adv* — **bad·ness** *n*

**bade** *past of* BID

**badge** \'baj\ *n* : a device or token usu. worn as a sign of status

**¹bad·ger** \'baj-ər\ *n* : a sturdy burrowing mammal with long claws on the forefeet

**²badger** *vb* **bad·gered; bad·ger·ing** \'baj-(ə-)riŋ\ : to harass or annoy persistently

**ba·di·nage** \,bad-°n-'äzh\ *n* : playful talk back and forth : BANTER

**bad·land** \'bad-,land\ *n* : a region marked by intricate erosional sculpturing and scanty vegetation — usu. used in pl.

**bad·min·ton** \'bad-,mint-°n\ *n* : a court game played with light rackets and a shuttlecock volleyed over a net

**Bae·de·ker** \'bād-i-kər\ *n* : GUIDEBOOK

**¹baf·fle** \'baf-əl\ *vb* **baf·fled; baf·fling** \-(ə-)liŋ\ : FRUSTRATE, THWART, FOIL; *also* : PERPLEX

**²baffle** *n* : a device (as a wall or screen) to deflect, check, or regulate flow (as of liquid or sound)

**¹bag** \'bag\ *n* : a flexible usu. closable container (as for storing or carrying)

**²bag** *vb* **bagged; bag·ging 1** : DISTEND, BULGE **2** : to put in a bag **3** : to get possession of; *esp* : to take in hunting **syn** trap, snare, catch

**ba·gasse** \bə-'gas\ *n* : plant residue (as of sugarcane) left after a product (as juice) has been extracted

**bag·a·telle** \,bag-ə-'tel\ *n* : TRIFLE

**ba·gel** \'bā-gəl\ *n* [Yiddish *beygel*, deriv. of Old High German *boug* ring] : a hard glazed doughnut-shaped roll

**bag·gage** \'bag-ij\ *n* **1** : the traveling bags and personal belongings of a traveler : LUGGAGE **2** : a worthless or contemptible woman

**bag·gy** \'bag-ē\ *adj* **bag·gi·er; -est** : puffed out or hanging like a bag — **bag·gi·ly** \'bag-ə-lē\ *adv* — **bag·gi·ness** \-ē-nəs\ *n*

**bag·man** \-mən\ *n* : a person who collects or distributes illicitly gained money on behalf of another

**ba·gnio** \'ban-yō\ *n, pl* **bagnios** : BROTHEL

**bag of waters** : a double-walled fluid-filled sac that encloses and protects the fetus in the womb and that breaks releasing its fluid during the process of birth

**bag·pipe** \'bag-,pīp\ *n* : a musical wind instrument consisting of a bag, a tube with valves, and sounding pipes — often used in pl.

**ba·guette** \ba-'get\ *n* : a gem having the shape of a long narrow rectangle; *also* : the shape itself

**baht** \'bät\ *n, pl* **bahts** *or* **baht** — see MONEY table

**¹bail** \'bāl\ *n* : security given to guarantee a prisoner's appearance when legally required; *also* : one giving such security or the release secured

**²bail** *vb* : to release under bail; *also* : to procure the release of by giving bail

**³bail** *n* : a container for ladling water out of a boat

**⁴bail** *vb* : to dip and throw out water from a boat

**⁵bail** *n* : the arched handle of a pail or kettle

**bail·able** \'bā-lə-bəl\ *adj* **1** : entitled to bail **2** : allowing bail ⟨a ~ offense⟩

**bai·liff** \'bā-ləf\ *n* **1** : an aide of a British sheriff employed esp. in serving writs and making arrests; *also* : a minor officer of a U.S. court **2** : an estate or farm manager esp. in Britain : STEWARD

**bai·li·wick** \'bā-li-,wik\ *n* : one's special province or domain **syn** territory, field, sphere

**bails·man** \'bālz-mən\ *n* : one who gives bail for another

**bairn** \'baərn\ *n, Scot* : CHILD

**¹bait** \'bāt\ *vb* **1** : to persecute by continued attacks **2** : to harass with dogs usu. for sport ⟨~ a bear⟩ **3** : ALLURE, ENTICE **4** : to furnish (as a hook) with bait **5** : to give food and drink to (as an animal) **syn** badger, heckle, hound

**²bait** *n* **1** : a lure for catching animals (as fish) : LURE, TEMPTATION **syn** snare, trap, decoy

**bai·za** \'bī-(,)zä\ *n* — see *rial* at MONEY table

**baize** \'bāz\ *n* : a coarse feltlike fabric

**¹bake** \'bāk\ *vb* **baked; bak·ing 1** : to cook or become cooked in dry heat esp. in an oven **2** : to dry and harden by heat ⟨~ bricks⟩ — **bak·er** *n*

**²bake** *n* : a social gathering featuring baked food

**baker's dozen** *n* : THIRTEEN

**bak·ery** \'bā-k(ə-)rē\ *n, pl* **-er·ies** : a place for baking or selling baked goods

**bake·shop** \'bāk-,shäp\ *n* : BAKERY

**baking powder** *n* : a powder that consists of a carbonate, an acid, and a starch and that makes the dough rise and become light in baking cakes and biscuits

**baking soda** *n* : BICARBONATE OF SODA

**bak·sheesh** \'bak-,shēsh\ *n, pl* **baksheesh** : TIP, GRATUITY

**bal** *abbr* balance

**bal·a·lai·ka** \,bal-ə-'lī-kə\ *n* : a triangular wooden instrument of the guitar kind used esp. in the U.S.S.R.

¹**bal·ance** \'bal-əns\ *n* [ME, fr. OF, fr. LL *bilanc-, bilanx* having two scalepans, fr. L *bi* two + *lanc-, lanx* plate] **1** : a weighing device : SCALE **2** : a weight, force, or influence counteracting the effect of another **3** : a vibrating wheel used to regulate a watch or clock **4** : a state of equilibrium **5** : REMAINDER, REST; *esp* : an amount in excess esp. on the credit side of an account — **bal·anced** \-ənst\ *adj*

²**balance** *vb* **bal·anced; bal·anc·ing 1** : to compute the balance of an account **2** : to arrange so that one set of elements equals another; *also* : to equal or equalize in weight, number, or proportions **3** : WEIGH **4** : to bring or come to a state or position of equipoise; *also* : to bring into harmony or proportion

**balance wheel** *n* : a wheel that regulates or stabilizes the motion of a mechanism

**bal·boa** \bal-'bō-ə\ *n* — see MONEY table

**bal·brig·gan** \bal-'brig-ən\ *n* : a knitted cotton fabric used esp. for underwear

**bal·co·ny** \'bal-kə-nē\ *n, pl* **-nies 1** : a platform projecting from the side of a building and enclosed by a railing **2** : a gallery inside a building

**bald** \'bold\ *adj* **1** : lacking a natural or usual covering (as of hair) **2** : UNADORNED, PLAIN   **syn** bare, barren, naked, nude — **bald·ness** *n*

**bal·da·chin** \'bȯl-də-kən, 'bal-\ *or* **bal·da·chi·no** \,bal-də-'kē-nō\ *n, pl* **baldachins** *or* **baldachinos** : a canopylike structure over an altar

**bald eagle** *n* : a common eagle of No. America that has a white head and neck feathers when mature and also a white tail when old

**bal·der·dash** \'bȯl-dər-,dash\ *n* : NONSENSE

**bald·ing** \'bȯld-iŋ\ *adj* : becoming bald

**bal·dric** \'bȯl-drik\ *n* : a belt worn over the shoulder to carry a sword or bugle

¹**bale** \'bāl\ *n* : a large bundle or closely packed package

²**bale** *vb* **baled; bal·ing** : to pack in a bale — **bal·er** *n*

**ba·leen** \bə-'lēn\ *n* : WHALEBONE

**bale·ful** \'bāl-fəl\ *adj* : DEADLY, HARMFUL; *also* : OMINOUS **syn** sinister

¹**balk** \'bȯk\ *n* **1** : HINDRANCE, CHECK, SETBACK **2** : an illegal motion of the pitcher in baseball while in position

²**balk** *vb* **1** : BLOCK, THWART **2** : to stop short and refuse to go on **3** : to commit a balk in sports **syn** frustrate

**balky** \'bȯ-kē\ *adj* **balk·i·er; -est**

: likely to balk

¹**ball** \'bȯl\ *n* **1** : a rounded body or mass (as at the base of the thumb or for use as a missile or in a game) **2** : a game played with a ball **3** : PITCH (a fast ~) **4** : a pitched baseball that misses the strike zone and is not swung at by the batter

²**ball** *vb* : to form into a ball

³**ball** *n* : a large formal dance

**bal·lad** \'bal-əd\ *n* **1** : a simple song : AIR **2** : a narrative poem of strongly marked rhythm suitable for singing **3** : a slow romantic dance song

**bal·lad·eer** \,bal-ə-'diər\ *n* : a singer of ballads

¹**bal·last** \'bal-əst\ *n* **1** : heavy material put in the hold of a ship to steady it or in the car of a balloon to steady it or control its ascent **2** : crushed stone laid in a railroad bed or used in making concrete

²**ballast** *vb* : to provide with ballast **syn** balance

**ball bearing** *n* : a bearing in which the journal turns upon steel balls that roll easily in a groove; *also* : one of the balls in such a bearing

**ball·car·ri·er** \'bȯl-,kar-ē-ər\ *n* : the football player carrying the ball in an offensive play

**bal·le·ri·na** \,bal-ə-'rē-nə\ *n* : a female ballet dancer

**bal·let** \'ba-,lā, ba-'lā\ *n* **1** : dancing in which fixed poses and steps are combined with light flowing movements often to convey a story; *also* : a theatrical art form using ballet dancing **2** : a company of ballet dancers

**bal·let·o·mane** \ba-'let-ə-,mān\ *n* : a devotee of ballet

**bal·lis·tic missile** \bə-'lis-tik-\ *n* : a self-powered missile that is guided during ascent and that falls freely during descent

**bal·lis·tics** \-tiks\ *n sing or pl* **1** : the science dealing with the motion of projectiles (as bullets) in flight **2** : the flight characteristics of a projectile — **ballistic** *adj*

**ball of fire** : an unusually energetic person

¹**bal·loon** \bə-'lün\ *n* **1** : a bag filled with gas or heated air so as to rise and float in the atmosphere **2** : a toy consisting of a rubber bag that can be inflated — **bal·loon·ist** *n*

²**balloon** *vb* **1** : to travel in a balloon **2** : to swell or puff out **3** : to increase rapidly

**balloon tire** *n* : a pneumatic tire with a flexible body and large cross section

¹**bal·lot** \'bal-ət\ *n* [It *ballotta* small ball used in secret voting, fr. It dial., dim. of *balla* ball] **1** : a piece of paper used to cast a vote **2** : the action or a system of voting; *also* : the right to vote

²**ballot** *vb* : to decide by ballot : VOTE

**ball-point pen** *n* : a pen having as the writing point a small rotating metal ball that inks itself by contact with an inner container

**ball·room** \'bȯl-,rüm, -,rùm\ *n* : a large room for dances

**bal·ly·hoo** \'bal-ē-,hü\ *n*, *pl* **-hoos**
**1** : a noisy attention-getting demonstration or talk  **2** : grossly exaggerated or sensational advertising or propaganda — **ballyhoo** *vb*

**balm** \'bäm, 'bälm\ *n*  **1** : a fragrant healing or soothing lotion or ointment  **2** : any of several spicy fragrant herbs  **3** : something that comforts or soothes

**balm·y** \'bäm-ē, 'bäl-mē\ *adj* **balm·i·er**; **-est**  **1** : gently soothing : MILD  **2** : FOOLISH, INSANE **syn** soft, bland — **balm·i·ness** *n*

**ba·lo·ney** \bə-'lō-nē\ *n* : NONSENSE

**bal·sa** \'bȯl-sə\ *n* : the extremely light strong wood of a tropical American tree

**bal·sam** \'bȯl-səm\ *n*  **1** : a fragrant aromatic and usu. resinous substance oozing from various plants; *also* : a preparation containing or smelling like balsam  **2** : a balsam-yielding plant  **3** : a common garden ornamental plant

**balsam fir** *n* : a resinous American evergreen tree that is widely used for pulpwood and as a Christmas tree

**Bal·ti·more oriole** \,bȯl-tə-,mȯr-\ *n* : a common American oriole in which the male is brightly colored with orange, black, and white

**bal·us·ter** \'bal-ə-stər\ *n* [F *balustre*, fr. It *balaustro*, fr. *balaustra* wild pomegranate flower, fr. L *balaustium*, fr. Gk *balaustion*; fr. its shape] : an upright support of a rail (as of a staircase)

**bal·us·trade** \-ə-,strād\ *n* : a row of balusters topped by a rail

**bam·boo** \bam-'bü\ *n*, *pl* **bamboos** : any of various woody mostly tall tropical grasses including some with strong hollow stems used for building, furniture, or utensils

**bamboo curtain** *n*, *often cap B&C* : a political, military, and ideological barrier in the Orient

**bam·boo·zle** \bam-'bü-zəl\ *vb* **bam·boo·zled**; **bam·boo·zling** \-'büz-(ə-)liŋ\ : TRICK, HOODWINK

**¹ban** \'ban\ *vb* **banned**; **ban·ning** : PROHIBIT, FORBID

**²ban** *n*  **1** : CURSE  **2** : a legal or official prohibiting

**³ban** \'bän\ *n*, *pl* **ba·ni** \'bän-ē\ — see *leu* at MONEY table

**ba·nal** \bə-'näl, -'nal; 'bān-ʔl\ *adj* : COMMONPLACE, TRITE — **ba·nal·i·ty** \bā-'nal-ət-ē\ *n*

**ba·nana** \bə-'nan-ə\ *n* : a treelike tropical plant bearing thick clusters of yellow or reddish fruit; *also* : this fruit

**¹band** \'band\ *n*  **1** : something (as a fetter or an obligation) that constrains or restrains  **2** : a strip serving to bind or hold together; *also* : one used to cover, protect, or finish something  **3** : a range of wavelengths (as in radio)  **4** : a group of grooves on a phonograph record containing recorded sound

**²band** *vb*  **1** : to tie up, finish, or enclose with a band  **2** : to gather or unite in a company or for some common end — **band·er** *n*

**³band** *n* : a group of persons, animals, or things; *esp* : a group of musicians organized for playing together

**¹ban·dage** \'ban-dij\ *n* : a strip of material used esp. in dressing wounds

**²bandage** *vb* **ban·daged**; **ban·dag·ing** : to dress or cover with a bandage

**ban·dan·na** *or* **ban·dana** \ban-'dan-ə\ *n* : a large colored figured handkerchief

**band·box** \'ban(d)-,bäks\ *n* : a usu. cylindrical box for carrying clothing

**band·ed** \'ban-dəd\ *adj* : having or marked with bands

**ban·de·role** *or* **ban·de·rol** \'ban-də-,rōl\ *n* : a long narrow forked flag or streamer

**ban·dit** \'ban-dət\ *n* [It *bandito*, fr. *bandire* to banish] **1** *pl also* **ban·dit·ti** \ban-'dit-ē\ : an outlaw who lives by plunder; *esp* : a member of a band of marauders  **2** : ROBBER — **ban·dit·ry** \'ban-də-trē\ *n*

**ban·do·lier** *or* **ban·do·leer** \,ban-də-'liər\ *n* : a belt slung over the shoulder esp. to carry ammunition

**band saw** *n* : a saw in the form of an endless steel belt running over pulleys

**band·stand** \'ban(d)-,stand\ *n* : a usu. roofed stand or raised platform on which a band or orchestra performs

**band w** *abbr* black and white

**band·wag·on** \'band-,wag-ən\ *n*  **1** : a wagon carrying musicians in a parade  **2** : a candidate, side, or movement that attracts open support or approval because it seems to be winning or gaining popularity — used in phrases like *climb on the bandwagon*

**¹ban·dy** \'ban-dē\ *vb* **ban·died**; **ban·dy·ing**  **1** : to exchange (as blows or quips) esp. in rapid succession  **2** : to use in a glib or offhand way

**²bandy** *adj* : curved outward ⟨~ legs⟩

**bane** \'bān\ *n*  **1** : POISON  **2** : WOE, HARM; *also* : a source of this — **bane·ful** *adj*

**¹bang** \'baŋ\ *vb*  **1** : BUMP ⟨fell and ~ed his knee⟩  **2** : to strike, thrust, or move usu. with a loud noise

**²bang** *n*  **1** : BLOW  **2** : a sudden loud noise

**³bang** *adv* : DIRECTLY, RIGHT

**⁴bang** *n* : a fringe of hair cut short (as across the forehead) — usu. used in pl.

**⁵bang** *vb* : to cut a bang in

**ban·gle** \'baŋ-gəl\ *n* : BRACELET; *also* : a loose-hanging ornament

**bang-up** \'baŋ-,əp\ *adj* : FIRST-RATE, EXCELLENT ⟨a ~ job⟩

**ban·ish** \'ban-ish\ *vb*  **1** : to require by authority to leave a country  **2** : to drive out : EXPEL **syn** exile, ostracize, deport — **ban·ish·ment** *n*

**ban·is·ter** *also* **ban·nis·ter** \'ban-ə-stər\ *n*  **1** : one of the upright supports of a handrail along a staircase  **2** : the handrail of a staircase

**ban·jo** \'ban-,jō\ *n*, *pl* **banjos** *also* **banjoes** : a musical instrument with a long neck, a drumlike body, and usu. 5 strings — **ban·jo·ist** *n*

**¹bank** \'baŋk\ *n*  **1** : a piled-up mass (as of cloud or earth)  **2** : an undersea elevation **3 :** rising ground bordering a lake, river, or sea **4 :** the sideways slope of a surface along a curve or of a vehicle as it rounds a curve

²**bank** *vb* **1 :** to form a bank about **2 :** to cover (as a fire) with fuel to keep inactive **3 :** to build (a curve) with the roadbed or track inclined laterally upward from the inside edge **4 :** to pile or heap in a bank; *also* **:** to arrange in a tier **5 :** to incline (an airplane) laterally

³**bank** *n* **1 :** a tier of oars **2 :** a group of objects arranged near together (as in a row or tier) ⟨a ~ of file drawers⟩

⁴**bank** *n* [ME, fr. MF or It; MF *banque*, fr. It *banca*, lit., bench] **1 :** an establishment concerned esp. with the custody, loan, exchange, or issue of money, the extension of credit, and the transmission of funds **2 :** a stock of or a place for holding something in reserve ⟨a blood ~⟩

⁵**bank** *vb* **1 :** to conduct the business of a bank **2 :** to deposit money or have an account in a bank — **bank·er** *n* — **bank·ing** *n*

**bank·book** \'baŋk-ˌbůk\ *n* **:** the depositor's book in which a bank records his deposits and withdrawals

**bank note** *n* **:** a promissory note issued by a bank and circulating as money

**bank·roll** \'baŋk-ˌrōl\ *n* **:** supply of money **:** FUNDS

¹**bank·rupt** \'baŋk-(ˌ)rəpt\ *n* **:** an insolvent person; *esp* **:** one whose property is turned over by court action to a trustee to be handled for the benefit of his creditors — **bankrupt** *vb*

²**bankrupt** *adj* **1 :** reduced to financial ruin; *esp* **:** legally declared a bankrupt **2 :** wholly lacking in or deprived of some essential ⟨~ soils⟩ — **bank·rupt·cy** \'baŋk-(ˌ)rəp-(t)sē\ *n*

¹**ban·ner** \'ban-ər\ *n* **1 :** a piece of cloth attached to a staff and used by a ruler or commander as his standard **2 :** FLAG

²**banner** *adj* **:** distinguished from all others esp. in excellence ⟨a ~ year⟩

**ban·nock** \'ban-ək\ *n* **:** a flat oatmeal or barley cake usu. cooked on a griddle

**banns** \'banz\ *n pl* **:** public announcement esp. in church of a proposed marriage

**ban·quet** \'baŋ-kwət\ *n* [MF, fr. It *banchetto*, fr. dim. of *banca* bench, bank] **:** a ceremonial dinner — **banquet** *vb*

**ban·quette** \baŋ-'ket\ *n* **1 :** a raised way along the inside of a parapet or trench for gunners or guns **2 :** a long upholstered seat esp. along a wall

**ban·shee** \'ban-shē\ *n* [ScGael *bean-sīth*, fr. or akin to Old Irish *ben sīde* woman of fairyland] **:** a female spirit in Gaelic folklore whose wailing warns a family of an approaching death

**ban·tam** \'bant-əm\ *n* **1 :** a small domestic fowl that is often a miniature of a standard breed **2 :** a small but pugnacious person

¹**ban·ter** \'bant-er\ *vb* **:** to speak to in a witty and teasing manner

²**banter** *n* **:** good-natured witty joking

**bant·ling** \'bant-liŋ\ *n* **:** a young child

**Ban·tu** \'ban-ˌtü\ *n, pl* **Bantu** or **Bantus 1 :** a member of a family of Negroid peoples occupying equatorial and southern Africa **2 :** a group of African languages spoken generally in equatorial and southern Africa — **Bantu** *adj*

**Ban·tu·stan** \ˌban-tù-'stan, ˌbän-tù-'stän\ *n* **:** an all-black enclave in the Republic of So. Africa with a limited degree of self-government

**ban·yan** \'ban-yən\ *n* [earlier *banyan* Hindu merchant, fr. Hindi *baniyā*; fr. a merchant's pagoda erected under a tree of the species in Iran] **:** a large East Indian tree whose aerial roots grow downward to the ground and form new trunks

**ban·zai** \bän-'zī\ *n* **:** a Japanese cheer or cry of triumph

**banzai attack** *n* **:** a mass attack by Japanese soldiers

**bao·bab** \'baů-ˌbab, 'bā-ə-\ *n* **:** an Old World tropical tree with short swollen trunk and sour edible gourdlike fruits

**bap·tism** \'bap-ˌtiz-əm\ *n* **1 :** a Christian sacrament signifying spiritual rebirth and symbolized by the ritual use of water **2 :** an act of baptizing — **bap·tis·mal** \bap-'tiz-məl\ *adj*

**baptismal name** *n* **:** CHRISTIAN NAME

**Bap·tist** \'bap-təst\ *n* **:** a member of a Protestant denomination emphasizing baptism of believers by immersion

**bap·tis·tery** or **bap·tis·try** \'bap-tə-strē\ *n, pl* **-ter·ies** or **-tries** **:** a place esp. in a church used for baptism

**bap·tize** \bap-'tīz, 'bap-ˌtīz\ *vb* **baptized; bap·tiz·ing** [ME *baptizen*, fr. OF *baptiser*, fr. L *baptizare*, fr. Gk *baptizein* to dip, baptize, fr. *baptos* dipped, fr. *baptein* to dip] **1 :** to administer baptism to; *also* **:** CHRISTEN **2 :** to purify esp. by an ordeal

¹**bar** \'bär\ *n* **1 :** a long narrow piece of material (as wood or metal) used esp. for a lever, fastening, or support **2 :** BARRIER, OBSTACLE **3 :** the railing in a law court at which prisoners are stationed; *also* **:** the legal profession or the whole body of lawyers **4 :** a stripe, band, or line much longer than wide **5 :** a counter at which food or esp. drink is served; *also* **:** BARROOM **6 :** a vertical line across the musical staff

²**bar** *vb* **barred; bar·ring 1 :** to fasten, confine, or obstruct with or as if with a bar or bars **2 :** to mark with bars **:** STRIPE **3 :** to shut or keep out **:** EXCLUDE **4 :** FORBID, PREVENT

³**bar** *prep* **:** EXCEPT

⁴**bar** *abbr* barometer

**barb** \'bärb\ *n* **1 :** a sharp projection extending backward (as from the point of an arrow or a fishhook) **2 :** a plant hair or bristle ending in a hook — **barbed** \'bärbd\ *adj*

**bar·bar·i·an** \bär-'ber-ē-ən\ *adj* **1 :** of, relating to, or being a land, culture, or people alien to and usu. believed to be inferior to one's own **2 :** lacking refinement, learning, or artistic or literary culture — **barbarian** *n*

**bar·bar·ic** \bär-'bar-ik\ *adj* **1** : BARBARIAN **2** : marked by a lack of restraint : WILD **3** : PRIMITIVE, UNSOPHISTICATED

**bar·ba·rism** \'bär-bə-,riz-əm\ *n* **1** : a word or expression that offends current standards of correctness or purity **2** : the social condition of barbarians; *also* : the use or display of barbarian or barbarous acts, attitudes, or ideas

**bar·ba·rous** \'bär-b(ə-)rəs\ *adj* **1** : using linguistic barbarisms **2** : lacking culture or refinement **3** : mercilessly harsh or cruel — **bar·bar·i·ty** \bär-'bar-ət-ē\ *n* — **bar·ba·rous·ly** *adv*

¹**bar·be·cue** \'bär-bi-,kyü\ *n* : a large animal (as an ox) roasted whole over an open fire; *also* : a social gathering at which barbecued food is served

²**barbecue** *vb* **-cued; -cu·ing 1** : to cook over hot coals or on a revolving spit **2** : to cook in a highly seasoned vinegar sauce

**bar·bell** \'bär-,bel\ *n* : a bar with adjustable weights attached to each end used for exercise and in weight-lifting competition

**bar·ber** \'bär-bər\ *n* [ME, fr. MF *barbeor*, fr. *barbe* beard, fr. L *barba*] : one whose business is cutting and dressing hair and shaving and trimming beards

**bar·ber·ry** \'bär-,ber-ē\ *n* : a spiny shrub bearing sour oblong red berries

**bar·bi·can** \'bär-bi-kən\ *n* : an outer defensive work

**bar·bi·tal** \'bär-bə-,tȯl\ *n* : a white crystalline addiction-causing hypnotic often administered in the form of its soluble sodium salt

**bar·bi·tu·rate** \bär-'bich-ə-rət\ *n* : a salt or ester of an organic acid (**bar·bi·tu·ric acid** \,bär-bə-,t(y)ůr-ik-\); *esp* : one used as a sedative or hypnotic

**bar·ca·role** *or* **bar·ca·rolle** \'bär-kə-,rōl\ *n* : a Venetian boat song characterized by a beat suggesting a rowing rhythm; *also* : a piece of music imitating this

**bard** \'bärd\ *n* : POET

¹**bare** \'baər\ *adj* **bar·er; bar·est 1** : NAKED **2** : UNCONCEALED, EXPOSED **3** : EMPTY **4** : leaving nothing to spare : MERE **5** : PLAIN, UNADORNED **syn** nude, bald — **bare·ness** *n*

²**bare** *vb* **bared; bar·ing** : to make or lay bare : REVEAL

**bare·back** \-,bak\ *or* **bare·backed** \-'bakt\ *adv or adj* : without a saddle

**bare·faced** \-'fāst\ *adj* **1** : having the face uncovered; *esp* : BEARDLESS **2** : not concealed : OPEN

**bare·foot** \-,fůt\ *or* **bare·foot·ed** \-'fůt-əd\ *adv or adj* : with bare feet

**bare·hand·ed** \-'han-dəd\ *adv or adj* **1** : without gloves **2** : without tools or weapons

**bare·head·ed** \-'hed-əd\ *adv or adj* : without a hat

**bare·ly** \'baər-lē\ *adv* **1** : by a narrow margin : SCARCELY ⟨~ enough money⟩

**2** : PLAINLY, MEAGERLY **syn** hardly

**bar·fly** \'bär-,flī\ *n* : a drinker who frequents bars

¹**bar·gain** \'bär-gən\ *n* **1** : AGREEMENT **2** : an advantageous purchase **3** : a transaction, situation, or event regarded in the light of its results

²**bargain** *vb* **1** : to negotiate over the terms of an agreement; *also* : to come to terms **2** : BARTER

¹**barge** \'bärj\ *n* **1** : a broad flat-bottomed boat for river or canal use usu. moved by towing **2** : a powerboat supplied to a flagship (as for use by an admiral) **3** : a ceremonial boat elegantly furnished — **barge·man** \-mən\ *n*

²**barge** *vb* **barged; barg·ing 1** : to carry by barge **2** : to move or thrust oneself clumsily or rudely

**bari·tone** \'bar-ə-,tōn\ *n* [F *baryton* or It *baritono*, fr. Gk *barytonos* deep sounding, fr. *barys* heavy + *tonos* tone] : a male voice between bass and tenor; *also* : a man with such a voice

**bar·i·um** \'bar-ē-əm\ *n* : a silver-white metallic chemical element that occurs only in combination

¹**bark** \'bärk\ *vb* **1** : to make the characteristic short sharp cry of a dog **2** : to speak or utter in a curt loud tone : SNAP

²**bark** *n* : the sound made by a barking dog

³**bark** *n* : the tough corky outer covering of a woody stem or root

⁴**bark** *vb* **1** : to strip the bark from **2** : to rub the skin from : ABRADE

⁵**bark** *n* : a 3-masted ship with foremast and mainmast square-rigged

**bar·keep·er** \'bär-,kē-pər\ *or* **bar·keep** \-,kēp\ *n* : BARTENDER

**bark·er** \'bär-kər\ *n* : a person who stands at the entrance esp. to a show and tries to attract customers to it

**bar·ley** \'bär-lē\ *n* : a cereal grass with seeds used as food and in making malt liquors; *also* : its seed

**bar mitz·vah** \bär-'mits-və\ *n, often cap B&M* [Heb *bar miṣwāh*, lit., son of the (divine) law] **1** : a Jewish boy who at about 13 years of age assumes religious responsibilities **2** : the ceremony recognizing a boy as a bar mitzvah

**barn** \'bärn\ *n* [ME *bern*, fr. OE *bereærn*, fr. *bere* barley + *ærn* place] : a building used esp. for storing hay and grain and for housing livestock

**bar·na·cle** \'bär-ni-kəl\ *n* : a marine crustacean free-swimming when young but fixed (as to rocks) when adult

**barn·storm** \'bärn-,stȯrm\ *vb* **1** : to tour through rural districts staging theatrical performances usu. in one-night stands **2** : to travel from place to place making brief stops (as in political campaigning)

**barn·yard** \-,yärd\ *n* : a usu. fenced area adjoining a barn

**baro·graph** \'bar-ə-,graf\ *n* : a self-registering barometer — **baro·graph·ic** \,bar-ə-'graf-ik\ *adj*

**ba·rom·e·ter** \bə-'räm-ət-ər\ *n* : an instrument for measuring atmospheric pressure — **baro·met·ric** \,bar-ə-'met-rik\ *or* **baro·met·ri·cal** \-ri-kəl\ *adj*

**bar·on** \'bar-ən\ *n* : a member of the lowest grade of the British peerage — **ba·ro·ni·al** \bə-'rō-nē-əl\ *adj* — **bar·ony** \'bar-ə-nē\ *n*

**bar·on·age** \-ə-nij\ *n* : PEERAGE

**bar·on·ess** \-ə-nəs\ *n* **1** : the wife or widow of a baron **2** : a woman holding a baronial title in her own right

**bar·on·et** \'bar-ə-nət\ *n* : a man holding a rank of honor below a baron but above a knight — **bar·on·et·cy** \-sē\ *n*

**ba·roque** \bə-rōk, -'räk\ *adj* : marked by elaborate and sometimes grotesque ornamentation and esp. by curved and plastic figures

**ba·rouche** \bə-'rüsh\ *n* [G barutsche, fr. It biroccio, deriv. of LL birotus two-wheeled, fr. L bi two + rota wheel] : a 4-wheeled carriage with a high driver's seat in front and a folding top

**bar·racks** \'bar-əks\ *n sing or pl* : a building or group of buildings for lodging soldiers

**bar·ra·cu·da** \,bar-ə-'küd-ə\ *n, pl* **-da** *or* **-das** : any of several large predaceous sea fishes related to the gray mullets

¹**bar·rage** \'bär-ij\ *n* : an artificial dam in a watercourse

²**bar·rage** \bə-'räzh, 'räj\ *n* : a heavy concentration of fire (as of artillery)

**bar·ra·try** \'bar-ə-trē\ *n, pl* **-tries 1** : the purchase or sale of office or preferment in church or state **2** : a fraudulent breach of duty by the master or crew of a ship intended to harm the owner or cargo **3** : the practice of inciting lawsuits or quarrels

**barred** \'bärd\ *adj* : STRIPED

¹**bar·rel** \'bar-əl\ *n* **1** : a round bulging cask with flat ends of equal diameter **2** : the amount contained in a barrel **3** : a cylindrical or tubular part ⟨gun ~⟩

²**barrel** *vb* **-reled** *or* **-relled; -rel·ing** *or* **-rel·ling 1** : to pack in a barrel **2** : to travel at high speed

**barrel roll** *n* : an airplane maneuver in which a complete revolution about the longitudinal axis is made

¹**bar·ren** \'bar-ən\ *adj* **1** : STERILE, UNFRUITFUL **2** : lacking interest or charm **3** : unproductive of results ⟨a ~ scheme⟩ **4** : DULL, STUPID — **bar·ren·ness** \-ən-nəs\ *n*

²**barren** *n* : a tract of barren land

**bar·rette** \bä-'ret, bə-\ *n* : a clasp for holding a woman's hair in place

¹**bar·ri·cade** \'bar-ə-,kād, ,bar-ə-'kād\ *vb* **-cad·ed; -cad·ing** : to block, obstruct, or fortify with a barricade

²**barricade** *n* [F, fr. MF, fr. barriquer to barricade, fr. barrique barrel] **1** : a hastily thrown-up obstruction or fortification **2** : BARRIER, OBSTACLE

**bar·ri·er** \'bar-ē-ər\ *n* : something that separates, demarcates, or serves as a barricade ⟨racial ~s⟩

**barrier reef** *n* : a coral reef roughly parallel to a shore and separated from it by a lagoon

**bar·ring** \'bär-iŋ\ *prep* : excluding by exception : EXCEPTING

**bar·rio** \'bär-ē-,ō, 'bar-\ *n, pl* **-ri·os 1** : a district of a city or town in a Spanish-speaking country **2** : a Spanish-speaking quarter in a U.S. city

**bar·ris·ter** \'bar-ə-stər\ *n* : a British counselor admitted to plead in the higher courts **syn** lawyer, attorney

**bar·room** \'bär-,rüm, -,rum\ *n* : a room or establishment whose main feature is a bar for the sale of liquor

¹**bar·row** \'bar-ō\ *n* : a large burial mound of earth and stones

²**barrow** *n* : a male hog castrated while young

³**barrow** *n* **1** : HANDBARROW **2** : WHEELBARROW **3** : a cart with a boxlike body and two shafts for pushing it

**Bart** *abbr* baronet

**bar·tend·er** \'bär-,ten-dər\ *n* : one that serves liquor at a bar

**bar·ter** \'bärt-ər\ *vb* : to trade by exchange of goods — **barter** *n*

**bas·al** \'bā-səl\ *adj* **1** : situated at or forming the base **2** : BASIC

**basal metabolism** *n* : the turnover of energy in a fasting and resting organism using energy solely to maintain vital cellular activity, respiration, and circulation as measured by the rate at which heat is given off

**ba·salt** \bə-'solt, 'bā-,solt\ *n* : a dark fine-grained igneous rock — **ba·sal·tic** \bə-'sol-tik\ *adj*

¹**base** \'bās\ *n, pl* **bas·es** \'bā-səz\ **1** : BOTTOM, FOUNDATION **2** : a side or face on which a geometrical figure stands **3** : a main ingredient or fundamental part **4** : the point of beginning an act or operation **5** : any of the four stations at the corners of a baseball diamond **6** : a place on which a force depends for supplies **7** : the number with reference to which a number system or a mathematical table is constructed **8** : a chemical compound (as lime or ammonia) that reacts with an acid to form a salt, has a salty taste, and turns litmus blue **syn** basis, ground

²**base** *vb* **based; bas·ing 1** : to form or serve as a base for **2** : ESTABLISH

³**base** *adj* **1** : of inferior quality : DEBASED, ALLOYED **2** : CONTEMPTIBLE, IGNOBLE **3** : MENIAL, DEGRADING **4** : of little value **syn** low, vile — **base·ly** *adv* — **base·ness** *n*

**base·ball** \'bās-,bol\ *n* : a game played with a bat and ball by 2 teams on a field with 4 bases arranged in a diamond; *also* : the ball used in this game

**base·board** \-,bord\ *n* : a line of boards or molding covering the joint of a wall and the adjoining floor

**base-born** \-'born\ *adj* **1** : of humble birth **2** : of illegitimate birth **3** : MEAN, IGNOBLE

**base exchange** *n* : a post exchange at a naval or air force base

**base hit** *n* : a hit in baseball that enables the batter to reach base safely with no error made and no base runner forced out

**base·less** \-ləs\ *adj* **:** having no base or basis **:** GROUNDLESS

**base·line** \'bās-,līn\ *n* **1 :** a line serving as a base **2 :** the area within which a baseball player must keep when running between bases

**base·ment** \-mənt\ *n* **1 :** the part of a building that is wholly or partly below ground level **2 :** the lowest or fundamental part of something

**base on balls :** an advance to first base given to a baseball player who receives four balls

**¹bash** \'bash\ *vb* **1 :** to strike violently **:** BEAT **2 :** to smash by a blow

**²bash** *n* **1 :** a heavy blow **2 :** a festive social gathering **:** PARTY

**bash·ful** \'bash-fəl\ *adj* **:** inclined to shrink from public attention — **bash·ful·ness** *n*

**ba·sic** \'bā-sik\ *adj* **1 :** of, relating to, or forming the base or essence **:** FUNDAMENTAL **2 :** of, relating to, or having the character of a chemical base ⟨a ~ substance⟩ **syn** underlying — **ba·si·cal·ly** \-si-k(ə-)lē\ *adv* — **ba·sic·i·ty** \bā-'sis-ət-ē\ *n*

**ba·sil** \'baz-əl, 'bās-\ *n* **:** an aromatic mint used in cookery

**ba·sil·i·ca** \bə-'sil-i-kə, -'zil-\ *n* [L, fr. Gk *basilikē*, fr. fem. of *basilikos* royal, fr. *basileus* king] **1 :** an early Christian church building consisting of nave and aisles with clerestory and apse **2 :** a church or cathedral given ceremonial privileges

**bas·i·lisk** \'bas-ə-,lisk, 'baz-\ *n* [ME, fr. L *basiliscus*, fr. Gk *basiliskos*, fr. dim. of *basileus* king] **:** a legendary reptile with fatal breath and glance

**ba·sin** \'bās-ⁿn\ *n* **1 :** an open usu. circular vessel with sloping sides for holding liquid (as water) **2 :** a hollow or enclosed place containing water; *also* **:** the region drained by a river

**ba·sis** \'bā-səs\ *n, pl* **ba·ses** \-,sēz\ **1 :** FOUNDATION, BASE **2 :** a fundamental principle

**bask** \'bask\ *vb* **1 :** to expose oneself to comfortable heat **2 :** to enjoy something warmly comforting ⟨~ing in his friends' admiration⟩

**bas·ket** \'bas-kət\ *n* **:** a container made of woven material (as twigs or grasses); *also* **:** any of various lightweight usu. wood containers — **bas·ket·ful** *n*

**bas·ket·ball** \-,bȯl\ *n* **:** a game played on a court by 2 teams who try to throw an inflated ball through a raised goal; *also* **:** the ball used in this game

**basket case** *n* **1 :** one who has all four limbs amputated **2 :** one that is totally incapacitated or inoperative

**basket weave** *n* **:** a textile weave resembling the checkered pattern of a plaited basket

**bas mitz·vah** \bäs-'mits-və\ *n, often cap B&M* [Heb *bath miṣwāh*, lit., daughter of the (divine) law] **1 :** a Jewish girl who at about 13 years of age assumes religious responsibilities **2 :** the ceremony recognizing a girl as a bas mitzvah

**Basque** \'bask\ *n* **1 :** a member of a people inhabiting a region bordering on the Bay of Biscay in northern Spain and southwestern France **2 :** the language of the Basque people — **Basque** *adj*

**bas–re·lief** \,bä-ri-'lēf\ *n* **:** a sculpture in relief with the design raised very slightly from the background

**¹bass** \'bas\ *n, pl* **bass** *or* **bass·es :** any of several spiny-finned sport and food fishes of eastern No. America

**²bass** \'bās\ *adj* **:** of low pitch

**³bass** \'bās\ *n* **1 :** a deep sound or tone **2 :** the lowest part in harmonic or polyphonic music **3 :** the lowest male singing voice **4 :** a singer or instrument having a bass voice or part

**bas·set hound** \'bas-ət-\ *n* **:** any of an old French breed of short-legged dogs with long ears and crooked front legs

**bas·si·net** \,bas-ə-'net\ *n* **:** a baby's bed that resembles a basket and often has a hood over one end

**bas·so** \'bas-ō\ *n, pl* **bassos** *or* **bas·si** \'bäs-,ē\ **:** a bass singer

**bas·soon** \bə-'sün, ba-\ *n* **:** a musical wind instrument lower in pitch than the oboe

**bass·wood** \'bas-,wu̇d\ *n* **1 :** a linden tree; *also* **:** its wood **2 :** TULIP TREE

**bast** \'bast\ *n* **:** strong woody plant fiber used esp. in making ropes

**¹bas·tard** \'bas-tərd\ *n* **1 :** an illegitimate child **2 :** an offensive or disagreeable person

**²bastard** *adj* **1 :** ILLEGITIMATE **2 :** of an inferior or nontypical kind, size, or form; *also* **:** SPURIOUS — **bas·tardy** *n*

**bas·tard·ize** \'bas-tər-,dīz\ *vb* **-ized; -iz·ing :** to reduce from a higher to a lower state **:** DEBASE

**¹baste** \'bāst\ *vb* **bast·ed; bast·ing :** to sew with long stitches so as to keep temporarily in place

**²baste** *vb* **bast·ed; bast·ing :** to moisten (as meat) at intervals with liquid while cooking

**³baste** *vb* **bast·ed; bast·ing :** to beat severely **:** THRASH

**bas·ti·na·do** \,bas-tə-'nād-ō, -'näd-\ *or* **bas·ti·nade** \,bas-tə-'nād, -'näd\ *n, pl* **-na·does** *or* **-nades 1 :** a blow or beating esp. with a stick **2 :** a punishment consisting of beating the soles of the feet

**bas·tion** \'bas-chən\ *n* **:** a projecting part of a fortification; *also* **:** a fortified position — **bas·tioned** \-chənd\ *adj*

**¹bat** \'bat\ *n* **1 :** a stout stick **:** CLUB **2 :** a sharp blow **3 :** an implement (as of wood) used to hit a ball (as in baseball) **4 :** a turn at batting — usu. used with *at*

**²bat** *vb* **bat·ted; bat·ting :** to hit with or as if with a bat

**³bat** *n* **:** any of a large group of flying mammals with forelimbs modified to form wings

**⁴bat** *vb* **bat·ted; bat·ting :** WINK, BLINK

**batch** \'bach\ *n* **1 :** a quantity (as of bread) baked at one time **2 :** a quantity of material for use at one time or produced at one operation

**bate** \'bāt\ *vb* **bat·ed; bat·ing** : MODERATE, REDUCE

**ba·teau** \ba-'tō\ *n, pl* **ba·teaux** \-'tōz\ : any of various small craft; *esp* : a flat-bottomed boat with overhanging bow and stern

**bath** \'bath, 'bȧth\ *n, pl* **baths** \'bathz, 'baths, 'bȧthz, 'bȧths\ **1** : a washing of the body **2** : water for washing the body **3** : a liquid in which objects are immersed so that it can act on them **4** : BATHROOM

**bathe** \'bāth\ *vb* **bathed; bath·ing 1** : to wash in liquid and esp. water; *also* : to apply water or a medicated liquid to ⟨*bathed* her eyes⟩ **2** : to wash along, over, or against so as to wet **3** : to suffuse with or as if with light **4** : to take a bath; *also* : to take a swim — **bath·er** *n*

**bath·house** \'bath-,haus, 'bȧth-\ *n* **1** : a building equipped for bathing **2** : a building containing dressing rooms for bathers

**batho·lith** \'bath-ə-,lith\ *n* : a great subsurface mass of intruded igneous rock — **batho·lith·ic** \,bath-ə-'lith-ik\ *adj*

**ba·thos** \'bā-,thäs\ *n* **1** : the sudden appearance of the commonplace in otherwise elevated matter or style **2** : insincere or overdone pathos — **ba·thet·ic** \bə-'thet-ik\ *adj*

**bath·robe** \'bath-,rōb, 'bȧth-\ *n* : a loose usu. absorbent robe worn before and after bathing or as a dressing gown

**bath·room** \-,rüm, -,rum\ *n* : a room containing a bathtub or shower and usu. a washbowl and toilet

**bath·tub** \-,təb\ *n* : a usu. fixed tub for bathing

**bathy·scaphe** \'bath-i-,skaf, -,skȧf\ *also* **bathy·scaph** \-,skaf\ *n* : a navigable submerging ship for deep-sea exploration having a spherical watertight cabin attached to its underside

**bathy·sphere** \-,sfiər\ *n* : a steel diving sphere for deep-sea observation

**ba·tik** \bə-'tēk, 'bat-ik\ *n* **1** : an Indonesian method of hand-printing textiles by coating with wax the parts not to be dyed; *also* : a design so executed **2** : a fabric printed by batik

**ba·tiste** \bə-'tēst\ *n* : a fine sheer fabric of plain weave

**bat·man** \'bat-mən\ *n* : an orderly of a British military officer

**ba·ton** \bə-'tän\ *n* : STAFF, ROD; *esp* : a stick with which the leader directs an orchestra or band

**ba·tra·chi·an** \bə-'trā-kē-ən\ *n* : a tailless leaping amphibian : FROG, TOAD — **batrachian** *adj*

**bats·man** \'bats-mən\ *n* : a batter esp. in cricket

**bat·tal·ion** \bə-'tal-yən\ *n* **1** : a large body of troops organized to act together : ARMY **2** : a military unit composed of a headquarters and two or more units (as companies)

**¹bat·ten** \'bat-ᵊn\ *vb* **bat·tened; bat·**

**ten·ing** \'bat-(ᵊ-)niŋ\ **1** : to grow or make fat **2** : THRIVE

**²batten** *n* : a strip of wood for nailing across other pieces to cover a crack or strengthen parts

**³batten** *vb* **bat·tened; bat·ten·ing** \'bat-(ᵊ-)niŋ\ : to fasten with battens

**¹bat·ter** \'bat-ər\ *vb* : to beat or damage with repeated blows

**²batter** *n* : a soft mixture (as for cake) basically of flour and liquid

**³batter** *n* : one that bats; *esp* : the player whose turn it is to bat

**battering ram** *n* : an ancient military machine for battering down walls

**bat·tery** \'bat-(ə-)rē\ *n, pl* **-ter·ies 1** : BEATING; *esp* : unlawful beating of or use of force on a person **2** : a grouping of artillery pieces for tactical purposes; *also* : the guns of a warship **3** : a group of electric cells for furnishing electric current; *also* : a single electric cell ⟨a flashlight ∼⟩ **4** : a number of similar items grouped or used as a unit ⟨a ∼ of tests⟩ **5** : the pitcher and the catcher of a baseball team

**bat·ting** \'bat-iŋ\ *n* : layers or sheets of cotton or wool (as for lining quilts)

**¹bat·tle** \'bat-ᵊl\ *n* [ME *batel*, fr. OF *bataille* battle, fortifying tower, battalion, fr. LL *battalia* combat, alter. of *battualia* fencing exercises, fr. L *battuere* to beat] : a general military engagement; *also* : an extended contest or controversy

**²battle** *vb* **bat·tled; bat·tling** \'bat-(ᵊ-)liŋ\ : to engage in battle : CONTEND, FIGHT

**bat·tle-ax** \'bat-ᵊl-,aks\ *n* **1** : a long-handled ax formerly used as a weapon **2** : a quarrelsome domineering woman

**bat·tle·field** \'bat-ᵊl-,fēld\ *n* : a place where a battle is fought

**bat·tle·ment** \-mənt\ *n* : a decorative or defensive parapet on top of a wall

**bat·tle·ship** \-,ship\ *n* : a warship of the most heavily armed and armored class

**bat·tle·wag·on** \-,wag-ən\ *n* : BATTLE-SHIP

**bat·ty** \'bat-ē\ *adj* **bat·ti·er; -est** : CRAZY, FOOLISH

**bau·ble** \'bȯ-bəl\ *n* : TRINKET

**baux·ite** \'bȯk-,sīt\ *n* : a clayey substance that is the chief ore of aluminum — **baux·it·ic** \bȯk-'sit-ik\ *adj*

**bawd** \'bȯd\ *n* **1** : MADAM **2** : PROSTITUTE

**bawdy** \'bȯd-ē\ *adj* **bawd·i·er; -est** : OBSCENE, LEWD — **bawd·i·ly** \'bȯd-ᵊl-ē\ *adv* — **bawd·i·ness** \-ē-nəs\ *n*

**¹bawl** \'bȯl\ *vb* : to cry or cry out loudly; *also* : to scold harshly

**²bawl** *n* : a long loud cry : BELLOW

**¹bay** \'bā\ *adj* : reddish brown

**²bay** *n* **1** : a bay-colored animal **2** : a moderate brown

**³bay** *n* : the Old World laurel; *also* : a shrub or tree resembling this

**⁴bay** *n* **1** : a compartment of a building set off from other parts (as by pillars) **2** : a compartment projecting outward from the wall of a building and containing a window (**bay window**)

⁵**bay** *vb* **:** to bark with deep long tones

⁶**bay** *n* **1 :** the position of one unable to escape and forced to face danger **2 : a** baying of dogs

⁷**bay** *n* **:** an inlet of a body of water (as the sea) usu. smaller than a gulf

**bay·ber·ry** \'bā-,ber-ē\ *n* **1 :** a West Indian tree related to the allspice tree **2 :** an American shrub bearing small hard berries coated with a white wax used for candles; *also* **:** its fruit

**bay leaf** *n* **:** the dried leaf of the European laurel used in cooking

¹**bay·o·net** \'bā-ə-nət, ,bā-ə-'net\ *n* **:** a daggerlike weapon made to fit on the muzzle end of a rifle

²**bayonet** *vb* **-net·ed** *also* **-net·ted; -net·ing** *also* **-net·ting :** to use or stab with a bayonet

**bay·ou** \'bī-ō, -ū\ *n* [Louisiana French, fr. Choctaw *bayuk*] **:** a minor or secondary stream that is tributary to a larger body of water; *also* **:** a marshy or sluggish body of water

**bay rum** *n* **:** a fragrant cosmetic and medicinal liquid distilled from the leaves of the West Indian bayberry or usu. prepared from essential oils, alcohol, and water

**ba·zaar** \bə-'zär\ *n* **1 :** a group of shops **:** MARKETPLACE **2 :** a fair for the sale of articles usu. for charity

**ba·zoo·ka** \bə-'zü-kə\ *n* [*bazooka* (a crude musical instrument made of pipes and a funnel)] **:** a weapon consisting of a tube and launching an explosive rocket able to pierce armor

¹**BB** \'bē-(,)bē\ *n* **:** a small round shot pellet

²**BB** *abbr* **1** bases on balls **2** best of breed

**BBA** *abbr* bachelor of business administration

**BBB** *abbr* Better Business Bureau

**BBC** *abbr* British Broadcasting Corporation

**bbl** *abbr* barrel; barrels

**BC** *abbr* **1** before Christ **2** British Columbia

**BCS** *abbr* bachelor of commercial science

**bd** *abbr* **1** board **2** bound

**BD** *abbr* **1** bachelor of divinity **2** bank draft **3** bills discounted **4** brought down

**bdl** *or* **bdle** *abbr* bundle

**bdrm** *abbr* bedroom

**be** \'(')bē\ *vb, past 1st & 3d sing* **was** \(')wəz, 'wäz\; *2d sing* **were** \(')wər\; *pl* **were;** *past subjunctive* **were;** *past part* **been** \(')bin\; *pres part* **be·ing** \'bē-iŋ\; *pres 1st sing* **am** \əm, (')am\; *2d sing* **are** \ər, (')är\; *3d sing* **is** \(')iz, əz\; *pl* **are;** *pres subjunctive* **be 1 :** to equal in meaning or symbolically ⟨God *is* love⟩; *also* **:** to have a specified qualification or relationship ⟨leaves *are* green⟩ ⟨this fish *is* a trout⟩ **2 :** to have objective existence ⟨there *was* once an old woman⟩; *also* **:** to have or occupy a particular place ⟨here *is* your pen⟩ **3 :** to take place **:** OCCUR ⟨the meeting *is* tonight⟩ **4 —** used with the past participle of transitive verbs as a passive voice auxiliary ⟨the door *was* opened⟩ **5 —** used as the auxiliary of the present participle in expressing continuous action ⟨he *is* sleeping⟩ **6 —** used as an auxiliary with the past participle of some intransitive verbs to form archaic perfect tenses **7 —** used as an auxiliary with *to* and the infinitive to express futurity, prearrangement, or obligation ⟨he *is* to come when called⟩

**Be** *symbol* beryllium

**BE** *abbr* bill of exchange

¹**beach** \'bēch\ *n* **:** the shore of the sea or of a lake or the bank of a river

²**beach** *vb* **:** to run or drive ashore

**beach buggy** *n* **:** a motor vehicle with oversize tires for use on a sand beach

**beach·comb·er** \'bēch-,kō-mər\ *n* **1 :** a drifter, loafer, or casual worker along the seacoast **2 :** one who searches along a shore for useful or salable flotsam and refuse

**beach flea** *n* **:** any of various small leaping crustaceans common on beaches

**beach·head** \'bēch-,hed\ *n* **:** an area on an enemy-held shore occupied by an advance attacking force to protect the later landing of troops or supplies

**bea·con** \'bē-kən\ *n* **1 :** a signal fire **2 :** a signal mark (as a lighthouse) for guidance **3 :** a radio transmitter emitting signals for guidance of airplanes — **beacon** *vb*

¹**bead** \'bēd\ *n* [ME *bede* prayer, prayer bead, fr. OE *bed, gebed* prayer] **1** *pl* **:** a series of prayers and meditations made with a rosary **2 :** a small piece of material pierced for threading on a line (as in a rosary) **3 :** a small globular body **4 :** a narrow projecting rim or band — **bead·ing** *n* — **beady** *adj*

²**bead** *vb* **:** to form into a bead

**bea·dle** \'bēd-ᵊl\ *n* **:** a usu. English parish officer whose duties include keeping order in church

**bea·gle** \'bē-gəl\ *n* **:** a small short-legged smooth-coated hound

**beak** \'bēk\ *n* **:** the bill of a bird and esp. of a bird of prey; *also* **:** a pointed projecting part — **beaked** \'bēkt\ *adj*

**bea·ker** \'bē-kər\ *n* **1 :** a large drinking cup with a wide mouth **2 :** a thin-walled laboratory vessel with a wide mouth

¹**beam** \'bēm\ *n* **1 :** a large long piece of timber or metal **2 :** the bar of a balance from which the scales hang **3 :** the breadth of a ship at its widest part **4 :** a ray or shaft of light **5 :** a collection of nearly parallel rays (as X rays) or particles (as electrons) **6 :** a directed flow of radio signals for the guidance of pilots; *also* **:** the course indicated by this flow

²**beam** *vb* **1 :** to send out light **2 :** to smile with joy **3 :** to aim (a radio broadcast) by directional antennas

¹**bean** \'bēn\ *n* **:** the edible seed borne in pods by some leguminous plants; *also* **:** a plant or a pod bearing these

²**bean** *vb* **:** to strike on the head with an object

**bean·ball** \'bēn-,bȯl\ *n* **:** a pitched baseball thrown at a batter's head

**bean curd** *n* **:** a soft vegetable cheese that is eaten extensively in the Orient and is prepared by treating soybean milk with coagulants

**bean·ie** \'bē-nē\ *n* : a small round tight-fitting skullcap worn esp. by schoolboys and college freshmen

**beano** \'bē-nō\ *n* : BINGO

**¹bear** \'baər\ *n, pl* **bears 1** *or pl* **bear** : a large heavy mammal with shaggy hair and a very short tail **2** : a surly uncouth person **3** : one who sells securities or commodities in expectation of a price decline — **bear·ish** *adj*

**²bear** *vb* **bore** \'bōr\; **borne** \'bōrn\ *also* **born** \'bȯrn\; **bear·ing 1** : CARRY **2** : to be equipped with **3** : to give as testimony ⟨∼ witness to the facts of the case⟩ **4** : to give birth to; *also* : PRODUCE, YIELD ⟨a tree that ∼s regularly⟩ **5** : ENDURE, SUSTAIN ⟨∼ pain⟩ ⟨bore the weight on piles⟩; *also* : to exert pressure or influence **6** : to be or become directed ⟨∼ to the right⟩ — **bear·able** *adj* — **bear·er** *n*

**¹beard** \'biərd\ *n* **1** : the hair that grows on the face of a man **2** : a growth of bristly hairs (as on rye or the chin of a goat) — **beard·ed** \-əd\ *adj* — **beard·less** *adj*

**²beard** *vb* : to confront boldly

**bear·ing** \'ba(ə)r-iŋ\ *n* **1** : manner of carrying oneself : COMPORTMENT **2** : a supporting object, purpose, or point **3** : an emblem in a coat of arms **4** : connection with or influence on something; *also* : SIGNIFICANCE **5** : a machine part in which another part (as an axle or pin) turns **6** : the position or direction of one point with respect to another or to the compass; *also* : a determination of position **7** *pl* : comprehension of one's situation

**bear·skin** \'baər-ˌskin\ *n* : an article made of the skin of a bear

**beast** \'bēst\ *n* **1** : ANIMAL 1; *esp* : a 4-footed animal **2** : a contemptible person **syn** brute

**¹beast·ly** \'bēst-lē\ *adj* **beast·li·er**; **-est 1** : of, relating to, or resembling a beast **2** : ABOMINABLE, DISAGREEABLE — **beast·li·ness** \-lē-nəs\ *n*

**²beastly** *adv* : VERY

**¹beat** \'bēt\ *vb* **beat**; **beat·en** \'bēt-ᵊn\ *or* **beat**; **beat·ing 1** : to strike repeatedly **2** : TREAD **3** : to affect or alter by beating ⟨∼ metal into sheets⟩ **4** : OVERCOME; *also* : SURPASS **5** : to sound (as an alarm) on a drum **6** : to act or arrive before ⟨∼ his brother home⟩ **7** : THROB — **beat·er** *n*

**²beat** *n* **1** : a single stroke or blow esp. of a series; *also* : PULSATION **2** : a rhythmic stress in poetry or music or the rhythmic effect of these **3** : a regularly traversed course

**³beat** *adj* **1** : EXHAUSTED **2** : of or relating to beatniks

**⁴beat** *n* : BEATNIK

**be·at·if·ic** \ˌbē-ə-'tif-ik\ *adj* : giving or indicative of great joy or bliss

**be·at·i·fy** \bē-'at-ə-ˌfī\ *vb* **-fied; -fy·ing 1** : to make supremely happy **2** : to declare to have attained the blessedness of heaven and authorize the title "Blessed" for — **be·at·i·fi·ca-**

**tion** \-ˌat-ə-fə-'kā-shən\ *n*

**be·at·i·tude** \bē-'at-ə-ˌt(y)üd\ *n* **1** : a state of utmost bliss **2** : any of the declarations made in the Sermon on the Mount (Mt 5:3–12) beginning "Blessed are"

**beat·nik** \'bēt-nik\ *n* : a person who behaves and dresses unconventionally and is inclined to exotic philosophizing and extreme self-expression

**beau** \'bō\ *n, pl* **beaux** \'bōz\ *or* **beaus** [F, fr. *beau* beautiful, fr. L *bellus* pretty] **1** : a man of fashion : DANDY **2** : SUITOR, LOVER

**beau geste** \bō-'zhest\ *n, pl* **beaux gestes** *or* **beau gestes** \bō-'zhest\ : a graceful or magnanimous gesture

**beau ide·al** \ˌbō-ī-'dē(-ə)l\ *n, pl* **beau ideals** : the perfect type or model

**Beau·jo·lais** \ˌbō-zhō-'lā\ *n* : a French red table wine

**beau monde** \bō-'mänd, -mōⁿd\ *n, pl* **beau mondes** \-'män(d)z\ *or* **beaux mondes** \bō-mōⁿd\ : the world of high society and fashion

**beau·te·ous** \'byüt-ē-əs\ *adj* : BEAUTIFUL — **beau·te·ous·ly** *adv*

**beau·ti·cian** \byü-'tish-ən\ *n* : COSMETOLOGIST

**beau·ti·ful** \'byüt-i-fəl\ *adj* : characterized by beauty : LOVELY **syn** pretty, fair — **beau·ti·ful·ly** \-f(ə-)lē\ *adv*

**beautiful people** *n pl, often cap B&P* : people who are identified with international society

**beau·ti·fy** \'byüt-ə-ˌfī\ *vb* **-fied; fy·ing** : to make more beautiful — **beau·ti·fi·ca·tion** \ˌbyüt-ə-fə-'kā-shən\ *n* — **beau·ti·fi·er** *n*

**beau·ty** \'byüt-ē\ *n, pl* **beauties** : qualities that give pleasure to the senses or exalt the mind : LOVELINESS; *also* : something having such qualities

**beauty shop** *n* : an establishment where hairdressing, facials, and manicures are done

**beaux arts** \bō-'zär\ *n pl* : FINE ARTS

**bea·ver** \'bē-vər\ *n, pl* **beavers** : a large fur-bearing rodent that builds dams and underwater houses of mud and sticks; *also* : its fur

**be·calm** \bi-'käm, -'kälm\ *vb* : to keep (as a ship) motionless by lack of wind

**be·cause** \bi-'kȯz, -'kəz\ *conj* : for the reason that

**because of** *prep* : by reason of

**Bech·u·a·na** \ˌbech-ə-'wän-ə\ *n* : a member of one of the various Bantu-speaking Negro peoples dwelling between the Orange and Zambezi rivers esp. in Botswana

**beck** \'bek\ *n* : a beckoning gesture; *also* : SUMMONS

**beck·on** \'bek-ən\ *vb* **beck·oned; beck·on·ing** \'bek-(ə-)niŋ\ : to summon or signal esp. by a nod or gesture; *also* : ATTRACT

**be·cloud** \bi-'klaùd\ *vb* : OBSCURE

**be·come** \bi-'kəm\ *vb* **-came** \-'kām\; **-come; -com·ing 1** : to come to be ⟨∼ tired⟩ **2** : to suit or be suitable to ⟨her dress ∼s her⟩

**be·com·ing** \-'kəm-iŋ\ *adj* : SUITABLE,

FIT; *also* : ATTRACTIVE — **be·com·ing·ly** *adv*

**¹bed** \'bed\ *n* **1** : an article of furniture to sleep on **2** : a plot of ground prepared for plants **3** : FOUNDATION, BOTTOM ⟨river ~⟩ **4** : LAYER, STRATUM

**²bed** *vb* **bed·ded; bed·ding 1** : to put or go to bed **2** : to fix in a foundation : EMBED **3** : to plant in beds **4** : to lay or lie flat or in layers

**be·daub** \bi-'dȯb\ *vb* : SMEAR

**be·daz·zle** \bi-'daz-əl\ *vb* : to confuse by or as if by a strong light — **be·daz·zle·ment** *n*

**bed·bug** \'bed-,bəg\ *n* : a wingless bloodsucking insect infesting houses and esp. beds

**bed·clothes** \'bed-,klō(th)z\ *n pl* : BEDDING 1

**bed·ding** \'bed-iŋ\ *n* **1** : materials for making up a bed **2** : FOUNDATION

**be·deck** \bi-'dek\ *vb* : ADORN

**be·dev·il** \bi-'dev-əl\ *vb* **1** : HARASS, TORMENT **2** : CONFUSE, MUDDLE

**be·dew** \bi-'d(y)ü\ *vb* : to wet with or as if with dew

**bed·fast** \'bed-,fast\ *adj* : BEDRIDDEN

**bed·fel·low** \'bed-,fel-ō\ *n* **1** : one sharing the bed of another **2** : a close associate : ALLY

**be·di·zen** \bi-'dīz-ᵊn, -'diz-\ *vb* [*be-* + *dizen*, fr. earlier *disen* to dress a distaff with flax, fr. D] : to dress or adorn with showy or vulgar finery

**bed·lam** \'bed-ləm\ *n* [*Bedlam*, popular name for the Hospital of St. Mary of Bethlehem, London, an insane asylum, fr. ME *Bedlem* Bethlehem] **1** *archaic* : an insane asylum **2** : a scene of uproar and confusion

**bed·ou·in** \'bed-(-ə)-wən\ *n, pl* **bedouin** *or* **bedouins** *often cap* : a nomadic Arab of the Arabian, Syrian, or No. African deserts

**bed·pan** \'bed-,pan\ *n* : a shallow vessel used by a person in bed for urination or defecation

**bed·post** \-,pōst\ *n* : the post of a bed

**be·drag·gled** \bi-'drag-əld\ *adj* : soiled and disordered as if by being drenched

**bed·rid·den** \'bed-,rid-ᵊn\ *or* **bed·rid** \-,rid\ *adj* : kept in bed by illness or weakness

**bed·rock** \-'räk\ *n* : the solid rock underlying surface materials (as soil) — **bedrock** *adj*

**bed·roll** \-,rōl\ *n* : bedding rolled up for carrying

**bed·room** \-,rüm, -,rum\ *n* : a room containing a bed and used esp. for sleeping

**bed·side** \'bed-,sīd\ *n* : the place beside a bed esp. of a sick or dying person

**bed·sore** \'bed-,sōr\ *n* : an ulceration of tissue deprived of nutrition by prolonged pressure

**bed·spread** \-,spred\ *n* : a usu. ornamental outer cover for a bed

**bed·stead** \-,sted, -,stid\ *n* : the framework of a bed

**bed·time** \-,tīm\ *n* : a time for going to bed

**bee** \'bē\ *n* **1** : a colonial 4-winged insect often kept in hives for the honey it produces; *also* : any of various related insects **2** : a neighborly gathering for work

**beech** \'bēch\ *n, pl* **beech·es** *or* **beech** : a deciduous hardwood tree with smooth gray bark and small sweet triangular nuts — **beech·en** \'bē-chən\ *adj*

**beech·nut** \'bēch-,nət\ *n* : the nut of a beech

**¹beef** \'bēf\ *n, pl* **beefs** \'bēfs\ *or* **beeves** \'bēvz\ **1** : the flesh of a steer, cow, or bull; *also* : the dressed carcass of a beef animal **2** : a steer, cow, or bull esp. when fattened for food **3** : MUSCLE, BRAWN **4** *pl* **beefs** : COMPLAINT

**²beef** *vb* **1** : STRENGTHEN — usu. used with *up* **2** : COMPLAIN

**beef·eat·er** \-,ēt-ər\ *n* : a yeoman of the guard of an English monarch

**beef·steak** \'bēf-,stāk\ *n* : a slice of beef suitable for broiling or frying

**beefy** \'bē-fē\ *adj* **beef·i·er; -est** : THICKSET, BRAWNY

**bee·hive** \'bē-,hīv\ *n* : HIVE

**bee·keep·er** \-,kē-pər\ *n* : a raiser of bees — **bee·keep·ing** *n*

**bee·line** \-,līn\ *n* : a straight direct course

**been** *past part of* BE

**beer** \'biər\ *n* : an alcoholic beverage brewed from malt and hops — **beery** *adj*

**bees·wax** \'bēz-,waks\ *n* : wax that bees secrete and use in making honeycomb

**beet** \'bēt\ *n* : a garden plant with edible leaves and a thick sweet root used as a vegetable, as a source of sugar, or as forage; *also* : its root

**¹bee·tle** \'bēt-ᵊl\ *n* : an insect with four wings of which the stiff outer pair covers the membranous inner pair when not in flight

**²beetle** *n* : a heavy tool for hammering or ramming

**³beetle** *vb* **bee·tled; bee·tling** : to jut out : PROJECT

**BEF** *abbr* British Expeditionary Force

**be·fall** \bi-'fȯl\ *vb* **-fell** \-'fel\; **-fall·en** \-'fȯ-lən\ : to happen to : OCCUR

**be·fit** \bi-'fit\ *vb* : to be suitable to

**be·fog** \bi-'fȯg, -'fäg\ *vb* : OBSCURE; *also* : CONFUSE

**¹be·fore** \bi-'fōr\ *adv* **1** : in front **2** : EARLIER

**²before** *prep* **1** : in front of ⟨stood ~ him⟩ **2** : earlier than ⟨got there ~ me⟩ **3** : in a more important category than ⟨put quality ~ quantity⟩

**³before** *conj* **1** : earlier than the time when ⟨he got here ~ I did⟩ **2** : more willingly than ⟨he'd starve ~ he'd steal⟩

**be·fore·hand** \bi-'fōr-,hand\ *adv or adj* : in advance

**be·foul** \bi-'faúl\ *vb* : SOIL

**be·friend** \bi-'frend\ *vb* : to act as friend to

**be·fud·dle** \bi-'fəd-ᵊl\ *vb* : MUDDLE, CONFUSE

**beg** \'beg\ *vb* **begged; beg·ging 1** : to ask as a charity; *also* : ENTREAT

**2** : EVADE **3** : to live by asking charity

**be·get** \bi-'get\ *vb* **-got** \-'gät\;
**-gotten** \-'gät-ᵊn\ *or* **-got; get·ting**
: to become the father of : SIRE

¹**beg·gar** \'beg-ər\ *n* : one that begs
esp. as a way of life

²**beggar** *vb* **beg·gared; beg·gar·ing**
\'beg-(ə-)riŋ\ : IMPOVERISH

**beg·gar·ly** \'beg-ər-lē\ *adj* **1** : marked
by unrelieved poverty ⟨a ~ life⟩ **2**
: contemptibly mean or inadequate

**beg·gary** \'beg-ə-rē\ *n, pl* **-gar·ies**
**1** : extreme poverty **2** : the class or
occupation of beggars

**be·gin** \bi-'gin\ *vb* **be·gan** \-'gan\;
**be·gun** \-'gən\; **be·gin·ning 1** : to
do the first part of an action; *also* : to
undertake or undergo initial steps
: COMMENCE **2** : to come into being
: ARISE; *also* : FOUND **3** : ORIGINATE,
INVENT — **be·gin·ner** *n*

**be·gone** \bi-'gòn\ *vb* : to go away
: DEPART — used esp. in the imperative

**be·go·nia** \bi-'gōn-yə\ *n* : any of a
genus of tropical herbs widely grown
for their showy leaves and waxy flowers

**be·grime** \bi-'grīm\ *vb* **be·grimed;
be·grim·ing** : to make dirty

**be·grudge** \bi-'grəj\ *vb* **1** : to give,
do, or concede reluctantly **2** : to take
little pleasure in : be annoyed by **3**
: to envy a person's possession or enjoyment of something

**be·guile** \-'gīl\ *vb* **be·guiled; be-
guil·ing 1** : DECEIVE, CHEAT **2** : to
while away **3** : to coax by wiles

**be·guine** \bi-'gēn\ *n* [AmerF *béguine*,
fr. F *béguin* flirtation] : a vigorous popular dance of the islands of Saint Lucia
and Martinique

**be·gum** \'bā-gəm, 'bē-\ *n* : a Muslim
woman of high rank

**be·half** \bi-'haf, -'hàf\ *n* : BENEFIT,
SUPPORT, DEFENSE

**be·have** \bi-'hāv\ *vb* **be·haved; be-
hav·ing 1** : to bear, comport, or
conduct oneself in a particular and esp.
a proper way **2** : to act, function, or
react in a particular way

**be·hav·ior** \bi-'hā-vyər\ *n* : way of
behaving; *esp* : personal conduct —
**be·hav·ior·al** \-vyə-rəl\ *adj*

**be·hav·ior·ism** \bi-'hā-vyə-,riz-əm\ *n*
: the doctrine that the proper concern of
psychology is the objective evidence of
behavior

**be·head** \bi-'hed\ *vb* : to cut off the
head of

**be·he·moth** \bi-'hē-məth, 'bē-ə-,mäth\
*n* : a huge powerful animal described in
Job 40:15–24 that is prob. the hippo-
potamus

**be·hest** \bi-'hest\ *n* **1** : COMMAND
**2** : an urgent prompting

¹**be·hind** \bi-'hīnd\ *adv* **1** : BACK,
BACKWARD **2** : LATE, SLOW

²**behind** *prep* **1** : in or to a place or situation in back of or to the rear of ⟨look
~ you⟩ ⟨the staff stayed ~ the troops⟩
**2** : inferior to (as in rank) : BELOW
⟨three games ~ the first-place team⟩
**3** : in support of : SUPPORTING ⟨we're
~ you all the way⟩

**be·hind·hand** \bi-'hīnd-,hand\ *adj*

**1** : being in arrears **2** : lagging behind
the times **syn** tardy, late, overdue

**be·hold** \bi-'hōld\ *vb* **-held** \-'held\;
**-hold·ing 1** : to have in sight : SEE
**2** — used imperatively to direct the
attention **syn** view, observe, notice,
contemplate — **be·hold·er** *n*

**be·hold·en** \bi-'hōl-dən\ *adj* : OBLI-
GATED, INDEBTED

**be·hoof** \bi-'hüf\ *n* : ADVANTAGE,
PROFIT

**be·hoove** \bi-'hüv\ *or* **be·hove**
\-'hōv\ *vb* **be·hooved** *or* **be·hoved;
be·hoov·ing** *or* **be·hov·ing** : to be
necessary, proper, or advantageous for

**beige** \'bāzh\ *n* : a pale dull yellowish
brown — **beige** *adj*

**be·ing** \'bē-iŋ\ *n* **1** : EXISTENCE; *also*
: LIFE **2** : the qualities or constitution
of an existent thing **3** : a living thing;
*esp* : PERSON

**be·la·bor** \bi-'lā-bər\ *vb* **1** : to beat
soundly **2** : to assail (as with words)
tiresomely or at length

**be·lat·ed** \bi-'lāt-əd\ *adj* : DELAYED,
LATE

**be·lay** \bi-'lā\ *vb* **1** : to wind (a rope)
around a pin or cleat in order to hold
secure **2** : QUIT, STOP — used in the
imperative

**belch** \'belch\ *vb* **1** : to expel (gas)
from the stomach through the mouth
**2** : to gush forth ⟨a volcano ~ing lava⟩
— **belch** *n*

**bel·dam** *or* **bel·dame** \'bel-dəm\ *n*
[ME *beldam* grandmother, fr. MF *bel*
beautiful + ME *dam* lady, mother] : an
old woman; *esp* : HAG

**be·lea·guer** \bi-'lē-gər\ *vb* **1** : BE-
SIEGE **2** : HARASS ⟨~ed parents⟩

**bel·fry** \'bel-frē\ *n, pl* **belfries** [ME
*belfrey*, alter. of *berfrey*, fr. MF *berfrei*,
deriv. of Gk *pyrgos phorētos* movable
war tower] : a tower for a bell (as on a
church); *also* : the part of the tower
in which the bell hangs

**Belg** *abbr* Belgian; Belgium

**Bel·gian** \'bel-jən\ *n* : a native or inhabitant of Belgium — **Belgian** *adj*

**be·lie** \bi-'lī\ *vb* **-lied; -ly·ing 1**
: MISREPRESENT **2** : to prove (something) false **3** : to be false to; *also* : to
run counter to

**be·lief** \bə-'lēf\ *n* **1** : CONFIDENCE,
TRUST **2** : something (as a tenet or
creed) believed **syn** conviction, opinion

**be·lieve** \bə-'lēv\ *vb* **be·lieved; be-
liev·ing 1** : to have religious convictions **2** : to have a firm conviction
about something : accept as true **3** : to
hold as an opinion : SUPPOSE — **be-
liev·able** *adj* — **be·liev·er** *n*

**be·like** \bi-'līk\ *adv, archaic* : PROB-
ABLY

**be·lit·tle** \bi-'lit-ᵊl\ *vb* **-lit·tled; -lit-
tling** \-'lit-(ᵊ-)liŋ\ : to make seem
little or less; *also* : DISPARAGE

¹**bell** \'bel\ *n* **1** : a hollow metallic device that makes a ringing sound when
struck **2** : the sounding or stroke of a
bell (as on shipboard to tell the time);
*also* : time so indicated **3** : something
with the flared form of a typical bell

²**bell** *vb* : to provide with a bell

**bel·la·don·na** \,bel-ə-'dän-ə\ *n* [It, lit., beautiful lady; fr. its cosmetic use] **:** a poisonous herb related to the potato that yields a drug used esp. to relieve spasms and pain or to dilate the eye; *also* **:** this drug

**bell·bot·toms** \'bel-'bät-əmz\ *n pl* **:** pants with wide flaring bottoms — **bell-bottom** *adj*

**bell·boy** \'bel-,bȯi\ *n* **:** a hotel or club employee who escorts guests to rooms, carries luggage, and runs errands

**belle** \'bel\ *n* **:** an attractive and popular girl or woman

**belles let·tres** \bel-letr³\ *n pl* **:** literature that is an end in itself and not practical or purely informative

**bel·le·trist** \bel-'le-trəst\ *n* **:** a writer of belles lettres — **bel·le·tris·tic** \,bel-ə-'tris-tik\ *adj*

**bell·hop** \'bel-,häp\ *n* **:** BELLBOY

**bel·li·cose** \'bel-i-,kōs\ *adj* **:** WARLIKE, PUGNACIOUS **syn** belligerent, quarrelsome — **bel·li·cos·i·ty** \,bel-i-'käs-ət-ē\ *n*

**bel·lig·er·en·cy** \bə-'lij-(ə)-rən-sē\ *n* **1 :** the status of a nation engaged in war **2 :** BELLIGERENCE, TRUCULENCE

**bel·lig·er·ent** \-rənt\ *adj* **1 :** waging war **2 :** TRUCULENT **syn** bellicose, pugnacious — **bel·lig·er·ence** \-rəns\ *n* — **belligerent** *n*

**bel·low** \'bel-ō\ *vb* **1 :** to make the deep hollow sound characteristic of a bull **2 :** to call or utter in a loud deep voice — **bellow** *n*

**bel·lows** \-ōz, -əz\ *n sing or pl* **:** a closed boxlike device with sides that can be spread apart or pressed together thereby drawing in air and then expelling it through a tube

**bells** \'belz\ *n pl* **:** BELL-BOTTOMS

**bell·weth·er** \'bel-'weth-ər, -,weth-\ *n* **:** one that takes the lead or initiative

**¹bel·ly** \'bel-ē\ *n, pl* **bellies** [ME *bely* bellows, belly, fr. OE *belg* bag, skin] **1 :** ABDOMEN; *also* **:** STOMACH **2 :** the under part of an animal's body

**²belly** *vb* **bel·lied; bel·ly·ing :** BULGE

**¹bel·ly·ache** \'bel-ē-,āk\ *n* **:** pain in the abdomen

**²bellyache** *vb* **:** COMPLAIN

**belly button** *n* **:** NAVEL

**belly dance** *n* **:** a usu. solo dance emphasizing movement of the belly — **belly dance** *vb* — **belly dancer** *n*

**belly laugh** *n* **:** a deep hearty laugh

**be·long** \bi-'lȯŋ\ *vb* **1 :** to be suitable or appropriate; *also* **:** to be properly situated ⟨shoes ~ in the closet⟩ **2 :** to be the property ⟨this ~s to me⟩; *also* **:** to be attached (as through birth or membership) ⟨~ to a club⟩ **3 :** to form an attribute or part ⟨this wheel ~s to the cart⟩ **4 :** to be classified ⟨whales ~ among the mammals⟩

**be·long·ings** \-'lȯŋ-iŋz\ *n pl* **:** GOODS, EFFECTS, POSSESSIONS

**be·loved** \bi-'ləv-(ə)d\ *adj* **:** dearly loved — **beloved** *n*

**¹be·low** \bi-'lō\ *adv* **1 :** in or to a lower place or rank **2 :** on earth **3 :** in hell **syn** under, beneath, underneath

**²below** *prep* **1 :** in or to a lower place than **2 :** inferior to (as in rank)

**¹belt** \'belt\ *n* **1 :** a strip (as of leather) worn about the waist **2 :** an endless band passing around pulleys or cylinders to communicate motion or convey material **3 :** a region marked by some distinctive feature; *esp* **:** one suited to a particular crop

**²belt** *vb* **1 :** to encircle or secure with a belt **2 :** to beat with or as if with a belt **3 :** to mark with an encircling band

**³belt** *n* **:** a jarring blow **:** WHACK **2 :** DRINK ⟨a ~ of whiskey⟩

**belt tightening** *n* **:** a reduction in spending

**belt·way** \'belt-,wā\ *n* **:** a highway skirting an urban area

**be·lu·ga** \bə-'lü-gə\ *n* **:** a white sturgeon of the Black sea, Caspian sea, and their tributaries that is a source of caviar

**bel·ve·dere** \'bel-və-,diər\ *n* [It, lit., beautiful view] **:** a structure (as a summerhouse) designed to command a view

**be·mire** \bi-'mī(ə)r\ *vb* **:** to cover or soil with or sink in mire

**be·moan** \bi-'mōn\ *vb* **:** LAMENT, DEPLORE **syn** bewail

**be·muse** \bi-'myüz\ *vb* **:** BEWILDER, CONFUSE

**¹bench** \'bench\ *n* **1 :** a long seat for two or more persons **2 :** a table for holding work and tools ⟨a carpenter's ~⟩ **3 :** the seat of a judge in court; *also* **:** the office or dignity of a judge **4 :** COURT; *also* **:** JUDGES

**²bench** \'bench\ *vb* **1 :** to furnish with benches **2 :** to seat on a bench **3 :** to remove from or keep out of a game **4 :** to exhibit (dogs) on a bench

**bench mark** *n* **1 :** a mark on a permanent object serving as an elevation reference in topographical surveys **2** *usu* **bench·mark :** a point of reference for measurement; *also* **:** STANDARD

**bench warrant** *n* **:** a warrant issued by a presiding judge or by a court against a person guilty of contempt or indicted for a crime

**¹bend** \'bend\ *n* **:** a knot by which a rope is fastened (as to another rope)

**²bend** *vb* **bent** \'bent\; **bend·ing** **1 :** to draw (as a bow) taut **2 :** to curve or cause a change of shape in ⟨~ a bar⟩ **3 :** to turn in a certain direction ⟨*bent* his steps toward town⟩ **4 :** to make fast **:** SECURE **5 :** SUBDUE **6 :** RESOLVE, DETERMINE ⟨*bent* on self-destruction⟩; *also* **:** APPLY ⟨*bent* themselves to the task⟩ **7 :** DEFLECT **8 :** to curve downward **9 :** YIELD, SUBMIT

**³bend** *n* **1 :** an act or process of bending **2 :** something bent; *esp* **:** CURVE **3** *pl* **:** a painful and dangerous disorder resulting from too sudden removal (as of a diver) from a compressed atmosphere

**bend·er** \'ben-dər\ *n* **:** SPREE

**¹be·neath** \bi-'nēth\ *adv* **:** BELOW, UNDERNEATH **syn** under

**²beneath** *prep* **1 :** BELOW, UNDER ⟨stood ~ a tree⟩ **2 :** unworthy of ⟨considered such behavior ~ her⟩

**ben·e·dict** \'ben-ə-,dikt\ *n* **:** a newly

married man who has long been a bachelor

**bene·dic·tion** \,ben-ə-'dik-shən\ n : the invocation of a blessing esp. at the close of a public worship service

**bene·fac·tion** \-'fak-shən\ n : a charitable donation **syn** contribution, alms

**bene·fac·tor** \'ben-ə-,fak-tər\ n : one that confers a benefit and esp. a benefaction — **bene·fac·tress** \-trəs\ n

**ben·e·fice** \'ben-ə-fəs\ n : an ecclesiastical office to which the revenue from an endowment is attached

**be·nef·i·cence** \bə-'nef-ə-səns\ n 1 : beneficent quality 2 : BENEFACTION

**be·nef·i·cent** \-sənt\ adj : doing or producing good (as by acts of kindness or charity); also : productive of benefit

**ben·e·fi·cial** \,ben-ə-'fish-əl\ adj : being of benefit or help : HELPFUL **syn** advantageous, profitable — **ben·e·fi·cial·ly** \-ē\ adv

**ben·e·fi·cia·ry** \,ben-ə-'fish-ē-,er-ē, -'fish-(ə-)rē\ n, pl -ries : one that receives a benefit (as the income of a trust or the proceeds of an insurance)

**¹ben·e·fit** \'ben-ə-,fit\ n 1 : ADVANTAGE ⟨the ~s of exercise⟩ 2 : useful aid : HELP; also : material aid provided or due (as in sickness or unemployment) as a right 3 : a performance or event to raise funds for some person or cause

**²benefit** vb **-fit·ed** \-,fit-əd\ or **-fit·ted**; **-fit·ing** or **-fit·ting** 1 : to be useful or profitable to 2 : to receive benefit

**be·nev·o·lence** \bə-'nev-(ə-)ləns\ n 1 : charitable nature : CHARITY 2 : an act of kindness — **be·nev·o·lent** \-lənt\ adj

**be·night·ed** \bi-'nīt-əd\ adj 1 : overtaken by darkness or night 2 : living in ignorance

**be·nign** \bi-'nīn\ adj 1 : of a gentle disposition; also : showing kindness 2 : of a mild kind; esp : not malignant ⟨~ tumors⟩ **syn** benignant, kind — **be·nig·ni·ty** \-'nig-nət-ē\ n

**be·nig·nant** \-'nig-nənt\ adj : BENIGN 1 **syn** kind, kindly

**ben·i·son** \'ben-ə-sən, -zən\ n : BLESSING, BENEDICTION

**ben·ny** \'ben-ē\ n, pl **bennies** : a tablet of amphetamine taken as a stimulant

**bent** \'bent\ n 1 : strong inclination or interest; also : TALENT 2 : power of endurance **syn** talent, aptitude, gift

**ben·thic** \'ben-thik\ or **ben·thal** \-thəl\ adj : of, relating to, or occurring at the bottom of a body of water

**ben·thos** \'ben-,thäs\ n : organisms that live on or in the bottom of bodies of water

**ben·ton·ite** \'bent-ᵊn-,īt\ n : an absorptive clay used esp. as a filler (as in paper) — **ben·ton·it·ic** \,bent-ᵊn-'it-ik\ adj

**bent·wood** \'bent-,wùd\ adj : made of wood bent into shape ⟨a ~ chair⟩

**be·numb** \bi-'nəm\ vb 1 : DULL, DEADEN 2 : to make numb esp. by cold

**ben·zene** \'ben-,zēn\ n : a colorless highly flammable liquid obtained chiefly in the distillation of coal and used as a

solvent and in making dyes and drugs

**benzene ring** n : a hexagonal structural arrangement of atoms held to exist in benzene

**ben·zine** \'ben-,zēn\ n 1 : BENZENE 2 : any of various flammable petroleum distillates used as solvents for fats or as motor fuels

**ben·zo·ate** \'ben-zə-,wāt\ n : a salt or ester of benzoic acid

**ben·zo·ic acid** \ben-,zō-ik-\ n : a white crystalline acid that occurs naturally in benzoin and cranberries and is used as a preservative and antiseptic

**ben·zo·in** \'ben-zə-wən, -,zȯin\ n : a balsamlike resin from trees of southern Asia used esp. in medicine and perfumes

**ben·zol** \'ben-,zȯl, -,zōl\ n : BENZENE

**be·queath** \bi-'kwēth, -'kwēth\ vb [ME bequethen, fr. OE becwethan, fr. be- + cwethan to say] 1 : to leave by will 2 : to hand down

**be·quest** \bi-'kwest\ n 1 : the action of bequeathing 2 : something bequeathed : LEGACY

**be·rate** \-'rāt\ vb : to scold harshly

**Ber·ber** \'bər-bər\ n : a member of a Caucasoid people of northwestern Africa

**ber·ceuse** \beər-'sœ(r)z\ n, pl **ber·ceuses** \-'sœ(r)z(-əz)\ 1 : LULLABY 2 : a musical composition of a tranquil nature

**¹be·reaved** \bi-'rēvd\ adj : suffering the death of a loved one — **be·reave·ment** n

**²bereaved** n, pl **bereaved** : one who is bereaved

**be·reft** \-'reft\ adj 1 : deprived of or lacking something — used with of 2 : BEREAVED

**be·ret** \bə-'rā\ n : a round soft cap with no visor

**berg** \'bərg\ n : ICEBERG

**beri·beri** \,ber-ē-'ber-ē\ n : a deficiency disease marked by weakness, wasting, and nerve damage and caused by lack of thiamine

**berke·li·um** \'bər-klē-əm\ n : an artificially prepared radioactive chemical element

**Ber·mu·das** \bər-'myüd-əz\ n pl : BERMUDA SHORTS

**Bermuda shorts** n pl : knee-length walking shorts

**ber·ry** \'ber-ē\ n, pl **berries** 1 : a small pulpy fruit; esp : a simple fruit (as a grape, tomato, or banana) with the wall of the ripened ovary thick and pulpy 2 : the dry seed of some plants (as coffee)

**ber·serk** \bə(r)-'sərk, -'zərk\ adj [ON berserkr warrior frenzied in battle, fr. björn bear + serkr shirt] : FRENZIED, CRAZED — **berserk** adv

**¹berth** \'bərth\ n 1 : room enough for a ship to maneuver 2 : the place where a ship lies at anchor 3 : a place to sit or sleep esp. on a ship or vehicle 4 : JOB, POSITION **syn** post, situation

**²berth** vb 1 : to bring or come into a berth 2 : to allot a berth to

**ber·yl** \'ber-əl\ n : a hard silicate

mineral occurring as green, yellow, pink, or white crystals

**be·ryl·li·um** \bə-'ril-ē-əm\ n : a light strong metallic chemical element used as a hardener in alloys

**be·seech** \bi-'sēch\ vb **-sought** \-'sȯt\ or **-seeched; -seech·ing** : to ask earnestly : ENTREAT syn implore, beg

**be·seem** \bi-'sēm\ vb, archaic : to be seemly or fitting : BEFIT

**be·set** \-'set\ vb 1 : TROUBLE, HARASS 2 : ASSAIL; also : to hem in : SURROUND

**be·set·ting** adj : persistently present or assailing

**be·shrew** \bi-'shrü\ vb, archaic : CURSE

¹**be·side** \-'sīd\ adv, archaic : BESIDES

²**beside** prep 1 : by the side of ⟨sit ~ me⟩ 2 : BESIDES

¹**be·sides** \bi-'sīdz\ adv 1 : in addition : ALSO 2 : MOREOVER

²**besides** prep 1 : other than ⟨there's nobody here ~ me⟩ 2 : in addition to ⟨~ being pretty, she's intelligent⟩

**be·siege** \bi-'sēj\ vb : to lay siege to; also : IMPORTUNE — **be·sieg·er** n

**be·smear** \-'smir\ vb : SMEAR

**be·smirch** \-'smərch\ vb : SMIRCH, SOIL

**be·som** \'bē-zəm\ n : BROOM

**be·sot** \bi-'sät\ vb **be·sot·ted; be·sot·ting** : to make dull or stupid; esp : to muddle with drunkenness

**be·span·gle** \-'span-gəl\ vb : to adorn with or as if with spangles

**be·spat·ter** \-'spat-ər\ vb : SPATTER

**be·speak** \bi-'spēk\ vb **-spoke** \-'spōk\; **-spo·ken** \-'spō-kən\; **-speak·ing** 1 : to hire or arrange for beforehand 2 : INDICATE, SIGNIFY 3 : FORETELL

**be·sprin·kle** \-'sprin-kəl\ vb : SPRINKLE

¹**best** \'best\ adj, superlative of GOOD 1 : excelling all others 2 : most productive (as of good or satisfaction) 3 : LARGEST, MOST

²**best** adv, superlative of WELL 1 : in the best way 2 : MOST

³**best** n : something that is best

⁴**best** vb : to get the better of : OUTDO

**bes·tial** \'bes-chəl\ adj 1 : of or relating to beasts 2 : resembling a beast esp. in lack of intelligence or reason

**bes·ti·al·i·ty** \,bes-chē-'al-ət-ē\ n, pl **-ties** 1 : the condition or status of a lower animal 2 : display or gratification of bestial traits or impulses

**bes·ti·ary** \'bes-chē-,er-ē\ n, pl **-aries** : a medieval allegorical or moralizing work on the appearance and habits of animals

**be·stir** \bi-'stər\ vb : to rouse to action

**best man** n : the principal groomsman at a wedding

**be·stow** \bi-'stō\ vb 1 : PUT, PLACE, STOW 2 : to present as a gift : CONFER — **be·stow·al** n

**be·stride** \bi-'strīd\ vb **-strode** \-'strōd\; **-strid·den** \-'strid-ᵊn\; **-strid·ing** \-'strīd-iŋ\ : to ride, sit, or stand astride

¹**bet** \'bet\ n 1 : an agreement requiring the person whose guess about a result

proves wrong to give something to a person whose guess proves right; also : the making of such an agreement 2 : the money or thing risked

²**bet** vb **bet** also **bet·ted; bet·ting** 1 : to stake on the outcome of an issue ⟨bet $2 on the race⟩ 2 : to make a bet with 3 : to lay a bet

³**bet** abbr between

**be·take** \bi-'tāk\ vb **-took** \-'tu̇k\; **-tak·en** \-'tā-kən\; **-tak·ing** : to cause (oneself) to go

**be·ta particle** \'bāt-ə-\ n : an electron or positron ejected from an atomic nucleus during radioactive transformation

**beta ray** n 1 : BETA PARTICLE 2 : a stream of beta particles

**be·ta·tron** \'bāt-ə-,trän\ n : an electron accelerator

**be·tel** \'bēt-ᵊl\ n : a climbing pepper whose leaves are chewed together with lime and the astringent seed (**betel nut**) of a palm esp. by southern Asians

**bête noire** \,bet-nə-'wär, ,bāt-\ n, pl **bêtes noires** \,bet-nə-'wär(z), ,bāt-\ [F, lit., black beast] : one that is an object of strong fear or aversion

**beth·el** \'beth-əl\ n [Heb bēth'ēl house of God] : a place of worship esp. for seamen

**be·think** \bi-'think\ vb **-thought** \-'thȯt\; **-think·ing** : to cause (oneself) to call to mind or consider

**be·tide** \bi-'tīd\ vb : to happen to

**be·times** \bi-'tīmz\ adv : in good time : EARLY syn soon, beforehand

**be·to·ken** \bi-'tō-kən\ vb **be·to·kened; be·to·ken·ing** \-'tōk-(ə-)niŋ\ 1 : to give evidence of 2 : PRESAGE syn indicate, prove

**be·tray** \bi-'trā\ vb 1 : to lead astray; esp : SEDUCE 2 : to deliver to an enemy by treachery 3 : to prove unfaithful to 4 : to reveal unintentionally; also : SHOW, INDICATE syn mislead, delude, deceive, disclose, divulge — **be·tray·al** n — **be·tray·er** n

**be·troth** \bi-'träth, -'troth, -'trȯth⟩ or with th\ vb : to promise to marry : AFFIANCE — **be·troth·al** n

**be·trothed** n : the person to whom one is betrothed

¹**bet·ter** \'bet-ər\ adj, comparative of GOOD 1 : more than half 2 : improved in health 3 : of higher quality

²**better** adv, comparative of WELL 1 : in a superior manner 2 : to a higher or greater degree; also : MORE

³**better** n 1 : something better; also : a superior esp. in merit or rank 2 : ADVANTAGE

⁴**better** vb 1 : to make or become better 2 : SURPASS, EXCEL

**bet·ter·ment** \'bet-ər-mənt\ n : IMPROVEMENT

**bet·tor** or **bet·ter** \'bet-ər\ n : one that bets

¹**be·tween** \bi-'twēn\ prep 1 : by the common action of ⟨earned $10,000 ~ the two of them⟩ 2 : in the interval separating ⟨an alley ~ two buildings⟩ 3 : in point of comparison of ⟨choose ~ two cars⟩ 4 : marking or constitut-

ing the interrelation or interaction of (hostility ~ nations)

**²between** *adv* : in an intervening space or interval

**be·twixt** \bi-'twikst\ *adv or prep*, *archaic* : BETWEEN

**¹bev·el** \'bev-əl\ *n* 1 : the angle or slant that one surface or line makes with another when not at right angles 2 : a device for adjusting the slant of the surfaces of a piece of work

**²bevel** *vb* **-eled** *or* **-elled**; **-el·ing** *or* **-el·ling** \'bev-(ə-)liŋ\ 1 : to cut or shape (as an edge or surface) to a bevel 2 : INCLINE, SLANT

**bev·er·age** \'bev-(ə-)rij\ *n* : liquid for drinking; *esp* : a liquid (as milk or coffee) other than water

**bevy** \'bev-ē\ *n, pl* **bev·ies** : a large group or collection (as of women or quail)

**be·wail** \bi-'wāl\ *vb* : LAMENT **syn** deplore, bemoan

**be·ware** \-'waər\ *vb* : to be on one's guard : be wary of

**be·wil·der** \bi-'wil-dər\ *vb* **be·wil·dered**; **be·wil·der·ing** \-d(ə-)riŋ\ : PERPLEX, CONFUSE **syn** mystify, distract, puzzle — **be·wil·der·ment** *n*

**be·witch** \-'wich\ *vb* 1 : to affect by witchcraft 2 : CHARM, FASCINATE **syn** enchant, attract — **be·witch·ment** *n*

**bey** \'bā\ *n* 1 : a former Turkish provincial governor 2 : the former ruler of Tunis or Tunisia

**¹be·yond** \bē-'änd\ *adv* 1 : FARTHER 2 : BESIDES

**²beyond** *prep* 1 : on or to the farther side of 2 : out of the reach or sphere of 3 : BESIDES

**be·zel** \'bē-zəl, 'bez-əl\ *n* 1 : a sloping edge on a cutting tool 2 : the top part of a ring setting 3 : the faceted part of a cut gem that rises above the setting 4 : a usu. grooved rim holding a transparent covering (as on a watch)

**bf** *abbr* boldface

**BF** *abbr* brought forward

**BFA** *abbr* bachelor of fine arts

**bg** *abbr* bag

**bhang** \'baŋ\ *n* : a narcotic and intoxicant product of the hemp plant

**bhd** *abbr* bulkhead

**Bi** *symbol* bismuth

**bi·an·nu·al** \(')bī-'an-yə-(-wə)l\ *adj* : occurring twice a year — **bi·an·nu·al·ly** \-ē\ *adv*

**¹bi·as** \'bī-əs\ *n* 1 : a line diagonal to the grain of a fabric : PREJUDICE, BENT

**²bias** *adv* : on the bias : DIAGONALLY

**³bias** *vb* **bi·ased** *or* **bi·assed**; **bi·as·ing** *or* **bi·as·sing** : PREJUDICE

**bi·ath·lon** \bī-'ath-lən, -,län\ *n* : a composite athletic contest consisting of cross-country skiing and rifle precision shooting

**¹bib** \'bib\ *n* : a protective cover tied under a child's chin to protect the clothes

**²bib** *abbr* Bible; biblical

**bi·be·lot** \'bē-bə-,lō\ *n, pl* **bibelots** \-,lō(z)\ : a small household ornament or decorative object

**Bi·ble** \'bī-bəl\ *n* [ME, fr. OF, fr. ML

*biblia*, fr. Gk, pl. of *biblion* book, fr. *byblos* papyrus, book, fr. *Byblos*, ancient Phoenician city from which papyrus was exported] 1 : the sacred scriptures of Christians comprising the Old and New Testaments 2 : the sacred scriptures of Judaism or of some other religion — **bib·li·cal** \'bib-li-kəl\ *adj, sometimes cap*

**bib·li·og·ra·phy** \,bib-lē-'äg-rə-fē\ *n, pl* **-phies** 1 : the history or description of writings or publications 2 : a list of writings (as on a subject or of an author) — **bib·li·og·ra·pher** \-fər\ *n* — **bib·li·o·graph·ic** \-lē-ə-'graf-ik\ *or* **bib·li·o·graph·i·cal** \-i-kəl\ *adj*

**bib·lio·phile** \'bib-lē-ə,fīl\ *n* : a lover of books

**bib·u·lous** \'bib-yə-ləs\ *adj* 1 : highly absorbent 2 : inclined to drink esp. to excess

**bi·cam·er·al** \'bī-'kam-(ə-)rəl\ *adj* : having or consisting of two legislative branches

**bi·car·bon·ate** \'bī-'kär-bə-,nāt, -nət\ *n* : an acid carbonate

**bicarbonate of soda** : SODIUM BICARBONATE

**bi·cen·te·na·ry** \,bī-sen-'ten-ə-rē, bī-'sent-ᵊn-,er-ē\ *n* : BICENTENNIAL — **bicentenary** *adj*

**bi·cen·ten·ni·al** \,bī-sen-'ten-ē-əl\ *n* : a 200th anniversary or its celebration — **bicentennial** *adj*

**bi·ceps** \'bī-,seps\ *n* [NL, fr. L, two-headed, fr. *bi-* two + *caput* head] : a muscle (as in the front of the upper arm) having two points of origin

**bi·chlo·ride** \bī-'klōr-,īd\ *n* : any of several chlorides; *esp* : one (**mercuric chloride** or **bichloride of mercury**) that is a poisonous compound of mercury and chlorine used as an antiseptic and fungicide

**¹bick·er** \'bik-ər\ *n* : QUARRELING, ALTERCATION

**²bicker** *vb* **bick·ered**; **bick·er·ing** \-(ə-)riŋ\ : to contend in petty altercation : SQUABBLE

**bi·con·cave** \,bī-(,)kän-'kāv, bī-'kän-,kāv\ *adj* : concave on both sides — **bi·con·cav·i·ty** \,bī-(,)kän-'kav-ət-ē\ *n*

**bi·con·vex** \,bī-(,)kän-'veks, 'bī-'kän-,veks\ *adj* : convex on both sides — **bi·con·vex·i·ty** \,bī-kən-'vek-sət-ē, -(,)kän-\ *n*

**bi·cus·pid** \bī-'kəs-pəd\ *n* : either of two double-pointed teeth next to the canine on each side of each jaw in man

**¹bi·cy·cle** \'bī-,sik-əl, -,sīk-\ *n* : a light 2-wheeled vehicle with a steering handle, saddle, and pedals

**²bicycle** *vb* **bi·cy·cled**; **bi·cy·cling** \-,sik-(ə-)liŋ, -,sīk-\ : to ride a bicycle — **bi·cy·cler** \-lər\ *n* — **bi·cy·clist** \-ləst\ *n*

**¹bid** \'bid\ *vb* **bade** \'bad, 'bād\ **bid**; **bid·den** \'bid-ᵊn\ *or* **bid** *also* **bade**; **bid·ding** 1 : COMMAND, ORDER 2 : INVITE 3 : to give expression to 4 : to make a bid : OFFER — **bid·der** *n*

**²bid** *n* 1 : an act of bidding; *also* : a

chance or turn to bid **2** : an offer (as at an auction) of what one will give for something; *also* : the thing or sum offered **3** : an announcement by a player in a card game of what he proposes to accomplish; *also* : an attempt to win or gain **4** : INVITATION

**BID** *abbr* [L *bis in die*] twice a day

**bid·da·ble** \'bid-ə-bəl\ *adj* **1** : OBEDIENT, DOCILE **2** : capable of being bid

**bid·dy** \'bid-ē\ *n* : a hen or young chicken

**bide** \'bīd\ *vb* **bode** \'bōd\ *or* **bid·ed; bid·ed; bid·ing 1** : WAIT, TARRY **2** : DWELL **3** : to wait for

**bi·det** \bi-'dā\ *n* : a fixture about the height of a chair seat used esp. for bathing the external genitals and the posterior parts of the body

**bi·en·ni·al** \bī-'en-ē-əl\ *adj* **1** : taking place once in two years **2** : lasting two years **3** : producing leaves the first year and fruiting and dying the second year — **biennial** *n* — **bi·en·ni·al·ly** \-ē\ *adv*

**bi·en·ni·um** \bī-'en-ē-əm\ *n, pl* **-ni·ums** *or* **-nia** \-ē-ə\ : a period of two years

**bier** \'biər\ *n* : a stand bearing a coffin or corpse

**bi·fo·cal** \bī-'fō-kəl\ *adj* : having two focal lengths

**bifocals** \bī-'fō-kəlz\ *n pl* : eyeglasses with lenses that have one part that corrects for near vision and one for distant vision

**bi·fur·cate** \'bī-fər-,kāt, bī-'fər-\ *vb* **-cat·ed; -cat·ing** : to divide into two branches or parts — **bi·fur·ca·tion** \,bī-fər-'kā-shən\ *n*

**big** \'big\ *adj* **big·ger; big·gest 1** : large in size, amount, or scope **2** : PREGNANT; *also* : SWELLING **3** : IMPORTANT, IMPOSING **syn** great — **big·ness** *n*

**big·a·my** \'big-ə-mē\ *n* : the act of marrying one person while still legally married to another — **big·a·mist** \-məst\ *n* — **big·a·mous** \-məs\ *adj*

**big bang theory** *n* : a theory in astronomy: the universe originated from the explosion of a single mass of material so that the pieces are still flying apart

**big brother** *n* **1** : an older brother **2** : a man who befriends a delinquent or friendless boy **3** *cap both Bs* : the leader of an authoritarian state or movement

**Big Dipper** *n* : the seven principal stars in the constellation of Ursa Major arranged in a form resembling a dipper

**big·horn** \'big-,hȯrn\ *n, pl* **bighorn** *or* **bighorns** : a wild sheep of mountainous western No. America

**bight** \'bīt\ *n* **1** : the slack part of a rope fastened at both ends **2** : a curve in a coast; *also* : the bay formed by such a curve

**big-name** \'big-'nām\ *adj* : widely popular (a ~ performer) — **big name** *n*

**big·ot** \'big-ət\ *n* : one intolerantly devoted to his own church, party, or opinion **syn** fanatic, enthusiast, zealot — **big·ot·ed** \-ət-əd\ *adj* — **big·ot·ry** \-ə-trē\ *n*

**big shot** \'big-,shät\ *n* : BIGWIG

**big time** \-,tīm\ *n* **1** : a high-paying vaudeville circuit requiring only two performances a day **2** : the top rank — **big-tim·er** \-,tī-mər\ *n*

**big top** *n* **1** : the main tent of a circus **2** : CIRCUS

**big·wig** \'big-,wig\ *n* : an important person

**bike** \'bīk\ *n* : BICYCLE

**bike·way** \'bīk-,wā\ *n* : a roadway for bicycles

**bi·ki·ni** \bə-'kē-nē\ *n* : a woman's brief 2-piece bathing suit

**bi·lat·er·al** \bī-'lat-(ə-)rəl\ *adj* **1** : having or involving two sides **2** : affecting reciprocally two sides or parties — **bi·lat·er·al·ly** \-ē\ *adv*

**bile** \'bīl\ *n* **1** : a bitter greenish fluid secreted by the liver that aids in the digestion of fats **2** : ill-humored state

**bilge** \'bilj\ *n* : the part of a ship that lies between the bottom and the point where the sides go straight up

**bi·lin·gual** \bī-'liŋ-gwəl\ *adj* : expressed in, knowing, or using two languages

**bil·ious** \'bil-yəs\ *adj* **1** : marked by or suffering from disordered liver function **2** : IRRITABLE, CHOLERIC — **bil·ious·ness** *n*

**bilk** \'bilk\ *vb* : CHEAT, SWINDLE

¹**bill** \'bil\ *n* : the jaws of a bird together with their horny covering; *also* : a mouth structure (as of a turtle) resembling these — **billed** \'bild\ *adj*

²**bill** *vb* : to caress fondly

³**bill** *n* **1** : a written document (as a memorandum); *esp* : a draft of a law presented to a legislature for enactment **2** : a written statement of a legal wrong suffered or of some breach of law **3** : a paper bearing a statement of particulars (as of a ship's crew members and their duties) **4** : a list of items (as of moneys due) **5** : an advertisement (as a poster or handbill) displayed or distributed **6** : a piece of paper money

⁴**bill** *vb* **1** : to enter in or prepare a bill; *also* : to submit a bill or account to **2** : to advertise by bills or posters

**bill·board** \-,bȯrd\ *n* : a flat surface on which advertising bills are posted

¹**bil·let** \'bil-ət\ *n* **1** : an order requiring a person to provide lodging for a soldier; *also* : quarters assigned by or as if by such an order **2** : POSITION, APPOINTMENT

²**billet** *vb* : to assign lodging to by billet

**bil·let–doux** \,bil-ā-'dü\ *n, pl* **billets–doux** \-ā-'dü(z)\ [F *billet doux*, lit., sweet letter] : a love letter

**bill·fold** \'bil-,fōld\ *n* : WALLET

**bill·head** \-,hed\ *n* : a printed form for making out a commercial bill

**bil·liards** \'bil-yərdz\ *n* : any of several games played on a rectangular table (**billiard table**) by driving balls against each other or into pockets with a cue

**bil·lings·gate** \'bil-iŋz-,gāt, *Brit usu* -git\ *n* [*Billingsgate*, old gate and fish market, London, England] : coarsely abusive language

**bil·lion** \'bil-yən\ *n, pl* **billions** *or* **billion** **1 :** a thousand millions **2** *Brit* **:** a million millions — **billion** *adj* — **bil·lionth** \-yənth\ *adj or n*

**bill of exchange :** a written order from one party to another to pay to a person named in the bill a specified sum of money

**¹bil·low** \'bil-ō\ *n* **1 :** WAVE; *esp* **:** a great wave **2 :** a rolling mass (as of fog or flame) like a great wave — **bil·lowy** \'bil-ə-wē\ *adj*

**²billow** *vb* **:** to rise and roll in waves; *also* **:** to swell out ⟨~*ing* sails⟩

**bil·ly** \'bil-ē\ *n, pl* **billies :** BILLY CLUB

**billy club** *n* **:** a heavy usu. wooden club; *esp* **:** a policeman's club

**bil·ly goat** \'bil-ē-\ *n* **:** a male goat

**bi·met·al** \'bī-,met-ᵊl\ *adj* **:** BIMETALLIC — **bimetal** *n*

**bi·me·tal·lic** \,bī-mə-'tal-ik\ *adj* **:** made of two different metals — often used of devices having a bonded expansive part — **bimetallic** *n*

**bi·met·al·lism** \bī-'met-ᵊl-,iz-əm\ *n* **:** the policy of using two metals at fixed ratios to form a standard of value for a monetary system

**¹bi·month·ly** \bī-'mənth-lē\ *adj* **1 :** occurring every two months **2 :** occurring twice a month **:** SEMIMONTHLY — **bimonthly** *adv*

**²bimonthly** *n* **:** a bimonthly publication

**bin** \'bin\ *n* **:** a box, crib, or enclosure used for storage

**bi·na·ry** \'bī-nə-rē\ *adj* **1 :** consisting of two things or parts **:** DOUBLE **2 :** involving a choice between or condition of two alternatives only (as on≠ off, yes-no) **3 :** involving binary notation — **binary** *n*

**binary digit** *n* **:** either of the two digits conventionally 0 and 1 used in a binary system of numeration

**binary notation** *n* **:** the writing of a number using only the digits 0 and 1 with each digital space representing a power of 2 instead of a power of 10 as in the usual decimal representation

**binary star** *n* **:** a system of two stars revolving around each other

**bin·au·ral** \bī-'nȯr-əl\ *adj* **:** of or relating to sound transmission, recording, or reproduction techniques that provide two separate transmission or recording paths to achieve an effect of hearing sound sources in their original positions

**bind** \'bīnd\ *vb* **bound** \'baùnd\; **bind·ing 1 :** TIE; *also* **:** to restrain as if by tying **2 :** to put under an obligation; *also* **:** to constrain with legal authority **3 :** to unite into a mass **4 :** BANDAGE **5 :** CONSTIPATE **6 :** to strengthen or decorate with a band **7 :** to fasten together and enclose in a cover ⟨~ books⟩ **8 :** to compel as if by a pledge **9 :** to exert a tying, restraining, or compelling effect — **bind·er** *n*

**bind·ing** \'bīn-diŋ\ *n* **:** something (as a ski fastening, a cover, or an edging fabric) used to bind

**binge** \'binj\ *n* **:** SPREE

**bin·go** \'biŋ-gō\ *n, pl* **bingos :** a game of chance played with cards having numbered squares corresponding to numbered balls drawn at random and won by covering five squares in a row

**bin·na·cle** \'bin-i-kəl\ *n* [alter. of ME *bitakle,* fr. Port or Sp; Port *bitácola* & Sp *bitácula,* fr. L *habitaculum* dwelling place, fr. *habitare* to inhabit] **:** a container holding a ship's compass

**¹bin·oc·u·lar** \bī-'näk-yə-lər, bə-\ *adj* **:** of, relating to, or adapted to the use of both eyes — **bin·oc·u·lar·ly** *adv*

**²bin·oc·u·lar** \bə-'näk-yə-lər, bī-\ *n* **1 :** a binocular optical instrument (as a microscope) **2 :** FIELD GLASS — usu. used in pl.

**bi·no·mi·al** \bī-'nō-mē-əl\ *n* **1 :** a mathematical expression consisting of two terms connected by the sign plus (+) or minus (−) **2 :** a biological species name consisting of two terms — **binomial** *adj*

**bio·chem·is·try** \,bī-ō-'kem-ə-strē\ *n* **:** chemistry that deals with the chemical compounds and processes in organisms — **bio·chem·i·cal** \-i-kəl\ *adj or n* — **bio·chem·ist** \-əst\ *n*

**bio·ci·dal** \,bī-ə-'sīd-ᵊl\ *adj* **:** destructive to life or living beings

**bio·de·grad·able** \-di-'grād-ə-bəl\ *adj* **:** capable of being broken down esp. into innocuous products by the actions of living beings (as microorganisms) ⟨a ~ detergent⟩ — **bio·de·grad·abil·i·ty** \-,grād-ə-'bil-ət-ē\ *n* — **bio·deg·ra·da·tion** \-,deg-rə-'dā-shən\ *n* — **bio·de·grade** \-di-'grād\ *vb*

**bio·feed·back** \-'fēd-,bak\ *n* **:** the technique of making unconscious or involuntary bodily processes (as heartbeat or brain waves) objectively perceptible to the senses (as by use of an oscilloscope) in order to manipulate them by conscious mental control

**biog** *abbr* biographical; biography

**bio·ge·og·ra·phy** \,bī-ō-jē-'äg-rə-fē\ *n* **:** a branch of biology that deals with the distribution of plants and animals — **bio·ge·og·ra·pher** \-fər\ *n* — **bio·geo·graph·ic** \-,jē-ə-'graf-ik\ *or* **bio·geo·graph·i·cal** \-i-kəl\ *adj*

**bi·og·ra·phy** \bī-'äg-rə-fē, bē-\ *n, pl* **-phies :** a written history of a person's life; *also* **:** such writings in general — **bi·og·ra·pher** \-fər\ *n* — **bio·graph·i·cal** \,bī-ə-'graf-i-kəl\ *or* **bi·o·graph·ic** \-ik\ *adj*

**biol** *abbr* biologic; biological; biology

**biological clock** *n* **:** an inherent timing mechanism responsible for various cyclical physiological and behavioral responses of living beings

**biological warfare** *n* **:** warfare in which living organisms (as bacteria) are used to harm the enemy or his livestock and crops

**bi·ol·o·gy** \bī-'äl-ə-jē\ *n* [G *biologie,* fr. Gk *bios* mode of life + *logos* word] **1 :** a science that deals with living beings and life processes **2 :** the laws and phenomena of life (as of a kind of organism) — **bi·o·log·ic** \ˌbī-ə-ˈläj-ik\ *or* **bi·o·log·i·cal** \-i-kəl\ *adj* — **bi·ol·o·gist** \bī-ˈäl-ə-jəst\ *n*

**bio·med·i·cal** \ˌbī-ō-ˈmed-i-kəl\ *adj* : of, relating to, or involving biological, medical, and physical science

**bio·phys·ics** \ˌbī-ō-ˈfiz-iks\ *n* : a branch of knowledge concerned with the application of physical principles and methods to biological problems — **bio·phys·i·cal** \-i-kəl\ *adj* — **bio·phys·i·cist** \-ˈfiz-ə-səst\ *n*

**bi·op·sy** \ˈbī-ˌäp-sē\ *n, pl* **-sies** : the removal of cells or tissue from the living body for examination

**bio·sat·el·lite** \ˌbī-ō-ˈsat-ᵊl-ˌīt\ *n* : an artificial satellite for carrying a living human, animal, or plant

**bio·sphere** \ˈbī-ə-ˌsfiər\ *n* **1** : the part of the world in which life can exist **2** : living beings together with their environment

**bio·te·lem·e·try** \ˌbī-ō-tə-ˈlem-ə-trē\ *n* : the remote detection and measurement of a condition, activity, or function relating to a man or animal — **bio·tel·e·met·ric** \-ˌtel-ə-ˈmet-rik\ *adj*

**bi·ot·ic** \bī-ˈät-ik\ *adj* : of or relating to life; *esp* : caused by living beings

**bi·o·tin** \ˈbī-ə-tən\ *n* : a member of the vitamin B complex found esp. in yeast, liver, and egg yolk and active in growth promotion

**bi·o·tite** \ˈbī-ə-ˌtīt\ *n* : a dark mica containing iron, magnesium, potassium, and aluminum

**bi·pa·ren·tal** \ˌbī-pə-ˈrent-ᵊl\ *adj* : involving or derived from two parents ⟨~ inheritance⟩

**bi·par·ti·san** \bī-ˈpärt-ə-zən\ *adj* : representing or composed of members of two parties

**bi·par·tite** \-ˈpär-ˌtīt\ *adj* **1** : being in two parts **2** : shared by two parties ⟨~ treaty⟩

**bi·ped** \ˈbī-ˌped\ *n* : a 2-footed animal

**bi·plane** \ˈbī-ˌplān\ *n* : an airplane with two main supporting surfaces placed one above the other

**bi·po·lar** \bī-ˈpō-lər\ *adj* : having or involving the use of two poles — **bi·po·lar·i·ty** \ˌbī-pō-ˈlar-ət-ē\ *n*

**bi·ra·cial** \bī-ˈrā-shəl\ *adj* : of, relating to, or involving members of two races

**¹birch** \ˈbərch\ *n* **1** : any of a genus of mostly short-lived deciduous shrubs and trees with membranous outer bark and pale close-grained wood; *also* : this wood **2** : a birch rod or bundle of twigs for flogging — **birch** *or* **birch·en** \ˈbər-chən\ *adj*

**²birch** *vb* : WHIP, FLOG

**Birch·er** \ˈbər-chər\ *n* : a member of or adherent of the John Birch Society — **Birch·ism** \ˈbər-ˌchiz-əm\ *n* — **Birch·ist** \-chəst\ *or* **Birch·ite** \-ˌchīt\ *n*

**bird** \ˈbərd\ *n* : a warm-blooded egg-laying vertebrate having the body feathered and the forelimbs modified to form wings

**bird·bath** \ˈbərd-ˌbath, -ˌbàth\ *n* : a usu. ornamental basin set up for birds to bathe in

**bird·house** \ˈbərd-ˌhaus\ *n* : an artificial nesting place for birds

**bird·ie** \ˈbərd-ē\ *n* : a score of one under par on a hole in golf

**bird·lime** \-ˌlīm\ *n* : a sticky substance smeared on twigs to snare small birds

**bird of paradise** : any of numerous brilliantly colored plumed birds of the New Guinea area

**bird·seed** \ˈbərd-ˌsēd\ *n* : a mixture of small seeds (as of hemp or millet) used chiefly for feeding cage birds

**bird's-eye** \ˈbərd-ˌzī\ *adj* **1** : seen from above as if by a flying bird ⟨~ view⟩; *also* : CURSORY **2** : marked with spots resembling birds' eyes ⟨~ maple⟩; *also* : made of bird's-eye wood

**bi·ret·ta** \bə-ˈret-ə\ *n* : a square cap with three ridges on top worn esp. by Roman Catholic clergymen

**birth** \ˈbərth\ *n* **1** : the act or fact of being born or of bringing forth young **2** : LINEAGE, DESCENT **3** : ORIGIN, BEGINNING

**birth control** *n* : control of the number of children born esp. by preventing or lessening the frequency of conception

**birth·day** \ˈbərth-ˌdā\ *n* : the day or anniversary of one's birth

**birth·mark** \-ˌmärk\ *n* : an unusual mark or blemish on the skin at birth

**birth·place** \ˈbərth-ˌplās\ *n* : place of birth or origin

**birth·rate** \-ˌrāt\ *n* : the number of births for every hundred or every thousand persons in a given area or group during a given time

**birth·right** \-ˌrīt\ *n* : a right, privilege, or possession to which one is entitled by birth **syn** prerogative, heritage, inheritance

**birth·stone** \-ˌstōn\ *n* : a gemstone associated symbolically with the month of one's birth

**bis·cuit** \ˈbis-kət\ *n* [ME *bisquite*, fr. MF *bescuit*, fr. (pain) *bescuit* twice-cooked bread] : an unraised bread formed into flat cakes and baked hard and crisp; *also* : a bread made with a leavening agent other than yeast baked in small cakes

**bi·sect** \ˈbī-ˌsekt\ *vb* : to divide into two usu. equal parts; *also* : CROSS, INTERSECT — **bi·sec·tion** \ˈbī-ˌsek-shən\ *n* — **bi·sec·tor** \-tər\ *n*

**bi·sex·u·al** \bī-ˈsek-sh(ə-w)əl\ *adj* **1** : possessing characters of or sexually oriented toward both sexes **2** : of, relating to, or involving two sexes

**bish·op** \ˈbish-əp\ *n* [ME *bisshop*, fr. OE *bisceop*, fr. L *episcopus*, fr. Gk *episkopos*, lit., overseer, fr. *epi-* on, over + *skeptesthai* to look] **1** : a clergyman ranking above a priest and typically governing a diocese **2** : any of various Protestant church officials who superintend other clergy **3** : a chess piece that can move diagonally across any number of unoccupied squares

**bish·op·ric** \ˈbish-ə-prik\ *n* **1** : DIOCESE **2** : the office of bishop

**bis·muth** \ˈbiz-məth\ *n* : a heavy brittle grayish white metallic chemical

element used in alloys and medicine —
**bis·mu·thic** \biz-'məth-ik, -'myü-
thik\ *adj*

**bi·son** \'bīs-ᵊn, 'bīz-\ *n, pl* **bison** : a
large shaggy-maned hump-shouldered
wild ox formerly abundant on the
plains of central U.S.

**bisque** \'bisk\ *n* **1** : a thick cream
soup **2** : ice cream containing powdered nuts or macaroons

**bis·tro** \'bēs-trō, 'bis-\ *n, pl* **bistros**
**1** : a small or unpretentious European
restaurant **2** : BAR; *also* : NIGHTCLUB

¹**bit** \'bit\ *n* **1** : the part of a bridle that
is placed in a horse's mouth **2** : a
drilling or boring tool used in a brace

²**bit** *n* **1** : a morsel of food; *also* : a small
piece or quantity of something **2** : a
small coin; *also* : a unit of value equal
to 12½ cents **3** : something small or
trivial; *also* : an indefinite usu. small
degree or extent (a ~ tired)

³**bit** *n* : a unit of computer information
equivalent to the result of a choice
between two alternatives; *also* : its
physical representation

¹**bitch** \'bich\ *n* **1** : the female of the
dog **2** : a lewd or immoral woman;
*also* : a malicious, spiteful, and domineering woman

²**bitch** *vb* : COMPLAIN

¹**bite** \'bīt\ *vb* **bit** \'bit\; **bit·ten** \'bit-
ᵊn\ *also* **bit**; **bit·ing** \'bīt-iŋ\ **1** : to
grip with teeth or jaws; *also* : to wound
or sting with or as if with fangs **2** : to
cut or pierce with or as if with a sharp-
edged instrument **3** : to cause to smart
or sting **4** : CORRODE **5** : to take bait

²**bite** *n* **1** : the act or manner of biting
**2** : MORSEL, SNACK **3** : a wound made
by biting; *also* : a biting sensation

**bit·ing** \'bīt-iŋ\ *adj* : SHARP, CUTTING

**bit·stock** \'bit-,stäk\ *n* : BRACE 1

**bit·ter** \'bit-ər\ *adj* **1** : having the
acrid lingering taste suggestive of worm-
wood or hops that is one of the basic
taste sensations **2** : marked by intensity or severity (as of distress or hatred)
**3** : extremely harsh or cruel — **bit-
ter·ly** *adv* — **bit·ter·ness** *n*

**bit·tern** \'bit-ərn\ *n* : a small heron
with a loud booming call

**bit·ters** \'bit-ərz\ *n sing or pl* : a usu.
alcoholic solution of bitter and often
aromatic plant products used in mixing
drinks and as a mild tonic

¹**bit·ter·sweet** \'bit-ər-,swēt\ *n* **1** : a
poisonous nightshade with purple
flowers and orange-red berries **2** : a
woody vine with yellow capsules that
open when ripe and disclose scarlet
seed coverings

²**bittersweet** *adj* : being at once both
bitter and sweet

**bi·tu·men** \bə-'t(y)ü-mən, bī-\ *n*
: any of various mixtures of hydrocarbons (as asphalt, tar, or petroleum)
— **bi·tu·mi·nize** \-t(y)ü-mə-,nīz\ *vb*

**bi·tu·mi·nous** \bə-'t(y)ü-mə-nəs, bī-\
*adj* **1** : resembling, mixed with, or
containing bitumen **2** : being coal
that when heated yields considerable
volatile bituminous matter

**bi·valve** \'bī-,valv\ *n* : an animal (as a
clam) with a shell composed of two

separate parts that open and shut —
**bivalve** *adj*

¹**biv·ouac** \'biv-(ə-),wak\ *n* [F, fr. LG
*biwake*, fr. *bi* at + *wake* guard] : a
temporary encampment or shelter

²**bivouac** *vb* **-ouacked; -ouack·ing**
: to form a bivouac : CAMP

¹**bi·week·ly** \bī-'wē-klē\ *adj* **1** : occurring every two weeks : FORTNIGHTLY
**2** : occurring twice a week — **biweekly** *adv*

²**biweekly** *n* : a biweekly publication

**bi·year·ly** \-'yiər-lē\ *adj* **1** : BIENNIAL
**2** : BIANNUAL

**bi·zarre** \bə-'zär\ *adj* : ODD, EC-
CENTRIC, FANTASTIC — **bi·zarre·ly** *adv*

**bk** *abbr* **1** bank **2** book

**Bk** *symbol* berkelium

**bkg** *abbr* banking

**bkgd** *abbr* background

**bks** *abbr* barracks

**bkt** *abbr* **1** basket **2** bracket

**bl** *abbr* **1** bale **2** blue

**blab** \'blab\ *vb* **blabbed; blab·bing**
: TATTLE, GOSSIP

¹**black** \'blak\ *adj* **1** : of the color
black; *also* : very dark **2** : SWARTHY
**3** : of or relating to a group of dark-
haired dark-skinned people **4** : NEGRO;
*also* : AFRO-AMERICAN **5** : SOILED,
DIRTY **6** : lacking light (a ~ night)
**7** : WICKED, EVIL (~ deeds) (~ magic)
**8** : DISMAL, GLOOMY (a ~ outlook)
**9** : SULLEN (a ~ mood) — **black·ish**
*adj* — **black·ly** *adv* — **black·ness** *n*

²**black** *n* **1** : a black pigment or dye;
*also* : something (as clothing) that is
black **2** : the color of least lightness
that characterizes objects which neither
reflect nor transmit light : the opposite
of white **3** : a person of a dark-
skinned race; *esp* : NEGRO

³**black** *vb* : BLACKEN

**black·a·moor** \'blak-ə-,mùr\ *n*
: NEGRO

**black-and-blue** \,blak-ən-'blü\ *adj*
: darkly discolored from blood effused
by bruising

**black art** *n* : MAGIC, WITCHCRAFT

**black·ball** \'blak-,bòl\ *n* : a black object used to cast a negative vote; *also*
: such a vote — **black·ball** *vb*

**black bass** *n* : any of several freshwater sunfishes native to eastern and
central No. America

¹**black belt** \'blak-,belt\ *n* : an area
densely populated by blacks

²**black belt** \-'belt\ *n* **1** : a rating of
expert (as in judo or karate) **2** : one
who holds a black belt

**black·ber·ry** \'blak-,ber-ē\ *n* : the
usu. black or purple juicy but seedy
edible fruit of various brambles; *also*
: a plant bearing this fruit

**black·bird** \'blak-,bərd\ *n* : any of
various birds (as the redwing blackbird) of which the male is largely or
wholly black

**black·board** \-,bòrd\ *n* : a dark
smooth surface (as of slate) used for
writing or drawing on usu. with chalk

**black·body** \'blak-'bäd-ē\ *n* : a body
or surface that completely absorbs
incident radiation

**black box** *n* : a usu. electronic device whose components are unknown to the user

**black·en** \'blak-ən\ *vb* **black·ened; black·en·ing** \-(ə-)niŋ\ **1** : to make or become black **2** : DEFAME, SULLY

**black eye** *n* : a discoloration of the skin around the eye from bruising

**black-eyed Su·san** \,blak-,īd-'süz-ᵊn\ *n* : either of two No. American plants that are related to the daisies and have deep yellow to orange flower heads with dark conical centers

**Black·foot** \'blak-,fút\ *n, pl* **Black-feet** *or* **Blackfoot** : a member of an Indian people of Montana, Alberta, and Saskatchewan

**black·guard** \'blag-ərd, -,ärd\ *n* : SCOUNDREL, RASCAL

**black·head** \'blak-,hed\ *n* : a small oily mass plugging the outlet of a skin gland

**black·ing** \'blak-iŋ\ *n* : a substance applied to something to make it black

¹**black·jack** \-,jak\ *n* **1** : a leather-covered club with a flexible handle **2** : a card game in which the object is to be dealt cards having a higher count than the dealer but not exceeding 21

²**blackjack** *vb* : to hit with or as if with a blackjack

**black light** *n* : invisible ultraviolet or infrared radiation

**black·list** \'blak-,list\ *n* : a list of persons who are disapproved of and are to be punished (as by refusal of jobs or a boycott) — **blacklist** *vb*

**black magic** *n* : WITCHCRAFT

**black·mail** \'blak-,māl\ *n* : extortion by threats esp. of public exposure; *also* : something so extorted — **blackmail** *vb* — **black·mail·er** *n*

**black market** *n* : illicit trade in goods; *also* : a place where such trade is carried on

**Black Mass** *n* : a travesty of the Christian mass ascribed to worshipers of Satan

**Black Muslim** *n* : a member of an exclusively black group that professes Islamic religious belief and advocates a strictly separate black community

**black nationalism** *n, often cap* B&N : a member of a group of militant blacks who advocate separatism from whites and the formation of self-governing black communities — **black nationalism** *n, often cap* B&N

**black·out** \'blak-,aút\ *n* **1** : a period of darkness due to electrical power failure **2** : a transitory loss or dulling of vision or consciousness — **black out** \-'aút\ *vb*

**Black Panther** *n* : a member of an organization of militant black Americans

**black power** *n* : the mobilization of the political and economic power of black Americans esp. to further racial equality

**black sheep** *n* : a discreditable member of an otherwise respectable group

**black·smith** \'blak-,smith\ *n* : a workman who shapes heated iron by hammering it

**black·thorn** \-,thórn\ *n* : a European thorny plum; *also* : an American hawthorn

**black·top** \'blak-,täp\ *n* : a blackish bituminous material used esp. for surfacing roads — **blacktop** *vb*

**black widow** *n* : a venomous spider having the female black with an hourglass-shaped red mark on the underside of the abdomen

**blad·der** \'blad-ər\ *n* : a sac in which liquid is stored; *esp* : one in a vertebrate into which urine passes from the kidneys

**blade** \'blād\ *n* **1** : a leaf of a plant and esp. of a grass; *also* : the flat part of a leaf as distinguished from its stalk **2** : something (as the flat part of an oar or an arm of a propeller) resembling the blade of a leaf **3** : the cutting part of an instrument or tool **4** : SWORD; *also* : SWORDSMAN **5** : a dashing fellow (a gay ~) **6** : the runner of an ice skate

**blain** \'blān\ *n* : an inflammatory swelling or sore

¹**blame** \'blām\ *vb* **blamed; blam·ing** [ME *blamen*, fr. OF *blamer*, fr. L *blasphemare* to blaspheme, fr. Gk *blasphēmein*] **1** : to find fault with **2** : to hold responsible or responsible for **syn** charge, condemn, criticize — **blam·able** *adj*

²**blame** *n* **1** : CENSURE, REPROOF **2** : responsibility for fault or error **syn** guilt — **blame·less** *adj* — **blame·less·ly** *adv*

**blame·wor·thy** \-,wər-thē\ *adj* : deserving blame — **blame·wor·thi·ness** *n*

**blanch** \'blanch\ *vb* **1** : BLEACH **2** : to make or become white or pale

**blanc·mange** \blə-'mänj, -'mä⁽ⁿ⁾zh\ *n* [ME *blancmanger*, fr. MF *blanc manger*, lit., white food] : a dessert made from gelatin or a starchy substance and milk usu. sweetened and flavored

**bland** \'bland\ *adj* **1** : smooth in manner : SUAVE **2** : gently soothing ⟨a ~ diet⟩; *also* : INSIPID **syn** diplomatic, mild, soft, balmy — **bland·ly** *adv* — **bland·ness** *n*

**blan·dish·ment** \'blan-dish-mənt\ *n* : flattering or coaxing speech or action : CAJOLERY

¹**blank** \'blaŋk\ *adj* **1** : showing or causing an appearance of dazed dismay; *also* : EXPRESSIONLESS **2** : DULL, COLORLESS ⟨~ moments⟩ **3** : EMPTY; *esp* : free from writing or marks **4** : ABSOLUTE, DOWNRIGHT ⟨a ~ refusal⟩ **5** : not shaped in final form — **blank·ly** *adv* — **blank·ness** *n*

²**blank** *n* **1** : an empty space **2** : a form with spaces for the entry of data **3** : the center of a target **4** : an unfinished form (as of a key) **5** : a cartridge with powder but no bullet

³**blank** *vb* **1** : to cover or close up : OBSCURE **2** : to keep from scoring

**blank check** *n* : complete freedom of action

¹**blan·ket** \'blaŋ-kət\ *n* **1** : a heavy woven often woolen covering **2** : a covering layer ⟨a ~ of snow⟩

²**blanket** *vb* : to cover with a blanket

³**blanket** *adj* : covering a group or class

⟨~ insurance⟩; *also* : applicable in all instances ⟨~ rules⟩

**blank verse** *n* : unrhymed iambic pentameter

**blare** \'blaər\ *vb* **blared; blar·ing** : to sound loud and harsh; *also* : to proclaim loudly — **blare** *n*

**blar·ney** \'blär-nē\ *n* [*Blarney stone*, a stone in Blarney Castle, near Cork, Ireland, held to bestow skill in flattery on those who kiss it] : skillful flattery : BLANDISHMENT

**bla·sé** \blä-'zā\ *adj* : not responsive to pleasure or excitement as a result of excessive indulgence; *also* : SOPHISTICATED

**blas·pheme** \blas-'fēm\ *vb* **blasphemed; blas·phem·ing 1** : to speak of or address with irreverence **2** : to utter blasphemy

**blas·phe·my** \'blas-fə-mē\ *n, pl* **-mies 1** : the act of expressing lack of reverence for God **2** : irreverence toward something considered sacred — **blas·phe·mous** *adj*

¹**blast** \'blast\ *n* **1** : a violent gust of wind; *also* : its effect **2** : sound made by a wind instrument **3** : a sudden withering esp. of plants : BLIGHT **4** : a current of air forced at high pressure through a hole in a furnace (**blast furnace**) **5** : EXPLOSION; *also* : the often destructive wave of increased air pressure that moves outward from an explosion

²**blast** *vb* **1** : to shrivel up : BLIGHT **2** : to shatter by or as if by an explosive

**blast off** \(')blast-'öf\ *vb* : to take off — used esp. of rocket-propelled devices — **blast-off** \'blast-,öf\ *n*

**bla·tant** \'blāt-ᵊnt\ *adj* : offensively obtrusive : vulgarly showy : vociferous, boisterous — **bla·tan·cy** \-ᵊn-sē\ *n*

**blath·er** \'blath-ər\ *vb* **blath·ered; blath·er·ing** \-(ə-)riŋ\ : to talk foolishly — **blather** *n*

**blath·er·skite** \'blath-ər-,skīt\ *n* : a blustering talkative person

¹**blaze** \'blāz\ *n* **1** : FIRE **2** : intense direct light (as of the sun at noon) **3** : something (as a dazzling display or sudden outburst) suggesting fire (a ~ of autumn leaves) *syn* glare, glow

²**blaze** *vb* **blazed; blaz·ing 1** : to burn brightly; *also* : to flare up **2** : to be conspicuously bright : GLITTER

³**blaze** *vb* **blazed; blaz·ing** : to make public

⁴**blaze** *n* **1** : a white mark on the face of an animal **2** : a mark made on a tree by chipping off a piece of bark

⁵**blaze** *vb* **blazed; blaz·ing** : to mark (as a tree or trail) with blazes

**blaz·er** \'blā-zər\ *n* : a sports jacket often with notched collar and pockets that are stitched on

¹**bla·zon** \'blāz-ᵊn\ *n* **1** : COAT OF ARMS **2** : ostentatious display

²**blazon** *vb* **bla·zoned; bla·zon·ing** \'blāz-(ə-)niŋ\ **1** : to publish abroad **2** : DECK, ADORN

**bldg** *abbr* building

**bldr** *abbr* builder

¹**bleach** \'blēch\ *vb* : to whiten or become white : BLANCH

²**bleach** *n* : a preparation used in bleaching

**bleach·ers** \'blē-chərz\ *n sing or pl* : a usu. uncovered stand containing lower-priced tiered seats for spectators

**bleak** \'blēk\ *adj* **1** : desolately barren and windswept **2** : lacking warm or cheering qualities — **bleak·ish** *adj* — **bleak·ly** *adv* — **bleak·ness** *n*

**blear** \'bliər\ *adj* : dim with water or tears (~ eyes) — **blear-eyed** \-'īd\ *adj*

**bleary** \'bli(ə)r-ē\ *adj* **1** : dull or dimmed esp. from fatigue or sleep **2** : poorly outlined or defined

**bleat** \'blēt\ *n* : the cry of a sheep or goat or a sound like it — **bleat** *vb*

**bleed** \'blēd\ *vb* **bled** \'bled\; **bleeding 1** : to lose or shed blood **2** : to be wounded; *also* : to feel pain or distress **3** : to flow or ooze from a wounded surface; *also* : to draw fluid from ⟨~ a tire⟩ **4** : to extort money from

**bleed·er** \'blēd-ər\ *n* : one that bleeds; *esp* : HEMOPHILIAC

**bleeding heart** *n* **1** : a garden plant related to the poppy that has deep pink drooping heart-shaped flowers **2** : one who shows extravagant sympathy esp. for an object of alleged persecution

¹**blem·ish** \'blem-ish\ *vb* : to spoil by a flaw : MAR

²**blemish** *n* : a noticeable flaw

¹**blench** \'blench\ *vb* [ME *blenchen* to deceive, blench, fr. OE *blencan* to deceive] : FLINCH, QUAIL *syn* shrink, recoil, wince

²**blench** *vb* : to grow or make pale

¹**blend** \'blend\ *vb* **blend·ed; blending 1** : to mix thoroughly **2** : to prepare (as coffee) by mixing different varieties **3** : to combine into an integrated whole **4** : HARMONIZE *syn* fuse, merge, mingle — **blend·er** *n*

²**blend** *n* : a product of blending *syn* compound, composite

**bless** \'bles\ *vb* **blessed** \'blest\ *also* **blest** \'blest\; **bless·ing** [ME *blessen*, fr. OE *blētsian*, fr. *blōd* blood; fr. the use of blood in consecration] **1** : to hallow or consecrate by religious rite or word **2** : to make the sign of the cross over **3** : to invoke divine care for **4** : PRAISE, GLORIFY **5** : to confer happiness upon

**bless·ed** \'bles-əd\ *or* **blest** \'blest\ *adj* **1** : HOLY **2** : BEATIFIED **3** : DELIGHTFUL — **bless·ed·ness** *n*

**bless·ing** \'bles-iŋ\ *n* **1** : the act of one who blesses **2** : a thing conducive to happinesss **3** : grace said at a meal

**blew** *past of* BLOW

**blight** \'blīt\ *n* **1** : a plant disorder marked by withering; *also* : an organism causing a blight **2** : an impairing or frustrating influence; *also* : an impaired condition

**blight** *vb* : to affect with or suffer from blight

**blimp** \'blimp\ *n* : a small nonrigid airship

¹**blind** \'blīnd\ *adj* **1** : lacking or

# blind • bloodless

grossly deficient in ability to see; *also* : intended for blind persons **2** : not based on reason, evidence, or knowledge ⟨∼ faith⟩ **3** : not intelligently controlled or directed ⟨∼ chance⟩ **4** : performed solely by the aid of instruments within an airplane and without looking outside ⟨a ∼ landing⟩ **5** : hard to discern or make out : HIDDEN ⟨a ∼ seam⟩ **6** : lacking an opening or outlet ⟨a ∼ alley⟩ — **blind·ly** *adv* — **blind·ness** \'blīn(d)-nəs\ *n*

²**blind** *vb* **1** : to make blind **2** : DAZZLE **3** : DARKEN; *also* : HIDE

³**blind** *n* **1** : something (as a shutter) to hinder vision or keep out light **2** : a place of concealment **3** : SUBTERFUGE

**blind date** *n* : a date between persons who have not previously met; *also* : either of these persons

**blind·er** \'blīn-dər\ *n* : either of two flaps on a horse's bridle to prevent sight of objects at his sides

**blind·fold** \'blīn(d)-ˌfōld\ *vb* : to cover the eyes of with or as if with a bandage — **blindfold** *n*

¹**blink** \'bliŋk\ *vb* **1** : WINK **2** : TWINKLE **3** : EVADE, SHIRK

²**blink** *n* **1** : GLIMMER, SPARKLE **2** : a usu. involuntary shutting and opening of the eyes

**blink·er** \'bliŋ-kər\ *n* : a blinking light used as a signal

**blin·tze** \'blint-sə\ *or* **blintz** \'blints\ *n* : a thin rolled pancake with a filling usu. of cream cheese

**blip** \'blip\ *n* : an image on a radar screen

**bliss** \'blis\ *n* **1** : complete happiness **2** : HEAVEN, PARADISE **syn** felicity

**bliss·ful** \'blis-fəl\ *adj* : full of or causing bliss — **bliss·ful·ly** \-ē\ *adv*

¹**blis·ter** \'blis-tər\ *n* **1** : a raised area of skin containing watery fluid; *also* : an agent that causes blisters **2** : something (as a raised spot in paint) suggesting a blister **3** : a disease of plants marked by large swollen patches on the leaves

²**blister** *vb* **blis·tered**; **blis·ter·ing** \-t(ə-)riŋ\ : to develop a blister; *also* : to cause blisters

**blithe** \'blīth, 'blīth\ *adj* **blith·er**; **blith·est** : happily lighthearted **syn** merry, jovial, jolly — **blithe·ly** *adv* — **blithe·some** \-səm\ *adj*

**blitz** \'blits\ *n* **1** : an intensive series of air raids **2** : a fast intensive campaign **3** : a rush of the passer by the defensive linebackers in football — **blitz** *vb*

**blitz·krieg** \-ˌkrēg\ *n* [G, lit., lightning war, fr. *blitz* lightning + *krieg* war] : war conducted with great speed and force

**bliz·zard** \'bliz-ərd\ *n* : a long severe snowstorm esp. with wind-driven snow and intense cold

**blk** *abbr* **1** black **2** block

**bloat** \'blōt\ *vb* : to swell by or as if by filling with water or air

**bloat·er** \'blōt-ər\ *n* : a fat herring or mackerel lightly salted and smoked

**blob** \'bläb\ *n* : a small lump or drop of a thick consistency

**bloc** \'bläk\ *n* : a combination of individuals or groups (as nations) working for a common purpose

¹**block** \'bläk\ *n* **1** : a solid piece of substantial material (as wood or stone) **2** : a frame enclosing one or more pulleys and having a hook or strap by which it may be attached to objects **3** : a quantity of things considered as a unit ⟨a ∼ of seats⟩ **4** : a large building divided into separate units (as apartments or offices) **5** : a row of houses or shops **6** : a city square; *also* : the distance along one of the sides of such a square **7** : HINDRANCE, OBSTRUCTION; *also* : interruption of normal function of body or mind ⟨heart ∼⟩ **8** : an engraved stamp from which impressions are made

²**block** *vb* **1** : OBSTRUCT, CHECK **2** : to outline roughly ⟨∼ out a statue⟩ **3** : to provide or support with a block ⟨∼ up a wheel⟩ **syn** bar, impede, hinder

¹**block·ade** \blä-'kād\ *n* : the shutting off of a place usu. by troops or ships to prevent entrance or exit

²**blockade** *vb* **block·ad·ed**; **block·ad·ing** : to subject to a blockade

**block·bust·er** \'bläk-ˌbəs-tər\ *n* : a very large high-explosive bomb

**block·bust·ing** \-tiŋ\ *n* : profiteering by inducing property owners to sell hastily and often at a loss by appeals to fears of depressed values because of threatened encroachment of minority groups and then reselling at inflated prices

**block·head** \'bläk-ˌhed\ *n* : DOLT, DUNCE

**block·house** \-ˌhaus\ *n* : a small strong building used as a shelter (as from enemy fire) or observation post (as of operations producing blast or radiation)

¹**blond** *or* **blonde** \'bländ\ *adj* : fair in complexion; *also* : of a light or bleached color ⟨∼ mahogany⟩

²**blond** *or* **blonde** *n* : a person having blond hair

**blood** \'bləd\ *n* **1** : the red liquid that circulates in the heart, arteries, and veins of animals **2** : LIFEBLOOD; *also* : LIFE **3** : LINEAGE, STOCK **4** : KINSHIP; *also* : KINDRED **5** : the taking of life **6** : TEMPER, PASSION **7** : DANDY 1 — **blood·less** *adj* — **blood·stained** \-ˌstānd\ *adj* — **bloody** *adj*

**blood bank** *n* : a place where blood or plasma is stored

**blood·bath** \'bləd-ˌbath, -ˌbäth\ *n* : MASSACRE

**blood count** *n* : the determination of the number of blood cells in a definite volume of blood; *also* : the number of cells so determined

**blood·cur·dling** \-ˌkərd-(ə-)liŋ\ *adj* : seeming to have the effect of congealing the blood through fear or horror

**blood·ed** \'bləd-əd\ *adj* **1** : entirely or largely of pure stock ⟨∼ horses⟩ **2** : having blood of a specified kind ⟨warm-*blooded* animals⟩

**blood·hound** \'bləd-ˌhaund\ *n* : a large powerful hound noted for keenness of smell

**blood·let·ting** \-,let-iŋ\ *n* **1 :** the letting of blood in the treatment of disease **2 :** BLOODSHED

**blood·line** \-,līn\ *n* **:** a sequence of direct ancestors esp. in a pedigree

**blood·mo·bile** \-,mō-,bēl\ *n* **:** an automobile equipped for collecting blood from donors

**blood poisoning** *n* **:** invasion of the bloodstream by virulent microorganisms from a focus of infection

**blood pressure** *n* **:** pressure of the blood on the walls of blood vessels and esp. arteries

**blood·root** \-,rüt, -,rut\ *n* **:** a plant related to the poppy that has a red root and sap, a solitary leaf, and a white flower in early spring

**blood·shed** \'bləd-,shed\ *n* **:** wounding or taking of life **:** CARNAGE, SLAUGHTER

**blood·shot** \-,shät\ *adj* **:** inflamed to redness ⟨~ eyes⟩

**blood·stain** \-,stān\ *n* **:** a discoloration caused by blood — **blood·stained** \-,stānd\ *adj*

**blood·stone** \-,stōn\ *n* **:** a green quartz sprinkled with red spots

**blood·stream** \-,strēm\ *n* **:** the flowing blood in a circulatory system

**blood·suck·er** \-,sək-ər\ *n* **:** an animal that sucks blood; *esp* **:** LEECH — **blood·suck·ing** \-iŋ\ *adj*

**blood test** *n* **:** a test of the blood; *esp* **:** one for syphilis

**blood·thirsty** \'bləd-,thər-stē\ *adj* **:** eager to shed blood — **blood·thirst·i·ly** \-,thər-stə-lē\ *adv* — **blood·thirst·i·ness** \-stē-nəs\ *n*

**blood vessel** *n* **:** a vessel (as a vein or artery) in which blood circulates in an animal

**Bloody Mary** \-'me(ə)r-ē\ *n*, *pl* **Bloody Marys :** a drink made essentially of vodka and tomato juice

**bloom** \'blüm\ *n* **1 :** FLOWER; *also* **:** flowers or amount of flowers (as of a plant) **2 :** the period or state of flowering **3 :** a state or time of beauty and vigor **4 :** a powdery coating esp. on fruits and leaves **5 :** rosy color; *also* **:** an appearance of freshness or health — **bloomy** *adj*

**bloom** *vb* **1 :** to produce or yield flowers **2 :** to glow esp. with healthy color **syn** flower, blossom

**bloo·mers** \'blü-mərz\ *n pl* [Amelia *Bloomer* d1894 Am pioneer in feminism] **:** a woman's garment of short loose trousers gathered at the knee

**bloop·er** \'blü-pər\ *n* **1 :** an embarrassing blunder made in public **2 :** a fly ball hit barely beyond a baseball infield

¹**blos·som** \'bläs-əm\ *n* **:** the flower of a plant **:** BLOOM

²**blossom** *vb* **:** FLOWER, BLOOM

¹**blot** \'blät\ *n* **1 :** SPOT, STAIN ⟨ink ~s⟩ **2 :** BLEMISH **syn** stigma, brand

²**blot** *vb* **blot·ted; blot·ting 1 :** SPOT, STAIN **2 :** OBSCURE, ECLIPSE ⟨his obs **:** MAR; *also* **:** DISGRACE **4 :** to dry or remove with or as if with blotting paper **5 :** to make a blot

**blotch** \'bläch\ *n* **:** a usu. large and irregular spot or mark (as of ink or color) — **blotch** *vb* — **blotchy** *adj*

**blot·ter** \'blät-ər\ *n* **1 :** a piece of blotting paper **2 :** a book for preliminary records (as of sales or arrests)

**blotting paper** *n* **:** a soft spongy paper used to absorb ink

**blouse** \'blaus, 'blauz\ *n* **1 :** a loose outer garment like a smock **2 :** a military uniform coat **3 :** a usu. loose garment reaching from the neck to about the waist level

¹**blow** \'blō\ *vb* **blew** \'blü\; **blown** \'blōn\; **blow·ing 1 :** to move forcibly ⟨the wind *blew*⟩ **2 :** to send forth a current of gas (as air) **3 :** to sound or cause to sound ⟨~ a horn⟩ **4 :** PANT, GASP; *also* **:** to expel moist air in breathing ⟨the whale *blew*⟩ **5 :** BOAST; *also* **:** BLUSTER **6 :** MELT — used of an electrical fuse **7 :** to act on with a current of gas or vapor; *esp* **:** to drive with such a current **8 :** to shape or form by blown or injected air ⟨~ glass⟩ **9 :** to shatter or destroy by or as if by explosion **10 :** to make breathless by exertion — **11 :** to spend recklessly — **blow·er** *n*

²**blow** *n* **1 :** a usu. strong blowing of air **:** GALE **2 :** BOASTING, BRAG **3 :** a blowing from the mouth or nose or through or from an instrument

³**blow** *vb* **blew** \'blü\; **blown** \'blōn\; **blow·ing :** FLOWER, BLOOM

⁴**blow** *n* **1 :** a forcible stroke **2** *pl* **:** COMBAT ⟨come to ~s⟩ **3 :** a severe and usu. unexpected calamity

**blow-by-blow** \-,bī-,-bə-\ *adj* **:** minutely detailed ⟨~ account⟩

**blow·gun** \-,gən\ *n* **:** a tube from which an arrow or a dart may be shot by the force of the breath

**blow·out** \'blō-,aut\ *n* **:** a bursting of something (as a tire) because of pressure of the contents (as air)

**blow·pipe** \'blō-,pīp\ *n* **:** an instrument for blowing gas (as air) into a flame so as to concentrate and increase the heat

**blow·sy** *also* **blow·zy** \'blau-zē\ *adj* **:** DISHEVELED, SLOVENLY

**blow·torch** \'blō-,torch\ *n* **:** a small portable burner in which combustion is intensified by means of a blast of air or oxygen

**blow·up** \'blō-,əp\ *n* **1 :** EXPLOSION **2 :** an outburst of temper **3 :** a photographic enlargement

**blowy** \'blō-ē\ *adj* **:** WINDY

**BLT** \,bē-,el-'tē\ *n* **:** a bacon, lettuce, and tomato sandwich

¹**blub·ber** \'bləb-ər\ *n* **1 :** the fat of large sea mammals (as whales) **2 :** a noisy crying

²**blubber** *vb* **blub·bered; blub·ber·ing** \'bləb-(ə-)riŋ\ **:** to cry noisily

**blu·cher** \'blü-chər, -kər\ *n* **:** a shoe with the tongue and vamp in one piece

¹**blud·geon** \'bləj-ən\ *n* **:** a short often loaded club

²**bludgeon** *vb* **:** to strike with or as if with a bludgeon

¹**blue** \'blü\ *adj* **blu·er; blu·est 1 :** of the color blue; *also* **:** BLUISH **2 :** MEL-

ANCHOLY; *also* : DEPRESSING 3 : PURITANICAL 4 : INDECENT

²**blue** n 1 : a color between green and violet in the spectrum : the color of the clear daytime sky 2 : something (as clothing or the sky) that is blue

**blue baby** n : a baby with bluish skin usu. due to a congenital heart defect

**blue-bell** \-,bel\ n : a plant with blue bell-shaped flowers

**blue-ber-ry** \'blü-,ber-ē, -b(ə-)rē\ n : the edible blue or blackish berry of various shrubs related to the heaths; *also* : one of these shrubs

**blue-bird** \-,bərd\ n : any of several small songbirds related to the robin and more or less blue above

**blue-black** \-'blak\ adj : being of a dark bluish hue

**blue-bon-net** \'blü-,bän-ət\ n : a low-growing annual lupine with silky foliage and blue flowers

**blue-bot-tle** \'blü-,bät-ᵊl\ n : any of several blowflies with iridescent blue bodies or abdomens

**blue cheese** n : cheese marked with veins of greenish blue mold

**blue-col-lar** \'blü-'käl-ər\ adj : of, relating to, or being the class of workers whose duties call for work clothes

**blue-fish** \-,fish\ n : a marine sport and food fish bluish above and silvery below

**blue-grass** \-,gras\ n : KENTUCKY BLUEGRASS

**blue-jack-et** \-,jak-ət\ n : an enlisted man in the navy : SAILOR

**blue jay** \-,jā\ n : an American crested jay with upper parts bright blue

**blue jeans** n pl : pants usu. made of blue denim

**blue-nose** \'blü-,nōz\ n : one who advocates a rigorous moral code

**blue-point** \'blü-,pȯint\ n : a small delicate oyster orig. from Long Island

**blue-print** \-,print\ n 1 : a photographic print in white on a blue ground used esp. for copying mechanical drawings and architects' plans 2 : a detailed plan of action — **blueprint** vb

**blues** \'blüz\ n pl 1 : MELANCHOLY 2 : music in a style of American Negro origin marked by recurrent minor intervals and melancholy lyrics

**blue-stock-ing** \'blü-,stäk-iŋ\ n : a woman having intellectual interests

**blu-et** \'blü-ət\ n : a low American herb with dainty solitary bluish flowers

¹**bluff** \'bləf\ adj 1 : having a broad flattened front 2 : rising steeply with a broad flat front 3 : OUTSPOKEN, FRANK **syn** blunt, brusque, curt, gruff

²**bluff** n : a high steep bank : CLIFF

³**bluff** vb : to frighten or deceive by pretense or a mere show of strength

⁴**bluff** n : an act or instance of bluffing; *also* : one who bluffs

**blu-ing** *or* **blue-ing** \'blü-iŋ\ n : a preparation of blue or violet dyes used in laundering to counteract yellowing of white fabrics

**blu-ish** \'blü-ish\ adj : somewhat blue

¹**blun-der** \'blən-dər\ vb **blun-dered**; **blun-der-ing** \-d(ə-)riŋ\ 1 : to move clumsily or unsteadily 2 : to make a stupid or needless mistake

²**blunder** n : an avoidable and usu. serious mistake

**blun-der-buss** \'blən-dər-,bəs\ n [by folk etymology fr. obs. D donderbus, fr. D donder thunder + obs. D bus gun] : an obsolete short-barreled firearm with a flaring muzzle

¹**blunt** \'blənt\ adj 1 : not sharp : DULL 2 : lacking in tact : BLUFF **syn** brusque, curt, gruff — **blunt-ly** adv — **blunt-ness** n

²**blunt** vb : to make or become dull

**blur** \'blər\ n 1 : a smear or stain that obscures 2 : something vaguely seen or perceived — **blur-ry** \-ē\ adj

²**blur** vb **blurred**; **blur-ring** : DIM, CLOUD, OBSCURE

**blurb** \'blərb\ n : a short publicity notice (as on a book jacket)

**blurt** \'blərt\ vb : to utter suddenly and impulsively

**blush** \'bləsh\ n : a reddening of the face (as from modesty or confusion) : FLUSH — **blush** vb — **blush-ful** adj

**blus-ter** \'bləs-tər\ vb **blus-tered**; **blus-ter-ing** \-t(ə-)riŋ\ 1 : to blow in stormy noisy gusts 2 : to talk or act with noisy swaggering threats — **bluster** n — **blus-tery** adj

**blvd** abbr boulevard

**BM** abbr 1 basal metabolism 2 bowel movement

**BMR** abbr basal metabolic rate

**bn** abbr battalion

**BO** abbr 1 body odor 2 branch office 3 buyer's option

**boa** \'bō-ə\ n 1 : a large snake (as the **boa con-stric-tor** \,bō-ə-kən-'strik-tər\ or the related anaconda) that crushes its prey in its coils 2 : a fluffy scarf usu. of fur or feathers

**boar** \'bōr\ n : a male swine; *also* : the Old World wild hog from which domestic swine are descended

¹**board** \'bōrd\ n 1 : the side of a ship 2 : a thin flat length of sawed lumber; *also* : material (as cardboard) or a piece of material formed as a thin flat firm sheet 3 pl : STAGE 1 4 : a table spread with a meal; *also* : daily meals esp. when furnished for pay 5 : a table at which a council or magistrates sit 6 : a group or association of persons organized for a special responsibility (as the management of a business or institution); *also* : an organized commercial exchange

²**board** vb 1 : to go aboard (~ a boat) 2 : to cover with boards 3 : to provide or be provided with meals and often lodging — **board-er** n

**board-ing-house** \'bōrd-iŋ-,haus\ n : a house at which persons are boarded

**board-walk** \'bōrd-,wȯk\ n : a promenade (as of planking) along a beach

**boast** \'bōst\ vb 1 : to praise oneself 2 : to mention or assert with excessive pride 3 : to prize as a possession; *also* : HAVE (the house ~s a fireplace) — **boast** n — **boast-er** n

**boast-ful** \-fəl\ adj : given to or marked by boasting — **boast-ful-ly** \-ē\ adv

**boat** \'bōt\ n : a vessel (as a canoe or ship) for traveling through water

**boat·er** \'bōt-ər\ *n* **1 :** one that travels in a boat **2 :** a stiff straw hat
**boat·man** \'bōt-mən\ *n* **:** a man who manages, works on, or deals in boats
**boat·swain** \'bōs-ᵊn\ *n* **:** a subordinate officer of a ship in charge of the hull and related matters (as rigging)
**¹bob** \'bäb\ *vb* **bobbed; bob·bing 1 :** to move up and down jerkily or repeatedly **2 :** to emerge, arise, or appear suddenly or unexpectedly
**²bob** *n* **:** a bobbing movement
**³bob** *n* **1 :** a knob, bunch, or tuft esp. of hair or angling bait **2 :** FLOAT 2 **3 :** a short haircut of a woman or child **4 :** a small usu. pendent weight (as on a pendulum or plumb line)
**⁴bob** *vb* **bobbed; bob·bing :** to cut hair in a bob
**⁵bob** *n, pl* **bob** *slang* **:** SHILLING
**bob·bin** \'bäb-ən\ *n* **:** a cylinder or spindle for holding or dispensing thread (as in a sewing machine)
**bob·ble** \'bäb-əl\ *vb* **bob·bled; bob·bling** \-(ə-)liŋ\ **:** FUMBLE — **bobble** *n*
**bob·by** \'bäb-ē\ *n, pl* **bobbies** [*Bobby,* nickname for *Robert,* after Sir Robert Peel, who organized the London police force] *Brit* **:** POLICEMAN
**bob·by pin** \'bäb-ē-\ *n* **:** a flat wire hairpin with prongs that press close together
**bob·by·sox·er** \-,säk-sər\ *n* **:** an adolescent girl
**bob·cat** \'bäb-,kat\ *n* **:** a small usu. rusty-colored American lynx
**bob·o·link** \'bäb-ə-,liŋk\ *n* **:** an American migratory songbird related to the meadowlarks
**bob·sled** \'bäb-,sled\ *n* **1 :** a short sled usu. used as one of a joined pair **2 :** a large usu. metal sled used in racing and equipped with two pairs of runners in tandem, a long seat for two or more people, a steering wheel, and a hand brake — **bobsled** *vb*
**bob·white** \(ˈ)bäb-ˈhwīt\ *n* **:** QUAIL
**boc·cie** *or* **boc·ci** *or* **boc·ce** \'bäch-ē\ *n* **:** Italian lawn bowling played on a long narrow court
**bock** \'bäk\ *n* **:** a dark heavy beer usu. sold in early spring
**¹bode** \'bōd\ *vb* **bod·ed; bod·ing :** to indicate by signs **:** PRESAGE
**²bode** *past of* BIDE
**bod·ice** \'bäd-əs\ *n* [alter. of *bodies,* pl. of *body*] **:** the usu. close-fitting part of a dress above the waist
**bodi·less** \'bäd-i-ləs, 'bäd-ᵊl-əs\ *adj* **:** lacking a body or material form
**¹bodi·ly** \'bäd-ᵊl-ē\ *adj* **:** of or relating to the body ⟨~ welfare⟩
**²bodily** *adv* **1 :** in the flesh **2 :** as a whole ⟨lifted the crate up ~⟩
**bod·kin** \'bäd-kən\ *n* **1 :** DAGGER **2 :** a pointed implement for punching holes in cloth **3 :** a blunt needle for drawing tape or ribbon through a loop or hem
**body** \'bäd-ē\ *n, pl* **bod·ies 1 :** the physical whole of a living or dead organism; *also* **:** the trunk or main mass of an organism as distinguished from its appendages **2 :** a human being

**:** PERSON **3 :** the main part of something **4 :** a mass of matter distinct from other masses **5 :** GROUP **6 :** VISCOSITY, FIRMNESS **7 :** richness of flavor — used esp. of wines
**body English** *n* **:** the instinctive attempt of a person to influence the movement of a propelled object (as a ball) by contorting his body in the right direction
**body·guard** \'bäd-ē-,gärd\ *n* **:** a personal guard; *also* **:** RETINUE
**body stocking** *n* **:** a sheer close-fitting one-piece garment for the torso that often has sleeves and legs
**body·work** \'bäd-ē-,wərk\ *n* **1 :** a vehicle body **2 :** the process of working on vehicle bodies
**Boer** \'bōr, 'bûr\ *n* **:** a South African of Dutch or Huguenot descent
**¹bog** \'bäg, 'bȯg\ *n* **:** wet, spongy, and usu. acid ground — **bog·gy** *adj*
**²bog** *vb* **bogged; bog·ging :** to sink into or as if into a bog
**bo·gey** *also* **bo·gy** *or* **bo·gie** \'bùg-ē, 'bō-gē *for 1;* 'bō-gē *for 2*\ *n, pl* **bogeys** *also* **bogies 1 :** SPECTER, HOBGOBLIN; *also* **:** a source of annoyance **2 :** a score of one over par on a hole in golf
**bo·gey·man** \'bùg-ē-,man, 'bō-gē-, 'bü-gē-\ *n* **:** a terrifying person or thing; *esp* **:** an imaginary figure used in threatening children
**bog·gle** \'bäg-əl\ *vb* **bog·gled; bog·gling** \-(ə-)liŋ\ **:** to overwhelm or to be overwhelmed with fright or amazement
**bo·gus** \'bō-gəs\ *adj* **:** SPURIOUS, SHAM
**Bo·he·mi·an** \bō-'hē-mē-ən\ *n* **1 :** a native or inhabitant of Bohemia **2** *often not cap* **:** VAGABOND, WANDERER **3** *often not cap* **:** a person (as a writer or artist) living an unconventional life — **bohemian** *adj, often cap*
**¹boil** \'bȯil\ *n* **:** an inflamed swelling on the skin containing pus
**²boil** *vb* **1 :** to heat or become heated to a temperature (**boiling point**) at which vapor is formed and rises in bubbles ⟨water ~s and changes to steam⟩; *also* **:** to act on or be acted on by a boiling liquid ⟨~ eggs⟩ **2 :** to be in a state of seething agitation
**³boil** *n* **:** the action or state of boiling
**boil·er** \'bȯi-lər\ *n* **1 :** a container in which something is boiled **2 :** the part of a steam-generating plant in which water is heated until it becomes steam **3 :** a tank holding hot water
**boil·er·mak·er** \'bȯi-lər-,mā-kər\ *n* **:** whiskey with a beer chaser
**bois·ter·ous** \'bȯi-st(ə-)rəs\ *adj* **:** noisily turbulent or exuberant — **bois·ter·ous·ly** *adv*
**bo·la** \'bō-lə\ *or* **bo·las** \-ləs\ *n, pl* **bolas** \-ləz\ *also* **bo·las·es :** a weapon consisting of balls attached to the ends of a cord for hurling at and entangling an animal
**bold** \'bōld\ *adj* **1 :** COURAGEOUS, INTREPID **2 :** IMPUDENT **3 :** STEEP **4 :** ADVENTUROUS, DARING ⟨a ~ thinker⟩ **syn** dauntless, brave — **bold·ly** *adv* — **bold·ness** \'bōl(d)-nəs\ *n*

**bold·face** \'bōl(d)-,fās\ *n* : a heavy-faced type; *also* : printing in boldface — **bold·faced** \-'fāst\ *adj*

**bole** \'bōl\ *n* : the trunk of a tree

**bo·le·ro** \bə-'le(ə)r-ō\ *n, pl* **-ros 1** : a Spanish dance or its music **2** : a short loose jacket open at the front

**bo·li·var** \bə-'lē-,vär, 'bäl-ə-vər\ *n, pl* **-vars** *or* **-va·res** \,bäl-ə-'vär-,ās, ,bō-li-\ — see MONEY table

**boll** \'bōl\ *n* : a seed pod (as of cotton)

**boll weevil** *n* : a small grayish weevil that infests the cotton plant both as a larva and as an adult

**boll·worm** \'bōl-,wərm\ *n* : any of several moths whose larvae feed on cotton bolls

**bo·lo** \'bō-lō\ *n, pl* **bolos** : a long heavy single-edged knife used in the Philippines

**bo·lo·gna** \bə-'lō-nē\ *n* : a large smoked sausage of beef, veal, and pork

**Bol·she·vik** \'bōl-shə-,vik\ *n, pl* **Bolsheviks** *also* **Bol·she·vi·ki** \,bōl-shə-'vik-ē\ [Russ *bol'shevik,* fr. *bol'she* larger] **1** : a member of the party that seized power in Russia in the revolution of November 1917 **2** : COMMUNIST — **Bolshevik** *adj*

**bol·she·vism** \'bōl-shə-,viz-əm\ *n, often cap* : the doctrine or program of the Bolsheviks advocating violent overthrow of capitalism

**¹bol·ster** \'bōl-stər\ *n* : a long pillow or cushion extending from side to side of a bed

**²bolster** *vb* **bol·stered; bol·ster·ing** \-st(ə-)riŋ\ : to support with or as if with a bolster; *also* : REINFORCE

**¹bolt** \'bōlt\ *n* **1** : a usu. short stout blunt missile for a crossbow or catapult **2** : a flash of lightning : THUNDERBOLT **3** : a sliding bar used to fasten a door **4** : a roll of cloth or wallpaper of specified length **5** : a rod with a head at one end and a screw thread at the other used to hold objects in place **6** : a short length or block of timber

**²bolt** *vb* **1** : to move suddenly (as in fright or hurry) : START, DASH **2** : to break away (as from association) ⟨∼ a political convention⟩ **3** : to secure or fasten with a bolt **4** : to swallow hastily or without chewing

**³bolt** *n* : an act of bolting

**⁴bolt** *vb* : SIFT ⟨∼ flour⟩

**bo·lus** \'bō-ləs\ *n* : a rounded mass (as of chewed food or medicine)

**¹bomb** \'bäm\ *n* **1** : an explosive-filled case that may be dropped (as from a plane) or projected (as by hand) and is designed to detonate under specified conditions (as impact) **2** : a container of material (as insecticide) under pressure for release in a fine spray **3** : a long pass in football

**²bomb** *vb* : to attack with bombs

**bom·bard** \bäm-'bärd, bəm-\ *vb* **1** : to attack with artillery **2** : to assail persistently **3** : to subject to the impact of rapidly moving particles (as electrons) — **bom·bard·ment** *n*

**bom·bar·dier** \,bäm-bə(r)-'diər\ *n* : a

bomber-crew member who releases the bombs

**bom·bast** \'bäm-,bast\ *n* [fr. *bombast* cotton padding, fr. MF *bombace,* fr. ML *bombax* cotton, alter. of L *bombyx* silkworm, silk, fr. Gk] : pretentious wordy speech or writing — **bom·bas·tic** \bäm-'bas-tik\ *adj*

**bom·ba·zine** \,bäm-bə-'zēn\ *n* **1** : a silk fabric in twill weave dyed black **2** : a twilled fabric with silk warp and worsted filling

**bomb·er** \'bäm-ər\ *n* **1** : one that bombs; *esp* : an airplane for dropping bombs

**bomb·proof** \'bäm-'prüf\ *adj* : safe against the explosive force of bombs

**bomb·shell** \'bäm-,shel\ *n* **1** : BOMB 1 **2** : one that stuns, amazes, or completely upsets

**bomb·sight** \-,sīt\ *n* : a sighting device on an airplane for aiming bombs

**bona fide** \'bō-nə-,fīd, 'bän-ə-; ,bō-nə-'fīd-ē, -'fīd-ə\ *adj* [L, in good faith] **1** : made in good faith ⟨a *bona fide* agreement⟩ **2** : GENUINE, REAL ⟨a *bona fide* bargain⟩ **syn** authentic

**bo·nan·za** \bə-'nan-zə\ *n* [Sp, lit., calm, fr. ML *bonacia,* alter. of L *malacia* calm at sea, fr. Gk *malakia,* lit., softness, fr. *malakos* soft] : something yielding a rich return

**bon·bon** \'bän-,bän\ *n* : a candy usu. with a creamy center in a cover (as of chocolate)

**¹bond** \'bänd\ *n* **1** *pl* : FETTERS **2** : a binding or uniting force or tie ⟨∼s of friendship⟩ **3** : an agreement or obligation often made binding by a pledge of money or goods **4** : a person who acts as surety for another **5** : an interest-bearing certificate of public or private indebtedness **6** : the state of goods subject to supervision pending payment of taxes or duties due ⟨imports held in ∼⟩

**²bond** *vb* **1** : to assure payment of duties or taxes on (goods) by giving a bond **2** : to insure against losses caused by the acts of ⟨∼ a salesman⟩ **3** : to make or become firmly united as if by bonds ⟨∼ iron to copper⟩

**bond·age** \'bän-dij\ *n* : SLAVERY, SERVITUDE

**bond·hold·er** \'bänd-,hōl-dər\ *n* : one that owns a government or corporation bond

**bond·man** \'bän(d)-mən\ *n* : SLAVE, SERF

**¹bonds·man** \'bän(d)z-mən\ *n* : BONDMAN

**²bondsman** *n* : SURETY

**bond·wom·an** \'bänd-,wùm-ən\ *n* : a female slave or serf

**¹bone** \'bōn\ *n* **1** : a hard largely calcareous tissue forming most of the skeleton of a vertebrate animal; *also* : one of the pieces in which bone naturally occurs **2** : a hard animal substance (as ivory or whalebone) similar to true bone **3** : something made of bone — **bone·less** *adj* — **bony** *or* **bon·ey** \'bō-nē\ *adj*

**²bone** *vb* **boned; bon·ing** : to free

from bones ⟨~ a chicken⟩

**bone black** n : the black carbon residue from calcined bones used esp. as a pigment

**bone meal** n : fertilizer or feed made of crushed or ground bone

**bon·er** \'bō-nər\ n : a stupid and ridiculous blunder

**bon·fire** \'bän-,fī(ə)r\ n [ME bonefire a fire of bones, fr. bon bone + fire] : a large fire built in the open air

**bon·go** \'bäŋ-gō\ n, pl **bongos** also **bongoes** : one of a pair of small tuned drums played with the hands

**bon·ho·mie** \,bän-ə-'mē\ n [F bonhomie, fr. bonhomme good-natured man, fr. bon good + homme man] : good-natured easy friendliness

**bo·ni·to** \bə-'nēt-ō\ n, pl **-tos** or **-to** : any of several medium-sized tunas

**bon mot** \bōⁿ-'mō\ n, pl **bons mots** \bōⁿ-'mō(z)\ or **bon mots** \-'mō(z)\ [F, lit., good word] : a clever remark

**bon·net** \'bän-ət\ n : a covering (as a cap) for the head; esp : a hat for a woman or infant tied under the chin

**bon·ny** \'bän-ē\ adj **bon·ni·er; -est** chiefly Brit : HANDSOME, PRETTY, FINE

**bon·sai** \bōn-'sī\ n, pl **bonsai** : a potted plant (as a tree) dwarfed by special methods of culture

**bo·nus** \'bō-nəs\ n : something extra and esp. money given in addition to what is usual or due  **syn** bounty, premium, reward

**bon vi·vant** \,bän-vē-'vänt, ,bōⁿ-vē-'väⁿ\ n, pl **bons vivants** \,bän-vē-'vänts, ,bōⁿ-vē-'väⁿ(z)\ or **bon vivants** \same\ [F, lit., good liver] : a person having cultivated, refined, and sociable tastes esp. in food and drink

**bon voy·age** \,bōⁿv-,wī-'äzh, -,wä-'yäzh; ,bän-\ n : FAREWELL — often used as an interjection

**bonze** \'bänz\ n : a Buddhist monk

**boo** \'bü\ n, pl **boos** : a shout of disapproval or contempt — **boo** vb

**boo·by** \'bü-bē\ n, pl **boobies** : an awkward ineffective person : DOPE

**booby hatch** n : an insane asylum

**booby prize** n : an award for the poorest performance in a contest

**booby trap** n : a concealed explosive device set to go off when some harmless-looking object is touched

**boo·dle** \'büd-⁹l\ n 1 : bribe money  2 : a large amount of money

¹**book** \'bük\ n 1 : a set of sheets bound into a volume  2 : a long written or printed narrative or record  3 : a subdivision of a long literary work  4 cap : BIBLE

²**book** vb 1 : to engage, reserve, or schedule by or as if by writing in a book ⟨~ seats on a plane⟩  2 : to enter charges against in a police register

**book·case** \-,kās\ n : a piece of furniture consisting of shelves to hold books

**book·end** \-,end\ n : a support to hold up of a row of books

**book·ie** \'bük-ē\ n : BOOKMAKER

**book·ish** \'bük-ish\ adj 1 : fond of books and reading  2 : inclined to rely unduly on book knowledge

**book·keep·er** \'bük-,kē-pər\ n : one who records the accounts or transactions of a business — **book·keep·ing** \-piŋ\ n

**book·let** \'bük-lət\ n : PAMPHLET

**book·mak·er** \'bük-,mā-kər\ n : one who determines odds and receives and pays off bets — **book·mak·ing** \-kiŋ\ n

**book·mark** \-,märk\ or **book·mark·er** \-,mär-kər\ n : a marker for finding a place in a book

**book·mo·bile** \'bük-mō-,bēl\ n : a truck that serves as a traveling library

**book·plate** \'bük-,plāt\ n : a label placed in a book to show who owns it

**book·sell·er** \'bük-,sel-ər\ n : the proprietor of a bookstore

**book·shelf** \-,shelf\ n : a shelf for books

**book·worm** \'bük-,wərm\ n 1 : an insect larva (as of a beetle) that feeds on the binding and paste of a book  2 : a person unusually devoted to reading and study

¹**boom** \'büm\ n 1 : a long spar used to extend the bottom of a sail  2 : a beam projecting from the upright pole of a derrick to support or guide the object lifted  3 : a line of floating timbers used to hold logs in a restricted water area

²**boom** vb 1 : to make a deep hollow sound : RESOUND  2 : to grow or cause to grow rapidly esp. in value, esteem, or importance

³**boom** n 1 : a booming sound or cry  2 : a rapid expansion or increase esp. of economic activity

**boo·mer·ang** \'bü-mə-,raŋ\ n : a bent or angular club that can be so thrown as to return near the starting point

¹**boon** \'bün\ n [ME, fr. ON bōn petition] : BENEFIT, BLESSING  **syn** favor, gift

²**boon** adj [ME bon, fr. MF, good] : INTIMATE, CONGENIAL

**boon·docks** \'bün-,däks\ n pl [Tagalog (language of the Philippines) bundok mountain] 1 : rough country filled with dense brush  2 : a rural area

**boon·dog·gle** \'bün-,däg-əl, -,dóg-\ n : a useless or wasteful project or activity

**boor** \'bùr\ n 1 : YOKEL  2 : a rude or insensitive person  **syn** churl, lout, bumpkin — **boor·ish** adj

**boost** \'büst\ vb 1 : to push up from below  2 : INCREASE, RAISE ⟨~ prices⟩  3 : AID, PROMOTE ⟨voted a bonus to ~ morale⟩ — **boost** n — **boost·er** n

¹**boot** \'büt\ n, dial : something to equalize a trade — **to boot** : BESIDES

²**boot** vb, archaic : AVAIL, PROFIT

³**boot** n 1 : a covering for the foot and leg  2 : a protective sheath (as of a flower) or liner (as in a tire)  3 Brit : an automobile trunk  4 : KICK; also : a discharge from employment  5 : a navy or marine trainee

⁴**boot** vb 1 : KICK  2 : to eject or discharge summarily

**boot·black** \'büt-,blak\ n : a person who shines shoes

**boo·tee** or **boo·tie** \'büt-ē\ n : an infant's knitted or crocheted sock

**booth** \'büth\ *n, pl* **booths** \'büthz, 'büths\ **1** : a small enclosed stall (as at a fair) **2** : a restaurant accommodation having a table between backed benches

**boot·leg** \'büt-,leg\ *vb* : to make, transport, or sell (as liquor) illegally — **boot·leg** *adj or n* — **boot·leg·ger** *n*

**boot·less** \'büt-ləs\ *adj* : USELESS **syn** futile, vain — **boot·less·ly** *adv*

**boo·ty** \'büt-ē\ *n, pl* **booties** : PLUNDER, SPOIL

¹**booze** \'büz\ *vb* **boozed; booz·ing** : to drink liquor to excess — **booz·er** *n*

²**booze** *n* : intoxicating liquor — **boozy** *adj*

**bop** \'bäp\ *vb* **bopped; bop·ping** : HIT, SOCK — **bop** *n*

**BOQ** *abbr* bachelor officers' quarters

**bor** *abbr* borough

**bo·rate** \'bōr-,āt\ *n* : a salt or ester of a boric acid

**bo·rax** \'bōr-,aks\ *n* : a crystalline compound of boron that occurs as a mineral and is used as a flux and cleanser

**bor·del·lo** \bòr-'del-ō\ *n, pl* **-los** : BROTHEL

¹**bor·der** \'bórd-ər\ *n* **1** : EDGE, MARGIN **2** : BOUNDARY, FRONTIER **syn** rim, brim, brink

²**border** *vb* **bor·dered; bor·der·ing** \'bórd-(ə-)riŋ\ **1** : to put a border on **2** : ADJOIN **3** : VERGE

**bor·der·land** \'bórd-ər-,land\ *n* **1** : territory at or near a border **2** : an outlying or intermediate region often not clearly defined

¹**bore** \'bōr\ *vb* **bored; bor·ing 1** : to make a hole in with or as if with a rotary tool **2** : to make (as a well) by piercing or drilling **syn** perforate, drill — **bor·er** *n*

²**bore** *n* **1** : a hole made by boring **2** : a lengthwise cylindrical cavity **3** : the diameter of a hole or tube; *esp* : the interior diameter of a gun barrel or engine cylinder

³**bore** *past of* BEAR

⁴**bore** *n* : a tidal wave with a high abrupt front

⁵**bore** *n* : one that causes boredom

⁶**bore** *vb* **bored; bor·ing** : to weary with tedious dullness

**bo·re·al** \'bōr-ē-əl\ *adj* : of, relating to, or located in northern regions

**bore·dom** \'bōrd-əm\ *n* : the condition of being bored

**boric acid** \,bōr-ik-\ *n* : a white crystalline weak acid that contains boron and is used as an antiseptic

**born** \'bórn\ *adj* **1** : brought into life by birth **2** : NATIVE ⟨American-*born*⟩ **3** : having special natural abilities or character from birth ⟨a ~ leader⟩

**borne** *past part of* BEAR

**bo·ron** \'bōr-,än\ *n* : a chemical element that occurs in nature only in combination and is used esp. in metallurgy

**bor·ough** \'bər-ō\ *n* **1** : a British town that sends one or more members to parliament; *also* : an incorporated British urban area **2** : an incorporated town or village in some U.S. states;

*also* : any of the five political divisions of New York City **3** : a civil division of the state of Alaska corresponding to a county in most other states

**bor·row** \'bär-ō\ *vb* **1** : to take or receive (something) temporarily and with intent to return **2** : to take into possession or use from another source : DERIVE, APPROPRIATE ⟨~ a metaphor⟩

**borscht** *or* **borsch** \'bórsh(t)\ *n* : a soup made mainly from beets

**bosh** \'bäsh\ *n* [Turk *boş* empty] : foolish talk : NONSENSE

**bosky** \'bäs-kē\ *adj* : covered with trees or shrubs

¹**bo·som** \'búz-əm, 'büz-\ *n* **1** : the front of the human chest; *esp* : the female breasts **2** : the part of a garment covering the breast **3** : the seat of secret thoughts and feelings — **bo·somed** \-əmd\ *adj*

²**bosom** *adj* : CLOSE, INTIMATE

¹**boss** \'bäs, 'bós\ *n* : a knoblike ornament : STUD

²**boss** *vb* : to ornament with bosses

³**boss** \'bós\ *n* **1** : one (as a foreman or manager) exercising control or supervision **2** : a politician who controls votes or dictates policies — **bossy** *adj*

⁴**boss** \'bós\ *vb* : to act as a boss : SUPERVISE

**bo·sun** \'bōs-ᵊn\ *var of* BOATSWAIN

**bot** *abbr* botanical; botany

**bot·a·ny** \'bät-(ᵊ-)nē\ *n, pl* **-nies** : a branch of biology dealing with plants and plant life — **bo·tan·i·cal** \bə-'tan-i-kəl\ *or* **bo·tan·ic** \-ik\ *adj* — **bot·a·nist** \'bät-(ᵊ-)nəst\ *n* — **bot·a·nize** \-ᵊn-,īz\ *vb*

**botch** \'bäch\ *vb* **1** : to patch clumsily **2** : BUNGLE — **botch** *n*

¹**both** \'bōth\ *adj* : the one and the other

²**both** *pron* : both ones : the one and the other

³**both** *conj* — used as a function word to indicate and stress the inclusion of each of two or more things specified by co-ordinated words, phrases, or clauses ⟨~ New York and London⟩

**both·er** \'bäth-ər\ *vb* **-ered; -er·ing** \-(ə-)riŋ\ : WORRY, PESTER, TROUBLE **syn** vex, annoy, irk — **bother** *n* — **both·er·some** \-səm\ *adj*

¹**bot·tle** \'bät-ᵊl\ *n* **1** : a container (as of glass) with a narrow neck and usu. no handles **2** : the quantity held by a bottle **3** : intoxicating liquor

²**bottle** *vb* **bot·tled; bot·tling** \'bät-(ᵊ-)liŋ\ : to put into a bottle

**bot·tle·neck** \'bät-ᵊl-,nek\ *n* **1** : a narrow passage or point of congestion **2** : something that obstructs or impedes

**bot·tom** \'bät-əm\ *n* **1** : an under or supporting surface; *also* : BUTTOCKS **2** : the bottom of a body of water **3** : the lowest part or place; *also* : an inferior position ⟨start at the ~⟩ **4** : low land along a river — **bottom** *adj* — **bot·tom·less** *adj*

**bot·tom·land** \'bät-əm-,land\ *n* : BOTTOM 4

**bottom out** *vb* : to decline to a point

where demand begins to exceed supply and a rise in prices is imminent ⟨a security market that *bottoms out*⟩

**bot·u·lism** \'bäch-ə-,liz-əm\ *n* : acute food poisoning caused by a bacterial toxin in food

**bou·doir** \'büd-,wär, 'bùd-\ *n* [F, fr. *bouder* to pout] : a woman's private room

**bouf·fant** \bü-'fänt, 'bü-,fänt\ *adj* : puffed out ⟨~ hairdos⟩

**bough** \'baù\ *n* : a usu. large or main branch of a tree

**bought** *past of* BUY

**bouil·la·baisse** \,bü-yə-'bäs\ *n* : a highly seasoned fish stew made of at least two kinds of fish

**bouil·lon** \'bü-,yän; 'bùl-,yän, -yən\ *n* : a clear soup made usu. from beef

**boul·der** \'bōl-dər\ *n* : a detached rounded or worn mass of rock — **bouldered** \-dərd\ *adj*

**boule** \'bül\ *n* : a synthetically formed pear-shaped mass (as of sapphire)

**bou·le·vard** \'bùl-ə-,värd, 'bül-\ *n* [F, modif. of Middle Dutch *bolwerc* bulwark; so called because the first boulevards were laid out on the sites of razed city fortifications] : a broad often landscaped thoroughfare

**bounce** \'baùns\ *vb* **bounced; bounc·ing** : BOUND, REBOUND — **bounce** *n*

**bounc·er** \'baùn-sər\ *n* : a man employed in a public place to remove disorderly persons

¹**bound** \'baùnd\ *adj* : intending to go

²**bound** *n* : LIMIT, BOUNDARY — **bound·less** *adj* — **bound·less·ness** *n*

³**bound** *vb* **1** : to set limits to **2** : to form the boundary of **3** : to name the boundaries of

⁴**bound** *adj* **1** : constrained by or as if by bonds : CONFINED, OBLIGED; *also* : held in combination ⟨~ water⟩ **2** : enclosed in a binding or cover **3** : RESOLVED, DETERMINED; *also* : SURE

⁵**bound** *n* **1** : LEAP, JUMP **2** : REBOUND, BOUNCE

⁶**bound** *vb* : SPRING, BOUNCE

**bound·ary** \'baùn-d(ə-)rē\ *n*, *pl* -**aries** : something that marks or fixes a limit (as of territory) **syn** border, frontier

**bound·en** \'baùn-dən\ *adj* : BINDING

**boun·te·ous** \'baùnt-ē-əs\ *adj* **1** : GENEROUS **2** : ABUNDANT — **boun·te·ous·ly** *adv*

**boun·ti·ful** \'baùnt-i-fəl\ *adj* **1** : giving freely **2** : PLENTIFUL — **boun·ti·ful·ly** *adv*

**boun·ty** \'baùnt-ē\ *n*, *pl* **bounties** [ME *bounte* goodness, fr. OF *bonté*, fr. L *bonitas*, fr. *bonus* good] **1** : GENEROSITY **2** : something given liberally **3** : a reward, premium, or subsidy given usu. for doing something **syn** award, prize, bonus

**bou·quet** \bō-'kā, bü-\ *n* [F, fr. MF, thicket, fr. OF *bosc* forest] **1** : flowers picked and fastened together in a bunch **2** : a distinctive aroma (as of wine) **syn** scent, fragrance

**bour·bon** \'bər-bən\ *n* : a whiskey distilled from a corn mash

**bour·geois** \'bùrzh-,wä, bùrzh-'wä\ *n*, *pl* **bourgeois** \-,wä(z), -'wä(z)\ [MF, lit., citizen of a town, fr. *borc* town, borough, fr. L *burgus* fortified place, of Gmc origin] : a middle-class person — **bourgeois** *adj*

**bour·geoi·sie** \,bùrzh-,wä-'zē\ *n*, *pl* **bourgeoisie** : a social order dominated by bourgeois

**bourn** *or* **bourne** \'bōrn, 'bùrn\ *n*, *archaic* : BOUNDARY; *also* : DESTINATION

**bourse** \'bùrs\ *n* : a European stock exchange

**bout** \'baùt\ *n* **1** : CONTEST, MATCH **2** : OUTBREAK, ATTACK ⟨a ~ of measles⟩ **3** : SESSION

**bou·tique** \bü-'tēk\ *n* : a small retail store; *esp* : a fashionable specialty shop for women

**bou·ton·niere** \,büt-²n-'iər\ *n* : a flower or bouquet worn in a buttonhole

**bo·vine** \'bō-,vīn, -,vēn\ *adj* : of, related to, or resembling the ox or cow — **bovine** *n*

¹**bow** \'baù\ *vb* **1** : SUBMIT, YIELD **2** : to bend the head or body (as in submission, courtesy, or assent)

²**bow** *n* : an act or posture of bowing

³**bow** \'bō\ *n* **1** : BEND, ARCH; *esp* : RAINBOW **2** : a weapon for shooting arrows; *also* : ARCHER **3** : a knot formed by doubling a line into two or more loops **4** : a wooden rod strung with horsehairs for playing an instrument of the violin family

⁴**bow** \'bō\ *vb* **1** : BEND, CURVE **2** : to play (an instrument) with a bow

⁵**bow** \'baù\ *n* : the forward part of a ship — **bow** *adj*

**bowd·ler·ize** \'bōd-lə-,rīz, 'baùd-\ *vb* -**ized; -iz·ing** : to expurgate by omitting parts considered vulgar

**bow·el** \'baù(-ə)l\ *n* **1** *pl* : INTESTINES **2** : one of the divisions of the intestine **3** *pl* : the inmost parts ⟨the ~s of the earth⟩

**bow·er** \'baù(-ə)r\ *n* : a shelter of boughs or vines : ARBOR

¹**bowl** \'bōl\ *n* **1** : a concave vessel used to hold liquids **2** : a drinking vessel **3** : a bowl-shaped part or structure — **bowl·ful** \-,fùl\ *n*

²**bowl** *n* **1** : a ball for rolling on a level surface in bowling **2** : a cast of the ball in bowling

³**bowl** *vb* **1** : to play a game of bowling; *also* : to roll a ball in bowling **2** : to travel in a vehicle rapidly and smoothly **3** : to strike or knock down with a moving object; *also* : to overwhelm with surprise

**bowlder** *var of* BOULDER

**bow·leg** \'bō-,leg, -'leg\ *n* : a leg bowed outward usu. at or below the knee — **bow-legged** \-'leg-əd\ *adj*

¹**bowl·er** \'bō-lər\ *n* : one that bowls

²**bowl·er** \'bō-lər\ *n* : DERBY 3

**bow·line** \'bō-lən, -,līn\ *n* : a knot used to form a loop that neither slips nor jams

**bowl·ing** \'bō-liŋ\ *n* : any of various games in which balls are rolled on a green (**bowling green**) or alley (**bowling alley**) at an object or a group of objects; *esp* : TENPINS

**bow·man** \'bō-mǝn\ *n* : ARCHER

**bow·sprit** \'baù-,sprit\ *n* : a spar projecting forward from the prow of a ship

**bow·string** \'bō-,striŋ\ *n* : the cord connecting the two ends of a bow

¹**box** \'bäks\ *n, pl* **box** *or* **box·es** : an evergreen shrub or small tree used esp. for hedges — **box·wood** \-,wùd\ *n*

²**box** *n* **1** : a rigid typically rectangular receptacle often with a cover; *also* : the quantity held by a box **2** : a small compartment (as for a group of theater patrons); *also* : a boxlike receptacle or division **3** : any of six spaces on a baseball diamond where the batter, pitcher, coaches, and catcher stand **4** : PREDICAMENT

³**box** *vb* : to furnish with or enclose in or as if in a box

⁴**box** *n* : SLAP, CUFF

⁵**box** *vb* **1** : to strike with the hand **2** : to engage in boxing with : fight with the fists **syn** smite, strike, slap

**box·car** \'bäks-,kär\ *n* : a roofed freight car usu. with sliding doors in the sides

¹**box·er** \'bäk-sǝr\ *n* : one that engages in boxing

²**boxer** *n* : a compact short-haired usu. fawn or brindle dog of German origin

**box·ing** \'bäk-siŋ\ *n* : the sport of fighting with the fists

**box office** *n* : an office (as in a theater) where admission tickets are sold

**boy** \'bòi\ *n* **1** : a male child : YOUTH **2** : a male servant — **boy·hood** \-,hùd\ *n* — **boy·ish** *adj* — **boy·ish·ly** *adv* — **boy·ish·ness** *n*

**boy·cott** \'bòi-,kät\ *vb* [Charles C. Boycott d1897 E land agent in Ireland who was ostracized for refusing to reduce rents] : to refrain from having any dealings with — **boycott** *n*

**boy scout** *n* : a member of the Boy Scouts of America

**boy·sen·ber·ry** \'bòiz-ᵊn-,ber-ē, 'bòis-\ *n* : a large bramble fruit with a raspberry flavor; *also* : the plant bearing it

**bp** *abbr* **1** bishop **2** boiling point

**BP** *abbr* **1** blood pressure **2** British Pharmacopoeia

**bpl** *abbr* birthplace

**BPOE** *abbr* Benevolent and Protective Order of Elks

**br** *abbr* **1** branch **2** brass **3** brown

¹**Br** *abbr* British

²**Br** *symbol* bromine

**BR** *abbr* bills receivable

**bra** \'brä\ *n* : BRASSIERE

¹**brace** \'brās\ *n, pl* **brac·es 1** : a crank-shaped device for turning a bit **2** : something (as a tie, prop, or clamp) that distributes, directs, or resists pressure or weight; *also* : an appliance for supporting a body part or for correcting position irregularities of the teeth **3** *pl* : SUSPENDERS **4** : a mark { or } or ⁓ used to connect words or items to be considered together

²**brace** *vb* **braced; brac·ing 1** *archaic*

: to make fast : BIND **2** : to tighten preparatory to use; *also* : to get ready for : prepare oneself **3** : INVIGORATE **4** : to furnish or support with a brace; *also* : STRENGTHEN **5** : to set firmly; *also* : to gain courage or confidence

**brace·let** \'brā-slǝt\ *n* [ME, fr. MF, dim. of *bras* arm, fr. L *bracchium*, fr. Gk *brachīon*] : an ornamental band or chain usu. worn around the wrist

**bra·ce·ro** \brä-'ser-(,)ō\ *n, pl* **-ros** : a Mexican laborer admitted to the U.S. esp. for seasonal farm work

**brack·en** \'brak-ǝn\ *n* : a large coarse fern; *also* : a growth of such ferns

¹**brack·et** \'brak-ǝt\ *n* **1** : a projecting framework or arm designed to support weight; *also* : a shelf on such framework **2** : one of a pair of punctuation marks [ ] used esp. to enclose interpolated matter **3** : a continuous section of a series; *esp* : one of a graded series of income groups

²**bracket** *vb* **1** : to furnish or fasten with brackets **2** : to place within brackets; *also* : to separate or group with or as if with brackets

**brack·ish** \'brak-ish\ *adj* : somewhat salty — **brack·ish·ness** *n*

**bract** \'brakt\ *n* : an often modified leaf on or at the base of a flower stalk

**brad** \'brad\ *n* : a slender nail with a small head

**brae** \'brā\ *n, chiefly Scot* : a hillside esp. along a river

**brag** *vb* **bragged; brag·ging** : to talk or assert boastfully — **brag** *n*

**brag·ga·do·cio** \,brag-ǝ-'dō-s(h)ē-,ō, -(,)shō\ *n, pl* **-cios 1** : BRAGGART, BOASTER **2** : empty boasting **3** : arrogant pretension : COCKINESS

**brag·gart** \'brag-ǝrt\ *n* : one who brags

**Brah·man** *or* **Brah·min** \'bräm-ǝn *for 1;* 'bräm-, 'bräm-, 'bram- *for 2*\ *n* **1** : a Hindu of the highest caste traditionally assigned to the priesthood **2** : any of the large vigorous humped cattle developed in the southern U.S. from Indian stock

**Brah·man·ism** \'bräm-ǝ-,niz-ǝm\ *n* : orthodox Hinduism

**Brah·min** \'bräm-ǝn\ *n* : an intellectually and socially cultivated and exclusive person

¹**braid** \'brād\ *vb* **1** : to form (strands) into a braid : PLAIT; *also* : to make by braiding **2** : to ornament with braid

²**braid** *n* **1** : a cord or ribbon of three or more interwoven strands; *also* : a length of braided hair **2** : a narrow ornamental fabric of intertwined threads

**braille** \'brāl\ *n, often cap* : a system of writing for the blind that uses characters made up of raised dots

¹**brain** \'brān\ *n* **1** : the part of the vertebrate nervous system that is the organ of thought and nervous coordination, is made up of nerve cells and their fibers, and is enclosed in the skull; *also* : a centralized mass of nerve tissue in an invertebrate **2** : INTELLECT, INTELLIGENCE — often used in pl. —

**brained** \'brānd\ *adj* — **brain·less** *adj* — **brainy** *adj*

²**brain** *vb* **1 :** to kill by smashing the skull **2 :** to hit on the head

**brain·child** \-,chīld\ *n* **:** a product of one's creative imagination

**brain drain** *n* **:** a migration of professional people (as scientists) from one country to another usu. for higher pay

**brain·storm** \-,stȯrm\ *n* **:** a sudden burst of inspiration

**brain·wash·ing** \'brān-,wȯsh-in, -,wäsh-\ *n* **1 :** a forcible attempt by indoctrination to induce someone to give up his basic political, social, or religious beliefs and attitudes and to accept contrasting regimented ideas **2 :** persuasion by propaganda or salesmanship

**brain wave** *n* **:** rhythmic fluctuation of voltage between parts of the brain; *also* **:** a current produced by brain waves

**braise** \'brāz\ *vb* **braised; brais·ing :** to cook (meat) slowly in fat and little moisture in a covered dish

¹**brake** \'brāk\ **:** BRACKEN

²**brake** *n* **:** a device for slowing up or checking motion — **brake·less** *adj*

³**brake** *vb* **braked; brak·ing 1 :** to slow or stop by or as if by a brake **2 :** to apply a brake

⁴**brake** *n* **:** rough or wet land heavily overgrown (as with thickets or reeds)

**brake fluid** *n* **:** the liquid used in a hydraulic brake system

**brake·man** \'brāk-mən\ *n* **:** a train crew member whose duties include operating hand brakes and switches and checking the train mechanically

**bram·ble** \'bram-bəl\ *n* **:** any of a large genus of prickly shrubs related to the roses

**bran** \'bran\ *n* **:** broken husks of cereal grain sifted from flour or meal

¹**branch** \'branch\ *n* [ME, fr. OF *branche*, fr. L *branca* paw] **1 :** a natural subdivision (as a bough or twig) of a plant stem **2 :** a division (as of an antler or a river) related to a whole like a plant branch to its stem **3 :** a discrete unit or element of a complex system (as of knowledge, people, or business); *esp* **:** a division of a family descended from one ancestor

²**branch** *vb* **1 :** to develop branches **2 :** DIVERGE

¹**brand** \'brand\ *n* **1 :** a piece of charred or burning wood **2 :** a mark made (as by burning) usu. to identify; *also* **:** a mark of disgrace **:** STIGMA **3 :** a class of goods identified as the product of a particular firm or producer **4 :** a distinctive kind ⟨his own ∼ of humor⟩

²**brand** *vb* **1 :** to mark with a brand **2 :** STIGMATIZE

**bran·dish** \'bran-dish\ *vb* **:** to shake or wave menacingly   **syn** flourish, swing

**brand-new** \'bran-'n(y)ü\ *adj* **:** conspicuously new and unused

**bran·dy** \'bran-dē\ *n, pl* **brandies** [short for *brandywine*, fr. D *brandewijn*, fr. Middle Dutch *brantwijn*, fr. *brant*

distilled + *wijn* wine] **:** a liquor distilled from wine or fermented fruit juice — **brandy** *vb*

**brash** \'brash\ *adj* **1 :** IMPETUOUS **2 :** aggressively self-assertive

**brass** \'bras\ *n* **1 :** an alloy of copper and zinc; *also* **:** an object of brass **2 :** brazen self-assurance — **brassy** *adj*

**bras·se·rie** \,bras-(ə-)'rē\ *n* **:** a restaurant that sells beer

**brass hat** *n* **:** a high-ranking military officer

**bras·siere** \brə-'zir\ *n* **:** a woman's close-fitting undergarment designed to support the breasts

**brat** \'brat\ *n* **:** an ill-behaved child — **brat·ty** *adj*

**bra·va·do** \brə-'väd-ō\ *n, pl* **-does** or **-dos 1 :** blustering swaggering conduct **2 :** a show of bravery

¹**brave** \'brāv\ *adj* **brav·er; brav·est** [MF, fr. It & Sp *bravo* courageous, wild, fr. L *barbarus* barbarous] **1 :** showing courage **2 :** EXCELLENT, SPLENDID **syn** bold, intrepid — **brave·ly** *adv*

²**brave** *vb* **braved; brav·ing :** to face or endure bravely

³**brave** *n* **:** a No. American Indian warrior

**brav·ery** \'brāv-(ə-)rē\ *n, pl* **-er·ies :** COURAGE

**bra·vo** \'bräv-ō\ *n, pl* **bravos :** a shout of approval — often used as an interjection in applauding

**bra·vu·ra** \brə-'v(y)ür-ə\ *n* **1 :** a florid brilliant musical style **2 :** self-assured brilliant performance

**brawl** \'brȯl\ *n* **:** a noisy quarrel **syn** fracas, row, rumpus, scrap — **brawl** *vb* — **brawl·er** *n*

**brawn** \'brȯn\ *n* **:** strong muscles; *also* **:** muscular strength — **brawny** *adj*

**bray** \'brā\ *n* **:** the characteristic harsh cry of a donkey — **bray** *vb*

**braze** \'brāz\ *vb* **brazed; braz·ing :** to solder with a relatively infusible alloy (as brass) — **braz·er** *n*

**bra·zen** \'brāz-²n\ *adj* **1 :** made of brass **2 :** sounding harsh and loud **3 :** of the color of brass **4 :** marked by contemptuous boldness — **bra·zen·ly** *adv* — **bra·zen·ness** \'brāz-²n-(n)əs\ *n*

¹**bra·zier** \'brā-zhər\ *n* **:** a worker in brass

²**brazier** *n* **1 :** a vessel holding burning coals (as for heating) **2 :** a device on which food is exposed to heat through a wire grill

**Bra·zil·ian** \brə-'zil-yən\ *n* **:** a native or inhabitant of Brazil — **Brazilian** *adj*

**Bra·zil nut** \brə-,zil-\ *n* **:** the triangular oily edible nut borne in large capsules by a tall So. American tree; *also* **:** the tree

¹**breach** \'brēch\ *n* **1 :** a breaking of a law, obligation, tie (as of friendship), or standard (as of conduct) **2 :** an interruption or opening made by or as if by breaking through **syn** violation, transgression, infringement

²**breach** *vb* **:** to make a breach in

**¹bread** \'bred\ *n* **1** : baked food made basically of flour or meal **2** : FOOD

**²bread** *vb* : to cover with bread crumbs before cooking

**bread·bas·ket** \'bred-,bas-kət\ *n* : a major cereal-producing region

**bread·board** \-,bōrd\ *vb* : to make an experimental arrangement of (as an electronic circuit) — **breadboard** *n*

**bread·fruit** \-,früt\ *n* : a round usu. seedless fruit resembling bread in color and texture when baked; *also* : a tall tropical tree bearing breadfruit

**bread·stuff** \-,stəf\ *n* : GRAIN, FLOUR

**breadth** \'bredth\ *n* **1** : WIDTH **2** : SPACIOUSNESS; *also* : liberality of taste or views

**bread·win·ner** \'bred-,win-ər\ *n* : a member of a family whose wages supply its livelihood

**¹break** \'brāk\ *vb* **broke** \'brōk\; **bro·ken** \'brō-kən\; **break·ing** **1** : to separate into parts usu. suddenly or violently : come or force apart **2** : TRANSGRESS ⟨~ a law⟩ **3** : to force a way into, out of, or through **4** : to disrupt the order or unity of ⟨~ ranks⟩ ⟨~ up a gang⟩; *also* : to bring to submission or helplessness **5** : EXCEED, SURPASS ⟨~ a record⟩ **6** : RUIN **7** : to make known **8** : HALT, INTERRUPT; *also* : to act or change abruptly (as a course or activity) **9** : to come esp. suddenly into being or notice ⟨as day ~s⟩ **10** : to fail under stress **11** : HAPPEN, DEVELOP — **break·able** *adj or n*

**²break** *n* **1** : an act of breaking **2** : a result of breaking; *esp* : an interruption of continuity **3** : an awkward social blunder **4** : a stroke of good luck

**break·age** \'brā-kij\ *n* **1** : the action of breaking **2** : articles or amount broken **3** : allowance for things broken

**break·down** \'brāk-,daün\ *n* **1** : functional failure; *esp* : a physical, mental, or nervous collapse **2** : DISINTEGRATION **3** : DECOMPOSITION **4** : ANALYSIS, CLASSIFICATION — **break down** \(')brāk-'daün\ *vb*

**break·er** \'brā-kər\ *n* **1** : one that breaks **2** : a wave that breaks into foam (as against the shore)

**break·fast** \'brek-fəst\ *n* : the first meal of the day — **breakfast** *vb*

**break·front** \'brāk-,frənt\ *n* : a large cabinet whose center section projects beyond the flanking end sections

**break in** \(')brāk-'in\ *vb* **1** : to enter a building by force **2** : INTERRUPT; *also* : INTRUDE **3** : TRAIN

**break·out** \'brāk-,aüt\ *n* : a military attack to break from encirclement

**break out** \(')brāk-'aüt\ *vb* : to become affected with a skin eruption

**break·through** \'brāk-,thrü\ *n* **1** : an act or point of breaking through an obstruction or defensive line **2** : a sudden advance in knowledge or technique

**break·up** \'brāk-,əp\ *n* **1** : DISSOLUTION **2** : a division into smaller units

**break·wa·ter** \'brāk-,wȯt-ər, -,wät-\

*n* : a structure built to break the force of waves

**bream** \'brim\ *n, pl* **bream** *or* **breams** : any of various small freshwater sunfishes

**breast** \'brest\ *n* **1** : either of two milk-producing glandular organs situated on the front of the chest esp. in the human female; *also* : the front part of the chest **2** : something resembling a breast

**breast·bone** \'bres(t)-'bōn, -,bōn\ *n* : STERNUM

**breast–feed** \'brest-,fēd\ *vb* : to feed (a baby) from a mother's breast rather than from a bottle

**breast·plate** \'bres(t)-,plāt\ *n* : a metal plate of armor for protecting the breast

**breast·stroke** \-,strōk\ *n* : a swimming stroke executed by extending the arms in front of the head while drawing the knees forward and outward and then sweeping the arms back with palms out while kicking backward and outward

**breast·work** \'brest-,wərk\ *n* : a temporary fortification

**breath** \'breth\ *n* **1** : the act or power of breathing **2** : a slight breeze **3** : air inhaled or exhaled in breathing **4** : spoken sound **5** : SPIRIT — **breath·less** *adj* — **breath·less·ly** *adv*

**breathe** \'brēth\ *vb* **breathed**; **breath·ing** **1** : to draw air into and expel it from the lungs in respiration **2** : LIVE **3** : to halt for rest **4** : to utter softly or secretly

**breath·tak·ing** \'breth-,tā-kiŋ\ *adj* **1** : making one out of breath **2** : EXCITING, THRILLING ⟨~ beauty⟩

**brec·cia** \'brech-(ē-)ə\ *n* : a rock consisting of sharp fragments held in fine-grained material

**breech** \'brēch\ *n* **1** *pl* \usu 'brich-əz\ : trousers ending near the knee; *also* : PANTS **2** : BUTTOCKS, RUMP **3** : the rear part of a firearm behind the bore

**¹breed** \'brēd\ *vb* **bred** \'bred\; **breed·ing 1** : BEGET; *also* : ORIGINATE **2** : to propagate sexually; *also* : MATE **3** : to bring up : NURTURE **4** : to produce (fissionable material) from nonradioactive material **syn** generate, reproduce — **breed·er** *n*

**²breed** *n* **1** : a strain of similar and presumably related plants or animals usu. developed under the influence of man **2** : KIND, SORT, CLASS

**breed·ing** *n* **1** : ANCESTRY **2** : training in polite social interaction **3** : sexual propagation of plants or animals

**¹breeze** \'brēz\ *n* : a light wind — **breezy** *adj*

**²breeze** *vb* **breezed**; **breez·ing** : to progress quickly and easily

**breeze·way** \'brēz-,wā\ *n* : a roofed open passage usu. connecting two buildings (as a house and garage)

**breth·ren** \'breth-(ə-)rən, -ərn\ *pl of* BROTHER — used esp. in formal or solemn address

**Brethren** *n pl* : members of one of several Protestant denominations originating chiefly in a German religious movement and stressing personal religious experience

**bre·vet** \brĭ-'vet\ n : a commission giving a military officer higher nominal rank than that for which he receives pay — **brevet** vb

**bre·via·ry** \'brē-v(y)ə-rē, -vē-,er-ē\ n, pl **-ries** : a book of prayers, hymns, psalms, and readings used by Roman Catholic priests

**brev·i·ty** \'brev-ət-ē\ n, pl **-ties** 1 : shortness of duration 2 : CONCISENESS

**brew** \'brü\ vb : to prepare (as beer) by steeping, boiling, and fermenting — **brew** n — **brew·er** n — **brew·ery** \'brü-ə-rē, 'brü(-)r-ē\ n

**bri·ar** \'brī(-ə)r\ n : a tobacco pipe made from the root of a brier

¹**bribe** \'brīb\ vb **bribed; brib·ing** : to corrupt or influence (one in a position of trust) by favors or gifts — **brib·ery** \'brī-b(ə-)rē\ n

²**bribe** n [ME, something stolen, fr. MF, bread given to a beggar] : something offered or given in bribing

**bric-a-brac** \'brik-ə-,brak\ n pl : small ornamental articles

¹**brick** \'brik\ n : a block molded from moist clay and hardened by heat used esp. for building

²**brick** vb : to close, cover, or pave with bricks

**brick·bat** \'brik-,bat\ n 1 : a piece of a broken brick esp. when thrown as a missile 2 : an uncomplimentary remark

**brick·lay·er** \'brik-,lā-ər\ n : a person who builds or paves with bricks — **brick·lay·ing** \-,lā-iŋ\ n

¹**brid·al** \'brīd-ᵊl\ n [ME bridale, fr. OE brȳdealu, fr. brȳd bride + ealu ale] : MARRIAGE, WEDDING

²**bridal** adj : of or relating to a bride or a wedding

**bride** \'brīd\ n : a woman just married or about to be married

**bride·groom** \'brīd-,grüm, -,grùm\ n : a man just married or about to be married

**brides·maid** \'brīdz-,mād\ n : a woman who attends a bride at her wedding

¹**bridge** \'brij\ n 1 : a structure built over a depression or obstacle for use as a passageway 2 : something (as the upper part of the nose) resembling a bridge in form or function; also : a platform over the deck of a ship 3 : an artificial replacement for missing teeth

²**bridge** vb **bridged; bridg·ing** : to build a bridge over — **bridge·able** adj

³**bridge** n : a card game for four players developed from whist and usu. played as either **contract bridge** or **auction bridge**

**bridge·head** \-,hed\ n : an advanced position seized in enemy territory as a foothold

**bridge·work** \-,wərk\ n : the dental bridges in a mouth

¹**bri·dle** \'brīd-ᵊl\ n 1 : headgear with

which a horse is controlled 2 : CURB, RESTRAINT

²**bridle** vb **bri·dled; bri·dling** \'brīd-(ᵊ-)liŋ\ 1 : to put a bridle on; also : to restrain with or as if with a bridle 2 : to show hostility or scorn usu. by tossing the head

¹**brief** \'brēf\ adj 1 : short in duration or extent 2 : CONCISE; also : CURT — **brief·ly** adv — **brief·ness** n

²**brief** n 1 : a concise statement or document; esp : one summarizing a law client's case or a legal argument 2 pl : short snug drawers

³**brief** vb : to give final instructions or essential information to

**brief·case** \'brēf-,kās\ n : a flat flexible case for carrying papers

¹**bri·er** or **bri·ar** \'brī(-ə)r\ n : a plant (as a bramble or rose) with a thorny or prickly woody stem; also : a group or mass of brier bushes — **bri·ery** \'brī(-ə)r-ē\ adj

²**brier** n : a heath of southern Europe with a root used for making pipes

¹**brig** \'brig\ n : a 2-masted square-rigged sailing ship

²**brig** n : the place of confinement for offenders on a naval ship

³**brig** abbr 1 brigade 2 brigadier

**bri·gade** \brig-'ād\ n 1 : a military unit composed of a headquarters, one or more units of infantry or armored forces, and supporting units 2 : a group organized for a particular purpose (as fire-fighting)

**brig·a·dier general** \,brig-ə-,diər-\ n : a commissioned officer (as in the army) ranking next below a major general

**brig·and** \'brig-ənd\ n : BANDIT — **brig·and·age** \-ən-dij\ n

**brig·an·tine** \'brig-ən-,tēn\ n : a 2-masted square-rigged ship not carrying a square mainsail

**bright** \'brīt\ adj 1 : SHINING, RADIANT 2 : ILLUSTRIOUS, GLORIOUS 3 : INTELLIGENT, CLEVER; also : LIVELY, CHEERFUL syn brilliant, lustrous, beaming, smart — **bright·ly** adv — **bright·ness** n

**bright·en** \'brīt-ᵊn\ vb **bright·ened; bright·en·ing** \'brīt-(ᵊ-)niŋ\ : to make or become bright or brighter — **bright·en·er** \-(ᵊ-)nər\ n

¹**bril·liant** \'bril-yənt\ adj [F brillant, prp. of briller to shine, fr. It brillare, fr. brillo beryl, fr. L beryllus] 1 : very bright 2 : DISTINGUISHED, SPLENDID 3 : very intelligent syn radiant, lustrous, beaming, clever, bright, smart — **bril·liance** \-yəns\ or **bril·lian·cy** \-yən-sē\ n — **bril·liant·ly** adv

²**brilliant** n : a gem cut in a particular form with many facets

**bril·lian·tine** \'bril-yən-,tēn\ n : a usu. oily dressing for the hair

**brim** \'brim\ n : EDGE, RIM syn brink, border, verge — **brim·less** adj

**brim·ful** \-'fùl\ adj : full to the brim

**brim·stone** \'brim-,stōn\ n : SULFUR

**brin·dled** \'brin-dᵊld\ adj : having dark streaks or flecks on a gray or tawny ground

**brine** \'brīn\ n 1 : water saturated

with salt 2 : OCEAN — **brin·i·ness** \'brī-nē-nəs\ n — **briny** \'brī-nē\ adj

**bring** \'briŋ\ vb **brought** \'brȯt\; **bring·ing** \'briŋ-iŋ\ 1 : to cause to come with one 2 : INDUCE, PERSUADE, LEAD 3 : PRODUCE, EFFECT 4 : to sell for — **bring·er** n

**bring up** vb 1 : to give a parent's fostering care to 2 : to come or bring to a sudden halt 3 : to call to notice 4 : VOMIT

**brink** \'briŋk\ n 1 : an edge at the top of a steep place 2 : the point of onset

**brio** \'brē-ō\ n : VIVACITY, SPIRIT

**bri·oche** \brē-'ōsh, -'ȯsh\ n : a roll baked from light yeast dough rich with eggs and butter

**bri·quette** or **bri·quet** \brik-'et\ n : a consolidated often brick-shaped mass of fine material ⟨a charcoal ∼⟩

**brisk** \'brisk\ adj 1 : ALERT, LIVELY 2 : INVIGORATING syn agile, spry — **brisk·ly** adv — **brisk·ness** n

**bris·ket** \'bris-kət\ n : the breast or lower chest of a quadruped

**bris·ling** or **bris·tling** \'briz-liŋ, 'bris-\ n : a small sardinelike herring

¹**bris·tle** \'bris-əl\ n : a short stiff coarse hair — **bris·tly** \-(ə-)lē\ adj

²**bristle** vb **bris·tled**; **bris·tling** \'bris-(ə-)liŋ\ 1 : to stand stiffly erect 2 : to show angry defiance 3 : to appear as if covered with bristles

**Brit** abbr 1 Britain 2 British

**Bri·tan·nia metal** \bri-,tan-yə-, -,tan-ē-ə-\ n : a silver-white alloy of tin, antimony, and copper similar to pewter

**Bri·tan·nic** \bri-'tan-ik\ adj : BRITISH

**britch·es** \'brich-əz\ n pl : BREECHES, TROUSERS

**Brit·ish** \'brit-ish\ n pl : the people of Great Britain or the British Commonwealth — **British** adj

**British thermal unit** n : the quantity of heat needed to raise one pound of water one degree Fahrenheit

**Brit·on** \'brit-ᵊn\ n 1 : a member of a people inhabiting Britain before the Anglo-Saxon invasion 2 : a native or inhabitant of Great Britain

**brit·tle** \'brit-ᵊl\ adj **brit·tler** \'brit-(ᵊ-)lər\; **brit·tlest** \-ləst, -ᵊl-əst\ : easily broken or snapped : FRAGILE syn crisp

**bro** abbr brother

¹**broach** \'brōch\ n 1 : a pointed tool (as for opening casks) 2 : a bitlike tool for enlarging or shaping a hole

²**broach** vb 1 : to pierce (as a cask) in order to draw the contents 2 : to shape or enlarge a hole with a broach 3 : to introduce as a topic of conversation

¹**broad** \'brȯd\ adj 1 : WIDE 2 : SPACIOUS 3 : CLEAR, OPEN 4 : OBVIOUS 5 : COARSE, CRUDE ⟨∼ stories⟩ 6 : liberal in outlook 7 : GENERAL 8 : dealing with essential points — **broad·ly** adv — **broad·ness** n

²**broad** n, slang : WOMAN

**broad·band** \'brȯd-,band\ adj : of, having, or operating with uniform efficiency over a wide band of frequencies

¹**broad·cast** \-,kast\ n 1 : the trans-

mitting of sound or images by radio waves 2 : a single radio or television program

²**broadcast** vb **broadcast** also **broad·cast·ed**; **broad·cast·ing** 1 : to scatter or sow broadcast; also : to make widely known 2 : to send out or speak or perform on a radio or television broadcast — **broad·cast·er** n

**broad·cloth** \-,klȯth\ n 1 : a smooth dense woolen cloth 2 : a fine soft cloth of cotton, silk, or synthetic fiber

**broad·en** \'brȯd-ᵊn\ vb **broad·ened**; **broad·en·ing** \'brȯd-(ᵊ-)niŋ\ : WIDEN

**broad·loom** \-,lüm\ adj : woven on a wide loom; also : so woven in solid color ⟨a ∼ carpet⟩

**broad-mind·ed** \-'mīn-dəd\ adj : free from prejudice — **broad-mind·ed·ly** adv — **broad-mind·ed·ness** n

**broad·side** \-,sīd\ n 1 : the part of a ship's side above the waterline 2 : simultaneous discharge of all the guns on one side of a ship; also : a volley of abuse or denunciation 3 : a sheet printed on one or both sides and folded; also : something printed on a broadside

**broad-spectrum** adj : having a wide range esp. of effectiveness ⟨∼ antibiotics⟩

**broad·sword** \'brȯd-,sōrd\ n : a broad-bladed sword

**broad·tail** \-,tāl\ n : a flat and wavy fur or skin of a very young or premature lamb of a breed from Bukhara

**bro·cade** \brō-'kād\ n : a usu. silk fabric with a raised design

**broc·co·li** or **broc·o·li** \'bräk-(ə-)lē\ n [It, pl. of broccolo flowering top of a cabbage, dim. of brocco small nail, sprout, fr. L broccus projecting] : an open branching cauliflower whose young flowering shoots are used as a vegetable

**bro·chette** \brō-'shet\ n : SKEWER

**bro·chure** \brō-'shùr\ n [F, fr. brocher to sew, fr. MF, to prick, fr. OF brochier, fr. broche pointed tool] : PAMPHLET, BOOKLET

**bro·gan** \'brō-gən, brō-'gan\ n : a heavy shoe; esp : a work shoe reaching to the ankle

**brogue** \'brōg\ n : a dialect or regional pronunciation; esp : an Irish accent

**broi·der** \'brȯid-ər\ vb : EMBROIDER — **broi·dery** \'brȯid-(ə-)rē\ n

**broil** \'brȯil\ vb : to cook by exposure to radiant heat : GRILL — **broil** n

**broil·er** \'brȯi-lər\ n 1 : a utensil for broiling 2 : a young chicken fit for broiling

¹**broke** \'brōk\ past of BREAK

²**broke** adj : PENNILESS

**bro·ken** \'brō-kən\ adj 1 : SHATTERED 2 : having gaps or breaks : INTERRUPTED, DISRUPTED 3 : SUBDUED, CRUSHED 4 : BANKRUPT 5 : imperfectly spoken — **bro·ken·ly** adv

**bro·ken·heart·ed** \,brō-kən-'härt-əd\ adj : overcome by grief or despair

**bro·ker** \'brō-kər\ n : an agent who negotiates contracts of purchase and sale for a fee or commission; *also* **: DEALER**

**bro·ker·age** \'brō-k(ə-)rij\ *n* **1 :** the business of a broker **2 :** the fee or commission on business transacted through a broker

**bro·mide** \'brō-,mīd\ *n* **1 :** a compound of bromine and another element or a radical including some (as **potassium bromide**) used as sedatives **2 :** a trite remark or notion

**bro·mid·ic** \brō-'mid-ik\ *adj* **:** DULL, TIRESOME ⟨~ remarks⟩

**bro·mine** \'brō-,mēn\ *n* [F *brome* bromine, fr. Gk *brōmos* stink] **:** a deep red liquid corrosive chemical element that gives off an irritating vapor and occurs naturally only in combination

**bron·chi·al** \'brän-kē-əl\ *adj* **:** of, relating to, or affecting the bronchi or their branches

∥**bron·chi·tis** \brän-'kīt-əs, bräŋ-\ *n* **:** inflammation of the bronchi and their branches — **bron·chit·ic** \-'kit-ik\ *adj*

**bron·chus** \'bräŋ-kəs\ *n, pl* **bron·chi** \'bräŋ-,kī, -,kē\ **:** either of the main divisions of the windpipe each leading to a lung

**bron·co** \'bräŋ-kō\ *n, pl* **broncos** [MexSp, fr. Sp, rough, wild] **:** a small half-wild horse of western No. America

**bron·to·saur** \'bränt-ə-,sôr\ *also* **bron·to·sau·rus** \,bränt-ə-'sôr-əs\ *n* **:** any of various large 4-footed and prob. herbivorous dinosaurs

**Bronx cheer** \'bräŋks-\ *n* **:** RASPBERRY 2

¹**bronze** \'bränz\ *vb* **bronzed; bronzing :** to give the appearance of bronze to

²**bronze** *n* **1 :** an alloy basically of copper and tin; *also* **:** something made of bronze **2 :** a yellowish brown color — **bronzy**∥\'brän-zē\ *adj*

**brooch** \'brōch, 'brüch\ *n* **:** an ornamental clasp or pin

¹**brood** \'brüd\ *n* **:** a family of young animals or children and esp. of birds

²**brood** *vb* **1 :** to sit on eggs to hatch them; *also* **:** to shelter (hatched young) with the wings **2 :** to think anxiously or gloomily about something **:** PONDER

³**brood** *adj* **:** kept for breeding ⟨a ~ mare⟩

**brood·er** \'brüd-ər\ *n* **1 :** one that broods **2 :** a heated structure for raising young birds

¹**brook** \'brük\ *vb* **:** TOLERATE, BEAR

²**brook** *n* **:** a small natural stream of water

**brook·let** \-lət\ *n* **:** a small brook

**brook trout** *n* **:** a common speckled cold-water char of eastern No. America

**broom** \'brüm, 'brùm\ *n* **1 :** a shrub of the pea group with long slender branches and yellow flowers **2 :** an implement for sweeping orig. made from twigs — **broom·stick** \-,stik\ *n*

**bros** *abbr* brothers

**broth** \'brôth\ *n, pl* **broths** \'brôths, 'brôthz\ **1 :** liquid in which meat or sometimes vegetable food has been cooked **2 :** a fluid culture medium

**broth·el** \'bräth-əl, 'brôth-\ *n* **:** an establishment housing prostitutes

**broth·er** \'brəth-ər\ *n, pl* **brothers** *also* **breth·ren** \'breth-(ə-)rən, 'breth-ərn\ **1 :** a male having one or both parents in common with another individual; *also* **:** KINSMAN **2 :** a kindred human being **3 :** a man who is a religious but not a priest — **broth·er·li·ness**∥\-lē-nəs\ *n* — **broth·er·ly** \-lē\ *adj*

**broth·er·hood** \'brəth-ər-,hùd\ *n* **1 :** the state of being brothers or a brother **2 :** ASSOCIATION, FRATERNITY **3 :** the whole body of persons in a business or profession

**broth·er-in-law** \'brəth-(ə-)rən-,lò, 'brəth-ərn-,lò\ *n, pl* **brothers-in-law** \'brəth-ərz-ən-\ **:** the brother of one's spouse; *also* **:** the husband of one's sister or of one's spouse's sister

**brougham** \'brü(-ə)m, 'brō(-ə)m\ *n* **1 :** a light closed horse-drawn carriage with the driver outside in front **2 :** a coupe automobile; *esp* **:** one electrically driven **3 :** a sedan having no roof over the driver's seat

**brought** *past of* BRING

**brou·ha·ha** \brü-'hä-hä\ *n* **:** HUBBUB, UPROAR

**brow** \'braù\ *n* **1 :** the eyebrow or the ridge on which it grows; *also* **:** FOREHEAD **2 :** the projecting upper part of a steep place

**brow·beat** \'braù-,bēt\ *vb* **-beat; -beat·en** \-,bēt-ᵊn\ *or* **-beat; -beat·ing :** to intimidate by sternness or arrogance **:** BULLY *syn* intimidate

¹**brown** \'braùn\ *adj* **:** of the color brown; *also* **:** of dark or tanned complexion

²**brown** *n* **:** a color like that of coffee or chocolate that is a blend of red and yellow darkened by black — **brown·ish** *adj*

³**brown** *vb* **:** to make or become brown

**brown bag·ging** \-'bag-iŋ\ *n* **:** the practice of carrying a bottle of liquor into a restaurant or club where setups are available — **brown bag·ger** \-'bag-ər\ *n*

**brown·ie** \'braù-nē\ *n* **1 :** a cheerful goblin believed to do good deeds at night **2** *cap* **:** a member of the Girl Scouts from 7 through 9 years

**brown·out** \'braùn-,aùt\ *n* **:** a curtailment in electrical power; *also* **:** a period of reduced illumination due to such curtailment

**brown·stone** \-,stōn\ *n* **:** a dwelling faced with reddish brown sandstone

¹**browse** \'braùz\ *n* **:** tender shoots, twigs, and leaves fit for food for cattle

²**browse** *vb* **browsed; brows·ing 1 :** to feed on browse; *also* **:** GRAZE **2 :** to read bits at random in a book or collection of books

**bru·in** \'brü-ən\ *n* **:** BEAR

¹**bruise** \'brüz\ *vb* **bruised; bruis·ing :** a surface injury to flesh **:** CONTUSION

²**bruise** *n* **1 :** to inflict a bruise on; *also* **:** to become bruised **2 :** to break down by pounding ⟨~ garlic for a salad⟩

**bruis·er** \'brü-zər\ *n* **:** a big husky man

**bruit** \'brüt\ *vb* : to noise abroad

**brunch** \'brənch\ *n* : a late breakfast, early lunch, or combination of both

**bru·net** *or* **bru·nette** \brü-'net\ *adj* : of dark or relatively dark pigmentation; *esp* : having brown or black hair and eyes — **brunet** *n*

**brunt** \'brənt\ *n* : the main shock, force, or stress esp. of an attack

¹**brush** \'brəsh\ *n* **1** : small branches lopped from trees or shrubs **2** :THICKET; *also* : coarse shrubby vegetation

²**brush** *n* **1** : a device composed of bristles set in a handle and used esp. for cleaning or painting **2** : a bushy tail (as of a fox) **3** : an electrical conductor that makes contact between a stationary and a moving part of a generator or motor **4** : a light rubbing or touching

³**brush** *vb* **1** : to treat (as in cleaning or painting) with a brush **2** : to remove with or as if with a brush; *also* : to dispose of in an offhand manner **3** : to touch gently in passing

⁴**brush** *n* : SKIRMISH **syn** encounter

**brush-off** \'brəsh-,ȯf\ *n* : an abrupt or offhand dismissal

**brush up** *vb* : to renew one's skill

**brush·wood** \'brəsh-,wu̇d\ *n* : ¹BRUSH

**brusque** \'brəsk\ *adj* [F *brusque*, fr. It *brusco*, fr. ML *bruscus* a plant with stiff twigs used for brooms] : CURT, BLUNT, ABRUPT **syn** gruff, bluff — **brusque·ly** *adv*

**brus·sels sprout** \,brəs-əl(z)-\ *n*, *often cap B* : one of the edible small heads borne on the stalk of a cabbage-like plant; *also*, *pl* : this plant

**bru·tal** \'brüt-ºl\ *adj* : resembling or befitting a brute (as in coarseness or cruelty) — **bru·tal·i·ty** \brü-'tal-ət-ē\ *n* — **bru·tal·ly** \'brüt-ºl-ē\ *adv*

**bru·tal·ize** \'brüt-ºl-,īz\ *vb* **-ized; -iz·ing 1** : to make brutal **2** : to treat brutally

¹**brute** \'brüt\ *adj* [ME, fr. MF *brut* rough, fr. L *brutus* stupid, lit., heavy] **1** : of, relating to, or typical of beasts **2** : BRUTAL **3** : UNREASONING; *also* : purely physical

²**brute** *n* **1** : BEAST **2** : a brutal person **syn** animal

**brut·ish** \'brüt-ish\ *adj* **1** : BRUTE **1 2** : stupidly cruel or sensual; *also* : UNREASONING

**BS** *abbr* **1** bachelor of science **2** bill of sale

**BSA** *abbr* Boy Scouts of America

**BSc** *abbr* bachelor of science

**bskt** *abbr* basket

**btry** *abbr* battery

**Btu** *abbr* British thermal unit

**bu** *abbr* bushel

¹**bub·ble** \'bəb-əl\ *vb* **bub·bled; bub·ling** \'bəb-(ə-)liŋ\ : to form, rise in, or give off bubbles

²**bubble** *n* **1** : a globule of gas in a liquid **2** : a thin film of liquid filled with gas **3** : something lacking firmness or solidity — **bub·bly** \-(ə-)lē\ *adj*

**bu·bo** \'b(y)ü-bō\ *n*, *pl* **buboes** : an inflammatory swelling of a lymph gland

**bu·bon·ic plague** \b(y)ü-,bän-ik-\ *n* : a bacterial plague transmitted to man by flea bites and marked esp. by chills and fever and by buboes usu. in the groin

**buc·ca·neer** \,bək-ə-'niər\ *n* : PIRATE

¹**buck** \'bək\ *n*, *pl* **bucks 1** *or pl* **buck** : a male animal (as a deer or antelope) **2** : DANDY **3** *slang* : DOLLAR

²**buck** *vb* **1** : to spring with a quick plunging leap (a ~*ing* horse) **2** : to charge against something; *also* : to strive for advancement sometimes without regard to ethical behavior **3** : to charge into (the line in football)

**buck·board** \-,bōrd\ *n* : a 4-wheeled vehicle with a springy platform carrying the seat

**buck·et** \'bək-ət\ *n* **1** : PAIL **2** : an object resembling a bucket in collecting, scooping, or carrying something — **buck·et·ful** *n*

**bucket seat** *n* : a low separate seat for one person (as in an automobile)

**buck·eye** \'bək-,ī\ *n* : a tree related to the horse chestnut that occurs chiefly in the central U.S.; *also* : its large nutlike seed

**buck fever** *n* : nervous excitement of an inexperienced hunter at the sight of game

¹**buck·le** \'bək-əl\ *n* : a clasp (as on a belt) for two loose ends

²**buckle** *vb* **buck·led; buck·ling** \'bək-(ə-)liŋ\ **1** : to fasten with a buckle **2** : to apply oneself with vigor **3** : to crumple up : BEND, COLLAPSE

³**buckle** *n* : BEND, FOLD, KINK

**buck·ler** \'bək-lər\ *n* : SHIELD

**buck·ram** \'bək-rəm\ *n* : a coarse stiff cloth used esp. for binding books

**buck·saw** \'bək-,sȯ\ *n* : a saw set in a deep often H-shaped frame and used for sawing wood

**buck·shot** \'bək-,shät\ *n* : coarse lead shot used in shotgun shells

**buck·skin** \-,skin\ *n* **1** : the skin of a buck **2** : a soft usu. suede-finished leather — **buckskin** *adj*

**buck·tooth** \-'tüth\ *n* : a large projecting front tooth — **buck-toothed** \-'tütht\ *adj*

**buck·wheat** \-,hwēt\ *n* : an herb grown for its triangular seeds which are used as a cereal grain; *also* : these seeds

**bu·col·ic** \byü-'käl-ik\ *adj* [L *bucolicus*, fr. Gk *boukolikos*, fr. *boukolos* one who tends cattle, fr. *bous* head of cattle + *-kolos* (akin to L *colere* to cultivate)] : RURAL, RUSTIC

¹**bud** \'bəd\ *n* **1** : an undeveloped plant shoot (as of a leaf or a flower); *also* : a partly opened flower **2** : an asexual reproductive structure **3** : something not yet mature

²**bud** *vb* **bud·ded; bud·ding 1** : to form or put forth buds; *also* : to reproduce by asexual buds **2** : to be or develop like a bud **3** : to propagate a desired variety (as of peach) by inserting a bud in a plant of a different variety

**Bud·dhism** \'bü-,diz-əm, 'büd-,iz-\ *n* : a religion of eastern and central Asia growing out of the teachings of Gautama Buddha — **Bud·dhist** \'büd-əst, 'bùd-\ *n or adj*

**bud·dy** \'bəd-ē\ *n, pl* **buddies** : COMPANION; *esp* : a fellow soldier

**budge** \'bəj\ *vb* **budged; budg·ing** : MOVE, STIR, SHIFT

**bud·ger·i·gar** \'bəj-(ə-)rē-,gär, ,bəj-ə-'rē-\ *n* : a small Australian parrot raised in many colors for a pet

¹**bud·get** \'bəj-ət\ *n* [ME *bowgette*, fr. MF *bougette*, dim. of *bouge* leather bag, fr. L *bulga*] **1** : STOCK, SUPPLY **2** : a financial report containing estimates of income and expenses; *also* : a plan for coordinating income and expenses

²**budget** *vb* **1** : to allow for in a budget **2** : to draw up a budget

**bud·gie** \'bəj-ē\ *n* : BUDGERIGAR

¹**buff** \'bəf\ *n* **1** : a fuzzy-surfaced usu. oil-tanned leather; *also* : a garment of this **2** : a dull yellow-orange color **3** : FAN, ENTHUSIAST

²**buff** *adj* : of the color buff

³**buff** *vb* : POLISH, SHINE

**buf·fa·lo** \'bəf-ə-,lō\ *n, pl* **-lo** *or* **-loes** *also* **-los** : any of several wild oxen; *esp* : BISON

¹**buff·er** \'bəf-ər\ *n* : one that buffs

²**buffer** *n* : something that lessens shock (as from a physical or financial blow)

¹**buf·fet** \'bəf-ət\ *n* : BLOW, SLAP

²**buffet** *vb* **1** : to strike with the hand; *also* : to pound repeatedly **2** : to struggle against or on **syn** beat

³**buf·fet** \(,)bə-'fā, bü-\ *n* **1** : SIDEBOARD **2** : a counter for refreshments; *also* : a meal at which people serve themselves (as from a buffet)

**buf·foon** \(,)bə-'fün\ *n* [MF *bouffon*, fr. It *buffone*, fr. ML *bufon-, bufo*, fr. L, toad] : CLOWN **syn** fool, jester — **buf·foon·ery** \-(ə-)rē\ *n*

¹**bug** \'bəg\ *n* **1** : a small usu. obnoxious creeping or crawling creature (as a louse or spider); *esp* : any of a group of 4-winged sucking insects that includes many serious plant pests **2** : a disease-producing germ **3** : a concealed microphone

²**bug** \'bəg\ *vb* **bugged; bug·ging 1** : BOTHER, ANNOY **2** : to plant a concealed microphone in

**bug·a·boo** \'bəg-ə-,bü\ *n, pl* **-boos** : BOGEY

**bug·bear** \'bəg-,baər\ *n* : BOGEY; *also* : a source of dread

**bug·gy** \'bəg-ē\ *n, pl* **buggies** : a light carriage

**bu·gle** \'byü-gəl\ *n* [ME, buffalo, instrument made of buffalo horn, bugle, fr. OF, fr. L *buculus*, dim. of *bos* head of cattle] : a brass wind instrument resembling a trumpet but shorter — **bu·gler** \-glər\ *n*

¹**build** \'bild\ *vb* **built** \'bilt\; **build·ing 1** : to form or have formed by ordering and uniting materials (~ a house); *also* : to bring into being or develop **2** : ESTABLISH, FOUND (~ an argument on facts) **3** : INCREASE, ENLARGE; *also* : ENHANCE **4** : to engage in building — **build·er** *n*

²**build** *n* : form or mode of structure; *esp* : PHYSIQUE

**build·ing** \'bil-diŋ\ *n* **1** : a usu. roofed and walled structure (as a house) for permanent use **2** : the art or business of constructing buildings

**built-in** \'bil-'tin\ *adj* **1** : forming an integral part of a structure **2** : INHERENT

**bulb** \'bəlb\ *n* **1** : a large underground plant bud or bud group from which a new plant (as a lily or onion) can grow; *also* : a fleshy plant structure (as a tuber) resembling a bud **2** : a plant having or growing from a bulb **3** : a rounded, spheroidal, or pear-shaped object or part (as an electric lamp) — **bul·bous** \'bəl-bəs\ *adj*

**bul·bul** \'bùl-,bùl\ *n* : a Persian songbird

**Bul·gar·i·an** \,bəl-'gar-ē-ən, bùl-\ *n* : a native or inhabitant of Bulgaria — **Bulgarian** *adj*

¹**bulge** \'bəlj\ *n* : a swelling projecting part

²**bulge** *vb* **bulged; bulg·ing** : to become or cause to become protuberant

¹**bulk** \'bəlk\ *n* **1** : MAGNITUDE, VOLUME **2** : material (as indigestible fibrous residues of food) that forms a mass in the intestine **3** : a large mass **4** : the major portion

²**bulk** *vb* **1** : to have a bulky appearance : LOOM **2** : to be impressive or important

**bulk·head** \'bəlk-,hed\ *n* **1** : a partition separating compartments on a ship **2** : a retaining wall along a waterfront **3** : a structure built to cover a shaft or a cellar stairway

**bulky** \'bəl-kē\ *adj* **bulk·i·er; -est** : having bulk; *esp* : being large and unwieldly

¹**bull** \'bùl\ *n* **1** : the adult male of a bovine animal; *also* : a usu. adult male of various other large animals (as the elephant or walrus) **2** : one who buys securities or commodities in expectation of a price increase — **bull·ish** *adj*

²**bull** *adj* **1** : MALE **2** : large of its kind **3** : RISING (a ~ market)

³**bull** *n* [ME *bulle*, fr. ML *bulla*, fr. L, bubble, amulet] **1** : a papal letter **2** : EDICT

⁴**bull** *n* **1** : a grotesque blunder **2** *slang* : NONSENSE

⁵**bull** *abbr* bulletin

¹**bull·dog** \'bùl-,dòg\ *n* : a compact muscular short-haired dog of English origin

²**bulldog** *vb* : to throw (a steer) by seizing the horns and twisting the neck

**bull·doze** \-,dōz\ *vb* **1** : to move, clear, gouge out, or level off with a tractor-driven machine (**bull·doz·er**) having a broad blade or a ram for pushing **2** : to force as if by using a bulldozer

**bul·let** \'bùl-ət\ *n* [MF *boulette* small ball & *boulet* missile, dims. of *boule* ball] : a missile to be shot from a firearm — **bul·let·proof** \,bùl-ət-'prüf\ *adj*

**bul·le·tin** \'bùl-ət-ᵊn\ *n* **1** : a brief public report of a matter of public interest **2** : a periodical publication (as of a college) — **bulletin** vb

**bull·fight** \'bŭl-,fīt\ n : a spectacle in which men ceremonially excite and kill bulls in an arena — **bull·fight·er** n

**bull·finch** \-,finch\ n : a red-breasted English songbird often kept as a pet

**bull·frog** \-,frŏg, -,fräg\ n : FROG; esp : a large deep-voiced frog

**bull·head** \-,hed\ n : a large-headed fish (as a catfish)

**bull·head·ed** \-'hed-əd\ adj : stupidly stubborn : HEADSTRONG

**bul·lion** \'bŭl-yən\ n : gold or silver esp. in bars or ingots

**bull·ock** \'bŭl-ək\ n : a young bull; also : STEER

**bull pen** n : a place on a baseball field where relief pitchers warm up; also : the relief pitchers of a baseball team

**bull session** n : an informal discussion

**bull's-eye** \'bŭl-,zī\ n, pl **bull's-eyes** : the center of a target; also : a shot that hits the bull's-eye

**¹bul·ly** \'bŭl-ē\ n, pl **bullies** : a blustering fellow oppressive to others weaker than himself

**²bully** adj : EXCELLENT, FIRST-RATE — often used interjectionally

**³bully** vb **bul·lied; bul·ly·ing** : to behave as a bully toward : DOMINEER **syn** browbeat, intimidate

**bul·rush** \'bŭl-,rəsh\ n : a tall coarse rush or sedge

**bul·wark** \'bŭl-(,)wərk, -,wŏrk; 'bəl-(,)wərk\ n 1 : a wall-like defensive structure 2 : a strong support or protection in danger

**¹bum** \'bəm\ vb **bummed; bum·ming** 1 : to wander as a tramp; also : LOAF 2 : to seek or gain by begging

**²bum** n : an idle worthless fellow : LOAFER

**³bum** adj 1 : WORTHLESS ⟨~ advice⟩ 2 : DISABLED ⟨a ~ knee⟩

**bum·ble·bee** \'bəm-bəl-,bē\ n : a large hairy social bee that makes a loud humming sound in flight

**bum·mer** \'bəm-ər\ n, slang : an unpleasant experience; esp : a bad reaction to a hallucinogenic drug

**¹bump** \'bəmp\ vb 1 : to strike or knock forcibly; also : to move or alter by bumping 2 : to collide with

**²bump** n 1 : a sudden forceful blow or impact 2 : a local bulge; esp : a swelling of tissue — **bumpy** adj

**¹bum·per** \'bəm-pər\ n 1 : a cup or glass filled to the brim 2 : something unusually large — **bumper** adj

**²bump·er** \'bəm-pər\ n : a device for absorbing shock or preventing damage; esp : a metal bar at either end of an automobile

**bump·kin** \'bəmp-kən\ n : an awkward and unsophisticated country person

**bump·tious** \'bəmp-shəs\ adj : obtusely and often noisily self-assertive

**bun** \'bən\ n : a sweet biscuit or roll

**¹bunch** \'bənch\ n 1 : SWELLING 2 : CLUSTER, GROUP — **bunchy** adj

**²bunch** vb : to form into a group or bunch

**bun·co** or **bun·ko** \'bəŋ-kō\ n, pl **buncos** or **bunkos** : a swindling scheme — **bunco** vb

**¹bun·dle** \'bən-d²l\ n 1 : several items bunched and fastened together; also : something wrapped for carrying 2 : a considerable amount 3 : GROUP

**²bundle** vb **bun·dled; bun·dling** \'bənd-(²-)liŋ\ : to gather or tie in a bundle

**bun·dling** \'bənd-(²-)liŋ\ n : a former custom of a courting couple's occupying the same bed without undressing

**bung** \'bəŋ\ n : the stopper in the bunghole of a cask

**bun·ga·low** \'bəŋ-gə-,lō\ n : a one-storied dwelling with a low-pitched roof

**bung·hole** \'bəŋ-,hōl\ n : a hole for emptying or filling a cask

**bun·gle** \'bəŋ-gəl\ vb **bun·gled; bun·gling** \-g(ə-)liŋ\ : to do badly : BOTCH — **bungle** n — **bun·gler** \-g(ə-)lər\ n

**bun·ion** \'bən-yən\ n : an inflamed swelling of the first joint of the big toe

**¹bunk** \'bəŋk\ n : BED; esp : a built-in bed that is often one of a tier

**²bunk** n : BUNKUM, NONSENSE

**bun·ker** \'bəŋ-kər\ n 1 : a bin or compartment for storage (as for coal on a ship) 2 : a protective embankment or dugout; also : an embankment constituting a hazard on a golf course

**bun·kum** or **bun·combe** \'bəŋ-kəm\ n [Buncombe County, N.C.; fr. the defense of a seemingly irrelevant speech made by its congressional representative that he was speaking to Buncombe] : insincere or foolish talk

**bun·ny** \'bən-ē\ n, pl **-nies** : RABBIT

**Bun·sen burner** \,bən-sən-\ n : a gas burner usu. consisting of a straight tube with air holes at the bottom

**¹bunt** vb 1 : BUTT 2 : to push or tap a baseball lightly without swinging the bat

**²bunt** n : an act or instance of bunting; also : a bunted ball

**¹bun·ting** \'bənt-iŋ\ n : any of numerous small stout-billed finches

**²bunting** n : a thin fabric used esp. for flags; also : FLAGS

**¹buoy** \'bü-ē, 'bói\ n 1 : a floating object anchored in water to mark something (as a channel, shoal, or rock) 2 : a float consisting of a ring of buoyant material to support a person who has fallen into the water

**²buoy** vb 1 : to mark by a buoy 2 : to keep afloat 3 : to raise the spirits of

**buoy·an·cy** \'bói-ən-sē, 'bü-yən-\ n 1 : the quality of being able to float 2 : upward force exerted by a liquid or gas upon a body in or on it 3 : resilience of spirit — **buoy·ant** \-ənt, -yənt\ adj

**buq·sha** \'bük-shə\ n — see rial at MONEY table

**¹bur** \'bər\ var of BURR

**²bur** abbr bureau

**¹bur·den** \'bərd-²n\ n 1 : LOAD; also : CARE, RESPONSIBILITY 2 : something oppressive : ENCUMBRANCE 3 : CARGO; also : capacity for cargo

**²burden** vb **bur·dened; bur·den·ing**

\\'bərd-(ə-)niŋ\\ **:** LOAD, OPPRESS — **bur·den·some** \\-səm\\ *adj*

³**burden** *n* 1 **:** REFRAIN, CHORUS 2 **:** a main theme or idea **:** GIST

**bur·dock** \\'bər-,däk\\ *n* **:** a tall coarse herb with prickly flower heads

**bu·reau** \\'byúr-ō\\ *n, pl* **bureaus** *also* **bu·reaux** \\-ōz\\ [F, desk, cloth covering for desks, fr. OF *burel* woolen cloth, fr. L *burra* shaggy cloth] 1 **:** a chest of drawers for bedroom use 2 **:** an administrative unit (as of a government department) 3 **:** a business office

**bu·reau·cra·cy** \\byú-'räk-rə-sē\\ *n, pl* **-cies** 1 **:** a body of appointive government officials 2 **:** administration characterized by specialization of functions under fixed rules and a hierarchy of authority; *also* **:** an unwieldy administrative system deficient in initiative and flexibility — **bu·reau·crat** \\'byúr-ə-,krat\\ *n* — **bu·reau·crat·ic** \\,byúr-ə-'krat-ik\\ *adj*

**bu·rette** *or* **bu·ret** \\byú-'ret\\ *n* **:** a graduated glass tube with a small aperture for measuring fluids

**bur·gee** \\'bər-,jē, ,bər-'jē\\ *n* **:** a swallow-tailed flag used esp. by ships for signals or identification

**bur·geon** \\'bər-jən\\ *vb* **:** to put forth fresh growth (as from buds) **:** GROW vigorously **:** FLOURISH

**bur·gess** \\'bər-jəs\\ *n* 1 **:** a citizen of a borough 2 **:** an official or representative usu. of a borough

**burgh** \\'bər-ō\\ *n* **:** a Scottish town

**bur·gher** \\'bər-gər\\ *n* 1 **:** TOWNSMAN 2 **:** a prosperous social citizen

**bur·glary** \\'bər-glə-rē\\ *n, pl* **-glaries :** forcible entry into a building and esp. a dwelling with intent to steal — **bur·glar** \\-glər\\ *n* — **bur·glar·i·ous** \\,bər-'glar-ē-əs\\ *adj* — **bur·glar·ize** \\'bər-glə-,rīz\\ *vb*

**bur·gle** \\'bər-gəl\\ *vb* **bur·gled; bur·gling** \\-g(ə-)liŋ\\ **:** to commit burglary on

**bur·go·mas·ter** \\'bər-gə-,mas-tər\\ *n* **:** the chief magistrate of a town in some European countries

**Bur·gun·dy** \\'bər-gən-dē\\ *n, pl* **-dies :** a dry red or white table wine

**buri·al** \\'ber-ē-əl\\ *n* **:** the act or process of burying

**burl** \\'bərl\\ *n* **:** a hard woody often flattened hemispherical outgrowth on a tree

**bur·lap** \\'bər-,lap\\ *n* **:** a coarse fabric usu. of jute or hemp used esp. for bags

¹**bur·lesque** \\(,)bər-'lesk\\ *n* [*burlesque*, adj. (comic, droll), fr. F, fr. It *burlesco*, fr. *burla* joke, fr. Sp] 1 **:** a witty or derisive literary or dramatic imitation 2 **:** broadly humorous theatrical entertainment consisting of several items (as songs, skits, or dances)

²**burlesque** *vb* **bur·lesqued; bur·lesqu·ing :** to make ludicrous by burlesque **:** MOCK  **syn** caricature, parody

**bur·ly** \\'bər-lē\\ *adj* **bur·li·er; -est :** strongly and heavily built **:** HUSKY **syn** muscular, brawny

**Bur·mese** \\,bər-'mēz, -'mēs\\ *n, pl* **Burmese :** a native or inhabitant of Burma — **Burmese** *adj*

¹**burn** \\'bərn\\ *vb* **burned** \\'bərnd, 'bərnt\\ *or* **burnt** \\'bərnt\\; **burn·ing** 1 **:** to be on fire 2 **:** to feel or look as if on fire 3 **:** to alter or become altered by or as if by the action of fire or heat 4 **:** to use as fuel ⟨~ coal⟩; *also* **:** to destroy by fire ⟨~ trash⟩ 5 **:** to cause or make by fire ⟨~ a hole⟩; *also* **:** to affect as if by heat

²**burn** *n* **:** an injury or effect produced by burning

**burn·er** \\'bər-nər\\ *n* **:** the part of a fuel-burning device where the flame is produced

**bur·nish** \\'bər-nish\\ *vb* **:** to polish usu. with something hard and smooth — **bur·nish·er** *n* — **bur·nish·ing** *adj or n*

**bur·noose** *or* **bur·nous** \\(,)bər-'nüs\\ *n* **:** a hooded cloak worn esp. by Arabs

**burn·out** \\'bərn-,aút\\ *n* **:** the cessation of operation of a jet or rocket engine

**burp** \\'bərp\\ *n* **:** an act of belching — **burp** *vb*

**burp gun** *n* **:** a small submachine gun

**burr** \\'bər\\ *n* 1 *usu* **bur :** a rough or prickly envelope of a fruit; *also* **:** a plant that bears burs 2 **:** a roughness left on metal that has been cut or shaped (as by a drill) 3 **:** WHIR — **bur·ry** *adj*

**bur·ro** \\'bər-ō, 'búr-\\ *n, pl* **burros :** a usu. small donkey

¹**bur·row** \\'bər-ō\\ *n* **:** a hole in the ground made by an animal (as a rabbit)

²**burrow** *vb* 1 **:** to form by tunneling ⟨~ a way through the snow⟩; *also* **:** to make a burrow 2 **:** to progress by or as if by digging — **bur·row·er** *n*

**bur·sar** \\'bər-sər\\ *n* **:** a treasurer esp. of a college

**bur·si·tis** \\(,)bər-'sīt-əs\\ *n* **:** inflammation of the serous sac (**bur·sa** \\'bər-sə\\) of a joint (as the elbow or shoulder)

¹**burst** \\'bərst\\ *vb* **burst** *or* **burst·ed; burst·ing** 1 **:** to fly apart or into pieces 2 **:** suddenly to give vent to **:** PLUNGE ⟨~ into song⟩ 3 **:** to enter or emerge suddenly **:** SPRING 4 **:** to be filled to the breaking point

²**burst** *n* 1 **:** a sudden outbreak or effort **:** SPURT 2 **:** EXPLOSION 3 **:** an act or result of bursting

**Bu·run·di·an** \\bú-'rün-dē-ən\\ *n* **:** a native or inhabitant of Burundi

**bury** \\'ber-ē\\ *vb* **bur·ied; bury·ing** 1 **:** to deposit in the earth; *also* **:** to inter with funeral ceremonies 2 **:** CONCEAL, HIDE

¹**bus** \\'bəs\\ *n, pl* **bus·es** *or* **bus·ses** [short for *omnibus*, fr. F, fr. L, for all, dat. pl. of *omnis* all] **:** a large motor-driven passenger vehicle

²**bus** *vb* **bused** *or* **bussed; bus·ing** *or* **bus·sing** 1 **:** to travel or transport by bus 2 **:** to work as a busboy

³**bus** *abbr* business

**bus·boy** \\'bəs-,bòi\\ *n* **:** a waiter's helper

**bus·by** \\'bəz-bē\\ *n, pl* **busbies :** a military full-dress fur hat

**bush** \\'búsh\\ *n* 1 **:** SHRUB 2 **:** rough uncleared country 3 **:** a thick tuft or mat — **bushy** *adj*

**bushed** \'bush̀t\ *adj* : TIRED, EXHAUSTED

**bush·el** \'bush̀-əl\ *n* — see WEIGHT table

**bush·ing** \'bush̀-iŋ\ *n* : a metal lining used as a guide or as a bearing (as for an axle or shaft)

**bush·mas·ter** \'bush̀-mas-tər\ *n* : a large venomous tropical American snake

**bush·whack** \-,hwak\ *vb* 1 : to live or hide out in the woods 2 : AMBUSH — **bush·whack·er** *n*

**busi·ly** \'biz-ə-lē\ *adv* : in a busy manner

**busi·ness** \'biz-nəs, -nəz\ *n* 1 : OCCUPATION, CALLING; *also* : TASK, MISSION 2 : a commercial or industrial enterprise; *also* : TRADE ⟨~ is good⟩ 3 : AFFAIR, MATTER 4 : personal concerns **syn** work, commerce, industry

**busi·ness·man** \-,man\ *n* : a man engaged in business esp. as an executive — **busi·ness·wom·an** \-,wùm-ən\ *n*

**bus·kin** \'bəs-kən\ *n* 1 : a laced half boot 2 : tragic drama

**bus·man's holiday** \,bəs-mənz-\ *n* : a holiday spent in following or observing the practice of one's usual occupation

**buss** \'bəs\ *n* : KISS — **buss** *vb*

¹**bust** \'bəst\ *n* [F *buste,* fr. It *busto,* fr. L *bustum* tomb] 1 : sculpture representing the upper part of the human figure 2 : the part of the human torso between the neck and the waist; *esp* : the breasts of a woman

²**bust** *vb* **bust·ed** *also* **bust; bust·ing** 1 : BREAK, SMASH; *also* : BURST 2 : DEMOTE 3 : TAME 4 *slang* : ARREST 5 : to go broke

³**bust** *n* 1 : PUNCH, SOCK 2 : a complete failure : FLOP 3 : a business depression 4 *slang* : a police raid

¹**bus·tle** \'bəs-əl\ *vb* **bus·tled; bus·tling** \'bəs-(ə-)liŋ\ : to move or work in a brisk fussy way

²**bustle** *n* : briskly energetic activity

³**bustle** *n* : a pad or frame formerly worn to swell out the fullness at the back of a women's skirt

¹**busy** \'biz-ē\ *adj* **busi·er; -est** 1 : engaged in action : not idle 2 : being in use ⟨~ telephones⟩ 3 : full of activity ⟨~ streets⟩ 4 : OFFICIOUS **syn** industrious, diligent

²**busy** *vb* **bus·ied; busy·ing** : to make or keep busy : OCCUPY

**busy·body** \'biz-ē-,bäd-ē\ *n* : MEDDLER

**busy·work** \-,wərk\ *n* : work that appears productive but only keeps one occupied

¹**but** \('))bət\ *conj* 1 : except for the fact ⟨would have protested ~ that he was afraid⟩ 2 : as to the following, namely ⟨there's no doubt ~ he's the guilty one⟩ 3 : without the concomitant that ⟨never rains ~ it pours⟩ 4 : on the contrary ⟨not one, ~ two job offers⟩ 5 : yet nevertheless ⟨would like to go, ~ I can't⟩; *also* : while on the contrary ⟨would like to go ~ he is busy⟩ 6 : yet also ⟨came home sadder ~ wiser⟩ ⟨poor ~ proud⟩

²**but** *prep* : other than : EXCEPT ⟨there's no one here ~ me⟩

**bu·tane** \'byü-,tān\ *n* : either of two gaseous hydrocarbons used as a fuel

¹**butch·er** \'bùch-ər\ *n* [ME *bocher,* fr. OF *bouchier,* fr. *bouc* he-goat] 1 : one who slaughters animals or dresses their flesh; *also* : a dealer in meat 2 : one who kills brutally or needlessly — **butch·ery** \-(ə-)rē\ *n*

²**butcher** *vb* **butch·ered; butch·er·ing** \-(ə-)riŋ\ 1 : to slaughter and dress for meat ⟨~ hogs⟩ 2 : to kill barbarously

**but·ler** \'bət-lər\ *n* [ME *buteler,* fr. OE *bouteillier* bottle bearer, fr. *bouteille* bottle] : the chief male servant of a household

¹**butt** \'bət\ *vb* : to strike with the head or horns

²**butt** *n* : a blow or thrust with the head or horns

³**butt** *n* 1 : TARGET 2 : an object of abuse or ridicule

⁴**butt** *vb* 1 : ABUT 2 : to place or join edge to edge without overlapping

⁵**butt** *n* : a large, thicker, or bottom end of something

⁶**butt** *n* 1 : a large cask 2 : a varying measure for liquid

**butte** \'byüt\ *n* : an isolated steep-sided hill

¹**but·ter** \'bət-ər\ *n* [ME, fr. OE *butere,* fr. L *butyrum* butter, fr. Gk *boutyron,* fr. *bous* cow + *tyros* cheese] 1 : a solid edible emulsion of fat obtained from cream by churning 2 : a substance resembling butter — **but·tery** *adj*

²**butter** *vb* : to spread with butter

**but·ter-and-eggs** \,bət-ə-rə-'negz\ *n sing or pl* : a common perennial herb related to the snapdragon that has showy yellow and orange flowers

**but·ter·cup** \'bət-ər-,kəp\ *n* : a usu. 5-petaled yellow-flowered herb

**but·ter·fat** \-,fat\ *n* : the natural fat of milk and chief constituent of butter

**but·ter·fin·gered** \-,fiŋ-gərd\ *adj* : likely to let things fall or slip through the fingers — **but·ter·fin·gers** \-gərz\ *n sing or pl*

**but·ter·fly** \-,flī\ *n* : any of a group of slender day-flying insects with four broad wings covered with brightly colored scales

**but·ter·milk** \'bət-ər-,milk\ *n* : the liquid remaining after butter is churned

**but·ter·nut** \-,nət\ *n* : the edible oily nut of an American tree related to the walnut; *also* : this tree

**but·ter·scotch** \-,skäch\ *n* : a candy made from sugar, corn syrup, and water; *also* : the flavor of such candy

**but·tock** \'bət-ək\ *n* 1 : the back of a hip that forms one of the fleshy parts on which a person sits 2 *pl* : the seat of the body : RUMP

¹**but·ton** \'bət-ᵊn\ *n* 1 : a small knob secured to an article (as of clothing) and used as a fastener by passing it through a buttonhole or loop 2 : a buttonlike part, object, or device

²**but·ton** \'bət-ᵊn\ *vb* **but·toned; but-**

**ton·ing** \'bət-(ə-)niŋ\ **:** to close or fasten with buttons

**¹but·ton·hole** \'bət-²n-,hōl\ *n* **:** a slip or loop for a button to pass through

**²buttonhole** *vb* **:** to detain in conversation by or as if by holding on to the outer garments of

**but·ton·hook** \'bət-²n-,hůk\ *n* **:** a hook for drawing small buttons through buttonholes

**¹but·tress** \'bət-rəs\ *n* **1 :** a projecting structure to support a wall **2 :** PROP, SUPPORT

**²buttress** *vb* **:** PROP, SUPPORT

**bu·tut** \bù-'tüt\ *n* — see *dalasi* at MONEY table

**bux·om** \'bək-səm\ *adj* **:** healthily plump; *esp* **:** full-bosomed

**¹buy** \'bī\ *vb* **bought** \'bȯt\; **buying :** to obtain for a price **:** PURCHASE; *also* **:** BRIBE — **buy·er** *n*

**²buy** *n* **1 :** PURCHASE 1, 2 **2 :** an exceptional value

**¹buzz** \'bəz\ *vb* **1 :** to make a buzz **2 :** to fly low and fast over in an airplane

**²buzz** *n* **:** a low humming sound (as of bees in flight)

**buz·zard** \'bəz-ərd\ *n* **1 :** a heavy slow-flying hawk **2 :** an American vulture

**buzz·er** \'bəz-ər\ *n* **:** a device that signals with a buzzing sound

**buzz saw** *n* **:** a circular saw having teeth on its periphery and revolving on a spindle

**BV** *abbr* Blessed Virgin

**BWI** *abbr* British West Indies

**bx** *abbr* box

**BX** *abbr* base exchange

**¹by** \(')bī, bə\ *prep* **1 :** NEAR ⟨stood ~ the window⟩ **2 :** through or through the medium of **:** VIA ⟨left ~ the door⟩ **3 :** PAST ⟨drove ~ the house⟩ **4 :** DURING, AT ⟨studied ~ night⟩ **5 :** no later than ⟨get here ~ 3 p.m.⟩ **6 :** through the means or direct agency of ⟨got it ~ fraud⟩ ⟨was seen ~ the others⟩ **7 :** in

conformity with **:** according to ⟨did it ~ the book⟩ **8 :** with respect to ⟨an electrician ~ trade⟩ **9 :** to the amount or extent of ⟨won ~ a nose⟩ ⟨overpaid ~ $3⟩ **10** — used to express relationship in multiplication, division, and in measurements ⟨divide $a \sim b$⟩ ⟨multiply ~ 6⟩ ⟨15 feet ~ 20 feet⟩

**²by** \'bī\ *adv* **1 :** near at hand; *also* **:** IN ⟨stopped ~ to chat⟩ **2 :** PAST **3 :** ASIDE, APART

**bye** \'bī\ *n* **:** a position of a participant in a tournament who has no opponent after pairs are drawn and advances to the next round without playing

**by-elec·tion** *also* **bye-election** \'bī-ə-,lek-shən\ *n* **:** a special election held between regular elections in order to fill a vacancy

**by·gone** \'bī-,gȯn\ *adj* **:** gone by **:** PAST — **bygone** *n*

**by·law** *or* **bye-law** \'bī-,lȯ\ *n* **:** a rule adopted by an organization for managing its internal affairs

**by-line** \'bī-,līn\ *n* **:** a line at the head of a newspaper or magazine article giving the writer's name

**¹by·pass** \'bī-,pas\ *n* **:** a way around something; *esp* **:** an alternate route

**²bypass** *vb* **:** to avoid by means of a bypass

**by-path** \-,path, -,päth\ *n* **:** BYWAY

**by-play** \'bī-,plā\ *n* **:** action engaged in at the side of a stage while the main action proceeds

**by-prod·uct** \-,präd-(,)əkt\ *n* **:** something produced (as in manufacturing) in addition to the main product

**by·stand·er** \-,stan-dər\ *n* **:** one present but not participating **syn** onlooker, witness, spectator

**byte** \'bīt\ *n* **:** a group of binary digits often shorter than a word that a computer processes as a unit ⟨an 8-bit ~⟩

**by·way** \'bī-,wā\ *n* **:** a side road; *also* **:** a secondary aspect

**by·word** \-,wərd\ *n* **1 :** PROVERB **2 :** an object of scorn

---

**¹c** \'sē\ *n, pl* **c's** *or* **cs** \'sēz\ *often cap* **1 :** the 3d letter of the English alphabet **2 :** a grade rating a student's work as fair

**²c** *abbr, often cap* **1** cape **2** carat **3** cent **4** centigrade **5** centimeter **6** century **7** chapter **8** circa **9** cobalt **10** cocaine **11** copyright

**C** *symbol* carbon

**ca** *abbr* circa

**Ca** *symbol* calcium

**CA** *abbr* **1** California **2** chartered accountant **3** chief accountant **4** chronological age

**cab** \'kab\ *n* **1 :** a light closed horse-drawn carriage **2 :** TAXICAB **3 :** the covered compartment for the engineer and operating controls of a locomotive; *also* **:** a similar structure (as on a truck) — **cab·man** \-mən\ *n*

**CAB** *abbr* Civil Aeronautics Board

**¹ca·bal** \kə-'bal\ *n* [F *cabale*, fr. ML

*cabbala* cabala, fr. Heb *quabbālāh*, lit., received (lore)] **:** a secret group of plotters or political conspirators

**²cabal** *vb* **ca·balled**; **ca·bal·ling :** to unite in or form a cabal

**ca·ba·la** \'kab-ə-lə, kə-'bäl-ə\ *n, often cap* **1 :** a medieval Jewish mysticism marked by belief in creation through emanation and a cipher method of interpreting scriptures **2 :** esoteric doctrine or belief

**ca·bana** \kə-'ban-(y)ə\ *n* **:** a shelter usu. with an open side facing a beach or swimming pool

**cab·a·ret** \,kab-ə-'rā\ *n* **:** a restaurant providing liquor and entertainment; *also* **:** the show provided

**cab·bage** \'kab-ij\ *n* [ME *caboche*, fr. OF head] **:** a vegetable related to the turnip and grown for its dense head of leaves

**cab·by** *or* **cab·bie** \'kab-ē\ *n, pl* **cabbies :** a driver of a cab

**cab·in** \'kab-ən\ *n* **1** : a private room on a ship; *also* : a compartment below deck on a small boat for passengers or crew **2** : a small simple one-story house **3** : an airplane compartment for passengers, crew, or cargo

**cabin boy** *n* : a boy acting as servant on a ship

**cabin class** *n* : a class of accommodations on a passenger ship superior to tourist class and inferior to first class

**cabin cruiser** *n* : CRUISER 2

**cab·i·net** \'kab-(ə-)nət\ *n* **1** : a case or cupboard for holding or displaying articles (as jewels, specimens, or documents) **2** : an upright case housing a radio or television receiver **3** *archaic* : a private room for consultations **4** : the advisory council of a head of state (as a president or sovereign)

**cab·i·net·mak·er** \-,mā-kər\ *n* : a woodworker who makes fine furniture — **cab·i·net·mak·ing** \-,mā-kiŋ\ *n*

**cab·i·net·work** \-,wərk\ *n* : the finished work of a cabinetmaker

**¹ca·ble** \'kā-bəl\ *n* **1** : a very strong rope, wire, or chain **2** : CABLEGRAM **3** : a bundle of insulated wires for carrying electric current

**²cable** *vb* **ca·bled; ca·bling** \'kā-b(ə-)liŋ\ : to telegraph by submarine cable

**cable car** *n* : a car moved along rails by an endless cable operated by a stationary engine or along an overhead cable

**ca·ble·gram** \'kā-bəl-,gram\ *n* : a message sent by a submarine telegraph cable

**cable TV** *n* : COMMUNITY ANTENNA TELEVISION

**cab·o·chon** \'kab-ə-,shän\ *n* : a gem or bead cut in convex form and highly polished but not given facets; *also* : this style of cutting — **cabochon** *adv*

**ca·boose** \kə-'büs\ *n* : a car usu. at the rear of a freight train for the use of the train crew and railroad workmen

**cab·ri·o·let** \,kab-rē-ə-'lā\ *n* **1** : a light 2-wheeled one-horse carriage **2** : a convertible coupe

**cab·stand** \'kab-,stand\ *n* : a place for cabs to park while waiting for passengers

**ca·cao** \kə-'kaù, -'kā-ō\ *n, pl* **cacaos** : a So. American tree whose seeds (**cacao beans**) are the source of cocoa and chocolate

**cac·cia·to·re** \,käch-ə-'tōr-ē\ *adj* : cooked with tomatoes and herbs ⟨veal ∼⟩

**¹cache** \'kash\ *n* : a hiding place esp. for concealing and preserving provisions; *also* : something hidden or stored in a cache

**²cache** *vb* **cached; cach·ing** : to place or store in a cache

**ca·chet** \ka-'shā\ *n* **1** : a seal used esp. as a mark of official approval **2** : a feature or quality conferring prestige; *also* : PRESTIGE **3** : a flour paste capsule for medicine **4** : a design, inscription, or advertisement printed or stamped on mail

**cack·le** \'kak-əl\ *vb* **cack·led; cack·ling** \-(ə-)liŋ\ **1** : to make the sharp

broken cry characteristic of a hen **2** : to laugh in a way suggestive of a hen's cackle **3** : CHATTER 2 — **cackle** *n* — **cack·ler** \-(ə-)lər\ *n*

**ca·coph·o·ny** \ka-'käf-ə-nē\ *n, pl* **-nies** : harsh or discordant sound — **ca·coph·o·nous** \-nəs\ *adj*

**cac·tus** \'kak-təs\ *n, pl* **cac·ti** \-,tī\ *or* **cac·tus·es** : any of a large group of drought-resistant flowering plants with fleshy usu. jointed stems and with leaves replaced by scales or prickles

**cad** \'kad\ *n* : an ungentlemanly person — **cad·dish** \-ish\ *adj* — **cad·dish·ly** *adv* — **cad·dish·ness** *n*

**ca·dav·er** \kə-'dav-ər\ *n* : a dead body : CORPSE

**ca·dav·er·ous** \kə-'dav-(ə-)rəs\ *adj* : suggesting a corpse esp. in gauntness or pallor **syn** wasted — **ca·dav·er·ous·ly** *adv*

**cad·die** *or* **cad·dy** \'kad-ē\ *n, pl* **caddies** [F *cadet* military cadet] : one that assists a golfer esp. by carrying his clubs — **caddie** *or* **caddy** *vb*

**cad·dy** \'kad-ē\ *n, pl* **caddies** [Malay *kati* a unit of weight] : a small box or chest; *esp* : one to keep tea in

**ca·dence** \'kād-°ns\ *n* : the measure or beat of a rhythmical flow : RHYTHM — **ca·denced** \-°nst\ *adj*

**ca·den·za** \kə-'den-zə\ *n* : a brilliant sometimes improvised passage usu. toward the close of a musical composition

**ca·det** \kə-'det\ *n* [F, fr. F dial. *capdet* chief, fr. L *capitellum*, fr. L *caput* head] **1** : a younger son or brother **2** : a student in a service academy

**Ca·dette scout** \kə-,det-\ *n* : a member of the Girl Scouts from 12 through 14 years of age

**cadge** \'kaj\ *vb* **cadged; cadg·ing** : SPONGE, BEG — **cadg·er** *n*

**cad·mi·um** \'kad-mē-əm\ *n* : a grayish metallic chemical element used in protective platings and bearing metals

**cad·re** \'kad-rē\ *n* **1** : FRAMEWORK **2** : a nucleus esp. of trained personnel capable of assuming control and training others

**ca·du·ceus** \kə-'d(y)ü-sē-əs, -shəs\ *n, pl* **-cei** \-sē-,ī\ **1** : the staff of a herald; *esp* : a representation of a staff with two entwined snakes and two wings at the top **2** : an insignia bearing a caduceus and symbolizing a physician

**cae·cum** *var of* CECUM

**Cae·sar** \'sē-zər\ *n* **1** : any of the Roman emperors succeeding Augustus Caesar — used as a title **2** *often not cap* : a powerful ruler : AUTOCRAT, DICTATOR; *also* : the civil or temporal power

**cae·sura** \si-'z(h)ùr-ə, -'zyùr-\ *n, pl* **-suras** *or* **-su·rae** \-'z(h)ùr-(,)ē\ : a break in the flow of sound usu. in the middle of a line of verse

**CAF** *abbr* cost and freight

**ca·fé** \ka-'fā, kə-\ *n* **1** : RESTAURANT **2** : BARROOM **3** : CABARET

**ca·fé au lait** \(,)ka-,fā-ō-'lā\ *n* : coffee with hot milk in about equal parts

**caf·e·te·ria** \,kaf-ə-'tir-ē-ə\ *n* [AmerSp *cafetería* retail coffee store, fr. Sp *café* coffee] **:** a restaurant in which the customers serve themselves or are served at a counter and take the food to tables

**caf·feine** \ka-'fēn, 'ka-ˌfēn\ *n* **:** a stimulating alkaloid found esp. in coffee and tea

**caf·tan** \kaf-'tan, 'kaf-ˌtan\ *n* [Russ *kaftan*, fr. Turk, fr. Per *qaftān*] **:** an ankle-length garment with long sleeves worn in the Levant

**¹cage** \'kāj\ *n* **1 :** an openwork enclosure for confining an animal **2 :** something resembling a cage **3 :** a sheer one-piece dress that has no waistline, is often gathered at the neck, and is worn over a close-fitting dress or slip

**²cage** *vb* **caged; cag·ing :** to put or keep in or as if in a cage

**cage·ling** \'kāj-liŋ\ *n* **:** a caged bird

**ca·gey** *also* **ca·gy** \'kā-jē\ *adj* **ca·gi·er; -est :** wary of being trapped or deceived **: SHREWD — ca·gi·ly** \'kā-jə-lē\ *adv* **— ca·gi·ness** \-jē-nəs\ *n*

**ca·hoot** \kə-'hüt\ *n* **:** PARTNERSHIP, LEAGUE — usu. used in pl. ⟨officials in ~s with the underworld⟩

**cai·man** \kā-'man, kī-; 'kā-mən\ *n* **:** any of several Central and So. American relatives of the crocodiles

**cairn** \'kaərn\ *n* **:** a heap of stones serving as a memorial or a landmark

**cais·son** \'kā-ˌsän, 'kās-ᵊn\ *n* **1 :** a usu. 2-wheeled vehicle for artillery ammunition **2 :** a watertight chamber used in underwater construction work or as a foundation

**caisson disease** *n* **: BEND 3**

**cai·tiff** \'kāt-əf\ *adj* [ME *caitif*, fr. OF, captive, vile, fr. L *captivus* captive] **:** being base, cowardly, or despicable — **caitiff** *n*

**ca·jole** \kə-'jōl\ *vb* **ca·joled; ca·jol·ing** [F *cajoler* to chatter like a caged jay, cajole, fr. MF *gaioler*, fr OF *gaiole* cage] **:** to persuade or coax esp. with flattery or false promises **: WHEEDLE — ca·jole·ment** *n* — **ca·jol·ery** \-'jōl-(ə-)rē\ *n*

**Ca·jun** \'kā-jən\ *n* **:** a Louisianan descended from French-speaking immigrants from Acadia

**¹cake** \'kāk\ *n* **1 :** batter that may be fried or baked into a usu. small round flat shape **2 :** sweet batter or dough usu. containing a leaven (as baking powder) that is first baked and then often coated with an icing

**²cake** *vb* **caked; cak·ing 1 :** to form or harden into a cake **2 : ENCRUST**

**cake·walk** \'kāk-ˌwȯk\ *n* **:** a stage dance typically involving a high prance with backward tilt

**cal** *abbr* **1** calendar **2** caliber **3** calorie

**Cal** *abbr* California

**cal·a·bash** \'kal-ə-ˌbash\ *n* **:** a gourd fruit; *also* **:** a utensil made from its shell

**cal·a·boose** \'kal-ə-ˌbüs\ *n* [Sp *calabozo* dungeon] *dial* **: JAIL**

**ca·la·di·um** \kə-'lād-ē-əm\ *n* **:** any of a genus of tropical American ornamental plants related to the arums

**cal·a·mine** \'kal-ə-ˌmīn\ *n* **:** a mixture of oxides of zinc and iron used in

lotions and ointments

**ca·lam·i·ty** \kə-'lam-ət-ē\ *n, pl* **-ties 1 :** great distress or misfortune **2 :** an event causing great harm or loss and affliction **: DISASTER — ca·lam·i·tous** \-ət-əs\ *adj* **— ca·lam·i·tous·ly** *adv* **— ca·lam·i·tous·ness** *n*

**calc** *abbr* calculate; calculated

**cal·car·e·ous** \kal-'kar-ē-əs\ *adj* **:** containing calcium or calcium carbonate; *also* **:** resembling calcium carbonate in hardness **— cal·car·e·ous·ness** *n*

**cal·cic** \'kal-sik\ *adj* **:** containing calcium or lime

**cal·cif·er·ous** \kal-'sif-(ə-)rəs\ *adj* **:** producing or containing calcium carbonate

**cal·ci·fy** \'kal-sə-ˌfī\ *vb* **-fied; fy·ing :** to make or become calcareous **— cal·ci·fi·ca·tion** \ˌkal-sə-fə-'kā-shən\ *n*

**cal·ci·mine** \'kal-sə-ˌmīn\ *n* **:** a thin water paint for plastering **— calci·mine** *vb*

**cal·cine** \kal-'sīn\ *vb* **cal·cined; cal·cin·ing :** to heat to a high temperature but without fusing to drive off volatile matter and often to reduce to powder **— cal·ci·na·tion** \ˌkal-sə-'nā-shən\ *n*

**cal·cite** \'kal-ˌsīt\ *n* **:** a crystalline mineral consisting of calcium carbonate **— cal·cit·ic** \kal-'sit-ik\ *adj*

**cal·ci·um** \'kal-sē-əm\ *n* **:** a silver-white soft metallic chemical element occurring in combination (as in limestone and bones)

**calcium carbonate** *n* **:** a substance found in nature as limestone and marble and in plant ashes, bones, and shells

**cal·cu·late** \'kal-kyə-ˌlāt\ *vb* **-lat·ed; -lat·ing** [L *calculare*, fr. *calculus* small stone, pebble used in reckoning] **1 :** to determine by mathematical processes **: COMPUTE 2 :** to reckon by exercise of practical judgment **: ESTIMATE 3 :** to design or adapt for a purpose **4 : COUNT, RELY — cal·cu·la·ble** \-lə-bəl\ *adj* **— cal·cu·la·bly** \-blē\ *adv* **— cal·cu·la·tor** \-ˌlāt-ər\ *n*

**cal·cu·lat·ed** \-ˌlāt-əd\ *adj* **:** undertaken after estimating the probability of success or failure ⟨a ~ risk⟩

**cal·cu·lat·ing** \-ˌlāt-iŋ\ *adj* **:** marked by shrewd consideration esp. of self-interest **— cal·cu·lat·ing·ly** *adv*

**cal·cu·la·tion** \ˌkal-kyə-'lā-shən\ *n* **1 :** the process or an act of calculating **2 :** the result of an act of calculating **3 :** studied care **: CAUTION**

**cal·cu·lus** \'kal-kyə-ləs\ *n, pl* **-li** \-ˌlī\ *also* **-lus·es 1 :** a concretion usu. of mineral salts esp. in hollow organs or ducts **2 :** a process or system of usu. mathematical reasoning through the use of symbols; *esp* **:** one dealing with rate of change and integrals of functions

**cal·de·ra** \kal-'der-ə, kȯl-, -'dir-\ *n* **:** a large crater usu. formed by the collapse of a volcanic cone

**cal·dron** \'kȯl-drən\ *n* **:** a large kettle or boiler

¹cal·en·dar \'kal-ən-dər\ n 1 : an arrangement of time into days, weeks, months, and years; also : a sheet or folder containing such an arrangement for a period 2 : an orderly list

²calendar vb -dared; -dar·ing \-d(ə-)riŋ\ : to enter in a calendar

¹cal·en·der \'kal-ən-dər\ vb : to press (as cloth or paper) between rollers or plates so as to make smooth or glossy or to thin into sheets

²calender n : a machine for calendering

cal·ends \'kal-əndz, 'kāl-\ n sing or pl : the first day of the ancient Roman month

ca·len·du·la \kə-'len-jə-lə\ n : any of a genus of yellow-flowered herbs related to the daisies

¹calf \'kaf, 'kàf\ n, pl calves \'kavz, 'kàvz\ 1 : the young of the domestic cow or of some related large mammals (as the whale) 2 : CALFSKIN

²calf n, pl calves \'kavz, 'kàvz\ : the fleshy back part of the leg below the knee

calf·skin \'kaf-,skin, 'kàf-\ n : leather made of the skin of a calf

cal·i·ber or cal·i·bre \'kal-ə-bər\ n [MF calibre, fr. It calibro, fr. Ar qālib shoemaker's last] 1 : the diameter of a projectile 2 : the diameter of the bore of a gun 3 : degree of mental capacity or moral quality : measure of excellence or importance

cal·i·brate \'kal-ə-,brāt\ vb -brat·ed; -brat·ing 1 : to measure the caliber of 2 : to determine, correct, or put the measuring marks on ⟨~ a thermometer⟩ — cal·i·bra·tion \,kal-ə-'brā-shən\ n — cal·i·bra·tor \'kal-ə-,brāt-ər\ n

cal·i·co \'kal-i-,kō\ n, pl -coes or -cos : cotton cloth; esp : a cheap cotton printed fabric — calico adj

Calif abbr California

Cal·i·for·nia poppy \,kal-ə-'fòr-nyə-\ n : a widely cultivated herb with pale yellow to red flowers that is related to the poppies

cal·i·for·ni·um \,kal-ə-'fòr-nē-əm\ n : an artificially prepared radioactive chemical element

cal·i·per or cal·li·per \'kal-ə-pər\ n 1 : an instrument with two adjustable legs used to measure the thickness of objects or distances between surfaces — usu. used in pl. ⟨a pair of ~s⟩ 2 : a device consisting of two plates lined with a frictional material that press against the sides of a rotating wheel or disk in certain brake systems

ca·liph or ca·lif \'kā-ləf, 'kal-əf\ n : a successor of Muhammad as head of Islam — used as a title — ca·liph·ate \-,āt, -ət\ n

cal·is·then·ics \,kal-əs-'then-iks\ n sing or pl [Gk kalos beautiful + sthenos strength] : systematic bodily exercises without apparatus or with light hand apparatus — cal·is·then·ic adj

calk \'kòk\ var of CAULK

¹call \'kòl\ vb 1 : SHOUT, CRY; also : to utter a characteristic cry 2 : to utter in a loud clear voice 3 : to announce authoritatively 4 : SUMMON 5 : to make a request or demand ⟨~ for an investigation⟩ 6 : to get or try to get into communication by telephone 7 : to demand payment of (a loan); also : to demand surrender of (as a bond issue) for redemption 8 : to make a brief visit 9 : to speak of or address by name : give a name to 10 : to estimate or consider for practical purposes ⟨~ it ten miles⟩ 11 : to halt because of unsuitable conditions — call·er n

²call n 1 : SHOUT 2 : the cry of an animal (as a bird) 3 : a request or a command to come or assemble : INVITATION, SUMMONS 4 : DEMAND, CLAIM; also : REQUEST 5 : a brief usu. formal visit 6 : an act of calling on the telephone

cal·la \'kal-ə\ n : a plant whose flowers form a fleshy yellow spike surrounded by a lilylike usu. white leaf

call·back \'kòl-,bak\ n : a recall by a manufacturer of a product to correct a defect

call·board \-,bòrd\ n : a board for posting notices (as of rehearsal calls in a theater)

call down vb : REPRIMAND

call girl n : a prostitute with whom appointments are made by phone

cal·lig·ra·phy \kə-'lig-rə-fē\ n 1 : beautiful or elegant handwriting; also : the art of producing such writing 2 : PENMANSHIP — cal·lig·ra·pher \-fər\ n

call in vb 1 : to order to return or be returned 2 : to summon to one's aid 3 : to report by telephone

call·ing \'kò-liŋ\ n 1 : a strong inner impulse toward a particular vocation 2 : the activity in which one customarily engages as an occupation

cal·li·ope \kə-'lī-ə-(,)pē, 'kal-ē-,ōp\ n [fr. Calliope, chief of the Muses, fr. L, fr. Gk Kalliopē] : a musical instrument consisting of a series of whistles played by keys arranged as in an organ

call number n : a combination of characters assigned to a library book to indicate its place on a shelf

call off vb : CANCEL

cal·los·i·ty \ka-'läs-ət-ē, kə-\ n, pl -ties 1 : the quality or state of being callous 2 : CALLUS 1

¹cal·lous \'kal-əs\ adj 1 : being thickened and usu. hardened ⟨~ skin⟩ 2 : hardened in feeling — cal·lous·ly adv — cal·lous·ness n

²callous vb : to make callous

cal·low \'kal-ō\ adj [ME calu bald, fr. OE] : lacking adult sophistication : IMMATURE — cal·low·ness n

call-up \'kòl-,əp\ n : an order to report for active military service

call up \(')kòl-'əp\ vb : to summon for active military duty

¹cal·lus \'kal-əs\ n 1 : a callous area on skin or bark 2 : tissue that is converted into bone in the healing of a bone fracture

²callus vb : to form a callus

¹calm \'käm, 'kälm\ n 1 : a period or a

condition of freedom from storms, high winds, or rough water **2** : complete or almost complete absence of wind **3** : a state of freedom from turmoil or agitation

²**calm** *adj* : marked by calm : STILL, PLACID, SERENE — **calm·ly** *adv* — **calm·ness** *n*

³**calm** *vb* : to make or become calm

**cal·o·mel** \'kal-ə-məl, -,mel\ *n* : a chloride of mercury used esp. as a purgative and fungicide

**ca·lor·ic** \kə-'lȯr-ik\ *adj* **1** : of or relating to heat **2** : of or relating to calories

**cal·o·rie** *also* **cal·o·ry** \'kal-(ə-)rē\ *n, pl* **-ries** : a unit for measuring heat; *esp* : one for measuring the value of foods for producing heat and energy in the human body equivalent to the amount of heat required to raise the temperature of one kilogram of water one degree centigrade

**cal·o·rif·ic** \,kal-ə-'rif-ik\ *adj* : CALORIC

**cal·o·rim·e·ter** \,kal-ə-'rim-ət-ər\ *n* : an apparatus for measuring quantities of heat — **ca·lo·ri·met·ric** \,kal-ə-rə-'me-trik; kə-,lȯr-ə-\ *adj* — **ca·lo·ri·met·ri·cal·ly** \-tri-k(ə-)lē\ *adv* — **cal·o·rim·e·try** \,kal-ə-'rim-ə-trē\ *n*

**cal·u·met** \'kal-yə-,met, -mət\ *n* : an American Indian ceremonial pipe

**ca·lum·ni·ate** \kə-'ləm-nē-,āt\ *vb* **-at·ed; -at·ing** : to accuse falsely and maliciously : SLANDER **syn** defame, malign, libel — **ca·lum·ni·a·tion** \-,ləm-nē-'ā-shən\ *n* — **ca·lum·ni·a·tor** \-'ləm-nē-,āt-ər\ *n*

**cal·um·ny** \'kal-əm-nē\ *n, pl* **-nies** : false and malicious accusation — **ca·lum·ni·ous** \kə-'ləm-nē-əs\ *adj* — **ca·lum·ni·ous·ly** *adv*

**calve** \'kav, 'kȧv\ *vb* **calved; calv·ing** : to give birth to a calf

**calves** *pl of* CALF

**Cal·vin·ism** \'kal-və-,niz-əm\ *n* : the theological system of Calvin and his followers — **Cal·vin·ist** \-və-nəst\ *n or adj* — **Cal·vin·is·tic** \,kal-və-'nis-tik\ *adj*

**ca·lyp·so** \kə-'lip-sō\ *n, pl* **-sos** : an improvised ballad usu. satirizing current events in a rhythmic style originating in the British West Indies

**ca·lyx** \'kā-liks, 'kal-iks\ *n, pl* **ca·lyx·es** *or* **ca·ly·ces** \'kā-lə-,sēz, 'kal-ə-\ : the outside usu. green or leaflike part of a flower

**cam** \'kam\ *n* : a rotating or sliding projection (as on a wheel) for receiving or imparting motion

**ca·ma·ra·de·rie** \,kam-(ə-)'rad-ə-rē, ,käm-(ə-)'räd-\ *n* : friendly feeling and goodwill among comrades

**cam·ber** \'kam-bər\ *n* : a slight convexity or arching (as of a road surface) — **camber** *vb*

**cam·bi·um** \'kam-bē-əm\ *n, pl* **-bi·ums** *or* **-bia** \-bē-ə\ : a thin cellular layer between xylem and phloem of most higher plants from which new tissues develop — **cam·bi·al** \-bē-əl\ *adj*

**cam·bric** \'kām-brik\ *n* : a fine thin white linen fabric or a cotton cloth resembling this

**came** *past of* COME

**cam·el** \'kam-əl\ *n* : a large hoofed cud-chewing mammal used esp. in desert regions of Asia and Africa for carrying burdens and for riding

**cam·el·back** \'kam-əl-,bak\ *n* : an uncured compound chiefly of reclaimed or synthetic rubber used for retreading or recapping pneumatic tires

**ca·mel·lia** *also* **ca·me·lia** \kə-'mēl-yə\ *n* : any of several shrubs or trees related to the tea plant and grown in warm regions for their showy roselike flowers

**ca·mel·o·pard** \kə-'mel-ə-,pärd\ *n* : GIRAFFE

**camel's hair** *n* **1** : the hair of a camel or a substitute for it **2** : cloth made of camel's hair or of camel's hair and wool

**Cam·em·bert** \'kam-əm-,be‸r\ *n* : a soft surface-ripened cheese with a grayish rind and yellow interior

**cam·eo** \'kam-ē-,ō\ *n, pl* **-eos 1** : a gem carved in relief; *also* : a small medallion with a profiled head in relief **2** : a brief appearance by a well-known actor in a play or movie

**cam·era** \'kam(ə-)rə\ *n* : a closed lightproof box with an aperture through which the image of an object can be recorded on a surface sensitive to light; *also* : the part of a television transmitter in which the image is formed — **cam·era·man** \'kam-(ə-)rə-,man, -mən\ *n*

**Cam·er·oo·ni·an** *or* **Cam·er·ou·ni·an** \,kam-ə-'rü-nē-ən\ *n* : a native or inhabitant of the Republic of Cameroon or the Cameroons region — **Cameroonian** *or* **Camerounian** *adj*

**cam·i·sole** \'kam-ə-,sōl\ *n* : a short sleeveless undergarment for women

**camomile** *var of* CHAMOMILE

**cam·ou·flage** \'kam-ə-,fläzh, -,fläj\ *n* **1** : the disguising of military equipment or installations with paint, nets, or foliage; *also* : the disguise itself **2** : a deceptive expedient — **camouflage** *vb*

¹**camp** \'kamp\ *n* **1** : a place where tents or buildings are erected for usu. temporary shelter **2** : a collection of tents or other shelters **3** : a body of persons encamped — **camp·ground** \-,graùnd\ *n* — **camp·site** \-,sīt\ *n*

²**camp** *vb* **1** : to make or occupy a camp **2** : to live in a camp or outdoors

³**camp** *n* **1** : exaggerated effeminate mannerisms **2** : something so outrageous or in such bad taste as to be considered amusing — **camp** *adj* — **camp·i·ly** \'kam-pə-lē\ *adv* — **camp·i·ness** \-pē-nəs\ *n* — **campy** \'kam-pē\ *adj*

⁴**camp** *vb* : to engage in camp : exhibit the qualities of camp

**cam·paign** \kam-'pān\ *n* **1** : a series of military operations forming one distinct stage in a war **2** : a series of activities designed to bring about a particular result ⟨advertising ∼⟩ — **campaign** *vb* — **cam·paign·er** *n*

**cam·pa·nile** \,kam-pə-'nē-lē\ *n, pl* **-ni·les** *or* **-ni·li** \-'nē-lē\ : a usu. freestanding bell tower

**cam·pa·nol·o·gy** \,kam-pə-'näl-ə-jē\ *n* : the art of bell ringing — **cam·pa·nol·o·gist** \-jəst\ *n*

**camp·er** \'kam-pər\ *n* **1** : one that camps **2** : a portable dwelling (as a specially equipped automotive vehicle) for use during casual travel and camping

**camp fire girl** *n* : a member of a national organization of girls from 7 to 18

**camp follower** *n* **1** : a civilian (as a prostitute) who follows a military unit to attend or exploit its personnel **2** : a follower who is not a member of the main body of adherents; *esp* : a politician who joins a movement solely for personal gain

**cam·phor** \'kam(p)-fər\ *n* : a gummy volatile fragrant compound obtained from an evergreen Asiatic tree (**camphor tree**) and used esp. in medicine and the chemical industry

**cam·phor·ate** \'kam(p)-fə-,rāt\ *vb* **-at·ed; -at·ing** : to impregnate with camphor ⟨*camphorated* oil⟩

**camp meeting** *n* : a series of evangelistic meetings held outdoors or in a tent

**camp·o·ree** \,kam-pə-'rē\ *n* : a gathering of boy scouts or girl scouts from a given geographic area

**camp·stool** \'kamp-,stül\ *n* : a folding backless seat

**cam·pus** \'kam-pəs\ *n* [L, plain] : the grounds and buildings of a college or school; *also* : a central grassy part of the grounds

**cam·shaft** \'kam-,shaft\ *n* : a shaft to which a cam is fastened

¹**can** \kən, (')kan\ *vb, past* **could** \kəd, (')kùd\; *pres sing & pl* **can 1** : be able to **2** : may perhaps ⟨~ he still be alive⟩ **3** : be permitted by conscience or feeling to ⟨you ~ hardly blame him⟩ **4** : have permission or liberty to ⟨you ~ go now⟩

²**can** \'kan\ *n* **1** : a typically cylindrical metal container or receptacle ⟨garbage ~⟩ ⟨coffee ~⟩ **2** *slang* : JAIL

³**can** \'kan\ *vb* **canned; can·ning 1** : to put in a can : preserve by sealing in airtight cans or jars **2** *slang* : to discharge from employment **3** *slang* : to put a stop or an end to **4** : to record on discs or tape — **can·ner** *n*

**Can** *or* **Canad** *abbr* **1** Canada **2** Canadian

**Can·a·da goose** \'kan-əd-ə-\ *n* : the common wild goose of No. America

**Ca·na·di·an** \kə-'nād-ē-ən\ *n* : a native or inhabitant of Canada — **Canadian** *adj*

**ca·naille** \kə-'nī, -'nāl\ *n* : RABBLE, RIFFRAFF

**ca·nal** \kə-'nal\ *n* **1** : a tubular passage in the body : DUCT **2** : a channel dug and filled with water (as for passage of boats or irrigation of land)

**ca·nal·boat** \kə-'nal-,bōt\ *n* : a boat for use on a canal

**can·a·lize** \'kan-ºl-,īz\ *vb* **-lized; -liz·ing 1** : to provide with a canal or make into or like a channel **2** : to provide with an outlet; *esp* : to direct into preferred channels — **ca·nal·iza·tion** \,kan-ºl-ə-'zā-shən\ *n*

**can·a·pé** \'kan-ə-pē, -,pā\ *n* [F, lit., sofa, fr. ML *canopeum, canapeum* mosquito net] : a piece of bread or toast or a cracker topped with a savory food

**ca·nard** \kə-'närd\ *n* : a false or unfounded report or story

**ca·nary** \kə-'ne(ə)r-ē\ *n, pl* **ca·nar·ies** [fr. the *Canary* islands] **1** : a usu. sweet wine similar to Madeira **2** : a usu. yellow or greenish finch often kept as a cage bird **3** : a bright yellow

**ca·nas·ta** \kə-'nas-tə\ *n* [Sp, lit., basket] : rummy played with two full decks of cards plus four jokers

**canc** *abbr* canceled

**can·can** \'kan-,kan\ *n* : a woman's dance of French origin characterized by high kicking

¹**can·cel** \'kan-səl\ *vb* **-celed** *or* **-celled; -cel·ing** *or* **-cel·ling** \-s(ə-)liŋ\ [ME *cancellen*, fr. MF *canceller*, fr. L *cancellare* to make like a lattice, fr. *cancer* lattice] **1** : to cross out : DELETE **2** : to destroy the force or validity of : ANNUL **3** : to match in force or effect : OFFSET **4** : to remove (a common divisor) from a numerator and denominator; *also* : to remove (equivalents) on opposite sides of an equation or account **5** : to cross (a postage stamp) with lines to invalidate for reuse **6** : to neutralize each other's strength or effect — **can·cel·la·tion** \,kan-sə-'lā-shən\ *n*

²**cancel** *n* **1** : CANCELLATION **2** : a deleted part **3** : a part (as a page) from which something has been deleted

**can·cer** \'kan-sər\ *n* [L, lit., crab] **1** : a malignant tumor that tends to spread in the body **2** : a malignant evil that corrodes slowly and fatally — **can·cer·ous** \'kans-(ə-)rəs\ *adj* — **can·cer·ous·ly** *adv*

**can·de·la·bra** \,kan-də-'läb-rə, -'lab-\ *n* : CANDELABRUM

**can·de·la·brum** \-rəm\ *n, pl* **-bra** \-rə\ *also* **-brums** : an ornamental branched candlestick or lamp with several lights

**can·des·cent** \kan-'des-ºnt\ *adj* : glowing or dazzling esp. from great heat - **can·des·cence** \-ºns\ *n*

**can·did** \'kan-dəd\ *adj* **1** : FRANK, STRAIGHTFORWARD **2** : relating to the informal recording (as in photography) of human subjects acting naturally or spontaneously without being posed — **can·did·ly** *adv* — **can·did·ness** *n*

**can·di·da·cy** \'kan-(d)əd-ə-sē\ *n, pl* **-cies** : the state of being a candidate

**can·di·date** \'kan-(d)ə-,dāt, -(d)əd-ət\ *n* [L *candidatus*, fr. *candidatus* clothed in white, fr. *candidus* white; fr. the white toga worn by candidates in ancient Rome] : one who seeks or is proposed for an office, honor, or membership

**can·di·da·ture** \'kan-(d)əd-ə-,chůr\ *n, chiefly Brit* : CANDIDACY

**can·died** \'kan-dēd\ *adj* : preserved in or encrusted with sugar

¹**can·dle** \'kan-d³l\ *n* : a usu. slender mass of tallow or wax molded around a wick and burned to give light

²**candle** *vb* **can·dled; can·dling** \'kan-(d)liŋ, -d³l-iŋ\ : to examine (as eggs) by holding between the eye and a light — **can·dler** \-d(°-)lər\ *n*

**can·dle·light** \'kan-d³l-,(l)īt\ *n* 1 : the light of a candle; *also* : any soft artificial light 2 : time for lighting up

**Can·dle·mas** \'kan-d³l-məs\ *n* : February 2 observed as a church festival in commemoration of the presentation of Christ in the temple

**can·dle·pin** \-,pin\ *n* : a slender bowling pin tapering toward top and bottom used in a bowling game (**candlepins**) with a smaller ball than that used in tenpins

**can·dle·stick** \-,stik\ *n* : a holder with a socket for a candle

**can·dle·wick** \-,wik\ *n* : a soft cotton yarn; *also* : embroidery made with this yarn usu. in tufts

**can·dor** \'kan-dər\ *n* : FRANKNESS, OUTSPOKENNESS

**C and W** *abbr* country and western

¹**can·dy** \'kan-dē\ *n, pl* **candies** : a confection made from sugar often with flavoring and filling

²**candy** *vb* **can·died; can·dy·ing** 1 : to encrust in sugar often by cooking in a syrup 2 : to crystallize into sugar 3 : to make attractive : SWEETEN

**candy strip·er** \-,strī-pər\ *n* : a teen-age volunteer nurse's aide

¹**cane** \'kān\ *n* 1 : a slender hollow or pithy stem (as of a reed or bramble) 2 : a tall woody grass or reed (as sugarcane) 3 : a walking stick; *also* : a rod for flogging

²**cane** *vb* **caned; can·ing** 1 : to beat with a cane 2 : to weave or make with cane — **can·er** *n*

**cane·brake** \'kān-,brāk\ *n* : a thicket of cane

¹**ca·nine** \'kā-,nīn\ *adj* [L *caninus*, fr. *canis* dog] 1 : of or relating to dogs or to the natural group to which they belong 2 : being the pointed tooth next to the incisors

²**canine** *n* 1 : a canine tooth 2 : DOG

**can·is·ter** \'kan-ə-stər\ *n* 1 : a small box for holding a dry product (as tea) 2 : a shell for close-range artillery fire 3 : a perforated box containing material to absorb or filter a harmful substance in the air

**can·ker** \'kaŋ-kər\ *n* : a spreading sore that eats into tissue — **can·ker·ous** \kaŋ-k(ə-)rəs\ *adj*

**can·ker·worm** \-,wərm\ *n* : an insect larva (as a caterpillar) that injures plants

**can·na** \'kan-ə\ *n* : any of a genus of tropical herbs with large leaves and racemes of irregular flowers

**can·na·bis** \'kan-ə-bəs\ *n* : the dried flowering spikes of the female hemp plant

**canned** \'kand\ *adj* 1 : preserved in cans or jars 2 : recorded for radio or television reproduction (~ laughter)

**can·nel coal** \,kan-³l-\ *n* : a bituminous coal containing much volatile matter that burns brightly

**can·nery** \'kan-(ə-)rē\ *n, pl* **-ner·ies** : a factory for the canning of foods

**can·ni·bal** \'kan-ə-bəl\ *n* [NL *Canibalis* a member of a Caribbean Indian people, fr. Sp *Caníbal*, fr. a native word *Caniba* or *Carib*] 1 : a human being who eats human flesh 2 : an animal that eats its own kind — **can·ni·bal·ism** \'kan-ə-bə-,liz-əm\ *n* — **can·ni·bal·is·tic** \,kan-ə-bə-'lis-tik\ *adj*

**can·ni·bal·ize** \'kan-ə-bə-,līz\ *vb* **-ized; -iz·ing** 1 : to dismantle (a machine) for parts for other machines 2 : to practice cannibalism

¹**can·non** \'kan-ən\ *n, pl* **cannons** *or* **cannon** [MF *canon*, fr. It *cannone*, lit., large tube, fr. *canna* reed, tube, fr. L, cane, reed] 1 : an artillery piece supported on a carriage or mount 2 : a heavy-caliber automatic gun on an airplane

²**cannon** *n, Brit* : a carom in billiards

**can·non·ade** \,kan-ə-'nād\ *n* : a heavy fire of artillery — **cannonade** *vb*

¹**can·non·ball** \'kan-ən-,bȯl\ *n* : a usu. round solid missile for firing from a cannon

²**cannonball** *vb* : to travel at great speed

**can·non·eer** \,kan-ə-'niər\ *n* : an artillery gunner

**can·not** \'kan-,ät; kə-'nät\ : can not — cannot but : to be bound to

**can·nu·la** \'kan-yə-lə\ *n, pl* **-las** *or* **-lae** \-,lē\ : a small tube for insertion into a body cavity or into a duct or vessel

**can·ny** \'kan-ē\ *adj* **can·ni·er; -est** : PRUDENT, SHREWD — **can·ni·ly** \'kan-³l-ē\ *adv* — **can·ni·ness** \'kan-ē-nəs\ *n*

**ca·noe** \kə-'nü\ *n* : a long narrow boat with sharp ends and curved sides that is usu. propelled by paddles — **canoe** *vb* — **ca·noe·ist** *n*

¹**can·on** \'kan-ən\ *n* 1 : a regulation decreed by a church council; *also* : a provision of canon law 2 : an accepted principle (the ~s of good taste) 3 : an official or authoritative list (as of the saints or the books of the Bible)

²**canon** *n* : a clergyman on the staff of a cathedral — **can·on·ry** \-rē\ *n*

**ca·ñon** \'kan-yən\ *var of* CANYON

**ca·non·i·cal** \kə-'nän-i-kəl\ *adj* 1 : of, relating to, or conforming to a canon 2 : conforming to a general rule : ORTHODOX 3 : of or relating to a clergyman who is a canon — **ca·non·i·cal·ly** \-k(ə-)lē\ *adv*

**ca·non·i·cals** \-kəlz\ *n pl* : the vestments prescribed by canon for an officiating clergyman

**can·on·ize** \'kan-ə-,nīz\ *vb* **can·on·ized** \-,nīzd\; **can·on·iz·ing** 1 : to declare an officially recognized saint 2 : GLORIFY, EXALT — **can·on·iza·tion** \,kan-ə-nə-'zā-shən\ *n*

**canon law** *n* : the law governing a church

**canon regular** *n, pl* **canons regular** : a member of one of several Roman Catholic religious institutes of regular priests living in community

**can·o·py** \'kan-ə-pē\ *n, pl* **-pies** [ME *canope*, fr. ML *canopeum* mosquito net, fr. L *conopeum*, fr. Gk *kōnōpion*, fr. *kōnōps* mosquito] : an overhanging cover, shelter, or shade — **canopy** *vb*

¹**cant** \'kant\ *n* **1** : an oblique or slanting surface **2** : TILT, SLANT

²**cant** *vb* **1** : to tip or tilt up or over **2** : to pitch to one side : LEAN **3** : SLOPE

³**cant** *vb* **1** : BEG **2** : to talk hypocritically

⁴**cant** *n* **1** : the special idiom of a profession or trade : JARGON **2** : the expression of conventional, trite, or unconsidered opinions or sentiment; *esp* : insincere use of pious phraseology

**can't** \'kant, 'kȧnt, 'känt\ : can not

**can·ta·bi·le** \kän-'täb-ə-,lā\ *adv or adj* : in a singing manner — used as a direction in music

**can·ta·loupe** \'kant-ᵊl-,ōp\ *n* : MUSKMELON; *esp* : one with orange flesh and rough skin

**can·tan·ker·ous** \kan-'taŋ-k(ə-)rəs\ *adj* : ILL-NATURED, QUARRELSOME — **can·tan·ker·ous·ly** *adv* — **can·tan·ker·ous·ness** *n*

**can·ta·ta** \kən-'tät-ə\ *n* : a choral composition usu. accompanied by organ, piano, or orchestra

**can·teen** \kan-'tēn\ *n* [F *cantine* bottle case, canteen (store), fr. It *cantina* wine cellar, fr. *canto* corner, fr. L *canthus* iron tire] **1** : a store (as in a camp or factory) in which food, drinks, and small supplies are sold **2** : a place of recreation and entertainment for servicemen **3** : a flask for water

**can·ter** \'kant-ər\ *n* : a horse's 3-beat gait resembling but easier and slower than a gallop — **canter** *vb*

**Can·ter·bury bell** \,kant-ə(r)-,ber-ē-\ *n* : any of several plants related to the bluebell that are cultivated for their showy flowers

**can·thar·is** \'kar-thə-rəs\ *n, pl* **can·thar·i·des** \kan-'thar-ə-,dēz\ : SPANISH FLY

**can·ti·cle** \'kant-i-kəl\ *n* : SONG; *esp* : any of several liturgical songs taken from the Bible

**can·ti·le·ver** \'kant-ᵊl-,ē-vər, -,ev-ər\ *n* : a projecting beam or structure supported only at one end; *also* : either of a pair of such structures projecting toward each other so that when joined they form a bridge

**can·tle** \'kant-ᵊl\ *n* : the upwardly projecting rear part of a saddle

**can·to** \'kan-,tō\ *n, pl* **cantos** : one of the major divisions of a long poem

¹**can·ton** \'kant-ᵊn, 'kan-,tän\ *n* : a small territorial division of a country; *esp* : one of the political divisions of Switzerland — **can·ton·al** \'kant-ᵊn-əl, kan-'tän-ᵊl\ *adj*

²**can·ton** \'kant-ᵊn, 'kan-,tän; 2 *usu* kan-'tōn or -'tän\ *vb* **1** : to divide into

cantons **2** : to allot quarters to

**can·ton·ment** \kan-'tōn-mənt, -'tän-\ *n* **1** : the quartering of troops **2** : a group of more or less temporary structures for housing troops

**can·tor** \'kant-ər\ *n* : a synagogue official who sings liturgical music and leads the congregation in prayer

**can·vas** *also* **can·vass** \'kan-vəs\ *n* **1** : a strong cloth used esp. for making tents and sails **2** : a set of sails **3** : a group of tents **4** : a surface prepared to receive oil paint; *also* : an oil painting **5** : the floor of a boxing or wrestling ring

**can·vas·back** \'kan-vəs-,bak\ *n* : a No. American wild duck with red head and gray back

¹**can·vass** *also* **can·vas** \'kan-vəs\ *vb* : to go through (a district) or to go to (persons) to solicit votes or orders for goods or to determine public opinion or sentiment — **can·vass·er** *n*

²**canvass** *n* : an act of canvassing (as the solicitation of votes or orders or an examination into public opinion)

**can·yon** \'kan-yən\ *n* : a deep valley with high steep slopes

**caou·tchouc** \'kaù-,chùk, -,chük\ : RUBBER 3

¹**cap** \'kap\ *n* **1** : a usu. tight-fitting covering for the head; *also* : something resembling such a covering **2** : a container holding an explosive charge

²**cap** *vb* **capped; cap·ping 1** : to provide or protect with or as if with a cap **2** : to form a cap over : CROWN **3** : OUTDO, SURPASS **4** : CLIMAX

³**cap** *abbr* **1** capacity **2** capital **3** capitalize; capitalized

**CAP** *abbr* Civil Air Patrol

**ca·pa·ble** \'kā-pə-bəl\ *adj* : having ability, capacity, or power to do something : ABLE, COMPETENT — **ca·pa·bil·i·ty** \,kā-pə-'bil-ət-ē\ *n* — **ca·pa·bly** \'kā-pə-blē\ *adv*

**ca·pa·cious** \kə-'pā-shəs\ *adj* : able to contain much — **ca·pa·cious·ly** *adv* — **ca·pa·cious·ness** *n*

**ca·pac·i·tance** \kə-'pas-ət-əns\ *n* **1** : the property of an electric nonconductor that permits the storage of energy **2** : a part of a circuit or network that possesses capacitance — **ca·pac·i·tive** \-'pas-ət-iv\ *adj* — **ca·pac·i·tive·ly** *adv*

**ca·pac·i·tate** \kə-'pas-ə-,tāt\ *vb* **-tat·ed; -tat·ing** : to make capable

**ca·pac·i·tor** \kə-'pas-ət-ər\ *n* : a device giving capacitance usu. consisting of conducting plates separated by a dielectric

¹**ca·pac·i·ty** \kə-'pas-ət-ē\ *n, pl* **-ties 1** : the ability to contain, receive, or accommodate **2** : extent of space : VOLUME **3** : legal qualification or fitness **4** : ABILITY **5** : position or character assigned or assumed

²**capacity** *adj* : equaling maximum capacity

**cap–a–pie** *or* **cap–à–pie** \,kap-ə-'pē\ *adv* : from head to foot : at all points

**ca·par·i·son** \kə-'par-ə-sən\ *n* **1** : an

ornamental covering for a horse
**2 :** TRAPPINGS, ADORNMENT — **capar-
ison** *vb*

**¹cape** \'kāp\ *n* **1 :** a point of land jutting out into water **2 :** CAPE COD
COTTAGE

**²cape** *n* **:** a sleeveless garment hanging
from the neck over the shoulders

**Cape Cod cottage** \,kāp-,käd-\ *n* **:** a
compact rectangular dwelling of one or
one-and-a-half stories usu. with a steep
gable roof

**¹ca·per** \'kā-pər\ *n* **:** the flower bud of a
Mediterranean shrub pickled for use as
a relish; *also* **:** this shrub

**²caper** *vb* **ca·pered; ca·per·ing**
\-p(ə-)riŋ\ **:** to leap about in a gay
frolicsome way **:** PRANCE

**³caper** *n* **1 :** a frolicsome leap or spring
**2 :** a capricious escapade **3 :** an illegal
escapade

**cape·skin** \'kāp-,skin\ *n* **:** a light flexible leather made from sheepskins

**cap·ful** \'kap-,fùl\ *n* **:** as much as a
cap will hold

**cap·il·lar·i·ty** \,kap-ə-'lar-ət-ē\ *n, pl*
**-ties :** the action by which the surface
of a liquid where (as in a slender tube)
it is in contact with a solid is raised or
lowered depending on the relative attraction of the molecules of the liquid
for each other and for those of the solid

**¹cap·il·lary** \'kap-ə-,ler-ē\ *adj* **1 :** resembling a hair; *esp* **:** having a very
small bore ⟨~ tube⟩ **2 :** of or relating
to capillaries or to capillarity

**²capillary** *n, pl* **-lar·ies :** any of the tiny
thin-walled tubes that carry blood be-
tween the smallest arteries and their
corresponding veins

**¹cap·i·tal** \'kap-ət-ᵊl\ *adj* **1 :** punishable by death ⟨a ~ crime⟩ **2 :** most
serious ⟨a ~ error⟩ **3 :** first in importance or position **:** CHIEF ⟨the ~ city⟩
**4 :** conforming to the series A, B, C
rather than a, b, c ⟨~ letters⟩ ⟨~ G⟩
**5 :** of or relating to capital ⟨~ expendi-
tures⟩ **6 :** FIRST-RATE, EXCELLENT

**²capital** *n* **1 :** a letter larger than the ordinary small letter and often different in
form **2 :** the capital city of a state or
country; *also* **:** a city preeminent in some
activity ⟨the fashion ~ of the world⟩
**3 :** accumulated wealth esp. as used to
produce more wealth **4 :** the total face
value of shares of stock issued by a company **5 :** capitalists considered as a
group **6 :** ADVANTAGE, GAIN

**³capital** *n* **:** the top part or piece of an
architectural column

**capital goods** *n pl* **:** machinery, tools,
factories, and commodities used in the
production of goods

**cap·i·tal·ism** \'kap-ət-ᵊl-,iz-əm\ *n* **:** an
economic system characterized by private or corporation ownership of capital goods and by prices, production,
and distribution of goods that are determined mainly in a free market

**¹cap·i·tal·ist** \-əst\ *n* **1 :** a person who
has capital esp. invested in business
**2 :** a person of great wealth **:** PLUTO-
CRAT **3 :** a believer in capitalism

**²capitalist** *or* **cap·i·tal·is·tic** \,kap-

ət-ᵊl-'is-tik\ *adj* **1 :** owning capital
**2 :** practicing or advocating capitalism
**3 :** marked by capitalism — **cap·i·tal·
is·ti·cal·ly** \-ti-k(ə-)lē\ *adv*

**cap·i·tal·iza·tion** \,kap-ət-ᵊl-ə-'zā-
shən\ *n* **1 :** the act or process of capi-
talizing **2 :** the total amount of money
used as capital in a business

**cap·i·tal·ize** \'kap-ət-ᵊl-,īz\ *vb* **-ized;
-iz·ing 1 :** to write or print with an
initial capital or in capitals **2 :** to convert into or use as capital **3 :** to supply
capital for **4 :** to gain by turning something to advantage **:** PROFIT

**cap·i·tal·ly** \'kap-ət-ᵊl-ē\ *adv* **1 :** in a
way involving sentence of death **2
:** ADMIRABLY, EXCELLENTLY

**capital ship** *n* **:** a warship of the first
rank in size and armament

**cap·i·ta·tion** \,kap-ə-'tā-shən\ *n* **:** a
direct uniform tax levied on each person

**cap·i·tol** \'kap-ət-ᵊl\ *n* **:** the building in
which a legislature holds its sessions

**ca·pit·u·late** \kə-'pich-ə-,lāt\ *vb* **-lat-
ed; -lat·ing 1 :** to surrender esp. on
conditions agreed upon **2 :** to cease
resisting **:** ACQUIESCE **syn** submit, yield,
succumb, relent — **ca·pit·u·la·tion**
\-,pich-ə-'lā-shən\ *n*

**ca·pon** \'kā-,pän, -pən\ *n* **:** a castrated
male chicken

**ca·po·re·gi·me** \,käp-ō-rā-'jē-mā\ *n*
**:** a lieutenant in a criminal mob

**cap pistol** *n* **:** a toy pistol that fires caps

**ca·pric·cio** \kə-'prē-ch(ē-,)ō\ *n, pl*
**-cios :** an instrumental piece in free
form usu. lively in tempo and brilliant
in style

**ca·price** \kə-'prēs\ *n* [F, fr. It *capriccio*, lit., head with hair standing on end,
shudder, fr. *capo* head + *riccio* hedge-
hog] **1 :** a sudden whim or fancy
**2 :** CAPRICCIO — **ca·pri·cious** \kə-
'prish-əs\ *adj* — **ca·pri·cious·ly** *adv*
— **ca·pri·cious·ness** *n*

**cap·ri·ole** \'kap-rē-,ōl\ *n* **:** CAPER; *esp*
**:** an upward leap of a horse without
forward motion — **capriole** *vi*

**caps** *abbr* **1** capitals **2** capsule

**cap·si·cum** \'kap-si-kəm\ *n* **:** PEPPER 2

**cap·size** \'kap-,sīz, kap-'sīz\ *vb* **cap-
sized; cap·siz·ing :** UPSET, OVER-
TURN

**cap·stan** \'kap-stən, -,stan\ *n* **1 :** an
upright revolving drum used on ships
to lift weights by use of a rope wound
around it **2 :** a rotating shaft that
drives recorder tape

**cap·su·lar** \'kap-sə-lər\ *adj* **:** of, relating to, or resembling a capsule

**cap·su·late** \-,lāt, -lət\ *or* **cap·su·
lat·ed** \-,lāt-əd\ *adj* **:** enclosed in a
capsule

**¹cap·sule** \'kap-səl, -sül\ *n* **1 :** an enveloping cover (as of a bodily joint) ⟨a
spore ~⟩; *esp* **:** an edible shell enclosing
medicine to be swallowed **2 :** a dry
fruit made of two or more united
carpels that splits open when ripe **3 :** a
small pressurized compartment for an
aviator or astronaut

**²capsule** *vb* **cap·suled; cap·sul·ing
:** to condense into or present in compact form ⟨~ the news⟩

³**cap·sule** adj **1 :** very brief **2 :** very compact

**Capt** abbr captain

¹**cap·tain** \'kap-tən\ n **1 :** a commander of a body of troops **2 :** an officer in charge of a ship **3 :** a commissioned officer in the navy ranking next below a rear admiral or a commodore **4 :** a commissioned officer (as in the army) ranking next below a major **5 :** a leader of a side or team **6 :** a dominant figure — **cap·tain·cy** n — **cap·tain·ship** n

²**captain** vb **:** to be captain of **:** LEAD

**cap·tion** \'kap-shən\ n **1 :** a heading esp. of an article or document **:** TITLE **2 :** the explanatory matter accompanying an illustration **3 :** a motion-picture subtitle — **cap·tion** vb

**cap·tious** \'kap-shəs\ adj **:** marked by an inclination to find fault — **cap·tious·ly** adv — **cap·tious·ness** n

**cap·ti·vate** \'kap-tə-,vāt\ vb **-vat·ed; -vat·ing :** to attract and hold irresistibly by some special charm or art — **cap·ti·va·tion** \,kap-tə-'vā-shən\ n — **cap·ti·va·tor** \'kap-tə-,vāt-ər\ n

**cap·tive** \'kap-tiv\ adj **1 :** made prisoner esp. in war **2 :** kept within bounds **:** CONFINED **3 :** held under control **4 :** of or relating to bondage — **captive** n — **cap·tiv·i·ty** \kap-'tiv-ət-ē\ n

**cap·tor** \'kap-tər\ n **:** one that captures

¹**cap·ture** \'kap-chər\ n **1 :** seizure by force or trickery **2 :** one that has been taken; esp **:** a prize ship

²**capture** vb **cap·tured; cap·tur·ing 1 :** to take captive **:** WIN, GAIN **2 :** to preserve in a relatively permanent form

**Ca·pu·chin** \'kap-yə-shən, kə-'p(y)ü-\ n **:** a member of an austere branch of the first order of St. Francis of Assisi engaged in missionary work and preaching

**car** \'kär\ n **1 :** a vehicle moved on wheels **2 :** the cage of an elevator **3 :** the part of a balloon or airship which carries passengers or equipment

**ca·ra·bao** \,kär-ə-'baù\ n **:** the water buffalo of the Philippines

**car·a·bi·neer** or **car·a·bi·nier** \,kar-ə-bə-'niər\ n **:** a soldier armed with a carbine

**car·a·cole** \'kar-ə-,kōl\ n **:** a half turn to right or left executed by a mounted horse — **caracole** vb

**ca·rafe** \kə-'raf, -'räf\ n **:** a water bottle with a flaring lip

**car·a·mel** \'kar-ə-məl, 'kär-məl\ n **1 :** burnt sugar used for flavoring and coloring **2 :** a firm chewy candy

**car·a·pace** \'kar-ə-,pās\ n **:** a protective case or shell on the back of an animal (as a turtle or crab)

¹**car·at** var of KARAT

²**car·at** \'kar-ət\ n **:** a unit of weight for precious stones equal to 200 milligrams

**car·a·van** \'kar-ə-,van\ n **1 :** a group of travelers journeying together through desert or hostile regions **2 :** a group of vehicles traveling in a file **3 :** VAN

**car·a·van·sa·ry** \,kar-ə-'van-sə-rē\ or **car·a·van·se·rai** \-sə-,rī\ n, pl **-ries** or **-rais** or **-rai** [fr. *kārwānsarāi*, fr. *kārwān* caravan + *sarāi* palace, inn] **1 :** an inn in eastern countries where caravans rest at night **2 :** HOTEL, INN

**car·a·vel** \'kar-ə-,vel\ n **:** a small 15th and 16th century ship with broad bows, high narrow poop, and lateen sails

**car·a·way** \'kar-ə-,wā\ n **:** an aromatic herb related to the carrot with seeds used in seasoning and medicine

**car bed** n **:** a portable bed for an infant

**car·bide** \'kär-,bīd\ n **:** a binary compound of carbon with another element

**car·bine** \'kär-,bēn, -,bīn\ n **:** a short-barreled lightweight rifle

**car·bo·hy·drate** \,kär-bō-hī-,drāt, -drət\ n **:** any of various compounds composed of carbon, hydrogen, and oxygen including the sugars and starches

**car·bo·lat·ed** \'kär-bə-,lāt-əd\ adj **:** impregnated with carbolic acid

**car·bol·ic acid** \,kär-,bäl-ik-\ n **:** a caustic crystalline compound usu. obtained from coal tar or by synthesis and used in solution as an antiseptic and disinfectant and in making plastics

**car·bon** \'kär-bən\ n **1 :** a chemical element occurring in nature as the diamond and graphite and forming a constituent of coal, petroleum, and limestone **2 :** a piece of carbon paper; also **:** a copy made with carbon paper — **car·bon·less** adj

**car·bo·na·ceous** \,kär-bə-'nā-shəs\ adj **:** relating to, containing, or composed of carbon

¹**car·bon·ate** \'kär-bə-,nāt, -nət\ n **:** a salt or ester of carbonic acid

²**car·bon·ate** \-,nāt\ vb **-at·ed; -at·ing :** to impregnate with carbon dioxide (a *carbonated* beverage) — **car·bon·ation** \,kär-bə-'nā-shən\ n

**carbon black** n **:** any of various colloidal black substances consisting chiefly of carbon used esp. as pigments

**carbon copy** n **1 :** a copy made by carbon paper **2 :** DUPLICATE

**carbon dating** n **:** the determination of the age of old material (as an archaeological specimen) by means of the content of carbon 14

**carbon dioxide** n **:** a heavy colorless gas that does not support combustion but is formed by the combustion and decomposition of organic substances

**carbon 14** n **:** a heavy radioactive form of carbon used in dating archaeological and geological materials

**car·bon·ic acid** \,kär-,bän-ik-\ n **:** a weak acid that decomposes readily into water and carbon dioxide

**car·bon·if·er·ous** \,kär-bə-'nif-(ə-)rəs\ adj **:** producing or containing carbon or coal

**carbon monoxide** n **:** a colorless odorless very poisonous gas formed by the incomplete burning of carbon

**carbon paper** n **:** a thin paper coated with a waxy substance containing pigment and used in making copies of written or printed matter

**carbon tet·ra·chlo·ride** \-,te-trə-'klōr-,īd\ n : a colorless nonflammable toxic liquid that is used as a solvent and a fire extinguisher

**car·boy** \'kär-,bȯi\ n [Per *qarāba*, fr. Ar *qarrābah* demijohn] : a large specially cushioned container for liquids

**car·bun·cle** \'kär-,bəŋ-kəl\ n : a painful inflammation of the skin and underlying tissue that discharges pus from several openings — **car·bun·cu·lar** \kär-'bəŋ-kyə-lər\ adj

**car·bu·re·tor** \'kär-b(y)ə-,rāt-ər\ n : an apparatus for supplying an internal-combustion engine with an explosive mixture of vaporized fuel and air

**car·bu·rize** \'kär-byə-,rīz\ vb -rized; -riz·ing : to combine or impregnate (as metal) with carbon — **car·bu·ri·za·tion** \,kär-byə-rə-'zā-shən\ n

**car·cass** \'kär-kəs\ n : a dead body; esp : one of an animal dressed for food

**car·cin·o·gen** \kär-'sin-ə-jən\ n : an agent causing or inciting cancer — **car·ci·no·gen·ic** \,kärs-ᵊn-ō-'jen-ik\ adj — **car·ci·no·ge·nic·i·ty** \-jə-'nis-ət-ē\ n

**car·ci·no·ma** \,kärs-ᵊn-'ō-mə\ n, pl -mas or ma·ta \-'mət-ə\ : a malignant tumor of epithelial origin — **car·ci·no·ma·tous** \-'ō-mət-əs\ adj

**¹card** \'kärd\ vb : to comb with a card : cleanse and untangle before spinning — **card·er** n

**²card** n 1 : an implement for raising a nap on cloth 2 : a toothed instrument for carding fibers (as wool or cotton)

**³card** n 1 : PLAYING CARD 2 pl : a game played with playing cards; also : card playing 3 : a usu. clownishly amusing person : WAG 4 : a small flat stiff piece of paper 5 : PROGRAM; esp : a sports program

**⁴card** vb 1 : to place or fasten on a card 2 : to list or record on a card 3 : SCORE

**⁵card** abbr cardinal

**car·da·mom** \'kärd-ə-məm\ n : the aromatic capsular fruit of an East Indian herb related to the ginger whose seeds are used as a condiment and in medicine; also : this plant

**card·board** \'kärd-,bōrd\ n : a stiff moderately thick board made of paper

**card-car·ry·ing** \'kärd-,kar-ē-iŋ\ adj : being a regularly enrolled member of an organized group and esp. of the Communist party and not merely a sympathizer with its ideals and programs

**card catalog** n : a catalog (as of books) in which the entries are arranged systematically on cards

**car·di·ac** \'kärd-ē-,ak\ adj 1 : of, relating to, or located near the heart 2 : of or relating to heart disease

**car·di·gan** \'kärd-i-gən\ n : a sweater or jacket usu. without a collar and with a full-length opening in the front

**¹car·di·nal** \'kärd-(ᵊ-)nəl\ adj [ME, fr. OF, fr. LL *cardinalis*, fr. L *cardo* hinge] 1 : of basic importance : CHIEF, MAIN, PRIMARY 2 : of cardinal red color — **car·di·nal·ly** \-ē\ adv

**²cardinal** n 1 : an ecclesiastical official of the Roman Catholic Church ranking next below the pope 2 : a bright red 3 : any of several American finches of which the male is bright red

**car·di·nal·ate** \-ət, -,āt\ n 1 : the office, rank, or dignity of a cardinal 2 : CARDINALS

**cardinal flower** n : a No. American plant that bears a spike of brilliant red flowers

**car·di·nal·i·ty** \,kärd-ᵊn-'al-ət-ē\ n, pl -ties : the number of elements in a given mathematical set

**cardinal number** n : a number (as 1, 5, 82, 357) that is used in simple counting and answers the question "how many?"

**cardinal point** n : one of the four principal compass points north, south, east, and west

**car·dio·gram** \'kärd-ē-ə-,gram\ n : the line made by a cardiograph

**car·dio·graph** \-,graf\ n : an instrument that graphically registers movements of the heart — **car·dio·graph·ic** \,kärd-ē-ə-'graf-ik\ adj — **car·di·og·ra·phy** \-'äg-rə-fē\ n

**car·di·ol·o·gy** \,kärd-ē-'äl-ə-jē\ n : the study of the heart and its action and diseases — **car·di·ol·o·gist** \-'äl-ə-jəst\ n

**car·dio·vas·cu·lar** \,kärd-ē-ō-'vas-kyə-lər\ adj : of or relating to the heart and blood vessels

**card·sharp** \'kärd-,shär-pər\ or **card·sharp** \-,shärp\ n : a cheater at cards

**¹care** \'keər\ n 1 : a heavy sense of responsibility : WORRY, ANXIETY 2 : watchful attention : HEED 3 : CHARGE, SUPERVISION 4 : a person or thing that is an object of anxiety or solicitude

**²care** vb cared; car·ing 1 : to feel anxiety 2 : to feel interest 3 : to have a liking, fondness, taste, or inclination 4 : to give care 5 : to be concerned about (~ what happens)

**CARE** abbr Cooperative for American Relief to Everywhere

**ca·reen** \kə-'rēn\ vb 1 : to cause (as a boat) to lean over on one side 2 : to heel over 3 : to sway from side to side

**¹ca·reer** \kə-'riər\ n [MF *carrière*, fr. Old Provençal *carriera* street, fr. ML *carraria* road for vehicles, fr. L *carrus* car] 1 : a course of action or events; esp : a person's progress in his chosen occupation 2 : an occupation or profession followed as a life's work

**²career** vb : to go at top speed esp. in a headlong manner

**care·free** \'keər-,frē\ adj : free from care or worry

**care·ful** \-fəl\ adj **care·ful·ler; care·ful·lest** 1 : using or taking care : VIGILANT 2 : marked by solicitude, caution, or prudence — **care·ful·ly** \-ē\ adv — **care·ful·ness** n

**care·less** \-ləs\ adj 1 : free from care : UNTROUBLED 2 : UNCONCERNED, INDIFFERENT 3 : not taking care 4 : not showing or receiving care — **care·less·ly** adv — **care·less·ness** n

¹**ca·ress** \kə-'res\ *n* : a tender or loving touch or embrace

²**caress** *vb* : to touch or stroke tenderly or lovingly — **ca·ress·er** *n*

**car·et** \'kar-ət\ *n* [L, is missing, fr. *carēre* to be lacking] : a mark ∧ used to indicate the place where something is to be inserted

**care·tak·er** \'keər-,tā-kər\ *n* **1** : one in charge usu. as occupant in place of an absent owner **2** : one temporarily fulfilling the functions of an office

**care·worn** \-,wōərn\ *adj* : showing the effects of grief or anxiety

**car·fare** \'kär-,faər\ *n* : passenger fare (as on a streetcar or bus)

**car·go** \'kär-gō\ *n, pl* **cargoes** or **cargos** : the goods carried in a ship, airplane, or vehicle : FREIGHT

**car·hop** \'kär-,häp\ *n* : one who serves customers at a drive-in restaurant

**Ca·rib·be·an** \,kar-ə-'bē-ən, kə-'rib-ē-\ *adj* : of or relating to the eastern and southern West Indies or the Caribbean sea

**car·i·bou** \'kar-ə-,bü\ *n, pl* **caribou** or **caribous** : a large No. American deer related to the reindeer

**car·i·ca·ture** \'kar-i-kə-,chùr\ *n* **1** : distorted representation of parts or features to produce a ridiculous effect **2** : a representation esp. in literature or art having the qualities of caricature — **caricature** *vb* — **car·i·ca·tur·ist** \-,chùr-əst\ *n*

**car·ies** \'ka(ə)r-ēz\ *n, pl* **caries** : tooth decay

**car·il·lon** \'kar-ə-,län\ *n* : a set of bells tuned to the chromatic scale and sounded by hammers controlled by a keyboard

**car·il·lon·neur** \,kar-ə-lə-'nər\ *n* : a carillon player

**car·i·ous** \'kar-ē-əs\ *adj* : affected with caries

**car·load** \'kär-'lōd, -,lōd\ *n* : a load that fills a car

**car·mi·na·tive** \kär-'min-ət-iv\ *adj* : expelling gas from the alimentary canal — **carminative** *n*

**car·mine** \'kär-mən, -,mīn\ *n* : a vivid red

**car·nage** \'kär-nij\ *n* : great destruction of life : SLAUGHTER

**car·nal** \'kärn-ᵊl\ *adj* **1** : of or relating to the body **2** : SENSUAL — **car·nal·i·ty** \kär-'nal-ət-ē\ *n* — **car·nal·ly** \'kärn-ᵊl-ē\ *adv*

**car·na·tion** \kär-'nā-shən\ *n* : a cultivated usu. double-flowered pink

**car·nau·ba** \kär-'nô-bə, ,kär-nə-'ü-bə\ *n* : a Brazilian palm that yields a brittle yellowish wax used esp. in polishes; *also* : this wax

**car·ne·lian** \kär-'nēl-yən\ *n* : a hard tough reddish quartz used as a gem

**car·ni·val** \'kär-nə-vəl\ *n* [It *carnevale*, fr. *carnelevare*, lit., removal of meat] **1** : a season of merrymaking just before Lent **2** : a boisterous merrymaking **3** : a traveling enterprise offering a variety of amusements **4** : an organized program of entertainment

**car·niv·o·ra** \kär-'niv-(ə)rə\ *n pl* : carnivorous mammals

**car·ni·vore** \'kär-nə-,vōr\ *n* : a flesh-eating animal; *esp* : any of a large group of mammals that feed mostly on flesh and include the dogs, cats, bears, minks, and seals

**car·niv·o·rous** \kär-'niv-(ə-)rəs\ *adj* **1** : feeding on animal tissues **2** : of or relating to the carnivores — **car·niv·o·rous·ly** *adv* — **car·niv·o·rous·ness** *n*

**car·ny** or **car·ney** or **car·nie** \'kär-nē\ *n, pl* **carnies** or **carneys** **1** : CARNIVAL 3 **2** : one who works with a carnival

**car·ol** \'kar-əl\ *n* : a song of joy, praise, or devotion — **carol** *vb*

**car·om** \'kar-əm\ *n* **1** : a shot in billiards in which the cue ball strikes each of two object balls **2** : a rebounding esp. at an angle — **carom** *vb*

**car·o·tene** \'kar-ə-,tēn\ *n* : any of several orange to red pigments formed esp. in plants and used as a source of vitamin A

**ca·rot·id** \kə-'rät-əd\ *adj* : of, relating to, or being the chief artery or pair of arteries that pass up the neck and supply the head — **carotid** *n*

**ca·rous·al** \kə-'raù-zəl\ *n* : CAROUSE

**ca·rouse** \kə-'raùz\ *n* [MF *carrousse*, fr. *carous*, adv., all out (in *boire carous* to empty the cup), fr. G *garaus*] : a drunken revel — **carouse** *vb* — **ca·rous·er** *n*

**car·ou·sel** \,kar-ə-'sel, 'kar-ə-,sel\ *n* : MERRY-GO-ROUND

¹**carp** \'kärp\ *vb* : to find fault : CAVIL, COMPLAIN — **carp·er** *n*

²**carp** *n, pl* **carp** or **carps** : a long-lived soft finned freshwater fish of sluggish waters

¹**car·pal** \'kär-pəl\ *adj* : relating to the wrist or the bones of the wrist

²**carpal** *n* : a carpal element (as a bone)

**car·pe di·em** \,kär-pē-'dē-,em, -'dī-, -əm\ *n* [L, enjoy the day] : enjoyment of the present without concern for the future

**car·pel** \'kär-pəl\ *n* : one of the highly modified leaves that together form the ovary of a flower

**car·pen·ter** \'kär-pən-tər\ *n* : one who builds or repairs wooden structures — **carpenter** *vb* — **car·pen·try** \-trē\ *n*

¹**car·pet** \'kär-pət\ *n* : a heavy fabric used esp. as a floor covering

²**carpet** *vb* : to cover with or as if with a carpet

**car·pet·bag** \-,bag\ *n* : a traveling bag common in the 19th century

**car·pet·bag·ger** \-,bag-ər\ *n* : a Northerner in the South during the reconstruction period seeking private gain by taking advantage of unsettled conditions and political corruption

**car·pet·ing** \'kär-pət-iŋ\ *n* : material for carpets; *also* : CARPETS

**car pool** *n* : a group of automobile owners each of whom in turn drives his own car and carries the others as passengers

**car·port** \'kär-,pōrt\ *n* : an open-sided automobile shelter

**car·ra·geen·an** *or* **car·ra·geen·in** \,kar-ə-'gē-nən\ *n* : a colloid extracted esp. from a dark purple branching seaweed and used esp. as a suspending agent (as in foods)

**car·rel** \'kar-əl\ *n* : a table with bookshelves often partitioned or enclosed for individual study in a library

**car·riage** \'kar-ij\ *n* **1** : conveyance esp. of goods **2** : manner of holding or carrying oneself **3** : a wheeled vehicle **4** *Brit* : a railway passenger coach **5** : a movable part of a machine for supporting some other moving part

**carriage trade** *n* : trade from well-to-do or upper-class people

**car·ri·er** \'kar-ē-ər\ *n* **1** : one that carries something; *esp* : one that spreads germs while remaining well himself **2** : a person or corporation in the transportation business **3** : a wave whose amplitude or frequency is varied in order to transmit a radio or television signal

**carrier pigeon** *n* : a pigeon used esp. to carry messages

**car·ri·on** \'kar-ē-ən\ *n* : dead and decaying flesh

**car·rot** \'kar-ət\ *n* : a vegetable widely grown for its elongated orange-red root; *also* : this root

**car·rou·sel** *var of* CAROUSEL

**¹car·ry** \'kar-ē\ *vb* **car·ried**; **car·ry·ing** **1** : to move while supporting : TRANSPORT, CONVEY, TAKE **2** : to influence by mental or emotional appeal **3** : to get possession or control of : CAPTURE, WIN **4** : to have or wear on one's person; *also* : to bear within one **5** : INVOLVE, IMPLY **6** : to hold or bear (oneself) in a specified way **7** : to sustain the weight or burden of : SUPPORT **8** : to keep in stock for sale **9** : to prolong in space, time, or degree **10** : to reach or penetrate to a distance **11** : to win adoption (as in a legislature) **12** : to succeed in (an election) **13** : PUBLISH, PRINT **14** : to keep on one's books as a debtor

**²carry** *n* **1** : the range of a gun or projectile or of a struck or thrown ball **2** : an act or method of carrying (fireman's ~) **3** : a portage esp. between two bodies of navigable water

**car·ry·all** \'kar-ē-,ól\ *n* **1** : a light covered carriage for four or more persons **2** : a passenger automobile similar to a station wagon **3** : a capacious bag or case **4** : a self-loading carrier esp. for hauling earth

**carry away** *vb* : to arouse to a high and often excessive degree of emotion

**carrying charge** *n* **1** : expense incident to ownership or use of property **2** : a charge added to the price of merchandise sold on the installment plan

**car·ry·on** \'kar-ē-,ón, -,än\ *n* : a piece of luggage suitable for being carried aboard an airplane by a passenger

**carry on** \,kar-ē-'ón, -'än\ *vb* **1** : CONDUCT, MANAGE **2** : to behave in a foolish, excited, or improper manner **3** : to

continue in spite of hindrance or discouragement

**carry out** *vb* **1** : to put into execution **2** : to bring to a successful conclusion

**car·sick** \'kär-,sik\ *adj* : affected with motion sickness esp. in an automobile — **car sickness** *n*

**¹cart** \'kärt\ *n* **1** : a 2-wheeled wagon **2** : a small wheeled vehicle

**²cart** *vb* : to convey in or as if in a cart — **cart·er** *n*

**cart·age** \'kärt-ij\ *n* : the act of or rate charged for carting

**carte blanche** \'kärt-'blänsh\ *n, pl* **cartes blanches** \'kärt-'blänsh(-əz)\ : full discretionary power

**car·tel** \kär-'tel\ *n* : a combination of independent business enterprises designed to limit competition **syn** pool, syndicate, monopoly

**car·ti·lage** \'kärt-°l-ij\ *n* : an elastic tissue composing most of the skeleton of embryonic and very young vertebrates and later mostly turning into bone — **car·ti·lag·i·nous** \,kärt-°l-'aj-ə-nəs\ *adj*

**car·tog·ra·phy** \kär-'täg-rə-fē\ *n* : the making of maps — **car·tog·ra·pher** \-fər\ *n*

**car·ton** \'kärt-°n\ *n* : a cardboard box or container

**car·toon** \kär-'tün\ *n* **1** : a preparatory sketch (as for a painting) **2** : a drawing intended as humor, caricature, or satire **3** : COMIC STRIP — **cartoon** *vb* — **car·toon·ist** *n*

**car·top** \'kär-,täp\ *adj* : suitable for carrying on top of an automobile

**car·tridge** \'kär-trij\ *n* **1** : a tube containing a complete charge for a firearm **2** : a container of material for insertion into an apparatus **3** : a phonograph part that translates stylus motion into voltage **4** : a case containing a reel of magnetic recording tape

**cart·wheel** \'kärt-,hwēl\ *n* **1** : a large coin (as a silver dollar) **2** : a lateral handspring with arms and legs extended

**carve** \'kärv\ *vb* **carved**; **carv·ing** **1** : to cut with care or precision : shape by cutting **2** : to cut into pieces or slices **3** : to slice and serve meat at table — **carv·er** *n*

**cary·at·id** \,kar-ē-'at-əd\ *n, pl* **-ids** *or* **-i·des** \-ə-,dēz\ : a sculptured draped female figure used as an architectural column

**ca·sa·ba** \kə-'säb-ə\ *n* : any of several winter melons with yellow rind and sweet flesh

**¹cas·cade** \kas-'kād\ *n* **1** : a steep usu. small waterfall **2** : something arranged in a series or succession of stages so that each stage derives from or acts upon the product of the preceding

**²cascade** *vb* **cas·cad·ed**; **cas·cad·ing** : to fall, pass, or connect in or as if in a cascade

**cas·ca·ra** \kas-'kar-ə\ *n* : the dried bark of a small Pacific coastal tree used as a laxative; *also* : this tree

**¹case** \'kās\ *n* **1** : a particular instance or situation **2** : a convincing argument **3** : an inflectional form esp. of a noun or pronoun indicating its grammatical relation to other words; *also* : such a relation whether indicated by inflection or not  **4** : what actually exists or happens : FACT  **5** : a suit or action in law : CAUSE  **6** : an instance of disease or injury; *also* : PATIENT  **7** : INSTANCE, EXAMPLE — **in case 1** : IF  **2** : as a precaution that — **in case of** : in the event of

²**case** *n*  **1** : a receptacle (as a box) for holding something  **2** : SET ⟨a ~ of instruments⟩; *esp* : PAIR  **3** : an outer covering  **4** : a shallow divided tray for holding printing type  **5** : the frame of a door or window : CASING

³**case** *vb* **cased; cas·ing  1** : to enclose in or cover with a case  **2** : to inspect esp. with intent to rob

**ca·sein** \'kā-'sēn, 'kā-sē-ən\ *n* : a whitish phosphorus-containing protein occurring in milk

**case·ment** \'kās-mənt\ *n* : a window sash that opens like a door; *also* : a window having such a sash

**case·work** \-,wərk\ *n* : social work that involves the individual person or family — **case·work·er** *n*

¹**cash** \'kash\ *n* [MF or It; MF *casse* money box, fr. It *cassa*, fr. L *capsa* chest]  **1** : ready money  **2** : money or its equivalent paid at the time of purchase or delivery

²**cash** *vb* : to pay or obtain cash for

**ca·shew** \'kash-ü, kə-'shü\ *n* : a tropical American tree related to the sumac; *also* : its edible nut

¹**ca·shier** \ka-'shiər\ *vb* : to dismiss from service; *esp* : to dismiss in disgrace

²**cash·ier** \ka-'shiər\ *n*  **1** : a bank official responsible for moneys received and paid out  **2** : an employee (as of a store or restaurant) who receives and records payments by customers

**cashier's check** *n* : a check drawn by a bank upon its own funds and signed by its cashier

**cash in** *vb*  **1** : to convert into cash ⟨*cash in* bonds⟩  **2** : to settle accounts and withdraw from a gambling game or business deal  **3** : to obtain financial profit or advantage

**cash·mere** \'kazh-,miər, 'kash-\ *n* : fine wool from the undercoat of an Indian goat or a yarn spun of this; *also* : a soft twilled fabric orig. woven from this yarn

**cash register** *n* : a business machine that indicates each sale and often records the money received

**cas·ing** \'kā-siŋ\ *n* : something that encases

**ca·si·no** \kə-'sē-nō\ *n, pl* **-nos  1** : a building or room for social amusements; *esp* : one used for gambling  **2** *or* **cas·si·no** : a card game

**cask** \'kask\ *n* [MF *casque* helmet, fr. Sp *casco* potsherd, skull, helmet, fr. *cascar* to break] : a barrel-shaped container usu. for liquids; *also* : the quantity held by such a container

**cas·ket** \'kas-kət\ *n*  **1** : a small box (as for jewels)  **2** : COFFIN

**casque** \'kask\ *n* : HELMET

**cas·sa·va** \kə-'säv-ə\ *n* : a tropical spurge whose rootstock yields a nutritious starch from which tapioca is prepared; *also* : its rootstock

**cas·se·role** \'kas-ə-,rōl, 'kaz-\ *n*  **1** : a dish in which food may be baked and served  **2** : a dish cooked and served in a casserole

**cas·sette** *or* **ca·sette** \kə-'set, ka-\ *n*  **1** : a lightproof container of films or plates for a camera  **2** : a plastic case containing two reels of magnetic tape

**cas·sia** \'kash-ə\ *n*  **1** : a coarse cinnamon bark  **2** : any of various East Indian leguminous herbs, shrubs, and trees of which several yield senna

**cas·sit·er·ite** \kə-'sit-ə-,rīt\ *n* : a dark mineral that is the chief source of metallic tin

**cas·sock** \'kas-ək\ *n* : an ankle-length garment worn esp. by Roman Catholic and Anglican clergy

**cas·so·wary** \'kas-ə-,wer-ē\ *n, pl* **-war·ies** : any of several large birds closely related to the emu

¹**cast** \'kast\ *vb* **cast; cast·ing  1** : THROW, FLING  **2** : DIRECT ⟨~ a glance⟩  **3** : to deposit (a ballot) formally  **4** : to throw off, out, or away : DISCARD, SHED  **5** : COMPUTE; *esp* : to add up  **6** : to assign the parts of (a play) to actors; *also* : to assign to a role or part  **7** : MOLD  **8** : to make (as a knot or stitch) by looping or catching up

²**cast** *n*  **1** : THROW, FLING  **2** : a throw of dice  **3** : something formed in or as if in a mold; *also* : a rigid surgical dressing (as for protecting and supporting a fractured bone)  **4** : TINGE, HUE  **5** : APPEARANCE, LOOK  **6** : something thrown out or off, shed, or expelled ⟨worm ~s⟩  **7** : the group of actors to whom parts in a play are assigned

**cas·ta·nets** \,kas-tə-'nets\ *n pl* [Sp *castañeta*, fr. *castaña* chestnut, fr. L *castanea*] : a rhythm instrument consisting of two small ivory or wooden shells held in the hand and clicked in accompaniment with music and dancing

**cast·away** \'kas-tə-,wā\ *adj*  **1** : thrown away : REJECTED  **2** : cast adrift or ashore as a survivor of a shipwreck — **castaway** *n*

**caste** \'kast\ *n* [Port *casta*, lit., race, lineage, fr. fem. of *casto* pure, chaste, fr. L *castus*]  **1** : one of the hereditary social classes in Hinduism  **2** : a division of society based on wealth, inherited rank, or occupation  **3** : social position : PRESTIGE  **4** : a system of rigid social stratification

**cas·tel·lat·ed** \'kas-tə-,lāt-əd\ *adj* : having battlements like a castle

**cast·er** *or* **cas·tor** \'kas-tər\ *n*  **1** : a small container to hold salt or pepper at the table  **2** : a small wheel usu. free to swivel used to support and move furniture, trucks, and machines

**cas·ti·gate** \'kas-tə-,gāt\ *vb* **-gat·ed; -gat·ing** : to punish, reprove, or criticize severely — **cas·ti·ga·tion** \,kas-tə-'gā-shən\ *n* — **cas·ti·ga·tor** \'kas-tə-,gāt-ər\ *n*

**cast·ing** \'kas-tiŋ\ *n* **1** : something cast in a mold **2** : something cast out or off

**casting vote** *n* : a deciding vote cast by a presiding officer to break a tie

**cast iron** *n* : a hard brittle alloy of iron, carbon, and silicon cast in a mold

**cas·tle** \'kas-əl\ *n* **1** : a large fortified building or set of buildings **2** : a large or imposing house **3** : ³ROOK

**cas·tled** \'kas-əld\ *adj* : CASTELLATED

**castle in the air** : an impracticable project

**cast-off** \'kas-,tȯf\ *adj* : thrown away or aside : DISCARDED — **cast·off** *n*

**cas·tor oil** \,kas-tər-\ *n* : a thick yellowish oil extracted from the poisonous seeds of an herb (**castor-oil plant**) and used as a lubricant and cathartic

**cas·trate** \'kas-,trāt\ *vb* **cas·trat·ed; cas·trat·ing** : to deprive of sex glands and esp. testes — **cas·trat·er** *n* — **cas·tra·tion** \ka-'strā-shən\ *n*

**ca·su·al** \'kazh-(ə-w)əl\ *adj* **1** : resulting from or occurring by chance **2** : OCCASIONAL, INCIDENTAL **3** : OFFHAND, NONCHALANT **4** : designed for informal use (~ clothing) — **ca·su·al·ly** \-ē\ *adv* — **ca·su·al·ness** *n*

**ca·su·al·ty** \'kazh-(ə-w)əl-tē\ *n, pl* **-ties 1** : serious or fatal accident : DISASTER **2** : a military person lost through death, injury, sickness, or capture or through being missing in action **3** : a person or thing injured, lost, or destroyed

**ca·su·ist·ry** \'kazh-ə-wə-strē\ *n, pl* **-ries** : adroit and esp. false or misleading argument or reasoning usu. about morals — **ca·su·ist** \-wəst\ *n* — **ca·su·is·tic** \,kazh-ə-'wis-tik\ *or* **ca·su·is·ti·cal** \-ti-kəl\ *adj*

**ca·sus bel·li** \,käs-əs-'bel-,ē, ,kā-səs-'bel-,ī\ *n, pl* **ca·sus belli** \,käs-,üs-, ,kā-,süs-\ : an event or action that justifies or allegedly justifies war

¹**cat** \'kat\ *n* **1** : a common domestic mammal long kept by man as a pet or for catching rats and mice **2** : any of various animals (as the lion, lynx, or leopard) that are related to the domestic cat **3** : a spiteful woman **4** : CAT-O'-NINE-TAILS **5** *slang* : a jazz musician; *also* : GUY

²**cat** *abbr* catalog

**ca·tab·o·lism** \kə-'tab-ə-,liz-əm\ *n* : destructive metabolism involving the release of energy and resulting in the breakdown of complex materials — **cat·a·bol·ic** \,kat-ə-'bäl-ik\ *adj* — **cat·a·bol·i·cal·ly** \-i-k(ə-)lē\ *adv*

**cat·a·clysm** \'kat-ə-,kliz-əm\ *n* : a violent change or upheaval — **cat·a·clys·mic** \,kat-ə-'kliz-mik\ *adj*

**cat·a·comb** \'kat-ə-,kōm\ *n* : an underground burial place with galleries and recesses for tombs

**cat·a·falque** \'kat-ə-,falk, -,fȯ(l)k\ *n* : an ornamental structure sometimes used in solemn funerals to hold the body

**cat·a·lep·sy** \'kat-ᵊl-,ep-sē\ *n, pl* **-sies** : a trancelike state of suspended animation — **cat·a·lep·tic** \,kat-ᵊl-'ep-tik\ *adj or n*

¹**cat·a·log** *or* **cat·a·logue** \'kat-ᵊl-,ȯg\ *n* **1** : LIST, REGISTER **2** : a systematic list of items with descriptive details; *also* : a book containing such a list

²**catalog** *or* **catalogue** *vb* **-loged** *or* **-logued; -log·ing** *or* **-logu·ing 1** : to make a catalog of **2** : to enter in a catalog — **cat·a·log·er** *or* **cat·a·logu·er** *n*

**ca·tal·pa** \kə-'tal-pə\ *n* : a broad-leaved tree with showy flowers and long slim pods

**ca·tal·y·sis** \kə-'tal-ə-səs\ *n, pl* **-y·ses** \-,sēz\ : the change and esp. increase in the rate of a chemical reaction brought about by a substance (**cat·a·lyst** \'kat-ᵊl-əst\) that is itself unchanged at the end — **cat·a·lyt·ic** \,kat-ᵊl-'it-ik\ *adj* — **cat·a·lyt·i·cal·ly** \-i-k-(ə-)lē\ *adv*

**cat·a·lyze** \'kat-ᵊl-,īz\ *vb* **-lyzed; -lyz·ing** : to bring about the catalysis of (a chemical reaction) — **cat·a·lyz·er** *n*

**cat·a·ma·ran** \,kat-ə-mə-'ran\ *n* [Tamil (a language of southern India) *kaṭṭumaram*, fr. *kaṭṭu* to tie + *maram* tree] **1** : a raft propelled by paddles or sails **2** : a boat with twin hulls

**cat·a·mount** \'kat-ə-,maȯnt\ *n* : COUGAR; *also* : LYNX

**cat·a·pult** \'kat-ə-,pəlt, -,pùlt\ *n* **1** : an ancient military machine for hurling missiles (as stones and arrows) **2** : a device for launching an airplane from the deck of a ship — **catapult** *vb*

**cat·a·ract** \'kat-ə-,rakt\ *n* **1** : a large waterfall; *also* : steep rapids in a river **2** : a cloudiness of the lens of the eye obstructing vision

**ca·tarrh** \kə-'tär\ *n* : inflammation of a mucous membrane esp. of the nose and throat — **ca·tarrh·al** \-əl\ *adj*

**ca·tas·tro·phe** \kə-'tas-trə-(,)fē\ *n* [Gk *katastrophē*, fr. *katastrephein* to overturn, fr. *kata-* down + *strephein* to turn] **1** : a great disaster or misfortune **2** : utter failure — **cat·a·stroph·ic** \,kat-ə-'sträf-ik\ *adj* — **cat·a·stroph·i·cal·ly** \-i-k(ə-)lē\ *adv*

¹**cat·a·ton·ic** \,kat-ə-'tän-ik\ *adj* : of, relating to, or marked by schizophrenia characterized by symptoms such as stupor, catalepsy, or negativism

²**catatonic** *n* : one who is catatonic

**cat·bird** \'kat-,bərd\ *n* : an American songbird with a call like the cry of a cat

**cat·boat** \'kat-,bōt\ *n* : a single-masted sailboat with the sail extended by a long boom

**cat·call** \-,kȯl\ *n* : a sound like the cry of a cat; *also* : a noise made to express disapproval — **catcall** *vb*

¹**catch** \'kach, 'kech\ *vb* **caught** \'kȯt\; **catch·ing 1** : to capture esp. after pursuit **2** : TRAP **3** : to discover esp. unexpectedly : SURPRISE, DETECT **4** : to become suddenly aware of **5** : to take hold of : SEIZE, GRASP **6** : SNATCH (~ at a straw) **7** : INTERCEPT **8** : to get entangled **9** : to become affected with or by (~ fire) (~ cold) **10** : to seize and hold firmly; *also* : FASTEN **11** : to take in and retain **12** : OVER-

TAKE 13 : to be in time for ⟨~ a train⟩ 14 : to look at or listen to

²catch n 1 : the act of catching; also : a game consisting of throwing and catching a ball 2 : something caught 3 : something that catches or checks or holds immovable ⟨a door ~⟩ 4 : one worth catching esp. in marriage 5 : FRAGMENT, SNATCH 6 : a concealed difficulty

catch·all \-,ȯl\ n : something to hold a variety of odds and ends

catch-as-catch-can \,kach-əz-,kach-'kan, ,kech-əz-,kech-\ adj : using any means available

catch·er \'kech-ər, 'kech-\ n : one that catches; esp : a player stationed behind home plate in baseball

catch·ing \-iŋ\ adj 1 : INFECTIOUS, CONTAGIOUS 2 : ALLURING, CATCHY

catch·ment \'kach-mənt, 'kech-\ n 1 : the action of catching water 2 : something that catches water; also : the amount of water caught

catch on vb 1 : UNDERSTAND 2 : to become popular

catch·pen·ny \-,pen-ē\ adj : designed esp. to get small sums of money from the ignorant ⟨a ~ plan⟩

catch·up \'kech-əp, 'kach-; 'kat-səp\ var of CATSUP

catch up vb : to travel or work fast enough to overtake or complete

catch·word \'kach-,wərd, 'kech-\ n 1 : GUIDE WORD 2 : a word or expression representative of a party, school, or point of view

catchy \'kach-ē, 'kech-\ adj catch·i·er; -est 1 : apt to catch the interest or attention 2 : TRICKY 3 : FITFUL, IRREGULAR

cat·e·chism \'kat-ə-,kiz-əm\ n : a summary or test (as of religious doctrine) usu. in the form of questions and answers — cat·e·chist \-,kist\ n — cat·e·chize \-,kīz\ vb

cat·e·chu·men \,kat-ə-'kyü-mən\ n : a religious convert receiving training before baptism

cat·e·gor·i·cal \,kat-ə-'gȯr-i-kəl\ adj 1 : ABSOLUTE, UNQUALIFIED 2 : of, relating to, or constituting a category — cat·e·gor·i·cal·ly \-i-k(ə-)lē\ adv

cat·e·go·rize \'kat-i-gə-,rīz\ vb -rized; -riz·ing : to put into a category : CLASSIFY — cat·e·go·ri·za·tion \,kat-i-gə-rə-'zā-shən\ n

cat·e·go·ry \'kat-ə-,gȯr-ē\ n, pl -ries : a division used in classification; also : CLASS, GROUP, KIND

ca·ter \'kāt-ər\ vb 1 : to provide a supply of food 2 : to supply what is wanted — ca·ter·er n

cat·er-cor·ner \'kat-ē-'kȯr-nər, ,kat-ə-, ,kit-ē-\ or cat·er-cor·nered adv or adj [obs. cater (four-spot of cards or dice) + E corner] : in a diagonal or oblique position

cat·er·pil·lar \'kat-ə(r)-,pil-ər\ n [ME catyrpel, fr. OF catepelose, lit., hairy cat] : a wormlike often hairy insect larva esp. of a butterfly or moth

cat·er·waul \'kat-ər-,wȯl\ vb : to make the characteristic harsh cry of a rutting cat — caterwaul n

cat·fish \'kat-,fish\ n : any of several big-headed stout-bodied fishes with fleshy sensory processes around the mouth

cat·gut \-,gət\ n : a tough cord made usu. from sheep intestines

ca·thar·sis \kə-'thär-səs\ n, pl ca·thar·ses \-,sēz\ 1 : an act of purging or purification 2 : elimination of a complex by bringing it to consciousness and affording it expression

ca·thar·tic \kə-'thärt-ik\ adj or n : PURGATIVE

ca·the·dral \kə-'thē-drəl\ n : the principal church of a diocese

cath·e·ter \'kath-ət-ər\ n : a tube for insertion into a bodily passage or cavity esp. for drawing off material (as urine)

cath·ode \'kath-,ōd\ n 1 : the negative electrode of an electrolytic cell 2 : the positive terminal of a battery 3 : the electron-emitting electrode of an electron tube — ca·thod·ic \ka-'thäd-ik\ adj

cath·o·lic \'kath-(ə-)lik\ adj 1 : GENERAL, UNIVERSAL 2 cap : of or relating to Catholics and esp. Roman Catholics

Cath·o·lic \'kath-(ə-)lik\ n : a member of a church claiming historical continuity from the ancient undivided Christian church; esp : a member of the Roman Catholic Church — Ca·thol·i·cism \kə-'thäl-ə-,siz-əm\ n

cath·o·lic·i·ty \,kath-ə-'lis-ət-ē\ n, pl -ties 1 cap : the character of being in conformity with a Catholic church 2 : liberality of sentiments or views 3 : comprehensive range

cat·ion \'kat-,ī-ən\ n 1 : the ion in an electrolyte that migrates to the cathode 2 : a positively charged ion

cat·kin \'kat-kən\ n : a long flower cluster (as of a willow) bearing crowded flowers and prominent bracts

cat·like \-,līk\ adj : resembling a cat; esp : STEALTHY

cat·nap \-,nap\ n : a very short light nap — catnap vb

cat·nip \-,nip\ n : an aromatic mint relished by cats

cat-o'-nine-tails \,kat-ə-'nīn-,tālz\ n, pl cat-o'-nine-tails : a whip made of usu. 9 knotted cords with a handle

cat's cradle n : a game played with a string looped on the fingers in such a way as to resemble a small cradle

cat's-eye \'kats-,ī\ n, pl cat's-eyes : any of various iridescent gems

cat's-paw \-,pȯ\ n, pl cat's-paws : a person used by another as a tool

cat·sup \'kech-əp, 'kach-; 'kat-səp\ n [Malay kĕchap spiced fish sauce] : a seasoned tomato puree

cat·tail \'kat-,tāl\ n : a tall reedlike marsh herb with furry brown spikes of tiny flowers

cat·tle \'kat-ᵊl\ n pl : LIVESTOCK; esp : domestic bovines (as cows, bulls, or calves) — cat·tle·man \-mən,-,-man\ n

cat·ty \'kat-ē\ adj cat·ti·er; -est : slyly spiteful — cat·ti·ly \'kat-ᵊl-e\ adv — cat·ti·ness \-ē-nəs\ n

**cat·ty-cor·ner** or **cat·ty-cor·nered** var of CATERCORNER

**CATV** abbr community antenna television

**cat·walk** \'kat-,wòk\ n : a narrow walk (as along a bridge)

**Cau·ca·sian** \kò-'kā-zhən, -'kazh-ən\ adj : of or relating to the white race — **Caucasian** n — **Cau·ca·soid** \'kò-kə-,sòid\ adj or n

**cau·cus** \'kò-kəs\ n : a meeting of a group of persons belonging to the same political party or faction usu. to decide upon policies and candidates — **caucus** vb

**cau·dal** \'kòd-ᵊl\ adj : of, relating to, or located near the tail or the hind end of the body — **cau·dal·ly** \-ē\ adv

**cau·di·llo** \kaù-'thē-(y)ō, -'thēl-yō\ n, pl -**llos** : a Spanish or Latin-American military dictator

**caught** \'kòt\ past of CATCH

**caul** \'kòl\ n : the inner fetal membrane of higher vertebrates (as man) esp. when covering the head at birth

**cauldron** var of CALDRON

**cau·li·flow·er** \'kò-li-,flaù-(-ə)r\ n [It cavolfiore, fr. cavolo cabbage (fr. L caulis stem, cabbage) + fiore flower] : a vegetable closely related to cabbage and grown for its compact head of undeveloped flowers; also : this head

**cauliflower ear** n : an ear deformed from injury and excessive growth of scar tissue

**caulk** \'kòk\ vb [ME caulken, fr. OF cauquer to trample, fr. L calcare, fr. calx heel] : to make the seams of (a boat) watertight by filling with waterproofing material; also : to make tight against leakage by a sealing substance (~ a pipe joint) — **caulk·er** n

**caus·al** \'kò-zəl\ adj 1 : expressing or indicating cause 2 : relating to or acting as a cause 3 : showing interaction of cause and effect — **cau·sal·i·ty** \kò-'zal-ət-ē\ n — **caus·al·ly** \'kò-zə-lē\ adv

**cau·sa·tion** \kò-'zā-shən\ n 1 : the act or process of causing 2 : the means by which an effect is produced

¹**cause** \'kòz\ n 1 : something that brings about a result; esp : a person or thing that is the agent of bringing something about 2 : REASON, MOTIVE 3 : a question or matter to be decided 4 : a suit or action in court : CASE 5 : a principle or movement earnestly supported — **cause·less** adj

²**cause** vb **caused; caus·ing** : to be the cause or occasion of — **caus·ative** \'kò-zət-iv\ adj — **caus·er** n

**cause cé·lè·bre** \,kòz-sā-'lebrᵊ, ,kòz-\ n, pl **causes cé·lè·bres** \same\ 1 : a legal case that excites widespread interest 2 : a notorious incident or episode

**cau·se·rie** \,kōz-(ə-)'rē\ n 1 : an informal conversation : CHAT 2 : a short informal composition

**cause·way** \'kòz-,wā\ n : a raised way across wet ground or water

**caus·tic** \'kò-stik\ adj 1 : CORROSIVE 2 : SHARP, INCISIVE (~ wit) — **caustic** n

**cau·ter·ize** \'kòt-ə-,rīz\ vb -**ized;** -**iz·ing** : to burn or sear usu. to prevent infection or bleeding — **cau·ter·i·za·tion** \,kòt-ə-rə-'zā-shən\ n

¹**cau·tion** \'kò-shən\ n 1 : a word or act that conveys a warning 2 : prudent forethought to minimize risk : WARINESS 3 : one that arouses astonishment — **cau·tion·ary** \-shə-,ner-ē\ adj

²**caution** vb **cau·tioned; cau·tion·ing** \'kò-sh(ə-)niŋ\ : to advise caution to : WARN

**cau·tious** \'kò-shəs\ adj : marked by or given to caution : CAREFUL — **cau·tious·ly** adv — **cau·tious·ness** n

**cav** abbr cavalry

**cav·al·cade** \,kav-əl-'kād\ n 1 : a procession of persons on horseback; also : a procession of vehicles 2 : a dramatic sequence or procession

¹**cav·a·lier** \,kav-ə-'lìor\ n [MF, fr. It cavaliere, fr. Old Provençal cavalier, fr. LL caballarius groom, fr. L caballus horse] 1 : a mounted soldier : KNIGHT 2 cap : a Royalist in the time of Charles I of England 3 : a debonair person

²**cavalier** adj 1 : gay and easy in manner : DEBONAIR 2 : DISDAINFUL, HAUGHTY — **cav·a·lier·ly** adv — **cav·a·lier·ness** n

**cav·al·ry** \'kav-əl-rē\ n, pl -**ries** : troops mounted on horseback or moving in motor vehicles — **cav·al·ry·man** \-mən, -,man\ n

**cave** \'kāv\ n : a natural underground chamber with an opening to the surface

**ca·ve·at** \'kav-ē-,at, -,ät; 'kāv-ē-,ät\ n : WARNING

**caveat emp·tor** \-'emp-tər, -,tòr\ n [NL, let the buyer beware] : a warning principle in trading that the buyer should be alert to see that he gets the quantity and quality paid for

**cave-in** \'kāv-,in\ n 1 : the action of caving in 2 : a place where earth has caved in

**cave in** \(')kāv-'in\ vb 1 : to collapse or cause to collapse 2 : to cease resisting : SUBMIT

**cave·man** \'kāv-,man\ n 1 : one who lives in a cave; esp : a man of the Stone Age 2 : a man who acts with rough or violent directness esp. toward women

**cav·ern** \'kav-ərn\ n : an underground chamber of large extent : CAVE — **cav·ern·ous** adj — **cav·ern·ous·ly** adv

**cav·i·ar** or **cav·i·are** \'kav-ē-,är, 'käv-\ n : the salted roe of a large fish (as sturgeon) used as an appetizer

**cav·il** \'kav-əl\ vb -**iled** or -**illed;** -**il·ing** or -**il·ling** \-(ə-)liŋ\ : to find fault without good reason : make frivolous objections — **cavil** n — **cav·il·er** or **cav·il·ler** n

**cav·i·ta·tion** \,kav-ə-'tā-shən\ n : the formation of partial vacuums in a liquid by a swiftly moving solid body (as a propeller) or by high-frequency sound waves; also : a cavity so formed

**cav·i·ty** \'kav-ət-ē\ n, pl -**ties** : an unfilled space within a mass : a hollow place

**ca·vort** \kə-'vòrt\ vb : PRANCE, CAPER

**ca·vy** \'kā-vē\ n, pl **cavies** : GUINEA PIG

**caw** \'kȯ\ *vb* **:** to utter the harsh raucous natural call of the crow or a similar cry — **caw** *n*

**cay** \'kē, 'kā\ *n* **:** a low island or reef of sand or coral

**cay·enne pepper** \,kī-,en-, ,kā-\ *n* **:** a pungent condiment consisting of ground dried fruits or seeds of a hot pepper

**cay·man** *var of* CAIMAN

**Ca·yu·ga** \kē-'ü-gə, 'kyü-, kā-'(y)ü-\ *n, pl* **Cayuga** *or* **Cayugas :** a member of an Indian people of New York

**Cay·use** \'kī-,(y)üs, kī-'(y)üs\ *n* **1** *pl* **Cayuse** *or* **Cayuses :** a member of an Indian people of Oregon and Washington **2** *not cap, pl* **cayuses** *West* **:** a native range horse of the western U.S.

**Cb** *symbol* columbium

**CBC** *abbr* Canadian Broadcasting Corporation

**CBD** *abbr* cash before delivery

**CBS** *abbr* Columbia Broadcasting System

**CBW** *abbr* chemical and biological warfare

**cc** *abbr* cubic centimeter

**CC** *abbr* carbon copy

**CCC** *abbr* **1** Civilian Conservation Corps **2** Commodity Credit Corporation

**CCTV** *abbr* closed-circuit television

**ccw** *abbr* counterclockwise

**cd** *abbr* cord

**Cd** *symbol* cadmium

**CD** *abbr* Civil Defense

**CDR** *abbr* commander

**Ce** *symbol* cerium

**CE** *abbr* **1** chemical engineer **2** civil engineer **3** Corps of Engineers

**cease** \'sēs\ *vb* **ceased; ceas·ing :** to come or bring to an end **:** STOP

**cease-fire** \'sēs-'fī(ə)r\ *n* **:** a suspension of active hostilities

**cease·less** \'sēs-ləs\ *adj* **:** being without pause or stop **:** CONTINUOUS — **cease·less·ly** *adv* — **cease·less·ness** *n*

**ce·cum** \'sē-kəm\ *n, pl* **ce·ca** \-kə\ **:** the blind pouch at the beginning of the large intestine into one side of which the small intestine opens — **ce·cal** \-kəl\ *adj*

**ce·dar** \'sēd-ər\ *n* **:** any of various cone-bearing trees noted for their fragrant durable wood; *also* **:** this wood

**cede** \'sēd\ *vb* **ced·ed; ced·ing 1 :** to yield or give up esp. by treaty **2 :** ASSIGN, TRANSFER — **ced·er** *n*

**ce·di** \'sād-ē\ *n* — see MONEY table

**ce·dil·la** \si-'dil-ə\ *n* **:** a mark placed under the letter *c* (as ç) to show that the *c* is to be pronounced like *s*

**ceil·ing** \'sē-liŋ\ *n* **1 :** the overhead inside surface of a room **2 :** the greatest height at which an airplane can operate efficiently **3 :** the height above the ground of the base of the lowest layer of clouds when over half of the sky is obscured **4 :** a prescribed upper limit ⟨price ~⟩

**cel·an·dine** \'sel-ən-,dīn, -,dēn\ *n* **:** a yellow-flowered herb related to the poppies

**cel·e·brate** \'sel-ə-,brāt\ *vb* **-brat·ed; -brat·ing 1 :** to perform (as a

sacrament) with appropriate rites **2 :** to honor (as a holy day) by solemn ceremonies or by refraining from ordinary business **3 :** to observe a notable occasion with festivities **4 :** EXTOL — **cel·e·brant** \-brənt\ *n* — **cel·e·bra·tion** \,sel-ə-'brā-shən\ *n* — **cel·e·bra·tor** \'sel-ə-,brāt-ər\ *n*

**cel·e·brat·ed** \-əd\ *adj* **:** widely known and often referred to **syn** distinguished, renowned, noted, famous, illustrious, notorious

**ce·leb·ri·ty** \sə-'leb-rət-ē\ *n, pl* **-ties 1 :** the state of being celebrated **:** RENOWN **2 :** a celebrated person

**ce·ler·i·ty** \sə-'ler-ət-ē\ *n* **:** SPEED, RAPIDITY

**cel·ery** \'sel-(ə-)rē\ *n, pl* **-er·ies :** an herb related to the carrot and widely grown for crisp edible petioles

**ce·les·ta** \sə-'les-tə\ *n* **:** a keyboard instrument with hammers that strike steel plates

**ce·les·tial** \sə-'les-chəl\ *adj* **1 :** of or relating to the sky **2 :** HEAVENLY, DIVINE — **ce·les·tial·ly** \-ē\ *adv*

**celestial navigation** *n* **:** navigation by observation of the positions of celestial bodies

**celestial sphere** *n* **:** an imaginary sphere of infinite radius against which the celestial bodies appear to be projected

**cel·i·ba·cy** \'sel-ə-bə-sē\ *n* **1 :** the state of being unmarried; *esp* **:** abstention by vow from marriage **2 :** CHASTITY

**cel·i·bate** \'sel-ə-bət\ *n* **:** one who lives in celibacy — **celibate** *adj*

**cell** \'sel\ *n* **1 :** a small room (as in a convent or prison) usu. for one person; *also* **:** a small compartment, cavity, or bounded space **2 :** a tiny mass of protoplasm that contains a nucleus, is enclosed by a membrane, and forms the fundamental unit of living matter **3 :** a container holding an electrolyte either for generating electricity or for use in electrolysis **4 :** a device for converting radiant energy into electrical energy or for varying an electric current in accordance with radiation received — **celled** \'seld\ *adj*

**cel·lar** \'sel-ər\ *n* **1 :** a room or group of rooms below the surface of the ground and usu. under a building **2 :** the lowest position (as in an athletic league) **3 :** a stock of wines

**cel·lar·age** \'sel-ə-rij\ *n* **1 :** a cellar esp. for storage **2 :** charge for storage in a cellar

**cel·lar·ette** *or* **cel·lar·et** \,sel-ə-'ret\ *n* **:** a case or cabinet for a few bottles of wine or liquor

**cel·lo** \'chel-ō\ *n, pl* **cellos :** a bass member of the violin family tuned an octave below the viola — **cel·list** \-əst\ *n*

**cel·lo·phane** \'sel-ə-,fān\ *n* **:** a thin transparent material made from cellulose and used as a wrapping

**cel·lu·lar** \'sel-yə-lər\ *adj* **1 :** of, relating to, or consisting of cells **2 :** porous in texture

**cel·lu·lose** \-ˌlōs\ *n* : a complex carbohydrate of the cell walls of plants used esp. in making paper or rayon — **cel·lu·los·ic** \ˌsel-yə-ˈlō-sik\ *adj or n*

**Cel·sius** \ˈsel-sē-əs\ *adj* : CENTIGRADE

**Celt** \ˈselt, ˈkelt\ *n* : a member of any of a group of peoples (as the Irish or Welsh) of western Europe — **Celt·ic** *adj*

**cem·ba·lo** \ˈchem-bə-ˌlō\ *n, pl* **-ba·li** \-ˌlē\ *or* **-balos** : HARPSICHORD

¹**ce·ment** \si-ˈment\ *n* 1 : a powder that is produced from a burned mixture chiefly of clay and limestone, that with water forms a paste that hardens into a stonelike mass, and that is used in mortars and concretes; *also* : CONCRETE 2 : a binding element or agency 3 : a substance for filling cavities in teeth

²**cement** *vb* : to unite or cover with cement — **ce·ment·er** *n*

**ce·men·ta·tion** \ˌsē-ˌmen-ˈtā-shən\ *n* 1 : the act or process of cementing 2 : the state of being cemented

**ce·men·tum** \si-ˈment-əm\ *n* : a specialized external bony layer of the part of a tooth normally within the gum

**cem·e·tery** \ˈsem-ə-ˌter-ē\ *n, pl* **-ter·ies** [ME *cimitery*, fr. MF *cimitiere*, fr. LL *coemeterium*, fr. Gk *koimētērion* sleeping chamber, burial place, fr. *koiman* to put to sleep] : a burial ground : GRAVEYARD

**cen** *abbr* central

**cen·o·bite** \ˈsen-ə-ˌbīt\ *n* : a member of a religious group living together in a monastic community — **cen·o·bit·ic** \ˌsen-ə-ˈbit-ik\ *or* **cen·o·bit·i·cal** \-i-kəl\ *adj*

**ceno·taph** \ˈsen-ə-ˌtaf\ *n* [F *cénotaphe*, fr. L *cenotaphium*, fr. Gk *kenotaphion*, fr. *kenos* empty + *taphos* tomb] : a tomb or a monument erected in honor of a person whose body is elsewhere

**cen·ser** \ˈsen-sər\ *n* : a vessel for burning incense (as in a religious ritual)

¹**cen·sor** \ˈsen-sər\ *n* 1 : one of two early Roman magistrates whose duties included taking the census 2 : an official who inspects printed matter or sometimes motion pictures with power to suppress anything objectionable — **cen·so·ri·al** \sen-ˈsōr-ē-əl\ *adj*

²**censor** *vb* : to subject to censorship

**cen·so·ri·ous** \sen-ˈsōr-ē-əs\ *adj* : marked by or given to censure : CRITICAL — **cen·so·ri·ous·ly** *adv* — **cen·so·ri·ous·ness** *n*

**cen·sor·ship** \ˈsen-sər-ˌship\ *n* 1 : the office of a Roman censor 2 : the action of a censor esp. in stopping the transmission or publication of matter considered objectionable

¹**cen·sure** \ˈsen-chər\ *n* 1 : the act of blaming or condemning sternly 2 : an official reprimand

²**censure** *vb* **cen·sured; cen·sur·ing** \ˈsench-(ə-)riŋ\ : to find fault with and criticize as blameworthy — **cen·sur·able** *adj* — **cen·sur·er** *n*

**cen·sus** \ˈsen-səs\ *n* 1 : a periodic governmental count of population 2 : COUNT, TALLY

¹**cent** \ˈsent\ *n* [MF, hundred, fr. L *centum*] 1 : a monetary unit equal to 1/100 of a basic unit of value — see *dollar, gulden, leone, piaster, rand, rupee, shilling* at MONEY table 2 : a coin, token, or note representing one cent

²**cent** *abbr* 1 centigrade 2 central 3 century

**cent·are** \ˈsen-ˌta(ə)r\ *n* — see METRIC SYSTEM table

**cen·taur** \ˈsen-ˌtȯr\ *n* : one of a race of creatures in Greek mythology half man and half horse

¹**cen·ta·vo** \sen-ˈtäv-(ˌ)ō\ *n, pl* **-vos** — see *colon, cordoba, lempira, peso, quetzal, sol, sucre* at MONEY table

²**cen·ta·vo** \-ˈtäv-(ˌ)ü, -(ˌ)ō\ *n, pl* **-vos** — see *cruzeiro, escudo* at MONEY table

**cen·te·nar·i·an** \ˌsent-ᵊn-ˈer-ē-ən\ *n* : a person who is 100 or more years old

**cen·te·na·ry** \sen-ˈten-ə-rē, ˈsent-ᵊn-ˌer-ē\ *n, pl* **-ries** : CENTENNIAL — **centenary** *adj*

**cen·ten·ni·al** \sen-ˈten-ē-əl\ *n* : a 100th anniversary or its celebration — **centennial** *adj* — **cen·ten·ni·al·ly** \-ē\ *adv*

¹**cen·ter** \ˈsent-ər\ *n* 1 : the point equally distant or at the average distance from the outside points of a figure or body 2 : the point about which an activity concentrates or from which something originates 3 : a region of concentrated population 4 : a middle part 5 *often cap* : political figures holding moderate views esp. between those of conservatives and liberals 6 : a player occupying a middle position (as in football or basketball)

²**center** *vb* 1 : to place or fix at or around a center or central area 2 : to gather to a center : CONCENTRATE 3 : to have a center

**cen·ter·board** \ˈsent-ər-ˌbȯrd\ *n* : a retractable keel used esp. in sailboats

**cen·tered** \ˈsent-ərd\ *adj* : having a center

**cen·ter·piece** \ˈsent-ər-ˌpēs\ *n* : an object in a central position; *esp* : an adornment in the center of a table

**center punch** *n* : a punch for making the centers of holes to be drilled

**cen·tes·i·mal** \sen-ˈtes-ə-məl\ *adj* : marked by or relating to division into hundredths

¹**cen·tes·i·mo** \chen-ˈtez-ə-ˌmō\ *n, pl* **-mi** \-(ˌ)mē\ — see *lira* at MONEY table

²**cen·tes·i·mo** \sen-ˈtes-ə-ˌmō\ *n, pl* **-mos** — see *balboa, escudo, peso* at MONEY table

**cen·ti·grade** \ˈsent-ə-ˌgrād, ˈsänt-\ *adj* : relating to, conforming to, or having a thermometer scale on which the interval between the freezing and boiling points of water is divided into 100 degrees with 0° representing the freezing point and 100° the boiling point ⟨10° ∼⟩

**cen·ti·gram** \-ˌgram\ *n* — see METRIC SYSTEM table

**cen·ti·li·ter** \ˈsent-i-ˌlēt-ər\ *n* — see METRIC SYSTEM table

**cen·time** \ˈsän-ˌtēm\ *n* — see *dinar, franc, gourde* at MONEY table

**cen·ti·me·ter** \ˈsent-ə-ˌmēt-ər, ˈsänt-\

*n* — see METRIC SYSTEM table

**cen·ti·me·ter-gram-second** *adj* **:** of, relating to, or being a system of units based on the centimeter as the unit of length, the gram as the unit of weight, and the second as the unit of time

**cen·ti·mo** \'sent-ə-,mō\ *n*, *pl* **-mos** — see *bolivar, colon, guarani, peseta* at MONEY table

**cen·ti·pede** \'sent-ə-,pēd\ *n* [L *centipeda*, fr. *centi-* hundred + *pes* foot] **:** a long flat many-legged arthropod

¹**cen·tral** \'sen-trəl\ *adj* **1 :** constituting a center **2 :** ESSENTIAL, PRINCIPAL **3 :** situated at, in, or near the center **4 :** centrally placed and superseding separate units (~ heating) — **cen·tral·ly** \-ē\ *adv*

²**central** *n* **1 :** a telephone exchange or an operator handling calls there **2 :** a central controlling office

**cen·tral·ize** \'sen-trə-,līz\ *vb* **-ized; -iz·ing :** to bring to a central point or under central control — **cen·tral·iza·tion** \,sen-trə-lə-'zā-shən\ *n* — **cen·tral·iz·er** \'sen-trə-,lī-zər\ *n*

**central nervous system** *n* **:** the part of the nervous system which supervises and coordinates the activity of the entire nervous system and which in vertebrates consists of the brain and spinal cord

**cen·tre** *chiefly Brit var of* CENTER

**cen·trif·u·gal** \sen-'trif-yə-gəl, -'trif-i-gəl\ *adj* [NL *centrifugus*, fr. *centr-* center + *fugere* to flee] **1 :** proceeding or acting in a direction away from a center or axis **2 :** using or acting by centrifugal force — **cen·trif·u·gal·ly** \-ē\ *adv*

**centrifugal force** *n* **1 :** the force that tends to impel a thing or parts of a thing outward from a center of rotation **2 :** the force that an orbiting body exerts on the object constraining it

**cen·tri·fuge** \'sen-trə-,fyüj\ *n* **:** a machine using centrifugal force (as for separating substances of different densities or for removing moisture)

**cen·trip·e·tal** \sen-'trip-ət-ᵊl\ *adj* [NL *centripetus*, fr. *centr-* center + L *petere* seek] **:** proceeding or acting in a direction toward a center or axis — **cen·trip·e·tal·ly** \-ē\ *adv*

**centripetal force** *n* **:** the force needed to constrain a body to a circular path

**cen·trist** \'sen-trəst\ *n* **1** *often cap* **:** a member of a center party **2 :** one that holds moderate views

**cen·tu·ri·on** \sen-'t(y)ùr-ē-ən\ *n* **:** an officer commanding a Roman century

**cen·tu·ry** \'sench-(ə-)rē\ *n*, *pl* **-ries** **1 :** a subdivision of a Roman legion **2 :** a group or sequence of 100 like things **3 :** a period of 100 years

**century plant** *n* **:** a Mexican agave (*Agave americana*) maturing and flowering only once and then dying

**ce·phal·ic** \sə-'fal-ik\ *adj* **1 :** of or relating to the head **2 :** directed toward or situated on or in or near the head

**ce·ram·ic** \sə-'ram-ik\ *n* **1** *pl* **:** the art or process of making articles from clay by shaping and hardening by fir-

ing; *also* **:** the process of making any product (as earthenware, brick, tile, or glass) from a nonmetallic mineral by firing **2 :** a product produced by ceramics — **ceramic** *adj*

**ce·ra·mist** \sə-'ram-əst\ *or* **ce·ram·i·cist** \sə-'ram-ə-səst\ *n* **:** one that engages in ceramics

¹**ce·re·al** \'sir-ē-əl\ *adj* [L *cerealis*, fr. *Ceres*, the Roman goddess of agriculture] **:** relating to grain or to the plants that produce it; *also* **:** made of grain

²**cereal** *n* **1 :** a grass (as wheat) yielding grain suitable for food; *also* **:** its grain **2 :** cereal grain prepared for use as a breakfast food

**cer·e·bel·lum** \,ser-ə-'bel-əm\ *n*, *pl* **-bellums** *or* **-bel·la** \-'bel-ə\ **:** a part of the brain that projects over the medulla and is concerned esp. with coordination of muscular action and with bodily equilibrium — **cer·e·bel·lar** \-'bel-ər\ *adj*

**ce·re·bral cortex** \sə-,rē-brəl-, ,ser-ə-\ *n* **:** the surface layer of gray matter of the cerebrum that functions chiefly in coordination of higher nervous activity

**cerebral palsy** *n* **:** a disorder caused by brain damage usu. before or during birth and marked esp. by defective muscle control

**cer·e·brate** \'ser-ə-,brāt\ *vb* **-brat·ed; -brat·ing :** THINK — **cer·e·bra·tion** \,ser-ə-'brā-shən\ *n*

**ce·re·brum** \sə-'rē-brəm, 'ser-ə-\ *n*, *pl* **-brums** *or* **-bra** \-brə\ **:** the enlarged front and upper part of the brain that contains the higher nervous centers — **ce·re·bral** \sə-'rē-brəl, 'ser-ə-\ *adj* — **ce·re·bral·ly** \-ē\ *adv*

**cere·cloth** \'sior-,klòth\ *n* **:** cloth treated with melted wax or gummy matter and formerly used esp. for wrapping a dead body

**cere·ment** \'ser-ə-mənt, 'sior-mənt\ *n* **:** a shroud for the dead

¹**cer·e·mo·ni·al** \,ser-ə-'mō-nē-əl\ *adj* **:** of, relating to, or forming a ceremony — **cer·e·mo·ni·al·ly** \-ē\ *adv*

²**ceremonial** *n* **:** a ceremonial act or system **:** RITUAL, FORM

**cer·e·mo·ni·ous** \,ser-ə-'mō-nē-əs\ *adj* **1 :** CEREMONIAL **2 :** devoted to forms and ceremony **3 :** according to formal usage or procedure **4 :** marked by ceremony — **cer·e·mo·ni·ous·ly** *adv* — **cer·e·mo·ni·ous·ness** *n*

**cer·e·mo·ny** \'ser-ə-,mō-nē\ *n*, *pl* **-nies** **1 :** a formal act or series of acts prescribed by law, ritual, or convention **2 :** a conventional act of politeness **3 :** a mere outward form **4 :** FORMALITY

**ce·re·us** \'sir-ē-əs\ *n* **:** any of various cacti of the western U.S. and tropical America

**ce·rise** \sə-'rēs\ *n* **:** a moderate red

**ce·ri·um** \'sir-ē-əm\ *n* **:** a malleable metallic chemical element

**cer·met** \'sər-,met\ *n* **:** a strong alloy of a heat-resistant compound and a metal used esp. for turbine blades

**cert** *abbr* certificate; certification; certified; certify

¹**cer·tain** \'sərt-ⁿn\ *adj* **1** : FIXED, SETTLED **2** : proved to be true **3** : of a specific but unspecified character (~ people in authority) **4** : DEPENDABLE, RELIABLE **5** : INDISPUTABLE, UNDENIABLE **6** : assured in mind or action — **cer·tain·ly** *adv*

²**certain** *pron* : certain ones

**cer·tain·ty** \-tē\ *n, pl* -**ties 1** : something that is certain **2** : the quality or state of being certain — **for a certainty** : beyond doubt : CERTAINLY

**cer·tif·i·cate** \sər-'tif-i-kət\ *n* **1** : a document testifying to the truth of a fact **2** : a document testifying that one has fulfilled certain requirements (as of a course or school) **3** : a document evidencing ownership or debt

**cer·ti·fi·ca·tion** \ˌsərt-ə-fə-'kā-shən\ *n* **1** : the act of certifying : the state of being certified **2** : a certified statement

**certified check** *n* : a check certified to be good by the bank on which it is drawn

**certified milk** *n* : milk produced in dairies that operate under the rules and regulations of an authorized medical milk commission

**certified public accountant** *n* : an accountant who has met the requirements of a state law and has been granted a state certificate

**cer·ti·fy** \'sərt-ə-ˌfī\ *vb* -**fied**; -**fy·ing 1** : VERIFY, CONFIRM **2** : to endorse officially **3** : to guarantee (a bank check) as good by a statement to that effect stamped on its face **4** : to attest officially to the insanity of **syn** attest, witness, accredit, approve, sanction — **cer·ti·fi·able** \-ˌfī-ə-bəl\ *adj* — **cer·ti·fi·ably** \-blē\ *adv* — **cer·ti·fi·er** *n*

**cer·ti·tude** \'sərt-ə-ˌt(y)üd\ *n* : the state of being or feeling certain

**ce·ru·le·an** \sə-'rü-lē-ən\ *adj* : AZURE

**ce·ru·men** \sə-'rü-mən\ *n* : EARWAX

**cer·vi·cal** \'sər-vi-kəl\ *adj* : of or relating to a neck or cervix

**cer·vix** \'sər-viks\ *n, pl* **cer·vi·ces** \-və-ˌsēz\ *or* **cer·vix·es 1** : NECK; *esp* : the back part of the neck **2** : a constricted portion of an organ or part; *esp* : the narrow outer end of the uterus

**ce·sar·e·an** *also* **ce·sar·i·an** \si-'zar-ē-ən, -'zer-\ *n* : surgical incision of the walls of the abdomen and uterus for delivery of offspring — **cesarean** *also* **cesarian** *adj*

**ce·si·um** \'sē-zē-əm\ *n* : a silver-white soft ductile chemical element

**ces·sa·tion** \se-'sā-shən\ *n* : a temporary or final ceasing (as of action)

**ces·sion** \'sesh-ən\ *n* : a yielding (as of rights) to another

**cess·pool** \'ses-ˌpül\ *n* : an underground pit or tank for receiving household sewage

**cf** *abbr* [L *confer*] compare

**Cf** *symbol* californium

**CF** *abbr* **1** carried forward **2** cost and freight

**CFI** *abbr* cost, freight, and insurance

**cg** *or* **cgm** *abbr* centigram

**CG** *abbr* **1** coast guard **2** commanding general

**cgs** *abbr* centimeter-gram-second

**ch** *abbr* **1** chain **2** champion **3** chapter **4** church

**CH** *abbr* **1** clearinghouse **2** courthouse **3** customhouse

**Cha·blis** \'shab-ˌlē; sha-'blē\ *n, pl* **Cha·blis** \-ˌlēz, -'blēz\ : a dry white table wine

**cha–cha** \'chä-ˌchä\ *n* : a fast rhythmic ballroom dance originating in Latin America

**Chad·ian** \'chad-ē-ən\ *n* : a native or inhabitant of Chad — **Chadian** *adj*

**chafe** \'chāf\ *vb* **chafed**; **chaf·ing 1** : IRRITATE, VEX **2** : FRET **3** : to warm by rubbing esp. with the hands **4** : to rub so as to wear away; *also* : to make sore by rubbing

**cha·fer** \'chā-fər\ *n* : any of various large beetles

¹**chaff** \'chaf\ *n* **1** : debris (as husks) separated from grain in threshing **2** : something light and worthless — **chaffy** *adj*

²**chaff** *n* : light jesting talk : BANTER

³**chaff** *vb* : to tease in a good-natured manner

**chaffer** \'chaf-ər\ *vb* : BARGAIN, HAGGLE — **chaf·fer·er** *n*

**chaf·finch** \'chaf-ˌinch\ *n* : a European finch with a cheerful song often kept as a cage bird

**chaf·ing dish** \'chā-fiŋ-\ *n* : a utensil for cooking food at the table

¹**cha·grin** \shə-'grin\ *n* : mental uneasiness or annoyance caused by failure, disappointment, or humiliation

²**chagrin** *vb* -**grined** \-'grind\; -**grin·ing** \-'grin-iŋ\ : to cause to feel chagrin

¹**chain** \'chān\ *n* **1** : a flexible series of connected links **2** *pl* : BONDS, FETTERS; *also* : BONDAGE **3** : a series of things linked together **4** : a chainlike measuring instrument 66 feet long; *also* : a unit of measurement equal to 66 feet **syn** train, string, set, sequence, succession

²**chain** *vb* : to fasten, bind, or connect with a chain; *also* : FETTER

**chain gang** *n* : a gang of convicts chained together

**chain letter** *n* **1** : a social letter sent to a series of persons in succession and often added to by each recipient **2** : a letter sent to several persons with a request that each send copies to an equal number of persons

**chain mail** *n* : flexible armor of interlocking metal rings

**chain reaction** *n* **1** : a series of events in which each event initiates the succeeding one **2** : a chemical or nuclear reaction yielding products that cause further reactions of the same kind — **chain–re·act** \ˌchān-rē-'akt\ *vb*

**chain saw** *n* : a portable power saw that has teeth linked together to form an endless chain

**chain–smoke** \'chān-'smōk\ *vb* : to smoke esp. cigarettes continuously

**chain store** *n* : one of numerous usu. retail stores under the same ownership and general management that sell the same lines of goods

**¹chair** \'cheər\ *n* 1 : a seat with a back for one person 2 : an official seat; *also* : an office or position of authority or dignity 3 : CHAIRMAN 4 : a sedan chair 5 : ELECTRIC CHAIR

**²chair** *vb* : to act as chairman of

**chair lift** *n* : a power-driven conveyor consisting of seats hung from a moving cable for carrying skiers and sightseers up or down a mountain slope

**chair·man** \'cheər-mən\ *n* 1 : the presiding officer of a meeting or of a committee 2 : a carrier of a sedan chair — **chair·man·ship** *n* — **chair·woman** \-,wŭm-ən\ *n*

**chaise** \'shāz\ *n* 1 : a 2-wheeled carriage with a folding top 2 : a light carriage or pleasure cart

**chaise longue** \'shāz-'lòŋ\ *n, pl* **chaise longues** \-'lòŋ(z)\ [F *chaise longue*, lit., long chair] : a long couchlike chair

**chaise lounge** \-'laùnj\ *n* : CHAISE LONGUE

**chal·ced·o·ny** \kal-'sed-ᵊn-ē\ *n, pl* **-nies** : a translucent pale blue or gray quartz

**chal·co·py·rite** \,kal-kə-'pī-,rīt\ *n* : a yellow mineral constituting an important ore of copper

**cha·let** \sha-'lā\ *n* 1 : a herdsman's cabin in the Swiss mountains 2 : a building in the style of a Swiss cottage with a wide roof overhang and balconies

**chal·ice** \'chal-əs\ *n* : a drinking cup; *esp* : the eucharistic cup

**¹chalk** \'chòk\ *n* 1 : a soft limestone 2 : chalk or chalky material used as a crayon — **chalky** *adj*

**²chalk** *vb* 1 : to rub or mark with chalk 2 : to record (an account) with or as if with chalk — usu. used with *up*

**chalk·board** \'chòk-,bòrd\ *n* : BLACKBOARD

**chalk up** *vb* 1 : ASCRIBE, CREDIT 2 : ATTAIN, ACHIEVE

**¹chal·lenge** \'chal-ᵊnj\ *vb* **challenged; chal·leng·ing** [ME *chalengen* to accuse, fr. OF *chalengier*, fr. L *calumniari* to accuse falsely, fr. *calumnia* calumny] 1 : to halt and demand the countersign of 2 : to take exception to : DISPUTE 3 : to issue an invitation to compete against one esp. in single combat : DARE, DEFY — **chal·leng·er** *n*

**²challenge** *n* 1 : a calling into question 2 : an exception taken to a juror 3 : a sentry's command to halt and prove identity 4 : a summons to a duel 5 : an invitation to compete in a sport

**chal·lis** \'shal-ē\ *n, pl* **chal·lises** \-ēz\ : a lightweight clothing fabric of wool, cotton, or synthetic yarns

**cham** \'kam\ *var of* KHAN

**cham·ber** \'chām-bər\ *n* 1 : ROOM; *esp* : BEDROOM 2 : an enclosed space or compartment 3 : a hall for meetings of a legislative body 4 *pl, chiefly Brit* : a set of rooms 5 : a judge's consultation room — usu. used in pl. 6 : a legisla-

tive or judicial body; *also* : a council for a business purpose 7 : a compartment in the cartridge cylinder of a revolver — **cham·bered** \-bərd\ *adj*

**cham·ber·lain** \'chām-bər-lən\ *n* 1 : a high court dignitary 2 : TREASURER

**cham·ber·maid** \-,mād\ *n* : a maid who takes care of bedrooms

**chamber music** *n* : music intended for performance by a few musicians before a small audience

**chamber of commerce** : an association of businessmen for promoting commercial and industrial interests in the community

**cham·bray** \'sham-,brā\ *n* : a lightweight clothing fabric of white and colored threads

**cha·me·leon** \kə-'mēl-yən\ *n* [ME *camelion*, fr. MF, fr. L *chamaeleon*, fr. Gk *chamaileōn*, fr. *chamai* on the ground + *leōn* lion] : a small lizard whose skin changes color esp. according to the surroundings

**¹cham·fer** \'cham-fər\ *n* : a beveled edge

**²chamfer** *vb* **chamfered; chamfering** \-f(ə-)riŋ\ 1 : to cut a furrow in (as a column) : GROOVE 2 : to make a chamfer on : BEVEL

**cham·ois** \'sham-ē\ *n, pl* **cham·ois** \-ē(z)\ 1 : a small goatlike antelope of Europe and the Caucasus 2 *also* **cham·my** \'sham-ē\ : a soft leather made esp. from the skin of the sheep or goat

**cham·o·mile** \'kam-ə-,mīl, -,mēl\ *n* : any of a genus of strong-scented herbs related to the daisy whose flower heads yield a bitter medicinal substance

**¹champ** \'champ, 'chimp\ *vb* 1 : to chew noisily 2 : to show impatience of delay or restraint

**²champ** \'champ\ *n* : CHAMPION

**cham·pagne** \sham-'pān\ *n* : a sparkling white wine

**cham·paign** \sham-'pān\ *n* : a stretch of flat open country

**¹cham·pi·on** \'cham-pē-ən\ *n* 1 : a militant advocate or defender 2 : one that wins first prize or place in a contest 3 : one that is acknowledged to be better than all others

**²champion** *vb* : to protect or fight for as a champion *syn* back, advocate, uphold, support

**cham·pi·on·ship** \-,ship\ *n* 1 : the position or title of a champion 2 : the act of championing : DEFENSE 3 : a contest held to determine a champion

**¹chance** \'chans\ *n* 1 : something that happens without apparent cause 2 : the unpredictable element in existence : LUCK, FORTUNE 3 : OPPORTUNITY 4 : the likelihood of a particular outcome in an uncertain situation : PROBABILITY 5 : RISK 6 : a ticket in a raffle — **chance** *adj* — **by chance** : in the haphazard course of events

**²chance** *vb* **chanced; chanc·ing** 1 : to take place by chance : HAPPEN 2 : to come casually and unexpectedly —used with *upon* 3 : to leave to chance 4 : to accept the risk of

**chan·cel** \'chan-səl\ *n* : the part of a church including the altar and choir

**chan·cel·lery** or **chan·cel·lory** \'chan-s(ə-)lə-rē\ n, pl **-ler·ies** or **-lor·ies** 1 : the position or office of a chancellor 2 : the building or room housing a chancellor's office 3 : the office or staff of an embassy or consulate

**chan·cel·lor** \'chan-s(ə-)lər\ n 1 : a high state official in various countries 2 : a judge in the equity court in various states of the U.S. 3 : the head of a university 4 : the chief minister of state in some European countries — **chan·cel·lor·ship** n

**chan·cery** \'chans-(ə-)rē\ n, pl **-cer·ies** 1 : any of various courts of equity in the U.S. and Britain 2 : a record office for public or diplomatic archives 3 : a chancellor's court or office 4 : the office of an embassy

**chan·cre** \'shaŋ-kər\ n : a primary sore or ulcer at the site of entry of an infective agent (as of syphilis)

**chan·croid** \'shaŋ-ˌkrȯid\ n : a venereal disease caused by a bacterium and characterized by chancres that differ from those of syphilis in lacking hardened margins

**chancy** \'chan-sē\ adj **chanc·i·er; -est** Scot : AUSPICIOUS 2 : RISKY

**chan·de·lier** \ˌshan-də-'lir\ n : a branched lighting fixture suspended from a ceiling

**chan·dler** \'chan-dlər\ n [ME chandeler a maker or seller of candles, fr. MF chandelier, fr. OF, fr. chandelle candle, fr. L candela] : a dealer in provisions and supplies of a specified kind ⟨ship's ∼⟩ — **chan·dlery** n

¹**change** \'chānj\ vb **changed; chang·ing** 1 : to make or become different : ALTER 2 : to replace with another 3 : EXCHANGE 4 : to give or receive an equivalent sum in notes or coins of usu. smaller denominations or of another currency 5 : to put fresh clothes or covering on ⟨∼ a bed⟩ 6 : to put on different clothes — **change·able** adj — **chang·er** n

²**change** n 1 : the act, process, or result of changing 2 : a fresh set of clothes to replace those being worn 3 : surplus money returned to a person who offers payment exceeding the sum due 4 : money given in exchange for other money of higher denomination 5 : coins esp. of small denominations — **change·ful** adj — **change·less** adj

**change·ling** \'chānj-liŋ\ n : a child secretly exchanged for another in infancy

**change of life** : MENOPAUSE

**change·over** \'chānj-ˌō-vər\ n : conversion to a different function or use of a different method

**change ringing** n : the art or practice of ringing a set of tuned bells in continually varying order

¹**chan·nel** \'chan-ᵊl\ n 1 : the bed of a stream 2 : the deeper part of a waterway 3 : DUCT, TUBE; also : PASSAGEWAY 4 : a long narrow depression (as a groove) 5 : STRAIT 6 : a means of passage or transmission 7 : a range of

frequencies of sufficient width for a single radio or television transmission

²**channel** vb **-neled** or **-nelled; -neling** or **-nel·ling** 1 : to make a channel in 2 : to direct into or through a channel

**chan·nel·ize** \'chan-ᵊl-ˌīz\ vb **-ized; -iz·ing** : CHANNEL — **chan·nel·ization** \ˌchan-ᵊl-ə-'zā-shən\ n

**chan·son** \shäⁿ-sōⁿ\ n, pl **chan·sons** \-sōⁿ(z)\ : SONG; esp : a cabaret song

¹**chant** \'chant\ vb 1 : SING; esp : to sing a chant 2 : to sing or speak in the manner of a chant 3 : to celebrate or praise in song — **chant·er** n

²**chant** n 1 : a repetitive melody in which several words are sung to one tone : SONG; esp : a liturgical melody 2 : a manner of singing or speaking in musical monotones

**chan·teuse** \shäⁿ-'tə(r)z, shan-'tüz\ n, pl **chan·teuses** \-'tə(r)z(-əz), -'tüz(-əz)\ : a female concert or night-club singer

**chan·tey** or **chan·ty** \'shant-ē, 'chant-\ n, pl **chanteys** or **chanties** : a song sung by sailors in rhythm with their work

**chan·ti·cleer** \ˌchant-ə-'kliər, ˌshant-\ n : COCK 1

**chan·try** \'chan-trē\ n, pl **chantries** 1 : an endowment for the chanting of masses 2 : a chapel endowed by a chantry

**Cha·nu·kah** \'kän-ə-kə, 'hän-\ var of HANUKKAH

**cha·os** \'kā-ˌäs\ n 1 often cap : the confused unorganized state existing before the creation of distinct forms 2 : complete disorder syn confusion, jumble, snarl, muddle — **cha·ot·ic** \kā-'ät-ik\ adj — **cha·ot·i·cal·ly** \-i-k(ə-)lē\ adv

¹**chap** \'chap\ n : FELLOW

²**chap** vb **chapped; chap·ping** : to dry and crack open usu. from wind and cold ⟨chapped lips⟩

³**chap** n : a jaw with its fleshy covering — usu. used in pl.

⁴**chap** abbr chapter

**chap·ar·ral** \ˌshap-ə-'ral\ n 1 : a dense impenetrable thicket of shrubs or dwarf trees 2 : an ecological community of southern California comprised of shrubby plants

**chap·book** \'chap-ˌbùk\ n : a small book of ballads, tales, or tracts

**cha·peau** \sha-'pō, shə-\ n, pl **cha·peaus** \-'pōz\ or **cha·peaux** \-'pō(z)\ : HAT

**cha·pel** \'chap-əl\ n [ME, fr. OF chapele, fr. ML cappella, fr. LL cappa cloak; fr. the cloak of St. Martin of Tours preserved as a sacred relic in a chapel built for that purpose] 1 : a private or subordinate place of worship 2 : an assembly at an educational institution usu. including devotional exercises 3 : a place of worship used by a Christian group other than the established church

¹**chap·er·on** or **chap·er·one** \'shap-ə-ˌrōn\ n [F chaperon, lit., hood, fr. MF, head covering, fr. chape] 1 : a

matron who accompanies young un-married women in public for propriety **2** : an older person who accompanies young people at a social gathering to ensure proper behavior

²**chaperon** or **chaperone** vb **-oned; -on·ing 1** : ESCORT, GUIDE **2** : to act as a chaperon to or for — **chap·er·on·age** \-,rō-nij\ n

**chap·fall·en** \'chap-,fò-lən, 'chãp-\ adj **1** : having the lower jaw hanging loosely **2** : DEJECTED, DEPRESSED

**chap·lain** \'chap-lən\ n **1** : a clergy-man officially attached to a special group (as the army) **2** : a person chosen to conduct religious exercises (as for a club) — **chap·lain·cy** \-sē\ n

**chap·let** \'chap-lət\ n **1** : a wreath for the head **2** : a string of beads : NECK-LACE — **chap·let·ed** \-lət-əd\ adj

**chap·man** \'chap-mən\ n, Brit : an itinerant dealer : PEDDLER

**chaps** \'shaps\ n pl [fr. MexSp chaparreras] : leather leggings resem-bling trousers without a seat that are worn esp. by western ranch hands

**chap·ter** \'chap-tər\ n **1** : a main divi-sion of a book **2** : a body of canons (as of a cathedral) **3** : a local branch of a society or fraternity

¹**char** \'chär\ n, pl **char** or **chars** : any of a genus of small-scaled trouts (as the brook trout of eastern No. America)

²**char** vb **charred; char·ring 1** : to burn to charcoal **2** : SCORCH **3** : to burn to a cinder

³**char** vb **charred; char·ring** : to work as a charwoman

**char·a·banc** \'shar-ə-baŋ\ n, Brit : a sight-seeing motor coach

**char·ac·ter** \'kar-ik-tər\ n [ME caracter, fr. MF caractère, fr. L char-acter mark, distinctive quality, fr. Gk charaktēr, fr. charassein to scratch, en-grave] **1** : a graphic symbol (as a letter) used in writing or printing **2** : a dis-tinguishing feature : ATTRIBUTE **3** : the complex of mental and ethical traits marking a person or a group **4** : a person marked by conspicuous often peculiar traits **5** : one of the persons in a novel or play **6** : REPUTATION **7** : moral excellence **8** : a symbol that represents information; also : a repre-sentation of such a character that may be accepted by a computer

¹**char·ac·ter·is·tic** \,kar-ik-tə-'ris-tik\ adj : serving to mark individual char-acter **syn** individual, peculiar, dis-tinctive — **char·ac·ter·is·ti·cal·ly** \-ti-k(ə-)lē\ adv

²**characteristic** n : a distinguishing trait, quality, or property

**char·ac·ter·ize** \'kar-ik-tə-,rīz\ vb **-ized; -iz·ing 1** : to describe the character of **2** : to be a characteristic of — **char·ac·ter·i·za·tion** \,kar-ik-t(ə-)rə-'zā-shən\ n

**char·ac·tery** \'kar-ik-t(ə-)rē\ n, pl **-ter·ies** : written letters or symbols

**cha·rades** \shə-'rādz\ n sing or pl : a guessing game in which contestants act out the syllables of a word to be guessed

¹**char·coal** \'chär-,kōl\ n **1** : a porous

carbon prepared from vegetable or animal substances **2** : a piece of fine charcoal used in drawing; also : a drawing made with charcoal

**chard** \'chärd\ n : a beet lacking the enlarged root but having leaves and stalks often cooked as a vegetable

¹**charge** \'chärj\ vb **charged; charg-ing 1** : to load or fill to capacity; also : IMPREGNATE **2** : to give an electric charge to; also : to restore the activity of (a storage battery) by means of an electric current **3** : to impose a task or responsibility on **4** : COMMAND, ORDER **5** : ACCUSE **6** : to rush against : rush forward in assault **7** : to make liable for payment; also : to record a debt or liability against **8** : to fix as a price — **charge·able** adj

²**charge** n **1** : a quantity (as of fuel or ammunition) required to fill something to capacity **2** : a store or accumulation of force **3** : an excess or deficiency of electrons in a body **4** : THRILL, KICK **5** : a task or duty imposed **6** : one given into another's care **7** : CARE, RESPONSIBILITY **8** : ACCUSATION, IN-DICTMENT **9** : instructions from a judge to a jury **10** : COST, EXPENSE, PRICE; also : a debit to an account **11** : AT-TACK, ASSAULT

**charge-a-plate** \'chär-jə-,plāt\ or **charge plate** n : an embossed address plate used by a customer when buying on credit

**char·gé d'af·faires** \shär-,zhãd-ə-'faer\ n, pl **chargés d'affaires** \-,zhā(z)d-ə-\ : a diplomat who sub-stitutes for an absent ambassador or minister

¹**char·ger** \'chär-jər\ n : a large platter

²**charg·er** n **1** : a device or a workman that charges something **2** : WAR-HORSE

**char·i·ot** \'char-ē-ət\ n **1** : a 2-wheeled vehicle of ancient times used in war and in races and processions — **char·i·o·teer** \,chär-ē-ə-'tiər\ n

**cha·ris·ma** \kə-'riz-mə\ also **char·ism** \'kar-,iz-əm\ n, pl **cha·ris·ma·ta** \kə-'riz-mət-ə\ also **charisms** : a personal quality of leadership arousing special popular loyalty or enthusiasm — **char·is·mat·ic** \,kar-əz-'mat-ik\ adj

**char·i·ta·ble** \'char-ət-ə-bəl\ adj **1** : liberal in giving to the poor **2** : mer-ciful or lenient in judging others **syn** benevolent, philanthropic — **char·i·ta·ble·ness** n — **char·i·ta·bly** \-blē\ adv

**char·i·ty** \'char-ət-ē\ n, pl **-ties 1** : Christian love for God and men **2** : an act or feeling of generosity **3** : the giving of aid to the poor; also : ALMS **4** : an institution engaged in relief of the poor **5** : leniency in judg-ing others **syn** mercy, clemency, philanthropy

**char·la·tan** \'shär-lə-tən\ n : a person pretending to knowledge or ability that he lacks : QUACK

**Charles·ton** \'chärl-stən\ n : a lively ballroom dance in which the knees are twisted in and out and the heels are swung sharply outward on each step

**char·ley horse** \'chär-lē-,hòrs\ *n* : pain and stiffness from muscular strain in an arm or leg

¹**charm** \'chärm\ *n* [ME *charme*, fr. OF, fr. L *carmen* song, fr. *canere* to sing] **1** : an act or expression believed to have magic power **2** : something worn about the person to ward off evil or bring good fortune : AMULET **3** : a trait that fascinates or allures **4** : physical grace or attraction **5** : a small ornament worn on a bracelet or chain

²**charm** *vb* **1** : to affect by or as if by a magic spell **2** : FASCINATE, ENCHANT **3** : to protect by or as if by charms **syn** allure, captivate, bewitch, attract

**charm·er** \'chär-mor\ *n* : one that charms; *esp* : an attractive woman

**charm·ing** \'chär-miŋ\ *adj* : greatly pleasing to the mind or senses : DELIGHTFUL — **charm·ing·ly** *adv*

**char·nel** \'chärn-ᵊl\ *n* : a building or chamber in which bodies or bones are deposited — **charnel** *adj*

¹**chart** \'chärt\ *n* **1** : MAP **2** : a sheet giving information in the form of a table, list, or diagram; *also* : GRAPH

²**chart** *vb* **1** : to make a chart of **2** : PLAN

¹**char·ter** \'chärt-ər\ *n* **1** : an official document granting rights or privileges (as to a colony, town, or college) from a sovereign or a governing body **2** : CONSTITUTION **3** : an instrument from a society creating a branch **4** : a mercantile lease of a ship

²**charter** *vb* **1** : to establish, enable, or convey by charter **2** *Brit* : CERTIFY (~ *ed* engineer) **3** : to hire, rent, or lease for temporary use — **char·ter·er** *n*

**charter member** *n* : an original member of an organization

**char·treuse** \shär-'trüz, -'trüs\ *n* **1** : a usu. green or yellow liqueur **2** : a variable color averaging a brilliant yellow green

**char·wom·an** \'chär-,wùm-ən\ *n* : a woman who does cleaning (as of houses and offices) by the hour or day

**chary** \'cha(ə)r-ē\ *adj* **chari·er; -est** [ME, sorrowful, dear, fr. OE *cearig* sorrowful, fr. *caru* sorrow] **1** : CAUTIOUS, CIRCUMSPECT **2** : SPARING — **char·i·ly** \'char-ə-lē\ *adv*

¹**chase** \'chās\ *vb* **chased; chas·ing** **1** : to follow rapidly : PURSUE **2** : HUNT **3** : to seek out (salesmen *chasing* orders) **4** : to cause to depart or flee : drive away **5** : RUSH, HASTEN

²**chase** *n* **1** : PURSUIT; *also* : HUNTING **2** : QUARRY **3** : a tract of unenclosed land used as a game preserve

³**chase** *vb* **chased; chas·ing** **1** : to decorate (a metal surface) by embossing or engraving

⁴**chase** *n* : FURROW, GROOVE

**chas·er** \'chā-sər\ *n* **1** : one that chases **2** : a mild drink taken after hard liquor

**chasm** \'kaz-əm\ *n* : GORGE

**chas·sis** \'shas-e, 'chas-ē\ *n, pl* **chassis** \-ēz\ : a supporting framework (as

for the body of an automobile or the parts of a radio set)

**chaste** \'chāst\ *adj* **chast·er; chastest** **1** : innocent of unlawful sexual intercourse : VIRTUOUS, PURE **2** : CELIBATE **3** : pure in thought : MODEST **4** : severe or simple in design — **chaste·ly** *adv* — **chaste·ness** *n*

**chas·ten** \'chās-ᵊn\ *vb* **chas·tened; chas·ten·ing** \'chās-(ᵊ-)niŋ\ : to correct through punishment or suffering : DISCIPLINE; *also* : PURIFY — **chas·ten·er** *n*

**chas·tise** \chas-'tīz\ *vb* **chas·tised; chas·tis·ing** [ME *chastisen*, alter. of *chasten*] : to punish esp. bodily — **chas·tise·ment** \-mənt, 'chast-təz-\ *n*

**chas·ti·ty** \'chas-tət-ē\ *n* : the quality or state of being chaste; *esp* : sexual purity

**cha·su·ble** \'chaz-ə-bəl, 'chas-\ *n* : the outer vestment of the celebrant at the Eucharist

**chat** \'chat\ *n* : light familiar informal talk — **chat** *vb*

**châ·teau** \sha-'tō\ *n, pl* **châ·teaus** \-'tōz\ *or* **châ·teaux** \-'tō(z)\ [F, fr. L *castellum* castle, dim. of *castra* camp] **1** : a feudal castle in France **2** : a large country house **3** : a French vineyard estate

**chat·e·laine** \'shat-ᵊl-,ān\ *n* **1** : the mistress of a chateau **2** : a clasp or hook for a watch, purse, or keys

**chat·tel** \'chat-ᵊl\ *n* **1** : an item of tangible property other than real estate **2** : SLAVE, BONDMAN

**chat·ter** \'chat-ər\ *vb* **1** : to utter speechlike but meaningless sounds **2** : to talk idly, incessantly, or fast **3** : to click repeatedly or uncontrollably — **chatter** *n* — **chat·ter·er** *n*

**chat·ter·box** \'chat-ər-,bäks\ *n* : one who talks incessantly

**chat·ty** \'chat-ē\ *adj* **chat·ti·er; -est** : TALKATIVE — **chat·ti·ly** \'chat-ᵊl-ē\ *adv* — **chat·ti·ness** \-ē-nəs\ *n*

¹**chauf·feur** \'shō-fər, shō-'fər\ *n* [F, lit., stoker, fr. *chauffer* to heat] : a person employed to drive an automobile

²**chauffeur** *vb* **chauf·feured; chauf·feur·ing** \'shō-f(ə-)riŋ, shō-'fər-iŋ\ **1** : to do the work of a chauffeur **2** : to transport in the manner of a chauffeur

**chaunt** \'chònt, 'chänt\ *archaic var of* CHANT

**chau·vin·ism** \'shō-və-,niz-əm\ *n* [F *chauvinisme*, fr. Nicolas *Chauvin* F soldier of excessive patriotism and devotion to Napoleon] : excessive or blind patriotism — **chau·vin·ist** \-və-nəst\ *n* — **chau·vin·is·tic** \,shō-və-'nis-tik\ *adj* — **chau·vin·is·ti·cal·ly** \-ti-k(ə-)lē\ *adv*

**cheap** \'chēp\ *adj* **1** : INEXPENSIVE **2** : costing little effort to obtain **3** : worth little **4** : SHODDY, TAWDRY **5** : worthy of scorn — **cheap** *adv* — **cheap·ly** *adv* — **cheap·ness** *n*

**cheap·en** \'chē-pən\ *vb* **cheapened; cheap·en·ing** \'chēp-(ə-)niŋ\ **1** : to make or become cheap or cheaper in price or value **2** : to make tawdry

**cheap·skate** \'chēp-,skāt\ *n* : a niggardly person; *esp* : one seeking to avoid his share of costs

¹**cheat** \'chēt\ *n* **1** : the act of deceiving : FRAUD, DECEPTION  **2** : a means of cheating : a deceitful trick  **3** : one that cheats : a dishonest person

²**cheat** *vb* **1** : to deprive of something through fraud or deceit  **2** : to practice fraud or trickery  **3** : to violate rules (as of a game) dishonestly — **cheat·er** *n*

¹**check** \'chek\ *n* **1** : a sudden stoppage of progress  **2** : a sudden pause or break  **3** : something that stops or restrains  **4** : a standard for testing or evaluation  **5** : EXAMINATION, INVESTIGATION  **6** : the act of testing or verifying  **7** : a written order to a bank to pay money  **8** : a ticket or token showing ownership or identity  **9** : a slip indicating an amount due  **10** : a pattern in squares; *also* : a fabric in such a pattern  **11** : a mark typically √ placed beside an item to show that it has been noted  **12** : CRACK, SPLIT

²**check** *vb* **1** : to slow down or stop : BRAKE  **2** : to restrain the action or force of : CURB  **3** : to compare with a source, original, or authority : VERIFY  **4** : to correspond point by point : TALLY  **5** : to inspect or test for satisfactory condition  **6** : to mark with a check as examined  **7** : to leave or accept for safekeeping in a checkroom  **8** : to consign for shipment for one holding a passenger ticket  **9** : to mark into squares  **10** : CRACK, SPLIT

**check·book** \'chek-,bůk\ *n* : a book containing blank checks

¹**check·er** \'chek-ər\ *n* : a piece in the game of checkers

²**checker** *vb* **check·ered; check·er·ing** \'chek-(ə-)riŋ\ **1** : to variegate with different colors or shades  **2** : to mark into squares  **3** : to subject to frequent changes (as of fortune)

³**checker** *n* : one that checks

**check·er·ber·ry** \'chek-ə(r)-,ber-ē\ *n* : the spicy red fruit of an American wintergreen; *also* : the plant

**check·er·board** \-ə(r)-,bōrd\ *n* : a board of 64 squares of alternate colors used in various games

**check·ers** \'chek-ərz\ *n* : a game for two played on a checkerboard with each player having 12 pieces

**check in** *vb* : to report one's presence or arrival (as at a hotel)

**check·list** \'chek-,list\ *n* : a list of items that may easily be referred to

**check·mate** \'chek-,māt\ *vb* [ME *chekmaten*, fr. *chekmate*, interj. used to announce checkmate, fr. MF *eschec mat*, fr. Ar *shāh māt*, fr. Per, lit., the king is left unable to escape]  **1** : to thwart completely : DEFEAT, FRUSTRATE  **2** : to attack (an opponent's king) in chess so that escape is impossible — **checkmate** *n*

**check·off** \'chek-,óf\ *n* : the deduction of union dues from a worker's paycheck by the employer

**check·out** \'chek-,aůt\ *n* **1** : the action or an instance of checking out

**2** : the process of examining and testing something as to readiness for intended use ⟨the ∼ of a spacecraft⟩  **3** : the process of familiarizing oneself with the operation of a mechanical thing (as an airplane)

**check out** \-'aůt\ *vb* : to settle one's account (as at a hotel) and leave

**check·point** \'chek-,póint\ *n* : a point at which vehicular traffic is halted for inspection or clearance

**check·room** \-,rüm, -,rům\ *n* : a room for temporary safekeeping of baggage, parcels, or clothing

**check·up** \-,əp\ *n* : EXAMINATION; *esp* : a general physical examination

**ched·dar** \'ched-ər\ *n*, *often cap* : a hard mild to sharp cheese of smooth texture

**cheek** \'chēk\ *n* **1** : the fleshy side part of the face  **2** : IMPUDENCE, BOLDNESS, AUDACITY  **3** : BUTTOCK 1 — **cheeked** \'chēkt\ *adj*

**cheek·bone** \'chēk-'bōn, -,bōn\ *n* : the bone or bony projection below the eye

**cheeky** \'chē-kē\ *adj* **cheek·i·er; -est** : IMPUDENT, SAUCY — **cheek·i·ly** \'chē-kə-lē\ *adv* — **cheek·i·ness** \-kē-nəs\ *n*

**cheep** \'chēp\ *vb* : to utter faint shrill sounds : PEEP — **cheep** *n*

¹**cheer** \'chiər\ *n* [ME *chere* face, cheer, fr. OF, face]  **1** : state of mind or heart : SPIRIT  **2** : ANIMATION, GAIETY  **3** : hospitable entertainment : WELCOME  **4** : food and drink for a feast  **5** : something that gladdens  **6** : a shout of applause or encouragement

²**cheer** *vb* **1** : to give hope or courage to : COMFORT  **2** : to make glad  **3** : to urge on esp. by shouts  **4** : to applaud with shouts  **5** : to grow or be cheerful — usu. used with *up* — **cheer·er** *n*

**cheer·ful** \'chiər-fəl\ *adj* **1** : having or showing good spirits  **2** : conducive to good spirits : pleasant and bright — **cheer·ful·ly** \-ē\ *adv* — **cheer·ful·ness** *n*

**cheer·lead·er** \'chiər-,lēd-ər\ *n* : a person who directs organized cheering esp. at a sports event

**cheer·less** \'chiər-ləs\ *adj* : BLEAK, DISPIRITING — **cheer·less·ly** *adv* — **cheer·less·ness** *n*

**cheery** \'chi(ə)r-ē\ *adj* **cheer·i·er; -est** : LIVELY, BRIGHT, GAY — **cheer·i·ly** \'chir-ə-lē\ *adv* — **cheer·i·ness** \-ē-nəs\ *n*

**cheese** \'chēz\ *n* : the curd of milk usu. pressed into cakes and cured for use as food — **cheesy** *adj*

**cheese·burg·er** \'chēz-,bər-gər\ *n* : a hamburger containing a slice of cheese

**cheese·cake** \-,kāk\ *n* **1** : a cake made with cream cheese or cottage cheese  **2** : photographs of attractive usu. scantily clad girls

**cheese·cloth** \-,klóth\ *n* : a lightweight coarse cotton gauze

**cheese·par·ing** \-,pa(ə)r-iŋ\ *n* : miserly or petty economizing — **cheeseparing** *adj*

**chee·tah** \'chēt-ə\ *n* [Hindi *cītā*, fr. Skt *citrakāya* tiger, fr. *citra* bright +

*kāya* body] **:** a long-legged spotted swift-moving African and formerly Asiatic cat

**chef** \'shef\ *n* **1 :** a male head cook **2 :** COOK

**chef d'oeu·vre** \shā-dœvr°\ *n, pl* **chefs d'oeuvre** \-dœvr°\ **:** MASTERPIECE

**che·la** \'kē-lə\ *n, pl* **che·lae** \-(,)lē\ **:** a large pincerlike organ esp. on a limb of a crustacean

**chem** *abbr* chemical; chemist; chemistry

¹**chem·i·cal** \'kem-i-kəl\ *adj* **1 :** of or relating to chemistry **2 :** acting or operated or produced by chemicals — **chem·i·cal·ly** \-i-k(ə-)lē\ *adv*

²**chemical** *n* **:** a substance obtained by a process involving the use of chemistry; *also* **:** a substance used for producing a chemical effect

**chemical engineering** *n* **:** engineering dealing with the industrial application of chemistry

**chemical warfare** *n* **:** warfare using incendiary mixtures, smokes, or irritant, burning, or asphyxiating gases

**che·mise** \shə-'mēz\ *n* **1 :** a woman's one-piece undergarment **2 :** a loose straight-hanging dress

**chem·ist** \'kem-əst\ *n* **1 :** one trained in chemistry **2** *Brit* **:** PHARMACIST

**chem·is·try** \'kem-ə-strē\ *n, pl* **-tries 1 :** a science that deals with the composition, structure, and properties of substances and of the changes they undergo **2 :** chemical composition or properties ⟨the ~ of gasoline⟩

**che·mo·ster·il·ant** \‚kē-mō-'ster-ə-lənt, ‚kem-ō-\ *n* **:** a substance that produces irreversible sterility (as of an insect) without evidently altering mating habits or life expectancy

**che·mo·ther·a·py** \-'ther-ə-pē\ *n* **:** the use of chemicals in the treatment or control of disease — **che·mo·ther·a·peu·tic** \-‚ther-ə-'pyüt-ik\ *or* **che·mo·ther·a·peu·ti·cal** \-i-kəl\ *adj*

**chem·ur·gy** \'kem-(,)ər-jē\ *n* **:** chemistry that deals with industrial utilization of organic raw materials esp. from farm products — **chem·ur·gic** \kə-'mər-jik, ke-\ *adj*

**che·nille** \shə-'nēl\ *n* [F, lit., caterpillar, fr. L *canicula*, dim. of *canis* dog] **:** a wool, cotton, silk, or rayon yarn with protruding pile; *also* **:** a fabric of such yarn

**cheque** \'chek\ *chiefly Brit var of* ¹CHECK 7

**cher·ish** \'cher-ish\ *vb* **1 :** to hold dear **:** treat with care and affection **2 :** to keep deeply in mind

**Cher·o·kee** \'cher-ə-(,)kē\ *n, pl* **Cherokee** *or* **Cherokees : **a member of an Indian people orig. of Tennessee and No. Carolina; *also* **:** their language

**che·root** \shə-'rüt\ *n* **:** a cigar cut square at both ends

**cher·ry** \'cher-ē\ *n, pl* **cherries** [ME *chery*, fr. OF *cherise* (taken as a plural), fr. LL *ceresia*, fr. L *cerasus* cherry tree, fr. Gk *kerasos*] **1 :** the small fleshy fruit of a tree related to the roses; *also* **:** the tree or its wood **2 :** a variable

color averaging a moderate red

**chert** \'chərt, 'chat\ *n* **:** a rock resembling flint and consisting essentially of fine crystalline quartz or fibrous chalcedony — **cherty** *adj*

**cher·ub** \'cher-əb\ *n, pl* **cherubs** *or* **cher·u·bim** \'cher-(y)ə-‚bim\ **1 :** an angel of the second highest rank **2 :** a chubby rosy child — **che·ru·bic** \chə-'rü-bik\ *adj*

**chess** \'ches\ *n* **:** a game for two played on a board of 64 squares of alternate colors with each player having 16 pieces — **chess·board** \-‚bōrd\ *n* — **chess·man** \-‚man, -mən\ *n*

**chest** \'chest\ *n* **1 :** a box, case, or boxlike receptacle for storage or shipping **2 :** the part of the body enclosed by the ribs and breastbone — **chested** \'ches-təd\ *adj*

**ches·ter·field** \'ches-tər-‚fēld\ *n* **:** an overcoat with a velvet collar

**chest·nut** \'ches-(,)nət\ *n* **1 :** the edible nut of a tree related to the beech and oak; *also* **:** this tree **2 :** a grayish brown **3 :** an old joke or story

**che·val glass** \shə-'val-\ *n* **:** a full-length mirror that may be tilted in a frame

**che·va·lier** \‚shev-ə-'liər, shə-'val-‚yā\ *n* **:** a member of one of various orders of knighthood or of merit

**chev·i·ot** \'shev-ē-ət\ *n, often cap* **1 :** a twilled fabric with a rough nap used for coats and suits **2 :** a sturdy soft-finished cotton fabric used for shirts

**chev·ron** \'shev-rən\ *n* **:** a sleeve badge of one or more V-shaped or inverted V-shaped stripes worn to indicate rank or service (as in the armed forces)

¹**chew** \'chü\ *vb* **:** to crush or grind with the teeth — **chew·able** *adj* — **chew·er** *n*

²**chew** *n* **1 :** an act of chewing **2 :** something that is chewed or is suitable for chewing

**chewy** \'chü-ē\ *adj* **:** requiring chewing ⟨~ candy⟩

**Chey·enne** \shī-'an, -'en\ *n, pl* **Cheyenne** *or* **Cheyennes** [CanF, fr. Dakota *Shaiyena*, fr. *shaia* to speak unintelligibly] **:** a member of an Indian people of the western plains of the U.S.; *also* **:** their language

**chg** *abbr* **1** change **2** charge

**Chi·an·ti** \kē-'änt-ē, -'ant-\ *n* **:** a dry usu. red table wine

**chiao** \'tyaù\ *n, pl* **chiao** — see *yuan* at MONEY table

**chiar·oscu·ro** \kē-‚är-ə-'sk(y)ùr-ō\ *n, pl* **-ros 1 :** pictorial representation in terms of light and shade without regard to color **2 :** the arrangement or treatment of light and dark parts in a pictorial work of art

¹**chic** \'shēk\ *n* **:** STYLISHNESS

²**chic** *adj* **:** cleverly stylish **:** SMART; *also* **:** currently fashionable

**chi·cane** \shik-'ān\ *n* **:** CHICANERY — **chicane** *vb*

**chi·ca·nery** \-'ān-(ə-)rē\ *n, pl* **-ner·ies :** TRICKERY, DECEPTION

**Chi·ca·no** \chi-'kän-ō\ *n, pl* **-nos**

[modif. of Sp *mejicano* Mexican] : an American of Mexican descent — **Chicano** *adj*

**chi·chi** \'shē-(,)shē, 'chē-(,)chē\ *adj* **1** : SHOWY, FRILLY **2** : ARTY, PRECIOUS **3** : CHIC — **chichi** *n*

**chick** \'chik\ *n* **1** : a young chicken; *also* : a young bird **2** : a young woman : GIRL

**chick·a·dee** \'chik-ə-(,)dē\ *n* : a small grayish American bird with a black cap

**Chick·a·saw** \'chik-ə-,sò\ *n*, *pl* **Chickasaw** *or* **Chickasaws** : a member of an Indian people of Mississippi and Alabama

¹**chick·en** \'chik-ən\ *n* **1** : a common domestic fowl esp. when young; *also* : its flesh used as food **2** : COWARD

²**chicken** *adj* **1** *slang* : CHICKEN-HEARTED **2** *slang* : insistent on petty esp. military discipline

**chicken feed** *n*, *slang* : an insignificant sum of money

**chick·en-heart·ed** \,chik-ən-'härt-əd\ *adj* : TIMID, COWARDLY

**chicken out** *vb* : to lose one's courage

**chicken pox** *n* : an acute contagious virus disease esp. of children characterized by fever and vesicles

**chick–pea** \'chik-,pē\ *n* : an Asiatic leguminous herb cultivated for its short pods; *also* : its seed

**chick·weed** \'chik-,wēd\ *n* : a low small-leaved weed related to the pinks that has seeds relished by birds

**chi·cle** \'chik-əl\ *n* : a gum from the latex of a tropical evergreen tree used as the chief ingredient of chewing gum

**chic·o·ry** \'chik-(ə-)rē\ *n*, *pl* **-ries** : an herb related to the thistles and used in salad; *also* : its dried ground root used for flavoring or adulterating coffee

**chide** \'chīd\ *vb* **chid** \'chid\ *or* **chid·ed** \'chīd-əd\; **chid** *or* **chid·den** \'chid-ⁿn\ *or* **chided**; **chid·ing** \'chīd-iŋ\ : to speak disapprovingly to **syn** reproach, reprove, reprimand, admonish, scold, rebuke

¹**chief** \'chēf\ *n* **1** : the leader of a body or organization : HEAD **2** : the principal or most valuable part — **chief·dom** *n* — **chief·ship** *n*

²**chief** *adj* **1** : highest in rank **2** : most eminent or important **syn** principal, main, leading — **chief·ly** *adv*

**chief master sergeant** *n* : a noncommissioned officer of the highest rank in the air force

**chief of staff 1** : the ranking officer of a staff in the armed forces **2** : the ranking office of the army or air force

**chief of state** : the formal head of a national state as distinguished from the head of the government

**chief petty officer** *n* : an enlisted man in the navy ranking next below a senior chief petty officer

**chief·tain** \'chēf-tən\ *n* : a chief esp. of a band, tribe, or clan — **chief·tain·cy** \-sē\ *n* — **chief·tain·ship** *n*

**chief warrant officer** *n* : a warrant officer of senior rank

**chif·fon** \shif-'än, 'shif-,\ *n* [F, lit., rag, fr. *chiffe* old rag, fr. MF *chipe*, fr. ME *chip* chip] : a sheer fabric esp. of silk

**chif·fo·nier** \,shif-ə-'niər\ *n* : a high narrow chest of drawers

**chig·ger** \'chig-ər\ *n* **1** : a tropical flea that burrows under the skin **2** : a blood-sucking larval mite that irritates the skin

**chi·gnon** \'shēn-,yän\ *n* : a knot of hair worn at the back of the head

**chil·blain** \'chil-,blān\ *n* : a sore or inflamed swelling (as on the feet or hands) caused by cold

**child** \'chīld\ *n*, *pl* **chil·dren** \'chil-drən\ **1** : an unborn or recently born person **2** : a young person between the periods of infancy and youth **3** : a male or female offspring : SON, DAUGHTER **4** : one strongly influenced by another or by a place or stage of affairs — **child·ish** *adj* — **child·ish·ly** *adv* — **child·ish·ness** *n* — **child·less** *adj* — **child·less·ness** *n* — **child·like** *adj*

**child·bear·ing** \'chīld-,bar-iŋ\ *n* : CHILDBIRTH — **childbearing** *adj*

**childbirth** \-,bərth\ *n* : the act or process of giving birth to offspring

**child·hood** \-,hùd\ *n* : the state or time of being a child

**child's play** *n* : a simple task or act

**chili** *or* **chile** *or* **chil·li** \'chil-ē\ *n*, *pl* **chil·ies** *or* **chil·es** *or* **chil·lies** **1** : a pungent pepper related to the tomato **2** : a thick sauce of meat and chilies **3** : CHILI CON CARNE

**chili con car·ne** \,chil-ē-,kän-'kär-nē, -kən-\ *n* : a spiced stew of ground beef and chilies or chili powder usu. with beans

¹**chill** \'chil\ *vb* **1** : to make or become cold or chilly **2** : to make cool esp. without freezing **3** : to harden the surface of (as metal) by sudden cooling — **chill·er** *n*

²**chill** *adj* **1** : moderately cold **2** : COLD, RAW **3** : DISTANT, FORMAL (a ~ reception) **4** : DEPRESSING, DISPIRITING

³**chill** *n* **1** : a feeling of coldness attended with shivering **2** : moderate coldness **3** : a check to enthusiasm or warmth of feeling

**chilly** \'chil-ē\ *adj* **chill·i·er; -est** **1** : noticeably cold **2** : unpleasantly affected by cold **3** : lacking warmth of feeling — **chill·i·ness** *n*

¹**chime** \'chīm\ *n* **1** : a set of bells musically tuned **2** : the sound of a set of bells — usu. used in pl. **3** : a sound suggesting bells

**chime** *vb* **chimed; chim·ing 1** : to make bell-like sounds **2** : to indicate (as the time of day) by chiming **3** : to be or act in accord : be in harmony

**chime in** *vb* : to break into or join in a conversation

**chi·me·ra** *or* **chi·mae·ra** \kī-'mir-ə, kə-\ *n* [L *chimaera*, fr. Gk *chimaira* she-goat, chimera] **1** : an imaginary monster made up of incongruous parts **2** : a frightful or foolish fancy

**chi·me·ri·cal** \-'mer-i-kəl\ *or* **chi-**

**me·ric** \-ik\ adj **1** : FANTASTIC, IMAGINARY **2** : inclined to fantastic schemes

**chim·ney** \'chim-nē\ n, pl **chimneys 1** : a passage for smoke that is usu. made of bricks, stone, or metal and often rises above the roof of a building **2** : a glass tube around a lamp flame

**chimp** \'chimp, 'shimp\ n : CHIMPANZEE

**chim·pan·zee** \,chim-,pan-'zē, ,shim-, -pən-; chim-'pan-zē, shim-\ n : an African manlike ape

**¹chin** \'chin\ n : the part of the face below the mouth including the prominence of the lower jaw — **chin·less** adj

**²chin** vb **chinned**; **chin·ning** : to raise (oneself) while hanging by the hands until the chin is level with the support

**Chin** abbr Chinese

**chi·na** \'chī-nə\ n : porcelain ware; also : domestic pottery in general

**chinch bug** \'chinch-\ n : a small black and white bug destructive to cereal grasses

**chin·chil·la** \chin-'chil-ə\ n **1** : a small So. American rodent with soft pearl-gray fur; also : its fur **2** : a heavy long-napped woolen cloth

**chine** \'chīn\ n **1** : BACKBONE, SPINE; also : a cut of meat or fish including the backbone or part of it and the surrounding flesh **2** : RIDGE, CREST

**Chi·nese** \chī-'nēz, -'nēs\ n, pl **Chinese 1** : a native or inhabitant of China **2** : any of a group of related languages of China — **Chinese** adj

**Chinese checkers** n : a game in which each player in turn transfers a set of marbles from a home point to the opposite point of a pitted 6-pointed star

**Chinese lantern** n : a collapsible lantern of thin colored paper

**Chinese wall** n : a strong barrier; esp : a serious obstacle to understanding

**¹chink** \'chiŋk\ n : a small crack or fissure

**²chink** vb : to fill the chinks : stop up

**³chink** n : a slight sharp metallic sound

**⁴chink** vb : to make a slight sharp metallic sound

**chi·no** \'chē-nō\ n, pl **chinos 1** : a usu. khaki cotton twill **2** : an article of clothing made of chino — usu. used in pl.

**Chi·nook** \shə-'nuk, chə-, -'nük\ n, pl **Chinook** or **Chinooks** : a member of an Indian people of Oregon

**chintz** \'chints\ n : a usu. glazed printed cotton cloth

**chintzy** \'chint-sē\ adj **chintz·i·er**; **-est 1** : decorated with or as if with chintz **2** : GAUDY, CHEAP

**chin-up** \'chin-,əp\ n : the act of chinning oneself

**¹chip** \'chip\ n **1** : a small usu. thin and flat piece (as of wood) cut or broken off **2** : a thin crisp morsel of food **3** : a counter used in games (as poker) **4** pl, slang : MONEY **5** : a flaw left after a chip is removed

**²chip** vb **chipped**; **chip·ping 1** : to cut or break chips from **2** : to break

off in small pieces at the edges **3** : to play a chip shot

**chip in** vb : CONTRIBUTE

**chip·munk** \'chip-,məŋk\ n : a small striped American ground-dwelling squirrel

**chipped beef** \'chip(t)-\ n : smoked dried beef sliced thin

**¹chip·per** \'chip-ər\ n : one that chips

**²chipper** adj : LIVELY, CHEERFUL

**Chip·pe·wa** \'chip-ə-,wo, -,wä, -,wā, -wə\ n, pl **Chippewa** or **Chippewas** : OJIBWA

**chip shot** n : a short usu. low shot to the green in golf

**chi·rog·ra·phy** \kī-'räg-rə-fē\ n : HANDWRITING, PENMANSHIP — **chi·rog·ra·pher** \-fər\ n — **chi·ro·graph·ic** \,kī-rə-'graf-ik\ or **chi·ro·graph·i·cal** \-i-kəl\ adj

**chi·ro·man·cy** \'kī-rə-,man-sē\ n : divination by examination of the hand

**chi·rop·o·dy** \kə-'räp-əd-ē, shə-\ n : professional care and treatment of the human foot — **chi·rop·o·dist** \-əd-əst\ n

**chi·ro·prac·tic** \'kī-rə-,prak-tik\ n : a system of healing based esp on manipulation of body structures — **chi·ro·prac·tor** \-tər\ n

**chirp** \'chərp\ n : a short sharp sound characteristic of a small bird or cricket — **chirp** vb

**¹chis·el** \'chiz-əl\ n : a sharp-edged metal tool used in cutting away and shaping wood, stone, or metal

**²chisel** vb **-eled** or **-elled**; **-el·ing** or **-el·ling** \'chiz-(ə-)liŋ\ **1** : to work with or as if with a chisel **2** : to obtain by shrewd often unfair methods; also : CHEAT — **chis·el·er** \-(ə-)lər\ n

**¹chit** \'chit\ n [ME chitte kitten, cub] **1** : CHILD **2** : a pert young woman

**²chit** n [Hindi ciṭṭhī letter, note] : a signed voucher for a small debt

**chit-chat** \'chit-,chat\ n : casual or trifling conversation

**chi·tin** \'kīt-ᵊn\ n : a sugar polymer that forms part of the hard outer integument esp. of insects — **chi·tin·ous** adj

**chit·ter·lings** or **chit·lings** or **chit·lins** \'chit-lənz\ n pl : the intestines of hogs esp. prepared as food

**chi·val·ric** \shə-'val-rik\ adj : relating to chivalry : CHIVALROUS

**chiv·al·rous** \'shiv-əl-rəs\ adj **1** : of or relating to chivalry **2** : marked by honor, courtesy, and generosity **3** : marked by especial courtesy to women — **chiv·al·rous·ly** adv — **chiv·al·rous·ness** n

**chiv·al·ry** \'shiv-əl-rē\ n, pl **-ries 1** : a body of knights **2** : the system or practices of knighthood **3** : the spirit or character of the ideal knight

**chive** \'chīv\ n : an herb related to the onion that has leaves used for flavoring

**chlo·ral hydrate** \,klor-əl-\ n : a white crystalline compound used as a hypnotic and sedative

**chlor·dane** \'klor-,dän\ or **chlor·dan** \-,dan\ n : a viscous liquid insecticide

**chlo·ride** \'klōr-,īd\ *n* : a compound of chlorine with another element or a radical

**chlo·ri·nate** \'klōr-ə-,nāt\ *vb* **-nat·ed; -nat·ing** : to treat or cause to combine with chlorine or a chlorine-containing compound — **chlo·ri·na·tion** \,klōr-ə-'nā-shən\ *n* — **chlo·ri·na·tor** \'klōr-ə-,nāt-ər\ *n*

**chlo·rine** \'klōr-,ēn\ *n* : a chemical element that is a heavy strong-smelling greenish yellow irritating gas used as a bleach, oxidizing agent, and disinfectant

**chlo·rite** \'klōr-,īt\ *n* : any of a group of usu. green minerals resembling the micas

**¹chlo·ro·form** \'klōr-ə-,fȯrm\ *n* : a colorless heavy fluid with etherlike odor used as a solvent and anesthetic

**²chloroform** *vb* : to treat with chloroform to produce anesthesia or death

**chlo·ro·phyll** \-,fil\ *n* : the green coloring matter of plants that functions in photosynthesis

**chm** *abbr* chairman

**chock** \'chäk\ *n* : a wedge for steadying something or for blocking the movement of a wheel — **chock** *vb*

**chock·a·block** \'chäk-ə-,bläk\ *adj* : very full : CROWDED

**chock-full** \'chək-'fùl, 'chäk-\ *adj* : full to the limit

**choc·o·late** \'chäk-(ə-)lət, 'chȯk-\ *n* [Sp, fr. Nahuatl (an Indian language of southern Mexico) *xocoatl*] **1** : processed ground and roasted cacao beans; *also* : a drink prepared from this **2** : a candy made of or with a coating of chocolate **3** : a dark brown color

**Choc·taw** \'chäk-,tȯ\ *n, pl* **Choctaw** *or* **Choctaws** : a member of an Indian people of Mississippi, Alabama, and Louisiana; *also* : their language

**¹choice** \'chȯis\ *n* **1** : the act of choosing : SELECTION **2** : the power or opportunity of choosing : OPTION **3** : a person or thing selected **4** : the best part **5** : a variety offered for selection

**²choice** *adj* **choic·er; choic·est 1** : worthy of being chosen **2** : selected with care **3** : of high quality

**choir** \'kwī(-ə)r\ *n* **1** : an organized company of singers esp. in a church **2** : the part of a church occupied by the singers

**choir·boy** \'kwī(-ə)r-,bȯi\ *n* : a boy member of a church choir

**choir·mas·ter** \-,mas-tər\ *n* : the director of a choir (as in a church)

**¹choke** \'chōk\ *vb* **choked; chok·ing 1** : to hinder breathing (as by obstructing the windpipe) : STRANGLE **2** : to check the growth or action of **3** : CLOG, OBSTRUCT **4** : to decrease or shut off the air intake of the carburetor of a gasoline engine to make the fuel mixture richer **5** : to perform badly in a critical situation

**²choke** *n* **1** : a choking or sound of choking **2** : a narrowing in size toward the muzzle in the bore of a gun **3** : a valve for choking a gasoline engine ■

**chok·er** \'chō-kər\ *n* : something (as a necklace) worn tightly around the neck

**cho·ler** \'käl-ər, 'kō-lər\ *n* : tendency toward anger : IRASCIBILITY

**chol·era** \'käl-ə-rə\ *n* : a disease marked by severe vomiting and dysentery; *esp* : an often fatal epidemic disease (**Asiatic cholera**) chiefly of southeastern Asia

**cho·ler·ic** \'käl-ə-rik, kə-'ler-ik\ *adj* **1** : IRASCIBLE **2** : ANGRY, IRATE

**cho·les·ter·ol** \kə-'les-tə-,rȯl, ,rōl\ *n* : a physiologically important waxy substance in animal tissues

**chomp** \'chämp, 'chȯmp\ *vb* : to chew or bite on something heavily

**chon** \'chän\ *n, pl* **chon** — see **won** at MONEY TABLE

**chon·drite** \'kän-,drīt\ *n* : a meteoric stone possessing chondrules — **chon·drit·ic** \kän-'drit-ik\ *adj*

**chon·drule** \'kän-(,)drül\ *n* : a rounded granule of cosmic origin often found embedded in meteoric stones

**choose** \'chüz\ *vb* **chose** \'chōz\; **cho·sen** \'chōz-²n\; **choos·ing** \'chü-ziŋ\ **1** : to select esp. after consideration **2** : to think proper : see fit : PLEASE **3** : DECIDE — **choos·er** *n*

**choosy** *or* **choos·ey** \'chü-zē\ *adj* **choos·i·er; -est** : very particular in making choices

**¹chop** \'chäp\ *vb* **chopped; chop·ping 1** : to cut by repeated blows **2** : to cut into small pieces : MINCE **3** : to strike (a ball) with a short quick downward stroke

**²chop** *n* **1** : a sharp downward blow or stroke **2** : a small cut of meat often including part of a rib **3** : a short abrupt motion (as of waves)

**³chop** *n* **1** : an official seal or stamp or its impression **2** : a mark on goods to indicate quality or kind; *also* : QUALITY, GRADE

**chop·house** \'chäp-,hau̇s\ *n* : RESTAURANT

**chop·per** \'chäp-ər\ *n* **1** : one that chops **2** : HELICOPTER

**¹chop·py** \'chäp-ē\ *adj* **chop·pi·er; -est** : CHANGEABLE, VARIABLE ⟨a ~ wind⟩ — **chop·pi·ness** \-nəs\ *n*

**²choppy** *adj* **1** : rough with small waves **2** : JERKY, DISCONNECTED — **chop·pi·ly** \'chäp-ə-lē\ *adv* — **chop·pi·ness** \-ē-nəs\ *n*

**chops** \'chäps\ *n pl* : the fleshy covering of the jaws

**chop·stick** \'chäp-,stik\ *n* : one of a pair of sticks used in oriental countries for lifting food to the mouth

**chop su·ey** \chäp-'sü-ē\ *n, pl* **chop sueys** : a dish made typically of bean sprouts, bamboo shoots, celery, onions, mushrooms, and meat or fish and served with rice

**cho·ral** \'kōr-əl\ *adj* : of, relating to, or sung by a choir or chorus or in chorus — **cho·ral·ly** \-ē\ *adv*

**cho·rale** *also* **cho·ral** \kə-'ral, -'räl\ *n* **1** : a hymn or psalm sung in church; *also* : a hymn tune or a harmonization of a traditional melody **2** : CHORUS, CHOIR

¹**chord** \'kȯrd\ n [alter. of ME cord, short for accord] : a combination of tones that blend harmoniously when sounded together

²**chord** n 1 : CORD, STRING; esp : a cord-like anatomical structure 2 : a straight line joining two points on a curve

**chore** \'chōr\ n 1 pl : the daily light work of a household or farm 2 : a routine task or job 3 : a difficult or disagreeable task

**cho·rea** \kə-'rē-ə\ n : a nervous disorder marked by spasmodic uncontrolled movements

**cho·re·og·ra·phy** \,kȯr-ē-'äg-rə-fē\ n, pl -phies : the art of dancing or of arranging dances and esp. ballets — **cho·reo·graph** \'kȯr-ē-ə-,graf\ vb — **cho·re·og·ra·pher** \,kȯr-ē-'äg-rə-fər\ n — **cho·reo·graph·ic** \,kȯr-ē-ə-'graf-ik\ adj — **cho·reo·graph·i·cal·ly** \-i-k(ə-)lē\ adv

**cho·ris·ter** \'kȯr-ə-stər\ n : a singer in a choir

**chor·tle** \'chȯrt-ᵊl\ vb **chor·tled; chor·tling** \'chȯrt-(ᵊ-)liŋ\ : to laugh or chuckle esp. in satisfaction or exultation — **chortle** n

¹**chorus** \'kȯr-əs\ n 1 : an organized company of singers : CHOIR 2 : a group of dancers and usu. singers supporting the featured players in a revue 3 : a part of a song repeated at intervals 4 : a composition to be sung by a number of voices in concert; also : group singing 5 : sounds uttered by a number of persons or animals together

²**chorus** vb : to sing or utter in chorus

**chose** past of CHOOSE

**cho·sen** \'chōz-ᵊn\ adj : selected or marked for special favor or privilege

¹**chow** \'chaù\ n : FOOD

²**chow** n : a thick-coated straight-legged muscular dog with a blue-black tongue and a short tail curled close to the back

**chow·chow** \'chaù-,chaù\ n : chopped mixed pickles in mustard sauce

**chow chow** \'chaù-,chaù\ n : ²CHOW

**chow·der** \'chaùd-ər\ n : a thick soup typically made from seafood and usu. containing milk

**chow mein** \'chaù-'mān\ n 1 : fried noodles 2 : a thick stew of shredded or diced meat, mushrooms, vegetables, and seasonings served with fried noodles

**chrism** \'kriz-əm\ n : consecrated oil used esp. in baptism and confirmation

**Christ** \'krīst\ n [L Christus, fr. Gk Christos, lit., anointed, trans. of Heb māshīah] : Jesus esp. in his character as the Messiah — **Christ·like** adj — **Christ·ly** adj

**chris·ten** \'kris-ᵊn\ vb **chris·tened; chris·ten·ing** \'kris-(ᵊ-)niŋ\ 1 : BAPTIZE 2 : to name at baptism 3 : to name or dedicate (as a ship) by a ceremony suggestive of baptism — **chris·ten·ing** n

**Chris·ten·dom** \'kris-ᵊn-dəm\ n 1 : the entire body of Christians 2 : the part of the world in which Christianity prevails

¹**Chris·tian** \'kris-chən\ n 1 : an adherent of Christianity 2 : a member of one of several Protestant religious bodies dedicated to the restoration of a united New Testament Christianity

²**Christian** adj 1 : of, relating to, or professing a belief in Christianity 2 : of or relating to Jesus Christ 3 : based on or conforming with Christianity 4 : of or relating to a Christian

**chris·ti·an·ia** \,kris-chē-'an-ē-ə, ,kris-tē-\ n : CHRISTIE

**Chris·ti·an·i·ty** \,kris-chē-'an-ət-ē\ n : the religion derived from Jesus Christ, based on the Bible as sacred scripture, and professed by Christians

**Chris·tian·ize** \'kris-chə-,nīz\ vb **-ized; -iz·ing** : to make Christian

**Christian name** n : a name that precedes one's surname

**Christian Science** n : a religion and system of healing founded by Mary Baker Eddy and taught by the Church of Christ, Scientist — **Christian Scientist** n

**chris·tie** or **chris·ty** \'kris-tē\ n, pl **christies** : a skiing turn used for altering direction of descent or for checking or stopping and executed usu. at high speed by shifting body weight forward and skidding into a turn with parallel skis

**Christ·mas** \'kris-məs\ n : December 25 celebrated as a church festival in commemoration of the birth of Christ and observed as a legal holiday

**Christmas club** n : a savings account in which regular deposits are made to provide money for Christmas shopping

**Christ·mas·tide** \'kris-mə-,stīd\ n : the season of Christmas

**chro·mat·ic** \krō-'mat-ik\ adj 1 : of or relating to color 2 : proceeding by half steps of the musical scale — **chro·mat·i·cism** \-'mat-ə-,siz-əm\ n

**chro·ma·tic·i·ty** \,krō-mə-'tis-ət-ē\ n 1 : the quality or state of being chromatic 2 : the quality of color characterized by its dominant or complementary wavelength and purity taken together

**chro·ma·tog·ra·phy** \,krō-mə-'täg-rə-fē\ n : the separation of complex solutions into chemically distinct layers by seepage through an adsorbent — **chro·mato·graph·ic** \krō-,mat-ə-'graf-ik\ adj — **chro·mato·graph·i·cal·ly** \-i-k(ə-)lē\ adv

**chrome** \'krōm\ n 1 : CHROMIUM 2 : a chromium pigment 3 : something plated with an alloy of chromium

**chrome green** n : any of various brilliant green pigments containing or consisting of chromium compounds

**chrome yellow** n : a pigment consisting of lead, chromium, and oxygen

**chro·mic** \'krō-mik\ adj : of, relating to, or derived from chromium

**chro·mi·um** \'krō-mē-əm\ n : a bluish white metallic element used esp. in alloys

**chro·mo** \'krō-mō\ n, pl **chromos** : a colored picture printed from lithographic surfaces

**chro·mo·some** \'krō-mə-,sōm, -,zōm\ n : one of the usu. elongated bodies in a

cel. nucleus that contains the genes —
**chro·mo·som·al** \,krō-mə-'sō-məl,
-'zō-\ *adj*
**chro·mo·sphere** \'krō-mə-,sfïər\ *n*
: the lower atmosphere of a star (as the
sun) — **chro·mo·spher·ic** \,krō-
mə-'sfïər-ik, -'sfer-\ *adj*
**chron** *abbr* 1 chronicle 2 chronological; chronology
**Chron** *abbr* Chronicles
**chron·ic** \'krän-ik\ *adj* : marked by
long duration or frequent recurrence ⟨a
~ disease⟩; *also* : affected by a chronic
condition ⟨a ~ grumbler⟩ — **chron·i-
cal·ly** \-i-k(ə-)lē\ *adv*
¹**chron·i·cle** \'krän-i-kəl\ *n* : HISTORY,
NARRATIVE
²**chronicle** *vb* -**cled; -cling** \-k(ə-)liŋ\
: to record in or as if in a chronicle —
**chron·i·cler** \-k(ə-)lər\ *n*
**chro·no·graph** \'krän-ə-,graf\ *n* : an
instrument for measuring and recording
time intervals with accuracy — **chro-
no·graph·ic** \,krän-ə-'graf-ik\ *adj* —
**chro·nog·ra·phy** \krə-'näg-rə-fē\ *n*
**chro·nol·o·gy** \krə-'näl-ə-jē\ *n, pl*
-**gies** 1 : the science that deals with
measuring time and dating events 2 : a
chronological list or table 3 : arrangement of events in the order of their
occurrence — **chron·o·log·i·cal**
\,krän-³l-'äj-i-kəl\ *adj* — **chron·o-
log·i·cal·ly** \-i-k(ə-)lē\ *adv* — **chro-
nol·o·gist** \krə-'näl-ə-jəst\ *n*
**chro·nom·e·ter** \krə-'näm-ət-ər\ *n*
: a very accurate timepiece
**chrys·a·lis** \'kris-ə-ləs\ *n, pl* **chry-
sal·i·des** \kris-'al-ə-,dēz\ *or* **chrys-
a·lis·es** : an insect pupa quiescent in a
firm case
**chry·san·the·mum** \kris-'an-thə-
məm\ *n* [L, fr. Gk *chrysanthemon*, fr.
*chrysos* gold + *anthemon* flower] : any
of a genus of plants related to the
daisies including some grown for their
showy bloom or for medicinal products
or insecticides; *also* : a chrysanthemum
bloom
**chrys·o·lite** \'kris-ə-,līt\ *n* : OLIVINE
**chub** \'chəb\ *n, pl* **chub** *or* **chubs** : a
small freshwater fish related to the carp
**chub·by** \'chəb-ē\ *adj* **chub·bi·er;
-est** : PLUMP — **chub·bi·ness** *n*
¹**chuck** \'chək\ *vb* 1 : to give a pat or
tap 2 : to toss or throw with a short
motion of the arms 3 : DISCARD; *also*
: EJECT 4 : to have done with
²**chuck** *n* 1 : a light pat under the chin
2 : TOSS
³**chuck** *n* 1 : a part of a side of dressed
beef 2 : a device for holding work or a
tool in a machine (as a lathe)
**chuck·hole** \'chək-,hōl\ *n* : a hole or
rut in a road
**chuck·le** \'chək-əl\ *vb* **chuck·led;
chuck·ling** \-(ə-)liŋ\ : to laugh in a
quiet hardly audible manner —
**chuckle** *n*
**chuck wagon** *n* : a wagon equipped
with a stove and provisions for cooking
¹**chug** \'chəg\ *n* : a dull explosive sound
made by or as if by a laboring engine
²**chug** *vb* **chugged; chug·ging** 1 : to
move or go with chugs

**chuk·ka** \'chək-ə\ *n* : a short usu.
ankle-length leather boot with two pairs
of eyelets
**chuk·ker** *or* **chuk·kar** \'chək-ər\ *or*
**chuk·ka** \-ə\ *n* : a playing period of a
polo game
¹**chum** \'chəm\ *n* : an intimate friend
²**chum** *vb* **chummed; chum·ming**
1 : to room together 2 : to go about
with as a friend
**chum·my** \'chəm-ē\ *adj* **chum·mi-
er; -est** : INTIMATE, SOCIABLE —
**chum·mi·ly** \'chəm-ə-lē\ *adv* —
**chum·mi·ness** \-ē-nəs\ *n*
**chump** \'chəmp\ *n* : FOOL, BLOCKHEAD
**chunk** \'chəŋk\ *n* 1 : a short thick
piece 2 : a sizable amount
**chunky** \'chəŋ-kē\ *adj* **chunk·i·er;
-est** 1 : STOCKY 2 : containing
chunks
**church** \'chərch\ *n* [OE *cirice*, fr. LGk
*kyriakon*, short for *kyriakon dōma*, lit.,
the Lord's house, fr. Gk *Kyrios* Lord +
*dōma* house] 1 : a building esp. for
Christian public worship 2 : the whole
body of Christians 3 : DENOMINATION
4 : CONGREGATION 5 : public divine
worship
**church·go·er** \'chərch-,gō(-ə)r\ *n*
: one who frequently attends church —
**church·go·ing** \-,gō-iŋ\ *adj or n*
**church·less** \'chərch-ləs\ *adj* : not
affiliated with a church
**church·man** \'chərch-mən\ *n* 1
: CLERGYMAN 2 : a member of a church
**church·war·den** \'chərch-,wòrd-³n\
*n* : WARDEN 5
**church·yard** \-,yärd\ *n* : a yard that
belongs to a church and is often used as
a burial ground
**churl** \'chərl\ *n* 1 : a medieval peasant
2 : RUSTIC 3 : a rude ill-bred person —
**churl·ish** *adj* — **churl·ish·ly** *adv* —
**churl·ish·ness** *n*
¹**churn** \'chərn\ *n* : a container in which
milk or cream is violently stirred in
making butter
²**churn** *vb* 1 : to stir in a churn; *also* : to
make (butter) by such stirring 2 : to
shake around violently
**churn out** *vb* : to produce mechanically
and in large quantity
**chute** \'shüt\ *n* 1 : an inclined surface,
trough, or passage down or through
which something may pass ⟨a coal ~⟩
⟨a mail ~⟩ 2 : PARACHUTE
**chut·ney** \'chət-nē\ *n, pl* **chutneys**
: a condiment of acid fruits with
raisins, dates, and onions
**chutz·pah** *or* **chutz·pa** \'hùt-spə,
'kùt-, -(,)spä\ *n* : supreme self-
confidence
**CI** *abbr* cost and insurance
**CIA** *abbr* Central Intelligence Agency
**cía** *abbr* [Sp *compañía*] company
**ciao** \'chaù\ *interj* [It, fr. It dial., alter.
of *schiavo* (I am your) slave, fr. ML
*sclavus*] — used to express greeting or
farewell
**ci·ca·da** \sə-'kād-ə\ *n* : a stout-bodied
insect related to the aphids that has a
wide blunt head and large transparent
wings
**ci·ca·trix** \'sik-ə-,triks\ *n, pl* **ci·ca-**

**tri·ces** \,sik-ə-'trī-,sēz\ : a scar resulting from formation and contraction of fibrous tissue in a flesh wound

**ci·ce·ro·ne** \,sis-ə-'rō-nē, ,chē-chə-\ n, pl **-ni** \-(,)nē\ : a guide who conducts sightseers

**CID** abbr **1** Criminal Investigation Department **2** cubic inch displacement

**ci·der** \'sīd-ər\ n : juice pressed from fruit (as apples) and used as a beverage, vinegar, or flavoring

**cie** abbr [F compagnie] company

**CIF** abbr cost, insurance, and freight

**ci·gar** \sig-'är\ n : a roll of tobacco for smoking

**cig·a·rette** \,sig-ə-'ret, 'sig-ə-,ret\ n : a small tube of cut tobacco enclosed in paper for smoking

**cig·a·ril·lo** \,sig-ə-'ril-ō, -'rē-ō\ n, pl **-los 1** : a very small cigar **2** : a cigarette wrapped in tobacco rather than paper

**cil·i·ate** \'sil-ē-,āt\ n : any of a group of protozoans characterized by cilia

**cil·i·um** \'sil-ē-əm\ n, pl **-ia** \-ē-ə\ **1** : EYELASH **2** : a minute short hairlike process; esp : one of a cell

**C in C** abbr commander in chief

**cinch** \'sinch\ n **1** : a strong strap for holding a saddle or a pack in place **2** : a sure or an easy thing — **cinch** vb

**cin·cho·na** \sin-'kō-nə\ n : a So. American tree; also : its bitter quinine-containing bark

**cinc·ture** \'sink-chər\ n : BELT, GIRDLE

**cin·der** \'sin-dər\ n **1** : SLAG **2** pl : ASHES **3** : a hot piece of partly burned wood or coal **4** : a fragment of lava from an erupting volcano — **cinder** vb — **cin·dery** adj

**cinder block** n : a building block made of cement and coal cinders

**cin·e·ma** \'sin-ə-mə\ n **1** chiefly Brit : a motion-picture theater **2** : MOVIES — **cin·e·mat·ic** \,sin-ə-'mat-ik\ adj

**cin·e·ma·theque** \,sin-ə-mə-'tek\ n : a small movie house specializing in avant-garde films

**cin·e·mat·o·graph** \,sin-ə-'mat-ə-,graf\ n [F cinématographe, fr. Gk kinēmat-, kinēma movement (fr. kinein to move) + -o- + -graphe -graph] : a motion-picture projector, camera, theater, or show

**cin·e·ma·tog·ra·phy** \,sin-ə-mə-'tägrə-fē\ n : motion-picture photography — **cin·e·ma·tog·ra·pher** \-fər\ n — **cin·e·mat·o·graph·ic** \-,mat-ə-'graf-ik\ adj

**cin·er·ar·i·um** \,sin-ə-'rer-ē-əm\ n, pl **-ia** \-ē-ə\ : a place to receive the ashes of the cremated dead — **cin·er·ary** \'sin-ə-,rer-ē\ adj

**cin·na·bar** \'sin-ə-,bär\ n : a red mineral that is the only important ore of mercury

**cin·na·mon** \'sin-ə-mən\ n : the aromatic inner bark of a tropical Asiatic tree related to the true laurel that is used as a spice

**cinque·foil** \'sink-,fóil, 'sank-\ n : any of a genus of plants related to the roses with leaves having five lobes

**¹ci·pher** \'sī-fər\ n [ME, fr. MF cifre, fr. ML cifra, fr. Ar ṣifr empty, cipher, zero] **1** : ZERO, NAUGHT **2** : a method of secret writing : CODE

**²cipher** vb **ci·phered; ci·pher·ing** \-f(ə-)riŋ\ : to compute arithmetically

**cir** or **circ** abbr circular

**cir·ca** \'sər-kə\ prep : ABOUT ⟨~ 1600⟩

**cir·ca·di·an** \,sər-'kad-ē-ən, ,sər-kə-'dī-ən\ adj : approximating 24 hours ; occurring at approximately 24-hour intervals

**¹cir·cle** \'sər-kəl\ n **1** : a closed curve every point of which is equally distant from a fixed point within it **2** : something in the form of a circle **3** : an area of action or influence **4** : CYCLE, ROUND **5** : a group bound by a common tie

**²circle** vb **cir·cled; cir·cling** \-k(ə-)liŋ\ **1** : to enclose in a circle **2** : to move or revolve around; also : to move in a circle

**cir·clet** \'sər-klət\ n : a small circle; esp : a circular ornament

**cir·cuit** \'sər-kət\ n **1** : a boundary around an enclosed space **2** : a moving or revolving around (as in an orbit) **3** : a regular tour (as by a judge) around an assigned territory **4** : LEAGUE; also : a chain of theaters **5** : the complete path of an electric current — **cir·cuit·al** \-kət-ᵊl\ adj

**circuit breaker** n : a switch that automatically interrupts an electric circuit under an abnormal condition

**circuit court** n : a court that sits at two or more places within one judicial district

**cir·cu·itous** \,sər-'kyü-ət-əs\ adj **1** : marked by a circular or winding course **2** : ROUNDABOUT, INDIRECT

**cir·cuit·ry** \'sər-kə-trē\ n, pl **-ries** : the plan or the components of an electric circuit

**cir·cu·ity** \,sər-'kyü-ət-ē\ n, pl **-ities** : INDIRECTION

**¹cir·cu·lar** \'sər-kyə-lər\ adj **1** : having the form of a circle : ROUND **2** : moving in or around a circle **3** : CIRCUITOUS **4** : sent around to a number of persons ⟨a ~ letter⟩ — **cir·cu·lar·i·ty** \,sər-kyə-'lar-ət-ē\ n

**²circular** n : a paper (as an advertising leaflet) intended for wide distribution

**cir·cu·lar·ize** \'sər-kyə-lə-,rīz\ vb **-ized; -iz·ing 1** : to send circulars to **2** : to poll by questionnaire

**cir·cu·late** \'sər-kyə-,lāt\ vb **-lat·ed; -lat·ing 1** : to move or cause to move in a circle, circuit, or orbit **2** : to pass from place to place or from person to person — **cir·cu·la·tion** \,sər-kyə-'lā-shən\ n — **cir·cu·la·to·ry** \'sər-kyə-lə-,tōr-ē\ adj

**cir·cum·am·bu·late** \,sər-kəm-'am-byə-,lāt\ vb **-lat·ed; -lat·ing** : to circle on foot esp. ritualistically

**cir·cum·cise** \'sər-kəm-,sīz\ vb **-cised; -cis·ing** : to cut off the foreskin of — **cir·cum·ci·sion** \,sər-kəm-'sizh-ən\ n

**cir·cum·fer·ence** \sər-'kəm-f(ə-)rəns\ *n* 1 : the perimeter of a circle 2 : the external boundary or surface of a figure or object

cir·cum·flex \'sər-kəm-,fleks\ *n* : a mark (as ^) used chiefly to indicate length, contraction, or a specific vowel quality

cir·cum·lo·cu·tion \,sər-kəm-lō-'kyü-shən\ *n* : the use of an unnecessarily large number of words to express an idea

cir·cum·lu·nar \-'lü-nər\ *adj* : revolving about or surrounding the moon

cir·cum·nav·i·gate \-'nav-ə-,gāt\ *vb* : to go completely around esp. by water — cir·cum·nav·i·ga·tion \-,nav-ə-'gā-shən\ *n*

cir·cum·po·lar \-'pō-lər\ *adj* 1 : continually visible above the horizon ⟨a ~ star⟩ 2 : surrounding or found in the vicinity of a terrestrial pole

cir·cum·scribe \'sər-kəm-,skrīb\ *vb* 1 : to draw a line around 2 : to limit narrowly the range or activity of — cir·cum·scrip·tion \,sər-kəm-'skrip-shən\ *n*

cir·cum·spect \'sər-kəm-,spekt\ *adj* : careful to consider all circumstances and consequences : PRUDENT — cir·cum·spec·tion \,sər-kəm-'spek-shən\ *n*

cir·cum·stance \'sər-kəm-,stans\ *n* 1 : a fact or event that must be considered along with another fact or event 2 *pl* : surrounding conditions 3 *pl* : situation with regard to wealth 4 : CEREMONY 5 : CHANCE, FATE

cir·cum·stan·tial \,sər-kəm-'stan-chəl\ *adj* 1 : consisting of or depending on circumstances 2 : INCIDENTAL 3 : containing full details — cir·cum·stan·tial·ly \-'ē\ *adv*

cir·cum·vent \,sər-kəm-'vent\ *vb* : to check or defeat esp. by ingenuity or stratagem

cir·cus \'sər-kəs\ *n* 1 : an often tent-covered arena used for shows that feature feats of physical skill and daring, wild animal acts, and performances by clowns 2 : a circus performance; *also* : the physical plant, livestock, and personnel of a circus

cirque \'sərk\ *n* : a deep steep-walled mountain basin shaped like half a bowl

cir·rho·sis \sə-'rō-səs\ *n, pl* -rho·ses \-,sēz\ [NL, fr. Gk *kirrhos* orange-colored] : fibrosis esp. of the liver — cir·rhot·ic \-'rät-ik\ *adj or n*

cir·rus \'sir-əs\ *n, pl* cir·ri \'sir-,ī\ : a wispy white cloud usu. of minute ice crystals at high altitudes

cis·lu·nar \('')sis-'lü-nər\ *adj* : lying between the earth and the moon or the moon's orbit

cis·tern \'sis-tərn\ *n* : an often underground tank for storing water

cit *abbr* 1 citation; cited 2 citizen

cit·a·del \'sit-əd-ªl, -ə-,del\ *n* 1 : a fortress commanding a city 2 : STRONGHOLD

ci·ta·tion \sī-'tā-shən\ *n* 1 : an official summons to appear (as before a court) 2 : QUOTATION 3 : a formal statement of the achievements of a

person; *also* : a specific reference in a military dispatch to meritorious performance of duty

cite \'sīt\ *vb* cit·ed; cit·ing 1 : to summon to appear before a court 2 : QUOTE 3 : to refer to esp. in commendation or praise

citi·fy \'sit-i-,fī\ *vb* -fied; -fy·ing : URBANIZE

cit·i·zen \'sit-ə-zən\ *n* 1 : an inhabitant of a city or town 2 : a person who owes allegiance to a government and is entitled to government protection — cit·i·zen·ship *n*

cit·i·zen·ry \-rē\ *n, pl* -ries : a whole body of citizens

cit·ric acid \'sit-rik-\ *n* : a sour acid substance obtained from lemon and lime juices or by fermentation of sugars and used as a flavoring

cit·ron \'sit-rən\ *n* 1 : the oval lemon-like fruit of an Asiatic citrus tree 2 : a small hard-fleshed watermelon used esp. in pickles and preserves

cit·ro·nel·la \,sit-rə-'nel-ə\ *n* : a fragrant Asiatic grass that yields an oil used esp. as an insect repellent; *also* : the oil

cit·rus \'sit-rəs\ *n, pl* citrus *or* cit·rus·es : any of a genus of often thorny evergreen trees or shrubs grown in warm regions for their fruits (as the orange, lemon, lime, and grapefruit)

city \'sit-ē\ *n, pl* cit·ies [ME *citie* large or small town, fr. OF *cité* capital city, fr. ML *civitas*, fr. L, citizenship, state, city of Rome, fr. *civis* citizen] 1 : an inhabited place larger or more important than a town 2 : a municipality in the U.S. governed under a charter granted by the state; *also* : an incorporated municipal unit of the highest class in Canada

city manager *n* : an official employed by an elected council to direct the administration of a city government

city-state \'sit-ē-'stāt, -,stāt\ *n* : an autonomous state consisting of a city and surrounding territory

civ *abbr* civil; civilian

civ·et \'siv-ət\ *n* : a yellowish strong-smelling substance obtained from a cat-like African mammal (civet cat) and used in making perfumes

civic \'siv-ik\ *adj* : of or relating to a city, citizenship, or civil affairs

civ·ics \-iks\ *n* : a social science dealing with the rights and duties of citizens

civ·il \'siv-əl\ *adj* 1 : of or relating to citizens or to the state as a political body 2 : of or relating to the general population : not military or ecclesiastical 3 : COURTEOUS, POLITE 4 : of or relating to legal proceedings in connection with private rights and obligations ⟨the ~ code⟩

civil defense *n* : the protective measures and emergency relief activities conducted by civilians in case of hostile attack, sabotage, or natural disaster

civil disobedience *n* : refusal to obey governmental commands esp. as a non-violent means of gaining concessions from the government

**civil engineering** *n* **:** engineering dealing chiefly with design and construction of public works (as roads or harbors) — **civil engineer** *n*

**ci·vil·ian** \sə-'vil-yən\ *n* **:** a person not on active duty in a military, police, or fire-fighting force

**ci·vil·i·ty** \sə-'vil-ət-ē\ *n, pl* **-ties** **1 :** POLITENESS, COURTESY **2 :** a polite act or expression

**civ·i·li·za·tion** \ˌsiv-ə-lə-'zā-shən\ *n* **1 :** a relatively high level of cultural and technological development **2 :** the culture characteristic of a time or place

**civ·i·lize** \'siv-ə-ˌlīz\ *vb* **-lized; -liz·ing 1 :** to raise from a primitive state to an advanced and ordered stage of cultural development **2 :** REFINE — **civ·i·lized** *adj*

**civil liberty** *n* **:** freedom from arbitrary governmental interference specif. by denial of governmental power — usu. used in pl.

**civ·il·ly** \'siv-ə(l)-lē\ *adv* **1 :** in a civil manner : POLITELY **2 :** in terms of civil rights, matters, or law ⟨~ dead⟩

**civil rights** *n pl* **:** the nonpolitical rights of a citizen; *esp* **:** those guaranteed by the 13th and 14th amendments to the Constitution and by acts of Congress

**civil servant** *n* **:** a member of a civil service

**civil service** *n* **:** the administrative service of a government

**civil war** *n* **:** a war between opposing groups of citizens of the same country

**civ·vies** \'siv-ēz\ *n pl* **:** civilian clothes as distinguished from a military uniform

**CJ** *abbr* chief justice

**ck** *abbr* **1** cask **2** check

**cl** *abbr* class

**Cl** *symbol* chlorine

**CL** *abbr* carload

**¹clack** \'klak\ *vb* **1 :** CHATTER, PRATTLE **2 :** to make or cause to make a clatter

**²clack** *n* **1 :** rapid continuous talk **:** CHATTER **2 :** a sound of clacking ⟨the ~ of a typewriter⟩

**¹clad** \'klad\ *adj* **:** CLOTHED, COVERED

**²clad** *n* **:** a coin with outer layers of one metal bonded to a core of a different metal

**¹claim** \'klām\ *vb* **1 :** to ask for as one's own; *also* **:** to take as the rightful owner **2 :** to call for : REQUIRE **3 :** to state as a fact : MAINTAIN

**²claim** *n* **1 :** a demand for something due **2 :** a right to something usu. in another's possession **3 :** an assertion open to challenge **4 :** something claimed

**claim·ant** \'klā-mənt\ *n* **:** a person making a claim

**clair·voy·ant** \klaər-'vȯi-ənt\ *adj* **1 :** unusually perceptive **2 :** having the power of discerning objects not present to the senses — **clair·voy·ance** \-əns\ *n* — **clairvoyant** *n*

**clam** \'klam\ *n* **:** any of numerous bivalve mollusks including many that are edible

**clam·bake** \-ˌbāk\ *n* **:** a party or gathering (as at the seashore) at which food is cooked usu. on heated rocks covered by seaweed

**clam·ber** \'klam-bər\ *vb* **clam·bered;** **clam·ber·ing** \'klam-b(ə-)riŋ, 'klam-(ə-)riŋ\ **:** to climb awkwardly (as by scrambling)

**clam·my** \'klam-ē\ *adj* **clam·mi·er;** **-est :** being damp, soft, sticky, and usu. cool — **clam·mi·ness** *n*

**¹clam·or** \'klam-ər\ *n* **1 :** a noisy shouting; *also* **:** a loud continuous noise **2 :** vigorous protest or demand — **clam·or·ous** *adj*

**²clamor** *vb* **clam·ored; clam·or·ing** \'klam-(ə-)riŋ\ **:** to make a clamor

**¹clamp** \'klamp\ *n* **:** a device for holding things together

**²clamp** *vb* **:** to fasten with or as if with a clamp

**clamp down** \(')klamp-'daùn\ *vb* **:** to impose restrictions **:** become repressive — **clamp·down** \'klamp-ˌdaùn\ *n*

**clam·shell** \'klam-ˌshel\ *n* **:** a bucket or grapple (as on a dredge) having two hinged jaws

**clam up** *vb* **:** to become silent

**clan** \'klan\ *n* [ME, fr. ScGael *clann* offspring, clan, fr. Old Irish *cland* plant, offspring, fr. L *planta* plant] **:** a group (as in the Scottish Highlands) made up of households whose heads claim descent from a common ancestor — **clan·nish** *adj* — **clan·nish·ness** *n*

**clan·des·tine** \klan-'des-tən\ *adj* **:** held in or conducted with secrecy

**clang** \'klaŋ\ *n* **:** a loud metallic ringing sound — **clang** *vb*

**clan·gor** \'klaŋ-(g)ər\ *n* **:** a resounding clang or medley of clangs

**clank** \'klaŋk\ *n* **:** a sharp brief metallic ringing sound — **clank** *vb*

**¹clap** \'klap\ *vb* **clapped; clap·ping 1 :** to strike noisily **2 :** APPLAUD

**²clap** *n* **1 :** a loud noisy crash **2 :** the noise made by clapping the hands

**³clap** *n* **:** GONORRHEA

**clap·board** \'klab-ərd; 'kla(p)-ˌbȯrd\ *n* **:** a narrow board thicker at one edge than the other used for siding — **clapboard** *vb*

**clap·per** \'klap-ər\ *n* **:** one that makes a clapping sound; *esp* **:** the tongue of a bell

**clap·trap** \'klap-ˌtrap\ *n* **:** pretentious nonsense

**claque** \'klak\ *n* **:** a group hired to applaud at a performance

**clar·et** \'klar-ət\ *n* **:** a dry red table wine

**clar·i·fy** \'klar-ə-ˌfī\ *vb* **-fied; -fy·ing :** to make or become pure or clear — **clar·i·fi·ca·tion** \ˌklar-ə-fə-'kā-shən\ *n*

**clar·i·net** \ˌklar-ə-'net\ *n* **:** a single-reed woodwind instrument in the form of a cylindrical tube with moderately flaring end — **clar·i·net·ist** *or* **clar·i·net·tist** \-əst\ *n*

**clar·i·on** \'klar-ē-ən\ *adj* **:** brilliantly clear ⟨a ~ call to action⟩

**clar·i·ty** \'klar-ət-ē\ *n* **:** CLEARNESS

**¹clash** \'klash\ *vb* **1 :** to make or cause to make a clash **2 :** CONFLICT, COLLIDE

²**clash** n 1 : a noisy usu. metallic sound of collision 2 : a hostile encounter; also : a conflict of opinion

¹**clasp** \'klasp\ n 1 : a device (as a hook) for holding objects or parts together 2 : EMBRACE, GRASP

²**clasp** vb 1 : to fasten with a clasp 2 : EMBRACE 3 : GRASP

¹**class** \'klas\ n 1 : a group of the same general status or nature 2 : social rank; also : high quality 3 : a course of instruction; also : the period when such a course is taught 4 : a group of students meeting regularly in a course; also : a group graduating together 5 : a division or rating based on grade or quality — **class·less** adj

²**class** vb : CLASSIFY

**class action** n : a legal action undertaken in behalf of the plaintiffs and all others having an identical interest in the alleged wrong

¹**clas·sic** \'klas-ik\ adj 1 : serving as a standard of excellence; also : TRADITIONAL 2 : CLASSICAL 2 3 : notable esp. as the best example 4 : AUTHENTIC

²**classic** n 1 : a work of enduring excellence and esp. of ancient Greece or Rome; also : its author 2 : a traditional event

**clas·si·cal** \'klas-i-kəl\ adj 1 : CLASSIC 2 : of or relating to the ancient Greek and Roman classics 3 : of or relating to a form or system of primary significance before modern times ⟨~ economics⟩ 4 : concerned with a general study of the arts and sciences — **clas·si·cal·ly** \-k(ə-)lē\ adv

**clas·si·cism** \'klas-ə-,siz-əm\ n 1 : the principles or style of the literature or art of ancient Greece and Rome 2 : adherence to traditional standards believed to be universally valid — **clas·si·cist** \-səst\ n

**clas·si·fied** \'klas-ə-,fīd\ adj : withheld from general circulation for reasons of national security

**clas·si·fy** \'klas-ə-,fī\ vb **-fied; -fy·ing** : to arrange in or assign to classes — **clas·si·fi·able** adj — **clas·si·fi·ca·tion** \,klas-ə-fə-'kā-shən\ n

**class·mate** \'klas-,māt\ n : a member of the same class (as in a college)

**class·room** \-,rüm-, -,rüm\ n : a room (as in a school) in which classes meet

**classy** \'klas-ē\ adj **class·i·er; -est** : ELEGANT, STYLISH

**clas·tic** \'klas-tik\ adj : made up of fragments of preexisting rocks ⟨a ~ sediment⟩ — **clastic** n

**clat·ter** \'klat-ər\ n : a rattling sound ⟨the ~ of dishes⟩ — **clatter** vb

**clause** \'klòz\ n 1 : a separate part of an article or document 2 : a group of words having its own subject and predicate but forming only part of a compound or complex sentence

**claus·tro·pho·bia** \,klò-strə-'fō-bē-ə\ n : abnormal dread of being in closed or narrow spaces

**clav·i·chord** \'klav-ə-,kòrd\ n : an early keyboard instrument in use before the piano

**clav·i·cle** \'klav-i-kəl\ n [F clavicule,

fr. NL clavicula, fr. L, dim. of L clavis key] : COLLARBONE

**cla·vier** \klə-'viər; 'klā-vē-ər\ n 1 : the keyboard of a musical instrument 2 : an early keyboard instrument

¹**claw** \'klò\ n 1 : a sharp usu. curved nail on the toe of an animal 2 : a sharp curved process (as on the foot of an insect); also : CHELA — **clawed** \'klòd\ adj

²**claw** vb : to rake, seize, or dig with or as if with claws

**clay** \'klā\ n 1 : plastic earthy material used in making pottery that consists largely of silicates of aluminum and becomes permanently hardened by firing; also : finely divided soil consisting largely of such clay 2 : EARTH, MUD 3 : the mortal human body — **clay·ey** \'klā-ē\ adj

**clay·more** \'klā-,mōr\ n : a large 2-edged sword formerly used by Scottish Highlanders

**clay pigeon** n : a saucer-shaped target thrown from a trap in trapshooting

**cld** abbr 1 called 2 cleared

¹**clean** \'klēn\ adj 1 : free from dirt or disease 2 : PURE; also : HONORABLE 3 : THOROUGH ⟨made a ~ sweep⟩ 4 : TRIM ⟨a ship with ~ lines⟩; also : EVEN 5 : habitually neat — **clean** adv — **clean·ly** \'klēn-lē\ adv — **clean·ness** \'klēn-nəs\ n

²**clean** vb : to make or become clean — **clean·er** n

**clean-cut** \'klēn-'kət\ adj 1 : cut so that the surface or edge is smooth and even 2 : sharply defined or outlined 3 : giving an effect of wholesomeness

**clean·ly** \'klen-lē\ adj **clean·li·er; -est** 1 : careful to keep clean 2 : habitually kept clean — **clean·li·ness** n

**clean room** \'klēn-,rüm, -,rùm\ n : an uncontaminated room maintained for the manufacture or assembly of objects (as precision parts)

**cleanse** \'klenz\ vb **cleansed; cleans·ing** : to make clean — **cleans·er** n

¹**clean·up** \'klēn-,əp\ n 1 : an act or instance of cleaning 2 : a very large profit

²**cleanup** adj : being fourth in the batting order of a baseball team

**clean up** \(')klēn-'əp\ vb : to make a spectacular business profit

¹**clear** \'kliər\ adj 1 : BRIGHT, LUMINOUS; also : UNTROUBLED, SERENE 2 : CLEAN, PURE; also : TRANSPARENT 3 : easily heard, seen, or understood 4 : capable of sharp discernment; also : free from doubt 5 : INNOCENT 6 : free from restriction, obstruction, or entanglement 7 : CLOUDLESS — **clear** adv — **clear·ly** adv — **clear·ness** n

²**clear** vb 1 : to make or become clear 2 : to go away : DISPERSE 3 : to free from accusation or blame; also : to certify as trustworthy 4 : EXPLAIN 5 : to get free from obstruction 6 : SETTLE 7 : NET 8 : to get rid of : REMOVE 9 : to jump or go by without touching; also : PASS

³**clear** n : a clear space or part

**clear·ance** \'klir-əns\ n 1 : an act or process of clearing 2 : the distance by which one object clears another

**clear–cut** \'kliər-'kət\ adj 1 : sharply outlined 2 : DEFINITE, UNEQUIVOCAL

**clear–head·ed** \-'hed-əd\ adj : having a clear understanding : PERCEPTIVE

**clear·ing** \'kli(ə)r-iŋ\ n 1 : a tract of land cleared of wood 2 : the passage of checks and claims through a clearing-house

**clear·ing·house** \-,haůs\ n : an institution maintained by banks for making an exchange of checks and claims held by each bank against other banks

**cleat** \'klēt\ n : a piece of wood or metal fastened on or projecting from something to give strength, provide a grip, or prevent slipping

**cleav·age** \'klē-vij\ n : a splitting apart : SPLIT

¹**cleave** \'klēv\ vb **cleaved** \'klēvd\ or **clove** \'klōv\; **cleav·ing** : ADHERE, CLING

²**cleave** vb **cleaved** \'klēvd\ also **cleft** \'kleft\ or **clove** \'klōv\; **cleaved** also **cleft** or **clo·ven** \'klō-vən\; **cleav·ing** 1 : to divide by force : split asunder 2 : DIVIDE

**cleav·er** \'klē-vər\ n : a heavy chopping knife for cutting meat

**clef** \'klef\ n : a sign placed on the staff in music to show what pitch is represented by each line and space

**cleft** \'kleft\ n : FISSURE, CRACK

**clem·a·tis** \'klem-ət-əs; kli-'mat-əs\ n : a vine related to the buttercups that has showy usu. white or purple flowers

**clem·en·cy** \'klem-ən-sē\ n 1 : disposition to be merciful 2 : mildness of weather

**clem·ent** \-ənt\ adj 1 : MERCIFUL, LENIENT 2 : TEMPERATE, MILD

**clench** \'klench\ vb 1 : CLINCH 2 : to hold fast 3 : to set or close tightly

**clere·sto·ry** or **clear·sto·ry** \'kliər-,stōr-ē\ n : an outside wall of a room or building that rises above an adjoining roof and contains windows

**cler·gy** \'klər-jē\ n : a body of religious officials authorized to conduct services

**cler·gy·man** \-ji-mən\ n : a member of the clergy

**cler·ic** \'kler-ik\ n : CLERGYMAN

**cler·i·cal** \'kler-i-kəl\ adj 1 : of or relating to the clergy or a clergyman 2 : of or relating to a clerk or office worker

**cler·i·cal·ism** \'kler-i-kə-,liz-əm\ n : a policy of maintaining or increasing the power of a religious hierarchy

**clerk** \'klərk, Brit 'klärk\ n 1 : CLERIC 2 : an official responsible for correspondence, records, and accounts; also : a person employed to perform general office work 3 : a store salesman — **clerk** vb — **clerk·ship** n

**clev·er** \'klev-ər\ adj 1 : showing skill or resourcefulness 2 : marked by wit or ingenuity — **clev·er·ly** adv — **clev·er·ness** n

**clev·is** \'klev-əs\ n : a U-shaped shackle used for attaching or suspending parts

**clew** var of CLUE

**cli·ché** \kli-'shā\ n : a trite phrase or expression — **cli·chéd** \-'shād\ adj

¹**click** \'klik\ n : a slight sharp noise

²**click** vb 1 : to make or cause to make a click 2 : to fit or work together smoothly

**cli·ent** \'klī-ənt\ n 1 : DEPENDENT 2 : a person who engages the professional services of another; also : PATRON, CUSTOMER

**cli·en·tele** \,klī-ən-'tel, ,klē-ən-\ n : a body of clients and esp. customers

**cliff** \'klif\ n : a high steep face of rock

**cliff–hang·er** \-,haŋ-ər\ n 1 : an adventure serial or melodrama usu. presented in installments each of which ends in suspense 2 : a contest whose outcome is in doubt up to the very end

**cli·mac·ter·ic** \klī-'mak-t(ə-)rik\ n 1 : a major turning point or critical stage 2 : MENOPAUSE; also : a corresponding period in the male

**cli·mate** \'klī-mət\ n [ME climat, fr. MF, fr. LL clima, fr. Gk klima inclination, latitude, climate, fr. klinein to lean] 1 : a region having specific climatic conditions 2 : the average weather conditions at a place over a period of years 3 : a prevailing atmosphere or environment ⟨the ~ of opinion⟩ — **cli·mat·ic** \klī-'mat-ik\ adj — **cli·mat·i·cal·ly** \-i-k(ə-)lē\ adv

**cli·ma·tol·o·gy** \,klī-mə-'täl-ə-jē\ n : the science that deals with climates — **cli·ma·to·log·i·cal** \,klī-mət-ᵊl-'äj-i-kəl\ adj — **cli·ma·to·log·i·cal·ly** \-k(ə-)lē\ adv — **cli·ma·tol·o·gist** \-mə-'täl-ə-jəst\ n

¹**cli·max** \'klī-,maks\ n [L, fr. Gk klimax ladder, fr. klinein to lean] 1 : a series of ideas or statements so arranged that they increase in force and power from the first to the last; also : the last member of such a series 2 : the highest point 3 : a relatively stable or the final stage in the development of an ecological community esp. of plants — **cli·mac·tic** \klī-'mak-tik\ adj

²**climax** vb : to come or bring to a climax

¹**climb** \'klīm\ vb 1 : to go up or down esp. by use of hands and feet; also : to ascend in growing 2 : to rise to a higher point — **climb·er** n

²**climb** n 1 : a place where climbing is necessary 2 : the act of climbing : ascent by climbing

**clime** \'klīm\ n : CLIMATE

¹**clinch** \'klinch\ vb 1 : to fasten securely 2 : to make final : SETTLE 3 : to hold fast or firmly

²**clinch** n 1 : a fastening by means of a clinched nail, rivet, or bolt 2 : an act or instance of clinching in boxing

**clinch·er** \'klin-chər\ n : one that clinches; esp : a decisive fact, argument, act, or remark

**cling** \'kliŋ\ vb **clung** \'kləŋ\; **cling·ing** 1 : to adhere as if glued firmly; also : to hold or hold on tightly 2 : to have a strong emotional attachment

**cling·stone** \'kliŋ-ˌstōn\ n : a fruit (as a peach) whose flesh adheres strongly to the pit

**clin·ic** \'klin-ik\ n 1 : medical instruction featuring the examination and discussion of actual cases 2 : a facility (as of a hospital) for diagnosis and treatment of outpatients

**clin·i·cal** \'klin-i-kəl\ adj 1 : of, relating to, or typical of a clinic; esp : involving direct observation of the patient 2 : scientifically detached and dispassionate — **clin·i·cal·ly** \-k(ə-)lē\ adv

**cli·ni·cian** \kli-'nish-ən\ n : one qualified in the clinical practice of medicine, psychiatry, or psychology as distinguished from one specializing in laboratory or research techniques

**¹clink** \'kliŋk\ vb : to make or cause to make a slight sharp short metallic sound

**²clink** n : a clinking sound

**clin·ker** \'kliŋ-kər\ n : stony matter fused by fire (as in a furnace from impurities in coal) : SLAG

**¹clip** \'klip\ vb clipped; clip·ping 1 : to clasp or fasten with a clip 2 : to illegally block (an opponent) in football

**²clip** n 1 : a device that grips, clasps, or hooks 2 : a cartridge holder for a rifle

**³clip** vb clipped; clip·ping 1 : to cut or cut off with shears 2 : CURTAIL, DIMINISH 3 : HIT, PUNCH

**⁴clip** n 1 : a 2-bladed instrument for cutting esp. the nails 2 : a sharp blow 3 : a rapid pace

**clip·board** \'klip-ˌbōrd\ n : a small writing board with a spring clip at the top for holding papers

**clip joint** n, slang : an establishment (as a nightclub) that makes a practice of defrauding its customers

**clip·per** \'klip-ər\ n 1 : an implement for clipping esp. the hair or nails — usu. used in pl. 2 : a fast sailing ship

**clip·ping** \'klip-iŋ\ n : a piece clipped from something (as a newspaper)

**clip·sheet** \'klip-ˌshēt\ n : a sheet of newspaper material issued by an organization and usu. printed on only one side to facilitate clipping and reprinting

**clique** \'klēk, 'klik\ n : a small exclusive group of people : COTERIE — **cliqu·ey** or **cliquy** \'klēk-ē, 'klik-\ adj — **cliqu·ish** \-ish\ adj

**cli·to·ris** \'klit-ə-rəs, 'klīt-\ n : a small organ at the anterior or ventral part of the vulva homologous to the penis — **cli·to·ral** \-rəl\ or **cli·tor·ic** \kli-'tōr-ik, klī-\ adj

**clk** abbr clerk

**clo** abbr clothing

**¹cloak** \'klōk\ n [ME cloke, fr. OF cloque bell, cloak, fr. ML clocca bell; fr. its shape] 1 : a loose outer garment 2 : something that conceals or covers

**²cloak** vb : to cover or hide with a cloak

**cloak-and-dag·ger** adj : involving or suggestive of espionage

**clob·ber** \'kläb-ər\ vb clob·bered; clob·ber·ing \-(ə-)riŋ\ 1 : to pound

or hit forcefully 2 : to defeat overwhelmingly

**cloche** \'klōsh\ n : a woman's small helmetlike hat

**¹clock** \'kläk\ n : a timepiece not intended to be carried on the person

**²clock** vb 1 : to time (a person or a performance) by a timing device 2 : to register (as speed) on a mechanical recording device — **clock·er** n

**³clock** n : an ornamental figure on a stocking or sock

**clock·wise** \'kläk-ˌwīz\ adv : in the direction in which the hands of a clock move — **clockwise** adj

**clock·work** \-ˌwərk\ n : machinery containing a train of wheels of small size

**clod** \'kläd\ n 1 : a lump esp. of earth or clay 2 : a dull or insensitive person

**clod·hop·per** \-ˌhäp-ər\ n 1 : an uncouth rustic 2 : a large heavy shoe

**¹clog** \'kläg\ n 1 : a weight so attached as to impede motion 2 : a thick-soled shoe

**²clog** vb clogged; clog·ging 1 : to impede with a clog : HINDER 2 : to obstruct passage through 3 : to become filled with extraneous matter

**cloi·son·né** \ˌklȯiz-ᵊn-'ā\ adj : a colored decoration made of enamels poured into the divided areas in a design outlined with wire or metal strips

**¹clois·ter** \'klȯi-stər\ n [ME cloistre, fr. OF, fr. ML claustrum, fr. L, bar, bolt, fr. claudere to close] 1 : a monastic establishment 2 : a covered usu. colonnaded passage on the side of a court — **clois·tral** \-strəl\ adj

**²cloister** vb : to shut away from the world

**clop** \'kläp\ n : a sound made by or as if by a hoof or wooden shoe against pavement — **clop** vb

**¹close** \'klōz\ vb closed; clos·ing 1 : to bar passage through : SHUT 2 : to suspend the operations (as of a school) 3 : END, TERMINATE 4 : to bring together the parts or edges of; also : to fill up 5 : GRAPPLE ⟨~ with the enemy⟩ 6 : to enter into an agreement — **clos·able** or **close·able** adj

**²close** \'klōz\ n : CONCLUSION, END

**³close** \'klōs\ adj clos·er; clos·est 1 : having no openings 2 : narrowly restricting or restricted 3 : limited to a privileged class 4 : SECLUDED; also : SECRETIVE 5 : RIGOROUS 6 : SULTRY, STUFFY 7 : STINGY 8 : having little space between items or units 9 : fitting tightly; also : SHORT ⟨~ haircut⟩ 10 : NEAR 11 : INTIMATE ⟨~ friends⟩ 12 : ACCURATE 13 : decided by a narrow margin ⟨a ~ game⟩ — **close** adv — **close·ly** adv — **close·ness** n

**closed circuit** n : television in which the signal is transmitted by wire

**close-fist·ed** \'klōs-'fis-təd\ adj : STINGY

**close-knit** \-'nit\ adj : closely bound together by social, cultural, economic, or political ties

**close-mouthed** \-'maùthd, -'maùtht\ adj : cautious in speaking

**close·out** \'klōz-ˌaůt\ *n* : a sale of a business's entire remaining stock at reduced prices

**close out** \'klōz-'aůt\ *vb* **1** : to dispose of by a closeout **2** : to dispose of a business ; sell out

¹**clos·et** \'kläz-ət, 'klóz-\ *n* **1** : a small room for privacy **2** : a small compartment for household utensils or clothing **3** : WATER CLOSET

²**closet** *vb* : to take into a private room for an interview

**close-up** \'klōs-ˌəp\ *n* **1** : a photograph or movie shot taken at close range **2** : an intimate view or examination of something

**clo·sure** \'klō-zhər\ *n* **1** : an act of closing : the condition of being closed **2** : something that closes **3** : CLOTURE

**clot** \'klät\ *n* : a mass formed by a portion of liquid (as blood or cream) thickening and sticking together — **clot** *vb*

**cloth** \'klóth\ *n, pl* **cloths** \'klóthz, 'klóths\ **1** : a pliable fabric made usu. by weaving or knitting natural or synthetic fibers and filaments **2** : TABLECLOTH **3** : distinctive dress of a profession and esp. of the clergy; *also* : CLERGY

**clothe** \'klōth\ *vb* **clothed** *or* **clad** \'klad\; **cloth·ing 1** : DRESS **2** : to express by suitably significant language

**clothes** \'klō(th)z\ *n pl* **1** : CLOTHING **2** : BEDCLOTHES

**clothes·horse** \-ˌhórs\ *n* **1** : a frame on which to hang clothes **2** : a conspicuously dressy person

**clothes·pin** \'klō(th)z-ˌpin\ *n* : a device for fastening clothes on a line

**clothes·press** \-ˌpres\ *n* : a receptacle for clothes

**cloth·ier** \'klōth-yər, 'klō-thē-ər\ *n* : a maker or seller of cloth or clothing

**cloth·ing** \'klō-thiŋ\ *n* : garments in general

**clo·ture** \'klō-chər\ *n* : the closing or limitation (as by calling for a vote) of debate in a legislative body

¹**cloud** \'klaůd\ *n* [ME *cloud*, cloud, fr. OE *clūd* rock, hill] **1** : a visible mass of water or ice particles in the air **2** : a usu. visible mass of minute airborne particles; *also* : a mass of obscuring matter in interstellar space **3** : CROWD, SWARM ⟨a ~ of mosquitoes⟩ **4** : something having a dark or threatening look — **cloud·i·ness** \-ē-nəs\ *n* — **cloud·less** *adj* — **cloudy** *adj*

²**cloud** *vb* **1** : to darken or hide with or as if with a cloud **2** : OBSCURE **3** : TAINT, SULLY

**cloud·burst** \-ˌbərst\ *n* : a sudden heavy rainfall

**cloud·let** \-lət\ *n* : a small cloud

**cloud nine** *n* : a feeling of extreme wellbeing or elation — usu. used with *on*

¹**clout** \'klaůt\ *n* **1** : a blow esp. with the hand **2** : PULL, INFLUENCE

²**clout** *vb* : to hit forcefully

¹**clove** *past of* CLEAVE

²**clove** \'klōv\ *n* [ME *clowe*, fr. OF *clou* (de girofle), lit., nail of clove, fr. L *clavus* nail] : the dried flower bud of an East Indian tree used esp. as a spice

**clo·ven** \'klō-vən\ *past part of* CLEAVE

**clo·ver** \'klō-vər\ *n* : any of numerous leguminous herbs with usu. 3-parted leaves and dense flower heads

**clo·ver·leaf** \-ˌlēf\ *n, pl* **cloverleafs** \-ˌlēfs\ *or* **clo·ver·leaves** \-ˌlēvz\ : a road plan passing one highway over another and routing turning traffic without left-hand turns or direct crossings

¹**clown** \'klaůn\ *n* **1** : BOOR **2** : a fool or comedian in an entertainment (as a circus) — **clown·ish** *adj* — **clown·ish·ly** *adv* — **clown·ish·ness** *n*

²**clown** *vb* : to act like a clown

**cloy** \'klói\ *vb* : to disgust or nauseate with excess of something orig. pleasing

**clr** *abbr* clear

**CLU** *abbr* chartered life underwriter

¹**club** \'kləb\ *n* **1** : a heavy wooden stick or staff used as a weapon; *also* : BAT **2** : any of a suit of playing cards marked with a black figure resembling a clover leaf **3** : a group of persons associated for a common purpose; *also* : the meeting place of such a group

²**club** *vb* **clubbed; club·bing 1** : to strike with a club **2** : to unite or combine for a common cause

**club·foot** \'kləb-ˌfůt\ *n* : a misshapen foot twisted out of position from birth; *also* : this deformity — **club·foot·ed** \-ˌfůt-əd\ *adj*

**club·house** \'kləb-ˌhaůs\ *n* **1** : a house occupied by a club **2** : locker rooms used by an athletic team

**club sandwich** *n* : a sandwich of three slices of bread with two layers of meat (as chicken) and lettuce, tomato, and mayonnaise

**club soda** *n* : SODA WATER 1

**club steak** *n* : a small steak cut from the end of the short loin

**cluck** \'klək\ *n* : the call of a hen esp. to her chicks — **cluck** *vb*

¹**clue** *or* **clew** \'klü\ *n* **1** : a guide through an intricate procedure or maze; *esp* : a piece of evidence leading to the solution of a problem **2** *usu* **clew** : a metal loop on a lower corner of a sail for holding ropes

²**clue** *or* **clew** *vb* **clued** *or* **clewed; clue·ing** *or* **clu·ing** *or* **clew·ing 1** : to provide with a clue; *also* : to give reliable information to ⟨~ me in⟩ **2** *usu* **clew** : to haul a sail up or down by ropes.through the clews

¹**clump** \'kləmp\ *n* **1** : a group of things clustered together **2** : a heavy tramping sound

²**clump** *vb* : to tread clumsily and noisily

**clum·sy** \'kləm-zē\ *adj* **clum·si·er; -est 1** : lacking dexterity, nimbleness, or grace **2** : not tactful or subtle — **clum·si·ly** \'kləm-zə-lē\ *adv* — **clum·si·ness** \-zē-nəs\ *n*

**clung** *past of* CLING

¹**clus·ter** \'kləs-tər\ *n* : GROUP, BUNCH

²**cluster** *vb* **clus·tered; clus·ter·ing** \-t(ə-)riŋ\ : to grow or gather in a cluster

**cluster college** *n* : a small residential college constituting a largely self-governing division of a university and usu.

specializing in one branch of knowledge

**¹clutch** \'klǝch\ *vb* : to grasp with or as if with the hand

**²clutch** *n* 1 : the claws or a hand in the act of grasping; *also* : CONTROL, POWER 2 : a device (as a coupling for connecting two working parts in machinery) for gripping an object 3 : a crucial situation

**³clutch** *adj* : made, done, or successful in a crucial situation

**¹clut·ter** \'klǝt-ǝr\ *vb* : to fill with scattered things that impede movement or reduce efficiency

**²clutter** *n* : crowded confusion

**cm** *abbr* centimeter

**CM** *abbr* Congregation of the Mission

**cmdg** *abbr* commanding

**cmdr** *abbr* commander

**cml** *abbr* commercial

**CMSgt** *abbr* chief master sergeant

**CN** *abbr* credit note

**CNO** *abbr* chief of naval operations

**CNS** *abbr* central nervous system

**co** *abbr* 1 company 2 county

**Co** *symbol* cobalt

**CO** *abbr* 1 cash order 2 Colorado 3 commanding officer 4 conscientious objector

**c/o** *abbr* care of

**¹coach** \'kōch\ *n* 1 : a closed 2-door 4-wheeled carriage with an elevated outside front seat for the driver 2 : a railroad passenger car esp. for day travel 3 : BUS 4 : an automobile body esp. of a closed model 5 : a private tutor; *also* : one who instructs or trains a team of performers

**²coach** *vb* 1 : to go in a horse-drawn coach 2 : to instruct, direct, or prompt as a coach — **coach·er** *n*

**coach·man** \-mǝn\ *n* : a man whose business is driving a coach or carriage

**co·ad·ju·tor** \ˌkō-ǝ-'jüt-ǝr, kō-'aj-ǝt-ǝr\ *n* : ASSISTANT; *esp* : an assistant bishop having the right of succession

**co·ag·u·lant** \kō-'ag-yǝ-lǝnt\ *n* : something that produces coagulation

**co·ag·u·late** \kō-'ag-yǝ-ˌlāt\ *vb* -lat·ed; -lat·ing : CLOT — **co·ag·u·la·tion** \ˌag-yǝ-'lā-shǝn\ *n*

**co·ag·u·lum** \kō-'ag-yǝ-lǝm\ *n, pl* -la \-lǝ\ *or* -lums : a coagulated mass or substance : CLOT, CURD

**¹coal** \'kōl\ *n* 1 : EMBER 2 : a black solid mineral used as fuel

**²coal** *vb* 1 : to supply with coal 2 : to take in coal

**co·alesce** \ˌkō-ǝ-'les\ *vb* **co·alesced**; **co·alesc·ing** : to grow together; *also* : FUSE **syn** merge, blend, mingle, mix — **co·ales·cence** \-'les-ǝns\ *n*

**coal·field** \'kōl-ˌfēld\ *n* : a region where deposits of coal occur

**coal gas** *n* : gas from coal; *esp* : gas distilled from bituminous coal and used for heating

**co·ali·tion** \ˌkō-ǝ-'lish-ǝn\ *n* : UNION; *esp* : a temporary union for a common purpose — **co·ali·tion·ist** *n*

**coal oil** *n* : KEROSENE

**coal tar** *n* : tar distilled from bituminous coal and used in dyes and drugs

**coarse** \'kōrs\ *adj* **coars·er**; **coars-**

**est** 1 : of ordinary or inferior quality 2 : composed of large parts or particles (~ sand) 3 : ROUGH, HARSH 4 : CRUDE (~ manners) — **coarse·ly** *adv* — **coarse·ness** *n*

**coars·en** \'kōrs-²n\ *vb* **coars·ened**; **coars·en·ing** \'kōrs-(²-)niŋ\ : to make or become coarse

**¹coast** \'kōst\ *n* [ME *cost*, fr. MF *coste*, fr. L *costa* rib, side] 1 : SEASHORE 2 : a slide down a slope — **coast·al** *adj*

**²coast** *vb* 1 : to sail along the shore 2 : to move (as downhill on a sled or as on a bicycle while not pedaling) without effort — **coast·er** *n*

**coaster brake** *n* : a brake in the hub of the rear wheel of a bicycle

**coast guard** *n* : a military force employed in guarding or patrolling a coast — **coast·guards·man** \'kōst-ˌgärdz-mǝn\ *n*

**coast·line** \'kōst-ˌlīn\ *n* : the outline or shape of a coast

**¹coat** \'kōt\ *n* 1 : an outer garment for the upper part of the body 2 : an external growth (as of fur or feathers) on an animal 3 : a covering layer

**²coat** *vb* : to cover usu. with a finishing or protective coat

**coat·ing** \'kōt-iŋ\ *n* : COAT, COVERING

**coat of arms** : the heraldic bearings (as of a person) usu. depicted on an escutcheon

**coat of mail** : a garment of metal scales or rings worn as armor

**co·au·thor** \'kō-'ȯ-thǝr\ *n* : a joint or associate author — **coauthor** *vb*

**coax** \'kōks\ *vb* : WHEEDLE; *also* : to gain by gentle urging or flattery — **coax·er** *n*

**co·ax·i·al** \'kō-'ak-sē-ǝl\ *adj* 1 : having coincident axes 2 : being an electrical cable that consists of a tube of conducting material surrounding a central conductor — **co·ax·i·al·ly** \-ē\ *adv*

**cob** \'käb\ *n* 1 : a male swan 2 : CORN COB 3 : a short-legged stocky horse

**co·balt** \'kō-ˌbȯlt\ *n* [G *kobalt*, alter. of *kobold*, lit., goblin, fr. its occurrence in silver ore, believed to be due to goblins] : a tough shiny silver-white magnetic metallic chemical element found with iron and nickel

**cob·ble** \'käb-ǝl\ *vb* **cob·bled**; **cob·bling** \-(ǝ-)liŋ\ : to make or put together roughly or hastily

**cob·bler** \'käb-lǝr\ *n* 1 : a mender or maker of shoes 2 : a deep-dish fruit pie with a thick crust

**cob·ble·stone** \'käb-ǝl-ˌstōn\ *n* : a naturally rounded stone larger than a pebble and smaller than a boulder

**co·bra** \'kō-brǝ\ *n* : a venomous snake of Asia and Africa that when excited expands the skin of the neck into a broad hood

**cob·web** \'käb-ˌweb\ *n* [ME *coppeweb*, fr. *coppe* spider, fr. OE *ātorcoppe*] 1 : the network spun by a spider; *also* : a thread of insect or spider silk 2 : something flimsy or entangling

**co·caine** \kō-'kān, 'kō-ˌkān\ *n* : a

drug that is obtained from the leaves of a So. American shrub (co·ca \'kō-kə\), can result in severe psychological dependence, and is sometimes used as a local anesthetic

**coc·cus** \'käk-əs\ n, pl **coc·ci** \'käk-,(s)ī\ : a spherical bacterium

**coc·cyx** \'käk-siks\ n, pl **coc·cy·ges** \'käk-sə-,jēz\ also **coc·cyx·es** \'käk-sik-səz\ : the end of the vertebral column beyond the sacrum esp. in man

**co·chi·neal** \'käch-ə-,nēl\ n : a red dye made from the dried bodies of a tropical American insect (**cochineal insect**)

**co·chlea** \'kō-klē-ə, 'käk-lē-\ n, pl **co·chle·as** or **co·chle·ae** \-(k)lē-,ē, -,ī\ : the usu. spiral part of the inner ear that is the seat of the organ of hearing — **coch·le·ar** \-lē-ər\ adj

¹**cock** \'käk\ n **1** : the male of a bird and esp. of the common domestic fowl **2** : VALVE, FAUCET **3** : LEADER **4** : the hammer of a firearm; also : the position of the hammer when ready for firing

²**cock** vb **1** : to draw back the hammer of a firearm **2** : to set erect **3** : to turn or tilt usu. to one side

³**cock** n : a small conical pile (as of hay)

**cock·ade** \kä-'käd\ n : an ornament worn on the hat as a badge

**cock·a·tiel** \,käk-ə-'tēl\ n : a small crested parrot often kept as a cage bird

**cock·a·too** \'käk-ə-,tü\ n, pl **-toos** [D kaketoe, fr. Malay kakatua, fr. kakak elder sibling + tua old] : a large crested brilliantly colored Australian parrot

**cock·a·trice** \'käk-ə-trəs, -,trīs\ n : a legendary serpent with a deadly glance

**cock·crow** \'käk-,krō\ n : DAWN

**cocked hat** \'käkt-\ n : a hat with the brim turned up on two or three sides

**cock·er·el** \'käk-(ə-)rəl\ n : a young cock

**cock·er spaniel** \,käk-ər-\ n : a small spaniel with long ears, square muzzle and silky coat

**cock·eye** \'käk-'ī, -,ī\ n : a squinting eye — **cock·eyed** \-'īd\ adj

**cock·fight** \-,fīt\ n : a contest of gamecocks usu. heeled with metal spurs

¹**cock·le** \'käk-əl\ n : any of several weeds found in fields where grain is grown

²**cockle** n : a bivalve mollusk with a heart-shaped shell

**cock·le·shell** \-,shel\ n **1** : the shell of a cockle **2** : a small shallow boat

**cock·ney** \'käk-nē\ n, pl **cockneys** [ME cokeney, lit., cock's egg, fr. cok cock + ey egg, fr. OE æg] : a native of London and esp. of the East End of London; also : the dialect of a cockney

**cock·pit** \'käk-,pit\ n **1** : a pit for cockfights **2** : an open space aft of a decked area from which a small boat is steered **3** : a space in an airplane fuselage for the pilot, pilot and passengers, or pilot and crew

**cock·roach** \'käk-,rōch\ n : an active nocturnal insect often infesting houses and ships

**cock·sure** \'käk-'shùr\ adj **1** : per-

fectly sure : CERTAIN **2** : COCKY

**cocktail** \'käk-,tāl\ n **1** : an iced drink made of liquor and flavoring ingredients **2** : an appetizer (as tomato juice) served as a first course of a meal

**cocky** \'käk-ē\ adj **cock·i·er; -est** : marked by overconfidence : PERT, CONCEITED — **cock·i·ly** \'käk-ə-lē\ adv — **cock·i·ness** \-ē-nəs\ n

**co·co** \'kō-kō\ n, pl **cocos** : the coconut palm or its fruit

**co·coa** \'kō-kō\ n **1** : CACAO **2** : chocolate deprived of some of its fat and powdered; also : a drink made of this cooked with water or milk

**co·co·nut** \'kō-kə-(,)nət\ n : a large edible nut produced by a tall tropical palm (**coconut palm**)

**co·coon** \kə-'kün\ n : a case which an insect larva forms and in which it passes the pupal stage

**cod** \'käd\ n, pl **cod** also **cods** : a soft-finned large-mouthed food fish of the No. Atlantic

**COD** abbr **1** cash on delivery **2** collect on delivery

**co·da** \'kōd-ə\ n : a closing section in a musical composition that is formally distinct from the main structure

**cod·dle** \'käd-ªl\ vb **cod·dled; cod·dling** \'käd-(ª-)liŋ\ **1** : to cook slowly in water below the boiling point **2** : PAMPER

**code** \'kōd\ n **1** : a systematic statement of a body of law **2** : a system of principles or rules (moral ~) **3** : a system of signals **4** : a system of letters or symbols used (as in secret communication or in a computing machine) with special meanings **5** : GENETIC CODE

**co·deine** \'kō-,dēn, 'käd-ē-ən\ n : a narcotic drug obtained from opium and used in cough remedies

**co·dex** \'kō-,deks\ n, pl **co·di·ces** \'kōd-ə-,sēz, 'käd-\ : a manuscript book (as of the Scriptures or classics)

**cod·fish** \'käd-,fish\ n : COD

**cod·ger** \'käj-ər\ n : an odd or cranky fellow

**cod·i·cil** \'käd-ə-səl, -,sil\ n : a legal instrument modifying an earlier will

**cod·i·fy** \'käd-ə-,fī, 'kōd-\ vb **-fied; -fy·ing** : to arrange in a systematic form — **cod·i·fi·ca·tion** \-fə-'kā-shən\ n

**cod·ling** \'käd-liŋ\ n **1** : a young cod **2** : HAKE

**co·ed** \'kō-,ed\ n : a female student in a coeducational institution — **coed** adj

**co·ed·u·ca·tion** \,kō-,ej-ə-'kā-shən\ n : the education of male and female students at the same institution — **co·ed·u·ca·tion·al** \-sh(ə-)nəl\ adj — **co·ed·u·ca·tion·al·ly** \-ē\ adv

**co·ef·fi·cient** \,kō-ə-'fish-ənt\ n **1** : any of the factors of a product considered in relation to a specific factor **2** : a number that serves as a measure of some property or characteristic (as of a substance or device)

**coel·en·ter·ate** \si-'lent-ə-,rāt, -rət\ n : any of a phylum of radially symmetrical invertebrate animals including the corals, sea anemones, and jellyfishes

**co·equal** \kō-'ē-kwəl\ *adj* **:** equal with another — **co·equal·i·ty** \,kō-ē-'kwäl-ət-ē\ *n* — **co·equal·ly** \kō-'ē-kwə-lē\ *adv*

**co·erce** \kō-'ərs\ *vb* **co·erced; co·erc·ing 1 :** REPRESS **2 :** COMPEL **3 :** ENFORCE — **co·er·cion** \-'ər-zhən, -shən\ *n* — **co·er·cive** \-'ər-siv\ *adj*

**co·eval** \kō-'ē-vəl\ *adj* **:** of the same age — **coeval** *n*

**co·ex·ist** \,kō-ig-'zist\ *vb* **1 :** to exist together or at the same time **2 :** to live in peace with each other — **co·ex·is·tence** \-'zis-təns\ *n*

**co·ex·ten·sive** \,kō-ik-'sten-siv\ *adj* **:** having the same scope or extent in space or time

**C of C** *abbr* Chamber of Commerce

**co·fea·ture** \'kō-,fē-chər\ *n* **:** a feature (as a movie) accompanying a main attraction

**cof·fee** \'kȯ-fē\ *n* [It & Turk; It *caffè*, fr. Turk *kahve*, fr. Ar *qahwa*] **:** a drink made from the roasted and ground seeds of a fruit of a tropical shrub or tree; *also* **:** these seeds (**coffee beans**) or a plant producing them

**cof·fee·house** \-,haùs\ *n* **:** CAFÉ

**coffee klatch** \-,klach\ *n* **:** KAFFEE-KLATSCH

**cof·fee·pot** \-,pät\ *n* **:** a utensil for preparing or serving coffee

**coffee shop** *n* **:** a small restaurant

**coffee table** *n* **:** a low table customarily placed in front of a sofa

**cof·fer** \'kȯ-fər\ *n* **:** a chest or box used esp. for valuables

**cof·fer·dam** \-,dam\ *n* **:** a watertight enclosure from which water is pumped to expose the bottom of a body of water and permit construction

**cof·fin** \'kȯ-fən\ *n* **:** a box or chest for a corpse to be buried in

**C of S** *abbr* chief of staff

**¹cog** \'käg\ *n* **:** a tooth on the rim of a wheel or gear — **cogged** \'kägd\ *adj*

**²cog** *abbr* cognate

**co·gent** \'kō-jənt\ *adj* **:** having power to compel or constrain **:** CONVINCING — **co·gen·cy** \-jən-sē\ *n*

**cog·i·tate** \'käj-ə-,tāt\ *vb* **-tat·ed; -tat·ing :** THINK, PONDER — **cog·i·ta·tion** \,käj-ə-'tā-shən\ *n* — **cog·i·ta·tive** \'käj-ə-,tāt-iv\ *adj*

**co·gnac** \'kōn-,yak\ *n* **:** a French brandy

**cog·nate** \'käg-,nāt\ *adj* **1 :** RELATED; *esp* **:** related by descent from the same ancestral language **2 :** of the same or similar nature — **cognate** *n*

**cog·ni·tion** \käg-'nish-ən\ *n* **:** the act or process of knowing — **cog·ni·tion·al** \-'nish-(ə-)nəl\ *adj* — **cog·ni·tive** \'käg-nət-iv\ *adj*

**cog·ni·zance** \'käg-nə-zəns\ *n* **1 :** apprehension by the mind **:** AWARENESS **2 :** NOTICE, HEED — **cog·ni·za·ble** \'käg-nə-zə-bəl, käg-'nī-\ *adj* — **cog·ni·zant** \'käg-nə-zənt\ *adj*

**cog·no·men** \käg-'nō-mən, 'käg-nə-\ *n, pl* **cognomens** *or* **cog·no·mi·na** \käg-'näm-ə-nə, -'nō-mə-\ **:** NAME; *esp* **:** NICKNAME

**cog·no·scen·te** \,kän-yə-'shent-ē\ *n, pl* **-scen·ti** \-ē\ **:** CONNOISSEUR

**cog railway** *n* **:** a mountain railroad with a cogged rail that engages a cogwheel on the locomotive

**cog·wheel** \'käg-,hwēl\ *n* **:** a wheel with cogs on the rim

**co·hab·it** \kō-'hab-ət\ *vb* **:** to live together as husband and wife — **co·hab·i·ta·tion** \-,hab-ə-'tā-shən\ *n*

**co·heir** \'kō-'aər\ *n* **:** a joint heir

**co·here** \kō-'hiər\ *vb* **co·hered; co·her·ing :** to stick together

**co·her·ent** \kō-'hir-ənt\ *adj* **1 :** having the quality of cohering **2 :** logically consistent — **co·her·ence** \-əns\ *n* — **co·her·ent·ly** *adv*

**co·he·sion** \kō-'hē-zhən\ *n* **1 :** a sticking together **2 :** molecular attraction by which the particles of a body are united — **co·he·sive** \-siv\ *adj*

**co·ho** \'kō-,hō\ *n, pl* **cohos** *or* **coho** **:** a rather small salmon with light-colored flesh

**co·hort** \'kō-,hȯrt\ *n* **1 :** a group of warriors or followers **2 :** COMPANION, ACCOMPLICE

**coif** \'kȯif; *2 usu* 'kwäf\ *n* **1 :** a close-fitting hat **2 :** COIFFURE

**coif·feur** \kwä-'fər\ *n* **:** HAIRDRESSER

**coif·feuse** \kwä-'fə(r)z, -'f(y)üz\ *n* **:** a female hairdresser

**coif·fure** \kwä-'fyùr\ *n* **:** a manner of arranging the hair

**¹coil** \'kȯil\ *vb* **:** to wind in a spiral shape

**²coil** *n* **:** a series of rings or loops (as of coiled rope, wire, or pipe) **:** RING, LOOP

**¹coin** \'kȯin\ *n* [ME, fr. MF, wedge, corner, fr. L *cuneus* wedge] **:** a piece of metal issued by government authority as money

**²coin** *vb* **1 :** to make (a coin) esp. by stamping **:** MINT **2 :** CREATE, INVENT ⟨~ a phrase⟩ — **coin·er** *n*

**coin·age** \'kȯi-nij\ *n* **1 :** the act or process of coining **2 :** COINS

**co·in·cide** \,kō-ən-'sīd, 'kō-ən-,sīd\ *vb* **-cid·ed; -cid·ing 1 :** to occupy the same place in space **2 :** to correspond or agree exactly

**co·in·ci·dence** \kō-'in-səd-əns\ *n* **1 :** exact agreement **2 :** occurrence together apparently without reason; *also* **:** an event that so occurs

**co·in·ci·dent** \-səd-ənt\ *adj* **1 :** occupying the same space or time **2 :** of similar nature — **co·in·ci·den·tal** \kō-,in-sə-'dent-ºl\ *adj*

**co·itus** \'kō-ət-əs\ *n* **:** SEXUAL INTERCOURSE — **co·ital** \-ət-ºl\ *adj*

**coke** \'kōk\ *n* **:** a hard gray porous fuel made by heating soft coal to drive off most of its volatile material

**col** *abbr* **1** colonel **2** colony **3** column

**Col** *abbr* Colossians

**COL** *abbr* cost of living

**co·la** \'kō-lə\ *n* **:** a carbonated soft drink

**col·an·der** \'kəl-ən-dər, 'käl-\ *n* **:** a perforated utensil for draining food

**¹cold** \'kōld\ *adj* **1 :** having a low or decidedly subnormal temperature **2**

: lacking warmth of feeling **3** : suffering or uncomfortable from lack of warmth — **cold·ly** adv — **cold·ness** \'kōl(d)-nəs\ n — **in cold blood** : with premeditation : DELIBERATELY

²**cold** n **1** : a condition marked by low temperature; also : cold weather **2** : a chilly feeling **3** : a bodily disorder (as a respiratory inflammation) popularly associated with chilling

³**cold** adv : TOTALLY, FINALLY

**cold-blood·ed** \'kōld-'bləd-əd\ adj **1** : lacking normal human feelings **2** : having a body temperature not internally regulated but approximately that of the environment **3** : sensitive to cold

**cold duck** n : a blend of sparkling burgundy and champagne

**cold feet** n : doubt or fear that prevents action

**cold shoulder** n : cold or unsympathetic behavior — **cold-shoul·der** vb

**cold sore** n : a group of blisters appearing in or about the mouth and caused by a virus

**cold sweat** n : concurrent perspiration and chill usu. associated with fear, pain, or shock

**cold turkey** n : abrupt complete cessation of the use of an addictive drug

**cold war** n : a conflict characterized by the use of means short of sustained overt military action

**cold weld** vb : to adhere upon contact without application of pressure or heat — used of metals in the vacuum of outer space

**cole·slaw** \'kōl-,slò\ n [D koolsla, fr. kool cabbage + sla salad] : a salad made of raw cabbage

**col·ic** \'käl-ik\ n : sharp sudden abdominal pain — **colicky** adj

**col·i·se·um** \,käl-ə-'sē-əm\ n : a large structure esp. for athletic contests

**coll** abbr college

**col·lab·o·rate** \kə-'lab-ə-,rāt\ vb **-rat·ed; -rat·ing 1** : to work jointly with others (as in writing a book) **2** : to cooperate with an enemy force occupying one's country — **col·lab·o·ra·tion** \-,lab-ə-'rā-shən\ n — **col·lab·o·ra·tor** \-'lab-ə-,rāt-ər\ n

**col·lage** \kə-'läzh\ n : an artistic composition of fragments (as of printed matter) pasted on a picture surface

¹**col·lapse** \kə-'laps\ vb **col·lapsed; col·laps·ing 1** : DISINTEGRATE; also : to fall in : give way **2** : to shrink together abruptly **3** : to break down physically or mentally; esp : to fall helpless or unconscious — **col·laps·ible** adj

²**collapse** n : BREAKDOWN

¹**col·lar** \'käl-ər\ n **1** : a band, strip, or chain worn around the neck or the neckline of a garment **2** : something resembling a collar — **col·lar·less** adj

²**collar** vd : to seize by the collar; also : CAPTURE, GRAB

**col·lar·bone** \-,bōn\ n : the bone of the shoulder that joins the breastbone and the shoulder blade

**col·lard** \'käl-ərd\ n : a stalked

smooth-leaved kale — usu. used in pl.

**collat** abbr collateral

**col·late** \kə-'lāt; 'käl-,āt, 'kōl-\ vb **col·lat·ed; col·lat·ing 1** : to compare (as two texts) carefully and critically **2** : to assemble in proper order

¹**col·lat·er·al** \kə-'lat-(ə-)rəl\ adj **1** : associated but of secondary importance **2** : descended from the same ancestors but not in the same line **3** : PARALLEL **4** : of, relating to, or being collateral used as security; also : secured by collateral

²**collateral** n : property (as stocks) used as security for the repayment of a loan

**col·la·tion** \kə-'lā-shən, kä-, kō-\ n **1** : a light meal **2** : the act, process, or result of collating

**col·league** \'käl-,ēg\ n : an associate esp. in a profession

¹**col·lect** \'käl-ikt, -,ekt\ n : a short prayer comprising an invocation, petition, and conclusion

²**col·lect** \kə-'lekt\ vb **1** : to bring or come together into one body or place : ASSEMBLE **2** : to gather from numerous sources (~ stamps) **3** : to gain control of (~ his thoughts) **4** : to receive payment for — **col·lect·ible** or **col·lect·able** adj — **col·lec·tion** \-'lek-shən\ n — **col·lec·tor** \-'lek-tər\ n

³**col·lect** \kə-'lekt\ adv or adj : to be paid for by the receiver

**col·lect·ed** \kə-'lek-təd\ adj : SELF-POSSESSED, CALM

¹**col·lec·tive** \kə-'lek-tiv\ adj **1** : of, relating to, or denoting a group of individuals considered as a whole **2** : formed by collecting **3** : shared or assumed by all members of the group — **col·lec·tive·ly** adv

²**collective** n **1** : GROUP **2** : a cooperative unit or organization

**collective bargaining** n : negotiation between an employer and union representatives

**col·lec·tiv·ism** \kə-'lek-tə-,viz-əm\ n : a political or economic theory advocating collective control esp. over production and distribution

**col·lec·tiv·ize** \-,vīz\ vb **-ized; -iz·ing** : to organize under collective control

**col·leen** \kä-'lēn, 'käl-,ēn\ n : an Irish girl

**col·lege** \'käl-ij\ n [ME, fr. MF, fr. L collegium society, fr. collega colleague, fr. com- with + legare to appoint] **1** : a building used for an educational or religious purpose **2** : an institution of higher learning granting a bachelor's degree; also : an institution offering instruction esp. in a vocational or technical field (barber ~) **3** : an organized body of persons having common interests or duties (~ of cardinals) — **col·le·giate** \kə-'lē-jət\ adj

**col·le·gi·al·i·ty** \kə-,lē-jē-'al-ət-ē\ n : the participation of bishops in the government of the Roman Catholic Church under the leadership of and in collaboration with the pope

**col·le·gian** \kə-'lē-jən\ n : a college student

**col·le·gi·um** \kə-'leg-ē-əm, -'lāg-\ *n*, *pl* **-gia** \-ē-ə\ *or* **-gi·ums** : a governing group in which each member has approximately equal power

**col·lide** \kə-'līd\ *vb* **col·lid·ed; col·lid·ing 1** : to come together with solid impact **2** : CLASH — **col·li·sion** \-'lizh-ən\ *n*

**col·lie** \'käl-ē\ *n* : a large usu. long-haired dog of a breed developed in Scotland for herding sheep

**col·lier** \'käl-yər\ *n* **1** : a coal miner **2** : a ship for carrying coal

**col·liery** \'käl-yə-rē\ *n*, *pl* **-lier·ies** : a coal mine

**col·li·mate** \'käl-ə-,māt\ *vb* **-mat·ed; -mat·ing** : to make (as rays of light) parallel

**col·lo·ca·tion** \,käl-ə-'kā-shən\ *n* **1** : a placing together or side by side; *also* : the result of such placing **2** : a noticeable arrangement or conjoining of linguistic elements (as words)

**col·lo·di·on** \kə-'lōd-ē-ən\ *n* : a sticky substance that hardens in the air and is used to cover wounds and coat photographic films

**col·loid** \'käl-,óid\ *n* : a substance in the form of submicroscopic particles that when in solution or suspension do not settle out; *also* : such a substance together with the gaseous, liquid or solid substance in which it is dispersed — **col·loi·dal** \kə-'lóid-ʼl\ *adj* — **col·loi·dal·ly** \-ē\ *adv*

**colloq** *abbr* colloquial

**col·lo·qui·al** \kə-'lō-kwē-əl\ *adj* : of, relating to, or characteristic of conversation and esp. of familiar and informal conversation

**col·lo·qui·al·ism** \-'lō-kwē-ə-,liz-əm\ *n* : a colloquial expression

**col·lo·qui·um** \kə-'lō-kwē-əm\ *n*, *pl* **-quiums** *or* **-quia** \-kwē-ə\ : CONFERENCE, SEMINAR

**col·lo·quy** \'käl-ə-kwē\ *n*, *pl* **-quies** : a usu. formal conversation or conference

**col·lu·sion** \kə-'lü-zhən\ *n* : secret agreement or cooperation for a fraudulent or deceitful purpose — **col·lu·sive** \-'lü-siv\ *adj*

**col·lu·vi·um** \kə-'lü-vē-əm\ *n*, *pl* **-via** \-vē-ə\ *or* **-vi·ums** : rock detritus accumulated at the foot of a slope — **col·lu·vi·al** \-vē-əl\ *adj*

**Colo** *abbr* Colorado

**co·logne** \kə-'lōn\ *n* : a perfumed liquid consisting of alcohol and aromatic oils — **co·logned** \-'lōnd\ *adj*

¹**co·lon** \'kō-lən\ *n*, *pl* **colons** *or* **co·la** \-lə\ : the part of the large intestine extending from the cecum to the rectum — **co·lon·ic** \kō-'län-ik\ *adj*

²**colon** *n*, *pl* **colons** *or* **co·la** \-lə\ : a punctuation mark : used esp. to direct attention to following matter

³**co·lon** \kō-'lōn\ *n*, *pl* **co·lo·nes** \-'lō-,näs\ — see MONEY table

**col·o·nel** \'kərn-ʼl\ *n* [alter. of *coronel*, fr. MF, fr. It *colonnello* column of soldiers, colonel, fr. L *columna*] : a commissioned officer (as in the army) ranking next below a brigadier general

¹**co·lo·nial** \kə-'lō-nē-əl, -nyəl\ *adj* **1** : of, relating to, or characteristic of a colony; *also* : possessing or composed of colonies **2** *often cap* : of or relating to the original 13 colonies forming the U.S.

²**colonial** *n* : a member or inhabitant of a colony

**co·lo·nial·ism** \-,iz-əm\ *n* : control by one power over a dependent area or people; *also* : a policy advocating or based on such control — **co·lo·nial·ist** \-əst\ *n or adj*

**col·o·nist** \'käl-ə-nəst\ *n* **1** : COLONIAL **2** : one who takes part in founding a colony

**col·o·nize** \'käl-ə-,nīz\ *vb* **-nized; -niz·ing 1** : to establish a colony in or on **2** : to settle in a colony — **col·o·ni·za·tion** \,käl-ə-nə-'zā-shən\ *n* — **col·o·niz·er** *n*

**col·on·nade** \,käl-ə-'nād\ *n* : a row of columns usu. supporting the base of the roof structure

**col·o·ny** \'käl-ə-nē\ *n*, *pl* **-nies 1** : a body of people sent out by a state to a new territory; *also* : the territory inhabited by these people **2** : a localized population of organisms ⟨a ~ of bees⟩ **3** : a group with common interests ⟨a writers' ~⟩; *also* : the section occupied by such group

**col·o·phon** \'käl-ə-fən, -,fän\ *n* : an inscription placed at the end of a book with facts relative to its production

¹**col·or** \'kəl-ər\ *n* **1** : a phenomenon of light (as red or blue) or visual perception that enables one to differentiate otherwise identical objects; *also* : a hue as contrasted with black, white, or gray **2** : APPEARANCE **3** : complexion tint **4** *pl* : FLAG; *also* : military service ⟨a call to the ~s⟩ **5** : VIVIDNESS, INTEREST — **col·or·ful** *adj* — **col·or·less** *adj*

²**color** *vb* **colored; col·or·ing** \'kəl-(ə-)riŋ\ **1** : to give color to; *also* : to change the color of **2** : BLUSH

**Col·o·ra·do potato beetle** \,käl-ə-'rad-ō-, -'räd-\ *n* : a black-and-yellow striped beetle that feeds on the leaves of the potato

**col·or·ation** \,kəl-ə-'rā-shən\ *n* : use or arrangement of colors

**col·or·a·tu·ra** \,kəl-ə-rə-'t(y)ůr-ə\ *n* **1** : florid ornamentation in vocal music **2** : a soprano specializing in coloratura

**col·or·blind** \'kəl-ər-,blīnd\ *adj* : partially or totally unable to distinguish one or more chromatic colors — **color blindness** *n*

**col·or·cast** \-,kast\ *n* : a telecast in color — **colorcast** *vb*

**col·or·cast·er** \-,kas-tər\ *n* : a broadcaster (as of a sports contest) who supplies picturesque details and gives statistical or analytical information

¹**col·ored** \'kəl-ərd\ *adj* **1** : having color **2** : SLANTED, BIASED **3** : of a race other than the white; *esp* : NEGRO

²**colored** *n*, *pl* **colored** *or* **coloreds** *often cap* : a colored person

**col·or·fast** \'kəl-ər-,fast\ *adj* : having color that does not fade or run — **col·or·fast·ness** *n*

**co·los·sal** \kə-ˈläs-əl\ *adj* **:** of very great size or degree

**co·los·sus** \kə-ˈläs-əs\ *n, pl* **co·los·sus·es** \-ˈläs-ə-səz\ *or* **co·los·si** \-ˈläs-ˌī\ **:** a gigantic statue; *also* **:** something of great size or scope

**col·por·teur** \ˈkäl-ˌpȯrt-ər\ *n* **:** a peddler of religious books

**colt** \ˈkōlt\ *n* **:** FOAL; *also* **:** a young male horse, ass, or zebra — **colt·ish** *adj*

**col·um·bine** \ˈkäl-əm-ˌbīn\ *n* [ME, fr. ML *columbina*, fr. L, fem. of *columbinus* dovelike, fr. *columba* dove] **:** a plant related to the buttercups that has showy spurred flowers

**Columbus Day** \kə-ˈləm-bəs-\ *n* **:** the 2d Monday in October or formerly October 12 observed as a legal holiday in many states in commemoration of the landing of Columbus

**col·umn** \ˈkäl-əm\ *n* **1 :** one of two or more vertical sections of a printed page; *also* **:** a special department (as in a newspaper) **2 :** a pillar supporting a roof or gallery; *also* **:** something resembling such a column ⟨a ~ of water⟩ **3 :** a long row (as of soldiers) — **co·lum·nar** \kə-ˈləm-nər\ *adj*

**col·um·nist** \ˈkäl-əm-(n)əst\ *n* **:** one who writes a newspaper column

**com** *or* **comm** *abbr* **1** command; commander **2** commerce; commercial **3** commission; commissioner **4** committee **5** common **6** commonwealth

**co·ma** \ˈkō-mə\ *n* **:** a state of deep unconsciousness caused by disease, injury, or poison — **co·ma·tose** \ˈkō-mə-ˌtōs, ˈkäm-ə-\ *adj*

**Co·man·che** \kə-ˈman-chē\ *n, pl* **Comanche** *or* **Comanches :** a member of an Indian people ranging from Wyoming and Nebraska south into New Mexico and Texas

**¹comb** \ˈkōm\ *n* **1 :** a toothed instrument for arranging the hair or for separating and cleaning textile fibers **2 :** a fleshy crest on the head of a fowl **3 :** HONEYCOMB — **comb** *vb* — **combed** \ˈkōmd\ *adj*

**²comb** *abbr* combination; combining

**com·bat** \kəm-ˈbat, ˈkäm-ˌbat\ *vb* **-bat·ed** *or* **-bat·ted; -bat·ing** *or* **-bat·ting** **1 :** FIGHT, CONTEND **2 :** to struggle or work against **:** OPPOSE — **com·bat** \ˈkäm-ˌbat\ *n* — **com·bat·ant** \kəm-ˈbat-ᵊnt, ˈkäm-bət-ənt\ *n* — **com·bat·ive** \kəm-ˈbat-iv\ *adj*

**combat fatigue** *n* **:** a traumatic neurotic or psychotic reaction occurring under conditions (as wartime combat) that cause intense stress

**comb·er** \ˈkō-mər\ *n* **1 :** one that combs **2 :** a long curling wave of the sea

**com·bi·na·tion** \ˌkäm-bə-ˈnā-shən\ *n* **1 :** the process of combining or being combined **2 :** a union or aggregation made by combining **3 :** a series of symbols which when dialed by a disk on a lock will open the lock

**¹com·bine** \kəm-ˈbīn\ *vb* **com·bined; com·bin·ing :** to become one **:** UNITE

**²com·bine** \ˈkäm-ˌbīn\ *n* **1 :** COMBINA-

TION; *esp* **:** one made to secure business or political advantage **2 :** a machine that harvests and threshes grain while moving over the field

**comb·ings** \ˈkō-miŋz\ *n pl* **:** loose hairs or fibers removed by a comb

**combining form** *n* **:** a linguistic form that occurs only in compounds or derivatives

**com·bo** \ˈkäm-bō\ *n, pl* **combos :** a small jazz or dance band

**com·bus·ti·ble** \kəm-ˈbəs-tə-bəl\ *adj* **:** apt to catch fire **:** FLAMMABLE — **com·bus·ti·bil·i·ty** \-ˌbəs-tə-ˈbil-ət-ē\ *n* — **combustible** *n*

**com·bus·tion** \kəm-ˈbəs-chən\ *n* **1 :** the process of burning **2 :** slow oxidation (as in the animal body) — **com·bus·tive** \-ˈbəs-tiv\ *adj*

**comdg** *abbr* commanding

**comdr** *abbr* commander

**comdt** *abbr* commandant

**come** \ˈ(ᵊ)kəm\ *vb* **came** \ˈkām\; **come; com·ing** \ˈkəm-iŋ\ **1 :** APPROACH **2 :** ARRIVE **3 :** to reach the point of being or getting ⟨~ to a boil⟩ **4 :** to have a place in a series, calendar, or scale **5 :** ORIGINATE, ARISE **6 :** to be available **7 :** REACH, EXTEND **8 :** AMOUNT **9 :** to experience orgasm — **come across :** to meet or find by chance — **come to pass :** HAPPEN — **come upon :** to come across

**come·back** \ˈkəm-ˌbak\ *n* **1 :** RETORT **2 :** a return to a former position or condition (as of health or prosperity) — **come back** \(ˌ)kəm-ˈbak\ *vb*

**co·me·di·an** \kə-ˈmēd-ē-ən\ *n* **1 :** an actor in comedy **2 :** an amusing person

**co·me·di·enne** \-ˌmēd-ē-ˈen\ *n* **:** a female comedian

**come·down** \ˈkəm-ˌdaȯn\ *n* **:** a descent in rank or dignity

**com·e·dy** \ˈkäm-əd-ē\ *n, pl* **-dies** [ME, fr. MF *comedie*, fr. L *comoedia*, fr. Gk *kōmōidia*, fr. *kōmos* revel + *aeidein* to sing] **1 :** a light amusing play with a happy ending **2 :** a literary work treating a comic theme or written in a comic style

**come·ly** \ˈkəm-lē\ *adj* **come·li·er; -est :** good-looking **:** HANDSOME — **come·li·ness** *n*

**come off** *vb* **:** SUCCEED

**come-on** \ˈkəm-ˌȯn, -ˌän\ *n* **:** INDUCEMENT, LURE

**come out** *vb* **:** to make a debut

**com·er** \ˈkəm-ər\ *n* **:** a promising beginner

**¹co·mes·ti·ble** \kə-ˈmes-tə-bəl\ *adj* **:** EDIBLE

**²comestible** *n* **:** FOOD — usu. used in pl.

**com·et** \ˈkäm-ət\ *n* [ME *comete*, fr. OE *cometa*, fr. L, fr. Gk *komētēs*, lit., long-haired, fr. *komē* hair] **:** a small bright celestial body that often develops a cloudy tail when in orbit around the sun

**come to** *vb* **:** to regain consciousness

**come-up·pance** \kə-ˈməp-əns\ *n* **:** a deserved rebuke or penalty

**com·fit** \ˈkəm-fət\ *n* **:** a candied fruit or nut

**¹com·fort** \ˈkəm-fərt\ *n* **1 :** CONSOLA-

TION **2** : freedom from pain, trouble, or anxiety; *also* : something that gives such freedom — **com·fort·less** *adj*

²**comfort** *vb* **1** : to give strength and hope to **2** : CONSOLE

**com·fort·able** \'kəm(f)t-ə-bəl, 'kəm-fərt-\ *adj* **1** : providing comfort **2** : more than adequate **3** : feeling at ease — **com·fort·ably** \-blē\ *adv*

**com·fort·er** \'kəm-fə(r)t-ər\ *n* **1** : one that comforts **2** : QUILT

**com·fy** \'kəm-fē\ *adj* **com·fi·er; -est** : COMFORTABLE

¹**com·ic** \'käm-ik\ *adj* **1** : relating to comedy **2** : provoking laughter **syn** laughable, funny — **com·i·cal** *adj*

²**comic** *n* **1** : COMEDIAN **2** : a magazine composed of comic strips

**comic book** *n* : a magazine containing sequences of comic strips

**comic strip** *n* : a group of cartoons in narrative sequence

**coming** \'kəm-iŋ\ *adj* **1** : APPROACHING, NEXT **2** : gaining importance

**co·mi·ty** \'käm-ət-ē, 'kō-mət-\ *n, pl* **-ties** : friendly civility : COURTESY

**coml** *abbr* commercial

**comm** *abbr* — see COM

**com·ma** \'käm-ə\ *n* : a punctuation mark, used esp. as a mark of separation within the sentence

¹**com·mand** \kə-'mand\ *vb* **1** : to direct authoritatively : ORDER **2** : DOMINATE, CONTROL, GOVERN **3** : to overlook from a strategic position

²**command** *n* **1** : the act of commanding **2** : an order given **3** : ability to control : MASTERY **4** : a body of troops under a commander; *also* : an area or position that one commands **5** : a position of highest authority **6** : an electrical signal that actuates a device (as a control mechanism in a spacecraft); *also* : the activation of a device by means of such a signal

**com·man·dant** \'käm-ən-,dant, -,dänt\ *n* : an officer in command

**com·man·deer** \,käm-ən-'diər\ *vb* : to seize for military purposes

**com·mand·er** \kə-'man-dər\ *n* **1** : LEADER, CHIEF; *esp* : an officer commanding an army or subdivision of an army **2** : a commissioned officer in the navy ranking next below a captain

**commander in chief** : one who holds supreme command of the armed forces of a nation

**com·mand·ment** \kə-'man(d)-mənt\ *n* : COMMAND, ORDER; *esp* : any of the Ten Commandments

**command module** *n* : a space vehicle module designed to carry the crew and reentry equipment

**com·man·do** \kə-'man-dō\ *n, pl* **-dos** *or* **-does** : a member of a military unit trained for surprise raids

**command sergeant major** *n* : a noncommissioned officer in the army ranking above a first sergeant

**com·mem·o·rate** \kə-'mem-ə-,rāt\ *vb* **-rat·ed; -rat·ing** **1** : to call or recall to mind **2** : to serve as a memorial of — **com·mem·o·ra·tion** \-,mem-ə-'rā-shən\ *n*

**com·mem·o·ra·tive** \kə-'mem-(ə-)rət-iv, -'mem-ə-,rāt-iv\ *adj* : intended to commemorate an event

**com·mence** \kə-'mens\ *vb* **com·menced; com·menc·ing** : BEGIN, START

**com·mence·ment** \-mənt\ *n* **1** : the act or time of a beginning **2** : the graduation exercises of a school or college

**com·mend** \kə-'mend\ *vb* **1** : to commit to one's care **2** : RECOMMEND **3** : PRAISE — **com·mend·able** \-'men-də-bəl\ *adj* — **com·mend·ably** \-blē\ *adv* — **com·men·da·tion** \,käm-ən-'dā-shən, ,en-\ *n*

**com·men·su·ra·ble** \kə-'mens-(ə-)rə-bəl\ *adj* : having a common measure; *esp* : divisible by a common unit an integral number of times

**com·men·su·rate** \kə-'mens-(ə-)rət, -'mench(-ə)-\ *adj* : equal in measure or extent; *also* : PROPORTIONATE, CORRESPONDING

**com·ment** \'käm-,ent\ *n* **1** : an expression of opinion **2** : an explanatory, illustrative, or critical note or observation : REMARK — **comment** *vb*

**com·men·tary** \'käm-ən-,ter-ē\ *n, pl* **-tar·ies** : a systematic series of comments

**com·men·ta·tor** \-,tāt-ər\ *n* : one who comments; *esp* : one who gives talks on news events on radio or television

**com·merce** \'käm-(,)ərs\ *n* : the buying and selling of commodities : TRADE

¹**com·mer·cial** \kə-'mər-shəl\ *adj* : having to do with commerce; *also* : designed for profit or for mass appeal — **com·mer·cial·ly** \-ē\ *adv*

²**commercial** *n* : an advertisement broadcast on radio or television

**com·mer·cial·ism** \kə-'mər-shə-,liz-əm\ *n* : a spirit, method, or practice characteristic of business

**com·mer·cial·ize** \-,līz\ *vb* **-ized; -iz·ing** : to manage on a business basis for profit

**com·mi·na·tion** \,käm-ə-'nā-shən\ *n* : DENUNCIATION — **com·mi·na·to·ry** \'käm-ə-nə-,tōr-ē\ *adj*

**com·min·gle** \kə-'miŋ-gəl\ *vb* : MINGLE, BLEND

**com·mis·er·ate** \kə-'miz-ə-,rāt\ *vb* **-at·ed; at·ing** : to feel or express pity : SYMPATHIZE — **com·mis·er·a·tion** \-,miz-ə-'rā-shən\ *n*

**com·mis·sar** \'käm-ə-,sär\ *n* : a Communist party official assigned to a military unit to teach and enforce party principles and policy

**com·mis·sar·i·at** \,käm-ə-'ser-ē-ət\ *n* **1** : a system for supplying troops with food **2** : a department headed by a commissar

**com·mis·sary** \'käm-ə-,ser-ē\ *n, pl* **-sar·ies** : a store for equipment and provisions esp. for military personnel

¹**com·mis·sion** \kə-'mish-ən\ *n* **1** : a warrant granting certain powers and imposing certain duties **2** : authority to act as agent for another; *also* : something to be done by an agent **3** : a body

of persons charged with performing a duty **4** : the doing of some act; *also* : the thing done **5** : the allowance made to an agent for transacting business for another **6** : a certificate conferring military rank and authority

²**commission** *vb* **com·mis·sioned**; **com·mis·sion·ing** \-'mish-(ə-)niŋ\ **1** : to give a commission to **2** : to order to be made **3** : to put (a ship) into a state of readiness for service

**commissioned officer** *n* : an officer of the armed forces holding rank from virtue of a commission from the president

**com·mis·sion·er** \kə-'mish-(ə-)nər\ *n* **1** : a person given a commission **2** : a member of a commission **3** : an official in charge of a department of public service — **com·mis·sion·er·ship** *n*

**com·mit** \kə-'mit\ *vb* **com·mit·ted**; **com·mit·ting** **1** : to put into charge or trust : ENTRUST **2** : TRANSFER, CONSIGN **3** : to put in a prison or mental institution **4** : PERPETRATE ⟨∼ a crime⟩ **5** : to pledge or assign to some particular course or use — **com·mit·ment** *n* — **com·mit·tal** *n*

**com·mit·tee** \kə-'mit-ē\ *n* : a body of persons selected to consider and act or report on some matter — **com·mit·tee·man** \-mən\ *n*

**commo** *abbr* commodore

**com·mode** \kə-'mōd\ *n* [F, fr. *commode*, adj., suitable, convenient, fr. L *commodus*, fr. *com-* with + *modus* measure] **1** : a movable washstand with cupboard underneath **2** : TOILET

**com·mo·di·ous** \kə-'mōd-ē-əs\ *adj* : comfortably spacious : ROOMY

**com·mod·i·ty** \kə-'mäd-ət-ē\ *n, pl* **-ties 1** : a product of agriculture or mining **2** : an article of commerce

**com·mo·dore** \'käm-ə-,dōr\ *n* **1** : a former commissioned officer in the navy ranking next below a rear admiral **2** : an officer commanding a group of merchant ships; *also* : the chief officer of a yacht club

¹**com·mon** \'käm-ən\ *adj* **1** : belonging to or serving the community : PUBLIC **2** : shared by a number in a group **3** : widely or generally known, found, or observed : FAMILIAR **4** : ORDINARY, USUAL **5** : not above the average esp. in social status **syn** universal, mutual, popular, vulgar — **com·mon·ly** *adv*

²**common** *n* **1** *pl* : the mass of people as distinguished from the nobility **2** : a piece of land held in common by a community **3** *pl* : a dining hall **4** *pl, cap* : the lower house of the British and Canadian parliaments — **in common** : shared together

**com·mon·al·ty** \'käm-ən-ºl-tē\ *n, pl* **-ties** : the common people

**common denominator** *n* **1** : a common multiple of the denominators of a number of fractions **2** : a common trait or theme

**common divisor** *n* : a number or expression that divides two or more numbers or expressions without remainder

**com·mon·er** \'käm-ə-nər\ *n* : one of the common people : one having no rank of nobility

**common fraction** *n* : a fraction in which both the numerator and denominator are expressed as numbers and are separated by a horizontal or slanted line

**common logarithm** *n* : a logarithm whose base is 10

**common market** *n* : an economic unit formed to remove trade barriers among members

**common multiple** *n* : a multiple of each of two or more numbers or expressions

¹**com·mon·place** \'käm-ən-,plās\ *n* : something that is ordinary or trite

²**commonplace** *adj* : ORDINARY

**common sense** *n* **1** : sound and prudent judgment **2** : the unreflective opinions of ordinary men

**com·mon·weal** \'käm-ən-,wēl\ *n* **1** : the general welfare **2** *archaic* : COMMONWEALTH

**com·mon·wealth** \-,welth\ *n* **1** : the body of people politically organized into a state **2** : STATE; *also* : an association or federation of autonomous states

**com·mo·tion** \kə-'mō-shən\ *n* **1** : AGITATION **2** : DISTURBANCE, UPRISING

**com·mu·nal** \kə-'myün-ºl, 'käm-yən-ºl\ *adj* **1** : relating to a commune or to organization in communes **2** : of or belonging to a community **3** : marked by collective ownership and use of property

¹**com·mune** \kə-'myün\ *vb* **com·muned**; **com·mun·ing** : to communicate intimately **syn** consult, negotiate

²**com·mune** \'käm-,yün; kə-'myün\ *n* **1** : the common people **2** : the smallest administrative district in some European countries **3** : a community organized on a communal basis

**com·mu·ni·ca·ble** \kə-'myü-ni-kə-bəl\ *adj* : capable of being communicated ⟨∼ diseases⟩ — **com·mu·ni·ca·bil·i·ty** \-,myü-ni-kə-'bil-ət-ē\ *n*

**com·mu·ni·cant** \-'myü-ni-kənt\ *n* **1** : a church member entitled to receive Communion **2** : one who communicates; *esp* : INFORMANT

**com·mu·ni·cate** \kə-'myü-nə-,kāt\ *vb* **-cat·ed**; **-cat·ing** **1** : TRANSMIT, IMPART **2** : to make known **3** : to receive Communion **4** : to be in communication **5** : JOIN, CONNECT

**com·mu·ni·ca·tion** \kə-,myü-nə-'kā-shən\ *n* **1** : an act of transmitting **2** : exchange of information or opinions **3** : MESSAGE **4** : a means of communicating — **com·mu·ni·ca·tive** \kə-'myü-nə-,kāt-iv, -ni-kət-iv\ *adj*

**com·mu·nion** \kə-'myü-nyən\ *n* **1** : a sharing of something with others **2** : intimate fellowship or rapport **3** *cap* : a Christian sacrament in which bread and wine are partaken of as a commemoration of the death of Christ **4** *cap* : the act of receiving the sacrament **5** : a body of Christians having a common faith and discipline

com·mu·ni·qué \kə-'myü-nə-,kā, -,myü-nə-'kā\ n : BULLETIN 1

com·mu·nism \'käm-yə-,niz-əm\ n 1 : social organization in which goods are held in common 2 : a theory of social organization advocating common ownership of means of production and a distribution of products of industry based on need 3 cap : a political doctrine based on revolutionary Marxian socialism that is the official ideology of the U.S.S.R. and some other countries — com·mu·nist \-nəst\ n or adj, often cap — com·mu·nis·tic \,käm-yə-'nis-tik\, adj, often cap

com·mu·ni·ty \kə-'myü-nət-ē\ n, pl -ties 1 : a body of people living in the same place under the same laws; also : a natural population of plants and animals occupying a common area 2 : society at large 3 : joint ownership 4 : AGREEMENT, CONCORD

community antenna television n : a system of television reception in which signals from distant stations are picked up by a single elevated antenna and sent by cable to the individual receivers of paying subscribers

community college n : a nonresidential 2-year college that is usu. government-supported

community property n : property held jointly by husband and wife

com·mu·ta·tion \,käm-yə-'tā-shən\ n : substitution of one form of payment or penalty for another

commutation ticket n : a transportation ticket sold at a reduced rate for a fixed number of trips over the same route

com·mu·ta·tive \'käm-yə-,tāt-iv, kə-'myüt-ət-\ adj : combining elements or having elements that combine in such a manner that the result is not affected by the order in which the elements are taken ⟨addition of positive integers is ~⟩ — com·mu·ta·tiv·i·ty \kə-myüt-ə-'tiv-ət-ē, ,käm-yə-tə-\ n

com·mu·ta·tor \'käm-yə-,tāt-ər\ n : a device (as on a generator or motor) for changing the direction of electric current

¹com·mute \kə-'myüt\ vb com·mut·ed; com·mut·ing 1 : EXCHANGE 2 : to substitute a less severe penalty for (one more severe) 3 : to travel back and forth regularly — com·mut·er n

²commute n : a trip made in commuting

comp abbr 1 comparative 2 compiled; compiler 3 composition 4 compound

¹com·pact \kəm-'pakt, (')käm-\ adj 1 : SOLID, DENSE 2 : BRIEF, SUCCINCT 3 : filling a small space or area — com·pact·ly adv — com·pact·ness n

²compact vb : to pack together

³com·pact \'käm-,pakt\ n 1 : a small case for cosmetics 2 : a small automobile

⁴com·pact \'käm-,pakt\ n : AGREEMENT, COVENANT

¹com·pan·ion \kəm-'pan-yən\ n [OF compagnon, fr. LL companion-, companio, lit., one who shares bread, fr. L com- together + panis bread] 1 : an intimate friend or associate : COMRADE 2 : one of a pair of matching things — com·pan·ion·able adj — com·pan·ion·less adj — com·pan·ion·ship n

²companion n : COMPANIONWAY

com·pan·ion·way \-,wā\ n : a ship's stairway from one deck to another

com·pa·ny \'kəmp-(ə-)nē\ n, pl -nies 1 : association with others : FELLOWSHIP; also : COMPANIONS 2 : RETINUE 3 : an association of persons for carrying on a business 4 : a group of musical or dramatic performers 5 : GUESTS 6 : an infantry unit normally commanded by a captain 7 : the officers and crew of a ship syn party, band, troop, troupe

compar abbr comparative

com·pa·ra·ble \'käm-p(ə-)rə-bəl\ adj : capable of being compared syn parallel, similar, like, alike — com·pa·ra·bil·i·ty \-'bil-ət-ē\ n

¹com·par·a·tive \kəm-'par-ət-iv\ adj 1 : of, relating to, or constituting the degree of grammatical comparison that denotes increase in quality, quantity, or relation 2 : RELATIVE ⟨a ~ stranger⟩ — com·par·a·tive·ly adv

²comparative n : the comparative degree or a comparative form in a language

¹com·pare \kəm-'paər\ vb compared; com·par·ing 1 : to represent as like something : LIKEN 2 : to examine for likenesses and differences 3 : to inflect or modify (an adjective or adverb) according to the degrees of comparison

²compare n : COMPARISON

com·par·i·son \-'par-ə-sən\ n 1 : the act of comparing : relative estimate 2 : change in the form of an adjective or adverb to show different levels of quality, quantity, or relation

com·part·ment \kəm-'pärt-mənt\ n 1 : a section of an enclosed space : ROOM 2 : a separate division

com·part·men·tal·ize \,kəm-,pärt-'ment-ᵊl-,īz\ vb -ized; -iz·ing : to separate into compartments

¹com·pass \'kəm-pəs, 'käm-\ vb [ME compassen, fr. OF compasser to measure, fr. (assumed) VL compassare to pace off, fr. L com- + passus pace] 1 : CONTRIVE, PLOT 2 : to bring about : ACHIEVE 3 : to make a circuit of; also : SURROUND

²compass n 1 : BOUNDARY, CIRCUMFERENCE 2 : an enclosed space 3 : RANGE, SCOPE 4 usu pl : an instrument for drawing circles or transferring measurements consisting of two legs joined at the top by a pivot 5 : a device for determining direction by means of a magnetic needle swinging freely and pointing to the magnetic north; also : a nonmagnetic device that indicates direction

com·pas·sion \kəm-'pash-ən\ n : sympathetic feeling : PITY, MERCY — com·pas·sion·ate \-(ə-)nət\ adj

com·pat·i·ble \kəm-'pat-ə-bəl\ adj : able to exist or act together harmoniously ⟨~ colors⟩ ⟨~ drugs⟩ syn consonant, congenial, sympathetic — com-

**pat·i·bil·i·ty** \-ˌpat-ə-'bil-ət-ē\ *n*

**com·pa·tri·ot** \kəm-'pā-trē-ət, -trē-ˌät\ *n* : a fellow countryman

**com·peer** \'käm-ˌpiər\ *n* : EQUAL, PEER

**com·pel** \kəm-'pel\ *vb* **com·pelled; com·pel·ling** : to drive or urge with force : CONSTRAIN

**com·pen·di·um** \kəm-'pen-dē-əm\ *n, pl* **-di·ums** *or* **-dia** \-dē-ə\ : a brief summary of a larger work or of a field of knowledge

**com·pen·sate** \'käm-pən-ˌsāt\ *vb* **-sat·ed; -sat·ing 1** : to be equivalent to in value or effect : COUNTERBALANCE **2** : PAY, REMUNERATE **syn** balance, offset, recompense, repay, satisfy — **com·pen·sa·tion** \ˌkäm-pən-'sā-shən\ *n* — **com·pen·sa·to·ry** \kəm-'pen-sə-ˌtōr-ē\ *adj*

**com·pete** \kəm-'pēt\ *vb* **com·pet·ed; com·pet·ing** : CONTEND, VIE

**com·pe·tence** \'käm-pət-əns\ *n* **1** : adequate means for subsistence **2** : FITNESS, ABILITY

**com·pe·ten·cy** \-pət-ən-sē\ *n, pl* **-cies** : COMPETENCE

**com·pe·tent** \-pət-ənt\ *adj* : CAPABLE, FIT, QUALIFIED

**com·pe·ti·tion** \ˌkäm-pə-'tish-ən\ *n* **1** : the act of competing : RIVALRY **2** : CONTEST, MATCH — **com·pet·i·tive** \kəm-'pet-ət-iv\ *adj* — **com·pet·i·tive·ly** *adv* — **com·pet·i·tive·ness** *n*

**com·pet·i·tor** \kəm-'pet-ət-ər\ *n* : one that competes; *esp* : a rival in business

**com·pile** \kəm-'pīl\ *vb* **com·piled; com·pil·ing** [ME *compilen,* fr. MF *compiler,* fr. L *compilare* to plunder] **1** : to collect (literary materials) into a volume **2** : to compose out of materials from other documents — **com·pi·la·tion** \ˌkäm-pə-'lā-shən\ *n* — **com·pil·er** \kəm-'pī-lər\ *n*

**com·pla·cence** \kəm-'plās-°ns\ *n* : SATISFACTION; *esp* : SELF-SATISFACTION — **com·pla·cent** \-°nt\ *adj* — **com·pla·cent·ly** *adv*

**com·pla·cen·cy** \-°n-sē\ *n, pl* **-cies** : COMPLACENCE

**com·plain** \kəm-'plān\ *vb* **1** : to express grief, pain, or discontent **2** : to make a formal accusation — **com·plain·ant** *n* — **com·plain·er** *n*

**com·plaint** \kəm-'plānt\ *n* **1** : expression of grief or discontent **2** : a bodily ailment or disease **3** : a formal accusation against a person

**com·plai·sance** \kəm-'plās-°ns, ˌkäm-plā-'zans\ *n* : disposition to please — **com·plai·sant** \-°nt, -'zant\ *adj*

**com·pleat** \kəm-'plēt\ *adj* : PROFICIENT

**com·plect·ed** \kəm-'plek-təd\ *adj* : having a specified facial complexion ⟨dark-*complected*⟩

**¹com·ple·ment** \'käm-plə-mənt\ *n* **1** : a quantity needed to make a thing complete **2** : full quantity, number, or amount **3** : an added word by which a predication is made complete — **com·ple·men·ta·ry** \ˌkäm-plə-'men-t(ə-)rē\ *adj*

**²com·ple·ment** \-ˌment\ *vb* : to be complementary to : fill out

**¹com·plete** \kəm-'plēt\ *adj* **com·plet·er; -est 1** : having no part lacking **2** : ENDED **3** : fully realized : THOROUGH — **com·plete·ly** *adv* — **com·plete·ness** *n* — **com·ple·tion** \-'plē-shən\ *n*

**²complete** *vb* **com·plet·ed; com·plet·ing 1** : to make whole or perfect **2** : FINISH, CONCLUDE

**¹com·plex** \käm-'pleks, kəm-'pleks, 'käm-ˌpleks\ *adj* **1** : composed of two or more parts **2** : consisting of a main clause and one or more subordinate clauses ⟨~ sentence⟩ **3** : COMPLICATED, INTRICATE — **com·plex·i·ty** \kəm-'plek-sət-ē, käm-\ *n*

**²com·plex** \'käm-ˌpleks\ *n* : something made up of or involving an often intricate combination of elements; *esp* : a system of repressed desires and memories that modify the personality or the individual's response to a subject or situation

**complex fraction** *n* : a fraction with a fraction or mixed number in the numerator or denominator or both

**com·plex·ion** \kəm-'plek-shən\ *n* **1** : the hue or appearance of the skin esp. of the face **2** : general appearance — **com·plex·ioned** \-shənd\ *adj*

**complex number** *n* : a number (as $3 + 4\sqrt{-1}$) formed by adding a real number to the product of a real number and the square root of minus one

**com·pli·ance** \kəm-'plī-əns\ *n* **1** : the act of complying to a demand or proposal **2** : a disposition to yield — **com·pli·ant** \-ənt\ *adj*

**com·pli·an·cy** \-ən-sē\ *n* : COMPLIANCE

**com·pli·cate** \'käm-plə-ˌkāt\ *vb* **-cat·ed; -cat·ing** : to make or become complex or intricate — **com·pli·ca·tion** \ˌkäm-plə-'kā-shən\ *n*

**com·pli·cat·ed** \'käm-plə-ˌkāt-əd\ *adj* **1** : consisting of parts intricately combined **2** : difficult to analyze, understand, or explain — **com·pli·cat·ed·ly** *adv* — **com·pli·cat·ed·ness** *n*

**com·plic·i·ty** \kəm-'plis-ət-ē\ *n, pl* **-ties** : the state of being an accomplice

**¹com·pli·ment** \'käm-plə-mənt\ *n* **1** : an expression of approval or courtesy; *esp* : a flattering remark **2** *pl* : formal greeting

**²com·pli·ment** \-ˌment\ *vb* : to pay a compliment to

**com·pli·men·ta·ry** \ˌkäm-plə-'men-t(ə-)rē\ *adj* **1** : containing or expressing a compliment **2** : given free as a courtesy ⟨~ ticket⟩

**com·ply** \kəm-'plī\ *vb* **com·plied; com·ply·ing** : ACQUIESCE, YIELD

**¹com·po·nent** \kəm-'pō-nənt, 'käm-ˌpō-\ *n* : a component part **syn** ingredient, element

**²component** *adj* : serving to form a part of : CONSTITUENT

**com·port** \kəm-'pōrt\ *vb* **1** : AGREE, ACCORD **2** : CONDUCT **syn** behave

**com·port·ment** \-mənt\ *n* : BEHAVIOR, BEARING

**com·pose** \kəm-'pōz\ *vb* **com·posed; com·pos·ing 1** : to form by putting together : FASHION  **2** : ADJUST, ARRANGE  **3** : CALM, QUIET  **4** : to set type for printing  **5** : to practice composition (~ music) — **com·posed** \-'pōzd\ adj — **com·pos·ed·ly** \-'pō-zəd-lē\ adv — **com·pos·er** n

**composing stick** n : a hand-held compositor's tray with an adjustable slide for setting type

¹**com·pos·ite** \käm-'päz-ət, kəm-\ adj **1** : made up of distinct parts or elements  **2** : of, relating to, or being a large group of flowering plants (as the daisy) that bear many small flowers united into compact heads resembling single flowers

²**composite** n **1** : something composite **2** : a plant of the composite group **syn** blend, compound, mixture

**com·po·si·tion** \,käm-pə-'zish-ən\ n **1** : the act of composing ; esp : arrangement of elements in artistic form **2** : the art or practice of writing **3** : MAKEUP, CONSTITUTION  **4** : a product of mixing various elements or ingredients  **5** : a literary, musical, or artistic product ; esp : ESSAY  **6** : the composing of type

**com·pos·i·tor** \kəm-'päz-ət-ər\ n : one who sets type

**com·post** \'käm-,pōst\ n : a fertilizing material consisting largely of decayed organic matter

**com·po·sure** \kəm-'pō-zhər\ n : CALMNESS, SELF-POSSESSION

**com·pote** \'käm-,pōt\ n **1** : fruits cooked in syrup  **2** : a bowl (as of glass) usu. with a base and stem from which compotes, fruits, nuts, or sweets are served

¹**com·pound** \(')käm-'paùnd, kəm-\ vb [ME compounen, fr. MF compondre, fr. L componere, fr. com- together + ponere to put]  **1** : COMBINE  **2** : to form by combining parts (~ a medicine)  **3** : SETTLE (~ a dispute)  **4** : to increase (as interest) by an amount that itself increases ; also : to add to  **5** : to forbear prosecution of (an offense) in return for some reward

²**com·pound** \'käm-,paùnd\ adj **1** : made up of two or more parts **2** : composed of united similar parts esp. of a kind usu. separate (a ~ plant ovary)  **3** : formed by the combination of two or more otherwise independent elements (~ sentence)

³**com·pound** \'käm-,paùnd\ n **1** : a compound substance ; esp : one formed by the union of two or more chemical elements  **2** : a solid or hyphenated word made up of two or more distinct words or word elements **syn** mixture, composite, blend

⁴**com·pound** \'käm-,paùnd\ n [by folk etymology fr. Malay kampong group of buildings, village] : an enclosure containing buildings

**compound interest** n : interest computed on the sum of an original principal and accrued interest

**com·pre·hend** \,käm-pri-'hend\ vb **1** : UNDERSTAND  **2** : INCLUDE — **com·pre·hen·si·ble** \-'hen-sə-bəl\ adj

**com·pre·hen·sion** \-'hen-chən\ n — **com·pre·hen·sive** \-'siv\ adj

¹**com·press** \kəm-'pres\ vb : to squeeze together : CONDENSE  **syn** constrict, contract, shrink — **com·pressed** adj — **com·pres·sion** \-'presh-ən\ n — **com·pres·sor** \-'pres-ər\ n

²**com·press** \'käm-,pres\ n : a soft often wet or medicated pad used to press upon an injured bodily part

**compressed air** n : air under pressure greater than that of the atmosphere

**com·prise** \kəm-'prīz\ vb **com·prised; com·pris·ing  1** : INCLUDE, CONTAIN  **2** : to be made up of  **3** : to make up : CONSTITUTE

¹**com·pro·mise** \'käm-prə-,mīz\ n : a settlement of differences reached by mutual concessions ; also : the agreement thus made

²**compromise** vb **-mised; -mis·ing  1** : to settle by compromise  **2** : to endanger the reputation of

**comp·trol·ler** \kən-'trō-lər, 'kämp-,trō-\ n : an official who audits and supervises expenditures and accounts

**com·pul·sion** \kəm-'pəl-shən\ n **1** : COERCION  **2** : an irresistible impulse **syn** constraint, force, violence, restraint — **com·pul·sive** \-siv\ adj — **com·pul·so·ry** \-'pəls-(ə-)rē\ adj

**com·punc·tion** \kəm-'pəŋk-shən\ n : anxiety arising from guilt : REMORSE

**com·pute** \kəm-'pyüt\ vb **com·put·ed; com·put·ing** : CALCULATE, RECKON — **com·pu·ta·tion** \,käm-pyü-'tā-shən\ n

**com·put·er** \kəm-'pyüt-ər\ n : an automatic electronic machine for calculating

**com·put·er·ize** \kəm-'pyüt-ə-,rīz\ vb **-ized; -iz·ing  1** : to carry out, control, or conduct by means of a computer — **com·put·er·iz·able** adj — **com·put·er·iza·tion** \-,pyüt-ə-rə-'zā-shən\ n

**comr** abbr commissioner

**com·rade** \'käm-,rad, -rəd\ n [MF comarade group sleeping in one room, roommate, companion, fr. Sp camarada, fr. cámara room, fr. LL camera] : COMPANION, ASSOCIATE — **com·rade·ly** adj — **com·rade·ship** n

**com·sat** \'käm-,sat\ n : an artificial earth satellite for intercontinental communication

¹**con** \'kän\ vb **conned; con·ning 1** : STUDY  **2** : MEMORIZE

²**con** adv : in opposition : AGAINST

³**con** n : an opposing argument, person, or position

⁴**con** vb **conned; con·ning  1** : SWINDLE  **2** : PERSUADE, CAJOLE

⁵**con** n : CONVICT

⁶**con** abbr consul

**con brio** \kän-'brē-ō, kōn-\ adv : with spirit : VIGOROUSLY — used as a direction in music

**conc** abbr concentrated

**con·cat·e·na·tion** \(,)kän-,kat-ə-'nā-shən\ n : a series connected like links in a chain — **con·cat·e·nate** \kän-'kat-ə-nət\ n

**con·cave** \(')kän-'kāv\ adj : curved or

rounded inward like the inside of a bowl — con·cav·i·ty \kän-'kav-ət-ē\ n

con·ceal \kən-'sēl\ vb : to place out of sight : HIDE — con·ceal·ment n

con·cede \kən-'sēd\ vb con·ced·ed; con·ced·ing 1 : to admit to be true 2 : GRANT, YIELD syn allow, accord, award

con·ceit \kən-'sēt\ n 1 : excessively high opinion of oneself, one's appearance, or ability : VANITY 2 : an elaborate or strained metaphor — con·ceit·ed \-əd\ adj

con·ceive \kən-'sēv\ vb con·ceived; con·ceiv·ing 1 : to become pregnant 2 : to form an idea of : THINK, IMAGINE — con·ceiv·able \-'sē-və-bəl\ adj — con·ceiv·ably \-blē\ adv

con·cel·e·brant \kən-'sel-ə-brənt\ n : one of two or more members of the clergy celebrating the Eucharist or Mass together

¹con·cen·trate \'kän-sən-,trāt\ vb -trat·ed; -trat·ing 1 : to gather into one body, mass, or force 2 : to make less dilute 3 : to fix one's powers, efforts, or attentions on one thing

²concentrate n : something concentrated

con·cen·tra·tion \,kän-sən-'trā-shən\ n 1 : the act or process of concentrating : the state of being concentrated; esp : direction of attention on a single object 2 : the relative content of a component : STRENGTH

concentration camp n : a camp where persons (as prisoners of war or political prisoners) are confined

con·cen·tric \kən-'sen-trik\ adj 1 : having a common center ⟨~ circles⟩ 2 : COAXIAL

con·cept \'kän-,sept\ n : THOUGHT, NOTION, IDEA — con·cep·tu·al \kən-'sep-chə(-wə)l\ adj

con·cep·tion \kən-'sep-shən\ n 1 : the act of conceiving or being conceived; also : BEGINNING 2 : the power to form ideas or concepts 3 : IDEA, CONCEPT

con·cep·tu·al·ize \-'sep-chə(-wə)-,līz\ vb -ized; -iz·ing : to form a conception of

¹con·cern \kən-'sərn\ vb 1 : to relate to 2 : to be the business of : INVOLVE 3 : ENGAGE, OCCUPY

²concern n 1 : AFFAIR, MATTER 2 : INTEREST, ANXIETY 3 : a business organization syn business, care, worry

con·cerned \-'sərnd\ adj : ANXIOUS, TROUBLED

con·cern·ing \-'sər-niŋ\ prep : relating to : REGARDING

con·cern·ment \kən-'sərn-mənt\ n 1 : something in which one is concerned 2 : IMPORTANCE, CONSEQUENCE

¹con·cert \kən-'sərt\ vb 1 : to plan together 2 : to act in conjunction or harmony

²con·cert \'kän-(,)sərt\ n 1 : agreement in a plan or design 2 : a concerted action 3 : a public performance of several musical compositions

con·cert·ed \kən-'sərt-əd\ adj : mutually agreed on

con·cer·ti·na \,kän-sər-'tē-nə\ n : an instrument of the accordion family

con·cert·mas·ter \'kän-sərt-,mastər\ or con·cert·meis·ter \-,mīstər\ n : the leader of the first violins of an orchestra and assistant to the conductor

con·cer·to \kən-'chert-ō\ n, pl -ti \-(,)ē\ or -tos : a symphonic piece for one or more solo instruments and orchestra

con·ces·sion \kən-'sesh-ən\ n 1 : an act of conceding or yielding 2 : something yielded 3 : a grant by a government of land or of a right to use it 4 : a grant of a portion of premises for some specific purpose — con·ces·sion·aire \-,sesh-ə-'nar\ n

con·ces·sive \-'ses-iv\ adj : tending toward, expressing, or being a concession

conch \'käŋk, 'känch\ n, pl conchs \'käŋks\ or conch·es \'kän-chəz\ : a large spiral-shelled marine mollusk

con·cierge \kōⁿ-'syerzh\ n, pl con·cierges \-'syerzh(-əz)\ [F, fr. L conservus fellow slave, fr. com- with + servus slave] : an attendant at the entrance of a building esp. in France who observes those entering and leaving, handles mail, and acts as a janitor

con·cil·i·ate \kən-'sil-ē-,āt\ vb -at·ed; -at·ing 1 : to win over from a state of hostility 2 : to gain the goodwill of — con·cil·i·a·tion \-,sil-ē-'ā-shən\ n — con·cil·i·a·to·ry \-'sil-yə-,tōr-ē, -'sil-ē-ə-\ adj

con·cise \kən-'sīs\ adj : expressing much in few words : TERSE, SUCCINCT — con·cise·ly adv — con·cise·ness n

con·clave \'kän-,klāv\ n [ML, fr. L, room that can be locked, fr. com- together + clavis key] : a private gathering (as of Roman Catholic cardinals); also : CONVENTION

con·clude \kən-'klüd\ vb con·clud·ed; con·clud·ing 1 : to bring to a close : END 2 : DECIDE, JUDGE 3 : to bring about as a result syn close, finish, terminate, complete, gather, infer

con·clu·sion \kən-'klü-zhən\ n 1 : the logical consequence of a reasoning process 2 : TERMINATION, END 3 : OUTCOME, RESULT — con·clu·sive \-siv\ adj — con·clu·sive·ly adv

con·coct \kən-'käkt, kän-\ vb 1 : to prepare by combining diverse ingredients 2 : DEVISE ⟨~ a scheme⟩ — con·coc·tion \-'käk-shən\ n

con·com·i·tant \-'käm-ət-ənt\ adj : ACCOMPANYING, ATTENDING — concomitant n

con·cord \'kän-,kòrd, 'käŋ-\ n : AGREEMENT, HARMONY

con·cor·dance \kän-'kòrd-ᵊns\ n 1 : AGREEMENT 2 : an alphabetical index of words in a book or in an author's works with the passages in which they occur

con·cor·dant \-ᵊnt\ adj : HARMONIOUS, AGREEING

con·cor·dat \kən-'kòr-,dat\ n : AGREEMENT, COVENANT

**con·course** \'kän-ˌkōrs\ *n* **1 :** a flocking together of people **:** GATHERING **2 :** an open space where roads meet **3 :** an open space or hall (as in a bus terminal) where crowds gather

**con·cres·cence** \kən-'kres-ᵊns\ *n* **:** a growing together — **con·cres·cent** \-ᵊnt\ *adj*

**¹con·crete** \kän-'krēt, 'kän-ˌkrēt\ *adj* **1 :** united in solid form **2 :** naming a real thing or class of things **:** not abstract **3 :** not theoretical **:** ACTUAL **4 :** made of or relating to concrete **syn** specific, particular, special

**²con·crete** \'kän-ˌkrēt, kän-'krēt\ *n* **:** a hard building material made by mixing cement, sand, and gravel with water

**³con·crete** \'kän-ˌkrēt, kän-'krēt\ *vb* **con·cret·ed; con·cret·ing 1 :** SOLIDIFY **2 :** to cover with concrete

**con·cre·tion** \kän-'krē-shən\ *n* **:** a hard mass esp. when formed abnormally in the body

**con·cu·bine** \'käŋ-kyù-ˌbīn\ *n* **:** a woman who is not legally a wife but lives with a man and has a recognized position in his household — **con·cu·bi·nage** \kän-'kyü-bə-nij\ *n*

**con·cu·pis·cence** \kän-'kyü-pə-səns\ *n* **:** ardent sexual desire **:** LUST

**con·cur** \kən-'kər\ *vb* **con·curred; con·cur·ring 1 :** COINCIDE **2 :** to act together **3 :** AGREE **syn** unite, combine, cooperate

**con·cur·rence** \-'kər-əns\ *n* **1 :** CONJUNCTION, COINCIDENCE **2 :** agreement in action or opinion

**con·cur·rent** \-'kər-ənt\ *adj* **1 :** happening or operating at the same time **2 :** joint and equal in authority

**con·cus·sion** \kən-'kəsh-ən\ *n* **1 :** SHOCK, SHAKING **2 :** a sharp sudden blow or collision; *also* **:** bodily injury (as to the brain) resulting from a sudden jar

**con·demn** \kən-'dem\ *vb* **1 :** to declare to be wrong **2 :** to convict of guilt **3 :** to sentence judicially **4 :** to pronounce unfit for use (~ a building) **5 :** to declare forfeited or taken for public use **syn** denounce, censure, blame, criticize, doom, damn — **con·dem·na·tion** \ˌkän-ˌdem-'nā-shən\ *n* — **con·dem·na·to·ry** \kən-'dem-nə-ˌtōr-ē\ *adj*

**¹con·den·sate** \'kän-dən-ˌsāt, kən-'den-\ *n* **:** a product of condensation

**con·dense** \kən-'dens\ *vb* **con·densed; con·dens·ing 1 :** to make or become more compact or dense **:** CONCENTRATE **2 :** to change from vapor to liquid **syn** contract, shrink, deflate — **con·den·sa·tion** \ˌkän-ˌden-'sā-shən, -dən-\ *n*

**con·dens·er** \kən-'den-sər\ *n* **1 :** one that condenses **2 :** CAPACITOR

**con·de·scend** \ˌkän-di-'send\ *vb* **:** to assume an air of superiority **syn** stoop, deign — **con·de·scend·ing·ly** \-'sen-diŋ-lē\ *adv* — **con·de·scen·sion** \-'sen-chən\ *n*

**con·dign** \kən-'dīn, 'kän-ˌdīn\ *adj* **:** DESERVED, APPROPRIATE (~ punishment)

**con·di·ment** \'kän-də-mənt\ *n* **:** something used to make food savory; *esp* **:** pungent seasoning (as pepper)

**¹con·di·tion** \kən-'dish-ən\ *n* **1 :** something essential to the occurrence of some other thing **2** *pl* **:** state of affairs **:** CIRCUMSTANCES **3 :** state of being **4 :** station in life **:** social rank **5 :** state in respect to fitness (as for action or use); *esp* **:** state of health

**²condition** *vb* **con·di·tioned; con·di·tion·ing 1 :** to limit or modify by a condition **2 :** to put into proper condition for action or use **3 :** to modify so that an act or response previously associated with one stimulus becomes associated with another

**con·di·tion·al** \kən-'dish-(ə-)nəl\ *adj* **:** containing, implying, or depending on a condition — **con·di·tion·al·ly** \-ē\ *adv*

**con·di·tioned** *adj* **:** determined or established by conditioning

**con·dole** \kən-'dōl\ *vb* **con·doled; con·dol·ing :** to express sympathetic sorrow — **con·do·lence** \kən-'dō-ləns, 'kän-də-\ *n*

**con·dom** \'kən-dəm, 'kän-\ *n* **:** a usu. membranous or rubber sheath worn over the penis to prevent conception or venereal infection during sexual intercourse

**con·do·min·i·um** \ˌkän-də-'min-ē-əm\ *n, pl* **-ums 1 :** joint sovereignty (as by two or more nations) **2 :** a politically dependent territory under condominium **3 :** individual ownership of a unit (as an apartment) in a multi-unit structure; *also* **:** a unit so owned

**con·done** \kən-'dōn\ *vb* **con·doned; con·don·ing :** to overlook or forgive (an offense) by treating the offender as if he had done nothing wrong **syn** excuse, pardon — **con·do·na·tion** \ˌkän-də-'nā-shən\ *n*

**con·dor** \'kän-dər, -ˌdȯr\ *n* [Sp *cóndor*, fr. Quechua (a So. American Indian language) *kúntur*] **:** a very large western American vulture

**con·duce** \kən-'d(y)üs\ *vb* **con·duced; con·duc·ing :** to lead or contribute to a result — **con·du·cive** *adj*

**¹con·duct** \'kän-(ˌ)dəkt\ *n* **1 :** MANAGEMENT, DIRECTION **2 :** BEHAVIOR

**²con·duct** \kən-'dəkt\ *vb* **1 :** GUIDE, ESCORT **2 :** MANAGE, DIRECT **3 :** to serve as a channel for **4 :** BEHAVE, BEAR — **con·duc·tion** \-'dək-shən\ *n*

**con·duc·tance** \kən-'dək-təns\ *n* **:** the reciprocal of electrical resistance

**con·duc·tive** \kən-'dək-tiv\ *adj* **:** having the power to conduct (as heat or electricity) — **con·duc·tiv·i·ty** \ˌkän-ˌdək-'tiv-ət-ē\ *n*

**con·duc·tor** \kən-'dək-tər\ *n* **1 :** one that conducts **2 :** a collector of fares in a public conveyance **3 :** the leader of a musical ensemble

**con·duit** \'kän-ˌd(y)ü-ət, -d(w)ət\ *n* **1 :** a channel for conveying fluid **2 :** a tube or trough for protecting electric wires or cables

**con·dyle** \'kän-,dīl, -d°l\ *n* **:** an articular prominence of a bone — **con·dy·lar** \-də-lər\ *adj*

**cone** \'kōn\ *n* **1 :** the scaly fruit of trees of the pine family **2 :** a solid figure whose base is a circle and whose sides taper evenly up to an apex; *also* **:** something having a similar shape

**Con·es·to·ga** \,kän-ə-'stō-gə\ *n* **:** a broad-wheeled covered wagon usu. drawn by six horses and used esp. for transporting freight across the prairies

**co·ney** \'kō-nē\ *n, pl* **coneys 1 :** a rabbit or its fur **2 :** a small short-eared mammal of the rocky parts of high mountains that is related to the rabbits

**conf** *abbr* conference

**con·fab** \'kän-,fab, kən-'fab\ *n* **:** CONFABULATION

**con·fab·u·la·tion** \kən-,fab-yə-'lā-shən\ *n* **:** CHAT; *also* **:** CONFERENCE

**con·fec·tion** \kən-'fek-shən\ *n* **:** a fancy dish or sweet; *also* **:** CANDY

**con·fec·tion·er** \-sh(ə-)nər\ *n* **:** a maker of or dealer in confections (as candies)

**con·fec·tion·ery** \-shə-,ner-ē\ *n, pl* **-er·ies 1 :** CANDIES **2 :** a confectioner's place of business

**Confed** *abbr* Confederate

**con·fed·er·a·cy** \kən-'fed-(ə-)rə-sē\ *n, pl* **-cies 1 :** LEAGUE, ALLIANCE **2** *cap* **:** the 11 southern states that seceded from the U. S. in 1860 and 1861

**1con·fed·er·ate** \kən-'fed-(ə-)rət\ *adj* **1 :** united in a league **:** ALLIED **2** *cap* **:** of or relating to the Confederacy

**2confederate** *n* **1 :** ALLY; *also* **:** ACCOMPLICE **2** *cap* **:** an adherent of the Confederacy

**3con·fed·er·ate** \-'fed-ə-,rāt\ *vb* **-at·ed; -at·ing :** to unite in a confederacy or a conspiracy

**con·fed·er·a·tion** \kən-,fed-ə-'rā-shən\ *n* **1 :** an act of confederating **2 :** ALLIANCE, LEAGUE

**con·fer** \kən-'fər\ *vb* **con·ferred; con·fer·ring 1 :** GRANT, BESTOW **2 :** to exchange views **:** CONSULT — **con·fer·ee** \,kän-fə-'rē\ *n*

**con·fer·ence** \'kän-f(ə-)rəns\ *n* **:** an interchange of views; *also* **:** a meeting for this purpose

**con·fess** \kən-'fes\ *vb* **1 :** to acknowledge or disclose one's misdeed, fault, or sin **2 :** to acknowledge one's sins to God or to a priest **3 :** to receive the confession of (a penitent) **syn** admit, own

**con·fessed·ly** \-'fes-əd-lē\ *adv* **:** by confession **:** ADMITTEDLY

**con·fes·sion** \-'fesh-ən\ *n* **1 :** an act of confessing (as in the sacrament of penance) **2 :** an acknowledgment of guilt **3 :** a formal statement of religious beliefs **4 :** a religious body having a common creed — **con·fes·sion·al** *adj*

**con·fes·sion·al** \-'fesh-(ə-)nəl\ *n* **:** a place where a priest hears confessions

**con·fes·sor** \kən-'fes-ər, 2 *also* 'kän-,fes-\ *n* **1 :** one that confesses **2 :** a priest who hears confessions

**con·fet·ti** \kən-'fet-ē\ *n* [It, pl, of

*confetto* sweetmeat, fr. ML *confectum*, fr. L *conficere* to prepare] **:** bits of colored paper or ribbon for throwing about in celebration

**con·fi·dant** \'kän-fə-,dant, -,dänt\ *n* **:** one to whom secrets are confided

**con·fide** \kən-'fīd\ *vb* **con·fid·ed; con·fid·ing 1 :** to have or show faith ⟨~ in a friend⟩ **2 :** to tell confidentially ⟨~ a secret⟩ **3 :** ENTRUST

**1con·fi·dence** \'kän-fəd-əns\ *n* **1 :** TRUST, RELIANCE **2 :** SELF-ASSURANCE, BOLDNESS **3 :** a state of trust or intimacy — **con·fi·dent** \-fəd-ənt\ *adj* — **con·fi·dent·ly** *adv*

**2confidence** *adj* **:** of or relating to swindling by false promises

**con·fi·den·tial** \,kän-fə-'den-chəl\ *adj* **1 :** SECRET, PRIVATE **2 :** enjoying or treated with confidence ⟨~ clerk⟩ — **con·fi·den·tial·ly** \-ē\ *adv*

**con·fig·u·ra·tion** \kən-,fig-yə-'rā-shən\ *n* **:** structural arrangement of parts **:** SHAPE

**con·fine** \kən-'fīn\ *vb* **con·fined; con·fin·ing 1 :** to keep within limits **:** RESTRAIN **2 :** IMPRISON **3 :** to restrict to a particular place or situation — **con·fine·ment** *n* — **con·fin·er** *n*

**con·fines** \'kän-,fīnz\ *n* **1 :** BOUNDS, BORDERS **2 :** outlying parts **3 :** TERRITORY

**con·firm** \kən-'fərm\ *vb* **1 :** to make firm or firmer **2 :** RATIFY **3 :** VERIFY, CORROBORATE **4 :** to administer the rite of confirmation to — **con·fir·ma·to·ry** \-'fər-mə-,tōr-ē\ *adj* — **confirmed** *adj*

**con·fir·ma·tion** \,kän-fər-'mā-shən\ *n* **1 :** an act of ratifying or corroborating; *also* **:** PROOF **2 :** a religious ceremony admitting a person to full membership in a church or synagogue

**con·fis·cate** \'kän-fə-,skāt\ *vb* **-cat·ed; -cat·ing** [L *confiscare*, fr. *com-* with + *fiscus* treasury] **:** to take possession of by or as if by public authority — **con·fis·ca·tion** \,kän-fə-'skā-shən\ *n* — **con·fis·ca·to·ry** \kən-'fis-kə-,tōr-ē\ *adj*

**con·fla·gra·tion** \,kän-flə-'grā-shən\ *n* **:** FIRE; *esp* **:** a large disastrous fire

**1con·flict** \'kän-,flikt\ *n* **1 :** WAR **2 :** a clash between hostile or opposing elements or ideas

**2con·flict** \kən-'flikt\ *vb* **:** to show antagonism or irreconcilability **:** CLASH

**con·flu·ence** \'kän-,flü-əns, kən-'flü-\ *n* **1 :** the meeting or place of meeting of two or more streams **2 :** a flocking together **:** CROWD — **con·flu·ent** \-ənt\ *adj*

**con·flux** \'kän-,fləks\ *n* **:** CONFLUENCE

**con·fo·cal** \kän-'fō-kəl\ *adj* **:** having the same foci — **con·fo·cal·ly** \-ē\ *adv*

**con·form** \kən-'fôrm\ *vb* **1 :** to make or be like **:** AGREE **2 :** to obey customs or standards — **con·form·able** *adj*

**con·for·mance** \kən-'fôr-məns\ *n* **:** CONFORMITY

**con·for·ma·tion** \,kän-fôr-'mā-shən\ *n* **:** arrangement and congruity of parts

**con·for·mi·ty** \kən-'fôr-mət-ē\ *n*

1 : HARMONY, AGREEMENT  2 : COMPLIANCE, OBEDIENCE

**con·found** \kən-'faund, kän-\ *vb* 1 : to throw into disorder or confusion : DISMAY  2 : to mix up : CONFUSE **syn** bewilder, puzzle, perplex, mistake

**con·fra·ter·ni·ty** \ˌkän-frə-'tər-nət-ē\ *n* : a society devoted to a religious or charitable cause

**con·frere** \'kän-ˌfreər, -'kōⁿ-\ *n* : COLLEAGUE, COMRADE

**con·front** \kən-'frənt\ *vb* 1 : to face esp. in challenge : OPPOSE  2 : to cause to face or meet — **con·fron·ta·tion** \ˌkän-frən-'tā-shən\ *n*

**Con·fu·cian·ism** \kən-'fyü-shən-ˌiz-əm\ *n* : a religion growing out of the teachings of the Chinese philosopher Confucius — **Con·fu·cian** *n or adj*

**con·fuse** \kən-'fyüz\ *vb* **con·fused; con·fus·ing** 1 : to make mentally unclear or uncertain; *also* : to disturb the composure of  2 : to mix up : JUMBLE  **syn** muddle, befuddle, mistake, confound — **con·fus·ed·ly** \-'fyü-zəd-lē\ *adv*

**con·fu·sion** \-'fyü-zhən\ *n* 1 : turmoil or uncertainty of mind  2 : DISORDER, JUMBLE

**con·fute** \kən-'fyüt\ *vb* **con·fut·ed; con·fut·ing** : to overwhelm by argument : REFUTE — **con·fu·ta·tion** \ˌkän-fyü-'tā-shən\ *n*

**cong** *abbr* congress; congressional

**con·ga** \'käŋ-gə\ *n* : a Cuban dance of African origin performed by a group usu. in single file

**con·geal** \kən-'jēl\ *vb* 1 : FREEZE  2 : to make or become hard or thick as if by freezing

**con·ge·ner** \'kän-jə-nər\ *n* : one related to another; *esp* : one of the same taxonomic genus as another plant or animal — **con·ge·ner·ic** \ˌkän-jə-'ner-ik\ *adj*

**con·ge·nial** \kən-'jē-nyəl\ *adj* 1 : KINDRED, SYMPATHETIC  2 : suited to one's taste or nature : AGREEABLE — **con·ge·ni·al·i·ty** \-ˌjē-nē-'al-ət-ē\ *n* — **con·ge·nial·ly** \-'jē-nyə-lē\ *adv*

**con·gen·i·tal** \kən-'jen-ə-tᵊl\ *adj* : existing at or dating from birth but usu. not hereditary  **syn** inborn, innate

**con·ger eel** \ˈkäŋ-gər-\ *n* : a large edible marine eel

**con·ge·ries** \'kän-jə-ˌ(ˌ)rēz\ *n, pl* **congeries** \*same*\ : AGGREGATION, COLLECTION

**con·gest** \kən-'jest\ *vb* 1 : to cause excessive fullness of the blood vessels of (as a lung)  2 : to obstruct by overcrowding — **con·ges·tion** \-'jes-chən\ *n* — **con·ges·tive** \-'jes-tiv\ *adj*

**¹con·glom·er·ate** \kən-'gläm-(ə-)rət\ *adj* [L *conglomerare* to roll together, fr. *com-* together + *glomerare* to wind into a ball, fr. *glomer-, glomus* ball] 1 : made up of parts from various sources  2 : densely massed or clustered

**²con·glom·er·ate** \-ə-ˌrāt\ *vb* **-at·ed; -at·ing** : to form into a ball or mass — **con·glom·er·a·tion** \-ˌgläm-ə-'rā-shən\ *n*

**³con·glom·er·ate** \-(ə-)rət\ *n* 1 : a mass formed of fragments from various sources; *esp* : a rock composed of fragments varying from pebbles to boulders held together by a cementing material  2 : a widely diversified corporation

**con·grat·u·late** \kən-'grach-ə-ˌlāt\ *vb* **-lat·ed; -lat·ing** : to express sympathetic pleasure to on account of success or good fortune : FELICITATE — **con·grat·u·la·tion** \-ˌgrach-ə-'lā-shən\ *n* — **con·grat·u·la·to·ry** \-'grach-ə-lə-ˌtōr-ē\ *adj*

**con·gre·gate** \'käŋ-gri-ˌgāt\ *vb* **-gat·ed; -gat·ing** [ME *congregaten*, fr. L *congregare*, fr. *com-* together + *greg-, grex* flock] : ASSEMBLE

**con·gre·ga·tion** \ˌkäŋ-gri-'gā-shən\ *n* 1 : an assembly of persons met esp. for worship; *also* : a group that habitually so meets  2 : a company or order of religious persons under a common rule  3 : the act or an instance of congregating

**con·gre·ga·tion·al** \-sh(ə-)nəl\ *adj* 1 : of or relating to a congregation  2 *cap* : observing the faith and practice of certain Protestant churches which recognize the independence of each congregation in church matters

**con·gre·ga·tion·al·ist** \-əst\ *n* : a member of one of several Protestant denominations that emphasize the autonomy of the local congregation — **con·gre·ga·tion·al·ism** \-ˌiz-əm\ *n*

**con·gress** \'käŋ-grəs\ *n* 1 : an assembly esp. of delegates for discussion and usu. action on some question  2 : the body of senators and representatives constituting a nation's legislature — **con·gres·sio·nal** \kən-'gresh-(ə-)nəl\ *adj*

**con·gress·man** \'käŋ-grəs-mən\ *n* : a member of a congress — **con·gress·wom·an** \-ˌwum-ən\ *n*

**con·gru·ence** \kən-'grü-əns, 'käŋ-grə-wəns\ *n* : the quality of according or coinciding : CONGRUITY — **con·gru·ent** \kən-'grü-ənt, 'käŋ-grə-wənt\ *adj*

**con·gru·en·cy** \-ən-sē, -wən-\ *n, pl* **-cies** : CONGRUENCE

**con·gru·ity** \kən-'grü-ət-ē, kän-\ *n* : correspondence between things — **con·gru·ous** \'käŋ-grə-wəs\ *adj*

**con·ic** \'kän-ik\ *adj* 1 : CONICAL  2 : of or relating to a cone

**con·i·cal** \'kän-i-kəl\ *adj* : resembling a cone

**co·ni·fer** \'kän-ə-fər, 'kōn-\ *n* : a cone-bearing tree or shrub (as a pine) — **co·nif·er·ous** \kō-'nif-(ə-)rəs\ *adj*

**conj** *abbr* conjunction

**con·jec·ture** \kən-'jek-chər\ *n* : GUESS, SURMISE — **con·jec·tur·al** \-chə-rəl\ *adj* — **conjecture** *vb*

**con·join** \kən-'jóin\ *vb* : to join together — **con·joint** \-'jóint\ *adj*

**con·ju·gal** \'kän-ji-gəl, kən-'jü-\ *adj* : of or relating to marriage : MATRIMONIAL

**¹con·ju·gate** \'kän-ji-gət, -jə-ˌgāt\ *adj* 1 : united esp. in pairs : COUPLED

2 : of kindred origin and meaning ⟨*sing* and *song* are ∼⟩

²con·ju·gate \-jə-,gāt\ *vb* -gat·ed; -gat·ing 1 : INFLECT ⟨∼ a verb⟩ 2 : to join together : COUPLE

con·ju·ga·tion \,kän-jə-'gā-shən\ *n* 1 : the act of conjugating : the state of being conjugated 2 : a schematic arrangement of the inflectional forms of a verb

con·junct \kən-'jəŋkt, kän-\ *adj* : JOINED, UNITED

con·junc·tion \kən-'jəŋk-shən\ *n* 1 : UNION, COMBINATION 2 : occurrence at the same time 3 : a word that joins together sentences, clauses, phrases, or words

con·junc·ti·va \,kän-,jəŋk-'tī-və\ *n*, *pl* -vas *or* -vae \-(,)vē\ : the mucous membrane lining the inner surface of the eyelids and continuing over the forepart of the eyeball

con·junc·tive \kən-'jəŋk-tiv\ *adj* 1 : CONNECTIVE 2 : CONJUNCT 3 : being or functioning like a conjunction

con·junc·ti·vi·tis \kən-,jəŋk-ti-'vīt-əs\ *n* : inflammation of the conjunctiva

con·junc·ture \kən-'jəŋk-chər\ *n* 1 : CONJUNCTION, UNION 2 : a combination of circumstances or events esp. producing a crisis

con·jure \'kän-jər, 'kən- *for* 1, 2; kən-'jür *for* 3\ *vb* con·jured; con·jur·ing \'känj-(ə-)riŋ, 'kənj-; kən-'jü(ə)r-iŋ\ 1 : to practice magic; *esp* : to summon (as a devil) by sorcery 2 : to practice sleight of hand 3 : to implore earnestly or solemnly — con·ju·ra·tion \,kän-jù-'rā-shən, ,kən-\ *n* — con·jur·er *or* con·ju·ror \'kän-jər-ər, 'kən-\ *n*

conk \'käŋk\ *vb* : to break down; *esp* : STALL ⟨the motor ∼ed out⟩

Conn *abbr* Connecticut

con·nect \kə-'nekt\ *vb* 1 : JOIN, LINK 2 : to associate in one's mind — con·nec·tor *n*

con·nec·tion \kə-'nek-shən\ *n* 1 : JUNCTION, UNION 2 : logical relationship : COHERENCE; *esp* : relation of a word to other words in a sentence 3 : BOND, LINK 4 : family relationship 5 : relationship in social affairs or in business 6 : a person related by blood or marriage 7 : an association of persons; *esp* : a religious denomination

¹con·nec·tive \kə-'nek-tiv\ *adj* : connecting or functioning in connecting

²connective *n* : a word (as a conjunction) that connects words or word groups

con·nip·tion \kə-'nip-shən\ *n* : a fit of rage, hysteria, or alarm

con·nive \kə-'nīv\ *vb* con·nived; con·niv·ing [F or L; F *conniver*, fr. L *conivere* to close the eyes, connive] 1 : to pretend ignorance of something one ought to oppose as wrong 2 : to cooperate secretly : give secret aid — con·niv·ance *n*

con·nois·seur \,kän-ə-'sər\ *n* : a critical judge in matters of art or taste

con·no·ta·tion \,kän-ə-'tā-shən\ *n* : a

meaning in addition to or apart from the thing explicitly named or described by a word

con·no·ta·tive \'kän-ə-,tāt-iv, kə-'nōt-ət-\ *adj* 1 : connoting or tending to connote 2 : relating to connotation

con·note \kə-'nōt\ *vb* con·noted; con·not·ing 1 : to suggest or mean along with or in addition to the exact explicit meaning 2 : to be associated with as a consequence or concomitant

con·nu·bi·al \kə-'n(y)ü-bē-əl\ *adj* : of or relating to marriage : CONJUGAL

con·quer \'käŋ-kər\ *vb* con·quered; con·quer·ing \-k(ə-)riŋ\ 1 : to gain by force of arms : WIN 2 : to get the better of : OVERCOME syn defeat, subjugate, subdue, overthrow — con·quer·or \-kər-ər\ *n*

con·quest \'kän-,kwest, 'käŋ-\ *n* 1 : an act of conquering : VICTORY 3 : something conquered

con·quis·ta·dor \kōŋ-'kēs-tə-,dór, kän-'k(w)is-\ *n*, *pl* con·quis·ta·do·res \-,kēs-tə-'dór-ēz, -,k(w)is-\ *or* con·quis·ta·dors \-'kēs-tə-,dórz\ : CONQUEROR; *esp* : a leader in the Spanish conquest of America and esp. of Mexico and Peru in the 16th century

cons *abbr* consonant

con·san·guin·i·ty \,kän-,san-'gwin-ət-ē, -,saŋ-\ *n*, *pl* -ties : blood relationship — con·san·guin·e·ous \-'gwin-ē-əs\ *adj*

con·science \'kän-chəns\ *n* : consciousness of the moral right and wrong of one's own acts or motives — con·science·less *adj*

con·sci·en·tious \,kän-chē-'en-chəs\ *adj* : guided by one's own sense of right and wrong syn scrupulous, honorable, honest, upright, just — con·sci·en·tious·ly *adv*

conscientious objector *n* : one who refuses to serve in the armed forces or to bear arms on moral or religious grounds

con·scious \'kän-chəs\ *adj* 1 : AWARE 2 : mentally awake or alert : not asleep or unconscious 3 : known or felt by one's inner self 4 : INTENTIONAL — con·scious·ly *adv* — con·scious·ness *n*

con·script \kən-'skript\ *vb* : to enroll by compulsion for military or naval service — con·script \'kän-,skript\ *n* — con·scrip·tion \kən-'skrip-shən\ *n*

con·se·crate \'kän-sə-,krāt\ *vb* -crat·ed; -crat·ing 1 : to induct (as a bishop) into an office with a religious rite 2 : to make or declare sacred ⟨∼ a church⟩ 3 : to devote solemnly to a purpose — con·se·cra·tion \,kän-sə-'krā-shən\ *n*

con·sec·u·tive \kən-'sek-(y)ət-iv\ *adj* : following in regular order : SUCCESSIVE — con·sec·u·tive·ly *adv*

con·sen·sus \kən-'sen-səs\ *n* 1 : agreement in opinion, testimony, or belief 2 : collective opinion

¹con·sent \kən-'sent\ *vb* : to give assent or approval

²consent *n* : approval or acceptance of

something done or proposed by another

**con·se·quence** \'kän-sə-,kwens\ *n*
**1 :** RESULT **2 :** IMPORTANCE **syn** effect, outcome, significance

**con·se·quent** \-kwənt, -,kwent\ *adj* **:** following as a result or effect — **con·se·quent·ly** \-,kwent-lē, -kwənt-\ *adv*

**con·se·quen·tial** \,kän-sə-'kwen-chəl\ *adj* **1 :** having significant consequences **2 :** showing self-importance

**con·ser·van·cy** \kən-'sər-vən-sē\ *n, pl* **-cies :** an organization or area designated to conserve and protect natural resources

**con·ser·va·tion** \,kän-sər-'vā-shən\ *n* **:** PRESERVATION; *esp* **:** planned management of natural resources

**con·ser·va·tion·ist** \-sh(ə-)nəst\ *n* **:** one who advocates conservation esp. of natural resources

**con·ser·va·tism** \kən-'sər-və-,tiz-əm\ *n* **:** disposition to keep to established ways **:** opposition to change

**¹con·ser·va·tive** \kən-'sər-vət-iv\ *adj* **1 :** PRESERVATIVE **2 :** disposed to maintain existing views, conditions, or institutions **3 :** MODERATE, CAUTIOUS — **con·ser·va·tive·ly** *adv*

**²conservative** *n* **:** one who adheres to traditional methods or views

**con·ser·va·tor** \kən-'sər-vət-ər, 'kän-sər-,vāt-\ *n* **1 :** PROTECTOR, GUARDIAN **2 :** one named by a court to protect the interests of an incompetent (as a child)

**con·ser·va·to·ry** \kən-'sər-və-,tōr-ē\ *n, pl* **-ries 1 :** GREENHOUSE **2 :** a place of instruction in one of the fine arts (as music)

**¹con·serve** \kən-'sərv\ *vb* **con-served; con·serv·ing :** to keep from losing or wasting **:** PRESERVE

**²con·serve** \'kän-,sərv\ *n* **1 :** CONFECTION; *esp* **:** a candied fruit **2 :** PRESERVE; *esp* **:** one prepared from a mixture of fruits

**con·sid·er** \kən-'sid-ər\ *vb* **con-sid-ered; con·sid·er·ing** \-(ə-)riŋ\ [ME *consideren*, fr. MF *considerer*, fr. L *considerare*, lit., to observe the stars, fr. *sider-, sidus* star] **1 :** THINK, PONDER **2 :** HEED, REGARD **3 :** JUDGE, BELIEVE — **con·sid·ered** *adj*

**con·sid·er·able** \-'sid-ər-(ə-)bəl, -'sid-rə-bəl\ *adj* **1 :** IMPORTANT **2 :** large in extent, amount, or degree — **con·sid·er·a·bly** \-blē\ *adv*

**con·sid·er·ate** \kən-'sid-(ə-)rət\ *adj* **:** observant of the rights and feelings of others **syn** thoughtful, attentive

**con·sid·er·ation** \kən-,sid-ə-'rā-shən\ *n* **1 :** careful thought **:** DELIBERATION **2 :** thoughtful attention **3 :** MOTIVE, REASON **4 :** JUDGMENT, OPINION **5 :** RECOMPENSE

**con·sid·er·ing** \-(ə-)riŋ\ *prep* **:** in view of **:** taking into account

**con·sign** \kən-'sīn\ *vb* **1 :** to deliver formally **2 :** ENTRUST, COMMIT **3 :** ALLOT **4 :** to send (goods) to an agent for sale — **con·sign·ee** \,kän-sə-'nē, ,sī-; kən-,sī-\ *n* — **con·sign·or** \,kän-sə-'nór, ,sī-; kən-,sī-\ *n*

**con·sign·ment** \kən-'sīn-mənt\ *n* **:** a

shipment of goods consigned to an agent

**con·sist** \kən-'sist\ *vb* **1 :** to be inherent **:** LIE — used with *in* **2 :** to be composed or made up

**con·sis·tence** \kən-'sis-təns\ *n* **:** CONSISTENCY

**con·sis·ten·cy** \-tən-sē\ *n, pl* **-cies 1 :** COHESIVENESS, FIRMNESS **2 :** agreement or harmony in parts or of different things **3 :** UNIFORMITY (〜 of behavior) — **con·sis·tent** \-tənt\ *adj* — **con·sis·tent·ly** *adv*

**con·sis·to·ry** \kən-'sis-t(ə-)rē\ *n, pl* **-ries :** a solemn assembly (as of Roman Catholic cardinals)

**consol** *abbr* consolidated

**¹con·sole** \kən-'sōl\ *vb* **con·soled; con·sol·ing :** to soothe the grief of **:** COMFORT, SOLACE — **con·so·la·tion** \,kän-sə-'lā-shən\ *n* — **con·so·la·to·ry** \kən-'sōl-ə-,tōr-ē, -'säl-\ *adj*

**²con·sole** \'kän-,sōl\ *n* **1 :** the desk-like part of an organ at which the organist sits **2 :** a panel or cabinet for the controls of an electrical or mechanical device **3 :** a cabinet for a radio or television set resting directly on the floor **4 :** a small storage cabinet between bucket seats in an automobile

**con·sol·i·date** \kən-'säl-ə-,dāt\ *vb* **-dat·ed; -dat·ing 1 :** to unite or become united into one whole **:** COMBINE **2 :** to make firm or secure **3 :** to form into a compact mass — **con·sol·i·da·tion** \-,säl-ə-'dā-shən\ *n*

**con·som·mé** \,kän-sə-'mā\ *n* **:** a clear soup made from well-seasoned meat broth

**con·so·nance** \'kän-s(ə-)nəns\ *n* **1 :** AGREEMENT, HARMONY **2 :** repetition of consonants esp. as an alternative to rhyme in verse

**¹con·so·nant** \-s(ə-)nənt\ *n* **1 :** a speech sound (as \p\, \g\, \n\, \l\, \s\, \r\) characterized by constriction or closure at one or more points in the breath channel **2 :** a letter other than *a, e, i, o,* and *u* — **con·so·nan·tal** \,kän-sə-'nant-ᵊl\ *adj*

**²consonant** *adj* **:** having consonance, harmony, or agreement **syn** consistent, compatible, congruous, congenial, sympathetic

**¹con·sort** \'kän-,sórt\ *n* **1 :** SPOUSE, MATE **2 :** a ship accompanying another for protection

**²con·sort** \kən-'sórt\ *vb* **1 :** to keep company **2 :** ACCORD, HARMONIZE

**con·sor·tium** \kən-'sórt-ē-əm, -'sórsh(ē-)əm\ *n, pl* **-sor·tia** \-'sórt-ē-ə, -'sórt-sh(ē-)ə\ **:** an international business or banking agreement or combination

**con·spec·tus** \kən-'spek-təs\ *n* **1 :** a brief survey or summary **2 :** OUTLINE, SYNOPSIS

**con·spic·u·ous** \kən-'spik-yə-wəs\ *adj* **:** attracting attention **:** PROMINENT, STRIKING **syn** noticeable, remarkable, outstanding — **con·spic·u·ous·ly** *adv*

**con·spir·a·cy** \kən-'spir-ə-sē\ *n, pl* **-cies :** an agreement among conspirators **:** PLOT

**con·spire** \kən-'spī(ə)r\ *vb* **con·spired; con·spir·ing :** to plan secretly an unlawful act **:** PLOT — **con·spir·a·tor** \-'spir-ət-ər\ *n*

**const** *abbr* **1** constant **2** constitution; constitutional

**con·sta·ble** \'kän-stə-bəl, 'kən-\ *n* [ME *conestable,* fr. OF, fr. LL *comes stabuli,* lit., officer of the stable] **:** POLICEMAN

**con·stab·u·lary** \kən-'stab-yə-ˌler-ē\ *n, pl* **-lar·ies 1 :** the police of a particular district or country **2 :** an armed police force organized on military lines but distinct from the army

**con·stan·cy** \'kän-stən-sē\ *n, pl* **-cies 1 :** firmness of mind **2 :** STABILITY

¹**con·stant** \-stənt\ *adj* **1 :** STEADFAST, FAITHFUL **2 :** FIXED, UNCHANGING **3 :** continually recurring **:** REGULAR — **con·stant·ly** *adv*

²**constant** *n* **:** something unchanging

**con·stel·la·tion** \ˌkän-stə-'lā-shən\ *n* **:** any of 88 groups of stars forming patterns

**con·ster·na·tion** \ˌkän-stər-'nā-shən\ *n* **:** amazed dismay and confusion

**con·sti·pa·tion** \ˌkän-stə-'pā-shən\ *n* **:** abnormally delayed or infrequent passage of usu. hard dry feces — **con·sti·pate** \'kän-stə-ˌpāt\ *vb*

**con·stit·u·en·cy** \kən-'stich-ə-wən-sē\ *n, pl* **-cies :** a body of constituents; *also* **:** an electoral district

¹**con·stit·u·ent** \-wənt\ *n* **1 :** COMPONENT **2 :** having power to elect **3 :** having power to frame or revise a constitution

²**constituent** *adj* **1 :** a component part **2 :** one entitled to vote for a representative for a district

**con·sti·tute** \'kän-stə-ˌt(y)üt\ *vb* **-tut·ed; -tut·ing 1 :** to appoint to an office or duty **2 :** to set up **:** ESTABLISH ⟨~ a law⟩ **3 :** to make up **:** COMPOSE

**con·sti·tu·tion** \ˌkän-stə-'t(y)ü-shən\ *n* **1 :** an established law or custom **2 :** the physical makeup of the individual **3 :** the structure, composition, or makeup of something ⟨~ of the sun⟩ **4 :** the basic law in a politically organized body; *also* **:** a document containing such law

¹**con·sti·tu·tion·al** \-sh(ə-)nəl\ *adj* **1 :** of or relating to the constitution of body or mind **2 :** of or relating to the constitution of a state or society — **con·sti·tu·tion·al·ly** \-ē\ *adv*

²**constitutional** *n* **:** an exercise (as a walk) taken for one's health

**con·sti·tu·tion·al·i·ty** \-ˌt(y)ü-shə-'nal-ət-ē\ *n* **:** the condition of being in accordance with the constitution of a state or society

**con·sti·tu·tive** \'kän-stə-ˌt(y)üt-iv, kən-'stich-ət-iv\ *adj* **:** CONSTITUENT, ESSENTIAL

**constr** *abbr* construction

**con·strain** \kən-'strān\ *vb* **1 :** COMPEL, FORCE **2 :** CONFINE **3 :** RESTRAIN

**con·straint** \-'strānt\ *n* **1 :** COMPULSION; *also* **:** RESTRAINT **2 :** unnaturalness of manner produced by a repression of one's natural feelings

**con·strict** \kən-'strikt\ *vb* **:** to draw together **:** SQUEEZE — **con·stric·tion** \-'strik-shən\ *n* — **con·stric·tive** \-'strik-tiv\ *adj*

**con·struct** \kən-'strəkt\ *vb* **:** BUILD, MAKE — **con·struc·tor** \-'strək-tər\ *n*

**con·struc·tion** \kən-'strək-shən\ *n* **1 :** the process, or manner of building; *also* **:** something built **:** STRUCTURE **2 :** INTERPRETATION **3 :** syntactical arrangement of words in a sentence — **con·struc·tive** \-tiv\ *adj*

**con·struc·tion·ist** \-sh(ə-)nəst\ *n* **:** one who construes a legal document (as the U.S. Constitution) in a specific way ⟨a strict ~⟩

**con·strue** \kən-'strü\ *vb* **con·strued; con·stru·ing 1 :** to explain the mutual relations of words in a sentence; *also* **:** TRANSLATE **2 :** EXPLAIN, INTERPRET — **con·stru·able** *adj*

**con·sub·stan·ti·a·tion** \ˌkän-səb-ˌstan-chē-'ā-shən\ *n* **:** the actual substantial presence and combination of the body of Christ with the eucharistic bread and wine

**con·sul** \'kän-səl\ *n* **1 :** a chief magistrate of the Roman republic **2 :** an official appointed by a government to reside in a foreign country to care for the commercial interests of that government's citizens — **con·sul·ar** \-sə-lər\ *adj* — **con·sul·ate** \-lət\ *n* — **con·sul·ship** *n*

**con·sult** \kən-'səlt\ *vb* **1 :** to ask the advice or opinion of **2 :** CONFER — **con·sul·tant** \-'nt\ *n* — **con·sul·ta·tion** \ˌkän-səl-'tā-shən\ *n*

**con·sume** \kən-'süm\ *vb* **con·sumed; con·sum·ing 1 :** DESTROY ⟨consumed by fire⟩ **2 :** to spend wastefully **3 :** to eat up **:** DEVOUR **4 :** to absorb the attention of **:** ENGROSS — **con·sum·able** *adj* — **con·sum·er** *n*

**con·sum·er·ism** \kən-'sü-mə-ˌriz-əm\ *n* **:** the promotion of consumers' interests (as against false advertising)

¹**con·sum·mate** \kən-'səm-ət\ *adj* **:** COMPLETE, PERFECT *syn* finished, accomplished

²**con·sum·mate** \'kän-sə-ˌmāt\ *vb* **-mat·ed; -mat·ing :** to make complete **:** FINISH, ACHIEVE — **con·sum·ma·tion** \ˌkän-sə-'mā-shən\ *n*

**con·sump·tion** \kən-'səmp-shən\ *n* **1 :** the act of consuming or using up **2 :** the use of economic goods **3 :** progressive bodily wasting away; *also* **:** TUBERCULOSIS

¹**con·sump·tive** \-'səmp-tiv\ *adj* **1 :** DESTRUCTIVE, WASTEFUL **2 :** relating to or affected with bodily consumption

²**consumptive** *n* **:** a consumptive person

**cont** *abbr* **1** containing **2** contents **3** continent; continental **4** continued **5** control

¹**con·tact** \'kän-ˌtakt\ *n* **1 :** a touching or meeting of bodies **2 :** ASSOCIATION, RELATIONSHIP; *also* **:** CONNECTION, COMMUNICATION **3 :** CONTACT LENS

²**contact** *vb* **1 :** to come or bring into contact **:** TOUCH **2 :** to get in communication with

**contact flying** *n* : airplane navigation by direct landmark observation

**contact lens** *n* : a thin lens fitting over the cornea

**con·ta·gion** \kən-'tā-jən\ *n* **1** : the passing of disease by contact **2** : a contagious disease; *also* : its causative agent **3** : transmission of an influence on the mind or emotions

**con·ta·gious** \-jəs\ *adj* : communicable by contact; *also* : relating to contagion or to contagious diseases

**con·tain** \kən-'tān\ *vb* **1** : ENCLOSE, INCLUDE **2** : to have within : HOLD **3** : RESTRAIN — **con·tain·ment** *n*

**con·tain·er** \kən-'tā-nər\ *n* : RECEPTACLE; *esp* : one for shipment of goods

**con·tain·er·iza·tion** \kən-ˌtā-nə-rə-'zā-shən\ *n* : a method of shipping large amounts of material in one container

**con·tain·er·ize** \kən-'tā-nə-ˌrīz\ *vb* **-ized; -iz·ing** : to ship by containerization

**con·tain·er·ship** \-nər-ˌship\ *n* : a ship esp. designed or equipped for carrying containerized cargo

**con·tam·i·nant** \kən-'tam-ə-nənt\ *n* : something that contaminates

**con·tam·i·nate** \kən-'tam-ə-ˌnāt\ *vb* **-nat·ed; -nat·ing** : to soil, stain, or infect by contact or association — **con·tam·i·na·tion** \-ˌtam-ə-'nā-shən\ *n*

**contd** *abbr* continued

**con·temn** \kən-'tem\ *vb* : to view or treat with contempt

**con·tem·plate** \'känt-əm-ˌplāt\ *vb* **-plat·ed; -plat·ing** [L *contemplari,* fr. *templum* space marked out for observation of auguries] **1** : to view or consider with continued attention **2** : INTEND — **con·tem·pla·tion** \ˌkänt-əm-'plā-shən\ *n* — **con·tem·pla·tive** \kən-'tem-plət-iv; 'känt-əm-ˌplāt-\ *adj*

**con·tem·po·ra·ne·ous** \kən-ˌtem-pə-'rā-nē-əs\ *adj* : CONTEMPORARY

**con·tem·po·rary** \kən-'tem-pə-ˌrer-ē\ *adj* **1** : occurring or existing at the same time **2** : being of the same age **3** : marked by characteristics of the present period — **contemporary** *n*

**con·tempt** \kən-'tempt\ *n* **1** : the act of despising : the state of mind of one who despises : DISDAIN **2** : the state of being despised **3** : disobedience to or open disrespect of a court or legislature

**con·tempt·ible** \kən-'temp-tə-bəl\ *adj* : deserving contempt : DESPICABLE — **con·tempt·ibly** \-blē\ *adv*

**con·temp·tu·ous** \-'temp-chə(-wə)s\ *adj* : feeling or expressing contempt — **con·temp·tu·ous·ly** *adv*

**con·tend** \kən-'tend\ *vb* **1** : to strive against rivals or difficulties; *also* : ARGUE, DEBATE **2** : MAINTAIN, CLAIM — **con·tend·er** *n*

**¹con·tent** \kən-'tent\ *adj* : SATISFIED

**²content** *vb* : SATISFY; *esp* : to limit (oneself) in requirements or actions

**³content** *n* : CONTENTMENT

**⁴con·tent** \'kän-ˌtent\ *n* **1** : something contained ⟨~s of a room⟩ ⟨~s of a bottle⟩ **2** : subject matter or topics treated (as in a book) **3** : essential meaning **4** : proportion contained

**con·tent·ed** \kən-'tent-əd\ *adj* : SATISFIED — **con·tent·ed·ly** *adv* — **con·tent·ed·ness** *n*

**con·ten·tion** \kən-'ten-chən\ *n* : CONTEST, STRIFE — **con·ten·tious** \-chəs\ *adj*

**con·tent·ment** \kən-'tent-mənt\ *n* : ease of mind : SATISFACTION

**con·ter·mi·nous** \kən-'tər-mə-nəs, kän-\ *adj* : having the same or a common boundary — **con·ter·mi·nous·ly** *adv*

**¹con·test** \kən-'test\ *vb* **1** : to engage in strife : FIGHT **2** : CHALLENGE, DISPUTE — **con·tes·tant** \-'tes-tənt\ *n*

**²con·test** \'kän-ˌtest\ *n* **1** : STRUGGLE, FIGHT **2** : COMPETITION

**con·text** \'kän-ˌtekst\ *n* [ME, weaving together of words, fr. L *contextus* coherence, fr. *contexere* to weave together] : the part of a discourse surrounding a word or group of words that helps to explain the meaning of the word or word group; *also* : the circumstances surrounding an act or event

**contg** *abbr* containing

**con·tig·u·ous** \kən-'tig-yə-wəs\ *adj* : being in contact : TOUCHING; *also* : NEXT, ADJOINING — **con·ti·gu·i·ty** \ˌkänt-ə-'gyü-ət-ē\ *n*

**con·ti·nence** \'känt-ᵊn-əns\ *n* **1** : SELF-RESTRAINT; *esp* : voluntary refraining from sexual intercourse **2** : ability to retain a bodily discharge — **con·ti·nent** \-ᵊn-ənt\ *adj*

**con·ti·nent** \'känt-(ᵊ-)nənt\ *n* **1** : one of the great divisions of land on the globe **2** *cap* : the continent of Europe as distinguished from the British Isles

**¹con·ti·nen·tal** \ˌkänt-ᵊn-'ent-ᵊl\ *adj* **1** : of or relating to a continent; *esp* : of or relating to the continent of Europe as distinguished from the British Isles **2** *often cap* : of or relating to the colonies later forming the U.S.

**²continental** *n* **1** *often cap* : a soldier in the Continental army **2** : the least bit ⟨not worth a ~⟩

**continental divide** *n* : a divide separating streams that flow to opposite sides of a continent

**continental shelf** *n* : a shallow submarine plain forming a border to a continent

**continental slope** *n* : a usu. steep slope from a continental shelf to the oceanic depths

**con·tin·gen·cy** \kən-'tin-jən-sē\ *n, pl* **-cies** : a chance or possible event

**¹con·tin·gent** \-jənt\ *adj* **1** : liable but not certain to happen : POSSIBLE **2** : happening by chance : not planned **3** : CONDITIONAL **4** : dependent on something that may or may not occur **syn** accidental, casual, incidental

**²contingent** *n* : a quota (as of troops) supplied from an area or group

**con·tin·u·al** \kən-'tin-yə(-wə)l\ *adj* **1** : CONTINUOUS, UNBROKEN **2** : steadily recurring — **con·tin·u·al·ly** \-ē\ *adv*

**con·tin·u·ance** \-yə-wəns\ *n* **1 :** a continuing in a state or course of action **:** DURATION **2 :** unbroken succession **3 :** adjournment of legal proceedings

**con·tin·u·a·tion** \kən-ˌtin-yə-'wā-shən\ *n* **1 :** extension or prolongation of a state or activity **2 :** resumption after an interruption; *also* **:** something that carries on after a pause or break

**con·tin·ue** \kən-'tin-yü\ *vb* **-tin·ued; -tinu·ing 1 :** to remain in a place or condition **:** ABIDE, STAY **2 :** ENDURE, LAST **3 :** PERSEVERE **4 :** to resume (as a story) after an intermission **5 :** EXTEND; *also* **:** to persist in **6 :** to allow to remain **7 :** to keep (a legal case) on the calendar or undecided

**con·ti·nu·ity** \ˌkänt-ᵊn-'(y)ü-ət-ē\ *n*, *pl* **-ities 1 :** the condition of being continuous **2 :** something that continues without a break; *esp* **:** a motion-picture scenario

**con·tin·u·ous** \kən-'tin-yə-wəs\ *adj* **:** continuing without interruption **:** UNBROKEN — **con·tin·u·ous·ly** *adv*

**con·tin·u·um** \-yə-wəm\ *n*, *pl* **-ua** \-yə-wə\ *also* **-ums 1 :** something that is the same throughout **2 :** something consisting of a series of variations or of a sequence of things in regular order

**con·tort** \kən-'tȯrt\ *vb* **:** to twist out of shape — **con·tor·tion** \-'tȯr-shən\ *n*

**con·tor·tion·ist** \-'tȯr-sh(ə-)nəst\ *n* **:** an acrobat who puts himself into unusual postures

**con·tour** \'kän-ˌtu̇r\ *n* [F, fr. It *contorno* fr. *contornare* to round off, sketch in outline, fr. L com- together + *tornare* to turn in a lathe, fr. *tornus* lathe] **1 :** OUTLINE **2 :** SHAPE, FORM — *usu.* used in pl. (the ~s of a statue)

**contr** *abbr* contract; contraction

**con·tra·band** \'kän-trə-ˌband\ *n* **:** goods legally prohibited in trade; *also* **:** smuggled goods

**con·tra·cep·tion** \ˌkän-trə-'sep-shən\ *n* **:** intentional prevention of conception — **con·tra·cep·tive** \-'sep-tiv\ *adj or n*

¹**con·tract** \'kän-ˌtrakt\ *n* **1 :** a binding agreement **:** COVENANT **2 :** an undertaking to win a specified number of tricks in contract bridge — **con·trac·tu·al** \kän-'trak-chə(-wə)l\ *adj* — **con·trac·tu·al·ly** \-ē\ *adv*

²**con·tract** \kən-'trakt, *1 usu* 'kän-ˌtrakt\ *vb* **1 :** to establish or undertake by contract **:** CATCH (~ a disease) **3 :** SHRINK, LESSEN; *esp* **:** to draw together esp. so as to shorten (~ a muscle) **4 :** to shorten (a word) by omitting letters or sounds in the middle — **con·trac·tion** \kən-'trak-shən\ *n* — **con·trac·tor** \'kän-ˌtrak-tər, kən-'trak-\ *n*

**con·trac·tile** \kən-'trak-tᵊl\ *adj* **:** able to contract — **con·trac·til·i·ty** \ˌkän-ˌtrak-'til-ət-ē\ *n*

**con·tra·dict** \ˌkän-trə-'dikt\ *vb* **:** to state the contrary of **:** deny the truth of — **con·tra·dic·tion** \-'dik-shən\ *n* — **con·tra·dic·to·ry** \-'dik-t(ə-)rē\ *adj*

**con·tra·dis·tinc·tion** \ˌkän-trə-dis-'tiŋk-shən\ *n* **:** distinction by contrast

**con·trail** \'kän-ˌtrāl\ *n* **:** streaks of condensed water vapor created in the air by an airplane or rocket at high altitudes

**con·tral·to** \kən-'tral-tō\ *n*, *pl* **-tos :** the lowest female voice; *also* **:** a singer having such a voice

**con·trap·tion** \kən-'trap-shən\ *n* **:** CONTRIVANCE, DEVICE

**con·tra·pun·tal** \ˌkän-trə-'pənt-ᵊl\ *adj* **:** of or relating to counterpoint

**con·tra·ri·ety** \ˌkän-trə-'rī-ət-ē\ *n*, *pl* **-eties :** the state of being contrary **:** DISAGREEMENT, INCONSISTENCY

**con·trari·wise** \'kän-ˌtrer-ē-ˌwīz, kən-'trer-\ *adv* **1 :** on the contrary **:** NO **2 :** OPPOSITELY, CONVERSELY

**con·trary** \'kän-ˌtrer-ē; *4 often* kən-'tre(ə)r-ē\ *adj* **1 :** opposite in nature or position **2 :** UNFAVORABLE **3 :** COUNTER, OPPOSED **4 :** tending to oppose or find fault — **con·trari·ly** \-ˌtrer-ə-lē, -'trer-\ *adv* — **con·trary** \n 'kän-ˌtrer-ē, *adv like adj*\ *n or adv*

¹**con·trast** \'kän-ˌtrast\ *n* **1 :** unlikeness as shown when things are compared **:** DIFFERENCE **2 :** diversity of adjacent parts in color, emotion, tone, or brightness (the ~ of a photograph)

²**con·trast** \kən-'trast\ *vb* [F *contraster*, fr. MF, to oppose, resist, fr. (assumed) VL *contrastare*, fr. L *contra-* against + *stare* to stand] **1 :** to show differences when compared **2 :** to compare in such a way as to show differences

**con·tra·vene** \ˌkän-trə-'vēn\ *vb* **-vened; -ven·ing 1 :** to go or act contrary to (~ a law) **2 :** CONTRADICT

**con·tre·temps** \'kän-trə-ˌtäⁿ, kōⁿ-trə-täⁿ\ *n*, *pl* **con·tre·temps** \-ˌtäⁿ(z)\ **:** an inopportune embarrassing occurrence

**contrib** *abbr* contribution; contributor

**con·trib·ute** \kən-'trib-yət\ *vb* **-uted; -ut·ing :** to give along with others (as to a fund) **:** supply or furnish a share to **:** HELP, ASSIST — **con·tri·bu·tion** \ˌkän-trə-'byü-shən\ *n* — **con·trib·u·tor** \kən-'trib-yət-ər\ *n* — **con·trib·u·to·ry** \-yə-ˌtōr-ē\ *adj*

**con·trite** \'kän-ˌtrīt, kən-'trīt\ *adj* **:** PENITENT, REPENTANT — **con·tri·tion** \kən-'trish-ən\ *n*

**con·triv·ance** \kən-'trī-vəns\ *n* **1 :** SCHEME, PLAN **2 :** a mechanical device **:** APPLIANCE

**con·trive** \kən-'trīv\ *vb* **con·trived; con·triv·ing 1 :** PLAN, DEVISE **2 :** FRAME, MAKE **3 :** to bring about with difficulty — **con·triv·er** *n*

¹**con·trol** \kən-'trōl\ *vb* **con·trolled; con·trol·ling 1 :** to exercise restraining or directing influence over **:** REGULATE **2 :** DOMINATE, RULE

²**control** *n* **1 :** power to direct or regulate **2 :** RESERVE, RESTRAINT **3 :** a device for regulating a mechanism

**con·trol·ler** \kən-'trō-lər, 'kän-ˌtrō-lər\ *n* **1 :** COMPTROLLER **2 :** one that controls

**con·tro·ver·sy** \'kän-trə-ˌvər-sē\ *n*, *pl* **-sies :** a clash of opposing views **:** DISPUTE — **con·tro·ver·sial** \ˌkän-trə-'vər-shəl, -sē-əl\ *adj* con·tro·vert \'kän-trə-,vərt, ,kän-trə-'vərt\ vb : DENY, CONTRADICT — con·tro·vert·ible adj

con·tu·ma·cious \,kän-t(y)ə-'mā-shəs\ adj : stubbornly resisting or disobeying authority syn rebellious, insubordinate — con·tu·ma·cy \kən-'t(y)ü-mə-sē, 'kän-t(y)ə-\ n — con·tu·ma·cious·ly adv

con·tu·me·li·ous \,kän-t(y)ə-'mē-lē-əs\ adj : insolently abusive and humiliating

con·tu·me·ly \kən-'t(y)ü-mə-lē, 'kän-t(y)ə-,mē-lē\ n : contemptuous treatment : INSULT

con·tu·sion \kən-'t(y)ü-zhən\ n : BRUISE — con·tuse \-'t(y)üz\ vb

co·nun·drum \kə-'nən-drəm\ n : RIDDLE

con·ur·ba·tion \,kän-(,)ər-'bā-shən\ n : a continuous network of urban communities

con·va·lesce \,kän-və-'les\ vb -lesced; -lesc·ing : to recover health gradually — con·va·les·cence \-'les-ⁿs\ n — con·va·les·cent \-ⁿt\ adj or n

con·vec·tion \kən-'vek-shən\ n : a circulatory motion in fluids due to warmer portions rising and colder denser portions sinking; also : the transfer of heat by such motion — con·vect \kən-'vekt\ vb — con·vec·tion·al \-'vek-sh(ə-)nəl\ adj — con·vec·tive \-'vek-tiv\ adj

con·vene \kən-'vēn\ vb con·vened; con·ven·ing : ASSEMBLE, MEET

con·ve·nience \kən-'vē-nyəns\ n 1 : SUITABLENESS 2 : personal comfort : EASE 3 : a laborsaving device 4 : a suitable time

con·ve·nient \-nyənt\ adj 1 : suited to one's comfort or ease 2 : placed near at hand — con·ve·nient·ly adv

con·vent \'kän-vənt, -,vent\ n [ME covent, fr. OF, fr. ML conventus, fr. L, assembly, fr. convenire come together] : a local community or house of a religious order esp. of nuns — con·ven·tu·al \kən-'ven-chə-wəl, kän-\ adj

con·ven·ti·cle \kən-'vent-i-kəl\ n : MEETING; esp : a secret meeting for worship

con·ven·tion \kən-'ven-chən\ n 1 : an agreement esp. between states on a matter of common concern 2 : MEETING, ASSEMBLY 3 : a body of delegates convened for some purpose 4 : fixed usage : accepted way of acting 5 : a social form sanctioned by general custom

con·ven·tion·al \-'vench-(ə-)nəl\ adj 1 : sanctioned by general custom 2 : COMMONPLACE, ORDINARY syn formal, ceremonial — con·ven·tion·al·i·ty \-,ven-chə-'nal-ət-ē\ n — con·ven·tion·al·ly \-'vench-(ə-)nəl-ē\ adv

con·ven·tion·al·ize \-'vench-(ə-)nə-,līz\ vb -ized; -iz·ing : to make conventional

con·verge \kən-'vərj\ vb con·verged; con·verg·ing : to approach one common center or single point —

con·ver·gence \kən-'vər-jəns\ or con·ver·gen·cy \-jən-sē\ n — con·ver·gent \-jənt\ adj

con·ver·sant \kən-'vərs-ⁿt\ adj : having knowledge and experience

con·ver·sa·tion \,kän-vər-'sā-shən\ n : an informal talking together — con·ver·sa·tion·al \-sh(ə-)nəl\ adj

¹con·verse \kən-'vərs\ vb con·versed; con·vers·ing : to engage in conversation

²con·verse \'kän-,vərs\ n : CONVERSATION

³con·verse \kən-'vərs, 'kän-,vərs\ adj : reversed in order or relation — con·verse·ly adv

⁴con·verse \'kän-,vərs\ n 1 : a statement related to another statement by having the parts reversed or interchanged 2 : OPPOSITE, REVERSE

con·ver·sion \kən-'vər-zhən\ n 1 : a change in nature or form 2 : an experience associated with a decisive adoption of religion 3 : illegal seizure and use of property of another person

¹con·vert \kən-'vərt\ vb 1 : to turn from one belief or party to another 2 : TRANSFORM, CHANGE 3 : MISAPPROPRIATE 4 : EXCHANGE — con·vert·er or con·ver·tor \-ər\ n — con·vert·ible adj

²con·vert \'kän-,vərt\ n : one who has undergone religious conversion

con·vert·ible \kən-'vərt-ə-bəl\ n : an automobile with a top that may be lowered or removed

con·vex \kän-'veks; 'kän-,veks, kən-'veks\ adj : curved or rounded like the exterior of a sphere or circle — con·vex·i·ty \kən-'vek-sət-ē, kän-\ n

con·vey \kən-'vā\ vb 1 : CARRY, TRANSPORT 2 : TRANSMIT, TRANSFER — con·vey·er or con·vey·or \-ər\ n

con·vey·ance \-'vā-əns\ n 1 : the act of conveying 2 : VEHICLE 3 : a legal paper transferring ownership of property

¹con·vict \kən-'vikt\ vb : to prove or find guilty

²con·vict \'kän-,vikt\ n : a person serving a prison sentence

con·vic·tion \kən-'vik-shən\ n 1 : the act of convicting esp. in a court 2 : the state of being convinced : strong belief

con·vince \kən-'vins\ vb con·vinced; con·vinc·ing : to bring by demonstration or argument to a sure belief — con·vinc·ing adj — con·vinc·ing·ly adv

con·viv·ial \kən-'viv-yəl, -'viv-ē-əl\ adj [LL convivialis, fr. L convivium banquet, fr. com- together + vivere to live] : enjoying companionship and the pleasures of feasting and drinking : JOVIAL, FESTIVE — con·viv·i·al·i·ty \-,viv-ē-'al-ət-ē\ n — con·viv·ial·ly \-'viv-yə-lē, -'viv-ē-ə-lē\ adv

con·vo·ca·tion \,kän-və-'kā-shən\ n 1 : a ceremonial assembly (as of clergymen) 2 : the act of convoking

con·voke \kən-'vōk\ vb con·voked; con·vok·ing : to call together to a meeting

con·vo·lut·ed \'kän-və-,lüt-əd\ adj

**1 :** folded in curved or tortuous windings **2 :** INVOLVED, INTRICATE

**con·vo·lu·tion** \,kän-və-'lü-shən\ *n* **1 :** a winding or coiling together **2 :** a tortuous or sinuous structure; *esp* **:** one of the ridges of the brain

**¹con·voy** \'kän-,vȯi, kən-'vȯi\ *vb* **:** to accompany for protection

**²con·voy** \'kän-,vȯi\ *n* **1 :** one that convoys; *esp* **:** a protective escort for ships, persons, or goods **2 :** a group of moving vehicles (as ships) with or without an escort

**con·vulse** \kən-'vəls\ *vb* **con·vulsed; con·vuls·ing :** to agitate violently

**con·vul·sion** \kən-'vəl-shən\ *n* **1 :** an abnormal and violent involuntary contraction or series of contractions of muscle **2 :** a violent disturbance — **con·vul·sive** \-'vəl-siv\ *adj* — **con·vul·sive·ly** *adv*

**cony** *var of* CONEY

**coo** \'kü\ *n* **:** a soft low sound made by doves or pigeons; *also* **:** a sound like this — **coo** *vb*

**¹cook** \'kùk\ *n* **:** one who prepares food for eating

**²cook** *vb* **1 :** to prepare food for eating **2 :** to subject to heat or fire — **cook·er** *n* — **cook·ware** \-,waər\ *n*

**cook·book** \-,bùk\ *n* **:** a book of cooking directions and recipes

**cook·ery** \'kùk-(ə-)rē\ *n, pl* **-er·ies** **:** the art or practice of cooking

**cook·ie** *or* **cooky** \'kùk-ē\ *n, pl* **cook·ies :** a small sweet flat cake

**cook·out** \'kùk-,aùt\ *n* **:** an outing at which a meal is cooked and served in the open

**¹cool** \'kül\ *adj* **1 :** moderately cold **2 :** protecting from heat **3 :** not excited **:** CALM **4 :** not ardent **5 :** indicating dislike **6 :** IMPUDENT **7** *slang* **:** very good **8 :** employing understatement **syn** chilly, composed, collected, unruffled, nonchalant — **cool·ly** \-'kül-(l)ē\ *adv* — **cool·ness** *n*

**²cool** *vb* **:** to make or become cool

**³cool** *n* **1 :** a cool time or place **2 :** INDIFFERENCE; *also* **:** SELF-ASSURANCE, COMPOSURE (kept his ~)

**cool·ant** \'kü-lənt\ *n* **:** a usu. fluid cooling agent

**cool·er** \'kü-lər\ *n* **1 :** REFRIGERATOR **2 :** JAIL, PRISON **3 :** an iced drink

**coo·lie** \'kü-lē\ *n* [Hindi *kulī*] **:** an unskilled laborer in the Far East

**coon** \'kün\ *n* **:** RACCOON

**coon·hound** \-,haùnd\ *n* **:** a sporting dog trained to hunt raccoons

**coon·skin** \-,skin\ *n* **:** the pelt of a raccoon; *also* **:** something (as a cap) made of this

**¹coop** \'küp, 'kùp\ *n* **:** a small enclosure or building usu. for poultry

**²coop** *vb* **:** to confine in or as if in a coop

**co-op** \'kō-,äp\ *n* **:** COOPERATIVE

**coo·per** \'kü-pər, 'kùp-ər\ *n* **:** one who makes or repairs barrels or casks — **cooper** *vb* — **coo·per·age** \'küp(ə-)rij, 'kùp-(ə-)\ *n*

**co·op·er·ate** \kō-'äp-ə-,rāt\ *vb* **:** to act jointly with another or others —

**co·op·er·a·tion** \-,äp-ə-'rā-shən\ *n* — **co·op·er·a·tor** \-'äp-ə-,rāt-ər\ *n*

**¹co·op·er·a·tive** \kō-'äp-(ə-)rət-iv, 'äp-ə-,rāt\ *adj* **1 :** willing to work with others **2 :** of or relating to an association formed to enable its members to buy or sell to better advantage by eliminating middlemen's profits

**²cooperative** *n* **:** a cooperative association

**co-opt** \kō-'äpt\ *vb* **1 :** to choose or elect as a colleague **2 :** ABSORB, ASSIMILATE; *also* **:** to take over

**¹co·or·di·nate** \kō-'ȯrd-(ə-)nət\ *adj* **1 :** equal in rank or order **2 :** of equal rank in a compound sentence ⟨~ clause⟩ **3 :** joining words or word groups of the same rank

**²coordinate** *n* **1 :** one of a set of numbers used in specifying the location of a point on a surface or in space **2** *pl* **:** articles (as of clothing) designed to be used together and to attain their effect through pleasing contrast

**³co·or·di·nate** \kō-'ȯrd-ᵊn-,āt\ *vb* **-nat·ed, -nat·ing** **1 :** to make or become coordinate **2 :** to work or act together harmoniously — **co·or·di·na·tion** \-,ȯrd-ᵊn-'ā-shən\ *n* — **co·or·di·na·tor** \-ᵊn-,āt-ər\ *n*

**coot** \'küt\ *n* **:** a dark-colored ducklike bird of the rail group

**coo·tie** \'küt-ē\ *n* **:** a body louse

**cop** \'käp\ *n* **:** POLICEMAN

**co·part·ner** \'kō-'pärt-nər\ *n* **:** PARTNER

**¹cope** \'kōp\ *n* **:** a long cloaklike ecclesiastical vestment

**²cope** *vb* **coped; cop·ing :** to struggle to overcome problems or difficulties

**cop·i·er** \'käp-ē-ər\ *n* **:** one that copies; *esp* **:** a machine for making copies

**co·pi·lot** \'kō-,pī-lət\ *n* **:** an assistant airplane pilot

**cop·ing** \'kō-piŋ\ *n* **:** the top layer of a wall

**co·pi·ous** \'kō-pē-əs\ *adj* **:** LAVISH, ABUNDANT — **co·pi·ous·ly** *adv* — **co·pi·ous·ness** *n*

**cop-out** \'käp-,aut\ *n* **:** an excuse for copping out; *also* **:** an act of copping out

**cop out** \(')käp-'aut\ *vb* **:** to back out (as of an unwanted responsibility)

**cop·per** \'käp-ər\ *n* **1 :** a malleable reddish metallic chemical element that is one of the best conductors of heat and electricity **2 :** something made of copper; *esp* **:** PENNY — **cop·pery** *adj*

**cop·per·as** \'käp-(ə-)rəs\ *n* **:** a green sulfate of iron used in dyeing and in making inks

**cop·per·head** \'käp-ər-,hed\ *n* **:** a largely coppery brown venomous snake esp. of uplands in the eastern U.S.

**cop·pice** \'käp-əs\ *n* **:** THICKET

**co·pra** \'kō-prə\ *n* **:** dried coconut meat yielding coconut oil

**copse** \'käps\ *n* **:** THICKET

**cop·ter** \'käp-tər\ *n* **:** HELICOPTER

**cop·u·la** \'käp-yə-lə\ *n* **:** a verb (as *be, seem, feel, grow, turn*) that links a subject with its predicate — **cop·u·la·tive** \-,lāt-iv\ *adj*

**cop·u·late** \\'käp-yə-ˌlāt\\ *vb* **-lat·ed;
-lat·ing :** to engage in sexual intercourse — **cop·u·la·tion** \\ˌkäp-yə-'lā-
shən\\ *n* — **cop·u·la·to·ry** \\'käp-yə-
lə-ˌtōr-ē\\ *adj*

¹**copy** \\'käp-ē\\ *n, pl* **cop·ies** **1 :** an
imitation or reproduction of an original
work **2 :** PATTERN **3 :** material to
be set up for printing **syn** duplicate

²**copy** *vb* **cop·ied; copy·ing** **1 :** to
make a copy of **2 :** IMITATE — **copy·
ist** *n*

**copy·book** \\'käp-ē-ˌbuk\\ *n* **:** a book
containing copies esp. of penmanship
for learners to imitate

**copy·boy** \\-ˌbȯi\\ *n* **:** one who carries
copy and runs errands (as in a newspaper office)

**copy·cat** \\-ˌkat\\ *n* **:** a slavish imitator

**copy·desk** \\-ˌdesk\\ *n* **:** the desk at
which newspaper copy is edited

**copy·read·er** \\-ˌrēd-ər\\ *n* **:** one who
edits and writes headlines for newspaper copy; *also* **:** one who reads and
corrects manuscript copy in a publishing house

¹**copy·right** \\-ˌrīt\\ *n* **:** the sole right to
reproduce, publish, and sell a literary or
artistic work

²**copyright** *vb* **:** to secure a copyright on

**copy·writ·er** \\'käp-ē-ˌrīt-ər\\ *n* **:** a
writer of advertising copy

**co·quet** *or* **co·quette** \\kō-'ket\\ *vb*
**-quet·ted; -quet·ting :** FLIRT — **co·
quet·ry** \\'kō-kə-trē, kō-'ke-trē\\ *n*

**co·quette** \\kō-'ket\\ *n* **:** FLIRT — **co·
quett·ish** *adj*

¹**cor** *abbr* corner

²**cor** *or* **corr** *abbr* **1** correct; corrected;
correction **2** correspondence; corresponding

**Cor** *abbr* Corinthians

**cor·a·cle** \\'kȯr-ə-kəl\\ *n* [W *corwgl*]
**:** a boat made of hoops covered with
horsehide or tarpaulin

**cor·al** \\'kȯr-əl\\ *n* **1 :** a stony or horny
material that forms the skeleton of
colonies of tiny sea polyps and includes
a red form used in jewelry; *also* **:** a
coral-forming polyp or polyp colony
**2 :** a deep pink color — **coral** *adj*

**coral snake** *n* **:** any of several venomous chiefly tropical New World snakes
brilliantly banded in red, black, and
yellow or white

**cor·bel** \\'kȯr-bəl\\ *n* **:** a bracket-shaped
architectural member that projects from
a wall and supports a weight

¹**cord** \\'kȯrd\\ *n* **1 :** a usu. heavy string
consisting of several strands woven or
twisted together **2 :** a long slender
anatomical structure (as a tendon or
nerve) **3 :** a cubic measure used esp.
for firewood and equal to a stack
4x4x8 feet **4 :** a rib or ridge on cloth
**5 :** a small flexible insulated electrical
cable used to connect an appliance
with a receptacle

²**cord** *vb* **1 :** to tie or furnish with a cord
**2 :** to pile (wood) in cords

**cord·age** \\'kȯrd-ij\\ *n* **:** ROPES, CORDS;
*esp* **:** ropes in the rigging of a ship

¹**cor·dial** \\'kȯr-jəl\\ *adj* [ME, fr. ML
*cordialis*, fr. L *cord-, cor* heart] **:** warmly

receptive or welcoming **:** HEARTFELT,
HEARTY — **cor·di·al·i·ty** \\ˌkȯr-jē-'al-
ət-ē, kȯr-'jal-; kȯrd-'yal-\\ *n* — **cor·
dial·ly** \\'kȯr-jə-lē\\ *adv*

²**cordial** *n* **1 :** a stimulating medicine or
drink **2 :** LIQUEUR

**cor·dil·le·ra** \\ˌkȯrd-ᵊl-'(y)er-ə, kȯr-
'dil-ə-rə\\ *n* **:** a group of mountain
ranges — **cor·dil·le·ran** *adj*

**cord·ite** \\'kȯr-ˌdīt\\ *n* **:** a smokeless
gunpowder composed of nitroglycerin,
guncotton, and a stabilizing jelly

**cord·less** \\'kȯrd-ləs\\ *adj* **:** having no
cord; *esp* **:** powered by a battery ⟨∼
tools⟩

**cor·do·ba** \\'kȯrd-ə-bə, -ə-və\\ *n* — see
MONEY table

**cor·don** \\'kȯrd-ᵊn\\ *n* **1 :** an ornamental cord **2 :** an encircling line
composed of individual units **:**
**cordon** *vb*

**cor·do·van** \\'kȯrd-ə-vən\\ *n* **:** a soft
fine-grained leather

**cor·du·roy** \\'kȯrd-ə-ˌrȯi\\ *n, pl* **-roys**
**:** a heavy ribbed fabric; *also, pl* **:** trousers of this material

**cord·wain·er** \\'kȯrd-ˌwā-nər\\ *n*
**:** SHOEMAKER

¹**core** \\'kōr\\ *n* **1 :** the central usu. inedible part of some fruits (as the apple);
*also* **:** an inmost part of something
**2 :** GIST, ESSENCE

²**core** *vb* **cored; cor·ing :** to take out
the core of — **cor·er** *n*

**CORE** \\'kōr\\ *abbr* Congress of Racial
Equality

**co·re·spon·dent** \\ˌkō-ri-'spän-dənt\\
*n* **:** a person named as guilty of adultery
with the defendant in a divorce suit

**co·ri·an·der** \\'kȯr-ē-ˌan-dər\\ *n* **:** an
herb related to the carrot; *also* **:** its
aromatic dried fruit used as a flavoring

¹**cork** \\'kȯrk\\ *n* **1 :** the tough elastic
bark of a European oak (**cork oak**)
used esp. for stoppers and insulation;
*also* **:** a stopper of this **2 :** a tissue
making up most of the bark of a woody
plant — **corky** *adj*

²**cork** *vb* **:** to furnish with or stop up with
cork or a cork

**cork·screw** \\'kȯrk-ˌskrü\\ *n* **:** a device
for drawing corks from bottles

**corm** \\'kȯrm\\ *n* **:** a thick rounded
underground stem base with membranous or scaly leaves and buds that
acts as a vegetative reproductive
structure

**cor·mo·rant** \\'kȯrm-(ə-)rənt, 'kȯr-mə-
ˌrant\\ *n* [ME *cormeraunt*, fr. MF
*cormorant*, fr. OF *cormareng*, fr. *corp*
raven + *marenc* of the sea, fr. L
*marinus*] **:** a dark seabird used in the
Orient to catch fish

¹**corn** \\'kȯrn\\ *n* **1 :** the seeds of a cereal
grass and esp. of the chief cereal crop
of a region; *also* **:** a cereal grass
**2 :** INDIAN CORN **3 :** sweet corn served
as a vegetable

²**corn** *vb* **:** to salt (as beef) in brine and
preservatives

³**corn** *n* **:** a local hardening and thickening of skin (as on a toe)

**corn bread** *n* **:** bread made with cornmeal

**corn·cob** \-ˌkäb\ *n* : the axis on which the kernels of Indian corn are arranged

**corn·crib** \-ˌkrib\ *n* : a crib for storing ears of Indian corn

**cor·nea** \ˈkȯr-nē-ə\ *n* : the transparent part of the coat of the eyeball covering the iris and the pupil — **cor·ne·al** *adj*

**corn earworm** *n* : a moth whose larva is esp. destructive to Indian corn

¹**cor·ner** \ˈkȯr-nər\ *n* [ME, fr. OF *cornere*, fr. *corne* horn, corner, fr. L *cornu* horn, point] **1** : the point or angle formed by the meeting of lines, edges, or sides **2** : the place where two streets come together **3** : a quiet secluded place **4** : a position from which retreat or escape is impossible **5** : control of enough of the available supply (as of a commodity) to permit manipulation of the price

²**cor·ner** *vb* **cor·nered; cor·ner·ing** \ˈkȯrn-(ə-)riŋ\ **1** : to drive into a corner **2** : to get a corner on ⟨~ the wheat market⟩ **3** : to turn a corner

**cor·ner·stone** \ˈkȯr-nər-ˌstōn\ *n* **1** : a stone forming part of a corner in a wall; *esp* : such a stone laid with special ceremonies **2** : something of basic importance

**cor·net** \kȯr-ˈnet\ *n* : a brass band instrument resembling the trumpet

**corn flour** *n, Brit* : CORNSTARCH

**corn·flow·er** \ˈkȯrn-ˌflau̇(-ə)r\ *n* : a pink-, blue-, or white-flowered garden plant related to the daisies

**cor·nice** \ˈkȯr-nəs\ *n* : the horizontal projecting part crowning the wall of a building

**corn·meal** \ˈkȯrn-ˈmēl, -ˌmēl\ *n* : meal ground from corn

**corn snow** *n* : granular snow formed by alternate thawing and freezing

**corn·stalk** \ˈkȯrn-ˌstȯk\ *n* : a stalk of Indian corn

**corn·starch** \-ˌstärch\ *n* : a starch made from corn and used in cookery as a thickening agent

**corn syrup** *n* : a syrup obtained by partial hydrolysis of cornstarch

**cor·nu·co·pia** \ˌkȯr-n(y)ə-ˈkō-pē-ə\ *n* [LL, fr. L *cornu copiae* horn of plenty] : a goat's horn shown filled with fruits and grain emblematic of abundance

**corny** \ˈkȯr-nē\ *adj* **corn·i·er; -est** : tiresomely simple or sentimental

**co·rol·la** \kə-ˈräl-ə\ *n* : the petals of a flower

**cor·ol·lary** \ˈkȯr-ə-ˌler-ē\ *n, pl* **-lar·ies** **1** : a deduction from a proposition already proved true **2** : CONSEQUENCE, RESULT

**co·ro·na** \kə-ˈrō-nə\ *n* **1** : a colored ring surrounding the sun or moon; *esp* : a shining ring around the sun seen during eclipses **2** : a faint glow adjacent to the surface of a conductor at high voltage

**cor·o·nach** \ˈkȯr-ə-nək\ *n* : DIRGE

**cor·o·nal** \ˈkȯr-ən-ᵊl\ *n* : a circlet for the head

¹**cor·o·nary** \ˈkȯr-ə-ˌner-ē\ *adj* : of or relating to the heart or its blood vessels

²**coronary** *n, pl* **-nar·ies** : coronary disease

**coronary thrombosis** *n* : the blocking by a thrombus of one of the arteries supplying the heart tissues

**cor·o·na·tion** \ˌkȯr-ə-ˈnā-shən\ *n* : the ceremony attending the crowning of a monarch

**cor·o·ner** \ˈkȯr-ə-nər\ *n* : a public official whose chief duty is to investigate the causes of deaths possibly not due to natural causes

**cor·o·net** \ˌkȯr-ə-ˈnet\ *n* **1** : a small crown indicating rank lower than sovereignty **2** : an ornamental band worn around the temples

**corp** *abbr* **1** corporal **2** corporation

¹**cor·po·ral** \ˈkȯr-p(ə-)rəl\ *adj* : BODILY PHYSICAL ⟨~ punishment⟩

²**corporal** *n* : a noncommissioned officer (as in the army) ranking next below a sergeant

**cor·po·rate** \ˈkȯr-p(ə-)rət\ *adj* **1** : combined into one body **2** : INCORPORATED; *also* : belonging to an incorporated body

**cor·po·ra·tion** \ˌkȯr-pə-ˈrā-shən\ *n* **1** : a political body legally authorized to act as a person **2** : a legal creation authorized to act with the rights and liabilities of a person ⟨a business ~⟩

**cor·po·re·al** \kȯr-ˈpōr-ē-əl\ *adj* **1** : PHYSICAL, MATERIAL **2** : BODILY — **cor·po·re·al·i·ty** \(ˌ)kȯr-ˌpōr-ē-ˈal-ət-ē\ *n* — **cor·po·re·al·ly** \-ē-ə-lē\ *adv*

**corps** \ˈkȯr\ *n, pl* **corps** \ˈkȯrz\ **1** : an organized subdivision of a country's military forces **2** : a group acting under common direction

**corpse** \ˈkȯrps\ *n* : a dead body

**corps·man** \ˈkȯr(z)-mən\ *n* : an enlisted man trained to give first aid and minor medical treatment

**cor·pu·lence** \ˈkȯr-pyə-ləns\ *or* **cor·pu·len·cy** \-lən-sē\ *n* : excessive fatness — **cor·pu·lent** \-lənt\ *adj*

**cor·pus** \ˈkȯr-pəs\ *n, pl* **cor·po·ra** \-pə-rə\ **1** : BODY; *esp* : CORPSE **2** : a body of writings

**cor·pus·cle** \ˈkȯr-(ˌ)pəs-əl\ *n* **1** : a minute particle **2** : a living cell; *esp* : one (as in blood or cartilage) not aggregated into continuous tissues — **cor·pus·cu·lar** \kȯr-ˈpəs-kyə-lər\ *adj*

**cor·pus de·lic·ti** \ˌkȯr-pəs-di-ˈlik-ˌtī, -tē\ *n, pl* **corpora delicti** [NL, lit., body of the crime] : the substantial fact establishing that a crime has been committed; *also* : the body of a victim of murder

**corr** *abbr* — see COR

**cor·ral** \kə-ˈral\ *n* [Sp, fr. (assumed) VL *currale* enclosure for vehicles, fr. L *currus* cart, fr. *currere* to run] : an enclosure for confining or capturing animals; *also* : an enclosure for defense — **corral** *vb*

¹**cor·rect** \kə-ˈrekt\ *vb* **1** : to make right **2** : REPROVE, CHASTISE — **cor·rec·tion** \-ˈrek-shən\ *n* — **cor·rec·tion·al** \-ˈrek-sh(ə-)nəl\ *adj* — **cor·rec·tive** \-ˈrek-tiv\ *adj*

²**correct** *adj* **1** : agreeing with fact or truth **2** : conforming to a conventional

standard — **cor·rect·able** adj —
**cor·rect·ly** \kə-'rek-(t)lē\ adv —
**cor·rect·ness** \-'rek(t)-nəs\ n

**cor·re·late** \'kȯr-ə-ˌlāt\ vb -lat·ed;
-lat·ing : to connect in a systematic
way : establish the mutual relations
of — **cor·re·late** \-lət, -ˌlāt\ n — **cor·re·la·tion** \ˌkȯr-ə-'lā-shən\ n

**cor·rel·a·tive** \kə-'rel-ət-iv\ adj 1
: reciprocally related 2 : regularly used
together (as either and or) — **correla·tive** n

**cor·re·spond** \ˌkȯr-ə-'spänd\ vb 1
: to be in agreement : SUIT, MATCH
2 : to communicate by letter — **cor·re·spond·ing·ly** \-'spän-diŋ-lē\ adv

**cor·re·spon·dence** \-'spän-dəns\ n
1 : agreement between particular things
2 : communication by letters; also : the
letters exchanged

¹**cor·re·spon·dent** \-'spän-dənt\ adj
1 : SIMILAR 2 : FITTING, CONFORMING

²**correspondent** n 1 : something that
corresponds to some other thing 2 : a
person with whom one communicates
by letter 3 : a person employed to
contribute news regularly from a place

**cor·ri·dor** \'kȯr-əd-ər, -ə-ˌdȯr\ n
1 : a passageway into which compartments or rooms open (as in a hotel or
school) 2 : a narrow strip of land esp.
through foreign-held territory 3 : an
elongated area of dense population
including two or more major cities

**cor·ri·gen·dum** \ˌkȯr-ə-'jen-dəm\ n,
pl -da \-də\ : an error in a printed
work discovered after printing and
shown with its correction on a separate
sheet

**cor·ri·gi·ble** \'kȯr-ə-jə-bəl\ adj : CORRECTABLE

**cor·rob·o·rate** \kə-'räb-ə-ˌrāt\ vb
-rat·ed; -rat·ing [L corroborare, fr.
robur strength] : to support with
evidence : CONFIRM — **cor·rob·o·ra·tion** \-ˌräb-ə-'rā-shən\ n — **cor·rob·o·ra·tive** \-'räb-ə-ˌrāt-iv, -'räb-
(ə-)rət-\ adj — **cor·rob·o·ra·to·ry** \-'räb-(ə-)rə-ˌtōr-ē\ adj

**cor·rode** \kə-'rōd\ vb cor·rod·ed;
cor·rod·ing : to eat or be eaten away
gradually (as by action of rust or of a
chemical) — **cor·ro·sion** \-'rō-zhən\
n — **cor·ro·sive** \-'rō-siv\ adj or n

**cor·ru·gate** \'kȯr-ə-ˌgāt\ vb -gat·ed;
-gat·ing : to form into wrinkles or
ridges and grooves — **cor·ru·gat·ed**
adj — **cor·ru·ga·tion** \ˌkȯr-ə-'gā-shən\ n

¹**cor·rupt** \kə-'rəpt\ vb 1 : to make evil
: DEPRAVE; esp : BRIBE 2 : TAINT —
**cor·rupt·ible** adj — **cor·rup·tion** \-'rəp-shən\ n

²**corrupt** adj : DEPRAVED, DEBASED

**cor·sage** \kȯr-'säzh, -'säj\ n [F, bust,
bodice, fr. OF, bust, fr. cors body, fr. L
corpus] 1 : the waist of a woman's
dress 2 : a bouquet worn or carried
by a woman

**cor·sair** \'kȯr-ˌsaər\ n 1 : PIRATE
2 : a pirate's ship

**cor·set** \'kȯr-sət\ n : a stiffened undergarment worn by women to give shape
to the waist and hips

**cor·tege** also **cor·tège** \kȯr-'tezh,
'kȯr-ˌtezh\ n : PROCESSION; esp : a
funeral procession

**cor·tex** \'kȯr-ˌteks\ n, pl cor·ti·ces
\'kȯrt-ə-ˌsēz\ or cor·tex·es : an
outer or covering layer of an organism
or one of its parts ⟨the kidney ∼⟩ ⟨∼ of
a plant stem⟩; esp : the outer layer of
gray matter of the brain — **cor·ti·cal**
\'kȯrt-i-kəl\ adj

**cor·ti·sone** \'kȯrt-ə-ˌsōn, -ˌzōn\ n : an
adrenal hormone used in treating
arthritis

**co·run·dum** \kə-'rən-dəm\ n : a very
hard aluminum-containing mineral used
as an abrasive or in some crystalline
forms as a gem

**cor·us·cate** \'kȯr-ə-ˌskāt\ vb -cat·ed; -cat·ing : FLASH, SPARKLE —
**cor·us·ca·tion** \ˌkȯr-ə-'skā-shən\ n

**cor·vette** \kȯr-'vet\ n 1 : a naval
sailing ship smaller than a frigate
2 : a lightly armed escort ship smaller
than a destroyer

**co·ry·za** \kə-'rī-zə\ n : an inflammatory disorder of the upper respiratory
tract : the common cold

**COS** abbr 1 cash on shipment 2 chief
of staff

**co·sig·na·to·ry** \kō-'sig-nə-ˌtōr-ē\ n
: a joint signer

**co·sign·er** \'kō-ˌsī-nər\ n : COSIGNATORY; esp : a joint signer of a promissory note

¹**cos·met·ic** \käz-'met-ik\ n : an external application intended to beautify
the complexion

²**cosmetic** adj [Gk kosmētikos skilled
in adornment, fr. kosmein to arrange,
adorn, fr. kosmos order, ornament,
universe] : relating to beautifying the
physical appearance

**cos·me·tol·o·gist** \ˌkäz-mə-'täl-ə-jəst\ n : one who gives beauty treatments — **cos·me·tol·o·gy** \-jē\ n

**cos·mic** \'käz-mik\ also **cos·mi·cal**
\-mi-kəl\ adj 1 : of or relating to the
cosmos 2 : VAST, GRAND — **cos·mi·cal·ly** \-mi-k(ə-)lē\ adv

**cosmic ray** n : a stream of very penetrating and high speed atomic nuclei
that enter the earth's atmosphere from
outer space

**cos·mo·chem·is·try** \ˌkäz-mō-'kem-ə-strē\ n : chemistry dealing with the
chemical composition and changes in
the universe — **cos·mo·chem·i·cal**
\-'kem-i-kəl\ adj

**cos·mog·o·ny** \käz-'mäg-ə-nē\ n : the
origin or creation of the world or universe — **cos·mo·gon·ic** \ˌkäz-mə-'gän-ik\ adj

**cos·mol·o·gy** \käz-'mäl-ə-jē\ n, pl
-gies : a study dealing with the origin
and structure of the universe — **cos·mo·log·i·cal** \ˌkäz-mə-'läj-i-kəl\ adj
— **cos·mol·o·gist** \käz-'mäl-ə-jəst\ n

**cos·mo·naut** \'käz-mə-ˌnȯt\ n : ASTRONAUT; specif : a Soviet astronaut

**cos·mop·o·lis** \käz-'mäp-ə-ləs\ n : a
cosmopolitan city — **cos·mop·o·lite**
\-ˌlīt\ n

**cos·mo·pol·i·tan** \ˌkäz-mə-'päl-ət-ᵊn\
adj : belonging to all the world : not

local **syn** universal — **cosmopolitan** n

**cos·mos** \'käz-məs, 1 also -,mōs, -,mäs\ n 1 : UNIVERSE 2 : a tall garden herb related to the daisies

**co·spon·sor** \'kō-,spän-sər, -'spän-\ n : a joint sponsor — **cosponsor** vb

**cos·sack** \'käs-,ak, -ək\ n [Russ kazak & Ukrainian kozak, fr. Turk kazak free person] : a member of a group of frontiersmen of southern Russia organized as cavalry in the czarist army

¹**cost** \'kȯst\ n 1 : the amount paid or asked for a thing : PRICE 2 : the loss or penalty incurred in gaining something 3 : OUTLAY

²**cost** vb **cost**; **cost·ing** 1 : to require a specified amount in payment 2 : to cause to pay, suffer, or lose

**co·star** \'kō-,stär\ n : one of two leading players in a motion picture or film — **co·star** vb

**cos·tive** \'käs-tiv\ adj : affected with or causing constipation

**cost·ly** \'kȯst-lē\ adj **cost·li·er; -est** : of great cost or value : not cheap **syn** dear, valuable — **cost·li·ness** n

**cos·tume** \'käs-,t(y)üm\ n : CLOTHES, ATTIRE; also : a suit or dress characteristic of a period or country — **cos·tum·er** \'käs-,t(y)ü-mər\ n — **cos·tu·mi·er** \käs-'t(y)ü-mē-ər\ n

**costume jewelry** n : inexpensive jewelry

**co·sy** \'kō-zē\ var of COZY

¹**cot** \'kät\ n : a small house : COTTAGE

²**cot** n : a small often collapsible bed

**cote** \'kōt, 'kät\ n : a small shed or coop (as for sheep or doves)

**co·te·rie** \'kōt-ə-,rē, ,kōt-ə-'rē\ n : an intimate often exclusive group of persons with a common interest

**co·ter·mi·nal** \kō-'ter-mən-°l\ adj : having the same or coincident boundaries

**co·ter·mi·nous** \-mə-nəs\ adj : coextensive in scope or duration

**co·til·lion** \kō-'til-yən\ n 1 : an elaborate dance with frequent changing of partners executed under the leadership of one couple at formal balls 2 : a formal ball

**cot·tage** \'kät-ij\ n : a small house — **cot·tag·er** n

**cottage cheese** n : a soft uncured cheese made from soured skim milk

**cot·ter** or **cot·tar** \'kät-ər\ n : a farm laborer occupying a cottage and often a small holding

**cotter pin** n : a metal strip bent into a pin whose ends can be flared after insertion through a hole

**cot·ton** \'kät-°n\ n [ME coton, fr. MF, fr. Ar quṭn] : a soft fibrous usu. white substance composed of hairs attached to the seeds of a plant related to the mallow; also : thread or cloth made of cotton — **cot·tony** adj

**cot·ton·mouth** \'kät-°n-,maůth\ n : WATER MOCCASIN

**cot·ton·seed** \-,sēd\ n : the seed of the cotton plant yielding a protein-rich meal and a fixed oil (**cottonseed oil**) used esp. in cooking

**cot·ton·tail** \-,tāl\ n : an American rabbit with a white-tufted tail

**cot·ton·wood** \-,wůd\ n : a poplar with cottony hair on its seed

**cot·y·le·don** \,kät-°l-'ēd-°n\ n : the first leaf or one of the first pair or whorl of leaves developed by a seed plant — **cot·y·le·don·ary** \-,er-ē\ adj

¹**couch** \'kaůch\ vb 1 : to lie or place on a couch 2 : to phrase in a certain manner

²**couch** n : a bed or sofa for resting or sleeping

**couch·ant** \'kaů-chənt\ adj : lying down with the head raised ⟨coat of arms with lion ~⟩

**cou·gar** \'kü-gər, -,gär\ n, pl **cougars** also **cougar** [F couguar, fr. NL cuguacuarana, modif. of Tupi (a Brazilian Indian language) suasuarana, lit., false deer, fr. suasú deer + rana false] : a large tawny wild American cat

**cough** \'kȯf\ vb : to force air from the lungs with short sharp noises; also : to expel by coughing — **cough** n

**could** \kəd, (')kůd\ past of CAN — used as an auxiliary in the past or as a polite or less forceful alternative to can in the present

**cou·lee** \'kü-lē\ n 1 : a small stream 2 : a dry stream bed 3 : GULLY

**cou·lomb** \'kü-,läm, -,lōm\ n : a unit of electric charge equal to the electricity transferred by a current of one ampere in one second

**coun·cil** \'kaůn-səl\ n 1 : ASSEMBLY, MEETING 2 : an official body of lawmakers ⟨a city ~⟩ — **coun·cil·lor** or **coun·cil·or** \-s(ə-)lər\ n — **coun·cil·man** \-səl-mən\ n — **coun·cil·wom·an** \-,wům-ən\ n

¹**coun·sel** \'kaůn-səl\ n 1 : ADVICE 2 : deliberation together 3 : a plan of action 4 pl **counsel** : LAWYER

²**counsel** vb **-seled** or **-selled**; **-sel·ing** or **-sel·ling** \-s(ə-)liŋ\ 1 : ADVISE, RECOMMEND 2 : to consult together

**coun·sel·or** or **coun·sel·lor** \'kaůn-s(ə-)lər\ n 1 : ADVISER 2 : LAWYER

¹**count** \'kaůnt\ vb [ME counten, fr. MF compter, fr. L computare, fr. com- with + putare to consider] 1 : to name or indicate one by one in order to find the total number 2 : to recite numbers in order 3 : CONSIDER, ESTEEM 4 : RELY ⟨you can ~ on him⟩ 5 : to be of value or account — **count·able** adj

²**count** n 1 : the act of counting; also : the total obtained by counting 2 : a particular charge in an indictment or legal declaration

³**count** n [MF comte, fr. LL comes, fr. L, companion, one of the imperial court, fr. com- with + ire to go] : a European nobleman whose rank corresponds to that of a British earl

**count·down** \'kaůnt-,daůn\ n : an audible backward counting off (as in seconds) to indicate the time remaining before an event (as the launching of a rocket) — **count down** \-'daůn\ vb

¹**coun·te·nance** \'kaůnt-(°-)nəns\ n

1 : the human face esp. as an indicator of mood or character  2 : FAVOR, APPROVAL

²**countenance** *vb* -nanced; -nancing : SANCTION, TOLERATE

¹**count·er** \'kaünt-ər\ *n* 1 : a piece (as of metal or ivory) used in reckoning or in games  2 : a level surface over which business is transacted, food is served, or work is conducted

²**count·er** *n* : a device for indicating a number or amount

³**coun·ter** *vb* : to act in opposition to

⁴**coun·ter** *adv* : in an opposite direction : CONTRARY

⁵**coun·ter** *n* 1 : OPPOSITE, CONTRARY  2 : an answering or offsetting force or blow

⁶**coun·ter** *adj* : CONTRARY, OPPOSITE

**coun·ter·act** \,kaünt-ər-'akt\ *vb* : to lessen the force of : OFFSET — **coun·ter·ac·tive** \-'ak-tiv\ *adj*

**coun·ter·at·tack** \'kaünt-ər-ə-,tak\ *n* : an attack made to oppose an enemy's attack — **counterattack** *vb*

¹**coun·ter·bal·ance** \'kaünt-ər-,bal-əns\ *n* : a weight or influence that balances another

²**counterbalance** \,kaünt-ər-'bal-əns\ *vb* : to oppose with equal weight or influence

**coun·ter·claim** \'kaünt-ər-,klām\ *n* : an opposing claim esp. in law

**coun·ter·clock·wise** \,kaünt-ər-'kläk-,wīz\ *adv* : in a direction opposite to that in which the hands of a clock rotate — **counterclockwise** *adj*

**coun·ter·cul·ture** \'kaünt-ər-,kəl-chər\ *n* : a culture esp. of the young with values and mores that run counter to those of established society

**coun·ter·es·pi·o·nage** \,kaünt-ər-'es-pē-ə-,näzh, -nij\ *n* : the attempt to discover and defeat enemy espionage

¹**coun·ter·feit** \'kaünt-ər-,fit\ *vb* 1 : to copy or imitate in order to deceive  2 : PRETEND, FEIGN — **coun·ter·feit·er** *n*

²**counterfeit** *adj* : SHAM, SPURIOUS; *also* : FORGED

³**counterfeit** *n* : something made to imitate another thing with a view to defraud  **syn** fraud, sham, fake, imposture, deceit, deception

**coun·ter·in·sur·gen·cy** \,kaünt-ər-in-'sər-jən-sē\ *n* : military activity designed to deal with insurgents

**coun·ter·in·tel·li·gence** \,kaünt-ər-in-'tel-ə-jəns\ *n* : organized activities of an intelligence service designed to counter the activities of an enemy's intelligence service

**count·er·man** \'kaünt-ər-,man, -mən\ *n* : one who tends a counter

**coun·ter·mand** \'kaünt-ər-,mand\ *vb* : to withdraw (an order already given) by a contrary order

**coun·ter·mea·sure** \-,mezh-ər\ *n* : an action undertaken to counter another

**coun·ter·of·fen·sive** \-ə-,fen-siv\ *n* : a military offensive undertaken by a force previously on the defensive

**coun·ter·pane** \'kaünt-ər-,pān\ *n* : BEDSPREAD

**coun·ter·part** \-,pärt\ *n* : a person or thing very closely like or corresponding to another person or thing

**coun·ter·point** \-,pöint\ *n* : music in which one melody is accompanied by one or more other melodies all woven into a harmonious whole

**coun·ter·poise** \-,pöiz\ *n* : COUNTERBALANCE

**coun·ter·rev·o·lu·tion** \,kaünt-ə(r)-,rev-ə-'lü-shən\ *n* : a revolution opposed to a former revolution

¹**coun·ter·sign** \'kaünt-ər-,sīn\ *n* 1 : a confirmatory signature added to a writing already signed by another person  2 : a secret signal that must be given by a person who wishes to pass a guard

²**countersign** *vb* : to add a confirmatory signature to — **coun·ter·sig·na·ture** \,kaünt-ər-'sig-nə-,chür\ *n*

**coun·ter·sink** \'kaünt-ər-,siŋk\ *vb* -sunk \-,səŋk\; -sink·ing : to form a flaring depression around the top of a drilled hole; *also* : to sink (a screw or bolt) in such a depression — **countersink** *n*

**coun·ter·spy** \-,spī\ *n* : a spy engaged in counterespionage

**coun·ter·ten·or** \-,ten-ər\ *n* : a tenor with an unusually high range

**coun·ter·vail** \,kaünt-ər-'vāl\ *vb* : COUNTERACT

**coun·ter·weight** \'kaünt-ər-,wāt\ *n* : COUNTERBALANCE

**count·ess** \'kaünt-əs\ *n* 1 : the wife or widow of a count or an earl  2 : a woman holding the rank of a count or an earl in her own right

**count·ing·house** \'kaünt-iŋ-,haüs\ *n* : a building or office for keeping books and conducting business

**count·less** \'kaünt-ləs\ *adj* : INNUMERABLE

**coun·tri·fied** *also* **coun·try·fied** \'kən-tri-,fīd\ *adj* 1 : RURAL, RUSTIC  2 : UNSOPHISTICATED

¹**coun·try** \'kən-trē\ *n, pl* **countries** [ME *contree*, fr. OF *contrée*, fr. ML *contrata*, fr. L *contra* against, on the opposite side] 1 : REGION, DISTRICT  2 : the territory of a nation  3 : FATHERLAND  4 : NATION  5 : rural regions as opposed to towns and cities

²**country** *adj* 1 : RURAL  2 : of or relating to country music (a ~ singer)

**country and western** *n* : COUNTRY MUSIC

**country club** *n* : a suburban club for social life and recreation

**coun·try-dance** \'kən-trē-,dans\ *n* : an English dance in which partners face each other esp. in rows

**coun·try·man** \'kən-trē-mən, 2 *often* -,man\ *n* 1 : an inhabitant of a certain country; *also* : COMPATRIOT  2 : one raised in the country : RUSTIC

**country music** *n* : music derived from or imitating the folk style of the southern U.S. or of the Western cowboy

**coun·try·side** \'kən-trē-,sīd\ *n* : a rural area or its people

**coun·ty** \'kaünt-ē\ *n, pl* **counties**

**1 :** the domain of a count or earl **2 :** a territorial division of a country or state for purposes of local government

**coup** \'kü\ *n, pl* **coups** \'küz\ **1 :** a brilliant sudden stroke or stratagem **2 :** COUP D'ETAT

**coup de grace** \,küd-ə-'gräs\ *n, pl* **coups de grace** \,küd-ə-\ [F *coup de grâce*, lit., stroke of mercy] **:** a deathblow or final decisive stroke or event

**coup d'etat** \,küd-ə-'tä\ *n, pl* **coups d'etat** \,küd-ə-'tä(z)\ **:** a sudden violent overthrow of a government by a small group

**cou·pé** *or* **coupe** \kü-'pā, *2 often* 'küp\ *n* [F *coupé*, fr. *couper* to cut] **1 :** a closed carriage for two persons inside with an outside seat for the driver in front **2** *usu coupe* **:** a 2-door automobile with an enclosed body and separate luggage compartment

¹**cou·ple** \'kəp-əl\ *vb* **cou·pled; cou·pling** \-(ə-)liŋ\ **:** to link together

²**couple** *n* **1 :** BOND, TIE **2 :** PAIR **3 :** two persons closely associated; *esp* **:** a man and a woman married or otherwise paired

**cou·plet** \'kəp-lət\ *n* **:** two successive rhyming lines of verse

**cou·pling** \'kəp-liŋ (*usual for* 2), -ə-liŋ\ *n* **1 :** CONNECTION **2 :** a device for connecting two parts or things

**cou·pon** \'k(y)ü-,pän\ *n* **1 :** a certificate attached to a bond showing interest due and designed to be cut off and presented for payment **2 :** a certificate given to a purchaser of goods and redeemable in merchandise, cash, or services; *also* **:** a similar ticket or form surrendered for other purposes ⟨a ration ∼⟩ **3 :** a part of an advertisement to be cut off for use as an order blank or inquiry form

**cour·age** \'kər-ij\ *n* **:** ability to conquer fear or despair **:** BRAVERY, VALOR — **cou·ra·geous** \kə-'rā-jəs\ *adj* — **cou·ra·geous·ly** *adv*

**cou·ri·er** \'kùr-ē-ər, 'kər-ē-\ *n* **1 :** one who bears messages or information esp. for the diplomatic or military services **2 :** a tourists' guide

¹**course** \'kōrs\ *n* **1 :** PROGRESS, PASSAGE; *also* **:** direction of progress **2 :** the ground or path over which something moves **3 :** the part of a meal served at one time **4 :** an ordered series of acts or proceedings **:** sequence of events **5 :** method of procedure **:** CONDUCT, BEHAVIOR **6 :** a series of instruction periods dealing with a subject **7 :** the series of studies leading to graduation from a school or college — **of course :** as might be expected

²**course** *vb* **coursed; cours·ing 1 :** to hunt with dogs ⟨∼ a rabbit⟩ **2 :** to run or go speedily

**cours·er** \'kōr-sər\ *n* **:** a swift or spirited horse

¹**court** \'kōrt\ *n* **1 :** the residence of a sovereign or similar dignitary **2 :** a sovereign and his officials and advisers as a governing power **3 :** an assembly of the retinue of a sovereign **4 :** an open space enclosed by a building or

buildings **5 :** a space walled or marked off for playing a game (as tennis or basketball) **6 :** the place where justice is administered; *also* **:** a judicial body or a meeting of a judicial body **7 :** HOMAGE, COURTSHIP

²**court** *vb* **1 :** to try to gain the favor of **2 :** WOO **3 :** ATTRACT, TEMPT

**cour·te·ous** \'kərt-ē-əs\ *adj* **:** marked by respect for others **:** CIVIL, POLITE — **cour·te·ous·ly** *adv*

**cour·te·san** \'kōrt-ə-zən, 'kərt-\ *n* **:** PROSTITUTE

**cour·te·sy** \'kərt-ə-sē\ *n, pl* **-sies 1 :** courteous behavior **:** POLITENESS **2 :** a favor courteously performed

**court·house** \'kōrt-,haùs\ *n* **1 :** a building in a town or city for holding courts of law **2 :** a building for housing county offices

**court·ier** \'kōrt-ē-ər, 'kōrt-yər\ *n* **:** a person in attendance at a royal court

**court·ly** \'kōrt-lē\ *adj* **court·li·er; -est :** REFINED, ELEGANT, POLITE **syn** courteous, civil — **court·li·ness** *n*

**court–mar·tial** \'kōrt-,mär-shəl\ *n, pl* **courts–martial :** a military or naval court for trial of offenses against military or naval law; *also* **:** a trial by this court — **court–martial** *vb*

**court·room** \-,rüm, -,rùm\ *n* **:** a room in which a court of law is held

**court·ship** \-,ship\ *n* **:** the act of courting **:** WOOING

**court·yard** \-,yärd\ *n* **:** an enclosure attached to a house or palace

**cous·in** \'kəz-ᵊn\ *n* [ME *cosin*, fr. OF, fr. L *consobrinus*, fr. *com-* with + *sobrinus* cousin on the mother's side, fr. *soror* sister] **:** a child of one's uncle or aunt

**cou·ture** \kü-'tùr, -'tȳr\ *n* **:** the business of designing fashionable custom-made women's clothing; *also* **:** the designers and establishments engaged in this business

**cou·tu·ri·er** \kü-'tùr-ē-ər, -ē-,ā\ *n* **:** the owner of an establishment engaged in couture

**co·va·lence** \(')kō-'vā-ləns\ *n* **:** valence characterized by the sharing of electrons — **co·va·lent** \-lənt\ *adj* — **co·va·lent·ly** *adv*

**cove** \'kōv\ *n* **1 :** a trough for lights at the upper part of a wall **2 :** a small sheltered inlet or bay

**co·ven** \'kəv-ən, 'kō-vən\ *n* **:** an assembly or band of witches

**cov·e·nant** \'kəv-(ə-)nənt\ *n* **:** a formal binding agreement **:** COMPACT — **cov·e·nant** \'kəv-(ə-)nənt, -ə-,nant\ *vb*

¹**cov·er** \'kəv-ər\ *vb* **cov·ered; cov·er·ing** \'kəv-(ə-)riŋ\ **1 :** to place something over or upon **2 :** CLOTHE **3 :** to bring or hold within range of a firearm **4 :** PROTECT, SHIELD **5 :** INCLUDE, COMPRISE **6 :** HIDE, CONCEAL **7 :** to have as one's field of activity ⟨one salesman ∼s the state⟩ **8 :** to buy (stocks) in order to have them for delivery on a previous short sale

²**cover** *n* **1 :** something that protects or shelters **2 :** LID, TOP **3 :** CASE, BINDING

4 : SCREEN, DISGUISE  5 : TABLECLOTH
6 : a cloth used on a bed  7 : an envelope or wrapper for mail

**cov·er·age** \'kəv-(ə-)rij\ n 1 : the act or fact of covering  2 : the total group covered : SCOPE

**cov·er·all** \'kəv-ər-,ȯl\ n : a one-piece outer garment worn to protect one's clothes — usu. used in pl.

**cover charge** n : a charge made by a restaurant or nightclub in addition to the charge for food and drink

**cover crop** n : a crop planted to prevent soil erosion and to provide humus

**cov·er·let** \'kəv-ər-lət\ n : BEDSPREAD

¹**cov·ert** \'kō-(,)vərt, 'kəv-ərt\ adj 1 : HIDDEN, SECRET  2 : SHELTERED — **cov·ert·ly** adv

²**co·vert** \'kəv-ərt, 'kō-vərt\ n 1 : a secret or sheltered place; esp : a thicket sheltering game  2 : a feather covering the bases of the quills of the wings and tail of a bird  3 : a wool or silk-and-wool cloth usu. of mixed-color yarns

**cov·er·up** \'kəv-ər-,əp\ n : a device for masking or concealing

**cov·et** \'kəv-ət\ vb : to desire enviously (what belongs to another) — **cov·et·ous** adj — **cov·et·ous·ness** n

**cov·ey** \'kəv-ē\ n, pl **coveys** [ME, fr. MF covee, fr. OF, fr. cover to sit on, brood over, fr. L cubare to lie]  1 : a bird with her brood of young  2 : a small flock (as of quail)

¹**cow** \'kau̇\ n 1 : the mature female of cattle or of an animal (as the moose) of which the male is called bull  2 : a domestic bovine animal irrespective of sex or age

²**cow** vb : INTIMIDATE, DAUNT, OVERAWE

**cow·ard** \'kau̇-(ə)rd\ n [ME, fr. OF coart, fr. coe tail, fr. L cauda] : one who lacks courage or shows shameful fear or timidity — **coward** adj — **cow·ard·ice** \-əs\ n — **cow·ard·ly** adv or adj

**cow·bird** \'kau̇-,bərd\ n : a small No. American bird that lays its eggs in the nests of other birds

**cow·boy** \-,bȯi\ n : one (as a mounted ranch hand) who tends or drives cattle — **cow·girl** \-,gərl\ n

**cow·er** \'kau̇-(ə)r\ vb : to shrink or crouch down from fear or cold : QUAIL

**cow·hand** \'kau̇-,hand\ n : COWBOY

**cow·hide** \-,hīd\ n 1 : the hide of a cow; also : leather made from it  2 : a coarse whip of braided rawhide

**cowl** \'kau̇l\ n 1 : a monk's hood  2 : the top part of the front of the body of an automobile to which the windshield is attached

**cow·lick** \'kau̇-,lik\ n : a turned-up tuft of hair that resists control

**cowl·ing** \'kau̇-liŋ\ n : a usu. metal covering over the engine or another part of an airplane

**cow·man** \'kau̇-mən, -,man\ n : COWBOY; also : a cattle owner or rancher

**co-work·er** \'kō-,wər-kər\ n : a fellow worker

**cow·poke** \'kau̇-,pōk\ n : COWBOY

**cow pony** n : a horse trained for herding cattle

**cow·pox** \'kau̇-,päks\ n : a mild disease of the cow that when communicated to man protects against smallpox

**cow·punch·er** \-,pən-chər\ n : COWBOY

**cow·slip** \'kau̇-,slip\ n 1 : MARSH MARIGOLD  2 : a yellow-flowered European primrose

**cox·comb** \'käks-,kōm\ n : a conceited foolish person : FOP

**cox·swain** \'käk-sən, -,swān\ n : the steersman of a ship's boat or a racing shell

**coy** \'kȯi\ adj [ME, quiet, shy, fr. MF coi calm, fr. L quietus quiet] : BASHFUL, SHY; esp : pretending shyness — **coy·ly** adv — **coy·ness** n

**coy·ote** \'kī-,ōt, kī-'ōt-ē\ n, pl **coyotes** or **coyote** : a small wolf native to western No. America

**coy·pu** \'kȯi-pü\ n 1 : a So. American aquatic rodent with webbed feet and dorsal mammary glands  2 : NUTRIA

**coz·en** \'kəz-ᵊn\ vb [obs. It cozzonare, fr. It cozzone horse trader, fr. L cocio trader] : CHEAT, DEFRAUD — **coz·en·age** \-ij\ n

¹**co·zy** \'kō-zē\ adj **co·zi·er; -est** : SNUG, COMFORTABLE — **co·zi·ly** \'kō-zə-lē\ adv — **co·zi·ness** \-zē-nəs\ n

²**cozy** n, pl **cozies** : a padded covering for a vessel (as a teapot) to keep the contents hot

**cp** abbr 1 compare  2 coupon

**CP** abbr 1 chemically pure  2 command post  3 communist party

**CPA** abbr certified public accountant

**cpd** abbr compound

**CPFF** abbr cost plus fixed fee

**Cpl** abbr corporal

**CPO** abbr chief petty officer

**CPOM** abbr master chief petty officer

**CPOS** abbr senior chief petty officer

**CPS** abbr cycles per second

**CPT** abbr captain

**CQ** abbr charge of quarters

**Cr** symbol chromium

¹**crab** \'krab\ n : a crustacean with a short broad shell and small abdomen

²**crab** n : an ill-natured person

**crab apple** n : a small sour apple

**crab·bed** \'krab-əd\ adj 1 : MOROSE, PEEVISH  2 : CRAMPED, IRREGULAR

**crab·by** \'krab-ē\ adj **crab·bi·er; -est** : ILL-NATURED

**crab·grass** \'krab-,gras\ n : a creeping grass often pestiferous in turf or cultivated lands

**crab louse** n : a louse infesting the pubic region in man

¹**crack** \'krak\ vb 1 : to break with a sharp sudden sound  2 : to fail in tone or become harsh ⟨his voice ~ed⟩  3 : to break without completely separating into parts  4 : to subject (as a petroleum oil) to heat for breaking down into lighter products (as gasoline)

²**crack** n 1 : a sudden sharp noise  2 : a witty or sharp remark  3 : a narrow break or opening : FISSURE  4 : a sharp blow  5 : ATTEMPT, TRY

³**crack** adj : extremely proficient

**crack·down** \'krak-,daůn\ *n* **:** an act or instance of taking positive disciplinary action ⟨a ~ on gambling⟩ — **crack down** \-'daůn\ *vb*

**crack·er** \'krak-ər\ *n* **1 :** FIRECRACKER **2 :** a dry thin crisp bakery product made of flour and water **3** *cap* **:** a native of Georgia or Florida

**crack·er·jack** \-,jak\ *n* **:** something very excellent — **crackerjack** *adj*

**crack·le** \'krak-əl\ *vb* **crack·led; crack·ling** \-(ə-)liŋ\ **1 :** to make small sharp snapping noises **2 :** to develop fine cracks in a surface — **crackle** *n* — **crack·ly** \-(ə-)lē\ *adj*

**crack·pot** \'krak-,pät\ *n* **:** an eccentric person

**crack–up** \'krak-,əp\ *n* **:** CRASH, WRECK; *also* **:** BREAKDOWN

¹**cra·dle** \'krād-ᵊl\ *n* **1 :** a baby's bed or cot **2 :** a place of origin and early development **3 :** a scythe for mowing grain **4 :** the support for a telephone receiver

²**cradle** *vb* **cra·dled; cra·dling** \'krād-(ᵊ-)liŋ\ **1 :** to place in or as if in a cradle **2 :** NURSE, REAR

**cra·dle·song** \'krād-ᵊl-,soŋ\ *n* **:** LULLABY

**craft** \'kraft\ *n* **1 :** ART, SKILL; *also* **:** an occupation requiring special skill **2 :** CUNNING, GUILE **3** *pl usu* **craft :** a boat esp. of small size; *also* **:** AIRCRAFT, SPACECRAFT

**crafts·man** \'krafts-mən\ *n* **:** a skilled artisan — **crafts·man·ship** *n*

**crafty** \'kraf-tē\ *adj* **craft·i·er; -est :** CUNNING, DECEITFUL, SUBTLE — **craft·i·ly** \'kraf-tə-lē\ *adv* — **craft·i·ness** \-tē-nəs\ *n*

**crag** \'krag\ *n* **:** a steep rugged cliff or point of rock — **crag·gy** \-ē\ *adj*

**cram** \'kram\ *vb* **crammed; cram·ming 1 :** to eat greedily **2 :** to pack in tight ⟨JAM **3 :** to study rapidly under pressure for an examination

¹**cramp** \'kramp\ *n* **1 :** a sudden painful contraction of muscle **2 :** sharp abdominal pains

²**cramp** *vb* **1 :** to affect with cramp **2 :** to restrain from free action **:** HAMPER **3 :** to turn (the front wheels) sharply to the side

**cran·ber·ry** \'kran-,ber-ē, -b(ə-)rē\ *n* **:** the red acid berry of a trailing plant related to the heaths; *also* **:** this plant

¹**crane** \'krān\ *n* **1 :** a tall wading bird related to the rails **2 :** a machine for lifting and carrying heavy objects

²**crane** *vb* **craned; cran·ing :** to stretch one's neck to see better

**crane fly** *n* **:** any of numerous long-legged slender two-winged flies that do not bite

**cra·ni·um** \'krā-nē-əm\ *n, pl* **-ni·ums** or **-nia** \-nē-ə\ **:** SKULL; *esp* **:** the part enclosing the brain — **cra·ni·al** \-əl\ *adj*

¹**crank** \'kraŋk\ *n* **1 :** a bent part of an axle or shaft or an arm at right angles to the end of a shaft by which circular motion is imparted to or received from it **2 :** a person with a mental twist esp. on some one subject **3 :** a bad-tempered person **:** GROUCH

²**crank** *vb* **:** to start or operate by turning a crank

**crank·case** \'kraŋk-,kās\ *n* **:** the housing of a crankshaft

**crank out** *vb* **:** to produce in a mechanical manner

**crank·shaft** \'kraŋk-,shaft\ *n* **:** a shaft turning or driven by a crank

**cranky** \'kraŋ-kē\ *adj* **crank·i·er; -est 1 :** operating uncertainly or imperfectly **2 :** IRRITABLE

**cran·ny** \'kran-ē\ *n, pl* **crannies :** CREVICE, CHINK

**crape** \'krāp\ *n* **:** CREPE; *esp* **:** black crepe used in mourning

**craps** \'kraps\ *n* **:** a gambling game played with two dice

**crap·shoot·er** \'krap-,shüt-ər\ *n* **:** a person who plays craps

¹**crash** \'krash\ *vb* **1 :** to break noisily **:** SMASH **2 :** to damage an airplane in landing **3 :** to enter or attend without invitation or without paying ⟨~ a party⟩

²**crash** *n* **1 :** a loud sound (as of things smashing) **2 :** SMASH; *also* **:** COLLISION **3 :** a sudden failure (as of a business) **4 :** the crashing of an airplane

³**crash** *adj* **:** marked by concerted effort over the shortest possible time

⁴**crash** *n* **:** coarse linen fabric used for towels and draperies

**crash–land** \'krash-'land\ *vb* **:** to land an airplane under emergency conditions usu. with damage to the craft — **crash landing** *n*

**crass** \'kras\ *adj* **:** STUPID, GROSS — **crass·ly** *adv*

**crate** \'krāt\ *n* **:** a container often of wooden slats — **crate** *vb*

**cra·ter** \'krāt-ər\ *n* [L, mixing bowl, crater, fr. Gk *kratēr*, fr. *kerannynai* to mix] **1 :** the depression around the opening of a volcano **2 :** a depression formed by the impact of a meteorite

**cra·ton** \'krā-,tän, 'kra-\ *n* **:** a stable area of the earth's crust forming a continental nuclear mass — **cra·ton·ic** \krə-'tän-ik, krā-, kra-\ *adj*

**cra·vat** \krə-'vat\ *n* **:** NECKTIE

**crave** \'krāv\ *vb* **craved; crav·ing 1 :** to ask for earnestly **:** BEG **2 :** to long for **:** DESIRE

**cra·ven** \'krā-vən\ *adj* **:** COWARDLY — **craven** *n*

**crav·ing** \'krā-viŋ\ *n* **:** an urgent or abnormal desire

**craw·fish** \'kro-,fish\ *n* **:** CRAYFISH; *also* **:** SPINY LOBSTER

¹**crawl** \'krol\ *vb* **1 :** to move slowly by drawing the body along the ground **2 :** to advance feebly, cautiously, or slowly **3 :** to swarm with or as if with creeping things **4 :** to feel as if crawling creatures were swarming over one

²**crawl** *n* **1 :** a very slow pace **2 :** a prone speed swimming stroke

**cray·fish** \'krā-,fish\ *n* **:** a freshwater crustacean like a lobster but smaller

**cray·on** \'krā-,än, -ən\ *n* **:** a stick of chalk or wax used for writing, drawing, or coloring; *also* **:** a drawing made with such material — **crayon** *vb*

¹**craze** \'krāz\ *vb* **crazed; craz·ing**

[ME *crasen* to crush, craze] : to make or become insane

²**craze** *n* : FAD, MANIA

**cra·zy** \'krā-zē\ *adj* **craz·i·er; -est**
**1** : mentally disordered : INSANE
**2** : wildly impractical; *also* : ERRATIC
— **cra·zi·ly** \'krā-zə-lē\ *adv* — **cra·zi·ness** \-zē-nəs\ *n*

**CRC** *abbr* Civil Rights Commission

**creak** \'krēk\ *vb* : to make a prolonged squeaking or grating sound — **creak** *n* — **creaky** *adj*

¹**cream** \'krēm\ *n* **1** : the yellowish fat rich part of milk **2** : a thick smooth sauce, confection, or cosmetic **3** : the choicest part **4** : a pale yellow color — **creamy** *adj*

²**cream** *vb* **1** : to prepare with a cream sauce **2** : to beat or blend (butter) into creamy consistency

**cream cheese** *n* : a cheese made from sweet milk enriched with cream

**cream·ery** \'krēm-(ə-)rē\ *n, pl* **-er·ies** : an establishment where butter and cheese are made or milk and cream are prepared for sale

**crease** \'krēs\ *n* : a mark or line made by or as if by folding — **crease** *vb*

**cre·ate** \krē-'āt\ *vb* **cre·at·ed; cre·at·ing** : to bring into being ; cause to exist : MAKE, PRODUCE — **cre·ative** \-'āt-iv\ *adj* — **cre·ativ·i·ty** \krē-(,)ā-'tiv-ət-ē, krē-ə-\ *n*

**cre·ation** \krē-'ā-shən\ *n* **1** : the act of creating or producing ⟨~ of the world⟩ **2** : something that is created **3** : all created things : WORLD

**cre·ator** \krē-'āt-ər\ *n* : one that creates : MAKER, AUTHOR

**crea·ture** \'krē-chər\ *n* : a lower animal; *also* : a human being

**crèche** \'kresh\ *n* : a representation of the Nativity scene in the stable at Bethlehem

**cre·dence** \'krēd-ᵊns\ *n* : BELIEF

**cre·den·tial** \kri-'den-chəl\ *n* : something that gives a basis for credit or confidence

**cre·den·za** \kri-'den-zə\ *n* : a sideboard, buffet, or bookcase usu. without legs

**cred·i·ble** \'kred-ə-bəl\ *adj* : TRUSTWORTHY, BELIEVABLE — **cred·i·bil·i·ty** \,kred-ə-'bil-ət-ē\ *n*

¹**cred·it** \'kred-ət\ *n* [MF, fr. It *credito*, fr. L *creditum* something entrusted to another, loan, fr. *credere* to believe, entrust] **1** : the balance (as in a bank) in a person's favor **2** : time given for payment for goods sold on trust **3** : an accounting entry of payment received **4** : BELIEF, FAITH **5** : financial trustworthiness **6** : ESTEEM **7** : a source of honor or distinction **8** : a unit of academic work

²**credit** *vb* **1** : BELIEVE **2** : to give credit to

**cred·it·able** \'kred-ət-ə-bəl\ *adj* : worthy of esteem or praise — **cred·it·ably** \-blē\ *adv*

**credit card** *n* : a card authorizing purchases on credit

**cred·i·tor** \'kred-ət-ər\ *n* : a person to whom money is owed

**cre·do** \'krēd-ō, 'krād-\ *n, pl* **credos** : CREED

**cred·u·lous** \'krej-ə-ləs\ *adj* : inclined to believe esp. on slight evidence — **cre·du·li·ty** \kri-'d(y)ü-lət-ē\ *n*

**Cree** \'krē\ *n, pl* **Cree** *or* **Crees** : a member of an Indian people of Manitoba and Saskatchewan

**creed** \'krēd\ *n* [ME *crede*, fr. OE *crēda*, fr. L *credo* I believe, first word of the Apostles' and Nicene Creeds] : a statement of the essential beliefs of a religious faith

**creek** \'krēk, 'krik\ *n* **1** *chiefly Brit* : a small inlet **2** : a stream smaller than a river and larger than a brook

**Creek** \'krēk\ *n* : a member of an Indian people of Alabama, Georgia, and Florida; *also* : their language

**creel** \'krēl\ *n* : a wickerwork basket esp. for carrying fish

**creep** \'krēp\ *vb* **crept** \'krept\; **creep·ing** **1** : CRAWL **2** : to grow over a surface like ivy **3** : to feel as though insects were crawling on the skin — **creep** *n* — **creep·er** *n*

**creep·ing** \'krē-piŋ\ *adj* : developing or advancing by imperceptible degrees

**creepy** \'krē-pē\ *adj* **creep·i·er; -est** : having or producing a nervous shivery fear

**cre·mains** \kri-'mānz\ *n pl* : the ashes of a cremated human body

**cre·mate** \'krē-māt\ *vb* **cre·mat·ed; cre·mat·ing** : to reduce (a dead body) to ashes with fire — **cre·ma·tion** \kri-'mā-shən\ *n*

**cre·ma·to·ry** \'krē-mə-,tōr-ē, 'krem-ə-\ *n, pl* **-ries** : a furnace for cremating; *also* : a structure containing such a furnace

**crème** \'krem, 'krēm\ *n, pl* **crèmes** \'krem(z), 'krēmz\ : a sweet liqueur

**cren·el·late** *or* **cren·el·ate** \'kren-ᵊl-,āt\ *vb* **-lat·ed** *or* **-at·ed; -lat·ing** *or* **-at·ing** : to furnish with battlements — **cren·el·la·tion** \,kren-ᵊl-'ā-shən\ *n*

**Cre·ole** \'krē-,ōl\ *n* : a descendant of early French or Spanish settlers of the U.S. Gulf states preserving their speech and culture; *also* : a person of mixed French or Spanish and Negro descent speaking a dialect of French or Spanish

**cre·o·sote** \'krē-ə-,sōt\ *n* : an oily liquid obtained by distillation of coal tar and used in preserving wood

**crepe** *or* **crêpe** \'krāp\ *n* : a light crinkled fabric of any of various fibers

**crepe su·zette** \,krāp-sü-'zet\ *n, pl* **crepes suzette** \,krāp(s)-sü-'zet\ *or* **crepe suzettes** \,krāp-sü-'zets\ : a thin folded or rolled pancake in a hot orange-butter sauce that is sprinkled with a liqueur and set ablaze for serving

**cre·pus·cu·lar** \kri-'pəs-kyə-lər\ *adj* **1** : of, relating to, or resembling twilight **2** : active in the twilight ⟨~ insects⟩

**cresc** *abbr* crescendo

**cre·scen·do** \krə-'shen-dō\ *adv or adj* : increasing in loudness — used as a direction in music — **crescendo** *n*

**cres·cent** \'kres-ᵊnt\ *n* [ME *cressant*, fr. MF *creissant*, fr. *creistre* to grow, increase, fr. L *crescere*] **:** the moon at any stage between new moon and first quarter and between last quarter and new moon; *also* **:** something shaped like the figure of the crescent moon with a convex and a concave edge — **cres·cen·tic** \kre-'sent-ik, krə-\ *adj*

**cress** \'kres\ *n* **:** any of several salad plants related to the mustards

¹**crest** \'krest\ *n* **1 :** a tuft or process on the head of an animal (as a bird) **2 :** the ridge at the top of a hill or a billow **3 :** a heraldic device — **crest·ed** \'kres-tə d\ *adj* — **crest·less** *adj*

²**crest** *vb* **1 :** CROWN **2 :** to reach the crest of **3 :** to rise to a crest

**crest·fall·en** \'krest-,fȯ-lən\ *adj* **:** DISPIRITED, DEJECTED

**cre·ta·ceous** \kri-'tā-shəs\ *adj* **:** having the nature of or abounding in chalk

**cre·tin** \'krēt-ᵊn\ *n* [F *crétin*, fr. F dial. *cretin* Christian, human being, kind of idiot found in the Alps, fr. L *christianus* Christian] **:** a person with marked mental deficiency

**cre·tin·ism** \-,iz-əm\ *n* **:** a usu. congenital abnormal condition characterized by physical stunting and mental deficiency

**cre·tonne** \'krē-,tän\ *n* **:** a strong unglazed cotton cloth for curtains and upholstery

**cre·vasse** \kri-'vas\ *n* **1 :** a deep fissure esp. in a glacier **2 :** a break in a levee

**crev·ice** \'krev-əs\ *n* **:** a narrow fissure

¹**crew** \'krü\ *chiefly Brit past of* CROW

²**crew** \'krü\ *n* [ME *crue*, lit., reinforcement, fr. MF *creue* increase, fr. *creistre* to grow, fr. L *crescere*] **1 :** a body of men trained to work together for certain purposes **2 :** the body of seamen who man a ship **3 :** the persons who man an airplane in flight **4 :** the body of men who man a racing shell; *also* **:** the sport of rowing engaged in by a crew — **crew·man** \-mən\ *n*

**crew cut** *n* **:** a very short bristly haircut

**crew·el** \'krü-əl\ *n* **:** slackly twisted worsted yarn used for embroidery — **crew·el·work** \-,wərk\ *n*

¹**crib** \'krib\ *n* **1 :** a manger for feeding animals **2 :** a building or bin for storage (as of grain) **3 :** a small bedstead for a child **4 :** a translation prepared to aid a student in preparing a lesson

²**crib** *vb* **cribbed; crib·bing 1 :** CONFINE **2 :** to put in a crib **3 :** STEAL; *esp* **:** PLAGIARIZE — **crib·ber** *n*

**crib·bage** \'krib-ij\ *n* **:** a card game usu. played by two players and scored on a board (**cribbage board**)

**crick** \'krik\ *n* **:** a painful spasm of muscles (as of the neck)

¹**crick·et** \'krik-ət\ *n* **:** a leaping insect noted for the chirping notes of the male

²**cricket** *n* **:** a game played with a bat and ball by two teams on a field centering upon two wickets each defended by a batsman

**cri·er** \'krī(-ə)r\ *n* **:** one who calls out proclamations and announcements

**crime** \'krīm\ *n* **:** a serious offense against the public law

¹**crim·i·nal** \'krim-ən-ᵊl\ *adj* **1 :** involving or being a crime **2 :** relating to crime or its punishment — **crim·i·nal·i·ty** \,krim-ə-'nal-ət-ē\ *n* — **crim·i·nal·ly** \'krim-ən-ᵊl-ē\ *adv*

²**criminal** *n* **:** one who has committed a crime

**crim·i·nol·o·gy** \,krim-ə-'näl-ə-jē\ *n* **:** the scientific study of crime and criminals — **crim·i·no·log·i·cal** \-ən-ᵊl-'äj-i-kəl\ *adj* — **crim·i·nol·o·gist** \,krim-ə-'näl-ə-jəst\ *n*

¹**crimp** \'krimp\ *vb* **:** to cause to become crinkled, wavy, or bent — **crimp·er** *n*

²**crimp** *n* **:** something (as a curl in hair) produced by or as if by crimping

¹**crim·son** \'krim-zən\ *n* **:** a deep purplish red — **crimson** *adj*

²**crimson** *vb* **:** to make or become crimson

**cringe** \'krinj\ *vb* **cringed; cring·ing :** to shrink in fear **:** WINCE, COWER

**crin·kle** \'kriŋ-kəl\ *vb* **crin·kled; crin·kling** \-k(ə-)liŋ\ **:** to turn or wind in many short bends or curves; *also* **:** WRINKLE, RIPPLE — **crinkle** *n* — **crin·kly** \-k(ə-)lē\ *adj*

**crin·o·line** \'krin-ᵊl-ən\ *n* **1 :** an open-weave cloth used for stiffening and lining **2 :** a full stiff skirt or underskirt

¹**crip·ple** \'krip-əl\ *n* **:** a lame or disabled person

²**cripple** *vb* **crip·pled; crip·pling** \-(ə-)liŋ\ **:** to make lame **:** DISABLE

**cri·sis** \'krī-səs\ *n, pl* **cri·ses** \'krī-,sēz\ [L, fr. Gk *krisis*, decision, fr. *krinein* to decide] **1 :** the turning point for better or worse in an acute disease or fever **2 :** a decisive or critical moment

**crisp** \'krisp\ *adj* **1 :** CURLY, WAVY **2 :** BRITTLE **3 :** being sharp and clear **4 :** LIVELY, SPARKLING **5 :** FIRM, FRESH (~ lettuce) **6 :** FROSTY, SNAPPY; *also* **:** BRACING — **crisp** *vb* — **crisp·ly** *adv* — **crisp·ness** *n* — **crispy** *adj*

¹**criss·cross** \'kris-,krȯs\ *n* **:** a pattern of crossed lines

²**crisscross** *vb* **1 :** to mark with crossed lines **2 :** to go or pass back and forth

³**crisscross** *adv* **:** CONTRARILY, AWRY

**crit** *abbr* critical; criticism

**cri·te·ri·on** \krī-'tir-ē-ən\ *n, pl* **-ria** \-ē-ə\ *also* **-rions :** a standard on which a judgment may be based

**crit·ic** \'krit-ik\ *n* **1 :** one skilled in judging literary or artistic works **2 :** one inclined to find fault

**crit·i·cal** \'krit-i-kəl\ *adj* **1 :** inclined to criticize **2 :** requiring careful judgment **3 :** being a crisis **4 :** UNCERTAIN **5 :** relating to criticism or critics — **crit·i·cal·ly** \-i-k(ə-)lē\ *adv*

**crit·i·cism** \'krit-ə-,siz-əm\ *n* **1 :** the act of criticizing; *esp* **:** CENSURE **2 :** a judgment or review **3 :** the art of judging expertly works of literature or art

**crit·i·cize** \'krit-ə-,sīz\ *vb* **-cized; -ciz·ing 1 :** to judge as a critic **:** EVALUATE **2 :** to find fault; express criticism **syn** blame, censure, condemn

**cri·tique** \krə-'tēk\ *n* **:** a critical estimate or discussion

**cǐt·ter** \'krit-ər\ *n, dial* : CREATURE

**croak** \'krōk\ *n* : a hoarse harsh cry (as of a frog) — **croak** *vb*

**cro·chet** \krō-'shā\ *n* [F, hook, crochet, fr. MF, dim. of *croche* hook] : needlework done with a single thread and hooked needle — **crochet** *vb*

**crock** \'kräk\ *n* : a thick earthenware pot or jar

**crock·ery** \'kräk-(ə-)rē\ *n* : EARTHENWARE

**croc·o·dile** \'kräk-ə-,dīl\ *n* [ME & L; ME *cocodrille*, fr. OF, fr. ML *cocodrillus*, alter. of L *crocodilus*, fr. Gk *krokodilos* lizard, crocodile, fr. *krokē* pebble + *drilos* worm] : a thick-skinned long-bodied reptile of tropical and subtropical waters

**cro·cus** \'krō-kəs\ *n, pl* **cro·cus·es** : a low herb related to the irises with brightly colored flowers borne singly in early spring

**crois·sant** \krə-,wä-'säⁿ\ *n, pl* **crois·sants** \-'säⁿ(z)\ : a rich crescent-shaped roll

**crone** \'krōn\ *n* : a withered old woman

**cro·ny** \'krō-nē\ *n, pl* **cronies** : a close friend esp. of long standing

¹**crook** \'krúk\ *n* 1 : a bent or curved implement 2 : a bent or curved part; *also* : BEND, CURVE 3 : SWINDLER, THIEF

²**crook** *vb* : to curve or bend sharply

**crook·ed** \'krúk-əd\ *adj* 1 : having a crook : BENT, CURVED 2 : DISHONEST — **crook·ed·ly** *adv* — **crook·ed·ness** *n*

**croon** \'krün\ *vb* 1 : to sing in a low soft voice 2 : to sing in a soft voice into a closely held microphone — **croon·er** *n*

¹**crop** \'kräp\ *n* 1 : a pouch in the throat of many birds and insects where food is received 2 : the handle of a whip; *also* : a short riding whip 3 : something that can be harvested; *also* : the yield at harvest

²**crop** *vb* **cropped; crop·ping** 1 : to remove the tips of : cut off short; *also* : TRIM 2 : to feed on by cropping 3 : to devote (land) to crops 4 : to appear unexpectedly

**crop–dust·ing** \'kräp-,dəs-tiŋ\ *n* : the application of fungicidal or insecticidal dusts to crops esp. from an airplane — **crop dust·er** *n*

**crop·land** \-,land\ *n* : land devoted to the production of plant crops

**crop·per** \'kräp-ər\ *n* : a raiser of crops; *esp* : SHARECROPPER

**cro·quet** \krō-'kā\ *n* : a game in which mallets are used to drive wooden balls through a series of wickets set out on a lawn

**cro·quette** \krō-'ket\ *n* : a roll or ball of hashed meat, fish, or vegetables fried in deep fat

**cro·sier** \'krō-zhər\ *n* : a staff carried by bishops and abbots

¹**cross** \'krós\ *n* 1 : a structure consisting of an upright beam and a crossbar used esp. by the ancient Romans for execution 2 *often cap* : a figure of the cross on which Christ was crucified used as a Christian symbol 3 : a hybridizing of unlike individuals or strains; *also* : a product of this 4 : a punch delivered with a circular motion over an opponent's lead

²**cross** *vb* 1 : to lie or place across; *also* : INTERSECT 2 : to cancel by marking a cross on or by lining through 3 : THWART, OBSTRUCT 4 : to go or extend across : TRAVERSE 5 : HYBRIDIZE 6 : to meet and pass on the way

³**cross** *adj* 1 : lying across 2 : CONTRARY, OPPOSED 3 : marked by bad temper 4 : HYBRID — **cross·ly** *adv*

**cross·bar** \'krós-,bär\ *n* : a transverse bar or piece

**cross·bones** \-,bōnz\ *n pl* : two leg or arm bones placed or depicted crosswise

**cross·bow** \-,bō\ *n* : a medieval weapon consisting of a strong bow mounted crosswise on a stock

**cross·breed** \'krós-,brēd, -'brēd\ *vb* **-bred** \-'bred\; **-breed·ing** : HYBRIDIZE

**cross–coun·try** \-'kən-trē\ *adj* 1 : extending or moving across a country 2 : proceeding over the countryside (as fields and woods) rather than by roads 3 : of or relating to racing over the countryside instead of over a track — **cross–country** *adv*

**cross·cur·rent** \-'kər-ənt\ *n* 1 : a current running counter to another 2 : a conflicting tendency

¹**cross·cut** \-,kət\ *vb* : to cut or saw crosswise esp. of the grain of wood

²**crosscut** *adj* 1 : made or used for crosscutting ⟨a ~ saw⟩ 2 : cut across the grain

³**crosscut** *n* : something that cuts through transversely ⟨a ~ through the park⟩

**cross–ex·am·ine** \,krós-ig-'zam-ən\ *vb* : to examine with questions as a check to answers to previous examination — **cross–ex·am·i·na·tion** \-,zam-ə-'nā-shən\ *n*

**cross–eye** \'krós-,ī\ *n* : an abnormality in which the eye turns toward the nose — **cross–eyed** \-'īd\ *adj*

**cross–file** \'krós-'fīl\ *vb* : to register as a candidate in the primary elections of more than one party

**cross fire** *n* 1 : crossing lines of fire in combat 2 : rapid or angry interchange

**cross hair** *n* : one of the fine wires or threads in the eyepiece of an optical instrument used as a reference line

**cross–hatch** \'krós-,hach\ *vb* : to mark with a series of parallel lines that cross esp. obliquely — **cross–hatch·ing** *n*

**cross·ing** \'kró-siŋ\ *n* 1 : a point of intersection (as of a street and a railroad track) 2 : a place for crossing something (as a street or river)

**cross·over** \'krós-,ō-vər\ *n* 1 : CROSSING 2 : one who votes in an election for a party other than the one he usu. votes for

**cross·piece** \'krós-,pēs\ *n* : a crosswise member

**cross–pol·li·na·tion** \,krós-,päl-ə-'nā-shən\ *n* : transfer of pollen from one flower to the stigma of another — **cross-pol·li·nate** \'kròs-'pàl-ə-,nãt\ *vb*

**cross-pur·pose** \'kròs-'pər-pəs\ *n* **:** a purpose usu. intentionally contrary to another purpose ⟨working at ∼s⟩

**cross-ques·tion** \-'kwes-chən\ *vb* **:** CROSS-EXAMINE

**cross-re·fer** \,kròs-ri-'fər\ *vb* **:** to refer by a notation or direction from one place to another (as in a book or list) — **cross-reference** \'kròs-'ref-(ə-)rəns\ *n*

**cross-road** \'kròs-,rõd\ *n* **1 :** a road that crosses a main road or runs between main roads **2 :** a place where roads meet — usu. used in pl.

**cross section** *n* **1 :** a section cut across something; *also* **:** a representation made by or as if by such cutting **2 :** a number of persons or things selected from a group that show the general nature of the whole group

**cross talk** *n* **:** interference in one track of a tape recording caused by another track

**cross·walk** \'kròs-,wòk\ *n* **:** a specially marked path for pedestrians crossing a street

**cross·ways** \-,wãz\ *adv* **:** CROSSWISE

**cross·wise** \-,wīz\ *adv* **:** so as to cross something **:** ACROSS — **crosswise** *adj*

**cross·word puzzle** \,kròs-,word-\ *n* **:** a puzzle in which words are fitted into a pattern of numbered squares in answer to clues

**crotch** \'kräch\ *n* **:** an angle formed by the parting of two legs, branches, or members

**crotch·et** \'kräch-ət\ *n* **:** an odd notion **:** WHIM — **crotch·ety** *adj*

**crouch** \'kraùch\ *vb* **1 :** to stoop over **2 :** CRINGE, COWER — **crouch** *n*

**croup** \'krüp\ *n* **:** laryngitis esp. of infants marked by a hoarse ringing cough and difficult breathing — **croupy** *adj*

**crou·pi·er** \'krü-pē-ər, -pē-,ā\ *n* [F, lit., rider on the rump of a horse, fr. *croupe* rump] **:** an employee of a gambling casino who collects and pays bets at a gaming table

**crou·ton** \'krü-,tän\ *n* **:** a small piece of toast

**¹crow** \'krõ\ *n* **1 :** a large glossy black bird **2** *cap* **:** a member of an Indian people of the region between the Platte and Yellowstone rivers; *also* **:** the language of the Crow people

**²crow** *vb* **1 :** to make the loud shrill sound characteristic of the cock **2 :** to utter a sound expressive of pleasure **3 :** EXULT, GLOAT; *also* **:** BRAG, BOAST

**³crow** *n* **:** the cry of the cock

**crow·bar** \'krõ-,bär\ *n* **:** a metal bar usu. wedge-shaped at the end for use as a pry or lever

**¹crowd** \'kraùd\ *vb* **1 :** to collect in numbers **:** THRONG **2 :** to press close **3 :** CRAM, STUFF

**²crowd** *n* **:** a large number of people gathered together at random **:** THRONG

**crow·foot** \'krõ-,fùt\ *n, pl* **crow·feet** \-,fēt\ **:** BUTTERCUP

**crown** \'kraùn\ *n* **1 :** GARLAND; *also*

**:** the title of champion in a sport **2 :** a royal headdress **3** *often cap* **:** sovereign power; *also* **:** MONARCH **4 :** the top of the head **5 :** a British silver coin **6 :** something resembling a crown; *esp* **:** a top part (as of a tree or tooth) — **crowned** \'kraùnd\ *adj*

**²crown** *vb* **1 :** to place a crown on **2 :** HONOR **3 :** TOP, SURMOUNT **4 :** to fit (a tooth) with an artificial crown

**crown vetch** *n* **:** a European herb with umbels of pink-and-white flowers and sharp-angled pods

**crow's-foot** \'krõz-,fùt\ *n, pl* **crow's-feet** \-,fēt\ **:** any of the wrinkles around the outer corners of the eyes — usu. used in pl.

**crow's nest** *n* **:** a partly enclosed platform high on a ship's mast for use as a lookout

**cru·cial** \'krü-shəl\ *adj* **:** DECISIVE; *also* **:** SEVERE, TRYING

**cru·ci·ble** \'krü-sə-bəl\ *n* **:** a heat-resisting container in which material can be subjected to great heat

**cru·ci·fix** \'krü-sə-,fiks\ *n* **:** a representation of Christ on the cross

**cru·ci·fix·ion** \,krü-sə-'fik-shən\ *n* **:** the act of crucifying; *esp, cap* **:** the execution of Christ on the cross

**cru·ci·form** \'krü-sə-,fòrm\ *adj* **:** cross-shaped

**cru·ci·fy** \'krü-sə-,fī\ *vb* **-fied; -fy·ing 1 :** to put to death by nailing or binding the hands and feet to a cross **2 :** MORTIFY **3 :** TORTURE, PERSECUTE

**¹crude** \'krüd\ *adj* **crud·er; crud·est 1 :** not refined **:** RAW ⟨∼ oil⟩ ⟨∼ statistics⟩ **2 :** lacking grace, taste, tact, or polish **:** RUDE — **crude·ly** *adv* — **cru·di·ty** \'krüd-ət-ē\ *n*

**²crude** *n* **:** unrefined petroleum

**cru·el** \'krü-əl\ *adj* **cru·el·er** or **cru·el·ler; cru·el·est** or **cru·el·lest :** causing pain and suffering to others **:** MERCILESS — **cru·el·ly** \-ē\ *adv* — **cru·el·ty** \-tē\ *n*

**cru·et** \'krü-ət\ *n* **:** a small usu. glass bottle for vinegar, oil, or sauce

**cruise** \'krüz\ *vb* **cruised; cruis·ing** [D *kruisen* to make a cross, cruise, fr. L *crux* cross] **1 :** to sail about touching at a series of ports **2 :** to travel for enjoyment **3 :** to travel about the streets at random **4 :** to travel at the most efficient operating speed ⟨the *cruising* speed of an airplane⟩ — **cruise** *n*

**cruis·er** \'krü-zər\ *n* **1 :** a fast moderately armored and gunned warship **2 :** a motorboat equipped for living aboard **3 :** SQUAD CAR

**crul·ler** \'krəl-ər\ *n* **1 :** a sweet cake made of egg batter fried in deep fat **2** *North & Midland* **:** an unraised doughnut

**¹crumb** \'krəm\ *n* **:** a small fragment

**²crumb** *vb* **1 :** to break into crumbs **2 :** to cover with crumbs

**crum·ble** \'krəm-bəl\ *vb* **crum·bled; crum·bling** \-b(ə-)liŋ\ **:** to break into small pieces **:** DISINTEGRATE — **crum·bly** \-b(ə-)lē\ *adj*

**crum·my** or **crumby** \'krəm-ē\ *adj*

**crum·mi·er** *or* **crumb·i·er; -est**
**1** : MISERABLE, FILTHY **2** : CHEAP,
WORTHLESS

**crum·pet** \'krəm-pət\ *n* : a small
round cake made of rich unsweetened
batter cooked on a griddle

**crum·ple** \'krəm-pəl\ *vb* **crum·pled;**
**crum·pling** \-p(ə-)liŋ\ **1** : to crush
together **2** : RUMPLE **2** : COLLAPSE

¹**crunch** \'krənch\ *vb* : to chew with a
grinding noise; *also* : to grind or press
with a crushing noise

²**crunch** *n* **1** : an act of or a sound made
by crunching **2** : a tight or critical
situation — **crunchy** *adj*

**cru·sade** \krü-'sād\ *n* **1** *cap* : any of
the expeditions in the 11th, 12th, and
13th centuries undertaken by Christian
countries to take the Holy Land from
the Muslims **2** : a reforming enterprise
undertaken with zeal — **crusade** *vb*
— **cru·sad·er** *n*

**cruse** \'krüz, 'krüs\ *n* : a jar for water
or oil

¹**crush** \'krəsh\ *vb* **1** : to squeeze out of
shape **2** : HUG, EMBRACE **3** : to grind
or pound to small bits **4** : OVERWHELM,
SUPPRESS

²**crush** *n* **1** : an act of crushing **2** : a
violent crowding **3** : INFATUATION

**crust** \'krəst\ *n* **1** : the outside part of
bread; *also* : a piece of old dry bread
**2** : the cover of a pie **3** : a hard surface
layer — **crust·al** *adj* — **crusty** *adj*

**crus·ta·cean** \,krəs-'tā-shən\ *n* : any
of a large group of mostly aquatic
arthropods (as lobsters or crabs) having
a firm crustlike shell

**crutch** \'krəch\ *n* : a supporting device; *esp* : a support fitting under the
armpit for use by the disabled in walking

**crux** \'krəks, 'krüks\ *n, pl* **crux·es**
**1** : a puzzling or difficult problem
**2** : a crucial point

**cru·zei·ro** \krü-'ze(ə)r-ō\ *n, pl* **-ros** —
see MONEY table

¹**cry** \'krī\ *vb* **cried; cry·ing 1** : to
call out : SHOUT **2** : WEEP **3** : to proclaim publicly; *also* : to advertise wares
by calling out

²**cry** *n, pl* **cries 1** : a loud outcry
**2** : APPEAL, ENTREATY **3** : a fit of weeping **4** : the characteristic sound uttered
by an animal

**cry·ba·by** \'krī-,bā-bē\ *n* : one who
cries easily or often

**cryo·gen·ic** \,krī-ə-'jen-ik\ *adj* **1** : of
or relating to the production of very
low temperatures **2** : produced or
stored at a very low temperature ⟨a ~
rocket fuel⟩ **3** : used or usable at a
very low temperature — **cryo·gen·i·**
**cal·ly** \-i-k(ə-)lē\ *adv*

**cryo·gen·ics** \-iks\ *n* : a branch of
physics that relates to the production
and effects of very low temperatures

**cryo·lite** \'krī-ə-,līt\ *n* : a usu. white
mineral used in making soda and
aluminum

**crypt** \'kript\ *n* : a chamber wholly or
partly underground

**cryp·tic** \'krip-tik\ *adj* : MYSTERIOUS,
ENIGMATIC

**cryp·to·gram** \'krip-tə-,gram\ *n* : a
communication in cipher or code

**cryp·tog·ra·phy** \krip-'täg-rə-fē\ *n*
: the enciphering and deciphering of
messages in secret code — **cryp·tog·**
**ra·pher** \-fər\ *n*

**cryst** *abbr* crystalline

**crys·tal** \'kris-t²l\ *n* [ME *cristal*, fr.
OF, fr. L *crystallum*, fr. Gk *krystallos*
ice, crystal] **1** : transparent quartz
**2** : something resembling crystal (as in
transparency); *esp* : a clear glass used
for table articles **3** : a body that is
formed by solidification of a substance
and has a regular repeating arrangement of atoms and often of external
plane faces ⟨a snow ~⟩ ⟨a salt ~⟩
**4** : the transparent cover of a watch
dial — **crys·tal·line** \-tə-lən\ *adj*

**crys·tal·lize** \'kris-tə-,līz\ *vb* **-lized;**
**-liz·ing 1** : to assume or cause to assume a crystalline structure or a fixed
and definite shape — **crys·tal·li·za·**
**tion** \,kris-tə-lə-'zā-shən\ *n*

**crys·tal·log·ra·phy** \,kris-tə-'läg-rə-
fē\ *n* : the science dealing with the
forms and structures of crystals —
**crys·tal·log·ra·pher** \-fər\ *n* —
**crys·tal·lo·graph·ic** \-lə-'graf-ik\
*adj*

**cs** *abbr* case; cases

**Cs** *symbol* cesium

**CS** *abbr* **1** civil service **2** county seat

**C/S** *abbr* cycles per second

**CSA** *abbr* Confederate States of
America

**CSM** *abbr* command sergeant major

**CSsR** *abbr* [L *Congregatio Sanctissimi*
*Redemptoris*] Congregation of the Most
Holy Redeemer

**CST** *abbr* central standard time

**ct** *abbr* **1** carat **2** cent **3** count **4** court

**CT** *abbr* **1** central time **2** Connecticut

**ctg** *or* **ctge** *abbr* cartage

**ctn** *abbr* carton

**ctr** *abbr* center

**cu** *abbr* cubic

**Cu** *symbol* [L *cuprum*] copper

**cub** \'kəb\ *n* : a young individual of
some animals (as a fox, bear, or lion)

**Cu·ban** \'kyü-bən\ *adj* : of, relating to,
or characteristic of Cuba or its people

**cub·by·hole** \'kəb-ē-,hōl\ *n* **1** : a
snug or confined place (as for hiding)
**2** : a small closet, cupboard, or compartment for storing things

¹**cube** \'kyüb\ *n* **1** : a solid having 6
equal square sides **2** : the product obtained by taking a number 3 times as a
factor ⟨27 is the ~ of 3⟩

²**cube** *vb* **cubed; cub·ing 1** : to raise
to the third power **2** : to form into a
cube **3** : to cut into cubes

**cube root** *n* : a number whose cube is a
given number

**cu·bic** \'kyü-bik\ *adj* **1** : having the
form of a cube **2** : having three dimensions **3** : being the volume of a cube
whose edge is a specified unit — **cu·bi·**
**cal** \-bi-kəl\ *adj*

**cu·bi·cle** \'kyü-bi-kəl\ *n* **1** : a sleeping compartment partitioned off from a
large room **2** : a small partitioned
space

**cubic measure** *n* : a unit (as cubic inch) for measuring volume — see METRIC SYSTEM table, WEIGHT table

**cub·ism** \'kyü-,biz-əm\ *n* : a style of art that stresses abstract structure esp. by displaying several aspects of the same object simultaneously and by fragmenting the form of depicted objects

**cu·bit** \'kyü-bət\ *n* : an ancient measure of length equal to about 18 inches

**cub scout** *n* : a member of the program of the Boy Scouts of America for boys 8–10 years of age

**cuck·old** \'kək-əld, 'kük-\ *n* : a man whose wife is unfaithful

¹**cuck·oo** \'kük-ü, 'kük-\ *n, pl* **cuckoos** : a European bird that lays its eggs in the nests of other birds for them to hatch

²**cuckoo** *adj* : SILLY, FOOLISH

**cu·cum·ber** \'kyü-(,)kəm-bər\ *n* : a fleshy fruit related to the gourds and eaten as a vegetable

**cud** \'kəd\ *n* : food brought up into the mouth by ruminating animals (as cows) from the first stomach to be chewed again

**cud·dle** \'kəd-ᵊl\ *vb* **cud·dled; cud·dling** \'kəd-(ᵊ-)liŋ\ : to lie close

**cud·gel** \'kəj-əl\ *n* : a short heavy club — **cudgel** *vb*

¹**cue** \'kyü\ *n* 1 : words or stage business serving as a signal for an entrance or for the next speaker to speak 2 : HINT — **cue** *vb*

²**cue** *n* : a tapered rod for striking the balls in billiards or pool

**cue ball** *n* : the ball a player strikes with a cue in billiards or pool

**cues·ta** \'kwes-tə\ *n* : a ridge with a steep face on one side and a gentle slope on the other

¹**cuff** \'kəf\ *n* 1 : a part (as of a sleeve or glove) encircling the wrist 2 : the folded hem of a trouser leg

²**cuff** *vb* : to strike esp. with the open hand : SLAP

³**cuff** *n* : a blow with the hand esp. when open

**cui·sine** \kwi-'zēn\ *n* : manner of cooking; *also* : the food so prepared

**cuke** \'kyük\ *n* : CUCUMBER

**cul–de–sac** \,kəl-di-'sak, ,kül-\ *n, pl* **culs–de–sac** \,kəl(z)-, ,kül(z)-\ *also* **cul–de–sacs** \,kəl-də-'saks, ,kül-\ [F, lit., bottom of the bag] : a street or passage closed at one end

**cu·li·nary** \'kəl-ə-,ner-ē, 'kyü-lə-\ *adj* : of or relating to cookery

¹**cull** \'kəl\ *vb* : to pick out from a group : CHOOSE

²**cull** *n* : something rejected from a group or lot as worthless or inferior

**cul·len·der** *var of* COLANDER

**cul·mi·nate** \'kəl-mə-,nāt\ *vb* **-nat·ed; -nat·ing** : to form a summit : rise to the highest point — **cul·mi·na·tion** \,kəl-mə-'nā-shən\ *n*

**cu·lotte** \'k(y)ü-,lät, k(y)ü-'lät\ *n* : a divided skirt; *also* : a garment having a divided skirt — often used in pl.

**cul·pa·ble** \'kəl-pə-bəl\ *adj* : deserving blame

**cul·prit** \'kəl-prət\ *n* [Anglo-French (the French of medieval England) *cul.* (abbr. of *culpable* guilty) + *prest, prit* ready (i.e. to prove it), fr. L *praestus*] : one accused or guilty of a crime

**cult** \'kəlt\ *n* 1 : formal religious veneration 2 : a religious system; *also* : its adherents 3 : faddish devotion; *also* : a group of persons showing such devotion — **cult·ist** *n*

**cul·ti·vate** \'kəl-tə-,vāt\ *vb* **-vat·ed; -vat·ing** 1 : to prepare for the raising of crops 2 : to foster the growth of ⟨~ vegetables⟩ 3 : REFINE, IMPROVE 4 : ENCOURAGE, FURTHER — **cul·ti·va·ble** \-və-bəl\ *adj* — **cul·ti·vat·able** \-,vāt-ə-bəl\ *adj* — **cul·ti·va·tion** \,kəl-tə-'vā-shən\ *n* — **cul·ti·va·tor** \'kel-tə-,vāt-ər\ *n*

**cul·ture** \'kəl-chər\ *n* 1 : TILLAGE, CULTIVATION; *also* : the growing of a particular crop ⟨grape ~⟩ 2 : the act of developing by education and training 3 : refinement of intellectual and artistic taste 4 : a particular form or stage of civilization; *also* : a society characterized by such a culture — **cul·tur·al** \'kəlch-(ə-)rəl\ *adj* — **cul·tur·al·ly** \-ē\ *adv* — **cul·tured** \'kəl-chərd\ *adj*

**cul·vert** \'kəl-vərt\ *n* : a drain crossing under a road or railroad

**cum** *abbr* cumulative

**cum·ber** \'kəm-bər\ *vb* **cum·bered; cum·ber·ing** \-b(ə-)riŋ\ : to weigh down : BURDEN — **cum·ber·some** *adj* — **cum·brous** \'kəm-brəs\ *adj*

**cum·mer·bund** \'kəm-ər-,bənd\ *n* [Hindi *kamarband*, fr. Per, fr. *kamar* waist + *band*] : a broad sash worn as a waistband

**cu·mu·la·tive** \'kyü-myə-lət-iv, -,lāt-\ *adj* : increasing in force or value by successive additions

**cu·mu·lo·nim·bus** \,kyü-mye-lō-'nim-bəs\ *n* : an anvil-shaped cumulus cloud extending to great heights

**cu·mu·lus** \'kyü-myə-ləs\ *n, pl* **-li** \-,lī, -,lē\ : a massive cloud having a flat base and rounded outlines

**cu·ne·i·form** \kyü-'nē-ə-,fȯrm\ *adj* 1 : wedge-shaped 2 : composed of wedge-shaped characters ⟨~ alphabet⟩

**cun·ner** \'kən-ər\ *n* : a small American food fish of the New England coast

¹**cun·ning** \'kən-iŋ\ *adj* 1 : contrived with skill 2 : CRAFTY, SLY 3 : CLEVER 4 : CUTE — **cun·ning·ly** *adv*

²**cunning** *n* 1 : SKILL 2 : CRAFTINESS, SLYNESS

¹**cup** \'kəp\ *n* 1 : a small bowl-shaped drinking vessel 2 : the contents of a cup 3 : communion wine 4 : something resembling a cup : a small bowl or hollow — **cup·ful** *n*

²**cup** *vb* **cupped; cup·ping** : to curve into the shape of a cup

**cup·bear·er** \'kəp-,bar-ər\ *n* : one who has the duty of filling and serving cups of wine

**cup·board** \'kəb-ərd\ *n* : a small storage closet

**cup·cake** \'kəp-,kāk\ *n* : a small cake baked in a cuplike mold

**Cu·pid** \'kyü-pəd\ *n* : a winged naked figure of an infant often with a bow and arrow that represents the god Cupid

**cu·pid·i·ty** \kyù-'pid-ət-ē\ *n, pl* **-ties** : excessive desire for money : AVARICE

**cu·po·la** \'kyü-pə-lə, -ˌlō\ *n* : a small structure on top of a roof or building

**cu·prite** \'k(y)ü-ˌprīt\ *n* : a mineral that is an oxide and ore of copper

¹**cur** \'kər\ *n* : a mongrel dog

²**cur** *abbr* **1** currency **2** current

**cu·rate** \'kyùr-ət\ *n* **1** : a clergyman in charge of a parish **2** : a clergyman who assists a rector or vicar — **cu·ra·cy** \-ə-sē\ *n*

**cu·ra·tive** \'kyùr-ət-iv\ *adj* : relating to or used in the cure of diseases — **curative** *n*

**cu·ra·tor** \kyù-'rāt-ər\ *n* : CUSTODIAN; *esp* : one in charge of a place of exhibit (as a museum or zoo)

¹**curb** \'kərb\ *n* **1** : a chain or strap on a bit used to check a horse **2** : CHECK, RESTRAINT **3** : a raised stone edging along a paved street **4** : a market for trading in securities not listed on the stock exchange

²**curb** *vb* : to hold in or back : RESTRAIN

**curb·ing** \'kər-biŋ\ *n* **1** : the material for a curb **2** : CURB

**curb service** *n* : service extended (as by a restaurant) to customers sitting in parked cars

**curd** \'kərd\ *n* : the thick protein-rich part of coagulated milk

**cur·dle** \'kərd-ᵊl\ *vb* **curd·led; curd·ling** \'kərd-(ᵊ-)liŋ\ : to form curds; *also* : SPOIL, SOUR

¹**cure** \'kyùr\ *n* **1** : spiritual care **2** : recovery or relief from disease **3** : a curative agent : REMEDY **4** : a course or period of treatment

²**cure** *vb* **cured; cur·ing 1** : to restore to health : HEAL, REMEDY **2** : to process for storage or use (~ bacon); *also* : to become cured — **cur·able** *adj*

**cu·ré** \kyù-'rā\ *n* : a parish priest

**cure-all** \'kyùr-ˌȯl\ *n* : a remedy for all ills : PANACEA

**cu·ret·tage** \ˌkyùr-ə-'täzh\ *n* : a surgical scraping and cleaning by means of a scoop, loop, or ring

**cur·few** \'kər-ˌfyü\ *n* [ME, fr. MF *covrefeu*, signal given to bank the hearth fire, curfew, fr. *covrir* to cover + *feu* fire, fr. L *focus* hearth] : a regulation that specified persons (as children) be off the streets at a set hour of the evening; *also* : the sounding of a signal (as a bell) at this hour

**cu·ria** \'k(y)ùr-ē-ə\ *n, pl* **cu·ri·ae** \'kyùr-ē-ˌē, 'kùr-ē-ˌī\ *often cap* : the body of congregations, tribunals, and offices through which the pope governs the Roman Catholic Church

**cu·rio** \'kyùr-ē-ˌō\ *n, pl* **cu·ri·os** : a small object valued for its rarity or beauty; *also* : an unusual or strange thing

**cu·ri·ous** \'kyùr-ē-əs\ *adj* **1** : having a desire to investigate and learn **2** : STRANGE, UNUSUAL **3** : ODD, ECCENTRIC — **cu·ri·os·i·ty** \ˌkyùr-ē-'äs-ət-ē\ *n* — **cu·ri·ous·ly** *adv*

**cu·ri·um** \'kyùr-ē-əm\ *n* : a metallic radioactive element produced artificially

¹**curl** \'kərl\ *vb* **1** : to form into ringlets **2** : CURVE, COIL — **curl·er** *n*

²**curl** *n* **1** : a lock of hair that coils : RINGLET **2** : something having a spiral or twisted form — **curly** *adj*

**cur·lew** \'kər-l(y)ü\ *n, pl* **curlews** or **curlew** : a long-legged brownish bird with a down-curved bill

**curli·cue** \'kər-li-ˌkyü\ *n* : a fancifully curved or spiral figure

**cur·rant** \'kər-ənt\ *n* **1** : a small seedless raisin **2** : the acid berry of a shrub related to the gooseberry; *also* : this plant

**cur·ren·cy** \'kər-ən-sē\ *n, pl* **-cies 1** : general use or acceptance **2** : something that is in circulation as a medium of exchange : MONEY

¹**cur·rent** \'kər-ənt\ *adj* **1** : occurring in or belonging to the present **2** : used as a medium of exchange **3** : generally accepted or practiced

²**current** *n* **1** : continuous onward movement of a fluid; *also* : the swiftest part of a stream **2** : a flow of electric charge; *also* : the rate of such flow

**cur·ric·u·lum** \kə-'rik-yə-ləm\ *n, pl* **-la** \-lə\ *also* **-lums** [L, racecourse, fr. *currere* to run] : a course of study offered by a school or one of its divisions

¹**cur·ry** \'kər-ē\ *vb* **cur·ried; cur·ry·ing 1** : to dress the coat of (a horse) with a currycomb **2** : to scrape (leather) until clean — **curry fa·vor** \-'fā-vər\ : to seek to gain favor by flattery or attention

²**cur·ry** \'kər-ē\ *n, pl* **curries** : a powder of blended spices used in cooking; *also* : a food seasoned with curry

**cur·ry·comb** \-ˌkōm\ *n* : a comb used esp. to curry horses — **currycomb** *vb*

¹**curse** \'kərs\ *n* **1** : a prayer for harm to come upon one **2** : something that is cursed **3** : something that comes as if in response to a curse : SCOURGE

²**curse** *vb* **cursed; curs·ing 1** : to call on divine power to send injury upon **2** : BLASPHEME **3** : AFFLICT *syn* execrate, damn, anathematize

**cur·sive** \'kər-siv\ *adj* : written or formed with the strokes of the letters joined together and the angles rounded

**cur·so·ry** \'kərs-(ə-)rē\ *adj* : hastily and often superficially done : HASTY — **cur·so·ri·ly** \-rə-lē\ *adv*

**curt** \'kərt\ *adj* : rudely short or abrupt — **curt·ly** *adv*

**cur·tail** \(ˌ)kər-'tāl\ *vb* : to cut off the end of : SHORTEN — **cur·tail·ment** *n*

**cur·tain** \'kərt-ᵊn\ *n* **1** : a hanging screen that can be drawn back esp. at a window **2** : the screen between the stage and auditorium of a theater — **curtain** *vb*

**curt·sy** or **curt·sey** \'kərt-sē\ *n, pl* **curtsies** or **curtseys** : a courteous bow made by women chiefly by bending the knees — **curtsy** *vb*

**cur·va·ceous** *also* **cur·va·cious** \ˌkər-'vā-shəs\ *adj* : having a well-proportioned feminine figure marked by pronounced curves

**cur·va·ture** \'kər-və-,chŭr\ n : a measure or amount of curving : BEND

¹**curve** \'kərv\ vb **curved**; **curv·ing** : to bend from a straight line or course

²**curve** n 1 : a bending without angles 2 : something curved 3 : a ball thrown so that it swerves from a normal course

**cur·vet** \(,)kər-'vet\ n : a prancing leap of a horse — **curvet** vb

¹**cush·ion** \'kŭsh-ən\ n 1 : a soft pillow or pad to rest on or against 2 : the springy pad inside the rim of a billiard table 3 : something soft that prevents discomfort or protects against injury

²**cushion** vb **cush·ioned**; **cush·ion·ing** (-(ə-)niŋ\ 1 : to provide (as a seat) with a cushion 2 : to soften or lessen the force or shock of

**cusp** \'kəsp\ n : a pointed end (as of a tooth)

**cus·pid** \'kəs-pəd\ n : a canine tooth

**cus·pi·dor** \'kəs-pə-,dór\ n : SPITTOON

**cus·tard** \'kəs-tərd\ n : a sweetened mixture of milk and eggs cooked until it is set

**cus·to·di·al** \,kəs-'tōd-ē-əl\ adj : marked by watching and protecting rather than seeking to cure (⟨~ care⟩

**cus·to·di·an** \,kəs-'tōd-ē-ən\ n : one who has custody (as of a building)

**cus·to·dy** \'kəs-təd-ē\ n, pl **-dies** : immediate care or charge

¹**cus·tom** \'kəs-təm\ n 1 : habitual course of action : recognized usage 2 pl : taxes levied on imports 3 : business patronage

²**custom** adj 1 : made to personal order 2 : doing work only on order

**cus·tom·ary** \'kəs-tə-,mer-ē\ adj 1 : based on or established by custom (⟨~ rent⟩ 2 : commonly practiced or observed : HABITUAL — **cus·tom·ar·i·ly** \,kəs-tə-'mer-ə-lē\ adv

**cus·tom-built** \,kəs-təm-'bilt\ adj : built to individual order

**cus·tom·er** \'kəs-tə-mər\ n : BUYER, PURCHASER; esp : a regular or frequent buyer

**cus·tom·house** \'kəs-təm-,haùs\ n : the building where customs are paid

**cus·tom·ize** \'kəs-tə-,mīz\ vb **-ized**; **-iz·ing** : to build, fit, or alter according to individual specifications

**cus·tom-made** \,kəs-təm-'(m)ād\ adj : made to individual order

¹**cut** \'kət\ vb **cut**; **cut·ting** 1 : to penetrate or divide with a sharp edge : CLEAVE, GASH; also : to experience the growth of (a tooth) through the gum 2 : SHORTEN, REDUCE 3 : to remove by severing or paring 4 : INTERSECT, CROSS 5 : to strike sharply 6 : to divide into parts 7 : to go quickly or change direction abruptly 8 : to cause to stop

²**cut** n 1 : something made by cutting : GASH, CLEFT 2 : an excavated channel or roadway 3 : SHARE 4 : a customary segment of a meat carcass 5 : a sharp stroke or blow 6 : the shape or manner in which a thing is cut 7 : REDUCTION (⟨~ in wages⟩ 8 : an engraved surface for printing; also : a picture printed from it 9 : BAND 4

**cut-and-dried** \,kət-ᵊn-'drīd\ also

**cut-and-dry** \-'drī\ adj : according to a plan, set procedure, or formula

**cu·ta·ne·ous** \kyù-'tā-nē-əs\ adj : of or relating to the skin — **cu·ta·ne·ous·ly** adv

**cut·back** \'kət-,bak\ n 1 : something cut back 2 : REDUCTION

**cute** \'kyüt\ adj **cut·er**; **cut·est** [short for acute] 1 : CLEVER, SHREWD 2 : daintily attractive : PRETTY

**cu·ti·cle** \'kyüt-i-kəl\ n : an outer layer (as of skin) — **cu·tic·u·lar** \kyù-'tik-yə-lər\ adj

**cut in** \,kət-'in\ vb 1 : to thrust oneself between others 2 : to interrupt a dancing couple and take one as one's partner

**cut·lass** \'kət-ləs\ n : a short heavy curved sword

**cut·ler** \'kət-lər\ n : one who makes, deals in, or repairs cutlery

**cut·lery** \'kət-lə-rē\ n : edged or cutting tools; esp : implements for cutting and eating food

**cut·let** \'kət-lət\ n : a slice of meat (as veal) for broiling or frying

**cut·off** \'kət-,óf\ n 1 : the channel formed when a stream cuts through the neck of an oxbow; also : SHORTCUT 2 : a device for cutting off

**cut·out** \'kət-,aùt\ n : something cut out or prepared for cutting out from something else ⟨a page of animal ~s⟩

**cut out** \,kət-'aùt\ vb 1 : to depart hastily 2 : to shut off

**cut-rate** \'kət-'rāt\ adj : relating to or dealing in goods sold at reduced rates

**cut·ter** \'kət-ər\ n 1 : a tool or a machine for cutting 2 : a ship's boat for carrying stores and passengers 3 : a small armed powerboat 4 : a light sleigh

¹**cut·throat** \'kət-,thrōt\ n : MURDERER

²**cutthroat** adj 1 : MURDEROUS, CRUEL 2 : MERCILESS, RUTHLESS (⟨~competition⟩

**cutthroat trout** n : a large American trout with a red mark under the jaw

**cut·ting** \'kət-iŋ\ n : a piece of a plant able to grow into a new plant

**cut·tle·fish** \'kət-ᵊl-,fish\ n : a 10-armed mollusk related to the squid with an internal shell (**cut·tle·bone** \-,bōn\) used in cage-bird feeding

**cut·up** \'kət-,əp\ n : one that clowns or acts boisterously — **cut up** \,kət-'əp\ vb

**cut·worm** \-,wərm\ n : a smooth-bodied moth larva that feeds on plants at night

**cw** abbr clockwise

**CWO** abbr 1 cash with order 2 chief warrant officer

**cwt** abbr hundredweight

**-cy** \sē\ n suffix : action : practice ⟨mendicancy⟩ : rank : office ⟨chaplaincy⟩ : body : class ⟨magistracy⟩ : state : quality ⟨accuracy⟩

**cy·an** \'sī-,an, -ən\ n : a greenish blue color

**cy·a·nide** \'sī-ə-,nīd, -nəd\ n : a poisonous substance containing potassium or sodium used esp. in electroplating

**cy·ber·na·tion** \,sī-bər-'nā-shən\ n : the automatic control of a process or operation by means of computers — **cy·ber·nat·ed** \'sī-bər-,nāt-əd\ adj

**cy·ber·net·ics** \,sī-bər-'net-iks\ n

: the science of communication and control theory that is concerned esp. with the comparative study of automatic control systems — **cy·ber·net·ic** *adj*

**cyc** *or* **cycl** *abbr* cyclopedia

**cy·cla·mate** \'sī-klə-ˌmāt\ *n* : an artificially produced salt of sodium or calcium

**cy·cla·men** \'sī-klə-mən\ *n* : an herb related to the primroses and grown for its showy nodding flowers

**¹cy·cle** \'sī-kəl, *6 & 7 also* 'sik-əl\ *n* **1** : a period of time occupied by a series of events that repeat themselves regularly and in the same order **2** : a recurring round of operations or events **3** : one complete series of changes of value of an alternating current or an electromagnetic wave; *also* : the number of such changes per second ⟨a current of 60 ~s⟩ **4** : a circular or spiral arrangement **5** : a long period of time : AGE **6** : BICYCLE **7** : MOTORCYCLE — **cy·clic** \'sī-klik, 'sik-lik\ *or* **cy·cli·cal** \'sī-kli-kəl, 'sik-li-\ *adj* — **cy·cli·cal·ly** \-k(ə-)lē\ *or* **cy·clic·ly** \'sī-kli-klē, 'sik-li-\ *adv*

**²cycle** \'sī-kəl, 'sik-əl\ *vb* **cy·cled**; **cy·cling** \'sī-k(ə-)liŋ, 'sik(-ə)-\ : to ride a cycle

**cy·clist** \'sī-k(ə-)ləst, 'sik(-ə)-\ *n* : one who rides a cycle

**cy·clom·e·ter** \sī-'kläm-ət-ər\ *n* : a device which records the revolutions of a wheel and the distance covered

**cy·clone** \'sī-ˌklōn\ *n* **1** : a storm or system of winds that rotates about a center of low atmospheric pressure and advances at 20 to 30 miles an hour **2** : TORNADO — **cy·clon·ic** \sī-'klän-ik\ *adj*

**cy·clo·pe·dia** *or* **cy·clo·pae·dia** \ˌsī-klə-'pēd-ē-ə\ *n* : ENCYCLOPEDIA

**cy·clo·tron** \'sī-klə-ˌträn\ *n* : a device for giving high speed to charged particles by magnetic and electric forces

**cyg·net** \'sig-nət\ *n* : a young swan

**cyl** *abbr* cylinder

**cyl·in·der** \'sil-ən-dər\ *n* **1** : the solid figure formed by turning a rectangle about one side as an axis; *also* : a body of this form **2** : the rotating chamber in a revolver **3** : the piston chamber in an engine — **cy·lin·dri·cal** \sə-'lin-dri-kəl\ *adj*

**cym·bal** \'sim-bəl\ *n* : one of a pair of concave brass plates clashed together

**cyme** \'sīm\ *n* : an inflorescence of several flowers each on a stem with the first-opening central flower on the main stem and later-opening flowers developing from lateral buds — **cy·mose** \'sī-ˌmōs\ *adj*

**cyn·ic** \'sin-ik\ *n* [MF *or* L, MF *cynique*, fr. L *cynicus*, fr. Gk *kynikos*, lit., like a dog, fr. *kyōn* dog] : one who attributes all actions to selfish motives — **cyn·i·cal** \-i-kəl\ *adj* — **cyn·i·cal·ly** \-k(ə-)lē\ *adv* — **cyn·i·cism** \'sin-ə-ˌsiz-əm\ *n*

**cy·no·sure** \'sī-nə-ˌshùr, 'sin-ə-\ *n* [MF & L; MF, fr. L *cynosura* Ursa Minor, guide, fr. L *cynosura* Ursa Minor, fr. Gk *kynosoura*, fr. *kynos oura* dog's tail] : a center of attraction

**CYO** *abbr* Catholic Youth Organization

**cy·press** \'sī-prəs\ *n* : a scaly-leaved evergreen tree related to the pines

**cyst** \'sist\ *n* : an abnormal closed bodily sac usu. containing liquid —**cys·tic** \'sis-tik\ *adj*

**cystic fibrosis** *n* : a common hereditary disease marked esp. by deficiency of pancreatic enzymes and by respiratory symptoms

**cy·tol·o·gy** \sī-'täl-ə-jē\ *n* : a branch of biology dealing with cells — **cy·to·log·i·cal** \ˌsīt-ʰl-'äj-i-kəl\ *or* **cy·to·log·ic** \-'äj-ik\ *adj* — **cy·tol·o·gist** \sī-'täl-ə-jəst\ *n*

**cy·to·plasm** \'sīt-ə-ˌplaz-əm\ *n* : the protoplasm of a cell that lies external to the nucleus — **cy·to·plas·mic** \ˌsīt-ə-'plaz-mik\ *adj*

**cy·to·sine** \'sīt-ə-ˌsēn\ *n* : a pyrimidine base that codes genetic information in DNA and RNA

**CZ** *abbr* Canal Zone

**czar** \'zär\ *n* : the ruler of Russia until 1917; *also* : one having great authority — **czar·ist** *n or adj*

**cza·ri·na** \zä-'rē-nə\ *n* : the wife of a czar

**Czech** \'chek\ *n* **1** : a native or inhabitant of Czechoslovakia **2** : the language of the Czechs — **Czech** *adj*

---

**D**

**¹d** \'dē\ *n, pl* **d's** *or* **ds** \'dēz\ *often cap* **1** : the 4th letter of the English alphabet **2** : a grade rating a student's work as poor

**²d** *abbr, often cap* **1** date **2** daughter **3** day **4** deceased **5** degree **6** [L *denarius*] penny **7** diameter **8** died **9** Dutch

**D** *symbol* deuterium

**DA** *abbr* **1** days after acceptance **2** Department of Agriculture **3** deposit account **4** district attorney **5** don't answer

**¹dab** \'dab\ *n* **1** : a sudden blow or thrust : POKE; *also* : PECK **2** : a gentle touch or stroke : PAT

**²dab** *vb* **dabbed**; **dab·bing** **1** : to strike or touch gently : PAT **2** : to apply lightly or irregularly : DAUB

**³dab** *n* **1** : DAUB **2** : a small amount

**dab·ble** \'dab-əl\ *vb* **dab·bled**; **dab·bling** \-(ə-)liŋ\ **1** : to wet by splashing : SPATTER **2** : to paddle or play in or as if in water **3** : to work or concern oneself without serious effort

**dace** \'dās\ *n, pl* **dace** : a small freshwater fish related to the carp

**da·cha** \'däch-ə\ *n* [Russ., lit., gift; fr. its frequently being the gift of a ruler] : a Russian country house

**dachs·hund** \'däks-ˌhùnt\ *n, pl* **dachshunds** *or* **dachs·hun·de** \'däks-ˌhùn-də\ [G, fr. *dachs* badger + *hund* dog] : a small dog of a breed of

German origin with a long body, short legs, and long drooping ears

**dac·tyl** \'dak-t⁹l\ *n* [ME *dactile*, fr. L *dactylus*, fr. Gk *daktylos*, lit., finger; fr. the fact that the three syllables have the first one longest like the joints of the finger] **:** a metrical foot of one accented syllable followed by two unaccented syllables — **dac·tyl·ic** \dak-'til-ik\ *adj or n*

**dad** \'dad\ *n* **:** FATHER

**da·da** \'däd-(,)ä\ *n, often cap* **:** a movement in art and literature based on deliberate irrationality and negation of traditional artistic values — **da·da·ism** \-,iz-əm\ *n, often cap* — **da·da·ist** \-,ist\ *n, often cap*

**dad·dy** \'dad-ē\ *n, -i pl* **daddies :** FATHER

**dad·dy long·legs** \,dad-ē-'lȯṅ-,legz\ *n sing or pl* **:** an arthropod that is related to the spiders and has a small rounded body and long slender legs

**dae·mon** *var of* DEMON

**daf·fo·dil** \'daf-ə-,dil\ *n* **:** a narcissus with usu. large flowers having a trumpetlike center

**daf·fy** \'daf-ē\ *adj* **daf·fi·er; -est :** DAFT

**daft** \'daft\ *adj* **:** FOOLISH; *also* **:** INSANE — **daft·ness** *n*

**dag·ger** \'dag-ər\ *n* **1 :** a short knifelike weapon used for stabbing **2 :** a character † used as a reference mark or to indicate a death date

**da·guerre·o·type** \də-'ger-(ē-)ə-,tīp\ *n* **:** an early photograph produced on a silver or a silver-covered copper plate

**dahl·ia** \'dal-yə, 'däl-\ *n* **:** a tuberous herb related to the daisies and widely grown for its showy flowers

**¹dai·ly** \'dā-lē\ *adj* **1 :** occurring, done, or used every day or every weekday **2 :** of or relating to every day ⟨~ visitors⟩ **3 :** computed in terms of one day ⟨~ wages⟩ — **daily** *adv*

**²daily** *n, pl* **dailies :** a newspaper published every weekday

**daily double** *n* **:** a system of betting on races in which the bettor must pick the winners of two stipulated races in order to win

**daily dozen** *n* **:** a set of exercises done daily

**¹dain·ty** \'dānt-ē\ *n, pl* **dainties** [ME *deinte*, fr. OF *deintié*, fr. L *dignitas* dignity, worth] **:** something delicious or pleasing to the taste **:** DELICACY

**²dainty** *adj* **dain·ti·er; -est 1 :** pleasing to the taste **2 :** delicately pretty **3 :** having or showing delicate taste; *also* **:** FASTIDIOUS — **dain·ti·ly** \'dānt-⁹l-ē\ *adv* — **dain·ti·ness** \-ē-nəs\ *n*

**dai·qui·ri** \'dī-kə-rē\ *n* **:** a cocktail made of rum, lime juice, and sugar

**dairy** \'de(ə)r-ē\ *n, pl* **dair·ies** [ME *deyerie*, fr. *deye* dairymaid, fr. OE *dæge* kneader of bread] **1 :** CREAMERY **2 :** a farm specializing in milk production

**dairy·ing** \'der-ē-iṅ\ *n* **:** the business of operating a dairy

**dairy·maid** \-,mād\ *n* **:** a woman employed in a dairy

**dairy·man** \-mən, -,man\ *n* **:** one who operates a dairy farm or works in a dairy

**da·is** \'dā-əs, 'dī-\ *n* **:** a raised platform usu. above the floor of a hall or large room

**dai·sy** \'dā-zē\ *n, pl* **daisies** [ME *dayeseye*, fr. OE *dægeseage*, fr. *dæg* day + *ēage* eye] **:** any of numerous composite plants having flower heads in which the marginal flowers resemble petals

**Da·ko·ta** \də-'kōt-ə\ *n, pl* **Dakotas** *also* **Dakota :** a member of an Indian people of the northern Mississippi valley; *also* **:** their language

**da·la·si** \dä-'läs-ē\ *n* — *see* MONEY table

**dale** \'dāl\ *n* **:** VALLEY

**dal·ly** \'dal-ē\ *vb* **dal·lied; dal·ly·ing 1 :** to act playfully; *esp* **:** to play amorously **2 :** to waste time **3 :** LINGER, DAWDLE — **dal·li·ance** \-əns\ *n*

**dal·ma·tian** \dal-'mā-shən\ *n, often cap* **:** a large dog of a breed characterized by a white short-haired coat with black or brown spots

**¹dam** \'dam\ *n* **:** a female parent — used esp. of a domestic animal

**²dam** *n* **:** a barrier (as across a stream) to prevent the flow of water — **dam** *vb*

**dam·age** \'dam-ij\ *n* **1 :** loss or harm due to injury to persons, property, or reputation **2** *pl* **:** compensation in money imposed by law for loss or injury ⟨bring a suit for ~s⟩

**²damage** *vb* **dam·aged; dam·ag·ing :** to cause damage to

**dam·a·scene** \'dam-ə-,sēn\ *vb* **-scened; -scen·ing :** to ornament (as iron or steel) with wavy patterns or with inlaid work of precious metals

**Da·mas·cus steel** \də-,mas-kəs-\ *n* **:** a hard elastic steel used esp. for sword blades

**dam·ask** \'dam-əsk\ *n* **1 :** a firm lustrous reversible figured fabric used for household linen **2 :** DAMASCUS STEEL

**dame** \'dām\ *n* **1 :** a woman of rank, station, or authority **2 :** an elderly woman **3** *slang* **:** WOMAN

**damn** \'dam\ *vb* **damned; damn·ing** \'dam-iṅ\ [ME *dampnen*, fr. OF *dampner*, fr. L *damnare*, fr. *damnum* damage, loss, fine] **1 :** to condemn esp. to hell **2 :** CURSE — **damned** *adj*

**dam·na·ble** \'dam-nə-bəl\ *adj* **1 :** liable to or deserving punishment **2 :** DETESTABLE ⟨~ weather⟩ — **dam·na·bly** \-blē\ *adv*

**dam·na·tion** \dam-'nā-shən\ *n* **1 :** the act of damning **2 :** the state of being damned

**¹damp** \'damp\ *n* **1 :** a noxious gas **2 :** MOISTURE

**²damp** *vb* **1 :** DEPRESS **2 :** CHECK, RESTRAIN **3 :** DAMPEN

**³damp** *adj* **:** MOIST — **damp·ness** *n*

**damp·en** \'dam-pən\ *vb* **dampened; damp·en·ing** \'damp-(ə)niṅ\ **1 :** to check or diminish in activity or vigor **2 :** to make or become damp

**damp·er** \'dam-pər\ *n* **:** one that

damps; *esp* **:** a valve or movable plate (as in the flue of a stove, furnace, or fireplace) to regulate the draft

**dam·sel** \\'dam-zəl\\ *n* **:** GIRL, MAIDEN

**dam·sel·fly** \\-,flī\\ *n* **:** any of a group of insects that are closely related to the dragonflies but fold their wings above the body when at rest

**dam·son** \\'dam-zən\\ *n* **:** a plum with acid purple fruit; *also* **:** its fruit

**Dan** *abbr* **1** Daniel **2** Danish

**¹dance** \\'dans\\ *vb* **danced; danc·ing 1 :** to glide, step, or move through a set series of movements usu. to music **2 :** to move quickly up and down or about **3 :** to perform or take part in as a dancer — **danc·er** *n*

**²dance** *n* **1 :** an act or instance of dancing **2 :** a social gathering for dancing **3 :** a piece of music (as a waltz) by which dancing may be guided **4 :** the art of dancing

**dan·de·li·on** \\'dan-dᵊl-,ī-ən\\ *n* [MF *dent de lion*, lit., lion's tooth] **:** a common yellow-flowered composite herb

**dan·der** \\'dan-dər\\ *n* **:** ANGER, TEMPER

**dan·di·fy** \\'dan-di-,fī\\ *vb* **-fied; -fy·ing :** to make characteristic of a dandy

**dan·dle** \\'dan-dᵊl\\ *vb* **dan·dled; dan·dling :** to move up and down in one's arms or on one's knee in affectionate play

**dan·druff** \\'dan-drəf\\ *n* **:** a whitish scurf on the scalp that comes off in small scales

**¹dan·dy** \\'dan-dē\\ *n, pl* **dandies 1 :** a man unduly attentive to dress **2 :** something excellent in its class

**²dandy** *adj* **dan·di·er; -est :** very good **:** FIRST-RATE

**Dane** \\'dān\\ *n* **:** a native or inhabitant of Denmark

**dan·ger** \\'dān-jər\\ *n* **1 :** exposure or liability to injury, harm, or evil **2 :** something that may cause injury or harm **syn** peril, hazard

**dan·ger·ous** \\'dānj-(ə-)rəs\\ *adj* **1 :** HAZARDOUS, PERILOUS **2 :** able or likely to inflict injury — **dan·ger·ous·ly** *adv*

**dan·gle** \\'daŋ-gəl\\ *vb* **dan·gled; dan·gling** \\-g(ə-)liŋ\\ **1 :** to hang loosely esp. with a swinging motion **:** SWING **2 :** to be a hanger-on or dependent **3 :** to be left without proper grammatical connection in a sentence **4 :** to keep hanging uncertainly

**Dan·ish** \\'dā-nish\\ *n* **:** the language of the Danes — **Danish** *adj*

**Danish pastry** *n* **:** a pastry made of a rich yeast-raised dough

**dank** \\'daŋk\\ *adj* **:** disagreeably wet or moist **:** DAMP

**dan·seuse** \\dänⁿ-'sə(r)z, dän-'süz\\ *n* **:** a female ballet dancer

**dap·per** \\'dap-ər\\ *adj* **1 :** SPRUCE, TRIM **2 :** being alert and lively in movement and manners **:** JAUNTY

**dap·ple** \\'dap-əl\\ *vb* **dap·pled; dap·pling :** to mark with different-colored spots

**DAR** *abbr* Daughters of the American Revolution

**¹dare** \\'daər\\ *vb* **dared; dar·ing 1 :** to have sufficient courage **:** be bold enough to **2 :** CHALLENGE **3 :** to confront boldly

**²dare** *n* **:** an invitation to contend

**dare·dev·il** \\-,dev-əl\\ *n* **:** a recklessly bold person

**dar·ing** \\'da(ə)r-iŋ\\ *n* **:** venturesome boldness — **daring** *adj* — **dar·ing·ly** *adv*

**¹dark** \\'dark\\ *adj* **1 :** being without light or without much light **2 :** not light in color ⟨a ~ suit⟩ **3 :** GLOOMY **4 :** being without knowledge and culture ⟨the Dark Ages⟩ **5 :** SECRETIVE — **dark·ly** *adv* — **dark·ness** *n*

**²dark** *n* **1 :** absence of light **:** DARKNESS; *esp* **:** NIGHT **2 :** a dark or deep color **3 :** IGNORANCE; *also* **:** SECRECY

**dark adaptation** *n* **:** the whole process by which the eye adapts to seeing in weak light — **dark-adapt·ed** \\,där-kə-'dap-təd\\ *adj*

**dark·en** \\'där-kən\\ *vb* **dark·ened; dark·en·ing** \\'därk-(ə-)niŋ\\ **1 :** to make or grow dark or darker **2 :** DIM **3 :** BESMIRCH, TARNISH **4 :** to make or become gloomy or forbidding

**dark horse** *n* **:** a contestant or a political figure whose abilities and chances as a contender are not known

**dark·ling** \\'där-kliŋ\\ *adv* **:** in the dark

**dark·room** \\'därk-,rüm, -,rùm\\ *n* **:** a room protected from rays of light that are harmful in the process of developing sensitive photographic plates and film

**dark·some** \\'därk-səm\\ *adj* **:** DARK

**¹dar·ling** \\'där-liŋ\\ *n* **1 :** a dearly loved person **2 :** FAVORITE

**²darling** *adj* **1 :** dearly loved **:** FAVORITE **2 :** very pleasing **:** CHARMING

**darn** \\'därn\\ *vb* **:** to mend with interlacing stitches — **darn·er** *n*

**dar·nel** \\'därn-ᵊl\\ *n* **:** a weedy grass with bristly flower clusters

**darning needle** *n* **1 :** a needle for darning **2 :** DRAGONFLY

**¹dart** \\'därt\\ *n* **1 :** a small pointed missile with a shaft pointed on one end and feathered on the other; *also, pl* **:** a game in which darts are thrown at a target **2 :** something projected with sudden speed; *esp* **:** a sharp glance **3 :** something causing a sudden pain **4 :** a stitched tapering fold in a garment **5 :** a quick movement

**²dart** *vb* **1 :** to throw with a sudden movement **2 :** to thrust or move suddenly or rapidly

**dart·er** \\'därt-ər\\ *n* **:** a small freshwater fish related to the perches

**Dar·win·ism** \\'där-wə-,niz-əm\\ *n* **:** a theory of the origin and perpetuation of new species of plants and animals through the action of natural selection on chance variations — **Dar·win·ist** \\-nəst\\ *n*

**¹dash** \\'dash\\ *vb* **1 :** to knock, hurl, or thrust violently **2 :** SMASH **3 :** SPLASH, SPATTER **4 :** RUIN **5 :** DEPRESS, SADDEN **6 :** to perform or finish hastily **7 :** to move with sudden speed

**²dash** *n* **1 :** a sudden burst or splash

**2** : a stroke of a pen **3** : a punctuation mark — that is used esp. to indicate a break in the thought or structure of a sentence **4** : a small addition ⟨add a ~ of salt⟩ **5** : flashy showiness **6** : animation in style and action **7** : a sudden rush or attempt ⟨made a ~ for the door⟩ **8** : a short foot race

**dash·board** \-ˌbȯrd\ *n* : an instrument panel below the windshield in an automobile or airplane

**dash·er** \'dash-ər\ *n* : a device (as in a churn) that agitates or stirs up something

**da·shi·ki** \də-'shē-kē\ *or* **dai·shi·ki** \dī-\ *n* : a usu. brightly colored loose-fitting pullover garment

**dash·ing** \'dash-iŋ\ *adj* **1** : marked by vigorous action **2** : marked by smartness esp. in dress and manners

**dash·pot** \'dash-ˌpät\ *n* : a device for damping a movement (as of a mechanical part) to avoid shock

**das·tard** \'das-tərd\ *n* : COWARD; *esp* : one who sneakingly commits malicious acts — **das·tard·ly** *adj*

**dat** *abbr* dative

**da·ta** \'dāt-ə, 'dat-, 'dät-\ *sing or pl* : factual information (as measurements or statistics) used as a basis for reasoning, discussion, or calculation

**da·ta·ma·tion** \ˌdāt-ə-'mā-shən, ˌdat-, ˌdät-\ *n* : automatic data processing

**data processing** *n* : the converting of crude information into usable form — **data processor** *n*

**¹date** \'dāt\ *n* [ME, fr. OF, deriv. of L *dactylus*, fr. Gk *daktylos*, lit., finger] : the edible fruit of a tall Old World palm; *also* : this plant

**²date** *n* [ME, fr. MF, fr. LL *data*, fr. *data* (as in *data Romae* given at Rome), fr. L *dare* to give] **1** : the day, month, or year of an event **2** : a statement giving the time of execution or making (as of a coin or check) **3** : the period to which something belongs **4** : APPOINTMENT; *esp* : a social engagement between two persons of opposite sex **5** : a person of the opposite sex with whom one has a social engagement — **to date** : up to the present moment

**³date** *vb* **dat·ed; dat·ing 1** : to determine the date of **2** : to record the date of or on **3** : to mark or reveal the date, age, or period of **4** : to make or have a date with **5** : ORIGINATE ⟨~s from ancient times⟩ **6** : EXTEND ⟨*dating* back to childhood⟩ **7** : to show qualities typical of a past period

**dat·ed** \'dāt-əd\ *adj* **1** : provided with a date **2** : OLD-FASHIONED

**date·less** \'dāt-ləs\ *adj* **1** : ENDLESS **2** : having no date **3** : too ancient to be dated **4** : TIMELESS

**date·line** \'dāt-ˌlīn\ *n* : a line in a publication giving the date and place of composition or issue — **dateline** *vb*

**dating bar** *n* : a bar that caters esp. to young unmarried men and women

**da·tive** \'dāt-iv\ *adj* : of, relating to, or constituting a grammatical case marking typically the indirect object of a verb — **dative** *n*

**da·tum** \'dāt-əm, 'dat-, 'dät-\ *n, pl* **da·ta** \-ə\ *or* **datums** : a single piece of data : FACT

**dau** *abbr* daughter

**¹daub** \'dȯb\ *vb* **1** : to cover with soft adhesive matter **2** : SMEAR, SMUDGE **3** : to paint crudely — **daub·er** *n*

**²daub** *n* **1** : something daubed on : SMEAR **2** : a crude picture

**daugh·ter** \'dȯt-ər\ *n* **1** : a female offspring esp. of human beings **2** : a human female having a specified ancestor or belonging to a group of common ancestry — **daugh·ter·ly** *adj*

**daugh·ter-in-law** \'dȯt-ə-rən-ˌlȯ, -ərn-ˌlȯ\ *n, pl* **daugh·ters-in-law** \-ər-zən-\ : the wife of one's son

**daunt** \'dȯnt\ *vb* [ME *daunten*, fr. OF *danter*, alter. of *donter*, fr. L *domitare* to tame] : to lessen the courage of

**daunt·less** \-ləs\ *adj* : FEARLESS, UNDAUNTED

**dau·phin** \'dȯ-fən\ *n, often cap* : the eldest son of a king of France

**dav·en·port** \'dav-ən-ˌpȯrt\ *n* : a large upholstered sofa

**da·vit** \'dā-vət, 'dav-ət\ *n* : either of a pair of small cranes for raising and lowering small boats

**daw·dle** \'dȯd-ᵊl\ *vb* **daw·dled; daw·dling** \'dȯd-(ᵊ-)liŋ\ **1** : to spend time wastefully or idly **2** : LOITER — **daw·dler** \'dȯd-(ᵊ-)lər\ *n*

**¹dawn** \'dȯn\ *vb* **1** : to begin to grow light as the sun rises **2** : to begin to appear or develop **3** : to begin to be understood ⟨the solution ~ed on him⟩

**²dawn** *n* **1** : the first appearance of light in the morning **2** : a first appearance : BEGINNING ⟨the ~ of a new era⟩

**day** \'dā\ *n* **1** : the period of light between one night and the next : DAYLIGHT **2** : the period of the earth's revolution on its axis **3** : a period of 24 hours beginning at midnight **4** : a specified day or date ⟨wedding ~⟩ **5** : a specified time or period : AGE ⟨in olden ~s⟩ **6** : the conflict or contention of the day ⟨carried the ~⟩ **7** : the time set apart by usage or law for work ⟨the 8-hour ~⟩

**day·bed** \'dā-ˌbed\ *n* : a couch that can be converted into a bed

**day·book** \-ˌbùk\ *n* : DIARY, JOURNAL

**day·break** \-ˌbrāk\ *n* : DAWN

**day–care** \'dā-ˌkeər\ *adj* : of, relating to, or providing supervision and facilities for preschool children during the day

**day·dream** \'dā-ˌdrēm\ *n* : a pleasant reverie — **daydream** *vb*

**day·light** \'dā-ˌlīt\ *n* **1** : the light of day **2** : DAWN **3** : understanding of something that has been obscure **4** *pl* : CONSCIOUSNESS; *also* : WITS

**daylight saving time** *n* : time usu. one hour ahead of standard time

**Day of Atonement** *n* : YOM KIPPUR

**day school** *n* : a private school without boarding facilities

**day student** *n* : a student who attends regular classes at a college or preparatory school but does not live at the institution

**day·time** \'dā-,tīm\ *n* : the period of daylight

**¹daze** \'dāz\ *vb* **dazed; daz·ing** **1** : to stupefy esp. by a blow **2** : DAZZLE

**²daze** *n* : the state of being dazed

**daz·zle** \'daz-əl\ *vb* **daz·zled; daz·zling** \-(ə-)liŋ\ **1** : to overpower with light **2** : to impress greatly or confound with brilliance — **dazzle** *n*

**db** *abbr* decibel

**dbl** *abbr* double

**DC** *abbr* **1** [It *da capo*] from the beginning **2** direct current **3** District of Columbia **4** doctor of chiropractic

**DD** *abbr* **1** days after date **2** demand draft **3** dishonorable discharge **4** doctor of divinity

**D day** *n* [*D*, abbr. for *day*] : a day set for launching an operation (as an invasion)

**DDS** *abbr* **1** doctor of dental science **2** doctor of dental surgery

**DDT** \,dē-(,)dē-'tē\ *n* : a persistent insecticide that tends to accumulate in ecosystems and has toxic effects on many vertebrates

**DE** *abbr* Delaware

**dea·con** \'dē-kən\ *n* [ME *dekene*, fr. OE *dēacon*, fr. LL *diaconus*, fr. Gk *diakonos*, lit., servant] : a subordinate officer in a Christian church — **dea·con·ess** *n*

**de·ac·ti·vate** \dē-'ak-tə-,vāt\ *vb* : to make inactive or ineffective

**¹dead** \'ded\ *adj* **1** : LIFELESS **2** : DEATHLIKE, DEADLY ⟨in a ~ faint⟩ **3** : NUMB **4** : very tired **5** : UNRESPONSIVE **6** : EXTINGUISHED ⟨~ coals⟩ **7** : INANIMATE, INERT **8** : no longer active or functioning : EXHAUSTED, EXTINCT ⟨a ~ battery⟩ ⟨a ~ volcano⟩ **9** : lacking power, significance, or effect ⟨a ~ custom⟩ **10** : OBSOLETE ⟨a ~ language⟩ **11** : lacking in gaiety or animation ⟨a ~ party⟩ **12** : QUIET, IDLE, UNPRODUCTIVE ⟨~ capital⟩ **13** : lacking elasticity ⟨a ~ tennis ball⟩ **14** : not circulating : STAGNANT ⟨~ air⟩ **15** : lacking warmth, vigor, or taste ⟨~ wine⟩ **16** : absolutely uniform ⟨~ level⟩ **17** : UNERRING, EXACT ⟨a ~ shot⟩ **18** : ABRUPT ⟨a ~ stop⟩ **19** : COMPLETE ⟨a ~ loss⟩

**²dead** *n, pl* **dead** **1** : one that is dead — usu. used collectively ⟨the living and the ~⟩ **2** : the time of greatest quiet ⟨the ~ of the night⟩

**³dead** *adv* **1** : UTTERLY ⟨~ right⟩ **2** : in a sudden and complete manner ⟨stopped ~⟩ **3** : DIRECTLY ⟨~ ahead⟩

**dead·beat** \-,bēt\ *n* : one who persistently fails to pay his debts or his way

**dead·en** \'ded-ᵊn\ *vb* **dead·ened; dead·en·ing** \'ded-(ᵊ-)niŋ\ **1** : to impair in force, activity, or sensation : BLUNT ⟨~ pain⟩ **2** : to lessen the luster or spirit of **3** : to make (as a wall) soundproof

**dead end** *n* **1** : an end (as of a street) without an exit **2** : a position, situation, or course of action that leads to nothing further — **dead-end** \,ded-,end\ *adj*

**dead heat** *n* : a contest in which two or more contestants tie (as by crossing the finish line simultaneously)

**dead letter** *n* **1** : something that has lost its force or authority without being formally abolished **2** : a letter that is not deliverable or returnable by the post office

**dead·line** \'ded-,līn\ *n* : a date or time before which something must be done

**dead·lock** \'ded-,läk\ *n* : a stoppage of action because neither of two equally strong factions in a struggle will give in — **deadlock** *vb*

**¹dead·ly** \'ded-lē\ *adj* **dead·li·er; -est** **1** : likely to cause or capable of causing death **2** : HOSTILE, IMPLACABLE **3** : very accurate : UNERRING **4** : fatal to spiritual progress **5** : tending to deprive of force or vitality ⟨a ~ habit⟩ **6** : suggestive of death **7** : very great : EXTREME — **dead·li·ness** *n*

**²deadly** *adv* **1** : suggesting death ⟨~ pale⟩ **2** : EXTREMELY ⟨~ dull⟩

**deadly sin** *n* : one of seven sins of pride, covetousness, lust, anger, gluttony, envy, and sloth held to be fatal to spiritual progress

**dead·pan** \'ded-,pan\ *adj* : marked by an impassive manner or expression — **deadpan** *vb*

**dead reckoning** *n* : the determination of the position of a ship or airplane solely from the record of the direction and distance of its course — **dead reckon** *vb*

**dead·weight** \'ded-'wāt\ *n* : the unrelieved weight of an inert mass

**dead·wood** \-,wud\ *n* **1** : wood dead on the tree **2** : useless personnel or material

**deaf** \'def\ *adj* **1** : unable to hear **2** : unwilling to hear or listen ⟨~ to all suggestions⟩ — **deaf·ness** *n*

**deaf·en** \'def-ən\ *vb* **deaf·ened; deaf·en·ing** \-(ə-)niŋ\ : to make deaf

**deaf-mute** \'def-,myüt\ *n* : a deaf person who cannot speak

**¹deal** \'dēl\ *n* **1** : an indefinite quantity or degree ⟨a great ~⟩; *also* : a large quantity ⟨a ~ of money⟩ **2** : the act or right of distributing cards to players in a card game; *also* : HAND

**²deal** *vb* **dealt** \'delt\; **deal·ing** \'dē-liŋ\ **1** : DISTRIBUTE; *esp* : to distribute playing cards to players in a game **2** : ADMINISTER, DELIVER ⟨*dealt* him a blow⟩ **3** : to concern itself with : TREAT ⟨the book ~s with crime⟩ **4** : to take action in regard to something ⟨~ with offenders⟩ **5** : TRADE; *also* : to sell or distribute something as a business ⟨~ in used cars⟩ — **deal·er** *n*

**³deal** *n* **1** : BARGAINING, NEGOTIATION; *also* : TRANSACTION **2** : treatment received ⟨a raw ~⟩ **3** : a secret or underhand agreement **4** : BARGAIN

**⁴deal** *n* : wood or a board of fir or pine

**deal·er·ship** \'dē-lər-,ship\ *n* : an authorized sales agency

**deal·ing** \'dē-liŋ\ *n* **1** *pl* : friendly or business transactions **2** : a way of acting or of doing business

**dean** \'dēn\ n [ME deen, fr. MF deien, fr. LL decanus, lit., chief of ten, fr. L decem ten] **1 :** a clergyman who is head of a group of canons or of joint pastors of a church **2 :** the head of a division, faculty, college, or school of a university **3 :** a college or secondary school administrator in charge of counseling and disciplining students **4 :** the senior member of a group ⟨the ~ of a diplomatic corps⟩ — **dean·ship** n

**dean·ery** \'dēn-(ə-)rē\ n, pl **-er·ies :** the office, jurisdiction, or official residence of a clerical dean

**¹dear** \'diər\ adj **1 :** highly valued **:** PRECIOUS **2 :** AFFECTIONATE, FOND **3 :** EXPENSIVE **4 :** HEARTFELT — **dear·ly** adv — **dear·ness** n

**²dear** n **:** a loved one **:** DARLING

**Dear John** \-'jän\ n **:** a letter (as to a soldier) in which a wife asks for a divorce or a girl friend breaks off an engagement or a friendship

**dearth** \'dərth\ n **:** SCARCITY, FAMINE

**death** \'deth\ n **1 :** the end of life **2 :** the cause of loss of life **3 :** the state of being dead **4 :** DESTRUCTION, EXTINCTION **5 :** SLAUGHTER — **death-like** adj

**death·bed** \'deth-'bed\ n **1 :** the bed in which a person dies **2 :** the last hours of life

**death·blow** \'deth-'blō\ n **:** a destructive or killing stroke or event

**death·less** \'deth-ləs\ adj **:** IMMORTAL, IMPERISHABLE ⟨~ fame⟩

**death·ly** \'deth-lē\ adj **1 :** FATAL **2 :** of, relating to, or suggestive of death ⟨a ~ pallor⟩ — **deathly** adv

**death rattle** n **:** a sound produced by air passing through mucus in the lungs and air passages of a dying person

**death's-head** \'deths-,hed\ n **:** a human skull emblematic of death

**¹death·watch** \'deth-,wäch\ n **:** a small insect that makes a ticking sound

**²deathwatch** n **:** a vigil kept with the dead or dying

**deb** \'deb\ n **:** DEBUTANTE

**de·ba·cle** \di-'bäk-əl, -'bak-əl\ n **:** DISASTER, FAILURE, ROUT ⟨stock market ~⟩

**de·bar** \di-'bär\ vb **:** to bar from having or doing something **:** PRECLUDE

**de·bark** \di-'bärk\ vb **:** DISEMBARK — **de·bar·ka·tion** \,dē-,bär-'kā-shən\ n

**de·base** \di-'bās\ vb **:** to lower in character, quality, or value **syn** degrade, corrupt, deprave — **de·base·ment** n

**de·bate** \di-'bāt\ vb **de·bat·ed; de·bat·ing 1 :** to discuss or examine a question by presenting and considering arguments on both sides **2 :** to take part in a debate — **de·bat·able** adj — **debate** n — **de·bat·er** n

**de·bauch** \di-'bóch\ vb [MF debaucher, fr. OF desbauchier to scatter, rough-hew (timber), fr. bauch beam] **:** SEDUCE, CORRUPT — **de·bauch·ery** \-(ə-)rē\ n

**de·ben·ture** \di-'ben-chər\ n **:** a certificate of indebtedness; esp **:** a bond secured only by the general assets of the issuing government or corporation

**de·bil·i·tate** \di-'bil-ə-,tāt\ vb **-tat·ed; -tat·ing :** to impair the health or strength of

**de·bil·i·ty** \di-'bil-ət-ē\ n, pl **-ties :** an infirm or weakened state

**¹deb·it** \'deb-ət\ n **1 :** an entry in an account showing money paid out or owed **2 :** a disadvantageous or unfavorable quality or character

**²debit** vb **:** to enter as a debit **:** charge with or as a debit

**deb·o·nair** \,deb-ə-'naər\ adj [ME debonere, fr. OF debonaire, fr. de bonne aire of good family or nature] **:** gaily and gracefully charming **:** LIGHTHEARTED

**de·bouch** \di-'bauch, -'büsh\ vb **:** to march or issue out into an open area

**de·brief** \di-'brēf\ vb **1 :** to question (as a pilot back from a mission) in order to obtain useful information **2 :** to instruct not to reveal any classified information

**de·bris** \də-'brē, dā-; 'dā-,brē\ n, pl **debris** \-'brēz, -,brēz\ **1 :** the remains of something broken down or destroyed **:** RUINS **2 :** an accumulation of fragments of rock

**debt** \'det\ n **1 :** SIN, TRESPASS **2 :** something owed **:** OBLIGATION **3 :** a condition of owing; esp **:** the state of owing money in amounts greater than one can pay

**debt·or** \'det-ər\ n **1 :** SINNER **2 :** one that owes a debt

**de·bunk** \dē-'bəŋk\ vb **:** to expose the sham or falseness of ⟨~ a rumor⟩

**de·but** \'dā-,byü, dā-'byü\ n **1 :** a first public appearance **2 :** a formal entrance into society

**deb·u·tante** \'deb-yu̇-,tänt\ n **:** a young woman making her formal entrance into society

**dec** abbr **1** deceased **2** decrease

**Dec** abbr December

**de·cade** \'dek-,ād, -əd; de-'kād\ n **:** a period of 10 years

**dec·a·dence** \'dek-əd-əns, di-'kād-²ns\ n **:** DETERIORATION, DECLINE — **dec·a·dent** \'dek-əd-ənt, di-'kād-²nt\ adj or n

**deca·gon** \'dek-ə-,gän\ n **:** a plane polygon of 10 angles and 10 sides

**de·cal** \'dē-,kal, di-'kal, 'dek-əl\ n **:** DECALCOMANIA

**de·cal·co·ma·nia** \di-,kal-kə-'mā-nē-ə\ n [F décalcomanie, fr. décalquer to copy by tracing (fr. calquer to trace, fr. It calcare, lit., to trample, fr. L) + manie mania, fr. LL mania] **:** a transferring (as to glass) of designs from specially prepared paper; also **:** a design prepared for such transferring

**Deca·logue** \'dek-ə-,lóg\ n **:** the ten commandments of God given to Moses on Mount Sinai

**de·camp** \di-'kamp\ vb **1 :** to break up a camp **2 :** to depart suddenly

**de·cant** \di-'kant\ vb **:** to pour (liquor) gently

**de·cant·er** \di-'kant-ər\ n **:** an ornamental glass bottle for serving wine

**de·cap·i·tate** \di-'kap-ə-,tāt\ vb **-tat·ed; -tat·ing :** BEHEAD — **de·cap·i·ta·tion** \-,kap-ə-'tā-shən\ n

**deca·syl·lab·ic** \,dek-ə-sə-'lab-ik\ *adj* : having or composed of verses having 10 syllables — **decasyllabic** *n*

**de·cath·lon** \di-'kath-lən, -,län\ *n* : an athletic contest in which each competitor participates in each of a series of 10 track-and-field events

**de·cay** \di-'kā\ *vb* 1 : to decline from a sound, prosperous, or healthy condition 2 : to cause or undergo decomposition ⟨radium ~s slowly⟩; *esp* : to break down in the course of spoiling : ROT — **decay** *n*

**de·cease** \di-'sēs\ *n* : DEATH — **decease** *vb*

**de·ce·dent** \di-'sēd-ᵊnt\ *n* : a deceased person

**de·ceit** \di-'sēt\ *n* 1 : DECEPTION 2 : TRICK 3 : DECEITFULNESS

**de·ceit·ful** \-fəl\ *adj* 1 : practicing or tending to practice deceit 2 : MISLEADING, DECEPTIVE ⟨a ~ answer⟩ — **de·ceit·ful·ly** *adv* — **de·ceit·ful·ness** *n*

**de·ceive** \di-'sēv\ *vb* **de·ceived**; **de·ceiv·ing** 1 : to cause to believe an untruth 2 : to deal with dishonestly 3 : to use or practice dishonesty — **de·ceiv·er** *n*

**de·cel·er·ate** \dē-'sel-ə-,rāt\ *vb* -**at·ed**; -**at·ing** : to slow down

**De·cem·ber** \di-'sem-bər\ *n* [ME *Decembre*, fr. OF, fr. L *December* (tenth month), fr. *decem* ten] : the 12th month of the year having 31 days

**de·cen·cy** \'dēs-ᵊn-sē\ *n*, *pl* -**cies** 1 : PROPRIETY 2 : conformity to standards of taste, propriety, or quality 3 : standard of propriety — usu. used in pl.

**de·cen·ni·al** \di-'sen-ē-əl\ *adj* 1 : consisting of 10 years 2 : happening every 10 years ⟨~ census⟩ — **decennial** *n* — **de·cen·ni·al·ly** \-ē\ *adv*

**de·cent** \'dēs-ᵊnt\ *adj* 1 : conforming to standards of propriety, good taste, or morality 2 : modestly clothed 3 : free from immodesty or obscenity 4 : ADEQUATE ⟨~ housing⟩ — **de·cent·ly** *adv*

**de·cen·tral·iza·tion** \dē-,sen-trə-lə-'zā-shən\ *n* 1 : the dispersion or distribution of functions and powers from a central authority to regional and local authorities 2 : the redistribution of population and industry from urban centers to outlying areas — **de·cen·tral·ize** \-'sen-trə-,līz\ *vb*

**de·cep·tion** \di-'sep-shən\ *n* 1 : the act of deceiving 2 : the fact or condition of being deceived 3 : FRAUD, TRICK — **de·cep·tive** \-'sep-tiv\ *adj* — **de·cep·tive·ly** *adv*

**deci·bel** \'des-ə-,bel, -bəl\ *n* 1 : a unit for expressing the ratio of two amounts of electric or acoustic signal power 2 : a unit for measuring the relative loudness of sounds

**de·cide** \di-'sīd\ *vb* **de·cid·ed**; **de·cid·ing** [ME *deciden*, fr. MF *decider*, fr. L *decidere*, lit., to cut off, fr. *caedere* to cut] 1 : to arrive at a solution that ends uncertainty or dispute about 2 : to bring to a definitive end ⟨one blow *decided* the fight⟩

3 : to induce to come to a choice 4 : to make a choice or judgment

**de·cid·ed** \dē-'sīd-əd\ *adj* 1 : CLEAR, UNMISTAKABLE 2 : FIRM, DETERMINED — **de·cid·ed·ly** *adv*

**de·cid·u·ous** \di-'sij-ə-wəs\ *adj* 1 : falling off usu. at the end of a period of growth or function ⟨~ leaves⟩ ⟨a ~ tooth⟩ 2 : having deciduous parts ⟨~ trees⟩

**deci·gram** \'des-ə-,gram\ *n* — see METRIC SYSTEM table

**deci·li·ter** \'des-ə-,lēt-ər\ *n* — see METRIC SYSTEM table

¹**dec·i·mal** \'des-ə-məl\ *adj* : based on the number 10 : reckoning by tens — **dec·i·mal·ly** \-ē\ *adv*

²**decimal** *n* : a fraction in which the denominator is a power of 10 usu. not expressed but signified by a point placed at the left of the numerator (as .2 = 2/10, .25 = 25/100, .025 = 25/1000)

**dec·i·mal·ize** \'des-ə-mə-,līz\ *vb* -**ized**; -**iz·ing** : to convert to a decimal system — **dec·i·mal·iza·tion** \,des-ə-mə-lə-'zā-shən\ *n*

**decimal point** *n* : the dot at the left of a decimal fraction

**dec·i·mate** \'des-ə-,māt\ *vb* -**mat·ed**; -**mat·ing** 1 : to take or destroy the 10th part of 2 : to destroy a large part of

**dec·i·meter** \'des-ə-,mēt-ər\ *n* — see METRIC SYSTEM table

**de·ci·pher** \di-'sī-fər\ *vb* 1 : to translate from secret writing (as code) 2 : to make out the meaning of despite indistinctness — **de·ci·pher·able** *adj*

**de·ci·sion** \di-'sizh-ən\ *n* 1 : the act or result of deciding esp. by giving judgment 2 : promptness and firmness in deciding : DETERMINATION

**de·ci·sive** \-'sī-siv\ *adj* 1 : having the power to decide ⟨the ~ vote⟩ 2 : CONCLUSIVE ⟨a ~ victory⟩ 3 : marked by or showing decision — **de·ci·sive·ly** *adv* — **de·ci·sive·ness** *n*

**deci·stere** \'des-ə-,sti(ə)r, -,ste(ə)r\ *n* — see METRIC SYSTEM table

¹**deck** \'dek\ *n* 1 : a floorlike platform of a ship; *also* : something resembling the deck of a ship 2 : a pack of playing cards

²**deck** *vb* 1 : ARRAY 2 : DECORATE 3 : to furnish with a deck 4 : to knock down : FLOOR

**deck·hand** \'dek-,hand\ *n* : a seaman who performs manual duties

**deck·le edge** \,dek-əl-\ *n* : the rough untrimmed edge of paper — **deck·le-edged** \,dek-ə-'lejd\ *adj*

**de·claim** \di-'klām\ *vb* : to speak or deliver loudly or impressively — **dec·la·ma·tion** \,dek-lə-'mā-shən\ *n* — **de·clam·a·to·ry** \di-'klam-ə-,tōr-ē\ *adj*

**de·clar·a·tive** \di-'klar-ət-iv\ *adj* : making a declaration ⟨~ sentence⟩

**de·clare** \di-'klaər\ *vb* **de·clared**; **de·clar·ing** 1 : to make known formally or explicitly : ANNOUNCE ⟨~ war⟩ 2 : to state emphatically : AFFIRM 3 : to make a full statement of — **dec·la·ra·tion** \,dek-lə-'rā-shən\ n — **de·clar·a·to·ry** \di-'klar-ə-,tōr-ē\ adj — **de·clar·er** n

**de·clas·si·fy** \dē-'klas-ə-,fī\ vb : to remove or reduce the security classification of

**de·clen·sion** \di-'klen-chən\ n 1 : a schematic arrangement of the inflectional forms esp. of a noun or pronoun 2 : DECLINE, DETERIORATION 3 : DESCENT, SLOPE

¹**de·cline** \di-'klīn\ vb **de·clined; de·clin·ing** 1 : to slope downward : DESCEND 2 : DROOP 3 : RECEDE 4 : WANE 5 : to withhold consent; also : REFUSE, REJECT 6 : INFLECT (~ a noun) — **de·clin·able** adj — **dec·li·na·tion** \,dek-lə-'nā-shən\ n

²**decline** n 1 : a gradual sinking and wasting away 2 : a change to a lower state or level 3 : the time when something is approaching its end 4 : a descending slope 5 : a wasting disease; esp : pulmonary tuberculosis

**de·cliv·i·ty** \di-'kliv-ət-ē\ n, pl **-ties** : a steep downward slope

**de·code** \dē-'kōd\ vb : to convert (a coded message) into ordinary language

**dé·col·le·té** \dā-,käl-ə-'tā\ adj 1 : wearing a strapless or low-necked gown 2 : having a low-cut neckline

**de·col·or·ize** \dē-'kəl-ə-,rīz\ vb **-ized; -iz·ing** : to remove color from — **de·col·or·iz·er** n

**de·com·mis·sion** \,dē-kə-'mish-ən\ vb : to take out of commission

**de·com·pen·sa·tion** \,dē-,käm-pən-'sā-shən\ n : loss of compensation; esp : inability of the heart to maintain adequate circulation — **de·com·pen·sate** \dē-'käm-pən-,sāt\ vb

**de·com·pose** \,dē-kəm-'pōz\ vb 1 : to separate into constituent parts 2 : to break down in decay : ROT — **de·com·po·si·tion** \dē-,käm-pə-'zish-ən\ n

**de·com·press** \,dē-kəm-'pres\ vb : to release (as a diver) from pressure or compression — **de·com·pres·sion** \-'presh-ən\ n

**de·con·ges·tant** \,dē-kən-'jes-tənt\ n : an agent that relieves congestion (as of mucous membranes)

**de·con·tam·i·nate** \,dē-kən-'tam-ə-,nāt\ vb : to rid of contamination — **de·con·tam·i·na·tion** \-,tam-ə-'nā-shən\ n

**de·con·trol** \,dē-kən-'trōl\ vb : to end control of (~ prices)

**de·cor** or **dé·cor** \dā-'kor, 'dā-,kor\ n : DECORATION; esp : the arrangement of accessories in interior decoration

**dec·o·rate** \'dek-ə-,rāt\ vb **-rat·ed; -rat·ing** 1 : to make more attractive by adding something beautiful or becoming : ADORN, EMBELLISH 2 : to award a mark of honor (as a medal) to

**dec·o·ra·tion** \,dek-ə-'rā-shən\ n 1 : the act or process of decorating 2 : ORNAMENT 3 : a badge of honor

**dec·o·ra·tive** \'dek-(ə-)rət-iv\ adj : ORNAMENTAL

**dec·o·ra·tor** \'dek-ə-,rāt-ər\ n : one that decorates; esp : a person who de-

signs or executes the interiors of buildings and their furnishings

**dec·o·rous** \'dek-ə-rəs, di-'kōr-əs\ adj : PROPER, SEEMLY, CORRECT

**de·co·rum** \di-'kōr-əm\ n 1 : conformity to accepted standards of conduct 2 : ORDERLINESS, PROPRIETY

**de·cou·page** or **dé·cou·page** \,dā-(,)kü-'päzh\ n : the art of decorating surfaces by applying cutouts (as of paper) and then coating with several layers of finish; also : work produced by decoupage

¹**de·coy** \'dē-,kȯi, di-'kȯi\ n : something that lures or entices; esp : an artificial bird used to attract live birds within shot

²**de·coy** \di-'kȯi, 'dē-,kȯi\ vb : to lure by or as if by a decoy : ENTICE

¹**de·crease** \di-'krēs\ vb **de·creased; de·creas·ing** : to grow or cause to grow less : DIMINISH

²**de·crease** \'dē-,krēs\ n 1 : DIMINISHING, LESSENING 2 : REDUCTION

¹**de·cree** \di-'krē\ n 1 : ORDER, EDICT 2 : a judicial decision

²**decree** vb **de·creed; de·cree·ing** 1 : COMMAND 2 : to determine or order judicially

**dec·re·ment** \'dek-rə-mənt\ n 1 : gradual decrease 2 : the quantity lost by diminution or waste

**de·crep·it** \di-'krep-ət\ adj : broken down with age : worn out — **de·crep·i·tude** \-ə-,t(y)üd\ n

**de·cre·scen·do** \,dā-krə-'shen-dō\ adv or adj : with a decrease in volume — used as a direction in music

**de·cry** \di-'krī\ vb 1 : to belittle publicly 2 : to find fault with : CONDEMN

**ded·i·cate** \'ded-i-,kāt\ vb **-cat·ed; -cat·ing** 1 : to devote to the worship of a divine being esp. with sacred rites 2 : to set apart for a definite purpose; also : to give over 3 : to inscribe or address as a compliment — **ded·i·ca·tion** \,ded-i-'kā-shən\ n — **ded·i·ca·to·ry** \'ded-i-kə-,tōr-ē\ adj

**de·duce** \di-'d(y)üs\ vb **de·duced; de·duc·ing** 1 : to trace the course of (~ their lineage) 2 : to derive by reasoning : INFER — **de·duc·ible** adj

**de·duct** \di-'dəkt\ vb : SUBTRACT — **de·duct·ible** adj

**de·duc·tion** \di-'dək-shən\ n 1 : SUBTRACTION 2 : the deriving of a conclusion by reasoning : the conclusion so reached 3 : something that is or may be subtracted : ABATEMENT — **de·duc·tive** \-'dək-tiv\ adj

¹**deed** \'dēd\ n 1 : something done 2 : FEAT, EXPLOIT 3 : a document containing some legal transfer, bargain, or contract

²**deed** vb : to convey or transfer by deed

**dee·jay** \'dē-'jā\ n : DISC JOCKEY

**deem** \'dēm\ vb : THINK, JUDGE

**de·em·pha·size** \dē-'em-fə-,sīz\ vb : to refrain from emphasizing — **de·em·pha·sis** \-fə-səs\ n

¹**deep** \'dēp\ adj 1 : extending far down, back, within, or outward 2 : having a specified extension down-

ward or backward **3 :** difficult to understand; *also* **:** MYSTERIOUS, OBSCURE ⟨a ~ dark secret⟩ **4 :** WISE **5 :** ENGROSSED, INVOLVED ⟨~ in thought⟩ **6 :** INTENSE, PROFOUND ⟨~ sleep⟩ **7 :** high in saturation and low in lightness ⟨a ~ red⟩ **8 :** having a low musical pitch or range ⟨a ~ voice⟩ **9 :** coming from or situated well within **10 :** covered, enclosed, or filled often to a specified degree — **deep·ly** *adv*

²**deep** *adv* **1 :** DEEPLY **2 :** far on **:** LATE ⟨~ in the night⟩

³**deep** *n* **1 :** an extremely deep place or part; *esp* **:** OCEAN **2 :** the middle or most intense part ⟨the ~ of winter⟩

**deep·en** \ˈdē-pən\ *vb* **deep·ened;** **deep·en·ing** \ˈdēp-(ə-)niŋ\ **:** to make or become deep or deeper

**deep-freeze** \ˈdēp-ˈfrēz\ *vb* **:** QUICK-FREEZE

**deep-root·ed** \-ˈrüt-əd, -ˈrüt-\ *adj* **:** deeply implanted or established

**deep-sea** \ˌdēp-ˈsē\ *adj* **:** of, relating to, or occurring in the deeper parts of the sea ⟨~ fishing⟩

**deep-seat·ed** \ˈdēp-ˈsēt-əd\ *adj* **1** **:** situated far below the surface **2 :** firmly established ⟨~ convictions⟩

**deep-set** \-ˈset\ *adj* **:** set far in

**deer** \ˈdiər\ *n, pl* **deer** [ME, deer, animal, fr. OE *dēor* beast] **:** any of a group of ruminant mammals with cloven hoofs and antlers in the males

**deer·fly** \-ˌflī\ *n* **:** any of numerous small horseflies

**deer·skin** \-ˌskin\ *n* **:** leather made from the skin of a deer; *also* **:** a garment of such leather

**de-es·ca·late** \dē-ˈes-kə-ˌlāt\ *vb* **:** to decrease in extent, volume, or scope **:** REDUCE ⟨~ the war⟩ — **de-es·ca·la·tion** \dē-ˌes-kə-ˈlā-shən\ *n*

**def** *abbr* **1** definite **2** definition

**de·face** \di-ˈfās\ *vb* **:** to destroy or mar the face or surface of — **de·face·ment** *n*

**de fac·to** \di-ˈfak-tō, dā-\ *adj or adv* **1 :** actually exercising power ⟨*de facto* government⟩ **2 :** actually existing ⟨*de facto* segregation⟩

**de·fal·ca·tion** \ˌdē-ˌfal-ˈkā-shən, ˌdē-fōl-; ˌdef-əl-\ *n* **:** EMBEZZLEMENT

**de·fame** \di-ˈfām\ *vb* **de·famed; de·fam·ing :** to injure or destroy the reputation of by libel or slander — **def·a·ma·tion** \ˌdef-ə-ˈmā-shən\ *n* — **de·fam·a·to·ry** \di-ˈfam-ə-ˌtōr-ē\ *adj*

**de·fault** \di-ˈfȯlt\ *n* **:** failure to do something required by duty or law ⟨the defendant failed to appear and was held in ~⟩; *also* **:** failure to compete in or to finish an appointed contest ⟨lose a race by ~⟩ — **default** *vb* — **de·fault·er** *n*

¹**de·feat** \di-ˈfēt\ *vb* **1 :** FRUSTRATE, NULLIFY **2 :** to win victory over **:** BEAT

²**defeat** *n* **1 :** FRUSTRATION **2 :** an overthrow of an army in battle **3 :** loss of a contest

**de·feat·ism** \-ˌiz-əm\ *n* **:** acceptance of or resignation to defeat — **de·feat·ist** \-əst\ *n or adj*

**def·e·cate** \ˈdef-i-ˌkāt\ *vb* **-cat·ed;**

**-cat·ing 1 :** to free from impurity or corruption **:** REFINE **2 :** to discharge feces from the bowels — **def·e·ca·tion** \ˌdef-i-ˈkā-shən\ *n*

¹**de·fect** \ˈdē-ˌfekt, di-ˈfekt\ *n* **:** BLEMISH, FAULT, IMPERFECTION

²**de·fect** \di-ˈfekt\ *vb* **:** to desert a cause or party esp. in order to espouse another — **de·fec·tion** \-ˈfek-shən\ *n* — **de·fec·tor** \-ˈfek-tər\ *n*

**de·fec·tive** \di-ˈfek-tiv\ *adj* **:** FAULTY, DEFICIENT — **defective** *n*

**de·fend** \di-ˈfend\ *vb* [ME *defenden*, fr. OF *defendre*, fr. L *defendere*, fr. *de-* from + *-fendere* to strike] **1 :** to repel danger or attack from **2 :** to act as attorney for **3 :** to oppose the claim of another in a lawsuit **:** CONTEST **4 :** to maintain against opposition ⟨~ an idea⟩ — **de·fend·er** *n*

**de·fen·dant** \di-ˈfen-dənt\ *n* **:** a person required to make answer in a legal action or suit

**de·fense** *or* **de·fence** \di-ˈfens\ *n* **1 :** the act of defending **:** resistance against attack **2 :** capability of resisting attack **3 :** means or method of defending **4 :** an argument in support or justification **5 :** a defending party, group, or team **6 :** the answer made by the defendant in a legal action — **de·fense·less** *adj* — **de·fen·si·ble** *adj* — **de·fen·sive** *adj*

**defense mechanism** *n* **:** an often unconscious mental process (as repression or sublimation) that assists in reaching compromise solutions to problems

**de·fen·sive** \di-ˈfen-siv\ *n* **:** a defensive position

¹**de·fer** \di-ˈfər\ *vb* **de·ferred; de·fer·ring** [ME *deferren, differren*, fr. MF *differer*, fr. L *differre* to postpone, be different] **:** to put off **:** DELAY

²**defer** *vb* **deferred; deferring** [ME *deferren, differren*, fr. MF *deferer*, *deferer*, fr. LL *deferre*, fr. L, to bring down, bring, fr. *ferre* to carry] **:** to submit or yield to the opinion or wishes of another

**def·er·ence** \ˈdef-(ə-)rəns\ *n* **:** courteous, respectful, or ingratiating regard for another's wishes — **def·er·en·tial** \ˌdef-ə-ˈren-chəl\ *adj*

**de·fer·ment** \di-ˈfər-mənt\ *n* **:** the act of delaying; *esp* **:** official postponement of military service

**de·fi·ance** \di-ˈfī-əns\ *n* **1 :** CHALLENGE **2 :** a willingness to resist **:** contempt of opposition

**de·fi·ant** \-ənt\ *adj* **:** full of defiance ⟨a ~ gesture⟩ — **de·fi·ant·ly** *adv*

**deficiency disease** *n* **:** a disease (as scurvy) caused by a lack of essential dietary elements and esp. a vitamin or mineral

**de·fi·cient** \di-ˈfish-ənt\ *adj* **:** lacking in something necessary (as for completeness or health) **:** DEFECTIVE — **de·fi·cien·cy** \-ˈfish-ən-sē\ *n*

**def·i·cit** \ˈdef-ə-sət\ *n* **:** a deficiency in amount; *esp* **:** an excess of expenditures over revenue

¹**de·file** \di-ˈfīl\ *vb* **de·filed; de·fil-**

**ing 1 :** to make filthy **2 :** CORRUPT **3 :** RAVISH, VIOLATE **4 :** to make ceremonially unclean **:** DESECRATE **5 :** DISHONOR — **de·file·ment** n

²**de·file** \di-'fīl, 'dē-,fīl\ n **:** a narrow passage or gorge

**de·fine** \di-'fīn\ vb **de·fined; de·fin·ing 1 :** to fix or mark the limits of **2 :** to clarify in outline or character **3 :** to discover and set forth the meaning of ⟨~ a word⟩ — **de·fin·able** adj — **de·fin·er** n

**def·i·nite** \'def-(ə-)nət\ adj **1 :** having distinct limits **:** FIXED **2 :** clear in meaning **3 :** typically designating an identified or immediately identifiable person or thing — **def·i·nite·ly** adv — **def·i·nite·ness** n

**def·i·ni·tion** \,def-ə-'nish-ən\ n **1 :** an act of determining or settling **2 :** a statement of the meaning of a word or word group; also **:** the action or process of stating such a meaning **3 :** the action or the power of making definite and clear **:** CLARITY, DISTINCTNESS

**de·fin·i·tive** \di-'fin-ət-iv\ adj **1 :** DECISIVE, CONCLUSIVE **2 :** being authoritative and apparently exhaustive **3 :** serving to define or specify precisely

**def·la·grate** \'def-lə-,grāt\ vb **-grat·ed; -grat·ing :** to burn rapidly with intense heat — **def·la·gra·tion** \,def-lə-'grā-shən\ n

**de·flate** \di-'flāt\ vb **de·flat·ed; de·flat·ing 1 :** to release air or gas from **2 :** to cause to contract from an abnormally high level **:** reduce from a state of inflation **3 :** to become deflated

**de·fla·tion** \-'flā-shən\ n **1 :** an act or instance of deflating **2 :** the state of being deflated **2 :** reduction in the volume of available money or credit resulting in a decline of the general price level

**de·flect** \di-'flekt\ vb **:** to turn aside — **de·flec·tion** \-'flek-shən\ n

**de·flo·ra·tion** \,def-lə-'rā-shən\ n **:** rupture of the hymen

**de·flow·er** \dē-'flau(-ə)r\ vb **:** to deprive of virginity **:** RAVISH

**de·fog** \dē-'fog, -'fäg\ vb **:** to remove fog or condensed moisture from — **de·fog·ger** n

**de·fo·li·ant** \dē-'fō-lē-ənt\ n **:** a chemical spray or dust applied to plants to cause the leaves to drop off prematurely

**de·fo·li·ate** \-lē-,āt\ vb **:** to deprive of leaves esp. prematurely — **de·fo·li·a·tion** \dē-,fō-lē-'ā-shən\ n — **de·fo·li·a·tor** \'fō-lē-,āt-ər\ n

**de·for·est** \dē-'for-əst\ vb **:** to clear of forests — **de·for·es·ta·tion** \dē-,fór-ə-'stā-shən\ n

**de·form** \di-'form\ vb **1 :** MISSHAPE, DISTORT **2 :** DISFIGURE, DEFACE — **de·for·ma·tion** \,dē-,fór-'mā-shən, ,def-ər-\ n

**de·for·mi·ty** \di-'fór-mət-ē\ n, pl **-ties 1 :** the state of being deformed **2 :** a physical blemish or distortion

**de·fraud** \di-'frod\ vb **:** CHEAT

**de·fray** \di-'frā\ vb **:** to provide for the payment of **:** PAY — **de·fray·al** n

**de·frost** \di-'fróst\ vb **1 :** to thaw out

**2 :** to free from ice — **de·frost·er** n

**deft** \'deft\ adj **:** quick and neat in action — **deft·ly** adv — **deft·ness** n

**de·funct** \di-'fəŋkt\ adj **:** DEAD, EXTINCT ⟨a ~ organization⟩

**de·fuse** \dē-'fyüz\ vb **1 :** to remove the fuse from (as a bomb) **2 :** to make less harmful, potent, or tense

**de·fy** \di-'fī\ vb **de·fied; de·fy·ing** [ME defyen to renounce faith in, challenge, fr. OF defier, fr. de- from + fier to entrust, fr. L fidere to trust] **1 :** CHALLENGE, DARE **2 :** to refuse boldly to obey or to yield to **:** DISREGARD ⟨~ the law⟩ **3 :** WITHSTAND, BAFFLE ⟨a scene that defies description⟩

**deg** abbr degree

**de·gas** \dē-'gas\ vb **:** to remove gas from

**de·gauss** \dē-'gaůs\ vb **:** DEMAGNETIZE

**de·gen·er·a·cy** \di-'jen-(ə-)rə-sē\ n, pl **-cies 1 :** the state of being degenerate **2 :** the process of becoming degenerate

¹**de·gen·er·ate** \di-'jen-(ə-)rət\ adj **:** fallen from a former, higher, or normal condition — **de·gen·er·a·cy** \-rə-sē\ n — **de·gen·er·a·tion** \-,jen-ə-'rā-shən\ n — **de·gen·er·a·tive** \-'jen-ə-,rāt-iv\ adj

²**degenerate** n **:** a degenerate person; esp **:** a sexual pervert

³**de·gen·er·ate** \di-'jen-ə-,rāt\ vb **:** to become degenerate **:** DETERIORATE

**de·grad·able** \di-'grād-ə-bəl\ adj **:** capable of being chemically degraded ⟨~ detergents⟩

**de·grade** \di-'grād\ vb **1 :** to reduce from a higher to a lower rank or degree **2 :** DEBASE, CORRUPT — **deg·ra·da·tion** \,deg-rə-'dā-shən\ n

**de·gree** \di-'grē\ n [ME, fr. OF degré, fr. (assumed) VL degradus, fr. L gradus step, grade] **1 :** a step in a series **2 :** the extent, intensity, or scope of something esp. as measured by a graded series **3 :** one of the forms or sets of forms used in the comparison of an adjective or adverb **4 :** a rank or grade of official, ecclesiastical, or social position; also **:** the civil condition of a person **5 :** a title conferred upon students by a college, university, or professional school upon completion of a unified program of study **6 :** a 360th part of the circumference of a circle **7 :** a line or space of the musical staff; also **:** a note or tone of a musical scale

**de·horn** \dē-'hórn\ vb **:** to deprive of horns

**de·hu·man·ize** \dē-'hyü-mə-,nīz\ vb **:** to divest of human qualities or personality — **de·hu·man·iza·tion** \,dē-,hyü-mə-nə-'zā-shən\ n

**de·hu·mid·i·fy** \,dē-hyu-'mid-ə-,fī\ vb **:** to remove moisture from (as the air) — **de·hu·mid·i·fi·ca·tion** \-,mid-ə-fə-'kā-shən\ n — **de·hu·mid·i·fi·er** \-'mid-ə-,fī(-ə)r\ n

**de·hy·drate** \dē-'hī-,drāt\ vb **:** to remove water from ⟨dehydrated by fever⟩ ⟨~ fruits⟩; also **:** to lose liquid — **de·hy·dra·tion** \,dē-hī-'drā-shən\ n de·hy·dro·ge·nate \,dē-hī'-'dräj-ə-,nāt\ *vb* : to remove hydrogen from — de·hy·dro·ge·na·tion \,dē-hī-,dräj-ə-'nā-shən\ *n*

de·ice \dē-'īs\ *vb* : to keep free of ice — de·ic·er *n*

de·i·fy \'dē-ə-,fī\ *vb* -fied; -fy·ing 1 : to make a god of 2 : WORSHIP, GLORIFY — de·i·fi·ca·tion \,dē-ə-fə-'kā-shən\ *n*

deign \'dān\ *vb* [ME *deignen*, fr. OF *deignier*, fr. L *dignare, dignari*, fr. *dignus* worthy] : CONDESCEND

de·in·dus·tri·al·iza·tion \,dē-in-,dəs-trē-ə-lə-'zā-shən\ *n* : the act or process of reducing or destroying the industrial organization and potential esp. of a defeated nation

de·ion·ize \dē-'ī-ə-,nīz\ *vb* : to remove ions from — de·ion·iza·tion \dē-,ī-ə-nə-'zā-shən\ *n*

de·ism \'dē-,iz-əm\ *n, often cap* : a system of thought advocating natural religion based on human reason rather than revelation — de·ist \'dē-əst\ *n, often cap* — de·is·tic \dē-'is-tik\ *adj*

de·i·ty \'dē-ət-ē\ *n, pl* -ties 1 : the rank or nature of a god or supreme being 2 *cap* : GOD 1 3 : a god or goddess

de·ject·ed \di-'jek-təd\ *adj* : low-spirited : SAD — de·ject·ed·ly *adv*

de·jec·tion \di-'jek-shən\ *n* : lowness of spirits : DEPRESSION

de ju·re \dē-'jur-ē\ *adv or adj* : existing or exercising power by legal right ⟨*de jure* government⟩

deka·gram \'dek-ə-,gram\ *n* — see METRIC SYSTEM table

deka·li·ter \-,lēt-ər\ *n* — see METRIC SYSTEM table

deka·me·ter \-,mēt-ər\ *n* — see METRIC SYSTEM table

deka·stere \-,sti(ə)r, -,ste(ə)r\ *n* — see METRIC SYSTEM table

del *abbr* delegate; delegation

Del *abbr* Delaware

Del·a·ware \'del-ə-,waər\ *n, pl* Dela·ware *or* Delawares : a member of an Indian people orig. of the Delaware valley; *also* : their language

¹de·lay \di-'lā\ *n* 1 : the act of delaying : the state of being delayed 2 : the time during which something is delayed

²delay *vb* 1 : to put off : POSTPONE 2 : to stop, detain, or hinder for a time 3 : to move or act slowly

de·le \'dē-lē\ *vb* de·led; de·le·ing [L, imper. sing. of *delēre*] : to remove (as a word) from typeset matter

de·lec·ta·ble \di-'lek-tə-bəl\ *adj* 1 : highly pleasing : DELIGHTFUL 2 : DELICIOUS

de·lec·ta·tion \,dē-,lek-'tā-shən\ *n* : DELIGHT, PLEASURE, DIVERSION

¹del·e·gate \'del-i-gət, -,gāt\ *n* 1 : DEPUTY, REPRESENTATIVE 2 : a member of the lower house of the legislature of Maryland, Virginia, or West Virginia

²del·e·gate \-,gāt\ *vb* -gat·ed; -gat·ing 1 : to entrust to another ⟨*delegated* his authority⟩ 2 : to appoint as one's delegate

del·e·ga·tion \,del-i-'gā-shən\ *n* 1 : the act of delegating 2 : one or more persons chosen to represent others

de·lete \di-'lēt\ *vb* de·leted; de·let·ing [L *delēre* to wipe out, destroy] : to eliminate esp. by blotting out, cutting out, or erasing — de·le·tion \-'lē-shən\ *n*

del·e·te·ri·ous \,del-ə-'tir-ē-əs\ *adj* : HARMFUL, NOXIOUS

delft \'delft\ *n* 1 : a Dutch brown pottery covered with an opaque white glaze upon which the predominantly blue decoration is painted 2 : glazed pottery esp. when blue and white

delft·ware \-,waər\ *n* : DELFT

deli \'del-ē\ *n, pl* del·is : DELICATESSEN

¹de·lib·er·ate \di-'lib-(ə-)rət\ *adj* [L *deliberare* to weigh in mind, ponder, fr. *libra* scale, pound] 1 : determined after careful thought 2 : careful and slow in deciding : weighing facts and arguments 3 : UNHURRIED, SLOW — de·lib·er·ate·ly *adv* — de·lib·er·ate·ness *n*

²de·lib·er·ate \di-'lib-ə-,rāt\ *vb* -at·ed; -at·ing : to consider carefully — de·lib·er·a·tion \-,lib-ə-'rā-shən\ *n*

de·lib·er·a·tive \-'lib-ə-,rāt-iv, -'lib-(ə)-rət-\ *adj* : of, relating to, or marked by deliberation ⟨~ assembly⟩ — de·lib·er·a·tive·ly *adv*

del·i·ca·cy \'del-i-kə-sē\ *n, pl* -cies 1 : something pleasing to eat because it is rare or luxurious 2 : FINENESS, DAINTINESS; *also* : FRAILTY 3 : nicety or expressiveness of touch 4 : precise perception and discrimination : SENSITIVITY 5 : sensibility in feeling or conduct; *also* : SQUEAMISHNESS 6 : the quality or state of requiring delicate treatment

del·i·cate \'del-i-kət\ *adj* 1 : pleasing to the senses of taste or smell esp. in a mild or subtle way 2 : marked by daintiness or charm : EXQUISITE 3 : FASTIDIOUS, SQUEAMISH, SCRUPULOUS 4 : marked by minute precision : very sensitive 5 : marked by or requiring meticulous technique or fine skill 6 : easily damaged : FRAGILE; *also* : SICKLY 7 : SUBTLE 8 : marked by or requiring tact — del·i·cate·ly *adv*

del·i·ca·tes·sen \,del-i-kə-'tes-ᵊn\ *n pl* [G, pl of *delicatesse* delicacy, fr. F *délicatesse*, prob. fr. It *delicatezza*, fr. *delicato* delicate] 1 : ready-to-eat food products (as cooked meats and prepared salads) 2 *sing, pl* delicatessens : a store where delicatessen are sold

de·li·cious \di-'lish-əs\ *adj* : affording great pleasure : DELIGHTFUL; *esp* : very pleasing to the taste or smell — de·li·cious·ly *adv*

¹de·light \di-'līt\ *n* 1 : great pleasure or satisfaction : JOY 2 : something that gives great pleasure — de·light·ful \-fəl\ *adj* — de·light·ful·ly \-ē\ *adv*

²delight *vb* 1 : to take great pleasure 2 : to satisfy greatly : PLEASE

de·light·ed \-əd\ *adj* : highly pleased : GRATIFIED — de·light·ed·ly *adv*

de·lim·it \di-'lim-ət\ *vb* : to fix the limits of : BOUND

**de·lin·eate** \di-'lin-ē-,āt\ vb **-eat·ed; -eat·ing 1 :** SKETCH, PORTRAY **2 :** to picture in words : DESCRIBE — **de·lin·ea·tion** \-,lin-ē-'ā-shən\ n

**de·lin·quen·cy** \di-'liŋ-kwən-sē\ n : the quality or state of being delinquent

¹**de·lin·quent** \-kwənt\ n : a delinquent person

²**delinquent** adj **1 :** offending by neglect or violation of duty or of law **2 :** being overdue in payment

**del·i·quesce** \,del-i-'kwes\ vb **-quesced; -quesc·ing 1 :** to become liquid by absorbing moisture from the air **2 :** MELT — **del·i·ques·cent** \-'kwes-ənt\ adj

**de·lir·i·um** \di-'lir-ē-əm\ n [L, fr. delirare to be crazy, fr. de- from + lira furrow] : mental disturbance marked by confusion, disordered speech, and hallucinations; also : violent excitement — **de·lir·i·ous** \-ē-əs\ adj — **de·lir·i·ous·ly** adv

**delirium tre·mens** \-'trē-mənz, -'trem-ənz\ n : a violent delirium with tremors that is induced by excessive and prolonged use of alcoholic liquors

**de·liv·er** \di-'liv-ər\ vb **de·liv·ered; de·liv·er·ing** \-(ə-)riŋ\ **1 :** to set free : SAVE **2 :** to hand over : CONVEY, SURRENDER **3 :** to assist in giving birth or at the birth of **4 :** UTTER, RELATE, COMMUNICATE **5 :** to send to an intended target or destination — **de·liv·er·ance** n — **de·liv·er·er** n

**de·liv·ery** \di-'liv-(ə-)rē\ n, pl **-er·ies 1 :** a freeing from restraint **2 :** the act of handing over **:** something delivered at one time or in one unit **3 :** CHILDBIRTH **4 :** UTTERANCE; also **:** manner of speaking or singing **5 :** the act or manner of discharging or throwing

**dell** \'del\ n : a small secluded valley

**de·louse** \dē-'laůs\ vb : to remove lice from

**del·phin·i·um** \del-'fin-ē-əm\ n : any of a genus of mostly perennial herbs related to the buttercups and grown for their tall branching spikes of irregular flowers

**del·ta** \'del-tə\ n [Gk, fr. delta, fourth letter of the Gk alphabet, Δ, which an alluvial delta resembles in shape] : triangular silt-formed land at the mouth of a river — **del·ta·ic** \del-'tā-ik\ adj

**delta ray** n : an electron ejected by an ionizing particle in its passage through matter

**de·lude** \di-'lüd\ vb **de·lud·ed; de·lud·ing :** MISLEAD, DECEIVE, TRICK

¹**del·uge** \'del-yüj\ n **1 :** a flooding of land by water **2 :** a drenching rain **3 :** an irresistible rush ⟨a ~ of Easter mail⟩

²**deluge** vb **de·luged; del·ug·ing 1 :** INUNDATE, FLOOD **2 :** to overwhelm as if with a deluge

**de·lu·sion** \di-'lü-zhən\ n : a deluding or being deluded; esp : a persistent belief in something false typical of some mental disorders — **de·lu·sion·al** \-'lüzh-(ə-)nəl\ adj — **de·lu·sive** \-'lü-siv\ adj

**de·luxe** \di-'lůks, -'ləks, 'lůks\ adj

**:** notably luxurious or elegant

**delve** \'delv\ vb **delved; delv·ing 1 :** DIG **2 :** to seek laboriously for information in written records

**dely** abbr delivery

**Dem** abbr Democrat; Democratic

**de·mag·ne·tize** \dē-'mag-nə-,tīz\ vb **:** to deprive of magnetic properties — **de·mag·ne·ti·za·tion** \dē-,mag-nət-ə-'zā-shən\ n

**dem·a·gogue** or **dem·a·gog** \'dem-ə-,gäg\ n [Gk dēmagōgos, fr. dēmos people + agōgos leading, fr. agein to lead] : a person who appeals to the emotions and prejudices of people esp. in order to advance his own political ends — **dem·a·gogu·ery** \-,gäg-(ə-)rē\ n — **dem·a·gogy** \-,gäg-ē, -,gäj-ē\ n

¹**de·mand** \di-'mand\ n **1 :** an act of demanding or asking esp. with authority; also **:** something claimed as due **2 :** an expressed desire to own or use something ⟨the ~ for new cars⟩ **3 :** the ability and desire to buy goods or services; also **:** the quantity of goods wanted at a stated price **4 :** a seeking or being sought after **5 :** urgent need **6 :** a pressing need or requirement

²**demand** vb **1 :** to ask for with authority : claim as due **2 :** to ask earnestly or in the manner of a command **3 :** REQUIRE, NEED ⟨an illness that ~s care⟩

**de·mar·cate** \di-'mär-,kāt, 'dē-,mär-\ vb **-cat·ed; -cat·ing 1 :** to mark the limits of **2 :** SEPARATE — **de·mar·ca·tion** \,dē-,mär-'kā-shən\ n

**de·marche** \dā-'märsh\ n : a course of action : MANEUVER

¹**de·mean** \di-'mēn\ vb **de·meaned; de·mean·ing :** to behave or conduct (oneself) usu. in a proper manner

²**demean** vb **de·meaned; de·mean·ing :** DEGRADE, DEBASE

**de·mean·or** \di-'mē-nər\ n : CONDUCT, BEARING

**de·ment·ed** \di-'ment-əd\ adj **:** MAD, INSANE — **de·ment·ed·ly** adv

**de·men·tia** \di-'men-chə\ n : mental deterioration : INSANITY

**de·mer·it** \di-'mer-ət\ n **1 :** FAULT **2 :** a mark placed against a person's record for some fault or offense

**de·mesne** \di-'mān, -'mēn\ n **1 :** manorial land actually possessed by the lord and not held by free tenants **2 :** ESTATE **3 :** REGION **4 :** REALM

**demi·god** \'dem-i-,gäd\ n : a mythological being with more power than a mortal but less than a god

**demi·john** \'dem-i-,jän\ n [F dame-jeanne, lit., Lady Jane] : a large glass or pottery bottle enclosed in wickerwork

**de·mil·i·ta·rize** \dē-'mil-ə-tə-,rīz\ vb **:** to strip of military forces, weapons, or fortifications — **de·mil·i·tar·i·za·tion** \dē-,mil-ə-t(ə-)rə-'zā-shən\ n

**demi·mon·daine** \,dem-i-,män-'dän\ n : a woman of the demimonde

**demi·monde** \'dem-i-,mänd\ n **1 :** a class of women on the fringes of respectable society supported by wealthy lovers **2 :** a group engaged in activity of doubtful legality or propriety

**de·min·er·al·ize** \dē-'min-(ə-)rə-,līz\ vb : to remove the mineral matter from

**de·mise** \di-'mīz\ n 1 : LEASE 2 : transfer of sovereignty to a successor ⟨~ of the crown⟩ 3 : DEATH

**demi·tasse** \'dem-i-,tas\ n [F demi-tasse, fr. demi- half + tasse cup, fr. MF, fr. Ar tass, fr. Per tast] : a small cup of black coffee; also : the cup used to serve it

**de·mo·bi·lize** \di-'mō-bə-,līz, dē-\ vb 1 : to disband from military service 2 : to change from a state of war to a state of peace — **de·mo·bi·li·za·tion** \di-,mō-bə-lə-'zā-shən, dē-\ n

**de·moc·ra·cy** \di-'mäk-rə-sē\ n, pl -cies 1 : government by the people; esp : rule of the majority 2 : a government in which the supreme power is held by the people 3 : a political unit that has a democratic government 4 cap : the principles and policies of the Democratic party in the U.S. 5 : the common people esp. when constituting the source of political authority 6 : the absence of hereditary or arbitrary class distinctions or privileges

**dem·o·crat** \'dem-ə-,krat\ n 1 : an adherent of democracy 2 : one who practices social equality 3 cap : a member of the Democratic party of the U.S.

**dem·o·crat·ic** \,dem-ə-'krat-ik\ adj 1 : of, relating to, or favoring democracy 2 often cap : of or relating to one of the two major political parties in the U.S. associated in modern times with policies of broad social reform and internationalism 3 : of, relating to, or appealing to the common people ⟨~ art⟩ 4 : not snobbish

**de·moc·ra·tize** \di-'mäk-rə-,tīz\ vb -tized; -tiz·ing : to make democratic

**dé·mo·dé** \,dā-mō-'dā\ adj : no longer fashionable : OUT-OF-DATE

**de·mog·ra·phy** \di-'mäg-rə-fē\ n : the statistical study of human populations and esp. their size and distribution and the number of births and deaths — **de·mog·ra·pher** \-fər\ n — **de·mo·graph·ic** \,dē-mə-'graf-ik, ,dem-ə-\ adj — **de·mo·graph·ic·al·ly** \-i-k(ə-)lē\ adv

**dem·oi·selle** \,dem-(w)ə-'zel\ n : a young woman

**de·mol·ish** \di-'mäl-ish\ vb 1 : to tear down : RAZE 2 : SMASH 3 : to put an end to

**de·mo·li·tion** \,dem-ə-'lish-ən, ,dē-mə-\ n : the act of demolishing; esp : destruction in war by means of explosives

**de·mon** or **dae·mon** \'dē-mən\ n 1 usu daemon : an attendant power or spirit 2 : an evil spirit : DEVIL 3 : one that has unusual drive or effectiveness

**de·mon·e·tize** \dē-'män-ə-,tīz, -'mən-\ vb : to stop using as money or as a monetary standard ⟨~ silver⟩ — **de·mon·e·ti·za·tion** \dē-,män-ət-ə-'zā-shən, -,mən-\ n

**de·mo·ni·ac** \di-'mō-nē-,ak\ also **de·mo·ni·a·cal** \,dē-mə-'nī-ə-kəl\ adj 1 : possessed or influenced by a demon 2 : DEVILISH, FIENDISH

**de·mon·ic** \di-'män-ik\ also **de·mon·i·cal** \-i-kəl\ adj : DEMONIAC 2

**de·mon·ol·o·gy** \,dē-mə-'näl-ə-jē\ n 1 : the study of demons 2 : belief in demons

**de·mon·stra·ble** \di-'män-strə-bəl\ adj 1 : capable of being demonstrated or proved 2 : APPARENT, EVIDENT

**dem·on·strate** \'dem-ən-,strāt\ vb -strat·ed; -strat·ing 1 : to show clearly 2 : to prove or make clear by reasoning or evidence 3 : to explain esp. with many examples 4 : to show publicly ⟨~ a new car⟩ 5 : to make a public display (as of feelings or military force) ⟨citizens demonstrated in protest⟩ — **dem·on·stra·tion** \,dem-ən-'strā-shən\ n — **dem·on·stra·tor** \'dem-ən-,strāt-ər\ n

¹**de·mon·stra·tive** \di-'män-strət-iv\ adj 1 : demonstrating as real or true 2 : characterized by demonstration 3 : pointing out the one referred to and distinguishing it from others of the same class ⟨~ pronoun⟩ ⟨~ adjective⟩ 4 : marked by display of feeling : EFFUSIVE — **de·mon·stra·tive·ly** adv — **de·mon·stra·tive·ness** n

²**demonstrative** n : a demonstrative word and esp. a pronoun

**de·mor·al·ize** \di-'mȯr-ə-,līz\ vb 1 : to corrupt in morals 2 : to weaken in discipline or spirit : DISORGANIZE — **de·mor·al·i·za·tion** \di-,mȯr-ə-lə-'zā-shən\ n

**de·mote** \di-'mōt\ vb **de·mot·ed**; **de·mot·ing** : to reduce to a lower grade or rank

**de·mot·ic** \di-'mät-ik\ adj : of or relating to the people ⟨~ Greek⟩

¹**de·mul·cent** \di-'məl-sənt\ adj : SOOTHING

²**demulcent** n : a usu. oily or somewhat thick and gelatinous preparation used to soothe or protect an irritated mucous membrane

**de·mur** \di-'mər\ vb **de·murred**; **de·mur·ring** [ME demeoren to linger, fr. OF demorer, fr. L demorari, fr. morari to linger, fr. mora delay] : to take exception : OBJECT — **de·mur** n

**de·mure** \di-'myu̇r\ adj 1 : quietly modest : DECOROUS 2 : affectedly modest, reserved, or serious : PRIM — **de·mure·ly** adv

**de·mur·rage** \di-'mər-ij\ n : the detention of a ship by the shipper or receiver beyond the time allowed for loading, unloading, or sailing; also : a charge for detaining a ship, freight car, or truck for such a delay

**de·mur·rer** \di-'mər-ər\ n : a claim by the defendant in a legal action that the pleadings of the plaintiff are defective

**den** \'den\ n 1 : a shelter or resting place of a wild animal 2 : a hiding place (as for thieves) 3 : a dirty wretched place in which people live or gather ⟨~s of misery⟩ 4 : a cozy private little room

**Den** abbr Denmark

**de·na·ture** \dē-'nā-chər\ vb **de·na·tured**; **de·na·tur·ing** \-'nāch-(ə-)riŋ\ : to change the nature of; esp

: to make (alcohol) unfit for drinking

**den·drol·o·gy** \den-'dräl-ə-jē\ *n* : the study of trees — **den·dro·log·ic** \,den-drə-'läj-ik\ *or* **den·dro·log·i·cal** \-i-kəl\ *adj* — **den·drol·o·gist** \den-'dräl-ə-jəst\ *n*

**den·gue** \'deŋ-gē, -,gā\ *n* : an acute infectious disease characterized by headache, severe joint pain, and rash

**de·ni·al** \di-'nī(-ə)l\ *n* **1** : rejection of a request **2** : refusal to admit the truth of a statement or charge; *also* : assertion that something alleged is false : DISAVOWAL **4** : restriction on one's own activity or desires

**de·nier** \'den-yər\ *n* : a unit of fineness for silk, rayon, or nylon yarn

**den·i·grate** \'den-i-,grāt\ *vb* **-grat·ed; -grat·ing** [L *denigrare*, fr. *nigrare* to blacken, fr. *niger* black] : to cast aspersions on : DEFAME

**den·im** \'den-əm\ *n* [F (*serge*) *de Nîmes* serge of Nîmes, France] **1** : a firm durable twilled usu. cotton fabric woven with colored warp and white filling threads **2** *pl* : overalls or trousers of usu. blue denim

**den·i·zen** \'den-ə-zən\ *n* : INHABITANT

**de·nom·i·nate** \di-'näm-ə-,nāt\ *vb* : to give a name to : DESIGNATE

**de·nom·i·nate number** \di-,näm-ə-nət-\ *n* : a number (as 7 in 7 *feet*) that specifies a quantity in terms of a unit of measurement

**de·nom·i·na·tion** \di-,näm-ə-'nā-shən\ *n* **1** : an act of denominating **2** : NAME, DESIGNATION; *esp* : a general name for a class of things **3** : a religious body comprising a number of local congregations having similar beliefs **4** : a value or size of a series of related values (as of money) — **de·nom·i·na·tion·al** \-sh(ə-)nəl\ *adj*

**de·nom·i·na·tor** \di-'näm-ə-,nāt-ər\ *n* : the part of a fraction that is below the line

**de·no·ta·tive** \'dē-nō-,tāt-iv, di-'nōt-ət-iv\ *adj* **1** : denoting or tending to denote **2** : relating to denotation

**de·note** \di-'nōt\ *vb* **1** : to mark out plainly : INDICATE **2** : to make known **3** : MEAN, NAME — **de·no·ta·tion** \,dē-nō-'tā-shən\ *n*

**de·noue·ment** \,dā-,nü-'mäⁿ\ *n* [F *dénouement*, lit., untying, fr. MF *desnouement*, fr. *desnouer* to untie, fr. OF *desnoer*, fr. *noer* to tie, fr. L *nodare*, fr. *nodus* knot] : the final outcome of the dramatic complications in a literary work

**de·nounce** \di-'naúns\ *vb* **de·nounced; de·nounc·ing 1** : to point out as deserving blame or punishment **2** : to inform against : ACCUSE **3** : to announce formally the termination of (as a treaty) — **de·nounce·ment** *n*

**de no·vo** \di-'nō-vō\ *adv* : ANEW, AGAIN

**dense** \'dens\ *adj* **dens·er; dens·est 1** : marked by compactness or crowding together of parts : THICK ⟨a ~ forest⟩ ⟨a ~ fog⟩ **2** : DULL, STUPID — **dense·ly** *adv* — **dense·ness** *n*

**den·si·tom·e·ter** \,den-sə-'täm-ət-ər\ *n* : an instrument for determining photographic density

**den·si·ty** \'den-sət-ē\ *n, pl* **-ties 1** : the quality or state of being dense **2** : the quantity of something per unit volume, unit area, or unit length ⟨population ~⟩

**dent** \'dent\ *n* **1** : a small depressed place made by a blow or by pressure **2** : an impression or effect made usu. against resistance **3** : initial progress — **dent** *vb*

**den·tal** \'dent-ᵊl\ *adj* : of or relating to the teeth or dentistry — **den·tal·ly** \-ē\ *adv*

**dental floss** *n* : a flat waxed thread used to clean between the teeth

**dental hygienist** *n* : one who assists a dentist esp. in cleaning teeth

**den·tate** \'den-,tāt\ *or* **den·tat·ed** \-,tāt-əd\ *adj* : having pointed projections : NOTCHED

**den·ti·frice** \'dent-ə-frəs\ *n* [MF, fr. L *dentifricium*, fr. *dent-, dens* tooth + *fricare* to rub] : a powder, paste, or liquid for cleaning the teeth

**den·tin** \'dent-ᵊn\ *or* **den·tine** \'den-,tēn, den-'tēn\ *n* : a calcareous material like bone but harder and denser that composes the principal mass of a tooth — **den·tin·al** \den-'tēn-ᵊl, 'dent-ᵊn-əl\ *adj*

**den·tist** \'dent-əst\ *n* : one whose profession is the care and replacement of teeth — **den·tist·ry** *n*

**den·ti·tion** \den-'tish-ən\ *n* : the number, kind, and arrangement of teeth (as of a person)

**den·ture** \'den-chər\ *n* : an artificial replacement for teeth

**de·nude** \di-'n(y)üd\ *vb* **de·nud·ed; de·nud·ing** : to strip the covering from — **de·nu·da·tion** \dē-(,)n(y)ü-'dā-shən\ *n*

**de·nun·ci·a·tion** \di-,nən-sē-'ā-shən\ *n* : the act of denouncing; *esp* : a public accusation

**de·ny** \di-'nī\ *vb* **de·nied; de·ny·ing 1** : to declare untrue : CONTRADICT **2** : to refuse to recognize or acknowledge : DISAVOW **3** : to refuse to grant ⟨~ a request⟩ **4** : to reject as false ⟨~ the theory of evolution⟩

**de·o·dar** \'dē-ə-,där\ *or* **de·o·da·ra** \,dē-ə-'där-ə\ *n* [Hindi *deodār*, fr. Skt *devadāru*, lit., timber of the gods, fr. *deva* god + *dāru* wood] : an East Indian cedar

**de·odor·ant** \dē-'ōd-ə-rənt\ *n* : a preparation that destroys or masks unpleasant odors

**de·odor·ize** \dē-'ōd-ə-,rīz\ *vb* : to eliminate the offensive odor of

**de·ox·i·dize** \dē-'äk-sə-,dīz\ *vb* : to remove oxygen from — **de·ox·i·diz·er** *n*

**de·oxy·ri·bo·nu·cle·ic acid** \dē-'äk-si-,rī-bō-n(y)ü,-klē-ik\ *n* : DNA

**dep** *abbr* **1** depart; departure **2** deposit **3** deputy

**de·part** \di-'pärt\ *vb* **1** : to go away : go away from : LEAVE **2** : DIE **3** : to turn aside : DEVIATE

**de·part·ment** \di-'pärt-mənt\ n 1 : a distinct sphere : PROVINCE 2 : a functional or territorial division (as of a government, business, or college) — **de·part·men·tal** \di-,pärt-'ment-ᵊl, ,dē-\ adj

**department store** n : a store selling a wide variety of goods arranged in several departments

**de·par·ture** \di-'pär-chər\ n 1 : the act of going away 2 : a starting out (as on a journey) 3 : DIVERGENCE

**de·pend** \di-'pend\ vb 1 : to hang down ⟨a vine ~ing from a tree⟩ 2 : to be dependent esp. for financial support 3 : to be determined by or based on some action or condition ⟨our success ~s on his cooperation⟩ 4 : TRUST, RELY ⟨you can ~ on me⟩

**de·pend·able** \di-'pen-də-bəl\ adj : TRUSTWORTHY, RELIABLE — **de·pend·abil·i·ty** \-,pen-də-'bil-ət-ē\ n

**de·pen·dence** also **de·pen·dance** \di-'pen-dəns\ n 1 : the quality or state of being dependent; esp : the quality or state of being influenced by or subject to another 2 : RELIANCE, TRUST 3 : something on which one relies 4 : drug addiction; also : HABITUATION 2

**de·pen·den·cy** \-dən-sē\ n, pl **-cies** 1 : DEPENDENCE 2 : a territory under the jurisdiction of a nation but not formally annexed by it

¹**de·pen·dent** \di-'pen-dənt\ adj 1 : hanging down 2 : determined or conditioned by another 3 : relying on another for support 4 : subject to another's jurisdiction : SUBORDINATE 4

²**dependent** also **de·pen·dant** \-dənt\ n : one that is dependent; esp : a person who relies on another for support

**de·pict** \di-'pikt\ vb 1 : to represent by a picture 2 : to describe in words — **de·pic·tion** \-'pik-shən\ n

**de·pil·a·to·ry** \di-'pil-ə-,tōr-ē\ n, pl **-ries** : an agent for removing hair, wool, or bristles

**de·plane** \dē-'plān\ vb : to get off an airplane

**de·plete** \di-'plēt\ vb **de·plet·ed; de·plet·ing** : to exhaust esp. of strength or resources — **de·ple·tion** \-'plē-shən\ n

**de·plor·able** \di-'plōr-ə-bəl\ adj 1 : LAMENTABLE 2 : WRETCHED — **de·plor·ably** \-blē\ adv

**de·plore** \-'plōr\ vb **de·plored; de·plor·ing** 1 : to feel or express grief for 2 : to regret strongly 3 : to consider unfortunate or deserving of disapproval

**de·ploy** \di-'ploi\ vb : to spread out (as troops or ships) in order for battle — **de·ploy·ment** \-mənt\ n

**de·po·lar·ize** \dē-'pō-lə-,rīz\ vb : to prevent, reduce, or remove polarization of — **de·po·lar·iza·tion** \dē-,pō-lə-rə-'zā-shən\ n — **de·po·lar·iz·er** \dē-'pō-lə-,rī-zər\ n

**de·po·nent** \di-'pō-nənt\ n : one who gives evidence esp. in writing

**de·pop·u·late** \dē-'päp-yə-,lāt\ vb : to reduce greatly the population of by

destroying or driving away the inhabitants — **de·pop·u·la·tion** \dē-,päp-yə-'lā-shən\ n

**de·port** \di-'pōrt\ vb 1 : CONDUCT, BEHAVE 2 : BANISH, EXILE — **de·por·ta·tion** \dē-,pōr-'tā-shən\ n

**de·port·ment** \di-'pōrt-mənt\ n : BEHAVIOR, BEARING

**de·pose** \di-'pōz\ vb **de·posed; de·pos·ing** 1 : to remove from a high office (as of king) 2 : to testify under oath or by affidavit

¹**de·pos·it** \di-'päz-ət\ vb **de·pos·it·ed** \-'päz-ət-əd\; **de·pos·it·ing** 1 : to place for safekeeping or as a pledge; esp : to put money in a bank 2 : to lay down : PUT 3 : to let fall or sink ⟨sand and silt ~ed by a flood⟩ — **de·pos·i·tor** \-'päz-ət-ər\ n

²**deposit** n 1 : the state of being deposited ⟨money on ~⟩ 2 : something placed for safekeeping; esp : money deposited in a bank 3 : money given as a pledge 4 : an act of depositing 5 : something laid or thrown down ⟨a ~ of silt by a river⟩ 6 : an accumulation of mineral matter (as ore, oil, or gas) in nature

**de·po·si·tion** \,dep-ə-'zish-ən, ,dēp-ə-\ n 1 : an act of removing from a position of authority 2 : TESTIMONY 3 : the process of depositing 4 : DEPOSIT

**de·pos·i·to·ry** \di-'päz-ə-,tōr-ē\ n, pl **-ries** : a place where something is deposited esp. for safekeeping

**de·pot** \1, 3 usu 'dep-ō, 2 usu 'dēp-\ n 1 : STOREHOUSE 2 : a building for railroad, bus, or airplane passengers : STATION 3 : a place where military supplies are kept or where troops are assembled and trained

**depr** abbr depreciation

**de·prave** \di-'prāv\ vb **de·praved; de·prav·ing** [ME depraven, fr. MF depraver, fr. L depravare to pervert, fr. pravus crooked, bad] : CORRUPT, PERVERT — **de·praved** adj — **de·prav·i·ty** \-'prav-ət-ē\ n

**dep·re·cate** \'dep-ri-,kāt\ vb **-cat·ed; -cat·ing** [L deprecari to avert by prayer, fr. precari to pray] 1 : to express disapproval of 2 : DEPRECIATE — **dep·re·ca·tion** \,dep-ri-'kā-shən\ n

**dep·re·ca·to·ry** \'dep-ri-kə-,tōr-ē\ adj 1 : serving to deprecate 2 : expressing deprecation : APOLOGETIC

**de·pre·ci·ate** \di-'prē-shē-,āt\ vb **-at·ed; -at·ing** [LL depretiare, fr. L pretium price] 1 : to lessen in price or value 2 : UNDERVALUE, BELITTLE, DISPARAGE — **de·pre·ci·a·tion** \-,prē-shē-'ā-shən\ n

**dep·re·da·tion** \,dep-rə-'dā-shən\ n : a laying waste or plundering

**de·press** \di-'pres\ vb 1 : to press down : cause to sink to a lower position 2 : to lessen the activity or force of 3 : SADDEN, DISCOURAGE 4 : to lessen in price or value — **de·pres·sor** \di-'pres-ər\ n

**de·pres·sant** \di-'pres-ᵊnt\ n : one that depresses; esp : an agent that

**depressant** *adj*

**de·pressed** \di-'prest\ *adj* **1** : affected with emotional depression **2** : suffering from economic depression

**de·pres·sion** \di-'presh-ən\ *n* **1** : an act of depressing **:** a state of being depressed **2** : a pressing down **:** LOWERING **3** : a state of feeling sad **4** : an emotional disorder marked by sadness, inactivity, difficulty in thinking and concentration, and feelings of dejection **5** : a depressed area or part **6** : a period of low general economic activity with widespread unemployment

¹**de·pres·sive** \di-'pres-iv\ *adj* **1** : tending to depress **2** : characterized by depression

²**depressive** *n* : one who is psychologically depressed

**de·pri·va·tion** \,dep-rə-'vā-shən\ *n* : an act or instance of depriving **:** LOSS; *also* : PRIVATION

**de·prive** \di-'prīv\ *vb* **de·prived; de·priv·ing 1** : to take something away from ⟨~ a king of his power⟩ **2** : to stop from having something

**dept** *abbr* department

**depth** \'depth\ *n, pl* **depths** \'dep(th)s\ **1** : something that is deep; *esp* : the deep part of a body of water **2** : a part that is far from the outside or surface ⟨the ~s of the woods⟩ **3** : ABYSS **4** : the middle or innermost part ⟨the ~ of winter⟩ **5** : an extreme state (as of misery); *also* : the worst part ⟨the ~s of despair⟩ **6** : the perpendicular distance downward from a surface; *also* : the distance from front to back **7** : the quality of being deep **8** : degree of intensity

**depth charge** *n* : an explosive projectile for use under water esp. against submarines

**dep·u·ta·tion** \,dep-yə-'tā-shən\ *n* **1** : the act of appointing a deputy **2** : DELEGATION

**de·pute** \di-'pyüt\ *vb* **de·put·ed; de·put·ing** : DELEGATE

**dep·u·tize** \'dep-yə-,tīz\ *vb* **-tized; -tiz·ing** : to appoint as deputy

**dep·u·ty** \'dep-yət-ē\ *n, pl* **-ties 1** : a person appointed to act for or in place of another **2** : an assistant empowered to act as a substitute in the absence of his superior **3** : a member of a lower house of a legislative assembly

**der** *or* **deriv** *abbr* derivation; derivative

**de·rail** \di-'rāl\ *vb* : to cause to run off the rails — **de·rail·ment** *n*

**de·range** \di-'rānj\ *vb* **de·ranged; de·rang·ing 1** : DISARRANGE, UPSET **2** : to make insane — **de·range·ment** *n*

**der·by** \'dər-bē, *Brit* 'där-\ *n, pl* **derbies 1** : a horse race usu. for three-year-olds held annually **2** : a race or contest open to all **3** : a man's stiff felt hat with dome-shaped crown and narrow brim

¹**der·e·lict** \'der-ə-,likt\ *adj* **1** : abandoned by the owner or occupant ⟨a ~ ship⟩ **2** : NEGLIGENT ⟨~ in his duty⟩

²**derelict** *n* **1** : something voluntarily abandoned; *esp* : a ship abandoned on the high seas **2** : one that is not a responsible or acceptable member of society

**der·e·lic·tion** \,der-ə-'lik-shən\ *n* **1** : the act of abandoning **:** the state of being abandoned **2** : a failure in duty

**de·ride** \di-'rīd\ *vb* **de·rid·ed; de·rid·ing** [L *deridēre*, fr. *ridēre* to laugh] **:** to laugh at scornfully **:** make fun of **:** RIDICULE — **de·ri·sion** \-'rizh-ən\ *n* — **de·ri·sive** \-'rī-siv\ *adj* — **de·ri·sive·ly** *adv* — **de·ri·so·ry** \-'rī-sə-rē\ *adj*

**de ri·gueur** \də-rē-'gər\ *adj* : prescribed or required by fashion, etiquette, or custom

**deriv** *abbr* derivation; derivative

**der·i·va·tion** \,der-ə-'vā-shən\ *n* **1** : the formation of a word from an earlier word or root; *also* : an act of ascertaining or stating the derivation of a word **2** : ETYMOLOGY **3** : SOURCE, ORIGIN; *also* : DESCENT **4** : an act or process of deriving

¹**de·riv·a·tive** \di-'riv-ət-iv\ *adj* : derived from something else

²**derivative** *n* **1** : a word formed by derivation **2** : something derived

**de·rive** \di-'rīv\ *vb* **de·rived; de·riv·ing** [ME *deriven*, fr. MF *deriver*, fr. L *derivare*, fr. *de-* from + *rivus* stream] **1** : to receive or obtain from a source **2** : to obtain from a parent substance **3** : to trace the origin, descent, or derivation of **4** : to come from a certain source **5** : INFER, DEDUCE

**der·mal** \'dər-məl\ *adj* : of or relating to the skin

**der·ma·ti·tis** \,dər-mə-'tīt-əs\ *n* : skin inflammation

**der·ma·tol·o·gy** \-'täl-ə-jē\ *n* : a branch of science dealing with the skin and its disorders — **der·ma·tol·o·gist** \-jəst\ *n*

**der·mis** \'dər-məs\ *n* : the sensitive vascular inner layer of the skin

**der·o·gate** \'der-ə-,gāt\ *vb* **-gat·ed; -gat·ing 1** : to cause to seem inferior **:** DISPARAGE **2** : DETRACT — **der·o·ga·tion** \,der-ə-'gā-shən\ *n*

**de·rog·a·to·ry** \di-'räg-ə-,tōr-ē\ *adj* : intended to lower the reputation of a person or thing **:** DISPARAGING

**der·rick** \'der-ik\ *n* [obs. *derrick* hangman, gallows, fr. *Derick*, name of 17th cent. E hangman] **1** : a hoisting apparatus **:** CRANE **2** : a framework over a drill hole (as for oil) supporting the tackle for boring and hoisting

**der·ri·ere** *or* **der·ri·ère** \,der-ē-'eər\ *n* : BUTTOCKS

**der·ring-do** \,der-iŋ-'dü\ *n* : daring action **:** DARING

**der·rin·ger** \'der-ən-jər\ *n* : a short-barreled pocket pistol

**der·ris** \'der-əs\ *n* : an insecticide obtained from several Old World legumes; *also* : one of these plants

**der·vish** \'dər-vish\ *n* [Turk *derviş*, lit., beggar, fr. Per *darvēsh*] : a member of a Muslim religious order noted for devotional exercises (as bodily movements leading to a trance)

**de·sal·i·nate** \dē-'sal-ə-ˌnāt\ vb **-nat·ed; -nat·ing :** DESALT — **de·sal·i·na·tion** \-ˌsal-ə-'nā-shən\ n

**de·sal·i·nize** \dē-'sal-ə-ˌnīz\ vb **-nized; -niz·ing :** DESALT — **de·sal·i·ni·za·tion** \-ˌsal-ə-nə-'zā-shən\ n

**de·salt** \dē-'sȯlt\ vb **:** to remove salt from \~ seawater\ — **de·salt·er** n

**des·cant** \'des-ˌkant\ vb **1 :** to sing or play part music **:** SING, WARBLE **2 :** to discourse or write at length

**de·scend** \di-'send\ vb **1 :** to pass from a higher to a lower place or level **:** pass, move, or climb down or down along **2 :** DERIVE \~ed from royalty\ **3 :** to pass by inheritance or transmission **4 :** to incline, bend, or extend downward **5 :** to swoop down in a sudden attack

¹**de·scen·dant** or **de·scen·dent** \di-'sen-dənt\ adj **1 :** DESCENDING **2 :** proceeding from an ancestor or source

²**descendant** or **descendent** n **1 :** one descended from another or or from a common stock **2 :** one deriving directly from a precursor or prototype

**de·scent** \di-'sent\ n **1 :** the act or process of descending **2 :** a downward step (as in station or value) **:** DECLINE **3 :** ANCESTRY, BIRTH, LINEAGE **4 :** SLOPE **5 :** a descending way (as a downgrade) **6 :** a sudden hostile raid or assault

**de·scribe** \di-'skrīb\ vb **de·scribed; de·scrib·ing 1 :** to represent or give an account of in words **2 :** to trace the outline of **— de·scrib·able** adj

**de·scrip·tion** \di-'skrip-shən\ n **1 :** an account of something; esp **:** an account that presents a picture to a person who reads or hears it **2 :** KIND, SORT — **de·scrip·tive** \-'skrip-tiv\ adj

**de·scry** \di-'skrī\ vb **de·scried; de·scry·ing 1 :** to catch sight of **2 :** to discover by observation or investigation

**des·e·crate** \'des-i-ˌkrāt\ vb **-crat·ed; -crat·ing :** PROFANE — **des·e·cra·tion** \ˌdes-i-'krā-shən\ n

**de·seg·re·gate** \dē-'seg-ri-ˌgāt\ vb **:** to eliminate segregation in; esp **:** to free of any law, provision, or practice requiring isolation of the members of a particular race in separate units — **de·seg·re·ga·tion** \dē-ˌseg-ri-'gā-shən\ n

**de·se·lect** \ˌdē-sə-'lekt\ vb **:** to dismiss from a training program

**de·sen·si·tize** \dē-'sen-sə-ˌtīz\ vb **:** to make (a sensitized or hypersensitive individual) insensitive or nonreactive to a sensitizing agent — **de·sen·si·ti·za·tion** \dē-ˌsen-sət-ə-'zā-shən\ n — **de·sen·si·tiz·er** n

¹**des·ert** \'dez-ərt\ n **:** a dry barren region incapable of supporting a population without an artificial water supply

²**des·ert** \'dez-ərt\ adj **:** of, relating to, or resembling a desert; esp **:** being barren and without life \a \~ island\

³**de·sert** \di-'zərt\ n **1 :** worthiness of reward or punishment **2 :** a just reward or punishment

⁴**de·sert** \di-'zərt\ vb **1 :** to withdraw from **2 :** FORSAKE — **de·sert·er** n — **de·ser·tion** \-'zər-shən\ n

**de·serve** \di-'zərv\ vb **de·served; de·serv·ing :** to be worthy of **:** MERIT — **de·serv·ing** adj

**de·serv·ed·ly** \-'zər-vəd-lē\ adv **:** according to merit **:** JUSTLY

**des·ic·cant** \'des-i-kənt\ n **:** a drying agent

**des·ic·cate** \'des-i-ˌkāt\ vb **-cat·ed; -cat·ing :** DRY, DEHYDRATE — **des·ic·ca·tion** \ˌdes-i-'kā-shən\ n — **des·ic·ca·tor** \'des-i-ˌkāt-ər\ n

**de·sid·er·a·tum** \di-ˌsid-ə-'rät-əm, -ˌzid-, -'rāt-\ n, pl **-ta** \-ə\ **:** something desired as essential or needed

¹**de·sign** \di-'zīn\ vb **1 :** to conceive and plan out in the mind; also **:** DEVOTE, CONSIGN **2 :** INTEND **3 :** to devise for a specific function or end **4 :** to make a pattern or sketch of **5 :** to conceive and draw the plans for \~ an airplane\ — **de·sign·er** n

²**design** n **1 :** a mental project or scheme **:** PLAN **2 :** a particular purpose **:** deliberate planning **3 :** a secret project or scheme **:** PLOT **4** pl **:** aggressive or evil intent — used with on or against **5 :** a preliminary sketch or plan **:** DELINEATION **6 :** an underlying scheme that governs functioning, developing, or unfolding **:** MOTIF **7 :** the arrangement of elements that make up a structure or a work of art **8 :** a decorative pattern

¹**des·ig·nate** \'dez-ig-ˌnāt, -nət\ adj **:** chosen for an office but not yet installed \ambassador \~\

²**des·ig·nate** \-ˌnāt\ vb **-nat·ed; -nat·ing 1 :** to mark or point out **:** INDICATE; also **:** SPECIFY, STIPULATE **2 :** to appoint or choose by name for a special purpose **3 :** to call by a name or title — **des·ig·na·tion** \ˌdez-ig-'nā-shən\ n

**de·sign·ing** \di-'zī-niŋ\ adj **:** CRAFTY, SCHEMING

**de·sir·able** \di-'zī-rə-bəl\ adj **1 :** PLEASING, ATTRACTIVE \a \~ woman\ **2 :** ADVISABLE \~ legislation\ — **de·sir·abil·i·ty** \-ˌzī-rə-'bil-ət-ē\ n

¹**de·sire** \di-'zī(ə)r\ vb **de·sired; de·sir·ing** [ME desiren, fr. OF desirer, fr. L desiderare, fr. sider-, sidus star] **1 :** to long, hope, or wish for **:** COVET **2 :** REQUEST

²**desire** n **1 :** a strong wish **:** LONGING, CRAVING **2 :** an expressed wish **:** REQUEST **3 :** something desired

**de·sir·ous** \di-'zīr-əs\ adj **:** eagerly wishing **:** DESIRING

**de·sist** \di-'zist, -'sist\ vb **:** to cease to proceed or act

**desk** \'desk\ n [ME deske, fr. ML desca, fr. It desco table, fr. L discus dish, disc] **1 :** a table, frame, or case esp. for writing and reading **2 :** a counter, stand, or booth at which a person performs his duties **3** : a specialized division of an organization (as a newspaper) ⟨city ~⟩

¹**des·o·late** \'des-ə-lət, 'dez-\ *adj* **1** : DESERTED, ABANDONED **2** : FORSAKEN, LONELY **3** : DILAPIDATED **4** : BARREN, LIFELESS **5** : CHEERLESS, GLOOMY — **des·o·late·ly** *adv*

²**des·o·late** \-ˌlāt\ *vb* **-lat·ed; -lat·ing** : to make desolate : lay waste : make wretched

**des·o·la·tion** \ˌdes-ə-'lā-shən, ˌdez-\ *n* **1** : the action of desolating **2** : DEVASTATION, RUIN **3** : barren wasteland **4** : GRIEF, SADNESS **5** : LONELINESS

**des·oxy·ri·bo·nu·cle·ic acid** \de-ˌzäk-sē-ˌrī-bō-n(y)ü-ˌklē-ik-\ *n* : DNA

¹**de·spair** \di-'spaər\ *vb* : to lose all hope or confidence — **de·spair·ing** *adj* — **de·spair·ing·ly** *adv*

²**despair** *n* **1** : utter loss of hope **2** : a cause of hopelessness

**des·patch** \dis-'pach\ *var of* DISPATCH

**des·per·a·do** \ˌdes-pə-'räd-ō, -'räd-\ *n, pl* **-does** *or* **-dos** : a bold or reckless criminal

**des·per·ate** \'des-p(ə-)rət\ *adj* **1** : being beyond or almost beyond hope : causing despair **2** : RASH **3** : extremely intense — **des·per·ate·ly** *adv*

**des·per·a·tion** \ˌdes-pə-'rā-shən\ *n* **1** : a loss of hope and surrender to despair **2** : a state of hopelessness leading to rashness

**de·spi·ca·ble** \di-'spik-ə-bel, 'des-pik-\ *adj* : deserving to be despised — **de·spi·ca·bly** \-blē\ *adv*

**de·spise** \di-'spīz\ *vb* **de·spised; de·spis·ing** **1** : to look down on with contempt or aversion : DISDAIN, DETEST **2** : to regard as negligible, worthless, or distasteful

**de·spite** \di-'spīt\ *prep* : in spite of

**de·spoil** \di-'spoil\ *vb* **:** to strip of belongings, possessions, or value — **de·spoil·er** *n* — **de·spoil·ment** *n*

**de·spo·li·a·tion** \di-ˌspō-lē-'ā-shən\ *n* : the act of plundering : the state of being despoiled

¹**de·spond** \di-'spänd\ *vb* **:** to become discouraged or disheartened

²**despond** *n* : DESPONDENCY

**de·spon·den·cy** \-'spän-dən-sē\ *n* : DEJECTION, HOPELESSNESS — **de·spon·dent** \-dənt\ *adj*

**des·pot** \'des-pət, -ˌpät\ *n* [MF *despote*, fr. Gk *despotēs* master] **1** : a ruler with absolute power and authority : AUTOCRAT, TYRANT **2** : a person exercising power abusively, oppressively, or tyrannously — **des·pot·ic** \des-'pät-ik\ *adj* — **des·po·tism** \'des-pə-ˌtiz-əm\ *n*

**des·sert** \di-'zərt\ *n* : a course of sweet food, fruit, or cheese served at the close of a meal

**des·ti·na·tion** \ˌdes-tə-'nā-shən\ *n* **1** : an act of appointing, setting aside for a purpose, or predetermining **2** : purpose for which something is destined **3** : a place set for the end of a journey or to which something is sent

**des·tine** \'des-tən\ *vb* **des·tined; des·tin·ing** **:** to settle in advance

**2** : to designate, assign, or dedicate in advance **3** : to be bound or directed

**des·ti·ny** \'des-tə-nē\ *n, pl* **-nies** **1** : something to which a person or thing is destined : FATE, FORTUNE **2** : a predetermined course of events

**des·ti·tute** \'des-tə-ˌt(y)üt\ *adj* **1** : lacking something needed or desirable **2** : extremely poor — **des·ti·tu·tion** \ˌdes-tə-'t(y)ü-shən\ *n*

**de·stroy** \di-'stroi\ *vb* **1** : to put an end to : RUIN **2** : KILL

**de·stroy·er** \di-'stroi(-ə)r\ *n* **1** : one that destroys **2** : a small speedy warship

**destroyer escort** *n* : a warship similar to but smaller than a destroyer

¹**de·struct** \di-'strəkt\ *vb* : DESTROY

²**destruct** *n* : the deliberate destruction of a rocket missile or vehicle after launching

**de·struc·ti·ble** \di-'strək-tə-bəl\ *adj* : capable of being destroyed — **de·struc·ti·bil·i·ty** \di-ˌstrək-tə-'bil-ət-ē\ *n*

**de·struc·tion** \di-'strək-shən\ *n* **1** : the action or process of destroying something **2** : RUIN **3** : a destroying agency — **de·struc·tive** \-'strək-tiv\ *adj* — **de·struc·tive·ly** *adv* — **de·struc·tive·ness** *n*

**de·struc·tor** \di-'strək-tər\ *n* : a furnace for burning refuse : INCINERATOR

**de·sue·tude** \'des-wi-ˌt(y)üd\ *n* : DISUSE

**des·ul·to·ry** \'des-əl-ˌtōr-ē\ *adj* : passing aimlessly from one thing or subject to another : DISCONNECTED

**det** *abbr* **1** detached; detachment **2** detail

**de·tach** \di-'tach\ *vb* **1** : to separate esp. from a larger mass **2** : DISENGAGE, WITHDRAW — **de·tach·able** *adj*

**de·tached** \di-'tacht\ *adj* **1** : not joined or connected : SEPARATE **2** : ALOOF, IMPARTIAL ⟨a ~ attitude⟩

**de·tach·ment** \di-'tach-mənt\ *n* **1** : SEPARATION **2** : the dispatching of a body of troops or part of a fleet from the main body for special service; *also* : the portion so dispatched **3** : a small permanent military unit different in composition from normal units **4** : indifference to worldly concerns : ALOOFNESS, UNWORLDLINESS **5** : IMPARTIALITY

¹**de·tail** \di-'tāl, 'dē-ˌtāl\ *n* [F *détail*, fr. OF *detail* slice, piece, fr. *detaillier* to cut in pieces, fr. *taillier* to cut] **1** : a dealing with something item by item ⟨go into ~⟩; *also* : ITEM, PARTICULAR ⟨the ~*s* of a story⟩ **2** : selection (as of soldiers) for special duty; *also* : the persons thus selected

²**detail** *vb* **1** : to report in detail **2** : ENUMERATE, SPECIFY **3** : to select for some special duty

**de·tain** \di-'tān\ *vb* **1** : to hold in or as if in custody **2** : STOP, DELAY

**de·tect** \di-'tekt\ *vb* : to discover the nature, existence, presence, or fact of — **de·tect·able** *adj* — **de·tec·tion** \-'tek-shən\ *n* — **de·tec·tor** \-tər\ *n*

¹**de·tec·tive** \di-'tek-tiv\ *adj* **1** : fitted for, employed for, or concerned with detection ⟨a ~ device for coal gas⟩

2 : of or relating to detectives

²**detective** n : a person employed or engaged in detecting lawbreakers or getting information that is not readily accessible

**dé·tente** \dā-tä<sup>n</sup>nt\ n : a relaxation of strained relations or tensions (as between nations)

**de·ten·tion** \di-'ten-chən\ n 1 : the act or fact of detaining : CONFINEMENT; esp : a period of temporary custody prior to disposition by a court 2 : a forced delay

**de·ter** \di-'tər\ vb **de·terred; de·ter·ring** [L deterrēre, fr. terrēre to frighten] 1 : to turn aside, discourage, or prevent from acting (as by fear) 2 : INHIBIT

**de·ter·gent** \di-'tər-jənt\ n : a cleansing agent; esp : any of numerous synthetic preparations chemically different from soap

**de·te·ri·o·rate** \di-'tir-ē-ə-,rāt\ vb -rat·ed; -rat·ing : to make or grow worse : DEGENERATE — **de·te·ri·o·ra·tion** \-,tir-ē-ə-'rā-shən\ n

**de·ter·min·able** \-'tər-mə-nə-bəl\ adj : capable of being determined; esp : ASCERTAINABLE

**de·ter·mi·nant** \-mə-nənt\ n 1 : something that determines or conditions 2 : a hereditary factor : GENE

**de·ter·mi·nate** \di-'tər-mə-nət\ adj 1 : having fixed limits : DEFINITE 2 : definitely settled — **de·ter·mi·na·cy** \-nə-sē\ n — **de·ter·mi·nate·ness** n

**de·ter·mi·na·tion** \di-,tər-mə-'nā-shən\ n 1 : the act of coming to a decision; also : the decision or conclusion reached 2 : the act of fixing the extent, position, or character of something 3 : accurate measurement (as of length or volume) 4 : firm or fixed purpose

**de·ter·mine** \di-'tər-mən\ vb **de·ter·mined; de·ter·min·ing** \-'tərm-(ə-)niŋ\ 1 : to fix conclusively or authoritatively 2 : to come to a decision : SETTLE, RESOLVE 3 : to fix the form or character of beforehand : ORDAIN; also : REGULATE 4 : to find out the limits, nature, dimensions, or scope of ⟨~ a position at sea⟩ 5 : to be the cause of or reason for : DECIDE

**de·ter·mined** \-'tər-mənd\ adj 1 : DECIDED, RESOLVED 2 : FIRM, RESOLUTE — **de·ter·mined·ly** \-mən-dlē, -mə-nəd-lē\ adv — **de·ter·mined·ness** \-mən(d)-nəs\ n

**de·ter·min·ism** \di-'tər-mə-,niz-əm\ n : a doctrine that acts of the will, natural events, or social changes are determined by preceding causes — **de·ter·min·ist** \-nəst\ n or adj

**de·ter·rence** \di-'tər-əns\ n : the act, process, or capacity of deterring

**de·ter·rent** \-ənt\ adj 1 : serving to deter 2 : relating to deterrence — **deterrent** n

**de·test** \di-'test\ vb [ME detesten, fr. L detestari, lit., to curse while calling a deity to witness, fr. de- from + testari to call to witness] : LOATHE, — HATE

**de·test·able** adj — **de·tes·ta·tion** \,dē-,tes-'tā-shən\ n

**de·throne** \di-'thrōn\ vb : to remove from a throne — **de·throne·ment** n

**det·o·nate** \'det-ə<sup>n</sup>-,āt, 'det-ə-,nāt\ vb -nat·ed; -nat·ing : to explode with violence — **det·o·na·tion** \,det-ə<sup>n</sup>-'ā-shən, ,det-ə-'nā-\ n

**det·o·na·tor** \'det-ə<sup>n</sup>-,āt-ər, -ə-,nāt-\ n : a device for detonating a high explosive

¹**de·tour** \'dē-,tùr\ n : a roundabout way temporarily replacing part of a route

²**detour** vb : to go by detour

**de·tox·i·fy** \dē-'täk-sə-,fī\ vb -fied; -fy·ing : to remove a poison or toxin or the effect of such from — **de·tox·i·fi·ca·tion** \dē-,täk-sə-fə-'kā-shən\ n

**de·tract** \di-'trakt\ vb 1 : to take away : WITHDRAW, SUBTRACT 2 : DISTRACT — **de·trac·tion** \-'trak-shən\ n — **de·trac·tor** \-'trak-tər\ n

**de·train** \dē-'trān\ vb : to leave or cause to leave a railroad train

**det·ri·ment** \'de-trə-mənt\ n : injury or damage or its cause : HURT — **det·ri·men·tal** \,de-trə-'ment-ᵊl\ adj — **det·ri·men·tal·ly** \-ē\ adv

**de·tri·tus** \di-'trīt-əs\ n, pl **de·tri·tus** : fragments resulting from disintegration (as of rocks acted on by frost)

**deuce** \'d(y)üs\ n 1 : a two in cards or dice 2 : a tie in tennis with both sides at 40 3 : DEVIL — used chiefly as a mild oath

**Deut** abbr Deuteronomy

**deu·te·ri·um** \d(y)ü-'tir-ē-əm\ n : a form of hydrogen that is of twice the mass of ordinary hydrogen

**deut·sche mark** \,dòi-chə-'märk\ n — see MONEY table

**dev** abbr deviation

**de·val·ue** \dē-'val-yü\ vb : to reduce the international exchange value of ⟨~ a currency⟩ — **de·val·u·a·tion** \dē-,val-yə-'wā-shən\ n

**dev·as·tate** \'dev-ə-,stāt\ vb -tat·ed; -tat·ing 1 : to reduce to ruin : lay waste 2 : to shatter completely — **dev·as·ta·tion** \,dev-ə-'stā-shən\ n

**de·vel·op** \di-'vel-əp\ vb 1 : to unfold gradually or in detail 2 : to place (exposed photographic material) in chemicals in order to make the image visible 3 : to bring out the possibilities of 4 : to make more available or usable ⟨~ natural resources⟩ 5 : to acquire gradually ⟨~ a taste for olives⟩ 6 : to go through a natural process of growth and differentiation : EVOLVE 7 : to become apparent — **de·vel·op·er** n — **de·vel·op·ment** n — **de·vel·op·men·tal** \-,vel-əp-'ment-ᵊl\ adj

**de·vi·ant** \'dē-vē-ənt\ adj 1 : deviating esp. from some accepted norm 2 : characterized by deviation — **de·vi·ance** \-əns\ n — **de·vi·an·cy** \-ən-sē\ n — **deviant** n

**de·vi·ate** \'dē-vē-,āt\ vb -at·ed; -at·ing [LL deviare, fr. L de- from + via way] : to turn aside from a course, standard, principle, or topic — **de·vi·ate** \-vē-ət, -vē-,āt\ n — **de·vi-**

**a·tion** \,dē-vē-'ā-shən\ n

**de·vice** \di-'vīs\ n 1 : SCHEME, STRATAGEM 2 : a piece of equipment or a mechanism for a special purpose 3 : WILL, DESIRE (left to his own ~s) 4 : an emblematic design

¹**dev·il** \'dev-əl\ n [ME devel, fr. OE dēofol, fr. LL diabolus, fr. Gk diabolos, lit., slanderer, fr. diaballein to throw across, slander, fr. dia- across + ballein to throw] 1 often cap : the personal supreme spirit of evil 2 : DEMON 3 : a wicked person 4 : a reckless or dashing person 5 : a pitiable person (poor ~) 6 : a printer's apprentice

²**devil** vb -iled or -illed; -il·ing or -il·ling \'dev-(ə-)liŋ\ 1 : TEASE, ANNOY 2 : to chop fine and season highly (~ed eggs)

**dev·il·ish** \'dev-(ə-)lish\ adj 1 : characteristic of or resembling the devil 2 : EXTREME, EXCESSIVE — **dev·il·ish·ly** adv — **dev·il·ish·ness** n

**dev·il·ment** \'dev-əl-mənt, -,ment\ n : MISCHIEF

**dev·il·ry** \-rē\ or **dev·il·try** \-trē\ n, pl -ilries or -iltries 1 : action performed with the help of the devil 2 : reckless mischievousness

**de·vi·ous** \'dē-vē-əs\ adj 1 : deviating from a straight line : ROUNDABOUT 2 : ERRING 3 : TRICKY

¹**de·vise** \di-'vīz\ vb **de·vised**; **de·vis·ing** 1 : INVENT 2 : PLOT 3 : to give (real estate) by will

²**devise** n 1 : a disposing of real property by will 2 : a will or clause of a will disposing of real property 3 : property given by will

**de·vi·tal·ize** \dē-'vīt-ᵊl-,īz\ vb : to deprive of life or vitality

**de·void** \di-'vȯid\ adj : entirely lacking : DESTITUTE (a book ~ of interest)

**de·voir** \dəv-'wär\ n 1 : DUTY 2 : a formal act of civility or respect — usu. used in pl.

**de·volve** \di-'välv\ vb **de·volved**; **de·volv·ing** : to pass from one person to another by succession or transmission — **dev·o·lu·tion** \,dev-ə-'lü-shən, ,dē-və-\ n

**de·vote** \di-'vōt\ vb **de·vot·ed**; **de·vot·ing** 1 : to set apart for a special purpose : DEDICATE 2 : to give up to wholly or chiefly

**de·vot·ed** \-'vōt-əd\ adj 1 : ARDENT, DEVOUT 2 : AFFECTIONATE

**dev·o·tee** \,dev-ə-'tē, -'tā\ n 1 : an esp ardent adherent of a religion or deity 2 : a zealous follower, supporter, or enthusiast (a ~ of sports)

**de·vo·tion** \di-'vō-shən\ n 1 : religious fervor 2 : an act of prayer or supplication — usu. used in pl. 3 pl : religious exercises for private use 4 : the act of devoting or quality of being devoted (~ to music) 5 : strong love or affection — **de·vo·tion·al** \-sh(ə-)nəl\ adj

**de·vour** \di-'vaů(ə)r\ vb 1 : to eat up greedily or ravenously 2 : WASTE, ANNIHILATE 3 : to take in eagerly by the senses or mind (~ a book) — **de·vour·er** n

**de·vout** \di-'vaůt\ adj 1 : devoted to religion : PIOUS 2 : expressing devotion or piety 3 : warmly devoted : SINCERE — **de·vout·ly** adv — **de·vout·ness** n

**dew** \'d(y)ü\ n : moisture condensed on the surfaces of cool bodies at night — **dewy** adj

**DEW** abbr distant early warning

**dew·ber·ry** \'d(y)ü-,ber-ē\ n : any of several sweet edible berries related to and resembling blackberries

**dew·claw** \-,klȯ\ n : a reduced digit on the foot of a mammal that does not reach the ground; also : its claw or hoof

**dew·drop** \-,dräp\ n : a drop of dew

**dew·lap** \-,lap\ n : a hanging fold of skin under the neck esp. of a bovine animal

**dew point** n : the temperature at which a vapor begins to condense

**dex·ter·i·ty** \dek-'ster-ət-ē\ n, pl -ties 1 : readiness and grace in physical activity; esp : skill and ease in using the hands 2 : mental skill or quickness

**dex·ter·ous** or **dex·trous** \'dek-st(ə-)rəs\ adj 1 : skillful and competent with the hands 2 : EXPERT 3 : done with skillfulness — **dex·ter·ous·ly** adv

**dex·trin** \'dek-strən\ n : any of various polymers of sugar obtained from starch and used as adhesives, as sizes for paper and textiles, and in syrups and beer

**dex·trose** \'dek-,strōs\ n : a sugar that occurs in plants and blood and may be made from starch

**DF** abbr damage free

**DFC** abbr Distinguished Flying Cross

**DFM** abbr Distinguished Flying Medal

**DG** abbr 1 [LL Dei gratia] by the grace of God 2 director general

**dhow** \'daů\ n : an Arab sailing ship usu. having a long overhang forward and a high poop

**dia** abbr diameter

**di·a·be·tes** \,dī-ə-'bēt-ēz, -'bēt-əs\ n : an abnormal state marked by passage of excessive amounts of urine; esp : one (**diabetes mel·li·tus** \-'mel-ət-əs\) in which insulin is deficient and the urine and blood contain excess sugar — **di·a·bet·ic** \-'bet-ik\ adj or n

**di·a·bol·ic** \,dī-ə-'bäl-ik\ or **di·a·bol·i·cal** \-i-kəl\ adj : DEVILISH, FIENDISH — **di·a·bol·i·cal·ly** \-k(ə-)lē\ adv

**di·a·crit·ic** \,dī-ə-'krit-ik\ n : a mark accompanying a letter and indicating a sound value different from that of the same letter when unmarked — **di·a·crit·i·cal** \-'krit-i-kəl\ adj

**di·a·dem** \'dī-ə-,dem\ n : CROWN; esp : a band worn on or around the head as a badge of royalty

**di·aer·e·sis** \dī-'er-ə-səs\ n, pl -e·ses \-,sēz\ : a mark ¨ placed over a vowel to show that it is pronounced in a separate syllable (as in naïve)

**diag** abbr 1 diagonal 2 diagram

**di·ag·no·sis** \,dī-ig-'nō-səs, -əg-\ n, pl -no·ses \-,sēz\ : the art or act of identifying a disease from its signs and symptoms — **di·ag·nose** \'dī-ig-

\ˌnōs, -əg-\ *vb* — **di·ag·nos·tic** \ˌdī-ig-ˈnäs-tik, -əg-\ *adj* — **di·ag·nos·ti·cian** \-ˌnäs-ˈtish-ən\ *n*

¹**di·ag·o·nal** \dī-ˈag-(ə-)nəl\ *adj* **1** : extending from one corner to the opposite corner in a 4-sided figure **2** : running in a slanting direction ⟨∼ stripes⟩ **3** : having slanting markings or parts ⟨a ∼ weave⟩ — **di·ag·o·nal·ly** \-ē\ *adv*

²**diagonal** *n* **1** : a diagonal line **2** : a diagonal direction **3** : a diagonal row, arrangement, or pattern

¹**di·a·gram** \ˈdī-ə-ˌgram\ *n* : a drawing, sketch, plan, or chart that makes something easier to understand — **di·a·gram·mat·ic** \ˌdī-ə-grə-ˈmat-ik\ *also* **di·a·gram·mat·i·cal** \-ˈmat-i-kəl\ *adj* — **di·a·gram·mat·i·cal·ly** \-i-k(ə-)lē\ *adv*

²**diagram** *vb* **-gramed** \-ˌgramd\ *or* **-grammed; -gram·ing** \-ˌgram-iŋ\ *or* **-gram·ming** : to represent by a diagram

¹**di·al** \ˈdī(-ə)l\ *n* [ME, fr. L *dies* day] **1** : SUNDIAL **2** : the face of a timepiece **3** : a plate or face with a pointer and numbers that indicate something ⟨the ∼ of a gauge⟩ **4** : a disk with a knob or slots that is turned for making connections (as on a telephone) or for regulating operation (as of a radio)

²**dial** *vb* **di·aled** *or* **di·alled; di·al·ing** *or* **di·al·ling** **1** : to manipulate a telephone dial so as to call **2** : to manipulate a dial so as to operate or select

³**dial** *abbr* dialect

**di·a·lect** \ˈdī-ə-ˌlekt\ *n* : a regional variety of a language

**di·a·lec·tic** \ˌdī-ə-ˈlek-tik\ *n* : the process or art of reasoning correctly

**di·a·logue** *or* **di·a·log** \ˈdī-ə-ˌlòg\ *n* **1** : a conversation between two or more persons **2** : the parts of a literary or dramatic composition that represent conversation

**di·al·y·sis** \dī-ˈal-ə-səs\ *n, pl* **-y·ses** \-ˌsēz\ : the separation of substances from solution by means of their unequal diffusion through semipermeable membranes

**dia·mag·net·ic** \ˌdī-ə-mag-ˈnet-ik\ *adj* : slightly repelled by a magnet — **dia·mag·ne·tism** \ˌdī-ə-ˈmag-nə-ˌtiz-əm\ *n*

**di·am·e·ter** \dī-ˈam-ət-ər\ *n* [ME *diametre*, fr. MF, fr. L *diametros*, fr. Gk, fr. *dia-* through + *metron* measure] **1** : a straight line that passes through the center of a circle and divides it in half **2** : THICKNESS ⟨∼ of a rope⟩

**di·a·met·ric** \ˌdī-ə-ˈme-trik\ *or* **di·a·met·ri·cal** \-tri-kəl\ *adj* **1** : of, relating to, or constituting a diameter **2** : completely opposed or opposite — **di·a·met·ri·cal·ly** \-tri-k(ə-)lē\ *adv*

**di·a·mond** \ˈdī-(ə-)mənd\ *n* **1** : a hard brilliant mineral that consists of crystalline carbon and is used as a gem **2** : a flat figure having four equal sides, two acute angles, and two obtuse angles **3** : any of a suit of playing cards marked with a red diamond **4** : INFIELD; *also* : the entire playing field in baseball

**di·a·mond·back** \ˈdī-(ə-)mən(d)-ˌbak\ *n* : a large and very deadly rattlesnake

**di·an·thus** \dī-ˈan-thəs\ *n* : ²PINK 1

**di·a·pa·son** \ˌdī-ə-ˈpāz-ᵊn, -ˈpās-\ *n* **1** : the range of notes sounded by a voice or instrument **2** : an organ stop covering the range of the organ

¹**di·a·per** \ˈdī(-ə)-pər\ *n* **1** : a cotton or linen fabric woven in a simple geometric pattern **2** : a piece of folded cloth drawn up between the legs of a baby and fastened about the waist

²**diaper** *vb* **di·a·pered; di·a·per·ing** \-p(ə-)riŋ\ **1** : to ornament with diaper designs **2** : to put a diaper on

**di·aph·a·nous** \dī-ˈaf-ə-nəs\ *adj* : so fine of texture as to be transparent

**di·a·pho·ret·ic** \ˌdī-ə-fə-ˈret-ik\ *adj* : having the power to increase perspiration — **diaphoretic** *n*

**di·a·phragm** \ˈdī-ə-ˌfram\ *n* **1** : a muscular bodily partition; *esp* : one between the chest and abdominal cavities of a mammal **2** : a vibrating disk (as in a telephone receiver) **3** : a molded cap usu. of thin rubber fitted over the uterine cervix to act as a mechanical contraceptive barrier — **di·a·phrag·mat·ic** \ˌdī-ə-frə(g)-ˈmat-ik, -ˌfrag-\ *adj*

**di·a·rist** \ˈdī-ə-rəst\ *n* : one who keeps a diary

**di·ar·rhea** *or* **di·ar·rhoea** \ˌdī-ə-ˈrē-ə\ *n* : abnormal looseness of the bowels

**di·a·ry** \ˈdī-(ə-)rē\ *n, pl* **-ries** : a daily record esp. of personal experiences and observations; *also* : a book for keeping such private notes and records

**di·as·to·le** \dī-ˈas-tə-(ˌ)lē\ *n* : a rhythmically recurrent expansion; *esp* : the dilatation of the cavities of the heart during which they fill with blood — **di·a·stol·ic** \ˌdī-ə-ˈstäl-ik\ *adj*

**di·as·tro·phism** \dī-ˈas-trə-ˌfiz-əm\ *n* : the process by which the major relief features of the earth are formed — **di·a·stroph·ic** \ˌdī-ə-ˈsträf-ik\ *adj*

**dia·ther·my** \ˈdī-ə-ˌthər-mē\ *n* : the generation of heat in tissue by electric currents for medical or surgical purposes

**di·a·tom** \ˈdī-ə-ˌtäm\ *n* : any of a class of planktonic one-celled or colonial algae with skeletons of silica

**di·atom·ic** \ˌdī-ə-ˈtäm-ik\ *adj* : having two atoms in the molecule

**di·at·o·mite** \dī-ˈat-ə-ˌmīt\ *n* : a light friable siliceous material used esp. as a filter

**di·a·tribe** \ˈdī-ə-ˌtrīb\ *n* : a bitter or violent attack in speech or writing : an angry criticism or denunciation

**dib·ble** \ˈdib-əl\ *n* : a pointed hand tool for making holes (as for planting bulbs) in the ground — **dibble** *vb*

¹**dice** \ˈdīs\ *n, pl* **dice** : a small cube marked on each face with one to six spots and used usu. in pairs in various games and in gambling

²**dice** *vb* **diced; dic·ing** **1** : to cut into small cubes ⟨∼ carrots⟩ **2** : to play games with dice

**di·chot·o·my** \dī-ˈkät-ə-mē\ *n, pl* **-mies** : a division or the process of dividing into two esp. mutually exclusive or contradictory groups — **di·chot·o·mous** \-məs\ *adj*

**dick·er** *vb* **dick·ered; dick·er·ing** \'dik-(ə-)riŋ\ : BARGAIN, HAGGLE

**dick·ey** *or* **dicky** \'dik-ē\ *n, pl* **dickeys** *or* **dick·ies 1 :** a small fabric insert worn to fill in the neckline **2** *chiefly Brit* **:** the driver's seat in a carriage; *also* **:** a seat at the back of a carriage or automobile

**di·cot·y·le·don** \ˌdī-ˌkät-ᵊl-'ēd-ᵊn\ : a seed plant having two cotyledons — **di·cot·y·le·don·ous** *adj*

**dict** *abbr* dictionary

**¹dic·tate** \'dik-ˌtāt\ *vb* **1 :** to speak or read for a person to transcribe or for a machine to record **2 :** COMMAND, ORDER — **dic·ta·tion** \dik-'tā-shən\ *n*

**²dic·tate** \'dik-ˌtāt\ *n* **:** an authoritative rule, prescription, or injunction **:** COMMAND ⟨the ∼s of conscience⟩

**dic·ta·tor** \'dik-ˌtāt-ər\ *n* **1 :** a person ruling absolutely and often brutally and oppressively **2 :** one that dictates

**dic·ta·to·ri·al** \ˌdik-tə-'tōr-ē-əl\ *adj* **:** of, relating to, or characteristic of a dictator or a dictatorship

**dic·ta·tor·ship** \dik-'tāt-ər-ˌship, 'dik-ˌtāt-\ *n* **1 :** the office or term of office of a dictator **2 :** autocratic rule, control, or leadership **3 :** a government or country in which absolute power is held by a dictator or a small clique

**dic·tion** \'dik-shən\ *n* **1 :** choice of words esp. with regard to correctness, clearness, or effectiveness **:** WORDING **2 :** ENUNCIATION

**dic·tio·nary** \'dik-shə-ˌner-ē\ *n, pl* **-nar·ies :** a reference book containing words usu. alphabetically arranged along with information about their forms, pronunciations, functions, etymologies, meanings, and syntactical and idiomatic uses

**dic·tum** \'dik-təm\ *n, pl* **dic·ta** \-tə\ *also* **dictums 1 :** an authoritative statement **:** PRONOUNCEMENT **2 :** a formal statement of an opinion

**did** *past of* DO

**di·dac·tic** \dī-'dak-tik\ *adj* **1 :** intended primarily to instruct; *esp* **:** intended to teach a moral lesson **2 :** having or showing a tendency to instruct or lecture others ⟨a ∼ manner⟩

**di·do** \'dīd-ō\ *n, pl* **didoes** *or* **didos :** a foolish or mischievous act

**¹die** \'dī\ *vb* **died; dy·ing** \'dī-iŋ\ **1 :** to stop living **:** EXPIRE **2 :** to pass out of existence ⟨a *dying* race⟩ **3 :** to disappear or subside gradually ⟨the wind *died* down⟩ **4 :** to long keenly ⟨*dying* to go⟩ **5 :** STOP ⟨the motor *died*⟩

**²die** \'dī\ *n, pl* **dice** \'dīs\ *or* **dies** \'dīz\ **1** *pl* **dice :** DICE **2** *pl usu* **dice :** something determined as if by a cast of dice **3** *pl* **dies :** a device used in shaping or stamping an object or material

**die·hard** \'dī-ˌhärd\ *n* **:** one who resists against hopeless odds

**diel·drin** \'dē(ə)l-drən\ *n* **:** a persistent chlorinated hydrocarbon insecticide

**di·elec·tric** \ˌdī-ə-'lek-trik\ *n* **:** an electrically nonconducting material

**die·sel** \'dē-zəl, -səl\ *n* **1 :** DIESEL ENGINE **2 :** a vehicle driven by a diesel engine

**diesel engine** *n* **:** an engine in which air is compressed to a temperature sufficiently high to ignite the fuel in the cylinder

**¹di·et** \'dī-ət\ *n* [ME *diete*, fr. OF, fr. L *diaeta* prescribed diet, fr. Gk *diaita*, lit., manner of living] **1 :** the food and drink regularly consumed (as by a person or group) **:** FARE **2 :** an allowance of food prescribed with reference to a particular state (as ill health) — **di·etary** \'dī-ə-ˌter-ē\ *adj or n*

**²diet** *vb* **:** to eat or cause to eat less or according to a prescribed rule — **di·et·er** *n*

**di·etet·ics** \ˌdī-ə-'tet-iks\ *n sing or pl* **:** the science or art of applying the principles of nutrition to diet — **di·etet·ic** *adj* — **di·eti·tian** *or* **di·eti·cian** \-'tish-ən\ *n*

**dif** *or* **diff** *abbr* difference

**dif·fer** \'dif-ər\ *vb* **dif·fered; dif·fer·ing** \-(ə-)riŋ\ **1 :** to be unlike **2 :** DISAGREE

**dif·fer·ence** \'dif-ərns, 'dif-(ə-)rəns\ *n* **1 :** UNLIKENESS ⟨∼ in their looks⟩ **2 :** distinction or discrimination in preference **3 :** DISAGREEMENT, DISSENSION; *also* **:** an instance or cause of disagreement ⟨unable to settle their ∼s⟩ **4 :** the amount by which one number or quantity differs from another

**dif·fer·ent** \'dif-ərnt, 'dif-(ə-)rənt\ *adj* **1 :** UNLIKE, DISSIMILAR **2 :** not the same ⟨∼ age groups⟩ ⟨seen at ∼ times⟩ ⟨try a ∼ book⟩ **3 :** UNUSUAL, SPECIAL — **dif·fer·ent·ly** *adv*

**¹dif·fer·en·tial** \ˌdif-ə-'ren-chəl\ *adj* **:** showing, creating, or relating to a difference

**²differential** *n* **1 :** the amount or degree by which things differ **2 :** DIFFERENTIAL GEAR

**differential gear** *n* **:** an arrangement of gears in an automobile that allows one wheel to go faster than another (as in rounding curves)

**dif·fer·en·ti·ate** \ˌdif-ə-'ren-chē-ˌāt\ *vb* **-at·ed; -at·ing 1 :** to make or become different **2 :** to recognize or state the difference ⟨∼ between two plants⟩ — **dif·fer·en·ti·a·tion** \-ˌren-chē-'ā-shən\ *n*

**dif·fi·cult** \'dif-i-(ˌ)kəlt\ *adj* **1 :** hard to do or make **2 :** hard to understand or deal with ⟨∼ reading⟩ ⟨a ∼ child⟩

**dif·fi·cul·ty** \-(ˌ)kəl-tē\ *n, pl* **-ties 1 :** difficult nature ⟨the ∼ of a task⟩ **2 :** great effort **3 :** OBSTACLE ⟨overcome *difficulties*⟩ **4 :** TROUBLE ⟨in financial *difficulties*⟩ **5 :** DISAGREEMENT ⟨settled their *difficulties*⟩ **syn** hardship, rigor, vicissitude

**dif·fi·dent** \'dif-əd-ənt\ *adj* **1 :** lacking confidence **:** TIMID **2 :** RESERVED, UNASSERTIVE — **dif·fi·dence** \-əns\ *n* — **dif·fi·dent·ly** *adv*

**dif·frac·tion** \dif-'rak-shən\ *n* **:** the deflecting of a light beam esp. when passing through narrow slits or when reflecting from a ruled surface

**¹dif·fuse** \dif-'yüs\ *adj* **1** : not concentrated ⟨~ light⟩ **2** : VERBOSE, WORDY ⟨~ writing⟩ **3** : SCATTERED

**²dif·fuse** \dif-'yüz\ *vb* **dif·fused; dif·fus·ing** : to pour out or spread widely — **dif·fu·sion** \-'yü-zhən\ *n*

**¹dig** \'dig\ *vb* **dug** \'dəg\; **dig·ging 1** : to turn up the soil (as with a spade) **2** : to hollow out or form by removing earth ⟨~ a hole⟩ **3** : to uncover or seek by turning up earth ⟨~ potatoes⟩ **4** : DISCOVER ⟨~ up information⟩ **5** : POKE, THRUST ⟨~ a person in the ribs⟩ **6** : to work hard **7** : NOTICE, APPRECIATE; *also* : LIKE, ADMIRE

**²dig** *n* **1** : THRUST, POKE **2** : a cutting remark : GIBE

**³dig** *abbr* digest

**¹di·gest** \'dī-,jest\ *n* : a summation or condensation of a body of information or of a literary creation

**²di·gest** \dī-'jest, də-\ *vb* **1** : to think over and arrange in the mind **2** : to convert (food) into a form that can be absorbed **3** : to compress into a short summary — **di·gest·ibil·i·ty** \-,jes-tə-'bil-ət-ē\ *n* — **di·gest·ible** *adj* — **di·ges·tion** \-'jes-chən\ *n* — **di·ges·tive** \-'jes-tiv\ *adj*

**dig in** *vb* **1** : to dig defensive trenches **2** : to go resolutely to work **3** : to begin eating

**dig·it** \'dij-ət\ *n* [ME, fr. L *digitus* finger, toe] **1** : any of the figures 1 to 9 inclusive and usu. the symbol 0 **2** : FINGER, TOE

**dig·i·tal** \'dij-ət-ᵊl\ *adj* **1** : of or relating to the fingers or toes **2** : of or relating to calculation directly with digits rather than through measurable physical quantities ⟨a ~ computer⟩ — **dig·i·tal·ly** \-ē\ *adv*

**dig·i·tal·is** \,dij-ə-'tal-əs\ *n* : a drug from the common foxglove that is a powerful heart stimulant; *also* : FOXGLOVE

**dig·ni·fied** \'dig-nə-,fīd\ *adj* : showing or expressing dignity

**dig·ni·fy** \-,fī\ *vb* **-fied; -fy·ing** : to give dignity or distinction to : HONOR

**dig·ni·tary** \'dig-nə-,ter-ē\ *n, pl* **-tar·ies** : a person of high position or honor

**dig·ni·ty** \'dig-nət-ē\ *n, pl* **-ties 1** : the quality or state of being worthy, honored, or esteemed : true worth : EXCELLENCE **2** : high rank, office, or position **3** : formal reserve of manner or language

**di·graph** \'dī-,graf\ *n* : a group of two successive letters whose phonetic value is a single sound

**di·gress** \dī-'gres, də-\ *vb* : to turn aside esp. from the main subject in writing or speaking — **di·gres·sion** \-'gresh-ən\ *n* — **di·gres·sive** \-'gres-iv\ *adj*

**dike** \'dīk\ *n* : a bank of earth to control water : LEVEE

**dil** *abbr* dilute

**di·lap·i·dat·ed** \də-'lap-ə-,dāt-əd\ *adj* : fallen into partial ruin or decay — **di·lap·i·da·tion** \-,lap-ə-'dā-shən\ *n*

**di·late** \dī-'lāt, 'dī-,lāt\ *vb* **di·lat·ed; di·lat·ing** : SWELL, DISTEND, EXPAND

— **dil·a·ta·tion** \,dil-ə-'tā-shən\ *n* — **di·la·tion** \dī-'lā-shən\ *n*

**dil·a·to·ry** \'dil-ə-,tōr-ē\ *adj* **1** : DELAYING **2** : TARDY, SLOW

**di·lem·ma** \də-'lem-ə\ *n* : a choice between equally undesirable alternatives

**dil·et·tante** \,dil-ə-'tänt-(ē), -'tant-(ē)\ *n, pl* **-tantes** *or* **-tan·ti** \-'tänt-ē, -'tant-ē\ [It, fr. *dilettare* to delight, fr. L *dilectare*] : a person having a superficial interest in an art or a branch of knowledge

**dil·i·gent** \'dil-ə-jənt\ *adj* : characterized by steady, earnest, and energetic application and effort : PAINSTAKING — **dil·i·gence** \-jəns\ *n* — **dil·i·gent·ly** *adv*

**dill** \'dil\ *n* : an herb related to the carrot with aromatic leaves and seeds used in pickles

**dil·ly·dal·ly** \'dil-ē-,dal-ē\ *vb* : to waste time by loitering or delay

**dil·u·ent** \'dil-yə-wənt\ *n* : a diluting agent

**¹di·lute** \dī-'lüt, də-\ *vb* **di·lut·ed; di·lut·ing** : to lessen the consistency or strength of by mixing with something else — **di·lu·tion** \-'lü-shən\ *n*

**²dilute** *adj* : DILUTED, WEAK

**¹dim** \'dim\ *adj* **dim·mer; dim·mest 1** : not bright or distinct : OBSCURE, FAINT **2** : LUSTERLESS, DULL **3** : not seeing or understanding clearly — **dim·ly** *adv* — **dim·ness** *n*

**²dim** *vb* **dimmed; dim·ming 1** : to make or become dim or lusterless **2** : to reduce the light from ⟨~ the headlights⟩

**³dim** *abbr* **1** dimension **2** diminished **3** diminutive

**dime** \'dīm\ *n* [ME, tenth part, tithe, fr. MF, fr. L *decima*, fr. fem. of *decimus* tenth, fr. *decem* ten] : a U.S. coin worth ¹/₁₀ dollar

**di·men·sion** \də-'men-chən, dī-\ *n* **1** : measurement of extension (as in length, height, or breadth) **2** : EXTENT, SCOPE, PROPORTIONS — **di·men·sion·al** \-'mench-(ə-)nəl\ *adj* — **di·men·sion·al·i·ty** \-,men-chə-'nal-ət-ē\ *n*

**di·min·ish** \də-'min-ish\ *vb* **1** : to make less or cause to appear less **2** : BELITTLE **3** : DWINDLE **4** : TAPER — **dim·i·nu·tion** \,dim-ə-'n(y)ü-shən\ *n*

**di·min·u·en·do** \də-,min-(y)ə-'wen-dō\ *adv or adj* : DECRESCENDO

**¹di·min·u·tive** \də-'min-yət-iv\ *n* **1** : a diminutive word or affix **2** : a diminutive object or individual

**²diminutive** *adj* **1** : indicating small size and sometimes the state or quality of being lovable, pitiable, or contemptible ⟨the ~ suffixes *-ette* and *-ling*⟩ **2** : extremely small : TINY

**dim·i·ty** \'dim-ət-ē\ *n, pl* **-ties** : a thin usu. corded cotton fabric

**dim·mer** \'dim-ər\ *n* **1** : one that dims **2** *pl* : automobile headlights that have been dimmed

**di·mor·phic** \(')dī-'mȯr-fik\ *adj* : occurring in two distinct forms — **di·mor·phism** \-,fiz-əm\ *n*

**¹dim·ple** \'dim-pəl\ *n* : a small depression esp. in the cheek or chin

**²dimple** *vb* **dim·pled; dim·pling** : to

form dimples (as in smiling)

**din** \'din\ *n* : a loud, confused, or clanging noise

**di·nar** \di-'när\ *n* 1 — see MONEY table 2 — see *rial* it MONEY table

**dine** \'dīn\ *vb* **dined; din·ing** [ME *dinen*, fr. OF *diner*, fr. (assumed) VL *disjejunare* to break one's fast, fr. L *jejunus* fasting] 1 : to eat dinner 2 : to give a dinner to : FEED

**din·er** \'dī-nər\ *n* 1 : one that dines 2 : railroad dining car; *also* : a restaurant usu. in the shape of a railroad car

**di·nette** \dī-'net\ *n* : an alcove or small room used for dining

**din·ghy** \'diŋ-(k)ē\ *n*, *pl* **dinghies** 1 : a light rowboat 2 : a rubber life raft

**din·gle** \'diŋ-gəl\ *n* : a narrow wooded valley

**din·go** \'diŋ-gō\ *n*, *pl* **dingoes** : a reddish brown wild dog of Australia

**din·gus** \'diŋ-(g)əs\ *n* : something whose proper name is unknown or forgotten

**din·gy** \'din-jē\ *adj* **din·gi·er; -est** 1 : DARK, DULL 2 : not fresh or clean : GRIMY — **din·gi·ness** *n*

**din·ky** \'diŋ-kē\ *adj* **din·ki·er; -est** : SMALL, INSIGNIFICANT

**din·ner** \'din-ər\ *n* : the main meal of the day; *also* : a formal banquet

**din·ner·ware** \'din-ər-,waər\ *n* : china, glassware, or tableware used in table service

**di·no·fla·gel·late** \,dī-nō-'flaj-ə-lət, -,lāt\ *n* : any of an order of planktonic plantlike flagellates of which some cause red tide

**di·no·saur** \'dī-nə-,sȯr\ *n* [fr. Gk *deinos* terrible + *sauros* lizard] : any of a group of extinct long-tailed reptiles often of huge size

**dint** \'dint\ *n* 1 *archaic* : BLOW, STROKE 2 : FORCE, POWER ⟨he reached the top by ~ of sheer grit⟩ 3 : DENT

**di·o·cese** \'dī-ə-səs, -,sēz, -,sēs\ *n*, *pl* **-ces·es** \-sə-səz, -,sē-zəz, -,sē-səz, -ə-,sēz\ : the territorial jurisdiction of a bishop — **di·oc·e·san** \dī-'äs-ə-sən, ,dī-ə-'sēz-²n\ *adj or n*

**di·ode** \'dī-,ōd\ *n* 1 : an electron tube having a cathode and anode 2 : a rectifier consisting of a semiconductor crystal

**dip** \'dip\ *vb* **dipped; dip·ping** 1 : to plunge temporarily or partially under the surface (as of a liquid) so as to moisten, cool, or coat 2 : to thrust in a way to suggest immersion 3 : to scoop up or out : LADLE 4 : to lower and then raise quickly ⟨~ a flag in salute⟩ 5 : to drop or slope down or out of sight esp. suddenly ⟨the moon *dipped* below the crest⟩ 6 : to decrease moderately and usu. temporarily ⟨prices *dipped*⟩ 7 : to reach down inside or as if inside or below a surface ⟨*dipped* into their savings⟩ 8 : to delve casually into something; *esp* : to read superficially ⟨~ into a book⟩

**dip** *n* 1 : an act of dipping; *esp* : a brief plunge into the water for sport or exer-

cise 2 : inclination downward : DROP 3 : something obtained by or used in dipping 4 : a liquid into which something may be dipped

**diph·the·ria** \dif-'thir-ē-ə, dip-\ *n* : an acute contagious bacterial disease marked by fever and by coating of the air passages with a membrane that interferes with breathing — **diph·the·rit·ic** \,dif-thə-'rit-ik, ,dip-\ *adj*

**diph·thong** \'dif-,thȯŋ, 'dip-\ *n* : two vowel sounds joined in one syllable to form one speech sound (as *ou* in *out*, *oi* in *oil*)

**dip·loid** \'dip-,lȯid\ *adj* : having the basic chromosome number doubled — **diploid** *n*

**di·plo·ma** \də-'plō-mə\ *n*, *pl* **diplomas** : an official paper bearing record of graduation from or of a degree conferred by an educational institution

**di·plo·ma·cy** \də-'plō-mə-sē\ *n* 1 : the art and practice of conducting negotiations between nations 2 : TACT

**dip·lo·mat** \'dip-lə-,mat\ *n* : one employed or skilled in diplomacy — **dip·lo·mat·ic** \,dip-lə-'mat-ik\ *adj*

**di·plo·ma·tist** \də-'plō-mət-əst\ *n* : DIPLOMAT

**dip·per** \'dip-ər\ *n* 1 : something (as a ladle or scoop) that dips or is used for dipping 2 *cap* : BIG DIPPER 3 *cap* : LITTLE DIPPER 4 : any of several birds skilled in diving

**dip·so·ma·nia** \,dip-sə-'mā-nē-ə\ *n* : an uncontrollable craving for alcoholic liquors — **dip·so·ma·ni·ac** \-nē-,ak\ *n*

**dip·stick** \'dip-,stik\ *n* : a graduated rod for indicating depth

**dip·ter·ous** \'dip-tə-rəs\ *adj* : having two wings; *also* : of or relating to the two-winged flies — **dip·ter·an** \-rən\ *adj or n*

**dir** *abbr* director

**dire** \'dī(-ə)r\ *adj* **dir·er; dir·est** 1 : very horrible : DREADFUL 2 : warning of disaster 3 : EXTREME

**¹di·rect** \də-'rekt, dī-\ *vb* 1 : ADDRESS ⟨~ a letter⟩; *also* : to impart orally : AIM ⟨~ a remark to the gallery⟩ 2 : to cause to turn, move, or point or to follow a certain course 3 : to point, extend, or project in a specified line or course 4 : to show or point out the way 5 : to regulate the activities or course of : guide the supervision, organizing, or performance of 6 : to request or instruct with authority

**²direct** *adj* 1 : leading from one point to another in time or space without turn or stop : STRAIGHT 2 : stemming immediately from a source, cause, or reason ⟨~ result⟩ 3 : operating without an intervening agency or step ⟨~ action⟩ 4 : being or passing in a straight line of descent : LINEAL ⟨~ ancestor⟩ 5 : NATURAL, STRAIGHTFORWARD ⟨a ~ manner⟩ 6 : effected by the action of the people or the electorate and not by representatives ⟨~ legislation⟩ 7 : consisting of or reproducing the exact words of a speaker ⟨~ discourse⟩ — **direct** *adv* — **di·rect·ly** \də-'rek-(t)lē, dī-\ *adv* —

**di·rect·ness** \-'rek(t)-nəs\ n

**direct current** n : an electric current flowing in one direction only

**di·rec·tion** \də-'rek-shən, dī\ n 1 : MANAGEMENT, GUIDANCE 2 archaic : SUPERSCRIPTION 3 : COMMAND, ORDER, INSTRUCTION 4 : the course or line along which something moves, lies, or points; also : TREND — **di·rec·tion·al** \-sh(ə-)nəl\ adj

**di·rec·tive** \də-'rek-tiv, dī-\ n : a general instruction as to procedure

**di·rec·tor** \də-'rek-tər, dī-\ n 1 : one that directs : MANAGER, SUPERVISOR, CONDUCTOR 2 : one of a group of persons who direct the affairs of an organized body — **di·rec·tor·ship** n — **di·rec·tress** \-trəs\ n

**di·rec·tor·ate** \də-'rek-t(ə-)rət, dī-\ n 1 : the office or position of director 2 : a board of directors; also : membership on such a board 3 : an executive staff

**di·rec·to·ry** \-t(ə-)rē\ n, pl -ries : an alphabetical or classified list of names and addresses

**dire·ful** \'dī(ə)r-fəl\ adj : producing dire effects

**dirge** \'dərj\ n : a song or hymn of lamentation; also : a slow mournful piece of music

**dir·ham** \də-'ram\ n 1 — see MONEY table 2 — see dinar at MONEY table

**di·ri·gi·ble** \'dir-ə-jə-bəl, də-'rij-ə-\ n : AIRSHIP

**dirk** \'dərk\ n : DAGGER

**dirndl** \'dərn-dᵊl\ n [short for G dirndlkleid, fr. G dial. dirndl girl + G kleid dress] : a full skirt with a tight waistband

**dirt** \'dərt\ n 1 : a filthy or soiling substance (as mud, dust, or grime) 2 : loose or packed earth : SOIL 3 : moral uncleanness 4 : scandalous gossip

¹**dirty** \'dərt-ē\ adj dirt·i·er; -est 1 : SOILED, FILTHY 2 : BASE, UNFAIR ⟨a ~ trick⟩ 3 : INDECENT, SMUTTY ⟨~ talk⟩ 4 : STORMY, FOGGY ⟨~ weather⟩ 5 : not clear in color : DULL ⟨a ~ red⟩ — **dirt·i·ness** \'dərt-ē-nəs\ n

²**dirty** vb dirt·ied; dirty·ing : to make or become dirty

**dis·able** \dis-'ā-bəl\ vb dis·abled; dis·abling \-b(ə-)liŋ\ 1 : to incapacitate by or as if by illness, injury, or wounds 2 : to disqualify legally — **dis·abil·i·ty** \,dis-ə-'bil-ət-ē\ n

**dis·abuse** \,dis-ə-'byüz\ vb : to free from error or fallacy

**di·sac·cha·ride** \dī-'sak-ə-,rīd\ n : a sugar that yields two molecules of simple sugar upon hydrolysis

**dis·ad·van·tage** \,dis-əd-'vant-ij\ n 1 : loss or damage esp. to reputation or finances 2 : an unfavorable, inferior, or prejudicial condition; also : HANDICAP — **dis·ad·van·ta·geous** \dis-,ad-,van-'tā-jəs, -vən-\ adj

**dis·af·fect** \,dis-ə-'fect\ vb : to alienate the affection or loyalty of : cause discontent in ⟨the troops were ~ed⟩ — **dis·af·fec·tion** \-'fek-shən\ n

**dis·agree** \,dis-ə-'grē\ vb 1 : to fail to agree 2 : to differ in opinion 3 : to be unsuitable ⟨fried foods ~ with her⟩ — **dis·agree·ment** n

**dis·agree·able** \-ə-bəl\ adj 1 : causing discomfort : UNPLEASANT, OFFENSIVE 2 : ILL-TEMPERED, PEEVISH — **dis·agree·able·ness** n — **dis·agree·ably** \-blē\ adv

**dis·al·low** \,dis-ə-'laů\ vb : to refuse to admit or recognize : REJECT ⟨~ a claim⟩ — **dis·al·low·ance** n

**dis·ap·pear** \,dis-ə-'piər\ vb 1 : to pass out of sight 2 : to cease to be : become lost — **dis·ap·pear·ance** n

**dis·ap·point** \,dis-ə-'pȯint\ vb : to fail to fulfill the expectation or hope of — **dis·ap·point·ment** n

**dis·ap·pro·ba·tion** \dis-,ap-rə-'bā-shən\ n : DISAPPROVAL

**dis·ap·prov·al** \,dis-ə-'prü-vəl\ n : adverse judgment : CENSURE

**dis·ap·prove** \-'prüv\ vb 1 : to CONDEMN 2 : REJECT 3 : to feel or express disapproval ⟨~s of smoking⟩

**dis·arm** \dis-'ärm\ vb 1 : to take arms or weapons from 2 : DISBAND; esp : to reduce the size and strength of the armed forces of a country 3 : to make harmless, peaceable, or friendly : win over ⟨a ~ing smile⟩ — **dis·ar·ma·ment** \-'är-mə-mənt\ n

**dis·ar·range** \,dis-ə-'rānj\ vb : to disturb the arrangement or order of — **dis·ar·range·ment** n

**dis·ar·ray** \-'rā\ n 1 : DISORDER, CONFUSION 2 : disorderly or careless dress

**dis·as·sem·ble** \,dis-ə-'sem-bəl\ vb : to take apart

**dis·as·so·ci·ate** \-'sō-s(h)ē-,āt\ vb : to detach from association

**di·sas·ter** \diz-'as-tər, dis-\ n [MF desastre, fr. It disastro, fr. astro star, fr. L astrum] : a sudden or great misfortune — **di·sas·trous** \-'as-trəs\ adj — **di·sas·trous·ly** adv

**dis·avow** \,dis-ə-'vaů\ vb : to deny responsibility for : REPUDIATE — **dis·avow·al** \-'vaů(-ə)l\ n

**dis·band** \dis-'band\ vb : to break up the organization of : DISPERSE

**dis·bar** \dis-'bär\ vb : to expel from the bar or the legal profession — **dis·bar·ment** n

**dis·be·lieve** \,dis-bə-'lēv\ vb 1 : to hold not to be true or real ⟨disbelieved his testimony⟩ 2 : to withhold or reject belief — **dis·be·lief** \-'lēf\ n — **dis·be·liev·er** n

**dis·bur·den** \dis-'bərd-ᵊn\ vb : to rid of a burden

**dis·burse** \dis-'bərs\ vb dis·bursed; dis·burs·ing : to pay out : EXPEND — **dis·burse·ment** n

¹**disc** var of DISK

²**disc** abbr discount

**dis·card** \dis-'kärd, 'dis-,kärd\ vb 1 : to let go a playing card from one's hand; also : to play (a card) from a suit other than a trump but different from the one led 2 : to get rid of as useless or unwanted — **dis·card** \'dis-,kärd\ n

**disc brake** n : a brake that operates by the friction of a pair of plates pressing against the sides of a rotating disc

**dis·cern** \dis-'ərn, diz-\ *vb* **1** : to detect with the eyes : make out : DISTINGUISH **2** : to come to know or recognize mentally **3** : DISCRIMINATE — **dis·cern·ible** *adj* — **dis·cern·ment** *n*

**dis·cern·ing** \-iŋ\ *adj* : revealing insight and understanding

**¹dis·charge** \dis-'chärj, 'dis-,chärj\ *vb* **1** : to relieve of a charge, load, or burden : UNLOAD **2** : SHOOT ⟨~ a gun⟩ ⟨~ an arrow⟩ **3** : to set free ⟨~ a prisoner⟩ **4** : to dismiss from service or employment ⟨~ a soldier⟩ **5** : to let go or let off ⟨~ passengers⟩ **6** : to give forth plainly ⟨the river ~s into the ocean⟩ **7** : to get rid of by paying or doing ⟨~ a debt⟩ **8** : to remove the electrical energy from ⟨~ a storage battery⟩

**²dis·charge** \'dis-,chärj, dis-'chärj\ *n* **1** : the act of discharging, unloading, or releasing **2** : something that discharges; *esp* : a certification of release or payment **3** : a firing off (as of a gun) : a flowing out (as of blood from a wound); *also* : something that is emitted ⟨a purulent ~⟩ **5** : release or dismissal esp. from an office or employment; *also* : complete separation from military service **6** : a flow of electricity (as through a gas)

**dis·ci·ple** \dis-'ī pəl\ *n* **1** : a pupil or follower who helps to spread his master's teachings; *also* : a convinced adherent **2** *cap* : a member of the Disciples of Christ

**dis·ci·pli·nar·i·an** \,dis-ə-plə-'ner-ē-ən\ *n* : one who disciplines or enforces order

**dis·ci·plin·ary** \'dis-ə-plə-,ner-ē\ *adj* : of or relating to discipline; *also* : CORRECTIVE ⟨take ~ action⟩

**¹dis·ci·pline** \'dis-ə-plən\ *n* **1** : a field of study : SUBJECT **2** : training that corrects, molds, or perfects **3** : PUNISHMENT **4** : control gained by obedience or training : orderly conduct **5** : a system of rules governing conduct

**²discipline** *vb* **-plined; -plin·ing 1** : PUNISH **2** : to train or develop by instruction and exercise esp. in self-control **3** : to bring under control ⟨~ troops⟩; *also* : to impose order upon

**disc jockey** *n* : a person who conducts a radio or television program of popular musical recordings

**dis·claim** \dis-'klām\ *vb* : to deny having a connection with or responsibility for : DISAVOW — **dis·claim·er** *n*

**dis·close** \dis-'klōz\ *vb* : to expose to view — **dis·clo·sure** \-'klō-zhər\ *n*

**dis·co** \'dis-kō\ *n, pl* **discos** : DISCOTHEQUE

**dis·col·or** \dis-'kəl-ər\ *vb* : to alter or change in hue or color : STAIN — **dis·col·or·ation** \dis-,kəl-ə-'rā-shən\ *n*

**dis·com·bob·u·late** \,dis-kəm-'bäb-(y)ə-,lāt\ *vb* **-lat·ed; -lat·ing** : UPSET, CONFUSE

**dis·com·fit** \dis-'kəm-fət, *esp South* ,dis-kəm-'fit\ *vb* : UPSET, FRUSTRATE — **dis·com·fi·ture** \dis-'kəm-fə-,chùr\ *n*

**¹dis·com·fort** \dis-'kəm-fərt\ *vb* : to

make uncomfortable or uneasy

**²discomfort** *n* : lack of comfort : uneasiness of mind or body : DISTRESS

**dis·com·mode** \,dis-kə-'mōd\ *vb* **-mod·ed; -mod·ing** : INCONVENIENCE, TROUBLE

**dis·com·pose** \-kəm-'pōz\ *vb* **1** : AGITATE **2** : DISARRANGE — **dis·com·po·sure** \-'pō-zhər\ *n*

**dis·con·cert** \,dis-kən-'sərt\ *vb* : CONFUSE, UPSET

**dis·con·nect** \,dis-kə-'nekt\ *vb* : to undo the connection of — **dis·con·nec·tion** \-'nek-shən\ *n*

**dis·con·nect·ed** \-əd\ *adj* : not connected : RAMBLING, INCOHERENT — **dis·con·nect·ed·ly** *adv*

**dis·con·so·late** \dis-'kän-sə-lət\ *adj* **1** : hopelessly sad **2** : CHEERLESS — **dis·con·so·late·ly** *adv*

**dis·con·tent** \,dis-kən-'tent\ *n* : uneasiness of mind : DISSATISFACTION — **dis·con·tent·ed** *adj*

**dis·con·tin·ue** \,dis-kən-'tin-yü\ *vb* **1** : to break the continuity of : cease to operate, use, or take **2** : END — **dis·con·tin·u·ance** \-yə-wəns\ *n* — **dis·con·ti·nu·i·ty** \dis-,känt-ə-n-'(y)ü-ət-ē\ *n* — **dis·con·tin·u·ous** \,dis-kən-'tin-yə-wəs\ *adj*

**dis·cord** \'dis-,kòrd\ *n* **1** : lack of agreement or harmony : DISSENSION, CONFLICT, OPPOSITION **2** : a harsh combination of musical sounds **3** : a harsh or unpleasant sound — **dis·cor·dant** \dis-'kòrd-ənt\ *adj*

**dis·co·theque** \'dis-kə-,tek\ *n* : a usu. small intimate nightclub for dancing to live or recorded music; *also* : a nightclub featuring psychedelic and multimedia attractions (as movies and special lighting effects)

**¹dis·count** \'dis-,kaúnt\ *n* **1** : a reduction made from a regular or list price **2** : a deduction of interest in advance when lending money

**²dis·count** \'dis-,kaúnt, dis-'kaúnt\ *vb* **1** : to deduct from the amount of a bill, debt, or charge usu. for cash or prompt payment; *also* : to sell or offer for sale at a discount **2** : to lend money after deducting the discount ⟨~ a note⟩ **3** : DISREGARD; *also* : MINIMIZE **4** : to make allowance for bias or exaggeration; *also* : DISBELIEVE **5** : to take into account (as a future event) in present calculations — **dis·count·able** *adj* — **dis·count·er** *n*

**dis·coun·te·nance** \dis-'kaúnt-(°-)nəns\ *vb* **1** : EMBARRASS, DISCONCERT **2** : to look with disfavor on

**dis·cour·age** \dis-'kər-ij\ *vb* **-aged; -ag·ing 1** : to deprive of courage or confidence : DISHEARTEN **2** : to hinder by inspiring fear of consequences : DETER **3** : to attempt to dissuade — **dis·cour·age·ment** *n* — **dis·cour·ag·ing·ly** \-ij-iŋ-lē\ *adv*

**¹dis·course** \'dis-,kōrs\ *n* [ME *discours*, fr. ML & LL *discursus*; ML, argument, fr. LL, conversation, fr. L, act of running about, fr. *discurrere* to run about, fr. *currere* to run] **1** : CONVERSATION **2** : formal and orderly and usu.

extended expression of thought on a subject

²**dis·course** \dis-'kōrs\ vb **dis·coursed; dis·cours·ing 1 :** to express oneself in esp. oral discourse **2 :** TALK, CONVERSE

**dis·cour·te·ous** \dis-'kərt-ē-əs\ adj **:** lacking courtesy **:** UNCIVIL, RUDE — **dis·cour·te·ous·ly** adv

**dis·cour·te·sy** \-'kərt-ə-sē\ n **:** RUDENESS; also **:** a rude act

**dis·cov·er** \dis-'kəv-ər\ vb **1 :** to make known or visible **2 :** to obtain sight or knowledge of for the first time **:** FIND — **dis·cov·er·er** n — **dis·cov·ery** \-(ə-)rē\ n

¹**dis·cred·it** \dis-'kred-ət\ vb **1 :** DISBELIEVE **2 :** to cause disbelief in the accuracy or authority of **:** DISGRACE — **dis·cred·it·able** adj

²**discredit** n **1 :** loss of credit or reputation **2 :** lack or loss of belief or confidence

**dis·creet** \dis-'krēt\ adj **:** showing good judgment **:** PRUDENT; esp **:** capable of observing prudent silence — **dis·creet·ly** adv

**dis·crep·an·cy** \dis-'krep-ən-sē\ n, pl **-cies 1 :** DIFFERENCE, DISAGREEMENT **2 :** an instance of being discrepant

**dis·crep·ant** \-ənt\ adj [L discrepans, prp of discrepare to sound discordantly, fr. crepare to rattle, creak] **:** being at variance **:** DISAGREEING

**dis·crete** \dis-'krēt, 'dis-ˌkrēt\ adj **1 :** individually distinct **2 :** NONCONTINUOUS

**dis·cre·tion** \dis-'kresh-ən\ n **1 :** the quality of being discreet **:** PRUDENCE **2 :** individual choice or judgment **3 :** power of free decision or latitude of choice — **dis·cre·tion·ary** adj

**dis·crim·i·nate** \dis-'krim-ə-ˌnāt\ vb **-nat·ed; -nat·ing 1 :** DISTINGUISH, DIFFERENTIATE **2 :** to make a distinction in favor of or against one person or thing as compared with others — **dis·crim·i·na·tion** \-ˌkrim-ə-'nā-shən\ n

**dis·crim·i·nat·ing** \-ˌnāt-iŋ\ adj **:** marked by discrimination; esp **:** DISCERNING, JUDICIOUS

**dis·crim·i·na·to·ry** \dis-'krim-ə-nə-ˌtōr-ē\ adj **:** marked by esp. unjust discrimination ⟨~ treatment⟩

**dis·cur·sive** \dis-'kər-siv\ adj **:** passing from one topic to another **:** RAMBLING — **dis·cur·sive·ly** adv — **dis·cur·sive·ness** n

**dis·cus** \'dis-kəs\ n, pl **dis·cus·es :** a disk (as of wood or rubber) that is hurled for distance in a track-and-field contest

**dis·cuss** \dis-'kəs\ vb [ME discussen, fr. L discutere, fr. dis- apart + quatere to shake] **1 :** to argue or consider carefully by presenting the various sides **2 :** to talk about — **dis·cus·sion** \-'kəsh-ən\ n

**dis·cus·sant** \dis-'kəs-ənt\ n **:** one who takes part in a formal discussion or symposium

¹**dis·dain** \dis-'dān\ n **:** CONTEMPT, SCORN — **dis·dain·ful** \-fəl\ adj — **dis·dain·ful·ly** \-ē\ adv

²**disdain** vb **1 :** to look upon with scorn **2 :** to reject or refrain from because of disdain

**dis·ease** \diz-'ēz\ n **:** an alteration of a living body that impairs its functioning **:** SICKNESS — **dis·eased** \-'ēzd\ adj

**dis·em·bark** \dis-əm-'bärk\ vb **:** to go or put ashore from a ship — **dis·em·bar·ka·tion** \dis-ˌem-ˌbär-'kā-shən\ n

**dis·em·body** \dis-əm-'bäd-ē\ vb **:** to divest of bodily existence

**dis·em·bow·el** \-'baù-(ə)l\ vb **:** EVISCERATE — **dis·em·bow·el·ment** n

**dis·en·chant** \dis-ᵊn-'chant\ vb **:** to free from enchantment **:** DISILLUSION — **dis·en·chant·ment** n

**dis·en·cum·ber** \dis-ᵊn-'kəm-bər\ vb **:** to free from something that burdens or obstructs

**dis·en·fran·chise** \dis-ᵊn-'fran-ˌchīz\ vb **:** DISFRANCHISE — **dis·en·fran·chise·ment** n

**dis·en·gage** \dis-ᵊn-'gāj\ vb **:** RELEASE, EXTRICATE, DISENTANGLE — **dis·en·gage·ment** n

**dis·en·tan·gle** \dis-ᵊn-'taŋ-gəl\ vb **:** to free from entanglement **:** UNRAVEL

**dis·equi·lib·ri·um** \dis-ˌē-kwə-'lib-rē-əm\ n **:** loss or lack of equilibrium

**dis·es·tab·lish** \dis-ə-'stab-lish\ vb **:** to end the establishment of; esp **:** to deprive of the status of an established church — **dis·es·tab·lish·ment** n

**dis·es·teem** \dis-ə-'stēm\ n **:** lack of esteem **:** DISFAVOR, DISREPUTE

**di·seuse** \dē-'zə(r)z, -'züz\ n, pl **di·seuses** \-'zə(r)z(-əz), -'züz(-əz)\ **:** a skilled and usu. professional woman reciter

**dis·fa·vor** \dis-'fā-vər\ n **1 :** DISAPPROVAL, DISLIKE **2 :** the state or fact of being deprived of favor

**dis·fig·ure** \dis-'fig-yər\ vb **:** to spoil the appearance of ⟨disfigured by a scar⟩ — **dis·fig·ure·ment** n

**dis·fran·chise** \dis-'fran-ˌchīz\ vb **:** to deprive of a franchise, a legal right, or a privilege; esp **:** to deprive of the right to vote — **dis·fran·chise·ment** n

**dis·gorge** \-'gòrj\ vb **:** VOMIT; also **:** to discharge forcefully or confusedly

¹**dis·grace** \dis-'grās\ vb **:** to bring reproach or shame to

²**disgrace** n **1 :** the condition of being out of favor **:** loss of respect **2 :** SHAME, DISHONOR; also **:** a cause of shame — **dis·grace·ful** \-fəl\ adj — **dis·grace·ful·ly** \-ē\ adv

**dis·grun·tle** \dis-'grənt-ᵊl\ vb **dis·grun·tled; dis·grun·tling :** to put in bad humor

¹**dis·guise** \dis-'gīz\ vb **dis·guise; dis·guis·ing 1 :** to change the dress or looks of so as to conceal the identity or so as to resemble another **:** ALTER **2 :** HIDE, CONCEAL

²**disguise** n **1 :** clothing put on to conceal one's identity or counterfeit another's **2 :** an outward form hiding or misrepresenting the true nature or identity of a person or thing **:** PRETENSE

¹**dis·gust** \dis-'gəst\ n **:** AVERSION, REPUGNANCE

²**dis·gust** vb : to provoke to loathing, repugnance, or aversion : be offensive to — **dis·gust·ed·ly** adv — **dis·gust·ing·ly** \-'gəs-tiŋ-lē\ adv

¹**dish** \'dish\ n [ME, fr. OE disc plate, fr. L discus quoit, disk, dish, fr. Gk diskos, fr. dikein to throw] 1 : a vessel used for serving food 2 : the food served in a dish ⟨a ～ of berries⟩ 3 : food prepared in a particular way 4 : something resembling a dish esp. in being shallow and concave

²**dish** vb 1 : to put into a dish 2 : to make concave like a dish

**dis·ha·bille** \,dis-ə-'bēl\ n : the state of being dressed in a casual or careless manner

**dis·har·mo·ny** \dis-'här-mə-nē\ n : lack of harmony — **dis·har·mo·ni·ous** \,dis-(,)här-'mō-nē-əs\ adj

**dish·cloth** \'dish-,klȯth\ n : a cloth for washing dishes

**dis·heart·en** \dis-'härt-ᵊn\ vb : DISCOURAGE, DEJECT

**dished** \'disht\ adj : CONCAVE

**di·shev·el** \dish-'ev-əl\ vb **di·shev·eled** or **di·shev·elled**; **di·shev·el·ing** or **di·shev·el·ling** [ME discheveled, fr. MF deschevelé, fr. descheveler to disarrange the hair, fr. chevel hair, fr. L capillus] : to let hang or fall loosely in disorder : DISARRAY — **di·shev·eled** or **di·shev·elled** adj

**dis·hon·est** \dis-'än-əst\ adj 1 : not honest : UNTRUSTWORTHY 2 : DECEITFUL, CORRUPT — **dis·hon·est·ly** adv — **dis·hon·es·ty** \-ə-stē\ n

¹**dis·hon·or** \dis-'än-ər\ n 1 : lack or loss of honor : SHAME, DISGRACE 2 : something dishonorable : a cause of disgrace 3 : the act of dishonoring a negotiable instrument when presented for payment — **dis·hon·or·able** \-'än-(ə-)rə-bəl, -'än-ər-bəl\ adj — **dis·hon·or·ably** \-blē\ adv

²**dishonor** vb 1 : DISGRACE 2 : to refuse to accept or pay ⟨～ a check⟩

**dish out** vb 1 : to serve (food) from a dish 2 : to give freely

**dish·rag** \'dish-,rag\ n : DISHCLOTH

**dish·wash·er** \-,wȯsh-ər, -,wäsh-\ n : one that washes dishes

**dish·wa·ter** \-,wȯt-ər, -,wät-\ n : water in which dishes have been or are to be washed

**dis·il·lu·sion** \,dis-ə-'lü-zhən\ vb — **dis·il·lu·sioned**; **dis·il·lu·sion·ing** \-'lüzh-(ə-)niŋ\ : to free from or deprive of illusion — **dis·il·lu·sion·ment** n

**dis·in·cli·na·tion** \dis-,in-klə-'nā-shən\ n : a feeling of unwillingness or aversion : DISTASTE

**dis·in·cline** \,dis-ᵊn-'klīn\ vb : to make or be unwilling

**dis·in·fect** \,dis-ᵊn-'fekt\ vb : to free from infection esp. by destroying disease germs — **dis·in·fec·tant** \-'fek-tənt\ adj or n — **dis·in·fec·tion** \-'fek-shən\ n

**dis·in·gen·u·ous** \-'jen-yə-wəs\ adj : lacking in candor : not frank or naive

**dis·in·her·it** \,dis-ᵊn-'her-ət\ vb : to prevent from inheriting property that would naturally be passed on

**dis·in·te·grate** \dis-'int-ə-,grāt\ vb 1 : to break or decompose into constituent parts or small particles 2 : to destroy the unity or integrity of — **dis·in·te·gra·tion** \dis-,int-ə-'grā-shən\ n

**dis·in·ter** \,dis-ᵊn-'tər\ vb 1 : to take from the grave or tomb 2 : UNEARTH

**dis·in·ter·est·ed** \dis-'in-t(ə-)rəs-təd, -tə-,res-\ adj 1 : not interested 2 : free from selfish motive or interest : UNBIASED — **dis·in·ter·est·ed·ness** n

**dis·in·tox·i·ca·tion** \,dis-ᵊn-,täk-sə-'kā-shən\ n : the freeing of an individual from an intoxicating agent (as an addict from a drug) stored in the body

**dis·join** \dis-'jȯin\ vb : SEPARATE

**dis·joint** \dis-'jȯint\ vb : to separate the parts of : DISCONNECT; also : to separate at the joints

**dis·joint·ed** \-əd\ adj 1 : separated at or as if at the joint 2 : DISCONNECTED; esp : INCOHERENT

**disk** or **disc** \'disk\ n 1 : something round and flat; esp : a flat rounded anatomical structure (as the central part of the flower head of a composite plant or a pad of cartilage between vertebrae) 2 usu **disc** : a phonograph record

¹**dis·like** \dis-'līk\ vb : to regard with dislike : DISAPPROVE

²**dislike** n : a feeling of distaste or disapproval

**dis·lo·cate** \'dis-lō-,kāt, dis-'lō-\ vb 1 : to put out of place; esp : to displace (a joint) from normal connections ⟨～ a shoulder⟩ 2 : DISRUPT — **dis·lo·ca·tion** \,dis-(,)lō-'kā-shən\ n

**dis·lodge** \dis-'läj\ vb 1 : to force out of a place 2 : to drive out from a place of hiding or defense

**dis·loy·al** \dis-'lȯi-(ə)l\ adj : lacking in loyalty — **dis·loy·al·ty** n

**dis·mal** \'diz-məl\ adj [ME, fr. dismal, n., days marked as unlucky in medieval calendars, fr. ML dies mali, lit., evil days] 1 : gloomy to the eye or ear : DREARY, DEPRESSING 2 : DEPRESSED — **dis·mal·ly** \-ē\ adv

**dis·man·tle** \dis-'mant-ᵊl\ vb **dis·man·tled**, **dis·man·tling** \-'mant-(ə-)liŋ\ 1 : to strip of furniture and equipment 2 : to take apart — **dis·man·tle·ment** n

**dis·may** \dis-'mā\ vb : to cause to lose courage or resolution from alarm or fear : DAUNT — **dismay** n — **dis·may·ing·ly** \-iŋ-lē\ adv

**dis·mem·ber** \dis-'mem-bər\ vb **dis·mem·bered**; **dis·mem·ber·ing** \-b(ə-)riŋ\ 1 : to cut off or separate the limbs, members, or parts of 2 : to break up or tear into pieces — **dis·mem·ber·ment** n

**dis·miss** \dis-'mis\ vb 1 : to send away 2 : to send or remove from office, service, or employment 3 : to put aside or out of mind 4 : to refuse further judicial hearing or consideration to ⟨the judge ～ed the charge⟩ — **dis·miss·al** n

**dis·mount** \dis-'maunt\ vb 1 : to get

down from something (as a horse or bicycle) **2** : UNHORSE **3** : to take (as a cannon) from the carriage or mountings **4** : to take apart (as a machine)

**dis·obe·di·ence** \,dis-ə-'bēd-ē-əns\ *n* : neglect or refusal to obey — **dis·o·be·di·ent** \-ənt\ *adj*

**dis·obey** \,dis-ə-'bā\ *vb* : to fail to obey : be disobedient

**dis·oblige** \,dis-ə-'blīj\ *vb* **1** : to go counter to the wishes of **2** : INCONVENIENCE

**¹dis·or·der** \dis-'ȯrd-ər\ *vb* **1** : to disturb the order of **2** : to cause disorder in ⟨a ~ed digestion⟩

**²disorder** *n* **1** : lack of order : CONFUSION **2** : breach of the peace or public order : TUMULT **3** : an abnormal state of body or mind : AILMENT

**dis·or·der·ly** \-lē\ *adj* **1** : UNRULY, TURBULENT **2** : offensive to public order or decency; *also* : guilty of disorderly conduct **3** : marked by disorder : DISARRANGED ⟨a ~ desk⟩ — **dis·or·der·li·ness** *n*

**dis·or·ga·nize** \dis-'ȯr-gə-,nīz\ *vb* : to break up the regular system of : throw into disorder — **dis·or·ga·ni·za·tion** \dis-,ȯrg-(ə-)nə-'zā-shən\ *n*

**dis·ori·ent** \dis-'ōr-ē-,ent\ *vb* : to cause to lose bearings or a sense of location or identity : CONFUSE — **dis·ori·en·tate** \-ē-ən-,tāt\ *vb* — **dis·ori·en·ta·tion** \dis-,ōr-ē-ən-'tā-shən\ *n*

**dis·own** \dis-'ōn\ *vb* : REPUDIATE, RENOUNCE, DISCLAIM

**dis·par·age** \dis-'par-ij\ *vb* **-aged; -ag·ing** [ME *disparagen* to degrade by marriage below one's class, disparage, fr. MF *desparagier* to marry below one's class, fr. OF, fr. *parage* extraction, lineage, fr. *per* peer] **1** : to lower in rank or reputation : DEGRADE **2** : BELITTLE — **dis·par·age·ment** *n* — **dis·par·ag·ing·ly** \-ij-iŋ-lē\ *adv*

**dis·pa·rate** \dis-'par-ət, 'dis-p(ə-)rət\ *adj* : distinct in quality or character — **dis·par·i·ty** \dis-'par-ət-ē\ *n*

**dis·pas·sion·ate** \dis-'pash-(ə-)nət\ *adj* : not influenced by strong feeling : CALM, IMPARTIAL — **dis·pas·sion** \-ən\ *n* — **dis·pas·sion·ate·ly** *adv*

**¹dis·patch** \dis-'pach\ *vb* **1** : to send off or away with promptness or speed esp. on official business **2** : to put to death **3** : to attend to rapidly or efficiently — **dis·patch·er** *n*

**²dispatch** *n* **1** : the sending of a message or messenger **2** : the shipment of goods **3** : MESSAGE **4** : the act of putting to death **5** : a news item sent in by a correspondent to a newspaper **6** : promptness and efficiency in performing a task

**dis·pel** \dis-'pel\ *vb* **dis·pelled; dis·pel·ling** : to drive away by scattering : DISSIPATE

**dis·pens·able** \dis-'pen-sə-bəl\ *adj* : capable of being dispensed with

**dis·pen·sa·ry** \dis-'pens-(ə-)rē\ *n, pl* **-ries** : a place where medicine or medical or dental aid is dispensed

**dis·pen·sa·tion** \,dis-pən-'sā-shən\ *n*

**1** : a system of rules for ordering affairs; *esp* : a system of revealed commands and promises regulating human affairs **2** : a particular arrangement or provision esp. of nature **3** : an exemption from a rule or from a vow or oath **4** : the act of dispensing **5** : something dispensed or distributed

**dis·pense** \dis-'pens\ *vb* **dis·pensed; dis·pens·ing** **1** : to portion out **2** : ADMINISTER ⟨~ justice⟩ **3** : EXEMPT **4** : to make up and give out (remedies) — **dis·pens·er** *n* — **dispense with** **1** : SUSPEND **2** : to do without

**dis·perse** \dis-'pərs\ *vb* **dis·persed; dis·pers·ing** **1** : to break up and scatter about : SPREAD **2** : DISSEMINATE, DISTRIBUTE — **dis·per·sal** \-'pər-səl\ *n* — **dis·per·sion** \-'pər-zhən\ *n*

**dis·pir·it** \dis-'pir-ət\ *vb* : DEPRESS, DISCOURAGE, DISHEARTEN

**dis·place** \dis-'plās\ *vb* **1** : to remove from the usual or proper place; *esp* : to expel or force to flee from home or native land ⟨*displaced* persons⟩ **2** : to remove from an office **3** : to take the place of : REPLACE

**dis·place·ment** \dis-'plās-mənt\ *n* **1** : the act of displacing : the state of being displaced **2** : the volume or weight of a fluid displaced by a floating body (as a ship) **3** : the difference between the initial position of an object and a later position

**¹dis·play** \dis-'plā\ *vb* : to present to view

**²display** *n* : a displaying of something

**dis·please** \dis-'plēz\ *vb* **1** : to arouse the disapproval and dislike of **2** : to be offensive to : give displeasure

**dis·plea·sure** \dis-'plezh-ər\ *n* : a feeling of annoyance and dislike accompanying disapproval

**dis·port** \dis-'pōrt\ *vb* **1** : DIVERT, AMUSE **2** : FROLIC **3** : DISPLAY

**dis·pos·able** \dis-'pō-zə-bəl\ *adj* **1** : remaining after deduction of taxes ⟨~ income⟩ **2** : designed to be used once and then thrown away ⟨~ diapers⟩ — **disposable** *n*

**dis·pos·al** \dis-'pō-zəl\ *n* **1** : ARRANGEMENT **2** : a getting rid of **3** : MANAGEMENT, ADMINISTRATION **4** : the transfer of something into new hands **5** : CONTROL, COMMAND

**dis·pose** \dis-'pōz\ *vb* **dis·posed; dis·pos·ing** **1** : to give a tendency to : INCLINE ⟨*disposed* to accept⟩ **2** : PREPARE ⟨troops *disposed* for withdrawal⟩ **3** : ARRANGE **4** : SETTLE — **dis·pos·er** *n* — **dispose of 1** : to settle or determine the fate, condition, or use of **2** : to get rid of **3** : to transfer to the control of another

**dis·po·si·tion** \,dis-pə-'zish-ən\ *n* **1** : the act or power of disposing : DISPOSAL ⟨funds at their ~⟩ **2** : RELINQUISHMENT **3** : ARRANGEMENT **4** : TENDENCY, INCLINATION **5** : natural attitude toward things ⟨a cheerful ~⟩

**dis·pos·sess** \dis-pə-'zes\ *vb* : to put out of possession or occupancy — **dis·pos·ses·sion** \-'zesh-ən\ *n*

**dis·praise** \dis-'prāz\ vb : DISPARAGE — **dispraise** n

**dis·pro·por·tion** \,dis-prə-'pōr-shən\ n : lack of proportion, symmetry, or proper relation — **dis·pro·por·tion·ate** \-sh(ə-)nət\ adj

**dis·prove** \dis-'prüv\ vb : to prove to be false — **dis·proof** \-'prüf\ n

**dis·pu·tant** \dis-'pyüt-ᵊnt, 'dis·pyət-ənt\ n : one that is engaged in a dispute

**dis·pu·ta·tion** \,dis-pyə-'tā-shən\ n 1 : DEBATE 2 : an oral defense of an academic thesis

**dis·pu·ta·tious** \-shəs\ adj : inclined to dispute : ARGUMENTATIVE

¹**dis·pute** \dis-'pyüt\ vb **dis·put·ed; dis·put·ing** 1 : ARGUE, DEBATE 2 : WRANGLE 3 : to deny the truth or rightness of 4 : to struggle against or over : CONTEST — **dis·put·able** \dis-'pyüt-ə-bəl, 'dis·pyət-ə-bəl\ adj — **dis·put·er** \dis-'pyüt-ər\ n

²**dispute** n 1 : DEBATE 2 : QUARREL

**dis·qual·i·fy** \dis-'kwäl-ə-,fī\ vb 1 : to make or declare unfit or ineligible 2 : to deprive of necessary qualifications — **dis·qual·i·fi·ca·tion** \-,kwäl-ə-fə-'kā-shən\ n

¹**dis·qui·et** \dis-'kwī-ət\ vb : to make uneasy or restless : DISTURB

²**disquiet** n : lack of peace or tranquillity : ANXIETY

**dis·qui·e·tude** \dis-'kwī-ə-,t(y)üd\ n : AGITATION, ANXIETY

**dis·qui·si·tion** \,dis-kwə-'zish-ən\ n : a formal inquiry or discussion

¹**dis·re·gard** \,dis-ri-'gärd\ vb : to pay no attention to : treat as unworthy of notice or regard

²**disregard** n : the act of disregarding : the state of being disregarded : NEGLECT — **dis·re·gard·ful** adj

**dis·re·pair** \,dis-ri-'paər\ n : the state of being in need of repair

**dis·rep·u·ta·ble** \dis-'rep-yət-ə-bəl\ adj : not reputable : DISCREDITABLE, DISGRACEFUL; esp : having a bad reputation

**dis·re·pute** \,dis-ri-'pyüt\ n : loss or lack of reputation : low esteem

**dis·re·spect** \,dis-ri-'spekt\ n : DISCOURTESY — **dis·re·spect·ful** adj

**dis·robe** \dis-'rōb\ vb : UNDRESS

**dis·rupt** \dis-'rəpt\ vb 1 : to break apart 2 : to throw into disorder : break up — **dis·rup·tion** \-'rəp-shən\ n — **dis·rup·tive** \-'rəp-tiv\ adj

**dis·sat·is·fac·tion** \dis-,at-əs-'fak-shən\ n : DISCONTENT

**dis·sat·is·fy** \dis-'at-əs-,fī\ vb : to fail to satisfy : DISPLEASE — **dis·sat·is·fied** adj

**dis·sect** \dis-'ekt; dī-'sekt\ vb 1 : to divide into parts esp. for examination and study 2 : ANALYZE — **dis·sec·tion** \-'ek-shən, -'sek-\ n

**dis·sect·ed** adj : cut deeply into narrow lobes ⟨a ~ leaf⟩

**dis·sem·ble** \dis-'em-bəl\ vb **dis·sem·bled; dis·sem·bling** \-b(ə-)liŋ\ 1 : to hide under or put on a false appearance : conceal facts, intentions, or feelings under some pre-

tense 2 : SIMULATE — **dis·sem·bler** \-b(ə-)lər\ n

**dis·sem·i·nate** \dis-'em-ə-,nāt\ vb **-nat·ed; -nat·ing** : to spread abroad as though sowing seed ⟨~ ideas⟩ — **dis·sem·i·na·tion** \-,em-ə-'nā-shən\ n

**dis·sen·sion** \dis-'en-chən\ n : disagreement in opinion : DISCORD

¹**dis·sent** \dis-'ent\ vb 1 : to withhold assent 2 : to differ in opinion

²**dissent** n 1 : difference of opinion; esp : religious nonconformity 2 : a written statement in which a justice disagrees with the opinion of the majority — **dis·sen·tient** \-'en-chənt\ adj or n

**dis·sent·er** \dis-'ent-ər\ n 1 : one that dissents 2 cap : an English Nonconformist

**dis·ser·ta·tion** \,dis-ər-'tā-shən\ n : an extended usu. written treatment of a subject; esp : one submitted for a doctorate

**dis·ser·vice** \dis-'ər-vəs\ n : INJURY, HARM, MISCHIEF

**dis·sev·er** \dis-'ev-ər\ vb : SEPARATE, DISUNITE

**dis·si·dent** \'dis-əd-ənt\ adj [L dissidens, prp. of dissidēre to sit apart, disagree, fr. dis- apart + sedēre to sit] : openly and often violently differing with an opinion or a group — **dis·si·dence** \-əns\ n — **dissident** n

**dis·sim·i·lar** \dis-'im-ə-lər\ adj : UNLIKE — **dis·sim·i·lar·i·ty** \dis-,im-ə-'lar-ət-ē\ n

**dis·sim·u·late** \dis-'im-yə-,lāt\ vb **-lat·ed; -lat·ing** : to hide under a false appearance : DISSEMBLE — **dis·sim·u·la·tion** \dis-,im-yə-'lā-shən\ n

**dis·si·pate** \'dis-ə-,pāt\ vb **-pat·ed; -pat·ing** 1 : to break up and drive off ⟨~ a crowd⟩ 2 : DISPEL, DISSOLVE ⟨the breeze dissipated the fog⟩ 3 : SQUANDER 4 : to break up and vanish 5 : to be dissolute; esp : to drink alcoholic beverages to excess 6 : to lose (as heat) irrecoverably — **dis·si·pat·ed** adj — **dis·si·pa·tion** \,dis-ə-'pā-shən\ n

**dis·so·ci·ate** \dis-'ō-s(h)ē-,āt\ vb **-at·ed; -at·ing** : DISCONNECT, DISUNITE — **dis·so·ci·a·tion** \dis-,ō-s(h)ē-'ā-shən\ n

**dis·so·lute** \'dis-ə-,lüt\ adj : loose in morals or conduct — **dis·so·lute·ly** adv — **dis·so·lute·ness** n

**dis·so·lu·tion** \,dis-ə-'lü-shən\ n 1 : separation of a thing into its parts 2 : DECAY; esp : DEATH 3 : the termination or breaking up of an assembly or a partnership

**dis·solve** \diz-'älv\ vb 1 : to separate into component parts 2 : to pass or cause to pass into solution ⟨sugar ~s in water⟩ 3 : TERMINATE, DISPERSE ⟨~ parliament⟩ 4 : to waste or fade away ⟨his courage dissolved⟩ 5 : to be overcome emotionally ⟨~ in tears⟩ 6 : to resolve itself as if by dissolution

**dis·so·nance** \'dis-ə-nəns\ n : DISCORD — **dis·so·nant** \-nənt\ adj

**dis·suade** \dis-'wād\ vb **dis·suad·ed; dis·suad·ing** : to advise against a course of action : persuade or try to persuade not to do something — **dis·sua·sion** \-'wā-zhən\ *n* — **dis·sua·sive** \-'wā-siv\ *adj*

**dist** *abbr* 1 distance 2 district

**¹dis·taff** \'dis-,taf\ *n, pl* **distaffs** \-,tafs, -,tavz\ 1 : a staff for holding the flax, tow, or wool in spinning 2 : a woman's work or domain 3 : the female branch or side of a family

**²distaff** *adj* : MATERNAL, FEMALE

**dis·tal** \'dis-t'l\ *adj* : away from the point of attachment or origin — **dis·tal·ly** \-ē\ *adv*

**¹dis·tance** \'dis-təns\ *n* 1 : measure of separation in space or time 2 : EXPANSE 3 : a full course ⟨go the ∼⟩ 4 : spatial remoteness 5 : COLDNESS, RESERVE 6 : DIFFERENCE, DISPARITY 7 : a distant point

**²distance** *vb* **dis·tanced; dis·tanc·ing** : to leave far behind : OUTSTRIP

**dis·tant** \'dis-tənt\ *adj* 1 : separate in space 2 : AWAY 3 : FAR-OFF 4 : being far apart 5 : different in kind ⟨a ∼ cousin⟩ 6 : RESERVED, ALOOF, COLD ⟨∼ politeness⟩ 7 : coming from or going to a distance — **dis·tant·ly** *adv* — **dis·tant·ness** *n*

**dis·taste** \dis-'tāst\ *n* : DISINCLINATION, DISLIKE — **dis·taste·ful** *adj*

**dis·tem·per** \dis-'tem-pər\ *n* : a bodily disorder usu. of a domestic animal; *esp* : a contagious often fatal virus disease of dogs

**dis·tend** \dis-'tend\ *vb* : EXPAND, SWELL — **dis·ten·si·ble** \-'ten-sə-bəl\ *adj* — **dis·ten·sion** *or* **dis·ten·tion** \-chən\ *n*

**dis·tich** \'dis-(,)tik\ *n* : a strophic unit of two lines

**dis·till** *also* **dis·til** \dis-'til\ *vb* **dis·tilled; dis·till·ing** 1 : to fall or let fall drop by drop 2 : to obtain or extract by distillation 3 : to undergo distillation — **dis·till·er** *n* — **dis·till·ery** \-(ə-)rē\ *n*

**dis·til·late** \'dis-tə-,lāt, -lət\ *n* : a liquid product condensed from vapor during distillation

**dis·til·la·tion** \,dis-tə-'lā-shən\ *n* : the driving off of gas or vapor from liquids or solids by heat into a retort and then condensing into a liquid product

**dis·tinct** \dis-'tiŋkt\ *adj* 1 : distinguished from others : SEPARATE, INDIVIDUAL 2 : clearly seen, heard, or understood : PLAIN, UNMISTAKABLE — **dis·tinct·ly** *adv* — **dis·tinct·ness** *n*

**dis·tinc·tion** \dis-'tiŋk-shən\ *n* 1 : the act of distinguishing a difference 2 : DIFFERENCE 3 : a distinguishing quality or mark 4 : a special recognition; *also* : a mark or sign of such recognition 5 : HONOR

**dis·tinc·tive** \dis-'tiŋk-tiv\ *adj* 1 : clearly marking a person or a thing as different from others 2 : CHARACTERISTIC 3 : having or giving style or distinction — **dis·tinc·tive·ly** *adv* — **dis·tinc·tive·ness** *n*

**dis·tin·guish** \dis-'tiŋ-gwish\ *vb* [MF *distinguer*, fr. L *distinguere*, lit., to

separate by pricking] 1 : to recognize by some mark or characteristic 2 : to hear or see clearly : DISCERN 3 : to make distinctions ⟨∼ between right and wrong⟩ 4 : to set apart : mark as different 5 : to make outstanding — **dis·tin·guish·able** *adj*

**dis·tin·guished** \-gwisht\ *adj* 1 : marked by eminence or excellence 2 : befitting an eminent person

**distn** *abbr* distillation

**dis·tort** \dis-'tȯrt\ *vb* 1 : to twist out of the true meaning 2 : to twist out of a natural, normal, or original shape or condition 3 : to reproduce improperly ⟨a radio ∼*ing* sound⟩ — **dis·tortion** \-'tȯr-shən\ *n*

**distr** *abbr* distribute; distribution

**dis·tract** \dis-'trakt\ *vb* 1 : DIVERT; *esp* : to draw (the attention or mind) to a different object 2 : to stir up or confuse with conflicting emotions or motives : HARASS — **dis·trac·tion** \-'trak-shən\ *n*

**dis·trait** \di-'strā\ *adj* : ABSENTMINDED, DISTRAUGHT

**dis·traught** \dis-'trȯt\ *adj* : PERPLEXED, CONFUSED; *also* : CRAZED

**¹dis·tress** \dis-'tres\ *n* 1 : suffering of body or mind : PAIN, ANGUISH 2 : TROUBLE, MISFORTUNE 3 : a condition of danger or desperate need — **dis·tress·ful** *adj*

**²distress** *vb* 1 : to subject to great strain or difficulties 2 : UPSET

**dis·trib·ute** \dis-'trib-yət\ *vb* **-ut·ed; -ut·ing** 1 : to divide among several or many : APPORTION 2 : to spread out : SCATTER; *also* : DELIVER 3 : CLASSIFY 4 : to market in a particular area usu. as a wholesaler — **dis·tri·bu·tion** \,dis-trə-'byü-shən\ *n*

**dis·trib·u·tive** \dis-'trib-yət-iv\ *adj* 1 : of or relating to distribution 2 : producing the same element when operating on the whole as when operating on each part and collecting the results ⟨multiplication is ∼ relative to addition since $a(b + c) = ab + ac$⟩ — **dis·trib·u·tive·ly** *adv* — **dis·trib·u·tiv·i·ty** \-,trib-yə-'tiv-ət-ē\ *n*

**dis·trib·u·tor** \dis-'trib-yət-ər\ *n* 1 : one that distributes 2 : a device for directing current to the spark plugs of an engine

**dis·trict** \'dis-(,)trikt\ *n* 1 : a fixed territorial division (as for administrative or electoral purposes) 2 : an area, region, or section with a distinguishing character

**district attorney** *n* : the prosecuting attorney of a judicial district

**¹dis·trust** \dis-'trəst\ *vb* : to feel no confidence in : SUSPECT

**²distrust** *n* : a lack of trust or confidence : SUSPICION, WARINESS — **dis·trust·ful** \-fəl\ *adj* — **dis·trust·ful·ly** \-ē\ *adv*

**dis·turb** \dis-'tərb\ *vb* 1 : to interfere with : INTERRUPT 2 : to alter the position or arrangement of 3 : to destroy the tranquillity or composure of : make uneasy 4 : to throw into disorder 5 : INCONVENIENCE — **dis·tur·bance** \-'tər-bəns\ *n* — **dis·turb·er** *n*

**dis·turbed** \-'tərbd\ *adj* **:** showing symptoms of mental or emotional illness

**dis·unite** \,dish-ü-'nīt, ,dis-yü-\ *vb* DIVIDE, SEPARATE

**dis·uni·ty** \dish-'ü-nət-ē, dis-'yü-\ *n* **:** lack of unity; *esp* **:** DISSENSION

**dis·use** \-'üs, -'yüs\ *n* **:** a cessation of use or practice

¹**ditch** \'dich\ *n* **:** a trench dug in the earth

²**ditch** *vb* **1 :** to enclose with a ditch; *also* **:** to dig a ditch in **2 :** to drive a car into a ditch **3 :** to get rid of **:** DISCARD **4 :** to make a forced landing of an airplane on water

**dith·er** \'dith-ər\ *n* **:** a highly nervous, excited, or agitated state

**dit·to** \'dit-ō\ *n, pl* **dittos** [It dial., pp. of It *dire* to say, fr. L *dicere*] **1 :** the same or more of the same **:** ANOTHER — used to avoid repeating a word 〈lost: one book (new); ~ (old)〉 **2 :** a mark composed of a pair of inverted commas or apostrophes used as a symbol for the word *ditto*

**dit·ty** \'dit-ē\ *n, pl* **ditties :** a short simple song

**di·uret·ic** \,dī-(y)ə-'ret-ik\ *adj* **:** tending to increase urine flow — **diuretic** *n*

**di·ur·nal** \dī-'ərn-ᵊl\ *adj* **1 :** DAILY **2 :** of, relating to, or occurring in the daytime

**div** *abbr* **1** divided **2** dividend **3** division **4** divorced

**di·va** \'dē-və\ *n, pl* **divas** or **di·ve** \-,vä\ [It, lit., goddess, fr. L, fem. of *divus* divine, god] **:** PRIMA DONNA

**di·va·gate** \'dī-və-,gāt\ *vb* **-gat·ed; -gat·ing 1 :** to wander about **2 :** DIVERGE — **di·va·ga·tion** \,dī-və-gā-shən\ *n*

**di·van** \'dī-,van, di-'van\ *n* **:** COUCH, SOFA

¹**dive** \'dīv\ *vb* **dived** \'dīvd\ or **dove** \'dōv\; **dived**; **div·ing 1 :** to plunge into water headfirst **2 :** SUBMERGE **3 :** to descend or fall precipitously **4 :** to descend in an airplane at a steep angle with or without power **5 :** to plunge into some matter or activity **6 :** DART, LUNGE — **div·er** *n*

²**dive** *n* **1 :** the act or an instance of diving **2 :** a sharp decline **3 :** a disreputable bar or place of amusement

**di·verge** \də-'vərj, dī-\ *vb* **di·verged; di·verg·ing 1 :** to move or extend in different directions from a common point **:** draw apart **2 :** to differ in character, form, or opinion **3 :** DEVIATE **4 :** DEFLECT — **di·ver·gence** \-'vər-jəns\ *n* — **di·ver·gent** \-jənt\ *adj*

**di·vers** \'dī-vərz\ *adj* **:** VARIOUS

**di·verse** \dī-'vərs, də-, 'dī-,vərs\ *adj* **1 :** UNLIKE **2 :** having various forms or qualities 〈the ~ nature of man〉 — **di·verse·ly** *adv*

**di·ver·si·fy** \də-'vər-sə-,fī, dī-\ *vb* **-fied; -fy·ing :** to make different or various in form or quality — **di·ver·si·fi·ca·tion** \-,vər-sə-fə-'kā-shən\ *n*

**di·ver·sion** \də-'vər-zhən, dī-\ *n* **1 :** a

turning aside from a course, activity, or use **:** DEVIATION **2 :** something that diverts or amuses **:** PASTIME

**di·ver·si·ty** \də-'vər-sət-ē, dī-\ *n, pl* **-ties 1 :** the condition of being different or having differences **:** VARIETY **2 :** an instance or a point of difference

**di·vert** \də-'vərt, dī-\ *vb* **1 :** to turn from a course or purpose **:** DEFLECT **2 :** DISTRACT **3 :** ENTERTAIN, AMUSE

**di·vest** \dī-'vest, də-\ *vb* **1 :** to strip esp. of clothing, ornament, or equipment **2 :** to deprive or dispossess esp. of property, authority, or rights

¹**di·vide** \də-'vīd\ *vb* **di·vid·ed; di·vid·ing 1 :** SEPARATE; *also* **:** CLASSIFY **2 :** CLEAVE, PART **3 :** DISTRIBUTE, APPORTION **4 :** to possess or make use of in common **:** share in **5 :** to cause to be separate, distinct, or apart from one another **6 :** to separate into opposing sides or parties **7 :** to mark divisions on **8 :** to subject to mathematical division **9 :** to branch out

²**divide** *n* **:** WATERSHED

**div·i·dend** \'div-ə-,dend\ *n* **1 :** a sum or amount to be divided and distributed; *also* **:** an individual share of such a sum **2 :** BONUS **3 :** a number to be divided by another

**di·vid·er** \də-'vīd-ər\ *n* **1 :** one that divides (as a partition) 〈room ~〉 **2** *pl* **:** COMPASSES

**div·i·na·tion** \,div-ə-'nā-shən\ *n* **1 :** the art or practice that seeks to foresee or foretell future events or discover hidden knowledge usu. by the study of omens or by the aid of supernatural powers **2 :** unusual insight or intuitive perception

¹**di·vine** \də-'vīn\ *adj* **di·vin·er; -est 1 :** of, relating to, or being God or a god **2 :** supremely good **:** SUPERB; *also* **:** HEAVENLY — **di·vine·ly** *adv*

²**divine** *n* **1 :** CLERGYMAN **2 :** THEOLOGIAN

³**divine** *vb* **di·vined; di·vin·ing 1 :** INFER, CONJECTURE **2 :** PROPHESY **3 :** DOWSE — **di·vin·er** *n*

**di·vin·ing rod** \də-'vī-niŋ-\ *n* **:** a forked rod believed to divine the presence of water or minerals by dipping downward when held over a vein

**di·vin·i·ty** \də-'vin-ət-ē\ *n, pl* **-ties 1 :** the quality or state of being divine **2 :** a divine being; *esp* **:** GOD **3 :** THEOLOGY

**di·vis·i·ble** \də-'viz-ə-bəl\ *adj* **:** capable of being divided — **di·vis·i·bil·i·ty** \-'bil-ət-ē\ *n*

**di·vi·sion** \də-'vizh-ən\ *n* **1 :** DISTRIBUTION, SEPARATION **2 :** one of the parts, sections, or groupings into which a whole is divided **3 :** a large self-contained military unit **4 :** a naval unit or subdivision **5 :** an administrative or operating unit of a governmental, business, or educational organization **6 :** something that divides or separates **7 :** DISAGREEMENT, DISUNITY **8 :** the process of finding how many times one number or quantity is contained in another — **di·vi·sion·al** \-'vizh-(ə-)nəl\ *adj*

**di·vi·sive** \də-'vī-siv, -'viz-iv\ *adj* : creating disunity or dissension — **di·vi·sive·ly** *adv* — **di·vi·sive·ness** *n*

**di·vi·sor** \də-'vī-zər\ *n* : the number by which a dividend is divided

**di·vorce** \də-'vōrs\ *n* 1 : a complete legal breaking up of a marriage 2 : SEPARATION, SEVERANCE — **divorce** *vb* — **di·vorce·ment** *n*

**di·vor·cée** \də-,vōr-'sā, -'sē\ *n* : a divorced woman

**div·ot** \'div-ət\ *n* : a piece of turf dug from a golf fairway in making a stroke

**di·vulge** \də-'vəlj, dī-\ *vb* **di·vulged**; **di·vulg·ing** : REVEAL, DISCLOSE

**dix·ie·land** \'dik-sē-,land\ *n* : jazz music in duple time usu. played by a small band and characterized by improvisation

**diz·zy** \'diz-ē\ *adj* **diz·zi·er**; **-est** [ME *disy*, fr. OE *dysig* stupid] 1 : having a sensation of whirling : GIDDY 2 : causing or caused by giddiness — **diz·zi·ly** \'diz-ə-lē\ *adv* — **diz·zi·ness** \-ē-nəs\ *n*

**DJ** *abbr* disc jockey

**dk** *abbr* 1 dark 2 deck 3 dock

**DLitt** *or* **DLit** *abbr* [L *doctor litterarum*] doctor of letters; doctor of literature

**DLO** *abbr* dead letter office

**DMD** *abbr* [NL *dentariae medicinae doctor*] doctor of dental medicine

**DMZ** *abbr* demilitarized zone

**dn** *abbr* down

**DNA** \,dē-,en-'ā\ *n* : any of various nucleic acids usu. of cell nuclei that are the molecular basis of heredity in many organisms

¹**do** \(')dü\ *vb* **did** \(')did\; **done** \'dən\; **do·ing** \'dü-iŋ\; **does** \(')dəz\ 1 : to bring to pass : ACCOMPLISH 2 : ACT, BEHAVE ⟨~ as I say⟩ 3 : to be active or busy ⟨up and ~ing⟩ 4 : HAPPEN ⟨what's ~ing?⟩ 5 : to work at ⟨he *does* tailoring⟩ 6 : PREPARE ⟨*did* his homework⟩ 7 : to put in order (as by cleaning or arranging) ⟨~ the dishes⟩ 8 : DECORATE ⟨*did* the hall in blue⟩ 9 : to get along ⟨he *does* well⟩ 10 : to carry on 11 : to feel or function better ⟨could ~ with some food⟩ 12 : RENDER 13 : FINISH ⟨when he had *done*⟩ 14 : EXERT ⟨*did* my best⟩ 15 : PRODUCE ⟨*did* a poem⟩ 16 : to play the part of 17 : CHEAT ⟨*did* him out of his share⟩ 18 : TRAVERSE, TOUR 19 : TRAVEL 20 : to serve out in prison 21 : to serve the needs or purpose of : SUIT 22 : to be fitting or proper 23 — used as an auxiliary verb (1) before the subject in an interrogative sentence ⟨*does* he work?⟩ and after some adverbs ⟨never *did* he say so⟩, (2) in a negative statement ⟨I *don't* know⟩, (3) for emphasis ⟨he *does* know⟩, and (4) as a substitute for a preceding predicate ⟨he works harder than I ~⟩ — **do away with** 1 : to get rid of 2 : DESTROY, KILL — **do by** : to act toward in a specified way : TREAT ⟨*did* right *by* her⟩ — **do for** : to bring about the death or ruin of — **do one's thing** : to do what is personally satisfying

²**do** *abbr* ditto

**DOA** *abbr* dead on arrival

**DOB** *abbr* date of birth

**dob·bin** \'däb-ən\ *n* 1 : a farm horse 2 : a quiet plodding horse

**Do·ber·man pin·scher** \,dō-bər-mən-'pin-chər\ *n* : a short-haired medium-sized dog of a breed of German origin

**dob·son·fly** \'däb-sən-,flī\ *n* : a winged insect with long slender mandibles in the male and a large carnivorous aquatic larva

¹**doc** \'däk\ *n* : DOCTOR — used chiefly as a familiar term of address

²**doc** *abbr* document

**do·cent** \'dōs-²nt, dō(t)-'sent\ *n* : TEACHER, LECTURER

**doc·ile** \'däs-əl\ *adj* [L *docilis*, fr. *docēre* to teach] : easily taught, led, or managed : TRACTABLE — **do·cil·i·ty** \dä-'sil-ət-ē\ *n*

¹**dock** \'däk\ *n* : a weedy herb related to buckwheat

²**dock** *vb* 1 : to cut off the end of : cut short 2 : to take away a part of : deduct from ⟨~ a man's wages⟩

³**dock** *n* 1 : an artificial basin to receive ships 2 : a slip between two piers to receive ships 3 : a wharf or platform for loading or unloading materials

⁴**dock** *vb* 1 : to bring or come into dock 2 : to join (as two spacecraft) mechanically in space

⁵**dock** *n* : the place in a court where a prisoner stands or sits during trial

**dock·age** \'däk-ij\ *n* : the provision or use of a dock; *also* : the charge for using a dock

**dock·et** \'däk-ət\ *n* 1 : a formal abridged record of the proceedings in a legal action; *also* : a register of such records 2 : a list of legal causes to be tried 3 : a calendar of matters to be acted on : AGENDA 4 : a label attached to a parcel containing identification or directions — **docket** *vb*

**dock·hand** \'däk-,hand\ *n* : LONGSHOREMAN

**dock·work·er** \-,wər-kər\ *n* : LONGSHOREMAN

**dock·yard** \-,yärd\ *n* : a storage place for naval supplies or materials used in building ships

¹**doc·tor** \'däk-tər\ *n* [ME *doctour* teacher, doctor, fr. MF & ML; MF, fr. ML *doctor*, fr. L, teacher, fr. *docēre* to teach] 1 : a person holding one of the highest academic degrees (as a PhD) conferred by a university 2 : one skilled in healing arts; *esp* : an academically and legally qualified physician, surgeon, dentist, or veterinarian — **doc·tor·al** \-t(ə-)rəl\ *adj*

²**doctor** *vb* **doc·tored**; **doc·tor·ing** \-t(ə-)riŋ\ 1 : to give medical treatment to 2 : to practice medicine 3 : REPAIR 4 : to adapt or modify for a desired end 5 : to alter deceptively

**doc·tor·ate** \'däk-t(ə-)rət\ *n* : the degree, title, or rank of a doctor

**doc·tri·naire** \,däk-trə-'naər\ *n* : one who attempts to put an abstract theory into effect without regard to practical difficulties

**doc·trine** \'däk-trən\ *n* **1** : something that is taught **2** : DOGMA, TENET — **doc·tri·nal** \-trən-ʔl\ *adj*

**doc·u·ment** \'däk-yə-mənt\ *n* : a paper that furnishes information, proof, or support of something else — **doc·u·ment** \-,ment\ *vb* — **doc·u·men·ta·tion** \,däk-yə-mən-'tā-shən\ *n*

**doc·u·men·ta·ry** \,däk yə-'men-t(ə-)rē\ *adj* **1** : of or relating to documents **2** : giving a factual presentation in artistic form ⟨a ~ movie⟩ — **documentary** *n*

¹**dod·der** \'däd-ər\ *n* : any of a genus of leafless elongated wiry parasitic herbs deficient in chlorophyll

²**dodder** *vb* **dod·dered; dod·der·ing** \'däd-(ə-)riŋ\ : to become feeble and shaky usu. from age

¹**dodge** \'däj\ *vb* **dodged; dodg·ing** **1** : to move suddenly aside; *also* : to avoid or evade by so doing **2** : to avoid by trickery or evasion

²**dodge** *n* **1** : an act of evading by sudden bodily movement **2** : an artful device to evade, deceive, or trick **3** : TECHNIQUE, METHOD

**do·do** \'dōd-ō\ *n, pl* **dodoes** *or* **dodos** [Port *doudo*, fr. *doudo* silly, stupid] **1** : a heavy flightless extinct bird related to the pigeons but larger than a turkey and formerly found on some of the islands of the Indian ocean **2** : one hopelessly behind the times; *also* : a stupid person

**doe** \'dō\ *n, pl* **does** *or* **doe** : an adult female deer; *also* : the female of a mammal of which the male is called buck — **doe·skin** \-,skin\ *n*

**do·er** \'dü-ər\ *n* : one that does

**does** *pres 3d sing of* DO

**doff** \'däf\ *vb* [ME *doffen*, fr. *don* to do + *of* off] **1** : to take off ⟨~ed his clothes⟩ *esp* : to take off or lift up ⟨he ~ed his hat⟩ **2** : to rid oneself of

¹**dog** \'dôg\ *n* **1** : a flesh-eating domestic mammal related to the wolves; *esp* : a male of this animal **2** : a worthless fellow **3** : FELLOW, CHAP ⟨a gay ~⟩ **4** : a mechanical device for holding something **5** : affected stylishness or dignity ⟨put on the ~⟩ **6** *pl* : RUIN ⟨gone to the ~s⟩

²**dog** *vb* **dogged; dog·ging** **1** : to hunt or track like a hound **2** : to worry as if by dogs : HOUND

**dog·bane** \'dôg-,bān\ *n* : any of a genus of mostly poisonous herbs with milky juice and often showy flowers

**dog·cart** \-,kärt\ *n* : a light one-horse carriage with two seats back to back

**dog·catch·er** \-,kach-ər, -,kech-\ *n* : a community official assigned to catch and dispose of stray dogs

**doge** \'dōj\ *n* : the chief magistrate in the republics of Venice and Genoa

**dog·ear** \'dôg-,iər\ *n* : the turned-down corner of a leaf of a book — **dog·eared** \-,iərd\ *adj*

**dog·fight** \'dôg-,fīt\ *n* : a fight between two or more fighter planes usu. at close quarters

**dog·fish** \-,fish\ *n* : any of various small sharks

**dog·ged** \'dôg-əd\ *adj* : stubbornly determined : TENACIOUS — **dog·ged·ly** *adv* — **dog·ged·ness** *n*

**dog·ger·el** \'dôg-(ə-)rəl\ *n* : verse that is loosely styled and irregular in measure esp. for comic effect

**dog·gie bag** \'dôg-ē-\ *n* : a bag provided by a restaurant to a customer for carrying home leftover food

¹**dog·gy** \'dôg-ē\ *adj* **dog·gi·er; -est** : resembling a dog ⟨a ~ odor⟩

²**dog·gy** *or* **dog·gie** \'dôg-ē\ *n, pl* **dog·gies** : a small dog

**dog·house** \'dôg-,haús\ *n* : a shelter for a dog — **in the doghouse** : in a state of disfavor

**do·gie** \'dō-gē\ *n, chiefly West* : a motherless calf

**dog·leg** \'dôg-,leg\ *n* : a sharp bend or angle (as in a road) — **dogleg** *vb*

**dog·ma** \'dôg-mə\ *n* **1** : a tenet or code of tenets **2** : a doctrine or body of doctrines formally proclaimed by a church

**dog·ma·tism** \'dôg-mə-,tiz-əm\ *n* : positiveness in stating matters of opinion esp. when unwarranted or arrogant — **dog·mat·ic** \dôg-'mat-ik\ *adj* — **dog·mat·i·cal·ly** \-i-k(ə-)lē\ *adv*

**dog·tooth violet** \'dôg-,tüth-\ *n* : a small spring-flowering bulbous herb related to the lilies

**dog·trot** \'dôg-,trät\ *n* : a gentle trot — **dogtrot** *vb*

**dog·wood** \'dôg-,wúd\ *n* : any of a genus of trees and shrubs having heads of small flowers often with showy bracts

**doi·ly** \'dói-lē\ *n, pl* **doilies** : a small often decorative mat

**do in** *vt* **1** : RUIN **2** : KILL **3** : TIRE, EXHAUST **4** : CHEAT

**do·ings** \'dü-iŋz\ *n pl* : ACTS, DEEDS, EVENTS

**do-it-yourself** \,dü-ə-chər-'self\ *adj* : of, relating to, or designed for use by or as if by an amateur or hobbyist — **do-it-your·self·er** \-'sel-fər\ *n*

**dol** *abbr* dollar

**dol·drums** \'dōl-drəmz, 'däl-\ *n pl* **1** : a spell of listlessness or despondency **2** : a part of the ocean near the equator abounding in calms **3** : a state of inactivity, stagnation, or slump ⟨business is in the ~⟩

¹**dole** \'dōl\ *n* **1** : a distribution esp. of food, money, or clothing to the needy; *also* : something so distributed **2** : a grant of government funds to the unemployed

²**dole** *vb* **doled; dol·ing** **1** : to give or distribute as a charity **2** : to give in small portions : PARCEL ⟨~ out food⟩

**dole·ful** \'dōl-fəl\ *adj* : full of grief : SAD — **dole·ful·ly** \-ē\ *adv*

**doll** \'däl, 'dôl\ *n* **1** : a small figure of a human being used esp. as a child's plaything **2** : a pretty woman

**dol·lar** \'däl-ər\ *n* [D or LG *daler*, fr. G *taler*, short for *joachimstaler*, fr. Sankt *Joachimsthal*, Bohemia, where talers were first made] **1** : any of various basic monetary units (as in the U.S. and Canada) — see MONEY table

2 : YUAN  3 : a coin, note, or token representing one dollar

**dol·lop** \'däl-əp\ n : LUMP, BLOB

**doll up** vb  1 : to dress elegantly or extravagantly  2 : to make more attractive

**dol·ly** \'däl-ē\ n, pl **dollies** : a small wheeled truck used in moving heavy loads; also : a wheeled platform for a television or movie camera

**dol·men** \'dōl-mən, 'däl-\ n : a prehistoric monument consisting of two or more upright stones supporting a horizontal stone slab

**do·lo·mite** \'dō-lə-,mīt, 'däl-ə-\ n : a mineral usu. found as a limestone or marble

**do·lor** \'dō-lər, 'däl-ər\ n : mental suffering or anguish : SORROW — **do·lor·ous** adj — **do·lor·ous·ly** adv — **do·lor·ous·ness** n

**dol·phin** \'däl-fən\ n  1 : a sea mammal related to the whales  2 : either of two active food fishes of tropical and temperate seas

**dolt** \'dōlt\ n : a stupid fellow — **dolt·ish** adj

**dom** abbr  1 domestic  2 dominant  3 dominion

**-dom** \dəm\ n suffix  1 : dignity : office ⟨dukedom⟩  2 : realm : jurisdiction ⟨kingdom⟩  3 : geographical area  4 : state or fact of being ⟨freedom⟩  5 : those having a (specified) office, occupation, interest, or character ⟨officialdom⟩

**do·main** \dō-'mān, də-\ n  1 : complete and absolute ownership of land  2 : land completely owned  3 : a territory over which dominion is exercised  4 : a sphere of influence or action ⟨the ~ of science⟩

**dome** \'dōm\ n : a large hemispherical roof or ceiling

**¹do·mes·tic** \də-'mes-tik\ adj  1 : of or relating to the household or the family  2 : relating and limited to one's own country or the country under consideration  3 : INDIGENOUS  4 : living near or about the habitations of man  5 : TAME, DOMESTICATED  6 : devoted to home duties and pleasures — **do·mes·ti·cal·ly** \-ti-k(ə-)lē\ adv

**²domestic** n : a household servant

**do·mes·ti·cate** \də-'mes-ti-,kāt\ vb **-cat·ed; -cat·ing** : to adapt to life in association with and to the use of man — **do·mes·ti·ca·tion** \-,mes-ti-'kā-shən\ n

**do·mes·tic·i·ty** \,dō-,mes-'tis-ət-ē, də-\ n, pl **-ties**  1 : the quality or state of being domestic or domesticated  2 : domestic activities or life

**dom·i·cile** \'däm-ə-,sīl, 'dōm-ə-; 'däm-ə-səl\ n : a dwelling place : HOME — **domicile** vb — **dom·i·cil·i·ary** \,däm-ə-'sil-ē-,er-ē, ,dō-mə-\ adj

**dom·i·nance** \'däm-ə-nəns\ n : AUTHORITY, CONTROL — **dom·i·nant** \-nənt\ adj

**dom·i·nate** \'däm-ə-,nāt\ vb **-nat·ed; -nat·ing**  1 : RULE, CONTROL  2 : to have a commanding position or controlling power over  3 : to rise high

above in a position suggesting power to dominate

**dom·i·na·tion** \,däm-ə-'nā-shən\ n  1 : supremacy or preeminence over another  2 : exercise of mastery or preponderant influence

**dom·i·neer** \,däm-ə-'niər\ vb  1 : to rule in an arrogant manner  2 : to be overbearing

**do·mi·nie** \¹ oftenest 'däm-ə-nē, ² oftenest 'dō-mə-\ n  1 : PEDAGOGUE  2 : CLERGYMAN

**do·min·ion** \də-'min-yən\ n  1 : supreme authority : SOVEREIGNTY  2 : DOMAIN  3 often cap : a self-governing nation of the British Commonwealth

**dom·i·no** \'däm-ə-,nō\ n, pl **-noes** or **-nos**  1 : a long loose hooded cloak usu. worn with a half mask as a masquerade costume  2 : a half mask worn with a masquerade costume  3 : a person wearing a domino  4 : a flat rectangular block used as a piece in a game (**dominoes**)

**¹don** \'dän\ n [Sp, fr. L dominus lord, master]  1 : a Spanish nobleman or gentleman — used as a title prefixed to the Christian name  2 : a head, tutor, or fellow in an English university

**²don** vb **donned; don·ning** [do + on] : to put on (as clothes)

**do·ña** \,dō-nyə\ n : a Spanish woman of rank — used as a title prefixed to the Christian name

**do·nate** \'dō-,nāt\ vb **do·nat·ed; do·nat·ing**  1 : to make a gift of : CONTRIBUTE  2 : to make a donation

**do·na·tion** \dō-'nā-shən\ n  1 : the action of making a gift esp. to a charity  2 : a free contribution : GIFT

**¹done** \'dən\ past part of DO

**²done** adj  1 : conformable to social convention  2 : gone by : OVER ⟨when day is ~⟩  3 : doomed to failure, defeat, or death  4 : cooked sufficiently

**dong** \'dȯŋ, 'däŋ\ n  1 — see MONEY table  2 : a coin of South Vietnam worth one plaster

**don·key** \'däŋ-kē, 'dəŋ-\ n, pl **donkeys**  1 : the domestic ass  2 : a stupid or obstinate person

**don·ny·brook** \'dän-ē-,brùk\ n, often cap : an uproarious brawl

**do·nor** \'dō-nər\ n : one that gives, donates, or presents

**donut** var of DOUGHNUT

**doo·dad** \'dü-,dad\ n : a small article whose common name is unknown or forgotten

**doo·dle** \'düd-¹l\ vb **doo·dled; doo·dling** \'düd-(°-)liŋ\ : to draw or scribble aimlessly while occupied with something else — **doodle** n — **doo·dler** \'düd-(°-)lər\ n

**doom** \'düm\ n  1 : JUDGMENT, SENTENCE; esp : a judicial condemnation or sentence  2 : DESTINY, FATE  3 : RUIN, DEATH — **doom** vb

**dooms·day** \'dümz-,dā\ n : the day of the Last Judgment

**door** \'dȯr\ n  1 : the movable frame by which a passageway for entrance can be opened or closed  2 : a passage for entrance  3 : a means of access

**door·jamb** \-,jam\ *n* : an upright piece forming the side of a door opening

**door·keep·er** \-,kē-pər\ *n* : one that tends a door

**door·knob** \-,näb\ *n* : a knob that when turned releases a door latch

**door·man** \-,man, -mən\ *n* 1 : DOOR-KEEPER 2 : one who tends a door and assists people by calling taxis and helping them in and out of cars

**door·mat** \-,mat\ *n* : a mat placed before or inside a door for wiping dirt from the shoes

**door·plate** \-,plāt\ *n* : a plate or plaque bearing a name (as of a resident) on a door

**door·step** \-,step\ *n* : a step or series of steps before an outer door

**door·way** \-,wā\ *n* 1 : the opening that a door closes 2 : a means of gaining access

**door·yard** \-,yärd\ *n* : a yard outside the door of a house

**do·pa** \'dō-pə\ *n* : a form of an amino acid that is used esp. in the treatment of Parkinson's disease

**dop·ant** \'dō-pənt\ *n* : an impurity added usu. in minute amounts to a pure substance to alter its properties

**dope** \'dōp\ *n* 1 : a preparation for giving a desired quality 2 : a narcotic preparation 3 : a stupid person 4 : INFORMATION

**dope** *vb* **doped; dop·ing** 1 : to treat with dope; *esp* : to give a narcotic to 2 *slang* : PREDICT, FIGURE ⟨~ out which team will win⟩

**dop·ey** *or* **dopy** \'dō-pē\ *adj* **dop·i·er; -est** 1 : dulled by alcohol or a narcotic 2 : SLUGGISH 3 : DULL, STUPID

**dorm** \'dòrm\ *n* : DORMITORY

**dor·mant** \'dòr-mənt\ *adj* 1 : INACTIVE; *esp* : not actively growing or functioning ⟨~ buds⟩ — **dor·man·cy** \-mən-sē\ *n*

**dor·mer** \'dòr-mər\ *n* [MF *dormeor* dormitory, fr. L *dormitorium*, fr. *dormire* to sleep] : a window built upright in a sloping roof

**dor·mi·to·ry** \'dòr-mə-,tōr-ē\ *n, pl* **-ries** 1 : a room for sleeping; *esp* : a large room containing a number of beds 2 : a residence hall providing sleeping rooms

**dor·mouse** \'dòr-,maùs\ *n* : an Old World squirrellike rodent

**dor·sal** \'dòr-səl\ *adj* : of, relating to, or located near or on the surface of the body that in man is the back but in most other animals is the upper surface — **dor·sal·ly** \-ē\ *adv*

**do·ry** \'dōr-ē\ *n, pl* **dories** : a flat-bottomed boat with flaring sides

**dose** \'dōs\ *n* [F, fr. LL *dosis*, fr. Gk, lit., act of giving, fr. *didonai* to give] 1 : a quantity (as of medicine) to be taken or administered at one time 2 : the quantity of radiation administered or absorbed — **dos·age** \'dō-sij\ *n*

**dose** *vb* **dosed; dos·ing** 1 : to give medicine to 2 : to give in doses

**do·sim·e·ter** \dō-'sim-ət-ər\ *n* : a device for measuring doses of X rays or of radioactivity — **do·sim·e·try** \-ə-trē\ *n*

**dos·sier** \'dòs-,yā, 'dòs-ē-,ā\ *n* [F, bundle of documents labeled on the back, dossier, fr. *dos* back, fr. L *dorsum*] : a file of papers containing a detailed report or detailed information

**dot** \'dät\ *n* 1 : a small spot : SPECK 2 : a small round mark made with or as if with a pen 3 : a precise point in time or space ⟨be here on the ~⟩

**dot** *vb* **dot·ted; dot·ting** 1 : to mark with a dot ⟨~ an *i*⟩ 2 : to cover with or as if with dots

**DOT** *abbr* Department of Transportation

**dot·age** \'dōt-ij\ *n* : feebleness of mind esp. in old age : SENILITY

**dot·ard** \-ərd\ *n* : a person in dotage

**dote** \'dōt\ *vb* **dot·ed; dot·ing** 1 : to be feebleminded esp. from old age 2 : to show excessive or foolish affection or fondness ⟨*doted* on her niece⟩

**dot·tle** \'dät-ᵊl\ *n* : unburned and partially burned tobacco caked in the bowl of a pipe

**dou·ble** \'dəb-əl\ *adj* 1 : TWOFOLD, DUAL 2 : consisting of two members or parts 3 : being twice as great or as many 4 : folded in two 5 : having more than one whorl of petals ⟨~ roses⟩

**double** *n* 1 : something twice another in size, strength, speed, quantity, or value 2 : a hit in baseball that enables the batter to reach second base 3 : COUNTERPART, DUPLICATE; *esp* : a person who closely resembles another 4 : UNDERSTUDY, SUBSTITUTE 5 : a sharp turn : REVERSAL 6 : FOLD 7 : a combined bet placed on two different contests 8 *pl* : a tennis match with two players on each side 9 : an act of doubling in a card game

**double** *adv* 1 : DOUBLY 2 : two together ⟨sleep ~⟩

**double** *vb* **dou·bled; dou·bling** \'dəb-(ə-)liŋ\ 1 : to make, be, or become twice as great or as many 2 : to make a call in bridge that increases the trick values and penalties of (an opponent's bid) 3 : FOLD 4 : CLENCH 5 : BEND 6 : to sail around (as a cape) 7 : to take the place of another 8 : to hit a double 9 : to turn sharply and suddenly; *esp* : to turn back on one's course

**dou·ble-cross** \,dəb-əl-'kròs\ *vb* : to deceive by double-dealing — **dou·ble-cross·er** *n*

**dou·ble-deal·ing** \-'dē-liŋ\ *n* : action contradictory to a professed attitude : DUPLICITY — **dou·ble-deal·er** \-'dē-lər\ *n* — **double-dealing** *adj*

**dou·ble-deck·er** \-'dek-ər\ *n* 1 : something (as a ship or bed) having two decks, levels, or layers 2 : a sandwich having two layers

**dou·ble en·ten·dre** \,düb-(ə)-,län-'tän²dr², ,dəb-ə-\, *n, pl* **double entendres** \-'tän²dr², -'tän²d-rəz\ [obs. F, lit., double meaning] : a word or expression capable of two interpretations one of which is usu. risqué

**dou·ble-head·er** \,dəb-əl-'hed-ər\ *n*

: two games played consecutively on the same day by the same teams or by different pairs of teams

**dou·ble-joint·ed** \-'jóint-əd\ *adj* : having a joint that permits an exceptional degree of freedom of motion of the parts joined

**double play** *n* : a play in baseball by which two players are put out

**dou·blet** \'dəb-lət\ *n* **1** : a man's close-fitting jacket worn in Europe esp. in the 16th century **2** : one of two similar or identical things

**dou·ble take** \'dəb-əl-,tāk\ *n* : a delayed reaction to a surprising or significant situation after an initial failure to notice anything unusual

**dou·ble-talk** \-,tók\ *n* : language that appears to be meaningful but in fact is a mixture of sense and nonsense

**double up** *vb* : to share accommodations designed for one

**dou·bloon** \,dəb-'lün\ *n* : a former gold coin of Spain and Spanish America

**dou·bly** \'dəb-lē\ *adv* **1** : to twice the degree **2** : in a twofold manner

**¹doubt** \'daút\ *vb* **1** : to be uncertain about **2** : to lack confidence in : DISTRUST, FEAR **3** : to consider unlikely — **doubt·able** *adj* — **doubt·er** *n*

**²doubt** *n* **1** : uncertainty of belief or opinion **2** : the condition of being uncertain ⟨the outcome was in ~⟩ **3** : DISTRUST **4** : an inclination not to believe or accept

**doubt·ful** \'daút-fəl\ *adj* **1** : not clear or certain as to fact **2** : QUESTIONABLE **3** : UNDECIDED **4** : not certain in outcome — **doubt·ful·ly** \-ē\ *adv*

**¹doubt·less** \'daút-ləs\ *adv* **1** : without doubt **2** : PROBABLY

**²doubtless** *adj* : free from doubt

**douche** \'düsh\ *n* : a jet of fluid (as water) directed against a part or into a cavity of the body; *also* : a cleansing with a douche

**dough** \'dō\ *n* **1** : a mixture of flour and other ingredients stiff enough to knead or roll **2** : something resembling dough esp. in consistency **3** : MONEY — **doughy** \'dō-ē\ *adj*

**dough·boy** \-,bói\ *n* : an American infantryman esp. in World War I

**dough·nut** \-,(,)nət\ *n* : a small usu. ring-shaped cake fried in fat

**dough·ty** \'daút-ē\ *adj* **dough·ti·er; -est** : ABLE, STRONG, VALIANT

**Doug·las fir** \,dəg-ləs-\ *n* : a tall evergreen timber tree of the western U.S.

**do up** *vb* **1** : LAUNDER, CLEAN **2** : to wrap up

**dour** \'daú(ə)r, 'dúr\ *adj* [ME, fr. L *durus* hard] **1** : STERN, HARSH **2** : GLOOMY, SULLEN

**douse** \'daús, 'daúz\ *vb* **doused; dous·ing 1** : to plunge into water **2** : DRENCH **3** : EXTINGUISH

**¹dove** \'dəv\ *n* **1** : PIGEON; *esp* : a small wild pigeon **2** : an advocate of peace or a peaceful policy — **dove·cote** \-,kōt, -,kät\ *or* **dove·cot** \-,kät\ *n* — **dov·ish** \'dəv-ish\ *adj*

**²dove** \'dōv\ *past of* DIVE

**¹dove·tail** \'dəv-,tāl\ *n* : something that resembles a dove's tail; *esp* : a flaring tenon and a mortise into which it fits tightly

**²dovetail** *vb* **1** : to join (as timbers) by means of dovetails **2** : to fit skillfully together to form a whole ⟨our plans ~ perfectly⟩

**dow·a·ger** \'daú-i-jər\ *n* **1** : a widow owning property or a title received from her deceased husband **2** : a dignified elderly woman

**dowdy** \'daúd-ē\ *adj* **dowd·i·er; -est** : lacking neatness and charm : SHABBY, UNTIDY; *also* : lacking smartness

**dow·el** \'daú-(ə)l\ *n* : a pin used for fastening together two pieces (as of board) — **dowel** *vb*

**¹dow·er** \'daú-(ə)r\ *n* **1** : the part of a deceased husband's real estate which the law gives for life to his widow **2** : DOWRY

**²dower** *vb* : to supply with a dower or dowry : ENDOW

**dow·itch·er** \'daú-i-chər\ *n, pl* **dowitchers** : a long-billed snipe

**¹down** \'daún\ *n* : a rolling usu. treeless upland with sparse soil — usu. used in pl.

**²down** *adv* **1** : toward or in a lower physical position **2** : to a lying or sitting position **3** : toward or to the ground, floor, or bottom **4** : in cash ⟨paid $5 ~⟩ **5** : on paper ⟨put ~ what he says⟩ **6** : to a source or place of concealment ⟨tracked him ~⟩ **7** : FULLY, COMPLETELY **8** : in a direction that is the opposite of up **9** : SOUTH **10** : toward or in the center of a city; *also* : away from a center **11** : to or in a lower or worse condition or status **12** : from a past time **13** : to or in a state of less activity **14** : from a thinner to a thicker consistency

**³down** *adj* **1** : occupying a low position; *esp* : lying on the ground **2** : directed or going downward **3** : being at a lower level ⟨sales were ~⟩ **4** : being in a state of reduced or low activity **5** : DEPRESSED, DEJECTED **6** : SICK ⟨~ with a cold⟩ **7** : having a low opinion or dislike ⟨~ on the boy⟩ **8** : FINISHED, DONE **9** : being the part of a price paid at the time of purchase or delivery ⟨a ~ payment⟩

**⁴down** *prep* : in a descending direction in, on, along, or through : to or toward the lower end or bottom of

**⁵down** *n* **1** : a low or falling period (as in activity, emotional life, or fortunes) **2** : one of a series of attempts to advance a football

**⁶down** *vb* **1** : to go or cause to go or come down **2** : DEFEAT

**⁷down** *n* **1** : a covering of soft fluffy feathers; *also* : such feathers **2** : a downlike covering or material

**down·beat** \'daún-,bēt\ *n* : the downward stroke of a conductor indicating the principally accented note of a measure of music

**down·cast** \-,kast\ *adj* **1** : DEJECTED **2** : directed down ⟨a ~ glance⟩

**down·er** \'daú-nər\ *n* **1** : a depressant

**drug**; *esp* : BARBITURATE **2** : a depressing experience or situation

**down·fall** \'daùn-,fòl\ *n* **1** : a sudden fall (as from high rank) : RUIN **2** : a fall (as of rain) esp. when sudden or heavy **3** : something that causes a downfall — **down·fall·en** \-,fó-lən\ *adj*

¹**down·grade** \'daùn-,grād\ *n* **1** : a downward grade or slope (as of a road) **2** : a decline toward a worse condition

²**downgrade** *vb* : to lower in grade, rank, position, or status

**down·heart·ed** \-'härt-əd\ *adj* : DEJECTED

**down·hill** \'daùn-'hil\ *adv* : toward the bottom of a hill — **downhill** \-,hil\ *adj*

**down payment** *n* : a part of the full price paid at the time of purchase or delivery with the balance to be paid later

**down·pour** \'daùn-,pōr\ *n* : a heavy rain

**down·range** \-'rānj\ *adv or adj* : toward the target area of a firing range

¹**down·right** \-,rīt\ *adv* : THOROUGHLY

²**downright** *adj* **1** : ABSOLUTE, THOROUGH ⟨a ~ lie⟩ **2** : PLAIN, BLUNT ⟨a ~ man⟩

**down·shift** \-,shift\ *vb* : to shift an automotive vehicle into a lower gear — **downshift** *n*

**down·stage** \'daùn-'stāj\ *adv or adj* : toward or at the front of a theatrical stage

**down·stairs** \'daùn-'staərz\ *adv* : on or to a lower floor and esp. the main or ground floor — **downstairs** *adj or n*

**down·stream** \'daùn-'strēm\ *adv or adj* : in the direction of flow of a stream

**down·stroke** \-,strōk\ *n* : a stroke made in a downward direction

**down·swing** \-,swiŋ\ *n* **1** : a swing downward **2** : DOWNTURN

**down–to–earth** \,daùn-tə-'(w)ərth\ *adj* : PRACTICAL, REALISTIC

¹**down·town** \'daùn-'taùn\ *adv* : to, toward, or in the lower part or business center of a town or city — **downtown** \,daùn-,taùn\ *adj*

²**downtown** \'daùn-,taùn\ *n* : the section of a town or city located downtown

**down·trod·den** \'daùn-'träd-³n\ *adj* : abused by superior power

**down·turn** \-,tərn\ *n* **1** : a turning downward **2** : a decline esp. in business activity

¹**down·ward** \'daùn-wərd\ *or* **downwards** \-wərdz\ *adv* **1** : from a higher to a lower place or condition **2** : from an earlier time **3** : from an ancestor or predecessor

²**downward** *adj* : directed toward or situated in a lower place or condition

**down·wind** \'daùn-'wind\ *adv or adj* : in the direction toward which the wind is blowing

**downy** \'daù-nē\ *adj* **down·i·er**; **-est** : resembling or covered with down

**downy mildew** *n* : a parasitic fungus producing whitish masses esp. on the underside of plant leaves; *also* : a plant disease caused by downy mildew

**downy woodpecker** *n* : a small black-and-white woodpecker of No. America

**dow·ry** \'daù(ə)r-ē\ *n, pl* **dowries** : the property that a woman brings to her husband in marriage

**dowse** \'daùz\ *vb* **dowsed**; **dows·ing** : to use a divining rod esp. to find water — **dows·er** *n*

**dox·ol·o·gy** \däk-'säl-ə-jē\ *n, pl* **-gies** : a usu. short hymn of praise to God

**doy·en** \'dòi-ən, 'dwä-,yaⁿ(n)\ *n* : the senior or most experienced person in a group

**doy·enne** \dòi-'(y)en, dwä-'yen\ *n* : a female doyen

**doz** *abbr* dozen

**doze** \'dōz\ *vb* **dozed**; **doz·ing** : to sleep lightly — **doze** *n*

**doz·en** \'dəz-³n\ *n, pl* **dozens** *or* **dozen** [ME *dozeine*, fr. OF *dozaine*, fr. *doze* twelve, fr. L *duodecim*, fr. *duo* two + *decem* ten] : a group of twelve — **doz·enth** \-³nth\ *adj*

¹**DP** \'dē-'pē\ *n, pl* **DP's** *or* **DPs** [*displaced person*] : a person expelled from his native land

²**DP** *abbr* **1** data processing **2** double play

**dpt** *abbr* department

**dr** *abbr* **1** debtor **2** dram **3** drive **4** drum

**Dr** *abbr* doctor

**DR** *abbr* **1** dead reckoning **2** dining room

**drab** \'drab\ *adj* **drab·ber**; **drab·best** **1** : being of a light olive-brown color **2** : DULL, MONOTONOUS, CHEERLESS — **drab·ness** *n*

**drach·ma** \'drak-mə\ *n, pl* **drach·mas** *or* **drach·mae** \-(,)mē\ *or* **drach·mai** \-,mī\ — see MONEY table

¹**draft** \'draft, 'dràft\ *n* **1** : the act of drawing or hauling : the thing or amount that is drawn **2** : the force required to pull an implement **3** : the act or an instance of drinking or inhaling; *also* : the portion drunk or inhaled in one such act **4** : DOSE, POTION **5** : DELINEATION, PLAN, DESIGN; *also* : a preliminary sketch, outline, or version ⟨a rough ~ of a speech⟩ **6** : the act of drawing (as from a cask); *also* : a portion of liquid so drawn **7** : the depth of water a ship draws esp. when loaded **8** : the selection of a person esp. for compulsory military service; *also* : the persons so selected **9** : an order for the payment of money drawn by one person or bank on another **10** : a heavy demand : STRAIN **11** : a current of air; *also* : a device to regulate air supply (as to a fire) — **on draft** : ready to be drawn from a receptacle ⟨beer *on draft*⟩

²**draft** *adj* **1** : used for drawing loads ⟨~ animals⟩ **2** : constituting a preliminary sketch, outline, or version **3** : being on draft; *also* : DRAWN ⟨~ beer⟩

³**draft** *vb* **1** : to select usu. on a compulsory basis; *esp* : to conscript for military service **2** : to draw the preliminary sketch, version, or plan of **3** : COMPOSE, PREPARE **4** : to draw up, off, or away — **draft·ee** \draf-'tē, dràf-\ *n*

**drafts·man** \'draft-smən, 'draft-\ *n*
: one who draws plans (as for buildings
or machinery)

**drafty** \'draf-tē, 'raf-\ *adj* **draft·i·er;
-est** : relating to or exposed to a draft

¹**drag** \'ag\ *n* **1** : something (as a
harrow, grapnel, sledge, or clog) that is
dragged along over a surface **2** : something
that hinders progress **3** : the
act or an instance of dragging **4**
: STREET 〈the main ~〉 **5** : woman's
dress worn by a man **6** : something
boring 〈the party was a ~〉

²**drag** *vb* **dragged; drag·ging 1** : HAUL
**2** : to move with painful slowness or
difficulty **3** : to force into or out of
some situation, condition, or course of
action **4** : to pass (time) in pain or
tedium **5** : PROTRACT 〈~ a story out〉
**6** : to hang or lag behind **7** : to trail
along on the ground **8** : to explore,
search, or fish with a drag **9** : DRAW,
PUFF 〈~ on a cigarette〉 — **drag·ger** *n*

**drag·net** \-,net\ *n* **1** : NET, TRAWL
**2** : a network of planned actions for
pursuing and catching 〈a police ~〉

**drag·o·man** \'drag-ə-mən\ *n, pl*
**-mans** *or* **-men** \-mən\ : an interpreter
(as of Arabic) employed esp. in
the Near East

**drag·on** \'drag-ən\ *n* [ME, fr. OF, fr.
L *dracon-, draco* serpent, dragon, fr. Gk
*drakōn* serpent] : a fabulous animal
usu. represented as a huge winged scaly
serpent with a crested head and large
claws

**drag·on·fly** \-,flī\ *n* : any of a group of
large harmless 4-winged insects

**dragon lizard** *n* : an **Indonesian**
lizard that is the largest of all known
lizards

¹**dra·goon** \drə-'gün, ra-\ *n* [F *dragon*
dragon, dragoon, fr. MF] : a heavily
armed mounted soldier

²**dragoon** *vb* : to force or attempt to
force into submission by violent measures

**drag race** *n* : an acceleration contest
between vehicles

**drag strip** *n* : a site for drag races

¹**drain** \'drān\ *vb* **1** : to draw off or
flow off gradually or completely **2** : to
exhaust physically or emotionally
**3** : to make or become gradually dry
or empty **4** : to carry away the surface
water of : discharge surface or surplus
water **5** : EMPTY, EXHAUST — **drain·er** *n*

²**drain** *n* **1** : a means (as a channel or
sewer) of draining **2** : the act of draining
**3** : DEPLETION **4** : BURDEN,
STRAIN 〈a ~ on his savings〉

**drain·age** \-ij\ *n* **1** : the act or process
of draining; *also* : something that is
drained off **2** : a means for draining
: DRAIN, SEWER **3** : an area drained

**drain·pipe** \'drān-,pīp\ *n* : a pipe for
drainage

**drake** \'drāk\ *n* : a male duck

**dram** \'dram\ *n* **1** — see WEIGHT table
**2** : FLUIDRAM **3** : a small drink

**dra·ma** \'dräm-ə, 'dram-\ *n* [LL, fr.
Gk, deed, drama, fr. *dran* to do, act]
**1** : a literary composition designed for

theatrical presentation **2** : PLAYS
**3** : a series of events involving conflicting
forces — **dra·mat·ic** \drə-'mat-ik\ *adj* — **dra·mat·i·cal·ly** \-i-k(ə-)lē\ *adv* — **dram·a·tist** \'dram-ət-əst, 'dräm-\ *n*

**dra·ma·tize** \'dram-ə-,tīz, 'dräm-\ *vb*
**-tized; -tiz·ing 1** : to adapt for or be
suitable for theatrical presentation
**2** : to present or represent in a dramatic
manner — **dram·a·ti·za·tion** \,dram-ət-ə-'zā-shən, ,dräm-\ *n*

**drank** *past of* DRINK

¹**drape** \'drāp\ *vb* **draped; drap·ing**
**1** : to cover or adorn with or as if with
folds of cloth **2** : to cause to hang or
stretch out loosely or carelessly **3** : to
arrange or become arranged in flowing
lines or folds

²**drape** *n* **1** : CURTAIN **2** : arrangement
in or of folds **3** : the cut or hang of
clothing

**drap·er** \'drā-pər\ *n, chiefly Brit* : a
dealer in cloth and sometimes in clothing
and dry goods

**drap·ery** \'drā-p(ə-)rē\ *n, pl* **-er·ies**
**1** *Brit* : DRY GOODS **2** : a decorative
fabric esp. when hung loosely and in
folds : HANGINGS **3** : the draping or
arranging of materials

**dras·tic** \'dras-tik\ *adj* : HARSH,
RIGOROUS, SEVERE 〈~ punishment〉 — **dras·ti·cal·ly** \-ti-k(ə-)lē\ *adv*

**draught** \'dráft\ *chiefly Brit var of*
DRAFT

**draughts** \'dráfts\ *n, Brit* : CHECKERS

¹**draw** \'dró\ *vb* **drew** \'drü\; **drawn**
\'drón\; **draw·ing 1** : HAUL, DRAG
**2** : to cause to go in a certain direction
〈*drew* him aside〉 **3** : to move or go
steadily or gradually 〈night ~s near〉
**4** : ATTRACT, ENTICE **5** : PROVOKE,
ROUSE 〈*drew* enemy fire〉 **6** : INHALE
〈~ a deep breath〉 **7** : to bring or pull
out **8** : to force out from cover or
possession 〈~ trumps〉 **9** : to extract
the essence from 〈~ tea〉 **10** : EVISCERATE
**11** : to require (a specified
depth) to float in **12** : ACCUMULATE,
GAIN 〈~ing interest〉 **13** : to take money
from a place of deposit : WITHDRAW
**14** : to receive regularly from a source
〈~ a salary〉 **15** : to take (cards) from
a stack or the dealer **16** : to receive or
take at random 〈~ a winning number〉
**17** : to bend (a bow) by pulling back
the string **18** : WRINKLE, SHRINK
**19** : to change shape by or as if by
pulling or stretching 〈a face *drawn* with
sorrow〉 **20** : to leave (a contest)
undecided : TIE **21** : DELINEATE,
SKETCH **22** : to write out in some form
: DRAFT 〈~ up a will〉 **23** : FORMULATE
〈~ comparisons〉 **24** : DEDUCE **25** : to
spread or elongate (metal) by hammering
or by pulling through dies **26** : to
produce or allow a draft or current of
air 〈the furnace ~s well〉 **27** : to
swell out in a wind 〈all sails ~ing〉

²**draw** *n* **1** : the act, process, or result of
drawing **2** : a lot or chance drawn at
random **3** : TIE **4** : ATTRACTION

**draw·back** \'dró-,bak\ *n* : HINDRANCE,
HANDICAP

**draw·bridge** \-ˌbrij\ *n* : a bridge made to be drawn up, down, or aside

**draw down** \(ˌ)drȯ-ˈdau̇n\ *vb* : to deplete by using or spending — **draw·down** \ˈdrȯ-ˌdau̇n\ *n*

**draw·er** \ˈdrȯ-(ə)r\ *n* **1** : one that draws **2** : a sliding boxlike compartment (as in a table or desk) **3** *pl* : an undergarment for the lower part of the body

**draw·ing** \ˈdrȯ(-)iŋ\ *n* **1** : an act or instance of drawing; *esp* : an occasion when something is decided by drawing lots **2** : the act or art of making a figure, plan, or sketch by means of lines **3** : a representation made by drawing : SKETCH

**drawing card** *n* : something that attracts attention or patronage

**drawing room** *n* **1** : a formal reception room **2** : a private room on a railroad car with three berths

**drawl** \ˈdrȯl\ *vb* : to speak or utter slowly with vowels greatly prolonged — **drawl** *n*

**draw on** *vb* : APPROACH

**draw out** *vb* **1** : PROLONG **2** : to cause to speak freely

**draw·string** \ˈdrȯ-ˌstriŋ\ *n* : a string, cord, or tape for use in closing a bag or controlling fullness in garments or curtains

**draw up** *vb* **1** : to draft in due form **2** : to pull oneself erect **3** : to bring or come to a stop

**dray** \ˈdrā\ *n* : a strong low cart for carrying heavy loads

**dread** \ˈdred\ *vb* **1** : to fear greatly **2** : to feel extreme reluctance to meet face to face

**dread** *n* : great fear esp. of some harm to come

**dread** *adj* **1** : causing great fear or anxiety **2** : inspiring awe

**dread·ful** \ˈdred-fəl\ *adj* **1** : inspiring dread or awe : FRIGHTENING **2** : extremely distasteful, unpleasant, or shocking — **dread·ful·ly** \-ē\ *adv*

**dread·nought** \ˈdred-ˌnȯt\ *n* : a battleship with big guns all of one caliber

**dream** \ˈdrēm\ *n* [ME *dreem*, fr. OE *drēam* noise, joy] **1** : a series of thoughts, images or emotions occurring during sleep **2** : a dreamlike vision : DAYDREAM, REVERIE **3** : something notable for its beauty, excellence, or enjoyable quality **4** : IDEAL — **dream·like** *adj* — **dreamy** *adj*

**dream** \ˈdrēm\ *vb* **dreamed** \ˈdremt, ˈdrēmd\ *or* **dreamt** \ˈdremt\; **dream·ing** **1** : to have a dream of **2** : to indulge in daydreams or fantasies : pass (time) in reverie or inaction **3** : IMAGINE — **dream·er** *n*

**dream·land** \ˈdrēm-ˌland\ *n* : an unreal delightful country that exists in imagination or in dreams

**dream up** *vb* : INVENT, CONCOCT

**dream·world** \-ˌwərld\ *n* : DREAMLAND; *also* : a world of illusion or fantasy

**drear** \ˈdriər\ *adj* : DREARY

**drea·ry** \ˈdri(ə)r-ē\ *adj* **drea·ri·er**;

**-est** [ME *drery*, fr. OE *drēorig* sad, bloody, fr. *drēor* gore] **1** : DOLEFUL, SAD **2** : DISMAL, GLOOMY — **drea·ri·ly** \ˈdrir-ə-lē\ *adv*

**¹dredge** \ˈdrej\ *n* : a machine or ship for removing earth or silt

**²dredge** *vb* **dredged; dredg·ing** : to gather or search with or as if with a dredge — **dredg·er** *n*

**³dredge** *vb* **dredged; dredg·ing** : to coat (food) by sprinkling (as with flour)

**dreg** \ˈdreg\ *n* **1** : LEES, SEDIMENT — usu. used in pl. **2** : the most worthless part of something — usu. used in pl.

**drench** \ˈdrench\ *vb* : to wet through

**¹dress** \ˈdres\ *vb* **1** : to make or set straight : ALIGN **2** : to put clothes on : CLOTHE; *also* : to put on or wear formal or fancy clothes **3** : TRIM, EMBELLISH ⟨∼ a store window⟩ **4** : to prepare for use; *esp* : BUTCHER **5** : to apply dressings or remedies to **6** : to arrange (the hair) by combing or curling **7** : to apply fertilizer to **8** : SMOOTH, FINISH ⟨∼ leather⟩

**²dress** *n* **1** : APPAREL, CLOTHING **2** : FROCK, GOWN — **dress·mak·er** \-ˌmā-kər\ — **dress·mak·ing** \-ˌmā-kiŋ\ *n*

**³dress** *adj* : suitable for a formal occasion; *also* : requiring formal dress

**dres·sage** \drə-ˈsäzh\ *n* : the execution by a horse of complex maneuvers in response to barely perceptible movements of a rider's hands, legs, and weight

**dress down** *vb* : to scold severely

**¹dress·er** \ˈdres-ər\ *n* : a chest of drawers or bureau with a mirror

**²dresser** *n* : one that dresses

**dress·ing** \-iŋ\ *n* **1** : the act or process of one who dresses **2** : a sauce for adding to a dish (as a salad **3** : a seasoned mixture usu. used as a stuffing (as for poultry) **4** : material used to cover an injury

**dressing gown** *n* : a loose robe worn esp. while dressing or resting

**dressy** \ˈdres-ē\ *adj* **dress·i·er**; **-est 1** : showy in dress **2** : STYLISH, SMART

**drew** *past of* DRAW

**¹drib·ble** \ˈdrib-əl\ *vb* **drib·bled; drib·bling** \-(ə-)liŋ\ **1** : to fall or flow in drops : TRICKLE **2** : DROOL **3** : to propel by successive slight taps or bounces

**²dribble** *n* **1** : a small trickling stream or flow **2** : a drizzling shower **3** : the dribbling of a ball or puck

**drib·let** \ˈdrib-lət\ *n* **1** : a trifling amount **2** : a falling drop

**dri·er** *also* **dry·er** \ˈdrī(-ə)r\ *n* **1** : a substance dissolved in paints, varnishes, or inks to speed drying **2** *usu* **dryer** : a device for drying

**¹drift** \ˈdrift\ *n* **1** : the motion or course of something drifting **2** : a mass of matter (as snow or sand) blown up by wind **3** : earth, gravel, and rock deposited by a glacier or by running water **4** : a general underlying design or tendency : MEANING

**²drift** *vb* **1 :** to float or be driven along by or as if by wind, waves, or currents **2 :** to pile up under the force of the wind or water

**drift·er** \'drif-tər\ *n* **:** a person without aim, ambition, or initiative

**drift·wood** \drift-,wùd\ *n* **:** wood drifted or floated by water

**¹drill** \'dril\ *vb* **1 :** to bore with a drill **2 :** to instruct and exercise by repetition **3 :** to train in or practice military drill — **drill·er** *n*

**²drill** *n* **1 :** a boring tool **2 :** the training of soldiers in marching and the manual of arms **3 :** strict training and instruction in a subject

**³drill** *n* **:** an agricultural implement for making furrows and dropping seed into them

**⁴drill** *n* **:** a firm cotton fabric in twill weave

**drill·mas·ter** \'dril-,mas-tər\ *n* **:** one who drills; *esp* **:** an instructor in military drill

**drill press** *n* **:** an upright drilling machine in which the drill is pressed to the work usu. by a hand lever

**drily** *var of* DRYLY

**¹drink** \'driŋk\ *vb* **drank** \'draŋk\; **drunk** \'drəŋk\ *or* **drank; drinking 1 :** to swallow liquid **:** IMBIBE **2 :** ABSORB **3 :** to take in through the senses ⟨~ in the beautiful scenery⟩ **4 :** to give or join in a toast **5 :** to drink alcoholic beverages esp. to excess — **drink·able** *adj* — **drink·er** *n*

**²drink** *n* **1 :** BEVERAGE **2 :** alcoholic liquor **3 :** a draft or portion of liquid **4 :** excessive consumption of alcoholic beverages

**¹drip** \'drip\ *vb* **dripped; drip·ping 1 :** to fall or let fall in drops **2 :** to let fall drops of moisture or liquid ⟨a *dripping* faucet⟩ **3 :** to overflow with or as if with moisture

**²drip** *n* **1 :** a falling in drops **2 :** liquid that falls, overflows, or is extruded in drops **3 :** the sound made by or as if by falling drops

**¹drive** \'drīv\ *vb* **drove** \'drōv\; **driv·en** \'driv-ən\; **driv·ing 1 :** to urge, push, or force onward **2 :** to direct the movement or course of **3 :** to convey in a vehicle **4 :** to set or keep in motion or operation **5 :** to carry through strongly ⟨~ a bargain⟩ **6 :** FORCE, COMPEL ⟨*driven* by hunger to steal⟩ **7 :** to project, inject, or impress forcefully ⟨*drove* the lesson home⟩ **8 :** to bring into a specified condition ⟨the noise ~s me crazy⟩ **9 :** to produce by opening a way ⟨~ a well⟩ **10 :** to rush and press with violence ⟨a *driving* rain⟩ **11 :** to propel an object of play (as a golf ball) by a hard blow — **driv·er** *n*

**²drive** *n* **1 :** a trip in a carriage or automobile **2 :** a driving together of animals (as for capture or slaughter) **3 :** the guiding of logs downstream to a mill **4 :** the act of driving a ball; *also* **:** the flight of a ball **5 :** DRIVEWAY **6 :** a public road for driving (as in a park) **7 :** an offensive or aggressive move **:** a military attack **8 :** an intensive campaign ⟨membership ~⟩ **9 :** the state of being hurried and under pressure **10 :** NEED, LONGING **11 :** dynamic quality **12 :** the apparatus by which motion is imparted to a machine

**drive-in** \'drī-,vin\ *adj* **:** accommodating patrons while they remain in their automobiles — **drive-in** *n*

**¹driv·el** \'driv-əl\ *vb* **-eled** *or* **-elled; -el·ling** *or* **-el·ling** \-(ə-)liŋ\ **1 :** DROOL, SLAVER **2 :** to talk or utter stupidly, carelessly, or in an infantile way — **driv·el·er** \-(ə-)lər\ *n*

**²drivel** *n* **:** NONSENSE

**drive shaft** *n* **:** a shaft that transmits mechanical power

**drive·way** \'drīv-,wā\ *n* **1 :** a road or way along which animals are driven **2 :** a short private road leading from the street to a house, garage, or parking lot

**¹driz·zle** \'driz-əl\ *vb* **driz·zled; driz·zling** \-(ə-)liŋ\ **:** to rain in very small drops

**²drizzle** *n* **:** a fine misty rain

**drogue** \'drōg\ *n* **:** a small parachute for slowing down or stabilizing something (as an astronaut's capsule)

**droll** \'drōl\ *adj* [F *drôle*, fr. *drôle* scamp, fr. MF *drolle*, fr. Middle Dutch *drol* imp] **:** having a humorous, whimsical, or odd quality ⟨a ~ expression⟩ — **droll·ery** \-(ə-)rē\ *n* — **drol·ly** \'drōl(l)-lē\ *adv*

**drom·e·dary** \'dräm-ə,der-ē\ *n, pl* **-dar·ies** [ME *dromedarie*, fr. MF *dromedaire*, fr. LL *dromedarius*, fr. L *dromad-, dromas*, fr. Gk. *dromad-, dromas* running] **:** CAMEL; *esp* **:** a usu. speedy one-humped camel used esp. for riding

**¹drone** \'drōn\ *n* **1 :** a male honeybee **2 :** one that lives on the labors of others **:** PARASITE **3 :** a pilotless airplane or ship controlled by radio

**²drone** *vb* **droned; dron·ing 1 :** to sound with a low dull monotonous murmuring sound **:** speak monotonously

**³drone** *n* **:** a deep monotonous sound

**drool** \'drül\ *vb* **1 :** to let liquid flow from the mouth **2 :** to talk foolishly

**droop** \'drüp\ *vb* **1 :** to hang or incline downward **2 :** to sink gradually **3 :** LANGUISH — **droop** *n*

**¹drop** \'dräp\ *n* **1 :** the quantity of fluid that falls in one spherical mass **2** *pl* **:** a dose of medicine measured by drops **3 :** a small quantity of drink **4 :** the smallest practical unit of liquid measure **5 :** something (as a pendant or a small round candy) that resembles a liquid drop **6 :** FALL **7 :** a decline in quantity or quality **8 :** a descent by parachute **9 :** the distance through which something drops **10 :** a slot into which something (as a coin) is dropped; *also* **:** a place where something is brought ⟨a mail ~⟩ **11 :** something that drops or has dropped

**²drop** *vb* **dropped; drop·ping 1 :** to fall or let fall in drops **2 :** to let fall **:** LOWER ⟨~ a glove⟩ ⟨*dropped* his voice⟩ **3 :** SEND ⟨~ me a note⟩ **4 :** to let go : DISMISS ⟨∼ the subject⟩ **5** : to knock down : cause to fall **6** : to go lower : become less ⟨prices *dropped*⟩ **7** : to come or go unexpectedly or informally ⟨∼ in to call⟩ **8** : to pass from one state into a less active one ⟨∼ off to sleep⟩ **9** : to move downward or with a current **10** : QUIT ⟨*dropped* out of the race⟩ — **drop back** : to move toward the rear — **drop behind** : to fail to keep up — **drop in** : to pay an unexpected visit

**drop·kick** \-'kik\ *n* : a kick made by dropping a football to the ground and kicking it at the moment it starts to rebound — **drop–kick** *vb*

**drop·let** \'dräp-lət\ *n* : a tiny drop

**drop–off** \'dräp-,óf\ *n* **1** : a steep or perpendicular descent **2** : a marked decline ⟨a ∼ in attendance⟩

**drop off** \dräp-'óf\ *vb* : to fall asleep

**drop out** \dräp-'aút\ *vb* **1** : to leave school before graduation **2** : to withdraw from conventional society out of disenchantment with its values and mores — **drop·out** \'dräp-,aút\ *n*

**drop·per** \'dräp-ər\ *n* **1** : one that drops **2** : a short glass tube with a rubber bulb used to measure out liquids by drops

**drop·sy** \'dräp-sē\ *n* [ME *dropesie*, short for *ydropesie*, fr. OF, fr. L *hydropisis*, fr. Gk *hydrōps*, fr. *hydōr* water] : an abnormal accumulation of serous fluid in the body — **drop·si·cal** \-si-kəl\ *adj*

**dross** \'dräs\ *n* **1** : the scum that forms on the surface of a molten metal **2** : waste matter : REFUSE

**drought** *or* **drouth** \'draut(h)\ *n* : a long spell of dry weather

**drove** \'drōv\ *n* **1** : a group of animals driven or moving in a body **2** : a crowd of people moving or acting together

**drov·er** \'drō-vər\ *n* : one that drives domestic animals usu. to market

**drown** \'draún\ *vb* **drowned** \'draúnd\; **drown·ing 1** : to suffocate by submersion esp. in water **2** : to become drowned **3** : to cover with water **4** : OVERCOME, OVERPOWER

**drowse** \'draúz\ *vb* **drowsed**; **drows·ing** : DOZE — **drowse** *n*

**drow·sy** \'draú-zē\ *adj* **drows·i·er; -est 1** : ready to fall asleep **2** : making one sleepy — **drows·i·ly** \'draú-zə-lē\ *adv* — **drows·i·ness** \-zē-nəs\ *n*

**drub** \'drəb\ *vb* **drubbed; drub·bing 1** : to beat severely : PUMMEL, THRASH **2** : to defeat decisively

**drudge** \'drəj\ *vb* **drudged; drudg·ing** : to do hard, menial, or monotonous work — **drudge** *n* — **drudg·ery** \-(ə-)rē\ *n*

¹**drug** \'drəg\ *n* **1** : a substance used as or in medicine **2** : NARCOTIC

²**drug** *vb* **drugged; drug·ging** : to affect with drugs; *esp* : to stupefy with a narcotic

**drug·gist** \'drəg-əst\ *n* : a dealer in drugs and medicines : PHARMACIST

**drug·store** \'drəg-,stōər\ *n* : a retail shop where medicines and miscellaneous articles are sold

**dru·id** \'drü-əd\ *n, often cap* : one of an ancient Celtic priesthood of Gaul, Britain, and Ireland appearing in legends as magicians and wizards

¹**drum** \'drəm\ *n* **1** : a musical percussion instrument usu. consisting of a hollow cylinder with a skin head stretched over each end that is beaten with sticks in playing **2** : EARDRUM **3** : the sound of a drum; *also* : a similar sound **4** : a drum-shaped object

²**drum** *vb* **drummed; drum·ming 1** : to beat a drum **2** : to sound rhythmically : THROB, BEAT **3** : to summon or assemble by or as if by beating a drum **4** : EXPEL ⟨*drummed* out of camp⟩ **5** : to drive or force by steady effort ⟨∼ a lesson into his head⟩ **6** : to strike or tap repeatedly so as to produce rhythmic sounds

**drum·beat** \'drəm-,bēt\ *n* : a stroke on a drum or its sound

**drum·lin** \'drəm-lən\ *n* : an oval hill of glacial drift

**drum major** *n* : the marching leader of a band

**drum ma·jor·ette** \,drəm-,mā jo 'rət\ *n* : a female drum major; *also* : a baton twirler who accompanies a marching band

**drum·mer** \'drəm-ər\ *n* **1** : one that plays a drum **2** : a traveling salesman

**drum·stick** \-,stik\ *n* **1** : a stick for beating a drum **2** : the lower segment of a fowl's leg

**drum up** *vb* **1** : to bring about by persistent effort ⟨*drum up* business⟩ **2** : INVENT, ORIGINATE

¹**drunk** \'drəŋk\ *adj* **1** : having the faculties impaired by alcohol **2** : controlled by some feeling as if under the influence of alcohol **3** : of, relating to, or caused by intoxication

²**drunk** *n* **1** : a period of excessive drinking **2** : a drunken person : DRUNKARD

**drunk·ard** \'drəŋ-kərd\ *n* : one who is habitually drunk

**drunk·en** \'drəŋ-kən\ *adj* **1** : DRUNK **2** : given to habitual excessive use of alcohol **3** : of, relating to, or resulting from intoxication **4** : unsteady or lurching as if from intoxication — **drunk·en·ly** *adv* — **drunk·en·ness** \-kən-nəs\ *n*

**drupe** \'drüp\ *n* : a partly fleshy one-seeded fruit that remains closed at maturity

¹**dry** \'drī\ *adj* **dri·er** \'drī(-ə-)r\; **dri·est** \'drī-əst\ **1** : free or freed from water or liquid **2** : characterized by loss or lack of water or moisture **3** : lacking freshness : WITHERED; *also* : low in or deprived of succulence ⟨∼ fruits⟩ **4** : not being in or under water ⟨∼ land⟩ **5** : THIRSTY **6** : marked by the absence of alcoholic beverages **7** : no longer liquid or sticky ⟨the ink is ∼⟩ **8** : containing or employing no liquid **9** : not givirg milk ⟨a ∼ cow⟩ **10** : lacking natural lubrication ⟨a ∼ cough⟩ **11** : solid as

opposed to liquid ⟨∼ groceries⟩ **12 :** SEVERE **13 :** not productive **:** BARREN **14 :** marked by a matter-of-fact, ironic, or terse manner of expression ⟨∼ humor⟩ **15 :** UNINTERESTING, WEARISOME **16 :** not sweet ⟨∼ wine⟩ **17 :** relating to, favoring, or practicing prohibition of alcoholic beverages — **dry·ly** *adv* — **dry·ness** *n*

²**dry** *vb* **dried; dry·ing :** to make or become dry

³**dry** *n, pl* **drys :** PROHIBITIONIST

**dry·ad** \'drī-əd, -ˌad\ *n* **:** WOOD NYMPH

**dry cell** *n* **:** a battery whose contents are not spillable

**dry–clean** \'drī-ˌklēn\ *vb* **:** to clean (fabrics) chiefly with solvents (as naphtha) other than water — **dry cleaning** *n*

**dry dock** \'drī-ˌdäk\ *n* **:** a dock that can be kept dry during ship construction or repair

**dry·er** *var of* DRIER

**dry farm·ing** *n* **:** farming without irrigation in areas of limited rainfall — **dry-farm** *vb* — **dry farm·er** *n*

**dry goods** \'drī-ˌgùdz\ *n pl* **:** textiles, ready-to-wear clothing, and notions as distinguished from other goods

**dry ice** *n* **:** solidified carbon dioxide used chiefly as a refrigerant

**dry measure** *n* **:** a series of units of capacity for dry commodities — see METRIC SYSTEM table, WEIGHT table

**dry run** *n* **1 :** a practice firing without ammunition **2 :** REHEARSAL, TRIAL

**DS** *abbr* **1** [ It *dal segno*] from the sign **2** days after sight

**DSC** *abbr* **1** Distinguished Service Cross **2** doctor of surgical chiropody

**DSM** *abbr* Distinguished Service Medal

**DSO** *abbr* Distinguished Service Order

**DSP** *abbr* [L *decessit sine prole*] died without issue

**DST** *abbr* **1** daylight saving time **2** doctor of sacred theology

**d.t.'s** \(')dē-'tēz\ *n pl, often cap D&T* **:** DELIRIUM TREMENS

**Du** *abbr* Dutch

**du·al** \'d(y)ü-əl\ *adj* **1 :** TWOFOLD, DOUBLE **2 :** having a double character or nature — **du·al·ism** \-ə-ˌliz-əm\ *n* — **du·al·i·ty** \d(y)ü-'al-ət-ē\ *n*

¹**dub** \'dəb\ *vb* **dubbed; dub·bing 1 :** to confer knighthood upon **2 :** NAME, NICKNAME

²**dub** *n* **:** a clumsy person **:** DUFFER

³**dub** *vb* **dubbed; dub·bing :** to add (sound effects) to a motion picture or to a radio or television production

**dub·bin** \'dəb-ən\ *also* **dub·bing** \-ən, -iŋ\ *n* **:** a dressing of oil and tallow for leather

**du·bi·ety** \d(y)ù-'bī-ət-ē\ *n, pl* **-eties 1 :** UNCERTAINTY **2 :** a matter of doubt

**du·bi·ous** \'d(y)ü-bē-əs\ *adj* **1 :** occasioning doubt **:** UNCERTAIN **2 :** feeling doubt **:** UNDECIDED **3 :** QUESTIONABLE — **du·bi·ous·ly** *adv* — **du·bi·ous·ness** *n*

**du·cal** \'d(y)ü-kəl\ *adj* **:** of or relating to a duke or dukedom

**duc·at** \'dək-ət\ *n* **:** a gold coin of vari-

---

ous European countries

**duch·ess** \'dəch-əs\ *n* **1 :** the wife or widow of a duke **2 :** a woman holding a ducal title in her own right

**duchy** \'dəch-ē\ *n, pl* **duch·ies :** the territory of a duke or duchess **:** DUKEDOM

¹**duck** \'dək\ *n, pl* **ducks :** any of various swimming birds related to but smaller than geese and swans

²**duck** *vb* **1 :** to thrust or plunge under water **2 :** to lower the head or body suddenly **3 :** BOW, BOB **4 :** DODGE **5 :** to evade a duty, question, or responsibility ⟨∼ the issue⟩

³**duck** *n* **1 :** a durable closely woven usu. cotton fabric **2** *pl* **:** clothes made of duck

**duck·bill** \'dək-ˌbil\ *n* **:** PLATYPUS

**duck·board** \-ˌbōrd\ *n* **:** a boardwalk or slatted flooring laid on a wet, muddy, or cold surface — usu. used in pl.

**duck·ling** \'dək-liŋ\ *n* **:** a young duck

**duck·pin** \-ˌpin\ *n* **1 :** a small bowling pin shorter and wider in the middle than a tenpin **2** *pl but sing in constr* **:** a bowling game using duckpins

**duct** \'dəkt\ *n* **:** a tube or canal for conveying a fluid; *also* **:** a pipe or tube for electrical conductors — **duct·less** \'dək-tləs\ *adj*

**duc·tile** \'dək-t°l\ *adj* **1 :** capable of being drawn out (as into wire) or hammered thin **2 :** DOCILE — **duc·til·i·ty** \ˌdək-'til-ət-ē\ *n*

**ductless gland** *n* **:** an endocrine gland

**dud** \'dəd\ *n* **1** *pl* **:** CLOTHES; *also* **:** personal belongings **2 :** one that fails completely **3 :** a missile that fails to explode

**dude** \'d(y)üd\ *n* **1 :** FOP, DANDY **2 :** a city man; *esp* **:** an Easterner in the West

**dude ranch** *n* **:** a vacation resort offering activities (as horseback riding) typical of western ranches

**dudgeon** \'dəj-ən\ *n* **:** ill humor **:** RESENTMENT ⟨in high ∼⟩

¹**due** \'d(y)ü\ *adj* [ME, fr. MF *deu*, pp. of *devoir* to owe, fr. L *debēre*] **1 :** owed or owing as a debt **2 :** owed or owing as a right **3 :** APPROPRIATE, FITTING **4 :** SUFFICIENT, ADEQUATE **5 :** REGULAR, LAWFUL ⟨∼ process of law⟩ **6 :** ATTRIBUTABLE, ASCRIBABLE ⟨∼ to negligence⟩ **7 :** PAYABLE ⟨a bill ∼ today⟩ **8 :** required or expected to happen ⟨∼ to arrive soon⟩

²**due** *n* **1 :** something that rightfully belongs to one ⟨give to each his ∼⟩ **2 :** something owed **3 :** DEBT **4** *pl* **:** a regular or legal charge or fee

³**due** *adv* **:** DIRECTLY, EXACTLY ⟨∼ north⟩

**du·el** \'d(y)ü-əl\ *n* **:** a combat between two persons; *esp* **:** one fought with weapons in the presence of witnesses — **duel** *vb* — **du·el·ist** *n*

**du·en·de** \dü-'en-dā\ *n* [Sp dial., charm, fr. Sp, ghost, goblin, fr. *duen de casa*, prob. fr. *dueño de casa* owner of a house] **:** the power to attract through personal magnetism and charm

**du·en·na** \d(y)ü-'en-ə\ *n* **1 :** an elderly woman in charge of the younger ladies in a Spanish or Portuguese family **2 :** GOVERNESS, CHAPERON

**du·et** \d(y)ü-'et\ *n* **:** a musical composition for two performers

**due to** *prep* **:** because of

**duffel bag** \'dəf-əl-\ *n* **:** a large cylindrical bag for personal belongings

**duf·fer** \'dəf-ər\ *n* **:** an incompetent or clumsy person

**dug** *past of* DIG

**dug·out** \'dəg-ˌaút\ *n* **1 :** a boat made by hollowing out a log **2 :** a shelter dug in a hillside or in the ground or in the side of a trench **3 :** a low shelter facing a baseball diamond that contains the players' bench

**duke** \'d(y)ük\ *n* **1 :** a sovereign ruler of a continental European duchy **2 :** a nobleman of the highest rank; *esp* **:** a member of the highest grade of the British peerage **3** *slang* **:** FIST — usu. used in pl. — **duke·dom** *n*

**dul·cet** \'dəl-sət\ *adj* **1 :** sweet to the ear **2 :** AGREEABLE, SOOTHING

**dul·ci·mer** \'dəl-sə-mər\ *n* **:** a wire-stringed instrument of trapezoidal shape played with light hammers held in the hands

**¹dull** \'dəl\ *adj* **1 :** mentally slow **:** STUPID **2 :** slow in perception or sensibility **3 :** LISTLESS **4 :** slow in action **:** SLUGGISH (a ~ market) **5 :** BLUNT **6 :** lacking brilliance or luster **7 :** DIM, INDISTINCT **8 :** not resonant or ringing **9 :** CLOUDY, OVERCAST **10 :|** TEDIOUS, UNINTERESTING **11 :** low in saturation and lightness (~ color) — **dull·ness** *or* **dul·ness** *n* — **dul·ly** \'dəl-(l)ē\ *adv*

**²dull** *vb* **:** to make or become dull

**dull·ard** \'dəl-ərd\ *n* **:** a stupid person

**du·ly** \'d(y)ü-lē\ *adv* **:** in a due manner, time, or degree

**du·ma** \'dü-mə\ *n* **:** the principal legislative assembly in czarist Russia

**dumb** \'dəm\ *adj* **1 :** lacking the power of speech **2 :** SILENT **3 :** STUPID — **dumb·ly** *adv*

**dumb·bell** \'dəm-ˌbel\ *n* **1 :** a weight of two rounded ends connected by a short bar and usu. used in pairs for gymnastic exercises **2 :** one who is dull or stupid **:** DUMMY

**dumb·found** *or* **dum·found** \ˌdəm-'faúnd\ *vb* **:** to strike dumb with astonishment **:** AMAZE

**dumb·waiter** \'dəm-ˌwāt-ər\ *n* **:** a small elevator for conveying food and dishes or small goods from one story of a building to another

**dum·dum** \'dəm-ˌdəm\ *n* **:** a soft-nosed bullet that expands upon hitting an object

**dum·my** \'dəm-ē\ *n, pl* **dummies** **1 :** a dumb person **2 :** the exposed hand in bridge played by the declarer in addition to his own hand; *also* **:** a bridge player whose hand is a dummy **3 :** an imitation or copy of something used as a substitute **4 :** one who seems to be acting for himself but is really acting for another **5 :** something usu. mechanically operated that serves to replace or aid a human being's work **6 :** a pattern arrangement of matter to be reproduced esp. by printing

**¹dump** \'dəmp\ *vb* **:** to let fall in a mass **:** UNLOAD (~ coal)

**²dump** *n* **1 :** a place for dumping something (as refuse) **2 :** a reserve supply; *esp* **:** one of military materials stored at one place (an ammunition ~) **3 :** a slovenly or dilapidated place

**dump·ing** \-iŋ\ *n* **:** the selling of goods in quantity at below market price esp. in international trade

**dump·ling** \'dəm-pliŋ\ *n* **1 :** a small mass of dough cooked by boiling or steaming **2 :** a dessert of fruit baked in biscuit dough

**dumps** \'dəmps\ *n pl* **:** a dull gloomy state of mind **:** low spirits (in the ~)

**dump truck** *n* **:** a truck for transporting and dumping loose materials

**dumpy** \'dəm-pē\ *adj* **dump·i·er**; **-est :** short and thick in build

**¹dun** \'dən\ *adj* **:** having a variable color averaging a nearly neutral slightly brownish dark gray

**²dun** *vb* **dunned; dun·ning 1 :** to ask repeatedly (as for payment of a debt) **2 :** PLAGUE, PESTER — **dun** *n*

**dunce** \'dəns\ *n* [John Duns Scotus, whose once accepted writings were ridiculed in the 16th cent.] **:** a dull-witted and stupid person

**dun·der·head** \'dən-dər-ˌhed\ *n* **:** DUNCE, BLOCKHEAD

**dune** \'d(y)ün\ *n* **:** a hill or ridge of sand piled up by the wind

**dune buggy** *n* **:** BEACH BUGGY

**¹dung** \'dəŋ\ *n* **:** MANURE

**²dung** *vb* **:** to dress (land) with dung

**dun·ga·ree** \ˌdəŋ-gə-'rē\ *n* **1 :** a heavy coarse cotton twill; *esp* **:** blue denim **2** *pl* **:** trousers or work clothes made of dungaree

**dun·geon** \'dən-jən\ *n* [ME *donjon*, fr. MF, fr. (assumed) ML *dominion-*, *dominio*, fr. L *dominus* lord] **:** a close dark prison commonly underground

**dung·hill** \'dəŋ-ˌhil\ *n* **:** a manure pile

**dunk** \'dəŋk\ *vb* **1 :** to dip (as bread) into liquid (as coffee) while eating **2 :** to dip or submerge temporarily in liquid **3 :** to submerge oneself in water

**duo** \'d(y)ü-(ˌ)ō\ *n, pl* **du·os 1 :** DUET **2 :** PAIR

**duo·dec·i·mal** \ˌd(y)ü-ə-'des-ə-məl\ *adj* **:** of, relating to, or proceeding by twelve or the scale of twelves

**du·o·de·num** \ˌd(y)ü-ə-'dē-nəm, d(y)ü-'äd-ᵊn-əm\ *n, pl* **-de·na** \-'dē-nə, ᵊn-ə\ *or* **-denums :** the part of the small intestine immediately below the stomach — **du·o·de·nal** \-'dēn-ᵊl, -ᵊn-əl\ *adj*

**dup** *abbr* **1** duplex **2** duplicate

**¹dupe** \'d(y)üp\ *n* **:** one who is easily deceived or cheated **:** FOOL

**²dupe** *vb* **duped; dup·ing :** to make a dupe of **:** DECEIVE, FOOL

**du·ple** \'d(y)ü-pəl\ *adj* **:** having two beats or a multiple of two beats to the measure (~ time)

**¹du·plex** \'d(y)ü-ˌpleks\ *adj* **:** DOUBLE

²**duplex** n : something duplex; esp : a 2-family house

¹**du·pli·cate** \'d(y)ü-pli-kət\ adj **1** : consisting of or existing in two corresponding or identical parts or examples **2** : being the same as another

²**duplicate** n : a thing that exactly resembles another in appearance, pattern, or content ⟨ COPY

³**du·pli·cate** \'d(y)ü-pli-ˌkāt\ vb -cated; -cat·ing **1** : to make double or twofold **2** : to make an exact copy of — **du·pli·ca·tion** \ˌd(y)ü-pli-'kā-shən\ n

**du·pli·ca·tor** \'d(y)ü-pli-ˌkāt-ər\ n : a machine for making copies of typed, drawn, or printed matter

**du·plic·i·ty** \d(y)ü-'plis-ət-ē\ n, pl -ties : deception by pretending to feel and act one way while acting another

**du·ra·ble** \'d(y)ùr-ə-bəl\ adj : able to exist for a long time without significant deterioration ⟨~ clothing⟩ — **du·ra·bil·i·ty** \ˌd(y)ùr-ə-'bil-ət-ē\ n

**durable press** n : the process of treating fabrics with chemicals (as resin) and heat for setting the shape and for aiding wrinkle resistance

**du·rance** \'d(y)ùr-əns\ n : IMPRISONMENT

**du·ra·tion** \d(y)ù-'rā-shən\ n **1** : continuance in time **2** : the time during which something exists or lasts

**du·ress** \d(y)ù-'res\ n **1** : forcible restraint or restriction **2** : compulsion by threat ⟨confession made under ~⟩

**dur·ing** \ˌd(y)ùr-iŋ\ prep **1** : throughout the course of ⟨there was rationing ~ the war⟩ **2** : at some point in the course of ⟨broke in ~ the night⟩

**dusk** \'dəsk\ n **1** : the darker part of twilight esp. at night **2** : GLOOM

**dusky** \'dəs-kē\ adj **dusk·i·er; -est** **1** : somewhat dark in color; esp : having dark skin **2** : SHADOWY — **dusk·i·ness** n

¹**dust** \'dəst\ n **1** : powdery particles (as of earth) **2** : the earthy remains of bodies once alive; esp : the human corpse **3** : something worthless **4** : a state of humiliation **5** : the surface of the ground — **dust·less** adj — **dusty** adj

²**dust** vb **1** : to make free of dust : remove dust **2** : to sprinkle with fine particles **3** : to sprinkle in the form of dust

**dust bowl** n : a region suffering from long droughts and dust storms

**dust devil** n : a small whirlwind containing sand or dust

**dust·er** \'dəs-tər\ n **1** : one that removes dust **2** : a lightweight garment to protect clothing from dust **3** : a dress-length housecoat **4** : one that scatters fine particles

**dust·pan** \'dəst-ˌpan\ n : a shovel-shaped pan for sweepings

**dust storm** n **1** : a dust-laden whirlwind moving across an arid region **2** : strong winds bearing clouds of dust

**dutch** \'dəch\ adv, often cap : with each person paying his own way ⟨go ~⟩

**Dutch** \'dəch\ n **1** **Dutch** pl : the people of the Netherlands **2** : the language of the Netherlands — **Dutch** adj — **Dutch·man** \-mən\ n

**Dutch elm disease** n : a fungous disease of elms characterized by yellowing of the foliage, defoliation, and death

**Dutch treat** n : an entertainment (as a meal) for which each person pays his own way

**du·te·ous** \'d(y)üt-ē-əs\ adj : DUTIFUL, OBEDIENT

**du·ti·able** \'d(y)üt-ē-ə-bəl\ adj : subject to a duty ⟨~ imports⟩

**du·ti·ful** \'d(y)üt-i-fəl\ adj **1** : filled with or motivated by a sense of duty ⟨a ~ son⟩ **2** : proceeding from or expressive of a sense of duty ⟨~ affection⟩ — **du·ti·ful·ly** \-f(ə-)lē\ adv — **du·ti·ful·ness** n

**du·ty** \'d(y)üt-ē\ n, pl **duties** **1** : conduct due to parents or superiors : RESPECT **2** : the action required by one's occupation or position **3** : assigned service or business; esp : active military service **4** : a moral or legal obligation **5** : TAX **6** : the service required (as of a machine) : USE ⟨a heavy-duty tire⟩

**DV** abbr **1** [L Deovo lente] God willing **2** Douay Version

**DVM** abbr doctor of veterinary medicine

¹**dwarf** \'dwórf\ n, pl **dwarfs** \'dwó(ə)rfs\ or **dwarves** \'dwórvz\ : a person, animal, or plant much below normal size — **dwarf·ish** adj

²**dwarf** vb **1** : to restrict the growth or development of : STUNT **2** : to cause to appear smaller

**dwell** \'dwel\ vb **dwelt** \'dwelt\ or **dwelled** \'dweld, 'dwelt\; **dwell·ing** [ME dwellen, fr. OE dwellan to go astray, hinder] **1** : ABIDE, REMAIN **2** : RESIDE, EXIST **3** : to keep the attention directed **4** : to write or speak at length or insistently — **dwell·er** n

**dwell·ing** \'dwel-iŋ\ n : RESIDENCE

**dwin·dle** \'dwin-d°l\ vb **dwin·dled; dwin·dling** \'dwin-d(ə-)liŋ\ : to make or become steadily less : DIMINISH

**dwt** abbr pennyweight

**DX** \(')dē-'eks\ n : DISTANCE — used of long-distance radio transmission

**dyb·buk** \'dib-ək\ n, pl **dyb·bu·kim** \ˌdib-ù-'kēm\ also **dybbuks** : a wandering soul believed in Jewish folklore to enter and possess a person

¹**dye** \'dī\ n **1** : color produced by dyeing **2** : material used for coloring or staining

²**dye** vb **dyed; dye·ing** **1** : to impart a new color to esp. by impregnating with a dye **2** : to take up or impart color in dyeing

**dye·stuff** \'dī-ˌstəf\ n : DYE 2

**dying** pres part of DIE

**dyke** var of DIKE

**dy·nam·ic** \dī-'nam-ik\ adj : of or relating to physical force producing motion : ENERGETIC, FORCEFUL

¹**dy·na·mite** \'dī-nə-ˌmīt\ n : an explosive made of nitroglycerin absorbed in a porous material; also : a blasting explosive

229

**²dy·na·mite** *vb* **-mit·ed; -mit·ing 1 :** to blow up with dynamite **2 :** to cause the complete failure or destruction of

**dy·na·mo** \'dī-nə-,mō\ *n, pl* **-mos :** an electrical generator

**dy·na·mom·e·ter** \,dī-nə-'mäm-ət-ər\ *n* **:** an instrument for measuring mechanical power

**dy·nas·ty** \'dī-nəs-tē, -,nas-\ *n, pl* **-ties 1 :** a succession of rulers of the same line of descent **2 :** a powerful group or family that maintains its position for a considerable time — **dy·nas·tic** \dī-'nas-tik\ *adj*

**dys·en·tery** \'dis-ᵊn-,ter-ē\ *n, pl* **-ter-**

**ies :** a disorder marked by diarrhea with blood and mucus in the feces

**dys·lex·ia** \dis-'lek-sē-ə\ *n* **:** a disturbance of the ability to read — **dys·lex·ic** \-sik\ *adj*

**dys·pep·sia** \dis-'pep-shə, -sē-ə\ *n* **:** INDIGESTION — **dys·pep·tic** \-'pep-tik\ *adj or n*

**dys·pro·si·um** \dis-'prō-zē-əm\ *n* **:** a metallic chemical element that forms highly magnetic compounds

**dys·tro·phy** \'dis-trə-fē\ *n, pl* **-phies :** any of several disorders involving nervous and muscular tissue

**dz** *abbr* dozen

---

**¹e** \'ē\ *n, pl* **e's** *or* **es** \'ēz\ *often cap* **1 :** the 5th letter of the English alphabet **2 :** the base of the system of natural logarithms having the approximate value 2.71828 **3 :** a grade rating a student's work as failing

**²e** *abbr, often cap* **1** east; eastern **2** error **3** excellent

**E** *symbol* einsteinium

**ea** *abbr* each

**¹each** \'ēch\ *adj* **:** being one of the class named ⟨~ man⟩

**²each** *pron* **:** each one **:** every individual one

**³each** *adv* **:** APIECE ⟨cost five cents ~⟩

**each other** *pron* **:** each of two or more in reciprocal action or reaction ⟨looked at *each other*⟩

**ea·ger** \'ē-gər\ *adj* **:** marked by urgent or enthusiastic desire or interest ⟨~ to learn⟩ *syn* avid, anxious — **ea·ger·ly** *adv* — **ea·ger·ness** *n*

**ea·gle** \'ē-gəl\ *n* **1 :** a large bird of prey related to the hawks **2 :** a U.S. 10-dollar gold coin **3 :** a score of two under par on a hole in golf

**ea·glet** \'ē-glət\ *n* **:** a young eagle

**-ean** — see -AN

**E and OE** *abbr* errors and omissions excepted

**¹ear** \'iər\ *n* **1 :** the organ of hearing; *also* **:** the outer part of this in a vertebrate **2 :** something resembling a mammal's ear in shape or position **3 :** sympathetic attention

**²ear** *n* **:** the fruiting spike of a cereal (as wheat)

**ear·ache** \-,āk\ *n* **:** an ache or pain in the ear

**ear·drum** \-,drəm\ *n* **:** a thin membrane that receives and transmits sound waves in the ear

**eared** \'iərd\ *adj* **:** having ears — used esp. in combination ⟨a big-*eared* man⟩

**earl** \'ərl\ *n* [ME *erl*, fr. OE *eorl* warrior, nobleman; akin to ON *jarl* warrior, nobleman] **:** a member of the British peerage ranking below a marquess and above a viscount — **earl·dom** \-dəm\ *n*

**ear·lobe** \'iər-,lōb\ *n* **:** the pendent part of the ear

**¹ear·ly** \'ər-lē\ *adv* **ear·li·er; -est :** at an early time (as in a period or series)

**²early** *adj* **ear·li·er; -est 1 :** of, relat-

ing to, or occurring near the beginning (as of a period, series, or development) **2 :** ANCIENT, PRIMITIVE **3 :** occurring before the usual time ⟨an ~ breakfast⟩; *also* **:** occurring in the near future

**ear·mark** \'iər-,märk\ *n* **:** a mark of identification orig. on the ear of an animal — **earmark** *vb*

**ear·muff** \-,məf\ *n* **:** one of a pair of ear coverings connected by a flexible band and worn as protection against cold

**earn** \'ərn\ *vb* **1 :** to receive as a return for service **2 :** DESERVE, MERIT *syn* gain, secure, get, obtain

**¹ear·nest** \'ər-nəst\ *n* **:** an intensely serious state of mind (spoken in ~)

**²earnest** *adj* **1 :** seriously intent and sober ⟨an ~ face⟩ ⟨an ~ attempt⟩ **2 :** GRAVE, IMPORTANT *syn* solemn, sedate, staid — **ear·nest·ly** *adv* — **ear·nest·ness** \-nəs(t)-nəs\ *n*

**³earnest** *n* **1 :** something of value given by a buyer to a seller to bind a bargain **2 :** PLEDGE

**earn·ings** \'ər-niŋz\ *n pl* **:** something earned **:** WAGES, PROFIT

**ear·phone** \'iər-,fōn\ *n* **:** a device that converts electrical energy into sound and is worn over or in the ear

**ear·plug** \-,pləg\ *n* **:** a protective or insulating device for insertion into the outer opening of the ear

**ear·ring** \-,riŋ\ *n* **:** an ornament for the earlobe

**ear·shot** \-,shät\ *n* **:** range of hearing

**ear·split·ting** \-,split-iŋ\ *adj* **:** intolerably loud or shrill

**earth** \'ərth\ *n* **1 :** SOIL, DIRT **2 :** LAND, GROUND **3 :** the planet inhabited by man **:** WORLD

**earth·en** \'ər-thən\ *adj* **:** made of earth or baked clay

**earth·en·ware** \-,waər\ *n* **:** slightly porous opaque pottery fired at low heat of the earth

**earth·ling** \'ərth-liŋ\ *n* **:** an inhabitant of the earth

**earth·ly** \'ərth-lē\ *adj* **:** typical of or belonging to this earth esp. as distinguished from heaven ⟨~ affairs⟩ — **earth·li·ness** \-lē-nəs\ *n*

**earth·quake** \-,kwāk\ *n* **:** a shaking or trembling of a portion of the earth

**earth science** *n* **:** any of the sciences (as geology or meteorology) that deal with the earth or one of its parts

**earth·shak·ing** \'ərth-,shā-kiŋ\ *adj*

: of fundamental importance

**earth·ward** \-word\ *or* **earth·wards** \-wordz\ *adv* : toward the earth

**earth·work** \'orth-,work\ *n* : an embankment or fortification of earth

**earth·worm** \-,worm\ *n* : a long segmented worm found in damp soil

**earthy** \'or-thē\ *adj* **earth·i·er; -est** **1** : consisting of or resembling soil **2** : PRACTICAL **3** : COARSE, GROSS — **earth·i·ness** \'or-thē-nəs\ *n*

**ear·wax** \'ier-,waks\ *n* : the yellow waxy secretion from the ear

**ear·wig** \-,wig\ *n* : any of an order of insects with slender many-jointed antennae and a pair of appendages resembling forceps at the end of the body

**¹ease** \'ēz\ *n* **1** : comfort of body or mind **2** : naturalness of manner **3** : freedom from difficulty or effort **syn** relaxation, rest, repose, comfort, leisure

**²ease** *vb* **eased; eas·ing 1** : to relieve from something (as pain or worry) that distresses **2** : to lessen the pressure or tension of **3** : to make or become less difficult ⟨~ credit⟩

**ea·sel** \'ē-zəl\ *n* [D *ezel* ass] : a frame to hold a painter's canvas or a picture

**¹east** \'ēst\ *adv* : to or toward the east

**²east** *adj* **1** : situated toward or at the east **2** : coming from the east

**³east** *n* **1** : the general direction of sunrise **2** : the compass point directly opposite to west **3** *cap* : regions or countries east of a specified or implied point — **east·er·ly** \'ē-stər-lē\ *adv or adj* — **east·ward** *adv or adj* — **east·wards** *adv*

**Eas·ter** \'ē-stər\ *n* : a church feast observed on a Sunday in March or April in commemoration of Christ's resurrection

**east·ern** \'ē-stərn\ *adj* **1** *often cap* : of, relating to, or characteristic of a region conventionally designated East **2** : lying toward or coming from the east **3** *cap* : of, relating to, or being the Christian churches originating in the church of the Eastern Roman Empire — **East·ern·er** *n*

**easy** \'ē-zē\ *adj* **eas·i·er; -est 1** : marked by ease ⟨an ~ life⟩; *esp* : not causing distress or difficulty ⟨~ tasks⟩ **2** : MILD, LENIENT ⟨be ~ on him⟩ **3** : TRANQUIL ⟨an ~ calm⟩ **4** : not less than ⟨weighs an ~ 200 pounds⟩ **5** : GRADUAL ⟨an ~ slope⟩ **syn** comfortable, restful, facile, simple, effortless — **eas·i·ly** \'ēz-(ə-)lē\ *adv* — **eas·i·ness** \-nəs\ *n*

**easy·go·ing** \,ē-zē-'gō-iŋ\ *adj* : taking life easily

**eat** \'ēt\ *vb* **ate** \'āt\; **eat·en** \'ēt-ⁿn\; **eat·ing 1** : to take in as food : take food **2** : to use up : DEVOUR **3** : CORRODE — **eat·able** *adj or n* — **eat·er** *n*

**eat·ery** \'ēt-ə-rē\ *n, pl* **-er·ies** : LUNCHEONETTE, RESTAURANT

**eaves** \'ēvz\ *n pl* : the overhanging lower edge of a roof

**eaves·drop** \'ēvz-,dräp\ *vb* : to listen secretly — **eaves·drop·per** *n*

**¹ebb** \'eb\ *n* **1** : the flowing back of water brought in by the tide **2** : a point or state of decline

**²ebb** *vb* **1** : to recede from the flood state **2** : DECLINE ⟨as his fortunes ~ed⟩

**eb·o·nite** \'eb-ə-,nīt\ *n* : hard rubber esp. when black or when lacking filler

**¹eb·o·ny** \'eb-ə-nē\ *n, pl* **-nies** : a hard heavy wood of Old World tropical trees (**ebony trees**) related to the persimmon

**²ebony** *adj* **1** : made of or resembling ebony **2** : BLACK, DARK

**ebul·lient** \i-'búl-yənt, -'bəl-\ *adj* **1** : BOILING, AGITATED **2** : EXUBERANT — **ebul·lience** \-yəns\ *n*

**eb·ul·li·tion** \,eb-ə-'lish-ən\ *n* **1** : boiling or bubbling up **2** : a seething excitement or outburst

**ec·cen·tric** \ik-'sen-trik\ *adj* **1** : deviating from a usual or accepted pattern **2** : deviating from a circular path ⟨~ orbits⟩ **3** : set with axis or support off center ⟨an ~ cam⟩; *also* : being off center **syn** erratic, queer, singular, curious — **eccentric** *n* — **ec·cen·tri·cal·ly** \-tri-k(ə-)lē\ *adv* — **ec·cen·tric·i·ty** \,ek-,sen-'tris-ət-ē\ *n*

**eccl** *abbr* ecclesiastic; ecclesiastical

**Eccles** *abbr* Ecclesiastes

**ec·cle·si·as·tic** \ik-,lē-zē-'as-tik\ *n* : CLERGYMAN

**ec·cle·si·as·ti·cal** \ti-kəl\ *adj* : of or relating to a church esp. as an institution ⟨~ art⟩ — **ecclesiastic** *adj*

**Ecclus** *abbr* Ecclesiasticus

**ECG** *abbr* electrocardiogram

**ech·e·lon** \'esh-ə-,län\ *n* [F *échelon*, lit., rung of a ladder] **1** : a steplike arrangement (as of troops or airplanes) **2** : a level (as of authority or responsibility) within a hierarchy

**echo** \'ek-ō\ *n, pl* **ech·oes** : repetition of a sound caused by a reflection of the sound waves; *also* : the reflection of a radar signal by an object — **echo** *vb*

**echo·lo·ca·tion** \,ek-o-lō-'kā-shən\ *n* : a process for locating distant or invisible objects by means of sound waves reflected back to the sender (as a bat or submarine) by the objects

**éclair** \ā-'klaər\ *n* [F, lit., lightning] : an oblong shell of light pastry with whipped cream or custard filling

**éclat** \ā-'klä\ *n* **1** : a dazzling effect or success **2** : ACCLAIM

**eclec·tic** \e-'klek-tik, i-\ *adj* : selecting or made up of what seems best of varied sources — **eclectic** *n*

**¹eclipse** \i-'klips\ *n* **1** : the total or partial obscuring of one heavenly body by another; *also* : a passing into the shadow of a heavenly body **2** : a failing into obscurity, decline, or disgrace

**²eclipse** *vb* **eclipsed; eclips·ing** : to cause an eclipse of

**eclip·tic** \i-'klip-tik\ *n* : the great circle of the celestial sphere that is the apparent path of the sun

**ec·logue** \'ek-,lóg, -,läg\ *n* : a pastoral poem

**ECM** *abbr* European Common Market

**ecol** *abbr* ecological; ecology

**ecol·o·gy** \i-'käl-ə-jē, e-\ *n, pl* **-gies** [G *ökologie*, fr. Gk *oikos* house] **1** : a branch of science concerned with the interaction of organisms and their environment **2 :** the pattern of relations between organisms and their environment — **eco·log·i·cal** \ˌē-kə-ˈläj-i-kəl, ˌek-ə-\ *also* **eco·log·ic** \-ik\ *adj* — **eco·log·i·cal·ly** \-i-k(ə-)lē\ *adv* — **ecol·o·gist** \i-ˈkäl-ə-jəst, e-\ *n*

**econ** *abbr* economics; economist; economy

**eco·nom·ic** \ˌek-ə-ˈnäm-ik, ˌē-kə-\ *adj* **:** of or relating to the satisfaction of man's material needs

**eco·nom·i·cal** \-ˈnäm-i-kəl\ *adj* **1 :** THRIFTY **2 :** operating with little waste or at a saving **syn** frugal, sparing — **eco·nom·i·cal·ly** \-k(ə-)lē\ *adv*

**eco·nom·ics** \ˌek-ə-ˈnäm-iks, ˌē-kə-\ *n* **:** a branch of knowledge dealing with the production, distribution, and consumption of goods and services — **econ·o·mist** \i-ˈkän-ə-məst\ *n*

**econ·o·mize** \i-ˈkän-ə-ˌmīz\ *vb* **-mized; -miz·ing :** to practice economy **:** be frugal

**econ·o·my** \i-ˈkän-ə-mē\ *n, pl* **-mies** [MF *yconomie,* fr. ML *oeconomia,* fr. Gk *oikonomia,* fr. *oikonomos* household manager, fr. *oikos* house + *nemein* to manage] **1 :** thrifty management or use of resources; *also* **:** an instance of this **2 :** manner of arrangement or functioning **:** ORGANIZATION ⟨the bodily ∼⟩ **3 :** an economic system ⟨a money ∼⟩ — **economy** *adj* **:** ECONOMICAL ⟨∼ cars⟩

**eco·sys·tem** \ˈē-kō-ˌsis-təm, ˈek-ō-\ *n* **:** the complex of a community and its environment functioning as a unit in nature

**ecru** \ˈek-rü, ˈā-krü\ *n* **:** BEIGE

**ec·sta·sy** \ˈek-stə-sē\ *n, pl* **-sies :** extreme and usu. rapturous emotional excitement — **ec·stat·ic** \ek-ˈstat-ik, ik-ˈstat-\ *adj* — **ec·stat·i·cal·ly** \-i-k(ə-)lē\ *adv*

**Ecua** *abbr* Ecuador

**ec·u·men·i·cal** \ˌek-yə-ˈmen-i-kəl\ *adj* **:** general in extent or influence; *esp* **:** promoting or tending toward worldwide Christian unity — **ec·u·men·i·cal·ly** \-k(ə-)lē\ *adv* — **ec·u·me·nic·i·ty** \-mə-ˈnis-ət-ē, -me-\ *n*

**ec·ze·ma** \ig-ˈzē-mə, ˈeg-zə-mə, ˈek-sə-\ *n* **:** an itching skin inflammation with crusted lesions — **ec·zem·a·tous** \ig-ˈzem-ət-əs\ *adj*

**ed** *abbr* **1** edited; ₂edition; editor **2** education

**-ed** \d *after a vowel or* b, g, j, l, m, n, ŋ, r, ₁th, v, z, zh; əd, id *after* d, t; t *after other sounds*\ *vb suffix or adj suffix* **1** — used to form the past participle of regular weak verbs ⟨end*ed*⟩ ⟨fad*ed*⟩ ⟨tri*ed*⟩ ⟨patt*ed*⟩ **2** — used to form adjectives of identical meaning from Latin-derived adjectives ending in *-ate* ⟨pinnat*ed*⟩ **3 :** having **:** characterized by ⟨cultur*ed*⟩ ⟨two-legg*ed*⟩; *also* **:** having the characteristics of ⟨bigot*ed*⟩

**-ed** *vb suffix* — used to form the past tense of regular weak verbs ⟨judg*ed*⟩ ⟨deni*ed*⟩ ⟨dropp*ed*⟩

**₁dam** \ˈēd-əm, ˈēˌdam\ *n* **:** a yellow Dutch pressed cheese made in balls

**d·dy** \ˈed-ē\ *n, pl* **eddies :** WHIRL-

POOL; *also* **:** a contrary or circular current — **eddy** *vb*

**edel·weiss** \ˈād-ᵊl-ˌwīs, -ˌvīs\ *n* **:** a small perennial woolly herb that is related to the thistles and grows high in the Alps

**ede·ma** \i-ˈdē-mə\ *n* **:** abnormal accumulation of watery fluid in connective tissue or in a serous cavity; *also* **:** a condition marked by such accumulation — **edem·a·tous** \-ˈdem-ət-əs\ *adj*

**Eden** \ˈēd-ᵊn\ *n* **:** PARADISE 2

**¹edge** \ˈej\ *n* **1 :** the cutting side of a blade **2 :** power to cut or penetrate **:** SHARPNESS **3 :** the line where something begins or ends; *also* **:** the area adjoining such an edge

**²edge** *vb* **edged; edg·ing 1 :** to give or form an edge **2 :** to move or force gradually ⟨∼ into a crowd⟩ — **edg·er** *n*

**edge·ways** \ˈej-ˌwāz\ *adv* **:** SIDEWAYS

**edg·ing** \ˈej-iŋ\ *n* **:** something that forms an edge or border ⟨a lace ∼⟩

**edgy** \ˈej-ē\ *adj* **edg·i·er; -est 1** ₂SHARP ⟨an ∼ tone⟩ **2 :** TENSE, NERVOUS — **edg·i·ness** \ˈej-ē-nəs\ *n*

**ed·i·ble** \ˈed-ə-bəl\ *adj* **:** fit or safe to be eaten — **ed·i·bil·i·ty** \ˌed-ə-ˈbil-ət-ē\ *n* — **edible** *n*

**edict** \ˈē-ˌdikt\ *n* **:** DECREE

**ed·i·fi·ca·tion** \ˌed-ə-fə-ˈkā-shən\ *n* **:** instruction and improvement esp. in morality — **ed·i·fy** \ˈed-ə-ˌfī\ *vb*

**ed·i·fice** \ˈed-ə-fəs\ *n* **:** a usu. large building

**ed·it** \ˈed-ət\ *vb* **1 :** to revise and prepare for publication **2 :** to direct the publication and policies of ⟨as a newspaper⟩ — **ed·i·tor** \ˈed-ət-ər\ *n* — **ed·i·tor·ship** *n*

**edi·tion** \i-ˈdish-ən\ *n* **1 :** the form in which a text is published **2 :** the total number of copies ⟨as of a book⟩ published at one time **3 :** VERSION

**¹ed·i·to·ri·al** \ˌed-ə-ˈtōr-ē-əl\ *adj* **1 :** of, relating to, or functioning as an editor **2 :** being an editorial; *also* **:** expressing opinion — **ed·i·to·ri·al·ly** \-ē\ *adv*

**²editorial** *n* **:** an article ⟨as in a newspaper⟩ expressing the views of an editor or publisher

**ed·i·to·ri·al·ize** \ˌed-ə-ˈtōr-ē-ə-ˌlīz\ *vb* **-ized; -iz·ing 1 :** to express an opinion in an editorial **2 :** to introduce opinions into factual reporting — **ed·i·to·ri·al·iza·tion** \-ˌtōr-ē-ə-lə-ˈzā-shən\ *n* — **ed·i·to·ri·al·iz·er** *n*

**EDP** *abbr* electronic data processing

**EDT** *abbr* Eastern daylight time

**educ** *abbr* education; educational

**ed·u·ca·ble** \ˈej-ə-kə-bəl\ *adj* **:** capable of being educated

**ed·u·cate** \ˈej-ə-ˌkāt\ *vb* **-cat·ed; -cat·ing 1 :** to provide with schooling **2 :** to develop and cultivate mentally and morally **syn** train, discipline, school, instruct — **ed·u·ca·tor** \-ˌkāt-ər\ *n*

**ed·u·ca·tion** \ˌej-ə-ˈkā-shən\ *n* **1 :** the action or process of educating or being educated **2 :** a field of knowledge dealing with technical aspects of teaching — **ed·u·ca·tion·al** \-sh(ə-)nəl\ *adj*

**educational television** *n* **1 :** PUBLIC TELEVISION **2 :** television that provides instruction esp. for students and sometimes by closed circuit

**educe** \i-'d(y)üs\ *vb* **educed; educing 1 :** ELICIT, EVOKE **2 :** to arrive at usu. through reasoning **syn** extract

**EE** *abbr* electrical engineer

**EEG** *abbr* electroencephalogram

**eel** \'ēl\ *n* **:** a snakelike fish with a smooth slimy skin

**ee·rie** *also* **ee·ry** \'i(ə)r-ē\ *adj* **ee·ri·er; -est** [ME *eri*, fr. OE *earg* cowardly, wretched] **:** WEIRD, UNCANNY — **ee·ri·ly** \'ir-ə-lē\ *adv*

**eff** *abbr* efficiency

**ef·face** \i-'fās, e-\ *vb* **ef·faced; ef·fac·ing :** to obliterate or obscure by or as if by rubbing out **syn** erase, delete — **ef·face·a·ble** *adj* — **ef·face·ment** *n*

**¹ef·fect** \i-'fekt\ *n* **1 :** RESULT **2 :** MEANING, INTENT **3 :** APPEARANCE **4 :** FULFILLMENT **5 :** REALITY **6 :** INFLUENCE **7** *pl* **:** GOODS, POSSESSIONS **8 :** the quality or state of being operative **:** OPERATION **syn** consequence, outcome, upshot

**²effect** *vb* **1 :** ACCOMPLISH ⟨~ repairs⟩ **2 :** PRODUCE ⟨~ changes⟩

**ef·fec·tive** \i-'fek-tiv\ *adj* **1 :** producing a decided, decisive, or desired effect **2 :** IMPRESSIVE, STRIKING **3 :** ready for service or action **4 :** being in effect — **ef·fec·tive·ly** *adv* — **ef·fec·tive·ness** *n*

**ef·fec·tu·al** \i-'fek-chə(-wə)l\ *adj* **:** producing an intended effect **:** ADEQUATE — **ef·fec·tu·al·ly** \-ē\ *adv*

**ef·fec·tu·ate** \i-'fek-chə-,wāt\ *vb* **-at·ed; -at·ing :** to bring about **:** EFFECT

**ef·fem·i·nate** \ə-'fem-ə-nət\ *adj* **:** marked by qualities more typical of and suitable to women than men **:** UNMANLY — **ef·fem·i·na·cy** \-nə-sē\ *n*

**ef·fen·di** \e-'fen-dē\ *n* [Turk *efendi* master, fr. NGk *aphentēs*, alter. of Gk *authentēs*] **:** a man of property, authority, or education in an eastern Mediterranean country

**ef·fer·ent** \'ef-ə-rənt\ *adj* **:** bearing or conducting outward from a more central part ⟨~ nerves⟩ — **efferent** *n*

**ef·fer·vesce** \,ef-ər-'ves\ *vb* **-vesced; -vesc·ing :** to bubble and hiss as gas escapes; *also* **:** to be exhilarated — **ef·fer·ves·cence** \-'ves-ⁿns\ *n* — **ef·fer·ves·cent** \-ⁿnt\ *adj* — **ef·fer·ves·cent·ly** *adv*

**ef·fete** \e-'fēt\ *adj* **:** worn out **:** EXHAUSTED; *also* **:** DECADENT

**ef·fi·ca·cious** \,ef-ə-'kā-shəs\ *adj* **:** producing an intended effect ⟨~ remedies⟩ **syn** effectual, effective — **ef·fi·ca·cy** \'ef-i-kə-sē\ *n*

**ef·fi·cient** \i-'fish-ənt\ *adj* **:** productive of desired effects usu. without loss or waste **:** COMPETENT — **ef·fi·cien·cy** \-ən-sē\ *n* — **ef·fi·cient·ly** *adv*

**ef·fi·gy** \'ef-ə-jē\ *n, pl* **-gies :** IMAGE; *esp* **:** a crude figure of a hated person

**ef·flo·resce** \,ef-lə-'res\ *vb* **-resced; -resc·ing :** to burst forth **:** BLOOM

**ef·flo·res·cence** \-'res-ⁿns\ *n* **1 :** the period or state of flowering **2 :** the action or process of developing **3 :** fullness of manifestation **:** CULMINATION — **ef·flo·res·cent** \-ⁿnt\ *adj*

**ef·flu·ence** \'ef-,lü-əns\ *n* **1 :** something that flows out **2 :** an action or process of flowing out — **ef·flu·ent** \-ənt\ *adj or n*

**ef·flu·vi·um** \e-'flü-vē-əm\ *n, pl* **-via** \-vē-ə\ *or* **-vi·ums 1 :** a usu. unpleasant emanation **2 :** a by-product usu. in the form of waste

**ef·fort** \'ef-ərt\ *n* **1 :** EXERTION, ENDEAVOR; *also* **:** a product of effort **2 :** active or applied force — **ef·fort·less** *adj* — **ef·fort·less·ly** *adv*

**ef·fron·tery** \i-'frənt-ə-rē\ *n, pl* **-ter·ies :** shameless boldness **:** IMPUDENCE **syn** temerity, audacity

**ef·ful·gence** \i-'fül-jəns, -'fəl-\ *n* **:** radiant splendor **:** BRILLIANCE — **ef·ful·gent** \-jənt\ *adj*

**ef·fu·sion** \i-'fyü-zhən, e-\ *n* **:** a gushing forth; *also* **:** unrestrained utterance — **ef·fuse** \i-'fyüz, e-\ *vb* — **ef·fu·sive** \i-'fyü-siv, e-\ *adj*

**eft** \'eft\ *n* **:** NEWT

**e.g.** \f(ə-)rig-'zam-pəl, (')ē-'jē\ *abbr* [L *exempli gratia*] for example

**Eg** *abbr* Egypt; Egyptian

**egal·i·tar·i·an·ism** \i-,gal-ə-'ter-ē-ə-,niz-əm\ *n* **:** a belief in human equality esp. in social, political, and economic affairs — **egal·i·tar·i·an** *adj or n*

**¹egg** \'eg, 'āg\ *vb* [ME *eggen*, fr. ON *eggja*; akin to OE *ecg* edge] **:** to urge to action

**²egg** *n* [ME *egge*, fr. ON *egg*; akin to OE *ǣg* egg, L *ovum*, Gk *ōion*] **1 :** a rounded usu. hard-shelled reproductive body esp. of birds and reptiles from which the young hatches; *also* **:** the egg of domestic poultry as an article of food ⟨allergic to ~s⟩ **2 :** EGG CELL

**egg·beat·er** \'eg-,bēt-ər, 'āg-\ *n* **:** a rotary beater operated by hand for beating eggs or liquids (as cream)

**egg cell** *n* **:** a female germ cell

**egg·head** \-,hed\ *n* **:** INTELLECTUAL, HIGHBROW

**egg·nog** \-,näg\ *n* **:** a drink consisting of eggs beaten up with sugar, milk or cream, and often alcoholic liquor

**egg·plant** \-,plant\ *n* **:** the edible usu. large and purplish fruit of a plant related to the potato; *also* **:** the plant

**egg roll** *n* **:** a thin egg-dough casing filled with minced vegetables and often bits of meat and usu. fried in deep fat

**egg·shell** \'eg-,shel\ *n* **:** the hard exterior covering of an egg

**egis** \'ē-jəs\ *var of* AEGIS

**eg·lan·tine** \'eg-lən-,tīn, -,tēn\ *n* **:** SWEETBRIER

**ego** \'ē-gō\ *n, pl* **egos** [L, I] **1 :** the self as distinguished from others **2 :** the one of the three divisions of the psyche in psychoanalytic theory that serves as the organized conscious mediator between the person and reality

**ego·cen·tric** \,ē-gō-'sen-trik\ *adj* **:** concerned or overly concerned with the self; *esp* **:** SELF-CENTERED

**ego ideal** *n* **:** the positive standards

ideals, and ambitions that according to psychoanalytic theory are assimilated from the superego

**ego·ism** \'ē-gə-,wiz-əm\ n 1 : a doctrine holding self-interest to be the motive or the valid end of action 2 : EGOTISM — **ego·ist** \-wəst\ n — **ego·is·tic** \,ē-gə-'wis-tik\ also **ego·is·ti·cal** \-ti-kəl\ adj — **ego·is·ti·cal·ly** \-ē\ adv

**ego·tism** \'ē-gə-,tiz-əm\ n : too frequent reference to oneself; also : an exaggerated sense of self-importance : CONCEIT — **ego·tist** \-təst\ n — **ego·tis·tic** \,ē-gə-'tis-tik\ or **ego·tis·ti·cal** \-ti-kəl\ adj — **ego·tis·ti·cal·ly** \-ē\ adv

**ego trip** n : an act that enhances and satisfies one's ego

**egre·gious** \i-'grē-jəs\ adj [L egregius outstanding from the herd, fr. ex, e out of + greg-, grex flock, herd] : notably bad : FLAGRANT — **egre·gious·ly** adv — **egre·gious·ness** n

**egress** \'ē-,gres\ n : a way out : EXIT

**egret** \'ē-grət, i-'gret, 'eg-rət\ n : any of various herons that bear long plumes during the breeding season

**Egyp·tian** \i-'jip-shən\ n 1 : a native or inhabitant of Egypt 2 : the language of the ancient Egyptians from earliest times to about the 3d century A.D.

**EHF** abbr extremely high frequency

**ei·der** \'ī-dər\ n : a northern sea duck that yields a soft down

**ei·der·down** \-,daùn\ n : the down of an eider

**ei·do·lon** \ī-'dō-lən\ n, pl **-lons** or **-la** \-lə\ 1 : an insubstantial image : PHANTOM 2 : IDEAL

**eight** \'āt\ n 1 : one more than seven 2 : the 8th in a set or series 3 : something having eight units; esp : an 8≠ cylinder engine or automobile — **eight** adj or pron — **eighth** \'āth\ adj or adv or n

**eight ball** n : a black pool ball numbered 8 — **behind the eight ball** : in a highly disadvantageous position or baffling situation

**eigh·teen** \'ā(t)-'tēn\ n : one more than 17 — see NUMBER table — **eigh·teen** adj or pron — **eigh·teenth** \-'tēnth\ adj or n

**eighty** \'āt-ē\ n, pl **eight·ies** : eight times 10 — **eight·i·eth** \'āt-ē-əth\ adj or n — **eighty** adj or pron

**ein·stei·ni·um** \īn-'stī-nē-əm\ n : an artificially produced radioactive element

**ei·stedd·fod** \ī-'steth-,vód\ n : a Welsh competitive festival of the arts esp. in singing

¹**ei·ther** \'ē-thər, 'ī-\ adj 1 : being the one and the other of two : BOTH ⟨trees on ~ side⟩ 2 : being the one or the other of two ⟨take ~ one of the two⟩

²**either** pron : one of two or more

³**either** conj — used as a function word before the first of two or more words or word groups of which the last is preceded by or to indicate that they represent alternatives ⟨a statement is ~ true or false⟩

**ejac·u·late** \i-'jak-yə-,lāt\ vb **-lat·ed; -lat·ing** 1 : to utter suddenly : EXCLAIM 2 : to eject a fluid (as semen) — **ejac·u·la·tion** \-,jak-yə-'lā-shən\ n — **ejac·u·la·to·ry** \-'jak-yə-lə-,tōr-ē\ adj

**eject** \i-'jekt\ vb : to drive or throw out or off syn expel, oust, evict — **ejec·tion** \-'jek-shən\ n

**ejection seat** n : an emergency escape seat for propelling an occupant out of an airplane

**eke** \'ēk\ vb **eked; ek·ing** : to gain, supplement, or extend usu. with effort — usu. used with out ⟨~ out a living⟩

**EKG** abbr [G elektrokardiogramm] electrocardiogram

**ekis·tics** \i-'kis-tiks\ n : a science dealing with human settlements and drawing on the research and experience of the architect, the engineer, the city planner, and the social scientist — **ekis·tic** \-tik\ adj

**el** abbr elevation

¹**elab·o·rate** \i-'lab-(ə-)rət\ adj 1 : planned or carried out with care and in detail 2 : being complex and usu. ornate — **elab·o·rate·ly** adv — **elab·o·rate·ness** n

²**elab·o·rate** \i-'lab-ə-,rāt\ vb **-rat·ed; -rat·ing** 1 : to work out in detail : develop fully 2 : to build up from simpler ingredients — **elab·o·ra·tion** \-,lab-ə-'rā-shən\ n

**élan** \ā-lä⁼\ n : ARDOR, SPIRIT

**eland** \'ē-lənd, -,land\ n : either of two large African antelopes with short spirally twisted horns

**elapse** \i-'laps\ vb **elapsed; elaps·ing** : to slip by : PASS

¹**elas·tic** \i-'las-tik\ adj 1 : SPRINGY 2 : FLEXIBLE, PLIABLE 3 : ADAPTABLE syn resilient, supple — **elas·tic·i·ty** \-,las-'tis-ət-ē, ,ē-,las-\ n

²**elastic** n 1 : elastic material 2 : a rubber band

**elas·to·mer** \i-'las-tə-mər\ n : any of various elastic substances resembling rubber — **elas·to·mer·ic** \-,las-tə-'mer-ik\ adj

**elate** \i-'lāt\ vb **elat·ed; elat·ing** : to fill with joy — **ela·tion** \-'lā-shən\ n

¹**el·bow** \'el-,bō\ n 1 : the joint of the arm; also : the outer curve of the bent arm 2 : a bend or joint resembling an elbow in shape

²**elbow** vb : to push or shove aside with the elbow; also : to make one's way by elbowing

**el·bow·room** \'el-,bō-,rüm, -,rùm\ n 1 : room for moving the elbows freely 2 : enough space for work or operation

¹**el·der** \'el-dər\ n : ELDERBERRY 2

²**elder** adj 1 : OLDER 2 : EARLIER, FORMER 3 : of higher ranking : SENIOR

³**elder** n 1 : an older individual : SENIOR 2 : one having authority by reason of age and experience 3 : a church officer

**el·der·ber·ry** \'el-də(r)-,ber-ē\ n 1 : the edible black or red fruit of a shrub or tree related to the honeysuckle and bearing flat clusters of small white or pink flowers 2 : a tree or shrub bearing elderberries

**el·der·ly** \'el-dər-lē\ *adj* **1** : rather old; *esp* : past middle age **2** : of, relating to, or characteristic of later life

**el·dest** \'el-dəst\ *adj* : OLDEST

**El Do·ra·do** \,el-də-'räd-ō, -'rād-\ *n* : a place of vast riches or abundance

¹**elect** \i-'lekt\ *adj* **1** : CHOSEN, SELECT **2** : elected but not yet installed in office ⟨the president-*elect*⟩

²**elect** *n, pl* **elect 1** : a selected person **2** *pl* : a select or exclusive group

³**elect** *vb* **1** : to select by vote (as for office or membership) **2** : CHOOSE, PICK **syn** designate, name

**elec·tion** \i-'lek-shən\ *n* **1** : an act or process of electing **2** : the fact of being elected

**elec·tion·eer** \i-,lek-shə-'niər\ *vb* : to work for the election of a candidate or party

¹**elec·tive** \i-'lek-tiv\ *adj* **1** : chosen or filled by election **2** : permitting a choice : OPTIONAL

²**elective** *n* : an elective course or subject of study

**elec·tor** \i-'lek-tər\ *n* **1** : one qualified to vote in an election **2** : one elected to an electoral college — **elec·tor·al** \i-'lek-t(ə-)rəl\ *adj*

**electoral college** *n* : a body of electors who elect the president and vice-president of the U.S.

**elec·tor·ate** \i-'lek-t(ə-)rət\ *n* : a body of persons entitled to vote

**elec·tric** \i-'lek-trik\ *adj* [NL *electricus* produced from amber by friction, electric, fr. ML, of amber, fr. L *electrum* amber, fr. Gk *ēlektron*] **1** : of, relating to, operated by, or produced by electricity **2** : ELECTRIFYING, THRILLING — **elec·tri·cal** \-tri-kəl\ *adj* — **elec·tri·cal·ly** \-k(ə-)lē\ *adv* — **elec·tri·cal·ness** \-kəl-nəs\ *n*

**electrical storm** *n* : THUNDERSTORM

**electric chair** *n* : a chair used in legal electrocution

**electric eye** *n* : PHOTOELECTRIC CELL

**elec·tri·cian** \i-,lek-'trish-ən\ *n* : one who designs, installs, operates, or repairs electrical equipment

**elec·tric·i·ty** \i-,lek-'tris-(ə-)tē\ *n, pl* **-ties** : a fundamental phenomenon of nature observable in the attractions and repulsions of bodies electrified by friction and in natural phenomena (as lightning) and utilized as a source of energy in the form of electric currents; *also* : such a current

**elec·tri·fy** \i-'lek-trə-,fī\ *vb* **-fied; -fy·ing 1** : to charge with electricity **2** : to equip for use of electric power **3** : THRILL — **elec·tri·fi·ca·tion** \-,lek-trə-fə-'kā-shən\ *n*

**elec·tro·car·dio·gram** \i-,lek-trō-'kärd-ē-ə-,gram\ *n* : the tracing made by an electrocardiograph

**elec·tro·car·dio·graph** \-,graf\ *n* : an instrument for recording the changes of electrical potential occurring during the heartbeat — **elec·tro·car·dio·graph·ic** \-,kärd-ē-ə-'graf-ik\ *adj* — **elec·tro·car·di·og·ra·phy** \-ē-'äg-rə-fē\ *n*

**elec·tro·chem·is·try** \-'kem-ə-strē\ *n* : a science that deals with the relation of electricity to chemical changes — **elec·tro·chem·i·cal** \-'kem-i-kəl\ *adj* — **elec·tro·chem·i·cal·ly** \-k(ə-)lē\ *adv*

**elec·tro·cute** \i-'lek-trə-,kyüt\ *vb* **-cut·ed; -cut·ing 1** : to execute (a criminal) by electricity **2** : to kill by an electric shock — **elec·tro·cu·tion** \-,lek-trə-'kyü-shən\ *n*

**elec·trode** \i-'lek-,trōd\ *n* : a conductor used to establish electrical contact with a nonmetallic part of a circuit

**elec·tro·de·pos·it** \i-,lek-trō-di-'päz-ət\ *vb* : to deposit (as a metal or rubber) by electrolysis — **elec·tro·de·po·si·tion** \-,dep-ə-'zish-ən, -,dē-pə-\ *n*

**elec·tro·dy·nam·ics** \-dī-'nam-iks\ *n* : physics dealing with the interactions of electric currents with magnets, with other currents, or with themselves — **elec·tro·dy·nam·ic** \-ik\ *adj*

**elec·tro·en·ceph·a·lo·gram** \-in-'sef-ə-lə-,gram\ *n* : the tracing of the electrical activity of the brain that is made by an electroencephalograph

**elec·tro·en·ceph·a·lo·graph** \-,graf\ *n* : an apparatus for detecting and recording the electrical activity of the brain — **elec·tro·en·ceph·a·lo·graph·ic** \-,sef-ə-lə-'graf-ik\ *adj* — **elec·tro·en·ceph·a·log·ra·phy** \-'läg-rə-fē\ *n*

**elec·tro·form** \i-'lek-trə-,fórm\ *vb* : to form shaped articles by electrodeposition on a mold

**elec·tro·hy·drau·lic** \i-,lek-trō-hī-'drô-lik\ *adj* : of, relating to, or involving a combination of electric and hydraulic mechanisms — **elec·tro·hy·drau·li·cal·ly** \-li-k(ə-)lē\ *adv*

**elec·trol·o·gist** \i-,lek-'träl-ə-jəst\ *n* : one that uses electrical means to remove hair, warts, moles, and birthmarks from the body

**elec·trol·y·sis** \i-,lek-'träl-ə-səs\ *n* **1** : the production of chemical changes by passage of an electric current through an electrolyte **2** : the destruction of hair roots with an electric current — **elec·tro·lyt·ic** \-trə-'lit-ik\ *adj*

**elec·tro·lyte** \i-'lek-trə-,līt\ *n* : a nonmetallic electric conductor in which current is carried by the movement of ions; *also* : a substance whose solution or molten form is such a conductor

**elec·tro·mag·net** \i-,lek-trō-'mag-nət\ *n* : a core of magnetic material surrounded by wire through which an electric current is passed to magnetize the core

**elec·tro·mag·net·ic** \-mag-'net-ik\ *adj* **1** : of, relating to, or produced by electromagnetism **2** : being a wave (as a light wave) propagated by regular variations of the intensity of an associated electric and magnetic effect — **elec·tro·mag·net·i·cal·ly** \-i-k(ə-)lē\ *adv*

**electromagnetic radiation** *n* : a series of electromagnetic waves

**elec·tro·mag·ne·tism** \i-,lek-trō-'mag-nə-,tiz-əm\ *n* **1** : magnetism developed by a current of electricity **2** : physics dealing with the relations between electricity and magnetism

**elec·tro·mo·tive force** \i-ˌlek-trə-ˌmōt-iv-\ *n* **1** : something that moves or tends to move electricity **2** : the energy derived from an electrical source per unit quantity of electricity passing through the source (as a generator)

**elec·tron** \i-'lek-ˌträn\ *n* : a negatively charged elementary particle that forms the part of an atom outside the nucleus

**elec·tron·ic** \i-ˌlek-'trän-ik\ *adj* : of or relating to electrons or electronics — **elec·tron·i·cal·ly** \-i-k(ə-)lē\ *adv*

**elec·tron·ics** \i-ˌlek-'trän-iks\ *n* : the physics of electrons and their utilization

**electron microscope** *n* : an instrument in which a focused beam of electrons is used to produce an enlarged image of a minute object on a fluorescent screen or photographic plate

**electron tube** *n* : a device in which electrical conduction by electrons takes place within a container and which is used for the controlled flow of electrons

**elec·tro·pho·re·sis** \i-ˌlek-trə-fə-'rē-səs\ *n* : the movement of suspended particles through a fluid by an electromotive force — **elec·tro·pho·ret·ic** \-'ret-ik\ *adj*

**elec·tro·plate** \i-'lek-trə-ˌplāt\ *vb* : to coat (as with metal) by electrolysis

**elec·tro·shock therapy** \-ˌtrō-ˌshäk-\ *n* : the treatment of mental disorder by the induction of coma with an electric current

**elec·tro·stat·ics** \i-ˌlek-trə-'stat-iks\ *n* : physics dealing with the interactions of stationary electric charges

**elec·tro·type** \i-'lek-trə-ˌtīp\ *n* : a printing plate made by electrodepositing a thin shell of metal on a typeset mold and then putting on a backing

**el·ee·mos·y·nary** \ˌel-i-'mäs-ᵊn-ˌer-ē\ *adj* : CHARITABLE

**el·e·gance** \'el-i-gəns\ *n* **1** : refined gracefulness; *also* : tasteful richness (as of design) **2** : something marked by elegance — **el·e·gant** \-gənt\ *adj* — **el·e·gant·ly** *adv*

**ele·gi·ac** \ˌel-ə-'jī-ək, -ˌak *also* i-'lē-jē-ˌak\ *adj* : of, relating to, or constituting an elegy; *esp* : expressing grief

**el·e·gy** \'el-ə-jē\ *n, pl* **-gies** : a poem expressing grief for one who is dead; *also* : a reflective poem usu. melancholy in tone

**elem** *abbr* elementary

**el·e·ment** \'el-ə-mənt\ *n* **1** *pl* : weather conditions; *esp* : severe weather ⟨boards exposed to the ~s⟩ **2** : natural environment ⟨in her ~⟩ **3** : a constituent part **4** *pl* : the simplest principles (as of an art or science) : RUDIMENTS **5** : a basic member of a mathematical set **6** : a substance not separable by ordinary chemical means into substances different from itself **syn** component, ingredient, factor — **el·e·men·tal** \ˌel-ə-'ment-ᵊl\ *adj*

**el·e·men·ta·ry** \ˌel-ə-'men-t(ə-)rē\ *adj* **1** : SIMPLE, RUDIMENTARY; *also* : of, relating to, or teaching the basic subjects of education **2** : of or relating to an element : consisting of a single chemical element : UNCOMBINED

**elementary particle** *n* : any of the submicroscopic constituents (as the electron or photon) of matter and energy whose existence has not been attributed to the combination of other more fundamental entities

**elementary school** *n* : a school usu. including the first six or the first eight grades

**el·e·phant** \'el-ə-fənt\ *n* : a huge mammal with the snout prolonged as a trunk and two long ivory tusks

**el·e·phan·ti·a·sis** \ˌel-ə-fən-'tī-ə-səs\ *n, pl* **-a·ses** \-ˌsēz\ : enlargement and thickening of tissues in response esp. to infection by minute parasitic worms

**el·e·phan·tine** \ˌel-ə-'fan-ˌtēn, -ˌtīn, 'el-ə-fən-\ *adj* **1** : of great size or strength **2** : CLUMSY, PONDEROUS

**el·e·vate** \'el-ə-ˌvāt\ *vb* **-vat·ed; -vat·ing 1** : to lift up **2** : RAISE **2** : EXALT, ENNOBLE **3** : ELATE

**el·e·va·tion** \ˌel-ə-'vā-shən\ *n* **1** : the height to which something is raised (as above sea level) **2** : a lifting up **3** : something (as a hill or swelling) that is elevated **syn** altitude

**el·e·va·tor** \'el-ə-ˌvāt-ər\ *n* **1** : a cage or platform for conveying something from one level to another **2** : a building for storing and discharging grain **3** : a movable surface on an airplane to produce motion up or down

**elev·en** \i-'lev-ən\ *n* **1** : one more than 10 **2** : the 11th in a set or series **3** : something having 11 units; *esp* : a football team — **eleven** *adj or pron* — **elev·enth** \-ənth\ *adj or n*

**elf** \'elf\ *n, pl* **elves** \'elvz\ : a mischievous fairy — **elf·in** \'el-fən\ *adj* — **elf·ish** \'el-fish\ *adj*

**elic·it** \i-'lis-ət\ *vb* : to draw out or forth **syn** evoke, educe, extract, extort

**elide** \i-'līd\ *vb* **elid·ed; elid·ing** : to suppress or alter by elision

**el·i·gi·ble** \'el-ə-jə-bəl\ *adj* : qualified to participate or to be chosen — **el·i·gi·bil·i·ty** \ˌel-ə-jə-'bil-ət-ē\ *n* — **eligible** *n*

**elim·i·nate** \i-'lim-ə-ˌnāt\ *vb* **-nat·ed; -nat·ing** [L *eliminatus*, pp. of *eliminare*, fr. *limen* threshold] **1** : EXCLUDE, EXPEL; *esp* : to pass (wastes) from the body **2** : to leave out : IGNORE — **elim·i·na·tion** \-ˌlim-ə-'nā-shən\ *n*

**eli·sion** \i-'lizh-ən\ *n* : the omission of a final or initial sound or a word; *esp* : the omission of an unstressed vowel or syllable in a verse to achieve a uniform rhythm

**elite** \ā-'lēt\ *n* **1** : the choice part; *also* : a superior group **2** : a typewriter type providing 12 characters to the inch

**elit·ism** \-'lēt-ˌiz-əm\ *n* : leadership or rule by an elite; *also* : advocacy of such elitism

**elix·ir** \i-'lik-sər\ *n* [ME, fr. ML, fr. Ar *al-iksīr* the elixir, fr. *al* the + *iksīr* elixir] **1** : a substance held capable of prolonging life indefinitely; *also*

: PANACEA **2** : a sweetened alcoholic medicinal solution

**Eliz·a·be·than** \i-,liz-ə-'bē-thən\ *adj* : of, relating to, or characteristic of Elizabeth I of England or her times

**elk** \'elk\ *n, pl* **elks** : a very large deer; *esp* : WAPITI

**¹ell** \'el\ *n* : a unit of length; *esp* : a former English cloth measure of 45 inches

**²ell** *n* : an extension at right angles to a building **syn** wing, annex

**el·lipse** \i-'lips, e-\ *n* : a closed curve of oval shape — **el·lip·tic** \-'lip-tik\ *or* **el·lip·ti·cal** \-ti-kəl\ *adj*

**el·lip·sis** \i-'lip-səs, e-\ *n, pl* **el·lip·ses** \-,sēz\ **1** : omission from an expression of a word clearly implied **2** : marks (as ... or ***) to show omission — **el·lip·ti·cal** \-ti-kəl\ *or* **el·lip·tic** \-'lip-tik\ *adj*

**el·lip·soid** \i-'lip-,sȯid, e-\ *n* : a surface all plane surfaces of which are circles or ellipses — **ellipsoid** *or* **el·lip·soi·dal** \-'lip-'sȯid-°l\ *adj*

**elm** \'elm\ *n* : a tall shade tree with spreading branches and broad top; *also* : its wood

**el·o·cu·tion** \,el-ə-'kyü-shən\ *n* : the art of effective public speaking — **el·o·cu·tion·ist** \-sh(ə-)nəst\ *n*

**elon·gate** \i-'lȯŋ-,gāt\ *vb* **-gat·ed; -gat·ing** : to make or grow longer **syn** extend, lengthen — **elon·ga·tion** \(,)ē-,lȯŋ-'gā-shən\ *n*

**elope** \i-'lōp\ *vb* **eloped; elop·ing** : to run away esp. to be married — **elope·ment** *n*

**el·o·quent** \'el-ə-kwənt\ *adj* **1** : speaking with ease and force **2** : of a kind to move the hearers **syn** articulate, fluent, glib — **el·o·quence** \-kwəns\ *n* — **el·o·quent·ly** *adv*

**¹else** \'els\ *adv* **1** : so as to differ (as in manner, place, or time) ⟨where ~ can we meet⟩ **2** : OTHERWISE ⟨obey or ~ you'll be sorry⟩

**²else** *adj* : OTHER; *esp* : being in addition ⟨what ~ do you want⟩

**else·where** \-,hweər\ *adv* : in or to another place

**elu·ci·date** \i-'lü-sə-,dāt\ *vb* **-dat·ed; -dat·ing** : to make clear usu. by explanation **syn** interpret — **elu·ci·da·tion** \-,lü-sə-'dā-shən\ *n*

**elude** \ē-'lüd\ *vb* **elud·ed; elud·ing** **1** : EVADE **2** : to escape the notice of

**elu·sive** \ē-'lü-siv\ *adj* : tending to elude : EVASIVE — **elu·sive·ly** *adv* — **elu·sive·ness** *n*

**el·ver** \'el-vər\ *n* [alter. of *eelfare* (migration of eels)] : a young eel

**elves** *pl of* ELF

**Ely·si·um** \i-'liz(h)-ē-əm\ *n, pl* **-si·ums** *or* **-sia** \-ē-ə\ **1** : PARADISE **2** — **Ely·sian** \-'lizh-ən\ *adj*

**em** \'em\ *n* : the width of the body of a piece of type bearing the letter *M* used as a unit of measure of printed matter

**EM** *abbr* enlisted man

**ema·ci·ate** \i-'mā-shē-,āt\ *vb* **-at·ed; -at·ing** : to become or cause to become very thin — **ema·ci·a·tion** \-,mā-s(h)ē-'ā-shən\ *n*

**em·a·nate** \'em-ə-,nāt\ *vb* **-nat·ed; -nat·ing** : to come out from a source **syn** proceed, spring, rise, arise, originate — **em·a·na·tion** \,em-ə-'nā-shən\ *n*

**eman·ci·pate** \i-'man-sə-,pāt\ *vb* **-pat·ed, -pat·ing** : to set free **syn** enfranchise, liberate, release, deliver, discharge — **eman·ci·pa·tion** \-,man-sə-'pā-shən\ *n* — **eman·ci·pa·tor** \-'man-sə-,pāt-ər\ *n*

**emas·cu·late** \i-'mas-kyə-,lāt\ *vb* **-lat·ed, -lat·ing** : CASTRATE, GELD; *also* : WEAKEN — **emas·cu·la·tion** \-,mas-kyə-'lā-shən\ *n*

**em·balm** \im-'bäm, -'bälm\ *vb* : to treat (a corpse) with preservative preparations — **em·balm·er** *n*

**em·bank** \im-'baŋk\ *vb* : to enclose or confine by an embankment

**em·bank·ment** \-mənt\ *n* : a raised structure (as of earth) to hold back water or carry a roadway

**em·bar·go** \im-'bär-gō\ *n, pl* **-goes** [Sp. fr. *embargar* to bar] : a prohibition on commerce — **embargo** *vb*

**em·bark** \im-'bärk\ *vb* **1** : to put or go on board a ship or airplane **2** : to make a start — **em·bar·ka·tion** \,em-,bär-'kā-shən\ *n*

**em·bar·rass** \im-'bar-əs\ *vb* **1** : HINDER **2** : CONFUSE, DISCONCERT **3** : to involve in financial difficulties — **em·bar·rass·ing·ly** *adv* — **em·bar·rass·ment** *n*

**em·bas·sy** \'em-bə-sē\ *n, pl* **-sies** **1** : the function or position of an ambassador; *also* : an official mission esp. of an ambassador **2** : a group of diplomatic representatives usu. headed by an ambassador **3** : the official residence and offices of an ambassador

**em·bat·tle** \im-'bat-°l\ *vb* **em·bat·tled; em·bat·tling** \-'bat-(ə-)liŋ\ : to arrange in order of battle

**em·bay·ment** \-'bā-mənt\ *n* **1** : formation of a bay **2** : a bay or something resembling a bay

**em·bed** \im-'bed\ *vb* **em·bed·ded; em·bed·ding** : to enclose closely in a surrounding mass

**em·bel·lish** \im-'bel-ish\ *vb* : ADORN, DECORATE **syn** beautify, deck, bedeck, garnish, ornament — **em·bel·lish·ment** *n*

**em·ber** \'em-bər\ *n* **1** : a glowing or smoldering fragment from a fire **2** *pl* : smoldering remains of a fire

**em·bez·zle** \im-'bez-əl\ *vb* **em·bez·zled; em·bez·zling** \-(ə-)liŋ\ : to take (as money) fraudulently by breach of trust — **em·bez·zle·ment** *n* — **em·bez·zler** \-(ə-)lər\ *n*

**em·bit·ter** \im-'bit-ər\ *vb* **1** : to make bitter **2** : to arouse bitter feelings in

**em·bla·zon** \-'blāz-°n\ *vb* **1** : to adorn with heraldic devices **2** : to make bright with color **3** : EXTOL

**em·blem** \'em-bləm\ *n* : something (as an object or picture) suggesting another object or an idea : SYMBOL — **em·blem·at·ic** \,em-blə-'mat-ik\ *also* **em·blem·at·i·cal** \-i-kəl\ *adj*

**em·body** \im-'bäd-ē\ *vb* **em·bod·ied;**

**em·bod·y·ing** **1** : INCARNATE **2** : to express in definite form **3** : to incorporate into a system or body **syn** materialize, assimilate, identify — **em·bodi·ment** \-'bäd-i-mənt\ n

**em·bold·en** \im-'bōl-dən\ vb : to inspire with courage

**em·bo·lism** \'em-bə-,liz-əm\ n : obstruction of a blood vessel by a foreign or abnormal particle (as an air bubble or blood clot) during life — **em·bol·ic** \em-'bäl-ik\ adj

**em·bon·point** \äⁿ-bōⁿ-pwäⁿ\ n : plumpness of person : STOUTNESS

**em·boss** \im-'bäs, -'bȯs\ vb **1** : to ornament with raised work **2** : to raise in relief from a surface

**em·bou·chure** \,äm-bù-'shùr\ n : the position and use of the lips in producing a musical tone on a wind instrument

**em·bow·er** \im-'baù(-ə)r\ vb : to shelter or enclose in a bower

¹**em·brace** \im-'brās\ vb **em·braced; em·brac·ing 1** : to clasp in the arms; also : CHERISH, LOVE **2** : ENCIRCLE **3** : to take up : ADOPT; also : WELCOME **4** : INCLUDE **5** : to participate in an embrace **syn** comprehend, involve

²**embrace** n : an encircling with the arms

**em·bra·sure** \im-'brā-zhər\ n **1** : a recess of a door or window **2** : an opening in a wall through which cannon are fired

**em·bro·cate** \'em-brə-,kāt\ vb **-cat·ed; -cat·ing** : to moisten and rub (a part of the body) with a medicinal lotion or liniment — **em·bro·ca·tion** \,em-brə-'kā-shən\ n

**em·broi·der** \im-'brȯid-ər\ vb **em·broi·dered; em·broi·der·ing** \-(ə-)riŋ\ **1** : to ornament with or do needlework **2** : to elaborate with florid detail

**em·broi·dery** \im-'brȯid-(ə-)rē\ n, pl **-der·ies 1** : the forming of decorative designs with needlework **2** : something embroidered

**em·broil** \im-'brȯil\ vb : to throw into confusion or strife — **em·broil·ment** n

**em·bryo** \'em-brē-,ō\ n : a living being in its earliest stages of development — **em·bry·on·ic** \,em-brē-'än-ik\ adj

**embryol** abbr embryology

**em·bry·ol·o·gy** \,em-brē-'äl-ə-jē\ n : a branch of biology dealing with embryos and their development — **em·bry·o·log·ic** \-brē-ə-'läj-ik\ or **em·bry·o·log·i·cal** \-i-kəl\ adj — **em·bry·ol·o·gist** \-orē-'äl-ə-jəst\ n

**em·cee** \'em-'sē\ n : MASTER OF CEREMONIES — **emcee** vb

**emend** \ē-'mend\ vb : to correct or alter usu. by altering the text of **syn** rectify, revise, amend — **emen·da·tion** \,ē-,men-'dā-shən\ n

**emer** abbr emeritus

¹**em·er·ald** \'em-(ə-)rəld\ n : a green beryl prized as a gem

²**emerald** adj : brightly or richly green

**emerge** \i-'mərj\ vb **emerged; emerg·ing** : to rise, come forth, or come out into view **syn** appear, loom — **emer·gence** \-'mər-jəns\ n —

**emer·gent** \-jənt\ adj

**emer·gen·cy** \i-'mər-jən-sē\ n, pl **-cies** : an unforeseen happening or state of affairs requiring prompt action **syn** exigency, contingency, crisis

**emer·i·ta** \i-'mer-ət-ə\ adj : EMERITUS — used of a woman

**emer·i·tus** \i-'mer-ət-əs\ adj : retired from active duty ⟨professor ∼⟩

**em·ery** \'em-(ə-)rē\ n, pl **em·er·ies** : a dark granular corundum used esp. for grinding

**emet·ic** \i-'met-ik\ n : an agent that induces vomiting — **emetic** adj

**EMF** abbr electromotive force

**em·i·grate** \'em-ə-,grāt\ vb **-grat·ed; -grat·ing** : to leave a place (as a country) to settle elsewhere — **em·i·grant** \-i-grənt\ n — **em·i·gra·tion** \,em-ə-'grā-shən\ n

**émi·gré** or **emi·gré** \'em-i-,grā, ,em-i-'grā\ n : a person who emigrates esp. because of political conditions

**em·i·nence** \'em-ə-nəns\ n **1** : high rank or position; also : a person of high rank or attainments **2** : a lofty place

**em·i·nent** \'em-ə-nənt\ adj **1** : CONSPICUOUS, EVIDENT **2** : LOFTY, HIGH **3** : DISTINGUISHED, PROMINENT ⟨∼ men⟩ — **em·i·nent·ly** adv

**eminent domain** n : a right of a government to take private property for public use

**emir** \i-'miər, ā-\ n [Ar amīr commander] : a native ruler in parts of Africa and Asia

**em·is·sary** \'em-ə-,ser-ē\ n, pl **-sar·ies** : AGENT; esp : a secret agent

**emit** \ē-'mit\ vb **emit·ted; emit·ting 1** : to give off or out ⟨∼ light⟩; also : EJECT **2** : to put (as money) into circulation **3** : EXPRESS, UTTER — **emis·sion** \-'mish-ən\ n

**emol·lient** \i-'mäl-yənt\ adj : making soft or supple; also : soothing esp. to the skin or mucous membrane — **emollient** n

**emol·u·ment** \i-'mäl-yə-mənt\ n [ME, fr. L emolumentum, lit., miller's fee, fr. emolere to grind up] : the product (as salary or fees) of an employment

**emote** \i-'mōt\ vb **emot·ed; emot·ing** : to give expression to emotion in or as if in a play

**emo·tion** \i-'mō-shən\ n : a usu. intense feeling (as of love, hate, or despair) — **emo·tion·al** \-sh(ə-)nəl\ adj — **emo·tion·al·ly** \-ē\ adv

**emp** abbr emperor; empress

**em·pa·thy** \'em-pə-thē\ n : capacity for participating in the feelings or ideas of another — **em·path·ic** \em-'path-ik\ adj

**em·pen·nage** \,äm-pə-'näzh, ,em-\ n : the tail assembly of an airplane

**em·per·or** \'em-pər-ər\ n : the sovereign ruler of an empire

**em·pha·sis** \'em-fə-səs\ n, pl **em·pha·ses** \-,sēz\ : particular stress or prominence given (as to a phrase in speaking or to a phase of action)

**em·pha·size** \-,sīz\ vb **-sized; -siz·ing** : STRESS

**em·phat·ic** \im-'fat-ik, em-\ adj

: uttered with emphasis : STRESSED —
**em·phat·i·cal·ly** \-'fat-i-k(ə-)lē\ adv
**em·phy·se·ma** \,em fə-'zē-mə, -'sē-\ n
: a condition of the lung marked by
distension and frequently by impairment of heart action
**em·pire** \'em-,pī(ə)r\ n 1 : a large
state or a group of states under a single
sovereign who is usu. an emperor
2 : imperial sovereignty or dominion
**em·pir·i·cal** \im-'pir-i-kəl\ also **em-
pir·ic** \-ik\ adj : depending or based
on experience or observation; also
: subject to verification by observation
or experiment ⟨~ laws⟩ — **em·pir·i-
cal·ly** \-i-k(ə-)lē\ adv
**em·pir·i·cism** \im-'pir-ə-,siz-əm, em-\
n : the practice of relying on observation and experiment esp. in the natural
sciences — **em·pir·i·cist** \-səst\ n
**em·place·ment** \im-'plās-mənt\ n
1 : a prepared position for weapons or
military equipment 2 : PLACEMENT
**¹em·ploy** \im-'ploi\ vb 1 : to make use
of 2 : to use the services of 3 : OC-
CUPY, DEVOTE — **em·ploy·er** n
**²employ** n : EMPLOYMENT
**em·ploy·ee** or **em·ploye** \im-,ploi-
'ē, ,em-; im-'ploi-,ē, em-\ n : a person
who works for another
**em·ploy·ment** \im-'ploi-mənt\ n
1 : the act of employing : the condition of being employed 2 : OCCUPA-
TION, ACTIVITY
**em·po·ri·um** \im-'pōr-ē-əm, em-\ n,
pl **-ri·ums** also **-ria** \-ē-ə\ [L, fr. Gk
emporion, fr. emporos traveler, trader,
fr. poros journey] : a commercial center; esp : a store carrying varied articles
**em·pow·er** \im-'pau̇(-ə)r\ vb : AU-
THORIZE
**em·press** \'em-prəs\ n 1 : the wife or
widow of an emperor 2 : a woman
holding an imperial title in her own
right
**¹emp·ty** \'emp-tē\ adj 1 : containing
nothing 2 : UNOCCUPIED, UNINHABITED
3 : lacking value, force, sense, or purpose **syn** vacant, blank, void, idle, hollow, vain — **emp·ti·ness** \-tē-nəs\ n
**²empty** vb **emp·tied; emp·ty·ing**
1 : to make or become empty 2 : to
discharge its contents; also : to transfer
by emptying
**³empty** n, pl **empties** : an empty container or vehicle
**emp·ty-hand·ed** \,emp-tē-'han-dəd\
adj 1 : having nothing in the hands
2 : having acquired or gained nothing
**em·py·re·an** \,em-,pī-'rē-ən, -pə-\ n
: the highest heaven; also : HEAVENS,
FIRMAMENT
**¹emu** \'ē-myü\ n : a flightless Australian
bird smaller than the related ostrich
**²emu** abbr electromagnetic unit
**em·u·late** \'em-yə-,lāt\ vb **-lat·ed;
-lat·ing** : to strive to equal or excel
— **em·u·la·tion** \,em-yə-'lā-shən\ n
— **em·u·lous** \-yə-ləs\ adj
**emul·si·fi·er** \i-'məl-sə-,fī(-ə)r\ n
: something promoting the formation
and stabilizing of an emulsion
**emul·si·fy** \-,fī\ vb **-fied; -fy·ing**
: to convert into or become an emul-

sion — **emul·si·fi·able** \-,fī-ə-bəl\
adj — **emul·si·fi·ca·tion** \-i-,məl-sə-
fə-'kā-shən\ n
**emul·sion** \i-'məl-shən\ n 1 : a mixture of mutually insoluble liquids in
which one is dispersed in droplets
throughout the other ⟨an ~ of oil in
water⟩ 2 : a light-sensitive coating on
photographic film or paper — **emul-
sive** \-'məl-siv\ adj
**¹-en** \ən, °n\ also **-n** \n\ adj suffix
: made of : consisting of ⟨earthen⟩
**²-en** vb suffix 1 : become or cause to be
⟨sharpen⟩ 2 : cause or come to have
⟨lengthen⟩
**en·able** \in-'ā-bəl\ vb **en·abled; enabling** \-b(ə-)liŋ\ 1 : to make able
or feasible 2 : to give legal power,
capacity, or sanction to
**en·act** \in-'akt\ vb 1 : to make into
law 2 : to act out — **en·act·ment** n
**enam·el** \in-'am-əl\ n 1 : a glasslike
substance used for coating the surface
of metal or pottery 2 : the hard outer
layer of a tooth 3 : a usu. glossy paint
that forms a hard coat — **enamel** vb
**enam·el·ware** \-,waər\ n : metal utensils coated with enamel
**en·am·or** \in-'am-ər\ vb **en·am-
ored; en·am·or·ing** \-(ə-)riŋ\ : to
inflame with love
**en·am·our** chiefly Brit var of ENAMOR
**en bloc** \än-'bläk\ adv or adj : as a
whole : in a mass
**encr** or **encl** abbr enclosure
**en·camp** \in-'kamp\ vb : to make
camp — **en·camp·ment** n
**en·cap·su·late** \in-'kap-sə-,lāt\ vb
**-lat·ed; -lat·ing** : to encase or become encased in a capsule — **en·cap-
su·la·tion** \-,kap-sə-'lā-shən\ n
**en·case** \in-'kās\ vb : to enclose in or
as if in a case
**-ence** \əns, °ns\ n suffix 1 : action or
process ⟨emergence⟩ : instance of an
action or process ⟨reference⟩ 2 : quality or state ⟨dependence⟩
**en·ceinte** \än"-'sant\ adj : PREGNANT
**en·ceph·a·li·tis** \in-,sef-ə-'līt-əs\ n,
pl **-lit·i·des** \-'lit-ə-,dēz\ : inflammation of the brain — **en·ceph·a·lit·ic**
\-'lit-ik\ adj
**en·ceph·a·lo·my·eli·tis** \in-,sef-ə-
lō-,mī-ə-'līt-əs\ n : concurrent inflammation of the brain and spinal cord
**en·chain** \in-'chān\ vb : FETTER, CHAIN
**en·chant** \in-'chant\ vb 1 : BEWITCH
2 : ENRAPTURE, FASCINATE — **en-
chant·er** n — **en·chant·ing·ly** adv
— **en·chant·ment** n — **en·chant-
ress** \-'chan-trəs\ n
**en·chi·la·da** \,en-chə-'läd-ə\ n : a
tortilla rolled with meat filling and
served with tomato sauce seasoned
with chili
**en·ci·pher** \in-'sī-fər, en-\ vb : to
convert (a message) into cipher — **en-
ci·pher·ment** n
**en·cir·cle** \in-'sər-kəl\ vb : to pass
completely around : SURROUND — **en-
cir·cle·ment** n
**en·clave** \'en-,klāv; 'än-,klāv\ n : a
territorial or culturally distinct unit
enclosed within foreign territory

**en·close** \in-'klōz\ *vb* **1** : to shut up or in; *esp* : to surround with a fence **2** : to include along with something else in a parcel or envelope ⟨~ a check⟩ — **en·clo·sure** \in-'klō-zhər\ *n*

**en·code** \in-'kōd, en-\ *vb* : to convert (a message) into code

**en·co·mi·um** \en-'kō-mē-əm\ *n, pl* **-mi·ums** *or* **-mia** \-mē-ə\ : high or glowing praise

**en·com·pass** \in-'kəm-pəs, -'käm-\ *vb* **1** : ENCIRCLE **2** : ENVELOP, INCLUDE

¹**en·core** \'än-ˌkōr\ *n* : a demand for repetition or reappearance; *also* : a further performance (as of a singer) in response to such a demand

²**encore** *vb* **en·cored; en·cor·ing** : to request an encore from

¹**en·coun·ter** \in-'kaunt-ər\ *vb* **1** : to meet as an enemy : FIGHT **2** : to meet usu. unexpectedly

²**encounter** *n* **1** : a hostile meeting; *esp* : COMBAT **2** : a chance meeting

**encounter group** *n* : a usu. leaderless and unstructured group that seeks by unrestrained personal confrontations (as physical contact or uninhibited speech) to develop a person's capacity to openly express his feelings and to form close emotional ties

**en·cour·age** \in-'kər-ij\ *vb* **-aged; -ag·ing 1** : to inspire with courage and hope **2** : STIMULATE, INCITE; *also* : FOSTER — **en·cour·age·ment** *n* — **en·cour·ag·ing·ly** *adv*

**en·croach** \in-'krōch\ *vb* [ME *encrochen* to seize, fr. MF *encrochier*, fr. OF, fr. *croche* hook] : to enter or force oneself gradually upon another's property or rights — **en·croach·ment** *n*

**en·crust** \in-'krəst\ *vb* : to provide with or form a crust

**en·cum·ber** \in-'kəm-bər\ *vb* **en·cum·bered; en·cum·ber·ing** \-b(ə-)riŋ\ **1** : to weigh down : BURDEN **2** : to hinder the function or activity of — **en·cum·brance** \-brəns\ *n*

**ency** *or* **encyc** *abbr* encyclopedia

**-en·cy** \ən-sē, ²n-\ *n suffix* : quality or state ⟨despond*ency*⟩

¹**en·cyc·li·cal** \in-'sik-li-kəl, en-\ *adj* : addressed to all the individuals of a group

²**encyclical** *n* : an encyclical letter; *esp* : a papal letter to the bishops of the church

**en·cy·clo·pe·dia** \in-ˌsī-klə-'pēd-ē-ə\ *n* [ML *encyclopaedia* course of general education, fr. Gk *enkyklios paideia* general education] · a work treating the various branches of learning — **en·cy·clo·pe·dic** \-'pēd-ik\ *adj*

**en·cyst** \in-'sist, en-\ *vb* : to form or become enclosed in a cyst — **en·cyst·ment** *n*

¹**end** \'end\ *n* **1** : the part of an area that lies at the boundary. *also* : a point which marks the extent or limit of something or at which something ceases to exist **2** : a ceasing of a course (as of action or activity); *also* : DEATH **3** : an ultimate state; *also* : RESULT, ISSUE **4** : REMNANT **5** : PURPOSE, OBJECTIVE

**6** : a share or phase esp. of an undertaking **7** : a player stationed at the extremity of a line (as in football)

²**end** *vb* **1** : to bring or come to an end **2** : to put to death, *also* : DIE **3** : to form or be at the end of **syn** close, conclude, terminate, finish

**en·dan·ger** \in-'dān-jər\ *vb* **en·dan·gered; en·dan·ger·ing** \-'dānj-(ə-)riŋ\ : to bring into danger

**en·dan·gered** \-jərd\ *adj* : threatened with extinction ⟨~ species⟩

**en·dear** \in-'diər\ *vb* : to cause to become an object of affection

**en·dear·ment** \-mənt\ *n* : a sign of affection : CARESS

**en·deav·or** \in-'dev-ər\ *vb* **en·deav·ored; en·deav·or·ing** \-(ə-)riŋ\ : TRY, ATTEMPT — **endeavor** *n*

**en·dem·ic** \en-'dem-ik, in-\ *adj* : restricted or peculiar to a particular place ⟨~ plants⟩ ⟨an ~ disease⟩ — **endemic** *n*

**end·ing** \'en-diŋ\ *n* : something that forms an end; *esp* : SUFFIX

**en·dive** \'en-ˌdīv\ *n* **1** : an herb related to chicory and grown as a salad plant **2** : the blanched shoot of chicory

**end·less** \'end-ləs\ *adj* **1** : having no end : ETERNAL **2** : united at the ends : CONTINUOUS ⟨an ~ belt⟩ **syn** interminable, everlasting, unceasing — **end·less·ly** *adv*

**end man** *n* : a man at each end of the line of performers in a minstrel show who engages in comic repartee with the interlocutor

**end·most** \'en(d)-ˌmōst\ *adj* : situated at the very end

**en·do·crine** \'en-də-krən, -ˌkrīn, -ˌkrēn\ *adj* : producing secretions that are distributed by way of the bloodstream ⟨~ glands⟩; *also* : HORMONAL ⟨~ effects⟩ — **endocrine** *n* — **en·do·cri·nol·o·gist** \ˌen-də-kri-'näl-ə-jəst\ *n* — **en·do·cri·nol·o·gy** \-jē\ *n*

**en·dog·e·nous** \en-'däj-ə-nəs\ *adj* : developing or originating inside the cell or body — **en·dog·e·nous·ly** *adv*

**en·dorse** \in-'dórs\ *vb* **en·dorsed; en·dors·ing 1** : to sign one's name on the back of (as a check) for some purpose **2** : APPROVE, SANCTION **syn** accredit — **en·dorse·ment** *n*

**en·do·scope** \'en-də-ˌskōp\ *n* : an instrument with which the interior of a hollow organ (as the rectum) may be visualized — **en·do·scop·ic** \ˌen-də-'skäp-ik\ *adj* — **en·dos·co·py** \en-s-kə-pē\ *n*

**en·do·ther·mic** \ˌen-də-'thər-mik\ *or* **en·do·ther·mal** \-məl\ *adj* : characterized by or formed with absorption of heat

**en·dow** \in-'dau\ *vb* **1** : to furnish with funds for support ⟨~ a school⟩ **2** : to furnish with something freely or naturally — **en·dow·ment** *n*

**en·drin** \'en-drən\ *n* : a chlorinated hydrocarbon insecticide that resembles dieldrin in toxicity

**end run** *n* : a football play in which the ballcarrier attempts to run wide around the end

**en·due** \in-'d(y)ü\ *vb* **en·dued; en·du·ing :** to provide with some quality or power

**en·dur·ance** \in-'d(y)ùr-əns\ *n* **1 :** DURATION **2 :** ability to withstand hardship or stress **:** FORTITUDE

**en·dure** \in-'d(y)ùr\ *vb* **en·dured; en·dur·ing 1 :** LAST, PERSIST **2 :** to suffer firmly or patiently **:** BEAR **3 :** TOLERATE **syn** continue, abide — **en·dur·able** *adj*

**en·duro** \in-'d(y)ùr-ō\ *n, pl* **en·dur·os :** a long race (as for motorcycles) stressing endurance rather than speed

**end·ways** \'end-,wāz\ *adv or adj* **1 :** with the end forward **2 :** LENGTHWISE **3 :** on end

**end·wise** \-,wīz\ *adv or adj* **:** ENDWAYS

**ENE** *abbr* east-northeast

**en·e·ma** \'en-ə-mə\ *n, pl* **enemas** *also* **ene·ma·ta** \,en-ə-'mät-ə, 'en-ə-mə-tə\ **:** injection of liquid into the rectum; *also* **:** material so injected

**en·e·my** \'en-ə-mē\ *n, pl* **-mies :** one that attacks or tries to harm another **:** FOE; *esp* **:** a military opponent

**en·er·get·ic** \,en-ər-'jet-ik\ *adj* **:** marked by energy **:** ACTIVE, VIGOROUS **syn** strenuous, lusty — **en·er·get·i·cal·ly** \-i-k(ə-)lē\ *adv*

**en·er·gize** \'en-ər-,jīz\ *vb* **-gized; -giz·ing :** to give energy to

**en·er·giz·er** \-,jī-zər\ *n* **:** ANTIDEPRESSANT

**en·er·gy** \'en-ər-jē\ *n, pl* **-gies 1 :** vitality of expression **2 :** capacity for action **:** VIGOR; *also* **:** vigorous action **3 :** capacity for performing work **syn** strength, might

**en·er·vate** \'en-ər-,vāt\ *vb* **-vat·ed; -vat·ing :** to lessen the strength or vigor of **:** weaken in mind or body — **en·er·va·tion** \,en-ər-'vā-shən\ *n*

**en·fee·ble** \in-'fē-bəl\ *vb* **en·fee·bled; en·fee·bling** \-b(ə-)liŋ\ **:** to make feeble **syn** weaken, debilitate sap, undermine — **en·fee·ble·ment** *n*

**en·fi·lade** \'en-fə-,lād, -,läd\ *n* **:** gunfire directed along the length of an enemy battle line

**en·fold** \in-'fōld\ *vb* **1 :** ENVELOP **2 :** EMBRACE

**en·force** \in-'fōrs\ *vb* **1 :** COMPEL ⟨∼ obedience by threats⟩ **2 :** to execute with vigor ⟨∼ the law⟩ — **en·force·able** *adj* — **en·force·ment** *n*

**en·fran·chise** \in-'fran-,chīz\ *vb* **-chised; -chis·ing 1 :** to set free (as from slavery) **2 :** to admit to citizenship; *also* **:** to grant the vote to — **en·fran·chise·ment** \-,chīz-mənt, -chəz-\ *n*

**eng** *abbr* engine; engineer; engineering

**Eng** *abbr* England; English

**en·gage** \in-'gāj\ *vb* **en·gaged; en·gag·ing 1 :** to offer as security **:** PLEDGE **2 :** to attract and hold esp. by interesting ⟨*engaged* his friend's attention⟩; *also* **:** to cause to participate **3 :** to connect or interlock with **:** MESH; *also* **:** to cause to mesh **4 :** to bind by a pledge to marry **5 :** EMPLOY, HIRE **6 :** to bring or enter into conflict **7 :** to

commence or take part in a venture

**en·gage·ment** \in-'gāj-mənt\ *n* **1 :** a mutual promise to marry **2 :** EMPLOYMENT **3 :** a hostile encounter **4 :** APPOINTMENT

**en·gag·ing** *adj* **:** ATTRACTIVE — **en·gag·ing·ly** *adv*

**en·gen·der** \in-'jen-dər\ *vb* **en·gen·dered; en·gen·der·ing** \-d(ə-)riŋ\ **1 :** BEGET **2 :** to bring into being **:** CREATE **syn** generate, breed, sire

**en·gine** \'en-jən\ *n* [ME *engin*, fr. OF, fr. L *ingenium* natural disposition, talent] **1 :** a mechanical device; *esp* **:** a machine used in war **2 :** a machine by which physical power is applied to produce a physical effect **3 :** LOCOMOTIVE

**¹en·gi·neer** \,en-jə-'niər\ *n* **1 :** a member of a military group devoted to engineering work **2 :** a designer or builder of engines **3 :** one trained in engineering **4 :** one that operates an engine

**²engineer** *vb* **:** to lay out or manage as an engineer **syn** guide, pilot, lead, steer

**en·gi·neer·ing** \-iŋ\ *n* **:** a science by which the properties of matter and sources of energy are made useful to man in structures, machines, and products

**En·glish** \'iŋ-glish\ *n* **1 English** *pl* **:** the people of England **2 :** the language of England, the U.S., and many areas now or formerly under British rule — **English** *adj* — **En·glish·man** \-mən\ *n* — **En·glish·wom·an** \-,wùm-ən\ *n*

**English horn** *n* **:** a woodwind instrument longer than and having a range lower than the oboe

**English sparrow** *n* **:** a sparrow native to Europe and parts of Asia that has been widely introduced elsewhere

**engr** *abbr* **1** engineer **2** engraved

**en·graft** \in-'graft\ *vb* **:** GRAFT 1; *also* **:** IMPLANT

**en·gram** \'en-,gram\ *n* **:** a hypothetical change in neural tissue postulated in order to account for persistence of memory

**en·grave** \in-'grāv\ *vb* **en·graved; en·grav·ing 1 :** to produce (as letters or lines) by incising a surface **2 :** to incise (as stone or metal) to produce a representation (as of letters or figures) esp. that may be printed from **3 :** PHOTOENGRAVE — **en·grav·er** *n*

**en·grav·ing** \in-'grā-viŋ\ *n* **1 :** the art of one who engraves **2 :** an engraved plate; *also* **:** a print made from it

**en·gross** \in-'grōs\ *vb* **1 :** to copy or write in a large hand; *also* **:** to prepare the final text of (an official document) **2 :** to occupy fully **syn** monopolize, absorb

**en·gulf** \in-'gəlf\ *vb* **:** to flow over and enclose

**en·hance** \in-'hans\ *vb* **en·hanced; en·hanc·ing :** to make greater (as in value or desirability) **syn** heighten, intensify — **en·hance·ment** *n*

**enig·ma** \i-'nig-mə\ *n* [L *aenigma*, fr.

Gk *ainigma*, fr. *ainissesthai* to speak in riddles, fr. *ainos* fable] : something obscure or hard to understand : PUZZLE

**enig·mat·ic** \,en-ig-'mat-ik, ,ē-nig-\ *adj* : resembling an enigma **syn** obscure, ambiguous, equivocal — **en·ig·mat·i·cal·ly** \-i-k(ə-)lē\ *adv*

**en·isle** \in-'īl\ *vb* 1 : ISOLATE 2 : to make an island of

**en·jamb·ment** \in-'jam-mənt\ *or* **en·jambe·ment** \*same, or* äⁿ-zhäⁿb(-ə)mäⁿ\ *n* : the running over of a sentence from one verse or couplet into another so that closely related words fall in different lines

**en·join** \in-'join\ *vb* 1 : COMMAND, ORDER 2 : FORBID **syn** direct, bid, charge, prohibit

**en·joy** \in-'joi\ *vb* 1 : to take pleasure or satisfaction in ⟨~ed the concert⟩ 2 : to have for one's benefit, use, or lot ⟨~ good health⟩ **syn** like, love, relish, fancy, possess, own — **en·joy·able** *adj* — **en·joy·ment** *n*

**enl** *abbr* 1 enlarged 2 enlisted

**en·large** \in-'lärj\ *vb* **en·larged**; **en·larg·ing** 1 : to make or grow larger 2 : to set free 3 : to speak or write at length **syn** increase, augment, multiply — **en·large·ment** *n*

**en·light·en** \in-'līt-ⁿn\ *vb* **en·light·ened**; **en·light·en·ing** \-'līt-(ə-)niŋ\ 1 : INSTRUCT, INFORM 2 : to give spiritual insight to **syn** illuminate — **en·light·en·ment** *n*

**en·list** \in-'list\ *vb* 1 : to engage for service in the armed forces 2 : to secure the aid or support of — **en·list·ee** \-,lis-'tē\ *n* — **en·list·ment** \-'lis(t)-mənt\ *n*

**enlisted man** *n* : a man or woman in the armed forces ranking below a commissioned or warrant officer

**en·liv·en** \in-'līˌ-vən\ *vb* : to give life, action, or spirit to : ANIMATE

**en masse** \äⁿ-'mas\ *adv* : in a body : as a whole

**en·mesh** \in-'mesh\ *vb* : to catch or entangle in or as if in meshes

**en·mi·ty** \'en-mət-ē\ *n, pl* **-ties** : ILL WILL; *esp* : mutual hatred **syn** hostility, antipathy, animosity, rancor

**en·no·ble** \in-'ō-bəl\ *vb* **en·no·bled**; **en·no·bling** \-b(ə-)liŋ\ : ELEVATE, EXALT, *esp* : to raise to noble rank — **en·no·ble·ment** *n*

**en·nui** \än-'wē\ *n* : BOREDOM

**enor·mi·ty** \i-'nor-mət-ē\ *n, pl* **-ties** 1 : great wickedness 2 : an outrageous act 3 : huge size

**enor·mous** \i-'nor-məs\ *adj* [L *enormis*, fr. *e*, *ex* out of + *norma* rule] 1 : exceedingly wicked 2 : great in size, number, or degree : HUGE **syn** immense, vast, gigantic, giant, colossal, mammoth, elephantine

¹**enough** \i-'nəf\ *adj* : SUFFICIENT **syn** adequate

²**enough** *adv* 1 : SUFFICIENTLY 2 : TOLERABLY

³**enough** *pron* : a sufficient number, quantity, or amount

**en·plane** \in-'plān\ *vb* : to board an airplane

**en·quire** \in-'kwī(ə)r\, **en·qui·ry** \'in-,kwī(ə)r-ē, in-'kwī(ə)r-; 'in-kwə-rē, i\ *var of* INQUIRE, INQUIRY

**en·rage** \in-'rāj\ *vb* : to fill with rage

**en·rap·ture** \in-'rap-chər\ *vb* **en·rap·tured**; **en·rap·tur·ing** : DELIGHT

**en·rich** \in-'rich\ *vb* 1 : to make rich or richer 2 : ORNAMENT, ADORN — **en·rich·ment** *n*

**en·roll** *or* **en·rol** \in-'rōl\ *vb* **en·rolled**; **en·roll·ing** 1 : to enter or register on a roll or list 2 : to offer (oneself) for enrolling — **en·roll·ment** *n*

**en route** \äⁿ-'rüt, en-, in-\ *adv or adj* : on or along the way

**ENS** *abbr* ensign

**en·sconce** \in-'skäns\ *vb* **en·sconced**; **en·sconc·ing** 1 : SHELTER, CONCEAL 2 : to settle snugly or securely **syn** secrete, hide

**en·sem·ble** \äⁿ-'säm-bəl\ *n* [F, fr. *ensemble* together, fr. L *insimul* at the same time] 1 : SET, WHOLE 2 : integrated music of two or more parts 3 : a complete costume of harmonizing garments 4 : a group of persons (as musicians acting together to produce a particular effect or end

**en·sheathe** \in-'shēth\ *vb* : to cover with or as if with a sheath

**en·shrine** \in-'shrīn\ *vb* 1 : to enclose in or as if in a shrine 2 : to cherish as sacred

**en·shroud** \in-'shraud\ *vb* : SHROUD, OBSCURE

**en·sign** \'en-sən, *1 also* 'en-,sīn\ *n* 1 : FLAG, *also* : BADGE, EMBLEM 2 : a commissioned officer in the navy ranking next below a lieutenant junior grade

**en·si·lage** \'en-sə-lij\ *n* : SILAGE

**en·sile** \en-'sīl\ *vb* **en·siled**; **en·sil·ing** : to prepare and store (fodder) for silage

**en·slave** \in-'slāv\ *vb* : to make a slave of — **en·slave·ment** *n*

**en·snare** \in-'snaər\ *vb* : SNARE, TRAP **syn** entrap, bag, catch, capture

**en·sue** \in-'sü\ *vb* **en·sued**; **en·su·ing** : to follow as a consequence or in time : RESULT

**en·sure** \in-'shùr\ *vb* **en·sured**; **en·sur·ing** : INSURE, GUARANTEE **syn** assure, secure

**en·tail** \in-'tāl\ *vb* 1 : to limit the inheritance of (property) to the owner's lineal descendants or to a class thereof 2 : to include or involve as a necessary result — **en·tail·ment** *n*

**en·tan·gle** \in-'taŋ-gəl\ *vb* : TANGLE, CONFUSE — **en·tan·gle·ment** *n*

**en·tente** \än-'tänt\ *n* : an understanding providing for joint action; *also* : parties linked by such an entente

**en·ter** \'ent-ər\ *vb* **en·tered**; **en·ter·ing** \'ent-ə-riŋ, 'en-triŋ\ 1 : to go or come in or into 2 : to become a member of : JOIN ⟨~ the ministry⟩ 3 : BEGIN 4 : to take part in : CONTRIBUTE 5 : to set down (as in a list) : REGISTER 6 : to place (a complaint) before a court; *also* : to put on record ⟨~ed his objections⟩ 7 : to go into or upon and take possession

**en·ter·i·tis** \,ent-ə-'rīt-əs\ n : intestinal inflammation

**en·ter·prise** \'ent-ər ,prīz\ n 1 : UNDERTAKING, PROJECT 2 : a business organization 3 : readiness for daring action : INITIATIVE

**en·ter·pris·ing** \-,prī-ziŋ\ adj : bold and vigorous in action : ENERGETIC

**en·ter·tain** \,ent-ər 'tān\ vb 1 : to treat or receive as a guest 2 : to hold in mind 3 : AMUSE, DIVERT syn harbor, shelter, lodge, house — **en·ter·tain·er** n — **en·ter·tain·ment** n

**en·thrall** or **en·thral** \in-'thról\ vb **en·thralled**; **en·thrall·ing** 1 : ENSLAVE 2 : to hold spellbound

**en·throne** \in-'thrōn\ vb 1 : to seat on or as if on a throne 2 : EXALT

**en·thuse** \in-'th(y)üz\ vb **en·thused**; **en·thus·ing** 1 : to make enthusiastic 2 : to show enthusiasm

**en·thu·si·asm** \in-'th(y)ü-zē-,az-əm\ n [Gk ‹nthousiasmos, fr. enthousiazein to be inspired, fr. entheos inspired, fr. theos god] 1 : strong warmth of feeling : keen interest : FERVOR 2 : a cause of fervor — **en·thu·si·ast** \-,ast, -əst\ n — **en·thu·si·as·tic** \in-,th(y)ü-zē-'as-tik\ adj — **en·thu·si·as·ti·cal·ly** \-ti-k-(ə )lē\ adv

**en·tice** \in-'tīs\ vb **en·ticed**; **en·tic·ing** : ALLURE, TEMPT — **en·tice·ment** n

**en·tire** \in-'tī(ə)r\ adj : COMPLETE, WHOLE syn total, all, gross, perfect, intact — **en·tire·ly** adv

**en·tire·ty** \in-'tī-rət-ē, -'tī-(ə)rt-ē\ n, pl **-ties** 1 : COMPLETENESS 2 : WHOLE, TOTALITY

**en·ti·tle** \in-'tīt-ºl\ vb **en·ti·tled**; **en·ti·tling** \-'tīt-(º )liŋ\ 1 : NAME, DESIGNATE 2 : to give a right or claim to

**en·ti·ty** \'ent-ət-ē\ n, pl **-ties** 1 : EXISTENCE, BEING 2 : something with separat‹ and rea‹ existence

**entom** or **entomol** abbr entomological; entomology

**en·tomb** \in-'tüm\ vb : to place in a tomb : BURY — **en·tomb·ment** \-'tüm-mənt\ n

**en·to·mol·o·gy** \,ent-ə-'mäl-ə-jē\ n : a branch of zoology that deals with insects — **en·to·m‹ ·lo·i·cal** \-mə-'läj-i-kəl\ adj — **en·to·mol·o·gist** \,ent-ə-'mäl-ə-jəst\ n

**en·tou·rage** \,än-tü-'räzh\ n : RETINUE

**en·tr'acte** \'ä"n ,trакt\ n 1 : the interval between two acts of a play 2 ‹omething (as a dance) performed between two acts of a play

**en·trails** \ en-trəlz -,trālz\ n pl : VISCERA; esp : INTESTINES

**en·train** \in tran\ vb · to put or go aboard a railroad train

¹**en·trance** \ en-trəns\ n 1 : the act of entering 2 : a means or place of entry 3 : peּ mission or right to enter

²**en·tı·ance** \in-'trans\ vb **en·tranced**; **en·tranc·ing** : CHARM, DELIGHT

**en·trant** \ en-trənt\ n : one that enters esp as a competitor

**en·trap** \in-'trap\ vb : ENSNARE, TRAP — **en·trap·ment** n

**en·treat** \in-'trēt\ vb : to ask earnestly or urgently : BESEECH syn beg, implore — **en·treaty** \-'trēt-ē\ n

**en·trée** or **en·tree** \'än-,trā\ n 1 : ENTRANCE 2 : the principal dish of the meal in the U.S. syn entry, access

**en·trench** \in-'trench\ vb 1 : to surround with a trench; also : to establish in a strong defensive position ⟨∼ed customs⟩ 2 : ENCROACH, TRESPASS — **en·trench·ment** n

**en·tre·pre·neur** \,än-trə-prə-'nər\ n : an organizer or promoter of an activity; esp : one that manages and assumes the risk of a business

**en·tro·py** \'en-trə-pē\ n, pl **-pies** 1 : a measure of the unavailable energy of a system 2 : an ultimate state of inert uniformity

**en·trust** \in-'trəst\ vb 1 : to commit something to as a trust 2 : to commit to another with confidence syn confide, consign, relegate

**en·try** \'en-trē\ n, pl **entries** 1 : ENTRANCE 1, 2; also : VESTIBULE 2 : an entering in a record; also : an item so entered 3 : a headword with its definition or identification; also : VOCABULARY ENTRY 4 : one entered for a contest

**en·twine** \in-'twīn\ vb : to twine together or around

**enu·mer·ate** \i-'n(y)ü-mə-,rāt\ vb **-at·ed**; **-at·ing** 1 : to determine the number of : COUNT 2 : LIST — **enu·mer·a·tion** \-,n(y)ü-mə-'rā-shən\ n

**enun·ci·ate** \ē-'nən-sē-,āt\ vb **-at·ed**; **-at·ing** 1 : tc state definitely; also : ANNOUNCE, PROCLAIM 2 : PRONOUNCE, ARTICULATE — **enun·ci·a·tion** \-,nən-sē-'ā-shən\ n

**en·ure·sis** \,en-yü-'rē-səs\ n : involuntary discharge of urine : bed-wetting

**env** abbr envelope

**en·vel·op** \in-'vel-əp\ vb : to enclose completely with or as if with a covering — **en·vel·op·ment** \-'tüm-mənt\ n

**en·ve·lope** \'en-və-,lōp, 'än-\ n 1 : WRAPPER, COVERING 2 : a usu. paper container for a letter 3 · the bag containing the gas in a balloon or airship

**en·ven·om** \in-'ven-əm\ vb 1 : to taint or fill with poison 2 : EMBITTER

**en·vi·able** \'en-vē-ə-bəl\ adj : highly desirable — **en·vi·ably** \-blē\ adv

**en·vi·ous** \'en-vē-əs\ adj : feeling or showing envy — **en·vi·ous·ly** adv — **en·vi·ous·ness** n

**en·vi·ron·ment** \in-'vī-rən-mənt\ n : SURROUNDINGS — **en·vi·ron·men·tal** \-,vī-rən-'ment-ºl\ adj

**en·vi·ron·men·tal·ist** \-'ºl-əst\ n : a person concerned about the quality of the human environment

**en·vi·rons** \in- vī-rənz\ n pl 1 : SUBURBS 2 : ENVIRONMENT; also : VICINITY

**en·vis·age** \in-'viz-ij\ vb **-aged**; **-ag·ing** : to have a mental picture of

**en·voi** or **en·voy** \'en-,voi, än-\ n : the concluding remarks to a poem, essay, or book

**en·voy** \'en-,vói, än-\ n 1 : a diplomatic agent 2 : REPRESENTATIVE, MESSENGER

¹**en·vy** \'en-vē\ *n, pl* **envies** [ME *envie*, fr. OF, fr. L *invidia*, fr. *invidus* envious, fr. *invidēre* to look askance at, envy, fr. *vidēre* to see] **:** grudging desire for or discontent at the sight of another's excellence or advantages; *also* **:** an object of envy

²**envy** *vb* **en·vied; en·vy·ing : to feel envy toward or on account of

**en·wreathe** \in-'rēth\ *vb* **:** WREATHE, ENVELOP

**en·zyme** \'en-,zīm\ *n* **:** a complex mostly protein product of living cells that induces or speeds chemical reactions in plants and animals without being itself permanently altered — **en·zy·mat·ic** \,en-zə-'mat-ik\ *adj*

**eo·lian** \ē-'ō-lē-ən\ *adj* **:** borne, deposited, or produced by the wind

**EOM** *abbr* end of month

**eon** \'ē-ən, 'ē-,än\ *var of* AEON

**ep·au·let** *also* **ep·au·lette** \,ep-ə-'let\ *n* **:** a shoulder ornament esp. on a uniform

**épée** \'ep-,ā, ā-'pā\ *n* **:** a fencing or dueling sword having a bowl-shaped guard and a tapering rigid blade with no cutting edge

**epergne** \i-'pərn, ā-\ *n* **:** a composite centerpiece of silver or glass used esp. on a dinner table

**Eph** *or* **Ephes** *abbr* Ephesians

**ephed·rine** \i-'fed-rən\ *n* **:** a drug used in relieving hay fever, asthma, and nasal congestion

**ephem·er·al** \i-'fem(-ə)-rəl\ *adj* [Gk *ephēmeros* lasting a day, daily, fr. *hēmera* day] **:** SHORT-LIVED, TRANSITORY **syn** passing, fleeting

**ep·ic** \'ep-ik\ *n* **:** a long poem in elevated style narrating the deeds of a hero — **epic** *adj*

**epi·cen·ter** \'ep-i-,sent-ər\ *n* **:** the earth's surface directly above the focus of an earthquake — **epi·cen·tral** \,ep-i-'sen-trəl\ *adj*

**ep·i·cure** \'ep-i-,kyur\ *n* **:** a person with sensitive and fastidious tastes esp. in food and wine

**ep·i·cu·re·an** \,ep-i-kyu-'rē-ən, -'kyur-ē-\ *n* **:** EPICURE — **epicurean** *adj*

¹**ep·i·dem·ic** \,ep-ə-'dem-ik\ *adj* **:** affecting many persons at one time ⟨∼ disease⟩; *also* **:** excessively prevalent

²**epidemic** *n* **:** an epidemic outbreak esp. of disease

**epi·der·mis** \,ep-ə-'dər-məs\ *n* **:** an outer layer esp. of skin — **epi·der·mal** \-məl\ *adj*

**epi·glot·tis** \-'glät-əs\ *n* **:** a thin plate of flexible tissue protecting the tracheal opening during swallowing

**ep·i·gram** \'ep-ə-,gram\ *n* **:** a short witty poem or saying — **ep·i·gram·mat·ic** \,ep-ə-grə-'mat-ik\ *adj*

**epig·ra·phy** \i-'pig-rə-fē\ *n* **:** the study of inscriptions and esp. of ancient inscriptions

**ep·i·lep·sy** \'ep-ə-,lep-sē\ *n, pl* **-sies :** a nervous disorder marked typically by convulsive attacks with loss of consciousness — **ep·i·lep·tic** \,ep-ə-'lep-tik\ *adj or n*

**ep·i·logue** \'ep-ə-,lòg, -,läg\ *n* **:** a

speech addressed to the spectators by an actor at the end of a play

**epi·neph·rine** *also* **epi·neph·rin** \,ep-ə-'nef-rən\ *n* **:** an adrenal hormone used medicinally esp. as a heart stimulant, a muscle relaxant, and a vasoconstrictor

**Epiph·a·ny** \i-'pif-ə-nē\ *n, pl* **-nies :** January 6 observed as a church festival in commemoration of the coming of the Magi to Jesus at Bethlehem

**epis·co·pa·cy** \i-'pis-kə-pə-sē\ *n, pl* **-cies 1 :** government of a church by bishops **2 :** EPISCOPATE

**epis·co·pal** \i-'pis-kə-pəl\ *adj* **1 :** of or relating to a bishop **2 :** of, having, or constituting government by bishops **3** *cap* **:** of or relating to the Protestant Episcopal Church

**Epis·co·pa·lian** \i-,pis-kə-'pāl-yən\ *n* **:** a member of the Protestant Episcopal Church

**epis·co·pate** \i-'pis-kə-pət, -,pāt\ *n* **1 :** the rank, office, or term of bishop **2 :** a body of bishops

**ep·i·sode** \'ep-ə-,sōd, -,zōd\ *n* [Gk *epeisodion,* fr. *epeisodios* coming in besides, fr. *eisodios* coming in, fr. *eis* into + *hodos* road, journey] **1 :** a unit of action in a dramatic or literary work **2 :** an incident in a course of events **:** OCCURRENCE ⟨a feverish ∼⟩ — **ep·i·sod·ic** \,ep-ə-'säd-ik, -'zäd-\ *adj*

**epis·tle** \i-'pis-əl\ *n* **1** *cap* **:** one of the letters of the New Testament **2 :** LETTER — **epis·to·lary** \i-'pis-tə-,ler-ē\ *adj*

**ep·i·taph** \'ep-ə-,taf\ *n* **:** an inscription in memory of a dead person

**ep·i·tha·la·mi·um** \,ep-ə-thə-'lā-mē-əm\ *or* **ep·i·tha·la·mi·on** \-mē-ən\ *n, pl* **-mi·ums** *or* **-mia** \-mē-ə\ **:** a song or poem in honor of a bride and bridegroom

**ep·i·the·li·um** \,ep-ə-'thē-lē-əm\ *n, pl* **-lia** \-lē-ə\ **:** a cellular membrane covering a bodily surface or lining a cavity — **ep·i·the·li·al** \-lē-əl\ *adj*

**ep·i·thet** \'ep-ə-,thet, -thət\ *n* **:** a characterizing and often abusive word or phrase

**epit·o·me** \i-'pit-ə-mē\ *n* **1 :** ABSTRACT, SUMMARY **2 :** EMBODIMENT — **epit·o·mize** \-,mīz\ *vb*

**ep·och** \'ep-ək, 'ep-,äk\ *n* **:** a usu. extended period **:** ERA, AGE — **ep·och·al** \'ep-ə-kəl, 'ep-,äk-əl\ *adj*

¹**ep·oxy** \'ep-,äk-sē, ep-'äk-sē\ *n* **:** EPOXY RESIN

²**epoxy** *vb* **ep·ox·ied** *or* **ep·oxyed; ep·oxy·ing : to glue with epoxy resin

**epoxy resin** *n* **:** a synthetic resin used in coatings and adhesives

**Ep·som salts** \'ep-səm-\ *n pl* **:** a bitter colorless or white magnesium salt with cathartic properties

**eq** *abbr* equation

**equa·ble** \'ek-wə-bəl, 'ē-kwə-\ *adj* **:** UNIFORM, EVEN; *esp* **:** free from unpleasant extremes — **equa·bil·i·ty** \,ek-wə-'bil-ət-ē, ,ē-kwə-\ *n* — **equa·bly** \'ek-wə-blē, 'ē-kwə-\ *adv*

¹**equal** \'ē-kwəl\ *adj* **1 :** of the same measure, quantity, value, quality, num-

ber, or degree as another **2** : IMPARTIAL **3** : free from extremes **4** : able to cope with a situation or task **syn** same, identical — **equal·i·ty** \i-'kwäl-ət-ē\ n — **equal·ly** \'ē-kwə-lē\ adv

²**equal** n : one that is equal; esp : a person of like rank, abilities, or age

³**equal** vb **equaled** or **equalled**; **equal·ing** or **equal·ling** : to be or become equal to : MATCH

**equal·ize** \'ē-kwə-,līz\ vb **-ized**; **-iz·ing** : to make equal, uniform, or constant — **equal·iza·tion** \,ē-kwə-lə-'zā-shən\ n — **equal·iz·er** \'ē-kwə-,lī-zər\ n

**equa·nim·i·ty** \,ē-kwə-'nim-ət-ē, ,ek-wə-\ n, pl **-ties** : COMPOSURE

**equate** \i-'kwāt\ vb **equat·ed**; **equat·ing** : to make, treat, or regard as equal or comparable

**equa·tion** \i-'kwā-zhən, -shən\ n **1** : an act of equaling : the state of being equated **2** : a usu. formal statement of equivalence (as between mathematical or logical expressions) with the relation typically symbolized by the sign =

**equa·tor** \i-'kwāt-ər\ n : an imaginary circle around the earth that is everywhere equally distant from the two poles and divides the earth's surface into the northern and southern hemispheres — **equa·to·ri·al** \,ē-kwə-'tōr-ē-əl, ,ek-wə-\ adj

**equer·ry** \'ek-wə-rē, i-'kwer-ē\ n, pl **-ries 1** : an officer in charge of the horses of a prince or nobleman **2** : a personal attendant of a member of the British royal family

¹**eques·tri·an** \i-'kwes-trē-ən\ adj **1** : of or relating to horses, horsemen, or horsemanship **2** : representing a person on horseback

²**equestrian** n : one that rides on horseback

**eques·tri·enne** \i-,kwes-trē-'en\ n : a female equestrian

**equi·dis·tant** \,ē-kwə-'dis-tənt\ adj : equally distant

**equi·lat·er·al** \,ē-kwə-'lat-(ə-)rəl\ adj : having equal sides

**equi·lib·ri·um** \,ē-kwə-'lib-rē-əm\ n, pl **-ri·ums** or **-ria** \-rē-ə\ : a state of balance between opposing forces or actions **syn** poise

**equine** \'ē-,kwīn, 'ek-,wīn\ adj [L equinus, fr. equus horse] : of or relating to the horse — **equine** n

**equi·nox** \'ē-kwə-,näks, 'ek-wə-\ n : either of the two times each year when the sun crosses the equator and day and night are everywhere of equal length that occur about March 21 and September 23 — **equi·noc·tial** \,ē-kwə-'näk-shəl, ,ek-wə-\ adj

¹**equip** \i-'kwip\ vb **equipped**; **equip·ping** : to supply with needed resources

²**equip** abb equipment

**eq·ui·page** \'ek-wə-pij\ n : a horse-drawn carriage usu. with its attendant servants

**equip·ment** \i-'kwip-mənt\ n **1** : the equipping of a person or thing : the state of being equipped **2** : things used in equipping : SUPPLIES, OUTFIT

**equi·poise** \'ek-wə-,pȯiz, 'ē-kwə-\ n **1** : BALANCE, EQUILIBRIUM **2** : COUNTERPOISE

**eq·ui·ta·ble** \'ek-wət-ə-bəl\ adj : JUST, FAIR — **eq·ui·ta·bly** \-blē\ adv

**eq·ui·ta·tion** \,ek-wə-'tā-shən\ n : the act or art of riding on horseback

**eq·ui·ty** \'ek-wət-ē\ n, pl **-ties 1** : JUSTNESS, IMPARTIALITY **2** : a legal system developed into a body of rules supplementing the common law **3** : value of a property or of an interest in it in excess of claims against it

**equiv** abbr equivalent

**equiv·a·lent** \i-'kwiv-(ə-)lənt\ adj : EQUAL; also : virtually identical **syn** same — **equiv·a·lence** \-ləns\ n — **equivalent** n

**equiv·o·cal** \i-'kwiv-ə-kəl\ adj **1** : AMBIGUOUS **2** : UNCERTAIN **3** : SUSPICIOUS, DUBIOUS (~ behavior) **syn** obscure, dark, vague, enigmatic — **equiv·o·cal·ly** \-ē\ adv

**equiv·o·cate** \i-'kwiv-ə-,kāt\ vb **-cat·ed**; **-cat·ing** : to use misleading language; also : PREVARICATE — **equiv·o·ca·tion** \-,kwiv-ə-'kā-shən\ n

¹**-er** \ər\ adj suffix or adv suffix — used to form the comparative degree of adjectives and adverbs of one syllable (hotter) (drier) and of some adjectives and adverbs of two syllables (completer) and sometimes of longer ones

²**-er** \ər\ also **-ier** \ē-ər, yər\ or **-yer** \yər\ n suffix **1** : a person occupationally connected with (batter) (lawyer) **2** : a person or thing belonging to or associated with (old-timer) **3** : a native of : resident of (New Yorker) **4** : one that has (three-decker) **5** : one that produces or yields (porker) **6** : one that does or performs (a specified action) (reporter) (builder-upper) **7** : one that is a suitable object of (a specified action) (broiler) **8** : one that is (foreigner)

**era** \'ir-ə, 'er-ə, 'ē-rə\ n [LL aera, fr. L counters, pl. of aes copper, money] **1** : a chronological order or system of notation reckoned from a given date as basis **2** : a period typified by some special feature **syn** age, epoch, aeon

**erad·i·cate** \i-'rad-ə-,kāt\ vb **-cat·ed**; **-cat·ing** [L eradicatus, pp. of eradicare, fr. e- out + radix root] : UPROOT, ELIMINATE **syn** exterminate — **erad·i·ca·ble** \-'rad-i-kə-bəl\ adj

**erase** \i-'rās\ vb **erased**; **eras·ing** : to rub or scratch out (as written words); also : OBLITERATE **syn** cancel, efface, delete — **eras·er** \i-'rā-sər\ n — **era·sure** \-shər\ n

¹**ere** \(,)eər\ prep : BEFORE

²**ere** conj : BEFORE

¹**erect** \i-'rekt\ adj : not leaning or lying down : UPRIGHT

²**erect** vb **1** : BUILD **2** : to fix or set in an upright position **3** : to set up; also : ESTABLISH, DEVELOP

**erec·tile** \i-'rek-t⁷l, -,tīl\ adj : composed largely of vascular sinuses and capable of dilating with blood to bring

**erec·tion** \i-'rek-shən\ *n* **1** : CON-STRUCTION **2** : the turgid state of a previously flaccid bodily part when it becomes dilated with blood

**ere·long** \eər-'lȯŋ\ *adv* : before long

**er·e·mite** \'er-ə-ˌmīt\ *n* : HERMIT

**er·go** \'eər-gō, 'ər-\ *adv* : THEREFORE

**er·gos·ter·ol** \(ˌ)ər-'gäs-tə-ˌrȯl, -ˌrōl\ *n* : a steroid alcohol that occurs esp. in yeast, molds, and ergot and that is converted by ultraviolet radiation ultimately into vitamin D

**er·got** \'ər-gət, -ˌgät\ *n* **1** : a disease of rye and other cereals caused by a fungus; *also* : this fungus **2** : a medicinal compound or preparation derived from an ergot fungus

**Erie** \'i(ə)r-ē\ *n, pl* **Eries** *or* **Erie** : a member of an Indian people of the Lake Erie region; *also* : their language

**er·mine** \'ər-mən\ *n, pl* **ermines** **1** : a weasel with winter fur mostly white; *also* : its fur **2** : a rank or office whose official robe is ornamented with ermine

**erode** \i-'rōd\ *vb* **erod·ed; erod·ing** : to diminish or destroy by degrees; *esp* : to gradually eat into or wear away ⟨soil *eroded* by wind and water⟩ — **erod·ible** \-'rōd-ə-bəl\ *adj*

**erog·e·nous** \i-'räj-ə-nəs\ *also* **er·o·gen·ic** \ˌer-ə-'jen-ik\ *adj* **1** : sexually sensitive ⟨∼ zones⟩ **2** : of, relating to, or arousing sexual feelings

**ero·sion** \i-'rō-zhən\ *n* : the process or state of being eroded — **ero·sion·al** \-'rōzh-(ə-)nəl\ *adj* — **ero·sion·al·ly** \-ē\ *adv*

**ero·sive** \i-'rō-siv\ *adj* : tending to erode — **ero·sive·ness** *n*

**erot·ic** \i-'rät-ik\ *adj* : relating to or dealing with sexual love : AMATORY — **erot·i·cal·ly** \-i-k(ə-)lē\ *adv*

**err** \'eər, 'ər\ *vb* : to be or do wrong

**er·rand** \'er-ənd\ *n* : a short trip taken to do something often for another; *also* : the object or purpose of this trip

**er·rant** \'er-ənt\ *adj* **1** : WANDERING **2** : going astray; *esp* : doing wrong **3** : moving aimlessly

**er·ra·ta** \e-'rät-ə\ *n* : a list of corrigenda

**er·rat·ic** \ir-'at-ik\ *adj* **1** : IRREGULAR, CAPRICIOUS **2** : ECCENTRIC, QUEER — **er·rat·i·cal·ly** \-i-k(ə-)lē\ *adv*

**er·ra·tum** \e-'rät-əm\ *n, pl* **-ta** \-ə\ : CORRIGENDUM

**er·ro·ne·ous** \ir-'ō-nē-əs, e-'rō-\ *adj* : INCORRECT — **er·ro·ne·ous·ly** *adv*

**er·ror** \'er-ər\ *n* **1** : a usu. ignorant or unintentional deviating from accuracy or rectitude ⟨made an ∼ in adding⟩ **2** : the state of one that errs ⟨to be in ∼⟩ **3** : a product of mistake ⟨a typographical ∼⟩ **4** : a defensive misplay in baseball — **er·ror·less** *adj*

**er·satz** \'er-ˌzäts\ *adj* : SUBSTITUTE, SYNTHETIC ⟨∼ flour⟩

**erst** \'ərst\ *adv, archaic* : FORMERLY

**erst·while** \-ˌhwīl\ *adv* : in the past

²**erstwhile** *adj* : FORMER, PREVIOUS

**er·u·di·tion** \ˌer-(y)ə-'dish-ən\ *n* : LEARNING, SCHOLARSHIP — **er·u·dite** \'er-(y)ə-ˌdīt\ *adj*

**erupt** \i-'rəpt\ *vb* **1** : to force out or release usu. suddenly and violently something (as lava or steam) that is pent up **2** : to become active or violent : EXPLODE **3** : to break out with or as if with a skin rash — **erup·tion** \-'rəp-shən\ *n* — **erup·tive** \-tiv\ *adj*

**-ery** \(ə-)rē\ *n suffix* **1** : qualities collectively : characte ⟨-NESS ⟨snobbery⟩ **2** : art : practice ⟨cookery⟩ **3** : place of doing, keeping, producing, or selling (the thing specified) ⟨fishery⟩ ⟨bakery⟩ **4** : collection : aggregate ⟨finery⟩ **5** : state or condition ⟨slavery⟩

**ery·sip·e·las** \ˌer-ə-'sip-(ə-)ləs, ˌir-\ *n* : an acute bacterial disease marked by fever and severe skin inflammation

**er·y·the·ma** \ˌer-ə-'thē-mə\ *n* : abnormal redness of the skin due to capillary congestion (as in inflammation)

**Es** *symbol* einsteinium

¹**-es** \əz, iz *after* s, z, sh, ch; z *after* v or a vowel\ *n pl suffix* **1** — used to form the plural of most nouns that end in *s* ⟨glasses⟩, *z* ⟨fuzzes⟩, *sh* ⟨bushes⟩, *ch* ⟨peaches⟩, or a final *y* that changes to *i* ⟨ladies⟩ and of some nouns ending in *f* that changes to *v* ⟨loaves⟩ **2** : ¹-s **2**

²**-es** *vb suffix* — used to form the third person singular present of most verbs that end in *s* ⟨blesses⟩, *z* ⟨fizzes⟩, *sh* ⟨hushes⟩, *ch* ⟨catches⟩, or a final *y* that changes to *i* ⟨defies⟩

**es·ca·late** \'es-kə-ˌlāt\ *vb* **-lat·ed; -lat·ing** : to increase in extent, volume, intensity, or scope — **es·ca·la·tion** \ˌes-kə-'lā-shən\ *n* — **es·ca·la·to·ry** \'es-kə-lə-ˌtȯr-ē\ *adj*

**es·ca·la·tor** \'es-kə-ˌlāt-ər\ *n* : a power-driven set of stairs arranged to ascend or descend continuously

**es·cal·lop** \is-'käl-əp, -'kal-\ *var of* SCALLOP

**es·ca·pade** \'es-kə-ˌpād\ *n* : a mischievous adventure : PRANK

¹**es·cape** \is-'kāp\ *vb* **es·caped; es·cap·ing** [ME *escapen*, fr. OF *escaper*, fr. (assumed) VL *excappare*, fr. L *ex-* out + LL *cappa* head covering, cloak] **1** : to get away **2** : to avoid a threatening evil **3** : to miss or succeed in averting ⟨∼ injury⟩ **4** : ELUDE ⟨his name ∼s me⟩ **5** : to be produced or uttered involuntarily by ⟨let a sob ∼ him⟩

²**escape** *n* **1** : flight from or avoidance of something unpleasant **2** : LEAKAGE **3** : a means of escape

³**escape** *adj* : providing a means or way of escape

**es·cap·ee** \is-ˌkā-'pē, ˌes-(ˌ)kā-\ *n* : one that has escaped esp. from prison

**escape velocity** *n* : the minimum velocity needed by a body (as a rocket) to escape from the gravitational field of a celestial body (as the earth)

**es·cap·ism** \is-'kā-ˌpiz-əm\ *n* : diversion of the mind to imaginative activity as an escape from routine — **es·cap·ist** \-pəst\ *adj or n*

**es·ca·role** \'es-kə-ˌrōl\ *n* : ENDIVE 1

**es·carp·ment** \is-'kärp-mənt\ *n* **1** : a steep slope in front of a fortification **2** : a long cliff

**es·chew** \is-'chü\ *vb* : SHUN, AVOID ▮

¹es·cort \'es-,kȯrt\ n : one (as a person or warship) accompanying another esp. as a protection or courtesy

²es·cort \is-'kȯrt, es-\ vb : to accompany as an escort

es·cri·toire \'es-krə-,twär\ n : a writing table or desk

es·crow \'es-,krō\ n : something (as a deed or a sum of money) delivered by one person to another to be delivered by him to a third party only upon the fulfillment of a condition; also : a fund or deposit serving as an escrow

es·cu·do \is-'küd-ō\ n, pl -dos — see MONEY table

es·cutch·eon \is-'kəch-ən\ n : the surface on which armorial bearings are displayed

**Esd** abbr Esdras

**ESE** abbr east-southeast

Es·ki·mo \'es-kə-,mō\ n 1 : a member of a group of peoples of northern Canada, Greenland, Alaska, and eastern Siberia 2 : the language of the Eskimo people

**Eskimo dog** n : a broad-chested powerful dog with a long shaggy coat

esoph·a·gus \i-'säf-ə-gəs\ n, pl -gi \-,gī, -,jī\ : a muscular tube connecting the mouth and stomach — esoph·a·geal \-,säf-ə-'jē-əl\ adj

es·o·ter·ic \,es-ə-'ter-ik\ adj 1 : designed for or understood only by the specially initiated 2 : PRIVATE, SECRET

esp abbr especially

**ESP** \,ē-,es-'pē\ n : extrasensory perception

es·pa·drille \'es-pə-,dril\ n : a flat sandal usu. having a fabric upper and a flexible sole

es·pal·ier \is-'pal-yər, -,yā\ n : a plant (as a fruit tree) trained to grow flat against a support — espalier vb

es·pe·cial \is-'pesh-əl\ adj : SPECIAL, PARTICULAR — es·pe·cial·ly \-'pesh-(ə-)lē\ adv

Es·pe·ran·to \,es-pə-'rant-ō, -'rän-tō\ n : an artificial international language based as far as possible on words common to the chief European languages

es·pi·o·nage \'es-pē-ə-,näzh, -nij\ n : the practice of spying

es·pla·nade \'es-plə-,näd, -,nād\ n : a level open stretch or area; esp : one designed for walking or driving along a shore

es·pous·al \is-'paů-zəl\ n 1 : BETROTHAL; also : WEDDING 2 : a taking up (as of a cause) as a supporter — es·pouse \-'paůz\ vb

espres·so \e-'spres-ō\ n, pl -sos [It (caffè) espresso, lit., pressed out coffee] : coffee brewed by forcing steam through finely ground darkly roasted coffee beans

es·prit \is-'prē\ n : sprightly wit

es·prit de corps \is-,prēd-ə-'kȯr\ n : the common spirit existing in the members of a group

es·py \is-'pī\ vb es·pied; es·py·ing : to catch sight of syn behold, see, perceive, discern, notice

**Esq** or **Esqr** abbr esquire

es·quire \'es-,kwī(ə)r\ n [ME, fr. MF esquier squire, fr. LL scutarius, fr. L scutum shield] 1 : a man of the English gentry ranking next below a knight 2 : a candidate for knighthood serving as attendant to a knight 3 — used as a title of courtesy

-ess \əs, ,es\ n suffix : female (authoress)

¹es·say \e-'sā, 'es-,ā\ vb : ATTEMPT, TRY

²es·say n 1 \'es-,ā, e-'sā\ : ATTEMPT 2 \'es-,ā\ : a literary composition usu. dealing with a subject from a limited or personal point of view — es·say·ist \'es-,ā-əst\ n

es·sence \'es-²ns\ n 1 : fundamental nature or quality 2 : a substance distilled or extracted from another substance (as a plant or drug) and having the special qualities of the original substance ⟨∼ of peppermint⟩ 3 : PERFUME

¹es·sen·tial \i-'sen-chəl\ adj 1 : containing or constituting an essence ⟨free speech is an ∼ right of citizenship⟩ ⟨∼ oils⟩ 2 : of the utmost importance : INDISPENSABLE syn requisite, needful — es·sen·tial·ly \-ē\ adv

²essential n : something essential

est abbr 1 established 2 estimate; estimated

**EST** abbr eastern standard time

¹-est \əst, ist\ adj suffix or adv suffix — used to form the superlative degree of adjectives and adverbs of one syllable ⟨fattest⟩ ⟨latest⟩, of some adjectives and adverbs of two syllables ⟨luckiest⟩ ⟨oftenest⟩, and less often of longer ones ⟨beggarliest⟩

²-est \-əst,-ist\ or -st \st\ vb suffix — used to form the archaic second person singular of English verbs (with thou) ⟨gettest⟩ ⟨didst⟩

es·tab·lish \is-'tab-lish\ vb 1 : to make firm or stable 2 : ORDAIN 3 : FOUND ⟨∼ a settlement⟩; also : EFFECT 4 : to put on a firm basis : set up ⟨∼ a son in business⟩ 5 : to gain acceptance or recognition of (as a claim or fact) ⟨∼ed his right to help⟩; also : PROVE

es·tab·lish·ment \-mənt\ n 1 : an organized force for carrying on public or private business 2 : a place of residence or business with its furnishings and staff 3 : an establishing or being established 4 : an established ruling or controlling group ⟨the literary ∼⟩

es·ta·mi·net \e-stá-mē-nȧ\ n, pl -nets \-nä(z)\ : a small café

es·tate \is-'tāt\ n 1 : STATE, CONDITION; also : social standing : STATUS 2 : a social or political class ⟨the three ∼s of nobility, clergy, and commons⟩ 3 : a person's possessions : FORTUNE 4 : a landed property

¹es·teem \is-'tēm\ n : high regard

²esteem vb 1 : REGARD 2 : to set a high value on syn respect, admire

es·ter \'es-tər\ n : an often fragrant organic compound formed by the reaction of an acid and an alcohol

**Esth** abbr Esther

esthete, esthetic, esthetics var of AESTHETE, AESTHETIC, AESTHETICS

es·ti·ma·ble \'es-tə-mə-bəl\ adj : worthy of esteem

¹es·ti·mate \'es-tə-ˌmāt\ vb -mat·ed; -mat·ing 1 : to give or form an approximation (as of value, size, or cost) 2 : JUDGE, CONCLUDE syn evaluate, value, rate, calculate — es·ti·ma·tor \-ˌmā-tər\ n

²es·ti·mate \'es-tə-mət\ n 1 : OPINION, JUDGMENT 2 : a rough or approximate calculation 3 : a statement of the cost of a job

es·ti·ma·tion \ˌes-tə-'mā-shən\ n 1 : JUDGMENT, OPINION 2 : ESTIMATE 3 : ESTEEM, HONOR

Es·to·nian \e-'stō-nē-ən\ n : a native or inhabitant of Estonia

es·trange \is-'trānj\ vb es·tranged; es·trang·ing : to alienate the affections or confidence of — es·trange·ment n

es·tro·gen \'es-trə-jən\ n : a substance (as a hormone) that promotes development of various female characteristics — es·tro·gen·ic \ˌes-trə-'jen-ik\ adj

es·tu·ary \'es-chə-ˌwer-ē\ n, pl -ar·ies : an arm of the sea at the mouth of a river

ET abbr eastern time

ETA abbr estimated time of arrival

et al \et-'al\ abbr [L et alii] and others

etc \ən-'sō-ˌforth, et-'set-ə-rə, -'se trə\ abbr et cetera

et cet·era \et-'set-ə-rə, -'se-trə\ [L] : and others esp. of the same kind

etch \'ecd\ vb [D etsen, fr G ätzen lit., to feed] 1 : to make lines on (as metal) usu. by the action of acid; also : to produce (as a design) by etching 2 : to delineate clearly — etch·er n

etch·ing \-iŋ\ n 1 : the act, process, or art of etching 2 : a design produced on or print made from an etched plate

ETD abbr estimated time of departure

eter·nal \i-'tərn-ᵊl\ adj : EVERLASTING, PERPETUAL — eter·nal·ly \-ē\ adv

eter·ni·ty \i-'tər-nət-ē\ n, pl -ties 1 : infinite duration 2 : IMMORTALITY

¹-eth \əth, ith\ or -th \th\ vb suffix — used to form the archaic third person singular present of verbs ⟨goeth⟩ ⟨doth⟩

²-eth — see ²-TH

eth·ane \'eth-ˌān\ n : a colorless odorless gaseous hydrocarbon found in natural gas and used esp. as a fuel

eth·a·nol \'eth-ə-ˌnòl, -ˌnōl\ n : ALCOHOL 1

ether \'ē-thər\ n 1 : the upper regions of space; also : the gaseous element formerly held to fill these regions 2 : a light flammable liquid used as an anesthetic and solvent

ethe·re·al \i-'thir-ē-əl\ adj 1 : CELESTIAL, HEAVENLY 2 : exceptionally delicate : AIRY, DAINTY — ethe·re·al·ly \-ē\ adv — ethe·re·al·ness n

eth·i·cal \'eth-i-kəl\ adj 1 : of or relating to ethics 2 : conforming to accepted and esp. professional standards of conduct syn virtuous, honorable, upright — eth·i·cal·ly \-i-k(ə-)lē\ adv

eth·ics \'eth-iks\ n sing or pl 1 : a discipline dealing with good and evil and with moral duty 2 : moral principles or practice

Ethi·o·pi·an \ˌē-thē-'ō-pē-ən\ n : a native or inhabitant of Ethiopia — Ethiopian adj

¹eth·nic \'eth-nik\ adj : of or relating to races or large groups of people classed according to common traits and customs — eth·ni·cal·ly \-ni-k(ə-)lē\ adv

²ethnic n : a member of a minority ethnic group who retains its customs, language, or social views

ethnol abbr ethnology

eth·nol·o·gy \eth-'näl-ə-jē\ n : a science dealing with the races of man, their origin, distribution, characteristics, and relations — eth·no·log·ic \ˌeth-nə-'läj-ik\ or eth·no·log·i·cal \-i-kəl\ adj — eth·nol·o·gist \eth-'näl-ə-jəst\ n

ethol·o·gy \ē-'thäl-ə-jē\ n : the scientific and objective study of animal behavior — etho·log·i·cal \ˌē-thə-'läj-i-kəl, ˌeth-ə-\ adj — ethol·o·gist \ē-'thäl-ə-jəst\ n

ethos \'ē-ˌthäs\ n : the distinguishing character, sentiment, moral nature, or guiding beliefs of a person, group, or institution

eth·yl \'eth-əl\ n : a hydrocarbon radical occurring in alcohol and ether — eth·yl·ic \e-'thil-ik\ adj

ethyl alcohol n : ALCOHOL 1

eti·ol·o·gy \ˌēt-ē-'äl-ə-jē\ n 1 : CAUSE, ORIGIN; also : the study of causes — eti·o·log·ic \ˌēt-ē-ə-'läj-ik\ or eti·o·log·i·cal \-i-kəl\ adj

et·i·quette \'et-i-kət, -ˌket\ n [F étiquette, lit., ticket] : the forms prescribed by custom or authority to be observed in social, official, or professional life syn propriety, decorum

Etrus·can \i-'trəs-kən\ n 1 : an inhabitant of ancient Etruria 2 : the language of the Etruscans

et seq abbr [L et sequens, et sequentes (masc. & fem. pl.), et sequentia (neut. pl.)] 1 and the following one 2 and the following ones

-ette \'et, ˌet, ət, it\ n suffix 1 : little one ⟨dinette⟩ 2 : female ⟨majorette⟩

étude \'ā-ˌt(y)üd\ n : a musical composition for practice to develop technical skill

ETV abbr educational television

ety abbr etymology

et·y·mol·o·gy \ˌet-ə-'mäl-ə-jē\ n, pl -gies 1 : the history of a linguistic form (as a word) shown by tracing its development and relationships 2 : a branch of linguistics dealing with etymologies — et·y·mo·log·i·cal \-mə-'läj-i-kəl\ adj — et·y·mol·o·gist \-'mäl-ə-jəst\ n

Eu symbol europium

eu·ca·lyp·tus \ˌyü-kə-'lip-təs\ n, pl -ti \-ˌtī\ or -tus·es : any of a genus of mostly Australian evergreen trees widely grown for shade or useful products

Eu·cha·rist \'yü-k(ə-)rəst\ n : COMMUNION 3 — eu·cha·ris·tic \ˌyü-kə-'ris-tik\ adj, often cap

¹eu·chre \'yü-kər\ n : a card game in which the side naming the trump must

take three of five tricks to win

²euchre \ˈ eu·chred; eu·chring \-k(ə-)riŋ\ : CHEAT, TRICK

eu·clid·e·an also u·clid·i·an \yu̇-ˈklid-ē-ən\ adj, often cap : of or relating to the geometry of Euclid or a geometry based on similar axioms

eu·gen·ics \yu̇-ˈjen-iks\ n : a science dealing with the improvement (as by selective breeding) of hereditary qualities esp. of human beings — eu·gen·ic \-ik\ adj

eu·lo·gy \ˈyü-lə-jē\ n, pl -gies 1 : a speech in praise of some person or thing 2 : high praise — eu·lo·gis·tic \ˌyü-lə-ˈjis-tik\ adj — eu·lo·gize \ˈyü-lə-ˌjīz\ vb

eu·nuch \ˈyü-nək\ n : a castrated man

eu·phe·mism \ˈyü-fə-ˌmiz-əm\ n [Gk euphēmismos, fr euphēmos auspicious, sounding good, fr. eu- good + phēmē speech, fr. phanai to speak] : the substitution of a pleasant expression for one offensive or unpleasant; also : the expression substituted — eu·phe·mis·tic \ˌyü-fə-ˈmis-tik\ adj

eu·pho·ni·ous \yu̇-ˈfō-nē-əs\ adj : pleasing to the ear

eu·pho·ny \ˈyü-fə-nē\ n, pl -nies : the effect produced by words so combined as to please the ear

eu·pho·ria \yu̇-ˈfōr-ē-ə\ n : a marked feeling of well-being or elation — eu·phor·ic \-ˈfor-ik\ adj

Eur abbr Europe; European

Eur·asian \yu̇-ˈrā-zhən, -shən\ adj : of or relating to Europe and Asia — Eurasian n

eu·re·ka \yu̇-ˈrē-kə\ interj [Gk heurēka I have found, fr. heuriskein to find; fr. the exclamation attributed to Archimedes on discovering a method for determining the purity of gold] — used to express triumph on a discovery

Eu·ro·bond \ˈyu̇r-ō-ˌbänd\ n : a bond of a U.S. corporation that is sold outside the U.S. but that is valued and paid for in dollars and yields interest in dollars

Eu·ro·dol·lar \ˈyu̇r-ō-ˌdäl-ər\ n : a U.S. dollar held (as by a bank) outside the U.S. and esp. in Europe

Eu·ro·pe·an \ˌyu̇r-ə-ˈpē-ən\ n : a native or inhabitant of Europe — European adj

European plan n : a hotel plan whereby the daily rates cover only the cost of the room

eu·ro·pi·um \yu̇-ˈrō-pē-əm\ n : a metallic chemical element

Eu·ro·po·cen·tric \yu̇-ˌrō-pə-ˈsen·trik\ adj : WESTERN; esp : centered on Europe and the Europeans

eu·sta·chian tube \yu̇-ˌstā-sh(ē-)ən-\ n, often cap E : a tube connecting the inner cavity of the ear with the throat and equalizing air pressure on both sides of the eardrum

eu·tha·na·sia \ˌyü-thə-ˈnā-zh(ē-)ə\ n [Gk, easy death, fr. eu- good + thanatos death] : the act or practice of killing (as an aged animal or incurable invalid) for reasons of mercy

eu·then·ics \yu̇-ˈthen-iks\ n : a

science dealing with the improvement of human qualities by changes in environment

eu·tro·phic \yu̇-ˈtrō-fik\ adj : rich in dissolved nutrients (as phosphates) but often shallow and seasonally deficient in oxygen ⟨a ~ lake⟩ — eu·tro·phi·ca·tion \-ˌtrō-fə-ˈkā-shən\ n — eu·tro·phy \ˈyü-trə-fē\

EVA abbr extravehicular activity

evac·u·ate \i-ˈvak-yə-ˌwāt\ vb -at·ed; -at·ing 1 : EMPTY 2 : to discharge wastes from the body 3 : to remove or withdraw from : VACATE — evac·u·a·tion \-ˌvak-yə-ˈwā-shən\ n

evac·u·ee \i-ˌvak-yə-ˈwē\ n : an evacuated person

evade \i-ˈvād\ vb evad·ed; evad·ing : to manage to avoid esp. by dexerity or slyness : ELUDE, ESCAPE

eval·u·ate \i-ˈval-ə-ˌwāt\ vb at·ed; -at·ing : APPRAISE, VALUE — eval·u·a·tion \-ˌval-yə-ˈwā-shən\ n

ev·a·nes·cent \ˌev-ə-ˈnes-ᵊnt\ adj : tending to vanish like vapor syn passing, transient, transitory, momentary — ev·a·nes·cence \-ᵊns\ n

evan·gel·i·cal \ˌē-ˌvan-ˈjel-i-kəl, ˌev-ən\ adj [LL evangelium gospel, fr. Gk evangelion, fr. eu- good + angelos messenger] 1 : of or relating to the Christian gospel esp. as presented in the four Gospels 2 : of or relating to certain Protestant churches emphasizing the authority of Scripture and the importance of preaching as contrasted with ritual 3 : ZEALOUS ⟨~ fervor⟩ — Evangelical n — Evan·gel·i·cal·ism \-kə-ˌliz-əm\ n — evan·gel·i·cal·ly \-k(ə-)lē\ adv

evan·ge·lism \i-ˈvan-jə-ˌliz-əm\ n 1 : the winning or revival of personal commitments to Christ 2 : militant or crusading zeal — evan·ge·lis·tic \-ˌvan-jə-ˈlis-tik\ adj — evan·ge·lis·ti·cal·ly \-ti-k(ə-)lē\ adv

evan·ge·list \i-ˈvan-jə-ləst\ n 1 often cap : the writer of any of the four Gospels 2 : one who evangelizes; esp : a preacher who conducts revival services

evan·ge·lize \i-ˈvan-jə-ˌlīz\ vb -lized; -liz·ing 1 : to preach the gospel 2 : to convert to Christianity

evap abbr evaporate

evap·o·rate \i-ˈvap-ə-ˌrāt\ vb -rat·ed; -rat·ing 1 : to pass off in vapor 2 : to convert into vapor 3 : to drive out the moisture from (as by heat) 4 : to disappear quickly — evap·o·ra·tion \-ˌvap-ə-ˈrā-shən\ n — evap·o·ra·tive \-ˈvap·ə-ˌrāt-iv\ adj — evap·o·ra·tor \-ˌrāt-ər\ n

evap·o·rite \i-ˈvap-ə-ˌrīt\ n : a sedimentary rock that originates by the evaporation of seawater in an enclosed basin — evap·o·rit·ic \-ˌvap-ə-ˈrit-ik\ adj

eva·sion \i-ˈvā-zhən\ n 1 : an act or instance of evading 2 : a means of evading; esp : an equivocal statement used in evading — eva·sive \i-ˈvā-siv\ adj — eva·sive·ness n

eve \ˈēv\ n 1 : EVENING 2 : the period just before some important event

**even** \'ē-vən\ *adj* **1** : LEVEL, FLAT **2** : REGULAR, SMOOTH **3** : EQUAL **4** : FAIR **5** : BALANCED; *also* : fully revenged **6** : divisible by two **7** : EXACT **syn** flush, uniform, steady, constant — **even·ly** *adv* — **even·ness** \-vən-nəs\ *n*

²**even** *adv* **1** : as well : PRECISELY, JUST **2** : FULLY, QUITE **3** : at the very time : ALREADY **4** — used as an intensive to stress identity ⟨~ we know that⟩ **5** — used as an intensive to stress the comparative degree

³**even** *vb* **evened; even·ing** \'ēv-(ə-)niŋ\ : to make or become even

**even-hand·ed** \‚ē-vən-'han-dəd\ *adj* : FAIR, IMPARTIAL

**eve·ning** \'ēv-niŋ\ *n* : the end of the day and early part of the night

**evening primrose** *n* : a coarse biennial herb with yellow flowers that open in the evening

**evening star** *n* : a bright planet seen esp. in the western sky at or after sunset

**even·song** \'ē-vən-,sȯŋ\ *n, often cap* **1** : VESPERS **2** : evening prayer esp. when sung

**event** \i-'vent\ *n* [MF or L; MF, fr. L *eventus*, fr. *evenire* to happen, fr. *venire* to come] **1** : OCCURRENCE **2** : a noteworthy happening **3** : CONTINGENCY **4** : a contest in a program of sports — **event·ful** *adj*

**even·tide** \'ē-vən-,tīd\ *n* : EVENING

**even·tu·al** \i-'vench-(ə-w)əl\ *adj* : LATER; *also* : ULTIMATE — **even·tu·al·ly** \-ē\ *adv*

**even·tu·al·i·ty** \i-,ven-chə-'wal-ət-ē\ *n, pl* **-ties** : a possible event or outcome

**even·tu·ate** \i-'ven-chə-‚wāt\ *vb* **-at·ed; -at·ing** : to result finally

**ev·er** \'ev-ər\ *adv* **1** : ALWAYS **2** : at any time **3** : in any case

**ev·er-bloom·ing** \‚ev-ər-'blü-miŋ\ *adj* : blooming more or less continuously throughout the growing season

**ev·er·glade** \'ev-ər-,glād\ *n* : a low-lying tract ot swampy or marshy land

**ev·er·green** \-,grēn\ *adj* : having foliage that remains green ⟨coniferous trees are mostly ~⟩ — **evergreen** *n*

¹**ev·er·last·ing** \‚ev-ər-'las-tiŋ\ *adj* : enduring forever : ETERNAL — **ev·er·last·ing·ly** *adv*

²**everlasting** *n* **1** : ETERNITY ⟨from ~⟩ **2** : a plant whose flowers may be dried without loss of form or color

**ev·er·more** \‚ev-ər-'mōr\ *adv* : FOREVER

**ev·ery** \'ev-rē\ *adj* **1** : being one of the total of members of a group or class **2** : all possible ⟨given ~ chance⟩; *also* : COMPLETE

**ev·ery·body** \'ev-ri-,bäd-ē, -,bəd-\ *pron* : every person

**ev·ery·day** \'ev-rē-,dā\ *adj* : used or fit for daily use : ORDINARY

**ev·ery·one** \-‚(,)wən\ *pron* : every person

**ev·ery·thing** \'ev-rē-,thiŋ\ *pron* : all that exists; *also* : all that is relevant

**ev·ery·where** \'ev-rē-,hwear\ *adv* : in every place or part

**evg** *abbr* evening

**evict** \i-'vikt\ *vb* : to put (a person) out from a property by legal process; *also* : EXPEL **syn** eject, oust — **evic·tion** \-'vik-shən\ *n*

**ev·i·dence** \'ev-əd-əns\ *n* **1** : an outward sign **2** : PROOF, TESTIMONY; *esp* : matter submitted in court to determine the truth of alleged facts

**ev·i·dent** \'ev-əd-ənt\ *adj* : clear to the vision and understanding **syn** manifest, distinct, obvious, apparent, plain — **ev·i·dent·ly** \'ev-əd-ənt-lē, -ə-‚dent-\ *adv*

¹**evil** \'ē-vəl\ *adj* **evil·er** *or* **evil·ler; evil·est** *or* **evil·lest** **1** : WICKED **2** : causing or threatening distress or harm : PERNICIOUS — **evil·ly** *adv*

²**evil** *n* **1** : SIN **2** : a source of sorrow or distress : CALAMITY — **evil·do·er** \‚ē-vəl-'dü-ər\ *n*

**evil-mind·ed** \‚ē-vəl-'mīn-dəd\ *adj* : having an evil disposition or evil thoughts

**evince** \i-'vins\ *vb* **evinced; evinc·ing** : SHOW, REVEAL

**evis·cer·ate** \i-'vis-ə-,rāt\ *vb* **-at·ed; -at·ing** **1** : to remove the entrails of **2** : to deprive of vital content or force — **evis·cer·a·tion** \-,vis-ə-'rā-shən\ *n*

**evoke** \i-'vōk\ *vb* **evoked; evok·ing** : to call forth or up — **evo·ca·tion** \‚ē-vō-'kā-shən ,ev-ə-\ *n* — **evoc·a·tive** \i-'väk-ət-iv\ *adj*

**evo·lu·tion** \‚ev-ə-'lü-shən\ *n* **1** : a process of change in a particular direction **2** : one of a series of prescribed movements (as in a dance or military exercise) **3** : the process by which through a series of steps something (as an organism) attains its distinctive character; *also* : a theory that existent types of animals and plants have developed from previously existing kinds — **evo·lu·tion·ary** \‚ sha-,ner-ē\ *adj* — **evo·lu·tion·ist** \-sh(ə-)nəst\ *n*

**evolve** \i-'välv\ *vb* **evolved; evolv·ing** [L *evolvere* to unroll] : to develop by or as if by evolution

**EW** *abbr* enlisted woman

**ewe** \'yü\ *n* : a female sheep

**ew·er** \'yü-ər\ *n* : a vase-shaped jug

¹**ex** \'eks\ *n* : a former spouse

²**ex** \(,)eks\ *prep* [L] : out of : from

³**ex** *abbr* **1** example **2** express **3** extra

**Ex** *abbr* Exodus

**ex-** \e *also occurs in this prefix where only i is shown below (as in* "express") *and* ks *sometimes occurs where only gz is shown (as in* "exact")\ *prefix* **1** : out of : outside **2** : former ⟨*ex* president⟩

**ex·ac·er·bate** \ig-'zas-ər-,bāt\ *vb* **-bat·ed; -bat·ing** : to make more violent, bitter, or severe — **ex·ac·er·ba·tion** \-,zas-ər-'bā-shən\ *n*

¹**ex·act** \ig-'zakt\ *vb* **1** : to compel to furnish : EXTORT **2** : to call for as suitable or necessary — **ex·ac·tion** \-'zak-shən\ *n*

²**exact** *adj* : precisely accurate or correct **syn** right, precise — **ex·act·ly** \-(t)lē\ *adv* — **ex·act·ness** \-'zak(t)-nəs\ *n*

**ex·act·ing** \ig-'zak-tiŋ\ *adj* **1** : greatly demanding ⟨an ~ taskmaster⟩ **2** : requiring close attention and precision

**ex·ac·ti·tude** \ig-'zak-tə-,t(y)üd\ *n* : the quality or an instance of being exact

**ex·ag·ger·ate** \ig-'zaj-ə-,rāt\ *vb* **-at·ed; -at·ing** [L *exaggeratus*, pp. of *exaggerare*, lit., to heap up, fr. *agger* heap] : to enlarge (as a statement) beyond bounds : OVERSTATE — **ex·ag·ger·at·ed·ly** *adv* — **ex·ag·ger·a·tion** \-,zaj-ə-'rā-shən\ *n* — **ex·ag·ger·a·tor** \-'zaj-ə-,rāt-ər\ *n*

**ex·alt** \ig-'zȯlt\ *vb* **1** : to raise up esp. in rank, power, or dignity **2** : GLORIFY **3** : to elate the mind or spirits — **ex·al·ta·tion** \,eg-,zȯl-'tā-shən, ,ek-,sȯl-\ *n*

**ex·am** \ig-'zam\ *n* : EXAMINATION

**ex·am·ine** \ig-'zam-ən\ *vb* **ex·am·ined; ex·am·in·ing** \-(ə-)niŋ\ **1** : to inspect closely : SCRUTINIZE, INVESTIGATE **2** : QUESTION; *esp* : to test by questioning syn scan, audit, quiz, catechize — **ex·am·i·na·tion** \-,zam-ə-'nā-shən\ *n*

**ex·am·ple** \ig-'zam-pəl\ *n* **1** : a representative sample **2** : something forming a model to be followed or avoided **3** : a problem to be solved in order to show the application of some rule

**ex·as·per·ate** \ig-'zas-pə-,rāt\ *vb* **-at·ed; -at·ing** : VEX, IRRITATE — **ex·as·per·a·tion** \ig-,zas-pə-'rā-shən\ *n*

**exc** *abbr* excellent, except

**ex·ca·vate** \'ek-skə-,vāt\ *vb* **-vat·ed; -vat·ing 1** : to hollow out; *also* : to form by hollowing out **2** : to dig out and remove (as earth) **3** : to reveal to view by digging away a covering — **ex·ca·va·tion** \,ek-skə-'vā-shən\ *n* — **ex·ca·va·tor** \'ek-skə-,vāt-ər\ *n*

**ex·ceed** \ik-'sēd\ *vb* **1** : to go or be beyond the limit of **2** : SURPASS

**ex·ceed·ing·ly** \-iŋ-lē\ *or* **ex·ceed·ing** *adv* : EXTREMELY, VERY

**ex·cel** \ik-'sel\ *vb* **ex·celled; ex·cel·ling** : SURPASS, OUTDO

**ex·cel·lence** \'ek-s(ə-)ləns\ *n* **1** : the quality of being excellent **2** : an excellent or valuable quality : VIRTUE **3** : EXCELLENCY 2

**ex·cel·len·cy** \-s(ə-)lən-sē\ *n, pl* **-cies 1** : EXCELLENCE **2** — used as a title of honor

**ex·cel·lent** \'ek-s(ə-)lənt\ *adj* : very good of its kind : FIRST-CLASS — **ex·cel·lent·ly** *adv*

**ex·cel·si·or** \ik-'sel-sē-ər\ *n* : fine curled wood shavings used esp. for packing fragile items

¹**ex·cept** \ik-'sept\ *vb* **1** : to take or leave out **2** : OBJECT

²**except** *also* **ex·cept·ing** *prep* **1** : not including ⟨daily ~ Sundays⟩ **2** : other than : BUT ⟨saw no one ~ him⟩

³**except** *also* **excepting** *conj* : ONLY ⟨I'd go, ~ it's too far⟩

**ex·cep·tion** \ik-'sep-shən\ *n* **1** : the act of excepting **2** : something excepted **3** : OBJECTION

**ex·cep·tion·able** \ik-'sep-sh(ə-)nə-bəl\ *adj* : liable to exception

**ex·cep·tion·al** \ik-'sep-sh(ə-)nəl\ *adj* : UNUSUAL; *esp* : SUPERIOR — **ex·cep-**

**tion·al·ly** \-'sep-sh(ə-)nə-lē\ *adv*

**ex·cerpt** \'ek-,sərpt, 'eg-,zərpt\ *n* : a passage selected or copied : EXTRACT — **excerpt** \ek-'sərpt, eg-'zərpt; 'ek-,sərpt, 'eg-,zərpt\ *vb*

**ex·cess** \ik-'ses, 'ek-,ses\ *n* **1** : SUPERFLUITY, SURPLUS **2** : the amount by which one quantity exceeds another **3** : INTEMPERANCE — **excess** *adj* — **ex·ces·sive** \ik-'ses-iv\ *adj* — **ex·ces·sive·ly** *adv*

**exch** *abbr* exchange; exchanged

¹**ex·change** \iks-'chānj, 'eks-,chānj\ *n* **1** : the giving or taking of one thing in return for another : TRADE **2** : a substituting of one thing for another **3** : interchange of valuables and esp. of bills of exchange or money of different countries **4** : a place where things and services are exchanged; *esp* : a marketplace esp. for securities **5** : a central office in which telephone lines are connected for communication

²**exchange** *vb* **ex·changed; ex·chang·ing** : to transfer in return for some equivalent : BARTER, SWAP — **ex·change·able** \iks-'chān-jə-bəl\ *adj*

**ex·che·quer** \'eks-,chek-ər\ *n* [ME *escheker* fr. OF *eschequier* chessboard, counting table] : TREASURY; *esp* : a national treasury

¹**ex·cise** \'ek-,sīz, -,sīs\ *n* : a tax on the manufacture, sale, or consumption of goods within a country

²**ex·cise** \ik-'sīz\ *vb* **ex·cised; ex·cis·ing** : to remove by cutting out — **ex·ci·sion** \-'sizh-ən\ *n*

**ex·cit·able** \ik-'sīt-ə-bəl\ *adj* : easily excited — **ex·cit·abil·i·ty** \-,sīt-ə-'bil-ət-ē\ *n*

**ex·cite** \ik-'sīt\ *vb* **ex·cit·ed; ex·cit·ing 1** : to rouse to activity : stir up **2** : to kindle the emotions of : STIMULATE syn provoke, stimulate, pique — **ex·ci·ta·tion** \,ek-,sī-'tā-shən, ,ek-sə-\ *n* — **ex·cit·ed·ly** *adv*

**ex·cite·ment** \ik-'sīt-mənt\ *n* : AGITATION, STIR

**ex·claim** \iks-'klām\ *vb* : to cry out, speak, or utter sharply or vehemently — **ex·cla·ma·tion** \,eks-klə-'mā-shən\ *n* — **ex·clam·a·to·ry** \iks-'klam-ə-,tōr-ē\ *adj*

**exclamation point** *n* : a punctuation mark ! used esp. after an interjection or exclamation

**ex·clude** \iks-'klüd\ *vb* **ex·clud·ed; ex·clud·ing 1** : to shut out (as from using or participating) : EJECT **2** : BAR — **ex·clu·sion** \-'klü-zhən\ *n*

**ex·clu·sive** \iks-'klü-siv\ *adj* **1** : reserved for particular persons **2** : snobbishly aloof; *also* : STYLISH **3** : SOLE ⟨~ rights⟩; *also* : UNDIVIDED syn select, elect, fashionable — **ex·clu·sive·ly** *adv* — **ex·clu·sive·ness** *n*

**exclusive of** *prep* : not taking into account

**ex·cog·i·tate** \ek-'skäj-ə-,tāt\ *vb* : to think out : DEVISE

**ex·com·mu·ni·cate** \,ek-skə-'myü-nə-,kāt\ *vb* **1** : to cut off officially from communion with the church **2** : to exclude from fellowship — **ex·com·mu-**

**ni·ca·tion** \-ˌmyü-nə-ˈkā-shən\ n

**ex·co·ri·ate** \ek-ˈskōr-ē-ˌāt\ vb **-at·ed; -at·ing :** to censure with harsh severity

**ex·cre·ment** \ˈek-skrə-mənt\ n **:** waste discharged from the body and esp. from the alimentary canal — **ex·cre·men·tal** \ˌek-skrə-ˈment-ᵊl\ adj

**ex·cres·cence** \ik-ˈskres-ᵊns\ n **:** OUT-GROWTH; esp **:** an abnormal outgrowth (as a wart) — **ex·cres·cent** \-ᵊnt\ adj

**ex·cre·ta** \ik-ˈskrēt-ə\ n pl **:** waste matter separated or eliminated from an organism

**ex·crete** \ik-ˈskrēt\ vb **ex·cret·ed; ex·cret·ing :** to separate and eliminate wastes from the body esp. in urine — **ex·cre·tion** \-ˈskrē-shən\ n — **ex·cre·to·ry** \ˈek-skrə-ˌtōr-ē\ adj

**ex·cru·ci·at·ing** \ik-ˈskrü-shē-ˌāt-iŋ\ adj [L excruciare, fr. cruciare to crucify, fr. crux cross] **:** intensely painful or distressing syn agonizing — **ex·cru·ci·at·ing·ly** adv

**ex·cul·pate** \ˈek-(ˌ)skəl-ˌpāt\ vb **-pat·ed; -pat·ing :** to clear from alleged fault or guilt syn absolve, exonerate, acquit, vindicate

**ex·cur·sion** \ik-ˈskər-zhən\ n **1 :** EX-PEDITION; esp **:** a pleasure trip **2 :** DI-GRESSION **3 :** an outward movement or a cycle of movement (as of a pendulum) — **ex·cur·sion·ist** \-ˈskərzh-(ə-)nəst\ n

**ex·cur·sive** \-ˈskər-siv\ adj **:** constituting or characterized by digression

**ex·cur·sus** \ik-ˈskər-səs\ n, pl **ex·cur·sus·es** also **ex·cur·sus** \-səs, -ˌsüs\ **:** an appendix or a digression containing further exposition of some point or topic

**¹ex·cuse** \ik-ˈskyüz\ vb **ex·cused; ex·cus·ing** [ME excusen, fr. OF excuser, fr. L excusare, fr. causa cause, explanation] **1 :** to offer excuse for **2 :** PARDON **3 :** to release from an obligation **4 :** JUSTIFY — **ex·cus·able** adj

**²ex·cuse** \ˈskyüs\ n **1 :** an act of excusing **2 :** grounds for being excused **:** JUSTIFICATION **3 :** APOLOGY

**exec** abbr executive

**ex·e·cra·ble** \ˈek-si-krə-bəl\ adj **1 :** DETESTABLE **2 :** very bad (~ spelling)

**ex·e·crate** \ˈek-sə-ˌkrāt\ vb **-crat·ed; -crat·ing** [L exsecratus, pp. of exsecrari to put under a curse, fr. ex- out of + sacer sacred] **:** to denounce as evil or detestable; also **:** DETEST — **ex·e·cra·tion** \ˌek-sə-ˈkrā-shən\ n

**ex·e·cute** \ˈek-si-ˌkyüt\ vb **-cut·ed; -cut·ing 1 :** to carry to completion **:** PERFORM **2 :** to do what is called for by (as a law) **3 :** to put to death in accordance with a legal sentence **4 :** to produce in accordance with a plan or design **5 :** to do what is needed to give legal force to (as a deed) — **ex·e·cu·tion** \ˌek-si-ˈkyü-shən\ n — **ex·e·cu·tion·er** \-sh(ə-)nər\ n

**¹ex·ec·u·tive** \ig-ˈzek-(y)ət-iv\ adj **1 :** designed for or related to carrying out plans or purposes **2 :** of or relating to the enforcement of laws and the conduct of affairs

**²executive** n **1 :** the branch of government with executive duties **2 :** one constituting the controlling element of an organization **3 :** one working as a manager or administrator

**ex·ec·u·tor** \ig-ˈzek-(y)ət-ər\ n **:** the person named by a testator to execute his will

**ex·ec·u·trix** \ig-ˈzek-(y)ə-ˌtriks\ n, pl **ex·ec·u·tri·ces** \-ˌzek-(y)ə-ˈtrī-ˌsēz\ or **ex·ec·u·trix·es** \-ˈzek-(y)ə-ˌtrik-səz\ **:** a female executor

**ex·e·ge·sis** \ˌek-sə-ˈjē-səs\ n, pl **-ge·ses** \-ˈjē-ˌsēz\ **:** explanation or critical interpretation of a text

**ex·e·gete** \ˈek-sə-ˌjēt\ n **:** one who practices exegesis

**ex·em·plar** \ig-ˈzem-ˌplär, -plər\ n **1 :** one that serves as a model or pattern; esp **:** an ideal model **2 :** a typical instance or example

**ex·em·pla·ry** \ig-ˈzem-plə-rē\ adj **:** serving as a pattern; also **:** COMMEND-ABLE

**ex·em·pli·fy** \ig-ˈzem-plə-ˌfī\ vb **-fied; -fy·ing :** to illustrate by example **:** serve as an example of — **ex·em·pli·fi·ca·tion** \-ˌzem-plə-fə-ˈkā-shən\ n

**¹ex·empt** \ig-ˈzempt\ adj **:** free from some liability to which others are subject

**²exempt** vb **:** to make exempt **:** EXCUSE — **ex·emp·tion** \ig-ˈzemp-shən\ n

**¹ex·er·cise** \ˈek-sər-ˌsīz\ n **1 :** EMPLOY-MENT, USE (~ of authority) **2 :** exertion made for the sake of training **3 :** a task or problem done to develop skill **4** pl **:** a public exhibition or ceremony

**²exercise** vb **-cised; -cis·ing 1 :** EX-ERT (~ control) **2 :** to train by or engage in exercise **3 :** WORRY, DISTRESS — **ex·er·cis·er** n

**ex·ert** \ig-ˈzert\ vb **:** to bring or put into action (~ a skill) (~ed himself) — **ex·er·tion** \-ˈzər-shən\ n

**ex·hale** \eks-ˈhāl\ vb **ex·haled; ex·hal·ing 1 :** to breathe out **2 :** to give or pass off in the form of vapor — **ex·ha·la·tion** \ˌeks-(h)ə-ˈlā-shən\ n

**¹ex·haust** \ig-ˈzȯst\ vb **1 :** to draw out completely (as air from a jar); also **:** EMPTY **2 :** to use up wholly **3 :** to tire or wear out **4 :** to develop (a subject) completely

**²exhaust** n **1 :** the escape of used steam or gas from an engine; also **:** the matter that escapes **2 :** a system for withdrawing fumes from an enclosure

**ex·haus·tion** \ig-ˈzȯs-chən\ n **:** extreme weariness **:** FATIGUE

**ex·haus·tive** \ig-ˈzȯ-stiv\ adj **:** covering all possibilities **:** THOROUGH

**ex·haust·less** \ig-ˈzȯst-ləs\ adj **:** IN-EXHAUSTIBLE

**¹ex·hib·it** \ig-ˈzib-ət\ vb **1 :** to display esp. publicly **2 :** to present to a court in legal form syn expose, show, parade, flaunt — **ex·hi·bi·tion** \ˌek-sə-ˈbish-ən\ n — **ex·hib·i·tor** \ig-ˈzib-ət-ər\ n

**²exhibit** n **1 :** an act or instance of ex-

# exhibitionism • expediency

hibiting; *also* : something exhibited **2** : something produced and identified in court for use as evidence

**ex·hi·bi·tion·ism** \,ek-sə-'bish-ə-,niz-əm\ *n* : the act or practice of so behaving as to attract undue attention sometimes by indecent exposure — **ex·hi·bi·tion·ist** \-'bish-(ə-)nəst\ *n or adj*

**ex·hil·a·rate** \ig-'zil-ə-,rāt\ *vb* **-at·ed; -rat·ing** : ENLIVEN, STIMULATE — **ex·hil·a·ra·tion** \-,zil-ə-'rā-shən\ *n*

**ex·hort** \ig-'zȯrt\ *vb* : to urge, advise, or warn earnestly — **ex·hor·ta·tion** \,eks-,ȯr-'tā-shən, ,egz-, -ər-\ *n*

**ex·hume** \igz-'(y)üm, iks-'(h)yüm\ *vb* **ex·humed; ex·hum·ing** [F or ML; F *exhumer*, fr. ML *exhumare*, fr. L *ex* out of + *humus* earth] : DISINTER — **ex·hu·ma·tion** \,eks-(h)yü-'mā-shən, ,egz-(y)ü \ *n*

**ex·i·gen·cy** \'ek-sə-jən-sē, ig-'zij-ən-\ *n, pl* **-cies 1** : urgent need **2** *pl* : REQUIREMENTS — **ex·i·gent** \'ek-sə-jənt\ *adj*

**ex·ig·u·ous** \ig-'zig-yə-wəs\ *adj* : scanty in amount — **ex·i·gu·i·ty** \,eg-zi-'gyü-ət-ē\ *n*

**¹ex·ile** \'eg-,zīl, 'ek-,sīl\ *n* **1** : BANISHMENT **2** : a person driven from his native place

**²exile** *vb* **ex·iled; ex·il·ing** : BANISH, EXPEL **syn** expatriate, deport

**ex·ist** \ig-'zist\ *vb* **1** : to have being **2** : to continue to be : LIVE

**ex·is·tence** \ig-'zis-təns\ *n* **1** : continuance in living **2** : actual occurrence **3** : something existing — **ex·is·tent** \-tənt\ *adj*

**ex·is·ten·tial·ism** \,eg-zis-ten-chə-,liz-əm\ *n* : a philosophy centered upon the analysis of existence and stressing the freedom, responsibility, and usu. the isolation of the individual — **ex·is·ten·tial·ist** \-ləst\ *adj or n*

**ex·it** \'eg-zət, 'ek-sət\ *n* **1** : a departure from a stage **2** : a going out or away; *also* : DEATH **3** : a way out of an enclosed space — **exit** *vb*

**exo·bi·ol·o·gy** \,ek-sō-bī-'äl-ə-jē\ *n* : biology concerned with life originating or existing outside the earth or its atmosphere — **exo·bi·o·log·i·cal** \-,bī-ə-'läj-i-kəl\ *adj* — **exo·bi·ol·o·gist** \-bī-'äl-ə-jəst\ *n*

**exo·crine gland** \'ek-sə-krən-, -,krīn-, -,krēn-\ *n* : a gland (as a sweat gland or a kidney) that releases a secretion externally by means of a canal or duct

**Exod** *abbr* Exodus

**ex·o·dus** \'ek-səd-əs\ *n* : a mass departure : EMIGRATION

**ex of·fi·cio** \,ek-sə-'fish-ē-,ō\ *adv or adj* : by virtue of or because of an office ⟨*ex officio* chairman⟩

**ex·og·e·nous** \ek-'säj-ə-nəs\ *adj* : developing or originating outside the cell or body — **ex·og·e·nous·ly** *adv*

**ex·on·er·ate** \ig-'zän-ə-,rāt\ *vb* **-at·ed; -at·ing** [ME *exoneraten*, fr. L *exonerare* to unburden, fr. *ex-* out + *onus* load] : to free from blame **syn** acquit, absolve, exculpate — **ex·on·er·a·tion** \-,zän-ə-'rā-shən\ *n*

**exor** *abbr* executor

**ex·or·bi·tant** \ig-'zȯr-bət-ənt\ *adj* : exceeding what is usual or proper

**ex·or·cise** \'ek-,sȯr-,sīz, -sər-\ *vb* **-cised; -cis·ing 1** : to get rid of by or as if by solemn command **2** : to free of an evil spirit — **ex·or·cism** \-,siz-əm\ *n* — **ex·or·cist** \-,sist\ *n*

**ex·or·di·um** \eg-'zȯrd-ē-əm\ *n, pl* **-diums** *or* **-dia** \-ē-ə\ : an introduction esp. to a discourse or composition

**exo·sphere** \'ek-sō-,sfiər\ *n* : the outer fringe region of the atmosphere — **exo·spher·ic** \,ek-sō-'sfiər-ik, -'sfer-\ *adj*

**exo·ther·mic** \,ek-sō-'thər-mik\ *or* **exo·ther·mal** \-məl\ *adj* : characterized by or formed with evolution of heat

**ex·ot·ic** \ig-'zät-ik\ *adj* : FOREIGN, STRANGE — **exotic** *n* — **ex·ot·i·cal·ly** \-i-k(ə-)lē\ *adv* — **ex·ot·i·cism** \-'zät-ə-,siz-əm\ *n*

**exp** *abbr* **1** expense **2** export **3** express

**ex·pand** \ik-'spand\ *vb* **1** : to spread out **2** : ENLARGE **3** : to develop in detail **syn** amplify, swell, distend, inflate, dilate — **ex·pand·er** *n*

**ex·panse** \ik-'spans\ *n* : a broad extent (as of land or sea)

**ex·pan·sion** \ik-'span-chən\ *n* **1** : the act or process of expanding **2** : the state or degree of being expanded **3** : an expanded part or thing

**ex·pan·sive** \ik-'span-siv\ *adj* **1** : tending to expand or to cause expansion **2** : warmly benevolent or emotional **3** : of large extent or scope — **ex·pan·sive·ly** *adv* — **ex·pan·sive·ness** *n*

**ex parte** \eks-'pärt-ē\ *adv or adj* : from a one-sided point of view

**ex·pa·ti·ate** \ek-'spā-shē-,āt\ *vb* **-at·ed; -at·ing** : to talk or write at length — **ex·pa·ti·a·tion** \ek-,spā-shē-'ā-shən\ *n*

**ex·pa·tri·ate** \ek-'spā-trē-,āt\ *vb* **-at·ed; -at·ing** : EXILE — **ex·pa·tri·ate** \-,āt, -ət\ *n* — **ex·pa·tri·a·tion** \ek-,spā-trē-'ā-shən\ *n*

**ex·pect** \ik-'spekt\ *vb* **1** : to look forward to **2** : to consider (one) in duty bound **3** : SUPPOSE, ASSUME

**ex·pec·tan·cy** \ik-'spek-tən-sē\ *n, pl* **-cies 1** : EXPECTATION **2** : something expected

**ex·pec·tant** \-tənt\ *adj* : EXPECTING; *esp* : expecting the birth of a child — **ex·pec·tant·ly** *adv*

**ex·pec·ta·tion** \,ek-,spek-'tā-shən\ *n* **1** : the act or state of expecting **2** : anticipation of future good **3** : something expected

**ex·pec·to·rant** \ik-'spek-t(ə-)rənt\ *adj* : tending to promote discharge of mucus from the respiratory tract — **expectorant** *n*

**ex·pec·to·rate** \-tə-,rāt\ *vb* **-rat·ed; -rat·ing** : SPIT — **ex·pec·to·ra·tion** \-,spek-tə-'rā-shən\ *n*

**ex·pe·di·ence** \ik-'spēd-ē-əns\ *n* : EXPEDIENCY

**ex·pe·di·en·cy** \-ən-sē\ *n, pl* **-cies 1** : fitness to some end **2** : use of expedient means and methods; *also* : something expedient

¹**ex·pe·di·ent** \ik-'spēd-ē-ənt\ adj [ME, fr. MF or L; MF, fr. L expediens prp. of expedire to extricate, arrange, be advantageous, fr. ex- out + ped-, pes foot] **1** : adapted for achieving a particular end **2** : marked by concern with what is advantageous without regard to fairness or rightness

²**expedient** n : something that is expedient; also : a means devised or used for want of something better

**ex·pe·dite** \'ek-spə-,dīt\ vb -**dit·ed; -dit·ing** : to carry out promptly; also : FACILITATE

**ex·pe·dit·er** \-,dīt-ər\ n : one that expedites; esp : one employed to ensure adequate supplies of raw materials and equipment or to coordinate the flow of materials, tools, parts, and processed goods within a plant

**ex·pe·di·tion** \,ek-spə-'dish-ən\ n **1** : a journey for a particular purpose; also : the persons making it **2** : efficient promptness

**ex·pe·di·tion·ary** \-'dish-ə-,ner-ē\ adj : of, relating to, or constituting an expedition; also : sent on military service abroad

**ex·pe·di·tious** \,ek-spə-'dish-əs\ adj : marked by or acting with prompt efficiency **syn** swift, fast, rapid

**ex·pel** \ik-'spel\ vb **ex·pelled; ex·pel·ling** : to drive or force out : EJECT

**ex·pend** \ik-'spend\ vb **1** : to pay out : SPEND **2** : to consume by use or use up — **ex·pend·able** adj

**ex·pen·di·ture** \ik-'spen-di-chər, -də-,chúr\ n **1** : the act or process of expending **2** : something expended

**ex·pense** \ik-'spens\ n **1** : EXPENDITURE **2** : COST **3** : a cause of expenditure **4** : SACRIFICE

**ex·pen·sive** \ik-'spen-siv\ adj : COSTLY, DEAR — **ex·pen·sive·ly** adv

¹**ex·pe·ri·ence** \ik-'spir-ē-əns\ n **1** : observation or practice resulting in or tending toward knowledge; also : the resulting state of enhanced comprehension and efficiency **2** : a state of being affected from without (as by events); also : an affecting event ⟨a startling ∼⟩ **3** : something or the totality experienced (as by a person or community)

²**experience** vb -**enced; -enc·ing 1** : to know as an experience : SUFFER, UNDERGO **2** : to find out : DISCOVER

**ex·pe·ri·enced** \-ənst\ adj : made capable by repeated experience

¹**ex·per·i·ment** \ik-'sper-ə-mənt\ n : a controlled procedure carried out to discover, test, or demonstrate something; also : the practice of experiments — **ex·per·i·men·tal** \-,sper-ə-'ment-ᵊl\ adj

²**ex·per·i·ment** \-,ment\ vb : to make experiments — **ex·per·i·men·ta·tion** \ik-,sper-ə-mən-'tā-shən\ n — **ex·per·i·men·ter** \-'sper-ə-,ment-ər\ n

¹**ex·pert** \'ek-,spərt\ adj : thoroughly skilled — **ex·pert·ly** adv — **ex·pert·ness** n

²**ex·pert** \'ek-,spərt\ n : an expert person : SPECIALIST

**ex·per·tise** \,ek-(,)spər-'tēz\ n : EXPERTNESS

**ex·pi·ate** \'ek-spē-,āt\ vb -**at·ed; -at·ing** : to make amends : ATONE — **ex·pi·a·tion** \,ek-spē-'ā-shən\ n

**ex·pi·a·to·ry** \'ek-spē-ə-,tōr-ē\ adj : serving to expiate

**ex·pire** \ik-'spī(ə)r, ek-\ vb **ex·pired; ex·pir·ing 1** : to breathe out from or as if from the lungs; also : to emit the breath **2** : DIE **3** : to come to an end — **ex·pi·ra·tion** \,ek-spə-'rā-shən\ n

**ex·plain** \ik-'splān\ vb [ME explanen, fr. L explanare, lit., to make level, fr. planus level, flat] **1** : to make clear or plain **2** : to give the reason for or cause of — **ex·pla·na·tion** \,ek-splə-'nā-shən\ n — **ex·plan·a·to·ry** \ik-'splan-ə-,tōr-ē\ adj

**ex·ple·tive** \'ek-splət-iv\ n : a usu. profane exclamation

**ex·pli·ca·ble** \ek-'splik-ə-bəl, 'ek-(,)splik-\ adj : capable of being explained

**ex·pli·cate** \'ek-splə-,kāt\ vb -**cat·ed; -cat·ing** : to give a detailed explanation of

**ex·plic·it** \ik-'splis-ət\ adj : clearly and precisely expressed — **ex·plic·it·ly** adv — **ex·plic·it·ness** n

**ex·plode** \ik-'splōd\ vb **ex·plod·ed; ex·plod·ing** [L explodere to drive off the stage by clapping, fr. ex- out + plaudere to clap] **1** : DISCREDIT ⟨∼ a belief⟩ **2** : to affect or be affected (as by driving or shattering) by or as if by the pressure of expanding gas ⟨∼ a bomb⟩ ⟨the boiler exploded⟩ **3** : to cause or undergo a rapid chemical or nuclear reaction with production of heat and violent expansion of gas ⟨∼ dynamite⟩ ⟨material that ∼s when jarred⟩; also : to react violently ⟨ready to ∼ with rage⟩

**ex·plod·ed** \-əd\ adj : showing the parts separated but in correct relationship to each other ⟨an ∼ view of a carburetor⟩

¹**ex·ploit** \'ek-,splòit\ n : a usu. heroic act : DEED

²**ex·ploit** \ik-'splòit\ vb **1** : to turn to economic account ⟨∼ resources⟩; also : UTILIZE **2** : to use unfairly for one's own advantage — **ex·ploi·ta·tion** \,ek-,splòi-'tā-shən\ n

**ex·plore** \ik-'splōr\ vb **ex·plored; ex·plor·ing** : to range over (a region) in order to discover facts about it; also : to examine in careful detail ⟨∼ a wound⟩ — **ex·plo·ra·tion** \,ek-splə-'rā-shən\ n — **ex·plor·a·to·ry** \ik-'splōr-ə-,tōr-ē\ adj — **ex·plor·er** n

**ex·plo·sion** \ik-'splō-zhən\ n : the process or an instance of exploding

**ex·plo·sive** \ik-'splō-siv\ adj **1** : relating to or prepared to cause explosion **2** : tending to explode — **explosive** n — **ex·plo·sive·ly** adv

**ex·po** \'ek-,spō\ n, pl **expos** : EXPOSITION

**ex·po·nent** \ik-'spō-nənt, 'ek-,spō-\ n **1** : a symbol written above and to the right of a mathematical expression to signify how many times it is to be repeated as a factor **2** : INTERPRETER, EXPOUNDER **3** : ADVOCATE, CHAMPION —

**ex·po·nen·tial** \,ek-spə-'nen-chəl\ *adj* — **ex·po·nen·tial·ly** \-ē\ *adv*

**¹ex·port** \ek-'spōrt, 'ek-,spōrt\ *vb* : to send (as merchandise) to foreign countries — **ex·por·ta·tion** \,ek-,spōr-'tā-shən, -spor-\ *n* — **ex·port·er** \ek-'spōrt-ər, 'ek-,spōrt-\ *n*

**²ex·port** \'ek-,spōrt\ *n* **1** : something exported esp. for trade **2** : an act or the business of exporting

**ex·pose** \ik-'spōz\ *vb* **ex·posed; ex·pos·ing** **1** : to deprive of shelter or protection **2** : to submit or subject to an action or influence; *esp* : to subject (a sensitive photographic film, plate, or paper) to the action of radiant energy (as light) **3** : to display esp. for sale **4** : to bring to light : DISCLOSE

**ex·po·sé** *or* **ex·po·se** \,ek-spō-'zā\ *n* : an exposure of something discreditable

**ex·po·si·tion** \,ek-spə-'zish-ən\ *n* **1** : a setting forth of the meaning or purpose (as of a writing); *also* : discourse designed to convey information **2** : a public exhibition

**ex·pos·i·tor** \ik-'späz-ət-ər\ *n* : one that explains or expounds

**ex·pos·tu·late** \ik-'späs-chə-,lāt\ *vb* : to reason earnestly with a person esp. in dissuading : REMONSTRATE — **ex·pos·tu·la·tion** \-,späs-chə-'lā-shən\ *n*

**ex·po·sure** \ik-'spō-zhər\ *n* **1** : an exposing or being exposed **2** : a section of a photographic film for one picture **3** : the time during which a film is subjected to the action of light

**ex·pound** \ik-'spaúnd\ *vb* **1** : STATE **2** : INTERPRET, EXPLAIN — **ex·pound·er** *n*

**¹ex·press** \ik-'spres\ *adj* **1** : EXPLICIT; *also* : EXACT, PRECISE **2** : SPECIFIC (his ~ purpose) **3** : traveling at high speed and usu. with few stops; *also* : adapted to high speed use (~ roads) **4** : being or relating to special transportation of goods at premium rates (~ delivery) — **ex·press·ly** *adv*

**²express** *adv* : by express (ship it ~)

**³express** *n* : an express system or vehicle

**⁴express** *vb* **1** : to make known : SHOW, STATE (~ regret); *also* : SYMBOLIZE **2** : to squeeze out : extract by pressing **3** : to send by express

**ex·pres·sion** \ik-'spresh-ən\ *n* **1** : UTTERANCE **2** : something that represents or symbolizes : SIGN; *esp* : a mathematical symbol or symbol group representing a quantity or operation **3** : a significant word or phrase; *also* : manner of expressing (as in writing or music) **4** : facial aspect or vocal intonation indicative of feeling — **ex·pres·sion·less** *adj* — **ex·pres·sive** \-'spres-iv\ *adj* — **ex·pres·sive·ness** *n*

**ex·pres·sion·ism** \ik-'spresh-ə-,niz-əm\ *n* : a theory or practice in art of seeking to depict the artist's subjective responses to objects and events — **ex·pres·sion·ist** \-'spresh-(ə-)nəst\ *n or adj* — **ex·pres·sion·is·tic** \-,spresh-ə-'nis-tik\ *adj*

**ex·press·man** \ik-'spres-,man, -mən\ *n* : a person employed in the express business

**ex·press·way** \ik-'spres-,wā\ *n* : a high-speed divided highway for through traffic with grade separations at intersections

**ex·pro·pri·ate** \ek-'sprō-prē-,āt\ *vb* **-at·ed; -at·ing** : to take away from a person the possession of or right to (property) — **ex·pro·pri·a·tion** \(,)ek-,sprō-prē-'ā-shən\ *n*

**expt** *abbr* experiment

**exptl** *abbr* experimental

**ex·pul·sion** \ik-'spəl-shən\ *n* : an expelling or being expelled : EJECTION

**ex·punge** \ik-'spənj\ *vb* **ex·punged; ex·pung·ing** [L *expungere* to mark for deletion by dots, fr. *ex-* out + *pungere* to prick] : OBLITERATE, ERASE

**ex·pur·gate** \'ek-spər-,gāt\ *vb* **-gat·ed; -gat·ing** : to clear (as a book) of objectionable passages — **ex·pur·ga·tion** \,ek-spər-'gā-shən\ *n*

**¹ex·qui·site** \ek-'skwiz-ət, 'ek-(,)skwiz-\ *adj* [ME *exquisit*, fr. L *exquisitus*, fr. pp. of *exquirere* to search out, fr. *quaerere* to seek] **1** : excellent in form or workmanship **2** : keenly appreciative **3** : pleasingly beautiful or delicate **4** : INTENSE

**²exquisite** *n* : an overly fastidious individual

**ext** *abbr* **1** extension **2** exterior **3** external **4** extra **5** extract

**ex·tant** \'ek-stənt; ek-'stant\ *adj* : EXISTENT; *esp* : not lost or destroyed

**ex·tem·po·ra·ne·ous** \ek-,stem-pə-'rā-nē-əs\ *adj* : not planned beforehand : IMPROMPTU — **ex·tem·po·ra·ne·ous·ly** *adv*

**ex·tem·po·rary** \ik-'stem-pə-,rer-ē\ *adj* : EXTEMPORANEOUS

**ex·tem·po·re** \ik-'stem-pə-(,)rē\ *adv* : EXTEMPORANEOUSLY

**ex·tem·po·rize** \ik-'stem-pə-,rīz\ *vb* **-rized; -riz·ing** : to do something extemporaneously

**ex·tend** \ik-'stend\ *vb* **1** : to spread or stretch forth or out (as in reaching or straightening) **2** : to exert or cause to exert to full capacity **3** : PROLONG (~ a note) **4** : PROFFER (~ credit) **5** : to make greater or broader (~ knowledge) (~ a business) **6** : to spread over (as space) or through (as time) *syn* lengthen, elongate — **ex·tend·a·ble** *or* **ex·tend·i·ble** \-'sten-də-bəl\ *adj*

**ex·ten·sion** \ik-'sten-chən\ *n* **1** : an extending or being extended **2** : an additional part (~ on a house) **3** : educational programs (as correspondence courses) that reach beyond the campus of a school

**ex·ten·sive** \ik-'sten-siv\ *adj* : of considerable extent : far-reaching : BROAD — **ex·ten·sive·ly** *adv*

**ex·tent** \ik-'stent\ *n* **1** : the size, length, or bulk of something (a property of large ~) **2** : the degree or measure of something (the ~ of his guilt)

**ex·ten·u·ate** \ik-'sten-yə-,wāt\ *vb* **-at·ed; -at·ing** : to treat (as a fault) as of less importance than is real or apparent : EXCUSE — **ex·ten·u·a·tion** \-,sten-yə-'wā-shən\ *n*

**¹ex·te·ri·or** \ek-'stir-ē-ər\ *adj* **1** : EX-

TERNAL **2 :** suitable for use on an outside surface ⟨~ paint⟩

**²exterior** *n* **:** an exterior part or surface

**ex·ter·mi·nate** \ik-'stər-mə-ˌnāt\ *vb* **-nat·ed; -nat·ing :** to destroy utterly **syn** extirpate, eradicate — **ex·ter·mi·na·tion** \-ˌstər-mə-'nā-shən\ *n* — **ex·ter·mi·na·tor** \-'stər-mə-ˌnāt-ər\ *n*

**ex·tern** \'ek-ˌstərn\ *n* **:** a person (as a doctor) professionally connected with an institution but not living in it

**¹ex·ter·nal** \ek-'stərn-ᵊl\ *adj* **1 :** outwardly perceivable; *also* **:** SUPERFICIAL **2 :** of, relating to, or located on the outside or an outer part **3 :** arising or acting from without; *also* **:** FOREIGN ⟨~ affairs⟩ — **ex·ter·nal·ly** \-ē\ *adv*

**²external** *n* **:** an external feature

**ex·tinct** \ik-'stiŋkt\ *adj* **1 :** EXTINGUISHED ⟨with hope ~⟩ **2 :** no longer existing (as a kind of plant) or active (as a volcano) or in use (as a language) — **ex·tinc·tion** \ik-'stiŋk-shən\ *n*

**ex·tin·guish** \ik-'stiŋ-gwish\ *vb* **:** to put out (as a fire); *also* **:** to bring to an end (as by destroying, checking, eclipsing, or nullifying) — **ex·tin·guish·able** *adj* — **ex·tin·guish·er** *n*

**ex·tir·pate** \'ek-stər-ˌpāt\ *vb* **-pat·ed; -pat·ing** [L *exstirpatus,* pp. of *stirpare,* fr. *ex-* out + *stirps* trunk, root] **1 :** UPROOT **2 :** to cut out by surgery **syn** exterminate, eradicate — **ex·tir·pa·tion** \ˌek-stər-'pā-shən\ *n*

**ex·tol** *also* **ex·toll** \ik-'stōl\ *vb* **ex·tolled; ex·tol·ling :** to praise highly **:** GLORIFY **syn** laud, eulogize, acclaim

**ex·tort** \ik-'stort\ *vb* [L *extortus,* pp. of *extorquēre* to wrench out, extort, fr. *ex-* out + *torquēre* to twist] **:** to obtain by force or improper pressure ⟨~ a bribe⟩ — **ex·tor·tion** \-'stor-shən\ *n* — **ex·tor·tion·er** *n* — **ex·tor·tion·ist** *n*

**ex·tor·tion·ate** \ik-'stor-sh(ə-)nət\ *adj* **:** EXCESSIVE, EXORBITANT — **ex·tor·tion·ate·ly** *adv*

**¹ex·tra** \'ek-strə\ *adj* **1 :** ADDITIONAL **2 :** SUPERIOR **syn** spare, surplus, superfluous

**²extra** *n* **1 :** something (as a charge) added **2 :** a special edition of a newspaper **3 :** an additional worker or performer (as in a group scene)

**³extra** *adv* **:** beyond what is usual

**¹ex·tract** \ik-'strakt, *esp for 3* 'ek-ˌstrakt\ *vb* **1 :** to draw out; *esp* **:** to pull out forcibly ⟨~ a tooth⟩ **2 :** to withdraw (as a juice or a constituent) by a physical or chemical process **3 :** to select for citation **:** QUOTE — **ex·tract·able** *adj* — **ex·trac·tion** \-'strak-shən\ *n* — **ex·trac·tor** \-tər\ *n*

**²ex·tract** \'ek-ˌstrakt\ *n* **1 :** EXCERPT, CITATION **2 :** a product (as a juice or concentrate) obtained by extracting

**ex·tra·cur·ric·u·lar** \ˌek-strə-kə-'rik-yə-lər\ *adj* **:** lying outside the regular curriculum, *esp* **:** of or relating to school-connected activities (as sports) carrying no academic credit

**ex·tra·dite** \'ek-strə-ˌdīt\ *vb* **-dit·ed; -dit·ing :** to obtain by or deliver up to extradition

**ex·tra·di·tion** \ˌek-strə-'dish-ən\ *n* **:** a surrendering of an alleged criminal to a different jurisdiction for trial

**ex·tra·dos** \'ek-strə-ˌdäs, ek-'strä-ˌdäs\ *n, pl* **ex·tra·dos** \-ˌdöz, -ˌdäs\ *or* **ex·tra·dos·es** \-ˌdäs-əz\ **:** the exterior curve of an arch

**ex·tra·ga·lac·tic** \ˌek strə-gə-'lak-tik\ *adj* **:** lying or coming from outside the Milky Way

**ex·tra·mar·i·tal** \ˌek-strə-'mar-ət-ᵊl\ *adj* **:** of or relating to a married person's sexual intercourse with other than his or her spouse

**ex·tra·mu·ral** \-'myúr-əl\ *adj* **:** relating to or taking part in informal contests between teams of different schools other than varsity teams

**ex·tra·ne·ous** \ek-'strā-nē-əs\ *adj* **1 :** coming from without ⟨~ moisture⟩ **2 :** not intrinsic ⟨~ incidents in a story⟩; *also* **:** IRRELEVANT ⟨~ digressions⟩ — **ex·tra·ne·ous·ly** *adv*

**ex·traor·di·nary** \ik-'strórd-ᵊn-ˌer-ē, ˌek-strə-'órd-\ *adj* **1 :** notably unusual or exceptional **2 :** employed on a special service — **ex·traor·di·nari·ly** \ik-ˌstrórd-ᵊn-'er-ə-lē, ˌek-strə-ˌórd-\ *adv*

**ex·trap·o·late** \ik-'strap-ə-ˌlāt\ *vb* **-lat·ed; -lat·ing :** to infer (unknown data) from known data — **ex·trap·o·la·tion** \-ˌstrap-ə-'lā-shən\ *n*

**ex·tra·sen·so·ry** \ˌek-strə-'sens-(ə-)rē\ *adj* **:** occurring beyond the known senses ⟨~ perception⟩

**ex·tra·ter·res·tri·al** \-tə-'res-trē-əl\ *adj* **:** originating or existing outside the earth or its atmosphere ⟨~ life⟩

**ex·tra·ter·ri·to·ri·al** \-ˌter-ə-'tōr-ē-əl\ *adj* **1 :** located outside the territorial limits of a jurisdiction **2 :** of or relating to extraterritoriality ⟨~ rights⟩

**ex·tra·ter·ri·to·ri·al·i·ty** \-ˌtōr-ē-'al-ət-ē\ *n* **:** exemption from the application or jurisdiction of local law or tribunals ⟨diplomats enjoy ~⟩

**ex·trav·a·gant** \ik-'strav-i-gənt\ *adj* **1 :** EXCESSIVE ⟨~ claims⟩ **2 :** unduly lavish **:** WASTEFUL **3 :** too costly **syn** immoderate, exorbitant, extreme — **ex·trav·a·gance** \-gəns\ *n* — **ex·trav·a·gant·ly** *adv*

**ex·trav·a·gan·za** \ik-ˌstrav-ə-'gan-zə\ *n* **1 :** a literary or musical work marked by extreme freedom of style and structure **2 :** a lavish or spectacular show or event

**ex·tra·ve·hic·u·lar** \ˌek-strə-vē-'hik-yə-lər\ *adj* **:** taking place outside a vehicle (as a spacecraft) ⟨~ activity⟩

**ex·tra·vert** *or* **ex·tro·vert** \'ek-strə-ˌvərt\ *n* **:** a person more interested in the world about him than in his inner self — **ex·tra·ver·sion** \ˌek-strə-'vər-ˌzhən\ *n* — **extravert** \'ek-strə-ˌvərt\ *adj* — **ex·tra·vert·ed** \-əd\ *adj*

**¹ex·treme** \ik-'strēm\ *adj* **1 :** very great or intense ⟨~ cold⟩ **2 :** very severe or drastic ⟨~ measures⟩ **3 :** going to great lengths or beyond normal limits ⟨politically ~⟩ **4 :** mos remote ⟨the ~ end⟩ **5 :** UTMOST; *also* **:** MAXIMUM ⟨an ~ effort⟩ — **ex·treme·ly** *adv*

**²extreme** *n* **1 :** an extreme state **2**

: something located at one end or the other of a range or series  **3** : EXTREMITY 4

**extremely high frequency** *n* : a radio frequency in the highest range of the radio frequency spectrum

**ex·trem·ism** \ik-'strē-₁miz-əm\ *n* : the quality or state of being extreme; *esp* : advocacy of extreme political measures : RADICALISM — **ex·trem·ist** \-məst\ *n or adj*

**ex·trem·i·ty** \ik-'strem-ət-ē\ *n, pl* **-ties 1** : the most remote part or point  **2** : a limb of the body; *esp* : a human hand or foot  **3** : the greatest need or danger  **4** : the utmost degree; *also* : a drastic or desperate measure

**ex·tri·cate** \'ek-strə-₁kāt\ *vb* **-cat·ed; -cat·ing** [L *extricatus*, pp. of *extricare*, fr. *ex-* out + *tricae* trifles, perplexities] : to free from an entanglement or difficulty  **syn** disentangle, untangle — **ex·tri·ca·ble** \ik-'strik-ə-bəl, ek-; 'ek-(₁)strik-\ *adj* — **ex·tri·ca·tion** \₁ek-strə-'kā-shən\ *n*

**ex·trin·sic** \ek-'strin-zik, -sik\ *adj* **1** : not forming part of or belonging to a thing  **2** : EXTERNAL — **ex·trin·si·cal·ly** \-zi-k(ə-)lē, -si-\ *adv*

**ex·trude** \ik-'strüd\ *vb* **ex·trud·ed; ex·trud·ing** : to force, press, or push out; *esp* : to form (as plastic) by forcing through a die — **ex·tru·sion** \-'strü-zhən\ *n* — **ex·trud·er** *n*

**ex·tru·sive** \ik-'strü-siv\ *adj* : formed by crystallization of lava poured out of the earth's surface

**ex·u·ber·ant** \ig-'zü-b(ə-)rənt\ *adj* **1** : joyously unrestrained  **2** : PROFUSE — **ex·u·ber·ance** \-b(ə-)rəns\ *n* — **ex·u·ber·ant·ly** *adv*

**ex·ude** \ig-'züd\ *vb* **ex·ud·ed; ex·ud·ing** [L *exsudare*, fr. *ex-* out + *sudare* to sweat]  **1** : to discharge slowly through pores or cuts  **2** : to spread out in all directions — **ex·u·date** \'ek-s(y)ü-₁dāt\ *n* — **ex·u·da·tion** \₁ek-s(y)ü-'dā-shən\ *n*

**ex·ult** \ig-'zəlt\ *vb* : to rejoice in triumph : GLORY — **ex·ul·tant** \-'zəlt-ᵊnt\ *adj* — **ex·ul·tant·ly** *adv* — **ex·ul·ta·tion** \₁ek-(₁)səl-'tā-shən, ₁eg-(₁)zəl-\ *n*

**ex·urb** \'ek-₁sərb, 'eg-₁zərb\ *n* : a region or district outside a city and usu. beyond its suburbs inhabited chiefly by well-to-do families — **ex·ur·bia** \ek-'sər-bē-ə, eg-'zər-\ *n*

**ex·ur·ban·ite** \ek-'sər-bə-₁nīt; eg-'zər-\ *n* : one who lives in an exurb

**-ey** — see -Y

¹**eye** \'ī\ *n* **1** : an organ of sight typical-

ly consisting of a globular structure in a socket of the skull with thin movable covers bordered with hairs  **2** : VISION, PERCEPTION; *also* : faculty of discrimination ⟨a good ∼ for bargains⟩  **3** : POINT OF VIEW, JUDGMENT — often used in pl. ⟨an offender in the ∼s of the law⟩  **4** : something suggesting an eye ⟨the ∼ of a needle⟩; *esp* : an undeveloped bud (as of a potato) — **eyed** \'īd\ *adj*

²**eye** *vb* **eyed; eye·ing** *or* **ey·ing** : to look at : WATCH

**eye·ball** \'ī-₁bȯl\ *n* : the globular capsule of the vertebrate eye

**eye·brow** \'ī-₁braů\ *n* : the bony arch forming the upper edge of the eye socket; *also* : the hairs growing on this

**eye·drop·per** \'ī-₁dräp-ər\ *n* : DROPPER 2

**eye·glass** \'ī-₁glas\ *n* **1** : a lens variously mounted for personal use as an aid to vision  **2** *pl* : GLASS 3

**eye·lash** \'ī-₁lash\ *n* : the fringe of hair edging the eyelid; *also* : a single hair of this fringe

**eye·let** \'ī-lət\ *n* **1** : a small reinforced hole in material intended for ornament or for passage of something (as a cord or lace)  **2** : a typically metal ring for reinforcing an eyelet

**eye·lid** \'ī-₁lid\ *n* : one of the movable lids of skin and muscle that can be closed over the eyeball

**eye·lin·er** \'ī-₁līn-ər\ *n* : makeup used to emphasize the contour of the eyes

**eye-open·er** \'ī-₁ōp(-ə)-nər\ *n* : something startling or surprising — **eye-open·ing** \-₁niŋ\ *adj*

**eye·piece** \'ī-₁pēs\ *n* : the lens or combination of lenses at the eye end of an optical instrument

**eye shadow** *n* : a colored cosmetic applied to the eyelids to accent the eyes

**eye·sight** \'ī-₁sīt\ *n* : SIGHT, VISION

**eye·sore** \'ī-₁sōr\ *n* : something displeasing to the sight

**eye·strain** \'ī-₁strān\ *n* : weariness or a strained state of the eye

**eye·tooth** \'ī-'tüth\ *n* : a canine tooth of the upper jaw

**eye·wash** \'ī-₁wȯsh, -₁wäsh\ *n* **1** : an eye lotion  **2** : misleading or deceptive statements, actions, or procedures

**eye·wit·ness** \'ī-'wit-nəs\ *n* : a person who sees an occurrence with his own eyes and is able to give a firsthand account of it

**ey·rie** \'ī(ə)r-ē, *or like* AERIE\ *var of* AERIE

**ey·rir** \'ā-₁riər\ *n, pl* **au·rar** \'aů-₁rär\ — see *krona* at MONEY table

**Ezek** *abbr* Ezekiel

---

**F**

¹**f** \'ef\ *n, pl* **f's** *or* **fs** \'efs\ *often cap* **1** : the 6th letter of the English alphabet  **2** : a grade rating a student's work as failing

²**f** *abbr, often cap* **1** Fahrenheit  **2** false  **3** family  **4** female  **5** feminine  **6** forte  **7** French  **8** frequency

³**f** *symbol* **1** focal length  **2** the relative

aperture of a photographic lens — often written f/  **3** function

**F** *symbol* fluorine

**FAA** *abbr* Federal Aviation Agency

**Fa·bi·an** \'fā-bē-ən\ *adj* : of, relating to, or being a society of socialists organized in England in 1884 to spread socialist principles gradually — **Fabian** *n* — **Fa·bi·an·ism** *n*

**fa·ble** \'fā-bəl\ *n* **1** : a legendary story

of supernatural happenings **2** : a narration intended to teach a lesson; *esp* : one in which animals speak and act like people **3** : FALSEHOOD

**fa·bled** \'fā-bəld\ *adj* **1** : FICTITIOUS **2** : told or celebrated in fable

**fab·ric** \'fab-rik\ *n* [MF *fabrique*, fr. L *fabrica* workshop, structure] **1** : STRUCTURE, FRAMEWORK ⟨the ~ of society⟩ **2** : CLOTH; *also* : a material that resembles cloth

**fab·ri·cate** \'fab-ri-ˌkāt\ *vb* **-cat·ed; -cat·ing 1** : CONSTRUCT, MANUFACTURE **2** : INVENT, CREATE **3** : to make up for the sake of deception — **fab·ri·ca·tion** \ˌfab-ri-'kā-shən\ *n*

**fab·u·lous** \'fab-yə-ləs\ *adj* **1** : resembling a fable : LEGENDARY **2** : told in or based on fable **3** : INCREDIBLE, MARVELOUS · **fab·u·lous·ly** *adv*

**fac** *abbr* **1** facsimile **2** faculty

**fa·cade** *also* **fa·çade** \fə-'säd\ *n* **1** : the principal face or front of a building **2** : a false, superficial, or artificial appearance ⟨a ~ of composure⟩

¹**face** \'fās\ *n* **1** : the front part of the head **2** : PRESENCE ⟨in the ~ of danger⟩ **3** : facial expression : LOOK ⟨put a sad ~ on⟩ **4** : GRIMACE ⟨made a ~⟩ **5** : outward appearance ⟨looks easy on the ~ of it⟩ **6** : BOLDNESS **7** : DIGNITY, PRESTIGE ⟨afraid to lose ~⟩ **8** : the surface of something; *esp* : the front or principal surface — **faced** \'fāsd\ *adj* — **face·less** *adj* — **face·less·ness** *n*

²**face** *vb* **faced; fac·ing 1** : to confront brazenly **2** : to line near the edge esp. with a different material; *also* : to cover the front or surface of ⟨~ a building with marble⟩ **3** : to bring face to face ⟨*faced* him with the proof⟩ **4** : to stand or sit with the face toward ⟨~ the sun⟩ **5** : to front on ⟨a house *facing* the park⟩ **6** : to oppose firmly ⟨*faced* up to his foe⟩ **7** : to turn the face or body in a specified direction

**face·down** \'fās-'daùn\ *adv* : with the face downward

**face-lift·ing** \-ˌlif-tiŋ\ *n* **1** : a plastic operation for removal of facial defects (as wrinkles or sagging) usu. associated with aging **2** : MODERNIZATION

**face-off** \'fās-ˌóf\ *n* **1** : a method of putting a puck in play in ice hockey by dropping it between two opposing players each of whom attempts to control it **2** : CONFRONTATION

**fac·et** \'fas-ət\ *n* [F *facette*, dim. of *face*] **1** : one of the small plane surfaces of a cut gem **2** : ASPECT, PHASE

**fa·ce·tious** \fə-'sē-shəs\ *adj* **1** : COMICAL **2** : JOCULAR **3** : FLIPPANT — **fa·ce·tious·ly** *adv* — **fa·ce·tious·ness** *n*

¹**fa·cial** \'fā-shəl\ *adj* : of or relating to the face

²**facial** *n* : a facial treatment or massage

**fac·ile** \'fas-əl\ *adj* **1** : easily accomplished, handled, or attained **2** : SUPERFICIAL **3** : readily manifested and often insincere ⟨~ prose⟩ **4** : mild or yielding in disposition : PLIANT **5** : READY, FLUENT ⟨a ~ writer⟩

**fa·cil·i·tate** \fə-'sil-ə-ˌtāt\ *vb* **-tat·ed; -tat·ing** : to make easier

**fa·cil·i·ty** \fə-'sil-ət-ē\ *n, pl* **-ties 1** : the quality of being easily performed **2** : ease in performance : APTITUDE **3** : PLIANCY **4** : something that makes easier an action, operation, or course of conduct **5** : something (as a hospital or plumbing) built, installed, or established to serve a purpose

**fac·ing** \'fā-siŋ\ *n* **1** : a lining at the edge esp. of a garment **2** *pl* : the collar, cuffs, and trimmings of a uniform coat **3** : an ornamental or protective covering; *esp* : one on the face of something **4** : material for facing

**fac·sim·i·le** \fak-'sim-ə-lē\ *n* [L *fac simile* make similar] **1** : an exact copy **2** : the transmitting of printed matter or pictures by wire or radio for reproduction

**fact** \'fakt\ *n* **1** : DEED; *esp* : CRIME ⟨accessory after the ~⟩ **2** : the quality of being actual **3** : something that exists or occurs : EVENT; *also* : a piece of information about such a fact

**fac·tion** \'fak-shən\ *n* **1** : a group or combination (as in a state or church) acting together within and usu. against a larger body · CLIQUE **2** : party spirit esp. when marked by dissension — **fac·tion·al·ism** \-sh(ə-)nə-ˌliz-əm\ *n*

**fac·tious** \'fak-shəs\ *adj* **1** : of, relating to, or caused by faction **2** : inclined to faction or the formation of factions : causing dissension

**fac·ti·tious** \fak-'tish-əs\ *adj* : ARTIFICIAL, SHAM ⟨a ~ display of grief⟩

¹**fac·tor** \'fak-tər\ *n* **1** : AGENT **2** : something that actively contributes to a result **3** : GENE **4** : a number or symbol in mathematics that when multiplied with another forms a product

²**factor** *vb* **fac·tored; fac·tor·ing** \-t(ə-)riŋ\ **1** : to resolve into factors **2** : to work as a factor

**fac·to·ri·al** \fak-'tōr-ē-əl\ *n* : the product of all the positive integers from one to a given integer

²**factorial** *adj* : of or relating to a factor or a factorial

**fac·to·ry** \'fak-t(ə-)rē\ *n, pl* **-ries 1** : a trading post where resident factors trade **2** : a building or group of buildings used for manufacturing

**fac·to·tum** \fak-'tōt-əm\ *n* [NL, lit., do everything, fr. L *fac* do + *totum* everything] : an employee with numerous varied duties

**facts of life** : the physiology of sex and reproduction

**fac·tu·al** \'fak-chə(-wə)l\ *adj* : of or relating to facts; *also* : based on fact — **fac·tu·al·ly** \-ē\ *adv*

**fac·u·la** \'fak-yə-lə\ *n, pl* **-lae** \-ˌlē, -ˌlī\ : any of the bright regions of the sun's photosphere

**fac·ul·ty** \'fak-əl-tē\ *n, pl* **-ties 1** : ability to act or do : POWER; *also* : natural aptitude **2** : one of the powers of the mind or body ⟨the ~ of hearing⟩ **3** : the teachers in a school or college **4** : a department of instruction in an educational institution **5** : the members of a profession

**fad** \'fad\ *n* : a practice or interest followed for a time with exaggerated zeal : CRAZE — **fad·dish** *adj* — **fad·dist** *n*

**fade** \'fād\ *vb* **fad·ed; fad·ing** 1 : WITHER 2 : to lose or cause to lose freshness or brilliance of color 3 : to grow dim or faint 4 : VANISH

**fade·less** \'fād-ləs\ *adj* : not susceptible to fading

**FADM** *abbr* fleet admiral

**fae·cal, fae·ces** *var of* FECAL, FECES

**fa·er·ie** *also* **fa·ery** \'fā-(ə-)rē, 'fa(ə)r-ē\ *n, pl* **fa·er·ies** 1 : FAIRYLAND 2 : FAIRY

**¹fag** \'fag\ *vb* **fagged; fag·ging** 1 : DRUDGE 2 : to act as a fag 3 : TIRE, EXHAUST

**²fag** *n* 1 : an English public-school boy who acts as servant to another 2 : MENIAL, DRUDGE

**³fag** *n* : CIGARETTE

**⁴fag** *n* : HOMOSEXUAL

**fag end** *n* 1 : the last part or coarser end of a web of cloth 2 : the untwisted end of a rope 3 : REMNANT 4 : the extreme end

**fag·got** \'fag-ət\ *n* : HOMOSEXUAL

**fag·ot** *or* **fag·got** \'fag-ət\ *n* : a bundle of sticks or twigs esp. as used for fuel

**fag·ot·ing** *or* **fag·got·ing** *n* : an embroidery produced by tying threads in hourglass-shaped clusters

**Fah** *or* **Fahr** *abbr* Fahrenheit

**Fahr·en·heit** \'far-ən-,hīt\ *adj* : relating to, conforming to, or having a thermometer scale on which the boiling point of water is at 212 degrees and the freezing point at 32 degrees above its zero point

**fa·ience** *or* **fa·ïence** \fā-'äns\ *n* : earthenware decorated with opaque colored glazes

**¹fail** \'fāl\ *vb* 1 : to become feeble; *esp* : to decline in health 2 : to die away 3 : to stop functioning 4 : to fall short 〈~ed in his duty〉 5 : to be or become absent or inadequate 6 : to be unsuccessful 7 : to become bankrupt 8 : DISAPPOINT, DESERT 9 : NEGLECT

**²fail** *n* 1 : FAILURE 〈without ~〉 2 : a failure (as by a broker) to deliver or receive securities within a prescribed period after a purchase or sale

**¹fail·ing** \'fā-liŋ\ *n* : WEAKNESS, SHORTCOMING

**²failing** *prep* : in the absence or lack of

**faille** \'fīl\ *n* : a somewhat shiny closely woven ribbed silk, rayon, or cotton fabric

**fail–safe** \'fāl-,sāf\ *adj* : incorporating a counteractive feature for a possible source of failure

**[fail·ure** \'fāl-yər\ *n* 1 : a failing to do or perform 2 : a state of inability to perform a normal function adequately 〈heart ~〉 3 : a lack of success 4 : BANKRUPTCY 5 : DEFICIENCY 6 : DETERIORATION, BREAKDOWN 7 : one that has failed

**¹fain** \'fān\ *adj, archaic* 1 : GLAD 2 : INCLINED 3 : OBLIGED

**²fain** *adv, archaic* 1 : WILLINGLY 2 : RATHER

**¹faint** \'fānt\ *adj* [ME *faint, feint,* fr. OF,

fr. *faindre, feindre* to feign, shirk] 1 : COWARDLY, SPIRITLESS 2 : weak and dizzy nearly to the loss of consciousness 3 : lacking vigor or strength : FEEBLE 〈~ praise〉 4 : INDISTINCT, DIM — **faint·ly** *adv* — **faint·ness** *n*

**²faint** *vb* : to lose consciousness

**³faint** *n* : an act or condition of fainting

**faint·heart·ed** \'fānt-'härt-əd\ *adj* : lacking courage : TIMID

**¹fair** \'faər\ *adj* 1 : attractive in appearance : BEAUTIFUL; *also* : FEMININE 2 : superficially pleasing : SPECIOUS 3 : CLEAN, PURE 4 : CLEAR, LEGIBLE 5 : not stormy or cloudy 〈~ weather〉 6 : JUST 7 : conforming with the rules : ALLOWED; *also* : being within the foul lines 〈~ ball〉 8 : open to legitimate pursuit or attack 〈~ game〉 9 : PROMISING, LIKELY 〈a ~ chance of winning〉 10 : favorable to a ship's course 〈a ~ wind〉 11 : light in coloring : BLOND 12 : ADEQUATE — **fair·ness** *n*

**²fair** *adv* : FAIRLY

**³fair** *n* 1 : a gathering of buyers and sellers at a stated time and place for trade 2 : a competitive exhibition (as of farm products) 3 : a sale of a collection of articles usu. for a charitable purpose

**fair·ground** \-,graund\ *n* : an area where outdoor fairs, circuses, or exhibitions are held

**fair·ing** \'fa(ə)r-iŋ\ *n* : a structure for producing a smooth outline and reducing drag (as on an airplane)

**fair·ly** \'fa(ə)r-lē\ *adv* 1 : HANDSOMELY, FAVORABLY 〈~ situated〉 2 : QUITE, COMPLETELY 3 : in a fair manner : JUSTLY 4 : MODERATELY, TOLERABLY 〈a ~ easy job〉

**fair-spok·en** \'faər-'spō-kən\ *adj* : using fair speech : COURTEOUS

**fair-trade** \-'trād\ *adj* : of, relating to, or being an agreement between a producer and a seller that branded merchandise will be sold at or above a specified price 〈~ items〉 — **fair-trade** *vb*

**fair·way** \-,wā\ *n* : the mowed part of a golf course between tee and green

**fairy** \'fa(ə)r-ē\ *n, pl* **fairies** [ME *fairie* fairyland, fairy people, fr. OF *faerie,* fr. *feie, fee* fairy, fr. L *Fata,* goddess of fate, fr. *fatum* fate] 1 : an imaginary being of folklore and romance usu. having diminutive human form and magic powers 2 : HOMOSEXUAL — **fairy tale** *n*

**fairy·land** \-,land\ *n* 1 : the land of fairies 2 : a place of delicate beauty or magical charm

**fait ac·com·pli** \'fāt-,ak-,ō°-'plē, ,fe-,tak-\ *n, pl* **faits accomplis** \*same, or* -'plēz\ : a thing accomplished and presumably irreversible

**faith** \'fāth\ *n, pl* **faiths** \'fāths, 'fāthz\ 1 : allegiance to duty or a person : LOYALTY 2 : belief and trust in God 3 : CONFIDENCE 4 : a system of religious beliefs — **faith·ful** \-fəl\ *adj* — **faith·ful·ly** \-ē\ *adv* — **faith·ful·ness** *n* — **faith·less** *adj* — **faith·less·ly** *adv* — **faith·less·ness** *n*

**¹fake** \'fāk\ *vb* **faked; fak·ing** 1 : to treat so as to falsify 2 : COUNTERFEIT

**3** : PRETEND, SIMULATE — **fak·er** n

**²fake** n **1** : IMITATION, FRAUD, COUNTERFEIT **2** : IMPOSTOR

**³fake** adj : COUNTERFEIT, SHAM

**fa·kir** \fə-'kiər\ n [Ar *faqīr*, lit., poor man] **1** : a Muslim mendicant : DERVISH **2** : a wandering beggar of India who performs tricks

**fal·chion** \'fȯl-chən\ n : a broad-bladed slightly curved medieval sword

**fal·con** \'fal-kən, 'fȯ(l)-\ n : a hawk trained to pursue game birds; *also* : any of various long-winged hawks — **fal·con·ry** \-rē\ n

**¹fall** \'fȯl\ vb **fell** \'fel\; **fall·en** \'fȯ-lən\; **fall·ing 1** : to descend freely by the force of gravity **2** : to hang freely **3** : to come as if by descending ⟨darkness *fell*⟩ **4** : to become uttered **5** : to lower or become lowered : DROP ⟨her eyes *fell*⟩ **6** : to leave an erect position suddenly and involuntarily **7** : STUMBLE, STRAY **8** : to drop down wounded or dead : die in battle **9** : to become captured or defeated **10** : to suffer ruin or failure **11** : to commit an immoral act **12** : to move or extend in a downward direction **13** : SUBSIDE, ABATE **14** : to decline in quality, activity, quantity, or value **15** : to assume a look of shame or dejection ⟨her face *fell*⟩ **16** : to occur at a certain time **17** : to come by chance **18** : DEVOLVE **19** : to have the proper place or station ⟨the accent ~s on the first syllable⟩ **20** : to come within the scope of something **21** : to pass from one condition to another ⟨*fell* ill⟩ **22** : to set about heartily or actively ⟨~ to work⟩ — **fall flat** : to produce no response or result — **fall for 1** : to fall in love with **2** : to become a victim of — **fall foul 1** : to have a collision **2** : to have a quarrel : CLASH — **fall from grace 1** : SIN **2** : BACKSLIDE — **fall into line** : to comply with a certain course of action — **fall over oneself** or **fall over backward** : to display excessive eagerness — **fall short 1** : to be deficient **2** : to fail to attain

**²fall** n **1** : the act of falling **2** : a falling out, off, or away : DROPPING **3** : AUTUMN **4** : a thing or quantity that falls ⟨a light ~ of snow⟩ **5** : COLLAPSE, DOWNFALL **6** : the surrender or capture of a besieged place **7** : departure from virtue or goodness : SLOPE **9** : WATERFALL - usu. used in pl. **10** : a decrease in size, quantity, activity, or value ⟨a ~ in price⟩ **11** : the distance which something falls : DROP **12** : an act of forcing a wrestler's shoulders to the mat; *also* : a bout of wrestling

**fal·la·cious** \fə-'lā-shəs\ adj **1** : embodying a fallacy ⟨a ~ argument⟩ **2** : MISLEADING, DECEPTIVE

**fal·la·cy** \'fal-ə-sē\ n, pl **-cies 1** : a false or mistaken idea **2** : false or illogical reasoning; *also* : an instance of such reasoning

**fall back** \'fȯl-'bak\ vb : RETREAT, RECEDE

**fall guy** n **1** : one that is easily duped **2** : SCAPEGOAT

**fal·li·ble** \'fal-ə-bəl\ adj **1** : liable to be erroneous **2** : capable of making a mistake

**fall·ing-out** \,fȯ-liŋ-'aút\ n, pl **fall·ings-out** or **falling-outs** : QUARREL

**falling star** n : METEOR

**fall line** n : the transition zone between an upland and a lowland

**fal·lo·pi·an tube** \fə-,lō-pē-ən-\ n, *often cap F* : either of the pair of anatomical tubes that carry the egg from the ovary to the uterus

**fall·out** \'fȯl-,aút\ n : the often radioactive particles that result from a nuclear explosion and descend through the air

**fall out** \(')fȯl-'aút\ vb : QUARREL

**fal·low** \'fal-ō\ n **1** : usu. cultivated land left idle during a growing season : land plowed but not tilled or sowed — **fallow** vb — **fallow** adj

**fallow deer** n : a small European deer with broad antlers and a pale yellow coat spotted white in the summer

**false** \'fȯls\ adj **fals·er; fals·est 1** : not true : ERRONEOUS, INCORRECT **2** : intentionally untrue **3** : DISHONEST, DECEITFUL **4** : adjusted or made so as to deceive ⟨~ scales⟩ **5** : inaccurate in pitch **6** : tending to mislead : DECEPTIVE ⟨~ promises⟩ **7** : not faithful or loyal : TREACHEROUS **8** : SHAM, ARTIFICIAL **9** : not essential or permanent ⟨~ front⟩ **10** : based on mistaken ideas — **false·ly** adv — **false·ness** n — **fal·si·ty** \'fȯl-sət-ē\ n

**false·hood** \'fȯls-,húd\ n **1** : LIE **2** : absence of truth or accuracy **3** : the practice of lying

**fal·set·to** \fȯl-'set-ō\ n, pl **-tos** : an artificially high voice; *esp* : an artificial singing voice that overlaps and extends above the range of the full voice esp. of a tenor

**fal·si·fy** \'fȯl-sə-,fī\ vb **-fied; -fy·ing 1** : to make false : change so as to deceive **2** : LIE **3** : MISREPRESENT **4** : to prove to be false — **fal·si·fi·ca·tion** \,fȯl-sə-fə-'kā-shən\ n

**falt·boat** \'fält-,bōt\ n : FOLDBOAT

**fal·ter** \'fȯl-tər\ vb **fal·tered; fal·ter·ing** \-t(ə-)riŋ\ **1** : to move unsteadily : STUMBLE, TOTTER **2** : to hesitate in speech : STAMMER **3** : to hesitate in purpose or action : WAVER, FLINCH — **fal·ter·ing·ly** \-t(ə-)riŋ-lē\ adv

**fame** \'fām\ n : public reputation : RENOWN — **famed** \'fāmd\ adj

**fa·mil·ial** \fə-'mil-yəl\ adj **1** : of, relating to, or characteristic of a family **2** : tending to occur in more members of a family than expected by chance alone ⟨a ~ disorder⟩

**¹fa·mil·iar** \fə-'mil-yər\ n **1** : COMPANION **2** : a spirit held to attend and serve or guard a person **3** : one that frequents a place

**²familiar** adj **1** : closely acquainted : INTIMATE **2** : of or relating to a family **3** : INFORMAL **4** : FORWARD, PRESUMPTUOUS **5** : frequently seen or experienced **6** : being of everyday occurrence — **fa·mil·iar·ly** adv

**fa·mil·iar·i·ty** \fə-,mil-'yar-ət-ē -,mil-ē-'(y)ar-\ *n, pl* **-ties 1 :** close friendship **:** INTIMACY **2 :** close acquaintance with or knowledge of something **3 :** INFORMALITY **4 :** an unduly bold or forward act or expression **:** IMPROPRIETY

**fa·mil·iar·ize** \fə-'mil-yə-,rīz\ *vb* **-ized; -iz·ing 1 :** to make known or familiar **2 :** to make thoroughly acquainted **:** ACCUSTOM

**fam·i·ly** \'fam-(ə-)lē\ *n, pl* **-lies 1 :** a group of persons of common ancestry **:** CLAN **2 :** a group of individuals living under one roof and under one head **:** HOUSEHOLD **3 :** a social group composed of parents and their children **4 :** a group of related persons, lower animals, or plants; *also* **:** a group of things having common characteristics

**family tree** *n* **:** GENEALOGY; *also* **:** a genealogical diagram

**fam·ine** \'fam-ən\ *n* **1 :** an extreme general scarcity of food **2 :** a great shortage

**fam·ish** \'fam-ish\ *vb* **1 :** STARVE **2 :** to suffer or cause to suffer from extreme hunger

**fa·mous** \'fā-məs\ *adj* **1 :** widely known **2 :** honored for achievement **3 :** EXCELLENT, FIRST-RATE **syn** renowned, celebrated, noted, notorious, distinguished, eminent, illustrious — **fa·mous·ly** *adv*

¹**fan** \'fan\ *n* **:** a device (as a hand-waved triangular piece or a mechanism with blades) for producing a current of air

²**fan** *vb* **fanned; fan·ning 1 :** to drive away the chaff from grain by winnowing **2 :** to move (air) with or as if with a fan **3 :** to direct a current of air upon ⟨~ a fire⟩ **4 :** to stir up to activity **:** STIMULATE **5 :** to spread like a fan **6 :** to strike out in baseball

³**fan** *n* **1 :** an enthusiastic follower of a sport or entertainment **2 :** an enthusiastic admirer (as of a celebrity)

**fa·nat·ic** \fə-'nat-ik\ *or* **fa·nat·i·cal** \-i-kəl\ *adj* [L *fanaticus* inspired by a deity, frenzied, fr. *fanum* temple] **:** marked or moved by excessive enthusiasm and intense uncritical devotion — **fanatic** *n* — **fa·nat·i·cism** \fə-'nat-ə-,siz-əm\ *n*

**fan·ci·er** \'fan-sē-ər\ *n* **:** a person who breeds or grows some kind of animal or plant for points of excellence

**fan·ci·ful** \'fan-si-fəl\ *adj* **1 :** full of fancy **:** guided by fancy **:** WHIMSICAL **2 :** coming from the fancy rather than from the reason **3 :** curiously made or shaped — **fan·ci·ful·ly** \-f(ə-)lē\ *adv*

¹**fan·cy** \'fan-sē\ *n, pl* **fancies** [ME *fantasie, fantsy* fantasy, fancy, fr. MF *fantasie*, fr. L *phantasia*, fr. Gk, appearance, imagination] **1 :** LIKING, INCLINATION; *also* **:** LOVE **2 :** NOTION, IDEA, WHIM ⟨a passing ~⟩ **3 :** IMAGINATION **4 :** TASTE, JUDGMENT

²**fancy** *vb* **fan·cied; fan·cy·ing 1 :** LIKE **2 :** IMAGINE **3 :** to believe without any evidence

³**fancy** *adj* **fan·ci·er; -est 1 :** WHIMSICAL **2 :** not plain **:** ORNAMENTAL **3 :** of particular excellence **4 :** bred for special qualities **5 :** being above

the usual price or the real value **:** EXTRAVAGANT **6 :** executed with technical skill and superior grace — **fan·ci·ly** \'fan-sə-lē\ *adv*

**fancy dress** *n* **:** a costume (as for a masquerade) chosen to suit the wearer's fancy

**fan·cy-free** \'fan-sē-,frē\ *adj* **:** not centering the attention on any one person or thing; *esp* **:** not in love

**fan·cy·work** \'fan-sē-,wərk\ *n* **:** ornamental needlework (as embroidery)

**fan·dan·go** \fan-'daŋ-gō\ *n, pl* **-gos :** a lively Spanish or Spanish-American dance

**fane** \'fān\ *n* **:** TEMPLE

**fan·fare** \'fan-,faər\ *n* **1 :** a flourish of trumpets **2 :** a showy outward display

**fang** \'faŋ\ *n* **:** a long sharp tooth; *esp* **:** a grooved or hollow tooth of a venomous snake

**fan-jet** \'fan-,jet\ *n* **1 :** a jet engine having a fan in its forward end that draws in extra air whose compression and expulsion provide extra thrust **2 :** an airplane powered by a fan-jet engine

**fan·light** \'fan-,līt\ *n* **:** a semicircular window with radiating sash bars like the ribs of a fan placed over a door or window

**fan·tail** \'fan-,tāl\ *n* **1 :** a fan-shaped tail or end **2 :** a fancy goldfish with the tail fins double **3 :** an overhang at the stern of a ship

**fan·ta·sia** \fan-'tā-zhə, -z(h)ē-ə; ,fant-ə-'zē-ə\ *also* **fan·ta·sie** \,fant-ə-'zē ,fänt-\ *n* **:** a musical composition free and fanciful in form

**fan·ta·size** \'fant-ə-,sīz\ *vb* **-sized; -siz·ing :** IMAGINE, DAYDREAM

**fan·tas·tic** \fan-'tas-tik\ *adj* **1 :** IMAGINARY, UNREAL, UNREALISTIC **2 :** conceived by unrestrained fancy **:** GROTESQUE **3 :** exceedingly or unbelievably great **4 :** ECCENTRIC — **fan·tas·ti·cal** \-ti-kəl\ *adj* — **fan·tas·ti·cal·ly** \-ti-k(ə-)lē\ *adv*

**fan·ta·sy** \'fant-ə-sē\ *n, pl* **-sies 1 :** IMAGINATION, FANCY **2 :** a product of the imagination **:** ILLUSION **3 :** FANTASIA **4 :** a coin unauth. intended for circulation as currency and often issued by a dubious authority (as a government-in-exile) — **fantasy** *vb*

**FAO** *abbr* Food and Agricultural Organization of the United Nations

¹**far** \'fär\ *adv* **far·ther** \-thər\ *or* **fur·ther** \'fər-\; **far·thest** *or* **fur·thest** \-thəst\ **1 :** at or to a considerable distance in space or time ⟨~ from home⟩ **2 :** by a broad interval **:** WIDELY, MUCH ⟨~ better⟩ **3 :** to or at a definite distance, point, or degree ⟨as ~ as I know⟩ **4 :** to an advanced point or extent ⟨go ~ in his field⟩ — **by far :** GREATLY — **far and away :** DECIDEDLY — **so far :** until now

²**far** *adj* **farther** *or* **further; farthest** *or* **furthest 1 :** remote in space or time **:** DISTANT **2 :** DIFFERENT ⟨a ~ cry from former methods⟩ **3 :** LONG ⟨a ~ journey⟩ **4 :** being the more distant

of two ⟨on the ∼ side of the lake⟩

**far-away** \,fär-ə-,wā\ adj **1** : DISTANT, REMOTE  **2** : DREAMY

**farce** \'färs\ n **1** : a play marked by broadly satirical comedy and improbable plot  **2** : the broad humor characteristic of farce or pretense  **3** : a ridiculous action, display, or pretense — **far·ci·cal** \'fär-si-kəl\ adj

¹**fare** \'faər\ vb **fared; far·ing 1** : GO, TRAVEL  **2** : to get along : SUCCEED  **3** : EAT, DINE

²**fare** n **1** : the price charged to transport a person  **2** : a person paying a fare : PASSENGER  **3** : range of food : DIET; also : material provided for use, consumption, or enjoyment

¹**fare-well** \faər-'wel\ vb imper : get along well — used interjectionally to or by one departing

²**farewell** n **1** : a wish of welfare at parting : GOOD-BYE  **2** : LEAVE-TAKING

³**fare-well** \,faər-,wel\ adj : PARTING, FINAL ⟨a ∼ concert⟩

**far·fetched** \'fär-'fecht\ adj : not easily or naturally deduced or introduced : IMPROBABLE

**far–flung** \-'fləŋ\ adj : widely spread or distributed

**fa·ri·na** \fə-'rē-nə\ n : a fine meal (as of wheat) used in puddings or as a breakfast cereal

**far·i·na·ceous** \,far-ə-'nā-shəs\ adj **1** : containing or rich in starch  **2** : having a mealy texture or surface

¹**farm** \'färm\ n [ME ferme rent, lease, fr. OF, lease, fr. fermer to fix, make a contract, fr. L firmare to make firm, fr. firmus firm] **1** : a tract of land used for raising crops or livestock  **2** : a minor-league subsidiary of a major-league baseball team

²**farm** vb : to use (land) as a farm ⟨∼ed 200 acres⟩; also : to raise crops or livestock esp. as a business — **farm·er** n

**farm·hand** \'färm-,hand\ n : a farm laborer

**farm·house** \-,haus\ n : a dwelling on a farm

**farm·ing** \'fär-miŋ\ n : the practice of agriculture

**farm·land** \'färm-,land\ n : land used or suitable for farming

**farm out** vb : to turn over (as a task) to another

**farm·stead** \'färm-,sted\ also **farm·stead·ing** \-iŋ\ n · the buildings and adjacent service areas of a farm

**farm·yard** \-,yärd\ n : space around or enclosed by farm buildings

**far–off** \'fär-'of\ adj : remote in time or space : DISTANT

**fa·rouche** \fə-'rüsh\ adj : marked by shyness and lack of polish; also : WILD

**far–out** \'fär-'aut\ adj : very unconventional : EXTREME ⟨∼ clothes⟩

**far·ra·go** \fə-'räg-ō, -'rä-gō\ n, pl **-goes** : a confused collection : MIXTURE

**far–reach·ing** \'fär-'rē-ch·ŋ\ adj : having a wide range or ..ect

**far·ri·er** \'fär-ē-ər\ n : a blacksmith who shoes horses; also : VETERINARIAN

¹**far·row** \'far-ō\ vb : to give birth to a farrow

²**farrow** n : a litter of pigs

**far·see·ing** \'fär-'sē-iŋ\ adj : FAR-SIGHTED

**far·sight·ed** \'fär-'sīt-əd\ adj **1** : able to see distant things more clearly than near  **2** : JUDICIOUS, WISE, SHREWD  **3** : having visual images focusing behind the retina — **far·sight·ed·ness** n

¹**far·ther** \'fär-thər\ adv **1** : at or to a greater distance or more advanced point  **2** : more completely

²**farther** adj **1** : more distant  **2** : ²FURTHER 2

**far·ther·most** \-,mōst\ adj : most distant

¹**far·thest** \'fär-thəst\ adj : most distant

²**farthest** adv **1** : to or at the greatest distance : REMOTEST  **2** : to the most advanced point  **3** : by the greatest degree or extent : MOST

**far·thing** \'fär-thiŋ\ n : a former British monetary unit equal to ¼ of a penny; also : a coin representing this unit

**far·thin·gale** \'fär-thən-,gāl, -thiŋ-\ n [modif. of MF verdugale, fr. Sp verdugado, fr. verdugo young shoot of a tree, fr. verde green, fr. L viridis] : a support (as of hoops) worn esp. in the 16th century to swell out a skirt

**FAS** abbr free alongside ship

**fas·ci·cle** \'fas-i-kəl\ n **1** : a small bundle or cluster (as of flowers or roots)  **2** : one of the divisions of a book published in parts — **fas·ci·cled** \-kəld\ adj

**fas·ci·nate** \'fas-ᵊn-,āt\ vb **-nat·ed; -nat·ing** [L fascinare, fr. fascinum witchcraft] **1** : to transfix and hold spellbound by an irresistable power  **2** : ALLURE  **3** : to be irresistibly attractive — **fas·ci·na·tion** \,fas-ᵊn-'ā-shən\ n

**fas·cism** \'fash-,iz-əm\ n **1** often cap : the body of principles held by Fascisti  **2** : a political philosophy, movement or regime that exalts nation and race and stands for a centralized autocratic government headed by a dictatorial leader, severe economic and social regimentation, and forcible suppression of opposition — **fas·cist** \-əst\ n or adj, often cap — **fas·cis·tic** \fa-'shis-tik\ adj, often cap

**Fa·sci·sta** \fä-'shē-stä\ n, pl **-sti** \-stē\ : a member of an Italian political organization under Mussolini governing Italy 1922–43 according to the principles of fascism

¹**fash·ion** \'fash-ən\ n **1** : the make or form of something  **2** : MANNER, WAY  **3** : a prevailing custom, usage, or style  **4** : the prevailing style (as in dress) syn mode, vogue

²**fashion** vb **fash·ioned; fash·ion·ing** \'fash-(ə-)niŋ\ : to MOLD, CONSTRUCT  **2** : FIT, ADAPT

**fash·ion·able** \'fash-(ə-)nə-bəl\ adj **1** : dressing or behaving according to fashion : STYLISH  **2** : of or relating to the world of fashion ⟨∼ resorts⟩ — **fash·ion·ably** \-blē\ adv

¹**fast** \'fast\ adj **1** : firmly fixed or

bound **2** : tightly shut **3** : adhering firmly : STUCK **4** : UNCHANGEABLE ⟨hard and ~ rules⟩ **5** : STAUNCH ⟨~ friends⟩ **6** : characterized by quick motion, operation, or effect ⟨a ~ trip⟩ ⟨a ~ track⟩ **7** : indicating ahead of the correct time ⟨the clock is ~⟩ **8** : not easily disturbed : SOUND ⟨a ~ sleep⟩ **9** : permanently dyed; *also* : being proof against fading ⟨colors ~ to sunlight⟩ **10** : DISSIPATED, WILD **11** : daringly unconventional esp. in sexual matters **syn** rapid, swift, fleet, quick, speedy, hasty

²**fast** *adv* **1** : in a fast or fixed manner ⟨stuck ~ in the mud⟩ **2** : SOUNDLY, DEEPLY ⟨~ asleep⟩ **3** : SWIFTLY **4** : RECKLESSLY

³**fast** *vb* **1** : to abstain from food **2** : to eat sparingly or abstain from some foods

⁴**fast** *n* **1** : the act or practice of fasting **2** : a time of fasting

⁵**fast** *n* : something that fastens or holds a fastening

**fast-back** \'fas(t)-ˌbak\ *n* : an automobile roof with a long curving slope to the rear; *also* : an automobile with such a roof

**fas-ten** \'fas-ᵊn\ *vb* **fas-tened; fas-ten-ing** \'fas-(ᵊ-)niŋ\ **1** : to attach or join by or as if by pinning, tying, or nailing **2** : to make fast : fix securely **3** : to fix or set steadily ⟨~ed his eyes on her⟩ **4** : to become fixed or joined — **fas-ten-er** \'fas-(ə-)nər\ *n*

**fas-ten-ing** \'fas-(ᵊ-)niŋ\ *n* : something that fastens : FASTENER

**fas-tid-i-ous** \fas-'tid-ē-əs\ *adj* **1** : overly difficult to please **2** : showing or demanding excessive delicacy or care — **fas-tid-i-ous-ly** *adv* — **fas-tid-i-ous-ness** *n*

**fast-ness** \'fas(t)-nəs\ *n* **1** : the quality or state of being fast **2** : a fortified or secure place : STRONGHOLD

**fast-talk** \'fas(t)-'tòk\ *vb* : to influence by persuasive and usu. deceptive talk

¹**fat** \'fat\ *adj* **fat-ter; fat-test 1** : FLESHY, PLUMP **2** : OILY, GREASY **3** : well filled out : BIG **4** : well stocked : ABUNDANT **5** : PROFITABLE — **fat-ness** *n*

²**fat** *n* **1** : animal tissue rich in greasy or oily matter **2** : any of numerous energy-rich esters that occur naturally in animal fats and in plants and are soluble in organic solvents (as ether) but not in water **3** : the best or richest portion ⟨lived on the ~ of the land⟩ **4** : OBESITY **5** : excess matter

**fa-tal** \'fāt-ᵊl\ *adj* **1** : MORTAL, DEADLY, DISASTROUS **2** : FATEFUL — **fa-tal-ly** \-ē\ *adv*

**fa-tal-ism** \-ˌiz-əm\ *n* : the belief that events are determined by fate — **fa-tal-ist** \-əst\ *n* — **fa-tal-is-tic** \ˌfāt-ᵊl-'is-tik\ *adj*

**fa-tal-i-ty** \fā-'tal-ət-ē, fə-\ *n, pl* **ties 1** : DEADLINESS **2** : the quality or state of being destined for disaster **3** : FATE **4** : death resulting from a disaster or accident

**fat-back** \'fat-ˌbak\ *n* : a fatty strip

from the back of the hog usu. cured by salting and drying

**fat cat** *n* **1** : a wealthy contributor to a political campaign **2** : a wealthy privileged person

**fate** \'fāt\ *n* [ME, fr. MF or L; MF, fr. L *fatum*, lit., what has been spoken, fr. *fari* to speak] **1** : the cause beyond man's control that is held to determine events : DESTINY **2** : LOT, FORTUNE **3** : END, OUTCOME **4** : DISASTER; *esp* : DEATH **5** *cap, pl* : the three goddesses of classical mythology who determine the course of human life

**fat-ed** \'fā-təd\ *adj* : decreed, controlled, or marked by fate

**fate-ful** \'fāt-fəl\ *adj* **1** : IMPORTANT **2** : OMINOUS, PROPHETIC **3** : determined by fate **4** : DEADLY, DESTRUCTIVE — **fate-ful-ly** \-ē\ *adv*

**fath** *abbr* fathom

¹**fa-ther** \'fäth-ər\ *n* **1** : a male parent **2** *cap* : God esp. as the first person of the Trinity **3** : ANCESTOR, FOREFATHER **4** : one deserving the respect and love given to a father **5** *often cap* : an early Christian writer accepted by the church as an authoritative witness to its teaching and practice **6** : ORIGINATOR ⟨the ~ of modern radio⟩; *also* : SOURCE **7** : PRIEST — used esp. as a title **8** : one of the leading men ⟨city ~s⟩ — **fa-ther-hood** \-ˌhud\ *n* — **fa-ther-land** \-ˌland\ *n* — **fa-ther-less** *adj* — **fa-ther-ly** *adj*

²**father** *vb* **1** : BEGET **2** : to be the founder, producer, or author of **3** : to treat or care for as a father

**father-in-law** \'fäth-(ə-)rən-ˌlò\ *n, pl* **fa-thers-in-law** \-ər-zən-\ : the father of one's husband or wife

**fa-ther-land** \'fäth-ər-ˌland\ *n* **1** : one's native land **2** : the native land of one's ancestors

¹**fath-om** \'fath-əm\ *n* [ME *fadme*, fr. OE *fæthm* outstretched arms, fathom] : a nautical unit of length equal to 6 feet

²**fathom** *vb* **1** : to measure by a sounding line **2** : PROBE **3** : to penetrate and come to understand — **fath-om-able** \'fath-ə-mə-bəl\ *adj*

**fath-om-less** \'fath-əm-ləs\ *adj* : incapable of being fathomed

¹**fa-tigue** \fə-'tēg\ *n* **1** : weariness from labor or use **2** : manual or menial work performed by military personnel **3** *pl* : the uniform or work clothing worn on fatigue and in the field **4** : the tendency of a material to break under repeated stress

²**fatigue** *vb* **fa-tigued; fa-tigu-ing** : WEARY, TIRE

**fat-ten** \'fat-ᵊn\ *vb* : to make or grow fat

¹**fat-ty** \'fat-ē\ *adj* **fat-ti-er; -est** : containing fat : GREASY

²**fatty** *n, pl* **fatties** : a fat person

**fatty acid** *n* : any of numerous acids that contain only carbon, hydrogen, and oxygen and that occur naturally in fats and various oils

**fa-tu-ity** \fə-'t(y)ü-ət-ē\ *n, pl* **-ities** : FOOLISHNESS, STUPIDITY

**fat·u·ous** \'fach-(ə-)wəs\ adj : FOOL-ISH, INANE, SILLY — **fat·u·ous·ly** adv

**fau·bourg** \fō-'bu̇r\ n 1 : SUBURB; esp : a suburb of a French city 2 : a city quarter

**fau·ces** \'fȯ-ˌsēz\ n pl : the narrow passage between the soft palate and the base of the tongue that joins the mouth to the pharynx

**fau·cet** \'fȯs-ət, 'fäs-\ n : a fixture for drawing off a liquid (as from a pipe or cask)

¹**fault** \'fȯlt\ n 1 : a weakness in character : FAILING 2 : IMPERFECTION, IM-PAIRMENT 3 : an error in a racket game 4 : MISDEMEANOR; also : MISTAKE 5 : responsibility for something wrong 6 : a fracture in the earth's crust accompanied by a displacement of one side relative to the other — **fault·i·ly** \'fȯl-tə-lē\ adv — **fault·less** adj — **fault·less·ly** adv — **faulty** adj

²**fault** vb 1 : to commit a fault : ERR 2 : to fracture so as to produce a geo-logic fault 3 : to find a fault in

**fault·find·er** \'fȯlt-ˌfīn-dər\ n : a person who is inclined to find fault or complain — **fault·find·ing** \-diŋ\ n or adj

**faun** \'fȯn\ n : an ancient Italian deity of fields and herds represented as part goat and part man

**fau·na** \'fȯn-ə\ n, pl **faunas** also **fau·nae** \-ˌē, -ˌī\ [LL Fauna, sister of Faunus (the Roman god of animals)] : animals or animal life esp. of a region or period — **fau·nal** \-ᵊl\ adj

**fau·vism** \'fō-ˌviz-əm\ n, often cap : a movement in painting characterized by vivid colors, free treatment of form, and a vibrant and decorative effect — **fau·vist** \-vəst\ n, often cap

**faux pas** \'fō-'pä\ n, pl **faux pas** \-'pä(z)\ [F, lit., false step] : BLUN-DER; esp : a social blunder

¹**fa·vor** \'fā-vər\ n 1 : friendly regard shown toward another esp. by a su-perior 2 : APPROVAL 3 : PARTIALITY 4 : POPULARITY 5 : gracious kind-ness; also : an act of such kindness 6 pl : effort in one's behalf : ATTENTION 7 : a token of love (as a ribbon) usu. worn conspicuously 8 : a small gift or decorative item given out at a party 9 : a special privilege 10 archaic : LETTER 11 : BEHALF, INTEREST

²**favor** vb **fa·vored; fa·vor·ing** \'fāv-(ə-)riŋ\ 1 : to regard or treat with favor 2 : OBLIGE 3 : ENDOW ⟨~ed by nature⟩ 4 : to treat gently or care-fully : SPARE ⟨~ a lame leg⟩ 5 : PREFER 6 : SUPPORT, SUSTAIN 7 : FACILITATE ⟨darkness ~s attack⟩ 8 : RESEMBLE ⟨he ~s his father⟩

**fa·vor·able** \'fāv-(ə-)rə-bəl\ adj 1 : APPROVING 2 : HELPFUL, PROMISING, ADVANTAGEOUS ⟨~ weather⟩ — **fa·vor·ably** \-blē\ adv

**fa·vor·ite** \'fāv-(ə-)rət\ n 1 : a person or a thing that is favored above others 2 : a competitor regarded as most likely to win — **favorite** adj

**favorite son** n : a candidate supported by the delegates of his state at a presi-dential nominating convention

**fa·vor·it·ism** \'fāv-(ə-)rət-ˌiz-əm\ n : PARTIALITY, BIAS

**fa·vour** chiefly Brit var of FAVOR

¹**fawn** \'fȯn\ vb 1 : to show affection ⟨a dog ~ing on its master⟩ 2 : to court favor by a cringing or flattering manner

²**fawn** n 1 : a young deer 2 : a variable color averaging a light grayish brown

**fay** \'fā\ n : FAIRY, ELF

**faze** \'fāz\ vb **fazed; faz·ing** : to disturb the composure or courage of : DAUNT

**FB** abbr freight bill

**FBI** abbr Federal Bureau of Investigation

**FCC** abbr Federal Communications Commission

**fcp** abbr foolscap

**fcy** abbr fancy

**FD** abbr fire department

**FDA** abbr Food and Drug Administra-tion

**FDIC** abbr Federal Deposit Insurance Corporation

**Fe** symbol [L ferrum] iron

**fe·al·ty** \'fē-(ə)l-tē\ n, pl **-ties** : LOY-ALTY, ALLEGIANCE

¹**fear** \'fiər\ n 1 : an unpleasant often strong emotion caused by expectation or awareness of danger; also : an in-stance of or a state marked by this emo-tion 2 : anxious concern : SOLICITUDE 3 : profound reverance esp. toward God **syn** dread, fright, alarm, panic, terror, trepidation

²**fear** vb 1 : to have a reverent awe of ⟨~ God⟩ 2 : to be afraid of : have fear 3 : to be apprehensive

**fear·ful** \-fəl\ adj 1 : causing fear 2 : filled with fear 3 : showing or caused by fear 4 : extremely bad, intense, or large — **fear·ful·ly** \-ē\ adv

**fear·less** \-ləs\ adj : free from fear : BRAVE — **fear·less·ly** adv — **fear·less·ness** n

**fear·some** \-səm\ adj 1 : causing fear 2 : TIMID

**fea·si·ble** \'fē-zə-bəl\ adj 1 : capable of being done or carried out ⟨a ~ plan⟩ 2 : SUITABLE 3 : REASONABLE, LIKELY — **fea·si·bil·i·ty** \ˌfē-zə-'bil-ət-ē\ n — **fea·si·bly** \'fē-zə-blē\ adv

¹**feast** \'fēst\ n 1 : an elaborate meal : BANQUET 2 : FESTIVAL 1

²**feast** vb 1 : to eat plentifully 2 : to entertain with rich and plentiful food 3 : DELIGHT, GRATIFY

**feat** \'fēt\ n : DEED, EXPLOIT, ACHIEVE-MENT; esp : an act notable for courage, skill, endurance, or ingenuity

¹**feath·er** \'feth-ər\ n 1 : one of the light horny outgrowths that form the external covering of the body of a bird 2 : PLUME 3 : PLUMAGE 4 : KIND, NATURE ⟨men of the same ~⟩ 5 : AT-TIRE, DRESS ⟨fine ~s⟩ 6 : CONDITION, MOOD ⟨feeling in good ~⟩ 7 : a feath-ery tuft or fringe of hair (as on the leg of a dog) — **feath·ered** \-ərd\ adj — **feath·er·less** adj — **feath·ery** adj — **a feather in one's cap** : a mark of distinction : HONOR

²**feather** vb 1 : to furnish with a feather

⟨~ an arrow⟩ **2** : to cover, clothe, line, or adorn with feathers — **feather one's nest** : to provide for oneself esp. while in a position of trust

**feath·er·bed·ding** \'feth-ər-,bed-iŋ\ *n* : the requiring of an employer usu under a union rule or safety statute to employ more workers than are needed or to limit production

**feath·er·edge** \-,e`\ *n* : a very thin sharp edge; *esp* : one that is easily broken or bent over

**feath·er·weight** \-,wāt\ *n* **1** : a very light weight **2** : one that is very light in weight; *esp* : a boxer weighing more than 118 but not over 126 pounds

¹**feature** \'fē-chər\ *n* **1** : the shape or appearance of the face or its parts **2** : a part of the face : LINEAMENT **3** : a specially prominent characteristic **4** : a special attraction (as in a motion picture or newspaper) **5** : something offered to the public or advertised as particularly attractive — **fea·ture·less** *adj*

²**feature** *vb* **1** : to outline or mark the features of **2** : to give special prominence to ⟨~ a story in a newspaper⟩ **3** : to play an important part

**feaze** \'fēz, 'fāz\ *var of* FAZE

**Feb** *abbr* February

**feb·ri·fuge** \'feb-rə-,fyüj\ *n* : a medicine for relieving fever — **febrifuge** *adj*

**fe·brile** \'feb-rəl, -,rīl; 'fēb-\ *adj* : FEVERISH

**Feb·ru·ary** \'feb-(y)ə-,wer-ē, 'feb-rə-\ *n* [ME *Februarie,* fr. L *Februarius,* fr. *Februa,* pl., feast of purification] : the second month of the year having 28 and in leap years 29 days

**fec** *abbr* [L *fecit*] he made it

**fe·ces** \'fē-,sēz\ *n pl* : bodily waste discharged from the intestine — **fe·cal** \-kəl\ *adj*

**feck·less** \'fek-ləs\ *adj* **1** : INEFFECTUAL, WEAK **2** : WORTHLESS, IRRESPONSIBLE

**fe·cund** \'fek-ənd, 'fēk-\ *adj* : FRUITFUL, PROLIFIC — **fe·cun·di·ty** \fi-'kən-dət-ē, fe-\ *n*

**fe·cun·date** \'fek-ən-,dāt, 'fē-kən-\ *vb* **-dated; -dat·ing** : FERTILIZE — **fe·cun·da·tion** \,fek-ən-'dā-shən, ,fē-kən-\ *n*

**fed** *abbr* federal; federation

**fed·er·al** \'fed-(ə)-rəl\ *adj* **1** : formed by a compact between political units that surrender individual sovereignty to a central authority but retain certain limited powers **2** : of or constituting a form of government in which power is distributed between a central authority and constituent territorial units **3** : of or relating to the central government of a federation **4** *often cap* : FEDERALIST **5** *often cap* : of, relating to, or loyal to the federal government or the Union armies of the U.S. in the American Civil War — **fed·er·al·ly** \-ē\ *adv*

**Federal** *n* : a supporter of the U.S. government in the Civil War; *esp* : a soldier in the federal armies

**federal district** *n* : a district (as the District of Columbia) set apart as the seat of the central government of a federation

**fed·er·al·ism** \'fed-(ə)-rə-,liz-əm\ *n* **1** *often cap* : the federal principle of organization **2** : support or advocacy of federalism **3** *cap* : the principles of the Federalists

**fed·er·al·ist** \-ləst\ *n* **1** : an advocate of federalism; *esp, often cap* : an advocate of a federal union between the American colonies after the Revolution and of adoption of the U.S. Constitution **2** *cap* : a member of a major political party in the early years of the U.S. favoring a strong centralized national government — **federalist** *adj, often cap*

**fed·er·al·ize** \'fed-(ə)-rə-,līz\ *vb* **-ized; -iz·ing** **1** : to unite in or under a federal system **2** : to bring under the jurisdiction of a federal government

**fed·er·ate** \'fed-ə-,rāt\ *vb* **-at·ed; -at·ing** : to join in a federation

**fed·er·a·tion** \,fed-ə-'rā-shən\ *n* **1** : the act of federating; *esp* : the formation of a federal union **2** : a federal government **3** : a union of organizations

**fedn** *abbr* federation

**fe·do·ra** \fi-'dōr-ə\ *n* : a low soft felt hat with the crown creased lengthwise

**fed up** *adj* : satiated, tired, or disgusted beyond endurance

**fee** \'fē\ *n* **1** : an estate in land held from a feudal lord **2** : an inherited or heritable estate in land **3** : a fixed charge; *also* : a charge for a professional service **4** : TIP

**fee·ble** \'fē-bəl\ *adj* **fee·bler** \-b(ə-)lər\; **fee·blest** \-b(ə-)ləst\ [ME *feble,* fr. OF, fr. L *flebilis* lamentable, wretched, fr. *flēre* to weep] **1** : DECREPIT, FRAIL **2** : INEFFECTIVE, INADEQUATE ⟨a ~ protest⟩ — **fee·ble·ness** *n* — **fee·bly** \-blē\ *adv*

**fee·ble·mind·ed** \,fē-bəl-'mīn-dəd\ *adj* : lacking normal intelligence — **fee·ble·mind·ed·ness** *n*

¹**feed** \'fēd\ *vb* **fed** \'fed\; **feed·ing** **1** : to give food to; *also* : to give as food **2** : to consume food; *also* : PREY **3** : to furnish what is necessary to the growth or function of — **feed·er** *n*

²**feed** *n* **1** : a usu. large meal; *also* : food for livestock **2** : material supplied (as to a furnace) **3** : a mechanism for feeding material to a machine

**feed·back** \'fēd-,bak\ *n* : the return to the input of a part of the output of a machine, system, or process

**feed·lot** \'fēd-,lät\ *n* : land on which cattle are fattened for market

**feed·stock** \-,stäk\ *n* : raw material supplied to a machine

**feed·stuff** \-,stəf\ *n* : food for livestock

¹**feel** \'fēl\ *vb* **felt** \'felt\; **feel·ing** **1** : to perceive or examine through physical contact : TOUCH, HANDLE **2** : EXPERIENCE; *also* : to suffer from **3** : to ascertain by cautious trial ⟨~ out public sentiment⟩ **4** : to be aware of **5** : BELIEVE, THINK **6** : to search for

something with the fingers **:** GROPE **7 :** to be conscious of an inward impression, state of mind, or physical condition **8 :** to seem esp. to the touch **9 :** to have sympathy or pity

²**feel** n **1 :** the sense of touch **2 :** SENSATION, FEELING **3 :** a quality of a thing as imparted through touch

**feel·er** \'fē-lər\ n **1 :** a tactile organ (as on the head of an insect) **2 :** a proposal or remark made to find out the views of other people

¹**feel·ing** \'fē-liŋ\ n **1 :** the sense of touch; also **:** a sensation perceived by this **2 :** an often indefinite state of mind ⟨a ~ of loneliness⟩ **3 :** EMOTION; also, pl **:** SENSIBILITIES **4 :** mental awareness **5 :** OPINION, BELIEF **6 :** unreasoned attitude **:** SENTIMENT **7 :** capacity to respond emotionally

²**feeling** adj **1 :** SENSITIVE; esp **:** easily moved emotionally **2 :** expressing emotion or sensitivity — **feel·ing·ly** adv

**feet** pl of FOOT

**feign** \'fān\ vb **1 :** to give a false appearance of **:** SHAM ⟨~ illness⟩ **2 :** to assert as if true **:** PRETEND

**feint** \'fānt\ n **:** something feigned; esp **:** a mock blow or attack at one point in order to distract attention from the point one really intends to attack — **feint** vb

**feld·spar** \'fel(d)-,spär\ n **:** any of a group of crystalline minerals consisting of silicates of aluminum with either potassium, sodium, calcium, or barium

**fe·lic·i·tate** \fi-'lis-ə-,tāt\ vb **-tat·ed; -tat·ing :** CONGRATULATE — **fe·lic·i·ta·tion** \-,lis-ə-'tā-shən\ n

**fe·lic·i·tous** \fi-'lis-ət-əs\ adj **1 :** suitably expressed **:** APT **2 :** possessing a talent for apt expression ⟨a ~ speaker⟩ — **fe·lic·i·tous·ly** adv

**fe·lic·i·ty** \fi-'lis-ət-ē\ n, pl **-ties 1 :** the quality or state of being happy; esp **:** great happiness **2 :** something that causes happiness **3 :** a pleasing faculty esp. in art or language **:** APTNESS **4 :** an apt expression

**fe·line** \'fē-,līn\ adj [L felinus, fr. felis cat] **1 :** of or relating to cats or their kin **2 :** SLY, TREACHEROUS, STEALTHY — **feline** n

¹**fell** \'fel\ n **:** SKIN, HIDE, PELT

²**fell** vb **1 :** to cut, beat, or knock down ⟨~ trees⟩; also **:** KILL **2 :** to sew (a seam) by folding down one raw edge under the other

³**fell** past of FALL

⁴**fell** adj **:** CRUEL, FIERCE; also **:** DEADLY

**fel·lah** \'fel-ə\ n, pl **fel·la·hin** or **fel·la·heen** \,fel-ə-'hēn\ **:** a peasant or agricultural laborer in Arab countries (as Egypt or Syria)

**fel·la·tio** \fə-'lā-shē-,ō\ also **fel·la·tion** \-'lā-shən\ n **:** oral stimulation of the penis

**fel·low** \'fel-ō\ n [ME felawe, fr. OE fēolaga, fr. ON fēlagi, fr. fēlag partnership, fr. fē cattle, money + lag act of laying] **1 :** COMRADE, ASSOCIATE **2 :** EQUAL, PEER **3 :** one of a pair **:** MATE **4 :** a member of an incorporated literary or scientific society **5 :** MAN, BOY **6 :** BEAU **7 :** a person granted a stipend for advanced study

**fel·low·man** \,fel-ō-'man\ n **:** a kindred human being

**fel·low·ship** \'fel-ō-,ship\ n **1 :** the condition of friendly relationship existing among persons **:** COMPANIONSHIP, COMRADESHIP **2 :** a community of interest or feeling **3 :** a group with similar interests **:** ASSOCIATION **4 :** the position of a fellow (as of a university) **5 :** the stipend granted a fellow; also **:** a foundation granting such a stipend

**fellow traveler** n **:** a person who sympathizes with and often furthers the ideals and program of an organized group (as the Communist party) without joining it or regularly participating in its activities

**fel·ly** \'fel-ē\ or **fel·loe** \ -ō\ n, pl **fellies** or **felloes :** the outside rim or a part of the rim of a wheel supported by the spokes

**fel·on** \'fel-ən\ n **1 :** CRIMINAL; esp **:** one who has committed a felony **2 :** a deep inflammation on a finger or toe

**fel·o·ny** \'fel-ə-nē\ n, pl **-nies :** a serious crime punishable by a heavy sentence — **fe·lo·ni·ous** \fə-'lō-nē-əs\ adj

¹**felt** \'felt\ n **1 :** a cloth made of wool and fur often mixed with natural or synthetic fibers **2 :** a material resembling felt

²**felt** past of FEEL

**fem** abbr **1** female **2** feminine

**fe·male** \'fē-,māl\ adj **:** of, relating to, or being the sex that bears young; also **:** PISTILLATE **syn** feminine, womanly, womanlike, womanish, effeminate, ladylike — **female** n

¹**fem·i·nine** \'fem-ə-nən\ adj **1 :** of the female sex; also **:** characteristic of or appropriate or peculiar to women **2 :** of, relating to, or constituting the gender that includes most words or grammatical forms referring to females — **fem·i·nin·i·ty** \,fem-ə-'nin-ət-ē\ n

²**feminine** n **1 :** WOMAN **2 :** a noun, pronoun, adjective, or inflectional form or class of the feminine gender; also **:** the feminine gender

**fem·i·nism** \'fem-ə-,niz-əm\ n **1 :** the theory of the political, economic, and social equality of the sexes **2 :** organized activity on behalf of women's rights and interests — **fem·i·nist** \-nəst\ n or adj

**femme fa·tale** \,fem-fə-'tal\ n, pl **femmes fa·tales** \-'tal(z)\ n **:** a seductive woman **:** SIREN

**fe·mur** \'fē-mər\ n, pl **fe·murs** or **fem·o·ra** \'fem-(ə-)rə\ **:** the long bone of the thigh — **fem·o·ral** \'fem-(ə-)rəl\ adj

¹**fen** \'fen\ n **:** low swampy land

²**fen** \'fən\ n, pl **fen** — see yuan at MONEY table

¹**fence** \'fens\ n [ME fens, short for defens defense] **1 :** a barrier intended to prevent escape or intrusion or to mark a boundary; esp **:** such a barrier

made of posts and wire or boards **2** : a person who receives stolen goods; *also* : a place where stolen goods are disposed of — **on the fence** : in a position of neutrality or indecision

²**fence** *vb* **fenced; fenc·ing 1** : to enclose with a fence **2** : to keep in or out with a fence **3** : to practice fencing **4** : to use tactics of attack and defense esp. in debate — **fenc·er** *n*

**fenc·ing** \'fen-siŋ\ *n* **1** : the art or practice of attack and defense with the sword or foil **2** : the fences of a property or region **3** : material used for building fences

**fend** \'fend\ *vb* **1** : to keep or ward off : REPEL **2** : SHIFT ⟨~ for himself⟩

**fend·er** \'fen-dər\ *n* : a protective device (as a guard over the wheel of an automobile or as a screen before a fire

**fen·es·tra·tion** \,fen-ə-'strā-shən\ *n* : the arrangement, proportioning, and design of windows and doors in a building

**Fe·ni·an** \'fē-nē-ən\ *n* : a member of a secret 19th century Irish and Irish-American organization dedicated to the overthrow of British rule in Ireland

**fen·nel** \'fen-ᵊl\ *n* : an herb related to the carrot and grown for its aromatic foliage and seeds

**FEPC** *abbr* Fair Employment Practices Commission

**fe·ral** \'fir-əl, 'fer-\ *adj* **1** : SAVAGE **2** : WILD **1 3** : having escaped from domestication and become wild

**fer-de-lance** \'ferd-ᵊl-'ans\ *n, pl* **fer-de-lance** [F. lit., lance iron, spearhead] : a large venomous pit viper of Central and So. America

¹**fer·ment** \fər-'ment\ *vb* **1** : to cause or undergo fermentation **2** : to be or cause to be in a state of agitation or intense activity

²**fer·ment** \'fər-,ment\ *n* **1** : an agent (as yeast or an enzyme) that causes fermentation **2** : AGITATION, TUMULT

**fer·men·ta·tion** \,fər-mən-'tā-shən, -,men-\ *n* **1** : chemical decomposition of an organic substance (as milk or fruit juice) in the absence of oxygen by enzymatic action often with formation of gas **2** : AGITATION, UNREST

**fer·mi·um** \'fer-mē-əm, 'fər-\ *n* : an artificially produced radioactive metallic chemical element

**fern** \'fərn\ *n* : any of a group of flowerless seedless vascular green plants

**fern·ery** \'fərn-(ə-)rē\ *n, pl* **-er·ies 1** : a place for growing ferns **2** : a collection of growing ferns

**fe·ro·cious** \fə-'rō-shəs\ *adj* **1** : FIERCE, SAVAGE **2** : unbearably intense : EXTREME ⟨~ heat⟩ — **fe·ro·cious·ly** *adv* — **fe·ro·cious·ness** *n*

**fe·roc·i·ty** \fə-'räs-ət-ē\ *n* : the quality or state of being ferocious

¹**fer·ret** \'fer-ət\ *n* : a usu. white European polecat used esp. for hunting rodents

²**ferret** *vb* **1** : to hunt game with ferrets **2** : to drive out of a hiding place **3** : to find and bring to light by searching ⟨~ out the truth⟩

**fer·ric** \'fer-ik\ *adj* : of, relating to, or containing iron

**ferric oxide** *n* : an oxide of iron that is found in nature as hematite and as rust and that is used as a pigment and for polishing

**Fer·ris wheel** \'fer-əs-\ *n* : an amusement device consisting of a large upright power-driven wheel carrying seats that remain horizontal around its rim

**fer·ro·mag·net·ic** \,fer-ō-mag-'net-ik\ *adj* : of or relating to substances that are easily magnetized — **ferromagnetic** *n* — **fer·ro·mag·ne·tism** \-'mag-nə-,tiz-əm\ *n*

**fer·rous** \'fer-əs\ *adj* : of, relating to, or containing iron

**fer·rule** \'fer-əl\ *n* : a metal ring or band around a slender shaft to prevent splitting

¹**fer·ry** \'fer-ē\ *vb* **fer·ried; fer·ry·ing** [ME *ferien*, fr. OE *ferian* to carry, convey] **1** : to carry by boat over a body of water **2** : to cross by a ferry **3** : to convey from one place to another

²**ferry** *n, pl* **ferries 1** : a place where persons or things are carried across a body of water (as a river) in a boat **2** : FERRYBOAT **3** : an organized service and route for flying airplanes

**fer·ry·boat** \'fer-ē-,bōt\ *n* : a boat used in ferrying

**fer·tile** \'fərt-ᵊl\ *adj* **1** : producing plentifully : PRODUCTIVE ⟨~ soils⟩ **2** : capable of developing or reproducing ⟨~ eggs⟩ ⟨a family⟩ **syn** fruitful, prolific — **fer·til·i·ty** \(,)fər-'til-ət-ē\ *n*

**fer·til·ize** \'fərt-ᵊl-,īz\ *vb* **-ized; -iz·ing 1** : to make fertile; *esp* : to apply fertilizer to **2** : to interact with to form a zygote ⟨one sperm ~s each egg⟩ — **fer·til·iza·tion** \,fərt-ᵊl-ə-'zā-shən\ *n*

**fer·til·iz·er** \-ᵊl-,ī-zər\ *n* : material (as manure or a chemical mixture) for enriching land

**fer·ule** \'fer-əl\ *also* **fer·u·la** \'fer-(y)ə-lə\ *n* : a rod or ruler used to punish children

**fer·ven·cy** \'fər-vən-sē\ *n, pl* **-cies** : FERVOR

**fer·vent** \'fər-vənt\ *adj* **1** : very hot : GLOWING **2** : marked by great warmth of feeling : ARDENT — **fer·vent·ly** *adv*

**fer·vid** \-vəd\ *adj* **1** : very hot **2** : ARDENT, ZEALOUS — **fer·vid·ly** *adv*

**fer·vor** \'fər-vər\ *n* **1** : intense heat **2** : intensity of feeling or expression

**fes·tal** \'fest-ᵊl\ *adj* : FESTIVE

¹**fes·ter** \'fes-tər\ *n* : a pus-filled sore

²**fester** *vb* **fes·tered; fes·ter·ing** \-t-(ə-)riŋ\ **1** : to form pus; *also* : to become inflamed **2** : RANKLE

**fes·ti·val** \'fes-tə-vəl\ *n* **1** : a time of celebration marked by special observances; *esp* : an occasion marked with religious ceremonies **2** : a periodic season or program of cultural events or entertainment ⟨a dance ~⟩ **3** : CONVIVIALITY, GAIETY

**fes·tive** \'fes-tiv\ *adj* **1** : of, relating to, or suitable for a feast or festival : JOYOUS, GAY — **fes·tive·ly** *adv*

**fes·tiv·i·ty** \fes-'tiv-ət-ē\ *n, pl* **-ties**

**1** : FESTIVAL 1 **2** : the quality or state of being festive **3** : festive activity

**¹fes·toon** \fes-'tün\ n **1** : a decorative chain or strip hanging in a curve between two points **2** : a carved, molded, or painted ornament representing a decorative chain

**²festoon** vb **1** : to hang or form festoons on **2** : to shape into festoons

**fe·tal** \'fēt-ᵊl\ adj : of, relating to, or being a fetus

**fetal position** n : a resting position with body curved, legs bent and drawn toward the chest, head bowed forward, and arms tucked in in the manner of the fetus in the womb that is assumed in some forms of psychic disorder

**fetch** \'fech\ vb **1** : to go or come after and bring or take back ⟨teach a dog to ~ a stick⟩ **2** : to cause to come : bring out ⟨~ed tears from the eyes⟩ **3** : DRAW ⟨~ing her breath⟩; also : HEAVE ⟨~ a sigh⟩ **4** : to sell for **5** : to give by striking ⟨~ him a blow⟩

**fetch·ing** \'fech-iŋ\ adj : ATTRACTIVE, PLEASING — **fetch·ing·ly** adv

**¹fete or fête** \'fāt, 'fet\ n **1** : FESTIVAL **2** : a lavish often outdoor entertainment **3** : a lavish usu. large party

**²fete or fête** vb **fet·ed** or **fêt·ed; fet·ing** or **fêt·ing 1** : to honor or commemorate with a fete **2** : to pay high honor to

**fet·id** \'fet-əd\ adj : having an offensive smell : STINKING

**fe·tish** also **fe·tich** \'fet-ish, 'fēt-\ n [F & Port; F fétiche, fr. Port feitiço, fr. feitiço artificial, false, fr. L facticius factitious] **1** : an object (as an idol or image) believed to have magical powers (as in curing disease) **2** : an object of unreasoning devotion or concern **3** : an object whose real or fantasied presence is psychologically necessary for sexual gratification

**fe·tish·ism** also **fe·tich·ism** \-ish-‚iz-əm\ n : belief in, devotion to, or pathological attachment to fetishes — **fe·tish·ist** \-ish-əst\ n — **fe·tish·is·tic** \‚fet-ish-'is-tik, ‚fēt-\ adj

**fet·lock** \'fet-‚läk\ n : a projection on the back of a horse's leg above the hoof; also : a tuft of hair on this

**fet·ter** \'fet-ər\ n **1** : a chain or shackle for the feet **2** : something that confines : RESTRAINT — **fetter** vb

**fet·tle** \'fet-ᵊl\ n : a state of fitness or order : CONDITION ⟨in fine ~⟩

**fe·tus** \'fēt-əs\ n : an unborn or unhatched vertebrate esp. after its basic structure is laid down

**feud** \'fyüd\ n : a prolonged quarrel; esp : a lasting conflict between families or clans marked by violent attacks undertaken for revenge — **feud** vb

**feu·dal** \'fyüd-ᵊl\ adj **1** : of, relating to, or having the characteristics of a medieval fee **2** : of, relating to, or characteristic of feudalism

**feu·dal·ism** \'fyüd-ᵊl-‚iz-əm\ n : a system of political organization prevailing in medieval Europe in which a vassal renders service to a lord and receives protection and land in return; also : a

similar political or social system — **feu·dal·is·tic** \‚fyüd-ᵊl-'is-tik\ adj

**¹feu·da·to·ry** \'fyüd-ə-‚tōr-ē\ adj : owing feudal allegiance : being in the relation of a vassal to his lord

**²feudatory** n, pl **-ries 1** : a person who holds lands by feudal law or usage **2** : FIEF

**fe·ver** \'fē-vər\ n **1** : a rise in body temperature above the normal; also : a disease of which this is a chief symptom **2** : a state of heightened emotion or activity **3** : a contagious transient enthusiasm : CRAZE — **fe·ver·ish** adj — **fe·ver·ish·ly** adv

**¹few** \'fyü\ pron : not many : a small number

**²few** adj **1** : consisting of or amounting to a small number **2** : not many but some ⟨caught a ~ fish⟩ — **few·ness** n

**³few** n **1** : a small number of units or individuals ⟨a ~ of them⟩ **2** : a special limited number ⟨among the ~⟩

**few·er** \'fyü-ər\ pron : a smaller number of persons or things

**fey** \'fā\ adj **1** chiefly Scot : fated to die; also : marked by a foreboding of death or calamity **2** : ELFIN **3** : VISIONARY **4** : marked by an otherworldly air or attitude **5** : CRAZY, TOUCHED

**fez** \'fez\ n, pl **fez·zes** also **fez·es** : a round flat-crowned hat that usu. has a tassel, is made of red felt, and is worn by men in eastern Mediterranean countries

**ff** abbr **1** folios **2** following **3** fortissimo

**FHA** abbr Federal Housing Administration

**fi·an·cé** \‚fē-‚än-'sā\ n [F, fr. MF, fr. fiancer to promise, betroth, fr. OF fiancier, fr. fiance promise, trust, fr. fier to trust, fr. L fidere] : a man engaged to be married

**fi·an·cée** \‚fē-‚än-'sā\ n : a woman engaged to be married

**fi·as·co** \fē-'as-kō\ n, pl **-coes** : a complete failure

**fi·at** \'fē-ət, -‚at, -‚ät; 'fī-ət, -‚at\ n [L, let it be done] : an authoritative and often arbitrary order or decree

**fiat money** n : paper currency backed only by the authority of the government and not by metal

**¹fib** \'fib\ n : a lie about some trivial matter

**²fib** vb **fibbed; fib·bing** : to tell a fib — **fib·ber** n

**fi·ber or fi·bre** \'fī-bər\ n **1** : a threadlike substance or structure (as a muscle cell or plant root fiber); esp : a natural (as wool or flax) or artificial (as rayon) filament capable of being spun or woven **2** : an element that gives texture or substance **3** : basic toughness : STRENGTH — **fi·brous** \-brəs\ adj

**fi·ber·board** \-‚bōrd\ n : a material made by compressing fibers (as of wood) into stiff sheets

**fi·ber·glass** \-‚glas\ n : glass in fibrous form used in making various products (as yarn and insulation)

**fiber optic** n : a transparent homogenous fiber of glass or plastic that is enclosed by a less refractive material so that it transmits light by internal reflection

**fi·bril** \'fīb-rəl, 'fib-\ *n* : a small fiber

**fi·bril·la·tion** \,fib-rə-'lā-shən, ,fīb-\ *n* : rapid irregular contractions of muscle fibers (as of the heart) — **fib·ril·late** \'fib-rə-,lāt, 'fīb-\ *vb*

**fi·brin** \'fī-brən\ *n* : a white insoluble fibrous protein formed from fibrinogen in the clotting of blood — **fi·brin·ous** \'fib-rə-nəs, 'fīb-\ *adj*

**fi·brin·o·gen** \fī-'brin-ə-jən\ *n* : a globulin produced in the liver, present esp. in blood plasma, and converted into fibrin during clotting of blood

**fi·broid** \'fī-,brȯid, 'fib-\ *adj* : resembling, forming, or consisting of fibrous tissue 〈~ tumors〉

**fi·bro·sis** \fī-'brō-səs\ *n* : a condition marked by abnormal increase of fiber-containing tissue

**fib·u·la** \'fib-yə-lə\ *n, pl* **-lae** \-,lē, -,lī\ *or* **-las** : the outer and usu. the smaller of the two bones of the hind limb below the knee — **fib·u·lar** \-lər\ *adj*

**FICA** *abbr* Federal Insurance Contributions Act

**fiche** \'fēsh, 'fish\ *n* : MICROFICHE

**fi·chu** \'fish-ü\ *n* : a woman's light triangular scarf draped over the shoulders and fastened in front

**fick·le** \'fik-əl\ *adj* : not firm or steadfast in disposition or character : INCONSTANT — **fick·le·ness** *n*

**fic·tion** \'fik-shən\ *n* 1 : something (as a story) invented by the imagination 2 : fictitious literature (as novels) — **fic·tion·al** \-sh(ə-)nəl\ *adj*

**fic·ti·tious** \fik-'tish-əs\ *adj* 1 : of, relating to, or characteristic of fiction : IMAGINARY 2 : FEIGNED **syn** fabulous, legendary, mythical

¹**fid·dle** \'fid-ᵊl\ *n* : VIOLIN

²**fiddle** *vb* **fid·dled; fid·dling** \'fid-(ᵊ-)liŋ\ 1 : to play on a fiddle 2 : to move the hands or fingers restlessly 3 : PUTTER 4 : MEDDLE, TAMPER — **fid·dler** \'fid-(ᵊ-)lər\ *n*

**fiddler crab** *n* : a burrowing crab with one claw much enlarged in the male

**fid·dle·stick** \'fid-ᵊl-,stik\ *n* 1 : a violin bow 2 *pl* : NONSENSE — used as an interjection

**fi·del·i·ty** \fə-'del-ət-ē, fī-\ *n, pl* **-ties** 1 : the quality or state of being faithful 2 : ACCURACY 〈~ of a news report〉 〈~ in sound reproduction〉 **syn** allegiance, loyalty, devotion

¹**fid·get** \'fij-ət\ *n* 1 *pl* : uneasiness or restlessness as shown by nervous movements 2 : one that fidgets — **fid·gety** *adj*

²**fidget** *vb* : to move or cause to move or act restlessly or nervously

**fi·do** \'fīd-ō\ *n, pl* **fidos** [*f*reaks + *i*rregulars + *d*efects + *o*ddities] : a coin having a minting error

**fi·du·cia·ry** \fə-'d(y)ü-shē-,er-ē, -shə-rē\ *adj* 1 : involving a confidence or trust 2 : held or holding in trust for another 〈~ accounts〉 — **fiduciary** *n*

**fie** \'fī\ *interj* — used to express disgust or shock

**fief** \'fēf\ *n* : a feudal estate : FEE

¹**field** \'fēld\ *n* 1 : open country 2 : a piece of cleared land for tillage or pasture 3 : a piece of land yielding some special product 4 : the place where a battle is fought; *also* : BATTLE 5 : an area, division, or sphere of activity 〈the ~ of science〉 〈salesmen in the ~〉 6 : an area for military exercises 7 : an area for sports 8 : a background on which something is drawn or projected 〈a flag with white stars on a ~ of blue〉 9 : a region or space in which a given effect (as magnetism) exists — **field** *adj*

²**field** *vb* 1 : to handle a batted or thrown baseball while on defense 2 : to put into the field 3 : to answer satisfactorily 〈~ a tough question〉 — **field·er** *n*

**field day** *n* 1 : a day devoted to outdoor sports and athletic competition 2 : a time of unusual pleasure or unexpected success

**field event** *n* : a track-and-field event (as weight-throwing) other than a race

**field glass** *n* : a hand-held binocular telescope — usu. used in pl.

**field hockey** *n* : a game played on a turfed field between two teams of 11 players whose object is to direct a ball into the opponent's goal with a hockey stick

**field marshal** *n* : an officer (as in the British army) of the highest rank

**field·piece** \'fēl(d)-,pēs\ *n* : a gun or howitzer for use in the field

**field-test** \-,test\ *vb* : to test (as a new product) in a natural environment — **field test** *n*

**fiend** \'fēnd\ *n* 1 : DEVIL, DEMON 2 : an extremely wicked or cruel person 3 : a person excessively devoted to a pursuit 4 : ADDICT 〈dope ~〉 — **fiend·ish** *adj* — **fiend·ish·ly** *adv*

**fierce** \'fiərs\ *adj* **fierc·er; fierc·est** 1 : violently hostile or aggressive in temperament 2 : PUGNACIOUS 3 : INTENSE 4 : furiously active or determined 5 : wild or menacing in aspect **syn** ferocious, barbarous, savage, cruel — **fierce·ly** *adv* — **fierce·ness** *n*

**fi·ery** \'fī(-ə)-rē\ *adj* **fi·er·i·er; -est** 1 : consisting of fire 2 : BURNING, BLAZING 3 : FLAMMABLE 4 : hot like a fire : INFLAMED, FEVERISH 5 : RED 6 : full of emotion or spirit 7 : IRRITABLE — **fi·er·i·ness** \'fī(-ə)-rē-nəs\ *n*

**fi·es·ta** \fē-'es-tə\ *n* : FESTIVAL

**fife** \'fīf\ *n* [G *pfeife* pipe, fife] : a small shrill flutelike musical instrument

**FIFO** *abbr* first in, first out

**fif·teen** \fif-'tēn\ *n* : one more than 14 — **fifteen** *adj or pron* — **fif·teenth** \-'tēnth\ *adj or n*

**fifth** \'fifth\ *n* 1 : one that is number five in a countable series 2 : one of five equal parts of something 3 : a unit of measure for liquor equal to ⅕ U.S. gallon — **fifth** *adj or adv*

**fifth column** *n* : a group of secret sympathizers or supporters of a nation's enemy that engage in espionage or sabotage within the country — **fifth col-**

**um·nist** \-'käl-əm-(n)əst\ *n*

**fifth wheel** *n* **1 :** a horizontal wheel on a tractor serving as a coupling and support for a semitrailer **2 :** one that is unnecessary and often burdensome

**fif·ty** \'fif-tē\ *n, pl* **fifties :** five times 10 — **fif·ti·eth** \-tē-əth\ *adj or n* — **fifty** *adj or pron*

**fif·ty–fif·ty** \,fif-tē-'fif-tē\ *adj* **1 :** shared equally ⟨a ~ proposition⟩ **2 :** half favorable and half unfavorable

**¹fig** \'fig\ *n* **:** a usu. pear-shaped edible fruit of warm regions; *also* **:** a tree related to the mulberry that bears this fruit

**²fig** *abbr* **1** figurative; figuratively **2** figure

**¹fight** \'fīt\ *vb* **fought** \'fȯt\; **fighting 1 :** to contend against another in battle or physical combat **2 :** BOX **3 :** to put forth a determined effort **4 :** STRUGGLE, CONTEND **5 :** to attempt to prevent the success or effectiveness of **6 :** WAGE **7 :** to gain by struggle

**²fight** *n* **1 :** a hostile encounter **:** BATTLE **2 :** a boxing match **3 :** a verbal disagreement **4 :** a struggle for a goal or an objective **5 :** strength or disposition for fighting ⟨full of ~⟩

**fight·er** \-ər\ *n* **1 :** one that fights; *esp* **:** WARRIOR **2 :** BOXER **3 :** an airplane of high speed and maneuverability with armament for destroying enemy aircraft

**fig·ment** \'fig-mənt\ *n* **:** something imagined or made up

**fig·u·ra·tion** \,fig-(y)ə-'rā-shən\ *n* **1 :** FORM, OUTLINE **2 :** an act or instance of representation in figures and shapes

**fig·u·ra·tive** \'fig-(y)ə-rət-iv\ *adj* **1 :** EMBLEMATIC **2 :** SYMBOLIC, METAPHORICAL ⟨~ language⟩ **3 :** characterized by figures of speech or elaborate expression — **fig·u·ra·tive·ly** *adv*

**¹fig·ure** \'fig-yər\ *n* **1 :** a symbol representing a number **:** NUMERAL **2** *pl* **:** arithmetical calculations **3 :** a written or printed character **4 :** PRICE, AMOUNT **5 :** SHAPE, FORM, OUTLINE **6 :** the graphic representation of a form and esp. of a person **7 :** a diagram or pictorial illustration of textual matter **8 :** an expression (as in metaphor) that uses words in other than a plain or literal way **9 :** PATTERN, DESIGN **10 :** appearance made or impression produced ⟨they cut quite a ~⟩ **11 :** a series of movements (as in a dance) **12 :** PERSONAGE

**²figure** *vb* **fig·ured; fig·ur·ing** \'fig-yə-riŋ\ **1 :** to represent by or as if by a figure or outline **:** PORTRAY **2 :** to decorate with a pattern **3 :** to indicate or represent by numerals **4 :** REGARD, CONSIDER **5 :** to be or appear important or conspicuous **6 :** COMPUTE, CALCULATE

**fig·ure·head** \'fig-(y)ər-,hed\ *n* **1 :** a carved figure on the bow of a ship **2 :** a person who is head or chief in name only

**fig·u·rine** \,fig-(y)ə-'rēn\ *n* **:** a small carved or molded figure

**fil·a·ment** \'fil-ə-mənt\ *n* **:** a fine thread or threadlike object, part, or process — **fil·a·men·tous** \-'ment-əs\ *adj*

**fi·lar** \'fī-lər\ *adj* **:** of or relating to a thread or line

**fil·bert** \'fil-bərt\ *n* **:** the oblong edible nut of a European hazel; *also* **:** this plant

**filch** \'filch\ *vb* **:** to steal furtively

**¹file** \'fīl\ *n* **:** a steel instrument with ridged surface used for rubbing down a hard substance

**²file** *vb* **filed; fil·ing :** to rub, smooth, or cut away with a file

**³file** *vb* **filed; fil·ing** [ME *filen*, fr. MF *filer* to string documents on a string or wire, fr. *fil* thread, fr. L *filum*] **1 :** to arrange in order for preservation or reference **2 :** to enter or record officially or as prescribed by law ⟨~ a lawsuit⟩ **3 :** to send (copy) to a newspaper

**⁴file** *n* **1 :** a device (as a folder or cabinet) by means of which papers or records may be kept in order **2 :** a collection of papers usu. arranged or classified

**⁵file** *n* **:** a row of persons, animals, or things arranged one behind the other

**⁶file** *vb* **filed; fil·ing :** to march or proceed in file

**fi·let mi·gnon** \fil-(,)ā-mēn-'yōⁿ, fi-,lā-\ *n, pl* **filets mignons** \-(,)ā-mēn-'yōⁿz, -,lā-\ **:** a fillet of beef cut from the thick end of a beef tenderloin

**fil·ial** \'fil-ē-əl, 'fil-yəl\ *adj* **:** of, relating to, or befitting a son or daughter

**fil·i·bus·ter** \'fil-ə-,bəs-tər\ *n* [Sp *filibustero*, lit., freebooter] **1 :** a military adventurer, *esp* **:** an American engaged in fomenting insurrections in Latin America in the mid-19th century **2 :** the use of delaying tactics (as extremely long speeches) esp. in a legislative assembly; *also* **:** an instance of this practice — **filibuster** *vb* — **fil·i·bus·ter·er** *n*

**fil·i·gree** \'fil-ə-,grē\ *n* **:** ornamental openwork (as of fine wire) — **fil·i·greed** \-,grēd\ *adj*

**fil·ing** \'fī-liŋ\ *n* **1 :** the act of one who files **2 :** a small piece scraped off by a file (iron ~s)

**Fil·i·pi·no** \,fil-ə-'pē-nō\ *n, pl* **Filipinos :** a native or inhabitant of the Philippines — **Filipino** *adj*

**¹fill** \'fil\ *vb* **1 :** to make or become full **2 :** to stop up **:** PLUG ⟨~ a cavity⟩ **3 :** FEED, SATIATE **4 :** SATISFY, FULFILL ⟨~ all requirements⟩ **5 :** to occupy fully **6 :** to spread through ⟨laughter ~ed the room⟩ **7 :** OCCUPY ⟨~ the office of president⟩ **8 :** to put a person in ⟨~ a vacancy⟩ **9 :** to supply as directed ⟨~ a prescription⟩

**²fill** *n* **:** a full supply; *esp* **:** a quantity that satisfies or satiates **2 :** material used esp. for filling a low place

**filled milk** *n* **:** skim milk with the fat content increased by the addition of vegetable oils

**¹fill·er** \'fil-ər\ *n* **1 :** one that fills **2 :** a substance added to another substance (as to increase bulk or weight) **3 :** a material used for filling cracks and pores in wood before painting

²**fil·ler** \'fil-ər\ *n, pl* **fillers** *or* **filler** — see *forint* at MONEY table

¹**fil·let** \'fil-ət, *in sense 2 also* fi-'lā, 'fil-(,)ā\ *also* **fi·let** \fi-'lā, 'fil-(,)ā\ *n* 1 : a narrow band, strip, or ribbon 2 : a piece or slice of boneless meat or fish; *esp* : the tenderloin of beef

²**fil·let** \'fil-ət, *in sense 2 also* fi-'lā, 'fil-(,)ā\ *vb* 1 : to bind or adorn with or as if with a fillet 2 : to cut into fillets

**fill in** \(')fil-'in\ *vb* 1 : to provide necessary or recent information 2 : to serve as a temporary substitute

**fill·ing** \'fil-iŋ\ *n* 1 : material used to fill something ⟨a ~ for a tooth⟩ 2 : the yarn interlacing the warp in a fabric 3 : a food mixture used to fill pastry or sandwiches

**filling station** *n* : SERVICE STATION

**fil·lip** \'fil-əp\ *n* 1 : a blow or gesture made by a flick or snap of the finger across the thumb 2 : something that serves to arouse or stimulate — **fillip** *vb*

**fil·ly** \'fil-ē\ *n, pl* **fillies** : a young female horse

¹**film** \'film\ *n* 1 : a thin skin or membrane 2 : a thin coating or layer 3 : a flexible strip of chemically treated material used in taking pictures 4 : MOTION PICTURE — **filmy** *adj*

²**film** *vb* 1 : to cover with a film 2 : PHOTOGRAPH 3 : to make a motion picture of

**film·dom** \'film-dəm\ *n* 1 : the motion-picture industry 2 : the personnel of the motion-picture industry

**film·og·ra·phy** \fil-'mäg-rə-fē\ *n, pl* **-phies** : a list or catalog of motion pictures relating usu. to a particular actor or director

**film·strip** \'film-,strip\ *n* : a strip of film bearing photographs, diagrams, or graphic matter for still projection upon a screen

**fils** \'fils\ *n, pl* **fils** — see *dinar* at MONEY table

¹**fil·ter** \'fil-tər\ *n* 1 : a porous material through which a fluid is passed to separate out matter in suspension; *also* : a device containing such material 2 : a device for suppressing waves or oscillations of certain frequencies; *esp* : one (as on a camera lens) that absorbs light of certain colors

²**filter** *vb* **fil·tered; fil·ter·ing** \-t(ə-)riŋ\ 1 : to pass through a filter 2 : to remove by means of a filter — **fil·ter·able** *also* **fil·tra·ble** \-t(ə-)rə-bəl\ *adj* — **fil·tra·tion** \fil-'trā-shən\ *n*

**filter bed** *n* : a bed of sand or gravel for filtering water or sewage

**filth** \'filth\ *n* [ME, fr. OE *fylth*, fr. *fūl* foul] 1 : foul matter; *esp* : loathsome dirt or refuse 2 : moral corruption 3 : OBSCENITY — **filth·i·ness** \'fil-thē-nəs\ *n* — **filthy** \'fil-thē\ *adj*

¹**fil·trate** \'fil-,trāt\ *vb* **fil·trat·ed; fil·trat·ing** : FILTER

²**filtrate** *n* : the fluid that has passed through a filter

¹**fin** \'fin\ *n* 1 : one of the thin external

processes by which an aquatic animal (as a fish) moves through water 2 : a fin-shaped part (as on an airplane) 3 : FLIPPER 2 — **finned** \'find\ *adj*

²**fin** *abbr* 1 : finance; financial 2 : finish

**fi·na·gle** \fə-'nā-gəl\ *vb* **fi·na·gled; fi·na·gling** \-g(ə-)liŋ\ 1 : to obtain by indirect or involved means 2 : to obtain by trickery 3 : to use devious dishonest methods to achieve one's ends — **fi·na·gler** \-g(ə-)lər\ *n*

¹**fi·nal** \'fīn-ᵊl\ *adj* 1 : not to be altered or undone : CONCLUSIVE 2 : ULTIMATE 3 : relating to or occurring at the end or conclusion — **fi·nal·i·ty** \fī-'nal-ət-ē, fə-\ *n* — **fi·nal·ly** \'fīn-(ᵊ-)lē\ *adv*

²**final** *n* 1 : a deciding match, game, or trial 2 : the last examination in a course

**fi·na·le** \fə-'nal-ē, fi-'nal-\ *n* : the close or termination of something; *esp* : the last section of a musical composition

**fi·nal·ist** \'fīn-ᵊl-əst\ *n* : a contestant in the finals of a competition

**fi·nal·ize** \'fīn-ᵊl-,īz\ *vb* **-ized; -iz·ing** : to put in final or finished form

¹**fi·nance** \fə-'nans, 'fī-,nans\ *n* [ME, payment, ransom, fr. MF, fr. *finer* to end, pay, fr. *fin* end, fr. L *finis* boundary, end] 1 *pl* : money resources available esp. to a government or business 2 : management of money affairs

²**finance** *vb* **fi·nanced; fi·nanc·ing** 1 : to raise or provide funds for 2 : to furnish with necessary funds 3 : to sell or supply on credit

**finance company** *n* : a company that finances businesses (as by buying installment notes at a discount) or individuals (as by making small loans at high rates of interest)

**fi·nan·cial** \fə-'nan-chəl, fī-\ *adj* : having to do with finance or financiers ⟨in ~ circles⟩ — **fi·nan·cial·ly** \-'nanch-(ə-)lē\ *adv*

**fi·nan·cier** \,fin-ən-'siər, ,fī-,nan-\ *n* 1 : a person skilled in managing large funds 2 : a person who invests large sums of money

**finch** \'finch\ *n* : any of a group of songbirds (as sparrows, linnets, or buntings) with strong conical bills

¹**find** \'find\ *vb* **found** \'faund\; **find·ing** 1 : to meet with either by chance or by searching or study : ENCOUNTER, DISCOVER 2 : to obtain by effort or management ⟨~ time to read⟩ 3 : to arrive at : REACH ⟨the bullet *found* its mark⟩ 4 : EXPERIENCE, DETECT, PERCEIVE, FEEL 5 : to gain or regain the use of ⟨*found* his voice again⟩ 6 : PROVIDE, SUPPLY 7 : to settle upon and make a statement about ⟨~ a verdict⟩

²**find** *n* 1 : an act or instance of finding 2 : something found; *esp* : a valuable item of discovery

**find·er** \'fīn-dər\ *n* : one that finds; *esp* : a device on a camera showing the view being photographed

**fin de siè·cle** \,fa⁻-də-sē-'eklᵊ\ *adj* : of, relating to, or characteristic of the close of the 19th century

**find·ing** \'fīn-diŋ\ *n* 1 : the act of

finding **2** : FIND 2 **3** : the result of a judicial proceeding or inquiry

¹**fine** \'fīn\ *n* : money exacted as a penalty for an offense

²**fine** *vb* **fined; fin·ing** : to impose a fine on : punish by a fine

³**fine** *adj* **fin·er; fin·est 1** : free from impurity **2** : very thin in gauge or texture **3** : not coarse **4** : SUBTLE, SENSITIVE ⟨a ~ distinction⟩ **5** : superior in quality, conception, or appearance **6** : ELEGANT, REFINED — **fine·ly** *adv* — **fine·ness** \'fīn-nəs\ *n*

⁴**fine** *adv* : FINELY

**fine art** *n* : art (as painting, sculpture, or music) concerned primarily with the creation of beautiful objects

**fin·ery** \'fīn-(ə-)rē\ *n, pl* **-er·ies** : ORNAMENT, DECORATION; *esp* : showy clothing and jewels

**fine·spun** \'fīn-'spən\ *adj* : developed with extremely or excessively fine delicacy or detail

**fi·nesse** \fə-'nes\ *n* **1** : delicate skill **2** : CUNNING, STRATAGEM, TRICK — **finesse** *vb*

**fin·fish** \'fin-,fish\ *n* : a true fish as distinguished from a shellfish

¹**fin·ger** \'fiŋ-gər\ *n* **1** : one of the five divisions at the end of the hand; *esp* : one other than the thumb **2** : something that resembles or does the work of a finger **3** : a part of a glove into which a finger is inserted — **fin·gered** \'fiŋ-gərd\ *adj*

²**finger** *vb* **fin·gered; fin·ger·ing** \-g(ə-)riŋ\ **1** : to touch with the fingers : HANDLE **2** : to perform with the fingers or with a certain fingering **3** : to mark the notes of a piece of music as a guide in playing **4** : to point out

**fin·ger·board** \'fiŋ-gər-,bōrd\ *n* : the part of a stringed instrument against which the fingers press the strings to vary the pitch

**finger bowl** *n* : a basin to hold water for rinsing the fingers at table

**fin·ger·ing** \'fiŋ-g(ə-)riŋ\ *n* **1** : the act or process of handling or touching with the fingers **2** : the act or method of using the fingers in playing an instrument **3** : the marking of the method of fingering

**fin·ger·ling** \'fiŋ-gər-liŋ\ *n* : a small fish

**fin·ger·nail** \'fiŋ-gər-,nāl\ *n* : the nail of a finger

**fin·ger·print** \-,print\ *n* : the pattern of marks made by pressing the tip of a finger or thumb on a surface; *esp* : an ink impression of such a pattern taken for the purpose of identification — **fingerprint** *vb*

**fin·ger·tip** \-,tip\ *n* : the tip of a finger

**fin·i·al** \'fin-ē-əl\ *n* : an ornamental projection or end (as on a spire)

**fin·ick·ing** \'fin-i-kiŋ\ *adj* : FINICKY

**fin·icky** \'fin-i-kē\ *adj* : excessively particular in taste or standards

**fi·nis** \'fin-əs, 'fī-nəs\ *n* : END, CONCLUSION

¹**fin·ish** \'fin-ish\ *vb* **1** : TERMINATE **2** : to use or dispose of entirely **3** : to bring to completion : ACCOMPLISH;

*also* : PERFECT **4** : to put a final coat or surface on **5** : to come to the end of a course or undertaking — **fin·ish·er** *n*

²**finish** *n* **1** : END, CONCLUSION **2** : something that completes or perfects **3** : the treatment given a surface; *also* : the result or product of a finishing process **4** : social polish

**fi·nite** \'fī-,nīt\ *adj* **1** : having definite or definable limits **2** : having a limited nature or existence **3** : being neither infinite nor infinitesimal

**fink** \'fiŋk\ *n* **1** : INFORMER **2** : STRIKEBREAKER **3** : a contemptible person

¹**Finn** \'fin\ *n* : a native or inhabitant of Finland

²**Finn** *abbr* Finnish

**fin·nan had·die** \,fin-ən-'had-ē\ *n* : smoked haddock

¹**Finn·ish** \'fin-ish\ *adj* : of or relating to Finland, the Finns, or Finnish

²**Finnish** *n* : the language of Finland

**fin·ny** \'fin-ē\ *adj* **1** : resembling or having fins **2** : of, relating to, or full of fish

**FIO** *abbr* frec in and out

**fiord** *var of* FJORD

**fir** \'fər\ *n* [ME, fr. OE *fyrh*; akin to L *quercus* oak] : an erect evergreen tree related to the pines; *also* : its light soft wood

¹**fire** \'fī(ə)r\ *n* **1** : the light or heat and esp. the flame of something burning **2** : fuel that is burning (as in a stove or fireplace) **3** : destructive burning of something (as a house) **4** : ENTHUSIASM, ZEAL **5** : the discharge of firearms — **fire·less** *adj*

²**fire** *vb* **fired; fir·ing 1** : KINDLE, IGNITE ⟨~ a house⟩ **2** : STIR, ENLIVEN ⟨~ the imagination⟩ **3** : to dismiss from employment **4** : SHOOT ⟨~ a gun⟩ ⟨~ an arrow⟩ **5** : to apply fire or fuel to something ⟨~ a furnace⟩ **6** : BAKE ⟨~ing pottery in a kiln⟩

**fire ant** *n* : any of a genus of fiercely stinging omnivorous ants

**fire·arm** \'fī(ə)r-,ärm\ *n* : a weapon (as a rifle or pistol) from which a shot is discharged by an explosion of gunpowder

**fire·ball** \'fī(ə)r-,bȯl\ *n* **1** : a ball of fire **2** : a brilliant meteor that may trail bright sparks **3** : the highly luminous cloud of vapor and dust created by a nuclear explosion (as of an atom bomb) **4** : a highly energetic person

**fire·boat** \'fī(ə)r-,bōt\ *n* : a ship equipped with apparatus (as pumps) for fighting fire

**fire·bomb** \-,bäm\ *n* : an incendiary bomb — **firebomb** *vb*

**fire·box** \-,bäks\ *n* **1** : a chamber (as of a furnace or steam boiler) that contains a fire **2** : a box containing an apparatus for transmitting an alarm to a fire station

**fire·brand** \-,brand\ *n* **1** : a piece of burning wood **2** : a person who creates unrest or strife : AGITATOR

**fire·break** \-,brāk\ *n* : a barrier of cleared or plowed land intended to check a forest or grass fire

**fire·brick** \-,brik\ *n* : a brick capable of withstanding great heat and used for lining furnaces or fireplaces

**fire·bug** \'fī(ə)r-,bəg\ *n* : a person who deliberately sets destructive fires

**fire·clay** \-,klā\ *n* : clay capable of withstanding high temperatures and used esp. for firebrick and crucibles

**fire·crack·er** \'fī(ə)r-,krak-ər\ *n* : a paper tube containing an explosive and a fuse and discharged to make a noise

**fire·damp** \-,damp\ *n* : a combustible mine gas that consists chiefly of methane

**fire engine** *n* : a mobile apparatus for extinguishing fires

**fire escape** *n* : a device for escape from a burning building; *esp* : a metal stairway attached to the outside of a building

**fire·fly** \'fī(ə)r-,flī\ *n* : a small night-flying beetle that produces a soft light

**fire·house** \'fī(ə)r-,haůs\ *n* : FIRE STATION

**fire irons** *n pl* : implements for tending a fire esp. in a fireplace

**fire·man** \-mən\ *n* **1** : a member of a company organized to put out fires **2** : STOKER; *also* : a locomotive crew member who services motors and assists the engineer

**fire·place** \'fī(ə)r-,plās\ *n* **1** : a framed opening made in a chimney to hold an open fire : HEARTH **2** : an outdoor structure of brick or stone made for an open fire

**fire·plug** \-,pləg\ *n* : HYDRANT

**fire·pow·er** \-,paů(-ə)r\ *n* : the relative ability to deliver gunfire or warheads on a target

¹**fire·proof** \-'prüf\ *adj* : proof against or resistant to fire

²**fireproof** *vb* : to make fireproof

**fire screen** *n* : a protecting wire screen before a fireplace

¹**fire·side** \'fī(ə)r-,sīd\ *n* **1** : a place near the fire or hearth **2** : HOME

²**fireside** *adj* : having an informal or intimate quality

**fire station** *n* : a building housing fire apparatus and usu. firemen

**fire tower** *n* : a tower from which a watch for fires is kept (as in a forest)

**fire·trap** \'fī(ə)r-,trap\ *n* : a building or place apt to catch on fire or difficult to escape from in case of fire

**fire truck** *n* : an automotive vehicle equipped with fire-fighting apparatus

**fire·wa·ter** \'fī(ə)r-,wòt-ər, -,wät-\ *n* : intoxicating liquor

**fire·wood** \-,wůd\ *n* : wood cut for fuel

**fire·work** \-,wərk\ *n* : a device designed to be lighted and produce a display of light, noise, and smoke

**firing line** *n* **1** : a line from which fire is delivered against a target **2** : the forefront of an activity

¹**firm** \'fərm\ *adj* **1** : securely fixed in place **2** : SOLID, VIGOROUS ⟨a ~ handshake⟩ **3** : having a solid or compact texture ⟨~ flesh⟩ **4** : not subject to change or fluctuation : STEADY ⟨~ prices⟩ **5** : STEADFAST **6** : indicating

firmness or resolution ⟨a ~ mouth⟩ — **firm·ly** *adv* — **firm·ness** *n*

²**firm** *vb* : to make or become firm

³**firm** *n* [G *firma*, fr. It, signature, deriv. of L *firmare* to make firm, confirm, fr. *firmus*] **1** : the name under which a company transacts business **2** : a business partnership of two or more persons **3** : a business enterprise

**fir·ma·ment** \'fər-mə-mənt\ *n* : the arch of the sky : HEAVENS

¹**first** \'fərst\ *adj* **1** : being number one in a countable series **2** : preceding all others

²**first** *adv* **1** : before any other **2** : for the first time **3** : in preference to something else

³**first** *n* **1** : number one in a countable series **2** : one that is first **3** : the lowest forward gear in an automotive vehicle

**first aid** *n* : emergency care or treatment given an injured or ill person

**first·born** \'fərs(t)-'bòrn\ *adj* : ELDEST — **firstborn** *n*

**first class** *n* : the best or highest group in a classification — **first-class** *adj or adv*

**first·hand** \'fərst-'hand\ *adj* : coming directly from the original source ⟨~ knowledge⟩ — **firsthand** *adv*

**first lady** *n*, *often cap F&L* : the wife or hostess of the chief executive of a political unit (as a country)

**first lieutenant** *n* : a commissioned officer (as in the army) ranking next below a captain

**first·ling** \'fərst-liŋ\ *n* **1** : the first of a class or kind **2** : the first produce or result

**first·ly** \-lē\ *adv* : in the first place : FIRST

**first-rate** \-'rāt\ *adj* : of the first order of size, importance, or quality — **first-rate** *adv*

**first sergeant** *n* **1** : a noncommissioned officer serving as the chief assistant to the commander of a military unit (as a company) **2** : a rank in the army below a command sergeant major and in the marine corps below a sergeant major

**first-string** \ fərs(t)-'striŋ\ *adj* : being a regular as distinguished from a substitute

**firth** \'fərth\ *n* [ME, fr. ON *fjörthr*] : a narrow arm of the sea

**fis·cal** \'fis-kəl\ *adj* [L *fiscalis*, fr. *fiscus* basket, treasury] **1** : of or relating to taxation, public revenues, or public debt **2** : of or relating to financial matters

¹**fish** \'fish\ *n*, *pl* **fish** *or* **fish·es** **1** : a water animal; *esp* : any of a large group of cold-blooded water-breathing vertebrates with fin, gills, and usu. scales **2** : the flesh of fish used as food

²**fish** *vb* **1** : to attempt to catch fish **2** : to seek something by roundabout means ⟨~ for praise⟩ **3** : to search (as with a hook) for something underwater **4** : to engage in a search by groping **5** : to draw forth

**fish-and-chips** \,fish-ən-'chips\ *n pl* : fried fish and french fried potatoes

**fish·bowl** \'fish-,bōl\ *n* **1** : a bowl for the keeping of live fish **2** : a place or condition that affords no privacy

**fish·er** \'fish-ər\ *n* **1** : one that fishes **2** : a large dark brown No. American arboreal carnivorous mammal

**fish·er·man** \-mən\ *n* : a person engaged in fishing; *also* : a fishing boat

**fish·ery** \'fish-(ə-)rē\ *n, pl* **-er·ies** : the business of catching fish; *also* : a place for catching fish

**fish·hook** \'fish-,hůk\ *n* : a usu. barbed hook for catching fish

**fish·ing** \'fish-iŋ\ *n* : the business or sport of catching fish

**fish ladder** *n* : an arrangement of pools by which fish can pass around a dam

**fish protein concentrate** *n* : flour made of pulverized dried fish

**fish·wife** \'fish-,wīf\ *n* **1** : a woman who sells fish **2** : a vulgar abusive woman

**fishy** \'fish-ē\ *adj* **fish·i·er; -est** **1** : of, relating to, or resembling fish **2** : QUESTIONABLE

**fis·sile** \'fis-əl, 'fis-,īl\ *adj* : capable of undergoing fission

**fis·sion** \'fish-ən, 'fizh-\ *n* [L *fissio*, fr. *fissus*, pp. of *findere* to split] **1** : a cleaving into parts **2** : the splitting of an atomic nucleus resulting in the release of large amounts of energy — **fis·sion·able** \'fish-(ə-)nə-bəl, 'fizh-\ *adj* — **fis·sion·al** \'fish-ən-əl, 'fizh-\ *adj*

**fis·sure** \'fish-ər\ *n* : a narrow opening or crack

**fist** \'fist\ *n* **1** : the hand with fingers doubled into the palm **2** : INDEX 6 — **fist·ed** \'fis-təd\ *adj*

**fist·ful** \-,fůl\ *n* : HANDFUL

**fist·i·cuffs** \'fis-ti-,kəfs\ *n pl* : a fight with usu. bare fists

**fis·tu·la** \'fis-chə-lə\ *n, pl* **-las** *or* **-lae** : an abnormal passage leading from an abscess or hollow organ — **fis·tu·lous** \-ləs\ *adj*

¹**fit** \'fit\ *n* **1** : a sudden violent attack (as of bodily disorder) **2** : a sudden outburst (as of laughter)

²**fit** *adj* **fit·ter; fit·test** **1** : adapted to a purpose **2** : APPROPRIATE, PROPER, RIGHT, BECOMING **3** : PREPARED, READY **4** : QUALIFIED, COMPETENT **5** : physically and mentally sound — **fit·ly** *adv* — **fit·ness** *n*

³**fit** *vb* **fit·ted** *also* **fit; fit·ting** **1** : to be suitable for or to : BEFIT **2** : to be correctly adjusted to or shaped for **3** : to insert or adjust until correctly in place **4** : to make a place or room for **5** : to be in agreement or accord with **6** : PREPARE **7** : ADJUST **8** : SUPPLY, EQUIP **9** : BELONG — **fit·ter** *n*

⁴**fit** *n* **1** : the state or manner of fitting or being fitted **2** : a piece of clothing that fits

**fit·ful** \'fit-fəl\ *adj* : RESTLESS ⟨~ sleep⟩ — **fit·ful·ly** \-ē\ *adv*

¹**fit·ting** \'fit-iŋ\ *adj* : APPROPRIATE, SUITABLE — **fit·ting·ly** *adv*

²**fitting** *n* **1** : the action or act of one that fits; *esp* : a trying on of clothes being made or altered **2** : a small ac-

cessory part ⟨a plumbing ~⟩

**five** \'fīv\ *n* **1** : one more than four **2** : the 5th in a set or series **3** : something having five units; *esp* : a male basketball team — **five** *adj or pron*

¹**fix** \'fiks\ *vb* **1** : to make firm, stable, or fast **2** : to give a permanent or final form to ⟨~ a photographic film⟩ **3** : AFFIX, ATTACH **4** : to hold or direct steadily ⟨~es his eyes on the horizon⟩ **5** : ESTABLISH ⟨~ a date⟩ **6** : ASSIGN ⟨~ blame⟩ **7** : to set in order : ADJUST **8** : PREPARE **9** : to make whole or sound again **10** : to get even with **11** : to influence by improper or illegal methods ⟨~ a horse race⟩ — **fix·er** *n*

²**fix** *n* **1** : PREDICAMENT **2** : a determination of position (as of a ship) **3** : an act of improper influence (as bribery) **4** : a shot of a narcotic

**fix·a·tion** \fik-'sā-shən\ *n* : an obsessive or unhealthy preoccupation or attachment — **fix·ate** \'fik-,sāt\ *vb*

**fix·a·tive** \'fik-sət-iv\ *n* : something (as a varnish for crayon drawings) that stabilizes or sets

**fixed** \'fikst\ *adj* **1** : securely placed or fastened : STATIONARY **2** : not volatile **3** : SETTLED, FINAL **4** : INTENT, CONCENTRATED ⟨a ~ stare⟩ **5** : supplied with a definite amount of something needed (as money) — **fixed·ly** \'fik-səd-lē\ *adv* — **fixed·ness** \-nəs\ *n*

**fixed star** *n* : a star so distant that its motion can be measured only by very precise observations over long periods

**fix·i·ty** \'fik-sət-ē\ *n, pl* **-ties** : the quality or state of being fixed or stable

**fix·ture** \'fiks-chər\ *n* : something firmly attached as a permanent part of some other thing ⟨an electrical ~⟩

¹**fizz** \'fiz\ *vb* : to make a hissing or sputtering sound

²**fizz** *n* : an effervescent beverage

**fiz·zle** \'fiz-əl\ *vb* **fiz·zled; fiz·zling** \-(ə-)liŋ\ **1** : FIZZ **2** : to fail after a good start

**fizzle** *n* : FAILURE

**fjord** \fē-'ôrd\ *n* : a narrow inlet of the sea between cliffs or steep slopes

**fl** *abbr* **1** flourished **2** fluid

**FL** *or* **Fla** *abbr* Florida

**flab** \'flab\ *n* : soft flabby body tissue

**flab·ber·gast** \'flab-ər-,gast\ *vb* : ASTOUND

**flab·by** \'flab-ē\ *adj* **flab·bi·er; -est** : lacking firmness and substance : FLACCID ⟨~ muscles⟩ — **flab·bi·ness** \'flab-ē-nəs\ *n*

**flac·cid** \'flak-səd, 'flas-əd\ *adj* : deficient in firmness ⟨~ plant stems⟩

**fla·con** \'flak-ən\ *n* : a small usu. ornamental bottle with a tight cap

¹**flag** \'flag\ *n* : a usu. wild iris or a related plant

²**flag** *n* : a hard flat stone suitable for paving

³**flag** *n* **1** : a usu. rectangular piece of fabric of distinctive design that is used as a symbol (as of nationality) or as a signaling device **2** : something used like a flag to signal or attract attention **3** : one of the cross strokes of a musical note less than a quarter note in value

⁴**flag** vb **flagged; flag·ging 1 :** to put a flag on **2 :** to signal with or as if with a flag; esp **:** to signal to stop ⟨∼ a taxi⟩

⁵**flag** vb **flagged; flag·ging 1 :** to be loose, yielding, or limp **:** DROOP **2 :** to become unsteady, feeble, or spiritless ⟨his interest flagged⟩ **3 :** to decline in interest or attraction ⟨the topic flagged⟩

**flag·el·late** \'flaj-ə-ˌlāt\ vb **-lat·ed; -lat·ing :** to punish by whipping — **flag·el·la·tion** \ˌflaj-ə-'lā-shən\ n

**fla·gel·lum** \flə-'jel-əm\ n, pl **-la** \-ə\ also **-lums 1 :** a long slender appendage **2 :** a tapering process that projects singly or in groups from a cell and is the primary organ of motion of many microorganisms — **fla·gel·lar** \-'jel-ər\ adj

**fla·geo·let** \ˌflaj-ə-'let, -'lā\ n **:** a small woodwind instrument belonging to the flute class

**fla·gi·tious** \flə-'jish-əs\ adj **:** grossly wicked **:** VILLAINOUS

**flag·on** \'flag-ən\ n **:** a container for liquids usu with a handle, spout, and lid

**flag·pole** \'flag-ˌpōl\ n **:** a pole to raise a flag on

**fla·grant** \'flā-grənt\ adj [L flagrans, prp. of flagrare to burn] **:** conspicuously bad — **fla·grant·ly** adv

**fla·gran·te de·lic·to** \flə-ˌgrant-ē-di-'lik-tō\ adv [ML, lit., while the crime is blazing] **:** in the very act of committing a misdeed

**flag·ship** \'flag-ˌship\ n **:** the ship that carries the commander of a fleet or subdivision thereof and flies his flag

**flag·staff** \-ˌstaf\ n **:** FLAGPOLE

**flag·stone** \-ˌstōn\ n **:** ²FLAG

¹**flail** \'flāl\ n **:** a tool for threshing grain by hand

²**flail** vb **:** to beat with or as if with a flail

**flair** \'flaər\ n [F, lit., sense of smell, fr. OF, odor, fr. flairier to give off an odor, fr. LL flagrare, fr. L fragrare] **1 :** discriminating sense **2 :** natural aptitude **:** BENT ⟨a ∼ for acting⟩

**flak** \'flak\ n, pl **flak** [G, fr. fliegerabwehrkanonen, fr. flieger flyer + abwehr defense + kanonen cannons] **:** antiaircraft guns or bursting shells fired from them

¹**flake** \'flāk\ n **1 :** a small loose mass or bit **2 :** a thin flattened piece or layer **:** CHIP — **flaky** adj

²**flake** vb **flaked; flak·ing :** to form or separate into flakes

**flam·beau** \'flam-ˌbō\ n, pl **flambeaux** \-ˌbōz\ or **flambeaus :** a flaming torch

**flam·boy·ant** \flam-'bȯi-ənt\ adj **:** FLORID, ORNATE, SHOWY — **flamboy·ance** \-əns\ also **flam·boy·an·cy** \-ən-sē\ n — **flam·boy·ant·ly** adv

**flame** \'flām\ n **1 :** the glowing gaseous part of a fire **2 :** a state of blazing combustion **3 :** a flamelike condition or appearance **4 :** BRILLIANCE **5 :** burning zeal or passion **6 :** SWEETHEART — **flame** vb — **flam·ing** \'flā-miŋ\ adj

**fla·men·co** \flə-'meŋ-kō\ n, pl **-cos** [Sp, Flemish, like a gypsy, fr. D Vlaminc Fleming] **:** a vigorous rhythmic dance style of the Andalusian gypsies

**flame-out** \'flām-ˌaut\ n **:** the cessation of operation of a jet airplane engine

**flame-throw·er** \'flām-ˌthrō-(ə)r\ n **:** a device that expels from a nozzle a burning stream of liquid or semiliquid fuel under pressure

**fla·min·go** \flə-'miŋ-gō\ n, pl **-gos** also **-goes** [obs. Sp flamengo, fr. D Vlaminc Fleming] **:** a long-legged long-necked tropical water bird with scarlet wings and a broad bill bent downward

**flam·ma·ble** \'flam-ə-bəl\ adj **:** easily ignited

**flange** \'flanj\ n **:** a rim used for strengthening or guiding something or for attachment to another object

¹**flank** \'flaŋk\ n **1 :** the fleshy part of the side between the ribs and the hip; also **:** the side of a quadruped **2 :** SIDE **3 :** the right or left of a formation

²**flank** vb **1 :** to attack or threaten the flank of **2 :** to get around the flank of **3 :** BORDER

**flank·er** \'flaŋ-kər\ n **1 :** one that flanks **2 :** a football player stationed wide of the end who serves chiefly as a pass receiver

**flan·nel** \'flan-ᵊl\ n **1 :** a soft twilled wool or worsted fabric with a napped surface **2 :** a stout cotton fabric napped on one side **3** pl **:** flannel underwear or trousers

**flan·nel·ette** \ˌflan-ᵊl-'et\ n **:** a napped cotton flannel

¹**flap** \'flap\ n **1 :** a stroke with something broad **:** SLAP **2 :** something broad, limber, or flat and usu. thin that hangs loose ⟨the ∼ of a pocket⟩ **3 :** the motion or sound of something broad and limber as it swings to and fro **4 :** a state of excitement or confusion

²**flap** vb **flapped; flap·ping 1 :** to beat with something broad and flat **2 :** FLING **3 :** to move (as wings) with a beating motion **4 :** to sway loosely usu. with a noise of striking

**flap·jack** \-ˌjak\ n **:** PANCAKE

**flap·per** \'flap-ər\ n **1 :** one that flaps **2 :** a young woman of the 1920s who showed bold freedom from conventions in conduct and dress

¹**flare** \'flaər\ vb **flared; flar·ing 1 :** to flame with a sudden unsteady light **2 :** to become suddenly excited or angry ⟨∼ up⟩ **3 :** to spread outward

²**flare** n **1 :** an unsteady glaring light **2 :** a blaze of light used to signal or illuminate; also **:** a device for producing such a blaze

**flare-up** \-ˌəp\ n **:** a sudden outburst or intensification

¹**flash** \'flash\ vb **1 :** to break forth in or like a sudden flame **2 :** to appear or pass suddenly or with great speed **3 :** to send out in or as if in flashes ⟨∼ a message⟩ **4 :** to make a sudden display (as of brilliance or feeling) **5 :** to gleam or glow intermittently **6 :** to fill by a sudden rush of water **7 :** to expose to view very briefly ⟨∼ a badge⟩

**syn** glance, glint, sparkle — **flash·er** n

²**flash** n **1 :** a sudden burst of light **2 :** a movement of a flag or light in signaling **3 :** a sudden and brilliant burst (as of wit) **4 :** a brief time **5 :** SHOW, DISPLAY; esp **:** ostentatious display **6 :** one that attracts notice; esp **:** an outstanding athlete **7 :** GLIMPSE, LOOK **8 :** a first brief news report **9 :** FLASHLIGHT **10 :** a quick-spreading flame or momentary intense outburst of radiant heat

³**flash** adj **1 :** of sudden origin and usu. short duration ⟨a ~ fire⟩ **2 :** involving brief exposure to an intense agent (as heat or cold) ⟨~ freezing of food⟩

**flash·back** \'flash-,bak\ n **:** injection into the chronological sequence of events in a literary or theatrical work of an event of earlier occurrence

**flash·bulb** \-,bəlb\ n **:** an electric flash lamp in which metal foil or wire is burned

**flash card** n **:** a card bearing words, numbers, or pictures briefly displayed by a teacher to a class during drills (as in reading, spelling, or arithmetic)

**flash·cube** \'flash-,kyüb\ n **:** a cubical device incorporating four flashbulbs for taking four successive photographs

**flash flood** n **:** a local flood of great volume and short duration generally resulting from heavy rainfall in the immediate vicinity

**flash·gun** \-,gən\ n **:** a device for holding and operating a flashbulb

**flash·ing** \'flash-iŋ\ n **:** sheet metal used in waterproofing roof valleys or the angle between a chimney and a roof

**flash lamp** n **:** a lamp producing a brief intense flash of light for taking photographs

**flash·light** \'flash-,līt\ n **1 :** a sudden bright artificial light used in photography; also **:** a photograph made by such a light **2 :** a small battery-operated portable electric light

**flash point** n **:** the lowest temperature at which vapors above a volatile combustible substance ignite in air when exposed to flame

**flash·tube** \'flash-,t(y)üb\ n **:** a gas-filled tube that produces a brief intense flash of light

**flashy** \'flash-ē\ adj **flash·i·er; -est 1 :** momentarily dazzling **2 :** BRIGHT **3 :** SHOWY - **flash·i·ly** \'flash-ə-lē\ adv — **flash·i·ness** \-ē-nəs\ n

**flask** \'flask\ n **:** a flattened bottle-shaped container ⟨a whiskey ~⟩

¹**flat** \'flat\ adj **flat·ter; flat·test 1 :** having a smooth, level, or even surface **2 :** spread out along a surface **3 :** having a broad smooth surface and little thickness **4 :** DOWNRIGHT, POSITIVE ⟨a ~ refusal⟩ **5 :** FIXED, UNCHANGING ⟨charge a ~ rate⟩ **6 :** EXACT, PRECISE **7 :** DULL, UNINTERESTING ⟨a ~ story⟩; also **:** INSIPID ⟨a ~ taste⟩ **8 :** DEFLATED **9 :** lower than the true pitch; also **:** lower by a half step ⟨a ~ note⟩ **10 :** lacking contrast ⟨a ~ photographic negative⟩ **11 :** free from gloss — **flat·ly** adv — **flat·ness** n

²**flat** n **1 :** a level surface of land **:** PLAIN **2 :** a flat part or surface **3 :** a flat note or tone in music; also **:** a character ♭ indicating a half step drop in pitch **4 :** something flat **5 :** a deflated tire

³**flat** adv **1 :** FLATLY **2 :** EXACTLY ⟨in one minute ~⟩ **3 :** below the true musical pitch

⁴**flat** vb **flat·ted; flat·ting 1 :** FLATTEN **2 :** to lower in pitch esp. by a half step **3 :** to sing or play below the true pitch

⁵**flat** n **1 :** a floor or story in a building **2 :** an apartment on one floor

**flat·bed** \'flat-,bed\ n **:** a motortruck with a body in the form of a platform or shallow box

**flat·boat** \-,bōt\ n **:** a flat-bottomed boat used esp. for carrying bulky freight

**flat·car** \-,kär\ n **:** a railroad freight car without permanent raised sides, ends, or covering

**flat·fish** \'flat-,fish\ n **:** any of a group of flattened bony sea fishes with both eyes on the upper side

**flat·foot** \-,fút, -'fút\ n, pl **flat·feet** \-,fēt, -'fēt\ **:** a condition in which the arch is flattened so that the entire sole rests upon the ground — **flat·foot·ed** \-'fút-əd\ adj

**Flat·head** \-,hed\ n, pl **Flatheads** or **Flathead :** a member of an Indian people of Montana

**flat·iron** \'flat-,ī(-ə)rn\ n **:** an iron for pressing clothes

**flat·land** \'flat-,land\ n **:** land lacking significant variation in elevation

**flat out** \-'aút\ adv **1 :** BLUNTLY, DIRECTLY **2 :** at top speed

**flat·ten** \'flat-ᵊn\ vb **flat·tened; flat·ten·ing** \'flat-(ᵊ-)niŋ\ **:** to make or become flat

**flat·ter** \'flat-ər\ vb [ME flateren, fr. OF flater to lick, flatter] **1 :** to praise too much or without sincerity **2 :** to represent too favorably ⟨the picture ~s her⟩ **3 :** to judge (oneself) favorably or too favorably — **flat·ter·er** n

**flat·tery** \'flat-ə-rē\ n, pl **-ter·ies :** flattering speech or attentions **:** insincere or excessive praise

**flat·top** \'flat-,täp\ n **1 :** AIRCRAFT CARRIER **2 :** CREW CUT

**flat·u·lent** \'flach-ə-lənt\ adj **1 :** full of gas ⟨a ~ stomach⟩ **2 :** TURGID ⟨~ oratory⟩ — **flat·u·lence** \-ləns\ n

**fla·tus** \'flāt-əs\ n **:** gas formed in the intestine or stomach

**flat·ware** \'flat-,waər\ n **:** tableware (as silver) more or less flat and usu. formed or cast in a single piece

**flaunt** \'flónt\ vb **1 :** to wave or flutter showily **2 :** to display oneself to public notice **3 :** to display ostentatiously or impudently **:** PARADE — **flaunt** n

**flau·tist** \'flót-əst, 'flaút-\ n **:** FLUTIST

¹**fla·vor** \'flā-vər\ n **1 :** the quality of something that affects the sense of taste or of taste and smell; also **:** the resulting sensation **2 :** something (as a condiment or extract) that adds flavor **3 :** characteristic or predominant quality — **fla·vor·ful** adj — **fla·vor·less** adj — **fla·vor·some** adj

²**flavor** vb **fla·vored; fla·vor·ing**

\flāv-(ə-)riŋ\ : to give or add flavor to
**fla·vor·ing** n : FLAVOR 2
**fla·vour** chiefly Brit var of FLAVOR
**flaw** \flȯ\ n : an imperfect part : CRACK, FAULT, DEFECT — **flaw·less** adj
**flax** \flaks\ n : a blue-flowered plant grown for its fiber and its oily seeds; also : its fiber that is the source of linen
**flax·en** \flak-sən\ adj 1 : made of flax 2 : resembling flax esp. in pale soft straw color
**flay** \flā\ vb 1 : to strip off the skin or surface of 2 : to criticize harshly : SCOLD
**flea** \flē\ n : any of a group of small wingless leaping bloodsucking insects
**flea·bane** \-ˌbān\ n : any of various plants of the daisy family believed to drive away fleas
**flea-bite** \flē-ˌbīt\ n : the bite of a flea
**flea–bit·ten** \-ˌbit-ᵊn\ adj : bitten by or infested with fleas
**flea market** n : a usu. open-air market for secondhand articles and antiques
**¹fleck** \flek\ vb : STREAK, SPOT
**²fleck** n 1 : SPOT, MARK 2 : FLAKE, PARTICLE
**fledg·ling** \flej-liŋ\ n : a young bird with feathers newly developed
**flee** \flē\ vb **fled** \fled\; **flee·ing** 1 : to run away from danger or evil 2 : to run away from 3 : VANISH
**¹fleece** \flēs\ n 1 : the coat of wool covering a sheep 2 : a soft or woolly covering — **fleecy** adj
**²fleece** vb **fleeced**; **fleec·ing** 1 : SHEAR 2 : to strip of money or property by fraud or extortion
**fleer** \fliər\ vb : to laugh or grimace in a coarse manner : SNEER
**¹fleet** \flēt\ vb : to pass rapidly
**²fleet** n [ME flete, fr. OE flēot ship, fr. flēotan to float] 1 : a group of warships under one command 2 : a group of ships or vehicles (as trucks or airplanes) under one management
**³fleet** adj 1 : SWIFT, NIMBLE 2 : not enduring : FLEETING — **fleet·ness** n
**fleet admiral** n : a commissioned officer of the highest rank in the navy
**fleet·ing** \flēt-iŋ\ adj : passing swiftly
**Flem** abbr Flemish
**Flem·ing** \flem-iŋ\ n : a member of a Germanic people inhabiting chiefly northern Belgium
**Flem·ish** \flem-ish\ n 1 : the Germanic language of the Flemings 2 **Flemish** pl : FLEMINGS — **Flemish** adj
**flesh** \flesh\ n 1 : the soft parts of an animal's body; esp : muscular tissue 2 : MEAT 3 : the physical being of man as distinguished from the soul 4 : human beings; also : living beings 5 : STOCK, KINDRED 6 : fleshy plant tissue (as fruit pulp) — **fleshed** \flesht\ adj
**flesh fly** n : a two-winged fly whose maggots feed on flesh
**flesh·ly** \flesh-lē\ adj 1 : CORPOREAL, BODILY 2 : CARNAL, SENSUAL 3 : not spiritual : WORLDLY
**flesh·pot** \flesh-ˌpät\ n 1 pl : bodily comfort : LUXURY 2 : a place of luxurious and esp. sexual entertainment

**fleshy** \flesh-ē\ adj **flesh·i·er; -est** : consisting of or resembling animal flesh; also : PLUMP, FAT
**flew** past of FLY
**flex** \fleks\ vb : to bend esp. repeatedly
**flex·i·ble** \flek-sə-bəl\ adj 1 : capable of being flexed : PLIANT, PLIABLE 2 : yielding to influence : TRACTABLE 3 : readily changed or changing : ADAPTABLE **syn** elastic, supple, resilient, springy — **flex·i·bil·i·ty** \ˌflek-sə-ˈbil-ət-ē\ n
**flex·ure** \flek-shər\ n : TURN, FOLD, BEND
**flib·ber·ti·gib·bet** \ˌflib-ərt-ē-ˈjib-ət\ n : a silly restless person
**¹flick** \flik\ n 1 : a light sharp jerky stroke or movement 2 : a sound produced by a flick 3 : DAUB, SPLOTCH
**²flick** vb 1 : to strike lightly with a quick sharp motion 2 : FLUTTER, DART, FLIT
**¹flick·er** \flik-ər\ vb **flick·ered; flick·er·ing** \-(ə-)riŋ\ 1 : to waver unsteadily; also : FLUTTER 2 : FLIT, DART 3 : to burn fitfully or with a fluctuating light ⟨a ∼ing candle⟩
**²flicker** n 1 : an act of flickering 2 : a sudden brief movement ⟨a ∼ of an eyelid⟩ 3 : a momentary stirring ⟨a ∼ of interest⟩ 4 : a brief interval of brightness 5 : a wavering light
**³flicker** n : a common large brightly marked woodpecker of eastern No. America; also : any of several related birds
**flied** past of FLY
**fli·er** \flī-(ə-)r\ n 1 : one that flies; esp : AVIATOR 2 : something (as an express train) that travels fast 3 : a reckless or speculative undertaking 4 : an advertising circular for mass distribution
**¹flight** \flīt\ n 1 : an act or instance of flying 2 : the ability to fly 3 : a passing through the air or through space 4 : the distance covered in a flight 5 : swift movement 6 : a trip made by or in an airplane 7 : a group of similar individuals (as birds or airplanes) flying as a unit 8 : a passing (as of the imagination) beyond ordinary limits 9 : a series of stairs from one landing to another — **flight·less** adj
**²flight** n : an act or instance of running away
**flight bag** n 1 : a canvas traveling bag with outside compartments for use esp. in air travel 2 : a small canvas satchel decorated with the name of an airline
**flight line** n : a parking and servicing area for airplanes
**flighty** \flīt-ē\ adj **flight·i·er; -est** 1 : subject to flights of fancy or sudden change of mind : CAPRICIOUS 2 : SKITTISH 3 : not stable; also : SILLY
**flim·flam** \flim-ˌflam\ n : DECEPTION, FRAUD
**flim·sy** \flim-zē\ adj **flim·si·er; -est** 1 : lacking strength or substance 2 : of inferior materials and workmanship 3 : having little worth or plausibility ⟨a ∼ excuse⟩ — **flim·si·ly** \flim-zə-lē\ adv — **flim·si·ness** \-zē-nəs\ n
**flinch** \flinch\ vb [MF flenchir to

bend\ **:** to shrink from or as if from physical pain **:** WINCE

¹fling \'fliŋ\ vb **flung** \'fləŋ\; **flinging** \'fliŋ-iŋ\ **1 :** to move hastily, brusquely, or violently ⟨*flung* out of the room⟩ **2 :** to kick or plunge vigorously **3 :** to throw with force or recklessness **:** HURL **4 :** DISCARD, DISREGARD **5 :** to put suddenly into a state or condition

²fling n **1 :** an act or instance of flinging **2 :** a casual try **:** ATTEMPT **3 :** a period of self-indulgence

flint \'flint\ n **1 :** a hard quartz that strikes fire with steel **2 :** an alloy used for striking fire in cigarette lighters — **flinty** adj

flint glass n **:** heavy glass containing oxide of lead that is used for optical structures

flint-lock \'flint-,läk\ n **1 :** a lock for a 17th and 18th century firearm using a flint to ignite the charge **2 :** a firearm fitted with a flintlock

¹flip \'flip\ vb **flipped; flip-ping 1 :** to turn by tossing ⟨∼ a coin⟩ **2 :** to turn over; *also* **:** to leaf through **3 :** FLICK, JERK ⟨∼ a light switch⟩ **4 :** to lose self-control — **flip** n

²flip adj **:** FLIPPANT, IMPERTINENT

flip-pant \'flip-ənt\ adj **:** treating lightly something serious or worthy of respect — **flip-pan-cy** \'flip-ən-sē\ n

flip-per \'flip-ər\ n **1 :** a broad flat limb (as of a seal) adapted for swimming **2 :** a paddlelike shoe used in swimming

flip side n **:** the reverse and usu. less popular side of a phonograph record

¹flirt \'flərt\ vb **1 :** to move erratically **:** FLIT **2 :** to behave amorously without serious intent **3 :** to deal lightly **:** TRIFLE — **flir-ta-tion** \,flər-'tā-shən\ n — **flir-ta-tious** \-shəs\ adj

²flirt n **1 :** an act or instance of flirting **2 :** a person who flirts

flit \'flit\ vb **flit-ted; flit-ting :** to pass or move quickly or abruptly from place to place **:** DART

flitch \'flich\ n **:** a side of pork cured and smoked as bacon

fliv-ver \'fliv-ər\ n **:** a small cheap usu. old automobile

¹float \'flōt\ n **1 :** something (as a raft) that floats **2 :** a cork buoying up the baited end of a fishing line **3 :** a hollow ball that floats at the end of a lever in a cistern or tank and regulates the level of the liquid **4 :** a vehicle with a platform to carry an exhibit **5 :** a drink consisting of ice cream floating in a beverage

²float vb **1 :** to rest on the surface of or be suspended in a fluid **2 :** to move gently on or through a fluid **3 :** to cause to float **4 :** to wander esp. without a permanent home ⟨the ∼ing population⟩ **5 :** FLOOD **6 :** to offer (securities) in order to finance an enterprise **7 :** to finance by floating an issue of stock or bonds **8 :** to arrange for ⟨∼ a loan⟩ — **float-er** n

¹flock \'fläk\ n **1 :** a group of birds or mammals assembled or herded together **2 :** a group of people under the

guidance of a leader; *esp* **:** CONGREGATION **3 :** a large number

²flock vb **:** to gather or move in a crowd

floe \'flō\ n **:** a flat mass of floating ice

flog \'fläg\ vb **flogged; flog-ging :** to beat severely with a rod or whip **:** LASH — **flog-ger** n

¹flood \'fləd\ n **1 :** a great flow of water over the land **2 :** the flowing in of the tide **3 :** an overwhelming volume

²flood vb **1 :** to cover or become filled with a flood; *esp* **:** to supply with too much fuel ⟨∼ a carburetor⟩ **2 :** to fill abundantly or excessively **3 :** to pour forth in a flood

flood-gate \'fləd-,gāt\ n **:** a gate for controlling a body of water **:** SLUICE

flood-light \-,līt\ n **:** a lamp that throws a broad beam of light; *also* **:** the beam itself — **floodlight** vb

flood-plain \'fləd-,plān\ n **:** a plain that may be submerged by floodwaters

flood-wa-ter \-,wot-ər, -,wät-\ n **:** the water of a flood

¹floor \'flōr\ n **1 :** the bottom of a room on which one stands **2 :** a ground surface **3 :** a story of a building **4 :** a main level space (as in a legislative chamber) distinguished from a platform or gallery **5 :** AUDIENCE **6 :** the right to speak from one's place in an assembly **7 :** a lower limit ⟨put a ∼ under wheat prices⟩ — **floor-ing** \-iŋ\ n

²floor vb **1 :** to furnish with a floor **2 :** to knock down **3 :** SHOCK, OVERWHELM **4 :** DEFEAT

floor-board \-,bōrd\ n **1 :** a board in a floor **2 :** the floor of an automobile

floor leader n **:** a member of a legislative body chosen by his party to have charge of its organization and strategy on the floor

floor show n **:** a series of acts presented in a nightclub

floor-walk-er \-,wò-kər\ n **:** a man employed in a retail store to oversee the sales force and aid customers

floo-zy or floo-zie \'flü-zē\ n, pl **floozies :** a tawdry or immoral woman

flop \'fläp\ vb **flopped; flop-ping 1 :** FLAP **2 :** to throw oneself down heavily, clumsily, or in a relaxed manner ⟨*flopped* into a chair⟩ **3 :** FAIL — **flop** n

flop-house \'fläp-,haůs\ n **:** a cheap hotel

flop-py \'fläp-ē\ adj **flop-pi-er; -est :** tending to flop; *esp* **:** soft and flexible

flo-ra \'flōr-ə\ n, pl **floras** also **flo-rae** \-,ē, -,ī\ [L *Flora*, Roman goddess of flowers] **:** plants or plant life esp. of a region or period

flo-ral \'flōr-əl\ adj **:** of or relating to flowers

flo-res-cence \flò-'res-⁰ns, flə-\ n **:** a state or period of being in bloom or flourishing — **flo-res-cent** \-⁰nt\ adj

flor-id \'flòr-əd\ adj **1 :** excessively flowery in style **:** ORNATE ⟨∼ writing⟩ **2 :** tinged with red **:** RUDDY

flo-rin \'flòr-ən\ n **1 :** an old gold coin first struck at Florence in 1252 **2 :** a gold coin of a European country patterned after the Florentine florin **3 :** a modern silver coin in the Netherlands and in Great Britain **4 :** GULDEN

**flo·rist** \'flōr-əst\ n : one who deals in flowers

**floss** \'fläs\ n **1 :** waste or short silk fibers that cannot be reeled **2 :** soft thread of silk or mercerized cotton used for embroidery **3 :** a lightweight wool knitting yarn **4 :** a fluffy filamentous mass esp. of plant fiber ⟨milkweed ∼⟩

**flossy** \'fläs-ē\ adj **floss·i·er; -est 1 :** of, relating to, or having the characteristics of floss; also **:** DOWNY **2 :** STYLISH, GLAMOROUS

**flo·ta·tion** \flō-'tā-shən\ n **:** the process or an instance of floating

**flo·til·la** \flō-'til-ə\ n **:** a small fleet or a fleet of small ships

**flot·sam** \'flät-səm\ n : floating wreckage of a ship or its cargo

**¹flounce** \'flauns\ vb **flounced; flounc·ing 1 :** to move with exaggerated jerky motions **2 :** to go with sudden determination **3 :** FLOUNDER, STRUGGLE

**²flounce** n : an act or instance of flouncing

**³flounce** n : a strip of fabric attached by one edge (as to a skirt)

**¹floun·der** \'flaun-dər\ n, pl **flounder** or **flounders :** FLATFISH; esp : one important as food

**²flounder** vb **floun·dered; floun·der·ing** \-d(ə-)riŋ\ **1 :** to struggle to move or obtain footing **2 :** to proceed clumsily ⟨∼ed through his speech⟩

**¹flour** \'flau(ə)r\ n **:** finely ground and sifted meal of a cereal (as wheat); also **:** a fine soft powder — **floury** adj

**²flour** vb : to coat with or as if with flour

**flour·ish** \'flər-ish\ vb **1 :** THRIVE, PROSPER **2 :** to be in a state of activity or production ⟨∼ed about 1850⟩ **3 :** to reach a height of development or influence **4 :** to make bold and sweeping gestures **:** BRANDISH

**²flourish** n **1 :** a florid embellishment or passage ⟨a ∼ of drums⟩ **2 :** WAVE ⟨with a ∼ of his cane⟩ **3 :** a dramatic action ⟨introduced her with a ∼⟩

**¹flout** \'flaut\ vb **1 :** SCORN **2 :** to indulge in scornful behavior **:** MOCK

**²flout** n : INSULT, MOCKERY

**¹flow** \'flō\ vb **1 :** to issue or move in a stream **2 :** RISE ⟨the tide ebbs and ∼s⟩ **3 :** ABOUND **4 :** to proceed smoothly and readily **5 :** to have a smooth uninterrupted continuity **6 :** to hang loose and billowing **7 :** COME, ARISE **8 :** MENSTRUATE

**²flow** n **1 :** an act or manner of flowing **2 :** FLOOD 1, 2 **3 :** a smooth uninterrupted movement **4 :** STREAM **5 :** the quantity that flows in a certain time **6 :** MENSTRUATION **7 :** YIELD, PRODUCTION **8 :** a continuous flow of energy

**flow·chart** \'flō-,chärt\ n : a symbolic diagram showing stepped progression through a procedure

**flow diagram** n : FLOWCHART

**¹flow·er** \'flau(-ə)r\ n **1 :** a plant branch modified for seed production and bearing leaves specialized into floral organs (as petals); also **:** a flowering plant **2 :** the best part or example

**3 :** the finest most vigorous period **4 : a** state of blooming or flourishing — **flow·ered** \'flau(-ə)rd\ adj — **flow·er·less** adj

**²flower** vb **1 :** to produce flowers **:** BLOOM **2 :** DEVELOP; also **:** FLOURISH

**flower girl** n : a little girl who carries flowers at a wedding

**flower head** n : a very short compact flower cluster suggesting a single flower

**flow·er·pot** \'flau(-ə)r-,pät\ n : a pot in which to grow plants

**flow·ery** \'flau(-ə)r-ē\ adj **1 :** full of or covered with flowers **2 :** full of fine words or phrases — **flow·er·i·ness** n

**flown** \'flōn\ past part of FLY

**fl oz** abbr fluidounce

**flu** \'flü\ n **1 :** INFLUENZA **2 :** a minor virus ailment usu. with respiratory symptoms

**flub** \'fləb\ vb **flubbed; flub·bing :** BOTCH, BLUNDER — **flub** n

**fluc·tu·ate** \'flək-chə-,wāt\ vb **-at·ed; -at·ing 1 :** to move up and down or back and forth like a wave **2 :** WAVER, VACILLATE — **fluc·tu·a·tion** \,flək-chə-'wā-shən\ n

**flue** \'flü\ n : a passage (as in a chimney) for gases, smoke, flame, or air

**flu·ent** \'flü-ənt\ adj **1 :** capable of flowing **:** FLUID **2 :** ready or facile in speech ⟨∼ in French⟩ **3 :** effortlessly smooth and rapid ⟨∼ speech⟩ — **flu·en·cy** \-ən-sē\ n — **flu·ent·ly** adv

**¹fluff** \'fləf\ n **1 :** NAP, DOWN ⟨∼ from a pillow⟩ **2 :** something fluffy **3 :** something inconsequential **4 :** BLUNDER; esp : an actor's lapse of memory

**²fluff** vb **1 :** to make or become fluffy ⟨∼ up a pillow⟩ **2 :** to make a mistake

**fluffy** \'fləf-ē\ adj **fluff·i·er; -est 1 :** having, covered with, or resembling fluff or down **2 :** being light and soft or airy ⟨a ∼ omelet⟩ **3 :** FATUOUS, SILLY

**flu·id** \'flü-əd\ adj **1 :** capable of flowing like a liquid or gas **2 :** likely to change or move **3 :** FLOWING, FLUENT ⟨∼ speech⟩ **4 :** available for various uses ⟨∼ capital⟩ **5 :** easily converted into cash ⟨∼ assets⟩ — **flu·id·i·ty** \flü-'id-ət-ē\ n

**²fluid** n : a substance tending to conform to the outline of its container ⟨liquids and gases are ∼s⟩

**fluid drive** n : an automotive system that depends on turbine blades in oil to transfer power from the engine to the transmission

**flu·id·ounce** \,flü-ə-'dauns\ n — see WEIGHT table

**flu·idram** \,flü-ə(d)-'dram\ n — see WEIGHT table

**¹fluke** \'flük\ n : a flattened trematode worm

**²fluke** n **1 :** the part of an anchor that fastens in the ground **2 :** a barbed head (as of a harpoon) **3 :** a lobe of a whale's tail

**³fluke** n : a stroke of luck ⟨won by a ∼⟩

**flume** \'flüm\ n **1 :** a ravine or gorge with a stream running through it **2 :** an inclined channel for carrying water (as for power)

**flung** past of FLING

**flunk** \'flǝŋk\ *vb* **:** to fail esp. in an examination or recitation

**flun·ky** *or* **flun·key** \'flǝŋ-kē\ *n, pl* **flunkies** *or* **flunkeys 1 :** a liveried servant; *esp* **:** FOOTMAN **2 :** TOADY

**flu·o·res·cence** \,flu̇-(ǝ)r-'es-ᵊns\ *n* **:** emission of radiation usu. as visible light from and only during the absorption of radiation from some other source; *also* **:** the emitted radiation — **flu·o·resce** \-'es\ *vb* — **flu·o·res·cent** \-'es-ᵊnt\ *adj*

**fluorescent lamp** *n* **:** a tubular electric lamp in which light is produced on the inside special coating by the action of invisible radiation

**flu·o·ri·date** \'flu̇r-ǝ-,dāt\ *vb* **-dat·ed; dat·ing :** to add a compound of fluorine to - **flu·o·ri·da·tion** \,flu̇r-ǝ-'dā-shǝn\ *n*

**flu·o·ride** \'flu̇(-ǝ)r-,īd\ *n* **:** a compound of fluorine with another chemical element or a radical

**flu·o·ri·nate** \'flu̇r-ǝ-,nāt\ *vb* **-nat·ed; -nat·ing :** to treat or cause to combine with fluorine or a compound of fluorine - **flu·o·ri·na·tion** \,flu̇r-ǝ-'nā-shǝn\ *n*

**flu·o·rine** \'flu̇(-ǝ)r-,ēn, -ǝn\ *n* **:** a pale yellowish flammable irritating toxic gaseous chemical element

**flu·o·rite** \'flu̇(-ǝ)r-,īt\ *n* **:** a mineral used as a flux and in making glass

**flu·o·ro·car·bon** \,flu̇(-ǝ)r-ō-'kär-bǝn\ *n* **:** any of various compounds containing fluorine and carbon used chiefly as a lubricant

**flu·o·ro·scope** \'flu̇r-ǝ-,skōp\ *n* **:** an instrument for observing the internal structure of an opaque object (as the living body) by means of X rays — **flu·o·ro·scop·ic** \,flu̇r-ǝ-'skäp-ik\ *adj* — **flu·o·ros·co·pist** \flu̇(-ǝ)r-'äs-kǝ-pǝst\ *n* — **flu·o·ros·co·py** \-pē\ *n*

**¹flur·ry** \'flǝr-ē\ *n, pl* **flurries 1 :** a gust of wind **2 :** a brief light snowfall **3 :** COMMOTION, BUSTLE **4 :** a brief outburst of activity ⟨a ~ of trading⟩

**²flurry** *vb* **flur·ried; flur·ry·ing :** AGITATE, EXCITE, FLUSTER

**¹flush** \'flǝsh\ *vb* **:** to cause (as a bird) to take wing suddenly

**²flush** *n* **1 :** a sudden flow (as of water) **2 :** a surge esp. of emotion ⟨a ~ of triumph⟩ **3 :** a tinge of red **:** BLUSH **4 :** a fresh and vigorous state ⟨in the ~ of youth⟩ **5 :** a passing sensation of extreme heat

**³flush** *vb* **1 :** to flow and spread suddenly and freely **:** RUSH **2 :** to glow brightly **3 :** BLUSH **4 :** to wash out with a rush of liquid **5 :** INFLAME, EXCITE **6 :** to make red or hot

**⁴flush** *adj* **1 :** filled to overflowing **2 :** fully supplied esp. with money **3 :** full of life and vigor **4 :** of a ruddy healthy color **5 :** readily available **:** ABUNDANT **6 :** having an unbroken or even surface **7 :** being on a level with an adjacent surface **8 :** directly abutting **:** immediately adjacent **9 :** set even with the left edge of the type page or column **10 :** DIRECT

**⁵flush** *adv* **1 :** in a flush manner

**2 :** SQUARELY ⟨a blow ~ on the chin⟩

**⁶flush** *vb* **:** to make flush

**⁷flush** *n* **:** a hand of cards all of the same suit

**flus·ter** \'flǝs-tǝr\ *vb* **:** to put into a state of agitated confusion **:** UPSET — **fluster** *n*

**flute** \'flüt\ *n* **1 :** a hollow pipelike musical instrument **2 :** a grooved pleat **3 :** CHANNEL, GROOVE — **fluted** *adj* — **flut·ing** *n*

**flut·ist** \'flüt-ǝst\ *n* **:** a flute player

**¹flut·ter** \'flǝt-ǝr\ *vb* [ME *floteren* to float, flutter, fr. OE *floterian*, fr. *flotian* to float] **1 :** to flap the wings rapidly without flying or in short flights **2 :** to move with quick wavering or flapping motions **3 :** to vibrate in irregular spasms **4 :** to move about or behave in an agitated aimless manner — **flut·tery** \-ǝ-rē\ *adj*

**²flutter** *n* **1 :** an act of fluttering **2 :** a state of nervous confusion **3 :** FLURRY, COMMOTION

**¹flux** \'flǝks\ *n* **1 :** an excessive fluid discharge esp. from the bowels **2 :** an act of flowing **3 :** a state of continuous change **4 :** a substance used to aid in fusing metals

**²flux** *vb* **:** FUSE

**¹fly** \'flī\ *vb* **flew** \'flü\; **flown** \'flōn\; **fly·ing 1 :** to move in or pass through the air with wings **2 :** to move through the air or before the wind **3 :** to float or cause to float, wave, or soar in the air **4 :** FLEE; *also* **:** AVOID, SHUN **5 :** to fade and disappear **:** VANISH **6 :** to move or pass swiftly **7 :** to become expended or dissipated rapidly **8 :** to pursue or attack in flight **9** *past or past part* **flied :** to hit a fly in baseball **10 :** to operate or travel in an airplane **11 :** to journey over by flying **12 :** to transport by flying

**²fly** *n, pl* **flies 1 :** the action or process of flying **:** FLIGHT **2 :** a horse drawn public coach or delivery wagon; *also, chiefly Brit* **:** a light covered carriage or cab **3** *pl* **:** the space over a theater stage **4 :** a garment closing concealed by a fold of cloth extending over the fastener **5 :** the outer canvas of a tent with double top **6 :** the length of an extended flag from its staff or support **7 :** a baseball hit high into the air — **on the fly :** while still in the air

**³fly** *n, pl* **flies 1 :** a winged insect; *esp* **:** any of a large group of typically stout-bodied mostly 2-winged insects **2 :** a fishhook dressed to suggest an insect

**fly·able** \'flī-ǝ-bǝl\ *adj* **:** suitable for flying or being flown

**fly ball** *n* **:** FLY 7

**fly·blown** \'flī-,blōn\ *adj* **:** TAINTED, SPOILED

**fly·by** \'flī-,bī\ *n, pl* **flybys :** a usu. low-altitude flight past a designated point by an aircraft or a space vehicle

**fly-by-night** \'flī-bǝ-,nīt\ *adj* **1 :** seeking a quick profit usu. by shady acts **2 :** TRANSITORY, PASSING

**fly casting** *n* **:** the act or practice of throwing the lure in angling with artificial flies

**fly·catch·er** \'flī-ˌkach-ər, -ˌkech-\ *n* : a small bird that feeds on insects caught in flight

**fly·er** *var of* FLIER

**flying boat** *n* : a seaplane with a hull adapted for floating

**flying buttress** *n* : a projecting arched structure to support a wall or building

**flying fish** *n* : any of numerous fishes with long fins suggesting wings that enable them to move some distance through the air

**flying saucer** *n* : any of various unidentified moving objects repeatedly reported as seen in the air and usu. alleged to be saucer-shaped or disk-shaped

**flying squirrel** *n* : a No. American squirrel with folds of skin connecting the forelegs and hind legs that enable it to make long gliding leaps

**fly·leaf** \'flī-ˌlēf\ *n* : a blank leaf at the beginning or end of a book

**fly·pa·per** \-ˌpā-pər\ *n* : paper poisoned or coated with a sticky substance for killing or catching flies

**fly·speck** \'flī-ˌspek\ *n* 1 : a speck of fly dung 2 : something small and insignificant — **flyspeck** *vb*

**fly·way** \'flī-ˌwā\ *n* : an established air route of migratory birds

**flywheel** \-ˌhwēl\ *n* : a heavy wheel that rotates steadily and thus regulates the speed of the machinery to which it is connected

**fm** *abbr* fathom

**Fm** *symbol* fermium

**FM** *abbr* frequency modulation

**fn** *abbr* footnote

**f-number** \'ef-ˌnəm-bər\ *n* [*focal length*] : a number following the symbol f/ that expresses the effectiveness of the aperture of a camera lens in relation to brightness of image

**fo** *or* **fol** *abbr* folio

**FO** *abbr* 1 foreign office 2 forward observer

**foal** \'fōl\ *n* : the young of an animal of the horse group; *esp* : one under one year — **foal** *vb*

**¹foam** \'fōm\ *n* 1 : a light mass of fine bubbles formed in or on the surface of a liquid : FROTH, SPUME 2 : material (as rubber) in a lightweight cellular form — **foamy** *adj*

**²foam** *vb* : to form foam : FROTH

**fob** \'fäb\ *n* 1 : a short strap, ribbon, or chain attached to a watch worn esp. in the watch pocket 2 : a small ornament worn on a fob

**FOB** *abbr* free on board

**fob off** *vb* 1 : to put off with a trick or excuse 2 : to pass or offer as genuine 3 : to put aside

**FOC** *abbr* free of charge

**focal length** *n* : the distance of a focus from a lens

**fo'·c'sle** *var of* FORECASTLE

**¹fo·cus** \'fō-kəs\ *n, pl* **fo·cus·es** *or* **fo·ci** \-ˌsī\ [L, hearth] 1 : a point at which rays (as of light, heat, or sound) meet or appear to meet after being reflected or refracted 2 : FOCAL LENGTH 3 : adjustment (as of eyes or eyeglasses) that gives clear vision

4 : central point : CENTER — **fo·cal** \'fō-kəl\ *adj* — **focally** \-ē\ *adv*

**²focus** *vb* **fo·cused** *also* **fo·cussed**; **fo·cus·ing** *also* **fo·cus·sing** 1 : to bring or come to a focus ⟨~ rays of light⟩ 2 : CENTER ⟨~ attention on a problem⟩ 3 : to adjust the focus of

**fod·der** \'fäd-ər\ *n* : coarse dry food (as cornstalks) for livestock

**foe** \'fō\ *n* [ME *fo*, fr. OE *fāh*, fr. *fāh* hostile] : ENEMY

**foehn** *or* **föhn** \'fā(r)n, 'fœn, 'fān\ *n* : a warm dry wind blowing down a mountainside

**foe·man** \'fō-mən\ *n* : FOE

**foe·tal, foe·tus** *var of* FETAL, FETUS

**¹fog** \'fog, 'fäg\ *n* 1 : fine particles of water suspended in the lower atmosphere 2 : mental confusion — **fog·gy** *adj*

**²fog** *vb* **fogged**; **fog·ging** : to obscure or become obscured with or as if with fog

**fog·horn** \-ˌhorn\ *n* : a horn sounded in a fog to give warning

**fo·gy** *also* **fo·gey** \'fō-gē\ *n, pl* **fogies** *also* **fogeys** : a person with old-fashioned ideas ⟨he's an old ~⟩

**foi·ble** \'foi-bəl\ *n* : a minor failing or weakness in character or behavior

**¹foil** \'foil\ *vb* [ME *foilen* to trample, full cloth, fr. MF *fouler*] 1 : to prevent from attaining an end : DEFEAT 2 : to bring to naught

**²foil** *n* : a fencing weapon with a light flexible blade tapering to a blunt point

**³foil** *n* [ME, leaf, fr. MF *foille*, foil, fr. L *folium*] 1 : a very thin sheet of metal 2 : something that by contrast sets off another thing to advantage

**foist** \'foist\ *vb* : to pass off (something false or worthless) as genuine

**¹fold** \'fōld\ *n* 1 : an enclosure for sheep 2 : a group of people with a common faith, belief, or interest

**²fold** *vb* : to house (sheep) in a fold

**³fold** *vb* 1 : to double or become doubled over itself 2 : to clasp together 3 : to lay one part over or against another part of something 4 : to enclose in or as if in a fold 5 : EMBRACE 6 : to incorporate into a mixture by repeated overturnings without stirring or beating 7 : FAIL, COLLAPSE

**⁴fold** *n* 1 : a doubling or folding over 2 : a part doubled or laid over another part

**fold·away** \ˌfōl-də-ˌwā\ *adj* : designed to fold out of the way or out of sight

**foldboat** \'fōl(d)-ˌbōt\ *n* : a small collapsible canoe made of rubberized sailcloth stretched over a framework

**fold·er** \'fōl-dər\ *n* 1 : one that folds 2 : a printed circular of folded sheets 3 : a folded cover or large envelope for loose papers

**fol·de·rol** \'fäl-də-ˌräl\ *n* 1 : a useless trifle 2 : NONSENSE

**fold·out** \'fōld-ˌaut\ *n* : a folded insert (as in a magazine) larger than the page

**fo·liage** \'fō-l(ē-)ij\ *n* : a mass of leaves (as of a plant or forest)

**fo·li·at·ed** \'fō-lē-ˌāt-əd\ *adj* : separable into layers

**fo·lio** \'fō-lē-ˌō\ *n*, *pl* **fo·li·os** 1 : a leaf of a book; *also* : a page number 2 : the size of a piece of paper cut two from a sheet 3 : a book printed on folio pages

¹**folk** \'fōk\ *n*, *pl* **folk** *or* **folks** 1 : a group of people forming a tribe or nation; *also* : the largest number or most characteristic part of such a group 2 : PEOPLE, PERSONS ⟨country ~⟩ ⟨old ~s⟩ 3 *folks pl* : the persons of one's own family

²**folk** *adj* : of, relating to, or originating among the common people ⟨~ music⟩

**folk·lore** \-ˌlōr\ *n* : customs, beliefs, stories, and sayings of a people handed down from generation to generation — **folk·lor·ist** \-əst\ *n*

**folk mass** *n* : a mass in which traditional liturgical music is replaced by folk music

**folk·sing·er** \'fōk-ˌsiŋ-ər\ *n* : a singer of folk songs — **folk·sing·ing** \-ˌsiŋ-iŋ\ *n*

**folk·sy** \'fōk-sē\ *adj* **folks·i·er**; **-est** [*folks* + *-y*] 1 : SOCIABLE, FRIENDLY 2 : informal, casual, or familiar in manner or style

**folk·way** \'fōk-ˌwā\ *n* : a way of thinking, feeling, or acting common to a people or to a social group; *esp* : a traditional social custom

**fol·li·cle** \'fäl-i-kəl\ *n* : a small anatomical cavity or gland ⟨a hair ~⟩

**fol·low** \'fäl-ō\ *vb* 1 : to go or come after 2 : PURSUE 3 : OBEY 4 : to proceed along 5 : to attend upon steadily ⟨~ the sea⟩ ⟨~ a profession⟩ 6 : to keep one's attention fixed on 7 : to result from **syn** succeed, ensue — **fol·low·er** *n* — **follow suit** 1 : to play a card of the same suit as the card led 2 : to follow an example set

¹**fol·low·ing** \'fäl-ə-wiŋ\ *adj* 1 : next after 2 : SUCCEEDING 2 : that immediately follows

²**following** *n* : a group of followers, adherents, or partisans

³**following** *prep* : subsequent to : AFTER

**follow-up** \'fäl-ə-ˌwəp\ *n* : a system or instance of pursuing an initial effort by supplementary action

**fol·ly** \'fäl-ē\ *n*, *pl* **follies** 1 : lack of good sense 2 : a foolish act or idea : FOOLISHNESS 3 : an excessively costly or unprofitable undertaking

**fo·ment** \fō-'ment\ *vb* 1 : to treat with moist heat (as for easing pain) 2 : to stir up : INSTIGATE — **fo·men·ta·tion** \ˌfō-mən-'tā-shən, -ˌmen-\ *n*

**fond** \'fänd\ *adj* [ME, fr. *fonne* fool] 1 : FOOLISH, SILLY ⟨~ pride⟩ 2 : prizing highly : DESIROUS ⟨~ of praise⟩ 3 : strongly attracted or predisposed ⟨~ of music⟩ 4 : foolishly tender : INDULGENT; *also* : LOVING, AFFECTIONATE 5 : CHERISHED, DEAR ⟨his ~est hopes⟩ — **fond·ly** \'fän-(d)lē\ *adv* — **fond·ness** \'fän(d)-nəs\ *n*

**fon·dant** \'fän-dənt\ *n* : a creamy preparation of sugar used as a basis for candies or icings

**fon·dle** \'fän-dºl\ *vb* **fon·dled**; **fon·dling** \-(d)liŋ, -dºl-iŋ\ : to touch or handle lovingly : CARESS, PET

**fon·due** *also* **fon·du** \fän-'d(y)ü\ *n* : a preparation of melted cheese usu. flavored with wine or brandy

¹**font** \'fänt\ *n* 1 : a receptacle for baptismal or holy water 2 : FOUNTAIN, SOURCE

²**font** *n* : an assortment of printing type of one size and style

**food** \'füd\ *n* 1 : material taken into an organism and used for growth, repair, and vital processes and as a source of energy; *also* : organic material produced by green plants and used by them as food 2 : solid nutritive material as distinguished from drink 3 : something that nourishes, sustains, or supplies ⟨~ for thought⟩

**food chain** *n* : a hierarchical arrangement of organisms in an ecological community such that each uses the next usu. lower member as a food source

**food poisoning** *n* : illness caused by food contaminated with bacteria or their products or with chemical residues

**food·stuff** \'füd-ˌstəf\ *n* : something with food value; *esp* : a specific nutrient (as fat or protein)

**food web** *n* : the interacting food chains of an ecological community

¹**fool** \'fül\ *n* [ME, fr. OF *fol*, fr. LL *follis*, fr. L, bellows, bag] 1 : a person who lacks sense or judgment 2 : JESTER 3 : DUPE 4 : IDIOT

²**fool** *vb* 1 : to spend time idly or aimlessly 2 : to meddle or tamper thoughtlessly or ignorantly 3 : JOKE 4 : DECEIVE 5 : FRITTER ⟨~ed away his time⟩

**fool·ery** \'fül-(ə-)rē\ *n*, *pl* **-er·ies** 1 : the habit of fooling : the behavior of a fool 2 : a foolish act : HORSEPLAY

**fool·har·dy** \'fül-ˌhärd-ē\ *adj* : foolishly daring : RASH — **fool·har·di·ness** \-ˌhärd-ē-nəs\ *n*

**fool·ish** \'fü-lish\ *adj* 1 : showing or arising from folly or lack of judgment 2 : ABSURD, RIDICULOUS 3 : ABASHED — **fool·ish·ly** *adv* — **fool·ish·ness** *n*

**fool·proof** \'fül-ˌprüf\ *adj* : so simple or reliable as to leave no opportunity for error, misuse, or failure

**fools·cap** *or* **fool's cap** \'fül-ˌskap\ *n* [fr. the watermark of a fool's cap formerly applied to such paper] : a size of paper typically 16x13 inches

¹**foot** \'fut\ *n*, *pl* **feet** \'fēt\ *also* **foot** 1 : the terminal part of a leg on which one stands 2 : see WEIGHT table 3 : a group of syllables forming the basic unit of verse meter 4 : something resembling an animal's foot in position or use 5 *foot pl*, *chiefly Brit* : INFANTRY 6 : the lowest part : BOTTOM 7 : the part at the opposite end from the head 8 : the part (as of a stocking) that covers the foot

²**foot** *vb* 1 : DANCE 2 : to go on foot 3 : to make speed : MOVE 4 : to add up 5 : to pay or provide for paying

**foot·age** \'fut-ij\ *n* : length expressed in feet

**foot·ball** \'fut-ˌbol\ *n* 1 : any of several games played by two teams on a rectangular field with goalposts at each end; *esp* : one in which the ball is in possession of one team at a time and is advanced by running or passing **2** : the ball used in football

**foot·board** \'fût-,bōrd\ *n* **1** : a narrow platform on which to stand or brace the feet **2** : a board forming the foot of a bed

**foot·bridge** \'fût-,brij\ *n* : a bridge for pedestrians

**foot·ed** \'fût-əd\ *adj* **1** : having a foot or feet ⟨a ~ stand⟩ ⟨~ creatures⟩ **2** : having such or so many feet ⟨flat-*footed*⟩ ⟨four-*footed*⟩

**-foot·er** \'fût-ər\ *comb form* : one that is a specified number of feet in height, length, or breadth ⟨a six-*footer*⟩

**foot·fall** \'fût-,fôl\ *n* : FOOTSTEP; *also* : the sound of a footstep

**foot·hill** \-,hil\ *n* : a hill at the foot of higher hills

**foot·hold** \-,hōld\ *n* **1** : a hold for the feet : FOOTING **2** : a position usable as a base for further advance

**foot·ing** \'fût-iŋ\ *n* **1** : the placing of one's foot in a position to secure a firm stand **2** : a place for the foot to rest on : FOOTHOLD **3** : a moving on foot **4** : position with respect to one another : STATUS **5** : BASIS **6** : the adding up of a column of figures; *also* : the total amount of such a column

**foot·less** \'fût-ləs\ *adj* **1** : having no feet **2** : UNSUBSTANTIAL **3** : STUPID, INEPT

**foot·lights** \-,līts\ *n pl* **1** : a row of lights along the front of a stage floor **2** : the stage as a profession

**foo·tling** \'fût-liŋ\ *adj* **1** : INEPT **2** : TRIVIAL

**foot·lock·er** \'fût-,läk-ər\ *n* : a small flat trunk designed to be placed at the foot of a bed (as in a barracks)

**foot·loose** \-,lüs\ *adj* : having no ties : FREE, UNTRAMMELED

**foot·man** \-mən\ *n* : a male servant who attends a carriage, waits on table, admits visitors, and runs errands

**foot·note** \-,nōt\ *n* **1** : a note of reference, explanation, or comment placed usu. at the bottom of a page **2** : COMMENTARY

**¹foot·pad** \-,pad\ *n* : a highwayman or robber on foot

**²footpad** *n* : a round somewhat flat foot on the leg of a spacecraft for distributing weight o minimize sinking into a surface

**foot·path** \'fût-,path, -,pȧth\ *n* : a narrow path for pedestrians

**foot·print** \'fût-,print\ *n* : an impression of the foot

**foot·race** \-,rās\ *n* : a race run on foot

**foot·rest** \-,rest\ *n* : a support for the feet

**foot·sore** \'fût-,sōr\ *adj* : having sore or tender feet (as from much walking)

**foot·step** \-,step\ *n* **1** : TREAD **2** : distance covered by a step : PACE **3** : the mark of the foot : TRACK **4** : a step on which to ascend or descend

**foot·stool** \-,stül\ *n* : a low stool to support the feet

**foot·wear** \-,waər\ *n* : apparel (as shoes or boots) for the feet

**foot·work** \-,wərk\ *n* : the management of the feet (as in boxing)

**fop** \'fäp\ *n* : DANDY — **fop·pery** \-(ə-)rē\ *n* — **fop·pish** *adj*

**¹for** \fər, (')fór\ *prep* **1** : as a preparation toward ⟨dress ~ dinner⟩ **2** : toward the purpose or goal of ⟨need time ~ study⟩ ⟨money ~ a trip⟩ **3** : so as to reach or attain ⟨run ~ cover⟩ **4** : as being ⟨took him ~ a fool⟩ **5** : because of ⟨cry ~ joy⟩ **6** — used to indicate a recipient ⟨a letter ~ you⟩ **7** : in support of ⟨fought ~ his country⟩ **8** : directed at : AFFECTING ⟨a cure ~ what ails you⟩ **9** — used with a noun or pronoun followed by an infinitive to form the equivalent of a noun clause ⟨~ you to go would be silly⟩ **10** : in exchange as equal to : so as to return the value of ⟨a lot of trouble ~ nothing⟩ ⟨pay $10 ~ a hat⟩ **11** : CONCERNING ⟨a stickler ~ detail⟩ **12** : CONSIDERING ⟨tall ~ his age⟩ **13** : through the period of ⟨served ~ three years⟩ **14** : in honor of

**²for** *conj* : BECAUSE

**³for** *abbr* **1** foreign **2** forestry

**FOR** *abbr* free on rail

**fora** *pl of* FORUM

**¹for·age** \'fȯr-ij\ *n* **1** : food for animals esp. when taken by browsing or grazing **2** : a search for provisions

**²forage** *vb* **for·aged; for·ag·ing** **1** : to collect forage from **2** : to wander in search of provisions **3** : to get by foraging **4** : RAVAGE, RAID **5** : to make a search : RUMMAGE

**for·ay** \'fȯr-,ā\ *vb* : to raid esp. in search of plunder : PILLAGE — **foray** *n*

**¹for·bear** \fór-'baər\ *vb* **-bore** \-'bōr\; **-borne** \-'bōrn\; **-bear·ing** **1** : to refrain from : ABSTAIN **2** : to be patient — **for·bear·ance** \-'bar-əns\ *n*

**²forbear** *var of* FOREBEAR

**for·bid** \fər-'bid\ *vb* **-bade** \-'bad, -'bād\ *or* **-bad** \-'bad\; **-bid·den** \-'bid-ᵊn\; **bid·ding** **1** : to command against : PROHIBIT **2** : to exclude or warn off by express command **3** : to bar from use **4** : HINDER, PREVENT **syn** enjoin, interdict, inhibit

**for·bid·ding** \-iŋ\ *adj* : DISAGREEABLE, REPELLENT

**forbode** *var of* FOREBODE

**¹force** \'fōrs\ *n* **1** : strength or energy esp. of an exceptional degree : active power **2** : capacity to persuade or convince **3** : military strength; *also*, *pl* : the whole military strength (as of a nation) **4** : a body (as of persons or ships) assigned to or available for a particular purpose **5** : VIOLENCE, COMPULSION **6** : an influence (as a push or pull) that causes motion or a change of motion — **force·ful** \-fəl\ *adj* — **force·ful·ly** \-ē\ *adv* — **in force 1** : in great numbers **2** : VALID, OPERATIVE

**²force** *vb* **forced; forc·ing** **1** : COMPEL, COERCE **2** : to cause through necessity ⟨*forced* to admit defeat⟩ **3** : to press, attain to, or effect against resistance or inertia ⟨~ your way through⟩ **4 :** to achieve or win by strength in struggle or violence **5 :** to raise or accelerate to the utmost ⟨∼ the pace⟩ **6 :** to produce with unnatural or unwilling effort ⟨forced laughter⟩ **7 :** to hasten (as in growth) by artificial means

**for·ceps** \'fôr-səps\ *n, pl* **forceps** [L, fr. *formus* warm + *capere* to take] **:** a hand-held instrument for grasping, holding, or pulling objects esp. for delicate operations

**forc·ible** \'fôr-sə-bəl\ *adj* **1 :** obtained or done by force **2 :** showing force or energy **:** POWERFUL — **forc·i·bly** \-blē\ *adv*

¹**ford** \'fôrd\ *n* **:** a place where a stream may be crossed by wading

²**ford** *vb* **:** to cross by a ford

¹**fore** \'fôr\ *adv* **:** in, toward, or adjacent to the front **:** FORWARD

²**fore** *adj* **:** being or coming before in time, order, or space

³**fore** *n* **1 :** FRONT **2 :** something that occupies a front position

⁴**fore** *interj* — used by a golfer to warn anyone within range of the probable line of flight of his ball

**fore-and-aft** \,fôr-ə-'naft\ *adj* **:** running in the line of the length (as of a ship) **:** LONGITUDINAL

¹**fore·arm** \fôr-'ärm\ *vb* **:** to arm in advance **:** PREPARE

²**fore·arm** \'fôr-,ärm\ *n* **:** the part of the arm between the elbow and the wrist

**fore·bear** *or* **for·bear** \-,baər\ *n* **:** ANCESTOR, FOREFATHER

**fore·bode** *also* **for·bode** \fôr-'bōd, fôr-\ *vb* **1 :** FORETELL, PORTEND **2 :** to have a premonition esp. of misfortune **syn** augur, predict — **fore·bod·ing** *n*

**fore·cast** \'fôr-,kast\ *vb* **-cast** *or* **-cast·ed; -cast·ing 1 :** PREDICT, CALCULATE ⟨∼ weather conditions⟩ **2 :** to indicate as likely to occur — **forecast** *n* — **fore·cast·er** *n*

**fore·cas·tle** \'fōk-səl\ *n* **1 :** the upper deck of a ship in front of the foremast **2 :** the forward part of a merchant ship where the sailors live

**fore·close** \fôr-'klōz\ *vb* **1 :** to shut out **:** DEBAR **2 :** to take legal measures to terminate a mortgage and take possession of the mortgaged property

**fore·clo·sure** \-'klō-zhər\ *n* **:** the act of foreclosing; *esp* **:** the legal procedure of foreclosing a mortgage

**fore·doom** \fôr-'düm\ *vb* **:** to doom beforehand

**fore·fa·ther** \'fôr-,fäth-ər\ *n* **1 :** ANCESTOR **2 :** a person of an earlier period and common heritage

**forefend** *var of* FORFEND

**fore·fin·ger** \-,fiŋ-gər\ *n* **:** the finger next to the thumb

**fore·foot** \-,fút\ *n* **:** either of the front feet of a quadruped

**fore·front** \-,frənt\ *n* **:** the foremost part or place **:** VANGUARD

**fore·gath·er** *var of* FORGATHER

¹**fore·go** \fôr-'gō\ *vb* **-went** \-'went\; **-gone** \-'gôn\; **-go·ing** \-'gō-iŋ\ **:** PRECEDE

²**forego** *var of* FORGO

**fore·go·ing** \-'gō-iŋ\ *adj* **:** PRECEDING

**fore·gone** \,fôr-,gôn\ *adj* **:** determined in advance ⟨a ∼ conclusion⟩

**fore·ground** \'fôr-,graúnd\ *n* **1 :** the part of a scene or representation that appears nearest to and in front of the spectator **2 :** a position of prominence

**fore·hand** \-,hand\ *n* **:** a stroke (as in tennis) made with the palm of the hand turned in the direction in which the hand is moving; *also* **:** the side on which such a stroke is made — **forehand** *adj*

**fore·hand·ed** \-'han-dəd\ *adj* **:** mindful of the future **:** THRIFTY, PRUDENT

**fore·head** \'fôr-əd, 'fôr-,hed\ *n* **:** the part of the face above the eyes

**for·eign** \'fôr-ən\ *adj* [ME *forein*, fr. OF, fr. LL *foranus* on the outside, fr. L *foris* outside] **1 :** situated outside a place or country and esp. one's own country **2 :** born in, belonging to, or characteristic of some place or country other than the one under consideration ⟨∼ language⟩ **3 :** not connected or pertinent **4 :** related to or dealing with other nations ⟨∼ affairs⟩ **5 :** occurring in an abnormal situation in the living body ⟨a ∼ body in the eye⟩

**for·eign·er** \'fôr-ə-nər\ *n* **:** a person belonging to or owing allegiance to a foreign country **:** ALIEN

**foreign minister** *n* **:** a governmental minister for foreign affairs

**fore·know** \fôr-'nō\ *vb* **-knew** \-'n(y)ü\; **-known** \-'nōn\; **-know·ing :** to have previous knowledge of — **fore·knowl·edge** \-'näl-ij\ *n*

**fore·la·dy** \'fôr-,lād-ē\ *n* **:** a woman who acts as a foreman

**fore·land** \'fôr-lənd\ *n* **:** PROMONTORY, HEADLAND

**fore·leg** \-,leg\ *n* **:** either of the front legs of a quadruped

**fore·limb** \-,lim\ *n* **:** either of an anterior pair of limbs (as wings, arms, or fins)

**fore·lock** \-,läk\ *n* **:** a lock of hair growing from the front part of the head

**fore·man** \'fôr-mən\ *n* **1 :** a spokesman of a jury **2 :** a workman in charge of a group of workers

**fore·mast** \-,mast\ *n* **:** the mast nearest the bow of a ship

**fore·most** \-,mōst\ *adj* **:** first in time, place, or order **:** most important **:** PREEMINENT — **foremost** *adv*

**fore·name** \-,nām\ *n* **:** a first name

**fore·named** \-,nāmd\ *adj* **:** previously named **:** AFORESAID

**fore·noon** \'fôr-,nün\ *n* **:** the period from morning to noon **:** MORNING

¹**fo·ren·sic** \fə-'ren-sik\ *adj* [L *forensis* public, forensic, fr. *forum* forum] **:** belonging to, used in, or suitable to courts of law or to public speaking or debate

²**forensic** *n* **1 :** an argumentative exercise **2 :** *pl* **:** the art or study of argumentative discourse

**fore·or·dain** \,fôr-ôr-'dān\ *vb* **:** to ordain or decree beforehand **:** PREDESTINE

**fore·part** \'fôr-,pärt\ *n* **1 :** the anterior part of something **2 :** the earlier part of a period of time

**fore·quar·ter** \-ˌkwȯrt-ər\ *n* **:** the front half of a lateral half of the body or carcass of a quadruped ⟨a ~ of beef⟩

**fore·run·ner** \'fōr-ˌrən-ər\ *n* **1 :** one that runs or is sent before to give notice of the approach of others **:** HARBINGER **2 :** PREDECESSOR, ANCESTOR *syn* precursor, herald

**fore·sail** \'fōr-ˌsāl, -səl\ *n* **1 :** the lowest sail on the foremast of a square-rigged ship **2 :** the lower sail set toward the stern on the foremast of a schooner

**fore·see** \fōr-'sē\ *vb* **·saw** \-'sȯ\; **-seen** \-'sēn\; **-see·ing :** to see or realize beforehand **:** EXPECT *syn* foreknow, divine, apprehend, anticipate — **fore·see·able** *adj*

**fore·shad·ow** \-'shad-ō\ *vb* **:** to give a hint or suggestion of beforehand **:** represent beforehand

**fore·sheet** \'fōr-ˌshēt\ *n* **1 :** one of the sheets of a foresail **2** *pl* **:** the forward part of an open boat

**fore·shore** \-ˌshȯr\ *n* **:** the part of a seashore between high-water and low-water marks

**fore·short·en** \fōr-'shȯrt-ᵊn\ *vb* **:** to shorten (a detail) in a drawing or painting so that the composition appears to have depth

**fore·sight** \'fōr-ˌsīt\ *n* **1 :** the act or power of foreseeing **2 :** an act of looking forward; *also* **:** a view forward **3 :** care or provision for the future **:** PRUDENCE — **fore·sight·ed** \-əd\ *adj* — **fore·sight·ed·ness** *n*

**fore·skin** \-ˌskin\ *n* **:** a fold of skin enclosing the end of the penis

**for·est** \'fȯr-əst\ *n* [ME, fr. OF, fr. ML *forestis*, fr. L *foris* outside] **:** a large thick growth of trees and underbrush — **for·est·ed** \'fȯr-ə-stəd\ *adj* — **for·est·land** \'fȯr-əst-ˌland\ *n*

**fore·stall** \fōr-'stȯl, fȯr-\ *vb* **1 :** to keep out, hinder, or prevent by measures taken in advance **2 :** ANTICIPATE

**forest ranger** *n* **:** a person in charge of the management and protection of a portion of a public forest

**for·est·ry** \'fȯr-ə-strē\ *n* **:** the science of growing and caring for forests — **for·est·er** \'fȯr-ə-stər\ *n*

**foreswear** *var of* FORSWEAR

**¹fore·taste** \'fōr-ˌtāst\ *n* **:** an advance indication, warning, or notion

**²fore·taste** \fōr-'tāst\ *vb* **:** to taste beforehand **:** ANTICIPATE

**fore·tell** \fōr-'tel\ *vb* **-told** \-'tōld\; **-tell·ing :** to tell of beforehand **:** PREDICT *syn* forecast, prophesy, prognosticate

**fore·thought** \'fōr-ˌthȯt\ *n* **1 :** PREMEDITATION **2 :** consideration for the future

**fore·to·ken** \fōr-'tō-kən\ *vb* **fore·to·kened; fore·to·ken·ing** \-'tōk-(ə-)niŋ\ **:** to indicate in advance

**fore·top** \'fōr-ˌtäp\ *n* **:** the platform at the head of a ship's foremast

**for·ev·er** \fȯr-'ev-ər\ *adv* **1 :** for a limitless time **2 :** at all times **:** ALWAYS

**for·ev·er·more** \-ˌev-ər-'mōr\ *adv* **:** FOREVER

**fore·warn** \fōr-'wȯrn\ *vb* **:** to warn beforehand

**fore wing** *n* **:** either of the anterior wings of a 4-winged insect

**fore·wom·an** \'fōr-ˌwùm-ən\ *n* **:** FORE-LADY

**fore·word** \-ˌwərd\ *n* **:** PREFACE

**¹for·feit** \'fȯr-fət\ *n* **1 :** something forfeited **:** PENALTY, FINE **2 :** FORFEITURE **3 :** something deposited and then redeemed on payment of a fine **4** *pl* **:** a game in which forfeits are exacted

**²forfeit** *vb* **:** to lose or lose the right to by some error, offense, or crime

**for·fei·ture** \'fȯr-fə-ˌchùr\ *n* **1 :** the act of forfeiting **2 :** something forfeited **:** PENALTY

**for·fend** *also* **fore·fend** \fȯr-'fend\ *vb* **1 :** to ward off **2 :** PROTECT, PRESERVE

**for·gath·er** *or* **fore·gath·er** \fȯr-'gath-ər, fōr-, -'geth-\ *vb* **1 :** to come together **:** ASSEMBLE **2 :** to meet someone usu. by chance

**¹forge** \'fōrj\ *n* [ME, fr. OF, fr. L *fabrica*, fr. *faber* smith] **:** SMITHY

**²forge** *vb* **forged; forg·ing 1 :** to form (metal) by heating and hammering **2 :** FASHION, SHAPE ⟨~ an agreement⟩ **3 :** to make or imitate falsely esp. with intent to defraud ⟨~ a signature⟩ — **forg·er** *n* — **forg·ery** \'fōrj-(ə-)rē\ *n*

**³forge** *vb* **forged; forg·ing :** to move ahead steadily but gradually

**for·get** \fər-'get\ *vb* **-got** \-'gät\; **-got·ten** \-'gät-ᵊn\ *or* **-got; -get·ting 1 :** to be unable to think of or recall **2 :** to fail to become mindful of at the proper time **3 :** NEGLECT, DISREGARD — **for·get·ful** \-'get-fəl\ *adj* — **for·get·ful·ly** \-ē\ *adv*

**for·get-me-not** \fər-'get-mē-ˌnät\ *n* **:** any of a genus of small herbs having bright-blue or white flowers usu. arranged in a curving spike

**forg·ing** \'fōr-jiŋ\ *n* **:** a piece of forged work

**for·give** \fər-'giv\ *vb* **-gave** \-'gāv\; **-giv·en** \-'giv-ən\; **-giv·ing 1 :** PARDON, ABSOLVE **2 :** to give up resentment of **3 :** to grant relief from payment of — **for·giv·able** *adj* — **for·give·ness** *n*

**for·giv·ing** \-iŋ\ *adj* **:** showing forgiveness **:** inclined or ready to forgive

**for·go** *or* **fore·go** \fȯr-'gō, fōr-\ *vb* **-went** \-'went\; **-gone** \-'gȯn\; **-go·ing** \-'gō-iŋ\ **:** to give up **:** abstain from **:** RENOUNCE

**fo·rint** \'fȯr-ˌint\ *n* — see MONEY table

**¹fork** \'fȯrk\ *n* **1 :** an implement with two or more prongs for taking up (as in eating), piercing, pitching, or digging **2 :** a forked part, tool, or piece of equipment **3 :** a dividing into branches or a place where something branches; *also* **:** a branch of such a fork

**²fork** *vb* **1 :** to divide into two or more branches **2 :** to give the form of a fork to ⟨~*ing* her fingers⟩ **3 :** to raise or pitch with a fork ⟨~ hay⟩

**forked** \'fȯrkt, 'fȯr-kəd\ *adj* **:** having a fork **:** shaped like a fork ⟨~ lightning⟩

**fork·lift** \'fȯrk-ˌlift\ *n* **:** a machine for hoisting heavy objects by means of steel fingers inserted under the load

**for·lorn** \fər-'lȯrn\ *adj* **1** : DESERTED, FORSAKEN **2** : WRETCHED **3** : nearly hopeless — **for·lorn·ly** *adv*

**forlorn hope** *n* [by folk etymology fr. D *verloren hoop*, lit., lost band] **1** : a body of men selected to perform a perilous service **2** : a desperate or extremely difficult enterprise

¹**form** \'fȯrm\ *n* **1** : SHAPE, STRUCTURE **2** : a body esp. of a person : FIGURE **3** : the essential nature of a thing **4** : established manner of doing or saying something **5** : FORMULA **6** : a printed or typed document with blank spaces for insertion of requested information ⟨tax ∼⟩ **7** : CEREMONY, CONVENTIONALITY **8** : manner or style of performing according to recognized standards **9** : a long seat : BENCH **10** : a frame model of the human figure used for displaying clothes **11** : MOLD ⟨a ∼ for concrete⟩ **12** : type or plates in a frame ready for printing **13** : MODE, KIND, VARIETY ⟨coal is a ∼ of carbon⟩ **14** : orderly method of arrangement; *also* : a particular kind or instance of such arrangement ⟨the sonnet ∼ in poetry⟩ **15** : the structural element, plan, or design of a work of art **16** : a bounded surface or volume **17** : a grade in a British secondary school or in some American private schools **18** : a table with information on the past performances of racehorses **19** : known ability to perform; *also* : condition (as of an athlete) suitable for performing **20** : one of the ways in which a word is changed to show difference in use ⟨the plural ∼ of a noun⟩

²**form** *vb* **1** : to give form or shape to : FASHION, MAKE **2** : to give a particular shape to : ARRANGE **3** : TRAIN, INSTRUCT **4** : DEVELOP, ACQUIRE ⟨∼ a habit⟩ **5** : to make up : CONSTITUTE **6** : to arrange in order ⟨∼ a battle line⟩ **7** : to take form : ARISE ⟨clouds are ∼ing⟩ **8** : to take a definite form, shape, or arrangement

¹**for·mal** \'fȯr-məl\ *adj* **1** : CONVENTIONAL **2** : done in due or lawful form ⟨a ∼ contract⟩ **3** : based on conventional forms and rules ⟨a ∼ reception⟩ **4** : CEREMONIOUS, PRIM ⟨a ∼ manner⟩ **5** : NOMINAL — **for·mal·ly** \-ē\ *adv*

²**formal** *n* : something (as a social event) formal in character

**form·al·de·hyde** \fȯr-'mal-də-ˌhīd\ *n* : a colorless pungent gas used in water solution as a preservative and disinfectant

**for·mal·ism** \'fȯr-mə-ˌliz-əm\ *n* : strict adherence to set forms

**for·mal·i·ty** \fȯr-'mal-ət-ē\ *n, pl* **-ties** **1** : the quality or state of being formal **2** : compliance with formal or conventional rules **3** : an established form that is required or conventional

**for·mal·ize** \'fȯr-mə-ˌlīz\ *vb* **-ized;** **-iz·ing 1** : to give a certain or definite form to **2** : to make formal; *also* : to give formal status or approval to

¹**for·mat** \'fȯr-ˌmat\ *n* **1** : the general composition or style of a publication

**2** : the general plan or arrangement of something

²**format** *vb* **for·mat·ted; for·mat·ting** : to produce (as a book, printed matter, or data) in a particular form

**for·ma·tion** \fȯr-'mā-shən\ *n* **1** : a giving form to something : DEVELOPMENT **2** : something that is formed **3** : STRUCTURE, SHAPE **4** : an arrangement of persons, ships, or airplanes

**for·ma·tive** \'fȯr-mət-iv\ *adj* **1** : giving or capable of giving form : CONSTRUCTIVE **2** : of, relating to, or characterized by important growth or formation ⟨a child's ∼ years⟩

**for·mer** \'fȯr-mər\ *adj* **1** : PREVIOUS, EARLIER **2** : FOREGOING **3** : being first mentioned or in order of two things

**for·mer·ly** \-lē\ *adv* : in time past : HERETOFORE, PREVIOUSLY

**form-fit·ting** \'fȯrm-ˌfit-iŋ\ *adj* : conforming to the outline of the body

**for·mi·da·ble** \'fȯr-məd-ə-bəl, fȯr-'mid-\ *adj* **1** : exciting fear, dread, or awe **2** : imposing serious difficulties — **for·mi·da·bly** \-blē\ *adv*

**form·less** \'fȯrm-ləs\ *adj* : having no definite shape or form

**form letter** *n* **1** : a letter on a frequently recurring topic that can be sent to different people at different times **2** : a letter sent out in many printed copies to a large number of people

**for·mu·la** \'fȯr-myə-lə\ *n, pl* **-las** *or* **-lae** \-ˌlē, -ˌlī\ **1** : a set form of words for ceremonial use **2** : a conventionalized statement intended to express some fundamental truth **3** : RECIPE **4** : a milk mixture or substitute for a baby **5** : a group of symbols or figures joined to express a single rule or idea **6** : a prescribed or set form or method

**for·mu·late** \-ˌlāt\ *vb* **-lat·ed; -lat·ing 1** : to express in a formula **2** : to state definitely and clearly **3** : to prepare according to a formula — **for·mu·la·tion** \ˌfȯr-myə-'lā-shən\ *n*

**for·ni·ca·tion** \ˌfȯr-nə-'kā-shən\ *n* : human sexual intercourse other than between a man and his wife — **for·ni·cate** \'fȯr-nə-ˌkāt\ *vb* — **for·ni·ca·tor** \-ˌkāt-ər\ *n*

**for·sake** \fər-'sāk\ *vb* **for·sook** \-'su̇k\; **for·sak·en** \-'sā-kən\; **for·sak·ing** [ME *forsaken*, fr. OE *forsacan*, fr. *sacan* to dispute] **1** : to give up : RENOUNCE **2** : to quit or leave entirely : ABANDON

**for·sooth** \fər-'süth\ *adv* : in truth : INDEED

**for·swear** *or* **fore·swear** \fȯr-'swaər, fōr-, -'swaar\ *vb* **-swore** \-'swōr\; **-sworn** \-'swōrn\; **-swear·ing 1** : to renounce earnestly or under oath **2** : to deny under oath **3** : to swear falsely : commit perjury

**for·syth·ia** \fər-'sith-ē-ə\ *n* : a shrub widely grown for its yellow bell-shaped flowers borne in early spring

**fort** \'fȯrt\ *n* [ME *forte*, fr. MF *fort*, fr. *fort* strong, fr. L *fortis*] **1** : a fortified place **2** : a permanent army post

¹**forte** \'fȯrt, 'fōrt, 'fȯr-ˌtā\ *n* : something in which a person excels

²**for·te** \'fȯr-,tā\ adv or adj **:** LOUDLY, POWERFULLY — used as a direction in music

**forth** \'fōrth\ adv **1 :** FORWARD, ONWARD ⟨from that day ~⟩ **2 :** out into view ⟨put ~ leaves⟩

**forth·com·ing** \fōrth-'kəm-iŋ\ adj **1 :** APPROACHING, COMING ⟨the ~ holidays⟩ **2 :** readily available or approachable ⟨the funds will be ~⟩

**forth·right** \'fōrth-,rīt\ adj **:** DIRECT, STRAIGHTFORWARD ⟨a ~ answer⟩ — **forth·right·ly** adv — **forth·right·ness** n

**forth·with** \fōrth-'with, -'with\ adv **:** IMMEDIATELY

**for·ti·fy** \'fȯrt-ə-,fī\ vb **-fied; -fy·ing 1 :** to strengthen and secure by military defenses **2 :** to give physical strength, courage, or endurance to **3 :** ENCOURAGE **4 :** ENRICH ⟨~ bread with vitamins⟩ — **for·ti·fi·ca·tion** \,fȯrt-ə-fə-'kā-shən\ n

**for·tis·si·mo** \fȯr-'tis-ə-,mō\ adv or adj **:** very loud — used as a direction in music

**for·ti·tude** \'fȯrt-ə-,t(y)üd\ n **:** strength of mind that enables a person to meet danger or bear pain or adversity with courage **syn** grit, backbone, pluck

**fort·night** \'fōrt-,nīt\ n [ME fourtenight, fr. fourtene night fourteen nights] **:** two weeks

**fort·night·ly** \-lē\ adj **:** occurring or appearing once in a fortnight — **fortnightly** adv

**for·tress** \'fȯr-trəs\ n **:** FORT 1

**for·tu·itous** \fȯr-'t(y)ü-ət-əs\ adj **:** happening by chance **:** ACCIDENTAL

**for·tu·ity** \-ət-ē\ n, pl **-ities 1 :** the quality or state of being fortuitous **2 :** a chance event or occurrence

**for·tu·nate** \'fȯrch-(ə-)nət\ adj **1 :** coming by good luck **2 :** LUCKY — **for·tu·nate·ly** adv

**for·tune** \'fȯr-chən\ n **1 :** an apparent cause of something that happens to one suddenly and unexpectedly **:** CHANCE, LUCK **2 :** what happens to a person **:** good or bad luck **3 :** FATE, DESTINY **4 :** RICHES, WEALTH

**fortune hunter** n **:** a person who seeks wealth esp. by marriage

**for·tune–tel·ler** \-,tel-ər\ n **:** a person who professes to tell future events — **for·tune–tell·ing** \-iŋ\ n or adj

**for·ty** \'fȯrt-ē\ n, pl **forties :** four times 10 — **for·ti·eth** \'fȯrt-ē-əth\ adj or n — **forty** adj or pron

**for·ty–five** \,fȯrt-ē-'fīv\ n **1 :** a .45 caliber pistol — usu. written .45 **2 :** a microgroove phonograph record designed to be played at 45 revolutions per minute

**for·ty–nin·er** \,fȯrt-ē-'nī-nər\ n **:** a person in the rush to California for gold in 1849

**forty winks** n sing or pl **:** a short sleep

**fo·rum** \'fōr-əm\ n, pl **forums** also **fo·ra** \-ə\ **1 :** the marketplace or central meeting place of an ancient Roman city **2 :** a medium (as a publication) of open discussion **3 :** COURT **4 :** a public assembly, lecture, or program involving audience or panel discussion

¹**for·ward** \'fȯr-wərd\ adj **1 :** being near or at or belonging to the front **2 :** EAGER, READY **3 :** BRASH, BOLD **4 :** notably advanced or developed **:** PRECOCIOUS **5 :** moving, tending, or leading toward a position **:** in front ⟨a ~ movement⟩ **6 :** EXTREME, RADICAL **7 :** of, relating to, or getting ready for the future — **for·ward·ness** n

²**forward** adv **:** to or toward what is before or in front

³**forward** n **:** a player stationed near the front of his team (as in hockey) or in the corner (as in basketball)

⁴**forward** vb **1 :** to help onward **:** ADVANCE **2 :** to send forward **:** TRANSMIT **3 :** to send or ship onward

**for·ward·er** \-wərd-ər\ n **:** one that forwards; esp **:** an agent who forwards goods — **for·ward·ing** \-iŋ\ n

**for·wards** \'fȯr-wərdz\ adv **:** FORWARD

**FOS** abbr free on steamer

¹**fos·sil** \'fäs-əl\ n [L fossilis dug up, fr. fossus, pp. of fodere to dig] **1 :** a trace or impression or the remains of a plant or animal preserved in the earth's crust from past ages **2 :** a person whose ideas are out-of-date — **fos·sil·ize** vb

²**fossil** adj **1 :** extracted from the earth ⟨~ fuels such as coal⟩ **2 :** being or resembling a fossil ⟨~ plants⟩

¹**fos·ter** \'fȯs-tər\ adj [ME, fr. OE fōstor-, fr. fōstor food, feeding] **:** affording, receiving, or sharing nourishment or parental care though not related by blood or legal ties ⟨~ parent⟩ ⟨~ child⟩

²**foster** vb **fos·tered; fos·ter·ing** \-t(ə-)riŋ\ **1 :** to give parental care to **:** NURTURE **2 :** to promote the growth or development of **:** ENCOURAGE

**fos·ter·ling** \-tər-liŋ\ n **:** a foster child

**FOT** abbr free on truck

**fought** past of FIGHT

¹**foul** \'faul\ adj **1 :** offensive to the senses **:** LOATHSOME; also **:** clogged with dirt **2 :** ODIOUS, DETESTABLE **3 :** OBSCENE, ABUSIVE **4 :** DISAGREEABLE, STORMY ⟨~ weather⟩ **5 :** TREACHEROUS, DISHONORABLE, UNFAIR **6 :** marking the bounds of a playing field ⟨~ lines⟩; also **:** being outside the foul line ⟨~ ball⟩ ⟨~ territory⟩ **7 :** marked up or defaced by changes **8 :** ENTANGLED — **foul·ly** \-ē\ adv — **foul·ness** n

²**foul** n **1 :** ENTANGLEMENT, COLLISION **2 :** an infraction of the rules in a game or sport; also **:** a baseball hit outside the foul line

³**foul** adv **:** FOULLY

⁴**foul** vb **1 :** to make or become foul or filthy **2 :** DISGRACE, DISHONOR **3 :** to make or hit a foul **4 :** to entangle or become entangled **5 :** OBSTRUCT, BLOCK **6 :** to collide with

**fou·lard** \fu̇-'lärd\ n **:** a lightweight silk of plain or twill weave usu. decorated with a printed pattern

**foul·ing** \'faul-iŋ\ n **:** DEPOSIT, INCRUSTATION

**foul-mouthed** \'faul-'maůthd, -'maůtht\ adj **:** given to the use of obscene, profane, or abusive language

**foul play** *n* : unfair play or dealing : dishonest conduct; *esp* : VIOLENCE

**foul-up** \'faùl-,əp\ *n* **1** : a state of confusion caused by ineptitude, carelessness, or error **2** : a mechanical difficulty

**foul up** \(')faùl-'əp\ *vb* **1** : to spoil by mistakes or poor judgment **2** : to make a mistake : BUNGLE

¹**found** \'faùnd\ *past of* FIND

²**found** *adj* : presented as or incorporated into an artistic work essentially as found by an artist

³**found** *vb* **1** : to take the first steps in building ⟨~ a colony⟩ **2** : to set or ground on something solid : BASE **3** : to establish and often to provide for the future maintenance of ⟨~ a college⟩ — **found·er** *n*

⁴**found** *vb* **1** : to melt (metal) and pour into a mold **2** : to make by founding metal — **found·er** *n*

**foun·da·tion** \faùn-'dā-shən\ *n* **1** : the act of founding **2** : the base or basis upon which something stands or is supported ⟨suspicions without ~⟩ **3** : funds given for the permanent support of an institution : ENDOWMENT; *also* : an institution so endowed **4** : supporting structure : BASE **5** : CORSET — **foun·da·tion·al** \-sh(ə-)nəl\ *adj*

**foun·der** \'faùn-dər\ *vb* **found·ered; foun·der·ing** \-d(ə-)riŋ\ **1** : to make or become lame ⟨~ a horse⟩ **2** : to give way : COLLAPSE **3** : SINK ⟨a ~ing ship⟩ **4** : FAIL

**found·ling** \'faùn-(d)liŋ\ *n* : an infant found after its unknown parents have abandoned it

**found object** *n* : OBJET TROUVÉ

**found·ry** \'faùn-drē\ *n, pl* **foundries** : a building or works where metal is cast

**fount** \'faùnt\ *n* : FOUNTAIN, SOURCE

**foun·tain** \'faùnt-ᵊn\ *n* **1** : a spring of water **2** : SOURCE **3** : an artificial jet of water **4** : a container for liquid that can be drawn off as needed

**foun·tain·head** \-,hed\ *n* : SOURCE

**fountain pen** *n* : a pen with a reservoir that feeds the writing point with ink

**four** \'fōr\ *n* **1** : one more than three **2** : the 4th in a set or series **3** : something having four units — **four** *adj or pron*

**four-flush** \-,fləsh\ *vb* : to make a false claim : BLUFF — **four-flush·er** *n*

**four·fold** \-,fōld, -'fōld\ *adj* **1** : having four units or members **2** : of or amounting to 400 percent — **four·fold** \-'fōld\ *adv*

**4-H** \'fōr-'āch\ *adj* : of or relating to a program set up by the U.S. Department of Agriculture to instruct rural young people in modern farm practices and in good citizenship — **4-H·er** \-ər\ *n*

**Four Hundred** *or* **400** *n* : the exclusive social set of a community — used with *the*

**four-in-hand** \'fōr-ən-,hand\ *n* **1** : a team of four horses driven by one person; *also* : a vehicle drawn by such a team **2** : a necktie tied in a slipknot with long ends overlapping vertically in front

**four-o'clock** \'fōr-ə-,kläk\ *n* : a garden plant with fragrant yellow, red, or white flowers without petals that open late in the afternoon

**four·pen·ny nail** \,fōr-,pen-ē\ *n* : a nail 1⅜ inches long

**four-post·er** \'fōr-'pō-stər\ *n* : a bed with tall corner posts orig. designed to support curtains or a canopy

**four·score** \'fōr-'skōr\ *adj* : being four times twenty : EIGHTY

**four·some** \'fōr-səm\ *n* **1** : a group of four persons or things **2** : a golf match between two pairs of partners

**four·square** \-'skwaər\ *adj* **1** : SQUARE **2** : marked by boldness and conviction; *also* : FORTHRIGHT — **foursquare** *adv*

**four·teen** \'fōr-'tēn\ *n* : one more than 13 — **fourteen** *adj or pron* — **four·teenth** \-'tēnth\ *adj or n*

**fourth** \'fōrth\ *n* **1** : one that is fourth **2** : one of four equal parts of something **3** : the 4th forward gear in an automotive vehicle — **fourth** *adj or adv*

**fourth estate** *n, often cap F&E* : the public press

**four-wheel** \,fōr-,hwēl\ *adj* : acting on or by means of four wheels of an automotive vehicle

¹**fowl** \'faùl\ *n, pl* **fowl** *or* **fowls** **1** : BIRD **2** : a domestic cock or hen; *also* : the flesh of these used as food

²**fowl** *vb* : to hunt wildfowl

¹**fox** \'fäks\ *n, pl* **fox·es** *or* **fox** **1** : a mammal related to the wolves but smaller and with shorter legs and pointed muzzle **2** : a clever crafty person **3** : a member of an American Indian people formerly living in Wisconsin

²**fox** *vb* : TRICK, OUTWIT

**foxed** \'fäkst\ *adj* : discolored with yellowish brown stains

**fox·glove** \'fäks-,gləv\ *n* : a plant grown for its showy spikes of dotted white or purple tubular flowers and as a source of digitalis

**fox·hole** \'fäks-,hōl\ *n* : a pit dug for protection against enemy fire

**fox·hound** \-,haùnd\ *n* : any of various large swift powerful hounds used in hunting foxes

**fox terrier** *n* : a small lively terrier that occurs in varieties with smooth dense coats or with harsh wiry coats

**fox-trot** \'fäks-,trät\ *n* **1** : a short broken slow trotting gait **2** : a ballroom dance in duple time

**foxy** \'fäk-sē\ *adj* **fox·i·er; -est** **1** : resembling or suggestive of a fox **2** : WILY; *also* : CLEVER

**foy·er** \'fòi-ər, 'fòi-,(y)ā\ *n* [F, lit., fireplace, fr. ML *focarius,* fr. L *jocus* hearth] : LOBBY; *also* : an entrance hallway

**fp** *abbr* freezing point

**FPC** *abbr* fish protein concentrate

**FPM** *abbr* feet per minute

**FPO** *abbr* fleet post office

**FPS** *abbr* feet per second

**fr** *abbr* **1** father **2** franc **3** friar **4** from

¹**Fr** *abbr* French

²**Fr** *symbol* francium

**fra·cas** \'frāk-əs  'frak-\ *n, pl* **fra-**

**cas·es** \-ə-səz\ [F, din, row, fr. It *fracasso*, fr. *fracassare* to shatter] : BRAWL

**frac·tion** \'frak-shən\ *n* 1 : a numerical representation of one or more equal parts of a unit (½, ⅜, .256 are ~s) 2 : FRAGMENT : PORTION — **frac·tion·al** \-sh(ə-)nəl\ *adj* — **frac·tion·al·ly** \-ē\ *adv*

**frac·tious** \'frak-shəs\ *adj* 1 : tending to be troublesome : hard to handle or control 2 : QUARRELSOME, IRRITABLE

**frac·ture** \'frak-chər\ *n* 1 : a breaking of something and esp. a bone 2 : CRACK, CLEFT — **fracture** *vb*

**frag·ile** \'fraj-əl, -,īl\ *adj* : easily broken : DELICATE — **fra·gil·i·ty** \frə-'jil-ət-ē\ *n*

¹**frag·ment** \'frag-mənt\ *n* : a part broken off, detached, or incomplete

²**frag·ment** \-,ment\ *vb* : to break into fragments — **frag·men·ta·tion** \,frag-mən-'tā-shən, -,men-\ *n*

**frag·men·tary** \'frag-mən-,ter-ē\ *adj* : made up of fragments : INCOMPLETE

**fra·grant** \'frā-grənt\ *adj* : sweet or agreeable in smell — **fra·grance** \-grəns\ *n* — **fra·grant·ly** *adv*

**frail** \'frāl\ *adj* 1 : morally or physically weak 2 : FRAGILE, DELICATE

**frail·ty** \'frā(-ə)l-tē\ *n, pl* **frailties** 1 : the quality or state of being frail 2 : a fault due to weakness

¹**frame** \'frām\ *vb* **framed; fram·ing** 1 : PLAN, CONTRIVE 2 : FORMULATE 3 : SHAPE, CONSTRUCT 4 : to draw up (~ a constitution) 5 : to fit or adjust for a purpose : ARRANGE 6 : to provide with or enclose in a frame 7 : to make appear guilty - **fram·er** *n*

²**frame** *n* 1 : something made of parts fitted and joined together 2 : the physical makeup of the body 3 : an arrangement of structural parts that gives form or support 4 : a supporting or enclosing border or open case (as for a window or picture) 5 : a particular state or disposition (as of mind) : MOOD 6 : one picture of a series (as in a comic strip, on a length of motion-picture film, or of television images) 7 : FRAME-UP

³**frame** *adj* : having a wood frame

**frame–up** \-,əp\ *n* : a scheme to cause an innocent person to be accused of a crime; *also* : the action resulting from such a scheme

**frame·work** \'frām-,wərk\ *n* 1 : a skeletal, openwork, or structural frame 2 : a basic structure (as of ideas)

**franc** \'fraŋk\ *n* 1 — see MONEY table 2 — see *dirham* at MONEY table

**fran·chise** \'fran-,chīz\ *n* [ME, fr. OF, fr. *franchir* to free, fr. *franc* free] 1 : a special privilege granted to an individual or group (a ~ to operate a ferry) 2 : a constitutional or statutory right or privilege; *esp* : the right to vote

**fran·chi·see** \,fran-,chī-'zē, -chə-\ *n* : one who is granted a marketing franchise

**fran·chis·er** \'fran-,chī-zər\ *n* 1 : FRANCHISEE 2 : FRANCHISOR

**fran·chi·sor** \,fran-,chī-'zór, -chə-\ *n*

: one that grants a marketing franchise

**fran·ci·um** \'fran-sē-əm\ *n* : a radioactive metallic chemical element

**Fran·co–Amer·i·can** \,fraŋ-kō-ə-'mer-ə-kən\ *n* : an American of French or esp. French-Canadian descent — **Franco–American** *adj*

**fran·gi·ble** \'fran-jə-bəl\ *adj* : BREAKABLE — **fran·gi·bil·i·ty** \,fran-jə-'bil-ət-ē\ *n*

¹**frank** \'fraŋk\ *adj* : marked by free, forthright, and sincere expression — **frank·ly** *adv* — **frank·ness** *n*

²**frank** *vb* : to mark (a piece of mail) with an official signature or sign indicating that it can be mailed free; *also* : to mail in this manner

³**frank** *n* 1 : a signature, mark, or stamp on a piece of mail indicating that it can be mailed free 2 : the privilege of sending mail free of charge

**Fran·ken·stein** \'fraŋ-kən-,stīn, -,stēn\ *n* 1 : a work or agency that ruins its originator 2 : a monster in the shape of a man

**frank·furt·er** *or* **frank·fort·er** \'fraŋk-fə(r)t-ər, -,fərt-\ *or* **frank·furt** *or* **frank·fort** \-fərt\ *n* : a seasoned sausage (as of beef or beef and pork)

**frank·in·cense** \'fraŋ-kən-,sens\ *n* : a fragrant resin burned as incense

**fran·tic** \'frant-ik\ *adj* : wildly excited — **fran·ti·cal·ly** \-i-k(ə-)lē\ *adv* — **fran·tic·ly** \-i-klē\ *adv*

**frap·pé** \fra-'pā\ *or* **frappe** \'frap, fra-'pā\ *n* 1 : an iced or frozen mixture or drink 2 : a thick milk shake — **frap·pé** *or* **frap·pe** \fra-'pā\ *adj*

**fra·ter·nal** \frə-'tərn-ᵊl\ *adj* 1 : of, relating to, or involving brothers 2 : of, relating to, or being a fraternity or society 3 : FRIENDLY, BROTHERLY — **fra·ter·nal·ly** \-ē\ *adv*

**fra·ter·ni·ty** \frə-'tər-nət-ē\ *n, pl* **-ties** 1 : a social, honorary, or professional organization; *esp* : a social club of male college students 2 : BROTHERLINESS, BROTHERHOOD 3 : men of the same class, profession, or tastes

**frat·er·nize** \'frat-ər-,nīz\ *vb* **-nized; -niz·ing** 1 : to associate or mingle as brothers or friends 2 : to associate on intimate terms with citizens or troops of a hostile nation — **frat·er·ni·za·tion** \,frat-ər-nə-'zā-shən\ *n*

**frat·ri·cide** \'fra-trə-,sīd\ *n* 1 : one that kills his brother or sister 2 : the act of a fratricide — **frat·ri·cid·al** \,fra-trə-'sīd-ᵊl\ *adj*

**fraud** \'fród\ *n* 1 : DECEIT, TRICKERY 2 : TRICK 3 : IMPOSTOR, CHEAT

**fraud·u·lent** \'fró-jə-lənt\ *adj* : characterized by, based on, or done by fraud : DECEITFUL - **fraud·u·lent·ly** *adv*

**fraught** \'frót\ *adj* 1 : ACCOMPANIED 2 : bearing promise or menace

¹**fray** \'frā\ *n* : BRAWL, FIGHT; *also* : DISPUTE

²**fray** *vb* 1 : to wear (as an edge of cloth) by rubbing 2 : to separate the threads at the edge of 3 : to wear out or into shreds 4 : STRAIN, IRRITATE (~ed nerves)

**fraz·zle** \'fraz-əl\ vb **fraz·zled; frazzling** \'fraz-(ə-)liŋ\ 1 : FRAY 2 : to put in a state of extreme physical or nervous fatigue — **frazzle** n

**freak** \'frēk\ n 1 : WHIM, CAPRICE 2 : a strange, abnormal, or unusual person or thing 3 : a person who uses an illicit drug 4 : an ardent enthusiast — **freak·ish** adj

**freak out** \'frēk-'aut\ vb 1 : to withdraw from reality esp. by taking drugs 2 : to experience nightmarish hallucinations as a result of taking drugs — **freak-out** \'frēk-,aut\ n

**freck·le** \'frek-əl\ n : a brownish spot on the skin - **freckle** vb

¹**free** \'frē\ adj **fre·er; fre·est** 1 : having liberty 2 : not controlled by others : INDEPENDENT; also : not allowing slavery 3 : not subject to a duty, tax, or other charge 4 : released or not suffering from something unpleasant 5 : given without charge 6 : made or done voluntarily : SPONTANEOUS 7 : LAVISH 8 : PLENTIFUL 9 : OPEN, FRANK 10 : not restricted by conventional forms 11 : not literal or exact 12 : not obstructed : CLEAR 13 : not being used or occupied 14 : not fastened or bound - **free·ly** adv

²**free** adv 1 : FREELY 2 : without charge

³**free** vb **freed; free·ing** 1 : to set free 2 : RELIEVE, RID 3 : DISENTANGLE, CLEAR **syn** release, liberate, discharge

**free·bie** or **free·bee** \'frē-bē\ n : something given without charge

**free·board** \'frē-,bōrd\ n : the vertical distance between the waterline and the deck of a ship

**free·boo·ter** \'frē-,büt-ər\ n [D *vrijbuiter*, fr. *vrijbuit* plunder, fr. *vrij* free + *buit* booty] : PLUNDERER, PIRATE

**free·born** \-'bórn\ adj 1 : not born in vassalage or slavery 2 : relating to or befitting one that is freeborn

**freed·man** \'frēd-mən, -,man\ n : a man freed from slavery

**free·dom** \'frēd-əm\ n 1 : the quality or state of being free : INDEPENDENCE 2 : EXEMPTION, RELEASE 3 : EASE, FACILITY 4 : FRANKNESS 5 : unrestricted use 6 : a political right; also : FRANCHISE, PRIVILEGE

**free-for-all** \'frē-fə-,ról\ n : a competition or fight open to all comers and usu. with no rules : BRAWL — **free-for-all** adj

**free·hand** \'frē-,hand\ adj : done without mechanical aids or devices

**free·hold** \'frē-,hōld\ n : ownership of an estate for life esp. with the right to bequeath it to one's heirs; also : an estate thus owned — **free·hold·er** n

**free lance** n : one who pursues a profession (as writing) without long-term contractual commitments to any one employer    **free–lance** adj or vb

**free·load** \'frē-'lōd\ vb : to impose upon another's generosity or hospitality without sharing in the cost — **free·load·er** n

**free love** n : the practice of living openly with one of the opposite sex without marriage

**free·man** \'frē-mən, -,man\ n 1 : one who has civil or political liberty 2 : one having the full rights of a citizen

**Free·ma·son** \-'mās-ᵊn\ n : a member of a secret fraternal society called Free and Accepted Masons — **Free·ma·son·ry** \-rē\ n

**free·stand·ing** \'frē-'stan-diŋ\ adj : standing alone or on its own foundation

**free·stone** \'frē-,stōn\ n 1 : a stone that may be cut freely without splitting 2 : a fruit stone to which the flesh does not cling; also : a fruit (as a peach or cherry) having such a stone

**free·think·er** \-'thiŋ-kər\ n : one who forms opinions on the basis of reason independently of authority; esp : one who doubts or denies religious do, ma — **free·think·ing** n or adj

**free trade** n : trade based upon the unrestricted international exchange of goods with tariffs used only as a source of revenue

**free university** n : an unaccredited institution established within a university by students to study subjects not included in the academic curriculum

**free verse** n : verse whose meter is irregular or whose rhythm is not metrical

**free·way** \'frē-,wā\ n : an expressway with fully controlled access

**free·wheel** \-'hwēl\ vb : to move, live, or drift along freely or irresponsibly

**free·will** \'frē-,wil\ adj : VOLUNTARY

**free will** n : the power to choose without restraint of physical or divine necessity or causal law

¹**freeze** \'frēz\ vb **froze** \'frōz\; **frozen** \'frōz-ᵊn\; **freez·ing** 1 : to harden into ice or a like solid by loss of heat 2 : to chill or become chilled with cold 3 : to act or become coldly formal in manner 4 : to act toward in a stiff and formal way 5 : to damage by frost 6 : to adhere solidly by freezing 7 : to cause to grip tightly or remain in immovable contact 8 : to clog with ice 9 : to become fixed or motionless 10 : to fix at a certain stage or level

²**freeze** n 1 : a state of weather marked by low temperature 2 : an act or instance of freezing ⟨a price ∼⟩ 3 : the state of being frozen

**freeze-dry** \'frēz-'drī\ vb : to dry in a frozen state under vacuum esp. for preservation - **freeze-dried** adj

**freez·er** \'frē-zər\ n : one that freezes or keeps something cool; esp : a cabinet or compartment for keeping food at a subfreezing temperature or for freezing perishable food rapidly

¹**freight** \'frāt\ n 1 : payment for carrying goods 2 : LOAD, CARGO 3 : the carrying of goods by a common carrier 4 : a train that carries freight

²**freight** vb 1 : to load with goods for transportation 2 : BURDEN, CHARGE 3 : to ship or transport by freight — **freight·er** n

**French** \'french\ n 1 **French** pl : the people of France 2 : the language of France — **French** adj — **French-**

man \-mən\ *n* — **French·wom·an** \-,wu̇m-ən\ *n*

**french fry** *vb, often cap 1st F* : to fry (as strips of potato) in deep fat until brown — **french fry** *n, often cap 1st F*

**French horn** *n* : a curved brass instrument with a funnel-shaped mouthpiece and a flaring bell

**fre·net·ic** \fri-'net-ik\ *adj* : FRENZIED, FRANTIC — **fre·net·i·cal·ly** \-i-k(ə-)lē\ *adv*

**fren·zy** \'fren-zē\ *n, pl* **frenzies** : temporary madness or a violently agitated state — **fren·zied** \-zēd\ *adj*

**freq** *abbr* frequency, frequent; frequently

**fre·quen·cy** \'frē-kwən-sē\ *n, pl* **-cies** **1** : the fact or condition of occurring frequently **2** : rate of occurrence **3** : the number of cycles per second of an alternating electric current **4** : the number of sound waves per second produced by a sounding body **5** : the number of complete oscillations per second of an electromagnetic wave

**frequency modulation** *n* : modulation of the frequency of a transmitting radio wave in accordance with the strength of the audio or video signal; *also* : a broadcasting system using such modulation

**¹fre·quent** \'frē-kwənt\ *adj* **1** : happening often or at short intervals **2** : HABITUAL, CONSTANT — **fre·quent·ly** *adv*

**²fre·quent** \frē-'kwent, 'frē-kwənt\ *vb* : to associate with, be in, or resort to habitually — **fre·quent·er** *n*

**fres·co** \'fres-kō\ *n, pl* **frescoes** *or* **frescos** : the art of painting on fresh plaster; *also* : a painting done by this method

**fresh** \'fresh\ *adj* **1** : not salt ⟨~ water⟩ **2** : PURE, INVIGORATING **3** : fairly strong : BRISK ⟨~ breeze⟩ **4** : not altered by processing (as freezing or canning) **5** : VIGOROUS, REFRESHED **6** : not stale, sour, or decayed ⟨~ bread⟩ **7** : not faded **8** : not worn or rumpled : SPRUCE **9** : experienced, made, or received newly or anew **10** : ADDITIONAL, ANOTHER ⟨made a ~ start⟩ **11** : ORIGINAL, VIVID **12** : INEXPERIENCED **13** : newly come or arrived ⟨~ from school⟩ **14** : IMPUDENT — **fresh·ly** *adv* — **fresh·ness** *n*

**fresh·en** \'fresh-ən\ *vb* **fresh·ened**; **fresh·en·ing** \-(ə-)niŋ\ : to make, grow, or become fresh

**fresh·et** \'fresh-ət\ *n* : an overflowing of a stream caused by heavy rains or melted snow

**fresh·man** \'fresh-mən\ *n* **1** : NOVICE, NEWCOMER **2** : a student in his first year (as of college)

**fresh·wa·ter** \,fresh-'wȯt-ər, -,wät-\ *adj* **1** : of, relating to, or living in water that is not salt **2** : accustomed to navigation only on fresh water; *also* : UNSKILLED ⟨a ~ sailor⟩

**¹fret** \'fret\ *vb* **fret·ted**; **fret·ting** [ME *freten* to devour, fret, fr. OE *fretan* to devour] **1** : to become irritated : WORRY, VEX **2** : WEAR, CORRODE **3**

: FRAY **4** : to make by wearing away **5** : GRATE, RUB, CHAFE **6** : AGITATE, RIPPLE

**²fret** *n* **1** : EROSION **2** : a worn or eroded spot **3** : IRRITATION

**³fret** *n* : ornamental work esp. of straight lines in symmetrical patterns

**⁴fret** *n* : a metal or ivory ridge across the fingerboard of a stringed musical instrument

**fret·ful** \'fret-fəl\ *adj* **1** : IRRITABLE **2** : TROUBLED ⟨~ waters⟩ **3** : GUSTY ⟨a ~ wind⟩ — **fret·ful·ly** \-ē\ *adv* — **fret·ful·ness** *n*

**fret·saw** \'fret-,sȯ\ *n* : a narrow-bladed saw used for cutting curved outlines

**fret·work** \-,wərk\ *n* **1** : decoration consisting of work adorned with frets **2** : ornamental openwork or work in relief

**Fri** *abbr* Friday

**fri·a·ble** \'frī-ə-bəl\ *adj* : easily pulverized

**fri·ar** \'frī(-ə)r\ *n* [ME *frere*, *fryer*, fr. OF *frere*, lit., brother, fr. L *frater*] : a member of a mendicant religious order

**fri·ary** \'frī(-ə)r-ē\ *n, pl* **-ar·ies** : a monastery of friars

**¹fric·as·see** \'frik-ə-,sē, ,frik-ə-'sē\ *n* : a dish made of meat (as chicken or veal) cut into pieces and stewed in a gravy

**²fricassee** *vb* **-seed**; **-see·ing** : to cook as a fricassee

**fric·tion** \'frik-shən\ *n* **1** : the rubbing of one body against another **2** : the resistance to motion between two surfaces that are touching each other in machinery **3** : clash in opinions between persons or groups : DISAGREEMENT — **fric·tion·al** *adj*

**friction tape** *n* : a usu. cloth tape impregnated with insulating material and an adhesive and used esp. to protect and insulate electrical conductors

**Fri·day** \'frīd-ē\ *n* : the sixth day of the week

**fried·cake** \'frīd-,kāk\ *n* : DOUGHNUT, CRULLER

**friend** \'frend\ *n* **1** : a person attached to another by respect or affection : ACQUAINTANCE **2** : one who is not hostile **3** : one who supports or favors something ⟨a ~ of art⟩ **4** *cap* : a member of the Society of Friends : QUAKER — **friend·less** \'fren-(d)ləs\ *adj* — **friend·li·ness** \'fren-(d)lē-nəs\ *n* — **friend·ly** *adj* — **friend·ship** \'fren(d)-,ship\ *n*

**frieze** \'frēz\ *n* : an ornamental often sculptured band extending around something (as a building or room)

**frig·ate** \'frig-ət\ *n* **1** : a square-rigged warship **2** : a British or Canadian escort ship between a corvette and a destroyer in size **3** : a U.S. warship smaller than a cruiser and larger than a destroyer

**fright** \'frīt\ *n* **1** : sudden terror : ALARM **2** : something that is ugly or shocking

**fright·en** \'frīt-ᵊn\ *vb* **fright·ened**; **fright·en·ing** \'frīt-(ᵊ-)niŋ\ **1** : to make afraid **2 :** to drive away or out by frightening **3 :** to become frightened — **fright·en·ing·ly** *adv*

**fright·ful** \'frīt-fəl\ *adj* **1 :** TERRIFYING **2 :** STARTLING **3 :** EXTREME ⟨~ thirst⟩ — **fright·ful·ly** \-ē\ *adv* — **fright·ful·ness** *n*

**frig·id** \'frij-əd\ *adj* **1 :** intensely cold **2 :** lacking warmth or ardor : INDIFFERENT — **fri·gid·i·ty** \frij-'id-ət-ē\ *n*

**frigid zone** *n* **:** the area or region between the arctic circle and the north pole or between the antarctic circle and the south pole

**frill** \'fril\ *n* **1 :** a gathered, pleated, or ruffled edging **2 :** an ornamental addition **:** something unessential — **frilly** \-ē\ *adj*

**fringe** \'frinj\ *n* **1 :** an ornamental border consisting of short threads or strips hanging from cut or raveled edges or from a separate band **2 :** something that resembles a fringe : BORDER **3 :** something on the margin of an activity, process, or subject matter — **fringe** *vb*

**fringe area** *n* **:** a region in which reception from a broadcasting station is weak or subject to serious distortion

**fringe benefit** *n* **:** an employment benefit paid for by an employer without affecting basic wage rates

**frip·pery** \'frip-(ə-)rē\ *n, pl* **-per·ies** [MF *friperie,* deriv. of ML *faluppa* piece of straw] **1 :** cheap showy finery **2 :** pretentious display

**frisk** \'frisk\ *vb* **1 :** to leap, skip, or dance in a lively or playful way **:** GAMBOL **2 :** to search (a person) esp. for concealed weapons by running the hand rapidly over the clothing

**frisky** \'fris-kē\ *adj* **frisk·i·er; -est :** FROLICSOME — **frisk·i·ly** \'fris-kə-lē\ *adv* - **frisk·i·ness** \-kē-nəs\ *n*

¹**frit·ter** \'frit-ər\ *n* **:** a small quantity of fried or sautéed batter often containing fruit or meat

²**fritter** *vb* **1 :** to reduce or waste piecemeal **2 :** to break into small fragments

**friv·o·lous** \'friv-(ə-)ləs\ *adj* **1 :** of little importance : TRIVIAL **2 :** lacking in seriousness — **fri·vol·i·ty** \friv-'äl-ət-ē\ *n* — **friv·o·lous·ly** *adv*

**frizz** \'friz\ *vb* **:** to curl in small tight curls — **frizz** *n* — **frizzy** *adj*

¹**friz·zle** \'friz-əl\ *vb* **friz·zled; friz·zling** \-(ə-)liŋ\ **:** FRIZZ, CURL — **frizzle** *n* — **friz·zly** \-(ə-)lē\ *adj*

²**frizzle** *vb* **friz·zled; friz·zling 1 :** to fry until crisp and curled **2 :** to cook with a sizzling noise

**fro** \'frō\ *adv* **:** BACK, AWAY — used in the phrase *to and fro*

**frock** \'fräk\ *n* **1 :** an outer garment worn by monks and friars **2 :** an outer garment worn esp. by men **3 :** a woolen jersey worn esp. by sailors **4 :** a woman's or child's dress

**frock coat** *n* **:** a man's usu. double-breasted coat with knee-length skirts

**frog** \'frȯg, 'fräg\ *n* **1 :** a largely aquatic smooth-skinned tailless leaping amphibian **2 :** a soreness in the throat causing hoarseness **3 :** an ornamental

braiding for fastening the front of a garment by a loop through which a button passes **4 :** an arrangement of rails where one railroad track crosses another **5 :** a small holder (as of metal, glass, or plastic) with perforations or spikes that is placed in a bowl or vase to keep cut flowers in position

**frog·man** \'frȯg-,man, 'fräg-, -mən\ *n* **:** a swimmer having equipment (as oxygen helmet and flippers) that permits an extended stay under water usu. for observation or demolition

¹**frol·ic** \'fräl-ik\ *vb* **frol·icked; frol·ick·ing 1 :** to make merry **2 :** to play about happily : ROMP

²**frolic** *n* **1 :** a playful mischievous action **2 :** FUN, MERRIMENT — **frol·ic·some** \-səm\ *adj*

**from** \(')frəm, 'främ\ *prep* **:** forth out of — used to indicate a physical or abstract point of origin or beginning

**frond** \'fränd\ *n* **:** a usu. large divided leaf (as of a fern)

¹**front** \'frənt\ *n* **1 :** FOREHEAD; *also* **:** the whole face **2 :** DEMEANOR, BEARING **3 :** external and often feigned appearance **4 :** a region of active fighting; *also* **:** a sphere of activity **5 :** the side of a building containing the main entrance **6 :** the forward part or surface **7 :** FRONTAGE **8 :** a boundary between two dissimilar masses **9 :** a position directly before or ahead of something else **10 :** a person, group, or thing used to mask the identity or true character or activity of the actual controlling agent — **fron·tal** \'frənt-ᵊl\ *adj*

²**front** *vb* **1 :** FACE **2 :** to serve as a front **3 :** CONFRONT

³**front** *abbr* frontispiece

**front·age** \'frənt-ij\ *n* **1 :** the front face (as of a building) **2 :** the direction in which something faces **3 :** the front boundary line of a lot on a street; *also* **:** the length of such a line

**fron·tier** \,frən-'tiər\ *n* **1 :** a border between two countries **2 :** a region that forms the margin of settled territory in a country being populated **3 :** the outer limits of knowledge or achievement ⟨the ~s of science⟩ — **fron·tiers·man** \-'tiərz-mən\ *n*

**fron·tis·piece** \'frənt-ə-,spēs\ *n* **:** an illustration preceding and usu. facing the title page of a book

**front man** *n* **:** a person serving as a front or figurehead

¹**frost** \'frȯst\ *n* **1 :** freezing temperature **2 :** a covering of minute ice crystals formed on a cold surface from atmospheric vapor — **frosty** *adj*

²**frost** *vb* **1 :** to cover with frost **2 :** to put icing on (as a cake) **3 :** to produce a slightly roughened surface on (as glass) **4 :** to injure or kill by frost **5 :** QUICK-FREEZE ⟨~ed food⟩

**frost·bite** \'frȯs(t)-,bīt\ *n* **:** the freezing or the local effect of a partial freezing of some part of the body — **frost·bit·ten** \-,bit-ᵊn\ *adj*

**frost heave** *n* **:** an upthrust of pavement caused by freezing of moist soil

**frost·ing** \'frȯ-stiŋ\ n 1 : ICING 2 : dull finish on metal or glass

**froth** \'frȯth\ n, pl **froths** \'frȯths, 'frȯthz\ 1 : bubbles formed in or on a liquid by fermentation or agitation 2 : something light or frivolous — **frothy** adj

**frou·frou** \'frü-frü\ 1 : a rustling esp. of a woman's skirts 2 : frilly ornamentation esp. in women's clothing

**fro·ward** \'frō-(w)ərd\ adj : PERVERSE, DISOBEDIENT, WILLFUL

**frown** \'fraün\ vb 1 : to wrinkle the forehead (as in anger, displeasure, or thought) : SCOWL 2 : to look with disapproval 3 : to express with a frown — **frown** n

**frow·sy** also **frow·zy** \'fraü-zē\ adj **frow·si·er** also **frow·zi·er**; **-est** : having a slovenly or uncared-for appearance

**froze** past of FREEZE

**fro·zen** \'frōz-ᵊn\ adj 1 : affected or crusted over by freezing 2 : subject to long and severe cold 3 : CHILLED, REFRIGERATED 4 : expressing or characterized by cold unfriendliness 5 : incapable of being changed, moved, or undone : FIXED ⟨~ wages⟩ 6 : not available for present use ⟨~ capital⟩

**FRS** abbr Federal Reserve System

**frt** abbr freight

**fruc·ti·fy** \'frək-tə-ˌfī, 'frük-\ vb **-fied; -fy·ing** 1 : to bear fruit 2 : to make fruitful or productive

**fru·gal** \'frü-gəl\ adj : ECONOMICAL, THRIFTY — **fru·gal·i·ty** \frü-'gal-ət-ē\ n — **fru·gal·ly** \'frü-gə-lē\ adv

¹**fruit** \'früt\ n [ME, fr. OF, fr. L fructus fruit, use, fr. frui to enjoy, have the use of] 1 : a usu. useful product of plant growth; esp : a usu. edible and sweet reproductive body of a seed plant 2 : a product of fertilization in a plant; esp : the ripe ovary of a seed plant with its contents and appendages 3 : CONSEQUENCE, RESULT — **fruit·ed** \-əd\ adj — **fruit·ful** adj — **fruit·ful·ness** n — **fruit·less** adj

²**fruit** vb : to bear or cause to bear fruit

**fruit·cake** \'früt-ˌkāk\ n : a rich cake containing nuts, dried or candied fruits, and spices

**fruit·er·er** \'früt-ər-ər\ n : one that deals in fruit

**fruit fly** n : any of various small two-winged flies whose larvae feed on fruit or decaying vegetable matter

**fru·ition** \frü-'ish-ən\ n 1 : ENJOYMENT 2 : the state of bearing fruit 3 : REALIZATION, ACCOMPLISHMENT

**fruity** \'früt-ē\ adj **fruit·i·er**; **-est** : resembling a fruit esp. in flavor

**frum·py** \'frəm-pē\ adj **frump·i·er**; **-est** : DRAB, DOWDY

**frus·trate** \'frəs-ˌtrāt\ vb **frus·trat·ed; frus·trat·ing** 1 : to balk in an endeavor : BLOCK 2 : to bring to nothing — **frus·trat·ing·ly** \-iŋ-lē\ adv — **frus·tra·tion** \ˌfrəs-'trā-shən\ n

**frus·tum** \'frəs-təm\ n, pl **frustums** or **frus·ta** \-tə\ : the part of a solid (as a cone) intersected between two usu. parallel planes

**frwy** abbr freeway

¹**fry** \'frī\ vb **fried; fry·ing** 1 : to cook in a pan or on a griddle over a fire esp. with the use of fat 2 : to undergo frying

²**fry** n, pl **fries** 1 : a dish of something fried 2 : a social gathering where fried food is eaten

³**fry** n, pl **fry** 1 : recently hatched fishes; also : very small adult fishes 2 : members of a group or class ⟨small ~⟩

**fry·er** \'frī-(ə)r\ n : something (as a pan) for frying; esp : a young chicken somewhat larger than a broiler

**FSLIC** abbr Federal Savings and Loan Insurance Corporation

**ft** abbr 1 feet; foot 2 fort

**FTC** abbr Federal Trade Commission

**fuch·sia** \'fyü-shə\ n 1 : a shrub grown for its showy nodding often red or purple flowers 2 : a vivid reddish purple

**fud·dle** \'fəd-ᵊl\ vb **fud·dled; fud·dling** : MUDDLE, CONFUSE

**fud·dy-dud·dy** \'fəd-ē-ˌdəd-ē\ n, pl **-dies** : a person who is old-fashioned, pompous, unimaginative, or concerned about trifles

¹**fudge** \'fəj\ vb **fudged; fudg·ing** 1 : to cheat or exaggerate by blurring or overstepping a boundary 2 : to avoid coming to grips with something

²**fudge** n 1 : NONSENSE 2 : a soft creamy candy of milk, sugar, butter, and flavoring

¹**fu·el** \'fyü-əl\ n : a substance (as coal) used to produce heat or power by combustion; also : a substance from which atomic energy can be liberated

²**fuel** vb **-eled** or **-elled; -el·ing** or **-el·ling** : to provide with or take in fuel

**fuel cell** n : a device that continuously changes the chemical energy of a fuel directly into electrical energy

¹**fu·gi·tive** \'fyü-jət-iv\ adj 1 : running away or trying to escape 2 : likely to vanish suddenly : not fixed or lasting

²**fugitive** n 1 : one who flees or tries to escape 2 : something elusive or hard to find

**fugue** \'fyüg\ n 1 : a musical composition in which different parts successively repeat the theme 2 : a disturbed state of consciousness characterized by acts that are not recalled upon recovery

**füh·rer** or **fueh·rer** \'fyùr-ər, 'fir-\ n : LEADER — used chiefly of the leader of the German Nazis

¹**-ful** \fəl\ adj suffix, sometimes **-ful·ler**; sometimes **-ful·lest** 1 : full of ⟨eventful⟩ 2 : characterized by ⟨peaceful⟩ 3 : having the qualities of ⟨masterful⟩ 4 : -ABLE ⟨mournful⟩

²**-ful** \ˌfùl\ n suffix : number or quantity that fills or would fill ⟨roomful⟩

**ful·crum** \'fùl-krəm, 'fəl-\ n, pl **crums** or **ful·cra** \-krə\ [LL, fr. L, bedpost, fr. fulcire to prop] : the support on which a lever turns

**ful·fill** or **ful·fil** \fùl-'fil\ vb **fulfilled; ful·fill·ing** 1 : to put into effect 2 : to bring to an end 3

: SATISFY — **ful·fill·ment** n

**¹full** \'fu̇l\ adj **1** : FILLED **2** : COMPLETE **3** : having all the distinguishing characteristics ⟨a ~ member⟩ **4** : MAXIMUM **5** : rounded in outline **6** : having an abundance of material ⟨a ~ skirt⟩ **7** : possessing or containing an abundance ⟨~ of wrinkles⟩ **8** : rich in detail ⟨a ~ report⟩ **9** : satisfied esp. with food or drink **10** : having volume or depth of sound **11** : completely occupied with a thought or plan — **full·ness** also **ful·ness** \'fu̇l-nəs\ n

**²full** adv **1** : VERY, EXTREMELY **2** : ENTIRELY **3** : EXACTLY **4** : STRAIGHT, SQUARELY ⟨hit him ~ in the face⟩

**³full** n **1** : the utmost extent **2** : the highest or fullest state or degree **3** : the requisite or complete amount

**⁴full** vb : to shrink and thicken (woolen cloth) by moistening, heating, and pressing — **full·er** n

**full·back** \'fu̇l-,bak\ n : a football back stationed between the halfbacks

**full-blood·ed** \'fu̇l-'bləd-əd\ adj : of unmixed ancestry : PUREBRED

**full-blown** \-'blōn\ adj **1** : being at the height of bloom **2** : fully mature or developed

**full-bod·ied** \-'bäd-ēd\ adj : marked by richness and fullness

**full dress** n : the style of dress prescribed for ceremonial or formal social occasions

**full-fledged** \'fu̇l-'flejd\ adj **1** : fully developed : MATURE **2** : having full plumage

**full moon** n : the moon with its whole disk illuminated

**full-scale** \'fu̇l-'skāl\ adj **1** : identical to an original in proportion and size ⟨~ drawing⟩ **2** : involving full use of available resources ⟨a ~ biography⟩

**full tilt** adv : at high speed

**ful·ly** \'fu̇l-(l)ē\ adv **1** : in a full manner or degree : COMPLETELY **2** : at least

**¹ful·mi·nate** \'fu̇l-mə-,nāt, 'fəl-\ vb **-nat·ed; -nat·ing** [ME fulminaten, fr. ML fulminare, fr. L, to flash with lightning, strike with lightning, fr. julmen lightning] **1** : to utter or send out censure or invective : condemn severely **2** : EXPLODE — **ful·mi·na·tion** \,fu̇l-mə-'nā-shən, ,fəl-\ n

**ful·some** \'fu̇l-səm\ adj : offensive esp. from insincerity or baseness of motive : DISGUSTING

**fu·ma·role** \'fyü-mə-,rōl\ n : a hole in a volcanic region from which hot gases issue — **fu·ma·rol·ic** \,fyü-mə-'rō-lik\ adj

**fum·ble** \'fəm-bəl\ vb **fum·bled; fum·bling** \-b(ə-)liŋ\ **1** : to grope about clumsily **2** : to fail to hold, catch, or handle properly — **fumble** n

**¹fume** \'fyüm\ n : a usu. irritating smoke, vapor, or gas

**²fume** vb **fumed; fum·ing 1** : to treat with fumes **2** : to give off fumes **3** : to express anger or annoyance

**fu·mi·gant** \'fyü-mi-gənt\ n : a substance used for fumigation

**fu·mi·gate** \'fyü-mə-,gāt\ vb **-gated; -gating** : to treat with fumes to disinfect or destroy pests — **fu·mi·ga·tion** \,fyü-mə-'gā-shən\ n

**fun** \'fən\ n [E dial. fun to hoax] **1** : something that provides amusement or enjoyment **2** : ENJOYMENT

**¹func·tion** \'fəŋk-shən\ n **1** : OCCUPATION **2** : special purpose **3** : a formal ceremony or social affair **4** : an action contributing to a larger action; esp : the normal contribution of a bodily part to the economy of the organism **5** : a mathematical quantity so related to another quantity that any change in the value of one is associated with a corresponding change in the other — **func·tion·al** \-sh(ə-)nəl\ adj — **func·tion·al·ly** \-ē\ adv — **func·tion·less** adj

**²function** vb **func·tioned; func·tion·ing** \-sh(ə-)niŋ\ **1** : SERVE **2** : OPERATE, WORK

**func·tion·ary** \'fəŋk-shə-,ner-ē\ n, pl **-ar·ies** : one who performs a certain function; esp : OFFICIAL

**function word** n : a word expressing primarily grammatical relationship

**¹fund** \'fənd\ n [L fundus bottom, piece of landed property] **1** : STORE, SUPPLY **2** : a sum of money or resources the income from which is set apart for a special purpose **3** pl : available money **4** : an organization administering a special fund

**²fund** vb **1** : to provide funds for **2** : to convert (a short-term obligation) into a long-term interest-bearing debt

**fun·da·men·tal** \,fən-də-'ment-ᵊl\ adj **1** : serving as an origin : PRIMARY **2** : BASIC, ESSENTIAL **3** : RADICAL ⟨~ change⟩ **4** : of central importance : PRINCIPAL — **fundamental** n — **fun·da·men·tal·ly** \-ē\ adv

**fun·da·men·tal·ism** \-,iz-əm\ n, often cap : a Protestant religious movement emphasizing the literal infallibility of the Scriptures — **fun·da·men·tal·ist** \-əst\ adj or n

**¹fu·ner·al** \'fyün-(ə-)rəl\ adj **1** : of, relating to, or constituting a funeral **2** : FUNEREAL 2

**²funeral** n : the ceremonies held for a dead person usu. before burial

**fu·ner·ary** \'fyü-nə-,rer-ē\ adj : of, used for, or associated with burial

**fu·ne·re·al** \fyù-'nir-ē-əl\ adj **1** : of or relating to a funeral **2** : suggesting a funeral

**fun·gi·cide** \'fən-jə-,sīd, 'fəŋ-gə-\ n : an agent that kills or checks the growth of fungi — **fun·gi·cid·al** \,fən-jə-'sīd-ᵊl, ,fəŋ-gə-\ adj

**fun·gus** \'fəŋ-gəs\ n, pl **fun·gi** \'fən-,jī, 'fəŋ-,gī\ also **fun·gus·es** \'fəŋ-gə-səz\ : any of a large group of lower plants that lack chlorophyll and include molds, mildews, mushrooms, and bacteria — **fun·gal** \-gəl\ adj — **fun·gous** \-gəs\ adj

**fu·nic·u·lar** \fyù-'nik-yə-lər, fə-\ n : a cable railway ascending a mountain; esp : one in which an ascending car counterbalances a descending car

**funk** \'fəŋk\ n : a state of paralyzed fear : PANIC

**funky** \ˈfəŋ-kē\ adj **funk·i·er; -est** : having an earthy, unsophisticated style and feeling; esp : having the style and feeling of blues

¹**fun·nel** \ˈfən-ᵊl\ n 1 : a cone-shaped utensil with a tube used for catching and directing a downward flow (as of liquid) 2 : FLUE, SMOKESTACK

²**funnel** vb **-neled** also **-nelled; -nel·ing** also **-nel·ling** 1 : to pass through or as if through a funnel 2 : to move to a central point or into a central channel

¹**fun·ny** \ˈfən-ē\ adj **fun·ni·er; -est** 1 : AMUSING 2 : FACETIOUS 3 : QUEER 4 : UNDERHANDED

²**funny** n, pl **funnies** : a comic strip or a comic section (as of a newspaper)

**funny bone** n : a place at the back of the elbow where a blow compresses a nerve and causes a painful tingling sensation

¹**fur** \ˈfər\ n 1 : the hairy coat of a mammal esp. when fine, soft, and thick; also : this coat dressed for human use 2 : an article of clothing made of or with fur — **fur** adj — **furred** \ˈfərd\ adj

²**fur** abbr furlong

**fur·be·low** \ˈfər-bə-ˌlō\ n 1 : FLOUNCE, RUFFLE 2 : showy trimming

**fur·bish** \ˈfər-bish\ vb 1 : to make lustrous : POLISH 2 : to give a new look to : RENOVATE

**fu·ri·ous** \ˈfyur-ē-əs\ adj 1 : FIERCE, ANGRY, VIOLENT 2 : BOISTEROUS 3 : INTENSE — **fu·ri·ous·ly** adv

**furl** \ˈfərl\ vb 1 : to wrap or roll (as a sail or a flag) close to or around something 2 : to curl or fold in furls — **furl** n

**fur·long** \ˈfər-ˌlȯŋ\ n : a unit of length equal to 220 yards

**fur·lough** \ˈfər-lō\ n : a leave of absence from duty granted esp. to a soldier — **furlough** vb

**fur·nace** \ˈfər-nəs\ n : an enclosed structure in which heat is produced

**fur·nish** \ˈfər-nish\ vb 1 : to provide with what is needed : EQUIP 2 : SUPPLY, GIVE

**fur·nish·ings** \-iŋs\ n pl 1 : articles or accessories of dress 2 : FURNITURE

**fur·ni·ture** \ˈfər-ni-chər\ n : equipment that is necessary, useful, or desirable; esp : movable articles (as chairs, tables, or beds) for a room

**fu·ror** \ˈfyur-ˌȯr\ n 1 : ANGER, RAGE 2 : a contagious excitement; esp : a fashionable craze 3 : UPROAR

**fu·rore** \-ˌȯr\ n : FUROR 2, 3

**fur·ri·er** \ˈfər-ē-ər\ n : one who prepares or deals in fur — **fur·ri·ery** \-ə-rē\ n

**fur·ring** \ˈfər-iŋ\ n : wood or metal strips applied to a wall or ceiling to form a level surface or an air space

**fur·row** \ˈfər-ō\ n 1 : a trench in earth made by or as if by a plow 2 : a narrow groove (as a wrinkle) — **furrow** vb

**fur·ry** \ˈfər-ē\ adj **fur·ri·er; -est** 1 : resembling or consisting of fur 2 : covered with fur

¹**fur·ther** \ˈfər-thər\ adv 1 : ¹FARTHER 1 2 : in addition : MOREOVER 3 : to a greater extent or degree

²**further** adj 1 : ²FARTHER 1 2 : ADDITIONAL

³**further** vb **fur·thered; fur·ther·ing** \ˈfərth-(ə-)riŋ\ : to help forward — **fur·ther·ance** \ˈfərth-(ə-)rəns\ n

**fur·ther·more** \ˈfər-thə(r)-ˌmȯr\ adv : in addition to what precedes : BESIDES

**fur·ther·most** \-thər-ˌmōst\ adj : most distant : FARTHEST

**fur·thest** \ˈfər-thəst\ adv or adj : FARTHEST

**fur·tive** \ˈfərt-iv\ adj [F or L; F furtif, fr. L furtivus, fr. furtum theft, fr. fur thief] : done by stealth : SLY — **fur·tive·ly** adv — **fur·tive·ness** n

**fu·ry** \ˈfyur-ē\ n, pl **furies** 1 : violent anger : RAGE 2 : extreme fierceness or violence 3 : FRENZY

**furze** \ˈfərz\ n : a common spiny evergreen Old World shrub with yellow flowers

¹**fuse** \ˈfyüz\ n 1 : a tube filled with something flammable and lighted to transmit fire to an explosive 2 usu **fuze** : a mechanical or electrical device for exploding the bursting charge of a projectile, bomb, or torpedo

²**fuse** or **fuze** \ˈfyüz\ vb **fused** or **fuzed; fus·ing** or **fuz·ing** : to equip with a fuse

³**fuse** vb **fused; fus·ing** 1 : MELT 2 : to unite by or as if by melting together — **fus·ible** adj

⁴**fuse** n : an electrical safety device in which metal melts and interrupts the circuit when the current becomes too strong

**fu·see** \fyu̇-ˈzē\ n 1 : a friction match with a bulbous head not easily blown out 2 : a red signal flare used esp. for protecting stalled trains and trucks

**fu·se·lage** \ˈfyü-sə-ˌläzh, -zə-\ n : the central body portion of an airplane that holds the crew, passengers, and cargo

**fu·sil·lade** \ˈfyü-sə-ˌläd, -ˌlād; ˌfyü-sə-ˌläd, -ˈläd; -zə-\ n : a number of shots fired simultaneously or in rapid succession

**fu·sion** \ˈfyü-zhən\ n 1 : the process of melting or melting together 2 : a merging by or as if by melting together 3 : the union of atomic nuclei to form heavier nuclei with the release of huge quantities of energy

¹**fuss** \ˈfəs\ n 1 : needless bustle or excitement : COMMOTION 2 : effusive praise 3 : a state of agitation 4 : OBJECTION, PROTEST 5 : DISPUTE

²**fuss** vb 1 : to create or be in a state of restless activity; esp : to shower flattering attention 2 : to pay undue attention to small details 3 : WORRY

**fuss·bud·get** \ˈfəs-ˌbəj-ət\ n : one who fusses about trifles

**fussy** \ˈfəs-ē\ adj **fuss·i·er; -est** 1 : IRRITABLE 2 : requiring or giving close attention to details 3 : revealing a concern for niceties : FASTIDIOUS ⟨not ~ about food⟩ — **fuss·i·ly** \ˈfəs-ə-lē\ adv — **fuss·i·ness** \-ē-nəs\ n

**fus·tian** \ˈfəs-chən\ n 1 : a strong cotton and linen cloth **2 :** pretentious writing or speech

**fus·ty** \'fəs-tē\ adj [ME, fr. just wine cask, fr. MF club, cask, fr. L justis] **1 :** MOLDY, MUSTY **2 :** OLD-FASHIONED

**fut** abbr future

**fu·tile** \'fyüt-ᵊl, 'fyü-,tīl\ adj **1 :** USE-LESS, VAIN **2 :** FRIVOLOUS, TRIVIAL — **fu·til·i·ty** \fyü-'til-ət-ē\ n

**¹fu·ture** \'fyü-chər\ adj **1 :** coming after the present **2 :** of, relating to, or constituting a verb tense that expresses time yet to come

**²future** n **1 :** time that is to come **2 :** what is going to happen **3 :** an expectation of advancement or progressive development **4 :** the future tense; also **:** a verb form in it

**fu·tur·ism** \'fyü-chə-,riz-əm\ n **:** a modern movement in art, music, and literature that tries esp. to express the energy and activity of contemporary life — **fu·tur·ist** \'fyüch-(ə-)rəst\ n

**fu·tur·is·tic** \,fyü-chə-'ris-tik\ adj **:** of or relating to the future or to futurism

**fu·tu·ri·ty** \fyü-'t(y)ür-ət-ē\ n, pl **-ties** **1 :** FUTURE **2 :** the quality or state of being future **3** pl **:** future events or prospects

**fuze, fu·zee** var of FUSE, FUSEE

**fuzz** \'fəz\ n **:** fine light particles or fibers (as of down or fluff)

**fuzzy** \'fəz-ē\ adj **fuzz·i·er; -est 1** **:** covered with or resembling fuzz **2** **:** INDISTINCT — **fuzz·i·ness** \'fəz-ē-nəs\ n

**fwd** abbr forward

**FWD** abbr front-wheel drive

**FY** abbr fiscal year

**-fy** \,fī\ vb suffix **1 :** make **:** form into ⟨dandify⟩ **2 :** invest with the attributes of **:** make similar to ⟨citify⟩ — **-fi·er** \-fī(-ə)r\ n suffix

**FYI** abbr for your information

---

**¹g** \'jē\ n, pl **g's** or **gs** \'jēz\ often cap **1 :** the 7th letter of the English alphabet **2 :** a unit of force equal to the force exerted by gravity on a body at rest and used to indicate the force to which a body is subjected when accelerated **3 :** a sum of $1000

**²g** abbr, often cap **1** game **2** gauge **3** German **4** good **5** gram **6** gravity

**ga** abbr gauge

**¹Ga** abbr Georgia

**²Ga** symbol gallium

**GA** abbr **1** general assembly **2** general average **3** general of the army **4** Georgia

**gab** \'gab\ vb **gabbed; gab·bing :** to talk in a rapid or thoughtless manner **:** CHATTER — **gab** n

**gab·ar·dine** \'gab-ər-,dēn\ n **1 :** GABERDINE **2 :** a firm durable twilled fabric having diagonal ribs and made of various fibers; also **:** a garment of gabardine

**gab·ble** \'gab-əl\ vb **gab·bled; gab·bling** \-(ə-)liŋ\ **:** JABBER, BABBLE

**gab·bro** \'gab-rō\ n, pl **gabbros :** a granular igneous rock rich in magnesium — **gab·bro·ic** \ga-'brō-ik\ adj

**gab·by** \'gab-ē\ adj **gab·bi·er; -est :** TALKATIVE, GARRULOUS

**gab·er·dine** \'gab-ər-,dēn\ n **1 :** a long coat or smock worn chiefly by Jews in medieval times **2 :** an English laborer's smock **3 :** GABARDINE

**gab·fest** \'gab-,fest\ n **1 :** an informal gathering for general talk **2 :** an extended conversation

**ga·ble** \'gā-bəl\ n **:** the triangular part of the end of a building formed by the sides of the roof sloping from the ridgepole down to the eaves — **ga·bled** \-bəld\ adj

**gad** \'gad\ vb **gad·ded; gad·ding :** to roam about **:** wander restlessly and without purpose — **gad·der** n

**gad·about** \'gad-ə-,baut\ n **:** a person who flits about in social activity

**gad·fly** \'gad-,flī\ n **1 :** a fly that bites or harasses (as livestock) **2 :** a usu.

intentionally annoying and persistently critical person

**gad·get** \'gaj-ət\ n **:** DEVICE, CONTRIVANCE — **gad·ge·teer** \,gaj-ə-'tiər\ n — **gad·get·ry** \'gaj-ə-trē\ n

**gad·o·lin·i·um** \,gad-ᵊl-'in-ē-əm\ n **:** a magnetic metallic chemical element

**¹Gael** \'gāl\ n **:** a Celtic inhabitant of Ireland or Scotland

**²Gael** abbr Gaelic

**Gael·ic** \'gāl-ik\ adj **:** of or relating to the Gaels or their languages — **Gaelic** n

**gaff** \'gaf\ n **1 :** a spear used in taking fish or turtles; also **:** a metal hook for holding or lifting heavy fish **2 :** the spar along the top of a fore-and-aft sail **3 :** rough treatment **:** ABUSE — **gaff** vb

**gaffe** \'gaf\ n **:** a social blunder

**gaf·fer** \'gaf-ər\ n **:** an old man

**¹gag** \'gag\ vb **gagged; gag·ging 1** **:** to prevent from speaking or crying out by stopping up the mouth **2 :** to prevent from speaking freely **3 :** to retch or cause to retch **4 :** OBSTRUCT, CHOKE **5 :** BALK **6 :** to make quips

**²gag** n **1 :** something thrust into the mouth esp. to prevent speech or outcry **2 :** a check to free speech **3 :** a laugh-provoking remark or act **4 :** HOAX, TRICK

**¹gage** \'gāj\ n **1 :** a token of defiance; esp **:** a glove or cap cast on the ground as a pledge of combat **2 :** SECURITY

**²gage** var of GAUGE

**gag·gle** \'gag-əl\ n [ME gagyll, fr. gagelen to cackle] **1 :** a flock of geese **2 :** GROUP, CLUSTER

**gai·ety** \'gā-ət-ē\ n, pl **-eties 1 :** MERRYMAKING **2 :** MERRIMENT **3 :** FINERY

**gai·ly** \'gā-lē\ adv **:** in a gay manner

**¹gain** \'gān\ n **1 :** PROFIT, ADVANTAGE **2 :** ACQUISITION, ACCUMULATION **3** **:** INCREASE

**²gain** vb **1 :** to get possession of **:** EARN **2 :** WIN ⟨∼ a victory⟩ **3 :** ACHIEVE ⟨∼ strength⟩ **4 :** to arrive at **5 :** PERSUADE **6 :** to increase in ⟨∼ momentum⟩ **7 :** to run fast ⟨the watch ∼s a minute a day⟩ **8 :** PROFIT **9 :** INCREASE

**10 :** to improve in health — **gain·er** n
**gain·ful** \'gān-fəl\ adj **:** PROFITABLE — **gain·ful·ly** \-ē\ adv
**gain·say** \gān-'sā\ vb **-said** \-'sād, -'sed\; **-say·ing** \-'sā-iŋ\; **-says** \-'sāz, -'sez\ **1 :** DENY, DISPUTE **2 :** to speak against — **gain·say·er** n
**gait** \'gāt\ n **:** manner of moving on foot; also **:** a particular pattern or style of such moving — **gait·ed** \-əd\ adj
**gai·ter** \'gāt-ər\ n **1 :** a leg covering reaching from the instep to ankle, mid calf, or knee **2 :** an ankle-high shoe with elastic gores in the sides **3 :** an overshoe with a fabric upper
¹**gal** \'gal\ n **:** GIRL
²**gal** abbr gallon
**Gal** abbr Galatians
**ga·la** \'gā-lə, 'gal-ə, 'gäl-ə\ n **:** a gay celebration **:** FESTIVITY — **gala** adj
**ga·lac·tose** \gə-'lak-,tōs\ n **:** a sugar less soluble and less sweet than glucose
**gal·axy** \'gal-ək-sē\ n, pl **-ax·ies** [ME galaxie, galaxias, fr. LL galaxias, fr. Gk, fr. galakt-, gala milk] **1** often cap **:** MILKY WAY GALAXY **2 :** one of billions of systems each including stars, nebulae, and dust that make up the universe **3 :** an assemblage of brilliant or famous persons or things — **ga·lac·tic** \gə-'lak-tik\ adj
**gale** \'gāl\ n **1 :** a strong wind **2 :** an emotional outburst (as of laughter)
**ga·le·na** \gə-'lē-nə\ n **:** a bluish gray mineral with metallic luster consisting of sulfide of lead
¹**gall** \'gól\ n **1 :** BILE **2 :** something bitter to endure **3 :** RANCOR **4 :** IMPUDENCE
²**gall** n **:** a sore on the skin caused by chafing
³**gall** vb **1 :** CHAFE; esp **:** to become sore or worn by rubbing **2 :** VEX, HARASS
⁴**gall** n **:** a swelling of plant tissue caused by parasites (as fungi or mites)
¹**gal·lant** \gə-'lant, gə-'länt, 'gal-ənt\ **1 :** a young man of fashion **2 :** a man who shows a marked fondness for the company of women and who is esp. attentive to them **3 :** SUITOR
²**gal·lant** \'gal-ənt (usual for 2, 3, 4); gə-'lant, gə-'länt (usual for 5)\ adj **1 :** showy in dress or bearing **:** SMART **2 :** SPLENDID, STATELY **3 :** SPIRITED; BRAVE **4 :** CHIVALROUS, NOBLE **5 :** polite and attentive to women — **gal·lant·ly** adv
**gal·lant·ry** \'gal-ən-trē\ n, pl **-ries 1** archaic **:** gallant appearance **2 :** an act of marked courtesy **3 :** courteous attention to a woman **4 :** conspicuous bravery
**gall·blad·der** \'gól-,blad-ər\ n **:** a pouch attached to the liver in which bile is stored
**gal·le·on** \'gal-ē-ən\ n **:** a former sailing vessel used for war or commerce esp. by the Spanish
**gal·lery** \'gal-(ə)-rē\ n, pl **-ler·ies 1 :** an outdoor balcony; also **:** PORCH, VERANDA **2 :** a balcony in a theater, auditorium, or church; esp **:** the highest one in a theater **3 :** a body of spectators (as at a tennis match) **4 :** a long

narrow room or hall; esp **:** one with windows along one side **5 :** a narrow passage (as one made underground by a miner or through wood by an insect) **6 :** a room where works of art are exhibited; also **:** an organization dealing in works of art **7 :** a photographer's studio — **gal·ler·ied** \-rēd\ adj
**gal·ley** \'gal-ē\ n, pl **galleys 1 :** a former ship propelled by both oars and sails **2 :** the kitchen of a ship, airplane, or trailer **3 :** a tray to hold printer's type that has been set; also **:** proof from type in such a tray
**Gal·lic** \'gal-ik\ adj **:** of or relating to Gaul or France
**gal·li·mau·fry** \,gal-ə-'mó-frē\ n, pl **-fries** [MF galimafree hash] **:** MEDLEY, JUMBLE
**gal·li·nule** \'gal-ə-,n(y)ü(ə)l\ n **:** any of several aquatic birds related to the rails
**gal·li·um** \'gal-ē-əm\ n **:** a rare bluish white metallic chemical element
**gal·li·vant** \'gal-ə-,vant\ vb **:** to go roaming about for pleasure
**gal·lon** \'gal-ən\ n — see WEIGHT table
**gal·lop** \'gal-əp\ n **:** a springing gait of a quadruped; esp **:** a fast 3-beat gait of a horse — **gal·lop** vb — **gal·lop·er** n
**gal·lows** \'gal-ōz\ n, pl **gallows** or **gal·lows·es 1 :** a frame usu. of two upright posts and a crosspiece from which criminals are hanged **2 :** a structure consisting of an upright frame with a crossbar
**gall·stone** \'gól-,stōn\ n **:** an abnormal concretion occurring in the gallbladder or bile passages
**gal·lus·es** \'gal-ə-səz\ n pl, chiefly dial **:** SUSPENDERS
**ga·lore** \gə-'lōr\ adj [IrGael go leor enough] **:** ABUNDANT, PLENTIFUL
**ga·losh** \gə-'läsh\ n **:** a high overshoe
**galv** abbr galvanized
**gal·va·nism** \'gal-və-,niz-əm\ n **:** electricity produced by chemical action — **gal·van·ic** \gal-'van-ik\ adj
**gal·va·nize** \'gal-və-,nīz\ vb **-nized; -niz·ing 1 :** to stimulate as if by an electric shock **2 :** to coat (iron or steel) with zinc — **gal·va·ni·za·tion** \,gal-və-nə-'zā-shən\ n — **gal·va·niz·er** \'gal-və-,nī-zər\ n
**gal·va·nom·e·ter** \,gal-və-'näm-ət-ər\ n **:** an instrument for detecting or measuring a small electric current — **gal·va·no·met·ric** \,gal-və-nō-'met-rik\ adj
**Gam·bi·an** \'gam-bē-ən\ n **:** a native or inhabitant of Gambia — **Gambian** adj
**gam·bit** \'gam-bət\ n [It gambetto, lit., act of tripping someone, fr. gamba leg, fr. LL] **1 :** a chess opening in which a player risks one or more minor pieces to gain an advantage in position **2 :** a calculated move **:** STRATAGEM
¹**gam·ble** \'gam-bəl\ vb **gam·bled; gam·bling** \-b(ə-)liŋ\ **1 :** to play a game for money or other stakes **2 :** SPECULATE, BET, WAGER **3 :** VENTURE, HAZARD — **gam·bler** \-blər\ n
²**gamble** n **:** a risky undertaking
**gam·bol** \'gam-bəl\ vb **-boled** or

-bolled; -bol·ing or -bol·ling \-b(ə-)liŋ\ : to skip about in play : FRISK — gambol n

gam·brel roof \,gam-brəl-\ n : a roof with a lower steeper slope and an upper flatter one on each side

¹game \'gām\ n 1 : AMUSEMENT, DIVERSION 2 : SPORT, FUN 3 : SCHEME, PROJECT 4 : a line of work : PROFESSION 5 : CONTEST 6 : animals hunted for sport or food; also : the flesh of a game animal

²game vb gamed; gam·ing : to play for a stake : GAMBLE

³game adj : PLUCKY — game·ly adv — game·ness n

⁴game adj : LAME ⟨a ~ leg⟩

game·cock \'gām-,käk\ n : a male domestic fowl of a strain bred to produce fighting cocks

game fish n : SPORT FISH

game·keep·er \'gām-,kē-pər\ n : one that has charge of the breeding and protection of game animals or birds on a private preserve

game·some \'gām-səm\ adj : GAY, FROLICSOME

game·ster \'gām-stər\ n : GAMBLER

ga·mete \gə-'mēt, 'gam-,ēt\ n : a matured germ cell — ga·met·ic \gə-'met-ik\ adj

game theory n : THEORY OF GAMES

gam·in \'gam-ən\ n 1 : a boy who roams the streets 2 : GAMINE 2

ga·mine \ga-'mēn\ n 1 : a girl who roams the streets : TOMBOY 2 : a girl of elfin appeal

gam·ma globulin \'gam-ə-\ n : a blood protein fraction rich in antibodies

gamma ray n : a quantum of penetrating radiation of the same nature as X rays but of shorter wavelength

gam·mer \'gam-ər\ n : an old woman

¹gam·mon \'gam-ən\ n : a cured ham or side of bacon

²gammon n : deceptive talk : HUMBUG

gam·ut \'gam-ət\ n [ML gamma, lowest note of a medieval scale (fr. LL, 3d letter of the Greek alphabet) + ut, lowest of each series of six tones in the scale] : an entire range or series

gamy or gam·ey \'gā-mē\ adj gam·i·er; -est 1 : GAME, PLUCKY 2 : having the flavor of game esp when slightly tainted ⟨~ meat⟩ 3 : SCANDALOUS; also : DISREPUTABLE — gam·i·ness \-mē-nəs\ n

¹gan·der \'gan-dər\ n : a male goose

²gander n : LOOK, GLANCE

¹gang \'gaŋ\ n 1 : a group of persons working or associated together; esp : a group of criminals or young delinquents 2 : a set of implements or devices arranged to operate together

²gang vb 1 : to attack in a gang — usu. used with up 2 : to form into or move or act as a gang

gang·land \'gaŋ-,land\ n : the world of organized crime

gan·gling \'gaŋ-gliŋ\ adj : LANKY, SPINDLING

gan·gli·on \'gaŋ-glē-ən\ n, pl -glia \-glē-ə\ also -gli·ons : a mass of nerve cells : a nerve center either in or outside of the brain — gan·gli·on·ic \,gaŋ-glē-'än-ik\ adj

gang·plank \'gaŋ-,plaŋk\ n : a movable platform used in boarding or leaving a ship

gang·plow \-,plaů\ n : a plow designed to turn two or more furrows at one time

gan·grene \'gaŋ-,grēn, gaŋ-'grēn; 'gan-,grēn, gan-'grēn\ n : the dying of a part of the body due to interference with its nutrition — gangrene vb — gan·gre·nous \'gaŋ-grə-nəs\ adj

gang·ster \'gaŋ-stər\ n : a member of a gang of criminals : RACKETEER

gang·way \'gaŋ-,wā\ n 1 : a passage into, through, or out of an enclosed place 2 : GANGPLANK

gan·net \'gan-ət\ n, pl gannets also gannet : any of several large fish-eating usu. white and black marine birds that breed on offshore islands

gant·let \'gónt-lət\ var of GAUNTLET

gan·try \'gan-trē\ n, pl gantries : a frame structure on side supports over or around something

GAO abbr General Accounting Office

gaol \'jāl\ chiefly Brit var of JAIL

gap \'gap\ n 1 : BREACH, CLEFT 2 : a mountain pass 3 : a blank space

gape \'gāp, 'gap\ vb gaped; gap·ing 1 : to open the mouth wide 2 : to open or part widely 3 : to stare with mouth open 4 : YAWN — gape n

¹gar \'gär\ n : any of several fishes that have a long body resembling that of a pike and long narrow jaws

²gar abbr garage

GAR abbr Grand Army of the Republic

¹ga·rage \gə-'räzh, -'räj\ n : a building for housing or repairing automobiles

²garage vb ga·raged; ga·rag·ing : to keep or put in a garage

garage sale n : a sale of discarded household articles held on one's own premises

¹garb \'gärb\ n 1 : style of dress 2 : CLOTHING, DRESS

²garb vb : CLOTHE, ARRAY

gar·bage \'gär-bij\ n 1 : food waste 2 : unwanted or useless material

gar·ble \'gär-bəl\ vb gar·bled; gar·bling \-b(ə-)liŋ\ [ME garbelen, fr. It garbellare to sift, fr. Ar ghirbāl sieve, fr. LL cribellum] : to distort the meaning or sound of ⟨~ a story⟩ ⟨~ words⟩

gar·çon \gär-'sōⁿ\ n, pl garçons \-'sōⁿ(z)\ : WAITER

¹gar·den \'gärd-ᵊn\ n 1 : a plot for growing fruits, flowers, or vegetables 2 : a fertile region 3 : a public recreation area; esp : one for displaying plants or animals

²garden vb gar·dened; gar·den·ing \'gärd-(ᵊ-)niŋ\ : to develop or work in a garden — gar·den·er \'gärd-(ᵊ-)nər\ n

gar·de·nia \gär-'dē-nyə\ n [NL, genus name, fr. Alexander Garden d1791 Sc naturalist] : a leathery-leaved tree or shrub with fragrant white or yellow flowers; also : its flowers

garden–variety adj : COMMONPLACE, ORDINARY

**gar·fish** \'gär-ˌfish\ n : GAR

**gar·gan·tuan** \gär-'ganch-(ə-)wən\ adj, often cap : of tremendous size or volume

**gar·gle** \'gär-gəl\ vb **gar·gled; gar·gling** \-g(ə-)liŋ\ : to rinse the throat with liquid agitated by air forced through it from the lungs — **gargle** n

**gar·goyle** \'gär-ˌgȯil\ n 1 : a waterspout in the form of a grotesque human or animal figure projecting from the roof or eaves of a building 2 : a grotesquely carved figure

**gar·ish** \'ga(ə)r-ish\ adj : FLASHY, GLARING, SHOWY, GAUDY

¹**gar·land** \'gär-lənd\ n : a wreath or rope of leaves or flowers

²**garland** vb : to form into or deck with a garland

**gar·lic** \'gär-lik\ n [ME garlek, fr. OE gārlēac, fr. gār spear + lēac leek] : an herb related to the lilies and grown for its pungent bulbs used in cooking; also : its bulb - **gar·licky** \-li-kē\ adj

**gar·ment** \'gär-mənt\ n : an article of clothing

**gar·ner** \'gär-nər\ vb **gar·nered; gar·ner·ing** \'gärn-(ə-)riŋ\ 1 : to gather into storage 2 : to acquire by effort 3 : ACCUMULATE, COLLECT

**gar·net** \'gär-nət\ n [ME grenat, fr. MF, fr. grenat, adj., red like a pomegranate, fr. (pomme) grenate pomegranate] : a transparent deep red mineral sometimes used as a gem

**gar·nish** \'gär-nish\ vb 1 : DECORATE, EMBELLISH 2 : to add decorative or savory touches to (food) — **garnish** n

**gar·nish·ee** \ˌgär-nə-'shē\ vb **-eed; -ee·ing** 1 : to serve with a garnishment 2 : to take (as a debtor's wages) by legal authority

**gar·nish·ment** \'gär-nish-mənt\ n 1 : GARNISH 2 : a legal warning to a party holding property of a debtor to give it to a creditor; also : the attachment of such property to satisfy a creditor

**gar·ni·ture** \-ni-chər, -nə-ˌchù(ə)r\ n : EMBELLISHMENT, TRIMMING

**gar·ret** \'gar-ət\ n [ME garette watchtower, fr. MF garite] : the part of a house just under the roof : ATTIC

**gar·ri·son** \'gar-ə-sən\ n 1 : a military post; esp : a permanent military installation 2 : the troops stationed at a garrison — **garrison** vb

**garrison state** n : a state organized on a primarily military basis

**gar·rote** or **ga·rotte** \gə-'rät, -'rōt\ n 1 : a method of execution by strangling with an iron collar; also : the iron collar used 2 : strangulation esp. for the purpose of robbery; also : an implement for this purpose — **garrote** or **garotte** vb

**gar·ru·lous** \'gar-ə-ləs\ adj : CHATTERING, TALKATIVE, WORDY — **gar·ru·li·ty** \gə-'rü-lət-ē\ n — **gar·ru·lous·ly** \'gar-ə-ləs-lē\ adv — **gar·ru·lous·ness** n

**gar·ter** \'gärt-ər\ n : a band or strap worn to hold up a stocking or sock

**garter snake** n : any of numerous

harmless American snakes with longitudinal stripes on the back

¹**gas** \'gas\ n, pl **gas·es** also **gas·ses** [NL, alter. of L chaos space, chaos] 1 : a fluid (as hydrogen or air) that tends to expand indefinitely 2 : a gas or mixture of gases used as a fuel or anesthetic 3 : a substance that can be used to produce a poisonous, asphyxiating, or irritant atmosphere 4 : GASOLINE — **gas** vb — **gas·eous** \-ē-əs, 'gash-əs\ adj

²**gas** vb **gassed; gas·sing** 1 : to treat with gas; also : to poison with gas 2 : to fill with gasoline

**gash** \'gash\ n : a deep long cut — **gash** vb

**gas·ket** \'gas-kət\ n : material (as asbestos, rubber, or metal) used to seal a joint against leakage of fluid

**gas·light** \'gas-ˌlīt\ n 1 : light made by burning illuminating gas 2 : a gas flame; also : a gas lighting fixture

**gas mask** n : RESPIRATOR 1

**gas·o·line** or **gas·o·lene** \'gas-ə-ˌlēn, ˌgas-ə-'lēn\ n : a flammable liquid made esp. by blending products from natural gas and petroleum and used as a motor fuel

**gasp** \'gasp\ vb 1 : to catch the breath with emotion (as shock) 2 : to breathe laboriously : PANT 3 : to utter in a gasping manner — **gasp** n

**gas·tric** \'gas-trik\ adj : of, relating to, or located near the stomach

**gastric juice** n : the acid digestive secretion of the stomach

**gas·tri·tis** \gas-'trīt-əs\ n : inflammatory disorder of the stomach

**gas·tro·en·ter·ol·o·gy** \ˌgas-trō-ˌent-ə-'räl-ə-jē\ n : a branch of medicine dealing with the alimentary canal — **gas·tro·en·ter·ol·o·gist** \-jəst\ n

**gas·tro·in·tes·ti·nal** \ˌgas-trō-in-'test-ən-ᵊl\ adj : of, relating to, or including both stomach and intestine

**gas·tron·o·my** \gas-'trän-ə-mē\ n [F gastronomie, fr. Gk Gastronomia, title of a 4th cent. B.C. poem, fr. gastēr belly] : the art of good eating — **gas·tro·nom·ic** \ˌgas-trə-'näm-ik\ also **gas·tro·nom·i·cal** \-i-kəl\ adj

**gas·tro·pod** \'gas-trə-ˌpäd\ n : any of a large group of mollusks (as snails, whelks, and slugs) with a muscular foot and a shell of one valve

**gas·works** \'gas-ˌwərks\ n pl : a plant for manufacturing gas

**gate** \'gāt\ n 1 : an opening for passage in a wall or fence 2 : a city or castle entrance often with defensive structures 3 : the frame or door that closes a gate 4 : a device (as a door or valve) for controlling the passage of a fluid or signal 5 : the total admission receipts or the number of spectators at a sports event

**gate–crash·er** \'gāt-ˌkrash-ər\ n : one who enters without paying admission or attends without invitation

**gate·keep·er** \-ˌkē-pər\ n : a person who tends or guards a gate

**gate·post** \'gāt-ˌpōst\ n : the post to which a gate is hung or the one against which it closes

**gate·way** \-,wā\ *n* **1** : an opening for a gate in a wall or fence **2** : a passage into or out of a place or state

**¹gath·er** \'gath-ər\ *vb* **gath·ered; gath·er·ing** \-(ə-)riŋ\ **1** : to bring together : COLLECT **2** : PICK, HARVEST **3** : to pick up little by little **4** : to gain or win by gradual increase ⟨~ speed⟩ **5** : ACCUMULATE **6** : to summon up ⟨~ courage to dive⟩ **7** : to draw about or close to something **8** : to pull (fabric) along a line of stitching into puckers **9** : GUESS, DEDUCE, INFER **10** : ASSEMBLE **11** : to swell out and fill with pus **12** : GROW, INCREASE — **gath·er·er** — **gath·er·ing** *n*

**²gather** *n* : a puckering in cloth made by gathering

**GATT** *abbr* General Agreement on Tariffs and Trade

**gauche** \'gōsh\ *adj* [F, lit., left] : lacking social experience or grace

**gau·che·rie** \,gōsh-(ə-)'rē\ *n* : a tactless or awkward action

**gau·cho** \'gaù-chō\ *n, pl* **gauchos** : a cowboy of the So. American pampas

**gaud** \'gȯd\ *n* : ORNAMENT, TRINKET

**gaudy** \'gȯd-ē\ *adj* **gaud·i·er; -est** : ostentatiously or tastelessly ornamented **syn** garish, flashy — **gaud·i·ly** \'gȯd-ᵊl-ē\ *adv* — **gaud·i·ness** \-ē-nəs\ *n*

**¹gauge** \'gāj\ *n* **1** : measurement according to some standard or system **2** : DIMENSIONS, SIZE **3** : an instrument for measuring, testing, or registering

**²gauge** *vb* **gauged; gaug·ing 1** : MEASURE **2** : to determine the capacity or contents of **3** : ESTIMATE, JUDGE

**gaunt** \'gȯnt\ *adj* **1** : being thin and angular : LANK, HAGGARD **2** : GRIM, BARREN, DESOLATE — **gaunt·ness** *n*

**¹gaunt·let** \'gȯnt-lət\ *n* **1** : a protective glove **2** : a challenge to combat **3** : a dress glove extending above the wrist

**²gauntlet** *n* **1** : a double file of men armed with weapons (as clubs) with which to strike at an individual who is made to run between them **2** : ORDEAL

**gauss** \'gaùs\ *n, pl* **gauss** *also* **gauss·es** : the cgs unit of magnetic induction

**gauze** \'gȯz\ *n* : a very thin often transparent fabric used esp. for draperies and surgical dressings — **gauzy** *adj*

**gave** *past of* GIVE

**gav·el** \'gav-əl\ *n* : the mallet of a presiding officer or auctioneer

**ga·votte** \gə-'vät\ *n* : a dance of French peasant origin marked by the raising rather than sliding of the feet

**GAW** *abbr* guaranteed annual wage

**gawk** \'gȯk\ *vb* : to gape or stare stupidly

**gawky** \'gȯ-kē\ *adj* **gawk·i·er; -est** : AWKWARD, CLUMSY

**gay** \'gā\ *adj* **1** : MERRY **2** : BRIGHT, LIVELY **3** : brilliant in color **4** : given to social pleasures; *also* : LICENTIOUS **5** : HOMOSEXUAL

**gay·ety, gay·ly** *var of* GAIETY, GAILY

**gaz** *abbr* gazette

**gaze** \'gāz\ *vb* **gazed; gaz·ing** : to fix the eyes in a steady intent look — **gaze** *n* — **gaz·er** *n*

**ga·ze·bo** \gə-'zā-bō, -'zē-\ *n, pl* **-bos** : BELVEDERE

**ga·zelle** \gə-'zel\ *n, pl* **gazelles** *also* **gazelle** : any of several small swift graceful antelopes

**¹ga·zette** \gə-'zet\ *n* **1** : NEWSPAPER **2** : an official journal

**²gazette** *vb* **ga·zett·ed; ga·zett·ing** *chiefly Brit* : to announce or publish in a gazette

**gaz·et·teer** \,gaz-ə-'tiər\ *n* **1** *archaic* : JOURNALIST, PUBLICIST **2** : a geographical dictionary

**GB** *abbr* Great Britain

**GCA** *abbr* ground-controlled approach

**GCT** *abbr* Greenwich civil time

**gd** *abbr* good

**Gd** *symbol* gadolinium

**Ge** *symbol* germanium

**ge·an·ti·cline** \jē-'ant-i-,klīn\ *also* **ge·an·ti·cli·nal** \(,)jē-,ant-i-'klīn-ᵊl\ *n* : a great upward flexure of the earth's crust

**gear** \'giər\ *n* **1** : CLOTHING **2** : EQUIPMENT ⟨fishing ~⟩ ⟨photographic ~⟩ **3** : movable property **4** : a mechanism that performs a specific function ⟨steering ~⟩ **5** : a toothed wheel that interlocks with another toothed wheel or shaft for transmitting motion **6** : working adjustment of gears ⟨in ~⟩ **7** : one of several adjustments of automobile transmission gears that determine direction of travel and relative speed between engine and motion of vehicle — **gear** *vb* — **gear·ing** \-iŋ\ *n*

**gear·box** \'giər-,bäks\ *n* : TRANSMISSION 3

**gear·shift** \-,shift\ *n* : a mechanism by which transmission gears are shifted

**gear wheel** *n* : COGWHEEL

**geese** *pl of* GOOSE

**gee·zer** \'gē-zər\ *n* : a queer, odd, or eccentric man

**Gei·ger counter** \,gī-gər-\ *or* **Gei·ger–Mül·ler counter** \-'myül-ər-, -'mil-, -'məl-\ *n* : an electronic instrument for indicating the presence of cosmic rays or radioactive substances

**gei·sha** \'gā-shə, 'gē-\ *n, pl* **geisha** *or* **geishas** [Jap, fr. *gei* art + *-sha* person] : a Japanese girl who is trained to provide entertaining company for men

**gel** \'jel\ *n* : a colloid in a more solid form than a sol — **gel** *vb*

**gel·a·tin** *also* **gel·a·tine** \'jel-ət-ᵊn\ *n* : a glutinous substance obtained from animal tissues by boiling and used as a food, in dyeing, and in photography — **ge·lat·i·nous** \jə-'lat-(ᵊ-)nəs\ *adj*

**geld** \'geld\ *vb* : CASTRATE

**geld·ing** \'gel-diŋ\ *n* : a gelded individual; *esp* : a castrated male horse

**gel·id** \'jel-əd\ *adj* : extremely cold

**gel·ig·nite** \'jel-ig-,nīt\ *n* : a dynamite having a potassium nitrate base

**gem** \'jem\ *n* **1** : JEWEL **2** : a more or less valuable stone cut and polished for ornament **3** : something valued for beauty or perfection

**gem·i·nate** \'jem-ə-,nāt\ *vb* **-nat·ed; -nat·ing** : DOUBLE — **gem·i·na·tion** \,jem-ə-'nā-shən\ *n*

**gem·ol·o·gy** *or* **gem·mol·o·gy** \je-

'māl-ə-jē, jə-\ n : the science of gems —
**gem·olog·i·cal** or **gem·mo·log·i·cal** \,jem-ə-'läj-i-kəl\ adj — **gem·ol·o·gist** or **gem·mol·o·gist** \-jəst\ n
**gem·stone** \'jem-,stōn\ n : a mineral or petrified material that when cut and polished can be used in jewelry
**gen** abbr 1 general 2 genitive
**Gen** abbr Genesis
**Gen AF** abbr general of the air force
**gen·darme** \'zhän-,därm, 'jän-\ n [F, intended as sing. of gensdarmes, pl. of gent d'armes, lit., armed people] : one of a body of soldiers esp. in France serving as an armed police force
**gen·dar·mer·ie** or **gen·dar·mery** \jän-'därm-ə-rē, zhän-\ n, pl **-mer·ies** : a body of gendarmes
**gen·der** \'jen-dər\ n 1 : SEX 2 : any of two or more divisions within a grammatical class that determine agreement with and selection of other words or grammatical forms
**gene** \'jēn\ n : one of the complex chemical units of a chromosome that are the actual carriers of heredity and consist of a specific sequence of purine and pyrimidine bases usu. in DNA — **gen·ic** \'jē-nik, 'jen-\ adj
**ge·ne·al·o·gy** \,jē-nē-'äl-ə-jē, ,jen-ē-, -'al-\ n, pl **-gies** : PEDIGREE, LINEAGE; also : the study of family pedigrees — **ge·ne·a·log·i·cal** \,jē-nē-ə-'läj-i-kəl, ,jen-ē-\ adj — **ge·ne·a·log·i·cal·ly** \-k(ə-)lē\ adv — **ge·ne·al·o·gist** \,jē-nē-'äl-ə-jəst, ,jen-ē-; -'al-\ n
**genera** pl of GENUS
¹**gen·er·al** \'jen-(ə-)rəl\ adj 1 : of or relating to the whole : not local 2 : taken as a whole 3 : relating to or covering all instances or individuals of a class or group ⟨a ~ conclusion⟩ 4 : not limited in meaning : not specific ⟨a ~ outline⟩ 5 : common to many ⟨a ~ custom⟩ 6 : not special or specialized 7 : not precise or definite 8 : holding superior rank ⟨inspector ~⟩ — **gen·er·al·ly** \-ē\ adv
²**general** n 1 : something that involves or is applicable to the whole 2 : a commissioned officer ranking next below a general of the army or a general of the air force 3 : a commissioned officer of the highest rank in the marine corps — **in general** : for the most part
**general assembly** n 1 : a legislative assembly; esp : a U.S. state legislature 2 cap G&A : the supreme deliberative body of the United Nations
**gen·er·a·lis·si·mo** \,jen-(ə-)rə-'lis-ə-,mō\ n, pl **-mos** : COMMANDER IN CHIEF
**gen·er·al·i·ty** \,jen-ə-'ral-ət-ē\ n, pl **-ties** 1 : the quality or state of being general 2 : GENERALIZATION 3 : a vague or inadequate statement 4 : the greatest part : BULK
**gen·er·al·iza·tion** \,jen-(ə-)rə-lə-'zā-shən\ n 1 : the act or process of generalizing 2 : a general statement, law, principle, or proposition
**gen·er·al·ize** \'jen-(ə-)rə-,līz\ vb **-ized; -iz·ing** 1 : to make general 2 : to draw general conclusions from 3 : to reach a general conclusion esp.

on the basis of particular instances 4 : to extend throughout the body
**general of the air force** : a commissioned officer of the highest rank in the air force
**general of the army** : a commissioned officer of the highest rank in the army
**general practitioner** n : a physician or veterinarian who does not limit his practice to a specialty
**gen·er·al·ship** \'jen-(ə-)rəl-,ship\ n 1 : office or tenure of office of a general 2 : military skill as a high commander 3 : LEADERSHIP
**general staff** n : a group of officers who assist a high-level commander in planning, coordinating, and supervising operations
**general store** n : a retail store that carries a wide variety of goods but is not divided into departments
**gen·er·ate** \'jen-ə-,rāt\ vb **-at·ed; -at·ing** : to bring into existence : PRODUCE; esp : to originate (as electricity) by a vital or chemical process
**gen·er·a·tion** \,jen-ə-'rā-shən\ n 1 : a body of living beings constituting a single step in the line of descent from an ancestor; also : the average period between generations 2 : PRODUCTION ⟨~ of electric current⟩ — **gen·er·a·tive** \'jen-ə-,rāt-iv, -(ə-)rət-\ adj
**gen·er·a·tor** \'jen-ə-,rāt-ər\ n : one that generates; esp : a machine by which mechanical energy is changed into electrical energy
**ge·ner·ic** \jə-'ner-ik\ adj 1 : not specific : GENERAL 2 : not protected by a trademark ⟨a ~ drug⟩ 3 : of or relating to a genus — **generic** n
**gen·er·ous** \'jen-(ə-)rəs\ adj 1 : free in giving or sharing 2 : HIGH-MINDED, NOBLE 3 : ABUNDANT, AMPLE, COPIOUS — **gen·er·os·i·ty** \,jen-ə-'räs-ət-ē\ n — **gen·er·ous·ly** \'jen-(ə-)rəs-lē\ adv — **gen·er·ous·ness** n
**gen·e·sis** \'jen-ə-səs\ n, pl **-e·ses** \-,sēz\ : the origin or coming into existence of something
**ge·net·ic** \jə-'net-ik\ adj : of or relating to the origin, development, or causes of something; also : of or relating to genetics — **ge·net·i·cal·ly** \-i-k(ə-)lē\ adv
**genetic code** n : the biochemical basis of the heredity of an organism consisting of specific sequences of nitrogenous bases in DNA and RNA
**ge·net·ics** \jə-'net-iks\ n : a branch of biology dealing with heredity and variation — **ge·net·i·cist** \-'net-ə-səst\ n
**ge·nial** \'jē-nyəl\ adj 1 : favorable to growth or comfort ⟨~ sunshine⟩ 2 : CHEERFUL, CHEERING, KINDLY ⟨a ~ host⟩ — **ge·nial·i·ty** \,jē-nē-'al-ət-ē, jēn-'yal-\ n — **ge·nial·ly** \'jē-nyə-lē\ adv
**-gen·ic** \'jen-ik\ adj comb form 1 : producing : forming 2 : produced by : formed from 3 : suitable for production or reproduction by (such) a medium
**ge·nie** \'jē-nē\ n, pl **ge·nies** also **ge·nii** \'jē-nē-,ī\ [F génie, fr. Ar jinnīy]

: a supernatural spirit that often takes human form

**gen·i·tal** \'jen-ə-t⁰l\ *adj* **1** : concerned with reproduction ⟨~ organs⟩ **2** : of, relating to, or characterized by the stage of psychosexual development in which oral and anal impulses are subordinated to adaptive interpersonal mechanisms — **gen·i·tal·ly** \-tə-lē\ *adv*

**gen·i·ta·lia** \,jen-ə-'tāl-yə\ *n pl* : reproductive organs; *esp* : the external genital organs — **gen·i·tal·ic** \-'tal-ik, -'tāl-\ *adj*

**gen·i·tals** \'jen-ə-t⁰lz\ *n pl* : GENITALIA

**gen·i·tive** \'jen-ət-iv\ *adj* : of, relating to, or constituting a grammatical case marking typically a relationship of possessor or source — **genitive** *n*

**gen·i·to·uri·nary** \,jen-ə-tō-'yùr-ə-,ner-ē\ *adj* : of or relating to the genital and urinary organs or functions

**ge·nius** \'jē-nyəs\ *n, pl* **ge·nius·es** or **ge·nii** \-nē-,ī\ [L, tutelary spirit, fondness for social enjoyment, fr. *gignere* to beget] **1** *pl* **genii** : an attendant spirit of a person or place **2** : a strong leaning or inclination **3** : a peculiar or distinctive character or spirit (as of a nation or a language) **4** : the associations and traditions of a place **5** *pl usu* **genii** : a nature spirit; *also* : a person who influences another for good or evil **6** : a single strongly marked capacity **7** : extraordinary intellectual power; *also* : a person having such power

**genl** *abbr* general

**geno·cide** \'jen-ə-,sīd\ *n* : the deliberate and systematic destruction of a racial, political, or cultural group

**-g·e·nous** \j-ə-nəs\ *adj comb form* **1** : producing : yielding **2** : having (such) an origin

**genre** \'zhän-rə, 'zhäⁿ-; 'zhäⁿ(-ə)r\ *n* **1** : a style of painting in which everyday subjects are treated realistically **2** : a distinctive type or category esp. of literary composition

**gens** \'jenz, 'gens\ *n, pl* **gen·tes** \'jen-,tēz, 'gen-,tās\ : a Roman clan embracing the families of the same stock in the male line

**gent** *n* : MAN, FELLOW

**gen·teel** \jen-'tēl\ *adj* **1** : ARISTOCRATIC **2** : ELEGANT, STYLISH **3** : POLITE, REFINED **4** : maintaining the appearance of superior or middle-class social status **5** : marked by false delicacy, prudery, or affectation

**gen·tian** \'jen-chən\ *n* : a fall-flowering herb with usu. blue flowers

**gen·tile** \'jen-,tīl\ *n* [LL *gentilis* heathen, pagan, lit., belonging to the nations, fr. L *gent-*, *gens* family, clan, nation] **1** *often cap* : a person who is not Jewish **2** : HEATHEN, PAGAN — **gentile** *adj, often cap*

**gen·til·i·ty** \jen-'til-ət-ē\ *n, pl* **-ties** **1** : good birth and family **2** : the qualities characteristic of a well-bred person **3** : good manners **4** : maintenance of the appearance of superior or middle-class social status

¹**gen·tle** \'jent-⁰l\ *adj* **gen·tler** \'jent-

(⁰-)lər\; **gen·tlest** \'jent-(⁰-)ləst\ **1** : belonging to a family of high social station **2** : of, relating to, or characteristic of a gentleman **3** : KIND, AMIABLE **4** : TRACTABLE, DOCILE **5** : not harsh, stern, or violent **6** : SOFT, DELICATE **7** : MODERATE — **gen·tly** \'jent-lē\ *adv*

²**gentle** *vb* **gen·tled; gen·tling** \'jent-(⁰-)liŋ\ **1** : to make mild, docile, soft, or moderate **2** : MOLLIFY, PLACATE

**gen·tle·folk** \'jent-⁰l-,fōk\ *also* **gen·tle·folks** \-,fōks\ *n* : persons of good family and breeding

**gen·tle·man** \'jent-⁰l-mən\ *n* **1** : a man of good family **2** : a well-bred man **3** : MAN — used in pl. as a form of address — **gen·tle·man·ly** *adj*

**gen·tle·wom·an** \'jent-⁰l-,wùm-ən\ *n* **1** : a woman of good family or breeding **2** : a woman attending a lady of rank

**gen·try** \'jen-trē\ *n, pl* **gentries** **1** : people of good birth, breeding, and education : ARISTOCRACY **2** : the class of English people between the nobility and the yeomanry **3** : PEOPLE; *esp* : persons of a designated class

**gen·u·flect** \'jen-yə-,flekt\ *vb* : to bend the knee esp. in worship — **gen·u·flec·tion** \,jen-yə-'flek-shən\ *n*

**gen·u·ine** \'jen-yə-wən\ *adj* **1** : AUTHENTIC, REAL **2** : SINCERE, HONEST — **gen·u·ine·ly** *adv* — **gen·u·ine·ness** \-wən-(n)əs\ *n*

**ge·nus** \'jē-nəs\ *n, pl* **gen·era** \'jen-ə-rə\ [L, birth, race, kind] : a category of biological classification comprising related organisms and usu. consisting of several species

**geo·cen·tric** \,jē-ō-'sen-trik\ *adj* **1** : relating to or measured from the earth's center **2** : having or relating to the earth as a center — **geo·cen·tri·cal·ly** \-tri-k(ə-)lē\ *adv*

**geo·chem·is·try** \-'kem-ə-strē\ *n* : a science that deals with the chemical composition of and chemical changes in the earth's crust — **geo·chem·i·cal** \-'kem-i-kəl\ *adj* — **geo·chem·ist** \-'kem-əst\ *n*

**geo·chro·nol·o·gy** \-krə-'näl-ə-jē\ *n* : the chronology of the past as indicated by geologic data — **geo·chro·no·log·ic** \-,krän-⁰l-'äj-ik\ or **geo·chro·no·log·i·cal** \-i-kəl\ *adj*

**ge·ode** \'jē-,ōd\ *n* : a nodule of stone having a mineral-lined cavity

¹**geo·de·sic** \,jē-ə-'des-ik, -'dēs-\ *adj* : made of a framework of light straight-sided polygons in tension ⟨a ~ dome⟩

²**geodesic** *n* : the shortest line between two points on a surface

**ge·od·e·sy** \jē-'äd-ə-sē\ *n* : a branch of applied mathematics that determines the exact positions of points and the figures and areas of large portions of the earth's surface, the shape and size of the earth, and the variations of terrestrial gravity and magnetism — **ge·od·e·sist** \-səst\ *n* — **geo·det·ic** \,jē-ə-'det-ik\ *adj*

**geog** *abbr* geographic; geographical; geography

**ge·og·ra·phy** \jē-'äg-rə-fē\ *n, pl* **-phies** **1** : a science that deals with the natural features of the earth and the climate, products, and inhabitants **2** : the natural features of a region — **ge·og·ra·pher** \-fər\ *n* — **geo·graph·ic** \ˌjē-ə-'graf-ik\ *or* **geo·graph·i·cal** \-i-kəl\ *adj* — **geo·graph·i·cal·ly** \-i-k(ə-)lē\ *adv*

**geol** *abbr* geologic; geological; geology

**ge·ol·o·gy** \jē-'äl-ə-jē\ *n, pl* **-gies 1** : a science that deals with the history of the earth and its life esp. as recorded in rocks **2** : the geologic features of an area **3** : a study of the solid matter of a celestial body (as the moon) — **ge·o·log·ic** \ˌjē-ə-'läj-ik\ *or* **ge·o·log·i·cal** \-i-kəl\ *adj* — **ge·ol·o·gist** \jē-'äl-ə-jəst\ *n*

**geom** *abbr* geometrical; geometry

**geo·mag·net·ic** \ˌjē-ō-mag-'net-ik\ *adj* : of or relating to the magnetism of the earth — **geo·mag·ne·tism** \-'mag-nə-ˌtiz-əm\ *n*

**geometric mean** *n* **1** : the square root of the product of two terms : a term between any two terms of a geometric progression **2** : the *n*th root of the product of *n* numbers

**geometric progression** *n* : a progression (as 1 ½, ¼) in which the ratio of a term to its predecessor is always the same

**ge·om·e·try** \jē-'äm-ə-trē\ *n, pl* **-tries** : a branch of mathematics dealing with the relations, properties, and measurements of solids, surfaces, lines, and angles — **ge·om·e·ter** \-'äm-ət-ər\ *n* — **ge·o·met·ric** \ˌjē-ə-'met-rik\ *or* **ge·o·met·ri·cal** \-ri-kəl\ *adj*

**geo·mor·phol·o·gy** \ˌjē-ə-mȯr-'fäl-ə-jē\ *n* : a science that deals with relief features and their genetic interpretation

**geo·phys·ics** \ˌjē-ə-'fiz-iks\ *n* : the physics of the earth including the fields of meteorology, hydrology, oceanography, seismology, volcanology, magnetism, radioactivity, and geodesy — **geo·phys·i·cal** \-i-kəl\ *adj* — **geo·phys·i·cist** \-'fiz-ə-səst\ *n*

**geo·pol·i·tics** \-'päl-ə-ˌtiks\ *n* : a science based on the theory that domestic and foreign politics of a country are dependent on physical geography

**geo·sci·ence** \ˌjē-ō-'sī-əns\ *n* : any of the sciences dealing with the earth — **geo·sci·en·tist** \-ənt-əst\ *n*

**geo·sta·tion·ary** \-'stā-shə-ˌner-ē\ *adj* : of, relating to, or being an artificial earth satellite that remains at a fixed position above the equator

**geo·syn·cline** \-'sin-ˌklīn\ *or* **geo·syn·cli·nal** \-sin-'klīn-ᵊl\ *n* : a great downward flexure of the earth's surface — **geosynclinal** *adj*

**geo·ther·mal** \-'thər-məl\ *or* **geo·ther·mic** \-mik\ *adj* : of or relating to the heat of the earth's interior

**ger** *abbr* gerund

**Ger** *abbr* German; Germany

**ge·ra·ni·um** \jə-'rā-nē-əm\ *n* [L, fr. Gk *geranion,* fr. *geranos* crane] **1** : a purple or pink wild flower with deeply cut leaves **2** : a garden plant with clusters of usu. white, pink, or scarlet flowers

**ger·bil** *also* **ger·bile** \'jər-bəl\ *n* : any of numerous Old World burrowing desert rodents with long hind legs

**ge·ri·at·ric** \ˌjer-ē-'a-trik\ *adj* : of or relating to aging, the aged, or geriatrics

**ge·ri·at·rics** \-triks\ *n* : a branch of medicine dealing with the aged and the problems of aging

**germ** \'jərm\ *n* **1** : a bit of living matter capable of growth and development (as into an organism); *also* : MICROBE **2** : SOURCE, RUDIMENT

**Ger·man** \'jər-mən\ *n* **1** : a native or inhabitant of Germany **2** : the language of Germany — **German** *adj* — **Ger·man·ic** \ˌjər-'man-ik\ *adj*

**ger·mane** \ˌjər-'mān\ *adj* [ME *germain,* lit., having the same parents, fr. MF] : RELEVANT, PERTINENT

**ger·ma·ni·um** \ˌjər-'mā-nē-əm\ *n* : a grayish white hard chemical element used as a semiconductor

**German measles** *n sing or pl* : an acute contagious virus disease milder than typical measles but damaging to the fetus when occurring early in pregnancy

**German shepherd** *n* : an intelligent responsive working dog often used in police work and as a guide dog for the blind

**germ cell** *n* : an egg or sperm or one of their antecedent cells

**ger·mi·cide** \'jər-mə-ˌsīd\ *n* : an agent that destroys germs — **ger·mi·cid·al** \ˌjər-mə-'sīd-ᵊl\ *adj*

**ger·mi·nal** \'jərm-(ə-)nəl\ *adj* : of or relating to a germ or germ cell; *also* : EMBRYONIC

**ger·mi·nate** \'jər-mə-ˌnāt\ *vb* **-nat·ed; -nat·ing** : to begin to develop : SPROUT — **ger·mi·na·tion** \ˌjər-mə-'nā-shən\ *n*

**germ plasm** *n* **1** : germ cells and their precursors serving as the bearers of heredity **2** : GENES

**ger·on·tol·o·gy** \ˌjer-ən-'täl-ə-jē\ *n* : a scientific study of aging and the problems of the aged — **ge·ron·to·log·i·cal** \jə-ˌränt-ᵊl-'äj-i-kəl\ *or* **ge·ron·to·log·ic** \-ik\ *adj* — **ger·on·tol·o·gist** \ˌjer-ən-'täl-ə-jəst\ *n*

**ger·ry·man·der** \ˌjer-ē-'man-dər, 'jer-ē-ˌman-dər; ˌger-, 'ger-\ *vb* **-man·dered; -man·der·ing** \-d(ə-)riŋ\ : to divide into election districts so as to give one political party an advantage — **gerrymander** *n*

**ger·und** \'jer-ənd\ *n* : a word having the characteristics of both verb and noun

**ge·sta·po** \gə-'stäp-ō\ *n, pl* **-pos** [G, fr. *Geheime Staats polizei,* lit., secret state police] : a secret-police organization operating esp. against suspected political criminals

**ges·ta·tion** \je-'stā-shən\ *n* : PREGNANCY, INCUBATION — **ges·tate** \'jes-ˌtāt\ *vb*

**ges·tic·u·late** \je-'stik-yə-ˌlāt\ *vb* **-lat·ed; -lat·ing** : to make gestures esp. when speaking — **ges·tic·u·la·tion** \-ˌstik-yə-'lā-shən\ *n*

**ges·ture** \'jes-chər\ *n* **1** : the use of

motions of the body or limbs as a means of expression **2** : a movement usu. of the body or limbs that expresses or emphasizes an idea, sentiment, or attitude **3** : something said or done by way of formality or courtesy, as a symbol or token, or for its effect on the attitudes of others — **ges·tur·al** \-chə-rəl\ *adj* — **gesture** *vb*

**ge·sund·heit** \gə-'zunt-,hīt\ *interj* — used to wish good health esp. to one who has just sneezed

¹**get** \'get\ *vb* **got** \'gät\; **got** *or* **got·ten** \'gät-ᵊn\; **get·ting** **1** : to gain possession of (as by receiving, acquiring, earning, buying, or winning) : PROCURE, OBTAIN, FETCH **2** : to succeed in coming or going **3** : to cause to come or go **4** : BEGET **5** : to cause to be in a certain condition or position **6** : BECOME ⟨~ sick⟩ **7** : PREPARE **8** : SEIZE **9** : to move emotionally; *also* : IRRITATE **10** : BAFFLE, PUZZLE **11** : HIT **12** : KILL **13** : to be subjected to ⟨~ the measles⟩ **14** : to receive as punishment **15** : to find out by calculation **16** : HEAR; *also* : UNDERSTAND **17** : PERSUADE, INDUCE **18** : HAVE ⟨he's *got* no money⟩ **19** : to have as an obligation or necessity ⟨he has *got* to come⟩ **20** : to establish communication with **21** : to be able : CONTRIVE, MANAGE **22** : to leave at once

²**get** \'get\ *n* : OFFSPRING, PROGENY

**get along** *vb* **1** : to get by **2** : to be on friendly terms

**get·away** \'get-ə-,wā\ *n* **1** : ESCAPE **2** : the action of starting or getting under way

**get by** *vb* : to meet one's needs

**get-to·geth·er** \'get-tə-,geth-ər\ *n* : an informal social gathering

**get-up** \'get-,əp\ *n* **1** : general composition or structure **2** : OUTFIT, COSTUME

**gew·gaw** \'g(y)ü-,gȯ\ *n* : a showy trifle : BAUBLE, TRINKET

**gey·ser** \'gī-zər\ *n* [Icelandic *geysir* gusher, fr. *geysa* to rush forth] : a spring that intermittently shoots up hot water and steam

**Gha·na·ian** \gä-'nā-(y)ən\ *n* : a native or inhabitant of Ghana — **Ghanaian** *adj*

**ghast·ly** \'gast-lē\ *adj* **ghast·li·er; -est 1** : HORRIBLE, SHOCKING **2** : resembling a ghost : DEATHLIKE, PALE **syn** gruesome, grim, lurid

**ghat** \'gȯt\ *n* : a broad flight of steps that is situated on an Indian riverbank and provides access to the water

**gher·kin** \'gər-kən\ *n* : a small spiny pale cucumber used for pickling; *also* : a young common cucumber similarly used

**ghet·to** \'get-ō\ *n*, *pl* **ghettos** *or* **ghettoes** : a quarter of a city in which members of a minority group live because of social, legal, or economic pressure

¹**ghost** \'gōst\ *n* **1** : the seat of life : SOUL **2** : a disembodied soul; *esp* : the soul of a dead person believed to be an inhabitant of the unseen world or to appear in bodily form to living people **3** : SPIRIT, DEMON **4** : a faint trace or suggestion ⟨a ~ of a smile⟩ **5** : a false image in a photographic negative or on a television screen — **ghost·ly** *adv*

²**ghost** *vb* : GHOSTWRITE

**ghost·write** \-,rīt\ *vb* **-wrote** \-,rōt\; **-writ·ten** \-,rit-ᵊn\ : to write for and in the name of another — **ghost·writ·er** *n*

**ghoul** \'gül\ *n* [Ar *ghūl*] : a legendary evil being that robs graves and feeds on corpses — **ghoul·ish** *adj*

**GHQ** *abbr* general headquarters

**gi** *abbr* gill

¹**GI** \('')jē-'ī\ *adj* [galvanized *iron*; fr. abbr. used in listing such articles as garbage cans, but taken as abbr. for *government issue*] **1** : provided by an official U.S. military supply department ⟨~ shoes⟩ **2** : of, relating to, or characteristic of U.S. military personnel **3** : conforming to military regulations or customs ⟨a ~ haircut⟩

²**GI** *n*, *pl* **GI's** *or* **GIs** \-'īz\ : a member or former member of the U.S. armed forces; *esp* : an enlisted man

³**GI** *abbr* **1** general issue **2** government issue

**gi·ant** \'jī-ənt\ *n* **1** : a huge legendary manlike being of great strength **2** : a living being or thing of extraordinary size or powers — **giant** *adj* — **gi·ant·ess** \-əs\ *n*

**gib·ber** \'jib-ər\ *vb* **gib·bered; gib·ber·ing** \-(ə-)riŋ\ : to speak rapidly, inarticulately, and often foolishly

**gib·ber·ish** \'jib-(ə-)rish\ *n* : unintelligible, confused, or meaningless speech or language

¹**gib·bet** \'jib-ət\ *n* : GALLOWS

²**gibbet** *vb* **1** : to hang on a gibbet **2** : to expose to public scorn **3** : to execute by hanging

**gib·bon** \'gib-ən\ *n* : a manlike ape of southeastern Asia and the East Indies

**gib·bous** \'jib-əs, 'gib-\ *adj* **1** : convexly rounded in form : PROTUBERANT **2** : seen with more than half but not all of the apparent disk illuminated ⟨~ moon⟩ **3** : swollen on one side **4** : having a hump : HUMPBACKED — **gib·bous·ly** *adv* — **gib·bous·ness** *n*

**gibe** \'jīb\ *vb* **gibed; gib·ing** : to utter taunting words : SNEER — **gibe** *n*

**gib·lets** \'jib-ləts\ *n pl* : the edible viscera of a fowl

**Gib·son** \'gib-sən\ *n* : a cocktail made of gin and dry vermouth and garnished with a small onion

**gid·dy** \'gid-ē\ *adj* **gid·di·er; -est 1** : DIZZY **2** : causing dizziness **3** : not serious : FRIVOLOUS, FICKLE — **gid·di·ness** \'gid-ē-nəs\ *n*

**gift** \'gift\ *n* **1** : the act or power of giving **2** : something given : PRESENT **3** : a special ability : TALENT

**gift·ed** \'gif-təd\ *adj* : TALENTED

¹**gig** \'gig\ *n* **1** : a long light ship's boat **2** : a light 2-wheeled carriage

²**gig** *n* : a pronged spear for catching fish — **gig** *vb*

³**gig** *n* : a military demerit — **gig** *vb*

⁴**gig** *n* : JOB; *esp* : a musician's engagement for a specified time

**gi·gan·tic** \jī-'gant-ik\ adj : resembling a giant : IMMENSE, HUGE

**gig·gle** \'gig-əl\ vb **gig·gled; gig·gling** \-(ə-)liŋ\ : to laugh with repeated short catches of the breath — **giggle** n — **gig·gly** \-(ə-)lē\ adj

**gig·o·lo** \'jig-ə-,lō\ n, pl **-los** 1 : a man living on the earnings of a woman 2 : a professional dancing partner or male escort

**Gi·la monster** \,hē-lə-\ n : a large orange and black venomous lizard of the southwestern U.S.

¹**gild** \'gild\ vb **gild·ed** \'gil-dəd\ or **gilt** \'gilt\; **gild·ing** 1 : to overlay with or as if with a thin covering of gold 2 : to give an attractive but often deceptive outward appearance to — **gild·ing** n

²**gild** var of GUILD

¹**gill** \'jil\ n — see WEIGHT table

²**gill** \'gil\ n : an organ (as of a fish) for obtaining oxygen from water

¹**gilt** \'gilt\ adj : of the color of gold

²**gilt** n : gold or a substance resembling gold laid on the surface of an object

³**gilt** n : a young female swine

**gim·bal** \'gim-bəl, 'jim-\ n : a device that allows a body to incline freely

**gim·crack** \'jim-,krak\ n : a showy object of little use or value

**gim·let** \'gim-lət\ n : a small tool with screw point and cross handle for boring

**gim·mick** \'gim-ik\ n 1 : CONTRIVANCE, GADGET; esp : one used secretly or illegally 2 : an important feature that is not immediately apparent : CATCH 3 : a new and ingenious scheme — **gim·micky** \-i-kē\ adj

**gim·mick·ry** \'gim-i-krē\ n, pl **-ries** : an array of or the use of gimmicks

**gimpy** \'gim-pē\ adj : CRIPPLED, LAME

¹**gin** \'jin\ n [ME gin, modif. of OF engin] 1 : TRAP, SNARE 2 : a machine to separate seeds from cotton — **gin** vb

²**gin** \'jin\ n [by shortening & alter. fr. geneva] : a liquor distilled from a grain mash and flavored with juniper berries

**gin·ger** \'jin-jər\ n : the pungent aromatic rootstock of a tropical plant used esp. as a spice and in medicine; also : this plant

**ginger ale** n : a sweetened carbonated nonalcoholic beverage flavored mainly with ginger extract

**gin·ger·bread** \'jin-jər-,bred\ n 1 : a cake made with molasses and flavored with ginger 2 : tawdry, gaudy, or superfluous ornament

**gin·ger·ly** \'jin-jər-lē\ adj : very cautious or careful — **gingerly** adv

**gin·ger·snap** \-,snap\ n : a thin brittle molasses cookie flavored with ginger

**ging·ham** \'giŋ-əm\ n : a clothing fabric usu. of yarn-dyed cotton in plain weave

**gin·gi·vi·tis** \,jin-jə-'vīt-əs\ n : inflammation of the gums

**gink·go** also **ging·ko** \'giŋ-(,)kō, 'giŋk-(,)gō\ n, pl **-goes** or **-gos** : a tree of eastern China with fan-shaped leaves often grown as a shade tree

**gin·seng** \'jin-,saŋ, -,seŋ, -,(,)siŋ\ n : a Chinese perennial herb with an

aromatic root valued locally as a medicine; also : its root

**Gipsy** var of GYPSY

**gi·raffe** \jə-'raf\ n, pl **giraffes** [It giraffa, fr. Ar zirāfah] : an African ruminant mammal with an extraordinarily long neck

**gird** \'gərd\ vb **gird·ed** \'gərd-əd\ or **girt** \'gərt\; **gird·ing** 1 : to encircle or fasten with or as if with a belt : GIRDLE (~ on a sword) 2 : SURROUND 3 : to clothe or invest esp. with power or authority 4 : PREPARE, BRACE

**gird·er** \'gərd-ər\ n : a strong horizontal main supporting beam

**gir·dle** \'gərd-əl\ n 1 : something (as a belt or sash) that encircles or confines 2 : a woman's supporting undergarment that extends from the waist to below the hips — **girdle** vb

**girl** \'gərl\ n 1 : a female child : a young unmarried woman; also : a woman of any age 2 : a female servant or employee 3 : SWEETHEART — **girl·hood** \-,hud\ n — **girl·ish** adj

**girl Friday** n : a female assistant (as in an office) entrusted with a wide variety of tasks

**girl friend** n 1 : a female friend 2 : a frequent or regular companion of a boy or man

**girl scout** n : a member of the Girl Scouts of America

**girth** \'gərth\ n 1 : a band around an animal by which something (as a saddle) may be fastened on its back 2 : a measure around something

**gist** \'jist\ n [MF, it lies, fr. gesir to lie, fr. L jacēre] : the main point of a matter

¹**give** \'giv\ vb **gave** \'gāv\; **giv·en** \'giv-ən\; **giv·ing** 1 : to make a present of 2 : to bestow by formal action 3 : to accord or yield to another 4 : to put into the possession or keeping of another 5 : PROFFER 6 : DELIVER; esp : to deliver in exchange 7 : PAY 8 : to present in public performance or to view 9 : PROVIDE 10 : ATTRIBUTE 11 : PRODUCE 12 : to deliver by some bodily action 13 : UTTER, PRONOUNCE 14 : DEVOTE 15 : to cause to have or receive 16 : CONTRIBUTE, DONATE 17 : to yield to force, strain, or pressure

²**give** n 1 : capacity or tendency to yield to force or strain 2 : the quality or state of being springy

**give–and–take** \,giv-ən-'tāk\ n : an exchange (as of remarks or ideas) esp. on fair or equal terms

**give·away** \'giv-ə-,wā\ n 1 : an unintentional revelation or betrayal 2 : something given away free; esp : PREMIUM 3 : a radio or television show on which prizes are given

**give in** vb : SUBMIT, SURRENDER

**giv·en** \'giv-ən\ adj 1 : DISPOSED, INCLINED (~ to swearing) 2 : SPECIFIED, FIXED (at a ~ time) 3 : granted as true : ASSUMED 4 : EXECUTED, DATED

**given name** n : CHRISTIAN NAME

**give out** vb 1 : to become used up (supplies give out) 2 : to become exhausted : COLLAPSE 3 : to break down

**give up** vb **1 :** SURRENDER **2 :** to cease from trying, hoping, or expecting

**giz·mo** or **gis·mo** \'giz-mō\ n, pl **gizmos** or **gismos :** GADGET

**giz·zard** \'giz-ərd\ n : a muscular usu. horny-lined enlargement following the crop of a bird

**Gk** abbr Greek

**gla·brous** \'glā-brəs\ adj : SMOOTH; esp : having a surface without hairs or projections

**gla·cial** \'glā-shəl\ adj **1 :** extremely cold **2 :** of or relating to glaciers **3 :** being or relating to a past period of time when a large part of the earth was covered by glaciers — **gla·cial·ly** \-ē\ adv

**gla·ci·ate** \'glā-shē-,āt\ vb **-at·ed; -at·ing 1 :** to subject to glacial action **2 :** to produce glacial effects in or on — **gla·ci·a·tion** \,glā-s(h)ē-'ā-shən\ n

**gla·cier** \'glā-shər\ n : a large body of ice moving slowly down a slope or valley or spreading outward on a land surface

**gla·ci·ol·o·gy** \,glā-s(h)ē-'äl-ə-jē\ n : a branch of geology dealing with snow or ice accumulation, glaciation, or glacial epochs — **gla·ci·ol·o·gist** \-jəst\ n

¹**glad** \'glad\ adj **glad·der; glad·dest 1 :** experiencing pleasure, joy, or delight **2 :** PLEASED **3 :** very willing **4 :** PLEASANT, JOYFUL **5 :** CHEERFUL — **glad·ly** adv — **glad·ness** n

²**glad** n : GLADIOLUS

**glad·den** \'glad-ᵊn\ vb : to make glad

**glade** \'glād\ n : a grassy open space in a forest

**glad·i·a·tor** \'glad-ē-,āt-ər\ n **1 :** a person engaged in a fight to the death for public entertainment in ancient Rome **2 :** a person engaging in a fierce fight or controversy — **glad·i·a·to·ri·al** \,glad-ē-ə-'tōr-ē-əl\ adj

**glad·i·o·lus** \,glad-ē-'ō-ləs\ n, pl **-li** \-,(,)lī, -,lī\ [L, fr. dim. of gladius sword] : a plant related to the irises and widely grown for its spikes of brilliantly colored flowers

**glad·some** \'glad-səm\ adj : giving or showing joy : CHEERFUL

**glad·stone** \'glad-,stōn\ n, often cap : a traveling bag with flexible sides on a rigid frame that opens flat into two compartments

**glam·or·ize** also **glam·our·ize** \'glam-ə-,rīz\ vb **-ized; -iz·ing 1 :** to make glamorous **2 :** GLORIFY

**glam·our** or **glam·or** \'glam-ər\ n [Sc glamour, alter. of E grammar; fr. the popular association of erudition with occult practices] : a romantic, exciting, and often illusory attractiveness; esp : alluring personal attraction — **glam·or·ous** also **glam·our·ous** \-(ə-)rəs\ adj

¹**glance** \'glans\ vb **glanced; glanc·ing 1 :** to strike and fly off to one side **2 :** GLEAM **3 :** to give a quick look

²**glance** n **1 :** a quick intermittent flash or gleam **2 :** a glancing impact or blow **3 :** a quick look

**gland** \'gland\ n : a cell or group of cells that prepares and secretes a substance (as saliva or sweat) for further use in or discharge from the body — **glan·du·lar** \'glan-jə-lər\ adj

**glans** \'glanz\ n, pl **glan·des** \'glan-,dēz\ : a conical vascular body forming the extremity of the penis or clitoris

¹**glare** \'glaər\ vb **glared; glar·ing 1 :** to shine with a harsh dazzling light **2 :** to gaze fiercely or angrily — **glar·ing** \'gla(ə)r-iŋ\ adj — **glar·ing·ly** adv

²**glare** n **1 :** a harsh dazzling light **2 :** an angry or fierce stare

**glass** \'glas\ n **1 :** a hard brittle usu. transparent or translucent substance made by melting sand and other materials and used for windows and lenses; also : a substance resembling glass **2 :** something made of glass **3** pl : a pair of lenses used to correct defects of vision : SPECTACLES **4 :** GLASSFUL — **glass** adj — **glassware** \-,waər\ n — **glassy** adj

**glass·blow·ing** \-,blō-iŋ\ n : the art of shaping a mass of glass that has been softened by heat by blowing air into it through a tube — **glass·blow·er** \-,blō-(ə)r\ n

**glass·ful** \-,fül\ n : the quantity held by a glass

**glass wool** n : glass fibers in a mass resembling wool used for insulation and air filters

**glau·co·ma** \glaù-'kō-mə, glô-\ n : a state of increased pressure within the eyeball resulting in damage to the retina and gradual loss of vision

¹**glaze** \'glāz\ vb **glazed; glaz·ing 1 :** to furnish (as a window frame) with glass **2 :** to apply glaze to

²**glaze** n : a smooth coating of thin ice **2 :** a glassy coating

**gla·zier** \'glā-zhər\ n : a person who sets glass in window frames

¹**gleam** \'glēm\ n **1 :** a transient subdued or partly obscured light **2 :** GLINT **3 :** a faint trace ⟨a ~ of hope⟩

²**gleam** vb **1 :** to shine with subdued light or moderate brightness **2 :** to appear briefly or faintly

**glean** \'glēn\ vb **1 :** to gather grain left by reapers **2 :** to collect little by little or with patient effort — **glean·able** adj — **glean·er** n

**glean·ings** \'glē-niŋz\ n pl : things acquired by gleaning

**glebe** \'glēb\ n : land belonging to or yielding revenue to a parish church or ecclesiastical benefice

**glee** \'glē\ n [ME, fr. OE glēo entertainment, music] **1 :** JOY, HILARITY **2 :** an unaccompanied song for three or more solo usu. male voices — **glee·ful** adj

**glee club** n : a chorus organized for singing usu. short choral pieces

**glee·man** \'glē-mən\ n : MINSTREL

**glen** \'glen\ n : a secluded narrow valley

**glen·gar·ry** \glen-'gar-ē\ n, pl **-ries** often cap : a woolen cap of Scottish origin

**glib** \'glib\ *adj* **glib·ber; glib·best** : speaking or spoken with careless ease — **glib·ly** *adv*

¹**glide** \'glīd\ *vb* **glid·ed; glid·ing** **1** : to move smoothly and effortlessly **2** : to descend smoothly without engine power (~ in an airplane)

²**glide** *n* **1** : smooth sliding motion **2** : smooth descent without engine power

**glid·er** \'glīd-ər\ *n* **1** : one that glides **2** : an aircraft resembling an airplane but having no engine **3** : a porch seat suspended from an upright framework by short chains or straps

¹**glim·mer** \'glim-ər\ *vb* **glim·mered; glim·mer·ing** \-(ə-)riŋ\ : to shine faintly or unsteadily

²**glimmer** *n* **1** : a faint unsteady light **2** : INKLING **3** : a small amount : BIT

¹**glimpse** \'glimps\ *vb* **glimpsed; glimps·ing** : to take a brief look : see momentarily or incompletely

²**glimpse** *n* **1** : a faint idea : GLIMMER **2** : a short hurried look

**glint** \'glint\ *vb* **1** : to shine by reflection : SPARKLE, GLITTER, GLEAM **2** : to appear briefly or faintly — **glint** *n*

**glis·san·do** \gli-'sän-(,)dō\ *n, pl* **-di** \-(,)dē\ *or* **-dos** : a rapid sliding up or down the musical scale

¹**glis·ten** \'glis-ᵊn\ *vb* **glis·tened; glis·ten·ing** \'glis-(ᵊ-)niŋ\ : to shine by reflection with a soft luster or sparkle

²**glisten** *n* : GLITTER, SPARKLE

**glis·ter** \'glis-tər\ *vb* : GLISTEN

**glitch** \'glich\ *n* : an unwanted brief surge of electric power : a false or spurious electronic signal

¹**glit·ter** \'glit-ər\ *vb* **1** : to shine with brilliant or metallic luster **2** : SPARKLE **3** : to shine with a cold glassy brilliance **4** : to be brilliantly attractive esp. in a superficial way

²**glitter** *n* **1** : sparkling brilliancy, showiness, or attractiveness **2** : small glittering objects used for ornamentation — **glit·tery** \'glit-ə-rē\ *adj*

**gloam·ing** \'glō-miŋ\ *n* : TWILIGHT, DUSK

**gloat** \'glōt\ *vb* **1** : to gaze at or think about with great self-satisfaction or joy **2** : to linger over or dwell upon something with malicious pleasure

**glob** \'gläb\ *n* **1** : a small drop **2** : a large rounded lump

**glob·al** \'glō-bəl\ *adj* **1** : WORLDWIDE **2** : COMPREHENSIVE, GENERAL — **glob·al·ly** \-ē\ *adv*

**globe** \'glōb\ *n* **1** : BALL, SPHERE; *also* : something nearly spherical **2** : EARTH; *also* : a spherical representation of the earth

**globe–trot·ter** \-,trät-ər\ *n* : one that travels widely — **globe–trot·ting** \-,trät-iŋ\ *n or adj*

**glob·ule** \'gläb-yül\ *n* : a tiny globe or ball — **glob·u·lar** \-yə-lər\ *adj*

**glob·u·lin** \'gläb-yə-lən\ *n* : any of a class of simple proteins insoluble in pure water but soluble in dilute salt solutions that occur widely in plant and animal tissues

**glock·en·spiel** \'gläk-ən-,s(h)pēl\ *n* [G, fr. *glocke* bell + *spiel* play] : a percussion musical instrument consisting of a series of graduated metal bars tuned to the chromatic scale and played with two hammers

**gloom** \'glüm\ *n* **1** : partial or total darkness **2** : lowness of spirits : DEJECTION **3** : an atmosphere of despondency — **gloom·i·ly** \'glü-mə-lē\ *adv* — **gloom·i·ness** \-mē-nəs\ *n* — **gloomy** \'glü-mē\ *adj*

**glop** \'gläp\ *n* : a messy mass or mixture

**glo·ri·fy** \'glōr-ə-,fī\ *vb* **-fied; -fy·ing** **1** : to raise to celestial glory **2** : to shed splendor on **3** : to make glorious by presentation in a favorable aspect **4** : to give glory to (as in worship) — **glo·ri·fi·ca·tion** \,glōr-ə-fə-'kā-shən\ *n*

**glo·ri·ous** \'glōr-ē-əs\ *adj* **1** : possessing or deserving glory : PRAISEWORTHY **2** : conferring glory **3** : RESPLENDENT, MAGNIFICENT **4** : DELIGHTFUL, WONDERFUL — **glo·ri·ous·ly** *adv*

¹**glo·ry** \'glōr-ē\ *n, pl* **glories** **1** : RENOWN **2** : honor and praise rendered in worship **3** : something that secures praise or renown **4** : a brilliant asset **5** : RESPLENDENCE, MAGNIFICENCE **6** : celestial bliss **7** : a height of prosperity or achievement

²**glory** *vb* **glo·ried; glo·ry·ing** : to rejoice proudly : EXULT

¹**gloss** \'gläs, 'glòs\ *n* **1** : LUSTER, SHEEN, BRIGHTNESS **2** : outward show — **glossy** *adj*

²**gloss** *vb* **1** : to give a deceptive appearance to **2** : to pass over quickly in an attempt to ignore (~ over inadequacies)

³**gloss** *n* [ME *glose*, fr. OF, fr. L *glossa* unusual word requiring explanation, fr. Gk *glōssa, glōtta* tongue, language, unusual word] **1** : an explanatory note (as in the margin of a text) **2** : GLOSSARY **3** : an interlinear translation **4** : a continuous commentary accompanying a text

⁴**gloss** *vb* : to furnish glosses for

**glos·sa·ry** \,gläs-(ə-)rē, 'glòs-\ *n, pl* **-ries** : a dictionary of the special terms found in a particular area of knowledge or usage — **glos·sar·i·al** \glä-'sar-ē-əl, glò-\ *adj*

**glos·so·la·lia** \,gläs-ə-'lā-lē-ə, ,glòs-\ *n* [Gk *glōssa* tongue, language + *lalia* chatter, fr. *lalein* to chatter, talk] : TONGUE 5

¹**glossy** \'gläs-ē, 'glòs-\ *adj* **gloss·i·er; -est** : having a surface luster or brightness — **gloss·i·ly** \-ə-lē\ *adv* — **gloss·i·ness** \-ē-nəs\ *n*

²**glossy** *n, pl* **gloss·ies** : a photograph printed on smooth shiny paper

**glot·tis** \'glät-əs\ *n, pl* **glot·tis·es** *or* **glot·ti·des** \-ə-,dēz\ : the slitlike opening between pharynx and windpipe — **glot·tal** \-ᵊl\ *adj*

**glove** \'gləv\ *n* **1** : a covering for the hand having separate sections for each finger **2** : a padded leather covering for the hand for use in a sport

¹**glow** \'glō\ *vb* **1** : to shine with or as

if with intense heat **2 :** to have a rich warm usu. ruddy color ; FLUSH, BLUSH **3 :** to feel hot **4 :** to show exuberance or elation ⟨~ with pride⟩

²**glow** *n* **1 :** brightness or warmth of color; *esp* **:** REDNESS **2 :** warmth of feeling or emotion **3 :** a sensation of warmth **4 :** light such as is emitted from a heated substance

**glow·er** \'glau̇(-ə)r\ *vb* **:** to look or stare with sullen annoyance or anger — **glower** *n*

**glow·worm** \'glō-ˌwərm\ *n* **:** an insect or insect larva that gives off light

**glox·in·ia** \gläk-'sin-ē-ə\ *n* **:** a tuberous herb widely cultivated for its showy bell-shaped flowers

**gloze** \'glōz\ *vb* **glozed; gloz·ing :** to make appear right or acceptable

**glu·cose** \'glü-ˌkōs\ *n* **1 :** a sugar known in three different forms; *esp* **:** DEXTROSE **2 :** a light-colored syrup obtained chiefly from cornstarch and used as a sweetening agent

**glue** \'glü\ *n* **:** a jellylike protein substance made from animal materials and used for sticking things together; *also* **:** any of various other strong adhesives — **glue** *vb* — **glu·ey** \'glü-ē\ *adj*

**glum** \'gləm\ *adj* **glum·mer; glummest 1 :** MOROSE, SULLEN **2 :** DREARY, GLOOMY

¹**glut** \'glət\ *vb* **glut·ted; glut·ting 1 :** to fill esp. with food to satiety **:** SATIATE **2 :** OVERSUPPLY

²**glut** *n* **:** an excessive supply

**glu·ten** \'glüt-ᵊn\ *n* **:** a gluey protein substance that causes dough to be sticky

**glu·ti·nous** \'glüt-(ᵊ-)nəs\ *adj* **:** STICKY

**glut·ton** \'glət-ᵊn\ *n* **:** one that eats to excess — **glut·ton·ous** \'glət-(ᵊ-)nəs\ *adj* — **glut·tony** \'glət-(ᵊ-)nē\ *n*

**glyc·er·in** *or* **glyc·er·ine** \'glis-(ə-)rən\ *n* **:** a sweet colorless syrupy liquid obtained from fats or synthesized and used as a solvent, moistener, and lubricant

**glyc·er·ol** \'glis-ə-ˌrȯl, -ˌrōl\ *n* **:** GLYCERIN

**gly·co·gen** \'glī-kə-jən\ *n* **:** a white tasteless substance that is the chief storage carbohydrate of animals

**gly·co·side** \'glī-kə-ˌsīd\ *n* **:** any of numerous derivatives of sugars that on hydrolysis yield a sugar (as glucose) — **gly·co·sid·ic** \ˌglī-kə-'sid-ik\ *adj*

**gm** *abbr* gram

**GM** *abbr* **1** general manager **2** guided missile

**G–man** \'jē-ˌman\ *n* **:** a special agent of the Federal Bureau of Investigation

**Gmc** *abbr* Germanic

**GMT** *abbr* Greenwich mean time

**gnarl** \'närl\ *n* **:** a hard enlargement with twisted grain on a tree — **gnarled** \'närld\ *adj*

**gnash** \'nash\ *vb* **:** to grind (as teeth) together

**gnat** \'nat\ *n* **:** any of various small usu. biting two-winged flies

**gnaw** \'nȯ\ *vb* **1 :** to consume, wear away, or make by persistent biting or nibbling **2 :** to affect as if by gnawing — **gnaw·er** \'nȯ(-ə)r\ *n*

**gneiss** \'nīs\ *n* **:** a granitelike rock in layers

**gnome** \'nōm\ *n* **:** a dwarf of folklore who lives inside the earth and guards precious ore or treasure — **gnom·ish** \'nō-mish\ *adj*

**GNP** *abbr* gross national product

**gnu** \'n(y)ü\ *n, pl* **gnu** *or* **gnus :** a large African antelope with oxlike head and horns and horselike mane and tail

¹**go** \'gō\ *vb* **went** \'went\; **gone** \'gȯn, 'gän\; **go·ing** \'gō-iŋ\; **goes** \'gōz\ **1 :** to move on a course **:** PROCEED ⟨~ slow⟩ **2 :** LEAVE, DEPART **3 :** to take a certain course **:** follow a certain procedure **4 :** EXTEND, RUN ⟨his land ~es to the river⟩; *also* **:** LEAD ⟨that door ~es to the cellar⟩ **5 :** to be habitually in a certain state ⟨~es armed after dark⟩ **6 :** to become lost, consumed, or spent; *also* **:** DIE **7 :** ELAPSE, PASS **8 :** to pass by sale ⟨went for a good price⟩ **9 :** to become impaired or weakened **10 :** to give way under force or pressure **:** BREAK **11 :** HAPPEN ⟨what's ~ing on⟩ **12 :** to be in general or on an average ⟨cheap, as yachts ~⟩ **13 :** to become esp. as the result of a contest ⟨the decision *went* against him⟩ **14 :** to put or subject oneself ⟨~ to great expense⟩ **15 :** RESORT ⟨*went* to court to recover damages⟩ **16 :** to begin or maintain an action or motion ⟨here ~es⟩ **17 :** to function properly ⟨the clock doesn't ~⟩ **18 :** to have currency **:** CIRCULATE ⟨the report ~es⟩ **19 :** to be or act in accordance ⟨a good rule to ~ by⟩ **20 :** to come to be applied **21 :** to pass by award, assignment, or lot **22 :** to contribute to a result ⟨qualities that ~ to make a hero⟩ **23 :** to be about, intending, or expecting something ⟨is ~ing to leave town⟩ **24 :** to arrive at a certain state or condition ⟨~ to sleep⟩ **25 :** to come to be ⟨the tire *went* flat⟩ **26 :** to be capable of being sung or played ⟨the tune ~es like this⟩ **27 :** to be suitable or becoming **:** HARMONIZE **28 :** to be capable of passing, extending, or being contained or inserted ⟨this coat will ~ in the trunk⟩ **29 :** to have a usual or proper place or position **:** BELONG ⟨these books ~ on the top shelf⟩ **30 :** to be capable of being divided ⟨3 ~es into 6 twice⟩ **31 :** to have a tendency ⟨that ~es to show that he is honest⟩ **32 :** to be acceptable, satisfactory, or adequate **33 :** to proceed along or according to **:** FOLLOW **34 :** TRAVERSE **35 :** BET, BID ⟨willing to ~ $50⟩ **36 :** to assume the function or obligation of ⟨~ bail for a friend⟩ **37 :** to participate to the extent of ⟨~ halves⟩ **38 :** WEIGH **39 :** ENDURE, TOLERATE **40 :** AFFORD ⟨can't ~ the price⟩ — **go at 1 :** ATTACK, ATTEMPT **2 :** UNDERTAKE — **go back on 1 :** ABANDON **2 :** BETRAY **3 :** FAIL — **go by the board :** to be discarded — **go down the line :** to give wholehearted support — **go for 1 :** to pass for or serve as **2 :** to try to secure **3 :** FAVOR — **go one better :** OUTDO, SURPASS — **go over 1 :** EXAMINE **2**

: REPEAT **3** : STUDY, REVIEW — **go places** : to be on the way to success — **go to bat for** : DEFEND, CHAMPION — **go to town 1** : to work or act efficiently **2** : to be very successful

²**go** \'gō\ *n, pl* **goes 1** : the act or manner of going **2** : the height of fashion ⟨boots are all the ~⟩ **3** : a turn of affairs : OCCURRENCE **4** : ENERGY, VIGOR **5** : ATTEMPT, TRY **6** : a spell of activity — **no go** : USELESS, HOPELESS — **on the go** : constantly active

³**go** *adj* : functioning properly

**GO** *abbr* general order

**goad** \'gōd\ *n* [ME *gode*, fr. OE *gād* spear, goad] **1** : a pointed rod used to urge on an animal **2** : something that urges : SPUR — **goad** *vb*

**go-ahead** \'gō-ə-,hed\ *n* : authority to proceed

**goal** \'gōl\ *n* **1** : the mark set as limit to a race **2** : AIM, PURPOSE **3** : an area or object toward which play is directed in order to score; *also* : a successful attempt to score

**goal•ie** \'gō-lē\ *n* : a player who defends the goal (as in soccer or hockey)

**goal•keep•er** \'gōl-,kē-pər\ *n* : GOALIE

**goal•post** \'gōl-,pōst\ *n* : one of the two vertical posts with a crossbar that constitute the goal (as in soccer)

**goat** \'gōt\ *n, pl* **goats** : a hollow-horned ruminant mammal related to the sheep that has backward-curving horns, short tail, and usu. straight hair

**goa•tee** \gō-'tē\ *n* : a small trim pointed or tufted beard on a man's chin

**goat•herd** \'gōt-,hərd\ *n* : one who tends goats

**goat•skin** \-,skin\ *n* : the skin of a goat used for making leather

¹**gob** \'gäb\ *n* : LUMP, MASS

²**gob** *n* : SAILOR

**gob•bet** \'gäb-ət\ *n* : LUMP, MASS

¹**gob•ble** \'gäb-əl\ *vb* **gob•bled; gob•bling** \-(ə-)liŋ\ **1** : to swallow or eat greedily **2** : to take eagerly : GRAB

²**gobble** *vb* **gob•bled; gob•bling** \-(ə-)liŋ\ : to make the natural guttural noise of a turkey cock

**gob•ble•dy•gook** *or* **gob•ble•degook** \,gäb-əl-dē-'gúk, -'gük\ *n* : generally unintelligible jargon

**gob•bler** \'gäb-lər\ *n* : a male turkey

**go-be•tween** \'gō-bə-,twēn\ *n* : a person who acts as a messenger or an intermediary between two parties

**gob•let** \'gäb-lət\ *n* : a drinking glass with a foot and stem

**gob•lin** \'gäb-lən\ *n* [ME *gobelin*, fr. MF, fr. ML *gobelinus*, deriv. of Gk *kobalos* rogue] : an ugly grotesque sprite that is mischievous and sometimes evil and malicious

**god** \'gäd, 'gòd\ *n* **1** *cap* : the supreme reality; *esp* : the Being whom men worship as the creator and ruler of the universe **2** : a being or object believed to have more than natural attributes and powers and to require man's worship **3** : a person or thing of supreme value

**god•child** \-,chīld\ *n* : a person for whom one stands as sponsor at baptism

**god•daugh•ter** \-,dòt-ər\ *n* : a female godchild

**god•dess** \'gäd-əs\ *n* **1** : a female god **2** : a woman whose charm or beauty arouses adoration

**god•fa•ther** \'gäd-,fäth-ər, 'gòd-\ *n* : a man who sponsors a person at baptism

**god•head** \-,hed\ *n* **1** : divine nature or essence **2** *cap* : GOD 1; *also* : the nature of God esp. as existing in three persons

**god•hood** \-,húd\ *n* : DIVINITY

**god•less** \'gäd-ləs, 'gòd-\ *adj* : not acknowledging a deity or divine law — **god•less•ness** *n*

**god•like** \-,līk\ *adj* : resembling or having the qualities of God or a god

**god•ly** \-lē\ *adj* **god•li•er; -est 1** : DIVINE **2** : PIOUS, DEVOUT — **god•li•ness** \-lē-nəs\ *n*

**god•moth•er** \-,məth-ər\ *n* : a woman who sponsors a person at baptism

**god•par•ent** \-,par-ənt\ *n* : a sponsor at baptism

**god•send** \-,send\ *n* : a desirable or needed thing that comes unexpectedly as if sent by God

**god•son** \-,sən\ *n* : a male godchild

**go-get•ter** \'gō-,get-ər\ *n* : an aggressively enterprising person — **go-get•ting** \-,get-iŋ\ *adj or n*

**gog•gle** \'gäg-əl\ *vb* **gog•gled; gog•gling** \-(ə-)liŋ\ : to stare with wide or protuberant eyes

**gog•gles** \'gäg-əlz\ *n pl* : protective glasses set in a flexible frame that fits snugly against the face

**go-go** \'gō-,gō\ *adj* **1** : related to, being, or employed to entertain in a discotheque ⟨~ dancers⟩ **2** : very up-to-date : HIP **3** : aggressively enterprising and energetic

**go•ings-on** \,gō-iŋz-'òn, -'än\ *n pl* : ACTIONS, EVENTS

**goi•ter** *also* **goi•tre** \'gòit-ər\ *n* : an abnormally enlarged thyroid gland visible as a swelling at the base of the neck — **goi•trous** \-(ə-)rəs\ *adj*

**gold** \'gōld\ *n* **1** : a malleable yellow metallic chemical element used esp. for coins and jewelry **2** : gold coins; *also* : MONEY **3** : a yellow color

**gold-beat•er** \'gōl(d)-,bēt-ər\ *n* : one that beats gold into gold leaf

**gold-brick** \-,brik\ *n* : a person (as a soldier) who shirks assigned work — **goldbrick** *vb*

**gold digger** *n* : a woman who uses feminine charm to extract money or gifts from men

**gold•en** \'gōl-dən\ *adj* **1** : made of or relating to gold **2** : abounding in gold **3** : having the color of gold; *also* : BLOND **4** : SHINING, LUSTROUS **5** : SUPERB **6** : FLOURISHING, PROSPEROUS **7** : radiantly youthful and vigorous **8** : FAVORABLE, ADVANTAGEOUS ⟨a ~ opportunity⟩ **9** : MELLOW, RESONANT

**gold•en•ag•er** \'gōl-dən-,ā-jər\ *n* : an elderly and often retired person usu. engaging in club activities

**golden hamster** *n* : a small tawny hamster often kept as a pet

**gold•en•rod** \'gōl-dən-,räd\ *n* : any of

numerous herbs related to the daisies but having tall slender stalks with many tiny usu. yellow flower heads

**gold·field** \'gōl(d)-ˌfēld\ *n* : a gold-mining district

**gold·finch** \-ˌfinch\ *n* : an American finch the male of which becomes bright yellow and black in summer

**gold·fish** \-ˌfish\ *n* : a small usu. yellow or golden carp often kept as an aquarium fish

**gold·smith** \'gōl(d)-ˌsmith\ *n* : one who makes or deals in articles of gold

**golf** \'gälf, 'gȯlf\ *n* : a game played with a small ball and various clubs on a course having 9 or 18 holes — **golf** *vb* — **golf·er** *n*

**-gon** \ˌgän, -gən\ *n comb form* : figure having (so many) angles ⟨hexagon⟩

**go·nad** \'gō-ˌnad\ *n* : a sex gland : OVARY, TESTIS — **go·nad·al** \gō-'nad-ᵊl\ *adj*

**go·nad·o·tro·phic** \ˌgō-ˌnad-ə-'trō-fik, -'träf-ik\ *or* **go·nad·o·trop·ic** \-'träp-ik\ *adj* : acting on or stimulating the gonads ⟨~ hormone⟩

**go·nad·o·tro·phin** \-'trō-fən\ *or* **go·nad·o·tro·pin** \-pən\ *n* : a gonadotrophic hormone

**gon·do·la** \'gän-də-lə (*usual for 1*), gän-'dō-\ *n* 1 : a long narrow boat used on the canals of Venice 2 : a railroad car with no top designed for bulky materials 3 : an enclosure attached to the undersurface of an airship or balloon 4 : an enclosed car suspended from a cable and used for transporting skiers

**gon·do·lier** \ˌgän-də-'liər\ *n* : one who propels a gondola

**gone** \'gȯn\ *adj* 1 : PAST 2 : ADVANCED, ABSORBED 3 : INFATUATED 4 : PREGNANT 5 : DEAD 6 : LOST, RUINED 7 : SINKING, WEAK 8 *slang* : GREAT, MARVELOUS

**gon·er** \'gȯn-ər\ *n* : one whose case is hopeless

**gon·fa·lon** \'gän-fə-ˌlän\ *n* : a flag that hangs from a crosspiece or frame

**gong** \'gäŋ, 'gȯŋ\ *n* : a metallic disk that produces a resounding tone when struck

**gono·coc·cus** \ˌgän-ə-'käk-əs\ *n, pl* **-coc·ci** \-'käk-ˌ(s)ī, -'käk-ˌ(ˌ)(s)ē\ : a pus-producing bacterium that causes gonorrhea — **gono·coc·cal** \-'käk-əl\ *or* **gono·coc·cic** \-'käk-(s)ik\ *adj*

**gon·or·rhea** \ˌgän-ə-'rē-ə\ *n* : a bacterial inflammatory venereal disease of the genital tract — **gon·or·rhe·al** \-'rē-əl\ *adj*

**goo** \'gü\ *n* 1 : a viscid or sticky substance 2 : sickly sentimentality — **goo·ey** \-ē\ *adj*

**goo·ber** \'gü-bər, 'gȯb-ər\ *n, South & Midland* : PEANUT

¹**good** \'gȯd\ *adj* **bet·ter** \'bet-ər\; **best** \'best\ 1 : of a favorable character or tendency 2 : BOUNTIFUL, FERTILE 3 : COMELY, ATTRACTIVE 4 : SUITABLE, FIT 5 : SOUND, WHOLE 6 : AGREEABLE, PLEASANT 7 : SALUTARY, WHOLESOME 8 : CONSIDERABLE, AMPLE 9 : FULL 10 : WELL-FOUNDED 11 : TRUE ⟨holds ~ for everybody⟩ 12

: REAL 13 : recognized or valid esp. in law 14 : ADEQUATE, SATISFACTORY 15 : conforming to a standard 16 : DISCRIMINATING 17 : COMMENDABLE, VIRTUOUS 18 : KIND 19 : UPPER-CLASS 20 : COMPETENT 21 : LOYAL — **good-heart·ed** \-'härt-əd\ *adj* — **good·ish** *adj* — **good-look·ing** \'gȯd-'lȯk-iŋ\ *adj* — **good-na·tured** \-'nā-chərd\ *adj* — **good-tem·pered** \-'tem-pərd\ *adj*

²**good** *n* 1 : something good 2 : GOODNESS 3 : BENEFIT, WELFARE ⟨for the ~ of mankind⟩ 4 : something that has economic utility 5 *pl* : personal property 6 *pl* : CLOTH 7 *pl* : WARES, COMMODITIES 8 : good persons ⟨the ~ die young⟩ — **for good** : FOREVER, PERMANENTLY — **to the good** : in a position of net gain or profit ⟨$10 *to the good*⟩

³**good** *adv* : WELL

**good-bye** *or* **good-by** \gȯd-'bī, gə(d)-\ *n* : a concluding remark at parting — often used interjectionally

**good-for-noth·ing** \'gȯd-fər-nəth-iŋ\ *n* : an idle worthless person

**Good Friday** *n* : the Friday before Easter observed as the anniversary of the crucifixion of Christ

**good·ly** \'gȯd-lē\ *adj* **good·li·er; -est** 1 : of pleasing appearance 2 : LARGE, CONSIDERABLE

**good·man** \'gȯd-mən\ *n, archaic* : MR.

**good·ness** \'gȯd-nəs\ *n* : EXCELLENCE, VIRTUE

**good·wife** \'gȯd-ˌwīf\ *n, archaic* : MRS.

**good·will** \'gȯd-'wil\ *n* 1 : BENEVOLENCE 2 : the value of the trade a business has built up over a considerable time 3 : cheerful consent 4 : willing effort

**goody** \'gȯd-ē\ *n, pl* **good·ies** : something that is good esp. to eat

**goody-goody** \ˌgȯd-ē-'gȯd-ē\ *adj* : affectedly good — **goody-goody** *n*

**goof** \'güf\ *vb* 1 : BLUNDER 2 : to spend time idly or foolishly; esp : to evade work — often used with *off* — **goof** *n*

**goof·ball** \'güf-ˌbȯl\ *n* 1 *slang* : a barbiturate sleeping pill 2 *slang* : a mentally abnormal person

**go off** *vb* 1 : EXPLODE 2 : to follow a course ⟨the party *went off* well⟩

**goof-off** \'güf-ˌȯf\ *n* : one who evades work or responsibility

**goofy** \'gü-fē\ *adj* **goof·i·er; -est** : CRAZY, SILLY — **goof·i·ness** \'gü-fē-nəs\ *n*

**goon** \'gün\ *n* : a man hired to terrorize or kill opponents

**go on** *vb* 1 : to continue in a course of action 2 : to be capable of being put on 3 : to come into operation or action

**goose** \'güs\ *n, pl* **geese** \'gēs\ 1 : a large web-footed bird related to the swans and ducks; *esp* : a female goose as distinguished from a gander 2 : a foolish person 3 *pl* **goos·es** : a tailor's smoothing iron

**goose·ber·ry** \'güs-ˌber-ē, 'güz-, -b(ə-)rē\ *n* : the acid berry of a shrub related to the currant and used esp. in jams and pies

**goose·flesh** \'güs-ˌflesh\ *n* : a roughening of the skin caused usu. by cold or fear

**goose pimples** *n pl* : GOOSEFLESH

**go out** *vb* **1** : to become extinguished **2** : to become a candidate

**go over** *vb* : SUCCEED

**GOP** *abbr* Grand Old Party (Republican)

**go·pher** \'gō-fər\ *n* **1** : a burrowing American land tortoise **2** : any of various American burrowing rodents (as a ground squirrel) many of which have cheek pouches

**¹gore** \'gōr\ *n* : BLOOD

**²gore** *n* : a tapering or triangular piece (as of cloth in a skirt)

**³gore** *vb* gored; gor·ing : to pierce or wound with a horn or tusk

**¹gorge** \'gȯrj\ *n* **1** : THROAT **2** : a narrow ravine **3** : a mass of matter that chokes up a passage

**²gorge** *vb* gorged; gorg·ing : to eat greedily : stuff to capacity : GLUT

**gor·geous** \'gȯr-jəs\ *adj* [ME *gorgayse*, fr. MF *gorgias* elegant, fr. *gorgias* neckerchief, fr. *gorge* throat] : resplendently beautiful

**Gor·gon·zo·la** \ˌgȯr-gən-'zō-lə\ *n* : a blue cheese of Italian origin

**go·ril·la** \gə-'ril-ə\ *n* [fr. Gk *Gorillai*, an African tribe of hairy women] : an African manlike ape related to but much larger than the chimpanzee

**gor·man·dize** \'gȯr-mən-ˌdīz\ *vb* -dized; -diz·ing : to eat ravenously — **gor·man·diz·er** *n*

**gorse** \'gȯrs\ *n* : FURZE, JUNIPER

**gory** \'gōr-ē\ *adj* gor·i·er; -est **1** : BLOODSTAINED **2** : HORRIBLE, SENSATIONAL

**gos·hawk** \'gäs-ˌhȯk\ *n* : any of several long-tailed hawks with short rounded wings

**gos·ling** \'gäz-liŋ, 'gȯz-\ *n* : a young goose

**¹gos·pel** \'gäs-pəl\ *n* [ME, fr. OE *gōdspel*, fr. *gōd* good + *spell* tale] **1** : the teachings of Christ and the apostles **2** *cap* : any of the first four books of the New Testament **3** : something accepted as infallible truth

**²gospel** *adj* **1** : of, relating to, or emphasizing the gospel **2** : relating to or being American religious songs associated with evangelism and popular devotion

**gos·sa·mer** \'gäs-ə-mər, gäz(-ə)-mər\ *n* [ME *gossomer*, fr. *gos* goose + *somer* summer] **1** : a film of floating cobweb **2** : a thin sheer fabric **3** : something light, delicate, or tenuous

**¹gos·sip** \'gäs-əp\ *n* **1** : a person who habitually reveals personal or sensational facts **2** : rumor or report of an intimate nature **3** : an informal conversation — **gos·sipy** *adj*

**²gossip** *vb* : to spread gossip

**got** *past of* GET

**¹Goth** \'gäth\ *n* : a member of a Germanic race that early in the Christian era overran the Roman Empire

**²Goth** *abbr* Gothic

**¹Goth·ic** \'gäth-ik\ *adj* **1** : of or relating to the Goths **2** : of or relating to a style of architecture prevalent in western Europe from the middle 12th to the early 16th century

**²Gothic** *n* **1** : the Germanic language of the Goths **2** : the Gothic architectural style or decoration

**gotten** *past part of* GET

**Gou·da** \'gaúd-ə, 'güd-\ *n* : a mild Dutch milk cheese shaped in balls

**¹gouge** \'gaúj\ *n* **1** : a rounded troughlike chisel **2** : a hole or groove made with or as if with a gouge

**²gouge** *vb* gouged; goug·ing **1** : to cut holes or grooves in with or as if with a gouge **2** : DEFRAUD, CHEAT

**gou·lash** \'gü-ˌläsh, -ˌlash\ *n* : a beef stew with onion, paprika, and caraway

**go under** *vb* : to be overwhelmed, defeated, or destroyed : FAIL

**gourd** \'gōrd, 'gúrd\ *n* **1** : any of a group of tendril-bearing vines including the cucumber, squash, and melon **2** : the fruit of a gourd; *esp* : any of various inedible hard-shelled fruits used esp. for ornament or implements

**gourde** \'gúrd\ *n* — see MONEY table

**gour·mand** \'gúr-ˌmänd\ *n* **1** : one who is excessively fond of eating and drinking **2** : GOURMET

**gour·met** \'gúr-ˌmā, gúr-'mā\ *n* [F, fr. MF, fr. *gromet* boy servant, vintner's assistant, fr. ME *grom* groom] : a connoisseur in eating and drinking

**gout** \'gaút\ *n* : a disease marked by painful inflammation and swelling of the joints — **gouty** *adj*

**gov** *abbr* **1** government **2** governor

**gov·ern** \'gəv-ərn\ *vb* **1** : to control and direct the making and administration of policy in : RULE **2** : CONTROL, DIRECT, INFLUENCE **3** : DETERMINE, REGULATE **4** : RESTRAIN — **gov·ernance** \'gəv-ər-nəns\ *n*

**gov·ern·ess** \'gəv-ər-nəs\ *n* : a woman who teaches and trains a child esp. in a private home

**gov·ern·ment** \'gəv-ər(n)-mənt\ *n* **1** : authoritative direction or control : RULE **2** : the making of policy **3** : the organization or agency through which a political unit exercises authority **4** : the complex of institutions, laws, and customs through which a political unit is governed **5** : the governing body — **gov·ern·men·tal** \ˌgəv-ər(n)-'ment-ᵊl\ *adj*

**gov·er·nor** \'gəv(-ə)-nər, 'gəv-ər-nər\ *n* **1** : one that governs; *esp* : a ruler, chief executive, or head of a political unit (as a state) **2** : an attachment to a machine for automatic control of speed — **gov·er·nor·ship** *n*

**govt** *abbr* government

**gown** \'gaún\ *n* **1** : a loose flowing outer garment **2** : an official robe worn esp. by a judge, clergyman, or teacher **3** : a woman's dress ⟨evening ~s⟩ **4** : a loose robe — **gown** *vb*

**gp** *abbr* group

**GP** *abbr* general practitioner

**GPO** *abbr* **1** general post office **2** Government Printing Office

**GQ** *abbr* general quarters

**gr** *abbr* **1** grade **2** grain **3** gram **4** gravity **5** gross

**grab** \'grab\ *vb* **grabbed; grab·bing** **:** to take hastily — **grab** *n*

**gra·ben** \'gräb-ən\ *n* **:** a depressed segment of the earth's crust bounded on at least two sides by faults

**¹grace** \'grās\ *n* **1 :** help given man by God (as in overcoming temptation) **2 :** freedom from sin through divine grace **3 :** a virtue coming from God **4 :** a short prayer before or after a meal **5 :** a temporary respite (as from the payment of a debt) **6 :** APPROVAL, ACCEPTANCE ⟨in his good ~s⟩ **7 :** CHARM **8 :** ATTRACTIVENESS, BEAUTY **9 :** fitness or proportion of line or expression **10 :** ease of movement **11 :** a musical trill or ornament **12** — used as a title for a duke, a duchess, or an archbishop — **grace·ful** \-fəl\ *adj* — **grace·ful·ly** \-ē\ *adv* — **grace·ful·ness** *n* — **grace·less** *adj*

**²grace** *vb* **graced; grac·ing 1 :** HONOR **2 :** ADORN, EMBELLISH

**gra·cious** \'grā-shəs\ *adj* **1 :** marked by kindness and courtesy **2 :** GRACEFUL **3 :** characterized by charm and good taste **4 :** MERCIFUL — **gra·cious·ly** *adv* — **gra·cious·ness** *n*

**grack·le** \'grak-əl\ *n* **1 :** an Old World starling **2 :** an American blackbird with glossy iridescent plumage

**grad** *abbr* graduate

**gra·da·tion** \grā-'dā-shən, grə-\ *n* **1 :** a series forming successive stages **2 :** a step, degree, or stage in a series **3 :** an advance by regular degrees **4 :** the act or process of grading

**¹grade** \'grād\ *n* **1 :** a degree or stage in a series, order, or ranking **2 :** a position in a scale of rank, quality, or order **3 :** a class of persons or things of the same rank or quality **4 :** a division of the school course representing one year's work; *also* **:** the pupils in such a division **5** *pl* **:** the elementary school system **6 :** a mark or rating esp. of accomplishment in school **7 :** the degree of slope (as of a road); *also* **:** SLOPE

**²grade** *vb* **grad·ed; grad·ing 1 :** to arrange in grades **:** SORT **2 :** to make level or evenly sloping ⟨~ a highway⟩ **3 :** to give a grade to ⟨~ a pupil in history⟩ **4 :** to assign to a grade

**grad·er** \'grād-ər\ *n* **:** a machine for leveling earth

**grade school** *n* **:** a public school including the first six or the first eight grades

**gra·di·ent** \'grād-ē-ənt\ *n* **:** SLOPE, GRADE

**grad·u·al** \'graj-(ə-w)əl\ *adj* **:** proceeding or changing by steps or degrees — **grad·u·al·ly** \-ē\ *adv*

**grad·u·al·ism** \-,iz-əm\ *n* **:** the policy of approaching a desired end by gradual stages

**¹grad·u·ate** \'graj-(ə-)wət, -ə-,wāt\ *n* **1 :** a holder of an academic degree or diploma **2 :** a receptacle marked with figures for measuring contents

**²graduate** *adj* **1 :** holding an academic degree or diploma **2 :** of or relating to

studies beyond the first or bachelor's degree ⟨~ school⟩

**³grad·u·ate** \'graj-ə-,wāt\ *vb* **-at·ed; -at·ing 1 :** to grant or receive an academic degree or diploma **2 :** to admit to a particular standing or grade **3 :** to mark with degrees of measurement **4 :** to divide into grades, classes, or intervals

**grad·u·a·tion** \,graj-ə-'wā-shən\ *n* **1 :** a mark that graduates something **2 :** an act or process of graduating **3 :** COMMENCEMENT

**graf·fi·to** \gra-'fēt-ō, grə-\ *n, pl* **-ti** \-(,)ē\ **:** an inscription or drawing made on a rock or wall

**¹graft** \'graft\ *vb* **1 :** to insert a shoot from one plant into another so that they join and grow; *also* **:** to join one thing to another as in plant grafting ⟨~ skin over a burn⟩ **2 :** to get (as money) dishonestly — **graft·er** *n*

**²graft** *n* **1 :** a grafted plant; *also* **:** the point of union in this **2 :** material (as skin) used in grafting **3 :** the getting of money or advantage dishonestly; *also* **:** the money or advantage so gained

**gra·ham flour** \'grā-əm-, ,gra-(ə)m-\ *n* **:** whole wheat flour

**Grail** \'grāl\ *n* **:** the cup or platter used according to medieval legend by Christ at the Last Supper and thereafter the object of knightly quests

**grain** \'grān\ *n* **1 :** a seed or fruit of a cereal grass **2 :** seeds or fruits of various food plants and esp. cereal grasses; *also* **:** a plant producing grain **3 :** a small hard particle **4 :** a unit of weight based on the weight of a grain of wheat — see WEIGHT table **5 :** TEXTURE; *also* **:** the arrangement of fibers in wood **6 :** natural disposition — **grained** \'grānd\ *adj*

**grain alcohol** *n* **:** ALCOHOL 1

**grain·field** \'grān-,fēld\ *n* **:** a field where grain is grown

**grainy** \'grā-nē\ *adj* **grain·i·er; -est 1 :** GRANULAR **2 :** resembling the grain of wood

**¹gram** *or* **gramme** \'gram\ *n* [F *gramme*, fr. LL *gramma*, a small weight, fr. Gk *gramma* letter, writing, a small weight, fr. *graphein* to write] **:** a metric unit of mass and weight equal to $1/1000$ kilogram and nearly equal to one cubic centimeter of water at its maximum density — see METRIC SYSTEM table

**²gram** *abbr* grammar; grammatical

**-gram** \,gram\ *n comb form* **:** drawing **:** writing **:** record ⟨telegram⟩

**gram·mar** \'gram-ər\ *n* **1 :** the study of the classes of words, their inflections, and their functions and relations in the sentence **2 :** a study of what is to be preferred and what avoided in inflection and syntax; *also* **:** speech or writing evaluated according to its conformity to the principles of grammar — **gram·mar·i·an** \grə-'mer-ē-ən, -'mar-\ *n* — **gram·mat·i·cal** \-'mat-i-kəl\ *adj* — **gram·mat·i·cal·ly** \-k-(ə-)lē\ *adv*

**grammar school** *n* **1 :** a British secondary school emphasizing Latin and Greek in preparation for college; *also*

: a British college preparatory school **2** : a school intermediate between the primary grades and high school **3** : GRADE SCHOOL

**gram·o·phone** \'gram-ə-ˌfōn\ *n* : PHONOGRAPH

**gra·na·ry** \'grān-(ə-)rē, 'grän-\ *n, pl* **-ries** : a storehouse for grain

¹**grand** \'grand\ *adj* **1** : higher in rank or importance : FOREMOST, CHIEF **2** : great in size **3** : INCLUSIVE, COMPLETE ⟨a ~ total⟩ **4** : MAGNIFICENT, SPLENDID **5** : showing wealth or high social standing **6** : IMPRESSIVE, STATELY — **grand·ly** \'gran-(d)lē\ *adv* — **grand·ness** \'gran(d)-nəs\ *n*

²**grand** *n, slang* : a thousand dollars

**gran·dam** \'gran-ˌdam, -dəm\ *or* **gran·dame** \-ˌdām, -dəm\ *n* : an old woman

**grand·child** \'gran(d)-ˌchīld\ *n* : a child of one's son or daughter

**grand·daugh·ter** \'gran-ˌdȯt-ər\ *n* : a daughter of one's son or daughter

**grande dame** \'grän-'däm, grä°d-däm\ *n* : a usu. elderly woman of great prestige or ability

**gran·dee** \gran-'dē\ *n* : a high-ranking Spanish or Portuguese nobleman

**gran·deur** \'gran-jər\ *n* **1** : the quality or state of being grand **2** : something grand or conducive to grandness

**grand·fa·ther** \'gran(d)-ˌfäth-ər\ *n* : the father of one's father or mother; *also* : ANCESTOR

**grandfather clock** *n* : a tall pendulum clock standing directly on the floor

**gran·dil·o·quence** \gran-'dil-ə-kwəns\ *n* : pompous eloquence — **gran·dil·o·quent** \-kwənt\ *adj*

**gran·di·ose** \'gran-dē-ˌōs, ˌgran-dē-'ōs\ *adj* : IMPRESSIVE, IMPOSING; *also* : affectedly splendid — **gran·di·ose·ly** *adv*

**grand mal** \'grän(d)-ˌmäl; 'gran(d)-ˌmal\ *n* : severe epilepsy

**grand·moth·er** \'gran(d)-ˌməth-ər\ *n* : the mother of one's father or mother; *also* : a female ancestor

**grand·par·ent** \-ˌpar-ənt\ *n* : a parent of one's father or mother

**grand piano** *n* : a piano with horizontal frame and strings

**grand prix** \'grä°-'prē\ *n, pl* **grand prix** \-'prē(z)\ *often cap* **G&P** : a long-distance auto race over a road course

**grand-slam** *adj* : being a home run with the bases loaded

**grand slam** *n* : a total victory or success

**grand·son** \'gran(d)-ˌsən\ *n* : a son of one's son or daughter

**grand·stand** \-ˌstand\ *n* : a usu. roofed stand for spectators at a race-course or stadium

**grange** \'grānj\ *n* : a farm or farmhouse with its various buildings

**gran·ite** \'gran-ət\ *n* : a hard igneous rock that takes a polish and is used for building — **gra·nit·ic** \gra-'nit-ik\ *adj*

**gran·ite·ware** \-ˌwaər\ *n* : enameled ironware

¹**grant** \'grant\ *vb* **1** : to consent to : ALLOW, PERMIT **2** : GIVE, BESTOW **3** : to admit as true — **grant·er** \-ər\

*n* — **grant·or** \'grant-ər, -ˌȯr\ *n*

²**grant** *n* **1** : the act of granting **2** : something granted; *esp* : a gift for a particular purpose ⟨a ~ for study abroad⟩ **3** : a transfer of property by deed or writing; *also* : the instrument by which such a transfer is made **4** : the property transferred by grant

**grant·ee** \grant-'ē\ *n* : one to whom a grant is made

**grants·man** \'grants-mən\ *n* : a specialist in grantsmanship

**grants·man·ship** \-ˌship\ *n* : the art of obtaining grants (as for research)

**gran·u·lar** \'gran-yə-lər\ *adj* : consisting of or appearing to consist of granules — **gran·u·lar·i·ty** \ˌgran-yə-'lar-ət-ē\ *n*

**gran·u·late** \'gran-yə-ˌlāt\ *vb* **-lat·ed; -lat·ing** : to form into grains or crystals — **gran·u·lat·ed** *adj* — **gran·u·la·tion** \ˌgran-yə-'lā-shən\ *n*

**gran·ule** \'gran-yül\ *n* : a small particle; *esp* : one of numerous particles forming a larger unit

**grape** \'grāp\ *n* [ME, fr. OF *crape, grape* hook, *grape* stalk, bunch of grapes, grape] **1** : a smooth juicy edible berry that is the chief source of wine **2** : a woody vine widely grown for its clustered grapes

**grape·fruit** \'grāp-ˌfrüt\ *n* : a large edible yellow-skinned citrus fruit

**grape hyacinth** *n* : a small bulbous spring-flowering herb with racemes of usu. blue flowers that is related to the lilies

**grape·shot** \'grāp-ˌshät\ *n* : a cluster of small iron balls used as a cannon charge

**grape·vine** \'grāp-ˌvīn\ *n* **1** : GRAPE 2 **2** : RUMOR; *also* : an informal means of circulating information or gossip

**graph** \'graf\ *n* : a diagram that by means of dots and lines shows a system of relationships between things — **graph** *vb*

**-graph** \ˌgraf\ *n comb form* **1** : something written ⟨autograph⟩ **2** : instrument for making or transmitting records ⟨seismograph⟩

**graph·ic** \'graf-ik\ *also* **graph·i·cal** \-i-kəl\ *adj* **1** : being written, drawn, or engraved **2** : vividly described **3** : of or relating to the arts (**graphic arts**) of representation, decoration, and printing on flat surfaces — **graph·i·cal·ly** \-i-k(ə-)lē\ *adv* — **graph·ics** \-iks\ *n*

**graph·ite** \'graf-ˌīt\ *n* [G *graphit,* fr. Gk *graphein* to write] : soft carbon used esp. for lead pencils and lubricants

**grap·nel** \'grap-n°l\ *n* : a small anchor with two or more claws used esp. in dragging or grappling operations

¹**grap·ple** \'grap-əl\ *n* [MF *grappelle,* dim. of *grape* hook] **1** : GRAPNEL **2** : a hand-to-hand struggle

²**grapple** *vb* **grap·pled; grap·pling** \'grap-(ə-)liŋ\ **1** : to seize or hold with or as if with a hooked implement **2** : to seize one another **3** : WRESTLE **4** : COPE ⟨~ with a problem⟩

¹**grasp** \'grasp\ *vb* **1** : to make the mo-

tion of seizing **2 :** to take or seize firmly **3 :** to enclose and hold with the fingers or arms **4 :** COMPREHEND

**²grasp** *n* **1 :** HANDLE **2 :** EMBRACE **3 :** HOLD, CONTROL **4 :** the reach of the arms **5 :** the power of seizing and holding **6 :** COMPREHENSION

**grasp·ing** \-iŋ\ *adj* : desiring material possessions urgently and excessively

**grass** \'gras\ *n* **1 :** herbage for grazing animals **2 :** any of a large group of plants with jointed stems and narrow leaves **3 :** grass-covered land **4 :** MARIJUANA — **grassy** *adj*

**grass·hop·per** \-,häp-ər\ *n* : any of a group of leaping plant-eating insects

**grass·land** \-,land\ *n* : land covered naturally or under cultivation with grasses and low-growing herbs

**grass roots** *n pl* **1 :** society at the local level as distinguished from the centers of political leadership **2 :** the very foundation or source

**¹grate** \'grāt\ *n* **1 :** a framework with bars across it (as in a window) **2 :** a frame of iron bars for holding fuel while it is burning

**²grate** *vb* **grat·ed; grat·ing 1 :** to pulverize by rubbing against something rough **2 :** to grind or rub against with a rasping noise **3 :** IRRITATE — **grater** *n* — **grat·ing·ly** \'grāt-iŋ-lē\ *adv*

**grate·ful** \'grāt-fəl\ *adj* **1 :** THANKFUL, APPRECIATIVE; *also* : expressing gratitude **2 :** PLEASING — **grate·ful·ly** \-ē\ *adv* — **grate·ful·ness** *n*

**grat·i·cule** \'grat-ə-,kyül\ *n* : a scale on clear material in the focal plane of an optical instrument

**grat·i·fy** \'grat-ə-,fī\ *vb* **-fied; -fy·ing :** to afford pleasure to — **grat·i·fi·ca·tion** \,grat-ə-fə-'kā-shən\ *n*

**grat·ing** \'grāt-iŋ\ *n* : GRATE

**gra·tis** \'grat-əs, 'grāt-\ *adv or adj* : without charge or recompense : FREE

**grat·i·tude** \'grat-ə-,t(y)üd\ *n* : THANKFULNESS

**gra·tu·itous** \grə-'t(y)ü-ət-əs\ *adj* **1 :** done or provided without recompense : FREE **2 :** UNWARRANTED

**gra·tu·ity** \-ət-ē\ *n, pl* **-ities :** TIP

**grau·pel** \'grau̇-pəl\ *n* : granular snow pellets

**gra·va·men** \grə-'vā-mən\ *n, pl* **-vamens** *or* **-vam·i·na** \-'vam-ə-nə\ : the basic or significant part of a grievance or complaint

**¹grave** \'grāv\ *vb* **graved; grav·en** \'grā-vən\ *or* **graved; grav·ing :** SCULPTURE, ENGRAVE

**²grave** *n* **:** an excavation in the earth as a place of burial; *also* : TOMB

**³grave** \'grāv; *5 also* 'gräv\ *adj* **1 :** IMPORTANT **2 :** threatening great harm or danger **3 :** DIGNIFIED, SOLEMN **4 :** drab in color : SOMBER **5 :** of, marked by, or being an accent mark having the form ` — **grave·ly** *adv* — **grave·ness** *n*

**grav·el** \'grav-əl\ *n* : loose rounded fragments of rock — **grav·el·ly** \-ē\ *adj*

**grave·stone** \'grāv-,stōn\ *n* : a burial monument

**grave·yard** \-,yärd\ *n* : CEMETERY

**grav·id** \'grav-əd\ *adj* : PREGNANT

**gra·vi·me·ter** \grə-'vim-ət-ər, 'grav-ə-,mēt-\ *n* **1 :** a device for determining specific gravity **2 :** a device for measuring variations in a gravitational field

**grav·i·tate** \'grav-ə-,tāt\ *vb* **-tat·ed; -tat·ing 1 :** to move or tend to move under the influence of gravitation **2 :** to move toward something

**grav·i·ta·tion** \,grav-ə-'tā-shən\ *n* : a natural force of attraction that tends to draw bodies together — **grav·i·ta·tion·al** \-sh(ə-)nəl\ *adj* — **grav·i·ta·tion·al·ly** \-ē\ *adv* — **grav·i·ta·tive** \'grav-ə-,tāt-iv\ *adj*

**grav·i·ty** \'grav-ət-ē\ *n, pl* **-ties 1 :** IMPORTANCE; *esp* : SERIOUSNESS **2 :** WEIGHT **3 :** the attraction of bodies toward the center of the earth — **gravity** *adj*

**gra·vure** \grə-'vyu̇r\ *n* : the process of printing from an intaglio plate

**gra·vy** \'grā-vē\ *n, pl* **gravies 1 :** a sauce made from the thickened and seasoned juices of cooked meat **2 :** unearned or illicit gain : GRAFT

**¹gray** \'grā\ *adj* **1 :** of the color gray; *also* : dull in color **2 :** having gray hair **3 :** CHEERLESS, DISMAL **4 :** intermediate in position or character — **gray·ish** *adj* — **gray·ness** *n*

**²gray** *n* **1 :** something of a gray color **2 :** a neutral color ranging between black and white

**³gray** *vb* : to make or become gray

**gray·beard** \'grā-,biərd\ *n* : an old man

**gray birch** *n* : a small No. American birch with many lateral branches, grayish white bark, and soft wood

**gray·ling** \'grā-liŋ\ *n, pl* **grayling** *also* **graylings :** any of several slender freshwater food and sport fishes related to the trouts

**gray matter** *n* : the grayish part of nervous tissue consisting mostly of nerve cell bodies

**¹graze** \'grāz\ *vb* **grazed; graz·ing 1 :** to feed (livestock) on grass or pasture **2 :** to feed on herbage or pasture — **graz·er** *n*

**²graze** *vb* **grazed; graz·ing 1 :** to touch lightly in passing **2 :** SCRATCH, ABRADE

**gra·zier** \'grā-zhər\ *n* : a person who grazes cattle; *also* : RANCHER

**¹grease** \'grēs\ *n* : rendered and usu. solid animal fat; *also* : oily material — **greasy** \'grē-sē, -zē\ *adj*

**²grease** \'grēs, 'grēz\ *vb* **greased; greas·ing :** to smear or lubricate with grease

**grease·paint** \'grēs-,pānt\ *n* : theater makeup

**great** \'grāt, *South also* 'gre(ə)t\ *adj* **1 :** large in size : BIG **2 :** ELABORATE, AMPLE **3 :** large in number : NUMEROUS **4 :** being beyond the average : MIGHTY, INTENSE ⟨a ~ weight⟩ ⟨in ~ pain⟩ **5 :** EMINENT, GRAND **6 :** long continued ⟨a ~ while⟩ **7 :** MAIN, PRINCIPAL **8 :** more distant in a family relationship by one generation ⟨a *great*-grandfather⟩

**9** : markedly superior in character, quality, or skill ⟨~ at bridge⟩ **10** : EXCELLENT, FINE ⟨had a ~ time⟩ — **great·ly** adv — **great·ness** n

**great circle** n : a circle that is formed on the surface of the earth by a plane passing through the center of the earth and that gives the shortest path on the earth's surface connecting any two points through which it passes

**great·coat** \'grāt-ˌkōt\ n : a heavy overcoat

**Great Dane** n : any of a breed of tall massive powerful smooth-coated dogs

**great-heart·ed** \'grāt-'härt-əd\ adj **1** : COURAGEOUS **2** : MAGNANIMOUS

**great power** n, often cap G&P : one of the nations that figure most decisively in international affairs

**grebe** \'grēb\ n : any of a group of lobe-toed diving birds related to the loons

**Gre·cian** \'grē-shən\ adj : GREEK

**greed** \'grēd\ n : acquisitive or selfish desire beyond reason — **greed·i·ly** \'grēd-°l-ē\ adv — **greed·i·ness** \-ē-nəs\ n — **greedy** \'grēd-ē\ adj

**¹Greek** \'grēk\ n **1** : a native or inhabitant of Greece **2** : the ancient or modern language of Greece

**²Greek** adj **1** : of, relating to, or characteristic of Greece, the Greeks, or Greek **2** : ORTHODOX **3**

**¹green** \'grēn\ adj **1** : of the color green **2** : covered with verdure; also : consisting of green plants or of the leafy parts of plants ⟨a ~ salad⟩ **3** : UNRIPE; also : IMMATURE **4** : having a sickly appearance **5** : not fully processed or treated ⟨~ liquor⟩ ⟨~ hides⟩ **6** : INEXPERIENCED; also : NAIVE — **green·ish** adj — **green·ness** \'grēn-nəs\ n

**²green** vb : to become green

**³green** n **1** : a color between blue and yellow in the spectrum : the color of growing fresh grass or of the emerald **2** : something of a green color **3** pl : leafy parts of plants **4** : a grassy plot; esp : a grassy area at the end of a golf fairway containing the hole into which the ball must be played

**green·back** \'grēn-ˌbak\ n : a U.S. legal-tender note

**green bean** n : a kidney bean that is used as a snap bean when the pods are colored green

**green·belt** \'grēn-ˌbelt\ n : a belt of parkways or farmlands that encircles a community and is designed to prevent undesirable encroachments

**green·ery** \'grēn-(ə-)rē\ n, pl **-er·ies** : green foliage or plants

**green–eyed** \'grēn-'īd\ adj : JEALOUS

**green·gro·cer** \'grēn-ˌgrō-sər\ n, chiefly Brit : a retailer of fresh vegetables and fruit

**green·horn** \-ˌhȯrn\ n : an inexperienced person; esp : one easily tricked or cheated

**green·house** \-ˌhau̇s\ n : a glass structure for the growing of tender plants

**green manure** n : an herbaceous crop (as clover) plowed under when green to enrich the soil

**green pepper** n : SWEET PEPPER

**green·room** \'grēn-ˌrüm, -ˌru̇m\ n : a room in a theater or concert hall where actors or musicians relax before, between, or after appearances

**green·sward** \-ˌswȯrd\ n : turf green with growing grass

**green thumb** n : an unusual ability to make plants grow

**Green·wich time** \'grin-ij-, 'gren-ˌich-\ n : the time of the meridian of Greenwich used as the basis of worldwide standard time

**green·wood** \'grēn-ˌwu̇d\ n : a forest green with foliage

**greet** \'grēt\ vb **1** : to address with expressions of kind wishes **2** : to meet or react to in a specified manner **3** : to be perceived by - **greet·er** n

**greet·ing** \-iŋ\ n **1** : a salutation on meeting **2** pl : best wishes : REGARDS

**gre·gar·i·ous** \gri-'gar-ē-əs, -'ger-\ adj [L gregarius of a flock or herd, fr. greg-, grex flock, herd] **1** : SOCIAL, COMPANIONABLE **2** : tending to flock together — **gre·gar·i·ous·ly** adv — **gre·gar·i·ous·ness** n

**grem·lin** \'grem-lən\ n : a small gnome held to be responsible for malfunction of equipment esp. in an airplane

**gre·nade** \grə-'nād\ n [MF, pomegranate, fr. LL granata, fr. L granatus seedy, fr. granum grain] : a case filled with a destructive agent (as an explosive) and designed to be hurled or launched against an enemy

**gren·a·dier** \ˌgren-ə-'dir\ n : a member of a European regiment formerly armed with grenades

**gren·a·dine** \ˌgren-ə-'dēn, 'gren-ə-ˌdēn\ n : a syrup flavored with pomegranates and used in mixed drinks

**grew** past of GROW

**grey** var of GRAY

**grey·hound** \'grā-ˌhau̇nd\ n : a tall slender dog noted for speed and keen sight

**grid** \'grid\ n **1** : GRATING **2** : a ridged or perforated metal plate for conducting current in a storage battery; also : an electron tube electrode with openings used for controlling the flow of electrons between other electrodes **3** : GRIDIRON **2**; also : FOOTBALL

**grid·dle** \'grid-°l\ n : a flat usu. metal surface for cooking food

**griddle cake** n : PANCAKE

**grid·iron** \'grid-ˌī(-ə)rn\ n **1** : a grate (as of parallel bars) for broiling food **2** : something resembling a gridiron in appearance; esp : a football field

**grief** \'grēf\ n **1** : emotional suffering caused by or as if by bereavement; also : a cause of such suffering **2** : MISHAP, DISASTER

**griev·ance** \'grē-vəns\ n **1** : a cause of distress affording reason for complaint or resistance **2** : COMPLAINT

**grieve** \'grēv\ vb **grieved; griev·ing** [ME greven, fr. OF grever, fr. L gravare to burden, fr. gravis heavy, grave] **1** : to cause grief or sorrow to : DISTRESS **2** : to feel grief : SORROW

**griev·ous** \'grē-vəs\ adj **1** : OPPRES-

SIVE, ONEROUS **2** : causing suffering : SEVERE ⟨a ~ wound⟩ **3** : causing grief or sorrow **4** : SERIOUS, GRAVE — **griev·ous·ly** adv

¹**grill** \'gril\ vb **1** : to broil on a grill; also : to fry or toast on a griddle **2** : to question intensely

²**grill** n **1** : GRIDIRON 1; also : GRIDDLE **2** : an informal restaurant

**grille** or **grill** \'gril\ n : a grating that forms a barrier or screen

**grill·work** \'gril-,wərk\ n : work constituting or resembling a grille

**grim** \'grim\ adj **grim·mer; grim·mest 1** : CRUEL, SAVAGE, FIERCE **2** : harsh and forbidding in appearance **3** : RELENTLESS **4** : ghastly, repellent, or sinister in character — **grim·ly** adv — **grim·ness** n

**gri·mace** \'grim-əs, grim-'ās\ n : a facial expression usu. of disgust or disapproval — **grimace** vb

**grime** \'grīm\ n : soot, smut, or dirt adhering to or embedded in a surface; also : accumulated dirtiness and disorder — **grimy** adj

**grin** \'grin\ vb **grinned; grin·ning** : to draw back the lips so as to show the teeth esp. in amusement — **grin** n

¹**grind** \'grīnd\ vb **ground** \'graùnd\; **grind·ing 1** : to reduce to small particles **2** : to wear down, polish, or sharpen by friction **3** : to press with a grating noise : GRIT ⟨~ the teeth⟩ **4** : OPPRESS **5** : to operate or produce by turning a crank **6** : to move with difficulty or friction ⟨gears ~ing⟩ **7** : DRUDGE; esp : to study hard

²**grind** n **1** : monotonous labor or routine; esp : intensive study **2** : a student who studies excessively

**grind·er** \'grīn-dər\ n **1** : MOLAR **2** pl : TEETH **3** : one that grinds **4** : SUBMARINE 2

**grind·stone** \'grīn-,stōn\ n : a flat circular stone of natural sandstone that revolves on an axle and is used for grinding, shaping, or smoothing

¹**grip** \'grip\ vb **gripped; grip·ping 1** : to seize or hold firmly **2** : to hold strongly the interest of

²**grip** n **1** : GRASP; also : strength in gripping **2** : CONTROL, MASTERY **3** : UNDERSTANDING **4** : a device for grasping and holding **5** : SUITCASE

**gripe** \'grīp\ vb **griped; grip·ing 1** : SEIZE, GRIP **2** : DISTRESS; also : VEX **3** : to cause or experience spasmodic pains in the bowels **4** : COMPLAIN — **gripe** n

**grippe** \'grip\ n : INFLUENZA

**gris-gris** \'grē-,grē\ n, pl **gris-gris** \-,grēz\ : an amulet or incantation used chiefly by people of African Negro ancestry

**gris·ly** \'griz-lē\ adj **gris·li·er; -est** : HORRIBLE, GRUESOME

**grist** \'grist\ n : grain to be ground or already ground

**gris·tle** \'gris-əl\ n : CARTILAGE — **gris·tly** \-(ə-)lē\ adj

**grist·mill** \'grist-,mil\ n : a mill for grinding grain

¹**grit** \'grit\ n **1** : a hard sharp granule

(as of sand); also : material composed of such granules **2** : unyielding courage — **grit·ty** adj

²**grit** vb **grit·ted; grit·ting** : GRIND, GRATE

**grits** \'grits\ n pl : coarsely ground hulled grain

**griz·zled** \'griz-əld\ adj : streaked or mixed with gray

**griz·zly** \'griz-lē\ adj **griz·zli·er; -est** : GRIZZLED

**grizzly bear** n : a large pale-coated bear of western No. America

**gro** abbr gross

**groan** \'grōn\ vb **1** : MOAN **2** : to make a harsh sound under sudden or prolonged strain ⟨the chair ~ed under his weight⟩ — **groan** n

**groat** \'grōt\ n : a former British coin worth four pennies

**gro·cer** \'grō-sər\ n [ME, fr. MF grossier wholesaler, fr. gros coarse, wholesale, fr. L grossus coarse] : a dealer esp. in staple foodstuffs — **gro·cery** \'grōs-(ə-)rē\ n

**grog** \'gräg\ n [Old Grog, nickname of Edward Vernon d1757 E admiral responsible for diluting the sailors' rum] : alcoholic liquor; esp : liquor (as rum) mixed with water

**grog·gy** \'gräg-ē\ adj **grog·gi·er; -est** : weak and dazed and unsteady on the feet or in action — **grog·gi·ly** \'gräg-ə-lē\ adv — **grog·gi·ness** \-ē-nəs\ n

**groin** \'gròin\ n **1** : the fold marking the juncture of abdomen and thigh; also : the region of this fold **2** : the curved line in a building formed by the meeting of two vaults

**grom·met** \'gräm-ət, 'grəm-\ n **1** : a ring of rope **2** : an eyelet of firm material to strengthen or protect an opening

¹**groom** \'grüm, 'grùm\ n **1** : a male servant; esp : one in charge of horses **2** : BRIDEGROOM

²**groom** vb **1** : to attend to the cleaning of (an animal) **2** : to make neat, attractive, or acceptable : POLISH

**grooms·man** \'grümz-mən, 'grùmz-\ n : a male friend who attends a bridegroom at his wedding

**groove** \'grüv\ n **1** : a long narrow channel **2** : a fixed routine — **groove** vb

**groovy** \'grü-vē\ adj **groov·i·er; -est** : WONDERFUL, EXCELLENT

**grope** \'grōp\ vb **groped; grop·ing 1** : to feel about blindly or uncertainly in search ⟨~ for the right word⟩ **2** : to feel one's way by groping

**gros·beak** \'grōs-,bēk\ n : any of several finches of Europe or America with large stout conical bills

**gro·schen** \'grō-shən\ n, pl **groschen** — see schilling at MONEY table

**gros·grain** \'grō-,grān\ n : a silk or rayon fabric with crosswise cotton ribs

¹**gross** \'grōs\ adj **1** : glaringly noticeable **2** : OUT-AND-OUT, UTTER **3** : BIG, BULKY; esp : excessively fat **4** : excessively luxuriant : RANK **5** : GENERAL, BROAD **6** : consisting of an overall total exclusive of deductions ⟨~ earnings⟩ **7** : EARTHY, CARNAL

⟨~ pleasures⟩ **8 :** UNDISCRIMINATING **9 :** lacking knowledge or culture **:** UNREFINED **10 :** OBSCENE — **gross·ly** *adv* — **gross·ness** *n*

²**gross** *n* **1 :** an overall total exclusive of deductions **2** *archaic* **:** main body **:** MASS — **gross** *vb*

³**gross** *n, pl* **gross :** a total of 12 dozen things ⟨a ~ of pencils⟩

**gross national product** *n* **:** the total value of the goods and services produced in a nation during a year

**grosz** \'grôsh\ *n, pl* **gro·szy** \'grô-shē\ – see *zloty* at MONEY table

**grot** \'grät\ *n* **:** GROTTO

**gro·tesque** \grō-'tesk\ *adj* **1 :** FANCIFUL, BIZARRE **2 :** absurdly incongruous **3 :** ECCENTRIC — **gro·tesque·ly** *adv*

**grot·to** \'grät-ō\ *n, pl* **grottoes** *also* **grottos 1 :** CAVE **2 :** an artificial cavelike structure

**grouch** \'graùch\ *n* **1 :** a fit of bad temper **2 :** an habitually irritable or complaining person — **grouch** *vb* — **grouchy** *adj*

¹**ground** \'graùnd\ *n* **1 :** the bottom of a body of water **2** *pl* **:** sediment at the bottom of a liquid **:** DREGS, LEES **3 :** a basis for belief, action, or argument **4 :** BACKGROUND **5 :** FOUNDATION **6 :** the surface of the earth; *also* **:** SOIL **7 :** an area of land with a particular use **8** *pl* **:** the area about and pertaining to a building **9 :** a conductor that makes electrical connection with the earth or a large body of zero potential — **ground·less** \'graùn-(d)ləs\ *adj*

²**ground** *vb* **1 :** to bring to or place on the ground **2 :** to provide a reason or justification for **3 :** to instruct in fundamental principles **4 :** to connect with an electrical ground **5 :** to restrict to the ground **6 :** to run aground

³**ground** *past of* GRIND

**ground cloth** *n* **:** GROUNDSHEET

**ground cover** *n* **:** low plants that grow over and cover the soil; *also* **:** a plant suitable for this use

**ground·er** \'graùn-dər\ *n* **:** a baseball hit on the ground

**ground glass** *n* **:** glass with a light-diffusing surface produced by etching or abrading

**ground·hog** \'graùnd-,hòg, -,häg\ *n* **:** WOODCHUCK

**ground·ling** \'graùn-(d)liŋ\ *n* **1 :** a spectator in the cheaper part of a theater **2 :** a person of inferior judgment or taste

**ground·mass** \'graùn(d)-,mas\ *n* **:** a fine-grained base of a porphyry in which larger crystals are embedded

**ground rule** *n* **1 :** a sports rule adopted to modify play on a particular field, court, or course **2 :** a rule of procedure

**ground·sheet** \'graùn(d)-,shēt\ *n* **:** a waterproof sheet placed on the ground for protection (as of a sleeping bag) against ground moisture

**ground swell** *n* **1 :** a broad deep ocean swell caused by an often distant gale or earthquake **2 :** a rapid spontaneous

growth (as of political opinion)

**ground·wa·ter** \'graùnd-,wòt-ər, -,wät-\ *n* **:** water within the earth that supplies wells and springs

**ground·work** \-,wərk\ *n* **:** FOUNDATION, BASIS

¹**group** \'grüp\ *n* **:** a number of individuals related by a common factor (as physical association, community of interests, or blood)

²**group** *vb* **:** to associate in groups **:** CLUSTER, AGGREGATE

**grou·per** \'grü-pər\ *n, pl* **groupers** *also* **grouper :** any of numerous large solitary bottom fishes of warm seas

**group·ie** \'grü-pē\ *n* **:** a female fan of a rock group who usu. follows the group around on concert tours

**group therapy** *n* **:** therapy in the presence of a therapist in which several patients discuss and share their personal problems

¹**grouse** \'graùs\ *n, pl* **grouse 1 :** a ground-dwelling game bird related to the pheasants

²**grouse** *vb* **groused; grous·ing :** COMPLAIN, GRUMBLE

**grout** \'graùt\ *n* **:** material (as mortar) used for filling spaces — **grout** *vb*

**grove** \'grōv\ *n* **:** a small wood usu. without underbrush

**grov·el** \'gräv-əl, 'grəv-\ *vb* **-eled** *or* **-elled, -el·ing** *or* **-el·ling** \-(ə-)liŋ\ **1 :** to creep or lie with the body prostrate in fear or humility **2 :** CRINGE

**grow** \'grō\ *vb* **grew** \'grü\; **grown** \'grōn\, **grow·ing 1 :** to spring up and come to maturity **2 :** to be able to grow **:** THRIVE **3 :** to unite by or as if by growth **4 :** INCREASE, EXPAND **5 :** RESULT, ORIGINATE **6 :** to come into existence **:** ARISE **7 :** BECOME **8 :** to obtain influence **9 :** to cause to grow — **grow·er** \'grō-(ə)r\ *n*

**growl** \'graùl\ *vb* **1 :** RUMBLE **2 :** to utter a deep throaty threatening sound **3 :** GRUMBLE **growl** *n*

**grown-up** \'grōn-,əp\ *adj* **:** not childish **:** ADULT **grown-up** *n*

**growth** \'grōth\ *n* **1 :** stage or condition attained in growing **2 :** a process of growing **:** progressive development or increase **3 :** a result or product of growing ⟨a fine ~ of hair⟩; *also* **:** an abnormal mass of tissue (as a tumor)

¹**grub** \'grəb\ *vb* **grubbed; grub·bing 1 :** to clear or root out by digging **2 :** DRUDGE **3 :** to dig in the ground usu. for a hidden object **4 :** RUMMAGE

²**grub** *n* **1 :** a soft thick wormlike larva ⟨beetle ~s⟩ **2 :** DRUDGE; *also* **:** a slovenly person **3 :** FOOD

**grub·by** \'grəb-ē\ *adj* **grub·bi·er; -est :** DIRTY, SLOVENLY — **grub·bi·ness** \'grəb-ē-nəs\ *n*

**grub·stake** \'grəb-,stāk\ *n* **:** supplies or funds furnished a mining prospector in return for a share in his finds

¹**grudge** \'grəj\ *vb* **grudged; grudg·ing :** to be reluctant to give **:** BEGRUDGE

²**grudge** *n* **:** a feeling of deep-seated resentment or ill will

**gru·el** \'grü-əl\ *n* **:** a thin porridge

**gru·el·ing** *or* **gru·el·ling** \-ə-liŋ\ *adj*

: requiring extreme effort : EXHAUSTING

**grue·some** \'grü-səm\ adj [fr. earlier growsome, fr. E dial. grow, grue to shiver, fr. ME gruen] : inspiring horror or repulsion : GRISLY

**gruff** \'grəf\ adj 1 : rough in speech or manner 2 : being deep and harsh : HOARSE — **gruff·ly** adv

**grum·ble** \'grəm-bəl\ vb **grum·bled**; **grum·bling** \-b(ə-)liŋ\ 1 : to mutter in discontent 2 : GROWL 3 : RUMBLE — **grum·bler** \-b(ə-)lər\ n

**grumpy** \'grəm-pē\ adj **grump·i·er**; **-est** : moodily cross : SURLY — **grump·i·ly** \'grəm-pə-lē\ adv — **grump·i·ness** \-pē-nəs\ n

**grun·ion** \'grən-yən\ n : a fish of the California coast notable for the regularity with which it comes inshore to spawn at nearly full moon

**grunt** \'grənt\ n : a deep throaty sound (as that of a hog) — **grunt** vb

**GSA** abbr 1 General Services Administration 2 Girl Scouts of America

**G suit** n [gravity|suit] : an astronaut's or aviator's suit designed to counteract the physiological effects of acceleration

**gt** abbr 1 great 2 [L gutta] drop

**GT** abbr gross ton

**Gt Brit** abbr Great Britain

**gtd** abbr guaranteed

**GU** abbr Guam

**gua·nine** \'gwän-ēn\ n : a purine base that codes genetic information in the molecular chain of DNA or RNA

**gua·no** \'gwän-ō\ n [Sp, fr. Quechua (a South American Indian language) huanu dung] : a substance composed chiefly of the excrement of seabirds and used as a fertilizer

**gua·ra·ni** \,gwär-ə-'nē\ n, pl **gua·ranis** or **guaranies** — see MONEY table

¹**guar·an·tee** \,gar-ən-'tē\ n 1 : GUARANTOR 2 : GUARANTY 3 : an agreement by which one person undertakes to secure another in the possession or enjoyment of something 4 : an assurance of the quality or of the length of use to be expected from a product offered for sale 5 : GUARANTY 3

²**guarantee** vb **-teed**; **-tee·ing** 1 : to undertake to answer for the debt, failure to perform, or faulty performance of (another) 2 : to undertake an obligation to establish, perform, or continue 3 : to give security to

**guar·an·tor** \,gar-ən-'tòr\ n : one who gives a guarantee

¹**guar·an·ty** \'gar-ən-tē\ n, pl **-ties** 1 : an undertaking to answer for another's failure to pay a debt or perform a duty 2 : GUARANTEE 3 3 : PLEDGE, SECURITY 4 : GUARANTOR

²**guaranty** vb **tied; ty·ing** : GUARANTEE

¹**guard** \'gärd\ n 1 : a defensive position (as in boxing) 2 : the act or duty of protecting or defending : PROTECTION 3 : a man or a body of men on sentinel duty 4 pl : troops attached to the person of the sovereign 5 : BRAKEMAN 6 Brit : CONDUCTOR 7 : a football lineman playing between center and tackle; also : a basketball player sta-

tioned toward the rear 8 : a protective or safety device

²**guard** vb 1 : PROTECT, DEFEND 2 : to watch over 3 : to be on guard

**guard·house** \'gärd-,haús\ n 1 : a building occupied by a guard or used as a headquarters by soldiers on guard duty 2 : a military jail

**guard·ian** \'gärd-ē-ən\ n 1 : CUSTODIAN 2 : one who has the care of the person or property of another — **guard·ian·ship** n

**guard·room** \'gärd-,rüm\ n 1 : a room used by a military guard while on duty 2 : a room where military prisoners are confined

**guards·man** \'gärdz-mən\ n : a member of a military body called guard or guards

**gua·va** \'gwäv-ə\ n : a shrubby tree widely cultivated for its sweet acid yellow fruit; also : the fruit of a guava

**gu·ber·na·to·ri·al** \,g(y)üb-ə(r)-nə-'tōr-ē-əl\ adj : of or relating to a governor

**guer·don** \'gərd-²n\ n [ME, fr. MF, fr. Old High German widarlōn, fr. widar back + lōn reward] : REWARD, RECOMPENSE

**guern·sey** \'gərn-zē\ n, pl **guernseys** often cap : any of a breed of fawn and white dairy cattle that produce rich yellowish milk

**guer·ril·la** or **gue·ril·la** \gə-'ril-ə\ n [Sp guerrilla, fr. dim. of guerra war, of Gmc origin] : one who engages in irregular warfare esp. as a member of an independent unit

**guerrilla theater** n : drama dealing with controversial social issues that is usu. performed outdoors

**guess** \'ges\ vb 1 : to form an opinion from little or no evidence 2 : to conjecture correctly about : DISCOVER 3 : BELIEVE, SUPPOSE — **guess** n

**guest** \'gest\ n 1 : a person to whom hospitality (as of a house or a club) is extended 2 : a patron of a commercial establishment (as a hotel or restaurant) 3 : a person not a regular member of a cast who appears on a program

**guf·faw** \(,)gə-'fò, 'gəf-,ò\ n : a loud burst of laughter — **guf·faw** \(,)gə-'fò\ vb

**guid·ance** \'gīd-²ns\ n 1 : the act or process of guiding 2 : ADVICE, DIRECTION

¹**guide** \'gīd\ n 1 : one who leads or directs another in his way or course 2 : one who exhibits and explains points of interest 3 : something that provides a person with guiding information; also : SIGNPOST 4 : a device on a machine to direct the motion of something

²**guide** vb **guid·ed; guid·ing** 1 : CONDUCT 2 : MANAGE, DIRECT 3 : to superintend the training of — **guid·able** \'gīd-ə-bəl\ adj

**guide·book** \'gīd-,búk\ n : a book of information for travelers

**guided missile** n : a missile whose course may be altered during flight

**guide·line** \'gīd-,līn\ n : an indication or outline of policy or conduct

**guide word** *n* : either of the terms at the head of a page of an alphabetical reference work that indicate the alphabetically first and last words on that page

**gui·don** \'gīd-,än, -ᵊn\ *n* : a small flag usu. borne by a military unit as a unit marker

**guild** \'gild\ *n* : an association of men with common aims and interests; *esp* : a medieval association of merchants or craftsmen — **guild·hall** \-,hól\ *n*

**guil·der** \'gil-dər\ *n* : GULDEN

**guile** \'gīl\ *n* : deceitful cunning : DUPLICITY — **guile·ful** *adj* — **guile·less** \'gīl-ləs\ *adj* — **guile·less·ness** *n*

**guil·lo·tine** \'gil-ə-,tēn; ,gē-(y)ə-'tēn, 'gē-(y)ə-,tēn\ *n* : a machine for beheading persons — **guillotine** *vb*

**guilt** \'gilt\ *n* 1 : the fact of having committed an offense esp. against the law 2 : BLAMEWORTHINESS 3 : a feeling of responsibility for offenses — **guilt·less** *adj*

**guilty** \'gil-tē\ *adj* **guilt·i·er; -est** 1 : having committed a breach of conduct 2 : suggesting or involving guilt 3 : aware of or suffering from guilt — **guilt·i·ly** \'gil-tə-lē\ *adv* — **guilt·i·ness** \-tē-nəs\ *n*

**guin·ea** \'gin-ē\ *n* 1 : a British gold coin no longer issued worth 21 shillings 2 : a unit of value equal to 21 shillings

**guinea fowl** *n* : a West African bird related to the pheasants and widely raised for food; *also* : any of several related birds

**guinea hen** *n* : a female guinea fowl; *also* : GUINEA FOWL

**guinea pig** *n* : a small stocky short-eared and nearly tailless So. American rodent

**guise** \'gīz\ *n* 1 : a form or style of dress : COSTUME 2 : external appearance : SEMBLANCE

**gui·tar** \gə-'tär, gi-\ *n* : a musical instrument with usu. six strings plucked with a pick or with the fingers

**gulch** \'gəlch\ *n* : RAVINE

**gul·den** \'gül-dən, 'gül-\ *n, pl* **guldens** *or* **gulden** — see MONEY table

**gulf** \'gəlf\ *n* [ME *goulf*, fr. MF *golfe*, fr. It *golfo*, fr. LL *colpus*, fr. Gk *kolpos* bosom, gulf] 1 : an extension of an ocean or a sea into the land 2 : ABYSS, CHASM 3 : a wide separation

**¹gull** \'gəl\ *n* : a usu. white and gray long-winged web-footed seabird

**²gull** *vb* : to make a dupe of : DECEIVE — **gull·ible** *adj*

**³gull** *n* : DUPE

**gul·let** \'gəl-ət\ *n* : ESOPHAGUS; *also* : THROAT

**gul·ly** \'gəl-ē\ *n, pl* **gullies** : a trench worn in the earth by running water after rains

**gulp** \'gəlp\ *vb* 1 : to swallow hurriedly or greedily 2 : SUPPRESS (~ down a sob) 3 : to catch the breath as if in taking a long drink — **gulp** *n*

**¹gum** \'gəm\ *n* : the tissue along the jaw that surrounds the necks of the teeth

**²gum** *n* 1 : a sticky plant exudate; *esp* : one that hardens on drying and is soluble in or swells in water and that includes substances used as emulsifiers, adhesives, and thickeners and in inks 2 : a sticky substance 3 : a preparation usu. of a plant gum sweetened and flavored and used as a chew — **gum·my** *adj*

**gum arabic** *n* : a water-soluble gum obtained from several acacias and used esp. in adhesives, in confectionery, and in pharmacy

**gum·bo** \'gəm-bō\ *n* [American French *gombo*, of Bantu origin] : a rich thick soup usu. thickened with okra

**gum·boil** \'gəm-,bóil\ *n* : an abscess in the gum

**gum·drop** \'gəm-,dräp\ *n* : a candy made usu. from corn syrup with gelatin and coated with sugar crystals

**gump·tion** \'gəmp-shən\ *n* 1 : shrewd common sense 2 : ENTERPRISE, INITIATIVE

**gum·shoe** \'gəm-,shü\ *n* : DETECTIVE — **gumshoe** *vb*

**¹gun** \'gən\ *n* 1 : CANNON 2 : a portable firearm 3 : a discharge of a gun 4 : something suggesting a gun in shape or function 5 : THROTTLE

**²gun** *vb* **gunned; gun·ning** 1 : to hunt with a gun 2 : SHOOT 3 : to open up the throttle of so as to increase speed

**gun·boat** \'gən-,bōt\ *n* : a small lightly armed ship for use in shallow waters

**gun·cot·ton** \-,kät-ᵊn\ *n* : an explosive usu. made by soaking cotton with nitric and sulfuric acids

**gun·fight** \-,fīt\ *n* : a duel with guns — **gun·fight·er** \-ər\ *n*

**gun·fire** \-,fī(ə)r\ *n* : the firing of guns

**gung ho** \'gəŋ-'hō\ *adj* [*Gung ho!*, motto (interpreted as meaning "work together") of certain U.S. marine raiders in World War II, fr. Chin *kung¹-ho²*, short for *chung¹-kuo² kung¹-yeh⁴ ho²-tso⁴ she⁴* Chinese Industrial Cooperatives Society] : extremely zealous

**gun·lock** \'gən-,läk\ *n* : a device on a firearm by which the charge is ignited

**gun·man** \-mən\ *n* : a man armed with a gun; *esp* : an armed bandit or gangster

**gun·ner** \'gən-ər\ *n* 1 : a soldier or airman who operates or aims a gun 2 : one that hunts with a gun

**gun·nery** \'gən-(ə-)rē\ *n* : the use of guns; *esp* : the science of the flight of projectiles and effective use of guns

**gunnery sergeant** *n* : a noncommissioned officer in the marine corps ranking next below a first sergeant

**gun·ny** \'gən-ē\ *n* : coarse jute or hemp material for making sacks

**gun·ny·sack** \-,sak\ *n* : a sack made of gunny

**gun·point** \-,póint\ *n* : the point of a gun — **at gunpoint** : under a threat of death by being shot

**gun·pow·der** \-,paùd-ər\ *n* : explosive powder used in guns and blasting

**gun·shot** \-,shät\ *n* 1 : shot or a projectile fired from a gun 2 : the range of a gun (within ~)

**gun-shy** \-ˌshī\ *adj* **1 :** afraid of a loud noise **2 :** markedly distrustful

**gun-sling-er** \-ˌsliŋ-ər\ *n* **:** a gunman esp. in the old West

**gun-smith** \-ˌsmith\ *n* **:** one who makes and repairs firearms

**gun-wale** *or* **gun-nel** \ˈgən-ᵊl\ *n* **:** the upper edge of a ship's or boat's side

**gup-py** \ˈgəp-ē\ *n, pl* **guppies** [after R.J.L. *Guppy* d1916 Trinidadian naturalist] **:** a tiny brightly colored tropical fish

**gur-gle** \ˈgər-gəl\ *vb* **gur-gled; gur-gling** \-g(ə-)liŋ\ **1 :** to flow in a broken irregular current **2 :** to make a sound like that of a gurgling liquid — **gurgle** *n*

**Gur-kha** \ˈgu̇(ə)r-kə, ˈgər-\ *n* **:** a soldier from Nepal in the British or Indian army

**gu-ru** \gə-ˈrü, ˈgu̇(ə)r-(ˌ)ü\ *n, pl* **gurus** **1 :** a personal religious teacher and spiritual guide in Hinduism **2 :** an intellectual guide in matters of fundamental concern

**gush** \ˈgəsh\ *vb* **1 :** to issue or pour forth copiously or violently **:** SPOUT **2 :** to make an effusive display of affection or enthusiasm

**gush-er** \ˈgəsh-ər\ *n* **:** one that gushes; *esp* **:** an oil well with a large natural flow

**gushy** \ˈgəsh-ē\ *adj* **gush-i-er; -est :** marked by effusive sentimentality

**gus-set** \ˈgəs-ət\ *n* [ME, piece of armor covering the joints in a suit of armor, fr. MF *gouchet*] **:** a triangular insert (as in a seam of a sleeve) to give width or strength — **gusset** *vb*

**gus-sy up** \ˌgəs-ē-\ *vb* **:** to dress up

¹**gust** \ˈgəst\ *n* **1 :** a sudden brief rush of wind **2 :** a sudden outburst **:** SURGE — **gusty** *adj*

²**gust** *vb* **:** to blow in gusts

**gus-ta-to-ry** \ˈgəs-tə-ˌtōr-ē\ *adj* **:** of, relating to, or being the sense or sensation of taste

**gus-to** \ˈgəs-tō\ *n, pl* **gustoes :** RELISH, ZEST

¹**gut** \ˈgət\ *n* **1** *pl* **:** BOWELS, ENTRAILS **2 :** the alimentary canal or a part of it (as the intestine); *also* **:** BELLY, ABDOMEN **3** *pl* **:** the inner essential parts **4** *pl* **:** COURAGE, STAMINA

²**gut** *vb* **gut-ted; gut-ting 1 :** EVISCERATE **2 :** to destroy the inside of

**gut-ter** \ˈgət-ər\ *n* **:** a channel for carrying off rainwater

**gut-ter-snipe** \-ˌsnīp\ *n* **:** a street urchin

**gut-tur-al** \ˈgət-ə-rəl\ *adj* **1 :** of or relating to the throat **3 :** sounded in the throat **3 :** being or marked by an utterance that is strange, unpleasant, or disagreeable — **guttural** *n*

**gut-ty** \ˈgət-ē\ *adj* **gut-ti-er; -est :** being vital, bold, and challenging

¹**guy** \ˈgī\ *n* **:** a rope, chain, or rod attached to something to steady it

²**guy** *vb* **:** to steady or reinforce with a guy

³**guy** *n* **:** MAN, FELLOW

⁴**guy** *vb* **:** to make fun of **:** RIDICULE

**Guy-a-nese** \ˌgī-ə-ˈnēz\ *n, pl* **Guya-nese :** a native or inhabitant of Guyana — **Guyanese** *adj*

**guy-ot** \ˈgē-(ˌ)ō\ *n* **:** a flat-topped seamount

**guz-zle** \ˈgəz-əl\ *vb* **guz-zled: guz-zling** \-(ə-)liŋ\ **:** to drink greedily

**gym** \ˈjim\ *n* **:** GYMNASIUM

**gym-kha-na** \jim-ˈkän-ə\ *n* **:** a meet featuring sports contests; *esp* **:** a contest designed to test automobile-driving skill

**gym-na-si-um** \*for 1* jim-ˈnā-zē-əm, -zhəm, *for 2* gim-ˈnä-zē-əm\ *n, pl* **-na-si-ums** *or* **-na-sia** \-ˈnā-zē-ə, -ˈnä-zhə; -ˈnä-zē-ə\ [L, exercise ground, school, fr. Gk *gymnasion*, fr. *gymnazein* to exercise naked, fr. *gymnos* naked] **1 :** a place or building for indoor sports activities **2 :** a German secondary school that prepares students for the university

**gym-nas-tics** \jim-ˈnas-tiks\ *n* **:** physical exercises performed in or adapted to performance in a gymnasium — **gym-nast** \ˈjim-ˌnast\ *n* — **gym-nas-tic** *adj*

**gym-no-sperm** \ˈjim-nə-ˌspərm\ *n* **:** any of a class or subdivision of woody vascular seed plants (as conifers) that produce naked seeds not enclosed in an ovary

**gy-ne-col-o-gy** \ˌgīn-ə-ˈkäl-ə-jē, ˌjin-\ *n* **:** a branch of medicine dealing with the diseases and hygiene of women — **gy-ne-co-log-ic** \ˌgīn-i-kə-ˈläj-ik, ˌjin-\ *or* **gy-ne-co-log-i-cal** \-i-kəl\ *adj* — **gy-ne-col-o-gist** \ˌgīn-ə-ˈkäl-ə-jəst, ˌjin-\ *n*

**gyp** \ˈjip\ *n* **1 :** CHEAT, SWINDLER **2 :** FRAUD, SWINDLE — **gyp** *vb*

**gyp-sum** \ˈjip-səm\ *n* **:** a calcium-containing mineral used in making plaster of paris

**Gyp-sy** \ˈjip-sē\ *n, pl* **Gypsies** [by shortening & alter. fr. *Egyptian*] **:** one of a dark Caucasian race coming orig. from India and living chiefly in Europe and the U.S.; *also* **:** the language of the Gypsies

**gypsy moth** *n* **:** an Old World moth that was introduced into the U.S. where its caterpillar is a destructive defoliator of many trees

**gy-rate** \ˈjī-ˌrāt\ *vb* **gy-rat-ed; gy-rat-ing 1 :** to revolve around a point or axis **2 :** to oscillate with or as if with a circular or spiral motion — **gy-ra-tion** \jī-ˈrā-shən\ *n*

**gyr-fal-con** \ˈjər-ˌfal-kən, -ˌfȯ(l)-\ *n* **:** an arctic falcon that is the largest of all falcons and occurs in several forms

**gy-ro** \ˈjī-rō\ *n, pl* **gyros 1 :** GYROSCOPE **2 :** GYROCOMPASS

**gy-ro-com-pass** \-ˌkəm-pəs, -ˌkäm-\ *n* **:** a compass in which the axis of a spinning gyroscope points to the north

**gy-ro-scope** \-ˌskōp\ *n* **:** a wheel or disk mounted to spin rapidly about an axis that is free to turn in various directions

**Gy Sgt** *abbr* gunnery sergeant

**gyve** \ˈjīv, ˈgīv\ *n* **:** FETTER — usu. used in pl. — **gyve** *vb*

**H** ¹h \'āch\ *n, pl* **h's** *or* **hs** \'ā-chəz\ *often cap* : the 8th letter of the English alphabet

⁴h *abbr, often cap* **1** hard; hardness **2** heroin **3** hit **4** husband

**H** *symbol* hydrogen

**ha** *abbr* hectare

**Hab** *abbr* Habakkuk

**ha·ba·ne·ra** \,(h)äb-ə-'ner-ə\ *n* [Sp (*danza*) *habanera* lit., dance of Havana] : a Cuban dance in slow time; *also* : the music for this dance

**ha·be·as cor·pus** \,hā-bē-əs-'kȯr-pəs\ *n* [ME, fr. ML, lit., you should have the body (the opening words of the writ)] : a writ issued to bring a party before a court

**hab·er·dash·er** \'hab-ə(r)-,dash-ər\ *n* : a dealer in men's furnishings

**hab·er·dash·ery** \-,dash-(ə-)rē\ *n, pl* **-er·ies 1** : goods sold by a haberdasher **2** : a haberdasher's shop

**ha·bil·i·ment** \hə-'bil-ə-mənt\ *n* **1** *pl* : TRAPPINGS, EQUIPMENT **2** : DRESS; *esp* : the dress characteristic of an occupation or occasion — usu. used in pl.

**hab·it** \'hab-ət\ *n* **1** : DRESS, GARB **2** : BEARING, CONDUCT **3** : PHYSIQUE **4** : mental makeup **5** : a usual manner of behavior : CUSTOM **6** : a behavior pattern acquired by frequent repetition **7** : ADDICTION **8** : mode of growth or occurrence

**hab·it·able** \'hab-ət-ə-bəl\ *adj* : capable of being lived in — **hab·it·abil·i·ty** \,hab-ət-ə-'bil-ət-ē\ *n* — **hab·it·able·ness** \'hab-ət-ə-bəl-nəs\ *n* — **hab·it·ably** \-blē\ *adv*

**hab·i·tant** \'hab-ət-ənt\ *n* : INHABITANT, RESIDENT

**hab·i·tat** \'hab-ə-,tat\ *n* [L, it inhabits] : the place or kind of place where a plant or animal naturally occurs

**hab·i·ta·tion** \,hab-ə-'tā-shən\ *n* **1** : OCCUPANCY **2** : a dwelling place : RESIDENCE **3** : SETTLEMENT

**hab·it-form·ing** \'hab-ət-,fȯr-miŋ\ *adj* : inducing the formation of an addiction

**ha·bit·u·al** \hə-'bich-(ə-w)əl\ *adj* **1** : CUSTOMARY **2** : doing, practicing, or acting in some manner by force of habit **3** : inherent in an individual — **ha·bit·u·al·ly** \-ē\ *adv* — **ha·bit·u·al·ness** *n*

**ha·bit·u·ate** \hə-'bich-ə-,wāt\ *vb* **-at·ed; -at·ing** : ACCUSTOM

**ha·bit·u·a·tion** \-,bich-ə-'wā-shən\ *n* **1** : the process of making habitual **2** : psychologic dependence on a drug after a period of use

**ha·bi·tué** \hə-'bich-ə-,wā\ *n* : one who frequents a place or class of places

**ha·ci·en·da** \,(h)äs-ē-'en-də\ *n* **1** : a landed estate in a Spanish-speaking country **2** : the main building of a farm or ranch

¹**hack** \'hak\ *vb* **1** : to cut with repeated irregular blows : CHOP **2** : to cough in a short dry manner **3** : to manage successfully — **hack·er** *n*

²**hack** *n* **1** : an implement for hacking;

*also* : a hacking blow **2** : a short dry cough

³**hack** *n* **1** : a horse let out for hire or used for varied work; *also* : a horse worn out in service **2** : a light easy often 3-gaited saddle horse **3** : HACKNEY 2, TAXICAB **4** : a writer who works mainly for hire — **hack** *adj*

⁴**hack** *vb* : to operate a taxicab

**hack·ie** \'hak-ē\ *n* : a taxicab driver

**hack·le** \'hak-əl\ *n* **1** : one of the long feathers on the neck or lower back of a bird **2** *pl* : hairs (as on the neck of a dog) that can be erected **3** *pl* : TEMPER, DANDER

**hack·man** \'hak-mən\ *n* : HACKIE

¹**hack·ney** \'hak-nē\ *n, pl* **hackneys 1** : a horse for riding or driving **2** : a carriage or automobile kept for hire

²**hackney** *vb* : to make trite or commonplace

**hack·neyed** \'hak-nēd\ *adj* : lacking in freshness or originality

**hack·saw** \'hak-,sȯ\ *n* : a fine-tooth saw in a frame for cutting metal

**hack·work** \-,wərk\ *n* : work done on order usu. according to a formula

**had** *past of* HAVE

**had·dock** \'had-ək\ *n, pl* **haddock** *also* **haddocks** : an Atlantic food fish usu. smaller than the related cod

**Ha·des** \'hād-(,)ēz\ *n* **1** : the abode of the dead in Greek mythology **2** *often not cap* : HELL

**haem·or·rhage** \'hem-(ə-)rij\ *var of* HEMORRHAGE

**haf·ni·um** \'haf-nē-əm\ *n* : a gray metallic chemical element

**haft** \'haft\ *n* : the handle of a weapon or tool

**hag** \'hag\ *n* **1** : WITCH **2** : an ugly, slatternly, or evil-looking old woman

**Hag** *abbr* Haggai

**hag·gard** \'hag-ərd\ *adj* : having a worn or emaciated appearance **syn** careworn, wasted - **hag·gard·ly** *adv*

**hag·gis** \'hag-əs\ *n* : a pudding popular esp. in Scotland made of the heart, liver, and lungs of a sheep or a calf minced with suet, onions, oatmeal

**hag·gle** \'hag-əl\ *vb* **hag·gled; hag·gling** \-(ə-)liŋ\ : to argue in bargaining — **hag·gler** \-(ə-)lər\ *n*

**ha·gi·og·ra·phy** \,hag-ē-'äg-rə-fē, ,hā-jē-\ *n* **1** : biography of saints or venerated persons **2** : idealizing or idolizing biography — **hag·i·og·ra·pher** \-fər\ *n*

**hai·ku** \'hī-(,)kü\ *n, pl* **haiku** : an unrhymed Japanese verse form of three lines containing 5, 7, and 5 syllables respectively; *also* : a poem in this form

¹**hail** \'hāl\ *n* **1** : precipitation in the form of small lumps of ice **2** : something that gives the effect of falling hail

²**hail** *vb* **1** : to precipitate hail **2** : to hurl forcibly

³**hail** *interj* [ME, fr. ON *heill*, fr. *heill* healthy] — used to express acclamation

⁴**hail** *vb* : SALUTE, GREET

⁵**hail** *n* **1** : an expression of greeting, approval, or praise **2** : hearing distance

**Hail Mary** *n* : a salutation and prayer to the Virgin Mary

**hail·stone** \-ˌstōn\ *n* : a pellet of hail

**hail·storm** \-ˌstȯrm\ *n* : a storm accompanied by hail

**hair** \'haər\ *n* : a threadlike outgrowth esp. of the skin of a mammal; *also* : a covering (as of the head) consisting of such hairs — **haired** \'haərd\ *adj* — **hair·less** *adj*

**hair·breadth** \-ˌbredth\ *or* **hairs·breadth** \'haərz-\ *n* : a very small distance or margin

**hair·brush** \-ˌbrəsh\ *n* : a brush for the hair

**hair·cloth** \-ˌklȯth\ *n* : a stiff wiry fabric used esp. for upholstery

**hair·cut** \-ˌkət\ *n* : the act, process, or style of cutting and shaping the hair

**hair·do** \'haər-ˌdü\ *n, pl* **hairdos** : a way of dressing a woman's hair

**hair·dress·er** \-ˌdres-ər\ *n* : one who dresses or cuts women's hair

**hair·line** \-'līn\ *n* 1 : a very slender line  2 : the outline of the scalp or of the hair on the head

**hair·piece** \-ˌpēs\ *n* 1 : TOUPEE  2 : supplementary hair (as a switch) used in some women's hairdos

**hair·pin** \-ˌpin\ *n* : a U-shaped pin to hold the hair in place

**hair·rais·ing** \'haər-ˌrā-ziŋ\ *adj* : causing terror or astonishment

**hair·split·ter** \-ˌsplit-ər\ *n* : a person who makes unnecessarily fine distinctions in reasoning or argument — **hair·split·ting** \-ˌsplit-iŋ\ *adj or n*

**hair·style** \-ˌstīl\ *n* : a way of wearing the hair

**hair·styl·ist** \-ˌstī-ləst\ *n* : HAIRDRESSER — **hair·styl·ing** \-ˌstī-liŋ\ *n*

**hair-trigger** *adj* : immediately responsive to the slightest stimulus

**hair trigger** *n* : a trigger adjusted to respond to very slight pressure

**hairy** \'ha(ə)r-ē\ *adj* **hair·i·er; -est** : covered with or as if with hair — **hair·i·ness** \'har-ē-nəs\ *n*

**hairy woodpecker** *n* : a common No. American woodpecker with a white back that is larger than the similarly marked downy woodpecker

**hajji** \'haj-ē\ *n* : one who has made a pilgrimage to Mecca—often used as a title

**hake** \'hāk\ *n* : a marine food fish related to the cod

**ha·la·la** \hə-'läl-ə\ *n, pl* **halala** *or* **halalas**    see *riyal* at MONEY table

**hal·berd** \'hal-bərd, 'hȯl-\ *or* **hal·bert** \-bərt\ *n* : a weapon esp. of the 15th and 16th centuries consisting of a battle-ax and pike on a long handle

**hal·cy·on** \'hal-sē-ən\ *adj* [Gk *halkyōn*, a mythical bird believed to nest at sea and to calm the waves] : CALM, PEACEFUL

¹**hale** \'hāl\ *adj* : free from defect, disease, or infirmity **syn** healthy, sound, robust, well

²**hale** *vb* **haled; hal·ing** 1 : HAUL, PULL  2 : to compel to go ⟨haled him into court⟩

**ha·ler** \'häl-ər\ *n, pl* **halers** *or* **ha·le·ru** \'häl-ə-ˌrü\ — see *koruna* at MONEY table

¹**half** \'haf, 'hȧf\ *n, pl* **halves** \'havz, 'hȧvz\ 1 : one of two equal parts into which something is divisible  2 : one of a pair

²**half** *adj* 1 : being one of two equal parts; *also* : amounting to nearly half  2 : of half the usual size or extent  3 : PARTIAL, IMPERFECT — **half** *adv*

**half·back** \'haf-ˌbak, 'hȧf-\ *n* 1 : a football back stationed on or near the flank  2 : a player stationed immediately behind the forward line

**half-baked** \-'bākt\ *adj* 1 : not thoroughly baked  2 : poorly planned; *also* : lacking intelligence or common sense

**half boot** *n* : a boot with a top reaching above the ankle

**half-breed** \'haf-ˌbrēd, 'hȧf-\ *n* : the offspring of parents of different races — **half-breed** *adj*

**half brother** *n* : a brother by one parent only

**half-caste** \'haf-ˌkast, 'hȧf-\ *n* : one of mixed racial descent — **half-caste** *adj*

**half·heart·ed** \'haf-'härt-əd, 'hȧf-\ *adj* : lacking spirit or interest — **half·heart·ed·ly** *adv* — **half·heart·ed·ness** *n*

**half-life** \-ˌlīf\ *n* : the time required for half of something to undergo a process

**half-mast** \-'mast\ *n* : a point some distance but not necessarily halfway down below the top of a mast or staff or the peak of a gaff ⟨flags hanging at ~⟩

**half·pen·ny** \'hāp-(ə)-nē\ *n, pl* **half·pence** \'hā-pəns\ *or* **halfpennies** : a British coin representing one half of a penny

**half-pint** \'haf-ˌpīnt, 'hȧf-\ *adj* : of less than average size — **half-pint** *n*

**half sister** *n* : a sister by one parent only

**half step** *n* : a pitch interval between any two adjacent keys on a keyboard instrument

**half-track** \'haf-ˌtrak, 'hȧf-\ *n* 1 : an endless chain-track drive system that propels a vehicle supported in front by a pair of wheels  2 : a motor vehicle propelled by half-tracks; *esp* : such a vehicle lightly armored for military use

**half-truth** \-ˌtrüth\ *n* : a statement that is only partially true; *esp* : one that mingles truth and falsehood and is deliberately intended to deceive

**half·way** \-'wā\ *adj* 1 : midway between two points  2 : PARTIAL — **half·way** *adv*

**half-wit** \'haf-ˌwit, 'hȧf-\ *n* : a foolish or imbecilic person — **half-wit·ted** \-'wit-əd\ *adj*

**hal·i·but** \'hal-ə-bət\ *n, pl* **halibut** *also* **halibuts** [ME *halybutte*, fr. *haly, holy* holy + *butte* flatfish, fr. its being eaten on holy days] : a large edible marine flatfish

**ha·lite** \'hal-ˌīt, 'hā-ˌlīt\ *n* : mineral sodium chloride

**hal·i·to·sis** \ˌhal-ə-'tō-səs\ *n* : a condition of having fetid breath

**hall** \'hȯl\ *n* 1 : the residence of a

medieval king or noble; *also* : the house of a landed proprietor **2** : a large public building **3** : a college or university building **4** : LOBBY; *also* : CORRIDOR **5** : AUDITORIUM

**hal·le·lu·jah** \,hal-ə-'lü-yə\ *interj* [Heb *halălūyāh* praise (ye) the Lord] — used to express praise, joy, or thanks

**hall·mark** \'hȯl-,märk\ *n* **1** : a mark put on an article to indicate origin, purity, or genuineness **2** : a distinguishing characteristic

**hal·lo** \hə-'lō, ha-\ *or* **hal·loo** \-'lü\ *var of* HOLLO

**hal·low** \'hal-ō\ *vb* **1** : CONSECRATE **2** : REVERE — **hal·lowed** \-ōd, -ə-wəd\ *adj*

**Hal·low·een** \,hal-ə-'wēn, ,häl-\ *n* : the evening of October 31 observed esp. by children in merrymaking and masquerading

**hal·lu·ci·nate** \hə-'lüs-ᵊn-,āt\ *vb* -**nat·ed**; -**nat·ing** : to perceive or experience as an hallucination

**hal·lu·ci·na·tion** \hə-,lüs-ᵊn-'ā-shən\ *n* : perception of objects or events with no existence in reality due usu. to use of drugs or to disorder of the nervous system; *also* : something so perceived **syn** delusion, illusion, mirage — **hal·lu·ci·na·tive** \-'lüs-ᵊn-,āt-iv\ *adj* — **hal·lu·ci·na·to·ry** \-ᵊn-ə-,tōr-ē\ *adj*

**hal·lu·ci·no·gen** \hə-'lüs-ᵊn-ə-jən\ *n* : a substance that induces hallucinations — **hal·lu·ci·no·gen·ic** \-,lüs-ᵊn-ə-'jen-ik\ *adj*

**hall·way** \'hȯl-,wā\ *n* : an entrance hall; *also* : CORRIDOR

**ha·lo** \'hā-lō\ *n, pl* **halos** *or* **haloes** [L *halos*, fr. Gk *halōs* threshing floor, disk, halo] **1** : a circle of light appearing to surround a shining body (as the sun) **2** : the aura of glory surrounding an idealized person or thing

**¹halt** \'hȯlt\ *adj* : LAME

**²halt** *n* : STOP

**³halt** *vb* **1** : to stop marching or traveling **2** : DISCONTINUE, END

**¹hal·ter** \'hȯl-tər\ *n* **1** : a rope or strap for leading or tying an animal; *also* : HEADSTALL **2** : NOOSE; *also* : death by hanging **3** : a brief blouse held in place by straps around the neck and across the back

**²halter** *vb* **hal·tered**; **hal·ter·ing** \-t(ə-)riŋ\ **1** : to catch with or as if with a halter; *also* : to put a halter on (as a horse) **2** : HAMPER, RESTRAIN

**halt·ing** \'hȯl-tiŋ\ *adj* **1** : LAME, LIMPING **2** : UNCERTAIN, FALTERING — **halt·ing·ly** *adv*

**halve** \'hav, 'hàv\ *vb* **halved**; **halv·ing** **1** : to divide into two equal parts; *also* : to share equally **2** : to reduce to one half

**halv·ers** \'hav-ərz, 'hàv-\ *n pl* : half shares

**halves** *pl of* HALF

**hal·yard** \'hal-yərd\ *n* : a rope or tackle for hoisting and lowering

**¹ham** \'ham\ *n* **1** : a buttock with its associated thigh; *also* : a cut of meat and esp. pork from this region **2** : an inept actor esp. in a highly theatrical style **3** : an operator of an amateur radio station — **ham** *adj*

**²ham** *vb* **hammed**; **ham·ming** : to overplay a part : OVERACT

**hama·dry·ad** \,ham-ə-'drī-əd, -,ad\ *n* : a nymph living in the woods

**ham·burg·er** \'ham-,bər-gər\ *or* **hamburg** \-,bərg\ *n* **1** : ground beef **2** : a sandwich consisting of a ground-beef patty in a round roll

**ham·let** \'ham-lət\ *n* : a small village

**¹ham·mer** \'ham-ər\ *n* **1** : a hand tool used for pounding; *also* : something resembling a hammer in form or function **2** : the part of a gun whose striking action causes explosion of the charge **3** : a metal sphere with a flexible wire handle that is hurled for distance in a track-and-field event (**hammer throw**)

**²hammer** *vb* **ham·mered**; **ham·mer·ing** \'ham-(ə-)riŋ\ **1** : to beat, drive, or shape with repeated blows of a hammer : POUND **2** : to produce or bring about as if by repeated blows

**ham·mer·head** \'ham-ər-,hed\ *n* **1** : the striking part of a hammer **2** : any of various medium-sized sharks with eyes at the ends of lateral extensions of the flattened head

**ham·mer·lock** \-,läk\ *n* : a wrestling hold in which an opponent's arm is held bent behind his back

**ham·mer·toe** \-'tō\ *n* : a deformed toe with the second and third joints permanently flexed

**ham·mock** \'ham-ək\ *n* [Sp *hamaca*, of AmerInd origin] : a swinging couch hung by cords at each end

**¹ham·per** \'ham-pər\ *vb* **ham·pered**; **ham·per·ing** \-p(ə-)riŋ\ : IMPEDE **syn** trammel, clog, fetter, shackle

**²hamper** *n* : a large basket

**ham·ster** \'ham-stər\ *n* : a stocky short-tailed Old World rodent with large cheek pouches

**ham·string** \'ham-,striŋ\ *vb* -**strung** \-,strəŋ\; -**string·ing** \-,striŋ-iŋ\ **1** : to cripple by cutting the leg tendons **2** : to make ineffective or powerless

**¹hand** \'hand\ *n* **1** : the end of a front limb when modified (as in man) for grasping **2** : personal possession — usu. used in pl; *also* : CONTROL **3** : SIDE **4** : a pledge esp. of betrothal **5** : HANDWRITING **6** : SKILL, ABILITY; *also* : a significant part **7** : SOURCE **8** : ASSISTANCE; *also* : PARTICIPATION **9** : an outburst of applause **10** : a single round in a card game; *also* : the cards held by a player after a deal **11** : WORKER, EMPLOYEE; *also* : a member of a ship's crew — **hand·less** \'han-(d)ləs\ *adj* — **at hand** : near in time or place

**²hand** *vb* **1** : to lead, guide, or assist with the hand **2** : to give, pass, or transmit with the hand

**hand·bag** \'hand(d)-,bag\ *n* : a woman's bag for carrying small personal articles and money

**hand·ball** \-,bȯl\ *n* : a game played by striking a small rubber ball against a wall with the hand

**hand·bar·row** \-,bar-ō\ *n* : a flat rectangular frame with handles at both ends that is carried by two persons

**hand·bill** \-,bil\ *n* **:** a small printed sheet for distribution by hand

**hand·book** \-,búk\ *n* **:** a concise reference book **:** MANUAL

**hand·car** \'han(d)-,kär\ *n* **:** a small 4-wheeled railroad car propelled by hand or by a small motor

**hand·clasp** \-,klasp\ *n* **:** HANDSHAKE

**hand·craft** \-,kraft\ *vb* **:** to fashion by manual skill

¹**hand·cuff** \-,kəf\ *vb* **:** MANACLE

²**handcuff** *n* **:** a metal fastening that can be locked around a wrist and is usu. connected with another such fastening

**hand·ful** \'han(d)-,fúl\ *n* **1 :** as much or as many as the hand will grasp **2 :** a small number ⟨a ∼ of people⟩ **3 :** as much as one can manage

**hand·gun** \-,gən\ *n* **:** a firearm held and fired with one hand

¹**hand·i·cap** \'han-di-,kap\ *n* [obs. E *handicap* (a game in which forfeits were held in a cap), fr. *hand in cap*] **1 :** a contest in which an artificial advantage is given or disadvantage imposed on a contestant to equalize chances of winning; *also* **:** the advantage given or disadvantage imposed **2 :** a disadvantage that makes achievement difficult

²**handicap** *vb* **-capped; -cap·ping 1 :** to give a handicap to **2 :** to put at a disadvantage

**hand·i·cap·per** \-,kap-ər\ *n* **:** one who predicts the winners in a horse race usu. for a publication

**hand·i·craft** \'han-di-,kraft\ *n* **1 :** manual skill **2 :** an occupation requiring manual skill **3 :** the articles fashioned by those engaged in handicraft — **hand·i·craft·er** *n* — **hand·i·crafts·man** \-,krafts-mən\ *n*

**hand in glove** *or* **hand and glove** *adv* **:** in an extremely close relationship

**hand·i·work** \-,wərk\ *n* **:** work done personally

**hand·ker·chief** \'haŋ-kər-chəf, -,chēf\ *n, pl* **-chiefs** \-chəfs, -,chēfs\ *also* **-chieves** \-,chēvz\ **:** a small piece of cloth used for various personal purposes (as the wiping of the face)

¹**han·dle** \'han-dᵊl\ *n* **:** a part (as of a tool) designed to be grasped by the hand — **off the handle :** into a state of sudden and violent anger

²**handle** *vb* **han·dled; han·dling** \'han-dliŋ\ **1 :** to touch, hold, or manage with the hands **2 :** to deal with **3 :** to deal or trade in — **han·dler** \'han-dlər\ *n*

**han·dle·bars** \-dᵊl-,bärz\ *n* **:** a straight or bent bar with a handle at each end (as for steering a bicycle)

**hand·made** \'han(d)-'mād\ *adj* **:** made by hand or a hand process

**hand·maid·en** \-,mād-ᵊn\ *or* **hand·maid** \-,mād\ *n* **:** a female attendant

**hand-me-down** \'han(d)-mē-,daún\ *adj* **:** used by one person after being used or discarded by another ⟨∼ clothes⟩ — **hand-me-down** *n*

**hand·out** \'hand-,aút\ *n* **1 :** a portion (as of food) given to a beggar **2 :** a

release sent to its subscribers by a news service; *also* **:** a prepared statement released to the press

**hand·pick** \'han(d)-'pik\ *vb* **:** to select personally ⟨a ∼*ed* candidate⟩

**hand·rail** \'hand-,rāl\ *n* **:** a narrow rail for grasping as a support

**hand·saw** \'han(d)-,só\ *n* **:** a saw usu. operated with one hand

**hands down** \'han(d)z-'daún\ *adv* **1 :** with little effort **2 :** without question

**hand·sel** \'han-səl\ *n* **1 :** a gift made as a token of good luck **2 :** a first installment **:** earnest money

**hand·set** \'han(d)-,set\ *n* **:** a combined telephone transmitter and receiver mounted on a handle

**hand·shake** \-,shāk\ *n* **:** a clasping of right hands by two people

**hand·some** \'han-səm\ *adj* [ME *handsom* easy to manipulate] **1 :** SIZABLE, AMPLE **2 :** GENEROUS, LIBERAL **3 :** pleasing and usu. impressive in appearance **:** beautiful, lovely, pretty, comely, fair — **hand·some·ly** *adv* — **hand·some·ness** *n*

**hand·spike** \'han(d)-,spīk\ *n* **:** a bar used as a lever

**hand·spring** \-,spriŋ\ *n* **:** an acrobatic feat in which the body turns forward or backward in a full circle from a standing position and lands first on the hands and then on the feet

**hand·stand** \-,stand\ *n* **:** an act of supporting the body on the hands with the trunk and legs balanced in the air

**hand-to-hand** \'han-tə-,hand\ *adj* **:** being at very close quarters — **hand to hand** *adv*

**hand-to-mouth** \-,maúth\ *adj* **:** having or providing nothing to spare

**hand·wo·ven** \'hand-,wō-vən\ *adj* **:** produced on a hand-operated loom

**hand·writ·ing** \-,rīt-iŋ\ *n* **:** writing done by hand; *also* **:** the form of writing peculiar to a person — **hand·writ·ten** \-,rit-ᵊn\ *adj*

**handy** \'han-dē\ *adj* **hand·i·er; -est 1 :** conveniently near **2 :** easily used **3 :** DEXTEROUS - **hand·i·ly** \'han-də-lē\ *adv* — **hand·i·ness** \-dē-nəs\ *n*

**handy·man** \-,man\ *n* **1 :** one who does odd jobs **2 :** one competent in a variety of small skills or repair work

¹**hang** \'haŋ\ *vb* **hung** \'həŋ\ *also* **hanged** \'haŋd\; **hang·ing** \'haŋ-iŋ\ **1 :** to fasten or remain fastened to an elevated point without support from below; *also* **:** to fasten or be fastened so as to allow free motion on the point of suspension ⟨a ∼ door⟩ **2 :** to put or come to death by suspension (as from a gallows) **3 :** to fasten to a wall ⟨∼ wallpaper⟩ **4 :** to prevent (a jury) from coming to a decision **5 :** to display (pictures) in a gallery **6 :** to remain stationary in the air **7 :** to be imminent **8 :** DEPEND **9 :** to take hold for support **10 :** to be burdensome **11 :** to undergo delay **12 :** to incline downward; *also* **:** to fit or fall from the figure in easy lines **13 :** to be raptly attentive **14 :** LINGER, LOITER — **hanger** *n*

²**hang** n **1** : the manner in which a thing hangs **2** : peculiar and significant meaning **3** : KNACK

**han·gar** \'haŋ-ər\ n : a covered and usu. enclosed area for housing and repairing airplanes

**hang-dog** \'haŋ-ˌdȯg\ adj **1** : ASHAMED, GUILTY **2** : ABJECT, COWED

**hang·er-on** \ˌhaŋ-ər-'ȯn, -'än\ n, pl **hangers–on** : one who hangs around a person or place esp. for personal gain

**hang in** vb : to persist tenaciously

**hang·ing** \'haŋ-iŋ\ n **1** : an execution by strangling or snapping the neck by a suspended noose **2** : something hung — **hanging** adj

**hang·man** \-mən\ n : a public executioner

**hang·nail** \-ˌnāl\ n : a bit of skin hanging loose at the side or base of a fingernail

**hang on** vb **1** : to hang in **2** : to keep a telephone connection open

**hang·out** \'haŋ-ˌaȯt\ n : a favorite or usual place of resort

**hang·over** \-ˌō-vər\ n **1** : something that remains from what is past **2** : disagreeable physical effects following heavy drinking

**hang–up** \'haŋ-ˌəp\ n : a source of mental or emotional difficulty

**hang up** \(')haŋ-'əp\ vb **1** : to place on a hook or hanger **2** : to end a telephone conversation by replacing the receiver on the cradle **3** : to keep delayed or suspended

**hank** \'haŋk\ n : COIL, LOOP

**han·ker** \'haŋ-kər\ vb **hankered**; **han·ker·ing** \-k(ə-)riŋ\ : to desire strongly or persistently — LONG — **han·ker·ing** n

**han·ky-pan·ky** \ˌhaŋ-kē-'paŋ-kē\ n : questionable or underhand activity

**han·sel** var of HANDSEL

**han·som** \'han-səm\ n : a 2-wheeled covered carriage with the driver's seat elevated at the rear

**Ha·nuk·kah** \'kän-ə-kə, 'hän-\ n [Heb ḥănukkāh dedication] : an 8-day Jewish holiday commemorating the rededication of the Temple of Jerusalem after its defilement by Antiochus of Syria

**hao·le** \'haȯ-lē\ n : one who is not a member of the native race of Hawaii; esp : WHITE

**hap** \'hap\ n **1** : HAPPENING **2** : CHANCE, FORTUNE

¹**hap·haz·ard** \hap-'haz-ərd\ n : CHANCE

²**haphazard** adj : marked by lack of plan or order : AIMLESS — **hap·haz·ard·ly** adv — **hap·haz·ard·ness** n

**hap·less** \'hap-ləs\ adj : UNFORTUNATE — **hap·less·ly** adv — **hap·less·ness** n

**hap·loid** \'hap-ˌlȯid\ adj : having the number of chromosomes characteristic of gametic cells — **haploid** n

**hap·ly** \'hap-lē\ adv : by chance

**hap·pen** \'hap-ən\ vb **hap·pened**; **hap·pen·ing** \-(ə-)niŋ\ **1** : to occur by chance **2** : to take place **3** : CHANCE

**hap·pen·ing** \'hap-(ə-)niŋ\ n **1**

: OCCURRENCE **2** : an event or series of events designed to evoke a spontaneous reaction to sensory, emotional, or spiritual stimuli

**hap·pi·ly** \'hap-ə-lē\ adv **1** : LUCKILY **2** : in a happy manner or state ⟨lived ~ ever after⟩ **3** : APTLY, SUCCESSFULLY

**hap·pi·ness** \'hap-i-nəs\ n **1** : a state of well-being and contentment; also : a pleasurable satisfaction **2** : APTNESS

**hap·py** \'hap-ē\ adj **hap·pi·er**; **-est** **1** : FORTUNATE **2** : APT, FELICITOUS **3** : enjoying well-being and contentment **4** : PLEASANT; also : PLEASED, GRATIFIED **syn** glad, cheerful, lighthearted, joyful, joyous

**hap·py–go–lucky** \ˌhap-ē-gō-'lək-ē\ adj : CAREFREE

**hara-kiri** \ˌhar-i-'kir-ē, -'kar-ē\ n : suicide by disembowelment

**ha·rangue** \hə-'raŋ\ n **1** : a bombastic ranting speech **2** : LECTURE — **harangue** vb — **ha·rangu·er** \-'raŋ-ər\ n

**ha·rass** \hə-'ras, 'har-əs\ vb [F harasser, fr. MF, fr. harer to set a dog on, fr. OF hare, interj. used to incite dogs] **1** : to worry and impede by repeated raids **2** : EXHAUST, FATIGUE **3** : to annoy continually **syn** harry, plague, pester, tease, tantalize — **ha·rass·ment** n

**har·bin·ger** \'här-bən-jər\ n : one that announces or foreshadows what is coming : PRECURSOR; also : PORTENT

¹**har·bor** \'här-bər\ n **1** : a place of security and comfort **2** : a part of a body of water protected and deep enough to furnish anchorage : PORT

²**harbor** vb **har·bored**; **har·bor·ing** \-b(ə-)riŋ\ **1** : to give or take refuge : SHELTER **2** : to be the home or habitat of; also : LIVE **3** : to hold a thought or feeling ⟨~ a grudge⟩

**har·bor·age** \-bə-rij\ n : HARBOR

**har·bour** chiefly Brit var of HARBOR

**hard** \'härd\ adj **1** : not easily penetrated **2** : having an alcoholic content of more than 22.5 percent; also : containing salts that prevent lathering with soap ⟨~ water⟩ **3** : stable in value ⟨~ currency⟩ **4** : physically fit; also : free from flaw **5** : FIRM, DEFINITE ⟨~ agreement⟩ **6** : CLOSE, SEARCHING ⟨~ look⟩ **7** : REALISTIC ⟨good ~ sense⟩ **8** : OBDURATE, UNFEELING ⟨~ heart⟩ **9** : difficult to bear ⟨~ times⟩; also : HARSH, SEVERE **10** : RESENTFUL ⟨~ feelings⟩ **11** : STRICT, UNRELENTING ⟨~ bargain⟩ **12** : INCLEMENT ⟨~ winter⟩ **13** : intense in force or manner ⟨~ blow⟩ **14** : ARDUOUS, STRENUOUS ⟨~ work⟩ **15** : TROUBLESOME ⟨~ problem⟩ **16** : having difficulty in doing something ⟨~ of hearing⟩ **17** : addictive and gravely detrimental to health ⟨~ drugs⟩ — **hard** adv — **hard·ness** n

**hard–and–fast** \ˌhärd-ən-'fast\ adj : rigidly binding : STRICT ⟨a ~ rule⟩

**hard·back** \'härd-ˌbak\ n : a book bound in hard covers

**hard–ball** \-ˌbȯl\ n : BASEBALL

**hard–bit·ten** \-'bit-ən\ adj : SEASONED, TOUGH ⟨~ campaigners⟩

**hard·board** \'härd-ˌbŏrd\ n : a composition board made from wood chips

**hard·boiled** \-'bóild\ adj **1 :** boiled until both white and yolk have solidified **2 :** lacking sentiment : CALLOUS; also : HARDHEADED

**hard·bound** \-ˌbaùnd\ adj **:** having rigid cloth- or paper-covered boards on the sides ⟨a ~ book⟩ — **hard·bound** n

**hard·core** \-'kŏr\ adj **1 :** extremely resistant to solution or improvement **2 :** being the most determined or dedicated members of a specified group

**hard·cov·er** \'härd-'kəv-ər\ adj : HARDBOUND

**hard·en** \'härd-ᵊn\ vb **hard·ened**; **hard·en·ing** \'härd-(ᵊ-)niŋ\ **1 :** to make or become hard or harder **2 :** to confirm or become confirmed in disposition, feelings, or action — **hard·en·er** n

**hard·hack** \'härd-ˌhak\ n **:** an American spirea with rusty hairy leaves and dense clusters of pink or white flowers

**hard hat** \-ˌhat\ n : a construction worker

**hard·head·ed** \-'hed-əd\ adj **1 :** STUBBORN, WILLFUL **2 :** SOBER, REALISTIC - **hard·head·ed·ly** adv - **hard·head·ed·ness** n

**hard·heart·ed** \'härd-'härt-əd\ adj : UNFEELING, PITILESS — **hard·heart·ed·ly** adv - **hard·heart·ed·ness** n

**har·di·hood** \'härd-ē-ˌhùd\ n **1 :** resolute courage and fortitude **2 :** VIGOR, ROBUSTNESS

**hard–line** \'härd-'līn\ adj : advocating or involving a persistently firm course of action — **hard–lin·er** \-'lī-nər\ n

**hard·ly** \'härd-lē\ adv **1 :** with force **2 :** SEVERELY **3 :** with difficulty **4 :** not quite : SCARCELY

**hard palate** n : the bony anterior part of the palate forming the roof of the mouth

**hard·pan** \'härd-ˌpan\ n : a compact often clayey layer in soil that is impenetrable by roots

**hard–shell** \-ˌshel\ adj : CONFIRMED, UNCOMPROMISING ⟨a ~ conservative⟩

**hard·ship** \'härd-ˌship\ n **1 :** SUFFERING, PRIVATION **2 :** something that causes suffering or privation

**hard·stand** \-ˌstand\ n : a hard-surfaced area for parking an airplane

**hard·sur·face** \-'sər-fəs\ vb : to provide (as a road) with a paved surface

**hard·tack** \-ˌtak\ n : a hard biscuit made of flour and water without salt

**hard·top** \-ˌtäp\ n : an automobile resembling a convertible but having a rigid top

**hard·ware** \-ˌwaər\ n **1 :** ware (as cutlery or tools) made of metal **2 :** the physical components (as electronic devices) of a vehicle (as a spacecraft) or an apparatus (as a computer)

¹**hard·wood** \'härd-ˌwùd\ n : the wood of a broad-leaved usu. deciduous tree as distinguished from that of a conifer; also : such a tree

²**hardwood** adj **1 :** having or made of hardwood ⟨~ floors⟩ **2 :** consisting of mature woody tissue ⟨~ cuttings⟩

**hard·work·ing** \-'wər-kiŋ\ adj : INDUSTRIOUS

**har·dy** \'härd-ē\ adj **har·di·er; -est 1 :** BOLD, BRAVE **2 :** AUDACIOUS, BRAZEN **3 :** ROBUST; also : able to withstand adverse conditions (as of weather) ⟨~ shrubs⟩ - **har·di·ly** \'härd-ə-lē\ adv — **har·di·ness** \-ē-nəs\ n

**hare** \'haər\ n, pl **hare** or **hares :** a swift timid long-eared mammal distinguished from the related rabbit by being open-eyed and furry at birth

**hare·bell** \-ˌbel\ n : a slender herb with blue bell-shaped flowers

**hare·brained** \-'brānd\ adj : FLIGHTY, FOOLISH

**hare·lip** \-'lip\ n : a deformity in which the upper lip is vertically split — **hare·lipped** \-'lipt\ adj

**ha·rem** \'har-əm\ n [Ar ḥarīm, lit., something forbidden & ḥaram, lit., sanctuary] **1 :** a house or part of a house allotted to women in a Muslim household **2 :** the women and servants occupying a harem **3 :** a group of females associated with one male

**hark** \'härk\ vb : LISTEN

**harken** var of HEARKEN

**har·le·quin** \'här-li-k(w)ən\ n **1** cap **:** a character (as in comedy) with a shaved head, masked face, variegated tights, and wooden sword **2 :** BUFFOON

**har·lot** \'här-lət\ n : PROSTITUTE

¹**harm** \'härm\ n **1 :** physical or mental damage : INJURY **2 :** MISCHIEF, HURT — **harm·ful** \-fəl\ adj — **harm·ful·ly** \-ē\ adv — **harm·ful·ness** n — **harm·less** adj - **harm·less·ly** adv — **harm·less·ness** n

²**harm** vb : to cause harm to : INJURE

¹**har·mon·ic** \här-'män-ik\ adj **1 :** of or relating to musical harmony or harmonics **2 :** pleasing to the ear — **har·mon·i·cal·ly** \-i-k(ə-)lē\ adv

²**harmonic** n : a musical overtone

**har·mon·i·ca** \här-'män-i-kə\ n **:** a small wind instrument played by breathing in and out through metallic reeds

**har·mon·ics** \här-'män-iks\ n : the study of the physical characteristics of musical sounds

**har·mo·ni·ous** \här-'mō-nē-əs\ adj **1 :** musically concordant **2 :** CONGRUOUS **3 :** marked by accord in sentiment or action - **har·mo·ni·ous·ly** adv — **har·mo·ni·ous·ness** n

**har·mo·ni·um** \här-'mō-nē-əm\ n : a keyboard wind instrument in which the wind acts on a set of metal reeds

**har·mo·nize** \'här-mə-ˌnīz\ vb **-nized; -niz·ing 1 :** to play or sing in harmony **2 :** to be in harmony **3 :** to bring into consonance or accord - **har·mo·ni·za·tion** \ˌhär-mə-nə-'zā-shən\ n

**har·mo·ny** \'här-mə-nē\ n, pl **-nies 1 :** musical agreement of sounds; esp : the combination of tones into chords and progressions of chords **2 :** a pleasing arrangement of parts; also : ACCORD **3 :** internal calm

¹**har·ness** \'här-nəs\ n **1 :** the gear

other than a yoke of a draft animal; *also* : something that resembles a harness **2** : occupational routine

²**harness** *vb* **1** : to put a harness on; *also* : YOKE **2** : UTILIZE

¹**harp** \'härp\ *n* : a musical instrument consisting of a triangular frame set with strings plucked by the fingers — **harpist** *n*

²**harp** *vb* **1** : to play on a harp **2** : to dwell on a subject tiresomely — **harper** *n*

**har·poon** \här-'pün\ *n* : a barbed spear used esp. in hunting large fish or whales — **harpoon** *vb* — **har·poon·er** *n*

**harp·si·chord** \'härp-si-,kord\ *n* : a keyboard instrument producing tones by the plucking of its strings with quills or with leather or plastic points

**har·py** \'här-pē\ *n, pl* **harpies** [L *Harpyia*, a mythical predatory monster having a woman's head and a vulture's body, fr. Gk] **1** : a predatory person : LEECH **2** : a shrewish woman

**har·ri·dan** \'har-əd-²n\ *n* : a scolding old woman

¹**har·ri·er** \'har-ē-ər\ *n* **1** : a small hound used esp. in hunting rabbits **2** : a runner on a cross-country team

²**harrier** *n* : a slender long-legged hawk

¹**har·row** \'har-ō\ *n* : an implement set with spikes, spring teeth, or disks and used esp. to pulverize and smooth the soil

²**harrow** *vb* **1** : to cultivate with a harrow **2** : TORMENT, VEX

**har·ry** \'har-ē\ *vb* **har·ried; har·ry·ing 1** : RAID, PILLAGE **2** : to torment by or as if by constant attack **syn** worry, annoy, plague, pester

**harsh** \'härsh\ *adj* **1** : disagreeably rough **2** : causing discomfort or pain **3** : unduly exacting : SEVERE — **harshly** *adv* — **harsh·ness** *n*

**hart** \'härt\ *n* : STAG

**harts·horn** \'härts-,horn\ *n* : a preparation of ammonia used as smelling salts

**har·um-scar·um** \,har-əm-'skar-əm\ *adj* : RECKLESS, IRRESPONSIBLE

¹**har·vest** \'här-vəst\ *n* **1** : the season for gathering in crops; *also* : the act of gathering in a crop **2** : a mature crop **3** : the product or reward of exertion

²**harvest** *vb* : to gather in a crop : REAP — **har·vest·er** *n*

**has** *pres 3d sing of* HAVE

**has-been** \'haz-,bin\ *n* : one that has passed the peak of ability, power, effectiveness, or popularity

¹**hash** \'hash\ *vb* [F *hacher*, fr. OF *hachier*, fr. *hache* battle-ax] **1** : to chop into small pieces **2** : to talk about

²**hash** *n* **1** : chopped meat mixed with potatoes and browned **2** : HODGE-PODGE, JUMBLE

³**hash** *n* : HASHISH

**hash·ish** \'hash-,ēsh, -(,)ish\ *n* : a narcotic and intoxicating preparation from the hemp plant

**hasp** \'hasp\ *n* : a fastener (as for a door) consisting of a hinged metal strap that fits over a staple and is secured by a pin or padlock

**has·sle** \'has-əl\ *n* **1** : WRANGLE; *also* : FIGHT **2** : a strenuous effort : STRUGGLE — **hassle** *vb*

**has·sock** \'has-ək\ *n* [ME, sedge, fr. OE *hassuc*] : a cushion that serves as a seat or leg rest; *also* : a cushion to kneel on in prayer

**haste** \'hāst\ *n* **1** : rapidity of motion or action : SPEED **2** : rash or headlong action **3** : undue eagerness to act : URGENCY — **hast·i·ly** \'hā-stə-lē\ *adv* — **hast·i·ness** \-stē-nəs\ *n* — **hasty** \'hā-stē\ *adj*

**has·ten** \'hās-²n\ *vb* **has·tened; has·ten·ing** \'hās-(²-)niŋ\ **1** : to urge on **2** : to move or act quickly : HURRY **syn** speed, accelerate, quicken

**hat** \'hat\ *n* : a covering for the head usu. having a shaped crown and brim

**hat·box** \-,bäks\ *n* : a round piece of luggage esp. for carrying hats

¹**hatch** \'hach\ *n* **1** : a small door or opening **2** : a door or cover for access down into a compartment of a ship

²**hatch** *vb* **1** : to produce young by incubation; *also* : to emerge from an egg or chrysalis **2** : ORIGINATE — **hatch·ery** \-(ə-)rē\ *n*

**hatch·et** \'hach-ət\ *n* **1** : a short-handled ax with a hammerlike part opposite the blade **2** : TOMAHAWK

**hatchet man** *n* : a person hired for murder, coercion, or unscrupulous attack

**hatch·ing** \'hach-iŋ\ *n* : the engraving or drawing of fine lines in close proximity chiefly to give an effect of shading; *also* : the pattern so created

**hatch·ment** \'hach-mənt\ *n* : a panel on which a coat of arms of a deceased person is temporarily displayed

**hatch·way** \'hach-,wā\ *n* : an opening having a hatch

¹**hate** \'hāt\ *n* **1** : intense hostility and aversion **2** : an object of hatred — **hate·ful** \-fəl\ *adj* — **hate·ful·ly** \-ē\ *adv* — **hate·ful·ness** *n*

²**hate** *vb* **hat·ed; hat·ing 1** : to express or feel extreme enmity **2** : to find distasteful **syn** detest, abhor, abominate, loathe — **hat·er** *n*

**ha·tred** \'hā-trəd\ *n* : HATE; *also* : prejudiced hostility or animosity

**hat·ter** \'hat-ər\ *n* : one that makes, sells, or cleans and repairs hats

**hau·berk** \'ho-bərk\ *n* : a coat of mail

**haugh·ty** \'hot-ē\ *adj* **haugh·ti·er; -est** [obs. *haught*, fr. ME *haute*, fr. MF *haut*, lit., high, fr. L *altus*] : disdainfully proud **syn** insolent, lordly, overbearing — **haugh·ti·ly** \'hot-ə-lē\ *adv* — **haugh·ti·ness** \-ē-nəs\ *n*

¹**haul** \'hol\ *vb* **1** : to exert traction on : DRAW, PULL **2** : to furnish transportation : CART — **haul·er** *n*

²**haul** *n* **1** : PULL, TUG **2** : the result of an effort to collect : TAKE **3** : the distance over which a load is transported; *also* : LOAD

**haul·age** \-ij\ *n* **1** : the act or process of hauling **2** : a charge for hauling

**haunch** \'honch\ *n* **1** : HIP 1 **2** : HINDQUARTER 2 — usu. used in pl. **3** : HINDQUARTER 1

¹haunt \'hȯnt\ *vb* 1 : to visit often : FREQUENT 2 : to recur constantly and spontaneously to; *also* : to reappear continually in 3 : to visit or inhabit as a ghost — **haunt·er** *n* — **haunt·ing·ly** \-iŋ-lē\ *adv*

²haunt \'hȯnt, 2 *is usu* 'hant\ *n* 1 : a place habitually frequented 2 *chiefly dial* : GHOST

**haut·bois** *or* **haut·boy** \'(h)ō-,bȯi\ *n, pl* **-bois** \-,bȯiz\ *or* **-boys** : OBOE

**haute cou·ture** \,ōt-kü-'tü(ə)r\ *n* : the establishments or designers that create fashions for women; *also* : the fashions created

**haute cul·sine** \-kwi-'zēn\ *n* : artful or elaborate cuisine •

**hau·teur** \hȯ-'tər, (h)ō-\ *n* : HAUGHTINESS

¹have \(')hav, (h)əv, v; *in sense 2 before "to" usu* 'haf\ *vb* **had** \(')had, (h)əd\; **hav·ing** \'hav-iŋ\; **has** \(')haz, (h)əz, *in sense 2 before "to" usu* 'has\ 1 : to hold in possession; *also* : to hold in one's use, service, or affection 2 : to be compelled or forced to 3 : to stand in relationship to ⟨*has* many enemies⟩ 4 : OBTAIN; *also* : RECEIVE, ACCEPT 5 : to be marked by 6 : SHOW; *also* : USE, EXERCISE 7 : EXPERIENCE; *also* : TAKE ⟨~ a look⟩ 8 : to entertain in the mind; *also* : MAINTAIN 9 : to cause to 10 : ALLOW 11 : to be competent in 12 : to hold in a disadvantageous position; *also* : TRICK 13 : BEGET 14 : to partake of 15 — used as an auxiliary with the past participle to form the present perfect, past perfect, or future perfect — **have at** : ATTACK — **have coming** : DESERVE — **have done with** : to be finished with — **have had it** : to have endured all one will permit or can stand — **have to do with** 1 : to deal with 2 : to have in the way of connection or relation with or effect on

²have \'hav\ *n* : one that has wealth as distinguished from one that is poor

**ha·ven** \'hā-vən\ *n* 1 : HARBOR, PORT 2 : a place of safety

**have–not** \'hav-,nät, -'nät\ *n* : one that is poor in material wealth as distinguished from one that is rich

**hav·er·sack** \'hav-ər-,sak\ *n* [F *havresac*, fr. G *habersack* bag for oats] : a bag similar to a knapsack but worn over one shoulder

**hav·oc** \'hav-ək\ *n* 1 : wide and general destruction 2 : great confusion and disorder

**haw** \'hȯ\ *n* : a hawthorn berry; *also* : HAWTHORN

**Ha·wai·ian** \hə-'wä-yən, -'wī-(y)ən\ *n* 1 : a native or resident of Hawaii; *esp* : one of Polynesian ancestry 2 : the Polynesian language of the Hawaiians

**hawk** \'hȯk\ *n* 1 : any of numerous mostly small or medium-sized day-flying birds of prey (as a falcon or kite) 2 : a supporter of a war or a warlike policy — **hawk·ish** *adj*

**hawk·er** \'hȯ-kər\ *n* : one who offers goods for sale by calling out in the street — **hawk** *vb*

**hawk·weed** \'hȯk-,wēd\ *n* : any of

several plants related to the daisies usu. having red or orange flower heads

**haw·ser** \'hȯ-zər\ *n* : a large rope for towing, mooring, or securing a ship

**haw·thorn** \'hȯ-,thȯrn\ *n* : a spiny shrub or tree related to the apple and noted for its white or pink fragrant flowers

¹hay \'hā\ *n* 1 : herbage (as grass) mowed and cured for fodder 2 : REWARD; *also* : a small amount of money 3 *slang* : BED ⟨hit the ~⟩

²hay *vb* : to cut, cure, and store for hay

**hay·cock** \'hā-,käk\ *n* : a small conical pile of hay

**hay fever** *n* : an acute allergic catarrh

**hay·fork** \-,fȯrk\ *n* : a hand or mechanically operated fork for loading or unloading hay

**hay·loft** \'hā-,lȯft\ *n* : a loft for hay

**hay·mow** \-,maù\ *n* : a mow of or for hay

**hay·rick** \-,rik\ *n* : a large sometimes thatched outdoor stack of hay

**hay·seed** \'hā-,sēd\ *n, pl* **hayseed** *or* **hayseeds** 1 : clinging bits of straw or chaff from hay 2 : BUMPKIN, YOKEL

**hay·stack** \-,stak\ *n* : a stack of hay

**hay·wire** \-,wī(ə)r\ *adj* 1 : being out of order ⟨the radio went ~⟩ 2 : emotionally or mentally upset : CRAZY

¹haz·ard \'haz-ərd\ *n* [ME, a dice game, fr. MF *hasard*, fr. Ar *az-zahr* the die] 1 : a source of danger 2 : CHANCE; *also* : ACCIDENT 3 : an obstacle on a golf course — **haz·ard·ous** *adj*

²hazard *vb* : VENTURE, RISK

¹haze \'hāz\ *n* 1 : fine dust, smoke, or light vapor causing lack of transparency in the air 2 : vagueness of mind or perception

²haze *vb* **hazed**; **haz·ing** : to harass by abusive and humiliating tricks

**ha·zel** \'hā-zəl\ *n* 1 : any of a genus of shrubs or small trees related to the birches and bearing edible nuts (**ha·zel·nuts** \-,nəts\) 2 : a light brown color

**hazy** \'hā-zē\ *adj* **haz·i·er; -est** 1 : obscured or darkened by haze 2 : VAGUE, INDEFINITE 3 : CLOUDED — **haz·i·ly** \'hā-zə-lē\ *adv* — **haz·i·ness** \-zē-nəs\ *n*

**Hb** *symbol* hemoglobin

**HBM** *abbr* Her Britannic Majesty; His Britannic Majesty

**H-bomb** \'āch-,bäm\ *n* : HYDROGEN BOMB

**hc** *abbr* [L *honoris causa*] for the sake of honor

**HC** *abbr* 1 Holy Communion 2 House of Commons

**HCL** *abbr* high cost of living

**hd** *abbr* head

**HD** *abbr* heavy-duty

**hdbk** *abbr* handbook

**hdkf** *abbr* handkerchief

**hdwe** *abbr* hardware

**he** \(')hē, ē\ *pron* 1 : that male one 2 : a or the person ⟨~ who hesitates is lost⟩

**He** *symbol* helium

**HE** *abbr* 1 His Eminence 2 His Excellency

¹head \'hed\ *n* 1 : the front or upper part of the body containing the brain, the chief sense organs, and the mouth 2 : MIND; *also* : natural aptitude 3 : POISE 4 : the obverse of a coin 5 : INDIVIDUAL; *also, pl* head : a unit of number (as of cattle) 6 : an upper or higher end; *also* : either end of something (as a drum) whose two ends need not be distinguished 7 : DIRECTOR, LEADER; *also* : a leading element (as of a procession) 8 : a projecting part; *also* : the striking part of a weapon 9 : the place of leadership or honor 10 : a separate part or topic 11 : the foam on a fermenting or effervescing liquid 12 : CRISIS 13 : one who uses a drug (as LSD or marijuana) — head•ed \-əd\ *adj* — head•less *adj*

²head *adj* 1 : PRINCIPAL, CHIEF 2 : coming from in front ⟨~ sea⟩

³head *vb* 1 : to cut back the upper growth of 2 : to provide with or form a head; *also* : to form the head of 3 : LEAD, CONDUCT 4 : to get in front of esp. so as to stop; *also* : SURPASS 5 : to put or stand at the head 6 : to point or proceed in a certain direction 7 : ORIGINATE

head•ache \-ˌāk\ *n* 1 : pain in the head 2 : a baffling situation or problem

head•band \'hed-ˌband\ *n* : a band worn on or around the head

head•board \-ˌbōrd\ *n* : a board forming the head (as of a bed)

head cold *n* : a common cold centered in the nasal passages and adjacent mucous tissues

head•dress \'hed-ˌdres\ *n* : an often elaborate covering for the head

head•first \-'fərst\ *adv* : HEADLONG — headfirst *adj*

head•gear \-ˌgiər\ *n* : a covering or protective device for the head

head•hunt•ing \-ˌhənt-iŋ\ *n* : the act or custom of seeking out and decapitating enemies and preserving their heads as trophies — head•hunt•er \-ər\ *n*

head•ing \'hed-iŋ\ *n* 1 : the compass direction in which the longitudinal axis of a ship or airplane points 2 : something that forms or serves as a head

head•land \'hed-lənd,, -ˌland\ *n* : PROMONTORY

head•light \-ˌlīt\ *n* : a light with a reflector and special lens mounted on the front of an automotive vehicle

head•line \-ˌlīn\ *n* : a head of a newspaper story or article usu. printed in large type

head•lock \'hed-ˌläk\ *n* : a wrestling hold in which one encircles his opponent's head with one arm

¹head•long \-'lȯŋ\ *adv* 1 : with the head foremost 2 : RECKLESSLY 3 : without delay

²head•long \-ˌlȯŋ\ *adj* 1 : PRECIPITATE, RASH 2 : plunging with the head foremost

head•man \'hed-'man, -ˌman\ *n* : one who is a leader : CHIEF

head•mas•ter \-ˌmas-tər\ *n* : a man heading the staff of a private school

head•mis•tress \-ˌmis-trəs\ *n* : a woman head of a private school

head•on \'hed-'ȯn, -'än\ *adj* : having the front facing in the direction of initial contact or line of sight ⟨~ collision⟩ — head•on *adv*

head•phone \'hed-ˌfōn\ *n* : an earphone held over the ear by a band worn on the head

head•piece \-ˌpēs\ *n* 1 : a covering for the head 2 : an ornament esp. at the beginning of a chapter

head•pin \-ˌpin\ *n* : the front pin in the triangular formation of pins in tenpins

head•quar•ters \'hed-ˌkwȯrt-ərz\ *n sing or pl* 1 : a place from which a commander performs the functions of command 2 : the administrative center of an enterprise

head•rest \-ˌrest\ *n* 1 : a support for the head 2 : a pad at the top of the back of an automobile seat for preventing whiplash injury

head restraint *n* : HEADREST 2

head•room \'hed-ˌrüm, -ˌrum\ *n* : vertical space in which to stand or move

head•set \-ˌset\ *n* : a pair of headphones

head•ship \-ˌship\ *n* : the position, office, or dignity of a head

heads•man \'hedz-mən\ *n* : EXECUTIONER

head•stall \'hed-ˌstȯl\ *n* : an arrangement of straps or rope encircling the head of an animal and forming part of a bridle or halter

head•stone \-ˌstōn\ *n* : a stone at the head of a grave

head•strong \-ˌstrȯŋ\ *adj* 1 : not easily restrained 2 : directed by ungovernable will **syn** unruly, intractable, willful

head•wait•er \'hed-ˌwāt-ər\ *n* : the head of the dining-room staff of a restaurant or hotel

head•wa•ter \-ˌwȯt-ər, -ˌwät-\ *n* : the source of a stream — usu. used in pl.

head•way \-ˌwā\ *n* 1 : forward motion; *also* : PROGRESS 2 : clear space (as under an arch)

head wind *n* : a wind blowing in a direction opposite to a course esp. in a ship or aircraft

head•word \-ˌwərd\ *n* 1 : a word or term placed at the beginning 2 : a word qualified by a modifier

head•work \-ˌwərk\ *n* : mental work or effort : THINKING

heady \'hed-ē\ *adj* head•i•er; -est 1 : WILLFUL, RASH; *also* : IMPETUOUS 2 : INTOXICATING 3 : SHREWD

heal \'hēl\ *vb* 1 : to make or become sound or whole; *also* : to restore to health 2 : CURE, REMEDY — heal•er *n*

health \'helth\ *n* 1 : sound physical or mental condition; *also* : personal functional condition ⟨in poor ~⟩ 2 : WELL-BEING 3 : a toast to someone's health or prosperity

health•ful \'helth-fəl\ *adj* 1 : beneficial to health 2 : HEALTHY — health•ful•ly \-ē\ *adv* — health•ful•ness *n*

**healthy** \'hel-thē\ *adj* **health·i·er; -est** **1** : enjoying or typical of good health : WELL **2** : evincing or conducive to health **3** : PROSPEROUS; *also* : CONSIDERABLE — **health·i·ly** \'hel-thə-lē\ *adv* — **health·i·ness** \-thē-nəs\ *n*

¹**heap** \'hēp\ *n* : PILE; *also* : LOT

²**heap** *vb* **1** : to throw or lay in a heap **2** : to fill more than full

**hear** \'hiər\ *vb* **heard** \'hərd\; **hear·ing** \'hi(ə)r-iŋ\ **1** : to perceive by the ear **2** : HEED; *also* : ATTEND **3** : to give a legal hearing to or take testimony from **4** : LEARN — **hear·er** \'hir-ər\ *n*

**hear·ing** *n* **1** : the process, function, or power of perceiving sound; *esp* : the special sense by which noises and tones are received as stimuli **2** : EARSHOT **3** : opportunity to be heard **4** : a listening to arguments (as in a court); *also* : a session in which witnesses are heard (as by a legislative committee)

**hear·ken** \'här-kən\ *vb* : to give attention : LISTEN **syn** hear, hark

**hear·say** \'hiər-,sā\ *n* : RUMOR

**hearse** \'hərs\ *n* [ME *herse*, fr. MF *herce* harrow, frame for holding candles] : a vehicle for carrying the dead to the grave

**heart** \'härt\ *n* **1** : a hollow muscular organ that by rhythmic contraction keeps up the circulation of the blood in the body **2** : any of a suit of playing cards marked with a red heart; *also, pl* : a card game in which the object is to avoid taking tricks containing hearts **3** : the whole personality; *also* : the emotional or moral as distinguished from the intellectual nature **4** : COURAGE **5** : one's innermost being **6** : CENTER; *also* : the essential part **7** : MEMORY, ROTE ⟨learn by ~⟩ — **heart·ed** \-əd\ *adj*

**heart·ache** \-,āk\ *n* : anguish of mind

**heart attack** *n* : an acute episode of heart disease; *esp* : CORONARY THROMBOSIS

**heart·beat** \'härt-,bēt\ *n* : one complete pulsation of the heart

**heart·break** \-,brāk\ *n* : crushing grief

**heart·break·ing** \-,brā-kiŋ\ *adj* : causing extreme sorrow or distress

**heart·bro·ken** \-,brō-kən\ *adj* : overcome by sorrow

**heart·burn** \-,bərn\ *n* : a burning distress behind the lower sternum usu. due to spasm of the esophagus or upper stomach

**heart disease** *n* : an abnormal organic condition of the heart or of the heart and circulation

**heart·en** \'härt-ᵊn\ *vb* **heart·ened; heart·en·ing** \'härt-(ᵊ-)niŋ\ : ENCOURAGE

**heart·felt** \'härt-,felt\ *adj* : deeply felt : SINCERE

**hearth** \'härth\ *n* **1** : an area (as of brick) in front of a fireplace; *also* : the floor of a fireplace **2** : HOME

**hearth·side** \-,sīd\ *n* : FIRESIDE

**hearth·stone** \-,stōn\ *n* **1** : a stone forming a hearth **2** : HOME

**heart·less** \-ləs\ *adj* : CRUEL

**heart·rend·ing** \'härt-,ren-diŋ\ *adj* : causing intense grief, anguish, or distress ⟨a ~ experience⟩

**heart·sick** \'härt-,sik\ *adj* : very despondent — **heart·sick·ness** *n*

**heart·strings** \-,striŋz\ *n pl* : the deepest emotions or affections

**heart·throb** \-,thräb\ *n* **1** : the throb of a heart **2** : sentimental emotion **3** : SWEETHEART

**heart-to-heart** \,härt-tə-,härt\ *adj* : SINCERE, FRANK ⟨a ~ talk⟩

**heart·warm·ing** \'härt-,wòr-miŋ\ *adj* : inspiring sympathetic feeling

**heart·wood** \-,wùd\ *n* : the older harder nonliving central portion of wood

¹**hearty** \'härt-ē\ *adj* **heart·i·er; -est** **1** : THOROUGHGOING; *also* : JOVIAL **2** : vigorously healthy **3** : ABUNDANT; *also* : NOURISHING **syn** sincere, wholehearted, unfeigned — **heart·i·ly** \'härt-ə-lē\ *adv* — **heart·i·ness** \-ē-nəs\ *n*

²**hearty** *n, pl* **heart·ies** : COMRADE; *also* : SAILOR

¹**heat** \'hēt\ *vb* **1** : to make or become warm or hot **2** : EXCITE — **heat·ed·ly** \-əd-lē\ *adv* — **heat·er** *n*

²**heat** *n* **1** : a condition of being hot : WARMTH **2** : a form of energy that causes a body to rise in temperature, to fuse, to evaporate, or to expand **3** : high temperature **4** : intensity of feeling; *also* : sexual excitement esp. in a female mammal **5** : pungency of flavor **6** : a single continuous effort; *also* : a preliminary race for eliminating less competent contenders **7** : PRESSURE — **heat·less** *adj*

**heat engine** *n* : a mechanism for converting heat energy into mechanical energy

**heat exhaustion** *n* : a condition marked by weakness, nausea, dizziness, and profuse sweating that results from physical exertion in a hot environment

**heath** \'hēth\ *n* **1** : any of a large group of often evergreen shrubby plants (as a blueberry or heather) of wet acid soils **2** : a tract of wasteland — **heathy** *adj*

**hea·then** \'hē-thən\ *n, pl* **heathens** *or* **heathen** **1** : an unconverted member of a people or nation that does not acknowledge the God of the Bible **2** : an uncivilized or irreligious person — **heathen** *adj* — **hea·then·dom** *n* — **hea·then·ish** *adj* — **hea·then·ism** *n*

**heath·er** \'heth-ər\ *n* : a northern evergreen heath with usu. lavender flowers — **heath·ery** *adj*

**heat lightning** *n* : flashes of light without thunder ascribed to distant lightning reflected by high clouds

**heat·stroke** \'hēt-,strōk\ *n* : a disorder marked esp. by high body temperature without sweating and by collapse that follows prolonged exposure to excessive heat

¹**heave** \'hēv\ *vb* **heaved** *or* **hove**

\‾hŏv\; **heav·ing 1 :** to rise or lift upward **2 :** THROW **3 :** to rise and fall rhythmically; *also :* PANT **4 :** PULL, PUSH **5 :** RETCH — **heav·er** *n*

²**heave** *n* **1 :** an effort to lift or raise **2 :** THROW, CAST **3 :** an upward motion **4** *pl* **:** a chronic lung disease of horses marked by difficult breathing and persistent cough

**heav·en** \‾hev-ən\ *n* **1 :** FIRMAMENT — usu. used in pl. **2** *often cap* **:** the abode of the Deity and of the blessed dead; *also* **:** a spiritual state of everlasting communion with God **3** *cap* **:** GOD 1 **4 :** a place of supreme happiness — **heav·en·ly** *adj* — **heav·en·ward** *adv or adj*

¹**heavy** \‾hev-ē\ *adj* **heavi·er; -est 1 :** having great weight **2 :** hard to bear **3 :** SERIOUS **4 :** DEEP, PROFOUND **5 :** burdened with something oppressive; *also* **:** PREGNANT **6 :** SLUGGISH **7 :** DRAB; *also* **:** DOLEFUL **8 :** DROWSY **9 :** greater than the average of its kind or class **10 :** digested with difficulty; *also* **:** not properly raised or leavened **11 :** producing goods (as steel) used in the production of other goods **12 :** heavily armed or armored — **heav·i·ly** \‾hev-ə-lē\ *adv* — **heavi·ness** \-ē-nəs\ *n*

²**heavy** *n, pl* **heav·ies :** a theatrical role representing a dignified or imposing person; *also* **:** a villain esp. in a story or a play

**heavy-du·ty** \‾hev-ē-‾d(y)üt-ē\ *adj* **:** able to withstand unusual strain

**heavy-hand·ed** \-‾han-dəd\ *adj* **1 :** CLUMSY, UNGRACEFUL **2 :** OPPRESSIVE

**heavy-heart·ed** \-‾härt-əd\ *adj* **:** SADDENED, DESPONDENT

**heavy·set** \‾hev-ē-‾set\ *adj* **:** stocky and compact in build

**heavy water** *n* **:** water enriched in deuterium

**heavy·weight** \‾hev-ē-‾wāt\ *n* **:** one above average in weight; *esp* **:** a boxer weighing over 175 pounds

**Heb** *abbr* **1** Hebrew **2** Hebrews

**He·bra·ism** \‾hē-brā-‾iz-əm\ *n* **:** the thought, spirit, or practice characteristic of the Hebrews — **He·bra·ic** \hi-‾brā-ik\ *adj* — **He·bra·ist** \‾hē-brā-əst\ *n*

**He·brew** \‾hē-brü\ *n* **1 :** a member of or descendant from a group of Semitic peoples, *esp* **:** ISRAELITE **2 :** the language of the Hebrews — **Hebrew** *adj*

**hec·a·tomb** \‾hek-ə-‾tōm\ *n* **:** an ancient Greek and Roman sacrifice of 100 oxen or cattle

**heck·le** \‾hek-əl\ *vb* **heck·led; heck·ling** \-(ə-)liŋ\ **:** to harass with questions or gibes **:** BADGER — **heck·ler** \-(ə-)lər\ *n*

**hect·are** \‾hek-‾taər\ *n* — see METRIC SYSTEM table

**hec·tic** \‾hek-tik\ *adj* **1 :** characteristic of a wasting disease esp. in being fluctuating but persistent \a ~ fever\; *also* **:** FLUSHED **2 :** RESTLESS — **hec·ti·cal·ly** \-ti-k(ə-)lē\ *adv*

**hec·to·gram** \‾hek-tə-‾gram\ *n* — see METRIC SYSTEM table

**hec·to·li·ter** \‾hek-tə-‾lēt-ər\ *n* — see METRIC SYSTEM table

**hec·to·me·ter** \‾hek-tə-‾mēt-ər, hek-‾täm-ət-ər\ *n* — see METRIC SYSTEM table

**hec·tor** \‾hek-tər\ *vb* **hec·tored; hec·tor·ing** \-t(ə-)riŋ\ **1 :** SWAGGER **2 :** to intimidate by bluster or personal pressure

¹**hedge** \‾hej\ *n* **1 :** a fence or boundary formed of shrubs or small trees **2 :** BARRIER **3 :** a means of protection (as against financial loss)

²**hedge** *vb* **hedged; hedg·ing 1 :** ENCIRCLE **2 :** HINDER **3 :** to protect oneself financially by a counterbalancing transaction **4 :** to evade the risk of commitment — **hedg·er** *n*

**hedge·hog** \-‾hóg, -‾häg\ *n* **:** a small Old World insect-eating mammal covered with spines; *also* **:** PORCUPINE

**hedge-hop** \-‾häp\ *vb* **:** to fly an airplane very close to the ground

**hedge·row** \-‾rō\ *n* **:** a row of shrubs or trees bounding or separating fields

**he·do·nism** \‾hēd-ᵊn-‾iz-əm\ *n* [Gk *hēdonē* pleasure] **:** the doctrine that pleasure is the chief good in life; *also* **:** a way of life based on this — **he·do·nist** \-ᵊn-əst\ *n* — **he·do·nis·tic** \‾hēd-ᵊn-‾is-tik\ *adj*

¹**heed** \‾hēd\ *vb* **:** to pay attention

²**heed** *n* **:** ATTENTION, NOTICE — **heed·ful** \-fəl\ *adj* — **heed·ful·ly** \-ē\ *adv* — **heed·ful·ness** *n* — **heed·less** *adj* — **heed·less·ly** *adv* — **heed·less·ness** *n*

¹**heel** \‾hēl\ *n* **1 :** the hind part of the foot **2 :** one of the crusty ends of a loaf of bread **3 :** a solid attachment forming the back of the sole of a shoe **4 :** a rear, low, or bottom part **5 :** a contemptible person — **heel·less** \‾hēl-ləs\ *adj*

²**heel** *vb* **:** to tilt to one side **:** LIST

¹**heft** \‾heft\ *n* **:** WEIGHT, HEAVINESS

²**heft** *vb* **:** to test the weight of by lifting

**hefty** \‾hef-tē\ *adj* **heft·i·er; -est 1 :** marked by bigness, bulk, and usu. strength **2 :** impressively large

**he·ge·mo·ny** \hi-‾jem-ə-nē\ *n* **:** preponderant influence or authority esp. of one nation over others

**he·gi·ra** \hi-‾jī-rə\ *n* [the *Hegira*, flight of Muhammad from Mecca in A.D. 622, fr. ML, fr. Ar *hijrah*, lit., flight] **:** a journey esp. when undertaken to seek refuge away from a dangerous or undesirable environment

**heif·er** \‾hef-ər\ *n* **:** a young cow; *esp* **:** one that has not had a calf

**height** \‾hīt, ‾hītth\ *n* **1 :** the highest part or point **2 :** the distance from the bottom to the top of something standing upright **3 :** ALTITUDE

**height·en** \‾hīt-ᵊn\ *vb* **height·ened; height·en·ing** \‾hīt-(ᵊ-)niŋ\ **1 :** to increase in amount or degree **:** AUGMENT **2 :** to make or become high or higher *syn* enhance, intensify

**hei·nous** \‾hā-nəs\ *adj* [ME, fr. MF *haineus*, fr. *haine* hate, fr. *hair* to hate] **:** hatefully or shockingly evil — **hei·nous·ly** *adv* — **hei·nous·ness** *n*

**heir** \‾aər\ *n* **:** one who inherits or is

entitled to inherit property — **heir-ship** n

**heir apparent** n, pl **heirs apparent** : an heir who cannot legally be deprived of his right to succeed (as to a throne or a title) if he survives the present holder

**heir-ess** \'ar-əs\ n : a female heir esp. to great wealth

**heir-loom** \'aər-,lüm\ n **1** : a piece of personal property that descends by inheritance **2** : something handed on from one generation to another

**heir presumptive** n, pl **heirs presumptive** : an heir whose present right to inherit could be lost through the birth of a nearer relative

**heist** \'hīst\ vb, slang : to commit armed robbery on; also : STEAL

**held** past of HOLD

**he-li-cal** \'hel-i-kəl, 'hē-li-\ adj : SPIRAL

**he-li-coid** \'hel-ə-,kȯid, 'hē-lə-\ or **he-li-coi-dal** \,hel-ə-'kȯid-ᵊl, ,hē-lə-\ adj : forming or arranged in a spiral

**he-li-cop-ter** \'hel-ə-,käp-tər, 'hē-lə-\ n [F hélicoptère, fr. Gk helix spiral + pteron wing] : an aircraft that is supported in the air by one or more rotors revolving on substantially vertical axes

**he-lio-cen-tric** \,hē-lē-ō-'sen-trik\ adj : having or relating to the sun as a center

**he-llo-graph** \'hē-lē-ə-,graf\ n : a device for telegraphing using the sun's rays reflected from a mirror

**he-lio-trope** \'hē-lyə-,trōp\ n : a hairy-leaved garden herb related to the forget-me-not that is grown for its clusters of small fragrant white or purple flowers

**he-li-port** \'hel-ə-,pōrt\ n : a landing and takeoff place for a helicopter

**he-li-um** \'hē-lē-əm\ n [NL, fr. Gk hēlios sun; so called from the fact that its existence in the sun's atmosphere was inferred before it was identified on the earth] : a very light nonflammable gaseous chemical element occurring in various natural gases

**he-lix** \'hē-liks\ n, pl **he-li-ces** \'hel-ə-,sēz, 'hē-lə-\ also **he-lix-es** \'hē-lik-səz\ : something spiral

**hell** \'hel\ n **1** : a nether world in which the dead continue to exist **2** : the realm of the devil in which the damned suffer everlasting punishment **3** : a place or state of torment or destruction — **hell-ish** adj

**hell-bent** \-,bent\ adj **1** : stubbornly determined **2** : going full speed

**hell-cat** \-,kat\ n **1** : WITCH 2 **2** : TORMENTOR; esp : SHREW

**hel-le-bore** \'hel-ə-,bōr\ n **1** : a plant related to the buttercup; also : its roots used formerly in medicine **2** : a poisonous plant related to the lilies; also : its dried roots used in medicine and insecticides

**Hel-lene** \'hel-,ēn\ n : GREEK

**Hel-le-nism** \'hel-ə-,niz-əm\ n : a body of humanistic and classical ideals associated with ancient Greece — **Hel-len-ic** \he-'len-ik\ adj — **Hel-le-nist** \'hel-ə-nəst\ n

**Hel-le-nis-tic** \,hel-ə-'nis-tik\ adj : of or relating to Greek history, culture, or art after Alexander the Great

**hell-for-leather** adv : at full speed

**hell-gram-mite** \'hel-grə-,mīt\ n : an aquatic insect larva used as bait in fishing

**hell-hole** \'hel-,hōl\ n : a place of extreme discomfort or squalor

**hel-lion** \'hel-yən\ n : a troublesome or mischievous person

**hel-lo** \hə-'lō, he-\ n, pl **hellos** : an expression of greeting — used interjectionally

**helm** \'helm\ n **1** : a lever or wheel for steering a ship **2** : a position of control

**hel-met** \'hel-mət\ n : a protective covering for the head

**helms-man** \'helmz-mən\ n : the man at the helm : STEERSMAN

**hel-ot** \'hel-ət\ n : SLAVE, SERF

**¹help** \'help\ vb **1** : AID, ASSIST **2** : REMEDY, RELIEVE **3** : to be of use; also : PROMOTE **4** : to change for the better **5** : to refrain from; also : PREVENT **6** : to serve with food or drink — **help-er** n

**²help** n **1** : AID, ASSISTANCE; also : a source of aid **2** : REMEDY, RELIEF **3** : one who assists another **4** : the services of a paid worker — **help-ful** \-fəl\ adj — **help-ful-ly** \-ē\ adv — **help-ful-ness** n — **help-less** adj — **help-less-ly** adv — **help-less-ness** n

**help-ing** \'hel-piŋ\ n : a portion of food (asked for a second ~ of potatoes)

**help-mate** \'help-,māt\ n **1** : HELPER **2** : WIFE

**help-meet** \-,mēt\ n : HELPMATE

**hel-ter-skel-ter** \,hel-tər-'skel-tər\ adv **1** : in headlong disorder **2** : HAPHAZARDLY

**helve** \'helv\ n : a handle of a tool or weapon

**Hel-ve-tian** \hel-'vē-shən\ adj : SWISS — Helvetian n

**¹hem** \'hem\ n **1** : a border of an article (as of cloth) doubled back and stitched down **2** : RIM, MARGIN

**²hem** vb hemmed; hem-ming **1** : to make a hem in sewing; also : BORDER, EDGE **2** : to surround restrictively

**he-man** \'hē-'man\ n : a strong virile man

**he-ma-tite** \'hē-mə-,tīt\ n : a mineral that consists of an oxide of iron and that constitutes an important iron ore

**he-ma-tol-o-gy** \,hē-mə-'täl-ə-jē\ n : a branch of biology that deals with the blood and blood-forming organs — **hem-a-to-log-ic** \-mət-ᵊl-'äj-ik\ or **hem-a-to-log-i-cal** \-i-kəl\ adj — **he-ma-tol-o-gist** \-'täl-ə-jəst\ n

**heme** \'hēm\ n : the deep red iron-containing part of hemoglobin

**hemi-sphere** \'hem-ə-,sfiər\ n **1** : one of the halves of the earth as divided by the equator into northern and southern parts (**northern hemisphere, southern hemisphere**) or by a meridian into two parts so that one half (**eastern hemisphere**) to the east of the Atlantic ocean includes Europe, Asia, and Africa and the half (**western hemisphere**) to the west includes No. and So. America and surrounding waters **2** : either of two half spheres formed by a plane through the sphere's center — **hemi·spher·ic** \,hem-ə-'sfiər-ik, -'sfer-\ or **hemi·spher·i·cal** \-'sfir-i-kəl, -'sfer-\ adj

**hemi·stitch** \'hem-i-,stik\ n : half a poetic line usu. divided by a caesura

**hem·line** \'hem-,līn\ n : the line formed by the lower edge of a dress, skirt, or coat

**hem·lock** \'hem-,läk\ n **1** : any of several poisonous herbs related to the carrot **2** : an evergreen tree related to the pines; also : its soft light wood

**he·mo·glo·bin** \'hē-mə-,glō-bən\ n : an iron-containing compound found in red blood cells that carries oxygen from the lungs to the body tissues

**he·mo·phil·ia** \,hē-mə-'fil-ē-ə\ n : a usu. hereditary tendency to severe prolonged bleeding — **he·mo·phil·i·ac** \-ē-,ak\ adj or n

**hem·or·rhage** \'hem-(ə-)rij\ n : a large discharge of blood from the blood vessels — **hemorrhage** vb — **hem·or·rhag·ic** \,hem-ə-'raj-ik\ adj

**hem·or·rhoid** \'hem-(ə-),ròid\ n : a swollen mass of dilated veins situated at or just within the anus — usu. used in pl.

**hemp** \'hemp\ n : a tall Asiatic herb related to the mulberry and grown for its tough fiber used in cordage and its flowers and leaves used in drugs — **hemp·en** \'hem-pən\ adj

**hem·stitch** \'hem-,stich\ vb : to embroider (fabric) by drawing out parallel threads and stitching the exposed threads in groups to form designs

**hen** \'hen\ n : a female domestic fowl esp. over a year old; also : a female bird

**hence** \'hens\ adv **1** : AWAY **2** : from this time **3** : CONSEQUENTLY **4** : from this source or origin

**hence·forth** \-,fòrth\ adv : from this point on

**hence·for·ward** \hens-'fòr-wərd\ adv : HENCEFORTH

**hench·man** \'hench-mən\ n [ME hengestman groom, fr. hengest stallion] **1** : a trusted follower **2** : a political follower whose support is chiefly for personal advantage

**hen·na** \'hen-ə\ n **1** : an Old World tropical shrub with fragrant white flowers; also : a reddish brown dye obtained from its leaves and used esp. for the hair **2** : the color of henna dye

**hen·peck** \'hen-,pek\ vb : to subject (one's husband) to persistent nagging and domination

**hep** \'hep\ var of HIP

**hep·a·rin** \'hep-ə-rən\ n : a compound found esp. in liver that slows the clotting of blood and is used medically

**he·pat·ic** \hi-'pat-ik\ adj : of, relating to, or resembling the liver

**he·pat·i·ca** \hi-'pat-i-kə\ n : any of a genus of herbs related to the buttercups that have lobed leaves and delicate flowers

**hep·a·ti·tis** \,hep-ə-'tīt-əs\ n, pl -tit-

i·des \-'tit-ə-,dēz\ : inflammation of the liver; also : an acute virus disease of which this is a feature

**hep·cat** \'hep-,kat\ n : HIPSTER

**hepped up** \'hept-'əp\ adj : ENTHUSIASTIC

**hep·tam·e·ter** \hep-'tam-ət-ər\ n : a line of verse containing seven metrical feet

¹**her** \(h)ər, ,hər\ adj : of or relating to her or herself

²**her** \ər, (')hər\ pron, objective case of SHE

¹**her·ald** \'her-əld\ n **1** : an official crier or messenger **2** : HARBINGER **3** : ANNOUNCER, SPOKESMAN

²**herald** vb **1** : to give notice of **2** : PUBLICIZE; also : HAIL

**he·ral·dic** \he-'ral-dik, hə-\ adj : of or relating to heralds or heraldry

**her·ald·ry** \'her-əl-drē\ n, pl -ries **1** : the practice of devising, blazoning, and granting armorial insignia and of tracing and recording genealogies **2** : an armorial ensign; also : INSIGNIA **3** : PAGEANTRY

**herb** \'(h)ərb\ n **1** : a seed plant that lacks woody tissue and dies to the ground at the end of a growing season **2** : a plant or plant part valued for medicinal or savory qualities — **her·ba·ceous** \,(h)ər-'bā-shəs\ adj

**herb·age** \'(h)ər-bij\ n : green plants esp. when used or fit for grazing

**herb·al·ist** \'(h)ər-bə-ləst\ n : one that collects, grows, or deals in herbs

**her·bar·i·um** \,(h)ər-'bar-ē-əm\ n, pl -ia \-ē-ə\ **1** : a collection of dried plant specimens **2** : a place that houses an herbarium

**her·bi·cide** \'(h)ər-bə-,sīd\ n : an agent used to destroy unwanted plants — **her·bi·cid·al** \,(h)ər-bə-'sīd-ᵊl\ adj

**her·biv·o·rous** \,(h)ər-'biv-ə-rəs\ adj : feeding on plants — **her·bi·vore** \'(h)ər-bə-,vōr\ n — **her·biv·o·rous·ly** adv

**her·cu·le·an** \,hər-kyə-'lē-ən, ,hər-'kyü-lē-\ adj, often cap : of extraordinary power, size, or difficulty

¹**herd** \'hərd\ n **1** : a group of animals of one kind kept or living together **2** : a group of people with a common bond **3** : MOB

²**herd** vb : to assemble or move in a herd — **herd·er** n

**herds·man** \'hərdz-mən\ n : one who manages, breeds, or tends livestock

¹**here** \'hiər\ adv **1** : in or at this place; also : NOW **2** : at or in this point or particular **3** : in the present life or state **4** : HITHER

²**here** n : this place (get away from ~)

**here·abouts** \'hir-ə-,baùts\ or **here·about** \-,baùt\ adv : in this vicinity : about or near this place

¹**here·af·ter** \hir-'af-tər\ adv **1** : after this in sequence or in time **2** : in some future time or state

²**hereafter** n, often cap **1** : FUTURE **2** : an existence beyond earthly life

**here·by** \hiər-'bī\ adv : by means of this

**he·red·i·tary** \hə-'red-ə-ˌter-ē\ *adj* **1** : genetically passed or passable from parent to offspring **2** : passing by inheritance; *also* : having title or possession through inheritance **3** : of a kind established by tradition **syn** innate, inborn, inbred

**he·red·i·ty** \-ət-ē\ *n* : the qualities and potentialities genetically derived from one's ancestors; *also* : the passing of these from ancestor to descendant

**Her·e·ford** \'hər-fərd, 'her-ə-\ *n* : any of an English breed of hardy red beef cattle with white faces and markings

**here·in** \hir-'in\ *adv* : in this

**here·of** \-'əv, -'äv\ *adv* : of this

**here·on** \-'ȯn, -'än\ *adv* : on this

**her·e·sy** \'her-ə-sē\ *n, pl* **-sies** [ME *heresie,* fr. OF, fr. LL *haeresis,* fr. LGk *hairesis,* fr. Gk, action of taking, choice, sect, fr. *hairein* to take] **1** : adherence to a religious opinion contrary to church dogma **2** : an opinion or doctrine contrary to church dogma **3** : dissent from a dominant theory or opinion — **her·e·tic** \-,tik\ *n* — **he·ret·i·cal** \hə-'ret-i-kəl\ *adj*

**here·to** \hir-'tü\ *adv* : to this document

**here·to·fore** \'hirt-ə-,fōr\ *adv* : up to this time

**here·un·der** \hir-'ən-dər\ *adv* : under this

**here·un·to** \hir-'ən-tü\ *adv* : to this

**here·upon** \'hir-ə-,pȯn, -,pän\ *adv* : on this

**here·with** \hiər-'with, -'with\ *adv* **1** : with this **2** : HEREBY

**her·i·ta·ble** \'her-ət-ə-bəl\ *adj* : capable of being inherited

**her·i·tage** \'her-ət-ij\ *n* **1** : property that descends to an heir **2** : LEGACY **3** : BIRTHRIGHT

**her·maph·ro·dite** \(ˌ)hər-'maf-rə-ˌdīt\ *n* : an animal or plant having both male and female reproductive organs — **hermaphrodite** *adj* — **her·maph·ro·dit·ic** \(ˌ)hər-ˌmaf-rə-'dit-ik\ *adj*

**her·met·ic** \hər-'met-ik\ *also* **her·met·i·cal** \-i-kəl\ *adj* **1** : RECONDITE **2** : tightly sealed : AIRTIGHT — **her·met·i·cal·ly** \-i-k(ə-)lē\ *adv*

**her·mit** \'hər-mət\ *n* [ME *eremite,* fr. OF, fr. LL *eremita,* fr. Gk *erēmitēs,* adj., living in the desert, fr. *erēmia* desert, fr. *erēmos* lonely] : one who lives in solitude esp. for religious reasons — **her·mit·age** \-ij\ *n* **1** : the dwelling of a hermit **2** : a secluded dwelling

**her·nia** \'hər-nē-ə\ *n, pl* **-ni·as** or **-ni·ae** \-nē-ˌō, -nē-ˌī\ : a protruding of a bodily part (as a loop of intestine) into a pouch of the weakened wall of a cavity in which it is normally enclosed; *also* : the protruded mass — **her·ni·al** \-nē-əl\ *adj* — **her·ni·ate** \-nē-ˌāt\ *vb* — **her·ni·a·tion** \ˌhər-nē-'ā-shən\ *n*

**he·ro** \'hē-rō\ *n, pl* **heroes 1** : a mythological or legendary figure of great strength or ability **2** : a man admired for his achievements and qualities **3** : the chief male character in a literary or dramatic work **4** *pl usu*

**heros** : SUBMARINE 2 — **he·ro·ic** \hi-'rō-ik\ *adj* — **he·ro·i·cal·ly** \-i-k(ə-)lē\ *adv*

**heroic couplet** *n* : a rhyming couplet in iambic pentameter

**he·ro·ics** \hi-'rō-iks\ *n pl* : heroic or showy behavior

**her·o·in** \'her-ə-wən\ *n* : an addictive narcotic drug made from morphine

**her·o·ine** \'her-ə-wən\ *n* : a woman of heroic achievements or qualities

**her·o·ism** \'her-ə-ˌwiz-əm\ *n* **1** : heroic conduct **2** : the qualities of a hero **syn** valor, prowess, gallantry

**her·on** \'her-ən\ *n, pl* **herons** *also* **heron** : a long-legged long-billed wading bird with soft plumage

**her·pes** \'hər-pēz\ *n* : any of several virus diseases characterized by the formation of blisters on the skin or mucous membranes

**herpes zos·ter** \-ˌhər-(ˌ)pē(z)-'zōs-tər, -'zäs-\ *n* : SHINGLES

**her·pe·tol·o·gy** \ˌhər-pə-'täl-ə-jē\ *n* : a branch of zoology dealing with reptiles and amphibians — **her·pe·to·log·ic** \-pət-ᵊl-'äj-ik\ *or* **her·pe·to·log·i·cal** \-i-kəl\ *adj* — **her·pe·tol·o·gist** \ˌhər-pə-'täl-ə-jəst\ *n*

**her·ring** \'her-iŋ\ *n, pl* **herring** *or* **herrings** : a soft-finned narrow-bodied food fish of the north Atlantic; *also* : any of various similar or related fishes

**her·ring·bone** \'her-iŋ-ˌbōn\ *n* : a pattern made up of rows of parallel lines with adjacent rows slanting in reverse directions; *also* : a twilled fabric with this pattern

**hers** \'hərz\ *pron* : one or the ones belonging to her

**her·self** \(h)ər-'self\ *pron* : SHE, HER — used reflexively, for emphasis, or in absolute constructions

**hertz** \'herts, 'hərts\ *n, pl* **hertz** : a unit of frequency equal to one cycle per second

**hes·i·tant** \'hez-ə-tənt\ *adj* : tending to hesitate — **hes·i·tan·cy** \-tən-sē\ *n* — **hes·i·tant·ly** *adv*

**hes·i·tate** \'hez-ə-ˌtāt\ *vb* **-tat·ed; -tat·ing 1** : to hold back (as in doubt) **2** : PAUSE **syn** waver, vacillate, falter — **hes·i·ta·tion** \ˌhez-ə-'tā-shən\ *n*

**het·ero·dox** \'het-(ə-)rə-ˌdäks\ *adj* **1** : differing from an acknowledged standard **2** : holding unorthodox opinions — **het·er·o·doxy** \-ˌdäk-sē\ *n*

**het·er·o·ge·neous** \ˌhet-(ə-)rə-'jē-nē-əs, -nyəs\ *adj* : consisting of dissimilar ingredients or constituents : MIXED — **het·er·o·ge·neous·ly** *adv* — **het·er·o·ge·neous·ness** *n*

**het·ero·sex·u·al** \ˌhet-ə-rō-'sek-sh(ə-w)əl\ *adj* : involving two sexes; *also* : oriented toward the opposite sex — **heterosexual** *n* — **het·ero·sex·u·al·i·ty** \-ˌsek-shə-'wal-ət-ē\ *n*

**hew** \'hyü\ *vb* **hewed; hewed** *or* **hewn** \'hyün\; **hew·ing 1** : to cut or fell with blows (as of an ax) **2** : to give shape to with or as if with an ax **3** : to conform strictly — **hew·er** *n*

**HEW** *abbr* Department of Health, Education, and Welfare

**¹hex** \'heks\ *vb* **1 :** to practice witchcraft **2 :** JINX

**²hex** *n* **:** SPELL, JINX

**³hex** *abbr* hexagon; hexagonal

**hexa·gon** \'hek-sə-,gän\ *n* **:** a polygon having six angles and six sides — **hex·ag·o·nal** \hek-'sag-ən-ᵊl\ *adj*

**hex·am·e·ter** \hek-'sam-ət-ər\ *n* **:** a line of verse containing six metrical feet

**hexa·pod** \'hek-sə-,päd\ *n* **:** INSECT

**hey·day** \'hā-,dā\ *n* **:** a period of greatest strength, vigor, or prosperity

**hf** *abbr* half

**Hf** *symbol* hafnium

**HF** *abbr* high frequency

**Hg** *symbol* [NL *hydrargyrum*, lit., water silver] mercury

**HG** *abbr* High German

**hgt** *abbr* height

**hgwy** *abbr* highway

**HH** *abbr* **1** Her Highness. His Highness **2** His Holiness

**hhd** *abbr* hogshead

**HI** *abbr* Hawaii

**hi·a·tus** \hī-'āt-əs\ *n* [L, fr. *hiatus*, pp. of *hiare* to yawn] **1 :** a break in an object **: GAP 2 :** a lapse in continuity

**hi·ba·chi** \hi-'bäch-ē\ *n* **:** a charcoal brazier

**hi·ber·nate** \'hī-bər-,nāt\ *vb* **-nat·ed; -nat·ing :** to pass the winter in a torpid or resting state — **hi·ber·na·tion** \,hī-bər-'nā-shən\ *n* — **hi·ber·na·tor** \'hī-bər-,nāt-ər\ *n*

**hi·bis·cus** \hī-'bis-kəs, hə-\ *n* **:** any of a genus of herbs, shrubs, and trees related to the mallows and noted for large showy flowers

**hic·cup** *also* **hic·cough** \'hik-(,)əp\ *n* **:** a spasmodic breathing movement checked by sudden closing of the glottis accompanied by a peculiar sound; *also* **:** this sound — **hiccup** *vb*

**hick** \'hik\ *n* [*Hick*, nickname for *Richard*] **:** an awkward provincial person — **hick** *adj*

**hick·o·ry** \'hik-(ə-)rē\ *n, pl* **-ries :** any of a genus of No. American hardwood trees related to the walnuts; *also* **:** the wood of a hickory — **hickory** *adj*

**hi·dal·go** \hid-'al-gō\ *n, pl* **-gos** *often cap* [Sp, fr. earlier *fijo dalgo*, lit., son of something, son of property] **:** a member of the lower nobility of Spain

**hidden tax** *n* **:** INDIRECT TAX

**¹hide** \'hīd\ *vb* **hid** \'hid\; **hid·den** \'hid-ᵊn\ *or* **hid; hid·ing** \'hīd-iŋ\ **1 :** to put or remain out of sight **2 :** to conceal for shelter or protection; *also* **:** to seek protection **3 :** to keep secret **4 :** to turn away in shame or anger

**²hide** *n* **:** the skin of an animal

**hide-and-seek** \,hīd-ᵊn-'sēk\ *n* **:** a children's game in which one player covers his eyes and after giving the others time to hide goes looking for and tries to catch them

**hide·away** \'hīd-ə-,wā\ *n* **:** HIDEOUT

**hide·bound** \-,baund\ *adj* **:** obstinately conservative

**hid·eous** \'hid-ē-əs\ *adj* [ME *hidous*, fr. OF, fr. *hisde*, *hide* terror] **1 :** offensive to one of the senses **: UGLY 2 :** morally offensive **: SHOCKING** — **hid·eous·ly** *adv* — **hid·eous·ness** *n*

**hide·out** \'hīd-,aut\ *n* **:** a place of refuge or concealment

**hie** \'hī\ *vb* **hied; hy·ing** *or* **hie·ing :** HASTEN

**hi·er·ar·chy** \'hī-(ə-),rär-kē\ *n, pl* **-chies 1 :** a ruling body of clergy organized into ranks **2 :** persons or things arranged in a graded series — **hi·er·ar·chi·cal** \,hī-ə-'rär-ki-kəl\ *adj* — **hi·er·ar·chi·cal·ly** \-k(ə-)lē\ *adv*

**hi·er·o·glyph·ic** \,hī-(ə-)rə-'glif-ik\ *n* [MF *hieroglyphique*, adj., fr. Gk *hieroglyphikos*, fr. *hieros* sacred + *glyphein* to carve] **1 :** a character in a system of picture writing (as of the ancient Egyptians) **2 :** a symbol or sign difficult to decipher

**hi·ero·phant** \'hī-(ə-)rə-,fant\ *n* **1 :** a priest in ancient Greece **2 :** EXPOSITOR; *also* **:** ADVOCATE

**hi-fi** \'hī-'fī\ *n* **1 :** HIGH FIDELITY **2 :** equipment for reproduction of sound with high fidelity

**hig·gle·dy-pig·gle·dy** \,hig-əl-dē-'pig-əl-dē\ *adv* **:** in confusion

**¹high** \'hī\ *adj* **1 :** ELEVATED; *also* **: TALL 2 :** advanced toward fullness or culmination; *also* **:** slightly tainted **3 :** long past **4 :** SHRILL, SHARP **5 :** far from the equator ⟨~ latitudes⟩ **6 :** exalted in character **7 :** of greater degree, size, or amount than average **8 :** of relatively great importance **9 :** FORCIBLE, STRONG ⟨~ winds⟩ **10 :** BOASTFUL, ARROGANT **11 :** showing elation or excitement **12 :** COSTLY, DEAR **13 :** advanced esp. in complexity ⟨~*er* mathematics⟩ **14 :** INTOXICATED; *also* **:** excited or stupefied by a drug (as heroin) — **high·ly** *adv*

**²high** *adv* **1 :** at or to a high place or degree **2 :** LUXURIOUSLY ⟨living ~⟩

**³high** *n* **1 :** an elevated place **2 :** a high point or level **3 :** the arrangement of gears in an automobile that gives the highest speed

**high·ball** \'hī-,bȯl\ *n* **:** a usu. tall drink of liquor mixed with water or a carbonated beverage

**high beam** *n* **:** the long-range focus of a vehicle headlight

**high-born** \-'bȯrn\ *adj* **:** of noble birth

**high·boy** \-,bȯi\ *n* **:** a high chest of drawers mounted on a base with legs

**high-bred** \-'bred\ *adj* **:** coming from superior stock

**high·brow** \-,braù\ *n* **:** a person of superior learning or culture — **highbrow** *adj*

**high·er-up** \,hī-ər-'əp\ *n* **:** a superior officer or official

**high·fa·lu·tin** \,hī-fə-'lüt-ᵊn\ *adj* **:** PRETENTIOUS, POMPOUS

**high fashion** *n* **1 :** HIGH STYLE **2 :** HAUTE COUTURE

**high fidelity** *n* **:** the reproduction of sound with a high degree of faithfulness to the original

**high-flown** \'hī-'flōn\ *adj* **1 :** EXALTED **2 :** BOMBASTIC

**high frequency** *n* **:** a radio frequency between 3 and 30 megacycles

**high gear** *n* **:** HIGH 3

**High German** *n* **:** German as used in southern and central Germany

**high-hand•ed** \'hī-'han-dəd\ *adj* **:** OVERBEARING — **high-hand•ed•ly** *adv* — **high-hand•ed•ness** *n*

**high-hat** \'hī-'hat\ *adj* **:** SUPERCILIOUS, SNOBBISH — **high-hat** *vb*

**high•land** \'hī-lənd\ *n* **:** elevated or mountainous land

**high•land•er** \-lən-dər\ *n* **1 :** an inhabitant of a highland **2** *cap* **:** an inhabitant of the Highlands of Scotland

¹**high•light** \'hī-,līt\ *n* **:** an event or detail of major importance

²**highlight** *vb* **1 :** EMPHASIZE **2 :** to constitute a highlight of

**high–mind•ed** \'hī-'mīn-dəd\ *adj* **:** marked by elevated principles and feelings — **high–mind•ed•ness** *n*

**high•ness** \'hī-nəs\ *n* **1 :** the quality or state of being high **2** — used as a title (as for kings)

**high–pressure** *adj* **:** using or involving aggressive and insistent sales techniques

**high–rise** \'hī-'rīz\ *adj* **:** having several stories and being equipped with elevators (~ apartments); *also* **:** of or relating to high-rise buildings

**high•road** \'hī-,rōd\ *n, chiefly Brit* **:** HIGHWAY

**high school** *n* **:** a secondary school usu. comprising the 9th to 12th or 10th to 12th years of study

**high sea** *n* **:** the open sea outside territorial waters — usu. used in pl.

**high–sounding** \'hī-'saùn-diŋ\ *adj* **:** POMPOUS, IMPOSING

**high–spir•it•ed** \-'spir-ət-əd\ *adj* **:** characterized by a bold or lofty spirit

**high–strung** \'hī-'streŋ\ *adj* **:** having an extremely nervous or sensitive temperament

**high style** *n* **:** the newest in fashion or design and usu. adopted by a limited number of people

**high•tail** \'hī-,tāl\ *vb* **:** to retreat at full speed

**high–tension** *adj* **:** having, using, or relating to high voltage

**high–test** *adj* **:** having a high volatility

**high–toned** \'hī-'tōnd\ *adj* **1 :** high in social, moral, or intellectual quality **2 :** PRETENTIOUS, POMPOUS

**high•way** \'hī-,wā\ *n* **:** a public road

**high•way•man** \-mən\ *n* **:** a person who robs travelers on a road

**hi•jack** *or* **high–jack** \'hī-,jak\ *vb* **:** to steal esp. by stopping a vehicle on the highway; *also* **:** to commandeer a flying airplane — **hijack** *n* — **hi•jack•er** *n*

¹**hike** \'hīk\ *vb* **hiked; hik•ing 1 :** to move or raise with a sudden motion **2 :** to take a long walk — **hik•er** *n*

²**hike** *n* **1 :** a long walk **2 :** RISE

**hi•lar•i•ous** \hil-'ar-ē-əs, hī-'lar-\ *adj* **:** marked by or providing boisterous merriment — **hi•lar•i•ous•ly** *adv* — **hi•lar•i•ty** \-ət-ē\ *n*

**hill** \'hil\ *n* **1 :** a usu. rounded elevation of land **2 :** a little heap or mound (as of earth) — **hilly** *adj*

**hill•bil•ly** \'hil-,bil-ē\ *n, pl* **-lies :** a person from a backwoods area

**hill•ock** \'hil-ək\ *n* **:** a small hill

**hill•side** \-,sīd\ *n* **:** the part of a hill between the summit and the foot

**hill•top** \-,täp\ *n* **:** the top of a hill

**hilt** \'hilt\ *n* **:** a handle esp. of a sword or dagger

**him** \im, (')him\ *pron, objective case of* HE

**him•self** \(h)im-'self\ *pron* **:** HE, HIM — us⋯ reflexively, for emphasis, or in at⋯lute constructions

¹**hind** \'hīnd\ *n, pl* **hinds** *also* **hind :** a female deer — **DOE**

²**hind** *n* **:** a British farmhand

³**hind** *adj* **:** REAR

¹**hin•der** \'hin-dər\ *vb* **hin•dered; hin•der•ing** \-d(ə-)riŋ\ **1 :** to impede the progress of **2 :** to hold back **syn** obstruct, block, bar

²**hind•er** \'hīn-dər\ *adj* **:** HIND

**Hin•di** \'hin-dē\ *n* **:** a literary and official language of northern India

**hind•most** \'hīn(d)-,mōst\ *adj* **:** farthest to the rear

**hind•quar•ter** \-,kwȯrt-ər\ *n* **1 :** the back half of a lateral half of the body or carcass of a quadruped **2** *pl* **:** the part of the body of a quadruped behind the junction of hind limbs and trunk

**hin•drance** \'hin-drəns\ *n* **1 :** the state of being hindered; *also* **:** the action of hindering **2 :** IMPEDIMENT

**hind•sight** \'hīn(d)-,sīt\ *n* **:** understanding of an event after it has happened

**Hin•du•ism** \'hin-dü-,iz-əm\ *n* **:** a body of religious beliefs and practices native to India — **Hin•du** *n or adj*

**hind wing** *n* **:** either of the posterior wings of a 4-winged insect

¹**hinge** \'hinj\ *n* **:** a jointed piece on which one piece (as a door, gate, or lid) turns or swings on another

²**hinge** *vb* **hinged; hing•ing 1 :** to attach by or furnish with hinges **2 :** to be contingent on a single consideration

**hint** \'hint\ *n* **1 :** an indirect or summary suggestion **2 :** CLUE **3 :** a very small amount — **hint** *vb*

**hin•ter•land** \'hint-ər-,land\ *n* **1 :** a region behind a coast **2 :** a region remote from cities

¹**hip** \'hip\ *n* **:** the fruit of a rose

²**hip** *n* **1 :** the part of the body on either side below the waist consisting of the side of the pelvis and the upper thigh **2 :** the joint between pelvis and femur

³**hip** *also* **hep** *adj* **hip•per; hip•pest 1 :** keenly aware of or interested in the newest developments **2 :** WISE, ALERT

**hip•bone** \-'bōn, -,bōn\ *n* **:** the large flaring bone that makes a lateral half of the pelvis in mammals

**hip joint** *n* **:** the articulation between the femur and the hipbone

¹**hipped** \'hipt\ *adj* **:** having hips esp. of a specified kind ⟨broad-*hipped*⟩

²**hipped** *adj* **1 :** DEPRESSED **2 :** extremely absorbed or interested

**hip·pie** or **hip·py** \'hip-ē\ n, pl **hippies** : a usu. young person who rejects established mores, advocates nonviolence, and often uses psychedelic drugs or marijuana; also : a long-haired unconventionally dressed young person — **hip·pie·dom** n — **hip·pie·hood** n

**hip·po·drome** \'hip-ə-ˌdrōm\ n : an arena for equestrian performances

**hip·po·pot·a·mus** \ˌhip-ə-'pät-ə-məs\ n, pl **-mus·es** or **-mi** \-ˌmī\ [L, fr. Gk hippopotamos, fr. hippos horse + potamos river] : a large thick-skinned African river animal related to the swine

**hip·ster** \'hip-stər\ n : one who is keenly aware of or interested in the newest developments esp. in jazz

¹**hire** \'hī(ə)r\ n 1 : payment for labor or personal services : WAGES 2 : EMPLOYMENT

²**hire** vb **hired; hir·ing** 1 : to employ for pay 2 : to engage the temporary use of for pay

**hire·ling** \'hī(ə)r-liŋ\ n : a hired person whose motives are mercenary

**hir·sute** \'hər-ˌsüt, 'hiər-\ adj : HAIRY

¹**his** \(h)iz, ˌhiz\ adj : of or relating to him or himself

²**his** \'hiz\ pron : one or the ones belonging to him

**His·pan·ic** \his-'pan-ik\ adj : of or relating to the people, speech, or culture of Spain or Latin America

**hiss** \'his\ vb : to make a sharp sibilant sound; also : to condemn by hissing — **hiss** n

**hist** abbr historian; historical; history

**his·ta·mine** \'his-tə-ˌmēn, -mən\ n : a chemical compound widespread in animal tissues and believed to play a role in allergic reactions

**his·to·gram** \'his-tə-ˌgram\ n : representation of statistical data by means of rectangles whose widths represent class intervals and whose heights represent corresponding frequencies

**his·to·ri·an** \his-'tōr-ē-ən\ n : a student or writer of history

**his·to·ric·i·ty** \ˌhis-tə-'ris-ət-ē\ n : historical actuality

**his·to·ri·og·ra·pher** \his-ˌtōr-ē-'äg-rə-fər\ n : a usu. official writer of history : HISTORIAN

**his·to·ry** \'his-t(ə-)rē\ n, pl **-ries** [L historia, fr. Gk, inquiry, history, fr. histōr, istōr knowing, learned] 1 : a chronological record of significant events usu. with an explanation of their causes 2 : a branch of knowledge that records and explains past events 3 : events that form the subject matter of history — **his·tor·ic** \his-'tōr-ik\ adj — **his·tor·i·cal** \-i-kəl\ adj — **his·tor·i·cal·ly** \-k(ə-)lē\ adv

**his·tri·on·ic** \ˌhis-trē-'än-ik\ adj [LL histrionicus, fr. L histrio actor] 1 : of or relating to actors or the theater 2 : deliberately affected — **his·tri·on·i·cal·ly** \-i-k(ə-)lē\ adv

**his·tri·on·ics** \-iks\ n pl 1 : theatrical performances 2 : deliberate display of emotion for effect

¹**hit** \'hit\ vb **hit; hit·ting** 1 : to reach with a blow : STRIKE 2 : to come or cause to come in contact : COLLIDE 3 : to affect detrimentally 4 : to make a request of 5 : to come upon 6 : to accord with : SUIT 7 : REACH, ATTAIN 8 : to indulge in often to excess — **hit·ter** n

²**hit** n 1 : BLOW; also : COLLISION 2 : something highly successful 3 : a stroke in an athletic contest; esp : BASE HIT

¹**hitch** \'hich\ vb 1 : to move by jerks 2 : to catch or fasten esp. by a hook or knot 3 : HITCHHIKE

²**hitch** n 1 : JERK 2 : a sudden halt 3 : a connection between a vehicle or implement and a detachable source of power 4 : KNOT

**hitch·hike** \'hich-ˌhīk\ vb : to travel by securing free rides from passing vehicles — **hitch·hik·er** n

¹**hith·er** \'hith-ər\ adv : to this place

²**hither** adj : being on the near or adjacent side

**hith·er·to** \-ˌtü\ adv : up to this time

**hive** \'hīv\ n 1 : a container for housing honeybees 2 : a colony of bees 3 : a place swarming with busy occupants — **hive** vb

**hives** \'hīvz\ n sing or pl : an allergic disorder marked by the presence of itching wheals

**HJ** abbr [L hic jacet] here lies — used in epitaphs

**HL** abbr House of Lords

**HM** abbr Her Majesty; His Majesty

**HMS** abbr Her Majesty's Ship; His Majesty's Ship

**Ho** symbol holmium

**hoa·gie** also **hoa·gy** \'hō-gē\ n, pl **hoagies** : SUBMARINE 2

**hoard** \'hōrd\ n : a hidden accumulation — **hoard** vb — **hoard·er** n

**hoard·ing** \'hōrd-iŋ\ n 1 : a temporary board fence put about a building being erected or repaired 2 Brit : BILLBOARD

**hoar·frost** \'hōr-ˌfrȯst\ n : FROST 2

**hoarse** \'hōrs\ adj **hoars·er; hoars·est** 1 : rough and harsh in sound 2 : having a grating voice — **hoarse·ly** adv — **hoarse·ness** n

**hoary** \'hōr-ē\ adj **hoar·i·er; -est** 1 : gray or white with age 2 : ANCIENT — **hoar·i·ness** n

**hoax** \'hōks\ n : an act intended to trick or dupe; also : something accepted or established by fraud — **hoax** vb — **hoax·er** n

¹**hob** \'häb\ n : MISCHIEF, TROUBLE

²**hob** n : a projection at the back or side of a fireplace on which something may be kept warm

¹**hob·ble** \'häb-əl\ vb **hob·bled; hob·bling** \-(ə-)liŋ\ 1 : to limp along; also : to make lame 2 : FETTER

²**hobble** n 1 : a hobbling movement 2 : something used to hobble an animal

**hob·by** \'häb-ē\ n, pl **hobbies** : a pursuit or interest engaged in for relaxation — **hob·by·ist** \-ē-əst\ n

**hob·by·horse** \'häb-ē-ˌhȯrs\ n 1 : a stick sometimes with a horse's head on which children pretend to ride 2 : a toy horse mounted on rockers **3** : something (as a favorite topic) to which one constantly reverts

**hob·gob·lin** \'häb-,gäb-lən\ *n* **1** : a mischievous goblin **2** : BOGEY

**hob·nail** \-,nāl\ *n* [²hob] : a short large-headed nail for studding shoe soles - **hob·nailed** \-,nāld\ *adj*

**hob·nob** \-,näb\ *vb* **hob·nobbed; hob·nob·bing** : to associate familiarly

**ho·bo** \'hō-bō\ *n, pl* **hoboes** *also* **hobos** : TRAMP

**¹hock** \'häk\ *n* : a joint or region in the hind limb of a quadruped corresponding to the human ankle

**²hock** *n* : a means (or prison) : PAWN; *also* : DEBT **3** — **hock** *vb*

**hock·ey** \'häk-ē\ *n* **1** : FIELD HOCKEY **2** : ICE HOCKEY

**ho·cus-po·cus** \,hō-kəs-'pō-kəs\ *n* **1** : SLEIGHT OF HAND **2** : nonsense or sham used to conceal deception

**hod** \'häd\ *n* **1** : a long-handled tray or trough for carrying a load esp. of mortar or bricks **2** : SCUTTLE

**hodge·podge** \'häj-,päj\ *n* : a heterogeneous mixture

**hoe** \'hō\ *n* : a long-handled implement with a thin flat blade used esp. for cultivating, weeding, or loosening the earth around plants — **hoe** *vb*

**hoe·cake** \'hō-,kāk\ *n* : a cornmeal cake often baked on a griddle

**hoe·down** \-,daùn\ *n* **1** : SQUARE DANCE **2** : a gathering featuring hoedowns

**¹hog** \'hòg, 'häg\ *n, pl* **hogs** *also* **hog** **1** : a domestic swine esp. when grown **2** : a selfish, gluttonous, or filthy person - **hog·gish** *adj*

**²hog** *vb* **hogged; hog·ging** : to take or hold selfishly

**ho·gan** \'hō-,gän\ *n* : an earth-covered dwelling of the Navaho Indians

**hog·back** \'hòg-,bak, 'häg-\ *n* : a ridge with a sharp summit and steep sides

**hog·nose snake** \,hòg-,nōz, 'häg-\ *or* **hog·nosed snake** \-,nōz(d)-\ *n* : any of several rather small harmless stout-bodied No. American snakes with an upturned snout that play dead when their threatening display is ineffective

**hogs·head** \'hògz-,hed, 'hägz-\ *n* **1** : a large cask or barrel; *esp* : one holding from 63 to 140 gallons **2** : a liquid measure equal to 63 U.S. gallons

**hog-tie** \'hòg-,tī\ *vb* **1** : to tie together the feet of ⟨~ a calf⟩ **2** : to make helpless

**hog·wash** \-,wòsh, -,wäsh\ *n* **1** : SWILL 1, SLOP 2 **2** : NONSENSE, BALONEY

**hog-wild** \-'wīld\ *adj* : lacking in restraint

**hoi pol·loi** \,hòi-pə-'lòi\ *n pl* [Gk, the many] : the general populace

**¹hoist** \'hòist\ *vb* : RAISE, LIFT

**²hoist** *n* **1** : LIFT **2** : an apparatus for hoisting **3** : the height of a flag when viewed flying

**hoke** \'hōk\ *vb* **hok·ed; hok·ing** : FAKE — usu. used with *up*

**ho·kum** \'hō-kəm\ *n* : NONSENSE

**¹hold** \'hōld\ *vb* **held** \'held\; **hold·ing** **1** : POSSESS; *also* : KEEP **2** : RE-

STRAIN **3** : to have or maintain a grasp on **4** : to remain or cause to remain in a particular situation or position **5** : SUSTAIN; *also* : RESERVE **6** : BEAR, COMFORT **7** : to maintain in being or action : PERSIST **8** : CONTAIN, ACCOMMODATE **9** : HARBOR, ENTERTAIN; *also* : CONSIDER, REGARD **10** : to carry on by concerted action; *also* : CONVOKE **11** : to occupy esp. by appointment or election **12** : to be valid **13** : HALT, PAUSE — **hold·er** *n* — **hold forth** : to speak at length — **hold to** : to adhere to : MAINTAIN — **hold with** : to agree with or approve of

**²hold** *n* **1** : STRONGHOLD **2** : CONFINEMENT; *also* : PRISON **3** : the act or manner of holding or clasping : GRIP **4** : a nonphysical bond which attaches or restrains or by which something is affected **5** : something that may be grasped as a support **6** : an order or indication that something is to be reserved or delayed

**³hold** *n* **1** : the interior of a ship below decks; *esp* : a ship's cargo deck **2** : an airplane's cargo compartment

**hold·ing** \'hōl-diŋ\ *n* **1** : land held esp. of a superior; *also* : property owned **2** : a ruling of a court esp. on an issue of law

**holding pattern** *n* : a course flown by an aircraft waiting to land

**hold out** \(')hōld-'aùt\ *vb* **1** : to continue to fight or work **2** : to refuse to come to an agreement — **hold·out** \-,aùt\ *n*

**hold·over** \'hōld-,ō-vər\ *n* : a person who continues in office

**hold-up** \'hōld-,əp\ *n* **1** : robbery at the point of a gun **2** : DELAY

**hole** \'hōl\ *n* **1** : an opening into or through something **2** : a hollow place (as a pit or cave) **3** : DEN, BURROW **4** : a unit of play from tee to cup in golf **5** : a mean or dingy place **6** : an awkward position - **hole** *vb*

**hol·i·day** \'häl-ə-,dā\ *n* [ME, fr. OE *hāligdæg*, fr. *hālig* holy + *dæg* day] **1** : a day observed in Judaism with commemorative ceremonies **2** : a day of freedom from work; *esp* : one in commemoration of an event **3** : VACATION — **holiday** *vb*

**ho·li·ness** \'hō-lē-nəs\ *n* : the quality or state of being holy — used as a title esp. for the pope

**hol·ler** \'häl-ər\ *vb* **hol·lered; hol·ler·ing** \-(ə-)riŋ\ : to cry out : SHOUT — **holler** *n*

**hol·lo** \hä-'lō, hə-; 'häl-ō\ *also* **hol·loa** \hä-'lō, hə-\ *or* **hol·la** \hə-'lä, 'häl-(,)ä\ *interj* — used esp. to attract attention

**¹hol·low** \'häl-ō\ *adj* **hol·low·er** \'häl-ə-wər\; **hol·low·est** \-ə-wəst\ **1** : CONCAVE, SUNKEN **2** : having a cavity within **3** : MUFFLED ⟨a ~ sound⟩ **4** : devoid of value or significance; *also* : FALSE — **hol·low·ness** *n*

**²hollow** *vb* : to make or become hollow

**³hollow** *n* **1** : a surface depression **2** : CAVITY

**hol·low·ware** *or* **hol·lo·ware** \'häl-ə-

,waǝr\ *n* : vessels (as bowls or cups) that have a significant depth and volume

**hol·ly** \'häl-ē\ *n, pl* **hollies** : a tree or shrub with usu. evergreen glossy spiny-margined leaves and red berries

**hol·ly·hock** \-,häk, -,hȯk\ *n* [ME *holihoc,* fr. *holi* holy + *hoc* mallow] : a tall perennial herb related to the mallows that is widely grown for its showy flowers

**hol·mi·um** \'hōl-mē-ǝm\ *n* : a metallic chemical element

**ho·lo·caust** \'häl-ǝ-,kȯst, 'hō-lǝ-, 'hȯ-lǝ-\ *n* : a thorough destruction esp. by fire

**ho·lo·gram** \'hō-lǝ-,gram,'häl-ǝ-\ *n* : a three-dimensional picture made by reflected laser light on a photographic film without the use of a camera

**ho·lo·graph** \'hō-lǝ-,graf, 'häl-ǝ-\ *n* : a document wholly in the handwriting of its author

**ho·log·ra·phy** \hō-'läg-rǝ-fē\ *n* : the process of making or using a hologram — **ho·lo·graph** \'hō-lǝ-,graf\ *vb* — **ho·lo·graph·ic** \,hō-lǝ-'graf-ik, ,häl-ǝ-\ *adj* — **ho·lo·graph·i·cal·ly** \-i-k(ǝ-)lē\ *adv*

**hol·stein** \'hōl-,stēn, -,stīn\ *n* : any of a breed of large black-and-white dairy cattle that produce large quantities of comparatively low-fat milk

**hol·stein-frie·sian** \-'frē-zhǝn\ *n* : HOLSTEIN

**hol·ster** \'hōl-stǝr\ *n* : a usu. leather case for a pistol

**ho·ly** \'hō-lē\ *adj* **ho·li·er; -est 1** : SACRED **2** : commanding absolute devotion **3** : spiritually pure **syn** divine, godly, hallowed, blessed, religious

**ho·ly·stone** \'hō-lē-,stōn\ *n* : a soft sandstone used to scrub a ship's decks — **holystone** *vb*

**hom·age** \'(h)äm-ij\ *n* [ME, fr. OF *hommage,* fr. *homme* man, vassal, fr. L *homo* man] : reverential regard

**hom·burg** \'häm-,bǝrg\ *n* : a man's felt hat with a stiff curled brim and a high crown creased lengthwise

¹**home** \'hōm\ *n* **1** : one's residence; *also* : HOUSE **2** : the social unit formed by a family living together **3** : a congenial environment; *also* : HABITAT **4** : a place of origin **5** : the objective in various games — **home·less** *adj*

²**home** *vb* **homed; hom·ing 1** : to go or return home **2** : to proceed to or toward a source of radiated energy used as a guide

**home·body** \'hōm-,bäd-ē\ *n* : one whose life centers in the home

**home·bred** \'hōm-'bred\ *adj* : produced at home : INDIGENOUS

**home·com·ing** \'hōm-,kǝm-iŋ\ *n* **1** : a return home **2** : the return of a group of people esp. on a special occasion to a place formerly frequented

**home economics** *n* : the theory and practice of homemaking

**home·grown** \'hōm-'grōn\ *adj* **1** : grown domestically (⁓ corn) **2** : LOCAL, INDIGENOUS

**home·land** \-,land\ *n* : native land

**home·ly** \'hōm-lē\ *adj* **home·li·er; -est 1** : FAMILIAR **2** : KINDLY **3** : unaffectedly natural **4** : lacking beauty or proportion — **home·li·ness** *n*

**home·made** \'hōm-,(m)ād\ *adj* : made in the home, on the premises, or by one's own efforts

**home·mak·er** \'hōm-,mā-kǝr\ *n* : one who manages a household esp. as a wife and mother — **home·mak·ing** \-,kiŋ\ *n*

**ho·me·op·a·thy** \,hō-mē-'äp-ǝ-thē\ *n* : a system of medical practice that treats disease esp. with minute doses of a remedy that would in healthy persons produce symptoms of the disease treated — **ho·meo·path** \'hō-mē-ǝ-,path\ *n* — **ho·meo·path·ic** \,hō-mē-ǝ-'path-ik\ *adj*

**ho·meo·sta·sis** \,hō-mē-ō-'stā-sǝs\ *n* : a tendency toward a stable state of equilibrium between interrelated physiological, psychological, or social factors characteristic of an individual or group — **ho·meo·stat·ic** \-'stat-ik\ *adj*

**home plate** *n* : a slab at the apex of a baseball diamond that a base runner must touch in order to score

**hom·er** \'hō-mǝr\ *n* : HOME RUN — **homer** *vb*

**home·room** \'hōm-,rüm, -,rǔm\ *n* : a schoolroom where pupils of the same class report at the opening of school

**home run** *n* : a hit in baseball that enables the batter to make a circuit of the bases and score a run

**home·sick** \'hōm-,sik\ *adj* : longing for home and family while absent from them — **home·sick·ness** *n*

**home·spun** \-,spǝn\ *adj* **1** : spun or made at home; *also* : made of a loosely woven usu. woolen or linen fabric **2** : SIMPLE, HOMELY

**home·stead** \'hōm-,sted\ *n* : the home and adjoining land occupied by a family

**home·stead·er** \-'ǝr\ *n* : one who acquires a tract of land from U.S. public lands by filing a record and living on and cultivating the tract

**home·stretch** \'hōm-'strech\ *n* **1** : the part of a racecourse between the last curve and the winning post **2** : a final stage (as of a project)

¹**home·ward** \'hōm-wǝrd\ *or* **home·wards** \-wǝrdz\ *adv* : in the direction of home

²**homeward** *adj* : being or going in the direction of home

**home·work** \'hōm-,wǝrk\ *n* **1** : an assignment given a student to be completed outside the classroom **2** : preparatory reading or research

**hom·ey** *also* **homy** \'hō-mē\ *adj* **hom·i·er; -est** : intimate or home-like in nature

**ho·mi·cide** \'häm-ǝ-,sīd, 'hō-mǝ-\ *n* [L *homicida* manslayer & *homicidium* manslaughter; both fr. *homo* man + *caedere* to cut, kill] **1** : a person who kills another **2** : a killing of one human being by another — **hom·i·cid·al** \,häm-ǝ-'sīd-ᵊl\ *adj*

**hom·i·ly** \'häm-ə-lē\ *n, pl* **-lies :** SERMON — **hom·i·let·ic** \,häm-ə-'let-ik\ *adj*

**homing pigeon** *n* **:** a racing pigeon trained to return home

**hom·i·ny** \'häm-ə-nē\ *n* **:** hulled corn with the germ removed

¹**ho·mo** \'hō-mō\ *n, pl* **homos :** any of the genus of primate mammals that includes all surviving and various extinct men

²**homo** *n, pl* **homos :** HOMOSEXUAL

**ho·mo·ge·neous** \,hō-mə-'jē-nē-əs, -nyəs\ *adj* **:** of the same or a similar kind; *also* **:** of uniform structure — **ho·mo·ge·ne·i·ty** \-jə-'nē-ət-ē\ *n* — **ho·mo·ge·neous·ly** *adv* — **ho·mo·ge·neous·ness** *n*

**ho·mo·ge·nize** \hō-'mäj-ə-,nīz, hə-\ *vb* **-nized; -niz·ing 1 :** to make homogeneous **2 :** to reduce the particles in (as milk or paint) to uniform size and distribute them evenly throughout the liquid — **ho·mog·e·niz·er** *n*

**ho·mo·graph** \'häm-ə-,graf, 'hō-mə-\ *n* **:** one of two or more words spelled alike but different in origin or meaning or pronunciation ⟨the noun *conduct* and the verb *conduct* are ~s⟩

**ho·mol·o·gous** \hō-'mäl-ə-gəs, hə-\ *adj* **:** corresponding in structure usu. because of community of origin ⟨wings and arms are ~ organs⟩ — **ho·mo·logue** *or* **ho·mo·log** \'hō-mə-,lòg, 'häm-ə-, -,läg\ *n* — **ho·mol·o·gy** \hō-'mäl-ə-jē, hə-\ *n*

**hom·onym** \'häm-ə-,nim, 'hō-mə-\ *n* **1 :** HOMOPHONE, HOMOGRAPH **2 :** one of two or more words spelled and pronounced alike but different in meaning ⟨*pool* of water and *pool* the game are ~s⟩

**ho·mo·phone** \'häm-ə-,fōn, 'hō-mə-\ *n* **:** one of two or more words (as *to, too, two*) pronounced alike but different in meaning or derivation or spelling

**Ho·mo sa·pi·ens** \,hō-mō-'sap-ē-ənz, -'sä-pē-\ *n* **:** MAN, MANKIND

**ho·mo·sex·u·al** \,hō-mō-'seksh(ə-w)əl\ *adj* **:** of, relating to, or exhibiting sexual desire toward a member of one's own sex

**hon** *abbr* honor; honorable; honorary

**hone** \'hōn\ *n* **:** a fine-grit stone for sharpening a cutting implement — **hone** *vb* — **hon·er** *n*

**hon·est** \'än-əst\ *adj* **1 :** free from deception **:** TRUTHFUL; *also* **:** GENUINE, REAL **2 :** REPUTABLE **3 :** CREDITABLE **4 :** marked by integrity **5 :** FRANK *syn* upright, just, conscientious, honorable — **hon·est·ly** *adv* — **hon·esty** \-ə-stē\ *n*

**hon·ey** \'hən-ē\ *n, pl* **honeys :** a sweet sticky substance made by bees (**hon·ey·bees** \-,bēz\) from the nectar of flowers

¹**hon·ey·comb** \-,kōm\ *n* **:** a mass of 6-sided wax cells built by honeybees; *also* **:** something of similar structure or appearance

²**honeycomb** *vb* **:** to make or become full of cavities like a honeycomb

**hon·ey·dew** \-,d(y)ü\ *n* **:** a sweetish

deposit secreted on plants by aphids, scales, or fungi

**honeydew melon** *n* **:** a smooth-skinned muskmelon with sweet green flesh

**honey locust** *n* **:** a tall usu. spiny No. American leguminous tree with hard durable wood and long twisted pods

**hon·ey·moon** \'hən-ē-,mün\ *n* **1 :** a holiday taken by a newly married couple **2 :** a period of harmony esp. just after marriage — **honeymoon** *vb*

**hon·ey·suck·le** \'hən-ē-,sək-əl\ *n* **:** any of various shrubs, vines, or herbs with tubular flowers rich in nectar

**honk** \'häŋk, 'hòŋk\ *n* **:** the cry of a goose; *also* **:** a similar sound (as of a horn) — **honk** *vb* — **honk·er** *n*

**hon·ky-tonk** \'häŋ-kē-,täŋk, 'hòŋ-kē-,tòŋk\ *n* **:** a cheap nightclub or dance hall

¹**hon·or** \'än-ər\ *n* **1 :** good name **:** REPUTATION; *also* **:** outward respect **2 :** PRIVILEGE **3 :** a person of superior standing — used esp. as a title **4 :** one whose worth brings respect or fame **5 :** an evidence or symbol of distinction **6 :** CHASTITY, PURITY **7 :** INTEGRITY *syn* homage reverence, deference, obeisance

²**honor** *vb* **hon·ored; hon·or·ing** \-(ə-)riŋ\ **1 :** to regard or treat with honor **2 :** to confer honor on **3 :** to fulfill the terms of — **hon·or·er** \'än-ər-ər\ *n*

**hon·or·able** \'än-(ə-)rə-bəl\ *adj* **1 :** deserving of honor **2 :** accompanied with marks of honor **3 :** of great renown **4 :** doing credit to the possessor **5 :** characterized by integrity — **hon·or·able·ness** *n* — **hon·or·ably** \-blē\ *adv*

**hon·o·rar·i·um** \,än-ə-'rer-ē-əm\ *n, pl* **-ia** \-ē-ə\ *also* **-i·ums :** a reward usu. for services on which custom or propriety forbids a price to be set

**hon·or·ary** \'än-ə-,rer-ē\ *adj* **1 :** having or conferring distinction **2 :** conferred in recognition of achievement without the usual prerequisites ⟨~ degree⟩ **3 :** UNPAID, VOLUNTARY — **hon·or·ar·i·ly** \,än-ə-'rer-ə-lē\ *adv*

**hon·or·if·ic** \,än-ə-'rif-ik\ *adj* **:** conferring or conveying honor ⟨~ titles⟩

**hon·our** \'än-ər\ *chiefly Brit var of* HONOR

¹**hood** \'hüd\ *n* **1 :** a covering for the head and neck and sometimes the face **2 :** an ornamental fold (as at the back of an ecclesiastical vestment) **3 :** a cover for parts of mechanisms; *esp* **:** the metal covering over an automobile engine — **hood·ed** \-əd\ *adj*

²**hood** \'hüd, 'hùd\ *n* **:** HOODLUM

**-hood** \,hùd\ *n suffix* **1 :** state **:** condition **:** quality **:** character ⟨boy*hood*⟩ ⟨hardi*hood*⟩ **2 :** instance of a (specified) state or quality ⟨false*hood*⟩ **3 :** individuals sharing a (specified) state or character ⟨brother*hood*⟩

**hood·lum** \'hüd-ləm, 'hùd-\ *n* **1 :** THUG **2 :** a young ruffian

**hoo·doo** \'hüd-ü\ *n, pl* **hoodoos 1 :** VOODOO **2 :** something that brings

bad luck — **hoodoo** vb
**hood·wink** \'hùd-,wiŋk\ vb : to deceive by false appearance
**hoo·ey** \'hü-ē\ n : NONSENSE
**hoof** \'hùf, 'hüf\ n, pl **hooves** \'hùvz, 'hüvz\ or **hoofs** : a horny covering that protects the ends of the toes of some mammals (as horses or cattle); also : a hoofed foot —**hoofed** \'hùft, 'hüft\ adj
¹**hook** \'hùk\ n 1 : a curved or bent device for catching, holding, or pulling 2 : something curved or bent like a hook 3 : a flight of a ball (as in golf) that curves in a direction opposite to the dominant hand of the player propelling it 4 : a short punch delivered with a circular motion and with the elbow bent and rigid
²**hook** vb 1 : CURVE, CROOK 2 : to seize or make fast with a hook 3 : STEAL
**hoo·kah** \'hùk-ə, 'hü-kə\ n : a pipe for smoking that has a long flexible tube whereby the smoke is cooled by passing through water
**hook·er** \'hùk-ər\ n 1 : one that hooks 2 : PROSTITUTE
**hook·up** \'hùk-,əp\ n : an assemblage (as of apparatus or circuits) used for a specific purpose (as in radio)
**hook·worm** \'hùk-,wərm\ n : a parasitic intestinal worm having hooks or plates around the mouth
**hoo·li·gan** \'hü-li-gən\ n : RUFFIAN, HOODLUM
**hoop** \'hùp, 'hüp\ n 1 : a circular strip used esp. for holding together the staves of a container (as a barrel) 2 : a circular figure or object : RING 3 : a circle of flexible material for expanding a woman's skirt
**hoop·la** \'hüp-,lä, 'hùp-,lä\ n [F houp∘là, interj.] 1 : TO-DO 2 : utterances designed to bewilder or confuse
**hoose·gow** \'hüs-,gaù\ n [Sp juzgado panel of judges, courtroom] slang : JAIL
**Hoo·sier** \'hü-zhər\ n : a native or resident of Indiana
**hoot** \'hüt\ vb 1 : to utter a loud shout usu. in contempt 2 : to make the characteristic cry of an owl — **hoot** n — **hoot·er** n
**hoo·te·nan·ny** \'hüt-ᵊn-,an-ē\ n, pl **-nies** : a gathering at which folk singers entertain
¹**hop** \'häp\ vb **hopped; hop·ping** 1 : to move by quick springy leaps 2 : to make a quick trip esp. by air 3 : to ride on esp. surreptitiously and without authorization
²**hop** n 1 : a short brisk leap esp. on one leg 2 : DANCE 3 : a short trip by air
³**hop** n : a vine related to the mulberry whose ripe dried pistillate catkins are used in medicine and in flavoring malt liquors; also : its pistillate catkin
⁴**hop** vb **hopped; hop·ping** : to increase the power of (~ up an engine)
¹**hope** \'hōp\ vb **hoped; hop·ing** : to desire with expectation of fulfillment
²**hope** n 1 : TRUST, RELIANCE 2 : desire accompanied by expectation of fulfillment; also : something hoped for 3 : one that gives promise for the future

— **hope·ful** \-fəl\ adj — **hope·ful·ly** \-ē\ adv — **hope·ful·ness** n — **hope·less** adj — **hope·less·ly** adv — **hope·less·ness** n
**HOPE** abbr Health Opportunity for People Everywhere
**hop·head** \'häp-,hed\ n, slang : a drug addict
**Ho·pi** \'hō-pē\ n, pl **Hopi** also **Hopis** [Hopi Hópi, lit., good, peaceful] 1 : a member of an Indian people of Arizona; also : the language of the Hopi people
**hop·per** \'häp-ər\ n 1 : a usu. immature hopping insect 2 : a box in which a bill to be considered by a legislative body is dropped 3 : a freight car with hinged doors in a sloping bottom 4 : a tank holding a liquid and having a device for releasing its contents through a pipe
**hop·scotch** \'häp-,skäch\ n : a child's game in which a player tosses an object (as a stone) consecutively into areas of a figure outlined on the ground and hops through the figure and back to regain the object
**hor** abbr horizontal
**horde** \'hôrd\ n : THRONG, SWARM
**hore·hound** \'hôr-,haùnd\ n : an aromatic bitter mint with downy leaves used esp. in candy
**ho·ri·zon** \hə-'rīz-ᵊn\ n [Gk horizont-, horizōn, fr. prp. of horizein to bound, fr. horos limit, boundary] 1 : the line marking the apparent junction of earth and sky 2 : range of outlook or experience
**hor·i·zon·tal** \,hôr-ə-'zänt-ᵊl\ adj : parallel to the horizon : LEVEL — **hor·i·zon·tal·ly** \-ē\ adv
**hor·mon·al** \'hôr-'mōn-ᵊl\ adj : of, relating to, or resembling a hormone
**hor·mone** \'hôr-,mōn\ n [Gk hormōn, prp. of horman to stir up, fr. hormē impulse, assault] : a product of living cells that circulates in body fluids and has a specific effect on some other cells; esp : the secretion of an endocrine gland
**horn** \'hôrn\ n 1 : one of the hard bony projections on the head of many hoofed animals 2 : something resembling or suggesting a horn 3 : a brass wind instrument 4 : a usu. electrical device that makes a noise ⟨automobile ~⟩ — **horn·less** adj — **horny** adj
**horn·book** \'hôrn-,bùk\ n 1 : a child's primer consisting of a sheet of parchment or paper protected by a sheet of transparent horn 2 : a rudimentary treatise
**horned toad** \'hôrnd-\ n : any of several small harmless insect-eating lizards with spines on the head resembling horns and spiny scales on the body
**hor·net** \'hôr-nət\ n : any of the larger social wasps
**horn in** vb : to participate without invitation : INTRUDE
**horn·pipe** \'hôrn-,pīp\ n : a lively folk dance of the British Isles
**ho·rol·o·gy** \hə-'räl-ə-jē\ n : the science of measuring time or constructing time-indicating instruments —

**hor·o·log·i·cal** \ˌhȯr-ə-'läj-i-kəl\ adj
— **ho·rol·o·gist** \hə-'räl-ə-jəst\ n
**horo·scope** \'hȯr-ə-ˌskōp\ n [MF, fr.
L horoscopus, fr. Gk hōroskopos, fr.
hōra hour + skopein to look at] : a diagram of the relative positions of planets
and signs of the zodiac at a particular
time for use by astrologers to foretell
events of a person's life
**hor·ren·dous** \hȯ-'ren-dəs\ adj
: DREADFUL, HORRIBLE
**hor·ri·ble** \'hȯr-ə-bəl\ adj 1 : marked
by or conducive to horror 2 : highly
disagreeable — **hor·ri·ble·ness** n —
**hor·ri·bly** \-blē\ adv
**hor·rid** \'hȯr-əd\ adj 1 : HIDEOUS
2 : REPULSIVE — **hor·rid·ly** adv
**hor·ri·fy** \'hȯr-ə-ˌfī\ vb **-fied; -fy·ing**
: to cause to feel horror syn appall,
daunt, dismay
**hor·ror** \'hȯr-ər\ n 1 : painful and intense fear, dread, or dismay 2 : intense
aversion or repugnance 3 : something
that horrifies
**hors de com·bat** \ˌȯrd-ə-kōⁿ-'bä\ adv
or adj : in a disabled condition
**hors d'oeuvre** \ȯr-'dərv\ n, pl hors
d'oeuvres also hors d'oeuvre
\-'dərv(z)\ [F hors-d'oeuvre, lit., outside of work] : any of various savory
foods usu. served as appetizers
**horse** \'hȯrs\ n, pl hors·es also
horse 1 : a large solid-hoofed herbivorous mammal domesticated as a draft
and saddle animal 2 : a supporting
framework usu. with legs — **horse-
less** adj
¹**horse·back** \'hȯrs-ˌbak\ n : the back
of a horse
²**horseback** adv : on horseback
**horse chestnut** n : a large Asiatic tree
with palmate leaves erect conical
clusters of showy flowers, and large
glossy brown seeds enclosed in a
prickly bur
**horse·flesh** \'hȯrs-ˌflesh\ n : horses
for riding, driving, or racing
**horse·fly** \-ˌflī\ n : any of a group of
large two-winged flies with bloodsucking females
**horse·hair** \-ˌhaər\ n 1 : the hair of a
horse esp. from the mane or tail 2
: cloth made from horsehair
**horse·hide** \-ˌhīd\ n 1 : the
dressed or raw hide of a horse 2 : the
ball used in baseball
**horse latitudes** n pl : either of two
calm regions near 30°N and 30°S latitude
**horse·laugh** \-ˌlaf, -ˌläf\ n : a loud
boisterous laugh
**horse·man** \-mən\ n 1 : one who
rides horseback; also : one skilled in
managing horses 2 : a breeder or
raiser of horses — **horse·man·ship** n
**horse·play** \-ˌplā\ n : rough boisterous
play
**horse·player** \-ər\ n : a bettor on
horse races
**horse·pow·er** \-ˌpau̇(-ə)r\ n : a unit
of power equal to the power necessary
to raise 33,000 pounds one foot in one
minute
**horse·rad·ish** \'hȯrs-ˌrad-ish\ n : a

tall white-flowered herb related to the
mustards whose pungent root is used as
a condiment
**horse·shoe** \'hȯrs(h)-ˌshü\ n 1 : a
protective metal plate fitted to the rim
of a horse's hoof 2 pl : a game in
which horseshoes are pitched at a fixed
object — **horse·sho·er** \-ˌshü-ər\ n
**horseshoe crab** n : any of several
marine arthropods with a broad crescent-shaped combined head and thorax
**horse·tail** \'hȯrs-ˌtāl\ n : any of a
genus of perennial flowerless plants related to the ferns
**horse·whip** \'hȯrs-ˌhwip\ vb : to flog
with a whip made to be used on a horse
**horse·wom·an** \-ˌwu̇m-ən\ n : a
woman skilled in riding horseback or in
caring for or managing horses
**hors·ey** or **horsy** \'hȯr-sē\ adj **hors-
i·er; -est** 1 : of, relating to, or suggesting a horse 2 : having to do with
horses or horse racing
**hort** abbr horticultural; horticulture
**hor·ta·tive** \'hȯrt-ət-iv\ adj : giving
exhortation
**hor·ta·to·ry** \'hȯrt-ə-ˌtōr-ē\ adj : HOR-
TATIVE
**hor·ti·cul·ture** \'hȯrt-ə-ˌkəl-chər\ n
: the science and art of growing fruits,
vegetables, flowers, and ornamental
plants — **hor·ti·cul·tur·al** \ˌhȯrt-ə-
'kəlch(-ə)-rəl\ adj — **hor·ti·cul·tur-
ist** \-rəst\ n
**Hos** abbr Hosea
**ho·san·na** \hō-'zan-ə, -'zän-\ interj
[Gk hōsanna, fr. Heb hōshī'āh-nnā
pray, save (us)!] — used as a cry of acclamation and adoration
¹**hose** \'hōz\ n, pl hose or hos·es 1 pl
hose : STOCKING, SOCK; also : a close-
fitting garment covering the legs and
waist 2 : a flexible tube for conveying
fluids (as from a faucet)
²**hose** vb **hosed; hos·ing** : to spray,
water, or wash with a hose
**ho·siery** \'hōzh-(ə)-rē, 'hōz(-ə)-\ n
: STOCKINGS, SOCKS
**hosp** abbr hospital
**hos·pice** \'häs-pəs\ n : a lodging for
travelers or for young persons or the
underprivileged
**hos·pi·ta·ble** \hä-'spit-ə-bəl, 'häs-
(ˌ)pit-\ adj 1 : given to generous and
cordial reception of guests 2 : readily
receptive — **hos·pi·ta·bly** \-blē\ adv
**hos·pi·tal** \'häs-ˌpit-ᵊl\ n [ME, fr. OF,
fr. ML hospitale, fr. LL, hospice, fr. L,
guest room, fr. hospit-, hospes guest,
host, fr. hostis stranger, enemy] : an
institution where the sick or injured
receive medical or surgical care
**hos·pi·tal·i·ty** \ˌhäs-pə-'tal-ət-ē\ n, pl
**-ties** : hospitable treatment, reception,
or disposition
**hos·pi·tal·ize** \'häs-ˌpit-ᵊl-ˌīz\ vb
**-ized; -iz·ing** : to place in a hospital
for care and treatment — **hos·pi·tal-
iza·tion** \ˌhäs-ˌpit-ᵊl-ə-'zā-shən\ n
¹**host** \'hōst\ n 1 : ARMY 2 : MULTI-
TUDE
²**host** n 1 : one who receives or enter-
tains guests 2 : an animal or plant on
or in which a parasite lives — **host** vb

³**host** *n, often cap* **:** the eucharistic bread

**hos·tage** \'häs-tij\ *n* **:** a person kept as a pledge pending the fulfillment of an agreement

**hos·tel** \'häs-t°l\ *n* **1 :** INN **2 : a** supervised lodging for youth — **hos·tel·er** *n*

**hos·tel·ry** \-rē\ *n, pl* **-ries :** INN, HOTEL

**host·ess** \'hō-stəs\ *n* **:** a woman who acts as host

**hos·tile** \'häs-t°l, -,tīl\ *adj* **:** marked by usu. overt antagonism **:** UNFRIENDLY — **hostile** *n* — **hos·tile·ly** \-ē\ *adv* — **hos·til·i·ty** \häs-'til-ət-ē\ *n*

**hos·tler** \'(h)äs-lər\ *n* **:** one who takes care of horses or mules

**hot** \'hät\ *adj* **hot·ter; hot·test 1 :** marked by a high temperature or an uncomfortable degree of body heat **2 :** giving a sensation of heat or of burning **3 :** ARDENT, FIERY **4 :** LUSTFUL **5 :** EAGER **6 :** newly made or received **7 :** PUNGENT **8 :** unusually lucky or favorable (~ dice) **9 :** recently and illegally obtained (~ jewels) — **hot** *adv* — **hot·ly** *adv* — **hot·ness** *n*

**hot·bed** \-,bed\ *n* **1 :** a glass-covered bed of soil heated (as by fermenting manure) and used esp. for raising seedlings **2 :** an environment that favors rapid growth or development

**hot–blood·ed** \-'bləd-əd\ *adj* **:** easily roused or excited

**hot·box** \-,bäks\ *n* **:** a journal bearing (as of a railroad car) overheated by friction

**hot·cake** \-,kāk\ *n* **:** PANCAKE

**hot dog** \'hät-,dog\ *n* **:** a cooked frankfurter usu. served in a long split roll

**ho·tel** \hō-'tel\ *n* [F *hôtel*, fr. OF *hostel*, fr. LL *hospitale* hospice] **:** a building where lodging and usu. meals, entertainment, and various personal services are provided for the public

**hot flash** *n* **:** a sudden brief flushing and sensation of heat caused by dilation of skin capillaries usu. associated with menopausal endocrine imbalance

**hot·foot** \'hät-,fut\ *n, pl* **hotfoots :** a practical joke in which a match is surreptitiously inserted into the side of a victim's shoe and lighted

**hot·head·ed** \-'hed-əd\ *adj* **:** FIERY, IMPETUOUS — **hot·head** \-,hed\ *n* — **hot·head·ed·ly** *adv* — **hot·head·ed·ness** *n*

**hot·house** \-,haus\ *n* **:** a heated glass-enclosed house for raising plants

**hot line** *n* **:** a direct telephone line constantly open so as to facilitate immediate communication

**hot plate** *n* **:** a simple portable appliance for heating or for cooking

**hot potato** *n* **:** an embarrassing or controversial issue

**hot rod** *n* **:** an automobile rebuilt or modified for high speed and fast acceleration — **hot-rod·der** \'hät-'räd-ər\ *n*

**hot seat** *n, slang* **:** ELECTRIC CHAIR

**hot·shot** \'hät-,shät\ *n* **:** a showily skillful person

¹**hound** \'haund\ *n* **1 :** a long-eared

hunting dog that follows its prey by scent **2 :** FAN, ADDICT

²**hound** *vb* **:** to pursue constantly and relentlessly

**hour** \'au(ə)r\ *n* **1 :** the 24th part of a day **2 :** the time of day **3 :** a particular or customary time **4 :** a class session — **hour·ly** *adv or adj*

**hour·glass** \'au(ə)r-,glas\ *n* **:** an instrument for measuring time consisting of a glass vessel with two compartments from the uppermost of which a quantity of sand, water, or mercury runs in an hour into the lower one

**hou·ri** \'hur-ē\ *n* [F, fr. Per *hūrī*, fr. Ar *ḥūrīyah*] **:** one of the beautiful maidens of the Muslim paradise

¹**house** \'haus\ *n, pl* **hous·es** \'hau-zəz\ **1 :** a building for human habitation **2 :** a shelter for an animal **3 :** a building in which something is stored **4 :** HOUSEHOLD; *also* **:** FAMILY **5 :** a residence for a religious community or for students; *also* **:** those in residence **6 :** a legislative body **7 :** a place of business or entertainment **8 :** a business organization **9 :** the audience in a theater or concert hall — **house·ful** *n* — **house·less** *adj*

²**house** \'hauz\ *vb* **housed; hous·ing 1 :** to provide with or take shelter **:** LODGE **2 :** STORE

**house·boat** \'haus-,bōt\ *n* **:** a barge fitted for use as a dwelling or for leisurely cruising

**house·boy** \-,boi\ *n* **:** a boy or man hired to act as a household servant

**house·break·ing** \'haus-,brā-kiŋ\ *n* **:** the act of breaking into and entering a person's dwelling house with the intent of committing a felony

**house·bro·ken** \-,brō-kən\ *adj* **:** trained to excretory habits acceptable in indoor living

**house·clean** \'haus-,klēn\ *vb* **:** to clean a house and its furniture — **house·clean·ing** \-,klē-niŋ\ *n*

**house·coat** \'haus-,kōt\ *n* **:** a woman's often long-skirted informal garment for wear around the house

**house·fly** \'haus-,flī\ *n* **:** a two-winged fly that is common about human habitations and acts as a vector of diseases (as typhoid fever)

¹**house·hold** \'haus-,hōld\ *n* **:** those who dwell as a family under the same roof — **house·hold·er** *n*

²**household** *adj* **1 :** DOMESTIC **2 :** FAMILIAR, COMMON

**house·keep·er** \-,kē-pər\ *n* **:** a woman employed to take care of a house — **house·keep·ing** \-,piŋ\ *n*

**house·lights** \-,līts\ *n pl* **:** the lights that illuminate the parts of a theater occupied by the audience

**house·maid** \-,mād\ *n* **:** a female servant employed to do housework

**house·moth·er** \-,məth-ər\ *n* **:** a woman acting as hostess, chaperon, and often housekeeper in a residence for young people

**house sparrow** *n* **:** ENGLISH SPARROW

**house·top** \-,täp\ *n* **:** ROOF

**house·wares** \'haus-,waərz\ *n pl*

: small articles of household equipment

**house·warm·ing** \-,wȯr-miŋ\ *n* : a party to celebrate the taking possession of a house or premises

**house·wife** \'haùs-,wīf, 2 *often* 'həz-əf, 'həs-\ *n* **1** : a married woman in charge of a household **2** : a small container (as for needles and thread) — **house·wife·li·ness** \-lē-nəs\ *n* — **house·wife·ly** \-lē\ *adj* — **house·wif·ery** \-,wīf-(ə-)rē\ *n*

**house·work** \'haùs-,wərk\ *n* : the work of housekeeping

**¹hous·ing** \'haù-ziŋ\ *n* **1** : SHELTER; *also* : dwellings provided for people **2** : something that covers or protects

**²housing** *n* **1** : an ornamental cover for a saddle **2** *pl* : TRAPPINGS

**hove** *past of* HEAVE

**hov·el** \'həv-əl, 'häv-\ *n* : a small, wretched, and often dirty house : HUT

**hov·er** \'həv-ər, 'həv-\ *vb* **hov·ered; hov·er·ing** \-(ə-)riŋ\ **1** : FLUTTER; *also* : to move to and fro **2** : to be in an uncertain state

**¹how** \(')haù\ *adv* **1** : in what way or manner ⟨~ was it done⟩ **2** : with what meaning ⟨~ do we interpret such behavior⟩ **3** : for what reason ⟨~ could you have done such a thing⟩ **4** : to what extent or degree ⟨~ deep is it⟩ **5** : in what state or condition ⟨~ are you⟩ — **how about** : what do you say to or think of ⟨*how about* coming with me⟩ — **how come** : why is it that

**²how** *conj* **1** : in what manner or condition ⟨remember ~ they fought⟩ **2** : HOWEVER ⟨do it ~ you like⟩

**¹how·be·it** \haù-'bē-ət\ *adv* : NEVERTHELESS

**²howbeit** *conj* : ALTHOUGH

**how·dah** \'haùd-ə\ *n* : a seat or covered pavilion on the back of an elephant or camel

**¹how·ev·er** \haù-'ev-ər\ *conj* : in whatever manner

**²however** *adv* **1** : to whatever degree; *also* : in whatever manner **2** : in spite of that

**how·it·zer** \'haù-ət-sər\ *n* : a short cannon that shoots shells at a high angle of fire

**howl** \'haùl\ *vb* **1** : to emit a loud long doleful sound characteristic of dogs **2** : to cry loudly — **howl** *n*

**howl·er** \'haù-lər\ *n* **1** : one that howls **2** : a stupid and ridiculous blunder

**howl·ing** \'haù-liŋ\ *adj* **1** : DESOLATE, WILD **2** : very great ⟨a ~ success⟩

**how·so·ev·er** \,haù-sə-'wev-ər\ *adv* : HOWEVER **1**

**hoy·den** \'hȯid-ᵊn\ *n* : a girl or woman of saucy, boisterous, or carefree behavior

**HP** *abbr* **1** high pressure **2** horsepower

**HQ** *abbr* headquarters

**hr** *abbr* hour

**HR** *abbr* House of Representatives

**HRH** *abbr* Her Royal Highness; His Royal Highness

**hrzn** *abbr* horizon

**HS** *abbr* high school

**HST** *abbr* Hawaiian standard time

**ht** *abbr* height

**HT** *abbr* high-tension

**hua·ra·che** \wə-'räch-ē\ *n* : a low-heeled sandal having an upper made of interwoven leather thongs

**hub** \'həb\ *n* **1** : the central part of a wheel, propeller, or fan **2** : a center of activity

**hub·bub** \'həb-,əb\ *n* : UPROAR; *also* : TURMOIL

**hub·cap** \'həb-,kap\ *n* : a removable metal cap over the end of an axle

**hu·bris** \'hyü-brəs\ *n* : overweening pride or self-confidence

**huck·le·ber·ry** \'hək-əl-,ber-ē\ *n* **1** : an American shrub related to the blueberry; *also* : its edible dark blue berry **2** : BLUEBERRY

**huck·ster** \'hək-stər\ *n* : PEDDLER, HAWKER

**HUD** *abbr* Department of Housing and Urban Development

**¹hud·dle** \'həd-ᵊl\ *vb* **hud·dled; hud·dling** \'həd-(ᵊ-)liŋ\ **1** : to crowd together **2** : CONFER

**²huddle** *n* **1** : a closely packed group **2** : MEETING, CONFERENCE

**hue** \'hyü\ *n* **1** : a color as distinct from white, gray, and black; *also* : gradation of color **2** : the attribute of colors that permits them to be classed as red, yellow, green, blue, or an intermediate color — **hued** \'hyüd\ *adj*

**hue and cry** *n* : a clamor of pursuit or protest

**huff** \'həf\ *n* : a fit of anger or pique — **huffy** *adj*

**hug** \'həg\ *vb* **hugged; hug·ging** **1** : EMBRACE **2** : to stay close to ⟨the road ~s the river⟩ — **hug** *n*

**huge** \'hyüj\ *adj* **hug·er; hug·est** : very large or extensive — **huge·ly** *adv* — **huge·ness** *n*

**hug·ger-mug·ger** \'həg-ər-,məg-ər\ *n* **1** : SECRECY **2** : CONFUSION, MUDDLE

**Hu·gue·not** \'hyü-gə-,nät\ *n* : a French Protestant in the 16th and 17th centuries

**hu·la** \'hü-lə\ *n* : a sinuous Polynesian dance usu. accompanied by chants

**hulk** \'həlk\ *n* **1** : a heavy clumsy ship **2** : a bulky or unwieldy person or thing **3** : an old ship unfit for service

**hulk·ing** \'həl-kiŋ\ *adj* : HUSKY, MASSIVE

**¹hull** \'həl\ *n* **1** : the outer covering of a fruit or seed **2** : the frame or body esp. of a ship

**²hull** *vb* : to remove the hulls of — **hull·er** *n*

**hul·la·ba·loo** \'həl-ə-bə-,lü\ *n*, *pl* **-loos** : a confused noise : UPROAR

**hum** \'həm\ *vb* **hummed; hum·ming** **1** : to utter a sound like that of the speech sound \m\ prolonged **2** : DRONE **3** : to be busily active **4** : to sing with closed lips — **hum** *n* — **hum·mer** *n*

**hu·man** \'(h)yü-mən\ *adj* **1** : of, relating to, being, or characteristic of man **2** : having human form or attributes — **human** *n* — **hu·man·ly** *adv* — **hu·man·ness** \-mən-nəs\ *n*

**hu·mane** \(h)yü-'mān\ *adj* **1** : marked by compassion, sympathy, or consideration for others **2** : HUMANISTIC —

**hu·mane·ly** adv — **hu·mane·ness** \-'mān-nəs\ n

**hu·man·ism** \'(h)yü-mə-,niz-əm\ n 1 : devotion to the humanities; also : the revival of classical letters characteristic of the Renaissance 2 : a doctrine or way of life centered on human interests or values — **hu·man·ist** \-nəst\ n or adj — **hu·man·is·tic** \,(h)yü-mə-'nis-tik\ adj

**hu·man·i·tar·i·an** \(h)yü-,man ə-'ter-ē-ən\ n : one who practices philanthropy — **humanitarian** adj — **hu·man·i·tar·i·an·ism** n

**hu·man·i·ty** \(h)yü-'man-ət-ē\ n, pl **-ties** 1 : the quality or state of being human or humane 2 pl : the branches of learning having primarily a cultural character 3 : MANKIND

**hu·man·ize** \'(h)yü-mə-,nīz\ vb -ized; -iz·ing : to make human or humane — **hu·man·iza·tion** \,(h)yü-mə-nə-'zā-shən\ n

**hu·man·kind** \'(h)yü-mən-,kīnd\ n : MANKIND

**hu·man·oid** \'(h)yü-mə-,nȯid\ adj : having human form or characteristics — **humanoid** n

¹**hum·ble** \'(h)əm-bəl\ adj **hum·bler** \-b(ə-)lər\; **hum·blest** \-b(ə-)ləst\ [ME, fr. OF, fr. L humilis low, humble, fr. humus earth] 1 : not proud or haughty 2 : not pretentious : UNASSUMING 3 : INSIGNIFICANT **syn** meek, modest, lowly — **hum·ble·ness** n — **hum·bly** \-blē\ adv

²**humble** vb **hum·bled; hum·bling** \-b(ə-)liŋ\ 1 : to make humble 2 : to destroy the power or prestige of — **hum·bler** \-b(ə-)lər\ n

¹**hum·bug** \'həm-,bəg\ n 1 : HOAX, FRAUD 2 : NONSENSE

²**humbug** vb **hum·bugged; hum·bug·ging** : DECEIVE

**hum·ding·er** \'həm-'diŋ-ər\ n : a person or thing of striking excellence

**hum·drum** \'həm-,drəm\ adj : MONOTONOUS, DULL

**hu·mer·us** \'hyüm-(ə-)rəs\ n, pl **-meri** \'hyü-mə-,rī, -,rē\ : the long bone extending from elbow to shoulder

**hu·mid** \'(h)yü-məd\ adj : containing or characterized by perceptible moisture : DAMP — **hu·mid·ly** adv

**hu·mid·i·fy** \hyü-'mid-ə-,fī\ vb **-fied; -fy·ing** : to make humid — **hu·mid·i·fi·ca·tion** \-,mid-ə-fə-'kā-shən\ n — **hu·mid·i·fi·er** \-'mid-ə-,fī(-ə)r\ n

**hu·mid·i·ty** \(h)yü-'mid-ət-ē\ n, pl **-ties** : the amount of atmospheric moisture

**hu·mi·dor** \'(h)yü-mə-,dȯr\ n : a case usu. for storing cigars in which the air is kept properly humidified

**hu·mil·i·ate** \(h)yü-'mil-ē-,āt\ vb **-at·ed; -at·ing** : to injure the self-respect of : MORTIFY — **hu·mil·i·at·ing·ly** \-,āt-iŋ-lē\ adv — **hu·mil·i·a·tion** \-,mil-ē-'ā-shən\ n

**hu·mil·i·ty** \(h)yü-'mil-ət-ē\ n : the quality or state of being humble

**hum·ming·bird** \'həm-iŋ-,bərd\ n : a tiny American bird related to the swifts

**hum·mock** \'həm-ək\ n : a rounded

mound : KNOLL

¹**hu·mor** \'(h)yü-mər\ n 1 : TEMPERAMENT 2 : MOOD 3 : WHIM 4 : a quality that appeals to a sense of the ludicrous or incongruous ⟨the ~ of his plight⟩; also : a keen perception of the ludicrous or incongruous 5 : something designed to be comical or amusing — **hu·mor·ist** \'(h)yüm-(ə-)rəst\ n — **hu·mor·less** \'(h)yü-mər-ləs\ adj — **hu·mor·less·ly** adv — **hu·mor·less·ness** n — **hu·mor·ous** \'(h)yüm-(ə-)rəs\ adj — **hu·mor·ous·ly** adv — **hu·mor·ous·ness** n

²**humor** vb **hu·mored; hu·mor·ing** \'(h)yüm-(ə-)riŋ\ : to comply with the wishes or mood of

**hu·mour** chiefly Brit var of HUMOR

**hump** \'həmp\ n 1 : a rounded protuberance (as on the back of a camel) 2 : a difficult phase ⟨over the ~⟩

**hump·back** \-,bak; 1 also -'bak\ n 1 : HUNCHBACK 2 : a large whalebone whale with very long flippers — **hump·backed** adj

**hu·mus** \'(h)yü-məs\ n : the dark organic part of soil formed from decaying matter

**Hun** \'hən\ n : a member of an Asian people that invaded Europe in the 5th century A.D.

¹**hunch** \'hənch\ vb 1 : to thrust oneself forward 2 : to assume or cause to assume a bent or crooked posture

²**hunch** n 1 : PUSH 2 : a strong intuitive feeling as to how something will turn out

**hunch·back** \'hənch-,bak\ n : a back with a hump; also : a person with a crooked back — **hunch·backed** \-'bakt\ adj

**hun·dred** \'hən-drəd\ n, pl **hundreds** or **hundred** : 10 times 10 — **hundred** adj — **hun·dredth** \-drədth\ adj or n

**hun·dred·weight** \-,wāt\ n, pl **hundredweight** or **hundredweights** — see WEIGHT table

**hung** past of HANG

**Hung** abbr Hungarian; Hungary

**Hun·gar·i·an** \,həŋ-'ger-ē-ən\ n 1 : a native or inhabitant of Hungary 2 : the language of Hungary — **Hungarian** adj

**hun·ger** \'həŋ-gər\ n 1 : a craving or urgent need for food 2 : a strong desire — **hunger** vb — **hun·gri·ly** \-grə-lē\ adv — **hun·gry** adj

**hung over** adj : having a hangover

**hunk** \'həŋk\ n : a large piece

**hun·ker** \'həŋ-kər\ vb **hun·kered; hun·ker·ing** \-k(ə-)riŋ\ : CROUCH, SQUAT

**hun·kers** \'həŋ-kərz\ n pl : HAUNCHES

**hun·ky-do·ry** \,həŋ-kē-'dōr-ē\ adj : quite satisfactory : FINE

¹**hunt** \'hənt\ vb 1 : to pursue for food or in sport; also : to take part in a hunt 2 : to try to find : SEEK 3 : to drive or chase esp. by harrying 4 : to traverse in search of prey — **hunt·er** n

²**hunt** n 1 : an act, practice, or instance of hunting 2 : a group of huntsmen

**hunt·ress** \'hən-trəs\ n : a female hunter

**hunts·man** \'hənts-mən\ n 1 : HUNT-ER 2 : one who manages a hunt and looks after the hounds

**hur·dle** \'hərd-°l\ n 1 : a movable frame for enclosing land or livestock 2 : an artificial barrier to leap over in a race 3 : OBSTACLE — **hurdle** vb — **hur·dler** \'hərd-(°-)lər\ n

**hur·dy-gur·dy** \,hərd-ē-'gərd-ē, 'hərd-ē-,gərd-ē\ n, pl **-gur·dies** : a musical instrument in which the sound is produced by turning a crank

**hurl** \'hərl\ vb 1 : to move or cause to move vigorously 2 : to throw down with violence 3 : FLING; also : PITCH — **hurl** n — **hurl·er** n

**hur·ly-bur·ly** \,hər-lē-'bər-lē\ n : UP-ROAR, TUMULT

**Hu·ron** \'hyūr-ən, 'hyūr-,än\ n, pl **Hurons** or **Huron** : a member of an Indian people orig. of the St. Lawrence valley

**hur·rah** \hù-'rò, -'rä\ also **hur·ray** \hù-'rä\ interj — used to express joy, approval, or encouragement

**hur·ri·cane** \'hər-ə-,kān\ n [Sp huracán, of AmerInd origin] : a tropical cyclone that has winds of 74 miles per hour or greater, and is usu. accompanied by rain, thunder, and lightning

¹**hur·ry** \'hər-ē\ vb **hur·ried; hur·ry·ing** 1 : to carry or cause to go with haste 2 : to impel to a greater speed 3 : to move or act with haste — **hur·ried·ly** adv — **hur·ried·ness** n

²**hurry** n : extreme haste or eagerness

¹**hurt** \'hərt\ vb **hurt; hurt·ing** 1 : to feel or cause to feel pain 2 : to do harm to : DAMAGE 3 : OFFEND 4 : HAMPER

²**hurt** n 1 : a bodily injury or wound 2 : SUFFERING 3 : HARM, WRONG — **hurt·ful** adj

**hur·tle** \'hərt-°l\ vb **hur·tled; hurt·ling** \'hərt-(°-)liŋ\ 1 : to move with a rushing sound 2 : HURL, FLING

¹**hus·band** \'həz-bənd\ n [ME husbonde, fr. OE hūsbonda master of a house, fr. ON hūsbōndi, fr. hūs house + bōndi householder] : a married man

²**husband** vb : to manage prudently

**hus·band·man** \'həz-bən(d)-mən\ n : FARMER

**hus·band·ry** \'həz-bən-drē\ n 1 : the control or judicious use of resources 2 : AGRICULTURE

¹**hush** \'həsh\ vb 1 : to make or become quiet or calm 2 : SUPPRESS

²**hush** n : SILENCE, QUIET

**hush-hush** \'həsh-,həsh\ adj : SECRET, CONFIDENTIAL

¹**husk** \'həsk\ n 1 : a usu. thin dry outer covering of a seed or fruit 2 : an outer layer : SHELL

²**husk** vb : to strip the husk from — **husk·er** n

**husk·ing** n : a gathering of farm families to husk corn

¹**hus·ky** \'həs-kē\ adj **hus·ki·er; -est** : HOARSE — **hus·ki·ly** \'həs-kə-lē\ adv — **hus·ki·ness** \-kē-nəs\ n

²**hus·ky** adj **hus·ki·er; -est** 1 : BURLY, ROBUST 2 : LARGE — **husk·i·ness** n

³**husky** n, pl **huskies** : a heavy-coated working dog of the New World arctic region

**hus·sar** \(,)hə-'zär\ n [Hung huszár hussar, (obs.) highway robber, fr. Serb husar pirate, fr. ML cursarius, fr. cursus course] : a member of any of various European cavalry units

**hus·sy** \'həz-ē, 'həs-\ n, pl **hussies** [alter. of housewife] 1 : a lewd or brazen woman 2 : a pert or mischievous girl

**hus·tings** \'həs-tiŋs\ n pl : a place where political campaign speeches are made; also : the proceedings in an election campaign

**hus·tle** \'həs-əl\ vb **hus·tled; hus·tling** \'həs-(ə-)liŋ\ 1 : JOSTLE, SHOVE 2 : HASTEN, HURRY 3 : to work energetically — **hustle** n — **hus·tler** \'həs-lər\ n

**hut** \'hət\ n : a small and often temporary dwelling : SHACK

**hutch** \'həch\ n 1 : a chest or compartment for storage 2 : a low cupboard usu. surmounted with open shelves 3 : a pen or coop for an animal 4 : HUT, SHACK

**hut·ment** \'hət-mənt\ n 1 : a collection of huts 2 : HUT

**huz·zah** or **huz·za** \(,)hə-'zä\ interj — used to express joy or approbation

**HV** abbr 1 high velocity 2 high voltage

**Hvy** abbr heavy

**hwy** abbr highway

**hy·a·cinth** \'hī-ə-(,)sinth\ n : a bulbous herb related to the lilies and widely grown for its spikes of fragrant bell-shaped flowers

**hy·ae·na** var of HYENA

**hy·brid** \'hī-brəd\ n 1 : an offspring of genetically differing parents (as members of different breeds or species) 2 : one of mixed origin or composition — **hybrid** adj — **hy·brid·iza·tion** \,hī-brəd-ə-'zā-shən\ n — **hy·brid·ize** \'hī-brəd-,īz\ vb — **hy·brid·iz·er** \-,īz-ər\ n

**hy·dra** \'hī-drə\ n : any of numerous small tubular freshwater polyps having at one end a mouth surrounded by tentacles

**hy·dran·gea** \hī-'drān-jə\ n : any of a genus of shrubs related to the currants and grown for their large clusters of white or tinted flowers

**hy·drant** \'hī-drənt\ n : a pipe with a valve and spout at which water may be drawn from a main pipe

**hy·drate** \'hī-,drāt\ n 1 : a compound formed by union of water with some other substance 2 : HYDROXIDE ⟨calcium ∼⟩ — **hydrate** vb

**hy·drau·lic** \hī-'drò-lik\ adj 1 : operated, moved, or effected by means of water 2 : of or relating to hydraulics 3 : operated by the resistance offered or the pressure transmitted when a quantity of liquid is forced through a small orifice or through a tube 4 : hardening or setting under water

**hy·drau·lics** \hī-'drò-liks\ n : a science that deals with practical applications of liquids in motion

**hydro** \'hī-drō\ adj : HYDROELECTRIC

**hy·dro·car·bon** \,hī-drə-'kär-bən\ n

: an organic compound (as acetylene) containing only carbon and hydrogen

**hy·dro·ceph·a·lus** \,hī-drō-'sef-ə-ləs\ *n* : abnormal increase in the amount of fluid in the cranial cavity accompanied by expansion of the ventricles, enlargement of the skull, and atrophy of the brain

**hy·dro·chlo·ric acid** \,hī-drə-,klōr-ik-\ *n* : a sharp-smelling corrosive acid used in the laboratory and in industry

**hy·dro·dy·nam·ics** \,hī-drō-dī-'nam-iks\ *n* : a science that deals with the motion of fluids and the forces acting on moving bodies immersed in fluids — **hy·dro·dy·nam·ic** *adj*

**hy·dro·elec·tric** \,hī-drō-i-'lek-trik\ *adj* : of, relating to, or used in the production of electricity by waterpower — **hy·dro·elec·tri·cal·ly** \-tri-k(ə-)lē\ *adv* — **hy·dro·elec·tric·i·ty** \-,lek-'tris-ət-ē\ *n*

**hy·dro·flu·or·ic acid** \,hī-drō-flü-,ōr-ik-\ *n* : a weak poisonous acid used esp. in finishing and etching glass

**hy·dro·foil** \'hī-drə-,fóil\ *n* : a body similar to an airfoil but designed for action in or on water

**hy·dro·gen** \'hī-drə-jən\ *n* [F *hydrogène,* fr. Gk *hydōr* water + *-genēs* born; fr. the fact that water is generated by its combustion] : a gaseous colorless odorless highly flammable chemical element that is the lightest of the elements — **hy·drog·e·nous** \hī-'dräj-ə-nəs\ *adj*

**hy·dro·ge·nate** \hī-'dräj-ə-,nāt, hī-drə-jə-\ *vb* **-nat·ed; -nat·ing** : to combine or treat with hydrogen; *esp* : to add hydrogen to the molecule of — **hy·dro·ge·na·tion** \hī-,dräj-ə-'nā-shən, ,hī-drə-jə-\ *n*

**hydrogen bomb** *n* : a bomb whose violent explosive power is due to the sudden release of atomic energy resulting from the union of light nuclei (as of hydrogen atoms)

**hydrogen peroxide** *n* : an unstable liquid compound of hydrogen and oxygen used as an oxidizing and bleaching agent, an antiseptic, and a propellant

**hy·drog·ra·phy** \hī-'dräg-rə-fē\ *n* : the description and study of bodies of water — **hy·drog·ra·pher** \-fər\ *n* — **hy·dro·graph·ic** \,hī-drə-'graf-ik\ *adj*

**hy·drol·o·gy** \hī-'dräl-ə-jē\ *n* : a science dealing with the properties, distribution, and circulation of water — **hy·dro·log·ic** \,hī-drə-'läj-ik\ *or* **hy·dro·log·i·cal** \-i-kəl\ *adj* — **hy·drol·o·gist** \hī-'dräl-ə-jəst\ *n*

**hy·dro·ly·sis** \hī-'dräl-ə-səs\ *n* : a chemical decomposition involving the addition of the elements of water

**hy·drom·e·ter** \hī-'dräm-ət-ər\ *n* : a floating instrument for determining specific gravities of liquids and hence the strength (as of alcoholic liquors)

**hy·dro·pho·bia** \,hī-drə-'fō-bē-ə\ *n* [LL, fr. Gk, fr. *hydōr* water + *phobos* fear] : RABIES

**hy·dro·phone** \'hī-drə-,fōn\ *n* : an underwater listening device

**hy·dro·plane** \'hī-drə-,plān\ *n* **1** : a speedboat with fins or a stepped bottom so that the hull is raised wholly or partly out of the water **2** : SEAPLANE

**hy·dro·pon·ics** \,hī-drə-'pän-iks\ *n* : the growing of plants in nutrient solutions — **hy·dro·pon·ic** *adj*

**hy·dro·sphere** \'hī-drə-,sfiər\ *n* : the water (as vapor or lakes) of the earth

**hy·dro·stat·ic** \,hī-drə-'stat-ik\ *also* **hy·dro·stat·i·cal** \-i-kəl\ *adj* : of or relating to liquids at rest or to the pressures they exert or transmit

**hy·dro·ther·a·py** \,hī-drə-'ther-ə-pē\ *n* : the external application of water in the treatment of disease or disability

**hy·dro·ther·mal** \,hī-drə-'thər-məl\ *adj* : of or relating to hot water

**hy·drous** \'hī-drəs\ *adj* : containing water

**hy·drox·ide** \hī-'dräk-,sīd\ *n* : a compound of an oxygen-and-hydrogen group with an element or radical

**hy·e·na** \hī-'ē-nə\ *n* [L *hyaena,* fr. Gk *hyaina,* fr. *hys* hog] : a large nocturnal carnivorous mammal of Asia and Africa

**hy·giene** \'hī-,jēn\ *n* **1** : a science dealing with the establishment and maintenance of health **2** : conditions or practices conducive to health — **hy·gien·ic** \,hī-jē-'en-ik, hī-'jen-, hī-'jēn-\ *adj* — **hy·gien·i·cal·ly** \-i-k(ə-)lē\ *adv* — **hy·gien·ist** \hī-'jēn-əst, 'hī-,jēn-, h -'jen-\ *n*

**hy·grom·e·ter** \hī-'gräm-ət-ər\ *n* : any of several instruments for measuring the humidity of the atmosphere — **hy·grom·e·try** \-ə-trē\ *n*

**hy·gro·scop·ic** \,hī-grə-'skäp-ik\ *adj* : readily taking up and retaining moisture

**hying** *pres part of* HIE

**hy·men** \'hī-mən\ *n* : a fold of mucous membrane partly closing the orifice of the vagina

**hy·me·ne·al** \,hī-mə-'nē-əl\ *adj* : NUPTIAL

**hymn** \'him\ *n* : a song of praise esp. to God — **hymn** *vb* — **hym·nal** \'him-n°l\ *n*

**hym·no·dy** \'him-nəd-ē\ *n* **1** : hymn singing or writing **2** : the hymns of a time, place, or church

**hyp** *abbr* hypothesis; hypothetical

**hype** \'hīp\ *n* **1** *slang* : HYPODERMIC **2** *slang* : DECEPTION, PUT-ON

**hy·per·acid·i·ty** \,hī-pə-rə-'sid-ət-ē\ *n* : excessive stomach acidity — **hy·per·ac·id** \-pə-'ras-əd\ *adj*

**hy·per·ac·tive** \,hī-pə-'rak-tiv\ *adj* : excessively or pathologically active — **hy·per·ac·tiv·i·ty** \,rak-'tiv-ət-ē\ *n*

**hy·per·bar·ic** \,hī-pər-'bar-ik\ *adj* : of, relating to, or utilizing greater than normal pressure esp. of oxygen

**hy·per·bo·la** \hī-'pər-bə-lə\ *n, pl* **-las** *or* **-lae** \-(,)lē\ : a curve formed by the intersection of a double right circular cone with a plane that cuts both halves of the cone — **hy·per·bol·ic** \,hī-pər-'bäl-ik\ *adj*

**hy·per·bo·le** \hī-'pər-bə-(,)lē\ *n* : extravagant exaggeration used as a figure of speech

**hy·per·bo·re·an** \,hī-pər-'bōr-ē-ən\ *adj* : of, relating to, or inhabiting a remote northern region

**hy·per·crit·i·cal** \-'krit-i-kəl\ *adj* : excessively critical — **hy·per·crit·i·cal·ly** \-k(ə-)lē\ *adv*

**hy·per·sen·si·tive** \-'sen-sət-iv\ *adj* **1** : excessively or abnormally sensitive **2** : abnormally susceptible to an antigen, drug, or other agent — **hy·per·sen·si·tive·ness** *n* — **hy·per·sen·si·tiv·i·ty** \-,sen-sə-'tiv-ət-ē\ *n*

**hy·per·ten·sion** \'hī-pər-,ten-chən\ *n* : abnormally high blood pressure — **hy·per·ten·sive** \,hī-pər-'ten-siv\ *adj or n*

**hy·per·thy·roid·ism** \,hī-pər-'thī-,ŕoid-,iz-əm\ *n* : excessive functional activity of the thyroid gland; *also* : the resulting bodily condition — **hy·per·thy·roid** \-'thī-,ŕoid\ *adj*

**hy·per·tro·phy** \hī-'pər-trə-fē\ *n* : excessive growth or development of a body part — **hy·per·tro·phic** \,hī-pər-'trō-fik\ *adj* — **hypertrophy** *vb*

**hy·phen** \'hī-fən\ *n* : a punctuation mark - used to divide or to compound words or word elements — **hyphen** *vb*

**hy·phen·ate** \'hī-fə-,nāt\ *vb* **-at·ed;** **-at·ing** : to connect or divide with a hyphen — **hy·phen·ation** \,hī-fə-'nā-shən\ *n*

**hyp·no·sis** \hip-'nō-səs\ *n, pl* **-no·ses** \-,sēz\ : an induced state which resembles sleep and in which the subject is responsive to suggestions of the inducer (**hyp·no·tist** \'hip-nə-təst\) — **hyp·no·tism** \'hip-nə-,tiz-əm\ *n* — **hyp·no·tiz·able** \'hip-nə-,tī-zə-bəl\ *adj* — **hyp·no·tize** \-,tīz\ *vb*

**hyp·not·ic** \hip-'nät-ik\ *adj* **1** : inducing sleep : SOPORIFIC **2** : of or relating to hypnosis or hypnotism — **hyp·not·i·cal·ly** \-i-k(ə-)lē\ *adv*

**hypnotic** *n* : a sleep-inducing drug

**hy·po** \'hī-pō\ *n, pl* **hypos** : sodium thiosulfate used as a fixing agent in photography

**hypo** *n, pl* **hypos** : HYPODERMIC

**hy·po·cen·ter** \'hī-pə-,sent-ər\ *n* : EPICENTER

**hy·po·chon·dria** \,hī-pə-'kän-drē-ə\ *n* [NL, fr. LL, upper abdomen (formerly regarded as the seat of hypochondria), fr. Gk, lit., the parts under the cartilage (of the breastbone), fr. *hypo-* under + *chondros* cartilage] : depression of mind usu. centered on imaginary physical ailments — **hy·po·chon·dri·ac** \-drē-,ak\ *adj or n*

**hy·poc·ri·sy** \hip·'äk-rə-sē\ *n, pl* **-sies** : a feigning to be what one is not or to believe what one does not; *esp* : the false assumption of an appearance of virtue or religion — **hyp·o·crite** \'hip-ə-,krit\ *n* — **hyp·o·crit·i·cal** \,hip-ə-'krit-i-kəl\ *adj* — **hyp·o·crit·i·cal·ly** \-k(ə-)lē\ *adv*

¹**hy·po·der·mic** \,hī-pə-'dər-mik\ *adj* : adapted for use in or administered by injection beneath the skin ⟨~ injection⟩ ⟨~ syringe⟩

²**hypodermic** *n* : a small syringe with a hollow needle for injecting material into or through the skin; *also* : an injection made with this

**hypodermic needle** *n* **1** : NEEDLE 5 **2** : a hypodermic syringe complete with needle

**hy·po·gly·ce·mia** \,hī-pō-glī-'sē-mē-ə\ *n* : abnormal decrease of sugar in the blood — **hy·po·gly·ce·mic** \-mik\ *adj*

**hy·pot·e·nuse** \hī-'pät-ᵊn-, (y)üs, -,(y)üz\ *n* : the side of a right-angled triangle that is opposite the right angle

**hy·poth·e·cate** \hī-'päth-ə-,kāt\ *vb* **-cat·ed; -cat·ing** : HYPOTHESIZE

**hy·poth·e·sis** \hī-'päth-ə-səs\ *n, pl* **-e·ses** \-,sēz\ : an assumption made esp. in order to test its logical or empirical consequences — **hy·po·thet·i·cal** \,hī-pə-'thet-i-kəl\ *adj* — **hy·po·thet·i·cal·ly** \-k(ə-)lē\ *adv*

**hy·poth·e·size** \-,sīz\ *vb* **-sized; -siz·ing** : to adopt as a hypothesis

**hy·po·thy·roid·ism** \,hī-pō-'thī-,ŕoid-,iz-əm\ *n* : deficient activity of the thyroid gland; *also* : a resultant lowered metabolic rate and general loss of vigor — **hy·po·thy·roid** *adj*

**hys·sop** \'his-əp\ *n* : a European mint used in medicine

**hys·ter·ec·to·my** \,his-tə-'rek-tə-mē\ *n, pl* **-mies** : surgical removal of the uterus — **hys·ter·ec·to·mize** \-,mīz\ *vb*

**hys·te·ria** \his-'ter-ē-ə, -'tir-\ *n* [NL, fr. E *hysteric*, adj., fr. L *hystericus*, fr. Gk *hysterikos*, fr. *hystera* womb; fr. the former notion that hysteric women were suffering from disturbances of the womb] **1** : a nervous disorder marked esp. by defective emotional control **2** : uncontrollable fear or emotion — **hys·ter·ic** \-'ter-ik\ *or* **hys·ter·i·cal** \-i-kəl\ *adj* — **hys·ter·i·cal·ly** \-k(ə-)lē\ *adv*

**hys·ter·ics** \-'ter-iks\ *n pl* : a fit of uncontrollable laughter or crying

---

**I**

¹**i** \'ī\ *n, pl* **i's** *or* **is** \'īz\ *often cap* : the 9th letter of the English alphabet

²**i** *abbr, often cap* island; isle

**I** \(')ī, ə\ *pron* : the one speaking or writing

²**I** *abbr* interstate highway

*symbol* iodine

**a** *or* **IA** *abbr* Iowa

**iamb** \'ī-,am\ *or* **iam·bus** \ī-'am-bəs\ *n, pl* **iambs** \'ī-,amz\ *or* **iam·bus·es** : a metrical foot of one unaccented syllable followed by one accented syllable — **iam·bic** \ī-'am-bik\ *adj or n*

**-ian** — see -AN

**-i·at·ric** \ē-'a-trik\ *also* **-i·at·ri·cal** \-tri-kəl\ *adj comb form* : of or relating to (such) medical treatment or healing

**-i·at·rics** \ē-'a-triks\ *n pl comb form* : medical treatment

**ib** *or* **ibid** *abbr* ibidem

**ibex** \'ī-,beks\ *n, pl* **ibex** *or* **ibex·es** : an Old World wild goat with large curved horns

**ibi·dem** \'ib-ə-,dem, ib-'īd-əm\ *adv* [L] : in the same place

**ibis** \'ī-bəs\ *n, pl* **ibis** *or* **ibis·es** [L, fr. Gk, fr. Egypt *hby*] : any of several wading birds related to the herons but having a down-curved bill

**-ible** — see -ABLE

**¹-ic** \ik\ *adj suffix* **1** : having the character or form of : being ⟨panoram*ic*⟩ : consisting of **2** : of or relating to ⟨alderman*ic*⟩ **3** : related to, derived from, or containing ⟨alcohol*ic*⟩ **4** : in the manner of : like that of : characteristic of **5** : associated or dealing with : utilizing ⟨electron*ic*⟩ **6** : characterized by : exhibiting ⟨nostalg*ic*⟩ : affected with ⟨allerg*ic*⟩ **7** : caused by **8** : tending to produce

**²-ic** *n suffix* : one having the character or nature of : one belonging to or associated with : one exhibiting or affected by : one that produces

**-i·cal** \i-kəl\ *adj suffix* : -IC ⟨symmetr*ical*⟩ ⟨geolog*ical*⟩ — **-i·cal·ly** \ik-(ə-)lē\ *adv suffix*

**ICBM** \,ī-,sē-(,)bē-'em\ *n, pl* **ICBM's** *or* **ICBMs** \-'emz\ : an intercontinental ballistic missile

**ICC** *abbr* Interstate Commerce Commission

**¹ice** \'īs\ *n* **1** : frozen water **2** : a state of coldness (as from formality or reserve) **3** : a substance resembling ice **4** : a frozen dessert; *esp* : one containing no milk or cream

**²ice** *vb* **iced; ic·ing 1** : FREEZE **2** : CHILL **3** : to cover with or as if with icing — **iced** *adj*

**ice age** *n* : a time of widespread glaciation

**ice bag** *n* : a waterproof bag to hold ice for local application of cold to the body

**ice·berg** \'īs-,bərg\ *n* : a large floating mass of ice broken off from a glacier; *also* : an emotionally cold person

**ice·boat** \-,bōt\ *n* **1** : a boatlike frame on runners propelled on ice usu. by sails **2** : ICEBREAKER 2

**ice·bound** \-,baúnd\ *adj* : surrounded or obstructed by ice

**ice·box** \-,bäks\ *n* : REFRIGERATOR

**ice·break·er** \-,brā-kər\ *n* **1** : a structure that protects a bridge pier from floating ice **2** : a ship equipped to make a channel through ice

**ice cap** *n* : a cover of perennial ice and snow; *esp* : a glacier forming on relatively level land and flowing outward from its center

**ice cream** *n* : a frozen food containing cream or butterfat, flavoring, sweetening, and usu. eggs

**ice hockey** *n* : a game played on an ice rink by two teams of six players on skates whose object is to drive a puck into the opponent's goal

**ice·house** \'īs-,haús\ *n* : a building for storing ice

**Ice·land·er** \-,lan-dər, -lən-\ *n* : a native or inhabitant of Iceland

**¹ice·lan·dic** \īs-'lan-dik\ *adj* : of, relating to, or characteristic of Iceland, the Icelanders, or their language

**²Icelandic** *n* : the language of Iceland

**ice·man** \'īs-,man\ *n* : one who sells or delivers ice

**ice milk** *n* : a sweetened frozen food made of skim milk

**ice pick** *n* : a hand tool ending in a spike for chipping ice

**ice-skate** \'īs-,skāt\ *vb* : to skate on ice — **ice skater** *n*

**ice storm** *n* : a storm in which falling rain freezes on contact

**ice water** *n* : chilled or iced water esp. for drinking

**ichor** \'ī-,kȯ(ə)r\ *n* : an ethereal fluid taking the place of blood in the veins of the ancient Greek gods

**ich·thy·ol·o·gy** \,ik-thē-'äl-ə-jē\ *n* : a branch of zoology dealing with fishes — **ich·thy·ol·o·gist** \-jəst\ *n*

**ici·cle** \'ī-,sik-əl\ *n* : a hanging mass of ice formed by the freezing of dripping water

**ic·ing** \'ī-siŋ\ *n* : a sweet usu. creamy mixture used to coat baked goods

**ICJ** *abbr* International Court of Justice

**icky** \'ik-ē\ *adj* **ick·i·er; -est** : OFFENSIVE, DISTASTEFUL

**icon** \'ī-,kän\ *n* **1** : IMAGE; *esp* : a religious image painted on a small wood panel

**icon·o·clasm** \ī-'kän-ə-,klaz-əm\ *n* : the doctrine, practice, or attitude of an iconoclast

**icon·o·clast** \-,klast\ *n* [ML *iconoclastes*, fr. MGk *eikonoklastēs*, lit., image destroyer, fr. Gk *eikōn* image + *klan* to break] **1** : one who destroys religious images or opposes their veneration **2** : one who attacks cherished beliefs or institutions

**-ics** \iks\ *n sing or pl suffix* **1** : study : knowledge : skill : practice ⟨linguist*ics*⟩ ⟨electron*ics*⟩ **2** : characteristic actions or activities ⟨acrobat*ics*⟩ **3** : characteristic qualities, operations, or phenomena ⟨mechan*ics*⟩

**ic·tus** \'ik-təs\ *n* : the recurring stress or beat in a rhythmic or metrical series of sounds

**icy** \'ī-sē\ *adj* **ic·i·er; -est 1** : covered with, abounding in, or consisting of ice **2** : intensely cold **3** : being cold and unfriendly — **ic·i·ly** \'ī-sə-lē\ *adv* — **ic·i·ness** \-sē-nəs\ *n*

**¹id** \'id\ *n* [L, it] : the part of the psyche in psychoanalytic theory that is completely unconscious and is the source of psychic energy derived from instinctual needs and drives

**²id** *abbr* idem

**ID** *abbr* **1** Idaho **2** identification

**idea** \ī-'dē-ə\ *n* **1** : a plan for action : DESIGN, PROJECT **2** : something imagined or pictured in the mind **3** : a central meaning or purpose **syn** concept, conception, notion, impression

**¹ide·al** \ī-'dē(-ə)l\ *adj* **1** : existing only in the mind : IMAGINARY; *also* : lacking practicality **2** : of or relating to an ideal or to perfection : PERFECT ⟨~ weather⟩

**²ideal** *n* **1** : a standard of perfection, beauty, or excellence **2** : one regarded as exemplifying an ideal and often taken as a model for imitation **3** : GOAL

**ide·al·ism** \ī-'dē-(ə-),liz-əm\ *n* **1** : the

practice of forming or living according to ideals **2** : the ability or tendency to see things as they should be rather than as they are — **ide·al·ist** \-(ə-)ləst\ n — **ide·al·is·tic** \ī-,dē-(ə-)'lis-tik\ adj

**ide·al·ize** \ī-'dē-(ə-),līz\ vb **-ized; -iz·ing** : to think of or represent as ideal — **ide·al·iza·tion** \-,dē-(ə-)lə-'zā-shən\ n

**ide·al·ly** \ī-'dē-(ə-)lē\ adv **1** : in idea or imagination : MENTALLY **2** : in agreement with an ideal : PERFECTLY

**ide·ation** \,īd-ē-'ā-shən\ n : the capacity for or process of forming ideas — **ide·ate** \'īd-ē-,āt\ vb — **ide·ation·al** \,īd-ē-'ā-sh(ə-)nəl\ adj

**idem** \'īd-,em, 'ēd-, 'id-\ pron [L, same] : something previously mentioned

**iden·ti·cal** \ī-'dent-i-kəl\ adj **1** : being the same **2** : exactly or essentially alike **syn** equivalent, equal

**iden·ti·fi·ca·tion** \ī-,dent-ə-fə-'kā-shən\ n **1** : an act of identifying : the state of being identified **2** : evidence of identity

**iden·ti·fy** \ī-'dent-ə-,fī\ vb **-fied; -fy·ing 1** : to be or cause to be or become identical **2** : ASSOCIATE **3** : to establish the identity of

**iden·ti·ty** \ī-'dent-ət-ē\ n, pl **-ties 1** : sameness of essential character **2** : INDIVIDUALITY **3** : the fact of being the same person or thing as one described

**ideo·gram** \'īd-ē-ə-,gram, 'id-\ n **1** : a picture or symbol used in a system of writing to represent a thing or an idea but not a particular word or phrase for it **2** : a character or symbol used in a system of writing to represent an entire word without providing separate representation of the individual sounds in it

**ide·ol·o·gy** \,īd-ē-'äl-ə-jē, ,id-\ also **ide·al·o·gy** \-'äl-ə-jē, -'al-\ n, pl **-gies** : the body of ideas characteristic of a particular individual, group, or culture **2** : the assertions, theories, and aims that constitute a political, social, and economic program — **ide·o·log·i·cal** \,īd-ē-ə-'läj-i-kəl, ,id-\ adj

**ides** \'īdz\ n sing or pl : the 15th day of March, May, July, or October or the 13th day of any other month in the ancient Roman calendar

**id·i·o·cy** \'id-ē-ə-sē\ n, pl **-cies 1** : extreme mental deficiency **2** : something notably stupid or foolish

**id·i·om** \'id-ē-əm\ n **1** : the language peculiar to an individual, a group, a class, or a district : DIALECT **2** : the characteristic form or structure of a language **3** : an expression in the usage of a language that is peculiar to itself either grammatically (as *it wasn't me*) or that cannot be understood from the meanings of its separate words (as *take cold*) — **id·i·om·at·ic** \,id-ē-ə-'mat-ik\ adj — **id·i·om·at·i·cal·ly** \-i-k(ə-)lē\ adv

**id·io·path·ic** \,id-ē-ō-'path-ik\ adj : arising spontaneously or from an obscure or unknown cause ⟨an ~ disease⟩

**id·i·op·a·thy** \,id-ē-'äp-ə-thē\ n

**id·io·syn·cra·sy** \,id-ē-ō-'siŋ-krə-sē\ n, pl **-sies** : personal peculiarity (as of

habit or of response to a drug) — **id·io·syn·crat·ic** \,id-ē-ō-sin-'krat-ik\ adj

**id·i·ot** \'id-ē-ət\ n [ME, fr. L idiota ignorant person, fr. Gk idiōtēs one in a private station, ignorant person, fr. idios one's own, private] **1** : a feebleminded person requiring complete custodial care **2** : a silly or foolish person — **id·i·ot·ic** \,id-ē-'ät-ik\ adj — **id·i·ot·i·cal·ly** \-i-k(ə-)lē\ adv

**¹idle** \'īd-ᵊl\ adj **idler** \'īd-(ə-)lər\; **idlest** \'īd-(ə-)ləst\ **1** : GROUNDLESS, WORTHLESS, USELESS ⟨~ rumor⟩ ⟨~ talk⟩ **2** : not occupied or employed : INACTIVE **3** : LAZY ⟨~ fellows⟩ — **idle·ness** n — **idly** \'īd-lē\ adv

**²idle** vb **idled; idling** \'īd-(ᵊ-)liŋ\ **1** : to spend time doing nothing **2** : to pass in idleness **3** : to make idle **4** : to run without being connected so that power is not used for useful work — **idler** \'īd-(ᵊ-)lər\ n

**idol** \'īd-ᵊl\ n **1** : a representation of a deity used as an object of worship **2** : a false god **3** : an object of passionate devotion

**idol·a·ter** \ī-'däl-ət-ər\ n : a worshiper of idols

**idol·a·try** \-ə-trē\ n, pl **-tries 1** : the worship of a physical object as a god **2** : immoderate devotion — **idol·a·trous** \-trəs\ adj

**idol·ize** \'īd-ᵊl-,īz\ vb **-ized; -iz·ing** : to make an idol of

**idyll** or **idyl** \'īd-ᵊl\ n **1** : a simple descriptive or narrative composition; esp : a poem about country life **2** : a fit subject for an idyll **3** : a romantic interlude — **idyl·lic** \ī-'dil-ik\ adj

**i.e.** \that-'iz, (')ī-'ē\ abbr [L id est] that is

**IE** abbr **1** Indo-European **2** industrial engineer

**-ier** — see -ER

**if** \(,)if, əf\ conj **1** : in the event that ⟨~ he stays, I leave⟩ **2** : WHETHER ⟨ask ~ he left⟩ **3** : even though ⟨an interesting ~ untenable argument⟩

**IF** abbr intermediate frequency

**if·fy** \'if-ē\ adj : abounding in contingencies or unknown qualities or conditions

**-i·fy** \ə-,fī\ vb suffix : -FY

**ig·loo** \'ig-lü\ n, pl **igloos** [Eskimo iglu, igdlu house] : an Eskimo house or hut often made of snow blocks and in the shape of a dome

**ig·ne·ous** \'ig-nē-əs\ adj **1** : FIERY **2** : formed by solidification of molten rock

**ig·nite** \ig-'nīt\ vb **ig·nit·ed; ig·nit·ing** : to set afire or catch fire

**ig·ni·tion** \ig-'nish-ən\ n **1** : a setting on fire **2** : the process or means (as an electric spark) of igniting the fuel mixture in an engine

**ig·no·ble** \ig-'nō-bəl\ adj **1** : of low birth : PLEBEIAN **2** : not honorable : BASE, MEAN — **ig·no·bly** \-blē\ adv

**ig·no·min·i·ous** \,ig-nə-'min-ē-əs\ adj **1** : DISHONORABLE **2** : DESPICABLE **3** : HUMILIATING, DEGRADING — **ig·no·min·i·ous·ly** adv — **ig·no·mi·ny** \'ig-nə-,min-ē, ig-'näm-ə-nē\ n

**ig·no·ra·mus** \,ig-nə-'rā-məs\ *n* [*Ignoramus*, ignorant lawyer in *Ignoramus* (1615), play by George Ruggle] **:** an utterly ignorant person **:** DUNCE

**ig·no·rance** \'ig-nə-rəns\ *n* **:** the state of being ignorant **:** lack of knowledge

**ig·no·rant** \'ig-nə-rənt\ *adj* **1 :** lacking knowledge **:** UNEDUCATED **2 :** resulting from or showing lack of knowledge or intelligence **3 :** UNAWARE, UNINFORMED — **ig·no·rant·ly** *adv*

**ig·nore** \ig-'nōr\ *vb* **ig·nored; ig·nor·ing :** to refuse to take notice of **syn** overlook, slight, neglect

**igua·na** \i-'gwän-ə\ *n* **:** a large edible tropical American lizard

**IGY** *abbr* International Geophysical Year

**IHP** *abbr* indicated horsepower

**IHS** \,ī-,ā-'ches\ [LL, part transliteration of Gk IHΣ, abbreviation for IHΣOYΣ *Iēsous* Jesus] — used as a Christian symbol and monogram for Jesus

**ikon** *var of* ICON

**IL** *abbr* Illinois

**il·e·itis** \,il-ē-'īt-əs\ *n* **:** inflammation of the ileum

**il·e·um** \'il-ē-əm\ *n, pl* **il·ea** \-ē-ə\ **:** the part of the small intestine between the jejunum and the large intestine — **il·e·al** \-ē-əl\ *adj*

**ilk** \'ilk\ *n* **:** SORT, FAMILY — used chiefly in the phrase *of that ilk*

**[1]ill** \'il\ *adj* **worse** \'wərs\; **worst** \'wərst\ **1 :** not normal or sound 〈~ health〉; *also* **:** suffering ill health **:** SICK **2 :** BAD, UNLUCKY 〈~ omen〉 **3 :** not meeting an accepted standard 〈~ manners〉 **4 :** UNFRIENDLY, HOSTILE 〈~ feeling〉 **5 :** HARSH, CRUEL

**[2]ill** *adv* **worse; worst 1 :** with displeasure or hostility **2 :** in a harsh manner **3 :** HARDLY, SCARCELY 〈can ~ afford it〉 **4 :** BADLY, UNLUCKILY **5 :** in a faulty or inefficient manner

**[3]ill** *n* **1 :** EVIL **2 :** MISFORTUNE, DISTRESS **3 :** AILMENT, SICKNESS; *also* **:** TROUBLE

**[4]ill** *abbr* illustrated; illustration

**Ill** *abbr* Illinois

**ill–ad·vised** \,il-əd-'vīzd\ *adj* **:** not well counseled 〈~ efforts〉 — **ill–ad·vis·ed·ly** \-'vī-zəd-lē\ *adv*

**ill–bred** \-'bred\ *adj* **:** badly brought up **:** IMPOLITE

**il·le·gal** \il-'(l)ē-gəl\ *adj* **:** not lawful; *also* **:** not sanctioned by official rules — **il·le·gal·i·ty** \,il-i-'gal-ət-ē\ *n* — **il·le·gal·ly** \il-'(l)ē-gə-lē\ *adv*

**il·leg·i·ble** \il-'(l)ej-ə-bəl\ *adj* **:** not legible — **il·leg·i·bil·i·ty** \il-,(l)ej-ə-'bil-ət-ē\ *n* — **il·leg·i·bly** \il-'(l)ej-ə-blē\ *adv*

**il·le·git·i·mate** \,il-i-'jit-ə-mət\ *adj* **1 :** born of parents not married to each other **2 :** ILLOGICAL **3 :** ERRATIC **4 :** ILLEGAL — **il·le·git·i·ma·cy** \-'jit-ə-mə-sē\ *n* — **il·le·git·i·mate·ly** \-'jit-ə-mət-lē\ *adv*

**ill–fat·ed** \'il-'fāt-əd\ *adj* **:** having or destined to an evil fate **:** UNFORTUNATE

**ill–fa·vored** \-'fā-vərd\ *adj* **1 :** UGLY, UNATTRACTIVE **2 :** OFFENSIVE, OBJECTIONABLE

**ill–got·ten** \-'gät-ᵊn\ *adj* **:** acquired by evil means 〈~ gains〉

**ill–hu·mored** \-'(h)yü-mərd\ *adj* **:** SURLY, IRRITABLE

**il·lib·er·al** \il-'(l)ib-(ə-)rəl\ *adj* **:** not liberal **:** NARROW, BIGOTED

**il·lic·it** \il-'(l)is-ət\ *adj* **:** not permitted **:** UNLAWFUL - **il·lic·it·ly** *adv*

**il·lim·it·able** \il-'(l)im-ət-ə-bəl\ *adj* **:** BOUNDLESS, MEASURELESS — **il·lim·it·ably** \-blē\ *adv*

**Il·li·nois** \,il-ə-'nói, -'nóiz\ *n, pl* **Illinois :** a member of an Indian people of Illinois, Iowa, and Wisconsin

**il·lit·er·ate** \il-'(l)it-(ə-)rət\ *adj* **1 :** having little or no education; *esp* **:** unable to read or write **2 :** showing a lack of familiarity with language and literature or with the fundamentals of a particular field of knowledge — **il·lit·er·a·cy** \-'(l)it-(ə-)rə-sē\ *n* — **illiterate** *n*

**ill–man·nered** \'il-'man-ərd\ *adj* **:** marked by bad manners **:** RUDE

**ill–na·tured** \-'nā-chərd\ *adj* **:** CROSS, SURLY — **ill–na·tured·ly** *adv*

**ill·ness** \'il-nəs\ *n* **:** SICKNESS

**il·log·i·cal** \il-'(l)äj-i-kəl\ *adj* **:** not according to good reasoning; *also* **:** SENSELESS — **il·log·i·cal·ly** \-k(ə-)lē\ *adv*

**ill–starred** \'il-'stärd\ *adj* **:** ILL-FATED, UNLUCKY

**ill–tem·pered** \-'tem-pərd\ *adj* **:** ILL-NATURED, QUARRELSOME

**ill–treat** \-'trēt\ *vb* **:** to treat cruelly or improperly **:** MALTREAT — **ill–treat·ment** \-mənt\ *n*

**il·lume** \il-'üm\ *vb* **il·lumed; il·lum·ing :** ILLUMINATE

**il·lu·mi·nate** \il-'ü-mə-,nāt\ *vb* **-nat·ed; -nat·ing 1 :** to supply or brighten with light **:** make luminous or shining **2 :** to make clear **:** ELUCIDATE **3 :** to decorate (as a manuscript) with gold or silver or brilliant colors or with often elaborate designs or pictures — **il·lu·mi·nat·ing·ly** \-,nāt-iŋ-lē\ *adv* — **il·lu·mi·na·tion** \-,ü-mə-'nā-shən\ *n* — **il·lu·mi·na·tor** \-'ü-mə-,nāt-ər\ *n*

**il·lu·mine** \il-'ü-mən\ *vb* **-mined; -min·ing :** ILLUMINATE

**ill–us·age** \'il-'yü-sij, -zij\ *n* **:** harsh, unkind, or abusive treatment

**ill–use** \-'yüz\ *vb* **:** MALTREAT, ABUSE — **ill–use** \-'yüs\ *n*

**il·lu·sion** \il-'ü-zhən\ *n* [ME, fr. MF, fr. LL *illusio*, fr. L, action of mocking, fr. *illudere* to mock at, fr. *ludere* to play, mock] **1 :** a mistaken idea **:** MISAPPREHENSION, MISCONCEPTION, FANCY **2 :** a misleading image presented to the vision **:** HALLUCINATION; *esp* **:** APPARITION

**il·lu·sion·ism** \il-'ü-zhə-,niz-əm\ *n* **:** the use of artistic techniques (as perspective or shading) to create the illusion of reality esp. in a work of art — **il·lu·sion·ist** \-'üzh-(ə-)nəst\ *n or adj*

**il·lu·sive** \il-'ü-siv\ *adj* **:** ILLUSORY

**il·lu·so·ry** \il-'üs-(ə-)rē, -'üz-\ *adj* **:** based on or producing illusion

**illust** *or* **illus** *abbr* illustrated; illustration

**il·lus·trate** \'il-əs-,trāt\ *vb* **-trat·ed;**

-trat·ing [L *illustrare*, fr. *lustrare* to purify, make bright] **1** : to make clear or explain (as by use of examples) : CLARIFY; *also* : DEMONSTRATE **2** : to provide with pictures or figures intended to explain or decorate **3** : to serve to explain or decorate — **il·lus·tra·tor** \'il-əs-ˌträt-ər\ *n*

**il·lus·tra·tion** \ˌil-əs-'trā-shən\ *n* **1** : the action of illustrating : the condition of being illustrated **2** : an example or instance that helps make something (as a statement or article) clear **3** : a picture, drawing, or diagram intended to explain or decorate a book or article

**il·lus·tra·tive** \il-'əs-trət-iv\ *adj* : serving, tending, or designed to illustrate — **il·lus·tra·tive·ly** *adv*

**il·lus·tri·ous** \il-'əs-trē-əs\ *adj* : notably outstanding because of rank or achievement : EMINENT, DISTINGUISHED — **il·lus·tri·ous·ness** *n*

**ill will** *n* : unfriendly feeling

**ILS** *abbr* instrument landing system

¹**im·age** \'im-ij\ *n* **1** : a likeness or imitation of a person or thing; *esp* : STATUE **2** : a visual counterpart of an object formed by a device (as a mirror or lens) **3** : a mental picture or conception : IMPRESSION, IDEA, CONCEPT **4** : a vivid representation or description **5** : a person strikingly like another person ⟨he is the ~ of his father⟩

²**image** *vb* **im·aged; im·ag·ing 1** : to describe or portray in words **2** : to bring up before the imagination : IMAGINE, FANCY **3** : REFLECT, MIRROR **4** : to make appear : PROJECT **5** : to create a representation of

**im·ag·ery** \'im-ij-(ə-)rē\ *n* **1** : IMAGES; *also* : the art of making images **2** : figurative language **3** : mental images; *esp* : the products of imagination

**imag·in·able** \im-'aj-(ə-)nə-bəl\ *adj* : capable of being imagined : CONCEIVABLE — **imag·in·ably** \-blē\ *adv*

**imag·i·nary** \im-'aj-ə-ˌner-ē\ *adj* **1** : existing only in the imagination : FANCIED **2** : containing or relating to the imaginary unit

**imaginary number** *n* : a complex number (as $2 + 3i$) whose imaginary part is not zero

**imaginary part** *n* : the part of a complex number (as $3i$ in $3 + 3i$) that has the imaginary unit as a factor

**imaginary unit** *n* : the positive square root of minus 1 : $+\sqrt{-1}$

**imag·i·na·tion** \im-ˌaj-ə-'nā-shən\ *n* **1** : the act or power of forming a mental image of something not present to the senses or not previously known or experienced **2** : creative ability **3** : RESOURCEFULNESS **4** : a mental image : a creation of the mind **5** : popular or traditional belief or conception — **imag·i·na·tive** \im-'aj-(ə-)nət-iv, -ə-ˌnāt-iv\ *adj* — **imag·i·na·tive·ly** *adv*

**imag·ine** \im-'aj-ən\ *vb* **imag·ined; imag·in·ing** \-'aj-(ə-)niŋ\ **1** : to form a mental picture of something not present : FANCY **2** : PLAN, SCHEME **3** : THINK, GUESS ⟨I ~ it will rain⟩

**im·ag·ism** \'im-ij-ˌiz-əm\ *n, often cap*

: a movement in poetry advocating free verse and the expression of ideas and emotions through clear precise images — **im·ag·ist** \-ij-əst\ *n*

**ima·go** \im-'ā-gō, -'äg-ō\ *n, pl* **imagoes** *or* **ima·gi·nes** \-'ā-gə-ˌnēz, -'äg-ə-\ [L, image] : an insect in its final adult stage — **ima·gi·nal** \im-'ā-gən-ᵊl, -'äg-ən-\ *adj*

**im·bal·ance** \(')im-'bal-əns\ *n* : lack of balance : the state of being out of equilibrium or out of proportion

**im·be·cile** \'im-bə-səl, -ˌsil\ *n* **1** : a feebleminded person; *esp* : one capable of performing routine personal care under supervision **2** : FOOL, IDIOT — **imbecile** *or* **im·be·cil·ic** \ˌim-bə-'sil-ik\ *adj* — **im·be·cil·i·ty** \ˌim-bə-'sil-ət-ē\ *n*

**imbed** *var of* EMBED

**im·bibe** \im-'bīb\ *vb* **im·bibed; im·bib·ing 1** : DRINK **2** : to receive and retain in the mind **3** : ASSIMILATE **4** : to drink in : ABSORB — **im·bib·er** *n*

**im·bi·bi·tion** \ˌim-bə-'bish-ən\ *n* : the act or action of imbibing; *esp* : the taking up of fluid by a colloidal system resulting in swelling — **im·bi·bi·tion·al** \-'bish-(ə-)nəl\ *adj*

**im·bri·ca·tion** \ˌim-brə-'kā-shən\ *n* **1** : an overlapping of edges (as of tiles) **2** : a pattern showing imbrication — **im·bri·cate** \'im-bri-kət\ *adj*

**im·bro·glio** \im-'brōl-yō\ *n, pl* **-glios** [It, fr. *imbrogliare* to entangle] **1** : a confused mass **2** : a difficult or embarrassing situation; *also* : a serious or embarrassing misunderstanding

**im·brue** \im-'brü\ *vb* **im·brued; im·bru·ing** : DRENCH, STAIN ⟨a nation *imbrued* with the blood of executed men⟩

**im·bue** \-'byü\ *vb* **im·bued; im·bu·ing 1** : to tinge or dye deeply **2** : to cause to become penetrated : PERMEATE

**IMF** *abbr* International Monetary Fund

**imit** *abbr* imitative

**im·i·ta·ble** \'im-ət-ə-bəl\ *adj* : capable or worthy of being imitated or copied

**im·i·tate** \'im-ə-ˌtāt\ *vb* **-tat·ed; -tat·ing 1** : to follow as a pattern or model : COPY **2** : REPRODUCE **3** : RESEMBLE **4** : MIMIC, COUNTERFEIT — **im·i·ta·tor** \-ˌtāt-ər\ *n*

**im·i·ta·tion** \ˌim-ə-'tā-shən\ *n* **1** : an act of imitating or mimicking **2** : COPY, COUNTERFEIT **3** : a literary work designed to reproduce the style of another author — **imitation** *adj*

**im·i·ta·tive** \'im-ə-ˌtāt-iv\ *adj* **1** : marked by imitation **2** : exhibiting mimicry **3** : inclined to imitate or copy **4** : COUNTERFEIT

**im·mac·u·late** \im-'ak-yə-lət\ *adj* **1** : being without stain or blemish : PURE **2** : spotlessly clean ⟨~ linen⟩ — **im·mac·u·late·ly** *adv*

**im·ma·nent** \'im-ə-nənt\ *adj* **1** : INDWELLING; *esp* : having existence only in the mind **2** : dwelling in nature and the souls of men — **im·ma·nence** \-nəns\ *n* — **im·ma·nen·cy** \-nən-sē\ *n*

**im·ma·te·ri·al** \ˌim-ə-'tir-ē-əl\ *adj* **1** : not consisting of matter : SPIRITUAL

**2 :** UNIMPORTANT, TRIFLING — **im·ma·te·ri·al·i·ty** \-ˌtir-ē-ˈal-ət-ē\ n

**im·ma·ture** \ˌim-ə-ˈt(y)u̇r\ adj : lacking complete development : not yet mature — **im·ma·tu·ri·ty** \-ˈt(y)u̇r-ət-ē\ n

**im·mea·sur·able** \(ˈ)im-ˈezh-(ə-)rə-bəl\ adj : not capable of being measured : indefinitely extensive : ILLIMITABLE - **im·mea·sur·ably** \-blē\ adv

**im·me·di·a·cy** \im-ˈēd-ē-ə-sē\ n, pl -cies **1 :** the quality or state of being immediate; esp : lack of an intervening object, place, time, or agent **2 :** URGENCY **3 :** something that is of immediate importance

**im·me·di·ate** \im-ˈēd-ē-ət\ adj **1 :** acting directly and alone : DIRECT ⟨the ∼ cause of death⟩ **2 :** being next in line or relation ⟨members of the ∼ family attended⟩ **3 :** made or done at once ⟨an ∼ response⟩ **4 :** near to or related to the present time ⟨the ∼ future⟩ **5 :** not distant : CLOSE ⟨the ∼ vicinity⟩ — **im·me·di·ate·ly** adv

**im·me·mo·ri·al** \ˌim-ə-ˈmȯr-ē-əl\ adj : extending beyond the reach of memory, record, or tradition

**im·mense** \im-ˈens\ adj [MF, fr. L immensus immeasurable, fr. mensus, pp. of metiri to measure] **1 :** marked by greatness esp. in size or degree : VAST, HUGE **2 :** EXCELLENT — **im·mense·ly** adv — **im·men·si·ty** \-ˈen-sət-ē\ n

**im·merse** \im-ˈərs\ vb **im·mersed; im·mers·ing 1 :** to plunge or dip esp. into a fluid **2 :** to baptize by immersing **3 :** ENGROSS, ABSORB — **im·mer·sion** \im-ˈər-zhən\ n

**im·mi·grant** \ˈim-i-grənt\ n **1 :** a person who immigrates **2 :** a plant or animal that becomes established where it was previously unknown

**im·mi·grate** \ˈim-ə-ˌgrāt\ vb -grat·ed; -grat·ing **:** to come into a foreign country and take up permanent residence there — **im·mi·gra·tion** \ˌim-ə-ˈgrā-shən\ n

**im·mi·nent** \ˈim-ə-nənt\ adj : ready to take place; esp : hanging threateningly over one's head — **im·mi·nence** \-nəns\ n — **im·mi·nent·ly** adv

**im·mis·ci·ble** \(ˈ)im-ˈis-ə-bəl\ adj : incapable of mixing — **im·mis·ci·bil·i·ty** \(ˌ)im-ˌis-ə-ˈbil-ət-ē\ n

**im·mit·i·ga·ble** \(ˈ)im-ˈit-i-gə-bəl\ adj : not capable of being mitigated

**im·mo·bile** \(ˈ)im-ˈō-bəl\ adj : incapable of being moved : IMMOVABLE, FIXED — **im·mo·bil·i·ty** \ˌim-ō-ˈbil-ət-ē\ n

**im·mo·bi·lize** \im-ˈō-bə-ˌlīz\ vb **:** to make immobile

**im·mod·er·ate** \(ˈ)im-ˈäd-(ə-)rət\ adj : lacking in moderation : EXCESSIVE — **im·mod·er·a·cy** \-(ə-)rə-sē\ n — **im·mod·er·ate·ly** adv

**im·mod·est** \(ˈ)im-ˈäd-əst\ adj : not modest : BRAZEN, INDECENT ⟨an ∼ dress⟩ ⟨∼ conduct⟩ — **im·mod·est·ly** adv — **im·mod·es·ty** \-ə-stē\ n

**im·mo·late** \ˈim-ə-ˌlāt\ vb -lat·ed; -lat·ing [L immolare, fr. mola grits; fr. the custom of sprinkling victims with sacrificial meal] **:** to offer in sacrifice;

esp : to kill as a sacrificial victim — **im·mo·la·tion** \ˌim-ə-ˈlā-shən\ n

**im·mor·al** \(ˈ)im-ˈȯr-əl\ adj : inconsistent with purity or good morals : WICKED — **im·mor·al·ly** \-ē\ adv

**im·mo·ral·i·ty** \ˌim-ȯ-ˈral-ət-ē, ˌim-ə-ˈral-\ n **1 :** WICKEDNESS; esp : UNCHASTITY **2 :** an immoral act or practice

**1im·mor·tal** \(ˈ)im-ˈȯrt-ᵊl\ adj **1 :** not mortal : exempt from death ⟨∼ gods⟩ **2 :** exempt from oblivion ⟨those ∼ words⟩ — **im·mor·tal·ly** \-ē\ adv

**2immortal** n **1 :** one exempt from death **2** pl, often cap **:** the gods in Greek and Roman mythology **3 :** a person whose fame is lasting ⟨an ∼ of baseball⟩

**im·mor·tal·i·ty** \ˌim-ȯr-ˈtal-ət-ē\ n : the quality or state of being immortal; esp : unending existence

**im·mor·tal·ize** \im-ˈȯrt-ᵊl-ˌīz\ vb -ized; -iz·ing **:** to make immortal

**im·mo·tile** \im-ˈōt-ᵊl\ adj : lacking motility — **im·mo·til·i·ty** \ˌim-ō-ˈtil-ət-ē\ n

**im·mov·able** \(ˈ)im-ˈü-və-bəl\ adj **1 :** firmly fixed, settled, or fastened : FAST, STATIONARY ⟨∼ mountains⟩ **2 :** STEADFAST, UNYIELDING **3 :** IMPASSIVE — **im·mov·abil·i·ty** \(ˌ)im-ˌü-və-ˈbil-ət-ē\ n — **im·mov·ably** \-blē\ adv

**im·mune** \im-ˈyün\ adj : EXEMPT; esp : having a special capacity for resistance (as to a disease) — **im·mu·ni·ty** \im-ˈyü-nət-ē\ n

**im·mu·nize** \ˈim-yə-ˌnīz\ vb -nized; -niz·ing **:** to make immune — **im·mu·ni·za·tion** \ˌim-yə-nə-ˈzā-shən\ n

**im·mu·nol·o·gy** \ˌim-yə-ˈnäl-ə-jē\ n : a science that deals with the phenomena and causes of immunity — **im·mu·no·log·ic** \-yən-ᵊl-ˈaj-ik\ or **im·mu·no·log·i·cal** \-i-kəl\ adj — **im·mu·nol·o·gist** \ˌim-yə-ˈnäl-ə-jəst\ n

**im·mu·no·sup·pres·sive** \ˌim-yə-nō-sə-ˈpres-iv\ adj : involving or intended to induce suppression of natural immune responses ⟨∼ techniques for kidney transplants⟩ — **im·mu·no·sup·pres·sant** \-ˈpres-ᵊnt\ n or adj

**im·mure** \im-ˈyu̇(ə)r\ vb **im·mured; im·mur·ing 1 :** to enclose within or as if within walls **2 :** to build into or entomb in a wall

**im·mu·ta·ble** \(ˈ)im-ˈyüt-ə-bəl\ adj : UNCHANGEABLE, UNCHANGING — **im·mu·ta·bil·i·ty** \(ˌ)im-ˌyüt-ə-ˈbil-ət-ē\ n — **im·mu·ta·bly** \-ˈyüt-ə-blē\ adv

**1imp** \ˈimp\ n **1 :** a small demon : FIEND **2 :** a mischievous child

**2imp** abbr **1** imperative **2** imperfect **3** imperial **4** import; imported

**1im·pact** \im-ˈpakt\ vb **1 :** to press close; also : to fill with impacted material **2 :** to have an impact on

**2im·pact** \ˈim-ˌpakt\ n **1 :** a forceful contact, collision, or onset; also : the impetus communicated in or as if in a collision **2 :** EFFECT

**im·pact·ed** \im-ˈpak-təd\ adj : wedged between the jawbone and another tooth

**im·pair** \im-ˈpa(ə)r\ vb : to diminish in quantity, value, excellence, or strength : DAMAGE, LESSEN — **im·pair·ment** n

**im·pa·la** \im-ˈpal-ə\ n : a large brownish African antelope that in the male has slender lyre-shaped horns

**im·pale** \im-ˈpāl\ vb **im·paled**; **im·pal·ing** : to pierce with or as if with something pointed; esp : to torture or kill by fixing on a sharp stake — **im·pale·ment** n

**im·pal·pa·ble** \(ˈ)im-ˈpal-pə-bəl\ adj **1** : incapable of being felt by the touch : INTANGIBLE **2** : not readily discerned or apprehended — **im·pal·pa·bly** \(ˌ)im-ˈpal-pə-blē\ adv

**im·pan·el** \im-ˈpan-ᵊl\ vb : to enter in or on a panel : ENROLL ⟨~ a jury⟩

**im·part** \im-ˈpärt\ vb **1** : to give, grant, or bestow from one's store or abundance ⟨the sun ~s warmth⟩ **2** : to make known : DISCLOSE

**im·par·tial** \(ˈ)im-ˈpär-shəl\ adj : not partial : UNBIASED, JUST — **im·par·tial·i·ty** \(ˌ)im-ˌpär-shē-ˈal-ət-ē, -ˌpär-ˈshal-\ n — **im·par·tial·ly** \(ˈ)im-ˈpärsh-(ə-)lē\ adv

**im·pass·able** \(ˈ)im-ˈpas-ə-bəl\ adj : incapable of being passed, traversed, or circulated ⟨~ roads⟩

**im·passe** \ˈim-ˌpas\ n **1** : an impassable road or way **2** : a predicament from which there is no obvious escape

**im·pas·si·ble** \(ˈ)im-ˈpas-ə-bəl\ adj : UNFEELING, IMPASSIVE

**im·pas·sioned** \im-ˈpash-ənd\ adj : filled with passion or zeal : showing great warmth or intensity of feeling **syn** passionate, ardent, fervent, fervid

**im·pas·sive** \(ˈ)im-ˈpas-iv\ adj : showing no signs of feeling, emotion, or interest : EXPRESSIONLESS, INDIFFERENT **syn** stoic, phlegmatic, apathetic, stolid — **im·pas·sive·ly** adv — **im·pas·siv·i·ty** \ˌim-ˌpas-ˈiv-ət-ē\ n

**im·pas·to** \im-ˈpas-tō, -ˈpäs-\ n : the thick application of a pigment to a canvas or panel in painting; also : the body of pigment so applied

**im·pa·tience** \(ˈ)im-ˈpā-shən(t)s\ n **1** : restlessness of spirit esp. under irritation, delay, or opposition **2** : restless or eager desire or longing

**im·pa·tiens** \im-ˈpā-shənz, -shəns\ n : any of a genus of watery-juiced annual herbs with spurred flowers and seed capsules that readily split open

**im·pa·tient** \(ˈ)im-ˈpā-shənt\ adj **1** : not patient : restless or short of temper esp. under irritation, delay, or opposition **2** : INTOLERANT ⟨~ of poverty⟩ **3** : prompted or marked by impatience **4** : ANXIOUS — **im·pa·tient·ly** adv

**im·peach** \im-ˈpēch\ vb [ME empechen, fr. MF empeechier to hinder, fr. LL impedicare to fetter, fr. L pedica fetter, fr. ped-, pes foot] **1** : to charge (a public official) before an authorized tribunal with misbehavior in office **2** : to challenge the credibility or validity of — **im·peach·ment** n

**im·pearl** \im-ˈpərl\ vb : to form into pearls; also : to form of or adorn with pearls

**im·pec·ca·ble** \(ˈ)im-ˈpek-ə-bəl\ adj **1** : not capable of sinning or wrongdoing **2** : FAULTLESS, FLAWLESS, IRREPROACHABLE ⟨a man of ~ character⟩ — **im·pec·ca·bly** \(ˈ)ˈpek-ə-blē\ adv

**im·pe·cu·nious** \ˌim-pi-ˈkyü-nyəs, -nē-əs\ adj : having little or no money — **im·pe·cu·nious·ness** n

**im·ped·ance** \im-ˈpēd-ᵊns\ n : the opposition in an electrical circuit to the flow of an alternating current

**im·pede** \im-ˈpēd\ vb **im·ped·ed**; **im·ped·ing** [L impedire, fr. ped-, pes foot] : to interfere with the progress of

**im·ped·i·ment** \im-ˈped-ə-mənt\ n : HINDRANCE, OBSTRUCTION; esp : a speech defect

**im·ped·i·men·ta** \im-ˌped-ə-ˈment-ə\ n pl : things that impede

**im·pel** \im-ˈpel\ vb **im·pelled**; **im·pel·ling** : to urge or drive forward or on : FORCE; also : PROPEL

**im·pel·ler** also **im·pel·lor** \im-ˈpel-ər\ n : ROTOR

**im·pend** \im-ˈpend\ vb **1** : to hover or hang over threateningly : MENACE **2** : to be about to occur

**im·pen·e·tra·ble** \(ˈ)im-ˈpen-ə-trə-bəl\ adj **1** : incapable of being penetrated or pierced ⟨an ~ jungle⟩ **2** : incapable of being comprehended : INSCRUTABLE ⟨an ~ mystery⟩ — **im·pen·e·tra·bil·i·ty** \(ˌ)im-ˌpen-ə-trə-ˈbil-ət-ē\ n — **im·pen·e·tra·bly** \(ˈ)im-ˈpen-ə-trə-blē\ adv

**im·pen·i·tent** \(ˈ)im-ˈpen-ə-tənt\ adj : not penitent : not repenting of sin — **im·pen·i·tence** \-təns\ n

**imper** abbr imperative

**im·per·a·tive** \im-ˈper-ət-iv\ adj **1** : expressing a command, entreaty, or exhortation ⟨~ sentence⟩ **2** : having power to restrain, control, or direct **3** : URGENT — **imperative** n — **im·per·a·tive·ly** adv

**im·per·cep·ti·ble** \ˌim-pər-ˈsep-tə-bəl\ adj : not perceptible by the senses or by the mind ⟨~ changes⟩ — **im·per·cep·ti·bly** \-ˈsep-tə-blē\ adv

**im·per·cep·tive** \ˌim-pər-ˈsep-tiv\ adj : not perceptive

**im·per·cip·i·ent** \-ˈsip-ē-ənt\ adj : UNPERCEPTIVE

**imperf** abbr imperfect

¹**im·per·fect** \(ˈ)im-ˈpər-fikt\ adj **1** : not perfect : DEFECTIVE, INCOMPLETE **2** : of, relating to, or constituting a verb tense used to designate a continuing state or an incomplete action esp. in the past — **im·per·fect·ly** adv

²**imperfect** n : the imperfect tense; also : a verb form in it

**im·per·fec·tion** \ˌim-pər-ˈfek-shən\ n : the quality or state of being imperfect; also : DEFICIENCY, FAULT, BLEMISH

**im·per·fo·rate** \im-ˈpər-fə-rət\ adj **1** : having no opening or aperture; esp : lacking the usual or normal opening **2** : lacking perforations or tiny slits ⟨~ postage stamps⟩

¹**im·pe·ri·al** \im-ˈpir-ē-əl\ adj **1** : of, relating to, or befitting an empire or an emperor; also : of or relating to the United Kingdom or to the British Commonwealth or Empire **2** : ROYAL, SOVEREIGN; also : REGAL, IMPERIOUS **3** : of unusual size or excellence

²**imperial** n : a pointed beard growing below the lower lip

**im·pe·ri·al·ism** \im-'pir-ē-ə-,liz-əm\ n 1 : imperial government, authority, or system 2 : the policy of seeking to extend the power, dominion, or territories of a nation — **im·pe·ri·al·ist** \-ləst\ n or adj — **im·pe·ri·al·is·tic** \-,pir-ē-ə-'lis-tik\ adj

**im·per·il** \im-'per-əl\ vb -iled or -illed; -il·ing or -il·ling : ENDANGER

**im·pe·ri·ous** \im-'pir-ē-əs\ adj 1 : COMMANDING, LORDLY 2 : ARROGANT, DOMINEERING 3 : IMPERATIVE, URGENT — **im·pe·ri·ous·ly** adv

**im·per·ish·able** \(')im-'per-ish-ə-bəl\ adj : not perishable or subject to decay

**im·per·ma·nent** \(')im-'pər-mə-nənt\ adj : not permanent : TRANSIENT — **im·per·ma·nent·ly** adv

**im·per·me·able** \(')im-'pər-mē-ə-bəl\ adj : not permitting passage (as of a fluid) through its substance

**im·per·mis·si·ble** \,im-pər-'mis-ə-bəl\ adj : not permissible

**im·per·son·al** \(')im-'pərs-(ə-)nəl\ adj 1 : not referring to any particular person or thing 2 : not involving human emotions — **im·per·son·al·ly** \-ē\ adv

**im·per·son·ate** \im-'pərs-ᵊn-,āt\ vb -at·ed; -at·ing : to assume or act the character of — **im·per·son·ation** \-,pərs-ᵊn-'ā-shən\ n — **im·per·son·ator** \-'pərs-ᵊn-,āt-ər\ n

**im·per·ti·nent** \(')im-'pərt-ᵊn-ənt\ adj 1 : IRRELEVANT 2 : not restrained within due or proper bounds : RUDE, INSOLENT, SAUCY — **im·per·ti·nence** \-ᵊn-əns\ n — **im·per·ti·nent·ly** adv

**im·per·turb·able** \,im-pər-'tər-bə-bəl\ adj : marked by extreme calm, impassivity, and steadiness : SERENE

**im·per·vi·ous** \(')im-'pər-vē-əs\ adj 1 : incapable of being penetrated (as by moisture) 2 : not capable of being affected or disturbed (~ to criticism)

**im·pe·ti·go** \,im-pə-'tē-gō, -'tī-\ n : a contagious skin disease

**im·pet·u·ous** \im-'pech-(ə-)wəs\ adj 1 : marked by force and violence (with ~ speed) 2 : marked by impulsive vehemence (~ temper) — **im·pet·u·os·i·ty** \(,)im-,pech-ə-'wäs-ət-ē\ n — **im·pet·u·ous·ly** adv

**im·pe·tus** \'im-pət-əs\ n [L, assault, impetus, fr. impetere to attack, fr. petere to go to, seek] 1 : a driving force : IMPULSE 2 : INCENTIVE 3 : the tendency of a moving body to keep moving after the force which has kept it in motion ceases to act

**im·pi·e·ty** \(')im-'pī-ət-ē\ n, pl -eties 1 : the quality or state of being impious 2 : an impious act

**im·pinge** \im-'pinj\ vb im·pinged; im·ping·ing 1 : to strike or dash esp. with a sharp collision 2 : ENCROACH, INFRINGE — **im·pinge·ment** \-'pinj-mənt\ n

**im·pi·ous** \'im-pē-əs, (')im-'pī-\ adj : not pious : IRREVERENT, PROFANE

**imp·ish** \'im-pish\ adj : of, relating to, or befitting an imp; esp : MISCHIEVOUS

— **imp·ish·ly** adv — **imp·ish·ness** n

**im·pla·ca·ble** \(')im-'plak-ə-bəl, -'plā-kə-\ adj : not capable of being appeased, pacified, mitigated, or changed (an ~ enemy) — **im·pla·ca·bil·i·ty** \(,)im-,plak-ə-'bil-ət-ē, -,plā-kə-\ n — **im·pla·ca·bly** \(')im-'plak-ə-blē\ adv

**im·plau·si·ble** \(')im-'plò-zə-bəl\ adj : not plausible — **im·plau·si·bil·i·ty** \(,)im-,plò-zə-'bil-ət-ē\ n

¹**im·ple·ment** \'im-plə-mənt\ n [ME, fr. LL implementum action of filling up, fr. L implēre to fill up] : TOOL, UTENSIL, INSTRUMENT

²**im·ple·ment** \-,ment\ vb 1 : to carry out : FULFILL; esp : to put into practice 2 : to provide implements for — **im·ple·men·ta·tion** \,im-plə-mən-'tā-shən\ n

**im·pli·cate** \'im-plə-,kāt\ vb -cat·ed; -cat·ing 1 : IMPLY 2 : INVOLVE — **im·pli·ca·tion** \,im-plə-'kā-shən\ n

**im·plic·it** \im-'plis-ət\ adj 1 : understood though not directly stated or expressed : IMPLIED; also : POTENTIAL 2 : COMPLETE, UNQUESTIONING, ABSOLUTE (~ faith) — **im·plic·it·ly** adv

**im·plode** \im-'plōd\ vb im·plod·ed; im·plod·ing : to burst inward — **im·plo·sion** \-'plō-zhən\ n — **im·plo·sive** \-'plō-siv\ adj

**im·plore** \im-'plōr\ vb im·plored; im·plor·ing : BESEECH, ENTREAT syn supplicate, beg

**im·ply** \im-'plī\ vb im·plied; im·ply·ing 1 : to involve or indicate by inference, association, or necessary consequence rather than by direct statement (war implies fighting) 2 : to express indirectly : hint at : SUGGEST

**im·po·lite** \,im-pə-'līt\ adj : not polite : RUDE, DISCOURTEOUS

**im·pol·i·tic** \(')im-'päl-ə-,tik\ adj : not politic : UNWISE

**im·pon·der·a·ble** \(')im-'pän-d(ə-)rə-bəl\ adj : incapable of being weighed or evaluated with exactness — **imponderable** n

¹**im·port** \im-'pōrt\ vb 1 : MEAN, SIGNIFY 2 : to bring (as merchandise) into a place or country from a foreign or external source — **im·port·er** n

²**im·port** \'im-,pōrt\ n 1 : MEANING, SIGNIFICATION 2 : IMPORTANCE, SIGNIFICANCE 3 : something (as merchandise) brought in from another country

**im·por·tance** \im-'pōrt-ᵊns\ n : the quality or state of being important : MOMENT, SIGNIFICANCE syn consequence, import, weight

**im·por·tant** \im-'pōrt-ᵊnt\ adj 1 : marked by importance : SIGNIFICANT 2 : giving an impression of importance — **im·por·tant·ly** adv

**im·por·ta·tion** \,im-,pōr-'tā-shən, -pər-\ n : the act or practice of importing 2 : something imported

**im·por·tu·nate** \im-'pōrch-(ə-)nət\ adj 1 : BURDENSOME, TROUBLESOME 2 : troublesomely persistent

**im·por·tune** \,im-pər-'t(y)ün, im-'pōr-chən\ vb -tuned; -tun·ing : to urge or beg with troublesome persistence — im·por·tu·ni·ty \,im-pər-'t(y)ü-nət-ē\ n

im·pose \im-'pōz\ vb im·posed; im·pos·ing 1 : to establish or apply as compulsory : LEVY ⟨~ a tax⟩; also : INFLICT ⟨imposed himself as leader⟩ 2 : to palm off ⟨~ fake antiques on buyers⟩ 3 : OBTRUDE ⟨imposed herself upon others⟩ 4 : to take unwarranted advantage of something ⟨~ on his good nature⟩ 5 : to practice deception ⟨~ on the public⟩ — im·po·si·tion \,im-pə-'zish-ən\ n

im·pos·ing \im-'pō-ziŋ\ adj : impressive because of size, bearing, dignity, or grandeur — im·pos·ing·ly adv

im·pos·si·ble \(')im-'päs-ə-bəl\ adj 1 : incapable of being or of occurring 2 : HOPELESS 3 : extremely undesirable : UNACCEPTABLE 4 : OBJECTIONABLE — im·pos·si·bil·i·ty \(,)im-,päs-ə-'bil-ət-ē\ n — im·pos·si·bly \(')im-'päs-ə-blē\ adv

¹im·post \'im-,pōst\ n : TAX, DUTY

²impost n : a block, capital, or molding from which an arch springs

im·pos·tor or im·pos·ter \im-'päs-tər\ n : one that assumes an identity or title not his own for the purpose of deception : PRETENDER

im·pos·ture \im-'päs-chər\ n : DECEPTION; esp : fraudulent impersonation

im·po·tent \'im-pət-ənt\ adj 1 : lacking in power, strength, or vigor : HELPLESS 2 : lacking the power of procreation : STERILE — im·po·tence \-pət-əns\ n — im·po·ten·cy \-ən-sē\ n — im·po·tent·ly adv

im·pound \im-'paùnd\ vb 1 : CONFINE, ENCLOSE ⟨~ stray dogs⟩ 2 : to seize and hold in legal custody 3 : to collect in a reservoir ⟨~ water for irrigation⟩ — im·pound·ment \-'paùn(d)-mənt\ n

im·pov·er·ish \im-'päv-(ə-)rish\ vb : to make poor; also : to deprive of strength, richness, or fertility — im·pov·er·ish·ment n

im·prac·ti·ca·ble \(')im-'prak-ti-kə-bəl\ adj : not practicable : incapable of being put into practice or use

im·prac·ti·cal \(')im-'prak-ti-kəl\ adj 1 : not practical 2 : IMPRACTICABLE

im·pre·cate \'im-pri-,kāt\ vb -cat·ed; -cat·ing : CURSE — im·pre·ca·tion \,im-pri-'kā-shən\ n

im·pre·cise \,im-pri-'sīs\ adj : not precise im·pre·cise·ly adv — im·pre·cise·ness n — im·pre·ci·sion \-'sizh-ən\ n

im·preg·na·ble \im-'preg-nə-bəl\ adj : able to resist attack : UNCONQUERABLE, UNASSAILABLE — im·preg·na·bil·i·ty \(,)im-,preg-nə-'bil-ət-ē\ n

im·preg·nate \im-'preg-,nāt\ vb -nat·ed; -nat·ing 1 : to make pregnant, also : to make fertile or fruitful 2 : to saturate, fill, or charge with some other substance — im·preg·na·tion \,im-,preg-'nā-shən\ n

im·pre·sa·rio \,im-prə-'sär-ē-,ō\ n, pl -ri·os [It, fr. impresa undertaking, fr. imprendere to undertake] 1 : the promoter, manager, or conductor of an opera or concert company 2 : one who puts on or sponsors an entertainment 3 : MANAGER, PRODUCER

¹im·press \im-'pres\ vb 1 : to apply with pressure so as to imprint 2 : to produce (as a mark) by pressure : IMPRINT 3 : to press, stamp, or print in or upon 4 : to produce a vivid impression of 5 : to affect esp. forcibly or deeply — im·press·ible adj

²im·press \'im-,pres\ n 1 : a mark made by pressure : IMPRINT 2 : an image of something formed by or as if by pressure; esp : SEAL 3 : a product of pressure or influence 4 : a characteristic or distinctive mark : STAMP 5 : IMPRESSION, EFFECT

³im·press \im-'pres\ vb 1 : to enlist forcibly into public service; esp : to force into naval service 2 : to get the aid or services of by forcible argument or persuasion - im·press·ment n

im·pres·sion \im-'presh-ən\ n 1 : a stamp, form, or figure made by impressing : IMPRINT 2 : an esp. marked influence or effect on feeling, sense, or mind 3 : a characteristic trait or feature resulting from influence : IMPRESS 4 : a single print or copy (as from type or from an engraved plate or book) 5 : all the copies of a publication (as a book) printed from one issue : PRINTING 6 : a usu. vague notion, recollection, belief, or opinion 7 : an imitation in caricature of a noted personality as a form of entertainment

im·pres·sion·able \im-'presh-(ə-)nə-bəl\ adj : capable of being easily impressed : easily molded or influenced

im·pres·sion·ism \im-'presh-ə-,niz-əm\ n 1 often cap : a theory or practice in modern art of depicting the natural appearances of objects by dabs or strokes of primary unmixed colors in order to simulate actual reflected light 2 : the depiction of scene, emotion, or character by details intended to achieve a vividness or effectiveness esp. by evoking subjective and sensory impressions - im·pres·sion·is·tic \(,)im-,presh-ə-'nis-tik\ adj

im·pres·sion·ist \im-'presh-(ə-)nəst\ n 1 often cap : a painter who practices impressionism 2 : an entertainer who does impressions

im·pres·sive \im-'pres-iv\ adj : making or tending to make a marked impression ⟨an ~ speech⟩ — im·pres·sive·ly adv — im·pres·sive·ness n

im·pri·ma·tur \,im-prə-'mä-,tù(ə)r\ n [NL, let it be printed] 1 : a license to print or publish; also : official approval of a publication by a censor 2 : SANCTION, APPROVAL

¹im·print \im-'print, 'im-,print\ vb 1 : to stamp or mark by or as if by pressure : IMPRESS 2 archaic : PRINT

²im·print \'im-,print\ n 1 : something imprinted or printed : IMPRESS 2 : a publisher's name often with place and date of publication printed at the foot of a title page 3 : an indelible distinguishing effect or influence

im·pris·on \im-'priz-ⁿn\ vb : to put in

or as if in prison : CONFINE — **im·pris·on·ment** \im-'priz-ən-mənt\ n

**im·prob·a·ble** \(')im-'präb-ə-bəl\ adj : unlikely to be true or to occur — **im·prob·a·bil·i·ty** \(,)im-,präb-ə-'bil-ət-ē\ n — **im·prob·a·bly** \(')im-'präb-ə-blē\ adv

**im·promp·tu** \im-'prämp-t(y)ü\ adj [F, fr. impromptu extemporaneously, fr. L in promptu in readiness] **1** : made or done on or as if on the spur of the moment **2** : EXTEMPORANEOUS, UNREHEARSED — **impromptu** adv or n

**im·prop·er** \(')im-'präp-ər\ adj **1** : not proper, fit, or suitable **2** : INCORRECT, INACCURATE **3** : not in accord with propriety, modesty, or good manners — **im·prop·er·ly** adv

**improper fraction** n : a fraction whose numerator is equal to or larger than the denominator

**im·pro·pri·e·ty** \,im-prə-'prī-ət-ē\ n, pl **-eties 1** : the quality or state of being improper **2** : an improper act or remark; esp : an unacceptable use of a word or of language

**im·prove** \im-'prüv\ vb **im·proved**; **im·prov·ing 1** : INCREASE, AUGMENT ⟨his education improved his chances⟩ **2** : to enhance or increase in value or quality ⟨~ farmlands by cultivation⟩ **3** : to grow or become better ⟨~ in health⟩ **4** : to make good use of ⟨~ the time by reading⟩ — **im·prov·able** \-'prü-və-bəl\ adj

**im·prove·ment** \im-'prüv-mənt\ n **1** : the act or process of improving **2** : increased value or excellence of something **3** : something that adds to the value or appearance of a thing

**im·prov·i·dent** \(')im-'präv-əd-ənt\ adj : not providing for the future — **im·prov·i·dence** \-əns\ n

**im·pro·vise** \'im-prə-'vīz, 'im-prə-,vīz\ vb **-vised**; **-vis·ing** [F improviser, fr. It improvvisare, fr. improvviso sudden, fr. L improvisus, lit., unforeseen] **1** : to compose, recite, or sing on the spur of the moment : EXTEMPORIZE ⟨~ on the piano⟩ **2** : to make, invent, or arrange offhand ⟨~ a sail out of shirts⟩ — **im·pro·vi·sa·tion** \im-,präv-ə-'zā-shən, ,im-prə-və-\ n — **im·pro·vis·er** or **im·pro·vi·sor** \,im-prə-'vīz-ər, 'im-prə-,vī-\ n

**im·pru·dent** \(')im-'prüd-ᵊnt\ adj : not prudent : lacking discretion — **im·pru·dence** \-ᵊns\ n

**im·pu·dent** \'im-pyəd-ənt\ adj : marked by contemptuous or cocky boldness or disregard of others — **im·pu·dence** \-əns\ n — **im·pu·dent·ly** adv

**im·pugn** \im-'pyün\ vb : to attack by words or arguments : oppose or attack as false ⟨~ the motives of an opponent⟩

**im·puis·sance** \im-'pwis-ᵊns, -'pyü-ə-səns\ n : the quality or state of being powerless : WEAKNESS

**¹im·pulse** \'im-,pəls\ n **1** : a force that starts a body into motion; also : the motion produced by such a force **2** : an arousing of the mind and spirit to action; also : a wave of nervous excita-

tion **3** : a natural tendency

**im·pul·sion** \im-'pəl-shən\ n **1** : the act of impelling : the state of being impelled **2** : a force that impels **3** : a sudden inclination **4** : IMPETUS

**im·pul·sive** \im-'pəl-siv\ adj **1** : having the power of or actually driving or impelling **2** : acting or prone to act on impulse ⟨~ buying⟩ — **im·pul·sive·ly** adv — **im·pul·sive·ness** n

**im·pu·ni·ty** \im-'pyü-nət-ē\ n [MF or L; MF impunité, fr. L impunitas, fr. impune without punishment, fr. poena pain, punishment] : exemption from punishment, harm, or loss

**im·pure** \(')im-'pyůr\ adj **1** : not pure : UNCHASTE, OBSCENE **2** : DIRTY, FOUL **3** : ADULTERATED, MIXED — **im·pu·ri·ty** \-'pyůr-ət-ē\ n

**im·pute** \im-'pyüt\ vb **im·put·ed**; **im·put·ing 1** : to lay the responsibility or blame for often falsely or unjustly : CHARGE **2** : to credit to a person or a cause : ATTRIBUTE — **im·pu·ta·tion** \,im-pyə-'tā-shən\ n

**¹in** \(')in, ən, ᵊn\ prep **1** — used to indicate physical surroundings ⟨swim ~ the lake⟩ **2** : INTO 1 ⟨ran ~ the house⟩ **3** : DURING ⟨~ the summer⟩ **4** : WITH ⟨written ~ pencil⟩ **5** — used to indicate one's situation or state of being ⟨~ luck⟩ ⟨~ love⟩ ⟨~ trouble⟩ **6** — used to indicate manner ⟨~ a hurry⟩ or purpose ⟨said ~ reply⟩ **7** : INTO 2 ⟨broke ~ pieces⟩

**²in** \'in\ adv **1** : to or toward the inside ⟨come ~⟩ : to or toward some destination or place ⟨flew ~ from the South⟩ **2** : at close quarters : NEAR ⟨the enemy closed ~⟩ **3** : into the midst of something ⟨mix ~ the flour⟩ **4** : to or at its proper place ⟨fit a piece ~⟩ **5** : WITHIN ⟨locked ~⟩ **6** : in vogue or season; also : at hand **7** : in a completed or terminated state

**³in** \'in\ adj **1** : located inside or within **2** : that is in position, connection, operation, or power ⟨the ~ party⟩ **3** : directed inward : INCOMING ⟨the ~ train⟩ **4** : keenly aware of and responsive to what is new and smart ⟨the ~ crowd⟩; also : extremely fashionable ⟨the ~ thing to do⟩

**⁴in** \'in\ n **1** : one who is in office or power or on the inside **2** : INFLUENCE, PULL ⟨he has an ~ with the owner⟩

**⁵in** abbr inch

**In** symbol indium

**IN** abbr Indiana

**in-** \(')in, ,in\ prefix **1** : not : NON-, UN- **2** : opposite of : contrary to

| | |
|---|---|
| inacceptable | inappropriate |
| inaccuracy | inapt |
| inaccurate | inartistic |
| inaction | inattentive |
| inactive | inaudible |
| inactivity | inaudibly |
| inadmissible | inauspicious |
| inadvisability | incautious |
| inadvisable | incomprehension |
| inapplicable | |
| inapposite | inconceivable |
| inappreciative | inconclusive |
| inapproachable | inconsistency |

inconsistent
incoordination
indefensible
indemonstrable
indestructible
indeterminable
indiscernible
indistinguish-
  able
inedible
ineducable
inefficacious
inelastic
inelasticity
inequitable
inequity

ineradicable
inexpedient
inexpensive
inexpressive
inextinguish-
  able
infeasible
inharmonious
inhospitable
injudicious
inoffensive
insanitary
insensitive
insignificant
insuppressible
insusceptible

**in·abil·i·ty** \‚in-ə-'bil-ət-ē\ n : the quality or state of being unable

**in ab·sen·tia** \‚in-ab-'sen-ch(ē-)ə\ adv : in one's absence

**in·ac·ti·vate** \(')in-'ak-tə-‚vāt\ vb : to make inactive — **in·ac·ti·va·tion** \(‚)in-‚ak-tə-'vā-shən\ n

**in·ad·e·quate** \(')in-'ad-i-kwət\ adj : not adequate : INSUFFICIENT — **in·ad·e·qua·cy** \-kwə-sē\ n — **in·ad·e·quate·ly** adv — **in·ad·e·quate·ness** n

**in·ad·ver·tent** \‚in-əd-'vərt-²nt\ adj 1 : HEEDLESS, INATTENTIVE 2 : UNINTENTIONAL — **in·ad·ver·tence** \-²ns\ n — **in·ad·ver·ten·cy** \-²n-sē\ n — **in·ad·ver·tent·ly** adv

**in·alien·able** \(')in-'āl-yə-nə-bəl, -'ā-lē-ə-nə-\ adj : incapable of being alienated, surrendered, or transferred ⟨~ rights of a citizen⟩ — **in·alien·abil·i·ty** \(‚)in-‚āl-yə-nə-'bil-ət-ē, -‚ā-lē-ə-nə-\ n — **in·alien·ably** \(')in-'āl-yə-nə-blē, -'ā-lē-ə-nə-\ adv

**in·amo·ra·ta** \‚in-‚am-ə-'rät-ə\ n : a woman with whom one is in love

**inane** \in-'ān\ adj inan·er; -est : EMPTY, INSUBSTANTIAL; also : SHALLOW, SILLY — **inan·i·ty** \in-'an-ət-ē\ n

**in·an·i·mate** \(')in-'an-ə-mət\ adj : not animate or animated : lacking the special qualities of living things — **in·an·i·mate·ly** adv — **in·an·i·mate·ness** n

**in·a·ni·tion** \‚in-ə-'nish-ən\ n : a weak state from or as if from lack of food and water

**in·ap·pre·cia·ble** \‚in-ə-'prē-shə-bəl\ adj : too small to be perceived — **in·ap·pre·cia·bly** \-blē\ adv

**in·ap·ti·tude** \(')in-'ap-tə-‚t(y)üd\ n : lack of aptitude

**in·ar·tic·u·late** \‚in-är-'tik-yə-lət\ adj 1 : uttered or formed without the definite articulations of intelligible speech 2 : MUTE 3 : incapable of being expressed by speech; also : UNSPOKEN 4 : not having the power of distinct utterance or effective expression — **in·ar·tic·u·late·ly** adv

**in·as·much as** \‚in-əz-‚məch-əz\ conj : seeing that : SINCE

**in·at·ten·tion** \‚in-ə-'ten-chən\ n : failure to pay attention : DISREGARD

¹**in·au·gu·ral** \in-'ȯ-gyə-rəl, -g(ə-)rəl\ adj 1 : of or relating to an inauguration 2 : marking a beginning

²**inaugural** n 1 : an inaugural address

2 : INAUGURATION

**in·au·gu·rate** \in-'ȯ-g(y)ə-‚rāt\ vb -rat·ed; -rat·ing 1 : to introduce into an office with suitable ceremonies : INSTALL 2 : to dedicate ceremoniously ⟨~ a new library⟩ 3 : BEGIN, INITIATE ⟨~ a new system⟩ — **in·au·gu·ra·tion** \-‚ȯ-g(y)ə-'rā-shən\ n

**in·board** \'in-‚bȯrd\ adv 1 : inside the hull of a ship 2 : toward, facing, or closer to the center line of a ship or airplane fuselage — **inboard** adj

**in·born** \'in-'bȯrn\ adj : present from birth rather than acquired : NATURAL syn innate, congenital, inbred

**in·bound** \'in-‚baund\ adj : inward bound ⟨~ traffic⟩

**in·bred** \'in-'bred\ adj 1 : INBORN, INNATE 2 : produced by breeding closely related individuals together

**in·breed·ing** \'in-‚brēd-iŋ\ n 1 : the interbreeding of closely related individuals esp. to preserve and fix desirable characters of and to eliminate unfavorable characters from a stock 2 : confinement to a narrow range or a local or limited field of choice — **in·breed** \-'brēd\ vb

**inc** abbr 1 incorporated 2 increase

**In·ca** \'iŋ-kə\ n 1 : a noble or a member of the ruling family of an Indian empire of Peru, Bolivia, and Ecuador until the Spanish conquest 2 : a member of any people under Inca influence

**in·cal·cu·la·ble** \(')in-'kal-kyə-lə-bəl\ adj : not capable of being calculated; esp : too large or numerous to be calculated — **in·cal·cu·la·bly** \-blē\ adv

**in·can·des·cent** \‚in-kən-'des-²nt\ adj 1 : glowing with heat 2 : SHINING, BRILLIANT — **in·can·des·cence** \-²ns\ n

**incandescent lamp** n : a lamp in which an electrically heated filament emits light

**in·can·ta·tion** \‚in-‚kan-'tā-shən\ n : a use of spells or verbal charms spoken or sung as a part of a ritual of magic; also : a formula of words chanted or recited in or as if in such a ritual

**in·ca·pa·ble** \(')in-'kā-pə-bəl\ adj : lacking capacity, ability, or qualification for the purpose or end in view; also : UNQUALIFIED — **in·ca·pa·bil·i·ty** \(‚)in-‚kā-pə-'bil-ət-ē\ n

**in·ca·pac·i·tate** \‚in-kə-'pas-ə-‚tāt\ vb -tat·ed; -tat·ing : to make incapable or unfit : DISQUALIFY, DISABLE

**in·ca·pac·i·ty** \‚in-kə-'pas-ət-ē\ n, pl -ties : the quality or state of being incapable

**in·car·cer·ate** \in-'kär-sə-‚rāt\ vb : IMPRISON, CONFINE — **in·car·cer·a·tion** \(‚)in-‚kär-sə-'rā-shən\ n

**in·car·na·dine** \in-'kär-nə-‚dīn, -‚dēn\ vb -dined; -din·ing : REDDEN

**in·car·nate** \in-'kär-nət, -‚nāt\ adj 1 : having bodily and esp. human form and substance 2 : PERSONIFIED — **in·car·nate** \-‚nāt\ vb

**in·car·na·tion** \‚in-kär-'nā-shən\ n

1 : the act of incarnating : the state of being incarnate 2 : the embodiment of a deity or spirit in an earthly form 3 : a person showing a trait or typical character to a marked degree

**incase** var of ENCASE

**in·cen·di·ary** \in-'sen-dē-,er-ē\ adj 1 : of or relating to a deliberate burning of property 2 : tending to excite or inflame 3 : designed to kindle fires ⟨an ~ bomb⟩ — **incendiary** n

¹**in·cense** \'in-,sens\ n 1 : material used to produce a fragrant odor when burned 2 : the perfume or smoke from some spices and gums when burned

²**in·cense** \in-'sens\ vb **in·censed; in·cens·ing** : to make extremely angry

**in·cen·tive** \in-'sent-iv\ n‡[ME, fr. LL incentivum, fr. incentivus stimulating, fr. L, setting the tune, fr. incinere to set the tune, fr. canere to sing] : something that incites or has a tendency to incite to determination or action

**in·cep·tion** \in-'sep-shən\ n : BEGINNING, COMMENCEMENT

**in·cer·ti·tude** \(')in-'sərt-ə-,t(y)üd\ n 1 : UNCERTAINTY, DOUBT, INDECISION 2 : INSECURITY, INSTABILITY

**in·ces·sant** \(')in-'ses-ᵊnt\ adj : continuing or flowing without interruption ⟨~ rains⟩ — **in·ces·sant·ly** adv

**in·cest** \'in-,sest\ n [ME, fr. L incestum, fr. incestus impure, fr. castus pure] : sexual intercourse between persons so closely related that marriage is illegal — **in·ces·tu·ous** \in-'ses-chə-wəs\ adj

¹**inch** \'inch\ n [ME, fr. OE ynce, fr. L uncia twelfth part, inch, ounce] — see WEIGHT table

²**inch** vb : to advance or retire a little at a time ⟨cars ~ing along⟩

**in·cho·ate** \in-'kō-ət, 'in-kə-,wāt\ adj [L inchoatus, pp. of inchoare, lit., to hitch up, fr. cohum strap fastening a plow beam to the yoke] : being recently begun or only partly in existence : INCOMPLETE, INCIPIENT

**inch·worm** \'inch-,wərm\ n : LOOPER

**in·ci·dence** \'in-səd-əns\ n : rate of occurrence or effect

¹**in·ci·dent** \'in-səd-ənt\ n 1 : OCCURRENCE, HAPPENING 2 : an action likely to lead to grave consequences esp. in diplomatic matters

²**incident** adj 1 : occurring or likely to occur esp. in connection with some other happening 2 : falling or striking on something ⟨~ light rays⟩

¹**in·ci·den·tal** \,in-sə-'dent-ᵊl\ adj 1 : subordinate, nonessential, or attendant in position or significance ⟨~ expenses⟩ 2 : CASUAL, CHANCE — **in·ci·den·tal·ly** \-ē\ adv

²**incidental** n 1 : something that is incidental 2 pl : minor items (as of expense) that are not individually accounted for

**in·cin·er·ate** \in-'sin-ə-,rāt\ vb **-at·ed; -at·ing** : to burn to ashes

**in·cin·er·a·tor** \in-'sin-ə-,rāt-ər\ n : a furnace for burning waste

**in·cip·i·ent** \in-'sip-ē-ənt\ adj : beginning to be or become apparent

**in·cise** \in-'sīz\ vb **in·cised; in·cis·ing** : to cut into : CARVE, ENGRAVE

**in·ci·sion** \in-'sizh-ən\ n : CUT, GASH; esp : a surgical wound

**in·ci·sive** \in-'sī-siv\ adj 1 : CUTTING, PENETRATING 2 : ACUTE, CLEAR-CUT ⟨~ comments⟩ — **in·ci·sive·ly** adv

**in·ci·sor** \in-'sī-zər\ n : a tooth adapted for cutting; esp : one of the cutting teeth in front of the canines of a mammal

**in·cite** \in-'sīt\ vb **in·cit·ed; in·cit·ing** : to arouse to action : stir up — **in·cite·ment** n

**in·ci·vil·i·ty** \,in-sə-'vil-ət-ē\ n 1 : DISCOURTESY, RUDENESS 2 : a rude or discourteous act

**incl** abbr including; inclusive

**in·clem·ent** \(')in-'klem-ənt\ adj 1 : SEVERE, STORMY ⟨~ weather⟩ 2 : UNMERCIFUL, RIGOROUS ⟨an ~ judge⟩ — **in·clem·en·cy** \-ən-sē\ n

**in·clin·able** \in-'klī-nə-bəl\ adj : having a tendency or inclination : DISPOSED; also : FAVORABLE

**in·cli·na·tion** \,in-klə-'nā-shən\ n 1 : BOW, NOD ⟨an ~ of the head⟩ 2 : a tilting of something 3 : PROPENSITY, BENT; esp : LIKING 4 : SLANT, SLOPE

¹**in·cline** \in-'klīn\ vb **in·clined; in·clin·ing** 1 : BOW, BEND 2 : to lean, tend, or become drawn toward an opinion or course of conduct 3 : to deviate from the vertical or horizontal : SLOPE 4 : INFLUENCE, PERSUADE

²**in·cline** \'in-,klīn\ n : SLOPE

**inclose, inclosure** var of ENCLOSE, ENCLOSURE

**in·clude** \in-'klüd\ vb **in·clud·ed; in·clud·ing** : to take in or comprise as a part of a whole ⟨the price ~s tax⟩ — **in·clu·sion** \in-'klü-zhən\ n — **in·clu·sive** \-'klü-siv\ adj

**incog** abbr incognito

¹**in·cog·ni·to** \,in-,käg-'nēt-ō, in-'käg-nə-,tō\ adv or adj [It, fr. L incognitus unknown, fr. cognoscere to know] : with one's identity concealed (as under an assumed name or title)

²**incognito** n, pl -tos 1 : one appearing or living incognito 2 : the state or disguise of an incognito

**in·co·her·ent** \,in-kō-'hir-ənt, -'her-\ adj 1 : not sticking closely or compactly together : LOOSE 2 : not clearly or logically connected : RAMBLING — **in·co·her·ence** \-əns\ n — **in·co·her·ent·ly** adv

**in·com·bus·ti·ble** \,in-kəm-'bəs-tə-bəl\ adj : not combustible — **incombustible** n

**in·come** \'in-kəm\ n : a gain usu. measured in money that derives from labor, business, or property

**income tax** \,in-(,)kəm-\ n : a tax on the net income of an individual or business concern

**in·com·ing** \'in-,kəm-iŋ\ adj : coming in ⟨the ~ tide⟩ ⟨~ freshmen⟩

**in·com·men·su·rate** \,in-kə-'mens-(ə-)rət, -'mench-(ə-)rət\ adj : not commensurate; esp : not adequate

**in·com·mode** \,in-kə-'mōd\ vb

**-mod·ed; -mod·ing :** INCONVENIENCE, DISTURB

**in·com·mu·ni·ca·ble** \,in-kə-'myü-ni-kə-bəl\ *adj* **:** not communicable **:** not capable of being communicated or imparted; *also* **:** UNCOMMUNICATIVE

**in·com·mu·ni·ca·do** \-,myü-nə-'käd-ō\ *adv or adj* **:** without means of communication; *also* **:** in solitary confinement ⟨a prisoner held ∼⟩

**in·com·pa·ra·ble** \(')in-'käm-p(ə-)rə-bəl\ *adj* **1 :** eminent beyond comparison **:** MATCHLESS **2 :** not suitable for comparison

**in·com·pat·i·ble** \,in-kəm-'pat-ə-bəl\ *adj* **:** incapable of or unsuitable for association ⟨∼ colors⟩ ⟨∼ drugs⟩ ⟨temperamentally ∼⟩ — **in·com·pat·i·bil·i·ty** \,in-kəm-,pat-ə-'bil-ət-ē\ *n*

**in·com·pe·tent** \(')in-'käm-pət-ənt\ *adj* **1 :** not competent **:** lacking sufficient knowledge, skill, strength, or ability **2 :** not legally qualified — **in·com·pe·tence** \-pət-əns\ *n* — **in·com·pe·ten·cy** \-ən-sē\ *n* — **incompetent** *n*

**in·com·plete** \,in-kəm-'plēt\ *adj* **:** lacking a part or parts **:** UNFINISHED, IMPERFECT — **in·com·plete·ly** *adv* — **in·com·plete·ness** *n*

**in·com·pre·hen·si·ble** \,in-,käm-prē-'hen-sə-bəl\ *adj* **:** impossible to comprehend **:** UNINTELLIGIBLE

**in·com·press·ible** \,in-kəm-'pres-ə-bəl\ *adj* **:** not capable of or resistant to compression — **in·com·press·ibil·i·ty** \-,pres-ə-'bil-ət-ē\ *n* — **in·com·press·ibly** \-'pres-ə-blē\ *adv*

**in·con·gru·ent** \,in-kən-'grü-ənt, (')in-'käŋ-grə-wənt\ *adj* **:** not congruent

**in·con·gru·ous** \(')in-'käŋ-grə-wəs\ *adj* **:** not consistent with or suitable to the surroundings or associations — **in·con·gru·i·ty** \,in-kən-'grü-ət-ē, -,kän-\ *n* — **in·con·gru·ous·ly** \(')in-'käŋ-grə-wəs-lē\ *adv*

**in·con·se·quen·tial** \,in-,kän-sə-'kwen-chəl\ *adj* **1 :** ILLOGICAL; *also* **:** IRRELEVANT **2 :** of no significance **:** UNIMPORTANT — **in·con·se·quence** \(')in-'kän-sə-,kwens\ *n* — **in·con·se·quen·tial·ly** \,in-,kän-sə-'kwench-(ə-)lē\ *adv*

**in·con·sid·er·able** \,in-kən-'sid-ər-(ə-)bəl, -'sid-rə-bəl\ *adj* **:** SLIGHT, TRIVIAL

**in·con·sid·er·ate** \,in-kən-'sid-(ə-)rət\ *adj* **:** HEEDLESS, THOUGHTLESS; *esp* **:** not duly respecting the rights or feelings of others — **in·con·sid·er·ate·ly** *adv* — **in·con·sid·er·ate·ness** *n*

**in·con·sol·able** \,in-kən-'sō-lə-bəl\ *adj* **:** incapable of being consoled — **in·con·sol·ably** \-blē\ *adv*

**in·con·spic·u·ous** \,in-kən-'spik-yə-wəs\ *adj* **:** not readily noticeable — **in·con·spic·u·ous·ly** *adv*

**in·con·stant** \(')in-'kän-stənt\ *adj* **:** not constant **:** CHANGEABLE *syn* fickle, capricious, mercurial, unstable — **in·con·stan·cy** \-stən-sē\ *n* — **in·con·stant·ly** *adv*

**in·con·test·able** \,in-kən-'tes-tə-bəl\ *adj* **:** not contestable **:** INDISPUTABLE — **in·con·test·ably** \-'tes-tə-blē\ *adv*

**in·con·ti·nent** \(')in-'känt-ʰn-ənt\ *adj* **1 :** lacking self-restraint **2 :** unable to contain, keep, or restrain — **in·con·ti·nence** \-ʰn-əns\ *n*

**in·con·tro·vert·ible** \,in-,kän-trə-'vərt-ə-bəl\ *adj* **:** not open to question **:** INDISPUTABLE ⟨∼ evidence⟩ — **in·con·tro·vert·ibly** \-blē\ *adv*

**¹in·con·ve·nience** \,in-kən-'vē-nyəns\ *n* **1 :** DISCOMFORT ⟨the ∼ of his quarters⟩ **2 :** something that is inconvenient

**²inconvenience** *vb* **:** to subject to inconvenience

**in·con·ve·nient** \,in-kən-'vē-nyənt\ *adj* **:** not convenient **:** causing trouble or annoyance **:** INOPPORTUNE — **in·con·ve·nient·ly** *adv*

**in·cor·po·rate** \in-'kòr-pə-,rāt\ *vb* **-rat·ed; -rat·ing 1 :** to unite closely or so as to form one body **:** BLEND **2 :** to form, form into, or become a corporation **3 :** to give material form to **:** EMBODY — **in·cor·po·rat·ed** *adj* — **in·cor·po·ra·tion** \-,kòr-pə-'rā-shən\ *n*

**in·cor·po·re·al** \,in-kòr-'pòr-ē-əl\ *adj* **:** having no material body or form — **in·cor·po·re·al·ly** \-ē\ *adv*

**in·cor·rect** \,in-kə-'rekt\ *adj* **1 :** INACCURATE, FAULTY **2 :** not true **:** WRONG **3 :** UNBECOMING, IMPROPER — **in·cor·rect·ly** \-'rek-(t)lē\ *adv* — **in·cor·rect·ness** \-'rek(t)-nəs\ *n*

**in·cor·ri·gi·ble** \(')in-'kòr-ə-jə-bəl\ *adj* **:** incapable of being corrected, amended, or reformed **:** DEPRAVED, DELINQUENT, UNMANAGEABLE, UNALTERABLE — **in·cor·ri·gi·bil·i·ty** \(,)in-,kòr-ə-jə-'bil-ət-ē\ *n* — **in·cor·ri·gi·bly** \(')in-'kòr-ə-jə-blē\ *adv*

**in·cor·rupt·ible** \,in-kə-'rəp-tə-bəl\ *adj* **1 :** not subject to decay or dissolution **2 :** incapable of being bribed or morally corrupted — **in·cor·rupt·ibil·i·ty** \-,rəp-tə-'bil-ət-ē\ *n* — **in·cor·rupt·ibly** \-'rəp-tə-blē\ *adv*

**incr** *abbr* increase; increased

**¹in·crease** \in-'krēs, 'in-,krēs\ *vb* **in·creased; in·creas·ing 1 :** to become greater **:** GROW **2 :** to multiply by the production of young ⟨rabbits ∼ rapidly⟩ **3 :** to make greater — **in·creas·ing·ly** \-'krē-siŋ-lē\ *adv*

**²in·crease** \'in-,krēs, in-'krēs\ *n* **1 :** addition or enlargement in size, extent, or quantity **:** GROWTH **2 :** something (as offspring, produce, or profit) that is added to the original stock by augmentation or growth

**in·cred·i·ble** \(')in-'kred-ə-bəl\ *adj* **:** too extraordinary and improbable to be believed; *also* **:** hard to eblieve — **in·cred·i·bil·i·ty** \(,)in-,kred-ə-'bil-ət-ē\ *n* — **in·cred·i·bly** \(')in-'kred-ə-blē\ *adv*

**in·cred·u·lous** \(')in-'krej-ə-ləs\ *adj* **:** SKEPTICAL; *also* **:** expressing disbelief — **in·cre·du·li·ty** \,in-kri-'d(y)ü-lət-ē\ *n* — **in·cred·u·lous·ly** *adv*

**in·cre·ment** \'iŋ-krə-mənt, 'in-\ *n* **1 :** an increase esp. in quantity or value

: ENLARGEMENT; *also* : QUANTITY  2
: something gained or added; *esp* : one
of a series of regular consecutive additions — **in·cre·men·tal** \,in-krə-
'ment-ᵊl, ,in-\ *adj*

**in·crim·i·nate** \in-'krim-ə-,nāt\ *vb*
**-nat·ed; -nat·ing** : to charge with or
involve in a crime or fault : ACCUSE —
**in·crim·i·na·tion** \-,krim-ə 'nā-
shən\ *n* — **in·crim·i·na·to·ry**
\-'krim-(ə-)nə-,tōr-ē\ *adj*

**incrust** *var of* ENCRUST

**in·crus·ta·tion** \,in-,krəs-'tā-shən\ *n*
**1** : the act of encrusting : the state of
being encrusted  **2** : CRUST; *also* : something resembling a crust

**in·cu·bate** \'in-kyə-,bāt, 'in-\ *vb*
**-bat·ed; -bat·ing** : to sit upon eggs
to hatch them; *also* : to keep (as eggs)
under conditions favorable for development — **in·cu·ba·tion** \,in-kyə-'bā-
shən, ,in-\ *n*

**in·cu·ba·tor** \'in-kyə-,bāt-ər, 'in-\ *n*
: one that incubates; *esp* : an apparatus
providing suitable conditions (as of
warmth and moisture) for incubating
something

**in·cu·bus** \'in-kyə-bəs, 'in-\ *n, pl* **-bi**
\-,bī, -,bē\ *also* **-bus·es** [ME, fr. LL,
fr. L *incubare* to lie on]  **1** : a spirit
supposed to work evil on persons in
their sleep  **2** : NIGHTMARE  **3** : a person or thing that oppresses or burdens
like a nightmare

**in·cul·cate** \in-'kəl-,kāt, 'in-(,)kəl-\
*vb* **-cat·ed; -cat·ing** [L *inculcare*, lit.,
to tread on, fr. *calcare* to trample, fr.
*calx* heel] : to teach and impress on the
mind by frequent repetitions or admoni-
tions — **in·cul·ca·tion** \,in-(,)kəl-
'kā-shən\ *n*

**in·cul·pa·ble** \(')in-'kəl-pə-bəl\ *adj*
: free from guilt : BLAMELESS

**in·cul·pate** \in-'kəl-,pāt, 'in-(,)kəl-\
*vb* **-pat·ed; -pat·ing** : to involve or
implicate in guilt : INCRIMINATE

**in·cum·ben·cy** \in-'kəm-bən-sē\ *n, pl*
**-cies**  **1** : the quality or state of being
incumbent  **2** : something that is incumbent  **3** : the office or period of
office of an incumbent

**¹in·cum·bent** \in-'kəm-bənt\ *n* : the
holder of an office or position

**²incumbent** *adj*  **1** : lying or resting on
something else  **2** : imposed as a duty
**3** : occupying a specified office

**incumber** *var of* ENCUMBER

**in·cu·nab·u·lum** \,in-kyə-'nab-yə-
ləm, -in\ *n, pl* **-la** \-lə\ [NL, fr. L *in-
cunabula*, pl., swaddling clothes, cradle,
fr. *cunae* cradle] : a book printed before
1501

**in·cur** \in-'kər\ *vb* **in·curred; in-
cur·ring  1** : to meet with (as an inconvenience)  **2** : to become liable or
subject to : bring down upon oneself

**in·cur·able** \(')in-'kyùr-ə-bəl\ *adj*
: not subject to cure — **in·cur·abil·i-
ty** \,(,)in-,kyùr-ə-'bil-ət-ē\ *n* — **incurable** *n* — **in·cur·ably** \(')in-'kyùr-ə-
blē\ *adv*

**in·cu·ri·ous** \(')in-'kyùr-ē-əs\ *adj*
: not curious or inquisitive

**in·cur·sion** \in-'kər-zhən\ *n* : a sud-

den usu. temporary invasion : RAID

**in·cus** \'in-kəs\ *n, pl* **in·cu·des**
\in-'kyüd-(,)ēz\ [NL, fr. L, anvil] : the
middle of a chain of three small bones
in the ear of a mammal

**Ind** *abbr*  **1** independent  **2** index  **3** industrial; industry

**Ind** *abbr* Indiana

**in·debt·ed** \in-'det-əd\ *adj*  **1** : owing
money  **2** : owing gratitude or recognition to another — **in·debt·ed·ness** *n*

**in·de·cent** \(')in-'dēs-ᵊnt\ *adj* : not
decent : UNBECOMING, UNSEEMLY; *also*
: morally offensive — **in·de·cen·cy**
\-ᵊn-sē\ *n* — **in·de·cent·ly** *adv*

**in·de·ci·sion** \,in-di-'sizh-ən\ *n* : a
wavering between two or more possible
courses of action : IRRESOLUTION

**in·de·ci·sive** \,in-di-'sī-siv\ *adj*  **1**
: not decisive : INCONCLUSIVE  **2**
: marked by or prone to indecision
**3** : INDEFINITE — **in·de·ci·sive·ly**
*adv* — **in·de·ci·sive·ness** *n*

**in·de·clin·able** \,in-di-'klī-nə-bəl\ *adj*
: having no grammatical inflections

**in·de·co·rous** \(')in-'dek-(ə-)rəs; ,in-
di-'kōr-əs\ *adj* : not decorous **syn** improper, unseemly, indecent, unbecoming, indelicate — **in·de·co·rous·ly**
*adv* — **in·de·co·rous·ness** *n*

**in·deed** \in-'dēd\ *adv*  **1** : without any
question : TRULY — often used interjectionally to express irony, disbelief, or
surprise  **2** : in reality  **3** : all things
considered

**indef** *abbr* indefinite

**in·de·fat·i·ga·ble** \,in-di-'fat-i-gə-
bəl\ *adj* : UNTIRING — **in·de·fat·i·ga-
bly** \-blē\ *adv*

**in·de·fea·si·ble** \-'fē-zə-bəl\ *adj*
: not capable of or not liable to being
annulled, made void, or forfeited — **in-
de·fea·si·bly** \-'fē-zə-blē\ *adv*

**in·de·fin·able** \-'fī-nə-bəl\ *adj* : incapable of being precisely described or
analyzed

**in·def·i·nite** \(')in-'def-(ə-)nət\ *adj*  **1**
: not defining or identifying ⟨an is an
~ article⟩  **2** : not precise : VAGUE
**3** : having no fixed limit or amount —
**in·def·i·nite·ly** *adv* — **in·def·i-
nite·ness** *n*

**in·del·i·ble** \in-'del-ə-bəl\ *adj* [ML
*indelibilis*, fr. L *indelebilis*, fr. *delēre* to
delete, destroy]  **1** : not capable of being removed, washed away, or erased
⟨~ impression⟩  **2** : making marks
that cannot easily be removed ⟨an ~
pencil⟩ — **in·del·i·bly** \in-'del-ə-
blē\ *adv*

**in·del·i·cate** \(')in-'del-i-kət\ *adj*
: not delicate; *esp* : IMPROPER, COARSE,
TACTLESS **syn** indecent, unseemly, in-
decorous, unbecoming — **in·del·i·ca-
cy** \in-'del-ə-kə-sē\ *n*

**in·dem·ni·fy** \in-'dem-nə-,fī\ *vb*
**-fied; -fy·ing  1** : to secure against
hurt, loss, or damage  **2** : to make
compensation to for some loss or damage  **3** : to make compensation for
: make good ⟨~ a loss⟩ — **in·dem·ni-
fi·ca·tion** \-,dem-nə-fə-'kā-shən\ *n*

**in·dem·ni·ty** \in-'dem-nət-ē\ *n, pl*
**-ties  1** : security against hurt, loss, or

damage; *also* **:** exemption from incurred penalties or liabilities **2 :** something that indemnifies

¹in·dent \in-'dent\ *vb* [ME *indenten*, fr. MF *endenter*, fr. OF, fr. *dent* tooth, fr. L *dent-, dens*] **1 :** to make a toothlike cut on the edge of **2 :** INDENTURE **3 :** to space in (as the first line of a paragraph) from the margin

²indent *vb* **1 :** to force inward so as to form a depression **:** IMPRESS ⟨~ a pattern in metal⟩ **2 :** to form a dent in

in·den·ta·tion \,in-,den-'tā-shən\ *n* **1 :** NOTCH; *also* **:** a usu. deep recess (as in a coastline) **2 :** the action of indenting **:** the condition of being indented **3 :** DENT **4 :** INDENTION 2

in·den·tion \in-'den-chən\ *n* **1 :** the action of indenting **:** the condition of being indented **2 :** the blank space produced by indenting

¹in·den·ture \in-'den-chər\ *n* **1 :** a written certificate or agreement; *esp* **:** a contract binding one person (as an apprentice) to work for another for a given period of time — usu. used in pl. **2 :** INDENTATION 1 **3 :** DENT

²indenture *vb* in·den·tured; in·den·tur·ing **:** to bind (as an apprentice) by indentures

in·de·pen·dence \,in-də-'pen-dəns\ *n* **:** the quality or state of being independent **:** FREEDOM

Independence Day *n* **:** July 4 observed as a legal holiday in commemoration of the adoption of the Declaration of Independence in 1776

in·de·pen·dent \,in-də-'pen-dənt\ *adj* **1 :** SELF-GOVERNING; *also* **:** not affiliated with a larger controlling unit **2 :** not requiring or relying on something else or somebody else ⟨an ~ conclusion⟩ ⟨an ~ source of income⟩ **3 :** not easily influenced **:** showing self-reliance ⟨an ~ mind⟩ **4 :** not committed to a political party ⟨an ~ voter⟩ **5 :** refusing or disliking to look to others for help ⟨too ~ to accept charity⟩; *also* **:** marked by impatience with or annoyance at restriction ⟨a bold and ~ manner of acting⟩ **6 :** MAIN ⟨an ~ clause⟩ — independent *n* — in·de·pen·dent·ly *adv*

in·de·scrib·able \,in-di-'skrī-bə-bəl\ *adj* **1 :** that cannot be described ⟨an ~ sensation⟩ **2 :** surpassing description — in·de·scrib·ably \-blē\ *adv*

in·de·ter·mi·nate \,in-di-'tərm-(ə-)nət\ *adj* **1 :** VAGUE; *also* **:** not known in advance **2 :** not limited in advance; *also* **:** not leading to a definite end or result — in·de·ter·mi·na·cy \-(ə-)nə-sē\ *n* — in·de·ter·mi·nate·ly *adv*

¹in·dex \'in-,deks\ *n, pl* in·dex·es *or* in·di·ces \-də-,sēz\ **1 :** a guide for facilitating references; *esp* **:** an alphabetical list of items (as topics or names) treated in a printed work with the page number where each item may be found **2 :** POINTER, INDICATOR **3 :** SIGN, TOKEN ⟨an ~ of character⟩ **4 :** a list of restricted or prohibited material ⟨an ~ of forbidden books⟩ **5** *pl usu* indices **:** a number or symbol or expression (as an

exponent) associated with another to indicate a mathematical operation or use or position in an arrangement or expansion **6 :** a character ☞ used to direct attention (as to a note)

²index *vb* **1 :** to provide with or put into an index **2 :** to serve as an index of

index finger *n* **:** FOREFINGER

index number *n* **:** a number used to indicate change in magnitude (as of cost or price) as compared with the magnitude at some specified time usu. taken as 100

index of refraction **:** the ratio of the velocity of radiation in the first of two media to its velocity in the second

in·dia ink \,in-dē-ə-\ *n, often cap 1st I* **1 :** a black solid pigment used in drawing **2 :** a fluid made from india ink

In·dia·man \'in-dē-ə-mən\ *n* **:** a large sailing ship formerly used in trade with India

In·di·an \'in-dē-ən\ *n* **1 :** a native or inhabitant of the Republic or the peninsula of India **2 :** a member of any of the aboriginal peoples of No. and So. America except the Eskimo — Indian *adj*

Indian corn *n* **:** a tall widely grown American cereal grass bearing seeds on long ears; *also* **:** its ears or seeds

Indian meal *n* **:** CORNMEAL

Indian paintbrush *n* **:** any of a genus of herbaceous plants with brightly colored bracts that are related to the snapdragon

Indian pipe *n* **:** a waxy white leafless saprophytic herb of Asia and the U.S.

Indian summer *n* **:** a period of warm or mild weather in late autumn or early winter

in·dia paper \,in-dē-ə-\ *n* **1 :** a thin absorbent paper used esp. for taking impressions (as of steel engravings) **2 :** a thin tough opaque printing paper

indic *abbr* indicative

in·di·cate \'in-də-,kāt\ *vb* -cat·ed; -cat·ing **1 :** to point out or to **2 :** to state briefly **:** show indirectly **:** SUGGEST — in·di·ca·tion \,in-də-'kā-shən\ *n* — in·di·ca·tor \'in-də-,kāt-ər\ *n*

¹in·dic·a·tive \in-'dik-ət-iv\ *adj* **1 :** of, relating to, or constituting a verb form that represents a denoted act or state as an objective fact ⟨~ mood⟩ **2 :** serving to indicate ⟨actions ~ of fear⟩

²indicative *n* **1 :** the indicative mood of a language **2 :** a form in the indicative mood

in·di·cia \in-'dish-(ē-)ə\ *n pl* **1 :** distinctive marks **2 :** postal markings often imprinted on mail or on labels to be affixed to mail

in·dict \in-'dīt\ *vb* **1 :** to charge with an offense **2 :** to charge with a crime by the finding of a grand jury — in·dict·able *adj* — in·dict·ment *n*

in·dif·fer·ent \in-'dif-ərnt, -'dif-(ə-)rənt\ *adj* **1 :** UNBIASED, UNPREJUDICED **2 :** of no importance one way or the other **3 :** marked by no special liking for or dislike of something **4 :** being neither excessive nor defective

**5** : PASSABLE, MEDIOCRE  **6** : being neither right nor wrong — **in·dif·fer-
ence** \in-'dif-ərns, -'dif-(ə-)rəns\ *n* —
**in·dif·fer·ent·ly** *adv*

**in·dig·e·nous** \in-'dij-ə-nəs\ *adj* : produced, growing, or living naturally in a
particular region

**in·di·gent** \'in-di-jənt\ *adj* : IMPOVER-
ISHED, NEEDY — **in·di·gence** \-jəns\ *n*

**in·di·gest·ible** \,in-dī-'jes-tə-bəl, -də\
*adj* : not readily digested

**in·di·ges·tion** \-'jes-chən\ *n* : inadequate or difficult digestion : DYSPEPSIA

**in·dig·nant** \in-'dig-nənt\ *adj* : filled
with or marked by indignation — **in-
dig·nant·ly** *adv*

**in·dig·na·tion** \,in-dig-'nā-shən\ *n*
: anger aroused by something unjust,
unworthy, or mean

**in·dig·ni·ty** \in-'dig-nət-ē\ *n, pl* **-ties**
: an offense against personal dignity or
self-respect; *also* : humiliating treatment

**in·di·go** \'in-di-gō\ *n, pl* **-gos** *or*
**-goes** [It dial., fr. L *indicum*, fr. Gk
*indikon*, fr. *indikos* Indic, fr. *Indos*
India] **1** : a blue dye obtained from
plants or synthesized  **2** : a color between blue and violet

**indigo bunting** *n* : a common small
finch of the eastern U.S. of which the
male is largely indigo blue

**indigo snake** *n* : a large harmless blue-
black snake of the southern U.S.

**in·di·rect** \,in-də-'rekt, -dī-\ *adj* **1**
: not straight ⟨an ~ route⟩  **2** : not
straightforward and open ⟨~ methods⟩
**3** : not having a plainly seen connection
⟨an ~ cause⟩  **4** : not directly to the
point ⟨an ~ answer⟩ — **in·di·rec-
tion** \-'rek-shən\ *n* — **in·di·rect·ly**
\-'rek-(t)lē\ *adv* — **in·di·rect·ness**
\-'rek(t)-nəs\ *n*

**indirect tax** *n* : a tax exacted from a
person other than the one on whom the
ultimate burden of the tax will fall

**in·dis·creet** \,in-dis-'krēt\ *adj* : not
discreet : IMPRUDENT — **in·dis·cre-
tion** \-dis-'kresh-ən\ *n*

**in·dis·crim·i·nate** \,in-dis-'krim-ə-
nət\ *adj* **1** : not marked by discrimination or careful distinction  **2** : HAPHAZ-
ARD, RANDOM  **3** : UNRESTRAINED  **4**
: JUMBLED, CONFUSED — **in·dis·crim-
i·nate·ly** *adv*

**in·dis·pens·able** \,in-dis-'pen-sə-bəl\
*adj* : absolutely essential : REQUISITE —
**in·dis·pens·abil·i·ty** \-,pen-sə-'bil-
ət-ē\ *n* — **indispensable** *n* — **in-
dis·pens·ably** \-'pen-sə-blē\ *adv*

**in·dis·posed** \-'pōzd\ *adj* **1** : slightly
ill  **2** : AVERSE — **in·dis·po·si·tion**
\(,)in-,dis-pə-'zish-ən\ *n*

**in·dis·put·able** \,in-dis-'pyüt-ə-bəl,
(')in-'dis-pyət-\ *adj* : not disputable
: UNQUESTIONABLE ⟨~ proof⟩ — **in-
dis·put·ably** \-blē\ *adv*

**in·dis·sol·u·ble** \,in-dis-'äl-yə-bəl\
*adj* : not capable of being dissolved, undone, or broken : PERMANENT

**in·dis·tinct** \,in-dis-'tiŋkt\ *adj* **1**
: not sharply outlined or separable
: BLURRED, FAINT, DIM  **2** : not readily
distinguishable : UNCERTAIN — **in·dis-
tinct·ly** *adv* — **in·dis·tinct·ness** *n*

**in·dite** \in-'dīt\ *vb* **in·dit·ed; in·dit-
ing** : COMPOSE ⟨~ a poem⟩; *also* : to
put in writing ⟨~ a letter⟩

**in·di·um** \'in-dē-əm\ *n* : a malleable
tarnish-resistant silvery metallic chemical element

¹**in·di·vid·u·al** \,in-də-'vij-(ə-w)əl\ *adj*
**1** : of, relating to, or used by an individual ⟨~ traits⟩  **2** : being an individual
: existing as an indivisible whole  **3**
: intended for one person ⟨an ~ serv-
ing⟩  **4** : SEPARATE ⟨~ copies⟩  **5**
: having marked individuality ⟨an ~
style⟩ — **in·di·vid·u·al·ly** \-ē\ *adv*

²**individual** *n* **1** : a single member of a
category : a particular person, animal,
or thing  **2** : PERSON ⟨a disagreeable ~⟩

**in·di·vid·u·al·ism** \,in-də-'vij-ə-(wə-)
,liz-əm\ *n* **1** : EGOISM  **2** : a doctrine
that the chief end of society is to promote the welfare of its individual members  **3** : a doctrine holding that the
individual has certain political or economic rights with which the state must
not interfere

**in·di·vid·u·al·ist** \-ləst\ *n* **1** : one
that pursues a markedly independent
course in thought or action  **2** : one
that advocates or practices individual-
ism — **individualist** *or* **in·di·vid·u-
al·is·tic** \-,vij-ə-(wə)-'lis-tik\ *adj*

**in·di·vid·u·al·i·ty** \-,vij-ə-'wal-ət-ē\
*n, pl* **-ties** **1** : the sum of qualities that
characterize and distinguish an individual from all others; *also* : PERSONALITY
**2** : INDIVIDUAL, PERSON  **3** : separate or
distinct existence

**in·di·vid·u·al·ize** \-'vij-ə-(wə)-,līz\
*vb* **-ized; -iz·ing** **1** : to make individual in character  **2** : to treat or notice
individually : PARTICULARIZE  **3** : to
adapt to the needs of an individual

**in·di·vid·u·ate** \,in-də-'vij-ə-,wāt\ *vb*
**-at·ed; -at·ing** : to give individuality
to : form into an individual — **in·di-
vid·u·a·tion** \-,vij-ə-'wā-shən\ *n*

**in·di·vis·i·ble** \,in-də-'viz-ə-bəl\ *adj*
: not divisible — **in·di·vis·i·bil·i·ty**
\-,viz-ə-'bil-ət-ē\ *n* — **in·di·vis·i·bly**
\-'viz-ə-blē\ *adv*

**in·doc·tri·nate** \in-'däk-trə-,nāt\ *vb*
**-nat·ed; -nat·ing** **1** : to instruct esp.
in fundamentals or rudiments : TEACH
**2** : to imbue with a usu. partisan or
sectarian opinion, point of view, or
principle — **in·doc·tri·na·tion** \(,)in-
,däk-trə-'nā-shən\ *n*

**In·do-Eu·ro·pe·an** \,in-dō-,yur-ə-'pē-
ən\ *adj* : of, relating to, or constituting
a family of languages comprising those
spoken in most of Europe and in the
parts of the world colonized by Europeans since 1500 and also in Persia,
the subcontinent of India, and some
other parts of Asia

**in·do·lent** \'in-də-lənt\ *adj* [LL *indo-
lens* insensitive to pain, fr. L *dolēre* to
feel pain] **1** : slow to develop or heal
⟨~ ulcers⟩  **2** : LAZY — **in·do·lence**
\-ləns\ *n*

**in·dom·i·ta·ble** \in-'däm-ət-ə-bəl\ *adj*
: UNCONQUERABLE ⟨~ courage⟩ — **in-
dom·i·ta·bly** \-blē\ *adv*

**In·do·ne·sian** \,in-də-'nē-zhən\ *n* : a

native or inhabitant of the Republic of Indonesia — **Indonesian** *adj*

**in·door** \'in-,dōr\ *adj* **1** : of, or relating to, the interior of a building **2** : done, living, or belonging within doors

**in·doors** \in-'dōrz\ *adv* : in or into a building

**indorse** *var of* ENDORSE

**in·du·bi·ta·ble** \(')in-'d(y)ü-bət-ə-bəl\ *adj* : UNQUESTIONABLE — **in·du·bi·ta·bly** \-blē\ *adv*

**in·duce** \in-'d(y)üs\ *vb* **in·duced; in·duc·ing** **1** : to prevail upon : PERSUADE, INFLUENCE **2** : to bring on or bring about ⟨illness *induced* by overwork⟩ **3** : to produce (as an electric current or charge) by induction **4** : to determine by induction; *esp* : to infer from particulars — **in·duc·er** *n*

**in·duce·ment** \in-'d(y)üs-mənt\ *n* **1** : the act or process of inducing **2** : something that induces : MOTIVE

**in·duct** \in-'dəkt\ *vb* **1** : to place in office **2** : to admit as a member **3** : to enroll for military training or service (as under a selective-service act)

**in·duc·tance** \in-'dək-təns\ *n* : a property of an electric circuit by which a varying current produces an electromotive force in that circuit or in a nearby circuit

**in·duct·ee** \(,)in-,dək-'tē\ *n* : a person inducted into military service

**in·duc·tion** \in-'dək-shən\ *n* **1** : INSTALLATION; *also* : INITIATION **2** : the formality by which a civilian is inducted into military service **3** : reasoning from a part to a whole or from particular instances to a general conclusion; *also* : the conclusion so reached **4** : the process by which an electric current, an electric charge, or magnetism is produced in a body by the proximity of an electric or magnetic field

**in·duc·tive** \in-'dək-tiv\ *adj* **1** : of, relating to, or employing reasoning by induction **2** : of or relating to inductance or electrical induction

**indue** *var of* ENDUE

**in·dulge** \in-'dəlj\ *vb* **in·dulged; in·dulg·ing** **1** : to give free rein to : GRATIFY ⟨~ a taste for exotic dishes⟩ **2** : to yield to the desire of ⟨~ a sick child⟩ **3** : to gratify one's taste or desire for ⟨~ in alcohol⟩

**in·dul·gence** \in-'dəl-jəns\ *n* **1** : remission of temporal punishment due in Roman Catholic doctrine for sins whose eternal punishment has been remitted by reception of the sacrifice of penance **2** : the act of indulging : the state of being indulgent **3** : an indulgent act **4** : the thing indulged in **5** : SELF-INDULGENCE — **in·dul·gent** \-jənt\ *adj* — **in·dul·gent·ly** *adv*

¹**in·du·rate** \'in-d(y)ə-rət\ *adj* : physically or morally hardened

²**in·du·rate** \in-d(y)ə-,rāt\ *vb* **-rat·ed; -rat·ing** **1** : to make unfeeling, stubborn, or obdurate **2** : to make hardy : INURE **3** : to make hard or fibrous ⟨great heat ~s clay⟩ ⟨*indurated* tissue⟩ **4** : to grow hard : HARDEN — **in·du·ra·tion** \,in-d(y)ə-'rā-shən\ *n* — **in-**

**du·ra·tive** \'in-d(y)ə-,rāt-iv, in-'d(y)ür-ət-\ *adj*

**in·dus·tri·al** \in-'dəs-trē-əl\ *adj* : of, relating to, or having to do with industry — **in·dus·tri·al·ly** \-ē\ *adv*

**in·dus·tri·al·ist** \-ə-ləst\ *n* : a person owning or engaged in the management of an industry : MANUFACTURER

**in·dus·tri·al·ize** \in-'dəs-trē-ə-,līz\ *vb* **-ized; -iz·ing** : to make or become industrial — **in·dus·tri·al·iza·tion** \-,dəs-trē-ə-lə-'zā-shən\ *n*

**in·dus·tri·ous** \in-'dəs-trē-əs\ *adj* : DILIGENT, BUSY — **in·dus·tri·ous·ly** *adv* — **in·dus·tri·ous·ness** *n*

**in·dus·try** \'in-(,)dəs-trē\ *n, pl* **-tries** **1** : DILIGENCE **2** : a department or branch of a craft, art, business, or manufacture; *esp* : one that employs a large personnel and capital **3** : a distinct group of productive enterprises **4** : manufacturing activity as a whole

**in·dwell** \(')in-'dwel\ *vb* : to exist within as an activating spirit, force, or principle

¹**ine·bri·ate** \in-'ē-brē-,āt\ *vb* **-at·ed; -at·ing** : to make drunk : INTOXICATE — **ine·bri·a·tion** \-,ē-brē-'ā-shən\ *n*

²**ine·bri·ate** \-ət\ *n* : one that is drunk; *esp* : an habitual drunkard

**in·ed·it·ed** \(')in-'ed-ət-əd\ *adj* : UNPUBLISHED

**in·ef·fa·ble** \(')in-'ef-ə-bəl\ *adj* **1** : incapable of being expressed in words : INDESCRIBABLE ⟨~ joy⟩ **2** : UNSPEAKABLE ⟨~ disgust⟩ **3** : not to be uttered : TABOO ⟨the ~ name of Jehovah⟩ — **in·ef·fa·bly** \-blē\ *adv*

**in·ef·face·able** \,in-ə-'fā-sə-bəl\ *adj* : not effaceable : INERADICABLE

**in·ef·fec·tive** \,in-ə-'fek-tiv\ *adj* **1** : not effective : INEFFECTUAL **2** : INCAPABLE — **in·ef·fec·tive·ly** *adv*

**in·ef·fec·tu·al** \,in-ə-'fek-chə(-wə)l\ *adj* : not producing the proper or usual effect — **in·ef·fec·tu·al·ly** \-ē\ *adv*

**in·ef·fi·cient** \,in-ə-'fish-ənt\ *adj* **1** : not producing the effect intended or desired **2** : INCAPABLE, INCOMPETENT — **in·ef·fi·cien·cy** \-'fish-ən-sē\ *n* — **in·ef·fi·cient·ly** *adv*

**in·el·e·gant** \(')in-'el-i-gənt\ *adj* : lacking in refinement, grace, or good taste — **in·el·e·gance** \-gəns\ *n*

**in·el·i·gi·ble** \(')in-'el-ə-jə-bəl\ *adj* : not qualified to be chosen for an office — **in·el·i·gi·bil·i·ty** \(,)in-,el-ə-jə-'bil-ət-ē\ *n* — **ineligible** *n*

**in·eluc·ta·ble** \,in-i-'lək-tə-bəl\ *adj* : not to be avoided, changed, or resisted

**in·ept** \in-'ept\ *adj* **1** : lacking in fitness or aptitude : UNFIT **2** : being out of place : INAPPROPRIATE **3** : FOOLISH **4** : generally incompetent : BUNGLING — **in·ep·ti·tude** \in-'ep-tə-,t(y)üd\ *n* — **in·ept·ly** *adv* — **in·ept·ness** *n*

**in·equal·i·ty** \,in-i-'kwäl-ət-ē\ *n* **1** : the quality of being unequal or uneven; *esp* : UNEVENNESS, DISPARITY, CHANGEABLENESS **2** : an instance of being unequal (as in position, proportion, evenness, or regularity)

**in·er·rant** \(')in-'er-ənt\ *adj* : INFALLIBLE

**in·ert** \in-'ərt\ *adj* [L *inert-, iners* unskilled, idle, fr. *art-, ars* skill] 1 : powerless to move itself 2 : lacking in active properties ⟨chemically ∼⟩ 3 : SLUGGISH — **in·ert·ly** *adv* — **in·ert·ness** *n*

**in·er·tia** \in-'ər-sh(ē-)ə\ *n* 1 : a property of matter whereby it remains at rest or continues in uniform motion unless acted upon by some outside force 2 : INERTNESS, SLUGGISHNESS — **in·er·tial** \-shəl\ *adj*

**in·es·cap·able** \,in-ə-'skā-pə-bəl\ *adj* : incapable of being escaped : INEVITABLE — **in·es·cap·ably** \-blē\ *adv*

**in·es·ti·ma·ble** \(')in-'es-tə-mə-bəl\ *adj* 1 : incapable of being estimated or computed ⟨∼ errors⟩ 2 : too valuable or excellent to be fully appreciated ⟨an ∼ service to his country⟩ — **in·es·ti·ma·bly** \-blē\ *adv*

**in·ev·i·ta·ble** \in-'ev-ət-ə-bəl\ *adj* : incapable of being avoided or evaded ⟨bound to happen — **in·ev·i·ta·bil·i·ty** \(,)in-,ev-ət-ə-'bil-ət-ē\ *n* — **in·ev·i·ta·bly** \in-'ev-ət-ə-blē\ *adv*

**in·ex·act** \,in-ig-'zakt\ *adj* 1 : not precisely correct or true : INACCURATE 2 : not rigorous and careful — **in·ex·act·ly** \-'zak-(t)lē\ *adv*

**in·ex·cus·able** \,in-ik-'skyü-zə-bəl\ *adj* : being without excuse or justification — **in·ex·cus·ably** \-blē\ *adv*

**in·ex·haust·ible** \,in-ig-'zȯ-stə-bəl\ *adj* 1 : incapable of being used up ⟨an ∼ supply⟩ 2 : UNTIRING — **in·ex·haust·ibly** \-blē\ *adv*

**in·ex·o·ra·ble** \(')in-'eks-(ə-)rə-bəl\ *adj* : not to be moved by entreaty : RELENTLESS — **in·ex·o·ra·bly** *adv*

**in·ex·pe·ri·ence** \,in-ik-'spir-ē-əns\ *n* : lack of experience or of knowledge or proficiency gained by experience — **in·ex·pe·ri·enced** \-ənst\ *adj*

**in·ex·pert** \(')in-'ek-,spərt\ *adj* 1 : INEXPERIENCED 2 : not expert : UNSKILLED — **in·ex·pert·ly** *adv*

**in·ex·pi·a·ble** \(')in-'ek-spē-ə-bəl\ *adj* : not capable of being atoned for

**in·ex·pli·ca·ble** \,in-ik-'splik-ə-bəl, (')in-'ek-(,)splik-\ *adj* : incapable of being explained or accounted for — **in·ex·pli·ca·bly** \-blē\ *adv*

**in·ex·press·ible** \,in-ik-'spres-ə-bəl\ *adj* : not capable of being expressed — **in·ex·press·ibly** \-blē\ *adv*

**in ex·tre·mis** \,in-ik-'strā-məs, -'strē-\ *adv* : in extreme circumstances; *esp* : at the point of death

**in·ex·tri·ca·ble** \,in-ik-'strik-ə-bəl, (')in-'ek-(,)strik-\ *adj* 1 : forming a maze or tangle from which it is impossible to get free 2 : incapable of being disentangled or untied : UNSOLVABLE — **in·ex·tri·ca·bly** \-blē\ *adv*

**inf** *abbr* 1 infantry 2 infinitive

**in·fal·li·ble** \(')in-'fal-ə-bəl\ *adj* 1 : incapable of error : UNERRING 2 : SURE, CERTAIN ⟨an ∼ remedy⟩ — **in·fal·li·bil·i·ty** \(,)in-,fal-ə-'bil-ət-ē\ *n* — **in·fal·li·bly** \(')in-'fal-ə-blē\ *adv*

**in·fa·mous** \'in-fə-məs\ *adj* 1 : having a reputation of the worst kind 2 : DISGRACEFUL — **in·fa·mous·ly** *adv*

**in·fa·my** \-mē\ *n, pl* **-mies** 1 : evil reputation brought about by something grossly criminal, shocking, or brutal 2 : an extreme and publicly known criminal or evil act 3 : the state of being infamous

**in·fan·cy** \'in-fən-sē\ *n, pl* **-cies** 1 : early childhood 2 : a beginning or early period of existence

**in·fant** \'in-fənt\ *n* [ME *enfaunt,* fr. MF *enfant,* fr. L *infant-, infans,* incapable of speech, young, fr. *fant-, fans,* prp. of *fari* to speak] : BABY; *also* : a person who is a legal minor

**in·fan·ti·cide** \in-'fant-ə-,sīd\ *n* : the killing of an infant; *also* : one who kills an infant

**in·fan·tile** \'in-fən-,tīl, -t'l, -,tēl\ *adj* : of or relating to infants; *also* : CHILDISH

**infantile paralysis** *n* : POLIOMYELITIS

**in·fan·try** \'in-fən-trē\ *n, pl* **-tries** [MF & It; MF *infanterie,* fr. It *infanteria,* fr. *infante* boy, foot soldier] : soldiers trained, armed, and equipped for service on foot

**in·farct** \'in-,färkt\ *n* : an area of dead tissue (as of the heart wall) caused by blocking of local blood circulation — **in·farc·tion** \in-'färk-shən\ *n*

**in·fat·u·ate** \in-'fach-ə-,wāt\ *vb* **-at·ed; -at·ing** : to inspire with a foolish or extravagant love or admiration — **in·fat·u·a·tion** \-,fach-ə-'wā-shən\ *n*

**in·fect** \in-'fekt\ *vb* 1 : to contaminate with disease-producing matter 2 : to communicate a germ or disease to 3 : to influence so as to induce sympathy, belief, or support

**in·fec·tion** \in-'fek-shən\ *n* 1 : an act of infecting : the state of being infected 2 : a communicable disease; *also* : an infective agent (as a germ) — **in·fec·tious** \-shəs\ *adj* — **in·fec·tive** \-'fek-tiv\ *adj*

**in·fe·lic·i·tous** \,in-fi-'lis-ət-əs\ *adj* : not apt in application or expression — **in·fe·lic·i·ty** \-ət-ē\ *n*

**in·fer** \in-'fər\ *vb* **in·ferred; in·fer·ring** 1 : to derive as a conclusion from facts or premises 2 : GUESS, SURMISE 3 : to lead to as a conclusion or consequence 4 : HINT, SUGGEST **syn** deduce, conclude, judge, gather — **in·fer·ence** \'in-f(ə-)rəns\ *n* — **in·fer·en·tial** \,in-fə-'ren-chəl\ *adj*

**in·fe·ri·or** \in-'fir-ē-ər\ *adj* : situated lower (as in position, degree, rank, or merit) — **inferior** *n* — **in·fe·ri·or·i·ty** \(,)in-,fir-ē-'ȯr-ət-ē\ *n*

**in·fer·nal** \in-'fərn-²l\ *adj* 1 : of or relating to hell ⟨∼ fires⟩ 2 : HELLISH, FIENDISH ⟨∼ schemes⟩ 3 : DAMNABLE, DAMNED — **in·fer·nal·ly** \-ē\ *adv*

**in·fer·no** \in-'fər-nō\ *n, pl* **-nos** [It, hell, fr. LL *infernus* hell, fr. L *infernus* lower] : a place or a state that resembles or suggests hell

**in·fer·tile** \(')in-'fərt-²l\ *adj* : not fertile or productive : BARREN — **in·fer·til·i·ty** \,in-fər-'til-ət-ē\ *n*

**in·fest** \in-'fest\ *vb* : to trouble by spreading or swarming in or over; *also* : to live in or on as a parasite — **in-**

fes·ta·tion \,in-,fes-'tā-shən\ n

in·fi·del \'in-fəd-'l, -fə,del\ n 1 : one who is not a Christian or opposes Christianity 2 : an unbeliever esp. in respect to a particular religion

in·fi·del·i·ty \,in-fə-'del-ət-ē, -fī-\ n, pl -ties 1 : lack of belief in a religion 2 : UNFAITHFULNESS, DISLOYALTY

in·field \'in-,fēld\ n : the part of a baseball field inside the base lines — in·field·er n

in·fight·ing \'in-,fīt-iŋ\ n : fighting or boxing at close quarters

in·fil·trate \in-'fil-,trāt, 'in-(,)fil-\ vb -trat·ed; -trat·ing 1 : to enter or filter into or through something 2 : to pass into or through by or as if by filtering or permeating — in·fil·tra·tion \,in-(,)fil-'trā-shən\ n

in·fi·nite \'in-fə-nət\ adj 1 : LIMITLESS, BOUNDLESS, ENDLESS ⟨~ space⟩ ⟨~ wisdom⟩ ⟨~ patience⟩ 2 : VAST, IMMENSE; also : INEXHAUSTIBLE ⟨~ wealth⟩ 3 : greater than any preassigned finite value however large ⟨~ number of positive integers⟩; also : extending to infinity ⟨~ plane surface⟩ — infinite n — in·fi·nite·ly adv

in·fin·i·tes·i·mal \(,)in,fin-ə-'tes-ə-məl\ adj : immeasurably or incalculably small : very minute — in·fin·i·tes·i·mal·ly \-ē\ adv

in·fin·i·tive \in-'fin-ət-iv\ n : a verb form having the characteristics of both verb and noun and in English usu. being used with to

in·fin·i·tude \in-'fin-ə-,t(y)üd\ n 1 : the quality or state of being infinite 2 : something that is infinite esp. in extent

in·fin·i·ty \in-'fin-ət-ē\ n, pl -ties 1 : the quality of being infinite 2 : unlimited extent of time, space, or quantity : BOUNDLESSNESS 3 : an indefinitely great number or amount

in·firm \in-'fərm\ adj 1 : deficient in vitality; esp : feeble from age 2 : not solid or stable : INSECURE

in·fir·ma·ry \in-'fərm-(ə-)rē\ n, pl -ries : a place for the care of the infirm or sick

in·fir·mi·ty \in-'fər-mət-ē\ n, pl -ties 1 : FEEBLENESS 2 : DISEASE, AILMENT 3 : a personal failing : FOIBLE

infl abbr influenced

in·flame \in-'flām\ vb in·flamed; in·flam·ing 1 : KINDLE 2 : to excite to excessive or unnatural action or feeling; also : INTENSIFY 3 : to affect or become affected with inflammation

in·flam·ma·ble \in-'flam-ə-bəl\ adj 1 : FLAMMABLE 2 : easily inflamed, excited, or angered : IRASCIBLE

in·flam·ma·tion \,in-flə-'mā-shən\ n : a bodily response to injury in which an affected area becomes red, hot, and painful and congested with blood

in·flam·ma·to·ry \in-'flam-ə-,tōr-ē\ adj 1 : tending to excite the senses or to arouse anger, disorder, or tumult : SEDITIOUS 2 : causing or accompanied by inflammation ⟨an ~ disease⟩

in·flate \in-'flāt\ vb in·flat·ed; in·flat·ing 1 : to swell with air or gas ⟨~ a balloon⟩ 2 : to puff up : ELATE ⟨inflated with pride⟩ 3 : to expand or increase abnormally ⟨inflated prices⟩ — in·flat·able adj

in·fla·tion \in-'flā-shən\ n 1 : an act of inflating : the state of being inflated 2 : empty pretentiousness : POMPOSITY 3 : an abnormal increase in the volume of money and credit resulting in a substantial and continuing rise in the general price level

in·fla·tion·ary \-shə-,ner-ē\ adj : of, characterized by, or productive of inflation

in·fla·tion·ism \-shə-,niz-əm\ n : the policy of economic inflation — in·fla·tion·ist \-sh(ə-)nəst\ n or adj

in·flect \in-'flekt\ vb 1 : to turn from a direct line or course : CURVE 2 : to vary a word by inflection 3 : to change or vary the pitch of the voice

in·flec·tion \in-'flek-shən\ n 1 : the act or result of curving or bending 2 : a change in pitch or loudness of the voice 3 : the change of form that words undergo to mark case, gender, number, tense, person, mood, or voice — in·flec·tion·al \-sh(ə-)nəl\ adj

in·flex·i·ble \(')in-'flek-sə-bəl\ adj 1 : RIGID 2 : UNYIELDING 3 : UNALTERABLE — in·flex·i·bil·i·ty \(,)in-,flek-sə-'bil-ət-ē\ n — in·flex·i·bly \(')in-'flek-sə-blē\ adv

in·flex·ion \in-'flek-shən\ chiefly Brit var of INFLECTION

in·flict \in-'flikt\ vb : to give or deliver by or as if by striking : IMPOSE, AFFLICT — in·flic·tion \-'flik-shən\ n

in·flo·res·cence \,in-flə-'res-'ns\ n : the manner of development and arrangement of flowers on a stem; also : a flowering stem with its appendages : a flower cluster

in·flow \'in-,flō\ n : INFLUX

¹in·flu·ence \'in-,flü-əns\ n 1 : the act or power of producing an effect without apparent force or direct authority 2 : the power or capacity of causing an effect in indirect or intangible ways ⟨under the ~ of liquor⟩ 3 : a person or thing that exerts influence — in·flu·en·tial \,in-flü-'en-chəl\ adj

²influence vb -enced; -enc·ing 1 : to affect or alter by influence : SWAY 2 : to have an effect on the condition or development of : MODIFY

in·flu·en·za \,in-flü-'en-zə\ n [It, lit., influence, fr. ML influentia; fr. the belief that epidemics were due to the influence of the stars] : an acute and very contagious virus disease marked by fever, prostration, aches and pains, and respiratory inflammation; also : any of various feverish usu. virus diseases typically with respiratory symptoms

in·flux \'in-,fləks\ n : a flowing in

in·fo \'in-(,)fō\ n : INFORMATION

in·fold \in-'fōld\ vb 1 : ENFOLD 2 : to fold inward or toward one another

in·form \in-'fōrm\ vb 1 : to communicate knowledge to : TELL 2 : to give information or knowledge 3 : to act as an informer syn acquaint, apprise, advise, notify

**in·for·mal** \(')in-'fȯr-məl\ *adj* **1** : conducted or carried out without formality or ceremony ⟨an ∼ party⟩ **2** : characteristic of or appropriate to ordinary, casual, or familiar use ⟨∼ clothes⟩ — **in·for·mal·i·ty** \,in-fȯr-'mal-ət-ē, -fər-\ *n* — **in·for·mal·ly** \(')in-'fȯr-mə-lē\ *adv*

**in·for·mant** \in-'fȯr-mənt\ *n* : one who gives information : INFORMER

**in·for·ma·tion** \,in-fər-'mā-shən\ *n* **1** : the communication or reception of knowledge or intelligence **2** : knowledge obtained from investigation, study, or instruction : FACTS, DATA — **in·for·ma·tion·al** \-sh(ə-)nəl\ *adj*

**in·for·ma·tive** \in-'fȯr-mət-iv\ *adj* : imparting knowledge : INSTRUCTIVE

**in·formed** \in-'fȯrmd\ *adj* : EDUCATED, INTELLIGENT

**in·form·er** \-'fȯr-mər\ *n* : one that informs; *esp* : a person who secretly provides information about the activities of another

**in·frac·tion** \in-'frak-shən\ *n* : the act of infringing : VIOLATION

**in·fra dig** \,in-frə-'dig\ *adj* [short for L *infra dignitatem*] : being beneath one's dignity

**in·fra·red** \,in-frə-'red\ *adj* : being, relating to, or using invisible heat rays having wavelengths longer than those of red light — **infrared** *n*

**in·fra·son·ic** \-'sän-ik\ *adj* : having a frequency below the audibility range of the human ear ⟨∼ vibration⟩

**in·fre·quent** \(')in-'frē-kwənt\ *adj* **1** : seldom happening : RARE **2** : placed or occurring at considerable distances or intervals : OCCASIONAL **syn** uncommon, scarce, rare, sporadic — **in·fre·quent·ly** *adv*

**in·fringe** \in-'frinj\ *vb* **in·fringed; in·fring·ing** **1** : VIOLATE, TRANSGRESS ⟨∼ a treaty⟩ **2** : ENCROACH, TRESPASS — **in·fringe·ment** *n*

**in·fu·ri·ate** \in-'fyu̇r-ē-,āt\ *vb* **-at·ed; -at·ing** : to make furious : ENRAGE — **in·fu·ri·at·ing·ly** \-,āt-iŋ-lē\ *adv*

**in·fuse** \in-'fyüz\ *vb* **in·fused; in·fus·ing** **1** : to instill a principle or quality in : INTRODUCE **2** : INSPIRE, ANIMATE **3** : to steep (as tea) without boiling — **in·fu·sion** \-'fyü-zhən\ *n*

**in·fus·ible** \(')in-'fyü-zə-bəl\ *adj* : incapable of being fused : very difficult to fuse

**¹-ing** \iŋ\ *vb suffix or adj suffix* — used to form the present participle ⟨sail*ing*⟩ and sometimes to form an adjective resembling a present participle but not derived from a verb ⟨swashbuckl*ing*⟩

**²-ing** *n suffix* : one of a (specified) kind

**³-ing** *n suffix* **1** : action or process ⟨sleep*ing*⟩ **2** : instance of an action or process ⟨a meet*ing*⟩ **2** : product or result of an action or process ⟨an engrav*ing*⟩ ⟨earn*ings*⟩ **3** : something used in an action or process ⟨a bed cover*ing*⟩ **4** : something connected with, consisting of, or used in making (a specified thing) ⟨scaffold*ing*⟩ **5** : something related to (a specified concept) ⟨off*ing*⟩

**in·gath·er·ing** \'in-,gath-(ə-)riŋ\ *n* **1** : COLLECTION, HARVEST **2** : ASSEMBLY

**in·ge·nious** \in-'jēn-yəs\ *adj* **1** : marked by special aptitude at discovering, inventing, or contriving **2** : marked by originality, resourcefulness, and cleverness in conception or execution — **in·ge·nious·ly** *adv* — **in·ge·nious·ness** *n*

**in·ge·nue** *or* **in·gé·nue** \'an-jə-,nü, 'än-; 'a²-zhə-, 'ä²-\ *n* : a naive girl or young woman; *esp* : an actress representing such a person

**in·ge·nu·ity** \,in-jə-'n(y)ü-ət-ē\ *n, pl* **-ities** : skill or cleverness in planning or inventing : INVENTIVENESS

**in·gen·u·ous** \in-'jen-yə-wəs\ *adj* [L *ingenuus* native, free born, fr. *gignere* to beget] **1** : STRAIGHTFORWARD, FRANK **2** : NAIVE — **in·gen·u·ous·ly** *adv* — **in·gen·u·ous·ness** *n*

**in·gest** \in-'jest\ *vb* : to take in for or as if for digestion : ABSORB — **in·ges·tion** \-'jes-chən\ *n*

**in·gle** \'iŋ-gəl\ *n* **1** : FLAME, BLAZE **2** : FIREPLACE

**in·gle·nook** \-,nu̇k\ *n* **1** : a corner by the fire or chimney **2** : a high-backed wooden settee placed close to a fireplace

**in·glo·ri·ous** \(')in-'glȯr-ē-əs\ *adj* **1** : not glorious : lacking fame or honor **2** : SHAMEFUL — **in·glo·ri·ous·ly** *adv*

**in·got** \'iŋ-gət\ *n* : a mass of metal cast in a form convenient for storage or transportation

**ingraft** *var of* ENGRAFT

**¹in·grain** \(')in-'grān\ *vb* : to work indelibly into the natural texture or mental or moral constitution : IMBUE — **in·grained** *adj*

**²in·grain** \,in-,grān\ *adj* **1** : made of fiber that is dyed before being spun into yarn **2** : made of yarn that is dyed before being woven or knitted **3** : INNATE — **in·grain** \'in-,grān\ *n*

**in·grate** \'in-,grāt\ *n* : an ungrateful person

**in·gra·ti·ate** \in-'grā-shē-,āt\ *vb* **-at·ed; -at·ing** : to gain favor by deliberate effort

**in·gra·ti·at·ing** *adj* **1** : capable of winning favor : PLEASING ⟨an ∼ smile⟩ **2** : FLATTERING ⟨an ∼ manner⟩

**in·grat·i·tude** \(')in-'grat-ə-,t(y)üd\ *n* : lack of gratitude : UNGRATEFULNESS

**in·gre·di·ent** \in-'grēd-ē-ənt\ *n* : one of the substances that make up a mixture or compound : CONSTITUENT

**in·gress** \'in-,gres\ *n* : ENTRANCE, ACCESS

**in·grow·ing** \'in-,grō-iŋ\ *adj* : grown in; *esp* : having the free tip or edge embedded in the flesh ⟨∼ toenail⟩

**in·grown** \-,grōn\ *adj* : grown in and esp. into the flesh ⟨an ∼ toenail⟩

**in·gui·nal** \'iŋ-gwən-ᵊl\ *adj* : of, relating to, or situated in the region of the groin

**in·hab·it** \in-'hab-ət\ *vb* : to live or dwell in — **in·hab·it·able** *adj*

**in·hab·it·ant** \in-'hab-ət-ənt\ *n* : a permanent resident in a place

**in·hal·ant** \in-'hā-lənt\ *n* : something (as a medicine) that is inhaled

**in·ha·la·tor** \'in-(h)ə-,lāt-ər\ *n* : an

apparatus used in inhaling something

**in·hale** \in-'hāl\ vb **in·haled; in·hal·ing** : to draw in in breathing : draw air into the lungs — **in·ha·la·tion** \,in-(h)ə-'lā-shən\ n

**in·hal·er** \in-'hā-lər\ n : a device by means of which material can be inhaled

**in·here** \in-'hiər\ vb **in·hered; in·her·ing** : to be inherent : BELONG

**in·her·ent** \in-'hir-ənt, -'her-\ adj : established as an essential part of something : INTRINSIC — **in·her·ent·ly** adv

**in·her·it** \in-'her-ət\ vb : to receive esp. from one's ancestors — **in·her·i·tance** \-ət-əns\ n — **in·her·i·tor** \-ət-ər\ n

**in·hib·it** \in-'hib-ət\ vb **1** : PROHIBIT, FORBID **2** : to hold in check : RESTRAIN

**in·hi·bi·tion** \,in-(h)ə-'bish-ən\ n **1** : PROHIBITION, RESTRAINT **2** : a usu. inner check on free activity, expression, or functioning

**in·house** \,in-,haus, 'in-'haus\ adj : of, relating to, or carried on within a group or organization ⟨~ training⟩

**in·hu·man** \(')in-'(h)yü-mən\ adj **1** : lacking pity or kindness : CRUEL, SAVAGE **2** : COLD, IMPERSONAL **3** : not worthy of or conforming to the needs of human beings **4** : of or suggesting a nonhuman class of beings — **in·hu·man·ly** adv

**in·hu·mane** \,in-(h)yü-'mān\ adj : not humane : INHUMAN **1**

**in·hu·man·i·ty** \-'man-ət-ē\ n, pl **-ities 1** : the quality or state of being cruel or barbarous **2** : a cruel or barbarous act

**in·hume** \in-'hyüm\ vb **in·humed; in·hum·ing** : BURY, INTER — **in·hu·ma·tion** \,in-hyü-'mā-shən\ n

**in·im·i·cal** \in-'im-i-kəl\ adj **1** : HOSTILE, UNFRIENDLY **2** : HARMFUL, ADVERSE — **in·im·i·cal·ly** \-ē\ adv

**in·im·i·ta·ble** \(')in-'im-ət-ə-bəl\ adj : not capable of being imitated

**in·iq·ui·ty** \in-'ik-wət-ē\ n, pl **-ties** [ME iniquite, fr. MF iniquité, fr. L iniquitas, fr. iniquus uneven, fr. aequus equal] **1** : WICKEDNESS **2** : a wicked act — **in·iq·ui·tous** \-wət-əs\ adj

**ini·tial** \in-'ish-əl\ adj **1** : of or relating to the beginning : INCIPIENT **2** : FIRST — **ini·tial·ly** \-ē\ adv

**initial** n : the first letter of a word or name

**initial** vb **ini·tialed** or **ini·tialled; ini·tial·ing** or **ini·tial·ling** \-'ish-(ə-)liŋ\ : to affix an initial to

**ini·ti·ate** \in-'ish-ē-,āt\ vb **-at·ed; -at·ing 1** : START, BEGIN **2** : to instruct in the first principles of something **3** : to induct into membership by or as if by special ceremonies — **ini·ti·a·tion** \-,ish-ē-'ā-shən\ n

**ini·ti·ate** \in-'ish-(ē-)ət\ n **1** : a person who is undergoing or has passed an initiation **2** : a person who is instructed or adept in some special field

**ini·tia·tive** \in-'ish-ət-iv\ n **1** : an introductory step **2** : self-reliant enterprise **3** : a process by which laws may be introduced or enacted directly by vote of the people

**ini·tia·to·ry** \in-'ish-(ē-)ə-,tōr-ē\ adj **1** : INTRODUCTORY **2** : tending or serving to initiate ⟨~ rites⟩

**in·ject** \in-'jekt\ vb **1** : to force into something ⟨~ serum with a needle⟩ **2** : to introduce into some situation or subject ⟨~ a note of suspicion⟩

**in·jec·tion** \in-'jek-shən\ n **1** : an act or instance of injecting **2** : the placing of an artificial satellite or a spacecraft into an orbit **3** : the time or place at which injection occurs

**in·junc·tion** \in-'jəŋk-shən\ n **1** : ORDER, ADMONITION **2** : a court writ whereby one is required to do or to refrain from doing a specified act

**in·jure** \'in-jər\ vb **in·jured; in·jur·ing** \'inj-(ə-)riŋ\ : WRONG, DAMAGE, HURT syn harm, impair, mar, spoil

**in·ju·ry** \'inj-(ə-)rē\ n, pl **-ries 1** : an act that damages or hurts : WRONG **2** : hurt, damage, or loss sustained — **in·ju·ri·ous** \in-'jür-ē-əs\ adj

**in·jus·tice** \(')in-'jəs-təs\ n **1** : violation of a person's rights : UNFAIRNESS, WRONG **2** : an unjust act or deed

**¹ink** \'iŋk\ n [ME enke, fr. OF, fr. LL encaustum, fr. L encaustus burned in, fr. Gk enkaustos, verbal of enkaiein to burn in] : a usu. liquid and colored material for writing and printing — **inky** adj

**²ink** vb : to put ink on; esp : SIGN

**ink·blot test** \-,blät-\ n : any of several psychological tests based on the interpretation of irregular figures

**ink·horn** \'iŋk-,hôrn\ n : a small bottle (as of horn) for holding ink

**in·kling** \'iŋ-kliŋ\ n **1** : HINT, INTIMATION **2** : a vague idea

**ink·stand** \'iŋk-,stand\ n INKWELL; also : a pen and ink stand

**ink·well** \-,wel\ n : a container for ink

**in·laid** \'in-'lād\ adj : decorated with material set into a surface

**¹in·land** \'in-,land, -lənd\ n : the interior of a country

**²inland** adj **1** chiefly Brit : not foreign : DOMESTIC ⟨~ revenue⟩ **2** : of or relating to the interior of a country

**³inland** adv : into or toward the interior

**in-law** \'in-,lȯ\ n : a relative by marriage

**¹in·lay** \'in-'lā, 'in-,lā\ vb **in·laid** \-'lād\; **in·lay·ing** : to set (one material into another) by way of decoration

**²in·lay** \'in-,lā\ n **1** : inlaid work **2** : a shaped filling cemented into a tooth

**in·let** \'in-,let, -lət\ n **1** : a bay in the shore of a sea, lake, or river **2** : a narrow strip of water running into the land

**in·mate** \'in-,māt\ n : a person who lives in the same house or institution with another; esp : a person confined to an asylum, prison, or poorhouse

**in me·di·as res** \in-,med-ē-əs-'rās, -,mēd-ē-əs-'rēz\ adv [L, lit., into the midst of things] : in or into the middle of a narrative or plot

**in me·mo·ri·am** \,in-mə-'mōr-ē-əm\ prep : in memory of

**in·most** \'in-,mōst\ adj : deepest within : INNERMOST

**inn** \'in\ *n* : HOTEL, TAVERN

**in·nards** \'in-ərdz\ *n pl* 1 : the internal organs of a man or animal; *esp* : VISCERA 2 : the internal parts of a structure or mechanism

**in·nate** \in-'āt\ *adj* 1 : existing in or belonging to an individual from birth : NATIVE 2 : belonging to the essential nature of something : INHERENT — **in·nate·ly** *adv*

**in·ner** \'in-ər\ *adj* 1 : situated farther in ⟨the ~ bark⟩ 2 : near a center esp. of influence ⟨the ~ circle⟩ 3 : of or relating to the mind or spirit

**in·ner-di·rect·ed** \,in-ər-də-'rek-təd, -(,)dī-\ *adj* : directed in thought and action by one's own scale of values as opposed to external norms

**inner ear** *n* : a cavity in the temporal bone that contains a complex membranous labyrinth containing sense organs of hearing and of awareness of position in space

**in·ner·most** \'in-ər-,mōst\ *adj* : farthest inward : INMOST

**in·ner·sole** \,in-ər-'sōl\ *n* : INSOLE

**in·ner·spring** \in-ər-,spriŋ\ *adj* : having coil springs inside a padded casing

**inner tube** *n* : TUBE 5

**in·ning** \'in-iŋ\ *n* : a baseball team's turn at bat; *also* : a division of a baseball game consisting of a turn at bat for each team

**in·nings** \'in-iŋz\ *n sing or pl* : a division of a cricket match

**inn·keep·er** \'in-,kē-pər\ *n* : the landlord of an inn

**in·no·cence** \'in-ə-səns\ *n* 1 : BLAMELESSNESS; *also* : freedom from legal guilt 2 : GUILELESSNESS, SIMPLICITY; *also* : IGNORANCE

**in·no·cent** \-sənt\ *adj* [ME, fr. MF, fr. L *innocens*, fr. *nocens*, wicked, fr. *nocēre* to harm] 1 : free from guilt or sin : BLAMELESS 2 : harmless in effect or intention; *also* : CANDID 3 : free from legal guilt or fault : LAWFUL 4 : DESTITUTE 5 : ARTLESS, IGNORANT — **innocent** *n* — **in·no·cent·ly** *adv*

**in·noc·u·ous** \in-'äk-yə-wəs\ *adj* 1 : HARMLESS 2 : INOFFENSIVE, INSIPID

**in·nom·i·nate** \in-'äm-ə-nət\ *adj* : having no name; *also* : ANONYMOUS

**in·no·vate** \'in-ə-,vāt\ *vb* **-vat·ed; -vat·ing** : to introduce as or as if new : make changes — **in·no·va·tive** \-,vāt-iv\ *adj* — **in·no·va·tor** \-,vāt-ər\ *n*

**in·no·va·tion** \,in-ə-'vā-shən\ *n* 1 : the introduction of something new 2 : a new idea, method, or device

**in·nu·en·do** \,in-yə-'wen-dō\ *n, pl* **-dos** *or* **-does** [L, by hinting, fr. *innuere* to hint, fr. *nuere* to nod] : HINT, INSINUATION; *esp* : a veiled reflection on character or reputation

**in·nu·mer·a·ble** \in-'(y)üm-(ə)-rə-bəl\ *adj* : too many to be numbered

**in·oc·u·late** \in-'äk-yə-,lāt\ *vb* **-lat·ed; -lat·ing** [ME *inoculaten* to insert a bud in a plant, fr. L *inoculare*, fr. *oculus* eye, bud] : to introduce something into; *esp* : to treat usu. with a serum or antibody to prevent or cure a disease — **in·oc·u·la·tion** \-,äk-yə-'lā-shən\ *n*

**in·op·er·a·ble** \(')in-'äp-(ə-)rə-bəl\ *adj* 1 : not suitable for surgery 2 : not operable

**in·op·er·a·tive** \-'äp-(ə-)rət-iv, -'äp-ə-,rāt-\ *adj* : not functioning

**in·op·por·tune** \(,)in-,äp-ər-'t(y)ün\ *adj* : happening or coming at the wrong time — **in·op·por·tune·ly** *adv*

**in·or·di·nate** \in-'órd-(ə-)nət\ *adj* 1 : UNREGULATED, DISORDERLY 2 : EXTRAORDINARY, IMMODERATE ⟨an ~ curiosity⟩ — **in·or·di·nate·ly** *adv*

**in·or·gan·ic** \,in-,ór-'gan-ik\ *adj* : being or composed of matter of other than plant or animal origin : MINERAL

**INP** *abbr* International News Photo

**in·pa·tient** \'in-,pā-shənt\ *n* : a hospital patient who receives lodging and food as well as treatment

**in pet·to** \in-'pet-ō\ *adv or adj* [It, lit., in the breast] : in private : SECRETLY

**in·put** \'in-,pút\ *n* 1 : something put in 2 : power or energy put into a machine or system 3 : information fed into a data processing system or computer — **input** *vb*

**in·quest** \'in-,kwest\ *n* 1 : an official inquiry or examination esp. before a jury 2 : INQUIRY, INVESTIGATION

**in·qui·etude** \(')in-'kwī-ə-,t(y)üd\ *n* : UNEASINESS, RESTLESSNESS

**in·quire** \in-'kwī(ə)r\ *vb* **in·quired; in·quir·ing** 1 : to ask about : ASK 2 : INVESTIGATE, EXAMINE — **in·quir·er** *n* — **in·quir·ing·ly** *adv*

**in·qui·ry** \in-'kwī(ə)r-ē, in-'kwī(ə)r-ē; 'in-kwə-rē, 'iŋ-\ *n, pl* **-ries** 1 : a request for information; *also* : a search for truth or knowledge 2 : a systematic investigation of a matter of public interest

**in·qui·si·tion** \,in-kwə-'zish-ən, ,iŋ-\ *n* 1 : a judicial or official inquiry esp. before a jury 2 *cap* : a former Roman Catholic tribunal for the discovery and punishment of heretics 3 : a severe questioning — **in·quis·i·tor** \in-'kwiz-ət-ər\ *n* — **in·quis·i·to·ri·al** \-,kwiz-ə-'tōr-ē-əl\ *adj*

**in·quis·i·tive** \in-'kwiz-ət-iv\ *adj* 1 : given to examination or investigation ⟨an ~ mind⟩ 2 : unduly curious — **in·quis·i·tive·ly** *adv* — **in·quis·i·tive·ness** *n*

**in re** \in-'rā, -'rē\ *prep* : in the matter of

**INRI** *abbr* [L *Iesus Nazarenus Rex Iudaeorum*] Jesus of Nazareth, King of the Jews

**in·road** \'in-,rōd\ *n* 1 : INVASION, RAID 2 : ENCROACHMENT

**in·rush** \'in-,rəsh\ *n* : a crowding or flooding in : INFLUX

**ins** *abbr* 1 inches 2 insurance

**in·sa·lu·bri·ous** \,in-sə-'lü-brē-əs\ *adj* : UNWHOLESOME, NOXIOUS

**in·sane** \in-'sān\ *adj* 1 : not mentally sound : MAD; *also* : used by or for the insane 2 : FOOLISH, WILD — **in·sane·ly** *adv* — **in·san·i·ty** \in-'san-ət-ē\ *n*

**in·sa·tia·ble** \(')in-'sā-shə-bəl\ *adj* : incapable of being satisfied

**in·sa·tiate** \(')in-'sā-sh(ē-)ət\ *adj*
: INSATIABLE

**in·scribe** \in-'skrīb\ *vb* 1 : to write, engrave, or print esp. as a lasting record 2 : ENROLL 3 : to write, engrave, or print characters upon 4 : to dedicate to someone 5 : to stamp deeply or impress esp. on the memory 6 : to draw within a figure so as to touch in as many places as possible — **in·scrip·tion** \-'skrip-shən\ *n*

**in·scru·ta·ble** \in-'skrüt-ə-bəl\ *adj* 1 : not readily comprehensible : MYSTERIOUS ⟨an ~ smile⟩ 2 : impossible to see or see through physically ⟨an ~ fog⟩ — **in·scru·ta·bly** \-blē\ *adv*

**in·seam** \'in-,sēm\ *n* : an inner seam of a garment or shoe

**in·sect** \'in-,sekt\ *n* [L *insectum,* fr. *insectus,* pp. of *insecare* to cut into, fr. *secare* to cut] : any of a major group of small usu. winged animals (as flies, bees, beetles, and moths) with three pairs of legs

**in·sec·ti·cide** \in-'sek-tə-,sīd\ *n* : a preparation for destroying insects — **in·sec·ti·cid·al** \(,)in-,sek-tə-'sīd-°l\ *adj*

**in·sec·tiv·o·rous** \,in-,sek-'tiv-(ə-)rəs\ *adj* : using insects as food

**in·se·cure** \,in-si-'kyur\ *adj* 1 : UNCERTAIN 2 : UNPROTECTED, UNSAFE 3 : LOOSE, SHAKY 4 : INFIRM 5 : beset by fear or anxiety — **in·se·cure·ly** *adv* — **in·se·cu·ri·ty** \-'kyur-ət-ē\ *n*

**in·sem·i·nate** \in-'sem-ə-,nāt\ *vb* **-nat·ed; -nat·ing** : to introduce semen into the genital tract of (a female) — **in·sem·i·na·tion** \-,sem-ə-'nā-shən\ *n*

**in·sen·sate** \(')in-'sen-,sāt, -sət\ *adj* 1 : INANIMATE 2 : lacking sense or understanding; *also* : FOOLISH 3 : BRUTAL, INHUMAN ⟨~ rage⟩

**in·sen·si·ble** \(')in-'sen-sə-bəl\ *adj* 1 : INANIMATE 2 : UNCONSCIOUS 3 : lacking sensory perception or ability to react ⟨~ to pain⟩ ⟨~ from cold⟩ 4 : IMPERCEPTIBLE; *also* : SLIGHT, GRADUAL 5 : APATHETIC, INDIFFERENT; *also* : UNAWARE ⟨~ of their danger⟩ 6 : MEANINGLESS 7 : lacking delicacy or refinement — **in·sen·si·bil·i·ty** \(,)in-,sen-sə-'bil-ət-ē\ *n* — **in·sen·si·bly** \(')in-'sen-sə-blē\ *adv*

**in·sen·tient** \(')in-'sen-ch(ē-)ənt\ *adj* : lacking perception, consciousness, or animation — **in·sen·tience** \-ch(ē-)əns\ *n*

**in·sep·a·ra·ble** \(')in-'sep-(ə-)rə-bəl\ *adj* : incapable of being separated or disjoined — **in·sep·a·ra·bil·i·ty** \(,)in-,sep-(ə-)rə-'bil-ət-ē\ *n* — **in·separable** *n* — **in·sep·a·ra·bly** \(')in-'sep-(ə-)rə-blē\ *adv*

¹**in·sert** \in-'sərt\ *vb* 1 : to put or thrust in ⟨~ a key in a lock⟩ ⟨~ a comma⟩ 2 : INTERPOLATE 3 : to set in (as a piece of fabric) and make fast

²**in·sert** \'in-,sərt\ *n* : something that is inserted or is for insertion; *esp* : written or printed material inserted (as between the leaves of a book)

**in·ser·tion** \in-'sər-shən\ *n* 1 : the act or process of inserting 2 : something that is inserted

**in·set** \'in-,set\ *vb* **inset** *or* **in·set·ted; in·set·ting** : to set in : INSERT — **inset** *n*

¹**in·shore** \'in-'shōr\ *adj* 1 : situated or carried on near shore 2 : moving toward shore

²**inshore** *adv* : to or toward shore

¹**in·side** \in-'sīd, 'in-,sīd\ *n* 1 : an inner side or surface : INTERIOR 2 : inward nature, thoughts, or feeling 3 *pl* : VISCERA, ENTRAILS 4 : a position of power or confidence — **inside** *adj*

²**inside** *prep* 1 : in or into the inside of 2 : before the end of ⟨~ an hour⟩

³**inside** *adv* 1 : on the inner side 2 : in or into the interior

**inside of** *prep* : INSIDE

**in·sid·er** \in-'sīd-ər\ *n* : a person who is in a position of power or has access to confidential information

**in·sid·i·ous** \in-'sid-ē-əs\ *adj* [L *insidiosus,* fr. *insidiae* ambush, fr. *insidēre* to sit in, sit on, fr. *sedēre* to sit] 1 : SLY, TREACHEROUS 2 : SEDUCTIVE 3 : having a gradual and cumulative effect : SUBTLE — **in·sid·i·ous·ly** *adv* — **in·sid·i·ous·ness** *n*

**in·sight** \'in-,sīt\ *n* : the power or act of seeing into a situation : UNDERSTANDING, PENETRATION; *also* : INTUITION — **in·sight·ful** \'in-,sīt-fəl, in-'sīt-\ *adj*

**in·sig·nia** \in-'sig-nē-ə\ *or* **in·sig·ne** \-(,)nē\ *n, pl* **-nia** *or* **-ni·as** : a distinguishing mark esp. of authority, office, or honor : BADGE, EMBLEM

**in·sin·cere** \,in-sin-'siər\ *adj* : not sincere : HYPOCRITICAL — **in·sin·cere·ly** *adv* — **in·sin·cer·i·ty** \-'ser-ət-ē\ *n*

**in·sin·u·ate** \in-'sin-yə-,wāt\ *vb* **-at·ed; -at·ing** [L *insinuare,* fr. *sinuare* to bend, curve, fr. *sinus* curve] 1 : to introduce (as an idea) gradually or in a subtle or indirect way 2 : HINT, IMPLY 3 : to introduce (as oneself) by stealthy, smooth, or artful means — **in·sin·u·a·tion** \(,)in-,sin-yə-'wā-shən\ *n*

**in·sin·u·at·ing** *adj* 1 : tending gradually to cause doubt, distrust, or change of outlook 2 : winning favor and confidence by imperceptible degrees

**in·sip·id** \in-'sip-əd\ *adj* 1 : lacking savor 2 : DULL, UNINTERESTING — **in·si·pid·i·ty** \,in-sə-'pid-ət-ē\ *n*

**in·sist** \in-'sist\ *vb* [MF or L; MF *insister,* fr. L *insistere* to stand upon, persist, fr. *sistere* to stand] : to take a resolute stand : PERSIST

**in·sis·tence** \in-'sis-təns\ *n* : the act of insisting; *also* : an insistent attitude or quality : URGENCY

**in·sis·tent** \in-'sis-tənt\ *adj* : disposed to insist — **in·sis·tent·ly** *adv*

**in si·tu** \in-'sī-tü\ *adv or adj* [L, in position] : in the natural or original position

**insofar as** \,in-sə-,fär-əz\ *conj* : to the extent or degree that

**insol** *abbr* insoluble

**in·so·la·tion** \,in-(,)sō-'lā-shən\ *n* : solar radiation that has been received

**in·sole** \'in-ˌsōl\ *n* **1** : an inside sole of a shoe **2** : a loose thin strip (as of felt or leather) placed inside a shoe for warmth or ease

**in·so·lent** \'in-sə-lənt\ *adj* : contemptuous, rude, disrespectful, or brutal in behavior or language : OVERBEARING, BOLD — **in·so·lence** \-ləns\ *n*

**in·sol·u·ble** \(')in-'säl-yə-bəl\ *adj* **1** : having or admitting of no solution or explanation **2** : that cannot readily be dissolved in a liquid — **in·sol·u·bil·i·ty** \(,)in-ˌsäl-yə-'bil-ət-ē\ *n* — **insoluble** *n*

**in·solv·able** \(')in-'säl-və-bəl\ *adj* : admitting no solution

**in·sol·vent** \(')in-'säl-vənt\ *adj* **1** : unable to pay one's debts **2** : insufficient to pay all debts charged against it (an ~ estate) **3** : IMPOVERISHED, DEFICIENT — **in·sol·ven·cy** \-vən-sē\ *n*

**in·som·nia** \in-'säm-nē-ə\ *n* : prolonged or abnormal sleeplessness

**in·so·much** \ˌin-sə-'məch\ *adv* : so much : to such a degree : so — used with *as* or *that*

**in·sou·ci·ance** \in-'sü-sē-əns, aⁿ-süs-yäⁿs\ *n* : a lighthearted unconcern — **in·sou·ci·ant** \in-'sü-sē-ənt, aⁿ-süs-yäⁿ\ *adj*

**insp** *abbr* inspector

**in·spect** \in-'spekt\ *vb* : to view closely and critically : EXAMINE — **in·spec·tion** \-'spek-shən\ *n* — **in·spec·tor** \-tər\ *n*

**in·spi·ra·tion** \ˌin-spə-'rā-shən\ *n* **1** : INHALATION **2** : the act or power of moving the intellect or emotions **3** : the quality or state of being inspired; *also* : something that is inspired **4** : an inspiring agent or influence — **in·spi·ra·tion·al** \-sh(ə-)nəl\ *adj*

**in·spire** \in-'spī(ə)r\ *vb* **in·spired; in·spir·ing 1** : INHALE **2** : to influence, move, or guide by divine or supernatural inspiration **3** : exert an animating, enlivening, or exalting influence upon **4** : AFFECT **5** : to communicate to an agent supernaturally; *also* : CREATE **6** : to bring about; *also* : INCITE **7** : to spread by indirect means — **in·spir·er** *n*

**in·spir·it** \in-'spir-ət\ *vb* : ANIMATE, HEARTEN

**inst** *abbr* **1** instant **2** institute; institution

**in·sta·bil·i·ty** \ˌin-stə-'bil-ət-ē\ *n* : lack of firmness or steadiness

**in·stall** or **in·stal** \in-'stól\ *vb* **in·stalled; in·stall·ing 1** : to place formally in office : induct into an office, rank, or order **2** : to establish in an indicated place, condition, or status **3** : to set up for use or service — **in·stal·la·tion** \ˌin-stə-'lā-shən\ *n*

**¹in·stall·ment** or **in·stal·ment** \in-'stól-mənt\ *n* : INSTALLATION

**²installment** *also* **instalment** *n* **1** : one of the parts into which a debt or sum is divided for payment **2** : one of several parts presented at intervals

**¹in·stance** \'in-stəns\ *n* **1** : INSTIGATION, REQUEST (entered the contest at the ~ of friends) **2** : EXAMPLE (an ~ of

heroism) (for ~) **3** : an event or step that is part of a process or series **syn** case, illustration, sample, specimen

**²instance** *vb* **in·stanced; in·stanc·ing** : to mention as a case or example

**¹in·stant** \'in-stənt\ *n* **1** : MOMENT (the ~ we met) **2** : the present or current month (your letter of the 10th ~)

**²instant** *adj* **1** : URGENT **2** : PRESENT, CURRENT **3** : IMMEDIATE (~ relief) **4** : partially prepared by the manufacturer to make final preparation easy (~ cake mix); *also* : immediately soluble in water (~ coffee)

**in·stan·ta·neous** \ˌin-stən-'tā-nē-əs\ *adj* : done or occurring in an instant or without delay — **in·stan·ta·neous·ly** *adv*

**in·stan·ter** \in-'stant-ər\ *adv* : at once

**in·stan·ti·ate** \in-'stan-chē-ˌāt\ *vb* **-at·ed; -at·ing** : to represent by a concrete example — **in·stan·ti·a·tion** \-ˌstan-chē-'ā-shən\ *n*

**in·stant·ly** \'in-stənt-lē\ *adv* : at once : IMMEDIATELY

**in·state** \in-'stāt\ *vb* : to establish in a rank or office : INSTALL

**in sta·tu quo** \in-ˌstä-tü-'kwō, -ˌsta-\ *adv* [NL, lit., in the state in which] : in the former or same state

**in·stead** \in-'sted\ *adv* **1** : as a substitute or equivalent **2** : as an alternative : RATHER

**instead of** \in-ˌsted-ə(v), -ˌstid-\ *prep* : as a substitute for or alternative to

**in·step** \'in-ˌstep\ *n* : the arched part of the human foot in front of the ankle joint

**in·sti·gate** \'in-stə-ˌgāt\ *vb* **-gat·ed; -gat·ing** : to goad or urge forward : PROVOKE, INCITE (~ a revolt) — **in·sti·ga·tion** \ˌin-stə-'gā-shən\ *n* — **in·sti·ga·tor** \'in-stə-ˌgāt-ər\ *n*

**in·still** *also* **in·stil** \in-'stil\ *vb* **in·stilled; in·still·ing 1** : to cause to enter drop by drop **2** : to impart gradually

**¹in·stinct** \'in-ˌstiŋkt\ *n* **1** : a natural aptitude **2** : a largely inheritable and unalterable tendency of an organism to make a complex and specific response to environmental stimuli; *also* : behavior originating below the conscious level — **in·stinc·tive** \in-'stiŋk-tiv\ *adj* — **in·stinc·tive·ly** *adv*

**²in·stinct** \in-'stiŋkt, 'in-ˌstiŋkt\ *adj* : IMBUED, INFUSED

**¹in·sti·tute** \'in-stə-ˌt(y)üt\ *vb* **-tut·ed; -tut·ing 1** : to establish in a position or office **2** : to originate and get established : ORGANIZE **3** : INAUGURATE, INITIATE

**²institute** *n* **1** : an elementary principle recognized as authoritative; *also*, *pl* : a collection of such principles and precepts **2** : an organization for the promotion of a cause : ASSOCIATION **3** : an educational institution **4** : a meeting for instruction or a brief course of such meetings

**in·sti·tu·tion** \ˌin-stə-'t(y)ü-shən\ *n* **1** : an act of originating, setting up, or founding **2** : an established practice, law, or custom **3** : a society or corporation esp. of a public character ⟨a charitable ~⟩; *also* : the building which houses it — **in·sti·tu·tion·al** \-'t(y)ü-sh(ə-)nəl\ *adj* — **in·sti·tu·tion·al·ize** \-,īz\ *vb* — **in·sti·tu·tion·al·ly** \-ē\ *adv*

**Instr** *abbr* 1 instructor 2 instrument

**in·struct** \in-'strəkt\ *vb* [ME *instructen,* fr. L *instructus,* pp. of *instruere,* fr. *struere* to build] 1 : TEACH 2 : INFORM 3 : to give directions or commands to

**in·struc·tion** \in-'strək-shən\ *n* 1 : LESSON, PRECEPT 2 : COMMAND, ORDER 3 *pl* : DIRECTIONS 4 : the action, practice, or profession of a teacher — **in·struc·tion·al** \-sh(ə-)nəl\ *adj*

**in·struc·tive** \in-'strək-tiv\ *adj* : carrying a lesson : ENLIGHTENING

**in·struc·tor** \in-'strək-tər\ *n* : one that instructs; *esp* : a college teacher below professorial rank — **in·struc·tor·ship** \-,ship\ *n*

**¹in·stru·ment** \'in-strə-mənt\ *n* 1 : a means by which something is done 2 : TOOL, UTENSIL 3 : a device used to produce music 4 : a legal document (as a deed) 5 : a device used in navigating an airplane

**²in·stru·ment** \-,ment\ *vb* : to equip with instruments

**in·stru·men·tal** \,in-strə-'ment-ᵊl\ *adj* 1 : acting as an agent or means 2 : of, relating to, or done with an instrument 3 : relating to, composed for, or performed on a musical instrument

**in·stru·men·tal·ist** \-əst\ *n* : a player on a musical instrument

**in·stru·men·tal·i·ty** \,in-strə-mən-'tal-ət-ē, -,men-\ *n, pl* **-ties** 1 : the quality or state of being instrumental 2 : MEANS, AGENCY

**in·stru·men·ta·tion** \,in-strə-mən-'tā-shən, -,men-\ *n* 1 : the use or application of instruments 2 : the arrangement or composition of music for instruments (as for an orchestra)

**instrument flying** *n* : airplane navigation by instruments only

**in·sub·or·di·nate** \,in-sə-'bórd-(ᵊ-)nət\ *adj* : unwilling to submit to authority : DISOBEDIENT — **in·sub·or·di·na·tion** \-,bórd-ᵊn-'ā-shən\ *n*

**in·sub·stan·tial** \,in-səb-'stan-chəl\ *adj* 1 : lacking substance or reality 2 : lacking firmness or solidity

**in·suf·fer·able** \(')in-'səf-(ə-)rə-bəl\ *adj* : incapable of being endured : INTOLERABLE ⟨an ~ bore⟩ — **in·suf·fer·ably** \-blē\ *adv*

**in·suf·fi·cient** \,in-sə-'fish-ənt\ *adj* : not sufficient; *also* : INCOMPETENT — **in·suf·fi·cien·cy** \-'fish-ən-sē\ *n* — **in·suf·fi·cient·ly** *adv*

**in·su·lar** \'ins-(y)ə-lər, 'in-shə-lər\ *adj* 1 : of, relating to, or forming an island 2 : ISOLATED, DETACHED 3 : of or relating to island people 4 : NARROW, PREJUDICED — **in·su·lar·i·ty** \,ins-(y)ə-'lar-ət-ē, ,in-shə-'lar-\ *n*

**in·su·late** \'in-sə-,lāt\ *vb* **-lat·ed; -lat·ing** [L *insula* island] : ISOLATE; *esp* : to separate a conductor of electricity,

heat, or sound from other conducting bodies by means of something that will not conduct electricity, heat, or sound — **in·su·la·tion** \,in-sə-'lā-shən\ *n* — **in·su·la·tor** \'in-sə-,lāt-ər\ *n*

**in·su·lin** \'in-s(ə-)lən\ *n* : a pancreatic hormone essential for bodily use of sugars and used in the control of diabetes

**insulin shock** *n* : hypoglycemia associated with the presence of excessive insulin in the system

**¹in·sult** \in-'səlt\ *vb* [MF or L; MF *insulter,* fr. L *insultare,* lit., to spring upon, fr. *saltare* to leap] : to treat with insolence or contempt : AFFRONT — **in·sult·ing·ly** \-iŋ-lē\ *adv*

**²in·sult** \'in-,səlt\ *n* : a gross indignity

**in·su·per·a·ble** \(')in-'sü-p(ə-)rə-bəl\ *adj* : incapable of being surmounted, overcome, or passed over — **in·su·per·a·bly** \-blē\ *adv*

**in·sup·port·able** \,in-sə-'pōrt-ə-bəl\ *adj* 1 : UNENDURABLE 2 : UNJUSTIFIABLE

**in·sur·able** \in-'shùr-ə-bəl\ *adj* : capable of being or proper to be insured against loss, damage, or death

**in·sur·ance** \in-'shùr-əns\ *n* 1 : the action or process of insuring : the state of being insured; *also* : means of insuring 2 : the business of insuring persons or property 3 : coverage by contract whereby one party agrees to indemnify or guarantee another against loss by a specified contingent event or peril 4 : the sum for which something is insured

**in·sure** \in-'shùr\ *vb* **in·sured; in·sur·ing** 1 : to give, take, or procure an insurance on or for : UNDERWRITE 2 : to make certain : ENSURE

**in·sured** \in-'shùrd\ *n* : a person whose life or property is insured

**in·sur·er** \in-'shùr-ər\ *n* : one that insures; *esp* : a company issuing insurance

**in·sur·gent** \in-'sər-jənt\ *n* 1 : a person who revolts against civil authority or an established government : REBEL 2 : one who acts contrary to the policies and decisions of his political party — **in·sur·gence** \-jəns\ *n* — **in·sur·gen·cy** \-jən-sē\ *n* — **in·sur·gent** *adj*

**in·sur·mount·able** \,in-sər-maùnt-ə-bəl\ *adj* : INSUPERABLE — **in·sur·mount·ably** \-blē\ *adv*

**in·sur·rec·tion** \,in-sə-'rek-shən\ *n* : an act or instance of revolting against civil authority or an established government — **in·sur·rec·tion·ist** *n*

**int** *abbr* 1 interest 2 interior 3 internal 4 international 5 intransitive

**in·tact** \in-'takt\ *adj* : untouched esp. by anything that harms or diminishes

**in·ta·glio** \in-'tal-yō\ *n, pl* **-glios** : an engraving or incised figure in a hard material (as stone) depressed below the surface of the material

**in·take** \'in-,tāk\ *n* 1 : an opening through which fluid enters an enclosure 2 : the act of taking in 3 : the amount taken in

**in·tan·gi·ble** \(')in-'tan-jə-bəl\ *adj*
**1** : incapable of being touched : not
tangible : IMPALPABLE **2** : incapable of
being defined or determined with certainty or precision : VAGUE — **in·
tangible** *n* — **in·tan·gi·bly** \-blē\
*adv*

**in·te·ger** \'int-i-jər\ *n* [L, adj., whole,
entire] : a number (as 1, 2, 3, 12, 432)
that is not a fraction and does not
include a fraction, is the negative of
such a number, or is 0

**in·te·gral** \'int-i-grəl\ *adj* **1** : essential to completeness : CONSTITUENT
**2** : formed as a unit with another part
**3** : composed of parts that make up a
whole **4** : ENTIRE

**in·te·grate** \'int-ə-,grāt\ *vb* **-grat·ed;
-grat·ing** **1** : to form into a whole
: UNITE **2** : to incorporate into a
larger unit **3** : to end the segregation
of and bring into common and equal
membership in society or an organization; *also* : DESEGREGATE — **in·te·gra·
tion** \,int-ə-'grā-shən\ *n*

**in·teg·ri·ty** \in-'teg-rət-ē\ *n* **1** : SOUND-
NESS **2** : adherence to a code of
values : utter sincerity, honesty, and
candor **3** : COMPLETENESS

**in·teg·u·ment** \in-'teg-yə-mənt\ *n* : a
covering layer (as a skin or cuticle) of
an organism

**in·tel·lect** \'int-ᵊl-,ekt\ *n* **1** : the power
of knowing : the capacity for knowledge
**2** : the capacity for rational or intelligent thought esp. when highly developed
**3** : a person of notable intellect

**in·tel·lec·tu·al** \,int-ᵊl-'ek-ch(ə-w)əl\
*adj* **1** : of, relating to, or performed by
the intellect : RATIONAL **2** : given to
study, reflection, and speculation
**3** : engaged in activity requiring the
creative use of the intellect — **intellectual** *n* — **in·tel·lec·tu·al·ly**
\-ē\ *adv*

**in·tel·lec·tu·al·ism** \-chə(-wə)-,liz-
əm\ *n* : devotion to the exercise of
intellect or to intellectual pursuits

**in·tel·li·gence** \in-'tel-ə-jəns\ *n* **1**
: ability to learn and understand or to
deal with new or trying situations
**2** : relative intellectual capacity **3** : IN-
FORMATION, NEWS **4** : an agency engaged in obtaining information esp.
concerning an enemy or possible enemy

**intelligence quotient** *n* : a number
expressing the intelligence of a person
determined by dividing his mental age
by his chronological age and multiply-
ing by 100

**in·tel·li·gent** \in-'tel-ə-jənt\ *adj* : having or showing intelligence or intellect
— **in·tel·li·gent·ly** *adv*

**in·tel·li·gen·tsia** \in ,tel-ə-'jent-sē-ə,
-'gent-\ *n* [Russ *intelligentsiya*, fr. L
*intelligentia* intelligence] : intellectual
people as a group : the educated class

**in·tel·li·gi·ble** \in-'tel-ə-jə-bəl\ *adj*
: capable of being understood or com-
prehended — **in·tel·li·gi·bil·i·ty**
\-,tel-ə-jə-'bil-ət-ē\ *n* — **in·tel·li·gi·
bly** \-'tel-ə-jə-blē\ *adv*

**in·tem·per·ance** \(')in-'tem-
p(ə-)rəns\ *n* : lack of moderation esp.

in satisfying an appetite or passion;
*esp* : habitual or excessive drinking
of intoxicants — **in·tem·per·ate**
\-p(ə-)rət\ *adj* — **in·tem·per·ate·
ness** *n*

**in·tend** \in-'tend\ *vb* [ME *entenden,
intenden,* fr. MF *entendre* to purpose,
fr. L *indendere* to stretch out, to purpose, fr. *tendere* to stretch] **1** : to have
in mind as a purpose or aim **2** : to
design for a specified use or future

**in·ten·dant** \in-'ten-dənt\ *n* : a governor or similar administrative official
esp. under the French, Spanish, or
Portuguese monarchies

¹**in·tend·ed** \-'ten-dəd\ *adj* **1** : PRO-
POSED; *esp* : BETROTHED **2** : INTEN-
TIONAL

²**intended** *n* : an affianced person

**in·tense** \in-'tens\ *adj* **1** : existing in
an extreme degree **2** : very large
: CONSIDERABLE **3** : strained or
straining to the utmost **4** : feeling
deeply; *also* : deeply felt — **in·tense·
ly** *adv*

**in·ten·si·fy** \in-'ten-sə-,fī\ *vb* **-fied;
-fy·ing** **1** : to make or become intense
or more intensive **2** : to make more
acute : SHARPEN **syn** aggravate,
heighten, enhance — **in·ten·si·fi·ca·
tion** \-,ten-sə-fə-'kā-shən\ *n*

**in·ten·si·ty** \in-'ten-sət-ē\ *n, pl* **-ties
1** : the quality or state of being intense
**2** : degree of strength, energy, or force

¹**in·ten·sive** \in-'ten-siv\ *adj* **1** : involving or marked by special effort
**2** : serving to give emphasis — **in·
ten·sive·ly** *adv*

²**intensive** *n* : an intensive word, particle, or prefix

¹**in·tent** \in-'tent\ *n* **1** : PURPOSE
**2** : the state of mind with which an act
is done : VOLITION **3** : AIM **4** : MEAN-
ING, SIGNIFICANCE

²**intent** *adj* **1** : directed with keen or
eager attention ⟨an ~ gaze⟩ **2** : EN-
GROSSED; *also* : DETERMINED — **in·
tent·ly** *adv* — **in·tent·ness** *n*

**in·ten·tion** \in-'ten-chən\ *n* **1** : a
determination to act in a certain way
**2** : PURPOSE, AIM, END **syn** intent,
design, object, objective, goal

**in·ten·tion·al** \in-'tench-(ə-)nəl\ *adj*
: done by intention or design : IN-
TENDED — **in·ten·tion·al·ly** *adv*

**in·ter** \in-'tər\ *vb* **in·terred; in·ter·
ring** [ME *enteren,* fr. OF *enterrer,* fr.
L *in* in + *terra* earth] : BURY

**in·ter·ac·tion** \,int-ər-'ak-shən\ *n*
: mutual or reciprocal action or influence — **in·ter·act** \-'akt\ *vb*

**in·ter alia** \,int-ər-'ā-lē-ə, -'äl-ē-\ *adv*
: among other things

**in·ter·atom·ic** \,int-ər-ə-'täm-ik\ *adj*
: existing or acting between atoms

**in·ter·breed** \-'brēd\ *vb* **-bred**
\-'bred\; **-breed·ing** : to breed
together

**in·ter·ca·la·ry** \in-'tər-kə-,ler-ē\ *adj*
**1** : INTERCALATED ⟨February 29 is an
~ day⟩ **2** : INTERPOLATED

**in·ter·ca·late** \-,lāt\ *vb* **-lat·ed;
-lat·ing** **1** : to insert (as a day) in a
calendar **2** : to insert between or

**in·ter·ca·la·tion** \-,tər-kə-'lā-shən\ n

**in·ter·cede** \,int-ər-'sēd\ vb -ced·ed; -ced·ing : to act between parties with a view to reconciling differences

**¹in·ter·cept** \,int-ər-'sept\ vb 1 : to stop or interrupt the progress or course of 2 : to cut through : INTERSECT — **in·ter·cep·tion** \-'sep-shən\ n

**²in·ter·cept** \'int-ər-,sept\ n : INTERCEPTION; esp : the interception of a target by an interceptor or missile

**in·ter·cep·tor** \,int-ər-'sep-tər\ n : a fighter plane or missile designed for defense against attacking bombers or missiles

**in·ter·ces·sion** \,int-ər-'sesh-ən\ n 1 : MEDIATION 2 : prayer or petition in favor of another — **in·ter·ces·sor** \-'ses-ər\ n — **in·ter·ces·so·ry** \-'ses-(ə-)rē\ adj

**¹in·ter·change** \,int-ər-'chānj\ vb 1 : to put each in the place of the other 2 : EXCHANGE 3 : to change places mutually — **in·ter·change·able** adj

**²in·ter·change** \'int-ər-,chānj\ n 1 : EXCHANGE 2 : a highway junction that by separated levels permits passage between highways without crossing traffic streams

**in·ter·col·le·giate** \,int-ər-kə-'lēj(ē-)ət\ adj : existing or carried on between colleges

**in·ter·com** \'int-ər-,käm\ n : INTERCOMMUNICATION SYSTEM

**in·ter·com·mun·i·ca·tion system** \,int-ər-kə-,myü-nə-'kā-shən-\ n : a two-way communication system with microphone and loudspeaker at each station for localized use

**in·ter·con·ti·nen·tal** \-,känt-ⁿn-'ent-ⁿl\ adj 1 : extending among or carried on between continents ⟨~ trade⟩ 2 : capable of traveling between continents ⟨~ ballistic missiles⟩

**in·ter·course** \'int-ər-,kōrs\ n 1 : connection or dealings between persons or nations 2 : COPULATION

**in·ter·cul·tur·al** \,int-ər-'kəlch-(ə-)rəl\ adj : occurring between or relating to two or more cultures

**in·ter·de·nom·i·na·tion·al** \,int-ər-di-,näm-ə-'nā-sh(ə-)nəl\ adj : involving or occurring between different denominations

**in·ter·de·part·men·tal** \,int-ər-di-,pärt-'ment-ⁿl, -,dē-\ adj : carried on between or involving different departments (as of a college)

**in·ter·de·pen·dent** \,int-ər-di-'pendənt\ adj : dependent upon one another — **in·ter·de·pen·dence** \-dəns\ n

**in·ter·dict** \,int-ər-'dikt\ vb : to prohibit by decree — **in·ter·dic·tion** \-'dik-shən\ n

**in·ter·dis·ci·plin·ary** \-'dis-ə-plə-,ner-ē\ adj : involving two or more academic disciplines

**¹in·ter·est** \'in-t(ə-)rəst, -tə-,rest\ n 1 : right, title, or legal share in something 2 : WELFARE, BENEFIT; esp : SELF-INTEREST 3 : a charge for borrowed money that is generally a percentage of the amount borrowed : the return received by capital on its investment 4 pl : a group financially interested in an industry or enterprise ⟨oil ~s⟩ 5 : CURIOSITY, CONCERN ⟨lifelong ~ in sports⟩ 6 : readiness to be concerned with or moved by an object or class of objects 7 : the quality in a thing that arouses interest

**²interest** vb 1 : AFFECT, CONCERN 2 : to persuade to participate or engage 3 : to engage the attention of

**in·ter·est·ing** adj : holding the attention — **in·ter·est·ing·ly** adv

**in·ter·face** \'int-ər-,fās\ n 1 : a surface forming a common boundary of two bodies, spaces, or phases ⟨an oil• water ~⟩ 2 : the place at which two independent systems meet and act on or communicate with each other ⟨the man-machine ~⟩ 3 : the means by which interaction or communication is affected at an interface — **in·ter·fa·cial** \,int-ər-'fā-shəl\ adj

**in·ter·faith** \,int-ər-'fāth\ adj : involving persons of different religious faiths

**in·ter·fere** \,int-ə(r)- fiər\ vb -fered; -fer·ing [MF (s')entreferir to strike one another, fr. OF, fr. entre between among + ferir to strike, fr. L ferire] 1 : to come in collision or in opposition : CLASH 2 : to enter into the affairs of others 3 : to affect one another 4 : to run ahead of and provide blocking for the ballcarrier in football; also : to hinder illegally an attempt of a football player to receive a pass

**in·ter·fer·ence** \-'fir-əns\ n 1 : the act or process of interfering 2 : something that interferes : OBSTRUCTION 3 : the mutual effect on meeting of two waves resulting in areas of increased and decreased amplitude

**in·ter·fer·om·e·ter** \,int-ə(r)-fə-'rämət-ər\ n : a device that uses interference phenomena for precise measurements — **in·ter·fer·om·e·try** \-fə-'räm-ə-trē\ n

**in·ter·fer·on** \,int-ər-'fiər-,än\ n : a protein produced in cells that protects an animal esp. by rendering invading viruses ineffective

**in·ter·fuse** \,int-ər-'fyüz\ vb 1 : to combine by fusing : BLEND 2 : INFUSE 3 : PERVADE, PERMEATE

**in·ter·ga·lac·tic** \,int-ər-gə-'lak-tik\ adj : situated in the spaces between galaxies

**in·ter·gen·er·a·tion·al** \-,jen-ə-'rā-'sh(ə-)nəl\ adj : existing or occurring between generations

**in·ter·gla·cial** \-'glā-shəl\ adj : occurring between successive glaciations

**in·ter·gov·ern·men·tal** \,gəv-ər(n)-'ment-ⁿl\ adj : existing or occurring between two governments or levels of government

**in·ter·im** \'in-tə-rəm\ n [L, adv., meanwhile, fr. inter between] : a time intervening : INTERVAL — **interim** adj

**¹in·te·ri·or** \in-'tir-ē-ər\ adj 1 : lying, occurring, or functioning within the limits : INSIDE, INNER 2 : remote from the surface, border, or shore : INLAND

²**interior** n 1 : INSIDE 2 : the inland part (as of a country) 3 : the internal affairs of a state or nation 4 : a scene or view of the interior of a building

**interior decoration** n : INTERIOR DESIGN — **interior decorator** n

**interior design** n : the art or practice of planning and supervising the design and execution of architectural interiors and their furnishings — **interior designer** n

**interj** abbr interjection

**in·ter·ject** \,int-ər-'jekt\ vb : to throw in between or among other things

**in·ter·jec·tion** \,int-ər-'jek-shən\ n : an exclamatory word (as ouch) — **in·ter·jec·tion·al·ly** \-sh(ə-)nəl-ē\ adv

**in·ter·lace** \,int-ər-'lās\ vb 1 : to unite by or as if by lacing together : INTERWEAVE, 2 : INTERSPERSE

**in·ter·lard** \,int-ər-'lärd\ vb : to insert or introduce at intervals : INTERSPERSE

**in·ter·leaf** \'int-ər-,lēf\ n : a leaf inserted between two leaves of a book

**in·ter·leave** \,int-ər-'lēv\ vb -**leaved; -leav·ing** : to equip with an interleaf

¹**in·ter·line** \,int-ər-'līn\ vb : to insert between lines already written or printed

²**interline** vb : to provide (as a coat) with an interlining

**in·ter·lin·ear** \,int-ər-'lin-ē-ər\ adj : inserted between lines already written or printed ⟨an ~ translation of a text⟩

**in·ter·lin·ing** \'int-ər-,lī-niŋ\ n : a lining (as of a coat) between the ordinary lining and the outside fabric

**in·ter·link** \,int-ər-'liŋk\ vb : to link together

**in·ter·lock** \,int-ər-'läk\ vb 1 : to engage or interlace together : lock together : UNITE 2 : to connect in such a way that action of one part affects action of another part — **in·ter·lock** \'int-ər-,läk\ n

**in·ter·loc·u·tor** \,int-ər-'läk-yət-ər\ n 1 : one who takes part in dialogue or conversation 2 : a man in a minstrel show who questions the end men

**in·ter·loc·u·to·ry** \-yə-,tōr-ē\ adj : pronounced during the progress of a legal action and having only provisional force ⟨an ~ decree⟩

**in·ter·lope** \,int-ər-'lōp\ vb -**loped; -lop·ing** 1 : to encroach on the rights of others (as in trade) 2 : INTRUDE, INTERFERE — **in·ter·lop·er** n

**in·ter·lude** \'int-ər-,lüd\ n 1 : a performance given between the acts of a play 2 : an intervening period, space, or event 3 : a short piece of music inserted between the parts of a longer composition or a religious service

**in·ter·lu·nar** \,int-ər-'lü-nər\ also **in·ter·lu·na·ry** \-nə-rē\ adj : relating to the interval between the old and new moon when the moon is invisible

**in·ter·mar·riage** \,int-ər-'mar-ij\ n : marriage between members of different groups; also : marriage within one's own group

**in·ter·mar·ry** \-'mar-ē\ vb 1 : to marry each other 2 : to marry within a group 3 : to become connected by intermarriage

**in·ter·med·dle** \,int-ər-'med-ᵊl\ vb : MEDDLE, INTERFERE

¹**in·ter·me·di·ary** \,int-ər-'mēd-ē-,er-ē\ adj 1 : INTERMEDIATE 2 : acting as a mediator

²**intermediary** n, pl -ar·ies : MEDIATOR, GO-BETWEEN

¹**in·ter·me·di·ate** \,int-ər-'mēd-ē-ət\ adj : being or occurring at the middle place or degree or between extremes

²**intermediate** n 1 : an intermediate term, object, or class 2 : INTERMEDIARY

**intermediate school** n 1 : JUNIOR HIGH SCHOOL 2 : a school usu. comprising grades 4–6

**in·ter·ment** \in-'tər-mənt\ n : BURIAL

**in·ter·mez·zo** \,int-ər-'met-sō, -'med-zō\ n, pl -zi \-sē, -zē\ or -zos [It, deriv. of L intermedius intermediate] : a short movement connecting major sections of an extended musical work (as a symphony); also : a short independent instrumental composition

**in·ter·mi·na·ble** \(')in-'tərm-(ə-)nə-bəl\ adj : ENDLESS; esp : wearisomely protracted — **in·ter·mi·na·bly** \-blē\ adv

**in·ter·min·gle** \,int-ər-'miŋ-gəl\ vb : to mingle or mix together

**in·ter·mis·sion** \,int-ər-'mish-ən\ n 1 : INTERRUPTION BREAK 2 : a temporary halt esp. in a public performance

**in·ter·mit** \-'mit\ vb -**mit·ted; -mit·ting** : DISCONTINUE; also : to be intermittent

**in·ter·mit·tent** \-'mit-ᵊnt\ adj : coming and going at intervals syn recurrent, periodic, alternate — **in·ter·mit·tent·ly** adv

**in·ter·mix** \,int-ər-'miks\ vb : to mix together : INTERMINGLE — **in·ter·mix·ture** \-'miks-chər\ n

**in·ter·mo·lec·u·lar** \-mə-'lek-yə-lər\ adj : existing or acting between molecules

¹**in·tern** \'in-,tərn, in-'tərn\ vb : to confine or impound esp. during a war

²**in·tern** or **in·terne** \'in-,tərn\ n : an advanced student or recent graduate (as in medicine) gaining supervised practical experience — **in·tern·ship** n

³**in·tern** \'in-,tərn\ vb : to act as an intern

**in·ter·nal** \in-'tərn-ᵊl\ adj 1 : INWARD, INTERIOR 2 : having to do with or situated in the inside of the body ⟨~ pain⟩ 3 : of, relating to, or existing within the mind 4 : INTRINSIC, INHERENT 5 : of or relating to the domestic affairs of a country or state ⟨~ revenue⟩ — **in·ter·nal·ly** \-ē\ adv

**internal–combustion engine** n : a heat engine in which the combustion that generates the heat takes place inside the engine proper

**internal medicine** n : a branch of medicine that deals with the diagnosis and treatment of nonsurgical diseases

¹**in·ter·na·tion·al** \,int-ər-'nash-(ə-)nəl\ adj 1 : common to or affecting two or more nations ⟨~ trade⟩ 2 : of, relating to, or constituting a group having members in two or more nations — **in·ter·na·tion·al·ly** \-ē\ adv

²**in·ter·na·tion·al** \*same, or* -,nash-ə-'nal *for l*\ *n* **1** : one of several socialist or communist organizations of international scope **2** : a labor union having locals in more than one country

**in·ter·na·tion·al·ism** \-'nash-(ə-)nəl-,iz-əm\ *n* : a policy of political and economic cooperation among nations; *also* : an attitude favoring such a policy

**in·ter·na·tion·al·ize** \,int-ər-'nash-(ə-)nəl-,īz\ *vb* : to make international; *esp* : to place under international control

**in·ter·ne·cine** \,int-ər-'nes-,ēn, -'nēs-,īn\ *adj* [L *internecinus,* fr. *internecare* to destroy, kill, fr. *necare* to kill, fr. *nec-, nex* violent death] **1** : DEADLY; *esp* : mutually destructive **2** : of, relating to, or involving conflict within a group ⟨~ feuds⟩

**in·tern·ee** \,in-,tər-'nē\ *n* : an interned person

**in·ter·nist** \'in-,tər-nəst\ *n* : a specialist in internal medicine esp. as distinguished from a surgeon

**in·tern·ment** \in-'tərn-mənt\ *n* : the act of interning : the state of being interned

**in·ter·node** \'int-ər-,nōd\ *n* : an interval or part between two nodes (as of a stem)

**in·ter·nun·cio** \,int-ər-'nən-sē-,ō, -'nún-\ *n* : a papal legate of lower rank than a nuncio

**in·ter·of·fice** \-'óf-əs\ *adj* : functioning or communicating between the offices of an organization ⟨an ~ memo⟩

**in·ter·per·son·al** \-'pərs-(ə-)nəl\ *adj* : being, relating to, or involving relations between persons — **in·ter·per·son·al·ly** \-ē\ *adv*

**in·ter·plan·e·tary** \,int-ər-'plan-ə-,ter-ē\ *adj* : existing, carried on, or operating between planets ⟨~ space⟩

**in·ter·play** \'int-ər-,plā\ *n* : INTERACTION

**in·ter·po·late** \in-'tər-pə-,lāt\ *vb* **-lat·ed; -lat·ing** **1** : to change (as a text) by inserting new or foreign matter **2** : to insert (as words) into a text or into a conversation — **in·ter·po·la·tion** \-,tər-pə-'lā-shən\ *n*

**in·ter·pose** \,int-ər-'pōz\ *vb* **-posed; -pos·ing** **1** : to place between **2** : to thrust in : INTRUDE, INTERRUPT **3** : to inject between parts of a conversation or argument **4** : to be or come between **syn** interfere, intercede — **in·ter·po·si·tion** \-pə-'zish-ən\ *n*

**in·ter·pret** \in-'tər-prət\ *vb* **1** : to explain the meaning of; *also* : to act as an interpreter : TRANSLATE **2** : to understand according to individual belief, judgment, or interest **3** : to represent artistically — **in·ter·pret·er** *n* — **in·ter·pre·tive** \-'tər-prət-iv\ *adj*

**in·ter·pre·ta·tion** \in-,tər-prə-'tā-shən\ *n* **1** : EXPLANATION **2** : an instance of artistic interpretation in performance or adaptation — **in·ter·pre·ta·tive** \-'tər-prə-,tāt-iv\ *adj*

**in·ter·ra·cial** \-'rā-shəl\ *adj* : of, involving, or designed for members of different races

**in·ter·reg·num** \,int-ə-'reg-nəm\ *n, pl* **-nums** *or* **-na** \-nə\ **1** : the time during which a throne is vacant between two successive reigns or regimes **2** : a pause in a continuous series

**in·ter·re·late** \,int-ə(r)-ri-'lāt\ *vb* : to bring into or have a mutual relationship — **in·ter·re·lat·ed·ness** \-'lāt-əd-nəs\ *n* — **in·ter·re·la·tion** \-'lā-shən\ *n* — **in·ter·re·la·tion·ship** *n*

**interrog** *abbr* interrogative

**in·ter·ro·gate** \in-'ter-ə-,gāt\ *vb* **-gat·ed; -gat·ing** : to question esp. formally and systematically : ASK — **in·ter·ro·ga·tion** \-,ter-ə-'gā-shən\ *n* — **in·ter·ro·ga·tor** \-'ter-ə-,gāt-ər\ *n*

**in·ter·rog·a·tive** \,int-ə-'räg-ət-iv\ *adj* : asking a question ⟨~ sentence⟩ — **interrogative** *n*

**in·ter·rog·a·to·ry** \,int-ə-'räg-ə-,tōr-ē\ *adj* : INTERROGATIVE

**in·ter·rupt** \,int-ə-'rəpt\ *vb* **1** : to stop or hinder by breaking in **2** : to break the uniformity or continuity of **3** : to break in upon an action; *esp* : to break in with questions or remarks while another is speaking — **in·ter·rupt·er** *n* — **in·ter·rup·tion** \-'rəp-shən\ *n* — **in·ter·rup·tive** \-'rəp-tiv\ *adv*

**in·ter·scho·las·tic** \,int-ər-skə-'las-tik\ *adj* : existing or carried on between schools

**in·ter·sect** \,int-ər-'sekt\ *vb* : to cut or divide by passing through : cut across : meet and cross : OVERLAP — **in·ter·sec·tion** \-'sek-shən\ *n*

**in·ter·sperse** \,int-ər-'spərs\ *vb* **-spersed; -spers·ing** **1** : to insert at intervals among other things **2** : to place something at intervals in or among — **in·ter·sper·sion** \-'spər-zhən\ *n*

**in·ter·state** \,int-ər-'stāt\ *adj* : relating to, including, or connecting two or more states esp. of the U.S.

**in·ter·stel·lar** \,int-ər-'stel-ər\ *adj* : located or taking place among the stars

**in·ter·stice** \in-'tər-stəs\ *n, pl* **-stic·es** \-stə-,sēz, -stə-səz\ : a space that intervenes between things : CHINK — **in·ter·sti·tial** \,int-ər-'stish-əl\ *adj*

**in·ter·tid·al** \,int-ər-'tīd-°l\ *adj* : of, relating to, or being the area that is above low-tide mark but exposed to tidal flooding

**in·ter·twine** \-'twīn\ *vb* : to twine or twist together one with another

**in·ter·twist** \-'twist\ *vb* : INTERTWINE

**in·ter·ur·ban** \-'ər-bən\ *adj* : going between or connecting cities or towns

**in·ter·val** \'int-ər-vəl\ *n* [ME *intervalle,* fr. MF, fr. L *intervallum* space between ramparts, interval, fr. *inter-* between + *vallum* rampart] **1** : a space of time between events or states : PAUSE **2** : a space between objects, units, or states **3** : difference in pitch between two tones

**in·ter·vene** \,int-ər-'vēn\ *vb* **-vened; -ven·ing** **1** : to enter or appear as an unrelated feature or circumstance ⟨rain *intervened* and we postponed the trip⟩ **2** : to occur, fall, or come between points of time or between events **3** : to come in or between in order to stop, settle, or modify ⟨~ in a quarrel⟩ **4** : to occur or lie between two things — **in·ter·ven·tion** \-'ven-chən\ n

**in·ter·ven·tion·ism** \-'ven-chə-,niz-əm\ n : interference by one country in the political affairs of another — **in·ter·ven·tion·ist** \-'vench-(ə-)nəst\ n or adj

**in·ter·view** \'int-ər-,vyü\ n **1** : a formal consultation **2** : a meeting at which a writer or reporter obtains information from a person; also : the written account of such a meeting — interview vb — **in·ter·view·er** n

**in·ter·vo·cal·ic** \,int-ər-vō-'kal-ik\ adj : immediately preceded and immediately followed by a vowel

**in·ter·weave** \,int-ər-'wēv\ vb **-wove** \-'wōv\ also **-weaved; -wo·ven** \-'wō-vən\ also **-weaved; -weav·ing** : to weave or blend together : INTERTWINE, INTERMINGLE — **in·ter·wo·ven** \-'wō-vən\ adj

**in·tes·tate** \in-'tes-,tāt, -tət\ adj **1** : having made no valid will ⟨died ~⟩ **2** : not disposed of by will ⟨~ estate⟩

**in·tes·tine** \in-'tes-tən\ n : the tubular part of the alimentary canal that extends from stomach to anus and consists of a long narrow upper part (**small intestine**) followed by a broader shorter lower part (**large intestine**) — **in·tes·ti·nal** \-tən-ᵊl\ adj

¹**in·ti·mate** \'int-ə-,māt\ vb **-mat·ed; -mat·ing 1** : ANNOUNCE, NOTIFY **2** : to communicate indirectly : HINT — **in·ti·ma·tion** \,int-ə-'mā-shən\ n

²**in·ti·mate** \'int-ə-mət\ adj **1** : INTRINSIC; also : INNERMOST **2** : marked by very close association, contact, or familiarity **3** : marked by a warm friendship **4** : suggesting informal warmth or privacy **5** : of a very personal or private nature — **in·ti·ma·cy** \'int-ə-mə-sē\ n — **in·ti·mate·ly** adv

³**in·ti·mate** \'int-ə-mət\ n : an intimate friend, associate, or confidant

**in·tim·i·date** \in-'tim-ə-,dāt\ vb **-dat·ed; -dat·ing** : to make timid or fearful : FRIGHTEN; esp : to compel or deter by or as if by threats **syn** cow, bulldoze, bully, browbeat — **in·tim·i·da·tion** \-,tim-ə-'dā-shən\ n

**in·tinc·tion** \in-'tiŋk-shən\ n : the administration of Communion by dipping the bread in the wine and giving it to the communicant

**intl** or **intnl** abbr international

**in·to** \,in-tə, 'in-tü\ prep **1** : to the inside of ⟨ran ~ the house⟩ **2** : to the state, condition, or form of ⟨got ~ trouble⟩ **3** : AGAINST ⟨ran ~ a wall⟩

**in·tol·er·a·ble** \(')in-'täl-(ə-)rə-bəl\ adj **1** : UNBEARABLE **2** : EXCESSIVE — **in·tol·er·a·bly** \-blē\ adv

**in·tol·er·ant** \(')in-'täl-ə-rənt\ adj **1** : unable to endure **2** : unwilling to endure **3** : unwilling to grant equal freedom of expression esp. in religious matters or social, political, or professional rights : BIGOTED — **in·tol·er·ance** \-rəns\ n

**in·to·na·tion** \,in-tə-'nā-shən\ n **1** : the act of intoning and esp. of chanting **2** : something that is intoned **3** : the manner of singing, playing, or uttering tones **4** : the rise and fall in pitch of the voice in speech

**in·tone** \in-'tōn\ vb **in·toned; in·ton·ing** : to utter in musical or prolonged tones : CHANT

**in to·to** \in-'tōt-ō\ adv [L, on the whole] : TOTALLY, ENTIRELY

**in·tox·i·cant** \in-'täk-si-kənt\ n : something that intoxicates; esp : an alcoholic drink

**in·tox·i·cate** \-sə-,kāt\ vb **-cat·ed; -cat·ing** [ML intoxicare, fr. L toxicum poison] **1** : to make drunk **2** : to excite or elate greatly — **in·tox·i·ca·tion** \-,täk-sə-'kā-shən\ n

**in·trac·ta·ble** \(')in-'trak-tə-bəl\ adj : not easily controlled : OBSTINATE

**in·tra·dos** \in-'trā-,däs, -,dōs; in-'trā-,däs\ n, pl **-dos** \-,dōz, -,däs\ or **-dos·es** \-,däs-əz\ : the interior curve of an arch

**in·tra·mo·lec·u·lar** \,in-trə-mə-'lek-yə-lər\ adj : exciting or acting within the molecule — **in·tra·mo·lec·u·lar·ly** adv

**in·tra·mu·ral** \-'myùr-əl\ adj : being or occurring within the walls or limits (as of a city or college) ⟨~ sports⟩

**in·tra·mus·cu·lar** \-'məs-kyə-lər\ adj : situated within or going into a muscle — **in·tra·mus·cu·lar·ly** adv

**intrans** abbr intransitive

**in·tran·si·geance** \in-'trans-ə-jəns, -'tranz-\ n : INTRANSIGENCE

**in·tran·si·gence** \-jəns\ n : the quality or state of being intransigent

**in·tran·si·gent** \-jənt\ adj : UNCOMPROMISING; also : IRRECONCILABLE — **intransigent** n

**in·tran·si·tive** \(')in-'trans-ət-iv, -'tranz-\ adj : not transitive; esp : not having or containing an object ⟨an ~ verb⟩ — **in·tran·si·tive·ly** adv — **in·tran·si·tive·ness** n

**in·tra·state** \,in-trə-'stāt\ adj : existing or occurring within a state

**in·tra·uter·ine device** \-'yüt-ə-rən-, -,rīn-\ n : a device (as a spiral of plastic or a ring of stainless steel) inserted and left in the uterus to prevent pregnancy

**in·tra·ve·nous** \,in-trə-'vē-nəs\ adj : being within or entering by way of the veins — **in·tra·ve·nous·ly** adv

**intrench** var of ENTRENCH

**in·trep·id** \in-'trep-əd\ adj : characterized by resolute fearlessness, fortitude, and endurance — **in·tre·pid·i·ty** \,in-trə-'pid-ət-ē\ n

**in·tri·cate** \'in-tri-kət\ adj [ME, fr. L intricatus, pp. of intricare to entangle, fr. tricae trifles, impediments] **1** : having many complexly interrelated parts : COMPLICATED **2** : difficult to follow, understand, or solve — **in·tri·ca·cy** \'in-tri-kə-sē\ n — **in·tri·cate·ly** adv

¹**in·trigue** \in-'trēg\ vb **in·trigued; in·trigu·ing 1** : to accomplish by intrigue **2** : to carry on an intrigue; esp : PLOT, SCHEME **3** : to arouse the interest, desire, or curiosity of —

**in·trigu·ing·ly** \-ĭg-lē\ *adv*

²**in·trigue** \'in-ˌtrēg, in-'trēg\ *n* **1** : a secret scheme : MACHINATION **2** : a clandestine love affair

**in·trin·sic** \in-'trin-zik, -sik\ *adj* **1** : belonging to the essential nature or constitution of a thing **2** : REAL, ACTUAL — **in·trin·si·cal·ly** \-zi-k(ə-)lē, -si-\ *adv*

**introd** *abbr* introduction

**in·tro·duce** \ˌin-trə-'d(y)üs\ *vb* -**duced**; -**duc·ing 1** : to lead or bring in esp. for the first time **2** : to bring into practice or use **3** : to cause to be acquainted **4** : to bring to notice **5** : to put in *syn* insinuate, interpolate, interpose, interject — **in·tro·duc·tion** \-'dək-shən\ *n* — **in·tro·duc·to·ry** \-'dək-t(ə-)rē\ *adj*

**in·troit** \'in-ˌtrō-ət, -ˌtrȯit\ *n* **1** *often cap* : the first part of the traditional proper of the Mass **2** : a piece of music sung or played at the beginning of a worship service

**in·tro·mit** \ˌin-trə-'mit\ *vb* -**mit·ted**; -**mit·ting** : to send or put in : INSERT — **in·tro·mis·sion** \-'mish-ən\ *n*

**in·tro·spec·tion** \-'spek-shən\ *n* : a reflective looking inward : an examination of one's own thoughts or feelings — **in·tro·spect** \ˌin-trə-'spekt\ *vb* — **in·tro·spec·tive** \-'spek-tiv\ *adj* — **in·tro·spec·tive·ly** *adv*

**in·tro·vert** \'in-trə-ˌvərt\ *n* : a person more interested in his own mental life than in the world about him — **in·tro·ver·sion** \ˌin-trə-'vər-zhən\ *n* — **introvert** *adj* — **in·tro·vert·ed** \'in-trə-ˌvərt-əd\ *adj*

**in·trude** \in-'trüd\ *vb* **in·trud·ed**; **in·trud·ing 1** : to thrust, enter, or force in or upon **2** : ENCROACH, TRESPASS — **in·trud·er** *n* — **in·tru·sion** \-'trü-zhən\ *n* — **in·tru·sive** \-'trü-siv\ *adj* — **in·tru·sive·ness** *n*

**intrust** *var of* ENTRUST

**in·tu·it** \in-'t(y)ü-ət\ *vb* : to apprehend by intuition

**in·tu·ition** \ˌin-t(y)ü-'ish-ən\ *n* **1** : the power or faculty of knowing things without conscious reasoning **2** : quick and ready insight — **in·tu·i·tive** \in-'t(y)ü-ət-iv\ *adj* — **in·tu·i·tive·ly** *adv*

**in·tu·mesce** \ˌin-t(y)ü-'mes\ *vb* -**mesced**; -**mesc·ing** : ENLARGE, SWELL — **in·tu·mes·cence** \-'mes-ᵊns\ *n* — **in·tu·mes·cent** \-ᵊnt\ *adj*

**in·un·date** \'in-ən-ˌdāt\ *vb* -**dat·ed**; -**dat·ing** : to cover with or as if with a flood : OVERFLOW — **in·un·da·tion** \ˌin-ən-'dā-shən\ *n*

**in·ure** \in-'(y)ur\ *vb* **in·ured**; **in·ur·ing** [ME *enuren*, fr. *en-* in + *ure*, n., use, custom, fr. MF *uevre* work, practice, fr. L *opera* work] **1** : to accustom to accept something undesirable **2** : to become of advantage : ACCRUE

**in·urn** \in-'ərn\ *vb* **1** : to enclose in an urn **2** : ENTOMB

**inv** *abbr* invoice

**in vac·uo** \in-'vak-yə-ˌwō\ *adv* : in a vacuum

**in·vade** \in-'vād\ *vb* **in·vad·ed**; **in·vad·ing 1** : to enter for conquest or plunder **2** : to encroach upon **3** : to spread through and usu. harm (germs ~ the tissues) — **in·vad·er** *n*

¹**in·val·id** \(')in-'val-əd\ *adj* : being without foundation or force in fact, reason, or law — **in·va·lid·i·ty** \ˌin-və-'lid-ət-ē\ *n* — **in·val·id·ly** *adv*

²**in·va·lid** \'in-və-ləd\ *adj* : defective in health : SICKLY

³**invalid** \'in-və-ləd\ *n* : a person in usu. chronic ill health — **in·va·lid·ism** \-ˌiz-əm\ *n*

⁴**in·va·lid** \in-və-ləd, -ˌlid\ *vb* **1** : to make sickly or disabled **2** : to remove from active duty by reason of sickness or disability

**in·val·i·date** \(')in-'val-ə-ˌdāt\ *vb* : to make invalid; *esp* : to weaken or make valueless

**in·valu·able** \(')in-'val-yə(-wə)-bəl\ *adj* : valuable beyond estimation

**in·vari·able** \(')in-'var-ē-ə-bəl\ *adj* : not changing or capable of change : CONSTANT — **in·vari·ably** \-blē\ *adv*

**in·va·sion** \in-'vā-zhən\ *n* : an act or instance of invading; *esp* : entry of an army into a country for conquest or plunder

**in·vec·tive** \in-'vek-tiv\ *n* **1** : an abusive expression or speech **2** : abusive language — **invec·tive** *adj*

**in·veigh** \in-'vā\ *vb* : to protest or complain bitterly or vehemently : RAIL

**in·vei·gle** \in-'vā-gəl, -'vē-\ *vb* **vei·gled**; **in·vei·gling** \-g(ə-)liŋ\ [modif. of MF *aveugler* to blind, hoodwink, fr. OF *avogler*, fr. *avogle* blind, fr. ML *ab oculis*, lit., lacking eyes] **1** : to win over by flattery : ENTICE **2** : to acquire by ingenuity or flattery

**in·vent** \in-'vent\ *vb* **1** : to think up **2** : to create or produce for the first time — **in·ven·tor** \-'vent-ər\ *n*

**in·ven·tion** \in-'ven-chən\ *n* **1** : INVENTIVENESS **2** : a creation of the imagination; *esp* : a false conception **3** : a device, contrivance, or process originated after study and experiment **4** : the act or process of inventing

**in·ven·tive** \in-'vent-iv\ *adj* **1** : CREATIVE, INGENIOUS ⟨an ~ composer⟩ **2** : characterized by invention ⟨an ~ turn of mind⟩ — **in·ven·tive·ness** *n*

**in·ven·to·ry** \'in-vən-ˌtōr-ē\ *n*, *pl* -**ries 1** : an itemized list of current goods or assets **2** : SURVEY, SUMMARY **3** : STOCK, SUPPLY **4** : the act or process of taking an inventory — **inventory** *vb*

**in·ver·ness** \ˌin-vər-'nes\ *n* : a loose belted coat having a cape with a close round collar

**in·verse** \(')in-'vərs, 'in-ˌvərs\ *adj* : opposite in order, nature, or effect : REVERSED — **in·verse·ly** *adv*

**in·ver·sion** \in-'vər-zhən\ *n* **1** : the act or process of inverting **2** : a reversal of position, order, or relationship; *esp* : a reversal of the normal atmospheric gradient

**in·vert** \in-'vərt\ *vb* **1** : to turn upside down or inside out **2** : to turn inward **3** : to reverse in position, order, or relationship

¹in·ver·te·brate \(')in-'vərt-ə-brət, -,brāt\ *adj* : lacking a spinal column; *also* : of or relating to invertebrates

²invertebrate *n* : an invertebrate animal

¹in·vest \in-'vest\ *vb* 1 : to install formally in an office or honor 2 : to furnish with power or authority : VEST 3 : to cover completely : ENVELOP 4 : CLOTHE, ADORN 5 : BESIEGE 6 : to endow with a quality or characteristic

²invest *vb* 1 : to commit money in order to earn a financial return 2 : to make use of for future benefits or advantages 3 : to make an investment — **in·ves·tor** \-'ves-tər\ *n*

in·ves·ti·gate \in-'ves-tə-,gāt\ *vb* -gat·ed; -gat·ing [L *investigare* to track, investigate, fr. *vestigium* footprint, track] : to observe or study by close examination and systematic inquiry — **in·ves·ti·ga·tion** \-,ves-tə-'gā-shən\ *n* — **in·ves·ti·ga·tor** \-'ves-tə-,gāt-ər\ *n*

in·ves·ti·ture \in-'ves-tə-,chùr, -,chər\ *n* 1 : the act of ratifying or establishing in office : CONFIRMATION 2 : something that covers or adorns

¹in·vest·ment \in-'ves(t)-mənt\ *n* 1 : an outer layer : ENVELOPE 2 : INVESTITURE 1 3 : BLOCKADE, SIEGE

²investment *n* : the outlay of money for income or profit; *also* : the sum invested or the property purchased

in·vet·er·ate \in-'vet-(ə-)rət\ *adj* 1 : firmly established by age or long persistence 2 : confirmed in a habit — **in·vet·er·a·cy** \-(ə-)rə-sē\ *n*

in·vi·a·ble \(')in-'vī-ə-bəl\ *adj* : incapable of surviving

in·vid·i·ous \in-'vid-ē-əs\ *adj* 1 : tending to cause discontent, animosity, or envy 2 : ENVIOUS 3 : INJURIOUS — **in·vid·i·ous·ly** *adv*

in·vig·o·rate \in-'vig-ə-,rāt\ *vb* -rat·ed; -rat·ing : to give life and energy to : ANIMATE — **in·vig·o·ra·tion** \-,vig-ə-'rā-shən\ *n*

in·vin·ci·ble \(')in-'vin-sə-bəl\ *adj* : incapable of being conquered, overcome, or subdued — **in·vin·ci·bil·i·ty** \(,)in-,vin-sə-'bil-ət-ē\ *n* — **in·vin·ci·bly** \(')in-'vin-sə-blē\ *adv*

in·vi·o·la·ble \(')in-'vī-ə-lə-bəl\ *adj* 1 : safe from violation or profanation 2 : UNASSAILABLE — **in·vi·o·la·bil·i·ty** \(,)in-,vī-ə-lə-'bil-ət-ē\ *n*

in·vi·o·late \(')in-'vī-ə-lət\ *adj* : not violated or profaned : PURE

in·vis·i·ble \(')in-'viz-ə-bəl\ *adj* 1 : incapable of being seen ⟨~ to the naked eye⟩ 2 : HIDDEN 3 : IMPERCEPTIBLE, INCONSPICUOUS — **in·vis·i·bil·i·ty** \(,)in-,viz-ə-'bil-ət-ē\ *n* — **in·vis·i·bly** \(')in-'viz-ə-blē\ *adv*

in·vi·ta·tion·al \,in-və-'tā-sh(ə-)nəl\ *adj* : limited to invited participants

in·vite \in-'vīt\ *vb* in·vit·ed; in·vit·ing 1 : ENTICE, TEMPT 2 : to increase the likelihood of 3 : to request the presence or participation of : ASK 4 : to request formally 5 : ENCOURAGE — **in·vi·ta·tion** \,in-və-'tā-shən\ *n*

in·vit·ing \in-'vīt-iŋ\ *adj* : ATTRACTIVE, TEMPTING

in·vo·ca·tion \,in-və-'kā-shən\ *n* 1 : SUPPLICATION; *esp* : a prayer at the beginning of a service 2 : a formula for conjuring : INCANTATION

¹in·voice \'in-,vòis\ *n* [modif. of MF *envois*, pl. of *envoi* message] 1 : an itemized list of goods shipped usu. specifying the price and the terms of sale : BILL 2 : a consignment of merchandise

²invoice *vb* in·voiced; in·voic·ing : to make an invoice of : BILL

in·voke \in-'vōk\ *vb* in·voked; in·vok·ing 1 : to petition for help or support 2 : to appeal to or cite as authority ⟨~ a law⟩ 3 : to call forth by incantation : CONJURE ⟨~ spirits⟩ 4 : to make an earnest request for : SOLICIT 5 : to put into effect or operation 6 : to bring about : CAUSE

in·vo·lu·cre \'in-və-,lü-kər\ *n* : one or more whorls of bracts below and close to a flower or fruit

in·vol·un·tary \(')in-'väl-ən-,ter-ē\ *adj* 1 : done contrary to or without choice 2 : COMPULSORY 3 : not subject to control by the will ⟨~ muscles⟩ — **in·vol·un·tari·ly** \(,)in-,väl-ən-'ter-ə-lē\ *adv*

in·vo·lute \'in-və-,lüt\ *adj* 1 : curled spirally and usu. closely ⟨~ shell⟩ 2 : INVOLVED, INTRICATE

in·vo·lu·tion \,in-və-'lü-shən\ *n* 1 : the act or an instance of enfolding or entangling 2 : COMPLEXITY, INTRICACY

in·volve \in-'välv\ *vb* in·volved; in·volv·ing 1 : to draw in as a participant 2 : ENVELOP 3 : to relate closely : CONNECT 4 : to have as part of itself : INCLUDE 5 : ENTAIL, IMPLY 6 : to have an effect on 7 : to occupy fully — **in·volve·ment** *n*

in·volved \-'välvd\ *adj* : INTRICATE, COMPLEX ⟨an ~ assassination plot⟩

in·vul·ner·a·ble \(')in-'vəl-nə-rə-bəl\ *adj* 1 : incapable of being wounded, injured, or damaged 2 : immune to or proof against attack — **in·vul·ner·a·bil·i·ty** \(,)in-,vəl-nə-rə-'bil-ət-ē\ *n* — **in·vul·ner·a·bly** \(')in-'vəl-nə-rə-blē\ *adv*

¹in·ward \'in-wərd\ *adj* 1 : situated on the inside 2 : MENTAL; *also* : SPIRITUAL 3 : directed toward the interior

²inward *or* in·wards \-wərdz\ *adv* 1 : toward the inside, center, or interior 2 : toward the inner being

in·ward·ly \'in-wərd-lē\ *adv* 1 : MENTALLY, SPIRITUALLY 2 : INTERNALLY ⟨bled ~⟩ 3 : to oneself ⟨cursed ~⟩ 4 : toward the center or interior

in·wrought \(')in-'ròt\ *adj* : having a decorative element worked or woven in : ORNAMENTED

io·dide \'ī-ə-,dīd\ *n* : a compound of iodine with another element or a radical

io·dine *also* io·din \'ī-ə-,dīn, -əd-ᵊn\ *n* : a nonmetallic chemical element used in medicine and photography

io·dize \'ī-ə-,dīz\ *vb* io·dized; io·diz·ing : to treat with iodine or an iodide

ion \'ī-ən, 'ī-,än\ *n* [Gk, neut. of *iōn*, prp. of *ienai* to go; so called because in electrolysis it goes to one of the two poles] **:** an electrically charged particle or group of atoms — **ion·ic** \ī-'än-ik\ adj

**ion·ize** \'ī-ə-‚nīz\ vb **ion·ized; ion·iz·ing 1 :** to convert wholly or partly into ions **2 :** to become ionized — **ion·iz·able** \-‚nī-zə-bəl\ adj — **ion·iza·tion** \‚ī-ə-nə-'zā-shən\ n — **ion·iz·er** \'ī-ə-‚nī-zər\ n

**ion·o·sphere** \ī-'än-ə-‚sfiər\ n **:** the part of the earth's atmosphere beginning at an altitude of about 25 miles and extending outward 250 miles or more that is responsible for long-distance radio transmission — **ion·o·spher·ic** \ī-‚än-ə-'sfi(ə)r-ik, -'sfer-\ adj

**IOOF** abbr Independent Order of Odd Fellows

**io·ta** \ī-'ōt-ə\ n [L, fr. Gk iōta, the 9th letter of the Greek alphabet] **:** a very small quantity **:** JOT

**IOU** \‚ī-(‚)ō-'yü\ n **:** an acknowledgment of a debt

**IP** abbr innings pitched

**ip·e·cac** \'ip-i-‚kak\ n **1 :** a tropical So. American creeping plant related to the madder **2 :** the dried rhizome and roots of ipecac used esp. as the source of an emetic

**IPS** abbr inches per second

**ip·so fac·to** \‚ip-sō-'fak-tō\ adv [NL, lit., by the fact itself] **:** by the very nature of the case

**iq** abbr [L idem quod] the same as

**IQ** \'ī-'kyü\ n **:** INTELLIGENCE QUOTIENT

**¹Ir** abbr Irish

**²Ir** symbol iridium

**IR** abbr **1** information retrieval **2** internal revenue

**IRA** abbr Irish Republican Army

**Ira·ni·an** \ir-'ā-nē-ən\ n **:** a native or inhabitant of Iran — **Iranian** adj

**Iraqi** \i-'räk-ē, -'rak-\ n **:** a native or inhabitant of Iraq — **Iraqi** adj

**iras·ci·ble** \ir-'as-ə-bəl, ī-'ras-\ adj **:** marked by hot temper and easily provoked anger **syn** choleric, testy, touchy, cranky, cross — **iras·ci·bil·i·ty** \-‚as-ə-'bil-ət-ē, -‚ras-\ n

**irate** \ī-'rāt\ adj **1 :** roused to or given to ire **:** INCENSED **2 :** arising from anger ⟨~ words⟩ — **irate·ly** adv

**IRBM** abbr intermediate range ballistic missile

**ire** \'ī(ə)r\ n **:** ANGER, WRATH — **ire·ful** adj

**Ire** abbr Ireland

**ire·nic** \ī-'ren-ik\ adj **:** conducive to or operating toward peace or conciliation

**ir·i·des·cence** \‚ir-ə-'des-³ns\ n **:** a rainbowlike play of colors — **ir·i·des·cent** \-³nt\ adj

**irid·i·um** \ir-'id-ē-əm\ n **:** a hard brittle very heavy metallic chemical element used in alloys

**iris** \'ī-rəs\ n, pl **iris·es** or **iri·des** \'ī-rə-‚dēz, 'ir-ə-\ [ME, fr. L iris rainbow, iris plant, fr. Gk, rainbow, iris plant, iris of the eye] **1 :** the colored part around the pupil of the eye **2 :** any of a large genus of plants with linear basal leaves and large showy flowers

**Irish** \'ī(ə)r-ish\ n **1 Irish** pl **:** the people of Ireland **2 :** the Celtic language of Ireland — **Irish** adj — **Irish·man** \-mən\ n

**Irish bull** n **:** an apparently congruous but actually incongruous expression (as "it was hereditary in his family to have no children")

**Irish coffee** n **:** hot sugared coffee with Irish whiskey and whipped cream

**Irish moss** n **:** the dried and bleached plants of two red algae

**Irish setter** n **:** any of a breed of bird dogs with a chestnut-brown or mahogany-red coat

**irk** \'ərk\ vb **:** to make weary, irritated, or bored **:** ANNOY

**irk·some** \'ərk-səm\ adj **:** tending to irk **:** ANNOYING — **irk·some·ly** adv

**¹iron** \'ī(ə)rn\ n **1 :** a metallic chemical element that rusts easily, is attracted by magnets, can be readily shaped, and is vital to biological processes **2 :** something (as a utensil) made of metal and esp. iron; also **:** something (as handcuffs) used to bind or restrain ⟨put them in ~s⟩ **3 :** STRENGTH, HARDNESS

**²iron** vb **1 :** to press or smooth with or as if with a heated flatiron **2 :** to remove by ironing — **iron·er** n

**iron-bound** \'ī(-ə)rn-'baùnd\ adj **1 :** HARSH, RUGGED ⟨~ coast⟩ **2 :** STERN, RIGOROUS ⟨~ traditions⟩

**¹iron·clad** \-'klad\ adj **1 :** sheathed in iron armor **2 :** RIGOROUS, EXACTING

**²iron·clad** \-‚klad\ n **:** an armored naval vessel

**iron curtain** n **:** a political, military, and ideological barrier that cuts off and isolates an area; esp **:** one between an area under Soviet Russian control and other areas

**iron·ic** \ī-'rän-ik\ or **iron·i·cal** \-i-kəl\ adj **1 :** of, relating to, or marked by irony **2 :** given to irony — **iron·i·cal·ly** \-i-k(ə-)lē\ adv

**iron·ing** \'ī(-ə)r-niŋ\ n **:** clothes ironed or to be ironed

**iron lung** n **:** a device for artificial respiration (as in polio) that encloses the chest or body in a chamber in which changes of pressure force air into and out of the lungs

**iron out** vb **:** to remove or lessen difficulties in or extremes of

**iron oxide** n **:** FERRIC OXIDE

**iron pyrites** n **:** PYRITE

**iron·stone** \'ī(-ə)rn-‚stōn\ n **1 :** a hard iron-rich sedimentary rock **2 :** a hard heavy durable pottery developed in England in the 19th century

**iron·ware** \-‚waər\ n **:** articles made of iron

**iron·weed** \-‚wēd\ n **:** any of several weedy American plants related to the daisy that have red or purple tubular flowers in terminal cymose heads

**iron·wood** \-‚wùd\ n **:** a tree or shrub with exceptionally hard wood; also **:** its wood

**iron·work** \-‚wərk\ n **1 :** work in iron **2** pl **:** a mill or building where iron or steel is smelted or heavy iron or steel products are made — **iron·work·er** n

**iro·ny** \'ī-rə-nē\ *n, pl* **-nies** [L *ironia*, fr. Gk *eirōnia*, fr. *eirōn* dissembler] **1** : the use of words to express the opposite of what one really means **2** : incongruity between the actual result of a sequence of events and the expected result

**Ir·o·quois** \'ir-ə-ˌkwöi\ *n, pl* **Iroquois** \-ˌkwöi(z)\ [F, fr. Algonquin (a No. American Indian dialect) *Irinakhoiw*, lit., real adders] **1** *pl* : an Indian confederacy of New York that consisted of the Cayuga, Mohawk, Oneida, Onondaga, and Seneca and later included the Tuscarora **2** : a member of any of the Iroquois peoples

**ir·ra·di·ate** \ir-'ād-ē-ˌāt\ *vb* **-at·ed;** **-at·ing** **1** : ILLUMINATE **2** : ENLIGHTEN **3** : to treat by exposure to radiation **4** : RADIATE *(~ damage)* — **ir·ra·di·a·tion** \-ˌād-ē-'ā-shən\ *n*

**¹ir·ra·tio·nal** \(')ir-'ash-(ə-)nəl\ *adj* **1** : incapable of reasoning *(~ beasts)*; *also* : defective in mental power *(~ with fever)* **2** : not based on reason *(~ fears)* **3** : relating to, consisting of, or being one or more irrational numbers — **ir·ra·tio·nal·i·ty** \(ˌ)ir-ˌash-ə-'nal-ət-ē\ *n* — **ir·ra·tio·nal·ly** \(')ir-'ash-(ə-)nə-lē\ *adv*

**²irrational** *n* : IRRATIONAL NUMBER

**irrational number** *n* : a real number that cannot be expressed as the quotient of two integers

**ir·re·claim·able** \ˌir-i-'klā-mə-bəl\ *adj* : incapable of being reclaimed

**ir·rec·on·cil·able** \(ˌ)ir-ˌek-ən-'sī-lə-bəl, (')ir-'ek-ən-ˌsī-\ *adj* : impossible to reconcile, adjust, or harmonize — **ir·rec·on·cil·abil·i·ty** \(ˌ)ir-ˌek-ən-ˌsī-lə-'bil-ət-ē\ *n*

**ir·re·cov·er·able** \ˌir-i-'kəv-(ə-)rə-bəl\ *adj* : not capable of being recovered or rectified : IRREPARABLE — **ir·re·cov·er·ably** \-blē\ *adv*

**ir·re·deem·able** \ˌir-i-'dē-mə-bəl\ *adj* **1** : not redeemable; *esp* : not terminable by payment of the principal *(an ~ bond)* **2** : not convertible into gold or silver at the will of the holder **3** : admitting of no change or reform

**ir·re·den·tism** \-'den-ˌtiz-əm\ *n* : a principle or policy directed toward the incorporation of a territory historically or ethnically part of another into that other — **ir·re·den·tist** \-'dent-əst\ *n or adj*

**ir·re·duc·ible** \ˌir-i-'d(y)ü-sə-bəl\ *adj* : not reducible — **ir·re·duc·ibly** \-'d(y)ü-sə-blē\ *adv*

**ir·re·fra·ga·ble** \(')ir-'(r)ef-rə-gə-bəl\ *adj* : impossible to deny or refute

**ir·re·fut·able** \ˌir-i-'fyüt-ə-bəl, (')ir-'(r)ef-yət-\ *adj* : impossible to refute

**irreg** *abbr* irregular

**ir·reg·u·lar** \(')ir-'eg-yə-lər\ *adj* **1** : not regular : not natural or uniform **2** : not conforming to the normal or usual manner of inflection *(~ verbs)* **3** : not belonging to a regular or organized army organization *(~ troops)* — irregular *n* — **ir·reg·u·lar·i·ty** \(ˌ)ir-ˌeg-yə-'lar-ət-ē\ *n* — **ir·reg·u·lar·ly** \(')ir-'eg-yə-lər-lē\ *adv*

**ir·rel·e·vant** \(')ir-'el-ə-vənt\ *adj* : not relevant — **ir·rel·e·vance** \-vəns\ *n*

**ir·re·li·gious** \ˌir-i-'lij-əs\ *adj* : lacking religious emotions, doctrines, or practices

**ir·re·me·di·a·ble** \ˌir-i-'mēd-ē-ə-bəl\ *adj* : impossible to remedy or correct : INCURABLE

**ir·re·mov·able** \-'mü-və-bəl\ *adj* : not removable

**ir·rep·a·ra·ble** \(')ir-'ep-(ə-)rə-bəl\ *adj* : impossible to make good, undo, repair, or remedy *(~ damage)*

**ir·re·place·able** \ˌir-i-'plā-sə-bəl\ *adj* : not replaceable

**ir·re·press·ible** \-'pres-ə-bəl\ *adj* : impossible to repress or control

**ir·re·proach·able** \-'prō-chə-bəl\ *adj* : not reproachable : BLAMELESS

**ir·re·sist·ible** \-'zis-tə-bəl\ *adj* : impossible to successfully resist — **ir·re·sist·ibly** \-blē\ *adv*

**ir·res·o·lute** \(')ir-'ez-ə-ˌlüt\ *adj* : uncertain how to act or proceed : VACILLATING — **ir·res·o·lute·ly** \-ˌlüt-lē\, \(ˌ)ir-ˌez-ə-'lüt-\ *adv* — **ir·res·o·lu·tion** \(ˌ)ir-ˌez-ə-'lü-shən\ *n*

**ir·re·spec·tive** \ˌir-i-'spek-tiv-\ *prep* : without regard to

**ir·re·spon·si·ble** \-'spän-sə-bəl\ *adj* : not responsible — **ir·re·spon·si·bil·i·ty** \-ˌspän-sə-'bil-ət-ē\ *n* — **ir·re·spon·si·bly** \-'spän-sə-blē\ *adv*

**ir·re·triev·able** \ˌir-i-'trē-və-bəl\ *adj* : not retrievable : IRRECOVERABLE

**ir·rev·er·ence** \(')ir-'ev-(ə-)rəns\ *n* **1** : lack of reverence **2** : an irreverent act or utterance — **ir·rev·er·ent** \-(ə-)rənt\ *adj*

**ir·re·vers·ible** \ˌir-i-'vər-sə-bəl\ *adj* : incapable of being reversed

**ir·rev·o·ca·ble** \(')ir-'ev-ə-kə-bəl\ *adj* : incapable of being revoked or recalled — **ir·rev·o·ca·bly** \-blē\ *adv*

**ir·ri·gate** \'ir-ə-ˌgāt\ *vb* **-gat·ed;** **-gat·ing** **1** : to supply (as land) with water by artificial means; *also* : to flush with liquid — **ir·ri·ga·tion** \ˌir-ə-'gā-shən\ *n*

**ir·ri·ta·ble** \'ir-ət-ə-bəl\ *adj* : capable of being irritated; *esp* : readily or easily irritated — **ir·ri·ta·bil·i·ty** \ˌir-ət-ə-'bil-ət-ē\ *n* — **ir·ri·ta·bly** \'ir-ət-ə-blē\ *adv*

**ir·ri·tate** \'ir-ə-ˌtāt\ *vb* **-tat·ed;** **-tat·ing** **1** : to excite to anger : EXASPERATE **2** : to act as a stimulus toward : STIMULATE; *also* : to make sore or inflamed — **ir·ri·tant** \'ir-ə-tənt\ *adj or n* — **ir·ri·tat·ing·ly** \-ˌtāt-iŋ-lē\ *adv* — **ir·ri·ta·tion** \ˌir-ə-'tā-shən\ *n*

**ir·rupt** \(')ir-'əpt\ *vb* **1** : to rush in forcibly or violently **2** : to increase suddenly in numbers *(rabbits ~ in cycles)* — **ir·rup·tion** \-'əp-shən\ *n*

**IRS** *abbr* Internal Revenue Service

**is** *pres 3d sing of* BE

**Isa** *or* **Is** *abbr* Isaiah

**-ish** \ish\ *adj suffix* **1** : of, relating to, or being *(Finnish)* **2** : characteristic of *(boyish)* : having the undesirable qualities of *(mulish)* **3** : having a touch or trace of : somewhat *(purplish)* **4** : having the approximate age of *(fortyish)*

**5** : being or occurring at the approximate time of ⟨eight*ish*⟩

**isin·glass** \'īz-ə-n-ˌglas, 'ī-ziŋ-\ *n* **1** : a gelatin obtained from the air bladders of various fish **2** : MICA

**isl** *abbr* island

**is·lam** \is-'läm, iz-, -'lam, 'is-ˌ, 'iz-ˌ\ *n* [Ar *islām* submission (to the will of God)] : the religious faith of Muslims; *also* : the civilization built on this faith — **Is·lam·ic** \is-'läm-ik, iz-, -'lam-\ *adj*

**is·land** \'ī-lənd\ *n* **1** : a body of land surrounded by water and smaller than a continent **2** : something resembling an island by its isolated or surrounded position

**is·land·er** \'ī-lən-dər\ *n* : a native or inhabitant of an island

**isle** \'īl\ *n* : ISLAND; *esp* : a small island

**is·let** \'ī-lət\ *n* : a small island

**ism** \'iz-əm\ *n* : a distinctive doctrine, cause, or theory

**-ism** \ˌiz-əm\ *n suffix* **1** : act : practice : process ⟨critic*ism*⟩ **2** : manner of action or behavior characteristic of a (specified) person or thing **3** : state : condition : property ⟨barbarian*ism*⟩ **4** : abnormal state or condition resulting from excess of a (specified) thing ⟨alcohol*ism*⟩ or marked by resemblance to (such) a person or thing ⟨mongol*ism*⟩ **5** : doctrine : theory : cult ⟨Buddh*ism*⟩ **6** : adherence to a system or a class of principles ⟨stoic*ism*⟩ **7** : characteristic or peculiar feature or trait ⟨colloquial*ism*⟩

**iso·bar** \'ī-sə-ˌbär\ *n* : a line on a map connecting places of equal barometric pressure — **iso·bar·ic** \ˌī-sə-'bär-ik, -'bar-\ *adj*

**iso·late** \'ī-sə-ˌlāt, 'is-ə-\ *vb* **-lat·ed; -lat·ing** [fr. *isolated* set apart, fr. F *isolé*, fr. It *isolato*, fr. *isola* island, fr. L *insula*] : to place or keep by itself : separate from others — **iso·la·tion** \ˌī-sə-'lā-shən, ˌis-ə-\ *n*

**iso·la·tion·ism** \ˌī-sə-'lā-shə-ˌniz-əm, ˌis-ə-\ *n* : a policy of national isolation by abstention from international political and economic relations — **iso·la·tion·ist** \-sh(ə )nəst\ *n or adj*

**iso·mer** \'ī-sə-mər\ *n* : any of two or more chemical compounds that contain the same numbers of atoms of the same elements but differ in structural arrangement and properties — **iso·mer·ic** \ˌī-sə-'mer-ik\ *adj* — **isom·er·ism** \ī-'säm-ə-ˌriz-əm\ *n*

**iso·met·rics** \ˌī-sə-'met-riks\ *n sing or pl* : exercise or a system of exercises involving contraction of muscles taking place against resistance but without significant shortening of muscle fibers — **isometric** *adj*

**iso·prene** \'ī-sə-ˌprēn\ *n* : a hydrocarbon used esp. in making synthetic rubber

**isos·ce·les** \ī-'säs-ə-ˌlēz\ *adj* : having two equal sides ⟨an ~ triangle⟩

**isos·ta·sy** \ī-'säs-tə-sē\ *n* : general equilibrium in the earth's crust maintained by the gravity-induced flow of deep rock material — **iso·stat·ic** \ˌī-sə-'stat-ik\ *adj* — **iso·stat·i·cal·ly** \-i-k(ə-)lē\ *adv*

**iso·therm** \'ī-sə-ˌthərm\ *n* : a line on a map connecting points having the same average temperature

**iso·ther·mal** \ˌī-sə-'thər-məl\ *adj* : of, relating to, or marked by equality of temperature

**iso·ton·ic** \ˌī-sə-'tän-ik\ *adj* : having the same or equal osmotic pressure ⟨a salt solution ~ with red blood cells⟩

**iso·tope** \'ī-sə-ˌtōp\ *n* [Gk *isos* equal + *topos* place] : any of two or more species of atoms of the same chemical element nearly identical in chemical behavior but differing in the number of neutrons — **iso·to·pic** \ˌī-sə-'täp-ik, -'tō-pik\ *adj* — **iso·to·pi·cal·ly** \-'täp-i-k(ə-)lē, -'tō-pi-\ *adv*

**Isr** *abbr* Israel, Israeli

**Is·rae·li** \iz-'rā-lē\ *n, pl* **Israelis** *also* **Israeli** : a native or inhabitant of the Republic of Israel — **Israeli** *adj*

**Is·ra·el·ite** \'iz-rē-ə-ˌlīt\ *n* : a member of the Hebrew people descended from Jacob — **Israelite** *adj*

**is·su·ance** \'ish-ə-wəns\ *n* : the act of issuing or giving out esp. officially

**¹is·sue** \'ish-ü\ *n* **1** *pl* : proceeds from a source of revenue (as an estate) **2** : the action of going, coming, or flowing out : EGRESS, EMERGENCE **3** : EXIT, OUTLET, VENT **4** : OFFSPRING, PROGENY **5** : OUTCOME, RESULT **6** : a point of debate or controversy; *also* : the point at which an unsettled matter is ready for a decision **7** : a discharge (as of blood) from the body **8** : something coming forth from a specified source **9** : the act of officially giving out or printing : PUBLICATION; *also* : the quantity of things given out at one time

**²issue** *vb* **is·sued; is·su·ing 1** : to go, come, or flow out **2** : to come forth or cause to come forth : EMERGE, DISCHARGE, EMIT **3** : ACCRUE **4** : to descend from a specified parent or ancestor **5** : EMANATE, RESULT **6** : to result in **7** : to put forth or distribute officially **8** : PUBLISH — **is·su·er** *n*

**-ist** \əst\ *n suffix* **1** : one that performs a (specified) action ⟨cycl*ist*⟩ : one that makes or produces ⟨novel*ist*⟩ **2** : one that plays a (specified) musical instrument ⟨harp*ist*⟩ **3** : one that operates a (specified) mechanical instrument or contrivance ⟨automobil*ist*⟩ **4** : one that specializes in a (specified) art or science or skill ⟨geolog*ist*⟩ **5** : one that adheres to or advocates a (specified) doctrine or system or code of behavior ⟨social*ist*⟩ or that of a (specified) individual ⟨Darwin*ist*⟩

**²-ist** *adj suffix* : of, relating to, or characteristic of ⟨dilettant*ist*⟩

**isth·mi·an** \'is-mē-ən\ *adj* : of, relating to, or situated in or near an isthmus

**isth·mus** \'is-məs\ *n* : a narrow strip of land connecting two larger portions of land

**¹it** \(')it, ət\ *pron* **1** : that one — used of a lifeless thing, a plant, a person or animal, or an abstract entity ⟨~'s a big building⟩ ⟨~'s a shade tree⟩ ⟨who is ~⟩

⟨beauty is everywhere and ∼ is a source of joy⟩ **2** — used as an anticipatory subject or object ⟨∼'s good to see you⟩

²**it** \'it\ *n* : the player in a game who performs a function (as trying to catch others in a game of tag) essential to the nature of the game

**It** *abbr* Italian; Italy

**ital** *abbr* italic; italicized

**Ital** *abbr* Italian

**Ital·ian** \ə-'tal-yən, i-\ *n* **1** : a native or inhabitant of Italy **2** : the language of Italy — **Italian** *adj*

**Italian sandwich** *n* : SUBMARINE 2

**ital·ic** \ə-'tal-ik, i-, ī-\ *adj* : relating to type in which the letters slope up toward the right (as in "*italic*") — **italic** *n*

**ital·i·cize** \ə-'tal-ə-₁sīz, i-, ī-\ *vb* **-cized; -ciz·ing** : to print in italics

**itch** \'ich\ *n* **1** : an uneasy irritating skin sensation related to pain **2** : a skin disorder accompanied by an itch **3** : a persistent desire — **itch** *vb* — **itchy** *adj*

**-ite** \₁īt\ *n suffix* **1** : native : resident ⟨Brooklyn*ite*⟩ **2** : descendant ⟨Ish-mael*ite*⟩ **3** : adherent : follower ⟨Lenin-*ite*⟩ **4** : product ⟨vulcan*ite*⟩ **5** : mineral : rock ⟨quartz*ite*⟩

**item** \'īt-əm\ *n* [L, likewise, also] **1** : a separate particular in a list, account, or series : ARTICLE **2** : a separate piece of news (as in a newspaper)

**item·ize** \'īt-ə-₁mīz\ *vb* **-ized; -iz·ing** : to set down in detail : LIST — **item·iza·tion** \₁īt-ə-mə-'zā-shən\ *n*

**it·er·ate** \'it-ə-₁rāt\ *vb* **-at·ed; -at·ing** : REITERATE, REPEAT — **it·er·a·tion** \₁it-ə-'rā-shən\ *n*

**itin·er·ant** \ī-'tin-ə-rənt, ə-\ *adj* : traveling from place to place; *esp* : covering a circuit ⟨an ∼ preacher⟩

**itin·er·ary** \ī-'tin-ə-₁rer-ē, ə-\ *n, pl* **-ar·ies** **1** : the route of a journey or

the proposed outline of one **2** : a travel diary **3** : GUIDEBOOK

**its** \(₁)its, əts\ *adj* : of or relating to it or itself

**it·self** \it-'self, ət-\ *pron* : its self : IT — used reflexively, for emphasis, or in absolute constructions

**-ity** \ət-ē\ *n suffix* : quality : state : degree ⟨alkalin*ity*⟩

**IUD** *abbr* intrauterine device

**IV** *abbr* intravenous

**-ive** \iv\ *adj suffix* : that performs or tends toward an (indicated) action ⟨correct*ive*⟩

**ivo·ry** \'īv-(ə-)rē\ *n, pl* **-ries** [ME *ivorie*, fr. OF *ivoire*, fr. L *eboreus* of ivory, fr. *ebur* ivory, fr. Eg *'b* elephant, ivory] **1** : the hard creamy-white material composing elephants' tusks **2** : a variable color averaging a pale yellow **3** : something made of ivory or of a similar substance

**ivory tower** *n* : an impractical lack of concern with urgent problems; *also* : a secluded place for meditation

**ivy** \'ī-vē\ *n, pl* **ivies** : a trailing woody vine with evergreen leaves and small black berries

**IW** *abbr* Isle of Wight

**IWW** *abbr* Industrial Workers of the World

**-ize** \₁īz\ *vb suffix* **1** : cause to be or conform to or resemble ⟨system*ize*⟩ : cause to be formed into ⟨union*ize*⟩ **2** : subject to a (specified) action ⟨satir*ize*⟩ **3** : saturate, treat, or combine with ⟨macadam*ize*⟩ **4** : treat like ⟨idol*ize*⟩ **5** : become : become like ⟨crystall*ize*⟩ **6** : be productive in or of : engage in a (specified) activity ⟨philosoph*ize*⟩ **7** : adopt or spread the manner of activity or the teaching of ⟨calvin*ize*⟩

---

¹**j** \'jā\ *n, pl* **j's** *or* **js** \'jāz\ *often cap* : the 10th letter of the English alphabet

²**j** *abbr, often cap* **1** jack **2** journal **3** justice

¹**jab** \'jab\ *vb* **jabbed; jab·bing** : to thrust quickly or abruptly : POKE

²**jab** *n* : a usu. short straight punch

**jab·ber** \'jab-ər\ *vb* **jab·bered; jab·ber·ing** \'jab-(ə-)riŋ\ : to talk rapidly, indistinctly, or unintelligibly : CHATTER — **jabber** *n*

**jab·ber·wocky** \'jab-ər-₁wäk-ē\ *n* : meaningless speech or writing

**ja·bot** \zha-'bō, 'jab-₁ō\ *n* : a ruffle worn down the front of a dress or shirt

**jac·a·ran·da** \₁jak-ə-'ran-də\ *n* : any of a genus of pinnate-leaved tropical American trees with clusters of showy blue flowers

**ja·cinth** \'jās-ᵊnth\ *n* : HYACINTH

¹**jack** \'jak\ *n* **1** : a mechanical device; *esp* : one used to raise a heavy body a short distance **2** : a small national flag flown by a ship **3** : a playing card bearing the figure of a man **4** : a small target ball in lawn bowling **5** : a small 6-pointed metal object used in a game

(**jacks**) **6** : a socket into which a plug is inserted for connecting electric circuits **7** : a male donkey

²**jack** *vb* **1** : to raise by means of a jack **2** : INCREASE ⟨∼ up prices⟩

**jack·al** \'jak-əl, -₁ol\ *n* [Turk *çakal*, fr. Per *shagāl*, fr. Skt *srgāla*] : an Old World wild dog smaller than the related wolves

**jack·a·napes** \'jak-ə-₁nāps\ *n* **1** : MONKEY, APE **2** : an impudent or conceited person

**jack·ass** \-₁as\ *n* **1** : a male ass; *also* : DONKEY **2** : a stupid person : FOOL

**jack·boot** \-₁büt\ *n* **1** : a heavy military boot of glossy black leather extending above the knee **2** : a military boot reaching to the calf and having no laces

**jack·daw** \'jak-₁dȯ\ *n* : a black and gray Eurasian crowlike bird

**jack·et** \'jak-ət\ *n* [ME *jaket*, fr. MF *jaquet*, dim. of *jaque* short jacket, fr. *jacque* peasant, fr. the name *Jacques* James] **1** : a garment for the upper body usu. having a front opening, collar, and sleeves **2** : an outer covering or casing ⟨a book ∼⟩ — **jack·et·ed** *adj*

**Jack Frost** *n* **:** frost or frosty weather personified

**jack·ham·mer** \'jak-,ham-ər\ *n* **:** a pneumatic percussion tool for drilling rock or breaking pavement

**jack-in-the-box** \'jak-ən-thə-,bäks\ *n, pl* **jack-in-the-box·es** *or* **jacks-in-the-box :** a small box out of which a figure springs when the lid is raised

**jack-in-the-pul·pit** \,jak-ən-thə-'pùl-,pit, -pət, -'pəl-\ *n, pl* **jack-in-the-pulpits** *or* **jacks-in-the-pulpit :** an American spring-flowering woodland herb having an upright club-shaped spadix arched over by a green and purple spathe

¹**jack·knife** \'jak-,nīf\ *n* **1 :** a large pocketknife **2 :** a dive in which the diver bends from the waist and touches his ankles before straightening out

²**jackknife** *vb* **:** to turn or rise and form an angle of 90 degrees or less with each other — used esp. of a pair of connected vehicles

**jack·leg** \'jak-,leg\ *adj* **1 :** lacking skill or training **2 :** MAKESHIFT

**jack-of-all-trades** \,jak-ə-'vòl-,trädz\ *n, pl* **jacks-of-all-trades :** one who is able to do passable work at various tasks

**jack-o'-lan·tern** \'jak-ə-,lant-ərn\ *n* **:** a lantern made of a pumpkin cut to look like a human face

**jack·pot** \'jak-,pät\ *n* **1 :** a large sum of money formed by the accumulation of stakes from previous play (as in poker) **2 :** an impressive and often unexpected success or reward

**jack·rab·bit** \-,rab-ət\ *n* **:** a large hare of western No. America with very long hind legs

**jack·screw** \'jak-,skrü\ *n* **:** a screw-operated jack

**jack·straw** \-,strò\ *n* **1 :** a straw or a thin strip used in the game of jackstraws **2** *pl* **:** a game in which jackstraws are let fall in a heap and each player in turn tries to remove them one at a time without disturbing the rest

**jack·tar** \-'tär\ *n, often cap* **:** SAILOR

**Ja·cob's ladder** \,jā-kəbz-\ *n* **:** any of several perennial herbs related to phlox that have pinnate leaves and bright blue or white bell-shaped flowers

**jac·quard** \'jak-,ärd\ *n, often cap* **:** a fabric of intricate variegated weave or pattern

¹**jade** \'jād\ *n* **1 :** a broken-down, vicious, or worthless horse **2 :** a disreputable woman

²**jade** *vb* **jad·ed; jad·ing 1 :** to wear out by overwork or abuse **2 :** to become weary **syn** EXHAUST, fatigue, tire

³**jade** *n* [F, fr. obs. Sp (*piedra de la*) *ijada*, lit., loin stone; fr. the belief that jade cures renal colic] **:** a usu. green gemstone that takes a high polish

**jad·ed** \'jād-əd\ *adj* **:** dulled by a surfeit or excess

¹**jag** \'jag\ *n* **:** a sharp projecting part

²**jag** *n* **:** SPREE

**jag·ged** \'jag-əd\ *adj* **:** sharply notched

**jag·uar** \'jag(-yə)-,wär\ *n* **:** a black-spotted tropical American cat that is larger and stockier than the Old World leopard

**jai alai** \'hī-,lī\ *n* [Sp, fr. Basque, fr. *jai* festival + *alai* merry] **:** a court game played by two or four players with a ball and a curved wicker basket strapped to the right wrist

¹**jail** \'jāl\ *n* [ME *jaiole*, fr. OF, fr. (assumed) VL *caveola*, dim. of L *cavea* cage] **:** PRISON; *esp* **:** one for persons held in temporary custody

²**jail** *vb* **:** to confine in a jail

**jail·bird** \-,bərd\ *n* **:** a person confined in jail

**jail·break** \-,brāk\ *n* **:** a forcible escape from jail

**jail·er** *or* **jail·or** \'jā-lər\ *n* **:** a keeper of a jail

**jal·ap** \'jal-əp, 'jäl-\ *n* **:** a purgative drug from the root of a Mexican plant related to the morning glory; *also* **:** this root or plant

**ja·lopy** \jə-'läp-ē\ *n, pl* **jalopies :** a dilapidated automobile

**jal·ou·sie** \'jal-ə-sē\ *n* **:** a blind, window, or door with adjustable horizontal slats or louvers

¹**jam** \'jam\ *vb* **jammed; jam·ming 1 :** to press into a close or tight position **2 :** to push forcibly ⟨~ on the brakes⟩ **3 :** CRUSH, BRUISE **4 :** to cause to become wedged so as to be unworkable; *also* **:** to become unworkable through the jamming of a movable part **5 :** to make unintelligible by sending out interfering signals or messages **6 :** to take part in a jam session

²**jam** *n* **1 :** a crowded mass that impedes or blocks ⟨traffic ~⟩ **2 :** a difficult state of affairs

³**jam** *n* **:** a food made by boiling fruit and sugar to a thick consistency

**Jam** *abbr* Jamaica

**jamb** \'jam\ *n* **:** an upright piece forming the side of an opening (as of a door)

**jam·bo·ree** \,jam-bə-'rē\ *n* **:** a large festive gathering

**jam session** *n* **:** an impromptu performance by jazz musicians

**Jan** *abbr* January

**jan·gle** \'jaŋ-gəl\ *vb* **jan·gled; jangling** \-g(ə-)liŋ\ **:** to make a harsh or discordant sound — **jangle** *n*

**jan·i·tor** \'jan-ət-ər\ *n* **:** a person who has the care of a building — **jan·i·to·ri·al** \,jan-ə-'tōr-ē-əl\ *adj* — **jan·i·tress** \'jan-ə-trəs\ *n*

**Jan·u·ary** \'jan-yə-,wer-ē\ *n* [ME *Januarie*, fr. L *Januarius*, first month of the ancient Roman year, fr. *Janus*, two-faced god of gates and beginnings] **:** the first month of the year having 31 days

**Jap** *abbr* Japan; Japanese

**ja·pan** \jə-'pan\ *n* **1 :** a varnish yielding a hard brilliant finish **2 :** work (as lacquer ware) finished and decorated in the Japanese manner — **japan** *vb*

**Jap·a·nese** \,jap-ə-'nēz, -'nēs\ *n, pl* **Japanese 1 :** a native or inhabitant of Japan **2 :** the language of Japan — **Japanese** *adj*

**Japanese beetle** *n* : a small metallic green and brown beetle introduced from Japan that is a pest on the roots of grasses as a grub and on foliage and fruits as an adult

¹**jape** \'jāp\ *vb* **japed; jap·ing** **1** : JOKE **2** : MOCK

²**jape** *n* : JEST, GIBE

¹**jar** \'jär\ *vb* **jarred; jar·ring** **1** : to make a harsh or discordant sound **2** : to have a harsh or disagreeable effect **3** : VIBRATE, SHAKE

²**jar** *n* **1** : a harsh discordant sound **2** : JOLT **3** : QUARREL, DISPUTE **4** : a painful effect : SHOCK

³**jar** *n* : a broad-mouthed container usu. of glass or earthenware

**jar·di·niere** \ˌjärd-ᵊn-'iər\ *n* : an ornamental stand or pot for plants or flowers

**jar·gon** \'jär-gən, -ˌgän\ *n* **1** : confused unintelligible language **2** : the special vocabulary of a particular group or activity **3** : obscure and often pretentious language

**Jas** *abbr* James

**jas·mine** \'jaz-mən\ *n* : any of various climbing shrubs with fragrant flowers

**jas·per** \'jas-pər\ *n* : a red, yellow, or brown opaque quartz

**ja·to unit** \'jāt-ō-\ *n* [*jet* assisted *takeoff*] : a special rocket engine to help an airplane take off

**jaun·dice** \'jȯn-dəs\ *n* : yellowish discoloration of skin, tissues, and body fluids by bile pigments; *also* : a disorder marked by jaundice

**jaun·diced** \-dəst\ *adj* **1** : affected with or as if with jaundice **2** : exhibiting envy, distaste, or hostility

**jaunt** \'jȯnt\ *n* : a short trip usu. for pleasure

**jaun·ty** \'jȯnt-ē\ *adj* **jaun·ti·er; -est** : sprightly in manner or appearance : LIVELY *syn* debonair, perky, cocky — **jaun·ti·ly** \'jȯnt-ᵊl-ē\ *adv* — **jaun·ti·ness** \-ē-nəs\ *n*

**jav·e·lin** \'jav-(ə-)lən\ *n* **1** : a light spear **2** : a slender usu. metal shaft thrown for distance in a track-and-field contest

¹**jaw** \'jȯ\ *n* **1** : either of the bony or cartilaginous structures that support the soft tissues enclosing the mouth and that usu. bear teeth; *also* : the parts forming the walls of the mouth and serving to open and close it — usu. used in pl. **2** : one of a pair of movable parts for holding or crushing something — **jaw·bone** \-ˌbōn, -ˌbōn\ *n* — **jawed** \'jȯd\ *adj*

²**jaw** *vb* : to talk abusively, indignantly, or at length

**jaw·break·er** \-ˌbrā-kər\ *n* **1** : a word difficult to pronounce **2** : a round hard candy

**jay** \'jā\ *n* : any of various noisy brightly colored birds smaller than the related crows

**jay·bird** \'jā-ˌbərd\ *n* : JAY

**Jay·cee** \'jā-'sē\ *n* : a member of a junior chamber of commerce

**jay·gee** \'jā-'jē\ *n* : LIEUTENANT JUNIOR GRADE

**jay·vee** \'jā-'vē\ *n* **1** : JUNIOR VARSITY **2** : a member of a junior varsity team

**jay·walk** \'jā-ˌwȯk\ *vb* : to cross a street carelessly without regard for traffic regulations — **jay·walk·er** *n*

¹**jazz** \'jaz\ *vb* : ENLIVEN ⟨~ things up⟩

²**jazz** *n* **1** : American music characterized by improvisation, syncopated rhythms, and contrapuntal ensemble playing **2** : empty talk : STUFF

**jazzy** \'jaz-ē\ *adj* **jazz·i·er; -est** **1** : having the characteristics of jazz **2** : marked by unrestraint, animation, or flashiness

**JCC** *abbr* junior chamber of commerce

**JCS** *abbr* joint chiefs of staff

**jct** *abbr* junction

**JD** *abbr* **1** doctor of jurisprudence; doctor of law **2** doctor of laws **3** justice department **4** juvenile delinquent

**jeal·ous** \'jel-əs\ *adj* **1** : demanding complete devotion **2** : suspicious of a rival or of one believed to enjoy an advantage **3** : VIGILANT **4** : distrustfully watchful — **jeal·ous·ly** *adv* — **jeal·ou·sy** \-ə-sē\ *n*

**jeans** \'jēnz\ *n pl* : pants made of durable twilled cotton cloth

**jeep** \'jēp\ *n* [alter. of *gee pee*, fr. general-*purpose*] : a ¼-ton four-wheel drive general-purpose motor vehicle used by the U.S. army in World War II

¹**jeer** \'jiər\ *vb* **1** : to speak or cry out in derision **2** : RIDICULE

²**jeer** *n* : TAUNT

**Je·ho·vah** \ji-'hō-və\ *n* : GOD 1

**je·hu** \'jē-h(y)ü\ *n* : a driver of a coach or cab

**je·june** \ji-'jün\ *adj* **1** : lacking interest or significance : DULL **2** : CHILDISH ⟨~ remarks⟩

**je·ju·num** \ji-'jü-nəm\ *n* : the section of the small intestine between the duodenum and the ileum — **je·ju·nal** \-'jün-ᵊl\ *adj*

**jell** \'jel\ *vb* **1** : to come to the consistency of jelly **2** : to take shape

**jel·ly** \'jel-ē\ *n, pl* **jellies** **1** : a food with a soft somewhat elastic consistency due usu. to the presence of gelatin or pectin; *esp* : a fruit product made by boiling sugar and the juice of a fruit **2** : a substance resembling jelly in consistency — **jelly** *vb*

**jel·ly·fish** \'jel-ē-ˌfish\ *n* : a sea animal with a saucer-shaped jellylike body

**jen·net** \'jen-ət\ *n* **1** : a small Spanish horse **2** : a female donkey

**jen·ny** \'jen-ē\ *n, pl* **jennies** **1** : a female bird or donkey

**jeop·ar·dy** \'jep-ərd-ē\ *n* [ME *jeopardie,* fr. OF *jeu parti* alternative, lit., divided game] : exposure to death, loss, or injury *syn* peril, hazard, risk, danger — **jeop·ar·dize** \-ər-ˌdīz\ *vb* — **jeop·ar·dous** \-ərd-əs\ *adj*

**Jer** *abbr* Jeremiah

**jer·e·mi·ad** \ˌjer-ə-'mī-əd, -ˌad\ *n* : a prolonged lamentation or complaint

¹**jerk** \'jərk\ *vb* **1** : to give a sharp quick push, pull, or twist **2** : to move in short abrupt motions

²**jerk** *n* **1 :** a short quick pull or twist **:** TWITCH **2 :** a stupid, foolish, or eccentric person — **jerk·i·ly** \'jər-kə-lē\ *adv* — **jerky** \-kē\ *adj*

**jer·kin** \'jər-kən\ *n* **:** a close-fitting sleeveless jacket

**jerk·wa·ter** \'jərk-,wȯt-ər, -,wät-\ *adj* [fr. *jerkwater* (rural train); fr. the fact that it took on water carried in buckets from the source of supply] **:** of minor importance **:** INSIGNIFICANT ⟨~ towns⟩

**jer·ry-built** \'jer-ē-,bilt\ *adj* **1 :** built cheaply and flimsily **2 :** carelessly or hastily put together

**jer·sey** \'jər-zē\ *n, pl* **jerseys** [*Jersey*, one of the Channel islands] **1 :** a plain weft-knitted fabric **2 :** a close fitting knitted garment for the upper body **3 :** any of a breed of minor usu. fawn-colored dairy cattle

**jess** \'jes\ *n* **:** a leg strap to which the leash of a falconer's hawk is attached

**jes·sa·mine** \'jes-ə-mən\ *var of* JASMINE

¹**jest** \'jest\ *n* **1 :** an act intended to provoke laughter **2 :** a witty remark **3 :** a frivolous mood ⟨spoken in ~⟩

²**jest** *vb* **:** JOKE, BANTER

**jest·er** \'jes-tər\ *n* **:** a retainer formerly kept to provide casual entertainment

¹**jet** \'jet\ *n* **:** a compact velvet-black coal that takes a good polish and is used for jewelry

²**jet** *vb* **jet·ted; jet·ting 1 :** to spout or emit in a stream **2 :** to travel by jet

³**jet** *n* **1 :** a forceful rush (as of liquid or gas) through a narrow opening; *also* **:** a nozzle for a jet of fluid **2 :** a jet-propelled airplane

**jet·port** \'jet-,pȯrt\ *n* **:** an airport designed to handle jet airplanes

**jet-propelled** \,jet-prə-'peld\ *adj* **:** driven by an engine (**jet engine**) that produces propulsion (**jet propulsion**) as a result of the rearward discharge of a jet of fluid (as heated air and exhaust gases)

**jet·sam** \'jet-səm\ *n* **:** goods thrown overboard to lighten a ship in distress; *esp* **:** such goods when washed ashore

**jet set** *n* **:** an international social group of wealthy individuals who frequent fashionable resorts

**jet stream** *n* **:** a long narrow high-altitude current of high-speed winds blowing generally from the west

**jet·ti·son** \'jet-ə-sən\ *vb* **1 :** to throw (goods) overboard to lighten a ship in distress **2 :** DISCARD — **jettison** *n*

**jet·ty** \'jet-ē\ *n, pl* **jetties 1 :** a pier built to influence the current or to protect a harbor **2 :** a landing wharf

**jeu d'es·prit** \zhœ̄-des-prē\ *n, pl* **jeux d'esprit** \*same*\ [F, lit., play of the mind] **:** a witty comment or composition

**Jew** \'jü\ *n* **1 :** ISRAELITE **2 :** one whose religion is Judaism — **Jew·ish** *adj*

¹**jew·el** \'jü-əl\ *n* [ME *juel*, fr. OF, dim. of *jeu* game, play, fr. L *jocus* game, joke] **1 :** an ornament of precious metal worn as an accessory of dress **2 :** GEMSTONE, GEM

²**jewel** *vb* **-eled** *or* **-elled; -el·ing** *or* **-el·ling :** to adorn or equip with jewels

**jew·el·er** *or* **jew·el·ler** \'jü-ə-lər\ *n* **:** a person who makes or deals in jewelry and related articles

**jew·el·ry** \'jü-əl-rē\ *n* **:** JEWELS; *esp* **:** objects of precious metal set with gems and worn for personal adornment

**jew·el·weed** \-,wēd\ *n* **:** IMPATIENS

**Jew·ry** \'jú(ə)r-ē, 'jü-rē\ *n* **:** the Jewish people

**jg** *abbr* junior grade

¹**jib** \'jib\ *n* **:** a triangular sail extending forward from the foremast of a ship

²**jib** *vb* **jibbed; jib·bing :** to refuse to proceed further

**jibe** \'jīb\ *vb* **jibed; jib·ing :** to be in accord **:** AGREE

**jif·fy** \'jif-ē\ *n, pl* **jiffies :** MOMENT, INSTANT (I'll be ready in a ~)

¹**jig** \'jig\ *n* **1 :** a lively dance in triple rhythm **2 :** TRICK, GAME ⟨the ~ is up⟩ **3 :** a device to hold work during manufacture or assembly

²**jig** *vb* **jigged; jig·ging :** to dance a jig

**jig·ger** \'jig-ər\ *n* **:** a measure usu. holding 1½ ounces and used in mixing drinks

**jig·gle** \'jig-əl\ *vb* **jig·gled; jig·gling** \(-ə-)liŋ\ **:** to move with quick little jerks — **jiggle** *n*

**jig·saw** \'jig-,sȯ\ *n* **:** a machine saw with a narrow vertically reciprocating blade for cutting curved or irregular lines

**jigsaw puzzle** *n* **:** a puzzle consisting of small irregularly cut pieces to be fitted together to form a picture

**ji·had** \ji-'häd, -'hȯd\ *n* **1 :** a Muslim holy war **2 :** CRUSADE 2

¹**jilt** \'jilt\ *n* **:** a woman who jilts a man

²**jilt** *vb* **:** to drop (one's lover) unfeelingly

**jim crow** \'jim-'krō\ *n, often cap J&C* **:** discrimination against the Negro esp. by legal enforcement or traditional sanctions — **jim crow** *adj, often cap J&C* — **jim crow·ism** *n, often cap J&C*

**jim-dan·dy** \'jim-'dan-dē\ *n* **:** something excellent of its kind

¹**jim·my** \'jim-ē\ *n, pl* **jimmies :** a small crowbar

²**jimmy** *vb* **jim·mied; jim·my·ing :** to force open with a jimmy

**jim·son·weed** \'jim-sən-,wēd\ *n, often cap* **:** a coarse poisonous weed of the nightshade group sometimes grown for its large trumpet-shaped white or violet flowers

¹**jin·gle** \'jiŋ-gəl\ *vb* **jin·gled; jin·gling** \-g(ə-)liŋ\ **:** to make a light clinking or tinkling sound

²**jingle** *n* **1 :** a light clinking or tinkling sound **2 :** a short verse or song with catchy repetition

**jin·go·ism** \'jiŋ-gō-,iz-əm\ *n* **:** extreme chauvinism or nationalism marked esp. by a belligerent foreign policy — **jin·go·ist** \-əst\ *n* — **jin·go·is·tic** \,jiŋ-gō-'is-tik\ *adj*

**jin·rik·i·sha** \jin-'rik-,shȯ\ *n* **:** RICKSHA

¹**jinx** \'jiŋks\ *n* **:** one that brings bad luck

²**jinx** vb : to foredoom to failure or misfortune

**jit·ney** \'jit-nē\ n, pl **jitneys** : a small bus that serves a regular route according to a flexible schedule

**jit·ter·bug** \'jit-ər-,bəg\ n 1 : a dance in which couples two-step, balance, and twirl vigorously in standardized patterns 2 : one who dances the jitterbug — **jitterbug** vb

**jit·ters** \'jit-ərz\ n pl : extreme nervousness — **jit·tery** \-ə-rē\ adj

¹**jive** \'jīv\ n 1 : swing music or dancing performed to it 2 : glib, deceptive, or foolish talk 3 : the jargon of hipsters

²**jive** vb **jived; jiv·ing** 1 : to dance to or play jive 2 : KID, TEASE; also : DECEIVE, SWINDLE

**Jn** or **Jno** abbr John

**Jo** abbr Joel

**job** \'jäb\ n 1 : a piece of work 2 : something that has to be done : DUTY 3 : a regular remunerative position — **job·less** adj

²**job** vb **jobbed; job·bing** 1 : to do occasional pieces of work for hire 2 : to hire or let by the job

**job action** n : a temporary refusal (as by policemen) to work as a means of forcing compliance with demands

**job·ber** \'jäb-ər\ n 1 : a person who buys goods and then sells them to other dealers : MIDDLEMAN 2 : a person who does work by the job

**job·hold·er** \'jäb-,hōl-dər\ n : one having a regular job

¹**jock·ey** \'jäk-ē\ n, pl **jockeys** : one who rides a horse esp. as a professional in a race

²**jockey** vb **jock·eyed; jock·ey·ing** : to maneuver or manipulate by adroit or devious means

**jo·cose** \jō-'kōs\ adj : MERRY, HUMOROUS **syn** jocular, facetious, witty

**joc·u·lar** \'jäk-yə-lər\ adj : marked by jesting : PLAYFUL — **joc·u·lar·i·ty** \,jäk-yə-'lar-ət-ē\ n

**jo·cund** \'jäk-ənd\ adj : marked by mirth or cheerfulness : GAY

**jodh·pur** \'jäd-pər\ n 1 pl : riding breeches loose above the knee and tight-fitting below 2 : an ankle-high boot fastened with a strap

¹**jog** \'jäg\ vb **jogged; jog·ging** 1 : to give a slight shake or push to 2 : to run or ride at a slow trot 3 : to go at a slow monotonous pace — **jog·ger** n

²**jog** n 1 : a slight shake 2 : a jogging movement or pace

³**jog** n 1 : a projecting or retreating part of a line or surface 2 : a brief abrupt change in direction

**jog·gle** \'jäg-əl\ vb **jog·gled; jog·gling** \-(ə-)liŋ\ : to shake slightly — **joggle** n

**john** \'jän\ n 1 : TOILET 2 : a prostitute's client

**john·ny** \'jän-ē\ n, pl **johnnies** : a short gown opening in the back that is used by hospital bed patients

**John·ny-jump-up** \,jän-ē-'jəm-,pəp\ n : any of various small-flowered cultivated pansies

**joie de vi·vre** \,zhwäd-ə-'vēvrⁿ\ n : keen enjoyment of life

**join** \'jóin\ vb 1 : to come or bring together so as to form a unit 2 : to come or bring into close association 3 : to become a member of ⟨~ a church⟩ 4 : to take part in a collective activity 5 : ADJOIN

**join·er** \'jói-nər\ n 1 : a worker who constructs articles by joining pieces of wood 2 : a gregarious person who joins many organizations

¹**joint** \'jóint\ n 1 : the point of contact between bones of an animal skeleton with the parts that surround and support it 2 : a cut of meat suitable for roasting 3 : a place where two things or parts are connected 4 : ESTABLISHMENT; esp : a shabby or disreputable establishment 5 : a marijuana cigarette

²**joint** adj 1 : UNITED 2 : common to two or more — **joint·ly** adv

³**joint** vb 1 : to unite by or provide with a joint 2 : to separate the joints of

**joist** \'jóist\ n : any of the small timbers or metal beams ranged parallel from wall to wall in a building to support the floor or ceiling

¹**joke** \'jōk\ n : something said or done to provoke laughter; esp : a brief narrative with a humorous climax

²**joke** vb **joked; jok·ing** : to make jokes — **jok·ing·ly** \'jō-kiŋ-lē\ adv

**jok·er** \'jō-kər\ n 1 : a person who jokes 2 : an extra card used in some card games 3 : a part (as of an agreement) meaning something quite different from what it seems to mean and changing the apparent intention of the whole

**jol·li·fi·ca·tion** \,jäl-i-fə-'kā-shən\ n : a festive celebration

**jol·li·ty** \'jäl-ət-ē\ n, pl **-ties** : GAIETY, MERRIMENT

**jol·ly** \'jäl-ē\ adj **jol·li·er; -est** : full of high spirits : MERRY

¹**jolt** \'jōlt\ vb 1 : to move with a sudden jerky motion 2 : to give a quick hard knock or blow to — **jolt·er** n

²**jolt** n 1 : an abrupt jerky blow or movement 2 : a sudden shock

**jon·gleur** \zhōⁿ-'glər\ n : an itinerant medieval minstrel providing entertainment chiefly by song or recitation

**jon·quil** \'jän-kwəl\ n [F jonquille, fr. Sp junquillo, dim. of junco reed, fr. L juncus] : a narcissus with fragrant clustered white or yellow flowers

**josh** \'jäsh\ vb : TEASE, JOKE

**Josh** abbr Joshua

**Josh·ua tree** \'jäsh-(ə-)wə-\ n : a tall branched yucca of the southwestern U.S.

**joss** \'jäs\ n [Pidgin E, fr. Port deus god, fr. L] : a Chinese idol or cult image

**jos·tle** \'jäs-əl\ vb **jos·tled; jos·tling** \-(ə-)liŋ\ 1 : to come in contact or into collision 2 : to make one's way by pushing and shoving

¹**jot** \'jät\ n : the least bit : IOTA

²**jot** vb **jot·ted; jot·ting** : to write briefly and hurriedly

**jot·ting** \'jät-iŋ\ n : a brief note

**jounce** \'jauns\ vb **jounced; jouncing** : JOLT — **jounce** n

**jour** abbr journal

**jour·nal** \'jərn-ºl\ n [ME, service book containing the day hours, fr. MF, fr. *journal* daily, fr. L *diurnalis*, fr. *dies* day] **1** : a brief account of daily events **2** : a record of proceedings (as of a legislative body) **3** : a periodical (as a newspaper) dealing esp. with current events **4** : the part of a rotating axle or spindle that turns in a bearing

**jour·nal·ese** \ˌjərn-ºl-'ēz, -'ēs\ n : a style of writing held to be characteristic of newspapers

**jour·nal·ism** \'jərn-ºl-ˌiz-əm\ n **1** : the business of writing for, editing, or publishing periodicals (as newspapers) **2** : writing designed for or characteristic of newspapers — **jour·nal·ist** \-əst\ n — **jour·nal·is·tic** \ˌjərn-ºl-'is-tik\ adj

¹**jour·ney** \'jər-nē\ n, pl **journeys** : travel from one place to another

²**journey** vb **jour·neyed; jour·ney·ing** : to go on a journey : TRAVEL

**jour·ney·man** \-mən\ n **1** : a worker who has learned a trade and works for another person **2** : an experienced reliable workman

¹**joust** \'jaust\ vb : to engage in a joust

²**joust** n : a combat on horseback between two knights with lances esp. as part of a tournament

**jo·vial** \'jō-vē-əl\ adj : marked by good humor — **jo·vi·al·i·ty** \ˌjō-vē-'al-ət-ē\ n — **jo·vi·al·ly** \'jō-vē-ə-lē\ adv

¹**jowl** \'jaul\ n **1** : the lower jaw **2** : CHEEK

²**jowl** n : loose flesh about the lower jaw or throat

¹**joy** \'jȯi\ n **1** : a feeling of happiness that comes from success, good fortune, or a sense of well-being **2** : a source of happiness **syn** bliss, delight, enjoyment, pleasure — **joy·less** adj

²**joy** vb : REJOICE

**joy·ance** \'jȯi-əns\ n : DELIGHT, ENJOYMENT

**joy·ful** \-fəl\ adj : experiencing, causing, or showing joy — **joy·ful·ly** \-ē\ adv

**joy·ous** \'jȯi-əs\ adj : JOYFUL — **joy·ous·ly** adv — **joy·ous·ness** n

**joy·ride** \-ˌrīd\ n : a ride for pleasure often marked by reckless driving — **joy·rid·er** n — **joy·rid·ing** n

**JP** abbr **1** jet propulsion **2** justice of the peace

**Jr** abbr junior

**JRC** abbr Junior Red Cross

**ju·bi·lant** \'jü-bə-lənt\ adj [L *jubilans*, prp. of *jubilare* to rejoice] : expressing great joy — **ju·bi·lant·ly** adv

**ju·bi·la·tion** \ˌjü-bə-'lā-shən\ n : EXULTATION

**ju·bi·lee** \'jü-bə-ˌlē\ n [ME, fr. MF & LL; MF *jubilé*, fr. LL *jubilaeus*, fr. LGk *iōbēlaios*, fr. Heb *yōbhēl* ram's horn, trumpet, jubilee] **1** : a 50th anniversary **2** : a season or occasion of celebration

**Ju·da·ic** \jü-'dā-ik\ also **Ju·da·ical** \-'dā-ə-kəl\ adj : of, relating to, or characteristic of Jews or Judaism

**Ju·da·ism** \'jüd-ə-ˌiz-əm\ n : a religion developed among the ancient Hebrews and marked by belief in one God and by the moral and ceremonial laws of the Old Testament and the rabbinic tradition

**Ju·das tree** \'jüd-əs-\ n : a Eurasian leguminous tree with purplish rosy flowers

**Judg** abbr Judges

¹**judge** \'jəj\ vb **judged; judg·ing** **1** : to form an authoritative opinion **2** : to decide as a judge : TRY **3** : to determine or pronounce after inquiry and deliberation **4** : to form an estimate or evaluation about something : THINK **syn** adjudge, adjudicate, arbitrate, conclude, deduce, gather

²**judge** n **1** : a public official authorized to decide questions brought before a court **2** : UMPIRE **3** : one who gives an authoritative opinion : CRITIC — **judge·ship** n

**judg·ment** or **judge·ment** \'jəj-mənt\ n **1** : a decision or opinion given after judging; esp : a formal decision given by a court **2** cap : the final judging of mankind by God **3** : the process of forming an opinion by discerning and comparing : DISCERNMENT **4** : the capacity for judging : DISCERNMENT

**ju·di·ca·ture** \'jüd-i-kə-ˌchur\ n **1** : the administration of justice **2** : JUDICIARY 1

**ju·di·cial** \jü-'dish-əl\ adj **1** : of or relating to the administration of justice or the judiciary **2** : ordered or enforced by a court **3** : CRITICAL — **ju·di·cial·ly** \-ē\ adv

**ju·di·cia·ry** \jü-'dish-ē-ˌer-ē, -'dish-ə-rē\ n **1** : a system of courts of law; *also* : the judges of these courts **2** : a branch of government in which judicial power is vested — **judiciary** adj

**ju·di·cious** \jü-'dish-əs\ adj : having, exercising, or characterized by sound judgment **syn** prudent, sage, sane, sensible, wise — **ju·di·cious·ly** adv

**ju·do** \'jüd-ō\ n : a sport derived from jujitsu that emphasizes the use of quick movement and leverage to throw an opponent — **judo·ist** n

¹**jug** \'jəg\ n **1** : a large deep usu. earthenware or glass container with a narrow mouth and a handle **2** : JAIL, PRISON

²**jug** vb **jugged; jug·ging** : JAIL, IMPRISON

**jug·ger·naut** \'jəg-ər-ˌnȯt\ n [Hindi *Jagannāth*, title of Vishnu (a Hindu god), lit., lord of the world] : a massive inexorable force or object that crushes everything in its path

**jug·gle** \'jəg-əl\ vb **jug·gled; jug·gling** \-(ə-)liŋ\ **1** : to keep several objects in motion in the air at the same time **2** : to manipulate esp. in order to achieve a desired and often fraudulent end — **jug·gler** \-lər\ n

**jug·u·lar** \'jəg-yə-lər\ adj : of, relating to, or situated in or on the throat or neck ⟨the ~ veins⟩

**juice** \'jüs\ n **1** : the extractable fluid contents of cells or tissues **2** pl : the natural fluids of an animal body **3** : a medium (as electricity) that supplies power

**juic·er** \'jü-sər\ *n* : an appliance for extracting juice (as from fruit)

**juice up** *vb* : to give life, energy, or spirit to

**juicy** \'jü-sē\ *adj* **juic·i·er; -est 1** : SUCCULENT **2** : rich in interest; *also* : RACY — **juic·i·ly** \'jü-sə-lē\ *adv* — **juic·i·ness** \-sē-nəs\ *n*

**ju·jit·su** *or* **ju·jut·su** \jü-'jit-sü\ *n* [Jap *jūjutsu,* fr. *jū* weakness, gentleness + *jutsu* art, skill] : an art of weaponless fighting employing holds, throws, and paralyzing blows to subdue or disable an opponent

**ju·jube** \'jü-,jüb, 'jü-jə-,bē\ *n* : a candy made from corn syrup with gelatin or gum arabic

**juke·box** \'jük-,bäks\ *n* : a coin-operated automatic record player

**Jul** *abbr* July

**ju·lep** \'jü-ləp\ *n* : a drink made of bourbon, sugar, and mint served over crushed ice in a tall glass

**Ju·ly** \jù-'lī\ *n* [ME *Julie,* fr. OE *Julius,* fr. L, fr. Gaius *Julius* Caesar] : the seventh month of the year having 31 days

**¹jum·ble** \'jəm-bəl\ *vb* **jum·bled; jum·bling** \-b(ə-)liŋ\ : to mix in a confused mass

**²jumble** *n* : a disorderly mass or pile

**jum·bo** \'jəm-bō\ *n, pl* **jumbos** [*Jumbo,* a huge elephant exhibited by P. T. Barnum] : a very large specimen of its kind — **jumbo** *adj*

**¹jump** \'jəmp\ *vb* **1** : to spring into the air : leap over **2** : to give a start **3** : to rise or increase suddenly or sharply **4** : to make a sudden attack **5** : ANTICIPATE ⟨~ the gun⟩ **6** : to leave hurriedly and often furtively ⟨~ town⟩ **7** : to act or move before (as a signal)

**²jump** *n* **1** : a spring into the air; *esp* : one made for height or distance in a track meet **2** : a sharp sudden increase **3** : an initial advantage

**¹jump·er** \'jəm-pər\ *n* **1** : one that jumps **2** : PARACHUTIST

**²jumper** *n* **1** : a loose blouse **2** : a sleeveless one-piece dress worn usu. with a blouse **3** *pl* : a child's sleeveless coverall

**jumping bean** *n* : a seed of any of several Mexican shrubs that tumbles about because of the movements of the larva of a small moth inside it

**jumping-off place** \,jəm-piŋ-'òf-\ *n* **1** : a remote or isolated place **2** : a place from which an enterprise is launched

**jump suit** *n* **1** : a uniform worn by parachutists in jumping **2** : a one-piece garment consisting of a blouse or shirt with attached trousers or shorts

**jumpy** \'jəm-pē\ *adj* **jump·i·er; -est** : NERVOUS, JITTERY

**¹jun** \'jən\ *n, pl* **jun** — see *won* at MONEY table

**²jun** *abbr* junior

**Jun** *abbr* June

**junc** *abbr* junction

**jun·co** \'jəŋ-kō\ *n, pl* **juncos** *or* **juncoes** : any of several small common pink-billed American finches that are largely gray with conspicuous white feathers in the tail

**junc·tion** \'jəŋk-shən\ *n* **1** : an act of joining **2** : a place or point of meeting ⟨a railroad ~⟩

**junc·ture** \'jəŋk-chər\ *n* **1** : UNION **2** : JOINT, CONNECTION **3** : a critical time or state of affairs

**June** \'jün\ *n* [ME, fr. L *Junius*] : the sixth month of the year having 30 days

**jun·gle** \'jəŋ-gəl\ *n* **1** : a thick tangled mass of tropical vegetation; *also* : a tract overgrown with rank vegetation **2** : a place of ruthless struggle for survival

**¹ju·nior** \'jü-nyər\ *n* **1** : a person who is younger or of lower rank than another **2** : a student in his next-to-last year (as at a college)

**²junior** *adj* **1** : YOUNGER **2** : lower in rank **3** : of or relating to juniors

**junior college** *n* : a school that offers studies corresponding to those of the first two years of college

**junior high school** *n* : a school usu. including grades 7–9

**junior varsity** *n* : a team whose members lack the experience or qualifications required for the varsity

**ju·ni·per** \'jü-nə-pər\ *n* : any of various evergreen shrubs or trees related to the pines

**¹junk** \'jəŋk\ *n* **1** : old iron, glass, paper, or waste; *also* : discarded articles **2** : a shoddy product **3** *slang* : NARCOTICS; *esp* : HEROIN — **junky** *adj*

**²junk** *vb* : DISCARD, SCRAP

**³junk** *n* : a flat-bottomed ship of Chinese waters with a high poop and overhanging stem

**junk·er** \'jəŋ-kər\ *n* : something (as an old automobile) ready for scrapping

**Jun·ker** \'yùn-kər\ *n* : a member of the Prussian landed aristocracy

**jun·ket** \'jəŋ-kət\ *n* **1** : a dessert of sweetened flavored milk set in a jelly **2** : a trip made by an official at public expense

**junk·ie** *or* **junky** \'jəŋ-kē\ *n, pl* **junk·ies 1** : a junk dealer **2** *slang* : a narcotics peddler or addict

**jun·ta** \'hùn-tə, 'jənt-ə, 'hən-tə\ *n* [Sp, fr. *junto* joined, fr. L *jungere* to join] : a group of persons controlling a government esp. after a revolutionary seizure of power

**jun·to** \'jənt-ō\ *n, pl* **juntos** : a group of persons joined for a common purpose

**Ju·pi·ter** \'jü-pət-ər\ *n* : the largest of the planets and the one fifth in order of distance from the sun

**ju·rid·i·cal** \jù-'rid-i-kəl\ *or* **ju·rid·ic** \-ik\ *adj* **1** : of or relating to the administration of justice **2** : LEGAL — **ju·rid·i·cal·ly** \-i-k(ə-)lē\ *adv*

**ju·ris·dic·tion** \,jùr-əs-'dik-shən\ *n* **1** : the power, right, or authority to interpret and apply the law **2** : the authority of a sovereign power **3** : the limits or territory within which authority may be exercised — **ju·ris·dic·tion·al** \-sh(ə-)nəl\ *adj*

**ju·ris·pru·dence** \-'prüd-°ns\ *n* **1** : a system of laws **2** : the science or philosophy of law

**ju·rist** \'jùr-əst\ *n* : one having a thorough knowledge of law

**ju·ris·tic** \jù-'ris-tik\ *adj* **1** : of or relating to a jurist or jurisprudence **2** : of, relating to, or recognized in law

**ju·ror** \'jùr-ər\ *n* : a member of a jury

**¹ju·ry** \'jùr-ē\ *n, pl* **juries 1** : a body of persons sworn to inquire into and test a matter submitted to them and to give their verdict according to the evidence presented **2** : a committee for judging and awarding prizes (as at a contest) — **ju·ry·man** \-mən\ *n*

**²jury** *adj* : improvised for temporary use esp. in an emergency ⟨a ~ mast⟩

**¹just** \'jəst\ *adj* **1** : having a basis in or conforming to fact or reason : REASONABLE ⟨~ comment⟩ **2** : CORRECT, PROPER ⟨~ proportions⟩ **3** : morally or legally right ⟨a ~ title⟩ **4** : DESERVED, MERITED ⟨~ punishment⟩ **syn** upright, honorable, conscientious, honest — **just·ly** *adv* — **just·ness** *n*

**²just** \(,)jəst, (,)jist\ *adv* **1** : EXACTLY ⟨~ right⟩ **2** : very recently ⟨has ~ left⟩ **3** : BARELY ⟨lives ~ outside the city⟩ **4** : DIRECTLY ⟨~ across the street⟩ **5** : ONLY ⟨~ a note⟩ **6** : VERY

**jus·tice** \'jəs-təs\ *n* **1** : the administration of what is just (as by assigning

merited rewards or punishments) **2** : JUDGE **3** : the administration of law **4** : FAIRNESS; *also* : RIGHTEOUSNESS

**justice of the peace** : a local magistrate empowered chiefly to try minor cases, to administer oaths, and to perform marriages

**jus·ti·fy** \'jəs-tə-,fī\ *vb* **-fied; -fy·ing 1** : to prove to be just, right, or reasonable **2** : to pronounce free from guilt or blame **3** : to adjust or arrange exactly — **jus·ti·fi·able** *adj* — **jus·ti·fi·ca·tion** \,jəs-tə-fə-'kā-shən\ *n*

**jut** \'jət\ *vb* **jut·ted; jut·ting** : PROJECT, PROTRUDE

**jute** \'jüt\ *n* : a strong glossy fiber from a tropical herb used esp. for making sacks and twine

**juv** *abbr* juvenile

**¹ju·ve·nile** \'jü-və-,nīl, -vən-°l\ *adj* **1** : showing incomplete development **2** : of, relating to, or characteristic of children or young people

**²juvenile** *n* **1** : a young person **2** : a young lower animal (as a fish or a bird) **3** : an actor or actress who plays youthful parts

**ju·ve·noc·ra·cy** \,jü-və-'näk-rə-sē\ *n, pl* **-cies** : a state ruled or greatly influenced by youth

**jux·ta·pose** \'jək-stə-,pōz\ *vb* **-posed; -pos·ing** : to place side by side — **jux·ta·po·si·tion** \,jək-stə-pə-'zish-ən\ *n*

**JV** *abbr* junior varsity

---

**¹k** \'kā\ *n, pl* **k's** *or* **ks** \'kāz\ *often cap* : the 11th letter of the English alphabet

**²k** *abbr* karat; kitchen

**K** *symbol* [NL *kalium*] potassium

**ka·bob** \'kā-,bäb, kə-'bäb\ *n* : cubes of meat cooked with vegetables usu. on a skewer

**Ka·bu·ki** \kə-'bü-kē\ *n* : traditional Japanese popular drama with highly stylized singing and dancing

**kad·dish** \'käd-ish\ *n, often cap* : a Jewish prayer recited in the daily synagogue ritual and by mourners at public services after the death of a close relative

**kaf·fee·klatsch** \'kòf-ē-,klach, 'käf-\ *n, often cap* : an informal social gathering for coffee and talk

**kai·ser** \'kī-zər\ *n* : EMPEROR; *esp* : the ruler of Germany from 1871 to 1918

**kale** \'kāl\ *n* : a hardy cabbage with curled leaves that do not form a head

**ka·lei·do·scope** \kə-'līd-ə-,skōp\ *n* : an instrument containing loose bits of colored glass between two flat plates and two plane mirrors so placed that changes of position of the bits of glass are reflected in an endless variety of patterns — **ka·lei·do·scop·ic** \-,līd-ə-'skäp-ik\ *or* **ka·lei·do·scop·i·cal** \-i-kəl\ *adj* — **ka·lei·do·scop·i·cal·ly** \-i-k(ə-)lē\ *adv*

**ka·ma·ai·na** \,käm-ə-'ī-nə\ *n* [Hawaiian *kama'āina*, fr. *kama* child + *'āina*

land] : one who has lived in Hawaii for a long time

**kame** \'kām\ *n* : a short ridge or mound of stratified drift deposited by glacial meltwater

**ka·mi·ka·ze** \,käm-i-'käz-ē\ *n* [Jap, lit., divine wind] : a member of a corps of Japanese pilots assigned to make a suicidal crash on a target; *also* : an airplane flown in such an attack

**kan·ga·roo** \,kaŋ-gə-'rü\ *n, pl* **-roos** : a large leaping marsupial mammal of Australia with powerful hind legs and a long thick tail

**kangaroo court** *n* : a court or an illegal self-appointed tribunal characterized by irresponsible, perverted, or irregular procedures

**Kans** *abbr* Kansas

**ka·olin** *also* **ka·oline** \'kā-ə-lən\ *n* : a fine usu. white clay used in ceramics and refractories and as an absorbent

**ka·pok** \'kā-,päk\ *n* : silky fiber from the seeds of a tropical tree used esp. as a filling (as for life preservers)

**ka·put** *also* **ka·putt** \kä-'pùt, kə-, -'püt\ *adj* [G, fr. F *capot* not having made a trick at piquet] **1** : utterly defeated or destroyed **2** : made useless or unable to function

**kar·a·kul** \'kar-ə-kəl\ *n* : the dark tightly curled pelt of the newborn lamb of an Asiatic fat-tailed sheep

**kar·at** \'kar-ət\ *n* : a unit for expressing proportion of gold in an alloy equal to ¹/₂₄ part of pure gold

**ka·ra·te** \kə-'rät-ē\ *n* [Jap, lit.,

empty hand] : an art of self-defense in which an attacker is disabled by crippling kicks and punches

**kar·ma** \'kär-mə\ *n, often cap* : the force generated by a person's actions held in Hinduism and Buddhism to perpetuate transmigration and to determine his destiny in his next existence — **kar·mic** \-mik\ *adj, often cap*

**karst** \'kärst\ *n* : an irregular limestone region with sinks, underground streams, and caverns

**kart** \'kärt\ *n* : a miniature motorcar used esp. for racing — **kart·ing** \-iŋ\ *n*

**ka·ty·did** \'kāt-ē-,did\ *n* : any of several large green tree-dwelling American grasshoppers

**kay·ak** \'kī-,ak\ *n* : a decked-in Eskimo canoe made of skin and propelled by a double-bladed paddle; *also* : a similar canvas-covered canoe

**kayo** \(')kā-'ō, 'kā-ō\ *n* : KNOCKOUT — **kayo** *vb*

**ka·zoo** \kə-'zü\ *n, pl* **kazoos** : a toy musical instrument consisting of a tube with a membrane sealing one end and a side hole to sing or hum into

**kc** *abbr* kilocycle

**KC** *abbr* 1 Kansas City 2 King's Counsel 3 Knights of Columbus

**kc/s** *abbr* kilocycles per second

**KD** *abbr* 1 kiln-dried 2 knocked down

**ke·bab** *or* **ke·bob** \kə-'bäb\ *var of* KABOB

¹**kedge** \'kej\ *vb* **kedged; kedg·ing** : to move a ship by hauling on a line attached to a small anchor dropped at the distance and in the direction desired — **kayo** *vb*

²**kedge** *n* : a small anchor

**keel** \'kēl\ *n* 1 : a timber or plate running lengthwise along the center of the bottom of a ship 2 : something (as a bird's breastbone) like a ship's keel in form or use — **keeled** \'kēld\ *adj*

**keel·boat** \'kēl-,bōt\ *n* : a shallow covered keeled riverboat for freight that is usu. rowed, poled, or towed

**keel·haul** \-,hȯl\ *vb* : to haul under the keel of a ship as punishment

**keel over** *vb* 1 : OVERTURN, CAPSIZE 2 : FAINT, SWOON

**keel·son** \'kel-sən, 'kēl-\ *n* : a reinforcing structure above and fastened to a ship's keel

¹**keen** \'kēn\ *adj* 1 : SHARP ⟨a ∼ knife⟩ 2 : SEVERE ⟨a ∼ wind⟩ 3 : ENTHUSIASTIC ⟨∼ about swimming⟩ 4 : mentally alert ⟨a ∼ mind⟩ 5 : STRONG, ACUTE ⟨∼ eyesight⟩ 6 : WONDERFUL, EXCELLENT ⟨∼ us from harm⟩ — **keen·ly** *adv* — **keen·ness** \'kēn-nəs\ *n*

²**keen** *n* : a lamentation for the dead uttered in a loud wailing voice or in a wordless cry — **keen** *vb*

¹**keep** \'kēp\ *vb* **kept** \'kept\; **keep·ing** 1 : FULFILL, OBSERVE ⟨∼ a promise⟩ ⟨∼ a holiday⟩ 2 : GUARD ⟨∼ us from harm⟩; *also* : to take care of ⟨∼ a neighbor's children⟩ 3 : MAINTAIN ⟨∼ silence⟩ 4 : to have in one's service or at one's disposal ⟨∼ a horse⟩ 5 : to preserve a record in ⟨∼ a diary⟩ 6 : to have in stock for sale 7 : to retain in one's possession ⟨∼ what you

find⟩ 8 : to carry on (as a business) : CONDUCT 9 : HOLD, DETAIN ⟨∼ him in jail⟩ 10 : to refrain from revealing ⟨∼ a secret⟩ 11 : to continue in good condition ⟨meat will ∼ in a freezer⟩ 12 : ABSTAIN, REFRAIN — **keep·er** *n*

²**keep** *n* 1 : FORTRESS 2 : the means or provisions by which one is kept — **for keeps** 1 : with the provision that one keeps what he wins ⟨play marbles *for keeps*⟩ 2 : PERMANENTLY

**keep·ing** \'kē-piŋ\ *n* : CONFORMITY ⟨in ∼ with good taste⟩

**keep·sake** \'kēp-,sāk\ *n* : MEMENTO

**keep up** *vb* 1 : to persevere in 2 : MAINTAIN, SUSTAIN 3 : to keep informed 4 : to continue without interruption

**keg** \'keg\ *n* : a small cask or barrel

**keg·ler** \'keg-lər\ *n* : ¹BOWLER

**kelp** \'kelp\ *n* : any of various coarse brown seaweeds; *also* : a mass of these or their ashes often used as fertilizer

**Kelt** \'kelt\ *var of* CELT

**Kel·vin** \'kel-vən\ *adj* : relating to, conforming to, or having a thermometer scale according to which absolute zero is 0°, the equivalent of −273.16° C

**ken** \'ken\ *n* 1 : range of vision : SIGHT 2 : range of understanding

**ken·nel** \'ken-ᵊl\ *n* : a shelter for a dog; *also* : an establishment for the breeding or boarding of dogs — **kennel** *vb*

**ke·no** \'kē-nō\ *n* : a game resembling bingo

**Ken·tucky bluegrass** \kən-,tək-ē-\ *n* : a valuable pasture and meadow grass of both Europe and America

**ke·pi** \'kā-pē, 'kep-ē\ *n* : a military cap with a round flat top sloping toward the front and a visor

**ker·a·tin** \'ker-ət-ᵊn\ *n* : any of various sulfur-containing fibrous proteins that form the chemical basis of hair and horny tissues — **ke·ra·ti·nous** \kə-'rat-ᵊn-əs, ,ker-ə-'tīn-əs\ *adj*

**kerb** \'kərb\ *n, Brit* : CURB

**ker·chief** \'kər-chəf, -,chēf\ *n, pl* **kerchiefs** \-chəfs, -,chēfs\ *also* **kerchieves** \-,chēvz\ [ME *courchef,* fr. OF *cuevrechief,* fr. *covrir* to cover + *chief* head] 1 : a square of cloth worn by women esp. as a head covering 2 : HANDKERCHIEF

**kerf** \'kərf\ *n* : a slit or notch made by a saw or cutting torch

**ker·nel** \'kərn-ᵊl\ *n* 1 : the inner softer part of a seed, fruit stone, or nut 2 : a whole seed of a cereal 3 : a central or essential part : CORE

**ker·o·sine** *or* **ker·o·sene** \'ker-ə-,sēn, ,ker-ə-'sēn, 'kar-, ,kar-\ *n* : a thin oil produced from petroleum and used for a fuel and as a solvent

**ketch** \'kech\ *n* : a fore-and-aft rigged ship with two masts

**ketch·up** *var of* CATSUP

**ket·tle** \'ket-ᵊl\ *n* : a metallic vessel for boiling liquids

**ket·tle·drum** \-,drəm\ *n* : a brass or copper drum with parchment stretched across the top

¹**key** \'kē\ *n* 1 : a usu. metal instrument by which the bolt of a lock is turned;

*also* **:** a device having the form or function of a key **2 :** a means of gaining or preventing entrance, possession, or control **3 :** EXPLANATION, SOLUTION **4 :** one of the levers pressed by a finger in operating or playing an instrument **5 :** a leading individual or principle **6 :** a system of seven tones based on their relationship to a tonic; *also* **:** the tone or pitch of a voice **7 :** a small switch for opening or closing an electric circuit

²**key** *vb* **1 :** SECURE, FASTEN **2 :** to regulate the musical pitch of; *also* **:** ATTUNE **3 :** to make nervous — usu. used with *up*

³**key** *adj* **:** BASIC, CENTRAL ⟨~ issues⟩

⁴**key** *n* **:** a low island or reef (as off the southern coast of Florida)

**key·board** \-ˌbȯrd\ *n* **1 :** a row of keys (as on a piano) **2 :** an assemblage of keys for operating a machine

**key club** *n* **:** a private club serving liquor and providing entertainment

**key·hole** \'kē-ˌhōl\ *n* **:** a hole for receiving a key

¹**key·note** \-ˌnōt\ *n* **1 :** the first and harmonically fundamental tone of a scale **2 :** the central fact, idea, or mood

²**keynote** *vb* **1 :** to set the keynote of **2 :** to deliver the major address (as at a convention) — **key·not·er** *n*

**key·punch** \'kē-ˌpənch\ *n* **:** a machine with a keyboard used to cut holes or notches in punch cards — **keypunch** *vb* — **key·punch·er** *n*

**key·stone** \'kē-ˌstōn\ *n* **:** the wedge-shaped piece at the crown of an arch that locks the other pieces in place

**key word** *n* **:** a word that is a key; *esp* **:** a word exemplifying the meaning or value of a letter or symbol

**kg** *abbr* kilogram

**kha·ki** \'kak-ē, 'käk-\ *n* [Hindi *k͟hākī* dust-colored, fr. *k͟hāk* dust, fr. Per] **1 :** a light yellowish brown **2 :** a khaki-colored cloth; *also* **:** a military uniform of this cloth

**khan** \'kän, 'kan\ *n* **:** a Mongol leader; *esp* **:** a successor of Genghis Khan

**khe·dive** \kə-'dēv\ *n* **:** a ruler of Egypt from 1867 to 1914 governing as a viceroy of the sultan of Turkey

**KIA** *abbr* killed in action

**kib·ble** \'kib-əl\ *vb* **kib·bled; kib·bling :** to grind coarsely — **kibble** *n*

**kib·butz** \kib-'ùts, -'üts\ *n, pl* **kib·but·zim** \-ˌùt-'sēm, -ˌüt-\ **:** a collective farm or settlement in Israel

**ki·bitz·er** \'kib-ət-sər, kə-'bit-\ *n* **:** one who looks on and usu. offers unwanted advice esp. at a card game — **kib·itz** \'kib-əts\ *vb*

**ki·bosh** \'kī-ˌbäsh\ *n* **:** something that serves as a check or stop ⟨put the ~ on his plan⟩

¹**kick** \'kik\ *vb* **1 :** to strike out or hit with the foot; *also* **:** to score by kicking a ball **2 :** to object strongly **3 :** to recoil when fired — **kick·er** *n*

²**kick** *n* **1 :** a blow or thrust with the foot; *esp* **:** a propelling of a ball with the foot **2 :** the recoil of a gun **3 :** a feeling or expression of objection

**4 :** stimulating effect esp. of pleasure

**kick·back** \'kik-ˌbak\ *n* **1 :** a sharp violent reaction **2 :** a secret return of a part of a sum received

**kick in** *vb* **1 :** CONTRIBUTE **2** *slang* **:** DIE

**kick·off** \'kik-ˌȯf\ *n* **1 :** a kick that puts the ball in play (as in football) **2 :** COMMENCEMENT — **kick off** *vb*

**kick over** *vb* **:** to begin or cause to begin to fire — used of an internal-combustion engine

**kick·shaw** \'kik-ˌshȯ\ *n* [fr. F *quelque chose* something] **1 :** DELICACY **2 :** BAUBLE

**kick·stand** \'kik-ˌstand\ *n* **:** a swiveling metal bar for holding up a 2-wheeled vehicle when not in use

¹**kid** \'kid\ *n* **1 :** a young goat **2 :** the flesh, fur, or skin of a young goat; *also* **:** something (as leather) made of kid **3 :** CHILD, YOUNGSTER — **kid·dish** \'kid-ish\ *adj*

²**kid** *vb* **kid·ded; kid·ding 1 :** FOOL **2 :** TEASE — **kid·der** *n* — **kid·ding·ly** \'kid-iŋ-lē\ *adv*

**kid·nap** \'kid-ˌnap\ *vb* **-napped** *or* **-naped** \-ˌnapt\; **-nap·ping** *or* **-nap·ing :** to carry a person away by unlawful force or by fraud and against his will — **kid·nap·per** *or* **kid·nap·er** *n*

**kid·ney** \'kid-nē\ *n, pl* **kidneys 1 :** either of a pair of organs lying near the spinal column that excrete waste products of the body in the form of urine **2 :** TEMPERAMENT; *also* **:** SORT

**kidney bean** *n* **1 :** an edible seed of the common cultivated bean; *esp* **:** one that is large and dark red **2 :** a plant bearing kidney beans

**kid·skin** \'kid-ˌskin\ *n* **:** the skin of a young goat used for leather

**kiel·ba·sa** \k(y)el-'bäs-ə, kil-\ *n, pl* **-basas** *also* **-ba·sy** \-'bäs-ē\ **:** a smoked sausage of Polish origin

**kie·sel·guhr** *or* **kie·sel·gur** \'kē-zəl-ˌgùr\ *n* **:** loose or porous diatomite

¹**kill** \'kil\ *vb* **1 :** to deprive of life **2 :** to put an end to ⟨~ competition⟩; *also* **:** DEFEAT ⟨~ a proposed amendment⟩ **3 :** to use up ⟨~ time⟩ **4 :** to mark for omission **syn** slay, murder, assassinate, execute — **kill·er** *n*

²**kill** *n* **1 :** an act of killing **2 :** an animal or animals killed (as in a hunt); *also* **:** an aircraft, ship, or vehicle destroyed by military action

**kill·deer** \'kil-ˌdiər\ *n, pl* **killdeers** *or* **killdeer :** a plover of temperate No. America with a plaintive penetrating cry

**kill·ing** \'kil-iŋ\ *n* **:** a sudden notable gain or profit

**kill·joy** \'kil-ˌjȯi\ *n* **:** one who spoils the pleasures of others

**kiln** \'kil(n)\ *n* **:** a heated enclosure (as an oven) for processing a substance by burning, firing, or drying — **kiln** *vb*

**ki·lo** \'kē-lō\ *n, pl* **kilos 1 :** KILOGRAM **2 :** KILOMETER

**kilo·cy·cle** \'kil-ə-ˌsī-kəl\ *n* **:** KILOHERTZ

**ki·lo·gram** \'kē-lə-ˌgram, 'kil-ə-\ *n*

: the basic metric unit of mass and weight — see METRIC SYSTEM table

**ki·lo·hertz** \'kil-ə-,hərts, 'kē-lə-, -,herts\ *n* : 1000 hertz

**kilo·li·ter** \'kil-ə-,lēt-ər\ *n* — see METRIC SYSTEM table

**ki·lo·me·ter** \kil-'äm-ət-ər, 'kil-ə-,mēt-\ *n* — see METRIC SYSTEM table

**ki·lo·ton** \'kē-lō-,tən, 'kil-ō-\ *n* 1 : 1000 tons 2 : an explosive force equivalent to that of 1000 tons of TNT

**ki·lo·volt** \-,vōlt\ *n* : a unit of electromotive force equal to 1000 volts

**kilo·watt** \'kil-ə-,wät\ *n* : a unit of electric power equal to 1000 watts

**kilowatt–hour** *n* : a unit of energy equal to that expended by one kilowatt in one hour

**kilt** \'kilt\ *n* : a knee-length pleated skirt usu. of tartan worn by Scotsmen

**kil·ter** \'kil-tər\ *n* : proper condition ⟨out of ∼⟩

**ki·mo·no** \kə-'mō-nə\ *n, pl* **-nos** 1 : a loose robe with wide sleeves and a broad sash traditionally worn as an outer garment by the Japanese 2 : a loose dressing gown worn esp. by women

**kin** \'kin\ *n* 1 : an individual's relatives 2 : KINSMAN

**¹kind** \'kīnd\ *n* 1 : essential quality or character 2 : a group united by common traits or interests : CATEGORY; *also* : VARIETY 3 : goods or commodities as distinguished from money

**²kind** *adj* 1 : of a sympathetic, forbearing, or pleasant nature ⟨∼ friends⟩ 2 : arising from sympathy or forbearance ⟨∼ deeds⟩ **syn** benevolent, benign, benignant, gracious — **kind·ness** \'kīn(d)-nəs\ *n*

**kin·der·gar·ten** \'kin-dər-,gärt-ᵊn\ *n* : a school or class for children usu. from four to six years old

**kin·der·gart·ner** \-,gärt-nər\ *n* 1 : a kindergarten pupil 2 : a kindergarten teacher

**kind·heart·ed** \'kīnd-'härt-əd\ *adj* : marked by a sympathetic nature

**kin·dle** \'kin-dᵊl\ *vb* **kin·dled; kin·dling** \-(d)liŋ, -dᵊl-iŋ\ 1 : to set on fire : start burning 2 : to stir up : AROUSE 3 : ILLUMINATE, GLOW

**kin·dling** \'kin-(d)liŋ, 'kin-lən\ : easily combustible material for starting a fire

**¹kind·ly** \'kīn-dlē\ *adj* **kind·li·er; -est** 1 : of an agreeable or beneficial nature 2 : of a sympathetic or generous nature ⟨∼ men⟩ — **kind·li·ness** *n*

**²kindly** *adv* 1 : READILY ⟨does not take ∼ to criticism⟩ 2 : SYMPATHETICALLY 3 : COURTEOUSLY, OBLIGINGLY

**kind of** \,kīn-də(v)\ *adv* : to a moderate degree ⟨it's kind of late to begin⟩

**¹kin·dred** \'kin-drəd\ *n* 1 : a group of related individuals 2 : one's relatives

**²kindred** *adj* : of a like nature or character

**kine** \'kīn\ *archaic pl of* COW

**ki·ne·mat·ics** \,kin-ə-'mat-iks, ,kī-nə-\ *n* : a science that deals with motion apart from aspects of mass and force — **ki·ne·mat·ic** \-ik\ *or* **ki·ne·mat·i·cal** \-i-kəl\ *adj*

**kin·e·scope** \'kin-ə-,skōp\ *n* 1 : PICTURE TUBE 2 : a moving picture made from the image on a picture tube

**kin·es·the·sia** \,kin-əs-'thē-zh(ē-)ə, ,kī-nəs-\ *or* **kin·es·the·sis** \-'thē-səs\ *n, pl* **-the·sias** *or* **-the·ses** \-,sēz\ : a sense mediated by nervous elements in muscles, tendons, and joints and stimulated by bodily movements and tensions; *also* : sensory experience derived from this source — **kin·es·thet·ic** \-'thet-ik\ *adj*

**ki·net·ic** \kə-'net-ik, kī-\ *adj* : of or relating to the motion of material bodies and the forces and energy **(kinetic energy)** associated therewith

**ki·net·ics** \kə-'net-iks, kī-\ *n sing or pl* : a science that deals with the effects of forces upon the motions of material bodies or with changes in a physical or chemical system

**kin·folk** \'kin-,fōk\ *or* **kinfolks** *n pl* : RELATIVES

**king** \'kiŋ\ *n* 1 : a male sovereign 2 : a chief among competitors ⟨home-run ∼⟩ 3 : the principal piece in the game of chess 4 : a playing card bearing the figure of a king 5 : a checker that has been crowned — **king·less** *adj* — **king·ly** *adj* — **king·ship** *n*

**king·bolt** \-,bōlt\ *n* : a vertical bolt by which the forward axle and wheels of a vehicle are connected to the other parts

**king crab** *n* 1 : HORSESHOE CRAB 2 : any of several very large crabs

**king·dom** \'kiŋ-dəm\ *n* 1 : a country whose head is a king or queen 2 : a realm or region in which something or someone is dominant ⟨a cattle ∼⟩ 3 : one of the three primary divisions of lifeless material, plants, and animals into which natural objects are grouped

**king·fish·er** \-,fish-ər\ *n* : a brightly colored crested bird that feeds chiefly on fish

**king·pin** \'kiŋ-,pin\ *n* 1 : any of several bowling pins 2 : the leader in a group or undertaking 3 : KINGBOLT

**king–size** \'kiŋ-,sīz\ *or* **king–sized** \-,sīzd\ *adj* 1 : longer than the regular or standard size 2 : unusually large 3 : having dimensions of about 76 by 80 inches ⟨a ∼ bed⟩; *also* : of a size that fits a king-size bed

**kink** \'kiŋk\ *n* 1 : a short tight twist or curl 2 : CRAMP ⟨a ∼ in the back⟩ 3 : an imperfection likely to cause difficulties in operation 4 : a mental peculiarity : QUIRK — **kinky** *adj*

**kin·ship** \'kin-,ship\ *n* : RELATIONSHIP

**kins·man** \'kinz-mən\ *n* : RELATIVE; *esp* : a male relative

**kins·wom·an** \-,wùm-ən\ *n* : a female relative

**ki·osk** \'kē-,äsk\ *n* : a small structure with one or more open sides

**Ki·o·wa** \'kī-ə-,wò, -,wä, -,wä\ *n, pl* **Kiowa** *or* **Kiowas** : a member of an Indian people of Colorado, Kansas, New Mexico, Oklahoma, and Texas

**¹kip** \'kip\ *n* : the undressed hide of a young or small animal

**²kip** \'kip, 'gip\ *n, pl* **kip** *or* **kips** — see MONEY table

**kip·per** \'kip-ər\ n : a fish (as a herring) preserved by salting and drying or smoking — **kipper** vb

**kirk** \'kiərk, 'kərk\ n, chiefly Scot : CHURCH

**kir·tle** \'kərt-ᵊl\ n : a long gown or dress worn by women

**kis·met** \'kiz-,met, -mət\ n, often cap [Turk, fr. Ar qismah portion, lot] : FATE

¹**kiss** \'kis\ vb 1 : to touch or caress with the lips as a mark of affection or greeting 2 : to touch gently or lightly

²**kiss** n 1 : a caress with the lips 2 : a gentle touch or contact 3 : a bite-size candy

**kiss·er** \'kis-ər\ n 1 : one that kisses 2 slang : MOUTH 3 slang : FACE

**kit** \'kit\ n 1 : a set of articles for personal use; also : a set of tools or implements or of parts to be assembled 2 : a container (as a case) for a kit

**kitch·en** \'kich-ən\ n 1 : a room with cooking facilities 2 : the personnel that prepares, cooks, and serves food

**kitch·en·ette** \,kich-ə-'net\ n : a small kitchen or an alcove containing cooking facilities

**kitchen police** n 1 : enlisted men detailed to assist the cooks in a military mess 2 : the work of kitchen police

**kitch·en·ware** \'kich·ən-,waər\ n : utensils and appliances for use in a kitchen

**kite** \'kīt\ n 1 : any of several small hawks 2 : a light frame covered with paper or cloth and designed to be flown in the air at the end of a long string

**kith** \'kith\ n [ME, fr. OE cȳthth, fr. cūth known] : familiar friends, neighbors, or relatives (~ and kin)

**kitsch** \'kich\ n : shoddy or cheap artistic or literary material

**kit·ten** \'kit-ᵊn\ n : a young cat — **kit·ten·ish** adj

¹**kit·ty** \'kit-ē\ n, pl **kitties** : CAT; esp : KITTEN

²**kitty** n, pl **kitties** : a fund in a poker game made up of contributions from each pot; also : POOL

**kit·ty-cor·ner** or **kit·ty-cor·nered** var of CATERCORNER

**ki·wi** \'kē-(,)wē\ n : a flightless New Zealand bird

**KJV** abbr King James Version

**KKK** abbr Ku Klux Klan

**klatch** or **klatsch** \'klach\ n [G klatsch gossip] : a gathering marked by informal conversation

**klep·to·ma·nia** \,klep-tə-'mā-nē-ə\ n : a persistent neurotic impulse to steal esp. without economic motive — **klep·to·ma·ni·ac** \-nē-,ak\ n

**klieg light** or **kleig light** \'klēg-\ n : a carbon arc lamp used in taking motion pictures

**km** abbr kilometer

**kn** abbr knot

**knack** \'nak\ n 1 : a clever way of doing something 2 : natural aptitude

**knap·sack** \'nap-,sak\ n : a usu. canvas or leather bag or case strapped on the back and used esp. for carrying supplies (as on a hike)

**knave** \'nāv\ n 1 : ROGUE 2 : JACK 3 — **knav·ery** \'nāv-(ə-)rē\ n — **knav·ish** \'nā-vish\ adj

**knead** \'nēd\ vb : to work and press into a mass with the hands; also : MASSAGE — **knead·er** n

**knee** \'nē\ n : the joint in the middle part of the leg — **kneed** \'nēd\ adj

**knee·cap** \'nē-,kap\ n : a thick flat movable bone forming the front of the knee

**knee·hole** \-,hōl\ n : a space (as under a desk) for the knees

**kneel** \'nēl\ vb **knelt** \'nelt\ or **kneeled**; **kneel·ing** : to bend the knee : fall or rest on the knees

¹**knell** \'nel\ vb 1 : to ring esp. for a death or disaster 2 : to summon, announce, or proclaim by a knell

²**knell** n 1 : a stroke of a bell esp. when tolled (as for a funeral) 2 : an indication of the end or failure of something

**knew** past of KNOW

**knick·ers** \'nik-ərz\ n pl : loose-fitting short pants gathered at the knee

**knick·knack** \'nik-,nak\ n : a small trivial article intended for ornament

¹**knife** \'nīf\ n, pl **knives** \'nīvz\ 1 : a cutting instrument consisting of a sharp blade fastened to a handle 2 : a sharp cutting tool in a machine

²**knife** vb **knifed**; **knif·ing** : to stab, slash, or wound with a knife

¹**knight** \'nīt\ n 1 : a mounted warrior of feudal times serving a king 2 : a man honored by a sovereign for merit and in Great Britain ranking below a baronet 3 : a man devoted to the service of a lady 4 : a member of any of various orders or societies 5 : a chess piece having a move of two squares to a square of the opposite color — **knight·ly** adj

²**knight** vb : to make a knight of

**knight·hood** \'nīt-,hùd\ n 1 : the rank, dignity, or profession of a knight 2 : CHIVALRY 3 : knights as a class or body

**knish** \kə-'nish\ n : a small round or square of dough stuffed with a filling (as of meat or fruit) and baked or fried

¹**knit** \'nit\ vb **knit** or **knit·ted**; **knit·ting** 1 : to link firmly or closely 2 : WRINKLE (~ her brows) 3 : to form a fabric by interlacing yarn or thread in connected loops with needles 4 : to grow together — **knit·ter** n

²**knit** n 1 : a basic knitting stitch 2 : a knitted garment or fabric

**knit·wear** \-,waər\ n : knitted clothing

**knob** \'näb\ n 1 : a rounded protuberance; also : a small rounded ornament or handle 2 : a rounded usu. isolated hill or mountain — **knobbed** \'näbd\ adj — **knob·by** \'näb-ē\ adj

¹**knock** \'näk\ vb 1 : to strike with a sharp blow 2 : BUMP, COLLIDE 3 : to make a pounding noise esp. as a result of abnormal ignition 4 : to find fault with

²**knock** n 1 : a sharp blow 2 : a pounding noise; esp : one caused by abnormal ignition

**knock·down** \'näk-,daùn\ *n* **1** : the action of knocking down **2** : something (as a blow) that knocks down **3** : something that can be easily assembled or disassembled

**knock down** \-'daùn\ *vb* **1** : to strike to the ground with or as if with a sharp blow **2** : to take apart : DISASSEMBLE **3** : to receive an income or salary : EARN **4** : to make a reduction in

**knock·er** \'näk-ər\ *n* : one that knocks; *esp* : a device hinged to a door for use in knocking

**knock-knee** \'näk-'nē, -,nē\ *n* : a condition in which the legs curve inward at the knees — **knock-kneed** \-'nēd\ *adj*

**knock off** *vb* **1** : to stop doing something **2** : to do quickly, carelessly, or routinely **3** : to deduct from a price **4** : KILL **5** : ROB

**knock·out** \'näk-,aùt\ *n* **1** : a blow that fells and immobilizes an opponent (as in boxing) **2** : something sensationally striking or attractive

**knock out** \-'aùt\ *vb* **1** : to defeat by a knockout **2** : to make unconscious or inoperative **3** : to tire out : EXHAUST

**knock·wurst** *or* **knack·wurst** \'näk-,wərst, -,vù(r)st\ *n* : a short thick heavily seasoned sausage

**knoll** \'nōl\ *n* : a small round hill

¹**knot** \'nät\ *n* **1** : an interlacing (as of string or ribbon) that forms a lump or knob **2** : PROBLEM **3** : a bond of union; *esp* : the marriage bond **4** : a protuberant lump or swelling in tissue; *also* : the base of a woody branch enclosed in the stem from which it arises **5** : GROUP, CLUSTER **6** : an ornamental bow of ribbon **7** : one nautical mile per hour; *also* : one nautical mile — **knot·ty** *adj*

²**knot** *vb* **knot·ted; knot·ting 1** : to tie in or with a knot **2** : ENTANGLE

**knot·hole** \-,hōl\ *n* : a hole in a board or tree trunk where a knot has come out

**knout** \'naùt, 'nüt\ *n* : a whip for flogging criminals

**know** \'nō\ *vb* **knew** \'n(y)ü\; **known** \'nōn\; **know·ing 1** : to perceive directly : have understanding or direct cognition of; *also* : to recognize the nature of **2** : to be acquainted or familiar with **3** : to be aware of the truth of **4** : to have a practical understanding of — **know·able** *adj* — **know·er** *n* — **in the know** : possessing confidential information

**know-how** \'nō-,haù\ *n* : knowledge of how to do something smoothly and efficiently

**know·ing** \'nō-iŋ\ *adj* **1** : having or reflecting knowledge, intelligence, or information **2** : shrewdly and keenly alert **3** : DELIBERATE, INTENTIONAL **syn** astute, bright, smart — **know·ing·ly** *adv*

**knowl·edge** \'näl-ij\ *n* **1** : understanding gained by actual experience ⟨a ~ of carpentry⟩ **2** : range of information ⟨within my ~⟩ **3** : clear perception of truth **4** : something learned and kept in the mind

**knowl·edge·able** \-ə-bəl\ *adj* : having or showing knowledge or intelligence

**knuck·le** \'nək-əl\ *n* : the rounded knob at a joint and esp. at a finger joint

**knuck·le·bone** \,nək-əl-'bōn, 'nək-əl-,bōn\ *n* : one of the bones forming a knuckle

**knuckle down** *vb* : to apply oneself earnestly

**knuckle under** *vb* : SUBMIT, SURRENDER

**knurl** \'nərl\ *n* **1** : KNOB **2** : one of a series of small ridges on a metal surface to aid in gripping — **knurled** \'nərld\ *adj*

**KO** \(')kā-'ō, 'kā-ō\ *n* : KNOCKOUT — **KO** *vb*

**ko·ala** \kō-'äl-ə, kə-'wäl-\ *n* : a gray furry Australian marsupial with large hairy ears that feeds on eucalyptus leaves

**ko·bo** \'kō-(,)bō\ *n* — see naira at MONEY table

**ko·bold** \'kō-,bold\ *n* : a gnome or spirit of German folklore

**K of C** *abbr* Knights of Columbus

**kohl·ra·bi** \kōl-'rab-ē, -'räb-\ *n, pl* **-bies** : a cabbage that forms no head but has a swollen fleshy edible stem

**ko·lin·sky** *or* **ko·lin·ski** \kə-'lin-skē\ *n, pl* **-skies** : the fur of various Asiatic minks

**kook** \'kük\ *n* : SCREWBALL

**kooky** *also* **kook·ie** \'kü-kē\ *adj* **kook·i·er; -est** : having the characteristics of a kook — **kook·i·ness** *n*

**ko·peck** *also* **ko·pek** \'kō-,pek\ *n* — see ruble at MONEY table

**Ko·ran** \kə-'ran, -'rän\ *n* : a book of writings accepted by Muslims as revelations made to Muhammad by Allah

**Ko·re·an** \kə-'rē-ən\ *n* : a native or inhabitant of Korea — **Korean** *adj*

**ko·ru·na** \'kȯr-ə-,nä\ *n, pl* **ko·ru·ny** \-ə-nē\ *or* **korunas** — see MONEY table

**ko·sher** \'kō-shər\ *adj* [Yiddish, fr. Heb *kāshēr* fit, proper] : ritually fit for use according to Jewish law; *also* : selling or serving such food

**kow·tow** \kaù-'taù, 'kaù-,taù\ *vb* [Chin *k'o¹ t'ou²*, fr. *k'o¹* to bump + *t'ou²* head] **1** : to kneel and touch the forehead to the ground as a sign of homage or deep respect **2** : to show obsequious deference

**KP** *abbr* kitchen police

**Kr** *symbol* krypton

**kraal** \'krȯl, 'kräl\ *n* **1** : a village of southern African natives **2** : an enclosure for domestic animals in southern Africa

**kraut** \'kraùt\ *n* : SAUERKRAUT

**Krem·lin** \'krem-lən\ *n* : the Russian government

**Krem·lin·ol·o·gist** \,krem-lə-'näl-ə-jəst\ *n* : a specialist in the policies and practices of the Soviet government

¹**kro·na** \'krō-nə\ *n, pl* **kro·nur** \-nər\ — see MONEY table

²**kro·na** \'krō-nə\ *n, pl* **kro·nor** \-,nȯər\ — see MONEY table

**kro·ne** \'krō-nə\ *n, pl* **kro·ner** \-nər\ — see MONEY table

**Kru·ger·rand** \'krü-gə(r)-,rand,

-,ränd\ *n* : a 1-ounce gold coin of the Republic of South Africa equal in bullion value to 25 rands and having an official price of 31 rands

**kryp·ton** \'krip-,tän\ *n* : a gaseous chemical element that occurs in small quantities in air and is used in electric lamps

**KS** *abbr* Kansas

**kt** *abbr* 1 karat 2 knight

**ku·do** \'k(y)üd-ō\ *n, pl* **kudos** [fr. *kudos* (taken as pl.)] 1 : AWARD, HONOR 2 : COMPLIMENT, PRAISE

**ku·dos** \'k(y)ü-,däs\ *n* : fame and renown resulting from achievement

**ku·lak** \k(y)ü-'lak\ *n* [Russ, lit., fist] 1 : a wealthy peasant farmer in 19th century Russia 2 : a farmer characterized by Communists as too wealthy

**kum·quat** \'kəm-,kwät\ *n* [Chin *kam kwat*, fr. *kam* gold + *kwat* orange] : a small citrus fruit with sweet spongy rind and acid pulp

**kung fu** \'kùŋ-'fü, 'gùŋ-\ *n* : a Chinese art of self-defense resembling karate

**ku·rus** \kə-'rüsh\ *n, pl* **kurus** — see *lira* at MONEY table

**kv** *abbr* kilovolt

**kw** *abbr* kilowatt

**kwa·cha** \'kwäch-ə\ *n, pl* **kwacha** — see MONEY table

**kwash·i·or·kor** \,kwäsh-ē-'ȯr-kər, -ȯr-'kȯr\ *n* : a disease of young children resulting from deficient intake of protein

**Ky** *or* **KY** *abbr* Kentucky

**kyat** \'chät\ *n* — see MONEY table

[1] **l** \'el\ *n, pl* **l's** *or* **ls** \'elz\ *often cap* : the 12th letter of the English alphabet

[2] *abbr, often cap* 1 lake 2 Latin 3 left 4 pound 5 line 6 liter

[1] **La** *abbr* Louisiana

[2] **La** *symbol* lanthanum

**LA** *abbr* 1 law agent 2 Los Angeles 3 Louisiana

**lab** \'lab\ *n* : LABORATORY

**Lab** *abbr* Labrador

[1] **la·bel** \'lā-bəl\ *n* 1 : a slip attached to something for identification or description 2 : a descriptive or identifying word or phrase 3 : BRAND 3

[2] **label** *vb* **la·beled** *or* **la·belled**; **la·bel·ing** *or* **la·bel·ling** \'lā-b(ə-)liŋ\ 1 : to affix a label to 2 : to describe or designate with a label

**la·bi·al** \'lā-bē-əl\ *adj* : of or relating to the lips or labia

**la·bia ma·jo·ra** \,lā-bē-ə-mə-'jōr-ə\ *n pl* : the outer fatty folds bounding the vulva

**labia mi·no·ra** \-mə-'nōr-ə\ *n pl* : the inner highly vascular folds bounding the vulva

**la·bile** \'lā-,bīl, -bəl\ *adj* 1 : ADAPTABLE 2 : UNSTABLE

**la·bi·um** \'lā-bē-əm\ *n, pl* **la·bia** \-ə\ : any of the folds at the margin of the vulva

[1] **la·bor** \'lā-bər\ *n* 1 : expenditure of physical or mental effort; *also* : human activity that provides the goods or services in an economy 2 : the physical activities involved in parturition 3 : TASK 4 : those who do manual labor or work for wages; *also* : labor unions or their officials

[2] **labor** *vb* **la·bored**; **la·bor·ing** \-b(ə-)riŋ\ 1 : WORK 2 : to move with great effort 3 : to be in the labor of giving birth 4 : to suffer from some disadvantage or distress ⟨~ under a delusion⟩ 5 : to treat or work out laboriously — **la·bor·er** *n*

**lab·o·ra·to·ry** \'lab-(ə-)rə-,tōr-ē\ *n, pl* **-ries** : a place equipped for experimental study in a science or for testing and analysis

**Labor Day** *n* : the 1st Monday in September observed as a legal holiday in recognition of the workingman

**la·bored** \'lā-bərd\ *adj* : not freely or easily done ⟨~ breathing⟩

**la·bo·ri·ous** \lə-'bōr-ē-əs\ *adj* 1 : INDUSTRIOUS 2 : requiring great effort — **la·bo·ri·ous·ly** *adv*

**la·bor·sav·ing** \'lā-bər-,sā-viŋ\ *adj* : designed to replace or decrease labor

**la·bour** *chiefly Brit var of* LABOR

**lab·ra·dor·ite** \'lab-rə-,dȯr-,īt\ *n* : a feldspar showing a play of several colors

**la·bur·num** \lə-'bər-nəm\ *n* : a leguminous shrub or tree with hanging clusters of yellow flowers

**lab·y·rinth** \'lab-ə-,rinth\ *n* : a place constructed of or filled with confusing intricate passageways : MAZE — **lab·y·rin·thine** \,lab-ə-'rin-thən\ *adj*

**lac** \'lak\ *n* : a resinous substance secreted by a scale insect and used in the manufacture of shellac and lacquers

**lac·co·lith** \'lak-ə-,lith\ *n* : a mass of intrusive igneous rock causing dome-shaped bulging

[1] **lace** \'lās\ *n* [ME, fr. OF *laz*, fr. L *laqueus* snare, noose] 1 : a cord or string used for drawing together two edges 2 : an ornamental braid 3 : a fine openwork usu. figured fabric made of thread — **lacy** \'lā-sē\ *adj*

[2] **lace** *vb* **laced**; **lac·ing** 1 : TIE 2 : INTERTWINE 3 : to adorn with lace 4 : BEAT, LASH 5 : to give zest or savor to

**lac·er·ate** \'las-ə-,rāt\ *vb* **-at·ed**; **-at·ing** : to tear roughly — **lac·er·a·tion** \,las-ə-'rā-shən\ *n*

**lace·wing** \'lās-,wiŋ\ *n* : any of various insects with delicate wing veins, long antennae, and brilliant eyes

**lach·ry·mose** \'lak-rə-,mōs\ *adj* 1 : TEARFUL 2 : MOURNFUL

[1] **lack** \'lak\ *vb* 1 : to be wanting or missing 2 : to be deficient in

[2] **lack** *n* : the fact or state of being wanting or deficient : NEED

**lack·a·dai·si·cal** \,lak-ə-'dā-zi-kəl\ *adj* : lacking life, spirit, or zest — **lack·a·dai·si·cal·ly** \-k(ə-)lē\ *adv*

**lack·ey** \'lak-ē\ *n, pl* **lackeys** 1 : a liveried retainer 2 : TOADY

**lack·lus·ter** \'lak-,ləs-tər\ *adj* : DULL

**la·con·ic** \lə-'kän-ik\ *adj* [L *laconicus* Spartan, fr. Gk *lakōnikos;* fr. the Spartan reputation for terseness of speech]

: sparing of words : TERSE — **la·con·i·cal·ly** \-i-k(ə-)lē\ adv

**lac·quer** \'lak-ər\ n : a clear or colored usu. glossy and quick-drying surface coating that contains natural or synthetic substances and dries by evaporation of the solvent — **lacquer** vb

**lac·ri·mal** also **lach·ry·mal** \'lak-rə-məl\ adj : of, relating to, or being the glands that produce tears

**lac·ri·ma·tion** \,lak-rə-'mā-shən\ n : secretion of tears

**la·crosse** \lə-'krós\ n : a game played on a field by two teams with a hard ball and long-handled rackets

**lac·tate** \'lak-,tāt\ vb **lac·tat·ed; lac·tat·ing** : to secrete milk — **lac·ta·tion** \lak-'tā-shən\ n

**lac·te·al** \'lak-tē-əl\ adj : consisting of, producing, or resembling milk

**lac·tic** \'lak-tik\ adj **1** : of or relating to milk **2** : formed in the souring of milk

**lactic acid** n : a syrupy acid present in blood and muscle tissue, produced by bacterial fermentation of carbohydrates, and used in food and medicine

**lac·tose** \'lak-,tōs\ n : a sugar present in milk

**la·cu·na** \lə-'k(y)ü-nə\ n, pl **la·cu·nae** \-(,)nē\ or **la·cu·nas** [L, pool, pit, gap, fr. lacus lake] : a blank space or missing part : GAP

**lad** \'lad\ n : YOUTH; also : FELLOW

**lad·der** \'lad-ər\ n : a structure for climbing up or down that consists usu. of two long parallel sidepieces joined at intervals by crosspieces

**lad·die** \'lad-ē\ n : a young lad

**lad·en** \'lād-ᵊn\ adj : LOADED, BURDENED

**lad·ing** \'lād-iŋ\ n : CARGO, FREIGHT

**la·dle** \'lād-ᵊl\ n : a deep-bowled long-handled spoon used in taking up and conveying liquids — **ladle** vb

**la·dy** \'lād-ē\ n, pl **ladies** [ME, fr. OE hlǣfdīge, fr. hlāf bread + -dīge (akin to dǣge kneader of bread)] **1** : a woman of property, rank, or authority; also : a woman of superior social position or of refinement **2** : WOMAN **3** : WIFE

**lady beetle** n : LADYBUG

**la·dy·bird** \'lād-ē-,bərd\ n : LADYBUG

**la·dy·bug** \-,bəg\ n : any of various small nearly hemispherical and usu. brightly colored beetles that mostly feed on other insects

**la·dy·fin·ger** \'lād-ē-,fiŋ-gər\ n : a small finger-shaped sponge cake

**la·dy–in–wait·ing** \,lād-ē-in-'wāt-iŋ\ n, pl **ladies–in–waiting** : a lady appointed to attend or wait on a queen or princess

**la·dy·like** \'lād-ē-,līk\ adj : WELL-BRED

**la·dy·love** \-,ləv\ n : SWEETHEART

**la·dy·ship** \'lād-ē-,ship\ n : the condition of being a lady : rank of lady

**lady's slipper** \'lād-ē(z)-,slip-ər\ n : any of several No. American orchids with slipper-shaped flowers

**¹lag** \'lag\ vb **lagged; lag·ging 1** : to fail to keep up : stay behind **2** : to slacken gradually **syn** dawdle

**²lag** n **1** : a slowing up or falling behind; also : the amount by which one lags **2** : INTERVAL

**la·ger** \'läg-ər\ n : a light-colored usu. dry beer

**¹lag·gard** \'lag-ərd\ adj : DILATORY, SLOW — **lag·gard·ly** adv or adj — **lag·gard·ness** n

**²laggard** n : one that lags or lingers; esp : a security whose price has lagged for no obvious reason behind the average of its group or of the market

**la·gniappe** \'lan-,yap\ n : something given without charge or by way of good measure

**la·goon** \lə-'gün\ n : a shallow sound, channel, or pond near or communicating with a larger body of water

**laid** past of LAY

**lain** past part of LIE

**lair** \'laər\ n : the resting or living place of a wild animal : DEN

**laird** \'laərd\ n, Scot : a landed proprietor

**lais·sez–faire** \,les-ā-'faər\ n [F laissez faire let do] : a doctrine opposing governmental interference in economic affairs beyond the minimum necessary to maintain peace and property rights

**la·ity** \'lā-ət-ē\ n **1** : the people of a religious faith who are distinguished from its clergy **2** : the mass of the people who are distinguished from those of a particular field

**lake** \'lāk\ n : an inland body of standing water of considerable size; also : a pool of liquid (as lava or pitch)

**¹lam** \'lam\ vb **lammed; lam·ming** : to flee hastily — **lam** n

**²lam** abbr laminated

**Lam** abbr Lamentations

**la·ma** \'läm-ə\ n : a Buddhist monk of Tibet or Mongolia

**la·ma·sery** \'läm-ə-,ser-ē\ n, pl **-ser·ies** : a monastery for lamas

**¹lamb** \'lam\ n **1** : a young sheep; also : its flesh used as food **2** : an innocent or gentle person

**²lamb** vb : to bring forth a lamb

**lam·baste** or **lam·bast** \lam-'bāst, -'bast\ vb **1** : BEAT **2** : EXCORIATE

**lam·bent** \'lam-bənt\ adj [L lambens, prp. of lambere to lick] **1** : FLICKERING **2** : softly radiant ⟨~ eyes⟩ **3** : marked by lightness or brilliance ⟨~ humor⟩ — **lam·ben·cy** \-bən-sē\ n — **lam·bent·ly** adv

**lamb·skin** \'lam-,skin\ n : a lamb's skin or a small fine-grade sheepskin or the leather made from either

**¹lame** \'lām\ adj **lam·er; lam·est 1** : having a body part and usu. a limb so disabled as to impair freedom of movement; also : marked by stiffness and soreness **2** : lacking substance : WEAK — **lame·ly** adv — **lame·ness** n

**²lame** vb **lamed; lam·ing** : to make lame : CRIPPLE

**la·mé** \lä-'mā, la-\ n : a brocaded clothing fabric with tinsel filling threads (as of gold or silver)

**lame·brain** \'lām-,brān\ n : a stupid person

**lame duck** *n* : an elected official continuing to hold office between the time of his defeat for reelection and the inauguration of a successor

¹**la·ment** \lə-'ment\ *vb* **1** : to mourn aloud : WAIL **2** : to express sorrow for : BEWAIL — **lam·en·ta·ble** \'lam-ən-tə-bəl, lə-'ment-ə-\ *adj* — **lam·en·ta·bly** \-blē\ *adv* — **lam·en·ta·tion** \,lam-ən-'tā-shən\ *n*

²**lament** *n* **1** : a crying out in grief : WAIL **2** : DIRGE, ELEGY

**la·mia** \'lā-mē-ə\ *n* : a female demon

**lam·i·na** \'lam-ə-nə\ *n, pl* **-nae** \-,nē\ *or* **-nas** : a thin plate or scale

**lam·i·nar** \'lam-ə-nər\ *adj* : arranged in or consisting of laminae

**lam·i·nat·ed** \-,nāt-əd\ *adj* : consisting of laminae; *esp* : composed of layers of firmly united material — **lam·i·nate** \-,nāt\ *vb* — **lam·i·nate** \-nət\ *n or adj* — **lam·i·na·tion** \,lam-ə-'nā-shən\ *n*

**lamp** \'lamp\ *n* **1** : a vessel with a wick for burning a flammable liquid (as oil) to produce artificial light **2** : a device for producing light or heat

**lamp·black** \-blak\ *n* : a fine black soot made by incomplete burning of carbonaceous matter and used esp. as a pigment

**lamp·light·er** \-,līt-ər\ *n* : a person employed to go about lighting street lights that burn gas

**lam·poon** \lam-'pün\ *n* : SATIRE; *esp* : one that is harsh and usu. directed against an individual — **lampoon** *vb*

**lam·prey** \'lam-prē\ *n, pl* **lampreys** : an eellike water animal with sucking mouth and no jaws

**la·nai** \lə-'nī\ *n* : a porch furnished for use as a living room

¹**lance** \'lans\ *n* **1** : a steel-headed spear **2** : any of various sharp-pointed implements; *esp* : LANCET

²**lance** *vb* **lanced; lanc·ing** : to pierce or open with a lance 〈~ a boil〉

**lance corporal** *n* : an enlisted man in the marine corps ranking above a private first class and below a corporal

**lanc·er** \'lan-sər\ *n* : a cavalryman of a unit formerly armed with lances

**lan·cet** \'lan-sət\ *n* : a sharp-pointed and usu. 2-edged surgical instrument

¹**land** \'land\ *n* **1** : the solid part of the surface of the earth; *also* : a part of the earth's surface in some way distinguishable (as by political boundaries) **2** : the people of a country; *also* : REALM, DOMAIN **3** *pl* : territorial possessions — **land·less** *adj*

²**land** *vb* **1** : DISEMBARK; *also* : to touch at a place on shore **2** : to bring to or arrive at a destination **3** : to catch with a hook and bring in 〈~ a fish〉; *also* : GAIN, SECURE 〈~ a job〉 **4** : to strike or meet the ground **5** : to alight or cause to alight on a surface

**lan·dau** \'lan-,daù\ *n* **1** : a 4-wheeled carriage with a top divided into two sections that can be lowered, thrown back, or removed **2** : an enclosed automobile with a top whose rear quarter can be opened or folded down

**land·ed** \'lan-dəd\ *adj* : having an estate in land 〈~ gentry〉

**land·er** \'lan-dər\ *n* : a space vehicle designed to land on a celestial body

**land·fall** \'lan(d)-,fȯl\ *n* : a sighting or making of land (as after a voyage); *also* : the land first sighted

**land·fill** \-,fil\ *n* : a low-lying area on which trash and garbage is buried between layers of earth

**land·form** \-,fȯrm\ *n* : a natural feature of the earth's surface

**land·hold·er** \'land-,hōl-dər\ *n* : a holder or owner of land — **land·hold·ing** \-diŋ\ *adj or n*

**land·ing** \'lan-diŋ\ *n* **1** : the action of one that lands; *also* : a place for discharging or taking on passengers and cargo **2** : a level part of a staircase

**landing gear** *n* : the part that supports the weight of an airplane or spacecraft

**land·locked** \'land-,läkt\ *adj* **1** : enclosed or nearly enclosed by land 〈a ~ harbor〉 **2** : confined to fresh water by some barrier 〈~ salmon〉

**land·lord** \-,lȯrd\ *n* **1** : the owner of property leased or rented to another **2** : a man who rents lodgings : INNKEEPER — **land·la·dy** \-,lād-ē\ *n*

**land·lub·ber** \-,ləb-ər\ *n* : one who knows little of the sea or seamanship

**land·mark** \'lan(d)-,märk\ *n* **1** : an object that marks the boundary of land **2** : a conspicuous object on land that marks a course or serves as a guide **3** : an event that marks a turning point **4** : a structure of unusual historical and usu. aesthetic interest

**land·mass** \-,mas\ *n* : a large area of land

**land·own·er** \'land-,ō-nər\ *n* : an owner of land

¹**land·scape** \'lan(d)-,skāp\ *n* **1** : a picture representing a view of natural inland scenery **2** : a portion of land that the eye can see in one glance

²**landscape** *vb* **land·scaped; land·scap·ing** : to improve the natural beauties of a tract of land by grading, clearing, or decorative planting

**land·slide** \'lan(d)-,slīd\ *n* **1** : the slipping down of a mass of rocks or earth on a steep slope; *also* : the mass of material that slides **2** : an overwhelming victory esp. in a political contest

**lands·man** \'lan(d)z-mən\ *n* : a person who lives or works on land

**land·ward** \'land-wərd\ *adj* : lying or being toward the land — **landward** *adv*

**lane** \'lān\ *n* **1** : a narrow passageway (as between fences) **2** : a relatively narrow way or track 〈traffic ~〉

**lang** *abbr* language

**lan·guage** \'laŋ-gwij\ *n* **1** : the words, their pronunciation, and the methods of combining them used and understood by a considerable community **2** : form or style of verbal expression

**lan·guid** \'laŋ-gwəd\ *adj* **1** : WEAK **2** : sluggish in character or disposition : LISTLESS **3** : SLOW — **lan·guid·ly** *adv* — **lan·guid·ness** *n*

**lan·guish** \'laŋ-gwish\ *vb* **1** : to become languid **2** : to become dispirited : PINE **3** : to appeal for sympathy by assuming an expression of grief

**lan·guor** \'laŋ-(g)ər\ n **1** : a languid feeling **2** : listless indolence **syn** lethargy, lassitude — **lan·guor·ous** adj — **lan·guor·ous·ly** adv

**lank** \'laŋk\ adj **1** : not well filled out **2** : hanging straight and limp

**lanky** \'laŋ-kē\ adj **lank·i·er; -est** : ungracefully tall and thin

**lan·o·lin** \'lan-ᵊl-ən\ n : the fatty coating of sheep's wool esp. when refined for use in ointments and cosmetics

**lan·ta·na** \lan-'tän-ə\ n : any of a genus of tropical shrubs related to the vervains with heads of small bright flowers

**lan·tern** \'lant-ərn\ n **1** : a usu. portable light with a protective transparent or translucent covering **2** : the chamber in a lighthouse containing the light **3** : a projector for slides

**lan·tha·num** \'lan-thə-nəm\ n : a soft malleable metallic chemical element

**lan·yard** \'lan-yərd\ n : a piece of rope for fastening something in ships; also : any of various cords

**Lao·tian** \lā-'ō-shən, 'laù-shən\ n : a member of a Buddhist people living in Laos and northeastern Thailand

¹**lap** \'lap\ n **1** : a loose panel or hanging flap of a garment **2** : the clothing that lies on the knees, thighs, and lower part of the trunk when one sits; also : the front part of the lower trunk and thighs of a seated person **3** : an environment of nurture ⟨the ~ of luxury⟩ **4** : CHARGE, CONTROL ⟨in the ~ of the gods⟩

²**lap** vb **lapped; lap·ping 1** : FOLD **2** : WRAP **3** : to lay over or near so as to partly cover

³**lap** n **1** : the amount by which an object overlaps another; also : the part of an object that overlaps another **2** : one circuit around a racecourse **3** : one complete turn (as of a rope around a drum) **4** : a smoothing and polishing tool

⁴**lap** vb **lapped; lap·ping 1** : to scoop up food or drink with the tip of the tongue; also : DEVOUR — usu. used with up **2** : to splash gently ⟨lapping waves⟩

⁵**lap** n **1** : an act or instance of lapping **2** : a gentle splashing sound

**lap·board** \'lap-,bōrd\ n : a board used on the lap as a table or desk

**lap·dog** \-,dȯg\ n : a small dog that may be held in the lap

**la·pel** \lə-'pel\ n : the fold of the front of a coat that is usu. a continuation of the collar

¹**lap·i·dary** \'lap-ə-,der-ē\ n, pl **-dar·ies** : one who cuts, polishes, and engraves precious stones

²**lapidary** adj **1** : of or relating to precious stones or the art of cutting them **2** : of, relating to, or suitable for engraved inscriptions

**lap·in** \'lap-ən\ n : rabbit fur usu. sheared and dyed

**la·pis la·zu·li** \,lap-əs-'laz(h)-ə-lē\ n : a usu. blue semiprecious stone often

having sparkling bits of an iron compound

**Lapp** \'lap\ n : a member of a people of northern Scandinavia, Finland, and the Kola peninsula of Russia

**lap·pet** \'lap-ət\ n : a fold or flap on a garment

¹**lapse** \'laps\ n [L lapsus, fr. labi to slip] **1** : a slight error **2** : a fall from a higher to a lower state **3** : the termination of a right or privilege through failure to meet requirements **4** : a passage of time; also : INTERVAL

²**lapse** vb **lapsed; laps·ing 1** : to commit apostasy **2** : to sink or slip gradually : SUBSIDE **3** : CEASE

**lap·wing** \'lap-,wiŋ\ n : an Old World crested plover

**lar·board** \'lär-bərd\ n **1** : ⁴PORT

**lar·ce·ny** \'lärs-(ᵊ)-nē\ n, pl **-nies** [ME, fr. MF larcin theft, fr. L latrocinium robbery, fr. latro mercenary soldier] : THEFT — **lar·ce·nous** \-nəs\ adj

**larch** \'lärch\ n : a conical tree related to the pines that sheds its needles in the fall

¹**lard** \'lärd\ vb **1** : to insert strips of usu. pork fat into (meat) before cooking; also : GREASE **2** : ENRICH

²**lard** n : a soft white fat obtained by rendering fatty tissue of the hog

**lar·der** \'lärd-ər\ n : a place where foods (as meat) are kept

**lar·es and pe·na·tes** \,lar-ēz-ən-pə-'nāt-ēz\ n pl **1** : household gods **2** : personal or household effects

**large** \'lärj\ adj **larg·er; larg·est 1** : having more than usual power, capacity, or scope **2** : exceeding most other things of like kind in quantity or size **syn** big, great — **large·ly** adv — **large·ness** n — **at large 1** : UNCONFINED **2** : as a whole

**lar·gess** or **lar·gesse** \lär-'zhes, -'jes; 'lär-jes\ n **1** : liberal giving **2** : a generous gift

¹**lar·go** \'lär-gō\ adv or adj [It, slow, broad, fr. L largus abundant] : in a very slow and broad manner — used as a direction in music

²**largo** n, pl **largos** : a largo movement

**lar·i·at** \'lar-ē-ət\ n [AmerSp la reata the lasso, fr. Sp la the + AmerSp reata lasso, fr. Sp reatar to tie again] : a long rope used to catch or tether livestock

¹**lark** \'lärk\ n : any of various small songbirds; esp : SKYLARK

²**lark** vb : FROLIC, SPORT

³**lark** n : FROLIC; also : PRANK

**lark·spur** \'lärk-,spər\ n : any of various mostly annual delphiniums

**lar·va** \'lär-və\ n, pl **lar·vae** \-(,)vē\ also **larvas** [L, specter, mask] : the wingless often wormlike form in which insects often hatch from the egg; also : any young animal (as a tadpole) that is fundamentally unlike its parent — **lar·val** \-vəl\ adj

**lar·yn·gi·tis** \,lar-ən-'jīt-əs\ n : inflammation of the larynx

**lar·ynx** \'lar-iŋks\ n, pl **la·ryn·ges** \lə-'rin-,jēz\ or **lar·ynx·es** : the upper part of the trachea containing the vocal cords — **la·ryn·ge·al** \,lar-ən-'je-əl, lə-'rin-jē-əl\ adj

**la·sa·gna** \lə-'zän-yə\ n : boiled broad flat noodles baked with a sauce usu. of tomatoes, cheese, and meat

**las·car** \'las-kər\ n : an East Indian sailor

**las·civ·i·ous** \lə-'siv-ē-əs\ adj : LEWD, LUSTFUL — **las·civ·i·ous·ness** n

**la·ser** \'lā-zər\ n [light amplification by stimulated emission of radiation] : a device that amplifies light and produces an intense monochromatic beam as a result of atoms being stimulated

¹**lash** \'lash\ vb 1 : to move vigorously 2 : WHIP 3 : to attack or retort verbally

²**lash** n 1 : a stroke esp. with a whip; also : the flexible part of a whip 2 : a verbal blow 3 : EYELASH

³**lash** vb : to bind with a rope, cord, or chain

**lass** \'las\ n : GIRL

**lass·ie** \'las-ē\ n : LASS

**las·si·tude** \'las-ə-,t(y)üd\ n 1 : WEARINESS, FATIGUE 2 : LISTLESSNESS, LANGUOR

**las·so** \'las-ō, la-'sü\ n, pl **lassos** or **lassoes** : a rope or long leather thong with a noose used for catching livestock — **lasso** vb

¹**last** \'last\ vb 1 : to continue in existence or operation 2 : to remain valid, valuable, or important : ENDURE 3 : to be enough for the needs of

²**last** adj 1 : following all the rest : FINAL 2 : next before the present 3 : least likely ⟨the ~ thing he wants⟩ 4 : CONCLUSIVE; also : SUPREME — **last·ly** adv

³**last** adv 1 : at the end 2 : most recently 3 : in conclusion

⁴**last** n : something that is last : END — **at last** : FINALLY

⁵**last** n : a foot-shaped form on which a shoe is shaped or repaired

⁶**last** vb : to shape with a last

**lat** abbr latitude

**Lat** abbr Latin

**lat·a·kia** \,lat-ə-'kē-ə\ n : an aromatic Turkish smoking tobacco

¹**latch** \'lach\ vb : to catch or get hold

²**latch** n : a catch that holds a door or gate closed

³**latch** vb : CATCH, FASTEN

**latch·et** \'lach-ət\ n : a strap, thong, or lace for fastening a shoe or sandal

**latch·key** \'lach-,kē\ n : a key by which a door latch may be opened from the outside

**latch·string** \-,striŋ\ n : a string on a latch that may be left hanging outside the door for raising the latch

¹**late** \'lāt\ adj **lat·er; lat·est** 1 : coming or remaining after the due, usual, or proper time : TARDY 2 : far advanced toward the close or end 3 : recently deceased ⟨her ~ husband⟩ 4 : holding a position recently but not now 5 : made, appearing, or happening just previous to the present : RECENT — **late·ly** adv — **late·ness** n

²**late** adv **lat·er; lat·est** 1 : after the usual or proper time; also : at or to an advanced point in time 2 : RECENTLY

**late·com·er** \'lāt-,kəm-ər\ n : one who arrives late

**la·tent** \'lāt-ᵊnt\ adj : present but not visible or active syn dormant, quiescent, potential — **la·ten·cy** \-ᵊn-sē\ n

¹**lat·er·al** \'lat-(ə-)rəl\ adj : situated on, directed toward, or coming from the side — **lat·er·al·ly** \-ē\ adv

²**lateral** n 1 : a lateral passage (as a drainage ditch) 2 : a football pass thrown parallel to the line of scrimmage or away from the opponent's goal

**la·tex** \'lā-,teks\ n, pl **la·ti·ces** \'lāt-ə-,sēz, 'lat-\ or **la·tex·es** 1 : a milky plant juice esp. of members of the milkweed group ⟨rubber is made from a ~⟩ 2 : a water emulsion of a synthetic rubber or plastic used esp. as a paint

**lath** \'lath, 'lath\ n, pl **laths** or **lath** : a thin narrow strip of wood used esp. as a base for plaster; also : a building material in sheets used for the same purpose — **lath·ing** \-iŋ\ n

**lathe** \'lāth\ n : a machine in which a piece of material is held and turned while being shaped by a tool

¹**lath·er** \'lath-ər\ n 1 : a foam or froth formed when a detergent is agitated in water; also : foam from profuse sweating (as by a horse) 2 : DITHER

²**lather** vb **lath·ered; lath·er·ing** \-(ə-)riŋ\ : to spread lather over; also : to form a lather

**Lat·in** \'lat-ᵊn\ n 1 : the language of ancient Rome 2 : a member of any of the peoples whose languages derive from Latin — **Latin** adj

**Latin American** n : a native or inhabitant of any of the countries of No., Central, or So. America whose official language is Spanish or Portuguese — **Latin-American** adj

**lat·i·tude** \'lat-ə-,t(y)üd\ n 1 : angular distance north or south from the earth's equator measured in degrees 2 : a region marked by its latitude 3 : freedom of action or choice

**lat·i·tu·di·nar·i·an** \,lat-ə-,t(y)üd-ᵊn-'er-ē-ən\ n : a person who is broad and liberal in religious belief and conduct

**la·trine** \lə-'trēn\ n : TOILET

**lat·ter** \'lat-ər\ adj 1 : more recent; also : FINAL 2 : of, relating to, or being the second of two things referred to — **lat·ter·ly** adv

**lat·ter-day** adj 1 : of a later or subsequent time 2 : of present or recent time

**lat·tice** \'lat-əs\ n 1 : a framework of crossed wood or metal strips; also : a window, door, or gate having a lattice 2 : a regular geometrical arrangement

**lat·tice·work** \-,wərk\ n : LATTICE; also : work made of lattices

**Lat·vi·an** \'lat-vē-ən\ n : a native or inhabitant of Latvia

¹**laud** \'lod\ n 1 : ACCLAIM, PRAISE

²**laud** vb : EXTOL, PRAISE — **laud·able** adj — **laud·ably** adv

**lau·da·num** \'lod-(ᵊ-)nəm\ n : OPIATE; esp : a tincture of opium

**lau·da·to·ry** \'lod-ə-,tōr-ē\ adj : of, relating to, or expressive of praise

¹**laugh** \'laf, 'laf\ vb : to show mirth,

joy, or scorn with a smile and chuckle or explosive sound; *also* : to become amused or derisive — **laugh·able** *adj* — **laugh·ing·ly** \-iŋ-lē\ *adv*

²**laugh** *n* **1** : the act of laughing **2** : JOKE; *also* : JEER

**laugh·ing·stock** \'laf-iŋ-,stäk, 'làf-\ *n* : an object of ridicule

**laugh·ter** \'laf-tor, 'làf-\ *n* : the action or sound of laughing

¹**launch** \'lonch\ *vb* [ME *launchen*, fr. OF *lancher*, fr. LL *lanceare* to wield a lance] **1** : THROW, HURL; *also* : to send off (~ a rocket) **2** : to set afloat **3** : to set in operation : START

²**launch** *n* : an act or instance of launching

³**launch** *n* : a small open or half-decked motorboat

**launch·er** \'lon-chər\ *n* **1** : one that launches **2** : a device for firing a grenade from a rifle **3** : a device for launching a rocket or rocket shell

**launch·pad** \'lonch-,pad\ *n* : a platform from which a rocket is launched

**laun·der** \'lon-dər\ *vb* **laun·dered**; **laun·der·ing** \-d(ə-)riŋ\ : to wash or wash and iron clothing and household linens — **laun·der·er** *n* — **laun·dress** \-drəs\ *n*

**laun·dry** \'lon-drē\ *n, pl* **laundries** [fr. obs. *launder* launderer, fr. MF *lavandier*, fr. ML *lavandarius*, fr. L *lavandus* needing to be washed, fr. *lavare* to wash] **1** : clothes or linens that have been or are to be laundered **2** : a place where laundering is done — **laun·dry·man** \-mən\ *n*

**lau·re·ate** \'lor-ē-ət\ *n* : the recipient of honor for achievement in an art or science — **lau·re·ate·ship** *n*

**lau·rel** \'lor-əl\ *n* **1** : any of several trees or shrubs related to the sassafras and cinnamon; *esp* : a small evergreen tree of southern Europe **2** : a crown of laurel leaves **3** : HONOR, DISTINCTION

**la·va** \'läv-ə, 'lav-\ *n* : melted rock coming from a volcano; *also* : such rock solidified

**la·vage** \lə-'väzh\ *n* : WASHING; *esp* : the washing out (as of an organ) for medicinal reasons

**la·va·liere** *or* **la·val·liere** \,läv-ə-'liər\ *n* [F *lavallière* necktie with a large bow] : a pendant on a fine chain that is worn as a necklace

**lav·a·to·ry** \'lav-ə-,tor-ē\ *n, pl* **-ries** **1** : a fixed washbowl with running water and drainpipe **2** : BATHROOM

**lave** \'läv\ *vb* **laved; lav·ing** : WASH

**lav·en·der** \'lav-ən-dər\ *n* **1** : a European mint or its dried leaves and flowers used to perfume clothing and bed linen **2** : a pale purple

¹**lav·ish** \'lav-ish\ *adj* [ME *lavas* abundant, fr. MF *lavasse* downpour, fr. *laver* to wash] **1** : expending or bestowing profusely **2** : expended or produced in abundance — **lav·ish·ly** *adv*

²**lavish** *vb* : to expend or give freely

**law** \'lo\ *n* **1** : a rule of conduct or action established by custom or laid down and enforced by a governing authority; *also* : the whole body of such

rules **2** : the control brought about by enforcing rules **3** : a rule or principle of construction or procedure **4** : a rule or principle stating something that always works in the same way under the same conditions; *also* : the observed regularity of nature **5** *cap* : the revelation of the divine will set forth in the Old Testament; *also* : the first part of the Jewish scriptures **6** : trial in a court to determine what is just and right **7** : the science that deals with laws and their interpretation and application **8** : the profession of a lawyer

**law·break·er** \'lo-,brā-kər\ *n* : one who violates the law

**law·ful** \'lo-fəl\ *adj* **1** : permitted by law **2** : RIGHTFUL — **law·ful·ly** \-ē\ *adv*

**law·giv·er** \-,giv-ər\ *n* : LEGISLATOR

**law·less** \'lo-ləs\ *adj* **1** : having no laws **2** : UNRULY, DISORDERLY (a ~ mob) — **law·less·ness** *n*

**law·mak·er** \-,mā-kər\ *n* : LEGISLATOR

**law·man** \'lo-mən\ *n* : a law enforcement official (as a sheriff or marshal)

¹**lawn** \'lon\ *n* : a fine sheer linen or cotton fabric

²**lawn** *n* : ground (as around a house) covered with closely mowed grass

**law·ren·ci·um** \lo-'ren-sē-əm\ *n* : a short-lived radioactive element

**law·suit** \'lo-,süt\ *n* : a suit in law

**law·yer** \'lo-yər\ *n* : one who conducts lawsuits for clients or advises as to legal rights and obligations in other matters

**lax** \'laks\ *adj* **1** : LOOSE, OPEN **2** : not strict (~ discipline) **3** : not tense **syn** remiss, negligent, neglectful — **lax·i·ty** \'lak-sət-ē\ *n* — **lax·ly** *adv*

¹**lax·a·tive** \'lak-sət-iv\ *adj* : relieving constipation

²**laxative** *n* : a usu. mild laxative drug

¹**lay** \'lā\ *vb* **laid** \'läd\; **lay·ing 1** : to beat or strike down **2** : to put on or against a surface : PLACE **3** : to produce and deposit eggs **4** : SETTLE; *also* : ALLAY **5** : WAGER **6** : SPREAD **7** : to set in order or position **8** : to impose esp. as a duty or burden **9** : PREPARE, CONTRIVE **10** : to bring to a specified condition **11** : to put forward : SUBMIT

²**lay** *n* : the way in which something lies or is laid in relation to something else

³**lay** *past of* LIE

⁴**lay** *n* **1** : a simple narrative poem **2** : SONG

⁵**lay** *adj* : of or relating to the laity

**lay·away** \'lā-ə-,wā\ *n* : an article of merchandise reserved for delivery to a customer on his completion of payment

**lay·er** \'lā-ər\ *n* **1** : one that lays **2** : one thickness, course, or fold laid or lying over or under another

**lay·er·ing** \'lā-ə-riŋ\ *n* : the production of new plants by surrounding a stem which is often partly cut through with a rooting medium (as soil) until new roots have formed

**lay·ette** \lā-'et\ *n* : an outfit of clothing and equipment for a newborn infant

**lay·man** \'lā-mən\ *n* : a member of the laity — **lay·wom·an** \-,wùm-ən\ *n*

**lay·off** \'lā-,of\ *n* **1** : the act of dismissing an employee temporarily **2** : a period of inactivity

**lay·out** \'lā-ˌaüt\ n **1** : ARRANGEMENT **2** : SET, OUTFIT

**la·zar** \'laz-ər, 'lā-zər\ n : LEPER

**laze** \'lāz\ vb **lazed; laz·ing** : to pass time in idleness or relaxation

**la·zy** \'lā-zē\ adj **la·zi·er; -est 1** : disliking activity or exertion **2** : SLUGGISH — **la·zi·ly** \'lā-zə-lē\ adv — **la·zi·ness** \-zē-nəs\ n

**la·zy·bones** \'lā-zē-ˌbōnz\ n : a lazy person

**lazy Su·san** \ˌlā-zē-'süz-ᵊn\ n : a revolving tray placed on a dining table

**lb** abbr [L libra] pound

**lc** abbr lowercase

**LC** abbr Library of Congress

**LCD** abbr least common denominator

**LCDR** abbr lieutenant commander

**LCL** abbr less-than-carload lot

**LCM** abbr least common multiple

**LCpl** abbr lance corporal

**ld** abbr **1** load **2** lord

**LD** abbr lethal dose

**ldg** abbr **1** landing **2** loading

**lea** \'lē, 'lā\ n : PASTURE, MEADOW

**leach** \'lēch\ vb : to pass a liquid (as water) through to carry off the soluble components; also : to dissolve out by such means ⟨~ alkali from ashes⟩

**¹lead** \'lēd\ vb **led** \'led\; **lead·ing 1** : to guide on a way; also : to run in a specified direction **2** : LIVE ⟨~ a quiet life⟩ **3** : to direct the operations, activity, or performance of ⟨~ an orchestra⟩ **4** : to go at the head of : be first ⟨~ a parade⟩ **5** : to begin play with; also : BEGIN, OPEN **6** : to tend toward a definite result ⟨study ~ing to a degree⟩ — **lead·er** n — **lead·er·less** adj — **lead·er·ship** n

**²lead** \'lēd\ n **1** : a position at the front; also : a margin by which one leads **2** : one that leads **3** : the privilege of leading in cards; also : the card or suit led **4** : a principal role (as in a play); also : one who plays such a role **5** : EXAMPLE **6** : INDICATION, CLUE **7** : an insulated electrical conductor

**³lead** \'led\ n **1** : a heavy bluish white chemical element that is easily bent and shaped **2** : an article made of lead; esp : a weight for sounding at sea **3** : a thin strip of metal used to separate lines of type in printing **4** : a thin stick of marking substance in or for a pencil

**⁴lead** \'led\ vb **1** : to cover, line, or weight with lead **2** : to fix (glass) in position with lead **3** : to treat or mix with lead or a lead compound

**lead·en** \'led-ᵊn\ adj **1** : made of lead; also : of the color of lead **2** : low in quality **3** : SLUGGISH, DULL

**lead off** \(')lēd-'óf\ vb : OPEN, BEGIN; esp : to bat first in an inning — **lead-off** \'lēd-ˌóf\ adj

**lead poisoning** n : chronic intoxication produced by the absorption of lead into the system

**¹leaf** \'lēf\ n, pl **leaves** \'lēvz\ **1** : a usu. flat and green outgrowth of a plant stem that is a unit of foliage and functions esp. in photosynthesis; also

: FOLIAGE **2** : PETAL **3** : something that is suggestive of a leaf — **leaf-less** adj — **leafy** adj

**²leaf** vb **1** : to produce leaves **2** : to turn the pages of a book

**leaf·age** \'lē-fij\ n : FOLIAGE

**leafed** \'lēft\ adj : LEAVED

**leaf·hop·per** \'lēf-ˌhäp-ər\ n : any of numerous small leaping insects related to the cicadas that suck the juices of plants

**leaf·let** \'lēf-lət\ n **1** : a division of a compound leaf **2** : PAMPHLET, FOLDER

**leaf mold** n : a compost or layer composed chiefly of decayed vegetable matter

**leaf·stalk** \'lēf-ˌstók\ n : PETIOLE

**¹league** \'lēg\ n : a measure of distance equal to about three miles

**²league** n **1** : an association or alliance for a common purpose **2** : CLASS, CATEGORY — **league** vb

**leagu·er** \'lē-gər\ n : a member of a league

**¹leak** \'lēk\ vb **1** : to enter or escape through a leak **2** : to let a substance in or out through an opening **3** : to become or make known

**²leak** n **1** : a crack or hole that accidentally admits a fluid or light or lets it escape; also : something that secretly or accidentally permits the admission or escape of something else **2** : LEAKAGE — **leaky** adj

**leak·age** \'lē-kij\ n **1** : the act of leaking **2** : the thing or amount that leaks

**leal** \'lēl\ adj, chiefly Scot : LOYAL

**¹lean** \'lēn\ vb **1** : to bend from a vertical position : INCLINE **2** : to cast one's weight to one side for support **3** : to rely on for support **4** : to incline in opinion, taste, or desire — **lean** n

**²lean** adj **1** : lacking or deficient in flesh and esp. in fat **2** : lacking richness or productiveness — **lean·ness** \'lēn-nəs\ n

**lean-to** \'lēn-ˌtü\ n, pl **lean-tos** \-ˌtüz\ : a wing or extension of a building having a roof of only one slope; also : a rough shed or shelter with a similar roof

**¹leap** \'lēp\ vb **leaped** or **leapt** \'lēpt, 'lept\; **leap·ing** : to spring free from a surface or over an obstacle : JUMP

**²leap** n : JUMP

**leap·frog** \'lēp-ˌfróg, -ˌfräg\ n : a game in which one player bends down and another leaps over him — **leapfrog** vb

**leap year** n : a year containing 366 days with February 29 as the extra day

**learn** \'lərn\ vb **learned** \'lərnd, 'lərnt\ also **learnt** \'lərnt\; **learn·ing 1** : to gain knowledge, understanding, or skill by study or experience; also : MEMORIZE **2** : to find out : ASCERTAIN — **learn·er** n

**learn·ed** \'lə-nəd\ adj : SCHOLARLY, ERUDITE

**learn·ing** \'lər-niŋ\ n : KNOWLEDGE, ERUDITION

**lease** \'lēs\ n : a contract by which one party conveys real estate to another for a term of years or at will usu. for a specified rent

**²lease** vb **leased; leas·ing 1 :** to grant by lease **2 :** to hold under a lease **syn** let, charter, hire, rent

**lease·hold** \'lēs-ˌhōld\ n **1 :** a tenure by lease **2 :** land held by lease — **lease·hold·er** n

**leash** \'lēsh\ n [ME lees, leshe, fr. OF laisse, fr. laissier to let go, fr. L laxare to loosen, fr. laxus slack] **:** a line for leading or restraining an animal — **leash** vb

**¹least** \'lēst\ adj **1 :** lowest in importance or position **2 :** smallest in size or degree **3 :** SLIGHTEST

**²least** n **:** one that is least **:** the smallest amount or degree

**³least** adv **:** in the smallest or lowest degree

**least common denominator** n **:** the least common multiple of two or more denominators

**least common multiple** n **:** the smallest common multiple of two or more numbers

**least·wise** \'lēst-ˌwīz\ adv **:** at least

**leath·er** \'leth-ər\ n **:** animal skin dressed for use — **leather** adj — **leath·ern** \-ərn\ adj — **leath·ery** adj

**leath·er·neck** \-ˌnek\ n **:** MARINE

**¹leave** \'lēv\ vb **left** \'left\; **leav·ing 1 :** BEQUEATH **2 :** to allow or cause to remain behind; also **:** DELIVER **3 :** to have as a remainder **4 :** to let stay without interference **5 :** to go away **:** depart from **6 :** to give up **:** ABANDON

**²leave** n **1 :** PERMISSION; also **:** authorized absence from duty **2 :** DEPARTURE

**³leave** vb **leaved; leav·ing :** LEAF

**leaved** \'lēvd\ adj **:** having leaves

**¹leav·en** \'lev-ən\ n **1 :** a substance (as yeast) used to produce fermentation (as in dough) **2 :** something that modifies or lightens a mass or aggregate

**²leaven** vb **leav·ened; leav·en·ing** \'lev-(ə-)niŋ\ **:** to raise (dough) with a leaven; also **:** to permeate with a modifying or vivifying element

**leav·en·ing** \'lev-(ə-)niŋ\ n **:** LEAVEN

**leaves** pl of LEAF

**leave–tak·ing** \'lēv-ˌtā-kiŋ\ n **:** DEPARTURE, FAREWELL

**leav·ings** \'lē-viŋz\ n pl **:** REMNANT, RESIDUE

**lech·ery** \'lech-ə-rē\ n **:** inordinate indulgence in sexual activity — **lech·er** \'lech-ər\ n — **lech·er·ous** adj — **lech·er·ous·ness** n

**lec·i·thin** \'les-ə-thən\ n **:** any of several waxy phosphorus-containing substances that are common in animals and plants, form colloidal solutions in water, and have emulsifying and wetting properties

**lect** abbr lecture

**lec·tern** \'lek-tərn\ n **:** a desk to support a book in a convenient position for a standing reader

**lec·tor** \-tər\ n **:** one whose chief duty is to read the lessons in a church service

**lec·ture** \'lek-chər\ n **1 :** a discourse given before an audience or a class esp. for instruction **2 :** REPRIMAND —

**lec·ture** vb — **lec·tur·er** n — **lec·ture·ship** n

**led** past of LEAD

**le·der·ho·sen** \'lād-ər-ˌhōz-ᵊn\ n pl **:** leather shorts often with suspenders worn esp. in Bavaria

**ledge** \'lej\ n [ME legge bar of a gate] **1 :** a shelflike projection from a top or an edge **2 :** REEF

**led·ger** \'lej-ər\ n **:** a book containing accounts to which debits and credits are transferred in final form

**lee** \'lē\ n **1 :** a protecting shelter **2 :** the side (as of a ship) that is sheltered from the wind — **lee** adj

**leech** \'lēch\ n [ME leche physician, fr. OE lǣce] **1 :** any of various segmented usu. freshwater worms related to the earthworms; esp **:** one formerly used by physicians to draw blood **2 :** a hanger-on who seeks gain

**leek** \'lēk\ n **:** an onionlike herb grown for its mildly pungent leaves and stalk

**leer** \'liər\ n **:** a suggestive, knowing, or malicious look — **leer** vb

**leery** \'li(ə)r-ē\ adj **:** SUSPICIOUS, WARY

**lees** \'lēz\ n pl **:** DREGS

**¹lee·ward** \'lē-wərd, 'lü-ərd\ adj **:** situated away from the wind — **leeward** adv

**²leeward** n **:** the lee side

**lee·way** \'lē-ˌwā\ n **1 :** off-course lateral movement of a ship when under way **2 :** an allowable margin of freedom or variation

**¹left** \'left\ adj [ME, fr. OE, weak; fr. the left hand's being the weaker in most individuals] **1 :** of, relating to, or being the side of the body in which the heart is mostly located; also **:** located nearer to this side than to the right **2** often cap **:** of, adhering to, or constituted by the political Left — **left** adv

**²left** n **1 :** the left hand; also **:** the side or part that is on or toward the left side **2** cap **:** those professing political views characterized by desire to reform the established order and usu. to give greater freedom to the common man

**³left** past of LEAVE

**left–hand** adj **1 :** situated on the left **2 :** LEFT-HANDED

**left–hand·ed** \'left-'han-dəd\ adj **1 :** using the left hand habitually **2 :** CLUMSY, AWKWARD

**left·ism** \'lef-ˌtiz-əm\ n **1 :** the principles and views of the Left; also **:** the movement embodying these principles **2 :** advocacy of or adherence to the doctrines of the Left — **left·ist** \-təst\ n or adj

**left·over** \'left-ˌō-vər\ n **:** an unused or unconsumed residue

**¹leg** \'leg\ n **1 :** a limb of an animal used esp. for supporting the body and in walking; esp **:** the part of the vertebrate leg between knee and foot **2 :** something resembling or analogous to an animal leg (table ~) **3 :** the part of an article of clothing that covers the leg **4 :** a portion of a trip — **legged** \'legd\ adj — **leg·less** adj

**²leg** vb **legged; leg·ging :** to use the legs in walking or esp. in running

³leg *abbr* 1 legal 2 legislative; legislature

leg·a·cy \'leg-ə-sē\ *n, pl* -cies : IN-HERITANCE, BEQUEST; *also* : something that has come from an ancestor or predecessor or the past

le·gal \'lē-gəl\ *adj* 1 : of or relating to law or lawyers 2 : LAWFUL; *also* : STATUTORY 3 : enforced in courts of law — le·gal·i·ty \li-'gal-ət-ē\ *n* — le·gal·ize \'lē-gə-,līz\ *vb* — le·gal·ly \-gə-lē\ *adv*

le·gal·ism \'lē-gə-,liz-əm\ *n* : strict, literal, or excessive conformity to the law or to a religious or moral code — le·gal·is·tic \,lē-gə-'lis-tik\ *adj*

leg·ate \'leg-ət\ *n* : an official representative; *esp* : AMBASSADOR

leg·a·tee \,leg-ə-'tē\ *n* : a person to whom a legacy is bequeathed

le·ga·tion \li-'gā-shən\ *n* 1 : a diplomatic mission headed by a minister 2 : the official residence and office of a minister to a foreign government

le·ga·to \li-'gät-ō\ *adv or adj* [It, lit., tied] : in a smooth and connected manner — used as a direction in music

leg·end \'lej-ənd\ *n* [ME *legende*, fr. MF & ML; MF *legende*, fr. ML *legenda*, fr. L *legere* to gather, select, read] 1 : a story coming down from the past; *esp* : one popularly accepted as historical though not verifiable 2 : an inscription on an object; *also* : CAPTION

leg·end·ary \'lej-ən-,der-ē\ *adj* : of, relating to, or characteristic of a legend

leg·er·de·main \,lej-ərd-ə-'mān\ *n* [ME, fr. MF *leger de main* light of hand] : SLEIGHT OF HAND

leg·ging *or* leg·gin \'leg-ən, -iŋ\ *n* : a covering for the leg — usu. used in pl.

leg·gy \'leg-ē\ *adj* leg·gi·er; -est 1 : having unusually long legs 2 : SPINDLY 3 : having attractive legs

leg·horn \'leg-,(h)ȯrn, 'leg-ərn\ *n* 1 : a fine plaited straw; *also* : a hat made of this straw 2 : any of a Mediterranean breed of small hardy fowls

leg·i·ble \'lej-ə-bəl\ *adj* : capable of being read : CLEAR — leg·i·bil·i·ty \,lej-ə-'bil-ət-ē\ *n* — leg·i·bly \'lej-ə-blē\ *adv*

¹le·gion \'lē-jən\ *n* 1 : a unit of the Roman army comprising 3000 to 6000 soldiers 2 : MULTITUDE 3 : an association of ex-servicemen — le·gion·ary \-,er-ē\ *n* — le·gion·naire \,lē-jən-'aər\ *n*

²legion *adj* : MANY, NUMEROUS

legis *abbr* legislative; legislature

leg·is·late \'lej-ə-,slāt\ *vb* -lat·ed; -lat·ing : to make or enact laws; *also* : to bring about by legislation — leg·is·la·tor \-,slāt-ər\ *n*

leg·is·la·tion \,lej-ə-'slā-shən\ *n* 1 : the action of legislating 2 : laws made by a legislative body

leg·is·la·tive \'lej-ə-,slāt-iv\ *adj* 1 : having the power of legislating 2 : of or relating to a legislature

leg·is·la·ture \'lej-ə-,slā-chər\ *n* : an organized body of persons having the authority to make laws

le·git \li-'jit\ *adj, slang* : LEGITIMATE

le·git·i·mate \li-'jit-ə-mət\ *adj* 1

: lawfully begotten 2 : GENUINE 3 : LAWFUL 4 : conforming to recognized principles or accepted rules or standards — le·git·i·ma·cy \-mə-sē\ *n* — le·git·i·mate·ly *adv*

leg·man \'leg-,man\ *n* 1 : a newspaperman assigned usu. to gather information 2 : an assistant who gathers information and runs errands

le·gume \'leg-,yüm, li-'gyüm\ *n* 1 : any of a large group of plants having fruits that are dry pods and split when ripe and including important food and forage plants (as beans and clover) 2 : the part of a legume used as food; *also* : VEGETABLE 2 — le·gu·mi·nous \li-'gyü-mə-nəs\ *adj*

¹lei \'lā(-,ē)\ *n* : a wreath or necklace usu. of flowers

²lei \'lā\ *pl of* LEU

lei·sure \'lēzh-ər, 'lezh-, 'lāzh-\ *n* 1 : time free from work or duties 2 : EASE; *also* : CONVENIENCE syn relaxation, rest, repose — lei·sure·ly *adj*

leit·mo·tiv *or* leit·mo·tif \'līt-mō-,tēf\ *n* [G *leitmotiv*, fr. *leiten* to lead + *motiv* motive] : a dominant recurring theme

lek \'lek\ *n* — see MONEY table

LEM *abbr* lunar excursion module

lem·ming \'lem-iŋ\ *n* : any of several short-tailed northern rodents

lem·on \'lem-ən\ *n* 1 : an acid yellow usu. nearly oblong citrus fruit 2 : something unsatisfactory (as an automobile) : DUD — lem·ony *adj*

lem·on·ade \,lem-ə-'nād\ *n* : a beverage of lemon juice, sugar, and water

lem·pi·ra \lem-'pir-ə\ *n* — see MONEY table

le·mur \'lē-mər\ *n* : any of numerous arboreal mammals largely of Madagascar usu. with a muzzle like a fox, large eyes, very soft woolly fur, and a long furry tail

lend \'lend\ *vb* lent \'lent\; lend·ing 1 : to give for temporary use on condition that the same or its equivalent be returned 2 : AFFORD, FURNISH 3 : ACCOMMODATE — lend·er *n*

lend-lease \-'lēs\ *n* : the transfer of goods and services to an ally to aid in a common cause with payment being made by a return of the original items or their use in the common cause or by a similar transfer of other goods and services

length \'leŋth\ *n* 1 : the longer or longest dimension of an object; *also* : a measured distance or dimension 2 : duration or extent in time or space 3 : the length of something taken as a unit of measure ⟨the horse won by a ∼⟩ 4 : PIECE; *esp* : one in a series of pieces designed to be joined — lengthy *adj*

length·en \'leŋ-thən\ *vb* length·ened; length·en·ing \'leŋth-(ə-)niŋ\ : to make or become longer syn extend, elongate, prolong, protract

length·wise \-,wīz\ *adv* : in the direction of the length — lengthwise *adj*

le·nient \'lē-nē-ənt, -nyənt\ *adj* : of mild and tolerant disposition or effect

**syn** soft, gentle, indulgent, forbearing — **le·ni·en·cy** \'lē-nē-ən-sē, -nyən-sē\ n — **le·ni·ent·ly** adv

**len·i·tive** \'len-ət-iv\ adj : alleviating pain or acrimony

**len·i·ty** \'len-ət-ē\ n : LENIENCY, MILDNESS

**lens** \'lenz\ n [L lent-, lens lentil; so called fr. the shape of a convex lens] 1 : a curved piece of glass or plastic used singly or combined in an optical instrument for forming an image; also : a device for focusing radiations other than light 2 : a transparent body in the eye that focuses light rays on receptors at the back of the eye

**Lent** \'lent\ n : a 40-day period of penitence and fasting observed from Ash Wednesday to Easter by many churches — **Lent·en** \-ᵊn\ adj

**len·til** \'lent-ᵊl\ n : an Old World legume grown for its flat edible seeds and for fodder; also : its seed

**le·one** \lē-'ōn\ n — see MONEY table

**le·o·nine** \'lē-ə-,nīn\ adj : of, relating to, or resembling a lion

**leop·ard** \'lep-ərd\ n : a large strong usu. tawny and black-spotted cat of southern Asia and Africa

**le·o·tard** \'lē-ə-,tärd\ n : a close-fitting garment worn esp. by dancers and acrobats

**lep·er** \'lep-ər\ n 1 : a person affected with leprosy 2 : OUTCAST

**lep·re·chaun** \'lep-rə-,kän\ n : a mischievous elf of Irish folklore

**lep·ro·sy** \'lep-rə-sē\ n : a chronic bacterial disease marked esp. by slow-growing swellings with deformity and loss of sensation of affected parts — **lep·rous** \-rəs\ adj

**lep·ton** \lep-'tän\ n, pl **lep·ta** \-'tä\ — see drachma at MONEY table

**les·bi·an** \'lez-bē-ən\ n, often cap : a female homosexual — **lesbian** adj — **les·bi·an·ism** \-,iz-əm\ n

**lese maj·es·ty** or **lèse ma·jes·té** \'lēz-'maj-ə-stē\ n [MF lese majesté, fr. L laesa majestas, lit., injured majesty] : an offense violating the dignity of a sovereign

**le·sion** \'lē-zhən\ n : an abnormal structural change in the body due to injury or disease

¹**less** \'les\ adj 1 : FEWER ⟨~ than six⟩ 2 : of lower rank, degree, or importance 3 : SMALLER; also : more limited in quantity

²**less** adv : to a lesser extent or degree

³**less** prep : diminished by : MINUS

⁴**less** n, pl **less** 1 : a smaller portion 2 : something of less importance

**-less** \ləs\ adj suffix 1 : destitute of : not having ⟨childless⟩ 2 : unable to be acted on or to act (in a specified way) ⟨dauntless⟩

**les·see** \le-'sē\ n : a tenant under a lease

**less·en** \'les-ᵊn\ vb **less·ened**; **less·en·ing** \'les-(ᵊ-)niŋ\ : to make or become less **syn** decrease, diminish, dwindle

**less·er** \'les-ər\ adj 1 : SMALLER 2 : INFERIOR

**les·son** \'les-ᵊn\ n 1 : a passage from sacred writings read in a service of worship 2 : a reading or exercise to be studied by a pupil; also : something learned 3 : a period of instruction 4 : an instructive example

**les·sor** \'les-,ȯr, le-'sȯr\ n : one who conveys property by a lease

**lest** \,lest\ conj : for fear that

¹**let** \'let\ n [ME lette, fr. letten to delay, hinder, fr. OE lettan] 1 : HINDRANCE, OBSTACLE 2 : a stroke in racket games that does not count

²**let** vb **let**; **let·ting** [ME leten, fr. OE lǣtan] 1 : to cause to : MAKE ⟨~ it be known⟩ 2 : RENT, LEASE; also : to assign esp. after bids 3 : ALLOW, PERMIT ⟨~ him go⟩

**-let** \lət\ n suffix 1 : small one ⟨booklet⟩ 2 : article worn on ⟨wristlet⟩

**let·down** \'let-,daùn\ n 1 : DISAPPOINTMENT 2 : a slackening of effort 3 : the descent of an aircraft to the beginning of a landing approach

**le·thal** \'lē-thəl\ adj : DEADLY, FATAL — **le·thal·ly** \-ē\ adv

**leth·ar·gy** \'leth-ər-jē\ n 1 : abnormal drowsiness 2 : the quality or state of being lazy or indifferent **syn** languor, lassitude — **le·thar·gic** \li-'thär-jik\ adj

**let on** vb 1 : REVEAL, ADMIT 2 : PRETEND

**Lett** \'let\ n : LATVIAN

¹**let·ter** \'let-ər\ n 1 : a symbol that stands for a speech sound and constitutes a unit of an alphabet 2 : a written or printed communication 3 pl : LITERATURE; also : LEARNING 4 : the literal meaning ⟨the ~ of the law⟩ 5 : a single piece of type

²**letter** vb : to mark with letters: INSCRIBE — **let·ter·er** n

**let·ter·head** \'let-ər-,hed\ n : stationery with a printed or engraved heading; also : the heading itself

**let·ter·per·fect** \,let-ər-'pər-fikt\ adj : correct to the smallest detail

**let·ter·press** \'let-ər-,pres\ n 1 : printing done directly by impressing the paper on an inked raised surface 2 : TEXT

**letters patent** n pl : a written grant from a government to a person in a form readily open for inspection by all

**let·tuce** \'let-əs\ n [ME letuse, fr. OF laitues, pl. of laitue, fr. L lactuca, fr. lac milk; fr. its milky juice] : a garden plant with crisp leaves used esp. in salads

**let·up** \'let-,əp\ n : a lessening of effort

**leu** \'leù\ n, pl **lei** \'lā\ — see MONEY table

**leu·ke·mia** \lü-'kē-mē-ə\ n : a cancerous disease in which white blood cells increase greatly — **leu·ke·mic** \-mik\ adj or n

**leu·ko·cyte** also **leu·co·cyte** \'lü-kə-,sīt\ n : WHITE BLOOD CELL

**lev** \'lef\ n, pl **le·va** \'lev-ə\ — see MONEY table

**Lev** abbr Leviticus

¹**le·vee** \'lev-ē; lə-'vē, -'vā\ n : a recep-

tion held by a person of distinction

²lev·ee \'lev-ē\ n : an embankment to prevent flooding (as by a river); also : a river landing place

¹lev·el \'lev-əl\ n 1 : a device for establishing a horizontal line or plane 2 : horizontal condition 3 : a horizontal position, line, or surface often taken as an index of altitude; also : a flat area of ground 4 : height, position, rank, or size in a scale

²level vb -eled or -elled; -el·ing or -el·ling \-(ə-)liŋ\ 1 : to make flat or level; also : to come to a level 2 : AIM, DIRECT 3 : EQUALIZE 4 : RAZE — lev·el·er n

³level adj 1 : having a flat even surface 2 : HORIZONTAL 3 : of the same height or rank; also : UNIFORM 4 : steady and cool in judgment — lev·el·ly \'lev-əl-(l)ē\ adv — lev·el·ness n

lev·el·head·ed \,lev-əl-'hed-əd\ adj : having sound judgment : SENSIBLE

le·ver \'lev-ər, 'lē-vər\ n 1 : a bar used for prying or dislodging something; also : a means for achieving one's purpose 2 : a rigid piece turning about an axis and used for transmitting and changing force and motion

le·ver·age \'lev-(ə-)rij, 'lēv-\ n : the action or mechanical effect of a lever

le·vi·a·than \li-'vī-ə-thən\ n 1 : a large sea animal 2 : something very large or formidable of its kind

lev·i·tate \'lev-ə-,tāt\ vb -tat·ed; -tat·ing : to rise or cause to rise in the air in seeming defiance of gravitation — lev·i·ta·tion \,lev-ə-'tā-shən\ n

lev·i·ty \'lev-ət-ē\ n : lack of earnestness syn lightness, flippancy

¹levy \'lev-ē\ n, pl lev·ies 1 : the imposition or collection of an assessment; also : an amount levied 2 : the enlistment of men for military service; also : troops raised by levy

²levy vb lev·ied; levy·ing 1 : to impose or collect by legal authority 2 : to enlist for military service 3 : WAGE (~ war) 4 : to seize property in satisfaction of a legal claim

lewd \'lüd\ adj [ME lewed vulgar, fr. OE lǣwede lay, ignorant] 1 : sexually unchaste 2 : OBSCENE, SALACIOUS — lewd·ly adv — lewd·ness n

lex·i·cog·ra·phy \,lek-sə-'käg-rə-fē\ n 1 : the editing or making of a dictionary 2 : the principles and practices of dictionary making — lex·i·cog·ra·pher \-fər\ n — lex·i·co·graph·i·cal \-kō-'graf-i-kəl\ or lex·i·co·graph·ic \-ik\ adj

lex·i·con \'lek-sə-,kän\ n, pl lex·i·ca \-si-kə\ or lexicons : DICTIONARY

LF abbr low frequency

lg abbr 1 large 2 long

LGk abbr Late Greek

LH abbr 1 left hand 2 lower half

LHD abbr [L litterarum humaniorum doctor] doctor of humane letters

li abbr link

Li symbol lithium

LI abbr Long Island

li·a·bil·i·ty \,lī-ə-'bil-ət-ē\ n, pl -ties 1 : the quality or state of being liable

2 pl : DEBTS 3 : DISADVANTAGE

li·a·ble \'lī-ə-bəl\ adj 1 : legally obligated : RESPONSIBLE 2 : LIKELY, APT ⟨~ to fall⟩ 3 : SUSCEPTIBLE

li·ai·son \'lē-ə-,zän, lē-'ā-\ n 1 : a close bond : INTERRELATIONSHIP 2 : an illicit sexual relationship 3 : communication esp. between parts of an armed force

li·ar \'lī-ər\ n : a person who lies

¹lib \'lib\ n : LIBERATION

²lib abbr 1 liberal 2 librarian; library

li·ba·tion \lī-'bā-shən\ n 1 : an act of pouring a liquid as a sacrifice (as to a god); also : the liquid poured 2 : DRINK — li·ba·tion·ary adj

¹li·bel \'lī-bəl\ n [ME, written declaration, fr. MF, fr. L libellus, dim. of liber book] 1 : the action or crime of injuring a person's reputation by something printed or written or by a visible representation 2 : a spoken or written statement or a representation that gives an unjustly unfavorable impression of a person or thing — li·bel·ous or li·bel·lous \-bə-ləs\ adj

²libel vb -beled or -belled; -bel·ing or -bel·ling : to make or publish a libel — li·bel·er n — li·bel·ist n

¹lib·er·al \'lib-(ə-)rəl\ adj [ME, fr. MF, fr. L liberalis suitable for a freeman, generous, fr. liber free] 1 : of, relating to, or based on the liberal arts 2 : GENEROUS, BOUNTIFUL 3 : not literal 4 : not narrow in opinion or judgment : TOLERANT; also : not orthodox 5 : not conservative — lib·er·al·i·ty \,lib-ə-'ral-ət-ē\ n — lib·er·al·ize \'lib-(ə-)rə-,līz\ vb — lib·er·al·ly \-rə-lē\ adv

²liberal n : a person who holds liberal views

liberal arts n pl : the studies (as language, philosophy, mathematics, history, literature, or abstract science) in a college or university intended to provide chiefly general knowledge and to develop the general intellectual capacities

lib·er·al·ism \'lib-(ə-)rə-,liz-əm\ n : liberal principles and theories

lib·er·ate \'lib-ə-,rāt\ vb -at·ed; -at·ing 1 : to free from bondage or restraint; also : to raise to equal rights and status 2 : to free (as a gas) from combination — lib·er·a·tion \,lib-ə-'rā-shən\ n — lib·er·a·tor \'lib-ə-,rāt-ər\ n

lib·er·tar·i·an \,lib-ər-'ter-ē-ən\ n 1 : an advocate of the doctrine of free will 2 : one who upholds the principles of liberty

lib·er·tine \'lib-ər-,tēn\ n : one who leads a life of dissoluteness

lib·er·ty \'lib-ərt-ē\ n, pl -ties 1 : FREEDOM 2 : an action going beyond normal limits; esp : FAMILIARITY 3 : a short leave from naval duty

li·bid·i·nous \lə-'bid-ᵊn-əs\ adj 1 : LASCIVIOUS 2 : LIBIDINAL

li·bi·do \lə-'bēd-ō, -'bid-\ n, pl -dos : psychic energy derived from basic biological urges; also : sexual drive — li·bid·i·nal \lə-'bid-ᵊn-əl\ adj

**li·brar·i·an** \lī-'brer-ē-ən\ *n* : a specialist in the management of a library

**li·brary** \'lī-,brer-ē\ *n, pl* **-brar·ies** **1** : a place in which books and related materials are kept for use but not for sale **2** : a collection of books

**li·bret·to** \lə-'bret-ō\ *n, pl* **-tos** *or* **-ti** \-ē\ [It, dim. of *libro* book, fr. L *liber*] : the text of a work (as an opera) for the musical theater; *also* : a book containing such a text — **li·bret·tist** \-əst\ *n*

**Lib·y·an** \'lib-ē-ən\ *n* : a native or inhabitant of Libya — **Libyan** *adj*

**lice** *pl of* LOUSE

**li·cense** *or* **li·cence** \'līs-°ns\ *n* **1** : permission to act; *esp* : legal permission to engage in a business, occupation, or activity **2** : a document, plate, or tag evidencing a license granted **3** : freedom used irresponsibly — **license** *vb*

**li·cens·ee** \,līs-°n-'sē\ *n* : a licensed person

**li·cen·ti·ate** \lī-'sen-chē-ət\ *n* : one licensed to practice a profession

**li·cen·tious** \lī-'sen-chəs\ *adj* : LEWD, LASCIVIOUS — **li·cen·tious·ly** *adv* — **li·cen·tious·ness** *n*

**li·chee** *var of* LITCHI

**li·chen** \'lī-kən\ *n* : any of various complex lower plants made up of an alga and a fungus growing as a unit on a solid surface (as of a stone or tree trunk) — **li·chen·ous** *adj*

**lic·it** \'lis-ət\ *adj* : LAWFUL

**¹lick** \'lik\ *vb* **1** : to draw the tongue over; *also* : to flicker over like a tongue **2** : THRASH; *also* : DEFEAT

**²lick** *n* **1** : a stroke of the tongue **2** : a small amount **3** : a hasty careless effort **4** : BLOW **5** : a place (as a spring) having a deposit of salt that animals regularly lick

**lick·e·ty-split** \,lik-ət-ē-'split\ *adv* : at great speed

**lick·spit·tle** \'lik-,spit-°l\ *n* : a fawning subordinate : TOADY

**lic·o·rice** \'lik-(ə)-rish, -rəs\ *n* [ME *licorice*, fr. OF, fr. LL *liquiritia*, alter. of L *glycyrrhiza*, fr. Gk *glykyrrhiza*, fr. *glykys* sweet + *rhiza* root] **1** : a European leguminous plant; *also* : its dried root or an extract from it used esp. as a flavoring and in medicine **2** : a confection flavored with licorice

**lid** \'lid\ *n* **1** : a movable cover **2** : EYELID **3** : RESTRAINT, CURB

**li·do** \'lēd-ō\ *n, pl* **lidos** : a fashionable beach resort

**¹lie** \'lī\ *vb* **lay** \'lā\; **lain** \'lān\; **ly·ing** \'lī-iŋ\ **1** : to be in, stay at rest in, or assume a horizontal position; *also* : to be in a helpless or defenseless state **2** : EXTEND **3** : to occupy a certain relative position **4** : to have an effect esp. through mere presence

**²lie** *n* : the position in which something lies

**³lie** *vb* **lied**; **ly·ing** \'lī-iŋ\ : to tell a lie

**⁴lie** *n* : an untrue statement made with intent to deceive

**lied** \'lēt\ *n, pl* **lie·der** \'lēd-ər\ : a German song esp. of the 19th century

**lief** \'lēv, 'lēf\ *adv* : GLADLY, WILLINGLY

**¹liege** \'lēj\ *adj* [ME, fr. OF, fr. LL *laeticus*, fr. *laetus* serf] : LOYAL, FAITHFUL

**²liege** *n* **1** : VASSAL **2** : a feudal superior

**lien** \'lēn, 'lē-ən\ *n* : a legal claim on the property of another for the satisfaction of a debt or the fulfillment of a duty

**lieu** \'lü\ *n, archaic* : PLACE, STEAD — **in lieu of** : in the place of

**lieut** *abbr* lieutenant

**lieu·ten·ant** \lü-'ten-ənt\ *n* [ME, fr. MF, fr. *lieu* place + *tenant* holding, fr. *tenir* to hold, fr. L *tenēre*] **1** : a representative of another in the performance of duty **2** : FIRST LIEUTENANT; *also* : SECOND LIEUTENANT **3** : a commissioned officer in the navy ranking next below a lieutenant commander — **lieu·ten·an·cy** \-ən-sē\ *n*

**lieutenant colonel** *n* : a commissioned officer (as in the army) ranking next below a colonel

**lieutenant commander** *n* : a commissioned officer in the navy ranking next below a commander

**lieutenant general** *n* : a commissioned officer (as in the army) ranking next below a general

**lieutenant governor** *n* : a deputy or subordinate governor

**lieutenant junior grade** *n, pl* **lieutenants junior grade** : a commissioned officer in the navy ranking next below a lieutenant

**life** \'līf\ *n, pl* **lives** \'līvz\ **1** : the quality that distinguishes a vital and functional being from a dead body or inanimate matter; *also* : a state of an organism characterized esp. by capacity for metabolism, growth, reaction to stimuli, and reproduction **2** : the physical and mental experiences of an individual **3** : BIOGRAPHY **4** : the period of existence **5** : manner of living **6** : PERSON **7** : ANIMATION, SPIRIT; *also* : LIVELINESS **8** : animate activity ⟨signs of ∼⟩ **9** : one providing interest and vigor — **life·less** *adj* — **life·like** *adj*

**life·blood** \'līf-'bləd, -,bləd\ *n* : a basic source of strength and vitality

**life·boat** \-,bōt\ *n* : a strong boat designed for use in saving lives at sea

**life·guard** \-,gärd\ *n* : a usu. expert swimmer employed to safeguard bathers

**life·line** \-,līn\ *n* **1** : a line to which persons may cling to save or protect their lives **2** : a land, sea, or air route considered indispensable

**life·long** \'līf-,lòŋ\ *adj* : continuing through life

**life preserver** *n* : a device designed to save a person from drowning by buoying up the body while in the water

**lif·er** \'lī-fər\ *n* **1** : a person sentenced to life imprisonment **2** : a career serviceman

**life raft** *n* : a raft for use by people forced into the water

**life·sav·ing** \'līf-,sā-viŋ\ *n* : the art or practice of saving or protecting lives esp. of drowning persons — **life·sav·er** \-,sā-vər\ *n*

**life·time** \'līf-,tīm\ *n* : the duration of an individual's existence

**life·work** \-'work\ *n* : the entire or principal work of one's lifetime; *also* : a work extending over a lifetime

**LIFO** *abbr* last in, first out

¹**lift** \'lift\ *vb* **1** : RAISE, ELEVATE; *also* : RISE, ASCEND **2** : to put an end to : STOP **3** : to pay off 〈~ a mortgage〉

²**lift** *n* **1** : LOAD **2** : the action or an instance of lifting **3** : HELP; *also* : a ride along one's way **4** : RISE, ADVANCE **5** *chiefly Brit* : ELEVATOR **6** : the upward force that is developed by a moving airplane and that opposes the pull of gravity **7** : an elevation of the spirits

**lift-off** \'lif-,tòf\ *n* : a vertical takeoff (as by an aircraft or rocket vehicle)

**lift truck** *n* : a small truck for lifting and transporting loads

**lig·a·ment** \'lig-ə-mənt\ *n* : a band of tough tissue that holds bones together

**li·gate** \'lī-,gāt\ *vb* **li·gat·ed; li·gat·ing** : to tie with a ligature — **li·ga·tion** \lī-'gā-shən\ *n*

**lig·a·ture** \'lig-ə-,chùr, -chər\ *n* **1** : something that binds or ties; *also* : a thread used in surgery esp. for tying blood vessels **2** : a printed or written character consisting of two or more letters or characters (as æ) united

¹**light** \'līt\ *n* **1** : something that makes vision possible : electromagnetic radiation visible to the human eye; *also* : BRIGHTNESS **2** : DAYLIGHT **3** : a source of light (as a candle) **4** : ENLIGHTENMENT; *also* : TRUTH **5** : public knowledge **6** : WINDOW **7** *pl* : STANDARDS (according to his ~s) **8** : CELEBRITY **9** : a lighthouse beacon; *also* : a traffic signal **10** : a flame for lighting something

²**light** *adj* **1** : BRIGHT **2** : PALE 〈~ blue〉 — **light·ness** *n*

³**light** *vb* **light·ed** *or* **lit** \'lit\; **light·ing** **1** : to make or become light **2** : to cause to burn : BURN **3** : to conduct with a light **4** : ILLUMINATE

⁴**light** *adj* **1** : not heavy **2** : not serious 〈~ reading〉 **3** : SCANTY 〈~ rain〉 **4** : GENTLE 〈a ~ blow〉 **5** : easily endurable 〈~ cold〉; *also* : requiring little effort 〈~ exercise〉 **6** : SWIFT, NIMBLE **7** : FRIVOLOUS **8** : DIZZY **9** : producing goods for direct consumption by the consumer 〈~ industry〉 — **light·ly** *adv* — **light·ness** *n*

⁵**light** *adv* **1** : LIGHTLY **2** : with little baggage 〈travel ~〉

⁶**light** *vb* **light·ed** *or* **lit** \'lit\; **light·ing** **1** : SETTLE, ALIGHT **2** : to fall unexpectedly **3** : HAPPEN

**light adaptation** *n* : the whole process by which the eye adapts to seeing in strong light — **light–adapt·ed** \'līt-ə-,dap-təd\ *adj*

¹**light·en** \'līt-ᵊn\ *vb* **light·ened; light·en·ing** \'līt-(ᵊ-)niŋ\ **1** : ILLUMINATE, BRIGHTEN **2** : to give out flashes of lightning

²**lighten** *vb* **light·ened; light·en·ing** \'līt-(ᵊ-)niŋ\ **1** : to relieve of a burden **2** : GLADDEN **3** : to become lighter

¹**light·er** \'līt-ər\ *n* : a barge used esp. in loading or unloading ships

²**light·er** \'līt-ər\ *n* : a device for lighting 〈a cigarette ~〉

**light·face** \'līt-,fās\ *n* : a type having light thin lines — **light·faced** \-'fāst\ *adj*

**light·heart·ed** \-'härt-əd\ *adj* : GAY — **light·heart·ed·ly** *adv* — **light·heart·ed·ness** *n*

**light·house** \'līt-,haùs\ *n* : a structure with a powerful light for guiding mariners

**light meter** *n* : a small portable device for measuring illumination; *esp* : a device for indicating correct photographic exposure

¹**light·ning** \'līt-niŋ\ *n* : the flashing of light produced by a discharge of atmospheric electricity from one cloud to another or between a cloud and the earth

²**lightning** *adj* : extremely fast

**lightning bug** *n* : FIREFLY

**lightning rod** *n* : a grounded metallic rod set up on a structure to protect it from lightning

**light out** *vb* : to leave in a hurry

**light-proof** \'līt-'prüf\ *adj* : impenetrable by light

**lights** \'līts\ *n pl* : the lungs esp. of a slaughtered animal

**light·ship** \'līt-,ship\ *n* : a ship with a powerful light moored at a place dangerous to navigation

**light show** *n* : a kaleidoscopic display (as of colored lights) imitating the effects of psychedelic drugs

**light·some** \'līt-səm\ *adj* **1** : NIMBLE **2** : CHEERFUL

¹**light·weight** \'līt-,wāt\ *n* : one of less than average weight; *esp* : a boxer weighing more than 126 but not over 135 pounds

²**lightweight** *adj* **1** : of less than average weight **2** : INCONSEQUENTIAL

**light–year** \'līt-,yiər\ *n* : an astronomical unit of distance equal to the distance that light travels in one year or about 5,878,000,000,000 miles

**lig·ne·ous** \'lig-nē-əs\ *adj* : WOODY

**lig·ni·fy** \'lig-nə-,fī\ *vb* **-fied; -fy·ing** : to convert into or become wood or woody tissue — **lig·ni·fi·ca·tion** \,lig-nə-fə-'kā-shən\ *n*

**lig·nite** \'lig-,nīt\ *n* : brownish black soft coal of a slightly woody texture

¹**like** \'līk\ *vb* **liked; lik·ing 1** : ENJOY 〈~s baseball〉 **2** : WANT **3** : CHOOSE 〈does as she ~s〉 — **lik·able** *or* **like·able** \'lī-kə-bəl\ *adj*

²**like** *n* : PREFERENCE

³**like** *adj* : SIMILAR **syn** alike, identical, comparable, parallel, uniform

⁴**like** *prep* **1** : similar or similarly to **2** : typical of **3** : inclined to 〈looks ~ rain〉 **4** : such as 〈a subject ~ physics〉

⁵**like** *n* : COUNTERPART

⁶**like** *conj* : in the same way that

**-like** \,līk\ *adj comb form* **1** : of a form, kind, appearance, or effect resembling or suggesting 〈a life*like* statue〉 **2** : of the kind befitting or characteristic of 〈lady*like* behavior〉

**like·li·hood** \'lī-klē-,húd\ n : PROBA-BILITY

**like·ly** \'lī-klē\ adj **like·li·er; -est 1** : PROBABLE **2** : BELIEVABLE **3** : PROMISING ⟨a ~ place to fish⟩

²**likely** adv : in all probability

**lik·en** \'lī-kən\ vb **lik·ened; lik·en·ing** \'līk-(ə-)niŋ\ : COMPARE

**like·ness** \'līk-nəs\ n **1** : RESEMBLANCE **2** : APPEARANCE, GUISE **3** : COPY, PORTRAIT

**like·wise** \-,wīz\ adv **1** : in like manner **2** : in addition : ALSO

**lik·ing** \'lī-kiŋ\ n : favorable regard; also : TASTE

**li·ku·ta** \li-'küt-ə\ n, pl **ma·ku·ta** \mä-\ — see zaire at MONEY table

**li·lac** \'lī-lək, -,lak, -,läk\ n [obs. F (now lilas), fr. Ar līlak, fr. Per nīlak bluish, fr. nīl blue, fr. Skt nīla dark blue] **1** : a shrub with large clusters of fragrant grayish pink, purple, or white flowers **2** : a moderate purple

**lil·li·pu·tian** \,lil-ə-'pyü-shən\ adj, often cap **1** : SMALL, MINIATURE **2** : PETTY

**lilt** \'lilt\ n **1** : a gay lively song or tune **2** : a rhythmical swing, flow, or cadence

**lily** \'lil-ē\ n, pl **lil·ies** : any of numerous tall bulbous herbs with leafy stems and usu. funnel-shaped flowers; also : any of various related plants (as the onion, amaryllis, or iris)

**lily of the valley** : a low perennial herb of the lily family that produces a raceme of fragrant nodding bell-shaped white flowers

**li·ma bean** \,lī-mə-\ n : any of various bushy or tall-growing beans cultivated for their flat edible usu. pale green or whitish seeds; also : the seed of a lima bean

**limb** \'lim\ n **1** : one of the projecting paired appendages (as legs, arms, or wings) that an animal uses esp. in moving or grasping **2** : a large branch of a tree : BOUGH — **limb·less** adj

**lim·beck** \'lim-,bek\ n : ALEMBIC

¹**lim·ber** \'lim-bər\ adj **1** : FLEXIBLE, SUPPLE **2** : LITHE, NIMBLE

²**limber** vb **lim·bered; lim·ber·ing** \-b(ə-)riŋ\ : to make or become limber

¹**lim·bo** \'lim-bō\ n, pl **limbos** [ME, fr. ML, abl. of limbus limbo, fr. L, border] **1** often cap : an abode of souls barred from heaven through no fault of their own **2** : a place or state of confinement or oblivion

²**limbo** n, pl **limbos** [native name in West Indies] : a West Indian acrobatic dance orig. for men

**Lim·burg·er** \'lim-,bər-gər\ n : a creamy semisoft surface-ripened cheese with a pungent odor and strong flavor

¹**lime** \'līm\ n : a caustic infusible white substance that consists of calcium and oxygen, is obtained by heating limestone or shells until they crumble to powder, and is used in making cement and in fertilizer — **limy** \'lī-mē\ adj

²**lime** n : a small lemonlike greenish yellow citrus fruit with juicy acid pulp

**lime·ade** \lī-'mād\ n : a beverage of lime juice, sugar, and water

**lime·kiln** \'līm-,kil(n)\ n : a kiln or furnace for making lime by burning limestone or shells

**lime·light** \'līm-,līt\ n **1** : a device in which flame is directed against a cylinder of lime formerly used in the theater to cast a strong white light on the stage **2** : the center of public attention

**lim·er·ick** \'lim-(ə-)rik\ n : a light or humorous poem of five lines

**lime·stone** \'līm-,stōn\ n : a rock that is formed by accumulation of organic remains (as shells), is used in building, and yields lime when burned

¹**lim·it** \'lim-ət\ n **1** : BOUNDARY; also, pl : BOUNDS **2** : something that restrains or confines; also : the utmost extent **3** : a prescribed maximum or minimum — **lim·it·less** adj

²**limit** vb **1** : to set limits to **2** : to reduce in quantity or extent — **lim·i·ta·tion** \,lim-ə-'tā-shən\ n

**lim·it·ed** \'lim-ət-əd\ adj **1** : confined within limits **2** : offering superior and faster service and transportation

**limited war** n : a war with an objective less than the total defeat of the enemy

**limn** \'lim\ vb **limned; limn·ing** \'lim-(n)iŋ\ **1** : DRAW; also : PAINT **2** : DELINEATE, DESCRIBE

**li·mo·nite** \'lī-mə-,nīt\ n : a ferric oxide that is a major ore of iron — **li·mo·nit·ic** \,lī-mə-'nit-ik\ adj

**lim·ou·sine** \'lim-ə-,zēn, ,lim-ə-'zēn\ n **1** : a large luxurious often chauffeur-driven sedan **2** : a small bus with doors along the side like those of a sedan

¹**limp** \'limp\ vb : to walk lamely; also : to proceed with difficulty

²**limp** n : a limping movement or gait

³**limp** adj **1** : having no defined shape; also : not stiff or rigid **2** : lacking in strength or firmness — **limp·ly** adv — **limp·ness** n

**lim·pet** \'lim-pət\ n : a sea mollusk with a conical shell that clings to rocks or timbers

**lim·pid** \'lim-pəd\ adj [F or L; F limpide, fr. L limpidus, fr. lympha, limpa water] : CLEAR, TRANSPARENT

**lin** abbr **1** lineal **2** linear

**lin·age** \'lī-nij\ n : the number of lines of written or printed matter

**linch·pin** \'linch-,pin\ n : a locking pin inserted crosswise (as through the end of an axle)

**lin·den** \'lin-dən\ n : any of a genus of trees with large heart-shaped leaves and clustered yellowish flowers rich in nectar

¹**line** \'līn\ vb **lined; lin·ing** : to cover the inner surface of

²**line** n **1** : CORD, ROPE, WIRE; also : a length of material used in measuring and leveling **2** : pipes for conveying a fluid ⟨a gas ~⟩ **3** : a horizontal row of written or printed characters; also : VERSE **4** : NOTE **5** pl : the words making up a part in a drama **6** : something distinct, long, and narrow; also : ROUTE **7** : a state of agreement **8** : a course of conduct, action, or thought;

*also* : OCCUPATION **9** : LIMIT **10** : an arrangement (as of cars) in or as if in a row or sequence; *also* : the football players who are stationed on the line of scrimmage **11** : a ransportation system **12** : a long narrow mark; *also* : EQUATOR **13** : CONTOUR **14** : a general plan **15** : an indication based on insight or investigation

³**line** *vb* **lined; lin·ing** **1** : to mark with a line **2** : to place or form a line along **3** : ALIGN

**lin·eage** \'lin-ē-ij\ *n* 1 : lineal descent from a common progenitor; *also* : FAMILY

**lin·eal** \'lin-ē-əl\ *adj* **1** : LINEAR **2** : consisting of or being in a direct line of ancestry; *also* : HEREDITARY

**lin·ea·ment** \'lin-ē-ə-mənt\ *n* : an outline, feature, or contour of a body and esp. of a face — usu. used in pl.

**lin·ear** \'lin-ē-ər\ *adj* **1** : of, relating to, or consisting of a line : STRAIGHT **2** : being long and uniformly narrow **3** : composed of simply drawn lines with little attempt at pictorial representation (~ script)

**line·back·er** \'līn-,bak-ər\ *n* : a defensive football player who lines up immediately behind the line of scrimmage

**line drive** *n* : a baseball hit in a nearly straight line and typically not far above the ground

**line graph** *n* : a graph in which the points representing specific values are connected by a broken line

**line·man** \'līn-mən\ *n* **1** : one who sets up or repairs communication or power lines **2** : a player in the line in football

**lin·en** \'lin-ən\ *n* **1** : cloth made of flax; *also* : thread or yarn spun from flax **2** : clothing or household articles made of linen cloth or similar fabric

**line of scrimmage** : an imaginary line in football parallel to the goal lines and tangent to the nose of the ball laid on the ground preparatory to a scrimmage

¹**lin·er** \'lī-nər\ *n* : a ship or airplane belonging to a regular transportation line

²**liner** *n* : one that lines or is used as a lining

**line score** *n* : a score of a baseball game giving the runs, hits, and errors made by each team

**lines·man** \'līnz-mən\ *n* **1** : LINEMAN **2** : an official who assists a referee

**line-up** \'līn-,əp\ *n* **1** : a line of persons arranged for inspection or identification **2** : a list of players taking part in a game (as of baseball)

**ling** \'liŋ\ *n* : any of several fishes related to the cod

**lin·ger** \'liŋ-gər\ *vb* **lin·gered; lin·ger·ing** \-g(ə-)riŋ\ : TARRY; *also* : PROCRASTINATE

**lin·ge·rie** \,län-jə-'rā, ,laⁿ-zhə-, -'rē\ *n* [F, fr. MF, fr. *linge* linen, fr. L *lineus* made of linen, fr. *linum* flax, linen] : women's intimate apparel

**lin·go** \'liŋ-gō\ *n, pl* **lingoes** : usu. strange or incomprehensible language

**lin·gua fran·ca** \,liŋ-gwə-'fraŋ-kə\ *n,*

*pl* **lingua francas** *or* **lin·guae fran·cae** \-gwē-'fraŋ-,kē\ **1** : a common language that consists of Italian mixed with French, Spanish, Greek, and Arabic and is spoken in Mediterranean ports **2** : any of various languages used as common or commercial tongues among speakers of different languages

**lin·gual** \'liŋ-gwəl\ *adj* : of, relating to, or produced by the tongue

**lin·guist** \'liŋ-gwəst\ *n* **1** : a person skilled in languages **2** : one who specializes in linguistics

**lin·guis·tics** \liŋ-'gwis-tiks\ *n* : the study of human speech including the units, nature, structure, and development of language or a language — **lin·guis·tic** *adj*

**lin·i·ment** \'lin-ə-mənt\ *n* : a liquid preparation rubbed on the skin esp. to relieve pain

**lin·ing** \'lī-niŋ\ *n* : material used to line esp. an inner surface

**link** \'liŋk\ *n* **1** : a connecting structure; *esp* : a single ring of a chain **2** : BOND, TIE — **link** *vb* — **link·er** *n*

**link·age** \'liŋ-kij\ *n* **1** : the manner or style of being united **2** : the quality or state of being linked **3** : a system of links

**links** \'liŋks\ *n pl* : a golf course

**link-up** \'liŋk-,əp\ *n* **1** : MEETING **2** : something that serves as a linking device or factor

**lin·net** \'lin-ət\ *n* : an Old World finch

**li·no·leum** \lə-'nō-lē-əm\ *n* [L *linum* flax + *oleum* oil] : a floor covering with a canvas back and a surface of hardened linseed oil and a filler (as cork dust)

**lin·seed** \'lin-,sēd\ *n* : the seeds of flax yielding a yellowish oil (**linseed oil**) used esp. in paints and linoleum

**lin·sey-wool·sey** \,lin-zē-'wùl-zē\ *n* : a coarse sturdy fabric of wool and linen or cotton

**lint** \'lint\ *n* **1** : linen made into a soft fleecy substance for use in surgical dressings **2** : fine ravels, fluff, or loose short fibers from yarn or fabrics **3** : the fibers that surround cotton seeds and form the cotton staple

**lin·tel** \'lint-²l\ *n* : a horizontal piece across the top of an opening (as of a door) that carries the weight of the structure above it

**li·on** \'lī-ən\ *n, pl* **lions** : a large flesh-eating cat of Africa and southern Asia with a shaggy mane in the male — **li·on·ess** \'lī-ə-nəs\ *n*

**li·on·heart·ed** \,lī-ən-'härt-əd\ *adj* : having a courageous heart : BRAVE

**li·on·ize** \'lī-ə-,nīz\ *vb* **-ized; -iz·ing** : to treat as an object of great interest or importance — **li·on·iza·tion** \,lī-ə-nə-'zā-shən\ *n*

**lip** \'lip\ *n* **1** : either of the two fleshy folds that surround the mouth; *also* : a part or projection suggesting such a lip **2** : the edge of a hollow vessel or cavity — **lipped** \'lipt\ *adj*

**lip·read·ing** \'lip-,rēd-iŋ\ *n* : the interpreting of a speaker's words without hearing his voice by watching his lip and facial movements

**lip service** n : avowal of allegiance that goes no further than verbal expression

**lip·stick** \'lip-,stik\ n : a waxy solid colored cosmetic in stick form for the lips

**liq** abbr **1** liquid **2** liquor

**liq·ue·fy** also **liq·ui·fy** \'lik-wə-,fī\ vb **-fied; -fy·ing** : to reduce to a liquid state : become liquid — **liq·ue·fac·tion** \,lik-wə-'fak-shən\ n — **liq·ue·fi·able** \-,fī-ə-bəl\ adj — **liq·ue·fi·er** \-,fī-(ə)r\ n

**li·queur** \li-'kər\ n : a distilled alcoholic liquor flavored with aromatic substances and usu. sweetened

**¹liq·uid** \'lik-wəd\ adj **1** : flowing freely like water **2** : neither solid nor gaseous **3** : shining clear ⟨large ~ eyes⟩ **4** : smooth and musical in tone; also : smooth and unconstrained in movement **5** : consisting of or capable of ready conversion into cash ⟨~ assets⟩ — **li·quid·i·ty** \lik-'wid-ət-ē\ n

**²liquid** n : a liquid substance

**liq·ui·date** \'lik-wə-,dāt\ vb **-dat·ed; -dat·ing 1** : to pay off ⟨~ a debt⟩ **2** : to settle the accounts and distribute the assets of (as a business) **3** : to get rid of; esp : KILL — **liq·ui·da·tion** \,lik-wə-'dā-shən\ n

**liquid measure** n : a unit or series of units for measuring liquid capacity — see METRIC SYSTEM table, WEIGHT table

**li·quor** \'lik-ər\ n : a liquid substance; esp : a distilled alcoholic beverage

**li·ra** \'lir-ə, 'lē-rə\ n — see MONEY table

**lisle** \'līl\ n : a smooth tightly twisted thread usu. made of long-staple cotton

**lisp** \'lisp\ vb : to pronounce s and z imperfectly esp. by giving them the sound of th; also : to speak childishly — **lisp** n

**lis·some** also **lis·som** \'lis-əm\ adj : LITHE; also : NIMBLE

**¹list** \'list\ vb, archaic : PLEASE; also : WISH

**²list** vb, archaic : LISTEN

**³list** n **1** : a simple series of names; also : an official roster **2** : INDEX, CATALOG

**⁴list** vb : to make a list of; also : to include on a list

**⁵list** vb : TILT

**⁶list** n : a heeling over : TILT

**lis·ten** \'lis-°n\ vb **lis·tened; lis·ten·ing** \'lis-(°-)niŋ\ **1** : to pay attention in order to hear **2** : HEED — **lis·ten·er** \'lis-(°-)nər\ n

**list·ing** \'lis-tiŋ\ n **1** : an act or instance of making or including in a list **2** : something that is listed

**list·less** \'list-ləs\ adj : LANGUID, SPIRITLESS — **list·less·ly** adv — **list·less·ness** n

**list price** n : the basic price of an item as published in a catalog, price list, or advertisement but subject to discounts

**lists** \'lists\ n pl : an arena for jousting or for combat

**¹lit** \'lit\ past of LIGHT

**²lit** abbr **1** liter **2** literal; literally **3** literary **4** literature

**lit·a·ny** \'lit-°n-ē\ n, pl **-nies** [ME letanie, fr. OF, fr. LL litania, fr. LGk litaneia, fr. Gk, entreaty, fr. litanos

entreating] **:** a prayer consisting of a series of supplications and responses said alternately by a leader and a group

**li·tchi** \'lē-chē, 'lē-\ n **1** : an oval fruit with a hard scaly outer covering, a small hard seed, and edible flesh **2** : a tree bearing litchis

**litchi nut** n : LITCHI 1

**li·ter** \'lēt-ər\ n — see METRIC SYSTEM table

**lit·er·al** \'lit-(ə-)rəl\ adj **1** : adhering to fact or to the ordinary or usual meaning (as of a word) **2** : UN-ADORNED; also : PROSAIC **3** : VERBATIM — **lit·er·al·ly** \-ē\ adv

**lit·er·al·ism** \'lit-(ə-)rə-,liz-əm\ n **1** : adherence to the explicit substance (as of an idea) **2** : fidelity to observable fact — **lit·er·al·is·tic** \,lit-(ə-)rə-'lis-tik\ adj

**lit·er·ary** \'lit-ə-,rer-ē\ adj **1** : of or relating to literature **2** : versed in literature : WELL-READ

**lit·er·ate** \'lit-(ə-)rət\ adj **1** : EDU-CATED; also : able to read and write **2** : LITERARY; also : POLISHED, LUCID — **lit·er·a·cy** \'lit-(ə-)rə-sē\ n

**li·te·ra·ti** \,lit-ə-'rät-ē\ n pl **1** : the educated class **2** : men of letters

**lit·er·a·tim** \,lit-ə-'rāt-əm, -'rät-\ adv or adj : letter for letter

**lit·er·a·ture** \'lit-(ə-)rə-,chur, -chər\ n **1** : the production of written works having excellence of form or expression and dealing with ideas of permanent interest **2** : writings in prose or verse

**lith** or **litho** abbr lithography

**lithe** \'līth, 'līth\ adj **1** : SUPPLE, RE-SILIENT **2** : characterized by effortless grace

**lithe·some** \'līth-səm, 'līth-\ adj : LIS-SOME

**lith·i·um** \'lith-ē-əm\ n : a light silver-white chemical element

**li·thog·ra·phy** \lith-'äg-rə-fē\ n : the process of printing from a plane surface (as a smooth stone or metal plate) on which the image to be printed is ink-receptive and the blank area ink-repellent — **lith·o·graph** \'lith-ə-,graf\ n — **lithograph** vb — **li·thog·ra·pher** \lith-'äg-rə-fər, 'lith-ə-,graf-ər\ n — **lith·o·graph·ic** \,lith-ə-'graf-ik\ adj — **lith·o·graph·i·cal·ly** \-i-k-(ə-)lē\ adv

**li·thol·o·gy** \lith-'äl-ə-jē\ n, pl **-gies** : the study of rocks — **lith·o·log·ic** \,lith-ə-'läj-ik\ adj

**lith·o·sphere** \'lith-ə-,sfiər\ n : the outer part of the solid earth

**Lith·u·a·nian** \,lith-(y)ə-'wā-nē-ən\ n **1** : a native or inhabitant of Lithuania **2** : the language of the Lithuanians — **Lithuanian** adj

**lit·i·gant** \'lit-i-gənt\ n : a party to a lawsuit

**lit·i·gate** \'lit-ə-,gāt\ vb **-gat·ed; -gat·ing** : to carry on a legal contest by judicial process; also : to contest at law — **lit·i·ga·tion** \,lit-ə-'gā-shən\ n

**li·ti·gious** \lə-'tij-əs, li-\ adj **1** : CON-TENTIOUS **2** : prone to engage in lawsuits **3** : of or relating to litigation — **li·ti·gious·ness** n

**lit·mus** \'lit-məs\ *n* **:** a coloring matter from lichens that turns red in acid solutions and blue in alkaline

**Litt D** *or* **Lit D** *abbr* [ML *litterarum doctor*] doctor of letters; doctor of literature

**lit·ter** \'lit-ər\ *n* [ME, fr. OF *litiere,* fr. *lit* bed, fr. L *lectus*] **1 :** a covered and curtained couch with shafts used to carry a single passenger; *also* **:** a device (as a stretcher) for carrying a sick or injured person **2 :** material used as bedding for animals; *also* **:** the uppermost layer of organic debris on the forest floor **3 :** the offspring of an animal at one birth **4 :** RUBBISH

**²litter** *vb* **1 :** to give birth to young **2 :** to strew with litter

**lit·ter·a·teur** \,lit-ə-rə-'tər\ *n* **:** a literary man; *esp* **:** a professional writer

**lit·ter·bug** \'lit-ər-,bəg\ *n* **:** one who litters a public area

**¹lit·tle** \'lit-ᵊl\ *adj* **lit·tler** \'lit-(ə-)lər\ *or* **less** \'les\ *or* **less·er** \'les-ər\; **lit·tlest** \'lit-(ə-)ləst\ *or* **least** \'lēst\ **1 :** not big **2 :** not much **3 :** not important **4 :** NARROW, MEAN — **lit·tle·ness** *n*

**²little** *adv* **less** \'les\; **least** \'lēst\ **1 :** SLIGHTLY; *also* **:** not at all **2 :** INFREQUENTLY

**³little** *n* **1 :** a small amount or quantity **2 :** a short time or distance

**Little Dipper** *n* **:** the seven principal stars in the constellation of Ursa Minor arranged in a form resembling a dipper with the North Star forming the outer end of the handle

**little theater** *n* **:** a small theater for low-cost experimental drama designed for a relatively limited audience

**lit·to·ral** \'lit-ə-rəl; ,lit-ə-'ral\ *adj* **:** of, relating to, or growing on or near a shore esp. of the sea — **littoral** *n*

**lit·ur·gy** \'lit-ər-jē\ *n, pl* **-gies :** a rite or body of rites prescribed for public worship — **li·tur·gi·cal** \lə-'tər-ji-kəl\ *adj* — **li·tur·gi·cal·ly** \-k(ə-)lē\ *adv* — **lit·ur·gist** \'lit-ər-jəst\ *n*

**liv·able** *also* **live·able** \'liv-ə-bəl\ *adj* **1 :** suitable for living in or with **2 :** ENDURABLE — **liv·a·bil·i·ty** \,liv-ə-'bil-ət-ē\ *n*

**¹live** \'liv\ *vb* **lived; liv·ing 1 :** to be or continue alive **2 :** SUBSIST **3 :** to conduct one's life **4 :** RESIDE **5 :** to remain in human memory or record

**²live** \'līv\ *adj* **1 :** having life **2 :** abounding with life **3 :** BURNING, GLOWING ⟨a ~ cigar⟩ **4 :** connected to electric power ⟨a ~ wire⟩ **5 :** UNEXPLODED ⟨a ~ bomb⟩ **6 :** of continuing interest ⟨a ~ issue⟩ **7 :** being in play ⟨a ~ ball⟩ **8 :** of or involving the actual presence of real people ⟨~ audience⟩; *also* **:** broadcast directly at the time of production ⟨a ~ radio program⟩

**live down** *vb* **:** to live so as to wipe out the memory or effects of

**live in** \(')liv-'in\ *vb* **:** to live in one's place of employment — used of a servant — **live-in** \,liv-,in\ *adj*

**live·li·hood** \'līv-lē-,hůd\ *n* **:** means of support or subsistence

**live·long** \,liv-,lȯŋ\ *adj* [ME *lef long,* fr. *lef* dear + *long* long] **:** WHOLE, ENTIRE ⟨the ~ day⟩

**live·ly** \'līv-lē\ *adj* **live·li·er; -est 1 :** full of life **2 :** KEEN, VIVID ⟨~ interest⟩ **3 :** ANIMATED ⟨~ debate⟩ **4 :** showing activity or vigor ⟨a ~ manner⟩ **5 :** quick to rebound ⟨a ~ ball⟩ **syn** vivacious, sprightly, gay — **live·li·ness** *n*

**liv·en** \'lī-vən\ *vb* **liv·ened; liv·en·ing** \'līv-(ə-)niŋ\ **:** ENLIVEN

**¹liv·er** \'liv-ər\ *n* **:** a large glandular organ of vertebrates that secretes bile and is a center of metabolic activity — **liv·ered** \'liv-ərd\ *adj*

**²liver** *n* **:** one that lives esp. in a specified way ⟨a fast ~⟩

**liv·er·ish** \'liv-(ə-)rish\ *adj* **1 :** resembling liver esp. in color **2 :** BILIOUS **3 :** MELANCHOLY

**liv·er·wort** \'liv-ər-,wərt\ *n* **:** any of various plants resembling the related mosses

**liv·er·wurst** \-,wərst, -,wů(r)st\ *n* **:** a sausage consisting chiefly of liver

**liv·ery** \'liv-(ə-)rē\ *n, pl* **-er·ies 1 :** a special uniform worn by the servants of a wealthy household; *also* **:** distinctive dress **2 :** the feeding, care, and stabling of horses for pay; *also* **:** the keeping of horses and vehicles for hire — **liv·er·ied** \-rēd\ *adj*

**liv·ery·man** \-mən\ *n* **:** the keeper of a livery stable

**lives** *pl of* LIFE

**live·stock** \'līv-,stäk\ *n* **:** farm animals kept for use and profit

**live wire** *n* **:** an alert active aggressive person

**liv·id** \'liv-əd\ *adj* [F *livide,* fr. L *lividus,* fr. *livēre* to be blue] **1 :** discolored by bruising **2 :** ASHEN, PALLID **3 :** REDDISH **4 :** ENRAGED

**¹liv·ing** \'liv-iŋ\ *adj* **1 :** having life **2 :** NATURAL **3 :** full of life and vigor; *also* **:** VIVID

**²living** *n* **1 :** the condition of being alive; *also* **:** manner of life **2 :** LIVELIHOOD

**living room** *n* **:** a room in a residence used for the common social activities of the occupants

**living wage** *n* **:** a wage sufficient to provide the necessities and comforts held to comprise an acceptable standard of living

**liz·ard** \'liz-ərd\ *n* **:** a 4-legged scaly reptile with a long tapering tail

**Lk** *abbr* Luke

**ll** *abbr* lines

**LL** *abbr* Late Latin

**lla·ma** \'läm-ə\ *n* **:** any of several wild or domesticated So. American mammals related to the camel but smaller and without a hump

**lla·no** \'län-ō\ *n, pl* **llanos :** an open grassy plain esp. of Spanish America

**LLB** *abbr* [NL *legum baccalaureus*] bachelor of laws

**LLD** *abbr* [NL *legum doctor*] doctor of laws

**LM** *abbr* lunar module

**LNG** *abbr* liquefied natural gas

**lo** \'lō\ *interj* — used to call attention

¹**load** \'lōd\ *n* **1** : PACK; *also* : CARGO **2** : a mass of weight supported by something **3** : something that burdens the mind or spirits **4** : a standard, expected, or authorized burden **5** : a large quantity — usu. used in pl.

²**load** *vb* **1** : to put a load in or on; *also* : to receive a load **2** : BURDEN **3** : to increase the weight of by adding something **4** : to supply abundantly **5** : to put a charge in (as a firearm)

**load·ed** \'lōd-əd\ *adj* **1** *slang* : DRUNK **2** : having a large amount of money

**load·stone** *var of* LODESTONE

¹**loaf** \'lōf\ *n, pl* **loaves** \'lōvz\ : a shaped or molded mass esp. of bread

²**loaf** *vb* : to spend time in idleness : LOUNGE — **loaf·er** *n*

**loam** \'lōm, 'lüm\ *n* : SOIL; *esp* : a loose soil of mixed clay, sand, and silt — **loamy** *adj*

¹**loan** \'lōn\ *n* **1** : money let out at interest; *also* : something furnished for the borrower's temporary use **2** : the grant of temporary use

²**loan** *vb* : LEND

**loan shark** *n* : a person who lends money at excessive rates of interest — **loan·shark·ing** \'lōn-,shär-kiŋ\ *n*

**loan·word** \'lōn-,wərd\ *n* : a word taken from another language and at least partly naturalized

**loath** \'lōth, 'lōth\ *also* **loathe** \ lōth, lōth\ *adj* : RELUCTANT

**loathe** \'lōth\ *vb* **loathed; loath·ing** : to dislike greatly **syn** abominate, abhor, detest

**loath·ing** \'lō-thiŋ\ *n* : extreme disgust

**loath·ly** \'lōth-lē, 'lōth-\ *adj* : LOATHSOME

**loath·some** \'lōth-səm, 'lōth-\ *adj* : exciting loathing : REPULSIVE

**lob** \'läb\ *vb* **lobbed; lob·bing** : to throw, hit, or propel something in a high arc — **lob** *n*

¹**lob·by** \'läb-ē\ *n, pl* **lobbies** **1** : a corridor or hall used esp. as a passageway or waiting room **2** : a group of persons engaged in lobbying

²**lobby** *vb* **lob·bied; lob·by·ing** : to try to influence public officials and esp. legislators — **lob·by·ist** *n*

**lobe** \'lōb\ *n* : a curved or rounded projection or division — **lo·bar** \'lō-bər\ *adj* — **lobed** \'lōbd\ *adj*

**lo·bot·o·my** \lō-'bät-ə-mē\ *n, pl* **-mies** : severance of nerve fibers by incision into the brain for the relief of some mental disorders and tensions

**lob·ster** \'läb-stər\ *n* [ME, fr. OE *loppestre*, fr. *loppe* spider] : an edible marine crustacean with two large pincerlike claws and four other pairs of legs; *also* : SPINY LOBSTER

**lob·ule** \'läb-yül\ *n* : a small lobe; *also* : a subdivision of a lobe — **lob·u·lar** \'läb-yə-lər\ *adj*

¹**lo·cal** \'lō-kəl\ *adj* **1** : of, relating to, or occupying a particular place **2** : affecting a small part of the body (~ infection) **3** : serving a particular limited district; *also* : making all stops (a ~ train) — **lo·cal·ly** \-ē\ *adv*

²**local** *n* : one that is local

**lo·cale** \lō-'kal\ *n* : a place that is the setting for a particular event

**lo·cal·i·ty** \lō-'kal-ət-ē\ *n, pl* **-ties** : a particular spot, situation, or location

**lo·cal·ize** \'lō-kə-,līz\ *vb* **-ized; -izing** : to fix in or confine to a definite place or locality — **lo·cal·iza·tion** \,lō-kə-lə-'zā-shən\ *n*

**lo·cate** \'lō-,kāt, lō-'kāt\ *vb* **lo·cated; lo·cat·ing 1** : STATION, SETTLE **2** : to determine the site of **3** : to find or fix the place of in a sequence

**lo·ca·tion** \lō-'kā-shən\ *n* **1** : the process of locating **2** : SITUATION, PLACE **3** : a place outside a studio where a motion picture is filmed

**loc cit** *abbr* [L *loco citato*] in the place cited

**loch** \'läk, 'läk\ *n, Scot* : LAKE; *also* : a bay or arm of the sea esp. when nearly landlocked

¹**lock** \'läk\ *n* : a tuft, strand, or ringlet of hair; *also* : a cohering bunch (as of wool or flax)

²**lock** *n* **1** : a fastening in which a bolt is operated **2** : an enclosure (as in a canal) used in raising or lowering boats from level to level **3** : the mechanism of a firearm by which the charge is exploded **4** : a wrestling hold

³**lock** *vb* **1** : to fasten the lock of; *also* : to make fast with a lock **2** : to confine or exclude by means of a lock **3** : INTERLOCK

**lock·er** \'läk-ər\ *n* **1** : a drawer, cupboard, or compartment for individual storage use **2** : an insulated compartment for storing frozen food

**lock·et** \'läk-ət\ *n* : a small usu. metal case for a memento worn suspended from a chain or necklace

**lock·jaw** \'läk-,jò\ *n* : TETANUS

**lock·nut** \-,nət, -'nət\ *n* **1** : a nut screwed tight on another to prevent it from slacking back **2** : a nut designed to lock itself when screwed tight

**lock·out** \'läk-,aút\ *n* : the suspension of work or closing of a plant by an employer during a labor dispute in order to make his employees accept his terms

**lock·smith** \'läk-,smith\ *n* : one who makes or repairs locks

**lock·step** \'läk-,step\ *n* : a mode of marching in step by a body of men moving in a very close single file

**lock·up** \'läk-,əp\ *n* : JAIL

**lo·co** \'lō-kō\ *adj, slang* : CRAZY, FRENZIED

**lo·co·mo·tion** \,lō-kə-'mō-shən\ *n* **1** : the act or power of moving from place to place **2** : TRAVEL

¹**lo·co·mo·tive** \,lō-kə-'mōt-iv\ *adj* : of or relating to locomotion or a locomotive

²**locomotive** *n* : a self-propelled vehicle used to move railroad cars

**lo·co·mo·tor** \,lō-kə-'mōt-ər\ *adj* : LOCOMOTIVE

**lo·co·weed** \'lō-kō-,wēd\ *n* : any of several leguminous plants of western No. America that are poisonous to livestock

**lo·cus** \'lō-kəs\ *n, pl* **lo·ci** \'lō-,sī\ **1** : PLACE, LOCALITY **2** : the set of all points whose location is determined by stated conditions

**lo·cust** \'lō-kəst\ n 1 : a usu. destructive migratory grasshopper 2 : CICADA 3 : any of various hard-wooded leguminous trees

**lo·cu·tion** \lō-'kyü-shən\ n : a particular form of expression; also : PHRASEOLOGY

**lode** \'lōd\ n : an ore deposit

**lode·star** \'lōd-ˌstär\ n [ME lode sterre, fr. lode course, fr. OE lād] a : a guiding star; esp : NORTH STAR

**lode·stone** \-ˌstōn\ n : an iron-containing rock with magnetic properties

¹**lodge** \'läj\ vb lodged; lodg·ing 1 : to provide quarters for; also : to settle in a place 2 : CONTAIN 3 : to come to a rest and remain 4 : to deposit for safekeeping 5 : to vest (as authority) in an agent 6 : FILE ⟨~ a complaint⟩

²**lodge** n 1 : a house set apart for residence in a special season or by an employee on an estate; also : INN 2 : a den or lair esp. of gregarious animals 3 : the meeting place of a branch of a fraternal organization; also : the members of such a branch

**lodg·er** \'läj-ər\ n : a person who occupies a rented room in another's house

**lodg·ing** \'läj-iŋ\ n 1 : DWELLING 2 : a room or suite of rooms in another's house rented as a dwelling place — usu. used in pl.

**lodg·ment** or **lodge·ment** \'läj-mənt\ n 1 : a lodging place 2 : the act or manner of lodging 3 : DEPOSIT

**loess** \'les, 'lə(r)s, 'lō-əs\ n : a usu. yellowish brown loamy deposit believed to be chiefly deposited by the wind — **loess·ial** \'les-ē-əl, 'lə(r)s-, lō-'es-\ adj

¹**loft** \'loft\ n [ME, fr. OE, fr. ON lopt air] 1 : ATTIC 2 : GALLERY ⟨organ ~⟩ 3 : an upper floor (as in a warehouse or barn) esp. when not partitioned

²**loft** vb : to strike or throw a ball so that it rises high in the air

**lofty** \'lof-tē\ adj loft·i·er; -est 1 : extremely proud 2 : NOBLE; also : SUPERIOR 3 : HIGH, TALL — **loft·i·ly** \'lof-tə-lē\ adv — **loft·i·ness** \-tē-nəs\ n

¹**log** \'log, 'läg\ n 1 : a bulky piece of unshaped timber 2 : an apparatus for measuring the rate of a ship's motion through the water 3 : the daily record of a ship's progress; also : a regularly kept record of performance (as of an airplane)

²**log** vb logged; log·ging 1 : to cut trees for lumber 2 : to enter in a log 3 : to sail a ship or fly an airplane for (an indicated distance or period of time) 4 : to have (an indicated record) to one's credit : ACHIEVE

³**log** n : LOGARITHM

**lo·gan·ber·ry** \'lō-gən-ˌber-ē\ n : a red-fruited upright-growing dewberry; also : its fruit

**log·a·rithm** \'log-ə-ˌrith-əm, 'läg-\ n : the exponent that indicates the power to which a base number is raised to produce a given number ⟨the ~ of 100 to

the base number 10 is 2⟩ — **log·a·rith·mic** \ˌlog-ə-'rith-mik, ˌläg-\ adj

**loge** \'lōzh\ n 1 : a small compartment; also : a box in a theater 2 : a small partitioned area; also : the forward section of a theater mezzanine

**log·ger·head** \'log-ər-ˌhed, 'läg-\ n : a large sea turtle of the warmer parts of the Atlantic — **at loggerheads** : in a state of quarrelsome disagreement

**log·gia** \'lō-jē-ə, 'lō-jä\ n, pl **loggias** \'lō-jē-əz, 'lō-jäz\ : a roofed open gallery

**log·ic** \'läj-ik\ n 1 : a science that deals with the rules and tests of sound thinking and proof by reasoning 2 : sound reasoning 3 : the fundamental principles and the connection of circuit elements for arithmetical computation in a computer — **log·i·cal** \-i-kəl\ adj — **log·i·cal·ly** \-i-k(ə-)lē\ adv — **lo·gi·cian** \lō-'jish-ən\ n

**lo·gis·tics** \lō-'jis-tiks\ n sing or pl : the procurement, maintenance, and transportation of matériel, facilities, and personnel — **lo·gis·tic** adj

**log·jam** \'log-ˌjam, 'läg-\ n 1 : a deadlocked jumble of logs in a watercourse 2 : DEADLOCK

**logo** \'log-ō, 'läg-\ n, pl **log·os** \-ōz\ : LOGOTYPE

**logo·type** \'log-ə-ˌtip, 'läg-\ n : an identifying symbol (as for advertising)

**log-roll·ing** \-ˌrō-liŋ\ n : the trading of votes by legislators to secure favorable action on projects of individual interest

**lo·gy** \'lō-gē\ also **log·gy** \'lóg-ē, 'läg-\ adj **lo·gi·er; -est** : deficient in vitality : SLUGGISH

**loin** \'lóin\ n 1 : the part of the body on each side of the spinal column and between the hip and the lower ribs; also : a cut of meat from this part of a meat animal 2 pl : the upper and lower abdominal regions and the region about the hips

**loin·cloth** \-ˌklóth\ n : a cloth worn about the loins often as the sole article of clothing in warm climates

**loi·ter** \'lóit-ər\ vb 1 : LINGER 2 : to hang around idly syn dawdle, dally, procrastinate — **loi·ter·er** n

**loll** \'läl\ vb 1 : DROOP, DANGLE 2 : LOUNGE

**lol·li·pop** or **lol·ly·pop** \'läl-ē-ˌpäp\ n : a lump of hard candy on a stick

**lol·ly·gag** \'läl-ē-ˌgag\ vb : DAWDLE

**Lond** abbr London

**lone** \'lōn\ adj 1 : SOLITARY ⟨a ~ sentinel⟩ 2 : SOLE, ONLY ⟨the ~ theater in town⟩ 3 : ISOLATED ⟨a ~ tree⟩

**lone·ly** \'lōn-lē\ adj **lone·li·er; -est** 1 : being without company 2 : UNFREQUENTED ⟨a ~ spot⟩ 3 : LONESOME — **lone·li·ness** n

**lon·er** \'lō-nər\ n : one that avoids others

**lone·some** \'lōn-səm\ adj 1 : sad from lack of companionship 2 : REMOTE; also : SOLITARY — **lone·some·ly** adv — **lone·some·ness** n

¹**long** \'loŋ\ adj **lon·ger** \'loŋ-gər\; **lon·gest** \'loŋ-gəst\ 1 : extending

for a considerable distance; *also* : TALL, ELONGATED  **2** : having a specified length  **3** : extending over a considerable time; *also* : TEDIOUS  **4** : containing many items in a series  **5** : being a syllable or speech sound of relatively great duration  **6** : extending far into the future  **7** : well furnished with something — used *with on*

²**long** *adv* : for or during a long time

³**long** *n* : a long period of time

⁴**long** *vb* **longed; long·ing** \'lȯŋ-iŋ\ : to feel a strong desire or wish  **syn** yearn, hanker, pine

⁵**long** *abbr* longitude

**long·boat** \'lȯŋ-ˌbōt\ *n* : the largest boat carried by a merchant sailing ship

**long·bow** \-ˌbō\ *n* : a wooden bow drawn by hand and usu. 5 to 6 feet long

**lon·gev·i·ty** \län-'jev-ət-ē\ *n* [LL *longaevitas*, fr. L *longaevus* long-lived, fr. *longus* long + *aevum* age] : a long duration of individual life; *also* : length of life

**long·hair** \'lȯŋ-ˌha͡ər\ *n* **1** : a lover of classical music  **2** : HIPPIE

**long·hand** \-ˌhand\ *n* : HANDWRITING

**long·horn** \-ˌhȯrn\ *n* : any of the cattle with long horns formerly common in the southwestern U.S.

**long hundredweight** *n* — see WEIGHT table

**long·ing** \'lȯŋ-iŋ\ *n* : an eager desire esp. for something unattainable — **long·ing·ly** *adv*

**lon·gi·tude** \'län-jə-ˌt(y)üd\ *n* : angular distance due east or west from a meridian and esp. from the meridian that runs between the north and south poles and passes through Greenwich, England, usu. expressed in degrees

**lon·gi·tu·di·nal** \ˌlän-jə-'t(y)üd-(ᵊ-)nᵊl\ *adj* **1** : of or relating to length  **2** : extending lengthwise — **lon·gi·tu·di·nal·ly** \-ē\ *adv*

**long·shore·man** \'lȯŋ-'shȯr-mən\ *n* : a laborer at a wharf who loads and unloads cargo

**long–suf·fer·ing** \-'səf-(ə-)riŋ\ *n* : long and patient endurance of offense

**long–term** \'lȯŋ-'tərm\ *adj* **1** : extending over or involving a long period of time  **2** : constituting a financial obligation based on a term usu. of more than 10 years ⟨a ~ mortgage⟩

**long·time** \ˌlȯŋ-ˌtīm\ *adj* : of long duration ⟨~ friends⟩

**long ton** *n* — see WEIGHT table

**lon·gueur** \lōⁿ-gœr\ *n, pl* **longueurs** \-gœr(z)\ [F, lit., length] : a dull tedious passage or section

**long–wind·ed** \'lȯŋ-'win-dəd\ *adj* : tediously long in speaking or writing

¹**look** \'lu̇k\ *vb* **1** : to exercise the power of vision : SEE  **2** : EXPECT  **3** : to have an appearance that befits ⟨~s the part⟩  **4** : SEEM ⟨~s thin⟩  **5** : to direct one's attention : HEED  **6** : POINT, FACE  **7** : to show a tendency — **look after** : to take care of — **look for 1** : EXPECT  **2** : to search for

²**look** *n* **1** : the action of looking : GLANCE  **2** : EXPRESSION; *also* : physical appearance  **3** : ASPECT

**look down** \(')lu̇k-'da͡un\ *vb* : DESPISE — used *with on* or *upon*

**looking glass** *n* : MIRROR

**look·out** \'lu̇k-ˌa͡ut\ *n* **1** : a person assigned to watch (as on a ship)  **2** : a careful watch  **3** : VIEW  **4** : a matter of concern

**look up** \(')lu̇k-'əp\ *vb* **1** : IMPROVE ⟨business is *looking up*⟩  **2** : to seek out for in or as if in a reference work  **3** : to seek out esp. for a brief visit

¹**loom** \'lüm\ *n* : a frame or machine for weaving together threads or yarns into cloth

²**loom** *vb* **1** : to come into sight in an unnaturally large, indistinct, or distorted form  **2** : to appear in an impressively exaggerated form

**loon** \'lün\ *n* : a web-footed black-and-white fish-eating diving bird

**loo·ny** *or* **loo·ney** \'lü-nē\ *adj* **loo·ni·er; -est** : CRAZY, FOOLISH

**loony bin** *n* : an insane asylum

**loop** \'lüp\ *n* **1** : a fold or doubling of a line leaving an aperture between the parts through which another line can be passed; *also* : a loop-shaped figure or course ⟨a ~ in a river⟩  **2** : a circular airplane maneuver involving flying upside down  **3** : a ring-shaped intrauterine device  **4** : a piece of film whose ends are spliced together to project continuously — **loop** *vb*

**loop·er** \'lü-pər\ *n* : any of numerous rather small hairless moth caterpillars that move with a looping movement

**loop·hole** \'lüp-ˌhōl\ *n* **1** : a small opening in a wall through which small firearms may be discharged  **2** : a means of escape

¹**loose** \'lüs\ *adj* **loos·er; loos·est 1** : not rigidly fastened  **2** : free from restraint or obligation  **3** : not dense or compact in structure  **4** : not chaste : LEWD  **5** : SLACK  **6** : not precise or exact — **loose·ly** *adv* — **loose·ness** *n*

²**loose** *vb* **loosed; loos·ing 1** : RELEASE  **2** : UNTIE  **3** : DETACH  **4** : DISCHARGE  **5** : RELAX, SLACKEN

³**loose** *adv* : LOOSELY

**loos·en** \'lüs-ᵊn\ *vb* **loos·ened; loos·en·ing** \'lüs-(ᵊ-)niŋ\ **1** : FREE  **2** : to make or become loose  **3** : to relax the severity of

**loot** \'lüt\ *n* [Hindi *lūṭ*, fr. Skt *luṇṭati* he robs] : goods taken in war or by robbery : PLUNDER — **loot** *vb* — **loot·er** *n*

¹**lop** \'läp\ *vb* **lopped; lop·ping 1** : to cut branches or twigs from : TRIM; *also* : to cut off

²**lop** *vb* **lopped; lop·ping** : to hang downward; *also* : to flop or sway loosely

**lope** \'lōp\ *n* : an easy bounding gait — **lope** *vb*

**lop·sid·ed** \'läp-'sīd-əd\ *adj* **1** : leaning to one side  **2** : UNSYMMETRICAL — **lop·sid·ed·ly** *adv* — **lop·sid·ed·ness** *n*

**loq** *abbr* [L *loquitur*] he speaks

**lo·qua·cious** \lō-'kwā-shəs\ *adj* : excessively talkative — **lo·quac·i·ty** \-'kwas-ət-ē\ *n*

¹**lord** \'lȯrd\ *n* [ME *loverd, lord*, fr. OE

hlāford, fr. hlāf loaf + weard keeper]
**1** : one having power and authority
over others; esp : a person from whom a
feudal fee or estate is held  **2** : a man of
rank or high position; esp : a British
nobleman  **3** pl, cap : the upper house
of the British parliament  **4** : a person
of great power in some field

²**lord** vb : to act as if one were a lord;
esp : to put on airs — usu. used with it

**lord chancellor** n, pl **lords chancel-**
**lor** : a British officer of state who presides over the House of Lords, serves
as the head of the British judiciary,
and is usu. a leading member of the
cabinet

**lord·ly** \-lē\ adj **lord·li·er; -est  1**
: DIGNIFIED; also : NOBLE  **2** : HAUGHTY

**lord·ship** \-,ship\ n  **1** : the rank or
dignity of a lord — used as a title  **2**
: the authority or territory of a lord

**Lord's Supper** n : COMMUNION

**lore** \'lōr\ n : KNOWLEDGE; esp : traditional knowledge or belief

**lor·gnette** \lȯrn-'yet\ n  [F, fr. lor-
gner to take a sidelong look at, fr. MF,
fr. lorgne cross-eyed] : a pair of eyeglasses or opera glasses with a handle

**lorn** \'lȯrn\ adj : FORSAKEN, DESOLATE

**lor·ry** \'lȯr-ē\ n, pl **lorries  1** : a large
low horse-drawn wagon without sides
**2** Brit : MOTORTRUCK

**lose** \'lüz\ vb **lost** \'lȯst\; **los·ing**
\'lü-ziŋ\  **1** : DESTROY  **2** : to miss
from a customary place : MISLAY  **3** : to
suffer deprivation of  **4** : to fail to use
: WASTE  **5** : to fail to win or obtain ⟨~
the game⟩  **6** : to fail to keep or maintain ⟨~ his balance⟩  **7** : to wander
from ⟨~ his way⟩  **8** : to get rid of ⟨~
weight⟩ — **los·er** n

**loss** \'lȯs\ n  **1** : the harm resulting
from losing  **2** : something that is lost
**3** pl : killed, wounded, or captured
soldiers  **4** : failure to win  **5** : an
amount by which the cost exceeds the
selling price  **6** : decrease in amount or
degree  **7** : RUIN

**loss leader** n : an article sold at a loss
in order to draw customers

**lost** \'lȯst\ adj  **1** : not used, won, or
claimed  **2** : unable to find the way;
also : HELPLESS  **3** : ruined or destroyed
physically or morally  **4** : no longer
possessed or known  **5** : DENIED; also
: HARDENED  **6** : ABSORBED, RAPT

**lot** \'lät\ n  **1** : an object used in deciding something by chance; also : the use
of lots to decide something  **2** : SHARE,
PORTION; also : FORTUNE, FATE  **3** : a
plot of land  **4** : a group of individuals
: SET  **5** : a considerable quantity

**loth** \'lōth, 'lōth\ var of LOATH

**lo·tion** \'lō-shən\ n : a liquid preparation for cosmetic and external medicinal
use

**lot·tery** \'lät-ə-rē\ n, pl **-ter·ies  1** : a
drawing of lots in which prizes are
given to the winning names or numbers
**2** : a matter determined by chance

**lo·tus** \'lōt-əs\ n  **1** : a fruit held in
Greek legend to cause dreamy content
and forgetfulness  **2** : a water lily used
in ancient Egyptian and Hindu art and

religious symbolism  **3** : any of several
forage plants related to the clovers

**loud** \'laùd\ adj  **1** : marked by intensity or volume of sound  **2** : CLAMOROUS,
NOISY  **3** : obtrusive or offensive in
color or pattern ⟨a ~ suit⟩ — **loud** adv
— **loud·ly** adv — **loud·ness** n

**loud-mouthed** \-'maùthd, -'maùtht\
adj  **1** : having an offensively loud voice
or a noisy manner  **2** : TACTLESS

**loud-speak·er** \'laùd-,spē-kər\ n : a
device similar to a telephone receiver in
operation but amplifying sound

¹**lounge** \'laùnj\ vb **lounged; loung-**
**ing** : to act or move lazily or listlessly

²**lounge** n  **1** : a room with comfortable
furniture; also : a room (as in a theater)
with lounging, smoking, and toilet facilities  **2** : a long couch

**lour** \'laù(-ə)r\, **loury** \'laù)r-ē\ var
of LOWER, LOWERY

**louse** \'laùs\ n, pl **lice** \'līs\  **1** : a
small wingless insect parasitic on warm-
blooded animals  **2** : a plant pest (as an
aphid)  **3** : a contemptible person

**lousy** \'laù-zē\ adj **lous·i·er; -est**
**1** : infested with lice  **2** : POOR, INFERIOR
**3** : amply supplied ⟨~ with money⟩ —
**lous·i·ly** \'laù-zə-lē\ adv — **lous·i·**
**ness** \-zē-nəs\ n

**lout** \'laùt\ n : a stupid awkward fellow
— **lout·ish** adj — **lout·ish·ly** adv

**lou·ver** or **lou·vre** \'lü-vər\ n  **1** : an
opening having parallel slanted slats to
allow flow of air but to exclude rain or
sun or to provide privacy; also : a slat
in such an opening  **2** : a device with
fins, vanes, or a grating for controlling
a flow of air or the radiation of light

¹**love** \'ləv\ n  **1** : strong affection
**2** : warm attachment ⟨~ of the sea⟩
**3** : attraction based on sexual desire
: a beloved person  **4** : a score of zero
in tennis — **love·less** adj

²**love** vb **loved; lov·ing  1** : CHERISH
**2** : to feel a passion, devotion, or tenderness for  **3** : CARESS  **4** : to take
pleasure in ⟨~s to play bridge⟩ —
**lov·able** \'ləv-ə-bəl\ adj — **lov·er** n

**love·bird** \'ləv-,bərd\ n : any of various small usu. gray or green parrots
that show great affection for their
mates

**love·lorn** \-,lȯrn\ adj : deprived of
love or of a lover

**love·ly** \'ləv-lē\ adj **love·li·er; -est**
: BEAUTIFUL — **love·li·ness** n

**love·mak·ing** \'ləv-,mā-kiŋ\ n  **1**
: COURTSHIP  **2** : sexual activity; esp
: COPULATION

**love·sick** \'ləv-,sik\ adj  **1** : YEARNING
**2** : expressing a lover's longing —
**love·sick·ness** n

**lov·ing** \'ləv-iŋ\ adj : AFFECTIONATE
— **lov·ing·ly** adv

¹**low** \'lō\ vb : MOO

²**low** n : MOO

³**low** adj **low·er** \'lō(-ə)r\; **low·est**
\'lō-əst\  **1** : not high or tall ⟨~ wall⟩;
also : DÉCOLLETÉ  **2** : situated or passing below the normal level or surface
⟨~ ground⟩; also : marking a nadir
**3** : STRICKEN, PROSTRATE  **4** : not loud
⟨~ voice⟩  **5** : being near the equator

**6** : humble in status **7** : WEAK; *also* : DEPRESSED **8** : less than usual **9** : falling short of a standard **10** : UNFAVORABLE — **low** *adv* — **low·ness** *n*

⁴**low** *n* **1** : something that is low **2** : a region of low barometric pressure **3** : an adjustment of gears in an automobile transmission that gives the slowest speed and greatest power

**low beam** *n* : the short-range focus of a vehicle headlight

**low·brow** \'lō-₊braù\ *n* : a person without intellectual interests or culture

**low-down** \'lō-₊daùn\ *n* : pertinent and esp. guarded information

**low-down** \'lō-daùn\ *adj* **1** : MEAN, CONTEMPTIBLE **2** : deeply emotional

¹**low·er** \'laù(-ə)r\ *vb* **1** : FROWN **2** : to become dark, gloomy, and threatening

²**low·er** \'lō(-ə)r\ *adj* **1** : relatively low (as in rank) **2** : constituting the popular and more representative branch of a bicameral legislative body **3** : situated beneath the earth's surface

³**low·er** \'lō(-ə)r\ *vb* **1** : DROP; *also* : DIMINISH **2** : to let descend by its own weight; *also* : to reduce the height of **3** : to reduce in value or amount **4** : DEGRADE; *also* : HUMBLE

**low·er·case** \₊lō(-ə)r-'kās\ *adj* : being a letter that belongs to or conforms to the series a, b, c, etc., rather than A, B, C, etc. — **lowercase** *n*

**lower class** *n* : a social class occupying a position below the middle class and having the lowest status in a society — **lower-class** \-'klas\ *adj*

**low·ery** \'laù-(ə-)rē\ *adj*, *NewEng* : GLOOMY, LOWERING

**lowest common denominator** *n* : LEAST COMMON DENOMINATOR

**lowest common multiple** *n* : LEAST COMMON MULTIPLE

**low frequency** *n* : a frequency of a radio wave in the range between 30 and 300 kilocycles

**low-key** \'lō-'kē\ *also* **low-keyed** \-'kēd\ *adj* : of low intensity : restrained

**low·land** \'lō-lənd, -₊land\ *n* : low and usu. level country

**low·ly** \'lō-lē\ *adj* **low·li·er; -est 1** : HUMBLE, MEEK **2** : ranking low in some hierarchy — **low·li·ness** *n*

**low-rise** \'lō-'rīz\ *adj* : being one or two stories and not equipped with elevators ⟨a ~ building⟩

**low-ten·sion** \'lō-'ten-chən\ *adj* : having or using low voltage

¹**lox** \'läks\ *n* : liquid oxygen

²**lox** *n*, *pl* **lox** *or* **lox·es** : smoked salmon

**loy·al** \'lòi(-ə)l\ *adj* [MF, fr. OF *leial, leel,* fr. L *legalis* legal] **1** : faithful in allegiance to one's government **2** : faithful esp. to a cause or ideal : CONSTANT — **loy·al·ly** \'lòi-ə-lē\ *adv* — **loy·al·ty** \'lòi(-ə)l-tē\ *n*

**loy·al·ist** \'lòi-ə-ləst\ *n* : one who is or remains loyal to a political party, government, or sovereign

**loz·enge** \'läz-ənj\ *n* **1** : a diamond-shaped figure **2** : a small flat often medicated candy

**LP** *abbr* low pressure

**LPG** *abbr* liquefied petroleum gas

**LPN** *abbr* licensed practical nurse

**LR** *abbr* living room

**LS** *abbr* **1** left side **2** letter signed **3** [L *locus sigilli*] place of the seal

**LSD** \₊el,-es-'dē\ *n* [*l*ysergic *a*cid *d*iethylamide] : a crystalline compound that causes psychotic symptoms similar to those of schizophrenia

**LSS** *abbr* life-support system

**lt** *abbr* light

**Lt** *abbr* lieutenant

**LT** *abbr* **1** long ton **2** low-tension

**LTC** *or* **Lt Col** *abbr* lieutenant colonel

**Lt Comdr** *abbr* lieutenant commander

**ltd** *abbr* limited

**LTG** *or* **Lt Gen** *abbr* lieutenant general

**LTJG** *abbr* lieutenant, junior grade

**LTL** *abbr* less-than-truckload lot

**ltr** *abbr* letter

**Lu** *symbol* lutetium

**lu·au** \'lü-₊aù\ *n* : a Hawaiian feast

**lub** *abbr* lubricant; lubricating

**lub·ber** \'ləb-ər\ *n* **1** : LOUT **2** : an unskilled seaman — **lub·ber·ly** *adj*

**lube** \'lüb\ *n* : LUBRICANT

**lu·bri·cant** \'lü-bri-kənt\ *n* : a material (as grease) used between moving parts of machinery to make the surfaces slippery and reduce friction

**lu·bri·cate** \'lü-brə-₊kāt\ *vb* **-cat·ed; -cat·ing** : to apply a lubricant to — **lu·bri·ca·tion** \₊lü-brə-'kā-shən\ *n* — **lu·bri·ca·tor** \'lü-brə-₊kāt-ər\ *n*

**lu·bri·cious** \lü-'brish-əs\ *or* **lu·bri·cous** \'lü-bri-kəs\ *adj* **1** : LECHEROUS; *also* : SALACIOUS **2** : SMOOTH, SLIPPERY — **lu·bric·i·ty** \lü-'bris-ət-ē\ *n*

**lu·cent** \'lüs-ᵊnt\ *adj* **1** : LUMINOUS **2** : CLEAR, LUCID

**lu·cerne** \lü-'sərn\ *n*, *chiefly Brit* : ALFALFA

**lu·cid** \'lü-səd\ *adj* **1** : SHINING **2** : clear-minded **3** : easily understood — **lu·cid·i·ty** \lü-'sid-ət-ē\ *n* — **lu·cid·ly** *adv* — **lu·cid·ness** *n*

**Lu·ci·fer** \'lü-sə-fər\ *n* [ME, the morning star, a fallen rebel archangel, the Devil, fr. OE, fr. L, the morning star, fr. *lucifer* light-bearing] : DEVIL, SATAN

¹**luck** \'lək\ *n* **1** : CHANCE, FORTUNE **2** : good fortune — **luck·less** *adj*

²**luck** *vb* **1** : to prosper or succeed esp. through chance or good fortune **2** : to come upon something desirable by chance — usu. used with *out, on, onto,* or *into*

**lucky** \'lək-ē\ *adj* **luck·i·er; -est 1** : favored by luck : FORTUNATE **2** : FORTUITOUS **3** : seeming to bring good luck — **luck·i·ly** \'lək-ə-lē\ *adv* — **luck·i·ness** \-ē-nəs\ *n*

**lu·cra·tive** \'lü-krət-iv\ *adj* : PROFITABLE — **lu·cra·tive·ly** *adv* — **lu·cra·tive·ness** *n*

**lu·cre** \'lü-kər\ *n* : PROFIT; *also* : MONEY

**lu·cu·bra·tion** \₊lü-k(y)ə-'brā-shən\ *n* : laborious study : MEDITATION

**lu·di·crous** \'lüd-ə-krəs\ *adj* : LAUGHABLE, RIDICULOUS — **lu·di·crous·ly** *adv* — **lu·di·crous·ness** *n*

**luff** \'ləf\ *vb* : to sail a ship closer to the wind — **luff** *n*

¹**lug** \'ləg\ *vb* **lugged; lug·ging 1**

: DRAG, PULL   **2 :** to carry laboriously

**²lug** *n* **:** a projecting piece (as for fastening or support)

**lug·gage** \'ləg-ij\ *n* **1 :** BAGGAGE **2 :** containers (as suitcases) for carrying personal belongings

**lu·gu·bri·ous** \lu̇-'gü-brē-əs\ *adj* **:** mournful often to an exaggerated degree — **lu·gu·bri·ous·ly** *adv* — **lu·gu·bri·ous·ness** *n*

**luke·warm** \'lük-'wȯrm\ *adj* **1 :** moderately warm **:** TEPID **2 :** not enthusiastic — **luke·warm·ly** *adv*

**¹lull** \'ləl\ *vb* **1 :** SOOTHE, CALM **2 :** to cause to relax vigilance

**²lull** *n* **1 :** a temporary calm (as during a storm) **2 :** a temporary drop in activity

**lul·la·by** \'ləl-ə-ˌbī\ *n, pl* **-bies :** a song to lull children to sleep

**lum·ba·go** \ˌləm-'bā-gō\ *n* **:** rheumatic pain in the lower back and loins

**lum·bar** \'ləm-bər, -ˌbär\ *adj* **:** of, relating to, or constituting the loins or the vertebrae between the thoracic vertebrae and sacrum (∼ region)

**¹lum·ber** \'ləm-bər\ *vb* **lum·bered; lum·ber·ing** \-b(ə-)riŋ\ **:** to move heavily or clumsily

**²lumber** *n* **1 :** surplus or disused articles that are stored away **2 :** timber esp. when dressed for use

**³lumber** *vb* **lum·bered; lum·ber·ing** \-b(ə-)riŋ\ **:** to cut logs; *also* **:** to saw logs into lumber — **lum·ber·man** \-mən\ *n*

**lum·ber·jack** \-ˌjak\ *n* **:** LOGGER

**lum·ber·yard** \-ˌyärd\ *n* **:** a place where lumber is kept for sale

**lu·mi·nary** \'lü-mə-ˌner-ē\ *n, pl* **-nar·ies 1 :** a very famous person **2 :** a source of light; *esp* **:** a celestial body

**lu·mi·nes·cence** \-'nes-ᵊns\ *n* **:** the low-temperature emission of light (as by a chemical or physiological process) — **lu·mi·nes·cent** \-ᵊnt\ *adj*

**lu·mi·nous** \'lü-mə-nəs\ *adj* **1 :** emitting light; *also* **:** LIGHTED **2 :** CLEAR, INTELLIGIBLE — **lu·mi·nance** \-nəns\ *n* — **lu·mi·nos·i·ty** \ˌlü-mə-'näs-ət-ē\ *n* — **lu·mi·nous·ly** *adv*

**lum·mox** \'ləm-əks\ *n* **:** a clumsy person

**¹lump** \'ləmp\ *n* **1 :** a piece or mass of irregular shape **2 :** AGGREGATE, TOTALITY **3 :** a usu. abnormal swelling — **lump·ish** *adj* — **lumpy** *adj*

**²lump** *vb* **1 :** to heap together in a lump **2 :** to form into lumps

**³lump** *adj* **:** not divided into parts ⟨a ∼ sum⟩

**lu·na·cy** \'lü-nə-sē\ *n, pl* **-cies 1 :** INSANITY **2 :** extreme folly

**lu·nar** \'lü-nər\ *adj* **:** of or relating to the moon

**lu·na·tic** \'lü-nə-ˌtik\ *adj* [ME *lunatik*, fr. LL *lunaticus*, fr. L *luna:* fr. the belief that lunacy fluctuated with the phases of the moon] **1 :** INSANE; *also* **:** used for insane persons **2 :** extremely foolish — **lunatic** *n*

**lunatic fringe** *n* **:** the members of a political or social movement espousing extreme, eccentric, or fanatical views

**¹lunch** \'lənch\ *n* **1 :** a light meal usu. eaten in the middle of the day **2 :** the food prepared for a lunch

**²lunch** *vb* **:** to eat lunch

**lun·cheon** \'lən-chən\ *n* **:** a usu. formal lunch

**lun·cheon·ette** \ˌlən-chə-'net\ *n* **:** a place where light lunches are sold

**lunch·room** \'lənch-ˌrüm, -ˌru̇m\ *n* **1 :** LUNCHEONETTE **2 :** a room (as in a school) where lunches are sold and eaten or lunches brought from home may be eaten

**lu·nette** \lü-'net\ *n* **:** something shaped like a crescent or half-moon

**lung** \'ləŋ\ *n* **1 :** one of the usu. paired baglike breathing organs in the chest of an air-breathing vertebrate **2 :** a mechanical device for introducing fresh air into and removing stale air from the lungs — **lunged** \'ləŋd\ *adj*

**lunge** \'lənj\ *n* **1 :** a sudden thrust or pass (as with a sword) **2 :** a sudden forward stride or leap — **lunge** *vb*

**lu·pine** \'lü-pən\ *n* **:** a leguminous plant with long upright clusters of pealike flowers

**lurch** \'lərch\ *n* **:** a sudden swaying or tipping movement — **lurch** *vb*

**¹lure** \'lu̇r\ *n* **1 :** ENTICEMENT; *also* **:** APPEAL **2 :** an artificial bait for catching fish

**²lure** *vb* **lured; lur·ing :** to draw on with a promise of pleasure or gain

**lu·rid** \'lu̇r-əd\ *adj* **1 :** LIVID **2 :** shining with the red glow of fire as seen through smoke or cloud **3 :** GRUESOME; *also* **:** SENSATIONAL   **syn** ghastly, grisly — **lu·rid·ly** *adv*

**lurk** \'lərk\ *vb* **1 :** to move furtively **:** SNEAK **2 :** to lie concealed

**lus·cious** \'ləsh-əs\ *adj* **1 :** having a pleasingly sweet taste or smell **2 :** sensually appealing — **lus·cious·ly** *adv* — **lus·cious·ness** *n*

**¹lush** \'ləsh\ *adj* **:** having or covered with abundant growth ⟨∼ pastures⟩

**²lush** *n* **:** an habitual heavy drinker

**lust** \'ləst\ *n* **1 :** sexual desire often to an intense or unrestrained degree **2 :** an intense longing — **lust** *vb* — **lust·ful** *adj*

**luster** *or* **lustre** \'ləs-tər\ *n* **1 :** a shine or sheen esp. from reflected light **2 :** BRIGHTNESS, GLITTER **3 :** GLORY, SPLENDOR — **lus·ter·less** *adj* — **lus·trous** \-trəs\ *adj*

**lus·tral** \'ləs-trəl\ *adj* **:** PURIFICATORY

**lusty** \'ləs-tē\ *adj* **lust·i·er; -est :** full of vitality **:** ROBUST — **lust·i·ly** \'ləs-tə-lē\ *adv* — **lust·i·ness** \-tē-nəs\ *n*

**lute** \'lüt\ *n* **:** a stringed musical instrument with a large pear-shaped body and a fretted fingerboard — **lu·te·nist** *or* **lu·ta·nist** \'lüt-ᵊn-əst\ *n*

**lu·te·tium** *also* **lu·te·cium** \lü-'tē-sh(ē-)əm\ *n* **:** a rare metallic chemical element

**Lu·ther·an** \'lü-th(ə-)rən\ *n* **:** a member of a Protestant denomination adhering to the doctrines of Martin Luther — **Lu·ther·an·ism** \-ˌiz-əm\ *n*

**lux·u·ri·ant** \lǝg-'zhŭr-ē-ǝnt, ˌlǝk-'shŭr-\ *adj* **1** : yielding or growing abundantly : LUSH, PRODUCTIVE **2** : exuberantly rich and varied; *also* : FLORID — **lux·u·ri·ance** \-ē-ǝns\ *n* — **lux·u·ri·ant·ly** *adv*

**lux·u·ri·ate** \-ē-ˌāt\ *vb* **-at·ed; -at·ing 1** : to grow profusely **2** : REVEL

**lux·u·ry** \'lǝksh-(ǝ-)rē 'lǝgzh-\ *n, pl* **-ries 1** : great ease or comfort **2** : something desirable but costly or hard to get **3** : something adding to pleasure or comfort but not absolutely necessary — **lux·u·ri·ous** \ˌlǝg-'zhŭr-ē-ǝs, ˌlǝk-'shŭr-\ *adj* — **lux·u·ri·ous·ly** *adv*

**lv** *abbr* leave

**¹-ly** \lē\ *adj suffix* **1** : like in appearance, manner, or nature ⟨queen*ly*⟩ **2** : characterized by regular recurrence in (specified) units of time • every ⟨hour*ly*⟩

**²-ly** \lē\ (*corresponding adjectives may end in əl, as "double"*); **-ical·ly** *is* i-k-(ǝ-)lē\ *adv suffix* **1** : in a (specified) manner ⟨slow*ly*⟩ **2** : from a (specified) point of view ⟨grammatical*ly*⟩

**ly·ce·um** \lī-'sē-ǝm, 'lī-sē-\ *n* **1** : a hall for public lectures **2** : an association providing public lectures, concerts, and entertainments

**lye** \'lī\ *n* : a white crystalline corrosive alkaline substance used in making rayon and soap

**ly·ing** \'lī-iŋ\ *adj* : UNTRUTHFUL, FALSE

**ly·ing-in** \ˌlī-iŋ-'in\ *n, pl* **lyings-in** *or* **lying-ins** : the state attending and consequent to childbirth : CONFINEMENT

**lymph** \'limf\ *n* [L *lympha,* water goddess, water, fr. Gk *nymphē* nymph] : a pale liquid consisting chiefly of blood plasma and white blood cells, circulating in thin-walled tubes (**lymphatic vessels**), and bathing the body tissues — **lym·phat·ic** \lim-'fat-ik\ *adj*

**lymph node** *n* : one of the rounded masses of lymphoid tissue surrounded by a capsule

**lym·phoid** \'lim-ˌfȯid\ *adj* **1** : of, relating to, or resembling lymph **2** : of, relating to, or constituting the tissue characteristic of the lymph nodes

**lynch** \'linch\ *vb* : to put to death by mob action without legal sanction or due process of law — **lynch·er** *n*

**lynx** \'liŋks\ *n, pl* **lynx** *or* **lynx·es** : a wildcat with a short tail, long legs, and usu. tufted ears

**lyre** \'lī(ǝ)r\ *n* : a stringed musical instrument of the harp class used by the ancient Greeks

**¹lyr·ic** \'lir-ik\ *adj* **1** : suitable for singing : MELODIC **2** : expressing direct and usu. intense personal emotion

**²lyric** *n* **1** : a lyric poem **2** *pl* : the words of a popular song — **lyr·i·cal** \-i-kǝl\ *adj*

**lysergic acid di·eth·yl·am·ide** \lǝ-ˌsǝr-jik . . . ˌdī-,eth-ǝ-'lam-ˌīd, lī-, -'lam-ǝd\ *n* : LSD

**LZ** *abbr* landing zone

---

**¹m** \'em\ *n, pl* **m's** *or* **ms** \'emz\ *often cap* : the 13th letter of the English alphabet

**²m** *abbr, often cap* **1** Mach **2** male **3** married **4** masculine **5** [L *meridies*] noon **6** meter **7** mile **8** [L *mille*] thousand **9** minute **10** month **11** moon

**ma** \'mä, 'mȯ\ *n* : MOTHER

**MA** *abbr* **1** Massachusetts **2** master of arts **3** mental age

**ma'am** \'mam, *after "yes" often* ǝm\ *n* : MADAM

**ma·ca·bre** \mǝ-'käb-(rǝ), -'käb-ǝr, -'käbrᵊ\ *adj* **1** : having death as a subject **2** : GRUESOME **3** : HORRIBLE

**mac·ad·am** \mǝ-'kad-ǝm\ *n* **1** : a roadway or pavement constructed of small closely packed broken stone usu. cemented with stone dust or bituminous material **2** : the broken stone used in macadamizing — **mac·ad·am·ize** \-ˌīz\ *vb*

**ma·caque** \mǝ-'kak, -'käk\ *n* : any of several short-tailed Asiatic and East Indian monkeys

**mac·a·ro·ni** \ˌmak-ǝ-'rō-nē\ *n* **1** : a food made chiefly of wheat flour dried in the form of usu. slender tubes **2** *pl* **-nis** *or* **-nies** : FOP, DANDY

**mac·a·roon** \ˌmak-ǝ-'rün\ *n* : a small cookie made chiefly of egg whites, sugar, and ground almonds or coconut

**ma·caw** \mǝ-'kȯ\ *n* : a large long-tailed parrot of Central and So. America

**Mc·Coy** \mǝ-'kȯi\ *n* [alter. of *Mackay* (in the phrase *the real Mackay* the true chief of the Mackay clan, a position often disputed)] : something that is neither imitation nor substitute ⟨the real ∼⟩

**¹mace** \'mās\ *n* **1** : a heavy often spiked club used as a weapon esp. in the Middle Ages **2** : an ornamental staff carried as a symbol of authority esp. before a public official

**²mace** *n* : a spice from the fibrous coating of the nutmeg

**mac·er·ate** \'mas-ǝ-ˌrāt\ *vb* **-at·ed; -at·ing 1** : to cause to waste away **2** : to soften by steeping or soaking so as to separate the parts — **mac·er·a·tion** \ˌmas-ǝ-'rā-shǝn\ *n*

**mach** *abbr* machine; machinery; machinist

**Mach** \'mäk\ *n* : MACH NUMBER

**ma·che·te** \mǝ-'shet-ē\ *n* : a large heavy knife used esp. in So. America and the West Indies for cutting sugarcane and underbrush

**ma·chic·o·la·tion** \mǝ-ˌchik-ǝ-'lā-shǝn\ *n* : an opening between the corbels of a projecting parapet (as of a medieval castle) or in the floor of a gallery or roof of a portal for discharging missiles upon assailants below

**mach·i·na·tion** \ˌmak-ǝ-'nā-shǝn, ˌmash-ǝ-\ *n* **1** : an act of planning esp. to do harm **2** : PLOT — **mach·i·nate** \'mak-ǝ-ˌnāt, 'mash-\ *vb*

¹**ma·chine** \mə 'shēn\ n 1 : CONVEY-
ANCE, VEHICLE; esp : AUTOMOBILE 2 : a
combination of mechanical parts that
transmit forces, motion, and energy one
to another to some desired end (as for
sewing, printing, or hoisting) 3 : an
instrument (as a pulley or lever) for
transmitting or modifying force or
motion 4 : an electrical, electronic, or
mechanical device for performing a task
⟨a calculating ∼⟩ 5 : a highly organized political group under the leadership of a boss and small clique

²**machine** vb ma·chined; ma·chin-
ing : to shape or finish by machine-
operated tools — **ma·chin·able**
\-'shē-nə-bəl\ adj

**machine gun** n : an automatic gun
using small-arms ammunition for rapid
continuous firing — **machine-gun**
vb — **machine gunner** /

**ma·chin·ery** \mə-'shēn-(ə-)rē\ n, pl
-er·ies 1 : MACHINES; also : the
working parts of a machine 2 : the
means by which something is done or
kept going

**ma·chin·ist** \mə-'shē-nəst\ n : a person who makes or works on machines
and engines

**ma·chis·mo** \mä-'chēz-(,)mō, -'chiz-\
n : a strong or exaggerated pride in
one's masculinity

**Mach number** \'mäk-\ n : a number
representing the ratio of the speed of a
body to the speed of sound in the surrounding atmosphere ⟨a Mach number
of 2 indicates a speed that is twice the
speed of sound⟩

**mack·er·el** \'mak-(ə-)rəl\ n, pl
**mackerel** or **mackerels** : a No.
Atlantic food fish greenish above and
silvery below

**mack·i·naw** \'mak-ə-,nȯ\ n : a short
heavy plaid coat

**mack·in·tosh** also **mac·in·tosh**
\'mak-ən-,täsh\ n 1 chiefly Brit : RAIN-
COAT 2 : a lightweight waterproof
fabric

**mac·ra·me** \,mak-rə-'mā\ n : a coarse
lace or fringe made by knotting threads
or cords in a geometrical pattern

**mac·ro** \'mak-(,)rō\ adj : very large;
also : involving large quantities or being
on a large scale

**mac·ro·bi·ot·ic** \,mak-rō-bī-'ät-ik,
-bē-\ adj : relating to or being a very
restricted diet (as one containing chiefly
whole grains) considered by its advocates to promote health

**mac·ro·cosm** \'mak-rə-,käz-əm\ n
: the great world : UNIVERSE

**ma·cron** \'mäk-,rän, 'mak-\ n : a
mark ¯ placed over a vowel (as in
\'māk\) to show that the vowel is long

**mac·ro·scop·ic** \,mak-rə-'skäp-ik\
also **mac·ro·scop·i·cal** \-i-kəl\ adj
: visible to the naked eye — **mac·ro·
scop·i·cal·ly** \-i-k(ə-)lē\ adv

**mad** \'mad\ adj **mad·der; mad·dest**
1 : disordered in mind : INSANE 2
: being rash and foolish 3 : FURIOUS,
ENRAGED 4 : FRANTIC 5 : carried
away by enthusiasm 6 : marked by
wild gaiety and merriment 7 : RABID

— **mad·ly** adv — **mad·ness** n

**mad·am** \'mad-əm\ n 1 pl **mesdames** \mā-'däm\ — used as a form
of polite address to a woman 2 pl
**madams** : the female head of a house
of prostitution

**ma·dame** \mə-'dam, before a surname
also ,mad-əm\ n, pl **mes·dames**
\mā-'däm\ : MISTRESS — used as a
title for a woman not of English-
speaking nationality

**mad·cap** \'mad-,kap\ adj : WILD,
RECKLESS — **madcap** n

**mad·den** \'mad-ᵊn\ vb **mad·dened;
mad·den·ing** \'mad-(ᵊ-)niŋ\ : to
make mad — **mad·den·ing·ly** adv

**mad·der** \'mad-ər\ n : a Eurasian
plant with yellow flowers and fleshy
red roots; also : its root or a dye prepared from it

**mad·ding** \'mad-iŋ\ adj 1 : acting as
if mad : FRENZIED ⟨the ∼ crowd⟩
2 : MADDENING

**made** past of MAKE

**Ma·dei·ra** \mə-'dir-ə\ n : an amber-
colored dessert wine

**ma·de·moi·selle** \,mad-(ə-)m(w)ə-
'zel, mam-'zel\ n, pl **ma·de·moi·
selles** \-'zelz\ or **mes·de·moi·
selles** \,mād-(ə-)m(w)ə- zel\ : an unmarried girl or woman — used as a title
for a woman not of English-speaking
and esp. of French nationality

**made-up** \'mād-'əp\ adj 1 : marked
by the use of makeup ⟨∼ eyelids⟩
2 : fancifully conceived or falsely devised ⟨a ∼ story⟩

**mad·house** \'mad-,haús\ n 1 : a
place for the detention and care of the
insane 2 : a place of great uproar or
confusion

**mad·man** \'mad-,man, -mən\ n
: LUNATIC — **mad·wom·an** \-,wúm-
ən\ n

**ma·dras** \'mad-rəs; mə-'dras, -'dräs\
n : a fine usu. corded or striped cotton
fabric

**mad·ri·gal** \'mad-ri-gəl\ n [It madri-
gale, fr. ML matricale, fr. (assumed)
matricalis simple, fr. LL, of the womb,
fr. L matrix womb] : a somewhat
elaborate part-song esp. of the 16th
century; also : a love poem suitable for
a musical setting

**mael·strom** \'māl-strəm\ n [obs. D
(now maalstroom), fr. malen to grind +
strom stream] : a violent whirlpool

**mae·nad** \'mē-,nad\ n 1 : a woman
participating in bacchanalian rites
2 : an unnaturally excited or distraught
woman

**mae·stro** \'mī-strō\ n, pl **maestros** or
**mae·stri** \-,strē\ : a master in an art;
esp : an eminent composer, conductor,
or teacher of music

**Ma·fia** \'mäf-ē-ə\ n 1 : a secret terror-
ist society in Sicily 2 : a secret criminal
organization

**ma·fi·o·so** \,mäf-ē-'ō-(,)sō\ n, pl -si
\-(,)sē,\ : a member of the Mafia

¹**mag** abbr 1 magnetism 2 magneto
3 magnitude

²**mag** \'mag\ n, slang : MAGAZINE

**mag·a·zine** \'mag-ə-,zēn\ n 1 : a

storehouse esp. for military supplies
**2 :** a place for keeping gunpowder in a
fort or ship **3 :** a publication usu. containing stories, articles, or poems and
issued periodically **4 :** a container in a
gun for holding cartridges; *also* **:** a
chamber (as on a camera) for film

**mag·da·len** \\'mag-də-lən\\ *or* **mag·da·lene** \\-,lēn\\ *n, often cap* **:** a reformed prostitute

**ma·gen·ta** \\mə-'jent-ə\\ *n* **:** a deep purplish red

**mag·got** \\'mag-ət\\ *n* **:** the legless wormlike larva of a two-winged fly — **mag·goty** *adj*

**ma·gi** \\'mā-,jī\\ *n pl, often cap* **:** the three wise men from the East who paid homage to the infant Jesus

**mag·ic** \\'maj-ik\\ *n* **1 :** the art of persons who claim to be able to do things by the help of supernatural powers or by their own knowledge of nature's secrets **2 :** an extraordinary power or influence seemingly from a supernatural force **3 :** SLEIGHT OF HAND — **magic** *or* **mag·i·cal** \\-i-kəl\\ *adj* — **mag·i·cal·ly** \\-i·k(ə-)lē\\ *adv*

**ma·gi·cian** \\mə-'jish-ən\\ *n* **:** one skilled in magic

**mag·is·te·ri·al** \\,maj-ə-'stir-ē-əl\\ *adj* **1 :** AUTHORITATIVE **2 :** of or relating to a magistrate or his office or duties

**mag·is·tral** \\'maj-ə-strəl\\ *adj* **:** AUTHORITATIVE

**mag·is·trate** \\'maj-ə-,strāt\\ *n* **:** an official entrusted with administration of the laws — **mag·is·tra·cy** \\-strə-sē\\ *n*

**mag·ma** \\'mag-mə\\ *n* **:** molten rock material within the earth from which an igneous rock results by cooling — **mag·mat·ic** \\mag-'mat-ik\\ *adj*

**mag·nan·i·mous** \\mag-'nan-ə-məs\\ *adj* **1 :** showing or suggesting a lofty and courageous spirit **2 :** NOBLE, GENEROUS — **mag·na·nim·i·ty** \\,mag-nə-'nim-ət-ē\\ *n* — **mag·nan·i·mous·ly** *adv* — **mag·nan·i·mous·ness** *n*

**mag·nate** \\'mag-,nāt\\ *n* **:** a person of rank, influence, or distinction

**mag·ne·sia** \\mag-'nē-shə, -zhə\\ *n* [NL, fr. *magnes carneus*, a white earth, lit., flesh magnet] **:** a light white substance that is an oxide of magnesium and is used as a laxative

**mag·ne·sium** \\mag-'nē-zē-əm, -zhəm\\ *n* **:** a silver-white light and easily worked metallic chemical element

**mag·net** \\'mag-nət\\ *n* **1 :** LODESTONE **2 :** a body having the property of attracting iron **3 :** something that attracts

**mag·net·ic** \\mag-'net-ik\\ *adj* **1 :** of or relating to a magnet or magnetism **2 :** magnetized or capable of being magnetized **3 :** having an unusual ability to attract ⟨a ~ leader⟩ — **mag·net·i·cal·ly** \\-i·k(ə-)lē\\ *adv*

**magnetic north** *n* **:** the northerly direction in the earth's magnetic field indicated by the north-seeking pole of the horizontal magnetic needle

**magnetic recording** *n* **:** the process of recording sound, data, or a television program by producing varying local

magnetization of a moving tape, wire, or disc — **magnetic recorder** *n*

**magnetic tape** *n* **:** a ribbon of thin material coated for use in magnetic recording

**mag·ne·tism** \\'mag-nə-,tiz-əm\\ *n* **1 :** the power to attract as possessed by a magnet **2 :** the property of a substance (as iron) that allows it to be magnetized **3 :** an ability to attract

**mag·ne·tite** \\'mag-nə-,tīt\\ *n* **:** a black mineral that is an important iron ore

**mag·ne·tize** \\'mag-nə-,tīz\\ *vb* **-tized; -tiz·ing 1 :** to attract like a magnet **:** CHARM **2 :** to communicate magnetic properties to — **mag·ne·tiz·able** *adj* — **mag·ne·ti·za·tion** \\,mag-nət-ə-'zā-shən\\ *n* — **mag·ne·tiz·er** *n*

**mag·ne·to** \\mag-'nēt-ō\\ *n, pl* **-tos :** a generator used to generate electricity for ignition in an internal-combustion engine

**mag·ne·tom·e·ter** \\,mag-nə-'täm-ət-ər\\ *n* **:** an instrument for measuring magnetic intensity esp. of the earth's magnetic field

**mag·ne·to·sphere** \\mag-'nēt-ə-,sfiər, -'net-\\ *n* **:** a region of the upper atmosphere that extends out for thousands of miles and is dominated by the earth's magnetic field so that charged particles are trapped in it — **mag·ne·to·spher·ic** \\-,nēt-ə-'sfiər-ik, -'sfer-\\ *adj*

**mag·nif·i·cent** \\mag-'nif-ə-sənt\\ *adj* **1 :** characterized by grandeur or beauty **:** SPLENDID **2 :** EXALTED, NOBLE **syn** imposing, stately, noble — **mag·nif·i·cence** \\-səns\\ *n* — **mag·nif·i·cent·ly** *adv*

**mag·nif·i·co** \\mag-'nif-i-,kō\\ *n, pl* **-coes** *or* **-cos 1 :** a nobleman of Venice **2 :** a person of high position or distinguished appearance

**mag·ni·fy** \\'mag-nə-,fī\\ *vb* **-fied; -fy·ing 1 :** EXTOL, LAUD; *also* **:** to cause to be held in greater esteem **2 :** INTENSIFY; *also* **:** EXAGGERATE **3 :** to enlarge in fact or in appearance ⟨a microscope *magnifies* an object⟩ — **mag·ni·fi·ca·tion** \\,mag-nə-fə-'kā-shən\\ *n* — **mag·ni·fi·er** \\'mag-nə-,fī-(-ə)r\\ *n*

**mag·nil·o·quent** \\mag-'nil-ə-kwənt\\ *adj* **:** characterized by an exalted and often bombastic style or manner — **mag·nil·o·quence** \\-kwəns\\ *n*

**mag·ni·tude** \\'mag-nə-,t(y)üd\\ *n* **1 :** greatness of size or extent **2 :** SIZE **3 :** QUANTITY; *also* **:** volume of sound **4 :** a number representing the relative brightness of a celestial body

**mag·no·lia** \\mag-'nōl-yə\\ *n* **:** any of several spring-flowering shrubs and trees with large often fragrant flowers

**mag·num opus** \\,mag-nəm-'ō-pəs\\ *n* **:** the greatest achievement of an artist or writer

**mag·pie** \\'mag-,pī\\ *n* **:** a long-tailed black-and-white bird related to the jays

**Mag·yar** \\'mag-,yär, 'måg-; 'mäj-,är\\ *n* **:** a member of the dominant people of Hungary — **Magyar** *adj*

**ma·ha·ra·ja** *or* **ma·ha·ra·jah** \\,mä-hə-'räj-ə\ *n* **:** a Hindu prince ranking above a raja

**ma·ha·ra·nee** *or* **ma·ha·ra·nee** \-'rän-ē\ *n* **:** the wife of a maharaja; *also* **:** a Hindu princess ranking above a rani

**ma·ha·ri·shi** \mə-'här-ə-shē\ **:** a Hindu teacher of mystical knowledge

**ma·hat·ma** \mə-'hät-mə, -'hat-\ *n* [Skt *mahātman*, fr. *mahātman* great-souled, fr. *mahat* great + *ātman* soul] **:** a person revered for high-mindedness, wisdom, and selflessness

**Ma·hi·can** \mə-'hē-kən\ *n, pl* **Mahican** *or* **Mahicans :** a member of an Indian people of the upper Hudson river valley

**ma·hog·a·ny** \mə-'häg-ə-nē\ *n, pl* **-nies :** any of various tropical trees with reddish wood used in furniture; *esp* **:** an American evergreen tree or its durable lustrous reddish brown wood

**ma·hout** \mə-'haůt\ *n* **:** a keeper and driver of an elephant

**maid** \'mād\ *n* **1 :** an unmarried girl or young woman **2 :** a female servant

¹**maid·en** \'mād-ᵊn\ *n* **:** MAID 1 — **maid·en·ly** *adj*

²**maiden** *adj* **1 :** UNMARRIED; *also* **:** VIRGIN **2 :** of, relating to, or befitting a maiden ⟨~ voyage⟩

**maid·en·hair** \-,haer\ *n* **:** a fern with delicate feathery fronds

**maid·en·head** \'mād-ᵊn-,hed\ *n* **1 :** VIRGINITY **2 :** HYMEN

**maid·en·hood** \-,hůd\ *n* **:** the condition or time of being a maiden

**maid-in-wait·ing** \,mād-ᵊn-'wāt-iŋ\ *n, pl* **maids-in-wait·ing** \,mād-zᵊn-\ **:** a young woman appointed to attend a queen or princess

**maid of honor :** a bride's principal unmarried wedding attendant

**maid·ser·vant** \'mād-,sər-vənt\ *n* **:** a female servant

¹**mail** \'māl\ *n* **1 :** the bags of postal matter conveyed under public authority from one post office to another **2 :** a nation's postal system **3 :** postal matter

²**mail** *vb* **:** to send by mail

³**mail** *n* **:** armor made of metal links or plates

**mail·box** \-,bäks\ *n* **1 :** a public box for the collection of mail **2 :** a private box for the delivery of mail

**mailed** \'māld\ *adj* **:** protected or armed with or as if with mail ⟨~ fist⟩

**mail·man** \-,man\ *n* **:** a man who delivers mail

**maim** \'mām\ *vb* **:** to mutilate, disfigure, or wound seriously **:** CRIPPLE

¹**main** \'mān\ *n* **1 :** FORCE ⟨with might and ~⟩ **2 :** MAINLAND; *also* **:** HIGH SEA **3 :** the chief part **4 :** a principal pipe, duct or circuit of a utility system

²**main** *adj* **1 :** CHIEF, PRINCIPAL **2 :** fully exerted ⟨~ force⟩ **3 :** expressing the chief predication in a complex sentence ⟨the ~ clause⟩ — **main·ly** *adv*

**main·land** \'mān-,land, -lənd\ *n* **:** a continuous body of land constituting the chief part of a country or continent

**main·line** \'mān-'līn\ *vb, slang* **:** to inject a narcotic drug into a vein

**main line** *n* **1 :** a principal highway or railroad line **2** *slang* **:** a principal vein; *also* **:** injection of a narcotic into a principal vein

**main·mast** \'mān-,mast, -məst\ *n* **:** the principal mast on a sailing ship

**main·sail** \'mān-,sāl, -səl\ *n* **:** the principal sail on the mainmast

**main·spring** \-,spriŋ\ *n* **1 :** the chief spring in a mechanism (as of a watch) **2 :** the chief motive, agent, or cause

**main·stay** \-,stā\ *n* **1 :** a stay extending forward from the head of the mainmast to the foot of the foremast **2 :** a chief support

**main·stream** \-,strēm\ *n* **:** a prevailing current or direction of activity or influence — **mainstream** *adj*

**main·tain** \mān-'tān\ *vb* [ME *mainteinen*, fr. OF *maintenir*, fr. ML *manutenēre*, fr. L *manu tenēre* to hold in the hand] **1 :** to keep in an existing state (as of repair) **2 :** to sustain against opposition or danger **3 :** to continue in **:** carry on **4 :** to provide for **:** SUPPORT **5 :** ASSERT — **main·tain·abil·i·ty** \-,tā-nə-'bil-ət-ē\ *n* — **main·tain·able** \-'tā-nə-bəl\ *adj* — **main·te·nance** \'mānt-(ᵊ-)nəns\ *n*

**main·top** \'mān-,täp\ *n* **:** a platform about the head of the mainmast of a square-rigged ship

**mai·son·ette** \,māz-ᵊn-'et\ *n* **1 :** a small house **2 :** an apartment often on two floors

**mai·tre d'hô·tel** \,mā-trə-dō-'tel, ,me-\ *n, pl* **maîtres d'hôtel** \*same*\ [F, lit., master of house] **1 :** MAJORDOMO **2 :** the head of a dining-room staff (as of a hotel)

**maize** \'māz\ *n* **:** INDIAN CORN

**Maj** *abbr* major

**maj·es·ty** \'maj-ə-stē\ *n, pl* **-ties 1 :** sovereign power, authority, or dignity; *also* **:** the person of a sovereign — used as a title **2 :** GRANDEUR, SPLENDOR — **ma·jes·tic** \mə-'jes-tik\ *or* **ma·jes·ti·cal** \-ti-kəl\ *adj* — **ma·jes·ti·cal·ly** \-ti-k(ə-)lē\ *adv*

**ma·jol·i·ca** \mə-'jäl-i-kə\ *also* **ma·iol·i·ca** \-'yäl-\ *n* **:** any of several faiences; *esp* **:** an Italian tin-glazed pottery

¹**ma·jor** \'mā-jər\ *adj* **1 :** greater in number, extent, or importance ⟨a ~ poet⟩ **2 :** notable or conspicuous in effect or scope ⟨a ~ improvement⟩ **3 :** SERIOUS ⟨a ~ illness⟩ **4 :** having half steps between the third and fourth and the seventh and eighth degrees ⟨~ scale⟩; *also* **:** based on a major scale ⟨~ key⟩ ⟨~ chord⟩

²**major** *n* **1 :** a commissioned officer (as in the army) ranking next below a lieutenant colonel **2 :** a subject of academic study chosen as a field of specialization; *also* **:** a student specializing in such a field

³**major** *vb* **ma·jored; ma·jor·ing** \'māj-(ə-)riŋ\ **:** to pursue an academic major

**ma·jor·do·mo** \,mā-jər-'dō-mō\ *n, pl* **-mos** [Sp *mayordomo* or obs. It *maiordomo*, fr. ML *major domus*, lit.,

chief of the house} **1 : a head steward
2 :** BUTLER

**majorette** *n* **:** DRUM MAJORETTE

**major general** *n* **:** a commissioned officer (as in the army) ranking next below a lieutenant general

**ma·jor·i·ty** \mə-'jȯr-ət-ē\ *n, pl* **-ties 1 :** the age at which full civil rights are accorded; *also* **:** the status of one who has attained this age **2 :** a number greater than half of a total; *also* **:** the excess of this greater number over the remainder **3 :** the military rank of a major

**major–medical** *adj* **:** of, relating to, or being a form of insurance designed to pay all or part of the medical bills of major illnesses usu. after deduction of a fixed initial sum

**ma·jus·cule** \'maj-əs-ˌkyül, mə-'jəs-\ *n* **:** a large letter (as a capital)

**¹make** \'māk\ *vb* **made** \'mād\; **mak·ing 1 :** to cause to exist, occur, or appear; *also* **:** DESTINE ⟨was *made* to be an actor⟩ **2 :** FASHION ⟨~ a dress⟩; *also* **:** COMPOSE **3 :** to formulate in the mind ⟨~ plans⟩ **4 :** CONSTITUTE ⟨house *made* of stone⟩ **5 :** to compute to be **6 :** to set in order **:** PREPARE ⟨~ a bed⟩ **7 :** APPOINT **8 :** ENACT; *also* **:** EXECUTE ⟨~ a will⟩ **9 :** CONCLUDE ⟨didn't know what to ~ of it⟩ **10 :** to carry out **:** PERFORM ⟨~ a speech⟩ **11 :** COMPEL **12 :** to assure the success of ⟨anyone he likes is *made*⟩ **13 :** to amount to in significance ⟨~s no difference⟩ **14 :** to be capable of developing or being fashioned into **15 :** REACH, ATTAIN; *also* **:** GAIN **16 :** to start out **:** GO **17 :** to have weight or effect ⟨courtesy ~s for safer driving⟩ **syn** form, shape, fabricate, manufacture — **mak·er** *n* — **make believe :** PRETEND — **make do :** to manage with the means at hand — **make fun of :** RIDICULE, MOCK — **make good 1 :** INDEMNIFY ⟨*make good* the loss⟩; *also* **:** FULFILL ⟨*make good* his promise⟩ **2 :** SUCCEED — **make way 1 :** to open a passage for someone or something **2 :** to make progress

**²make** *n* **1 :** the manner or style of construction; *also* **:** BRAND **3 2 :** MAKE-UP **3 :** the action or process of manufacturing — **on the make :** in search of wealth, social status, or sexual adventure

**¹make–be·lieve** \'māk-bə-ˌlēv\ *n* **:** a pretending to believe **:** PRETENSE

**²make–believe** *adj* **:** IMAGINED, PRETENDED

**make–do** \-ˌdü\ *adj* **:** MAKESHIFT

**make out** *vb* **1 :** to draw up in writing ⟨*make out* a shopping list⟩ **2 :** to find or grasp the meaning of ⟨how do you *make* that out⟩ **3 :** to pretend to be true **4 :** DISCERN ⟨*make out* a form in the fog⟩ **5 :** to get along **:** FARE ⟨*make out* well in business⟩ **6 :** to engage in amorous kissing and caressing

**make over** *vb* **:** REMAKE, REMODEL

**make·shift** \'māk-ˌshift\ *n* **:** a temporary expedient — **makeshift** *adj*

**make–up** \-ˌəp\ *n* **1 :** the way in which something is put together; *also* **:** physical, mental, and moral constitution **2 :** cosmetics esp. for the face; *also* **:** materials (as wigs and cosmetics) used in costuming (as for a play)

**make up** \(')māk-'əp\ *vb* **1 :** INVENT, IMPROVISE **2 :** SETTLE ⟨*made up* his mind⟩ **3 :** to put on makeup **4 :** to become reconciled **5 :** to compensate for a deficiency

**make–work** \'māk-ˌwərk\ *n* **:** assigned busywork

**mak·ings** \'mā-kiŋs\ *n pl* **:** the material from which something is made

**makuta** *pl of* ¹IKUTA

**Mal** *abbr* Malachi

**mal·a·chite** \'mal-ə-ˌkīt\ *n* **:** a mineral that is a green carbonate of copper used for making ornamental objects

**mal·adapt·ed** \ˌmal-ə-'dap-təd \ *adj* **:** poorly suited to a particular use, purpose, or situation

**mal·ad·just·ed** \ˌmal-ə-'jəs-təd\ *adj* **:** poorly or inadequately adjusted (as to one's environment) — **mal·ad·just·ment** \-'jəs(t)-mənt\ *n*

**mal·ad·min·is·ter** \ˌmal-əd-'min-ə-stər\ *vb* **:** to administer badly

**mal·adroit** \ˌmal-ə-'drȯit\ *adj* **:** not adroit **:** INEPT

**mal·a·dy** \'mal-əd-ē\ *n, pl* **-dies :** a disease or disorder of body or mind

**mal·aise** \mə-'lāz, ma-\ *n* **:** a sense of physical ill-being

**mal·a·mute** \'mal-ə-ˌmyüt\ *n* **:** a dog often used to draw sleds esp. in northern No. America

**mal·apert** \ˌmal-ə-'pərt\ *adj* **:** impudently bold **:** SAUCY

**mal·a·prop·ism** \'mal-ə-ˌpräp-ˌiz-əm\ *n* **:** a usu. humorous misuse of a word

**mal·ap·ro·pos** \ˌmal-ˌap-rə-'pō, malˈap-rə-ˌpō\ *adv* **:** in an inappropriate or inopportune way — **malapropos** *adj*

**ma·lar·ia** \mə-'ler-ē-ə\ *n* [It, fr. *mala aria* bad air] **:** a disease marked by recurring chills and fever and caused by a parasite carried by a mosquito — **ma·lar·i·al** \-əl\ *adj*

**ma·lar·key** \mə-'lär-kē\ *n* **:** insincere or foolish talk

**mal·a·thi·on** \ˌmal-ə-'thī-ən, -ˌän\ *n* **:** an insecticide with a relatively low toxicity for mammals

**Ma·la·wi·an** \mə-'lä-wē-ən\ *n* **:** a native or inhabitant of Malawi — **Malawian** *adj*

**Ma·lay** \mə-'lā, 'mā-ˌlā\ *n* **1 :** a member of a people of the Malay peninsula and archipelago **2 :** the language of the Malays — **Malay** *adj* — **Ma·lay·an** \mə-'lā-ən, 'mā-ˌlā-\ *n or adj*

**Ma·lay·sian** \mə-'lā-zhən, -shən\ *n* **:** a native or inhabitant of Malaysia — **Malaysian** *adj*

**mal·con·tent** \ˌmal-kən-'tent\ *adj* **:** marked by a dissatisfaction with the existing state of affairs **:** DISCONTENTED — **malcontent** *n*

**mal de mer** \ˌmal-də-'meər\ *n* **:** SEA-SICKNESS

**¹male** \'māl\ *adj* **1 :** of, relating to, or being the sex that begets young; *also*

: STAMINATE **2** : MASCULINE — **male·ness** *n*

²**male** *n* : a male individual

**male·dic·tion** \,mal-ə-'dik-shən\ *n* : CURSE, EXECRATION

**male·fac·tor** \'mal-ə-,fak-tər\ *n* : EVILDOER; *esp* : one who commits an offense against the law — **mal·e·fac·tion** \,mal-ə-'fak-shən\ *n*

**ma·lef·ic** \mə-'lef-ik\ *adj* **1** : BALEFUL **2** : MALICIOUS

**ma·lef·i·cent** \-ə-sənt\ *adj* : working or productive of harm or evil — **ma·lef·i·cence** \-səns\ *n*

**ma·lev·o·lent** \mə-'lev-ə-lənt\ *adj* : having, showing, or arising from ill will, spite, or hatred **syn** malignant, malign, malicious, spiteful — **ma·lev·o·lence** \-ləns\ *n*

**mal·fea·sance** \mal-'fēz-ᵊns\ *n* : wrongful conduct esp. by a public official

**mal·for·ma·tion** \,mal-fòr-'mā-shən\ *n* : an irregular or faulty formation or structure — **mal·formed** \mal-'fòrmd\ *adj*

**mal·func·tion** \mal-'fəŋk-shən\ *vb* : to fail to operate in the normal or usual manner — **malfunction** *n*

**Ma·li·an** \'mäl-ē-ən\ *n* : a native or inhabitant of Mali — **Malian** *adj*

**mal·ice** \'mal-əs\ *n* : ILL WILL — **ma·li·cious** \mə-'lish-əs\ *adj* — **ma·li·cious·ly** *adv*

¹**ma·lign** \mə-'līn\ *adj* **1** : evil in nature, influence, or effect ⟨hindered by ∼ influences⟩; *also* : MALIGNANT **2** **2** : moved by ill will toward others

²**malign** *vb* : to speak evil of : DEFAME

**ma·lig·nant** \mə-'lig-nənt\ *adj* **1** : INJURIOUS, MALIGN **2** : tending or likely to cause death : VIRULENT — **ma·lig·nan·cy** \-nən-sē\ *n* — **ma·lig·nant·ly** *adv* — **ma·lig·ni·ty** \-nət-ē\ *n*

**ma·lin·ger** \mə-'liŋ-gər\ *vb* **ma·lin·gered; ma·lin·ger·ing** \-g(ə-)riŋ\ [F *malingre* sickly] : to pretend illness so as to avoid duty — **ma·lin·ger·er** *n*

**mal·i·son** \'mal-ə-sən, -zən\ *n* : CURSE, EXECRATION

**mall** \'mòl, 'mal\ *n* **1** : a shaded area designed esp. as a promenade **2** : a usu. paved or grassy strip esp. between two roadways **3** : an open or covered concourse providing access to rows of shops; *also* : a group of shops with such a concourse and a parking area

**mal·lard** \'mal-ərd\ *n, pl* **mallard** or **mallards** : a common wild duck that is the ancestor of domestic ducks

**mal·lea·ble** \'mal-ē-ə-bəl\ *adj* **1** : capable of being extended or shaped by beating with a hammer or by the pressure of rollers **2** : ADAPTABLE, PLIABLE **syn** plastic, pliant, ductile — **mal·le·a·bil·i·ty** \,mal-ē-ə-'bil-ət-ē\ *n*

**mal·let** \'mal-ət\ *n* **1** : a tool with a large head for driving another tool or for striking a surface without marring it **2** : a hammerlike implement for striking a ball (as in polo or croquet)

**mal·le·us** \'mal-ē-əs\ *n, pl* **mal·lei** \-ē-,ī, -ē-,ē\ : the outermost of the three small bones of the mammalian ear

**mal·low** \'mal-ō\ *n* : any of several tall herbs with lobed leaves and 5-petaled white, yellow, rose, or purplish flowers

**malm·sey** \'mä(l)m-zē\ *n, often cap* : the sweetest variety of Madeira wine

**mal·nour·ished** \mal-'nər-isht\ *adj* : poorly nourished

**mal·nu·tri·tion** \,mal-n(y)ù-'trish-ən\ *n* : faulty and esp. inadequate nutrition

**mal·oc·clu·sion** \,mal-ə-'klü-zhən\ *n* : faulty coming together of teeth in biting

**mal·odor·ous** \mal-'ōd-ə-rəs\ *adj* : ill-smelling — **mal·odor·ous·ly** *adv* — **mal·odor·ous·ness** *n*

**mal·prac·tice** \-'prak-təs\ *n* : a dereliction of professional duty or a failure of professional skill that results in injury, loss, or damage

**malt** \'mòlt\ *n* **1** : grain and esp. barley steeped in water until it has sprouted and used in brewing and distilling **2** : liquor made with malt — **malty** *adj*

**malted milk** \,mòl-təd-\ *n* : a powder prepared from dried milk and an extract from malt; *also* : a beverage of this powder in milk or other liquid

**Mal·thu·sian** \mal-'th(y)ü-zhən\ *adj* : of or relating to Malthus or to his theory that population unless checked (as by war or disease) tends to increase at a faster rate than its means of subsistence — **Malthusian** *n* — **Mal·thu·sian·ism** \-zhə-,niz-əm\ *n*

**malt·ose** \'mòl-,tōs\ *n* : a sugar formed esp. from starch by the action of enzymes and used in brewing and distilling

**mal·treat** \mal-'trēt\ *vb* : to treat cruelly or roughly : ABUSE — **mal·treat·ment** *n*

**malt·ster** \'mòlt-stər\ *n* : a maker of malt

**ma·ma** or **mam·ma** \'mäm-ə\ *n* : MOTHER

**mam·bo** \'mäm-bō\ *n, pl* **mambos** : a dance of Haitian origin related to the rumba — **mambo** *vb*

**mam·mal** \'mam-əl\ *n* : any of the group of vertebrate animals that includes man and all others which nourish their young with milk — **mam·ma·li·an** \mə-'mā-lē-ən, ma-\ *adj or n*

**mam·ma·ry** \'mam-ə-rē\ *adj* : of, relating to, or being the glands (**mammary glands**) that in female mammals secrete milk

**mam·mon** \'mam-ən\ *n, often cap* : material wealth having a debasing influence — **mam·mon·ish** *adj*

¹**mam·moth** \'mam-əth\ *n* : any of various large hairy extinct elephants

²**mammoth** *adj* : of very great size : GIGANTIC **syn** colossal, enormous, immense, vast

¹**man** \'man\ *n, pl* **men** \'men\ **1** : a human being; *esp* : an adult male **2** : MANKIND **3** : one possessing in high degree the qualities considered distinctive of manhood; *also* : HUSBAND **4** : an adult male servant or employee **5** : one of the pieces with which various

games (as chess) are played **6** *often cap* **:** white society or people

**²man** *vb* **manned; man·ning 1 :** to supply with men (~ a fleet) **2 :** FORTIFY, BRACE

**³man** *abbr* manual

**Man** *abbr* Manitoba

**man–about–town** \,man-ə-,baut-'taun\ *n, pl* **men–about–town** \,men-\ **:** a worldly and socially active man

**man·a·cle** \'man-i-kəl\ *n* **1 :** a shackle for the hand or wrist **2 :** something used as a restraint — usu. used in pl. — **manacle** *vb*

**man·age** \'man-ij\ *vb* **man·aged; man·ag·ing 1 :** HANDLE, CONTROL; *also* **:** to direct or carry on business or affairs **2 :** to make and keep submissive **3 :** to treat with care **:** HUSBAND **4 :** to achieve one's purpose **:** CONTRIVE — **man·age·abil·i·ty** \,man-ij-ə-'bil-ət-ē\ *n* — **man·age·able** \'man-ii-ə-bəl\ *adj* — **man·age·able·ness** *n* — **man·age·ably** \-blē\ *adv*

**man·age·ment** \'man-ij-mənt\ *n* **1 :** the act or art of managing **:** CONTROL **2 :** judicious use of means to accomplish an end **3 :** executive ability **4 :** the group of those who manage or direct an enterprise — **man·age·men·tal** \,man-ij-'ment-ᵊl\ *adj*

**man·ag·er** \'man-ij-ər\ *n* **:** one that manages; *esp* **:** a person who directs a team or athlete — **man·a·ge·ri·al** \,man-ə-'jir-ē-əl\ *adj*

**ma·ña·na** \mən-'yän-ə\ [Sp., lit., tomorrow, fr. earlier *cras mañana* early tomorrow, fr. *cras* tomorrow + *mañana* early] *n* **:** an indefinite time in the future

**man–at–arms** \,man-ət-'ärmz\ *n, pl* **men–at–arms** \,men-\ **:** SOLDIER; *esp* **:** one who is heavily armed and mounted

**man·ci·ple** \'man-sə-pəl\ *n* **:** a steward or purveyor esp. for a college or monastery

**man·da·mus** \man-'dā-məs\ *n* [L, we enjoin, fr. *mandare*] **:** a writ issued by a superior court commanding that a specified official act or duty be performed

**man·da·rin** \'man-də-rən\ *n* **1 :** a public official of high rank under the Chinese Empire **2** *cap* **:** the chief dialect of China **3 :** a small loose-skinned citrus fruit **:** TANGERINE

**man·date** \'man-,dāt\ *n* **1 :** an authoritative command **:** an authorization to act given to a representative **3 :** a commission granted by the League of Nations to a member nation for governing conquered territory; *also* **:** a territory so governed

**man·da·to·ry** \'man-də-,tōr-ē\ *adj* **1 :** containing or constituting a command **:** OBLIGATORY **2 :** of or relating to a League of Nations mandate

**man·di·ble** \'man-də-bəl\ *n* **1 :** JAW; *esp* **:** a lower jaw **2 :** either segment of a bird's bill — **man·dib·u·lar** \man-'dib-yə-lər\ *adj*

**man·do·lin** \,man-də-'lin, 'man-dᵊl-ən\ *n* **:** a stringed musical instrument

with a pear-shaped body and a fretted neck

**man·drag·o·ra** \man-'drag-ə-rə\ *n* **:** MANDRAKE 1

**man·drake** \'man-,drāk\ *n* **1 :** an Old World herb of the nightshade group with a large forked root superstitiously credited with human and medicinal attributes **2 :** MAYAPPLE

**man·drel** *also* **man·dril** \'man-drəl\ *n* **1 :** an axle or spindle inserted into a hole in a piece of work to support it during machining **2 :** a metal bar used as a core around which material may be cast, shaped, or molded

**man·dril** \'man-drəl\ *n* **:** a large fierce gregarious baboon of western Africa

**mane** \'mān\ *n* **:** long heavy hair growing about the neck of some mammals (as a horse) — **maned** \'mānd\ *adj*

**man–eat·er** \'man-,ēt-ər\ *n* **:** one (as a shark or cannibal) that has or is thought to have an appetite for human flesh — **man–eat·ing** \-,ēt-iŋ\ *adj*

**ma·nege** \ma-'nezh, mə-\ *n* **:** the art of horsemanship or of training horses

**ma·nes** \'män-,ās, 'mā-,nēz\ *n pl, often cap* **:** the spirits of the dead and gods of the lower world in ancient Roman belief

**ma·neu·ver** \mə-'n(y)ü-vər\ *n* [F *manœuvre*, fr. OF *maneuvre* work done by hand, fr. ML *manuopera*, fr. L *manu operare* to work by hand] **1 :** a military or naval movement; *also* **:** an armed forces training exercise — often used in pl **2 :** a procedure involving expert physical movement **3 :** an evasive movement or shift of tactics; *also* **:** an action taken to gain a tactical end — **maneuver** *vb* — **ma·neu·ver·abil·i·ty** \-,n(y)üv-(ə-)rə-'bil-ət-ē\ *n*

**man Fri·day** \'man-'frīd-ē\ *n* **:** an efficient and devoted aide or employee

**man·ful** \'man-fəl\ *adj* **:** having or showing courage and resolution — **man·ful·ly** \-ē\ *adv*

**man·ga·nese** \'maŋ-gə-,nēz, -,nēs\ *n* **:** a grayish white metallic chemical element resembling iron but not magnetic — **man·ga·ne·sian** \,maŋ-gə-'nē-zhən, -shən\ *adj*

**mange** \'mānj\ *n* **:** a contagious itchy skin disease esp. of domestic animals — **mangy** \'mān-jē\ *adj*

**man·gel–wur·zel** \'maŋ-gəl-,wər-zəl\ *n* **:** a large coarse yellow to reddish orange beet grown as food for cattle

**man·ger** \'mān-jər\ *n* **:** a trough or open box for livestock feed or fodder

**¹man·gle** \'maŋ-gəl\ *vb* **man·gled; man·gling** \-g(ə-)liŋ\ **1 :** to cut, bruise, or hack with repeated blows **2 :** to spoil or injure in making or performing — **man·gler** \-g(ə-)lər\ *n*

**²mangle** *n* **:** a machine for ironing laundry by passing it between heated rollers

**man·go** \'maŋ-gō\ *n, pl* **mangoes** *or* **mangos :** a yellowish red tropical fruit with juicy slightly acid pulp; *also* **:** an evergreen tropical tree related to the sumacs that bears this fruit

**man·grove** \'man-,grōv\ *n* **:** a tropical

maritime tree that sends out many prop roots and forms dense thickets important in coastal land building

**man·han·dle** \'man-,han-d²l\ *vb* : to handle roughly

**man·hat·tan** \man-'hat-²n\ *n, often cap* : a cocktail made of whiskey and sweet vermouth

**man·hole** \'man-,hōl\ *n* : a hole through which a man may go esp. to gain access to an underground or enclosed structure

**man·hood** \'man-,hùd\ *n* 1 : the condition of being a man and esp. an adult male 2 : manly qualities : COURAGE 3 : MEN ⟨the nation's ~⟩

**man–hour** \'man-'aù-(ə)r\ *n* : a unit of one hour's work by one man used esp. as a basis for wages and cost accounting

**man·hunt** \'man-,hənt\ *n* : an organized hunt for a person and esp. for one charged with a crime

**ma·nia** \'mā-nē-ə, -nyə\ *n* 1 : insanity esp. when marked by extreme excitement 2 : excessive enthusiasm

**ma·ni·ac** \'mā-nē-,ak\ *n* 1 : LUNATIC, MADMAN

**ma·ni·a·cal** \mə-'nī-ə-kəl\ *also* **ma·ni·ac** \'mā-nē-ak\ *adj* 1 : affected with or suggestive of madness 2 : FRANTIC

**man·ic** \'man-ik\ *adj* : affected with, relating to, or resembling mania — **manic** *n*

**man·ic–de·pres·sive** \,man-ik-di-'pres-iv\ *adj* : characterized by alternating mania and depression — **manic–depressive** *n*

**¹man·i·cure** \'man-ə-,kyùər\ *n* 1 : MANICURIST 2 : a treatment for the care of the hands and nails

**²manicure** *vb* **-cured; -cur·ing** 1 : to do manicure work on 2 : to trim closely and evenly

**man·i·cur·ist** \-,kyùr-əst\ *n* : a person who gives manicure treatments

**¹man·i·fest** \'man-ə-,fest\ *adj* [ME, fr. MF or L; MF *manifeste*, fr. L *manifestus*, lit., hit by the hand, fr. *manus* hand + *-festus* (akin to L *infestus* hostile)] 1 : readily perceived by the senses and esp. by the sight 2 : easily understood : OBVIOUS — **man·i·fest·ly** *adv*

**²manifest** *vb* : to make evident or certain by showing or displaying **syn** evidence, evince, demonstrate

**³manifest** *n* : a list of passengers or an invoice of cargo for a ship or plane

**man·i·fes·ta·tion** \,man-ə-fə-'stā-shən\ *n* : DISPLAY, DEMONSTRATION

**man·i·fes·to** \,man-ə-'fes-tō\ *n, pl* **-tos** *or* **-toes** : a public declaration of intentions, motives, or views

**¹man·i·fold** \'man-ə-,fōld\ *adj* 1 : marked by diversity or variety 2 : consisting of or operating many of one kind combined

**²manifold** *n* : a pipe fitting with several lateral outlets for connecting it with other pipes

**³manifold** *vb* 1 : to make a number of copies of (as a letter) 2 : MULTIPLY

**man·i·kin** *or* **man·ni·kin** \'man-i-kən\ *n* 1 : MANNEQUIN 2 : a little man : DWARF, PYGMY

**Ma·nila hemp** \mə-,nil-ə-\ *n* : a tough fiber from a Philippine banana plant used esp. for cordage

**manila paper** \mə-,nil-ə-\ *n, often cap M* : a tough brownish paper made orig. from Manila hemp

**man·i·oc** \'man-ē-,äk\ *or* **man·i·o·ca** \,man-ē-'ō-kə\ *n* : CASSAVA

**ma·nip·u·late** \mə-'nip-yə-,lāt\ *vb* **-lat·ed; -lat·ing** [fr. *manipulation*, fr. F, fr. *manipule* handful, fr. L *manipulus*] 1 : to treat or operate manually or mechanically esp. with skill 2 : to manage skillfully 3 : to control or change esp. by artful or unfair means so as to achieve a desired end — **ma·nip·u·la·tion** \mə-nip-yə-'lā-shən\ *n* — **ma·nip·u·la·tive** \-'nip-yə-,lāt-iv\ *adj* — **ma·nip·u·la·tor** \-,lāt-ər\ *n*

**man·kind** *n* 1 \'man-'kīnd\ : the human race 2 \-,kīnd\ : men as distinguished from women

**man·like** \'man-,līk\ *adj* : resembling or characteristic of a man

**¹man·ly** \'man-lē\ *adj* **man·li·er; -est** : having qualities appropriate to a man : BOLD, RESOLUTE — **man·li·ness** *n*

**²manly** *adv* : in a manly manner

**man–made** \'man-'mād\ *adj* : made by man rather than nature ⟨~ systems⟩; *also* : SYNTHETIC ⟨~ fibers⟩

**man·na** \'man-ə\ *n* 1 : food miraculously supplied to the Israelites in their journey through the wilderness 2 : something of value that comes one's way : WINDFALL

**manned** \'mand\ *adj* : carrying or performed by a man ⟨~ spaceflight⟩

**man·ne·quin** \'man-i-kən\ *n* 1 : an artist's, tailor's, or dressmaker's figure or model of the human body; *also* : a form representing the human figure used esp. for displaying clothes 2 : a woman who models clothing

**man·ner** \'man-ər\ *n* 1 : KIND, SORT 2 : a characteristic or customary mode of acting ⟨worked in a brisk ~⟩; *also* : MODE, FASHION ⟨spoke bluntly as was his ~⟩ 3 : a method of artistic execution 4 *pl* : social conduct; *also* : BEARING 5 *pl* : BEHAVIOR ⟨taught the child good ~s⟩

**man·nered** \'man-ərd\ *adj* 1 : having manners of a specified kind ⟨well-mannered⟩ 2 : having an artificial character ⟨a highly ~ style⟩

**man·ner·ism** \'man-ə-,riz-əm\ *n* 1 : ARTIFICIALITY, PRECIOSITY 2 : a characteristic mode or peculiarity of action, bearing, or treatment **syn** pose, air, affectation

**man·ner·ly** \'man-ər-lē\ *adj* : showing good manners : POLITE — **man·ner·li·ness** *n*

**man·nish** \'man-ish\ *adj* 1 : resembling or suggesting a man rather than a woman 2 : suitable to or characteristic of a man **syn** male, masculine, manly, manlike, manful, virile — **man·nish·ly** *adv* — **man·nish·ness** *n*

**ma·noeu·vre** \mə-'n(y)ü-vər\ *chiefly Brit var of* MANEUVER

**man-of-war** \,man-ə(v)-'wòr\ *n, pl* **men-of-war** \,men-\ **:** a combatant warship

**ma·nom·e·ter** \ma-'näm-ət-ər\ *n* **:** an instrument for measuring the pressure of gases — **mano·met·ric** \,man-ə-'met-rik\ *adj*

**man·or** \'man-ər\ *n* **1 :** the house or hall of an estate; *also* **:** a landed estate **2 :** an English estate of a feudal lord — **ma·no·ri·al** \mə-'nōr-ē-əl\ *adj* — **ma·no·ri·al·ism** \-ə-,liz-əm\ *n*

**man power** *n* **1 :** power available from or supplied by the physical effort of man **2** *usu* **man·pow·er :** the total supply of persons available and fitted for service

**man·qué** \mäⁿ-'kā\ *adj* [F, fr. pp. of *manquer* to lack, fail] **:** short of or frustrated in the fulfillment of one's aspirations or talents ⟨a poet ∼⟩

**man·sard** \'man-,särd\ *n* **:** a roof having two slopes on all sides with the lower slope steeper than the upper one

**manse** \'mans\ *n* **:** the residence esp. of a Presbyterian clergyman

**man·ser·vant** \'man-,sər-vənt\ *n, pl* **men·ser·vants** \'men-,sər-vənts\ **:** a male servant

**man·sion** \'man-chən\ *n* **:** a large imposing residence; *also* **:** a separate apartment in a large structure

**man–size** \'man-,sīz\ *or* **man–sized** \-,sīzd\ *adj* **:** suitable for or requiring a man

**man·slaugh·ter** \'man-,slòt-ər\ *n* **:** the unlawful killing of a human being without express or implied malice

**man·slay·er** \-,slā-ər\ *n* **:** one who slays a man

**man·sue·tude** \'man-swi-,t(y)üd\ *n* **:** GENTLENESS

**man·ta** \'mant-ə\ *n* **:** a square piece of cloth or blanket used in southwestern U.S. and Latin America as a cloak or shawl

**man·teau** \man-'tō\ *n* **:** a loose cloak, coat, or robe

**man·tel** \'mant-ᵊl\ *n* **:** a beam, stone, or arch serving as a lintel to support the masonry above a fireplace; *also* **:** a shelf above a fireplace

**man·te·let** \'mant-lət, -ᵊl-ət\ *n* **:** a very short cape or cloak

**man·tel·piece** \'mant-ᵊl-,pēs\ *n* **:** the shelf of a mantel

**man·til·la** \man-'tē-(y)ə, -'til-ə\ *n* **:** a light scarf worn over the head and shoulders esp. by Spanish and Latin American women

**man·tis** \'mant-əs\ *n, pl* **man·tis·es** *or* **man·tes** \'man-,tēz\ [NL, fr. Gk, lit., diviner, prophet] **:** a large insect related to the grasshoppers that feeds on other insects which it holds in forelimbs folded as if in prayer

**man·tis·sa** \man-'tis-ə\ *n* **:** the decimal part of a logarithm

**¹man·tle** \'mant-ᵊl\ *n* **1 :** a loose sleeveless garment worn over other clothes **2 :** something that covers, enfolds, or envelopes **3 :** a lacy hood of refractory material that gives light by incandescence when placed over a flame **4 :** MANTEL **5 :** the portion of the earth lying between the crust and the core

**²mantle** *vb* **man·tled; man·tling** \'mant-(ᵊ-)liŋ\ **1 :** to cover with a mantle **2 :** BLUSH

**man·tle–rock** \-,räk\ *n* **:** unconsolidated residual or transported material that overlies the earth's solid rock

**man·tra** \'man-trə\ *n* **:** a Hindu or Buddhist mystical formula of incantation

**¹man·u·al** \'man-yə-(-wə)l\ *adj* **1 :** of, relating to, or involving the hands; *also* **:** worked by hand ⟨a ∼ choke⟩ **2 :** requiring or using physical skill and energy — **man·u·al·ly** \-ē\ *adv*

**²manual** *n* **1 :** a small book; *esp* **:** HANDBOOK **2 :** the prescribed movements in the handling of a military item and esp. a weapon during a drill or ceremony **3 :** a keyboard esp. of a pipe-organ console

**manuf** *abbr* manufacture; manufacturing

**man·u·fac·to·ry** \,man-(y)ə-'fak-t(ə-)rē\ *n* **:** FACTORY

**¹man·u·fac·ture** \,man-(y)ə-'fak-chər\ *n* [MF, fr. L *manu factus* made by hand] **1 :** something made from raw materials **2 :** the process of making wares by hand or by machinery; *also* **:** a productive industry using mechanical power and machinery

**²manufacture** *vb* **man·u·fac·tured; man·u·fac·tur·ing 1 :** to make from raw materials by hand or by machinery; *also* **:** to engage in manufacture **2 :** INVENT, FABRICATE; *also* **:** CREATE — **man·u·fac·tur·er** *n*

**man·u·mit** \,man-yə-'mit\ *vb* **-mit·ted; -mit·ting :** to free from slavery — **man·u·mis·sion** \-'mish-ən\ *n*

**¹ma·nure** \mə-'n(y)ùr\ *vb* **ma·nured; ma·nur·ing :** to fertilize land with manure

**²manure** *n* **:** FERTILIZER; *esp* **:** refuse from stables and barnyards — **ma·nu·ri·al** \-'n(y)ùr-ē-əl\ *adj*

**man·u·script** \'man-yə-,skript\ *n* **1 :** a written or typewritten composition or document **2 :** writing as opposed to print

**Manx** \'maŋks\ *n pl* **:** the people of the Isle of Man — **Manx** *adj*

**¹many** \'men-ē\ *adj* **more** \'mōr\; **most** \'mōst\ **:** consisting of or amounting to a large but indefinite number

**²many** *pron* **:** a large number

**³many** *n* **:** a large but indefinite number

**many·fold** \,men-ē-'fōld\ *adv* **:** by many times

**many–sid·ed** \,men-ē-'sīd-əd\ *adj* **1 :** having many sides or aspects **2 :** VERSATILE

**Mao·ism** \'maù-,iz-əm\ *n* **:** the theory and practice of Communism developed in China chiefly by Mao Tse-tung — **Mao·ist** \'maù-əst\ *n or adj*

**Mao·ri** \'maù(ə)-rē\ *n, pl* **Maori** *or* **Maoris :** a member of a Polynesian people native to New Zealand — **Maori** *adj*

**¹map** \'map\ *n* [ML *mappa*, fr. L, napkin, towel] **1 :** a representation usu. on a flat surface of the whole or part of an area **2 :** a representation of the celestial sphere or part of it

**²map** *vb* **mapped; map·ping 1 :** to make a map of **2 :** to plan in detail ⟨∼ out a program⟩ — **map·pa·ble** \'map-ə-bəl\ *adj* — **map·per** *n*

**ma·ple** \'mā-pəl\ *n* **:** any of various trees or shrubs with 2-winged dry fruit and opposite leaves; *also* **:** the hard light-colored wood of a maple used esp. for floors and furniture

**maple sugar** *n* **:** sugar made by boiling maple syrup

**maple syrup** *n* **:** syrup made by concentrating the sap of maple trees and esp. the sugar maple

**¹mar** \'mär\ *vb* **marred; mar·ring :** to detract from the wholeness or perfection of **:** SPOIL **syn** injure, hurt, harm, damage, impair

**²mar** *abbr* maritime
**Mar** *abbr* March

**ma·ra·ca** \mə-'räk-ə, -'rak-\ *n* **:** a dried gourd or a rattle like a gourd that contains dried seeds or pebbles and is used as a percussion instrument

**mar·a·schi·no** \,mar-ə-'skē-nō, -'shē-\ *n, pl* **-nos** *often cap* **:** a cherry preserved in or as if in a sweet cherry liqueur

**mar·a·thon** \'mar-ə-,thän\ *n* [*Marathon*, Greece, site of a victory of Greeks over Persians in 490 B.C. the news of which was carried to Athens by a long-distance runner] **1 :** a long-distance race esp. on foot **2 :** an endurance contest

**ma·raud** \mə-'ròd\ *vb* **:** to roam about and raid in search of plunder **:** PILLAGE — **ma·raud·er** *n*

**mar·ble** \'mär-bəl\ *n* **1 :** a limestone that can be polished and used in fine building work **2 :** something resembling marble (as in coldness) **3 :** a small ball (as of glass) used in various games; *also, pl* **:** a children's game played with these small balls — **marble** *adj*

**mar·bling** \-b(ə-)liŋ\ *n* **:** an intermixture of fat through the lean of a cut of meat

**mar·cel** \mär-'sel\ *n* **:** a deep soft wave made in the hair by the use of a heated curling iron — **marcel** *vb*

**¹march** \'märch\ *n* **:** a border region **:** FRONTIER

**²march** *vb* **1 :** to move along in or as if in military formation **2 :** to walk in a direct purposeful manner; *also* **:** PROGRESS, ADVANCE **3 :** TRAVERSE — **march·er** *n*

**³march** *n* **1 :** the action of marching; *also* **:** the distance covered (as by a military unit) in a march **2 :** a regular measured stride or rhythmic step used in marching **3 :** forward movement **4 :** a piece of music with marked rhythm suitable for marching to

**March** *n* [ME, fr. OF, fr. L *martius*, fr. *Mart-, Mars*, Roman god of war] **:** the third month of the year having 31 days

**mar·chio·ness** \'mär-shə-nəs\ *n* **1 :** the wife or widow of a marquess

**2 :** a woman holding the rank of a marquess in her own right

**march–past** \'märch-,past\ *n* **:** a marching by esp. of troops in review

**Mar·di Gras** \'märd-ē-,grä\ *n* [F, lit., fat Tuesday] **:** the Tuesday before Ash Wednesday often observed with parades and merrymaking

**¹mare** \'maər\ *n* **:** a female of an animal of the horse group

**²ma·re** \'mär-(,)ā\ *n, pl* **ma·ria** \'mär-ē-ə\ **:** one of several large dark areas on the surface of the moon or Mars

**mar·ga·rine** \'märj-(ə-)rən, -ə-,rēn\ *n* **:** a food product made usu. from vegetable oils churned with skimmed milk and used as a spread and as a cooking fat

**marge** \'märj\ *n, archaic* **:** MARGIN

**mar·gent** \'mär-jənt\ *n, archaic* **:** MARGIN

**mar·gin** \'mär-jən\ *n* **1 :** the part of a page outside the main body of printed or written matter **2 :** EDGE **3 :** a spare amount, measure, or degree allowed for use if needed **4 :** measure or degree of difference ⟨passed the bill by a ∼ of one vote⟩ — **mar·gin·al** \-ᵊl\ *adj* — **mar·gin·al·ly** \-ē\ *adv*

**mar·gi·na·lia** \,mär-jə-'nā lē-ə\ *n pl* **:** marginal notes

**mar·grave** \'mär-,grāv\ *n* **:** the military governor esp. of a medieval German border province

**mar·gue·rite** \,mär-g(y)ə-'rēt\ *n* **:** any of several daisies or chrysanthemums

**ma·ri·a·chi** \,mär-ē-'äch-ē\ *n* **:** a Mexican street band; *also* **:** a member of or the music performed by such a band

**mari·gold** \'mar-ə-,gōld, 'mer-\ *n* **:** a garden plant related to the daisies with double yellow, orange, or reddish flower heads

**mar·i·jua·na** *or* **mar·i·hua·na** \,mar-ə-'(h)wän-ə\ *n* **:** an intoxicating drug obtained from the hemp plant and smoked in cigarettes; *also* **:** this plant

**ma·rim·ba** \mə-'rim-bə\ *n* **:** a xylophone of southern Africa and Central America; *also* **:** a modern version of it

**ma·ri·na** \mə-'rē-nə\ *n* **:** a dock or basin providing secure moorings for motorboats and yachts

**mar·i·nate** \'mar-ə-,nāt\ *vb* **-nat·ed; -nat·ing :** to steep (as meat or fish) in a brine or pickle

**¹ma·rine** \mə-'rēn\ *adj* **1 :** of or relating to the sea, the navigation of the sea, or the commerce of the sea **2 :** of or relating to marines

**²marine** *n* **1 :** the mercantile and naval shipping of a country **2 :** one of a class of soldiers serving on shipboard **3 :** a picture representing marine scenery

**mar·i·ner** \'mar-ə-nər\ *n* **:** SAILOR

**mar·i·o·nette** \,mar-ē-ə-'net, ,mer-\ *n* **:** a puppet moved by strings or by hand

**mar·i·tal** \'mar-ət-ᵊl\ *adj* **:** of or relating to marriage **:** CONJUGAL **syn** matrimonial, connubial, nuptial

**mar·i·time** \'mar-ə-ˌtīm\ *adj* **1** : of or relating to navigation or commerce on the sea **2** : of, relating to, or bordering on the sea

**mar·jo·ram** \'märj-(ə-)rəm\ *n* : a fragrant aromatic mint used esp. as a seasoning

¹**mark** \'märk\ *n* **1** : TARGET; *also* : GOAL, OBJECT **2** : something (as a line or fixed object) designed to record position; *also* : the starting line or position in a track event **3** : an object of abuse or ridicule **4** : the question under discussion **5** : NORM ⟨not up to the ~⟩ **6** : a visible sign : INDICATION; *also* : CHARACTERISTIC **7** : a written or printed symbol **8** : GRADE ⟨a ~ of B+⟩ **9** : IMPORTANCE, DISTINCTION **10** : a lasting impression ⟨made his ~ in the world⟩; *also* : a damaging impression left on a surface

²**mark** *vb* **1** : to set apart by a line or boundary **2** : to designate by a mark or make a mark on **3** : CHARACTERIZE ⟨the vehemence that ~s his speeches⟩; *also* : SIGNALIZE ⟨this year ~s the 50th anniversary⟩ **4** : to take notice of : OBSERVE — **mark·er** *n*

³**mark** *n* — see MONEY table

**mark·down** \'märk-ˌdaun\ *n* **1** : a lowering of price **2** : the amount by which an original price is reduced

**mark down** \'märk-'daun\ *vb* : to put a lower price on

**marked** \'märkt\ *adj* : NOTICEABLE — **mark·ed·ly** \'mär-kəd-lē\ *adv*

¹**mar·ket** \'mär-kət\ *n* **1** : a meeting together of people for trade by purchase and sale; *also* : a public place where such a meeting is held **2** : the rate or price offered for a commodity or security **3** : a geographical area of demand for commodities; *also* : extent of demand **4** : a retail establishment usu. of a specific kind ⟨a meat ~⟩

²**market** *vb* : to go to a market to buy or sell; *also* : SELL — **mar·ket·able** *adj*

**mar·ket·place** \'mär-kət-ˌplās\ *n* **1** : an open square in a town where markets are held **2** : the world of trade or economic activity

**mark·ka** \'mär-ˌkä\ *n, pl* **mark·kaa** \'mär-ˌkä\ *or* **markkas** \-ˌkäz\ — see MONEY table

**marks·man** \'märks-mən\ *n* : a person skillful at hitting a target — **marks·man·ship** *n*

**mark·up** \'märk-ˌəp\ *n* **1** : a raising of price **2** : an amount added to the cost price of an article to determine the selling price

**mark up** \(')märk-'əp\ *vb* : to put a higher price on

**marl** \'märl\ *n* : an earthy deposit rich in lime used as fertilizer — **marly** \'mär-lē\ *adj*

**mar·lin** \'mär-lən\ *n* : a large oceanic sport fish

**mar·line·spike** *also* **mar·lin·spike** \'mär-lən-ˌspīk\ *n* : a pointed iron tool used to separate strands of rope or wire (as in splicing)

**mar·ma·lade** \'mär-mə-ˌlād\ *n* : a clear jelly holding in suspension pieces of fruit and fruit rind

**mar·mo·re·al** \mär-'mōr-ē-əl\ *or* **mar·mo·re·an** \-ē-ən\ *adj* : of, relating to, or resembling marble

**mar·mo·set** \'mär-mə-ˌset\ *n* : any of various small bushy-tailed tropical American monkeys

**mar·mot** \'mär-mət\ *n* : a stout short-legged burrowing No. American rodent

¹**ma·roon** \mə-'rün\ *vb* **1** : to put ashore (as on a desolate island) and leave to one's fate **2** : to leave in isolation and without hope of escape

²**maroon** *n* : a dark red

**mar·plot** \'mär-ˌplät\ *n* : one who endangers the success of an enterprise by his meddling

**mar·quee** \mär-'kē\ *n* [modif. of F *marquise*, lit., marchioness] **1** : a large tent set up (as for an outdoor party) **2** : a usu. metal and glass canopy over an entrance (as of a theater)

**mar·quess** \'mär-kwəs\ *n* **1** : a nobleman of hereditary rank in Europe and Japan **2** : a member of the British peerage ranking below a duke and above an earl

**mar·que·try** \'mär-kə-trē\ *n* : inlaid work of wood, shell, or ivory (as on a table or cabinet)

**mar·quis** \'mär-kwəs, mär-'kē\ *n* : MARQUESS

**mar·quise** \mär-'kēz\ *n, pl* **marquises** \-'kēz(-əz)\ : MARCHIONESS

**mar·qui·sette** \ˌmär-k(w)ə-'zet\ *n* : a sheer meshed fabric

**mar·riage** \'mar-ij\ *n* **1** : the state of being married **2** : a wedding ceremony and attendant festivities **3** : a close union — **mar·riage·able** *adj*

**mar·row** \'mar-ō\ *n* : a soft vascular tissue that fills the cavities of most bones

**mar·row·bone** \'mar-ə-ˌbōn, -ō-ˌbōn\ *n* : a bone (as a shinbone) rich in marrow

**mar·ry** \'mar-ē\ *vb* **mar·ried; mar·ry·ing 1** : to join as husband and wife according to law or custom **2** : to take as husband or wife : WED **3** : to enter into a close union — **mar·ried** *adj or n*

**Mars** \'märz\ *n* : the planet fourth in order of distance from the sun conspicuous for the redness of its light

**marsh** \'märsh\ *n* : a tract of soft wet land — **marshy** *adj*

¹**mar·shal** \'mär-shəl\ *n* **1** : a high official in a medieval household; *also* : a person in charge of the ceremonial aspects of a gathering **2** : a general officer of the highest military rank **3** : an administrative officer (as of a U.S. judicial district) having duties similar to a sheriff's **4** : the administrative head of a city police or fire department

²**marshal** *vb* **mar·shaled** *or* **marshalled; mar·shal·ing** *or* **mar·shal·ling** \'märsh-(ə-)liŋ\ **1** : to arrange in order, rank, or position **2** : to lead with ceremony : USHER

**marsh gas** *n* : METHANE

**marsh·mal·low** \'märsh-ˌmel-ō, -ˌmal-\ *n* : a light creamy confection made from corn syrup, sugar, albumen, and gelatin

**marsh marigold** n : a swamp herb related to the buttercups that has bright yellow flowers

**mar·su·pi·al** \mär-'sü-pē-əl\ n : any of a large group of mostly Australian primitive mammals that bear very immature young which are nourished in a pouch on the abdomen of the female — **marsupial** adj

**mart** \'märt\ n : MARKET

**mar·ten** \'märt-ᵊn\ n, pl **marten** or **martens :** a slender weasel-like mammal with fine gray or brown fur; also : this fur

**mar·tial** \'mär-shəl\ adj [L martialis of Mars, fr. Mart-, Mars Mars, Roman god of war] **1 :** of, relating to, or suited for war or a warrior ⟨~ music⟩ **2 :** of or relating to an army or military life **3 :** WARLIKE

**martial law** n **1 :** the law applied in occupied territory by the military forces of the occupying power **2 :** the established law of a country administered by military forces in an emergency when civilian law enforcement agencies are unable to maintain public order and safety

**mar·tian** \'mär-shən\ adj, often cap : of or relating to the planet Mars or its hypothetical inhabitants — **martian** n, often cap

**mar·tin** \'märt-ᵊn\ n : any of several small swallows and flycatchers

**mar·ti·net** \,märt-ᵊn-'et\ n : a strict disciplinarian

**mar·tin·gale** \'märt-ᵊn-,gāl\ n : a strap connecting a horse's girth to the bit or reins so as to hold down its head

**mar·ti·ni** \mär-'tē-nē\ n : a cocktail made of gin or vodka and dry vermouth

**¹mar·tyr** \'märt-ər\ n [ME, fr. OE, fr. LL, fr. Gk martyr, martys, lit., witness] **1 :** a person who dies rather than renounce his religion; also : one who makes a great sacrifice for the sake of principle **2 :** a great or constant sufferer

**²martyr** vb **1 :** to put to death for adhering to a belief **2 :** TORTURE

**mar·tyr·dom** \'märt-ər-dəm\ n **1 :** the suffering and death of a martyr **2 :** TORTURE

**¹mar·vel** \'mär-vəl\ n **1 :** something that causes wonder or astonishment **2 :** intense surprise or interest

**²marvel** vb **mar·veled** or **mar·velled; mar·vel·ing** or **mar·vel·ling** \'märv-(ə-)liŋ\ : to feel surprise, wonder, or amazed curiosity

**mar·vel·ous** or **mar·vel·lous** \'märv-(ə-)ləs\ adj **1 :** causing wonder **2 :** of the highest kind or quality : SPLENDID — **mar·vel·ous·ly** adv — **mar·vel·ous·ness** n

**Marx·ism** \'märk-,siz-əm\ n : the political, economic, and social principles and policies advocated by Karl Marx — **Marx·ist** \-səst\ n or adj

**mar·zi·pan** \'märt-sə-,pän, -,pan; 'mär-zə-,pan\ n : a confection of

almond paste, sugar, and egg whites

**masc** abbr masculine

**mas·ca·ra** \mas-'kar-ə\ n : a cosmetic for coloring the eyelashes and eyebrows

**mas·con** \'mas-,kän\ n : one of the concentrations of large mass under the moon's maria

**mas·cot** \'mas-,kät, -kət\ n [F mascotte, fr. Provençal mascoto, fr. masco witch, fr. ML masca] : a person, animal, or object believed to bring good luck

**¹mas·cu·line** \'mas-kyə-lən\ adj **1 :** MALE; also : MANLY **2 :** of, relating to, or constituting the gender that includes most words or grammatical forms referring to males — **mas·cu·lin·i·ty** \,mas-kyə-'lin-ət-ē\ n

**²masculine** n **1 :** a male person **2 :** a noun, pronoun, adjective, or inflectional form or class of the masculine gender; also : the masculine gender

**ma·ser** \'mā-zər\ n [microwave amplification by stimulated emission of radiation] : a device that utilizes the natural oscillation of atoms or molecules between energy levels for generating microwaves

**¹mash** \'mash\ n **1 :** crushed malt or grain steeped in hot water to make wort **2 :** a mixture of ground feeds for livestock **3 :** a soft pulpy mass

**²mash** vb **1 :** to reduce to a soft pulpy state **2 :** CRUSH, SMASH ⟨~ a finger⟩ — **mash·er** n

**MASH** abbr mobile army surgical hospital

**¹mask** \'mask\ n **1 :** a cover for the face usu. for disguise or protection **2 :** MASQUE **3 :** a figure of a head worn on the stage in antiquity **4 :** a copy of a face made by means of a mold ⟨death ~⟩ **5 :** something that conceals or disguises **6 :** the face of an animal (as a fox)

**²mask** vb **1 :** to take part in a masquerade **2 :** to conceal from view : DISGUISE **3 :** to cover for protection — **mask·er** n

**mas·och·ism** \'mas-ə-'kiz-əm, 'maz-\ n **1 :** abnormal sexual passion charterized by pleasure in being abused **2 :** pleasure in being abused or dominated — **mas·och·ist** \-kəst\ n — **mas·och·is·tic** \,mas-ə-'kis-tik, ,maz-\ adj

**ma·son** \'mās-ᵊn\ n **1 :** a skilled workman who builds with stone or similar material (as brick or concrete) **2** cap : FREEMASON

**Ma·son·ic** \mə-'sän-ik\ adj : of or relating to Freemasons or Freemasonry

**ma·son·ry** \'mās-ᵊn-rē\ n, pl **-ries 1 :** something constructed of materials used by masons **2 :** the art, trade, or work of a mason **3** cap : FREEMASONRY

**masque** \'mask\ n **1 :** MASQUERADE **2 :** a short allegorical dramatic performance (as of the 17th century)

**¹mas·quer·ade** \,mas-kə-'rād\ n **1 :** a social gathering of persons wearing masks; also : a costume for wear at such a gathering **2 :** DISGUISE

**²masquerade** vb **-ad·ed; -ad·ing 1 :** to disguise oneself : POSE **2 :** to take part in a masquerade — **mas·quer·ad·er** n

**¹mass** \'mas\ n 1 cap : a sequence of prayers and ceremonies forming the eucharistic office of the Roman Catholic Church 2 often cap : a celebration of the Eucharist 3 : a musical setting for parts of the Mass

**²mass** n 1 : a quantity or aggregate of matter usu. of considerable size 2 : EXPANSE, BULK; also : MASSIVENESS 3 : the principal part 4 : AGGREGATE, WHOLE ⟨people in the ∼⟩ 5 : the quantity of matter that a body possesses as evidenced by inertia 6 : a large quantity, amount, or number 7 : the great body of people — usu. used in pl. — **massy** adj

**³mass** vb : to form or collect into a mass

**Mass** abbr Massachusetts

**Mas·sa·chu·set** \,mas-(ə-)'chü-sət, -zət\ n, pl **Massachuset** or **Massachusets** also **Massachusetts** : a member of an Indian people of Massachusetts

**mas·sa·cre** \'mas-i-kər\ n 1 : the killing of many persons under cruel or atrocious circumstances 2 : a wholesale slaughter — **massacre** vb

**mas·sage** \mə-'säzh, -'säj\ n : remedial or hygienic treatment of the body by manipulation (as rubbing and kneading) — **massage** vb

**mas·seur** \ma-'sər\ n : a man who practices massage

**mas·seuse** \-'sə(r)z, -'süz\ n : a woman who practices massage

**mas·sif** \ma-'sēf\ n : a principal mountain mass

**mas·sive** \'mas-iv\ adj 1 : forming or consisting of a large mass 2 : large in structure, scope, or degree — **mas·sive·ly** adv — **mas·sive·ness** n

**mass·less** \'mas-ləs\ adj : having no mass : lacking in mass ⟨∼ particles⟩ — **mass·less·ness** n

**mass medium** n, pl **mass media** : a medium of communication (as the newspapers or television) that is designed to reach the mass of the people

**mass-pro·duce** \,mas-prə-'d(y)üs\ vb : to produce in quantity usu. by machinery — **mass production** n

**¹mast** \'mast\ n 1 : a long pole or spar rising from the keel or deck of a ship and supporting the yards, booms, and rigging 2 : a vertical pole — **mast·ed** \'mas-təd\ adj

**²mast** n : nuts (as acorns) accumulated on the forest floor and often serving as food for hogs

**¹mas·ter** \'mas-tər\ n 1 : a male teacher; also : a person holding an academic degree higher than a bachelor's but lower than a doctor's 2 : one highly skilled (as in an art or profession) 3 : one having authority or control 4 : VICTOR, SUPERIOR 5 : the commander of a merchant ship 6 : a youth or boy too young to be called mister — used as a title 7 : an officer of court appointed to assist a judge 8 : an original (as of a phonograph record) from which copies are made

**²master** vb **mas·tered**; **mas·ter·ing** \-t(ə-)riŋ\ 1 : OVERCOME, SUBDUE 2 : to become skilled or proficient in

**master chief petty officer** n : a petty officer of the highest rank in the navy

**mas·ter·ful** \'mas-tər-fəl\ adj 1 : inclined and usu. competent to act as a master 2 : having or reflecting the skill of a master ⟨did a ∼ job of reporting⟩ — **mas·ter·ful·ly** \-ē\ adv

**master gunnery sergeant** n : a noncommissioned officer in the marine corps ranking above a master sergeant

**master key** n : a key designed to open several different locks

**mas·ter·ly** \'mas-tər-lē\ adj : indicating thorough knowledge or superior skill ⟨∼ performance⟩

**mas·ter·mind** \-,mīnd\ n : a person who provides the directing or creative intelligence for a project — **mastermind** vb

**master of ceremonies** : a person who acts as host at a formal event or a program of entertainment

**mas·ter·piece** \'mas-tər-,pēs\ n : a work done with extraordinary skill

**master plan** n : an overall plan

**master sergeant** n 1 : a noncommissioned officer in the army ranking next below a sergeant major 2 : a noncommissioned officer in the air force ranking next below a senior master sergeant 3 : a noncommissioned officer in the marine corps ranking next below a master gunnery sergeant

**mas·ter·ship** \'mas-tər-,ship\ n 1 : DOMINION, SUPERIORITY 2 : the status, office, or function of a master 3 : MASTERY

**mas·ter·stroke** \-,strōk\ n : a masterly performance or move

**mas·ter·work** \-,wərk\ n : MASTERPIECE

**mas·tery** \'mas-t(ə-)rē\ n 1 : DOMINION; also : SUPERIORITY 2 : possession or display of great skill or knowledge

**mast·head** \'mast-,hed\ n 1 : the top of a mast 2 : the printed matter in a newspaper giving the title and details of ownership and rates

**mas·tic** \'mas-tik\ n : a pasty material used as a protective coating or cement

**mas·ti·cate** \'mas-tə-,kāt\ vb **-cat·ed**; **-cat·ing** : CHEW — **mas·ti·ca·tion** \,mas-tə-'kā-shən\ n

**mas·tiff** \'mas-təf\ n : a large smooth-coated dog used esp. as a guard dog

**mast·odon** \'mas-tə-,dän\ n [NL, fr. Gk mastos breast + odōn, odous tooth] : a huge elephantlike extinct animal

**mas·toid** \'mas-,tȯid\ n : a bony prominence behind the ear; also : an infection of this area — **mastoid** adj

**mas·tur·ba·tion** \,mas-tər-'bā-shən\ n : stimulation of the genital organs to a climax of excitement by contact (as manual) exclusive of sexual intercourse — **mas·tur·bate** \'mas-tər-,bāt\ vb

**¹mat** \'mat\ n 1 : a piece of coarse

woven or plaited fabric **2 :** something made up of many intertwined or tangled strands **3 :** a large thick pad used as a surface for wrestling and gymnastics

²**mat** vb **mat·ted; mat·ting : to** form into a tangled mass

³**mat** or **matt** or **matte** adj [F, fr. OF, defeated, fr. L mattus drunk] **:** not shiny **:** DULL

⁴**mat** or **matt** or **matte** n **1 :** a border going around a picture between picture and frame or serving as the frame **2 :** a dull finish

**mat·a·dor** \'mat-ə-,dȯr\ n. [Sp, fr. matar to kill] **:** a bullfighter whose role is to kill the bull in a bullfight

¹**match** \'mach\ n **1 :** a person or thing equal or similar to another **:** COUNTERPART **2 :** a pair of persons or objects that harmonize **3 :** a contest or game between two or more individuals **4 :** a marriage union; also **:** a prospective marriage partner — **match·less** adj

²**match** vb **1 :** to meet as an antagonist; also **:** PIT ⟨~ing his strength against his enemy's⟩ **2 :** to provide with a worthy competitor; also **:** to set in comparison with **3 :** MARRY **4 :** to combine as being suitable or congenial; also **:** ADAPT, SUIT **5 :** to provide with a counterpart

³**match** n **:** a short slender piece of flammable material (as wood) tipped with a combustible mixture that ignites through friction

**match·book** \-,bùk\ n **:** a small folder containing rows of paper matches

**match·lock** \-,läk\ n **:** a musket equipped with a slow-burning cord lowered over a hole in the breech to ignite the charge

**match·mak·er** \-,mā-kər\ n **:** one who arranges a match and esp. a marriage

**match·wood** \'mach-,wùd\ n **:** small pieces of wood

¹**mate** \'māt\ vb **mated; mat·ing :** CHECKMATE — **mate** n

²**mate** n **1 :** ASSOCIATE, COMPANION; also **:** HELPER **2 :** a deck officer on a merchant ship ranking below the captain **3 :** one of a pair; esp **:** either member of a married couple

³**mate** vb **mated; mat·ing : 1 :** to join or fit together **:** COUPLE **2 :** to come or bring together as mates

**maté** or **ma·te** \'mä-,tā\ n **:** an aromatic beverage used esp. in So. America

¹**ma·te·ri·al** \mə-'tir-ē-əl\ adj **1 :** PHYSICAL ⟨~ world⟩; also **:** BODILY ⟨~ needs⟩ **2 :** of or relating to matter rather than form ⟨~ cause⟩; also **:** EMPIRICAL ⟨~ knowledge⟩ **3 :** highly important ⟨~ significant⟩ **4 :** of a physical or worldly nature ⟨~ progress⟩ — **ma·te·ri·al·ly** \-ē\ adv

²**material** n **1 :** the elements or substance of which something is composed or made **2 :** apparatus necessary for doing or making something

**ma·te·ri·al·ism** \mə-'tir-ē-ə-,liz-əm\ n **1 :** a theory that physical matter is the only reality and that all being and processes and phenomena can be ex-

plained as manifestations or results of matter **2 :** a preoccupation with material rather than intellectual or spiritual things — **ma·te·ri·al·ist** \-ləst\ n or adj — **ma·te·ri·al·is·tic** \-,tir-ē-ə-'lis-tik\ adj — **ma·te·ri·al·is·ti·cal·ly** \-ti-k(ə-)lē\ adv

**ma·te·ri·al·ize** \mə-'tir-ē-ə-,līz\ vb **-ized; -iz·ing 1 :** to give material form to; also **:** to assume bodily form **2 :** to make an often unexpected appearance — **ma·te·ri·al·i·za·tion** \mə-,tir-ē-ə-lə-'zā-shən\ n

**ma·té·ri·el** or **ma·te·ri·el** \mə-,tir-ē-'el\ n **:** equipment, apparatus, and supplies used by an organization

**ma·ter·nal** \mə-'tərn-ᵊl\ adj **1 :** MOTHERLY **2 :** related through or inherited or derived from a mother — **ma·ter·nal·ly** \-ē\ adv

**ma·ter·ni·ty** \mə-'tər-nət-ē\ n, pl **-ties 1 :** the quality or state of being a mother; also **:** MOTHERLINESS **2 :** a hospital facility for the care of women before and during childbirth and for the care of newborn babies — **maternity** adj

¹**math** \'math\ n **:** MATHEMATICS

²**math** abbr mathematical; mathematician; mathematics

**math·e·mat·ics** \,math-ə-'mat-iks\ n pl **:** the science of numbers and their operations and the relations between them and of space configurations and their structure and measurement — **math·e·mat·i·cal** \-'mat-i-kəl\ adj — **math·e·mat·i·cal·ly** \-i-k(ə-)lē\ adv — **math·e·ma·ti·cian** \,math-ə-mə-'tish-ən\ n

**mat·i·nee** or **mat·i·née** \,mat-ᵊn-'ā\ n [F matinée, lit., morning, fr. OF, fr. matin morning, fr. L matutinum, fr. neut of matutinus of the morning, fr. Matuta, goddess of morning] **:** a musical or dramatic performance usu. in the afternoon

**mat·ins** \'mat-ᵊnz\ n, often cap **1 :** special prayers said between midnight and 4 a.m. **2 :** a morning service of liturgical prayer in Anglican churches

**ma·tri·arch** \'mā-trē-,ärk\ n **:** a woman who rules a family, group, or state — **ma·tri·ar·chal** \,mā-trē-'är-kəl\ adj — **ma·tri·ar·chy** \'mā-trē-,är-kē\ n

**ma·tri·cide** \'ma-trə-,sīd, 'mā-\ n **1 :** the murder of a mother by her child **2 :** one who kills his mother — **ma·tri·cid·al** \,ma-trə-'sīd-ᵊl, ,mā-\ adj

**ma·tric·u·late** \mə-'trik-yə-,lāt\ vb **-lat·ed; -lat·ing :** to enroll as a member of a body and esp. of a college or university — **ma·tric·u·la·tion** \-,trik-yə-'lā-shən\ n

**mat·ri·mo·ny** \'mat-rə-,mō-nē\ n [ME, fr. MF matremoine fr. L matrimonium, fr. mater mother, matron] **:** MARRIAGE — **mat·ri·mo·ni·al** \,mat-rə-'mō-nē-əl\ adj — **mat·ri·mo·ni·al·ly** \-ē\ adv

**ma·trix** \'mā-triks\ n, pl **ma·tri·ces** \'mā-trə-,sēz, 'ma-\ or **ma·trix·es** \'mā-trik-səz\ **1 :** something within which something else originates or develops **2 :** a mold from which a relief surface (as a stereotype) is made

**ma·tron** \'mā-trən\ n **1 :** a married woman usu. of dignified maturity or social distinction **2 :** a woman supervisor (as in a school or police station) — **ma·tron·ly** adj

**Matt** abbr Matthew

**¹mat·ter** \'mat-ər\ n **1 :** a subject of interest or concern **2** pl **:** events or circumstances of a particular situation; also **:** elements that constitute material for treatment (as in writing) **3 :** TROUBLE, DIFFICULTY ⟨what's the ∼⟩ **4 :** the substance of which a physical object is composed **5 :** PUS **6 :** an indefinite amount or quantity ⟨a ∼ of a few days⟩ **7 :** something written or printed **8 :** MAIL

**²matter** vb **1 :** to be of importance : SIGNIFY **2 :** to form or discharge pus

**mat·ter-of-fact** \,mat-ə-rə(v)-'fakt\ adj **:** adhering to or concerned with fact — **mat·ter-of-fact·ly** adv — **mat·ter-of-fact·ness** n

**mat·tins** often cap, chiefly Brit var of MATINS

**mat·tock** \'mat-ək\ n **:** a digging and grubbing implement with features of an adz, ax, and pick

**mat·tress** \'ma-trəs\ n **1 :** a fabric case filled with resilient material used either alone as a bed or on a bedstead **2 :** an inflatable airtight sack for use as a mattress

**mat·u·rate** \'mach-ə-,rāt\ vb **-rat·ed; -rat·ing :** MATURE

**mat·u·ra·tion** \,mach-ə-'rā-shən\ n **1 :** the process of becoming mature **2 :** the emergence of personal and behavioral characteristics through growth processes — **mat·u·ra·tion·al** \-sh(ə-)nəl\ adj — **ma·tur·a·tive** \mə-'t(y)ùr-ət-iv\ adj

**¹ma·ture** \mə-'t(y)ùr\ adj **ma·tur·er; -est 1 :** based on slow careful consideration **2 :** having attained a final or desired state ⟨∼ wine⟩ **3 :** of or relating to a condition of full development **4 :** due for payment ⟨a ∼ loan⟩

**²mature** vb **ma·tured; ma·tur·ing :** to bring to maturity or completion

**ma·tu·ri·ty** \mə-'t(y)ùr-ət-ē\ n **1 :** the quality or state of being mature; esp **:** full development **2 :** the second of the three principal stages in a cycle of geologic change (as erosion)

**ma·tu·ti·nal** \,mach-ù-'tīn-ºl; mə-'t(y)üt-(ª-)nəl\ adj **:** of, relating to, or occurring in the morning : EARLY

**mat·zo** \'mät-sə, -(,)sō\ n, pl **mat·zoth** \-,sōt(h), -sōs\ or **mat·zos** \-səz, -səs, -,sōz\ **:** unleavened bread eaten at the Passover

**maud·lin** \'mȯd-lən\ adj [alter. of Mary Magdalene; fr. the practice of depicting her as a weeping, penitent sinner] **1 :** weakly and effusively sentimental **2 :** drunk enough to be emotionally silly : FUDDLED

**¹maul** \'mȯl\ n **:** a heavy hammer often with a wooden head used esp. for driving wedges or piles

**²maul** vb **1 :** BEAT, BRUISE; also **:** MANGLE

**2 :** to handle roughly

**maun·der** \'mȯn-dər\ vb **maundered; maun·der·ing** -d(ə-)riŋ\ **1 :** to wander slowly and idly **2 :** to speak indistinctly or disconnectedly

**mau·so·le·um** \,mȯ-sə-'lē-əm, ,mȯ-zə-\ n, pl **-leums** or **-lea** \-'lē-ə\ [L, fr. Gk mausōleion, fr. Mausōlos Mausolus d. ab. 353 B.C. ruler of Caria whose tomb was one of the seven wonders of the ancient world] **:** a large tomb; esp **:** a usu. stone building with places for entombment of the dead above ground

**mauve** \'mōv, 'mȯv\ n **:** a moderate purple, violet, or lilac color

**ma·ven** or **ma·vin** or **may·vin** \'mā-vən\ n **:** EXPERT

**mav·er·ick** \'mav-(ə-)rik\ n [Samuel A Maverick d 1870 Amer pioneer who did not brand his calves] **1 :** an unbranded range animal **2 :** NONCONFORMIST

**ma·vis** \'mā-vəs\ n **:** an Old World thrush

**maw** \'mȯ\ n **1 :** STOMACH; also **:** the crop of a bird **2 :** the throat, gullet, or jaws usu. of a carnivore

**mawk·ish** \'mȯ-kish\ adj [ME mawke maggot, fr. ON mathkr] **:** sickly or puerilely sentimental — **mawk·ish·ly** adv — **mawk·ish·ness** n

**max** abbr maximum

**maxi** \'mak-sē\ n, pl **max·is :** a long skirt or coat that usu. extends to the ankle

**maxi-** comb form **1 :** extra long ⟨maxi-kilt⟩ **2 :** extra large ⟨maxi-problems⟩

**max·il·la** \mak-'sil-ə\ n, pl **max·il·lae** \-'sil-(,)ē\ or **maxillas :** JAW; esp **:** an upper jaw — **max·il·lary** \'mak-sə-,ler-ē\ adj

**max·im** \'mak-səm\ n **:** a proverbial saying

**max·i·mal** \'mak-s(ə-)məl\ adj **:** MAXIMUM — **max·i·mal·ly** \-ē\ adv

**max·i·mize** \'mak-sə-,mīz\ vb **-mized; -miz·ing 1 :** to increase to a maximum **2 :** to assign maximum importance to

**max·i·mum** \'mak-s(ə-)məm\ n, pl **max·i·ma** \-sə-mə\ or **maximums** \-s(ə-)məmz\ **1 :** the greatest quantity, value, or degree **2 :** an upper limit allowed by authority **3 :** the largest of a set of numbers — **maximum** adj

**may** \(')mā\ verbal auxiliary, past **might** \(')mīt\; pres sing & pl **may 1 :** have permission or liberty to ⟨you ∼ go now⟩ **2 :** be in some degree likely to ⟨you ∼ be right⟩ **3 :** — used as an auxiliary to express a wish or desire, purpose or expectation, or contingency or concession

**May** \'mā\ n [ME, fr. OF mai, fr. L Maius, fr. Maia, Roman goddess] **:** the fifth month of the year having 31 days

**Ma·ya** \'mī-ə\ n, pl Maya or **Mayas :** a member of a group of peoples of the Yucatan peninsula and adjacent areas — **Ma·yan** \'mī-ən\ adj

**may·ap·ple** \'mā-,ap-əl\ n **:** a No. American woodland herb related to the barberry that has a poisonous root, large leaf, and edible but insipid yellow fruit

**may·be** \'mā-bē, 'meb-ē\ adv : PERHAPS

**May Day** \'mā-,dā\ n : May 1 celebrated as a springtime festival and in some countries as Labor Day

**may·flow·er** \'mā-,flaù(-ə)r\ n : any of several spring blooming herbs (as the trailing arbutus or anemone)

**may·fly** \'mā-flī\ n : any of an order of insects with an aquatic immature stage and a short-lived fragile adult having membranous wings

**may·hem** \'mā-,hem, 'mā-əm\ n : willful and permanent crippling, mutilation, or disfigurement of a person

**may·on·naise** \'mā-ə-,nāz\ n : a dressing of raw eggs or egg yolks, vegetable oil, and vinegar or lemon juice

**may·or** \'mā-ər\ n : an official elected to act as chief executive or nominal head of a city or borough — **may·or·al** \-əl\ adj — **may·or·al·ty** \-əl-tē\ n — **may·or·ess** \'mā-ə-rəs\ n

**may·pole** \'mā-,pōl\ n, often cap : a tall flower-wreathed pole forming a center for May Day sports and dances

**maze** \'māz\ n : a confusing intricate network of passages — **mazy** adj

**ma·zur·ka** \mə-'zər-kə\ n : a Polish dance in moderate triple measure

**MBA** abbr master of business administration

**mc** abbr megacycle

¹**MC** n : MASTER OF CEREMONIES

²**MC** abbr member of congress

**MCPO** abbr master chief petty officer

¹**Md** abbr Maryland

²**Md** symbol mendelevium

**MD** abbr 1 doctor of medicine 2 Maryland 3 months after date

**mdnt** abbr midnight

**mdse** abbr merchandise

**me** \(')mē\ pron, objective case of I

**Me** abbr Maine

**ME** abbr 1 Maine 2 mechanical engineer 3 Middle English

¹**mead** \'mēd\ n : an alcoholic beverage brewed from water and honey, malt, and yeast

²**mead** n, archaic : MEADOW

**mead·ow** \'med-ō\ n : land in or mainly in grass; esp : a tract of moist low-lying usu. level grassland — **mead·ow·land** \-,land\ n — **mead·owy** \'med-ə-wē\ adj

**mead·ow·lark** \'med-ō-,lärk\ n : any of several No. American songbirds that are largely brown and buff above and have a yellow breast marked with a black crescent

**mead·ow·sweet** \-,swēt\ n : a No. American native or naturalized spirea

**mea·ger** or **mea·gre** \'mē-gər\ adj 1 : THIN 2 : lacking richness, fertility, or strength : POOR syn scanty, scant, spare, sparse — **mea·ger·ly** adv — **mea·ger·ness** n

¹**meal** \'mēl\ n 1 : the portion of food taken at one time : REPAST 2 : an act or the time of eating a meal

²**meal** n 1 : usu. coarsely ground seeds of a cereal (as Indian corn) 2 : a product resembling seed meal — **mealy** adj

**meal·time** \'mēl-,tīm\ n : the usual time at which a meal is served

**mealy·bug** \'mē-lē-,bəg\ n : any of numerous scale insects with a white powdery covering that are destructive pests esp. of fruit trees

**mealy·mouthed** \,mē-lē-'maùthd, -'maùtht\ adj : smooth, plausible, and insincere in speech; also : affectedly unwilling to use strong or coarse language

¹**mean** \'mēn\ adj 1 : HUMBLE 2 : lacking power or acumen : ORDINARY 3 : SHABBY, CONTEMPTIBLE 4 : IGNOBLE, BASE 5 : STINGY 6 : pettily selfish or malicious — **mean·ly** adv — **mean·ness** \'mēn-nəs\ n

²**mean** \'mēn\ vb **meant** \'ment\; **mean·ing** \'mē-niŋ\ 1 : to have in the mind as a purpose 2 : to serve to convey, show, or indicate : SIGNIFY 3 : to direct to a particular individual 4 : to be of a specified degree of importance 〈music ∼s little to him〉

³**mean** n 1 : a middle point between extremes 2 pl : something helpful in achieving a desired end 3 pl : material resources affording a secure life 4 : a value computed by dividing the sum of a set of terms by the number of terms 5 : a value computed by dividing the sum of two extremes of a range of values by two

⁴**mean** adj 1 : occupying a middle position (as in space, order, or time) 2 : being a mean 〈a ∼ value〉

¹**me·an·der** \mē-'an-dər\ n [L maeander, fr. Gk maiandros, fr. Maiandros (now Menderes), river in Asia Minor] 1 : a turn or winding of a stream 2 : a winding course

²**meander** vb **me·an·dered; me·an·der·ing** \-d(ə-)riŋ\ 1 : to follow a winding course 2 : to wander aimlessly or casually

**mean·ing** \'mē-niŋ\ n 1 : the thing one intends to convey esp. by language; also : the thing that is thus conveyed 2 : PURPOSE 3 : SIGNIFICANCE 4 : CONNOTATION; also : DENOTATION — **mean·ing·ful** \-fəl\ adj — **mean·ing·ful·ly** \-ē\ adv — **mean·ing·less** adj

¹**mean·time** \'mēn-,tīm\ n : the intervening time

²**meantime** adv : MEANWHILE

¹**mean·while** \-,hwīl\ n : MEANTIME

²**meanwhile** adv : during the intervening time

**meas** abbr measure

**mea·sles** \'mē-zəlz\ n pl : an acute virus disease marked by fever and an eruption of distinct circular red spots

**mea·sly** \'mēz-(ə-)lē\ adj **mea·sli·er; -est** : contemptibly small or insignificant

¹**mea·sure** \'mezh-ər, 'māzh-\ n 1 : an adequate or moderate portion; also : a suitable limit 2 : the dimensions, capacity, or amount of something ascertained by measuring; also : an instrument or utensil for measuring 3 : a unit of measurement; also : a system of such units 〈metric ∼〉 4 : the act or

process of measuring **5** : rhythmic structure or movement **6** : CRITERION **7** : a means to an end **8** : a legislative bill **9** : the part of a musical staff between two adjacent bars — **mea·sure·less** *adj*

²**measure** *vb* **mea·sured; mea·sur·ing** \'mezh-(ə-)riŋ, 'māzh-\ **1** : to regulate esp. by a standard **2** : to apportion by measure **3** : to lay off by making measurements **4** : to ascertain the measurements of **5** : to bring into comparison or competition **6** : to serve as a measure of **7** : to have a specified measurement — **mea·sur·able** \'mezh-(ə-)rə-bəl, 'māzh-\ *adj* — **mea·sur·ably** \-blē\ *adv* — **mea·sur·er** *n*

**mea·sure·ment** \'mezh-ər-mənt, 'māzh-\ *n* **1** : the act or process of measuring **2** : a figure, extent, or amount obtained by measuring

**measure up** *vb* **1** : to have necessary qualifications **2** : to equal esp. in ability

**meat** \'mēt\ *n* **1** : FOOD; *esp* : solid food as distinguished from drink **2** : animal and esp. mammal flesh used as food **3** : the edible part inside a covering (as a shell or rind) — **meaty** *adj*

**meat·ball** \-,bȯl\ *n* : a small ball of chopped or ground meat

**meat·man** \'mēt-,man\ *n* : BUTCHER

**mec·ca** \'mek-ə\ *n, often cap* : a place sought as a goal by numerous people

**mech** *abbr* mechanical; mechanics

¹**me·chan·ic** \mi-'kan-ik\ *adj* **1** : of or relating to manual work or skill **2** : of the nature of or resembling a machine (as in automatic performance)

²**mechanic** *n* **1** : a manual worker **2** : MACHINIST; *esp* : one who repairs machines

**me·chan·i·cal** \mi-'kan-i-kəl\ *adj* **1** : of or relating to machinery or tools, to manual operations, or to mechanics **2** : done as if by a machine : AUTOMATIC **syn** instinctive, impulsive, spontaneous — **me·chan·i·cal·ly** \-k(ə-)lē\ *adv*

**mechanical drawing** *n* : drawing done with the aid of instruments

**me·chan·ics** \mi-'kan-iks\ *n sing or pl* **1** : a branch of physical science that deals with energy and forces and their effect on bodies **2** : the practical application of mechanics (as to the operation of machines) **3** : mechanical or functional details

**mech·a·nism** \'mek-ə-,niz-əm\ *n* **1** : a piece of machinery; *also* : a process or technique for achieving a result **2** : mechanical operation or action **3** : the fundamental processes involved in or responsible for a natural phenomenon ⟨the visual ∼⟩

**mech·a·nis·tic** \,mek-ə-'nis-tik\ *adj* **1** : mechanically determined ⟨∼ universe⟩ **2** : MECHANICAL — **mech·a·nis·ti·cal·ly** \-ti-k(ə-)lē\ *adv*

**mech·a·nize** \'mek-ə-,nīz\ *vb* **-nized; -niz·ing 1** : to make mechanical **2** : to equip with machinery esp. in order to replace human or ani-

mal labor **3** : to equip with armed and armored motor vehicles — **mech·a·ni·za·tion** \,mek-ə-nə-'zā-shən\ *n* — **mech·a·niz·er** \'mek-ə-,nī-zər\ *n*

**med** *abbr* **1** medical; medicine **2** medieval **3** medium

**MEd** *abbr* master of education

**med·al** \'med-ᵊl\ *n* [MF *medaille,* fr. OIt *medaglia* coin worth half a denarius, medal, fr. (assumed) VL *medalis* half, fr. LL *medialis* middle, fr. L *medius*] **1** : a metal disk bearing a religious emblem or picture **2** : a piece of metal issued to commemorate a person or event or awarded for excellence or achievement

**med·al·ist** *or* **med·al·list** \'med-ᵊl-əst\ *n* **1** : a designer or maker of medals **2** : a recipient of a medal

**me·dal·lion** \mə-'dal-yən\ *n* **1** : a large medal **2** : a tablet or panel bearing a portrait or an ornament

**med·dle** \'med-ᵊl\ *vb* **med·dled; med·dling** \'med-(ᵊ-)liŋ\ : to interfere without right or propriety — **med·dler** \'med-(ᵊ-)lər\ *n*

**med·dle·some** \'med-ᵊl-səm\ *adj* : inclined to meddle in the affairs of others

**me·dia** \'mēd-ē-ə\ *n, pl* **me·di·as** : MEDIUM **4**

**me·di·al** \'mēd-ē-əl\ *adj* **1** : occurring in or extending toward the middle : MEDIAN **2** : MEAN, AVERAGE

¹**me·di·an** \'mēd-ē-ən\ *n* **1** : a medial part **2** : a value in an ordered set of values below and above which there are an equal number of values

²**median** *adj* **1** : MEDIAL **1 2** : relating to or constituting a statistical median

**median strip** *n* : a strip dividing a highway into lanes according to the direction of travel

¹**me·di·ate** \'mēd-ē-ət\ *adj* **1** : occupying a middle or mediating position **2** : acting through a mediate agency — **me·di·ate·ly** *adv*

²**me·di·ate** \'mēd-ē-,āt\ *vb* **-at·ed; -at·ing** : to act as an intermediary in settling a dispute **syn** intercede, intervene, interpose — **me·di·a·tion** \,mēd-ē-'ā-shən\ *n* — **me·di·a·tor** \,mēd-ē-,āt-ər\ *n* — **me·di·a·trix** \,mēd-ē-'ā-triks\ *n*

**med·ic** \'med-ik\ *n* : one engaged in medical work; *esp* : CORPSMAN

**med·i·ca·ble** \'med-i-kə-bəl\ *adj* : CURABLE, REMEDIABLE — **med·i·ca·bly** \-blē\ *adv*

**med·ic·aid** \'med-i-,kād\ *n* : a program of medical aid designed for those unable to afford regular medical service and financed jointly by the state and federal governments

**med·i·cal** \'med-i-kəl\ *adj* : of or relating to the science or practice of medicine or the treatment of disease — **med·i·cal·ly** \-k(ə-)lē\ *adv*

**medical examiner** *n* : a public officer who makes postmortem examinations of bodies to find the cause of death

**me·di·ca·ment** \mi-'dik-ə-mənt, 'med-i-kə-\ *n* : a medicine or healing application

**medi·care** \'med-i-,keər\ *n* : a government program of medical care esp. for the aged

**med·i·cate** \'med-ə-,kāt\ vb **-cat·ed; -cat·ing :** to treat with medicine — **med·i·ca·tion** \,med-ə-'kā-shən\ n

**me·dic·i·nal** \mə-'dis-(ə-)nəl\ adj **:** tending or used to relieve or cure disease or pain — **me·dic·i·nal·ly** \-ē\ adv

**med·i·cine** \'med-ə-sən\ n **1 :** a substance or preparation used in treating disease **2 :** a science or art dealing with the prevention or cure of disease

**medicine ball** n **:** a heavy stuffed leather ball used for conditioning exercises

**medicine man** n **:** a priestly healer or sorcerer esp. among the American Indians

**med·i·co** \'med-i-,kō\ n, pl **-cos :** a medical practitioner or student

**me·di·eval** or **me·di·ae·val** \,mēd-ē-'ē-vəl, ,med-, mē-'dē-vəl\ adj **:** of, relating to, or characteristic of the Middle Ages — **me·di·e·val·ism** \-,iz-əm\ n — **me·di·e·val·ist** \-əst\ n

**me·di·o·cre** \,mēd-ē-'ō-kər\ adj [MF, fr. L mediocris, lit., halfway up a mountain, fr. medius middle + ocris stony mountain] **:** of moderate or low excellence **:** ORDINARY — **me·di·oc·ri·ty** \-'äk-rət-ē\ n

**med·i·tate** \'med-ə-,tāt\ vb **-tat·ed; -tat·ing 1 :** to muse over **:** CONTEMPLATE, PONDER **2 :** INTEND, PURPOSE — **med·i·ta·tion** \,med-ə-'tā-shən\ n — **med·i·ta·tive** \'med-ə-,tāt-iv\ adj — **med·i·ta·tive·ly** adv

**¹me·di·um** \'mēd-ē-əm\ n, pl **medi·ums** or **me·dia** \-ē-ə\ **1 :** something in a middle position; also **:** a middle position or degree **2 :** a means of effecting or conveying something **3 :** a surrounding or enveloping substance **4 :** a channel of communication; esp **:** a means of disseminating ideas or advertising (as broadcasting, publishing, or motion pictures) **5 :** a mode of artistic expression **6 :** an individual held to be a channel of communication between the earthly world and a world of spirits **7 :** a condition in which something may function or flourish

**²medium** adj **:** intermediate in amount, quality, position, or degree

**me·di·um·is·tic** \,mēd-ē-ə-'mis-tik\ adj **:** of, relating to, or being a spiritualistic medium

**med·ley** \'med-lē\ n, pl **medleys 1 :** HODGEPODGE **2 :** a musical composition made up esp. of a series of songs

**me·dul·la** \mə-'dəl-ə\ n, pl **-las** or **-lae** \-(,)ē, -,ī\ **:** an inner or deep anatomical part; also **:** the posterior part (**medulla ob·lon·ga·ta** \-,äb-,lóŋ-'gät-ə\) of the brain

**meed** \'mēd\ n **1** archaic **:** REWARD **2 :** a fitting return

**meek** \'mēk\ adj **1 :** characterized by patience and long-suffering **2 :** deficient in spirit and courage **3 :** MODERATE — **meek·ly** adv — **meek·ness** n

**meer·schaum** \'miər-shəm, -,shòm\ n

[G, fr. meer sea + schaum foam] **:** a tobacco pipe made of a light white clayey mineral

**¹meet** \'mēt\ vb **met** \'met\; **meet·ing 1 :** to come upon **:** FIND **2 :** JOIN, INTERSECT **3 :** to appear to the perception of **4 :** OPPOSE, FIGHT **5 :** to join in conversation or discussion; also **:** ASSEMBLE **6 :** to conform to **7 :** to pay fully **8 :** to cope with **9 :** to provide for **10 :** to be introduced to

**²meet** n **:** an assembling esp. for a hunt or for competitive sports

**³meet** adj **:** SUITABLE, PROPER

**meet·ing** \'mēt-iŋ\ n **1 :** an act of coming together **:** ASSEMBLY **2 :** JUNCTION, INTERSECTION

**meet·ing·house** \-,haùs\ n **:** a building for public assembly and esp. for Protestant worship

**meg** abbr megohm

**mega·cy·cle** \'meg-ə-,sī-kəl\ n **:** MEGAHERTZ

**mega·death** \-,deth\ n **:** one million deaths — used as a unit in reference to atomic warfare

**mega·hertz** \'meg-ə-,hərts, -,heərts\ n **:** a unit of frequency equal to one million hertz

**mega·lith** \'meg-ə-,lith\ n **:** one of the huge stones used in various prehistoric monuments — **mega·lith·ic** \,meg-ə-'lith-ik\ adj

**meg·a·lo·ma·nia** \,meg-ə-lō-'mā-nē-ə, -nyə\ n **:** a disorder of mind marked by feelings of personal omnipotence and grandeur — **meg·a·lo·ma·ni·ac** \-'mā-nē-,ak\ adj or n

**meg·a·lop·o·lis** \,meg-ə-'läp-ə-ləs\ n **:** a very large urban unit

**mega·phone** \'meg-ə-,fōn\ n **:** a cone-shaped device used to intensify or direct the voice — **megaphone** vb

**mega·ton** \'meg-ə-,tən\ n **:** an explosive force equivalent to that of a million tons of TNT

**meg·ohm** \'meg-,ōm\ n **:** one million ohms

**mei·o·sis** \mī-'ō-səs\ n **:** the cellular process that results in the number of chromosomes in gamete-producing cells being reduced to one half — **mei·ot·ic** \mī-'ät-ik\ adj

**mel·an·cho·lia** \,mel-ən-'kō-lē-ə\ n **:** a mental condition marked by extreme depression often with delusions

**mel·an·chol·ic** \,mel-ən-'käl-ik\ adj **1 :** DEPRESSED **2 :** of or relating to melancholia

**mel·an·choly** \'mel-ən-,käl-ē\ n, pl **-chol·ies** [ME malencolie, fr. MF melancolie, fr. LL melancholia, fr. Gk, fr. melan-, melas black + cholē bile; so called fr. the former belief that it was caused by an excess in the system of black bile, a substance supposedly secreted by the kidneys or spleen] **:** depression of spirits **:** DEJECTION, GLOOM — **melancholy** adj

**Mel·a·ne·sian** \,mel-ə-'nē-zhən\ n **:** a member of the dominant native group of Melanesia — **Melanesian** adj

**mé·lange** \mā-'lläⁿzh, -'länj\ n **:** a mixture esp. of incongruous elements

**me·lan·ic** \mə-'lan-ik\ *adj* **1** : having black pigment **2** : affected with or characterized by melanism — **melanic** *n*

**mel·a·nin** \'mel-ə-nən\ *n* : a dark brown or black animal or plant pigment

**mel·a·nism** \'mel-ə-,niz-əm\ *n* : an increased amount of black or nearly black pigmentation

**mel·a·no·ma** \,mel-ə-'nō-mə\ *n, pl* **-mas** *also* **-ma·ta** \-'mät-ə\ : a usu. malignant tumor containing black pigment

**¹meld** \'meld\ *vb* : to show or announce for a score in a card game

**²meld** *n* : a card or combination of cards that is or can be melded

**me·lee** \'mā-,lā, mā-'lā\ *n* : a confused struggle **syn** fracas, row, brawl

**me·lio·rate** \'mēl-yə-,rāt, 'mē-lē-ə-\ *vb* **-rat·ed; -rat·ing** : to make or become better — **me·lio·ra·tion** \,mēl-yə-'rā-shən, ,mē-lē-ə-\ *n* — **me·lio·ra·tive** \'mēl-yə-,rāt-iv, 'mē-lē-ə-\ *adj*

**mel·lif·lu·ous** \me-'lif-lə-wəs, mə-\ *adj* [LL *mellifluus*, fr. L *mel* honey + *fluere* to flow] : sweetly flowing — **mel·lif·lu·ous·ly** *adv* — **mel·lif·lu·ous·ness** *n*

**¹mel·low** \'mel-ō\ *adj* **1** : soft and sweet because of ripeness ⟨~ apple⟩; *also* : well aged and pleasingly mild ⟨~ wine⟩ **2** : made gentle by age or experience **3** : of soft loamy consistency ⟨~ soil⟩ **4** : being rich and full but not garish or strident ⟨~ colors⟩ — **mel·low·ness** *n*

**²mellow** *vb* : to make or become mellow

**me·lo·de·on** \mə-'lōd-ē-ən\ *n* : a small reed organ in which a suction bellows draws air inward through the reeds

**me·lo·di·ous** \mə-'lōd-ē-əs\ *adj* : pleasing to the ear — **me·lo·di·ous·ly** *adv* — **me·lo·di·ous·ness** *n*

**me·lo·dra·ma** \'mel-ə-,dräm-ə, -,dram-\ *n* : an extravagantly theatrical play in which action and plot predominate over characterization — **melo·dra·mat·ic** \,mel-ə-drə-'mat-ik\ *adj* — **melo·dra·ma·tist** \,mel-ə-'dram-ət-əst, -'dräm-\ *n*

**mel·o·dy** \'mel-əd-ē\ *n, pl* **-dies 1** : sweet or agreeable sound ⟨birds making ~⟩ **2** : a particular succession of notes : TUNE, AIR — **me·lod·ic** \mə-'läd-ik\ *adj* — **me·lod·i·cal·ly** \-i-k(ə-)lē\ *adv*

**mel·on** \'mel-ən\ *n* : any of certain gourds (as a muskmelon or watermelon) usu. eaten raw as fruits

**melt** \'melt\ *vb* **1** : to change from a solid to a liquid state usu. by heat **2** : DISSOLVE, DISINTEGRATE; *also* : to cause to disperse or disappear **3** : to make or become tender or gentle

**²melt** *n* : a melted substance

**melt·wa·ter** \'melt-,wót-ər, -,wät-\ *n* : water derived from the melting of ice and snow

**mem** *abbr* **1** member **2** memoir **3** memorial

**mem·ber** \'mem-bər\ *n* **1** : a part (as an arm, leg, or branch) of a person, lower animal, or plant **2** : one of the individuals composing a group **3** : a constituent part of a whole

**mem·ber·ship** \-,ship\ *n* **1** : the state or status of being a member **2** : the body of members (as of a church)

**mem·brane** \'mem-,brān\ *n* : a thin pliable layer esp. of animal or plant tissue — **mem·bra·nous** \-brə-nəs\ *adj*

**me·men·to** \mi-'ment-ō\ *n, pl* **-tos** *or* **-toes** : something that serves to warn or remind : SOUVENIR

**memo** \'mem-ō\ *n, pl* **mem·os** : MEMORANDUM

**mem·oir** \'mem-,wär\ *n* **1** : MEMORANDUM **2** : AUTOBIOGRAPHY — usu. used in pl. **3** : an account of something noteworthy; *also* : the record of the proceedings of a learned society

**mem·o·ra·bil·ia** \,mem-ə-rə-'bil-ē-ə, -'bil-yə\ *n pl* : things worthy of remembrance; *also* : a record of such things

**mem·o·ra·ble** \'mem-(ə-)rə-bəl\ *adj* : worth remembering : NOTABLE — **mem·o·ra·bil·i·ty** \,mem-ə-rə-'bil-ət-ē\ *n* — **mem·o·ra·ble·ness** \'mem-(ə-)rə-bəl-nəs\ *n* — **mem·o·ra·bly** \-blē\ *adv*

**mem·o·ran·dum** \,mem-ə-'ran-dəm\ *n, pl* **-dums** *or* **-da** \-də\ **1** : an informal record; *also* : a written reminder **2** : an informal written note

**¹me·mo·ri·al** \mə-'mōr-ē-əl\ *adj* : serving to preserve remembrance

**²memorial** *n* **1** : something designed to keep remembrance alive; *esp* : MONUMENT **2** : a statement of facts often accompanied with a petition — **me·mo·ri·al·ize** *vb*

**Memorial Day** *n* : the last Monday in May or formerly May 30 observed as a legal holiday in commemoration of dead servicemen

**mem·o·rize** \'mem-ə-,rīz\ *vb* **-rized; -riz·ing** : to learn by heart — **mem·o·ri·za·tion** \,mem-(ə-)rə-'zā-shən\ *n* — **mem·o·riz·er** \'mem-ə-,rīz-ər\ *n*

**mem·o·ry** \'mem-(ə-)rē\ *n, pl* **-ries 1** : the power or process of remembering **2** : the store of things remembered; *also* : a particular act of recollection **3** : commemorative remembrance **4** : the time within which past events are remembered **5** : a device (as in a computer) in which information can be stored **syn** remembrance, recollection, reminiscence

**men** *pl of* MAN

**¹men·ace** \'men-əs\ *n* **1** : THREAT **2** : DANGER; *also* : NUISANCE

**²menace** *vb* **men·aced; men·ac·ing 1** : THREATEN **2** : ENDANGER — **men·ac·ing·ly** *adv*

**mé·nage** \mā-'näzh\ *n* : HOUSEHOLD

**me·nag·er·ie** \mə-'naj-(ə-)rē\ *n* : a collection of wild animals esp. for exhibition

**¹mend** \'mend\ *vb* **1** : to improve in manners or morals **2** : to put into good shape : REPAIR **3** : to restore to health : HEAL — **mend·er** *n*

**²mend** *n* **1** : an act of mending **2** : a mended place

**men·da·cious** \men-'dā-shəs\ *adj*

: given to deception or falsehood : UN-TRUTHFUL **syn** dishonest, deceitful —
**men·da·cious·ly** \-'das-ət-ē\ *adv* — **men·dac·i·ty** \-'das-ət-ē\ *n*

**men·de·le·vi·um** \,men-də-'lē-vē-əm, -'lā-\ *n* : a radioactive chemical element artificially produced

**men·di·cant** \'men-di-kənt\ *n* **1** : BEGGAR **2** *often cap* : FRIAR — **mendi·can·cy** \-kən-sē\ *n* — **mendicant** *adj*

**men·folk** \'men-,fōk\ *or* **men·folks** -,fōks\ *n pl* **1** : men in general **2** : the men of a family or community

**men·ha·den** \men-'hād-ᵊn, mən-\ *n, pl* **-den** *also* **-dens** : a marine fish related to the herring that is abundant along the Atlantic coast of the U.S.

¹**me·nial** \'mē-nē-əl, -nyəl\ *adj* **1** : of or relating to servants **2** : HUMBLE; *also* : SERVILE — **me·ni·al·ly** \-ē\ *adv*

²**menial** *n* : a domestic servant

**men·in·gi·tis** \,men-ən-'jīt-əs\ *n, pl* **-git·i·des** \-'jit-ə,dēz\ : inflammation of the membranes enclosing the brain and spinal cord; *also* : a usu. bacterial disease marked by this

**me·ninx** \'mē-niŋks, 'men-iŋks\ *n, pl* **me·nin·ges** \mə-'nin-(,)jēz\ : any of the three membranes that envelop the brain and spinal cord — **men·in·ge·al** \,men-ən-'jē-əl\ *adj*

**me·nis·cus** \mə-'nis-kəs\ *n, pl* **me·nis·ci** \-'nis-,(k)ī, -,kē\ *also* **me·nis·cus·es 1** : a crescent-shaped body : CRESCENT **2** : a lens that is convex on one side and concave on the other **3** : the curved upper surface of a liquid column that is concave when the containing walls are wetted by the liquid and convex when not

**meno·pause** \'men-ə-,pöz\ *n* : the period of natural cessation of menstruation — **meno·paus·al** \,men-ə-'pö-zəl\ *adj*

**men·ses** \'men-,sēz\ *n pl* : the menstrual period or flow

**men·stru·a·tion** \,men-strə-'wā-shən, men-'strā-\ *n* : a discharging of bloody matter at approximately monthly intervals from the uterus of breeding-age primate females that are not pregnant — **men·stru·al** \'men-strə-(-wə)l\ *adj* — **men·stru·ate** \'men-strə-,wāt, -,strāt\ *vb*

**men·su·ra·ble** \'mens-(ə-)rə-bəl, 'mench-(ə-)rə-\ *adj* : MEASURABLE

**men·su·ra·tion** \,men-sə-'rā-shən, ,mench-ə-\ *n* : MEASUREMENT

**-ment** \mənt\ *n suffix* **1** : concrete result, object, or agent of a (specified) action ⟨embank*ment*⟩ ⟨entangle*ment*⟩ **2** : concrete means or instrument of a (specified) action ⟨entertain*ment*⟩ **3** : action : process ⟨encircle*ment*⟩ ⟨develop*ment*⟩ **4** : place of a (specified) action ⟨encamp*ment*⟩ **5** : state : condition ⟨amaze*ment*⟩

**men·tal** \'ment-ᵊl\ *adj* **1** : of or relating to the mind **2** : of, relating to, or affected with a disorder of the mind — **men·tal·ly** \-ē\ *adv*

**mental age** *n* : a measure used in psychological testing that expresses an individual's mental attainment in terms of the number of years it takes the average child to reach the same level

**mental deficiency** *n* : failure in intellectual development that results in social incompetence and is considered to be the result of a defective central nervous system

**men·tal·i·ty** \men-'tal-ət-ē\ *n, pl* **-ties 1** : mental power or capacity **2** : mode or way of thought

**men·thol** \'men-,thöl, -,thōl\ *n* : a white soothing substance from oil of peppermint — **men·tho·lat·ed** \-thə-,lāt-əd\ *adj*

¹**men·tion** \'men-chən\ *n* **1** : a brief or casual reference **2** : a formal citation for outstanding achievement

²**mention** *vb* **men·tioned; men·tion·ing** \'mench-(ə-)niŋ\ **1** : to refer to : CITE **2** : to cite for outstanding achievement

**men·tor** \'men-,tòr, 'ment-ər\ *n* : a trusted counselor or guide; *also* : TUTOR, COACH

**menu** \'men-yü, 'mān-\ *n, pl* **menus** [F, fr. *menu* small, detailed, fr. L *minutus* minute (adj.)] **1** : a list of the dishes available (as in a restaurant) for a meal; *also* : the dishes served

**me·ow** \mē-'aů\ *vb* : to make the characteristic cry of a cat — **meow** *n*

**me·phit·ic** \mə-'fit-ik\ *adj* : foulsmelling

**mer** *abbr* meridian

**mer·can·tile** \'mər-kən-,tēl, -,tīl\ *adj* : of or relating to merchants or trading

¹**mer·ce·nary** \'mərs-ᵊn-,er-ē\ *n, pl* **-nar·ies** : one who serves merely for wages; *esp* : a soldier serving in a foreign army

²**mercenary** *adj* **1** : serving merely for pay or gain **2** : hired for service in a foreign army — **mer·ce·nari·ly** \,mərs-ᵊn-'er-ə-lē\ *adv* — **mer·ce·nari·ness** \'mərs-ᵊn-,er-ē-nəs\ *n*

**mer·cer** \'mər-sər\ *n* : a dealer in textile fabrics

**mer·cer·ize** \'mər-sə-,rīz\ *vb* **-ized; -iz·ing** : to treat cotton yarn or cloth with alkali so that it looks silky or takes a better dye

¹**mer·chan·dise** \'mər-chən-,dīz, -,dīs\ *n* : the commodities or goods that are bought and sold in business

²**mer·chan·dise** \-,dīz\ *vb* **-dised; -dis·ing** : to buy and sell in business : TRADE — **mer·chan·dis·er** *n*

**mer·chant** \'mər-chənt\ *n* **1** : a buyer and seller of commodities for profit **2** : STOREKEEPER

**mer·chant·able** \'mər-chənt-ə-bəl\ *adj* : acceptable to buyers : MARKETABLE

**mer·chant·man** \'mər-chənt-mən\ *n* : a ship used in commerce

**merchant marine** *n* : the commercial ships of a nation

**merchant ship** *n* : MERCHANTMAN

**mer·cu·ri·al** \,mər-'kyúr-ē-əl\ *adj* **1** : unpredictably changeable **2** : MERCURIC — **mer·cu·ri·al·ly** \-ē\ *adv* — **mer·cu·ri·al·ness** *n*

**mer·cu·ric** \,mər-'kyúr-ik\ *adj* : of, relating to, or containing mercury

**mer·cu·rous** \,mər-'kyûr-əs, 'mər-kyə-rəs\ *adj* : of, relating to, or containing mercury

**mer·cu·ry** \'mər-kyə-rē\ *n, pl* **-ries** 1 : a heavy silver-white liquid metallic chemical element used in thermometers and medicine 2 *cap* : the smallest of the planets and the one nearest the sun

**mer·cy** \'mər-sē\ *n, pl* **mercies** [ME, fr. OF *merci*, fr. ML *merces*, fr. L, price paid, wages, fr. *merc-, merx* merchandise] 1 : compassion shown to an offender; *also* : imprisonment rather than death for first-degree murder 2 : a blessing resulting from divine favor or compassion; *also* : a fortunate circumstance 3 : compassion shown to victims of misfortune — **mer·ci·ful** \-si-fəl\ *adj* — **mer·ci·ful·ly** \-ē\ *adv* — **mer·ci·less** \-si-ləs\ *adj* — **mer·ci·less·ly** *adv* — **mercy** *adj*

**¹mere** \'miər\ *n* : LAKE, POOL

**²mere** *adj* **mer·est** 1 : apart from anything else : BARE 2 : not diluted : PURE — **mere·ly** *adv*

**mer·e·tri·cious** \,mer-ə-'trish-əs\ *adj* [L *meretricius*, fr. *meretrix* prostitute, fr. *merēre* to earn] : tawdrily attractive; *also* : SPECIOUS — **mer·e·tri·cious·ly** *adv* — **mer·e·tri·cious·ness** *n*

**mer·gan·ser** \(,)mər-'gan-sər\ *n* : any of various fish-eating ducks with a crested head and a slender bill hooked at the end and serrated along the margins

**merge** \'mərj\ *vb* **merged; merg·ing** 1 : to combine, unite, or coalesce into one 2 : to blend gradually **syn** mingle, amalgamate, fuse

**merg·er** \'mər-jər\ *n* 1 : absorption by a corporation of one or more others 2 : the combination of two or more groups (as churches)

**me·rid·i·an** \mə-'rid-ē-ən\ *n* [ME, fr. MF *meridien*, fr. *meridien* of noon, fr. L *meridianus*, fr. *meridies* noon, south, irreg. fr. *medius* mid + *dies* day] 1 : the highest point : CULMINATION 2 : one of the imaginary circles on the earth's surface passing through the north and south poles and any particular place — **meridian** *adj*

**me·ringue** \mə-'raŋ\ *n* : a dessert topping of baked beaten egg whites and powdered sugar

**me·ri·no** \mə-'rē-nō\ *n, pl* **-nos** 1 : any of a breed of sheep noted for fine soft wool; *also* : its wool or fleece 2 : a fine soft fabric or yarn of wool or wool and cotton

**¹mer·it** \'mer-ət\ *n* 1 : laudable or blameworthy traits or actions 2 : a praiseworthy quality; *also* : character or conduct deserving reward or honor 3 *pl* : the intrinsic rights and wrongs of a legal case; *also* : legal significance

**²merit** *vb* : EARN, DESERVE

**mer·i·toc·ra·cy** \,mer-ə-'täk-rə-sē\ *n, pl* **-cies** : an educational system whereby the talented are chosen and moved ahead on the basis of their achievement (as in competitive examinations); *also* : leadership by the talented

**mer·i·to·ri·ous** \,mer-ə-'tōr-ē-əs\ *adj*

: deserving reward or honor — **mer·i·to·ri·ous·ly** *adv* — **mer·i·to·ri·ous·ness** *n*

**mer·maid** \'mər-,mād\ *n* : a legendary sea creature with a woman's body and a fish's tail

**mer·man** \-,man, -mən\ *n* : a legendary sea creature with a man's body and a fish's tail

**mer·ri·ment** \'mer-i-mənt\ *n* 1 : HILARITY 2 : FESTIVITY

**mer·ry** \'mer-ē\ *adj* **mer·ri·er; -est** 1 : full of gaiety or high spirits 2 : marked by festivity 3 : BRISK ⟨a ~ pace⟩ **syn** blithe, jocund, jovial, jolly — **mer·ri·ly** \'mer-ə-lē\ *adv*

**merry-go-round** \'mer-ē-gō-,raúnd\ *n* 1 : a circular revolving platform with benches and figures of animals on which people sit for a ride 2 : a rapid round of activities

**mer·ry·mak·ing** \'mer-ē-,mā-kiŋ\ *n* 1 : CONVIVIALITY 2 : a festive occasion — **mer·ry·mak·er** \-,mā-kər\ *n*

**me·sa** \'mā-sə\ *n* [Sp, lit., table, fr. L *mensa*] : a flat-topped hill with steep sides

**més·al·li·ance** \,mā-,zal-'yäⁿs, ,mā-zə-'lī-əns\ *n, pl* **més·al·li·ances** \-'yäⁿs(-əz), -'lī-ən-səz\ : a marriage with a person of inferior social position

**mes·cal** \me-'skal, mə-\ *n* 1 : a small cactus that is the source of a stimulant used esp. by Mexican Indians 2 : a usu. colorless liquor distilled from the leaves of an agave; *also* : AGAVE

**mes·ca·line** \'mes-kə-lən, -,lēn\ *n* : a hallucinatory alkaloid from the mescal cactus

**mesdames** *pl of* MADAM *or of* MADAME

**mesdemoiselles** *pl of* MADEMOISELLE

**¹mesh** \'mesh\ *n* 1 : one of the openings between the threads or cords of a net; *also* : one of the similar spaces in a network 2 : the fabric of a net 3 : NETWORK 4 : working contact (as of the teeth of gears) ⟨in ~⟩ — **meshed** \'mesht\ *adj*

**²mesh** *vb* 1 : to catch in or as if in a mesh 2 : to be in or come into mesh : ENGAGE 3 : to fit together properly

**mesh·work** \'mesh-,wərk\ *n* : MESHES, NETWORK

**mes·mer·ize** \'mez-mə-,rīz\ *vb* **-ized; -iz·ing** : HYPNOTIZE — **mes·mer·ic** \mez-'mer-ik\ *adj* — **mes·mer·ism** \'mez-mə-,riz-əm\ *n*

**me·so·sphere** \'mez-ə-,sfiər\ *n* : a layer of the atmosphere above the stratosphere — **me·so·spher·ic** \,mez-ə-'sfiər-ik, -'sfer-\ *adj*

**mes·quite** \mə-'skēt, me-\ *n* : a thorny leguminous shrub of Mexico and the southwestern U.S. with sugar-rich pods important as fodder

**¹mess** \'mes\ *n* 1 : a quantity of food; *also* : enough food of a specified kind for a dish or meal ⟨a ~ of beans⟩ 2 : a group of persons who regularly eat together; *also* : a meal eaten by such a group 3 : a confused, dirty, or offensive state — **messy** *adj*

**²mess** *vb* 1 : to supply with meals; *also* : to take meals with a mess 2 : to make dirty or untidy; *also* **:** BUNGLE **3 :** PUTTER, TRIFLE **4 :** INTERFERE, MEDDLE

**mes·sage** \'mes-ij\ *n* **:** a communication sent by one person to another

**messeigneurs** *pl of* MONSEIGNEUR

**mes·sen·ger** \'mes-ᵊn-jər\ *n* **:** one who carries a message or does an errand

**messenger RNA** *n* **:** an RNA that carries the code for a particular protein from the nuclear DNA to the ribosome and acts as a nplate for the formation of that protein

**Mes·si·ah** \mə-'sī-ə\ *n* **1 :** the expected king and deliverer of the Jews **2 :** Jesus **3** *not cap* **:** a professed or accepted leader — **mes·si·an·ic** \,mes-ē-'an-ik\ *adj*

**messieurs** *pl of* MONSIEUR

**mess·mate** \'mes-,māt\ *n* **:** a member of a group who eat regularly together

**Messrs.** \,mes-ərz\ *pl of* MR.

**mes·ti·zo** \me-'stē-zō\ *n, pl* **-zos** [Sp, fr. *mestizo* mixed, fr. LL *mixticius*, fr. L *mixtus*, pp. of *miscēre* to mix] **:** a person of mixed blood

**¹met** *past of* MEET

**²met** *abbr* metropolitan

**me·tab·o·lism** \mə-'tab-ə-,liz-əm\ *n* **:** the sum of the processes in the building up and breaking down of the substance of plants and animals incidental to life; *also* **:** the processes by which a substance is handled in the body ⟨∼ of sugar⟩ — **met·a·bol·ic** \,met-ə-'bäl-ik\ *adj* — **me·tab·o·lize** \mə-'tab-ə-,līz\ *vb*

**me·tab·o·lite** \-,līt\ *n* **1 :** a product of metabolism **2 :** a substance essential to the metabolism of a particular organism

**meta·car·pus** \,met-ə-'kär-pəs\ *n* **:** the part of the hand or forefoot that typically contains five more or less elongated bones when all the digits are present

**meta·gal·axy** \-'gal-ək-sē\ *n* **:** UNIVERSE

**met·al** \'met-ᵊl\ *n* **1 :** any of various opaque, fusible, ductile, and typically lustrous substances; *esp* **:** one that is a chemical element **2 :** METTLE; *also* **:** the material out of which a person or thing is made — **me·tal·lic** \mə-'tal-ik\ *adj* — **met·al·lif·er·ous** \,met-ᵊl-'if-(ə-)rəs\ *adj* — **met·al·loid** \'met-ᵊl-,òid\ *n or adj*

**met·al·lur·gy** \'met-ᵊl-,ər-jē\ *n* **:** the science and technology of metals — **met·al·lur·gi·cal** \,met-ᵊl-'ər-ji-kəl\ *adj* — **met·al·lur·gi·cal·ly** \-k(ə-)lē\ *adv* — **met·al·lur·gist** \'met-ᵊl-,ər-jəst\ *n*

**met·al·ware** \'met-ᵊl-,waər\ *n* **:** metal utensils for household use

**met·al·work** \-,wərk\ *n* **1 :** the process or occupation of making things from metal **2 :** work and esp. artistic work made of metal — **met·al·work·er** \-,wər-kər\ *n* — **met·al·work·ing** \-,wər-kiŋ\ *n*

**meta·mor·phism** \,met-ə-'mòr-,fiz-əm\ *n* **1 :** METAMORPHOSIS **2 :** a change in the structure of rock; *esp* **:** a

change to a more compact and more highly crystalline condition produced by pressure, heat, and water — **meta·mor·phic** \-'mòr-fik\ *adj*

**meta·mor·pho·sis** \,met-ə-'mòr-fə-səs\ *n, pl* **-pho·ses** \-,sēz\ **1 :** a change of physical form, structure, or substance esp. by supernatural means; *also* **:** a striking alteration as in appearance or character) **2 :** a fundamental change in form and often habits of an animal accompanying the transformation of a larva into an adult — **meta·mor·phose** \-,fōz, -,fōs\ *vb*

**meta·phor** \'met-ə-,fòr, -fər\ *n* **:** a figure of speech in which a word denoting one subject or idea is used in place of another to suggest a likeness between them (as in "the ship plows the sea") — **meta·phor·i·cal** \,met-ə-'fòr-i-kəl\ *adj*

**meta·phys·ics** \,met-ə-'fiz-iks\ *n* [ML *Metaphysica*, title of Aristotle's treatise on the subject, fr. Gk *(ta) meta (ta) physika*, lit., the (works) after the physical (works); fr. its position in his collected works] **:** the part of philosophy concerned with the study of the ultimate causes and the underlying nature of things — **meta·phys·i·cal** \-'fiz-i-kəl\ *adj* — **meta·phy·si·cian** \-fə-'zish-ən\ *n*

**me·tas·ta·sis** \mə-'tas-tə-səs\ *n, pl* **-ta·ses** \-,sēz\ **:** transfer of a health-impairing agency (as tumor cells) to a new site in the body; *also* **:** a secondary growth of a malignant tumor — **meta·stat·ic** \,met-ə-'stat-ik\ *adj*

**meta·tar·sal** \,met-ə-'tär-səl\ *adj* **:** of or relating to the metatarsus — **metatarsal** *n*

**meta·tar·sus** \,met-ə-'tär-səs\ *n* **:** the part of the foot in man or of the hind foot in quadrupeds between the tarsus and the bones of the digits

**¹mete** \'mēt\ *vb* **met·ed; met·ing 1** *archaic* **:** MEASURE **2 :** ALLOT

**²mete** *n* **:** BOUNDARY ⟨∼s and bounds⟩

**me·tem·psy·cho·sis** \mə-,tem(p)-si-'kō-səs, ,met-əm-,sī-\ *n* **:** the passing of the soul at death into another body either human or animal

**me·te·or** \'mēt-ē-ər, -ē-,òr\ *n* **1 :** a usu. small particle of matter in the solar system observable only when it falls into the earth's atmosphere where friction causes it to glow **2 :** the streak of light produced by passage of a meteor

**me·te·or·ic** \,mēt-ē-'òr-ik\ *adj* **1 :** of, relating to, or resembling a meteor **2 :** transiently brilliant ⟨a ∼ career⟩ — **me·te·or·i·cal·ly** \-i-k(ə-)lē\ *adv*

**me·te·or·ite** \'mēt-ē-ə-,rīt\ *n* **:** a meteor that reaches the earth without being completely vaporized — **me·te·or·it·ic** \,mēt-ē-ə-'rit-ik\ *adj*

**me·te·or·oid** \'mēt-ē-ə-,ròid\ *n* **:** METEOR 1 — **me·te·or·oi·dal** \,mēt-ē-ə-'ròid-ᵊl\ *adj*

**me·te·o·rol·o·gy** \,mēt-ē-ə-'räl-ə-jē\ *n* **:** a science that deals with the atmosphere and its phenomena and esp. with weather and weather forecasting — **me·te·o·ro·log·i·cal** \-ē-,òr-ə-'läj-i-kəl\ *adj* — me·te·o·rol·o·gist \-ē-ə-'räl-ə-jəst\ *n*

¹me·ter \'mēt-ər\ *n* : rhythm in verse or music

²met·er \'mēt-ər\ *n* : the basic metric unit of length — see METRIC SYSTEM table

³me·ter \'mēt-ər\ *n* : a measuring and sometimes recording instrument

⁴me·ter *vb* 1 : to measure by means of a meter 2 : to print postal indicia on by means of a postage meter ⟨~ed mail⟩

meter–kilogram–second *adj* : of, relating to, or being a system of units based on the meter as the unit of length, the kilogram as the unit of mass, and the second as the unit of time

meter maid *n* : a female member of a police department who is assigned to write tickets for parking violations

meth·a·done \'meth-ə-ˌdōn\ *or* meth·a·don \-ˌdän\ *n* : a synthetic addictive narcotic drug used esp. as a substitute narcotic in the treatment of heroin addiction

⎮meth·am·phet·amine \ˌmeth-am-'fet-ə-ˌmēn, ˌmeth-əm-, -mən\ *n* : a drug used in the form of its hydrochloride as a stimulant for the central nervous system and in the treatment of obesity

meth·ane \'meth-ˌān\ *n* : a colorless odorless flammable gas produced by decomposition of organic matter (as in marshes) or from coal and used as a fuel

meth·a·nol \'meth-ə-ˌnȯl, -ˌnōl\ *n* : a volatile flammable poisonous liquid that consists of carbon, hydrogen, and oxygen and that is used esp. as a solvent and as an antifreeze

meth·od \'meth-əd\ *n* [MF *methode*, fr. L *methodus*, fr. Gk *methodos*, fr. *meta* with + *hodos* way] 1 : a procedure or process for achieving an end 2 : orderly arrangement : PLAN *syn* mode, manner, way, fashion, system — me·thod·i·cal \mə-'thäd-i-kəl\ *adj* — me·thod·i·cal·ly \-k-(ə-)lē\ *adv* — me·thod·i·cal·ness *n*

Meth·od·ist \'meth-əd-əst\ *n* : a member of a Protestant denomination adhering to the doctrines of John Wesley — Meth·od·ism \-ə-ˌdiz-əm\ *n*

meth·od·ize \'meth-ə-ˌdīz\ *vb* -ized; -iz·ing : SYSTEMATIZE

meth·od·ol·o·gy \ˌmeth-ə-'däl-ə-jē\ *n*, *pl* -gies 1 : a body of methods and rules followed in a science of discipline 2 : the study of the principles or procedures of inquiry in a particular field

meth·yl \'meth-əl\ *n* : a chemical radical consisting of carbon and hydrogen

methyl alcohol *n* : METHANOL

me·tic·u·lous \mə-'tik-yə-ləs\ *adj* [L *meticulosus* timid, fr. *metus* fear] : extremely careful in attending to details — me·tic·u·lous·ly *adv* — me·tic·u·lous·ness *n*

mé·tier \'me-ˌtyā, me-'tyā\ *n* : an area of activity in which one is expert or successful

me·tre \'mēt-ər\ *chiefly Brit var of* METER

met·ric \'met-rik\ *or* met·ri·cal \-ri-kəl\ *adj* : of or relating to the meter; *esp* : of or relating to the metric system — met·ri·cal·ly \-ri-k(ə-)lē\ *adv*

## Metric System¹

### LENGTH

| unit | number of meters | approximate U.S. equivalent |
|---|---|---|
| myriameter | 10,000 | 6.2 miles |
| kilometer | 1,000 | 0.62 mile |
| hectometer | 100 | 109.36 yards |
| dekameter | 10 | 32.81 feet |
| meter | 1 | 39.37 inches |
| decimeter | 0.1 | 3.94 inches |
| centimeter | 0.01 | 0.39 inch |
| millimeter | 0.001 | 0.04 inch |

### AREA

| unit | number of square meters | approximate U.S. equivalent |
|---|---|---|
| square kilometer | 1,000,000 | 0.3861 square mile |
| hectare | 10,000 | 2.47 acres |
| are | 100 | 119.60 square yards |
| centare | 1 | 10.76 square feet |
| square centimeter | 0.0001 | 0.155 square inch |

### VOLUME

| unit | number of cubic meters | approximate U.S. equivalent |
|---|---|---|
| dekastere | 10 | 13.10 cubic yards |
| stere | 1 | 1.31 cubic yards |
| decistere | 0.10 | 3.53 cubic feet |
| cubic centimeter | 0.000001 | 0.061 cubic inch |

**met·ri·cal** \'met-ri-kəl\ *or* **met·ric** \-rik\ *adj* **1** : of, relating to, or composed in meter **2** : of or relating to measurement — **met·ri·cal·ly** \-ri-k(ə-)lē\ *adv*

**met·ri·ca·tion** \,me-tri-'kā-shən\ *n* : the act or process of converting into or expressing in the metric system

**met·ri·cize** \'met-rə-,sīz\ *vb* **-cized; -cizing** : to change into or express in the metric system

**metric system** *n* : a decimal system of weights and measures based on the meter and on the kilogram

**metric ton** *n* — see METRIC SYSTEM table

**met·ro** \'met-rō\ *n, pl* **metros** : SUBWAY

**me·trol·o·gy** \me-'träl-ə-jē\ *n* : the science of weights and measures or of measurement

**met·ro·nome** \'met-rə-,nōm\ *n* : an instrument for marking exact time by a regularly repeated tick

**me·trop·o·lis** \mə-'träp-(ə-)ləs\ *n* [LL, fr. Gk *mētropolis*, fr. *mētēr* mother + *polis* city] : the chief or capital city of a country, state, or region — **met·ro·pol·i·tan** \,met-rə-'päl-ət-ᵊn\ *adj*

**met·tle** \'met-ᵊl\ *n* **1** : quality of temperament **2** : SPIRIT, COURAGE

**met·tle·some** \'met-ᵊl-səm\ *adj* : full of mettle

**MEV** *abbr* million electron volts

**mew** \'myü\ *vb* : CONFINE

**mews** \'myüz\ *n pl, chiefly Brit* : stables usu. with living quarters built around a court; *also* : a narrow street with dwellings converted from stables

**Mex** *abbr* Mexican; Mexico

**Mex·i·can** \'mek-si-kən\ *n* : a native or inhabitant of Mexico — **Mexican** *adj*

**mez·za·nine** \'mez-ᵊn-,ēn, ,mez-ᵊn-'ēn\ *n* **1** : a low-ceilinged story between two main stories of a building **2** : the lowest balcony in a theater; *also* : the first few rows of such a balcony

**mez·zo–so·pra·no** \,met-sō-sə-'pran-ō, ,me(d)z-\ *n* : a woman's voice having a full deep quality between that of the soprano and contralto; *also* : a singer having such a voice

**MF** *abbr* **1** Middle French **2** medium frequency

**MFA** *abbr* master of fine arts

**mfd** *abbr* manufactured

**mfg** *abbr* manufacturing

**mfr** *abbr* manufacture; manufacturer

**mg** *abbr* milligram

**Mg** *symbol* magnesium

**MG** *abbr* **1** machine gun **2** major general **3** military government

**mgr** *abbr* **1** manager **2** monseigneur **3** monsignor

**mgt** *abbr* management

**MGy Sgt** *abbr* master gunnery sergeant

**MHz** *abbr* megahertz

**mi** *abbr* **1** mile **2** mill

**MI** *abbr* **1** Michigan **2** military intelligence

**MIA** *abbr* missing in action

**Mi·ami** \mī-'am-ē, -'am-ə\ *n, pl* **Miami** *or* **Mi·am·is** : a member of an Indian people orig. of Wisconsin and Indiana

---

## Metric System¹, continued

### CAPACITY

| unit | number of liters | cubic | approximate U.S. equivalent dry | liquid |
|---|---|---|---|---|
| kiloliter | 1,000 | 1.31 cubic yards | 2.84 bushels | |
| hectoliter | 100 | 3.53 cubic feet | 2.84 bushels | |
| dekaliter | 10 | 0.35 cubic foot | 1.14 pecks | 2.64 gallons |
| liter | 1 | 61.02 cubic inches | 0.908 quart | 1.057 quarts |
| deciliter | 0.10 | 6.1 cubic inches | 0.18 pint | 0.21 pint |
| centiliter | 0.01 | 0.6 cubic inch | | 0.338 fluidounce |
| milliliter | 0.001 | 0.06 cubic inch | | 0.27 fluidram |

### MASS AND WEIGHT

| unit | number of grams | approximate U.S. equivalent |
|---|---|---|
| metric ton | 1,000,000 | 1.1 tons |
| quintal | 100,000 | 220.46 pounds |
| kilogram | 1,000 | 2.2046 pounds |
| hectogram | 100 | 3.527 ounces |
| dekagram | 10 | 0.353 ounce |
| gram | 1 | 0.035 ounce |
| decigram | 0.10 | 1.543 grains |
| centigram | 0.01 | 0.154 grain |
| milligram | 0.001 | 0.015 grain |

¹For metric equivalents of U.S. units see Weights and Measures table

**mi·as·ma** \mī-'az-mə, mē-\ *n, pl* -mas *also* -ma·ta \-mət-ə\ : an exhalation (as of a swamp) formerly held to cause disease : a noxious vapor — **mi·as·mic** \-mik\ *adj*

**Mic** *abbr* Micah

**mi·ca** \'mī-kə\ *n* [NL, fr. L, grain, crumb] : any of various minerals readily separable into thin transparent sheets

**mice** *pl of* MOUSE

**Mich** *abbr* Michigan

**Mic·mac** \'mik-,mak\ *n, pl* Micmac *or* Micmacs : a member of an Indian people of eastern Canada

**mi·cro** \'mī-krō\ *adj* : very small; *esp* : MICROSCOPIC

**mi·crobe** \'mī-,krōb\ *n* : MICROORGANISM; *esp* : one causing disease — **mi·cro·bi·al** \mī-'krō-bē-əl\ *adj*

**mi·cro·bi·ol·o·gy** \,mī-krō-bī-'äl-ə-jē\ *n* : a branch of biology dealing esp. with microscopic forms of life — **mi·cro·bi·o·log·i·cal** \'mī-krō-,bī-ə-'läj-i-kəl\ *adj* — **mi·cro·bi·ol·o·gist** \,mī-krō-bī-'äl-ə-jəst\ *n*

**mi·cro·bus** \'mī-krō-,bəs\ *n* : a station wagon shaped like a bus

**mi·cro·cap·sule** \-,kap-səl, -sül\ *n* : a tiny capsule containing a liquid or solid substance (as a chemical or medicine) that is released when the capsule is broken, melted, or dissolved

**mi·cro·cir·cuit** \'mī-krō-,sər-kət\ *n* : a compact electronic circuit consisting of elements of small size

**mi·cro·cli·mate** \'mī-krō-,klī-mət\ *n* : the essentially uniform local climate of a usu. small site or habitat — **mi·cro·cli·ma·tol·o·gy** \'mī-krō-,klī-mə-'täl-ə-jē\ *n*

**mi·cro·copy** \'mī-krō-,käp-ē\ *n* : a photographic copy (as of print) on a reduced scale — **microcopy** *vb*

**mi·cro·cosm** \'mī-krə-,käz-əm\ *n* : a little world; *esp* : man or human nature that is an epitome of the world or the universe

**mi·cro·elec·tron·ics** \'mī-krō-i-,lek-'trän-iks\ *n* : a branch of electronics that deals with the miniaturization of electronic circuits and components — **mi·cro·elec·tron·ic** \-ik\ *adj*

**mi·cro·en·cap·su·late** \,mī-krō-in-'kap-sə-,lāt\ *vb* : to enclose a small amount of a substance in a microcapsule — **mi·cro·en·cap·su·la·tion** \-in-,kap-sə-'lā-shən\ *n*

**mi·cro·fiche** \'mī-krō-,fēsh, -,fish\ *n, pl* -fiche *or* -fiches \-,fēsh(-əz), -,fish(-əz)\ : a fiche containing rows of images of pages of printed matter

**mi·cro·film** \-,film\ *n* : a film bearing a photographic record (as of print) on a reduced scale — **microfilm** *vb*

**mi·cro·gram** \'mī-krə-,gram\ *n* : one millionth of a gram

**mi·cro·graph** \-,graf\ *n* : a graphic reproduction of the image of an object formed by a microscope — **micrograph** *vb*

**mi·cro·me·te·or·ite** \,mī-krō-'mēt-ē-ə-,rīt\ *n* **1** : a meteorite particle of very small size **2** : a very small particle in interplanetary space — **mi·cro·me·te·or·it·ic** \-,mēt-ē-ə-'rit-ik\ *adj*

**mi·cro·me·te·or·oid** \-'mēt-ē-ə-,ròid\ *n* : MICROMETEORITE 2

**mi·crom·e·ter** \mī-'kräm-ət-ər\ *n* : an instrument used with a telescope or microscope for measuring minute distances

**mi·cro·min·ia·ture** \,mī-krō-'min-ē-ə-,chúr, -'min-i-,chùr, -chər\ *adj* **1** : MICROMINIATURIZED **2** : suitable for use with microminiaturized parts

**mi·cro·min·ia·tur·iza·tion** \-,min-ē-ə-,chùr-ə-'zā-shən, -,min-i-,chùr-, -chər-\ *n* : the process of producing microminiaturized things

**mi·cro·min·ia·tur·ized** \-īzd\ *adj* : reduced to or produced in a very small size and esp. in a size smaller than one considered miniature

**mi·cron** \'mī-,krän\ *n, pl* microns *also* mi·cra \-krə\ : a unit of length equal to one thousandth of a millimeter

**mi·cro·or·gan·ism** \,mī-krō-'òr-gə-,niz-əm\ *n* : a living being (as a bacterium) too tiny to be seen by the unaided eye

**mi·cro·phone** \'mī-krə-,fōn\ *n* : an instrument for converting sound waves into variations of an electric current for transmitting or recording sound

**mi·cro·pho·to·graph** \,mī-krə-'fōt-ə-,graf\ *n* : PHOTOMICROGRAPH

**mi·cro·probe** \'mī-krə-,prōb\ *n* : a device for chemical analysis on a small scale that operates by exciting radiation in a minute area or volume of material so that the composition may be determined from the emission spectrum

**mi·cro·scope** \'mī-krə-,skōp\ *n* : an optical instrument for making magnified images of minute objects — **mi·cros·co·py** \mī-'kräs-kə-pē\ *n*

**mi·cro·scop·ic** \,mī-krə-'skäp-ik\ *or* **mi·cro·scop·i·cal** \-i-kəl\ *adj* **1** : of, relating to, or involving the use of the microscope **2** : too tiny to be seen without the use of a microscope : very small — **mi·cro·scop·i·cal·ly** \-i-k(ə-)lē\ *adv*

**mi·cro·sec·ond** \,mī-krō-'sek-ənd\ *n* : one millionth of a second

**mi·cro·state** \'mī-krō-,stāt\ *n* : a newly independent nation that is extremely small in area and population and poor in resources

**mi·cro·sur·gery** \,mī-krō-'sərj-(ə-)rē\ *n* : minute dissection or manipulation (as by a laser beam) of living structures (as cells) for surgical or experimental purposes — **mi·cro·sur·gi·cal** \-'sər-ji-kəl\ *adj*

**mi·cro·wave** \'mī-krə-,wāv\ *n* : a radio wave between 1 and 100 centimeters in wavelength

**microwave oven** *n* : an oven in which food is cooked by the heat produced as a result of microwave penetration of the food

**¹mid** \'mid\ *adj* : MIDDLE

**²mid** *abbr* middle

**mid·air** \'mid-'aər\ *n* : a point or region in the air well above the ground

**mid·day** \'mid-,dā, -'dā\ *n* : NOON

**mid·den** \'mid-ᵊn\ *n* : a refuse heap

**¹mid·dle** \'mid-ᵊl\ *adj* **1** : equally distant from the extremes : MEDIAL, CENTRAL **2** : being at neither extreme : INTERMEDIATE **3** *cap* : constituting an intermediate period ⟨*Middle* Dutch⟩

**²middle** *n* **1** : a middle part, point, or position **2** : WAIST

**middle age** *n* : the period of life from about 40 to about 60 — **mid·dle-aged** \,mid-ᵊl-'ājd\ *adj*

**Middle Ages** *n pl* : the period of European history from about A.D. 500 to about 1500

**mid·dle·brow** \'mid-ᵊl-,braú\ *n* : a person who is moderately but not highly cultivated

**middle class** *n* : a social class occupying a position between the upper class and the lower class — **middle-class** *adj*

**middle ear** *n* : a small membrane-lined cavity of the ear through which sound waves are transmitted by a chain of tiny bones

**middle finger** *n* : the midmost of the five digits of the hand

**mid·dle·man** \'mid-ᵊl-,man\ *n* : INTERMEDIARY; *esp* : one intermediate between the producer of goods and the retailer or consumer

**middle-of-the-road** *adj* : standing for or following a course of action midway between extremes; *esp* : being neither liberal nor conservative in politics — **mid·dle-of-the-road·er** \-'rōd-ǝr\ *n* — **mid·dle-of-the-road·ism** \-'rōd-,iz-ǝm\ *n*

**middle school** *n* : a school usu. including grades 5–8

**mid·dle·weight** \'mid-ᵊl-,wāt\ *n* : one of average weight; *esp* : a boxer weighing more than 147 but not over 160 pounds

**mid·dling** \'mid-liŋ, -lǝn\ *adj* **1** : of middle, medium, or moderate size, degree, or quality **2** : MEDIOCRE

**mid·dy** \'mid-ē\ *n, pl* **middies** : MIDSHIPMAN

**midge** \'mij\ *n* : a very small fly : GNAT

**midg·et** \'mij-ǝt\ *n* **1** : a very small person : DWARF **2** : something (as an animal) very small of its kind

**midi** \'mid-ē\ *n* : a calf-length dress, coat, or skirt

**mid·land** \'mid-lǝnd, -,land\ *n* : the interior or central region of a country

**mid·most** \-,mōst\ *adj* : being in or near the exact middle — **midmost** *adv*

**mid·night** \'mid-,nīt\ *n* : 12 o'clock at night

**midnight sun** *n* : the sun above the horizon at midnight in the arctic or antarctic summer

**mid·point** \'mid-,point, -'point\ *n* : a point at or near the center or middle

**mid·riff** \'mid-,rif\ *n* [ME *midrif*, fr. OE *midhrif*, fr. *midde* mid + *hrif* belly] **1** : DIAPHRAGM 1 **2** : the mid-region of the human torso

**mid·ship·man** \'mid-,ship-mǝn, (')mid-'ship-mǝn\ *n* : a student naval officer

**mid·ships** \'mid-,ships\ *adv* : AMIDSHIPS

**midst** \'midst\ *n* **1** : the interior or central part or point **2** : a position of proximity to the members of a group ⟨in our ~⟩ **3** : the condition of being surrounded or beset — **midst** *prep*

**mid·stream** \'mid-'strēm, -,strēm\ *n* : the middle of a stream

**mid·sum·mer** \'mid-'sǝm-ǝr, -,sǝm-\ *n* : the middle of summer; *esp* : the summer solstice

**mid·town** \'mid-,taún, -'taún\ *n* : a central section of a city; *esp* : one situated between sections conventionally called *downtown* and *uptown* — **midtown** *adj*

**¹mid·way** \'mid-,wā, -'wā\ *adv* : in the middle of the way or distance

**²mid·way** \-,wā\ *n* : an avenue (as at a carnival) for concessions and light amusements

**mid·week** \-,wēk\ *n* : the middle of the week — **mid·week·ly** \-,wē-klē, -'wē-\ *adj or adv*

**mid·wife** \'mid-,wīf\ *n* : a woman who helps other women in childbirth — **mid·wife·ry** \-,wī-f(ǝ-)rē\ *n*

**mid·win·ter** \'mid-'wint-ǝr, -,wint-\ *n* : the middle of winter; *esp* : the winter solstice

**mid·year** \-,yiǝr\ *n* **1** : the middle of a year **2** : a midyear examination — **midyear** *adj*

**mien** \'mēn\ *n* **1** : air or bearing esp. as expressive of mood or personality : DEMEANOR **2** : APPEARANCE, ASPECT

**miff** \'mif\ *vb* : to put into an ill humor

**¹might** \(')mīt\ *past of* MAY — used as an auxiliary to express permission, liberty, probability, or possibility in the past, a present condition contrary to fact, less probability or possibility than *may*, or as a polite alternative to *may*, *ought*, or *should*

**²might** \'mīt\ *n* : the power, authority, or resources of an individual or a group

**mighty** \'mīt-ē\ *adj* **might·i·er; -est 1** : very strong : POWERFUL **2** : GREAT, NOTABLE — **might·i·ly** \'mīt-ǝ-lē\ *adv* — **might·i·ness** \-ē-nǝs\ *n* — **mighty** *adv*

**mi·gnon·ette** \,min-yǝ-'net\ *n* : a garden plant with spikes of tiny fragrant flowers

**mi·graine** \'mī-,grān\ *n* [F, fr. LL *hemicrania* pain in one side of the head, fr. Gk *hēmikrania*, fr. *hēmi-* half + *kranion* cranium] : a condition marked by recurrent severe headache and often nausea

**mi·grant** \'mī-grǝnt\ *n* : one that migrates; *esp* : a person who moves in order to find work (as in harvesting crops)

**mi·grate** \'mī-,grāt\ *vb* **mi·grat·ed; mi·grat·ing 1** : to move from one country, place, or locality to another **2** : to pass usu. periodically from one region or climate to another for feeding or breeding — **mi·gra·tion** \mī-'grā-shǝn\ *n* — **mi·gra·tion·al** \-sh(ǝ-)nǝl\ *adj* — **mi·gra·to·ry** \'mī-grǝ-,tōr-ē\ *adj*

**mi·ka·do** \mə-'käd-ō\ n, pl **-dos** : an emperor of Japan

**mike** \'mīk\ n **1** : MICROPHONE **2** : MICROGRAM — used esp. with relation to illicit drugs

**¹mil** \'mil\ n **1** : a unit of length equal to ¹/₁₀₀₀ inch **2** : THOUSAND **3** — see *pound* at MONEY table

**²mil** abbr military

**milch** \'milk, 'milch\ adj : giving milk ⟨~ cow⟩

**mild** \'mīld\ adj **1** : gentle in nature or behavior **2** : moderate in action or effect **3** : TEMPERATE **syn** soft, bland, lenient — **mild·ly** adv — **mild·ness** n

**mil·dew** \'mil-,d(y)ü\ n : a superficial usu. whitish growth produced on organic matter and on plants by a fungus; also : a fungus producing this growth — **mildew** vb

**mile** \'mīl\ n [ME, fr. OE mīl, fr. L milia miles, fr. milia passuum, lit., thousands of paces] **1** — see WEIGHT table **2** : NAUTICAL MILE

**mile·age** \'mī-lij\ n **1** : an allowance for traveling expenses at a certain rate per mile **2** : distance in miles traveled (as in a day); also : the amount of service yielded (as by a tire) expressed in terms of miles of travel

**mile·post** \'mīl-,pōst\ n : a post indicating the distance in miles from a given point

**mi·le·si·mo** \mi-'les-ə-,mō, -'läs-\ n, pl **-mos** — see escudo at MONEY table

**mile·stone** \'mīl-,stōn\ n **1** : a stone serving as a milepost **2** : a significant point in development

**mi·lieu** \mēl-'yə(r), -'yü\ n, pl **milieus** or **mi·lieux** \-'yə(r)(z), -'yüz\ : ENVIRONMENT, SETTING

**mil·i·tant** \'mil-ə-tənt\ adj **1** : engaged in warfare **2** : aggressively active esp. in a cause — **mil·i·tan·cy** \-tən-sē\ n — **militant** n — **mil·i·tant·ly** adv

**mil·i·ta·rism** \'mil-ə-tə-,riz-əm\ n : predominance of the military class or its ideals **2** : a policy of aggressive military preparedness — **mil·i·ta·rist** \-rəst\ n — **mil·i·ta·ris·tic** \,mil-ə-tə-'ris-tik\ adj

**mil·i·ta·rize** \'mil-ə-tə-,rīz\ vb **-rized; -riz·ing 1** : to equip with military forces and defenses **2** : to give a military character to

**¹mil·i·tary** \'mil-ə-,ter-ē\ adj **1** : of or relating to soldiers, arms, or war **2** : performed by armed forces; also : supported by armed force **3** : of or relating to the army **syn** martial, warlike — **mil·i·tar·i·ly** \,mil-ə-'ter-ə-lē\ adv

**²military** n, pl **military** also **mil·i·tar·ies 1** : the military, naval, and air forces of a nation **2** : military persons

**mil·i·tate** \'mil-ə-,tāt\ vb **-tat·ed; -tat·ing** : to have weight or effect

**mi·li·tia** \mə-'lish-ə\ n : a part of the organized armed forces of a country liable to call only in emergency — **mi·li·tia·man** \-mən\ n

**¹milk** \'milk\ n **1** : a nutritive usu. whitish fluid secreted by female mam-

mals for feeding their young **2** : a milklike liquid (as a plant juice) — **milk·i·ness** \-ē-nəs\ n — **milky** adj

**²milk** vb : to draw off the milk of ⟨~ a cow⟩; also : to draw or yield milk ⟨a cow that ~s 30 pounds⟩ — **milk·er** n

**milk·maid** \'milk-,mād\ n : DAIRYMAID

**milk·man** \-,man, -mən\ n : a man who sells or delivers milk

**milk of magnesia** : a milk-white mixture of hydroxide of magnesium and water used as an antacid and laxative

**milk shake** n : a thoroughly blended drink made of milk, a flavoring syrup, and often ice cream

**milk·sop** \'milk-,säp\ n : an unmanly man

**milk·weed** \-,wēd\ n : a coarse herb with milky juice and clustered flowers

**Milky Way** n **1** : a broad irregular band of light that stretches across the sky and is caused by the light of myriads of faint stars **2** : MILKY WAY GALAXY

**Milky Way galaxy** n : the huge system of stars of which the sun is a member and which includes the myriads of stars that comprise the Milky Way

**¹mill** \'mil\ n **1** : a building with machinery for grinding grain into flour; also : a machine for grinding grain **2** : a building with machinery for manufacturing **3** : a machine used esp. for crushing, stamping, grinding, cutting, shaping, or polishing

**²mill** vb **1** : to subject to an operation or process in a mill **2** : to move in a circle or in an eddying mass

**³mill** n : a money of account equal to ¹/₁₀ cent

**mill·age** \'mil-ij\ n : a rate (as of taxation) expressed in mills

**mill·dam** \'mil-,dam\ n : a dam to make a millpond; also : MILLPOND

**mil·len·ni·um** \mə-'len-ē-əm\ n, pl **-nia** \-ē-ə\ or **-niums 1** : a period of 1000 years; also : a 1000th anniversary or its celebration **2** : the 1000 years mentioned in Revelation 20 when holiness is to prevail and Christ is to reign on earth **3** : a period of great happiness or perfect government

**mill·er** \'mil-ər\ n **1** : one that operates a mill and esp. a flour mill **2** : any of various moths having powdery wings

**mil·let** \'mil-ət\ n : any of several small-seeded cereal and forage grasses long cultivated for grain or hay; also : the grain of a millet

**mil·li·am·pere** \,mil-ē-'am-,piər\ n : one thousandth of an ampere

**mil·liard** \'mil-,yärd, 'mil-ē-,ärd\ n, Brit : a thousand millions

**mil·li·bar** \'mil-ə-,bär\ n : a unit of atmospheric pressure

**mil·lieme** \mē(l)-'yem\ n, pl **mil·liemes** \-'yem(z)\ — see pound at MONEY table

**mil·li·gram** \'mil-ə-,gram\ n — see METRIC SYSTEM table

**mil·li·li·ter** \'mil-ə-,lēt-ər\ n — see METRIC SYSTEM table

**mil·lime** \mə-'lēm\ n — see dinar at MONEY table

**mil·li·me·ter** \'mil-ə-,mēt-ər\ *n* — see METRIC SYSTEM table

**mil·li·ner** \'mil-ə-nər\ *n* [fr. *Milan*, Italy; fr. the importation of women's linery from Italy in the 16th century] : one who designs, makes, trims, or sells women's hats

**mil·li·nery** \'mil-ə-,ner-ē\ *n* **1** : women's apparel for the head **2** : the business or work of a milliner

**mill·ing** \'mil-iŋ\ *n* : a corrugated edge on a coin

**mil·lion** \'mil-yən\ *n*, *pl* **millions** *or* **million** : a thousand thousands — **million** *adj* — **mil·lionth** \-yənth\ *adj or n*

**mil·lion·aire** \,mil-yə-'naər, 'mil-yə-,naer\ *n* : one whose wealth is estimated at a million or more (as of dollars or pounds)

**mil·li·pede** \'mil-ə-,pēd\ *n* : any of a group of arthropods that are related to the centipedes but have two pairs of legs on most apparent segments and no poison fangs

**mil·li·sec·ond** \'mil-ə-,sek-ond\ *n* : one thousandth of a second

**mil·li·volt** \-,vōlt\ *n* : one thousandth of a volt

**mill·pond** \'mil-,pänd\ *n* : a pond made by damming a stream to produce a fall of water for operating a mill

**mill·race** \-,rās\ *n* : a canal in which water flows to and from a mill wheel

**mill·stone** \-,stōn\ *n* : either of two round flat stones used for grinding grain

**mill·stream** \-,strēm\ *n* : a stream whose flow is used to run a mill; *also* : the stream in a millrace

**mill wheel** *n* : a waterwheel that drives a mill

**mill·wright** \'mil-,rīt\ *n* : one whose occupation is planning and building mills or setting up their machinery

**milt** \'milt\ *n* : the male reproductive glands of fishes when filled with secretion; *also* : the secretion itself

**mime** \'mīm, 'mēm\ *n* **1** : MIMIC **2** : the art of characterization or of narration by body movement; *also* : a performance of mime — **mime** *vb*

**mim·eo·graph** \'mim-ē-ə-,graf\ *n* : a machine for making many copies by means of a stencil through which ink is pressed — **mimeograph** *vb*

**mi·me·sis** \mə-'mē-səs, mī-\ *n* : IMITATION, MIMICRY

**mi·met·ic** \-'met-ik\ *adj* **1** : IMITATIVE **2** : relating to, characterized by, or exhibiting mimicry

**¹mim·ic** \'mim-ik\ *n* : one that mimics

**²mimic** *vb* **mim·icked** \-ikt\; **mim·ick·ing** **1** : to imitate closely **2** : to ridicule by imitation **3** : to resemble by biological mimicry

**mim·ic·ry** \'mim-i-krē\ *n*, *pl* **-ries** **1** : an instance of mimicking **2** : a superficial resemblance of one organism to another or to natural objects among which it lives that secures it a selective advantage (as protection from predation)

**mi·mo·sa** \mə-'mō-sə, mī-, -zə\ *n* : any of various leguminous trees, shrubs, and herbs of warm regions with globular heads of small white or pink flowers

**min** *abbr* **1** minimum **2** mining **3** minister **4** minor **5** minute

**min·a·ret** \,min-ə-'ret\ *n* [F, fr. Turk *minare*, fr. Ar *manārah* lighthouse] : a slender lofty tower attached to a mosque

**mi·na·to·ry** \'min-ə-,tōr-ē, 'mī-nə-\ *adj* : THREATENING, MENACING

**mince** \'mins\ *vb* **minced**; **minc·ing** **1** : to cut into small pieces **2** : to restrain (words) within the bounds of decorum **3** : to walk in a prim affected manner — **minc·ing** *adj*

**mince·meat** \'mins-,mēt\ *n* : a finely chopped mixture esp. of raisins, apples, spices, and often meat used as a filling for a pie

**mince pie** *n* : a pie filled with mincemeat

**¹mind** \'mīnd\ *n* **1** : MEMORY **2** : the part of an individual that feels, perceives, thinks, wills, and esp. reasons **3** : INTENTION, DESIRE **4** : the normal condition of the mental faculties **5** : OPINION, VIEW **6** : a person or group embodying mental qualities **7** : intellectual ability

**²mind** *vb* **1** *chiefly dial* : REMEMBER **2** : to attend to (~ your own business) **3** : HEED, OBEY **4** : to be concerned about : WORRY; *also* : DISLIKE **5** : to be careful or cautious **6** : to take charge of **7** : to regard with attention

**mind–blow·ing** \'mīn(d)-,blō-iŋ\ *adj* **1** : PSYCHEDELIC; *also* : causing a mental state similar to that produced by a psychedelic drug **2** : OVERWHELMING

**mind·ed** \'mīn-dəd\ *adj* **1** : having a mind of a specified kind — usu. used in combination (narrow-*minded*) **2** : INCLINED, DISPOSED

**mind–ex·pand·ing** \'mīn-dik-,spanding\ *adj* : causing an exposure of normally repressed psychic elements : PSYCHEDELIC (~ drugs)

**mind·ful** \'mīnd-fəl\ *adj* : bearing in mind : AWARE — **mind·ful·ly** \-ē\ *adv* — **mind·ful·ness** *n*

**mind·less** \'mīn-dləs\ *adj* **1** : destitute of mind or consciousness **2** : UNINTELLIGENT **3** : HEEDLESS — **mind·less·ly** *adv* — **mind·less·ness** *n*

**¹mine** \'mīn\ *pron* : one or the ones belonging to me

**²mine** \'mīn\ *n* **1** : an excavation in the earth from which mineral substances are taken; *also* : an ore deposit **2** : a subterranean passage under an enemy position; *also* : an encased explosive for destroying enemy personnel, vehicles, or ships **3** : a rich source of supply

**³mine** \'mīn\ *vb* **mined**; **min·ing** **1** : to dig a mine **2** : UNDERMINE **3** : to get ore from the earth **4** : to place military mines in — **min·er** *n*

**mine·lay·er** \'mīn-,lā-ər\ *n* : a naval vessel for laying underwater mines

**min·er·al** \'min-(ə)-rəl\ *n* **1** : a solid homogeneous crystalline substance (as diamond, gold, or quartz) not of animal or vegetable origin; *also* : ORE **2** : any of various naturally occurring homogeneous substances (as coal, salt, water, or gas) obtained for man's use usu. from the ground **3** *pl, Brit* : MINERAL WATER — **mineral** *adj*

**min·er·al·ize** \'min-(ə-)rə-,līz\ *vb* -ized; -iz·ing **1** : to transform (a metal) into an ore **2** : to impregnate or supply with minerals

**min·er·al·o·gy** \,min-ə-'räl-ə-jē, -'ral-\ *n* : a science dealing with minerals — **min·er·al·og·i·cal** \,min-(ə-)rə-'läj-i-kəl\ *adj* — **min·er·al·o·gist** \,min-ə-'räl-ə-jəst, -'ral-\ *n*

**mineral oil** *n* : an oil of mineral origin; *esp* : a refined petroleum oil used as a laxative

**mineral water** *n* : water impregnated with mineral salts or gases

**min·e·stro·ne** \,min-ə-'strō-nē, -'strōn\ *n* [It, fr. *minestra*, fr. *minestrare* to serve, dish up, fr. L *ministrare*, fr. *minister* servant] : a rich thick vegetable soup

**mine·sweep·er** \'mīn-,swē-pər\ *n* : a warship designed for removing or neutralizing underwater mines

**min·gle** \'miŋ-gəl\ *vb* **min·gled; min·gling** \-g(ə-)liŋ\ **1** : to bring or combine together : MIX **2** : CONCOCT

**ming tree** \'miŋ-\ *n* : a dwarfed usu. evergreen tree grown in a pot; *also* : an artificial imitation of this made from plant materials

**mini** \'min-ē\ *n, pl* **min·is** : something small of its kind — **mini** *adj*

**mini-** *comb form* : miniature : of small dimensions

**min·ia·ture** \'min-ē-ə-,chur, 'min-i-,chur, -chər\ *n* [It *miniatura* art of illuminating a manuscript, fr. ML, fr. L *miniare* to color with red lead, fr. *minium* red lead] **1** : a copy on a much reduced scale; *also* : something small of its kind **2** : a small painting (as on ivory or metal) — **miniature** *adj* — **min·ia·tur·ist** \-,chur-əst, -chər-\ *n*

**min·ia·tur·ize** \'min-ē-ə-,chə-,rīz, 'min-i-\ *vb* -ized; -iz·ing : to design or construct in small size — **min·ia·tur·iza·tion** \,min-ē-ə-,chur-ə-'zā-shən, ,min-i-, -chər-\ *n*

**mini·bike** \'min-i-,bīk\ *n* : a small one-passenger motorcycle

**mini·bus** \-,bəs\ *n* : a small bus for comparatively short trips

**mini·com·put·er** \,min-i-kəm-'pyüt-ər\ *n* : a small and relatively inexpensive computer

**min·im** \'min-əm\ *n* — see WEIGHT table

**min·i·mal** \'min-ə-məl\ *adj* **1** : relating to or being a minimum : LEAST **2** : of or relating to minimal art — **min·i·mal·ly** \-ē\ *adv*

**minimal art** *n* : an impersonal style of abstract art and esp. sculpture consisting primarily of simple geometric forms — **minimal artist** *n*

**min·i·mize** \'min-ə-,mīz\ *vb* -mized; -miz·ing **1** : to reduce to a minimum **2** : to estimate at a minimum; *also* : BELITTLE **syn** depreciate, decry, disparage

**min·i·mum** \'min-ə-məm\ *n, pl* **-ma** \-mə\ *or* **-mums** **1** : the least quantity assignable, admissible, or possible **2** : the least of a set of numbers **3** : the lowest degree or amount reached or recorded — **minimum** *adj*

**min·ion** \'min-yən\ *n* [MF *mignon* darling] **1** : a servile dependent **2** : one highly favored **3** : a subordinate official

**min·is·cule** \'min-əs-,kyül\ *var of* MINUSCULE

**mini·skirt** \'min-i-,skərt\ *n* : a woman's short skirt with the hemline several inches above the knee

**mini·state** \-,stāt\ *n* : MICROSTATE

¹**min·is·ter** \'min-ə-stər\ *n* **1** : AGENT **2** : CLERGYMAN; *esp* : a Protestant clergyman **3** : a high officer of state entrusted with the management of a division of governmental activities **4** : a diplomatic representative to a foreign state — **min·is·te·ri·al** \,min-ə-'stir-ē-əl\ *adj*

²**minister** *vb* **min·is·tered; min·is·ter·ing** \-st(ə-)riŋ\ **1** : to perform the functions of a minister of religion **2** : to give aid — **min·is·tra·tion** \,min-ə-'strā-shən\ *n*

**min·is·trant** \'min-ə-strənt\ *adj, archaic* : performing service as a minister — **ministrant** *n*

**min·is·try** \'min-ə-strē\ *n, pl* **-tries** **1** : MINISTRATION **2** : the office, duties, or functions of a minister; *also* : his period of service or office **3** : CLERGY **4** : AGENCY **5** *often cap* : the body of ministers governing a nation or state; *also* : a government department headed by a minister

**mink** \'miŋk\ *n, pl* **mink** *or* **minks** : a slender mammal resembling the related weasels. *also* : its soft lustrous typically dark brown fur

**Minn** *abbr* Minnesota

**min·ne·sing·er** \'min-i-,siŋ-ər, 'min-ə-,ziŋ-\ *n* [G, fr. Middle High German, fr. *minne* love + *singer*] : one of a class of German lyric poets and musicians of the 12th to the 14th centuries

**min·now** \'min-ō\ *n, pl* **minnows** *also* **minnow** : any of numerous small freshwater fishes

¹**mi·nor** \'mī-nər\ *adj* **1** : inferior in importance, size, or degree **2** : not having reached majority **3** : having the third, sixth, and sometimes the seventh degrees lowered by a half step (∼ scale); *also* : based on a minor scale (∼ key)

²**minor** *n* **1** : a person who has not attained majority **2** : a subject of academic study chosen as a secondary field of specialization

³**minor** *vb* : to pursue an academic minor

**mi·nor·i·ty** \mə-'nȯr-ət-ē, mī-\ *n, pl* **-ties** **1** : the period or state of being a minor **2** : the smaller in number of two groups; *esp* : a group having less than the number of votes necessary for control **3** : a part of a population differing from others (as in race or religion)

**min·ster** \'min-stər\ *n* **1** : a church attached to a monastery  **2 :** a large or important church

**min·strel** \'min-strəl\ *n* **1 :** a medieval singer of verses; *also* : MUSICIAN, POET  **2 :** one of a group of performers in a program usu of Negro songs, jokes, and impersonations — **min·strel·sy** \-sē\ *n*

**¹mint** \'mint\ *n* **1 :** a place where coins are made  **2 :** a vast sum — **mint** *vb* — **mint·age** \-ij\ *n* — **mint·er** *n*

**²mint** *adj* **:** unmarred as if fresh from a mint  〈~ coins〉

**³mint** *n* **:** any of a large group of square-stemmed herbs and shrubs; *esp* : one (as spearmint with fragrant aromatic foliage used in flavoring — **minty** *adj*

**min·u·end** \'min-yə-,wend\ *n* **:** a number from which another is to be subtracted

**min·u·et** \,min-yə-'wet\ *n* **:** a slow graceful dance

**¹mi·nus** \'mī-nəs\ *prep* **1 :** diminished by : LESS 〈7 ~ 3 equals 4〉  **2 :** LACKING, WITHOUT 〈~ his hat〉

**²minus** *n* **:** a negative quantity or quality

**³minus** *adj* **1 :** requiring subtraction  **2 :** algebraically negative 〈~ quantity〉  **3 :** having negative qualities

**¹mi·nus·cule** \'min-əs-,kyül, min-'əs-\ *n* **:** a lowercase letter

**²minuscule** *adj* **:** very small

**minus sign** *n* **:** a sign — used in mathematics to indicate subtraction or a negative quantity

**¹min·ute** \'min-ət\ *n* **1 :** the 60th part of an hour or of a degree  **2 :** a short space of time  **3** *pl* **:** the official record of the proceedings of a meeting

**²mi·nute** \mī-'n(y)üt, mə-\ *adj* **mi·nut·er; -est  1 :** very small  **2 :** of little importance: TRIFLING  **3 :** marked by close attention to details  **syn** diminutive, tiny, miniature, wee — **mi·nute·ly** *adv* — **mi·nute·ness** *n*

**min·ute·man** \'min-ət-,man\ *n* **:** a member of a group of armed men pledged to take the field at a minute's notice during and immediately before the American Revolution

**mi·nu·tia** \mə-'n(y)ü-sh(ē-)ə, mī-\ *n*, *pl* **-ti·ae** \-shē-,ē\ **:** a minute or minor detail — usu. used in pl.

**minx** \'minks\ *n* **:** a pert girl

**mir·a·cle** \'mir-i-kəl\ *n* **1 :** an extraordinary event manifesting a supernatural work of God  **2 :** an unusual event, thing, or accomplishment : WONDER, MARVEL — **mi·rac·u·lous** \mə-'rak-yə-ləs\ *adj* — **mi·rac·u·lous·ly** *adv*

**mi·rage** \mə-'räzh\ *n* **1 :** a reflection visible at sea, in deserts, or above a hot pavement of some distant object often in distorted form as a result of atmospheric conditions  **2 :** something illusory and unattainable

**¹mire** \'mī(ə)r\ *n* **:** heavy and often deep mud or slush — **miry** *adj*

**²mire** *vb* **: mired, mir·ing :** to stick or sink in or as if in mire

**¹mir·ror** \'mir-ər\ *n* **1 :** a polished or smooth substance (as of glass) that forms images by reflection  **2 :** a true representation; *also* : MODEL

**²mirror** *vb* **:** to reflect in or as if in a mirror

**mirth** \'mərth\ *n* **:** gladness or gaiety accompanied with laughter  **syn** glee, jollity, hilarity — **mirth·ful** \-fəl\ *adj* — **mirth·ful·ly** \-ē\ *adv* — **mirth·ful·ness** *n* — **mirth·less** *adj*

**mis·ad·ven·ture** \,mis-əd-'ven-chər\ *n* **:** MISFORTUNE, MISHAP

**mis·aligned** \,mis-ə-'līnd\ *adj* **:** not properly aligned — **mis·align·ment** \-'līn-mənt\ *n*

**mis·al·li·ance** \,mis-ə-'lī-əns\ *n* **:** MÉSALLIANCE; *also* : a marriage between persons unsuited to each other

**mis·al·lo·ca·tion** \,mis-,al-ə-'kā-shən\ *n* **:** faulty or improper allocation

**mis·an·thrope** \'mis-°n-,thrōp\ *n* **:** one who hates mankind — **mis·an·throp·ic** \,mis-°n-'thräp-ik\ *adj* — **mis·an·throp·i·cal·ly** \-i-k(ə-)lē\ *adv* — **mis·an·thro·py** \mis-'an-thrə-pē\ *n*

**mis·ap·ply** \,mis-ə-'plī\ *vb* **:** to apply wrongly — **mis·ap·pli·ca·tion** \,mis-,ap-lə-'kā-shən\ *n*

**mis·ap·pre·hend** \,mis-,ap-ri-'hend\ *vb* **:** MISUNDERSTAND — **mis·ap·pre·hen·sion** \-'hen-chən\ *n*

**mis·ap·pro·pri·ate** \,mis-ə-'prō-prē-,āt\ *vb* **:** to appropriate wrongly; *esp* **:** to take dishonestly for one's own use — **mis·ap·pro·pri·a·tion** \-,prō-prē-'ā-shən\ *n*

**mis·be·got·ten** \,mis-bi-'gät-°n\ *adj* **:** ILLEGITIMATE

**mis·be·have** \,mis-bi-'hāv\ *vb* **:** to behave improperly — **mis·be·hav·er** *n* — **mis·be·hav·ior** \-'hā-vyər\ *n*

**mis·be·liev·er** \,mis-bə-'lē-vər\ *n* **:** one who holds a false or unorthodox belief

**mis·brand** \mis-'brand\ *vb* **:** to brand falsely or in a misleading manner; *also* **:** to label in violation of statutory requirements

**misc** *abbr* miscellaneous

**mis·cal·cu·late** \mis-'kal-kyə-,lāt\ *vb* **:** to calculate wrongly — **mis·cal·cu·la·tion** \,mis-,kal-kyə-'lā-shən\ *n*

**mis·call** \mis-'kol\ *vb* **:** MISNAME

**mis·car·ry** \mis-'kar-ē\ *vb* **1 :** to give birth prematurely and esp. before the fetus is capable of living independently  **2 :** to go wrong; *also* : to be unsuccessful — **mis·car·riage** \-'kar-ij\ *n*

**mis·ce·ge·na·tion** \,mis-,ej-ə-'nā-shən, ,mis-i-jə-'nā-\ *n* [L *miscēre* to mix + *genus* race] **:** a mixture of races; *esp* **:** marriage or cohabitation between a white person and a member of another race

**mis·cel·la·neous** \,mis-ə-'lā-nē-əs\ *adj* **1 :** consisting of diverse things or members; *also* : having various traits  **2 :** dealing with or interested in diverse subjects — **mis·cel·la·neous·ly** *adv* — **mis·cel·la·neous·ness** *n*

**mis·cel·la·ny** \'mis-ə-,lā-nē\ *n*, *pl* **-nies  1 :** HODGEPODGE  **2 :** a collection of writings on various subjects

**mis·chance** \mis-'chans\ *n* **:** bad luck; *also* : MISHAP

**mis·chief** \'mis-chəf\ *n* **1 :** injury

caused by a human agency **2** : a source of harm or irritation **3** : action that annoys; *also* : MISCHIEVOUSNESS

**mis·chie·vous** \'mis-chə-vəs\ *adj* **1** : HARMFUL, INJURIOUS **2** : causing annoyance or minor injury **3** : irresponsibly playful — **mis·chie·vous·ly** *adv* — **mis·chie·vous·ness** *n*

**mis·ci·ble** \'mis-ə-bəl\ *adj* : capable of being mixed; *esp* : soluble in each other

**mis·com·mu·ni·ca·tion** \,mis-kə-,myü-nə-'kā-shən\ *n* : failure to communicate clearly

**mis·con·ceive** \,mis-kən-'sēv\ *vb* : to interpret incorrectly — **mis·con·cep·tion** \-'sep-shən\ *n*

**mis·con·duct** \mis-'kän-(,)dəkt\ *n* **1** : MISMANAGEMENT **2** : intentional wrongdoing **3** : improper behavior

**mis·con·strue** \,mis-kən-'strü\ *vb* : MISINTERPRET — **mis·con·struc·tion** \-'strək-shən\ *n*

**mis·count** \mis-'kaůnt\ *vb* : to count incorrectly : MISCALCULATE

**mis·cre·ant** \'mis-krē-ənt\ *n* : one who behaves criminally or viciously — **mis·creant** *adj*

**mis·cue** \mis-'kyü\ *n* : MISTAKE, ERROR — **miscue** *vb*

**mis·deed** \mis-'dēd\ *n* : a wrong deed

**mis·de·mean·or** \,mis-di-'mē-nər\ *n* **1** : a crime less serious than a felony **2** : MISDEED

**mis·di·rect** \,mis-də-'rekt, -dī-\ *vb* : to give a wrong direction to — **mis·di·rec·tion** \-'rek-shən\ *n*

**mis·do·ing** \mis-'düi-iŋ\ *n* : WRONGDOING — **mis·do·er** \-'dü-ər\ *n*

**mise-en-scène** \,mē-,zän̈-'sen, -'sän̈\ *n, pl* **mise-en-scènes** \-'sen(z), -'sän̈(z)\ **1** : the arrangement of the scenery, property, and actors on a stage **2** : SETTING; *also* : ENVIRONMENT

**mi·ser** \'mī-zər\ *n* [L *miser* miserable] : a person who hoards his money — **mi·ser·li·ness** \-lē-nəs\ *n* — **mi·ser·ly** *adj*

**mis·er·a·ble** \'miz-ər-bəl, 'miz-(ə-)rə-bəl\ *adj* **1** : wretchedly deficient; *also* : causing extreme discomfort **2** : extremely poor **3** : SHAMEFUL — **mis·er·a·ble·ness** *n* — **mis·er·a·bly** \-blē\ *adv*

**mis·ery** \'miz-(ə-)rē\ *n, pl* **-er·ies** **1** : a state of suffering and want caused by poverty or affliction **2** : a cause of suffering or discomfort **3** : a state of emotional distress

**mis·fea·sance** \mis-'fēz-ʰns\ *n* : the performance of a lawful action in an illegal or improper manner

**mis·file** \mis-'fīl\ *vb* : to file in an inappropriate place

**mis·fire** \mis-'fī(ə)r\ *vb* **1** : to fail to fire **2** : to miss an intended effect — **misfire** *n*

**mis·fit** \'mis-,fit, mis-'fit\ *n* **1** : an imperfect fit **2** : a person poorly adjusted to his environment

**mis·for·tune** \mis-'fȯr-chən\ *n* **1** : bad fortune : ill luck **2** : an unfortunate condition or event

**mis·giv·ing** \-'giv-iŋ\ *n* : a feeling of doubt or suspicion esp. concerning a future event

**mis·gov·ern** \-'gəv-ərn\ *vb* : to govern badly — **mis·gov·ern·ment** \-'gəv-ər(n)-mənt\ *n*

**mis·guid·ance** \mis-'gīd-ʰns\ *n* : faulty guidance — **mis·guide** \-'gīd\ *vb* — **mis·guid·ed·ly** \-'gīd-əd-lē\ *adv*

**mis·han·dle** \-'han-dʰl\ *vb* **1** : MALTREAT **2** : to manage wrongly

**mis·hap** \'mis-,hap\ *n* : an unfortunate accident

**mish·mash** \'mish-,mäsh, -,mash\ *n* : HODGEPODGE, JUMBLE

**mis·in·form** \,mis-ʰn-'fȯrm\ *vb* : to give false or misleading information to — **mis·in·for·ma·tion** \,mis-,in-fər-'mā-shən\ *n*

**mis·in·ter·pret** \,mis-ʰn-'tər-prət\ *vb* : to understand or explain wrongly — **mis·in·ter·pre·ta·tion** \-,tər-prə-'tā-shən\ *n*

**mis·judge** \mis-'jəj\ *vb* **1** : to estimate wrongly **2** : to have an unjust opinion of — **mis·judg·ment** \-'jəj-mənt\ *n*

**mis·la·bel** \-'lā-bəl\ *vb* : to label incorrectly or falsely

**mis·lay** \mis-'lā\ *vb* **-laid** \-'lād\; **-lay·ing** : MISPLACE, LOSE

**mis·lead** \-'lēd\ *vb* **-led** \-'led\; **-lead·ing** : to lead in a wrong direction or into a mistaken action or belief — **mis·lead·ing·ly** *adv*

**mis·like** \-'līk\ *vb* : DISLIKE — **mislike** *n*

**mis·man·age** \-'man-ij\ *vb* : to manage badly — **mis·man·age·ment** *n*

**mis·match** \-'mach\ *vb* : to match unsuitably or badly — **mis·match** \mis-'mach, 'mis-,mach\ *n*

**mis·name** \-'nām\ *vb* : to name incorrectly : MISCALL

**mis·no·mer** \mis-'nō-mər\ *n* : a wrong name or designation

**mi·sog·a·mist** \mə-'säg-ə-məst\ *n* : one who hates marriage — **mi·sog·a·my** \-ə-mē\ *n*

**mi·sog·y·nist** \mə-'säj-ə-nəst\ *n* : one who hates or distrusts women — **mi·sog·y·ny** \-nē\ *n*

**mis·ori·ent** \mis-'ȯr-ē-,ent\ *vb* : to orient improperly or incorrectly — **mis·ori·en·ta·tion** \mis-,ȯr-ē-ən-'tā-shən\ *n*

**mis·place** \-'plās\ *vb* **1** : to put in a wrong place; *also* : MISLAY **2** : to set on a wrong object ⟨~ trust⟩

**mis·play** \-'plā\ *n* : a wrong or unskillful play — **mis·play** \mis-'plā, 'mis-,plā\ *vb*

**mis·print** \mis-'print\ *vb* : to print incorrectly — **mis·print** \'mis-,print, mis-'print\ *n*

**mis·pro·nounce** \,mis-prə-'naůns\ *vb* : to pronounce incorrectly — **mis·pro·nun·ci·a·tion** \-,nən-sē-'ā-shən\ *n*

**mis·quote** \mis-'kwōt\ *vb* : to quote incorrectly — **mis·quo·ta·tion** \,mis-kwō-'tā-shən\ *n*

**mis·read** \-'rēd\ *vb* **-read** \-'red\; **-read·ing** \-'rēd-iŋ\ : to read or interpret incorrectly

**mis·rep·re·sent** \,mis-,rep-ri-'zent\ *vb* : to represent falsely or unfairly — **mis·rep·re·sen·ta·tion** \-,zen-'tā-shən\ *n*

¹**misrule** \mis-'rül\ *vb* : MISGOVERN

²**misrule** *n* **1** : MISGOVERNMENT **2** : DISORDER

¹**miss** \'mis\ *vb* **1** : to fail to hit, reach, or contact **2** : to feel the absence of **3** : to fail to obtain **4** : AVOID ⟨just ~ed hitting the other car⟩ **5** : OMIT **6** : to fail to understand **7** : to fail to perform or attend; *also* : MISFIRE

²**miss** *n* **1** : a failure to hit or to attain a result **2** : MISFIRE

³**miss** *n* **1** — used as a title prefixed to the name of an unmarried woman or girl **2** : a young unmarried woman or girl

**Miss** *abbr* Mississippi

**mis·sal** \'mis-əl\ *n* : a book containing all that is said or sung at mass during the entire year

**mis·send** \mis(h)-'send\ *vb* : to send incorrectly ⟨*missent* mail⟩

**mis·shape** \mis(h)-'shāp\ *vb* : DEFORM — **mis·shap·en** \-'shā-pən\ *adj*

**mis·sile** \'mis-əl\ *n* [L, fr. neut. of *missilis* capable of being thrown, fr. *mittere* to let go, send] **1** : an object (as a stone, bullet, or weapon) thrown or projected **2** : a self-propelled unmanned weapon (as a rocket)

**mis·sile·man** \'mis-əl-mən\ *n* : one who designs, manufactures, or uses a guided missile

**mis·sile·ry** *also* **mis·sil·ry** \'mis-əl-rē\ *n* **1** : MISSILES **2** : the science of the making and use of guided missiles

**miss·ing** \'mis-iŋ\ *adj* : ABSENT; *also* : LOST

**mis·sion** \'mish-ən\ *n* **1** : a ministry commissioned by a church (as to propagate its faith); *also* : a place where such a ministry is carried out **2** : a group of envoys to a foreign country; *also* : a team of specialists or cultural leaders sent to a foreign country **3** : TASK

¹**mis·sion·ary** \'mish-ə-,ner-ē\ *adj* : of, relating to, or engaged in church missions

²**missionary** *n, pl* **-ar·ies** : a person commissioned by a church to propagate its faith or carry on humanitarian work

**mis·sion·er** \'mish-(ə-)nər\ *n* : a person undertaking a mission and esp. a religious mission

**mis·sive** \'mis-iv\ *n* : LETTER

**mis·spell** \mis-'spel\ *vb* : to spell incorrectly — **mis·spell·ing** *n*

**mis·spend** \mis-'spend\ *vb* **-spent** \-'spent\; **-spend·ing** : WASTE, SQUANDER ⟨a *misspent* youth⟩

**mis·state** \-'stāt\ *vb* : to state incorrectly — **mis·state·ment** *n*

**mis·step** \-'step\ *n* **1** : a wrong step **2** : MISTAKE, BLUNDER

**mist** \'mist\ *n* **1** : water in the form of particles suspended or falling in the air **2** : something that dims or obscures

**mis·tak·able** \mə-'stā-kə-bəl\ *adj* : capable of being misunderstood or mistaken

**mis·take** \mə-'stāk\ *n* **1** : a misunder-

standing of the meaning or implication of something **2** : a wrong action or statement : ERROR — **mistake** *vb*

**mis·tak·en** \-'stā-kən\ *adj* **1** : MISUNDERSTOOD **2** : having a wrong opinion or incorrect information **3** : ERRONEOUS — **mis·tak·en·ly** *adv*

**mis·ter** \,mis-tər *for 1;* 'mis- *for 2*\ *n* **1** — used sometimes instead of *Mr.* **2** : SIR — used without a name in addressing a man

**mis·tle·toe** \'mis-əl-,tō\ *n* : a parasitic green plant with yellowish flowers and waxy white berries that grows on trees

**mis·tral** \'mis-trəl, mi-'sträl\ *n* [F, fr. Provençal, fr. *mistral* masterful, fr. L *magistralis*, fr. *magister* master] : a strong cold dry northerly wind of southern Europe

**mis·treat** \mis-'trēt\ *vb* : to treat badly : ABUSE — **mis·treat·ment** *n*

**mis·tress** \'mis-trəs\ *n* **1** : a woman who has power, authority, or ownership ⟨~ of the house⟩ **2** : a country or state having supremacy ⟨~ of the seas⟩ **3** : a woman with whom a man cohabits without benefit of marriage; *also, archaic* : SWEETHEART **4** — used archaically as a title prefixed to the name of a married or unmarried woman

**mis·tri·al** \mis-'trī-(-ə)l\ *n* : a trial that has no legal effect (as by reason of an error)

¹**mis·trust** \-'trəst\ *n* : a lack of confidence : DISTRUST — **mis·trust·ful** \-fəl\ *adj* — **mis·trust·ful·ly** \-ē\ *adv* — **mis·trust·ful·ness** *n*

²**mistrust** *vb* : to have no trust or confidence in : SUSPECT

**misty** \'mis-tē\ *adj* **mist·i·er; -est** **1** : obscured by or as if by mist : INDISTINCT — **mist·i·ly** \'mis-tə-lē\ *adv* — **mist·i·ness** \-tē-nəs\ *n*

**mis·un·der·stand** \,mis-,ən-dər-'stand\ *vb* **1** : to fail to understand **2** : to interpret incorrectly

**mis·un·der·stand·ing** \-'stan-diŋ\ *n* **1** : MISINTERPRETATION **2** : DISAGREEMENT, QUARREL

**mis·us·age** \mish-'ü-sij, mis(h)-'yü-, -zij\ *n* **1** : bad treatment : ABUSE **2** : wrong or improper use

**mis·use** \mish-'üz, mis(h)-'yüz\ *vb* **1** : to use incorrectly **2** : ABUSE, MISTREAT — **mis·use** \-'yüs\ *n*

**mite** \'mīt\ *n* **1** : any of various tiny animals related to the spiders that often live and feed on animals or plants **2** : a small coin or sum of money **3** : a small amount : BIT

¹**mi·ter** *or* **mi·tre** \'mīt-ər\ *n* [ME *mitre*, fr. MF, fr. L *mitra* headband, turban, fr. Gk] **1** : a headdress worn by bishops and abbots **2** : a joint or corner made by cutting two pieces of wood at an angle and fitting the cut edges together

²**miter** *or* **mitre** *vb* **mi·tered** *or* **mi·tred; mi·ter·ing** *or* **mi·tring** \'mīt-ə-riŋ\ **1** : to match or fit together in a miter joint **2** : to bevel the ends of for making a miter joint

**mit·i·gate** \'mit-ə-,gāt\ *vb* **-gat·ed; -gat·ing** **1** : to make less harsh or hostile   **2 :** to make less severe or painful — **mit·i·ga·tion** \,mit-ə-'gā-shən\ *n* — **mit·i·ga·tive** \'mit-ə-,gāt-iv\ *adj* — **mit·i·ga·tor** \-,gāt-ər\ *n* — **mit·i·ga·to·ry** \-gə-,tōr-ē\ *adj*

**mi·to·sis** \mī-'tō-səs\ *n, pl* **-to·ses** \-,sēz\ **:** a process that takes place in the nucleus of a dividing cell and results in the formation of two new nuclei each having the same number of chromosomes as the parent nucleus; *also* **:** cell division in which mitosis occurs — **mi·tot·ic** \-'tät-ik\ *adj*

**mitt** \'mit\ *n* **:** a baseball glove (as for a catcher)

**mit·ten** \'mit-ᵊn\ *n* **:** a covering for the hand having a separate section for the thumb only

**¹mix** \'miks\ *vb* **1 :** to combine into one mass   **2 :** ASSOCIATE   **3 :** to form by mingling components   **4 :** CROSSBREED   **5 :** CONFUSE  ⟨∼es up the facts⟩   **6 :** to become involved   **syn** blend  merge, coalesce, amalgamate, fuse — **mix·able** *adj* — **mix·er** *n*

**²mix** *n* **:** a product of mixing; *esp* **:** a commercially prepared mixture of food ingredients

**mixed number** *n* **:** a number (as 5⅔) composed of an integer and a fraction

**mixed–up** \'miks-'təp\ *adj* **:** marked by bewilderment, perplexity, or disorder **:** CONFUSED

**mixt** *abbr* mixture

**mix·ture** \'miks-chər\ *n* **1 :** the act or process of mixing; *also* **:** the state of being mixed   **2 :** a product of mixing

**mix–up** \'miks-,əp\ *n* **:** an instance of confusion ⟨a ∼ about the train⟩

**miz·zen** *or* **miz·en** \'miz-ᵊn\ *n* **1 :** a fore-and-aft sail set on the mizzenmast   **2 :** MIZZENMAST — **mizzen** *or* **mizen** *adj*

**miz·zen·mast** \-,mast, -məst\ *n* **:** the mast aft or next aft of the mainmast

**mk** *abbr* mark

**Mk** *abbr* Mark

**mks** *abbr* meter-kilogram-second

**mktg** *abbr* marketing

**ml** *abbr* milliliter

**ML** *abbr* Middle Latin

**MLD** *abbr* minimum lethal dose

**Mlle** *abbr* mademoiselle

**Mlles** *abbr* mesdemoiselles

**mm** *abbr* millimeter

**MM** *abbr* **1** Maryknoll Missioners **2** messieurs

**Mme** *abbr* madame

**Mn** *symbol* manganese

**MN** *abbr* Minnesota

**mne·mon·ic** \ni-'män-ik\ *adj* **:** assisting or designed to assist memory

**mo** *abbr* month

**¹Mo** *abbr* Missouri

**²Mo** *symbol* molybdenum

**MO** *abbr* **1** mail order **2** medical officer **3** Missouri **4** modus operandi **5** money order

**moan** \'mōn\ *n* **:** a low prolonged sound indicative of pain or grief — **moan** *vb*

**moat** \'mōt\ *n* **:** a deep wide usu. water-filled trench around the rampart of a castle

**¹mob** \'mäb\ *n* [L *mobile vulgus* vacillating crowd]   **1 :** MASSES, RABBLE   **2 :** a large disorderly crowd   **3 :** a criminal set **:** GANG

**²mob** *vb* **mobbed; mob·bing   1 :** to crowd around and attack or annoy   **2 :** to crowd into or around ⟨shoppers *mobbed* the stores⟩

**¹mo·bile** \'mō-bəl, -,bēl, -,bīl\ *adj*   **1 :** capable of moving or being moved   **2 :** changeable in appearance, mood, or purpose; *also* **:** ADAPTABLE   **3 :** using vehicles for transportation ⟨∼ warfare⟩   **4 :** having the opportunity for or undergoing a shift in social status

**²mo·bile** \'mō-,bēl\ *n* **:** a construction or sculpture (as of wire and sheet metal) with parts that can be set in motion by air currents; *also* **:** a similar structure suspended so that it is moved by a current of air

**mobile home** *n* **:** a trailer used as a permanent dwelling

**mo·bi·lize** \'mō-bə-,līz\ *vb* **-lized; -liz·ing   1 :** to put into movement or circulation   **2 :** to assemble and make ready for war duty; *also* **:** to marshal for action — **mo·bi·li·za·tion** \,mō-bə-lə-'zā-shən\ *n* — **mo·bi·liz·er** \'mō-bə-,lī-zər\ *n*

**mob·ster** \'mäb-stər\ *n* **:** a member of a criminal gang

**moc·ca·sin** \'mäk-ə-sən\ *n* **1 :** a soft leather heelless shoe   **2 :** a venomous snake of the southeastern U.S.

**¹mock** \'mäk, 'mȯk\ *vb* **1 :** to treat with contempt or ridicule   **2 :** DELUDE   **3 :** DEFY   **4 :** to mimic in sport or derision **:** IMITATE — **mock·er** *n* — **mock·ery** \-(ə-)rē\ *n* — **mock·ing·ly** *adv*

**²mock** *adj* **:** SHAM, PSEUDO

**mock–he·ro·ic** \,mäk-hi-'rō-ik,,mȯk-\ *adj* **:** ridiculing or burlesquing the heroic style or heroic character or action ⟨a ∼ poem⟩

**mock·ing·bird** \'mäk-iŋ-,bərd, 'mȯk-\ *n* **:** a songbird of the southern U.S. noted for its ability to mimic the calls of other birds

**mock–up** \'mäk-,əp, 'mȯk-\ *n* **:** a full-sized structural model built accurately to scale chiefly for study, testing, or display ⟨a ∼ of an airplane⟩

**¹mod** \'mäd\ *adj* **:** MODERN; *esp* **:** bold, free, and unconventional in style, behavior, or dress

**²mod** *n* **:** one who wears mod clothes or who follows current trends

**³mod** *abbr* **1** moderate **2** modern

**mode** \'mōd\ *n* **1 :** a particular form or variety of something; *also* **:** STYLE   **2 :** a manner of doing something   **3 :** the most frequent value of a set of data — **mod·al** \'mōd-ᵊl\ *adj*

**¹mod·el** \'mäd-ᵊl\ *n* **1 :** structural design   **2 :** a miniature representation; *also* **:** a pattern of something to be made   **3 :** an example for imitation or emulation   **4 :** one who poses for an artist; *also* **:** MANNEQUIN   **5 :** TYPE, DESIGN — **model** *adj*

**²model** *vb* **mod·eled** *or* **mod·elled; mod·el·ing** *or* **mod·el·ling** \'mäd-(ə-)liŋ\   **1 :** SHAPE, FASHION, CONSTRUCT

**2 :** to work as a fashion model

**³mod·el** *adj* **1 :** serving as or worthy of being a pattern ⟨a ~ student⟩ **2 :** being a miniature representation of something ⟨a ~ airplane⟩

**¹mod·er·ate** \'mäd-(ə-)rət\ *adj* **1 :** avoiding extremes; *also* **:** TEMPERATE **2 :** AVERAGE; *also* **:** MEDIOCRE **3 :** limited in scope or effect **4 :** not expensive — **moderate** *n* — **mod·er·ate·ly** *adv* — **mod·er·ate·ness** *n*

**²mod·er·ate** \'mäd-ə-,rāt\ *vb* **-at·ed; -at·ing 1 :** to lessen the intensity of **:** TEMPER **2 :** to act as a moderator — **mod·er·a·tion** \,mäd-ə-'rā-shən\ *n*

**mod·er·a·tor** \'mäd-ə-,rāt-ər\ *n* **1 :** MEDIATOR **2 :** one who presides over an assembly, meeting, or discussion

**mod·ern** \'mäd-ərn\ *adj* [LL *modernus,* fr. L *modo* just now, fr. *modus* measure] **:** of, relating to, or characteristic of the present or the immediate past **:** CONTEMPORARY — **modern** *n* — **mo·der·ni·ty** \mə-'dər-nət-ē\ *n* — **mod·ern·ly** \'mäd-ərn-lē\ *adv* — **mod·ern·ness** \-ərn-nəs\ *n*

**mod·ern·ism** \'mäd-ər-,niz-əm\ *n* **:** a practice, movement, or belief peculiar to modern times

**mod·ern·ize** \'mäd-ər-,nīz\ *vb* **-ized; -iz·ing :** to make or become modern — **mod·ern·i·za·tion** \,mäd-ər-nə-'zā-shən\ *n* — **mod·ern·iz·er** \'mäd-ər-,nī-zər\ *n*

**mod·est** \'mäd-əst\ *adj* **1 :** having a moderate estimate of oneself; *also* **:** DIFFIDENT **2 :** observing the proprieties of dress and behavior **3 :** limited in size, amount, or aim — **mod·est·ly** *adv* — **mod·es·ty** \-ə-stē\ *n*

**mod·i·cum** \'mäd-i-kəm\ *n* **:** a small amount

**modif** *abbr* modification

**mod·i·fy** \'mäd-ə-,fī\ *vb* **-fied; -fy·ing 1 :** MODERATE **2 :** to limit the meaning of esp. in a grammatical construction **3 :** CHANGE, ALTER — **mod·i·fi·ca·tion** \,mäd-ə-fə-'kā-shən\ *n* — **mod·i·fi·er** \'mäd-ə-,fī(-ə)r\ *n*

**mod·ish** \'mōd-ish\ *adj* **:** FASHIONABLE, STYLISH — **mod·ish·ly** *adv* — **mod·ish·ness** *n*

**mo·diste** \mō-'dēst\ *n* **:** a maker of fashionable dresses

**mod·u·lar** \'mäj-ə-lər\ *adj* **:** constructed with standardized units

**mod·u·lar·ized** \'mäj-ə-lə-,rīzd\ *adj* **:** containing or consisting of modules

**mod·u·late** \'mäj-ə-,lāt\ *vb* **-lat·ed; -lat·ing 1 :** to tune to a key or pitch **2 :** to keep in proper measure or proportion **:** TEMPER **3 :** to vary the amplitude, frequency, or phase of a carrier wave for the transmission of intelligence (as in radio or television) — **mod·u·la·tion** \,mäj-ə-'lā-shən\ *n* — **mod·u·la·tor** \'mäj-ə-,lāt-ər\ *n* — **mod·u·la·to·ry** \-lə-,tōr-ē\ *adj*

**mod·ule** \'mäj-ül\ *n* **1 :** any in a series of standardized units for use together **2 :** an independent unit that constitutes a part of the total structure of a space vehicle ⟨a propulsion ~⟩ **3 :** an assembly of wired electronic parts for use with other such assemblies

**mo·dus ope·ran·di** \,mōd-əs-,äp-ə-'ran-dē, -,dī\ *n, pl* **mo·di operandi** \'mō-,dē-,äp-, 'mō-,dī-\ **:** a method of procedure

**¹mo·gul** \'mō-gəl, mō-'gəl\ *n* [fr. *Mogul,* one of the Mongol conquerors of India or their descendants, fr. Per *Mughul* Mongol, fr. Mongolian *Moṅgol*] **:** an important person **:** MAGNATE

**²mogul** \'mo-gəl\ *n* **:** a bump in a ski run

**mo·hair** \'mō-,haər\ *n* [modif. of obs. It *mocaiarro,* fr. Ar *mukhayyar,* lit., choice] **:** a fabric or yarn made wholly or in part from the long silky hair of the Angora goat

**Mo·ham·med·an** *var of* MUHAMMADAN

**Mo·hawk** \'mō-,hȯk\ *n, pl* **Mohawk** *or* **Mohawks :** a member of an Indian people of the Mohawk river valley, New York; *also* **:** the language of the Mohawk people

**Mo·he·gan** \mō-'hē-gən, mə-\ *or* **Mo·hi·can** \-'hē-kən\ *n, pl* **Mohegan** *or* **Mohegans** *or* **Mohican** *or* **Mohicans :** a member of an Indian people of southeastern Connecticut

**Mo·hi·can** \mō-'hē-kən, mə-\ *var of* MAHICAN

**Mohs' scale** \'mōz-, 'mōs-, ,mō-səz-\ *n* **:** a scale of hardness for minerals ranging from 1 for the softest to 10 for the hardest

**moi·ety** \'mȯi-ət-ē\ *n, pl* **-eties :** one of two equal or approximately equal parts

**moil** \'mȯil\ *vb* **:** to work hard **:** DRUDGE — **moil** *n* — **moil·er** *n*

**moi·ré** \mȯ-'rā, mwä-\ *or* **moire** \*same,* *or* 'mȯi(-ə)r, 'mwär\ *n* **:** a fabric (as silk) having a watered appearance

**moist** \'mȯist\ *adj* **:** slightly or moderately wet — **moist·ly** *adv* — **moist·ness** *n*

**moist·en** \'mȯis-ᵊn\ *vb* **moist·ened; moist·en·ing** \'mȯis-(ᵊ-)niŋ\ **:** to make or become moist — **moist·en·er** \'mȯis-(ᵊ-)nər\ *n*

**mois·ture** \'mȯis-chər\ *n* **:** the small amount of liquid that causes dampness

**mol** *abbr* molecular; molecule

**mo·lar** \'mō-lər\ *n* [L *molaris,* fr. *molaris* of a mill, fr. *mola* millstone] **:** one of the broad teeth adapted to grinding food and located in the back of the jaw — **molar** *adj*

**mo·las·ses** \mə-'las-əz\ *n* **:** the thick brown syrup that is separated from raw sugar in sugar manufacture

**¹mold** \'mōld\ *n* **:** crumbly soil rich in organic matter

**²mold** *n* **1 :** distinctive nature or character **2 :** the frame on or around which something is constructed **3 :** a cavity in which something is shaped; *also* **:** an object so shaped **4 :** MOLDING

**³mold** *vb* **1 :** to shape in or as if in a mold **2 :** to ornament with molding — **mold·er** *n*

**⁴mold** *n* **:** a surface growth of fungus on damp or decaying matter; *also* **:** a fungus that forms molds — **mold·i·ness** \'mōl-dē-nəs\ *n* — **moldy** *adj*

**⁵mold** *vb* **:** to become moldy

**mold·board** \'mōl(d)-ˌbōrd\ *n* : a curved iron plate attached above the plowshare to lift and turn the soil

**mold·er** \'mōl-dər\ *vb* **mold·ered; mold·er·ing** \-d(ə-)riŋ\ : to crumble into small pieces

**mold·ing** \'mōl-diŋ\ *n* **1** : an act or process of shaping in a mold; *also* : an object so shaped **2** : a decorative surface, plane, or curved strip

**¹mole** \'mōl\ *n* : a small often pigmented spot or protuberance on the skin

**²mole** *n* : a small burrowing mammal with tiny eyes, hidden ears, and soft fur

**³mole** *n* : a massive breakwater or jetty

**mo·lec·u·lar biology** \mə-'läk-yə-lər-\ *n* : a branch of biology dealing with the ultimate physical and chemical organization of living matter and esp with the molecular basis of inheritance and protein synthesis — **molecular biologist** *n*

**mol·e·cule** \'mäl-i-ˌkyül\ *n* : the smallest particle of matter that is the same chemically as the whole mass — **mo·lec·u·lar** \mə-'lek-yə-lər\ *adj*

**mole·hill** \'mōl-ˌhil\ *n* : a little ridge of earth thrown up by a mole

**mole·skin** \-ˌskin\ *n* **1** : the skin of the mole used as fur **2** : a heavy durable cotton fabric for industrial, medical, or clothing use

**mo·lest** \mə-'lest\ *vb* **1** : ANNOY, DISTURB **2** : to make annoying sexual advances to — **mo·les·ta·tion** \ˌmōl-ˌes-'tā-shən\ *n* — **mo·lest·er** \mə-'les-tər\ *n*

**moll** \'mäl\ *n* : a gangster's girl friend

**mol·li·fy** \'mäl-ə-ˌfī\ *vb* **-fied; -fy·ing** **1** : to soothe in temper : APPEASE **2** : SOFTEN **3** : to reduce in intensity : ASSUAGE — **mol·li·fi·ca·tion** \ˌmäl-ə-fə-'kā-shən\ *n*

**mol·lusk** *or* **mol·lusc** \'mäl-əsk\ *n* : any of a large group of mostly shelled and aquatic invertebrate animals including snails, clams, and squids — **mol·lus·can** *also* **mol·lus·kan** \mə-'ləs-kən\ *adj*

**¹mol·ly·cod·dle** \'mäl-ē-ˌkäd-ᵊl\ *n* : a pampered man or boy

**²mollycoddle** *vb* **mol·ly·cod·dled; mol·ly·cod·dling** \-ˌkäd-(ᵊ-)liŋ\ : PAMPER

**Mo·lo·tov cocktail** \ˌmäl-ə-ˌtof, ˌmōl-\ *n* : a crude hand grenade made of a bottle filled with a flammable liquid (as gasoline) and fitted with a wick and saturated rag taped to the bottom and ignited at the moment of hurling

**¹molt** \'mōlt\ *vb* : to shed hair, feathers, outer skin, or horns periodically with the parts being replaced by new growth — **molt·er** *n*

**²molt** *n* : the act or process of molting

**mol·ten** \'mōlt-ᵊn\ *adj* : fused or liquefied by heat; *also* : GLOWING

**mo·ly** \'mō-lē\ *n* : a mythical herb with black root, white flowers, and magic powers

**mo·lyb·de·num** \mə-'lib-də-nəm\ *n* : a metallic chemical element used in strengthening and hardening steel

**mom** \'mäm, 'məm\ *n* : MOTHER

**MOM** *abbr* middle of month

**mo·ment** \'mō-mənt\ *n* **1** : a minute portion of time : INSTANT **2** : a time of excellence ⟨he has his ∼*s*⟩ **3** : IMPORTANCE **syn** consequence, significance

**mo·men·tar·i·ly** \ˌmō-mən-'ter-ə-lē\ *adv* **1** : for a moment **2** : INSTANTLY **3** : at any moment : SOON

**mo·men·tary** \'mō-mən-ˌter-ē\ *adj* **1** : continuing only a moment; *also* : EPHEMERAL **2** : recurring at every moment — **mo·men·tar·i·ness** \'mō-mən-ˌter-ē-nəs\ *n*

**mo·men·tous** \mō-'ment-əs\ *adj* : very important — **mo·men·tous·ly** *adv* — **mo·men·tous·ness** *n*

**mo·men·tum** \mō-'ment-əm\ *n, pl* **mo·men·ta** \-'ment-ə\ *or* **momentums** : the force which a moving body has because of its weight and motion

**Mon** *abbr* Monday

**mon·arch** \'män-ərk, -ˌärk\ *n* **1** : a person who reigns over a kingdom or an empire **2** : one holding preeminent position or power **3** : a large orange and black migratory American butterfly whose larva feeds on milkweed — **mo·nar·chi·cal** \mə-'när-ki-kəl\ *or* **mo·nar·chic** \-'när-kik\ *adj*

**mon·ar·chist** \'män-ər-kəst\ *n* : a believer in monarchical government — **mon·ar·chism** \-ˌkiz-əm\ *n*

**mon·ar·chy** \'män-ər-kē\ *n, pl* **-chies** : a nation or state governed by a monarch

**mon·as·tery** \'män-ə-ˌster-ē\ *n, pl* **-ter·ies** : a house for persons under religious vows (as monks) — **mon·as·te·ri·al** \ˌmän-ə-'stir-ē-əl\ *adj*

**mo·nas·tic** \mə-'nas-tik\ *adj* : of or relating to monasteries or to monks or nuns — **monastic** *n* — **mo·nas·ti·cal·ly** \-ti-k(ə-)lē\ *adv*

**mo·nas·ti·cism** \mə-'nas-tə-ˌsiz-əm\ *n* : the monastic life, system, or condition

**mon·au·ral** \mä-'nȯr-əl\ *adj* : MONOPHONIC — **mon·au·ral·ly** \-ē\ *adv*

**Mon·day** \'mən-dē\ *n* : the second day of the week

**mon·e·tary** \'män-ə-ˌter-ē, 'mən-\ *adj* : of or relating to money or to the mechanisms by which it is supplied and circulated in the economy

**mon·ey** \'mən-ē\ *n, pl* **moneys** *or* **mon·ies** \'mən-ēz\ **1** : something (as metal currency) accepted as a medium of exchange **2** : wealth reckoned in monetary terms **3** : the 1st, 2d, and 3d place in a horse or dog race ☞ see table on next page

**mon·eyed** \'mən-ēd\ *adj* **1** : having money : WEALTHY **2** : consisting in or derived from money

**mon·ey·lend·er** \'mən-ē-ˌlen-dər\ *n* : one whose business is lending money; *specif* : PAWNBROKER

**mon·ey·mak·er** \'mən-ē-ˌmā-kər\ *n* **1** : one who accumulates wealth **2** : a plan or product that produces profit — **mon·ey·mak·ing** \-kiŋ\ *adj or n*

**money of account** : a denominator of value or basis of exchange used in keeping accounts

# Money

| name | subdivisions | country |
|---|---|---|
| afghani | 100 puls | Afghanistan |
| baht *or* tical | 100 satang | Thailand |
| balboa | 100 centesimos | Panama |
| bolivar | 100 centimos | Venezuela |
| cedi | 100 pesewas | Ghana |
| colon | 100 centimos | Costa Rica |
| colon | 100 centavos | El Salvador |
| cordoba | 100 centavos | Nicaragua |
| cruzeiro | 100 centavos | Brazil |
| dalasi | 100 bututs | Gambia |
| deutsche mark | 100 pfennigs | West Germany |
| dinar | 100 centimes | Algeria |
| dinar | 1000 fils | Bahrain |
| dinar | 5 riyals 20 dirhams 1000 fils | Iraq |
| dinar | 1000 fils | Jordan |
| dinar | 1000 fils | Kuwait |
| dinar | 1000 dirhams | Libya |
| dinar | 1000 fils | Southern Yemen (People's Democratic Republic of Yemen) |
| dinar | 1000 millimes | Tunisia |
| dinar | 100 paras | Yugoslavia |
| dirham | 100 francs | Morocco |
| dollar | 100 cents | Australia |
| dollar | 100 cents | Bahamas |
| dollar | 100 cents | Barbados |
| dollar | 100 cents | Bermuda |
| dollar | 100 cents | British Honduras (Belize) |
| dollar | 100 sen | Brunei |
| dollar | 100 cents | Canada |
| dollar | 100 cents | Ethiopia |
| dollar | 100 cents | Fiji |
| dollar | 100 cents | Guyana |
| dollar | 100 cents | Hong Kong |
| dollar | 100 cents | Jamaica |
| dollar | 100 cents | Liberia |
| dollar | 100 cents | Malaysia |
| dollar | 100 cents | New Zealand |
| dollar | 100 cents | Rhodesia |
| dollar | 100 cents | Singapore |
| dollar | 100 cents | Trinidad and Tobago |
| dollar | 100 cents | United States |
| dollar—see YUAN, below | | |
| dong | 100 xu | North Vietnam |
| drachma | 100 lepta | Greece |
| escudo | 100 centesimos 1000 milesimos | Chile |
| escudo | 100 centavos | Portugal |
| florin—see GULDEN, below | | |
| forint | 100 filler | Hungary |
| franc | 100 centimes | Belgium |
| franc | 100 centimes | Burundi |
| franc | 100 centimes | Cameroon |
| franc | 100 centimes | Central African Republic |
| franc | 100 centimes | Chad |
| franc | 100 centimes | Congo (Brazzaville) |
| franc | 100 centimes | Dahomey |
| franc | 100 centimes | France |
| franc | 100 centimes | Gabon |
| franc | 100 centimes | Guinea |
| franc | 100 centimes | Ivory Coast |
| franc | 100 centimes | Luxembourg |
| franc | 100 centimes | Malagasy Republic |
| franc | 100 centimes | Mali |
| franc | 100 centimes | Mauritania |
| franc | 100 centimes | Niger |
| franc | 100 centimes | Rwanda |
| franc | 100 centimes | Senegal |
| franc | 100 centimes *or* rappen | Switzerland |
| franc | 100 centimes | Togo |
| franc | 100 centimes | Upper Volta |
| gourde | 100 centimes | Haiti |
| guarani | 100 centimos | Paraguay |
| gulden *or* guilder *or* florin | 100 cents | Netherlands |
| kip | 100 at | Laos |
| koruna | 100 halers | Czechoslovakia |
| krona | 100 aurar | Iceland |
| krona | 100 öre | Sweden |
| krone | 100 öre | Denmark |
| krone | 100 öre | Norway |
| kwacha | 100 tambala | Malawi |
| kwacha | 100 ngwee | Zambia |
| kyat | 100 pyas | Burma |
| lek | 100 qintar | Albania |
| lempira | 100 centavos | Honduras |
| leone | 100 cents | Sierra Leone |
| leu | 100 bani | Rumania |
| lev | 100 stotinki | Bulgaria |
| lira | 100 centesimi | Italy |
| lira *or* pound | 100 kurus *or* piasters | Turkey |
| lira—see POUND, below | | |
| mark *or* ostmark | 100 pfennigs | East Germany |
| mark—see DEUTSCHE MARK, above | | |
| markka | 100 pennia | Finland |
| naira | 100 kobo | Nigeria |
| ostmark—see MARK, above | | |
| pa'anga | 100 seniti | Tonga |
| pataca | 100 avos | Macao |
| peseta | 100 centimos | Equatorial Guinea |
| peseta | 100 centimos | Spain |
| peso | 100 centavos | Argentina |
| peso | 100 centavos | Bolivia |
| peso | 100 centavos | Colombia |
| peso | 100 centavos | Cuba |
| peso | 100 centavos | Dominican Republic |
| peso | 100 centavos | Mexico |
| peso | 100 sentimos *or* centavos | Philippines |
| peso | 100 centesimos | Uruguay |
| piaster | 100 cents | South Vietnam |

table continued page 454

## Money, continued

| name | subdivisions | country | name | subdivisions | country |
|------|-------------|---------|------|-------------|---------|
| pound | 1000 mils | Cyprus | rupee | 100 cents | Mauritius |
| pound | 100 piasters | Egypt | rupee | 100 paise | Nepal |
| | 1000 milliemes | | rupee | 100 paisa | Pakistan |
| pound | 100 pence | Ireland | rupee | 100 cents | Seychelles |
| pound *or* | 100 agorot | Israel | rupee | 100 cents | Sri Lanka |
| lira | | | rupiah | 100 sen | Indonesia |
| pound | 100 piasters | Lebanon | | | |
| pound | 100 pence | Malta | schilling | 100 groschen | Austria |
| pound | 20 shillings | Rhodesia | shilingi *or* | 100 senti | Tanzania |
| | 240 pence | | shilling | | |
| pound | 100 piasters | Sudan | shilling | 100 cents | Kenya |
| pound *or* | 100 piasters | Syria | shilling | 100 cents | Somalia |
| lira | | | shilling | 100 cents | Uganda |
| pound | 100 pence | United | sol | 100 centavos | Peru |
| | | Kingdom | sucre | 100 centavos | Ecuador |
| pound—see LIRA, above | | | taka | 100 paisa | Bangladesh |
| quetzal | 100 centavos | Guatemala | tala | 100 senes | Western |
| | | | | | Samoa |
| rand | 100 cents | Botswana | | | |
| rand | 100 cents | Lesotho | tical—see BAHT, above | | |
| rand | 100 cents | South Africa | tugrik | 100 mongo | Outer |
| rand | 100 cents | Swaziland | | | Mongolia |
| rial | 100 dinars | Iran | won | 100 jun | North Korea |
| rial | 1000 baizas | Oman | won | 100 chon | South Korea |
| rial | 40 buqshas | Yemen Arab | yen | 100 sen | Japan |
| | | Republic | yuan | 10 chiao | China |
| riel | 100 sen | Cambodia | | 100 fen | (mainland) |
| | | (Khmer | yuan *or* | 10 chiao | China |
| | | Republic) | dollar | | (Taiwan) |
| riyal | 20 qursh | Saudi Arabia | zaire | 100 makuta | Zaire |
| | 100 halala | | | (*sing*, likuta) | |
| ruble | 100 kopecks | U.S.S.R. | | 10,000 sengi | |
| rupee | 100 paise | Bhutan | zloty | 100 groszy | Poland |
| rupee | 100 paise | India | | | |

**money order** *n* : an order purchased at a post office, bank, or telegraph office directing another office to pay a specified sum of money to a person or firm named on it

**mon·ger** \'məŋ-gər, 'mäŋ-\ *n* **1** : DEALER **2** : one who tries to stir up or spread something

**mon·go** \'mäŋ-(,)gō\ *n, pl* **mongo**—see *tugrik* at MONEY table

**Mon·go·lian** \män-'gōl-yən, mäŋ-, -'gō-lē-ən\ *n* **1** : a native or inhabitant of Mongolia **2** : a member of a racial stock comprising chiefly the peoples of northern and eastern Asia — **Mon·gol** \'mäŋ-gəl, 'män-,gōl, 'mäŋ-\ *adj or n* — **Mongolian** *adj*

**mon·gol·ism** \'mäŋ-gə-,liz-əm\ *n* : a congenital idiocy associated with the presence of an extra chromosome in man

**Mon·gol·oid** \'mäŋ-gə-,lȯid\ *adj* : of, relating to, or affected with mongolism — **Mongoloid** *n*

**mon·goose** \'män-,güs, 'mäŋ-\ *n, pl* **mon·goos·es** *also* **mon·geese** \-,gēs\ : a small agile Indian mammal that is related to the civet cats and feeds on snakes and rodents

**mon·grel** \'məŋ-grəl, 'mäŋ-\ *n* : an offspring of parents of different breeds or uncertain ancestry

**mo·nism** \'mō-,niz-əm, 'män- iz-\ *n* : a view that reality is basically one — **mo·nist** \'mō-nəst, 'män-əst\ *n*, **mo-\**

**mo·ni·tion** \mō-'nish-ən, mə-\ *n* : WARNING, CAUTION

**¹mon·i·tor** \'män-ət-ər\ *n* **1** : a student appointed to assist a teacher **2** : one that monitors; *esp* : a screen used by television personnel for viewing the picture being picked up by a camera

**²monitor** *vb* **mon·i·tored; mon·i·tor·ing** \'män-ət-ə-riŋ, 'män-ə-triŋ\ **1** : to check or adjust the quality of (as a radio or television broadcast); *also* : to check (a broadcast or a telephone conversation) for political, military, or criminal significance **2** : to test for intensity of radiation esp. from radioactivity ⟨~ the upper air⟩ **3** : to watch or observe for a special purpose ⟨the engineer ~*ing* the dials⟩

**mon·i·to·ry** \'män-ə-,tōr-ē\ *adj* : giving admonition : WARNING

**¹monk** \'məŋk\ *n* [ME, fr. OE *munuc*, fr. LL *monachus*, fr. LGk *monachos*, fr. Gk, adj., single, fr. *monos* single, alone] : a man belonging to a religious order and living in a monastery — **monk·ish** *adj* — **monk·ish·ly** *adv* — **monk·ish·ness** *n*

**²monk** *n* : MONKEY

**¹mon·key** \'məŋ-kē\ *n, pl* **monkeys** : a primate mammal other than man; *esp* : one of the smaller, longer-tailed, and usu. more arboreal primates as contrasted with the apes

²**monkey** vb **mon·keyed; mon·key·ing 1** : FOOL, TRIFLE **2** : TAMPER

**mon·key·shine** \-,shīn\ n : PRANK — usu. used in pl.

**monkey wrench** n : a wrench with one adjustable jaw

**monks·hood** \'məŋks-,hùd\ n : a poisonous herb related to the buttercups and often grown for its showy hood⸗ shaped white or purple flowers

¹**mono** \'män-ō\ adj : MONOPHONIC

²**mono** n : MONONUCLEOSIS

**mono·chro·mat·ic** \,män-ə-krō-'mat-ik\ adj **1** : having or consisting of one color **2** : consisting of radiation (as light) of a single wavelength — **mono·chro·mat·i·cal·ly** \-i-k(ə-)lē\ adv — **mono·chro·ma·tic·i·ty** \-,krō-mə-'tis-ət-ē\ n

**mono·chrome** \'män-ə-,krōm\ adj : characterized by the reproduction or transmission of visual images in tones of gray ⟨∼ television⟩

**mon·o·cle** \'män-i-kəl\ n : an eyeglass for one eye

**mono·cot·y·le·don** \,män-ə-,kät-ºl-'ēd-ºn\ n : any of a subclass of seed plants having an embryo with a single cotyledon and usu. parallell-veined leaves — **mono·cot·y·le·don·ous** adj

**mon·o·dy** \'män-əd-ē\ n, pl **-dies** : ELEGY, DIRGE — **mo·nod·ic** \mə-'näd-ik\ adj — **mon·o·dist** \'män-əd-əst\ n

**mono·fil·a·ment** \,män-ə-'fil-ə-mənt\ n : a single untwisted synthetic filament

**mo·nog·a·my** \mə-'näg-ə-mē\ n : marriage with but one person at a time — **mono·gam·ic** \,män-ə-'gam-ik\ adj — **mo·nog·a·mist** \mə-'näg-ə-məst\ n — **mo·nog·a·mous** \mə-'näg-ə-məs\ adj

**mono·gram** \'män-ə-,gram\ n : a sign of identity composed of the combined initials of a name — **monogram** vb

**mono·graph** \'män-ə-,graf\ n : a learned treatise on a small area of learning

**mono·lin·gual** \,män-ə-'liŋ-gwəl\ adj : expressed in or knowing or using only one language

**mono·lith** \'män-ºl-,ith\ n **1** : a single great stone often in the form of a monument or column **2** : something (as a social structure) held to be a single massive whole exhibiting solid uniformity — **mono·lith·ic** \,män-ºl-'ith-ik\ adj

**mono·logue** also **mono·log** \'män-ºl-,óg\ n : a dramatic soliloquy; also : a long speech monopolizing conversation — **mono·logu·ist** \-,óg-əst\ or **mo·nol·o·gist** \mə-'näl-ə-jəst; 'män-ºl-,óg-əst\ n

**mono·ma·nia** \,män-ə-'mā-nē-ə, -nyə\ n **1** : mental derangement involving a single idea or area of thought **2** : excessive concentration on a single object or idea — **mono·ma·ni·ac** \-nē-,ak\ n or adj

**mono·mer** \'män-ə-mər\ n : one of the molecular units of a polymer

**mono·nu·cle·o·sis** \,män-ō-,n(y)ü-klē-'ō-səs\ n : an acute infectious disease characterized by fever, swelling of lymph glands, and increased numbers of lymph cells in the blood

**mono·phon·ic** \,män-ə-'fän-ik\ adj : of or relating to sound transmission, recording, or reproduction by techniques that provide a single transmission path as contrasted with binaural techniques — **mono·pho·ni·cal·ly** \-i-k(ə-)lē\ adv

**mono·plane** \'män-ə-,plān\ n : an airplane with only one main supporting surface

**mo·nop·o·ly** \mə-'näp-(ə-)lē\ n, pl **-lies** [L monopolium, fr. Gk monopōlion, fr. monos alone, single + pōlein to sell] **1** : exclusive ownership (as through command of supply) **2** : a commodity controlled by one party **3** : a person or group having a monopoly — **mo·nop·o·list** \-ləst\ n — **mo·nop·o·lis·tic** \mə-,näp-ə-'lis-tik\ adj — **mo·nop·o·li·za·tion** \-lə-'zā-shən\ n — **mo·nop·o·lize** \mə-'näp-ə-,līz\ vb

**mono·rail** \'män-ə-,rāl\ n : a single rail serving as a track for a wheeled vehicle; also : a vehicle traveling on such a track

**mono·so·di·um glu·ta·mate** \,män-ə-,sōd-ē-əm-'glüt-ə-,māt\ n : a crystalline salt used for seasoning foods

**mono·syl·la·ble** \'män-ə-,sil-ə-bəl\ n : a word of one syllable — **mono·syl·lab·ic** \,män-ə-sə-'lab-ik\ adj — **mono·syl·lab·i·cal·ly** \-i-k(ə-)lē\ adv

**mono·the·ism** \'män-ə-(,)thē-,iz-əm\ n : a doctrine or belief that there is only one deity — **mono·the·ist** \-,thē-əst\ n

**mono·tone** \'män-ə-,tōn\ n : a succession of syllables, words, or sentences in one unvaried key or pitch

**mo·not·o·nous** \mə-'nät-ºn-əs\ adj **1** : uttered or sounded in one unvarying tone **2** : tediously uniform — **mo·not·o·nous·ly** adv — **mo·not·o·nous·ness** n — **mo·not·o·ny** \-ºn-ē\ n

**mon·ox·ide** \mə-'näk-,sīd\ n : an oxide containing one atom of oxygen in the molecule

**mon·sei·gneur** \mōⁿ-,sān-'yər\ n, pl **mes·sei·gneurs** \,mā-,sān-'yər(z)\ : a French dignitary — used as a title

**mon·sieur** \məs(h)-(')yə(r),mə-'si(ə)r\ n, pl **mes·sieurs** \məs(h)-(')yə(r)(z), mäs-; mə-'si(ə)r(z)\ : a Frenchman of high rank or station — used as a title equivalent to Mr.

**mon·si·gnor** \män-'sē-nyər\ n, pl **monsignors** or **mon·si·gno·ri** \,män-,sēn-'yōr-ē\ : a Roman Catholic prelate — used as a title

**mon·soon** \män-'sün\ n [obs. D monssoen, fr. Port monção, fr. Ar mawsim time, season] : a periodic wind esp. in the Indian ocean and southern Asia; also : the season of the southwest monsoon esp. in India — **mon·soon·al** \-ºl\ adj

**mon·ster** \'män-stər\ *n* **1** : an abnormally developed plant or animal **2** : an animal of strange or terrifying shape; *also* : one unusually large of its kind **3** : an extremely ugly, wicked, or cruel person — **mon·stros·i·ty** \män-'sträs-ət-ē\ *n* — **mon·strous** \'män-strəs\ *adj* — **mon·strous·ly** *adv*

**mon·strance** \'män-strəns\ *n* : a vessel in which the consecrated Host is exposed for the adoration of the faithful

**Mont** *abbr* Montana

**mon·tage** \män-'täzh\ *n* **1** : a composite photograph made by combining several separate pictures **2** : an artistic composition made up of several different kinds of items (as strips of newspaper, pictures, bits of wood) arranged together

**month** \'mənth\ *n, pl* **months** \'məns, 'mənths\ [OE *mōnath*, fr. *mōna* moon] : one of the 12 parts into which the year is divided — **month·ly** *adv or adj or n*

**mon·u·ment** \'män-yə-mənt\ *n* **1** : a lasting reminder; *esp* : a structure erected in remembrance of a person or event **2** : a natural feature or area of special interest set aside by the government as public property

**mon·u·men·tal** \,män-yə-'ment-ᵊl\ *adj* **1** : MASSIVE; *also* : OUTSTANDING **2** : of or relating to a monument **3** : very great — **mon·u·men·tal·ly** \-ē\ *adv*

**moo** \'mü\ *vb* : to make the natural throat noise of a cow — **moo** *n*

**¹mood** \'müd\ *n* **1** : a conscious state of mind or predominant emotion : FEELING **2** : a prevailing attitude : DISPOSITION

**²mood** *n* : distinction of form of a verb to express whether its action or state is conceived as fact or in some other manner (as wish)

**moody** \'müd-ē\ *adj* **mood·i·er; -est** **1** : GLOOMY **2** : subject to moods : TEMPERAMENTAL — **mood·i·ly** \'müd-ᵊl-ē\ *adv* — **mood·i·ness** \-ē-nəs\ *n*

**¹moon** \'mün\ *n* : a celestial body that revolves around the earth

**²moon** *vb* : to engage in idle reverie

**moon·beam** \'mün-,bēm\ *n* : a ray of light from the moon

**¹moon·light** \-,līt\ *n* : the light of the moon **moon·lit** \-,lit\ *adj*

**²moonlight** *vb* **moon·light·ed; moon·light·ing** : to hold a second job in addition to a regular one — **moon·light·er** *n*

**moon·scape** \-,skāp\ *n* : the surface of the moon as seen or as pictured

**moon·shine** \'mün-,shīn\ *n* **1** : MOONLIGHT **2** : empty talk **3** : intoxicating liquor usu. illegally distilled

**moon shot** *also* **moon shoot** *n* : the launching of a spacecraft to the moon or its vicinity

**moon·stone** \'mün-,stōn\ *n* : a transparent or translucent feldspar of pearly luster used as a gem

**moon·struck** \-,strək\ *adj* **1** : mentally unbalanced **2** : romantically sentimental

**¹moor** \'mur\ *n* : an area of open and usu. infertile and wet or peaty wasteland

**²moor** *vb* : to make fast with cables, lines, or anchors

**Moor** \'mur\ *n* : one of a No. African people of Arab and Berber ancestry conquering Spain in the 8th century — **Moor·ish** *adj*

**moor·ing** \-iŋ\ *n* **1** : a place where or an object to which a craft can be made fast **2** : moral or spiritual resources — usu. used in pl.

**moor·land** \-lənd, -,land\ *n* : land consisting of moors

**moose** \'müs\ *n, pl* **moose** : a large heavy-antlered American deer; *also* : the European elk

**¹moot** \'müt\ *vb* : to bring up for debate or discussion; *also* : DEBATE

**²moot** *adj* **1** : open to question; *also* : DISPUTED **2** : having no practical significance

**¹mop** \'mäp\ *n* : an implement made of absorbent material fastened to a handle and used esp. for cleaning floors

**²mop** *vb* **mopped; mopping** : to use a mop on : clean with a mop

**mope** \'mōp\ *vb* **moped; mop·ing** **1** : to become dull, dejected, or listless **2** : DAWDLE

**mop·pet** \'mäp-ət\ *n* [obs. E *mop* fool, child] : CHILD

**mop-up** \'mäp-,əp\ *n* : a final clearance or disposal

**mo·raine** \mə-'rān\ *n* : an accumulation of earth and stones left by a glacier

**¹mor·al** \'mor-əl\ *adj* **1** : of or relating to principles of right and wrong **2** : conforming to a standard of right behavior; *also* : capable of right and wrong action **3** : probable but not proved ⟨a ~ certainty⟩ **4** : of, relating to, or acting on the mind, character, or will ⟨a ~ victory⟩ **syn** virtuous, righteous, noble — **mor·al·ly** \-ē\ *adv*

**²moral** *n* **1** : the practical meaning (as of a story) **2** *pl* : moral practices or teachings

**mo·rale** \mə-'ral\ *n* **1** : MORALITY **2** : the mental and emotional attitudes of an individual to the tasks expected of him; *also* : ESPRIT DE CORPS

**mor·al·ist** \'mor-ə-ləst\ *n* **1** : a teacher or student of morals **2** : one concerned with regulating the morals of others — **mor·al·is·tic** \,mor-ə-'lis-tik\ *adj* — **mor·al·is·ti·cal·ly** \-ti-k(ə-)lē\ *adv*

**mo·ral·i·ty** \mə-'ral-ət-ē\ *n, pl* **-ties** : moral conduct : VIRTUE

**mor·al·ize** \'mor-ə-,līz\ *vb* **-ized; -izing** : to make moral reflections — **mor·al·iza·tion** \,mor-ə-lə-'zā-shən\ *n* — **mor·al·iz·er** \'mor-ə-,lī-zər\ *n*

**mo·rass** \mə-'ras\ *n* : SWAMP

**mor·a·to·ri·um** \,mor-ə-'tōr-ē-əm\ *n, pl* **-ri·ums** *or* **-ria** \-ē-ə\ : a suspension of activity

**mo·ray** \mə-'rā, 'mor-,ā\ *n* : any of numerous often brightly colored savage eels occurring in warm seas

**mor·bid** \'mor-bəd\ *adj* **1** : of, relating to, or typical of disease; *also* : DISEASED, SICKLY **2** : characterized by gloomy or unwholesome ideas or feelings **3** : GRISLY, GRUESOME ⟨~ details⟩ — **mor·bid·i·ty** \mȯr-'bid-ət-ē\ *n* — **mor·bid·ly** \'mȯr-bəd-lē\ *adv* — **mor·bid·ness** *n*

**mor·dant** \'mȯrd-ᵊnt\ *adj* **1** : INCISIVE **2** : BURNING, PUNGENT — **mor·dant·ly** *adv*

¹**more** \'mȯr\ *adj* **1** : GREATER **2** : ADDITIONAL

²**more** *adv* **1** : in addition ⟨not much ~ to do⟩ **2** : to a greater or higher degree

³**more** *n* **1** : a greater quantity, number, or amount ⟨the ~ the merrier⟩ **2** : an additional amount ⟨too full to eat ~⟩

⁴**more** *pron* : additional persons or things ⟨~ were found in the road⟩

**mo·rel** \mə-'rel\ *n* : any of several pitted edible fungi

**more·over** \mōr-'ō-vər\ *adv* : in addition : FURTHER

**mo·res** \'mȯr-,āz, -,(,)ēz\ *n pl* **1** : the fixed morally binding customs of a group **2** : HABITS, MANNERS

**Mor·gan** \'mȯr-gən\ *n* : any of an American breed of lightly built horses

**morgue** \'mȯrg\ *n* : a place where the bodies of persons found dead are kept until released for burial

**mor·i·bund** \'mȯr-ə-(,)bənd\ *adj* : being in a dying condition — **mor·i·bun·di·ty** \,mȯr-ə-'bən-dət-ē\ *n*

**Mor·mon** \'mȯr-mən\ *n* : a member of the Church of Jesus Christ of Latter-Day Saints — **Mor·mon·ism** \-mə-,niz-əm\ *n*

**morn** \'mȯrn\ *n* : MORNING

**morn·ing** \'mȯr-niŋ\ *n* **1** : the early part of the day; *esp* : the time from sunrise to noon **2** : BEGINNING

**morning glory** *n* : any of various twining plants related to the sweet potato that have often showy bell-shaped or funnel-shaped flowers

**morning sickness** *n* : nausea and vomiting that occur on rising in the morning esp. during the earlier months of pregnancy

**morning star** *n* : a bright planet (as Venus) seen in the eastern sky before or at sunrise

**Mo·roc·can** \mə-'räk-ən\ *n* : a native or inhabitant of Morocco

**mo·roc·co** \mə-'räk-ō\ *n* : a fine leather made of goatskins tanned with sumac

**mo·ron** \'mȯr-,än\ *n* : a defective person having a mental capacity equivalent to that of a normal 8 to 12 year old and being able to do routine work under supervision; *also* : a stupid person — **mo·ron·ic** \mə-'rän-ik\ *adj* — **mo·ron·i·cal·ly** \-i-k(ə-)lē\ *adv*

**mo·rose** \mə-'rōs\ *adj* [L *morosus,* lit., capricious, fr. *mor-, mos* will] : having a sullen disposition; *also* : GLOOMY — **mo·rose·ly** *adv* — **mo·rose·ness** *n*

**mor·pheme** \'mȯr-,fēm\ *n* : a meaningful linguistic unit that contains no smaller meaningful parts — **mor·phe·mic** \mȯr-'fē-mik\ *adj*

**mor·phia** \'mȯr-fē-ə\ *n* : MORPHINE

**mor·phine** \'mȯr-,fēn\ *n* [F, fr. Gk *Morpheus* Greek god of dreams] : an addictive drug obtained from opium and used to ease pain or induce sleep

**mor·phol·o·gy** \mȯr-'fäl-ə-jē\ *n* **1** : a branch of biology dealing with the form and structure of organisms **2** : a study and description of word formation in a language — **mor·pho·log·i·cal** \,mȯr-fə-'läj-i-kəl\ *adj* — **mor·pho·log·ist** \mȯr-'fäl-ə-jəst\ *n*

**mor·ris** \'mȯr-əs\ *n* : a vigorous English dance performed by men wearing costumes and bells

**mor·row** \'mär-ō\ *n* : the next day

**Morse code** \'mȯrs-\ *n* : either of two codes consisting of dots and dashes or long and short sounds used for transmitting messages

**mor·sel** \'mȯr-səl\ *n* [ME, fr. OF, dim. of *mors* bite, fr. L *morsus,* fr. *mordēre* to bite] **1** : a small piece or quantity **2** : a tasty dish

**mor·tal** \'mȯrt-ᵊl\ *adj* **1** : causing death : FATAL; *also* : leading to eternal punishment ⟨~ sin⟩ **2** : subject to death ⟨~ man⟩ **3** : implacably hostile ⟨~ foe⟩ **4** : very great : EXTREME ⟨~ fear⟩ **5** : HUMAN ⟨~ limitations⟩ — **mortal** *n* — **mor·tal·i·ty** \mȯr-'tal-ət-ē\ *n* — **mor·tal·ly** \'mȯrt-ᵊl-ē\ *adv*

¹**mor·tar** \'mȯrt-ər\ *n* **1** : a strong bowl in which substances may be broken or powdered with a pestle **2** : a short-barreled cannon used to hurl projectiles at high angles

²**mortar** *n* : a plastic building material (as a mixture of cement, lime, or gypsum plaster with sand and water) that hardens and is used in masonry or plastering — **mortar** *vb*

**mor·tar·board** \'mȯrt-ər-,bȯrd\ *n* **1** : a board or platform about three feet square for holding mortar **2** : an academic cap with a broad square top

**mort·gage** \'mȯr-gij\ *n* [ME *morgage,* fr. MF, fr. OF, fr. *mort* dead + *gage*] : a transfer of rights to a piece of property usu. as security for the payment of a loan or debt that becomes void when the debt is paid — **mortgage** *vb* — **mort·gag·ee** \,mȯr-gi-'jē\ *n* — **mort·ga·gor** \,mȯr-gi-'jȯr\ *n*

**mor·ti·cian** \mȯr-'tish-ən\ *n* [L *mort-, mors* death + E *-ician* (as in *physician*)] : UNDERTAKER

**mor·ti·fy** \'mȯrt-ə-,fī\ *vb* **-fied; -fy·ing 1** : to subdue (as the body) esp. by abstinence or self-inflicted pain **2** : HUMILIATE **3** : to become necrotic or gangrenous — **mor·ti·fi·ca·tion** \,mȯrt-ə-fə-'kā-shən\ *n*

**mor·tise** *also* **mor·tice** \'mȯrt-əs\ *n* : a hole cut in a piece of wood into which another piece fits to form a joint

**mor·tu·ary** \'mȯr-chə-,wer-ē\ *n, pl* **-ar·ies** : a place in which dead bodies are kept until burial

**mo·sa·ic** \mō-'zā-ik\ *n* : a surface decoration made by inlaying small pieces (as of colored glass or stone) to form figures or patterns; *also* : a design made in mosaic

**mo·sey** \'mō-zē\ *vb* **mo·seyed; mo·sey·ing** : SAUNTER

**Mos·lem** \'mäz-ləm\ *var of* MUSLIM

**mosque** \'mäsk\ *n* : a building used for public worship by Muslims

**mos·qui·to** \mə-'skēt-ō\ *n, pl* -**toes** *also* -**tos** : a two-winged fly the female of which sucks the blood of man and lower animals

**mosquito net** *n* : a net or screen for keeping out mosquitoes

**moss** \'mȯs\ *n* : any of a large group of green plants without flowers but with small leafy stems growing in clumps — **mossy** *adj*

**moss·back** \'mȯs-,bak\ *n* : an extremely conservative person : FOGY

¹**most** \'mōst\ *adj* **1** : the majority of ⟨~ men⟩ **2** : GREATEST ⟨the ~ ability⟩

²**most** *adv* **1** : to the greatest or highest degree ⟨~ beautiful⟩ **2** : to a very great egree ⟨a ~ careful driver⟩

³**most** *n* : the greatest amount ⟨the ~ he can do⟩

⁴**most** *pron* : the greatest number or part ⟨~ became discouraged⟩

-**most** \,mōst\ *adj suffix* : most ⟨inner*most*⟩ : most toward ⟨head*most*⟩

**most·ly** \'mōst-lē\ *adv* : MAINLY

**mot** \'mō\ *n, pl* **mots** \'mō(z)\ [F, wor , saying, fr. L *muttum* grunt] : a witty saying

**mote** \'mōt\ *n* : a small particle

**mo·tel** \mō-'tel\ *n* : a hotel in which the rooms are accessible from an outdoor parking area

**mo·tet** \mō-'tet\ *n* : a choral work on a sacred text for several voices usu. without instrumental accompaniment

**moth** \'mȯth\ *n, pl* **moths** \'mȯthz, 'mȯths\ : any of various insects related to the butterflies but usu. nightflying and with a stouter body and smaller wings; *esp* : a small pale insect **(clothes moth** whose larvae eat wool, fur, and feathers

**moth·ball** \'mȯth-,bȯl\ *n* **1** : a ball (as of naphthalene) used to keep moths out of clothing **2** *pl* : protective storage ⟨ships put in ~s after the war⟩

¹**moth·er** \'məth-ər\ *n* **1** : a female parent **2** : a woman in authority **3** : SOURCE, ORIGIN — **moth·er·less** *adj* — **moth·er·li·ness** \-lē-nəs\ *n* — **moth·er·ly** *adj*

²**mother** *vb* **moth·ered; moth·er·ing** \'məth-(ə-)riŋ\ **1** : to give birth to; *also* : PRODUCE **2** : to protect like a mother

**moth·er·hood** \'məth-ər-,hùd\ *n* : the state of being a mother

**moth·er-in-law** \'məth-(ə-)rən-,lȯ, 'məth-ərn-,lȯ\ *n, pl* **mothers-in-law** \'məth-ər-zən-\ : the mother of one's spouse

**moth·er·land** \'məth-ər-,land\ *n* **1** : the land of origin of something **2** : the native land of one's ancestors

**moth·er-of-pearl** \,məth-ə-rə(v)-'pərl\ *n* : the hard pearly substance forming the inner layer of a mollusk shell

**mo·tif** \mō-'tēf\ *n* : a dominant idea or central theme (as in a work of art)

**mo·tile** \'mōt-ᵊl, 'mō-,tīl\ *adj* : capable of spontaneous movement — **mo·til·i-**

ty \mō-'til-ət-ē\ *n*

¹**mo·tion** \'mō-shən\ *n* **1** : a proposal for action (as by a deliberative body) **2** : an act, process, or instance of moving **3** *pl* : ACTIVITIES, MOVEMENTS — **mo·tion·less** *adj* — **mo·tion·less·ly** *adv* — **mo·tion·less·ness** *n*

²**motion** *vb* **mo·tioned; mo·tion·ing** \'mō-sh(ə-)niŋ\ : to direct or signal by a motion

**motion picture** *n* : a series of pictures thrown on a screen so rapidly that they produce a continuous picture in which persons and objects seem to move

**motion sickness** *n* : sickness induced by motion and characterized by nausea

**mo·ti·vate** \'mōt-ə-,vāt\ *vb* -**vat·ed;** -**vat·ing** : to provide with a motive : IMPEL — **mo·ti·va·tion** \,mōt-ə-'vā-shən\ *n*

¹**mo·tive** \'mōt-iv, 2 *also* mō-'tēv\ *n* **1** : something (as a need or desire) that causes a person to act **2** : a recurrent theme in a musical composition — **mo·tive·less** *adj*

²**mo·tive** \'mōt-iv\ *adj* **1** : moving to action **2** : of or relating to motion

**mot·ley** \'mät-lē\ *adj* **1** : variegated in color **2** : made up of diverse often incongruous elements **syn** heterogeneous, miscellaneous, assorted

¹**mo·tor** \'mōt-ər\ *n* **1** : one that imparts motion **2** : a small compact engine **3** : AUTOMOBILE

²**motor** *vb* : to travel or transport by automobile : DRIVE — **mo·tor·ist** *n*

**mo·tor·bike** \'mōt-ər-,bīk\ *n* : a small lightweight motorcycle

**mo·tor·boat** \-,bōt\ *n* : a boat propelled by an internal-combustion engine or an electric motor

**mo·tor·cade** \'mōt-ər-,kād\ *n* : a procession of motor vehicles

**mo·tor·car** \-,kär\ *n* : AUTOMOBILE

**motor court** *n* : MOTEL

**mo·tor·cy·cle** \'mōt-ər-,sī-kəl\ *n* : a 2-wheeled automotive vehicle — **mo·tor·cy·clist** \-k(ə-)ləst\ *n*

**motor home** *n* : an automotive vehicle built on a truck or bus chassis and equipped as a self-contained traveling home

**mo·tor·ize** \'mōt-ə-,rīz\ *vb* -**ized;** -**iz·ing** **1** : to equip with a motor **2** : to equip with motor-driven vehicles — **mo·tor·iza·tion** \,mōt-ə-rə-'zā-shən\ *n*

**mo·tor·man** \'mōt-ər-mən\ *n* : an operator of a motor-driven vehicle (as a streetcar or subway train)

**motor scooter** *n* : a low 2- or 3-wheeled automotive vehicle resembling a child's scooter but having a seat

**mo·tor·truck** \'mōt-ər-,trək\ *n* : an automotive truck for transporting freight

**motor vehicle** *n* : an automotive vehicle not operated on rails; *esp* : one with rubber tires for use on highways

**mot·tle** \'mät-ᵊl\ *vb* **mot·tled, mot·tling** \'mät-(ᵊ-)liŋ\ : to mark with spots of different color : BLOTCH

**mot·to** \'mät-ō\ *n, pl* **mottoes** *also* **mottos** [It, fr. L *muttum* grunt, fr.

*muttire* to mutter] **1** : a sentence, phrase, or word inscribed on something to indicate its character or use **2** : a short expression of a guiding rule of conduct

**moue** \'mu\ *n* : a little grimace

**mould** \'mōld\ *var of* MOLD

**moult** \'mōlt\ *var of* MOLT

**mound** \'maund\ *n* **1** : an artificial bank or hill of earth or stones **2** : KNOLL

¹**mount** \'maunt\ *n* : a high hill

²**mount** *vb* **1** : to increase in amount or extent; *also* : RISE, ASCEND **2** : to get up on something above ground level; *esp* : to seat oneself on (as a horse) for riding **3** : to put in position (~ artillery) **4** : to set on something that elevates **5** : to attach to a support **6** : to prepare esp. for examination or display : ARRANGE — **mount·able** *adj* — **mount·er** *n*

³**mount** *n* **1** : FRAME, SUPPORT **2** : a means of conveyance; *esp* : SADDLE HORSE

**moun·tain** \'maunt-°n\ *n* : a landmass higher than a hill — **moun·tain·ous** \-(°-)nəs\ *adj*

**mountain ash** *n* : any of various trees related to the roses that have pinnate leaves and red or orange-red fruits

**moun·tain·eer** \,maunt-°n-'iər\ *n* **1** : a native or inhabitant of a mountainous region **2** : one who climbs mountains for sport — **mountaineer** *vb*

**mountain goat** *n* : an antelope of mountainous northwestern No. America that resembles a goat

**mountain laurel** *n* : a No. American evergreen shrub related to the heaths that has glossy leaves and clusters of rose-colored or white flowers

**mountain lion** *n* : COUGAR

**moun·tain·side** \'maunt-°n-,sīd\ *n* : the side of a mountain

**moun·tain·top** \'maunt-°n-,täp\ *n* : the summit of a mountain

**moun·te·bank** \'maunt-i-,baŋk\ *n* [It *montimbanco*, fr. *montare* to mount + *in* in, on + *banco*, *banca* bench] : QUACK, CHARLATAN

**Mount·ie** \'maunt-ē\ *n* : a member of the Royal Canadian Mounted Police

**mount·ing** \'maunt-iŋ\ *n* : something that serves as a frame or support

**mourn** \'mōrn\ *vb* : to feel or express grief or sorrow — **mourn·er** *n*

**mourn·ful** \-fəl\ *adj* : expressing, feeling, or causing sorrow — **mourn·ful·ly** \-ē\ *adv* — **mourn·ful·ness** *n*

**mourn·ing** \'mōr-niŋ\ *n* **1** : an outward sign (as black clothes) of grief for a person's death **2** : a period of time during which signs of grief are shown

**mouse** \'maus\ *n, pl* **mice** \'mīs\ : any of various small rodents with pointed snout, long body, and slender tail

**mous·er** \'mau-zər\ *n* : a cat proficient at catching mice

**mouse·trap** \'maus-,trap\ *n* **1** : a trap for catching mice **2** : a stratagem that lures one to defeat or destruction — **mousetrap** *vb*

**mousse** \'müs\ *n* : a molded chilled dessert made with sweetened and flavored whipped cream or egg whites and gelatin

**mous·tache** \'məs-,tash, (,)məs-'tash\ *var of* MUSTACHE

**mousy** *or* **mous·ey** \'mau-sē, -zē\ *adj* **mous·i·er; -est 1** : QUIET, STEALTHY **2** : TIMID, COLORLESS — **mous·i·ness** \'mau-sē-nəs, -zē-\ *n*

¹**mouth** \'mauth\ *n, pl* **mouths** \'mauthz, 'mauths\ **1** : the opening through which an animal takes in food; *also* : the space between the mouth and the pharynx **2** : something resembling a mouth (as in affording entrance) — **mouthed** \'mauthd, 'mautht\ *adj* — **mouth·ful** *n*

²**mouth** \'mauth\ *vb* : SPEAK; *also* : DECLAIM

**mouth·part** \'mauth-,pärt\ *n* : a structure or appendage near the mouth

**mouth·piece** \-,pēs\ *n* **1** : a part (as of a musical instrument) that goes in the mouth or to which the mouth is applied **2** : SPOKESMAN

**mouth·wash** \-,wȯsh, -,wäsh\ *n* : a usu. antiseptic liquid preparation for cleaning the mouth and teeth

**mou·ton** \'mü-,tän\ *n* : processed sheepskin that has been sheared or dyed to resemble beaver or seal

¹**move** \'müv\ *vb* **moved; mov·ing 1** : to go or cause to go from one point to another : ADVANCE; *also* : DEPART **2** : to change one's residence **3** : to change or cause to change position or posture : SHIFT **4** : to show marked activity **5** : to take or cause to take action : PROMPT **6** : to make a formal request, application, or appeal **7** : to stir the emotions **8** : EVACUATE **2** — **mov·able** *or* **move·able** \-ə-bəl\ *adj*

²**move** *n* **1** : an act of moving **2** : a calculated procedure : MANEUVER

**move·ment** \'müv-mənt\ *n* **1** : the act or process of moving : MOVE **2** : TENDENCY, TREND; *also* : a series of organized activities working toward an objective **3** : the moving parts of a mechanism (as of a watch) **4** : RHYTHM, CADENCE **5** : a unit or division of an extended musical composition **6** : an act of voiding the bowels; *also* : STOOL **3**

**mov·er** \'mü-vər\ *n* : one that moves; *esp* : a person or company that moves the belongings of others from one home or place of business to another

**mov·ie** \'mü-vē\ *n* **1** : MOTION PICTURE **2** *pl* : a showing of a motion picture; *also* : the motion-picture industry

¹**mow** \'mau\ *n* : the part of a barn where hay or straw is stored

²**mow** \'mō\ *vb* **mowed, mowed** *or* **mown** \'mōn\; **mow·ing 1** : to cut (as grass) with a scythe or machine **2** : to cut the standing herbage of (~ the lawn) — **mow·er** *n*

**moz·za·rel·la** \,mat-sə-'rel-ə\ *n* : a moist white unsalted unripened mild cheese of a smooth rubbery texture

**MP** *abbr* **1** melting point **2** member of parliament **3** metropolitan police **4** military police; military policeman

**MPG** *abbr* miles per gallon

**MPH** *abbr* miles per hour

**Mr.** \ˌmis-tər\ *n*, *pl* **Messrs.** \ˌmes-ərz\ — used as a conventional title of courtesy before a man's surname or his title of office

**Mrs.** \ˌmis-əz, -əs, *esp South* ˌmiz-əz, -əs, *or* (ˌ)miz, *or before given names* (ˌ)mis\ *n*, *pl* **Mes·dames** \mā-'däm, -'dam\ — used as a conventional title of courtesy before a married woman's surname

**Ms.** \(ˈ)miz\ *n* — used instead of *Miss* or *Mrs.*

**MS** *abbr* **1** manuscript **2** master of science **3** military science **4** Mississippi **5** motor ship **6** multiple sclerosis

**msec** *abbr* millisecond

**msg** *abbr* message

**MSG** *abbr* monosodium glutamate

**msgr** *abbr* monseigneur; monsignor

**MSgt** *abbr* master sergeant

**MSL** *abbr* mean sea level

**MSS** *abbr* manuscripts

**MST** *abbr* mountain standard time

**mt** *abbr* mount; mountain

**Mt** *abbr* Matthew

**MT** *abbr* **1** metric ton **2** Montana **3** mountain time

**mtg** *abbr* **1** meeting **2** mortgage

**mtge** *abbr* mortgage

**¹much** \ˈməch\ *adj* **more** \ˈmōr\ **most** \ˈmōst\ : great in quantity, amount, extent, or degree ⟨~ money⟩

**²much** *adv* **more; most** **1** : to a great degree or extent ⟨~ happier⟩ **2** : APPROXIMATELY, NEARLY ⟨looks ~ as he did years ago⟩

**³much** *n* **1** : a great quantity, amount, extent, or degree **2** : something considerable or impressive

**mu·ci·lage** \ˈmyü-s(ə-)lij\ *n* : a watery sticky solution (as of a gum) used esp. as an adhesive — **mu·ci·lag·i·nous** \ˌmyü-sə-'laj-ə-nəs\ *adj*

**muck** \ˈmək\ *n* **1** : soft moist barnyard manure **2** : FILTH, DIRT **3** : a dark richly organic soil; *also* : MUD, MIRE — **mucky** *adj*

**muck·rak·er** \-ˌrā-kər\ *n* : one who exposes publicly real or apparent misconduct of prominent individuals — **muck·rak·ing** \-ˌrā-kiŋ\ *n*

**mu·cus** \ˈmyü-kəs\ *n* : a slimy slippery protective secretion of membranes (**mucous membranes**) lining some body cavities — **mu·cous** \-kəs\ *adj*

**mud** \ˈməd\ *n* : soft wet earth : MIRE — **mud·di·ly** \ˈməd-ˀl-ē\ *adv* — **mud·di·ness** \-ē-nəs\ *n* — **mud·dy** *adj or vb*

**mud·dle** \ˈməd-ˀl\ *vb* **mud·dled; mud·dling** \ˈməd-(ˀ-)liŋ\ **1** : to make muddy **2** : to confuse esp. with liquor **3** : to mix up or make a mess of **4** : to think or act in a confused way

**mud·dle·head·ed** \ˌməd-ˀl-'hed-əd\ *adj* **1** : mentally confused **2** : INEPT

**mud·guard** \ˈməd-ˌgärd\ *n* : a guard over a wheel of a vehicle to catch or deflect mud

**mud·room** \ˈməd-ˌrüm, -ˌrüm\ *n* : a room in a house for removing dirty or wet footwear and clothing

**mud·sling·er** \-ˌsliŋ-ər\ *n* : one who uses invective esp. against a political opponent — **mud·sling·ing** \-ˌsliŋ-iŋ\ *n*

**Muen·ster** \ˈmən-stər, 'm(y)ün-, 'mùn-\ *n* : a semisoft bland or sharp cheese

**mu·ez·zin** \m(y)ü-'ez-ˀn\ *n* : a Muslim crier who calls the hour of daily prayer

**¹muff** \ˈməf\ *n* : a warm tubular covering for the hands

**²muff** *n* : a bungling performance; *esp* : a failure to hold a ball in attempting a catch — **muff** *vb*

**muf·fin** \ˈməf-ən\ *n* : a small soft biscuit baked in a small cup-shaped container

**muf·fle** \ˈməf-əl\ *vb* **muf·fled; muf·fling** \ˈməf-(ə-)liŋ\ **1** : to wrap up so as to conceal or protect **2** : to wrap or pad with something to dull the sound of **3** : to keep down : SUPPRESS

**muf·fler** \ˈməf-lər\ *n* **1** : a scarf worn around the neck **2** : a device to deaden noise

**muf·ti** \ˈməf-tē\ *n* : civilian clothes

**¹mug** \ˈməg\ *n* : a usu. metal or earthenware cylindrical drinking cup

**²mug** *vb* **mugged; mug·ging 1** : to make faces esp. in order to attract the attention of an audience **2** : PHOTOGRAPH

**³mug** *vb* **mugged; mug·ging** : to assault usu. with intent to rob — **mugger** *n*

**mug·gy** \ˈməg-ē\ *adj* **mug·gi·er; -est** : being warm, damp, and close — **mug·gi·ness** \ˈməg-ē-nəs\ *n*

**mug·wump** \ˈməg-ˌwəmp\ *n* [obs. slang *mugwump* (kingpin), fr. Natick (a No. American Indian dialect) *mugwomp* captain] : an independent in politics

**Mu·ham·mad·an** \mō-'ham-əd-ən, -'häm-; mü-\ *n* : MUSLIM — **Mu·ham·mad·an·ism** \-ˌiz-əm\ *n*

**muk·luk** \ˈmək-ˌlək\ *n* [Eskimo *muklok* large seal] **1** : an Eskimo boot of sealskin or reindeer skin **2** : a boot with a soft leather sole worn over several pairs of socks

**mu·lat·to** \m(y)ù-'lat-ō, -'lät-\ *n*, *pl* **-toes** *or* **-tos** [Sp *mulato*, fr. *mulo* mule, fr. L *mulus*; so called because the mule is the offspring of parents of different species] : a first-generation offspring of a Negro and a white; *also* : a person of mixed Caucasian and Negro ancestry

**mul·ber·ry** \ˈməl-ˌber-ē\ *n* : a tree grown for its leaves that are used as food for silkworms or for its edible berrylike fruit; *also* : this fruit

**mulch** \ˈməlch\ *n* : a protective covering (as of straw or leaves) spread on the ground esp. to reduce evaporation and erosion, control weeds, or improve the soil — **mulch** *vb*

**¹mulct** \ˈməlkt\ *n* : FINE, PENALTY

**²mulct** *vb* **1** : FINE **2** : DEFRAUD

**¹mule** \ˈmyül\ *n* **1** : a hybrid offspring of a male ass and a female horse **2** : a very stubborn person — **mul·ish** \ˈmyü-lish\ *adj* — **mul·ish·ly** *adv* — **mu·lish·ness** *n*

²**mule** n : a slipper whose upper does not extend around the heel of the foot

**mule deer** n : a long-eared deer of western No. America

**mu·le·teer** \,myü-lə-'tiər\ n : one who drives mules

¹**mull** \'məl\ vb : PONDER, MEDITATE

²**mull** vb : to heat, sweeten, and flavor (as wine) with spices

**mul·lein** also **mul·len** \'məl-ən\ n : a tall herb with coarse woolly leaves and flowers in spikes

**mul·let** \'məl-ət\ n, pl **mullet** or **mullets** 1 : any of various largely gray marine food fishes 2 : any of various red or golden mostly tropical marine food fishes

**mul·li·gan stew** \,məl-i-gən-\ n : a stew chiefly of vegetables and meat or fish

**mul·li·ga·taw·ny** \,məl-i-gə-'tò-nē\ n : a soup usu. of chicken stock seasoned with curry

**mul·lion** \'məl-yən\ n : a vertical strip separating windowpanes

**multi-** comb form 1 : many : multiple ⟨multi-unit⟩ 2 : many times over ⟨multimillionaire⟩

**mul·ti·col·ored** \,məl-ti-'kəl-ərd\ adj : having many colors

**mul·ti·di·men·sion·al** \-ti-də-'mench-nəl, -dī-; -,tī-də-\ adj : of, relating to, or having many dimensions ⟨a ~ problem⟩

**mul·ti·fac·et·ed** \-'fas-ət-əd\ adj : having several distinct facets

**mul·ti·fam·i·ly** \-'fam-(ə-)lē\ adj : designed for several families

**mul·ti·far·i·ous** \,məl-tə-'far-ē-əs\ adj : having great variety : DIVERSE — **mul·ti·far·i·ous·ly** adv

**mul·ti·flo·ra rose** \,məl-tə-,flōr-ə-\ n : a vigorous thorny rose with clusters of small flowers that is used for hedges

**mul·ti·form** \'məl-ti-,fòrm\ adj : having many forms or appearances — **mul·ti·for·mi·ty** \,məl-ti-'fòr-mət-ē\ n

**mul·ti·lat·er·al** \,məl-ti-'lat-ə-rəl, -,tī-, -'la-trəl\ adj : having many sides or participants ⟨~ treaty⟩

**mul·ti·lev·el** \-'lev-əl\ adj : having several levels

**mul·ti·lin·gual** \-'liŋ-gwəl\ adj : containing, expressed in, or able to use several languages — **mul·ti·lin·gual·ism** \-gwə-,liz-əm\ n

**mul·ti·me·dia** \-'mēd-ē-ə\ adj : using, involving, or encompassing several media ⟨a ~ advertising campaign⟩

**mul·ti·mil·lion·aire** \,məl-ti-,mil-yə-'naər, -,ti-, -'mil-yə,naər\ n : a person worth several million dollars

**mul·ti·na·tion·al** \-'nash-(ə-)nəl\ adj 1 : relating to or involving several nations 2 : having divisions in several countries 3 : of or relating to several nationalities ⟨a ~ society⟩

¹**mul·ti·ple** \'məl-tə-pəl\ adj 1 : more than one; also : MANY 2 : VARIOUS, COMPLEX

²**multiple** n : the product of a quantity by an integer ⟨35 is a ~ of 7⟩

**multiple–choice** adj : having several answers given from which the correct one is to be chosen ⟨~ examination⟩

**multiple sclerosis** n : a disease marked by patches of hardened tissue in the brain or spinal cord resulting in partial or complete paralysis and muscular twitching

**mul·ti·pli·cand** \,məl-tə-pli-'kand\ n : a number that is to be multiplied by another

**mul·ti·pli·ca·tion** \,məl-tə-plə-'kā-shən\ n 1 : INCREASE 2 : a short method of finding out what would be the result of adding a figure the number of times indicated by another figure

**multiplication sign** n 1 : TIMES SIGN 2 : a centered dot used to indicate multiplication

**mul·ti·plic·i·ty** \,məl-tə-'plis-ət-ē\ n, pl **-ties** : a great number or variety

**mul·ti·pli·er** \'məl-tə-,plī(-ə)r\ n : one that multiplies; esp : a number by which another number is multiplied

**mul·ti·ply** \'məl-tə-,plī\ vb **-plied; -ply·ing** 1 : to increase in number (as by breeding) 2 : to find the product of by a process of multiplication

**mul·ti·pur·pose** \,məl-ti-'pər-pəs, -,tī-\ adj : having or serving several purposes

**mul·ti·ra·cial** \-'rā-shəl\ adj : composed of, involving, or representing several races

**mul·ti·sense** \-,sen(t)s\ adj : having several meanings ⟨~ words⟩

**mul·ti·stage** \-,stāj\ adj : having successive operating stages ⟨~ rockets⟩

**mul·ti·story** \-,stōr-ē\ adj : having several stories ⟨~ buildings⟩

**mul·ti·tude** \'məl-tə-,t(y)üd\ n : a great number — **mul·ti·tu·di·nous** \,məl-tə-'t(y)üd-(ə-)nəs\ adj

**mul·ti·ver·si·ty** \,məl-ti-'vər-s(ə-)tē\ n, pl **-ties** : a very large university with many divisions and diverse functions

**mul·ti·vi·ta·min** \,məl-ti-'vīt-ə-mən\ adj : containing several vitamins and esp. all known to be essential to health

¹**mum** \'məm\ adj : SILENT

²**mum** n : CHRYSANTHEMUM

**mum·ble** \'məm-bəl\ vb **mum·bled; mum·bling** \-b(ə-)liŋ\ : to speak in a low indistinct manner — **mumble** n — **mum·bler** \-b(ə-)lər\ n

**mum·ble·ty·peg** or **mum·ble·the·peg** \'məm-bəl-(tē)-,peg\ n : a game in which the players try to flip a knife from various positions so that the blade will stick into the ground

**mum·bo jum·bo** \,məm-bō-'jəm-bō\ n 1 : a complicated ritual with elaborate trappings 2 : complicated activity or language that obscures and confuses

**mum·mer** \'məm-ər\ n 1 : an actor esp. in a pantomime 2 : one who goes merrymaking in disguise during festivals — **mum·mery** n

**mum·my** \'məm-ē\ n, pl **mummies** [ME mummie powdered parts of a mummified body used as a drug, fr. MF momie, fr. ML mumia mummy, powdered mummy, fr. Ar mūmiyah bitumen, mummy, fr. Per mūm wax] : a body embalmed for burial in the manner of the ancient Egyptians — **mum·mi-**

fi·ca·tion \,məm-i-fə-'kā-shən\ n —
mum·mi·fy \'məm-i,fī\ vb

mumps \'məmps\ n sing or pl : a virus disease marked by fever and swelling esp. of the salivary glands

mun or munic abbr municipal

munch \'mənch\ vb : to chew with a crunching sound

mun·dane \,mən-'dān, 'mən-,dān\ adj 1 : of or relating to the world 2 : having no concern for the ideal or heavenly — mun·dane·ly adv

mu·nic·i·pal \myù-'nis-ə-pəl\ adj 1 : of, relating to, or characteristic of a municipality 2 : restricted to one locality — mu·nic·i·pal·ly \-ē\ adv

mu·nic·i·pal·i·ty \myù-,nis-ə-'pal-ət-ē\ n, pl -ties : an urban political unit with corporate status and usu. powers of self-government

mu·nif·i·cent \myù-'nif-ə-sənt\ adj : liberal in giving : GENEROUS — mu·nif·i·cence \-səns\ n

mu·ni·tion \myù-'nish-ən\ n : material used in war for defense or attack : ARMAMENT — usu. used in pl.

¹mu·ral \'myùr-əl\ adj 1 : of or relating to a wall 2 : applied to and made part of a wall surface

²mural n : a mural painting — mu·ral·ist n

¹mur·der \'mərd-ər\ n 1 : the crime of unlawfully killing a person esp. with malice aforethought 2 : something unusually difficult or dangerous

²murder vb 1 : to commit a murder; also : to kill brutally 2 : to put an end to 3 : to spoil by performing poorly ⟨~ a song⟩ — mur·der·er n — mur·der·ess \-əs\ n

mur·der·ous \-əs\ adj 1 : marked by or causing murder or bloodshed ⟨~ gunfire⟩ 2 : having or appearing to have the purpose of murder — mur·der·ous·ly adv

mu·ri·at·ic acid \,myùr-ē-,at-ik-\ n : HYDROCHLORIC ACID

murk \'mərk\ n : DARKNESS, GLOOM — murk·i·ly \'mər-kə-lē\ adv — murk·i·ness \-kē-nəs\ n — murky adj

mur·mur \'mər-mər\ n 1 : a muttered complaint 2 : a low indistinct and often continuous sound — murmur vb — mur·mur·er n — mur·mur·ous adj

mur·rain \'mər-ən\ n : PLAGUE

mus abbr 1 museum 2 music

mus·ca·tel \,məs-kə-'tel\ n : a sweet dessert wine

¹mus·cle \'məs-əl\ n [MF, fr. L musculus, fr. dim. of mus mouse] 1 : body tissue consisting of long cells that contract when stimulated; also : an organ consisting of this tissue and functioning in moving a body part 2 : STRENGTH, BRAWN — muscled \'məs-əld\ adj — mus·cu·lar \'məs-kyə-lər\ adj — mus·cu·lar·i·ty \,məs-kyə-'lar-ət-ē\ n

²muscle vb muscled; mus·cling \'məs-(ə-)liŋ\ : to force one's way ⟨~ in on another racketeer⟩

mus·cle-bound \'məs-əl-,baùnd\ adj : having some of the muscles abnor-

mally enlarged and lacking in elasticity (as from excessive athletic exercise)

muscular dystrophy n : a disease characterized by progressive wasting of muscles

mus·cu·la·ture \'məs-kyə-lə-,chùr\ n : the muscles of the body or one of its parts

¹muse \'myüz\ vb mused; mus·ing [ME musen, fr. MF muser to gape, idle, muse, fr. muse mouth of an animal, fr. ML musus] : to become absorbed in thought — mus·ing·ly adv

²muse n [fr. Muse any of the nine sister goddesses of learning and the arts in Greek mythology, fr. ME, fr. MF, fr. L Musa, fr. Gk Mousa] : a source of inspiration

mu·sette \myù-'zet\ n : a small knapsack with a shoulder strap used esp. by soldiers for carrying provisions and personal belongings

musette bag n : MUSETTE

mu·se·um \myù-'zē-əm\ n : an institution devoted to the procurement, care, and display of objects of lasting interest or value

¹mush \'məsh\ n 1 : cornmeal boiled in water 2 : sentimental drivel

²mush vb : to travel esp. over snow with a sled drawn by dogs

¹mush·room \'məsh-,rüm, -,rùm\ n : the fleshy usu. caplike spore-bearing organ of various fungi esp. when edible

²mushroom vb 1 : to grow rapidly 2 : to spread out : EXPAND

mushy \'məsh-ē\ adj mush·i·er; -est 1 : soft like mush 2 : weakly sentimental

mu·sic \'myü-zik\ n 1 : the science or art of combining tones into a composition having structure and continuity; also : vocal or instrumental sounds having rhythm, melody, or harmony 2 : an agreeable sound 3 : punishment for a misdeed — mu·si·cal \-zi-kəl\ adj — mu·si·cal·ly \-ē\ adv

¹mu·si·cal \'myü-zi-kəl\ adj 1 : of or relating to music or musicians 2 : having the pleasing tonal qualities of music 3 : having an interest in or a talent for music — mu·si·cal·ly \-k(ə-)lē\ adv

²musical n : a film or theatrical production consisting of musical numbers and dialogue based on a unifying plot

mu·si·cale \,myü-zi-'kal\ n : a usu. private social gathering featuring music

mu·si·cian \myù-'zish-ən\ n : a composer or performer of music — mu·si·cian·ly adj — mu·si·cian·ship n

mu·si·col·o·gy \,myü-zi-'käl-ə-jē\ n : a study of music as a branch of knowledge or field of research — mu·si·co·log·i·cal \-kə-'läj-i-kəl\ adj — mu·si·col·o·gist \-'käl-ə-jəst\ n

musk \'məsk\ n : a substance obtained esp. from a small Asiatic deer (musk deer) and used as a perfume fixative — musk·i·ness \'məs-kē-nəs\ n — musky adj

mus·keg \'məs-,keg\ n : BOG; esp : a mossy bog in northern No. America

**mus·kel·lunge** \'məs-kə-ˌlənj\ *n, pl* **muskellunge** : a large No. American pike prized as a sport fish

**mus·ket** \'məs-kət\ *n* [MF *mousquet*, fr. It *moschetto* arrow for a crossbow, musket, fr. dim. of *mosca* fly, fr. L *musca*] : a heavy large-caliber shoulder firearm — **mus·ke·teer** \ˌməs-kə-'tiər\ *n*

**mus·ket·ry** \'məs-kə-trē\ *n* 1 : MUS-KETS; *also* : musket fire 2 : MUSKETEERS

**musk·mel·on** \'məsk-ˌmel-ən\ *n* : a small round to oval melon related to the cucumber that has usu. a sweet edible green or orange flesh

**musk-ox** \'məsk-ˌäks\ *n* : a heavy-set shaggy-coated wild ox of Greenland and the arctic tundra of northern No. America

**musk·rat** \'məs-ˌkrat\ *n, pl* **muskrat** *or* **muskrats** : a large No. American water rodent with webbed feet and dark brown fur; *also* : its fur

**Mus·lim** \'məz-ləm\ *n* : an adherent of the religion founded by the Arab prophet Muhammad

**mus·lin** \'məz-lən\ *n* : a plain-woven sheer to coarse cotton fabric

**¹muss** \'məs\ *n* : a state of disorder — **muss·i·ly** \'məs-ə-lē\ *adv* — **muss·i·ness** \-ē-nəs\ *n* — **mussy** *adj*

**²muss** *vb* : to make untidy : DISARRANGE

**mus·sel** \'məs-əl\ *n* 1 : a dark edible saltwater bivalve mollusk 2 : any of various freshwater bivalve mollusks of central U.S. having shells with a pearly lining

**Mus·sul·man** \'məs-əl-mən\ *n, pl* **Mus·sul·men** \-mən\ *or* **Mussul-mans** : MUSLIM

**¹must** \(')məst\ *vb* — used as an auxiliary esp. to express a command, requirement, obligation, or necessity

**²must** \'məst\ *n* 1 : an imperative duty 2 : an indispensable item

**mus·tache** \'məs-ˌtash, (ˌ)məs-'tash\ *n* : the hair growing on the human upper lip

**mus·tang** \'məs-ˌtaŋ\ *n* [MexSp *mestengo*, fr. Sp, stray, fr. *mesteño* strayed, fr. *mesta* annual roundup of cattle that disposed of strays, fr. ML *(animalia) mixta* mixed animals] : a small hardy naturalized horse of the western plains of America

**mus·tard** \'məs-tərd\ *n* 1 : a pungent yellow powder obtained from the seeds of an herb related to the turnips and used as a condiment or in medicine 2 : the mustard plant; *also* : a closely related plant

**mustard gas** *n* : an irritant vesicant oily liquid used in warfare

**¹mus·ter** \'məs-tər\ *vb* **mus·tered**; **mus·ter·ing** \-t(ə-)riŋ\ [ME *mustren* to show, muster, fr. OF *monstrer*, fr. L *monstrare* to show, fr. *monstrum* evil omen, monster] 1 : CONVENE, AS-SEMBLE; *also* : to call the roll of 2 : ACCUMULATE 3 : to call forth : ROUSE 4 : to amount to : COMPRISE

**²muster** *n* 1 : an act of assembling (as for military inspection); *also* : critical examination 2 : an assembled group

**muster out** *vb* : to discharge from military service

**musty** \'məs-tē\ *adj* **mus·ti·er**; **-est** 1 : MOLDY, STALE; *also* : tasting or smelling of damp or decay — **must·i·ly** \'məs-tə-lē\ *adv* — **must·i·ness** \-tē-nəs\ *n*

**mu·ta·ble** \'myüt-ə-bəl\ *adj* 1 : prone to change : FICKLE 2 : liable to muta-tion : VARIABLE — **mu·ta·bil·i·ty** \ˌmyüt-ə-'bil-ət-ē\ *n*

**mu·tant** \'myüt-ʰnt\ *adj* : of, relating to, or produced by mutation — **mu-tant** *n*

**mu·tate** \'myü-ˌtāt\ *vb* **mu·tat·ed**; **mu·tat·ing** : to undergo or cause to undergo mutation — **mu·ta·tive** \'myü-ˌtāt-iv, 'myüt-ət-\ *adj*

**mu·ta·tion** \myü-'tā-shən\ *n* 1 : CHANGE 2 : a sudden and relatively permanent change in a hereditary character; *also* : one marked by such a change — **mu·ta·tion·al** *adj*

**¹mute** \'myüt\ *adj* **mut·er**; **mut·est** 1 : unable to speak : DUMB 2 : SILENT — **mute·ly** *adv* — **mute·ness** *n*

**²mute** *n* 1 : a person who cannot or does not speak 2 : a device on a musical instrument that reduces, softens, or muffles the tone

**³mute** *vb* **mut·ed**; **mut·ing** : to muffle or reduce the sound of

**mu·ti·late** \'myüt-ʰl-ˌāt\ *vb* **-lat·ed**; **-lat·ing** 1 : MAIM, CRIPPLE 2 : to cut up or alter radically so as to make im-perfect — **mu·ti·la·tion** \ˌmyüt-ʰl-'ā-shən\ *n* — **mu·ti·la·tor** \'myüt-ʰl-ˌāt-ər\ *n*

**mu·ti·ny** \'myüt-(ə-)nē\ *n, pl* **-nies** : willful refusal to obey constituted authority; *esp* : revolt against a superior officer — **mu·ti·neer** \ˌmyüt-ʰn-'iər\ *n* — **mu·ti·nous** \'myüt-ʰn-əs\ *adj* — **mu·ti·nous·ly** *adv*

**mutt** \'mət\ *n* : MONGREL, CUR

**mut·ter** \'mət-ər\ *vb* 1 : to speak in-distinctly or with a low voice and lips partly closed 2 : GRUMBLE — **mutter** *n*

**mut·ton** \'mət-ʰn\ *n* : the flesh of a ma-ture sheep — **mut·tony** *adj*

**mut·ton-chops** \'mət-ʰn-ˌchäps\ *n pl* : whiskers on the side of the face that are narrow at the temple and broad and round by the lower jaws

**mu·tu·al** \'myü-chə(-wə)l\ *adj* 1 : given and received in equal amount (~ trust) 2 : having the same feelings one for the other (~ enemies) 3 : COMMON, JOINT (a ~ friend) — **mu·tu·al·ly** \-ē\ *adv*

**mutual fund** *n* : an investment com-pany that invests money of its share-holders in a usu. diversified group of securities of other corporations

**muu·muu** \'mü-ˌmü\ *n* : a loose dress of Hawaiian origin for informal wear

**¹muz·zle** \'məz-əl\ *n* 1 : the nose and jaws of an animal; *also* : a covering for the muzzle to prevent the animal from biting or eating 2 : the mouth of a gun

**²muzzle** *vb* **muz·zled**; **muz·zling** \-(ə-)liŋ\ 1 : to put a muzzle on 2 : to restrain from expression : GAG

**Mv** *symbol* mendelevium

**MV** *abbr* motor vessel

**MVP** *abbr* most valuable player

**my** \(')mī, mə\ *adj* **1 :** of or relating to me or myself **2** — used interjectionally esp. to express surprise

**my·col·o·gy** \mī-'käl-ə-jē\ *n* **:** the study of fungi — **my·co·log·i·cal** \,mī-kə-'läj-i-kəl\ *adj* — **my·col·o·gist** \mī-'käl-ə-jəst\ *n*

**my·eli·tis** \,mī-ə-'līt-əs\ *n* **:** inflammation of the spinal cord or of the bone marrow

**my·na** *or* **my·nah** \'mī-nə\ *n* **:** any of several Asiatic starlings; *esp* **:** a dark brown slightly crested bird sometimes taught to mimic speech

**my·o·pia** \mī-'ō-pē-ə\ *n* **:** SHORTSIGHTEDNESS — **my·o·pic** \-'ō-pik, -'äp-ik\ *adj* — **my·o·pi·cal·ly** \-(ə-)lē\ *adv*

**¹myr·i·ad** \'mir-ē-əd\ *n* [Gk *myriad-, myrias,* fr. *myrioi* countless, ten thousand] **:** an indefinitely large number

**²myriad** *adj* **:** consisting of a very great but indefinite number

**myr·ia·me·ter** \'mir-ē-ə-,mēt-ər\ *n* — see METRIC SYSTEM table

**myr·mi·don** \'mər-mə-,dän\ *n* **:** a loyal follower; *esp* **:** one who executes orders without protest or pity

**myrrh** \'mər\ *n* **:** a fragrant aromatic plant gum used in perfumes and formerly for incense

**myr·tle** \'mərt-ᵊl\ *n* **:** an evergreen shrub of southern Europe with shiny leaves, fragrant flowers, and black berries; *also* **:** PERIWINKLE

**my·self** \mī-'self, mə-\ *pron* **:** I, ME — used reflexively, for emphasis, or in absolute constructions (I hurt ∼) (I ∼ did it) (∼ busy, I sent him instead)

**mys·tery** \'mis-t(ə-)rē\ *n, pl* **-ter·ies** **1 :** a religious truth known by revelation alone **2 :** something not understood or beyond understanding **3 :** enigmatic quality or character **4 :** a work of fiction dealing with the solution of a mysterious crime — **mys·te·ri·ous** \mis-'tir-ē-əs\ *adj* — **mys·te·ri·ous·ly** *adv* — **mys·te·ri·ous·ness** *n*

**¹mys·tic** \'mis-tik\ *adj* **1 :** of or relating to mystics or mysticism **2 :** MYSTERIOUS; *also* **:** MYSTIFYING

**²mystic** *n* **:** a person who experiences mystical union or direct communion with God or ultimate reality

**mys·ti·cal** \'mis-ti-kəl\ *adj* **1 :** SPIRITUAL, SYMBOLIC **2 :** of or relating to an intimate knowledge of or direct communion with God (as through contemplation or visions)

**mys·ti·cism** \'mis-tə-,siz-əm\ *n* **:** the belief that direct knowledge of God or ultimate reality is attainable through immediate intuition or insight

**mys·ti·fy** \'mis-tə-,fī\ *vb* **-fied; -fy·ing** **1 :** to perplex the mind of **2 :** to make mysterious — **mys·ti·fi·ca·tion** \,mis-tə-fə-'kā-shən\ *n*

**mys·tique** \mis-'tēk\ *n* **1 :** a set of beliefs and attitudes developing around an object or associated with a particular group **:** CULT **2 :** the special esoteric skill essential in a calling or activity

**myth** \'mith\ *n* **1 :** a usu. legendary narrative that presents part of the beliefs of a people or explains a practice or natural phenomenon **2 :** an imaginary or unverifiable person or thing — **myth·i·cal** \-i-kəl\ *adj*

**my·thol·o·gy** \mith-'äl-ə-jē\ *n, pl* **-gies :** a body of myths and esp. of those dealing with the gods and heroes of a people — **myth·o·log·i·cal** \,mith-ə-'läj-i-kəl\ *adj* — **my·thol·o·gist** \mith-'äl-ə-jəst\ *n*

---

**¹n** \'en\ *n, pl* **n's** *or* **ns** \'enz\ *often cap* **:** the 14th letter of the English alphabet

**²n** *abbr, often cap* **1** net **2** neuter **3** noon **4** normal **5** north **6** note **7** noun **8** number

**N** *symbol* nitrogen

**-n** — see -EN

**Na** *symbol* [NL *natrium*] sodium

**NA** *abbr* **1** no account **2** North America **3** not applicable

**NAACP** \,en-,dəb-əl-,ā-,sē-'pē, ,en-,ā-,ā-,sē-\ *abbr* National Association for the Advancement of Colored People

**nab** \'nab\ *vb* **nabbed; nab·bing :** SEIZE; *esp* **:** ARREST

**na·bob** \'nā-,bäb\ *n* [Hindi & Urdu *nawwāb,* fr. Ar *nuwwāb,* pl. of *nā'ib* governor] **:** a man of great wealth or prominence

**na·celle** \nə-'sel\ *n* **:** an enclosed shelter on an aircraft (as for an engine)

**na·cre** \'nā-kər\ *n* **:** MOTHER-OF-PEARL

**na·dir** \'nā-,diər, 'nād-ər\ *n* [ME, fr. MF, fr. Ar *nazīr* opposite] **1 :** the point of the celestial sphere that is directly opposite the zenith and vertically downward from the observer **2 :** the lowest point

**¹nag** \'nag\ *n* **:** HORSE; *esp* **:** an old or decrepit horse

**²nag** *vb* **nagged; nag·ging** **1 :** to find fault incessantly **:** COMPLAIN **2 :** to irritate by constant scolding or urging **3 :** to be a continuing source of annoyance (a nagging toothache)

**³nag** *n* **:** one who nags habitually

**Nah** *abbr* Nahum

**na·iad** \'nā-əd, 'nī-, -,ad\ *n, pl* **na·iads** *or* **na·ia·des** \-ə-,dēz\ **1 :** one of the nymphs in ancient mythology living in lakes, rivers, springs, and fountains **2 :** an aquatic young of some insects (as a dragonfly)

**na·if** \nä-'ēf\ *adj* **:** NAIVE

**¹nail** \'nāl\ *n* **1 :** a horny sheath protecting the end of each finger and toe in man and related primates **2 :** a slender pointed and headed piece of metal driven into or through something for fastening

²**nail** *vb* **:** to fasten with or as if with a nail — **nail·er** *n*

**nail down** *vb* **:** to settle or establish clearly and unmistakably

**nain·sook** \'nān-ˌsu̇k\ *n* [Hindi *nainsukh*, fr. *nain* eye + *sukh* delight] **:** a soft lightweight muslin

**nai·ra** \'nī-rə\ *n* - see MONEY table

**na·ive** *or* **na·ïve** \nä-'ēv\ *adj* **na·iv·er; -est** [F *naïve*, fem. of *naïf*, fr. OF, inborn, natural, fr. L *nativus* native] **1 :** marked by unaffected simplicity **:** ARTLESS, INGENUOUS **2 :** CREDULOUS — **na·ive·ly** *adv* **na·ive·ness** *n*

**na·ive·té** *or* **na·ïve·té** *or* **na·ive·te** \ˌnä-ˌēv-(ə)-'tā, nä-'ē-və-ˌtā\ *n* **1 :** the quality or state of being naive **2 :** a naive remark or action

**na·ive·ty** *also* **na·ïve·ty** \nä-'ēv-(ə-)tē\ *n, pl* **-ties :** NAIVETÉ

**na·ked** \'nā-kəd, 'nek-əd\ *adj* **1 :** having no clothes on **:** NUDE **2 :** UNSHEATHED ⟨a ~ sword⟩ **3 :** lacking a usual or natural covering (as of foliage or feathers) **4 :** PLAIN, UNADORNED ⟨the ~ truth⟩ **5 :** not aided by artificial means ⟨seen by the ~ eye⟩ — **na·ked·ly** *adv* - **na·ked·ness** *n*

**nam·by-pam·by** \ˌnam-bē-'pam-bē\ *adj* **1 :** INSIPID **2 :** WEAK, INDECISIVE

¹**name** \'nām\ *n* **1 :** a word or combination of words by which a person or thing is regularly known **2 :** a descriptive often disparaging epithet ⟨call someone ~*s*⟩ **3 :** REPUTATION; *esp* **:** distinguished reputation ⟨made a ~ for himself⟩ **4 :** FAMILY, CLAN ⟨was a disgrace to his ~⟩ **5 :** semblance as opposed to reality ⟨a friend in ~ only⟩

²**name** *vb* **named; nam·ing 1 :** to give a name to **:** CALL **2 :** to mention or identify by name **3 :** NOMINATE, APPOINT **4 :** to decide upon **:** CHOOSE **5 :** to speak about **:** MENTION ⟨~ a price⟩ — **name·able** *adj*

³**name** *adj* **1 :** of, relating to, or bearing a name ⟨~ tag⟩ **2 :** having an established reputation ⟨~ brands⟩

**name day** *n* **:** the day of the saint whose name one bears

**name·less** \'nām-ləs\ *adj* **1 :** having no name **2 :** not marked with a name ⟨a ~ grave⟩ **3 :** not known by name ⟨a ~ hero⟩ **4 :** not to be described ⟨~ fears⟩ — **name·less·ly** *adv*

**name·ly** \'nām-lē\ *adv* **:** that is to say **:** AS ⟨the cat family, ~, lions, tigers, and similar animals⟩

**name·plate** \-ˌplāt\ *n* **:** a plate or plaque bearing a name (as of a resident)

**name·sake** \-ˌsāk\ *n* **:** one that has the same name as another; *esp* **:** one named after another

**nan·keen** \nan-'kēn\ *n* **:** a durable brownish yellow cotton fabric orig. woven by hand in China

**nan·ny goat** \'nan-ē-\ *n* **:** a female domestic goat

**nano·me·ter** \'nan-ə-ˌmēt-ər\ *n* **:** one billionth of a meter

**nano·sec·ond** \-ˌsek-ənd\ *n* **:** one billionth of a second

¹**nap** \'nap\ *vb* **napped; nap·ping 1 :** to sleep briefly esp. during the day **:** DOZE **2 :** to be off guard ⟨was caught napping⟩

²**nap** *n* **:** a short sleep esp. during the day

³**nap** *n* **:** a soft downy fibrous surface (as on yarn and cloth) — **nap·less** *adj*

**na·palm** \'nā-ˌpä(l)m\ *n* **1 :** a thickener used in jelling gasoline (as for incendiary bombs) **2 :** fuel jelled with napalm

**nape** \'nāp, 'nap\ *n* **:** the back of the neck

**na·pery** \'nā-p(ə-)rē\ *n* **:** household linen esp. for the table

**naph·tha** \'naf-thə, 'nap-\ *n* **1 :** PETROLEUM **2 :** any of various liquid hydrocarbon mixtures used chiefly as solvents

**naph·tha·lene** \-ˌlēn\ *n* **:** a crystalline substance obtained from coal tar used in organic synthesis and as a moth repellent

**nap·kin** \'nap-kən\ *n* **1 :** a piece of material (as cloth) used at table to wipe the lips or fingers and protect the clothes **2 :** a small cloth or towel

**na·po·leon** \nə-'pōl-yən, -'pō-lē-ən\ *n* **1 :** a French 20-franc gold coin **2 :** an oblong pastry with a filling of cream, custard, or jelly between layers of puff paste

**Na·po·le·on·ic** \nə-ˌpō-lē-'än-ik\ *adj* **:** of, relating to, or characteristic of Napoleon I or his family

**narc** *or* **nark** \'närk\ *n, slang* **:** one (as a government agent) who investigates narcotics violations

**nar·cis·sism** \'när-sə-ˌsiz-əm\ *n* [G *narzissismus*, fr. *Narziss* Narcissus, fr. L *Narcissus*, fr. Gk *Narkissos*, beautiful youth of Greek mythology who fell in love with his own image] **1 :** undue dwelling on one's own self or attainments **2 :** love of or sexual desire for one's own body — **nar·cis·sist** \-səst\ *n or adj*

**nar·cis·sus** \när-'sis-əs\ *n, pl* **-cis·sus** *or* **-cis·sus·es** *or* **-cis·si** \-'sis-ˌī, -ē\ **:** DAFFODIL; *esp* **:** one with short-tubed flowers usu. borne separately

**nar·co·sis** \när-'kō-səs\ *n, pl* **-co·ses** \-ˌsēz\ **:** a state of stupor, unconsciousness, or arrested activity produced by the influence of chemicals (as narcotics)

**nar·cot·ic** \när-'kät-ik\ *n* [MB *narkotik*, fr. MF *narcotique*, fr. *narcotique*, adj., fr. ML *narcoticus*, fr. Gk *narkōtikos*, fr. *narkoun* to benumb, fr. *narkē* numbness] **:** a drug (as opium) that dulls the senses and induces sleep — **narcotic** *adj*

**nar·co·tize** \'när-kə-ˌtīz\ *vb* **-tized; -tiz·ing 1 :** to treat with or subject to a narcotic; *also* **:** to put into a state of narcosis **2 :** to soothe to unconsciousness or unawareness

**nard** \'närd\ *n* **:** a fragrant ointment of the ancients

**na·ris** \'nar-əs\ *n, pl* **na·res** \'nar-(ˌ)ēz\ **:** an opening of the nose **:** NOSTRIL

**Nar·ra·gan·set** \ˌnar-ə-'gan-sət\ *n, pl* **Narraganset** *or* **Narragansets :** a member of an Indian people of Rhode Island

**nar·rate** \'nar-,āt\ *vb* **nar·rat·ed; nar·rat·ing** : to recite the details of (as a story) : RELATE, TELL — **nar·ra·tion** \'nar-,āt-ər\ *n* — **nar·ra·tor** \'nar-,āt-ər\ *n*

**nar·ra·tive** \'nar-ət-iv\ *n* 1 : something that is narrated : STORY 2 : the art or practice of narrating

¹**nar·row** \'nar-ō\ *adj* 1 : of slender or less than standard width 2 : limited in size or scope : RESTRICTED 3 : not liberal in views : PREJUDICED 4 : interpreted or interpreting strictly 5 : CLOSE ⟨a ~ escape⟩; *also* : barely successful ⟨won by a ~ margin⟩ — **nar·row·ly** *adv* — **nar·row·ness** *n*

²**narrow** *n* : a narrow passage : STRAIT — usu. used in pl.

³**narrow** *vb* : to lessen in width or extent

**nar·row-mind·ed** \,nar-ō-'mīn-dəd\ *adj* : not liberal or broad-minded

**nar·thex** \'när-,theks\ *n* : a vestibule in a church

**nar·whal** \'när-,hwäl, 'när-wəl\ *n* : an arctic sea animal about 20 feet long that is related to the dolphin and in the male has a long twisted ivory tusk

**NAS** *abbr* naval air station

**NASA** \'nas-ə\ *abbr* National Aeronautics and Space Administration

¹**na·sal** \'nā-zəl\ *n* 1 : a nasal part 2 : a nasal consonant or vowel

²**nasal** *adj* 1 : of or relating to the nose 2 : uttered through the nose — **na·sal·ly** \-ē\ *adv*

**na·sal·ize** \'nā-zə-,līz\ *vb* **-ized; -iz·ing** 1 : to make nasal 2 : to speak in a nasal manner — **na·sal·iza·tion** \,nā-zə-lə-'zā-shən\ *n*

**na·scent** \'nas-ᵊnt, 'nās-\ *adj* : coming into existence : beginning to grow or develop — **na·scence** \-ᵊns\ *n*

**nas·tur·tium** \nə-'stər-shəm, na-\ *n* : a watery-stemmed herb with showy spurred flowers and pungent seeds

**nas·ty** \'nas-tē\ *adj* **nastier; -est** 1 : FILTHY 2 : INDECENT, OBSCENE 3 : DISAGREEABLE ⟨~ weather⟩ 4 : MEAN, ILL-NATURED ⟨a ~ temper⟩ 5 : DISHONORABLE ⟨a ~ trick⟩ 6 : HARMFUL, DANGEROUS ⟨took a ~ fall⟩ — **nas·ti·ly** \'nas-tə-lē\ *adv* — **nas·ti·ness** \-tē-nəs\ *n*

**nat** *abbr* 1 national 2 native 3 natural

**na·tal** \'nāt-ᵊl\ *adj* 1 : NATIVE 2 : of, relating to, or present at birth

**na·tal·i·ty** \nā-'tal-ət-ē, nə-\ *n*, *pl* **-ties** : BIRTHRATE

**na·ta·to·ri·um** \,nāt-ə-'tōr-ē-əm, ,nat-\ *n* : a swimming pool esp. indoors

**na·tion** \'nā-shən\ *n* [ME *nacioun*, fr. MF *nation*, fr. L *nation-, natio* birth, race, nation, fr. *natus*, pp. of *nasci* to be born] 1 : NATIONALITY 5; *also* : a politically organized nationality 2 : a community of people composed of one or more nationalities with its own territory and government 3 : a territorial division containing a body of people of one or more nationalities 4 : a federation of tribes (as of American Indians) — **na·tion·hood** *n*

¹**na·tion·al** \'nash-(ə-)nəl\ *adj* 1 : of or relating to a nation 2 : comprising

or characteristic of a nationality 3 : FEDERAL 3 — **na·tion·al·ly** \-ē\ *adv*

²**national** *n* 1 : one who is under the protection of a nation without regard to the more formal status of citizen or subject 2 : an organization (as a labor union) having local units throughout a nation 3 : a competition that is national in scope — usu. used in pl.

**National Guard** *n* : a militia force recruited by each state, equipped by the federal government, and jointly maintained subject to the call of either

**na·tion·al·ism** \'nash-(ə-)nəl-,iz-əm\ *n* : devotion to national interests, unity, and independence esp. of one nation above all others

**na·tion·al·ist** \-əst\ *n* 1 : an advocate of or believer in nationalism 2 *cap* : a member of a political party or group advocating national independence or strong national government — **nationalist** *adj, often cap* — **na·tion·al·is·tic** \,nash-(ə-)nəl-'is-tik\ *adj*

**na·tion·al·i·ty** \,nash-(ə-)'nal-ət-ē\ *n*, *pl* **-ties** 1 : national character 2 : national status; *esp* : a legal relationship involving allegiance of an individual and his protection by the state 3 : membership in a particular nation 4 : political independence or existence as a separate nation 5 : a people having a common origin, tradition, and language and capable of forming a state 6 : an ethnic group within a larger unit (as a nation)

**na·tion·al·ize** \'nash-(ə-)nəl-,īz\ *vb* **-ized; -iz·ing** 1 : to make national 2 : to remove from private ownership and place under government control — **na·tion·al·iza·tion** \,nash-(ə-)nəl-ə-'zā-shən\ *n*

**national park** *n* : an area of special scenic, historical, or scientific importance set aside and maintained by a national government esp. for recreation or study

**national seashore** *n* : a recreational area adjacent to a seacoast and maintained by the federal government

**na·tion·wide** \,nā-shən-'wīd\ *adj* : extending throughout a nation

¹**na·tive** \'nāt-iv\ *adj* 1 : INBORN, NATURAL 2 : born in a particular place or country 3 : belonging to a person because of the place or circumstances of his birth ⟨his ~ language⟩ 4 : grown, produced, or originating in a particular place : INDIGENOUS

²**native** *n* : one that is native; *esp* : a person who belongs to a particular country by birth

**na·tiv·ism** \'nāt-iv-,iz-əm\ *n* 1 : a policy of favoring native inhabitants over immigrants 2 : the revival or perpetuation of a native culture esp. in opposition to acculturation

**Na·tiv·i·ty** \nə-'tiv-ət-ē, nā-\ *n*, *pl* **-ties** 1 : the birth of Christ 2 : CHRISTMAS 3 *not cap* : the process or circumstances of being born : BIRTH

**natl** *abbr* national

**NATO** \'nāt-(,)ō\ *abbr* North Atlantic Treaty Organization

**nat·ty** \'nat-ē\ *adj* **nat·ti·er; -est** : trimly neat and tidy : SMART — **nat·ti·ly** \'nat-ᵊl-ē\ *adv* — **nat·ti·ness** \-ē-nəs\ *n*

¹**nat·u·ral** \'nach-(ə-)rəl\ *adj* **1** : determined by nature : INBORN, INNATE ⟨~ ability⟩ **2** : BORN ⟨a ~ fool⟩ **3** : ILLEGITIMATE **4** : HUMAN **5** : of or relating to nature **6** : not artificial **7** : being simple and sincere : not affected **8** : LIFELIKE **9** : having neither sharps nor flats in the key signature **syn** ingenuous, naive, unsophisticated, artless — **nat·u·ral·ness** *n*

²**natural** *n* **1** : IDIOT **2** : a character placed on a line or space of the musical staff to nullify the effect of a preceding sharp or flat **3** : one obviously suitable for a specific purpose **4** : AFRO

**natural gas** *n* : gas issuing from the earth's crust through natural openings or bored wells; *esp* : a combustible mixture of hydrocarbons and esp. methane used chiefly as a fuel and raw material

**natural history** *n* **1** : a treatise on some aspect of nature **2** : the study of natural objects esp. from an amateur or popular point of view

**nat·u·ral·ism** \'nach-(ə-)rə-,liz-əm\ *n* **1** : action, inclination, or thought based only on natural desires and instincts **2** : a doctrine that denies a supernatural explanation of the origin, development, or end of the universe and holds that scientific laws account for everything in nature **3** : realism in art and literature that emphasizes photographic exactness in portraying what actually exists — **nat·u·ral·is·tic** \,nach-(ə-)rə-'lis-tik\ *adj*

**nat·u·ral·ist** \-ləst\ *n* **1** : one that advocates or practices naturalism **2** : a student of animals or plants esp. in the field

**nat·u·ral·ize** \-,līz\ *vb* **-ized; -iz·ing** **1** : to become or cause to become established as if native ⟨~ new forage crops⟩ **2** : to confer the rights and privileges of a native citizen on - **nat·u·ral·iza·tion** \,nach-(ə-)rə-lə-'zā-shən\ *n*

**nat·u·ral·ly** \'nach-(ə-)rə-lē, 'nach-ər-lē\ *adv* **1** : by nature : by natural character or ability **2** : as might be expected **3** : without artificial aid; *also* : without affectation **4** : REALISTICALLY

**natural science** *n* : a science (as physics, chemistry, or biology) that deals with matter, energy, and their interrelations and transformations or with objectively measurable phenomena — **natural scientist** *n*

**natural selection** *n* : a natural process that tends to result in the survival of individuals or groups best adjusted to the conditions under which they live

**na·ture** \'nā-chər\ *n* [ME, fr. MF, fr. L *natura*, fr. *natus*, pp. of *nasci* to be born] **1** : the peculiar quality or basic constitution of a person or thing **2** : KIND, SORT **3** : DISPOSITION, TEMPERAMENT **4** : the physical universe **5** : one's natural instincts or way of life ⟨quirks of human ~⟩; *also* : primitive state ⟨a

return to ~⟩ **6** : natural scenery or environment ⟨beauties of ~⟩

**naught** \'nȯt, 'nät\ *n* **1** : NOTHING **2** : the arithmetical symbol 0 : ZERO

**naugh·ty** \'nȯt-ē, 'nät-\ *adj* **naugh·ti·er; -est** **1** : guilty of disobedience or misbehavior **2** : lacking in taste or propriety — **naught·i·ly** \'nȯt-ə-lē, 'nät-\ *adv* — **naught·i·ness** \-ē-nəs\ *n*

**nau·sea** \'nȯ-zē-ə, -shə\ *n* [L, seasickness, nausea, fr. Gk *nautia, nausia*, fr. *nautēs* sailor] **1** : sickness of the stomach with a desire to vomit **2** : extreme disgust — **nau·seous** \-shəs, -zē-əs\ *adj*

**nau·se·ate** \'nȯ-z(h)ē-,āt, -s(h)ē-\ *vb* **-at·ed; -at·ing** : to affect or become affected with nausea — **nau·se·at·ing·ly** \-,āt-iŋ-lē\ *adv*

**naut** *abbr* nautical

**nautch** \'nȯch\ *n* : an entertainment in India consisting chiefly of dancing by professional dancing girls

**nau·ti·cal** \'nȯt-i-kəl\ *adj* : of or relating to seamen, navigation, or ships — **nau·ti·cal·ly** \-k(ə-)lē\ *adv*

**nautical mile** *n* : an international unit of distance equal to about 6076.115 feet

**nau·ti·lus** \'nȯt-ᵊl-əs\ *n, pl* **-lus·es** or **-li** \-ᵊl-,ī, -,ē\ : a sea mollusk related to the octopuses but having a spiral shell divided into chambers

**nav** *abbr* **1** naval **2** navigable; navigation

**Na·va·ho** or **Na·va·jo** \'nav-ə-,hō, 'näv-\ *n, pl* **Navaho** or **Navahos** or **Navajo** or **Navajos** : a member of an Indian people of northern New Mexico and Arizona; *also* : their language

**na·val** \'nā-vəl\ *adj* : of, relating to, or possessing a navy

**naval stores** *n pl* : products (as pitch, turpentine, or rosin) obtained from resinous conifers (as pines)

**nave** \'nāv\ *n* [ML *navis*, fr. L, ship] : the central part of a church running lengthwise

**na·vel** \'nā-vəl\ *n* : a depression in the middle of the abdomen that marks the point of attachment of fetus and mother

**navel orange** *n* : a seedless orange having a pit at the apex where the fruit encloses a small secondary fruit

**nav·i·ga·ble** \'nav-i-gə-bəl\ *adj* **1** : capable of being navigated ⟨a ~ river⟩ **2** : capable of being steered ⟨a ~ balloon⟩ — **nav·i·ga·bil·i·ty** \,nav-i-gə-'bil-ət-ē\ *n* — **nav·i·ga·bly** \'nav-i-gə-blē\ *adv*

**nav·i·gate** \'nav-ə-,gāt\ *vb* **-gat·ed; -gat·ing** **1** : to sail on or through ⟨~ the Atlantic ocean⟩ **2** : to steer or direct the course of a ship or aircraft **3** : MOVE; *esp* : WALK ⟨could hardly ~⟩ — **nav·i·ga·tion** \,nav-ə-'gā-shən\ *n* — **nav·i·ga·tor** \'nav-ə-,gāt-ər\ *n*

**na·vy** \'nā-vē\ *n, pl* **navies** **1** : FLEET; *also* : the warships belonging to a nation **2** *often cap* : a nation's organization for naval warfare

**navy exchange** *n* : a post exchange at a navy installation

**navy yard** *n* : a yard where naval vessels are built or repaired

¹**nay** \'nā\ *adv* **1** : NO — used in oral voting **2** : not merely this but also : not only so but ⟨the letter made him happy, ~, ecstatic⟩

²**nay** *n* : a negative vote; *also* : a person casting such a vote

**Na·zi** \'nät-sē, 'nat-\ *n* : a member of a German fascist party controlling Germany from 1933 to 1945 under Adolf Hitler — **Nazi** *adj* — **Na·zism** \'nät-,siz-em, 'nat-\ *or* **Na·zi·ism** \-sē-,iz-əm\ *n*

**Nb** *symbol* niobium

**NB** *abbr* **1** New Brunswick **2** : nota bene

**NBC** *abbr* National Broadcasting Company

**NBS** *abbr* National Bureau of Standards

**NC** *abbr* **1** no charge **2** North Carolina

**NCE** *abbr* New Catholic Edition

**NCO** \,en-,sē-'ō\ *n* : NONCOMMISSIONED OFFICER

**NCV** *abbr* no commercial value

**Nd** *symbol* neodymium

**ND** *abbr* **1** no date **2** North Dakota

**N Dak** *abbr* North Dakota

**NDEA** *abbr* National Defense Education Act

**Ne** *symbol* neon

**NE** *abbr* **1** Nebraska **2** New England **3** northeast

**Ne·an·der·thal** \nē-'an-dər-,t(h)öl, nā-'än-dər-,täl\ *adj* : of, relating to, or being an extinct primitive Old World man; *also* : crudely primitive (as in manner or conduct) — **Neanderthal** *n*

**neap** \'nēp\ *adj* : being either of two tides that are the least in the lunar month

¹**near** \'nir\ *adv* **1** : at, within, or to a short distance or time **2** : ALMOST

²**near** *prep* : close to

³**near** *adj* **1** : closely related or associated; *also* : INTIMATE **2** : not far away; *also* : being the closer or left-hand member of a pair **3** : barely avoided ⟨a ~ accident⟩ **4** : DIRECT, SHORT ⟨by the ~*est* route⟩ **5** : STINGY **6** : not real but very like ⟨~ silk⟩ — **near·ly** *adv* — **near·ness** *n*

⁴**near** *vb* : APPROACH

**near beer** *n* : any of various malt liquors considered nonalcoholic because they contain less than a specified percentage of alcohol

**near·by** \nir-'bī, -,bī\ *adv or adj* : close at hand

**near·sight·ed** \'nir-'sīt-əd\ *adj* : seeing distinctly at short distances only : SHORTSIGHTED — **near·sight·ed·ly** *adv* — **near·sight·ed·ness** *n*

**neat** \'nēt\ *adj* [MF *net*, fr. L *nitēre* to shine] **1** : not mixed or diluted ⟨~ brandy⟩ **2** : marked by tasteful simplicity **3** : PRECISE, SYSTEMATIC **4** : SKILLFUL, ADROIT **5** : being orderly and clean **6** : CLEAR, NET ⟨~ profit⟩ **7** *slang* : FINE, ADMIRABLE — **neat** *adv* — **neat·ly** *adv* — **neat·ness** *n*

**neath** \'nēth\ *prep, dial* : BENEATH

**neat's-foot oil** \'nēts-,füt-\ *n* : a pale yellow fatty oil made esp. from the bones of cattle and used chiefly as a leather dressing

**neb** \'neb\ *n* **1** : the beak of a bird or tortoise; *also* : NOSE, SNOUT **2** : NIB

**Neb** *or* **Nebr** *abbr* Nebraska

**NEB** *abbr* New English Bible

**neb·u·la** \'neb-yə-lə\ *n, pl* **-las** *or* **-lae** \-,lē, -,lī\ **1** : any of many vast cloudlike masses of gas or dust among the stars **2** : GALAXY — **neb·u·lar** \-lər\ *adj*

**neb·u·lize** \'neb-yə-,līz\ *vb* **-lized; -liz·ing** : to reduce to a fine spray — **neb·u·liz·er** \-,lī-zər\ *n*

**neb·u·los·i·ty** \,neb-yə-'läs-ət-ē\ *n, pl* **-ties 1** : the quality or state of being nebulous **2** : nebulous matter

**neb·u·lous** \'neb-yə-ləs\ *adj* **1** : HAZY, INDISTINCT ⟨a ~ memory⟩ **2** : of or relating to a nebula

¹**nec·es·sary** \'nes-ə-,ser-ē\ *n, pl* **-saries** : an indispensable item

²**necessary** *adj* [ME *necessarie*, fr. L *necessarius*, fr. *necesse* necessary, fr. *ne-* not + *cedere* to withdraw] **1** : INEVITABLE, INESCAPABLE; *also* : CERTAIN **2** : PREDETERMINED **3** : COMPULSORY **4** : positively needed : INDISPENSABLE *syn* requisite, essential — **nec·es·sar·i·ly** \,nes-ə-'ser-ə-lē\ *adv*

**ne·ces·si·tate** \ni-'ses-ə-,tāt\ *vb* **-tat·ed; -tat·ing** : to make necessary

**ne·ces·si·tous** \ni-'ses-ət-əs\ *adj* **1** : NEEDY, IMPOVERISHED **2** : URGENT **3** : NECESSARY

**ne·ces·si·ty** \ni-'ses-ət-ē\ *n, pl* **-ties 1** : very great need **2** : something that is necessary **3** : WANT, POVERTY **4** : conditions that cannot be changed

¹**neck** \'nek\ *n* **1** : the part of the body connecting the head and the trunk **2** : the part of a garment covering or near to the neck **3** : a relatively narrow part suggestive of a neck ⟨~ of a bottle⟩ ⟨~ of land⟩ **4** : a narrow margin esp. of victory ⟨won by a ~⟩ — **necked** \'nekt\ *adj*

²**neck** *vb* **1** : to reduce in diameter **2** : to kiss and caress amorously

**neck·er·chief** \'nek-ər-chəf, -,chēf\ *n, pl* **-chiefs** \-chəfs, -,chēfs\ *also* **-chieves** \-,chēvz\ : a square of cloth worn folded about the neck like a scarf

**neck·lace** \'nek-ləs\ *n* : an ornamental chain or a string (as of jewels or beads) worn around the neck

**neck·line** \-,līn\ *n* : the outline of the neck opening of a garment

**neck·tie** \-,tī\ *n* : a narrow length of material worn about the neck and tied in front

**ne·crol·o·gy** \nə-'kräl-ə-jē\ *n, pl* **-gies 1** : a list of the recently dead **2** : OBITUARY

**nec·ro·man·cy** \'nek-rə-,man-sē\ *n* **1** : the art or practice of conjuring up the spirits of the dead for purposes of magically revealing the future **2** : MAGIC, SORCERY — **nec·ro·man·cer** \-sər\ *n*

**ne·crop·o·lis** \nə-'kräp-ə-ləs, ne-\ *n, pl* **-lis·es** *or* **-les** \-,lēz\ *or* **-leis** \-,läs\ *or* **-li** \-,lī, -,lē\ : CEMETERY; *esp* : a large elaborate cemetery of an ancient city

**ne·cro·sis** \nə-'krō-səs, ne-\ *n, pl* **ne·cro·ses** \-ˌsēz\ : usu. local death of body tissue — **ne·crot·ic** \-'krät-ik\ *adj*

**nec·tar** \'nek-tər\ *n* **1** : the drink of the Greek and Roman gods; *also* : any delicious drink **2** : a sweet plant secretion that is the raw material of honey

**nec·tar·ine** \ˌnek-tə-'rēn\ *n* : a smooth-skinned peach

**née** *or* **nee** \'nā\ *adj* : BORN — used to identify a woman by her maiden family name

**¹need** \'nēd\ *n* **1** : OBLIGATION ⟨no ~ to hurry⟩ **2** : a lack of something requisite, desirable, or useful **3** : a condition requiring supply or relief ⟨when the ~ arises⟩ **4** : POVERTY **syn** necessity, exigency

**²need** *vb* **1** : to be in want **2** : to have cause or occasion for : REQUIRE ⟨he ~s advice⟩ **3** : to be under obligation or necessity ⟨we ~ to know the truth⟩

**need·ful** \'nēd-fəl\ *adj* : NECESSARY, REQUISITE

**¹nee·dle** \'nēd-ᵊl\ *n* **1** : a slender pointed usu. steel implement used in sewing **2** : a slender rod (as for knitting, controlling a small opening, or transmitting vibrations to or from a recording) ⟨a phonograph ~⟩ **3** : a needle-shaped leaf (as of a pine) **4** : a slender bar of magnetized steel used in a compass; *also* : an indicator on a dial **5** : a slender hollow instrument by which material is introduced into or withdrawn from the body

**²needle** *vb* **nee·dled; nee·dling** \'nēd-(ᵊ-)liŋ\ : PROD, GOAD; *esp* : to incite to action by repeated gibes

**nee·dle·point** \'nēd-ᵊl-ˌpöint\ *n* **1** : lace worked with a needle over a paper pattern **2** : embroidery done on canvas across counted threads — **needlepoint** *adj*

**need·less** \'nēd-ləs\ *adj* : UNNECESSARY — **need·less·ly** *adv* — **need·less·ness** *n*

**nee·dle·wom·an** \'nēd-ᵊl-ˌwùm-ən\ *n* : a woman who does needlework; *esp* : SEAMSTRESS

**nee·dle·work** \-ˌwərk\ *n* : work done with a needle; *esp* : work (as embroidery) other than plain sewing

**needs** \'nēdz\ *adv* : of necessity : NECESSARILY ⟨must ~ be recognized⟩

**needy** \'nēd-ē\ *adj* **need·i·er; -est** : being in want : POVERTY-STRICKEN

**ne'er** \'neər\ *adv* : NEVER

**ne'er-do-well** \'neər-dü-ˌwel\ *n* : an idle worthless person — **ne'er-do-well** *adj*

**ne·far·i·ous** \ni-'far-ē-əs\ *adj* [L *nefarius*, fr. *nefas* crime, fr. *ne-* not + *fas* right, divine law] : very wicked : EVIL — **ne·far·i·ous·ly** *adv*

**neg** *abbr* negative

**ne·gate** \ni-'gāt\ *vb* **ne·gat·ed; ne·gat·ing 1** : to deny the existence or truth of **2** : to cause to be ineffective or invalid : NULLIFY

**ne·ga·tion** \ni-'gā-shən\ *n* **1** : the action of negating : DENIAL **2** : a negative doctrine or statement

**¹neg·a·tive** \'neg-ət-iv\ *adj* **1** : marked by denial, prohibition, or refusal ⟨a ~ reply⟩ **2** : not positive or constructive; *esp* : not affirming the presence of what is sought or suspected to be present ⟨a ~ test⟩ **3** : less than zero ⟨a ~ number⟩ **4** : being, relating to, or charged with electricity of which the electron is the elementary unit ⟨a ~ particle⟩ **5** : having lights and shadows opposite to what they were in the original photographic subject — **neg·a·tive·ly** *adv*

**²negative** *n* **1** : a negative word or statement **2** : a negative vote or reply; *also* : REFUSAL **3** : something that is the opposite or negation of something else **4** : the side that votes or argues for the opposition (as in a debate) **5** : the platelike part to which the current flows from the external circuit in a discharging storage battery **6** : a negative photographic image on transparent material

**³negative** *vb* **-tived; -tiv·ing 1** : to refuse to accept or approve **2** : to vote against : VETO **3** : DISPROVE

**negative income tax** *n* : a system of federal subsidy payments to families with incomes below a stipulated level

**neg·a·tiv·ism** \'neg-ət-iv-ˌiz-əm\ *n* : an attitude of skepticism and denial of nearly everything affirmed or suggested by others

**¹ne·glect** \ni-'glekt\ *vb* [L *neglegere, neclegere,* fr. *nec-* not + *legere* to gather] **1** : DISREGARD **2** : to leave undone or unattended to esp. through carelessness **syn** omit, ignore, overlook, slight, forget

**²neglect** *n* **1** : an act or instance of neglecting something **2** : the condition of being neglected — **ne·glect·ful** *adj*

**neg·li·gee** *or* **neg·li·gé** \ˌneg-lə-'zhā\ *n* **1** : a woman's long flowing dressing gown **2** : carelessly informal or incomplete attire

**neg·li·gent** \'neg-li-jənt\ *adj* : marked by neglect **syn** neglectful, remiss — **neg·li·gence** \-jəns\ *n* — **neg·li·gent·ly** *adv*

**neg·li·gi·ble** \'neg-li-jə-bəl\ *adj* : fit to be neglected or disregarded

**ne·go·tiant** \ni-'gō-sh(ē-)ənt\ *n* : NEGOTIATOR

**ne·go·ti·ate** \ni-'gō-shē-ˌāt\ *vb* **-at·ed; -at·ing** [L *negotiari* to carry on business, fr. *negotium* business, fr. *neg-* not + *otium* leisure] **1** : to confer with another so as to arrive at the settlement of some matter; *also* : to arrange for or bring about by such conferences ⟨~ a treaty⟩ **2** : to transfer to another by delivery or endorsement in return for equivalent value ⟨~ a check⟩ **3** : to get through, around, or over successfully ⟨~ a turn⟩ — **ne·go·tia·ble** \-sh(ē-)ə-bəl\ *adj* — **ne·go·ti·a·tion** \ni-ˌgō-s(h)ē-'ā-shən\ *n* — **ne·go·ti·a·tor** \-'gō-shē-ˌāt-ər\ *n*

**ne·gri·tude** \'neg-rə-ˌt(y)üd, 'nē-grə-\ *n* : a consciousness of and pride in one's African heritage

**Ne·gro** \'nē-grō\ *n, pl* **Negroes** : a member of the black race — **Negro** *adj*

— **Ne·groid** \'nē-ˌgroid\ *n or adj,
often not cap*

**ne·gus** \'nē-gəs\ *n* : a beverage of wine, hot water, sugar, lemon juice, and nutmeg

**Neh** *abbr* Nehemiah

**NEI** *abbr* not elsewhere included

**neigh** \'nā\ *n* : a loud prolonged cry of a horse — **neigh** *vb*

¹**neigh·bor** \'nā-bər\ *n* **1** : one living or located near another **2** : FELLOW-MAN

²**neighbor** *vb* **neigh·bored; neigh·bor·ing** \-b(ə-)riŋ\ : to be next to or near to : border on

**neigh·bor·hood** \'nā-bər-ˌhu̇d\ *n* **1** : NEARNESS **2** : a place or region near : VICINITY; *also* : an approximate amount, extent, or degree (costs in the ∼ of $10) **3** : the people living near one another **4** : a section lived in by neighbors and usu. having distinguishing characteristics

**neigh·bor·ly** \-lē\ *adj* : befitting congenial neighbors; *esp* : FRIENDLY — **neigh·bor·li·ness** *n*

¹**nei·ther** \'nē-thər, 'nī-\ *pron* : neither one : not the one and not the other (∼ of the two)

²**neither** *conj* **1** : not either (∼ good nor bad) **2** : NOR (∼ did I)

³**neither** *adj* : not either (∼ hand)

**nel·son** \'nel-sən\ *n* : a wrestling hold marked by the application of leverage against an opponent's arm, neck, and head

**nem·a·tode** \'nem-ə-ˌtōd\ *n* : any of a group of elongated cylindrical worms parasitic in animals or plants or free-living in soil or water

**nem·e·sis** \'nem-ə-səs\ *n, pl* **-e·ses** \-ə-ˌsēz\ [L *Nemesis*, goddess of divine retribution, fr. Gk] **1** : one that inflicts retribution or vengeance **2** : a formidable and usu. victorious rival **3** : an act or effect of retribution; *also* : CURSE

**neo·clas·sic** \ˌnē-ō-'klas-ik\ *adj* : of or relating to a revival or adaptation of the classical style esp. in literature, art, or music — **neo·clas·si·cal** \-i-kəl\ *adj*

**neo·co·lo·nial·ism** \ˌnē-ō-kə-'lō-nyəl-ˌiz-əm, -'lō-nē-ə-ˌliz-əm\ *n* : the economic and political policies by which a great power indirectly maintains or extends its influence over other areas or peoples — **neo·co·lo·nial** *adj* — **neo·co·lo·nial·ist** \-əst\ *n or adj*

**neo·dym·i·um** \ˌnē-ō-'dim-ē-əm\ *n* : a yellow metallic chemical element

**neo–im·pres·sion·ism** \ˌnē-ō-im-'presh-ə-ˌniz-əm\ *n, often cap N&I* : a late 19th century French art movement that attempted to make impressionism more precise and to use a pointillist painting technique

**ne·ol·o·gism** \nē-'äl-ə-ˌjiz-əm\ *n* : a new word or expression

**ne·ol·o·gy** \-jē\ *n, pl* **-gies** : the use of a new word or expression or of an established word in a new or different sense

**ne·on** \'nē-ˌän\ *n* [Gk, neut. of *neos* new] **1** : a gaseous colorless chemical element used in electric lamps **2** : a lamp in which a discharge through neon gives a reddish glow — **neon** *adj*

**neo·na·tal** \ˌnē-ō-'nāt-°l\ *adj* : of, relating to, or affecting the newborn — **neo·na·tal·ly** \-ē\ *adv* — **ne·o·nate** \'nē-ō-ˌnāt\ *n*

**neo·phyte** \'nē-ə-ˌfīt\ *n* **1** : a new convert : PROSELYTE **2** : BEGINNER, NOVICE

**neo·plasm** \'nē-ə-ˌplaz-əm\ *n* : TUMOR — **neo·plas·tic** \ˌnē-ə-'plas-tik\ *adj*

**ne·pen·the** \nə-'pen-thē\ *n* **1** : a potion used by the ancients to dull pain and sorrow **2** : something capable of making one forget grief or suffering

**neph·ew** \'nef-yü, *chiefly Brit* 'nev-\ *n* : a son of one's brother, sister, brother-in-law, or sister-in-law

**ne·phrit·ic** \ni-'frit-ik\ *adj* **1** : RENAL **2** : of, relating to, or affected with nephritis

**ne·phri·tis** \ni-'frīt-əs\ *n, pl* **ne·phrit·i·des** \-'frit-ə-ˌdēz\ : kidney inflammation

**ne plus ul·tra** \ˌnē-ˌpləs-'əl-trə\ *n* [NL, (go) no more beyond] : the highest point capable of being attained

**nep·o·tism** \'nep-ə-ˌtiz-əm\ *n* [F *népotisme*, fr. It *nepotismo*, fr. *nepote* nephew, fr. L *nepot-*, *nepos* grandson, nephew] : favoritism shown to a relative (as in the distribution of political offices)

**Nep·tune** \'nep-ˌt(y)ün\ *n* : the fourth largest of the planets and the one eighth in order of distance from the sun — **Nep·tu·ni·an** \nep-'t(y)ü-nē-ən\ *adj*

**nep·tu·ni·um** \nep-'t(y)ü-nē-əm\ *n* : a short-lived radioactive chemical element artificially produced as a by-product in the production of plutonium

**Ne·re·id** \'nir-ē-əd\ *n* : any of the sea nymphs held in Greek mythology to be the daughters of the sea-god Nereus

¹**nerve** \'nərv\ *n* **1** : one of the strands of nervous tissue that carry nervous impulses to and fro between the brain and spinal cord and every part of the body **2** : power of endurance or control : FORTITUDE; *also* : BOLDNESS, DARING **3** *pl* : NERVOUSNESS, HYSTERIA **4** : a vein of a leaf or insect wing — **nerved** \'nərvd\ *adj* — **nerve·less** *adj*

²**nerve** *vb* **nerved; nerv·ing** : to give strength or courage to

**nerve cell** *n* : NEURON; *also* : a nerve cell body exclusive of its processes

**nerve gas** *n* : a war gas damaging esp. to the nervous and respiratory systems

**nerve–rack·ing** or **nerve–wrack·ing** \'nərv-ˌrak-iŋ\ *adj* : extremely trying on the nerves

**ner·vous** \'nər-vəs\ *adj* **1** : FORCIBLE, SPIRITED **2** : of, relating to, or made up of nerve cells or nerves **3** : easily excited or annoyed : JUMPY **4** : TIMID, APPREHENSIVE (a ∼ smile) **5** : UNEASY, UNSTEADY — **ner·vous·ly** *adv* — **ner·vous·ness** *n*

**nervous breakdown** *n* : an emotional and psychic disorder that is characterized by impaired functioning in interpersonal relationships and often by fatigue, depression, feelings of inadequacy, headaches, hypersensitivity to sensory stimulation (as by light or noise) and psychosomatic symptoms (as disturbances of digestion and circulation)

**nervous system** *n* **:** a bodily system that in vertebrates is made up of the brain and spinal cord, nerves, ganglia, and parts of the sense organs and that receives and interprets stimuli and transmits impulses

**nervy** \'nər-vē\ *adj* **nerv·i·er; -est** **1 :** showing calm courage **2 :** marked by impudence or presumption ⟨a ~ salesman⟩ **3 :** EXCITABLE, NERVOUS

**NES** *abbr* not elsewhere specified

**-ness** \nəs\ *n suffix* **:** state **:** condition **:** quality **:** degree ⟨good*ness*⟩

**¹nest** \'nest\ *n* **1 :** the bed or shelter prepared by a bird for its eggs and young **2 :** a place where eggs (as of insects, fish, or turtles) are laid and hatched **3 :** a place of rest, retreat, or lodging **4 :** DEN, HANGOUT ⟨a ~ of thieves⟩ **5 :** the occupants of a nest **6 :** a series of objects (as bowls or tables) made to fit into or under the next larger one

**²nest** *vb* **1 :** to build or occupy a nest **2 :** to fit compactly together or within one another

**nest egg** *n* **1 :** a natural or artificial egg left in a nest to induce a fowl to continue to lay there **2 :** a fund of money accumulated as a reserve

**nes·tle** \'nes-əl\ *vb* **nes·tled; nes·tling** \-(ə-)liŋ\ **1 :** to settle snugly or comfortably **2 :** to settle, shelter, or house as if in a nest **3 :** to press closely and affectionately **:** CUDDLE

**nest·ling** \'nest-liŋ\ *n* **:** a bird too young to leave its nest

**¹net** \'net\ *n* **1 :** a meshed fabric twisted, knotted, or woven together at regular intervals; *esp* **:** a device of net used esp. to catch birds, fish, or insects **2 :** something made of net used esp. for protecting, confining, carrying, or dividing ⟨a tennis ~⟩ **3 :** SNARE, TRAP

**²net** *vb* **net·ted; net·ting 1 :** to cover or enclose with or as if with a net **2 :** to catch in or as if in a net

**³net** *adj* **:** free from all charges or deductions ⟨~ profit⟩ ⟨~ weight⟩

**⁴net** *vb* **net·ted; net·ting :** to gain or produce as profit **:** CLEAR, YIELD ⟨his business *netted* $10,000 a year⟩

**⁵net** *n* **:** a net amount, profit, weight, or price

**NET** *abbr* National Educational Television

**Neth** *abbr* Netherlands

**neth·er** \'neth-ər\ *adj* **:** situated down or below ⟨the ~ regions of the earth⟩

**neth·er·most** \-,mōst\ *adj* **:** LOWEST

**neth·er·world** \-,wərld\ *n* **1 :** the world of the dead **2 :** UNDERWORLD

**net·ting** \'net-iŋ\ *n* **1 :** NETWORK **2 :** the act or process of making a net or network **3 :** the act, process, or right of fishing with a net

**¹net·tle** \'net-ᵊl\ *n* **:** any of various coarse herbs with stinging hairs

**²nettle** *vb* **net·tled; net·tling :** PROVOKE, VEX, IRRITATE

**net·tle·some** \'net-ᵊl-səm\ *adj* **:** causing vexation **:** IRRITATING

**net·work** \'net-,wərk\ *n* **1 :** NET **2 :** a system of elements (as lines or channels) that cross in the manner of the threads in a net **3 :** a chain of radio or television stations

**neu·ral** \'n(y)ùr-əl\ *adj* **:** of, relating to, or involving a nerve or the nervous system

**neu·ral·gia** \n(y)ù-'ral-jə\ *n* **:** acute pain that follows the course of a nerve — **neu·ral·gic** \-jik\ *adj*

**neur·as·the·nia** \,n(y)ùr-əs-'thē-nē-ə\ *n* **:** a neurotic state marked by tension and malaise; *also* **:** NERVOUS BREAKDOWN — **neur·as·then·ic** \-'then-ik\ *adj or n*

**neu·ri·tis** \n(y)ù-'rīt-əs\ *n, pl* **-rit·i·des** \-'rit-ə-,dēz\ *or* **-ri·tis·es :** inflammation of a nerve — **neu·rit·ic** \-'rit-ik\ *adj or n*

**neurol** *abbr* neurology

**neu·rol·o·gy** \n(y)ù-'räl-ə-jē\ *n* **:** scientific study of the nervous system — **neu·ro·log·i·cal** \,n(y)ùr-ə-'läj-i-kəl\ *or* **neu·ro·log·ic** \-ik\ *adj* — **neu·ro·log·i·cal·ly** \-i-k(ə-)lē\ *adv* — **neu·rol·o·gist** \n(y)ù-'räl-ə-jəst\ *n*

**neu·ron** \'n(y)ü-,rän\ *also* **neu·rone** \-,rōn\ *n* **:** a nerve cell with all of its processes

**neu·ro·sci·ence** \,n(y)ùr-ō-'sī-ən(t)s\ *n* **:** a branch of the life sciences that deals with the anatomy, physiology, biochemistry, or molecular biology of nerves and nervous tissue and esp. with their relation to behavior and learning — **neu·ro·sci·en·tist** \-ənt-əst\ *n*

**neu·ro·sis** \n(y)ù-'rō-səs\ *n, pl* **-ro·ses** \-,sēz\ **:** a functional nervous disorder without demonstrable physical lesions

**¹neu·rot·ic** \n(y)ù-'rät-ik\ *adj* **:** of, relating to, being, or affected with a neurosis; *also* **:** NERVOUS — **neu·rot·i·cal·ly** \-i-k(ə-)lē\ *adv*

**²neurotic** *n* **:** an emotionally unstable or neurotic person

**neut** *abbr* neuter

**¹neu·ter** \'n(y)üt-ər\ *adj* [ME *neutre*, fr. MF & L; MF *neutre*, fr. L *neuter*, lit., neither, fr. *ne-* not + *uter* which of two] **1 :** of, relating to, or constituting the gender that includes most words of grammatical forms referring to things classed as neither masculine nor feminine **2 :** having imperfectly developed or no sex organs

**²neuter** *n* **1 :** a noun, pronoun, adjective, or inflectional form or class of the neuter gender; *also* **:** the neuter gender **2 :** WORKER 2; *also* **:** a spayed or castrated animal

**¹neu·tral** \'n(y)ü-trəl\ *adj* **1 :** not favoring either side in a quarrel, contest, or war **2 :** of or relating to a neutral state or power **3 :** being neither one thing nor the other **:** MIDDLING, INDIFFERENT **4 :** having no hue **:** GRAY; *also* **:** not decided in color **5 :** neither acid nor basic ⟨a ~ solution⟩ **6 :** not electrically charged

**²neutral** *n* **1 :** one that is neutral **2 :** a neutral color **3 :** the position of machine gears in which the motor imparts no motion

**neu·tral·ism** \'n(y)ü-trə-‚liz-əm\ *n* **:** a policy or the advocacy of neutrality esp. in international affairs

**neu·tral·i·ty** \n(y)ü-'tral-ət-ē\ *n* **:** the quality or state of being neutral; *esp* **:** immunity from invasion or from use by belligerents

**neu·tral·ize** \'n(y)ü-trə-‚līz\ *vb* **-ized; -iz·ing :** to make neutral; *esp* **:** COUNTERACT — **neu·tral·iza·tion** \‚n(y)ü-trə-lə-'zā-shən\ *n*

**neu·tri·no** \n(y)ü-'trē-nō\ *n, pl* **-nos :** an uncharged elementary particle held to be massless

**neu·tron** \'n(y)ü-‚trän\ *n* **:** an uncharged elementary particle that is nearly equal in mass to the proton and that is present in all atomic nuclei except hydrogen

**Nev** *abbr* Nevada

**nev·er** \'nev-ər\ *adv* **1 :** not ever **2 :** not in any degree, way, or condition

**nev·er·more** \‚nev-ər-'mōr\ *adv* **:** never again

**nev·er–nev·er land** \‚nev-ər-'nev-ər-\ *n* **:** an ideal or imaginary place

**nev·er·the·less** \‚nev-ər-thə-'les\ *adv* **:** in spite of that **:** HOWEVER

**ne·vus** \'nē-vəs\ *n, pl* **ne·vi** \-‚vī\ **:** a usu. pigmented birthmark

**¹new** \'n(y)ü\ *adj* **1 :** not old **:** RECENT, MODERN **2 :** different from the former **3 :** recently discovered, recognized, or learned about ⟨~ drugs⟩ **4 :** not formerly known or experienced **:** UNFAMILIAR **5 :** not accustomed ⟨~ to the work⟩ **6 :** beginning as a repetition of a previous act or thing ⟨a ~ year⟩ **7 :** REFRESHED, REGENERATED ⟨rest made a ~ man of him⟩ **8 :** being in a position or place for the first time ⟨a ~ member⟩ **9** *cap* **:** having been in use after medieval times **:** MODERN ⟨*New* Latin⟩ **syn** novel, original, fresh — **new·ish** *adj* — **new·ness** *n*

**²new** *adv* **:** NEWLY ⟨*new*-mown hay⟩

**¹new·born** \-'bȯrn\ *adj* **1 :** recently born **2 :** born anew ⟨~ hope⟩

**²newborn** *n, pl* **newborn** *or* **newborns :** a newborn individual

**new·com·er** \'n(y)ü-‚kəm-ər\ *n* **1 :** one recently arrived **2 :** BEGINNER

**New Deal** *n* **:** the legislative and administrative program of President F. D. Roosevelt designed to promote economic recovery and social reform during the 1930s — **New Deal·er** \-'dē-lər\ *n*

**new·el** \'n(y)ü-əl\ *n* [ME *nowell,* fr. MF *nouel* stone of a fruit, fr. LL *nucalis* like a nut, fr. L *nuc-, nux* nut] **:** an upright post about which the steps of a circular staircase wind; *also* **:** a post at the foot of a stairway or one at a landing

**new·fan·gled** \'n(y)ü-'faŋ-gəld\ *adj* [ME, fr. *newefangel,* fr. *new* + OE *fangen,* pp. of *fōn* to take, seize] **1 :** attracted to novelty **2 :** of the newest style **:** NOVEL

**new–fash·ioned** \-'fash-ənd\ *adj* **1 :** made in a new fashion or form **2 :** UP-TO-DATE

**new·found** \-'faund\ *adj* **:** newly found

**New Left** *n* **:** a political movement originating in the 1960s that is composed chiefly of students and advocates radical change in prevailing political, social, and educational practices

**new·ly** \'n(y)ü-lē\ *adv* **1 :** LATELY, RECENTLY **2 :** ANEW, AFRESH **3 :** in a new way

**new·ly·wed** \-‚wed\ *n* **:** one recently married

**new math** *n* **:** mathematics based on the theory of sets

**new mathematics** *n* **:** NEW MATH

**new moon** *n* **1 :** the phase of the moon with its dark side toward the earth **2 :** the thin crescent moon seen for a few days after the new moon phase

**news** \'n(y)üz\ *n* **1 :** a report of recent events **:** TIDINGS **2 :** material reported in a newspaper or news periodical or on a newscast

**news·boy** \'n(y)üz-‚bȯi\ *n* **:** a person who delivers or sells newspapers

**news·cast** \-‚kast\ *n* **:** a radio or television broadcast of news — **news·cast·er** \-‚kas-tər\ *n*

**news·let·ter** \-‚let-ər\ *n* **:** a newspaper containing news or information of interest chiefly to a special group

**news·mag·a·zine** \'n(y)üz-‚mag-ə-‚zēn\ *n* **:** a usu. weekly magazine devoted chiefly to summarizing and analyzing the news

**news·man** \-‚mən, -‚man\ *n* **:** one who gathers, reports, or comments on the news

**news·pa·per** \-‚pā-pər\ *n* **:** a paper that is printed and distributed at regular intervals and contains news, articles of opinion, features, and advertising

**news·pa·per·man** \'n(y)üz-‚pā-pər-‚man\ *n* **:** one who owns or is employed by a newspaper

**news·print** \'n(y)üz-‚print\ *n* **:** cheap machine-finished paper made chiefly from wood pulp and used mostly for newspapers

**news·reel** \-‚rēl\ *n* **:** a short motion picture portraying current events

**news·stand** \-‚stand\ *n* **:** a place where newspapers and periodicals are sold

**news·wor·thy** \-‚wər-thē\ *adj* **:** sufficiently interesting to the general public to warrant reporting (as in a newspaper)

**newsy** \'n(y)ü-zē\ *adj* **news·i·er; -est :** filled with news; *esp* **:** CHATTY

**newt** \'n(y)üt\ *n* **:** any of various small salamanders living chiefly in the water

**new town** *n* **:** an urban development consisting of a small to medium-sized city with a broad range of housing and planned industrial, commercial, and recreational facilities

**new wave** *n, often cap N&W* **:** a cinematic movement characterized by improvisation, abstraction, subjective symbolism, and often experimental photographic techniques

**New World** *n* **:** the western hemisphere; *esp* **:** the continental landmass of No. and So. America

**New Year** *n* **:** NEW YEAR'S DAY; *also* **:** the first days of the year

**New Year's Day** *n* **:** January 1 observed as a legal holiday

**New Zea·land·er** \n(y)ü-'zē-lən-dər\ *n* **:** a native or inhabitant of New Zealand

**¹next** \'nekst\ *adj* **:** immediately preceding or following: NEAREST

**²next** *adv* **1** **:** in the time, place, or order nearest or immediately succeeding **2** **:** on the first occasion to come

**³next** *prep* **:** nearest or adjacent to

**nex·us** \'nek-səs\ *n, pl* **nex·us·es** \-sə-səz\ *or* **nex·us** \-səs, -,süs\ **:** CONNECTION, LINK

**Nez Per·cé** \'nez-'pərs, *F* nā-per-sā\ *n, pl* **Nez Percé** *or* **Nez Percés** **:** a member of an Indian people of Idaho, Washington, and Oregon

**NF** *abbr* no funds

**Nfld** *abbr* Newfoundland

**NG** *abbr* **1** National Guard **2** no good

**NGk** *abbr* New Greek

**ngwee** \en-'gwē\ *n, pl* **ngwee** — see *kwacha* at MONEY table

**NH** *abbr* New Hampshire

**NHI** *abbr* national health insurance

**Ni** *symbol* nickel

**ni·a·cin** \'nī-ə-sən\ *n* **:** NICOTINIC ACID

**Ni·ag·a·ra** \nī-'ag-(ə-)rə\ *n* **:** an overwhelming flood: TORRENT ⟨a ~ of protests⟩

**nib** \'nib\ *n* **:** POINT; *esp* **:** a pen point

**¹nib·ble** \'nib-əl\ *vb* **nib·bled; nib·bling** \-(ə-)liŋ\ **:** to bite gently or bit by bit

**²nibble** *n* **:** a small or cautious bite

**nice** \'nīs\ *adj* **nic·er; nic·est** [ME, foolish, wanton, fr. OF, fr. L *nescius* ignorant, fr. *nescire* not to know] **1** **:** FASTIDIOUS, DISCRIMINATING **2** **:** marked by delicate discrimination or treatment **3** **:** PLEASING, AGREEABLE; *also* **:** well-executed **4** **:** WELL-BRED ⟨~ people⟩ **5** **:** VIRTUOUS, RESPECTABLE — **nice·ly** *adv* — **nice·ness** *n*

**nice–nel·ly** \'nīs-'nel-ē\ *adj, often cap 2d N* **1** **:** PRUDISH **2** **:** having the nature of or containing a euphemism — **nice nelly** *n, often cap 2d N* — **nice–nel·ly·ism** \-,iz-əm\ *n, often cap 2d N*

**nice·ty** \'nī-sət-ē\ *n, pl* **-ties** **1** **:** a dainty, delicate, or elegant thing ⟨enjoy the *niceties* of life⟩ **2** **:** a fine detail ⟨*niceties* of workmanship⟩ **3** **:** EXACTNESS, PRECISION, ACCURACY

**niche** \'nich\ *n* **1** **:** a recess (as for a statue) in a wall **2** **:** a place, work, or use for which a person or thing is best fitted

**¹nick** \'nik\ *n* **1** **:** a small groove **2** **:** CHIP ⟨a ~ in a cup⟩ **3** **:** the final critical moment ⟨in the ~ of time⟩

**²nick** *vb* **:** NOTCH, CHIP

**¹nick·el** *also* **nick·le** \'nik-əl\ *n* **1** **:** a hard silver-white metallic chemical element capable of a high polish and used in alloys **2** **:** the U.S. 5-cent piece made of copper and nickel; *also* **:** the Canadian 5-cent piece

**²nickel** *vb* **nick·eled** *or* **nick·elled; nick·el·ing** *or* **nick·el·ling** **:** to plate with nickel

**nick·el·ode·on** \,nik-ə-'lōd-ē-ən\ *n* **1** **:** a theater presenting entertainment for an admission price of five cents **2** **:** a coin-operated musical device

**nickel silver** *n* **:** a silver-white alloy of copper, zinc, and nickel

**nick·er** \'nik-ər\ *vb* **nick·ered; nick·er·ing** **:** NEIGH, WHINNY

**nick·name** \'nik-,nām\ *n* [ME *nekename* additional name, alter. (resulting from incorrect division of *an ekename*) of *ekename*, fr. *eke* addition + *name*] **1** **:** a usu. descriptive name given instead of or in addition to the one belonging to a person, place, or thing **2** **:** a familiar form of a proper name — **nickname** *vb*

**nic·o·tine** \'nik-ə-,tēn\ *n* **:** a poisonous substance found in tobacco and used as an insecticide

**nic·o·tin·ic** \,nik-ə-'tē-nik, -'tin-ik\ *adj* **:** of or relating to nicotine or nicotinic acid

**nicotinic acid** *n* **:** an organic acid of the vitamin B complex found in plants and animals and used against pellagra

**niece** \'nēs\ *n* **:** a daughter of one's brother, sister, brother-in-law, or sister-in-law

**nif·ty** \'nif-tē\ *adj* **nif·ti·er; -est** **:** FINE, SWELL

**Ni·ge·ri·an** \nī-'jir-ē-ən\ *n* **:** a native or inhabitant of Nigeria — **Nigerian** *adj*

**Ni·ge·rois** \,nē-zhər-'wä\ *n, pl* **Nigerois** **:** a native or inhabitant of the Republic of Niger

**nig·gard** \'nig-ərd\ *n* **:** a stingy person **:** MISER — **nig·gard·li·ness** \-lē-nəs\ *n* — **nig·gard·ly** *adv*

**nig·gling** \'nig-(ə-)liŋ\ *adj* **1** **:** PETTY **2** **:** demanding meticulous care

**¹nigh** \'nī\ *adv* **1** **:** near in place, time, or relationship **2** **:** NEARLY, ALMOST

**²nigh** *adj* **:** CLOSE, NEAR

**³nigh** *prep* **:** NEAR

**night** \'nīt\ *n* **1** **:** the period between dusk and dawn **2** **:** NIGHTFALL **3** **:** the darkness of night **4** **:** a period of misery or unhappiness — **night** *adj*

**night blindness** *n* **:** reduced visual capacity in faint light (as at night)

**night·cap** \'nīt-,kap\ *n* **1** **:** a cloth cap worn with nightclothes **2** **:** a usu. alcoholic drink taken at bedtime

**night·clothes** \-,klō(th)z\ *n pl* **:** garments worn in bed

**night·club** \-,kləb\ *n* **:** a place of entertainment open at night usu. serving food and liquor and providing music for dancing

**night crawler** *n* **:** EARTHWORM; *esp* **:** a large earthworm found on the soil surface at night

**night·dress** \'nīt-,dres\ *n* **:** NIGHTGOWN

**night·fall** \-,fȯl\ *n* : the coming of night

**night·gown** \-,gaùn\ *n* : a loose garment designed for wear in bed

**night·hawk** \-,hȯk\ *n* **1** : any of several birds related to and resembling the whippoorwill **2** : a person who habitually stays up late at night

**night·in·gale** \'nīt-ᵊn-,gāl, -iŋ-\ *n* [ME, fr. OE *nihtegale*, fr. *niht* night + *galan* to sing] : any of several Old World thrushes noted for the sweet nocturnal song of the male

**night·life** \'nīt-,līf\ *n* : the activity of pleasure-seekers at night

**night·ly** \'nīt-lē\ *adj* **1** : of or relating to the night or every night **2** : happening, done, or produced by night or every night — **nightly** *adv*

**night·mare** \'nīt-,mar\ *n* **1** : a frightening oppressive dream or state occurring during sleep — **nightmare** *adj* — **night·mar·ish** \-,mar-ish\ *adj*

**night rider** *n* : a member of a secret band that ride masked at night doing acts of violence for the purpose of punishing or terrorizing

**night·shade** \'nīt-,shād\ *n* : any of a large group of woody or herbaceous plants having alternate leaves, flowers in clusters, and fruits that are berries and including poisonous forms (as belladonna) and important food plants (as potato, tomato, or eggplant)

**night·shirt** \-,shərt\ *n* : a nightgown esp. for a man or a boy

**night soil** *n* : human excrement collected for fertilizing the soil

**night·stick** \-,stik\ *n* : a policeman's club

**night·time** \-,tīm\ *n* : the time from dusk to dawn

**night·walk·er** \-,wȯ-kər\ *n* : a person who roves about at night esp. with criminal or immoral intent

**ni·gri·tude** \'nī-grə-,t(y)üd, 'nig-rə-\ *n* : intense darkness : BLACKNESS

**ni·hil·ism** \'nī-(h)ə-,liz-əm, 'nē-\ *n* **1** : an attitude or doctrine that traditional values and beliefs are unfounded and that existence is senseless and useless **2** : ANARCHISM **3** : TERRORISM — **ni·hil·ist** \-ləst\ *n or adj* — **ni·hil·is·tic** \,nī-(h)ə-'lis-tik, ,nē-\ *adj*

**nil** \'nil\ *n* : NOTHING, ZERO

**nim·ble** \'nim-bəl\ *adj* **nim·bler** \-b(ə-)lər\; **nim·blest** \-b(ə-)ləst\ [ME *nimel*, fr. OE *numol* holding much, fr. *niman* to take] **1** : quick and light in motion : AGILE ⟨a ∼ dancer⟩ **2** : quick in understanding and learning : CLEVER ⟨a ∼ mind⟩ — **nim·ble·ness** *n* — **nim·bly** \-blē\ *adv*

**nim·bus** \'nim-bəs\ *n, pl* **nim·bi** \-,bī, -bē\ *or* **nim·bus·es** \-əz\ **1** : a figure (as a disk) suggesting radiant light about the head of a drawn or sculptured divinity, saint, or sovereign **2** : a rain cloud of uniform grayness and extends over the entire sky **3** : a cloud from which rain is falling

**nim·rod** \'nim-,räd\ *n* : HUNTER

**nin·com·poop** \'nin-kəm-,püp\ *n* : FOOL, SIMPLETON

**nine** \'nīn\ *n* **1** : one more than eight **2** : the 9th in a set or series **3** : something having nine units; *esp* : a baseball team — **nine** *adj or pron* — **ninth** \'nīnth\ *adj or adv or n*

**nine days' wonder** *n* : something that creates a short-lived sensation

**nine·pins** \'nīn-,pinz\ *n* : tenpins played without the headpin

**nine·teen** \'nīn-'tēn\ *n* : one more than 18 · **nineteen** *adj or pron* — **nine·teenth** \-'tēnth\ *adj or n*

**nine·ty** \'nīnt-ē\ *n, pl* **nineties** : nine times 10 — **nine·ti·eth** \-ē-əth\ *adj or n* – **ninety** *adj or pron*

**nin·ny** \'nin-ē\ *n, pl* **ninnies** : FOOL

**nin·ny·ham·mer** \-,ham-ər\ *n* : NINNY

**ni·o·bi·um** \nī-'ō-bē-əm\ *n* : a gray metallic chemical element used in alloys

**¹nip** \'nip\ *vb* **nipped**; **nip·ping 1** : to catch hold of and squeeze tightly between two surfaces, edges, or points **2** : CLIP **3** : to destroy the growth, progress, or fulfillment of ⟨*nipped* in the bud⟩ **4** : to injure or make numb with cold : CHILL **5** : SNATCH, STEAL

**²nip** *n* **1** : a sharp stinging cold **2** : a biting or pungent flavor **3** : PINCH, BITE **4** : a small portion : BIT

**³nip** *n* : a small quantity of liquor : SIP

**⁴nip** *vb* **nipped**; **nip·ping** : to take liquor in nips : TIPPLE

**nip and tuck** \,nip-ən-'tək\ *adj or adv* : so close that the lead shifts rapidly from one contestant to another

**nip·per** \'nip-ər\ *n* **1** : one that nips **2** *pl* : PINCERS **3** : CHELA **4** : a small boy

**nip·ple** \'nip-əl\ *n* : the protuberance of a mammary gland through which milk is drawn off : TEAT; *also* : something resembling a nipple

**nip·py** \'nip-ē\ *adj* **nip·pi·er; -est 1** : PUNGENT, SHARP **2** : CHILLY

**nir·va·na** \nir-'vän-ə\ *n, often cap* [Skt *nirvāṇa*, lit., act of extinguishing, fr. *nis-* out + *vāti* it blows] **1** : the final freeing of a soul from all that enslaves it; *esp* : the supreme happiness that according to Buddhism comes when all passion, hatred, and delusion die out and the soul is released from the necessity of further purification **2** : OBLIVION, PARADISE

**ni·sei** \nē-'sā\ *n, pl* **nisei** *also* **niseis** : a son or daughter of immigrant Japanese parents who is born and educated in America

**ni·si** \'nī-,sī\ *adj* [L, unless, fr. *ne-* not + *si* if] : taking effect at a specified time unless previously modified or voided ⟨a divorce decree ∼⟩

**nit** \'nit\ *n* : the egg of a parasitic insect (as a louse); *also* : the young insect

**ni·ter** *also* **ni·tre** \'nīt-ər\ *n* **1** : POTASSIUM NITRATE **2** : SODIUM NITRATE

**nit·pick·ing** \'nit-,pik-iŋ\ *n* : minute and usu. unjustified criticism — **nit·pick·er** \-ər\ *n*

**¹ni·trate** \'nī-,trāt, -trət\ *n* **1** : a salt or ester of nitric acid **2** : sodium nitrate or potassium nitrate used as a fertilizer

**²ni·trate** \-,trāt\ *vb* **ni·trat·ed; ni·trat·ing** : to treat or combine with nitric acid or a nitrate — **ni·tra·tion**

\nī-'trā-shən\ *n* — **ni·tra·tor** \'nī-
,trāt-ər\ *n*

**ni·tric** \'nī-trik\ *adj* : of, relating to,
or containing nitrogen

**nitric acid** *n* : a corrosive liquid used
in making dyes, explosives, and fertilizers

**ni·tri·fi·ca·tion** \,nī-trə-fə-'kā-shən\
*n* : the process of nitrifying; *esp* : the
oxidation (as by bacteria) of ammonium
salts to nitrites and then to nitrates

**ni·tri·fy** \'nī-trə-,fī\ *vb* **-fied; -fy·ing**
**1** : to combine with nitrogen or a
nitrogen compound  **2** : to subject to
or produce by nitrification

**ni·trite** \'nī-,trīt\ *n* : a salt or ester of
nitrous acid

**ni·tro** \'nī-trō\ *n, pl* **nitros** : any of
various nitrated products; *esp* : NITRO-
GLYCERIN

**ni·tro·cel·lu·lose** \nī-trō-'sel-yə-lōs\
*n* : GUNCOTTON — **ni·tro·cel·lu·los-
ic** \-,sel-yə-'lō-sik\ *adj*

**ni·tro·gen** \'nī-trə-jən\ *n* : a tasteless
odorless gaseous chemical element constituting 78 percent of the atmosphere
by volume — **ni·trog·e·nous** \nī-
'träj-ə-nəs\ *adj* — **ni·trous** \'nī-trəs\
*adj*

**ni·tro·glyc·er·in** or **ni·tro·glyc·er-
ine** \,nī-trə-'glis-(ə-)rən\ *n* : a heavy
oily explosive liquid used in making
dynamite and in medicine

**nitrous acid** *n* : an unstable nitrogen=
containing acid known only in solution
or in the form of its salts

**nitrous oxide** *n* : a colorless gas used
esp. as an anesthetic in dentistry

**nit·ty-grit·ty** \'nit-ē-,grit-ē, ,nit-ē-
'grit-ē\ *n* : the actual state of things
: what is ultimately essential and true

**nit·wit** \'nit-,wit\ *n* : a flighty stupid
person

**¹nix** \'niks\ *n, slang* : NOTHING

**²nix** *adv, slang* : NO

**³nix** *vb, slang* : VETO, FORBID

**NJ** *abbr* New Jersey

**NL** *abbr* **1** New Latin **2** [L *non licet*] it
is not permitted

**NLRB** *abbr* National Labor Relations
Board

**NM** *abbr* **1** nautical mile **2** New Mexico
**3** night message **4** no mark; not marked

**N Mex** *abbr* New Mexico

**NNE** *abbr* north-northeast

**NNW** *abbr* north-northwest

**¹no** \(')nō\ *adv* **1** — used to express the
negative of an alternative choice or
possibility ⟨shall we continue or ~⟩
**2** : in no respect or degree ⟨he is ~
better than the others⟩  **3** : not so
⟨~, I'm not ready⟩  **4** — used with a
following adjective to imply a meaning
expressed by the opposite positive statement ⟨in ~ uncertain terms⟩  **5** — used
to emphasize a following negative or to
introduce a more emphatic or explicit
statement ⟨has the right, ~, the duty to
continue⟩  **6** — used as an interjection
to express surprise or doubt ⟨~ — you
don't say⟩

**²no** *adj* **1** : not any; *also* : hardly any
**2** : not a ⟨he's a ~ expert⟩

**³no** \'nō\ *n, pl* **noes** or **nos** \'nōz\

**1** : REFUSAL, DENIAL  **2** : a negative
vote or decision; *also, pl* : persons voting in the negative

**⁴no** *abbr* **1** north **2** [L *numero*, abl. of
*numerus*] number

**¹No** or **Noh** \'nō\ *n, pl* **No** or **Noh**
: classic Japanese dance-drama having
a heroic theme, a chorus, and highly
stylized action, costuming, and scenery

**²No** *symbol* nobelium

**No·bel·ist** \nō-'bel-əst\ *n* : a winner of
a Nobel prize

**no·bel·i·um** \nō-'bel-ē-əm\ *n* : a
radioactive chemical element produced
artificially

**Nobel prize** \(,)nō-,bel-\ *n* : any of
various annual prizes (as in peace, literature, or medicine) established by the
will of Alfred Nobel for the encouragement of persons who work for the
interests of humanity

**no·bil·i·ty** \nō-'bil-ət-ē\ *n* **1** : NOBLE-
NESS ⟨~ of character⟩  **2** : noble rank
**3** : nobles considered as forming a class

**¹no·ble** \'nō-bəl\ *adj* **no·bler**
\-b(ə-)lər\; **no·blest** \-b(ə-)ləst\
[ME, fr. OF, fr. L *nobilis* knowable,
well known, noble, fr. *noscere* to come
to know]  **1** : ILLUSTRIOUS; *also* : FA-
MOUS, NOTABLE  **2** : of high birth, rank,
or station : ARISTOCRATIC  **3** : EXCELLENT
**4** : STATELY, IMPOSING ⟨a ~ edifice⟩  **5**
: of a magnanimous nature — **no·ble-
ness** *n* — **no·bly** \-blē\ *adv*

**²no·ble** *n* : a person of noble rank or
birth

**no·ble·man** \'nō-bəl-mən\ *n* : a member of the nobility : PEER

**no·blesse oblige** \nō-,bles-ə-'blēzh\
*n* : the obligation of honorable, generous, and responsible behavior associated with high rank or birth

**¹no·body** \'nō-,bäd-ē, -,bäd-ē\ *pron* : no
person

**²nobody** *n, pl* **no·bod·ies** : a person of
no influence, importance, or worth

**noc·tur·nal** \näk-'tərn-²l\ *adj* **1** : of,
relating to, or occurring in the night  **2**
: active at night ⟨a ~ bird⟩

**noc·turne** \'näk-,tərn\ *n* : a work of
art dealing with night; *esp* : a dreamy
pensive instrumental composition

**noc·u·ous** \'näk-yə-wəs\ *adj* : likely
to cause injury : HARMFUL

**nod** \'näd\ *vb* **nod·ded; nod·ding**
**1** : to bend the head downward or forward (as in bowing or going to sleep or
as a sign of assent)  **2** : to move up and
down ⟨the tulips nodded in the breeze⟩
**3** : to show by a nod of the head ⟨~
agreement⟩  **4** : to make a slip or error
in a moment of abstraction — **nod** *n*

**nod·dle** \'näd-²l\ *n* : HEAD

**nod·dy** \'näd-ē\ *n, pl* **noddies 1**
: SIMPLETON  **2** : a stout-bodied tropical tern

**node** \'nōd\ *n* **1** : a thickened, swollen, or differentiated area (as of tissue);
*esp* : the part of a stem from which a
leaf arises  **2** : an area of a vibrating
body that is free from vibrating motion
— **nod·al** \-²l\ *adj*

**nod·ule** \'näj-ül\ *n* : a small lump or
swelling — **nod·u·lar** \'näj-ə-lər\ *adj*

**no·el** \nō-'el\ n **1 :** a Christmas carol **2** cap **:** the Christmas season

**noes** pl of NO

**no–fault** adj **:** of, relating to, or being a motor vehicle insurance plan under which an accident victim is compensated usu. up to a stipulated limit for actual losses by his own insurance company regardless of who is responsible

**nog·gin** \'näg-ən\ n **1 :** a small mug or cup; also **:** a small quantity of drink usu. equivalent to a gill **2 :** a person's head

**no–good** \,nō-,gùd\ adj **:** having no worth, use, or chance of success — **no–good** \'nō-,gùd\ n

**Noh** var of NO

**no–hit·ter** \(')nō-'hit-ər\ n **:** a baseball game or a part of a game in which a pitcher allows the opposition no base hits

**no·how** \'nō-,haù\ adv **:** in no manner

**¹noise** \'nòiz\ n [ME, fr. OF, strife, quarrel, noise, fr. L nausea nausea] **1 :** loud, confused, or senseless shouting or outcry **2 :** SOUND; esp **:** one that lacks agreeable musical quality or is noticeably unpleasant **3 :** unwanted electronic signal or disturbance — **noise·less** adj – **noise·less·ly** adv

**²noise** vb **noised; nois·ing :** to spread by rumor or report ⟨the story was noised abroad⟩

**noise·mak·er** \'nòiz-,mā-kər\ n **:** one that makes noise; esp **:** a device used to make noise at parties

**noise pollution** n **:** environmental pollution consisting of annoying or harmful noise

**noi·some** \'nòi-səm\ adj **1 :** HARMFUL, UNWHOLESOME **2 :** offensive to the senses (as smell) **:** DISGUSTING

**noisy** \'nòi-zē\ adj **nois·i·er; -est :** making loud noises **2 :** full of noises **:** LOUD — **nois·i·ly** \'nòi-zə-lē\ adv — **nois·i·ness** \-zē-nəs\ n

**nol·le pro·se·qui** \,näl-ē-'präs-ə-,kwī\ n [L, to be unwilling to pursue] **:** an entry on the record of a legal action denoting that the prosecutor or plaintiff will proceed no further in his action or suit either as a whole or as to some count or as to one or more of several defendants

**no·lo con·ten·de·re** \,nō-lō-kən-'ten-də-rē\ n [L, I do not wish to contend] **:** a plea by the defendant in a criminal prosecution that without admitting guilt subjects him to conviction but does not preclude him from denying the charges in another proceeding

**nol–pros** \'näl-'präs\ vb **nol–prossed; nol–pros·sing :** to discontinue by entering a nolle prosequi

**nom** abbr nominative

**no·mad** \'nō-,mad\ n **1 :** one of a people that has no fixed location but wanders from place to place **2 :** an individual who roams about aimlessly — **nomad** adj

**no·mad·ic** \nō-'mad-ik\ adj **:** of, relating to, or suggestive of nomads

**no–man's–land** \'nō-,manz-,land\ n **1 :** an area of unowned, unclaimed, or uninhabited land **2 :** an unoccupied area between opposing troops

**nom de guerre** \,näm-di-'geər\ n, pl **noms de guerre** \,näm(z)-di-\ [F, lit., war name] **:** PSEUDONYM

**nom de plume** \-'plüm\ n, pl **noms de plume** \,näm(z)-di-\ [F nom name + de of + plume pen] **:** PSEUDONYM

**no·men·cla·ture** \'nō-mən-,klā-chər\ n **1 :** NAME, DESIGNATION **2 :** a system of names used in a science or art

**nom·i·nal** \'näm-ən-ˀl\ adj **1 :** being something in name or form only ⟨~ head of a party⟩ **2 :** TRIFLING ⟨a ~ price⟩ — **nom·i·nal·ly** \-ē\ adv

**nom·i·nate** \'näm-ə-,nāt\ vb **-nat·ed; -nat·ing :** to choose as a candidate for election, appointment, or honor — **nom·i·na·tion** \,näm-ə-'nā-shən\ n

**nom·i·na·tive** \'näm-(ə-)nət-iv\ adj **:** of, relating to, or constituting a grammatical case marking typically the subject of a verb — **nominative** n

**nom·i·nee** \,näm-ə-'nē\ n **:** a person nominated for an office, duty, or position

**non-** \(')nän, ,nän\ prefix **:** not **:** reverse of **:** absence of

nonabrasive
nonabsorbent
nonacademic
nonacceptance
nonacid
nonactive
nonadaptive
nonaddictive
nonadherence
nonadhesive
nonadjacent
nonadjustable
nonadministra-
tive
nonaggression
nonalcoholic
nonaligned
nonappearance
nonaromatic
nonathletic
nonattendance
nonattributive
nonbeliever
nonbelligerent
nonbreakable
nonburning
noncancerous
noncandidate
noncellular
nonchargeable
nonclerical
noncoital
noncollapsible
noncombat
noncombusti-
ble
noncommercial
noncommuni-
cable
non–Commu-
nist
noncompeting
noncompetitive
noncompliance
noncomplying
nonconcur-
rence
nonconcurrent
nonconducting
nonconflicting
nonconfor-
mance
nonconforming
nonconstruc-
tive
noncontagious
noncontinuous
noncontraband
noncontribut-
ing
noncorroding
noncorrosive
noncrystalline
nondeductible
nondefense
nondelivery
nondemocratic
nondenomi-
national
nondepart-
mental
nondevelop-
ment
nondiscrimina-
tion
nondistinctive
nondistribution
nondivided
nondrying
nondurable
noneducational
nonelastic
nonelection
nonelective
nonelectric
nonemotional
nonenforceable
nonenforce-
ment
nonessential

nonethical
nonexchange-
able
nonexempt
nonexistence
nonexistent
nonexplosive
nonfarm
nonfattening
nonfederated
nonferrous
nonfiction
nonfictional
nonfilament-
ous
nonfilterable
nonflammable
nonflowering
nonfreezing
nonfulfillment
nonfunctional
nongraded
nonhereditary
nonhomogene-
ous
nonhomolog-
ous
nonhuman
nonidentical
nonimportation
nonindustrial
noninfectious
noninflamma-
ble
nonintellectu-
al
nonintercourse
noninterfer-
ence
nonintoxicant
nonintoxicating
nonionized
nonirritating
nonlegal
nonlife
nonlinear
nonliterary
nonliving
nonlogical
nonmagnetic
nonmalignant
nonmarketable
nonmaterial
nonmember
nonmember-
ship
nonmigratory
nonmilitary
nonmoral
nonmotile
nonmoving
nonnegotiable
nonobservance
nonoccurrence
nonofficial
nonoily
nonorthodox
nonparallel
nonparasitic
nonparticipant
nonparticipat-
ing
nonpathogenic
nonpaying

nonpayment
nonperform-
ance
nonperishable
nonpermanent
nonphysical
nonpoisonous
nonpolar
nonpolitical
nonporous
nonproductive
nonprofession-
al
nonprotein
nonradioactive
nonrandom
nonreactive
nonreciprocal
nonrecognition
nonrecoverable
nonrecurrent
nonrecurring
nonrefillable
nonreligious
nonremovable
nonrenewable
nonresidential
nonrestricted
nonreturnable
nonreversible
nonruminant
nonsalable
nonscientific
nonscientist
nonseasonal
nonsectarian
nonsegregated
nonselective
non-self-
governing
nonsexual
nonshrinkable
nonsignificant
nonsinkable
nonskid
nonslip
nonsmoker
nonsocial
nonspeaking
nonspecialized
nonsporting
nonstaining
nonstandard
nonstriated
nonstriker
nonsubscriber
nonsuccess
nonsurgical
nonsustaining
nontaxable
nonteaching
nontechnical
nontemporal
nontenured
nontheistic
nontoxic
nontransfera-
ble
nontranspar-
ency
nontransparent
nontypical
nonuniform
nonuser

nonvascular
nonvenomous
nonviable
nonviolation
nonvirulent
nonvocal
nonvolatile

**non·age** \'nän-ij, 'nō-nij\ *n* **1** : legal minority **2** : a period of youth **3** : IM-MATURITY

**no·na·ge·nar·i·an** \,nō-nə-jə-'ner-ē-ən, ,nän-ə-\ *n* : a person who is in his nineties

**non·book** \'nän-,bůk\ *n* : a book of little literary merit which is often a compilation (as of press clippings)

¹**nonce** \'näns\ *n* : the one, particular, or present occasion or purpose ⟨for the ∼⟩

²**nonce** *adj* : occurring, used, or made only once or for a special occasion ⟨a ∼ word⟩

**non·cha·lant** \,nän-shə-'länt\ *adj* [F, fr. OF, fr. prp. of *nonchaloir* to disregard, fr. *non-* not + *chaloir* to concern, fr. L *calēre* to be warm] : giving an effect of unconcern or indifference — **non·cha·lance** \-'läns\ *n* — **non·cha·lant·ly** *adv*

**non·com** \'nän-,käm\ *n* : NONCOM-MISSIONED OFFICER

**non·com·ba·tant** \,nän-kəm-'bat-ᵊnt, nän-'käm-bət-ənt\ *n* : a member (as a chaplain) of the armed forces whose duties do not include fighting; *also* : CI-VILIAN — **noncombatant** *adj*

**non·com·mis·sioned officer** \,nän-kə-,mish-ənd-\ *n* : a subordinate officer in a branch of the armed forces appointed from enlisted personnel and holding one of various grades (as staff sergeant)

**non·com·mit·tal** \,nän-kə-'mit-ᵊl\ *adj* : indicating neither consent nor dissent

**non com·pos men·tis** \,nän-,käm-pəs-'ment-əs\ *adj* : not of sound mind

**non·con·duc·tor** \,nän-kən-'dək-tər\ *n* : a substance that is a very poor conductor of heat, electricity, or sound

**non·con·form·ist** \-'fȯr-məst\ *n* **1** *often cap* : a person who does not conform to an established church and esp. the Church of England **2** : a person who does not conform to a generally accepted pattern of thought or action — **non·con·for·mi·ty** \-'fȯr-mət-ē\ *n*

**non·co·op·er·a·tion** \,nän-kō-,äp-ə-'rā-shən\ *n* : failure or refusal to cooperate; *esp* : refusal through civil disobedience of a people to cooperate with the government of a country

**non·cred·it** \(')nän-'kred-ət\ *adj* : not offering credit toward a degree

**non·dairy** \'nän-'de(ə)r-ē\ *adj* : containing no milk or milk products

**non·de·script** \,nän-di-'skript\ *adj* : not belonging to any particular class or kind : not easily described

**non·drink·er** \-'driŋ-kər\ *n* : one who abstains from alcoholic beverages

¹**none** \'nən\ *pron* **1** : not any ⟨∼ of them went⟩ **2** : not one ⟨∼ of the family⟩ **3** : not any such thing or person ⟨half a loaf is better than ∼⟩

**²none** *adj, archaic* **:** not any **:** NO

**³none** *adv* **:** by no means **:** not at all 〈he got there ~ too soon〉

**non·en·ti·ty** \nä-'nent-ət-ē\ *n* **1 :** something that does not exist or exists only in the imagination **2 :** one of no consequence or significance

**nones** \'nōnz\ *n sing or pl* **:** the 7th day of March, May, July, or October or the 5th day of any other month in the ancient Roman calendar

**none·such** \'nən-ˌsəch\ *n* **:** one without an equal — **nonesuch** *adj*

**none·the·less** \ˌnən-thə-'les\ *adv* **:** NEVERTHELESS

**non·eu·clid·e·an** \ˌnän-yü-'klid-ē-ən\ *adj, often cap E* **:** not assuming or in accordance with the postulates of Euclid's *Elements* 〈~ geometry〉

**non·event** \'nän-i-ˌvent\ *n* **:** an event that fails to take place or to satisfy expectations **:** an event of little or no consequence

**non·fat** \'nän-'fat\ *adj* **:** lacking fat solids **:** having fat solids removed 〈~ milk〉

**non·he·ro** \-'hē-rō\ *n* **:** ANTI-HERO

**non·in·ter·ven·tion** \ˌnän-ˌint-ər-'ven-chən\ *n* **:** refusal or failure to intervene (as in the affairs of another state)

**non·met·al** \'nän-'met-ᵊl\ *n* **:** a chemical element (as carbon, phosphorus nitrogen, or oxygen) that lacks metallic properties — **non·me·tal·lic** \ˌnän-mə-'tal-ik\ *adj*

**non·neg·a·tive** \-'neg-ət-iv\ *adj* **:** not negative **:** being either positive or zero

**non·ob·jec·tive** \ˌnän-əb-'jek-tiv\ *adj* **1 :** not objective **2 :** representing no natural or actual object, figure, or scene 〈~ art〉

**¹non·pa·reil** \ˌnän-pə-'rel\ *adj* **:** having no equal **:** PEERLESS

**²nonpareil** *n* **1 :** an individual of unequaled excellence **:** PARAGON **2 :** a small flat disk of chocolate covered with white sugar pellets

**non·par·ti·san** \'nän-'pärt-ə-zən\ *adj* **:** not partisan; *esp* **:** not influenced by political party spirit or interests

**non·per·son** \'nän-'pərs-ᵊn\ *n* **1 :** a person who is regarded as nonexistent or as never having existed **2 :** UN-PERSON

**non·plus** \'nän-'pləs\ *vb* **-plussed** *also* **-plused** \-'pləst\; **-plus·sing** *also* **-plus·ing :** PUZZLE, PERPLEX

**non·pre·scrip·tion** \ˌnän-pri-'skrip-shən\ *adj* **:** available for sale legally without a doctor's prescription

**non·prof·it** \'nän-'präf-ət\ *adj* **:** not conducted or maintained for the purpose of making a profit

**non·pro·lif·er·a·tion** \ˌnän-prə-ˌlif-ə-'rā-shən\ *adj* **:** providing for the stoppage of proliferation (as of nuclear arms) 〈a ~ treaty〉

**non·read·er** \'nän-'rēd-ər\ *n* **:** one who does not read; *esp* **:** a child who is very slow in learning to read

**non·rep·re·sen·ta·tion·al** \ˌnän-ˌrep-ri-ˌzen-'tā-sh(ə-)nəl\ *adj* **:** NON-OBJECTIVE 2

**non·res·i·dent** \'nän-'rez-əd-ənt\ *adj* **:** not living in a particular place — **non·res·i·dence** \-əd-əns\ *n* — **nonresident** *n*

**non·re·sis·tance** \ˌnän-ri-'zis-təns\ *n* **:** the principles or practice of passive submission to authority even when unjust or oppressive

**non·re·stric·tive** \ˌnän-ri-'strik-tiv\ *adj* **1 :** not serving or tending to restrict **2 :** not limiting the reference of the word or phrase modified 〈a ~ clause〉

**non·rig·id** \ˌnän-'rij-əd\ *adj* **:** maintaining form by pressure of contained gas 〈a ~ airship〉 — **non·ri·gid·i·ty** \ˌnän-rə-'jid-ət-ē\ *n*

**non·sched·uled** \'nän-'skej-üld\ *adj* **:** licensed to carry passengers or freight by air without a regular schedule

**non·sense** \'nän-ˌsens, -səns\ *n* **1 :** foolish or meaningless words or actions **2 :** things of no importance or value **:** TRIFLES — **non·sen·si·cal** \nän-'sen-si-kəl\ *adj* — **non·sen·si·cal·ly** \-k(ə-)lē\ *adv*

**non seq** *abbr* non sequitur

**non se·qui·tur** \nän-'sek-wət-ər\ *n* [L, it does not follow] **:** an inference that does not follow from the premises

**non·sked** \'nän-'sked\ *n* **:** a nonscheduled airline or transport plane

**non·start·er** \-'stärt-ər\ *n* **:** one that does not start or gets off to a poor start

**non·stick** \'nän-'stik\ *adj* **:** allowing of easy removal of food particles

**non·stop** \'nän-'stäp\ *adj* **:** done or made without a stop — **nonstop** *adv*

**non·sup·port** \ˌnän-sə-'pōrt\ *n* **:** failure to support; *esp* **:** failure on the part of one under obligation to provide maintenance

**non trop·po** \'nän-'trò-pō\ *adv or adj* **:** not too much so **:** moderately so — used as a direction in music

**non-U** \'nän-'yü\ *adj* **:** not characteristic of the upper classes

**non·union** \'nän-'yü-nyən\ *adj* **1 :** not belonging to a trade union 〈~ carpenters〉 **2 :** not recognizing or favoring trade unions or their members 〈~ employers〉

**non·us·er** \-'yü-zər\ *n* **:** one who does not make use of something (as drugs)

**non·vi·o·lence** \'nän-'vī-ə-ləns\ *n* **1 :** abstention from violence as a matter of principle **2 :** avoidance of violence **3 :** nonviolent political demonstrations — **non·vi·o·lent** \-lənt\ *adj*

**noo·dle** \'nüd-ᵊl\ *n* **:** a food paste made with egg and shaped typically in ribbon form

**nook** \'nuk\ *n* **1 :** an interior angle or corner formed usu. by two walls 〈a chimney ~〉 **2 :** a sheltered or hidden place 〈a shady ~〉

**noon** \'nün\ *n* **:** the middle of the day **:** 12 o'clock in the daytime — **noon** *adj*

**noon·day** \-ˌdā\ *n* **:** NOON, MIDDAY

**no one** *pron* **:** NOBODY

**noon·tide** \'nün-ˌtīd\ *n* **:** NOON

**noon·time** \-ˌtīm\ *n* **:** NOON

**noose** \'nüs\ *n* **:** a loop with a running knot (as in a lasso) that binds closer the more it is drawn

**no-par** or **no-par-val-ue** adj : having no nominal value ⟨~ stock⟩

**nope** \'nōp\ adv : NO

**nor** \nər, (')nȯr\ conj : and not ⟨not for you ~ for me⟩ — used esp. to introduce and negate the second member and each later member of a series of items preceded by neither ⟨neither here ~ there⟩

**Nor** abbr Norway, Norwegian

**Nor-dic** \'nȯrd-ik\ adj 1 : of or relating to the Germanic peoples of northern Europe and esp. of Scandinavia 2 : of or relating to a physical type characterized by tall stature, long head, light skin and hair, and blue eyes — **Nordic** n

**norm** \'nȯrm\ n [L norma, lit., carpenter's square] : AVERAGE, esp : a set standard of development or achievement usu. derived from the average or median achievement of a large group

¹**nor-mal** \'nȯr-məl\ adj 1 : REGULAR, STANDARD, NATURAL 2 : of average intelligence; also : sound in mind and body — **nor-mal-cy** \-sē\ n — **nor-mal-i-ty** \nȯr-'mal-ət-ē\ n — **nor-mal-ly** \'nȯr-mə-lē\ adv

²**normal** n 1 : one that is normal 2 : the usual condition, level, or quantity

**nor-mal-ize** \'nȯr-mə-,līz\ vb -ized; -iz-ing : to make normal or average — **nor-mal-iza-tion** \,nȯr-mə-lə-'zā-shən\ n

**normal school** n : a usu. 2-year school for training chiefly elementary teachers

**Nor-man** \'nȯr-mən\ n 1 : a native or inhabitant of Normandy 2 : one of the 10th century Scandinavian conquerors of Normandy 3 : one of the Norman-French conquerors of England in 1066 — **Norman** adj

**nor-ma-tive** \'nȯr-mət-iv\ adj : of, relating to, or prescribing norms — **nor-ma-tive-ly** adv — **nor-ma-tive-ness** n

**Norse** \'nȯrs\ n, pl **Norse** 1 pl : SCANDINAVIANS; also : NORWEGIANS 2 : NORWEGIAN; also : any of the western Scandinavian dialects or languages

**Norse-man** \-mən\ n : one of the ancient Scandinavians

¹**north** \'nȯrth\ adv : to or toward the north

²**north** adj 1 : situated toward or at the north 2 : coming from the north

³**north** n 1 : the direction to the left of one facing east 2 : the compass point directly opposite to south 3 cap : regions or countries north of a specified or implied point — **north-er-ly** \'nȯrth-ər-lē\ adv or adj — **north-ern** \-ərn\ adj — **North-ern-er** \-ə(r)n-ər\ n — **north-ern-most** \-ərn-,mōst\ adj — **north-ward** \'nȯrth-wərd\ adv or adj — **north-wards** \-wərdz\ adv

**north-east** \nȯrth-'ēst\ n 1 : the general direction between north and east 2 : the compass point midway between north and east 3 cap : regions or countries northeast of a specified or implied point — **northeast** adj or adv — **north-east-er-ly** \-ər-lē\ adv or adj — **north-east-ern** \-ərn\ adj

**north-east-er** \-ər\ n 1 : a strong northeast wind 2 : a storm with northeast winds

**north-er** \'nȯr-thər\ n 1 : a strong north wind 2 : a storm with north winds

**northern lights** n pl : AURORA BOREALIS

**north pole** n, often cap N&P : the northernmost point of the earth

**North Star** n : the star toward which the northern end of the earth's axis points

**north-west** \nȯrth-'west\ n 1 : the general direction between north and west 2 : the compass point midway between north and west 3 cap : regions or countries northwest of a specified or implied point — **northwest** adj or adv — **north-west-er-ly** \-ər-lē\ adv or adj — **north-west-ern** \-ərn\ adj

**Norw** abbr Norway, Norwegian

**Nor-we-gian** \nȯr-'wē-jən\ n 1 : a native or inhabitant of Norway 2 : the language of Norway — **Norwegian** adj

**nos** abbr numbers

**NOS** abbr not otherwise specified

¹**nose** \'nōz\ n 1 : the part of the face containing the nostrils and covering the front of the nasal cavity 2 : the organ or sense of smell 3 : something (as a point, edge, or projecting front part) that resembles a nose ⟨the ~ of a plane⟩ — **nosed** \'nōzd\ adj

²**nose** vb **nosed**; **nos-ing** 1 : to detect by or as if by smell : SCENT 2 : to push or move with the nose 3 : to touch or rub with the nose : NUZZLE 4 : to defeat by a narrow margin in a contest ⟨nosed out his opponent⟩ 5 : PRY 6 : to move ahead slowly ⟨the ship nosed into her berth⟩

**nose-bleed** \-,blēd\ n : a bleeding from the nose

**nose cone** n : a protective cone constituting the forward end of a rocket or missile

**nose dive** n 1 : a downward nose-first plunge (as of an airplane) 2 : a sudden extreme drop (as in prices)

**nose-gay** \'nōz-,gā\ n : a small bunch of flowers : POSY

**nose-piece** \-,pēs\ n 1 : a piece of armor for protecting the nose 2 : a fitting at the lower end of a microscope tube to which the objectives are attached 3 : the bridge of a pair of eyeglasses

**no-show** \'nō-'shō\ n : a person who reserves space esp. on an airplane but neither uses nor cancels the reservation

**nos-tal-gia** \nä-'stal-jə, nə-\ n [NL, fr. Gk nostos return home + algos pain, grief] 1 : HOMESICKNESS 2 : a wistful yearning for something past or irrecoverable — **nos-tal-gic** \-jik\ adj

**nos-tril** \'näs-trəl\ n : an external naris usu. with the adjoining nasal wall and passage

**nos-trum** \'näs-trəm\ n [L, neut. of noster our, ours, fr. nos we] : a questionable medicine or remedy

**nosy** or **nos-ey** \'nō-zē\ adj **nos-i-er; -est** : INQUISITIVE, PRYING

**not** \\(')nät\\ *adv* **1** — used to make negative a group of words or a word ⟨the boys are ~ here⟩ **2** — used to stand for the negative of a preceding group of words ⟨sometimes hard to see and sometimes ~⟩

**no·ta be·ne** \\‚nōt-ə-'bē-nē, -'ben-ē\\ [L, mark well] — used to call attention to something important

**no·ta·bil·i·ty** \\‚nōt-ə-'bil-ət-ē\\ *n, pl* **-ties 1** : the quality or state of being notable **2** : NOTABLE

**¹no·ta·ble** \\'nōt-ə-bəl\\ *adj* **1** : NOTE-WORTHY, REMARKABLE ⟨a ~ achievement⟩ **2** : DISTINGUISHED, PROMINENT ⟨several ~ politicians had been invited⟩ — **no·ta·bly** \\-blē\\ *adv*

**²no·ta·ble** *n* : a person of note

**no·tar·i·al** \\nō-'ter-ē-əl\\ *adj* : of, relating to, or done by a notary public

**no·ta·rize** \\'nōt-ə-‚rīz\\ *vb* **-rized; -riz·ing** : to acknowledge or make legally authentic as a notary public

**no·ta·ry public** \\‚nōt-ə-rē-\\ *n, pl* **notaries public** *or* **notary publics** : a public official who attests or certifies writings (as deeds) to make them legally authentic

**no·ta·tion** \\nō-'tā-shən\\ *n* **1** : ANNO-TATION, NOTE **2** : the act, process, or method of representing data by marks, signs, figures, or characters; *also* : a system of symbols (as letters, numerals, or musical notes) used in such notation

**¹notch** \\'näch\\ *n* **1** : a V-shaped hollow in an edge or surface **2** : a narrow pass between two mountains

**²notch** *vb* **1** : to cut or make notches in **2** : to score or record by or as if by cutting a series of notches ⟨~ed 20 points for the team⟩

**notch·back** \\'näch-‚bak\\ *n* **1** : a back on a closed passenger automobile having a distinct deck as distinguished from a fastback **2** : an automobile having a notchback

**¹note** \\'nōt\\ *vb* **not·ed; not·ing 1** : to notice or observe with care; *also* : to record or preserve in writing **2** : to make special mention of : REMARK

**²note** *n* **1** : a musical sound **2** : a cry, call, or sound esp. of a bird **3** : a special tone in a person's words or voice ⟨a ~ of fear⟩ **4** : a character in music used to indicate duration of a tone by its shapes and pitch by its position on the staff **5** : a characteristic feature : MOOD, QUALITY ⟨a ~ of optimism⟩ **6** : MEMORANDUM **7** : a brief and informal record; *also* : a written or printed comment or explanation **8** : a written promise to pay a debt **9** : a piece of paper money **10** : a short informal letter **11** : a formal diplomatic or official communication **12** : DIS-TINCTION, REPUTATION ⟨a man of ~⟩ **13** : OBSERVATION, NOTICE, HEED ⟨take ~ of the exact time⟩

**note·book** \\'nōt-‚bùk\\ *n* : a book for notes or memoranda

**not·ed** \\'nōt-əd\\ *adj* : well known by reputation : EMINENT, CELEBRATED

**note·wor·thy** \\-‚wər-t͟hē\\ *adj* : worthy of note : REMARKABLE

**¹noth·ing** \\'nəth-iŋ\\ *pron* **1** : no thing ⟨leaves ~ to the imagination⟩ **2** : no part **3** : one of no interest, value, or importance ⟨she's ~ to me⟩

**²nothing** *adv* : not at all : in no degree ⟨~ daunted by his fall, he got up and continued the race⟩

**³nothing** *n* **1** : something that does not exist **2** : ZERO **3** : a person or thing of little or no value or importance

**⁴nothing** *adj* : of no account : worthless

**noth·ing·ness** \\-nəs\\ *n* **1** : the quality or state of being nothing **2** : NON-EXISTENCE; *also* : utter insignificance **3** : something insignificant or valueless

**¹no·tice** \\'nōt-əs\\ *n* **1** : WARNING, AN-NOUNCEMENT **2** : notification of the termination of an agreement or con-tract at a specified time **3** : ATTENTION, HEED ⟨brought the matter to my ~⟩ **4** : a written or printed announcement **5** : a short critical account or examina-tion (as of a play) : REVIEW

**²notice** *vb* **no·ticed; no·tic·ing 1** : to make mention of : remark on : NOTE **2** : to take notice of : OBSERVE, MARK

**no·tice·able** \\'nōt-ə-sə-bəl\\ *adj* **1** : worthy of notice **2** : capable of being or likely to be noticed — **no·tice·ably** \\-blē\\ *adv*

**no·ti·fy** \\'nōt-ə-‚fī\\ *vb* **-fied; -fy·ing 1** : to give notice of : report the occur-rence of **2** : to give notice to — **no·ti·fi·ca·tion** \\‚nōt-ə-fə-'kā-shən\\ *n*

**no·tion** \\'nō-shən\\ *n* **1** : IDEA, CON-CEPTION ⟨have a ~ of what he means⟩ **2** : a belief held : OPINION, VIEW **3** : WHIM, FANCY ⟨a sudden ~ to go⟩ **4** *pl* : small useful articles (as pins, needles, or thread).

**no·tion·al** \\'nō-sh(ə-)nəl\\ *adj* **1** : existing in the mind only : IMAGINARY, UNREAL **2** : given to foolish or fanciful moods or ideas : WHIMSICAL

**no·to·ri·ous** \\nō-'tōr-ē-əs\\ *adj* : gener-ally known and talked of; *esp* : widely and unfavorably known — **no·to·ri·ety** \\‚nōt-ə-'rī-ət-ē\\ *n* — **no·to·ri·ous·ly** \\nō-'tōr-ē-əs-lē\\ *adv*

**¹not·with·stand·ing** \\‚nät-with-'stan-diŋ, -with-\\ *prep* : in spite of

**²notwithstanding** *adv* : NEVERTHELESS

**³notwithstanding** *conj* : ALTHOUGH

**nou·gat** \\'nü-gət\\ *n* [F, fr. Provençal, fr. Old Provençal *nogat*, fr. *noga* nut, fr. L *nuc-, nux*] : a confection of nuts or fruit pieces in a sugar paste

**nought** \\'nòt, 'nät\\ *var of* NAUGHT

**noun** \\'naùn\\ *n* : a word that is the name of a subject of discourse (as a person or place)

**nour·ish** \\'nər-ish\\ *vb* : to cause to grow and develop (as by care and feed-ing)

**nour·ish·ing** \\-iŋ\\ *adj* : giving nour-ishment

**nour·ish·ment** \\'nər-ish-mənt\\ *n* **1** : FOOD, NUTRIMENT **2** : the action or process of nourishing

**nou·veau riche** \\‚nü-‚vō-'rēsh\\ *n, pl* **nou·veaux riches** \\*same*\\ : a person newly rich : PARVENU

**Nov** *abbr* November

**no·va** \\'nō-və\\ *n, pl* **novas** *or* **no·vae**

\-(,)vē, -,vī\ **:** a star that suddenly increases greatly in brightness and then within a few months or years grows dim again

¹**nov·el** \'näv-əl\ *adj* **1 :** having no precedent **:** NEW **2 :** STRANGE, UNUSUAL

²**novel** *n* **:** a long invented prose narrative dealing with human experience through a connected sequence of events — **nov·el·ist** \-(ə-)ləst\ *n*

**nov·el·ette** \,näv-ə-'let\ *n* **:** a brief novel or long short story

**nov·el·ize** \'näv-ə-,līz\ *vb* **-ized; -iz·ing :** to convert into the form of a novel — **nov·el·iza·tion** \,näv-ə-lə-'zā-shən\ *n*

**no·vel·la** \nō-'vel-ə\ *n, pl* **novellas** *or* **no·vel·le** \-'vel-ē\ **:** NOVELETTE

**nov·el·ty** \'näv-əl-tē\ *n, pl* **-ties 1 :** something new or unusual **2 :** NEWNESS **3 :** a small manufactured article intended mainly for personal or household adornment - usu. used in pl.

**No·vem·ber** \nō-'vem-bər\ *n* [ME *Novembre*, fr. OF fr. L *November* (ninth month), fr. *novem* nine] **:** the 11th month of the year having 30 days

**no·ve·na** \nō-'vē-nə\ *n* **:** a Roman Catholic nine days' devotion

**nov·ice** \'näv-əs\ *n* **1 :** a new member of a religious order who is preparing to take the vows of religion **2 :** one who is inexperienced or untrained

**no·vi·tiate** \nō-'vish-ət, nə-\ *n* **1 :** the period or state of being a novice **2 :** NOVICE **3 :** a house where novices are trained

¹**now** \(')naù\ *adv* **1 :** at the present time or moment **2 :** in the time immediately before the present **3 :** FORTHWITH **4** — used with the sense of present time weakened or lost (as to express command, introduce an important point, or indicate a transition) ⟨~ this would be treason⟩ **5 :** SOMETIMES ⟨~ one and ~ another⟩ **6 :** under the present circumstances **7 :** at the time referred to

²**now** *conj* **:** in view of the fact ⟨~ that you're here, we'll start⟩

³**now** \'naù\ *n* **:** the present time or moment **:** PRESENT

⁴**now** \'naù\ *adj* **1 :** of or relating to the present time ⟨the ~president⟩ **2 :** excitingly new ⟨~ clothes⟩; *also* **:** constantly aware of what is new ⟨~ people⟩

**now·a·days** \'naù-(ə-),dāz\ *adv* **:** at the present time

**no·way** \'nō-,wā\ *or* **no·ways** \-,wāz\ *adv* **:** NOWISE

**no·where** \-,hwear\ *adv* **:** not anywhere — **no·where** *n*

**nowhere near** *adv* **:** not nearly

**no·wise** \'nō-,wīz\ *adv* **:** in no way

**nox·ious** \'näk-shəs\ *adj* **:** harmful esp. to health or morals

**noz·zle** \'näz-əl\ *n* **:** a projecting part with an opening for an outlet; *esp* **:** a tube on a hose to direct flow of liquid

**np** *abbr* **1** no pagination **2** no place (of publication)

**Np** *symbol* neptunium

**NP** *abbr* **1** no protest **2** notary public **3** noun phrase

**NPN** *abbr* nonprotein nitrogen

**NS** *abbr* **1** not specified **2** Nova Scotia **3** nuclear ship

**NSA** *abbr* National Security Agency

**NSC** *abbr* National Security Council

**NSF** *abbr* **1** National Science Foundation **2** not sufficient funds

**NSW** *abbr* New South Wales

**NT** *abbr* **1** New Testament **2** Northern Territory

**nth** \'enth\ *adj* **1 :** numbered with an unspecified or indefinitely large ordinal number **2 :** EXTREME, UTMOST ⟨to the ~ degree⟩

**NTP** *abbr* normal temperature and pressure

**nt wt** *or* **n wt** *abbr* net weight

**NU** *abbr* name unknown

**nu·ance** \ n(y)ü-,äns, n(y)ü-'äns\ *n* [F, fr. MF, shade of color, fr. *nuer* to make shades of color, fr. *nue* cloud, fr. L *nubes*] **:** a shade of difference **:** a delicate variation (as in tone or meaning)

**nub** \'nəb\ *n* **1 :** KNOB, LUMP **2 :** GIST, POINT ⟨the ~ of the story⟩

**nub·bin** \'nəb-ən\ *n* **1 :** something (as an ear of Indian corn) that is small for its kind, stunted, undeveloped, or imperfect **2 :** a small projecting bit

**nub·ble** \'nəb-əl\ *n* **:** a small knob or lump — **nub·bly** \-(ə-)lē\ *adj*

**nu·bile** \'n(y)ü-bəl, -,bīl\ *adj* **:** of marriageable condition or age ⟨~ girls⟩

**nu·cle·ar** \'n(y)ü-klē-ər\ *adj* **1 :** of, relating to, or constituting a nucleus **2 :** of, relating to, or utilizing the atomic nucleus, atomic energy, the atom bomb, or atomic power

**nu·cle·ate** \'n(y)ü-klē-,āt\ *vb* **-at·ed; -at·ing :** to form, act as, or have a nucleus — **nu·cle·ation** \,n(y)ü-klē-'ā-shən\ *n*

**nu·cle·ic acid** \n(y)ü-,klē-ik-\ *n* **:** any of various complex organic acids (as DNA) found esp. in cell nuclei

**nu·cle·on** \'n(y)ü-klē-,än\ *n* **:** a proton or a neutron esp. in the atomic nucleus — **nu·cle·on·ic** \,n(y)ü-klē-'än-ik\ *adj*

**nu·cle·on·ics** \,n(y)ü-klē-'än-iks\ *n* **:** a branch of physical science that deals with nucleons or with all phenomena of the atomic nucleus

**nu·cle·us** \'n(y)ü-klē-əs\ *n, pl* **nu·clei** \-klē-,ī\ *also* **nu·cle·us·es** [NL, fr. L, kernel, dim. of *nuc-, nux* nut] **1 :** a central mass or part about which matter gathers or is collected **:** CORE **2 :** the part of a cell that contains chromosomes and is the seat of the mechanisms of heredity **3 :** the central part of an atom that comprises nearly all of the atomic mass

**nu·clide** \'n(y)ü-,klīd\ *n* **:** a species of atom characterized by the constitution of its nucleus — **nu·clid·ic** \n(y)ü-'klid-ik\ *adj*

¹**nude** \'n(y)üd\ *adj* **nud·er; nud·est :** BARE, NAKED, UNCLOTHED — **nu·di·ty** \'n(y)üd-ət-ē\ *n*

²**nude** *n* **1 :** a nude human figure esp. as depicted in art **2 :** the condition of being nude (in the ~)

**nudge** \'nəj\ *vb* **nudged; nudg·ing**

**:** to touch or push gently (as with the elbow) usu. in order to seek attention — **nudge** n

**nud·ism** \'n(y)üd-,iz-əm\ n **:** tne practice of going nude esp. in mixed groups at specially secluded places — **nud·ist** \'n(y)üd-əst\ n

**nu·ga·to·ry** \'n(y)ü-gə-,tōr-ē\ adj **1 :** INCONSEQUENTIAL, WORTHLESS **2 :** having no force **:** INOPERATIVE

**nug·get** \'nəg-ət\ n **:** a lump of precious metal (as gold)

**nui·sance** \'n(y)üs-²ns\ n **:** an annoying or troublesome person or thing

**nuisance tax** n **:** an excise tax collected in small amounts from the consumer

**null** \'nəl\ adj **1 :** having no legal or binding force **:** INVALID, VOID **2 :** amounting to nothing **3 :** INSIGNIFICANT — **nul·li·ty** \'nəl-ət-ē\ n

**null and void** adj **:** having no force, binding power, or validity

**nul·li·fy** \'nəl-ə-,fi\ vb **-fied; -fy·ing :** to make null or valueless; also **:** ANNUL — **nul·li·fi·ca·tion** \,nəl-ə-fə-'kā-shən\ n

**num** abbr numeral

**Num** or **Numb** abbr Numbers

**numb** \'nəm\ adj **:** lacking sensation or emotion **:** BENUMBED — **numb** vb — **numb·ly** adv — **numb·ness** n

**¹num·ber** \'nəm-bər\ n **1 :** the total of individuals or units taken together **2 :** a group or aggregate not specif. enumerated ⟨a small ~ of tickets remain unsold⟩ **3 :** a numerable state ⟨times without ~⟩ **4 :** a distinction of word form to denote reference to one or more than one **5 :** a unit belonging to a mathematical system and subject to its laws; also, pl **:** ARITHMETIC **6 :** a symbol used to represent a mathematical number; also **:** such a number used to identify or designate ⟨a phone ~⟩ **7 :** one in a sequence or series ⟨the best ~ on the program⟩

**²number** vb **num·bered; num·ber·ing** \-b(ə-)riŋ\ **1 :** COUNT, ENUMERATE **2 :** to include with or be one of a group **3 :** to restrict to a small or definite number **4 :** to assign a number to **5 :** to comprise in number **:** TOTAL

**num·ber·less** \-ləs\ adj **:** INNUMERABLE, COUNTLESS

**nu·mer·al** \'n(y)üm-(ə-)rəl\ n **:** a word or symbol representing a number — **numeral** adj

**nu·mer·ate** \'n(y)ü-mə-,rāt\ vb **-at·ed; -at·ing :** ENUMERATE

**nu·mer·a·tor** \'n(y)ü-mə-,rāt-ər\ n **:** the part of a fraction above the line

**nu·mer·ic** \n(y)ù-'mer-ik\ adj **:** NUMERICAL; esp **:** denoting a number or a system of numbers

**nu·mer·i·cal** \n(y)ù-'mer-i-kəl\ adj **1 :** of or relating to numbers **2 :** denoting a number or expressed in numbers — **nu·mer·i·cal·ly** \-k(ə-)lē\ adv

**nu·mer·ol·o·gy** \,n(y)ü-mə-'räl-ə-jē\ n **:** the study of the occult significance of numbers — **nu·mer·ol·o·gist** \-jəst\ n

**nu·mer·ous** \'n(y)üm-(ə-)rəs\ adj

**:** consisting of, including, or relating to a great number **:** MANY

**numis** abbr numismatic; numismatics

**nu·mis·mat·ics** \,n(y)ü-məz-'mat-iks\ n **:** the study or collection of monetary objects — **nu·mis·mat·ic** \-ik\ adj — **nu·mis·ma·tist** \n(y)ü-'miz-mət-əst\ n

**num·skull** \'nəm-,skəl\ n **:** a stupid person **:** DUNCE

**nun** \'nən\ n **:** a woman belonging to a religious order; esp **:** one under solemn vows of poverty, chastity, and obedience — **nun·nery** \-(ə-)rē\ n

**nun·cio** \'nən-sē-,ō, 'nün-\ n, pl **-ci·os :** a papal representative of the highest rank permanently accredited to a civil government

**¹nup·tial** \'nəp-shəl\ adj **:** of or relating to marriage or a wedding

**²nuptial** n **:** MARRIAGE, WEDDING — usu. used in pl.

**¹nurse** \'nərs\ n **1 :** a girl or woman employed to take care of children **2 :** a person trained to care for sick people

**²nurse** vb **nursed; nurs·ing 1 :** SUCKLE **2 :** to take charge of and watch over **3 :** TEND ⟨~ an invalid⟩ **4 :** to treat with special care ⟨~ a headache⟩ **5 :** to hold in one's mind or consideration ⟨~ a grudge⟩ **6 :** to act or serve as a nurse

**nurse·maid** \-,mād\ n **:** a girl employed to look after children

**nurs·ery** \'nərs-(ə-)rē\ n, pl **-er·ies 1 :** a room for children **2 :** a place where children are temporarily cared for in their parents' absence **3 :** a place where young plants are grown usu. for transplanting

**nurs·ery·maid** \-,mād\ n **:** NURSE-MAID

**nurs·ery·man** \-mən\ n **:** a man who keeps or works in a plant nursery

**nursery school** n **:** a school for children under kindergarten age

**nursing home** n **:** a private establishment where care is provided for persons who are unable to care for themselves

**nurs·ling** \'nərs-liŋ\ n **1 :** one that is solicitously cared for **2 :** a nursing child

**¹nur·ture** \'nər-chər\ n **1 :** TRAINING, UPBRINGING; also **:** the influences that modify the expression of an individual's heredity **2 :** FOOD, NOURISHMENT

**²nurture** vb **nur·tured; nur·tur·ing 1 :** to care for **:** FEED, NOURISH **2 :** EDUCATE, TRAIN **3 :** FOSTER

**nut** \'nət\ n **1 :** a dry fruit or seed with a hard shell and a firm inner kernel; also **:** its kernel **2 :** a metal block with a hole through it with the hole having a screw thread enabling the block to be screwed on a bolt or screw **3 :** the ridge on the upper end of the fingerboard in a stringed musical instrument over which the strings pass **4 :** a foolish, eccentric, or crazy person **5 :** ENTHUSIAST

**nut·crack·er** \-,krak-ər\ n **:** an instrument for cracking nuts

**nut·hatch** \'nət-,hach\ n [ME note-

*hache,* fr. *note* nut + *hache* ax, fr. OF, battle-ax] **:** any of various small birds that creep on tree trunks in search of food and resemble titmice

**nut·meg** \'nət-ˌmeg, -ˌmäg\ *n* [ME *notemuge,* deriv. of Old Provençal *noz muscada,* fr. *noz* nut (fr. L *nuc-, nux*) + *muscada,* fem. of *muscat* musky] **:** the nutlike aromatic seed of a tropical tree that is ground for use as a spice; *also* **:** this spice

**nut·pick** \'nət-ˌpik\ *n* **:** a small sharp-pointed table implement for extracting the kernels from nuts

**nu·tria** \'n(y)ü-trē-ə\ *n* **1 :** COYPU **1 2 :** the durable usu. light brown fur of the coypu

¹**nu·tri·ent** \'n(y)ü-trē-ənt\ *adj* **:** NOURISHING

²**nutrient** *n* **:** a nutritive substance or ingredient

**nu·tri·ment** \-trə-mənt\ *n* **:** NUTRIENT

**nu·tri·tion** \n(y)ù-'trish-ən\ *n* **:** the act or process of nourishing; *esp* **:** the processes by which an individual takes in and utilizes food material — **nu·tri·tion·al** \-'trish-(ə-)nəl\ *adj* — **nu·tri·tious** \-'trish-əs\ *adj* — **nu·tri·tive** \'n(y)ü-ˌtrət-iv\ *adj*

**nuts** \'nəts\ *adj* **1 :** ENTHUSIASTIC, KEEN **2 :** CRAZY, DEMENTED

**nut·shell** \'nət-ˌshel\ *n* **:** the shell of a nut — **in a nutshell :** in a few words ⟨that's the story *in a nutshell*⟩

**nut·ty** \'nət-ē\ *adj* **nut·ti·er; -est 1 :** containing or suggesting nuts ⟨a ~ flavor⟩ **2 :** mentally unbalanced

**nuz·zle** \'nəz-əl\ *vb* **nuz·zled; nuz·zling** \-(ə-)liŋ\ **1 :** to root around, push, or touch with or as if with the nose **2 :** NESTLE, SNUGGLE

**NV** *abbr* Nevada

**NW** *abbr* northwest

**NWT** *abbr* Northwest Territories

**NY** *abbr* New York

**NYC** *abbr* New York City

**ny·lon** \'nī-ˌlän\ *n* **1 :** any of numerous strong tough elastic synthetic materials used esp. in textiles and plastics **2** *pl* **:** stockings made of nylon

**nymph** \'nimf\ *n* **1** one of the lesser goddesses in ancient mythology represented as maidens living in the mountains, forests, meadows, and waters **2 :** an immature insect; *esp* **:** one that resembles the adult but is smaller and less differentiated and usu. lacks wings

**nym·pho·ma·nia** \ˌnim-fə-'mā-nē-ə, -nyə\ *n* **:** excessive sexual desire by a female — **nym·pho·ma·ni·ac** \-nē-ˌak\ *n or adj*

**NZ** *abbr* New Zealand

---

**O**

¹**o** \'ō\ *n, pl* **o's** *or* **os** \'ōz\ *often cap* **:** the 15th letter of the English alphabet

²**o** *abbr, often cap* **1** ocean **2** Ohio **3** ohm

¹**O** \'ō\ *var of* OH

²**O** *symbol* oxygen

**o/a** *abbr* on or about

**oaf** \'ōf\ *n* **:** a stupid or awkward person — **oaf·ish** \'ō-fish\ *adj*

**oak** \'ōk\ *n, pl* **oaks** *or* **oak :** any of various trees or shrubs related to the beech and chestnut and having a rounded thin-shelled nut; *also* **:** the usu. tough durable wood of an oak — **oak·en** \'ō-kən\ *adj*

**oa·kum** \'ō-kəm\ *n* **:** loosely twisted hemp or jute fiber impregnated with tar and used esp. in caulking ships

**oar** \'ōr\ *n* **:** a long slender broad-bladed implement for propelling or steering a boat

**oar·lock** \-ˌläk\ *n* **:** a U-shaped device for holding an oar in place

**oars·man** \'ōrz-mən\ *n* **:** one who rows esp. in a racing crew

**OAS** *abbr* Organization of American States

**oa·sis** \ō-'ā-səs\ *n, pl* **oa·ses** \-ˌsēz\ **:** a fertile or green area in an arid region

**oat** \'ōt\ *n* **:** a cereal grass widely grown for its edible seed; *also* **:** this seed — **oat·en** \-ᵊn\ *adj*

**oat·cake** \'ōt-ˌkāk\ *n* **:** a thin flat oatmeal cake

**oath** \'ōth\ *n, pl* **oaths** \'ōthz, 'ōths\ **1 :** a solemn appeal to God to witness to the truth of a statement or the sacredness of a promise **2 :** an irreverent or careless use of a sacred name

**oat·meal** \'ōt-ˌmēl\ *n* **1 :** meal made

from oats **2 :** porridge made from ground or rolled oats

**ob** *abbr* [L *obiit*] he died

**Ob** *or* **Obad** *abbr* Obadiah

**ob·bli·ga·to** \ˌäb-lə-'gät-ō\ *n, pl* **-tos** *also* **-ti** \-'gät-ē\ **:** an accompanying part usu. played by a solo instrument

**ob·du·rate** \'äb-d(y)ə-rət\ *adj* **:** stubbornly resistant **:** UNYIELDING **syn** inflexible, adamant — **ob·du·ra·cy** \-rə-sē\ *n*

**obe·di·ent** \ō-'bēd-ē-ənt\ *adj* **:** submissive to the restraint or command of authority **syn** docile, tractable, amenable — **obe·di·ence** \-əns\ *n* — **obe·di·ent·ly** *adv*

**obei·sance** \ō-'bās-əns, -'bēs-\ *n* **:** a bow made to show respect or submission; *also* **:** DEFERENCE, HOMAGE

**obe·lisk** \'äb-ə-ˌlisk\ *n* [MF *obelisque,* fr. L *obeliscus,* fr. Gk *obeliskos,* fr. dim. of *obelos* spit, pointed pillar] **:** a 4-sided pillar that tapers toward the top and ends in a pyramid

**obese** \ō-'bēs\ *adj* [L *obesus,* fr. pp. of *obedere* to eat up, fr. *ob-* against + *edere* to eat] **:** extremely fat — **obe·si·ty** \-'bē-sət-ē\ *n*

**obey** \ō-'bā\ *vb* **obeyed; obey·ing 1 :** to follow the commands or guidance of **:** behave obediently **2 :** to comply with ⟨~ orders⟩

**ob·fus·cate** \'äb-fə-ˌskāt\ *vb* **-cat·ed; -cat·ing 1 :** to make dark or obscure **2 :** CONFUSE — **ob·fus·ca·tion** \ˌäb-fəs-'kā-shən\ *n*

**obi** \'ō-bē\ *n* **:** a broad sash worn with a Japanese kimono

**obit** \ō-'bit, 'ō-bət\ *n* **:** OBITUARY

**obi·ter dic·tum** \ˌō-bət-ər-'dik-təm\ *n, pl* **obiter dic·ta** \-tə\ [LL, lit., something said in passing] : an incidental remark or observation

**obit·u·ary** \ə-'bich-ə-,wer-ē\ *n, pl* **-ar·ies** : a notice of a person's death usu. with a short biographical account

**obj** *abbr* object; objective

¹**ob·ject** \'äb-jikt\ *n* **1** : something that may be seen or felt; *also* : something that may be perceived or examined mentally **2** : something that arouses an emotional response (as of affection or pity) **3** : AIM, PURPOSE **4** : a word or word group denoting that on or toward which the action of a verb is directed; *also* : a noun or noun equivalent in a prepositional phrase

²**ob·ject** \əb-'jekt\ *vb* **1** : to offer in opposition **2** : to oppose something; *also* : DISAPPROVE **syn** protest, remonstrate, expostulate — **ob·jec·tion** \-'jek-shən\ *n* — **ob·jec·tion·able** \-sh(ə-)nə-bəl\ *adj* — **ob·jec·tor** \-'jek-tər\ *n*

**ob·jec·ti·fy** \əb-'jek-tə-,fī\ *vb* **-fied; -fy·ing** : to make objective

¹**ob·jec·tive** \əb-'jek-tiv\ *adj* **1** : of or relating to an object or end **2** : existing outside and independent of the mind **3** : treating or dealing with facts without distortion by personal feelings or prejudices **4** : of, relating to, or constituting a grammatical case marking typically the object of a verb or preposition — **ob·jec·tive·ly** *adv* — **ob·jec·tive·ness** *n* — **ob·jec·tiv·i·ty** \,äb-,jek-'tiv-ət-ē\ *n*

²**objective** *n* **1** : an aim or end of action : GOAL **2** : the objective case; *also* : a word in it **3** : the lens (as in a microscope) nearest the object being viewed and forming an image of it

**ob·jet d'art** \,öb-,zhä-'där\ *n, pl* **ob·jets d'art** \*same*\ : an article of artistic worth; *also* : CURIO

**ob·jet trou·vé** \'öb-,zhä-trü-'vā\ *n* [F, lit., found object] : a natural object (as a piece of driftwood) found by chance and held to have aesthetic value; *also* : an artifact not orig. intended as art but displayed as a work of art

**ob·jur·gate** \'äb-jər-,gāt\ *vb* **-gat·ed; -gat·ing** : to denounce harshly — **ob·jur·ga·tion** \,äb-jər-'gā-shən\ *n*

**obl** *abbr* **1** oblique **2** oblong

**ob·late** \äb-'lāt\ *adj* : flattened or depressed at the poles ⟨an ∼ spheroid⟩

**ob·la·tion** \ə-'blā-shən\ *n* : a religious offering

**ob·li·gate** \'äb-lə-,gāt\ *vb* **-gat·ed; -gat·ing** : to bind legally or morally; *also* : to bind by a favor

**ob·li·ga·tion** \,äb-lə-'gā-shən\ *n* **1** : an act of obligating oneself to a course of action **2** : something (as a promise or a contract) that binds one to a course of action **3** : DUTY **4** : INDEBTEDNESS; *also* : LIABILITY — **oblig·a·to·ry** \ə-'blig-ə-,tōr-ē, 'äb-li-gə-\ *adj*

**oblige** \ə-'blīj\ *vb* **obliged; oblig·ing 1** : FORCE, COMPEL **2** : to bind by a favor; *also* : to do a favor for or do something as a favor — **oblig·ing** *adj* — **oblig·ing·ly** *adv*

**oblique** \ō-'blēk, -'blīk\ *adj* **1** : neither perpendicular nor parallel : SLANTING **2** : not straightforward : INDIRECT — **oblique·ly** *adv* — **oblique·ness** *n* — **obliq·ui·ty** \ō-'blik-wət-ē\ *n*

**oblit·er·ate** \ə-'blit-ə-,rāt\ *vb* **-at·ed; at·ing** [L *oblitterare*, fr. *ob* in the way of + *littera* letter] **1** : to make undecipherable by wiping out or covering over **2** : to remove from recognition or memory **3** : CANCEL — **oblit·er·a·tion** \-,blit-ə-'rā-shən\ *n*

**obliv·i·on** \ə-'bliv-ē-ən\ *n* **1** : FORGETFULNESS **2** : the quality or state of being forgotten

**obliv·i·ous** \-ē-əs\ *adj* **1** : lacking memory or mindful attention **2** : UNAWARE — **obliv·i·ous·ly** *adv* — **obliv·i·ous·ness** *n*

**ob·long** \'äb-,lóŋ\ *adj* : longer in one direction than in the other with opposite sides parallel — **oblong** *n*

**ob·lo·quy** \'äb-lə-kwē\ *n, pl* **-quies 1** : strongly condemnatory utterance or language **2** : bad repute : DISGRACE **syn** dishonor, shame, infamy

**ob·nox·ious** \äb-'näk-shəs, əb-\ *adj* : REPUGNANT, OFFENSIVE — **ob·nox·ious·ly** *adv* — **ob·nox·ious·ness** *n*

**oboe** \'ō-bō\ *n* [It, fr. F *hautbois*, fr. *haut* high + *bois* wood] : a woodwind instrument shaped like a slender conical tube with holes and keys and a reed mouthpiece — **obo·ist** \'o-,bō-əst\ *n*

**obs** *abbr* obsolete

**ob·scene** \äb-'sēn, əb-\ *adj* **1** : REPULSIVE **2** : deeply offensive to morality or decency; *esp* : designed to incite to lust or depravity **syn** gross, vulgar, coarse — **ob·scene·ly** *adv* — **ob·scen·i·ty** \-'sen-ət-ē\ *n*

**ob·scu·ran·tism** \äb-'skyùr-ən-,tiz-əm, əb-; ,äb-skyù-'ran-\ *n* **1** : opposition to the spread of knowledge **2** : deliberate vagueness or abstruseness — **ob·scu·ran·tist** \-ən-təst, -'rant-əst\ *n or adj*

¹**ob·scure** \äb-'skyùr, əb-\ *adj* **1** : DIM, GLOOMY **2** : REMOTE; *also* : HUMBLE **3** : not readily understood : VAGUE — **ob·scure·ly** *adv* — **ob·scu·ri·ty** \-'skyùr-ət-ē\ *n*

²**obscure** *vb* **obscured; obscur·ing 1** : to make dark, dim, or indistinct **2** : to conceal or hide by or as if by covering

**ob·se·qui·ous** \əb-'sē-kwē-əs\ *adj* : humbly or excessively attentive (as to a person in authority) : FAWNING, SYCOPHANTIC — **ob·se·qui·ous·ly** *adv* — **ob·se·qui·ous·ness** *n*

**ob·se·quy** \'äb-sə-kwē\ *n, pl* **-quies** : a funeral or burial rite — usu. used in pl.

**ob·serv·able** \əb-'zər-və-bəl\ *adj* **1** : necessarily or customarily observed **2** : NOTICEABLE

**ob·ser·vance** \-'zər-vəns\ *n* **1** : a customary practice or ceremony **2** : an act or instance of following a custom, rule, or law **3** : OBSERVATION

**ob·ser·vant** \-vənt\ *adj* **1** : WATCHFUL ⟨∼ spectators⟩ **2** : MINDFUL ⟨∼ of the amenities⟩ **3** : quick to observe

**ob·ser·va·tion** \,äb-sər-'vā-shən, -zər-\ *n* **1** : an act or the power of observing **2** : the gathering of information (as for scientific studies) by noting facts or occurrences **3** : a conclusion drawn from observing; *also* : REMARK, STATEMENT **4** : the fact of being observed

**ob·ser·va·to·ry** \əb-'zər-və-,tōr-ē\ *n*, *pl* **-ries** : a place or institution equipped for observation of natural phenomena (as in astronomy)

**ob·serve** \əb-'zərv\ *vb* **ob·served; ob·serv·ing 1** : to conform one's action or practice to **2** : CELEBRATE **3** : to see or sense esp. through careful attention **4** : to come to realize esp. through consideration of noted facts **5** : REMARK **6** : to make a scientific observation — **ob·serv·er** *n*

**ob·sess** \əb-'ses\ *vb* : to preoccupy intensely or abnormally

**ob·ses·sion** \äb-'sesh-ən, əb-\ *n* : a persistent disturbing preoccupation with an idea or feeling; *also* : an emotion or idea causing such a preoccupation — **ob·ses·sive** \-'ses-iv\ *adj* — **ob·ses·sive·ly** *adv*

**ob·sid·i·an** \əb-'sid-ē-ən\ *n* : a dark natural glass formed by the cooling of molten lava

**ob·so·les·cent** \,äb-sə-'les-ᵊnt\ *adj* : going out of use : becoming obsolete — **ob·so·les·cence** \-ᵊns\ *n*

**ob·so·lete** \,äb-sə-'lēt, 'äb-sə-,lēt\ *adj* : no longer in use : OUTMODED **syn** old, antiquated, ancient

**ob·sta·cle** \'äb-sti-kəl\ *n* : something that stands in the way or opposes

**ob·stet·rics** \əb-'stet-riks\ *n sing or pl* : a branch of medicine that deals with childbirth — **ob·stet·ri·cal** \-ri-kəl\ *also* **ob·stet·ric** \-rik\ *adj* — **ob·ste·tri·cian** \,äb-stə-'trish-ən\ *n*

**ob·sti·nate** \'äb-stə-nət\ *adj* : fixed and unyielding (as in an opinion or course) despite reason or persuasion : STUBBORN — **ob·sti·na·cy** \-nə-sē\ *n* — **ob·sti·nate·ly** *adv*

**ob·strep·er·ous** \əb-'strep-(ə-)rəs\ *adj* **1** : uncontrollably noisy **2** : stubbornly defiant : UNRULY — **ob·strep·er·ous·ness** *n*

**ob·struct** \əb-'strəkt\ *vb* **1** : to block by an obstacle **2** : to impede the passage, action, or operation of **3** : to shut off from sight — **ob·struc·tive** \-'strək-tiv\ *adj* — **ob·struc·tor** \-tər\ *n*

**ob·struc·tion** \əb-'strək-shən\ *n* **1** : an act of obstructing : the state of being obstructed **2** : something that obstructs : HINDRANCE

**ob·struc·tion·ist** \-sh(ə-)nəst\ *n* : a person who hinders progress or business esp. in a legislative body — **ob·struc·tion·ism** \-shə,niz-əm\ *n*

**ob·tain** \əb-'tān\ *vb* **1** : to gain or attain usu. by planning or effort **2** : to be generally recognized or established **syn** procure, secure, win, earn — **ob·tain·able** *adj*

**ob·trude** \əb-'trüd\ *vb* **ob·trud·ed; ob·trud·ing 1** : to thrust out **2** : to

thrust forward without warrant or request **3** : INTRUDE — **ob·tru·sion** \-'trü-zhən\ *n* — **ob·tru·sive** \-'trü-siv\ *adj* — **ob·tru·sive·ly** *adv* — **ob·tru·sive·ness** *n*

**ob·tuse** \äb-'t(y)üs, əb-\ *adj* **1** : not sharp or quick of wit **2** : exceeding 90 degrees but less than 180 degrees ⟨~ angle⟩ **3** : not pointed or acute : BLUNT — **ob·tuse·ly** *adv* — **ob·tuse·ness** *n*

**obv** *abbr* obverse

¹**ob·verse** \äb-'vərs, 'äb-,\ *adj* **1** : facing the observer or opponent **2** : having the base narrower than the top **3** : being a counterpart or complement — **ob·verse·ly** *adv*

²**ob·verse** \'äb-,vərs, äb-'vərs\ *n* **1** : the side (as of a coin) bearing the principal design and lettering **2** : a front or principal surface **3** : COUNTERPART

**ob·vi·ate** \'äb-vē-,āt\ *vb* **-at·ed; -at·ing** : to anticipate and dispose of beforehand : make unnecessary **syn** prevent, avert — **ob·vi·a·tion** \,äb-vē-'ā-shən\ *n*

**ob·vi·ous** \'äb-vē-əs\ *adj* [L *obvius*, fr. *obviam* in the way, fr. *ob* in the way of + *viam*, acc. of *via* way] : easily discovered, seen, or understood : PLAIN **syn** evident, manifest, patent, clear — **ob·vi·ous·ly** *adv* — **ob·vi·ous·ness** *n*

**oc·a·ri·na** \,äk-ə-'rē-nə\ *n* [It, fr. *oca* goose, fr. LL *auca*, deriv. of L *avis* bird] : a simple wind instrument with a mouthpiece and holes that may be opened or closed by the finger to vary the pitch

**occas** *abbr* occasionally

¹**oc·ca·sion** \ə-'kā-zhən\ *n* **1** : a favorable opportunity **2** : a direct or indirect cause **3** : the time of an event **4** : EXIGENCY **5** *pl* : AFFAIRS, BUSINESS **6** : a special event : CELEBRATION

²**occasion** *vb* **oc·ca·sioned; oc·ca·sion·ing** \-'kāzh-(ə-)niŋ\ : CAUSE

**oc·ca·sion·al** \-'kāzh-(ə-)nəl\ *adj* **1** : happening or met with now and then ⟨~ references to the war⟩ **2** : used or designed for a special occasion ⟨~ verse⟩ **syn** infrequent, rare, sporadic — **oc·ca·sion·al·ly** \-ē\ *adv*

**oc·ci·den·tal** \,äk-sə-'dent-ᵊl\ *adj*, *often cap* [fr. *Occident* West, fr. ME, fr. L *occident-*, *occidens*, fr. prp. of *occidere* to fall, set (of the sun)] : WESTERN — **Occidental** *n*

**oc·clude** \ə-'klüd\ *vb* **oc·clud·ed; oc·clud·ing 1** : OBSTRUCT **2** : to shut in or out **3** : to take up and hold by absorption or adsorption **4** : to come together with opposing surfaces in contact — **oc·clu·sion** \-'klü-zhən\ *n* — **oc·clu·sive** \-'klü-siv\ *adj*

¹**oc·cult** \ə-'kəlt, 'äk-,əlt\ *adj* **1** : not revealed : SECRET **2** : ABSTRUSE, MYSTERIOUS **3** : of or relating to supernatural agencies, their effects, or knowledge of them

²**occult** *n* : occult matters — used with the

**oc·cult·ism** \ə-'kəl-,tiz-əm\ n : occult theory or practice — **oc·cult·ist** \-təst\ n

**oc·cu·pan·cy** \'äk-yə-pən-sē\ n, pl **-cies 1 :** OCCUPATION **2 :** an occupied building or part of a building

**oc·cu·pant** \-pənt\ n : one who occupies something; esp : RESIDENT

**oc·cu·pa·tion** \,äk-yə-'pā-shən\ n **1 :** an activity in which one engages; esp **:** VOCATION **2 :** the taking possession of property; also : the taking possession of an area by a foreign military force — **oc·cu·pa·tion·al** \-sh(ə-)nəl\ adj — **oc·cu·pa·tion·al·ly** \-ē\ adv

**occupational therapy** n : therapy by means of activity; esp : creative activity prescribed for its effect in promoting recovery or rehabilitation — **occupational therapist** n

**oc·cu·py** \'äk-yə-,pī\ vb **-pied; -py·ing 1 :** to engage the attention or energies of **2 :** to fill up (a extent in space or time) **3 :** to take or hold possession of **4 :** to reside in as owner or tenant — **oc·cu·pi·er** \-,pī(-ə)r\ n

**oc·cur** \ə-'kər\ vb **oc·curred; oc·cur·ring** \-'kər-iŋ\ **1 :** to be found or met with **:** APPEAR **2 :** to take place **3 :** to come to mind

**oc·cur·rence** \ə-'kər-əns\ n **1 :** something that takes place **2 :** APPEARANCE

**ocean** \'ō-shən\ n **1 :** the whole body of salt water that covers nearly three fourths of the surface of the earth **2 :** one of the large bodies of water into which the great ocean is divided — **oce·an·ic** \,ō-shē-'an-ik\ adj

**ocean·ar·i·um** \,ō-shə-'nar-ē-əm\ n, pl **-iums** or **-ia** \-ē-ə\ : a large marine aquarium

**ocean·front** \'ō-shən-,frənt\ n : an area that fronts on the ocean

**ocean·go·ing** \-,gō-iŋ\ adj : of, relating to, or suitable for ocean travel

**ocean·og·ra·phy** \,ō-shə-'näg-rə-fē\ n : a science dealing with the ocean and its phenomena — **ocean·og·ra·pher** \-fər\ n — **ocean·o·graph·ic** \-nə-'graf-ik\ adj

**ocean·ol·o·gy** \,ō-shə-'näl-ə-jē\ n **:** OCEANOGRAPHY — **ocean·ol·o·gist** \-jəst\ n

**oce·lot** \'äs-ə-,lät, 'ō-sə-\ n : a medium-sized American wildcat ranging southward from Texas and having a tawny yellow or gray coat with black markings

**ocher** or **ochre** \'ō-kər\ n : an earthy usu. red or yellow iron ore used as a pigment; also : the color esp. of yellow ocher

**o'·clock** \ə-'kläk\ adv : according to the clock

**OCS** abbr officer candidate school

**oct** abbr octavo

**Oct** abbr October

**oc·ta·gon** \'äk-tə-,gän\ n : a polygon of eight angles and eight sides — **oc·tag·o·nal** \äk-'tag-ən-ᵊl\ adj

**oc·tane** \'äk-,tān\ n **1 :** any of several isometric liquid hydrocarbons **2 :** OCTANE NUMBER

**octane number** n : a number that is used to measure or indicate the antiknock properties of a liquid motor fuel and that increases as the likelihood of knocking decreases

**oc·tave** \'äk-tiv\ n **1 :** a musical interval embracing eight degrees; also **:** a tone or note at this interval or the whole series of notes, tones, or keys within this interval **2 :** a group of eight

**oc·ta·vo** \äk-'tā-vō, -'täv-ō\ n, pl **-vos 1 :** the size of a piece of paper cut eight from a sheet **2 :** a book printed on octavo pages

**oc·tet** \äk-'tet\ n **1 :** a musical composition for eight voices or eight instruments; also : the performers of such a composition **2 :** a group or set of eight

**Oc·to·ber** \äk-'tō-bər\ n [ME Octobre, fr. OF, fr. L October (eighth month), fr. octo eight] : the 10th month of the year having 31 days

**oc·to·ge·nar·i·an** \,äk-tə-jə-'ner-ē-ən\ n : a person who is in his eighties

**oc·to·pus** \'äk-tə-pəs\ n, pl **-pus·es** or **-pi** \-,pī\ : any of various sea mollusks with eight long arms furnished with two rows of suckers for seizing and holding prey

**oc·to·syl·lab·ic** \,äk-tə-sə-'lab-ik\ adj **:** having or composed of verses having eight syllables — **octosyllabic** n

**¹oc·u·lar** \'äk-yə-lər\ adj **1 :** of or relating to the eye or the eyesight **2 :** VISUAL

**²ocular** n : EYEPIECE

**oc·u·list** \'äk-yə-ləst\ n **1 :** OPHTHALMOLOGIST **2 :** OPTOMETRIST

**¹OD** \(')ō-'dē\ n : an overdose of a narcotic

**²OD** abbr **1** doctor of optometry **2** [L oculus dexter] right eye **3** officer of the day **4** olive drab **5** overdraft **6** overdrawn

**odd** \'äd\ adj [ME odde, fr. ON oddi point of land, triangle, odd number] **1 :** being only one of a pair or set (an ~ shoe) **2 :** not divisible by two without leaving a remainder (~ numbers) **3 :** somewhat more than the number mentioned (forty ~ years ago) **4 :** additional to what is usual (~ jobs) **5 :** STRANGE (an ~ way of behaving) — **odd·ly** adv — **odd·ness** n

**odd·ball** \'äd-,bòl\ n : one whose behavior is eccentric

**odd·i·ty** \'äd-ət-ē\ n, pl **-ties 1 :** one that is odd **2 :** the quality or state of being odd

**odd·ment** \'äd-mənt\ n : something left over **:** REMNANT

**odds** \'ädz\ n pl **1 :** a difference by which one thing is favored over another **2 :** an equalizing allowance made to one believed to have a smaller chance of winning **3 :** DISAGREEMENT

**odds and ends** n pl : miscellaneous things or matters

**odds·on** \'ädz-'òn, -'än\ adj : having a better than even chance to win

**ode** \'ōd\ n : a lyric poem marked by nobility of feeling and solemnity of style

**odi·ous** \'ōd-ē-əs\ adj : causing or deserving hatred or repugnance — **odi-ous-ly** adv — **odi-ous-ness** n

**odi-um** \'ōd-ē-əm\ n **1 :** merited loathing **:** HATRED **2 :** DISGRACE

**odom-e-ter** \ō-'däm-ət-ər\ n [F *odomètre,* fr. Gk *hodometron,* fr. *hodos* way, road + *metron* measure] **:** an instrument for measuring distance traversed (as by a vehicle)

**odor** \'ōd-ər\ n **1 :** the quality of something that stimulates the sense of smell; *also* **:** a sensation resulting from such stimulation **2 :** REPUTE, ESTIMATION — **odor-less** adj — **odor-ous** adj

**od-ys-sey** \'äd-ə-sē\ n, pl **-seys** [the *Odyssey,* epic poem attributed to Homer recounting the long wanderings of Odysseus] **:** a long wandering marked usu. by many changes of fortune

**OE** abbr Old English

**OED** abbr Oxford English Dictionary

**oe-di-pal** \'ed-ə-pəl, 'ēd-\ adj, often cap **:** of or relating to the Oedipus complex

**Oe-di-pus complex** \-pəs-\ n **:** a positive sexual orientation of a child toward the parent of the opposite sex that may persist as a source of adult personality disorder

**OEO** abbr Office of Economic Opportunity

**o'er** \'ō(ə)r\ adv or prep **:** OVER

**OES** abbr Order of the Eastern Star

**oe-soph-a-gus** var of ESOPHAGUS

**oeu-vre** \'œvr'\ n, pl **oeuvres** \same\ **:** a substantial body of work constituting the lifework of a writer, an artist, or a composer

**¹of** \(')əv, 'äv\ prep **1 :** FROM ⟨a man ~ the West⟩ **2 :** having as a significant background or character element ⟨a man ~ noble birth⟩ ⟨a man ~ ability⟩ **3 :** owing to ⟨died ~ flu⟩ **4 :** BY ⟨the plays ~ Shakespeare⟩ **5 :** having as component parts or material, contents, or members ⟨a house ~ brick⟩ ⟨a glass ~ water⟩ ⟨a pack ~ fools⟩ **6 :** belonging to or included by ⟨the front ~ the house⟩ ⟨a time ~ life⟩ ⟨one ~ you⟩ ⟨the best ~ his kind⟩ ⟨the son ~ a doctor⟩ **7 :** connected with **:** OVER ⟨the king ~ England⟩ **8 :** marked by **:** having as a significant or the chief element ⟨a tale ~ woe⟩ **9 :** ABOUT ⟨tales ~ the West⟩ **10 :** that is **:** signified as ⟨the city ~ Rome⟩ **11** — used to indicate apposition of the words it joins ⟨that fool ~ a husband⟩ **12 :** as concerns **:** FOR ⟨love ~ country⟩ **13** — used to indicate the application of an adjective ⟨fond ~ candy⟩ **14 :** BEFORE ⟨five minutes ~ ten⟩

**OF** abbr Old French

**¹off** \'of\ adv **1 :** from a place or position ⟨drove ~ in a new car⟩; *also* **:** ASIDE ⟨turned ~ into a side road⟩ **2 :** so as to be unattached or removed ⟨the lid blew ~⟩ **3 :** to a state of discontinuance, exhaustion, or completion ⟨shut the radio ~⟩ **4 :** away from regular work ⟨took time ~ for lunch⟩ **5 :** at a distance in time or space ⟨stood ~ a few yards⟩ ⟨several years ~⟩

**²off** \(')of\ prep **1 :** away from the surface or top of ⟨take it ~ the table⟩ **2 :** FROM ⟨borrowed a dollar ~ me⟩ **3 :** at the expense of ⟨lives ~ his sister⟩ **4 :** to seaward of ⟨sail ~ the Maine coast⟩ **5 :** not engaged in ⟨~ duty⟩ **6 :** abstaining from ⟨~ liquor⟩ **7 :** below the usual level of ⟨~ his game⟩ **8 :** away from ⟨just ~ the highway⟩

**³off** \(')of\ adj **1 :** more removed or distant **2 :** started on the way **3 :** not operating **4 :** not correct **5 :** REMOTE, SLIGHT **6 :** INFERIOR **7 :** provided for ⟨well ~⟩

**⁴off** abbr office; officer; official

**of-fal** \'o-fəl\ n **:** the waste or by-product of a process; *esp* **:** the viscera and trimmings of a butchered animal removed in dressing

**off and on** adv **:** with periodic cessation

**¹off-beat** \'of-,bēt\ n **:** the unaccented part of a musical measure

**²offbeat** adj **:** ECCENTRIC, UNCONVENTIONAL

**off-col-or** \'of-'kəl-ər\ or **off-col-ored** \-ərd\ adj **1 :** not having the right or standard color **2 :** of doubtful propriety **:** RISQUÉ

**of-fend** \ə-'fend\ vb **1 :** SIN, TRANSGRESS **2 :** to cause discomfort or pain **:** HURT **3 :** to cause dislike or vexation **:** ANNOY syn affront, insult — **of-fend-er** n

**of-fense** or **of-fence** \ə-'fens, *esp for* 2 & 3 'äf-,ens\ n **1 :** something that outrages the senses **2 :** ATTACK, ASSAULT **3 :** the offensive team or members of a team playing offensive positions **4 :** DISPLEASURE **5 :** SIN, MISDEED **6 :** an infraction of law **:** CRIME

**¹of-fen-sive** \ə-'fen-siv *esp for* 1 & 2 'äf-,en-\ adj **1 :** AGGRESSIVE **2 :** of or relating to an attempt to score in a game or contest; *also* **:** of or relating to a team in possession of the ball or puck **3 :** OBNOXIOUS **4 :** INSULTING — **of-fen-sive-ly** adv — **of-fen-sive-ness** n

**²offensive** n **:** ATTACK

**¹of-fer** \'of-ər\ vb **of-fered**; **of-fer-ing** \-(ə-)riŋ\ **1 :** SACRIFICE **2 :** to present for acceptance **:** TENDER; *also* **:** to propose as payment **3 :** PROPOSE, SUGGEST; *also* **:** to declare one's readiness **4 :** to put up ⟨~ resistance⟩ **5 :** to place on sale — **of-fer-ing** n

**²offer** n **1 :** PROPOSAL **2 :** BID **3 :** TRY

**of-fer-to-ry** \'of-ə(r)-,tōr-ē\ n, pl **-ries** **:** the presentation of offerings at a church service; *also* **:** the musical accompaniment during it

**off-hand** \'of-'hand\ adv or adj **:** without previous thought or preparation

**off-hour** \'of-,aù(-ə)r\ n **:** a period of time other than a rush hour; *also* **:** a period of time other than business hours

**of-fice** \'of-əs\ n **1 :** a special duty or position; *esp* **:** a position of authority in government ⟨run for ~⟩ **2 :** a prescribed form or service of worship; *also* **:** RITE **3 :** an assigned or assumed duty or role **4 :** a place where a business is transacted or a service is supplied

**of·fice·hold·er** \-ˌhōl-dər\ *n* **:** one holding a public office

**of·fi·cer** \'òf-ə-sər\ *n* **1 :** one charged with the enforcement of law **2 :** one who holds an office of trust or authority **3 :** one who holds a commission in the armed forces

**¹of·fi·cial** \ə-'fish-əl\ *n* **:** OFFICER

**²official** *adj* **1 :** of or relating to an office or to officers **2 :** AUTHORIZED, AUTHORITATIVE **3 :** FORMAL — **of·fi·cial·ly** \-ē\ *adv*

**of·fi·cial·dom** \ə-'fish-əl-dəm\ *n* **:** officials as a class

**of·fi·cial·ism** \ə-'fish-ə-ˌliz-əm\ *n* **:** lack of flexibility and initiative combined with excessive adherence to regulations (as in the behavior of government officials)

**of·fi·ci·ant** \ə-'fish-ē-ənt\ *n* **:** an officiating clergyman

**of·fi·ci·ate** \ə-'fish-ē-ˌāt\ *vb* **-at·ed; -at·ing 1 :** to perform a ceremony, function, or duty **2 :** to act in an official capacity

**of·fi·cious** \ə-'fish-əs\ *adj* **:** volunteering one's services where they are neither asked for nor needed **:** MEDDLESOME — **of·fi·cious·ly** *adv* — **of·fi·cious·ness** *n*

**off·ing** \'òf-iŋ\ *n* **1 :** the part of the deep sea seen from the shore **2 :** the near or foreseeable future

**off·ish** \'òf-ish\ *adj* **:** inclined to stand aloof

**off–line** \'òf-'līn\ *adj* **:** not controlled directly by a computer

**off of** *prep* **:** OFF

**off·print** \'òf-ˌprint\ *n* **:** a separately printed excerpt (as from a magazine)

**off–sea·son** \'òf-ˌsēz-ᵊn\ *n* **:** a time of suspended or reduced activity

**¹off·set** \'òf-ˌset\ *n* **1 :** a sharp bend (as in a pipe) by which one part is turned aside out of line **2 :** a printing process in which an inked impression is first made on a rubber-blanketed cylinder and then transferred to the paper

**²off·set** *vb* **-set; -set·ting 1 :** to place over against **:** BALANCE **2 :** to compensate for **3 :** to form an offset in (as a wall)

**off·shoot** \'òf-ˌshüt\ *n* **1 :** a branch of a main stem (as of a plant) **2 :** a collateral or derived branch, descendant, or member

**¹off·shore** \'òf-'shōr\ *adv* **:** at a distance from the shore

**²off·shore** \'òf-ˌshōr\ *adj* **1 :** moving away from the shore **2 :** situated off the shore and esp. within a zone extending three miles from low-water line

**off·side** \'òf-'sīd\ *adv or adj* **:** illegally in advance of the ball or puck

**off·spring** \'òf-ˌspriŋ\ *n, pl* **offspring** *also* **offsprings :** PROGENY, YOUNG

**off·stage** \'òf-'stāj, -ˌstāj\ *adv or adj* **:** off or away from the stage

**off–the–record** *adj* **:** given or made in confidence and not for publication

**off–the–shelf** *adj* **:** available as a stock item **:** not specially designed or made

**off–white** \'òf-'hwīt\ *n* **:** a yellowish or grayish white

**off year** *n* **1 :** a year in which no major election is held **2 :** a year of diminished activity or production

**OFM** *abbr* Order of Friars Minor

**OFS** *abbr* Orange Free State

**oft** \'òft\ *adv* **:** OFTEN

**of·ten** \'òf-(t)ən\ *adv* **:** many times **:** FREQUENTLY

**of·ten·times** \-ˌtīmz\ *or* **oft·times** \'òf(t)-ˌtīmz\ *adv* **:** OFTEN

**OG** *abbr* original gum

**ogle** \'ōg-əl\ *vb* **ogled; ogling** \-(ə-)liŋ\ **:** to look at in a flirtatious way — **ogle** *n* — **ogler** \-(ə-)lər\ *n*

**ogre** \'ō-gər\ *n* **1 :** a monster of fairy tales and folklore that feeds on human beings **2 :** a dreaded person or object — **ogress** \'ō-g(ə-)rəs\ *n*

**oh** \(')ō\ *interj* **1 :** used to express an emotion **2 :** used in direct address

**OH** *abbr* Ohio

**ohm** \'ōm\ *n* **:** a unit of electrical resistance equal to the resistance of a circuit in which a potential difference of one volt produces a current of one ampere — **ohm·ic** \'ō-mik\ *adj*

**ohm·me·ter** \'ō(m)-ˌmēt-ər\ *n* **:** an instrument for indicating resistance in ohms directly

**¹oil** \'òil\ *n* [ME *oile*, fr. OF, fr. L *oleum* olive oil, fr. Gk *elaion*, fr. *elaia* olive] **1 :** a fatty or greasy liquid substance obtained from plants, animals, or minerals and used for fuel, lighting, food, medicines and manufacturing **2 :** PETROLEUM **3 :** artists' colors made with oil; *also* **:** a painting in such colors — **oil·i·ness** \'òi-lē-nəs\ *n* — **oily** \'òi-lē\ *adj*

**²oil** *vb* **:** to treat, furnish, or lubricate with oil — **oil·er** *n*

**oil·cloth** \-ˌklòth\ *n* **:** cloth treated with oil or paint and used for table and shelf coverings

**oil shale** *n* **:** shale from which oil can be recovered by distillation

**oil·skin** \'òil-ˌskin\ *n* **1 :** an oiled waterproof cloth **2 :** clothing (as a raincoat) made of oilskin

**oink** \'òiŋk\ *n* **:** the natural noise of a hog — **oink** *vb*

**oint·ment** \'òint-mənt\ *n* **:** a medicinal or cosmetic preparation usu. with a fatty or greasy base for use on the skin

**Ojib·wa** *or* **Ojib·way** \ō-'jib-ˌwā\ *n, pl* **Ojibwa** *or* **Ojibwas** *or* **Ojibway** *or* **Ojibways :** a member of an Indian people orig. of Michigan

**OJT** *abbr* on-the-job training

**¹OK** *or* **okay** \ō-'kā\ *adv or adj* **:** all right

**²OK** *or* **okay** *vb* **OK'd** *or* **okayed; OK'·ing** *or* **okay·ing :** APPROVE, AUTHORIZE — **OK** *or* **okay** *n*

**³OK** *abbr* Oklahoma

**Okla** *abbr* Oklahoma

**okra** \'ō-krə, *South also* -krē\ *n* **:** a tall annual plant related to the hollyhocks and grown for its edible green pods used esp. in soups and stews; *also* **:** these pods

**¹old** \'ōld\ *adj* **1 :** ANCIENT; *also* **:** of long standing **2** *cap* **:** belonging to an early period ⟨*Old* Irish⟩ **3 :** having existed for a specified period of time **4** : of or relating to a past era **5** : advanced in years **6** : showing the effects of age or use **7** : no longer in use — **old•ish** \'ōl-dish\ adj

**²old** n : old or earlier time ⟨days of ∼⟩

**old•en** \'ōl-dən\ adj : of or relating to a bygone era : ANCIENT

**¹old-fash•ioned** \'ōl(d)-'fash-ənd\ adj **1** : ANTIQUATED **2** : CONSERVATIVE

**²old-fashioned** n : a cocktail usu. made with whiskey, bitters, sugar, a twist of lemon peel, and water or soda water

**old guard** n, often cap O&G : the conservative members of an organization

**old hat** adj **1** : OLD-FASHIONED **2** : STALE, TRITE

**old•ie** \'ōl-dē\ n : something old; esp : a popular song of an earlier day

**old-line** \'ōl(d)-'līn\ adj **1** : ORIGINAL, ESTABLISHED ⟨an ∼ business⟩ **2** : adhering to old policies or practices

**old maid** n **1** : SPINSTER **2** : a prim fussy person — **old-maid•ish** \'ōl(d)-'mād-ish\ adj

**old man** n **1** : HUSBAND **2** : FATHER

**old•ster** \'ōl(d)-stər\ n : an old or elderly person

**old-time** \‚ōl(d)-‚tīm\ adj **1** : of, relating to, or characteristic of an earlier period **2** : of long standing

**old-tim•er** \'ōl(d)-'tī-mər\ n : VETERAN; also : OLDSTER

**old-world** \'ōl(d)-'wərld\ adj : OLD-FASHIONED, PICTURESQUE

**Old World** n : the eastern hemisphere; esp : continental Europe

**ole•ag•i•nous** \‚ō-lē-'aj-ə-nəs\ adj : OILY

**ole•an•der** \'ō-lē-‚an-dər\ n : a poisonous evergreen shrub often grown for its fragrant red or white flowers

**oleo** \'ō-lē-‚ō\ n : MARGARINE

**oleo•mar•ga•rine** \‚ō-lē-ō-'märj-(ə-)rən, -'märj-ə-‚rēn\ n : MARGARINE

**ol•fac•to•ry** \äl-'fak-t(ə-)rē, ōl-\ adj : of or relating to the sense of smell

**oli•gar•chy** \'äl-ə-‚gär-kē, 'ō-lə-\ n, pl -chies **1** : a government in which power is in the hands of a few **2** : a state having an oligarchy; also : the group holding power in such a state — **oli•garch** \-‚gärk\ n — **oli•gar•chic** \‚äl-ə-'gär-kik, ‚ō-lə-\ or **oli•gar•chi•cal** \-ki-kəl\ adj

**olio** \'ō-lē-‚ō\ n, pl **oli•os** : HODGEPODGE, MEDLEY

**ol•ive** \'äl-iv, -əv\ n **1** : an Old World evergreen tree grown in warm regions for its fruit that is important as food and for its edible oil (**olive oil**) **2** : a dull yellow to yellowish green color

**olive drab** n **1** : a variable color averaging a grayish olive **2** : a wool or cotton fabric of an olive drab color; also : a uniform of this fabric

**ol•iv•ine** \'äl-ə-‚vēn\ n : a usu. greenish mineral that is a complex silicate of magnesium and iron

**Olym•pic Games** \ə-'lim-pik-, ō-\ n pl : a modified revival of an ancient Greek festival held every four years and consisting of international athletic contests

**om** \'ōm\ n : a mantra consisting of the sound "om" used in contemplating ultimate reality

**Oma•ha** \'ō-mə-‚hò, -‚hä\ n, pl **Omaha** or **Omahas** : a member of an Indian people of northeastern Nebraska

**om•buds•man** \'äm-‚budz-mən, äm-'budz-\ n, pl **-men** \-mən\ **1** : a government official appointed to investigate complaints made by individuals against abuses or capricious acts of public officials **2** : one that investigates reported complaints (as from students or consumers)

**om•elet** or **om•elette** \'äm-(ə-)lət\ n [F omelette, alter. of MF alumelle, lit., knife blade, modif. of L lamella, dim. of lamina thin plate] : eggs beaten with milk or water, cooked without stirring until set, and folded over

**omen** \'ō-mən\ n : an event or phenomenon believed to be a sign or warning of a future occurrence

**om•i•nous** \'äm-ə-nəs\ adj : foretelling evil : THREATENING — **om•i•nous•ly** adv — **om•i•nous•ness** n

**omit** \ō-'mit\ vb **omit•ted; omit•ting 1** : to leave out or leave unmentioned **2** : to fail to perform : NEGLECT — **omis•sion** \-'mish-ən\ n

**¹om•ni•bus** \'äm-ni-(‚)bəs\ n : BUS

**²omnibus** adj : of, relating to, or providing for many things at once ⟨an ∼ bill⟩

**om•nip•o•tent** \äm-'nip-ət-ənt\ adj : having unlimited authority or influence : ALMIGHTY — **om•nip•o•tence** \-əns\ n — **om•nip•o•tent•ly** adv

**om•ni•pres•ent** \‚äm-ni-'prez-ᵊnt\ adj : present in all places at all times — **om•ni•pres•ence** \-ᵊns\ n

**om•ni•scient** \äm-'nish-ənt\ adj : having infinite awareness, understanding, and insight — **om•ni•science** \-əns\ n — **om•ni•scient•ly** adv

**om•ni•um-gath•er•um** \‚äm-nē-əm-'gath-ə-rəm\ n, pl **omnium-gatherums** : a miscellaneous collection

**om•niv•o•rous** \äm-'niv-(ə-)rəs\ adj : feeding on both animal and vegetable substances; also ⟨an ∼ reader⟩ — **om•niv•o•rous•ly** adv — **om•niv•o•rous•ness** n

**¹on** \(')òn, (')än\ prep **1** : in or to a position over and in contact with ⟨a book ∼ the table⟩ ⟨jumped ∼ his horse⟩ **2** : touching the surface of ⟨shadows ∼ the wall⟩ **3** : IN, ABOARD ⟨went ∼ the train⟩ **4** : AT, TO ⟨∼ the right were the mountains⟩ **5** : at or toward as an object ⟨crept up ∼ him⟩ ⟨smiled ∼ her⟩ **6** : ABOUT, CONCERNING ⟨a book ∼ minerals⟩ **7** — used to indicate a basis, source, or standard of computation ⟨has it ∼ good authority⟩ ⟨10 cents ∼ the dollar⟩ **8** : with regard to ⟨a monopoly ∼ wheat⟩ **9** : connected with as a member or participant ⟨∼ a committee⟩ ⟨∼ tour⟩ **10** : in a state or process of ⟨∼ fire⟩ ⟨∼ the wane⟩ **11** : during or at the time of ⟨came ∼ Monday⟩ ⟨every hour ∼ the hour⟩ **12** : through the agency of ⟨was cut ∼ a tin can⟩

²**on** \'ȯn, 'än\ *adv* **1 :** in or into a position of contact with or attachment to a surface **2 :** FORWARD **3 :** into operation

³**on** \'ȯn, 'än\ *adj* **:** being in operation or in progress

**ON** *abbr* Old Norse

**once** \'wəns\ *adv* **1 :** one time only **2 :** at any one time **3 :** FORMERLY **4 :** by one degree of relationship

**once–over** \-,ō-vər\ *n* **:** a swift examination or survey

**on·com·ing** \'ȯn-,kəm-iŋ, 'än-\ *adj* **:** APPROACHING ⟨~ traffic⟩

¹**one** \'wən\ *adj* **1 :** being a single unit or thing ⟨~ man went⟩ **2 :** being one in particular ⟨early ~ morning⟩ **3 :** being the same in kind or quality ⟨members of ~ race⟩; *also* **:** UNITED **4 :** being not specified or fixed ⟨at ~ time or another⟩

²**one** *pron* **1 :** a single member or specimen ⟨saw ~ of his friends⟩ **2 :** a person in general ⟨~ never knows⟩ **3 :** — used in place of a first-person pronoun

³**one** *n* **1 :** the number denoting unity **2 :** the 1st in a set or series **3 :** a single person or thing — **one·ness** \'wən-nəs\ *n*

**Onei·da** \ō-'nīd-ə\ *n, pl* **Oneida** *or* **Oneidas :** a member of an Indian people orig. of New York

**oner·ous** \'än-ə-rəs, 'ō-nə-\ *adj* **:** imposing or constituting a burden **:** TROUBLESOME **syn** oppressive, exacting

**one·self** \(,)wən-'self\ *also* **one's self** \(,)wən-, ,wənz-\ *pron* **:** one's own self — usu. used reflexively or for emphasis

**one–sid·ed** \'wən-'sīd-əd\ *adj* **1 :** having or occurring on one side only; *also* **:** having one side prominent or more developed **2 :** UNEQUAL ⟨a ~ game⟩ **3 :** PARTIAL ⟨a ~ attitude⟩

**one·time** \-,tīm\ *adj* **:** FORMER

**one–to–one** \,wən-tə-'wən\ *adj* **:** pairing each element of a class uniquely with an element of another class

**one up** *adj* **:** being in a position of advantage ⟨was *one up* on the competition⟩

**one–way** *adj* **1 :** moving, allowing movement, or functioning in only one direction ⟨~ streets⟩

**on·go·ing** \'ȯn-,gō-iŋ, 'än-\ *adj* **:** continuously moving forward

**on·ion** \'ən-yən\ *n* **:** a plant related to the lilies and grown for its pungent edible bulb; *also* **:** this bulb

**on·ion·skin** \-,skin\ *n* **:** a thin strong translucent paper of very light weight

**on–line** *adj* **:** controlled directly by a computer ⟨~ equipment⟩ — **on–line** *adv*

**on·look·er** \'ȯn-,lu̇k-ər, 'än-\ *n* **:** SPECTATOR

¹**on·ly** \'ōn-lē\ *adj* **1 :** unquestionably the best **2 :** SOLE

²**only** *adv* **1 :** MERELY, JUST ⟨~ $2⟩ **2 :** SOLELY ⟨known ~ to me⟩ **3 :** at the very least ⟨was ~ too true⟩ **4 :** as a final result ⟨will ~ make you sick⟩

³**only** *conj* **:** except that

**on·o·mato·poe·ia** \,än-ə-,mat-ə-'pē-**

**(y)ə\ *n* **1 :** formation of words in imitation of natural sounds (as *buzz* or *hiss*) **2 :** the use of words whose sound suggests the sense — **on·o·mato·poe·ic** \-'pē-ik\ *or* **on·o·mato·po·et·ic** \-,pō-'et-ik\ *adj* — **on·o·mato·poe·i·cal·ly** \-'pē-ə-k(ə-)lē\ *or* **on·o·mato·po·et·i·cal·ly** \-,pō-'et-i-k(ə-)lē\ *adv*

**On·on·da·ga** \,än-ə(n)-'dȯ-gə\ *n, pl* **Onondaga** *or* **Onondagas :** a member of an Indian people of New York and Canada

**on·rush** \'ȯn-,rəsh, 'än-\ *n* **:** a rushing onward — **on·rush·ing** \-iŋ\ *adj*

**on·set** \-,set\ *n* **1 :** ATTACK **2 :** BEGINNING

**on·shore** \-,shȯr\ *adj* **1 :** moving toward the shore **2 :** situated on or near the shore — **on·shore** \-'shȯr\ *adv*

**on·slaught** \'än-,slȯt, 'ȯn-\ *n* **:** a fierce attack

**Ont** *abbr* Ontario

**on·to** \,ȯn-tə, 'än-; 'ȯn-tü, 'än-\ *prep* **:** to a position or point on

**onus** \'ō-nəs\ *n* **1 :** BURDEN; *also* **:** OBLIGATION **2 :** BLAME

¹**on·ward** \'ȯn-wərd, 'än-\ *also* **onwards** \-wərdz\ *adv* **:** FORWARD

²**onward** *adj* **:** directed or moving onward **:** FORWARD

**on·yx** \'än-iks\ *n* [ME *onix*, fr. OF & L; OF, fr. L *onyx*, fr. Gk, lit., claw, nail] **:** a translucent chalcedony in parallel layers of different colors

**oo·dles** \'üd-ᵊlz\ *n pl* **:** a great quantity

**oo·lite** \'ō-ə-,līt\ *n* **:** a rock consisting of small round grains cemented together — **oo·lit·ic** \,ō-ə-'lit-ik\ *adj*

¹**ooze** \'üz\ *n* **1 :** a soft deposit (as of mud) on the bottom of a body of water **2 :** MUD, SLIME — **oozy** \'ü-zē\ *adj*

²**ooze** *n* **:** something that oozes

³**ooze** *vb* **oozed; ooz·ing 1 :** to flow or leak out slowly or imperceptibly **2 :** EXUDE

¹**op** \'äp\ *n* **:** OPTICAL ART

²**op** *abbr* opus

**OP** *abbr* **1** observation post **2** Order of Preachers **3** out of print

**opac·i·ty** \ō-'pas-ət-ē\ *n, pl* **-ties 1 :** the quality or state of being opaque to radiant energy **2 :** obscurity of meaning **3 :** mental dullness **4 :** an opaque spot on an otherwise or normally transparent structure

**opal** \'ō-pəl\ *n* **:** a noncrystalline silica mineral that is sometimes classed as a gem and has delicate changeable colors

**opal·es·cent** \,ō-pə-'les-ᵊnt\ *adj* **:** IRIDESCENT — **opal·es·cence** \-ᵊns\ *n*

**opaque** \ō-'pāk\ *adj* **1 :** not pervious to radiant energy and esp. light **2 :** not easily understood **3 :** OBTUSE, STUPID — **opaque·ly** *adv* — **opaque·ness** *n*

**op art** \'äp-\ *n* **:** OPTICAL ART — **op artist** *n*

**op cit** *abbr* [L *opere citato*] in the work cited

**ope** \'ōp\ *vb* **oped; op·ing** *archaic* **:** OPEN

¹**open** \'ō-pən\ *adj* **open·er** \'ōp-(ə-)nər\; **open·est** \'ōp-(ə-)nəst\ **1**

**:** not shut or shut up ⟨an ∼ door⟩ **2 :** not secret or hidden; *also* **:** FRANK **3 :** not enclosed or covered ⟨an ∼ fire⟩; *also* **:** not protected **4 :** free to be entered or used ⟨an ∼ tournament⟩ **5 :** easy to get through or see ⟨∼ country⟩ **6 :** spread out **:** EXTENDED **7 :** free from restraints or controls ⟨∼ season⟩ **8 :** readily accessible and cooperative; *also* **:** GENEROUS **9 :** not decided **:** UNCERTAIN ⟨an ∼ question⟩ **10 :** ready to operate ⟨stores are ∼⟩ **11 :** having components separated by a space in writing and printing ⟨the name *Spanish mackerel* is an ∼ compound⟩ — **open·ly** *adv* — **open·ness** \-pən-nəs\ *n*

**²open** \'ō-pən\ *vb* **opened** \'ō-pənd\; **open·ing** \'ōp-(ə-)niŋ\ **1 :** to change or move from a shut position; *also* **:** to make open by clearing away obstacles **2 :** to make or become functional ⟨∼ a store⟩ **3 :** REVEAL; *also* **:** ENLIGHTEN **4 :** to make openings in **5 :** BEGIN **6 :** to give access — **open·er** \'ōp-(ə-)nər\ *n*

**³open** *n* **1 :** OUTDOORS **2 :** a contest or tournament open to all

**open–air** *adj* **:** OUTDOOR ⟨∼ theaters⟩

**open–hand·ed** \,ō-pən-'han-dəd\ *adj* **:** GENEROUS

**open–heart** *adj* **:** of, relating to, or performed on a heart temporarily relieved of circulatory function and laid open for inspection and treatment

**open–hearth** *adj* **:** of, relating to, or being a process of making steel in a furnace that reflects the heat from the roof onto the material

**open·ing** \'ōp-(ə-)niŋ\ *n* **1 :** an act or instance of making or becoming open **2 :** something that is open **3 :** BEGINNING **4 :** OCCASION; *also* **:** an opportunity for employment

**open–mind·ed** \,ō-pən-'mīn-dəd\ *adj* **:** free from rigidly fixed preconceptions

**open sentence** *n* **:** a statement (as in mathematics) containing at least one blank or unknown so that when the blank is filled or a quantity substituted for the unknown the statement becomes a complete statement that is either true or false

**open shop** *n* **:** an establishment employing and retaining on the payroll members and nonmembers of a labor union

**open·work** \'ō-pən-,wərk\ *n* **:** work so made as to show openings through its substance ⟨a railing of wrought-iron ∼⟩ — **open–worked** \-,wərkt\ *adj*

**¹opera** *pl of* OPUS

**²op·era** \'äp-(ə-)rə\ *n* **:** a drama set to music — **op·er·at·ic** \,äp-ə-'rat-ik\ *adj*

**op·er·a·ble** \'äp-(ə-)rə-bəl\ *adj* **1 :** fit, possible, or desirable to use **2 :** suitable for surgical treatment

**opera glass** *n* **:** a small binocular adapted for use at an opera — often used in pl.

**op·er·ate** \'äp-ə-,rāt\ *vb* **-at·ed; -at·ing 1 :** to perform work **:** FUNCTION **2 :** to produce an effect **3 :** to perform an operation **4 :** to put or keep in operation — **op·er·a·tor** \-,rāt-ər\ *n*

**op·er·a·tion** \,äp-ə-'rā-shən\ *n* **1 :** a doing or performing of a practical work **2 :** an exertion of power or influence; *also* **:** method or manner of functioning **3 :** a surgical procedure **4 :** a process of deriving one mathematical expression from others according to a rule **5 :** a military action or mission — **op·er·a·tion·al** \-sh(ə-)nəl\ *adj*

**¹op·er·a·tive** \'äp-(ə-)rət-iv, 'äp-ə-,rāt-\ *adj* **1 :** producing an appropriate effect **2 :** OPERATING ⟨an ∼ force⟩ **3 :** having to do with physical operations; *also* **:** WORKING ⟨an ∼ craftsman⟩ **4 :** based on or consisting of an operation

**²operative** *n* **:** OPERATOR; *esp* **:** a secret agent

**op·er·et·ta** \,äp-ə-'ret-ə\ *n* **:** a light musical-dramatic work with a romantic plot, spoken dialogue, and dancing scenes

**oph·thal·mic** \äf-'thal-mik, äp-\ *adj* **:** of, relating to, or located near the eye

**oph·thal·mol·o·gy** \,äf-,thal-'mäl-ə-jē, ,äp-\ *n* **:** a branch of medicine dealing with the structure, functions, and diseases of the eye — **oph·thal·mol·o·gist** \-jəst\ *n*

**oph·thal·mo·scope** \äf-'thal-mə-,skōp, äp-\ *n* **:** an instrument with a mirror centrally perforated for use in viewing the interior of the eye and esp. the retina

**opi·ate** \'ō-pē-ət, -pē-,āt\ *n* **:** a preparation or derivative of opium; *also* **:** NARCOTIC

**opine** \ō-'pīn\ *vb* **opined; opin·ing :** to express an opinion **:** STATE

**opin·ion** \ə-'pin-yən\ *n* **1 :** a belief stronger than impression and less strong than positive knowledge **2 :** JUDGMENT **3 :** a formal statement by an expert after careful study

**opin·ion·at·ed** \-yə-,nāt-əd\ *adj* **:** obstinately adhering to personal opinions

**opi·um** \'ō-pē-əm\ *n* [ME, fr. L, fr. Gk *opion*, fr. dim. of *opos* sap] **:** an addictive narcotic drug that is the dried juice of a poppy

**opos·sum** \ə-'päs-əm\ *n, pl* **opossums** *also* **opossum** [fr. *ăpăsŭm*, lit., white animal (in some Indian language of Virginia)] **:** any of various American marsupial mammals; *esp* **:** a common omnivorous tree-dwelling animal of the eastern U.S.

**opp** *abbr* opposite

**op·po·nent** \ə-'pō-nənt\ *n* **:** one that opposes **:** ADVERSARY

**op·por·tune** \,äp-ər-'t(y)ün\ *adj* [ME, fr. MF *opportun*, fr. L *opportunus*, fr. *ob-* toward + *portus* port, harbor] **:** SUITABLE — **op·por·tune·ly** *adv*

**op·por·tun·ism** \-'t(y)ü-,niz-əm\ *n* **:** a taking advantage of opportunities or circumstances esp. with little regard for principles or ultimate consequences — **op·por·tun·ist** \-nəst\ *n* — **op·por·tu·nis·tic** \-,t(y)ü-'nis-tik\ *adj*

**op·por·tu·ni·ty** \-'t(y)ü-nət-ē\ *n, pl* **-ties 1 :** a favorable combination of circumstances, time, and place **2 :** a chance for advancement or progress

**op·pose** \ə-'pōz\ *vb* **op·posed; op·pos·ing** **1 :** to place opposite or against something (as to provide resistance or contrast) **2 :** to strive against **:** RESIST — **op·po·si·tion** \‚äp-ə-'zish-ən\ *n*

¹**op·po·site** \'äp-ə-zət\ *n* **:** one that is opposed or contrary

²**opposite** *adj* **1 :** set over against something that is at the other end or side **2 :** OPPOSED, HOSTILE; *also* **:** CONTRARY **3 :** contrarily turned or moving — **op·po·site·ly** *adv* — **op·po·site·ness** *n*

³**opposite** *adv* **:** on opposite sides

⁴**opposite** *prep* **:** across from and usu. facing (the house ~ ours)

**op·press** \ə-'pres\ *vb* **1 :** to crush by abuse of power or authority **2 :** to weigh down **:** BURDEN **syn** depress wrong, persecute — **op·pres·sive** \-'pres-iv\ *adj* — **op·pres·sive·ly** *adv* — **op·pres·sor** \-'pres-ər\ *n*

**op·pres·sion** \ə-'presh-ən\ *n* **1 :** unjust or cruel exercise of power or authority **2 :** DEPRESSION

**op·pro·bri·ous** \ə-'prō-brē-əs\ *adj* **:** expressing or deserving opprobrium — **op·pro·bri·ous·ly** *adv*

**op·pro·bri·um** \-brē-əm\ *n* **1 :** something that brings disgrace **2 :** INFAMY

¹**opt** \'äpt\ *vb* **:** to make a choice

²**opt** *abbr* **1** optical; optician; optics **2** optional

**op·tic** \'äp-tik\ *adj* **:** of or relating to vision or the eye

**op·ti·cal** \'äp-ti-kəl\ *adj* **1 :** relating to optics **2 :** OPTIC **3 :** of or relating to optical art

**optical art** *n* **:** nonobjective art characterized by the use of geometric patterns often for an illusory effect

**op·ti·cian** \äp-'tish-ən\ *n* **1 :** a maker of or dealer in optical items and instruments **2 :** one that grinds spectacle lenses to prescription and dispenses spectacles

**op·tics** \'äp-tiks\ *n pl* **1 :** a science that deals with the nature and properties of light and the effects that it undergoes and produces **2 :** optical properties

**op·ti·mal** \'äp-tə-məl\ *adj* **:** most desirable or satisfactory — **op·ti·mal·ly** \-ē\ *adv*

**op·ti·mism** \'äp-tə-‚miz-əm\ *n* [F *optimisme*, fr. L *optimum*, n., best, fr. neut. of *optimus* best] **1 :** a doctrine that this world is the best possible world **2 :** an inclination to anticipate the best possible outcome of actions or events — **op·ti·mist** \-məst\ *n* — **op·ti·mis·tic** \‚äp-tə-'mis-tik\ *adj* — **op·ti·mis·ti·cal·ly** \-tə-mə-'mis-tik(ə-)lē\ *adv*

**op·ti·mum** \'äp-tə-məm\ *n, pl* **-ma** \-mə\ *also* **-mums** **:** the amount or degree of something most favorable to an end; *also* **:** greatest degree attained under implied or specified conditions

**op·tion** \'äp-shən\ *n* **1 :** the power or right to choose **2 :** a right to buy or sell something at a specified price during a specified period **3 :** something offered for choice — **op·tion·al** \-sh(ə-)nəl\ *adj*

**op·tom·e·try** \äp-'täm-ə-trē\ *n* **:** the art or profession of examining the eyes for defects of refraction and of prescribing lenses to correct these — **op·tom·e·trist** \-trəst\ *n*

**opt out** *vb* **:** to choose not to participate

**op·u·lent** \'äp-yə-lənt\ *adj* **1 :** WEALTHY **2 :** richly abundant — **op·u·lence** \-ləns\ *n*

**opus** \'ō-pəs\ *n, pl* **opera** \'ō-pə-rə, 'äp-ə-\ *also* **opus·es** \'ō-pə-səz\ **:** WORK; *esp* **:** a musical composition

**opus·cule** \ō-'pəs-‚(,)kyül\ *n* **:** a minor work (as of literature)

**or** \ər, (,)ȯr\ *conj* — used as a function word to indicate an alternative (sink ~ swim)

**OR** *abbr* **1** operating room **2** Oregon **3** owner's risk

**-or** \ər\ *n suffix* **:** one that does a (specified) thing (calculator) (elevator)

**or·a·cle** \'ȯr-ə-kəl\ *n* **1 :** one held to give divinely inspired answers or revelations **2 :** an authoritative or wise utterance; *also* **:** a person of great authority or wisdom — **orac·u·lar** \ȯ-'rak-yə-lər\ *adj*

¹**oral** \'ōr-əl, 'ȯr-\ *adj* **1 :** SPOKEN **2 :** of or relating to the mouth **3 :** of, relating to, or characterized by the first stage of psychosexual development in which libidinal gratification is derived from intake (as of food), by sucking, and later by biting **4 :** relating to or characterized by personality traits of passive dependency and aggressiveness — **oral·ly** \'ōr-ə-lē, 'ȯr-\ *adv*

²**oral** *n* **:** an oral examination — usu. used in pl.

**or·ange** \'ȯr-inj\ *n* **1 :** a juicy citrus fruit with reddish yellow rind; *also* **:** the evergreen tree with fragrant white flowers that bears this fruit **2 :** a color between red and yellow

**or·ange·ade** \‚ȯr-inj-'ād\ *n* **:** a beverage of orange juice, sugar, and water

**orange hawkweed** *n* **:** a weedy herb related to the daisies with bright orange-red flower heads

**or·ange·ry** \'ȯr-inj-(ə-)rē\ *n, pl* **-ries** **:** a protected place (as a greenhouse) for raising oranges in cool climates

**orang·utan** or **orang·ou·tan** \ə-'raŋ-ə-‚taŋ, -‚tan\ *n* [Malay *orang hutan*, fr. *orang* man + *hutan* forest] **:** a reddish brown manlike tree-living ape of Borneo and Sumatra

**orate** \ȯ-'rāt\ *vb* **orat·ed; orat·ing** **:** to speak in a declamatory manner

**ora·tion** \ə-'rā-shən\ *n* **:** an elaborate discourse delivered in a formal dignified manner

**or·a·tor** \'ȯr-ət-ər\ *n* **:** one noted for his skill and power as a public speaker

**or·a·tor·i·cal** \‚ȯr-ə-'tȯr-i-kəl\ *adj* **:** of, relating to, or characteristic of an orator or oratory

**or·a·to·rio** \‚ȯr-ə-'tōr-ē-‚ō\ *n, pl* **-ri·os** **:** a choral work usu. on a scriptural subject

¹**or·a·to·ry** \'ȯr-ə-‚tōr-ē\ *n, pl* **-ries** **:** a private or institutional chapel

²**oratory** *n* **:** the art of speaking eloquently and effectively in public **syn** elo-

quence, elocution — **or·a·tor·i·cal** \ˌȯr-ə-ˈtȯr-i-kəl\ *adj*

**orb** \ˈȯrb\ *n* **:** a spherical body; *esp* **:** a celestial body (as a planet) — **or·bic·u·lar** \ȯr-ˈbik-yə-lər\ *adj*

**¹or·bit** \ˈȯr-bət\ *n* [L *orbita*, lit., track, rut] **1** **:** a path described by one body or object in its revolution about another **2** **:** range or sphere of activity — **or·bit·al** \-ᵊl\ *adj*

**²orbit** *vb* **1** **:** CIRCLE **2** **:** to send up and make revolve in an orbit ⟨∼ a satellite⟩

**or·bit·er** \-bət-ər\ *n* **:** one that orbits; *esp* **:** a spacecraft designed only to orbit a celestial body

**orch** *abbr* orchestra

**or·chard** \ˈȯr-chərd\ *n* [ME, fr. OE *ortgeard*, fr. L *hortus* garden + OE *geard* yard, both fr. the same prehistoric IE noun meaning an enclosure] **:** a place where fruit trees or nut trees are grown; *also* **:** the trees of such a place — **or·chard·ist** \-əst\ *n*

**or·ches·tra** \ˈȯr-kə-strə\ *n* [L, fr. Gk *orchēstra*, fr. *orcheisthai* to dance] **1** **:** a group of instrumentalists organized to perform ensemble music **2** **:** the front section of seats on the main floor of a theater — **or·ches·tral** \ȯr-ˈkes-trəl\ *adj*

**or·ches·trate** \ˈȯr-kə-ˌstrāt\ *vb* **-trat·ed; -trat·ing** **:** to compose or arrange for an orchestra — **or·ches·tra·tion** \ˌȯr-kə-ˈstrā-shən\ *n*

**or·chid** \ˈȯr-kəd\ *n* **:** any of numerous related plants having often showy flowers with three petals of which the middle one is enlarged into a lip; *also* **:** a flower of an orchid

**ord** *abbr* **1** order **2** ordnance

**or·dain** \ȯr-ˈdān\ *vb* **1** **:** to admit to the ministry or priesthood by the ritual of a church **2** **:** DECREE, ENACT; *also* **:** DESTINE

**or·deal** \ȯr-ˈdē(-ə)l, ˈȯr-ˌdē(-ə)l\ *n* **:** a severe trial or experience

**¹or·der** \ˈȯrd-ər\ *n* **1** **:** a group of people formally united; *also* **:** a badge or medal of such a group **2** **:** any of the several grades of the Christian ministry; *also, pl* **:** ORDINATION **3** **:** a rank, class, or special group of persons or things **4** **:** ARRANGEMENT, SEQUENCE; *also* **:** the prevailing mode of things **5** **:** a customary mode of procedure; *also* **:** the rule of law or proper authority **6** **:** a specific rule, regulation, or authoritative direction **7** **:** a style of building; *also* **:** an architectural column forming the unit of a style **8** **:** condition esp. with regard to repair **9** **:** a written direction to pay money or to buy or sell goods; *also* **:** goods bought or sold

**²order** *vb* **or·dered; or·der·ing** \ˈȯrd-(ə-)riŋ\ **1** **:** ARRANGE, REGULATE **2** **:** COMMAND **3** **:** to place an order

**¹or·der·ly** \ˈȯrd-ər-lē\ *adj* **1** **:** arranged according to some order; *also* **:** NEAT, TIDY **2** **:** well behaved ⟨an ∼ crowd⟩ **syn** methodical, systematic — **or·der·li·ness** *n*

**²orderly** *n, pl* **-lies** **1** **:** a soldier who attends a superior officer **2** **:** a hospital attendant who does general work

**¹or·di·nal** \ˈȯrd-(ᵊ-)nəl\ *n* **:** an ordinal number

**²ordinal** *adj* **:** indicating order or rank (as sixth) in a series

**or·di·nance** \ˈȯrd-(ᵊ-)nəns\ *n* **:** an authoritative decree or law; *esp* **:** a municipal regulation

**or·di·nary** \ˈȯrd-ᵊn-ˌer-ē\ *adj* **1** **:** to be expected **:** USUAL **2** **:** of common quality, rank, or ability; *also* **:** POOR, INFERIOR **syn** customary, routine, normal — **or·di·nar·i·ly** \ˌȯrd-ᵊn-ˈer-ə-lē\ *adv*

**or·di·nate** \ˈȯrd-(ᵊ-)nət, ˈȯrd-ᵊn-ˌāt\ *n* **:** the coordinate of a point in a plane obtained by measuring parallel to the vertical axis

**or·di·na·tion** \ˌȯrd-ᵊn-ˈā-shən\ *n* **:** the act or ceremony by which a person is ordained

**ord·nance** \ˈȯrd-nəns\ *n* **1** **:** military supplies (as weapons, ammunition, or vehicles) **2** **:** CANNON, ARTILLERY

**or·dure** \ˈȯr-jər\ *n* **:** EXCREMENT

**ore** \ˈȯr\ *n* **:** a mineral containing a constituent for which it is mined and worked

**öre** \ˈər-ə\ *n, pl* **öre** — see *krona, krone* at MONEY table

**Oreg** *or* **Ore** *abbr* Oregon

**oreg·a·no** \ə-ˈreg-ə-ˌnō\ *n* **:** a bushy perennial mint used as a seasoning and a source of oil

**org** *abbr* organization; organized

**or·gan** \ˈȯr-gən\ *n* **1** **:** a musical instrument having sets of pipes sounded by compressed air and controlled by keyboards; *also* **:** an instrument in which the sounds of the pipe organ are approximated by electronic devices **2** **:** a differentiated animal or plant structure made up of cells and tissues and performing some bodily function **3** **:** a means of performing a function or accomplishing an end **4** **:** PERIODICAL

**or·gan·dy** *also* **or·gan·die** \ˈȯr-gən-dē\ *n, pl* **-dies** **:** a fine transparent muslin with a stiff finish

**or·gan·ic** \ȯr-ˈgan-ik\ *adj* **1** **:** of, relating to, or arising in a bodily organ **2** **:** ORGANIZED ⟨an ∼ whole⟩ **3** **:** of, relating to, or derived from living things; *also* **:** containing carbon or its compounds **4** **:** of or relating to a branch of chemistry (**organic chemistry**) dealing with carbon compounds formed or related to those formed by living things — **or·gan·i·cal·ly** \-i-k(ə-)lē\ *adv*

**or·gan·ism** \ˈȯr-gə-ˌniz-əm\ *n* **:** a living person, animal, or plant — **or·gan·is·mic** \ˌȯr-gə-ˈniz-mik\ *adj*

**or·gan·ist** \ˈȯr-gə-nəst\ *n* **:** one who plays an organ

**or·ga·ni·za·tion** \ˌȯrg-(ə-)nə-ˈzā-shən\ *n* **1** **:** the act or process of organizing or of being organized; *also* **:** the condition or manner of being organized **2** **:** SOCIETY **3** **:** MANAGEMENT — **or·ga·ni·za·tion·al** *adj*

**or·ga·nize** \ˈȯr-gə-ˌnīz\ *vb* **-nized; -niz·ing** **1** **:** to develop an organic structure **2** **:** to arrange or form into a complete and functioning whole **3** **:** to set up an administrative structure for **4 :** to arrange by systematic planning and united effort **5 :** to join in a union; *also* **:** UNIONIZE **syn** institute, found, establish — **or·ga·niz·er** *n*

**or·gano·chlo·rine** \ȯr-,gan-ə-'klȯr-,ēn\ *adj* **:** of or relating to the chlorinated hydrocarbon pesticides (as DDT) — **organochlorine** *n*

**or·gano·phos·phate** \-'fäs-,fāt\ *n* **:** an organophosphorus pesticide — **organophosphate** *adj*

**or·gano·phos·pho·rus**\-'fäs-f(ə-)rəs\ *also* **or·gano·phos·pho·rous** \-fäs-'fōr-əs\ *adj* **:** of, relating to, or being a phosphorus-containing organic pesticide (as malathion) — **organophosphorus** *n*

**or·gan·za** \ȯr-'gan-zə\ *n* **:** a sheer dress fabric resembling organdy and usu. made of silk, rayon, or nylon

**or·gasm** \'ȯr-,gaz-əm\ *n* **:** a climax of sexual excitement

**or·gi·as·tic** \,ȯr-jē-'as-tik\ *adj* **:** of, relating to, or marked by orgies

**or·gu·lous** \'ȯr-g(y)ə-ləs\ *adj* **:** PROUD

**or·gy** \'ȯr-jē\ *n, pl* **orgies :** a gathering marked by unrestrained indulgence in alcohol, drugs, or sexual practices

**ori·el** \'ȯr-ē-əl\ *n* **:** a window built out from a wall and usu. supported by a bracket

**ori·ent** \'ȯr-ē-,ent\ *vb* **1 :** to set or arrange in a definite position esp. in relation to the points of the compass **2 :** to acquaint with an existing situation or environment — **ori·en·ta·tion** \,ȯr-ē-ən-'tā-shən\ *n*

**ori·en·tal** \,ȯr-ē-'ent-ᵊl\ *adj* [fr. *Orient* East, fr. ME, fr. MF, fr. L *orient-, oriens*, fr. prp. of *oriri* to rise] *often cap* **:** of or situated in the Orient — **Oriental** *n*

**ori·en·tate** \'ȯr-ē-ən-,tāt\ *vb* **-tat·ed; -tat·ing 1 :** ORIENT **2 :** to face east

**or·i·fice** \'ȯr-ə-fəs\ *n* **:** OPENING, MOUTH

**ori·flamme** \'ȯr-ə-,flam\ *n* **:** a brightly colored banner used as a standard or ensign in battle

**orig** *abbr* original; originally

**ori·ga·mi** \,ȯr-ə-'gäm-ē\ *n* **:** the art or process of Japanese paper folding

**or·i·gin** \'ȯr-ə-jən\ *n* **1 :** ANCESTRY **2 :** rise, beginning, or derivation from a source; *also* **:** CAUSE **3 :** the intersection of coordinate axes

¹**orig·i·nal** \ə-'rij-(ə-)nəl\ *n* **:** something from which a copy, reproduction, or translation is made **:** PROTOTYPE

²**original** *adj* **1 :** FIRST, INITIAL **2 :** not copied from something else **:** FRESH **3 :** INVENTIVE — **orig·i·nal·i·ty** \-,rij-ə-'nal-ət-ē\ *n* — **orig·i·nal·ly** \-'rij-ən-ᵊl-ē\ *adv*

**orig·i·nate** \ə-'rij-ə-,nāt\ *vb* **-nat·ed; -nat·ing 1 :** to give rise to **:** INITIATE **2 :** to come into existence **:** BEGIN — **orig·i·na·tor** \-,nāt-ər\ *n*

**ori·ole** \'ȯr-ē-,ōl\ *n* [F *oriol*, fr. L *aureolus*, dim. of *aureus* golden, fr. *aurum* gold] **:** any of several American songbirds about the size of a thrush; *esp* **:** BALTIMORE ORIOLE

**or·i·son** \'ȯr-ə-sən\ *n* **:** PRAYER

**or·mo·lu** \'ȯr-mə-,lü\ *n* **:** a brass made to imitate gold and used for decorative purposes

¹**or·na·ment** \'ȯr-nə-mənt\ *n* **:** something that lends grace or beauty — **or·na·men·tal** \,ȯr-nə-'ment-ᵊl\ *adj*

²**or·na·ment** \-,ment\ *vb* **:** to provide with ornament **:** ADORN — **or·na·men·ta·tion** \,ȯr-nə-mən-'tā-shən\ *n*

**or·nate** \ȯr-'nāt\ *adj* **:** elaborately decorated — **or·nate·ly** *adv* — **or·nate·ness** *n*

**or·nery** \'ȯrn-(ə-)rē, 'än-\ *adj* **:** having an irritable disposition

**ornith** *abbr* ornithology

**or·ni·thol·o·gy** \,ȯr-nə-'thäl-ə-jē\ *n, pl* **-gies :** a branch of zoology dealing with birds — **or·ni·tho·log·i·cal** \-thə-'läj-i-kəl\ *adj* — **or·ni·thol·o·gist** \-'thäl-ə-jəst\ *n*

**orog·e·ny** \ȯ-'räj-ə-nē\ *n* **:** the process of mountain formation — **oro·gen·ic** \,ȯr-ə-'jen-ik\ *adj*

**oro·tund** \'ȯr-ə-,tənd\ *adj* **1 :** SONOROUS **2 :** POMPOUS

**or·phan** \'ȯr-fən\ *n* **:** a child deprived by death of one or usu. both parents — **orphan** *vb*

**or·phan·age** \'ȯrf-(ə-)nij\ *n* **:** an institution for the care of orphans

**or·ris** \'ȯr-əs\ *n* **:** a European iris with a fragrant rootstock (**orrisroot**) used in perfume and sachets

**orth·odon·tia** \,ȯr-thə-'dän-ch(ē-)ə\ *n* **:** ORTHODONTICS

**or·tho·don·tics** \'dänt-iks\ *n* **:** a branch of dentistry dealing with faulty tooth occlusion and its correction — **or·tho·don·tist** \-'dänt-əst\ *n*

**or·tho·dox** \'ȯr-thə-,däks\ *adj* [MF or LL; MF *orthodoxe*, fr. LL *orthodoxus*, fr. LGk *orthodoxos*, fr. Gk *orthos* right + *doxa* opinion] **1 :** conforming to established doctrine esp. in religion **2 :** CONVENTIONAL **3** *cap* **:** of or relating to a Christian church originating in the church of the Eastern Roman Empire — **or·tho·doxy** \-,däk-sē\ *n*

**or·tho·epy** \'ȯr-thə-,wep-ē, ȯr-'thō-ə-pē\ *n* **:** the customary pronunciation of a language — **or·tho·ep·ist** \'ȯr-thə-,wep-əst, ȯr-'thō-ə-pəst\ *n*

**or·thog·ra·phy** \ȯr-'thäg-rə-fē\ *n* **:** SPELLING — **or·tho·graph·ic** \,ȯr-thə-'graf-ik\ *adj*

**or·tho·pe·dics** \,ȯr-thə-'pēd-iks\ *n sing or pl* **:** the correction or prevention of skeletal deformities — **or·tho·pe·dic** \-ik\ *adj* — **or·tho·pe·dist** \-'pēd-əst\ *n*

**or·to·lan** \'ȯrt-ᵊl-ən\ *n* **:** a European bunting valued as a table delicacy

**Os** *symbol* osmium

**OS** *abbr* **1** [L *oculus sinister*] left eye **2** ordinary seaman **3** out of stock

**Osage** \ō-'sāj\ *n, pl* **Osag·es** or **Osage :** a member of an Indian people orig. of Missouri

**OSB** *abbr* Order of St. Benedict

**os·cil·late** \'äs-ə-,lāt\ *vb* **-lat·ed; -lat·ing 1 :** to swing backward and forward like a pendulum **2 :** VARY, FLUCTUATE **3 :** to increase and decrease in magnitude or reverse direction periodically ⟨an *oscillating* current⟩ — os·cil·la·tion \ˌäs-ə-ˈlā-shən\ *n* — os·cil·la·tor \ˈäs-ə-ˌlāt-ər\ *n* — os·cil·la·to·ry \ˈä-ˈsil-ə-ˌtōr-ē\ *adj*

os·cil·lo·scope \ä-ˈsil-ə-ˌskōp\ *n* : an instrument in which variations in current or voltage appear as visible waves of light on a fluorescent screen — os·cil·lo·scop·ic \ˌä-ˌsil-ə-ˈskäp-ik, ˌäs-ə-lə-\ *adj* — os·cil·lo·scop·i·cal·ly \-i-k(ə-)lē\ *adv*

os·cu·late \ˈäs-kyə-ˌlāt\ *vb* -lat·ed; -lat·ing : KISS — os·cu·la·tion \ˌäs-kyə-ˈlā-shən\ *n*

OSF *abbr* Order of St. Francis

osier \ˈō-zhər\ *n* : a willow tree with pliable twigs used esp. in making baskets and furniture; *also* : a twig from an osier

os·mi·um \ˈäz-mē-əm\ *n* : a heavy hard brittle metallic chemical element used in alloys

os·mo·sis \äz-ˈmō-səs, äs-\ *n* : diffusion through a partially permeable membrane separating a solvent and a solution that tends to equalize their concentrations — os·mot·ic \-ˈmät-ik\ *adj*

os·prey \ˈäs-prē, -ˌprā\ *n, pl* ospreys : a large brown and white fish-eating hawk

os·si·fy \ˈäs-ə-ˌfī\ *vb* -fied; -fy·ing : to change into bone — os·si·fi·ca·tion \ˌäs-ə-fə-ˈkā-shən\ *n*

os·su·ary \ˈäsh-ə-ˌwer-ē, ˈäs-(y)ə-\ *n, pl* -ar·ies : a depository for the bones of the dead

os·ten·si·ble \ä-ˈsten-sə-bəl\ *adj* : shown outwardly : PROFESSED, APPARENT — os·ten·si·bly \-blē\ *adv*

os·ten·ta·tion \ˌäs-tən-ˈtā-shən\ *n* : pretentious or excessive display — os·ten·ta·tious \-shəs\ *adj* — os·ten·ta·tious·ly *adv*

os·te·op·a·thy \ˌäs-tē-ˈäp-ə-thē\ *n* : a system of healing that emphasizes manipulation (as of joints) but does not exclude other agencies (as the use of medicine and surgery) — os·te·o·path \ˈäs-tē-ə-ˌpath\ *n* — os·te·o·path·ic \ˌäs-tē-ə-ˈpath-ik\ *adj*

ostler *var of* HOSTLER

ost·mark \ˈōst-ˌmärk, ˈóst-\ *n* — see MONEY table

os·tra·cize \ˈäs-trə-ˌsīz\ *vb* -cized; -ciz·ing [Gk *ostrakizein* to banish by voting with potsherds, fr. *ostrakon* shell, potsherd] : to exclude from a group by common consent — os·tra·cism \-ˌsiz-əm\ *n*

os·trich \ˈäs-trich, ˈós-\ *n* : a very large swift-footed flightless bird of Africa and Arabia

Os·we·go tea \ä-ˌswē-gō-\ *n* : a No. American mint with showy scarlet flowers

OT *abbr* 1 Old Testament 2 overtime

¹oth·er \ˈəth-ər\ *adj* 1 : being the one left; *also* : being the ones distinct from those first mentioned 2 : ALTERNATE ⟨every ~ day⟩ 3 : DIFFERENT 4 : ADDITIONAL 5 : recently past ⟨the ~ night⟩

²other *pron* 1 : remaining one or ones ⟨one foot and then the ~⟩ 2 : a different or additional one ⟨something or ~⟩

oth·er·wise \-ˌwīz\ *adv* 1 : in a different way 2 : in different circumstances 3 : in other respects — otherwise *adj*

oth·er·world \-ˌwərld\ *n* : a world beyond death or beyond present reality

oth·er·world·ly \-ˌwərl-(d)lē\ *adj* : not worldly : concerned with spiritual, intellectual, or imaginative matters

oti·ose \ˈō-shē-ˌōs, ˈōt-ē-\ *adj* 1 : IDLE 2 : STERILE 3 : USELESS

oto·lar·yn·gol·o·gy \ˈōt-ō-ˌlar-ən-ˈgäl-ə-jē\ *n* : a branch of medicine dealing with the ear, nose, and throat — oto·lar·yn·gol·o·gist \-jəst\ *n*

OTS *abbr* officers' training school

Ot·ta·wa \ˈät-ə-wə, -ˌwä, -ˌwó\ *n, pl* Ottawas *or* Ottawa : a member of an Indian people of Michigan and southern Ontario

ot·ter \ˈät-ər\ *n, pl* otters *also* otter : a web-footed fish-eating mammal that is related to the weasels and has dark brown fur; *also* : its fur

ot·to·man \ˈät-ə-mən\ *n* : an upholstered seat or couch; *also* : an overstuffed footstool

ou·bli·ette \ˌü-blē-ˈet\ *n* [F, fr. MF, fr. *oublier* to forget, fr. L *oblivisci*] : a dungeon with an opening at the top

ought \ˈót\ *verbal auxiliary* — used to express moral obligation, advisability, natural expectation, or logical consequence

ounce \ˈaúns\ *n* [ME, fr. MF *unce*, fr. L *uncia* twelfth part, ounce, fr. *unus* one] — see WEIGHT table

our \ˈär, (ˈ)aú(ə)r\ *adj* : of or relating to us or ourselves

ours \(ˈ)aú(ə)rz, ärz\ *pron* : one or the ones belonging to us

our·selves \är-ˈselvz, aú(ə)r-\ *pron* : our own selves — used reflexively, for emphasis, or in absolute constructions ⟨we pleased ~⟩ ⟨we'll do it ~⟩ ⟨~ tourists, we avoided other tourists⟩

-ous \əs\ *adj suffix* : full of : abounding in : having : possessing the qualities of ⟨clamorous⟩ ⟨poisonous⟩

oust \ˈaúst\ *vb* : to eject from or deprive of property or position : EXPEL *syn* evict, dismiss

oust·er \ˈaús-tər\ *n* : EXPULSION

¹out \ˈaút\ *adv* 1 : in a direction away from the inside or center 2 : beyond control 3 : to extinction, exhaustion, or completion 4 : in or into the open 5 : so as to retire a batter or base runner; *also* : so as to be retired

²out *vb* : to become known ⟨the truth will ~⟩

³out *adj* 1 : situated outside or at a distance 2 : not in : ABSENT; *also* : not being in power 3 : not successful in reaching base 4 : not being in vogue or fashion : not up-to-date

⁴out \(ˌ)aút\ *prep* 1 : out through ⟨looked ~ the window⟩ 2 : outward on or along ⟨drive ~ the river road⟩

⁵out \ˈaút\ *n* 1 : one who is out of office 2 : a batter or base runner who has been retired

**out-and-out** \,aùt-ᵊn(d)-'aùt\ *adj* **1** : OPEN, UNDISGUISED **2** : COMPLETE, THOROUGHGOING

**out-bal-ance** \aùt-'bal-əns\ *vb* : OUTWEIGH

**out-bid** \-'bid\ *vb* : to make a higher bid than

¹**out-board** \'aùt-,bōrd\ *adj* **1** : situated outboard **2** : having or using an outboard motor

²**outboard** *adv* **1** : outside the lines of a ship's hull **2** : facing outward from the median line **2** : in a position closer to closest to either of the wing tips of an airplane

**outboard motor** *n* : a small internal-combustion engine with propeller attached for mounting at the stern of a small boat

**out-bound** \'aùt-,baùnd\ *adj* : outward bound (~ traffic)

**out-break** \'aùt-,brāk\ *n* **1** : a sudden or violent breaking out **2** : something (as an epidemic) that breaks out

**out-build-ing** \'aùt-,bil-diŋ\ *n* : a building separate from but accessory to a main house

**out-burst** \-,bərst\ *n* : ERUPTION; *esp* : a violent expression of feeling

**out-cast** \'aùt-,kast\ *n* : one who is cast out by society : PARIAH

**out-class** \aùt-'klas\ *vb* : SURPASS

**out-come** \'aùt-,kəm\ *n* : a final consequence : RESULT

**out-crop** \'aùt-,kräp\ *n* : the coming out of a stratum to the surface of the ground; *also* : the part of a stratum that thus appears — **outcrop** *vb*

**out-cry** \-,krī\ *n* : a loud cry : CLAMOR

**out-dat-ed** \aùt-'dāt-əd\ *adj* : OUTMODED

**out-dis-tance** \-'dis-təns\ *vb* : to go far ahead of (as in a race) : OUTSTRIP

**out-do** \-'dü\ *vb* **-did** \-'did\; **-done** \-'dən\; **-do-ing** \-'dü-iŋ\; **-does** \-'dəz\ : to go beyond in action or performance : EXCEL

**out-door** \,aùt-,dōr\ *also* **out-doors** \-,dōrz\ *adj* **1** : of or relating to the outdoors **2** : performed outdoors **3** : not enclosed (as by a roof)

¹**out-doors** \aùt-'dōrz\ *adv* : in or into the open air

²**outdoors** *n* **1** : the open air **2** : the world away from human habitation

**out-draw** \aùt-'drò\ *vb* **-drew** \-'drü\, **-drawn** \-'dròn\; **-drawing 1** : to attract a larger audience than **2** : to draw a handgun more quickly than

**out-er** \'aùt-ər\ *adj* **1** : EXTERNAL **2** : situated farther out; *also* : being away from a center

**out-er-most** \-,mōst\ *adj* : farthest out

▌**outer space** *n* : space outside the earth's atmosphere

**out-face** \aùt-'fās\ *vb* **1** : to cause to waver or submit **2** : DEFY

**out-field** \'aùt-,fēld\ *n* : the part of a baseball field beyond the infield and within the foul lines; *also* : players in the outfield — **out-field-er** \-,fēl-dər\ *n*

**out-fight** \aùt-'fīt\ *vb* : to surpass in fighting : DEFEAT

¹**out-fit** \'aùt-,fit\ *n* **1** : the equipment or apparel for a special purpose or occasion **2** : GROUP

²**outfit** *vb* **out-fit-ted; out-fit-ting** : EQUIP — **out-fit-ter** *n*

**out-flank** \aùt-'flaŋk\ *vb* : to get around the flank of (an opposing force)

**out-flow** \'aùt-,flō\ *n* **1** : a flowing out **2** : something that flows out

**out-fox** \aùt-'fäks\ *vb* : OUTSMART

**out-gen-er-al** \aùt-'jen-(ə-)rəl\ *vb* : to surpass in generalship

**out-go** \'aùt-,gō\ *n, pl* **outgoes** : EXPENDITURES, OUTLAY

**out-go-ing** \'aùt-,gō-iŋ\ *adj* **1** : going out (~ tide) **2** : retiring from a place or position **3** : FRIENDLY

**out-grow** \aùt-'grō\ *vb* **-grew** \-'grü\; **-grown** \-'grōn\; **-grow-ing 1** : to grow faster than **2** : to grow too large for

**out-growth** \'aùt-,grōth\ *n* : a product of growing out : OFFSHOOT 1; *also* : CONSEQUENCE

**out-guess** \aùt-'ges\ *vb* : OUTWIT

**out-gun** \-'gən\ *vb* : to surpass in firepower

**out-house** \'aùt-,haùs\ *n* : OUTBUILDING; *esp* : an outdoor toilet

**out-ing** \'aùt-iŋ\ *n* **1** : EXCURSION **2** : a brief stay or trip in the open

**out-land-ish** \aùt-'lan-dish\ *adj* **1** : of foreign appearance or manner; *also* : BIZARRE **2** : remote from civilization — **out-land-ish-ly** *adv*

**out-last** \-'last\ *vb* : to last longer than

¹**out-law** \'aùt-,lò\ *n* **1** : a person excluded from the protection of the law **2** : a lawless person

²**outlaw** *vb* **1** : to deprive of the protection of the law **2** : to make illegal — **out-law-ry** \'aùt-,lò(ə)r-ē\ *n*

**out-lay** \'aùt-,lā\ *n* **1** : the act of spending **2** : EXPENDITURE

**out-let** \'aùt-,let, -lət\ *n* **1** : EXIT, VENT **2** : a means of release (as for an emotion) **3** : a market for a commodity **4** : an electrical receptacle

¹**out-line** \'aùt-,līn\ *n* **1** : a line marking the outer limits of an object or figure **2** : a drawing in which only contours are marked **3** : SUMMARY, SYNOPSIS **4** : PLAN

²**outline** *vb* **1** : to draw the outline of **2** : to indicate the chief features or parts of

**out-live** \aùt-'liv\ *vb* : to live longer than **syn** outlast, survive

**out-look** \'aùt-,lùk\ *n* **1** : a place offering a view; *also* : VIEW **2** : STANDPOINT **3** : the prospect for the future

**out-ly-ing** \'aùt-,lī-iŋ\ *adj* : distant from a center or main body

**out-ma-neu-ver** \,aùt-mə-'n(y)ü-vər\ *vb* **1** : to defeat by more skillful maneuvering **2** : to surpass in maneuverability

**out-mod-ed** \aùt-'mōd-əd\ *adj* **1** : being out of style **2** : no longer acceptable or approved

**out-num-ber** \-'nəm-bər\ *vb* : to exceed in number

**out of** *prep* **1 :** out from within or behind⟨walk *out of* the room⟩ ⟨look *out of* the window⟩ **2 :** from a state of ⟨wake up *out of* a deep sleep⟩ **3 :** beyond the limits of ⟨*out of* sight⟩ **4 :** from among ⟨one *out of* four⟩ **5 :** in or into a state of loss or not having ⟨cheated him *out of* $5000⟩ ⟨we're *out of* matches⟩ **6 :** because of ⟨came *out of* curiosity⟩ **7 :** FROM, WITH ⟨built it *out of* scrap — **out of it :** SQUARE, OLD-FASHIONED

**out-of-bounds** \,aút-ə(v)-'baún(d)z\ *adv or adj* **:** outside the prescribed area of play

**out-of-date** \-'dāt\ *adj* **:** no longer in fashion or in use **:** OUTMODED

**out-of-door** \-'dōr\ *or* **out-of-doors** \-'dōrz\ *adj* **:** OUTDOOR

**out-of-the-way** \-thə-'wā\ *adj* **1 :** being off the beaten track **2 :** UNUSUAL

**out-pa-tient** \'aút-,pā-shənt\ *n* **:** a person not an inmate of a hospital who visits it for diagnosis or treatment

**out-per-form** \,aút-pər-'fòrm\ *vb* **:** to do better than

**out-play** \aút-'plā\ *vb* **:** to play more skillfully than

**out-point** \-'pòint\ *vb* **:** to win more points than

**out-post** \'aút-,pōst\ *n* **1 :** a military detachment stationed at some distance from a camp as a guard against enemy attack; *also* **:** a military base established (as by treaty) in a foreign country **2 :** an outlying or frontier settlement

**out-pour-ing** \-,pōr-iŋ\ *n* **:** something that pours out or is poured out

**out-pull** \aút-'púl\ *vb* **:** OUTDRAW 1

¹**out-put** \'aút-,pút\ *n* **1 :** the amount produced (as by a machine or factory) **:** PRODUCTION **2 :** the terminal for the output of an electrical device **3 :** the information fed out by a computer

²**output** *vb* **out-put-ted** *or* **output; out-put-ting :** to produce as output

¹**out-rage** \'aút-,rāj\ *n* [ME, fr. OF, excess, outrage, fr. *outre* beyond, in excess, fr. L *ultra*] **1 :** a violent or shameful act **2 :** INJURY, INSULT

²**outrage** *vb* **out-raged; out-rag-ing 1 :** RAPE **2 :** to subject to violent injury or gross insult **3 :** to arouse to extreme resentment

**out-ra-geous** \aút-'rā-jəs\ *adj* **:** extremely offensive, insulting, or shameful **:** SHOCKING — **out-ra-geous-ly** *adv*

**out-rank** \-'raŋk\ *vb* **:** to rank higher than

**ou-tré** \ü-'trā\ *adj* **:** violating convention or propriety **:** BIZARRE

¹**out-reach** \aút-'rēch\ *vb* **1 :** to surpass in reach **2 :** to get the better of by trickery

²**out-reach** \'aút-,rēch\ *n* **1 :** the act of reaching out **2 :** the extent of reach

**out-rid-er** \-,rīd-ər\ *n* **:** a mounted attendant

**out-rig-ger** \'aút-,rig-ər\ *n* **1 :** a projecting device (as a light spar with a log at the end) fastened at the side or sides of a boat to prevent upsetting **2 :** a boat equipped with an outrigger

**out-right** \('),aút-'rīt\ *adv* **1 :** COM-

PLETELY **2 :** INSTANTANEOUSLY

**out-run** \aút-'rən\ *vb* **-ran** \-'ran\; **-run; -run-ning :** to run faster than; *also* **:** EXCEED

**out-sell** \-'sel\ *vb* **-sold** \-'sōld\; **-sell-ing :** to exceed in sales

**out-set** \'aút-,set\ *n* **:** BEGINNING, START

**out-shine** \aút-'shīn\ *vb* **-shone** \-'shōn\ *or* **-shined; -shin-ing 1 :** to shine brighter than **2 :** SURPASS

¹**out-side** \aút-'sīd, 'aút-,sīd\ *n* **1 :** a place or region beyond an enclosure or boundary **2 :** EXTERIOR **3 :** the utmost limit or extent

²**outside** *adj* **1 :** OUTER **2 :** coming from without ⟨~ influences⟩ **3 :** being apart from one's regular duties ⟨~ activities⟩ **4 :** REMOTE ⟨an ~ chance⟩

³**outside** *adv* **:** on or to the outside

⁴**outside** *prep* **1 :** on or to the outside of **2 :** beyond the limits of **3 :** EXCEPT

**outside of** *prep* **1 :** OUTSIDE **2 :** BESIDES

**out-sid-er** \aút-'sīd-ər\ *n* **:** one who does not belong to a group

**out-size** \'aút-,sīz\ *n* **:** an unusual size; *esp* **:** a size larger than the standard

**out-skirts** \-,skərts\ *n pl* **:** the outlying parts (as of a city) **:** BORDERS

**out-smart** \aút-'smärt\ *vb* **:** OUTWIT

**out-spend** \-'spend\ *vb* **1 :** to exceed the limits of in spending ⟨~s his income⟩ **2 :** to surpass in spending

**out-spo-ken** \aút-'spō-kən\ *adj* **:** direct and open in speech or expression — **out-spo-ken-ness** \-kən-nəs\ *n*

**out-spread** \aút-'spred\ *vb* **-spread; -spread-ing :** to spread out **:** EXTEND

**out-stand-ing** \aút-'stan-diŋ\ *adj* **1 :** PROJECTING **2 :** UNPAID; *also* **:** UNRESOLVED **3 :** publicly issued and sold **4 :** CONSPICUOUS; *also* **:** DISTINGUISHED — **out-stand-ing-ly** *adv*

**out-stay** \aút-'stā\ *vb* **1 :** OVERSTAY **2 :** to surpass in endurance

**out-stretched** \-'strecht\ *adj* **:** stretched out **:** EXTENDED

**out-strip** \aút-'strip\ *vb* **1 :** to go faster than **2 :** EXCEL, SURPASS

**out-vote** \-'vōt\ *vb* **:** to defeat by a majority of votes

¹**out-ward** \'aút-wərd\ *adj* **1 :** moving or directed toward the outside **2 :** showing outwardly

²**outward** *or* **out-wards** \-wərdz\ *adv* **:** toward the outside

**out-ward-ly** \-aút-wərd-lē\ *adv* **:** on the outside **:** EXTERNALLY

**out-wear** \aút-'waər\ *vb* **-wore** \-'wōr\; **-worn** \-'wōrn\; **-wear-ing :** to wear longer than **:** OUTLAST

**out-weigh** \-'wā\ *vb* **:** to exceed in weight, value, or importance

**out-wit** \aút-'wit\ *vb* **:** to get the better of by superior cleverness

¹**out-work** \aút-'wərk\ *vb* **:** to outdo in working

²**out-work** \'aút-,wərk\ *n* **:** a minor defensive position outside a fortified area

**out-worn** \aút-'wōrn\ *adj* **:** OUTMODED

**ou-zo** \'ü-(,)zō, -(,)zò\ *n* **:** a colorless anise-flavored unsweetened Greek liqueur

**ova** *pl of* OVUM

**oval** \'ō-vəl\ *adj* [ML *ovalis*, fr. LL,

of an egg, fr. L *ovum*] **:** egg-shaped; *also* **:** broadly elliptical — **oval** *n*
**ova·ry** \'ōv-(ə-)rē\ *n, pl* **-ries 1 :** a usu. paired organ of a female animal in which eggs and often sex hormones are produced **2 :** the part of a flower in which seeds are produced — **ovar·i·an** \ō-'var-ē-ən, -'ver-\ *adj*
**ovate** \'ō-,vāt\ *adj* **:** egg-shaped
**ova·tion** \ō-'vā-shən\ *n* [L *ovation-, ovatio,* fr. *ovare,* pp. of *ovare* to exult] **:** an enthusiastic popular tribute
**ov·en** \'əv-ən\ *n* **:** a chamber (as in a stove) for baking, heating, or drying
**oven·bird** \-,bərd\ *n* **:** a large American warbler that builds its dome-shaped nest on the ground
¹**over** \'ō-vər\ *adv* **1 :** across a barrier or intervening space **2 :** across the brim (boil ∼) **3 :** so as to bring the underside up **4 :** out of a vertical position **5 :** beyond some quantity, limit, or norm **6 :** ABOVE **7 :** at an end **8 :** THROUGH; *also* **:** THOROUGHLY **9 :** AGAIN
²**over** \,ō-vər, 'ō-\ *prep* **1 :** above in position, authority, or scope (towered ∼ her) (obeyed those ∼ him) (the talk was ∼ their heads) **2 :** more than (paid ∼ $100 for it) **3 :** ON, UPON (a cape ∼ his shoulders) **4 :** along the length of (∼ the road) **5 :** through the medium of **:** ON (spoke ∼ TV) **6 :** all through (showed me ∼ the house) **7 :** on or above so as to cross (walk ∼ the bridge) (jump ∼ a ditch) **8 :** DURING (∼ the past 25 years) **9 :** on account of (fought ∼ a woman)
³**over** \'ō-vər, ,ō-\ *adj* **1 :** UPPER, HIGHER **2 :** REMAINING **3 :** ENDED
**over-** *prefix* **1 :** so as to exceed or surpass **2 :** excessive; excessively

overabundance
overabundant
overactive
overaggressive
overambitious
overanxious
overbid
overbold
overbuild
overburden
overbuy
overcapacity
overcapitalize
overcareful
overcautious
overcompensation
overconfidence
overconfident
overconscientious
overcooked
overcritical
overcrowd
overdecorated
overdetermined
overdevelop
overdose
overdress
overdue
overeager
overeat

overemphasis
overemphasize
overenthusiastic
overestimate
overexcite
overexert
overexertion
overextend
overfatigued
overfeed
overfill
overgenerous
overgraze
overhasty
overheat
overindulge
overindulgence
overindulgent
overissue
overlarge
overlearn
overliberal
overload
overlong
overman
overmodest
overnice
overoptimism
overoptimistic
overpay
overpopulated

overpopulation
overpraise
overprice
overproduce
overproduction
overproportion
overprotect
overproud
overrate
overreact
overrefinement
overrepresented
overripe
oversell
oversensitive
oversensitiveness
oversimple

oversimplification
oversimplify
overspecialization
overspecialize
overspend
overstock
overstrict
oversubtle
oversupply
overtax
overtired
overtrain
overuse
overvalue
overweight
overwork
overzealous

**over·act** \,ō-vər-'akt\ *vb* **:** to exaggerate in acting
¹**over·age** \,ō-vər-'āj\ *adj* **1 :** too old to be useful **2 :** older than is normal for one's position, function, or grade
²**over·age** \'ōv-(ə-)rij\ *n* **:** SURPLUS
**over·all** \,ō-vər-'ȯl\ *adj* **:** including everything (∼ expenses)
**over·alls** \'ō-vər-,ȯlz\ *n pl* **:** trousers of strong material usu. with a piece extending up to cover the chest
**over·arm** \'ō-vər-,ärm\ *adj* **:** done with the arm raised above the shoulder
**over·awe** \,ō-vər-'ȯ\ *vb* **:** to restrain or subdue by awe
**over·bal·ance** \-'bal-əns\ *vb* **1 :** OUTWEIGH **2 :** to cause to lose balance
**over·bear·ing** \-'ba(ə)r-iŋ\ *adj* **:** ARROGANT, DOMINEERING
**over·blown** \,ō-vər-'blōn\ *adj* **1 :** PORTLY **2 :** INFLATED, PRETENTIOUS
**over·board** \'ō-vər-,bōrd\ *adv* **1 :** over the side of a ship into the water **2 :** to extremes of enthusiasm
¹**over·cast** \'ō-vər-,kast\ *adj* **:** clouded over **:** GLOOMY
²**over·cast** *n* **:** COVERING; *esp* **:** a covering of clouds
**over·charge** \,ō-vər-'chärj\ *vb* **1 :** to charge too much **2 :** to fill or load too full — **over·charge** \'ō-vər-,chärj\ *n*
**over·cloud** \,ō-vər-'klaùd\ *vb* **:** to overspread with clouds
**over·coat** \'ō-vər-,kōt\ *n* **:** a warm coat worn over indoor clothing
**over·come** \,ō-vər-'kəm\ *vb* **-came** \-'kām\; **-come; -com·ing 1 :** CONQUER **2 :** to make helpless or exhausted
**over·do** \,ō-vər-'dü\ *vb* **-did** \-'did\; **-done** \-'dən\; **-do·ing** \-'dü-iŋ\; **-does** \-'dəz\ **1 :** to do too much; *also* **:** to tire oneself **2 :** EXAGGERATE **3 :** to cook too long
**over·draft** \'ō-vər-,draft, -,dráft\ *n* **:** an overdrawing of a bank account; *also* **:** the sum overdrawn
**over·draw** \,ō-vər-'drȯ\ *vb* **-drew** \-'drü\; **-drawn** \-'drȯn\; **-draw·ing 1 :** to draw checks on a bank account for more than the balance **2 :** EXAGGERATE
**over·drive** \'ō-vər-,drīv\ *n* **:** an automotive transmission gear that transmits to the drive shaft a speed greater than the engine speed

**over·ex·pose** \,ō-vər-ik-'spōz\ *vb* : to expose (a photographic plate or film) for more time than is needed — **over·ex·po·sure** \-'spō-zhər\ *n*

¹**over·flow** \,ō-vər-'flō\ *vb* 1 : INUNDATE; *also* : to pour forth in a flood 2 : to flow over the brim or top of

²**over·flow** \'ōvər-,flō\ *n* 1 : FLOOD; *also* : SURPLUS 2 : an outlet for surplus liquid

**over·fly** \,ō-vər-'flī\ *vb* **-flew** \-'flü\; **flown** \-'flōn\; **-fly·ing** : to fly over in an airplane — **over·flight** \'ō-vər-,flīt\ *n*

**over·grow** \,ō-vər-'grō\ *vb* **-grew** \-'grü\; **-grown** \-'grōn\; **-grow·ing** 1 : to grow over so as to cover 2 : OUTGROW 3 : to grow excessively

**over·hand** \'ō-vər-,hand\ *adj* : made with the hand brought down from above — **overhand** *adv*

¹**over·hang** \'ō-vər-,haŋ, ,ō-vər-'haŋ\ *vb* **-hung** \-,həŋ, -'həŋ\; **-hang·ing** 1 : to project over : jut out 2 : to hang over threateningly

²**over·hang** \'ō-vər-,haŋ\ *n* : a part (as of a roof) that overhangs

**over·haul** \,ō-vər-'hól\ *vb* 1 : to examine thoroughly and make necessary repairs and adjustments 2 : OVERTAKE

¹**over·head** \,ō-vər-'hed\ *adv* : ALOFT

²**over·head** \'ō-vər-,hed\ *adj* : operating or lying above (~ door)

³**over·head** \'ō-vər-,hed\ *n* : business expenses not chargeable to a particular part of the work

**over·hear** \,ō-vər-'hiər\ *vb* **-heard** \-'hərd\; **-hear·ing** \-'hi(ə)r-iŋ\ : to hear without the speaker's knowledge or intention

**over·joy** \,ō-vər-'jói\ *vb* : to fill with great joy

**over·kill** \,ō-vər-'kil\ *vb* : to obliterate (a target) with more nuclear force than required — **over·kill** \'ō-vər-,kil\ *n*

**over·land** \'ō-vər-,land, -lənd\ *adv* or *adj* : by, on, or across land

**over·lap** \,ō-vər-'lap\ *vb* 1 : to lap over 2 : to have something in common

**over·lay** \,ō-vər-'lā\ *vb* **-laid** \-'lād\; **-lay·ing** : to lay or spread over or across — **overlay** \'ō-vər-,lā\ *n*

**over·leap** \,ō-vər-'lēp\ *vb* **-leaped** or **-leapt** \-'lēpt, -'lept\; **-leap·ing** \-'lē-piŋ\ 1 : to leap over or across 2 : to defeat (oneself) by going too far

¹**over·look** \,ō-vər-'lùk\ *vb* 1 : INSPECT 2 : to look down on from above 3 : to fail to see 4 : IGNORE; *also* : EXCUSE 5 : SUPERVISE

²**over·look** \'ō-vər-,lúk\ *n* : a place from which to look down upon a scene below

**over·lord** \-,lórd\ *n* : a lord who has supremacy over other lords

**over·ly** \'ō-vər-lē\ *adv* : EXCESSIVELY

**over·mas·ter** \,ō-vər-'mas-tər\ *vb* : OVERPOWER, SUBDUE

**over·match** \-'mach\ *vb* : to be more than a match for : DEFEAT

**over·much** \-'məch\ *adj* or *adv* : too much

¹**over·night** \,ō-vər-'nīt\ *adv* 1 : on or

during the night 2 : SUDDENLY (became famous ~)

²**overnight** *adj* : of, lasting, or staying the night (~ guests)

**over·pass** \'ō-vər-,pas\ *n* : a crossing (as by a bridge) of two highways or of a highway and pedestrian path or railroad at different levels

**over·play** \,ō-vər-'plā\ *vb* 1 : EXAGGERATE; *also* : OVEREMPHASIZE 2 : to rely too much on the strength of

**over·pow·er** \,ō-vər-'paù-(ə)r\ *vb* 1 : to overcome by superior force 2 : OVERWHELM (~ed by hunger)

**over·print** \-'print\ *vb* : to print over with something additional — **over·print** \'ō-vər-,print\ *n*

**over·qual·i·fied** \-'kwäl-ə-,fīd\ *adj* : having more education, training, or experience than a job calls for

**over·reach** \,ō-və(r)-'rēch\ *vb* 1 : to reach above or beyond 2 : to defeat (oneself) by too great an effort

**over·ride** \-'rīd\ *vb* **-rode** \-'rōd\; **-rid·den** \-'rid-²n\; **-rid·ing** \-'rīd-iŋ\ 1 : to ride over or across 2 : to prevail over; *also* : to set aside

**over·rule** \-'rül\ *vb* 1 : to prevail over 2 : to rule against 3 : to set aside

¹**over·run** \-'rən\ *vb* **-ran** \-'ran\; **-run·ning** 1 : to defeat and occupy the positions of 2 : OVERSPREAD; *also* : INFEST 3 : to go beyond 4 : to flow over

²**over·run** \'ō-və(r)-,rən\ *n* 1 : an act or instance of overrunning; *esp* : an exceeding of the costs estimated in a contract 2 : the amount by which something overruns

**over·sea** \,ō-vər-'sē, 'ō-vər-,sē\ *adj* or *adv* : OVERSEAS

**over·seas** \,ō-vər-'sēz, -,sēz\ *adv* or *adj* : beyond or across the sea : ABROAD

**over·see** \,ō-vər-'sē\ *vb* **-saw** \-'só\; **-seen** \-'sēn\; **-see·ing** 1 : OVERLOOK 2 : INSPECT; *also* : SUPERVISE — **over·seer** \'ō-vər-,siər\ *n*

**over·sexed** \,ō-vər-'sekst\ *adj* : exhibiting excessive sexual drive or interest

**over·shad·ow** \-'shad-ō\ *vb* 1 : DARKEN 2 : to exceed in importance

**over·shoe** \'ō-vər-,shü\ *n* : a protective outer shoe; *esp* : GALOSH

**over·shoot** \,ō-vər-'shüt\ *vb* **-shot** \-'shät\; **-shoot·ing** 1 : to pass swiftly beyond 2 : to shoot over or beyond (as a target)

**over·sight** \'ō-vər-,sīt\ *n* 1 : SUPERVISION 2 : an inadvertent omission or error

**over·size** \,ō-vər-'sīz\ or **over·sized** \-'sīzd\ *adj* : of more than ordinary size

**over·sleep** \,ō-vər-'slēp\ *vb* **-slept** \-'slept\; **-sleep·ing** : to sleep beyond the time for waking

**over·spread** \,ō-vər-'spred\ *vb* **-spread**; **-spread·ing** : to spread over or above

**over·state** \-'stāt\ *vb* : EXAGGERATE — **over·state·ment** *n*

**over·stay** \-'stā\ *vb* : to stay beyond the time or limits of

**over·step** \ˌō-vər-'step\ vb : EXCEED

**over·stuffed** \-'stəft\ adj 1 : stuffed too full 2 : covered completely and deeply with upholstery

**over·sub·scribe** \-səb-'skrīb\ vb : to subscribe for more of than is available, asked for, or offered for sale

**overt** \ō-'vərt, 'ō-ˌvərt\ adj [ME, fr. MF ouvert, overt, fr. pp. of ouvrir to open] : not secret

**over·take** \ˌō-vər-'tāk\ vb -took \-'tùk\; -tak·en \-'tā-kən\; -tak·ing : to catch up with

**over·throw** \ˌō-vər-'thrō\ vb -threw \-'thrü\; -thrown \-'thrōn\; -throw·ing 1 : UPSET 2 : to bring down : DEFEAT ⟨~ a government⟩ 3 : to throw over or past — **over·throw** \'ō-vər-ˌthrō\ n

**over·time** \ˌō-vər-ˌtīm\ n : time beyond a set limit; esp : working time in excess of a standard day or week — **overtime** adv

**over·tone** \-ˌtōn\ n 1 : one of the higher tones in a complex musical tone 2 : IMPLICATION, SUGGESTION

**over·top** \ˌō-vər-'täp\ vb 1 : to tower above 2 : SURPASS

**over·trick** \'ō-vər-ˌtrik\ n : a card trick won in excess of the number bid

**over·ture** \'ō-vər-ˌchür, -chər\ n [ME, lit., opening, fr. MF, fr. (assumed) VL opertura, alter. of L apertura] 1 : an opening offer 2 : an orchestral introduction to a musical dramatic work

**over·turn** \ˌō-vər-'tərn\ vb 1 : to turn over 2 : UPSET 3 : OVERTHROW

**over·view** \'ō-vər-ˌvyü\ n : a brief survey : SUMMARY

**over·ween·ing** \ˌō-vər-'wē-niŋ\ adj 1 : ARROGANT 2 : IMMODERATE

**over·weigh** \-'wā\ vb 1 : to exceed in weight 2 : OPPRESS

**over·whelm** \ˌō-vər-'hwelm\ vb 1 : OVERTHROW 2 : SUBMERGE 3 : to overcome completely — **over·whelm·ing·ly** \-'hwel-miŋ-lē\ adv

**over·win·ter** \-'wint-ər\ vb : to survive the winter

**over·wrought** \ˌō-və(r)-'ròt\ adj 1 : extremely excited 2 : elaborated to excess

**ovi·duct** \'ō-və-ˌdəkt\ n : a tube that serves for the passage of eggs from an ovary

**ovip·a·rous** \ō-'vip-ə-rəs\ adj : reproducing by eggs that hatch outside the parent's body

**ovoid** \'ō-ˌvòid\ or **ovoi·dal** \ō-'vòid-ᵊl\ adj : egg-shaped : OVAL

**ovu·late** \'äv-yə-ˌlāt, 'ōv-\ vb -lat·ed; -lat·ing : to produce eggs or discharge them from an ovary — **ovu·la·tion** \ˌäv-yə-'lā-shən, ˌōv-\ n

**ovule** \'äv-yül, 'ōv-\ n : any of the bodies in a plant ovary that after fertilization become seeds

**ovum** \'ō-vəm\ n, pl **ova** \-və\ : a female germ cell : EGG

**owe** \'ō\ vb owed; ow·ing 1 : to be under obligation to pay or render 2 : to be indebted to or for; also : to be in debt

**owing to** prep : because of

**owl** \'aùl\ n : a nocturnal bird of prey with large head and eyes and strong talons — **owl·ish** adj — **owl·ish·ly** adv

**owl·et** \'aù-lət\ n : a young or small owl

¹**own** \'ōn\ adj : belonging to oneself — used as an intensive after a possessive adjective ⟨his ~ car⟩

²**own** vb 1 : to have or hold as property 2 : ACKNOWLEDGE; also : CONFESS — **own·er** n — **own·er·ship** n

³**own** pron : one or ones belonging to oneself

**ox** \'äks\ n, pl **ox·en** \'äk-sən\ also **ox** : an adult castrated male of the common domestic cattle

**ox·al·ic acid** \ˌäk-ˌsal-ik-\ n : a poisonous strong organic acid used esp. as a bleaching or cleaning agent and in making dyes

**ox·blood** \'äks-ˌbləd\ n : a moderate reddish brown

**ox·bow** \'äks-ˌbō\ n 1 : a U-shaped collar worn by a draft ox 2 : a U-shaped bend in a river — **oxbow** adj

**ox·ford** \'äks-fərd\ n : a low shoe laced or tied over the instep

**ox·i·dant** \'äk-səd-ənt\ n : OXIDIZING AGENT — **oxidant** adj

**ox·i·da·tion** \ˌäk-sə-'dā-shən\ n : the act or process of oxidizing : the condition of being oxidized — **ox·i·da·tive** \'äk-sə-ˌdāt-iv\ adj

**ox·ide** \'äk-ˌsīd\ n : a compound of oxygen with an element or radical

**ox·i·dize** \'äk-sə-ˌdīz\ vb -dized; -diz·ing : to combine with oxygen ⟨iron rusts because it is oxidized by exposure to the air⟩ — **ox·i·diz·able** \-ˌdī-zə-bəl\ adj — **ox·i·diz·er** n

**oxidizing agent** n : a substance (as oxygen or nitric acid) that oxidizes by taking up electrons

**oxy·acet·y·lene** \ˌäk-sē-ə-'set-ᵊl-ən, -ᵊl-ˌēn\ adj : of, relating to, or utilizing a mixture of oxygen and acetylene

**ox·y·gen** \'äk-si-jən\ n [F oxygène, fr. Gk oxys, adj., acid, lit., sharp + -genēs born; so called because it was once thought to be an essential element of all acids] : a colorless odorless gaseous chemical element that is found in the air, is essential to life, and is involved in combustion — **ox·y·gen·ic** \ˌäk-si-'jen-ik\ adj

**ox·y·gen·ate** \'äk-si-jə-ˌnāt\ vb -at·ed; -at·ing : to impregnate, combine, or supply with oxygen — **ox·y·gen·ation** \ˌäk-si-jə-'nā-shən\ n

**oxygen tent** n : a canopy which can be placed over a bedridden person and within which a flow of oxygen can be maintained

**oys·ter** \'òi-stər\ n : any of various mollusks with an irregular 2-valved shell that live on stony bottoms in shallow seas and include edible shellfish and pearl producers — **oys·ter·ing** \'òi-st(ə-)riŋ\ n — **oys·ter·man** \'òi-stər-mən\ n

**oz** abbr [It onza] ounce; ounces

**ozone** \'ō-ˌzōn\ n 1 : a faintly blue form of oxygen that is produced by the silent discharge of electricity in air or oxygen, has a faint chlorinelike odor, and is used for sterilizing water, purifying air, and bleaching **2 :** pure and refreshing air

**ozo·no·sphere** \ō-'zō-nə-,sfiər\ *n* **:** an atmospheric layer at heights of approximately 20 to 30 miles characterized by high ozone content

[P]

¹**p** \'pē\ *n, pl* **p's** *or* **ps** \'pēz\ *often cap* **:** the 16th letter of the English alphabet

²**p** *abbr, often cap* **1** page **2** participle **3** past **4** pawn **5** pence; penny **6** per **7** pint **8** pressure **9** puri

**P** *symbol* phosphorus

**pa** \'pä, 'pö\ *n* **:** FATHER

¹**Pa** *abbr* Pennsylvania

²**Pa** *symbol* protactinium

**PA** *abbr* **1** Pennsylvania **2** per annum **3** power of attorney **4** press agent **5** private account **6** public address **7** purchasing agent

**pa·'an·ga** \pä-'äṇ-(g)ə\ *n* — see MONEY table

**pab·u·lum** \'pab-yə-ləm\ *n* **:** usu. soft digestible food

**Pac** *abbr* Pacific

¹**pace** \'pās\ *n* **1 :** a step in walking; *also* **:** the length of such a step **2 :** rate of movement or progress (as in walking or working) **3 :** GAIT; *esp* **:** a horse's gait in which the legs on the same side move together

²**pace** *vb* **paced; pac·ing 1 :** to go or cover at a pace or with slow steps **2 :** to measure off by paces **3 :** to set or regulate the pace of

³**pace** \'pā-sē\ *prep* **:** with due respect to

**pace·mak·er** \'pās-,mā-kər\ *n* **1 :** one that sets the pace for another **2 :** a body part (as of the heart) that serves to establish and maintain a rhythmic activity **3 :** an electrical device for stimulating or steadying the heartbeat

**pac·er** \'pā-sər\ *n* **1 :** a horse that paces **2 :** PACEMAKER

**pachy·derm** \'pak-i-,dərm\ *n* [F *pachyderme*, fr. Gk *pachydermos* thickskinned, fr. *pachys* thick + *derma* skin] **:** any of various thick-skinned hoofed mammals (as an elephant)

**pach·ys·an·dra** \,pak-i-'san-drə\ *n* **:** any of a genus of low evergreen plants used as a ground cover

**pa·cif·ic** \pə-'sif-ik\ *adj* **1 :** tending to lessen conflict **:** CALM, PEACEFUL

**pac·i·fi·er** \'pas-ə-,fī(-ə)r\ *n* **:** one that pacifies; *esp* **:** a device for a baby to chew or suck on

**pac·i·fism** \'pas-ə-,fiz-əm\ *n* **:** opposition to war or violence as a means of settling disputes — **pac·i·fist** \-fəst\ *n or adj* — **pac·i·fis·tic** \,pas-ə-'fis-tik\ *adj*

**pac·i·fy** \'pas-ə-,fī\ *vb* **-fied; -fy·ing 1 :** to allay anger or agitation in **2 :** SETTLE; *also* **:** SUBDUE — **pac·i·fi·ca·tion** \,pas-ə-fə-'kā-shən\ *n*

¹**pack** \'pak\ *n* **1 :** a compact bundle (as a packet or package); *also* **:** a flexible container for carrying a bundle esp. on the back **2 :** a large amount or number **:** HEAP **3 :** a set of playing cards **4 :** a group or band of people or animals **5 :** wet absorbent material for application to the body

²**pack** *vb* **1 :** to make into a pack **2 :** to put into a protective container **3 :** to fill completely **:** CRAM **4 :** to load with a pack ⟨~ a mule⟩ **5 :** to stow goods for transportation **6 :** to crowd together **7 :** to cause to go without ceremony ⟨~ them off to school⟩ **8 :** to fill in or surround so as to prevent passage of air, steam, or water **9 :** WEAR, CARRY ⟨~ a gun⟩

³**pack** *vb* **:** to make up fraudulently so as to secure a desired result ⟨~ a jury⟩

¹**pack·age** \'pak-ij\ *n* **1 :** BUNDLE, PARCEL **2 :** something (as a group of related things offered as a whole) resembling a package

²**package** *vb* **pack·aged; pack·ag·ing :** to make into or enclose in a package

**package deal** *n* **:** an offer or agreement involving more than one item or making acceptance of one item dependent on the acceptance of another

**package store** *n* **:** a store that sells alcoholic beverages in sealed containers whose contents may not lawfully be drunk on the premises

**pack·er** \'pak-ər\ *n* **:** one that packs; *esp* **:** a wholesale food dealer

**pack·et** \'pak-ət\ *n* **1 :** a small bundle or package **2 :** a passenger boat carrying mail and cargo on a regular schedule

**pack·horse** \'pak-,hörs\ *n* **:** a horse used to carry goods or supplies

**pack·ing** \'pak-iṇ\ *n* **:** material used to pack something

**pack·ing·house** \-,haûs\ *n* **:** an establishment for processing and packing foodstuffs and esp. meat and its by-products

**pack rat** *n* **:** a bushy-tailed rodent of the Rocky Mountain area that hoards food and miscellaneous objects

**pack·sad·dle** \'pak-,sad-ʰl\ *n* **:** a saddle for supporting packs on the back of an animal

**pack·thread** \-,thred\ *n* **:** strong thread for tying

**pact** \'pakt\ *n* **:** AGREEMENT, TREATY

¹**pad** \'pad\ *n* **1 :** a cushioning part or thing **:** CUSHION **2 :** the cushioned part of the foot of some mammals **3 :** the floating leaf of a water plant **4 :** a writing tablet **5 :** LAUNCHPAD **6 :** living quarters; *also* **:** BED

²**pad** *vb* **pad·ded; pad·ding 1 :** to furnish with a pad or padding **2 :** to expand with needless or fraudulent matter

**pad·ding** \'pad-iṇ\ *n* **:** the material with which something is padded

¹**pad·dle** \'pad-ʰl\ *n* **1 :** an implement with a flat blade often shaped like an oar and used in propelling and steering

a small craft (as a canoe) **2 :** an implement used for stirring, mixing, or beating **3 :** a broad board on the outer rim of a waterwheel or a paddle wheel of a boat

²**paddle** *vb* **pad·dled; pad·dling** \'pad-(°-)liŋ\ **1 :** to move on or through water by or as if by using a paddle **2 :** to beat or stir with a paddle

³**paddle** *vb* **pad·dled; pad·dling** \'pad-(°-)liŋ\ **:** to move the hands and feet about in shallow water

**paddle wheel** *n* **:** a wheel with blades around its rim used to propel a boat

**pad·dock** \'pad-ək\ *n* **:** a usu. enclosed area for pasturing or exercising animals; *esp* **:** one where racehorses are saddled and paraded before a race

**pad·dy** \'pad-ē\ *n, pl* **paddies 1 :** RICE **2 :** wet land where rice is grown

**pad·dy wagon** \'pad-ē-\ *n* **:** PATROL WAGON

**pad·lock** \'pad-,läk\ *n* **:** a lock with a bow-shaped piece that can be snapped in or out of a catch (as by use of a key) — **padlock** *vb*

**pa·dre** \'päd-rā\ *n* [Sp or It or Port, lit., father, fr. L *pater*] **1 :** PRIEST, CLERGYMAN **2 :** a military chaplain

**pae·an** \'pē-ən\ *n* **:** an exultant song of praise or thanksgiving

**pa·gan** \'pā-gən\ *n* [ME, fr. LL *paganus*, fr. L, country dweller, fr. *pagus* country district] **:** HEATHEN — **pagan** *adj* — **pa·gan·ism** \-,iz-əm\ *n*

¹**page** \'pāj\ *n* **:** ATTENDANT; *esp* **:** one employed to deliver messages

²**page** *vb* **paged; pag·ing :** to summon by repeatedly calling out the name of

³**page** *n* **:** a single leaf (as of a book); *also* **:** a single side of such a leaf

⁴**page** *vb* **paged; pag·ing :** to mark or number the pages of

**pag·eant** \'paj-ənt\ *n* [ME *pagyn, padgeant*, lit., scene of a play, fr. ML *pagina*, fr. L, page] **:** an elaborate spectacle, show, or procession esp. with tableaux or floats — **pag·eant·ry** \-ən-trē\ *n*

**page·boy** \'pāj-,bòi\ *n* **:** an often shoulder-length hairdo with the ends of the hair turned under in a smooth roll

**pag·i·nate** \'paj-ə-,nāt\ *vb* **-nat·ed; -nat·ing :** ⁴PAGE

**pag·i·na·tion** \,paj-ə-'nā-shən\ *n* **1 :** the paging of written or printed matter **2 :** the number and arrangement of pages (as of a book)

**pa·go·da** \pə-'gōd-ə\ *n* **:** a tower with roofs curving upward at the division of each of several stories ⟨Chinese ∼⟩

**paid** *past of* PAY

**pail** \'pāl\ *n* **:** a usu. cylindrical vessel with a handle — **pail·ful** \-,fúl\ *n*

¹**pain** \'pān\ *n* **1 :** PUNISHMENT, PENALTY **2 :** suffering or distress of body or mind; *also* **:** a basic sensation caused by harmful stimuli and marked by discomfort (as throbbing or aching) **3** *pl* **:** CARE, TROUBLE — **pain·ful** \-fəl\ *adj* — **pain·ful·ly** \-ē\ *adv* — **pain·less** *adj* — **pain·less·ly** *adv*

²**pain** *vb* **:** to cause or experience pain

**pain·kil·ler** \'pān-,kil-ər\ *n* **:** something (as a drug) that relieves pain — **pain·kill·ing** \-iŋ\ *adj*

**pains·tak·ing** \'pān-,stā-kiŋ\ *adj* **:** taking pains : showing care — **pains·taking** *n* — **pains·tak·ing·ly** *adv*

¹**paint** \'pānt\ *vb* **1 :** to apply color, pigment, or paint to **2 :** to produce or portray in lines or colors on a surface; *also* **:** to practice the art of painting **3 :** to decorate with colors **4 :** to use cosmetics **5 :** to describe vividly **6 :** SWAB — **paint·er** *n*

²**paint** *n* **1 :** something produced by painting **2 :** MAKEUP **3 :** a mixture of a pigment and a liquid that forms a thin adherent coating when spread on a surface; *also* **:** the dry pigment used in making this mixture **4 :** an applied coating of paint

**paint·brush** \'pānt-,brəsh\ *n* **:** a brush for applying paint

**paint·ing** \'pānt-iŋ\ *n* **1 :** a work (as a picture) produced through the art of painting **2 :** the art or occupation of painting

¹**pair** \'paər\ *n, pl* **pairs** *also* **pair** [ME *paire*, fr. OF, fr. L *paria* equal things, fr. neut. pl. of *par* equal] **1 :** two things of a kind designed for use together **2 :** something made up of two corresponding pieces ⟨a ∼ of trousers⟩ **3 :** a set of two people or animals ⟨a carriage ∼⟩ ⟨a married ∼⟩

²**pair** *vb* **1 :** to arrange in pairs **2 :** to form a pair : MATCH **3 :** to become associated with another

**pai·sa** \pī-'sä\ *n, pl* **pai·se** \-'sä\ *or* **paisa** *or* **paisas** — see **rupee, taka** at MONEY table

**pais·ley** \'pāz-lē\ *adj, often cap* **:** made typically of soft wool with colorful curved abstract figures ⟨a ∼ shawl⟩

**Pai·ute** \'pī-,(y)üt\ *n* **:** a member of an Indian people orig. of Utah, Arizona, Nevada, and California

**pa·ja·mas** \pə-'jäm-əz, -'jam-\ *n pl* **:** a loose usu. 2-piece lightweight suit designed for sleeping or lounging

**Pak·i·stani** \,pak-i-'stan-ē, ,päk-i-'stän-ē\ *n* **:** a native or inhabitant of Pakistan — **Pakistani** *adj*

**pal** \'pal\ *n* **:** a close friend

**pal·ace** \'pal-əs\ *n* [ME *palais*, fr. OF, fr. L *palatium*, fr. *Palatium*, the Palatine Hill in Rome where the emperors' residences were built] **1 :** the official residence of a sovereign **2 :** MANSION — **pa·la·tial** \pə-'lā-shəl\ *adj*

**pal·a·din** \'pal-əd-ən\ *n* **:** a knightly supporter of a medieval prince

**pa·laes·tra** \pə-'les-trə\ *n, pl* **-trae** \-(,)trē\ **:** a school in ancient Greece or Rome for sports (as wrestling)

**pa·lan·quin** \,pal-ən-'kēn\ *n* **:** an enclosed couch for one person borne on the shoulders of men by means of poles

**pal·at·able** \'pal-ət-ə-bəl\ *adj* **:** agreeable to the taste **syn** appetizing, savory, tasty, toothsome

**pal·a·tal·ize** \'pal-ət-°l-,īz\ *vb* **-ized; -iz·ing :** to pronounce as or change into a palatal sound — **pal·a·tal·iza·tion** \,pal-ət-°l-ə-'zā-shən\ *n*

**pal·ate** \'pal-ət\ *n* **1** : the roof of the mouth consisting of an anterior bony part and a posterior membranous fold **2** : TASTE — **pa·la·tal** \-ət-ᵊl\ *adj*

**pa·lat·i·nate** \pə-'lat-ᵊn-ət\ *n* : the territory of a palatine

¹**pal·a·tine** \'pal-ə-ˌtīn\ *adj* **1** : of or relating to a palace : PALATIAL **2** : possessing royal privileges; *also* : of or relating to a palatine or a palatinate

²**palatine** \-ˌtīn\ *n* **1** : a high officer of an imperial palace **2** : a feudal lord having sovereign power within his domains

**pa·la·ver** \pə-'lav-ər, -'läv-\ *n* [Port *palavra* word, speech, fr. LL *parabola* parable, speech] : a long parley : TALK — **palaver** *vb*

¹**pale** \'pāl\ *adj* **pal·er; pal·est 1** : deficient in color : WAN ⟨~ face⟩ **2** : lacking in brightness : DIM ⟨~ star⟩ **3** : light in color or shade ⟨~ blue⟩ — **pale·ness** *n*

²**pale** *vb* **paled; pal·ing** : to make or become pale

³**pale** *vb* **paled; pal·ing** : to enclose with or as if with pales : FENCE

⁴**pale** *n* **1** : a stake or picket of a fence **2** : an enclosed place; *also* : a district or territory within certain bounds or under a particular jurisdiction **3** : LIMITS, BOUNDS ⟨conduct beyond the ~⟩

**pale·face** \'pāl-ˌfās\ *n* : a white person

**pa·le·og·ra·phy** \ˌpā-lē-'äg-rə-fē\ *n* : the study of ancient writings and inscriptions — **pa·le·og·ra·pher** \-fər\ *n*

**pa·leo·mag·ne·tism** \ˌpā-lē-ō-'mag-nə-ˌtiz-əm\ *n* **1** : the residual magnetization in ancient rocks **2** : a study that deals with paleomagnetism — **pa·leo·mag·net·ic** \-mag-'net-ik\ *adj* — **pa·leo·mag·net·i·cal·ly** \-i-k(ə-)lē\ *adv*

**paleon** *abbr* paleontology

**pa·le·on·tol·o·gy** \ˌpā-lē-ˌän-'täl-ə-jē\ *n* : a science dealing with the life of past geologic periods esp. as known from fossil remains — **pa·le·on·to·lo·gist** \-ˌän-'täl-ə-jəst, -ən-\ *n*

**pal·ette** \'pal-ət\ *n* : a thin often oval board or tablet on which a painter lays and mixes his colors; *also* : the colors on a palette

**pal·frey** \'pȯl-frē\ *n, pl* **palfreys** : a saddle horse; *esp* : one suitable for a woman

**pa·limp·sest** \'pal-əmp-ˌsest\ *n* : writing material (as a parchment) used after the erasure of earlier writing

**pal·in·drome** \'pal-ən-ˌdrōm\ *n* : a word, verse, or sentence (as "Able was I ere I saw Elba") that reads the same backward or forward

**pal·ing** \'pā-liŋ\ *n* **1** : a fence of pales **2** : material for pales **3** : PALE, PICKET

**pal·in·ode** \'pal-ə-ˌnōd\ *n* : an ode or song of recantation or retraction

**pal·i·sade** \ˌpal-ə-'sād\ *n* **1** : a high fence of stakes esp. for defense **2** : a line of bold cliffs

¹**pall** \'pȯl\ *n* **1** : a heavy cloth draped over a coffin **2** : something that produces a gloomy atmosphere

²**pall** *vb* **1** : to lose in interest or attraction **2** : SATIATE, CLOY

**pal·la·di·um** \pə-'lād-ē-əm\ *n* : a silver-white metallic chemical element used esp. as a catalyst and in alloys

**pall·bear·er** \'pȯl-ˌbar-ər\ *n* : a person who attends the coffin at a funeral

¹**pal·let** \'pal-ət\ *n* : a small, hard, or makeshift bed

²**pallet** *n* : a portable platform for transporting and storing materials

**pal·li·ate** \'pal-ē-ˌāt\ *vb* **-at·ed; -at·ing 1** : to ease without curing **2** : to cover by excuses and apologies — **pal·li·a·tion** \ˌpal-ē-'ā-shən\ *n* — **pal·li·a·tive** \'pal-ē-ˌāt-iv\ *adj or n*

**pal·lid** \'pal-əd\ *adj* : PALE, WAN

**pal·lor** \'pal-ər\ *n* : PALENESS

¹**palm** \'päm, 'pälm\ *n* **1** : any of a group of mostly tropical trees, shrubs, or vines usu. with a tall unbranched stem topped by a crown of large leaves **2** : a symbol of victory; *also* : VICTORY

²**palm** *n* : the underpart of the hand between the fingers and the wrist

³**palm** *vb* **1** : to conceal in or with the hand ⟨~ a card⟩ **2** : to impose by fraud ⟨~ off a fake⟩

**pal·mate** \'pal-ˌmāt, 'päl-\ *also* **pal·mat·ed** \-ˌmāt-əd, -ˌāt-\ *adj* : resembling a hand with the fingers spread

**palm·er** \'päm-ər, 'päl-mər\ *n* : a person wearing two crossed palm leaves as a sign of his pilgrimage to the Holy Land

**pal·met·to** \pal-'met-ō\ *n, pl* **-tos** *or* **-toes** : any of several usu. small palms with fan-shaped leaves

**palm·is·try** \'päm-ə-strē, 'päl-mə-\ *n* : the practice of reading a person's character or future from the markings on his palms — **palm·ist** \'päm-əst, 'päl-məst\ *n*

**Palm Sunday** *n* : the Sunday preceding Easter and commemorating Christ's triumphal entry into Jerusalem

**palmy** \'päm-ē, 'päl-mē\ *adj* **palm·i·er; -est 1** : abounding in or bearing palms **2** : FLOURISHING, PROSPEROUS ⟨during the ~ days⟩

**pal·o·mi·no** \ˌpal-ə-'mē-nō\ *n, pl* **-nos** [AmerSp, fr. Sp, like a dove, fr. L *palumbinus*, fr. *palumbes* wood pigeon] : a light tan or cream-colored horse with lighter mane and tail

**pal·pa·ble** \'pal-pə-bəl\ *adj* **1** : capable of being touched or felt : TANGIBLE **2** : OBVIOUS, PLAIN **syn** perceptible, sensible, appreciable, evident, manifest — **pal·pa·bly** \-blē\ *adv*

**pal·pate** \'pal-ˌpāt\ *vb* **pal·pat·ed; pal·pat·ing** : to examine by touch esp. medically — **pal·pa·tion** \pal-'pā-shən\ *n*

**pal·pi·tate** \'pal-pə-ˌtāt\ *vb* **-tat·ed; -tat·ing** : to beat strongly and irregularly : THROB, QUIVER — **pal·pi·ta·tion** \ˌpal-pə-'tā-shən\ *n*

**pal·sy** \'pȯl-zē\ *n, pl* **palsies 1** : PARALYSIS **2** : a condition marked by tremor — **pal·sied** \-zēd\ *adj*

**pal·ter** \'pȯl-tər\ *vb* **pal·tered; pal·ter·ing** \-t-(ə-)riŋ\ **1** : to act insincerely : EQUIVOCATE **2** : HAGGLE

**pal·try** \'pȯl-trē\ *adj* **pal·tri·er; -est 1 :** TRASHY ⟨a ~ pamphlet⟩ **2 :** MEAN ⟨a ~ trick⟩ **3 :** TRIVIAL ⟨~ excuses⟩ ⟨a ~ sum⟩

**pam** *abbr* pamphlet

**pam·pa** \'pam-pə\ *n, pl* **pam·pas** \-pəz, -pəs\ **:** a large grassy So. American plain

**pam·per** \'pam-pər\ *vb* **pam·pered; pam·per·ing** \-p(ə-)riŋ\ **:** to treat with excessive attention **:** INDULGE **syn** coddle, humor, baby, spoil

**pam·phlet** \'pam-flət\ *n* [ME *pamflet* unbound booklet, fr. *Pamphilus seu De Amore* Pamphilus or On Love, popular Latin love poem of the 12th cent.] **:** an unbound printed publication with no cover or a paper cover — **pam·phle·teer** \,pam-flə-'tir\ *n*

¹**pan** \'pan\ *n* **1 :** a usu. broad, shallow, and open container for domestic use; *also* **:** something resembling such a container **2 :** a basin or depression in land **3 :** HARDPAN

²**pan** *vb* **panned; pan·ning 1 :** to wash earth or gravel in a pan in searching for gold **2 :** to cook or wash in a pan **3 :** to criticize severely ⟨a new play *panned* by the critics⟩

**Pan** *abbr* Panama

**pan·a·cea** \,pan-ə-'sē-ə\ *n* **:** a remedy for all ills or difficulties

**pa·nache** \pə-'nash, -'näsh\ *n* **1 :** an ornamental tuft esp. of feathers) esp. on a helmet **2 :** dash or flamboyance in style and action

**pan·a·ma** \'pan-ə-,mä, -,mȯ\ *n, often cap* **:** a handmade hat braided from strips of the leaves from a tropical American tree

**pan·a·tela** \,pan-ə-'tel-ə\ *n* **:** a long slender cigar with straight sides rounded off at the sealed end

**pan·cake** \'pan-,kāk\ *n* **:** a flat cake made of thin batter and fried on both sides

**pan·chro·mat·ic** \,pan-krō-'mat-ik\ *adj* **:** sensitive to light of all colors ⟨~ film⟩

**pan·cre·as** \'paŋ-krē-əs, 'pan-\ *n* **:** a large gland that produces insulin and discharges enzymes into the intestine — **pan·cre·at·ic** \,paŋ-krē-'at-ik, ,pan-\ *adj*

**pan·da** \'pan-də\ *n* **:** either of two Asiatic mammals related to the raccoon; *esp* **:** a large black-and-white animal resembling a bear

**pan·dem·ic** \pan-'dem-ik\ *n* **:** a widespread outbreak of disease — **pandemic** *adj*

**pan·de·mo·ni·um** \,pan-də-'mō-nē-əm\ *n* **:** a wild uproar **:** TUMULT

¹**pan·der** \'pan-dər\ *n* **1 :** a go-between in love intrigues **2 :** PIMP **3 :** someone who caters to or exploits others' desires or weaknesses

²**pander** *vb* **pan·dered; pan·der·ing** \-d(ə-)riŋ\ **:** to act as a pander

**P and L** *abbr* profit and loss

**pan·dow·dy** \pan-'daȯd-ē\ *n, pl* **-dies :** a deep-dish apple dessert spiced, sweetened, and covered with a rich crust

**pane** \'pān\ *n* **:** a sheet of glass (as in a door or window)

**pan·e·gyr·ic** \,pan-ə-'jir-ik\ *n* **:** a eulogistic oration or writing — **pan·e·gyr·ist** \-'jir-əst\ *n*

¹**pan·el** \'pan-²l\ *n* **1 :** a list of persons appointed for special duty ⟨a jury ~⟩ **2 :** a group of people taking part in a discussion or quiz program **3 :** a section of something (as a wall or door) often sunk below the level of the frame **4 :** a flat piece of construction material; *also* **:** a flat piece of wood on which a picture is painted **5 :** a board mounting instruments or controls

²**panel** *vb* **-eled** *or* **-elled; -el·ing** *or* **-el·ling :** to decorate with panels

**pan·el·ing** \'pan-²l-iŋ\ *n* **:** decorative panels

**pan·el·ist** \'pan-²l-əst\ *n* **:** a member of a discussion or quiz panel

**panel truck** *n* **:** a small motortruck with a fully enclosed body

**pang** \'paŋ\ *n* **:** a sudden sharp attack (as of pain)

¹**pan·han·dle** \'pan-,han-d²l\ *n* **:** a narrow projection of a larger territory (as a state)

²**panhandle** *vb* **pan·han·dled; pan·han·dling** \-,han-d(²-)liŋ\ **:** to stop people on the street and ask for money — **pan·han·dler** \-d(²-)lər\ *n*

¹**pan·ic** \'pan-ik\ *n* **:** a sudden overpowering fright **syn** terror, consternation, dismay, alarm, dread, fear — **pan·icky** \-i-kē\ *adj*

²**panic** *vb* **pan·icked** \-ikt\; **pan·ick·ing :** to affect or be affected with panic

**pan·i·cle** \'pan-i-kəl\ *n* **:** a loosely branched often pyramidal flower cluster (as of the oat)

**pan·jan·drum** \pan-'jan-drəm\ *n, pl* **-drums** *also* **-dra** \-drə\ **:** a powerful personage or pretentious official

**pan·nier** *or* **pan·ier** \'pan-yər\ *n* **:** a large basket esp. for bearing on the back

**pan·o·ply** \'pan-ə-plē\ *n, pl* **-plies 1 :** a full suit of armor **2 :** something forming a protective covering **3 :** an impressive array

**pan·ora·ma** \,pan-ə-'ram-ə, -'räm-\ *n* **1 :** a view or picture unrolled before one's eyes **2 :** a complete view in every direction — **pan·oram·ic** \-'ram-ik\ *adj*

**pan out** *vb* **:** to turn out; *esp* **:** SUCCEED

**pan·sy** \'pan-zē\ *n, pl* **pansies** [MF *pensée*, fr. *pensée* thought, fr. *penser* to think, fr. L *pensare* to ponder] **:** a low-growing garden herb related to the violet; *also* **:** its showy flower

¹**pant** \'pant\ *vb* [ME *panten*, fr. MF *pantaisier*, fr. (assumed) VL *phantasiare* to have hallucinations, fr. Gk *phantasioun*, fr. *phantasia* appearance, imagination] **1 :** to breathe in a labored manner **2 :** YEARN **3 :** THROB

²**pant** *n* **:** a panting breath or sound

**pan·ta·loons** \,pant-²l-'ünz\ *n pl* **:** TROUSERS

**pan·the·ism** \'pan-thē-,iz-əm\ *n* **:** a doctrine that equates God with the forces and laws of the universe — **pan-**

**the·ist** \-əst\ *n* — **pan·the·is·tic** \,pan-thē-'is-tik\ *adj*

**pan·the·on** \'pan-thē-,än, -ən\ *n* **1 :** a temple dedicated to all the gods **2 :** a building serving as the burial place of or containing memorials to famous dead **3 :** the gods of a people

**pan·ther** \'pan-thər\ *n, pl* **panthers** *also* **panther :** a large wild cat (as a leopard or cougar)

**pant·ie** *or* **panty** \'pant-ē\ *n, pl* **pant·ies :** a woman's or child's undergarment covering the lower trunk and made with closed crotch and short legs — usu. used in pl.

**pan·to·mime** \'pant-ə-,mīm\ *n* **1 :** a play in which the actors use no words **2 :** expression of something by bodily or facial movements only — **pan·to·mim·ic** \,pant-ə-'mim-ik\ *adj*

**pan·try** \'pan-trē\ *n, pl* **pantries :** a room or closet used for storing provisions and dishes or for serving

**pants** \'pants\ *n pl* **:** TROUSERS; *also* **:** PANTIE

**pant·suit** \'pant-,süt\ *n* **:** a woman's ensemble consisting usu. of a long jacket and tailored pants of the same material

**panty hose** *n pl* **:** a one-piece undergarment for women consisting of hosiery combined with a panty

**panty·waist** \'pant-ē-,wāst\ *n* **:** SISSY

**pap** \'pap\ *n* **:** soft food for infants or invalids

**pa·pa** \'päp-ə\ *n* **:** FATHER

**pa·pa·cy** \'pā-pə-sē\ *n, pl* **-cies 1 :** the office of pope **2 :** a succession of popes **3 :** the term of a pope's reign **4** *cap* **:** the system of government of the Roman Catholic Church

**pa·pa·in** \pə-'pā-ən, -'pī-ən\ *n* **:** an enzyme in the juice of unripe papayas that is used esp. as a meat tenderizer and in medicine

**pa·pal** \'pā-pəl\ *adj* **:** of or relating to the pope or to the Roman Catholic Church

**pa·paw** *n* **1** \pə-'pò\ **:** PAPAYA **2** \'pàp-,ò\ **:** a No. American tree with yellow edible fruit; *also* **:** its fruit

**pa·pa·ya** \pə-'pī-ə\ *n* **:** a tropical American tree with large yellow black-seeded edible fruit; *also* **:** its fruit

**pa·per** \'pā-pər\ *n* [ME *papir,* fr. MF *papier,* fr. L *papyrus* papyrus, paper, fr. Gk *papyros* papyrus] **1 :** a pliable substance made usu. of vegetable matter and used to write or print on, to wrap things in, or to cover walls; *also* **:** a single sheet of this substance **2 :** a printed or written document **3 :** NEWSPAPER **4 :** WALLPAPER — **paper** *adj or vb* — **pa·pery** \'pā-p(ə-)rē\ *adj*

**pa·per·back** \'pā-pər-,bak\ *n* **:** a paper-covered book

**pa·per·board** \'pā-pər-,bòrd\ *n* **:** CARDBOARD — **paperboard** *adj*

**pa·per·hang·er** \'pā-pər-,haŋ-ər\ *n* **:** one that applies wallpaper — **pa·per·hang·ing** \-iŋ\ *n*

**pa·per·weight** \'pā-pər-,wāt\ *n* **:** an object used to hold down loose papers by its weight

**pa·pier–mâ·ché** \,pā-pər-mə-'shā, ,pap-,yä-mə-, -ma-\ *n* [F, lit., chewed paper] **:** a molding material of wastepaper and additives (as glue)

**pa·pil·la** \pə-'pil-ə\ *n, pl* **pa·pil·lae** \-'pil-(,)ē, -,ī\ **:** a small projecting bodily part — **pap·il·lary** \'pap-ə-,ler-ē, pə-'pil-ə-rē\ *adj*

**pa·pil·lote** \,päp-ē-'(y)ōt\ *n* **:** a greased paper wrapper in which food is cooked

**pa·pist** \'pā-pəst\ *n, often cap* **:** ROMAN CATHOLIC — usu. used disparagingly

**pa·poose** \pa-'püs, pə-\ *n* **:** a young child of No. American Indian parents

**pa·pri·ka** \pə-'prē-kə, pa-\ *n* **:** a mild red spice made from the fruit of some sweet peppers

**Pap smear** \'pap-\ *n* **:** a method for the early detection of cancer

**Pap test** \'pap-\ *n* **:** PAP SMEAR

**pap·ule** \'pap-yül\ *n* **:** a small solid usu. conical lesion of the skin — **pap·u·lar** \-yə-lər\ *adj*

**pa·py·rus** \pə-'pī-rəs\ *n, pl* **pa·py·rus·es** *or* **pa·py·ri** \-(,)rē, -,rī\ **1 :** a tall grassy Egyptian sedge **2 :** paper made from papyrus pith

**¹par** \'pär\ *n* **1 :** a stated value (as of a security) **2 :** a common level **:** EQUALITY **3 :** an accepted standard or normal condition **4 :** the score standard set for each hole of a golf course — **par** *adj*

**²par** *abbr* **1** paragraph **2** parallel **3** parish

**pa·ra** \'pär-ə\ *n, pl* **paras** *or* **para** — see *dinar* at MONEY table

**par·a·ble** \'par-ə-bəl\ *n* **:** a simple story told to illustrate a moral truth

**pa·rab·o·la** \pə-'rab-ə-lə\ *n* **:** a curve formed by the intersection of a cone with a plane parallel to its side — **par·a·bol·ic** \,par-ə-'bäl-ik\ *adj*

**para·chute** \'par-ə-,shüt\ *n* **:** a large umbrella-shaped device used esp. for making a descent from an airplane — **parachute** *vb* — **par·a·chut·ist** \-,shüt-əst\ *n*

**¹pa·rade** \pə-'rād\ *n* **1 :** a pompous display **:** EXHIBITION ⟨a ~ of wealth⟩ **2 :** MARCH, PROCESSION; *esp* **:** a ceremonial formation and march (as of troops) **3 :** a place for strolling

**²parade** *vb* **pa·rad·ed; pa·rad·ing 1 :** to march in a parade **2 :** PROMENADE **3 :** to show off **4 :** MASQUERADE

**par·a·digm** \'par-ə-,dīm, -,dim\ *n* **1 :** MODEL, PATTERN **2 :** a systematic inflection of a verb or noun showing a complete conjugation or declension

**par·a·dise** \'par-ə-,dīs, -,dīz\ *n* [ME *paradis,* fr. OF, fr. LL *paradisus,* fr. Gk *paradeisos,* lit., enclosed park, of Iranian origin] **1** *often cap* **:** HEAVEN **2 :** a place of bliss

**par·a·di·si·a·cal** \,par-ə-də-'sī-ə-kəl\ *or* **par·a·dis·i·ac** \-'dīz-ē-,ak, -'dis-\ *adj* **:** of, relating to, or resembling paradise — **par·a·di·si·a·cal·ly** \-də-'sī-ə-k(ə-)lē\ *adv*

**par·a·dox** \'par-ə-,däks\ *n* **:** a statement that seems contrary to common sense and yet is perhaps true — **par·a·dox·i·cal** \,par-ə-'däk-si-kəl\ *adj* — **par·a·dox·i·cal·ly** \-k(ə-)lē\ *adv* par·af·fin \'par-ə-fən\ n 1 : a waxy substance used esp. for making candles and sealing foods 2 *chiefly Brit* : KEROSENE — paraffin vb — par·af·fin·ic \,par-ə-'fin-ik\ adj

par·a·gon \'par-ə-,gän, -gən\ n : a model of perfection : PATTERN

¹par·a·graph \'par-ə-,graf\ n : a subdivision of a written composition that consists of one or more sentences and deals with one point or gives the words of one speaker; *also* : a character (as ¶) marking the beginning of such a subdivision

²paragraph vb : to divide into paragraphs

par·a·keet \'par-ə-,kēt\ n : any of numerous usu. small slender parrots with a long graduated tail

par·al·lax \'par-ə-,laks\ n : the difference in apparent direction of an object as seen from two different points

¹par·al·lel \'par-ə-,lel\ adj [L *parallelus*, fr. Gk *parallēlos*, fr. *para* beside + *allēlon* of one another, fr. *allos . . . allos* one . . . another, fr. *allos* other] 1 : lying or moving in the same direction but always the same distance apart 2 : similar in essential parts : LIKE — par·al·lel·ism \-,iz-əm\ n

²parallel n 1 : a parallel line, curve, or surface 2 : one of the imaginary circles on the earth's surface paralleling the equator and marking the latitude 3 : something essentially similar to another 4 : LIKENESS, SIMILARITY

³parallel vb 1 : COMPARE 2 : to correspond to 3 : to extend in a parallel direction with

par·al·lel·o·gram \,par-ə-'lel-ə-,gram\ n : a 4-sided geometrical figure with opposite sides equal and parallel

pa·ral·y·sis \pə-'ral-ə-səs\ n, pl -y·ses \-,sēz\ : loss of function and esp. of feeling or the power or voluntary motion — par·a·lyt·ic \,par-ə-'lit-ik\ adj or n

par·a·lyze \'par-ə-,līz\ vb -lyzed; -lyz·ing 1 : to affect with paralysis 2 : to make powerless or inactive — par·a·lyz·ing·ly \-,lī-ziŋ-lē\ adv

par·a·me·cium \,par-ə-'mē-sh(ē-)əm, -sē-əm\ n, pl -cia \-sh(ē-)ə, -sē-ə\ *also* -ci·ums : any of a genus of slipper-shaped protozoans that move by cilia

para·med·i·cal \,par-ə-'med-i-kəl\ adj : concerned with supplementing the work of trained medical professionals — para·med·ic \'par-ə,med-ik\ n

pa·ram·e·ter \pə-'ram-ət-ər\ n 1 : an arbitrary constant whose value characterizes a member of a system (as a family of curves) 2 : any of a set of physical properties whose values determine the characteristics or behavior of a system 3 : a characteristic element : FACTOR — para·met·ric \,par-ə-'met-rik\ adj

para·mil·i·tary \,par-ə-'mil-ə-,ter-ē\ adj : formed on a military pattern esp. as an auxiliary military force

par·a·mount \'par-ə-,maunt\ adj : superior to all others : SUPREME syn preponderant, predominant, dominant,

chief, sovereign

par·amour \'par-ə-,mur\ n : an illicit lover; *esp* : MISTRESS

para·noia \,par-ə-'noi-ə\ n : mental disorder marked by delusions and irrational suspicion — para·noid \'par-ə,noid\ adj or n

par·a·pet \'par-ə-pət, -,pet\ n 1 : a protecting rampart in a fort 2 : a low wall or railing (as at the edge of a platform or bridge)

par·a·pher·na·lia \,par-ə-fə(r)-'nāl-yə\ n sing or pl 1 : personal belongings 2 : EQUIPMENT, APPARATUS

para·phrase \'par-ə-,frāz\ n : a restatement of a text giving the meaning in different words — paraphrase vb

para·ple·gia \,par-ə-'plē-j(ē-)ə\ n : paralysis of the lower trunk and legs — para·ple·gic \-jik\ adj or n

para·pro·fes·sion·al \-prə-'fesh-(ə-)nəl\ n : a trained aide who assists a professional

para·psy·chol·o·gy \,par-ə-sī-'käl-ə-jē\ n : a branch of study involving the investigation of telepathy and related subjects — para·psy·chol·o·gist \-jəst\ n

par·a·site \'par-ə-,sīt\ n [MF, fr. L *parasitus*, fr. Gk *parasitos*, fr. *para*-beside + *sitos* grain, food] 1 : a plant or animal living in or on another organism usu. to its harm 2 : one depending on another and not making adequate return — par·a·sit·ic \,par-ə-'sit-ik\ adj — par·a·sit·ism \'par-ə-sə-,tiz-əm, -,sīt-,iz-\ n — par·a·sit·ize \-sə-,tīz\ vb

par·a·si·tol·o·gy \,par-ə-sə-'täl-ə-jē\ n : a branch of biology dealing with parasites and parasitism esp. among animals — par·a·si·tol·o·gist \-jəst\ n

para·sol \'par-ə-,sol\ n [F, fr. It *parasole*, fr. *parare* to shield + *sole* sun, fr. L *sol*] : a lightweight umbrella used as a shield against the sun

para·sym·pa·thet·ic nervous system \,par-ə-,sim-pə-'thet-ik-\ n : the part of the autonomic nervous system that tends to induce secretion, to increase the tone and contractility of smooth muscle, and to cause the dilatation of blood vessels

para·thi·on \,par-ə-'thī-ən, -,än\ n : an extremely toxic insecticide

para·thy·roid \-'thī-,roid\ n : PARATHYROID GLAND — parathyroid adj

parathyroid gland n : any of usu. four small endocrine glands that are adjacent to or embedded in the thyroid gland and produce a hormone concerned with calcium metabolism

para·troop·er \'par-ə-,trü-pər\ n : a member of the paratroops

para·troops \-,trüps\ n pl : troops trained to parachute from an airplane

para·ty·phoid \,par-ə-'tī-,foid, -'tī-'foid\ n : a food poisoning resembling typhoid fever

par·boil \'pär-,boil\ vb : to boil briefly

¹par·cel \'pär-səl\ n 1 : a tract or plot of land 2 : COLLECTION, LOT 3 : a wrapped bundle : PACKAGE

³**parcel** *vb* **par·celed** *or* **par·celled;**
**par·cel·ing** *or* **par·cel·ling** \'pär-s(ə-)liŋ\ **:** to divide into portions

**parcel post** *n* **1 :** a mail service handling parcels **2 :** packages handled by parcel post

**parch** \'pärch\ *vb* **1 :** to toast under dry heat **2 :** to shrivel with heat

**parch·ment** \'pärch-mənt\ *n* **:** the skin of a sheep or goat prepared for writing on; *also* **:** a writing on such material

**pard** \'pärd\ *n* **:** LEOPARD

¹**par·don** \'pärd-ᵊn\ *n* **:** excuse of an offense without penalty; *esp* **:** an official release from legal punishment

²**pardon** *vb* **par·doned; par·don·ing** \'pärd-(ᵊ-)niŋ\ **:** to free from penalty **:** EXCUSE, FORGIVE — **par·don·able** \-(ᵊ-)nə-bəl\ *adj*

**par·don·er** \'pärd-(ᵊ-)nər\ *n* **1 :** a medieval preacher delegated to raise money for religious works by soliciting offerings and granting indulgences **2 :** one that pardons

**pare** \'paər\ *vb* **pared; par·ing 1 :** to trim or shave off an outside part (as the skin or rind) of ⟨∼ an apple⟩ **2 :** to reduce as if by paring ⟨∼ expenses⟩ — **par·er** *n*

**par·e·gor·ic** \,par-ə-'gȯr-ik\ *n* **:** an alcoholic preparation of opium and camphor

**par·ent** \'par-ənt\ *n* **1 :** one that begets or brings forth offspring **:** FATHER, MOTHER **2 :** SOURCE, ORIGIN — **par·ent·age** \-ij\ *n* — **pa·ren·tal** \pə-'rent-ᵊl\ *adj* — **par·ent·hood** *n*

**pa·ren·the·sis** \pə-'ren-thə-səs\ *n, pl* **-the·ses** \-,sēz\ **1 :** a word, phrase, or sentence inserted in a passage to explain or modify the thought **2 :** one of a pair of punctuation marks ( ) used esp. to enclose parenthetic matter — **par·en·thet·ic** \,par-ən-'thet-ik\ *or* **par·en·thet·i·cal** \-i-kəl\ *adj* — **par·en·thet·i·cal·ly** \-k(ə-)lē\ *adv*

**pa·ren·the·size** \pə-'ren-thə-,sīz\ *vb* **-sized; -siz·ing :** to make a parenthesis of

**pa·re·sis** \pə-'rē-səs, 'par-ə-\ *n, pl* **pa·re·ses** \-,sēz\ **1 :** a usu. incomplete paralysis; *also* **:** a syphilitic disorder marked by mental and paralytic symptoms

**par ex·cel·lence** \,pär-,ek-sə-'läⁿs\ *adj* [F, lit., by excellence] **:** being the best of a kind **:** PREEMINENT

**par·fait** \pär-'fā\ *n* [F, lit., something perfect, fr. *parfait* perfect, fr. L *perfectus*] **1 :** a flavored custard containing whipped cream and a syrup frozen without stirring **2 :** a cold dessert made of layers of fruit, syrup, ice cream, and whipped cream

**par·fo·cal** \(')pär-'fō-kəl\ *adj* **:** being or having lenses with focal points in the same plane

**pa·ri·ah** \pə-'rī-ə\ *n* **:** OUTCAST

**pa·ri·etal** \pə-'rī-ət-ᵊl\ *adj* **1 :** of, relating to, or forming the walls of an anatomical structure **2 :** of or relating to college living or its regulation

**pari-mu·tu·el** \,par-i-'myü-**

cho(-wə)l\ *n* **:** a system of betting in which those with winning bets share the total stakes minus a percentage for the management

**par·ing** \'par-iŋ\ *n* **:** something pared off ⟨potato ∼s⟩

**pa·ri pas·su** \,par-i-'pas-ü\ *adv or adj* [L, with equal step] **:** at an equal rate or pace

**Par·is green** \,par-əs-\ *n* **:** a poisonous bright green powder used as a pigment and as an insecticide

**par·ish** \'par-ish\ *n* **1 :** the ecclesiastical area in the charge of one pastor; *also* **:** the residents of such an area **2 :** a local church community **3 :** a civil division of the state of Louisiana **:** COUNTY

**pa·rish·io·ner** \pə-'rish-(ə-)nər\ *n* **:** a member or resident of a parish

**par·i·ty** \'par-ət-ē\ *n, pl* **-ties :** EQUALITY, EQUIVALENCE

¹**park** \'pärk\ *n* **1 :** a tract of ground kept as a game preserve or recreation area **2 :** a place where vehicles (as automobiles) are parked **3 :** an enclosed stadium used esp. for ball games **4 :** a level valley between mountain ranges

²**park** *vb* **1 :** to enclose in a park **2 :** to keep (as an automobile) standing for a time at the edge of a public way or in a place reserved for the purpose

**par·ka** \'pär-kə\ *n* **:** a hooded fur pullover garment for arctic wear; *also* **:** a similar garment for sports or military wear

**Par·kin·son's disease** \'pär-kən-sənz-\ *n* **:** a chronic progressive nervous disease of later life that is marked by tremor and weakness of resting muscles and by a peculiar gait

**Par·kin·son's Law** \,pär-\ *n* **1 :** an observation in office organization: the number of subordinates increases at a fixed rate regardless of the amount of work produced **2 :** an observation in office organization: work expands so as to fill the time available for its completion

**park·way** \'pärk-,wā\ *n* **:** a broad landscaped thoroughfare

**par·lance** \'pär-ləns\ *n* **1 :** SPEECH **2 :** manner of speaking ⟨military ∼⟩

**par·lay** \'pär-,lā\ *n* **:** a series of bets in which the original stake plus its winnings are risked on the successive wagers — **parlay** *vb*

**par·ley** \'pär-lē\ *n, pl* **parleys :** a conference usu. over matters in dispute **:** DISCUSSION — **parley** *vb*

**par·lia·ment** \'pär-lə-mənt\ *n* **1 :** a formal governmental conference **2** *cap* **:** an assembly that constitutes the supreme legislative body of a country (as the United Kingdom) — **par·lia·men·ta·ry** \,pär-lə-'men-t(ə-)rē\ *adj*

**par·lia·men·tar·i·an** \,pär-lə-,men-'ter-ē-ən\ *n* **1** *often cap* **:** an adherent of the parliament in opposition to the king during the English Civil War **2 :** an expert in parliamentary procedure

**par·lor** \'pär-lər\ *n* **1 :** a room for

conversation or the reception of guests **2** : a place of business (beauty ~)

**par·lour** \'pär-lər\ *chiefly Brit var of* PARLOR

**par·lous** \'pär-ləs\ *adj* : full of danger or risk : PRECARIOUS (~ state of a country's finances) — **par·lous·ly** *adv*

**Par·me·san** \'pär-mə-,zän, -,zan\ *n* : a hard dry cheese with a sharp flavor

**par·mi·gia·na** \,pär-mi-'jän-ə\ *or* **par·mi·gia·no** \-'jän-(,)ō\ *adj* : made or covered with Parmesan cheese (veal ~)

**pa·ro·chi·al** \pə-'rō-kē-əl\ *adj* **1** : of or relating to a church parish **2** : limited in scope : NARROW, PROVINCIAL — **pa·ro·chi·al·ism** \-ə-,liz-əm\ *n*

**parochial school** *n* : a school maintained by a religious body

**par·o·dy** \'par-əd-ē\ *n, pl* **-dies** [L *parodia*, fr. Gk *parōidia*, fr. *para-* beside + *aidein* to sing] : a composition (as a poem or song) that imitates another work humorously or satirically — **parody** *vb*

**pa·role** \pə-'rōl\ *n* **1** : pledged word; *esp* : the promise of a prisoner of war to fulfill stated conditions in return for release **2** : a conditional release of a prisoner before his sentence expires — **parole** *vb* — **pa·rol·ee** \-,rō-'lē, -'rō-,lē\ *n*

**par·ox·ysm** \'par-ək-,siz-əm, pə-'räk-\ *n* : a sudden sharp attack (as of pain or coughing) : SPASM **syn** convulsion, fit — **par·ox·ys·mal** \,par-ək-'siz-məl, pə-,räk-\ *adj*

**par·quet** \'pär-,kā, pär-'kā\ *n* **1** : a flooring of parquetry **2** : the lower floor of a theater; *esp* : the forward part of the orchestra

**par·que·try** \'pär-kə-trē\ *n, pl* **-tries** : fine woodwork inlaid in patterns

**par·ra·keet** *var of* PARAKEET

**par·ri·cide** \'par-ə-,sīd\ *n* **1** : one that murders his father, mother, or a close relative **2** : the act of a parricide

**par·rot** \'par-ət\ *n* : a bright-colored tropical bird with a strong hooked bill

**parrot fever** *n* : an infectious disease of birds that is marked by diarrhea and wasting and is transmissible to man

**par·ry** \'par-ē\ *vb* **par·ried; par·ry·ing 1** : to ward off a weapon or blow **2** : to evade esp. by an adroit answer — **parry** *n*

**parse** \'pärs, 'pärz\ *vb* **parsed; pars·ing** : to give a grammatical description of a word or a group of words

**par·sec** \'pär-,sek\ *n* : a unit of measure for interstellar space equal to 19.2 trillion miles

**par·si·mo·ny** \'pär-sə-,mō-nē\ *n* : extreme or excessive frugality — **par·si·mo·ni·ous** \,pär-sə-'mō-nē-əs\ *adj* — **par·si·mo·ni·ous·ly** *adv*

**pars·ley** \'pär-slē\ *n* : a garden plant with finely divided leaves used as a seasoning or garnish

**pars·nip** \'pär-snəp\ *n* : a garden plant with a long edible root; *also* : this root

**par·son** \'pärs-ᵊn\ *n* [ME *persone*, fr. OF, fr. ML *persona*, lit., person, fr. L] : a usu. Protestant clergyman

**par·son·age** \'pärs-(ᵊ-)nij\ *n* : a house provided by a church for its pastor

**¹part** \'pärt\ *n* **1** : a division or portion of a whole **2** : a spare piece for a machine **3** : the melody or score for a particular voice or instrument (the alto ~) **4** : DUTY, FUNCTION **5** : one of the sides in a dispute (took his friend's ~) **6** : ROLE; *also* : an actor's lines in a play **7** *pl* : TALENTS, ABILITY **8** : the line where one's hair divides (as in combing)

**²part** *vb* **1** : to take leave of someone **2** : to divide or break into parts : SEPARATE **3** : to go away : DEPART; *also* : DIE **4** : to give up possession (~ed with her jewels) **5** : APPORTION, SHARE

**³part** *abbr* **1** participial; participle **2** particular

**par·take** \pär-'tāk, pər-\ *vb* **-took** \-'tůk\; **-tak·en** \-'tā-kən\; **-tak·ing 1** : to have a share or part **2** : to take a portion (as of food) — **par·tak·er** *n*

**par·terre** \pär-'teər\ *n* [F, fr. MF, fr. *par terre* on the ground] **1** : an ornamental arrangement of flower beds **2** : the part of a theater floor behind the orchestra

**par·the·no·gen·e·sis** \,pär-thə-nō-'jen-ə-səs\ *n* : development of a new individual from an unfertilized egg — **par·the·no·ge·net·ic** \-jə-'net-ik\ *adj*

**par·tial** \'pär-shəl\ *adj* **1** : favoring one party over the other : BIASED **2** : markedly or foolishly fond — used with *to* **3** : not total or general : affecting a part only — **par·tial·i·ty** \,pärsh-(ē-)'al-ət-ē\ *n* — **par·tial·ly** \'pärsh-(ə-)lē\ *adv*

**par·ti·ble** \'pärt-ə-bəl\ *adj* : capable of being parted

**par·tic·i·pate** \pər-'tis-ə-,pāt, pär-\ *vb* **-pat·ed; -pat·ing 1** : to take part in something (~ in a game) **2** : SHARE — **par·tic·i·pant** \-pənt\ *adj or n* — **par·tic·i·pa·tion** \-,tis-ə-'pā-shən\ *n* — **par·tic·i·pa·tor** \-'tis-ə-,pāt-ər\ *n* — **par·tic·i·pa·to·ry** \-'tis-ə-pə-,tōr-ē\ *adj*

**par·ti·ci·ple** \'pärt-ə-,sip-əl\ *n* : a word having the characteristics of both verb and adjective — **par·ti·cip·i·al** \,pärt-ə-'sip-ē-əl\ *adj*

**par·ti·cle** \'pärt-i-kəl\ *n* **1** : a very small bit of matter **2** : ELEMENTARY PARTICLE **3** : a unit of speech (as an article, preposition, or conjunction) expressing some general aspect of meaning or some connective or limiting relation

**particle board** *n* : a board made of very small pieces of wood bonded together

**par·ti-col·ored** \,pärt-ē-'kəl-ərd\ *adj* : showing different colors or tints

**¹par·tic·u·lar** \pə(r)-'tik-yə-lər\ *adj* **1** : of or relating to a specific person or thing (the laws of a ~ state) **2** : DISTINCTIVE, SPECIAL (the ~ point of his talk) **3** : SEPARATE, INDIVIDUAL (each ~ hair) **4** : attentive to details : PRECISE **5** : hard to please : EXACTING **syn** single, sole, unique, lone, solitary, specific, concrete, fussy, squeamish, nice — **par·tic·u·lar·i·ty** \-,tik-yə-

'lar-ət-ē\ *n* — **par·tic·u·lar·ly** \-'tik-yə-lər-lē\ *adv*

²**particular** *n* **:** an individual fact or detail

**par·tic·u·lar·ize** \pə(r)-'tik-yə-lə-,rīz\ *vb* **-ized; -iz·ing** 1 **:** to state in detail **:** SPECIFY 2 **:** to go into details

**par·tic·u·late** \pər-'tik-yə-lət, pär-, -,lāt\ *adj* **:** relating to or existing as minute separate particles

¹**part·ing** \'pärt-iŋ\ *n* 1 **:** SEPARATION, DIVISION 2 **:** the action of leaving one another ⟨lovers' ∼⟩ 3 **:** a place of separation or divergence

²**parting** *adj* 1 **:** DEPARTING; *esp* **:** DYING 2 **:** FAREWELL ⟨∼ words⟩ 3 **:** serving to part **:** SEPARATING

**par·ti pris** \,pär-,tē-'prē\ *n, pl* **par·tis pris** \-,tē-'prē(z)\ [F, lit., side taken] **:** a preconceived opinion

**par·ti·san** *or* **par·ti·zan** \'pärt-ə-zen, -sən\ *n* 1 **:** one that takes the part of another **:** ADHERENT 2 **:** GUERRILLA — **partisan** *adj* — **par·ti·san·ship** *n*

**par·tite** \'pär-,tīt\ *adj* **:** divided into a usu. specified number of parts

**par·ti·tion** \pər-'tish-ən, pär-\ *n* 1 **:** DIVISION 2 **:** something that divides or separates; *esp* **:** an interior wall dividing one part of a house from another — **partition** *vb*

**par·ti·tive** \'pärt-ət-iv\ *adj* **:** of, relating to, or denoting a part ⟨a ∼ construction⟩

**part·ly** \'pärt-lē\ *adv* **:** in part **:** in some measure or degree

**part·ner** \'pärt-nər\ *n* 1 **:** ASSOCIATE, COLLEAGUE 2 **:** either of a couple who dance together 3 **:** one who plays on the same team with another 4 **:** HUSBAND, WIFE 5 **:** one of two or more persons contractually associated as joint principals in a business — **part·ner·ship** *n*

**part of speech :** a traditional class of words distinguished according to the kind of idea denoted and the function performed in a sentence

**par·tridge** \'pär-trij\ *n, pl* **partridge** *or* **par·tridg·es :** any of various stout-bodied game birds

**part-song** \'pärt-,sȯŋ\ *n* **:** a song with two or more voice parts

**par·tu·ri·tion** \,pärt-ə-'rish-ən, ,pär-chə-, ,pärt-yu̇-\ *n* **:** CHILDBIRTH

**part·way** \'pärt-'wā\ *adv* **:** to some extent **:** PARTLY

**par·ty** \'pärt-ē\ *n, pl* **parties** 1 **:** a person or group taking one side of a question; *esp* **:** a group of persons organized for the purpose of directing the policies of a government 2 **:** a person or group concerned in an action or affair **:** PARTICIPANT 3 **:** a group of persons detailed for a common task 4 **:** a social gathering

**par·ve·nu** \'pär-və-,n(y)ü\ *n* [F, fr. pp. of *parvenir* to arrive, fr. L *pervenire*, fr. *per* through + *venire* to come] **:** one who has recently or suddenly risen to wealth or power and has not yet secured the social position appropriate to it

**pas** \'pä\ *n, pl* **pas** \'pä(z)\ *n* **:** a dance

step or combination of steps

**pa·sha** \'päsh-ə, 'pash-; pə-'shä\ *n* **:** a man (as formerly a governor in Turkey) of high rank

¹**pass** \'pas\ *vb* 1 **:** MOVE, PROCEED 2 **:** to go away; *also* **:** DIE 3 **:** to move past, beyond, or over 4 **:** to allow to elapse **:** SPEND 5 **:** to go or make way through 6 **:** to go or allow to go unchallenged 7 **:** to undergo transfer 8 **:** to render a legal judgment 9 **:** OCCUR 10 **:** to secure the approval of (as a legislature) 11 **:** to go or cause to go through an inspection, test, or course of study successfully 12 **:** to be regarded 13 **:** CIRCULATE 14 **:** VOID 15 **:** to transfer the ball or puck to another player 16 **:** to decline to bid or bet on one's hand in a card game 17 **:** to permit to reach first base by a base on balls — **pass·er** *n* — **pass·er·by** \,pas-ər-'bī, 'pas-ər-,bī\ *n*

²**pass** *n* **:** a gap in a mountain range

³**pass** *n* 1 **:** the act or an instance of passing 2 **:** REALIZATION, ACCOMPLISHMENT 3 **:** a state of affairs 4 **:** a written authorization to leave, enter, or move about freely 5 **:** a transfer of a ball or puck from one player to another 6 **:** BASE ON BALLS 7 **:** EFFORT, TRY 8 **:** a sexually inviting gesture or approach

⁴**pass** *abbr* 1 passenger 2 passive

**pass·able** \'pas-ə-bəl\ *adj* 1 **:** capable of being passed or traveled on 2 **:** barely good enough **:** TOLERABLE — **pass·ably** \-blē\ *adv*

**pas·sage** \'pas-ij\ *n* 1 **:** the action or process of passing 2 **:** a means (as a road or corridor) of passing 3 **:** a voyage esp. by sea or air 4 **:** a right or permission to pass 5 **:** ENACTMENT 6 **:** a mutual act (as an exchange of blows) 7 **:** a usu. brief portion or section (as of a book)

**pas·sage·way** \-,wā\ *n* **:** a way that allows passage

**pass·book** \'pas-,bu̇k\ *n* **:** BANKBOOK

**pas·sé** \pa-'sā\ *adj* 1 **:** past one's prime 2 **:** not up-to-date **:** OUTMODED

**pas·sel** \'pas-əl\ *n* **:** a large number

**pas·sen·ger** \'pas-ⁿn-jər\ *n* **:** a traveler in a public or private conveyance

**passe-par·tout** \,pas-pər-'tü\ *n* **:** something that passes or enables one to pass everywhere

**pas·ser·ine** \'pas-ə-,rīn\ *adj* **:** of or relating to the great group of birds comprising singing birds that perch

**pas·sim** \'pas-əm\ *adv* [L, fr. *passus* scattered, fr. pp. of *pandere* to spread] **:** here and there **:** THROUGHOUT

**pass·ing** \'pas-iŋ\ *n* **:** the act of one that passes or causes to pass; *esp* **:** DEATH

**pas·sion** \'pash-ən\ *n* 1 *often cap* **:** the sufferings of Christ between the night of the Last Supper and his death 2 **:** strong feeling; *also pl* **:** the emotions as distinguished from reason 3 **:** RAGE, ANGER 4 **:** LOVE; *also* **:** an object of affection or enthusiasm 5 **:** sexual desire — **pas·sion·ate** \'pash-(ə-)nət\ *adj* — **pas·sion·ate·ly** *adv* — **pas·sion·less** *adj*

**pas·sive** \'pas-iv\ adj **1 :** not active **:** acted upon **2 :** asserting that the grammatical subject is subjected to or affected by the action represented by the verb ⟨~ voice⟩ **3 :** SUBMISSIVE, PATIENT — **passive** n — **pas·sive·ly** adv — **pas·siv·i·ty** \pa-'siv-ət-ē\ n

**pass·key** \'pas-ˌkē\ n **:** a key for opening two or more locks

**pass out** vb **:** to lose consciousness

**Pass·over** \'pas-ˌō-vər\ n [fr. the exemption of the Israelites from the slaughter of the first-born in Egypt (Exod 12:23–27)] **:** a Jewish holiday celebrated in March or April in commemoration of the Hebrews' liberation from slavery in Egypt

**pass·port** \'pas-ˌpōrt\ n **:** an official document issued by a country upon request to a citizen requesting protection for him during travel abroad

**pass up** vb **:** DECLINE, REJECT

**pass·word** \'pas-ˌwərd\ n **:** a word or phrase that must be spoken by a person before he is allowed to pass a guard

**¹past** \'past\ adj **1 :** AGO ⟨10 years ~⟩ **2 :** just gone or elapsed ⟨the ~ month⟩ **3 :** having existed or taken place in a period before the present **:** BYGONE **4 :** of, relating to, or constituting a verb tense that expresses time gone by

**²past** prep or adv **:** BEYOND

**³past** n **1 :** time gone by **2 :** something that happened or was done in former time **3 :** the past tense; also **:** a verb form in it **4 :** a secret past life

**pas·ta** \'päs-tə\ n **1 :** a paste in processed form (as spaghetti) or in the form of fresh dough (as ravioli) **2 :** a dish of cooked pasta

**¹paste** \'pāst\ n **1 :** DOUGH **2 :** a smooth food product made by evaporation or grinding (almond ~) **3 :** a preparation (as of flour and water) for sticking things together **4 :** a brilliant glass of high lead content used in imitation gems

**²paste** vb **past·ed; past·ing :** to cause to adhere by paste **:** STICK

**paste·board** \'pās(t)-ˌbōrd\ n **1 :** a stiff material made of sheets of paper pasted together **2 :** medium-thick cardboard

**¹pas·tel** \pas-'tel\ n **1 :** a paste made of ground color; also **:** a crayon of such paste **2 :** a drawing in pastel **3 :** a pale or light color

**²pastel** adj **1 :** of or relating to a pastel **2 :** pale and light in color

**pas·tern** \'pas-tərn\ n **:** the part of a horse's foot between the fetlock and the joint at the hoof

**pas·teur·ize** \'pas-chə-ˌrīz, 'pas-tə-\ vb **-ized; -iz·ing :** to heat (as milk) to a point where harmful germs are killed — **pas·teur·i·za·tion** \ˌpas-chə-rə-'zā-shən, ˌpas-tə-\ n — **pas·teur·iz·er** n

**pas·tiche** \pas-'tēsh\ n **:** a composition (as in literature or music) made up of selections from different works

**pas·tille** \pas-'tēl\ also **pas·til** \'pas-tᵊl\ n **1 :** a small mass of aromatic paste for fumigating or scenting the air

of a room **2 :** an aromatic or medicated lozenge

**pas·time** \'pas-ˌtīm\ n **:** DIVERSION

**pas·tor** \'pas-tər\ n [ME pastour, fr. OF, fr. L pastor, herdsman, fr. pastus, pp. of pascere to feed] **:** a clergyman serving a local church or parish — **pas·tor·ate** \-t(ə-)rət\ n

**¹pas·to·ral** \'pas-t(ə-)rəl\ adj **1 :** of or relating to shepherds or to rural life **2 :** of or relating to spiritual guidance esp. of a congregation **3 :** of or relating to the pastor of a church

**²pastoral** \'pas-t(ə-)rəl\ n **:** a literary work dealing with shepherds or rural life

**pas·to·rale** \ˌpas-tə-'räl, -'ral\ n **:** a musical composition having a pastoral theme

**past participle** n **:** a participle that typically expresses completed action, that is one of the principal parts of the verb, and that is used in the formation of perfect tenses in the active voice and of all tenses in the passive voice

**pas·tra·mi** also **pas·tro·mi** \pə-'sträm-ē\ n **:** a highly seasoned smoked beef prepared esp. from shoulder cuts

**pas·try** \'pā-strē\ n, pl **pastries :** sweet baked goods made of dough or with a crust made of enriched dough

**pas·tur·age** \'pas-chə-rij\ n **:** PASTURE

**¹pas·ture** \'pas-chər\ n **1 :** plants (as grass) for the feeding of grazing livestock **2 :** land or a plot of land used for grazing

**²pasture** vb **pas·tured; pas·tur·ing 1 :** GRAZE **2 :** to use as pasture

**pasty** \'pā-stē\ adj **past·i·er; -est :** resembling paste; esp **:** pallid and unhealthy in appearance

**¹pat** \'pat\ n **1 :** a light tap esp. with the hand or a flat instrument; also **:** the sound made by it **2 :** something (as butter) shaped into a small flat usu. square individual portion

**²pat** vb **pat·ted; pat·ting 1 :** to strike lightly with a flat instrument **2 :** to flatten, smooth, or put into place or shape with a pat **3 :** to tap gently or lovingly with the hand

**³pat** adj or adv **1 :** exactly suited to the occasion **2 :** memorized exactly **3 :** UNYIELDING

**⁴pat** abbr patent

**pa·ta·ca** \pə-'täk-ə\ n — see MONEY table

**¹patch** \'pach\ n **1 :** a piece of cloth used to cover a torn or worn place in a garment; also **:** one worn on a garment as an ornament or insignia **2 :** a small area (as of land) distinct from that about it **3 :** a shield worn over the socket of an injured or missing eye

**²patch** vb **1 :** to mend or cover with a patch **2 :** to make of fragments **3 :** to repair usu. in hasty fashion

**patch test** n **:** a test for allergic sensitivity made by applying to the unbroken skin small pads soaked with the allergen to be tested

**patch·work** \'pach-ˌwərk\ n **:** something made of pieces of different materials, shapes, or colors

**pate** \'pāt\ *n* **:** HEAD, *esp* **:** the crown of the head

**pâ·té** \pä-'tā\ *n* **1 :** a meat or fish pie or patty **2 :** a spread of finely mashed seasoned and spiced meat

**pa·tel·la** \pə-'tel-ə\ *n, pl* **pa·tel·lae** \-'tel-(,)ē, -,ī\ *or* **patellas :** KNEECAP

**pat·en** \'pat-ᵊn\ *n* **1 :** PLATE; *esp* **:** one of precious metal for the eucharistic bread **2 :** a thin disk

**¹pa·tent** \ *1 & 4 are* 'pat-ᵊnt, *Brit also* 'pāt-; *2 & 3 are* 'pat-ᵊnt, 'pāt-\ *adj* **1 :** open to public inspection — used chiefly in the phrase *letters patent* **2 :** free from obstruction **3 :** EVIDENT, OBVIOUS **4 :** protected by a patent **syn** manifest, distinct, apparent, palpable, plain, clear

**²pat·ent** \'pat-ᵊnt, *Brit also* 'pāt-\ *n* **1 :** an official document conferring a right or privilege **2 :** a document securing to an inventor for a term of years exclusive right to his invention **3 :** something patented — **pat·en·tee** \,pat-ᵊn-'tē, *Brit also* ,pāt-\ *n*

**³pat·ent** *vb* **:** to secure by patent

**pa·ter·fa·mil·i·as** \,pāt-ər-fə-'mil-ē-əs\ *n, pl* **pa·tres·fa·mil·i·as** \,pä-,trēz-\ **:** the father of a family **:** the male head of a household

**pa·ter·nal** \pə-'tərn-ᵊl\ *adj* **1 :** FATHERLY **2 :** related through or inherited or derived from a father — **pa·ter·nal·ly** \-ē\ *adv*

**pa·ter·nal·ism** \-,iz-əm\ *n* **:** a system under which an authority treats those under its control paternally (as by regulating their conduct and supplying their needs)

**pa·ter·ni·ty** \pə-'tər-nət-ē\ *n* **1 :** FATHERHOOD **2 :** descent from a father

**¹path** \'path, 'pȧth\ *n, pl* **paths** \'pa*th*z, 'paths, 'pȧ*th*z, 'pȧths\ **1 :** a trodden way **2 :** ROUTE, COURSE — **path·less** *adj*

**²path** *or* **pathol** *abbr* pathology

**pa·thet·ic** \pə-'thet-ik\ *adj* **:** evoking tenderness, pity, or sorrow **syn** poignant, affecting, moving, touching, impressive — **pa·thet·i·cal·ly** \-i-k(ə-)lē\ *adv*

**path·find·er** \'path-,fīn-dər, 'pȧth-\ *n* **:** one that discovers a way; *esp* **:** one that explores untraveled regions to mark out a new route

**patho·gen** \'path-ə-jən\ *n* **:** a specific cause (as a bacterium or virus) of disease — **patho·gen·ic** \,path-ə-'jen-ik\ *adj* — **patho·ge·nic·i·ty** \-jə-'nis-ət-ē\ *n*

**pa·thol·o·gy** \pə-'thäl-ə-jē\ *n, pl* **-gies 1 :** the study of the essential nature of disease **2 :** the abnormality of structure and function characteristic of a disease — **path·o·log·i·cal** \,path-ə-'läj-i-kəl\ *adj* — **pa·thol·o·gist** \pə-'thäl-ə-jəst\ *n*

**pa·thos** \'pā-,thäs\ *n* **:** an element in experience or artistic representation evoking pity or compassion

**path·way** \'path-,wā, 'pȧth-\ *n* **:** PATH

**pa·tience** \'pā-shəns\ *n* **1 :** the capacity, habit, or fact of being patient **2** *chiefly Brit* **:** SOLITAIRE 2

**¹pa·tient** \'pā-shənt\ *adj* **1 :** bearing pain or trials without complaint **2 :** showing self-control **:** CALM **3 :** STEADFAST, PERSEVERING — **pa·tient·ly** *adv*

**²patient** *n* **:** a person under medical care

**pa·ti·na** \'pat-ə-nə, pə-'tē-nə\ *n, pl* **pa·ti·nas** \-nəz\ *or* **pa·ti·nae** \'pat-ə-,nē, -,nī\ **:** a green film formed on copper and bronze by long exposure to moist air

**pa·tio** \'pat-ē-,ō, 'pät-\ *n, pl* **pa·ti·os 1 :** COURTYARD **2 :** a paved recreation area near a house

**pa·tois** \'pa-,twä\ *n, pl* **pa·tois** \-,twäz\ **1 :** a dialect other than the standard or literary dialect; *esp* **:** illiterate or provincial speech **2 :** JARGON 2

**pa·tri·arch** \'pā-trē-,ärk\ *n* **1 :** a man revered as father or founder (as of a tribe) **2 :** a venerable old man **3 :** an ecclesiastical dignitary (as the bishop of an Eastern Orthodox see) — **pa·tri·ar·chal** \,pā-trē-'är-kəl\ *adj* — **pa·tri·arch·ate** \'pā-trē-,är-kət, -,kāt\ *n* — **pa·tri·ar·chy** \-,är-kē\ *n*

**pa·tri·cian** \pə-'trish-ən\ *n* **:** a person of high birth **:** ARISTOCRAT — **patrician** *adj*

**pat·ri·cide** \'pa-trə-,sīd\ *n* **1 :** one who murders his own father **2 :** the murder of one's own father

**pat·ri·mo·ny** \'pa-trə-,mō-nē\ *n* **:** something (as an estate) inherited or derived esp. from one's father **:** HERITAGE — **pat·ri·mo·ni·al** \,pat-rə-'mō-nē-əl\ *adj*

**pa·tri·ot** \'pā-trē-ət, -,ät\ *n* [MF *patriote*, fr. LL *patriota*, fr. Gk *patriōtēs*, fr. *patrios* of one's father, fr. *patr-, patēr* father] **:** one who loves his country — **pa·tri·ot·ic** \,pā-trē-'ät-ik\ *adj* — **pa·tri·ot·i·cal·ly** \-i-k(ə-)lē\ *adv* — **pa·tri·o·tism** \'pā-trē-ə-,tiz-əm\ *n*

**pa·tris·tic** \pə-'tris-tik\ *adj* **:** of or relating to the church fathers or their writings

**¹pa·trol** \pə-'trōl\ *n* **:** the action of going the rounds (as of an area) for observation or the maintenance of security; *also* **:** a person or group performing such an action

**²patrol** *vb* **pa·trolled; pa·trol·ling** [F *patrouiller*, fr. MF, to tramp around in the mud, fr. *patte* paw] **:** to carry out a patrol

**pa·trol·man** \pə-'trōl-mən\ *n* **:** a policeman assigned to a beat

**patrol wagon** *n* **:** an enclosed motortruck for carrying prisoners

**pa·tron** \'pā-trən\ *n* [ME, fr. MF, fr. ML & L; ML *patronus* patron saint, patron of a benefice, pattern, fr. L, defender, fr. *patr-, pater* father] **1 :** a person chosen or named as special protector **2 :** a wealthy or influential supporter (~ of poets); *also* **:** BENEFACTOR **3 :** a regular client or customer **syn** sponsor, guarantor — **pa·tron·ess** \-trə-nəs\ *n*

**pa·tron·age** \'pa-trə-nij, 'pā-\ *n* **1 :** the support or influence of a patron

2 : the trade of customers  3 : control of appointment to government jobs

**pa·tron·ize** \'pā-trə-ˌnīz, 'pa-\ *vb* **-ized; -iz·ing** 1 : to act as patron of; *esp* : to be a customer of  2 : to treat condescendingly

**pat·ro·nym·ic** \ˌpa-trə-'nim-ik\ *n* : a name derived from the name of one's father or paternal ancestor usu. by the addition of a prefix or suffix

**pa·troon** \pə-'trün\ *n* : the proprietor of a manorial estate esp. in New York under Dutch rule

**pat·sy** \'pat-sē\ *n, pl* **pat·sies** : one who is duped or victimized

¹**pat·ter** \'pat-ər\ *vb* : to talk glibly or mechanically **syn** chatter, prate, chat, prattle

²**patter** *n* 1 : a specialized lingo  2 : extremely rapid talk ⟨a comedian's ~⟩

³**patter** *vb* : to strike, pat, or tap rapidly

⁴**patter** *n* : a quick succession of taps or pats ⟨the ~ of rain⟩

¹**pattern** \'pat-ərn\ *n* [ME *patron*, fr. MF, fr. ML *patronus*, fr. L, defender, fr. *patr-, pater* father] 1 : an ideal model  2 : something used as a model for making things ⟨a dressmaker's ~⟩  3 : SAMPLE  4 : an artistic design  5 : CONFIGURATION

²**pattern** *vb* : to form according to a pattern

**pat·ty** *also* **pat·tie** \'pat-ē\ *n, pl* **patties** 1 : a little pie  2 : a small flat cake esp. of chopped food

**pau·ci·ty** \'pȯ-sət-ē\ *n* : smallness of number or quantity

**paunch** \'pȯnch\ *n* : a usu. large belly : POTBELLY — **paunchy** *adj*

**pau·per** \'pȯ-pər\ *n* : a person without means of support except from charity — **pau·per·ism** \-pə-ˌriz-əm\ *n* — **pau·per·ize** \-pə-ˌrīz\ *vb*

¹**pause** \'pȯz\ *n* 1 : a temporary stop; *also* : a period of inaction  2 : a brief suspension of the voice  3 : a sign ∩ or ∪ above or below a musical note or rest to show it is to be prolonged  4 : a reason for pausing

²**pause** *vb* **paused; paus·ing** : to stop, rest, or linger for a time

**pave** \'pāv\ *vb* **paved; pav·ing** : to cover (as a road) with hard material (as stone or asphalt) in order to smooth or firm the surface

**pave·ment** \'pāv-mənt\ *n* 1 : a paved surface  2 : the material with which something is paved

**pa·vil·ion** \pə-'vil-yən\ *n* [ME *pavilon*, fr. OF *paveillon*, fr. L *papilion-, papilio* butterfly] 1 : a large tent  2 : a light structure (as in a park) used for entertainment or shelter

**pav·ing** \'pā-viŋ\ *n* : PAVEMENT

¹**paw** \'pȯ\ *n* : the foot of a quadruped (as a dog or lion) having claws

²**paw** *vb* 1 : to feel or handle clumsily or rudely  2 : to touch or strike with a paw; *also* : to scrape with a hoof  3 : to flail about or grab for with the hands

**pawl** \'pȯl\ *n* : a pivoted tongue or sliding bolt adapted to fall into notches on another machine part to permit motion in one direction only

¹**pawn** \'pȯn\ *n* 1 : goods deposited with another as security for a loan; *also* : HOSTAGE  2 : the state of being pledged

²**pawn** *vb* : to deposit as a pledge

³**pawn** *n* [ME *pown*, fr. MF *poon*, fr. ML *pedon-, pedo* foot soldier, fr. LL, one with broad feet, fr. L *ped-, pes* foot] : a chessman of the least value

**pawn·bro·ker** \'pȯn-ˌbrō-kər\ *n* : one who loans money on goods pledged

**Paw·nee** \pȯ-'nē\ *n, pl* **Pawnee** *or* **Pawnees** : a member of an Indian people orig. of Kansas and Nebraska

**pawn·shop** \'pȯn-ˌshäp\ *n* : a pawnbroker's place of business

**paw·paw** *var of* PAPAW

¹**pay** \'pā\ *vb* **paid** \'pād\ *also in sense* 7 **payed; pay·ing** [ME *payen*, fr. OF *paier*, fr. L *pacare* to pacify, fr. *pac-, pax* peace] 1 : to make due return to for goods or services  2 : to discharge indebtedness for : SETTLE ⟨~ a bill⟩  3 : to give in forfeit ⟨~ the penalty⟩  4 : REQUITE  5 : to give, offer, or make freely or as fitting ⟨~ attention⟩  6 : to be profitable to : RETURN  7 : to make slack and allow to run out ⟨~ out a rope⟩ — **pay·able** *adj* — **pay·ee** \pā-'ē\ *n* — **pay·er** *n*

²**pay** *n* 1 : the status of being paid by an employer : EMPLOY  2 : something paid; *esp* : WAGES

³**pay** *adj* 1 : containing something valuable (as gold) ⟨~ dirt⟩  2 : equipped to receive a fee for use ⟨~ telephone⟩

**pay·check** \'pā-ˌchek\ *n* 1 : a check in payment of wages or salary  2 : WAGES, SALARY

**pay·load** \'pā-ˌlōd\ *n* : the load (as passengers or cargo) carried by a vehicle (as a spacecraft) in addition to what is necessary for its operation

**pay·mas·ter** \-ˌmas-tər\ *n* : one who distributes the payroll

**pay·ment** \'pā-mənt\ *n* 1 : the act of paying  2 : something paid

**pay·off** \-ˌȯf\ *n* 1 : payment at the outcome of an enterprise ⟨a big ~ from an investment⟩  2 : the climax of an incident or enterprise ⟨the ~ of a story⟩

**pay·roll** \'pā-ˌrōl\ *n* : a list of persons entitled to receive pay; *also* : the money to pay those on such a list

**payt** *abbr* payment

**pay up** *vb* : to pay in full; *also* : to pay what is due

**Pb** *symbol* [L *plumbum*] lead

**PBX** *abbr* private branch exchange

**PC** *abbr* 1 Peace Corps  2 percent; percentage  3 postcard  4 [L *post cibum*] after meals

**pct** *abbr* percent

**pd** *abbr* paid

**Pd** *symbol* palladium

**PD** *abbr* 1 per diem  2 police department  3 potential difference

**PDQ** \ˌpē-ˌdē-'kyü\ *adv, often not cap* [abbr. of *pretty damned quick*] : IMMEDIATELY

**PDT** *abbr* Pacific daylight time

**PE** *abbr* 1 physical education  2 printer's error  3 professional engineer  4 Protestant Episcopal

**pea** \'pē\ *n*, *pl* **peas** *also* **pease** \'pēz\ **1** : the round edible protein-rich seed borne in the pod of a widely grown leguminous vine; *also* : this vine **2** : any of various plants resembling or related to the pea

**peace** \'pēs\ *n* **1** : a state of calm and quiet; *esp* : public security under law **2** : freedom from disturbing thoughts or emotions **3** : a state of concord (as between persons or governments); *also* : an agreement to end hostilities — **peace·able** \-ə-bəl\ *adj* — **peace·ably** \-blē\ *adv* — **peace·ful** \-fəl\ *adj* — **peace·ful·ly** \-ē\ *adv*

**peace corps** *n* : a body of trained personnel sent out as volunteers to assist underdeveloped nations

**peace·keeping** \'pēs-,kē-piŋ\ *n* : the preserving of peace; *esp* : international enforcement and supervision of a truce — **peace·keep·er** \-pər\ *n*

**peace·mak·er** \'pēs-,mā-kər\ *n* : one who settles an argument or stops a fight

**peace·time** \-,tīm\ *n* : a time when a nation is not at war

**peach** \'pēch\ *n* [ME *peche*, fr. MF (the fruit), fr. LL *persica*, fr. L *persicum*, fr. neut. of *persicus* Persian, fr. *Persia*] : a sweet juicy fruit borne by a low tree with pink blossoms; *also* : this tree

**pea·cock** \'pē-,käk\ *n* : the male peafowl having long tail coverts which can be spread at will displaying brilliant colors

**pea·fowl** \'pē-,faůl\ *n* : a very large domesticated Asiatic pheasant

**pea·hen** \'pē-,hen\ *n* : the female peafowl

**¹peak** \'pēk\ *n* **1** : a pointed or projecting part **2** : the top of a hill or mountain; *also* : MOUNTAIN **3** : the front projecting part of a cap **4** : the narrow part of a ship's bow or stern **5** : the highest level or greatest degree — **peak** *adj*

**²peak** *vb* : to bring to or reach a maximum

**peak·ed** \'pē-kəd\ *adj* : THIN, SICKLY

**¹peal** \'pēl\ *n* **1** : the loud ringing of bells **2** : a set of tuned bells **3** : a loud sound or succession of sounds

**²peal** *vb* : to give out peals : RESOUND

**pea·nut** \'pē-(,)nət\ *n* : an annual herb related to the pea but having pods that ripen underground; *also* : this pod or one of the edible seeds it bears

**pear** \'paər\ *n* : the fleshy fruit of a tree related to the apple; *also* : this tree

**pearl** \'pərl\ *n* **1** : a small hard often lustrous body formed within the shell of some mollusks and used as a gem **2** : one that is choice or precious ⟨~s of wisdom⟩ **3** : a slightly bluish medium gray — **pearly** \'pər-lē\ *adj*

**peas·ant** \'pez-ᵊnt\ *n* **1** : one of a chiefly European class of tillers of the soil **2** : a person of low social or cultural status — **peas·ant·ry** \-ᵊn-trē\ *n*

**pea·shoot·er** \'pē-,shüt-ər, -,shüt-\ *n* : a toy blowgun for shooting peas

**peat** \'pēt\ *n* : a dark substance formed by partial decay of plants (as mosses) in wet ground; *also* : a piece of this cut and dried for fuel — **peaty** *adj*

**peat moss** *n* : SPHAGNUM

**¹peb·ble** \'peb-əl\ *n* : a small usu. round stone — **peb·bly** \-(ə-)lē\ *adj*

**²pebble** *vb* **peb·bled**; **peb·bling** \-(ə-)liŋ\ : to produce a rough surface texture in ⟨~ leather⟩

**pe·can** \pi-'kän, -'kan\ *n* : a large American hickory tree bearing a smooth-shelled edible nut; *also* : this nut

**pec·ca·dil·lo** \,pek-ə-'dil-ō\ *n*, *pl* **-loes** *or* **-los** : a slight offense

**pec·ca·ry** \'pek-ə-rē\ *n*, *pl* **-ries** : an American chiefly tropical mammal resembling but smaller than the related pigs

**pec·ca·vi** \pe-'kä-,wē\ *n* [L, I have sinned, fr. *peccare*] : an acknowledgment of sin

**¹peck** \'pek\ *n* — see WEIGHT table

**²peck** *vb* **1** : to strike or pierce with or as if with the bill **2** : to pick up with or as if with the bill

**³peck** *n* **1** : an impression made by pecking **2** : a quick sharp stroke; *also* : KISS

**pecking order** *or* **peck order** *n* : a basic pattern of social organization within a flock of poultry in which each bird pecks another lower in the scale without fear of retaliation and submits to pecking by one of higher rank; *also* : a hierarchy of social dominance, prestige, or authority

**pec·tin** \'pek-tən\ *n* : any of various water-soluble substances found in plant tissues that cause fruit jellies to set — **pec·tic** \-tik\ *adj*

**pec·to·ral** \'pek-t(ə-)rəl\ *adj* : of or relating to the breast or chest

**pec·u·late** \'pek-yə-,lāt\ *vb* **-lat·ed**; **-lat·ing** : EMBEZZLE — **pec·u·la·tion** \,pek-yə-'lā-shən\ *n*

**pe·cu·liar** \pi-'kyül-yər\ *adj* [ME *peculier*, fr. L *peculiaris* of private property, special, fr. *peculium* private property, fr. *pecu* cattle] **1** : belonging exclusively to one person or group **2** : CHARACTERISTIC, DISTINCTIVE **3** : QUEER, ODD **syn** individual, eccentric, singular, strange, unique — **pe·cu·liar·i·ty** \-,kyül-'yar-ət-ē, -ē-'ar-\ *n* — **pe·cu·liar·ly** \-'kyül-yər-lē\ *adv*

**pe·cu·ni·ary** \pi-'kyü-nē-,er-ē\ *adj* : of or relating to money : MONETARY

**ped·a·gogue** *also* **ped·a·gog** \'ped-ə-,gäg\ *n* : TEACHER, SCHOOLMASTER

**ped·a·go·gy** \'ped-ə-,gōj-ē, -,gäj-\ *n* : the art or profession of teaching; *esp* : EDUCATION **2** — **ped·a·gog·ic** \,ped-ə-'gäj-ik, -'gōj-\ *or* **ped·a·gog·i·cal** \-i-kəl\ *adj*

**¹ped·al** \'ped-ᵊl\ *n* : a lever worked by the foot

**²ped·al** *adj* : of or relating to the foot

**³ped·al** \'ped-ᵊl\ *vb* **ped·aled** *also* **ped·alled**; **ped·al·ing** *also* **ped·al·ling** \'ped-(ᵊ-)liŋ\ **1** : to use or work a pedal (as of a piano or bicycle) **2** : to ride a bicycle

**ped·ant** \'ped-ʰnt\ *n* **1** : a person who makes a display of his learning **2** : a formal uninspired teacher — **pe·dan·tic** \pi-'dant-ik\ *adj* — **ped·ant·ry** \'ped-ʰn-trē\ *n*

**ped·dle** \'ped-ᵊl\ *vb* **ped·dled; ped·dling** \'ped-(ᵊ-)liŋ\ : to sell or offer for sale from place to place — **ped·dler** *or* **ped·lar** \'ped-lər\ *n*

**ped·er·ast** \'ped-ə-,rast\ *n* : one that practices anal intercourse esp. with a boy — **ped·er·as·ty** \'ped-ə-,ras-tē\ *n*

**ped·es·tal** \'ped-əs-tᵊl\ *n* **1** : the support or foot of something (as a column, statue, or vase) that is upright **2** : a raised platform or dais

**¹pe·des·tri·an** \pə-'des-trē-ən\ *adj* **1** : COMMONPLACE **2** : going on foot

**²pedestrian** *n* : WALKER

**pe·di·at·rics** \,pēd-ē-'a-triks\ *n* : a branch of medicine dealing with the care and diseases of children — **pe·di·at·ric** \-trik\ *adj* — **pe·di·a·tri·cian** \,pēd-ē-ə-'trish-ən\ *n*

**pedi·cab** \'ped-i-,kab\ *n* : a small 3-wheeled hooded passenger vehicle that is pedaled

**ped·i·cure** \'ped-i-,kyür\ *n* : care of the feet, toes, and nails; *also* : a single treatment of these parts — **ped·i·cur·ist** \-,kyür-əst\ *n*

**ped·i·gree** \'ped-ə-,grē\ *n* [ME pedegru, fr. MF pie de grue crane's foot; fr. the shape made by the lines of genealogical chart] **1** : a record of a line of ancestors **2** : an ancestral line

**ped·i·ment** \'ped-ə-mənt\ *n* : a low triangular gablelike decoration (as over a door or window) on a building

**pe·dom·e·ter** \pi-'däm-ət-ər\ *n* : an instrument that measures the distance one walks

**pe·dun·cle** \'pē-,dəŋ-kəl\ *n* : a narrow supporting stalk

**peek** \'pēk\ *vb* **1** : to peek furtively **2** : to peer from a place of concealment **3** : GLANCE — **peek** *n*

**¹peel** \'pēl\ *vb* [ME pelen, fr. MF peler, fr. L pilare to remove the hair from, fr. pilus hair] **1** : to strip the skin, bark, or rind from **2** : to strip off (as a coat); *also* : to come off **3** : to lose the skin, bark, or rind

**²peel** *n* : a skin or rind esp. of a fruit

**peel·ing** \'pē-liŋ\ *n* : a peeled-off piece or strip (as of skin or rind)

**peen** *or* **pein** \'pēn\ *n* : the usu. hemispherical or wedge-shaped end of the head of a hammer opposite the face

**¹peep** \'pēp\ *vb* : to utter a feeble shrill sound

**²peep** *n* : a feeble shrill sound

**³peep** *vb* **1** : to look slyly esp. through an aperture : PEEK **2** : to begin to emerge — **peep·er** *n*

**⁴peep** *n* **1** : the first faint appearance **2** : a brief or furtive look

**peep·hole** \'pēp-,hōl\ *n* : a hole to peep through

**¹peer** \'piər\ *n* **1** : one of equal standing with another : EQUAL **2** : NOBLE — **peer·age** \-ij\ *n* — **peer·ess** \-əs\ *n*

**²peer** *vb* **1** : to look intently or curiously

**2** : to come slightly into view

**peer·less** \'piər-ləs\ *adj* : having no equal : MATCHLESS **syn** supreme, superlative, incomparable

**¹peeve** \'pēv\ *vb* **peeved; peev·ing** : to make resentful : AGGRIEVE

**²peeve** *n* **1** : a feeling or mood of resentment **2** : a particular grievance

**pee·vish** \'pē-vish\ *adj* : querulous in temperament : FRETFUL **syn** irritable, petulant, complaining — **pee·vish·ly** *adv* — **pee·vish·ness** *n*

**pee·wee** \'pē-(,)wē\ *n* : one that is diminutive or tiny

**¹peg** \'peg\ *n* **1** : a small pointed piece (as of wood) used to pin down or fasten things or to fit into holes **2** : a projecting piece used as a support or boundary marker **3** : SUPPORT, PRETEXT **4** : STEP, DEGREE **5** : THROW

**²peg** *vb* **pegged; peg·ging 1** : to put a peg into : fasten, pin down, or attach with or as if with pegs **2** : to work hard and steadily : PLUG **3** : HUSTLE **4** : to mark by pegs **5** : to hold (as prices) at a set level **6** : THROW

**peg·board** \'peg-,bōrd\ *n* : material (as fiberboard) with evenly spaced holes into which hooks or pegs are inserted

**peg·ma·tite** \'peg-mə-,tīt\ *n* : a coarse variety of granite occurring in veins — **peg·ma·tit·ic** \,peg-mə-'tit-ik\ *adj*

**PEI** *abbr* Prince Edward Island

**pei·gnoir** \pān-'wär, pen-\ *n* [F, lit., garment worn while combing the hair, fr. MF, fr. peigner to comb the hair, fr. L pectinare, fr. pectin-, pecten comb] : NEGLIGEE

**pe·jo·ra·tive** \pi-'jòr-ət-iv, 'pej-(ə-)rət-\ *adj* : having a tendency to make or become worse : DISPARAGING

**Pe·king·ese** *or* **Pe·kin·ese** \,pē-kə-'ēz, -kiŋ-, -'ēs\ *n*, *pl* **Pekingese** *or* **Pekinese** : a small short-legged long-haired Chinese dog

**pel·age** \'pel-ij\ *n* : the hairy covering of a mammal

**pe·lag·ic** \pə-'laj-ik\ *adj* : OCEANIC

**pelf** \'pelf\ *n* : MONEY, RICHES

**pel·i·can** \'pel-i-kən\ *n* : a large web-footed bird having a pouched lower bill used to scoop in fish

**pel·la·gra** \pə-'lag-rə, -'läg-\ *n* : a chronic disease marked by skin and digestive disorders and nervous symptoms and caused by a faulty diet

**pel·let** \'pel-ət\ *n* **1** : a little ball (as of medicine) **2** : BULLET — **pel·let·al** \-ᵊl\ *adj* — **pel·let·ize** \-,īz\ *vb*

**pell-mell** \'pel-'mel\ *adv* **1** : in mingled confusion **2** : HEADLONG

**pel·lu·cid** \pə-'lü-səd\ *adj* : extremely clear : LIMPID, TRANSPARENT **syn** translucent, lucid

**¹pelt** \'pelt\ *n* : a skin esp. of a fur-bearing animal

**²pelt** *vb* : to strike with a succession of blows or missiles

**pel·vis** \'pel-vəs\ *n*, *pl* **pel·vis·es** \-və-səz\ *or* **pel·ves** \-,vēz\ : a basin-shaped part of the vertebrate skeleton consisting chiefly of the two large bones of the hip — **pel·vic** \-vik\ *adj*

**pem·mi·can** also **pem·i·can** \'pem-i-kən\ n : dried meat pounded fine and mixed with melted fat

¹**pen** \'pen\ n 1 : a small enclosure for animals 2 : a small place of confinement or storage

²**pen** vb **penned; pen·ning** : to shut in a pen : ENCLOSE

³**pen** n : an instrument with a split point to hold ink used for writing; also : a fluid-using writing instrument

⁴**pen** vb **penned; pen·ning** : WRITE

⁵**pen** n : PENITENTIARY

⁶**pen** abbr peninsula

**pe·nal** \'pēn-ᵊl\ adj : of or relating to punishment

**pe·nal·ize** \'pēn-ᵊl-,īz, 'pen-\ vb **-ized; -iz·ing** : to put a penalty on

**pen·al·ty** \'pen-ᵊl-tē\ n, pl **-ties** 1 : punishment for crime or offense 2 : something forfeited when a person fails to do what he agreed to do 3 : disadvantage, loss, or hardship due to some action

**pen·ance** \'pen-əns\ n 1 : an act performed to show sorrow or repentance for sin 2 : a sacrament (as in the Roman Catholic Church) consisting of repentance, confession, satisfaction as imposed by the confessor, and absolution

**Pe·na·tes** \pə-'nāt-ēz\ n pl : the Roman gods of the household

**pence** \'pens\ pl of PENNY

**pen·chant** \'pen-chənt\ n [F, fr. prp. of pencher to incline, fr. (assumed) VL pendicare, fr. L pendere to weigh] : a strong inclination : LIKING **syn** leaning, propensity, flair

¹**pen·cil** \'pen-səl\ n : an implement for writing or drawing consisting of or containing a slender cylinder of a solid marking substance

²**pencil** vb **-ciled** or **-cilled; -cil·ing** or **-cil·ling** \-s(ə-)liŋ\ : to paint, draw, or write with a pencil

**pen·dant** also **pen·dent** \'pen-dənt\ n : a hanging ornament (as an earring)

**pen·dent** or **pen·dant** \'pen-dənt\ adj : SUSPENDED, OVERHANGING

¹**pend·ing** \'pen-diŋ\ prep 1 : DURING 2 : while awaiting

²**pending** adj 1 : not yet decided 2 : IMMINENT

**pen·du·lous** \'pen-jə-ləs, -də-\ adj : hanging loosely : DROOPING

**pen·du·lum** \-ləm\ n : a body suspended from a fixed point so that it may swing freely

**pe·ne·plain** also **pe·ne·plane** \'pēn-i-,plān\ n : an erosional land surface of large area and slight relief

**pen·e·trate** \'pen-ə-,trāt\ vb **-trat·ed; -trat·ing** 1 : to enter into : PIERCE 2 : PERMEATE 3 : to see into : UNDERSTAND 4 : to affect deeply — **pen·e·tra·ble** \-trə-bəl\ adj — **pen·e·tra·tion** \,pen-ə-'trā-shən\ n — **pen·e·tra·tive** \'pen-ə-,trāt-iv\ adj

**pen·e·trat·ing** \-,trāt-iŋ\ adj 1 : having the power of entering, piercing, or pervading ⟨a ~ shriek⟩ ⟨a ~ odor⟩ 2 : ACUTE, DISCERNING ⟨a ~ look⟩

**pen·guin** \'pen-gwən, 'peŋ-\ n : any of several erect short-legged flightless seabirds of the southern hemisphere

**pen·hold·er** \'pen-,hōl-dər\ n : a holder or handle for a pen

**pen·i·cil·lin** \,pen-ə-'sil-ən\ n : an antibiotic produced by a green mold and used against various bacteria

**pen·in·su·la** \pə-'nin-sə-lə, -'nin-chə-\ n [L paeninsula, fr. paene almost + insula island] : a long narrow portion of land extending out into the water from the main land body — **pen·in·su·lar** \-lər\ adj

**pe·nis** \'pē-nəs\ n, pl **pe·nes** \-,nēz\ or **pe·nis·es** : a male organ of copulation

¹**pen·i·tent** \'pen-ə-tənt\ adj : feeling sorrow for sins or offenses : REPENTANT — **pen·i·tence** \-təns\ n — **pen·i·ten·tial** \,pen-ə-'ten-chəl\ adj

²**penitent** n : a penitent person

¹**pen·i·ten·tia·ry** \,pen-ə-'tench-(ə-)rē\ n, pl **-ries** : a state or federal prison

²**pen·i·ten·tia·ry** adj : of, relating to, or incurring confinement in a penitentiary

**pen·knife** \'pen-,nīf\ n : a small pocketknife

**pen·light** or **pen·lite** \'pen-,līt\ n : a small flashlight resembling a fountain pen in size or shape

**pen·man** \'pen-mən\ n 1 : COPYIST 2 : one skilled in penmanship 3 : AUTHOR

**pen·man·ship** \-,ship\ n : the art or practice of writing with the pen

**Penn** or **Penna** abbr Pennsylvania

**pen name** n : an author's pseudonym

**pen·nant** \'pen-ənt\ n 1 : a small tapering nautical flag used for identification or signaling 2 : a long narrow flag 3 : a flag emblematic of championship

**pen·ni** \'pen-ē\ n, pl **pen·nia** \-ē-ə\ or **pen·nis** \-ēz\ — see markka at MONEY table

**pen·non** \'pen-ən\ n 1 : BANNER; esp : a long narrow ribbonlike flag borne on a lance 2 : WING

**pen·ny** \'pen-ē\ n, pl **pennies** \-ēz\ or **pence** \'pens\ 1 : a British monetary unit formerly equal to ¹/₁₂ shilling but now equal to ¹/₁₀₀ pound; also : a coin of this value — see pound at MONEY table 2 pl **pennies** : a cent of the U.S. or Canada — **pen·ni·less** \'pen-i-ləs\

**pen·ny-pinch** \'pen-ē-,pinch\ vb : to give money to in a niggardly manner — **penny pincher** n

**pen·ny·roy·al** \,pen-ē-'rói-əl, 'pen-i-,rīl\ n : a hairy perennial mint with small pungently aromatic leaves

**pen·ny·weight** \'pen-ē-,wāt\ n : a unit of troy weight equal to ¹/₂₀ troy ounce

**pen·ny-wise** \'pen-ē-,wīz\ adj : wise or prudent only in small matters

**pe·nol·o·gy** \pi-'näl-ə-jē\ n : a branch of criminology dealing with prison management and the treatment of offenders

¹pen·sion \'pen-chən\ n : a fixed sum paid regularly esp. to a person retired from service

²pen·sion \'pen-chən\ vb pen·sioned; pen·sion·ing \'pench-(ə-)niŋ\ : to pay a pension to — pen·sion·er n

pen·sive \'pen-siv\ adj : musingly, dreamily, or sadly thoughtful syn reflective, speculative, contemplative, meditative — pen·sive·ly adv

pen·stock \'pen-,stäk\ n 1 : a sluice or gate for regulating a flow 2 : a conduit for conducting water

pent \'pent\ adj : shut up : CONFINED

pent·a·gon \'pent-ə-,gän\ n : a polygon of 5 angles and 5 sides — pen·tag·o·nal \pen-'tag-ən-ˀl\ adj

pen·tam·e·ter \pen-'tam-ət-ər\ n : a line consisting of five metrical feet

Pen·te·cost \'pent-i-,kȯst\ n : the 7th Sunday after Easter observed as a church festival commemorating the descent of the Holy Spirit on the apostles — Pen·te·cos·tal \,pent-i-'käst-ˀl\ adj

Pentecostal n : a member of a Christian religious body that is ardently evangelistic — Pen·te·cos·tal·ism \,pent-i-'käst-ˀl-,iz-əm\ n

pent·house \'pent-,haůs\ n [ME pentis, pentice, fr. MF appentis, prob. fr. ML appenticium appendage, fr. L appendic-, appendix] 1 : a shed or roof attached to and sloping from a wall or building 2 : an apartment built on the roof of a building

pen·ul·ti·mate \pi-'nəl-tə-mət\ adj : next to the last (~ syllable)

pen·um·bra \pə-'nəm-brə\ n, pl -brae \-(,)brē\ or -bras : the partial shadow surrounding a complete shadow (as in an eclipse)

pe·nu·ri·ous \pə-'n(y)ůr-ē-əs\ adj 1 : marked by penury 2 : MISERLY syn stingy, close

pen·u·ry \'pen-yə-rē\ n : extreme poverty

pe·on \'pē-,än, -ən\ n, pl peons or pe·o·nes \pā-'ō-nēz\ 1 : a member of the landless laboring class in Spanish America 2 : one bound to service for payment of a debt — pe·on·age \-ə-nij\ n

pe·o·ny \'pē-ə-nē\ n, pl -nies : a garden plant with large usu. double red, pink, or white flowers; also : its flower

¹peo·ple \'pē-pəl\ n, pl people 1 pl : human beings not individually known (~ are funny) 2 pl : human beings making up a group or linked by a common characteristic or interest 3 pl : the mass of persons in a community : POPULACE; also : ELECTORATE (the ~'s choice) 4 pl peoples : a body of persons (as a tribe, nation, or race) united by a common culture, sense of kinship, or political organization

²people vb peo·pled; peo·pling \-p(ə-)liŋ\ : to supply or fill with or as if with people

¹pep \'pep\ n : brisk energy or initiative — pep·py adj

²pep vb pepped; pep·ping : to put pep into : STIMULATE

¹pep·per \'pep-ər\ n 1 : a pungent condiment from the berry of an East Indian climbing plant; also : this plant 2 : a plant related to the tomato and widely grown for its hot or mild sweet fruit used as a vegetable or in salads and pickles; also : this fruit

²pepper vb pep·pered; pep·per·ing \'pep-(ə-)riŋ\ 1 : to sprinkle or season with or as if with pepper 2 : to shower with missiles or rapid blows

pep·per·corn \-,kȯrn\ n : a dried berry of the East Indian pepper

pep·per·mint \-,mint, -mənt\ n : a pungent aromatic mint; also : candy flavored with its oil

pep·pery \'pep-(ə-)rē\ adj 1 : having the qualities of pepper : PUNGENT, HOT 2 : having a hot temper 3 : FIERY

pep·sin \'pep-sən\ n : an enzyme of the stomach that begins the digestion of proteins; also : a preparation of this used medicinally

pep·tic \'pep-tik\ adj 1 : relating to or promoting digestion 2 : resulting from the action of digestive juices (a ~ ulcer)

Pe·quot \'pē-,kwät\ n : a member of an Indian people of eastern Connecticut

¹per \(')pər\ prep 1 : by means of 2 : to or for each 3 : according to

²per abbr period

Per abbr Persian

¹per·ad·ven·ture \'pər-əd-,ven-chər\ adv, archaic : PERHAPS

²peradventure n : DOUBT, CHANCE

per·am·bu·late \pə-'ram-byə-,lāt\ vb -lat·ed; -lat·ing : to travel over esp. on foot — per·am·bu·la·tion \-,ram-byə-'lā-shən\ n

per·am·bu·la·tor \pə-'ram-byə-,lāt-ər\ n, chiefly Brit : a baby carriage

per an·num \(,)pər-'an-əm\ adv : in or for each year : ANNUALLY

per·cale \(,)pər-'kāl, 'pər-,; (,)pər-'kal\ n : a fine closely woven cotton cloth

per cap·i·ta \(,)pər-'kap-ət-ə\ adv or adj [ML, by heads] : by or for each person

per·ceive \pər-'sēv\ vb per·ceived; per·ceiv·ing 1 : to attain awareness : REALIZE 2 : to become aware of through the senses — per·ceiv·able adj

¹per·cent \pər-'sent\ adv : in each hundred

²percent n, pl percent or percents 1 : one part in a hundred : HUNDREDTH 2 : PERCENTAGE

per·cent·age \pər-'sent-ij\ n 1 : a part of a whole expressed in hundredths 2 : ADVANTAGE, PROFIT 3 : PROBABILITY; also : favorable odds

per·cen·tile \pər-'sen-,tīl\ n : a statistical measure expressing an individual's standing (as in a test) in terms of the percentage of individuals falling below him

per·cept \'pər-,sept\ n : a sense impression of an object accompanied by an understanding of what it is

per·cep·ti·ble \pər-'sep-tə-bəl\ adj : capable of being perceived — per·cep·ti·bly \-blē\ adv

per·cep·tion \pər-'sep-shən\ n 1 : an

act or result of perceiving **2** : awareness of environment through physical sensation **3** : ability to perceive : INSIGHT, COMPREHENSION **syn** penetration, discernment, discrimination

**per·cep·tive** \per-'sep-tiv\ *adj* : of or relating to perception : having perception; *also* : DISCERNING — **per·cep·tive·ly** *adv*

**per·cep·tu·al** \-chə-(-wə)l\ *adj* : of, relating to, or involving sensory stimulus as opposed to abstract concept — **per·cep·tu·al·ly** \-ē\ *adv*

¹**perch** \'pərch\ *n* **1** : a roost for birds **2** : a high station or vantage point

²**perch** *vb* : ROOST

³**perch** *n, pl* **perch** *or* **perch·es** : either of two small freshwater spiny-finned food fishes; *also* : any of various fishes resembling or related to these

**per·chance** \pər-'chans\ *adv* : PERHAPS

**per·cip·i·ent** \pər-'sip-ē-ənt\ *adj* : capable of or characterized by perception — **per·cip·i·ence** \-əns\ *n*

**per·co·late** \'pər-kə-,lāt\ *vb* -**lat·ed**; -**lat·ing** **1** : to trickle or filter through a permeable substance **2** : to filter hot water through to extract the essence ⟨~ coffee⟩ — **per·co·la·tor** \-,lāt-ər\ *n*

**per con·tra** \(,)pər-'kän-trä\ *adv* [It, by the opposite side (of the ledger)] **1** : on the contrary **2** : by way of contrast

**per·cus·sion** \pər-'kəsh-ən\ *n* **1** : a sharp blow : IMPACT; *esp* : a blow upon a cap (**percussion cap**) filled with powder and designed to explode the charge in a firearm **2** : the beating or striking of a musical instrument; *also* : instruments sounded by striking, shaking, or scraping

**per di·em** \-'dē-əm, -'dī-\ *adv* : by the day — **per diem** *adj or n*

**per·di·tion** \pər-'dish-ən\ *n* [ME *perdicion*, fr. LL *perdition-, perditio*, fr. L *perdere* to destroy, fr. *per-* to destruction + *dare* to give] **1** : eternal damnation **2** : HELL

**per·du·ra·ble** \(,)pər-'d(y)ùr-ə-bəl\ *adj* : very durable — **per·du·ra·bil·i·ty** \-,d(y)ùr-ə-'bil-ət-ē\ *n*

**per·e·gri·na·tion** \,per-ə-grə-'nā-shən\ *n* : a journeying about from place to place

**pe·remp·to·ry** \pə-'remp-t(ə-)rē\ *adj* **1** : barring a right of action or delay : FINAL **2** : expressive of urgency or command : IMPERATIVE **3** : marked by self-assurance : DECISIVE **syn** imperious, masterful, domineering — **pe·remp·to·ri·ly** \-t(ə-)rə-lē\ *adv*

¹**pe·ren·ni·al** \pə-'ren-ē-əl\ *adj* **1** : present at all seasons of the year ⟨~ streams⟩ **2** : continuing to live from year to year ⟨~ plants⟩ **3** : recurring regularly : PERMANENT ⟨~ problems⟩ **syn** lasting, perpetual, stable, everlasting — **pe·ren·ni·al·ly** \-ē\ *adv*

²**perennial** *n* : a plant that lives for an indefinite number of years

**perf** *abbr* **1** perfect **2** perforated

¹**per·fect** \'pər-fikt\ *adj* **1** : being without fault or defect **2** : EXACT, PRECISE

**3** : COMPLETE **4** : of, relating to, or constituting a verb tense that expresses an action or state completed at the time of speaking or at a time spoken of **syn** whole, entire, intact — **per·fect·ly** \-fik-(t)lē\ *adv* — **per·fect·ness** \-fik(t)-nəs\ *n*

²**per·fect** \pər-'fekt, 'pər-fikt\ *vb* : to make perfect

³**per·fect** \'pər-fikt\ *n* : the perfect tense; *also* : a verb form in it

**per·fect·ible** \pər-'fek-tə-bəl, 'pər-fik-\ *adj* : capable of improvement or perfection — **per·fect·ibil·i·ty** \pər-,fek-tə-'bil-ət-ē, ,pər-fik-\ *n*

**per·fec·tion** \pər-'fek-shən\ *n* **1** : the quality or state of being perfect **2** : the highest degree of excellence **3** : the act or process of perfecting **syn** virtue, merit

**per·fec·tion·ist** \-sh(ə-)nəst\ *n* : a person who will not accept or be content with anything less than perfection

**per·fec·to** \pər-'fek-tō\ *n, pl* -**tos** : a cigar that is thick in the middle and tapers almost to a point at each end

**per·fi·dy** \'pər-fəd-ē\ *n* [L *perfidia*, fr. *perfidus* faithless, fr. *per fidem decipere* to betray, lit., to deceive by trust] : violation of faith or loyalty : TREACHERY — **per·fid·i·ous** \pər-'fid-ē-əs\ *adj* — **per·fid·i·ous·ly** *adv*

**per·fo·rate** \'pər-fə-,rāt\ *vb* -**rat·ed**; -**rat·ing** : to bore through : PIERCE; *esp* : to make a line of holes in to facilitate separation **syn** puncture, punch, prick — **per·fo·ra·tion** \,pər-fə-'rā-shən\ *n*

**per·force** \pər-'fōrs\ *adv* : of necessity

**per·form** \pə(r)-'form\ *vb* **1** : FULFILL **2** : to carry out : ACCOMPLISH **3** : to do in a set manner **4** : FUNCTION **5** : to give a performance : PLAY **syn** execute, discharge, achieve, effect — **per·form·er** *n*

**per·for·mance** \pər-'fòr-məns\ *n* **1** : the act or process of performing **2** : DEED, FEAT **3** : a public presentation or exhibition

¹**per·fume** \'pər-,fyüm, pər-'fyüm\ *n* **1** : a usu. pleasant odor : FRAGRANCE **2** : a preparation used for scenting

²**per·fume** \pər-'fyüm, 'pər-,fyüm\ *vb* **per·fumed**; **per·fum·ing** : to treat with a perfume; *also* : SCENT

**per·fum·ery** \pər-'fyüm-(ə-)rē\ *n, pl* -**er·ies** : PERFUMES

**per·func·to·ry** \pər-'fəŋk-t(ə-)rē\ *adj* : done merely as a duty — **per·func·to·ri·ly** \-t(ə-)rə-lē\ *adv*

**per·go·la** \'pər-gə-lə\ *n* : a structure consisting of posts supporting an open roof in the form of a trellis

**perh** *abbr* perhaps

**per·haps** \pər-'(h)aps, 'praps\ *adv* : possibly but not certainly

**peri·cyn·thi·on** \,per-ə-'sin-thē-ən\ *n* : the point in the path of a body orbiting the moon that is nearest to the center of the moon

**per·i·gee** \'per-ə-,jē\ *n* [fr. *perigee* point in the orbit of a satellite of the earth when it is nearest the earth, fr. NL *perigeum*, fr. Gk *perigeion*, fr. *peri* around, near + *gē* earth] **:** the point at which an orbiting object is nearest the body (as the earth) being orbited

**peri·he·lion** \,per-ə-'hēl-yən\ *n, pl* **-he·lia** \-'hēl-yə\ **:** the point in the path of a celestial body (as a planet) that is nearest to the sun

**per·il** \'per-əl\ *n* **:** DANGER; *also* **:** a source of danger **:** RISK **syn** jeopardy, hazard — **per·il·ous** *adj* — **per·il·ous·ly** *adv*

**peri·lune** \'per-ə-,lün\ *n* **:** PERICYN-THION

**pe·rim·e·ter** \pə-'rim-ət-ər\ *n* **:** the outer boundary of a body or figure

**¹pe·ri·od** \'pir-ē-əd\ *n* **1 :** a well-rounded sentence; *also* **:** the full pause closing the utterance of a sentence **2 :** END, STOP **3 :** a punctuation mark **.** used esp. to mark the end of a declarative sentence or an abbreviation **4 :** a portion or division of time in which something comes to an end and is ready to begin again **5 :** MENSES **6 :** an extent of time; *esp* **:** one regarded as a stage or division in a process or development **syn** epoch, era, age, aeon

**²period** *adj* **:** of or relating to a particular historical period ⟨~ furniture⟩

**pe·ri·od·ic** \,pir-ē-'äd-ik\ *adj* **1 :** occurring at regular intervals of time **2 :** happening repeatedly **3 :** of or relating to a sentence that has no trailing elements following full grammatical statement of the essential idea

**¹pe·ri·od·i·cal** \,pir-ē-'äd-i-kəl\ *adj* **1 :** PERIODIC **2 :** published at regular intervals **3 :** of or relating to a periodical — **pe·ri·od·i·cal·ly** \-k(ə-)lē\ *adv*

**²periodical** *n* **:** a periodical publication

**peri·odon·tal** \,per-ē-ō-'dänt-ºl\ *adj* **:** surrounding or occurring about the teeth

**per·i·pa·tet·ic** \,per-ə-pə-'tet-ik\ *adj* **:** performed or performing while moving about **:** ITINERANT

**pe·riph·er·al** \pə-'rif-(ə-)rəl\ *n* **:** a device connected to a computer to provide communication or auxiliary functions

**pe·riph·ery** \pə-'rif-(ə-)rē\ *n, pl* **-er·ies 1 :** the boundary of a rounded figure **2 :** outward bounds **:** border area — **pe·riph·er·al** \-(ə-)rəl\ *adj*

**pe·riph·ra·sis** \pə-'rif-rə-səs\ *n, pl* **-ra·ses** \-,sēz\ **:** CIRCUMLOCUTION

**pe·rique** \pə-'rēk\ *n* **:** a strong-flavored Louisiana tobacco used in smoking mixtures

**peri·scope** \'per-ə-,skōp\ *n* **:** a tubular optical instrument enabling an observer to get an otherwise obstructed field of view

**per·ish** \'per-ish\ *vb* **:** to become destroyed or ruined **:** DIE

**per·ish·able** \'per-ish-ə-bəl\ *adj* **:** easily spoiled ⟨~ foods⟩ — **perishable** *n*

**peri·stal·sis** \,per-ə-'stȯl-səs, -'stal-\ *n* **:** waves of contraction passing along the intestine and forcing its contents onward — **per·i·stal·tic** \-'stȯl-tik, -'stal-\ *adj*

**peri·style** \'per-ə-,stīl\ *n* **:** a row of columns surrounding a building or court

**peri·to·ne·um** \,per-ət-ºn-'ē-əm\ *n* **:** the smooth transparent serous membrane that lines the cavity of the abdomen

**peri·to·ni·tis** \,per-ət-ºn-'īt-əs\ *n* **:** inflammation of the membrane lining the cavity of the abdomen

**peri·wig** \'per-i-,wig\ *n* **:** WIG

**¹peri·win·kle** \'per-i-,wiŋ-kəl\ *n* **:** a usu. blue-flowered creeping plant much grown as a ground cover

**²periwinkle** *n* **:** any of various small edible seashore snails

**per·ju·ry** \'pərj-(ə-)rē\ *n* **:** the voluntary violation of an oath to tell the truth **:** false swearing — **per·jure** \'pər-jər\ *vb* — **per·jur·er** *n*

**¹perk** \'pərk\ *vb* **1 :** to thrust (as the head) up impudently or jauntily **2 :** to make trim or brisk **:** FRESHEN **3 :** to regain vigor or spirit — **perky** *adj*

**²perk** *vb* **:** PERCOLATE

**per·lite** \'pər-,līt\ *n* **:** volcanic glass that when expanded by heat forms a lightweight material used esp. in concrete and plaster

**¹perm** \'pərm\ *n* **:** PERMANENT

**²perm** *abbr* permanent

**per·ma·frost** \'pər-mə-,frȯst\ *n* **:** a permanently frozen layer at variable depth below the earth's surface in frigid regions

**¹per·ma·nent** \'pər-mə-nənt\ *adj* **:** LASTING, STABLE — **per·ma·nence** \-nəns\ *n* — **per·ma·nen·cy** \-nən-sē\ *n* — **per·ma·nent·ly** *adv*

**²permanent** *n* **:** a long-lasting hair wave or straightening

**permanent press** *n* **:** DURABLE PRESS

**per·me·able** \'pər-mē-ə-bəl\ *adj* **:** having pores or small openings that permit liquids or gases to seep through — **per·me·a·bil·i·ty** \,pər-mē-ə-'bil-ət-ē\ *n*

**per·me·ate** \'pər-mē-,āt\ *vb* **-at·ed; -at·ing 1 :** to seep through the pores of **:** PENETRATE **2 :** PERVADE — **per·me·ation** \,pər-mē-'ā-shən\ *n*

**per·mis·si·ble** \pər-'mis-ə-bəl\ *adj* **:** that may be permitted **:** ALLOWABLE

**per·mis·sion** \pər-'mish-ən\ *n* **:** formal consent **:** AUTHORIZATION

**per·mis·sive** \pər-'mis-iv\ *adj* **:** granting permission; *esp* **:** INDULGENT ⟨pampered progeny of ~ parents⟩ **per·mis·sive·ness** *n*

**¹per·mit** \pər-'mit\ *vb* **per·mit·ted; per·mit·ting 1 :** to consent to **:** ALLOW **2 :** to make possible

**²per·mit** \'pər-,mit, pər-'mit\ *n* **:** a written permission **:** LICENSE

**per·mu·ta·tion** \,pər-myü-'tā-shən\ *n* **1 :** TRANSFORMATION **2 :** any one of the total number of changes in position or order possible among the units or members of a group ⟨~s of the alphabet⟩ **syn** alteration

**per·ni·cious** \pər-'nish-əs\ *adj* [MF *pernicieus,* fr. L *perniciosus,* fr. *pernicies* destruction, fr. *per-* through + *nec-, nex* violent death] **:** very destructive or injurious — **per·ni·cious·ly** *adv*

**per·o·ra·tion** \'per-ə-,rā-shən, ,pər-\ *n* **:** the concluding part of a speech

¹**per·ox·ide** \pə-'räk-,sīd\ *n* **:** an oxide containing a large proportion of oxygen; *esp* **:** a compound (as hydrogen peroxide) in which oxygen is joined to oxygen

²**peroxide** *vb* **-id·ed; -id·ing :** to bleach with hydrogen peroxide

**perp** *abbr* perpendicular

**per·pen·dic·u·lar** \,pər-pən-'dik-yə-lər\ *adj* **1 :** standing at right angles to the plane of the horizon **2 :** meeting another line at a right angle — **perpendicular** *n* — **per·pen·dic·u·lar·i·ty** \-,dik-yə-'lar-ət-ē\ *n* — **per·pen·dic·u·lar·ly** *adv*

**per·pe·trate** \'pər-pə-,trāt\ *vb* **-trated; -trat·ing :** to be guilty of **:** COMMIT — **per·pe·tra·tion** \,pər-pə-'trā-shən\ *n* — **per·pe·tra·tor** \'pər-pə-,trāt-ər\ *n*

**per·pet·u·al** \pər-'pech-(ə-w)əl\ *adj* **1 :** continuing forever **:** EVERLASTING **2 :** occurring continually **:** CONSTANT ⟨~ annoyance⟩ *syn* lasting, permanent, continual, continuous, incessant, perennial — **per·pet·u·al·ly** \-ē\ *adv*

**per·pet·u·ate** \pər-'pech-ə-,wāt\ *vb* **-at·ed; -at·ing :** to make perpetual **:** cause to last indefinitely — **per·pet·u·a·tion** \-,pech-ə-'wā-shən\ *n*

**per·pe·tu·ity** \,pər-pə-'t(y)ü-ət-ē\ *n, pl* **-ities 1 :** endless time **:** ETERNITY **2 :** the quality or state of being perpetual

**per·plex** \pər-'pleks\ *vb* **:** to disturb mentally; *esp* **:** CONFUSE — **per·plex·i·ty** \-ət-ē\ *n*

**per·plexed** \-'plekst\ *adj* **1 :** filled with uncertainty **:** PUZZLED **2 :** full of difficulty **:** COMPLICATED — **perplexed·ly** \-'plek-səd-lē\ *adv*

**per·qui·site** \'pər-kwə-zət\ *n* **:** a privilege or profit incidental to regular salary or wages

**pers** *abbr* person; personal

**Pers** *abbr* Persia; Persian

**per se** \(,)pər-'sā\ *adv* **:** by, of, or in itself **:** as such

**per·se·cute** \'pər-si-,kyüt\ *vb* **-cuted; -cut·ing :** to pursue in such a way as to injure or afflict **:** HARASS; *esp* **:** to cause to suffer because of belief *syn* oppress, wrong, aggrieve — **per·se·cu·tion** \,pər-si-'kyü-shən\ *n* — **per·se·cu·tor** \'pər-si-,kyüt-ər\ *n*

**per·se·vere** \,pər-sə-'viər\ *vb* **-vered; -ver·ing :** to persist (as in an undertaking) in spite of difficulties — **per·se·ver·ance** \-'vir-əns\ *n*

**Per·sian** \'pər-zhən\ *n* **1 :** a native or inhabitant of ancient Persia or modern Iran **2 :** the language of the Persians

**Persian cat** *n* **:** a stocky round-headed domestic cat that has long and silky fur

**Persian lamb** *n* **:** a pelt that is obtained from lambs of the same variety as but older than those yielding broadtail and that is characterized by very silky tightly curled fur

**per·si·flage** \'pər-si-,fläzh, 'per-\ *n* [F, fr. *persifler* to banter, fr. *per-* thoroughly + *siffler* to whistle, hiss, boo fr. L *sibilare*, of imit. origin] **:** lightly jesting or mocking talk

**per·sim·mon** \pər-'sim-ən\ *n* **:** a tree

related to the ebony; *also* **:** its edible orange-red plumlike fruit

**per·sist** \pər-'sist, -'zist\ *vb* **1 :** to go on resolutely or stubbornly in spite of difficulties **:** PERSEVERE **2 :** to continue to exist · **per·sis·tence** \-'sis-təns, -'zis-\ *n* — **per·sis·ten·cy** \-tən-sē\ *n* — **per·sis·tent** \-tənt\ *adj* — **per·sis·tent·ly** *adv*

**per·snick·e·ty** \pər-'snik-ət-ē\ *adj* **:** fussy about small details

**per·son** \'pərs-²n\ *n* [ME, fr. OF *persone*, fr. L *persona* actor's mask, character in a play, person, prob. fr. Etruscan *phersu* mask] **1 :** a human being **:** INDIVIDUAL **2 :** the body of a human being **3 :** the individual personality of a human being **:** SELF **4 :** reference of a segment of discourse to the speaker, to one spoken to, or to one spoken of esp. as indicated by certain pronouns **5 :** one of the three modes of being in the Godhead as understood by Trinitarians

**per·son·able** \'pərs-(²-)nə-bəl\ *adj* **:** pleasing in person **:** ATTRACTIVE

**per·son·age** \'pərs-(²-)nij\ *n* **:** a person of rank, note, or distinction

¹**per·son·al** \'pərs-(²-)nəl\ *adj* **1 :** of, relating to, or affecting a person **:** PRIVATE ⟨~ correspondence⟩ **2 :** done in person ⟨a ~ inquiry⟩ **3 :** relating to the person or body ⟨~ injuries⟩ **4 :** relating to an individual esp. in an offensive way ⟨resented such ~ remarks⟩ **5 :** of or relating to temporary or movable property as distinguished from real estate **6 :** denoting grammatical person — **person·al·ly** \-ē\ *adv*

²**personal** *n* **:** a short newspaper paragraph relating to a person or group or to personal matters

**per·son·al·i·ty** \,pərs-²n-'al-ət-ē\ *n, pl* **-ties 1 :** an offensively personal remark ⟨indulges in *personalities*⟩ **2 :** distinctive personal character **3 :** distinction of personal and social traits; *also* **:** a person having such quality *syn* individuality, temperament, disposition

**per·son·al·ize** \'pərs-(²-)nə-,līz\ *vb* **-ized; -iz·ing :** to make personal or individual; *esp* **:** to mark as belonging to a particular person

**per·son·al·ty** \'pərs-(²-)nəl-tē\ *n, pl* **-ties :** personal propery

**per·so·na non gra·ta** \pər-,sō-nə-,nän-'grat-ə, -'grät-\ *adj* **:** being personally unacceptable or unwelcome

**per·son·ate** \'pərs-²n-,āt\ *vb* **-at·ed; -at·ing :** IMPERSONATE, REPRESENT

**per·son·i·fy** \pər-'sän-ə-,fī\ *vb* **-fied; -fy·ing 1 :** to think of or represent as a person **2 :** to be the embodiment of **:** INCARNATE ⟨~ the law⟩ — **per·son·i·fi·ca·tion** \-,sän-ə-fə-'kā-shən\ *n*

**per·son·nel** \,pərs-²n-'el\ *n* **:** a body of persons employed in a service or an organization

**per·spec·tive** \pər-'spek-tiv\ *n* **1 :** the science of painting and drawing so that objects represented have apparent depth and distance **2 :** the aspect in which a subject or its parts are mentally viewed; *esp* : a view of things (as objects or events) in their true relationship or relative importance

**per·spi·cac·i·ty** \,pər-spə-'kas-ət-ē\ *n* : acuteness of mental vision or discernment — **per·spi·ca·cious** \-'kā-shəs\ *adj*

**per·spic·u·ous** \pər-'spik-yə-wəs\ *adj* : plain to the understanding — **per·spi·cu·i·ty** \,pər-spə-'kyü-ət-ē\ *n*

**per·spire** \pər-'spīr\ *vb* **per·spired; per·spir·ing** : SWEAT — **per·spi·ra·tion** \,pər-spə-'rā-shən\ *n*

**per·suade** \pər-'swād\ *vb* **per·suaded; per·suad·ing** : to move by argument or entreaty to a belief or course of action — **per·sua·sive** \-'swā-siv, -ziv\ *adj* — **per·sua·sive·ly** *adv* — **per·sua·sive·ness** *n*

**per·sua·sion** \pər-'swā-zhən\ *n* **1** : the act or process of persuading **2** : OPINION, BELIEF

**¹pert** \'pərt\ *adj* [ME, open, bold, pert, modif. of OF *apert*, fr. L *apertus* open, fr. pp. of *aperire* to open] **1** : saucily free and forward : IMPUDENT **2** : stylishly trim : JAUNTY **3** : LIVELY

**²pert** *abbr* pertaining

**per·tain** \pər-'tān\ *vb* **1** : to belong to as a part, quality, or function ⟨duties ~ing to the office⟩ **2** : to have reference : RELATE ⟨facts that ~ to the case⟩ **syn** bear, appertain, apply

**per·ti·na·cious** \,pərt-ᵊn-'ā-shəs\ *adj* **1** : holding resolutely to an opinion or purpose **2** : obstinately persistent : TENACIOUS ⟨a ~ bill collector⟩ **syn** obstinate, dogged mulish — **per·ti·nac·i·ty** \-'as-ət-ē\ *n*

**per·ti·nent** \'pərt-ᵊn-ənt\ *adj* : relating to the matter under consideration ⟨all ~ information⟩ **syn** relevant, germane, applicable, apropos — **per·ti·nence** \-əns\ *n*

**per·turb** \pər-'tərb\ *vb* : to disturb greatly in mind : UPSET — **per·tur·ba·tion** \,pərt-ər-'bā-shən\ *n*

**pe·ruke** \pə-'rük\ *n* : WIG

**pe·ruse** \pə-'rüz\ *vb* **pe·rused; pe·rus·ing** : READ; *esp* : to read attentively — **pe·rus·al** \-'rü-zəl\ *n*

**per·vade** \pər-'vād\ *vb* **per·vad·ed; per·vad·ing** : to spread through every part of : PERMEATE, PENETRATE — **per·va·sive** \-'vā-siv, -ziv\ *adj*

**per·verse** \pər-'vərs\ *adj* **1** : turned away from what is right or good : CORRUPT **2** : obstinate in opposing what is reasonable or accepted — **per·verse·ly** *adv* — **per·verse·ness** *n* — **per·ver·si·ty** \-'vər-sət-ē\ *n*

**per·ver·sion** \pər-'vər-zhən\ *n* **1** : the action of perverting : the condition of being perverted **2** : a perverted form of something; *esp* : aberrant sexual behavior

**¹per·vert** \pər-'vərt\ *vb* **1** : to lead astray : CORRUPT ⟨~ the young⟩ **2** : to divert to a wrong purpose : MISAPPLY ⟨~ evidence⟩ **syn** deprave, debase

**²per·vert** \'pər-,vərt\ *n* : one that is perverted; *esp* : a person given to sexual perversion

**pe·se·ta** \pə-'sāt-ə\ *n* — see MONEY table

**pe·se·wa** \pə-'sā-wə\ *n* — see *cedi* at MONEY table

**pes·ky** \'pes-kē\ *adj* **pes·ki·er; -est** : causing annoyance : TROUBLESOME

**pe·so** \'pā-sō\ *n*, *pl* **pesos** — see MONEY table

**pes·si·mism** \'pes-ə-,miz-əm\ *n* [F *pessimisme*, fr. L *pessimus* worst] : an inclination to take the least favorable view (as of events) or to expect the worst possible outcome — **pes·si·mist** \-məst\ *n* — **pes·si·mis·tic** \,pes-ə-'mis-tik\ *adj*

**pest** \'pest\ *n* **1** : a destructive epidemic disease : PLAGUE **2** : one that pesters : NUISANCE **3** : a plant or animal detrimental to man

**pes·ter** \'pes-tər\ *vb* **pes·tered; pes·ter·ing** \-t(ə-)riŋ\ : to harass with petty irritations : ANNOY

**pest·house** \'pest-,haús\ *n* : a shelter or hospital for those infected with a contagious disease

**pes·ti·cide** \'pes-tə-,sīd\ *n* : an agent used to kill pests

**pes·tif·er·ous** \pes-'tif-(ə-)rəs\ *adj* **1** : PESTILENT **2** : ANNOYING

**pes·ti·lence** \'pes-tə-ləns\ *n* : a destructive infectious swiftly spreading disease; *esp* : PLAGUE

**pes·ti·lent** \-lənt\ *adj* **1** : dangerous to life : DEADLY; *also* : spreading or causing pestilence **2** : PERNICIOUS, HARMFUL **3** : TROUBLESOME

**pes·ti·len·tial** \,pes-tə-'len-chəl\ *adj* **1** : causing or tending to cause pestilence : DEADLY **2** : morally harmful — **pes·ti·len·tial·ly** \-ē\ *adv*

**pes·tle** \'pes-əl, 'pes-tᵊl\ *n* : an implement for grinding substances in a mortar

**¹pet** \'pet\ *n* **1** : a domesticated animal kept for pleasure rather than utility **2** : FAVORITE, DARLING

**²pet** *adj* **1** : kept or treated as a pet ⟨~ dog⟩ **2** : expressing fondness ⟨~ name⟩ **3** : particularly liked or favored

**³pet** *vb* **pet·ted; pet·ting 1** : to stroke gently or lovingly **2** : to make a pet of : PAMPER **3** : to engage in amorous kissing and caressing

**⁴pet** *n* : a fit of peevishness, sulkiness, or anger

**⁵pet** *abbr* petroleum

**Pet** *abbr* Peter

**pet·al** \'pet-ᵊl\ *n* : one of the modified leaves of a flower's corolla

**pe·tard** \pə-'tär(d)\ *n* : a case containing an explosive to break down a door or gate or breach a wall

**pe·ter** \'pēt-ər\ *vb* : to diminish gradually and come to an end ⟨his energy ~ed out⟩

**pet·i·ole** \'pet-ē-,ōl\ *n* : a stalk that supports a leaf

**pe·tite** \pə-'tēt\ *adj* : small and trim of figure ⟨a ~ woman⟩

**pe·tit four** \,pet-ē-'fór\ *n*, *pl* **petits fours** *or* **petit fours** \-'fórz\ [F, lit., small oven] : a small cake cut from pound or sponge cake and frosted

**¹pe·ti·tion** \pə-'tish-ən\ *n* : an earnest

request : ENTREATY; *esp* : a formal written request made to a superior

²**petition** *vb* **pe·ti·tioned; pe·ti·tion·ing** \-'tish-(ə-)niŋ\ : to make a petition — **pe·ti·tion·er** \-'(ə)nər-\ *n*

**pet·nap·ping** \'pet-,nap-iŋ\ *n* : the act of stealing a pet

**pe·trel** \'pe-trəl\ *n* : any of various small seabirds that fly far from land

**pet·ri·fy** \'pe-trə-,fī\ *vb* **-fied; -fy·ing 1** : to change into stony material **2** : to make rigid or inactive (as from fear or awe) — **pet·ri·fac·tion** \,pe-trə-'fak-shən\ *n*

**pet·ro·chem·i·cal** \,pe-trō-'kem-i-kəl\ *n* : a chemical isolated or derived from petroleum or natural gas — **pet·ro·chem·is·try** \-'kem-ə-strē\ *n*

**pe·trog·ra·phy** \pə-'träg-rə-fē\ *n* : the description and systematic classification of rocks — **pe·trog·ra·pher** \-fər\ *n* — **pet·ro·graph·ic** \,pe-trə-'graf-ik\ *or* **pet·ro·graph·i·cal** \-i-kəl\ *adj*

**pet·rol** \'pe-trəl\ *n, Brit* : GASOLINE

**pet·ro·la·tum** \,pe-trə-'lāt-əm\ *n* : a tasteless, odorless, and oily or greasy substance from petroleum that is used esp. in ointments and dressings

**pe·tro·leum** \pə-'trō-lē-əm\ *n* [ML, fr. L *petr-* stone, rock (fr. Gk, fr. *petros* stone & *petra* rock) + *oleum* oil] : a dark oily liquid found at places in the earth's upper strata and processed into useful products (as gasoline and oil)

**petroleum jelly** *n* : PETROLATUM

**pe·trol·o·gy** \pə-'träl-ə-jē\ *n* : a science that deals with the history, occurrence, composition, and classification of rocks — **pet·ro·log·ic** \,pe-trə-'läj-ik\ *or* **pet·ro·log·i·cal** \-i-kəl\ *adj* — **pet·ro·log·i·cal·ly** \-i-k(ə-)lē\ *adv* — **pe·trol·o·gist** \pə-'träl-ə-jəst\ *n*

¹**pet·ti·coat** \'pet-ē-,kōt\ *n* **1** : a skirt worn under a dress **2** : an outer skirt

²**petticoat** *adj* : FEMALE (~ government)

**pet·ti·fog** \'pet-ē-,fóg, -,fäg\ *vb* **-fogged; -fog·ging 1** : to engage in legal trickery **2** : to quibble over insignificant details — **pet·ti·fog·ger** *n*

**pet·tish** \'pet-ish\ *adj* : PEEVISH syn irritable, petulant, fretful

**pet·ty** \'pet-ē\ *adj* **pet·ti·er; -est** [ME *pety* small, minor, alter. of *petit*, fr. MF, small] **1** : having secondary rank : MINOR (~ prince) **2** : of little importance : TRIFLING (~ faults) **3** : marked by narrowness or meanness — **pet·ti·ly** \'pet-ᵊl-ē\ *adv* — **pet·ti·ness** \-ē-nəs\ *n*

**petty officer** *n* : a subordinate officer in the navy or coast guard appointed from among the enlisted men

**petty officer first class** *n* : a petty officer ranking below a chief petty officer

**petty officer second class** *n* : a petty officer ranking below a petty officer first class

**petty officer third class** *n* : a petty officer ranking below a petty officer second class

**pet·u·lant** \'pech-ə-lənt\ *adj* : marked

by capricious ill humor syn irritable, peevish, fretful — **pet·u·lance** \-ləns\ *n* — **pet·u·lant·ly** *adv*

**pe·tu·nia** \pi-'t(y)ün-yə\ *n* : a garden plant with bright funnel-shaped flowers

**pew** \'pyü\ *n* [ME *pewe*, fr. MF *puie* balustrade, fr. L *podia*, pl. of *podium* parapet, podium, fr. Gk *podion* base, dim. of *pod-, pous* foot] : one of the benches with backs fixed in rows in a church

**pe·wee** \'pē-(,)wē\ *n* : any of various small flycatchers

**pew·ter** \'pyüt-ər\ *n* : an alloy of tin usu. with lead and sometimes also copper or antimony used esp. for kitchen or table utensils

**pey·o·te** \pā-'ōt-ē\ *or* **pey·otl** \-'ōt-ᵊl\ *n* : a stimulant drug derived from an American cactus; *also* : this cactus

**pf** *abbr* **1** pfennig **2** preferred

**PFC** *abbr* private first class

**pfd** *abbr* preferred

**pfen·nig** \'fen-ig\ *n, pl* **pfen·nigs** *or* **pfen·ni·ge** \'fen-i-gə\ — see *deutsche mark, mark* at MONEY table

**pg** *abbr* page

**PG** *abbr* postgraduate

**pH** \(')pē-'āch\ *n* : a value used to express relative acidity and alkalinity; *also* : the condition represented by such a value

**pha·eton** \'fā-ət-ᵊn\ *n* [F *phaéton*, fr. Gk Phaethōn, son of the sun god who persuaded his father to let him drive the chariot of the sun but who lost control of the horses with disastrous consequences] **1** : a light 4-wheeled horse-drawn vehicle **2** : an open automobile with two cross seats

**phage** \'fāj\ *n* : BACTERIOPHAGE

**pha·lanx** \'fā-,laŋks\ *n, pl* **pha·lanx·es** *or* **pha·lan·ges** \fə-'lan-,jēz\ **1** : a group or body (as of troops) in compact formation **2** *pl* **phalanges** : one of the digital bones of the hand or foot of a vertebrate

**phal·a·rope** \'fal-ə-,rōp\ *n, pl* **phalaropes** *also* **phalarope** : any of several small shorebirds

**phal·lic** \'fal-ik\ *adj* **1** : of, relating to, or resembling a phallus **2** : relating to or being the stage of psychosexual development in psychoanalytic theory during which a child becomes interested in his own sexual organs

**phal·lus** \'fal-əs\ *n, pl* **phal·li** \'fal-,ī\ *or* **phal·lus·es** : PENIS; *also* : a symbolic representation of the penis

**phan·tasm** \'fan-,taz-əm\ *n* : a product of the imagination : ILLUSION

**phan·tas·ma·go·ria** \fan-,taz-mə-'gōr-ē-ə\ *n* : a constantly shifting complex succession of things seen or imagined; *also* : a scene that constantly changes or fluctuates

**phantasy** *var of* FANTASY

**phan·tom** \'fant-əm\ *n* **1** : something (as a specter) that is apparent to sense but has no substantial existence **2** : a mere show : SHADOW **3** : a representation of something abstract, ideal, or incorporeal — **phantom** *adj* **phan·tom·like** *adv or adj*

**pha·raoh** \'fe(ə)r-ō, 'fā-rō\ *n, often cap* : a ruler of ancient Egypt

**phar·i·sa·ical** \,far-ə-'sā-ə-kəl\ *adj* : hypocritically self-righteous — **phar·i·sa·ical·ly** \-k(ə-)lē\ *adv*

**phar·i·see** \'far-ə-,sē\ *n* **1** *cap* : a member of an ancient Jewish sect noted for strict observance of rites and ceremonies of the traditional law **2** : a self-righteous or hypocritical person — **phar·i·sa·ic** \,far-ə-'sā-ik\ *adj*

**pharm** *abbr* pharmaceutical; pharmacist; pharmacy

**phar·ma·ceu·ti·cal** \,fär-mə-'süt-i-kəl\ *also* **phar·ma·ceu·tic** \-ik\ *adj* **1** : of or relating to pharmacy or pharmacists **2** : MEDICINAL — **pharmaceutical** *n*

**phar·ma·col·o·gy** \,fär-mə-'käl-ə-jē\ *n* **1** : the science of drugs esp. as related to medicinal uses **2** : the reactions and properties of a drug — **phar·ma·co·log·ic** \-kə-'läj-ik\ *or* **phar·ma·co·log·i·cal** \-i-kəl\ *adj* — **phar·ma·col·o·gist** \-'käl-ə-jəst\ *n*

**phar·ma·co·poe·ia** *also* **phar·ma·co·pe·ia** \-kə-'pē-(y)ə\ *n* **1** : a book describing drugs and medicinal preparations **2** : a stock of drugs

**phar·ma·cy** \'fär-mə-sē\ *n, pl* **-cies** **1** : the art or practice of preparing and dispensing drugs **2** : DRUGSTORE — **phar·ma·cist** \-səst\ *n*

**phar·os** \'faər-,äs\ *n* : LIGHTHOUSE

**phar·ynx** \'far-iŋks\ *n, pl* **pha·ryn·ges** \fə-'rin-,jēz\ *also* **phar·ynx·es** : the space just back of the mouth into which the nostrils, esophagus, and trachea open — **pha·ryn·ge·al** \fə-'rin-j(ē-)əl, ,far-ən-'jē-əl\ *adj*

**phase** \'fāz\ *n* **1** : a particular appearance in a recurring series of changes ⟨~s of the moon⟩ **2** : a stage or interval in a process or cycle ⟨first ~ of an experiment⟩ **3** : an aspect or part under consideration

**phase in** *vb* : to introduce in stages

**phase·out** \'fāz-,aút\ *n* : a gradual stopping of operations or production

**phase out** \'fāz-'aút\ *vb* : to stop production or use of in stages

**PhD** *abbr* [L *philosophiae doctor*] doctor of philosophy

**pheas·ant** \'fez-²nt\ *n, pl* **pheasant** *or* **pheasants** : any of various longtailed brilliantly colored game birds related to the domestic fowl

**phe·no·bar·bi·tal** \,fē-nō-'bär-bə-,tól\ *n* : a crystalline drug used as a hypnotic and sedative

**phe·nol** \'fē-,nól, -,nól, fi-'nól, -'nól\ *n* : a caustic poisonous acidic compound in tar used as a disinfectant and in making plastics

**phe·no·lic** \fi-'nō-lik, 'näl-ik\ *n* : a resin or plastic made from a phenol and used esp. for molding and insulating and in coatings and adhesives

**phe·nom·e·non** \fi-'näm-ə-,nän, -nən\ *n, pl* **-na** \-nə\ *or* **-nons** [LL *phaenomenon*, fr. Gk *phainomenon*, fr. neut. of *phainomenos*, prp. of *phainesthai* to appear] **1** : an observable fact or event **2** : an outward sign of the working of a law of nature **3** *pl* **-nons** : an extraordinary person or thing : PRODIGY — **phe·nom·e·nal** \-'näm-ən-²l\ *adj*

**pher·o·mone** \'fer-ə-,mōn\ *n* : a chemical substance that is produced by an animal and serves to stimulate a behavioral response in other individuals of the same species — **pher·o·mon·al** \,fer-ə-'mōn-²l\ *adj*

**phi·al** \'fī-(-ə)l\ *n* : VIAL

**phil** *or* **philol** *abbr* philological; philology

**Phil** *abbr* Philippians

**phi·lan·der** \fə-'lan-dər\ *vb* **phi·lan·dered; phi·lan·der·ing** \-d(ə-)riŋ\ : to make love without serious intent : FLIRT — **phi·lan·der·er** *n*

**phi·lan·thro·py** \fə-'lan-thrə-pē\ *n, pl* **-pies** **1** : goodwill to fellowmen; *esp* : effort to promote human welfare **2** : a charitable act or gift; *also* : an organization that distributes or is supported by donated funds — **phil·an·throp·ic** \,fil-ən-'thräp-ik\ *adj* — **phi·lan·thro·pist** \fə-'lan-thrə-pəst\ *n*

**phi·lat·e·ly** \fə-'lat-²l-ē\ *n* : the collection and study of postage and imprinted stamps — **phi·lat·e·list** \-²l-əst\ *n*

**phil·har·mon·ic** \,fil-ər-'män-ik, ,fil-(h)är-\ *adj* : of or relating to a symphony orchestra

**phi·lip·pic** \fə-'lip-ik\ *n* : TIRADE

**phi·lis·tine** \'fil-ə-,stēn; fə-'lis-tən\ *n, often cap* : a materialistic person; *esp* : one who is smugly insensitive or indifferent to intellectual or artistic values — **philistine** *adj*

**philo·den·dron** \,fil-ə-'den-drən\ *n; pl* **-drons** *or* **-dra** \-drə\ [NL, fr. Gk, neut. of *philodendros* loving trees, fr. *philos* dear, friendly + *dendron* tree] : any of various arums grown for their showy foliage

**phi·lol·o·gy** \fə-'läl-ə-jē\ *n* **1** : the study of literature and relevant fields **2** : LINGUISTICS; *esp* : historical and comparative linguistics — **phil·o·log·i·cal** \,fil-ə-'läj-i-kəl\ *adj* — **phi·lol·o·gist** \fə-'läl-ə-jəst\ *n*

**philos** *abbr* philosopher; philosophy

**phi·los·o·pher** \fə-'läs-ə-fər\ *n* **1** : a reflective thinker : SCHOLAR **2** : a student of or specialist in philosophy **3** : one whose philosophical perspective enables him to meet trouble calmly

**phi·los·o·phize** \fə-'läs-ə-,fīz\ *vb* **-phized; -phiz·ing** **1** : to reason like a philosopher : THEORIZE **2** : to expound a philosophy esp. superficially

**phi·los·o·phy** \fə-'läs-ə-fē\ *n, pl* **-phies** **1** : a critical study of fundamental beliefs and the grounds for them **2** : sciences and liberal arts exclusive of medicine, law, and theology ⟨doctor of ~⟩ **3** : a system of philosophical concepts ⟨Aristotelian ~⟩ **4** : a basic theory concerning a particular subject or sphere of activity **5** : the sum of the ideas and convictions of an individual or group ⟨his ~ of life⟩ **6** : calmness of temper and judgment — **phil·o·soph·ic** \,fil-ə-'säf-ik\ *or*

**phil·o·soph·i·cal** \-i-kəl\ adj —
**phil·o·soph·i·cal·ly** \-k(ə-)lē\ adv
**phil·ter** or **phil·tre** \'fil-tər\ n 1 : a
potion, drug, or charm held to arouse
sexual passion 2 : a magic potion
**phle·bi·tis** \fli-'bīt-əs\ n : inflammation of a vein
**phle·bot·o·my** \fli-'bät-ə-mē\ n, pl
**-mies** : the letting of blood in the
treatment of disease
**phlegm** \'flem\ n : thick mucus secreted in abnormal quantity esp. in the
nose and throat
**phleg·mat·ic** \fleg-'mat-ik\ adj : having or showing a slow and stolid temperament    **syn** impassive, apathetic,
stoic
**phlo·em** \'flō-,em\ n : a vascular plant
tissue external to the xylem that carries
dissolved food material downward
**phlox** \'fläks\ n, pl **phlox** or **phlox·**
**es** : any of several American herbs;
esp : one grown for its tall stalks with
showy spreading terminal clusters of
flowers
**pho·bia** \'fō-bē-ə\ n : an irrational
persistent fear or dread
**phoe·be** \'fē-(,)bē\ n : a flycatcher of
the eastern U.S. that has a slight crest
and is grayish brown above and yellowish white below
**phoe·nix** \'fē-niks\ n : a legendary
bird held to live for centuries and then
to burn itself to death and rise fresh
and young from its ashes
**phon** abbr phonetics
¹**phone** \'fōn\ n 1 : EARPHONE 2
: TELEPHONE
²**phone** vb **phoned; phon·ing** : TELE-
PHONE
**pho·neme** \'fō-,nēm\ n : one of the
smallest units of speech that distinguish
one utterance from another — **pho·**
**ne·mic** \fō-'nē-mik\ adj
**pho·net·ics** \fə-'net-iks\ n : the study
and systematic classification of the
sounds made in spoken utterance —
**pho·net·ic** \-ik\ adj — **pho·ne·ti·**
**cian** \,fō-nə-'tish-ən\ n
**pho·nic** \'fän-ik\ adj 1 : of, relating
to, or producing sound 2 : of or relating to the sounds of speech or to pho-
nics — **pho·ni·cal·ly** \-i-k(ə-)lē\ adv
**pho·nics** \'fän-iks\ n : a method of
teaching beginners to read and pronounce words by learning the phonetic
value of letters, letter groups, and syllables
**pho·no** \'fō-(,)nō\ n, pl **phonos**
: PHONOGRAPH
**pho·no·graph** \'fō-nə-,graf\ n : an instrument for reproducing sounds by
means of the vibration of a needle following a spiral groove on a revolving
disc — **pho·no·graph·ic** \,fō-nə-
'graf-ik\ adj — **pho·no·graph·i·cal·**
**ly** \-i-k(ə-)lē\ adv
**pho·nol·o·gy** \fə-'näl-ə-jē\ n : a study
and description of the sound changes in
a language — **pho·no·log·i·cal**
\,fōn-ᵊl-'äj-i-kəl\ adj — **pho·nol·o·**
**gist** \fə-'näl-ə-jəst\ n
**pho·ny** or **pho·ney** \'fō-nē\ adj
**pho·ni·er; -est** : marked by empty

pretension : FAKE — **phony** n
**phosph-** or **phospho-** comb form 1
: phosphorus 2 : phosphate
**phos·phate** \'fäs-,fāt\ n 1 : a chemical salt obtained esp. from various rocks
and bones and widely used in fertilizers
2 : an effervescent drink of carbonated
water flavored with fruit syrup —
**phos·phat·ic** \fäs-'fat-ik\ adj
**phos·phor** \'fäs-fər\ also **phos·**
**phore** \-,fōr, -,for\ n : a phosphores-
cent substance
**phos·pho·res·cence** \,fäs-fə-'res-
ᵊns\ n 1 : luminescence caused by
radiation absorption that continues
after the radiation has stopped 2 : an
enduring luminescence without sensible
heat — **phos·pho·res·cent** \-ᵊnt\
adj — **phos·pho·res·cent·ly** adv
**phosphoric acid** \,fäs-,fōr-ik-, -,fär-\
n : a syrupy or crystalline acid used in
making fertilizers and flavoring soft
drinks
**phos·pho·rus** \'fäs-f(ə-)rəs\ n [NL,
fr. Gk phōsphoros light-bearing, fr.
phōs light + pherein to carry, bring] : a
waxy nonmetallic chemical element that
is found combined with other elements
in phosphates, soils, and bones and
that has a faint glow in moist air —
**phos·phor·ic** \fäs-'fōr-ik, -'fär-\ adj
— **phos·pho·rous** \'fäs-f(ə-)rəs; fäs-
'fōr-əs, -'fōr-\ adj
**phot-** or **photo-** comb form 1 : light 2
: photograph : photographic 3
: photoelectric
**pho·to** \'fōt-ō\ n, pl **photos** : PHOTO-
GRAPH — **photo** vb or adj
**pho·to·cell** \'fōt-ō-,sel\ n : PHOTO-
ELECTRIC CELL
**pho·to·chem·i·cal** \,fōt-ō-'kem-i-
kəl\ adj : of, relating to, or resulting
from the chemical action of radiant
energy
**pho·to·com·pose** \-kəm-'pōz\ vb : to
compose reading matter for reproduction by means of characters photographed on film — **pho·to·com·po·**
**si·tion** \-,käm-pə-'zish-ən\ n
**pho·to·copy** \'fōt-ə-,käp-ē\ n : a
photographic reproduction of graphic
matter — **photocopy** vb
**pho·to·de·com·po·si·tion** \-,dē-
,käm-pə-'zish-ən\ n : chemical breaking
down by means of radiant energy
**pho·to·elec·tric** \,fōt-ō-i-'lek-trik\
adj : relating to an electrical effect due
to the interaction of light with matter —
**pho·to·elec·tri·cal·ly** \-tri-k(ə-)lē\
adv
**photoelectric cell** n : a device in
which variations in light are converted
into variations in an electric current
**pho·to·elec·tron** \,fōt-ō-i-'lek-,trän\
n : an electron released in photoemis-
sion
**pho·to·emis·sion** \-i-'mish-ən\ n
: the release of electrons from a metal
when exposed to radiation (as light)
**pho·to·en·grave** \-in-'grāv\ vb : to
make a photoengraving of
**pho·to·en·grav·ing** \-'grā-viŋ\ n : a
process by which an etched printing
plate is made from a photograph or

drawing; *also* **:** a print made from such a plate

**photo finish** *n* **:** a race finish so close that a photograph of the finish is used to determine the winner

**pho·to·flash** \'fōt-ə-,flash\ *n* **:** FLASH-BULB

¹**pho·tog** \fə-'täg\ *n* **:** PHOTOGRAPHER

²**photog** *abbr* photographic; photography

**pho·to·ge·nic** \,fōt-ə-'jen-ik\ *adj* **:** eminently suitable esp. aesthetically for being photographed

**pho·to·graph** \'fōt-ə-,graf\ *n* **:** a picture taken by photography — **pho·to-graph** *vb* — **pho·tog·ra·pher** \fə-'täg-rə-fər\ *n*

**pho·tog·ra·phy** \fə-'täg-rə-fē\ *n* **:** the art or process of producing images on a sensitized surface (as film in a camera) by the action of light — **pho·to-graph·ic** \,fōt-ə-'graf-ik\ *adj* — **pho·to·graph·i·cal·ly** \-i-k(ə-)lē\ *adv*

**pho·to·gra·vure** \,fōt-ə-grə-'vyùr\ *n* **:** a process for making prints from an intaglio plate prepared by photographic methods

**pho·to·mi·cro·graph** \,fōt-ə-'mī-krə-,graf\ *n* **:** a photograph of a magnified image of a small object — **photomi-crograph** *vb* — **pho·to·mi·cro-graph·ic** \-,mī-krə-'graf-ik\ *adj* — **pho·to·mi·crog·ra·phy** \-mī-'kräg-rə-fē\ *n*

**pho·tom·e·ter** \fō-'täm-ət-ər\ *n* **:** an instrument for measuring luminous intensity — **pho·to·met·ric** \,fōt-ə-'met-rik\ *adj* — **pho·tom·e·try** \fō-'täm-ə-trē\ *n*

**pho·to·mu·ral** \,fōt-ō-'myùr-əl\ *n* **:** an enlarged photograph used on walls esp. as decoration

**pho·ton** \'fō-,tän\ *n* **:** a quantum of radiant energy

**pho·to·play** \'fōt-ō-,plā\ *n* **:** MOTION PICTURE

**pho·to·sen·si·tive** \,fōt-ə-'sen-sət-iv\ *adj* **:** sensitive or sensitized to the action of radiant energy — **pho·to·sen·si·ti·za·tion** \-,sen-sət-ə-'zā-shən\ *n*

**pho·to·sphere** \'fōt-ə-,sfiər\ *n* **1 :** a sphere of light **2 :** the luminous surface of a star — **pho·to·spher·ic** \,fōt-ə-'sfi(ə)r-ik, -'sfer-\ *adj*

**pho·to·syn·the·sis** \,fōt-ō-'sin-thə-səs\ *n* **:** formation of carbohydrates by chlorophyll-containing plants exposed to sunlight — **pho·to·syn·the·size** \-,sīz\ *vb* — **pho·to·syn·thet·ic** \-sin-'thet-ik\ *adj*

¹**phr** *abbr* phrase

¹**phrase** \'frāz\ *n* **1 :** a brief expression **2 :** a group of two or more grammatically related words that form a sense unit expressing a thought

²**phrase** *vb* **phrased; phras·ing :** to express in words

**phrase·ol·o·gy** \,frā-zē-'äl-ə-jē\ *n, pl* **-gies :** a manner of phrasing **:** STYLE

**phras·ing** \'frā-ziŋ\ *n* **:** style of expression

**phre·net·ic** \fri-'net-ik\ *adj* **:** FRENETIC

**phren·ic** \'fren-ik\ *adj* **:** of or relating to the diaphragm ⟨~ nerves⟩

**phre·nol·o·gy** \fri-'näl-ə-jē\ *n* **:** the study of the conformation of the skull as indicative of mental faculties and character traits

**PHS** *abbr* Public Health Service

**phy·lac·tery** \fə-'lak-t(ə-)rē\ *n, pl* **-ter·ies 1 :** one of two small square leather boxes containing slips inscribed with scripture passages and traditionally worn on the left arm and forehead by Jewish men during morning weekday prayers **2 :** AMULET

**phy·lum** \'fī-ləm\ *n, pl* **phy·la** \-lə\ **:** a group (as of people) apparently of common origin; *also* **:** a major division of the plant or animal kingdom

**phys** *abbr* **1** physical **2** physician **3** physics

¹**phys·ic** \'fiz-ik\ *n* **1 :** the profession of medicine **2 :** MEDICINE; *esp* **:** CATHARTIC

²**physic** *vb* **phys·icked; phys·ick·ing :** PURGE

¹**phys·i·cal** \'fiz-i-kəl\ *adj* **1 :** of or relating to nature or the laws of nature **2 :** material as opposed to mental or spiritual **3 :** of, relating to, or produced by the forces and operations of physics **4 :** of or relating to the body — **phys·i·cal·ly** \-k(ə-)lē\ *adv*

²**physical** *n* **:** an examination of the bodily functions and condition of an individual

**physical education** *n* **:** instruction in the development and care of the body ranging from simple calisthenics to training in hygiene, gymnastics, and the performance and management of athletic games

**physical examination** *n* **:** PHYSICAL

**physical science** *n* **:** the sciences (as physics and astronomy) that deal primarily with nonliving materials — **physical scientist** *n*

**physical therapy** *n* **:** the treatment of disease by physical and mechanical means (as massage, exercise, water, or heat) — **physical therapist** *n*

**phy·si·cian** \fə-'zish-ən\ *n* **:** a doctor of medicine

**phys·i·cist** \'fiz-ə-səst\ *n* **:** a specialist in physics

**phys·ics** \'fiz-iks\ *n* **1 :** a science that deals with matter and motion and includes mechanics, heat, light, electricity, and sound **2 :** physical properties and composition

**phys·i·og·no·my** \,fiz-ē-'ä(g)-nə-mē\ *n, pl* **-mies :** facial appearance esp. as a reflection of inner character

**phys·i·og·ra·phy** \,fiz-ē-'äg-rə-fē\ *n* **:** geography dealing with physical features of the earth — **phys·io·graph·ic** \,fiz-ē-ō-'graf-ik\ *adj*

**physiol** *abbr* physiologist; physiology

**phys·i·ol·o·gy** \,fiz-ē-'äl-ə-jē\ *n* **1 :** a science dealing with the functions and functioning of living matter and beings **2 :** functional processes in an organism or any of its parts — **phys·i·o·log·i·cal** \-ē-ə-'läj-i-kəl\ *or* **phys·i·o·log·ic** \-ik\ *adj* — **phys·i·ol·o·gist** \-ē-'äl-ə-jəst\ *n*

**phys·io·ther·a·py** \,fiz-ē-ō-'ther-ə-pē\ *n* : treatment of disease by physical means (as massage or exercise) — **phys·io·ther·a·pist** \-pəst\ *n*

**phy·sique** \fə-'zēk\ *n* : the build of a person's body ; bodily constitution

¹**pi** \'pī\ *n, pl* **pis** \'pīz\ : the symbol π denoting the ratio of the circumference of a circle to its diameter; *also* : the ratio itself

²**pi** *also* **pie** \'pī\ *n, pl* **pies** : jumbled type

**pi·a·nis·si·mo** \,pē-ə-'nis-ə-,mō\ *adv or adj* : very softly — used as a direction in music

**pi·a·nist** \pē-'an-əst, 'pē-ə-nəst\ *n* : one who plays the piano

¹**pi·a·no** \pē-'än-ō\ *adv or adj* : SOFTLY — used as a direction in music

²**piano** \pē-'an-ō\ *n, pl* **pianos** [It, short for *pianoforte,* fr. *piano e forte* soft and loud, fr. *piano* soft (fr. L *planus* level, flat) + *forte* loud, fr. L *fortis* strong; fr. the fact that its tones could be varied in loudness] : a musical instrument having steel strings sounded by felt-covered hammers operated from a keyboard

**pi·ano·forte** \pē-'an-ə-,fōrt, ,an-ə-'fōrt-ē\ *n* : PIANO

**pi·as·ter** *or* **pi·as·tre** \pē-'as-tər\ *n* 1 — see MONEY table 2 — see *lira, pound* at MONEY table

**pi·az·za** \pē-'az-ə, *esp for 1* -'at-sə\ *n, pl* **piazzas** *or* **pi·az·ze** \-'at-(,)sā, -'ät-\ [It, fr. L *platea* broad street] 1 : an open square esp. in an Italian town 2 : an arcaded and roofed gallery; *also, chiefly North & Midland* : VERANDA

**pi·broch** \'pē-,bräk\ *n* : a set of martial or mournful variations for the bagpipe

**pic** \'pik\ *n, pl* **pics** *or* **pix** \'piks\ 1 : PHOTOGRAPH 2 : MOTION PICTURE

**pi·ca** \'pī-kə\ *n* : a typewriter type providing 10 characters to the inch

**pi·ca·resque** \,pik-ə-'resk, ,pē-kə-\ *adj* : of or relating to rogues (~ fiction)

**pic·a·yune** \,pik-ē-'(y)ün\ *adj* : of little value : TRIVIAL; *also* : PETTY

**pic·ca·lil·li** \,pik-ə-'lil-ē\ *n* : a pungent relish of chopped vegetables and spices

**pic·co·lo** \'pik-ə-,lō\ *n, pl* **-los** [It, short for *piccolo flauto* small flute] : a small shrill flute pitched an octave higher than the ordinary flute

**pice** \'pīs\ *n, pl* **pice** : PAISA

¹**pick** \'pik\ *vb* 1 : to pierce or break up with a pointed instrument 2 : to remove bit by bit (~ meat from bones); *also* : to remove covering matter from 3 : to gather by plucking (~ apples) 4 : CULL, SELECT 5 : ROB (~ a pocket) 6 : PROVOKE (~ a quarrel) 7 : to dig into or pull lightly at 8 : to pluck with fingers or a plectrum 9 : to loosen or pull apart with a sharp point (~ wool) 10 : to unlock with a wire 11 : to eat sparingly — **pick·er** *n*

²**pick** *n* 1 : the act or privilege of choosing 2 : the best or choicest one 3 : the part of a crop gathered at one time

³**pick** *n* 1 : PICKAX 2 : a pointed implement used for picking 3 : a small thin piece (as of metal) used to pluck the strings of a stringed instrument

**pick·a·back** \'pig-ē-,bak, 'pik-ə-\ *var of* PIGGYBACK

**pick·a·nin·ny** *or* **pic·a·nin·ny** \'pik-ə-,nin-ē\ *n, pl* **-nies** : a Negro child

**pick·ax** \'pik-,aks\ *n* : a tool with a wooden handle and a blade pointed at one end or at both ends that is used by diggers and miners

**pick·er·el** \'pik-(ə)-rəl\ *n, pl* **pickerel** *or* **pickerels** : any of various small pikes; *also* : WALLEYE 3

**pick·er·el·weed** \-rəl-,wēd\ *n* : a blue-flowered American shallow-water herb

¹**pick·et** \'pik-ət\ *n* 1 : a pointed stake (as for a fence) 2 : a detached body of soldiers on outpost duty; *also* : SENTINEL 3 : a person posted by a labor union where workers are on strike; *also* : a person posted for a demonstration

²**picket** *vb* 1 : to guard with pickets 2 : TETHER 3 : to post pickets at (~ a factory) 4 : to serve as a picket

**pick·ings** \'pik-iŋz, -ənz\ *n pl* 1 : gleanable or eatable fragments : SCRAPS 2 : yield for effort expended : RETURN; *also* : share of spoils

**pick·le** \'pik-əl\ *n* 1 : a brine or vinegar solution for preserving foods; *also* : a food preserved in a pickle 2 : a difficult situation : PLIGHT — **pickle** *vb*

**pick·lock** \'pik-,läk\ *n* 1 : a tool for picking locks 2 : BURGLAR, THIEF

**pick·pock·et** \'pik-,päk-ət\ *n* : one who steals from pockets

**pick·up** \'pik-,əp\ *n* 1 : a picking up 2 : revival of activity : IMPROVEMENT 3 : ACCELERATION 4 : a temporary chance acquaintance 5 : the conversion of mechanical movements into electrical impulses in the reproduction of sound; *also* : a device for making such conversion 6 : a light truck with open body and low sides

**pick up** \(')pik-'əp\ *vb* 1 : IMPROVE 2 : to put in order

**picky** \'pik-ē\ *adj* **pick·i·er; -est** : FUSSY, FINICKY

¹**pic·nic** \'pik-,nik\ *n* : an outing with food usu. provided by members of the group and eaten in the open

²**picnic** *vb* **pic·nicked; pic·nick·ing** : to go on a picnic : eat in picnic fashion

**pi·co·sec·ond** \,pē-kō-'sek-ənd\ *n* : one trillionth of a second

**pi·cot** \'pē-,kō\ *n* : one of a series of small loops forming an edging on ribbon or lace

**pic·to·ri·al** \pik-'tōr-ē-əl\ *adj* : of, relating to, or consisting of pictures

¹**pic·ture** \'pik-chər\ *n* 1 : a representation made by painting, drawing, or photography 2 : a vivid description in words 3 : IMAGE, COPY 4 : a transitory visual image or reproduction 5 : MOTION PICTURE 6 : SITUATION

²**picture** *vb* **pic·tured; pic·tur·ing** 1 : to paint or draw a picture of 2 : to describe vividly in words 3 : to form a mental image of

**pic·tur·esque** \,pik-chə-'resk\ *adj* **1** : resembling a picture ⟨a ~ landscape⟩ **2** : CHARMING, QUAINT ⟨a ~ character⟩ **3** : GRAPHIC, VIVID ⟨a ~ account⟩ — **pic·tur·esque·ness** *n*

**picture tube** *n* : a vacuum tube having at one end a screen of luminescent material on which are produced visible images

**pid·dle** \'pid-ᵊl\ *vb* **pid·dled; pid·dling** \'pid-(ᵊ-)liŋ\ : to act or work idly : DAWDLE

**pid·dling** \-(ᵊ-)lən, -(ᵊ-)liŋ\ *adj* : TRIVIAL, PALTRY

**pid·gin** \'pij-ən\ *n* [fr. *Pidgin English*, Pidgin E, modif. of E *business English*] : a simplified speech used for communication between people with different languages; *esp* : an English-based pidgin used in the Orient

¹**pie** \'pī\ *n* : a dish consisting of a pastry crust and a filling (as of fruit or meat)

²**pie** *var of* PI

¹**pie·bald** \'pī-,bȯld\ *adj* : of different colors; *esp* : blotched with white and black

²**piebald** *n* : a piebald animal (as a horse)

¹**piece** \'pēs\ *n* **1** : a part of a whole : FRAGMENT **2** : one of a group, set, or mass ⟨chess ~⟩; *also* : a single item ⟨a ~ of news⟩ **3** : a length, weight, or size in which something is made or sold **4** : a product (as an essay) of creative work **5** : FIREARM **6** : COIN

²**piece** *vb* **pieced; piec·ing 1** : to repair or complete by adding pieces : PATCH **2** : to join into a whole

**pièce de ré·sis·tance** \pē-,es-də-rə-,zē-'stäns, -rā-, -'stäⁿs\ *n, pl* **pièces de ré·sis·tance** \*same*\ **1** : the chief dish of a meal **2** : an outstanding item

**piece·meal** \'pēs-,mēl\ *adv or adj* : one piece at a time : GRADUALLY

**piece·work** \-,wərk\ *n* : work done and paid for by the piece — **piece·work·er** *n*

**pied** \'pīd\ *adj* : of two or more colors in blotches : VARIEGATED

**pied-à-terre** \pē-,ād-ə-'tear\ *n, pl* **pieds-à-terre** \*same*\ [F, lit., foot to the ground] : a temporary or second lodging

**pie·plant** \'pī-,plant\ *n* : RHUBARB

**pier** \'piər\ *n* **1** : a support for a bridge span **2** : a structure built out into the water for use as a landing place or a promenade or to protect or form a harbor **3** : PILLAR

**pierce** \'piərs\ *vb* **pierced; pierc·ing 1** : to enter or thrust into sharply or painfully : STAB **2** : to make a hole in or through : PERFORATE **3** : to force or make a way into or through : PENETRATE **4** : to see through : DISCERN

**pies** *pl of* PI *or of* PIE

**pi·ety** \'pī-ət-ē\ *n, pl* **pi·eties 1** : fidelity to natural obligations (as to parents) **2** : dutifulness in religion : DEVOUTNESS **3** : a pious act **syn** allegiance, devotion, loyalty

**pi·ezo·elec·tric·i·ty** \pē-,ā-zō-ə-,lek-'tris-(ə-)tē\ *n* : electricity due to pressure esp. in a crystalline substance (as

quartz) — **pi·ezo·elec·tric** \-'lek-trik\ *n or adj*

**pif·fle** \'pif-əl\ *n* : trifling talk or action

¹**pig** \'pig\ *n* **1** : SWINE; *esp* : a young swine **2** : PORK **3** : one resembling a pig (as in dirtiness or greed) **4** : a casting of metal (as iron or lead) run directly from a smelting furnace into a mold **5** *slang* : POLICEMAN

**pi·geon** \'pij-ən\ *n* : any of numerous stout-bodied short-legged birds with smooth thick plumage

¹**pi·geon·hole** \'pij-ən-,hōl\ *n* : a small open compartment (as in a desk) for keeping letters or documents

²**pigeonhole** *vb* **1** : to place in or as if in a pigeonhole : FILE **2** : to lay aside **3** : CLASSIFY

**pi·geon-toed** \,pij-ən-'tōd\ *adj* : having the toes turned in

**pig·gish** \'pig-ish\ *adj* **1** : GREEDY **2** : STUBBORN

**pig·gy·back** \'pig-ē-,bak\ *adv or adj* **1** : up on the back and shoulders **2** : on a railroad flatcar

**pig·head·ed** \'pig-'hed-əd\ *adj* : OBSTINATE, STUBBORN

**pig latin** *n, often cap L* : a jargon that is made by systematic mutilation of English

**pig·let** \'pig-lət\ *n* : a small usu. young hog

**pig·ment** \'pig-mənt\ *n* **1** : coloring matter **2** : a powder mixed with a suitable liquid to give color (as in paints and enamels)

**pig·men·ta·tion** \,pig-mən-'tā-shən\ *n* : coloration with or deposition of pigment; *esp* : an excessive deposition of bodily pigment

**pigmy** *var of* PYGMY

**pig·nut** \'pig-,nət\ *n* : any of several bitter hickory nuts; *also* : a tree bearing these

**pig·pen** \-,pen\ *n* **1** : a pen for pigs **2** : a dirty place

**pig·skin** \-,skin\ *n* **1** : the skin of a pig; *also* : leather made from it **2** : FOOTBALL 2

**pig·sty** \'pig-,stī\ *n* : PIGPEN

**pig·tail** \-,tāl\ *n* : a tight braid of hair

¹**pike** \'pīk\ *n* : a sharp point or spike

²**pike** *n, pl* **pike** *or* **pikes** : a large slender long-snouted freshwater food fish; *also* : a related fish

³**pike** *n* : a long wooden shaft with a pointed steel head formerly used as a foot soldier's weapon

⁴**pike** *n* : TURNPIKE

**pik·er** \'pī-kər\ *n* **1** : one who does things in a small way or on a small scale **2** : TIGHTWAD, CHEAPSKATE

**pike·staff** \'pīk-,staf\ *n* : the staff of a foot soldier's pike

**pi·laf** *or* **pi·laff** \pi-'läf, 'pē-,läf\ *or* **pi·lau** \pi-'lȯ, -'lȯ, 'pē-lȯ, -lȯ\ *n* : a dish made of seasoned rice often with meat

**pi·las·ter** \'pī-,las-tər, pə-'las-\ *n* : a slightly projecting upright column that ornaments or helps to support a wall

**pil·chard** \'pil-chərd\ *n* : any of several fishes related to the herrings and often packed as sardines

**¹pile** \'pīl\ *n* : a long slender column (as of wood or steel) driven into the ground to support a vertical load

**²pile** *n* **1** : a quantity of things heaped together **2** : PYRE **3** : a great number or quantity : LOT **4** : a large building

**³pile** *vb* **piled; pil·ing** **1** : to lay in a pile : STACK **2** : to heap up : ACCUMULATE **3** : to press forward in a mass : CROWD

**⁴pile** *n* : a velvety surface of fine short hairs or threads (as on cloth) — **piled** \'pīld\ *adj*

**piles** \'pīlz\ *n pl* : HEMORRHOIDS

**pil·fer** \'pil-fər\ *vb* **pil·fered; pil·fer·ing** \-f(ə-)riŋ\ : to steal in small quantities

**pil·grim** \'pil-grəm\ *n* [ME, fr. OF *peligrin*, fr. LL *pelegrinus*, alter. of L *peregrinus* foreigner, fr. *peregrinus* foreign, fr. *pereger* being abroad, fr. *per* through + *ager* land] **1** : one who journeys in foreign lands : WAYFARER **2** : one who travels to a shrine or holy place as an act of devotion **3** *cap* : one of the English settlers founding Plymouth colony in 1620

**pil·grim·age** \-grə-mij\ *n* : a journey of a pilgrim esp. to a shrine or holy place

**pil·ing** \'pī-liŋ\ *n* : a structure of piles

**pill** \'pil\ *n* **1** : a medicine prepared in a little ball to be taken whole **2** : a disagreeable or tiresome person **3** : an oral contraceptive — usu. used with *the*

**pil·lage** \'pil-ij\ *vb* **pil·laged; pil·lag·ing** : to take booty : LOOT, PLUNDER — **pillage** *n*

**pil·lar** \'pil-ər\ *n* : a column or shaft standing alone esp. as a monument; *also* : one used as an upright support in a building — **pil·lared** \-ərd\ *adj*

**pill·box** \'pil-,bäks\ *n* **1** : a low usu. round box to hold pills **2** : something (as a low concrete emplacement for machine guns) shaped like a pillbox

**pil·lion** \'pil-yən\ *n* **1** : a pad or cushion placed behind a saddle for an extra rider **2** : a motorcycle riding saddle for a passenger

**¹pil·lo·ry** \'pil-(ə-)rē\ *n, pl* **-ries** : a wooden frame for public punishment having holes in which the head and hands can be locked

**²pillory** *vb* **-ried; -ry·ing** **1** : to set in a pillory **2** : to expose to public scorn

**¹pil·low** \'pil-ō\ *n* : a case filled with springy material (as feathers) and used to support the head of a resting person

**²pillow** *vb* : to rest or place on or as if on a pillow; *also* : to serve as a pillow for

**pil·low·case** \'pil-ə-,kās, -ō-\ *n* : a removable covering for a pillow

**¹pi·lot** \'pī-lət\ *n* **1** : HELMSMAN, STEERSMAN **2** : a person qualified and licensed to take ships into and out of a port **3** : GUIDE, LEADER **4** : one that flies an aircraft or spacecraft **5** : a television show filmed or taped as a sample of a proposed series — **pi·lot·less** *adj*

**²pilot** *vb* : CONDUCT, GUIDE; *esp* : to act as pilot of

**³pilot** *adj* : serving as a guiding or activating device or as a testing or trial

unit ⟨a ~ light⟩ ⟨a ~ burner⟩ ⟨a ~ factory⟩

**pi·lot·age** \'pī-lət-ij\ *n* : the act or business of piloting

**pi·lot·house** \'pī-lət-,haůs\ *n* : an enclosed place forward on the upper deck of a ship that shelters the steering gear and the helmsman

**pil·sner** *also* **pil·sen·er** \'pilz-(ə-)nər\ *n* **1** : a light beer with a strong flavor of hops **2** : a tall slender footed glass for beer

**pi·men·to** \pə-'ment-ō\ *n, pl* **pi·mentos** *or* **pimento** [Sp *pimienta* allspice, pepper, fr. LL *pigmenta*, pl. of *pigmentum* plant juice, fr. L, pigment] **1** : PIMIENTO **2** : ALLSPICE

**pi·mien·to** \pə-'m(y)ent-ō\ *n, pl* **-tos** : a mild red sweet pepper fruit that yields paprika

**pimp** \'pimp\ *n* : a man who solicits clients for a prostitute — **pimp** *vb*

**pim·per·nel** \'pim-pər-,nel, -pər-nəl\ *n* : a weedy herb related to the primroses with flowers that close in cloudy or rainy weather

**pim·ple** \'pim-pəl\ *n* : a small inflamed swelling on the skin often containing pus — **pim·ply** \-p(ə-)lē\ *adj*

**¹pin** \'pin\ *n* **1** : a piece of wood or metal used esp. for fastening articles together or as a support by which one article may be suspended from another; *esp* : a small pointed piece of wire with a head used for fastening clothes or attaching papers **2** : an ornament or emblem fastened to clothing with a pin **3** : one of the wooden pieces constituting the target (as in bowling); *also* : the staff of the flag marking a hole on a golf course **4** : LEG

**²pin** *vb* **pinned; pin·ning** **1** : to fasten with a pin **2** : to press together and hold fast **3** : to make dependent ⟨*pinned* their hopes on one man⟩ **4** : to assign the blame for ⟨~ a crime on someone⟩ **5** : to define clearly : ESTABLISH ⟨~ down an idea⟩ **6** : to hold fast or immobile in a spot or position

**pin·afore** \'pin-ə-,fōr\ *n* : a sleeveless dress or apron fastened at the back

**pince-nez** \'paⁿs-'nā, pans-\ *n, pl* **pince-nez** \-'nā(z)\ : eyeglasses clipped to the nose by a spring

**pin·cer** \'pin-sər\ *n* **1** *pl* : a gripping instrument with two handles and two grasping jaws **2** : a claw (as of a lobster) resembling pincers

**¹pinch** \'pinch\ *vb* **1** : to squeeze between the finger and thumb or between the jaws of an instrument **2** : to compress painfully : CRAMP **3** : CONTRACT, SHRIVEL **4** : to be miserly; *also* : to subject to strict economy **5** : STEAL **6** : ARREST

**²pinch** *n* **1** : a critical point **2** : painful effect **3** : an act of pinching **4** : a very small quantity **5** : ARREST

**³pinch** *adj* : SUBSTITUTE ⟨a ~ runner⟩

**pinch-hit** \'(')pinch-'hit\ *vb* **1** : to bat in the place of another player esp. when a hit is particularly needed **2** : to act or serve in place of another — **pinch hit** *n* — **pinch hitter** *n*

**pin curl** *n* : a curl made usu. by dampening a strand of hair, coiling it, and securing it by a hairpin or clip

**pin·cush·ion** \'pin-,kush-ən\ *n* : a cushion for pins not in use

¹**pine** \'pīn\ *vb* **pined; pin·ing 1** : to lose vigor or health through distress **2** : to long for something intensely

²**pine** *n* : any of numerous evergreen cone-bearing trees; *also* : the light durable resinous wood of pines

**pi·ne·al** \'pī-nē-əl, pī-'nē-əl\ *adj* : of, relating to, or being a small usu. conical appendage of the brain of all vertebrates with a cranium that is variously postulated to be a vestigial third eye, an endocrine organ, or the seat of the soul

**pine·ap·ple** \'pīn-,ap-əl\ *n* : a tropical plant bearing an edible juicy fruit; *also* : its fruit

**pin·feath·er** \'pin-,feth-ər\ *n* : a new feather just coming through the skin

**ping** \'piŋ\ *n* **1** : a sharp sound like that of a bullet striking **2** : ignition knock

**pin·hole** \'pin-,hōl\ *n* : a small hole made by, for, or as if by a pin

¹**pin·ion** \'pin-yən\ *n* : the end section of a bird's wing; *also* : WING

²**pinion** *vb* : to restrain by binding the arms; *also* : SHACKLE

³**pinion** *n* : a gear with a small number of teeth designed to mesh with a larger wheel or rack

¹**pink** \'piŋk\ *vb* **1** : PIERCE, STAB **2** : to perforate in an ornamental pattern **3** : to cut a saw-toothed edge on

²**pink** *n* **1** : any of various plants with narrow leaves often grown for their showy flowers **2** : the highest degree : HEIGHT ⟨the ~ of condition⟩

³**pink** *adj* **1** : of the color pink **2** : holding socialistic views — **pink·ish** *adj*

⁴**pink** *n* **1** : a light tint of red **2** : a person who holds socialistic views

**pink elephants** *n pl* : any of various hallucinations arising esp. from heavy drinking or use of narcotics

**pink·eye** \'piŋk-,ī\ *n* : an acute contagious eye inflammation

**pin·kie** *or* **pin·ky** \'piŋ-kē\ *n, pl* **pinkies** : the smallest finger of the hand

**pin·nace** \'pin-əs\ *n* **1** : a light sailing ship **2** : a ship's boat

**pin·na·cle** \'pin-i-kəl\ *n* [ME *pinacle,* fr. MF, fr. LL *pinnaculum* gable, fr. dim. of L *pinna* wing, battlement] **1** : a turret ending in a small spire **2** : a lofty peak **3** : the highest point : ACME

**pin·nate** \'pin-,āt\ *adj* : having similar parts arranged on each side of an axis — **pin·nate·ly** *adv*

**pi·noch·le** \'pē-,nək-əl\ *n* : a card game played with a 48-card deck

**pi·ñon** *or* **pin·yon** \'pin-,yōn, -yän\ *n, pl* **pi·ñons** *or* **pin·yons** *or* **pi·ño·nes** \pin-'yō-nēz\ : any of various low-growing pines of western No. America with edible seeds; *also* : the edible seed of a piñon

**pin·point** \'pin-,pöint\ *vb* : to locate, hit, or aim with great precision

**pin·prick** \'pin-,prik\ *n* **1** : a small

puncture made by or as if by a pin **2** : a petty irritation or annoyance

**pin·stripe** \-,strīp\ *n* : a narrow stripe on a fabric; *also* : a suit with such stripes — **pin-striped** \-,strīpt\ *adj*

**pint** \'pīnt\ *n* — see WEIGHT table

**pin·to** \'pin-,tō\ *n, pl* **pintos** *also* **pintoes** : a spotted horse

**pin·up** \'pin-,əp\ *adj* : suitable for pinning up on an admirer's wall ⟨~ photo⟩; *also* : suited (as by beauty) to be the subject of a pinup photograph ⟨~ girl⟩

**pin·wheel** \-,hwēl\ *n* **1** : a toy consisting of lightweight vanes that revolve at the end of a stick **2** : a fireworks device in the form of a revolving wheel of colored fire

**pin·worm** \-,wərm\ *n* : a small worm parasitic in the intestines of man

**pinx** *abbr* [L *pinxit*] he painted it

¹**pi·o·neer** \,pī-ə-'niər\ *n* [MF *pionier,* fr. OF *peonier* foot soldier, fr. *peon* foot soldier, fr. ML *pedon-, pedo,* fr. LL. one with broad feet, fr. L *ped-, pes* foot] **1** : one that originates or helps open up a new line of thought or activity **2** : an early settler in a territory

²**pioneer** *vb* **1** : to act as a pioneer **2** : to open or prepare for others to follow; *esp* : SETTLE

**pi·ous** \'pī-əs\ *adj* **1** : marked by reverence for deity : DEVOUT **2** : excessively or affectedly religious **3** : SACRED, DEVOTIONAL **4** : showing loyal reverence for a person or thing : DUTIFUL **5** : marked by sham or hypocrisy — **pi·ous·ly** *adv*

¹**pip** \'pip\ *n* **1** : a disease of birds **2** : a usu. minor human ailment

²**pip** *n* : one of the dots or figures used chiefly to indicate numerical value (as of a playing card)

³**pip** *n* : a small fruit seed (as of an apple)

¹**pipe** \'pīp\ *n* **1** : a musical instrument consisting of a tube played by forcing a blast of air through it **2** : BAGPIPE **3** : a long tube designed to conduct something (as water, steam, or oil) **4** : a device for smoking consisting of a tube with a bowl at one end and a mouthpiece at the other

²**pipe** *vb* **piped; pip·ing 1** : to play on a pipe **2** : to speak in a high or shrill voice **3** : to convey by or as if by pipes — **pip·er** *n*

**pipe down** *vb* : to stop talking or making noise

**pipe dream** *n* : an illusory or fantastic hope

**pipe·line** \'pīp-,līn\ *n* **1** : a line of pipe with pumps, valves, and control devices for conveying liquids, gases, or finely divided solids **2** : a direct channel for information

**pi·pette** *or* **pi·pet** \pī-'pet\ *n* : a device for measuring and transferring small volumes of liquid

**pipe up** *vb* : to begin to play, sing, or speak

**pip·ing** \'pī-piŋ\ *n* **1** : the music of pipes **2** : a narrow fold of material used to decorate edges or seams

**piping hot** adj : so hot as to sizzle or hiss : very hot

**pip·kin** \'pip-kən\ n : a small earthenware or metal pot

**pip·pin** \'pip-ən\ n : any of several yellowish apples

**pip–squeak** \'pip-ˌskwēk\ n : a small or insignificant person

**pi·quant** \'pē-kənt\ adj 1 : pleasantly savory : PUNGENT 2 : engagingly provocative; also : having a lively charm — **pi·quan·cy** \-kən-sē\ n

¹**pique** \'pēk\ n : offense taken by one slighted; also : a fit of resentment

²**pique** vb **piqued; piqu·ing** 1 : to offend esp. by slighting 2 : to arouse by a provocation or challenge : GOAD

**pi·qué** or **pi·que** \pi-'kā\ n : a durable ribbed clothing fabric of cotton, rayon, or silk

**pi·quet** \pi-'kā\ n : a two-handed card game played with 32 cards

**pi·ra·cy** \'pī-rə-sē\ n, pl **-cies** 1 : robbery on the high seas or in the air 2 : the unauthorized use of another's production or invention

**pi·ra·nha** \pə-'ran-yə, -'rän-(y)ə\ n : a small So. American fish that often attacks men and large animals

**pi·rate** \'pī-rət\ n [ME, fr. MF or L; MF, fr. L pirata, fr. Gk peiratēs, fr. peiran to attempt, attack] : one who commits piracy — **pirate** vb — **pi·rat·i·cal** \pə-'rat-i-kəl, pī-\ adj

**pir·ou·ette** \ˌpir-ə-'wet\ n : a full turn on the toe or ball of one foot in ballet; also : a rapid whirling about of the body — **pirouette** vb

**pis** pl of PI

**pis·ca·to·ri·al** \ˌpis-kə-'tōr-ē-əl\ adj : of or relating to fishing

**pis·mire** \'pis-ˌmī(ə)r\ n : ANT

**pis·ta·chio** \pə-'stash-(e-ˌ)ō, -'stäsh-\ n, pl **-chios** : a small tree related to the sumac whose fruit contains a greenish edible seed; also : its seed

**pis·til** \'pis-t²l\ n : the female reproductive organ in a flower — **pis·til·late** \'pis-tə-ˌlāt\ adj

**pis·tol** \'pis-t²l\ n : a firearm held and fired with one hand

**pistol-whip** \-ˌhwip\ vb : to beat with a pistol

**pis·ton** \'pis-tən\ n : a sliding piece that receives and transmits motion and that usu. consists of a short cylinder inside a larger cylinder

¹**pit** \'pit\ n 1 : a hole, shaft, or cavity in the ground 2 : an often sunken area designed for a particular use; also : an enclosed place (as for cockfights) 3 : HELL 4 : a hollow or indentation esp. in the surface of the body 5 : a small indented scar (as from smallpox)

²**pit** vb **pit·ted; pit·ting** 1 : to form pits in or become marred with pits 2 : to match (as cocks) for fighting

³**pit** n : the stony seed of some fruits (as the cherry, peach, and date)

⁴**pit** vb **pit·ted; pit·ting** : to remove the pit from

**pit-a-pat** \ˌpit-i-'pat\ n : PITTER-PATTER — **pit-a-pat** adv or adj

¹**pitch** \'pich\ n 1 : a dark sticky substance left over esp. from distilling tar or petroleum 2 : resin from various conifers — **pitchy** adj

²**pitch** vb 1 : to erect and fix firmly in place ⟨~ a tent⟩ 2 : THROW, FLING 3 : to deliver a baseball to a batter 4 : to toss (as coins) toward a mark 5 : to set at a particular level ⟨~ the voice low⟩ 6 : to fall headlong 7 : to have the front end (as of a ship) alternately plunge and rise 8 : to choose something casually ⟨~ed on a likely spot⟩ 9 : to incline downward : SLOPE

³**pitch** n 1 : the action or a manner of pitching 2 : degree of slope ⟨~ of a roof⟩ 3 : the relative level of some quality or state ⟨a high ~ of excitement⟩ 4 : highness or lowness of sound 5 : an often high-pressure sales talk 6 : the delivery of a baseball to a batter; also : the baseball delivered

**pitch·blende** \'pich-ˌblend\ n : a dark mineral that is the chief source of uranium

¹**pitch·er** \'pich-ər\ n : a container for holding and pouring liquids that usu. has a lip and a handle

²**pitcher** n : one that pitches esp. in a baseball game

**pitcher plant** n : a plant with leaves modified to resemble pitchers in which insects are trapped and digested

**pitch·fork** \'pich-ˌfȯrk\ n : a long-handled fork used esp. in pitching hay

**pitch in** vb 1 : to begin to work 2 : to contribute to a common effort

**pitch·man** \'pich-mən\ n : SALESMAN; esp : one who vends novelties on the streets or from a concession

**pit·e·ous** \'pit-ē-əs\ adj : arousing pity : PITIFUL — **pit·e·ous·ly** adv

**pit·fall** \'pit-ˌfȯl\ n 1 : TRAP, SNARE; esp : a flimsily covered pit used for capturing animals 2 : a hidden danger or difficulty

**pith** \'pith\ n 1 : loose spongy tissue in the center of the stem of vascular plants 2 : the essential part : CORE

**pith·ec·an·thro·pus** \ˌpith-i-'kan-thrə-pəs\ n, pl **-pi** \-ˌpī\ : any of several primitive extinct men from Java

**pithy** \'pith-ē\ adj **pith·i·er; -est** 1 : consisting of or filled with pith 2 : being brief and to the point

**piti·able** \'pit-ē-ə-bəl\ adj : PITIFUL

**piti·ful** \'pit-i-fəl\ adj 1 : arousing or deserving pity ⟨a ~ sight⟩ 2 : MEAN, MEAGER — **piti·ful·ly** \-f-(ə-)lē\ adv

**piti·less** \'pit-i-ləs\ adj : devoid of pity : MERCILESS — **piti·less·ly** adv

**pi·ton** \'pē-ˌtän\ n : a spike, wedge, or peg that can be driven into a rock or ice surface as a support often with an eye through which a rope may pass

**pit·tance** \'pit-²ns\ n : a small portion, amount, or allowance

**pit·ter-pat·ter** \'pit-ər-ˌpat-ər, 'pit-ē-\ n : a rapid succession of light taps or sounds — **pitter-patter** \ˌpit-ər-'pat-ər, ˌpit-ē-\ adv or adj — **pitter-patter** \like adv\ vb

**pi·tu·itary** \pə-'t(y)ü-ə-ˌter-ē\ adj : of, relating to, or being a small oval endocrine gland attached to the brain

**pit viper** *n* : any of various mostly New World specialized venomous snakes with a sensory pit on each side of the head and hollow perforated fangs

¹**pity** \'pit-ē\ *n, pl* **pi·ties** [ME *pite*, fr. OF *pité*, fr. L *pietas* piety, pity, fr. *pius* pious] **1** : sympathetic sorrow : COMPASSION **2** : something to be regretted

²**pity** *vb* **pit·ied; pity·ing** : to feel pity for

¹**piv·ot** \'piv-ət\ *n* : a fixed pin on the end of which something turns — **pivot** *adj* — **piv·ot·al** *adj*

²**pivot** *vb* : to turn on or as if on a pivot

**pix** *pl of* PIC

**pix·ie** *or* **pixy** \'pik-sē\ *n, pl* **pix·ies** : FAIRY; *esp* : a mischievous sprite

**piz·za** \'pēt-sə\ *n* : an open pie made typically of thinly rolled bread dough spread with a spiced mixture (as of tomatoes, cheese, and ground meat) and baked

**piz·zazz** *or* **pi·zazz** \pə-'zaz\ *n* **1** : GLAMOUR **2** : VITALITY

**piz·ze·ria** \,pēt-sə-'rē-ə\ *n* : an establishment where pizzas are made and sold

**piz·zi·ca·to** \,pit-si-'kät-ō\ *adv or adj* : by means of plucking instead of bowing — used as a direction in music

**pj's** \(')pē-'jāz\ *n pl* : PAJAMAS

**pk** *abbr* **1** park **2** peak **3** peck

**pkg** *abbr* package

**pkt** *abbr* **1** packet **2** pocket

**pkwy** *abbr* parkway

**pl** *abbr* **1** place **2** plate **3** plural

¹**plac·ard** \'plak-ərd, -,ärd\ *n* : a notice posted in a public place : POSTER

²**plac·ard** \-,ärd, -ərd\ *vb* **1** : to cover with or as if with placards **2** : to announce by posting

**pla·cate** \'plā-,kāt, 'plak-,āt\ *vb* **pla·cat·ed; pla·cat·ing** : to soothe esp. by concessions : APPEASE — **plac·a·ble** \'plak-ə-bəl, 'plā-kə-\ *adj*

¹**place** \'plās\ *n* [ME, fr. MF, open space, fr. L *platea* broad street, fr. Gk *plateia* (*hodos*), fr. fem. of *platys* broad, flat] **1** : SPACE, ROOM **2** : an indefinite region : AREA **3** : a building or locality used for a special purpose **4** : a center of population **5** : a particular part of a surface : SPOT **6** : relative position in a scale or sequence; *also* : high and esp. second position in a competition **7** : ACCOMMODATION; *esp* : SEAT **8** : JOB; *esp* : public office **9** : a public square

²**place** *vb* **placed; plac·ing** **1** : to distribute in an orderly manner : ARRANGE **2** : to put in a particular place : SET **3** : IDENTIFY **4** : to give an order for ⟨~ a bet⟩ **5** : to rank high and esp. second in a competition

**pla·ce·bo** \plə-'sē-bō\ *n, pl* **-bos** [L, I shall please!] : an inert medication used for its psychological effect or for purposes of comparison in an experiment

**place·hold·er** \'plās-,hōl-dər\ *n* : a symbol in a mathematical or logical expression that may be replaced by the name of any element of a set

**place·kick** \-,kik\ *n* : the kicking of a ball (as a football) placed or held in a stationary position on the ground —

**placekick** *vb* — **place·kick·er** *n*

**place·ment** \'plās-mənt\ *n* : an act or instance of placing

**pla·cen·ta** \plə-'sent-ə\ *n, pl* **-centas** *or* **-cen·tae** \-'sent-(,)ē\ : the structure by which a mammal is nourished and joined to the mother before birth — **pla·cen·tal** \-'sent-ᵊl\ *adj*

**plac·er** \'plas-ər\ *n* : an alluvial or glacial deposit containing particles of valuable mineral

**plac·id** \'plas-əd\ *adj* : UNDISTURBED, PEACEFUL **syn** tranquil, serene, calm — **pla·cid·i·ty** \pla-'sid-ət-ē\ *n* — **plac·id·ly** \'plas-əd-lē\ *adv*

**plack·et** \'plak-ət\ *n* : a slit in a garment

**pla·gia·rize** \'plā-jə-,rīz\ *vb* **-rized; -riz·ing** : to pass off as one's own the ideas or words of another — **pla·gia·rism** \-,riz-əm\ *n* — **pla·gia·rist** \-rəst\ *n*

¹**plague** \'plāg\ *n* **1** : a disastrous evil or influx; *also* : NUISANCE **2** : PESTILENCE; *esp* : a destructive contagious bacterial disease (as bubonic plague)

²**plague** *vb* **plagued; plagu·ing** **1** : to afflict with or as if with disease or disaster **2** : TEASE, TORMENT, HARASS

**plaid** \'plad\ *n* **1** : a rectangular length of tartan worn esp. over the left shoulder as part of the Scottish national costume **2** : a twilled woolen fabric with a tartan pattern **3** : a pattern of unevenly spaced repeated stripes crossing at right angles — **plaid** *adj*

¹**plain** \'plān\ *n* : an extensive area of level or rolling treeless country

²**plain** *adj* **1** : lacking ornament ⟨a ~ dress⟩ **2** : free of extraneous matter **3** : OPEN, UNOBSTRUCTED ⟨~ view⟩ **4** : EVIDENT, OBVIOUS **5** : easily understood : CLEAR **6** : CANDID, BLUNT **7** : SIMPLE, UNCOMPLICATED ⟨~ cooking⟩ **8** : lacking beauty — **plain·ly** *adv* — **plain·ness** \'plān-nəs\ *n*

**plain·clothes·man** \'plān-'klō(th)z-mən, -,man\ *n* : a police officer who does not wear a uniform while on duty : DETECTIVE

**plain·spo·ken** \-'spō-kən\ *adj* : speaking or spoken plainly and esp. bluntly

**plaint** \'plānt\ *n* **1** : LAMENTATION, WAIL **2** : PROTEST, COMPLAINT

**plain·tiff** \'plānt-əf\ *n* : the complaining party in a lawsuit

**plain·tive** \'plānt-iv\ *adj* : expressive of suffering or woe : MELANCHOLY — **plain·tive·ly** *adv*

**plait** \'plāt, 'plat\ *n* **1** : PLEAT **2** : a braid esp. of hair or straw — **plait** *vb*

¹**plan** \'plan\ *n* **1** : a drawing or diagram drawn on a plane **2** : a method for accomplishing something **3** : GOAL, AIM — **plan·less** *adj*

²**plan** *vb* **planned; plan·ning** **1** : to form a plan of : DESIGN ⟨~ a new city⟩ **2** : to devise the accomplishment of ⟨~ the day's work⟩ **3** : INTEND ⟨planned to go⟩ — **plan·ner** *n*

¹**plane** \'plān\ *vb* **planed; plan·ing** : to smooth or level off with or as if with a plane — **plan·er** *n*

²**plane** *n* : any of several shade trees

with large 5-lobed leaves and flowers in globe-shaped heads

³**plane** n : a tool for smoothing or shaping a wood surface

⁴**plane** n 1 : a level or flat surface 2 : a level of existence, consciousness, or development 3 : AIRPLANE 4 : one of the main supporting surfaces of an airplane

⁵**plane** adj 1 : FLAT, LEVEL 2 : dealing with flat surfaces or figures ⟨∼ geometry⟩

**plane·load** \'plān-,lōd\ n : a load that fills an airplane

**plan·et** \'plan-ət\ n [ME planete, fr. OF, fr. LL planeta, modif. of Gk planēt-, planēs, lit., wanderer, fr. planasthai to wander] : a celestial body other than a comet, meteor, or satellite that revolves around the sun — **plan·e·tary** \-ə-,ter-ē\ adj

ception) designed to regulate the number and spacing of children in a family

¹**plant** \'plant\ vb 1 : to set in the ground to grow 2 : ESTABLISH, SETTLE 3 : to stock or provide with something 4 : to place firmly or forcibly 5 : to hide or arrange with intent to deceive

²**plant** n 1 : any of the great group of living things (as mushrooms, seaweeds, or trees) that usu. have no locomotor ability or obvious sense organs and have cellulose cell walls and usu. capacity for indefinite growth 2 : the land, buildings, and machinery used in carrying on a trade or business

¹**plan·tain** \'plant-ᵊn\ n [ME, fr. OF, fr. L plantagin-, plantago, fr. planta sole of the foot; fr. its broad leaves] : any of several short-stemmed weedy herbs with spikes of tiny greenish flowers

## Planets

| symbol | name | mean distance from the sun astronomical units | million miles | period of revolution in days or years | | equatorial diameter in miles |
|---|---|---|---|---|---|---|
| ☿ | Mercury | 0.387 | 36.0 | 88.0 | d. | 3,100 |
| ♀ | Venus | 0.723 | 67.2 | 224.7 | d. | 7,700 |
| ⊕ | Earth | 1.000 | 92.9 | 365.26 | d. | 7,926 |
| ♂ | Mars | 1.524 | 141.5 | 687.0 | d. | 4,200 |
| ♃ | Jupiter | 5.203 | 483.4 | 11.86 | y. | 88,700 |
| ♄ | Saturn | 9.539 | 886.0 | 29.46 | y. | 75,100 |
| ♅ | Uranus | 19.18 | 1782.0 | 84.01 | y. | 29,200 |
| ♆ | Neptune | 30.06 | 2792.0 | 164.8 | y. | 27,700 |
| ♇ | Pluto | 39.44 | 3664.0 | 247.7 | y. | 3,500 |

**plan·e·tar·i·um** \,plan-ə-'ter-ē-əm\ n, pl -iums or -ia \-ē-ə\ 1 : an optical device to project moving images of celestial bodies 2 : a building or room housing a planetarium

**plan·e·tes·i·mal** \,plan-ə-'tes-ə-məl\ n : one of numerous small solid celestial bodies which may have existed during the genesis of the solar system

**plan·e·toid** \'plan-ə-,tȯid\ n : a body resembling a planet; esp : ASTEROID

**plan·e·tol·o·gy** \,plan-ə-'täl-ə-jē\ n, pl -gies : a study that deals with planets and natural satellites — **plan·e·tol·o·gist** \-jəst\ n

**plan·gent** \'plan-jənt\ adj 1 : having a loud reverberating sound 2 : having an expressive esp. plaintive quality — **plan·gen·cy** \-jən-sē\ n

¹**plank** \'plaŋk\ n 1 : a heavy thick board 2 : an article in the platform of a political party

²**plank** vb 1 : to cover with planks 2 : to set or lay down forcibly 3 : to cook and serve on a board

**plank·ing** \'plaŋ-kiŋ\ n : a quantity or covering of planks

**plank·ton** \'plaŋk-tən\ n : the passively floating or weakly swimming animal and plant life of a body of water — **plank·ton·ic** \plaŋk-'tän-ik\ adj

**planned parenthood** n : the practice of birth control measures (as contra-

²**plantain** n [Sp plántano plane tree, banana tree, fr. ML platanus plane tree, alter. of L platanus] : a banana plant with starchy greenish fruit; also : its fruit

**plan·tar** \'plant-ər, 'plan-,tär\ adj : of or relating to the sole of the foot

**plan·ta·tion** \plan-'tā-shən\ n 1 : a large group of trees under cultivation 2 : an agricultural estate worked by resident laborers

**plant·er** \'plant-ər\ n 1 : one that plants or sows; esp : an owner or operator of a plantation 2 : a container for a plant

**plant louse** n : APHID

**plaque** \'plak\ n 1 : an ornamental brooch 2 : a flat thin piece (as of metal) used for decoration; also : a commemorative tablet 3 : a bacteria-harboring film on a tooth

**plash** \'plash\ n : SPLASH — **plash** vb

**plas·ma** \'plaz-mə\ n 1 : the watery part of blood, lymph, or milk 2 : a gas composed of ionized particles — **plas·mat·ic** \plaz-'mat-ik\ adj

¹**plas·ter** \'plas-tər\ n 1 : a dressing consisting of a backing spread with an often medicated substance that clings to the skin (adhesive ∼) 2 : a paste that hardens as it dries and is used for coating walls and ceilings — **plas·tery** \-t(ə-)rē\ adj

**²plaster** *vb* **plas·tered; plas·ter·ing** \-t(ə-)riŋ\ : to cover with plaster — **plas·ter·er** *n*

**plas·ter·board** \'plas-tər-,bōrd\ *n* : a wallboard consisting of fiberboard, paper, or felt over a plaster core

**plaster of par·is** \-'par-əs\ *often cap 2d P* : a white powder made from gypsum and used as a quick-setting paste with water for casts and molds

**¹plas·tic** \'plas-tik\ *adj* [L *plasticus* of molding, fr. Gk *plastikos*, fr. *plassein* to mold, form] **1** : CREATIVE ⟨~ forces in nature⟩ **2** : capable of being molded ⟨~ clay⟩ **3** : characterized by or using modeling ⟨~ arts⟩ *syn* pliable, pliant, ductile, malleable, adaptable — **plas·tic·i·ty** \plas-'tis-ət-ē\ *n*

**²plastic** *n* : a plastic substance; *esp* : a synthetic or processed material that can be formed into rigid objects or into films or filaments

**plastic surgery** *n* : surgery intended to repair or restore lost, mutilated, or deformed parts chiefly by the transfer of tissue — **plastic surgeon** *n*

**¹plat** \'plat\ *n* **1** : a small plot of ground **2** : a plan of a piece of land with actual or proposed features (as lots)

**²plat** *vb* **plat·ted; plat·ting** : to make a plat of

**¹plate** \'plāt\ *n* **1** : a flat thin piece of material **2** : domestic hollowware made of or plated with gold, silver, or base metals **3** : DISH **4** : a rubber slab at the apex of a baseball diamond that must be touched by a base runner in order to score **5** : the molded metal or plastic cast of a page of type to be printed from **6** : a thin sheet of material (as glass) that is coated with a chemical sensitive to light and is used in photography **7** : the part of a denture that fits to the mouth and holds the teeth **8** : something printed from an engraving

**²plate** *vb* **plat·ed; plat·ing** **1** : to arm with armor plate **2** : to overlay with metal (as gold or silver) **3** : to make a printing plate of

**pla·teau** \pla-'tō\ *n, pl* **plateaus** *or* **pla·teaux** \-'tōz\ : a large level area raised above adjacent land on at least one side : TABLELAND

**plate glass** *n* : rolled, ground, and polished sheet glass

**plat·en** \'plat-ᵊn\ *n* **1** : a flat plate of metal; *esp* : one (as the part of a printing press which presses the paper against the type) that exerts or receives pressure **2** : the roller of a typewriter

**plat·form** \'plat-,fȯrm\ *n* **1** : a raised flooring or stage for speakers, performers, or workers **2** : a declaration of the principles on which a group of persons (as a political party) stands

**plat·ing** \'plāt-iŋ\ *n* : a coating of metal plates or plate ⟨the ~ of a ship⟩

**plat·i·num** \'plat-(ᵊ-)nəm\ *n* : a heavy silver-white metallic chemical element used esp. in jewelry

**plat·i·tude** \'plat-ə-,t(y)üd\ *n* : a flat or trite remark — **plat·i·tu·di·nous** \-'t(y)üd-(ᵊ-)nəs\ *adj*

**pla·ton·ic love** \plə-,tän-ik-, plā-\ *n, often cap P* : a close relationship between two persons in which sexual desire has been suppressed or sublimated

**pla·toon** \plə-'tün\ *n* [F *peloton* small detachment, lit., ball, fr. *pelote* little ball, fr. L *pila* ball] **1** : a subdivision of a company-size military unit usu. consisting of two or more squads or sections **2** : a group of football players trained either for offense or for defense and sent into the game as a body

**platoon sergeant** *n* : a noncommissioned officer in the army ranking below a first sergeant

**plat·ter** \'plat-ər\ *n* **1** : a large plate used esp. for serving meat **2** : a phonograph record

**platy** \'plat-ē\ *n, pl* **platy** *or* **plat·ys** *or* **plat·ies** : any of various small stocky often brilliantly colored fish that are popular for tropical aquariums

**platy·pus** \'plat-i-pəs\ *n, pl* **platy·pus·es** *also* **platy·pi** \-,pī\ [NL, fr. Gk *platypous* flat-footed, fr. *platys* broad, flat + *pous* foot] : a small aquatic egg-laying mammal of Australia with webbed feet and a fleshy bill like a duck's

**plau·dit** \'plȯd-ət\ *n* : an act of applause

**plau·si·ble** \'plȯ-zə-bəl\ *adj* [L *plausibilis* worthy of applause, fr. *plausus*, pp. of *plaudere*] : seemingly worthy of belief : PERSUASIVE — **plau·si·bil·i·ty** \,plȯ-zə-'bil-ət-ē\ *n* — **plau·si·bly** \-blē\ *adv*

**¹play** \'plā\ *n* **1** : brisk handling of something (as a weapon) **2** : the course of a game; *also* : a particular act or maneuver in a game **3** : recreational activity; *esp* : the spontaneous activity of children **4** : JEST ⟨said in ~⟩ **5** : the act or an instance of punning **6** : a stage representation of a drama; *also* : a dramatic composition **7** : GAMBLING **8** : OPERATION ⟨bring extra force into ~⟩ **9** : a brisk, fitful, or light movement **10** : free motion (as of part of a machine); *also* : the length of such motion **11** : scope for action **12** : PUBLICITY ⟨made a ~ for her⟩ — **play·ful** \-fəl\ *adj* — **play·ful·ly** \-ē\ *adv* — **play·ful·ness** *n* — **in play** : in condition or position to be played

**²play** *vb* **1** : to engage in recreation : FROLIC **2** : to move aimlessly about : TRIFLE **3** : to deal in a light manner : JEST **4** : to make a pun ⟨~ on words⟩ **5** : to take advantage ⟨~ on fears⟩ **6** : to move or operate in a brisk, irregular, or alternating manner ⟨a flashlight ~ed over the wall⟩ **7** : to perform music ⟨~ on a violin⟩; *also* : to perform (music) on an instrument ⟨~ a waltz⟩ **8** : to perform music upon ⟨~ the piano⟩; *also* : to sound in performance ⟨the organ is ~ing⟩ **9** : to cause to emit sounds ⟨~ a radio⟩ **10** : to act in a dramatic medium; *also* : to act in the character of ⟨~ the hero⟩ **11** : GAMBLE **12** : to behave in a specified way ⟨~ safe⟩; *also* : COOPERATE ⟨~

along with him⟩ **13 :** to deal with; *also* **:** EMPHASIZE ⟨~ up his good qualities⟩ **14 :** to perform for amusement ⟨~ a trick⟩ **15 :** WREAK **16 :** to contend with in a game; *also* **:** to fill a (certain position) on a team **17 :** to make wagers on ⟨~ the races⟩ **18 :** WIELD, PLY **19 :** to keep in action — **play·er** *n*

**pla·ya** \'plī-ə\ *n* **:** the flat bottom of a desert basin that is not drained and becomes a shallow lake at times

**play-act·ing** \'plā-,ak-tiŋ\ *n* **1 :** performance in theatrical productions **2 :** insincere or artificial behavior

**play·back** \'plā-,bak\ *n* **:** an act of reproducing a sound recording often immediately after recording — **play back** \'(')plā-'bak\ *vb*

**play·bill** \'plā-,bil\ *n* **:** a poster advertising the performance of a play; *also* **:** a theater program

**play·book** \-,buk\ *n* **:** a notebook containing diagramed football plays

**play·boy** \-,boi\ *n* **:** a man whose chief interest is the pursuit of pleasure

**play·go·er** \-,gō(-ə)r\ *n* **:** a person who frequently attends plays

**play·ground** \-,graund\ *n* **:** a piece of ground used for games and recreation esp. by children

**play·house** \-,haus\ *n* **1 :** THEATER **2 :** a small house for children to play in

**playing card :** one of a set of 24 to 78 cards marked to show its rank and suit and used to play a game of cards

**play·let** \-lət\ *n* **:** a short play

**play·mate** \-,māt\ *n* **:** a companion in play

**play-off** \'plā-,óf\ *n* **:** a contest or series of contests to break a tie or determine a championship

**play·pen** \'plā-,pen\ *n* **:** a portable enclosure in which a baby or young child may play

**play·suit** \-,süt\ *n* **:** a sports and play outfit for women and children

**play·thing** \-,thiŋ\ *n* **:** TOY

**play·wright** \-,rīt\ *n* **:** a writer of plays

**pla·za** \'plaz-ə, 'pläz-\ *n* [Sp, fr. L *platea* broad street] **1 :** a public square in a city or town **2 :** a shopping center

**plea** \'plē\ *n* **1 :** a defendant's answer in law to charges made against him **2 :** something alleged as an excuse **:** PRETEXT **3 :** ENTREATY, APPEAL

**plead** \'plēd\ *vb* **plead·ed** \'plēd-əd\ *or* **pled** \'pled\; **plead·ing 1 :** to argue before a court or authority ⟨~ a case⟩ **2 :** to answer to a charge or indictment ⟨~ guilty⟩ **3 :** to argue for or against something ⟨~ for acquittal⟩ **4 :** to appeal earnestly ⟨~s for help⟩ **5 :** to offer as a plea (as in defense) ⟨~ed illness⟩ — **plead·er** *n*

**pleas·ant** \'plez-ᵊnt\ *adj* **1 :** giving pleasure **:** AGREEABLE ⟨a ~ experience⟩ **2 :** marked by pleasing behavior or appearance ⟨a ~ person⟩ — **pleas·ant·ly** *adv* — **pleas·ant·ness** *n*

**pleas·ant·ry** \-ᵊn-trē\ *n, pl* **-ries :** a playful or humorous act or speech

**please** \'plēz\ *vb* **pleased; pleas-**

**ing 1 :** to give pleasure or satisfaction to **2 :** LIKE ⟨do as you ~⟩ **3 :** to be the will or pleasure of ⟨may it ~ your Majesty⟩ **4 :** to be willing to ⟨~ come in⟩

**pleas·ing** \'plē-ziŋ\ *adj* **:** giving pleasure — **pleas·ing·ly** *adv*

**plea·sur·able** \'plezh-(ə-)rə-bəl\ *adj* **:** PLEASANT, GRATIFYING — **plea·sur·ably** \-blē\ *adv*

**plea·sure** \'plezh-ər\ *n* **1 :** DESIRE, INCLINATION ⟨await your ~⟩ **2 :** a state of gratification **:** ENJOYMENT **3 :** a source of delight or joy

¹**pleat** \'plēt\ *vb* **1 :** FOLD; *esp* **:** to arrange in pleats **2 :** BRAID

²**pleat** *n* **:** a fold in cloth made by doubling material over on itself **:** PLAIT

**plebe** \'plēb\ *n* **:** a freshman at a military or naval academy

¹**ple·be·ian** \pli-'bē-ən\ *n* **1 :** a member of the Roman plebs **2 :** one of the common people

²**plebeian** *adj* **1 :** of or relating to plebeians **2 :** COMMON, VULGAR

**pleb·i·scite** \'pleb-ə-,sīt, -sət\ *n* **:** a vote of the people (as of a country) on a proposal submitted to them

**plebs** \'plebz\ *n, pl* **ple·bes** \'plē-bēz\ **1 :** the common people of ancient Rome **2 :** the general populace

**plec·trum** \'plek-trəm\ *n, pl* **plec·tra** \-trə\ *or* **plec·trums :** PICK 3

¹**pledge** \'plej\ *n* **1 :** something given as security for the performance of an act **2 :** the state of being held as a security or guaranty **3 :** TOAST **4 :** PROMISE, VOW

²**pledge** *vb* **pledged; pledg·ing 1 :** to deposit as a pledge **2 :** TOAST **3 :** to bind by a pledge **:** PLIGHT **4 :** PROMISE

**ple·na·ry** \'plē-nə-rē, 'plen-ə-\ *adj* **1 :** FULL ⟨~ power⟩ **2 :** including all entitled to attend ⟨~ session⟩

**ple·ni·po·ten·tia·ry** \,plen-ə-pə-'tench-(ə-)rē, -'ten-chē-,er-ē\ *n* **:** a diplomatic agent having full authority — **plenipotentiary** *adj*

**plen·i·tude** \'plen-ə-,t(y)üd\ *n* **1 :** COMPLETENESS **2 :** ABUNDANCE

**plen·te·ous** \'plent-ē-əs\ *adj* **1 :** FRUITFUL **2 :** existing in plenty

**plen·ti·ful** \'plent-i-fəl\ *adj* **1 :** containing or yielding plenty **2 :** ABUNDANT — **plen·ti·ful·ly** \-ē\ *adv*

**plen·ty** \'plent-ē\ *n* [ME *plente*, fr. OF *plenté*, fr. LL *plenitat-, plenitas,* fr. L, fullness, fr. *plenus* full] **:** a more than adequate number or amount

**ple·num** \'plen-əm, 'plēn-əm\ *n, pl* **-nums** *or* **-na** \-ə\ **1 :** a space or all space that is full of matter **2 :** a general assembly of all members esp. of a legislative body

**pleth·o·ra** \'pleth-ə-rə\ *n* **:** an excessive quantity or fullness; *also* **:** PROFUSION

**pleu·ri·sy** \'plùr-ə-sē\ *n* **:** inflammation of the membrane that lines the chest and covers the lungs

**plex·us** \'plek-səs\ *n* **:** an interlacing network esp. of blood vessels or nerves

**pli·able** \'plī-ə-bəl\ *adj* **1 :** FLEXIBLE **2 :** yielding easily to others **syn** plastic, pliant, ductile, malleable, adaptable

**pli·ant** \'plī-ənt\ *adj* 1 : FLEXIBLE 2 : easily influenced : PLIABLE — **pli·an·cy** \-ən-sē\ *n*

**pli·ers** \'plī-(ə)rz\ *n pl* : small pincers with long jaws for bending wire or handling small objects

¹**plight** \'plīt\ *vb* : to put or give in pledge : ENGAGE

²**plight** *n* : CONDITION, STATE; *esp* : a bad state

**plinth** \'plinth\ *n* : the lowest part of the base of an architectural column

**plod** \'pläd\ *vb* **plod·ded; plod·ding** 1 : to walk heavily or slowly : TRUDGE 2 : to work laboriously and monotonously : DRUDGE — **plod·der** *n* — **plod·ding·ly** \-iŋ-lē\ *adv*

**plop** \'pläp\ *vb* **plopped; plop·ping** 1 : to make or move with a sound like that of something dropping into water 2 : to allow the body to drop heavily 3 : to set, drop, or throw heavily — **plop** *n*

¹**plot** \'plät\ *n* 1 : a small area of ground 2 : a ground plan (as of an area) 3 : the main story of a literary work 4 : a secret scheme : INTRIGUE

²**plot** *vb* **plot·ted; plot·ting** 1 : to make a plot or plan of 2 : to mark on or as if on a chart 3 : to plan or contrive esp. secretly — **plot·ter** *n*

**plo·ver** \'pləv-ər, 'plō-vər\ *n, pl* **plover** *or* **plovers** : any of various shorebirds related to the sandpipers but with shorter stouter bills

¹**plow** *or* **plough** \'plaů\ *n* 1 : an implement used to cut, turn over, and partly break up soil 2 : a device operating like a plow; *esp* : SNOWPLOW

²**plow** *or* **plough** *vb* 1 : to open, break up, or work with a plow 2 : to cleave or move through like a plow ⟨a ship ~*ing* the waves⟩ 3 : to proceed laboriously — **plow·able** *adj* — **plow·er** *n*

**plow·boy** \'plaů-,bȯi\ *n* : a boy who guides a plow or leads the horse drawing it

**plow·man** \-mən, -,man\ *n* 1 : a man who guides a plow 2 : a farm laborer

**plow·share** \-,she(ə)r\ *n* : the part of a plow that cuts the earth

**ploy** \'plȯi\ *n* : a tactic intended to embarrass or frustrate an opponent

¹**pluck** \'plək\ *vb* 1 : to pull off or out : PICK; *also* : to pull something from 2 : to pick, pull, or grasp at; *also* : to play (an instrument) in this manner 3 : TUG, TWITCH

²**pluck** *n* 1 : an act or instance of plucking 2 : SPIRIT, COURAGE

**plucky** \'plək-ē\ *adj* **pluck·i·er; -est** : COURAGEOUS, SPIRITED

¹**plug** \'pləg\ *n* 1 : STOPPER; *also* : an obstructing mass 2 : a cake of tobacco 3 : a poor or worn-out horse 4 : a device on the end of a cord for making an electrical connection 5 : a piece of favorable publicity

²**plug** *vb* **plugged; plug·ging** 1 : to stop, make tight, or secure by inserting a plug 2 : HIT, SHOOT 3 : to publicize insistently 4 : PLOD, DRUDGE

**plum** \'pləm\ *n* [ME, fr. OE *plūme*, fr.

L *prunum* plum, fr. Gk *proumnon*] 1 : a smooth-skinned juicy fruit borne by trees related to the peach and cherry; *also* : a tree bearing plums 2 : RAISIN 3 : something excellent; *esp* : something given as recompense esp. for political service

**plum·age** \'plü-mij\ *n* : the feathers of a bird

¹**plumb** \'pləm\ *n* : a weight on the end of a line used esp. by builders to show vertical direction

²**plumb** *adv* 1 : VERTICALLY 2 : EXACTLY; *also* : IMMEDIATELY 3 : COMPLETELY

³**plumb** *vb* : to sound, adjust, or test with a plumb ⟨~ the depth of a well⟩

⁴**plumb** *adj* 1 : VERTICAL 2 : DOWNRIGHT

**plumb·er** \'pləm-ər\ *n* : a workman who fits or repairs water and gas pipes and fixtures

**plumb·ing** \'pləm-iŋ\ *n* : a system of pipes in a building for supplying and carrying off water

¹**plume** \'plüm\ *n* : FEATHER; *esp* : a large, conspicuous, or showy feather — **plumed** \'plümd\ *adj* — **plumy** \'plü-mē\ *adj*

²**plume** *vb* **plumed; plum·ing** 1 : to provide or deck with feathers 2 : to indulge (oneself) in pride

¹**plum·met** \'pləm-ət\ *n* : PLUMB; *also* : a line with a plumb at one end

²**plummet** *vb* : to drop or plunge straight down

¹**plump** \'pləmp\ *vb* 1 : to drop or fall suddenly or heavily 2 : to favor something strongly ⟨~s for the new method⟩

²**plump** *adv* 1 : straight down; *also* : straight ahead 2 : UNQUALIFIEDLY

³**plump** *n* : a sudden heavy fall or blow; *also* : the sound made by it

⁴**plump** *adj* : having a full rounded usu. pleasing form : CHUBBY **syn** fleshy, stout — **plump·ness** *n*

¹**plun·der** \'plən-dər\ *vb* **plun·dered; plun·der·ing** \-d(ə-)riŋ\ : to take the goods of by force or wrongfully : PILLAGE — **plun·der·er** *n*

²**plunder** *n* : something taken by force or theft : LOOT

¹**plunge** \'plənj\ *vb* **plunged; plung·ing** 1 : IMMERSE, SUBMERGE 2 : to enter or cause to enter a state or course of action suddenly or violently ⟨~ into war⟩ 3 : to cast oneself into or as if into water 4 : to gamble heavily and recklessly 5 : to descend suddenly

²**plunge** *n* : an act or instance of plunging

**plung·er** \'plən-jər\ *n* 1 : one that plunges 2 : a sliding piece driven by or against fluid pressure : PISTON 3 : a rubber cup on a handle pushed against an opening to free a waste outlet of an obstruction

**plunk** \'pləŋk\ *vb* 1 : to make or cause to make a hollow metallic sound 2 : to drop heavily or suddenly — **plunk** *n*

**plu·per·fect** \(')plü-'pər-fikt\ *adj* : of, relating to, or constituting a verb tense that denotes an action or state as completed at or before a past time spoken of — **pluperfect** *n*

**plu·ral** \'plur-əl\ *adj* [ME, fr. MF & L; MF *plurel*, fr. L *pluralis*, fr. *plur-*, *plus* more] : of, relating to, or constituting a word form used to denote more than one — **plural** *n*

**plu·ral·i·ty** \plu-'ral-ət-ē\ *n, pl* -**ties** **1** : the state of being plural **2** : an excess of votes over those cast for an opposing candidate **3** : a number of votes cast for one candidate that is greater than the number cast for any other in the contest but less than a majority

**plu·ral·ize** \'plur-ə-,līz\ *vb* -**ized**; -**iz·ing** : to make plural or express in the plural form — **plu·ral·iza·tion** \,plur-ə-lə-'zā-shən\ *n*

**¹plus** \'pləs\ *prep* [L, more] : increased by : with the addition of ⟨3 ∼ 4 equals 7⟩

**²plus** *n, pl* **plus·es** \'pləs-əz\ *also* **plus·ses** **1** : a sign + (**plus sign**) used in mathematics to require addition or designate a positive quantity **2** : an added quantity; *also* : a positive quantity **3** : ADVANTAGE

**³plus** *adj* **1** : requiring addition **2** : having or being in addition to what is anticipated or specified ⟨∼ values⟩

**¹plush** \'pləsh\ *n* : a fabric with a pile longer and less dense than velvet pile — **plushy** *adj*

**²plush** *adj* : notably luxurious — **plush·ly** *adv*

**Plu·to** \'plüt-ō\ *n* : the planet most remote from the sun

**plu·toc·ra·cy** \plü-'täk-rə-sē\ *n, pl* -**cies** **1** : government by the wealthy **2** : a controlling class of rich men — **plu·to·crat** \'plüt-ə-,krat\ *n* — **plu·to·crat·ic** \,plüt-ə-'krat-ik\ *adj*

**plu·ton** \'plü-,tän\ *n* : a large body of intrusive igneous rock

**plu·to·ni·um** \plü-'tō-nē-əm\ *n* : a radioactive chemical element formed by the decay of neptunium

**plu·vi·al** \'plü-vē-əl\ *adj* **1** : of or relating to rain **2** : characterized by abundant rain

**¹ply** \'plī\ *vb* **plied**; **ply·ing** : to twist together ⟨∼ yarns⟩

**²ply** *n, pl* **plies** : one of the folds, thicknesses, or strands of which something (as plywood or yarn) is made

**³ply** *vb* **plied**; **ply·ing** **1** : to use, practice, or work diligently ⟨plies her needle⟩ ⟨∼ a trade⟩ **2** : to keep supplying something to ⟨plied him with liquor⟩ **3** : to go or travel regularly esp. by sea

**Plym·outh Rock** \,plim-əth-\ *n* : any of an American breed of medium-sized single-combed domestic fowls

**ply·wood** \'plī-,wud\ *n* : material made of thin sheets of wood glued and pressed together

**pm** *abbr* premium

**Pm** *symbol* promethium

**PM** *abbr* **1** paymaster **2** police magistrate **3** postmaster **4** post meridiem **5** postmortem **6** prime minister **7** provost marshal

**pmk** *abbr* postmark

**pmt** *abbr* payment

**PN** *abbr* promissory note

**pneu·mat·ic** \n(y)u-'mat-ik\ *adj* **1** : of, relating to, or using air or wind **2** : moved by air pressure **3** : filled with compressed air — **pneu·mat·i·cal·ly** \-i-k(ə-)lē\ *adv*

**pneu·mo·co·ni·o·sis** \'n(y)ü-mō-,kō-nē-'ō-səs\ *n* : a disease of the lungs caused by habitual inhalation of irritant mineral or metallic particles

**pneu·mo·nia** \n(y)u-'mō-nyə\ *n* : an inflammatory disease of the lungs

**pnxt** *abbr* [L *pinxit*] he painted it

**Po** *symbol* polonium

**PO** *abbr* **1** petty officer **2** postal order **3** post office

**¹poach** \'pōch\ *vb* [ME *pochen*, fr. MF *pocher*, fr. OF *pochier*, lit., to put into a bag, fr. *poche* bag, pocket, of Gmc origin] : to cook (as an egg or fish) in simmering liquid

**²poach** *vb* : to hunt or fish unlawfully — **poach·er** *n*

**POC** *abbr* port of call

**pock** \'päk\ *n* : a small swelling on the skin (as in smallpox); *also* : its scar

**¹pock·et** \'päk-ət\ *n* **1** : a small bag open at the top or side inserted in a garment **2** : supply of money : MEANS **3** : RECEPTACLE, CONTAINER **4** : a small isolated area or group **5** : a small body of ore — **pock·et·ful** *n*

**²pocket** *vb* **1** : to put in or as if in a pocket **2** : STEAL **3** : to put up with ⟨∼ an insult⟩

**³pocket** *adj* **1** : small enough to fit in a pocket; *also* : SMALL, MINIATURE **2** : of or relating to money **3** : carried in or paid from one's own pocket

**pock·et·book** \-,buk\ *n* **1** : PURSE; *also* : HANDBAG **2** : financial resources

**pocket gopher** *n* : any of several burrowing American rodents with small eyes, short ears, and large cheek pouches opening beside the mouth

**pock·et·knife** \-,nīf\ *n* : a knife with a folding blade to be carried in the pocket

**pocket veto** *n* : an indirect veto of a legislative bill by an executive through retention of the bill unsigned until after adjournment of the legislature

**pock·mark** \'päk-,märk\ *n* : the scar left by a pock — **pock·marked** \-,märkt\ *adj*

**po·co** \,pō-kō, 'pō-\ *adv* [It, little, fr. L *paucus*] : SOMEWHAT — used to qualify a direction in music ⟨∼ allegro⟩

**po·co a po·co** \,pō-kō-ä-'pō-kō, ,pō-kō-ä-'pō-\ *adv* : little by little : by small degrees : GRADUALLY

**po·co·sin** \pə-'kōs-ᵊn\ *n* : an upland swamp of the coastal plain of the southeastern U.S.

**pod** \'päd\ *n* **1** : a dry fruit (as of a pea) that splits open when ripe **2** : a compartment (as for a jet engine) under an airplane **3** : a detachable compartment (as for personnel, a power unit, or an instrument) on a spacecraft

**POD** *abbr* pay on delivery

**po·di·a·try** \pə-'dī-ə-trē, pō-\ *n* : the care and treatment of the human

# podium • pol

**foot** in health and disease — **po·di·a·trist** \pə-ˈdī-ə-trəst, pō-\ n

**po·di·um** \ˈpōd-ē-əm\ n, pl **podiums** or **po·dia** \-ē-ə\ **1** : a dais esp. for an orchestral conductor **2** : LECTERN

**POE** abbr **1** port of embarkation **2** port of entry

**po·em** \ˈpō-əm\ n : a composition in verse

**po·esy** \ˈpō-ə-zē\ n, : POETRY

**po·et** \ˈpō-ət\ n [ME, fr. OF poete, fr. L poeta, fr. Gk poiētēs maker, poet, fr. poiein to make, create] : a writer of poetry; also : a creative artist of great sensitivity — **po·et·ess** \-əs\ n

**po·et·as·ter** \ˈpō-ət-ˌas-tər\ n : an inferior poet

**poetic justice** n : an outcome in which vice is punished and virtue rewarded usu. in a manner peculiarly or ironically appropriate

**po·et·ry** \ˈpō-ə-trē\ n **1** : metrical writing **2** : POEMS — **po·et·ic** \pō-ˈet-ik\ or **po·et·i·cal** \-i-kəl\ adj

**po·grom** \pə-ˈgräm, ˈpō-grəm, ˈpäg-rəm\ n [Yiddish, fr. Russ, lit., devastation] : an organized massacre of helpless people and esp. of Jews

**poi** \ˈpȯi\ n, pl **poi** or **pois** : a Hawaiian food of taro root cooked, pounded, and kneaded to a paste and often allowed to ferment

**poi·gnant** \ˈpȯi-nyənt\ adj **1** : painfully affecting the feelings (~ grief) **2** : deeply moving (~ scene) — **poi·gnan·cy** \-nyən-sē\ n

**poi·lu** \pwäl-ˈ(y)ü\ n : a French soldier

**poin·ci·ana** \ˌpȯin-sē-ˈan-ə\ n : any of a genus of ornamental tropical leguminous trees or shrubs with bright orange or red flowers

**poin·set·tia** \pȯin-ˈset-ē-ə, -ˈset-ə\ n : a showy tropical American spurge that has scarlet bracts around its small greenish flowers

**¹point** \ˈpȯint\ n **1** : an individual detail; also : the most important essential **2** : PURPOSE **3** : a geometric element that has position but no size **4** : a particular place : LOCALITY **5** : a particular stage or degree **6** : a sharp end : TIP **7** : a projecting piece of land **8** : a punctuation mark; esp : PERIOD **9** : a decimal mark **10** : one of the divisions of the compass **11** : a unit of counting (as in a game score) — **pointless** adj — **beside the point** : IRRELEVANT — **in point** : to the point — **to the point** : RELEVANT, PERTINENT

**²point** vb **1** : to furnish with a point : SHARPEN **2** : PUNCTUATE **3** : to separate (a decimal fraction) from an integer by a decimal point **4** : to indicate the position of esp. by extending a finger **5** : to direct attention to (~ out an error) **6** : AIM, DIRECT **7** : to lie extended, aimed, or turned in a particular direction : FACE, LOOK

**point-blank** \ˈpȯint-ˈblaŋk\ adj **1** : so close to the target that a missile fired will travel in a straight line to the mark **2** : DIRECT, BLUNT

**point·ed** \ˈpȯint-əd\ adj **1** : having a point **2** : being to the point : DIRECT **3** : aimed at a particular person or group; also : CONSPICUOUS, MARKED — **point·ed·ly** adv

**point·er** \ˈpȯint-ər\ n **1** : one that points out : INDICATOR **2** : a large short-haired hunting dog **3** : HINT, TIP

**poin·til·lism** \ˈpwa(n)-tē-ˌ(y)iz-əm, ˈpȯint-ˈl-ˌiz-əm\ n : the theory or practice in painting of applying small strokes or dots of color to a surface so that from a distance they blend together — **poin·til·list** also **poin·til·liste** \ˌpwa(n)-tē-ˈ(y)ēst, ˈpȯint-ˈl-əst\ n or adj

**point of no return** : a critical point (as in a course of action) at which turning back or reversal is not possible

**point of view** : a position from which something is considered or evaluated

**¹poise** \ˈpȯiz\ vb **poised; pois·ing** : BALANCE

**²poise** n **1** : BALANCE **2** : self-possessed composure of bearing; also : a particular way of carrying oneself

**¹poi·son** \ˈpȯiz-ᵊn\ n [ME, fr. OF, drink, poisonous drink, poison, fr. L potion-, potio drink, fr. potare to drink] : a substance that through its chemical action can injure or kill — **poi·son·ous** \-(ᵊ-)nəs\ adj

**²poison** vb **poi·soned; poi·son·ing** \ˈpȯiz-(ᵊ-)niŋ\ **1** : to injure or kill with poison **2** : to treat or taint with poison **3** : to affect destructively : CORRUPT (~ed her mind) — **poi·son·er** \ˈpȯiz-(ᵊ-)nər\ n

**poison hemlock** n : a large branching poisonous herb of the carrot family with finely divided leaves and white flowers

**poison ivy** n : a usu. climbing plant related to sumac that has shiny 3-parted leaves and may irritate the skin of one who touches it

**poison oak** n : any of several plants closely related to poison ivy and with similar properties

**poison sumac** n : a smooth shrubby American swamp plant with pinnate leaves, greenish flowers, greenish white berries, and irritating properties similar to the related poison ivy

**¹poke** \ˈpōk\ n : BAG, SACK

**²poke** vb **pok·ing 1** : PROD; also : to stir up by prodding **2** : to make a prodding or jabbing movement esp. repeatedly **3** : HIT, PUNCH **4** : to thrust forward obtrusively **5** : RUMMAGE **6** : MEDDLE, PRY **7** : DAWDLE

**³poke** n : a quick thrust; also : PUNCH

**¹pok·er** \ˈpō-kər\ n : a metal rod for stirring a fire

**²pok·er** \ˈpō-kər\ n : any of several card games played with a deck of 52 cards in which each player bets on the superiority of his hand

**poke·weed** \ˈpōk-ˌwēd\ n : a coarse American perennial herb with clusters of white flowers and dark purple juicy berries

**poky** also **pok·ey** \ˈpō-kē\ aaj **pok·i·er; -est 1** : being small and cramped **2** : SHABBY, DULL **3** : annoyingly slow

**pol** \ˈpäl\ n : POLITICIAN

**Pol** *abbr* Poland; Polish

**po·lar** \'pō-lər\ *adj* **1 :** of or relating to a pole (as of a sphere or magnet) **2 :** of or relating to a geographical pole

**polar bear** *n* **:** a large creamy-white bear that inhabits arctic regions

**Po·lar·is** \pə-'lar-əs\ *n* **:** NORTH STAR

**po·lar·i·ty** \pō-'lar-ət-ē, pə-\ *n, pl* **-ties :** the quality or state of having poles; *esp* **:** the quality of having opposite negative and positive charges of electricity or of having opposing magnetic poles

**po·lar·iza·tion** \,pō-lə-rə-'zā-shən\ *n* **1 :** the action of polarizing **:** the state of being polarized **2 :** concentration about opposing extremes

**po·lar·ize** \'pō-lə-,rīz\ *vb* **-ized; -iz·ing 1 :** to cause to have magnetic poles **2 :** to cause (light waves) to vibrate in a definite way

**pol·der** \'pōl-dər, 'päl-\ *n* **:** a tract of low land reclaimed from the sea

**¹pole** \'pōl\ *n* **:** a long slender piece of wood or metal ⟨telephone ∼⟩

**²pole** *n* **1 :** either end of an axis esp. of the earth **2 :** either of the terminals of an electric battery **3 :** one of two or more regions in a magnetized body at which the magnetism is concentrated

**Pole** \'pōl\ *n* **:** a native or inhabitant of Poland

**pole·ax** \'pōl-,aks\ *n* **:** a battle-ax with a short handle and a cutting edge or point opposite the blade

**pole·cat** \'pōl-,kat\ *n, pl* **polecats** *or* **polecat 1 :** a European carnivorous mammal of which the ferret is considered a domesticated variety **2 :** SKUNK

**po·lem·ic** \pə-'lem-ik\ *n* **:** the art or practice of disputation — usu. used in pl. — **polemic** *or* **po·lem·i·cal** \-i-kəl\ *adj* — **po·lem·i·cist** \-səst\ *n*

**pole·star** \'pōl-,stär\ *n* **1 :** NORTH STAR **2 :** a directing principle **:** GUIDE

**pole vault** *n* **:** a track-and-field contest in which each contestant uses a pole to vault for height — **pole-vault** *vb* — **pole-vault·er** *n*

**¹po·lice** \pə-'lēs\ *n, pl* **police** [MF, government, fr. LL *politia*, fr. Gk *politeia*, fr. *politeuein* to be a citizen, engage in political activity, fr. *politēs* citizen, fr. *polis* city, state] **1 :** the department of government that keeps public order and safety, enforces the laws, and detects and prosecutes lawbreakers; *also* **:** the members of this department **2 :** a private organization resembling a police force; *also* **:** its members **3 :** the action or process of cleaning and putting in order; *also* **:** military personnel detailed to perform this function

**²police** *vb* **po·liced; po·lic·ing 1 :** to control, regulate, or keep in order esp. by use of police ⟨∼ a highway⟩ **2 :** to make clean and put in order ⟨∼ a camp⟩

**po·lice·man** \-mən\ *n* **:** a member of a police force — **po·lice·wom·an** \-,wum-ən\ *n*

**police state** *n* **:** a state characterized by repressive, arbitrary, totalitarian rule by means of secret police

**¹pol·i·cy** \'päl-ə-sē\ *n, pl* **-cies 1 :** wisdom in the management of affairs **2 :** a definite course or method of action selected to guide and determine present and future decisions

**²policy** *n, pl* **-cies :** a writing whereby a contract of insurance is made

**pol·i·cy·hold·er** \'päl-ə-sē-,hōl-dər\ *n* **:** one granted an insurance policy

**po·lio** \'pō-lē-,ō\ *n* **:** POLIOMYELITIS — **polio** *adj*

**po·lio·my·eli·tis** \-,mī-ə-'līt-əs\ *n* **:** an acute virus disease marked by inflammation of the nerve cells of the spinal cord

**¹pol·ish** \'päl-ish\ *vb* **1 :** to make smooth and glossy usu. by rubbing **2 :** to refine or improve in manners or condition **3 :** to bring to a highly developed, finished, or refined state

**²polish** *n* **1 :** a smooth glossy surface **:** LUSTER **2 :** REFINEMENT, CULTURE **3 :** the action or process of polishing

**Pol·ish** \'pō-lish\ *n* **:** the language of Poland — **Polish** *adj*

**polit** *abbr* political; politician

**po·lit·bu·ro** \'päl-ət-,byùr-ō, 'pō-lət-, pə-'lit-\ *n* **:** the principal policymaking committee of a Communist party

**po·lite** \pə-'līt\ *adj* **po·lit·er; -est 1 :** REFINED, CULTIVATED ⟨∼ society⟩ **2 :** marked by correct social conduct **:** COURTEOUS; *also* **:** CONSIDERATE, TACTFUL — **po·lite·ly** *adv* — **po·lite·ness** *n*

**po·li·tesse** \,päl-i-'tes\ *n* **:** formal politeness

**pol·i·tic** \'päl-ə-,tik\ *adj* **1 :** wise in promoting a policy ⟨a ∼ statesman⟩ **2 :** shrewdly tactful ⟨a ∼ move⟩

**po·lit·i·cal** \pə-'lit-i-kəl\ *adj* **1 :** of or relating to government or politics **2 :** involving or charged or concerned with acts against a government or a political system ⟨∼ criminals⟩ — **po·lit·i·cal·ly** \-k(ə-)lē\ *adv*

**pol·i·ti·cian** \,päl-ə-'tish-ən\ *n* **:** a person actively engaged in government or politics

**pol·i·tick** \'päl-ə-,tik\ *vb* **:** to engage in political discussion or activity

**po·lit·i·co** \pə-'lit-i-,kō\ *n, pl* **-cos** *also* **-coes :** POLITICIAN

**pol·i·tics** \'päl-ə-,tiks\ *n sing or pl* **1 :** the art or science of government, of guiding or influencing governmental policy, or of winning and holding control over a government **2 :** political affairs or business; *esp* **:** competition between groups or individuals for power and leadership **3 :** political opinions

**pol·i·ty** \'päl-ət-ē\ *n, pl* **-ties :** a politically organized unit; *also* **:** the form or constitution of such a unit

**pol·ka** \'pōl-kə\ *n* [Czech, fr. Pol *Polka* Polish woman, fem. of *Polak* Pole] **:** a lively couple dance of Bohemian origin; *also* **:** music for this dance — **polka** *vb*

**¹poll** \'pōl\ *n* **1 :** HEAD **2 :** the casting and recording of votes; *also* **:** the total vote cast **3 :** the place where votes are cast — usu. used in pl. **4 :** a questioning of persons to obtain information or opinions to be analyzed

²**poll** vb **1 :** to cut off or shorten a growth or part of **:** CLIP, SHEAR **2 :** to receive and record the votes of **3 :** to receive (as votes) in an election **4 :** to question in a poll

**pol·lack** or **pol·lock** \'päl-ək\ n, pl **pollack** or **pollock :** an important Atlantic food fish that is related to the cods

**pol·len** \'päl-ən\ n [NL fr. L, fine flour] **:** a mass of male spores of a seed plant usu. appearing as a yellow dust

**pol·li·na·tion** \,päl-ə-'nā-shən\ n **:** the carrying of pollen to the female part of a plant to fertilize the seed — **pol·li·nate** \'päl-ə-,nāt\ vb — **pol·li·na·tor** \-ər\ n

**pol·li·wog** or **pol·ly·wog** \'päl-ē-,wäg\ n **:** TADPOLE

**poll·ster** \'pōl-stər\ n **:** one that conducts a poll or compiles data obtained by a poll

**poll tax** n **:** a tax of a fixed amount per person levied on adults and often payable as a requirement for voting

**pol·lute** \pə-'lüt\ vb **pol·lut·ed; pol·lut·ing :** to make impure; esp **:** to contaminate with man-made waste — **pol·lut·ant** \-'lüt-ᵊnt\ n — **pol·lut·er** n — **pol·lu·tion** \-'lü-shən\ n

**po·lo** \'pō-lō\ n **:** a game played by two teams of players on horseback using long-handled mallets to drive a wooden ball

**po·lo·ni·um** \pə-'lō-nē-əm\ n [NL, fr. ML Polonia Poland, birthplace of its discoverer, Mme. Curie] **:** a radioactive metallic chemical element

**pol·ter·geist** \'pōl-tər-,gīst\ n [G, fr. poltern to knock + geist spirit, fr. Old High German] **:** a noisy usu. mischievous ghost held to be responsible for unexplained noises (as rappings)

**pol·troon** \päl-'trün\ n **:** COWARD

**poly·clin·ic** \,päl-i-'klin-ik\ n **:** a clinic or hospital treating diseases of many sorts

**poly·crys·tal·line** \-'kris-tə-lən\ adj **:** composed of more than one crystal — **poly·crys·tal** \'päl-i,kris-tᵊl\ n

**poly·es·ter** \'päl-ē-,es-tər\ n **:** a complex ester used esp. in making fibers or plastics

**poly·eth·yl·ene** \,päl-ē-'eth-ə-,lēn\ n **:** one of various lightweight plastics resistant to chemicals and moisture that are used in packaging

**po·lyg·a·my** \pə-'lig-ə-mē\ n **:** the practice of having more than one wife or husband at one time — **po·lyg·a·mist** \-məst\ n — **po·lyg·a·mous** \-məs\ adj

**poly·glot** \'päl-i-,glät\ adj **1 :** speaking or writing several languages **2 :** containing or made up of several languages — **polyglot** n

**poly·gon** \'päl-i-,gän\ n **:** a closed plane figure bounded by straight lines — **po·lyg·o·nal** \pə-'lig-ən-ᵊl\ adj

**poly·graph** \'päl-i-,graf\ n **:** an instrument for recording variations of several different pulsations (as of physiological variables) simultaneously

**poly·he·dron** \,päl-i-'hē-drən\ n **:** a solid formed by plane faces — **poly·he·dral** \-drəl\ adj

**poly·math** \'päl-i-,math\ n **:** a person of encyclopedic learning

**poly·mer** \'päl-ə-mər\ n **:** a substance formed by union of small molecules of the same kind — **pol·y·mer·ic** \,päl-ə-'mer-ik\ adj — **po·ly·mer·iza·tion** \pə-,lim-ə-rə-'zā-shən\ n

**Poly·ne·sian** \,päl-ə-'nē-zhən\ n **1 :** a member of any of the native peoples of Polynesia **2 :** a group of Austronesian languages spoken in Polynesia — **Polynesian** adj

**poly·no·mi·al** \,päl-ə-'nō-mē-əl\ n **:** an algebraic expression having two or more terms — **polynomial** adj

**pol·yp** \'päl-əp\ n **1 :** an animal (as a coral) with a hollow cylindrical body closed at one end **2 :** a projecting mass of overgrown membrane (a rectal ~)

**po·lyph·o·ny** \pə-'lif-ə-nē\ n **:** music consisting of two or more melodically independent but harmonizing voice parts — **poly·phon·ic** \,päl-i-'fän-ik\ adj

**poly·sty·rene** \,päl-i-'stīr-,ēn\ n **:** a rigid transparent nonconducting thermoplastic used esp. in molded products and foams

**poly·syl·lab·ic** \,päl-i-sə-'lab-ik\ adj **1 :** having more than three syllables **2 :** characterized by polysyllabic words

**poly·syl·la·ble** \'päl-i-,sil-ə-bəl\ n **:** a polysyllabic word

**poly·tech·nic** \,päl-i-'tek-nik\ adj **:** of, relating to, or instructing in many technical arts or applied sciences

**poly·the·ism** \'päl-i-thē-,iz-əm\ n **:** belief in or worship of many gods — **poly·the·ist** \-,thē-əst\ adj or n — **poly·the·is·tic** \,päl-i-thē-'is-tik\ adj

**poly·un·sat·u·rat·ed** \'päl-ē-,ən-'sach-ə-,rāt-əd\ adj, of an oil or fatty acid **:** rich in carbon atoms that can combine with other atoms to form a new compound

**po·made** \pō-'mäd, -'mād\ n **:** a perfumed unguent esp. for the hair or scalp

**pome·gran·ate** \'päm-(ə-),gran-ət\ n [ME poumgarnet, fr. MF pomme grenate, lit., seedy apple, fr. pomme apple (fr. LL pomum, fr. L, fruit) + grenate seedy, fr. L granatus, fr. granum grain] **:** a tropical reddish fruit with many seeds and an edible crimson pulp; also **:** the tree that bears it

¹**pom·mel** \'pəm-əl, 'päm-\ n **1 :** the knob on the hilt of a sword **2 :** the knoblike bulge at the front and top of a saddlebow

²**pom·mel** \'pəm-əl\ vb **-meled** or **-melled; -mel·ing** or **-mel·ling** \-(ə-)liŋ\ **:** PUMMEL

**pomp** \'pämp\ n **1 :** brilliant display **:** SPLENDOR **2 :** OSTENTATION

**pom·pa·dour** \'päm-pə-,dōr\ n **:** a style of dressing the hair high over the forehead

**pom·pa·no** \'päm-pə-,nō, 'pəm-\ n, pl **-no** or **-nos :** a food fish of the southern Atlantic coast

**pom–pom** \'päm-,päm\ n **:** an ornamental ball or tuft used on a cap or costume

**pom·pon** \'päm-,pän\ *n* **1** : POM-POM **2** : a chrysanthemum or dahlia with small rounded flower heads

**pomp·ous** \'päm-pəs\ *adj* **1** : suggestive of pomp; *esp* : OSTENTATIOUS **2** : pretentiously dignified : SELF-IMPORTANT **3** : excessively elevated or ornate **syn** showy, pretentious — **pom·pos·i·ty** \päm-'päs-ət-ē\ *n* — **pomp·ous·ly** *adv*

**pon·cho** \'pän-chō\ *n, pl* **ponchos 1** : a cloak resembling a blanket with a slit in the middle for the head **2** : a waterproof garment resembling a poncho

**pond** \'pänd\ *n* : a small body of water

**pon·der** \'pän-dər\ *vb* **pon·dered; pon·der·ing** \-d(ə-)riŋ\ **1** : to weigh in the mind **2** : MEDITATE **3** : to deliberate over

**pon·der·o·sa pine** \,pän-də-,rō-sə-, -zə-\ *n* : a tall timber tree of western No. America with long needles; *also* : its wood

**pon·der·ous** \'pän-d(ə-)rəs\ *adj* **1** : of very great weight ⟨a ~ stone⟩ **2** : UNWIELDY, CLUMSY ⟨a ~ weapon⟩ **3** : oppressively dull ⟨a ~ speech⟩ **syn** cumbrous, cumbersome, weighty

**pone** \'pōn\ *n, South & Midland* : an oval-shaped cornmeal cake; *also* : corn bread in the form of pones

**pon·gee** \pän-'jē\ *n* : a thin soft tan fabric

**pon·iard** \'pän-yərd\ *n* : DAGGER

**pon·tiff** \'pänt-əf\ *n* : BISHOP; *esp* : POPE — **pon·tif·i·cal** \pän-'tif-i-kəl\ *adj*

**pon·tif·i·cals** \pän-'tif-i-kəlz\ *n pl* : the insignia worn by a bishop when celebrating a pontifical mass

**¹pon·tif·i·cate** \pän-'tif-i-kət, -ə-,kāt\ *n* : the state, office, or term of office of a pontiff

**²pon·tif·i·cate** \pän-'tif-ə-,kāt\ *vb* **-cat·ed; -cat·ing** : to deliver dogmatic opinions

**pon·toon** \pän-'tün\ *n* **1** : a flat-bottomed boat; *esp* : a flat-bottomed boat, float, or frame used in building floating temporary bridges **2** : a float esp. of an airplane

**po·ny** \'pō-nē\ *n, pl* **ponies** : a small horse

**po·ny·tail** \-,tāl\ *n* : a style of arranging hair to resemble the tail of a pony

**pooch** \'püch\ *n* : DOG

**poo·dle** \'püd-ᵊl\ *n* [G *pudel*, short for *pudelhund*, fr. *pudeln* to splash (fr. *pudel* puddle + *hund* dog] : an active dog with a heavy curly coat

**pooh–pooh** \'pü-,pü\ *also* **pooh** \'pü\ *vb* **1** : to express contempt or impatience **2** : DERIDE, SCORN

**¹pool** \'pül\ *n* **1** : a small and rather deep body of usu. fresh water **2** : a small body of standing liquid

**²pool** *n* **1** : all the money bet on the result of a particular event **2** : any of several games of billiards played on a table (**pool table**) having six pockets **3** : the amount contributed by the

participants in a joint venture **4** : a combination between competing firms for mutual profit **5** : a readily available supply

**³pool** *vb* : to contribute to a common fund or effort

**¹poop** \'püp\ *n* : an enclosed superstructure at the stern of a ship

**²poop** *n, slang* : INFORMATION

**poop deck** *n* : a partial deck above a ship's main afterdeck

**poor** \'pu̇r\ *adj* **1** : lacking material possessions ⟨~ people⟩ **2** : less than adequate : MEAGER ⟨~ crop⟩ **3** : arousing pity ⟨~ fellows⟩ **4** : inferior in quality or value ⟨~ sportsmanship⟩ **5** : UNPRODUCTIVE, BARREN ⟨~ soil⟩ **6** : fairly unsatisfactory ⟨~ prospects⟩; *also* : UNFAVORABLE ⟨~ opinion⟩ **syn** bad, wrong — **poor·ly** *adv*

**poor boy** \'pō(r)-,bȯi\ *n* : SUBMARINE 2

**poor·house** \'pu̇r-,hau̇s\ *n* : a publicly supported home for needy or dependent persons

**poor-mouth** \-,mau̇th, -,mau̇th\ *vb* : to plead poverty as a defense

**¹pop** \'päp\ *vb* **popped; pop·ping 1** : to go, come, enter, or issue forth suddenly or quickly ⟨~ into bed⟩ **2** : to put or thrust suddenly ⟨~ questions⟩ **3** : to burst or cause to burst with or make a sharp sound **4** : to protrude from the sockets **5** : SHOOT **6** : to hit a pop-up

**²pop** *n* **1** : a sharp explosive sound **2** : SHOT **3** : a flavored soft drink

**³pop** *n* : FATHER

**⁴pop** *adj* **1** : POPULAR ⟨~ music⟩ **2** : of or relating to pop music ⟨~ singer⟩ **3** : of, relating to, or constituting a mass culture esp. of the young widely disseminated through the mass media ⟨~ society⟩ **4** : of, relating to, or imitating pop art ⟨~ painter⟩

**⁵pop** *n* : pop music, art, or culture

**⁶pop** *abbr* population

**pop art** *n* : art in which commonplace objects (as road signs, comic strips, or soup cans) are used as subject matter and are often physically incorporated in the work — **pop artist** *n*

**pop·corn** \'päp-,kȯrn\ *n* : an Indian corn whose kernels burst open into a white starchy mass when heated; *also* : the burst kernels

**pope** \'pōp\ *n, often cap* : the head of the Roman Catholic Church

**pop-eyed** \'päp-'īd\ *adj* : having eyes that bulge (as from disease)

**pop fly** *n* : a short high fly in baseball

**pop·gun** \'päp-,gən\ *n* : a toy gun for shooting pellets with compressed air

**pop·in·jay** \'päp-ən-,jā\ *n* [ME *papejay* parrot, fr. MF *papegai, papejai*, fr. Ar *babghā*] : a strutting supercilious person

**pop·lar** \'päp-lər\ *n* : any of various slender quick-growing trees related to the willows

**pop·lin** \'päp-lən\ *n* : a strong plain-woven fabric with crosswise ribs

**pop-off** \'päp-,ȯf\ *n* : one who talks loosely or loudly

**pop·over** \'päp-,ō-vər\ *n* : a biscuit

made from a thin batter rich in egg and expanded by baking into a hollow shell

**pop·per** \'päp-ər\ n : a utensil for popping corn

**pop·py** \'päp-ē\ n, pl **pop·pies** : any of several herbs that have showy flowers including one that yields opium

**pop·py·cock** \'päp-ē-,käk\ n : empty talk : NONSENSE

**pop·u·lace** \'päp-yə-ləs\ n 1 : the common people 2 : POPULATION

**pop·u·lar** \'päp-yə-lər\ adj 1 : of or relating to the general public ⟨~ government⟩ 2 : easy to understand ⟨PLAIN ⟨~ style⟩ 3 : INEXPENSIVE ⟨~ rates⟩ 4 : widely accepted ⟨~ notion⟩ 5 : commonly liked or approved ⟨~ teacher⟩ — **pop·u·lar·i·ty** \,päp-yə-'lar-ət-ē\ n — **pop·u·lar·ize** \'päp-yə-lə-,rīz\ vb — **pop·u·lar·ly** \-lər-lē\ adv

**pop·u·late** \'päp-yə-,lāt\ vb -**lat·ed**; -**lat·ing** 1 : to have a place in : INHABIT 2 : PEOPLE

**pop·u·la·tion** \,päp-yə-'lā-shən\ n 1 : the people or number of people in a country or area 2 : the individuals under consideration (as in statistical sampling)

**population explosion** n : a pyramiding of a living population; esp : the great increase in human numbers that is usu. related to both increased survival and increased reproduction

**pop·u·list** \'päp-yə-ləst\ n : a believer in or advocate of the rights, wisdom, or virtues of the common people — **pop·u·lism** \-,liz-əm\ n

**pop·u·lous** \'päp-yə-ləs\ adj 1 : densely populated 2 : CROWDED — **pop·u·lous·ness** n

**pop-up** \'päp-,əp\ n : a short high fly in baseball

**POR** abbr pay on return

**por·ce·lain** \'pȯr-s(ə-)lən\ n : a fine-grained translucent ceramic ware

**por·ce·lain·ize** \'pȯr-s(ə-)lə-,nīz\ vb -**ized**; -**iz·ing** : to fire a vitreous coating on (as steel)

**porch** \'pȯrch\ n : a covered entrance usu. with a separate roof : VERANDA

**por·cine** \'pȯr-,sīn\ adj : of, relating to, or suggesting swine

**por·cu·pine** \'pȯr-kyə-,pīn\ n [ME porkepin, fr. MF porc espin, fr. It porcospino, fr. L porcus pig + spina spine, prickle] : a mammal having stiff sharp easily detachable spines mingled with its hair

¹**pore** \'pȯr\ vb **pored**; **por·ing** 1 : to read studiously or attentively ⟨~ over a book⟩ 2 : PONDER, REFLECT

²**pore** n : a tiny hole or space (as in the skin or soil) — **pored** \'pȯrd\ adj

**pork** \'pȯrk\ n : the flesh of swine dressed for use as food

**pork barrel** n : a government project or appropriation yielding rich patronage benefits

**pork·er** \'pȯr-kər\ n : HOG; esp : a young pig suitable for use as fresh pork

**por·nog·ra·phy** \pȯr-'näg-rə-fē\ n : the depiction (as in writing) of erotic behavior designed primarily to cause sexual excitement — **por·no·graph·ic** \,pȯr-nə-'graf-ik\ adj

**po·rous** \'pȯr-əs\ adj 1 : full of pores 2 : permeable to fluids : ABSORPTIVE — **po·ros·i·ty** \pə-'räs-ət-ē\ n

**por·phy·ry** \'pȯr-f(ə-)rē\ n, pl -**ries** : a rock consisting of feldspar crystals embedded in a compact fine-grained groundmass — **por·phy·rit·ic** \,pȯr-fə-'rit-ik\ adj

**por·poise** \'pȯr-pəs\ n [ME porpoys, fr. MF porpois, fr. ML porcopiscis, fr. L porcus pig + piscis fish] 1 : any of several small blunt-snouted whales 2 : any of several dolphins

**por·ridge** \'pȯr-ij\ n : a soft food made by boiling meal of grains or legumes in milk or water

**por·rin·ger** \-ən-jər\ n : a low one-handled metal bowl or cup for children

¹**port** \'pȯrt\ n 1 : HARBOR 2 : a city with a harbor 3 : AIRPORT

²**port** n 1 : an inlet or outlet (as in an engine) for a fluid 2 : PORTHOLE

³**port** n : BEARING, CARRIAGE

⁴**port** n : the left side of a ship or airplane looking forward — **port** adj

⁵**port** vb : to turn or put a helm to the left

⁶**port** n : a fortified sweet wine

**Port** abbr Portugal; Portuguese

**por·ta·ble** \'pȯrt-ə-bəl\ adj : capable of being carried — **portable** n

¹**por·tage** \'pȯrt-ij, pȯr-'täzh\ n : the carrying of boats and goods overland between navigable bodies of water; also : a route for such carrying

²**por·tage** \'pȯrt-ij, pȯr-'täzh\ vb **por·taged**; **por·tag·ing** : to carry gear over a portage

**por·tal** \'pȯrt-²l\ n : DOOR, ENTRANCE; esp : a grand or imposing one

**portal-to-portal** adj : of or relating to the time spent by a workman in traveling from the entrance to his employer's property to his actual working place (as in a mine) and in returning after the work shift

**port·cul·lis** \pȯrt-'kəl-əs\ n : a grating at the gateway of a castle or fortress that can be let down to stop entrance

**porte co·chere** \,pȯrt-kō-'shear\ n [F porte cochère, lit., coach door] : a roofed structure extending from the entrance of a building over an adjacent driveway and sheltering those getting in or out of vehicles

**por·tend** \pȯr-'tend\ vb 1 : to give a sign or warning of beforehand 2 : INDICATE, SIGNIFY syn augur, prognosticate, foretell, predict, forecast, prophesy, forebode

**por·tent** \'pȯr-,tent\ n 1 : something that foreshadows a coming event : OMEN 2 : MARVEL, PRODIGY

**por·ten·tous** \pȯr-'tent-əs\ adj 1 : of, relating to, or constituting a portent 2 : PRODIGIOUS 3 : self-consciously weighty : POMPOUS

¹**por·ter** \'pȯrt-ər\ n, chiefly Brit : DOORKEEPER

²**porter** n 1 : one that carries burdens; esp : one employed (as at a terminal) to carry baggage 2 : an attendant in a railroad car 3 : a dark heavy ale

**por·ter·house** \'pȯrt-ər-,haȯs\ n : a choice beefsteak with a large tenderloin

**port·fo·lio** \pȯrt-'fō-lē-,ō\ n, pl **-lios** 1 : a portable case for papers or drawings 2 : the office and functions of a minister of state 3 : the securities held by an investor

**port·hole** \'pȯrt-,hōl\ n : an opening in the side of a ship or aircraft

**por·ti·co** \'pȯrt-i-,kō\ n, pl **-coes** or **-cos** : a row of columns supporting a roof around or at the entrance of a building

**por·tiere** \pȯr-'tye(ə)r, -'ti(ə)r; 'pȯrt-ē-ər\ n : a curtain hanging across a doorway

**¹por·tion** \'pȯr-shən\ n 1 : an individual's part or share ⟨her ~ of worldly goods⟩ 2 : DOWRY 3 : an individual's lot ⟨sorrow was his ~⟩ 4 : a part of a whole

**²portion** vb **por·tioned; por·tion·ing** \-sh(ə-)niŋ\ 1 : to divide into portions 2 : to allot to as a portion

**por·tion·less** \-shən-ləs\ adj : having no portion; esp : having no dowry or inheritance

**port·land cement** \,pȯrt-lən(d)-\ n : a cement made by calcining and grinding a mixture of clay and limestone

**port·ly** \'pȯrt-lē\ adj **port·li·er; -est** : somewhat stout

**port·man·teau** \pȯrt-'man-,tō\ n, pl **-teaus** or **-teaux** \-,tōz\ [MF *portemanteau,* fr. *porter* to carry + *manteau* mantle, fr. L *mantellum*] : a large traveling bag

**port of call** : an intermediate port where ships customarily stop for supplies, repairs, or transshipment of cargo

**port of entry** 1 : a place where foreign goods may be cleared through a customhouse 2 : a place where an alien may enter a country

**por·trait** \'pȯr-trət, -,trāt\ n : a picture (as a painting or photograph) of a person usu. showing the face

**por·trait·ist** \-əst\ n : a maker of portraits

**por·trai·ture** \'pȯr-trə-,chùr\ n : the practice or art of making portraits

**por·tray** \pȯr-'trā\ vb 1 : to make a picture of : DEPICT 2 : to describe in words 3 : to play the role of — **por·tray·al** n

**Por·tu·guese** \,pȯr-chə-'gēz, -'gēs\ n, pl **Portuguese** 1 : a native or inhabitant of Portugal 2 : the language of Portugal and Brazil — **Portuguese** adj

**Portuguese man-of-war** n : any of several large colonial invertebrate animals that are related to the jellyfishes and have a large sac or cyst resembling a bladder by means of which the colony floats at the surface of the sea

**por·tu·laca** \,pȯr-chə-'lak-ə\ n : a tropical succulent herb cultivated for its showy flowers

**pos** abbr 1 position 2 positive

**pose** \'pōz\ vb **posed; pos·ing** 1 : to put or set in place 2 : to assume or cause to assume a posture usu. for artistic purposes 3 : to set forth : PROPOSE ⟨~ a question⟩ 4 : to affect an attitude or character

**²pose** n 1 : a sustained posture; esp : one assumed by a model 2 : an attitude assumed for effect : PRETENSE

**¹pos·er** \'pō-zər\ n : a puzzling question

**²poser** n : a person who poses

**po·seur** \pō-'zər\ n : an affected person

**posh** \'päsh\ adj : FASHIONABLE

**pos·it** \'päz-ət\ vb : to assume the existence of : POSTULATE

**po·si·tion** \pə-'zish-ən\ n 1 : an arranging in order 2 : the stand taken on a question 3 : the point or area occupied by something : SITUATION 4 : the arrangement of parts (as of the body) in relation to one another : POSTURE 5 : RANK, STATUS 6 : EMPLOYMENT, JOB — **position** vb

**¹pos·i·tive** \'päz-ət-iv\ adj 1 : expressed definitely ⟨~ views⟩ 2 : CONFIDENT, CERTAIN 3 : of, relating to, or constituting the degree of grammatical comparison that denotes no increase in quality, quantity, or relation 4 : not fictitious : REAL 5 : active and effective in function ⟨~ leadership⟩ 6 : having the light and shade as existing in the original subject ⟨a ~ photograph⟩ 7 : numerically greater than zero ⟨a ~ number⟩ 8 : being, relating to, or charged with electricity of which the proton is the elementary unit 9 AFFIRMATIVE ⟨a ~ response⟩ — **pos·i·tive·ly** adv — **pos·i·tive·ness** n

**²positive** n 1 : the positive degree or a positive form in a language 2 : a positive photograph

**pos·i·tron** \'päz-ə-,trän\ n : a positively charged particle having the same mass and magnitude of charge as the electron

**poss** abbr possessive

**pos·se** \'päs-ē\ n [ML *posse comitatus,* lit., power or authority of the country] : a body of persons organized to assist a sheriff in an emergency

**pos·sess** \pə-'zes\ vb 1 : to have as property : OWN 2 : to have as an attribute, knowledge, or skill 3 : to enter into and control firmly ⟨~ed by a devil⟩ — **pos·ses·sor** \-'zes-ər\ n

**pos·ses·sion** \-'zesh-ən\ n 1 : control or occupancy of property 2 : OWNERSHIP 3 : something owned : PROPERTY 4 : domination by something 5 : SELF-CONTROL

**pos·ses·sive** \pə-'zes-iv\ adj 1 : of, relating to, or constituting a grammatical case denoting ownership 2 : showing the desire to possess ⟨a ~ nature⟩ — **possessive** n — **pos·ses·sive·ness** n

**pos·si·ble** \'päs-ə-bəl\ adj 1 : being within the limits of ability, capacity, or realization ⟨a ~ task⟩ 2 : being something that may or may not occur ⟨~ dangers⟩ 3 : able or fitted to become ⟨a ~ site for a bridge⟩ — **pos·si·bil·i·ty** \,päs-ə-'bil-ət-ē\ n — **pos·si·bly** \-blē\ adv

**pos·sum** \'päs-əm\ n : OPOSSUM

**¹post** \'pōst\ *n* **1 :** an upright piece of timber or metal serving esp. as a support : PILLAR **2 :** a pole or stake set up as a mark or indicator

**²post** *vb* **1 :** to affix to a usual place (as a wall) for public notices ⟨~ no bills⟩ **2 :** to publish or announce by or as if by a public notice ⟨~ grades⟩ **3 :** to forbid (property) to trespassers by putting up a notice **4 :** SCORE 4

**³post** *n* **1** *obs* : COURIER **2** *chiefly Brit* : MAIL; *also* : POST OFFICE

**⁴post** *vb* **1 :** to ride or travel with haste : HURRY **2 :** MAIL ⟨~ a letter⟩ **3 :** INFORM ⟨kept him ~ed on new developments⟩ **4 :** to enter in a ledger

**⁵post** *n* **1 :** the place at which a soldier is stationed; *esp* : a sentry's beat or station **2 :** a station or task to which a person is assigned **3 :** the place at which a body of troops is stationed : CAMP **4 :** OFFICE, POSITION **5 :** a trading settlement or station

**⁶post** *vb* **1 :** to station in a given place **2 :** to put up (as bond)

**post·age** \'pōs-tij\ *n* **:** the fee for postal service; *also* : stamps representing this fee

**post·al** \'pōs-t⁸l\ *adj* **:** of or relating to the mails or the post office

**postal card** *n* : POSTCARD

**postal service** *n* **:** a government agency or department handling the transmission of mail

**post·boy** \'pōs(t)-,bȯi\ *n* : POSTILION

**post·card** \'pōs(t)-,kärd\ *n* **:** a card on which a message may be written for mailing without an envelope

**post chaise** *n* **:** a 4-wheeled closed carriage for two to four persons

**post·con·so·nan·tal** \,pōst-,kän-sə-'nant-⁸l\ *adj* **:** immediately following a consonant

**post·date** \(')pōs(t)-'dāt\ *vb* **:** to date with a date later than that of execution

**post·doc·tor·al** \(')pōs(t)-'däk-t(ə-)rəl\ *also* **post·doc·tor·ate** \-t(ə-)rət\ *adj* **:** of, relating to, or engaged in advanced academic or professional work beyond a doctor's degree

**post·er** \'pō-stər\ *n* **:** a bill or placard for posting in a public place

**¹pos·te·ri·or** \po-'stir-ē-ər, pä-\ *adj* **1 :** later in time **2 :** situated behind

**²pos·te·ri·or** \pä-'stir-ē-ər, pō-\ *n* **:** the hinder parts of the body : BUTTOCKS

**pos·ter·i·ty** \pä-'ster-ət-ē\ *n* **1 :** all the descendants from one ancestor **2 :** succeeding generations; *also* : future time

**pos·tern** \'pōs-tərn, 'päs-\ *n* **1 :** a back door or gate **2 :** a private or side entrance

**post exchange** *n* **:** a store at a military post that sells to military personnel and authorized civilians

**post·grad·u·ate** \(')pōs(t)-'graj-ə-wət, -,wāt\ *adj* **:** of or relating to studies beyond the bachelor's degree — **postgraduate** *n*

**post·haste** \'pōst-'hāst\ *adv* **:** with all possible speed

**post·hole** \'pōst-,hōl\ *n* **:** a hole for a post and esp. a fence post

**post–horse** \'pōst-,hȯrs\ *n* **:** a horse for use esp. by couriers or mail carriers

**post·hu·mous** \'päs-chə-məs\ *adj* **1 :** born after the death of the father **2 :** published after the death of the author

**post·hyp·not·ic** \,pōst-hip-'nät-ik\ *adj* **:** of, relating to, or characteristic of the period following a hypnotic trance

**pos·til·ion** *or* **pos·til·lion** \pō-'stil-yən, pə-\ *n* **:** a rider on the left-hand horse of a pair drawing a coach

**Post·im·pres·sion·ism** \,pōst-im-'presh-ə-,niz-əm\ *n* **:** a late 19th century French theory or practice of art that stresses variously volume, picture structure, or expressionism

**post·lude** \'pōst-,lüd\ *n* **:** an organ solo played at the end of a church service

**post·man** \'pōs(t)-mən, -,man\ *n* : MAILMAN

**post·mark** \-,märk\ *n* **:** an official postal marking on a piece of mail; *esp* : the mark canceling the postage stamp — **postmark** *vb*

**post·mas·ter** \-,mas-tər\ *n* **:** one who has charge of a post office

**postmaster general** *n*, *pl* **postmasters general** **:** an official in charge of a national postal service

**post me·rid·i·em** \'pōs(t)-mə-'rid-ē-əm, -ē-,em\ *adj* [L] **:** being after noon

**post·mis·tress** \'pōs(t)-,mis-trəs\ *n* **:** a woman in charge of a post office

**¹post·mor·tem** \(')pōs(t)-'mȯrt-əm\ *adj* [L *post mortem* after death] **1 :** occurring, made, or done after death **2 :** relating to a postmortem examination

**²postmortem** *n* **:** a postmortem examination of a body esp. to find the cause of death

**post·na·sal drip** \-'nā-zəl-\ *n* **:** flow of mucous secretion from the posterior part of the nasal cavity onto the wall of the pharynx occurring usu. as a chronic accompaniment of an allergic state

**post·na·tal** \(')pōs(t)-'nāt-⁸l\ *adj* **:** subsequent to birth

**post office** *n* **1 :** POSTAL SERVICE **2 :** a local branch of a post office department

**post·op·er·a·tive** \(')pōst-'äp-(ə-)rət-iv, -'äp-ə-,rāt-\ *adj* **:** following a surgical operation ⟨~ care⟩

**post·paid** \'pōst-'pād\ *adv* **:** with the postage paid by the sender and not chargeable to the receiver

**post·par·tum** \(')pōs(t)-'pärt-əm\ *adj* [NL *post partum* after birth] **:** following parturition — **postpartum** *adv*

**post·pone** \pōs(t)-'pōn\ *vb* **post·poned; post·pon·ing :** to hold back to a later time — **post·pone·ment** *n*

**post road** *n* **:** a road over which mail is carried

**post·script** \'pō(s)-,skript\ *n* **:** a note added esp. to a completed letter

**post time** *n* **:** the designated time for the start of a horse race

**pos·tu·lant** \'päs-chə-lənt\ *n* **:** a probationary candidate for membership in a religious house

**¹pos·tu·late** \'päs-chə-,lāt\ *vb* **-lat·ed; -lat·ing :** to assume as true

²pos·tu·late \-lət, -ˌlāt\ n : a proposition taken for granted as true and made the starting point in a chain of reasoning

¹pos·ture \'päs-chər\ n 1 : the position or bearing of the body or one of its parts 2 : STATE, CONDITION 3 : ATTITUDE

²posture vb pos·tured; pos·tur·ing : to strike a pose esp. for effect

post·war \'pōst-'wòr\ adj : of or relating to the period after a war ⟨~ inflation⟩

po·sy \'pō-zē\ n, pl posies 1 : a brief sentiment ; MOTTO 2 : a bunch of flowers; also : FLOWER

¹pot \'pät\ n 1 : a rounded container used chiefly for domestic purposes 2 : the total of the bets at stake at one time 3 : RUIN ⟨go to ~⟩ 4 : MARIJUANA — pot·ful n

²pot vb pot·ted; pot·ting 1 : to preserve in a pot 2 : SHOOT

po·ta·ble \'pōt-ə-bəl\ adj : suitable for drinking

po·tage \pó-'täzh\ n : a thick soup

pot·ash \'pät-ˌash\ n [sing. of pot ashes] : a potassium carbonate esp. from wood ashes; also : potassium or any of its various compounds

po·tas·si·um \pə-'tas-ē-əm\ n : a silver-white metallic chemical element used in making glass, gunpowder, and fertilizer

potassium bromide n : a crystalline salt used as a sedative and in photography

potassium carbonate n : a white salt used in making glass and soap

potassium nitrate n : a soluble salt that occurs in some soils and is used in making gunpowder, in preserving meat, and in medicine

po·ta·tion \pō-'tā-shən\ n : a usu. alcoholic drink; also : the act of drinking

po·ta·to \pə-'tāt-ō\ n, pl -toes : the edible starchy tuber of a plant related to the tomato; also : this plant

potato beetle n : COLORADO POTATO BEETLE

potato bug n : COLORADO POTATO BEETLE

pot·bel·ly \'pät-ˌbel-ē\ n : a protruding abdomen — pot·bel·lied \-ēd\ adj

pot·boil·er \-ˌbói-lər\ n : a usu. inferior work of art or literature produced only to earn money

pot·boy \-ˌbói\ n : a boy who serves drinks in a tavern

po·teen also po·theen \pə-'tēn, -'chēn, -'tyēn, -'thēn\ n : illicitly distilled whiskey of Ireland

po·tent \'pōt-ᵊnt\ adj 1 : having authority or influence : POWERFUL 2 : chemically or medicinally effective 3 : able to copulate syn forceful, forcible — po·ten·cy \-ᵊn-sē\ n

po·ten·tate \'pōt-ᵊn-ˌtāt\ n : one who wields controlling power : RULER

¹po·ten·tial \pə-'ten-chəl\ adj : existing in possibility : capable of becoming actual ⟨a ~ champion⟩ syn dormant, latent — po·ten·ti·al·i·ty \pə-ˌten-

chē-'al-ət-ē\ n — po·ten·tial·ly \-'tench-(ə-)lē\ adv

²potential n 1 : something that can develop or become actual 2 : degree of electrification with reference to a standard (as of the earth)

po·ten·ti·ate \pə-'ten-chē-ˌāt\ vb -at·ed; -at·ing : to make potent; esp : to augment (as a drug) synergistically — po·ten·ti·a·tion \-ˌten-chē-'ā-shən\ n

pot·head \'pät-ˌhed\ n : an individual who smokes marijuana

poth·er \'päth-ər\ n : a noisy disturbance; also : FUSS

pot·herb \'pät-ˌ(h)ərb\ n : an herb whose leaves or stems are boiled for greens or used to season food

pot·hole \'pät-ˌhōl\ n : a large pit or hole (as in a road surface)

pot·hook \-ˌhùk\ n : an S-shaped hook for hanging pots and kettles over an open fire

po·tion \'pō-shən\ n : DRINK; esp : a dose of liquid medicine or poison

pot·luck \'pät-'lək\ n : the regular meal available to a guest for whom no special preparations have been made

pot·pie \'pät-'pī\ n : meat or fowl stew served with a crust or dumplings

pot·pour·ri \ˌpō-pù-'rē\ n [F pot pourri, lit., rotten pot] : a miscellaneous collection : MEDLEY

pot·sherd \'pät-ˌshərd\ n : a pottery fragment

pot·shot \-ˌshät\ n 1 : a shot taken in a casual manner or at an easy target 2 : a critical remark made in a random or sporadic manner

pot·tage \'pät-ij\ n : a thick soup of vegetables or vegetables and meat

¹pot·ter \'pät-ər\ n : one that makes pottery

²potter vb : PUTTER

pot·tery \'pät-ə-rē\ n, pl -ter·ies 1 : a place where earthen pots and dishes are made 2 : the art of the potter 3 : dishes, pots, and vases made from clay

¹pouch \'paùch\ n 1 : a small bag (as for tobacco) carried on the person 2 : a bag for storing or transporting goods ⟨mail ~⟩ ⟨diplomatic ~⟩ 3 : an anatomical sac; esp : one in which a marsupial carries her young

²pouch vb : to make puffy or protuberant

poult \'pōlt\ n : a young fowl; esp : a young turkey

poul·ter·er \'pōl-tər-ər\ n : one that deals in poultry

poul·tice \'pōl-təs\ n : a soft usu. heated and medicated mass spread on cloth and applied to a sore or injury — poultice vb

poul·try \'pōl-trē\ n : domesticated birds kept for eggs or meat

poul·try·man \-mən\ n 1 : one that raises domestic fowls esp. on a commercial scale 2 : a dealer in poultry or poultry products

pounce \'paùns\ vb pounced; pounc·ing : to spring or swoop upon and seize something

¹pound \'paùnd\ n, pl pounds also

**pound 1** — see WEIGHT table **2** — see MONEY table

**²pound** *vb* **1 :** to crush to a powder or pulp by beating **2 :** to strike or beat heavily or repeatedly **3 :** DRILL **4 :** to move or move along heavily

**³pound** *n* **:** a public enclosure where stray animals are kept

**pound·age** \'paún-dij\ *n* **:** POUNDS; *also* **:** weight in pounds

**pound cake** *n* **:** a rich cake made with a large amount of eggs and shortening in proportion to the flour used

**pound–fool·ish** \'paún(d)-'fü-lish\ *adj* **:** imprudent in dealing with large sums or large matters

**pour** \'pōr\ *vb* **1 :** to flow or cause to flow in a stream or flood **2 :** to rain hard **3 :** to supply freely and copiously

**pour·boire** \pùr-'bwär\ *n* [F, fr. *pour boire* for drinking] **:** TIP, GRATUITY

**pour·par·ler** \pùr-pär-'lā\ *n* **:** a discussion preliminary to negotiations

**pout** \'paút\ *vb* **:** to show displeasure by thrusting out the lips; *also* **:** to look sullen — **pout** *n*

**pov·er·ty** \'päv-ərt-ē\ *n* [ME *poverte*, fr. OF *poverté*, fr. L *paupertat-, paupertas*, fr. *pauper* poor] **1 :** lack of money or material possessions **:** WANT **2 :** poor quality (as of soil)

**pov·er·ty–strick·en** \-,strik-ən\ *adj* **:** very poor **:** DESTITUTE

**POW** \,pē-(,)ō-'dəb-əl-(,)yü\ *abbr* prisoner of war

**¹pow·der** \'paúd-ər\ *n* **1 :** dry material made up of fine particles; *also* **:** a usu. medicinal or cosmetic preparation in this form **2 :** a solid explosive (as gunpowder) — **pow·dery** *adj*

**²powder** *vb* **pow·dered; pow·der·ing** \'paúd-(ə-)riŋ\ **1 :** to sprinkle or cover with or as if with powder **2 :** to reduce to powder

**powder room** *n* **:** a rest room for women

**¹pow·er** \'paú(-ə)r\ *n* **1 :** a position of ascendancy over others **:** AUTHORITY **2 :** the ability to act or produce an effect **3 :** one that has control or authority; *esp* **:** a sovereign state **4 :** physical might; *also* **:** mental or moral vigor **5 :** the number of times as indicated by an exponent a number is to be multiplied by itself **6 :** force or energy used to do work; *also* **:** the time rate at which work is done or energy transferred **7 :** the amount by which an optical lens magnifies — **pow·er·ful** \-fəl\ *adj* — **pow·er·ful·ly** \-ē\ *adv* — **pow·er·less** *adj*

**²power** *vb* **:** to supply with power and esp. motive power

**pow·er·boat** \-,bōt\ *n* **:** MOTORBOAT

**pow·er·house** \-,haús\ *n* **:** a building in which electric power is generated

**power plant** *n* **1 :** POWERHOUSE **2 :** an engine and related parts supplying the motive power of a self-propelled vehicle

**pow·wow** \'paú-,waú\ *n* **1 :** a No. American Indian ceremony (as for victory in war) **2 :** a meeting for discussion **:** CONFERENCE

**pox** \'päks\ *n, pl* **pox** *or* **pox·es :** any of various diseases (as smallpox or syphilis) marked by eruptions

**pp** *abbr* **1** pages **2** pianissimo

**PP** *abbr* **1** parcel post **2** past participle

**PPC** *abbr* [F *pour prendre congé*] to take leave

**ppd** *abbr* **1** postpaid **2** prepaid

**ppt** *abbr* precipitate

**pptn** *abbr* precipitation

**PQ** *abbr* Province of Quebec

**pr** *abbr* **1** pair **2** price

**Pr** *symbol* praseodymium

**PR** *abbr* **1** payroll **2** public relations **3** Puerto Rico

**prac·ti·ca·ble** \'prak-ti-kə-bəl\ *adj* **:** capable of being put into practice, done, or accomplished — **prac·ti·ca·bil·i·ty** \,prak-ti-kə-'bil-ət-ē\ *n*

**prac·ti·cal** \'prak-ti-kəl\ *adj* **1 :** of, relating to, or shown in practice ⟨~ questions⟩ **2 :** VIRTUAL ⟨~ control⟩ **3 :** capable of being put to use or account ⟨a ~ knowledge of French⟩ **4 :** inclined to action as opposed to speculation ⟨a ~ person⟩ **5 :** qualified by practice ⟨a good ~ mechanic⟩ — **prac·ti·cal·i·ty** \,prak-ti-'kal-ət-ē\ *n* — **prac·ti·cal·ly** \'prak-ti-k(ə-)lē\ *adv*

**practical joke** *n* **:** a joke whose humor stems from the tricking or abuse of an individual placed somehow at a disadvantage

**practical nurse** *n* **:** a nurse who cares for the sick professionally without having the training or experience required of a registered nurse

**¹prac·tice** *or* **prac·tise** \'prak-təs\ *vb* **prac·ticed** *or* **prac·tised; prac·tic·ing** *or* **prac·tis·ing 1 :** to perform or work at repeatedly so as to become proficient ⟨~ tennis strokes⟩ **2 :** to carry out **:** APPLY ⟨~ s what he preaches⟩ **3 :** to do or perform customarily ⟨~ politeness⟩ **4 :** to be professionally engaged in ⟨~ law⟩

**²practice** *also* **practise** *n* **1 :** actual performance or application **2 :** customary action **:** HABIT **3 :** systematic exercise for proficiency **4 :** the exercise of a profession; *also* **:** a professional business

**prac·ti·tion·er** \prak-'tish-(ə-)nər\ *n* **:** one that practices a profession

**prae·tor** \'prēt-ər\ *n* **:** an ancient Roman magistrate ranking below a consul — **prae·to·ri·an** \prē-'tōr-ē-ən, -'tòr-\ *adj*

**prag·mat·ic** \prag-'mat·ik\ *also* **prag·mat·i·cal** \-i-kəl\ *adj* **1 :** of or relating to practical affairs **2 :** concerned with the practical consequences of actions or beliefs

**prag·ma·tism** \'prag-mə-,tiz-əm\ *n* **:** a practical approach to problems and affairs

**prai·rie** \'pre(ə)r-ē\ *n* **:** a broad tract of level or rolling land (as in the Mississippi valley) covered by coarse grass but with few trees

**prairie dog** *n* **:** a colonial American burrowing rodent related to the marmots

**prairie schooner** *n* **:** a covered wagon used by pioneers in cross-country travel

**praise** \\'prāz\\ *vb* **praised; prais·ing**
**1** : to express approval of : COMMEND
**2** : to glorify (a divinity or a saint) esp.
in song — **praise** *n* — **praise·wor·thy** \\-,wər-thē\\ *adj*

**pra·line** \\'prä-,lēn, 'prā-, 'prò-\\ *n* : a
candy of nut kernels embedded in
boiled brown sugar or maple sugar

**pram** \\'pram\\ *n, chiefly Brit* : PERAM-
BULATOR

**prance** \\'prans\\ *vb* **pranced; pranc·ing** **1** : to spring from the hind legs ⟨a
*prancing* horse⟩ **2** : SWAGGER; *also*
: CAPER — **prance** *n* — **pranc·er** *n*

**prank** \\'praŋk\\ *n* : a playful or mildly
mischievous act : TRICK — **prank·ster**
\\-stər\\ *n*

**pra·seo·dym·i·um** \\,prā-zē-ō-'dim-
ē-əm\\ *n* : a white metallic chemical element

**prate** \\'prāt\\ *vb* **prat·ed; prat·ing**
: to talk long and idly : chatter foolishly

**prat·fall** \\'prat-,fòl\\ *n* : a fall on the
buttocks

**pra·tique** \\pra-'tēk\\ *n* : clearance
given an incoming ship by the health
authority of a port

¹**prat·tle** \\'prat-ªl\\ *vb* **prat·tled; prat·tling** \\'prat-(ª-)liŋ\\ : PRATE, BABBLE

²**prattle** *n* : trifling or childish talk

**prawn** \\'pròn\\ *n* : any of various
edible shrimplike crustaceans

**pray** \\'prā\\ *vb* **1** : ENTREAT, IMPLORE
**2** : to ask earnestly for something **3**
: to address a divinity esp. with supplication

**prayer** \\'praər\\ *n* **1** : an earnest request **2** : the act or practice of addressing a divinity esp. in petition **3** : a religious service consisting chiefly of prayers — often used in pl. **4** : a set order
of words used in praying **5** : something
prayed for **6** : a slight chance

**prayer book** *n* : a book containing
prayers and often directions for worship

**prayer·ful** \\'praər-fəl\\ *adj* **1** : DEVOUT
**2** : EARNEST — **prayer·ful·ly** \\-ē\\ *adv*

**praying man·tid** \\-'mant-əd\\ *n*
: MANTIS

**praying mantis** *n* : MANTIS

**preach** \\'prēch\\ *vb* **1** : to deliver a
sermon **2** : to set forth in a sermon **3**
: to advocate earnestly — **preach·er** *n*
— **preach·ment** *n*

**pre·ad·o·les·cence** \\'prē-,ad-ªl-'es-
ªns\\ *n* : the period of human development just preceding adolescence —
**pre·ad·o·les·cent** \\-ªnt\\ *adj or n*

**pre·am·ble** \\'prē-,am-bəl\\ *n* [ME, fr.
MF *preambule*, fr. ML *preambulum*, fr.
LL, neut. of *praeambulus* walking in
front of, fr. L *prae* in front of +
*ambulare* to walk] : an introductory
part ⟨the ~ to a constitution⟩

**pre·am·pli·fi·er** \\(')prē-'am-plə-
,fī(-ə)r\\ *n* : an amplifier designed to increase extremely weak signals before
they are fed to additional amplifier
circuits

**pre·ar·range** \\,prē-ə-'rānj\\ *vb* : to arrange beforehand — **pre·ar·range·ment** *n*

**pre·as·signed** \\,prē-ə-'sīnd\\ *adj* : assigned beforehand

**preb·end** \\'preb-ənd\\ *n* : an endowment held by a cathedral or collegiate
church for the maintenance of a preb-
endary; *also* : the stipend paid from
this endowment

**preb·en·dary** \\'preb-ən-,der-ē\\ *n, pl*
**-dar·ies** **1** : a clergyman receiving a
prebend for officiating and serving in
the church **2** : an honorary canon

**prec** *abbr* preceding

**pre·can·cel** \\(')prē-'kan-səl\\ *vb* : to
cancel (a postage stamp) in advance of
use — **pre·can·cel·la·tion** \\,prē-
,kan-sə-'lā-shən\\ *n*

**pre·can·cer·ous** \\(')prē-'kans-(ə-)
rəs\\ *adj* : likely to become cancerous

**pre·car·i·ous** \\pri-'kar-ē-əs\\ *adj* : dependent on uncertain conditions : dangerously insecure : UNSTABLE ⟨a ~ foot-
hold⟩ ⟨~ prosperity⟩ **syn** dangerous,
hazardous, perilous, jeopardous, risky
— **pre·car·i·ous·ly** *adv* — **pre·car·i·ous·ness** *n*

**pre·cau·tion** \\pri-'kò-shən\\ *n* : a
measure taken beforehand to prevent
harm or secure good — **pre·cau·tion·ary** \\-shə-,ner-ē\\ *adj*

**pre·cede** \\pri-'sēd\\ *vb* **pre·ced·ed;
pre·ced·ing** : to be, go, or come
ahead or in front of (as in rank, sequence, or time) — **prec·e·dence**
\\'pres-əd-əns, pri-'sēd-ªns\\ *n*

¹**prec·e·dent** \\pri-'sēd-ªnt, 'pres-əd-
ənt\\ *adj* : prior in time, order, or significance

²**prec·e·dent** \\'pres-əd-ənt\\ *n* : something said or done that may serve to
authorize or justify further words or
acts of the same or a similar kind

**pre·ced·ing** \\pri-'sēd-iŋ\\ *adj* : that
precedes **syn** antecedent, foregoing,
prior, former, anterior

**pre·cen·tor** \\pri-'sent-ər\\ *n* : a leader
of the singing of a choir or congregation

**pre·cept** \\'prē-,sept\\ *n* : a command or
principle intended as a general rule of
action or conduct

**pre·cep·tor** \\pri-'sep-tər, 'prē-,sep-\\ *n*
: TUTOR — **pre·cep·tress** \\-trəs\\ *n*

**pre·ces·sion** \\prē-'sesh-ən\\ *n* : a slow
gyration of the rotation axis of a spinning body (as the earth) — **pre·cess**
\\prē-'ses\\ *vb* — **pre·ces·sion·al**
\\-'sesh-(ə-)nal\\ *adj*

**pre·cinct** \\'prē-,siŋkt\\ *n* **1** : an administrative subdivision (as of a city)
: DISTRICT ⟨police ~⟩ ⟨electoral ~⟩ **2**
: an enclosure bounded by the limits of
a building or place — often used in pl.
**3** *pl* : ENVIRONS

**pre·ci·os·i·ty** \\,pres(h)-ē-'äs-ət-ē\\ *n,
pl* **-ties** : fastidious refinement

**pre·cious** \\'presh-əs\\ *adj* **1** : of great
value ⟨~ jewels⟩ **2** : greatly cherished
: DEAR ⟨~ memories⟩ **3** : AFFECTED ⟨~
language⟩

**prec·i·pice** \\'pres-ə-pəs\\ *n* : a steep
cliff

**pre·cip·i·tan·cy** \\pri-'sip-ət-ən-sē\\ *n*
: precipitate action : PRECIPITATION

¹**pre·cip·i·tate** \\pri-'sip-ə-,tāt\\ *vb*
**-tat·ed; -tat·ing** **1** : to throw violently **2** : to throw down **3** : to cause

to happen quickly or abruptly ⟨~ a quarrel⟩ **4** : to cause to separate out of a liquid and fall to the bottom **5** : to fall as rain, snow, or hail **syn** speed, accelerate, quicken, hasten, hurry

**²pre·cip·i·tate** \pri-'sip-ət-ət, -ə-,tāt\ n : the solid matter that separates out and usu. falls to the bottom of a liquid

**³pre·cip·i·tate** \pri-'sip-ət-ət\ adj **1** : showing extreme or unwise haste : RASH **2** : falling with steep descent; also : PRECIPITOUS — **pre·cip·i·tate·ly** adv — **pre·cip·i·tate·ness** n

**pre·cip·i·ta·tion** \pri-,sip-ə-'tā-shən\ n **1** : rash haste **2** : the causing of solid matter to separate from a liquid and usu. fall to the bottom **3** : water that falls as rain, snow, or hail; also : the quantity of this water

**pre·cip·i·tous** \pri-'sip-ət-əs\ adj **1** : PRECIPITATE **2** : having the character of a precipice : very steep ⟨a ~ slope⟩; also : containing precipices ⟨~ trails⟩ — **pre·cip·i·tous·ly** adv

**pré·cis** \prā-'sē\ n, pl **pré·cis** \-'sēz\ : a concise summary of essential points

**pre·cise** \pri-'sīs\ adj **1** : exactly defined or stated : DEFINITE **2** : highly accurate : EXACT **3** : conforming strictly to a standard : SCRUPULOUS — **pre·cise·ly** adv — **pre·cise·ness** n

**pre·ci·sian** \pri-'sizh-ən\ n : a person who stresses or practices scrupulous adherence to a strict standard esp. of religious observance or morality

**pre·ci·sion** \pri-'sizh-ən\ n : the quality or state of being precise

**pre·clude** \pri-'klüd\ vb **pre·clud·ed; pre·clud·ing** : to make impossible : BAR, PREVENT

**pre·co·cious** \pri-'kō-shəs\ adj [L praecoc-, praecox early ripening, precocious, fr. prae- ahead + coquere to cook] : early in development and esp. in mental development — **pre·co·cious·ly** adv — **pre·coc·i·ty** \pri-'käs-ət-ē\ n

**pre·con·ceive** \,prē-kən-'sēv\ vb : to form an opinion of beforehand — **pre·con·cep·tion** \-'sep-shən\ n

**pre·con·cert·ed** \-'sərt-əd\ adj : arranged or agreed on in advance

**pre·con·di·tion** \-'dish-ən\ vb : to put in proper or desired condition or frame of mind in advance

**pre·cook** \'prē-'kúk\ vb : to cook partially or entirely before final cooking or reheating

**pre·cur·sor** \pri-'kər-sər\ n : one that precedes and indicates the approach of another : FORERUNNER

**pred** abbr predicate

**pre·da·ceous** or **pre·da·cious** \pri-'dā-shəs\ adj : living by preying on others : PREDATORY

**pre·date** \'prē-'dāt\ vb : ANTEDATE

**pre·da·tion** \pri-'dā-shən\ n **1** : the act of preying or plundering **2** : a mode of life in which food is primarily obtained by killing and consuming animals — **pred·a·tor** \'pred-ət-ər\ n

**pred·a·to·ry** \'pred-ə-,tōr-ē\ adj **1** : of or relating to plunder ⟨~ warfare⟩ **2** : disposed to exploit others **3** : prey-

ing upon other animals — **pred·a·tor** \'pred-ət-ər\ n

**pre·de·cease** \,prē-di-'sēs\ vb **-ceased; -ceas·ing** : to die before another person

**pre·de·ces·sor** \'pred-ə-,ses-ər, 'prēd-\ n : one who has previously held a position to which another has succeeded

**pre·des·ig·nate** \(')prē-'dez-ig-,nāt\ vb : to designate beforehand

**pre·des·ti·na·tion** \,prē-,des-tə-'nā-shən\ n : the act of foreordaining to an earthly lot or eternal destiny by divine decree; also : the state of being so foreordained — **pre·des·ti·nate** \prē-'des-tə-,nāt\ vb

**pre·des·tine** \prē-'des-tən\ vb : to settle beforehand : FOREORDAIN

**pre·de·ter·mine** \,prē-di-'tər-mən\ vb : to determine beforehand

**pred·i·ca·ble** \'pred-i-kə-bəl\ adj : capable of being predicated or affirmed

**pre·dic·a·ment** \pri-'dik-ə-mənt\ n : a difficult or trying situation **syn** dilemma, quandary

**¹pred·i·cate** \'pred-i-kət\ n : the part of a sentence or clause that expresses what is said of the subject

**²pred·i·cate** \'pred-ə-,kāt\ vb **-cat·ed; -cat·ing 1** : AFFIRM **2** : to assert to be a quality or attribute ⟨~ intelligence of man⟩ **3** : FOUND, BASE — **pred·i·ca·tion** \,pred-ə-'kā-shən\ n

**pre·dict** \pri-'dikt\ vb : to declare in advance — **pre·dict·able** \-'dik-tə-bəl\ adj — **pre·dict·ably** \-blē\ adv — **pre·dic·tion** \-'dik-shən\ n

**pre·di·ges·tion** \,prē-dī-'jes-chən, -də-\ n : artificial partial digestion of food esp. for use in illness — **pre·di·gest** \-'jest\ vb

**pre·di·lec·tion** \,pred-ᵊl-'ek-shən, ,prēd-\ n : a favorable inclination

**pre·dis·pose** \,prē-dis-'pōz\ vb : to incline in advance : make susceptible — **pre·dis·po·si·tion** \,prē-,dis-pə-,zish-ən\ n

**pre·dom·i·nate** \pri-'däm-ə-,nāt\ vb : to be superior esp. in power or numbers : PREVAIL — **pre·dom·i·nance** \-nəns\ n — **pre·dom·i·nant** \-nənt\ adj — **pre·dom·i·nant·ly** adv

**pree·mie** \'prē-mē\ n : a baby born prematurely

**pre·em·i·nent** \prē-'em-ə-nənt\ adj : having highest rank : OUTSTANDING — **pre·em·i·nence** \-nəns\ n — **pre·em·i·nent·ly** adv

**pre·empt** \prē-'empt\ vb **1** : to settle upon (public land) with the right to purchase before others; also : to take by such right **2** : to seize upon before someone else can **3** : to take the place of **syn** usurp, confiscate — **pre·emp·tion** \-'emp-shən\ n

**pre·emp·tive** \prē-'emp-tiv\ adj : marked by the seizing of the initiative : initiated by oneself ⟨~ attack⟩

**preen** \'prēn\ vb **1** : to trim or dress with the beak **2** : to dress or smooth up : PRIMP **3** : to pride (oneself) for achievement

**pre·ex·ist** \,prē-ig-'zist\ vb : to exist

before — **pre·ex·is·tence** \-'zis-təns\ *n* — **pre·ex·is·tent** \-tənt\ *adj*

**pref** *abbr* **1** preface **2** preference **3** preferred **4** prefix

**pre·fab** \'prē-'fab, 'prē-ˌfab\ *n* : a prefabricated structure

**pre·fab·ri·cate** \'prē-'fab-rə-ˌkāt\ *vb* : to fabricate the parts of (as a house) at the factory for rapid assembly elsewhere — **pre·fab·ri·ca·tion** \ˌprē-ˌfab-ri-'kā-shən\ *n*

**¹pref·ace** \'pref-əs\ *n* **:** introductory comments — FOREWORD — **pref·a·to·ry** \'pref-e-ˌtōr-ē\ *adj*

**²preface** *vb* **pref·aced; pref·ac·ing** : to introduce with a preface

**pre·fect** \'prē-ˌfekt\ *n* **1** : a high official; *esp* : a chief officer or magistrate **2** : a student monitor — **pre·fec·ture** \-ˌfek-chər\ *n*

**pre·fer** \pri-'fər\ *vb* **pre·ferred; pre·fer·ring 1** *archaic* : PROMOTE **2** : to like better : choose above another **3** : to bring (as a charge) against a person — **pref·er·a·ble** \'pref-(ə-)rə-bəl\ *adj* — **pref·er·a·bly** \-blē\ *adv*

**pref·er·ence** \'pref-(ə-)rəns\ *n* **1** : a special liking for one thing over another **2** : CHOICE, SELECTION — **pref·er·en·tial** \ˌpref-ə-'ren-chəl\ *adj*

**pre·fer·ment** \pri-'fər-mənt\ *n* : PROMOTION, ADVANCEMENT

**pre·fig·ure** \prē-'fig-yər\ *vb* **1** : FORESHADOW **2** : to imagine beforehand

**¹pre·fix** \'prē-ˌfiks, prē-'fiks\ *vb* : to place before (as a title to a name)

**²pre·fix** \'prē-ˌfiks\ *n* : an affix occurring at the beginning of a word

**pre·flight** \'prē-'flīt\ *adj* : preparing for or preliminary to airplane flight (~ training)

**pre·form** \'prē-'fȯrm\ *vb* : to form or shape beforehand

**preg·na·ble** \'preg-nə-bəl\ *adj* : vulnerable to capture (a ~ fort) — **preg·na·bil·i·ty** \ˌpreg-nə-'bil-ət-ē\ *n*

**preg·nant** \'preg-nənt\ *adj* **1** : containing unborn young **2** : rich in significance : MEANINGFUL — **preg·nan·cy** \-nən-sē\ *n*

**pre·heat** \'prē-'hēt\ *vb* : to heat beforehand; *esp* : to heat (an oven) to a designated temperature before placing food therein

**pre·hen·sile** \prē-'hen-səl, -ˌsīl\ *adj* : adapted for grasping esp. by wrapping around (a monkey with a ~ tail)

**pre·his·tor·ic** \ˌprē-(h)is-'tȯr-ik\ *or* **pre·his·tor·i·cal** \-i-kəl\ *adj* : of, relating to, or existing in the period before written history began

**pre·ig·ni·tion** \ˌprē-ig-'nish-ən\ *n* : ignition in an internal-combustion engine when the inlet valve is open or before compression is completed

**pre·in·duc·tion** \ˌprē-in-'dək-shən\ *adj* : occurring prior to induction into military service

**pre·judge** \'prē-'jəj\ *vb* : to judge before full hearing or examination

**¹prej·u·dice** \'prej-əd-əs\ *n* **1** : DAMAGE; *esp* : detriment to one's rights or claims **2** : an opinion for or against

something without adequate basis — **prej·u·di·cial** \ˌprej-ə-'dish-əl\ *adj*

**²prejudice** *vb* **-diced; -dic·ing 1** : to damage by a judgment or action esp. at law **2** : to cause to have prejudice

**prel·ate** \'prel-ət\ *n* : an ecclesiastic (as a bishop) of high rank — **prel·a·cy** \-ə-sē\ *n*

**pre·launch** \'prē-'lȯnch\ *adj* : preparing for or preliminary to launch

**pre·lim** \'prē-ˌlim, pri-'lim\ *n or adj* : PRELIMINARY

**¹pre·lim·i·nary** \pri-'lim-ə-ˌner-ē\ *n, pl* **-nar·ies** : something that precedes or introduces the main business or event

**²preliminary** *adj* : preceding the main discourse or business

**pre·lude** \'prel-ˌyüd, 'prā-ˌlüd, 'prel-ˌüd\ *n* **1** : an introductory performance or event **2** : a musical section or movement introducing the main theme; *also* : an organ solo played at the beginning of a church service

**prem** *abbr* premium

**pre·mar·i·tal** \(')prē-'mar-ət-ᵊl\ *adj* : existing or occurring before marriage

**pre·ma·ture** \ˌprē-mə-'t(y)u̇r, -'chu̇(ə)r\ *adj* : happening, coming, born, or done before the usual or proper time **syn** untimely, advanced — **pre·ma·ture·ly** *adv*

**pre·med** \'prē-'med\ *adj* : PREMEDICAL — **premed** *n*

**pre·med·i·cal** \(')prē-'med-i-kəl\ *adj* : preceding and preparing for the professional study of medicine

**pre·med·i·tate** \pri-'med-ə-ˌtāt\ *vb* : to consider and plan beforehand — **pre·med·i·ta·tion** \-ˌmed-ə-'tā-shən\ *n*

**pre·men·stru·al** \(')prē-'men-strə(-wə)l\ *adj* : of, relating to, or occurring in the period just preceding menstruation

**¹pre·mier** \pri-'m(y)ər, 'prē-mē-ər\ *adj* [ME *primier*, fr. MF *premier* first, chief, fr. L *primarius* of the first rank] : first in rank or importance : CHIEF; *also* : first in time : EARLIEST

**²premier** *n* : PRIME MINISTER — **pre·mier·ship** *n*

**¹pre·miere** \pri-'myeər, -'miər\ *n* : a first performance

**²premiere** *or* **pre·mier** \like ¹PREMIERE\ *vb* **pre·miered; pre·mier·ing** : to give or receive a first public performance

**prem·ise** \'prem-əs\ *n* **1** : a statement of fact or a supposition made or implied as a basis of argument **2** *pl* : a piece of land with the structures on it; *also* : the place of business of an enterprise

**pre·mi·um** \'prē-mē-əm\ *n* **1** : REWARD, PRIZE **2** : a sum over and above the stated value **3** : something paid over and above a fixed wage or price **4** : something given with a purchase **5** : the sum paid for a contract of insurance **6** : an unusually high value

**pre·mix** \'prē-'miks\ *vb* : to mix before use

**pre·mo·lar** \(')prē-'mō-lər\ *adj* : situated in front of or preceding the molar teeth

**pre·mo·ni·tion** \,prē-mə-'nish-ən, ,prem-ə-\ n : previous notice : FORE-WARNING; also : PRESENTIMENT — **pre·mon·i·to·ry** \pri-'män-ə-,tōr-ē\ adj

**pre·na·tal** \'prē-'nāt-ªl\ adj : occurring or existing before birth

**pre·oc·cu·pa·tion** \prē-,äk-yə-'pā-shən\ n : complete absorption of the mind or interests; also : something that causes such absorption

**pre·oc·cu·pied** \prē-'äk-yə-,pīd\ adj 1 : lost in thought : ENGROSSED 2 : already occupied **syn** abstracted, absent, absentminded, distraught

**pre·oc·cu·py** \-,pī\ vb 1 : to occupy the attention of beforehand 2 : to take possession of before another

**pre·op·er·a·tive** \(')prē-'äp-(ə-)rət-iv, -'äp-ə-,rāt-\ adj : occurring during the period preceding a surgical operation

**pre·or·dain** \,prē-ȯr-'dān\ vb : FORE-ORDAIN

**prep** abbr 1 preparatory 2 preposition

**pre·pack·age** \(')prē-'pak-ij\ vb : to package (as food) before offering for sale to the customer

**preparatory school** n 1 : a usu. private school preparing students primarily for college 2 Brit : a private elementary school preparing students primarily for public schools

**pre·pare** \pri-'paər\ vb **pre·pared**; **pre·par·ing** 1 : to make or get ready ⟨~ dinner⟩ ⟨~ a boy for college⟩ 2 : to get ready beforehand : PROVIDE ⟨~ equipment for a trip⟩ 3 : to put together : COMPOUND ⟨~ a vaccine⟩ 4 : to put into written form ⟨~ a document⟩ — **prep·a·ra·tion** \,prep-ə-'rā-shən\ n — **pre·par·a·to·ry** \pri-'par-ə-,tōr-ē\ adj

**pre·pared·ness** \pri-'par-əd-nəs\ n : a state of adequate preparation esp. for war

**pre·pay** \'prē-'pā\ vb **-paid** \-'pād\; **-pay·ing** : to pay or pay the charge on in advance

**pre·pon·der·ate** \pri-'pän-də-,rāt\ vb **-at·ed**; **-at·ing** [L praeponderare, fr. prae- ahead + ponder-, pondus weight] : to exceed in weight, power, importance, or numbers : PREDOMINATE — **pre·pon·der·ance** \-d(ə-)rəns\ n — **pre·pon·der·ant** \-d(ə-)rənt\ adj — **pre·pon·der·ant·ly** adv

**prep·o·si·tion** \,prep-ə-'zish-ən\ n : a word that combines with a noun or pronoun to form a phrase — **prep·o·si·tion·al** \-'zish-(ə-)nəl\ adj

**pre·pos·sess** \,prē-pə-'zes\ vb 1 : to influence beforehand for or against someone or something 2 : to induce to a favorable opinion beforehand

**pre·pos·sess·ing** adj : tending to create a favorable impression : ATTRAC-TIVE ⟨a ~ manner⟩

**pre·pos·ses·sion** \-'zesh-ən\ n 1 : PREJUDICE 2 : an exclusive concern with one idea or object

**pre·pos·ter·ous** \pri-'päs-t(ə-)rəs\ adj : contrary to nature or reason : ABSURD

**pre·puce** \'prē-,pyüs\ n : FORESKIN

**pre·re·cord** \,prē-ri-'kȯrd\ vb : to record (as a radio or television program) in advance of presentation or use

**pre·req·ui·site** \prē-'rek-wə-zət\ n : something required beforehand or for the end in view — **prerequisite** adj

**pre·rog·a·tive** \pri-'räg-ət-iv\ n : an exclusive or special right, power, or privilege

**pres** abbr 1 present 2 president

¹**pres·age** \'pres-ij\ n 1 : something that foreshadows a future event : OMEN 2 : FOREBODING

²**pre·sage** \'pres-ij, pri-'sāj\ vb **pre·saged**; **pre·sag·ing** 1 : to give an omen or warning of : FORESHADOW 2 : FORETELL, PREDICT

**pres·by·opia** \,prez-bē-'ō-pē-ə\ n : FARSIGHTEDNESS — **pres·by·opic** \-'ō-pik, -'äp-ik\ adj or n

**pres·by·ter** \'prez-bət-ər\ n 1 : PRIEST, MINISTER 2 : an elder in a Presbyterian church

¹**Pres·by·te·ri·an** \,prez-bə-'tir-ē-ən\ adj 1 often not cap : characterized by a graded system of representative ecclesiastical bodies (as presbyteries) exercising legislative and judicial powers 2 : of or relating to a group of Protestant Christian bodies that are presbyterian in government

²**Presbyterian** n : a member of a Presbyterian church — **Pres·by·te·ri·an·ism** \-,iz-əm\ n

**pres·by·tery** \'prez-bə-,ter-ē\ n, pl **-ter·ies** 1 : the part of a church reserved for the officiating clergy 2 : a ruling body in Presbyterian churches consisting of the ministers and representative elders of a district

**pre·school** \'prē-'skül\ adj : of, relating to, or constituting the period in a child's life from infancy to the age of five or six — **pre·school·er** \-'skü-lər\ n

**pre·science** \'prēsh-(ē-)əns, 'presh-\ n : foreknowledge of events; also : FORE-SIGHT — **pre·scient** \-(ē-)ənt\ adj

**pre·scribe** \pri-'skrīb\ vb **pre·scribed**; **pre·scrib·ing** 1 : to lay down as a guide or rule of action 2 : to direct the use of something as a remedy

**pre·scrip·tion** \pri-'skrip-shən\ n 1 : the action of prescribing 2 : a written direction for the preparation and use of a medicine; also : a medicine prescribed

**pres·ence** \'prez-ªns\ n 1 : the fact or condition of being present 2 : the space immediately around a person 3 : one that is present 4 : the bearing of a person; esp : stately bearing

¹**pres·ent** \'prez-ªnt\ n : something presented : GIFT

²**pre·sent** \pri-'zent\ vb 1 : to bring into the presence or acquaintance of : INTRODUCE 2 : to bring before the public ⟨~ a play⟩ 3 : to make a gift to 4 : to give formally 5 : to lay (as a charge) before a court for inquiry 6 : to aim or direct (as a weapon) so as to face in a particular direction — **pre·sent·able** adj — **pre·sen·ta·tion** \,prē-,zen-'tā-shən, ,prez-ªn-\ n — **pre·sent·ment** \pri-'zent-mənt\ n

³**pres·ent** \'prez-ᵊnt\ *adj* **1** : now existing or in progress ⟨~ conditions⟩ **2** : being in view or at hand ⟨~ at the meeting⟩ **3** : constituting the one actually involved ⟨the ~ writer⟩ **4** : of, relating to, or constituting a verb tense that expresses present time or the time of speaking

⁴**pres·ent** \'prez-ᵊnt\ *n* **1** *pl* : the present legal document **2** : the present tense; *also* : a verb form in it **3** : the present time

**pres·ent-day** \'prez-ᵊnt-'dā\ *adj* : now existing or occurring : CURRENT

**pre·sen·ti·ment** \pri-'zent-ə-mənt\ *n* : a feeling that something is about to happen : PREMONITION

**pres·ent·ly** \'prez-ᵊnt-lē\ *adv* **1** : SOON **2** : NOW

**present participle** *n* : a participle that typically expresses present action and that in English is formed with the suffix *-ing* and is used in the formation of the progressive tenses

¹**pre·serve** \pri-'zərv\ *vb* **pre·served; pre·serv·ing 1** : to keep safe : GUARD, PROTECT **2** : to keep from decaying; *esp* : to process food (as by canning or pickling) to prevent spoilage **3** : MAINTAIN ⟨~ silence⟩ — **pres·er·va·tion** \,prez-ər-'vā-shən\ *n* — **pre·ser·va·tive** \pri-'zər-vət-iv\ *adj or n* — **pre·serv·er** \-'zər-vər\ *n*

²**preserve** *n* **1** : preserved fruit — often used in pl. **2** : an area for the protection of natural resources (as animals)

**pre·set** \'prē-'set\ *vb* **-set; -set·ting** : to set beforehand

**pre·shrunk** \'prē-'shrəŋk\ *adj* : of, relating to, or constituting a fabric subjected to a shrinking process during manufacture usu. to reduce later shrinking

**pre·side** \pri-'zīd\ *vb* **pre·sid·ed; pre·sid·ing** [L *praesidēre* to guard, preside over, lit., to sit in front of, sit at the head of, fr. *prae* in front of + *sedēre* to sit] **1** : to occupy the place of authority; *esp* : to act as chairman **2** : to exercise guidance or control

**pres·i·dent** \'prez-əd-ənt\ *n* **1** : one chosen to preside ⟨~ of the assembly⟩ **2** : the chief officer of an organization (as a corporation or society) **3** : an elected official serving as both chief of state and chief political executive; *also* : a chief of state often with only minimal political powers — **pres·i·den·cy** \-ən-sē\ *n* — **pres·i·den·tial** \,prez-ə-'den-chəl\ *adj*

**pre·si·dio** \pri-'sēd-ē-,ō, -'sid-\ *n, pl* **-di·os** : a garrisoned place; *esp* : a military post or fortified settlement in areas currently or orig. under Spanish control

**pre·sid·i·um** \pri-'sid-ē-əm\ *n, pl* **-ia** \-ē-ə\ *or* **-iums** : a permanent executive committee selected in Communist countries to act for a larger body

¹**pre·soak** \(')prē-'sōk\ *vb* : to soak beforehand

²**pre·soak** \'prē-'sōk\ *n* **1** : a preparation used in presoaking clothes **2** : an instance of presoaking

¹**press** \'pres\ *n* **1** : a crowded condition : THRONG **2** : a machine for exerting pressure; *esp* : PRINTING PRESS **3** : CLOSET, CUPBOARD **4** : PRESSURE **5** : the properly creased condition of a freshly pressed garment **6** : the act or the process of printing **7** : a printing or publishing establishment **8** : the media (as newspapers) of public news and comment; *also* : persons (as reporters) employed in these media **9** : comment in newspapers and periodicals **10** : a pressure device (as for keeping a tennis racket from warping)

²**press** *vb* **1** : to bear down upon : push steadily against **2** : ASSAIL, COMPEL **3** : to squeeze out the juice or contents of ⟨~ grapes⟩ **4** : to squeeze to a desired density, shape, or smoothness; *esp* : IRON **5** : to try hard to persuade : URGE **6** : to follow through : PROSECUTE **7** : CROWD **8** : to make (a phonograph record) from a matrix — **press·er** *n*

**press agent** *n* : an agent employed to maintain good public relations through publicity

**press·ing** \'pres-iŋ\ *adj* : URGENT

**press·man** \'pres-mən, -,man\ *n* : the operator of a press and esp. a printing press

**press·room** \'pres-,rüm, -,rûm\ *n* : room in a printing plant containing the printing presses; *also* : a room for the use of reporters

¹**pres·sure** \'presh-ər\ *n* **1** : the burden of physical or mental distress : OPPRESSION **2** : the action of pressing; *esp* : the application of force to something by something else in direct contact with it **3** : the condition of being pressed or of exerting force over a surface **4** : the stress or urgency of matters demanding attention **syn** stress, strain, tension

²**pressure** *vb* **pres·sured; pres·sur·ing** \-(ə-)riŋ\ : to apply pressure to

**pressure group** *n* : a group that seeks to influence governmental policy but not to elect candidates to office

**pressure suit** *n* : an inflatable suit for protection (as of an aviator) against low pressure

**pres·sur·ize** \'presh-ə-,rīz\ *vb* **-ized; -iz·ing** : to maintain normal atmospheric pressure within (an airplane cabin) during high-level flight — **pres·sur·iza·tion** \,presh-(ə-)rə-'zā-shən\ *n*

**pres·ti·dig·i·ta·tion** \,pres-tə-,dij-ə-'tā-shən\ *n* : SLEIGHT OF HAND

**pres·tige** \pres-'tēzh, -'tēj\ *n* [F, fr. MF, conjuror's trick, illusion, fr. LL *praestigium*, fr. L *praestigiae*, pl., conjuror's tricks, irreg. fr. *praestringere* to tie up, blindfold, fr. *prae-* in front of + *stringere* to bind tight] : standing or estimation in the eyes of people : REPUTATION **syn** influence, authority — **pres·ti·gious** \-'tij-əs\ *adj*

**pres·to** \'pres-tō\ *adv or adj* : at once

**pre·stress** \(')prē-'stres\ *vb* : to introduce internal stresses into (as a structural beam) to counteract later load stresses

**pre·sume** \pri-'züm\ vb **pre·sumed;**
**pre·sum·ing 1 :** to take upon oneself without leave or warrant **:** DARE
**2 :** to take for granted **:** ASSUME **3 :** to
act or behave with undue boldness —
**pre·sum·able** \-'zü-mə-bəl\ adj —
**pre·sum·ably** \-blē\ adv

**pre·sump·tion** \pri-'zəmp-shən\ n **1**
**:** presumptuous attitude or conduct
**:** AUDACITY **2 :** an attitude or belief
dictated by probability; also **:** the
grounds lending probability to a belief
— **pre·sump·tive** \-tiv\ adj

**pre·sump·tu·ous** \pri-'zəmp-chə-
(wə)s\ adj **:** overstepping due bounds
**:** taking liberties **:** OVERBOLD

**pre·sup·pose** \prē-sə-'pōz\ vb **1 :** to
suppose beforehand **2 :** to require
beforehand as a necessary condition
syn presume, assume — **pre·sup·po·**
**si·tion** \(,)prē-,səp-ə-'zish-ən\ n

**pre·teen** \'prē-'tēn\ n **:** a preadoles-
cent child — **preteen** adj

**pre·tend** \pri-'tend\ vb **1 :** PROFESS
⟨doesn't ~ to be scientific⟩ **2 :** FEIGN
⟨~ to be angry⟩ **3 :** to lay claim
⟨~ to a throne⟩ — **pre·tend·er** n

**pre·tense** or **pre·tence** \'prē-,tens,
pri-'tens\ n **1 :** CLAIM; esp **:** one not
supported by fact **2 :** mere display
**:** SHOW **3 :** an attempt to attain a
certain condition ⟨made a ~ at disci-
pline⟩ **4 :** false show **:** PRETEXT —
**pre·ten·sion** \pri-'ten-chən\ n

**pre·ten·tious** \pri-'ten-chəs\ adj **1**
**:** making or possessing claims (as to
excellence) **:** OSTENTATIOUS ⟨a ~ literary style⟩ **2 :** making demands on one's
ability or means **:** AMBITIOUS ⟨too ~ an
undertaking⟩ — **pre·ten·tious·ly**
adv — **pre·ten·tious·ness** n

**pret·er·it** or **pret·er·ite** \'pret-ə-rət\
adj **:** PAST **4** — **preterit** n

**pre·ter·mi·nal** \(')prē-'tər-mən-ᵊl\ adj
**:** occurring before death

**pre·ter·nat·u·ral** \,prēt-ər-'nach-(ə-)
rəl\ adj **1 :** exceeding what is natural
**2 :** inexplicable by ordinary means —
**pre·ter·nat·u·ral·ly** \-ē\ adv

**pre·text** \'prē-,tekst\ n **:** a purpose
stated or assumed to cloak the real
intention or state of affairs

**pret·ti·fy** \'prit-i-,fī, 'pùrt-\ vb **-fied;**
**-fy·ing :** to make pretty — **pret·ti·fi·**
**ca·tion** \,prit-i-fə-'kā-shən, ,pùrt-\ n

¹**pret·ty** \'prit-ē, 'pùrt-\ adj **pret·ti·er;**
**-est** [ME praty, prety, fr. OE prættig
tricky, fr. prætt trick] **1 :** pleasing by
delicacy or grace **:** superficially appealing rather than strikingly beautiful ⟨~
flowers⟩ ⟨a ~ girl⟩ ⟨~ verses⟩ **2 :** FINE,
GOOD ⟨a ~ profit⟩ — often used ironically ⟨a ~ state of affairs⟩ syn comely,
fair — **pret·ti·ly** \'prit-ᵊl-ē\ adv —
**pret·ti·ness** \-ē-nəs\ n

²**pret·ty** \,pùrt-ē, pərt-, ,prit-\ adv **:** in
some degree **:** MODERATELY

³**pret·ty** \'prit-ē, 'pùrt-ē\ vb **pret·tied;**
**pret·ty·ing :** to make pretty

**pret·zel** \'pret-səl\ n [G brezel, deriv.
of L brachiatus having branches like
arms, fr. brachium arm] **:** a hard,
glazed, salted, and usu. twisted cracker

**prev** abbr previous; previously

**pre·vail** \pri-'vāl\ vb **1 :** to win
mastery **:** TRIUMPH **2 :** to be or become effective **:** SUCCEED **3 :** to urge
successfully ⟨~ed upon her to sing⟩ **4**
**:** to be frequent **:** PREDOMINATE — **pre·**
**vail·ing·ly** \-iŋ-lē\ adv

**prev·a·lent** \'prev-ə-lənt\ adj **:** generally or widely existent **:** WIDESPREAD
— **prev·a·lence** \-ləns\ n

**pre·var·i·cate** \pri-'var-ə-,kāt\ vb
**-cat·ed; -cat·ing :** to deviate from
the truth **:** EQUIVOCATE — **pre·var·i·**
**ca·tion** \-,var-ə-'kā-shən\ n — **pre·**
**var·i·ca·tor** \-'var-ə-,kāt-ər\ n

**pre·vent** \pri-'vent\ vb **1 :** to keep
from happening or existing ⟨steps to ~
war⟩ **2 :** to hold back **:** HINDER, STOP
⟨tried to ~ us from going⟩ — **pre·**
**vent·able** also **pre·vent·ible** \-ə-
bəl\ adj — **pre·ven·tion** \-'ven-chən\
n — **pre·ven·tive** \-'vent-iv\ or
**pre·ven·ta·tive** \-'vent-ət-iv\ adj or
n

**pre·ver·bal** \(')prē-'vər-bəl\ adj **:** hav-
ing not yet acquired the faculty of
speech

¹**pre·view** \'prē-,vyü\ vb **:** to see or
discuss beforehand; esp **:** to view or
show in advance of public presentation

²**preview** n **1 :** an advance showing or
viewing **2** also **pre·vue** \-,vyü\ **:** a
showing of snatches from a motion
picture advertised for future appearance
**3 :** FORETASTE

**pre·vi·ous** \'prē-vē-əs\ adj **:** going before **:** EARLIER, FORMER syn foregoing,
prior, preceding — **pre·vi·ous·ly** adv

**pre·vi·sion** \prē-'vizh-ən\ n **1 :** FORE-
SIGHT, PRESCIENCE **2 :** FORECAST, PRE-
DICTION

**pre·war** \'prē-'wòr\ adj **:** occurring or
existing before a war

¹**prey** \'prā\ n, pl **preys 1 :** an animal
taken for food by another; also **:** VICTIM
**2 :** the act or habit of preying

²**prey** vb **1 :** to raid for booty **2 :** to
seize and devour something as prey **3**
**:** to have a harmful or wearing effect

**prf** abbr proof

¹**price** \'prīs\ n **1** archaic **:** VALUE
**2 :** the amount of money paid or asked
for the sale of a specified thing; also
**:** the cost at which something is obtained

²**price** vb **priced; pric·ing 1 :** to set a
price on **2 :** to ask the price of **3 :** to
drive by raising prices ⟨priced themselves out of the market⟩

**price·less** \'prīs-ləs\ adj **:** having a
value beyond any price **:** INVALUABLE
syn precious, costly, expensive

**price support** n **:** artificial maintenance
of prices of a commodity at a level usu.
fixed through government action

**price war** n **:** a period of commercial
competition in which prices are repeatedly cut by the competitors

¹**prick** \'prik\ n **1 :** a mark or small
wound made by a pointed instrument
**2 :** something sharp or pointed **3 :** an
instance of pricking; also **:** a sensation
of being pricked

²**prick** vb **1 :** to pierce slightly with a
sharp point; also **:** to have or cause a
sensation of this **2 :** to affect with

anguish or remorse ⟨∼s his conscience⟩ **3** : to outline with punctures ⟨∼ out a pattern⟩ **4** : to cause to stand erect ⟨the dog ∼ed up his ears⟩ **syn** punch, puncture, perforate, bore, drill

**prick·er** \'prik-ər\ n : BRIAR, THORN

**¹prick·le** \'prik-əl\ n **1** : a small sharp point (as on a plant) **2** : a slight stinging pain — **prick·ly** \'prik-lē\ adj

**²prickle** vb **prick·led; prick·ling** \-(ə-)liŋ\ **1** : to prick lightly **2** : TINGLE

**prickly heat** n : a red cutaneous eruption with intense itching and tingling caused by inflammation around the sweat ducts

**prickly pear** n : any of a genus of cacti with usu. yellow flowers and prickly flat or rounded joints; also : the pulpy pear-shaped edible fruit of a prickly pear

**¹pride** \'prīd\ n **1** : CONCEIT **2** : justifiable self-respect **3** : elation over an act or possession **4** : haughty behavior : DISDAIN **5** : ostentatious display — **pride·ful** adj

**²pride** vb **prid·ed; prid·ing** : to indulge in pride : PLUME

**prie-dieu** \(')prē-'dyə(r)\ n, pl **prie-dieux** \-'dyə(r)(z)\ : a small kneeling bench designed for use by a person at prayer and fitted with a raised shelf on which the elbows or a book may be rested

**priest** \'prēst\ n [ME preist, fr. OE prēost, fr. LL presbyter, fr. Gk presbyteros elder, priest, fr. compar. of presbys old] : a person having authority to perform the sacred rites of a religion; esp : an Anglican, Eastern, or Roman Catholic clergyman ranking below a bishop and above a deacon — **priest·ess** \-əs\ n — **priest·hood** n — **priest·li·ness** \-lē-nəs\ n — **priest·ly** adj

**prig** \'prig\ n : one who irritates by rigid or pointed observance of proprieties — **prig·gish** \'prig-ish\ adj — **prig·gish·ly** adv

**¹prim** \'prim\ adj **prim·mer; prim·mest** : stiffly formal and precise — **prim·ly** adv — **prim·ness** n

**²prim** abbr **1** primary **2** primitive

**pri·ma·cy** \'prī-mə-sē\ n **1** : the state of being first (as in rank) **2** : the office, rank, or character of an ecclesiastical primate

**pri·ma don·na** \,prim-ə-'dän-ə\ n, pl **prima donnas** [It, lit., first lady] **1** : a principal female singer (as in an opera company) **2** : an extremely sensitive, vain, or undisciplined person

**pri·ma fa·cie** \,prī-mə-'fā-shə, -s(h)ē\ adj or adv **1** : based on immediate impression : APPARENT **2** : SELF-EVIDENT

**pri·mal** \'prī-məl\ adj **1** : ORIGINAL, PRIMITIVE **2** : first in importance

**pri·mar·i·ly** \prī-'mer-ə-lē\ adv **1** : FUNDAMENTALLY **2** : ORIGINALLY

**¹pri·ma·ry** \'prī-,mer-ē, 'prīm-(ə-)rē\ adj **1** : first in order of time or development; also : PREPARATORY **2** : of first rank or importance; also : FUNDAMENTAL **3** : not derived from or de-

pendent on something else ⟨∼ sources⟩

**²primary** n, pl **-ries 1** : something that stands first in order or importance — usu. used in pl. **2** : a preliminary election in which voters nominate or express a preference among candidates usu. of their own party

**primary school** n **1** : a school usu. including grades 1-3 and sometimes kindergarten **2** : ELEMENTARY SCHOOL

**pri·mate** \'prī-,māt or esp for 1 -mət\ n **1** often cap : the highest-ranking bishop of a province or nation **2** : any of the group of mammals that includes man, the apes, and monkeys

**¹prime** \'prīm\ n **1** : the earliest stage of something; esp : SPRINGTIME **2** : the most active, thriving, or successful stage or period (as of one's life) **3** : the best individual; also : the best part of something **4** : a positive integer that has no factor except itself and 1

**²prime** adj **1** : standing first (as in time, rank, significance, or quality) ⟨∼ requisite⟩ **2** : not capable of being divided by any number except itself or 1 ⟨a ∼ number⟩

**³prime** vb **primed; prim·ing 1** : FILL, LOAD **2** : to lay a preparatory coating upon (as in painting) **3** : to put in working condition **4** : to instruct beforehand : COACH

**prime meridian** n : the meridian of 0° longitude from which other longitudes are reckoned east and west

**prime minister** n **1** : the chief minister of a ruler or state **2** : the chief executive of a parliamentary government

**¹prim·er** \'prim-ər\ n **1** : a small book for teaching children to read **2** : a small introductory book on a subject

**²prim·er** \'prī-mər\ n **1** : one that primes **2** : a device for igniting an explosive **3** : material for priming a surface

**pri·me·val** \prī-'mē-vəl\ adj : of or relating to the earliest ages : PRIMITIVE

**¹prim·i·tive** \'prim-ət-iv\ adj **1** : ORIGINAL, PRIMEVAL **2** : of, relating to, or characteristic of an early stage of development or a relatively simple people or culture **3** : ELEMENTAL, NATURAL **4** : SELF-TAUGHT; also : produced by a self-taught artist — **prim·i·tive·ly** adv — **prim·i·tive·ness** n — **prim·i·tiv·i·ty** \,prim-ə-'tiv-ət-ē\ n

**²primitive** n **1** : a primitive artist **2** : a member of a primitive people

**prim·i·tiv·ism** \'prim-ət-iv-,iz-əm\ n : the style of art of primitive peoples or primitive artists

**pri·mo·gen·i·tor** \,prī-mō-'jen-ət-ər\ n : ANCESTOR, FOREFATHER

**pri·mo·gen·i·ture** \-'jen-ə-,chùr, -,l-chər\ n **1** : the state of being the first-born of a family **2** : an exclusive right of inheritance belonging to the eldest son

**pri·mor·di·al** \prī-'mord-ē-əl\ adj : first created or developed : existing in its original state : PRIMEVAL

**primp** \'primp\ vb : to dress in a careful or finicky manner

**prim·rose** \\'prim-ˌrōz\\ n : any of several low herbs with clusters of showy flowers

**prin** abbr 1 principal 2 principle

**prince** \\'prins\\ n [ME, fr. OF, fr. L princeps, lit., one who takes the first part, fr. primus first + capere to take] **1 :** MONARCH, KING **2 :** a male member of a royal family; esp : a son of the king **3 :** a person of high standing (as in a class) ⟨a ~ of poets⟩ — **prince·dom** \\-dəm\\ n — **prince·ly** adj

**prince·ling** \\-liŋ\\ n : a petty prince

**prin·cess** \\'prin-səs, -ˌses\\ n **1 :** a female member of a royal family **2 :** the consort of a prince

¹**prin·ci·pal** \\'prin-sə-pəl\\ adj : most important — **prin·ci·pal·ly** \\-ē\\ adv

²**principal** n **1 :** a leading person (as in a play) **2 :** the chief officer of an educational institution **3 :** the person from whom an agent's authority derives **4 :** a capital sum placed at interest or used as a fund

**prin·ci·pal·i·ty** \\ˌprin-sə-'pal-ət-ē\\ n, pl **-ties :** the position, territory, or jurisdiction of a prince

**prin·ci·ple** \\'prin-sə-pəl\\ n **1 :** a general or fundamental law, doctrine, or assumption **2 :** a rule or code of conduct; also : devotion to such a code **3 :** the laws or facts of nature underlying the working of an artificial device **4 :** a primary source : ORIGIN; also : an underlying faculty or endowment **5 :** the active part (as of a drug)

**prin·ci·pled** \\-sə-pəld\\ adj : exhibiting, based on, or characterized by principle ⟨high-principled⟩

**principal parts** n pl : the inflected forms of a verb

**prink** \\'priŋk\\ vb : PRIMP

¹**print** \\'print\\ n **1 :** a mark made by pressure **2 :** something stamped with an impression **3 :** printed state or form **4 :** printed matter **5 :** a copy made by printing **6 :** cloth upon which a figure is stamped

²**print** vb **1 :** to stamp (as a mark) in or on something **2 :** to produce impressions of (as from type) **3 :** to write in letters like those of printer's type **4 :** to make (a positive picture) from a photographic negative — **print·er** n

**print·able** \\'print-ə-bəl\\ adj **1 :** capable of being printed or of being printed from **2 :** worthy or fit to be published

**printed circuit** n : a circuit for electronic apparatus made by depositing conductive material on an insulating surface

**print·ing** \\'print-iŋ\\ n **1 :** reproduction in printed form **2 :** the art, practice, or business of a printer **3 :** IMPRESSION 5

**printing press** n : a machine by which printing is done from type or plates

**print·out** \\'print-ˌaút\\ n : a printed record produced by a computer — **print out** \\(ˈ)print-ˈaút\\ vb

¹**pri·or** \\'prī(-ə)r\\ n : the superior of a religious house — **pri·or·ess** \\'prī-ə-rəs\\ n

²**prior** adj **1 :** earlier in time or order

**2 :** taking precedence logically or in importance — **pri·or·i·ty** \\prī-'ȯr-ət-ē\\ n

**prior to** prep : in advance of : BEFORE

**pri·o·ry** \\'prī-(ə-)rē\\ n, pl **-ries :** a religious house under a prior or prioress

**prism** \\'priz-əm\\ n [LL prisma, fr. Gk, lit., anything sawed, fr. priein to saw] **1 :** a solid whose sides are parallelograms and whose ends are parallel and alike in shape and size **2 :** a 3-sided glass or crystal object of prism shape that breaks up light into rainbow colors — **pris·mat·ic** \\priz-'mat-ik\\ adj

**pris·on** \\'priz-ᵊn\\ n : a place or state of confinement esp. for criminals

**pris·on·er** \\'priz-(ᵊ-)nər\\ n : a person deprived of his liberty; esp : one on trial or in prison

**pris·sy** \\'pris-ē\\ adj **pris·si·er; -est** : being prim and precise — **pris·si·ness** \\'pris-ē-nəs\\ n

**pris·tine** \\'pris-ˌtēn\\ adj **1 :** PRIMITIVE **2 :** having the purity of its original state : UNSPOILED

**prith·ee** \\'prith-ē\\ interj, archaic — used to express a wish or request

**pri·va·cy** \\'prī-və-sē\\ n, pl **-cies 1 :** the quality or state of being apart from others **2 :** SECRECY

¹**pri·vate** \\'prī-vət\\ adj **1 :** belonging to or intended for a particular individual or group ⟨~ property⟩ **2 :** restricted to the individual : PERSONAL ⟨~ opinion⟩ **3 :** carried on by the individual independently ⟨~ study⟩ **4 :** not holding public office ⟨a ~ citizen⟩ **5 :** withdrawn from company or observation ⟨a ~ place⟩ **6 :** not known publicly ⟨~ dealings⟩ — **pri·vate·ly** adv

²**private** n **1 :** PRIVACY **2 :** an enlisted man of the lowest rank in the marine corps or of one of the two lowest ranks in the army

**pri·va·teer** \\ˌprī-və-'tiər\\ n : an armed private ship commissioned to cruise against enemy ships and commerce; also : the commander or one of the crew of such a ship

**private first class** n : an enlisted man ranking next below a corporal in the army and next below a lance corporal in the marine corps

**pri·va·tion** \\prī-'vā-shən\\ n **1 :** DEPRIVATION **2 :** the state of being deprived; esp : lack of what is needed for existence

**priv·et** \\'priv-ət\\ n : a nearly evergreen shrub related to the olive and widely used for hedges

¹**priv·i·lege** \\'priv-(ə-)lij\\ n [ME, fr. OF, fr. L privilegium law for or against a private person, fr. privus private + leg-, lex law] : a right or immunity granted as an advantage or favor esp. to some and not others

²**privilege** vb **-leged; -leg·ing :** to grant a privilege to

**priv·i·leged** \\-lijd\\ adj **1 :** having or enjoying one or more privileges ⟨~ classes⟩ **2 :** not subject to disclosure in a court of law ⟨a ~ communication⟩

**priv·y** \\'priv-ē\\ adj **1 :** PERSONAL, PRIVATE **2 :** SECRET **3 :** admitted as one sharing in a secret ⟨~ to the conspiracy⟩ — **priv·i·ly** \'priv-ə-lē\ *adv*

²**privy** *n, pl* **priv·ies** : TOILET; *esp* : OUT-HOUSE

¹**prize** \'prīz\ *n* **1** : something offered or striven for in competition or in contests of chance **2** : something exceptionally desirable

²**prize** *adj* **1** : awarded or worthy of a prize ⟨a ~ essay⟩; *also* : awarded as a prize ⟨a ~ medal⟩ **2** : OUTSTANDING

³**prize** *vb* **prized; priz·ing** : to value highly : ESTEEM **syn** treasure, cherish, appreciate

⁴**prize** *n* : property (as a ship) lawfully captured in time of war

⁵**prize** \'prīz\ *vb* **prized; priz·ing** : PRY

**prize·fight** \'prīz-,fīt\ *n* : a professional boxing match — **prize·fight·er** *n* — **prize·fight·ing** \-iŋ\ *n*

**prize·win·ner** \'prīz-,win-ər\ *n* : a winner of a prize — **prize·win·ning** \-,win-iŋ\ *adj*

**PRN** *abbr* [L *pro re nata*] for the emergency; as needed

¹**pro** \'prō\ *n* : a favorable argument, person, or position

²**pro** *adv* : in favor : FOR

³**pro** *n or adj* : PROFESSIONAL

**PRO** *abbr* public relations officer

**prob** *abbr* **1** probable; probably **2** problem

**prob·a·ble** \'präb-ə-bəl\ *adj* **1** : apparently or presumably true ⟨a ~ hypothesis⟩ **2** : likely to be or become true or real ⟨a ~ result⟩ — **prob·a·bil·i·ty** \,präb-ə-'bil-ət-ē\ *n* — **prob·a·bly** \'präb-ə-blē, 'präb-lē\ *adv*

¹**pro·bate** \'prō-,bāt\ *n* : the judicial determination of the validity of a will

²**pro·bate** *vb* **pro·bat·ed; pro·bat·ing** : to establish (a will) by probate as genuine and valid

**pro·ba·tion** \prō-'bā-shən\ *n* **1** : subjection of an individual to a period of testing and trial to ascertain fitness (as for a job) **2** : the action of giving a convicted offender freedom during good behavior under the supervision of a probation officer — **pro·ba·tion·ary** \-shə,ner-ē\ *adj*

**pro·ba·tion·er** \-sh(ə-)nər\ *n* **1** : one (as a newly admitted student nurse) whose fitness is being tested during a trial period **2** : a convicted offender on probation

**pro·ba·tive** \'prō-bət-iv\ *adj* **1** : serving to test or try **2** : serving to prove

¹**probe** \'prōb\ *n* **1** : a slender instrument for examining a cavity (as a wound) **2** : a penetrating investigation **3** : an information-gathering device sent into outer space **syn** inquiry, inquest, research

²**probe** *vb* **probed; prob·ing 1** : to examine with a probe **2** : to investigate thoroughly

**pro·bi·ty** \'prō-bət-ē\ *n* : UPRIGHTNESS, HONESTY

**prob·lem** \'präb-ləm\ *n* **1** : a question raised for consideration or solution **2** : an intricate unsettled question **3** : a source of perplexity or vexation — **problem** *adj*

**prob·lem·at·ic** \,präb-lə-'mat-ik\ *or* **prob·lem·at·i·cal** \-i-kəl\ *adj* **1** : difficult to solve or decide : PUZZLING **2** : DUBIOUS, QUESTIONABLE

**pro·bos·cis** \prə-'bäs-əs\ *n, pl* **-boscises** *also* **-bos·ci·des** \-'bäs-ə-,dēz\ [L, fr. Gk *proboskis*, fr. *pro-* before + *boskein* to feed] : a long flexible snout (as the trunk of an elephant)

**proc** *abbr* proceedings

**pro·caine** \'prō-,kān\ *n* : a compound used esp. as a local anesthetic

**pro·ca·the·dral** \,prō-kə-'thē-drəl\ *n* : a parish church used as a cathedral

**pro·ce·dure** \prə-'sē-jər\ *n* **1** : a particular way of doing something ⟨democratic ~⟩ **2** : a series of steps followed in a regular order ⟨surgical ~⟩ — **pro·ce·dur·al** \-'sēj-(ə-)rəl\ *adj*

**pro·ceed** \prō-'sēd\ *vb* **1** : to come forth : ISSUE **2** : to go on in an orderly way; *also* : CONTINUE **3** : to begin and carry on an action **4** : to take legal action **5** : to go forward : ADVANCE

**pro·ceed·ing** \-iŋ\ *n* **1** : PROCEDURE **2** *pl* : DOINGS **3** *pl* : legal action **4** : TRANSACTION **5** *pl* : an official record of things said or done

**pro·ceeds** \'prō-,sēdz\ *n pl* : the total amount or the profit arising from a business deal : RETURN

¹**pro·cess** \'präs-,es, 'prōs-\ *n, pl* **process·es** \-,es-əz, -ə-səz, -ə-,sēz\ **1** : PROGRESS, ADVANCE **2** : something going on : PROCEEDING **3** : a natural phenomenon marked by gradual changes that lead toward a particular result ⟨the ~ of growth⟩ **4** : a series of actions or operations directed toward a particular result ⟨a manufacturing ~⟩ **5** : legal action **6** : a mandate issued by a court; *esp* : SUMMONS **7** : a projecting part of an organism or organic structure

²**process** *vb* : to subject to a special process — **pro·ces·sor** \-ər\ *n*

**pro·ces·sion** \prə-'sesh-ən\ *n* : a group of individuals moving along in an orderly often ceremonial way : PARADE

**pro·ces·sion·al** \-'sesh-(ə-)nəl\ *n* **1** : music for a procession **2** : a ceremonial procession

**pro·claim** \prō-'klām\ *vb* : to make known publicly : DECLARE — **proc·la·ma·tion** \,präk-lə-'mā-shən\ *n*

**pro·cliv·i·ty** \prō-'kliv-ət-ē\ *n, pl* **-ties** : an inherent inclination esp. toward something objectionable

**pro·con·sul** \prō-'kän-səl\ *n* **1** : a governor or military commander of an ancient Roman province **2** : an administrator in a modern colony, dependency, or occupied area usu. with wide powers — **pro·con·su·lar** \-sə-lər\ *adj* — **pro·con·su·late** \-sə-lət\ *n* — **pro·con·sul·ship** *n*

**pro·cras·ti·nate** \prə-'kras-tə-,nāt\ *vb* **-nat·ed; -nat·ing** [L *procrastinare*, fr. *pro-* forward + *crastinus* of tomorrow, fr. *cras* tomorrow] : to put off usu. habitually the doing of something that should be done **syn** dawdle, delay, loiter — **pro·cras·ti·na·tion** \-,kras-tə-'nā-shən\ *n* — **pro·cras·ti·na·tor** \-'kras-tə-,nāt-ər\ *n*

**pro·cre·ate** \'prō-krē-ˌāt\ *vb* **-at·ed; -at·ing** : to beget or bring forth offspring **syn** reproduce — **pro·cre·ation** \ˌprō-krē-'ā-shən\ *n* — **pro·cre·ative** \'prō-krē-ˌāt-iv\ *adj* — **pro·cre·ator** \-ˌāt-ər\ *n*

**pro·crus·te·an** \prə-'krəs-tē-ən\ *adj, often cap* : marked by arbitrary often ruthless disregard of individual differences or special circumstances

**proc·tor** \'präk-tər\ *n* : one appointed to supervise students (as at an examination) — **proctor** *vb* — **proc·to·ri·al** \präk-'tōr-ē-əl\ *adj*

**proc·u·ra·tor** \'präk-yə-ˌrāt-ər\ *n* : ADMINISTRATOR; *esp* : an official of ancient Rome administering a province

**pro·cure** \prə-'kyu̇ər\ *vb* **pro·cured; pro·cur·ing 1** : to get possession of : OBTAIN **2** : to make women available for promiscuous sexual intercourse **3** : to bring about : ACHIEVE **syn** secure, acquire, gain, win, earn — **pro·cur·able** \-'kyu̇r-ə-bəl\ *adj* — **pro·cur·er** *n*

¹**prod** \'präd\ *vb* **prod·ded; prod·ding 1** : to thrust a pointed instrument into : GOAD **2** : INCITE, STIR — **prod** *n*

²**prod** *abbr* production

**prod·i·gal** \'präd-i-gəl\ *adj* **1** : recklessly extravagant; *also* : LUXURIANT **2** : WASTEFUL, LAVISH **syn** profuse — **prodigal** *n* — **prod·i·gal·i·ty** \ˌpräd-ə-'gal-ət-ē\ *n*

**pro·di·gious** \prə-'dij-əs\ *adj* **1** : exciting wonder **2** : extraordinary in size or degree : ENORMOUS **syn** monstrous, tremendous, stupendous, monumental — **pro·di·gious·ly** *adv*

**prod·i·gy** \'präd-ə-jē\ *n, pl* **-gies 1** : something extraordinary : WONDER **2** : a highly talented child

¹**pro·duce** \prə-'d(y)üs\ *vb* **pro·duced; pro·duc·ing 1** : to present to view : EXHIBIT **2** : to give birth or rise to : YIELD **3** : EXTEND, PROLONG **4** : to give being or form to : bring about : MAKE; *esp* : MANUFACTURE **5** : to cause to accrue (⟨~ a profit⟩) — **pro·duc·er** *n*

²**pro·duce** \'präd-(ˌ)üs, 'prōd- *also* -(ˌ)yüs\ *n* : PRODUCT **1**; *also* : agricultural products and esp. fresh fruits and vegetables

**prod·uct** \'präd-(ˌ)əkt\ *n* **1** : the number resulting from multiplication **2** : something produced (as by labor, thought, or growth)

**pro·duc·tion** \prə-'dək-shən\ *n* : something produced : PRODUCT **2** : the act or process of producing — **pro·duc·tive** \-'dək-tiv\ *adj* — **pro·duc·tive·ness** *n* — **pro·duc·tiv·i·ty** \(ˌ)prō-ˌdək-'tiv-ət-ē, ˌpräd-(ˌ)ək-\ *n*

**pro·em** \'prō-ˌem\ *n* **1** : preliminary comment : PREFACE **2** : PRELUDE

**prof** *abbr* professor

**pro·fa·na·to·ry** \prō-'fan-ə-ˌtōr-ē, prə-\ *adj* : tending to profane

¹**pro·fane** \prō-'fān\ *vb* **pro·faned; pro·fan·ing 1** : to treat (something sacred) with irreverence or contempt : DESECRATE **2** : to debase by an unworthy use — **prof·a·na·tion** \ˌpräf-ə-'nā-shən\ *n*

²**profane** *adj* [ME *prophane,* fr. MF, fr. L *profanus,* fr. *pro-* before + *fanum* temple] **1** : not concerned with religion : SECULAR **2** : not holy because unconsecrated, impure, or defiled **3** : serving to debase what is holy : IRREVERENT (⟨~ language⟩) — **pro·fane·ly** *adv* — **pro·fane·ness** \-'fān-nəs\ *n*

**pro·fan·i·ty** \prō-'fan-ət-ē\ *n, pl* **-ties 1** : the quality or state of being profane **2** : the use of profane language **3** : profane language

**pro·fess** \prə-'fes\ *vb* **1** : to declare or admit openly : AFFIRM **2** : to declare in words only : PRETEND **3** : to confess one's faith in **4** : to practice or claim to be versed in (a calling or occupation) — **pro·fess·ed·ly** \-əd-lē\ *adv*

**pro·fes·sion** \prə-'fesh-ən\ *n* **1** : an open declaration or avowal of a belief or opinion **2** : a calling requiring specialized knowledge and often long academic preparation **3** : the whole body of persons engaged in a calling

¹**pro·fes·sion·al** \prə-'fesh-(ə-)nəl\ *adj* **1** : of, relating to, or characteristic of a profession **2** : engaged in one of the learned professions **3** : participating for gain in an activity often engaged in by amateurs — **pro·fes·sion·al·ly** \-ē\ *adv*

²**professional** *n* : one that engages in an activity professionally

**pro·fes·sion·al·ism** \-ˌiz-əm\ *n* **1** : the conduct, aims, or qualities that characterize or mark a profession or a professional person **2** : the following of a profession (as athletics) for gain or livelihood

**pro·fes·sion·al·ize** \-ˌīz\ *vb* **-ized; -iz·ing** : to give a professional character to

**pro·fes·sor** \prə-'fes-ər\ *n* : a teacher at a university or college; *esp* : a faculty member of the highest academic rank — **pro·fes·so·ri·al** \ˌprō-fə-'sōr-ē-əl, ˌpräf-ə-\ *adj* — **pro·fes·sor·ship** *n*

**pro·fes·sor·ate** \prə-'fes-ə-rət\ *n* : the office, term of office, or position of a professor

**prof·fer** \'präf-ər\ *vb* **prof·fered; prof·fer·ing** \-(ə-)riŋ\ : to present for acceptance : OFFER — **proffer** *n*

**pro·fi·cient** \prə-'fish-ənt\ *adj* : well advanced in an art, occupation, or branch of knowledge **syn** adept, skillful — **pro·fi·cien·cy** \-ən-sē\ *n* — **proficient** *n* — **pro·fi·cient·ly** *adv*

¹**pro·file** \'prō-ˌfīl\ *n* [It *profilo,* fr. *profilare* to draw in outline, fr. *pro-* forward (fr. L) + *filare* to spin, fr. LL, fr. L *filum* thread] **1** : a representation of something in outline; *esp* : a human head seen in side view **2** : a concise biographical sketch **syn** contour, silhouette

²**profile** *vb* **pro·filed; pro·fil·ing** : to write or draw a profile of

¹**prof·it** \'präf-ət\ *n* **1** : a valuable return : GAIN **2** : the excess of the selling price of goods over their cost — **prof·it·less** *adj*

³**profit** vb **1** : to be of use : BENEFIT **2** : to derive benefit : GAIN — **prof·it·able** \'präf-ət-ə-bəl, 'präf-tə-bəl\ adj — **prof·it·ably** \-blē\ adv

**prof·i·teer** \,präf-ə-'tiər\ n : one who makes what is considered an unreasonable profit — **profiteer** vb

**prof·li·gate** \'präf-li-gət, -lə-,gāt\ adj **1** : completely given up to dissipation and licentiousness **2** : wildly extravagant — **prof·li·ga·cy** \-gə-sē\ n — **profligate** n — **prof·li·gate·ly** adv

**pro for·ma** \prō-'fȯr-mə\ adj : as a matter of form

**pro·found** \prə-'faund\ adj **1** : marked by intellectual depth or insight ⟨a ~ thought⟩ **2** : coming from or reaching to a depth : DEEP-SEATED ⟨a ~ sigh⟩ **3** : deeply felt : INTENSE ⟨~ sympathy⟩ — **pro·found·ly** adv — **pro·fun·di·ty** \-'fən-dət-ē\ n

**pro·fuse** \prə-'fyüs\ adj : pouring forth liberally : ABUNDANT **syn** lavish, prodigal, luxuriant, exuberant — **pro·fuse·ly** adv — **pro·fu·sion** \-'fyü-zhən\ n

**pro·gen·i·tor** \prō-'jen-ət-ər\ n **1** : a direct ancestor : FOREFATHER **2** : ORIGINATOR, PRECURSOR

**prog·e·ny** \'präj-ə-nē\ n, pl **-nies** : OFFSPRING, CHILDREN, DESCENDANTS

**prog·na·thous** \'präg-nə-thəs\ adj : having the jaws projecting beyond the upper part of the face

**prog·no·sis** \präg-'nō-səs\ n, pl **-no·ses** \-,sēz\ : a forecast esp. of the course of a disease

**prog·nos·tic** \präg-'näs-tik\ n **1** : PORTENT **2** : PROPHECY — **prognostic** adj

**prog·nos·ti·cate** \präg-'näs-tə-,kāt\ vb **-cat·ed; -cat·ing** : to foretell from signs or symptoms — **prog·nos·ti·ca·tion** \-,näs-tə-'kā-shən\ n — **prog·nos·ti·ca·tor** \-'näs-tə-,kāt-ər\ n

¹**pro·gram** or **pro·gramme** \'prō-,gram, -grəm\ n **1** : a brief outline of the order to be pursued or the subjects included (as in a public entertainment); also : PERFORMANCE **2** : a plan of procedure **3** : coded instructions for a mechanism (as a computer) **4** : matter for programmed instruction — **pro·gram·mat·ic** \,prō-grə-'mat-ik\ adj

²**program** also **programme** vb **-grammed** or **-gramed; -gram·ming** or **-gram·ing 1** : to enter in a program **2** : to provide (as a computer) with a program — **pro·gram·ma·bil·i·ty** \(,)prō-,gram-ə-'bil-ət-ē\ n — **pro·gram·ma·ble** \'prō-,gram-ə-bəl\ adj — **pro·gram·mer** also **pro·gram·er** \'prō-,gram-ər, -grə-mər\ n

**pro·grammed** or **pro·gramed** \'prō-,gramd, -grəmd\ adj **1** : being instruction or learning by means of a program **2** : produced in the form of a program ⟨a ~ textbook of physics⟩

**programmed instruction** n : instruction through information given in small steps with each requiring a correct response by the learner before going on to the next step

**pro·gram·ming** or **pro·gram·ing**

\-,gram-iŋ, -grə-miŋ\ n **1** : the process of instructing or learning by means of an instruction program **2** : the process of preparing an instruction program

¹**prog·ress** \'präg-rəs, -,res\ n **1** : a forward movement : ADVANCE **2** : a gradual betterment

²**pro·gress** \prə-'gres\ vb **1** : to move forward : PROCEED **2** : to develop to a more advanced stage : IMPROVE

**pro·gres·sion** \prə-'gresh-ən\ n **1** : an act of progressing : ADVANCE **2** : a continuous and connected series

¹**pro·gres·sive** \prə-'gres-iv\ adj **1** : of, relating to, or characterized by progress ⟨a ~ city⟩ **2** : advancing by stages ⟨a ~ disease⟩ **3** often cap : of or relating to political Progressives **4** : of, relating to, or constituting a verb form that expresses action at the time of speaking or a time spoken of — **pro·gres·sive·ly** adv

²**progressive** n **1** : one that is progressive **2** : a person believing in moderate political change and social improvement by government action; esp, cap : a member of a Progressive Party (as in the presidential campaigns of 1912, 1924, and 1948) in the U.S.

**pro·hib·it** \prō-'hib-ət\ vb **1** : to forbid by authority **2** : to prevent from doing something

**pro·hi·bi·tion** \,prō-ə-'bish-ən\ n **1** : the act of prohibiting **2** : the forbidding by law of the sale or manufacture of alcoholic beverages — **pro·hi·bi·tion·ist** \-'bish-(ə-)nəst\ n — **pro·hib·i·tive** \prō-'hib-ət-iv\ adj — **pro·hib·i·tive·ly** adv — **pro·hib·i·to·ry** \-'hib-ə-,tōr-ē\ adj

¹**proj·ect** \'präj-,ekt, -ikt\ n **1** : a specific plan or design : SCHEME **2** : a planned undertaking ⟨a research ~⟩

²**pro·ject** \prə-'jekt\ vb **1** : to devise in the mind : DESIGN **2** : to throw forward **3** : to cause to protrude **4** : to cause (light or shadow) to fall into space or (an image) to fall on a surface ⟨~ a beam of light⟩ — **pro·jec·tion** \-'jek-shən\ n

**pro·jec·tile** \prə-'jek-t²l\ n **1** : a body hurled or projected by external force; esp : a missile for a firearm **2** : a self-propelling weapon

**pro·jec·tion·ist** \prə-'jek-sh(ə-)nəst\ n : one that operates a motion-picture projector or television equipment

**pro·jec·tor** \-'jek-tər\ n : one that projects; esp : a device for projecting pictures on a screen

**pro·le·gom·e·non** \,prō-li-'gäm-ə-,nän, -nən\ n, pl **-e·na** \-nə\ : prefatory remarks

**pro·le·tar·i·an** \,prō-lə-'ter-ē-ən\ n : a member of the proletariat — **proletarian** adj

**pro·le·tar·i·at** \-ē-ət\ n, pl **proletariat** : the laboring class : wage earners

**pro·lif·er·ate** \prə-'lif-ə-,rāt\ vb **-at·ed; -at·ing** : to grow or increase by rapid production of new units (as cells or offspring) — **pro·lif·er·a·tion** \-,lif-ə-'rā-shən\ n

**pro·lif·ic** \prə-'lif-ik\ adj **1** : produc-

ing young or fruit abundantly **2**
: marked by abundant inventiveness or
productivity ⟨a ~ writer⟩ — **pro·lif·i·cal·ly** \-i-k(ə-)lē\ *adv*

**pro·lix** \prō-'liks, 'prō-,liks\ *adj* : VERBOSE **syn** wordy, diffuse, redundant — **pro·lix·i·ty** \prō-'lik-sət-ē\ *n*

**pro·logue** *also* **pro·log** \'prō-,lòg, -,läg\ *n* : PREFACE ⟨~ of a play⟩

**pro·long** \prə-'lòŋ\ *vb* **1** : to lengthen in time : CONTINUE ⟨~ a meeting⟩ **2** : to lengthen in extent or range **syn** protract, extend, elongate — **pro·lon·ga·tion** \,prō-,lòŋ-'gā-shən\ *n*

**prom** \'präm\ *n* : a formal dance given by a high school or college class

**¹prom·e·nade** \,präm-ə-'nād, -'näd\ *n* [F, fr. *promener* to take for a walk, fr. L *prominare* to drive forward, fr. *pro-* forward + *minare* to drive] **1** : a leisurely walk for pleasure or display **2** : a place for strolling **3** : an opening grand march at a formal ball

**²promenade** *vb* **-nad·ed; -nad·ing 1** : to take a promenade **2** : to walk about, in, or on

**pro·me·thi·um** \prə-'mē-thē-əm\ *n* : a metallic chemical element obtained from uranium or neodymium

**prom·i·nence** \'präm-(ə)-nəns\ *n* **1** : the quality, state, or fact of being prominent or conspicuous **2** : something prominent **3** : a mass of cloudlike gas that arises from the sun's chromosphere

**prom·i·nent** \-nənt\ *adj* **1** : jutting out : PROJECTING **2** : readily noticeable : CONSPICUOUS **3** : DISTINGUISHED, EMINENT **syn** remarkable, outstanding, striking — **prom·i·nent·ly** *adv*

**pro·mis·cu·ous** \prə-'mis-kyə-wəs\ *adj* **1** : consisting of various sorts and kinds : MIXED **2** : not restricted to one class or person; *esp* : not restricted to one sexual partner **syn** miscellaneous — **prom·is·cu·i·ty** \,präm-is-'kyü-ət-ē, ,prō-,mis-\ *n* — **pro·mis·cu·ous·ly** *adv* — **pro·mis·cu·ous·ness** *n*

**¹prom·ise** \'präm-əs\ *n* **1** : a pledge to do or not to do something specified **2** : ground for expectation usu. of success or improvement **3** : something promised

**²promise** *vb* **prom·ised; prom·is·ing 1** : to engage to do, bring about, or provide ⟨~ help⟩ **2** : to suggest beforehand ⟨dark clouds ~ rain⟩ **3** : to give ground for expectation ⟨the book ~s to be good⟩

**prom·is·ing** \'präm-ə-siŋ\ *adj* : likely to succeed or yield good results — **prom·is·ing·ly** *adv*

**prom·is·so·ry** \'präm-ə-,sōr-ē\ *adj* : containing a promise

**prom·on·to·ry** \'präm-ən-,tōr-ē\ *n, pl* **-ries** : a point of land jutting into the sea : HEADLAND

**pro·mote** \prə-'mōt\ *vb* **pro·mot·ed; pro·mot·ing 1** : to advance in station, rank, or honor **2** : to contribute to the growth or prosperity of : FURTHER **3** : LAUNCH — **pro·mo·tion** \-'mō-shən\ *n* — **pro·mo·tion·al** \-'mōsh-(ə-)nəl\ *adj*

**pro·mot·er** \-'mōt-ər\ *n* **1** : one that promotes; *esp* : one that takes the first steps in launching an enterprise **2** : one that assumes the financial responsibilities of a sports event

**¹prompt** \'prämpt\ *vb* **1** : INCITE **2** : to assist (one acting or reciting) by suggesting the next words **3** : INSPIRE, URGE — **prompt·er** *n*

**²prompt** *adj* **1** : being ready and quick to act; *also* : PUNCTUAL **2** : performed readily or immediately ⟨~ service⟩ — **prompt·ly** *adv* — **prompt·ness** *n*

**prompt·book** \-,bùk\ *n* : a copy of a play with directions for performance used by a theater prompter

**promp·ti·tude** \'prämp-tə-,t(y)üd\ *n* : the quality or habit of being prompt : PROMPTNESS

**pro·mul·gate** \'präm-əl-,gāt; prō-'məl-\ *vb* **-gat·ed; -gat·ing** : to make known or put into force by open declaration — **prom·ul·ga·tion** \,präm-əl-'gā-shən, ,prō-(,)məl-\ *n*

**pron** *abbr* **1** pronoun **2** pronounced **3** pronunciation

**prone** \'prōn\ *adj* **1** : having a tendency or inclination : DISPOSED **2** : lying face downward; *also* : lying flat or prostrate **syn** subject, exposed, open, liable, susceptible — **prone·ness** \'prōn-nəs\ *n*

**prong** \'pròŋ\ *n* : one of the sharp points of a fork : TINE; *also* : a slender projecting part (as of an antler)

**prong·horn** \'pròŋ-,hòrn\ *n, pl* **pronghorn** *also* **pronghorns** : a ruminant animal of treeless parts of western No. America that resembles an antelope

**pro·noun** \'prō-,naùn\ *n* : a word used as a substitute for a noun

**pro·nounce** \prə-'naùns\ *vb* **pro·nounced; pro·nounc·ing 1** : to utter officially or as an opinion ⟨~ sentence⟩ **2** : to employ the organs of speech in order to produce ⟨~ a word⟩; *esp* : to say or speak correctly ⟨she can't ~ his name⟩ — **pro·nounce·able** *adj* — **pro·nun·ci·a·tion** \-,nən-sē-'ā-shən\ *n*

**pro·nounced** \-'naùnst\ *adj* : strongly marked : DECIDED

**pro·nounce·ment** \prə-'naùns-mənt\ *n* : a formal declaration of opinion; *also* : ANNOUNCEMENT

**pron·to** \'prän-,tō\ *adv* [Sp, fr. L *promptus* prompt] : QUICKLY

**pro·nun·ci·a·men·to** \prō-,nən-sē-ə-'ment-ō\ *n, pl* **-tos** *or* **-toes** : PROCLAMATION, MANIFESTO

**¹proof** \'prüf\ *n* **1** : the evidence that compels acceptance by the mind of a truth or fact **2** : a process or operation that establishes validity or truth : TEST **3** : a trial print from a photographic negative **4** : a trial impression (as from type) **5** : alcoholic content (as of a beverage) indicated by a number that is twice the percent by volume of alcohol present ⟨whiskey of 90 ~ is 45% alcohol⟩

**²proof** *adj* **1** : successful in resisting or repelling ⟨~ against tampering⟩ **2** : of standard strength or quality or alcoholic content

**proof·read** \-‚rēd\ *vb* **:** to read and mark corrections in (printer's proof) — **proof·read·er** *n*

¹**prop** \'präp\ *n* **:** something that props

²**prop** *vb* **propped; prop·ping** **1 :** to support by placing something under or against ⟨~ up a wall⟩ **2 :** SUSTAIN, STRENGTHEN

³**prop** *n* **:** PROPERTY 4

⁴**prop** *n* **:** PROPELLER

⁵**prop** *abbr* **1** property **2** proposition **3** proprietor

**pro·pa·gan·da** \‚präp-ə-'gan-də, ‚prō-pə-\ *n* [NL, fr. *Congregatio de propaganda fide* Congregation for propagating the faith, organization established by Pope Gregory XV] **:** the spreading of ideas or information deliberately to further one's cause or damage an opposing cause; *also* **:** ideas, facts, or allegations spread for such a purpose — **prop·a·gan·dist** \-dəst\ *n*

**pro·pa·gan·dize** \-‚dīz\ *vb* **-dized; -diz·ing :** to subject to or carry on propaganda

**prop·a·gate** \'präp-ə-‚gāt\ *vb* **-gated; -gat·ing** **1 :** to reproduce or cause to reproduce biologically **:** MULTIPLY **2 :** to cause to spread — **prop·a·ga·tion** \‚präp-ə-'gā-shən\ *n*

**pro·pane** \'prō-‚pān\ *n* **:** a heavy flammable gas found in petroleum and natural gas and used as a fuel

**pro·pel** \prə-'pel\ *vb* **pro·pelled; pro·pel·ling** **1 :** to drive forward or onward **2 :** to urge on **:** MOTIVATE **syn** push, shove, thrust

**pro·pel·lant** *or* **pro·pel·lent** \-'pel-ənt\ *n* **:** something (as an explosive or fuel) that propels — **propellant** *or* **propellent** *adj*

**pro·pel·ler** *also* **pro·pel·lor** \prə-'pel-ər\ *n* **:** a device consisting of a hub fitted with revolving blades that imparts motion to a vehicle (as a motorboat or an airplane)

**pro·pen·si·ty** \prə-'pen-sət-ē\ *n, pl* **-ties :** a particular disposition of mind or character **:** BENT

¹**prop·er** \'präp-ər\ *adj* **1 :** marked by suitability or rightness ⟨~ punishment⟩ **2 :** referring to one individual only ⟨~ noun⟩ **3 :** belonging characteristically to a species or individual **:** PECULIAR **4 :** very satisfactory **:** EXCELLENT **5 :** strictly limited to a specified thing ⟨the city ~⟩ **6 :** CORRECT ⟨the ~ way to proceed⟩ **7 :** strictly decorous **:** GENTEEL **syn** meet, appropriate, fitting, seemly — **prop·er·ly** *adv*

²**proper** *n* **:** the parts of the Mass that vary according to the liturgical calendar

**prop·er·tied** \'präp-ərt-ēd\ *adj* **:** owning property and esp. much property

**prop·er·ty** \'präp-ərt-ē\ *n, pl* **-ties** **1 :** a quality peculiar to an individual or thing **2 :** something owned; *esp* **:** a piece of real estate **3 :** OWNERSHIP **4 :** an article or object used in a play other than painted scenery and actors' costumes

**proph·e·cy** *also* **proph·e·sy** \'präf-ə-

sē\ *n, pl* **-cies** *also* **-sies** **1 :** an inspired utterance of a prophet **2 :** PREDICTION

**proph·e·sy** \-‚sī\ *vb* **-sied; -sy·ing** **1 :** to speak or utter by divine inspiration **2 :** PREDICT — **proph·e·si·er** \-‚sī-(-ə)r\ *n*

**proph·et** \'präf-ət\ *n* [ME *prophete*, fr. OF, fr. L *propheta*, fr. Gk *prophētēs*, fr. *pro* for + *phanai* to speak] **1 :** one who utters divinely inspired revelations **2 :** one who foretells future events — **proph·et·ess** \-əs\ *n*

**pro·phet·ic** \prə-'fet-ik\ *or* **pro·phet·i·cal** \-i-kəl\ *adj* **:** of, relating to, or characteristic of a prophet or prophecy — **pro·phet·i·cal·ly** \-i-k(ə-)lē\ *adv*

¹**pro·phy·lac·tic** \‚prō-fə-'lak-tik, ‚präf-ə-\ *adj* **1 :** preventing or guarding against disease **2 :** PREVENTIVE

²**prophylactic** *n* **:** something (as a drug or device) that protects from disease

**pro·phy·lax·is** \-'lak-səs\ *n, pl* **-lax·es** \-'lak-‚sēz\ **:** measures designed to preserve health and prevent the spread of disease

**pro·pin·qui·ty** \prə-'piŋ-kwət-ē\ *n* **1 :** KINSHIP **2 :** nearness in place or time **:** PROXIMITY

**pro·pi·ti·ate** \prō-'pish-ē-‚āt\ *vb* **-ated; -at·ing :** to gain or regain the favor of **:** APPEASE — **pro·pi·ti·a·tion** \-‚pis(h)-ē-'ā-shən\ *n* — **pro·pi·tia·to·ry** \-'pish-(ē-)ə-‚tōr-ē\ *adj*

**pro·pi·tious** \prə-'pish-əs\ *adj* **1 :** favorably disposed ⟨~ deities⟩ **2 :** being of good omen ⟨~ circumstances⟩

**prop·jet engine** \‚präp-‚jet-\ *n* **:** TURBO-PROPELLER ENGINE

**prop·man** \'präp-‚man\ *n* **:** one who is in charge of theater or motion-picture stage properties

**pro·po·nent** \prə-'pō-nənt\ *n* **:** one who argues in favor of something

¹**pro·por·tion** \prə-'pōr-shən\ *n* **1 :** the relation of one part to another or to the whole with respect to magnitude, quantity, or degree **:** RATIO **2 :** BALANCE, SYMMETRY **3 :** SHARE, QUOTA **4 :** SIZE, DEGREE — **pro·por·tion·al** \-sh(ə-)nəl\ *adj* — **pro·por·tion·al·ly** \-ē\ *adv* — **pro·por·tion·ate** \-sh(ə-)nət\ *adj* — **pro·por·tion·ate·ly** *adv*

²**proportion** *vb* **pro·por·tioned; pro·por·tion·ing** \-sh(ə-)niŋ\ **1 :** to adjust (a part or thing) in size relative to other parts or things **2 :** to make the parts of harmonious

**pro·pose** \prə-'pōz\ *vb* **pro·posed; pro·pos·ing** **1 :** PLAN, INTEND ⟨~s to buy a house⟩ **2 :** to make an offer of marriage **3 :** to offer for consideration **:** SUGGEST ⟨~ a policy⟩ — **pro·pos·al** \-'pō-zəl\ *n* — **pro·pos·er** *n*

¹**prop·o·si·tion** \‚präp-ə-'zish-ən\ *n* **1 :** something proposed for consideration **:** PROPOSAL; *esp* **:** a suggesting of sexual intercourse **2 :** a statement of something to be discussed, proved, or explained **3 :** SITUATION, AFFAIR ⟨a tough ~⟩ — **prop·o·si·tion·al** \-'zish-(ə-)nəl\ *adj*

²**proposition** *vb* **prop·o·si·tioned;
prop·o·si·tion·ing** \-'zish-(ə-)niŋ\
: to make a proposal to; *esp* : to suggest
sexual intercourse to

**pro·pound** \prə-'paùnd\ *vb* : to set
forth for consideration or debate ⟨~ a
doctrine⟩

**pro·pri·e·tary** \prə-'prī-ə-,ter-ē\ *adj*
**1** : of, relating to, or characteristic of a
proprietor ⟨~ control⟩ **2** : made and
sold by one with the sole right to do so
⟨~ medicines⟩

**pro·pri·e·tor** \prə-'prī-ət-ər\ *n* : OWNER
— **pro·pri·e·tor·ship** *n* — **pro·pri·
etress** \-'prī-ə-trəs\ *n*

**pro·pri·e·ty** \prə-'prī-ət-ē\ *n, pl* -**eties**
**1** : the standard of what is socially acceptable in conduct or speech **2** *pl* : the
customs of polite society

**pro·pul·sion** \prə-'pəl-shən\ *n* **1** : the
action or process of propelling : a driving forward **2** : driving power — **pro·
pul·sive** \-siv\ *adj*

**pro ra·ta** \prō-'rāt-ə, -'rät-\ *adv* : in
proportion : PROPORTIONATELY

**pro·rate** \'prō-'rāt\ *vb* **pro·rat·ed;
pro·rat·ing** : to divide, distribute, or
assess proportionately

**pro·rogue** \prə-'rōg\ *vb* **pro·rogued;
pro·rogu·ing** : to suspend or end a
session of (a legislative body) **syn** adjourn, dissolve — **pro·ro·ga·tion**
\,prōr-ō-'gā-shən\ *n*

¹**pros** *pl of* PRO

²**pros** *abbr* prosody

**pro·sa·ic** \prō-'zā-ik\ *adj* : lacking
imagination or excitement : DULL

**pro·sce·ni·um** \prō-'sē-nē-əm\ *n* : the
wall that separates the stage from the
auditorium and provides the arch that
frames it

**pro·scribe** \prō-'skrīb\ *vb* **pro·
scribed; pro·scrib·ing 1** : OUTLAW
**2** : to condemn or forbid as harmful
— **pro·scrip·tion** \-'skrip-shən\ *n*

**prose** \'prōz\ *n* [ME, fr. MF, fr. L
*prosa,* fr. fem. of *prorsus, prosus,*
straightforward, being in prose, fr.
*proversus,* pp. of *provertere* to turn forward, fr. *pro-* forward + *vertere* to
turn] : the ordinary language of men in
speaking or writing

**pros·e·cute** \'präs-i-,kyüt\ *vb* **-cut-
ed; -cut·ing 1** : to follow to the end
⟨~ an investigation⟩ **2** : to pursue before a legal tribunal for punishment of a
violation of law ⟨~ a forger⟩ — **pros·
e·cu·tion** \,präs-i-'kyü-shən\ *n* —
**pros·e·cu·tor** \'präs-i-,kyüt-ər\ *n*

¹**pros·e·lyte** \'präs-ə-,līt\ *n* : a new
convert to a religion, belief, or party
— **pros·e·lyt·ism** \-,līt-,iz-əm\ *n*

²**proselyte** *vb* **-lyt·ed; -lyt·ing** : to
convert from one religion, belief, or
party to another

**pros·e·ly·tize** \'präs-(ə-)lə-,tīz\ *vb*
**-tized; -tiz·ing** : PROSELYTE

**pros·o·dy** \'präs-əd-ē\ *n, pl* -**dies**
: the study of versification and esp. of
metrical structure

¹**pros·pect** \'präs-,pekt\ *n* **1** : an extensive view; *also* : OUTLOOK **2** : the
act of looking forward **3** : a mental
vision of something to come **4** : some-

thing that is awaited or expected
: POSSIBILITY **5** : a potential buyer or
customer; *also* : a likely candidate —
**pro·spec·tive** \prə-'spek-tiv, 'präs-
,pek-\ *adj* — **pro·spec·tive·ly** *adv*

²**pros·pect** \'präs-,pekt\ *vb* : to explore esp. for mineral deposits — **pros·
pec·tor** \-,pek-tər, -'pek-\ *n*

**pro·spec·tus** \prə-'spek-təs\ *n* : a preliminary statement that describes an
enterprise and is distributed to prospective buyers or participants

**pros·per** \'präs-pər\ *vb* **pros·pered;
pros·per·ing** \-p(ə-)riŋ\ : SUCCEED;
*esp* : to achieve economic success

**pros·per·i·ty** \präs-'per-ət-ē\ *n*
: thriving condition : SUCCESS; *esp*
: economic well-being

**pros·per·ous** \'präs-p(ə-)rəs\ *adj* **1**
: FAVORABLE ⟨~ winds⟩ **2** : marked by
success or economic well-being ⟨a ~
business⟩

**pros·tate** \'präs-,tāt\ *n* : a glandular
body about the base of the male urethra
— **prostate** *also* **pros·tat·ic** \prä-
'stat-ik\ *adj*

**pros·ta·ti·tis** \,präs-tə-'tīt-əs\ *n* : inflammation of the prostate gland

**pros·the·sis** \präs-'thē-səs, 'präs-thə-\
*n, pl* -**the·ses** \-,sēz\ : an artificial
device to replace a missing part of the
body — **pros·thet·ic** \präs-'thet-ik\
*adj*

**pros·thet·ics** \-'thet-iks\ *n pl* : the
surgical and dental specialties concerned with the artificial replacement of
missing parts

¹**pros·ti·tute** \'präs-tə-,t(y)üt\ *vb* **-tut-
ed; -tut·ing 1** : to offer indiscrimi-
nately for sexual intercourse esp. for
money **2** : to devote to corrupt or unworthy purposes — **pros·ti·tu·tion**
\,präs-tə-'t(y)ü-shən\ *n*

²**prostitute** *n* : a woman who engages in
promiscuous sexual intercourse esp. for
pay

¹**pros·trate** \'präs-,trāt\ *adj* **1**
: stretched out with face on the ground
in adoration or submission **2** : EX-
tended in a horizontal position : FLAT
⟨a ~ shrub⟩ **3** : laid low : OVERCOME
⟨~ with a cold⟩

²**pros·trate** \'präs-,trāt\ *vb* **pros·trat-
ed; pros·trat·ing 1** : to throw or put
into a prostrate position **2** : to reduce
to submission, helplessness, or exhaustion — **pros·tra·tion** \präs-'trā-
shən\ *n*

**prosy** \'prō-zē\ *adj* **pros·i·er; -est 1**
: PROSAIC **2** : TEDIOUS

**Prot** *abbr* Protestant

**prot·ac·tin·i·um** \,prōt-,ak-'tin-ē-
əm\ *n* : a metallic radioactive element
of relatively short life

**pro·tag·o·nist** \prō-'tag-ə-nəst\ *n* **1**
: one who takes the leading part in a
drama or story **2** : a spokesman for a
cause : CHAMPION

**pro·te·an** \'prōt-ē-ən\ *adj* : readily assuming different shapes or roles

**pro·tect** \prə-'tekt\ *vb* : to shield from
injury : GUARD

**pro·tec·tion** \prə-'tek-shən\ *n* **1** : the
act of protecting : the state of being

protected **2** : one that protects ⟨wear a helmet as a ∼⟩ **3** : the oversight or support of one that is smaller and weaker **4** : the freeing of the producers of a country from foreign competition in their home market by high duties on foreign competitive goods — **pro·tec·tive** \-'tek-tiv\ adj

**pro·tec·tion·ist** \-sh(ə-)nəst\ n : an advocate of government economic protection for domestic producers through restrictions on foreign competitors — **pro·tec·tion·ism** \-sha-,niz-əm\ n

**pro·tec·tor** \prə-'tek-tər\ n **1** : one that protects : GUARDIAN **2** : a device used to prevent injury : GUARD **3** : REGENT — **pro·tec·tress** \-trəs\ n

**pro·tec·tor·ate** \-t(ə-)rət\ n **1** : government by a protector **2** : the relationship of superior authority assumed by one state over a dependent one; also : the dependent political unit in such a relationship

**pro·té·gé** \'prōt-ə-,zhā\ n : one who is under the care and protection of an influential person — **pro·té·gée** \-,zhā\ n

**pro·tein** \'prō-,tēn, 'prōt-ē-ən\ n [F protéine, fr. LGk prōteios primary, fr. Gk prōtos first] : any of a great class of complex usu. linear combinations of amino acids that contain carbon, hydrogen, nitrogen, oxygen, and sometimes other elements, are present in all living matter, and are an essential food item

**pro tem** \prō-'tem\ adv : for the time being

**pro tem·po·re** \prō-'tem-pə-rē\ adv : for the present : TEMPORARILY

¹**pro·test** \'prō-,test\ n **1** : the act of protesting; esp : an organized public demonstration of disapproval **2** : a complaint or objection against an idea, an act, or a course of action

²**pro·test** \prə-'test\ vb **1** : to assert positively : make solemn declaration of ⟨∼s his innocence⟩ **2** : to object strongly : make a protest against ⟨∼ a ruling⟩ — **prot·es·ta·tion** \,prät-əs-'tā-shən\ n — **pro·test·er** or **pro·tes·tor** \-ər\ n

**Prot·es·tant** \'prät-əs-tənt, 3 also prə-'tes-\ n **1** : a member or adherent of one of the Christian churches deriving from the Reformation **2** : a Christian not of a Catholic or Orthodox church **3** not cap : one who makes a protest — **Prot·es·tant·ism** \'prät-əs-tənt-,iz-əm\ n

**pro·tha·la·mi·on** \,prō-thə-'lā-mē-ən\ or **pro·tha·la·mi·um** \-mē-əm\ n, pl -mia \-mē-ə\ : a song in celebration of a marriage

**pro·to·col** \'prōt-ə-,kȯl\ n [MF prothocole, fr. ML protocollum, fr. LGk prōtokollon first sheet of a papyrus roll bearing data of manufacture, fr. Gk prōtos first + kollan to glue together, fr. kolla glue] **1** : an original draft or record **2** : a preliminary memorandum of diplomatic negotiation **3** : a code of diplomatic or military etiquette and precedence

**pro·to·mar·tyr** \'prōt-ō-,märt-ər\ n : the first martyr in a cause or region

**pro·ton** \'prō-,tän\ n [Gk prōton, neut. of prōtos first] : an elementary particle that is present in all atomic nuclei and carries a positive charge of electricity

**pro·to·plasm** \'prōt-ə-,plaz-əm\ n : the complex colloidal largely protein living substance of plant and animal cells — **pro·to·plas·mic** \,prōt-ə-'plaz-mik\ adj

**pro·to·type** \'prōt-ə-,tīp\ n : an original model : ARCHETYPE

**pro·to·zo·an** \,prōt-ə-'zō-ən\ n : any of a great group of lower invertebrate animals that are essentially single cells

**pro·tract** \prō-'trakt\ vb : to prolong in time or space **syn** extend, lengthen

**pro·trac·tor** \-'trak-tər\ n : an instrument for constructing and measuring angles

**pro·trude** \prō-'trüd\ vb **pro·trud·ed; pro·trud·ing** : to stick out or cause to stick out : jut out — **pro·tru·sion** \-'trü-zhən\ n — **pro·tru·sive** \-'trü-siv\ adj

**pro·tu·ber·ance** \prō-'t(y)ü-b(ə-)rəns\ n : something that is protuberant

**pro·tu·ber·ant** \-b(ə-)rənt\ adj : extending beyond the surrounding surface in a bulge

**proud** \'praud\ adj **1** : having or showing excessive self-esteem : HAUGHTY **2** : highly pleased : EXULTANT **3** : having proper self-respect ⟨too ∼ to beg⟩ **4** : GLORIOUS ⟨a ∼ occasion⟩ **5** : SPIRITED ⟨a ∼ steed⟩ **syn** arrogant, insolent, overbearing, disdainful — **proud·ly** adv

**prov** abbr **1** province; provincial **2** provisional

**Prov** abbr Proverbs

**prove** \'prüv\ vb **proved; proved** or **prov·en** \'prü-vən\; **prov·ing** \'prü-viŋ\ **1** : to test by experiment or by a standard **2** : to establish the truth of by argument or evidence **3** : to show to be correct, valid, or genuine **4** : to turn out esp. after trial or test ⟨the car proved to be a good choice⟩ — **prov·able** \'prü-və-bəl\ adj

**prov·e·nance** \'präv-ə-nəns\ n : ORIGIN, SOURCE

**Pro·ven·çal** \,präv-ən-'säl, ,prōv-\ n **1** : a native or inhabitant of Provence **2** : a Romance language spoken in southeastern France — **Provençal** adj

**prov·en·der** \'präv-ən-dər\ n **1** : dry food for domestic animals : FEED **2** : FOOD, VICTUALS

**pro·ve·nience** \prə-'vē-nyəns\ n : ORIGIN, SOURCE

**prov·erb** \'präv-,ərb\ n : a pithy popular saying : ADAGE — **pro·ver·bi·al** \prə-'vər-bē-əl\ adj

**pro·vide** \prə-'vīd\ vb **pro·vid·ed; pro·vid·ing** [ME providen, fr. L providēre, lit., to see ahead, fr. pro- forward + vidēre to see] **1** : to take measures beforehand ⟨∼ against inflation⟩ **2** : to make a proviso or stipulation **3** : to supply what is needed ⟨∼ for a

## provided • psychedelic

family⟩ **4** : EQUIP **5** : to supply for use : YIELD — **pro·vid·er** *n*

**pro·vid·ed** \prə-'vīd-əd\ *conj* : on condition that : IF

**prov·i·dence** \'präv-əd-əns\ *n* **1** *often cap* : divine guidance or care **2** *cap* : GOD **1** **3** : the quality or state of being provident

**prov·i·dent** \-əd-ənt\ *adj* **1** : making provision for the future : PRUDENT **2** : FRUGAL — **prov·i·dent·ly** *adv*

**prov·i·den·tial** \,präv-ə-'den-chəl\ *adj* **1** : of, relating to, or determined by Providence **2** : OPPORTUNE, LUCKY

**prov·ince** \'präv-əns\ *n* **1** : an administrative district or division of a country **2** *pl* : all of a country except the metropolis **3** : proper business or scope : SPHERE

**pro·vin·cial** \prə-'vin-chəl\ *adj* **1** : of or relating to a province **2** : confined to a region : NARROW ⟨∼ ideas⟩ — **pro·vin·cial·ism** \-,iz-əm\ *n*

**proving ground** *n* : a place for scientific experimentation or testing

**¹pro·vi·sion** \prə-'vizh-ən\ *n* **1** : the act or process of providing; *also* : a measure taken beforehand **2** : a stock of needed supplies; *esp* : a stock of food — usu. used in pl. **3** : PROVISO

**²provision** *vb* **pro·vi·sioned; pro·vi·sion·ing** \-'vizh-(ə-)niŋ\ : to supply with provisions

**pro·vi·sion·al** \-'vizh-(ə-)nəl\ *adj* : provided for a temporary need : CONDITIONAL

**pro·vi·so** \prə-'vī-zō\ *n, pl* **-sos** *or* **-soes** [ME, fr. ML *proviso quod* provided that] : an article or clause that introduces a condition : STIPULATION

**pro·voke** \prə-'vōk\ *vb* **pro·voked; pro·vok·ing** **1** : to incite to anger : INCENSE **2** : to bring on : EVOKE ⟨a sally that *provoked* laughter⟩ **3** : to stir up on purpose ⟨∼ an argument⟩ **syn** irritate, exasperate, excite, stimulate, pique — **prov·o·ca·tion** \,präv-ə-'kā-shən\ *n* — **pro·voc·a·tive** \prə-'väk-ət-iv\ *adj*

**pro·vo·lo·ne** \,prō-və-'lō-nē\ *n* : a hard smooth Italian cheese that is made from heated and kneaded curd, molded into various shapes, hung in strings to be cured, and often smoked

**pro·vost** \'prō-,vōst, 'präv-əst\ *n* : a high official : DIGNITARY; *esp* : a high-ranking university administrative officer

**provost marshal** \,prō-,vō-'mär-shəl\ *n* : an officer who supervises the military police of a command

**prow** \'prau̇\ *n* : the bow of a ship

**prow·ess** \'prau̇-əs\ *n* **1** : military valor and skill **2** : extraordinary ability

**prowl** \'prau̇l\ *vb* : to roam about stealthily — **prowl** *n* — **prowl·er** *n*

**prowl car** *n* : SQUAD CAR

**prox·i·mate** \'präk-sə-mət\ *adj* **1** : very near **2** : DIRECT ⟨the ∼ cause⟩

**prox·im·i·ty** \präk-'sim-ət-ē\ *n* : NEARNESS

**proximity fuze** *n* : an electronic device that detonates a projectile

**prox·i·mo** \'präk-sə-,mō\ *adj* [L *proximo mense* in the next month] : of

or occurring in the next month after the present

**proxy** \'präk-sē\ *n, pl* **prox·ies** : the authority or power to act for another; *also* : a document giving such authorization — **proxy** *adj*

**prp** *abbr* present participle

**prude** \'prüd\ *n* : one who shows or affects extreme modesty — **prud·ery** \'prüd-ə-rē\ *n* — **prud·ish** \'prüd-ish\ *adj*

**pru·dent** \'prüd-²nt\ *adj* **1** : shrewd in the management of practical affairs **2** : CAUTIOUS, DISCREET **3** : PROVIDENT, FRUGAL **syn** judicious, foresighted, sensible, sane — **pru·dence** \-²ns\ *n* — **pru·den·tial** \prü-'den-chəl\ *adj* — **pru·dent·ly** \'prüd-²nt-lē\ *adv*

**¹prune** \'prün\ *n* : a plum dried or capable of being dried without fermentation

**²prune** *vb* **pruned; prun·ing** : to cut off unwanted parts (as of a tree)

**pru·ri·ent** \'prür-ē-ənt\ *adj* : LASCIVIOUS; *also* : exciting to lasciviousness — **pru·ri·ence** \-ē-əns\ *n*

**¹pry** \'prī\ *vb* **pried; pry·ing** : to look closely or inquisitively; *esp* : SNOOP

**²pry** *vb* **pried; pry·ing** **1** : to raise, move, or pull apart with a pry or lever **2** : to detach or open with difficulty

**³pry** *n* : a tool for prying

**Ps** *or* **Psa** *abbr* Psalms

**PS** *abbr* **1** postscript **2** public school

**psalm** \'säm, 'sälm\ *n, often cap* [ME, fr. OE *psealm*, fr. LL *psalmus*, fr. Gk *psalmos*, lit., twanging of a harp, fr. *psallein* to pluck, play a stringed instrument] : a sacred song or poem; *esp* : one of the hymns collected in the Book of Psalms — **psalm·ist** *n*

**psalm·o·dy** \'säm-əd-ē, 'säl-məd-\ *n* : the singing of psalms in worship; *also* : a collection of psalms

**Psal·ter** \'sȯl-tər\ *n* : the Book of Psalms; *also* : a collection of the Psalms arranged for devotional use

**pseud** *abbr* pseudonym

**pseu·do** \'süd-ō\ *adj* **1** : SPURIOUS, SHAM

**pseud·onym** \'süd-²n-,im\ *n* : a fictitious name — **pseud·on·y·mous** \sü-'dän-ə-məs\ *adj*

**PSG** *abbr* platoon sergeant

**psi** *abbr* pounds per square inch

**pso·ri·a·sis** \sə-'rī-ə-səs\ *n* : a chronic skin disease characterized by circumscribed red patches covered with white scales

**PST** *abbr* Pacific standard time

**¹psych** *also* **psyche** \'sīk\ *vb* **1** : OUTGUESS; *also* : to analyze beforehand **2** : INTIMIDATE; *also* : to prepare oneself psychologically ⟨get *psyched* up for the game⟩

**²psych** *abbr* psychology

**psy·che** \'sī-kē\ *n* : SOUL, SELF; *also* : MIND

**psy·che·de·lia** \,sī-kə-'dēl-yə\ *n* : the world of people or items associated with psychedelic drugs

**psy·che·del·ic** \,sī-kə-'del-ik\ *adj* **1** : of, relating to, or causing abnormal psychic effects ⟨∼ drugs⟩ **2** : relating to the taking of psychedelic drugs ⟨∼

experience⟩ **3 :** imitating the effects of psychedelic drugs ⟨∼ art⟩ **4 :** FLUO-RESCENT ⟨∼ colors⟩ — **psychedelic** *n* — **psy·che·del·i·cal·ly** \-i-k(ə-)lē\ *adv*

**psy·chi·a·try** \sə-'kī-ə-trē, sī-\ *n* **:** a branch of medicine dealing with mental disorders — **psy·chi·at·ric** \ˌsī-kē-'a-trik\ *adj* — **psy·chi·a·trist** \sə-'kī-ə-trəst, sī-\ *n*

¹**psy·chic** \'sī-kik\ *also* **psy·chi·cal** \-ki-kəl\ *adj* **1 :** of or relating to the psyche    **2 :** lying outside the sphere of physical science    **3 :** sensitive to non-physical or supernatural forces — **psy·chi·cal·ly** \-k(ə-)lē\ *adv*

²**psychic** *n* **:** a person apparently sensitive to nonphysical forces; *also* **:** MEDIUM 6

**psychic energizer** *n* **:** a drug with marked antidepressant properties

**psy·cho** \'sī-kō\ *n, pl* **psychos :** a mentally disturbed person — **psycho** *adj*

**psy·cho·ac·tive** \ˌsī-kō-'ak-tiv\ *adj* **:** affecting the mind or behavior

**psy·cho·anal·y·sis** \ˌsī-kō-ə-'nal-ə-səs\ *n* **:** a method of dealing with psychic disorders by study of the normally hidden content of the mind esp. to resolve conflicts — **psy·cho·an·a·lyst** \-'an-ᵊl-əst\ *n* — **psy·cho·an·al·yt·ic** \-ˌan-ᵊl-'it-ik\ *adj* — **psy·cho·an·a·lyze** \-'an-ᵊl-ˌīz\ *vb*

**psy·cho·chem·i·cal** \-'kem-i-kəl\ *n* **:** a chemical that alters mental functioning; *esp* **:** a gas that acts on nervous centers and makes affected individuals temporarily helpless — **psychochemical** *adj*

**psy·cho·dra·ma** \ˌsī-kə-'dräm-ə, -'dram-\ *n* **:** an extemporized dramatization designed esp. to afford catharsis for one or more of the participants from whose life history the plot is abstracted

**psy·cho·gen·ic** \-'jen-ik\ *adj* **:** originating in the mind or in mental or emotional conflict

**psychol** *abbr* psychologist; psychology

**psy·chol·o·gy** \sī-'käl-ə-jē\ *n, pl* **-gies 1 :** the science of mind and behavior    **2 :** the mental and behavioral aspect (as of an individual) — **psy·cho·log·i·cal** \ˌsī-kə-'läj-i-kəl\ *adj* — **psy·cho·log·i·cal·ly** \-i-k(ə-)lē\ *adv* — **psy·chol·o·gist** \sī-'käl-ə-jəst\ *n*

**psy·cho·path** \'sī-kə-ˌpath\ *n* **:** a mentally ill or unstable person — **psy·cho·path·ic** \ˌsī-kə-'path-ik\ *adj*

**psy·cho·sex·u·al** \ˌsī-kō-'sek-sh(ə-w)əl\ *adj* **1 :** of or relating to the mental, emotional, and behavioral aspects of sexual development    **2 :** of or relating to the physiological psychology of sex

**psy·cho·sis** \sī-'kō-səs\ *n, pl* **-cho·ses** \-ˌsēz\ **:** fundamental mental derangement (as paranoia) characterized by defective or lost contact with reality — **psy·chot·ic** \-'kät-ik\ *adj or n*

**psy·cho·so·mat·ic** \ˌsī-kə-sə-'mat-ik\ *adj* **:** of, relating to, or caused by the interaction of mental and bodily phenomena ⟨∼ ulcers⟩

**psy·cho·ther·a·py** \ˌsī-kō-'ther-ə-pē\ *n* **:** treatment of mental or emotional disorder or of related bodily ills by psychological means — **psy·cho·ther·a·pist** \-pəst\ *n*

**psy·cho·tro·pic** \ˌsī-kə-'trō-pik\ *adj* **:** acting on the mind

**pt** *abbr* **1** part **2** payment **3** pint **4** point **5** port

**Pt** *symbol* platinum

**PT** *abbr* **1** Pacific time **2** physical therapy **3** physical training

**PTA** *abbr* Parent-Teacher Association

**ptar·mi·gan** \'tär-mi-gən\ *n, pl* **-gan** *or* **-gans :** any of various grouses of northern regions with completely feathered feet

**P T boat** \(')pē-'tē-\ *n* [patrol torpedo] **:** a high-speed 60 to 100 foot motorboat equipped for battle

**pte** *abbr, Brit* private

**ptg** *abbr* printing

**PTO** *abbr* please turn over

**pto·maine** \'tō-ˌmān\ *n* **:** a chemical substance formed by bacteria in decaying matter (as meat)

**ptomaine poisoning** *n* **:** a disorder of the stomach and intestines caused by food contaminated usu. with bacteria or their products

**PTV** *abbr* public television

**Pu** *symbol* plutonium

¹**pub** \'pəb\ *n, chiefly Brit* **:** PUBLIC HOUSE, TAVERN

²**pub** *abbr* **1** public **2** publication **3** published; publisher; publishing

**pu·ber·ty** \'pyü-bərt-ē\ *n* **:** the condition of being or period of becoming capable of reproducing sexually — **pu·ber·tal** \-bərt-ᵊl\ *adj*

**pu·bes** \'pyü-bēz\ *n, pl* **pubes 1 :** the hair that appears upon the lower middle region of the abdomen at puberty    **2 :** the pubic region

**pu·bes·cence** \pyü-'bes-ᵊns\ *n* **1 :** the quality or state of being pubescent    **2 :** a pubescent covering or surface

**pu·bes·cent** \-ᵊnt\ *adj* **1 :** arriving at or having reached puberty    **2 :** covered with fine soft short hairs

**pu·bic** \'pyü-bik\ *adj* **:** of, relating to, or situated near the pubes or the pubis

**pu·bis** \'pyü-bəs\ *n, pl* **pu·bes** \-bēz\ **:** the ventral and anterior of the three principal bones composing either half of the pelvis

**publ** *abbr* **1** publication **2** published; publisher

¹**pub·lic** \'pəb-lik\ *adj* **1 :** of, relating to, or affecting the people as a whole ⟨∼ opinion⟩    **2 :** CIVIC, GOVERNMENTAL ⟨∼ expenditures⟩    **3 :** not private **:** SOCIAL ⟨∼ morality⟩    **4 :** of, relating to, or serving the community ⟨∼ officials⟩    **5 :** open to all ⟨∼ library⟩    **6 :** exposed to general view ⟨the story became ∼⟩    **7 :** well known **:** PROMINENT ⟨∼ figures⟩ — **pub·lic·ly** *adv*

²**public** *n* **1 :** the people as a whole **:** POPULACE    **2 :** a group of people having common interests ⟨wrote for his ∼⟩

**pub·li·can** \'pəb-li-kən\ *n* **1 :** a Jewish tax collector for the ancient Romans

**2** *chiefly Brit* : the licensee of a public house

**pub·li·ca·tion** \,pəb-lə-'kā-shən\ *n* **1** : the act or process of publishing **2** : a published work

**public house** *n* **1** : INN **2** *chiefly Brit* : a licensed saloon or bar

**pub·li·cist** \'pəb-lə-səst\ *n* : one that publicizes; *esp* : PRESS AGENT

**pub·lic·i·ty** \(,)pə-'blis-ət-ē\ *n* **1** : information with news value issued to gain public attention or support **2** : public attention or acclaim

**pub·li·cize** \'pəb-lə-,sīz\ *vb* -cized; -ciz·ing : to give publicity to

**public relations** *n pl but usu sing in constr* : the business of fostering public goodwill toward a person, firm, or institution; *also* : the degree of goodwill and understanding achieved

**public school** *n* **1** : an endowed secondary boarding school in Great Britain offering a classical curriculum and preparation for the universities or public service **2** : a free tax-supported school controlled by a local governmental authority

**pub·lic-spir·it·ed** \,pəb-lik-'spir-ət-əd\ *adj* : motivated by devotion to the general or national welfare

**public television** *n* : television that provides cultural, informational, and instructive programs for the public and that does not promote the sale of a product or service except for identifying the donors of program funds

**pub·lish** \'pəb-lish\ *vb* **1** : to make generally known : announce publicly **2** : to produce or release literature, information, musical scores or sometimes recordings, or art for sale to the public — **pub·lish·er** *n*

**¹puck** \'pək\ *n* : a mischievous sprite — **puck·ish** *adj*

**²puck** *n* : a disk used in ice hockey

**¹puck·er** \'pək-ər\ *vb* **puck·ered; puck·er·ing** \-(ə-)riŋ\ : to contract into folds or wrinkles

**²pucker** *n* : FOLD, WRINKLE

**pud·ding** \'pu̇d-iŋ\ *n* : a dessert of a soft, spongy, or thick creamy consistency

**pud·dle** \'pəd-ᵊl\ *n* : a very small pool of usu. dirty or muddy water

**pud·dling** \'pəd-(ᵊ-)liŋ\ *n* : the process of converting pig iron into wrought iron by subjecting it to heat and stirring in the presence of oxidizing substances

**pu·den·dum** \pyu̇-'den-dəm\ *n, pl* -da \-də\ : the external genital organs of a human being and esp. of a woman

**pudgy** \'pəj-ē\ *adj* **pudg·i·er; -est** : being short and plump : CHUBBY

**pueb·lo** \pü-'eb-lō, 'pweb-\ *n, pl* -los [Sp, village, lit., people, fr. L *populus*] **1** : an Indian village of Arizona or New Mexico consisting of flat-roofed stone or adobe houses **2** *cap* : a member of an Indian people of the southwestern U.S.

**pu·er·ile** \'pyu̇-ə-rəl\ *adj* : CHILDISH, SILLY — **pu·er·il·i·ty** \,pyü-ə-'ril-ət-ē\ *n*

**pu·er·per·al** \pyü-'ər-p(ə-)rəl\ *adj*

: of or relating to parturition ⟨~ infection⟩

**puerperal fever** *n* : an abnormal condition that results from infection of the placental site following childbirth or abortion

**Puer·to Ri·can** \,pȯrt-ə-'rē-kən, ,pwert-\ *n* : a native or inhabitant of Puerto Rico — **Puerto Rican** *adj*

**¹puff** \'pəf\ *vb* **1** : to blow in short gusts **2** : PANT **3** : to emit small whiffs or clouds **4** : BLUSTER, BRAG **5** : INFLATE, SWELL **6** : to make proud or conceited **7** : to praise extravagantly

**²puff** *n* **1** : a short discharge (as of air or smoke); *also* : a slight explosive sound accompanying it **2** : a light fluffy pastry **3** : a slight swelling **4** : a fluffy mass; *esp* : a small pad for applying cosmetic powder **5** : a laudatory notice or review — **puffy** *adj*

**puff·ball** \'pəf-,bȯl\ *n* : any of various globose and often edible fungi

**puf·fin** \'pəf-ən\ *n* : a seabird having a short neck and a red-tipped triangular bill

**¹pug** \'pəg\ *n* **1** : a small stocky short-haired dog **2** : a close coil of hair

**²pug** *n* : ¹BOXER

**pu·gi·lism** \'pyü-jə-,liz-əm\ *n* : BOXING — **pu·gi·list** \-ləst\ *n* — **pu·gi·lis·tic** \,pyü-jə-'lis-tik\ *adj*

**pug·na·cious** \,pəg-'nā-shəs\ *adj* : fond of fighting : COMBATIVE **syn** belligerent, quarrelsome — **pug·nac·i·ty** \-'nas-ət-ē\ *n*

**puis·sance** \'pwis-ᵊns, 'pyü-ə-səns\ *n* : POWER, STRENGTH — **puis·sant** \-ᵊnt, -sənt\ *adj*

**puke** \'pyük\ *vb* **puked; puk·ing** : VOMIT — **puke** *n*

**puk·ka** \'pək-ə\ *adj* [Hindi *pakkā* cooked, ripe, solid, fr. Skt *pakva*] : GENUINE, AUTHENTIC; *also* : FIRST-CLASS, COMPLETE

**pul** \'pül\ *n, pl* **puls** \'pülz\ *or* **pu·li** \'pü-lē\ — see *afghani* at MONEY table

**pul·chri·tude** \'pəl-krə-,t(y)üd\ *n* : BEAUTY — **pul·chri·tu·di·nous** \,pəl-krə-'t(y)üd-(ᵊ-)nəs\ *adj*

**pule** \'pyül\ *vb* **puled; pul·ing** : WHINE, WHIMPER

**¹pull** \'pu̇l\ *vb* **1** : PLUCK; *also* : EXTRACT ⟨~ a tooth⟩ **2** : to exert force so as to draw (something) toward the force; *also* : MOVE ⟨~ out of a driveway⟩ **3** : STRETCH, STRAIN ⟨~ a tendon⟩ **4** : to draw apart : TEAR **5** : to make (as a proof) by printing **6** : REMOVE **7** : DRAW ⟨~ a gun⟩ **8** : to carry out esp. with daring ⟨~ a robbery⟩ **9** : to be guilty of : PERPETRATE **10** : ATTRACT **11** : to express strong sympathy — **pull·er** *n*

**²pull** *n* **1** : the act or an instance of pulling **2** : the effort expended in moving **3** : ADVANTAGE; *esp* : special influence **4** : a device for pulling something or for operating by pulling **5** : a force that attracts or compels

**pull·back** \'pu̇l-,bak\ *n* : an orderly withdrawal of troops

**pul·let** \'pu̇l-ət\ *n* : a young hen

**pul·ley** \'pu̇l-ē\ *n, pl* **pulleys** **1** : a

wheel with a grooved rim that forms part of a tackle for hoisting or for changing the direction of a force 2 : a wheel used to transmit power by means of a band, belt, rope, or chain

**Pull·man** \'pùl-mən\ n : a railroad passenger car with specially comfortable furnishings; esp : one with berths

**pull off** vb : to accomplish successfully

**pull·out** \'pùl-ˌaút\ n : PULLBACK

**pull·over** \ˌpùl-ˌō-vər\ adj : put on by being pulled over the head ⟨~ sweater⟩ — **pull·over** \'pùl-ˌō-vər\ n

**pull-up** \'pùl-ˌəp\ n : CHIN-UP

**pull up** \'pùl-'əp\ vb : to bring or come to a halt : STOP

**pul·mo·nary** \'pùl-mə-ˌner-ē, 'pəl-\ adj : of or relating to the lungs

**pul·mo·tor** \-ˌmōt-ər\ n : an apparatus for pumping oxygen or air into and out of the lungs (as of an asphyxiated person)

**pulp** \'pəlp\ n 1 : the soft juicy or fleshy part of a fruit or vegetable 2 : a soft moist mass 3 : a material (as from wood or rags) used in making paper 4 : a magazine using rough-surfaced paper and often dealing with sensational material — **pulpy** adj

**pul·pit** \'pùl-ˌpit\ n : a raised platform or high reading desk used in preaching or conducting a worship service

**pulp·wood** \'pəlp-ˌwùd\ n : wood suitable for paper pulp

**pul·sar** \'pəl-ˌsär\ n : a celestial source of pulsating radio waves

**pul·sate** \'pəl-ˌsāt\ vb **pul·sat·ed; pul·sat·ing** : to expand and contract rhythmically : BEAT — **pul·sa·tion** \ˌpəl-'sā-shən\ n

**pulse** \'pəls\ n 1 : the regular throbbing in the arteries caused by the contractions of the heart 2 : a brief change in electrical current or voltage — **pulse** vb

**pul·ver·ize** \'pəl-və-ˌrīz\ vb **-ized; -iz·ing** 1 : to reduce (as by crushing or grinding) or be reduced to very small particles 2 : DEMOLISH

**pu·ma** \'p(y)ü-mə\ n, pl **pumas** also **puma** : COUGAR

**pum·ice** \'pəm-əs\ n : a light porous volcanic glass used in polishing and erasing

**pum·mel** \'pəm-əl\ vb **-meled** or **-melled; -mel·ing** or **-mel·ling** \-(ə-)liŋ\ : POUND, BEAT

¹**pump** \'pəmp\ n : a device for raising, transferring, or compressing fluids or gases esp. by suction or pressure

²**pump** vb 1 : to raise (as water) with a pump 2 : to draw water or air from by means of a pump; also : to fill by means of a pump ⟨~ up a tire⟩ 3 : to force or propel in the manner of a pump — **pump·er** n

³**pump** n : a low shoe that is not fastened on and that grips the foot chiefly at the toe and heel

**pum·per·nick·el** \'pəm-pər-ˌnik-əl\ n : a dark coarse somewhat sour rye bread

**pump·kin** \'pəŋ-kən, 'pəm(p)-kən\ n : the large yellow fruit of a vine related

to the gourd grown for food; also : this vine

**pun** \'pən\ n : the humorous use of a word in a way that suggests two interpretations — **pun** vb

¹**punch** \'pənch\ vb 1 : PROD, POKE; also : DRIVE, HERD ⟨~ing cattle⟩ 2 : to strike with the fist 3 : to emboss, perforate, or make with a punch — **punch·er** n

²**punch** n 1 : a quick blow with or as if with the fist 2 : energy that commands attention : EFFECTIVENESS

³**punch** n : a tool for piercing, stamping, cutting, or forming

⁴**punch** n [perh. fr. Hindi pāc five, fr. Skt pañca: fr. the number of ingredients] : a beverage usu. composed of wine or alcoholic liquor, citrus juice, spices, tea, and water; also : a beverage composed of nonalcoholic liquids (as fruit juices)

**punch card** n : a data card with holes punched in particular positions each with its own signification

**pun·cheon** \'pən-chən\ n : a large cask

**punch line** n : the sentence or phrase in a joke that makes the point

**punc·til·io** \ˌpəŋk-'til-ē-ˌō\ n, pl **-i·os** 1 : a nice detail of conduct in a ceremony or in observance of a code 2 : careful observance of forms (as in social conduct)

**punc·til·i·ous** \-ē-əs\ adj : marked by precise accordance with the details of codes or conventions syn meticulous, scrupulous, careful, punctual

**punc·tu·al** \'pəŋk-chə-(-wə)l\ adj : acting or habitually acting at an appointed time : PROMPT — **punc·tu·al·i·ty** \ˌpəŋk-chə-'wal-ət-ē\ n — **punc·tu·al·ly** \'pəŋk-chə-(-wə)-lē\ adv

**punc·tu·ate** \'pəŋk-chə-ˌwāt\ vb **-at·ed; -at·ing** 1 : to mark or divide (written matter) with punctuation marks 2 : to break into at intervals 3 : EMPHASIZE

**punc·tu·a·tion** \ˌpəŋk-chə-'wā-shən\ n : the act, practice, or system of inserting standardized marks in written matter to clarify the meaning and separate structural units

¹**punc·ture** \'pəŋk-chər\ n 1 : an act of puncturing 2 : a small hole made by puncturing

²**puncture** vb **punc·tured; punc·tur·ing** 1 : to make a hole in : PIERCE 2 : to make useless as if by a puncture

**pun·dit** \'pən-dət\ n 1 : a learned man : TEACHER 2 : AUTHORITY

**pun·gent** \'pən-jənt\ adj 1 : having a sharp incisive quality : CAUSTIC ⟨a ~ editorial⟩ 2 : causing a sharp or irritating sensation; esp : ACRID ⟨~ smell of burning leaves⟩ — **pun·gen·cy** \-jən-sē\ n — **pun·gent·ly** adv

**pun·ish** \'pən-ish\ vb 1 : to impose a penalty on for a fault or crime ⟨~ an offender⟩ 2 : to inflict a penalty for ⟨~ treason with death⟩ 3 : to inflict injury on : HURT syn chastise, castigate, chasten, discipline, correct — **pun·ish·able** adj

**pun·ish·ment** \-mənt\ *n* **1** : retributive suffering, pain, or loss : PENALTY **2** : rough treatment

**pu·ni·tive** \'pyü-nət-iv\ *adj* : inflicting, involving, or aiming at punishment

¹**punk** \'pəŋk\ *n* **1** : a young inexperienced person **2** : a petty hoodlum

²**punk** *adj* : very poor : INFERIOR

³**punk** *n* : dry crumbly wood useful for tinder; *also* : a substance made from fungi for use as tinder

**pun·kin** *var of* PUMPKIN

**pun·ster** \'pən-stər\ *n* : one who is given to punning

¹**punt** \'pənt\ *n* : a long narrow flat-bottomed boat

²**punt** *vb* : to propel (as a punt) by pushing with a pole against the bottom of a body of water

³**punt** *vb* : to kick a football dropped from the hands before it touches the ground

⁴**punt** *n* : the act or an instance of punting a ball

**pu·ny** \'pyü-nē\ *adj* **pu·ni·er; -est** [MF *puisné* younger, lit., born afterward, fr. *puis* afterward (fr. L *post*) + *né* born, fr. L *natus*] : slight in power, size, or importance : WEAK

**pup** \'pəp\ *n* : a young dog; *also* : one of the young of some other animals

**pu·pa** \'pyü-pə\ *n, pl* **-pae** \-(,)pē, -,pī\ *or* **-pas** [NL, fr. L *pupa* girl, doll] : an insect (as a bee, moth, or beetle) in an intermediate stage of its growth when it is in a case or cocoon — **pu·pal** \-pəl\ *adj*

¹**pu·pil** \'pyü-pəl\ *n* **1** : a child or young person in school or in the charge of a tutor **2** : DISCIPLE

²**pupil** *n* : the dark central opening of the iris of the eye

**pup·pet** \'pəp-ət\ *n* **1** : a small figure of a person or animal moved by hand or by strings or wires **2** : DOLL **3** : one whose acts are controlled by an outside force

**pup·pe·teer** \,pəp-ə-'tiər\ *n* : one who manipulates puppets

**pup·py** \'pəp-ē\ *n, pl* **puppies** : a young dog

**pur·blind** \'pər-,blīnd\ *adj* **1** : partly blind **2** : lacking in insight : OBTUSE

¹**pur·chase** \'pər-chəs\ *vb* **pur·chased; pur·chas·ing** : to obtain by paying money or its equivalent : BUY — **pur·chas·er** *n*

²**purchase** *n* **1** : an act or instance of purchasing **2** : something purchased **3** : a secure hold or grasp; *also* : advantageous leverage

**pur·dah** \'pərd-ə\ *n* : seclusion of women from public observation among Muslims and some Hindus esp. in India

**pure** \'pyūr\ *adj* **pur·er; pur·est 1** : unmixed with any other matter : free from taint (~ gold) (~ water) **2** : SHEER, ABSOLUTE (~ nonsense) **3** : ABSTRACT, THEORETICAL (~ mathematics) **4** : free from what vitiates, weakens, or pollutes (speaks a ~ French) **5** : free from moral fault : INNOCENT **6** : CHASTE, CONTINENT — **pure·ly** *adv*

**pure·blood** \-,bləd\ *or* **pure-blood-**

ed \-'bləd-əd\ *adj* : of unmixed ancestry : PUREBRED — **pureblood** *n*

**pure·bred** \-'bred\ *adj* : bred from members of a recognized breed, strain, or kind without admixture of other blood over many generations — **purebred** \-,bred\ *n*

**pu·ree** \pyü-'rā, -'rē\ *n* [F, fr. MF, fr. fem of *puré*, pp. of *purer* to purify, strain, fr. L *purare* to purify, fr. *purus* pure] : a paste or thick liquid suspension usu. produced by rubbing cooked food through a sieve; *also* : a thick soup having vegetables so prepared as a base

**pur·ga·tion** \,pər-'gā-shən\ *n* : the act or result of purging

¹**pur·ga·tive** \'pər-gət-iv\ *adj* : purging or tending to purge; *also* : being a purgative

²**purgative** *n* : a vigorously laxative drug : CATHARTIC

**pur·ga·to·ry** \'pər-gə-,tōr-ē\ *n, pl* **-ries 1** : an intermediate state after death for expiatory purification **2** : a place or state of temporary punishment — **pur·ga·tor·i·al** \,pər-gə-'tōr-ē-əl\ *adj*

¹**purge** \'pərj\ *vb* **purged; purg·ing 1** : to cleanse or purify esp. from sin **2** : to have or cause free evacuation from the bowels **3** : to rid (as a political party) by a purge

²**purge** *n* **1** : an act or result of purging; *esp* : a ridding of persons regarded as treacherous or disloyal **2** : something that purges; *esp* : PURGATIVE

**pu·ri·fy** \'pyür-ə-,fī\ *vb* **-fied; -fy·ing** : to make or become pure — **pu·ri·fi·ca·tion** \,pyür-ə-fə-'kā-shən\ *n* — **pu·rif·i·ca·to·ry** \pyü-'rif-i-kə-,tōr-ē\ *adj* — **pu·ri·fi·er** \-,fī(-ə)r\ *n*

**Pu·rim** \'pùr-(,)im\ *n* : a Jewish holiday celebrated in February or March in commemoration of the deliverance of the Jews from the massacre plotted by Haman

**pu·rine** \'pyü(ə)r-,ēn\ *n* : a base (as adenine or guanine) that is a constituent of DNA or RNA

**pur·ism** \'pyür-,iz-əm\ *n* : rigid adherence to or insistence on purity or nicety esp. in use of words — **pur·ist** \-əst\ *n*

**pu·ri·tan** \'pyür-ət-°n\ *n* **1** *cap* : a member of a 16th and 17th century Protestant group in England and New England opposing formal usages of the Church of England **2** : one who practices or preaches a stricter or professedly purer moral code than that which prevails — **pu·ri·tan·i·cal** \,pyür-ə-'tan-i-kəl\ *adj*

**pu·ri·ty** \'pyür-ət-ē\ *n* : the quality or state of being pure

¹**purl** \'pərl\ *n* : a stitch in knitting

²**purl** *vb* : to knit in purl stitch

³**purl** *n* : a gentle murmur or movement (as of purling water)

⁴**purl** *vb* **1** : EDDY, SWIRL **2** : to make a soft murmuring sound

**pur·lieu** \'pərl-(y)ü\ *n* **1** : an outlying district : SUBURB **2** *pl* : ENVIRONS

**pur·loin** \(,)pər-'lȯin, 'pər-,lȯin\ *vb* : to appropriate wrongfully : FILCH

¹**pur·ple** \'pər-pəl\ *adj* **pur·pler**

\-p(ə-)lər\; **pur·plest** \-p(ə-)ləst\
**1** : of the color purple **2** : highly
rhetorical ⟨a ~ passage⟩ **3** : PROFANE
⟨~ language⟩ — **pur·plish** \'pər-
p(ə-)lish\ *adj*

²**purple** *n* **1** : a bluish red color **2** : a
purple robe emblematic esp. of regal
rank or authority

¹**pur·port** \'pər-ˌpōrt\ *n* : meaning conveyed or implied; *also* : GIST

²**pur·port** \(ˌ)pər-'pōrt\ *vb* : to convey
or profess outwardly as the meaning or
intention : CLAIM — **pur·port·ed·ly**
\-əd-lē\ *adv*

¹**pur·pose** \'pər-pəs\ *n* **1** : an object or
result aimed at : INTENTION **2** : RESO-
LUTION, DETERMINATION — **pur·pose·**
**ful** \-fəl\ *adj* — **pur·pose·ful·ly**
\-ē\ *adv* — **pur·pose·less** *adj* —
**pur·pose·ly** *adv*

²**purpose** *vb* **pur·posed; pur·pos·ing**
: to propose as an aim to oneself

**purr** \'pər\ *n* : a low murmur typical of
a contented cat — **purr** *vb*

¹**purse** \'pərs\ *n* **1** : a receptacle (as a
pouch) to carry money and often other
small objects in **2** : RESOURCES **3** : a sum
of money offered as a prize or present

²**purse** *vb* **pursed; purs·ing** : PUCKER

**purs·er** \'pər-sər\ *n* : an official on a
ship who keeps accounts and attends to
the comfort of passengers

**purs·lane** \'pər-slən, -ˌslān\ *n* : a
fleshy-leaved weedy trailing plant with
tiny yellow flowers that is sometimes
used in salads

**pur·su·ance** \pər-'sü-əns\ *n* : the act
of carrying into effect

**pursuant to** \-'sü-ənt\ *prep* : in carrying out : according to ⟨*pursuant to*
your instructions⟩

**pur·sue** \pər-'sü\ *vb* **pur·sued; pur-**
**su·ing** **1** : to follow in order to overtake or overcome : CHASE **2** : to seek to
accomplish ⟨~s his aims⟩ **3** : to proceed along ⟨~ a course⟩ **4** : to engage
in ⟨~ a vocation⟩ — **pur·su·er** *n*

**pur·suit** \pər-'süt\ *n* **1** : the act of
pursuing **2** : OCCUPATION, BUSINESS

**pu·ru·lent** \'pyùr-(y)ə-lənt\ *adj* : containing or accompanied by pus — **pu-**
**ru·lence** \-ləns\ *n*

**pur·vey** \(ˌ)pər-'vā\ *vb* **pur·veyed;**
**pur·vey·ing** : to supply (as provisions) usu. as a business — **pur·vey-**
**ance** \-əns\ *n* — **pur·vey·or** \-ər\ *n*

**pur·view** \'pər-ˌvyü\ *n* **1** : the range
or limit esp. of authority, responsibility,
or intention **2** : range of vision, understanding, or cognizance

**pus** \'pəs\ *n* : thick yellowish fluid (as
in a boil) containing germs, blood cells,
and tissue debris

¹**push** \'pùsh\ *vb* [ME *pusshen*, fr. OF
*poulser* to beat, push, fr. L *pulsare*, fr.
*pulsus*, pp. of *pellere* to drive, strike]
**1** : to press against with force in order
to drive or impel **2** : to thrust forward,
downward, or outward **3** : to urge on
: press forward **4** : to urge or press the
advancement, adoption, or practice of;
*esp* : to make aggressive efforts to sell **5**
: to engage in the illicit sale of narcotics

²**push** *n* **1** : a vigorous effort : DRIVE

**2** : an act of pushing : SHOVE **3** : vigorous enterprise : ENERGY

**push–button** *adj* : using or dependent
on complex and more or less automatic
mechanisms ⟨~ warfare⟩

**push button** *n* : a small button or knob
that when pushed operates something
esp. by closing an electric circuit

**push·cart** \'pùsh-ˌkärt\ *n* : a cart or
barrow pushed by hand

**push·er** \-ər\ *n* : one that pushes;
*esp* : one that pushes illegal drugs

**push·over** \'pùsh-ˌō-vər\ *n* **1** : an
opponent easy to defeat **2** : SUCKER
**3** : something easily accomplished

**push–up** \'pùsh-ˌəp\ *n* : a conditioning exercise performed in a prone position by raising and lowering the body
with the straightening and bending of
the arms while keeping the back straight
and supporting the body on the hands
and toes

**pushy** \'pùsh-ē\ *adj* **push·i·er; -est**
: aggressive often to an objectionable
degree

**pu·sil·lan·i·mous** \ˌpyü-sə-'lan-ə-
məs\ *adj* [LL *pusillanimis*, fr. L *pusillus*
very small (dim. of *pusus* small child) +
*animus* spirit] : contemptibly timid
: COWARDLY — **pu·sil·la·nim·i·ty**
\ˌpyü-sə-lə-'nim-ət-ē\ *n*

¹**puss** \'pùs\ *n* : CAT

²**puss** *n* : FACE

**pussy** \'pùs-ē\ *n, pl* **puss·ies** : CAT

²**pus·sy** \'pəs-ē\ *adj* **pus·si·er; -est**
: full of or resembling pus

**pussy·cat** \'pùs-ē-ˌkat\ *n* : CAT

**pussy·foot** \'pùs-ē-ˌfùt\ *vb* **1** : to
tread or move warily or stealthily **2**
: to refrain from committing oneself

**pussy willow** \ˌpùs-ē-\ *n* : a willow
having large silky cylindrical inflores-
cences

**pus·tule** \'pəs-chül\ *n* : a pus-filled
pimple

**put** \'pùt\ *vb* **put; put·ting** **1** : to
bring into a specified position : PLACE
⟨~ the book on the table⟩ **2** : SEND,
THRUST **3** : to throw with an upward
pushing motion ⟨~ the shot⟩ **4** : to
bring into a specified state ⟨~ the
matter right⟩ **5** : SUBJECT ⟨~ him to
expense⟩ **6** : IMPOSE **7** : to set before
one for decision ⟨~ the question⟩ **8**
: EXPRESS, STATE **9** : TRANSLATE, ADAPT
**10** : APPLY, ASSIGN ⟨~ them to work⟩
**11** : to give as an estimate ⟨~ the
number at 20⟩ **12** : ATTACH, ATTRIBUTE
⟨~ a high value on it⟩ **13** : to take a
specified course ⟨the ship ~ out to sea⟩

**pu·ta·tive** \'pyüt-ət-iv\ *adj* **1** : commonly accepted **2** : INFERRED

**put–down** \'pùt-ˌdaùn\ *n* : a humiliating remark : SQUELCH

**put in** *vb* **1** : to come in with : INTER-
POSE **2** : to spend time at some occupation or job

¹**put–on** \ˌpùt-ˌòn, -ˌän\ *adj* : PRE-
TENDED, ASSUMED

²**put–on** \'pùt-ˌòn, -ˌän\ *n* : a deliberate
act of misleading someone; *also* : PAR-
ODY, SPOOF

**put·out** \'pùt-ˌaùt\ *n* : the retiring of a
base runner or batter in baseball

**put out** \,pùt-'aùt\ *vb* **1 :** ANNOY; *also* **:** INCONVENIENCE **2 :** to cause to be out (as in baseball)

**pu·tre·fy** \'pyü-trə-,fī\ *vb* **-fied; -fy·ing :** to make or become putrid **:** ROT — **pu·tre·fac·tion** \,pyü-trə-'fak-shən\ *n* — **pu·tre·fac·tive** \-tiv\ *adj*

**pu·tres·cent** \pyü-'tres-ᵊnt\ *adj* **:** becoming putrid **:** ROTTING — **pu·tres·cence** \-ᵊns\ *n*

**pu·trid** \'pyü-trəd\ *adj* **1 :** ROTTEN, DECAYED **2 :** VILE, CORRUPT — **pu·trid·i·ty** \pyü-'trid-ət-ē\ *n*

**putsch** \'pùch\ *n* **:** a secretly plotted and suddenly executed attempt to overthrow a government

**putt** \'pət\ *n* **:** a golf stroke made on the green to cause the ball to roll into the hole — **putt** *vb*

**put·tee** \,pə-'tē, 'pət-ē\ *n* **1 :** a cloth strip wrapped around the lower leg **2 :** a leather legging

¹**put·ter** \'pùt-ər\ *n* **:** one that puts

²**putt·er** \'pət-ər\ *n* **1 :** a golf club used in putting **2 :** one that putts

³**put·ter** \'pət-ər\ *vb* **1 :** to move or act aimlessly or idly **2 :** TINKER

**put·ty** \'pət-ē\ *n, pl* **putties** [F *potée*, lit., potful, fr. OF, fr. *pot*, of Gmc origin] **:** a doughlike cement usu. of whiting and linseed oil used esp. to fasten glass in sashes — **putty** *vb*

¹**puz·zle** \'pəz-əl\ *vb* **puz·zled; puz·zling** \-(ə-)liŋ\ **1 :** to bewilder mentally **:** CONFUSE, PERPLEX **2 :** to solve with difficulty or ingenuity ⟨∼ out a mystery⟩ **3 :** to be in a quandary ⟨∼ over what to do⟩ **4 :** to attempt a solution of a puzzle ⟨∼ over a person's words⟩ *syn* mystify, bewilder, nonplus, confound — **puz·zle·ment** *n* — **puz·zler** \-(ə-)lər\ *n*

²**puzzle** *n* **1 :** something that puzzles **2 :** a question, problem, or contrivance designed for testing ingenuity

**pvt** *abbr* private

**PW** *abbr* prisoner of war

**PX** *abbr* post exchange

**pya** \pē-'ä\ *n* — see *kyat* at MONEY table

**pyg·my** \'pig-mē\ *n, pl* **pygmies** [ME *pigmei*, fr. L *pygmaeus* of a pygmy, dwarfish, fr. Gk *pygmaios*, fr. *pygmē* fist, measure of length] **1** *cap* **:** one of a small people of equatorial Africa **2 :** DWARF — **pygmy** *adj*

**py·ja·mas** \pə-'jä-məz\ *chiefly Brit var of* PAJAMAS

¹**py·lon** \'pī-,län, -lən\ *n* **1 :** a usu. massive gateway; *esp* **:** an Egyptian one flanked by flat-topped pyramids **2 :** a tower that supports a long span of wire **3 :** a post or tower marking a prescribed course of flight for an airplane

**py·or·rhea** \,pī-ə-'rē-ə\ *n* **:** an inflammation of the sockets of the teeth

¹**pyr·a·mid** \'pir-ə-,mid\ *n* **1 :** a massive structure with a square base and four triangular faces meeting at a point **2 :** a geometrical figure having for its base a polygon and for its sides several triangles meeting at a common point — **py·ra·mi·dal** \pə-'ram-əd-ᵊl, ,pir-ə-'mid-\ *adj*

²**pyramid** *vb* **1 :** to build up in the form of a pyramid **:** heap up **2 :** to increase rapidly on a broadening base

**pyre** \'pī(ə)r\ *n* **:** a combustible heap for burning a dead body as a funeral rite

**py·re·thrum** \pī-'rē-thrəm\ *n* **:** an insecticide consisting of the dried heads of any of several Old World chrysanthemums

**py·rim·i·dine** \pī-'rim-ə-,dēn\ *n* **:** a base (as cytosine, thymine, or uracil) that is a constituent of DNA or RNA

**py·rite** \'pī-,rīt\ *n* **:** a mineral containing sulfur and iron that is brass-yellow in color

**py·rites** \pə-'rīt-ēz, pī-; 'pī-,rīts\ *n, pl* **pyrites :** any of various metallic-looking sulfides — **py·rit·ic** \-'rit-ik\ *adj*

**py·rol·y·sis** \pī-'räl-ə-səs\ *n* **:** chemical change brought about by the action of heat

**py·ro·ma·nia** \,pī-rō-'mā-nē-ə\ *n* **:** an irresistible impulse to start fires — **py·ro·ma·ni·ac** \-nē-,ak\ *n*

**py·rom·e·ter** \pī-'räm-ət-ər\ *n* **:** an instrument for measuring high temperatures

**py·ro·tech·nics** \,pī-rə-'tek-niks\ *n pl* **1 :** a display of fireworks **2 :** a spectacular display (as of oratory) — **py·ro·tech·nic** \-nik\ *also* **py·ro·tech·ni·cal** \-ni-kəl\ *adj*

**Pyr·rhic victory** \,pir-ik-\ *n* [*Pyrrhus*, king of Epirus who sustained heavy losses in defeating the Romans] **:** a victory won at excessive cost

**py·thon** \'pī-,thän, -thən\ *n* [L, monstrous serpent killed by the god Apollo, fr. Gk *Pythōn*] **:** any of several very large Old World constricting snakes

**pyx** \'piks\ *n* **:** a small case used to carry the Eucharist to the sick

---

¹**q** \'kyü\ *n, pl* **q's** *or* **qs** \'kyüz\ *often cap* **:** the 17th letter of the English alphabet

²**q** *abbr, often cap* **1** quart **2** quarto **3** queen **4** query **5** question **6** quire

**QC** *abbr* Queen's Counsel

**QD** *abbr* [L *quaque die*] daily

**QDA** *abbr* quantity discount agreement

**QED** *abbr* [L *quod erat demonstrandum*] which was to be demonstrated

**QEF** *abbr* [L *quod erat faciendum*] which was to be done

**QEI** *abbr* [L *quod erat inveniendum*] which was to be found out

**QID** *abbr* [L *quater in die*] four times a day

**qin·tar** \kin-'tär\ *n* — see *lek* at MONEY table

**qi·vi·ut** \'kē-vē-,üt\ *n* **:** the wool of the undercoat of the musk-ox

**Qld** *or* **Q'land** *abbr* Queensland

**QM** *abbr* quartermaster

**QMC** *abbr* quartermaster corps

**QMG** *abbr* quartermaster general

**qq** *v abbr* [L *quae vide*] which (*pl*) see

**qr** *abbr* **1** quarter **2** quire

**¹qt** \'kyü-'tē\ *n, often cap Q & T* : QUIET — usu. used in the phrase *on the qt*

**²qt** *abbr* **1** quantity **2** quart

**qto** *abbr* quarto

**qty** *abbr* quantity

**qu** *or* **ques** *abbr* question

**¹quack** \'kwak\ *vb* : to make the characteristic cry of a duck

**²quack** *n* : the cry of a duck

**³quack** *n* **1** : a pretender to medical skill **2** : CHARLATAN **syn** faker, impostor — **quack** *adj* — **quack·ery** \-ə-rē\ *n* — **quack·ish** *adj*

**quack·sal·ver** \'kwak-ˌsal-vər\ *n* : CHARLATAN, QUACK

**¹quad** \'kwäd\ *n* : QUADRANGLE

**²quad** *n* : QUADRUPLET

**³quad** *abbr* quadrant

**quad·ran·gle** \'kwäd-ˌraŋ-gəl\ *n* **1** : a flat geometrical figure having four angles and four sides **2** : a 4-sided courtyard or enclosure — **quad·ran·gu·lar** \kwä-'draŋ-gyə-lər\ *adj*

**quad·rant** \'kwäd-rənt\ *n* **1** : one quarter of a circle : an arc of 90° **2** : an instrument for measuring heights used esp. in astronomy and surveying **3** : any of the four quarters into which something is divided by two lines intersecting each other at right angles

**qua·drat·ic** \kwä-'drat-ik\ *adj* : involving no higher power of terms than a square ⟨a ~ equation⟩ — **quadratic** *n*

**qua·drat·ics** \kwä-'drat-iks\ *n* : a branch of algebra dealing with quadratic equations

**qua·dren·ni·al** \kwä-'dren-ē-əl\ *adj* **1** : consisting of or lasting for four years **2** : occurring every four years

**qua·dren·ni·um** \-ē-əm\ *n* : a period of four years

**¹quad·ri·lat·er·al** \ˌkwäd-rə-'lat-(ə-)rəl\ *adj* : having four sides

**²quadrilateral** *n* : a polygon of four sides

**qua·drille** \kwä-'dril, k(w)ə-\ *n* : a square dance made up of five or six figures in various rhythms

**quad·ri·par·tite** \ˌkwäd-rə-'pär-ˌtīt\ *adj* **1** : consisting of four parts **2** : shared by four parties or persons

**qua·driv·i·um** \kwä-'driv-ē-əm\ *n* : the four liberal arts of arithmetic, music, geometry, and astronomy in a medieval university

**qua·droon** \kwä-'drün\ *n* : a person of one-quarter Negro ancestry

**quad·ru·ped** \'kwäd-rə-ˌped\ *n* : an animal having four feet — **qua·dru·pe·dal** \kwä-'drüp-əd-ᵊl, ˌkwäd-rə-'ped-\ *adj*

**¹qua·dru·ple** \kwä-'drüp-əl, -'drəp-; 'kwäd-rəp-\ *vb* **qua·dru·pled; qua·dru·pling** \-(ə-)liŋ\ **1** : to multiply by four : increase fourfold **2** : to total four times as many

**²quadruple** *adj* : FOURFOLD

**qua·dru·plet** \kwä-'drəp-lət, -'drüp-; 'kwäd-rəp-\ *n* **1** : one of four off-

spring born at one birth **2** : a group of four of a kind

**¹qua·dru·pli·cate** \kwä-'drü-pli-kət\ *adj* **1** : repeated four times **2** : FOURTH

**²qua·dru·pli·cate** \-plə-ˌkāt\ *vb* -**cat·ed; -cat·ing 1** : QUADRUPLE **2** : to provide in quadruplicate — **qua·dru·pli·ca·tion** \-ˌdrü-plə-'kā-shən\ *n*

**³qua·dru·pli·cate** \-'drü-pli-kət\ *n* **1** : one of four like things **2** : four copies all alike ⟨typed in ~⟩

**quaff** \'kwäf, 'kwaf\ *vb* : to drink deeply or repeatedly — **quaff** *n*

**quag·mire** \'kwag-ˌmī(ə)r, 'kwäg-\ *n* : soft miry land that yields under the foot

**qua·hog** \'kō-ˌhȯg, 'kwȯ-, 'kwō-, -ˌhäg\ *n* : a round thick-shelled American clam

**quai** \'kā\ *n* : QUAY

**¹quail** \'kwāl\ *n, pl* **quail** *or* **quails** [ME *quaille*, fr. MF, fr. ML *quaccula*, of imit. origin] : any of various short-winged stout-bodied game birds related to the grouse

**²quail** *vb* [ME *quailen* to curdle, fr. MF *quailler*, fr. L *coagulare*, fr. *coagulum* curdling agent, fr. *cogere* to drive together] : to lose heart : COWER **syn** recoil, shrink, flinch, wince

**quaint** \'kwānt\ *adj* **1** : unusual or different in character or appearance **2** : pleasingly old-fashioned or unfamiliar **syn** odd, queer, outlandish — **quaint·ly** *adv* — **quaint·ness** *n*

**¹quake** \'kwāk\ *vb* **quaked; quak·ing 1** : to shake usu. from shock or instability **2** : to tremble usu. from cold or fear

**²quake** *n* : a tremendous agitation; *esp* : EARTHQUAKE

**Quak·er** \'kwā-kər\ *n* : FRIEND 4

**Quaker meeting** *n* **1** : a meeting of Friends for worship marked often by long periods of silence **2** : a social gathering marked by many periods of silence

**quaking aspen** *n* : an aspen of the U.S. and Canada that has small nearly circular leaves with flattened petioles and finely serrate margins

**qual·i·fi·ca·tion** \ˌkwäl-ə-fə-'kā-shən\ *n* **1** : LIMITATION, MODIFICATION **2** : a special skill that fits a person for some work or position

**qual·i·fy** \'kwäl-ə-ˌfī\ *vb* -**fied; -fy·ing 1** : to reduce from a general to a particular form : MODIFY **2** : to make less harsh **3** : to fit by skill or training for some purpose **4** : to give or have a legal right to do something **5** : to demonstrate the necessary ability (as in a preliminary race) **6** : to limit the meaning of (as a noun) **syn** moderate, temper — **qual·i·fied** *adj* — **qual·i·fi·er** \-ˌfī(-ə)r\ *n*

**qual·i·ta·tive** \'kwäl-ə-ˌtāt-iv\ *adj* : of, relating to, or involving quality — **qual·i·ta·tive·ly** *adv*

**qual·i·ty** \'kwäl-ət-ē\ *n, pl* -**ties 1** : peculiar and essential character **2** : NATURE **3** : degree of excellence **3** : high social status **4** : a distinguishing attribute

**qualm** \'kwäm, 'kwälm, 'kwȯm\ *n*
**1** : a sudden attack (as of nausea)
**2** : a sudden misgiving **3** : SCRUPLE

**qualm·ish** \-ish\ *adj* **1** : feeling qualms : NAUSEATED **2** : overly scrupulous : SQUEAMISH **3** : of, relating to, or producing qualms — **qualm·ish·ly** *adv* — **qualm·ish·ness** *n*

**quan·da·ry** \'kwän-d(ə-)rē\ *n, pl* **-ries** : a state of perplexity or doubt **syn** predicament, dilemma, plight

**quan·ti·ta·tive** \'kwän-tə-,tāt-iv\ *adj* : of, relating to, or involving quantity — **quan·ti·ta·tive·ly** *adv*

**quan·ti·ty** \'kwän-tət-ē\ *n, pl* **-ties**
**1** : AMOUNT, NUMBER **2** : a considerable amount

**quan·tize** \'kwän-,tīz\ *vb* **quantized; quan·tiz·ing** : to subdivide (as energy) into small units — **quan·ti·za·tion** \,kwänt-ə-'zā-shən\ *n*

**quan·tum** \'kwänt-əm\ *n, pl* **quan·ta** \-ə\ [L, neut. of *quantus* how much]
**1** : QUANTITY, AMOUNT **2** : an elemental unit of energy

**quantum mechanics** *n sing or pl* : a general mathematical theory dealing with the interactions of matter and radiation in terms of observable quantities only — **quantum mechanical** *adj* — **quantum mechanically** *adv*

**quar·an·tine** \'kwȯr-ən-,tēn\ *n* [It *quarantina*, lit., period of forty days, fr. MF *quarantaine*, fr. OF, fr. *quarante* forty, fr. L *quadraginta*, fr. *quadra-* (akin to *quattuor* four) + *-ginta* (akin to *viginti* twenty)] **1** : a term during which a ship arriving in port and suspected of carrying contagious disease is forbidden contact with the shore **2** : a restraint on the movements of persons or goods intended to prevent the spread of pests or disease **3** : a place or period of quarantine — **quarantine** *vb*

¹**quar·rel** \'kwȯr(-ə)l\ *n* **1** : a ground of dispute **2** : a verbal clash : CONFLICT — **quar·rel·some** \-səm\ *adj*

²**quarrel** *vb* **-reled** *or* **-relled; -rel·ing** *or* **-rel·ling** **1** : to find fault **2** : to dispute angrily : WRANGLE

¹**quar·ry** \'kwȯr-ē\ *n, pl* **quarries** [ME *querre* entrails of game given to the hounds, fr. MF *cuirée*] **1** : game hunted with hawks **2** : PREY

²**quarry** *n, pl* **quarries** [ME *quarey*, alter. of *quarrere*, fr. MF *quarriere*, fr. (assumed) OF *quarre* squared stone, fr. L *quadrum* square] : an open excavation usu. for obtaining building stone, slate, or limestone — **quarry** *vb*

**quart** \'kwȯrt\ *n* — see WEIGHT table

¹**quar·ter** \'kwȯrt-ər\ *n* **1** : a fourth part **2** : a fourth of a dollar; *also* : a coin of this value **3** : a district of a city **4** *pl* : LODGINGS (moved into new ~s) **5** : MERCY, CLEMENCY (no ~)

²**quarter** *vb* **1** : to divide into four equal parts **2** : to provide with shelter

¹**quar·ter·back** \-,bak\ *n* : a football player who calls the signals for his team

²**quarterback** *vb* **1** : to direct the offensive play of a football team **2** : LEAD, BOSS

**quarter day** *n, chiefly Brit* : the day which begins a quarter of the year and on which a quarterly payment falls due

**quar·ter·deck** \'kwȯrt-ər-,dek\ *n* : the stern area of a ship's upper deck

**quarter horse** *n* : an alert stocky muscular horse capable of high speed for short distances and of great endurance under the saddle

¹**quar·ter·ly** \'kwȯrt-ər-lē\ *adv* : at 3-month intervals

²**quarterly** *adj* : occurring, issued, or payable at 3-month intervals

³**quarterly** *n, pl* **-lies** : a periodical published four times a year

**quar·ter·mas·ter** \-,mas-tər\ *n* **1** : a petty officer who attends to a ship's helm, binnacle, and signals **2** : an army officer who provides clothing and subsistence for troops

**quar·ter·staff** \-,staf\ *n, pl* **-staves** \-,stavz, -,stāvz\ : a long stout staff formerly used as a weapon

**quar·tet** *also* **quar·tette** \kwȯr-'tet\ *n* **1** : a musical composition for four instruments or voices **2** : a group of four and esp. of four musicians

**quar·to** \'kwȯrt-ō\ *n, pl* **quartos** **1** : the size of a piece of paper cut four from a sheet **2** : a book printed on quarto pages

**quartz** \'kwȯrts\ *n* : a common often transparent crystalline mineral that is a form of silica

**quartz·ite** \'kwȯrt-,sīt\ *n* : a compact granular rock composed of quartz and derived from sandstone

**qua·sar** \'kwā-,zär, -,sär\ *n* : QUASI-STELLAR RADIO SOURCE

**quash** \'kwäsh, 'kwȯsh\ *vb* **1** : to set aside by judicial action : VOID **2** : to suppress or extinguish summarily and completely : QUELL

**qua·si** \'kwā-,zī, -,sī; 'kwäz-ē, 'kwäs-; 'kwā-zē\ *adj* : having a likeness to something else

**qua·si-** *comb form* [L, as if, as it were, approximately, fr. *quam* as + *si* if] : in some sense or degree (*quasi*-historical)

**qua·si-stel·lar radio source** \,kwā-,zī-'stel-ər-, -,sī-; ,kwäz-ē-\ *n* : any of various distant celestial objects that resemble a star but emit unusually bright blue and ultraviolet light and radio waves

**qua·train** \'kwä-,trān\ *n* : a unit of four lines of verse

**qua·tre·foil** \'kat-ər-,fȯil, 'kat-rə-\ *n* : a conventionalized representation of a flower with four petals or of a leaf with four leaflets

**qua·ver** \'kwā-vər\ *vb* **qua·vered; qua·ver·ing** \'kwāv-(ə-)riŋ\ **1** : TREMBLE, SHAKE **2** : TRILL **3** : to speak in tremulous tones **syn** shudder, quake, totter, quiver, shiver — **quaver** *n*

**quay** \'kē, 'k(w)ā\ *n* : WHARF

**Que** *abbr* Quebec

**quean** \'kwēn\ *n* : a disreputable woman

**quea·sy** \'kwē-zē\ *adj* **quea·si·er; -est** : NAUSEATED — **quea·si·ly** \-zə-lē\ *adv* — **quea·si·ness** \-zē-nəs\ *n*

**queen** \\'kwēn\ *n* **1** : the wife or widow of a king **2** : a female monarch **3** : a woman notable for rank, power, or attractiveness **4** : the most privileged piece in the game of chess **5** : a playing card bearing the figure of a queen **6** : the fertile female of a social insect (as a bee or termite) — **queen·ly** *adj*

**Queen Anne's lace** \\-'anz-\ *n* : WILD CARROT

**queen consort** *n, pl* **queens consort** : the wife of a reigning king

**queen mother** *n* : a dowager queen who is mother of the reigning sovereign

**queen-size** *adj* : having dimensions of approximately 60 inches by 80 inches (~ bed); *also* : of a size that fits a queen-size bed

¹**queer** \\'kwir\ *adj* **1** : differing from the usual or normal : PECULIAR, STRANGE **2** : HOMOSEXUAL **3** : COUNTERFEIT   **syn** erratic, eccentric, curious — **queer·ly** *adv* — **queer·ness** *n*

²**queer** *vb* : DISRUPT (~*ed* our plans)

³**queer** *n* : one that is queer; *esp* : HOMOSEXUAL

**quell** \\'kwel\ *vb* : to put down : CRUSH (~ a riot)

**quench** \\'kwench\ *vb* **1** : to put out : EXTINGUISH **2** : SUBDUE **3** : SLAKE, SATISFY (~*ed* his thirst) **4** : to cool (as heated steel) suddenly esp. by immersion esp. in water or oil — **quench·able** *adj* — **quench·less** *adj*

**quer·u·lous** \\'kwer-(y)ə-ləs\ *adj* **1** : constantly complaining **2** : FRETFUL, WHINING   **syn** petulant, pettish, irritable, peevish — **quer·u·lous·ly** *adv* — **quer·u·lous·ness** *n*

**que·ry** \\'kwi(ə)r-ē, 'kwe(ə)r-\ *n, pl* **queries** : QUESTION — **query** *vb*

**quest** \\'kwest\ *n* : SEARCH — **quest** *vb*

¹**ques·tion** \\'kwes-chən\ *n* **1** : an interrogative expression : QUERY **2** : a subject for discussion or debate; *also* : a proposition to be voted on in a meeting **3** : INQUIRY **4** : DISPUTE

²**question** *vb* **1** : to ask questions **2** : DOUBT, DISPUTE **3** : to subject to analysis : EXAMINE   **syn** ask, interrogate, quiz — **ques·tion·er** *n*

**ques·tion·able** \\'kwes-chə-nə-bəl\ *adj* **1** : not certain or exact : DOUBTFUL **2** : not believed to be true, sound, or moral   **syn** dubious, problematical

**question mark** *n* : a punctuation mark ? used esp. at the end of a sentence to indicate a direct question

**ques·tion·naire** \\,kwes-chə-'na(ə)r\ *n* : a set of questions for obtaining information

**quet·zal** \ket-'säl, -'sal\ *n, pl* **quetzals** *or* **quet·za·les** \\-'säl-ās, -'sal-\ **1** : a Central American bird with brilliant plumage **2** — see MONEY table

¹**queue** \\'kyü\ *n* [F, lit., tail, fr. L *cauda*, *coda*] **1** : a braid of hair usu. worn hanging at the back of the head **2** : a line esp. of persons or vehicles

²**queue** *vb* **queued**; **queu·ing** *or* **queue·ing** : to line up in a queue

**quib·ble** \\'kwib-əl\ *n* **1** : an evasion of or shifting from the point at issue **2** : a minor objection — **quibble** *vb*

¹**quick** \\'kwik\ *adj* **1** *archaic* : LIVING **2** : RAPID, SPEEDY (~ steps) **3** : prompt to understand, think, or perceive : ALERT **4** : easily aroused (a ~ temper) **5** : turning or bending sharply (a ~ turn in the road)   **syn** fleet, fast, prompt, ready — **quick** *adv* — **quick·ly** *adv* — **quick·ness** *n*

²**quick** *n* **1** : sensitive living flesh **2** : a vital part : HEART

**quick bread** *n* : a bread made with a leavening agent that permits immediate baking of the dough or batter mixture

**quick·en** \\'kwik-ən\ *vb* **quick·ened**; **quick·en·ing** \\-(ə-)niŋ\ **1** : to come to life : REVIVE **2** : AROUSE, STIMULATE **3** : to increase in speed : HASTEN **4** : to show vitality (as by growing or moving)   **syn** animate, enliven, excite, provoke

**quick-freeze** \\'kwik-'frēz\ *vb* **-froze** \\-'frōz\ **-fro·zen** \\-'frōz-ᵊn\; **-freez·ing** : to freeze (food) for preservation so rapidly that ice crystals formed are too small to rupture the cells

**quick·ie** \\'kwik-ē\ *n* : something hurriedly done or made

**quick·lime** \\'kwik-,līm\ *n* : the first solid product obtained by calcining limestone

**quick-lunch** \\-'lənch\ *n* : a luncheonette specializing in short-order food

**quick·sand** \\'kwik-,sand\ *n* : a deep mass of loose sand mixed with water

**quick·sil·ver** \\-,sil-vər\ *n* : MERCURY

**quick·step** \\-,step\ *n* : a spirited march tune esp. accompanying a march in quick time

**quick time** *n* : a rate of marching in which 120 steps each 30 inches in length are taken in one minute

**quick-wit·ted** \\'kwik-'wit-əd\ *adj* : mentally alert   **syn** clever, bright, smart, intelligent

**quid** \\'kwid\ *n* : a cut or wad of something chewable (a ~ of tobacco)

**quid pro quo** \\,kwid-,prō-'kwō\ *n* [NL, something for something] : something given or received for something else

**qui·es·cent** \kwī-'es-ᵊnt\ *adj* : being at rest : QUIET   **syn** latent, dormant, potential — **qui·es·cence** \\-ᵊns\ *n*

¹**qui·et** \\'kwī-ət\ *n* : REPOSE

²**quiet** *adj* **1** : marked by little motion or activity : CALM **2** : GENTLE, MILD (a man of ~ disposition) **3** : enjoyed in peace and relaxation (a ~ cup of tea) **4** : free from noise or uproar **5** : not showy : MODEST (~ clothes) **6** : SECLUDED (a ~ nook) — **quiet** *adv* — **qui·et·ly** *adv* — **qui·et·ness** *n*

³**quiet** *vb* **1** : CALM, PACIFY **2** : to become quiet (~ down)

**qui·etude** \\'kwī-ə-,t(y)üd\ *n* : QUIETNESS, REPOSE

**qui·etus** \kwī-'ēt-əs\ *n* [ME *quietus est*, fr. ML, he is quit, formula of discharge from obligation] **1** : final settlement (as of a debt) **2** : DEATH

**quill** \\'kwil\ *n* **1** : a large stiff feather; *also* : the hollow barrel of a feather **2** : a spine of a hedgehog or porcupine

¹**quilt** \'kwilt\ *n* **:** a padded bed coverlet

²**quilt** *vb* **1 :** to fill, pad, or line like a quilt **2 :** to stitch or sew in layers with padding in between **3 :** to make quilts

**quince** \'kwins\ *n* **:** a hard yellow applelike fruit; *also* **:** a tree related to the roses that bears this fruit

**qui·nine** \'kwī-,nīn\ *n* **:** a bitter white salt obtained from cinchona bark and used esp. in treating malaria

**quin·sy** \'kwin-zē\ *n* **:** a severe inflammation of the throat or adjacent parts with swelling and fever

**quint** \'kwint\ *n* **:** QUINTUPLET

**quin·tal** \'kwint-ᵊl, 'kant-\ *n* — see METRIC SYSTEM table

**quin·tes·sence** \kwin-'tes-ᵊns\ *n* **1 :** the purest essence of something **2 :** the most typical example or representative — **quint·es·sen·tial** \,kwint-ə-'sen-chəl\ *adj*

**quin·tet** *also* **quin·tette** \kwin-'tet\ *n* **1 :** a musical composition for five instruments or voices **2 :** a group of five and esp. of five musicians; *also* **:** a basketball team

¹**quin·tu·ple** \kwin-'t(y)üp-əl, -'təp-; 'kwint-əp-\ *adj* **1 :** having five units or members **2 :** being five times as great or as many — **quintuple** *n*

²**quintuple** *vb* **quin·tu·pled; quin·tu·pling :** to make or become five times as great or as many

**quin·tu·plet** \kwin-'təp-lət, -'t(y)üp-; 'kwint-əp-\ *n* **1 :** a group of five of a kind **2 :** one of five offspring born at one birth

¹**quin·tu·pli·cate** \kwin-'t(y)ü-pli-kət\ *adj* **1 :** repeated five times **2 :** FIFTH

²**quintuplicate** *n* **1 :** one of five like things **2 :** five copies all alike ⟨typed in ∼⟩

³**quin·tu·pli·cate** \-plə-,kāt\ *vb* -cat·ed; -cat·ing **1 :** QUINTUPLE **2 :** to provide in quintuplicate

¹**quip** \'kwip\ *n* **:** a clever remark **:** GIBE

²**quip** *vb* **quipped; quip·ping 1 :** to make quips **:** GIBE **2 :** to jest or gibe at

**quire** \'kwī(ə)r\ *n* **:** a set of 24 or sometimes 25 sheets of paper of the same size and quality

**quirk** \'kwərk\ *n* **:** a peculiarity of action or behavior — **quirky** *adj*

**quirt** \'kwərt\ *n* **:** a riding whip with a short handle and a rawhide lash

**quis·ling** \'kwiz-liŋ\ *n* **:** a traitor who collaborates with the invaders of his country esp. by serving in a puppet government

**quit** \'kwit\ *vb* **quit** *also* **quit·ted; quit·ting 1 :** CONDUCT, BEHAVE ⟨∼ themselves well⟩ **2 :** to depart from **:** LEAVE, ABANDON **syn** acquit, comfort, deport, demean — **quit·ter** *n*

**quite** \'kwīt\ *adv* **1 :** COMPLETELY, WHOLLY **2 :** to an extreme **:** POSITIVELY **3 :** to a considerable extent **:** RATHER

**quits** \'kwits\ *adj* **:** even or equal with another (as by repaying a debt, returning a favor, or retaliating for an injury)

**quit·tance** \'kwit-ᵊns\ *n* **:** REQUITAL

¹**quiv·er** \'kwiv-ər\ *n* **:** a case for carrying arrows

²**quiver** *vb* **quiv·ered; quiv·er·ing** \-(ə-)riŋ\ **:** to shake with a slight trembling motion **syn** shiver, shudder, quaver, quake

³**quiver** *n* **:** the act or action of quivering **:** TREMOR

**qui vive** \kē-'vēv\ *n* [F *qui-vive*, fr. *qui vive?* long live who?, challenge of a French sentry] **1 :** CHALLENGE **2 :** ALERT ⟨on the *qui vive* for prowlers⟩

**quix·ot·ic** \kwik-'sät-ik\ *adj* [fr. Don *Quixote*, hero of the novel *Don Quixote de la Mancha* by Cervantes] **:** idealistic to an impractical degree

¹**quiz** \'kwiz\ *n, pl* **quiz·zes 1 :** an eccentric person **2 :** a practical joke **3 :** a short oral or written test

²**quiz** *vb* **quizzed; quiz·zing 1 :** MOCK **2 :** to look at inquisitively **3 :** to question closely **:** EXAMINE **syn** ask, interrogate, query

**quiz·zi·cal** \'kwiz-i-kəl\ *adj* **1 :** slightly eccentric **2 :** marked by bantering or teasing **3 :** INQUISITIVE, QUESTIONING

**quoit** \'kwät, 'k(w)òit\ *n* **1 :** a flattened ring of iron or circle of rope used in a throwing game **2** *pl* **:** a game in which quoits are thrown at an upright pin in an attempt to ring the pin

**quon·dam** \'kwän-dəm, -,dam\ *adj* [L, at one time, formerly, fr. *quom, cum* when] **:** FORMER

**quo·rum** \'kwōr-əm\ *n* **:** the number of members of a body required to be present for business to be legally transacted

**quot** *abbr* quotation

**quo·ta** \'kwōt-ə\ *n* **:** a proportional part esp. when assigned **:** SHARE

**quot·able** \'kwōt-ə-bəl\ *adj* **:** fit for or worth quoting

**quo·ta·tion mark** \kwō-'tā-shən-\ *n* **:** one of a pair of punctuation marks " " or ' ' used esp. to indicate the beginning and the end of a quotation in which the exact phraseology of another is directly cited

**quote** \'kwōt\ *vb* **quot·ed; quot·ing** [ML *quotare* to mark the number of, number references, fr. L *quotus* of what number or quantity, fr. *quot* how many, (as) many as] **1 :** to speak or write a passage from another usu. with acknowledgment; *also* **:** to repeat a passage in substantiation or illustration **2 :** to state the market price of a commodity, stock, or bond **3 :** to inform a hearer or reader that matter following is quoted — **quo·ta·tion** \kwō-'tā-shən\ *n* — **quote** *n*

**quoth** \(')kwōth\ *vb past* [ME, past of *quethen* to say, fr. OE *cwethan*] *archaic* **:** SAID — usu. used in the 1st and 3d persons with the subject following

**quo·tid·i·an** \kwō-'tid-ē-ən\ *adj* **1 :** DAILY **2 :** COMMONPLACE, ORDINARY

**quo·tient** \'kwō-shənt\ *n* **:** the number resulting from the division of one number by another

**qursh** *n, pl* **qursh** \'kùrsh\ — see *riyal* at MONEY table

**qv** *abbr* [L *quod vide*] which see

**qy** *abbr* query

**R** ¹r \\'är\ *n, pl* **r's** *or* **rs** \\'ärz\ *often cap* **:** the 18th letter of the English alphabet
²r *abbr, often cap* **1** rabbi **2** radius **3** rare **4** Republican **5** resistance **6** right **7** river **8** roentgen **9** rook **10** run

**Ra** *symbol* radium

**RA** *abbr* **1** regular army **2** Royal Academy

**RAAF** *abbr* Royal Australian Air Force

¹**rab·bet** \\'rab-ət\ *n* **:** a groove in the edge or face of a board esp. to receive another piece

²**rabbet** *vb* **:** to cut a rabbet in; *also* **:** to joint by means of a rabbet

**rab·bi** \\'rab-,ī\ *n* [LL, fr. Gk *rhabbi*, fr. Heb *rabbī* my master, fr. *rabh* master + -*ī* my] **1** : MASTER, TEACHER — used by Jews as a term of address **2** : a Jew trained and ordained for professional religious leadership — **rab·bin·ic** \rə-'bin-ik\ *or* **rab·bin·i·cal** \-i-kəl\ *adj*

**rab·bin·ate** \\'rab-ə-nət, -,nāt\ *n* **1** : the office of a rabbi **2** : the whole body of rabbis

**rab·bit** \\'rab-ət\ *n, pl* **rabbit** *or* **rabbits** : a long-eared burrowing mammal related to the hare

**rabbit brush** *n* : any of several low branched shrubs of the alkali plains of western No. America with clusters of golden yellow flowers

**rab·ble** \\'rab-əl\ *n* **1** : MOB **2** **2** : the lowest class of people

**ra·bid** \\'rab-əd\ *adj* **1** : VIOLENT, FURIOUS **2** : being fanatical or extreme (as in opinion or partnership) **3** : affected with rabies — **ra·bid·ly** *adv*

**ra·bies** \\'rā-bēz\ *n, pl* **rabies** : an acute deadly virus disease transmitted by the bite of an affected animal

**rac·coon** \ra-'kün\ *n, pl* **raccoon** *or* **raccoons** : a tree-dwelling gray No. American mammal with a bushy ringed tail; *also* : its fur

¹**race** \\'rās\ *n* **1** : a strong current of running water; *also* : its channel **2** : an onward course (as of time or life) **3** : a contest in speed **4** : a contest for a desired end (as election to office)

²**race** *vb* **raced; rac·ing** **1** : to run in a race **2** : to run swiftly : RUSH **3** : to engage in a race with **4** : to drive at high speed — **rac·er** *n*

³**race** *n* **1** : a family, tribe, people, or nation of the same stock; *also* : MANKIND **2** : a group of individuals within a biological species able to breed together — **ra·cial** \\'rā-shəl\ *adj* — **ra·cial·ly** \-ē\ *adv*

**race·course** \\'rās-,kōrs\ *n* : a course for racing

**race·horse** \-,hórs\ *n* : a horse bred or kept for racing

**ra·ceme** \rā-'sēm\ *n* [L *racemus* bunch of grapes] : a flower cluster with flowers borne along a stem and blooming from the base toward the tip — **rac·e·mose** \\'ras-ə-,mōs\ *adj*

**race·track** \\'rās-,trak\ *n* : a usu. oval course on which races are run

**race·way** \-,wā\ *n* **1** : a channel for a current of water **2** : RACECOURSE

**ra·cial·ism** \\'rā-shə-,liz-əm\ *n* : RACISM — **ra·cial·ist** \-ləst\ *n* — **ra·cial·is·tic** \,rā-shə-'lis-tik\ *adj*

**racing form** *n* : an information sheet giving data about horse races

**rac·ism** \\'rās-,iz-əm\ *n* : a belief that some races are by nature superior to others; *also* : discrimination based on such belief — **rac·ist** \-əst\ *n*

¹**rack** \\'rak\ *n* **1** : a framework on or in which something may be placed (as for display or storage) **2** : an instrument of torture on which a body is stretched **3** : a bar fitted with teeth to gear with a pinion or worm

²**rack** *vb* **1** : to torture with or as if with a rack **2** : to stretch or strain by force **3** : TORMENT **4** : to place on or in a rack

¹**rack·et** *also* **rac·quet** \\'rak-ət\ *n* [MF *raquette*, fr. Ar *rāḥah* palm of the hand] : a light bat made of netting stretched across an oval open frame and used for striking a ball (as in tennis

²**racket** *n* **1** : confused noise : DIN **2** : a fraudulent or dishonest scheme or activity

³**racket** *vb* **1** : to make a racket **2** : to engage in active social life (~ around)

**rack·e·teer** \,rak-ə-'tiər\ *n* : a person who extorts money or advantages esp. from businessmen by threats of violence or unlawful interference — **rack·e·teer·ing** *n*

**rack up** *vb* : SCORE

**ra·con·teur** \,rak-,än-'tər\ *n* : one good at telling anecdotes

**racy** \\'rā-sē\ *adj* **rac·i·er; -est** **1** : having the distinctive quality of something in its original or most characteristic form **2** : full of zest **3** : PUNGENT, SPICY **4** : RISQUÉ, SUGGESTIVE — **rac·i·ly** \\'rā-sə-lē\ *adv* — **rac·i·ness** \-sē-nəs\ *n*

**rad** *abbr* **1** radical **2** radio **3** radius

**ra·dar** \\'rā-,där\ *n* [*ra*dio *d*etecting *a*nd *r*anging] : a detecting device that establishes through reception and timing of reflected radio waves the distance, height, and direction of motion of an object in the path of the beam

**ra·dar·scope** \\'rā-,där-,skōp\ *n* : a device that gives the visual indication in a radar receiver

¹**ra·di·al** \\'rād-ē-əl\ *adj* : arranged or having parts arranged like rays coming from a common center — **ra·di·al·ly** \-ē\ *adv*

²**radial** *n* : a pneumatic tire with cords laid perpendicular to the center line

**radial engine** *n* : an internal-combustion engine with cylinders arranged radially like the spokes of a wheel

**ra·di·ant** \\'rād-ē-ənt\ *adj* **1** : SHINING, GLOWING **2** : beaming with happiness **3** : transmitted by radiation **syn** brilliant, bright, luminous, lustrous — **ra·di·ance** \-əns\ *n* — **ra·di·an·cy** \-ən-sē\ *n* — **ra·di·ant·ly** *adv*

**radiant energy** *n* : energy transmitted as electomagnetic waves

**ra·di·ate** \'rād-ē-ˌāt\ *vb* **-at·ed; -at·ing** **1** : to send out rays : SHINE, GLOW **2** : to issue in rays ⟨light ~s⟩ ⟨heat ~s⟩ **3** : to spread around as from a center — **ra·di·a·tion** \ˌrād-ē-'ā-shən\ *n*

**radiation sickness** *n* : sickness that results from exposure to radiation and is commonly marked by fatigue, nausea, vomiting, loss of teeth and hair, and in more severe cases by damage to blood-forming tissue

**ra·di·a·tor** \'rād-ē-ˌāt-ər\ *n* : a device to heat air (as in a room) or to cool water (as in an automobile engine)

¹**rad·i·cal** \'rad-i-kəl\ *adj* [ME, fr. LL *radicalis*, fr. L *radic-, radix* root] **1** : FUNDAMENTAL, EXTREME, THOROUGHGOING **2** : of or relating to radicals in politics — **rad·i·cal·ism** \-ˌiz-əm\ *n* — **rad·i·cal·ly** \-ē\ *adv*

²**radical** *n* **1** : a person who favors rapid and sweeping changes in laws and methods of government **2** : a group of atoms that is replaceable by a single atom or remains unchanged during reactions **3** : the indicated root of a mathematical expression; *also* : the sign √‾ placed before an expression to indicate that its root is to be taken

**rad·i·cal·ize** \-kə-ˌlīz\ *vb* **-ized; -iz·ing** : to make radical esp. in politics — **rad·i·cal·iza·tion** \ˌrad-i-kə-lə-'zā-shən\ *n*

**radii** *pl of* RADIUS

¹**ra·dio** \'rād-ē-ˌō\ *n, pl* **ra·di·os 1** : transmission or reception of electric impulses or signals esp. by sound by means of electric waves without a connecting wire **2** : a radio receiving set **3** : the radio broadcasting industry — **radio** *adj*

²**radio** *vb* : to communicate or send a message to by radio

**ra·dio·ac·tiv·i·ty** \ˌrād-ē-ō-ˌak-'tiv-ət-ē\ *n* : the property that some elements have of spontaneously emitting rays of radiant energy by the disintegration of the nuclei of atoms — **ra·dio·ac·tive** \-'ak-tiv\ *adj*

**radio astronomy** *n* : astronomy dealing with radio waves received from outside the earth's atmosphere

**ra·dio·car·bon** \ˌrād-ē-ō-'kär-bən\ *n* : CARBON 14

**radio frequency** *n* : an electromagnetic wave frequency intermediate between audio frequency and infrared frequency used esp. in radio and television transmission

**radio galaxy** *n* : a galaxy containing a source from which radio energy is detected

**ra·dio·gen·ic** \ˌrād-ē-ō-'jen-ik\ *adj* : produced by radioactivity

**ra·dio·gram** \'rād-ē-ō-ˌgram\ *n* **1** : RADIOGRAPH **2** : a message transmitted by radiotelegraphy

¹**ra·dio·graph** \-ˌgraf\ *n* : a photograph made by some form of radiation other than light; *esp* : an X-ray photograph — **ra·dio·graph·ic** \ˌrād-ē-ō-'graf-ik\ *adj* — **ra·dio·graph·i·cal·ly** \-i-k(ə-)lē\ *adv* — **ra·di·og·ra·phy** \ˌrād-ē-'äg-rə-fē\ *n*

²**radiograph** *vb* : to make a radiograph of

**ra·dio·iso·tope** \ˌrād-ē-ō-'ī-sə-ˌtōp\ *n* : a radioactive isotope

**ra·di·ol·o·gy** \ˌrād-ē-'äl-ə-jē\ *n* : the science of high-energy radiations; *also* : the use of radiant energy (as X rays and radium radiations) in medicine — **ra·di·ol·o·gist** \-jəst\ *n*

**ra·dio·man** \'rād-ē-ō-ˌman\ *n* : a radio operator or technician

**ra·di·om·e·ter** \ˌrād-ē-'äm-ət-ər\ *n* : an instrument for measuring the intensity of radiant energy — **ra·di·om·e·try** \-ə-trē\ *n*

**ra·dio·met·ric** \ˌrād-ē-ō-'met-rik\ *adj* **1** : related to or measured by a radiometer **2** : of or relating to the measurement of geologic time by means of the rate of disintegration of radioactive elements — **ra·dio·met·ri·cal·ly** \-tri-k(ə-)lē\ *adv*

**ra·dio·phone** \'rād-ē-ə-ˌfōn\ *n* : RADIO-TELEPHONE

**ra·dio·sonde** \'rād-ē-ō-ˌsänd\ *n* : a small radio transmitter carried aloft (as by balloon) and used to transmit meteorological data

**ra·dio·tele·graph** \ˌrād-ē-ō-'tel-ə-ˌgraf\ *n* : wireless telegraphy — **ra·dio·tele·graph·ic** \-ˌtel-ə-'graf-ik\ *adj* — **ra·dio·te·leg·ra·phy** \-tə-'leg-rə-fē\ *n*

**ra·dio·te·lem·e·try** \-tə-'lem-ə-trē\ *n* : the science or process of using a telemeter

**ra·dio·tele·phone** \-'tel-ə-ˌfōn\ *n* : an apparatus for wireless telephony using radio waves — **ra·dio·te·le·pho·ny** \-tə-'lef-ə-nē, -'tel-ə-ˌfō-nē\ *n*

**radio telescope** *n* : a radio receiver-antenna combination used in radio astronomy

**ra·dio·ther·a·py** \ˌrād-ē-ō-'ther-ə-pē\ *n* : treatment of disease by radiation (as X rays) — **ra·dio·ther·a·pist** \-pəst\ *n*

**rad·ish** \'rad-ish\ *n* [ME, alter. of OE *rædic*, fr. L *radic-, radix* root, radish] : a pungent fleshy root usu. eaten raw; *also* : a plant related to the mustards that produces this root

**ra·di·um** \'rād-ē-əm\ *n* : a metallic chemical element that is notable for its emission of radiant energy by the disintegration of the nuclei of atoms and is used in luminous materials and in the treatment of cancer

**ra·di·us** \'rād-ē-əs\ *n, pl* **ra·dii** \-ē-ˌī\ *also* **ra·di·us·es 1** : a straight line extending from the center of a circle or a sphere to the circumference or surface **2** : a circular area defined by the length of its radius **syn** range, reach, scope, compass

**RADM** *abbr* rear admiral

**ra·don** \'rā-ˌdän\ *n* : a heavy radioactive gaseous chemical element

**RAF** *abbr* Royal Air Force

**raf·fia** \'raf-ē-ə\ *n* : fiber used esp. for baskets and hats and obtained from the stalks of the leaves of a Madagascar palm (**raffia palm**)

**raff·ish** \'raf-ish\ *adj* : jaunty or sporty

esp. in a flashy or vulgar manner — **raff·ish·ly** \ adv — **raff·ish·ness** n

**¹raf·fle** \'raf-əl\ n : a lottery in which the prize is won by one of a number of persons buying chances

**²raffle** vb **raf·fled; raf·fling** \'raf-(ə-)liŋ\ : to dispose of by a raffle

**¹raft** \'raft\ n **1** : a number of logs or timbers fastened together to form a float **2** : a flat structure for support or transportation on water

**²raft** vb **1** : to travel or transport by raft **2** : to make into a raft

**³raft** n : a large amount or number

**raf·ter** \'raf-tər\ n : a usu. sloping timber of a roof

**¹rag** \'rag\ n : a waste piece of cloth

**²rag** n : a composition in ragtime

**ra·ga** \'räg-ə\ n **1** : an ancient traditional melodic pattern or mode in Indian music **2** : an improvisation based on a raga

**rag·a·muf·fin** \'rag-ə-,məf-ən\ n [Ragamoffyn, a demon in Piers Plowman (1393), attributed to William Langland] : a ragged dirty man or child

**¹rage** \'rāj\ n **1** : violent and uncontrolled anger **2** : VOGUE, FASHION

**²rage** vb **raged; rag·ing 1** : to be furiously angry : RAVE **2** : to be in violent tumult 〈the storm raged〉 **3** : to continue out of control

**rag·ged** \'rag-əd\ adj **1** : TORN, TATTERED; also : wearing tattered clothes **2** : done in an uneven way 〈a ~ performance〉 — **rag·ged·ly** adv — **rag·ged·ness** n

**rag·lan** \'rag-lən\ n : an overcoat with sleeves (raglan sleeves) sewn in with seams slanting from neck to underarm

**ra·gout** \ra-'gü\ n [F ragoût, fr. ragoûter to revive the taste, fr. re- + a-to (fr. L ad-) + goût taste, fr L gustus] : a highly seasoned meat stew with vegetables

**rag·pick·er** \'rag-,pik-ər\ n : one who collects rags and refuse for a livelihood

**rag·tag and bob·tail** \,rag-,tag-ən-'bäb-,tāl\ n : RABBLE

**rag·time** \'rag-,tīm\ n : rhythm in which there is more or less continuous syncopation in the melody

**rag·weed** \-,wēd\ n : any of several coarse weedy herbs with allergenic pollen

**¹raid** \'rād\ n : a sudden usu. surprise attack or invasion : FORAY

**²raid** vb : to make a raid on — **raid·er** n

**¹rail** \'rāl\ n [ME raile, fr. MF reille ruler, bar, fr. L regula ruler, fr. regere to keep straight, direct, rule] **1** : a bar extending from one support to another as a guard or barrier **2** : a bar forming a track for wheeled vehicles **3** : RAILROAD

**²rail** vb : to provide with a railing : FENCE

**³rail** n, pl **rail** or **rails** : any of several small wading birds related to the cranes

**⁴rail** vb [ME railen, fr. MF railler to mock, fr. Old Provençal ralhar to babble, joke, fr. (assumed) VL ragulare to bray, fr. LL ragere to neigh] : to complain angrily : SCOLD, REVILE — **rail·er** n

**rail·ing** \'rā-liŋ\ n : a barrier of rails

**rail·lery** \'rā-lə-rē\ n, pl **-ler·ies** : good-natured ridicule : BANTER

**¹rail·road** \'rāl-,rōd\ n : a permanent road with rails fixed to ties and laid on a roadbed providing a track for cars; also : such a road and its assets constituting a property

**²railroad** vb **1** : to send by rail **2** : to work on a railroad **3** : to put through (as a law) too hastily **4** : to convict hastily or with insufficient or improper evidence — **rail·road·er** n — **rail·road·ing** n

**rail·way** \-,wā\ n **1** : RAILROAD **2** : a line of track providing a runway for wheels

**rai·ment** \'rā-mənt\ n : CLOTHING

**¹rain** \'rān\ n **1** : water falling in drops from the clouds **2** : a shower of objects 〈a ~ of bullets〉 — **rainy** adj

**²rain** vb **1** : to fall as or like rain **2** : to send down rain **3** : to pour down

**rain·bow** \-,bō\ n : an arc of colors formed opposite the sun by the refraction and reflection of the sun's rays in rain, spray, or mist

**rainbow trout** n : a large stout-bodied black-dotted trout of western No. America with a pink, red, or lavender stripe along each side of the body

**rain check** n **1** : a ticket stub good for a later performance when the scheduled one is rained out **2** : an assurance of a deferred extension of an offer

**rain·coat** \'rān-,kōt\ n : a waterproof or water-resistant coat

**rain·drop** \-,dräp\ n : a drop of rain

**rain·fall** \-,fol\ n : a fall of rain; esp : the amount that falls measured by depth in inches

**rain forest** n : a tropical woodland that has an annual rainfall of at least 100 inches and that is marked by lofty broad-leaved evergreen trees forming a continuous canopy

**rain·mak·ing** \'rān-,mā-kiŋ\ n : the action or process of producing or attempting to produce rain by artificial means — **rain·mak·er** \-kər\ n

**rain out** vb : to interrupt or prevent by rain

**rain·spout** \-,spaùt\ n : a pipe, duct, or orifice draining a roof gutter

**rain·storm** \'rān-,stórm\ n : a storm of or with rain

**rain·wa·ter** \-,wòt-ər, -,wät-\ n : water fallen as rain

**¹raise** \'rāz\ vb **raised; rais·ing 1** : to cause or help to rise : LIFT 〈~ a window〉 **2** : AWAKEN, AROUSE 〈enough to ~ the dead〉 **3** : BUILD, ERECT 〈~ a monument〉 **4** : PROMOTE 〈was raised to captain〉 **5** : COLLECT 〈~ money〉 **6** : BREED, GROW 〈~ cattle〉 〈~ corn〉; also : to bring up 〈~ a family〉 **7** : PROVOKE 〈~ a laugh〉 **8** : to bring to notice 〈~ an objection〉 **9** : INCREASE 〈~ prices〉; also : to bet more than **10** : to make light and spongy 〈~ dough〉 **11** : END 〈~ a siege〉 **12** : to cause to form 〈~ a blister〉 **syn** lift, hoist, boost — **rais·er** n

**²raise** n : an increase in amount (as of a

bid or bet); *also* : an increase in pay

**rai·sin** \'rāz-ᵊn\ *n* [ME, fr. MF, grape, fr. L *racemus* cluster of grapes or berries] : a grape usu. of a special kind dried for food

**rai·son d'être** \ˌrā-ˌzōⁿ-'detr³\ *n* : reason or justification for existence

**ra·ja** *or* **ra·jah** \'räj-ə\ *n* [Hindi *rājā*, fr. Skt *rājan* king] : an Indian prince

**¹rake** \'rāk\ *n* : a long-handled garden tool having a crossbar with prongs

**²rake** *vb* **raked; rak·ing 1** : to gather, loosen, or smooth with or as if with a rake **2** : to sweep the length of (as a trench or ship) with gunfire

**³rake** *n* : a dissolute man : LIBERTINE

**⁴rake** *n* : inclination from either perpendicular or horizontal : SLANT, SLOPE

**rake-off** \'rāk-ˌôf\ *n* : a percentage or cut taken often unlawfully

**¹rak·ish** \'rā-kish\ *adj* : DISSOLUTE — **rak·ish·ly** *adv* — **rak·ish·ness** *n*

**²rakish** *adj* **1** : having a smart appearance indicative of speed ⟨a ∼ sloop⟩ ⟨∼ masts⟩ **2** : JAUNTY, SPORTY — **rak·ish·ly** *adv* — **rak·ish·ness** *n*

**¹ral·ly** \'rai-ē\ *vb* **ral·lied; ral·ly·ing 1** : to bring together for a common purpose; *also* : to bring back to order ⟨a leader ∼*ing* his forces⟩ **2** : to arouse to activity or from depression or weakness : REVIVE, RECOVER **3** : to come together again to renew an effort **syn** stir, rouse, awaken, waken

**²rally** *n, pl* **rallies 1** : an act of rallying **2** : a mass meeting to arouse enthusiasm **3** : a competitive automobile run over public roads

**³rally** *vb* **ral·lied; ral·ly·ing** : BANTER

**¹ram** \'ram\ *n* **1** : a male sheep **2** : a wooden beam or metal bar used in battering down walls or doors (as in a siege)

**²ram** *vb* **rammed; ram·ming 1** : to force or drive in or through **2** : CRAM, CROWD **3** : to strike against violently

**¹ram·ble** \'ram-bəl\ *vb* **ram·bled; ram·bling** \-b(ə-)liŋ\ : to go about aimlessly : ROAM, WANDER

**²ramble** *n* : a leisurely excursion; *esp* : an aimless walk

**ram·bler** \'ram-blər\ *n* : one that rambles; *esp* : a hardy climbing rose with large clusters of small flowers

**ram·bunc·tious** \ram-'bəŋk-shəs\ *adj* : UNRULY

**ra·mie** \'rā-mē, 'ram-ē\ *n* : a strong lustrous bast fiber from an Asiatic nettle

**ram·i·fy** \'ram-ə-ˌfī\ *vb* **-fied; -fy·ing** : to branch out — **ram·i·fi·ca·tion** \ˌram-ə-fə-'kā-shən\ *n*

**ramp** \'ramp\ *n* : a sloping passage or roadway connecting different levels

**¹ram·page** \'ram-ˌpāj, (')ram-'pāj\ *vb* **ram·paged; ram·pag·ing** : to rush about wildly

**²ram·page** \'ram-pāj\ *n* : a course of violent or riotous action or behavior — **ram·pa·geous** \ram-'pā-jəs\ *adj*

**ram·pant** \'ram-pənt\ *adj* : unchecked in growth or spread : RIFE ⟨fear was ∼ in the town⟩ — **ram·pant·ly** *adv*

**ram·part** \'ram-ˌpärt\ *n* **1** : a broad embankment raised as a fortification **2** : a protective barrier **3** : a wall-like ridge

**ram·rod** \'ram-ˌräd\ *n* **1** : a rod used to ram a charge into a muzzle-loading gun **2** : a cleaning rod for small arms

**ram·shack·le** \'ram-ˌshak-əl\ *adj* : RICKETY, TUMBLEDOWN

**ran** *past of* RUN

**¹ranch** \'ranch\ *n* [MexSp *rancho* small ranch, fr. Sp, camp, hut & Sp dial., small farm, fr. Old Spanish *ranchear* (se) to take up quarters, fr. MF (se) *ranger* to take up a position, fr. *ranger* to set in a row] **1** : an establishment for the raising and grazing of cattle, sheep, or horses **2** : a large farm devoted to a specialty — **ranch·er** *n*

**²ranch** *vb* : to live or work on a ranch

**ranch house** *n* : a one-story house typically with a low-pitched roof

**ranch·land** \-ˌland\ *n* : land suitable for ranching

**ran·cho** \'ran-chō, 'rän-\ *n, pl* **ran·chos** : RANCH

**ran·cid** \'ran-səd\ *adj* **1** : having a rank smell or taste **2** : ROTTEN, SPOILED — **ran·cid·i·ty** \ran-'sid-ət-ē\ *n* — **ran·cid·ness** \'ran-səd-nəs\ *n*

**ran·cor** \'raŋ-kər\ *n* : deep hatred : intense ill will **syn** antagonism, animosity, antipathy, enmity, hostility — **ran·cor·ous** *adj*

**rand** \'rand, 'ränd, 'ränt\ *n, pl* **rand** — see MONEY table

**R & B** *abbr* rhythm and blues

**R and D** *abbr* research and development

**ran·dom** \'ran-dəm\ *adj* : CHANCE, HAPHAZARD — **ran·dom·ly** *adv* — **ran·dom·ness** *n*

**random-access** *adj* : permitting access to stored data in any order the user desires

**ran·dom·ize** \'ran-də-ˌmīz\ *vb* **-ized; -iz·ing** : to distribute, treat, or perform in a random way — **ran·dom·iza·tion** \ˌran-də-mə-'zā-shən\ *n*

**R and R** *abbr* rest and recreation; rest and recuperation

**rang** *past of* RING

**¹range** \'rānj\ *n* **1** : a series of things in a row **2** : the act of ranging or roaming **3** : open land where cattle may roam and graze **4** : a cooking stove **5** : a variation within limits **6** : the distance a weapon will shoot or is to be shot **7** : a place where shooting is practiced; *also* : a course over which missiles are tested **8** : the space or extent included, covered, or used : SCOPE **syn** reach, compass, radius

**²range** *vb* **ranged; rang·ing 1** : to set in a row or in proper order **2** : to set in place among others of the same kind **3** : to roam over or through : EXPLORE **4** : to roam at large or freely **5** : to correspond in direction or line **6** : to vary within limits

**range·land** \'rānj-ˌland\ *n* : land used or suitable for range

**rang·er** \'rān-jər\ *n* **1** : a warden who patrols forest lands **2** : one that ranges **3** : a member of a body of armed men who range over a region **4** : an expert in close-range fighting and raiding attached to a special unit of assault troops

**rang·y** \'rān-jē\ *adj* **rang·i·er**; **-est** : being long-limbed and slender — **rang·i·ness** \'rān-jē-nəs\ *n*

**ra·ni** *or* **ra·nee** \rä-'nē, 'rän,-ē\ *n* : a raja's wife

**¹rank** \'raŋk\ *adj* **1** : strong and vigorous and usu. coarse in growth ⟨∼ weeds⟩ **2** : unpleasantly strong-smelling — **rank·ly** *adv* — **rank·ness** *n*

**²rank** *n* **1** : ROW **2** : a line of soldiers ranged side by side **3** *pl* : the body of enlisted men ⟨rose from the ∼s⟩ **4** : an orderly arrangement **5** : CLASS, DIVISION **6** : a grade of official standing (as in an army) **7** : position in a group **8** : superior position

**³rank** *vb* **1** : to arrange in lines or in regular formation **2** : to arrange according to classes **3** : to take or have a relative position **4** : to rate above (as in official standing)

**rank and file** *n* **1** : the enlisted men of an armed force **2** : the general membership of a body as contrasted with its leaders

**rank·ing** \'raŋ-kiŋ\ *adj* **1** : having a high position : FOREMOST **2** : being next to the chairman in seniority

**ran·kle** \'raŋ-kəl\ *vb* **ran·kled**; **ran·kling** \-k(ə-)liŋ\ [ME *ranclen* to fester, fr. MF *rancler*, fr. OF *draoncler*, *raoncler*, fr. *draoncle*, *raoncle* festering sore, fr. (assumed) VL *dracunculus*, fr. L, dim. of *draco* serpent] **1** : to become inflamed : FESTER **2** : to cause anger, irritation, or bitterness

**ran·sack** \'ran-ˌsak\ *vb* : to search thoroughly; *esp* : to search through and rob

**¹ran·som** \'ran-səm\ *n* [ME *ransoun*, fr. OF *rançon*, fr. L *redemption-*, *redemptio* act of buying back, fr. *redimere* to buy back, redeem] **1** : something paid or demanded for the freedom of a captive **2** : the act of ransoming

**²ransom** *vb* : to free from captivity or punishment by paying a price — **ran·som·er** *n*

**rant** \'rant\ *vb* **1** : to talk loudly and wildly **2** : to scold violently — **rant·er** *n* — **rant·ing·ly** \-iŋ-lē\ *adv*

**¹rap** \'rap\ *n* **1** : a sharp blow **2** : a sharp rebuke **3** *slang* : responsibility for or consequences of an action

**²rap** *vb* **rapped**; **rap·ping 1** : to strike sharply : KNOCK **2** : to utter sharply **3** : to criticize sharply

**³rap** *vb* **rapped**; **rap·ping** : to talk freely and frankly

**ra·pa·cious** \rə-'pā-shəs\ *adj* **1** : excessively greedy or covetous **2** : living on prey **3** : RAVENOUS — **ra·pa·cious·ly** *adv* — **ra·pa·cious·ness** *n* — **ra·pac·i·ty** \-'pas-ət-ē\ *n*

**¹rape** \'rāp\ *n* : a European herb related to the mustards that is grown as a forage crop and for its seeds (**rape·seed** \-ˌsēd\)

**²rape** *vb* **raped**; **rap·ing** : to commit rape on : RAVISH — **rap·er** *n* — **rap·ist** \'rā-pəst\ *n*

**³rape** *n* **1** : a carrying away by force **2** : unlawful sexual intercourse with a woman without her consent and chiefly by force or deception

**¹rap·id** \'rap-əd\ *adj* [L *rapidus* seizing, sweeping, rapid, fr. *rapere* to seize, sweep away] : very fast : SWIFT **syn** fleet, quick, speedy — **ra·pid·i·ty** \rə-'pid-ət-ē\ *n* — **rap·id·ly** \'rap-əd-lē\ *adv*

**²rapid** *n* : a place in a stream where the current flows very fast usu. over obstructions — usu. used in pl.

**rapid eye movement** *n* : rapid conjugate movement of the eyes associated with a state of sleep occurring approximately at 90-minute intervals that is characterized by changes in the electrical activity of the brain, changes in heart rhythm, relaxed muscles, vascular congestion of the sex organs, and dreaming

**rapid transit** *n* : fast passenger transportation (as by subway) in urban areas

**ra·pi·er** \'rā-pē-ər\ *n* : a straight 2-edged sword with a narrow pointed blade

**rap·ine** \'rap-ən, -ˌīn\ *n* : PILLAGE, PLUNDER

**rap·pen** \'räp-ən\ *n*, *pl* **rappen** : the centime of Switzerland

**rap·port** \ra-'pōr\ *n* : RELATION; *esp* : relation characterized by harmony

**rap·proche·ment** \ˌrap-ˌrōsh-'mäⁿ, ra-'prōsh-ˌmäⁿ\ *n* : the establishment or a state of cordial relations

**rap·scal·lion** \rap-'skal-yən\ *n* : RASCAL, SCAMP

**rapt** \'rapt\ *adj* **1** : carried away with emotion **2** : ABSORBED, ENGROSSED — **rapt·ly** \'rap-(t)lē\ *adv* — **rapt·ness** \'rap(t)-nəs\ *n*

**rap·ture** \'rap-chər\ *n* : spiritual or emotional ecstasy — **rap·tur·ous** \-chə-rəs\ *adj*

**rapture of the deep** *n* : a confused mental state caused by nitrogen forced into a diver's bloodstream from atmospheric air under pressure

**rapture of the depths** : RAPTURE OF THE DEEP

**ra·ra avis** \ˌrar-ə-'ā-vəs\ *n* [L, rare bird] : a rare person or thing : RARITY

**¹rare** \'ra(ə)r\ *adj* **rar·er**; **rar·est** : not thoroughly cooked

**²rare** *adj* **rar·er**; **rar·est 1** : not thick or dense : THIN ⟨∼ air⟩ **2** : unusually fine : EXCELLENT, SPLENDID **3** : seldom met with — **rare·ly** *adv* — **rare·ness** *n* — **rar·i·ty** \'rar-ət-ē\ *n*

**rare·bit** \'ra(ə)r-bət\ *n* : WELSH RABBIT

**rar·efy** *also* **rar·i·fy** \'rar-ə-ˌfī\ *vb* **-efied**; **-efy·ing** : to make or become rare, thin, or less dense — **rar·efac·tion** \ˌrar-ə-'fak-shən\ *n*

**rar·ing** \'ra(ə)r-ən, -iŋ\ *adj* : full of enthusiasm or eagerness

**ras·cal** \'ras-kəl\ *n* **1** : a mean or dishonest person **2** : a mischievous person — **ras·cal·i·ty** \ras-'kal-ət-ē\ *n* — **ras·cal·ly** \'ras-kə-lē\ *adj*

**¹rash** \'rash\ *adj* : having or showing little regard for consequences : too hasty in decision, action, or speech **: RECKLESS syn** daring, foolhardy, adventurous, venturesome — **rash·ly** *adv* — **rash·ness** *n*

²**rash** *n* **:** an eruption on the body

**rash·er** \'rash-ər\ *n* **:** a thin slice of bacon or ham broiled or fried; *also* **:** a portion consisting of several such slices

¹**rasp** \'rasp\ *vb* **1 :** to rub with or as if with a rough file **2 :** to grate harshly on (as one's nerves) **3 :** to speak in a grating tone

²**rasp** *n* **:** a coarse file with cutting points instead of ridges

**rasp·ber·ry** \'raz-,ber-ē, -b(ə)rē\ *n* **1 :** an edible red or black berry produced by some brambles; *also* **:** such a bramble **2 :** a sound of contempt made by protruding the tongue through the lips and expelling air forcibly

**ras·ter** \'ras-tər\ *n* **:** an area on which the image is produced in a picture tube

¹**rat** \'rat\ *n* **1 :** a scaly-tailed destructive rodent larger than the mouse **2 :** a contemptible person; *esp* **:** one that betrays his associates

²**rat** *vb* **rat·ted; rat·ting 1 :** to betray one's associates **2 :** to hunt or catch rats

**rat cheese** *n* **:** CHEDDAR

**ratch·et** \'rach-ət\ *n* **:** a device that consists of a notched wheel held or moved by a separate projection and is used esp. in a hand tool (as a drill) for giving motion in one direction

**ratchet wheel** *n* **:** a toothed wheel held in position or turned by an engaging pawl

¹**rate** \'rāt\ *vb* **rat·ed; rat·ing :** to scold violently

²**rate** *n* **1 :** quantity, amount, or degree measured by some standard **2 :** an amount (as of payment) measured by its relation to some other amount (as of time) **3 :** a charge, payment, or price fixed according to a ratio, scale, or standard 〈tax ~〉 **4 :** RANK, CLASS

³**rate** *vb* **rat·ed; rat·ing 1 :** CONSIDER, REGARD **2 :** ESTIMATE **3 :** to settle the relative rank or class of **4 :** to be classed **:** RANK **5 :** to be of consequence **6 :** to have a right to **:** DESERVE — **rat·er** *n*

**rath·er** \'rath-ər, 'rəth-, 'räth-\ *adv* [ME, fr. OE *hrathor,* compar. of *hrathe* quickly] **1 :** PREFERABLY **2 :** on the other hand **3 :** more properly **4 :** more correctly speaking **5 :** SOMEWHAT

**raths·kel·ler** \'rät-,skel-ər, 'rat(h)-\ *n* [obs. G (now *ratskeller*), city-hall basement restaurant, fr. *rat* council + *keller* cellar] **:** a restaurant which is patterned after the cellar of a German city hall and in which beer is sold

**rat·i·fy** \'rat-ə-,fī\ *vb* **-fied; -fy·ing :** to approve and accept formally — **rat·i·fi·ca·tion** \,rat-ə-fə-'kā-shən\ *n*

**rat·ing** \'rāt-iŋ\ *n* **1 :** a classification according to grade **:** RANK **2** Brit **:** a naval enlisted man **3 :** an estimate of the credit standing and business responsibility of a person or firm

**ra·tio** \'rā-sh(ē-)ō\ *n, pl* **ra·tios 1**

**:** the quotient of one quantity divided by another **2 :** the relation in number, quantity, or degree between things

**ra·ti·o·ci·na·tion** \,rat-ē-,ōs-ᵊn-'ā-shən, ,rash-, -,äs-\ *n* **:** exact thinking **: REASONING** — **ra·ti·o·ci·nate** \-'ōs-ᵊn-,āt, -'äs-\ *vb* — **ra·ti·o·ci·na·tive** \-'ōs-ᵊn-,āt-iv, -'äs-\ *adj* — **rat·i·o·ci·na·tor** \-'ōs-ᵊn-,āt-ər, -'äs-\ *n*

¹**ra·tion** \'rash-ən, 'rā-shən\ *n* **1 :** a food allowance for one day **2 :** FOOD, PROVISIONS, DIET — usu. used in pl. **3 :** SHARE, ALLOTMENT

²**ration** *vb* **ra·tioned; ra·tion·ing** \'rash-(ə)niŋ, 'rāsh-\ **1 :** to supply with or allot as rations **2 :** to use or allot sparingly **syn** apportion, portion

¹**ra·tio·nal** \'rash-(ə)nəl\ *adj* **1 :** having reason or understanding; *also* **:** SANE **2 :** of or relating to reason **3 :** relating to, consisting of, or being one or more rational numbers — **ra·tio·nal·ly** \-ē\ *adv*

²**rational** *n* **:** RATIONAL NUMBER

**ra·tio·nale** \,rash-ə-'nal\ *n* **1 :** an explanation of controlling principles of belief or practice **2 :** an underlying reason

**ra·tio·nal·ism** \'rash-(ə)nə-,liz-əm\ *n* **:** the practice of guiding one's actions and opinions solely by what seems reasonable — **ra·tio·nal·ist** \-ləst\ *n* — **rationalist** *or* **ra·tio·nal·is·tic** \,rash-(ə)nə-'lis-tik\ *adj*

**ra·tio·nal·i·ty** \,rash-ə-'nal-ət-ē\ *n, pl* **-ties :** the quality or state of being rational

**ra·tio·nal·ize** \'rash-(ə)nə-,līz\ *vb* **-ized; -iz·ing 1 :** to make (something irrational) appear rational or reasonable **2 :** to provide a natural explanation of (as a myth) **3 :** to justify (as one's behavior or weaknesses) esp. to oneself **4 :** to find plausible but untrue reasons for conduct — **ra·tio·nal·iza·tion** \,rash-(ə)nə-lə-'zā-shən\ *n*

**rational number** *n* **:** an integer or the quotient of two integers

**rat·line** \'rat-lən\ *n* **:** one of the small transverse ropes fastened to the shrouds and forming a rope ladder

**rat race** *n* **:** strenuous, tiresome, and usu. competitive activity or rush

**rat·tan** \ra-'tan, rə-\ *n* **:** an Asiatic climbing palm with long stems used esp. for canes and wickerwork

**rat·ter** \'rat-ər\ *n* **:** a rat-catching dog or cat

¹**rat·tle** \'rat-ᵊl\ *vb* **rat·tled; rat·tling** \'rat-(ᵊ-)liŋ\ **1 :** to make or cause to make a series of clattering sounds **2 :** to move with a clattering sound **3 :** to say or do in a brisk lively fashion 〈~ off the answers〉 **4 :** CONFUSE, UPSET 〈~ a witness〉

²**rattle** *n* **1 :** a series of clattering and knocking sounds **2 :** a toy that produces a rattle when shaken **3 :** one of the horny pieces on a rattlesnake's tail or the organ made of these

**rat·tler** \'rat-lər\ *n* **:** RATTLESNAKE

**rat·tle·snake** \'rat-ᵊl-,snāk\ *n* **:** any of various American venomous snakes with a rattle at the end of the tail

**rat·tle·trap** \'rat-ᵊl-,trap\ *n* : something rickety and full of rattles; *esp* : an old car

**rat·tling** \'rat-liŋ\ *adj* **1** : LIVELY, BRISK **2** : FIRST-RATE, SPLENDID

**rat-trap** \'rat-,trap\ *n* **1** : a trap for rats **2** : a dilapidated building **3** : a hopeless situation

**rat·ty** \'rat-ē\ *adj* **rat·ti·er; -est 1** : infested with rats **2** : of, relating to, or suggestive of rats

**rau·cous** \'rò-kəs\ *adj* **1** : HARSH, HOARSE, STRIDENT **2** : boisterously disorderly — **rau·cous·ly** *adv* — **rau·cous·ness** *n*

**raun·chy** \'ròn-chē, 'rän-\ *adj* **raun·chi·er; -est 1** : SLOVENLY, DIRTY **2** : OBSCENE, SMUTTY — **raun·chi·ness** \-chē-nəs\ *n*

**rau·wol·fia** \raù-'wùl-fē-ə, rò-\ *n* : a medicinal extract from the root of an Indian tree; *also* : this tree

**¹rav·age** \'rav-ij\ *n* : an act or result of ravaging : DEVASTATION

**²ravage** *vb* **rav·aged; rav·ag·ing** : to lay waste : DEVASTATE — **rav·ag·er** *n*

**¹rave** \'rāv\ *vb* **raved; rav·ing** [ME *raven*] **1** : to talk wildly in or as if in delirium : STORM, RAGE **2** : to talk with extreme enthusiasm

**²rave** *n* **1** : an act or instance of raving **2** : an extravagantly favorable criticism

**¹rav·el** \'rav-əl\ *vb* **-eled** *or* **-elled; -el·ing** *or* **-el·ling** \-(ə-)liŋ\ **1** : UNRAVEL, UNTWIST **2** : TANGLE, CONFUSE

**²ravel** *n* **1** : something tangled **2** : something raveled out; *esp* : a loose thread

**¹ra·ven** \'rā-vən\ *n* : a large black bird related to the crow

**²raven** *adj* : black and glossy like a raven's feathers

**rav·en·ing** \'rav-(ə-)niŋ\ *adj* : GREEDY

**rav·en·ous** \'rav-(ə-)nəs\ *adj* **1** : RAPACIOUS, VORACIOUS **2** : eager for food : very hungry — **rav·en·ous·ly** *adv* — **rav·en·ous·ness** *n*

**ra·vine** \rə-'vēn\ *n* : a small narrow steep-sided valley larger than a gully and smaller than a canyon

**rav·i·o·li** \,rav-ē-'ō-lē\ *n* [It, pl. of *raviolo*, lit., little turnip, dim. of *rava* turnip, fr. L *rapa*] : small cases of dough with a savory filling (as of meat or cheese)

**rav·ish** \'rav-ish\ *vb* **1** : to seize and take away by violence **2** : to overcome with emotion and esp. with joy or delight **3** : RAPE — **rav·ish·er** *n* — **rav·ish·ment** *n*

**¹raw** \'rò\ *adj* **raw·er** \'rò(-ə)r\; **rawest** \'rò-əst\ **1** : not cooked **2** : changed little from the original form : not processed 〈~ materials〉 **3** : not trained or experienced 〈~ recruits〉 **4** : having the skin abraded or irritated 〈a ~ sore〉 **5** : disagreeably cold and damp 〈a ~ day〉 **6** : VULGAR, COARSE **7** : UNFAIR 〈~ deal〉 — **raw·ness** *n*

**²raw** *n* : a raw place or state; *esp* : NUDITY

**raw·boned** \'rò-'bōnd\ *adj* **1** : THIN, LEAN, GAUNT **2** : having a coarse heavy frame that seems inadequately covered by flesh

**raw·hide** \'rò-,hīd\ *n* : the untanned skin of cattle; *also* : a whip made of this

**¹ray** \'rā\ *n* : any of various large flat fishes that are related to the sharks and have the hind end of the body slender and taillike

**²ray** *n* [ME, fr. MF *rai*, fr. L *radius* rod, ray] **1** : one of the lines of light that appear to radiate from a bright object **2** : a thin beam of radiant energy (as light) **3** : light from a beam **4** : a tiny bit : PARTICLE 〈a ~ of hope〉 **5** : a thin line like a beam of light **6** : an animal or plant structure resembling a ray

**ray·on** \'rā-,än\ *n* : a shiny fabric that resembles silk and is made from fibers produced chemically from cellulose

**raze** \'rāz\ *vb* **razed; raz·ing 1** : to destroy to the ground : DEMOLISH **2** : to scrape, cut, or shave off

**ra·zor** \'rā-zər\ *n* : a sharp cutting instrument used to shave off hair

**ra·zor–backed** \,rā-zər-'bakt\ *or* **ra·zor–back** \'rā-zər-,bak\ *adj* : having a sharp narrow back 〈~ horse〉

**razor clam** *n* : any of numerous marine bivalve mollusks having a long narrow curved thin shell

**¹razz** \'raz\ *n* : RASPBERRY 2

**²razz** *vb* : RIDICULE, TEASE

**Rb** *symbol* rubidium

**RBC** *abbr* red blood cells; red blood count

**RBI** \,är-(,)bē-'ī, 'rib-ē\ *n, pl* **RBIs** *or* **RBI** [*run batted in*] : a run scored in baseball by an action by a batter (as a base hit)

**RC** *abbr* **1** Red Cross **2** Roman Catholic

**RCAF** *abbr* Royal Canadian Air Force

**RCMP** *abbr* Royal Canadian Mounted Police

**rct** *abbr* recruit

**rd** *abbr* **1** road **2** rod **3** round

**RD** *abbr* rural delivery

**re** \(')rā, (')rē\ *prep* : with regard to

**Re** *symbol* rhenium

**re-** \rē, ,rē, 'rē\ *prefix* **1** : again : anew **2** : back : backward

| | |
|---|---|
| reabsorb | reappear |
| reaccommo-date | reappearance |
| | reapplication |
| reacquire | reapply |
| reactuate | reappoint |
| readapt | reappoint-ment |
| readdress | |
| readjust | reapportion |
| readjustment | reapportion-ment |
| readmission | |
| readmit | reappraisal |
| readmittance | reappraise |
| readopt | rearm |
| readoption | rearmament |
| reaffirm | rearouse |
| reaffirmation | rearrange |
| realign | rearrangement |
| realignment | rearrest |
| reallocate | reascend |
| reallocation | reassail |
| reanalysis | reassemble |
| reanalyze | reassembly |
| reanimate | reassert |
| reanimation | reassess |
| reannex | reassessment |
| reannexation | reassign |

| | | | |
|---|---|---|---|
| reassignment | recontaminate | reexport | renegotiate |
| reassort | recontamina- | refashion | renegotiation |
| reassume | tion | refasten | renominate |
| reattach | recontract | refight | renomination |
| reattachment | reconvene | refigure | renumber |
| reattack | reconvert | refilm | reoccupy |
| reattain | recook | refilter | reopen |
| reattainment | recopy | refinance | reorder |
| reattempt | recouple | refinish | reorganization |
| reauthorization | recross | refit | reorganize |
| reauthorize | recrystallize | refix | reorient |
| reawake | recurve | refloat | reorientation |
| reawaken | recut | reflow | repack |
| rebaptism | redecorate | reflower | repackage |
| rebaptize | redecoration | refly | repaint |
| rebid | rededicate | refocus | repass |
| rebind | rededication | refold | repeople |
| reboil | redefine | reforge | rephotograph |
| rebroadcast | redefinition | reformulate | rephrase |
| rebuild | redemand | reformulation | replant |
| reburial | redeploy | refortify | reprice |
| rebury | redeployment | refound | reprocess |
| recalculate | redeposit | refreeze | republication |
| recalculation | redesign | refuel | republish |
| recapitalization | redetermina- | refurnish | repurchase |
| recapitalize | tion | regather | reradiate |
| recapture | redetermine | regild | reread |
| recast | redevelop | regive | rerecord |
| rechannel | redevelopment | reglow | resay |
| recharge | redigest | reglue | rescore |
| recharter | redip | regrade | rescreen |
| recheck | redirect | regrind | reseal |
| rechristen | rediscount | regrow | reseed |
| reclean | rediscover | rehandle | resell |
| recoat | rediscovery | rehear | reset |
| recoin | redissolve | reheat | resettle |
| recolonization | redistill | rehouse | resettlement |
| recolonize | redistillation | reimpose | resew |
| recolor | redistribute | reimposition | reshipment |
| recomb | redistribution | reincorporate | reshow |
| recombination | redo | reinsert | resilver |
| recombine | redomesticate | reinsertion | resitting |
| recommence | redouble | reintegrate | resmooth |
| recommission | redraw | reinterpret | resow |
| recommit | reecho | reinterpreta- | respell |
| recommittal | reedit | tion | respring |
| recompile | reeducate | reintroduce | restaff |
| recomplete | reeducation | reintroduction | restate |
| recompose | reelect | reinvent | restatement |
| recompound | reelection | reinvention | restock |
| recompress | reembark | reinvest | restraighten |
| recompression | reembodiment | reinvestment | restrengthen |
| recomputation | reembody | reinvigorate | restrike |
| recompute | reemerge | reinvigoration | restring |
| reconceive | reemergence | reissue | restructure |
| reconcentrate | reemphasis | rejudge | restudy |
| reconception | reemphasize | rekindle | restuff |
| recondensation | reemploy | reknit | restyle |
| recondense | reemployment | relearn | resubmit |
| recondition | reenact | relet | resummon |
| reconfine | reenactment | reletter | resupply |
| reconfirm | reenlist | relight | resurface |
| reconfirmation | reenlistment | reline | resurvey |
| reconnect | reenter | reload | resynthesis |
| reconquer | reequip | remake | resynthesize |
| reconquest | reestablish | remanufacture | retaste |
| reconsecrate | reestablish- | remap | retell |
| reconsecration | ment | remarriage | retest |
| reconsign | reevaluate | remarry | rethink |
| reconsignment | reevaluation | remelt | retool |
| reconstructive | reevoke | remigrate | retrain |
| reconsult | reexamination | remix | retransmission |
| reconsultation | reexamine | remold | retransmit |
| recontact | reexchange | rename | retraverse |

retrial
reunification
reunify
reunite
reuse
revaluate
revaluation
revalue
reverification
reverify
revictual
revisit

rewarm
rewash
rewater
reweave
rewed
reweigh
reweld
rewind
rewire
rework
rewrite
rezone

**REA** *abbr* **1** Railway Express Agency **2** Rural Electrification Administration

**¹reach** \'rēch\ *vb* **1 :** to stretch out **2 :** to touch or attempt to touch or seize **3 :** to extend to **4 :** to arrive at **5 :** to communicate with **syn** gain, compass, achieve, attain — **reach-able** *adj* — **reach-er** *n*

**²reach** *n* **1 :** the act of reaching **2 :** the distance or extent of reaching or of ability to reach **3 :** an unbroken stretch or expanse; *esp* **:** a straight part of a river **4 :** power to comprehend

**re-act** \rē-'akt\ *vb* **1 :** to exert a return or counteracting influence **2 :** to respond to a stimulus **3 :** to act in opposition to a force or influence **4 :** to turn back or revert to a former condition **5 :** to undergo chemical reaction

**re-ac-tance** \rē-'ak-təns\ *n* **:** impedance due to inductance and capacitance

**re-ac-tant** \-tənt\ *n* **:** a chemically reacting substance

**re-ac-tion** \rē-'ak-shən\ *n* **1 :** a return or reciprocal action **2 :** a counter tendency; *esp* **:** a tendency toward a former esp. outmoded political or social order or policy **3 :** bodily, mental, or emotional response to a stimulus **4 :** chemical change

**¹re-ac-tion-ary** \rē-'ak-shə-,ner-ē\ *adj* **:** relating to, marked by, or favoring esp. political reaction

**²reactionary** *n, pl* **-ar-ies :** a reactionary person

**re-ac-ti-vate** \rē-'ak-tə-,vāt\ *vb* **:** to make or become activated again — **re-ac-ti-va-tion** \rē-,ak-tə-'vā-shən\ *n*

**re-ac-tive** \rē-'ak-tiv\ *adj* **:** reacting or tending to react

**re-ac-tor** \rē-'ak-tər\ *n* **1 :** one that reacts **2 :** a vat for a chemical reaction **3 :** an apparatus in which a chain reaction of fissionable material is initiated and controlled

**¹read** \'rēd\ *vb* read \'red\; read-ing \'rēd-iŋ\ **1 :** to understand language by interpreting written symbols for speech sounds **2 :** to utter aloud written or printed words **3 :** to learn by observing ⟨~ nature's signs⟩ **4 :** to discover the meaning of ⟨~ a riddle⟩ **5 :** to attribute (a meaning) to something ⟨~ guilt in his manner⟩ **6 :** to study by a course of reading ⟨~ law⟩ **7 :** to consist in phrasing or meaning ⟨the two versions ~ differently⟩ — **read-a-bil-i-ty** \,rēd-ə-'bil-ət-ē\ *n* — **read-able** \'rēd-ə-bəl\ *adj* — **read-ably** \-blē\ *adv* — **read-er** *n*

**²read** \'red\ *adj* **:** informed by reading ⟨a widely ~ man⟩

**read-er-ship** \'rēd-ər-,ship\ *n* **1 :** the office or position of a reader **2 :** the mass or a particular group of readers

**read-ing** \'rēd-iŋ\ *n* **1 :** something read or for reading **2 :** a particular version **3 :** a particular interpretation (as of a law) **4 :** a particular performance (as of a musical work) **5 :** an indication of a certain state of affairs; *also* **:** an indication of data made by an instrument ⟨thermometer ~⟩

**read-out** \'rēd-,aút\ *n* **1 :** the process of removing information from an automatic device (as a computer) and displaying it in an understandable form; *also* **:** the information removed from such a device **2 :** the radio transmission of data or pictures from a space vehicle

**read out** \(')rēd-'aút\ *vb* **:** to expel from an organization

**¹ready** \'red-ē\ *adj* read-i-er; -est **1 :** prepared for use or action **2 :** likely to do something indicated; *also* **:** willingly disposed **:** INCLINED **3 :** spontaneously prompt **4 :** notably dexterous, adroit, or skilled **5 :** immediately available **:** HANDY — **read-i-ly** \'red-ə-lē\ *adv* — **read-i-ness** \-ē-nəs\ *n*

**²ready** *vb* read-ied; ready-ing **:** to make ready **:** PREPARE

**³ready** *n* **:** the state of being ready

**ready-made** \,red-ē-'mād\ *adj* **:** already made up for general sale **:** not specially made — **ready-made** *n*

**ready room** *n* **:** a room in which pilots are briefed and await orders

**re-agent** \rē-'ā-jənt\ *n* **:** a substance that takes part in or brings about a particular chemical reaction

**¹re-al** \'rē(-ə)l\ *adj* [ME, real, relating to things (in law), fr. MF, fr. ML & LL; ML *realis* relating to things (in law), fr. LL, real, fr. L *res* thing, fact] **1 :** actually being or existent **2 :** not artificial **:** GENUINE — **re-al-ness** *n* — for **real 1 :** in earnest **2 :** GENUINE

**²real** *adv* **:** VERY

**real estate** *n* **:** property in houses and land

**real focus** *n* **:** a point at which rays (as of light) converge or from which they diverge

**real image** *n* **:** an optical image formed of real foci

**re-al-ism** \'rē-ə-,liz-əm\ *n* **1 :** the disposition to face facts and to deal with them practically **2 :** true and faithful portrayal of nature and of men in art or literature — **re-al-ist** \-ləst\ *adj or n* — **re-al-is-tic** \,rē-ə-'lis-tik\ *adj* — **re-al-is-ti-cally** \-ti-k(ə-)lē\ *adv*

**re-al-i-ty** \rē-'al-ət-ē\ *n, pl* **-ties 1 :** the quality or state of being real **2 :** something real **3 :** the totality of real things and events

**re-al-ize** \'rē-ə-,līz\ *vb* **-ized; -iz-ing 1 :** to make actual **:** ACCOMPLISH **2 :** OBTAIN, GAIN ⟨~ a profit⟩ **3 :** to convert into money ⟨~ assets⟩ **4 :** to be aware of **:** UNDERSTAND — **re-al-iz-able** *adj* — **re-al-i-za-tion** \,rē-ə-lə-'zā-shən\ *n*

**re·al·ly** \'rē-(ə-)lē\ *adv* **:** in truth **:** in fact **:** ACTUALLY

**realm** \'relm\ *n* **1 :** KINGDOM **2 :** SPHERE, DOMAIN

**real number** *n* **:** one of the numbers that have no imaginary parts and comprise the rationals and the irrationals

**re·al·po·li·tik** \rā-'äl-,pō-li-,tēk\ *n* **:** politics based on practical and material factors rather than on theoretical or ethical objectives

**real time** *n* **:** the actual time in which a physical process takes place — **real-time** *adj*

**re·al·ty** \'rē-(ə)l-tē\ *n* **:** REAL ESTATE

**¹ream** \'rēm\ *n* [ME *reme*, fr. MF *raime*, fr. Ar *rizmah*, lit., bundle] **:** a quantity of paper that is variously 480, 500, or 516 sheets

**²ream** *vb* **1 :** to enlarge or shape with a reamer **2 :** to clean or clear with a reamer

**ream·er** \'rē-mər\ *n* **:** a tool with cutting edges that is used to enlarge or shapea hole

**reap** \'rēp\ *vb* **1 :** to cut or clear with a scythe, sickle, or machine **2 :** to gather by or as if by cutting **:** HARVEST ⟨~ a reward⟩ — **reap·er** *n*

**¹rear** \'riər\ *vb* **1 :** to set or raise upright **2 :** to erect by building **3 :** to breed and rear for use or market ⟨~ livestock⟩ **4 :** to bring up (as offspring) **:** FOSTER **5 :** to lift or rise up; *esp* **:** to rise on the hind legs

**²rear** *n* **1 :** the unit (as of an army) or area farthest from the enemy **2 :** BACK; *also* **:** the position at the back of something

**³rear** *adj* **:** being at the back

**rear admiral** *n* **:** a commissioned officer in the navy or coast guard ranking next below a vice admiral

**¹rear·ward** \'riər-wərd\ *adj* **1 :** being at or toward the rear **2 :** directed to the rear

**²rear·ward** \-wərd\ *also* **rear·wards** \-wərdz\ *adv* **:** at or to the rear

**¹rea·son** \'rēz-ⁿn\ *n* [ME *resoun*, fr. OF *raison*, fr. L *ration-, ratio* reason, computation] **1 :** a statement offered in explanation or justification **2 :** GROUND, CAUSE **3 :** the power to think **:** INTELLECT **4 :** a sane or sound mind **5 :** due exercise of the faculty of logical thought

**²reason** *vb* **rea·soned; rea·son·ing** \'rēz-(ᵊ-)niŋ\ **1 :** to use the faculty of reason **:** THINK **2 :** to talk with another so as to influence his actions or opinions **3 :** to discover or formulate by the use of reason — **rea·son·er** *n* — **rea·son·ing** *n*

**rea·son·able** \'rēz-(ᵊ-)nə-bəl\ *adj* **1 :** being within the bounds of reason **:** not extreme **:** MODERATE, FAIR **2 :** INEXPENSIVE **3 :** able to reason **:** RATIONAL — **rea·son·able·ness** *n* — **rea·son·ably** \-blē\ *adv*

**re·as·sure** \,rē-ə-'shúr\ *vb* **1 :** to assure again **2 :** to restore confidence to **:** free from fear — **re·as·sur·ance** \-'shúr-əns\ *n* — **re·as·sur·ing·ly** \-'shúr-iŋ-lē\ *adv*

**¹re·bate** \'rē-,bāt\ *vb* **re·bat·ed; re·bat·ing :** to make or give a rebate

**²re·bate** *n* **:** a return of part of a payment **syn** deduction, abatement, discount

**¹reb·el** \'reb-əl\ *adj* [ME, fr. OF *rebelle*, fr. L *rebellis*, fr. *re-* + *bellum* war, fr. OL *duellum*] **:** of or relating to rebels

**²rebel** *n* **:** one that rebels against authority

**³rebel** \ri-'bel\ *vb* **re·belled; re·bel·ling 1 :** to resist the authority of one's government **2 :** to act in or show disobedience **3 :** to feel or exhibit anger or revulsion

**re·bel·lion** \ri-'bel-yən\ *n* **:** resistance to authority; *esp* **:** open defiance of established government through uprising or revolt

**re·bel·lious** \-yəs\ *adj* **1 :** given to or engaged in rebellion **2 :** inclined to resist authority — **re·bel·lious·ly** *adv* — **re·bel·lious·ness** *n*

**re·birth** \'rē-'bərth\ *n* **1 :** a new or second birth **2 :** RENAISSANCE, REVIVAL

**re·born** \-'bórn\ *adj* **:** born again **:** REGENERATED, REVIVED

**¹re·bound** \'rē-,baúnd, ri-\ *vb* **1 :** to spring back on or as if on striking another body **2 :** to recover from a setback or frustration

**²re·bound** \'rē-,baúnd\ *n* **1 :** the action of rebounding **2 :** a rebounding ball (as in basketball) **3 :** immediate spontaneous reaction to setback or frustration

**re·buff** \ri-'bəf\ *vb* **1 :** to refuse or repulse curtly **:** SNUB **2 :** to drive or beat back **:** REPULSE — **rebuff** *n*

**¹re·buke** \ri-'byük\ *vb* **re·buked; re·buk·ing :** to reprimand sharply **:** REPROVE

**²rebuke** *n* **:** a sharp reprimand

**re·bus** \'rē-bəs\ *n* [L, by things, abl. pl. of *res* thing] **:** a representation of syllables or words by means of pictures; *also* **:** a riddle composed of such pictures

**re·but** \ri-'bət\ *vb* **re·but·ted; re·but·ting :** to refute esp. formally (as in debate) by evidence and arguments **syn** disprove, controvert — **re·but·ter** *n*

**re·but·tal** \ri-'bət-ᵊl\ *n* **:** the act of rebutting

**rec** *abbr* **1** receipt **2** record; recording **3** recreation

**re·cal·ci·trant** \ri-'kal-sə-trənt\ *adj* [LL *recalcitrant-, recalcitrans*, prp. of *recalcitrare* to be stubbornly disobedient, fr. L, to kick back, fr. *re-* back, again + *calcitrare* to kick, fr. *calc-, calx* heel] **1 :** stubbornly resisting authority **2 :** resistant to handling or treatment **syn** refractory, headstrong, willful, unruly, ungovernable — **re·cal·ci·trance** \-trəns\ *n*

**¹re·call** \ri-'kól\ *vb* **1 :** to call back **2 :** REMEMBER, RECOLLECT **3 :** REVOKE, ANNUL **4 :** RESTORE, REVIVE

**²re·call** \ri-'kól, 'rē-,kól\ *n* **1 :** a summons to return **2 :** the right or procedure of removing an official by popular vote **3 :** remembrance of things learned or experienced **4 :** the act of revoking

**re·cant** \ri-'kant\ *vb* **:** to take back (something one has said) publicly **:** make an open confession of error — **re·can·ta·tion** \,rē-,kan-'tā-shən\ *n*

¹**re·cap** \'rē-,kap\ *vb* **re·capped; re·cap·ping :** to vulcanize a strip of rubber upon the outer surface of (a worn tire) — **re·cap** \'rē-,kap\ *n* — **re·cap·pa·ble** *adj*

²**re·cap** \'rē-,kap, ri-'kap\ *vb* **re·capped; re·cap·ping :** RECAPITU- LATE — **recap** *n*

**re·ca·pit·u·late** \,rē-kə-'pich-ə-,lāt\ *vb* **-lat·ed; -lat·ing :** to restate briefly **:** SUMMARIZE — **re·ca·pit·u·la·tion** \-,pich-ə-'lā-shən\ *n*

**recd** *abbr* received

**re·cede** \ri-'sēd\ *vb* **re·ced·ed; re- ced·ing 1 :** to move back or away **:** WITHDRAW **2 :** to slant backward **3 :** DIMINISH, CONTRACT

¹**re·ceipt** \ri-'sēt\ *n* **1 :** RECIPE **2 :** the act of receiving **3 :** something received — usu. used in pl. **4 :** a writing acknowledging the receiving of money or goods

²**receipt** *vb* **1 :** to give a receipt for **2 :** to mark as paid

**re·ceiv·able** \ri-'sē-və-bəl\ *adj* **1 :** capable of being received; *esp* **:** acceptable as legal ⟨~ certificates⟩ **2 :** subject to call for payment ⟨notes ~⟩

**re·ceive** \ri-'sēv\ *vb* **re·ceived; re- ceiv·ing 1 :** to take in or accept (as something sent or paid) **:** come into possession of **:** GET **2 :** CONTAIN, HOLD **3 :** to permit to enter **:** GREET, WELCOME **4 :** to be at home to visitors **5 :** to accept as true or authoritative **6 :** to be the subject of **:** UNDERGO, EXPERIENCE ⟨~ a shock⟩ **7 :** to change incoming radio waves into sounds or pictures

**re·ceiv·er** \ri-'sē-vər\ *n* **1 :** one that receives **2 :** a person legally appointed to receive and have charge of property or money involved in a lawsuit **3 :** an apparatus for receiving and changing an electrical signal into an audible or visible character ⟨telephone ~⟩

**re·ceiv·er·ship** \-,ship\ *n* **1 :** the office or function of a receiver **2 :** the condition of being in the hands of a receiver

**re·cen·cy** \'rēs-ᵊn-sē\ *n* **:** the quality or state of being recent

**re·cent** \'rēs-ᵊnt\ *adj* **1 :** lately made or used **:** NEW, FRESH **2 :** of the present time or time just past ⟨~ history⟩ — **re·cent·ly** *adv* — **re·cent·ness** *n*

**re·cep·ta·cle** \ri-'sep-ti-kəl\ *n* **1 :** something used to receive and hold something else **:** CONTAINER **2 :** the enlarged end of a stalk bearing a flower **3 :** an electrical fitting containing the live parts of a circuit

**re·cep·tion** \ri-'sep-shən\ *n* **1 :** the act of receiving **2 :** a social gathering; *esp* **:** one at which guests are formally welcomed

**re·cep·tion·ist** \-sh(ə-)nəst\ *n* **:** one employed to greet callers

**re·cep·tive** \ri-'sep-tiv\ *adj* **:** able or inclined to receive; *esp* **:** open and responsive to ideas, impressions, or suggestions — **re·cep·tive·ly** *adv* — **re·cep·tive·ness** *n* — **re·cep·tiv·i·ty** \,rē-,sep-'tiv-ət-ē\ *n*

**re·cep·tor** \ri-'sep-tər\ *n* **:** one that receives; *esp* **:** SENSE ORGAN

¹**re·cess** \'rē-,ses, ri-'ses\ *n* **1 :** an indentation in a line or surface (as an alcove in a room) **2 :** a secret or secluded place **3 :** a suspension of business or procedure for rest or relaxation

²**recess** *vb* **1 :** to put into a recess **2 :** to make a recess in **3 :** to interrupt for a recess **4 :** to take a recess

**re·ces·sion** \ri-'sesh-ən\ *n* **1 :** the act of receding **:** WITHDRAWAL **2 :** a departing procession (as at the end of a church service) **3 :** a period of reduced economic activity

**re·ces·sion·al** \-(ə-)nəl\ *n* **1 :** a hymn or musical piece at the conclusion of a service or program **2 :** RECESSION 2

**re·ces·sive** \ri-'ses-iv\ *adj* **:** tending to go back **:** RECEDING

**re·cher·ché** \rə-,sher-'shā, -'she(ə)r-,shā\ *adj* **1 :** CHOICE, RARE **2 :** excessively refined

**re·cid·i·vism** \ri-'sid-ə-,viz-əm\ *n* **:** a tendency to relapse into a previous condition; *esp* **:** relapse into criminal behavior — **re·cid·i·vist** \-vəst\ *n*

**recip** *abbr* reciprocal; reciprocity

**rec·i·pe** \'res-ə-(,)pē\ *n* [L, take, imperative of *recipere* to receive, fr. *re- back + capere* to take] **1 :** a set of instructions for making something (as a food dish) from various ingredients **2 :** a method of procedure **:** FORMULA

**re·cip·i·ent** \ri-'sip-ē-ənt\ *n* **:** one that receives

¹**re·cip·ro·cal** \ri-'sip-rə-kəl\ *adj* **1 :** inversely related **2 :** MUTUAL, JOINT, SHARED **3 :** so related to each other that one completes the other or is equivalent to the other **syn** common, correspondent, complementary — **re·cip·ro·cal·ly** \-k(ə-)lē\ *adv*

²**reciprocal** *n* **1 :** something in a reciprocal relationship to another **2 :** one of a pair of numbers (as ²/₃, ³/₂) whose product is one

**re·cip·ro·cate** \-,kāt\ *vb* **-cat·ed; -cat·ing 1 :** to move backward and forward alternately ⟨a *reciprocating* piston⟩ **2 :** to make a return for something done or given **3 :** to give and take mutually — **re·cip·ro·ca·tion** \-,sip-rə-'kā-shən\ *n*

**rec·i·proc·i·ty** \,res-ə-'präs-ət-ē\ *n*, *pl* **-ties 1 :** the quality or state of being reciprocal **2 :** mutual exchange of privileges; *esp* **:** a trade policy by which special advantages are granted by one country in return for special advantages granted it by another

**re·cit·al** \ri-'sīt-ᵊl\ *n* **1 :** an act or instance of reciting **:** ACCOUNT **2 :** a public reading or recitation ⟨a poetry ~⟩ **3 :** a concert given by an individual musician or dancer or by a dance troupe **4 :** a public exhibition of skill given by music or dance pupils — **re·cit·al·ist** \-ᵊl-əst\ *n*

**rec·i·ta·tion** \,res-ə-'tā-shən\ n 1 : RECITING, RECITAL 2 : delivery before an audience of something memorized 3 : a classroom exercise in which pupils answer questions on a lesson they have studied; also : a class period

**re·cite** \ri-'sīt\ vb **re·cit·ed; re·cit·ing** 1 : to repeat verbatim (as something memorized) 2 : to recount in some detail : RELATE 3 : to reply to a teacher's questions on a lesson — **re·cit·er** n

**reck·less** \'rek-ləs\ adj : lacking caution : RASH **syn** hasty, headlong, impetuous — **reck·less·ly** adv — **reck·less·ness** n

**reck·on** \'rek-ən\ vb **reck·oned; reck·on·ing** \-(ə-)niŋ\ 1 : COUNT, CALCULATE, COMPUTE 2 : CONSIDER, REGARD 3 chiefly dial : THINK, SUPPOSE, GUESS — **reck·on·er** n

**reck·on·ing** \-iŋ\ n 1 : an act or instance of reckoning 2 : calculation of a ship's position 3 : a settling of accounts ⟨day of ∼⟩

**re·claim** \ri-'klām\ vb 1 : to recall from wrong conduct : REFORM 2 : to put into a desired condition (as by labor or discipline) ⟨∼ marshy land⟩ 3 : to obtain (as rubber) from a waste product or by-product like save, redeem, rescue — **re·claim·able** adj — **rec·la·ma·tion** \,rek-lə-'mā-shən\ n

**ré·clame** \rā-'kläm\ n : public acclaim : FAME

**re·cline** \ri-'klīn\ vb **re·clined; re·clin·ing** 1 : to lean or incline backward 2 : to lie down : REST

**rec·luse** \'rek-,lüs, ri-'klüis\ n : a person who lives in seclusion or leads a solitary life : HERMIT

**rec·og·ni·tion** \,rek-ig-'nish-ən, -əg-\ n 1 : the act of recognizing : the state of being recognized : ACKNOWLEDGMENT 2 : special notice or attention

**re·cog·ni·zance** \ri-'kä(g)-nə-zəns\ n : a promise recorded before a court or magistrate to do something (as to appear in court or to keep the peace) usu. under penalty of a money forfeiture

**rec·og·nize** \'rek-ig-,nīz, -əg-\ vb **-nized; -niz·ing** 1 : to identify as previously known 2 : to perceive clearly : REALIZE 3 : to take notice of 4 : to acknowledge with appreciation 5 : to acknowledge acquaintance with 6 : to acknowledge (as a speaker in a meeting) as one entitled to be heard at the time 7 : to acknowledge the existence or the independence of (a country or government) — **rec·og·niz·able** \'rek-əg-,nī-zə-bəl, -ig-\ adj — **rec·og·niz·ably** \-blē\ adv

**¹re·coil** \ri-'kȯil\ vb 1 : to draw back : RETREAT 2 : to spring back to or as if to a starting point **syn** shrink, flinch, wince

**²re·coil** \'rē-,kȯil, ri-'kȯil\ n : the action of recoiling (as by a gun or spring)

**re·coil·less** \-,kȯil-ləs, -'kȯil-\ adj : having a minimum of recoil ⟨∼ gun⟩

**rec·ol·lect** \,rek-ə-'lekt\ vb : to recall to mind : REMEMBER **syn** recall, remind, reminisce, bethink

**rec·ol·lec·tion** \,rek-ə-'lek-shən\ n 1 : the act of recollecting 2 : the power of recollecting 3 : the time within which things can be recollected : MEMORY 4 : something recollected

**rec·om·mend** \,rek-ə-'mend\ vb 1 : to present as deserving of acceptance or trial 2 : to give in charge : COMMIT 3 : to cause to receive favorable attention 4 : ADVISE, COUNSEL — **rec·om·mend·able** \-'men-də-bəl\ adj — **rec·om·men·da·to·ry** \-də-,tōr-ē, -,tȯr-\ adj — **rec·om·mend·er** n

**rec·om·men·da·tion** \,rek-ə-mən-'dā-shən\ n 1 : the act of recommending 2 : something that recommends 3 : a thing or a course of action recommended

**¹re·com·pense** \'rek-əm-,pens\ vb **-pensed; -pens·ing** 1 : to give compensation to : pay for 2 : to return in kind : REQUITE **syn** reimburse, indemnify, repay

**²recompense** n : COMPENSATION

**rec·on·cile** \'rek-ən-,sīl\ vb **-ciled; -cil·ing** 1 : to cause to be friendly or harmonious again 2 : ADJUST, SETTLE ⟨∼ differences⟩ 3 : to bring to submission or acceptance **syn** conform, accommodate, adapt — **rec·on·cil·able** adj — **rec·on·cile·ment** n — **rec·on·cil·er** n — **rec·on·cil·i·a·tion** \,rek-ən-,sil-ē-'ā-shən\ n

**re·con·dite** \'rek-ən-,dīt\ adj 1 : hard to understand : PROFOUND, ABSTRUSE 2 : little known : OBSCURE

**re·con·nais·sance** \ri-'kän-ə-zəns, -səns\ n : a preliminary survey of an area; esp : an exploratory military survey of enemy territory

**re·con·noi·ter** \,rē-kə-'nȯit-ər, ,rek-ə-\ vb : to make a reconnaissance of : engage in reconnaissance

**re·con·sid·er** \,rē-kən-'sid-ər\ vb : to consider again with a view to changing or reversing; esp : to take up again in a meeting — **re·con·sid·er·a·tion** \-,sid-ə-'rā-shən\ n

**re·con·sti·tute** \'rē-'kän-stə-,t(y)üt\ vb 1 : to constitute again 2 : to restore to a former condition by adding water ⟨∼ powdered milk⟩

**re·con·struct** \,rē-kən-'strəkt\ vb : to construct again : REBUILD

**re·con·struc·tion** \,rē-kən-'strək-shən\ n 1 : the action of reconstructing : the state of being reconstructed 2 often cap : the reorganization and reestablishment of the seceded states in the Union after the American Civil War 3 : something reconstructed

**¹re·cord** \ri-'kȯrd\ vb 1 : to set down (as proceedings in a meeting) in writing 2 : to register permanently 3 : INDICATE, READ 4 : to cause (as sound or visual images) to be registered (as on magnetic tape) in a form that permits reproduction 5 : to give evidence of

**²rec·ord** \'rek-ərd\ n 1 : the act of recording 2 : a written account of proceedings 3 : known facts about a person 4 : an attested top performance 5 : something on which sound or visual images have been recorded

**re·cord·er** \ri-'kȯrd-ər\ *n* **1** : a person who records (transactions) officially ⟨~ of deeds⟩ **2** : a judge in some city courts **3** : a conical wind instrument with a whistle mouthpiece and eight fingerholes **4** : a recording instrument or device

**re·cord·ing** \ri-'kȯrd-iŋ\ *n* : RECORD 5

**re·cord·ist** \ri-'kȯrd-əst\ *n* : one who records sound esp. on film

**¹re·count** \ri-'kaůnt\ *vb* **1** : to relate in detail : TELL **2** : ENUMERATE **syn** recite, rehearse, narrate, describe, state, report

**²re·count** \'rē-'kaůnt\ *vb* : to count again

**³re·count** \'rē-,kaůnt, (')rē-'kaůnt\ *n* : a second or fresh count

**re·coup** \ri-'küp\ *vb* : to get an equivalent or compensation for : make up for something lost **syn** retrieve, regain, recover

**re·course** \'rē-,kōrs, ri-'kōrs\ *n* **1** : a turning to someone or something for assistance or protection : RESORT **2** : a source of aid

**re·cov·er** \ri-'kəv-ər\ *vb* **1** : to get back again : REGAIN, RETRIEVE **2** : to regain normal health, poise, or status **3** : RECLAIM ⟨~ land from the sea⟩ **4** : to make up for : RECOUP ⟨~ed all his losses⟩ **5** : to obtain a legal judgment in one's favor — **re·cov·er·able** *adj* — **re·cov·ery** \-'kəv-(ə-)rē\ *n*

**re·cov·er** \'rē-'kəv-ər\ *vb* : to cover again

**¹rec·re·ant** \'rek-rē-ənt\ *adj* [ME, fr. MF, fr. prp. of *recroire* to renounce one's cause in a trial by battle, fr. *re-* back + *croire* to believe, fr. L *credere*] **1** : COWARDLY, CRAVEN **2** : UNFAITHFUL, FALSE

**²recreant** *n* **1** : COWARD **2** : DESERTER

**¹rec·re·ate** \'rek-rē-,āt\ *vb* **-at·ed; -at·ing** : to give new life or freshness to

**²re·cre·ate** \,rē-krē-'āt\ *vb* : to create again — **re·cre·ative** \-'āt-iv\ *adj*

**¹rec·re·ation** \,rek-rē-'ā-shən\ *n* : a refreshing of strength or spirits after work; *also* : a means of refreshment **syn** diversion, relaxation — **rec·re·ation·al** \-sh(ə-)nəl\ *adj* — **rec·re·ative** \'rek-rē-,āt-iv\ *adj*

**²re·cre·ation** \,rē-krē-'ā-shən\ *n* : the act of creating over again : RENEWAL

**re·crim·i·nate** \ri-'krim-ə-,nāt\ *vb* **-nat·ed; -nat·ing** : to make an accusation against an accuser — **re·crim·i·na·tion** \-,krim-ə-'nā-shən\ *n* — **re·crim·i·na·tive** \-'krim-ə-,nāt-iv\ *adj* — **re·crim·i·na·to·ry** \-'krim-(ə-)nə-,tōr-ē\ *adj*

**re·cru·des·cence** \,rē-krü-'des-²ns\ *n* : a new outbreak after a period of abatement or inactivity — **re·cru·desce** \,rē-krü-'des\ *vb*

**¹re·cruit** \ri-'krüt\ *n* [F *recrute, recrue* fresh growth, new levy of soldiers, fr. MF, fr. *recroistre* to grow up again, fr. L *recrescere*, fr. *re-* again + *crescere* to grow] : a newcomer to an activity or field; *esp* : a newly enlisted member of the armed forces

**²recruit** *vb* **1** : to form or strengthen with new members ⟨~ an army⟩ **2** : to secure the services of ⟨~ engineers⟩ **3** : to restore or increase in health or vigor ⟨resting to ~ his strength⟩ — **re·cruit·er** *n* — **re·cruit·ment** *n*

**rec sec** *abbr* recording secretary

**rect** *abbr* **1** rectangle; rectangular **2** receipt **3** rectified

**rec·tal** \'rek-t²l\ *adj* : of or relating to the rectum — **rec·tal·ly** \-ē\ *adv*

**rect·an·gle** \'rek-,taŋ-gəl\ *n* : a 4-sided figure with four right angles — **rect·an·gu·lar** \rek-'taŋ-gyə-lər\ *adj*

**rec·ti·fi·er** \'rek-tə-,fī(-ə)r\ *n* : one that rectifies; *esp* : a device for converting alternating current into direct current

**rec·ti·fy** \'rek-tə-,fī\ *vb* **-fied; -fy·ing** **1** : to make or set right : CORRECT **2** : to convert alternating current into direct current **syn** emend, amend, remedy, redress — **rec·ti·fi·ca·tion** \,rek-tə-fə-'kā-shən\ *n*

**rec·ti·lin·ear** \,rek-tə-'lin-ē-ər\ *adj* **1** : moving in a straight line **2** : characterized by straight lines

**rec·ti·tude** \'rek-tə-,t(y)üd\ *n* **1** : moral integrity **2** : correctness of procedure **syn** virtue, goodness, morality

**rec·to** \'rek-tō\ *n, pl* **rectos** : a right-hand page

**rec·tor** \'rek-tər\ *n* **1** : a clergyman in charge of a parish **2** : the head of a university or school — **rec·tor·ate** \-t(ə-)rət\ *n* — **rec·to·ri·al** \rek-'tōr-ē-əl\ *adj*

**rec·to·ry** \'rek-t(ə-)rē\ *n, pl* **-ries** : the residence of a rector

**rec·tum** \'rek-təm\ *n, pl* **rectums** or **rec·ta** \-tə\ : the last part of the intestine joining colon and anus

**re·cum·bent** \ri-'kəm-bənt\ *adj* : lying down : RECLINING

**re·cu·per·ate** \ri-'k(y)ü-pə-,rāt\ *vb* **-at·ed; -at·ing** : to get back (as health, strength, or losses) : RECOVER — **re·cu·per·a·tion** \-,k(y)ü-pə-'rā-shən\ *n* — **re·cu·per·a·tive** \-'k(y)ü-pə-,rāt-iv\ *adj*

**re·cur** \ri-'kər\ *vb* **re·curred; re·cur·ring** **1** : to go or come back in thought or discussion **2** : to occur or appear again esp. after an interval — **re·cur·rence** \-'kər-əns\ *n* — **re·cur·rent** \-ənt\ *adj*

**re·cy·cle** \rē-'sī-kəl\ *vb* **1** : to pass again through a cycle of changes or treatment **2** : to pass (as liquid body wastes) continuously through a purification process to produce a product fit for human use

**¹red** \'red\ *adj* **red·der; red·dest** **1** : of the color red **2** : endorsing radical social or political change esp. by force **3** : of or relating to the U.S.S.R. or its allies — **red·ly** *adv* — **red·ness** *n*

**²red** *n* **1** : the color of blood or of the ruby **2** : a revolutionary in politics **3** *cap* : COMMUNIST **4** : the condition of showing a loss ⟨in the ~⟩

**re·dact** \ri-'dakt\ *vb* **1** : to put in writing : FRAME **2** : EDIT — **re·dac·tor** \-'dak-tər\ *n*

**re·dac·tion** \-'dak-shən\ *n* **1** : an act

or instance of redacting 2 : EDITION — **re·dac·tion·al** \-sh(ə-)nəl\ adj

**red alga** n : an alga with red pigmentation

**red blood cell** n : one of the hemoglobin-containing cells that carry oxygen to the tissues and are responsible for the red color of vertebrate blood

**red·breast** \'red-,brest\ n : ROBIN

**red·cap** \'red-,kap\ n : a baggage porter at a railroad station

**red–carpet** adj : marked by ceremonial courtesy

**red cedar** n : an American juniper with fragrant close-grained red wood; also : its wood

**red clover** n : a Eurasian clover with globose heads of reddish flowers widely cultivated for hay and forage

**red·coat** \'red-,kōt\ n : a British soldier esp. during the Revolutionary War

**red·den** \'red-ᵊn\ vb : to make or become red or reddish : FLUSH, BLUSH

**red·dish** \'red-ish\ adj : tinged with red — **red·dish·ness** n

**re·deem** \ri-'dēm\ vb [ME redemen, modif. of MF redimer, fr. L redimere, fr. re-, red- re- + emere to take, buy] 1 : to recover (property) by discharging an obligation 2 : to ransom, free, or rescue by paying a price 3 : to atone for 4 : to make good (a promise) by performing : FULFILL 5 : to free from the bondage of sin 6 : to remove the obligation of by payment (the government ~s savings bonds); also : to convert into something of value — **re·deem·able** adj — **re·deem·er** n

**re·demp·tion** \ri-'demp-shən\ n : the act of redeeming : the state of being redeemed — **re·demp·tive** \-tiv\ adj — **re·demp·to·ry** \-t(ə-)rē\ adj

**red fox** n : a fox with bright orange-red to dusky reddish brown fur

**red–hand·ed** \'red-'han-dəd\ adv or adj : in the act of committing a misdeed

**red·head** \-,hed\ n : a person having red hair — **red·head·ed** \-'hed-əd\ adj

**red herring** n : a diversion intended to distract attention from the real issue

**red–hot** \'red-'hät\ adj 1 : glowing red with heat (~ iron) 2 : EXCITED, FURIOUS 3 : very new (~ news)

**re·dis·trict** \'rē-'dis-(,)trikt\ vb : to organize into new territorial and esp. political divisions

**red–let·ter** \,red-'let-ər\ adj : of special significance : MEMORABLE

**red–light district** n : a district with many houses of prostitution

**red oak** n : any of various American oaks with leaves usu. having spiny-tipped lobes

**red·o·lent** \'red-ᵊl-ənt\ adj 1 : FRAGRANT, AROMATIC 2 : having a specified fragrance 3 : REMINISCENT, SUGGESTIVE — **red·o·lence** \-əns\ n — **red·o·lent·ly** adv

**re·doubt** \ri-'daut\ n [F redoute, fr. It ridotto, fr. ML reductus secret place, fr. L, withdrawn, fr. reducere to lead back, fr. re- back + ducere to lead] : a small usu. temporary fortification

**re·doubt·able** \ri-'daut-ə-bəl\ adj [ME redoutable, fr. MF, fr. redouter to dread, fr. re- re- + douter to doubt] : arousing dread or fear : FORMIDABLE

**re·dound** \ri-'daund\ vb 1 : to have an effect : CONDUCE 2 : to become added or transferred : ACCRUE

**red pepper** n : a powdered condiment made from the dried red pods of a pepper of the nightshade family; also : a plant producing this

¹**re·dress** \ri-'dres\ vb 1 : to set right : REMEDY 2 : COMPENSATE 3 : to remove the cause of (a grievance) 4 : AVENGE

²**re·dress** n 1 : relief from distress 2 : a means or possibility of seeking a remedy 3 : compensation for loss or injury 4 : an act or instance of redressing

**red·skin** \'red-,skin\ n : a No. American Indian

**red snapper** n : any of various fishes including several food fishes

**red spider** n : any of several small web-spinning mites that attack forage and crop plants

**red squirrel** n : a common American squirrel with the upper parts chiefly red

**red–tailed hawk** \,red-,tāld-\ n : a common rodent-eating hawk of eastern No. America with a rather short typically reddish tail

**red tape** n [fr. the red tape formerly used to bind legal documents in England] : official routine or procedure marked by excessive complexity which results in delay or inaction

**red tide** n : seawater discolored by the presence of large numbers of dino-flagellates in a density fatal to many forms of marine life

**re·duce** \ri-'d(y)üs\ vb **re·duced**; **re·duc·ing** 1 : LESSEN 2 : to put in a lower rank or grade 3 : CONQUER (~ a fort) 4 : to bring into a certain order or classification 5 : to bring to a specified state or condition (~ chaos to order) 6 : to correct (as a fracture) by restoration of displaced parts 7 : to lessen one's weight **syn** decrease, diminish, abate, dwindle, vanquish, defeat, subjugate, beat — **re·duc·er** n — **re·duc·ible** \-'d(y)üs-ə-bəl\ adj

**re·duc·tion** \ri-'dək-shən\ n 1 : the act of reducing : the state of being reduced 2 : the amount taken off in reducing something 3 : something made by reducing

**re·dun·dan·cy** \ri-'dən-dən-sē\ n, pl -cies 1 : the quality or state of being redundant : SUPERFLUITY 2 : something redundant or in excess 3 : the use of surplus words

**re·dun·dant** \-dənt\ adj : exceeding what is needed or normal : SUPERFLUOUS; esp : using more words than necessary — **re·dun·dant·ly** adv

**red·wing blackbird** \,red-,wiŋ-\ n : a No. American blackbird with a patch of bright scarlet and yellow or buff on the wings

**red·wood** \'red-,wůd\ n : a tall coniferous timber tree of California or its durable wood

**reed** \'rēd\ *n* **1** : any of various tall slender grasses of wet areas; *also* : a stem or growth of reed **2** : a musical instrument made from the hollow stem of a reed **3** : an elastic tongue of cane, wood, or metal by which tones are produced in organ pipes and certain other wind instruments — **reedy** *adj*

¹**reef** \'rēf\ *n* **1** : a part of a sail taken in or let out in regulating the size of the sail **2** : the reduction in sail area made by reefing

²**reef** *vb* **1** : to reduce the area of a sail by rolling or folding part of it **2** : to lower or bring inboard a spar

³**reef** *n* : a ridge of rocks or sand at or near the surface of the water — **reefy** *adj*

¹**reef·er** \'rē-fər\ *n* **1** : one that reefs **2** : a close-fitting thick jacket

²**reefer** *n* : a marijuana cigarette

**reek** \'rēk\ *n* : a strong or disagreeable fume or odor — **reeky** *adj*

²**reek** *vb* **1** : to give off or become permeated with a strong or offensive odor **2** : to give a strong impression of some constituent quality — **reek·er** *n*

¹**reel** \'rēl\ *n* : a revolvable device on which something flexible (as yarn, thread, or wire) may be wound; *also* : a quantity of something (as motion-picture film) wound on such a device

²**reel** *vb* **1** : to wind on or as if on a reel **2** : to pull or draw (as a fish) by reeling a line — **reel·able** *adj* — **reel·er** *n*

³**reel** *vb* **1** : WHIRL; *also* : to be giddy **2** : to waver or fall back from a blow : RECOIL **3** : to walk or move unsteadily

⁴**reel** *n* : a reeling motion

⁵**reel** *n* : a lively Scottish dance or its music

**re·en·force** \,rē-ən-'fōrs\ *var of* REINFORCE

**re·en·try** \rē-'en-trē\ *n* **1** : a second or new entry **2** : the action of reentering the earth's atmosphere after traveling into space

**reeve** \'rēv\ *vb* **rove** \'rōv\ or **reeved; reev·ing** : to pass (as a rope) through a hole in a block or cleat

**ref** *abbr* **1** referee **2** reference **3** referred **4** reformed **5** refunding

**re·fec·tion** \ri-'fek-shən\ *n* **1** : refreshment esp. after hunger or fatigue **2** : food and drink together : REPAST

**re·fec·to·ry** \ri-'fek-t(ə-)rē\ *n, pl* **-ries** : a dining hall esp. in a monastery

**re·fer** \ri-'fər\ *vb* **re·ferred; re·fer·ring** **1** : to assign to a certain source, cause, or relationship **2** : to direct or send to some person or place (as for treatment, information, or help) **3** : to submit to someone else for consideration or action **4** : to have recourse (as for information or aid) **5** : to have connection : RELATE **6** : to direct attention : speak of : MENTION, ALLUDE **syn** credit, accredit, ascribe, attribute, resort, apply, go, turn — **re·fer·able** \'ref-(ə-)rə-bəl, ri-'fər-ə-\ *adj*

¹**ref·er·ee** \,ref-ə-'rē\ *n* **1** : a person to whom an issue esp. in law is referred for investigation or settlement **2** : an umpire in certain games

²**referee** *vb* **-eed; -ee·ing** : to act as referee

**ref·er·ence** \'ref-ərns, 'ref-(ə-)rəns\ *n* **1** : the act of referring **2** : RELATION, RESPECT **3** : a direction of the attention to another passage or book **4** : ALLUSION, MENTION **5** : consultation esp. for obtaining information ⟨books for ~⟩ **6** : a person of whom inquiries as to character or ability can be made **7** : a written recommendation of a person for employment

**ref·er·en·dum** \,ref-ə-'ren-dəm\ *n, pl* **-da** \-də\ *or* **-dums** : the principle or practice of referring legislative measures to the voters for approval or rejection; *also* : a vote on a measure so submitted

**ref·er·ent** \'ref-(ə-)rənt\ *n* [L *referent-, referens*, prp. of *referre*] : one that refers or is referred to; *esp* : the thing a word stands for — **referent** *adj*

**re·fer·ral** \ri-'fər-əl\ *n* **1** : the act or an instance of referring **2** : one that is referred

¹**re·fill** \'rē-'fil\ *vb* : to fill again : REPLENISH — **re·fill·able** *adj*

²**re·fill** \'rē-,fil\ *n* : a new or fresh supply of something

**re·fine** \ri-'fīn\ *vb* **re·fined; re·fin·ing** **1** : to free from impurities or waste matter **2** : IMPROVE, PERFECT **3** : to free or become free of what is coarse or uncouth **4** : to make improvements by introducing subtle changes — **re·fin·er** *n*

**re·fined** \ri-'fīnd\ *adj* **1** : freed from impurities **2** : CULTURED, CULTIVATED **3** : SUBTLE

**re·fine·ment** \ri-'fīn-mənt\ *n* **1** : the action of refining **2** : the quality or state of being refined **3** : a refined feature or method; *also* : a device or contrivance intended to improve or perfect

**re·fin·ery** \ri-'fīn-(ə-)rē\ *n, pl* **-er·ies** : a building and equipment for refining metals, oil, or sugar

**refl** *abbr* reflex; reflexive

**re·flect** \ri-'flekt\ *vb* [ME *reflecten*, fr. L *reflectere* to bend back, fr. re- back + *flectere* to bend] **1** : to bend or cast back (as light, heat, or sound) **2** : to give back a likeness or image of as a mirror does **3** : to bring as a result ⟨~ed credit on him⟩ **4** : to cast reproach or blame ⟨their bad conduct ~ed on their training⟩ **5** : PONDER, MEDITATE — **re·flec·tion** \-'flek-shən\ *n* — **re·flec·tive** \-tiv\ *adj*

**re·flec·tor** \ri-'flek-tər\ *n* **1** : one that reflects; *esp* : a polished surface for reflecting radiation (as light) **2** : a telescope in which the principal focusing element is a mirror

¹**re·flex** \'rē-,fleks\ *n* : an automatic and usu. inborn response to a stimulus not involving higher mental centers

²**reflex** *adj* **1** : bent or directed back **2** : of or relating to a reflex — **re·flex·ly** *adv*

**reflex camera** *n* : a camera in which the image is reflected onto a usu. ground-glass screen for viewing

¹re·flex·ive \ri-'flek-siv\ adj : of or relating to an action directed back upon the doer or the grammatical subject ⟨a ~ verb⟩ ⟨the ~ pronoun *himself*⟩ — re·flex·ive·ly *adv* — re·flex·ive·ness *n*

²reflexive *n* : a reflexive verb or pronoun

re·flux \ri-'fləks, 'rē-,fləks\ *vb* : to heat so that vapors formed condense and return to be heated again — reflux \'rē-,fləks\ *n*

re·for·est \rē-'fȯr-əst\ *vb* : to renew forest cover on by seeding or planting — re·for·es·ta·tion \,rē-,fȯr-ə-'stā-shən\ *n*

¹re·form \ri-'fȯrm\ *vb* 1 : to make better or improve by removal of faults 2 : to correct or improve one's own character or habits **syn** correct, rectify, emend, remedy, redress, revise — re·form·able *adj* — re·for·ma·tive \-'fȯr-mət-iv\ *adj*

²reform *n* : improvement or correction of what is corrupt or defective

re–form \'rē-'fȯrm\ *vb* : to form again — re–for·ma·tion \,rē-fȯr-'mā-shən\ *n*

ref·or·ma·tion \,ref-ər-'mā-shən\ *n* 1 : the act of reforming 2 : the state of being reformed 2 *cap* : a 16th century religious movement marked by the establishment of the Protestant churches

¹re·for·ma·to·ry \ri-'fȯr-mə-,tōr-ē\ *adj* : aiming at or tending toward reformation : REFORMATIVE

²reformatory *n*, *pl* -ries : a penal institution for reforming young or first offenders or women

re·form·er \ri-'fȯr-mər\ *n* 1 : one that works for or urges reform 2 *cap* : a leader of the Protestant Reformation

refr *abbr* refraction

re·fract \ri-'frakt\ *vb* [L *refractus*, pp. of *refringere* to break open, break up, refract, fr. *re-* back + *frangere* to break] : to subject to refraction

re·frac·tion \ri-'frak-shən\ *n* : the bending of a ray of light, heat, or sound when it passes obliquely from one medium into another in which its velocity is different — re·frac·tive \-tiv\ *adj*

re·frac·tor \-tər\ *n* : a telescope in which the principal focusing element is a lens

re·frac·to·ry \ri-'frak-t(ə-)rē\ *adj* 1 : OBSTINATE, STUBBORN, UNMANAGEABLE 2 : difficult to melt, corrode, or draw out; *esp* : capable of enduring high temperature ⟨~ bricks⟩ **syn** recalcitrant, intractable, ungovernable, unruly, headstrong, willful — re·frac·to·ri·ly \-t(ə-)rə-lē; ,rē-,frak-'tōr-ə-lē\ *adv* — re·frac·to·ri·ness \ri-'frak-t(ə-)rē-nəs\ *n* — refractory *n*

¹re·frain \ri-'frān\ *vb* : to hold oneself back : FORBEAR — re·frain·ment *n*

²refrain *n* : a phrase or verse recurring regularly in a poem or song

re·fresh \ri-'fresh\ *vb* 1 : to make or become fresh or fresher 2 : to revive by or as if by renewal of supplies ⟨~ one's memory⟩ 3 : to freshen up 4 : to supply or take refreshment **syn** restore, rejuvenate, renovate, refurbish — re·fresh·er *n* — re·fresh·ing·ly *adv*

re·fresh·ment \-mənt\ *n* 1 : the act of refreshing : the state of being refreshed 2 : something that refreshes 3 *pl* : a light meal

refrig *abbr* refrigerating; refrigeration

re·frig·er·ate \ri-'frij-ə-,rāt\ *vb* -at·ed; -at·ing : to make cool; *esp* : to chill or freeze (food) for preservation — re·frig·er·ant \-(ə-)rənt\ *adj or n* — re·frig·er·a·tion \-,frij-ə-'rā-shən\ *n* — re·frig·er·a·tor \-'frij-ə-,rāt-ər\ *n*

re·frin·gent \ri-'frin-jənt\ *adj* : REFRACTIVE, REFRACTING

ref·uge \'ref-,yüj\ *n* 1 : shelter or protection from danger or distress 2 : a place that provides protection

ref·u·gee \,ref-yu̇-'jē\ *n* : one who flees for safety esp. to a foreign country

re·ful·gence \ri-'fu̇l-jəns, -'fəl-\ *n* : radiant or shining quality or state — re·ful·gent \-jənt\ *adj*

¹re·fund \ri-'fənd, 'rē-,fənd\ *vb* : to give or put back (money) : REPAY — re·fund·able *adj*

²re·fund \'rē-,fənd\ *n* 1 : the act of refunding 2 : a sum refunded

re·fur·bish \ri-'fər-bish\ *vb* : to brighten or freshen up : RENOVATE

¹re·fuse \ri-'fyüz\ *vb* re·fused; re·fus·ing 1 : to decline to accept : REJECT 2 : to decline to do, give, or grant : DENY — re·fus·al \-'fyü-zəl\ *n*

²ref·use \'ref-,yüs, -,yüz\ *n* : rejected or worthless matter : RUBBISH, TRASH

re·fute \ri-'fyüt\ *vb* re·fut·ed; re·fut·ing [L *refutare*, fr. *re-* back + *-futare* to beat] : to prove to be false by argument or evidence — ref·u·ta·tion \,ref-yu̇-'tā-shən\ *n* — re·fut·er \ri-'fyüt-ər\ *n*

reg *abbr* 1 region 2 register; registered 3 regular 4 regulation

re·gain \ri-'gān\ *vb* 1 : to gain or get again : get back ⟨~ed his health⟩ 2 : to get back to : reach again ⟨~ the shore⟩ **syn** recover, retrieve

re·gal \'rē-gəl\ *adj* 1 : of, relating to, or befitting a king : ROYAL 2 : STATELY, SPLENDID — re·gal·ly \-ē\ *adv*

re·gale \ri-'gāl\ *vb* re·galed; re·gal·ing 1 : to entertain richly or agreeably 2 : to give pleasure or amusement to **syn** gratify, delight, please, rejoice, gladden — re·gale·ment *n*

re·ga·lia \ri-'gāl-yə\ *n pl* 1 : the emblems, symbols, or paraphernalia of royalty (as the crown and scepter) 2 : the insignia of an office or order 3 : special costume : FINERY

¹re·gard \ri-'gärd\ *n* 1 : CONSIDERATION, HEED; *also* : CARE, CONCERN 2 : GAZE, GLANCE, LOOK 3 : RESPECT, ESTEEM 4 *pl* : friendly greetings implying respect and esteem 5 : an aspect to be considered : PARTICULAR — re·gard·ful *adj* — re·gard·less *adj*

²regard *vb* 1 : to pay attention to 2 : to show respect for : HEED 3 : to hold in high esteem : care for 4 : to look at : gaze upon 5 : to relate to

: touch on **6** : to think of : CONSIDER

**re·gard·ing** \-iŋ\ *prep* : CONCERNING

**regardless of** \ri-'gärd-ləs-\ *prep* : in spite of

**re·gat·ta** \ri-'gät-ə, -'gat-\ *n* : a rowing, speedboat, or sailing race or a series of such races

**re·gen·cy** \'rē-jən-sē\ *n, pl* **-cies 1** : the office or government of a regent or body of regents **2** : a body of regents **3** : the period during which a regent governs

**re·gen·er·a·cy** \ri-'jen-(ə-)rə-sē\ *n* : the state of being regenerated

¹**re·gen·er·ate** \ri-'jen-(ə-)rət\ *adj* **1** : formed or created again **2** : spiritually reborn or converted

²**re·gen·er·ate** \ri-'jen-ə-,rāt\ *vb* **1** : to reform completely **2** : to give or gain new life; *also* : to renew by a new growth of tissue **3** : to subject to spiritual renewal — **re·gen·er·a·tion** \-,jen-ə-'rā-shən\ *n* — **re·gen·er·a·tive** \-'jen-ə-,rāt-iv\ *adj* — **re·gen·er·a·tor** \-,rāt-ər\ *n*

**re·gent** \'rē-jənt\ *n* **1** : a person who rules during the childhood, absence, or incapacity of the sovereign **2** : a member of a governing board (as of a state university)

**reg·i·cide** \'rej-ə-,sīd\ *n* **1** : one who murders a king **2** : murder of a king — **reg·i·cid·al** \,rej-ə-'sīd-ᵊl\ *adj*

**re·gime** *also* **ré·gime** \rā-'zhēm, ri-\ *n* **1** : REGIMEN **2** : a form or system of government **3** : a government in power; *also* : a period of rule

**reg·i·men** \'rej-ə-mən\ *n* **1** : a systematic course of treatment or behavior (a strict dietary ~) **2** : GOVERNMENT

¹**reg·i·ment** \'rej-ə-mənt\ *n* : a military unit consisting usu. of a number of battalions — **reg·i·men·tal** \,rej-ə-'ment-ᵊl\ *adj*

²**reg·i·ment** \'rej-ə-,ment\ *vb* : to organize rigidly esp. for regulation or central control — **reg·i·men·ta·tion** \,rej-ə-mən-'tā-shən\ *n*

**reg·i·men·tals** \,rej-ə-'ment-ᵊlz\ *n pl* **1** : a regimental uniform **2** : military dress

**re·gion** \'rē-jən\ *n* [ME, fr. MF, fr. L *region-, regio*, fr. *regere* to rule] : an often indefinitely defined part or area

**re·gion·al** \'rēj-(ə-)nəl\ *adj* **1** : of or relating to a geographical region **2** : of or relating to a bodily region : LOCALIZED — **re·gion·al·ly** \-ē\ *adv*

¹**reg·is·ter** \'rej-ə-stər\ *n* **1** : a record of items or details; *also* : a book or system for keeping such a record **2** : a device to regulate ventilation or heated air **3** : a mechanical device recording a number or quantity **4** : the range of a voice or instrument

²**register** *vb* **reg·is·tered; reg·is·ter·ing** \-st(ə-)riŋ\ **1** : to enter or enroll in a register (as in a list of guests) **2** : to record automatically **3** : to secure special care for (mail matter) by paying additional postage **4** : to show (emotions) by facial expression or gestures **5** : to correspond or adjust so as to correspond exactly

**registered nurse** *n* : a graduate trained nurse who has been licensed to practice by a state authority after passing qualifying examinations

**reg·is·trant** \'rej-ə-strənt\ *n* : one that registers or is registered

**reg·is·trar** \-,strär\ *n* : an official recorder or keeper of records (as at an educational institution)

**reg·is·tra·tion** \,rej-ə-'strā-shən\ *n* **1** : the act of registering **2** : an entry in a register **3** : the number of persons registered : ENROLLMENT **4** : a document certifying an act of registering

**reg·is·try** \'rej-ə-strē\ *n, pl* **-tries 1** : ENROLLMENT, REGISTRATION **2** : the state or fact of being entered in a register **3** : a place of registration **4** : an official record book or an entry in one

**reg·nal** \'reg-nᵊl\ *adj* : of or relating to a king or his reign (his fifth ~ year)

**reg·nant** \'reg-nənt\ *adj* **1** : REIGNING **2** : DOMINANT **3** : of common or widespread occurrence : PREVALENT

**rego·lith** \'reg-ə-,lith\ *n* : MANTLEROCK

¹**re·gress** \'rē-,gres\ *n* **1** : WITHDRAWAL **2** : RETROGRESSION

²**re·gress** \ri-'gres\ *vb* : to go or cause to go back or to a lower level — **re·gres·sive** *adj* — **re·gres·sor** \-'gres-ər\ *n*

**re·gres·sion** \ri-'gresh-ən\ *n* : the act or an instance of regressing; *esp* : reversion to an earlier mental or behavioral level

¹**re·gret** \ri-'gret\ *vb* **re·gret·ted; re·gret·ting 1** : to mourn the loss or death of **2** : to be keenly sorry for **3** : to experience regret — **re·gret·ta·ble** \-ə-bəl\ *adj* — **re·gret·ta·bly** \-blē\ *adv* — **re·gret·ter** *n*

²**regret** *n* **1** : distress of mind on account of something beyond one's power to remedy **2** : an expression of sorrow **3** *pl* : a note or oral message politely declining an invitation — **re·gret·ful** \-fəl\ *adj* — **re·gret·ful·ly** \-ē\ *adv*

**re·group** \(')rē-'grüp\ *vb* : to form into a new grouping

**regt** *abbr* regiment

¹**reg·u·lar** \'reg-yə-lər\ *adj* [ME *reguler*, fr. MF, fr. LL *regularis* regular, fr. L, of a bar, fr. *regula* rule, straightedge, fr. *regere* to guide straight, rule] **1** : belonging to a religious order **2** : made, built, or arranged according to a rule, standard, or type; *also* : even or symmetrical in form or structure **3** : ORDERLY, METHODICAL (~ habits); *also* : not varying : STEADY (a ~ pace) **4** : made, selected, or conducted according to rule or custom **5** : properly qualified (not a ~ lawyer) **6** : conforming to the normal or usual manner of inflection **7** : belonging to a permanent standing army and esp. to one maintained by a national government **syn** systematic, typical, natural — **reg·u·lar·i·ty** \,reg-yə-'lar-ət-ē\ *n* — **reg·u·lar·ize** \'reg-yə-lə-,rīz\ *vb* — **reg·u·lar·ly** *adv*

²**regular** *n* **1** : one that is regular (as in attendance) **2** : a member of the regu-

lar clergy **3** : a soldier in a regular army **4** : a player on an athletic team who is usu. in the starting lineup

**reg·u·late** \'reg-yə-ˌlāt\ *vb* **-lat·ed;** **-lat·ing 1** : to govern or direct according to rule : CONTROL **2** : to bring under the control of law or authority **3** : to put in good order **4** : to fix or adjust the time, amount, degree, or rate of — **reg·u·la·tive** \-ˌlāt-iv\ *adj* — **reg·u·la·tor** \-ˌlāt-ər\ *n* — **reg·u·la·to·ry** \-lə-ˌtōr-ē\ *adj*

**reg·u·la·tion** \ˌreg-yə-'lā-shən\ *n* **1** : the act of regulating : the state of being regulated **2** : a rule dealing with details of procedure **3** : an order issued by an executive authority of a government and having the force of law

**re·gur·gi·tate** \rē-'gər-jə-ˌtāt\ *vb* **-tat·ed; -tat·ing** [ML *regurgitare,* fr. L *re-* re- + LL *gurgitare* to engulf, fr. L *gurgit-, gurges* whirlpool] : to throw or be thrown back or out; *esp* : VOMIT — **re·gur·gi·ta·tion** \-ˌgər-jə-'tā-shən\ *n*

**re·ha·bil·i·tate** \ˌrē-(h)ə-'bil-ə-ˌtāt\ *vb* **-tat·ed; tat·ing 1** : to restore to a former capacity, rank, or right : REIN-STATE **2** : to put into good condition again — **re·ha·bil·i·ta·tion** \-ˌbil-ə-'tā-shən\ *n* — **re·ha·bil·i·ta·tive** \-ˌtāt-iv\ *adj*

**re·hash** \'rē-'hash\ *vb* : to present again in another form without real change or improvement — **rehash** *n*

**re·hear·ing** \'rē-'hi(ə)r-iŋ\ *n* : a second or new hearing by the same tribunal

**re·hears·al** \ri-'hər-səl\ *n* **1** : something told again : RECITAL **2** : a private performance or practice session preparatory to a public appearance

**re·hearse** \ri-'hərs\ *vb* **re·hearsed; re·hears·ing 1** : to say again : RE-PEAT **2** : to recount in order : ENUMER-ATE **3** : to give a rehearsal of (~ a play) **4** : to train by rehearsal (~ an actor) **5** : to engage in a rehearsal — **re·hears·er** *n*

¹**reign** \'rān\ *n* **1** : the authority or rule of a sovereign **2** : the time during which a sovereign rules

²**reign** *vb* **1** : to rule as a sovereign **2** : to be predominant or prevalent

**re·im·burse** \ˌrē-əm-'bərs\ *vb* **-bursed; -burs·ing** [re- re- + obs. E *imburse* (to put in the pocket, pay), fr. ML *imbursare* to put into a purse, fr. L *in-* in- + ML *bursa* purse, fr. LL, oxhide, fr. Gk *byrsa*] : to pay back : make restitution : REPAY **syn** indemnify, recompense, requite — **re·im·burs·able** *adj* — **re·im·burse·ment** *n*

¹**rein** \'rān\ *n* **1** : a line of a bridle by which a rider or driver directs an animal **2** : a restraining influence : CHECK **3** : position of control or command **4** : complete freedom : SCOPE — usu. used in the phrase *give rein to*

²**rein** *vb* : to check or direct by reins

**re·in·car·na·tion** \ˌrē-ˌin-ˌkär-'nā-shən\ *n* : rebirth of the soul in a new body — **re·in·car·nate** \ˌrē-in-'kär-ˌnāt\ *vb*

**rein·deer** \'rān-ˌdiər\ *n* [ME *reindere,* fr. ON *hreinn* reindeer + ME *deer*] : any of several large deer of northern regions used for draft and meat

**reindeer moss** *n* : a gray, erect, tufted, and much-branched lichen of northern regions that is consumed by reindeer and sometimes by man

**re·in·fec·tion** \ˌrē-ən-'fek-shən\ *n* : infection following another infection of the same type

**re·in·force** \ˌrē-ən-'fōrs\ *vb* **1** : to strengthen with new force, aid, material, or support **2** : to strengthen with additional forces (as troops or ships) — **re·in·force·ment** — **re·in·forc·er** *n*

**re·in·state** \ˌrē-ən-'stāt\ *vb* **-stat·ed;** **-stat·ing** : to restore to a former position, condition, or capacity — **re·in·state·ment** *n*

**re·it·er·ate** \rē-'it-ə-ˌrāt\ *vb* **-at·ed;** **-at·ing** : to say or do over again or repeatedly **syn** repeat, iterate — **re·it·er·a·tion** \-ˌit-ə-'rā-shən\ *n*

¹**re·ject** \ri-'jekt\ *vb* **1** : to refuse to acknowledge or submit to **2** : to refuse to take or accept **3** : to refuse to grant, consider, or accede to **4** : to throw out esp. as useless or unsatisfactory — **re·jec·tion** \-'jek-shən\ *n*

²**re·ject** \'rē-ˌjekt\ *n* : a rejected person or thing

**re·joice** \ri-'jóis\ *vb* **re·joiced; re·joic·ing 1** : to give joy to : GLADDEN **2** : to feel joy or great delight — **re·joic·er** *n* — **re·joic·ing** *n*

**re·join** \'rē-'jóin *for 1,* ri- *for 2*\ *vb* **1** : to join again : come together again : REUNITE **2** : to say in answer (as to a plaintiff's plea in court) : REPLY

**re·join·der** \ri-'jóin-dər\ *n* : REPLY; *esp* : an answer to a reply

**re·ju·ve·nate** \ri-'jü-və-ˌnāt\ *vb* **-nat·ed; -nat·ing** : to make young or youthful again : give new vigor to **syn** renew, refresh — **re·ju·ve·na·tion** \-ˌjü-və-'nā-shən\ *n*

**rel** *abbr* relating; relative

¹**re·lapse** \ri-'laps, 'rē-ˌlaps\ *n* : the action or process of relapsing; *esp* : a recurrence of illness after a period of improvement

²**re·lapse** \ri-'laps\ *vb* **re·lapsed; re·laps·ing** : to slip back into a former condition (as of illness) after a change for the better

**re·late** \ri-'lāt\ *vb* **re·lat·ed; re·lat·ing 1** : to give an account of : TELL, NARRATE **2** : to show or establish logical or causal connection between **3** : to be connected : have reference **4** : to have meaningful social relationships **5** : to respond favorably — **re·lat·able** *adj* — **re·lat·er** *n*

**re·lat·ed** \-əd\ *adj* **1** : connected by some understood relationship **2** : connected through membership in the same family — **re·lat·ed·ness** *n*

**re·la·tion** \ri-'lā-shən\ *n* **1** : NARRA-TION, ACCOUNT **2** : CONNECTION, RE-LATIONSHIP **3** : connection by blood or marriage : KINSHIP **4** : REFERENCE, RESPECT (in ~ to this matter) **5** : the state of being mutually interested or involved (as in social or commercial matters) **6** *pl* : DEALINGS, AFFAIRS **7** *pl* : SEXUAL INTERCOURSE

**re·la·tion·ship** \-,ship\ *n* : the state of being related or interrelated

**¹rel·a·tive** \'rel-ət-iv\ *n* **1** : a word referring grammatically to an antecedent **2** : a thing having a relation to or a dependence upon another thing **3** : a person connected with another by blood or marriage; *also* : an animal or plant related to another by common descent

**²relative** *adj* **1** : introducing a subordinate clause qualifying an expressed or implied antecedent (~ pronoun); *also* : introduced by such a connective (~ clause) **2** : PERTINENT, RELEVANT **3** : not absolute or independent : COMPARATIVE **4** : expressed as the ratio of the specified quantity to the total magnitude or to the mean of all quantities involved **syn** dependent, contingent, conditional — **rel·a·tive·ly** *adv* — **rel·a·tive·ness** *n*

**relative humidity** *n* : the ratio of the amount of water vapor actually present in the air to the greatest amount possible at the same temperature

**rel·a·tiv·is·tic** \,rel-ət-iv-'is-tik\ *adj* : moving at a velocity such that there is a significant change in mass and other properties in accordance with the theory of relativity (a ~ electron) — **rela·tiv·is·ti·cal·ly** \-ti-k(ə-)lē\ *adv*

**rel·a·tiv·i·ty** \,rel-ə-'tiv-ət-ē\ *n, pl* **-ties 1** : the quality or state of being relative **2** : a theory leading to the assertion of the equivalence of mass and energy and of the increase in mass, dimension, and time with increased velocity

**re·la·tor** \ri-'lāt-ər\ *n* : NARRATOR

**re·lax** \ri-'laks\ *vb* **1** : to make or become less firm, tense, or rigid **2** : to make less severe or strict **3** : to seek rest or recreation — **re·lax·er** *n*

**¹re·lax·ant** \ri-'lak-sənt\ *adj* : producing relaxation

**²relaxant** *n* : a relaxing agent; *esp* : a drug that induces muscular relaxation

**re·lax·ation** \,rē-,lak-'sā-shən\ *n* **1** : the act or fact of relaxing or of being relaxed : a lessening of tension **2** : DIVERSION, RECREATION **syn** rest, repose, leisure, ease, comfort

**¹re·lay** \'rē-,lā\ *n* **1** : a fresh supply (as of horses or men) arranged beforehand to relieve or replace others at various stages **2** : a race between teams in which each team member covers a specified part of a course **3** : an electromagnetic device for remote or automatic control of other devices (as switches) in the same or a different circuit **4** : the act of passing along by stages

**²re·lay** \'rē-,lā, ri-'lā\ *vb* **re·layed**; **re·lay·ing 1** : to place in or provide with relays **2** : to pass along by relays **3** : to control or operate by a relay

**³re·lay** \'rē-'lā\ *vb* : to lay again

**¹re·lease** \ri-'lēs\ *vb* **re·leased**; **re·leas·ing 1** : to set free from confinement or restraint **2** : to relieve from something (as pain, trouble, or penalty) that oppresses or burdens **3** : RELINQUISH (~ a claim) **4** : to permit publication or performance (as of a news story or a motion picture) on but not before a specified date **syn** emancipate, discharge

**²release** *n* **1** : relief or deliverance from sorrow, suffering, or trouble **2** : discharge from an obligation or responsibility **3** : an act of setting free : the state of being freed **4** : a document effecting a legal release **5** : a device for holding or releasing a mechanism as required **6** : a releasing for performance or publication; *also* : the matter released (as to the press)

**rel·e·gate** \'rel-ə-,gāt\ *vb* **-gat·ed; -gat·ing 1** : to send into exile : BANISH **2** : to remove or dismiss to some less prominent position **3** : to assign to a particular class or sphere **4** : to submit or refer for judgment, decision, or execution : DELEGATE **syn** commit, entrust, consign — **rel·e·ga·tion** \,rel-ə-'gā-shən\ *n*

**re·lent** \ri-'lent\ *vb* **1** : to become less stern, severe, or harsh **2** : SLACKEN

**re·lent·less** \-ləs\ *adj* : mercilessly hard or harsh : immovably stern or persistent — **re·lent·less·ly** *adv* — **re·lent·less·ness** *n*

**rel·e·vance** \'rel-ə-vəns\ *n* : relation to the matter at hand : practical and esp. social applicability

**rel·e·van·cy** \-vən-sē\ *n* : RELEVANCE

**rel·e·vant** \'rel-ə-vənt\ *adj* : bearing upon the matter at hand : PERTINENT **syn** germane, material, applicable, apropos — **rel·e·vant·ly** *adv*

**re·li·able** \ri-'lī-ə-bəl\ *adj* : fit to be trusted or relied on : DEPENDABLE, TRUSTWORTHY — **re·li·a·bil·i·ty** \-,lī-ə-'bil-ət-ē\ *n* — **re·li·able·ness** *n* — **re·li·ably** \-'lī-ə-blē\ *adv*

**re·li·ance** \ri-'lī-əns\ *n* **1** : the act of relying **2** : the state or attitude of one that relies : DEPENDENCE **3** : one relied on — **re·li·ant** \-ənt\ *adj*

**rel·ic** \'rel-ik\ *n* **1** : an object venerated because of its association with a saint or martyr **2** *pl* : REMAINS, RUINS **3** : a remaining trace : SURVIVAL, VESTIGE **4** : SOUVENIR, MEMENTO

**rel·ict** \'rel-ikt\ *n* **1** : WIDOW **2** : something (as an organism or a rock) left unchanged in a process of change

**re·lief** \ri-'lēf\ *n* **1** : removal or lightening of something oppressive, painful, or distressing **2** : aid in the form of money or necessities (as for the aged or handicapped) **3** : military assistance in or rescue from a position of difficulty **4** : release from a post or from performance of a duty; *also* : one that relieves another by taking his place **5** : legal remedy or redress **6** : projection of figures or ornaments from the background (as in sculpture) **7** : the elevations of a land surface

**relief pitcher** *n* : a baseball pitcher who takes over for another during a game

**re·lieve** \ri-'lēv\ vb **re·lieved; re·liev·ing 1 :** to free partly or wholly from a burden or from distress **2 :** to bring about the removal or alleviation of **: MITIGATE 3 :** to release from a post or duty; *also* **:** to take the place of **4 :** to break the monotony of (as by contrast in color) **5 :** to raise in relief **syn** alleviate, lighten, assuage, allay — **re·liev·er** n

**relig** abbr religion

**re·li·gion** \ri-'lij-ən\ n **1 :** the service and worship of God or the supernatural **2 :** devotion to a religious faith **3 :** an organized system of faith and worship; *also* **:** a personal set of religious beliefs and practices **4 :** a cause, principle, or belief held to with faith and ardor — **re·li·gion·ist** n

**¹re·li·gious** \ri-'lij-əs\ adj **1 :** relating or devoted to the divine or that which is held to be of ultimate importance **2 :** of or relating to religious beliefs or observances **3 :** scrupulously and conscientiously faithful **4 :** FERVENT, ZEALOUS — **re·li·gious·ly** adv

**²religious** n, pl **religious :** one (as a monk) bound by vows and devoted to a life of piety

**re·lin·quish** \ri-'liŋ-kwish, -'lin-\ vb **1 :** to withdraw or retreat from **:** ABANDON, QUIT **2 :** RENOUNCE **3 :** to let go of **:** RELEASE **syn** yield, leave, resign, surrender, cede, waive — **re·lin·quish·ment** n

**rel·i·quary** \'rel-ə-ˌkwer-ē\ n, pl **-quar·ies :** a container for religious relics

**re·lique** \ri-'lēk, 'rel-ik\ archaic var of RELIC

**¹rel·ish** \'rel-ish\ n [ME reles aftertaste, fr. OF, release, something left over, fr. relessier to relax, release, fr. L relaxare] **1 :** a characteristic flavor (as of food) **:** SAVOR **2 :** keen enjoyment or delight in something **:** GUSTO **3 :** APPETITE, INCLINATION **4 :** a highly seasoned sauce (as of pickles) eaten with other food to add flavor

**²relish** vb **1 :** to add relish to **2 :** to take pleasure in **:** ENJOY **3 :** to eat with pleasure — **rel·ish·able** adj

**re·live** \(ˈ)rē-'liv\ vb **:** to live again or over again; esp **:** to experience again in the imagination

**re·lo·cate** \(ˈ)rē-'lō-ˌkāt, ˌrē-lō-'kāt\ vb **1 :** to locate again **2 :** to move to a new location — **re·lo·ca·tion** \ˌrē-lō-'kā-shən\ n

**re·luc·tance** \ri-'lək-təns\ n **1 :** the quality or state of being reluctant **2 :** the opposition offered by a magnetic substance to magnetic flux

**re·luc·tant** \ri-'lək-tənt\ adj **:** holding back (as from acting) **:** UNWILLING; also **:** showing unwillingness (~ obedience) **syn** disinclined, indisposed, hesitant, loath, averse — **re·luc·tant·ly** adv

**re·ly** \ri-'lī\ vb **re·lied; re·ly·ing** [ME relien to rally, fr. MF relier to connect, rally, fr. L religare to tie back, fr. re- back + ligare to tie] **:** to place faith or confidence in **:** DEPEND **syn** trust, count

**REM** \'rem\ n **:** RAPID EYE MOVEMENT

**re·main** \ri-'mān\ vb **1 :** to be left after others have been removed, subtracted, or destroyed **2 :** to be something yet to be shown, done, or treated (it ~s to be seen) **3 :** to stay after others have gone **4 :** to continue unchanged

**re·main·der** \ri-'mān-dər\ n **1 :** that which is left over **:** a remaining group, part, or trace **2 :** the number left after subtraction **3 :** a book sold at a reduced price by the publisher after sales have slowed **syn** leavings, rest, balance, remnant, residue

**re·mains** \-'mānz\ n pl **1 :** a remaining part or trace (the ~ of a meal) **2 :** writings left unpublished at an author's death **3 :** a dead body

**re·mand** \ri-'mand\ vb **:** to order back; esp **:** to return to custody pending trial or for further detention

**¹re·mark** \ri-'märk\ vb **1 :** to take notice of **:** OBSERVE **2 :** to express as an observation or comment **:** SAY

**²remark** n **1 :** the act of remarking **:** OBSERVATION, NOTICE **2 :** a passing observation or comment

**re·mark·able** \ri-'mär-kə-bəl\ adj **:** worthy of being or likely to be noticed **:** UNUSUAL, EXTRAORDINARY, NOTEWORTHY — **re·mark·able·ness** n — **re·mark·ably** \-blē\ adv

**re·me·di·a·ble** \ri-'mēd-ē-ə-bəl\ adj **:** capable of being remedied (~ speech defects)

**re·me·di·al** \ri-'mēd-ē-əl\ adj **:** intended to remedy or improve — **re·me·di·al·ly** \-ē\ adv

**¹rem·e·dy** \'rem-əd-ē\ n, pl **-dies 1 :** a medicine or treatment that cures or relieves **2 :** something that corrects or counteracts an evil or compensates for a loss

**²remedy** vb **-died; -dy·ing :** to provide or serve as a remedy for

**re·mem·ber** \ri-'mem-bər\ vb **re·mem·bered; re·mem·ber·ing** \-b(ə-)riŋ\ **1 :** to have come into the mind again **:** think of again **:** RECOLLECT **2 :** to keep from forgetting **:** keep in mind **3 :** to convey greetings from **4 :** COMMEMORATE

**re·mem·brance** \-brəns\ n **1 :** an act of remembering **:** RECOLLECTION **2 :** the state of being remembered **:** MEMORY **3 :** the power of remembering; also **:** the period over which one's memory extends **4 :** a memory of a person, thing, or event **5 :** something that serves to bring to mind **:** REMINDER, MEMENTO **6 :** a greeting or gift recalling or expressing friendship or affection

**re·mind** \ri-'mīnd\ vb **:** to put in mind of someone or something **:** cause to remember — **re·mind·er** n

**rem·i·nisce** \ˌrem-ə-'nis\ vb **-nisced; -nisc·ing :** to indulge in reminiscence

**rem·i·nis·cence** \-'nis-ᵊns\ n **1 :** a recalling or telling of a past experience **2 :** an account of a memorable experience **3 :** something so like another as to suggest unconscious repetition or imitation

**rem·i·nis·cent** \-³nt\ *adj* **1 :** of or relating to reminiscence **2 :** marked by or given to reminiscence **3 :** serving to remind — **rem·i·nis·cent·ly** *adv*

**re·miss** \ri-'mis\ *adj* **1 :** negligent or careless in the performance of work or duty **2 :** showing neglect or inattention **syn** lax, neglectful — **re·miss·ly** *adv* — **re·miss·ness** *n*

**re·mis·sion** \ri-'mish-ən\ *n* **1 :** the act or process of remitting (as from sin) **2 :** a state or period during which something is remitted

**re·mit** \ri-'mit\ *vb* **re·mit·ted; re·mit·ting 1 :** FORGIVE, PARDON **2 :** to give or gain relief from (as pain) **3 :** to refer for consideration, report, or decision **4 :** to refrain from exacting or enforcing (as a penalty) **5 :** to send (money) in payment of a bill **syn** excuse, condone

**re·mit·tal** \ri-'mit-³l\ *n* **:** REMISSION

**re·mit·tance** \ri-'mit-³ns\ *n* **1 :** a sum of money remitted **2 :** transmittal of money (as to a distant place)

**rem·nant** \'rem-nənt\ *n* **1 :** a usu. small part or trace remaining **2 :** an unsold or unused end of fabrics that are sold by the yard **syn** remainder, residue, rest

**re·mod·el** \'rē-'mäd-³l\ *vb* **:** to alter the structure of **:** make over

**re·mon·strance** \ri-'män-strəns\ *n* **:** an act or instance of remonstrating

**re·mon·strant** \-strənt\ *adj* **:** vigorously objecting or opposing — **remonstrant** *n* — **re·mon·strant·ly** *adv*

**re·mon·strate** \ri-'män-‚strāt\ *vb* **-strat·ed; -strat·ing :** to plead in opposition to something **:** speak in protest or reproof **syn** expostulate, object — **re·mon·stra·tion** \ri-‚män-'strā-shən, ‚rem-ən-\ *n* — **re·mon·stra·tive** \ri-'män-strət-iv\ *adj* — **re·mon·stra·tor** \ri-'män-‚strāt-ər\ *n*

**rem·o·ra** \'rem-ə-rə\ *n* **:** any of several fishes with sucking organs on the head by means of which they cling to sharks and ships

**re·morse** \ri-'mȯrs\ *n* [ME, fr. MF *remors*, fr. ML *remorsus*, fr. LL, act of biting again, fr. L *remorsus*, pp. of *remordēre* to bite again, fr. *re-* again *+ mordēre* to bite] **:** regret for one's sins or for acts that wrong others **:** distress arising from a sense of guilt **syn** penitence, repentance, contrition — **re·morse·ful** *adj* — **re·morse·less** *adj*

**re·mote** \ri-'mōt\ *adj* **re·mot·er; -est 1 :** far off in place or time **:** not near **2 :** not closely related **:** DISTANT **3 :** located out of the way **:** SECLUDED **4 :** small in degree **:** SLIGHT ⟨a ∼ chance⟩ **5 :** distant in manner — **re·mote·ly** *adv* — **re·mote·ness** *n*

**¹re·mount** \'rē-'maunt\ *vb* **1 :** to mount again **2 :** to furnish remounts to

**²re·mount** \'rē-‚maunt\ *n* **:** a fresh horse to replace one disabled or exhausted

**¹re·move** \ri-'müv\ *vb* **re·moved;**

**re·mov·ing 1 :** to move from one place to another **:** TRANSFER **2 :** to move by lifting or taking off or away **3 :** DISMISS, DISCHARGE **4 :** to get rid of **:** ELIMINATE ⟨∼ a fire hazard⟩ **5 :** to change one's residence or location **6 :** to go away **:** DEPART **7 :** to be capable of being removed — **re·mov·able** *adj* — **re·mov·al** \-vəl\ *n* — **re·mov·er** *n*

**²remove** *n* **1 :** a transfer from one location to another **:** MOVE **2 :** a degree or stage of separation

**re·mu·ner·ate** \ri-'myü-nə-‚rāt\ *vb* **-at·ed; -at·ing :** to pay an equivalent for or to **:** RECOMPENSE — **re·mu·ner·a·tor** \-‚rāt-ər\ *n* — **re·mu·ner·a·to·ry** \-rə-‚tōr-ē\ *adj*

**re·mu·ner·a·tion** \ri-‚myü-nə-'rā-shən\ *n* **:** COMPENSATION, PAYMENT

**re·mu·ner·a·tive** \ri-'myü-nə-rət-iv, -‚rāt-\ *adj* **:** serving to remunerate **:** GAINFUL — **re·mu·ner·a·tive·ly** *adv* — **re·mu·ner·a·tive·ness** *n*

**re·nais·sance** \‚ren-ə-'säns, -'zäns\ *n* **1** *cap* **:** the revival in art and literature in Europe in the 14th–17th centuries; *also* **:** the period of the Renaissance **2** *often cap* **:** a movement or period of vigorous artistic and intellectual activity **3 :** REBIRTH, REVIVAL

**re·nal** \'rēn-³l\ *adj* **:** of, relating to, or located in or near the kidneys

**re·na·scence** \ri-'nas-³ns, -'nās-\ *n, often cap* **:** RENAISSANCE

**ren·con·tre** \rä⁻-'kō⁻tr⁰, ren-'känt-ər\ *or* **ren·coun·ter** \ren-'kaunt-ər\ *n* **1 :** a hostile meeting or contest **:** COMBAT **2 :** a casual meeting

**rend** \'rend\ *vb* **rent** \'rent\; **rend·ing 1 :** to remove by violence **:** WREST **2 :** to tear forcibly apart **:** SPLIT

**ren·der** \'ren-dər\ *vb* **ren·dered; ren·der·ing** \-d(ə-)riŋ\ **1 :** to extract (as lard) by heating **2 :** DELIVER, GIVE; *also* **:** YIELD **3 :** to give in return **4 :** to do (a service) for another ⟨∼ aid⟩ **5 :** to cause to be or become **:** MAKE **6 :** to reproduce or represent by artistic or verbal means **7 :** TRANSLATE ⟨∼ into English⟩

**¹ren·dez·vous** \'rän-di-‚vü, -dā-\ *n, pl* **ren·dez·vous** \-‚vüz\ [MF, fr. *rendez vous* present yourselves] **1 :** a place appointed for a meeting; *also* **:** a meeting at an appointed place **2 :** a place of popular resort **3 :** the process of bringing two spacecraft together **syn** tryst, engagement, appointment

**²rendezvous** *vb* **ren·dez·voused** \-‚vüd\; **ren·dez·vous·ing** \-‚vü-iŋ\; **ren·dez·vouses** \-‚vüz\ **:** to come or bring together at a rendezvous

**ren·di·tion** \ren-'dish-ən\ *n* **:** an act or a result of rendering **:** first ∼ of the work into English

**ren·e·gade** \'ren-i-‚gād\ *n* [Sp *renegado*, fr. ML *renegatus*, fr. pp. of *renegare* to deny, fr. L *re-* re- *+ negare* to deny] **:** one who deserts a faith, cause, principle, or party for another

**re·nege** \ri-'nig, -'neg, -'nēg, -'nāg\ *vb* **re·neged; re·neg·ing 1 :** to fail to follow suit when able in a card game in violation of the rules **2 :** to go back on a promise or commitment — **re·neg·er** n

**re·new** \ri-'n(y)ü\ vb **1 :** to make or become new, fresh, or strong again **2 :** to restore to existence : RECREATE, REVIVE **3 :** to make or do again : REPEAT 〈~ a complaint〉 **4 :** to begin again : RESUME 〈~ed his efforts〉 **5 :** REPLACE 〈~ the lining of a coat〉 **6 :** to grant or obtain an extension of or on 〈~ a lease〉 〈~ a subscription〉 — **re·new·a·ble** adj — **re·new·er** n

**re·new·al** \ri-'n(y)ü-əl\ n **1 :** the act of renewing : the state of being renewed **2 :** something renewed

**ren·net** \'ren-ət\ n **1 :** the contents of the stomach of an unweaned calf (as a calf) or the lining membrane of the stomach used for curdling milk **2 :** rennin or a substitute used to curdle milk

**ren·nin** \'ren-ən\ n : a stomach enzyme that coagulates casein and is used commercially to curdle milk in the making of cheese

**re·nounce** \ri-'naùns\ vb **re·nounced; re·nounc·ing 1 :** to give up, refuse, or resign usu. by formal declaration **2 :** to refuse further to follow, obey, or recognize : REPUDIATE **syn** abdicate, forswear — **re·nounce·ment** n

**ren·o·vate** \'ren-ə-ˌvāt\ vb **-vat·ed; -vat·ing 1 :** to restore to vigor or activity **2 :** to make like new again : put in good condition : REPAIR — **ren·o·va·tion** \ˌren-ə-'vā-shən\ n — **ren·o·va·tor** \'ren-ə-ˌvāt-ər\ n

**re·nown** \ri-'naùn\ n : a state of being widely acclaimed and honored : FAME, CELEBRITY **syn** honor, glory, reputation, repute — **re·nowned** \-'naùnd\ adj

¹**rent** \'rent\ n **1 :** money or the amount of money paid or due (as monthly) for the use of another's property **2 :** property rented or for rent

²**rent** vb **1 :** to take and hold under an agreement to pay rent **2 :** to give possession and use of in return for rent **3 :** to be for or bring in as rent 〈~s for $100 a month〉 — **rent·er** n

³**rent** n **1 :** a tear in cloth **2 :** a split in a party or organized group : SCHISM

¹**rent·al** \'rent-ᵊl\ n **1 :** an amount paid or collected as rent **2 :** a property rented **3 :** an act of renting

²**rental** adj **:** of or relating to rent

**re·nun·ci·a·tion** \ri-ˌnən-sē-'ā-shən\ n : the act of renouncing : REPUDIATION

**rep** abbr Republican

**Rep** abbr **1** report; reporter **2** representative **3** republic

**Rep** abbr Republican

¹**re·pair** \ri-'paər\ vb [ME repairen, fr. MF repairier to go back to one's country, fr. LL repatriare, fr. L re- + patria native country] : to betake oneself : GO 〈~ed to his den〉

²**repair** vb [ME repairen, fr. MF reparer, fr. L reparare, fr. re- re- + parare to prepare] **1 :** to restore to good condition esp. by replacing parts or putting together something torn or broken

**2 :** to restore to a healthy state **3** : REMEDY 〈~ a wrong〉 — **re·pair·er** n

³**repair** n **1 :** an act of repairing **2 :** an instance or result of repairing **3 :** condition with respect to soundness or need of repairing 〈in bad ~〉

**re·pair·man** \-ˌman\ n : one whose occupation is making repairs

**rep·a·ra·tion** \ˌrep-ə-'rā-shən\ n **1 :** the act of making amends for a wrong **2 :** amends made for a wrong; esp : money paid by a defeated nation in compensation for damages caused during hostilities — usu. used in pl. **syn** redress, restitution, indemnity

**re·par·a·tive** \ri-'par-ət-iv\ adj **1 :** of, relating to, or effecting repairs **2 :** serving to make amends

**rep·ar·tee** \ˌrep-ər-'tē\ n **1 :** a witty reply **2 :** a succession of clever replies; also **:** skill in making such replies

**re·past** \ri-'past, 're-ˌpast\ n : something taken as food; esp **:** a supply of food and drink served as a meal

**re·pa·tri·ate** \rē-'pā-trē-ˌāt\ vb **-at·ed; -at·ing :** to send or bring back to one's own country or to the country of which one is a citizen — **re·pa·tri·ate** \-trē-ət, -trē-ˌāt\ n — **re·pa·tri·a·tion** \-ˌpā-trē-'ā-shən\ n

**re·pay** \rē-'pā\ vb **-paid** \-'pād\; **-pay·ing 1 :** to pay back : REFUND **2 :** to give or do in return or requital **3 :** to make a return payment to : RECOMPENSE, REQUITE **syn** remunerate, satisfy, reimburse, indemnify — **re·pay·able** adj — **re·pay·ment** n

**re·peal** \ri-'pēl\ vb **:** to rescind or annul by authoritative and esp. legislative action — **repeal** n — **re·peal·er** n

¹**re·peat** \ri-'pēt\ vb **1 :** to say again **2 :** to do again **3 :** to say over from memory **syn** iterate, reiterate — **re·peat·able** adj — **re·peat·er** n

²**re·peat** \ri-'pēt, 'rē-ˌpēt\ n **1 :** the act of repeating **2 :** something repeated or to be repeated (as a radio or television program)

**re·peat·ed** \ri-'pēt-əd\ adj **:** done or recurring again and again : FREQUENT — **re·peat·ed·ly** adv

**repeating decimal** n : a decimal in which after a certain point a particular digit or sequence of digits repeats itself indefinitely

**re·pel** \ri-'pel\ vb **re·pelled; re·pel·ling 1 :** to drive away : REPULSE **2 :** to fight against : RESIST **3 :** REJECT **4 :** to cause aversion in : DISGUST

¹**re·pel·lent** also **re·pel·lant** \ri-'pel-ənt\ adj **1 :** tending to drive away 〈a mosquito-repellent spray〉 **2 :** arousing aversion or disgust

²**repellent** also **repellant** n **:** something that repels; esp **:** a substance used to prevent insect attacks

**re·pent** \ri-'pent\ vb **1 :** to turn from sin and resolve to reform one's life **2 :** to feel sorry for (something done) : REGRET — **re·pen·tance** \ri-'pent-ᵊns\ n — **re·pen·tant** \-ᵊnt\ adj

**re·per·cus·sion** \ˌrē-pər-'kəsh-ən, ˌrep-ər-\ n **1 :** REVERBERATION **2 :** a reciprocal action or effect **3 :** a widespread, indirect, or unforeseen effect of something done or said

**rep·er·toire** \'rep-ə(r)-,twär\ n 1 : a list of plays, operas, pieces, or parts which a company or performer is prepared to present 2 : a list of the skills or devices possessed by a person or needed in his occupation

**rep·er·to·ry** \'rep-ə(r)-,tōr-ē\ n, pl -ries 1 : REPOSITORY 2 : REPERTOIRE 3 : the practice of presenting several plays successively or alternately in the same season by a resident company

**rep·e·ti·tion** \,rep-ə-'tish-ən\ n 1 : the act or an instance of repeating 2 : the fact of being repeated

**rep·e·ti·tious** \-'tish-əs\ adj : marked by repetition; esp : tediously repeating — **rep·e·ti·tious·ly** adv — **rep·e·ti·tious·ness** n

**re·pet·i·tive** \ri-'pet-ət-iv\ adj : REPETITIOUS — **re·pet·i·tive·ly** adv — **re·pet·i·tive·ness** n

**re·pine** \ri-'pīn\ vb re·pined; re·pin·ing : to feel or express discontent or dejection : COMPLAIN, FRET

**repl** abbr replace; replacement

**re·place** \ri-'plās\ vb 1 : to restore to a former place or position 2 : to take the place of : SUPPLANT 3 : to put something new in the place of — **re·place·able** adj — **re·plac·er** n

**re·place·ment** \ri-'plās-mənt\ n 1 : the act of replacing : the state of being replaced : SUBSTITUTION 2 : one that replaces; esp : one assigned to a military unit to replace a loss or fill a quota

¹**re·play** \rē-'plā\ vb : to play again or over

²**re·play** \'rē-,plā\ n 1 : an act or instance of replaying 2 : the playing of a tape (as a videotape)

**re·plen·ish** \ri-'plen-ish\ vb : to fill or build up again : stock or supply anew — **re·plen·ish·ment** n

**re·plete** \ri-'plēt\ adj 1 : fully provided 2 : FILL; esp : full of food — **re·plete·ness** n

**re·ple·tion** \ri-'plē-shən\ n : the state of being replete

**rep·li·ca** \'rep-li-kə\ n [It, repetition, fr. replicare to repeat, fr. LL, fr. L, to fold back, fr. re- back · plicare to fold] 1 : a close reproduction or facsimile (as of a painting or statue) esp. by the maker of the original. 2 : COPY, DUPLICATE

¹**rep·li·cate** \'rep-lə-,kāt\ vb -cat·ed; -cat·ing : DUPLICATE, REPEAT

²**rep·li·cate** \-li-kət\ n : one of several identical experiments or procedures

**rep·li·ca·tion** \,rep-lə-'kā-shən\ n 1 : ANSWER, REPLY 2 : precise copying or reproduction; also : an act or process of this

¹**re·ply** \ri-'plī\ vb re·plied; re·ply·ing : to say or do in answer : RESPOND

²**reply** n, pl replies : ANSWER, RESPONSE

¹**re·port** \ri-'pōrt\ n [ME, fr. MF, fr. OF, fr. reporter to report, fr. L reportare, fr. re- back + portare to carry] 1 : common talk : RUMOR 2 : FAME, REPUTATION 3 : a usu. detailed account or statement 4 : an explosive noise

²**report** vb 1 : to give an account of : RELATE, TELL 2 : to serve as carrier of (a message) 3 : to prepare or present an account of (an event) for a newspaper or for broadcast 4 : to make a charge of misconduct against 5 : to present oneself (as for work) 6 : to make known to the proper authorities ⟨~ a fire⟩ 7 : to return or present (as a matter officially referred to a committee) with conclusions and recommendations — **re·port·able** adj

**re·port·age** \ri-'pōrt-ij, esp for 2 ,repər-'täzh, ,rep-,ör-'\ n 1 : the act or process of reporting news 2 : writing intended to give an account of observed or documented events

**report card** n : a periodical report on a student's grades

**re·port·ed·ly** \ri-'pōrt-əd-lē\ adv : according to report

**re·port·er** \ri-'pōrt-ər\ n : one that reports, esp : a person who gathers and reports news for a newspaper — **re·por·to·ri·al** \,rep-ə(r)-'tōr-ē-əl\ adj

¹**re·pose** \ri-'pōz\ vb re·posed; re·pos·ing 1 : to place (as trust) in someone or something 2 : to place for control, management, or use

²**repose** vb re·posed; re·pos·ing 1 : to lay at rest 2 : to lie at rest 3 : to lie dead 4 : to take a rest 5 : to rest for support : LIE

³**repose** n 1 : a state of resting (as after exertion); esp : SLEEP 2 : CALM, PEACE 3 : cessation or absence of activity, movement, or animation 4 : composure of manner : POISE — **re·pose·ful** adj

**re·pos·i·to·ry** \ri-'päz-ə-,tōr-ē\ n, pl -ries 1 : a place where something is deposited or stored 2 : a person to whom something is entrusted

**re·pos·sess** \,rē-pə-'zes\ vb 1 : to regain possession of 2 : to resume possession of in default of the payments of installments due — **re·pos·ses·sion** \-'zesh-ən\ n

**rep·re·hend** \,rep-ri-'hend\ vb : to express disapproval of : CENSURE syn criticize, condemn, denounce, blame, reprimand — **rep·re·hen·sion** \-'hen-chən\ n

**rep·re·hen·si·ble** \-'hen-sə-bəl\ adj : deserving blame or censure : CULPABLE — **rep·re·hen·si·bly** \-blē\ adv

**rep·re·sent** \,rep-ri-'zent\ vb 1 : to present a picture or a likeness of : PORTRAY, DEPICT 2 : to serve as a sign or symbol of 3 : to act the role of 4 : to stand in the place of : act or speak for 5 : to be a member or example of : TYPIFY 6 : to describe as having a specified quality or character 7 : to state with the purpose of affecting judgment or action 8 : to serve as an elected representative of

**rep·re·sen·ta·tion** \,rep-ri-,zen-'tāshən\ n 1 : the act of representing 2 : one (as a picture or image) that represents something else 3 : the state of being represented in a legislative body; also : the body of persons representing a constituency **4** : a usu. formal statement made to effect a change

**¹rep·re·sen·ta·tive** \,rep-ri-'zent-ət-iv\ *adj* **1** : serving to represent **2** : standing or acting for another **3** : founded on the principle of representation : carried on by elected representatives ⟨~ government⟩ — **rep·re·sen·ta·tive·ly** *adv* — **rep·re·sen·ta·tive·ness** *n*

**²representative** *n* **1** : a typical example of a group, class, or quality **2** : one that represents another; *esp* : one representing a district or a state in a legislative body usu. as a member of a lower house

**re·press** \ri-'pres\ *vb* **1** : CURB, SUBDUE **2** : RESTRAIN, SUPPRESS; *esp* : to exclude from consciousness — **re·pres·sion** \-'presh-ən\ *n* — **re·pres·sive** \-'pres-iv\ *adj*

**¹re·prieve** \ri-'prēv\ *vb* **re·prieved**; **re·priev·ing 1** : to delay the punishment or execution of **2** : to give temporary relief to

**²reprieve** *n* **1** : the act of reprieving : the state of being reprieved **2** : a formal temporary suspension of a sentence esp. of death **3** : a temporary respite

**¹rep·ri·mand** \'rep-rə-,mand\ *n* : a severe or formal reproof

**²reprimand** *vb* : to reprove severely or formally

**¹re·print** \'rē-'print\ *vb* : to print again

**²re·print** \'rē-,print\ *n* : a reproduction of printed matter

**re·pri·sal** \ri-'prī-zəl\ *n* : action or an act in retaliation for something done by another person

**re·prise** \ri-'prēz\ *n* : a recurrence, renewal, or resumption of an action; *also* : a musical repetition

**¹re·proach** \ri-'prōch\ *n* : a cause or occasion of blame or disgrace **2** : DISGRACE, DISCREDIT **3** : the act of reproaching : REBUKE — **re·proach·ful** \-fəl\ *adj* — **re·proach·ful·ly** \-ē\ *adv* — **re·proach·ful·ness** *n*

**²reproach** *vb* **1** : CENSURE, REBUKE **2** : to cast discredit upon **syn** chide, admonish, reprove, reprimand — **re·proach·able** *adj*

**rep·ro·bate** \'rep-rə-,bāt\ *n* : a thoroughly bad person : SCOUNDREL — **reprobate** *adj*

**rep·ro·ba·tion** \,rep-rə-'bā-shən\ *n* : strong disapproval : CONDEMNATION

**re·pro·duce** \,rē-prə-'d(y)üs\ *vb* **1** : to produce again or anew **2** : to bear offspring — **re·pro·duc·ible** \-'d(y)üs-ə-bəl\ *adj* — **re·pro·duc·tion** \-'dək-shən\ *n* — **re·pro·duc·tive** \-'dək-tiv\ *adj*

**re·proof** \ri-'prüf\ *n* : blame or censure for a fault

**re·prove** \ri-'prüv\ *vb* **re·proved**; **re·prov·ing 1** : to administer a rebuke to **2** : to express disapproval of **syn** reprimand, admonish, reproach, chide — **re·prov·er** *n*

**rept** *abbr* report

**rep·tile** \'rep-t²l, -,tīl\ *n* [ME *reptil*, fr. MF or LL; MF *reptile* fr. LL *reptile*

fr. L *repere* to creep] : any of a large group of air-breathing scaly vertebrates including snakes, lizards, alligators, and turtles — **rep·til·i·an** \rep-'til-ē-ən\ *adj or n*

**re·pub·lic** \ri-'pəb-lik\ *n* [F *république*, fr. MF *republique*, fr. L *respublica*, fr. *res* thing, wealth + *publica*, fem. of *publicus* public] **1** : a government having a chief of state who is not a monarch and is usu. a president; *also* : a nation or other political unit having such a government **2** : a government in which supreme power is held by the citizens entitled to vote and is exercised by elected officers and representatives governing according to law; *also* : a nation or other political unit having such a form of government

**¹re·pub·li·can** \-li-kən\ *adj* **1** : of, relating to, or resembling a republic **2** : favoring or supporting a republic **3** *cap* : of, relating to, or constituting one of the two major political parties in the U.S. evolving in the mid-19th century — **re·pub·li·can·ism** *n, often cap*

**²republican** *n* **1** : one that favors or supports a republican form of government **2** *cap* : a member of a republican party and esp. of the Republican party of the U.S.

**re·pu·di·ate** \ri-'pyüd-ē-,āt\ *vb* **-at·ed; -at·ing** [L *repudiare* to cast off, divorce, fr. *repudium* divorce] **1** : to cast off : DISOWN **2** : to refuse to have anything to do with : refuse to acknowledge, accept, or pay ⟨~ a charge⟩ ⟨~ a debt⟩ **syn** spurn, reject, decline — **re·pu·di·a·tion** \-,pyüd-ē-'ā-shən\ *n* — **re·pu·di·a·tor** \-'pyüd-ē-,āt-ər\ *n*

**re·pug·nance** \ri-'pəg-nəns\ *n* **1** : the quality or fact of being contradictory or inconsistent **2** : strong dislike, distaste, or antagonism

**re·pug·nant** \-nənt\ *adj* **1** : marked by repugnance **2** : contrary to a person's tastes or principles : exciting distaste or aversion **syn** repellent, abhorrent, distasteful, obnoxious, revolting, offensive, loathsome — **re·pug·nant·ly** *adv*

**¹re·pulse** \ri-'pəls\ *vb* **re·pulsed**; **re·puls·ing 1** : to drive or beat back : REPEL **2** : to repel by discourtesy or denial : REBUFF **3** : to cause a feeling of repulsion in : DISGUST

**²repulse** *n* **1** : REBUFF, REJECTION **2** : a repelling or being repelled in hostile encounter

**re·pul·sion** \ri-'pəl-shən\ *n* **1** : the action of repulsing : the state of being repulsed **2** : the force with which bodies, particles, or like forces repel one another **3** : a feeling of aversion

**re·pul·sive** \-siv\ *adj* **1** : serving or tending to repel or reject **2** : arousing aversion or disgust **syn** repugnant, revolting, loathsome — **re·pul·sive·ly** *adv* — **re·pul·sive·ness** *n*

**rep·u·ta·ble** \'rep-yət-ə-bəl\ *adj* : having a good reputation : ESTIMABLE — **rep·u·ta·bly** \-blē\ *adv*

**rep·u·ta·tion** \,rep-yə-'tā-shən\ *n* **1** : overall quality or character as seen or judged by people in general **2** : place in public esteem or regard

¹**re·pute** \ri-'pyüt\ *vb* **re·put·ed; re·put·ing** : CONSIDER, ACCOUNT

²**repute** *n* **1** : the character commonly ascribed to one **2** : the state of being favorably known or spoken of

**re·put·ed** \ri-'pyüt-əd\ *adj* **1** : REPUTABLE **2** : according to reputation : SUPPOSED — **re·put·ed·ly** *adv*

**req** *abbr* **1** require; required **2** requisition

¹**re·quest** \ri-'kwest\ *n* **1** : an act or instance of asking for something **2** : a thing asked for **3** : the fact or condition of being asked for ⟨available on ∼⟩

²**request** *vb* **1** : to make a request to or of **2** : to ask for — **re·quest·er** *n*

**re·qui·em** \'rek-wē-əm, 'rāk-\ *n* [ME, fr. L (first word of the requiem mass), acc. of *requies* rest, fr. *quies* quiet, rest] **1** : a mass for a dead person; *also* : a musical setting for this **2** : a musical service or hymn in honor of the dead

**re·quire** \ri-'kwī(ə)r\ *vb* **re·quired; re·quir·ing** **1** : to insist upon : DEMAND **2** : to call for as essential

**re·quire·ment** \-mənt\ *n* **1** : something (as a condition or quality) required ⟨entrance ∼⟩ **2** : NECESSITY

**req·ui·site** \'rek-wə-zət\ *adj* : REQUIRED, NECESSARY — **req·uisite** *n*

**req·ui·si·tion** \,rek-wə-'zish-ən\ *n* **1** : formal application or demand (as for supplies) **2** : the state of being in demand or use — **requisition** *vb*

**re·quite** \ri-'kwīt\ *vb* **re·quit·ed; re·quit·ing** **1** : to make return for : REPAY **2** : to make retaliation for : AVENGE **3** : to make return to for a benefit or service or for an injury — **re·quit·al** \-'kwīt-²l\ *n*

**rere·dos** \'rer-ə-,däs\ *n* : a usu. ornamental wood or stone screen or partition wall behind an altar

**re·run** \'rē-,rən, 'rē-'rən\ *n* : the act or an instance of running again or anew; *esp* : a showing of a motion picture or television film after its first run — **rerun** \'rē-'rən\ *vb*

**res** *abbr* **1** research **2** reserve **3** residence **4** resolution

**re·sale** \'rē-,sāl, -'sāl\ *n* : the act of selling again usu. to a new party — **re·sal·able** \'rē-'sā-lə-bəl\ *adj*

**re·scind** \ri-'sind\ *vb* : REPEAL, CANCEL, ANNUL — **re·scind·er** *n* — **re·scis·sion** \-'sizh-ən\ *n*

**re·script** \'rē-,skript\ *n* : an official or authoritative order or decree

**res·cue** \'res-kyü\ *vb* **res·cued; res·cu·ing** [ME *rescuen*, fr. MF *rescourre*, fr. OF, fr. *re-* re- + *escourre* to shake out, fr. L *excutere*, fr. *ex-* out + *quatere* to shake] : to free from danger, harm, or confinement **syn** deliver, redeem, ransom, reclaim, save — **res·cue** *n* — **res·cu·er** *n*

**re·search** \ri-'sərch, 'rē-,sərch\ *n* **1** : careful or diligent search **2** : studious and critical inquiry and examination aimed at the discovery and inter-

pretation of new knowledge — **re·search** *vb* — **re·search·er** *n*

**re·sec·tion** \ri-'sek-shən\ *n* : the surgical removal of part of an organ or structure

**re·sem·blance** \ri-'zem-bləns\ *n* : the quality or state of resembling

**re·sem·ble** \ri-'zem-bəl\ *vb* **re·sem·bled; re·sem·bling** \-b(ə-)liŋ\ : to be like or similar to

**re·sent** \ri-'zent\ *vb* : to feel or exhibit annoyance or indignation at — **re·sent·ful** \-fəl\ *adj* — **re·sent·ful·ly** \-ē\ *adv* — **re·sent·ment** *n*

**re·ser·pine** \ri-'sər-,pēn, -pən\ *n* : a drug obtained from rauwolfia and used in treating high blood pressure and nervous tension

**res·er·va·tion** \,rez-ər-'vā-shən\ *n* **1** : an act of reserving **2** : something reserved; *esp* : a tract of public land set aside for a special use **3** : something (as a room in a hotel) arranged for in advance **4** : a limiting condition

¹**re·serve** \ri-'zərv\ *vb* **re·served; re·serv·ing** **1** : to store for future or special use **2** : to hold back for oneself **3** : to set aside or arrange to have set aside or held for special use

²**reserve** *n* **1** : something reserved : STOCK, STORE **2** : a tract set apart : RESERVATION **3** : a military force withheld from action for later decisive use — usu. used in pl. **4** : the military forces of a country not part of the regular services; *also* : RESERVIST **5** : an act of reserving : a state of being reserved **6** : restraint, caution, or closeness in one's words or bearing **7** : money or its equivalent kept in hand or set apart to meet liabilities

**re·served** \ri-'zərvd\ *adj* **1** : restrained in words and actions **2** : set aside for future or special use — **re·serv·ed·ly** \-'zər-vəd-lē\ *adv* — **re·serv·ed·ness** \-vəd-nəs\ *n*

**re·serv·ist** \ri-'zər-vəst\ *n* : a member of a military reserve

**res·er·voir** \'rez-ə(r)v-,wär, -ə(r)v-,(w)ȯr, -ər-,vȯi\ *n* : a place where something is kept in store; *esp* : a place where water is collected and kept for use when wanted (as by a city)

**re·shuf·fle** \rē-'shəf-əl\ *vb* **1** : to shuffle again **2** : to reorganize usu. by redistribution of existing elements — **reshuffle** *n*

**re·side** \ri-'zīd\ *vb* **re·sid·ed; re·sid·ing** **1** : to make one's home : DWELL **2** : to be present as a quality or vested as a right

**res·i·dence** \'rez-əd-əns\ *n* **1** : the act or fact of residing in a place as a dweller or in discharge of a duty or an obligation **2** : the place where one actually lives **3** : a building used as a home : DWELLING **4** : the period of living in a place

**res·i·den·cy** \'rez-əd-ən-sē\ *n*, *pl* **-cies** **1** : the residence of or the territory under a diplomatic resident **2** : a period of advanced training in a medical specialty

¹**res·i·dent** \-ənt\ *adj* **1** : RESIDING

**2** : being in residence **3** : not migratory

²**resident** n **1** : one who resides in a place **2** : a diplomatic representative with governing powers (as in a protectorate) **3** : a physician serving a residency

**res·i·den·tial** \,rez-ə-'den-chəl\ adj **1** : used as a residence or by residents **2** : occupied by or restricted to residences — **res·i·den·tial·ly** \-ē\ adv

¹**re·sid·u·al** \ri-'zij-(ə-w)əl\ adj : being a residue or remainder

²**residual** n **1** : a residual product or substance **2** : a payment (as to an actor or writer) for each rerun after an initial showing (as of a taped TV show)

**re·sid·u·ary** \ri-'zij-ə-,wer-ē\ adj : of, relating to, or constituting a residue esp. of an estate

**res·i·due** \'rez-ə-,d(y)ü\ n : a part remaining after another part has been taken away : REMAINDER

**re·sid·u·um** \ri-'zij-ə-wəm\ n, pl **re·sid·ua** \-ə-wə\ **1** : something remaining or residual after certain deductions are made **2** : a residual product **syn** remainder, rest, balance, remnant

**re·sign** \ri-'zīn\ vb [ME resignen, fr. MF resigner, fr. L resignare, lit., to unseal, cancel, fr. signare to sign, seal] **1** : to give up deliberately (as one's position) esp. by a formal act **2** : to give (oneself) over (as to grief or despair) without resistance

**res·ig·na·tion** \,rez-ig-'nā-shən\ n **1** : an act or instance of resigning; also : a formal notification of such an act **2** : the quality or state of being resigned

**re·signed** \ri-'zīnd\ adj : SUBMISSIVE — **re·sign·ed·ly** \-'zī-nəd-lē\ adv

**re·sil·ience** \ri-'zil-yəns\ n : an ability to recover from or adjust easily to change or misfortune

**re·sil·ien·cy** \-yən-sē\ n : RESILIENCE

**re·sil·ient** \-yənt\ adj : ELASTIC, SPRINGY **syn** flexible, supple

**res·in** \'rez-ᵊn\ n : a substance obtained from the gum or sap of some trees and used esp. in varnishes, plastics, and medicine; also : a comparable synthetic product — **res·in·ous** adj

¹**re·sist** \ri-'zist\ vb **1** : to withstand the force or effect of ⟨~ disease⟩ **2** : to fight against : OPPOSE ⟨~ aggression⟩ **syn** combat, withstand, antagonize — **re·sist·ible** or **re·sist·able** \-'zis-tə-bəl\ adj — **re·sist·less** adj

²**resist** n : something (as a coating) that resists or prevents a particular action

**re·sis·tance** \ri-'zis-təns\ n **1** : the act or an instance of resisting : OPPOSITION **2** : the opposition offered by a body to the passage through it of a steady electric current

**re·sis·tant** \-tənt\ adj : giving or capable of resistance

**re·sis·tiv·i·ty** \ri-,zis-'tiv-ət-ē, ,rē-\ n, pl -ties : capacity for resisting

**re·sis·tor** \ri-'zis-tər\ n : a device used to provide resistance to the flow of an electric current

**res·o·lute** \'rez-ə-,lüt\ adj : firmly determined in purpose : RESOLVED **syn**

steadfast, staunch, faithful, true, loyal — **res·o·lute·ly** adv — **res·o·lute·ness** n

**res·o·lu·tion** \,rez-ə-'lü-shən\ n **1** : the act or process of resolving **2** : the action of solving ; also : SOLUTION **3** : the quality of being resolute : FIRMNESS, DETERMINATION **4** : a formal statement expressing the opinion, will, or intent of a body of persons

¹**re·solve** \ri-'zälv\ vb **re·solved**; **re·solv·ing 1** : to break up into constituent parts : ANALYZE **2** : to find an answer to : SOLVE **3** : DETERMINE, DECIDE **4** : to make or pass a formal resolution — **re·solv·able** adj

²**resolve** n **1** : something resolved : RESOLUTION **2** : fixity of purpose

**res·o·nance** \'rez-ᵊn-əns\ n **1** : the quality or state of being resonant **2** : the prolongation or increase of sound in one body caused by sound waves from another vibrating body

**res·o·nant** \'rez-ᵊn-ənt\ adj **1** : continuing to sound : RESOUNDING **2** : relating to or exhibiting resonance **3** : intensified and enriched by or as if by resonance — **res·o·nant·ly** adv

**res·o·nate** \'rez-ᵊn-,āt\ vb **-nat·ed**; **-nat·ing 1** : to produce or exhibit resonance **2** : REECHO, RESOUND

**res·o·na·tor** \-ᵊn-,āt-ər\ n : something that resounds or exhibits resonance

**re·sorp·tion** \rē-'sȯrp-shən, -'zȯrp-\ n : the action or process of breaking down and assimilating something (as a tooth or an embryo)

¹**re·sort** \ri-'zȯrt\ n [ME, fr. MF, resource, recourse, fr. resortir to rebound, resort, fr. OF, fr. sortir to escape, sally] **1** : one looked to for help : REFUGE **2** : RECOURSE **3** : frequent or general visiting ⟨place of ~⟩ **4** : a frequently visited place : HAUNT **5** : a place providing recreation esp. to vacationers

²**resort** vb **1** : to go often or habitually **2** : to have recourse (as for aid)

**re·sort·er** \ri-'zȯrt-ər\ n : a frequenter of resorts

**re·sound** \ri-'zaund\ vb **1** : to become filled with sound : REVERBERATE, RING **2** : to sound loudly

**re·sound·ing** \-iŋ\ adj **1** : RESONATING, RESONANT **2** : impressively sonorous ⟨~ name⟩ **3** : EMPHATIC, UNEQUIVOCAL ⟨a ~ success⟩ — **re·sound·ing·ly** adv

**re·source** \'rē-,sȯrs, ri-'sȯrs\ n [F ressource, fr. OF ressourse relief, resource, fr. resourdre to relieve, lit., to rise again, fr. L resurgere, fr. re- again + surgere to rise] **1** : a new or a reserve source of supply or support **2** pl : available funds **3** : a possibility of relief or recovery **4** : a means of spending leisure time **5** : ability to meet and handle situations — **re·source·ful** adj — **re·source·ful·ness** n

**resp** abbr respective; respectively

¹**re·spect** \ri-'spekt\ n **1** : relation to something usu. specified : REFERENCE, REGARD **2** : high or special regard : ESTEEM **3** pl : an expression of respect

or deference **4 :** DETAIL, PARTICULAR — re·spect·ful \-fəl\ *adj* — re·spect·ful·ly \-ē\ *adv* — re·spect·ful·ness *n*

²respect *vb* **1 :** to consider deserving of high regard **:** ESTEEM **2 :** to refrain from interfering with ⟨~ another's privacy⟩ **3 :** to have reference to **:** CONCERN — re·spect·er *n*

re·spect·a·ble \ri-'spek-tə-bəl\ *adj* **1 :** worthy of respect **:** ESTIMABLE **2 :** decent or correct in conduct **:** PROPER **3 :** fair in size, quantity, or quality **:** MODERATE, TOLERABLE **4 :** fit to be seen **:** PRESENTABLE — re·spect·a·bil·i·ty \-,spek-tə-'bil-ət-ē\ *n* — re·spect·ably \-'spek-tə-blē\ *adv*

re·spect·ing \-tiŋ\ *prep* **:** with regard to

re·spec·tive \-tiv\ *adj* **:** PARTICULAR, SEPARATE ⟨returned to their ~ homes⟩ syn individual, special, specific

re·spec·tive·ly \-lē\ *adv* **1 :** as relating to each **2 :** each in the order given

res·pi·ra·tion \,res-pə-'rā-shən\ *n* **1 :** an act or the process of breathing **2 :** an energy-yielding oxidation in living matter — re·spi·ra·to·ry \'res-p(ə-)rə-,tōr-ē, ri-'spī-rə-\ *adj* — re·spire \ri-'spī(ə)r\ *vb*

res·pi·ra·tor \'res-pə-,rāt-ər\ *n* **1 :** a device covering the mouth or nose esp. to prevent the inhaling of harmful vapors **2 :** a device for artificial respiration

re·spite \'res-pət\ *n* **1 :** a temporary delay **2 :** an interval of rest or relief

re·splen·dent \ri-'splen-dənt\ *adj* **:** shining brilliantly **:** gloriously bright **:** SPLENDID — re·splen·dence \-dəns\ *n* — re·splen·dent·ly *adv*

re·spond \ri-'spänd\ *vb* **1 :** ANSWER, REPLY **2 :** REACT ⟨~ to a stimulus⟩ **3 :** to show favorable reaction ⟨~ to medication⟩ — re·spond·er *n*

re·spon·dent \ri-'spän-dənt\ *n* **:** one who responds; *esp* **:** one who answers in various legal proceedings — respondent *adj*

re·sponse \ri-'späns\ *n* **1 :** an act of responding **2 :** something constituting a reply or a reaction

re·spon·si·bil·i·ty \ri-,spän-sə-'bil-ət-ē\ *n*, *pl* -ties **1 :** the quality or state of being responsible **2 :** something for which one is responsible

re·spon·si·ble \ri-'spän-sə-bəl\ *adj* **1 :** liable to be called upon to answer for one's acts or decisions **:** ANSWERABLE **2 :** able to fulfill one's obligations **:** RELIABLE, TRUSTWORTHY **3 :** able to choose for oneself between right and wrong **4 :** involving accountability or important duties ⟨~ position⟩ — re·spon·si·ble·ness *n* — re·spon·si·bly \-blē\ *adv*

re·spon·sive \-siv\ *adj* **1 :** RESPONDING **2 :** quick to respond **:** SENSITIVE **3 :** using responses ⟨~ readings⟩ — re·spon·sive·ly *adv* — re·spon·sive·ness *n* or device

¹rest \'rest\ *n* **1 :** REPOSE, SLEEP **2 :** freedom from work or activity **3 :** a

state of motionlessness or inactivity **4 :** a place of shelter or lodging **5 :** something used as a support **6 :** a silence in music equivalent in duration to a note of the same value; *also* **:** a character indicating this — rest·ful \-fəl\ *adj* — rest·ful·ly \-ē\ *adv*

²rest *vb* **1 :** to get rest by lying down; *esp* **:** SLEEP **2 :** to cease from action or motion **3 :** to give rest to **:** set at rest **4 :** to sit or lie fixed or supported **5 :** to place on or against a support **6 :** to remain based or founded **7 :** to cause to be firmly fixed **:** GROUND **8 :** to remain for action **:** DEPEND

³rest *n* **:** something that remains over

res·tau·rant \'res-t(ə-)rənt, -tə-,ränt\ *n* [F, fr. prp. of *restaurer* to restore, fr. L *restaurare*] **:** a public eating place

res·tau·ra·teur \,res-tə-rə-'tər\ *also* res·tau·ran·teur \-,rän-\ *n* **:** the operator or proprietor of a restaurant

rest home *n* **:** an establishment that provides care for the aged or convalescent

res·ti·tu·tion \,res-tə-'t(y)ü-shən\ *n* **:** the act of restoring **:** the state of being restored; *esp* **:** restoration of something to its rightful owner syn amends, redress, reparation, indemnity

res·tive \'res-tiv\ *adj* [ME, fr. MF *restif*, fr. *rester* to stop behind, remain, fr. L *restare*, fr. *re-* back + *stare* to stand] **1 :** BALKY **2 :** UNEASY, FIDGETY syn restless, impatient, nervous — res·tive·ly *adv* — res·tive·ness *n*

rest·less \'rest-ləs\ *adj* **1 :** lacking rest **2 :** giving no rest **3 :** never resting or ceasing **:** UNQUIET ⟨the ~ sea⟩ **4 :** lacking in repose **:** averse to inaction **:** DISCONTENTED syn restive, impatient, nervous, fidgety — rest·less·ly *adv* — rest·less·ness *n*

re·stor·able \ri-'stōr-ə-bəl\ *adj* **:** fit for restoring or reclaiming

res·to·ra·tion \,res-tə-'rā-shən\ *n* **1 :** an act of restoring **:** the state of being restored **2 :** something that is restored; *esp* **:** a reconstruction or representation of an original form (as of a building)

re·stor·a·tive \ri-'stōr-ət-iv\ *n* **:** something that restores esp. to consciousness or health — restorative *adj*

re·store \ri-'stōr\ *vb* re·stored; re·stor·ing **1 :** to give back **:** RETURN **2 :** to put back into use or service **3 :** to put or bring back into a former or original state **:** REPAIR, RENEW **4 :** to put again in possession of something — re·stor·er *n*

re·strain \ri-'strān\ *vb* **1 :** to prevent from doing something **2 :** to limit, restrict, or keep under control **:** CURB **3 :** to place under restraint or arrest — re·strain·able *adj* — re·strain·er *n*

re·strained \ri-'strānd\ *adj* **:** marked by restraint **:** DISCIPLINED — re·strain·ed·ly \-'strā-nəd-lē\ *adv*

re·straint \ri-'strānt\ *n* **1 :** an act of restraining **:** the state of being restrained **2 :** a restraining force, agency, or device **3 :** deprivation or limitation of liberty **:** CONFINEMENT **4 :** control over one's feelings **:** RESERVE

**re·strict** \ri-'strikt\ *vb* **1 :** to confine within bounds **:** LIMIT **2 :** to place under restriction as to use — **re·stric·tive** *adj* — **re·stric·tive·ly** *adv*

**re·stric·tion** \ri-'strik-shən\ *n* **1 :** something (as a law or rule) that restricts **2 :** an act of restricting **:** the state of being restricted

**rest room** *n* **:** a room or suite of rooms providing personal facilities (as toilets)

¹**re·sult** \ri-'zəlt\ *vb* [ME *resulten*, fr. ML *resultare*, fr. L, to rebound, fr. *re-* + *saltare* to leap] **:** to proceed or come about as an effect or consequence — **re·sul·tant** \-'zəlt-ᵊnt\ *adj or n*

²**result** *n* **1 :** something that results **:** EFFECT, CONSEQUENCE **2 :** beneficial or discernible effect **3 :** something obtained by calculation or investigation

**re·sume** \ri-'züm\ *vb* **re·sumed; re·sum·ing 1 :** to take or assume again **2 :** to return to or begin again after interruption **3 :** to take back to oneself — **re·sump·tion** \-'zəmp-shən\ *n*

**ré·su·mé** *or* **re·su·me** *or* **re·su·mé** \'rez-ə-ˌmā, ˌrez-ə-'\ *n* **:** SUMMARY; *esp* **:** a short account of one's career and qualifications prepared typically by an applicant for a position

**re·sur·gence** \ri-'sər-jəns\ *n* **:** a rising again into life, activity, or prominence — **re·sur·gent** \-jənt\ *adj*

**res·ur·rect** \ˌrez-ə-'rekt\ *vb* **1 :** to raise from the dead **2 :** to bring to attention or use again

**res·ur·rec·tion** \ˌrez-ə-'rek-shən\ *n* **1** *cap* **:** the rising of Christ from the dead **2** *often cap* **:** the rising to life of all human dead before the final judgment **3 :** REVIVAL

**re·sus·ci·tate** \ri-'səs-ə-ˌtāt\ *vb* **-tat·ed; -tat·ing :** to revive from a condition resembling death — **re·sus·ci·ta·tion** \ri-ˌsəs-ə-'tā-shən, ˌrē-\ *n* — **re·sus·ci·ta·tor** \-ˌtāt-ər\ *n*

**ret** *abbr* **1** retain **2** retired **3** return

¹**re·tail** \'rē-ˌtāl, *esp for 2 also* ri-'tāl\ *vb* **1 :** to sell in small quantities directly to the ultimate consumer **2 :** to tell in detail or to one person after another — **re·tail·er** *n*

²**re·tail** \'rē-ˌtāl\ *n* **:** the sale of goods in small amounts to ultimate consumers — **retail** *adj or adv*

**re·tain** \ri-'tān\ *vb* **1 :** to keep in a fixed place or position **2 :** to hold in possession or use **3 :** to engage (as a lawyer) by paying a fee in advance **syn** detain, withhold, reserve

**re·tain·er** \-ər\ *n* **1 :** one that retains **2 :** a servant in a wealthy household; *also* **:** EMPLOYEE **3 :** a fee paid to secure services (as of a lawyer)

¹**re·take** \'rē-ˈtāk\ *vb* **-took** \-ˈtùk\; **-tak·en** \-ˈtā-kən\; **-tak·ing 1 :** to take or seize again **2 :** to photograph again

²**re·take** \'rē-ˌtāk\ *n* **:** a second photograph of a motion-picture scene

**re·tal·i·ate** \ri-'tal-ē-ˌāt\ *vb* **-at·ed; -at·ing :** to return like for like; *esp* **:** to get revenge — **re·tal·i·a·tion** \-ˌtal-ē-'ā-shən\ *n* — **re·tal·i·a·to·ry** \-'tal-yə-ˌtōr-ē\ *adj*

**re·tard** \ri-'tärd\ *vb* **:** to hold back **:** delay the progress of **syn** slow, slacken, detain — **re·tar·da·tion** \ˌrē-ˌtär-'dā-shən, ri-\ *n* — **re·tard·er** *n*

**re·tar·date** \-'tärd-ˌāt, -ət\ *n* **:** a mentally retarded person

**re·tard·ed** \ri-'tärd-əd\ *adj* **:** slow or limited in intellectual development, in emotional development, or in academic progress ⟨a ~ child⟩

**retch** \'rech, 'rēch\ *vb* **:** to try to vomit

**retd** *abbr* **1** retained **2** retired **3** returned

**re·ten·tion** \ri-'ten-chən\ *n* **1 :** the act of retaining **:** the state of being retained **2 :** the power of retaining esp. in the mind **:** RETENTIVENESS

**re·ten·tive** \-'tent-iv\ *adj* **:** having the power of retaining; *esp* **:** retaining knowledge easily — **re·ten·tive·ness** *n*

**ret·i·cent** \'ret-ə-sənt\ *adj* **:** inclined to be silent or secretive **:** UNCOMMUNICATIVE **syn** reserved, taciturn — **ret·i·cence** \-səns\ *n* — **ret·i·cent·ly** *adv*

**ret·i·na** \'ret-ᵊn-ə\ *n, pl* **retinas** *or* **ret·i·nae** \-ᵊn-ˌē\ **:** the sensory membrane lining the eye and receiving the image formed by the lens — **ret·i·nal** \'ret-ᵊn-əl\ *adj*

**ret·i·nue** \'ret-ᵊn-ˌ(y)ü\ *n* **:** the body of attendants or followers of a distinguished person

**re·tire** \ri-'tī(ə)r\ *vb* **re·tired; re·tir·ing 1 :** RETREAT **2 :** to withdraw esp. for privacy **3 :** to withdraw from one's occupation or position **4 :** to go to bed **5 :** to withdraw from circulation or from the market or from usual use or service **6 :** to cause to be out in baseball — **re·tire·ment** *n*

**re·tired** \ri-'tī(ə)rd\ *adj* **1 :** SECLUDED, QUIET **2 :** withdrawn from active duty or from one's occupation **3 :** received by or due to one who has retired

**re·tir·ee** \ri-ˌtī-'rē\ *n* **:** a person who has retired from his occupation

**re·tir·ing** \ri-'tī(ə)r-iŋ\ *adj* **:** SHY, RESERVED

¹**re·tort** \ri-'tòrt\ *vb* [L *retortus*, pp. of *retorquēre*, lit., to twist back, hurl back, fr. *re-* back + *torquēre* to twist] **1 :** to say in reply **:** answer back usu. sharply **2 :** to answer (an argument) by a counter argument **3 :** RETALIATE

²**retort** *n* **:** a quick, witty, or cutting reply

³**re·tort** \ri-'tòrt, 'rē-ˌtòrt\ *n* [MF *retorte*, fr. ML *retorta*, fr. L, fem. of *retortus*, pp. of *retorquēre* to twist back; fr. its shape] **:** a vessel in which substances are distilled or broken up by heat

**re·touch** \'rē-'təch\ *vb* **:** to touch or treat again (as a picture, film, or essay) in an effort to improve

**re·trace** \(')rē-'trās\ *vb* **1 :** to trace over again **2 :** to go over again in a reverse direction ⟨*retraced* his steps⟩

**re·tract** \ri-'trakt\ *vb* **1 :** to draw back or in **2 :** to withdraw (as a charge or promise) **:** DISAVOW — **re·tract·able** *adj* — **re·trac·tion** \-'trak-shən\ *n*

**re·trac·tile** \ri-'trak-tᵊl, -ˌtīl\ *adj* **:** capable of being drawn back or in ⟨~ claws⟩

¹re·tread \'rē-'tred\ vb re·tread·ed; re·tread·ing : to put a new tread on the bare cord fabric of (a tire)

²re·tread \'rē,tred\ n 1 : a new tread on a tire 2 : a retreaded tire 3 : one pressed into service again; also : RE-MAKE

¹re·treat \ri-'trēt\ n 1 : an act of withdrawing esp. from something dangerous, difficult, or disagreeable 2 : a military signal for withdrawal; also : a military flag-lowering ceremony 3 : a place of privacy or safety : REFUGE 4 : a period of group withdrawal for prayer, meditation, and study

²retreat vb : to make a retreat : WITH-DRAW; also : to slope backward

re·trench \ri-'trench\ vb [obs. F retrencher (now retrancher), fr. MF retrenchier, fr. re- + trenchier to cut] 1 : to cut down or pare away : REDUCE, CURTAIL ~ : to cut down expenses : ECONOMIZE — re·trench·ment n

ret·ri·bu·tion \,re-trə-'byü-shən\ n : something administered or exacted in recompense; esp : PUNISHMENT syn reprisal, vengeance, revenge, retaliation — re·trib·u·tive \ri-'trib-yət-iv\ adj — re·trib·u·to·ry \-yə-,tōr-ē\ adj

re·trieve \ri-'trēv\ vb re·trieved; re·triev·ing 1 : to search about for and bring in (killed or wounded game) 2 : RECOVER, RESTORE re·triev·able adj — re·triev·al \-'trē-vəl\ n

re·triev·er \ri-'trē-vər\ n : one that retrieves; esp : a dog bred or trained for retrieving game

ret·ro·ac·tive \,re-trō-'ak-tiv\ adj : made effective as of a date prior to enactment (a ~ pay raise) — ret·ro·ac·tive·ly adv

ret·ro·fire \'re-trō-,fī(ə)r\ vb : to ignite a retro-rocket — retrofire n

ret·ro·fit \,re-trō-'fit\ vb : to furnish (as an aircraft) with newly available equipment

¹ret·ro·grade \'re-trə-,grād\ adj 1 : moving or tending backward 2 : tending toward or resulting in a worse condition

²retrograde vb 1 : RETREAT 2 : DE-TERIORATE, DEGENERATE

ret·ro·gress \,re-trə-'gres\ vb : to move backward : DECLINE — ret·ro·gres·sion \,re-trə-'gresh-ən\ n

ret·ro·rock·et \'re-trō-,räk-ət\ n : an auxiliary rocket on an airplane, missile, or spacecraft that produces thrust for decelerating

ret·ro·spect \'re-trə-,spekt\ n : a review of past events — ret·ro·spec·tion \,re-trə-'spek-shən\ n — ret·ro·spec·tive \-'spek-tiv\ adj — ret·ro·spec·tive·ly adv

¹re·turn \ri-'tərn\ vb 1 : to go or come back 2 : to pass, give, or send back to an earlier possessor 3 : to put back to or in a former place or state 4 : REPLY, ANSWER 5 : to report esp. officially 6 : to elect (a candidate) as shown by an official report 7 : to bring in (as profit) : YIELD 8 : to give or perform in return — re·turn·able adj — re·turn·er n

²return n 1 : an act of coming or going back to or from a former place or state 2 : RECURRENCE 3 : a report of the results of balloting 4 : a formal statement of taxable income 5 : the act of returning something 6 : something that returns or is returned; also : a means (as a pipe) of returning 7 : the profit from labor, investment, or business : YIELD 8 : something given in repayment or reciprocation; also : AN-SWER, RETORT 9 : an answering play — return adj

re·turn·ee \ri-,tər-'nē\ n : one who returns; esp : one returning to the U.S. after military service abroad

re·union \rē-'yü-nyən\ n 1 : an act of reuniting : the state of being reunited 2 : a meeting again of persons who have been separated

¹rev \'rev\ n : a revolution of a motor

²rev vb revved; rev·ving : to increase the number of revolutions per minute of (a motor)

³rev abbr 1 revenue 2 reverse 3 review; reviewed 4 revised; revision 5 revolution

Rev abbr 1 Revelation 2 Reverend

re·vamp \(')rē-'vamp\ vb : RECON-STRUCT, REVISE; esp : to give a new form to old materials

re·vanche \rə-'väⁿsh\ n : REVENGE; esp : a usu. political policy designed to recover lost territory or status

re·veal \ri-'vēl\ vb 1 : to make known 2 : to show plainly : open up to view

rev·eil·le \'rev-ə-lē\ n [modif. of F réveillez, imper. pl. of réveiller to awaken, fr. éveiller to awaken, fr. (assumed) VL exvigilare, fr. L vigilare to keep watch, stay awake] : a military signal sounded at about sunrise

¹rev·el \'rev-əl\ vb -eled or -elled; -el·ing or -el·ling \-(ə-)liŋ\ 1 : to take part in a revel 2 : to take great delight — rev·el·er or rev·el·ler \-ər\ n — rev·el·ry \-əl-rē\ n

²revel n : a usu. wild party or celebration

rev·e·la·tion \,rev-ə-'lā-shən\ n 1 : an act of revealing 2 : something revealed; esp : an enlightening or astonishing disclosure

re·venge \ri-'venj\ vb re·venged; re·veng·ing : to inflict harm or injury in return for (a wrong) : AVENGE — re·veng·er n

²revenge n 1 : the act of revenging 2 : a desire to return evil for evil 3 : an opportunity for getting satisfaction syn vengeance, retaliation, retribution — re·venge·ful adj

rev·e·nue \'rev-ə-,n(y)ü\ n [ME, fr. MF, fr. revenir to return, fr. L revenire, fr. re- back + venire to come] 1 : investment income 2 : money collected by a government (as through taxes)

rev·e·nu·er \'rev-ə-,n(y)ü-ər\ n : a revenue officer or boat

re·verb \ri-'vərb, 'rē-,vərb\ n : an electronically produced echo effect in recorded music; also : a device for producing reverb

re·ver·ber·ate \ri-'vər-bə-,rāt\ vb -at·ed; -at·ing 1 : REFLECT ⟨~ light or heat⟩  **2 :** to resound in or as if in a series of echoes — **re·ver·ber·a·tion** \-ˌvər-bə-'rā-shən\ *n*

¹**re·vere** \ri-'vir\ *vb* **re·vered; re·ver·ing :** to show honor and devotion to **:** VENERATE **syn** reverence, worship, adore

²**revere** *n* **:** REVERS

¹**rev·er·ence** \ rev-(ə-)rəns\ *n* **1 :** honor and respect mixed with love and awe **2 :** a sign (as a bow or curtsy) of respect

²**reverence** *vb* **-enced; -enc·ing :** to regard or treat with reverence

¹**rev·er·end** \-rənd\ *adj* **1 :** worthy of reverence **:** REVERED **2 :** being a member of the clergy — used as a title

²**reverend** *n* **:** a member of the clergy

**rev·er·ent** \-rənt\ *adj* **:** expressing reverence — **rev·er·ent·ly** *adv*

**rev·er·en·tial** \ˌrev-ə-'ren-chəl\ *adj* **:** REVERENT

**rev·er·ie** *or* **rev·ery** \'rev-(ə-)rē\ *n, pl* **rev·er·ies 1 :** DAYDREAM **2 :** the state of being lost in thought

**re·vers** \ri-'vir, -'veər\ *n, pl* **re·vers** \-'virz, -'veərz\ **:** a lapel esp. on a woman's garment

**re·ver·sal** \ri-'vər-səl\ *n* **:** an act or process of reversing

¹**re·verse** \ri-'vərs\ *adj* **1 :** opposite to a previous or normal condition **2 :** acting or operating in a manner opposite or contrary **3 :** effecting reverse movement — **re·verse·ly** *adv*

²**reverse** *vb* **re·versed; re·vers·ing 1 :** to turn upside down or completely about in position or direction **2 :** to set aside or change (as a legal decision) **3 :** to change to the contrary ⟨~ a policy⟩ **4 :** to turn or move in the opposite direction **5 :** to put a mechanism (as an engine) in reverse — **re·vers·ible** \-'vər-sə-bəl\ *adj*

³**reverse** *n* **1 :** something contrary to something else **:** OPPOSITE **2 :** an act or instance of reversing; *esp* **:** a change for the worse **3 :** the back of something **4 :** a gear that reverses something

**re·ver·sion** \ri-'vər-zhən\ *n* **1 :** the right of succession or future possession (as to a title or property) **2 :** return toward some former or ancestral condition; *also* **:** a product of this — **re·ver·sion·ary** \-zhə-ˌner-ē\ *adj*

**re·vert** \ri-'vərt\ *vb* **1 :** to come or go back ⟨~ed to savagery⟩ **2 :** to return to a proprietor or his heirs **3 :** to return to an ancestral type

¹**re·view** \ri-'vyü\ *n* **1 :** an act of revising **2 :** a formal military inspection **3 :** a general survey **4 :** INSPECTION, EXAMINATION; *esp* **:** REEXAMINATION **5 :** a critical evaluation (as of a book) **6 :** a magazine devoted to reviews and essays **7 :** a renewed study of previously studied material **8 :** REVUE

²**re·view** \ri-'vyü, *l also* 'rē-\ *vb* **1 :** to examine or study again; *esp* **:** to reexamine judicially **2 :** to view retrospectively **:** look back over ⟨~ed his life⟩ **3 :** to write a critical examination of ⟨~ a novel⟩ **4 :** to hold a review of ⟨~ troops⟩ **5 :** to study material again

**re·view·er** \ri-'vyü-ər\ *n* **:** one that re-

views; *esp* **:** a writer of critical reviews

**re·vile** \ri-'vīl\ *vb* **re·viled; re·vil·ing :** to abuse verbally **:** rail at **syn** vituperate, berate, rate, upbraid, scold — **re·vile·ment** *n* — **re·vil·er** *n*

**re·vise** \ri-'vīz\ *vb* **re·vised; re·vis·ing 1 :** to look over something written in order to correct or improve **2 :** to make a new version of — **re·vis·able** *adj* — **re·vise** *n* — **re·vis·er** *or* **re·vi·sor** \-'vī-zər\ *n* — **re·vi·sion** \-'vizh-ən\ *n*

**re·vi·tal·ize** \'rē-'vīt-ᵊl-ˌīz\ *vb* **-ized; -iz·ing :** to give new life or vigor to — **re·vi·tal·i·za·tion** \ˌrē-ˌvīt-ᵊl-ə-'zā-shən\ *n*

**re·viv·al** \ri-'vī-vəl\ *n* **1 :** an act of reviving **:** the state of being revived **2 :** a new publication or presentation (as of a book or play) **3 :** an evangelistic meeting or series of meetings **4 :** REVITALIZATION

**re·vive** \ri-'vīv\ *vb* **re·vived; re·viv·ing 1 :** to return or restore to consciousness or life **:** become or make active or flourishing again **2 :** to bring back into use **3 :** to renew mentally **:** RECALL — **re·viv·er** *n*

**re·viv·i·fy** \rē-'viv-ə-ˌfī\ *vb* **:** REVIVE — **re·viv·i·fi·ca·tion** \-ˌviv-ə-fə-'kā-shən\ *n*

**re·vo·ca·ble** \'rev-ə-kə-bəl\ *adj* **:** capable of being revoked

**re·vo·ca·tion** \ˌrev-ə-'kā-shən\ *n* **:** an act or instance of revoking

**re·voke** \ri-'vōk\ *vb* **re·voked; re·vok·ing 1 :** to annul by recalling or taking back **:** REPEAL, RESCIND **2 :** RENEGE 1 — **re·vok·er** *n*

¹**re·volt** \ri-'vōlt\ *vb* **1 :** to throw off allegiance to a ruler or government **:** REBEL **2 :** to experience disgust or shock **3 :** to turn or cause to turn away with disgust or abhorrence — **re·volt·er** *n*

²**revolt** *n* **:** REBELLION, INSURRECTION

**re·volt·ing** \-iŋ\ *adj* **:** extremely offensive — **re·volt·ing·ly** *adv*

**rev·o·lu·tion** \ˌrev-ə-'lü-shən\ *n* **1 :** ROTATION **2 :** progress (as that of a planet) around in an orbit **3 :** CYCLE **4 :** a sudden, radical, or complete change; *esp* **:** the overthrow or renunciation of one ruler or government and substitution of another by the governed

¹**rev·o·lu·tion·ary** \-shə-ˌner-ē\ *adj* **1 :** of or relating to revolution **2 :** tending to or promoting revolution **3 :** RADICAL

²**revolutionary** *n, pl* **-ar·ies :** REVOLUTIONIST

**rev·o·lu·tion·ist** \ˌrev-ə-'lüsh(ə-)nəst\ *n* **:** one who takes part in a revolution or who advocates revolutionary doctrines — **revolutionist** *adj*

**rev·o·lu·tion·ize** \-shə-ˌnīz\ *vb* **-ized; -iz·ing :** to change fundamentally or completely **:** make revolutionary — **rev·o·lu·tion·iz·er** *n*

**re·volve** \ri-'välv\ *vb* **re·volved; re·volv·ing 1 :** to turn over in the mind **:** reflect upon **:** PONDER **2 :** to move in an orbit; *also* **:** ROTATE — **re·volv·able** *adj*

**re·volv·er** \ri-'väl-vər\ n : a pistol with a revolving cylinder of several chambers

**re·vue** \ri-'vyü\ n : a theatrical production consisting typically of brief often satirical sketches and songs

**re·vul·sion** \ri-'vəl-shən\ n 1 : a strong sudden reaction or change of feeling 2 : a feeling of complete distaste or repugnance

**¹re·ward** \ri-'wȯrd\ vb 1 : to give a reward to or for 2 : RECOMPENSE

**²reward** n : something given in return for good or evil done or received; esp : something given or offered for some service or attainment **syn** premium, prize, award

**RF** abbr radio frequency

**RFD** abbr rural free delivery

**Rh** symbol rhodium

**RH** abbr right hand

**rhap·so·dy** \'rap-səd-ē\ n, pl **-dies** [L rhapsodia portion of an epic poem adapted for recitation, fr. Gk rhapsōidia recitation of selections from epic poetry, rhapsody, fr. rhaptein to sew, stitch together + aidein to sing] 1 : a highly emotional utterance or literary composition : extravagantly rapturous discourse 2 : an instrumental composition of irregular form — **rhap·sod·ic** \rap-'säd-ik\ adj — **rhap·sod·i·cal·ly** \-i-k(ə-)lē\ adv — **rhap·so·dize** \'rap-sə-,dīz\ vb

**rhea** \'rē-ə\ n : any of several large tall flightless So. American birds that resemble but are smaller than the African ostrich

**rhe·ni·um** \'rē-nē-əm\ n : a heavy hard metallic chemical element

**rhe·ol·o·gy** \rē-'äl-ə-jē\ n : a science dealing with the deformation and flow of matter — **rhe·o·log·i·cal** \,rē-ə-'läj-i-kəl\ adj — **rhe·ol·o·gist** \rē-'äl-ə-jəst\ n

**rhe·om·e·ter** \rē-'äm-ət-ər\ n : an instrument for measuring the flow of viscous substances

**rheo·stat** \'rē-ə-,stat\ n : a variable resistor that controls the flow of electric current — **rheo·stat·ic** \,rē-ə-'stat-ik\ adj

**rhe·sus monkey** \,rē-səs-\ n : a pale brown Indian monkey

**rhet·o·ric** \'ret-ə-rik\ n [ME rethorik, fr. MF rethorique, fr. L rhetorica, fr. Gk rhētorikē, lit., art of oratory, fr. rhētōr orator, rhetorician] : the art of speaking or writing effectively — **rhe·tor·i·cal** \ri-'tor-i-kəl\ adj — **rhet·o·ri·cian** \,ret-ə-'rish-ən\ n

**rheum** \'rüm\ n : a watery discharge from the mucous membranes esp. of the eyes or nose — **rheumy** adj

**rheu·mat·ic fever** \ru-'mat-ik-\ n : an acute disease chiefly of children and young adults that is characterized by fever and by inflammation and pain in and around the joints and heart

**rheu·ma·tism** \'rü-mə-,tiz-əm, 'rüm-ə-,\ n : a disorder marked by inflammation or pain in muscles or joints — **rheu·mat·ic** \rü-'mat-ik\ adj

**rheu·ma·toid arthritis** \-,tȯid-\ n : a progressive constitutional disease characterized by inflammation and swelling of joint structures

**Rh factor** \'är-'āch-\ n [rhesus monkey (in which it was first detected)] : a substance in blood cells that may cause dangerous reactions in some infants or in transfusions

**rhine·stone** \'rīn-,stōn\ n : a colorless imitation stone of high luster made of glass, paste, or gem quartz

**rhi·no** \'rī-nō\ n, pl rhino or rhinos : RHINOCEROS

**rhi·noc·er·os** \rī-'näs-(ə-)rəs\ n, pl **-noc·er·os·es** or **-noc·eros** or **-noc·eri** \-'näs-ə-,rī\ [ME rinoceros, fr. L rhinoceros, fr. Gk rhinokerōs, fr. rhin-, rhis nose + keras horn] : a large thick-skinned mammal of Africa and Asia with one or two upright horns on the snout

**rhi·zome** \'rī-,zōm\ n : a specialized rootlike plant stem that forms shoots above and roots below — **rhi·zom·a·tous** \rī-'zäm-ət-əs\ adj

**Rh-neg·a·tive** \,är-,āch-'neg-ət-iv\ adj : lacking Rh factor in the blood

**rho·di·um** \'rōd-ē-əm\ n : a hard ductile metallic chemical element

**rho·do·den·dron** \,rōd-ə-'den-drən\ n : any of various shrubs or trees related to the heaths and grown for their clusters of large bright flowers

**rhom·boid** \'ram-,bȯid\ n : a parallelogram with unequal adjacent sides and oblique angles

**rhom·bus** \'räm-bəs\ n, pl **rhom·bus·es** or **rhom·bi** \-,bī\ : a parallelogram with equal sides and usu. oblique angles

**Rh-pos·i·tive** \,är-,āch-'päz-ət-iv\ adj : containing Rh factor in the red blood cells

**rhu·barb** \'rü-,bärb\ n [ME rubarbe, fr. MF reubarbe, fr. ML reubarbarum, alter. of rha barbarum, lit, barbarian rhubarb] : a garden plant with edible juicy petioles

**¹rhyme** \'rīm\ n 1 : correspondence in terminal sounds (as of two lines of verse) 2 : a composition in verse that rhymes; also : POETRY

**²rhyme** vb rhymed, rhym·ing 1 : to make rhymes; also : to write poetry 2 : to have rhymes : be in rhyme

**rhy·o·lite** \'rī-ə-,līt\ n : a very acid volcanic rock

**rhythm** \'rith-əm\ n 1 : regular rise and fall in the flow of sound in speech 2 : a movement or activity in which some action or element recurs regularly — **rhyth·mic** \'rith-mik\ or **rhyth·mi·cal** \-mi-kəl\ adj — **rhyth·mi·cal·ly** \-k(ə-)lē\ adv

**rhythm and blues** n : popular music based on blues and Negro folk music

**rhythm method** n : a method of birth control involving continence during the most fertile period of the female

**RI** abbr Rhode Island

**ri·al** \rē-'ȯl, -'äl\ n — see MONEY table

**¹rib** \'rib\ n 1 : one of the series of curved paired bony rods that are joined to the spine and stiffen the body wall of most vertebrates **2 :** something resembling a rib in shape or function **3 :** an elongated ridge

**²rib** vb **ribbed; rib·bing 1 :** to furnish or strengthen with ribs **2 :** to mark with ridges ⟨*ribbed* fabrics⟩ **3 :** to make fun of **:** TEASE — **rib·ber** n

**rib·ald** \'rib-əld\ adj **:** coarse or indecent esp. in language ⟨~ jokes⟩ — **rib·ald·ry** \-əl-drē\ n

**rib·and** \'rib-ənd\ n **:** RIBBON

**rib·bon** \'rib-ən\ n **1 :** a narrow fabric typically of silk or velvet used for trimming and for badges **2 :** a narrow strip or shred ⟨torn to ~s⟩ **3 :** a strip of inked cloth (as in a typewriter)

**ri·bo·fla·vin** \,rī-bə-'flā-vən, 'rī-bə-,flā-vən\ n **:** a growth-promoting vitamin of the B complex occurring in milk and liver

**ri·bo·nu·cle·ic acid** \,rī-bō-n(y)ü-,klē-ik-, -,klā-\ n **:** RNA

**ri·bo·some** \'rī-bə-,sōm\ n **:** one of the RNA-rich cytoplasmic granules that are sites of protein synthesis — **ri·bo·som·al** \,rī-bə-'sō-məl\ adj

**rice** \'rīs\ n, pl **rice :** an annual cereal grass grown in warm wet areas for its edible seed; also **:** this seed

**rich** \'rich\ adj **1 :** possessing or controlling great wealth **:** WEALTHY **2 :** COSTLY, VALUABLE **3 :** containing much sugar, fat, or seasoning; also **:** high in combustible content **4 :** deep and pleasing in color or tone **5 :** ABUNDANT **6 :** FRUITFUL, FERTILE — **rich·ly** adv — **rich·ness** n

**rich·es** \'rich-əz\ n pl [ME, sing. or pl., fr. richesse, lit., richness, fr. OF, fr. riche rich, of Gmc origin] **:** things that make one rich **:** WEALTH

**Rich·ter scale** \'rik-tər-\ n **:** a logarithmic scale for expressing the magnitude of a seismic disturbance (as an earthquake) in terms of the energy dissipated in it

**rick** \'rik\ n **:** a large stack (as of hay) in the open air

**rick·ets** \'rik-əts\ n **:** a children's disease marked esp. by soft deformed bones and caused by vitamin D deficiency

**rick·ett·sia** \rik-'et-sē-ə\ n, pl **-si·as** or **-si·ae** \-sē-,ē\ **:** any of a family of rod-shaped microorganisms that cause various diseases (as typhus)

**rick·ety** \'rik-ət-ē\ adj **1 :** affected with rickets **2 :** SHAKY, FEEBLE

**rick·sha** or **rick·shaw** \'rik-,shȯ\ n **:** a small covered 2-wheeled vehicle pulled by one man and used orig. in Japan

**¹ric·o·chet** \'rik-ə-,shā, Brit also -,shet\ n **:** a glancing rebound or skipping (as of a bullet off a wall)

**²ricochet** vb **-cheted** \-,shād\ or **-chet·ted** \-,shed- əd\; **-chet·ing** \-,shā-iŋ\ or **-chet·ting** \-,shet-iŋ\ **:** to skip with or as if with glancing rebounds

**rid** \'rid\ vb **rid** also **rid·ded; rid·ding :** to make free **:** CLEAR, RELIEVE — **rid·dance** \'rid-°ns\ n

**rid·den** \'rid-°n\ adj **1 :** extremely

concerned with or bothered by ⟨conscience-*ridden*⟩ **2 :** excessively full of or supplied with ⟨slum-*ridden*⟩

**¹rid·dle** \'rid-°l\ n **:** a puzzling question to be solved or answered by guessing

**²riddle** vb **rid·dled; rid·dling 1 :** EXPLAIN, SOLVE **2 :** to speak in riddles

**³riddle** n **:** a coarse sieve

**⁴riddle** vb **rid·dled; rid·dling 1 :** to sift with a riddle **2 :** to fill as full of holes as a sieve

**¹ride** \'rīd\ vb **rode** \'rōd\; **rid·den** \'rid-°n\; **rid·ing** \'rīd-iŋ\ **1 :** to go on an animal's back or in a conveyance (as a boat, car, or airplane); also **:** to sit on and control so as to be carried along ⟨~ a bicycle⟩ **2 :** to float or move on water ⟨~ at anchor⟩; also **:** to move like a floating object **3 :** to travel over a surface ⟨car ~s well⟩ **4 :** to proceed over on horseback **5 :** to bear along **:** CARRY ⟨rode him on their shoulders⟩ **6 :** OBSESS, OPPRESS ⟨*ridden* with anxiety⟩ **7 :** to torment by nagging or teasing — **ride roughshod over :** to treat with disdain or abuse

**²ride** n **1 :** an act of riding; esp **:** a trip on horseback or by vehicle **2 :** a way (as a lane) suitable for riding **3 :** a mechanical device (as a merry-go-round) for riding on **4 :** a means of transportation

**rid·er** \'rīd-ər\ n **1 :** one that rides **2 :** an addition to a document often attached on a separate piece of paper **3 :** a clause dealing with an unrelated matter attached to a legislative bill during passage — **rid·er·less** adj

**¹ridge** \'rij\ n **1 :** a range of hills **2 :** a raised line or strip **3 :** the line made where two sloping surfaces meet — **ridgy** adj

**²ridge** vb **ridged; ridg·ing 1 :** to form into a ridge **2 :** to extend in ridges

**ridge·pole** \'rij-,pōl\ n **:** the highest horizontal timber in a sloping roof to which the upper ends of the rafters are fastened

**¹rid·i·cule** \'rid-ə-,kyül\ n **:** the act of exposing to laughter **:** DERISION

**²ridicule** vb **-culed; -cul·ing :** to laugh at or make fun of mockingly or contemptuously **syn** deride, taunt, twit, mock

**ri·dic·u·lous** \rə-'dik-yə-ləs\ adj **:** arousing or deserving ridicule **:** ABSURD, PREPOSTEROUS **syn** laughable, ludicrous — **ri·dic·u·lous·ly** adv — **ri·dic·u·lous·ness** n

**ri·el** \rē-'el\ n — see MONEY table

**rife** \'rīf\ adj **:** WIDESPREAD, PREVALENT, ABOUNDING — **rife** adv — **rife·ness** n

**riff** \'rif\ n **:** a repeated phrase in jazz typically supporting a solo improvisation; also **:** a piece based on such a phrase — **riff** vb

**riff·raff** \'rif-,raf\ n [ME riffe raffe, fr. rif and raf every single one, fr. MF rif et raf completely, fr. rifler to plunder + raffe act of sweeping] **1 :** RABBLE **2 :** REFUSE, RUBBISH

**¹ri·fle** \'rī-fəl\ vb **ri·fled; ri·fling** \-f(ə-)liŋ\ **:** to ransack esp. in order to steal — **ri·fler** \-f(ə-)lər\ n

²**rifle** *vb* **ri·fled; ri·fling** \-f(ə-)liŋ\ : to cut spiral grooves into the bore of ⟨*rifled* arms⟩ — **rifling** *n*

³**rifle** *n* **1** : a shoulder weapon with a rifled bore **2** *pl* : a body of soldiers armed with rifles — **ri·fle·man** \-fəl-mən\ *n*

**rift** \'rift\ *n* **1** : CLEFT, FISSURE **2** : ESTRANGEMENT, SEPARATION — **rift** *vb*

¹**rig** \'rig\ *vb* **rigged; rig·ging 1** : to fit out (as a ship) with rigging **2** : CLOTHE, DRESS **3** : EQUIP **4** : to set up esp. as a makeshift ⟨~ up a shelter⟩

²**rig** *n* **1** : the distinctive shape, number, and arrangement of sails and masts of a ship **2** : CLOTHING, DRESS **3** : EQUIPMENT **4** : a carriage with its horse or horses **5** : APPARATUS

³**rig** *vb* **rigged; rig·ging 1** : to manipulate or control esp. by deceptive or dishonest means **2** : to fix in advance for a desired result

**rig·ger** \'rig-ər\ *n* **1** : one that rigs **2** : a ship of a specified rig

**rig·ging** \'rig-iŋ, -ən\ *n* **1** : the lines (as ropes and chains) that hold and move masts, sails, and spars of a ship **2** : a network (as in theater scenery) used for support and manipulation

¹**right** \'rīt\ *adj* **1** : RIGHTEOUS, UPRIGHT **2** : JUST, PROPER **3** : conforming to truth or fact : CORRECT **4** : APPROPRIATE, SUITABLE **5** : STRAIGHT ⟨a ~ line⟩ **6** : GENUINE, REAL **7** : NORMAL, SOUND ⟨not in his ~ mind⟩ **8** : of, relating to, or being the stronger hand in most persons **9** : located nearer to the right hand; *esp* : being on the right when facing in the same direction as the observer **10** : made to be placed or worn outward ⟨~ side of a rug⟩ **syn** good, accurate, exact, precise, nice — **right·ness** *n*

²**right** *n* **1** : something that is correct, just, proper, or honorable **2** : just action or decision : the cause of justice **3** : something (as a power or privilege) to which one has a just or lawful claim **4** : the side or part that is on or toward the right side **5** *often cap* : political conservatives; *also* : the beliefs they hold — **right·ward** \-wərd\ *adj*

³**right** *adv* **1** : according to what is right ⟨live ~⟩ **2** : EXACTLY, PRECISELY ⟨~ here and now⟩ **3** : DIRECTLY ⟨went ~ home⟩ **4** : according to fact or truth ⟨guess ~⟩ **5** : all the way : COMPLETELY ⟨~ to the end⟩ **6** : IMMEDIATELY ⟨~ after lunch⟩ **7** : on or to the right ⟨looked ~ and left⟩ **8** : QUITE, VERY ⟨~ nice weather⟩

⁴**right** *vb* **1** : to relieve from wrong **2** : to adjust or restore to a proper state or position **3** : to bring or restore to an upright position **4** : to become upright — **right·er** *n*

**right angle** *n* : an angle bounded by two lines perpendicular to each other — **right–an·gled** \'rīt-'aŋ-gəld\ *or* **right–an·gle** \-gəl\ *adj*

**right circular cone** *n* : a cone generated by rotating a right triangle about one of its legs

**righ·teous** \'rī-chəs\ *adj* : acting or being in accordance with what is just, honorable, and free from guilt or wrong : UPRIGHT **syn** virtuous, noble, moral, ethical — **righ·teous·ly** *adv* — **righ·teous·ness** *n*

**right·ful** \'rīt-fəl\ *adj* **1** : JUST; *also* : FITTING **2** : having or held by a legally just claim — **right·ful·ly** \-ē\ *adv* — **right·ful·ness** *n*

**right–hand** \'rīt-,hand\ *adj* **1** : situated on the right **2** : RIGHT-HANDED **3** : chiefly relied on ⟨his ~ man⟩

**right–hand·ed** \-'han-dəd\ *adj* **1** : using the right hand habitually or better than the left **2** : designed for or done with the right hand **3** : CLOCKWISE ⟨a ~ twist⟩ — **right–handed** *adv* — **right–hand·ed·ly** *adv* — **right–hand·ed·ness** *n*

**right·ly** \'rīt-lē\ *adv* **1** : FAIRLY, JUSTLY **2** : PROPERLY **3** : CORRECTLY, EXACTLY

**right–of–way** \,rīt-ə(v)-'wā\ *n* *pl* **rights–of–way 1** : a legal right of passage over another person's ground **2** : the area over which a right-of-way exists **3** : the land on which a public road is built **4** : the land occupied by a railroad **5** : the land used by a public utility **6** : the right of traffic to take precedence over other traffic

**right on** *interj* — used to express agreement or give encouragement

**rig·id** \'rij-əd\ *adj* **1** : lacking flexibility : STIFF **2** : STRICT **syn** tense, rigorous, stringent — **ri·gid·i·ty** \rə-'jid-ət-ē\ *n* — **rig·id·ly** \'rij-əd-lē\ *adv*

**rig·ma·role** \'rig-(ə-)mə-,rōl\ *n* **1** : confused or senseless talk **2** : a complex largely meaningless procedure

**rig·or** \'rig-ər\ *n* **1** : the quality of being inflexible or unyielding : STRICTNESS **2** : HARSHNESS, SEVERITY **3** : a tremor caused by a chill **4** : strict precision : EXACTNESS **syn** difficulty, hardship — **rig·or·ous** *adj* — **rig·or·ous·ly** *adv*

**rig·or mor·tis** \,rig-ər-'mȯrt-əs\ *n* [NL, stiffness of death] : temporary rigidity of muscles occurring after death

**rile** \'rīl\ *vb* **riled, ril·ing 1** : ROIL 1 **2** : to make angry

¹**rill** \'ril\ *n* : a very small brook

²**rill** \'ril\ *or* **rille** \'ril, 'ril-ə\ *n* : a long narrow valley on the moon

¹**rim** \'rim\ *n* **1** : an outer edge esp. of something curved : BORDER, MARGIN **2** : the outer part of a wheel

²**rim** *vb* **rimmed; rim·ming 1** : to furnish with a rim **2** : to run around the rim of

¹**rime** \'rīm\ *n* **1** : FROST 2 **2** : frostlike ice tufts formed from fog or cloud on the windward side of exposed objects — **rimy** \'rī-mē\ *adj*

²**rime** *var of* RHYME

**rind** \'rīnd\ *n* : a usu. hard or tough outer layer (as of skin) ⟨bacon ~⟩

¹**ring** \'riŋ\ *n* **1** : a circular band worn as an ornament or token or used for holding or fastening ⟨wedding ~⟩ ⟨key ~⟩ **2** : something circular in shape ⟨smoke ~⟩ **3** : a place for contest or display ⟨boxing ~⟩; *also* : PRIZEFIGHT-

ING **4** : a group of people who work together for selfish or dishonest purposes — **ring·like** \'riŋ-,līk\ adj

²**ring** vb **ringed; ring·ing** \'riŋ-iŋ\ **1** : ENCIRCLE **2** : to move in a ring or spirally **3** : to throw a ring over (a mark) in a game (as quoits)

³**ring** vb **rang** \'raŋ\; **rung** \'rəŋ\; **ring·ing** \'riŋ-iŋ\ **1** : to sound resonantly when struck; also : to feel as if filled with such sound **2** : to cause to make a clear metallic sound by striking **3** : to sound a bell (~ for the maid) **4** : to announce or call by or as if by striking a bell (~ an alarm) **5** : to repeat loudly and persistently

⁴**ring** n **1** : a set of bells **2** : the clear resonant sound of vibrating metal **3** : resonant tone : SONORITY **4** : a sound or character expressive of a particular quality **5** : an act or instance of ringing; esp : a telephone call

¹**ring·er** \'riŋ-ər\ n **1** : one that sounds by ringing **2** : one that enters a competition under false representations **3** : one that closely resembles another

²**ringer** n : one that encircles or puts a ring around

**ring·lead·er** \'riŋ-,lēd-ər\ n : a leader esp. of a group of troublemakers

**ring·let** \'riŋ-lət\ n : a long curl

**ring·mas·ter** \'riŋ-,mas-tər\ n : one in charge of performances in a ring (as of a circus)

**ring up** vb **1** : to total and record esp. by means of a cash register **2** : RECORD, SCORE

**ring·worm** \'riŋ-,wərm\ n : a contagious skin disease caused by fungi

**rink** \'riŋk\ n : a level extent of ice marked off for skating or various games; also : a similar surface (as of wood) marked off or enclosed for a sport or game (roller-skating ~)

¹**rinse** \'rins\ vb **rinsed; rins·ing** [ME rincen, fr. MF rincer, fr. (assumed) VL recentiare, fr. L recent-, recens fresh, recent] **1** : to wash lightly or in water only **2** : to cleanse (as of soap) with clear water **3** : to treat (hair) with a rinse — **rins·er** n

²**rinse** n **1** : an act of rinsing **2** : a liquid used for rinsing **3** : a solution that temporarily tints hair

**ri·ot** \'rī-ət\ n **1** : disorderly behavior **2** : disturbance of the public peace; esp : a violent public disorder **3** : random or disorderly profusion (a ~ of color) — **riot** vb — **ri·ot·er** n — **ri·ot·ous** adj

¹**rip** \'rip\ vb **ripped; rip·ping 1** : to cut or tear open **2** : to saw or split (wood) with the grain — **rip·per** n

²**rip** n : a rent made by ripping

**RIP** abbr [L requiescat in pace] may he rest in peace

**ri·par·i·an** \rə-'per-ē-ən\ adj : of or relating to the bank of a stream or lake

**rip cord** n : a cord that is pulled to release the pilot parachute which lifts a main parachute out of its container

¹**ripe** \'rīp\ adj **rip·er; rip·est 1** : fully grown and developed : MATURE (~ fruit) **2** : fully prepared for some

use or object : READY — **ripe·ly** adv — **ripe·ness** n

**rip·en** \'rī-pən\ vb **rip·ened; rip·en·ing** \'rīp-(ə-)niŋ\ **1** : to grow or make ripe **2** : to bring to completeness or perfection; also : to age or cure (cheese) to develop characteristic flavor, odor, body, texture, and color

**rip-off** \'rip-,óf\ n : an act of stealing : THEFT — **rip off** \(')rip-'óf\ vb

**ri·poste** \ri-'pōst\ n **1** : a fencer's return thrust after a parry **2** : a retaliatory maneuver or response; esp : a quick retort — **riposte** vb

**rip·ple** \'rip-əl\ vb **rip·pled; rip·pling** \-(ə-)liŋ\ **1** : to become lightly ruffled on the surface **2** : to make a sound like that of rippling water — **ripple** n

**rip·saw** \'rip-,só\ n : a coarse-toothed saw used to cut wood in the direction of the grain

¹**rise** \'rīz\ vb **rose** \'rōz\; **ris·en** \'riz-ᵊn\; **ris·ing** \'rī-ziŋ\ **1** : to get up from sitting, kneeling, or lying **2** : to get up from sleep or from one's bed **3** : to return from death **4** : to end a session : ADJOURN **5** : to take up arms : go to war; also : REBEL **6** : to appear above the horizon **7** : to move upward : ASCEND **8** : to extend above other objects **9** : to attain a higher level or rank **10** : to increase in quantity or in intensity **11** : to come into being : HAPPEN, BEGIN, ORIGINATE

²**rise** n **1** : an act of rising : a state of being risen **2** : BEGINNING, ORIGIN **3** : the elevation of one point above another **4** : an increase in amount, number, or volume **5** : an upward slope **6** : a spot higher than surrounding ground **7** : an angry reaction

**ris·er** \'rī-zər\ n **1** : one that rises **2** : the upright part between stair treads

**ris·i·bil·i·ty** \,riz-ə-'bil-ət-ē\ n, pl **-ties** : the ability or inclination to laugh — often used in pl.

**ris·i·ble** \'riz-ə-bəl\ adj **1** : able or inclined to laugh **2** : arousing laughter : FUNNY **3** : of or relating to laughter (~ muscles)

¹**risk** \'risk\ n : exposure to possible loss or injury : DANGER, PERIL — **risk·i·ness** \'ris-kē-nəs\ n — **risky** adj

²**risk** vb **1** : to expose to danger (~ed his life) **2** : to incur the danger of

**ris·qué** \ris-'kā\ adj : verging on impropriety or indecency

**rite** \'rīt\ n **1** : a set form of conducting a ceremony **2** : the liturgy of a church **3** : a ceremonial act or action

**rit·u·al** \'rich-(ə-w)əl\ n **1** : the established form esp. for a religious ceremony **2** : a system of rites **3** : a ceremonial act or action **4** : a customarily repeated act or series of acts — **ritual** adj — **rit·u·al·ism** \-,iz-əm\ n — **rit·u·al·is·tic** \,rich-(ə-w)əl-'is-tik\ adj — **rit·u·al·is·ti·cal·ly** \-ti-k(ə-)lē\ adv — **rit·u·al·ly** \'rich-(ə-w)ə-lē\ adv

**riv** abbr river

¹**ri·val** \'rī-vəl\ n [MF or L; MF, fr. L rivalis one using the same stream as

another, rival in love, fr. *rivalis* of a stream, fr. *rivus* stream] **1** : one of two or more trying to get what only one can have **2** : one who tries to excel another **3** : one that equals another esp. in desired qualities : MATCH, PEER

**²rival** *adj* : COMPETING

**³rival** *vb* **ri·valed** or **ri·valled; ri·val·ing** or **ri·val·ling** \'rīv-(ə-)liŋ\ **1** : to be in competition with **2** : to try to equal or excel **3** : to have qualities that equal another's : MATCH

**ri·val·ry** \'rī-vəl-rē\ *n, pl* **-ries** : COMPETITION

**rive** \'rīv\ *vb* **rived** \'rīvd\; **riv·en** \'riv-ən\ *also* **rived; riv·ing** \'rī-viŋ\ **1** : SPLIT, REND **2** : SHATTER

**riv·er** \'riv-ər\ *n* : a natural stream larger than a brook

**riv·er·bank** \-,baŋk\ *n* : the bank of a river

**riv·er·bed** \-,bed\ *n* : the channel occupied by a river

**riv·er·boat** \-,bōt\ *n* : a boat for use on a river

**riv·er·side** \'riv-ər-,sīd\ *n* : the side or bank of a river

**¹riv·et** \'riv-ət\ *n* : a headed metal bolt or pin for fastening things together by being put through holes in them and then being flattened on the plain end to make another head

**²rivet** *vb* : to fasten with a rivet — **riv·et·er** *n*

**riv·u·let** \'riv-(y)ə-lət\ *n* : a small stream

**ri·yal** \rē-'(y)ól, -'(y)äl\ *n* **1** — see *dinar* at MONEY table **2** — see MONEY table

**rm** *abbr* **1** ream **2** room

**Rn** *symbol* radon

**RN** *abbr* **1** registered nurse **2** Royal Navy

**RNA** \,är-,en-'ā\ *n* : a complex single-stranded biological molecule that is the intermediary between DNA and proteins in their synthesis and is the ultimate molecular basis of heredity in some organisms

**rnd** *abbr* round

**RNZAF** *abbr* Royal New Zealand Air Force

**¹roach** \'rōch\ *n, pl* **roach** *also* **roach·es** : a European freshwater fish related to the carp

**²roach** *n* **1** : COCKROACH **2** : the butt of a marijuana cigarette

**road** \'rōd\ *n* **1** : an anchorage for ships usu. less sheltered than a harbor — often used in pl. **2** : an open way for vehicles, persons, and animals : HIGHWAY **3** : ROUTE, PATH

**road·bed** \'rōd-,bed\ *n* **1** : the foundation of a road or railroad **2** : the traveled surface of a road

**road·block** \-,bläk\ *n* **1** : a barricade on a road ⟨a police ~⟩ **2** : an obstruction to progress

**road·run·ner** \-,rən-ər\ *n* : a largely terrestrial bird of the southwestern U.S. and Mexico that is a speedy runner

**road·side** \'rōd-,sīd\ *n* : the strip of land along a road — **roadside** *adj*

**road·stead** \-,sted\ *n* : ROAD 1

**road·ster** \'rōd-stər\ *n* **1** : a driving horse **2** : an open automobile with one cross seat

**road·way** \'rōd-,wā\ *n* : ROAD; *esp* : ROADBED

**road·work** \-,wərk\ *n* : conditioning for an athletic contest (as a boxing match) consisting mainly of long runs

**roam** \'rōm\ *vb* **1** : WANDER, ROVE **2** : to range or wander over or about

**¹roan** \'rōn\ *adj* : having a dark (as bay or black) coat with white hairs interspersed ⟨a ~ horse⟩

**²roan** *n* : an animal with a roan coat; *also* : its color

**¹roar** \'rōr\ *vb* **1** : to utter a full loud prolonged sound **2** : to make a loud confused sound (as of wind or waves) — **roar·er** *n*

**²roar** *n* : a sound of roaring

**¹roast** \'rōst\ *vb* **1** : to cook by dry heat (as before a fire or in an oven) **2** : to criticize severely

**²roast** *n* **1** : a piece of meat suitable for roasting **2** : an outing for roasting food ⟨corn ~⟩

**³roast** *adj* : ROASTED

**roast·er** \'rō-stər\ *n* **1** : one that roasts **2** : a device for roasting **3** : something (as a chicken) adapted to roasting

**rob** \'räb\ *vb* **robbed, rob·bing** **1** : to steal from **2** : to deprive of something due or expected **3** : to commit robbery — **rob·ber** *n*

**robber fly** *n* : any of numerous predaceous flies

**rob·bery** \'räb-(ə-)rē\ *n, pl* **-ber·ies** : the act or practice of robbing; *esp* : theft of something from a person by use of violence or threat

**¹robe** \'rōb\ *n* **1** : a long flowing outer garment; *esp* : one used for ceremonial occasions **2** : a wrap or covering for the lower body (as for sitting outdoors)

**²robe** *vb* **robed; rob·ing** **1** : to clothe with or as if with a robe **2** : DRESS

**rob·in** \'räb-ən\ *n* **1** : a small European thrush with a yellowish red breast **2** : a large No. American thrush with blackish head and tail and reddish breast

**ro·bot** \'rō-,bät, -bət\ *n* [Czech, fr. *robota* work] **1** : a machine that looks and acts like a human being **2** : an efficient but insensitive person **3** : an automatic apparatus **4** : something guided by automatic controls

**ro·bust** \rō-'bəst, 'rō-(,)bəst\ *adj* [L *robustus* oaken, strong, fr. *robur* oak, strength] : strong and vigorously healthy — **ro·bust·ly** *adv* — **ro·bust·ness** *n*

**¹rock** \'räk\ *vb* **1** : to move back and forth in or as if in a cradle **2** : to sway or cause to sway back and forth

**²rock** *n* **1** : a rocking movement **2** : popular music usu. playe on electronically amplified instruments and characterized by a strong beat and much repetition

**³rock** *n* **1 :** a mass of stony material; *also* **:** broken pieces of stone **2 :** solid mineral deposits **3 :** something like a rock in firmness — **rock** *adj* — **rock-like** *adj* — **rocky** *adj*

**rock·bound** \'räk-baúnd\ *adj* **:** fringed or covered with rocks

**rock·er** \'räk-ər\ *n* **1 :** one of the curved pieces on which something (as a chair or cradle) rocks **2 :** a device that works in a rocking motion

**¹rock·et** \'räk-ət\ *n* **1 :** a firework consisting of a case containing a combustible substance that is propelled through the air by the reaction to the rearward discharge of gases produced by burning **2 :** a jet engine that operates on the same principle as a firework rocket but carries the oxygen needed for burning its fuel **3 :** a rocket-propelled bomb or missile

**²rock·et** \'räk-ət\ *vb* **1 :** to convey by means of a rocket **2 :** to rise abruptly and rapidly

**rock·et·ry** \'räk-ə-trē\ *n* **:** the study or use of rockets

**rocket ship** *n* **:** a rocket-propelled spacecraft

**rock·fall** \'räk-,fȯl\ *n* **:** a mass of falling or fallen rocks

**rock 'n' roll** \,räk-ən-'rōl\ *n* **:** ²ROCK 2

**rock salt** *n* **:** common salt in rocklike masses or large crystals

**rock wool** *n* **:** woollike insulation made from molten rock or slag

**Rocky Mountain sheep** *n* **:** BIGHORN

**rod** \'räd\ *n* **1 :** a straight slender stick **2 :** a stick or bundle of twigs used in punishing a person; *also* **:** PUNISHMENT **3 :** a staff borne to show rank **4 —** see WEIGHT table **5** *slang* **:** PISTOL

**rode** *past of* RIDE

**ro·dent** \'rōd-ⁿt\ *n* [fr. L *rodent-, rodens,* prp *of rodere* to gnaw] **:** any of a large group of small gnawing mammals (as mice and squirrels)

**ro·deo** \'rōd-ē-,ō, rə-'dā-ō\ *n, pl* **ro·de·os** [Sp, fr. *rodear* to surround, fr. *rueda* wheel, fr. L *rota*] **1 :** ROUNDUP **1 2 :** a public performance representing features of cowboy life

**¹roe** \'rō\ *n, pl* **roe** *or* **roes 1 :** a small nimble European deer **2 :** DOE

**²roe** *n* **:** the eggs of a fish esp. while bound together in a mass

**roe·buck** \'rō-,bək\ *n* **:** a male roe deer

**roent·gen·ol·o·gy** \,rent-gən-'äl-ə-jē\ *n* **:** a branch of radiology that deals with the use of X rays for diagnosis or treatment of disease — **roent·gen·o·log·ic** \-ə-'läj-ik\ *or* **roent·gen·o·log·i·cal** \-i-kəl\ *adj* — **roent·gen·ol·o·gist** \-'äl-ə-jəst\ *n*

**roentgen ray** \,rent-gən-\ *n, often cap 1st R* **:** X RAY

**ROG** *abbr* receipt of goods

**rog·er** \'räj-ər\ *interj* — used esp. in radio and signaling to indicate that a message has been received and understood

**rogue** \'rōg\ *n* **1 :** a dishonest person **:** SCOUNDREL **2 :** a mischievous person **:** SCAMP — **rogu·ery** \'rō-gə-rē\ *n* —

**rogu·ish** \'rō-gish\ *adj* — **rogu·ish·ly** *adv* — **rogu·ish·ness** *n*

**roil** \'rȯil, *for 2 also* 'rīl\ *vb* **1 :** to make cloudy or muddy by stirring up **2 :** RILE 2

**rois·ter** \'rȯi-stər\ *vb* **rois·tered; rois·ter·ing** \-st(ə-)riŋ\ **:** to engage in noisy revelry **:** CAROUSE — **rois·ter·er** \-stər-ər\ *n*

**role** *also* **rôle** \'rōl\ *n* **1 :** an assigned or assumed character; *also* **:** a part played (as by an actor) **2 :** FUNCTION

**¹roll** \'rōl\ *n* **1 :** a document containing an official record **2 :** an official list of names **3 :** something (as a bun) that is rolled up or rounded as if rolled **4 :** something that rolls **:** ROLLER

**²roll** *vb* **1 :** to move by turning over and over **2 :** to move on wheels **3 :** to move onward as if by completing a revolution (years ~ *ed* by) **4 :** to flow or seem to flow in a continuous stream or with a rising and falling motion (the river ~ed *on*) **5 :** to swing or sway from side to side **6 :** to shape or become shaped in rounded form **7 :** to press with a roller **8 :** to sound with a full reverberating tone **9 :** to make a continuous beating sound (as on a drum) **10 :** to utter with a trill

**³roll** *n* **1 :** a sound produced by rapid strokes on a drum **2 :** a heavy reverberating sound **3 :** a rolling movement or action **4 :** a swaying movement (as of a ship) **5 :** SOMERSAULT

**roll·back** \'rōl-,bak\ *n* **:** the act or an instance of rolling back

**roll back** \'rōl-'bak\ *vb* **1 :** to reduce (as a commodity price) on a national scale by government action **2 :** to cause to withdraw **:** push back

**roll bar** *n* **:** an overhead metal bar in an automobile designed to protect riders in case of a turnover

**roll call** *n* **:** the act or an instance of calling off a list of names (as of soldiers); *also* **:** a time for a roll call

**roll·er** \'rō-lər\ *n* **1 :** a revolving cylinder used for moving, pressing, shaping, or smoothing **2 :** a rod on which something is rolled up **3 :** a long heavy wave on a coast **4 :** a tumbler pigeon

**roll·er coast·er** \'rō-lər-,kō-stər\ *n* **:** an elevated railway (as in an amusement park) constructed with curves and inclines

**roller derby** *n* **:** a contest between two roller-skating teams on a banked oval track

**roller skate** *n* **:** a skate with wheels instead of a runner for skating on a surface other than ice — **roller-skate** *vb* — **roller skater** *n*

**rol·lick** \'räl-ik\ *vb* **:** ROMP, FROLIC

**rol·lick·ing** \-iŋ\ *adj* **1 :** BOISTEROUS, SWAGGERING **2 :** lightheartedly gay — **rol·lick·ing·ly** *adv*

**roly-poly** \,rō-lē-'pō-lē\ *adj* **:** ROTUND

**Rom** *abbr* **1** Roman **2** Romance **3** Romania; Romanian **4** Romans

**¹Ro·man** \'rō-mən\ *n* **1 :** a native or resident of Rome **2 :** a citizen of the Roman Empire

²**Roman** adj **1 :** of or relating to Rome or the Romans **2 :** of or relating to the Roman Catholic Church

**Roman candle** n **:** a cylindrical firework that discharges balls or stars of fire

**Roman Catholic** adj **:** of or relating to the body of Christians in communion with the pope and having a liturgy centered in the Mass — **Roman Catholicism** n

¹**ro·mance** \rō-'mans, 'rō-,mans\ n [ME romauns, fr. OF romans French, fr. L romanice in the Roman manner, fr. romanicus Roman, fr Romanus] **1 :** a medieval tale of knightly adventure **2 :** a prose narrative dealing with heroic or mysterious events set in a remote time or place **3 :** a love story **4 :** a love affair — **ro·manc·er** n

²**romance** vb **ro·manced; ro·manc·ing 1 :** to exaggerate or invent detail or incident **2 :** to have romantic fancies **3 :** to carry on a love affair with

**Ro·mance** \rō-'mans, 'rō-,mans\ adj **:** of or relating to the languages developed from Latin

**Ro·ma·nian** \rù-'mā-nē-ən, rō-, -nyən\ var of RUMANIAN

**Roman numeral** n **:** a numeral in a system of notation that is based on the ancient Roman system

**Ro·ma·no** \rə-'män-ō, rō-\ n **:** a hard Italian cheese that is sharper than Parmesan

**ro·man·tic** \rō-'mant-ik\ adj **1 :** IMAGINARY **2 :** VISIONARY **3 :** having an imaginative or emotional appeal **4 :** ARDENT, FERVENT — **ro·man·ti·cal·ly** \-i-k(ə-)lē\ adv

**ro·man·ti·cism** \rō-'mant-ə-,siz-əm\ n, often cap **:** a literary movement (as in early 19th century England) marked esp. by emphasis on the imagination and the emotions and by the use of autobiographical material — **ro·man·ti·cist** \-səst\ n, often cap

**romp** \'rämp\ vb **1 :** to play actively and noisily **2 :** to run or play so as to win easily — **romp** n

**romp·er** \'räm-pər\ n **1 :** one that romps **2 :** a child's one-piece garment with the lower part shaped like bloomers — usu. used in pl.

**rood** \'rüd\ n **1 :** CROSS, CRUCIFIX **2 :** a unit of area equal to ¼ acre

¹**roof** \'rüf, 'rúf\ n, pl **roofs** \'rüfs, 'rúfs; 'rüvz, 'rúvz\ **1 :** the upper covering part of a building **2 :** something suggesting a roof of a building — **roofed** \'rüft, 'rúft\ adj — **roof·ing** n — **roof·less** adj

²**roof** vb **:** to cover with a roof

**roof·top** \-,täp\ n **:** a roof esp. of a house

**roof·tree** \-,trē\ n **:** RIDGEPOLE

¹**rook** \'rùk\ n **:** an Old World bird resembling the related crow

²**rook** vb **:** CHEAT, SWINDLE

³**rook** n **:** a chess piece that can move parallel to the sides of the board across any number of unoccupied squares

**rook·ery** \'rùk-ə-rē\ n, pl **-er·ies :** a breeding ground or haunt of gregarious birds or mammals; also **:** a colony of such birds or mammals

**rook·ie** \'rùk-ē\ n **:** RECRUIT; also **:** NOVICE

¹**room** \'rüm, 'rúm\ n **1 :** an extent of space occupied by or sufficient for available for something **2 :** a partitioned part of a building **:** CHAMBER; also **:** the people in a room **3 :** OPPORTUNITY, CHANCE (∼ to develop his talents) — **room·ful** n — **roomy** adj

²**room** vb **:** to occupy lodgings **:** LODGE — **room·er** n

**room·ette** \rü-'met, rùm-'et\ n **:** a small private room on a sleeping car

**room·mate** \'rüm-,māt, 'rúm-\ n **:** one of two or more persons occupying the same room

¹**roost** \'rüst\ n **:** a support on which or a place where birds perch

²**roost** vb **:** to settle on or as if on a roost

**roost·er** \'rüs-tər, 'rùs-\ n **:** an adult male domestic fowl **:** COCK

¹**root** \'rüt, 'rùt\ n **1 :** the leafless usu. underground part of a seed plant that functions in absorption, aeration, and storage or as a means of anchorage; also **:** an underground plant part **2 :** something (as the basal part of a tooth or hair) resembling a root **3 :** SOURCE, ORIGIN **4 :** the essential core **:** HEART ⟨get to the ∼ of the matter⟩ **5 :** a number that when taken as a factor an indicated number of times gives a specified number **6 :** the lower part — **root·less** adj — **root·like** adj

²**root** vb **1 :** to form roots **2 :** to fix or become fixed by or as if by roots **:** ESTABLISH **3 :** UPROOT

³**root** vb **1 :** to turn up or dig with the snout ⟨pigs ∼ing⟩ **2 :** to poke or dig around (as in search of something)

⁴**root** \'rüt, 'rùt\ vb **1 :** to applaud or encourage noisily **:** CHEER **2 :** to wish success or lend support to — **root·er** n

**root beer** n **:** a sweetened effervescent beverage flavored with extracts of roots and herbs

**root·let** \-lət\ n **:** a small root

**root·stock** \-,stäk\ n **:** a rootlike underground stem **:** RHIZOME

¹**rope** \'rōp\ n **1 :** a large strong cord made of strands of fiber **2 :** a hangman's noose **3 :** a thick string (as of pearls) made by twisting or braiding

²**rope** vb **roped; rop·ing 1 :** to bind, tie, or fasten together with a rope **2 :** to separate or divide off by means of a rope **3 :** LASSO

**Ror·schach inkblot test** \'rór-,shäk-\ n **:** RORSCHACH TEST

**Rorschach test** n **:** a personality and intelligence test in which a subject interprets inkblot designs in terms that reveal intellectual and emotional factors

**ro·sa·ry** \'rō-zə-rē\ n, pl **-ries** [ML rosarium, fr. L, rose garden, fr. neut. of rosarius of roses, fr rosa rose] **1 :** a string of beads used in praying **2 :** often cap **:** a Roman Catholic devotion consisting of meditation on sacred mysteries during recitation of Hail Marys

¹**rose** *past of* RISE

²**rose** \'rōz\ *n* **1** : any of various prickly shrubs with divided leaves and bright often fragrant flowers; *also* : one of these flowers **2** : something resembling a rose in form **3** : a variable color averaging a moderate purplish red — **rose** *adj*

**ro·sé** \rō-'zā\ *n* : a light pink table wine

**rose·ate** \'rō-zē-ət, -zē-,āt\ *adj* **1** : resembling a rose esp. in color **2** : OPTIMISTIC (a ~ view of the future)

**rose·bud** \'rōz-,bəd\ *n* : the flower of a rose when it is at most partly open

**rose·bush** \ ,bush\ *n* : a shrubby rose

**rose·mary** \'rōz-,mer-ē\ *n, pl* -**maries** [ME *rosmarine*, fr L *rosmarinus*, fr. *ros* dew + *marinus* of the sea, fr. *mare* sea] : a fragrant shrubby mint with evergreen leaves used in perfumery and cooking

**ro·sette** \rō-'zet\ *n* **1** : a usu. small badge or ornament of ribbon gathered in the shape of a rose **2** : a circular architectural ornament filled with representations of leaves

**rose·wa·ter** \'rōz-,wȯt-ər, -,wät-\ *adj* : a watery solution of the fragrant constituents of the rose used as a perfume

**rose·wood** \-,wu̇d\ *n* : any of various tropical trees with dark red wood streaked with black, *also* : this wood

**Rosh Ha·sha·nah** \,rȯsh-(h)ə-'shō-nə\ *n* [Heb *rōsh hashshānāh*, lit., beginning of the year] : the Jewish New Year observed as a religious holiday in September or October

**ros·in** \'räz-ən\ *n* : a hard brittle resin obtained esp. from pine trees and used in varnishes and on violin bows

**ros·ter** \'räs-tər\ *n* **1** : a list of personnel; *also* : the persons listed on a roster **2** : an itemized list

**ros·trum** \'räs-trəm\ *n, pl* **rostrums** *or* **ros·tra** \-trə\ [L *Rostra*, pl., a platform for speakers in the Roman Forum decorated with the beaks of captured ships, fr. pl of *rostrum* beak, ship's beak, fr. *rodere* to gnaw] : a stage or platform for public speaking

**rosy** \'rō-zē\ *adj* **ros·i·er; -est 1** : of the color rose **2** : HOPEFUL, PROMISING — **ros·i·ly** \'rō-sə-lē\ *adv* — **ros·i·ness** \-zē-nəs\ *n*

¹**rot** \'rät\ *vb* **rot·ted; rot·ting** : to undergo decomposition : DECAY

²**rot** *n* **1** : DECAY **2** : a disease of plants or animals in which tissue breaks down

¹**ro·ta·ry** \'rōt-ə-rē\ *adj* **1** : turning on an axis like a wheel **2** : having a rotating part

²**rotary** *n, pl* -**ries 1** : a rotary machine **2** : a circular road at a road junction

**ro·tate** \'rō-,tāt\ *vb* **ro·tat·ed; ro·tat·ing 1** : to turn about an axis or a center : REVOLVE **2** : to alternate in a series syn turn, circle, spin, whirl, twirl — **ro·ta·tion** \rō-'tā-shən\ *n* — **ro·ta·tor** \'rō-,tāt-ər\ *n* — **ro·ta·to·ry** \'rōt-ə-,tōr ē\ *adj*

**ROTC** *abbr* Reserve Officers' Training Corps

**rote** \'rōt\ *n* **1** : repetition from memory of forms or phrases often without attention to meaning **2** : fixed routine or repetition

**ro·tis·ser·ie** \rō-'tis-(ə-)rē\ *n* **1** : a restaurant specializing in broiled and barbecued meats **2** : an appliance fitted with a spit on which food is rotated before or over a source of heat

**ro·to·gra·vure** \,rōt-ə-grə-'vyur\ *n* : a photogravure process in which the impression is made by a rotary printing press, *also* : an illustration so printed

**ro·tor** \'rōt-ər\ *n* **1** : a part that rotates **2** : a system of rotating horizontal blades for supporting a helicopter

**rot·ten** \'rät-ᵊn\ *adj* **1** : having rotted : SPOILED, UNSOUND **2** : CORRUPT **3** : extremely unpleasant or inferior — **rot·ten·ness** \-ᵊn-(n)əs\ *n*

**rot·ten·stone** \'rät-ᵊn-,stōn\ *n* : a decomposed siliceous limestone used for polishing

**ro·tund** \rō-'tənd\ *adj* : rounded out syn plump, chubby, portly, stout — **ro·tun·di·ty** \-'tən-dət-ē\ *n*

**ro·tun·da** \rō-'tən-də\ *n* **1** : a round building; *esp* : one covered by a dome **2** : a large round room

**rou·ble** \'rü-bəl\ *var of* RUBLE

**roué** \rü-'ā\ *n* [F, lit., broken on the wheel, fr. pp. of *rouer* to break on the wheel, fr. ML *rotare*, fr. L, to rotate; fr. the feeling that such a person deserves this punishment] : a man given to debauched living : RAKE

**rouge** \'rüzh, 'rüj\ *n* **1** : a cosmetic used to give a red color to cheeks and lips **2** : a red powder used in polishing glass, gems, and metal — **rouge** *vb*

¹**rough** \'rəf\ *adj* **rough·er; rough·est 1** : uneven in surface : not smooth **2** : SHAGGY **3** : not calm : TURBULENT, TEMPESTUOUS **4** : marked by harshness or violence **5** : DIFFICULT, TRYING **6** : coarse or rugged in character or appearance **7** : marked by lack of refinement **8** : CRUDE, UNFINISHED **9** : done or made hastily or tentatively — **rough·ly** *adv* — **rough·ness** *n*

²**rough** *n* **1** : uneven ground covered with high grass esp. along a golf fairway **2** : a crude, unfinished, or preliminary state; *also* : something in such a state **3** : ROWDY, TOUGH

³**rough** *vb* **1** : ROUGHEN **2** : MANHANDLE **3** : to make or shape roughly esp. in a preliminary way — **rough·er** *n*

**rough·age** \'rəf-ij\ *n* : coarse bulky food (as bran) whose bulk stimulates the activity of the intestines

**rough-and-ready** \,əf-ən-'red-ē\ *adj* : rude or unpolished in nature, method, or manner but effective in action or use

**rough-and-tum·ble** \-'təm-bəl\ *n* : rough unrestrained fighting or struggling — **rough-and-tumble** *adj*

**rough·en** \'rəf-ən\ *vb* **rough·ened; rough·en·ing** \-(ə-)niŋ\ : to make or become rough

**rough-hew** \'rəf-'hyü\ *vb* -**hewed; -hewn** \-'hyün\; -**hew·ing 1** : to hew (as timber) coarsely without smoothing **2** : to form crudely or roughly

**rough·house** \'rəf-ˌha͝us\ *n* **:** rough noisy behavior — **roughhouse** *vb*

**rough·neck** \'rəf-ˌnek\ *n* **1 :** ROWDY, TOUGH **2 :** a member of an oil-well-drilling crew other than the driller

**rou·lette** \rü-'let\ *n* **1 :** a gambling game in which a whirling wheel is used **2 :** a toothed wheel or disk for making rows of dots or small holes

**Rou·ma·nian** \rü-'mā-nē-ən, -nyən\ *var of* RUMANIAN

**¹round** \'ra͝und\ *adj* **1 :** having every part of the surface or circumference the same distance from the center **2 :** CYLINDRICAL **3 :** COMPLETE, FULL **4 :** approximately correct **:** being in even units **:** being without fractions **5 :** liberal or ample in size or amount **6 :** BLUNT, OUTSPOKEN **7 :** moving in or forming a circle **8 :** curved or predominantly curved rather than angular — **round·ish** *adj* — **round·ly** \'ra͝un-(d)lē\ *adv* — **round·ness** \'ra͝un-(d)-nəs\ *n*

**²round** *prep or adv* **:** AROUND

**³round** *n* **1 :** something round (as a circle, globe, or ring) **2 :** a curved or rounded part (as a rung of a ladder) **3 :** a circuitous path or course; *also* **:** an habitually covered route (as of a watchman) **4 :** a series or cycle of recurring actions or events **5 :** a period of time or a unit of play in a game or contest **6 :** one shot fired by a soldier or a gun; *also* **:** ammunition for one shot **7 :** a cut of beef esp. between the rump and the lower leg — **in the round 1 :** FREESTANDING **2 :** with a center stage surrounded by an audience on all sides 〈theater *in the round*〉

**⁴round** *vb* **1 :** to make or become round **2 :** to go or pass around or part way around **3 :** to follow a winding course **:** BEND **4 :** COMPLETE, FINISH **5 :** to become plump or shapely **6 :** to express as a round number

**⁵round·about** \'ra͝un-də-ˌba͝ut\ *n, Brit* **:** MERRY-GO-ROUND

**²roundabout** *adj* **:** INDIRECT, CIRCUITOUS

**roun·de·lay** \'ra͝un-də-ˌlā\ *n* **1 :** a simple song with refrain **2 :** a poem with a refrain recurring frequently or at fixed intervals

**round·house** \'ra͝und-ˌha͝us\ *n* **1 :** a circular building for housing and repairing locomotives **2 :** a cabin on the after part of the quarterdeck of an old sailing ship

**round–shoul·dered** \'ra͝un(d)-'shōl-dərd\ *adj* **:** having the shoulders stooping or rounded

**round trip** *n* **:** a trip to a place and back

**round–up** \'ra͝und-ˌəp\ *n* **1 :** the gathering together of cattle on the range by riding around them and driving them in; *also* **:** the men and horses engaged in a roundup **2 :** a gathering in of scattered persons or things **3 :** SUMMARY, RÉSUMÉ 〈news ~〉 — **round up** \'ra͝und-'əp\ *vb*

**round·worm** \-ˌwərm\ *n* **:** NEMATODE

**rouse** \'ra͝uz\ *vb* **roused; rous·ing 1 :** to wake from sleep **2 :** to excite to activity **:** stir up

**roust·about** \'ra͝us-tə-ˌba͝ut\ *n* **:** one who does heavy unskilled labor (as on a dock or in an oil field)

**¹rout** \'ra͝ut\ *n* **1 :** MOB 1, 2 **2 :** DISTURBANCE **3 :** a fashionable gathering

**²rout** *vb* **1 :** RUMMAGE **2 :** to gouge out **3 :** to turn out by compulsion

**³rout** *n* **1 :** a state of wild confusion or disorderly retreat **2 :** a disastrous defeat

**⁴rout** *vb* **1 :** to put to flight **2 :** to defeat decisively

**¹route** \'rüt, 'ra͝ut\ *n* **1 :** a traveled way **2 :** CHANNEL **3 :** a line of travel

**²route** *vb* **rout·ed; rout·ing 1 :** to send by a selected route **2 :** to arrange and direct the order of

**route·man** \-mən, -ˌman\ *n* **:** one who sells and makes deliveries on an assigned route

**rou·tine** \rü-'tēn\ *n* [F, fr. MF, fr. *route* traveled way, fr. OF, fr. (assumed) VL *rupta (via)*, lit., broken way, fr. L *ruptus*, pp. of *rumpere* to break] **1 :** a round (as of work or play) regularly followed **2 :** any regular course of action — **routine** *adj* — **rou·tine·ly** *adv* — **rou·tin·ize** \-'tēn-ˌīz\ *vb*

**¹rove** \'rōv\ *vb* **roved; rov·ing :** to wander over or through **:** RAMBLE, ROAM — **rov·er** *n*

**²rove** *past of* REEVE

**¹row** \'rō\ *vb* **1 :** to propel a boat with oars **2 :** to travel or convey in a rowboat **3 :** to match rowing skill against — **row·er** \'rō-(ə)r\ *n*

**²row** *n* **:** an act or instance of rowing

**³row** *n* **1 :** a number of objects in an orderly sequence **2 :** WAY, STREET

**⁴row** \'ra͝u\ *n* **:** a noisy quarrel

**⁵row** \'ra͝u\ *vb* **:** to engage in a row

**row·boat** \'rō-ˌbōt\ *n* **:** a small boat designed to be rowed

**row·dy** \'ra͝ud-ē\ *adj* **row·di·er; -est :** coarse or boisterous in behavior **:** ROUGH — **row·di·ness** \'ra͝ud-ē-nəs\ *n* — **rowdy** *n* — **row·dy·ish** *adj* — **row·dy·ism** *n*

**row·el** \'ra͝u(-ə)l\ *n* **:** a small pointed wheel on a spur used to urge on a horse — **rowel** *vb*

**roy·al** \'rȯi-əl\ *adj* **1 :** of or relating to a king or sovereign **2 :** resembling or befitting a king — **roy·al·ly** \-ē\ *adv*

**roy·al·ist** \-ə-ləst\ *n* **:** an adherent of a king or of monarchical government

**roy·al·ty** \'rȯi-əl-tē\ *n, pl* **-ties 1 :** the state of being royal **2 :** a royal person **:** royal persons **3 :** a share of a product or profit (as of a mine or oil well) claimed by the owner for allowing another person to use the property **4 :** payment made to the owner of a patent or copyright for the use of it

**RPM** *abbr* revolutions per minute

**RPO** *abbr* railway post office

**RPS** *abbr* revolutions per second

**rpt** *abbr* **1** repeat **2** report

**RR** *abbr* **1** railroad **2** rural route

**RS** *abbr* **1** recording secretary **2** revised statutes **3** right side **4** Royal Society

**RSV** *abbr* Revised Standard Version

**RSVP** *abbr* [F *répondez s'il vous plaît*] please reply

**RSWC** *abbr* right side up with care
**rt** *abbr* right
**RT** *abbr* radiotelephone
**rte** *abbr* route
**Ru** *symbol* ruthenium

¹**rub** \'rəb\ *vb* **rubbed; rub·bing 1** : to use pressure and friction on a body or object **2** : to scour, polish, erase, or smear by pressure and friction **3** : to fret or chafe with friction

²**rub** *n* **1** : an act or instance of rubbing **2** : a place roughened or injured by rubbing **3** : DIFFICULTY, OBSTRUCTION **4** : something grating to the feelings

¹**rub·ber** \'rəb-ər\ *n* **1** : one that rubs **2** : ERASER **3** : a flexible waterproof elastic substance made from the juice of various tropical plants or synthetically; *also* : something made of this material — **rubber** *adj* — **rub·ber·ize** \-,īz\ *vb* — **rub·bery** *adj*

²**rubber** *n* **1** : a contest that consists of an odd number of games and is won by the side that takes a majority **2** : an extra game played to decide a tie

¹**rub·ber·neck** \-,nek\ *also* **rub·ber·neck·er** \-ər\ *n* **1** : an inquisitive person **2** : a person on a guided tour

²**rubberneck** *vb* : to look about, stare, or listen with excessive curiosity

**rub·bish** \'rəb-ish\ *n* **1** : useless waste or rejected matter : TRASH **2** : something worthless or nonsensical

**rub·ble** \'rəb-əl\ *n* : broken stones or bricks used in masonry; *also* : a mass of such material

**ru·bel·la** \rü-'bel-ə\ *n* : GERMAN MEASLES

**ru·bi·cund** \'rü-bi-(,)kənd\ *adj* : RED, RUDDY

**ru·bid·i·um** \rü-'bid-ē-əm\ *n* : a soft silvery metallic chemical element

**ru·ble** \'rü-bəl\ *n* — see MONEY table

**ru·bric** \'rü-brik\ *n* [ME *rubrike* red ocher, heading in red letters of part of a book, fr. MF *rubrique*, fr. L *rubrica*, fr. *ruber* red] **1** : HEADING, TITLE; *also* : CLASS, CATEGORY **2** : a rule esp. for the conduct of a religious service

**ru·by** \'rü-bē\ *n, pl* **rubies** : a precious stone of a clear red color

**ru·by–throat·ed hummingbird** \,rü-bē-,thrōt-əd-\ *n* : a bright green and whitish hummingbird of eastern No. America with a red throat in the male

**ruck·us** \'rək-əs\ *n* : ROW, DISTURBANCE

**rud·der** \'rəd-ər\ *n* : a movable flat piece attached vertically at the rear of a boat or aircraft for steering

**rud·dy** \'rəd-ē\ *adj* **rud·di·er; -est** : REDDISH; *esp* : of a healthy reddish complexion — **rud·di·ness** \'rəd-ē-nəs\ *n*

**rude** \'rüd\ *adj* **rud·er; rud·est 1** : roughly made : CRUDE **2** : UNDEVELOPED, PRIMITIVE **3** : UNSKILLED **4** : IMPOLITE, DISCOURTEOUS — **rude·ly** *adv* — **rude·ness** *n*

**ru·di·ment** \'rüd-ə-mənt\ *n* **1** : something not fully developed **2** : an elementary principle or basic skill — **ru·di·men·ta·ry** \,rüd-ə-'men-t(ə-)rē\ *adj*

¹**rue** \'rü\ *vb* **rued; ru·ing** : to feel regret, remorse, or penitence for

²**rue** *n* : REGRET, SORROW — **rue·ful** \-fəl\ *adj* — **rue·ful·ly** \-ē\ *adv* — **rue·ful·ness** *n*

³**rue** *n* : a European strong-scented woody herb with bitter-tasting leaves

**rue anemone** *n* : a delicate herb of the buttercup family with white flowers

**ruff** \'rəf\ *n* **1** : a wheel-shaped frilled collar worn about 1600 **2** : a fringe of hair or feathers around the neck of an animal — **ruffed** \'rəft\ *adj*

**ruf·fi·an** \'rəf-ē-ən\ *n* [MF *rufian*] : a brutal person — **ruf·fi·an·ly** *adj*

¹**ruf·fle** \'rəf-əl\ *vb* **ruf·fled; ruf·fling** \-(ə-)liŋ\ **1** : to draw into or provide with plaits or folds **2** : to roughen the surface of **3** : to erect (as hair or feathers) in or like a ruff **4** : IRRITATE, VEX **5** : to flip through (as pages)

²**ruffle** *n* **1** : RIPPLE **2** : a strip of fabric gathered or pleated on one edge **3** : RUFF 2

**rug** \'rəg\ *n* **1** : a piece of heavy fabric usu. with a nap or pile used as a floor covering **2** : a lap robe

**rug·by** \'rəg-bē\ *n, often cap* [*Rugby* School, Rugby, England, where it was first played] : a football game in which play is continuous and interference and forward passing are not permitted

**rug·ged** \'rəg-əd\ *adj* **1** : having a rough uneven surface **2** : TURBULENT, STORMY **3** : HARSH, STERN **4** : ROBUST, STURDY — **rug·ged·ly** *adv* — **rug·ged·ness** *n*

¹**ru·in** \'rü-ən\ *n* **1** : complete collapse or destruction **2** : the remains of something destroyed — usu. used in pl. **3** : a cause of destruction **4** : the action of destroying

²**ruin** *vb* **1** : DESTROY **2** : to damage beyond repair **3** : BANKRUPT

**ru·in·ation** \,rü-ə-'nā-shən\ *n* : RUIN, DESTRUCTION

**ru·in·ous** \'rü-ə-nəs\ *adj* **1** : RUINED, DILAPIDATED **2** : causing ruin — **ru·in·ous·ly** *adv* — **ru·in·ous·ness** *n*

¹**rule** \'rül\ *n* **1** : a guide or principle for governing action : REGULATION **2** : the usual way of doing something **3** : GOVERNMENT, CONTROL **4** : a straight strip of material (as wood or metal) marked off in units and used for measuring or as a straightedge

²**rule** *vb* **ruled; rul·ing 1** : CONTROL, GOVERN **2** : to be preeminent in : DOMINATE, PREVAIL **3** : to give or state as a considered decision **4** : to mark on paper with or as if with a rule

**rul·er** \'rü-lər\ *n* **1** : SOVEREIGN **2** : RULE 4

**rum** \'rəm\ *n* **1** : a liquor distilled from a fermented cane product (as molasses) **2** : alcoholic liquor

**Rum** *abbr* Rumania; Rumanian

**Ru·ma·nian** \rù-'mā-nē-ən, -nyən\ *n* **1** : a native or inhabitant of Rumania **2** : the language of Rumania — **Rumanian** *adj*

**rum·ba** \'rəm-bə, 'rùm-\ *n* : a Cuban Negro dance or an imitation of it

¹**rum·ble** \'rəm-bəl\ *vb* **rum·bled;**

**rum·bling** \-b(ǝ-)liŋ\ : to make a low heavy rolling sound; *also* : to travel or move along with such a sound — **rumbler** \-b(ǝ-)lǝr\ *n*

²**rumble** *n* **1** : a low heavy rolling sound **2** : a seat behind and outside a carriage body; *also* : a folding seat located behind the regular seating space in the back of an automobile and not covered by the top **3** *slang* : a street fight esp. among teenage gangs

**rum·bling** \'rǝm-bliŋ\ *n* **1** : RUMBLE **2** : widespread talk or complaints — usu. used in pl.

**ru·mi·nant** \'rü-mǝ-nǝnt\ *n* : any of a great group of hoofed mammals (as cattle, deer, and camels) that chew the cud — **ruminant** *adj*

**ru·mi·nate** \'rü-mǝ-ˌnāt\ *vb* **-nat·ed; -nat·ing** [L *ruminari* to chew the cud, muse upon, fr. *rumin-, rumen* gullet] **1** : MEDITATE, MUSE **2** : to chew the cud — **ru·mi·na·tion** \ˌrü-mǝ-'nā-shǝn\ *n*

¹**rum·mage** \'rǝm-ij\ *n* **1** : an act of rummaging **2** : things found by rummaging : miscellaneous old things

²**rummage** *vb* **rum·maged; rum·mag·ing** : to poke around in all corners looking for something — **rum·mag·er** *n*

**rum·my** \'rǝm-ē\ *n* : any of several card games for two or more players

**ru·mor** \'rü-mǝr\ *n* **1** : common talk **2** : a statement or report current but not authenticated — **rumor** *vb*

**rump** \'rǝmp\ *n* **1** : the rear part of an animal; *also* : a cut of beef behind the upper sirloin **2** : a small remaining fragment : REMNANT

**rum·ple** \'rǝm-pǝl\ *vb* **rum·pled; rum·pling** \-p(ǝ-)liŋ\ : TOUSLE, MUSS, WRINKLE — **rumple** *n* — **rum·ply** \'rǝm-p(ǝ-)lē\ *adj*

**rum·pus** \'rǝm-pǝs\ *n* : DISTURBANCE, FRACAS

**rumpus room** *n* : a room usu. in the basement of a home that is used for games, parties, and recreation

**rum·run·ner** \'rǝm-ˌrǝn-ǝr\ *n* : a person or ship engaged in bringing prohibited liquor ashore or across a border — **rum·run·ning** \-ˌrǝn-iŋ\ *adj*

¹**run** \'rǝn\ *vb* **ran** \'ran\; **run; run·ning 1** : to go at a pace faster than a walk **2** : to take to flight : FLEE **3** : to go without restraint (lets his children ∼) **4** : to go rapidly or hurriedly : HASTEN, RUSH **5** : to make a quick or casual trip or visit **6** : to contend in a race; *esp* : to enter an election **7** : to move on or as if on wheels : pass or slide freely **8** : to go back and forth : PLY **9** : FUNCTION, OPERATE (left his car *running*) **10** : to continue in force (two years to ∼) **11** : to flow rapidly or under pressure : MELT, FUSE, DISSOLVE; *also* : DISCHARGE **12** : to tend to produce or to recur (family ∼s to blonds) **13** : to take a certain direction **14** : to be current (rumors *running* wild) **15** : to move in schools esp. to a spawning ground (shad are *running*) **16** : to be worded or written **17** : to

cause to run **18** : to perform or bring about by running **19** : TRACE (∼ down a rumor) **20** : to put forward as a candidate for office **21** : to cause to pass (∼ a wire from the antenna) **22** : to cause to collide **23** : SMUGGLE **24** : MANAGE, CONDUCT, OPERATE (∼ a business) **25** : INCUR (∼ a risk) **26** : to permit to accumulate before settling (∼ a charge account)

²**run** *n* **1** : an act or the action of running **2** : BROOK, CREEK **3** : a continuous series esp. of similar things **4** : persistent heavy demands from depositors, creditors, or customers **5** : the quantity of work turned out in a continuous operation; *also* : a period of operation (as of a machine or plant) **6** : the usual or normal kind (the ordinary ∼ of men) **7** : the distance covered in continuous travel or sailing **8** : a regular course or route; *also* : TRIP, JOURNEY **9** : a school of migrating fish **10** : an enclosure for animals **11** : a lengthwise ravel (as in a stocking) **12** : a score in baseball **13** : an inclined course (as for skiing) — **run·less** *adj*

**run·about** \'rǝn-ǝ-ˌbaut\ *n* : a light wagon, automobile, or motorboat

**run·a·gate** \'rǝn-ǝ-ˌgāt\ *n* **1** : FUGITIVE **2** : VAGABOND

**run·around** \'rǝn-ǝ-ˌraund\ *n* : evasive or delaying action esp. in reply to a request

¹**run·away** \'rǝn-ǝ-ˌwā\ *n* **1** : FUGITIVE **2** : the act of running away or out of control

²**runaway** *adj* **1** : FUGITIVE **2** : accomplished by elopement (∼ marriage) **3** : won by a long lead **4** : subject to uncontrolled changes (∼ inflation)

**run·down** \'rǝn-ˌdaun\ *n* : an item-by-item report : SUMMARY

**run-down** \'rǝn-'daun\ *adj* **1** : being in poor repair : DILAPIDATED **2** : EXHAUSTED **3** : completely unwound

**run down** \'rǝn-'daun\ *vb* **1** : to collide with and knock down **2** : to chase until exhausted or captured **3** : to find by search **4** : DISPARAGE **5** : to cease to operate for lack of motive power **6** : to decline in physical condition

**rune** \'rün\ *n* **1** : a character of an alphabet formerly used by the Germanic peoples **2** : MYSTERY, MAGIC **3** : a poem esp. in Finnish or Old Norse — **ru·nic** \'rü-nik\ *adj*

¹**rung** *past part of* RING

²**rung** \'rǝŋ\ *n* **1** : a round of a chair or ladder **2** : a spoke of a wheel

**run-in** \'rǝn-ˌin\ *n* **1** : something run in **2** : ALTERCATION, QUARREL

**run in** \'rǝn-'in\ *vb* **1** : to arrest esp. for a minor offense **2** : to pay a casual visit

**run·let** \'rǝn-lǝt\ *n* : RUNNEL, BROOK

**run·nel** \'rǝn-ᵊl\ *n* : BROOK, RIVULET, STREAMLET

**run·ner** \'rǝn-ǝr\ *n* **1** : one that runs **2** : BALLCARRIER **3** : a baseball player on base or attempting to reach base **4** : either of the longitudinal pieces on which a sled or sleigh rides **5** : the part of an ice skate that slides on the ice **6** : the support of a drawer or a sliding door **7** : a horizontal branch from the base of a plant that produces new plants **8** : a plant producing runners

**run·ner-up** \'rən-ər-,əp\ *n, pl* **runners-up** *also* **runner-ups** : the competitor in a contest who finishes next to the winner

¹**run·ning** \'rən-iŋ\ *adj* **1** : FLUID, RUNNY **2** : CONTINUOUS, INCESSANT **3** : measured in a straight line ⟨cost per ∼ foot⟩ **4** : FLOWING **5** : of or relating to an act of running **6** : fitted or trained for running ⟨∼ horse⟩

²**running** *adv* : in succession

**running light** *n* : one of the lights carried by a vehicle at night

**run·ny** \'rən-ē\ *adj* : having a tendency to run

**run·off** \'rən-,óf\ *n* : a final contest to a previous indecisive contest

**run-of-the-mill** \,rən-ə-(v)-thə-'mil\ *adj* : not outstanding : AVERAGE

**run on** \'rən-'ón, -'än\ *vb* **1** : to continue (matter in type) without a break or a new paragraph **2** : to place or add (as an entry in a dictionary) at the end of a paragraphed item — **run-on** \-,ón, -,än\ *n*

**runt** \'rənt\ *n* : an unusually small person or animal : DWARF — **runty** *adj*

**run·way** \'rən-,wā\ *n* **1** : a beaten path made by animals, *also* : a passage for animals **2** : a surfaced strip of ground for the landing and takeoff of airplanes **3** : a narrow platform from a stage into an auditorium **4** : a support on which something runs

**ru·pee** \rü-'pē, 'rü-,pē\ *n* — see MONEY table

**ru·pi·ah** \rü-'pē-ə\ *n, pl* **rupiah** *or* **rupiahs** — see MONEY table

¹**rup·ture** \'rəp-chər\ *n* : a breaking or tearing apart; *also* : HERNIA

²**rupture** *vb* **rup·tured; rup·tur·ing** : to cause or undergo rupture

**ru·ral** \'rür-əl\ *adj* : of or relating to the country, country people, or agriculture

**ruse** \'rüs, 'rüz\ *n* : a wily subterfuge : TRICK, ARTIFICE

¹**rush** \'rəsh\ *n* : a hollow-stemmed grasslike marsh plant — **rushy** *adj*

²**rush** *vb* [ME *russhen*, fr. MF *ruser* to put to flight, repel, deceive, fr. L *recusare* to refuse, fr. re- back + *causari* to give a reason, fr. *causa* cause, reason] **1** : to move forward or act with too great haste or eagerness or without preparation **2** : to perform in a short time or at high speed **3** : ATTACK, CHARGE — **rush·er** *n*

³**rush** *n* **1** : a violent forward motion **2** : a crowding of people to one place **3** : unusual demand or activity

⁴**rush** *adj* : requiring or marked by special speed or urgency ⟨∼ orders⟩

**rush hour** *n* : a time when the amount of traffic or business is at a peak

**rusk** \'rəsk\ *n* : a sweet or plain bread baked, sliced, and baked again until dry and crisp

**Russ** *abbr* Russia, Russian

**rus·set** \'rəs-ət\ *n* **1** : a variable reddish brown or yellowish brown color **2** : a coarse cloth of the color russet **3** : any of various winter apples with rough russet skins — **russet** *adj*

**Rus·sian** \'rəsh-ən\ *n* **1** : a native or inhabitant of Russia or the U.S.S.R. **2** : the chief language of the U.S.S.R. — **Russian** *adj*

**rust** \'rəst\ *n* **1** : a reddish coating formed on metal (as iron) when it is exposed to air **2** : the reddish orange color of rust **3** : any of various diseases causing reddish spots on plants — **rust** *n* — **rusty** *adj*

¹**rus·tic** \'rəs-tik\ *adj* **1** : RURAL **2** : AWKWARD, BOORISH **3** : PLAIN, SIMPLE **4** : made of the rough limbs of trees ⟨∼ furniture⟩ — **rus·ti·cal·ly** \'rəs-ti-k(ə-)lē\ *adv* — **rus·tic·i·ty** \,rəs-'tis-ət-ē\ *n*

²**rustic** *n* : a rustic person

**rus·ti·cate** \'rəs-ti-,kāt\ *vb* **-cat·ed; -cat·ing** **1** : to go into or reside in the country **2** : to suspend from school or college — **rus·ti·ca·tion** \,rəs-ti-'kā-shən\ *n* — **rus·ti·ca·tor** \'rəs-ti-,kāt-ər\ *n*

¹**rus·tle** \'rəs-əl\ *vb* **rus·tled; rus·tling** \'rəs-(ə-)liŋ\ **1** : to make or cause a rustle **2** : to cause to rustle ⟨∼ a newspaper⟩ **3** : to act or move with energy or speed; *also* : to procure in this way **4** : to forage food **5** : to steal cattle from the range — **rus·tler** \-(ə-)lər\ *n*

²**rustle** *n* : a quick succession or confusion of small sounds ⟨∼ of leaves⟩

¹**rut** \'rət\ *n* : state or period of sexual excitement esp. in male deer — **rut** *vb*

²**rut** *n* **1** : a track worn by wheels or by habitual passage of something **2** : a usual way of doing something from which one is not easily stirred — **rutted** *adj*

**ru·ta·ba·ga** \,rüt-ə-'bā-gə, ,rüt-\ *n* : a turnip with a large yellowish root

**ru·the·ni·um** \rü-'thē-nē-əm\ *n* : a hard brittle metallic chemical element

**ruth·less** \'rüth-ləs\ *adj* [fr. *ruth* compassion, pity, fr. ME *ruthe*, fr. *ruen* to rue, fr. OE *hrēowan*] : having no pity : MERCILESS, CRUEL — **ruth·less·ly** *adv* — **ruth·less·ness** *n*

**RW** *abbr* **1** right worshipful **2** right worthy

**rwy** *or* **ry** *abbr* railway

**-ry** \rē\ *n suffix* : -ERY ⟨bigot*ry*⟩

**rye** \'rī\ *n* **1** : a hardy cereal grass grown for grain or as a cover crop; *also* : its seed **2** : a whiskey distilled from a rye mash

S

¹s \'es\ n, pl s's or ss \'es-əz\ often cap : the 19th letter of the English alphabet

²s abbr, often cap 1 saint 2 second 3 semi- 4 senate 5 series 6 shilling 7 singular 8 small 9 son 10 south; southern

¹-s \ after sounds f, k, ḳ, p, t, th; əz after sounds ch, j, s, sh, z, zh; z after other sounds\ 1 — used to form the plural of most nouns that do not end in s, z, sh, ch, or postconsonantal y \heads\ \books\ \boys\ \beliefs\, to form the plural of proper nouns that end in postconsonantal y \Marys\, and with or without a preceding apostrophe to form the plural of abbreviations, numbers, letters, and symbols used as nouns \MC's\ \4's\ \#s\ \B's\ 2 — used to form adverbs denoting usual or repeated action or state \works nights\

²-s vb suffix —used to form the third person singular present of most verbs that do not end in s, z, sh, ch, or postconsonantal y \falls\ \takes\ \plays\

S symbol sulfur

SA abbr 1 Salvation Army 2 seaman apprentice 3 sex appeal 4 [L sine anno] without date 5 South Africa 6 subject to approval

Sab·bath \'sab-əth\ n [ME sabat, fr. OF & OE, fr. L sabbatum, fr. Gk sabbaton, fr. Heb shabbāth, lit., rest] 1 : the seventh day of the week observed as a day of worship by Jews and some Christians 2 : Sunday observed among Christians as a day of worship

sab·bat·i·cal year \sə-,bat-i-kəl-\ n : a leave often with pay granted (as to a college professor) usu. every seventh year for rest, travel, or research

sa·ber or sa·bre \'sā-bər\ n : a cavalry sword with a curved blade and thick back

saber saw n : a light portable electric saw with a pointed reciprocating blade

Sa·bin vaccine \,sā-bən-\ n [after Albert B. Sabin b1906 American pediatrician] : a polio vaccine taken by mouth

sa·ble \'sā-bəl\ n, pl sables 1 : the color black 2 pl : mourning garments 3 : a dark brown mammal of northern Europe and Asia valued for its fur; also : this fur

¹sab·o·tage \'sab-ə-,täzh\ n 1 : deliberate destruction of an employer's property or hindering of production by workmen 2 : destructive or hampering action by enemy agents or sympathizers in time of war

²sabotage vb -taged; -tag·ing : to practice sabotage on : WRECK

sab·o·teur \,sab-ə-'tər\ n : a person who commits sabotage

sac \'sak\ n : a baglike part of an animal or plant

SAC \'sak\ abbr Strategic Air Command

sac·cha·rin \'sak-(ə-)rən\ n : a very sweet white crystalline substance made from coal tar

sac·cha·rine \'sak-(ə-)rən\ adj : nauseatingly sweet \~ poetry\

sac·er·do·tal \,sas-ər-'dōt-ᵊl, ,sak-\ adj : PRIESTLY — sac·er·do·tal·ism n — sac·er·do·tal·ly \-ē\ adv

sa·chem \'sā-chəm\ n : a No. American Indian chief

sa·chet \sa-'shā\ n : a small bag filled with perfumed powder (sachet powder) for scenting clothes

¹sack \'sak\ n 1 : a large coarse bag; also : a small container esp. of paper 2 : a loose jacket or short coat

²sack vb : DISMISS, FIRE

³sack n [modif. of MF sec dry, fr. L siccus] : a white wine popular in England in the 16th and 17th centuries

⁴sack vb : to plunder a captured town

sack·cloth \-,klóth\ n : a garment worn as a sign of mourning or penitence

sac·ra·ment \'sak-rə-mənt\ n 1 : a formal religious act or rite; esp : one (as baptism or the Eucharist) held to have been instituted by Christ 2 : the elements of the Eucharist — sac·ra·men·tal \,sak-rə-'ment-ᵊl\ adj

sa·cred \'sā-krəd\ adj 1 : set apart for the service or worship of deity 2 : devoted exclusively to one service or use 3 : worthy of veneration or reverence 4 : of or relating to religion : RELIGIOUS syn blessed, divine, hallowed, holy, spiritual — sa·cred·ly adv — sa·cred·ness n

sacred cow n : a person or thing immune from criticism

¹sac·ri·fice \'sak-rə-,fīs\ n 1 : the offering of something precious to deity 2 : something offered in sacrifice 3 : LOSS, DEPRIVATION 4 : a bunt allowing a base runner to advance while the batter is put out; also : a fly ball allowing a runner to score after the catch — sac·ri·fi·cial \,sak-rə-'fish-əl\ adj — sac·ri·fi·cial·ly \-ē\ adv

²sac·ri·fice vb -ficed; -fic·ing 1 : to offer up or kill as a sacrifice 2 : to accept the loss or destruction of for an end, cause, or ideal 3 : to make a sacrifice in baseball

sac·ri·lege \'sak-rə-lij\ n [ME, fr. OF, fr. L sacrilegium, fr. sacrilegus one who steals sacred things, fr. sacr-, sacer sacred + legere to gather, steal] 1 : violation of something consecrated to God 2 : gross irreverence toward a hallowed person, place, or thing — sac·ri·le·gious \,sak-rə-'lij-əs, -'lē-jəs\ adj — sac·ri·le·gious·ly adv

sac·ris·tan \'sak-rə-stən\ n 1 : a church officer in charge of the sacristy 2 : SEXTON

sac·ris·ty \'sak-rə-stē\ n, pl -ties : VESTRY

sac·ro·il·i·ac \,sak-rō-'il-ē-,ak\ n : the joint between the bone of the hip and the fused vertebrae near the base of the spine

sac·ro·sanct \'sak-rō-,saŋkt\ adj : SACRED, INVIOLABLE

sa·crum \'sak-rəm, 'sā-krəm\ n, pl sa·cra \'sak-rə, 'sā-krə\ : the part of the vertebral column that is directly connected with or forms a part of the pelvis

**sad** \'sad\ *adj* **sad·der; sad·dest** **1 :** GRIEVING, MOURNFUL, DOWNCAST **2 :** causing sorrow **3 :** DULL, SOMBER — **sad·ly** *adv* — **sad·ness** *n*

**sad·den** \'sad-ᵊn\ *vb* **sad·dened; sad·den·ing** \'sad-(ᵊ-)niŋ\ **:** to make sad

**¹sad·dle** \'sad-ᵊl\ *n* **1 :** a usu. padded leather-covered seat (as for a rider on horseback) **2 :** the upper back portion of a carcass (as of mutton)

**²saddle** *vb* **sad·dled; sad·dling** \'sad-(ᵊ-)liŋ\ **1 :** to put a saddle on **2 :** BURDEN

**sad·dle·bow** \'sad-ᵊl-,bō\ *n* **:** the arch in the front of a saddle

**saddle horse** *n* **:** a horse suited for or trained for riding

**Sad·du·cee** \'saj-ə-,sē, 'sad-yə-\ *n* **:** a member of an ancient Jewish sect opposed to the Pharisees — **Sad·du·ce·an** \,saj-ə-'sē-ən, ,sad-yə-\ *adj*

**sad-iron** \'sad-,ī(-ə)rn\ *n* **:** a flatiron with a removable handle

**sa·dism** \'sā-,diz-əm, 'sad-,iz-\ *n* **:** abnormal delight in cruelty — **sa·dist** \'sād-əst, 'sad-\ *n* — **sa·dis·tic** \sə-'dis-tik\ *adj* — **sa·dis·ti·cal·ly** \-ti-k(ə-)lē\ *adv*

**sa·fa·ri** \sə-'fär-ē, -'far-\ *n* **1 :** the caravan and equipment of a hunting expedition esp. in eastern Africa; *also* **:** the expedition itself **2 :** JOURNEY, TRIP

**¹safe** \'sāf\ *adj* **saf·er; saf·est** **1 :** freed from injury or risk **2 :** affording safety; *also* **:** secure from danger or loss **3 :** RELIABLE, TRUSTWORTHY — **safe·ly** *adv*

**²safe** *n* **:** a container for keeping articles (as valuables) safe

**safe-con·duct** \-'kän-(,)dəkt\ *n* **:** a pass permitting a person to go through enemy lines

**¹safe·guard** \-,gärd\ *n* **:** a measure or device for preventing accident or injury

**²safeguard** *vb* **:** to provide a safeguard for **:** PROTECT

**safe·keep·ing** \'sāf-'kē-piŋ\ *n* **:** a keeping or being kept in safety

**safe·ty** \'sāf-tē\ *n, pl* **safeties** **1 :** freedom from danger **:** SECURITY **2 :** a protective device **3 :** a football play in which the ball is downed by the offensive team behind its own goal line **4 :** a defensive football back in the deepest position — **safety** *adj*

**safety glass** *n* **:** shatter-resistant material formed of two sheets of glass with a sheet of clear plastic between them

**safety match** *n* **:** a match that ignites only when struck on a special surface

**saf·flow·er** \'saf-,laủ(-ə)r\ *n* **:** a widely grown Old World herb related to the daisies that has large orange or red flower heads yielding a dyestuff and seeds rich in edible oil

**saf·fron** \'saf-rən\ *n* **:** an aromatic deep orange powder from the flower of a crocus used to color and flavor foods

**sag** \'sag\ *vb* **sagged; sag·ging** **1 :** to bend down at the middle **2 :** to become flabby **:** DROOP — **sag** *n*

**sa·ga** \'säg-ə\ *n* **:** a narrative of heroic deeds; *esp* **:** one recorded in Iceland in the 12th and 13th centuries

**sa·ga·cious** \sə-'gā-shəs\ *adj* **:** of keen mind **:** SHREWD — **sa·gac·i·ty** \-'gas-ət-ē\ *n*

**sag·a·more** \'sag-ə-,mōr\ *n* **:** a subordinate No. American Indian chief

**¹sage** \'sāj\ *adj* [ME, fr. OF, fr. (assumed) VL *sapius*, fr. L *sapere* to taste, have good taste, be wise] **:** WISE, PRUDENT — **sage·ly** *adv*

**²sage** *n* **:** a wise man **:** PHILOSOPHER

**³sage** *n* [ME, fr. MF *sauge*, fr. L *salvia*, fr. *salvus* healthy; fr. its use as a medicinal herb] **1 :** a shrublike mint with leaves used in flavoring **2 :** SAGEBRUSH

**sage·brush** \-,brəsh\ *n* **:** a low shrub of the western U.S. with a sagelike odor

**sa·go** \'sā-gō\ *n, pl* **sagos :** a dry granulated starch esp. from the pith of an East Indian palm (**sago palm**)

**sa·gua·ro** \sə-'wär-ə\ *n, pl* **-ros :** a desert cactus of the southwestern U.S. and Mexico with a tall columnar simple or sparsely branched trunk of up to 60 feet

**said** *past of* SAY

**¹sail** \'sāl\ *n* **1 :** a piece of fabric by means of which the wind is used to propel a ship **2 :** a sailing ship **3 :** something resembling a sail **4 :** a trip on a sailboat

**²sail** *vb* **1 :** to travel on a sailing ship **2 :** to pass over in a ship **3 :** to manage or direct the course of a ship **4 :** to glide through the air

**sail·boat** \-,bōt\ *n* **:** a boat usu. propelled by a sail

**sail·cloth** \-,klòth\ *n* **:** a heavy canvas used for sails, tents, or upholstery

**sail·fish** \-,fish\ *n* **:** any of a genus of large fishes with a very large dorsal fin

**sail·ing** \'sā-liŋ\ *n* **:** the action, fact, or pastime of cruising or racing in a sailboat

**sail·or** \'sā-lər\ *n* **:** one that sails; *esp* **:** a member of a ship's crew

**sail·plane** \'sāl-,plān\ *n* **:** a glider designed to rise in an upward current of air

**saint** \'sānt, *before a name* (,)sānt or sənt\ *n* **1 :** one officially recognized as preeminent for holiness **2 :** one of the spirits of the departed in heaven **3 :** a holy or godly person — **saint·ed** \-əd\ *adj* — **saint·hood** \-,hùd\ *n*

**Saint Ber·nard** \-bər-'närd\ *n* **:** any of a Swiss alpine breed of tall powerful working dogs used esp. formerly in aiding lost travelers

**saint·ly** \'sānt-lē\ *adj* **:** relating to, resembling, or befitting a saint — **saint·li·ness** *n*

**¹sake** \'sāk\ *n* **1 :** MOTIVE, PURPOSE **:** personal or social welfare, safety, or well-being

**²sa·ke** *or* **sa·ki** \'säk-ē\ *n* **:** a Japanese alcoholic beverage of fermented rice

**sa·laam** \sə-'läm\ *n* [Ar *salām*, lit., peace] **1 :** a salutation or ceremonial greeting in the East **2 :** an obeisance performed by bowing very low and placing the right palm on the forehead — salaam vb

sa•la•cious \sə-'lā-shəs\ adj : OBSCENE, PORNOGRAPHIC

sal•ad \'sal-əd\ n : a cold dish (as of lettuce, vegetables, or fruit) served with dressing

sal•a•man•der \'sal-ə-,man-dər\ n : a small lizardlike animal related to the frogs

sa•la•mi \sə-'läm-ē\ n : highly seasoned sausage of pork and beef

sal•a•ry \'sal-(ə)-rē\ n, pl -ries [ME salarie, fr. L salarium salt money, pension, salary, fr. neut. of salarius of salt, fr. sal salt] : payment made at regular intervals for services

sale \'sāl\ n 1 : transfer of ownership of property from one person to another in return for money 2 : ready market : DEMAND 3 : AUCTION 4 : a selling of goods at bargain prices — sale•able or sale•able \'sā-lə-bəl\ adj

sales•girl \'sālz-,gərl\ n : SALESWOMAN

sales•man \-mən\ n : a person who sells in a store or to outside customers — sales•man•ship n

sales•wom•an \-,wum-ən\ n : a woman who sells merchandise

sal•i•cyl•ic acid \,sal-ə-,sil-ik-\ n : a crystalline organic acid used in the form of its salts to relieve pain and fever

¹sa•lient \'sāl-yənt\ adj : jutting forward beyond a line; also : PROMINENT
syn conspicuous, striking, noticeable

²salient n : a projecting part in a line of defense

¹sa•line \'sā-,lēn, -,līn\ adj : consisting of or containing salt : SALTY — sa•lin•i•ty \sā-'lin-ət-ē, sə-\ n

²saline n 1 : a metallic salt esp. with a purgative action 2 : a saline solution

sa•li•va \sə-'lī-və\ n : a liquid secreted into the mouth that helps digestion — sal•i•vary \'sal-ə-,ver-ē\ adj

sal•i•vate \'sal-ə-,vāt\ vb -vat•ed; -vat•ing : to produce saliva esp. in excess — sal•i•va•tion \,sal-ə-'vā-shən\ n

Salk vaccine \'sò(l)k-\ n [after Jonas Salk b1914 American physician] : a polio vaccine taken by injection

sal•low \'sal-ō\ adj : of a yellowish sickly color ⟨a ~ liverish skin⟩

sal•ly \'sal-ē\ n, pl sallies 1 : a rushing attack on besiegers by troops of a besieged place 2 : a witty remark or retort 3 : a brief excursion — sally vb

salm•on \'sam-ən\ n, pl salmon also salmons 1 : any of several soft-finned food fishes with pinkish flesh 2 : a strong yellowish pink

sa•lon \sə-'län, 'sal-,än, sa-'lōⁿ\ n : an elegant drawing room; also : a fashionable shop ⟨beauty ~⟩

sa•loon \sə-'lün\ n 1 : a large drawing room or ballroom esp. on a passenger ship 2 : a place where liquors are sold and drunk : BARROOM 3 Brit : SEDAN

sal soda \'sal-'söd-ə\ n : WASHING SODA

¹salt \'sòlt\ n 1 : a white crystalline substance that consists of sodium and chlorine and is used in seasoning foods 2 : a saltlike cathartic substance 3 : a compound formed usu. by action of an acid on metal 4 : SAILOR — salt•i•ness \'sòl-tē-nəs\ n — salty \'sòl-tē\ adj

²salt vb : to preserve, season, or feed with salt

³salt adj : preserved or treated with salt; also : SALTY

salt away vb : to lay away safely

salt•box \'sòlt-,bäks\ n : a frame dwelling with two stories in front and one behind and a long sloping roof

salt•cel•lar \'sòlt-,sel-ər\ n : a small vessel for holding salt at the table

sal•tine \sòl-'tēn\ n : a thin crisp cracker sprinkled with salt

salt lick n : LICK 5

salt•pe•ter \'sòlt-'pēt-ər\ n [fr. earlier saltpeter, fr. ME, fr. MF saltpetre, fr. ML sal petrae, lit., salt of the rock] 1 : POTASSIUM NITRATE 2 : SODIUM NITRATE

salt•wa•ter \-,sòlt-,wòt-ər, -,wät-\ adj : of, relating to, or living in salt water

sa•lu•bri•ous \sə-'lü-brē-əs\ adj : favorable to health

sal•u•tary \'sal-yə-,ter-ē\ adj : healthgiving; also : BENEFICIAL

sal•u•ta•tion \,sal-yə-'tā-shən\ n : an expression of greeting, goodwill, or courtesy usu. by word or gesture

¹sa•lute \sə-'lüt\ vb sa•lut•ed; sa•lut•ing 1 : GREET 2 : to honor by special ceremonies 3 : to show respect to (a superior officer) by a formal position of hand, rifle, or sword

²salute n 1 : GREETING 2 : the formal position assumed in saluting a superior

¹sal•vage \'sal-vij\ n 1 : money paid for saving a ship, its cargo, or passengers when the ship is wrecked or in danger 2 : the saving of a ship 3 : the saving of possessions in danger of being lost 4 : things saved from loss or destruction (as by fire or wreck)

²salvage vb sal•vaged; sal•vag•ing : to rescue from destruction

sal•va•tion \sal-'vā-shən\ n 1 : the saving of a person from sin or its consequences esp. in the life after death 2 : the saving from danger, difficulty, or evil 3 : something that saves

¹salve \'sav, 'sàv\ n : a medicinal ointment

²salve vb salved; salv•ing : EASE, SOOTHE

sal•ver \'sal-vər\ n [F salve, fr. Sp salva sampling of food to detect poison, tray, fr. salvar to save, sample food to detect poison, fr. LL salvare to save, fr. L salvus safe] : a small serving tray

sal•vo \'sal-vō\ n, pl -vos or -voes : a simultaneous discharge of guns

Sam or Saml abbr Samuel

SAM \'sam, ,es-(,)ā-'em\ abbr surface-to-air-missile

sa•mar•i•um \sə-'mer-ē-əm\ n : a pale gray lustrous metallic chemical element

¹same \'sām\ adj 1 : being the one referred to : not different 2 : SIMILAR
syn identical, equivalent, equal — same•ness n

²**same** *pron* : the same one or ones

³**same** *adv* : in the same manner

**sam·o·var** \'sam-ə-,vär\ *n* [Russ, fr. *samo-* self + *varit'* to boil] : an urn with a spigot at the base used esp. in Russia to boil water for tea

**sam·pan** \'sam-,pan\ *n* : a flat-bottomed skiff of the Far East usu. propelled by two short oars

¹**sam·ple** \'sam-pəl\ *n* : a piece or item that shows the quality of the whole from which it was taken : EXAMPLE, SPECIMEN

²**sample** *vb* **sam·pled; sam·pling** \-p(ə-)liŋ\ : to judge the quality of by a sample

**sam·pler** \'sam-plər\ *n* : a piece of needlework; *esp* : one testing skill in embroidering

**sam·u·rai** \'sam-(y)ə-,rī\ *n, pl* **samurai** : a member of a Japanese feudal warrior class practicing a chivalric code

**san·a·to·ri·um** \,san ə-'tōr-ē-əm\ *n, pl* **-riums** *or* **-ria** \-ē-ə\ : an establishment for the care esp. of convalescents or the chronically ill : a health resort

**sanc·ti·fy** \'saŋk-tə-,fī\ *vb* **-fied; -fying 1** : to make holy : CONSECRATE **2** : to free from sin — **sanc·ti·fi·ca·tion** \,saŋk-tə-fə-'kā shən\ *n*

**sanc·ti·mo·nious** \,saŋk-tə-'mō-nē-əs\ *adj* : hypocritically pious — **sanc·ti·mo·ni·ous·ly** *adv*

¹**sanc·tion** \'saŋk-shən\ *n* **1** : authoritative approval **2** : a measure (as a threat or fine) designed to enforce a law or standard ⟨economic ~s⟩

²**sanction** *vb* **sanc·tioned; sanc·tion·ing** \-sh(ə-)niŋ\ : to give approval to : RATIFY **syn** endorse, accredit, certify

**sanc·ti·ty** \'saŋk-tət-ē\ *n, pl* **-ties 1** : GODLINESS **2** : SACREDNESS

**sanc·tu·ary** \'saŋk-chə ,wer-ē\ *n, pl* **-ar·ies 1** : a consecrated place (as the part of a church in which the altar is placed) **2** : a place of refuge ⟨bird ~⟩

**sanc·tum** \'saŋk-təm\ *n, pl* **sanctums** *also* **sanc·ta** \-tə\ : a private office or study : DEN ⟨an editor's ~⟩

¹**sand** \'sand\ *n* : loose particles of hard broken rock — **sandy** *adj*

²**sand** *vb* **1** : to cover or fill with sand **2** : to scour, smooth, or polish with an abrasive (as sandpaper) — **sand·er** *n*

**san·dal** \'san-d⁰l\ *n* : a shoe consisting of a sole strapped to the foot; *also* : a low or open slipper or rubber overshoe

**san·dal·wood** \-,wúd\ *n* : the fragrant yellowish heartwood of a parasitic tree of southeastern Asia that is much used in ornamental carving and cabinetwork; *also* : the tree

**sand·bag** \'san(d)-,bag\ *n* : a bag filled with sand and used in fortifications, as ballast, or as a weapon

**sand·bank** \-,baŋk\ *n* : a deposit of sand (as in a bar or shoal)

**sand·bar** \-,bär\ *n* : a ridge of sand formed in water by tides or currents

**sand·blast** \-,blast\ *n* : sand blown (as for cleaning stone) by air or steam — **sandblast** *vb* — **sand·blast·er** *n*

**sand·hog** \'sand ,hóg, -,häg\ *n* : a laborer who builds underwater tunnels

**sand·lot** \'san(d)-,lät\ *n* : a vacant lot esp. when used for the unorganized sports of boys — **sand·lot** *adj* — **sand·lot·ter** *n*

**sand·man** \'san(d)-,man\ *n* : the genie of folklore who makes children sleepy

**sand·pa·per** \-,pā-pər\ *n* : paper with abrasive (as sand) glued on one side used in smoothing and polishing surfaces — **sandpaper** *vb*

**sand·pip·er** \-,pī-pər\ *n* : a long-billed shorebird related to the plovers

**sand·stone** \-,stōn\ *n* : rock made of sand held together by some natural cement

**sand·storm** \-,stórm\ *n* : a windstorm that drives clouds of sand

¹**sand·wich** \'sand-(,)wich\ *n* [after John Montagu, 4th Earl of *Sandwich* †1792 E diplomat] **1** : two or more slices of bread with a layer (as of meat or cheese) spread between them **2** : something resembling a sandwich

²**sandwich** *vb* : to squeeze or crowd in

**sandwich coin** *n* : a coin with a core of one metal between layers of another

**sane** \'sān\ *adj* **san·er; san·est 1** : mentally sound and healthy; *also* : SENSIBLE, RATIONAL — **sane·ly** *adv*

**sang** *past of* SING

**sang·froid** \'sä<sup>n</sup>-'frwä\ *n* [F *sang-froid* lit., cold blood] : self-possession or an imperturbable state esp under strain

**san·gui·nary** \'saŋ-gwə-,ner-ē\ *adj* : BLOODY ⟨~ battle⟩

**san·guine** \'saŋ-gwən\ *adj* **1** : RUDDY **2** : CHEERFUL, HOPEFUL

**sanit** *abbr* sanitary; sanitation

**san·i·tar·i·an** \,san-ə 'ter-ē-ən\ *n* : a specialist in sanitary science and public health

**san·i·tar·i·um** \,san-ə-'ter-ē-əm\ *n, pl* **-i·ums** *or* **-ia** \-ē-ə\ : SANATORIUM

**san·i·tary** \'san-ə-,ter-ē\ *adj* **1** : of or relating to health : HYGIENIC **2** : free from filth or infective matter

**sanitary napkin** *n* : a disposable absorbent pad used to absorb a uterine flow (as during menstruation)

**san·i·ta·tion** \,san-ə-'tā shən\ *n* : a making sanitary; *also* : protection of health by maintenance of sanitary conditions

**san·i·tize** \'san-ə-,tīz\ *vb* **-tized; -tiz·ing 1** : to make sanitary **2** : to make more acceptable by removing unpleasant features

**san·i·ty** \'san-ət-ē\ *n* : soundness of mind

**sank** *past of* SINK

**sans** \(,)sanz\ *prep* : WITHOUT

**San·skrit** \'san-,skrit\ *n* : an ancient language that is the classical language of India and of Hinduism — **Sanskrit** *adj*

¹**sap** \'sap\ *n* **1** : a vital fluid; *esp* : a watery fluid that circulates through a vascular plant — **sap·less** *adj*

²**sap** *vb* **sapped; sap·ping 1** : UNDERMINE **2** : to weaken or exhaust gradually

**sa·pi·ent** \'sā pē-ənt, 'sap-ē-\ *ad*

: WISE, DISCERNING — **sa·pi·ence** \-əns\ n

**sap·ling** \'sap-liŋ\ n : a young tree

**sap·phire** \'saf-,ī(ə)r\ n [ME safir, fr. OF, fr. L sapphirus, fr Gk sappheiros, fr. Heb sappīr, fr Skt śanipriya, lit., dear to the planet Saturn, fr. Śani Saturn + priya dear] : a hard transparent bright blue precious stone

**sap·py** \'sap-ē\ adj **sap·pi·er, -est** 1 : full of sap 2 : SILLY, FOOLISH

**sap·ro·phyte** \'sap-rə-,fīt\ n : a plant living on dead or decaying organic matter — **sap·ro·phy·tic** \,sap-rə-'fit-ik\ adj

**sap·suck·er** \'sap-,sək-ər\ n : any of several small American woodpeckers

**sap·wood** \-,wůd\ n : the younger active and usu. lighter and softer outer layer of wood (as of a tree trunk)

**sar·casm** \'sär-,kaz-əm\ n 1 : a cutting or contemptuous remark 2 : ironical criticism or reproach — **sar·cas·tic** \sär-'kas-tik\ adj — **sar·cas·ti·cal·ly** \-ti-k(ə-)lē\ adv

**sar·coph·a·gus** \sär-'käf-ə-gəs\ n, pl **-gi** \-,gī, -,jī\ also **-gus·es** [L sarcophagus (lapis) limestone used for coffins, fr. Gk (lithos) sarkophagos, lit., flesh-eating stone, fr. sark-, sarx flesh + phagein to eat] : a large stone coffin

**sar·dine** \sär-'dēn\ n, pl **sardines** also **sardine** : a young or small fish preserved esp. in oil for use as food

**sar·don·ic** \sär-'dän-ik\ adj : expressing scorn or mockery : bitterly disdainful syn ironic, satiric, sarcastic — **sar·don·i·cal·ly** \-i-k(ə-)lē\ adv

**sa·ri** or **sa·ree** \'sär-ē\ n : a garment of Hindu women that consists of a long cloth draped around the body and head or shoulder

**sa·rong** \sə-'roŋ, -'räŋ\ n : a loose skirt wrapped around the body and worn by men and women of the Malay archipelago and the Pacific islands

**sar·sa·pa·ril·la** \,sas-(ə-)pə-'ril-ə, ,särs-\ n : the root of a tropical American smilax used esp. for flavoring

**sar·to·ri·al** \sär-'tōr-ē-əl\ adj : of or relating to a tailor or men's clothes — **sar·to·ri·al·ly** \-ē\ adv

¹**sash** \'sash\ n : a broad band worn around the waist or over the shoulder

²**sash** n, pl **sash** also **sash·es** : a frame for a pane of glass in a door or window; also : the movable part of a window

**sa·shay** \sa-'shā, sī-\ vb 1 : WALK, GLIDE, GO 2 : to strut or move about in an ostentatious manner 3 : to proceed in a diagonal or sideways manner

**Sask** abbr Saskatchewan

**sas·sa·fras** \'sas-ə-,fras\ n : a No. American tree related to the laurel; also : its dried bark used in medicine and as flavoring

**sassy** \'sas-ē\ adj **sass·i·er; -est** : SAUCY

¹**sat** past of SIT

²**sat** abbr saturate; saturated; saturation

**Sat** abbr Saturday

**Sa·tan** \'sāt-ᵊn\ n : DEVIL

**sa·tang** \sə-'täŋ\ n, pl **satang** or **satangs** — see baht at MONEY table

**sa·tan·ic** \sə-'tan-ik, sā-\ adj 1 : of or resembling Satan 2 : extremely malicious or wicked — **sa·tan·i·cal·ly** \-i-k(ə-)lē\ adv

**satch·el** \'sach-əl\ n : TRAVELING BAG

**sate** \'sāt\ vb **sat·ed; sat·ing** : to satisfy to the full; also : SURFEIT, GLUT

**sa·teen** \sa-'tēn, sə-\ n : a cotton cloth finished to resemble satin

**sat·el·lite** \'sat-ᵊl-,īt\ n 1 : an obsequious follower of a prince or distinguished person : TOADY 2 : a smaller celestial body that revolves around a larger body 3 : a man-made object that orbits a celestial body

**sa·ti·ate** \'sā-shē-,āt\ vb **-at·ed, -at·ing** 1 : to satisfy fully 2 : SURFEIT

**sa·ti·ety** \sə-'tī-ət-ē\ n : fullness to the point of excess

**sat·in** \'sat-ᵊn\ n : a fabric (as of silk) with a glossy surface — **sat·iny** adj

**sat·in·wood** \'sat-ᵊn-,wůd\ n : a hard yellowish brown wood of satiny luster; also : a tree yielding this wood

**sat·ire** \'sa-,tī(ə)r\ n : biting wit, irony, or sarcasm used to expose vice or folly; also : a literary work having these qualities — **sa·tir·ic** \sə-'tir-ik\ or **sa·tir·i·cal** \-i-kəl\ adj — **sa·tir·i·cal·ly** \-ē\ adv — **sat·i·rist** \'sat-ə rəst\ n — **sat·i·rize** \-ə-,rīz\ vb

**sat·is·fac·tion** \,sat-əs-'fak-shən\ n 1 : payment through penance of punishment incurred by sin 2 : CONTENTMENT, GRATIFICATION 3 : reparation for an insult 4 : settlement of a claim

**sat·is·fac·to·ry** \-'fak-t(ə-)rē\ adj : giving satisfaction — **sat·is·fac·to·ri·ly** \-'fak-t(ə-)rə-lē\ adv

**sat·is·fy** \'sat-əs-,fī\ vb **-fied, -fy·ing** 1 : to make happy : GRATIFY 2 : to pay what is due to 3 : to answer or discharge (a claim) in full 4 : CONVINCE 5 : to meet the requirements of — **sat·is·fy·ing·ly** adv

**sa·trap** \'sā-,trap, 'sa-\ n [ME, fr. L satrapes, fr. Gk satrapēs, fr. Per xshahrapāvan, lit., protector of the dominion] : a petty prince : subordinate ruler

**sat·u·rate** \'sach-ə-,rāt\ vb **-rat·ed; -rat·ing** 1 : to soak thoroughly 2 : to treat or charge with something to the point (**saturation point**) where no more can be absorbed, dissolved, or retained ⟨water saturated with salt⟩ — **sat·u·ra·ble** \'sach-(ə-)rə-bəl\ adj — **sat·u·ra·tion** \,sach-ə-'rā-shən\ n

**Sat·ur·day** \'sat-ərd-ē\ n : the seventh day of the week : the Jewish Sabbath

**Sat·urn** \'sat-ərn\ n : the second largest of the planets and the one sixth in order of distance from the sun

**sat·ur·nine** \'sat-ər-,nīn\ adj : SULLEN, SARDONIC

**sa·tyr** \'sāt-ər, 'sat-\ n 1 : a woodland deity of Greek mythology having certain characteristics of a horse or goat 2 : a lecherous man

¹**sauce** \'sòs, 3 usu 'sas\ n 1 : a dressing for salads, meats, or puddings 2 : stewed fruit 3 : IMPUDENCE

²**sauce** \'sòs, 2 usu 'sas\ vb **sauced; sauc·ing** 1 : to add zest to 2 : to be impudent to

**sauce·pan** \'sȯs-ˌpan\ n : a cooking pan with a long handle

**sau·cer** \'sȯ-sər\ n : a rounded shallow dish for use under a cup

**saucy** \'sas-ē, 'sȯs-ē\ adj **sauc·i·er; -est** : IMPUDENT, PERT — **sauc·i·ly** \-ə-lē\ adv — **sauc·i·ness** \-ē-nəs\ n

**sau·er·kraut** \'sau̇(-ə)r-ˌkrau̇t\ n [G, fr. sauer sour + kraut cabbage] : finely cut cabbage fermented in brine

**sau·na** \'sau̇-nə\ n 1 : a Finnish steam bath in which the steam is provided by water thrown on hot stones 2 : a dry heat bath; also : a room or cabinet used for such a bath

**saun·ter** \'sȯnt-ər, 'sänt-\ vb : STROLL

**sau·sage** \'sȯ-sij\ n : minced and highly seasoned meat (as pork) usu. enclosed in a tubular casing

**S Aust** abbr South Australia

**sau·té** \sȯ-'tā, sō-\ vb **sau·téed** or **sau·téd; sau·té·ing** : to fry lightly in a little fat **sauté** n

**sau·terne** \sō-'tərn, sȯ-\ n, often cap : a usu. semisweet white table wine

¹**sav·age** \'sav-ij\ adj [ME sauvage, fr. MF, fr. ML salvaticus, fr. L silvaticus of the woods, wild, fr. silva wood, forest] 1 : WILD, UNTAMED 2 : UNCIVILIZED, BARBAROUS 3 : CRUEL, FIERCE — **sav·age·ly** adv — **sav·age·ness** n — **sav·age·ry** \-(ə-)rē\ n

²**savage** n 1 : member of a primitive human society 2 : a rude, unmannerly, or brutal person

**sa·van·na** or **sa·van·nah** \sə-'van-ə\ n : grassland containing scattered trees

**sa·vant** \sa-'vänt, sə-, 'sav-ənt\ n : a learned man : SCHOLAR

¹**save** \'sāv\ vb **saved; sav·ing** 1 : to rescue from danger 2 : to preserve or guard from destruction or loss 3 : to redeem from sin 4 : to put aside as a store or reserve **sav·er** n

²**save** n : a play that prevents an opponent from scoring or winning

³**save** \(ˌ)sāv\ prep : EXCEPT

⁴**save** \(ˌ)sāv\ conj : BUT

**sav·ior** or **sav·iour** \'sāv-yər\ n 1 : one who saves 2 cap : Jesus Christ

**sa·voir faire** \ˌsav-ˌwär-'faər\ n [F savoir-faire, lit. knowing how to do] : readiness in knowing how to act : TACT

¹**sa·vor** also **sa·vour** \'sā-vər\ n 1 : the taste and odor of something 2 : a special flavor or quality **sa·vory** adj

²**savor** also **savour** vb **sa·vored; sa·vor·ing** \'sāv-(ə-)riŋ\ 1 : to have a specified taste, smell, or quality 2 : to taste with pleasure

¹**sav·vy** \'sav-ē\ vb **sav·vied; sav·vy·ing** : COMPREHEND, UNDERSTAND

²**savvy** n : practical grasp ⟨political ~⟩

¹**saw** past of SEE

²**saw** \'sȯ\ n : a cutting tool with a thin flat blade having a line of teeth along its edge

³**saw** vb **sawed** \'sȯd\; **sawed** or **sawn** \'sȯn\; **saw·ing** \'sȯ(-)iŋ\ : to cut or divide with or as if with a saw — **saw·yer** \-yər\ n

⁴**saw** n : a common saying : MAXIM

**saw·dust** \'sȯ-(ˌ)dəst\ n : fine particles made by a saw in cutting

**saw·horse** \'sȯ-ˌhȯrs\ n : a rack on which wood is rested while being sawed by hand

**saw·mill** \-ˌmil\ n : a mill for sawing logs

**saw palmetto** n : any of several shrubby palms with spiny-toothed petioles

¹**say** \'sā\ vb **said** \'sed\; **say·ing** \'sā-iŋ\; **says** \'sez\ 1 : to express in words ⟨~ what you mean⟩; also : PRONOUNCE 2 : ALLEGE ⟨said to be rich⟩ 3 : to state positively ⟨can't ~ what will happen⟩ 4 : RECITE

²**say** n, pl **says** 1 : an expression of opinion 2 : power of decision

**say·ing** \'sā-iŋ\ n : a commonly repeated statement

**say-so** \'sā-(ˌ)sō\ n : an esp. authoritative assertion or decision; also : the right to decide

**sb** abbr substantive

**Sb** symbol [L stibium] antimony

**SB** abbr bachelor of science

**SBA** abbr Small Business Administration

**sc** abbr 1 scale 2 scene 3 science

¹**Sc** abbr Scots

²**Sc** symbol scandium

**SC** abbr South Carolina

¹**scab** \'skab\ n 1 : a disease of plants or animals marked by crusted lesions 2 : a protective crust over a sore or wound 3 : a worker who replaces a striker or works under conditions not authorized by a union **scab·by** adj

²**scab** vb **scabbed; scab·bing** 1 : to become covered with a scab 2 : to work as a scab

**scab·bard** \'skab-ərd\ n : a sheath for the blade of a weapon (as a sword)

**sca·brous** \'skab-rəs, 'skāb-\ adj 1 : DIFFICULT, KNOTTY 2 : rough to the touch : SCALY, SCURFY ⟨a ~ leaf⟩ 3 : dealing with suggestive, indecent, or scandalous themes; also : SQUALID

**scad** \'skad\ n 1 : a large number or quantity 2 pl : a great abundance

**scaf·fold** \'skaf-əld, -ˌōld\ n 1 : a raised platform for workmen to sit or stand on 2 : a platform on which a criminal is executed (as by hanging)

**scaf·fold·ing** \-iŋ\ n : a system of scaffolds; also : materials for scaffolds

**scal·a·wag** \'skal-i-ˌwag\ n : RASCAL

¹**scald** \'skȯld\ vb 1 : to burn with or as if with hot liquid or steam 2 : to heat up to the boiling point

²**scald** n : a burn caused by scalding

¹**scale** \'skāl\ n 1 : either pan of a balance 2 : BALANCE — usu. used in pl. 3 : a weighing machine

²**scale** vb **scaled; scal·ing** : WEIGH

³**scale** n 1 : one of the small thin plates that cover the body esp. of a fish or reptile 2 : a thin plate 3 : a thin coating, layer, or incrustation — **scaled** \'skāld\ adj — **scale·less** \'skāl-ləs\ adj — **scaly** adj

⁴**scale** vb **scaled; scal·ing** : to strip of scales

⁵**scale** n [ME, fr. LL scala ladder, staircase, fr. L scalae, pl., stairs, rungs, ladder] 1 : something divided into regular spaces as a help in drawing or measur-

ing **2** : a graduated series **3** : the size of a sample (as a model) in proportion to the size of the actual thing **4** : a standard of estimation or judgment **5** : a series of musical tones going up or down in pitch according to a specified scheme

⁶**scale** *vb* **scaled; scal·ing 1** : to go up by or as if by a ladder **2** : to arrange in a graded series

**scale insect** *n* : any of numerous small insects that live on plants and have wingless scale-covered females

**scale·pan** \'skāl-,pan\ *n* : a pan of a scale for weighing

**scal·lion** \'skal-yon\ *n* : an onion without an enlarged bulb

¹**scal·lop** \'skäl-əp, 'skal-\ *n* **1** : a marine mollusk with radially ridged shell valves; *also* : a large edible muscle of this mollusk **2** : one of a continuous series of rounded projections forming an edge (as in lace)

²**scallop** *vb* **1** : to edge (as lace) with scallops **2** : to bake in a casserole

¹**scalp** \'skalp\ *n* : the part of the skin and flesh of the head usu. covered with hair

²**scalp** *vb* **1** : to tear the scalp from **2** : to obtain for the sake of reselling at greatly increased prices — **scalp·er** *n*

**scal·pel** \'skal-pəl\ *n* : a small straight knife with a thin blade used esp. in surgery

**scamp** \'skamp\ *n* : RASCAL

**scam·per** \'skam-pər\ *vb* **scam·pered; scam·per·ing** \-p(ə-)riŋ\ : to run nimbly and playfully — **scamper** *n*

**scam·pi** \'skam-pē\ *n, pl* **scampi** : SHRIMP; *esp* : large shrimp prepared with a garlic-flavored sauce

**scan** \'skan\ *vb* **scanned; scan·ning 1** : to read (verses) so as to show metrical structure **2** : to examine closely **3** : to direct a succession of radar beams over in searching for a target — **scan** *n* — **scan·ner** *n* syn scrutinize, inspect

**Scand** *abbr* Scandinavia; Scandinavian

**scan·dal** \'skan-dᵊl\ *n* [LL *scandalum* stumbling block, offense, fr. Gk *skandalon*] **1** : DISGRACE, DISHONOR **2** : malicious gossip : SLANDER — **scan·dal·ize** *vb* — **scan·dal·ous** *adj* — **scan·dal·ous·ly** *adv*

**scan·dal·mon·ger** \-,məŋ-gər, -,mäŋ-\ *n* : a person who circulates scandal

**Scan·di·na·vian** \,skan-də-'nā-vē-ən\ *n* : a native or inhabitant of Scandinavia — **Scandinavian** *adj*

**scan·di·um** \'skan-dē-əm\ *n* : a white metallic chemical element

¹**scant** \'skant\ *adj* **1** : barely sufficient **2** : having scarcely enough syn scanty, skimpy, meager, sparse

²**scant** *vb* **1** : STINT **2** : SKIMP

**scant·ling** \-liŋ\ *n* : a piece of lumber; *esp* : one used for an upright in building

**scanty** \'skant-ē\ *adj* **scant·i·er; -est** : barely sufficient — **SCANT** — **scant·i·ly** \'skant-ə-lē\ *adv* — **scant·i·ness** \-ē-nəs\ *n*

**scape·goat** \'skāp-,gōt\ *n* : one that bears the blame for others

**scape·grace** \-,grās\ *n* : an incorrigible rascal

**scap·u·la** \'skap-yə-lə\ *n, pl* **-lae** \-,lē\ *or* **-las** : SHOULDER BLADE

**scap·u·lar** \-lər\ *adj* : of or relating to the shoulder or shoulder blade

**scar** \'skär\ *n* : a mark left after injured tissue has healed — **scar** *vb*

**scar·ab** \'skar-əb\ *n* : a large dark beetle; *also* : an ornament (as a gem) representing such a beetle

**scarce** \'skeərs\ *adj* **scarc·er; scarc·est 1** : not plentiful **2** : RARE — **scar·ci·ty** \'sker-sət-ē\ *n*

**scarce·ly** \'skeərs-lē\ *adv* **1** : BARELY **2** : almost not **3** : very probably not

¹**scare** \'skeər\ *vb* **scared; scar·ing** : FRIGHTEN, STARTLE

²**scare** *n* : FRIGHT — **scary** *adj*

**scare·crow** \'skeər-,krō\ *n* : a crude figure set up to scare birds away from crops

**scarf** \'skärf\ *n, pl* **scarves** \'skärvz\ *or* **scarfs 1** : a broad band (as of cloth) worn about the shoulders, around the neck, over the head, or about the waist **2** : a long narrow strip of fabric

**scar·i·fy** \'skar-ə-,fī\ *vb* **-fied; -fy·ing 1** : to make scratches or small cuts in : wound superficially ⟨~ skin for vaccination⟩ ⟨~ seeds to help them germinate⟩ **2** : to lacerate the feelings of : FLAY — **scar·i·fi·ca·tion** \,skar-ə-fə-'kā-shən\ *n*

**scar·la·ti·na** \,skär-lə-'tē-nə\ *n* : a usu. mild scarlet fever

**scar·let** \'skär-lət\ *n* : a bright red — **scarlet** *adj*

**scarlet fever** *n* : an acute contagious disease marked by fever, sore throat, and red rash

**scarp** \'skärp\ *n* : a line of cliffs produced by faulting or erosion

**scath·ing** \'skā-thiŋ\ *adj* : bitterly severe

**scat·o·log·i·cal** \,skat-ᵊl-'äj-i-kəl\ *adj* : concerned with obscene matters

**scat·ter** \'skat-ər\ *vb* **1** : to distribute or strew about irregularly **2** : DISPERSE

**scav·enge** \'skav-ənj\ *vb* **scav·enged. scav·eng·ing** : to work or function as a scavenger

**scav·en·ger** \'skav-ən-jər\ *n* [alter. of earlier *scavager*, fr. ME *skawager* collector of a toll on goods sold by nonresident merchants, fr. *skawage* toll on goods sold by nonresident merchants, fr. OF *escauwage* inspection] : a person or animal that collects or disposes of refuse or waste

**sce·nar·io** \sə-'nar-ē-,ō\ *n, pl* **-i·os** : the plot of a motion picture

**scene** \'sēn\ *n* [MF, stage, fr. L *scena, scaena* stage, scene, fr. Gk *skēnē* temporary shelter, tent, building forming the background for a dramatic performance, stage] **1** : a division of one act of a play **2** : a single situation or sequence in a play or motion picture **3** : a stage setting **4** : VIEW, PROSPECT **5** : the place of an occurrence or action

6 • a display of strong feeling and esp. anger 7 : a sphere of activity ⟨the drug ∼⟩ — **sce·nic** \'sēn-ik\ adj

**scen·ery** \'sēn-(ə-)rē\ n, pl **er·ies** 1 : the painted scenes or hangings of a stage and the fittings that go with them 2 : a picturesque view or landscape

¹**scent** \'sent\ vb 1 : SMELL 2 : to imbue or fill with odor

²**scent** n 1 : ODOR, SMELL 2 : sense of smell 3 : course of pursuit : TRACK 4 : PERFUME 2 — **scent·less** adj

**scep·ter** \'sep-tər\ n : a staff borne by a sovereign as an emblem of authority

**scep·tic** \skep-tik\ var of SKEPTIC

**sch** abbr school

¹**sched·ule** \'skej-ül, esp Brit 'shed-yül\ n 1 : a list of items or details 2 : TIMETABLE

²**schedule** vb sched·uled; sched·ul·ing : to make a schedule of; also : to enter on a schedule

**schee·lite** \'shā-,līt\ n : a mineral source of tungsten

**sche·mat·ic** \ski-'mat-ik\ adj : of or relating to a scheme or diagram : DIAGRAMMATIC — **schematic** n — **sche·mat·i·cal·ly** \-i-k(ə-)lē\ adv

¹**scheme** \'skēm\ n 1 : a plan for doing something; esp : a crafty plot 2 : a systematic design

²**scheme** vb schemed; schem·ing : to form a plot : INTRIGUE — **schem·er** n — **schem·ing** adj

**Schick test** \'shik-\ n : a serological test for susceptibility to diphtheria

**schil·ling** \'shil-iŋ\ n — see MONEY table

**schism** \'siz-əm, 'skiz-\ n 1 : DIVISION, SPLIT; also : DISCORD, DISSENSION 2 : a formal division in or separation from a religious body 3 : the offence of promoting schism

**schis·mat·ic** \siz-'mat-ik, skiz-\ n : one who creates or takes part in schism — **schismatic** adj

**schist** \'shist\ n : a metamorphic crystalline rock — **schis·tose** \'shis-,tōs\ adj

**schizo·phre·nia** \,skit-sə-'frē-nē-ə\ n [NL, fr. Gk schizein to split + phrēn diaphragm, mind] : mental disorder marked by loss of contact with reality, personality disintegration, and often hallucination — **schiz·oid** \'skit-,sȯid\ adj or n — **schizo·phren·ic** \,skit-sə-'fren-ik\ adj or n

**schle·miel** \shlə-'mēl\ n : an unlucky bungler : CHUMP

**schmaltz** or **schmalz** \'shmȯlts, 'shmälts\ n : sentimental or florid music or art — **schmaltzy** adj

**schnau·zer** \'shnaȯt-sər, 's(h)naȯzər\ n : a dog of any of three breeds that are characterized by a long head, small ears, heavy eyebrows, mustache and beard, and a wiry coat

**schol·ar** \'skäl-ər\ n 1 : STUDENT, PUPIL 2 : a learned man : SAVANT — **schol·ar·ly** adj

**schol·ar·ship** \-,ship\ n 1 : the qualities or learning of a scholar 2 : money given to a student to help him pay for his education

**scho·las·tic** \skə-'las-tik\ adj : of or relating to schools, scholars, or scholarship

¹**school** \'skül\ n 1 : an institution for teaching and learning; also : the pupils in a.tendance 2 : a body of persons of like opinions or beliefs ⟨the radical ∼⟩

²**school** vb : TEACH, DRILL

³**school** n : a large number of one kind of water animal and esp. of fish swimming and feeding together

**school·boy** \-,bȯi\ n : a boy attending school

**school·fel·low** \-,fel-ō\ n : SCHOOLMATE

**school·girl** \-,gərl\ n : a girl attending school

**school·house** \-,haȯs\ n : a building used as a school

**school·marm** \-,mä(r)m\ or **school·ma'am** \-,mäm, -,mam\ n 1 : a woman schoolteacher 2 : a person who exhibits characteristics popularly attributed to schoolteachers

**school·mas·ter** \-,mas-tər\ n : a male schoolteacher

**school·mate** \-,māt\ n : a school companion

**school·mis·tress** \-,mis-trəs\ n : a woman schoolteacher

**school·room** \-,rüm, -,rüm\ n : CLASSROOM

**school·teach·er** \-,tē-chər\ n : a person who teaches in a school

**schoo·ner** \'skü-nər\ n : a fore-and-aft rigged sailing ship

**schuss** \'shùs, 'shüs\ n 1 : a straight high-speed run on skis 2 : a straight skiing course running downhill — **schuss** vb

**sci** abbr science; scientific

**sci·at·i·ca** \sī-'at-i-kə\ n : pain in the region of the hips or along the course of the nerve at the back of the thigh

**sci·ence** \'sī-əns\ n [ME, fr. MF, fr. L scientia fr. scient-, sciens having knowledge, fr. prp. of scire to know] 1 : a branch of study concerned with observation and classification of facts and esp. with the establishment of verifiable general laws 2 : accumulated systematized knowledge esp. when it relates to the physical world — **sci·en·tif·ic** \,sī-ən-'tif-ik\ adj — **sci·en·tif·i·cal·ly** \-i-k(ə-)lē\ adv — **sci·en·tist** \'sī-ənt-əst\ n

**science fiction** n : fiction dealing principally with the impact of actual or imagined science on society or individuals

**scil** abbr scilicet

**sci·li·cet** \'skē-li-,ket, 'sī-lə-,set\ adv : that is to say : NAMELY

**scim·i·tar** \'sim-ət-ər\ n : a curved sword used by Arabs

**scin·til·la** \sin-'til-ə\ n : SPARK, TRACE

**scin·til·late** \'sint- l-,āt\ vb **-lat·ed; -lat·ing** : SPARKLE, GLEAM — **scin·til·la·tion** \,sint-ᵊl-'ā-shən\ n

**sci·on** \'sī-ən\ n 1 : a shoot of a plant joined to a stock in grafting 2 : DESCENDANT

**scis·sors** \'siz-ərz\ n pl : a cutting instrument like shears but usu. smaller

**scissors kick** *n* : a swimming kick in which the legs move like scissors

**scle·ro·sis** \sklə-'rō-səs\ *n* : a usu. abnormal hardening of tissue (as of an artery) — **scle·rot·ic** \-'rät-ik\ *adj*

**scoff** \'skäf\ *vb* : MOCK, JEER — **scoffer** *n*

**scoff·law** \-ˌlȯ\ *n* : a contemptuous law violator

¹**scold** \'skōld\ *n* : a person who scolds

²**scold** *vb* : to censure severely or angrily

**sconce** \'skäns\ *n* : a candlestick or an electric light fixture bracketed to a wall

**scone** \'skōn, 'skän\ *n* : a biscuit (as of oatmeal) baked on a griddle

¹**scoop** \'sküp\ *n* 1 : a large shovel; *also* : a shovellike utensil ⟨a sugar ∼⟩ 2 : a bucket of a dredge or grain elevator 3 : an act of scooping 4 : publication of a news story ahead of a competitor

²**scoop** *vb* 1 : to take out or up or empty with or as if with a scoop 2 : to dig out : make hollow 3 : to gather in as if with a scoop 4 : to get a scoop on

**scoot** \'sküt\ *vb* : to go suddenly and swiftly

**scoot·er** \'sküt-ər\ *n* 1 : a child's foot-operated vehicle consisting of a narrow board mounted between two wheels tandem with an upright steering handle 2 : MOTOR SCOOTER

¹**scope** \'skōp\ *n* [It *scopo* purpose, goal, fr. Gk *skopos*, fr. *skeptesthai* to watch, look at] 1 : mental range 2 : extent covered : RANGE 3 : room for development

²**scope** *n* : an instrument (as a microscope or radarscope) for viewing

**scorch** \'skȯrch\ *vb* : to burn the surface of; *also* : to dry or shrivel with heat ⟨∼ed lawns⟩

¹**score** \'skōr\ *n*, *pl* **scores** 1 *or pl* **score** : TWENTY 2 : CUT, SCRATCH, SLASH 3 : a record of points made (as in a game) 4 : DEBT 5 : REASON 6 : the music of a composition or arrangement with different parts indicated 7 : success esp. in obtaining narcotics

²**score** *vb* **scored; scor·ing** 1 : RECORD 2 : to mark with lines, scratches, or notches 3 : to keep score in a game 4 : to gain or tally in or as if in a game ⟨*scored* a point⟩ 5 : to assign a grade or score to ⟨∼ the tests⟩ 6 : to compose a score for 7 : SUCCEED — **score·less** *adj* — **scor·er** *n*

**sco·ria** \'skōr-ē-ə\ *n*, *pl* **-ri·ae** \-ē-ˌē\ : a rough vesicular lava

¹**scorn** \'skȯrn\ *n* : an emotion involving both anger and disgust : CONTEMPT — **scorn·ful** \-fəl\ *adj* — **scorn·ful·ly** \-ē\ *adv*

²**scorn** *vb* : to hold in contempt : DISDAIN — **scorn·er** *n*

**scor·pi·on** \'skȯr-pē-ən\ *n* : a spiderlike animal with a poisonous sting at the tip of its long jointed tail

¹**Scot** \'skät\ *n* : a native or inhabitant of Scotland — **Scots·man** \'skäts-mən\ *n*

²**Scot** *abbr* Scotland; Scottish

**Scotch** \'skäch\ *n* 1 Scotch *pl* : the people of Scotland 2 : SCOTS 3 : a whiskey distilled in Scotland esp. from malted barley — **Scotch** *adj* — **Scotch·man** \-mən\ *n*

**Scotch pine** *n* : a pine that is naturalized in the U.S. from northern Europe and Asia and is a valuable timber tree

**scot-free** \'skät-'frē\ *adj* : free from obligation, harm, or penalty

**Scots** \'skäts\ *n* : the English language of Scotland

**Scot·tish** \'skät-ish\ *adj* : SCOTCH

**scoun·drel** \'skaùn-drəl\ *n* : a mean worthless fellow : VILLAIN

¹**scour** \'skaù(ə)r\ *vb* 1 : to move rapidly through : RUSH 2 : to examine thoroughly

²**scour** *vb* 1 : to rub (as with a gritty substance) in order to clean 2 : to cleanse by or as if by rubbing 3 : to suffer from diarrhea

¹**scourge** \'skərj\ *n* 1 : LASH, WHIP 2 : PUNISHMENT; *also* : a cause of affliction (as a plague)

²**scourge** *vb* **scourged; scourg·ing** 1 : LASH, FLOG 2 : to punish severely

¹**scout** \'skaùt\ *vb* [ME *scouten*, fr. MF *escouter* to listen, fr. L *auscultare*] 1 : to look around : RECONNOITER 2 : to inspect or observe to get information

**scout** *n* 1 : a person sent out to get information; *also* : a soldier, airplane, or ship sent out to reconnoiter 2 : a member of either of two youth organizations (Boy Scouts, Girl Scouts) — **scout·mas·ter** \-ˌmas-tər\ *n*

³**scout** *vb* : SCORN, SCOFF

**scow** \'skaù\ *n* : a large flat-bottomed boat with square ends

**scowl** \'skaùl\ *vb* : to draw down the forehead and make a face in expression of displeasure — **scowl** *n*

**SCPO** *abbr* senior chief petty officer

**scrab·ble** \'skrab-əl\ *vb* **scrab·bled; scrab·bling** \-(ə-)liŋ\ 1 : SCRAPE, SCRATCH 2 : CLAMBER, SCRAMBLE 3 : to work hard and long 4 : SCRIBBLE — **scrabble** *n* — **scrab·bler** \-(ə-)lər\ *n*

**scrag·gly** \'skrag-lē\ *adj* : IRREGULAR; *also* : RAGGED, UNKEMPT

**scram** \'skram\ *vb* **scrammed; scram·ming** : to go away at once

**scram·ble** \'skram-bəl\ *vb* **scram·bled; scram·bling** \-b(ə-)liŋ\ 1 : to clamber clumsily around 2 : to struggle for or as if for possession of something 3 : to spread irregularly 4 : to mix together 5 : to prepare (eggs) by stirring during frying — **scramble** *n*

¹**scrap** \'skrap\ *n* 1 : FRAGMENT, PIECE 2 : discarded material : REFUSE

²**scrap** *vb* **scrapped; scrap·ping** 1 : to make into scrap ⟨∼ a battleship⟩ 2 : to get rid of as useless

³**scrap** *n* : FIGHT

⁴**scrap** *vb* **scrapped; scrap·ping** : FIGHT, QUARREL — **scrap·per** *n*

**scrap·book** \'skrap-ˌbùk\ *n* : a blank book in which mementos are kept

¹**scrape** \'skrāp\ *vb* **scraped; scrap·ing** 1 : to remove by drawing a knife

over; *also* : to clean or smooth by rubbing off the covering **2** : GRATE; *also* : to damage or injure the surface of by contact with something rough **3** : to scrape something with a grating sound **4** : to get together ⟨money⟩ by strict economy **5** : to get along with difficulty — **scrap·er** *n*

²**scrape** *n* **1** : the act or the effect of scraping **2** : a bow accompanied by a drawing back of the foot **3** : an unpleasant predicament

¹**scrap·py** \'skrap-ē\ *adj* **scrap·pi·er; -est** : DISCONNECTED, FRAGMENTARY

²**scrappy** *adj* **scrap·pi·er; -est 1** : QUARRELSOME **2** : aggressive and determined in spirit

¹**scratch** \'skrach\ *vb* **1** : to scrape, dig, or rub with or as if with claws or nails ⟨a dog ~ing at the door⟩ ⟨~ed his arm on thorns⟩ **2** : to cause to move or strike roughly and gratingly ⟨~ed his nails across the blackboard⟩ **3** : to scrape ⟨as money⟩ together **4** : to cancel or erase by or as if by drawing a line through — **scratchy** *adj*

²**scratch** *n* **1** : a mark made by or as if by scratching; *also* : a sound so made **2** : the starting line in a race

³**scratch** *adj* **1** : made as or used for a trial attempt ⟨~ paper⟩ **2** : made or done by chance ⟨a ~ hit⟩

**scrawl** \'skról\ *vb* : to write hastily and carelessly — **scrawl** *n*

**scraw·ny** \'skró-nē\ *adj* **scraw·ni·er; -est** : very thin : SKINNY

¹**scream** \'skrēm\ *vb* : to cry out loudly and shrilly

²**scream** *n* : a loud shrill cry

**screech** \'skrēch\ *vb* : SHRIEK — **screech** *n*

¹**screen** \'skrēn\ *n* **1** : a device or partition used to hide, restrain, protect, or decorate ⟨a wire-mesh window ~⟩; *also* : something that shelters, protects, or conceals **2** : a sieve or perforated material for separating finer from coarser parts ⟨as of sand⟩ **3** : a surface on which pictures appear ⟨as in movies or television⟩; *also* : the motion-picture industry

²**screen** *vb* **1** : to shield with or as if with a screen **2** : to separate with or as if with a screen **3** : to present ⟨as a motion picture⟩ on the screen **syn** hide, conceal, secrete

**screen·ing** \-iŋ\ *n* : metal or plastic mesh ⟨as for window screens⟩

¹**screw** \'skrü\ *n* [ME, fr. MF *escroe* nut, fr. ML *scrofa*, fr. L, sow] **1** : a naillike metal piece with a spiral groove and a head with a slot twisted into or through pieces of solid material to hold them together; *also* : a device with a spirally grooved cylinder used in a machine **2** : a wheellike device with a central hub and radiating blades for propelling vehicles ⟨as motorboats or airplanes⟩

²**screw** *vb* **1** : to fasten or close by means of a screw **2** : to operate or adjust by means of a screw **3** : to move or cause to move spirally; *also* : to close or set in position by such an action

**screw·ball** \'skrü-,ból\ *n* **1** : a baseball pitch breaking in a direction opposite to a curve **2** : a whimsical, eccentric, or crazy person

**screw·driv·er** \'skrü-,drī-vər\ *n* **1** : a tool for turning screws **2** : a drink made of vodka and orange juice

**screwy** \'skrü-ē\ *adj* **screw·i·er; -est 1** : crazily absurd, eccentric, or unusual **2** : CRAZY, INSANE

**scrib·ble** \'skrib-əl\ *vb* **scrib·bled; scrib·bling** \-(ə-)liŋ\ : to write hastily or carelessly — **scribble** *n* — **scrib·bler** \-(ə-)lər\ *n*

**scribe** \'skrīb\ *n* **1** : one of a learned class in ancient Palestine serving as copyists, teachers, and jurists **2** : a person whose business is the copying of writing **3** : AUTHOR; *esp* : JOURNALIST

**scrim** \'skrim\ *n* : a light loosely woven cotton or linen cloth

**scrim·mage** \'skrim-ij\ *n* : the play between two football teams beginning with the snap of the ball; *also* : practice play between a team's squads — **scrimmage** *vb*

**scrimp** \'skrimp\ *vb* : to be niggardly : economize greatly ⟨~ and save⟩

**scrim·shaw** \'skrim-,shó\ *n* : carved or engraved articles made esp. by American whalers usu. from whalebone or whale ivory — **scrimshaw** *vb*

**scrip** \'skrip\ *n* **1** : paper money for an amount less than one dollar **2** : a certificate showing its holder is entitled to something ⟨as stock or land⟩

¹**script** \'skript\ *n* : written matter ⟨as lines for a play or broadcast⟩

²**script** *abbr* scripture

**scrip·ture** \'skrip-chər\ *n* **1** *cap* : BIBLE — often used in pl. **2** : the sacred writings of a religion — **scrip·tur·al** \'skrip-chə-rəl\ *adj* — **scrip·tur·al·ly** \-ē\ *adv*

**scriv·en·er** \'skriv-(ə-)nər\ *n* : SCRIBE, WRITER, AUTHOR

**scrod** \'skräd\ *n* : a young fish ⟨as a cod or haddock⟩; *esp* : one split and boned for cooking

**scrof·u·la** \'skróf-yə-lə\ *n* : tuberculosis of lymph glands esp. in the neck

**scroll** \'skrōl\ *n* : a roll of paper or parchment for writing a document; *also* : a spiral or coiled ornamental form suggesting a loosely or partly rolled scroll

**scroll saw** *n* : JIGSAW

**scro·tum** \'skrōt-əm\ *n*, *pl* **scro·ta** \-ə\ *or* **scrotums** : a pouch that in most mammals contains the testes

**scrounge** \'skraùnj\ *vb* **scrounged; scroung·ing** : to collect by or as if by foraging

¹**scrub** \'skrəb\ *n* : a stunted tree or shrub; *also* : a growth of these **2** : an inferior domestic animal **3** : a person of insignificant size or standing; *esp* : a player not on the first team — **scrub** *adj* — **scrub·by** *adj*

²**scrub** *vb* **scrubbed; scrub·bing 1** : to rub in washing ⟨~ clothes⟩ **2** : to wash by rubbing ⟨~ out a spot⟩ **3** : to call off : CANCEL

**scruff** \'skrəf\ *n* : the loose skin of the back of the neck : NAPE

**scruffy** \'skrəf-ē\ *ad* **scruff·i·er;**
**-est** : SHABBY, CONTEMPTIBLE

**scrump·tious** \'skrəm(p)-shəs\ *adj*
: DELIGHTFUL, EXCELLENT — **scrump·tious·ly** *adv*

¹**scru·ple** \'skrü-pəl\ *n* **1** — see WEIGHT
table   **2** : a tiny part or quantity

²**scruple** *n* [MF *scrupule*, fr. L *scrupulus*
small sharp stone, cause of mental discomfort, scruple, dim. of *scrupus* sharp
stone] **1** : a point of conscience or
honor   **2** : hesitation due to ethical
considerations — **scru·pu·lous**
\-pyə-ləs\ *adj* — **scru·pu·lous·ly** *adv*

³**scruple** *vb* **scru·pled; scru·pling**
\-p(ə-)liŋ\ : to be reluctant on grounds
of conscience : HESITATE

**scru·ti·nize** \'skrüt-ən-ˌīz\ *vb* **-nized;**
**-niz·ing** : to examine closely

**scru·ti·ny** \'skrüt-ᵊn-ē\ *n, pl* **-nies** [L
*scrutinium*, fr. *scrutari* to search, examine, fr. *scruta* trash] : a careful looking
over   *syn* inspection

**scu·ba** \'sk(y)ü-bə\ *n* [*self-contained
underwater breathing apparatus*] : an
apparatus for breathing while swimming under water

**scuba diver** *n* : one who swims under
water with the aid of scuba gear

¹**scud** \'skəd\ *vb* **scud·ded; scud·ding** : to move speedily

²**scud** *n* : loose vaporlike clouds driven
by the wind

¹**scuff** \'skəf\ *vb* **1** : to scrape the feet
while walking : SHUFFLE **2** : to scratch
or become scratched, gouged, or worn
away

²**scuff** *n* **1** : a mark or injury caused by
scuffing **2** : a flat-soled slipper without quarter or heel strap

**scuf·fle** \'skəf-əl\ *vb* **scuf·fled;**
**scuf·fling** \-(ə-)liŋ\ **1** : to struggle
confusedly at close quarters **2** : to
shuffle one's feet — **scuffle** *n*

¹**scull** \'skəl\ *n* **1** : an oar for use in
sculling; *also* : one of a pair of short
oars for a single oarsman **2** : a racing
shell propelled by one or two persons
using sculls

²**scull** *vb* : to propel (a boat) by an oar
over the stern

**scul·lery** \'skəl-(ə-)rē\ *n, pl* **-ler·ies**
[ME, department of household in
charge of dishes, fr. MF *escuelerie*, fr.
*escuelle* bowl, fr. L *scutella* drinking
bowl, dim. of *scutra* platter] : a small
room near the kitchen used for cleaning
dishes, culinary utensils, and vegetables

**scul·lion** \'skəl-yən\ *n* [ME *sculion*, fr.
MF *escouillon* dishcloth, alter. of
*escouvillon*, fr. *escouve* broom, fr. L
*scopa*, lit., twig] : a kitchen helper

**sculpt** \'skəlpt\ *vb* : CARVE, SCULPTURE

**sculp·tor** \'skəlp-tər\ *n* : one who produces works of sculpture

¹**sculp·ture** \'skəlp-chər\ *n* : the act,
process, or art of carving or molding
material (as stone, wood, or plastic);
*also* : work produced this way —
**sculp·tur·al** \'skəlp-chə-rəl\ *adj*

²**sculpture** *vb* **sculp·tured, sculp·tur·ing** : to form or alter as or as if a
work of sculpture

**scum** \'skəm\ *n* **1** : a foul filmy cover-

ing on the surface of a liquid **2** : waste
matter **3** : RABBLE

**scup·per** \'skəp-ər\ *n* : an opening in
the side of a ship through which water
on deck is drained overboard

**scurf** \'skərf\ *n* : thin dry scales of skin
(as dandruff); *also* : a scaly deposit or
covering — **scurfy** \'skər-fē\ *adj*

**scur·ri·lous** \'skər-ə-ləs\ *adj* : coarsely
jesting : OBSCENE, VULGAR

**scur·ry** \'skər-ē\ *vb* **scur·ried; scur·ry·ing** : SCAMPER

¹**scur·vy** \'skər-vē\ *adj* : MEAN, CONTEMPTIBLE — **scur·vi·ly** *adv*

²**scurvy** *n* : a vitamin-deficiency disease
marked by spongy gums, loosened teeth,
and bleeding into the tissues

**scutch·eon** \'skəch-ən\ *n* : ESCUTCHEON

¹**scut·tle** \'skət-ᵊl\ *n* : a pail for carrying coal

²**scuttle** *n* : a small opening with a lid
esp. in the deck, side, or bottom of a
ship

³**scuttle** *vb* **scut·tled; scut·tling**
\'skət-(ᵊ-)liŋ\ : to cut a hole in the
deck, side, or bottom of (a ship) in
order to sink

⁴**scuttle** *vb* **scut·tled; scut·tling**
\'skət-(ᵊ-)liŋ\ : SCURRY, SCAMPER

**scut·tle·butt** \'skət-ᵊl-ˌbət\ *n* : GOSSIP

**scythe** \'sīth\ *n* : an implement for
mowing (as grass or grain) by hand —
**scythe** *vb*

**SD** *abbr* **1** sea-damaged **2** sine die
**3** South Dakota **4** special delivery

**S Dak** *abbr* South Dakota

**Se** *symbol* selenium

**SE** *abbr* southeast

**sea** \'sē\ *n* **1** : a large body of salt
water **2** : OCEAN **3** : rough water;
*also* : a heavy wave **4** : something like
or likened to a large body of water —
**sea** *adj* — **at sea** : LOST, BEWILDERED

**sea anemone** *n* : any of numerous
solitary polyps whose form, bright and
varied colors, and cluster of tentacles
superficially resemble a flower

**sea·bed** \-ˌbed\ *n* : the floor of a sea
or ocean

**sea·bird** \'sē-ˌbərd\ *n* : a bird (as a
gull) frequenting the open ocean

**sea·board** \-ˌbōrd\ *n* : a seacoast with
the country bordering it

**sea·coast** \'sē-ˌkōst\ *n* : land at and
near the edge of a sea

**sea·far·er** \'sē-ˌfar-ər\ *n* : SEAMAN

**sea·far·ing** \-ˌfar-iŋ\ *n* : a mariner's
calling - **seafaring** *adj*

**sea·food** \-ˌfüd\ *n* : edible marine fish
and shellfish

**sea·go·ing** \-ˌgō-iŋ\ *adj* : OCEANGOING

**sea horse** *n* : a small sea fish with a
head suggesting that of a horse

¹**seal** \'sēl\ *n, pl* **seals** *also* **seal 1**
: any of various large sea mammals of
cold regions with limbs adapted for
swimming **2** : the pelt of a seal

²**seal** *vb* : to hunt seals

³**seal** *n* **1** : a device having a raised design that can be stamped on clay or
wax; *also* : the impression made by
stamping with such a device **2** : something that fastens or secures as a

stamped wax impression fastens a letter; *also* : GUARANTY, PLEDGE **3** : a mark acceptable as having the legal effect of an official seal

**⁴seal** *vb* **1** : to affix a seal to; *also* : AUTHENTICATE **2** : to fasten with a seal; *esp* : to enclose securely **3** : to determine irrevocably

**sea-lane** \'sē-,lān\ *n* : an established sea route

**seal·ant** \'sē-lənt\ *n* : a sealing agent

**seal·er** \'sē-lər\ *n* : a coat applied to prevent subsequent coats of paint or varnish from sinking in

**sea level** *n* : the level of the surface of the sea esp. at its mean position midway between mean high and low water

**sea lion** *n* : any of several large Pacific seals with external ears

**seal·skin** \'sēl-,skin\ *n* **1** : ¹SEAL 2 **2** : a garment of sealskin

**¹seam** \'sēm\ *n* **1** : the line of junction of two edges and esp. of edges of fabric sewn together **2** : WRINKLE **3** : a layer of mineral matter ⟨coal ∼s⟩ — **seam·less** *adj*

**²seam** *vb* **1** : to join by or as if by sewing **2** : WRINKLE, FURROW

**sea·man** \'sē-mən\ *n* **1** : one who assists in the handling of ships : MARINER **2** : an enlisted man in the navy ranking next below a petty officer third class

**seaman apprentice** *n* : an enlisted man in the navy ranking next below a seaman

**seaman recruit** *n* : an enlisted man of the lowest rank in the navy

**sea·man·ship** \'sē-mən-,ship\ *n* : the art or skill of handling a ship

**sea·mount** \'sē-,maùnt\ *n* : a submarine mountain

**seam·stress** \'sēm-strəs\ *n* : a woman who does sewing

**seamy** \'sē-mē\ *adj* **seam·i·er; -est** **1** : UNPLEASANT **2** : DEGRADED, SORDID

**sé·ance** \'sā-,äns\ *n* : a spiritualist meeting to receive communications from spirits

**sea·plane** \'sē-,plān\ *n* : an airplane that can take off from and land on the water

**sea·port** \-,pōrt\ *n* : a port for oceangoing ships

**sear** \'siər\ *vb* **1** : to dry up : WITHER **2** : to burn or scorch esp. on the surface; *also* : BRAND

**¹search** \'sərch\ *vb* [ME *cerchen* fr. MF *cerchier* to go about, survey, search, fr. LL *circare* to go about, fr. L *circum* round about] **1** : to look through in trying to find something : SEEK **3** : PROBE — **search·er** *n*

**²search** *n* **1** : the act of searching **2** : critical examination **3** : an act of boarding and inspecting a ship on the high seas in exercise of right of search

**search·light** \-,līt\ *n* **1** : an apparatus for projecting a beam of light; *also* : the light projected **2** : FLASHLIGHT

**sea·scape** \'sē-,skāp\ *n* **1** : a view of the sea **2** : a picture representing a scene at sea

**sea·shore** \-,shōr\ *n* : the shore of a sea

**sea·sick** \-,sik\ *adj* : nauseated by or as if by the motion of a ship — **sea·sick·ness** *n*

**sea·side** \'sē-,sīd\ *n* : SEASHORE

**¹sea·son** \'sēz-ᵊn\ *n* [ME, fr. OF *saison*, fr. L *sation-, satio* action of sowing, fr. *satus*, pp. of *serere* to sow] **1** : one of the divisions of the year (as spring, summer, autumn, or winter) **2** : a special period (the Easter ∼) — **sea·son·al** \'sēz-(ᵊ-)nəl\ *adj* — **sea·son·al·ly** \-ē\ *adv*

**²season** *vb* **sea·soned; sea·son·ing** \'sēz-(ᵊ-)niŋ\ **1** : to make pleasant to the taste by use of salt, pepper, or spices **2** : to make (as by aging or drying) suitable for use **3** : to accustom or habituate to something (as hardship) *syn* harden, inure, acclimatize — **sea·son·er** \'sēz-(ᵊ-)nər\ *n*

**sea·son·able** \'sēz-(ᵊ-)nə-bəl\ *adj* : occurring at a fit time *syn* timely — **sea·son·ably** \-blē\ *adv*

**sea·son·ing** \'sēz-(ᵊ-)niŋ\ *n* : something that seasons : CONDIMENT

**¹seat** \'sēt\ *n* **1** : a place on or at which a person sits **2** : a chair, bench, or stool for sitting on **3** : a place which serves as a capital or center

**²seat** *vb* **1** : to place in or on a seat **2** : to provide seats for

**seat belt** *n* : straps designed to hold a person steady in a seat

**seat·ing** \-iŋ\ *n* : accommodations for sitting : SEATS

**SEATO** \'sē-,tō\ *abbr* Southeast Asia Treaty Organization

**sea urchin** *n* : any of a class of oblate spiny marine animals with thin brittle shells

**sea·wall** \'sē-,wól\ *n* : an embankment to protect the shore from erosion or to act as a breakwater

**¹sea·ward** \'sē-wərd\ *also* **sea·wards** \-wərdz\ *adv* : toward the sea

**²seaward** *n* : the direction or side away from land and toward the open sea

**³seaward** *adj* **1** : directed or situated toward the sea **2** : coming from the sea

**sea·wa·ter** \'sē-,wót-ər, -,wät-\ *n* : water in or from the sea

**sea·way** \-,wā\ *n* : an inland waterway that admits ocean shipping

**sea·weed** \-,wēd\ *n* : a marine alga : a mass of marine algae

**sea·wor·thy** \'sē-,wər-thē\ *adj* : fit for a sea voyage

**se·ba·ceous** \si-'bā-shəs\ *adj* : of, relating to, or secreting fatty material

**sec** *abbr* **1** second; secondary **2** secretary **3** section **4** [L *secundum*] according to

**SEC** *abbr* Securities and Exchange Commission

**se·cede** \si-'sēd\ *vb* **-ced·ed; -ced·ing** : to withdraw from an organized body and esp. from a political body

**se·ces·sion** \si-'sesh-ən\ *n* : the act of seceding — **se·ces·sion·ist** *n*

**se·clude** \si-'klüd\ *vb* **se·clud·ed; se·clud·ing** : to shut off by oneself

**se·clu·sion** \si-'klü-zhən\ *n* : the act of secluding : the state of being secluded — **se·clu·sive** \-siv\ *adj*

¹sec·ond \'sek-ənd\ *adj* [ME, fr. OF, fr. L *secundus* second, following, favorable, fr. *sequi* to follow] **1** : being number two in a countable series **2** : next after the first **3** : ALTERNATE ⟨every ~ year⟩ — **second** *or* **sec·ond·ly** *adv*

²second *n* **1** : one that is second **2** : one who assists another (as in a duel) **3** : an inferior or flawed article (as of merchandise) **4** : the second forward gear in a motor vehicle

³second *n* [ME *secunde* fr. ML *secunda*, fr. L, fem. of *secundus* second; fr. its being the second division of a unit into 60 parts, as a minute is the first] **1** : a 60th part of a minute either of time or of a degree **2** : an instant of time

⁴second *vb* **1** : to act as a second to **2** : to encourage or give support to **3** : to support (a motion) by adding one's voice to that of a proposer

sec·ond·ar·y \'sek-ən-,der-ē\ *adj* **1** : second in rank, value, or occurrence : INFERIOR, LESSER **2** : coming after the primary or elementary ⟨~ schools⟩ **3** : belonging to a second or later stage of development **syn** subordinate

sec·ond-guess \,sek-ᵊn-'ges, -ən-\ *vb* : to think out other strategies or explanations for after the event

sec·ond·hand \,sek-ən-'hand\ *adj* **1** : not original **2** : not new : USED ⟨~ clothes⟩ **3** : dealing in used goods

second lieutenant *n* : a commissioned officer (as in the army) ranking next below a first lieutenant

sec·ond-rate \,sek-ən(d)-'rāt\ *adj* : INFERIOR

second-story man *n* : a burglar who enters by an upstairs window

sec·ond-string \,sek-ən-,striŋ, ,sek-ᵊn-\ *adj* : being a substitute (as on a ball team)

se·cre·cy \'sē-krə-sē\ *n, pl* -cies **1** : the habit or practice of being secretive **2** : the quality or state of being secret

¹se·cret \'sē-krət\ *adj* **1** : HIDDEN, CONCEALED ⟨a ~ panel⟩ **2** : COVERT, STEALTHY; *also* : engaged in detecting or spying ⟨a ~ agent⟩ **3** : kept from general knowledge — se·cret·ly *adv*

²secret *n* **1** : something kept from the knowledge of others **2** : MYSTERY **3** : CONCEALMENT

sec·re·tar·i·at \,sek-rə-'ter-ē-ət\ *n* **1** : the office of a secretary **2** : the body of secretaries in an office **3** : the administrative department of a governmental organization ⟨the UN ~⟩

sec·re·tary \'sek-rə-,ter-ē\ *n, pl* -tar·ies **1** : a confidential clerk **2** : a corporation or business official who is in charge of correspondence or records **3** : an official at the head of a department of government **4** : a writing desk — sec·re·tar·i·al \,sek-rə-'ter-ē-əl\ *adj* — sec·re·tary·ship \'sek-rə-,ter-ē-,ship\ *n*

¹se·crete \si-'krēt\ *vb* se·cret·ed; se·cret·ing : to produce and emit as a secretion

²se·crete \si-'krēt, 'sē-krət\ *vb* -cret·ed; -cret·ing : HIDE, CONCEAL

se·cre·tion \si-'krē-shən\ *n* **1** : an act or process of secreting **2** : a product of glandular activity; *esp* : one (as a hormone) useful in the organism — se·cre·to·ry \-'krēt-ə-rē\ *adj*

se·cre·tive \'sē-krət-iv, si-'krēt-\ *adj* : tending to keep secrets or to act secretly — se·cre·tive·ly *adv* — se·cre·tive·ness *n*

¹sect \'sekt\ *n* **1** : a dissenting religious body **2** : a religious denomination **3** : a group adhering to a distinctive doctrine or to a leader

²sect *abbr* section

¹sec·tar·i·an \sek-'ter-ē-ən\ *adj* **1** : of or relating to a sect or sectarian **2** : limited in character or scope — sec·tar·i·an·ism *n*

²sectarian *n* **1** : an adherent of a sect **2** : a narrow or bigoted person

sec·ta·ry \'sek-tə-rē\ *n, pl* -ries : a member of a sect

sec·tion \'sek-shən\ *n* **1** : a cutting apart; *also* : a part cut off or separated **2** : a distinct part **3** : the appearance that a thing has or would have if cut straight through

sec·tion·al \'sek-sh(ə-)nəl\ *adj* **1** : of, relating to, or characteristic of a section **2** : local or regional rather than general in character **3** : divided into sections — sec·tion·al·ism *n*

section gang *n* : a gang or crew of track workers employed to maintain a section of a railroad

sec·tor \'sek-tər\ *n* **1** : a part of a circle between two radii **2** : a definite part of a region assigned to a military leader as his area of operations

sec·u·lar \'sek-yə-lər\ *adj* **1** : not sacred or ecclesiastical **2** : not bound by monastic vows ⟨~ priest⟩

sec·u·lar·ism \'sek-yə-lə-,riz-əm\ *n* : indifference to or exclusion of religion — sec·u·lar·ist \-rəst\ *n* — secularist *or* sec·u·lar·is·tic \,sek-yə-lə-'ris-tik\ *adj*

sec·u·lar·ize \'sek-yə-lə-,rīz\ *vb* -ized; -iz·ing **1** : to make secular **2** : to transfer from ecclesiastical to civil or lay use, possession, or control — sec·u·lar·iza·tion \,sek-yə-lə-rə-'zā-shən\ *n* — sec·u·lar·iz·er \'sek-yə-lə-,rī-zər\ *n*

¹se·cure \si-'kyùr\ *adj* se·cur·er; -est [L *securus* safe, secure, fr. *se* without + *cura* care] **1** : easy in mind : free from fear **2** : free from danger or risk of loss : SAFE **3** : CERTAIN, SURE — se·cure·ly *adv*

²secure *vb* se·cured; se·cur·ing **1** : to make safe : GUARD **2** : to assure payment of by giving a pledge or collateral **3** : to fasten safely ⟨~ a door⟩ **4** : GET, ACQUIRE

se·cu·ri·ty \si-'kyùr-ət-ē\ *n, pl* -ties **1** : SAFETY **2** : CERTAINTY **3** : freedom from worry **4** : PROTECTION, SHELTER **5** : something (as collateral) given as pledge of payment **6** *pl* : bond or stock certificates

secy *abbr* secretary

se·dan \si-'dan\ *n* **1** : a covered chair borne on poles by two men **2** : an enclosed automobile usu. with front and back seats  **3** : a motorboat with one passenger compartment

**se·date** \si-'dāt\ *adj* : quiet and dignified in behavior **syn** staid, sober, serious, solemn — **se·date·ly** *adv*

**¹sed·a·tive** \'sed-ət-iv\ *adj* : serving or tending to relieve tension — **se·da·tion** \si-'dā-shən\ *n*

**²sedative** *n* : a sedative drug

**sed·en·tary** \'sed-ºn-ter-ē\ *adj* : characterized by or requiring much sitting

**sedge** \'sej\ *n* : a grasslike plant with solid stems growing in tufts in marshes — **sedgy** \'sej-ē\ *adj*

**sed·i·ment** \'sed-ə-mənt\ *n* **1** : the material that settles to the bottom of a liquid : LEES, DREGS **2** : material (as stones and sand) deposited by water, wind, or a glacier — **sed·i·men·ta·ry** \,sed-ə-'men-t(ə-)rē\ *adj* — **sed·i·men·ta·tion** \-,mən-'tā-shən, ,men-\ *n*

**se·di·tion** \si-'dish-ən\ *n* : the causing of discontent, insurrection, or resistance against a government — **se·di·tious** \-əs\ *adj*

**se·duce** \si-'d(y)üs\ *vb* **se·duced; se·duc·ing 1** : to persuade to disobedience or disloyalty **2** : to lead astray **3** : to entice to unlawful sexual intercourse without the use of force **syn** tempt, entice, inveigle, lure — **se·duc·er** *n* — **se·duc·tion** \-'dək-shən\ *n* — **se·duc·tive** \-tiv\ *adj*

**sed·u·lous** \'sej-ə-ləs\ *adj* [L *sedulus*, fr. *sedulo* sincerely, diligently, fr. *se* without + *dolus* guile] : DILIGENT, PAINSTAKING

**¹see** \'sē\ *vb* **saw** \'sò\; **seen** \'sēn\; **see·ing** \'sē-iŋ\ **1** : to perceive by the eye : have the power of sight **2** : EXPERIENCE **3** : NOTICE, HEED **4** : UNDERSTAND **5** : to meet with **syn** behold, descry, espy, view, note, discern

**²see** *n* : the authority or jurisdiction of a bishop

**¹seed** \'sēd\ *n, pl* **seed** *or* **seeds 1** : a ripened ovule of a plant that may develop into a new plant **2** : a part (as a small seedlike fruit) by which a plant is propagated **3** : DESCENDANTS **4** : SOURCE, ORIGIN — **seed·less** *adj* — **go to seed** *or* **run to seed 1** : to develop seed **2** : DECAY

**²seed** *vb* **1** : SOW, PLANT ⟨~ land to grass⟩ **2** : to bear or shed seeds **3** : to remove seeds from — **seed·er** *n*

**seed·ling** \'sēd-liŋ\ *n* **1** : a plant grown from seed **2** : a young plant; *esp* : a tree smaller than a sapling

**seed·time** \'sēd-,tīm\ *n* : the season for sowing

**seedy** \'sēd-ē\ *adj* **seed·i·er; -est 1** : containing or full of seeds **2** : inferior in condition or quality

**seek** \'sēk\ *vb* **sought** \'sòt\; **seek·ing 1** : to search for **2** : to try to reach or obtain ⟨~ fame⟩ **3** : ATTEMPT — **seek·er** *n*

**seem** \'sēm\ *vb* **1** : to give the impression of being : APPEAR **2** : to appear to the observation or understanding **3**

: to give evidence of existing or being present

**seem·ing** \-iŋ\ *adj* : outwardly apparent — **seem·ing·ly** *adv*

**seem·ly** \'sēm-lē\ *adj* **seem·li·er; -est** : PROPER, DECENT

**seep** \'sēp\ *vb* : to leak through fine pores or cracks : percolate slowly — **seep·age** \'sē-pij\ *n*

**seer** \'siər\ *n* : a person who foresees or predicts events : PROPHET

**seer·suck·er** \'siər-,sək-ər\ *n* [Hindi *śīrśaker*, fr. Per *shīr-o-shakar*, lit., milk and sugar] : a light fabric of linen, cotton, or rayon usu. striped and slightly puckered

**see·saw** \'sē-,sò\ *n* **1** : a children's sport of riding up and down on the ends of a plank supported in the middle; *also* : the plank so used **2** : a contest in which now one side now the other has the lead — **seesaw** *vb*

**seethe** \'sēth\ *vb* **seethed; seeth·ing** : to become violently agitated

**seg·ment** \'seg-mənt\ *n* **1** : a division of a thing : SECTION ⟨~ of an orange⟩ **2** : a part cut off from a geometrical figure (as a circle) by a line — **seg·ment·ed** \-,ment-əd\ *adj*

**seg·re·gate** \'seg-ri-,gāt\ *vb* **-gat·ed; -gat·ing** [L *segregare*, fr. *se-* apart + *greg-, grex* herd, flock] : to cut off from others : ISOLATE — **seg·re·ga·tion** \,seg-ri-'gā-shən\ *n*

**seg·re·ga·tion·ist** \'seg-ri-'gā-sh(ə-)nəst\ *n* : one who believes in or practices the segregation of races

**sei·gneur** \sān-'yər\ *n, often cap* : a feudal lord

**¹seine** \'sān\ *n* : a large weighted fishing net

**²seine** *vb* **seined; sein·ing** : to fish or catch with a seine

**seism** \'sī-zəm\ *n* : EARTHQUAKE

**seis·mic** \'sīz-mik, 'sīs-\ *adj* : of, relating to, resembling, or caused by an earthquake — **seis·mic·i·ty** \sīz-'mis-ət-ē, sīs-\ *n*

**seis·mo·gram** \'sīz-mə-,gram, 'sīs-\ *n* : the record of an earth tremor by a seismograph

**seis·mo·graph** \-,graf\ *n* : an apparatus for recording the intensity, direction, and duration of earthquakes — **seis·mog·ra·pher** \sīz-'mäg-rə-fər, sīs-\ *n* — **seis·mo·graph·ic** \,sīz-mə-'graf-ik, ,sīs-\ *adj* — **seis·mog·ra·phy** \sīz-'mäg-rə-fē, sīs-\ *n*

**seis·mol·o·gy** \sīz-'mäl-ə-jē, sīs-\ *n* : a science that deals with earthquakes and with artificially produced vibrations of the earth — **seis·mo·log·i·cal** \,sīz-mə-'läj-i-kəl, ,sīs-\ *adj* — **seis·mol·o·gist** \sīz-'mäl-ə-jəst, sīs-\ *n*

**seis·mom·e·ter** \sīz-'mäm-ət-ər, sīs-\ *n* : a seismograph measuring the actual movement of the ground — **seis·mo·met·ric** \,sīz-mə-'me-trik, ,sīs-\ *adj*

**seize** \'sēz\ *vb* **seized; seiz·ing 1** : to lay hold of or take possession of by force **2** : ARREST **3** : UNDERSTAND **4** : to attack or overwhelm physically : AFFLICT **syn** take, grasp, clutch snatch, grab — **sei·zure** \'sē-zhər\ n

**sel** abbr select; selected; selection

**sel·dom** \'sel-dəm\ adv : not often : RARELY

¹**se·lect** \sə-'lekt\ adj 1 : CHOSEN, PICKED; also : CHOICE 2 : judicious or restrictive in choice : DISCRIMINATING

²**select** vb : to take by preference from a number or group : pick out : CHOOSE — **se·lec·tive** \sə-'lek-tiv\ adj

**se·lect·ee** \sə-,lek-'tē\ n : one inducted into military service under selective service

**se·lec·tion** \sə-'lek-shən\ n 1 : the act of selecting : CHOICE 2 : something selected 3 : a natural or artificial process that increases the chance of propagation of some organisms and decreases that of others

**selective service** n : a system for calling men up for military service

**se·lect·man** \si-'lek(t)-,man, -mən\ n : one of a board of officials elected in towns of most New England states to administer town affairs

**sel·e·nite** \'sel-ə-,nīt\ n [L selenites, fr. Gk selēnitēs (lithos), lit., stone of the moon, fr. selēnē moon; fr. the belief that it waxed and waned with the moon] : a variety of transparent crystalline gypsum

**se·le·ni·um** \sə-'lē-nē-əm\ n : a nonmetallic chemical element that varies in electrical conductivity with the intensity of its illumination

**sel·e·nog·ra·phy** \,sel-ə-'näg-rə-fē\ n 1 : the science of the physical features of the moon 2 : the physical features of the moon — **sel·e·nog·ra·pher** \-fər\ n

**sel·e·nol·o·gy** \,sel-ə-'näl-ə-jē\ n : astronomy that deals with the moon

**self** \'self\ n, pl **selves** \'selvz\ 1 : the essential person distinct from all other persons in identity 2 : a particular side of a person's character 3 : personal interest : SELFISHNESS

**self-** comb form 1 : oneself : itself 2 : of oneself or itself 3 : by oneself; also : automatic 4 : to, for, or toward oneself

self-abasement
self-accusation
self-acting
self-addressed
self-adjusting
self-administered
self-advancement
self-aggrandizement
self-aggrandizing
self-analysis
self-appointed
self-asserting
self-assertion
self-assertive
self-assurance
self-assured
self-awareness
self-betrayal
self-closing
self-command
self-complacent
self-conceit
self-concerned
self-condemned
self-confessed
self-confidence
self-confident
self-congratulation
self-congratulatory
self-constituted
self-contradiction
self-contradictory
self-control
self-correcting
self-created
self-criticism
self-cultivation
self-deceit
self-deceiving
self-deception
self-defeating
self-defense
self-delusion
self-denial
self-denying
self-depreciation
self-destruction
self-determination
self-discipline
self-distrust
self-doubt
self-driven
self-educated
self-employed
self-employment
self-esteem
self-evident
self-examination
self-explaining
self-explanatory
self-expression
self-forgetful
self-fulfilling
self-giving
self-governing
self-government
self-help
self-hypnosis
self-image
self-importance
self-important
self-imposed
self-improvement
self-incrimination
self-induced
self-indulgence
self-inflicted
self-interest
self-limiting
self-love
self-lubricating
self-mastery
self-operating
self-perpetuating
self-pity
self-portrait
self-possessed
self-possession
self-preservation
self-proclaimed
self-propelled
self-propelling
self-protection
self-realization
self-regard
self-registering
self-reliance
self-reliant
self-reproach
self-respect
self-respecting
self-restraint
self-rule
self-sacrifice
self-satisfaction
self-satisfied
self-seeking
self-service
self-serving
self-starting
self-styled
self-sufficiency
self-sufficient
self-supporting
self-sustaining
self-taught
self-torment
self-winding

**self-cen·tered** \'self-'sent-ərd\ adj : concerned only with one's own self — **self-cen·tered·ness** n

**self-com·posed** \,self-kəm-'pōzd\ adj : having control over one's emotions

**self-con·scious** \'self-'kän-chəs\ adj 1 : aware of oneself as an individual 2 : uncomfortably conscious of oneself as an object of the observation of others : ill at ease — **self-con·scious·ly** adv — **self-con·scious·ness** n

**self-con·tained** \,self-kən-'tānd\ adj 1 : showing self-command; also : reserved in manner 2 : complete in itself

**self-de·struct** \-di-'strəkt\ vb : to destroy itself

**self-ef·fac·ing** \-ə-'fā-siŋ\ adj : RETIRING, SHY

**self-fer·til·iza·tion** \,self-,fərt-ºl-ə-'zā-shən\ n : fertilization effected by union of ova with pollen or sperm from the same individual

**self·ish** \'sel-fish\ adj : taking care of one's own comfort, pleasure, or interest excessively or without regard for others

— **self·ish·ly** \ adv — **self·ish·ness** n

**self·less** \'self-ləs\ adj : UNSELFISH — **self·less·ness** n

**self-load·er** \'self-'lōd-ər\ n : a semiautomatic firearm

**self-load·ing** \-'lōd-iŋ\ adj, of a fire-arm : SEMIAUTOMATIC

**self-lu·mi·nous** \-'lü-mə-nəs\ adj : having in itself the property of emitting light

**self-made** \'self-'mād\ adj : rising from poverty or obscurity by one's own efforts ⟨~ man⟩

**self-pol·li·na·tion** \,self-,päl-ə-'nā-shən\ n : pollination of a flower with pollen from the same or a genetically identical flower

**self-reg·u·lat·ing** \'self-'reg-yə-,lāt-iŋ\ adj : AUTOMATIC

**self-righ·teous** \-rī'-chəs\ adj : strongly convinced of one's own righteousness — **self-righ·teous·ly** adv

**self·same** \'self-,sām\ adj : precisely the same : IDENTICAL

**self-seal·ing** \'self-'sē-liŋ\ adj : capable of sealing itself (as after puncture)

**self-start·er** \-'stärt-ər\ n : an electric motor used to start an internal-combustion engine

**self-will** \'self-'wil\ n : OBSTINACY

**sell** \'sel\ vb **sold** \'sōld\; **sell·ing** **1** : to transfer (property) in return for money or something else of value **2** : to deal in as a business **3** : to be sold ⟨cars are ~ing well⟩ — **sell·er** n

**selling climax** n : a sharp decline in stock prices for a short time on very heavy trading volume followed by a rally

**sell out** \(')sel-'aút\ vb **1** : to dispose of entirely by sale; esp **1** : to sell one's business **2** : BETRAY — **sell·out** \'sel-,aút\ n

**selt·zer** \'selt-sər\ n [modif. of G Selterser (wasser) water of Selters, fr. Nieder Selters, Germany] : an artificially prepared water charged with carbon dioxide and used in mixing alcoholic drinks

**sel·vage** or **sel·vedge** \'sel-vij\ n : the edge of a woven fabric so formed as to prevent raveling

**selves** pl of SELF

**sem** abbr seminary

**se·man·tic** \si-'mant-ik\ also **se·man·ti·cal** \-i-kəl\ adj : of or relating to meaning

**se·man·tics** \si-'mant-iks\ n sing or pl **1** : the study of meanings in language **2** : connotative meaning

**sema·phore** \'sem-ə-,fōr\ n **1** : a visual signaling apparatus with movable arms **2** : signaling by hand-held flags

**sem·blance** \'sem-bləns\ n **1** : outward appearance **2** : IMAGE, LIKENESS

**se·men** \'sē-mən\ n : male reproductive fluid consisting of secretions and germ cells

**se·mes·ter** \sə-'mes-tər\ n [G, fr. L semestris half-yearly, fr. sex six + mensis month] : half a year; esp : one of the two terms into which many colleges divide the school year — **se·mes-**

**tral** \-trəl\ or **se·mes·tri·al** \-trē-əl\ adj

**semi-** \,sem-i, 'sem-, -,ī\ prefix **1** : precisely half of **2** : half in quantity or value; also : half of or occurring halfway through a specified period **3** : partly : incompletely **4** : partial : incomplete **5** : having some of the characteristics of

semiannual
semiarid
semicentennial
semicircle
semicircular
semicivilized
semiclassical
semiconscious
semidarkness
semidivine
semiformal
semigloss
semi-independent
semiliquid
semiliterate
semimonthly
semiofficial
semipermanent
semipolitical
semiprecious
semiprivate
semiprofessional
semireligious
semiretired
semiskilled
semisweet
semitransparent
semiweekly
semiyearly

**semi·au·to·mat·ic** \,sem-ē-,ót-ə-'mat-ik\ adj, of a firearm : employing recoil or gas pressure to eject an empty cartridge case and to load before firing again

**semi·co·lon** \'sem-i-,kō-lən\ n : a punctuation mark ; used esp. in a coordinating function between major sentence elements

**semi·con·duc·tor** \,sem-i-kən-'dək-tər, -,ī-\ n : a substance whose electrical conductivity is between that of a conductor and an insulator and increases with temperature increase — **semi·con·duct·ing** \-'dək-tiŋ\ adj

**semi·dry·ing** \,sem-i-'drī-iŋ\ adj : that dries imperfectly or slowly ⟨a ~ oil⟩

¹**semi·fi·nal** \,sem-i-'fīn-ºl\ adj : being next to the last in an elimination tournament

²**semi·fi·nal** \'sem-i-,fīn-ºl\ n : a semifinal round or match

**semi·flu·id** \,sem-i-'flü-əd, -,ī-\ adj : having the qualities of both a fluid and a solid

**semi·lu·nar** \-'lü-nər\ adj : crescent-shaped

**sem·i·nal** \'sem-ən-ºl\ adj **1** : of, relating to, or consisting of seed or semen **2** : containing or contributing the seeds of later development : CREATIVE, ORIGINAL — **sem·i·nal·ly** \-ē\ adv

**sem·i·nar** \'sem-ə-,när\ n **1** : a course of study pursued by a group of advanced students doing original research under a professor **2** : CONFERENCE

**sem·i·nary** \'sem-ə-,ner-ē\ n, pl **-nar·ies** [ME, seedbed, nursery, fr. L seminarium, fr. semen seed] : an educational institution; esp : one that gives theological training — **sem·i·nar·i·an** \,sem-ə-'ner-ē-ən\ n

**Sem·i·nole** \'sem-ə-,nōl\ n, pl Seminoles or Seminole : a member of an Indian people of Florida

**semi·per·me·able** \,sem-i-'pər-mē-ə-bəl\ adj : partially but not freely or wholly permeable; esp : permeable to some usu. small molecules but not to other usu. larger particles ⟨a ~ membrane⟩ — **semi·per·me·abil·i·ty** \-ˌpər-mē-ə-'bil-ət-ē\ n

**semi·soft** \-'sȯft\ adj : moderately soft; esp : firm but easily cut ⟨~ cheese⟩

**Sem·ite** \'sem-ˌīt\ n : a member of any of a group of peoples (as the Jews or Arabs) of southwestern Asia — **Se·mit·ic** \sə-'mit-ik\ adj

**semi·trail·er** \'sem-i-ˌtrā-lər, 'sem-ˌī-\ n : a freight trailer that when attached is supported at its forward end by the truck tractor; also : a semitrailer with attached tractor

**semi·works** \'sem-i-ˌwərks, 'sem-ˌī-\ n pl : a manufacturing plant operating on a limited commercial scale to provide final tests of a new product or process

**semp·stress** \'semp-strəs\ var of SEAMSTRESS

¹**sen** \'sen\ n, pl **sen** — see yen at MONEY table

²**sen** n, pl **sen** — see dollar, riel, rupiah at MONEY table

³**sen** abbr **1** senate; senator **2** senior

**sen·ate** \'sen-ət\ n [ME senat, fr. OF, fr. L senatus, lit., council of elders, fr. senex old, old man] : the upper branch of a legislature

**sen·a·tor** \'sen-ət-ər\ n : a member of a senate — **sen·a·to·ri·al** \ˌsen-ə-'tōr-ē-əl\ adj

**send** \'send\ vb **sent** \'sent\; **send·ing 1** : to cause to go **2** : EMIT **3** : to propel or drive esp. with force **4** : DELIGHT, THRILL - **send·er** n

**send-off** \'send-ˌȯf\ n : a demonstration of goodwill and enthusiasm for the beginning of a new venture (as a trip)

**se·ne** \'sā-(ˌ)nā\ n — see tala at MONEY table

**Sen·e·ca** \'sen-i-kə\ n, pl **Seneca** or **Senecas** : a member of an Indian people of western New York

**Sen·e·ga·lese** \ˌsen-i-gə-'lēz, -'lēs\ n, pl **Senegalese** : a native or inhabitant of Senegal - **Senegalese** adj

**se·nes·cence** \si-'nes-ᵊns\ n : the state of being old; also : the process of becoming old — **se·nes·cent** \-ᵊnt\ adj

**sen·gi** \'seŋ-gē\ n, pl **sengi** — see zaire at MONEY table

**se·nile** \'sēn-ˌīl, 'sen-\ adj : OLD, AGED — **se·nil·i·ty** \si-'nil-ət-ē\ n

¹**se·nior** \'sē-nyər\ n **1** : a person older or of higher rank than another **2** : a member of the graduating class of a high school or college

²**senior** adj [ME, fr. L, fr. senex old, compar. of senex old] **1** : ELDER **2** : more advanced in dignity or rank **3** : belonging to the final year of a school or college course

**senior chief petty officer** n : a petty officer in the navy ranking next below a master chief petty officer

**senior high school** n : a school usu. including grades 10–12

**se·nior·i·ty** \sēn-'yȯr-ət-ē\ n **1** : the quality or state of being senior **2** : a privileged status owing to length of continuous service

**senior master sergeant** n : a non-commissioned officer in the air force ranking next below a chief master sergeant

**sen·i·ti** \'sen-ə-tē\ n, pl **seniti** — see pa'anga at MONEY table

**sen·na** \'sen-ə\ n **1** : any of various cassias **2** : the dried leaflets of a cassia used as a purgative

**sen·sa·tion** \sen-'sā-shən\ n **1** : awareness (as of noise or heat) or a mental process (as seeing or hearing) due to stimulation of a sense organ; also : an indefinite bodily feeling **2** : a condition of excitement; also : the thing that causes this condition

**sen·sa·tion·al** \-sh(ə-)nəl\ adj **1** : of or relating to sensation or the senses **2** : arousing an intense and usu. superficial interest or emotional reaction — **sen·sa·tion·al·ly** \-ē\ adv

**sen·sa·tion·al·ism** \-ˌiz-əm\ n : the use or effect of sensational subject matter or treatment

¹**sense** \'sens\ n **1** : semantic content : MEANING **2** : the faculty of perceiving by means of sense organs, also : a bodily function or mechanism based on this ⟨the pain ~⟩ **3** : JUDGMENT, UNDERSTANDING **4** : OPINION ⟨the ~ of the meeting⟩ — **sense·less** adj — **sense·less·ly** adv

²**sense** vb **sensed**; **sens·ing 1** : to be or become aware of : perceive by the senses **2** : to detect (as radiation) automatically

**sense organ** n : a bodily structure that responds to a stimulus (as heat or light) and sends impulses to the brain where they are interpreted as corresponding sensations

**sen·si·bil·i·ty** \ˌsen-sə-'bil-ət-ē\ n, pl **-ties** : delicacy of feeling : SENSITIVITY

**sen·si·ble** \'sen-sə-bəl\ adj **1** : capable of being perceived by the senses or by reason; also : capable of receiving sense impressions **2** : AWARE, CONSCIOUS **3** : REASONABLE, INTELLIGENT — **sen·si·bly** \-blē\ adv

**sen·si·tive** \'sen-sət-iv\ adj **1** : subject to excitation by or responsive to stimuli **2** : having power of feeling **3** : of such a nature as to be easily affected — **sen·si·tive·ness** n — **sen·si·tiv·i·ty** \ˌsen-sə-'tiv-ət-ē\ n

**sensitive plant** n : any of several mimosas with leaves that fold or droop when touched

**sen·si·tize** \'sen-sə-ˌtīz\ vb **-tized**; **-tiz·ing** : to make or become sensitive or hypersensitive — **sen·si·ti·za·tion** \ˌsen-sət-ə-'zā-shən\ n

**sen·si·tom·e·ter** \ˌsen-sə-'täm-ət-ər\ n : an instrument for measuring sensitivity of photographic material — **sen·si·to·met·ric** \-sət-ə-'met-rik\ adj — **sen·si·tom·e·try** \-sə-'täm-ə-trē\ n

**sen·sor** \'sen-ˌsȯr, -sər\ n : a device that responds to a physical stimulus

**sen·so·ry** \'sens-(ə-)rē\ adj : of or relating to sensation or the senses

**sen·su·al** \'sench-(ə )wəl, 'sen-shəl\ adj **1** : relating to the pleasing of the senses **2** : devoted to the pleasures of the senses — **sen·su·al·ist** n — **sen-**

**su·al·i·ty** \,sen-chə-'wal-ət-ē\ n —
**sen·su·al·ly** \'sench-(ə-)wə-lē, 'sen-shə-lē\ adv
**sen·su·ous** \'sench-(ə-)wəs\ adj 1 : relating to the senses or to things that can be perceived by the senses 2 : VOLUPTUOUS — **sen·su·ous·ly** adv — **sen·su·ous·ness** n
**sent** past of SEND
**¹sen·tence** \'sent-ᵊns, -ᵊnz\ n [ME, fr. OF, fr. L sententia, lit., feeling, opinion, fr. sentire to feel] 1 : DECISION, JUDGMENT ⟨pass ∼⟩ 2 : a grammatically self-contained speech unit that expresses an assertion, a question, a command, a wish, or an exclamation
**²sentence** vb **sen·tenced**; **sen·tenc·ing** : to impose a sentence on syn condemn, damn, doom
**sen·ten·tious** \sen-'ten chəs\ adj : using wise sayings or proverbs; also : using pompous language
**sen·ti** \'sent-ē\ n, pl **senti** — see shilingi at MONEY table
**sen·tient** \'sen-ch(ē-)ənt\ adj : capable of feeling : having perception
**sen·ti·ment** \'sent-ə mənt\ n 1 : FEELING; also : thought and judgment influenced by feeling : emotional attitude 2 : OPINION, NOTION
**sen·ti·men·tal** \,sent-ə-'ment-ᵊl\ adj 1 : influenced by tender feelings 2 : affecting the emotions syn romantic — **sen·ti·men·tal·ism** n — **sen·ti·men·tal·ist** n — **sen·ti·men·tal·i·ty** \-,men-'tal-ət-ē, -mən-\ n — **sen·ti·men·tal·ly** \-'ment-ᵊl-ē\ adv
**sen·ti·men·tal·ize** \-'ment-ᵊl-,īz\ vb **-ized**; **-iz·ing** 1 : to indulge in sentiment 2 : to look upon or imbue with sentiment — **sen·ti·men·tal·iza·tion** \-,ment-ᵊl-ə-'zā-shən\ n
**sen·ti·mo** \sen-'tē-(,)mō\ n, pl **-mos** — see peso at MONEY table
**sen·ti·nel** \'sent-(ᵊ-)nəl\ n [MF sentinelle, fr. It sentinella, fr. sentina vigilance, fr. sentire to perceive, fr. L] : one that watches or guards
**sen·try** \'sen-trē\ n, pl **sentries** : SENTINEL, GUARD
**sep** abbr separate; separated
**Sep** abbr September
**se·pal** \'sēp-əl, 'sep-\ n : one of the modified leaves comprising a flower calyx
**sep·a·ra·ble** \'sep-(ə-)rə-bəl\ adj : capable of being separated
**¹sep·a·rate** \'sep-ə-,rāt\ vb **-rat·ed**; **-rat·ing** 1 : to set or keep apart : DISUNITE, DISCONNECT, SEVER 2 : to keep apart by something intervening 3 : to cease to be together : PART
**²sep·a·rate** \'sep-(ə-)rət\ adj 1 : not connected 2 : divided from each other 3 : SINGLE, PARTICULAR ⟨the ∼ pieces of the puzzle⟩ — **sep·a·rate·ly** adv
**³sep·a·rate** n : an article of dress designed to be worn interchangeably with others to form various combinations
**sep·a·ra·tion** \,sep-ə-'rā-shən\ n 1 : the act or process of separating : the state of being separated 2 : a point, line, means, or area of division
**sep·a·rat·ist** \'sep-(ə-)rət-əst, 'sep-ə-,rāt-\ n, often cap : an advocate of separation (as from a political body)
**sep·a·ra·tive** \'sep-ə-,rāt-iv, 'sep-(ə-)rət-\ adj : tending toward, causing, or expressing separation
**sep·a·ra·tor** \'sep-(ə-),rāt-ər\ n : one that separates; esp : a device for separating cream from milk
**se·pia** \'sē-pē-ə\ n : a brownish gray to dark brown
**sepn** abbr separation
**sep·sis** \'sep-səs\ n, pl **sep·ses** \'sep-,sēz\ : a poisoned condition due to spread of bacteria or their products in the body
**Sept** abbr September
**Sep·tem·ber** \sep-'tem-bər\ n : the ninth month of the year having 30 days
**sep·tic** \'sep-tik\ adj 1 : PUTREFACTIVE 2 : relating to or characteristic of sepsis
**sep·ti·ce·mia** \,sep-tə-'sē-mē-ə\ n : invasion of the bloodstream by virulent microorganisms from a focus of infection accompanied esp. by chills, fever, and prostration
**septic tank** n : a tank in which sewage is disintegrated by bacteria
**sep·tu·a·ge·nar·i·an** \sep-,t(y)ü-ə-jə-'ner-ē-ən\ n : a person who is 70 or more but less than 80 years old — **septuagenarian** adj
**Sep·tu·a·gint** \sep-'t(y)ü-ə-jənt, 'sep-tə-wə-,jint\ n : a Greek version of the Old Testament used by Greek-speaking Christians
**¹sep·ul·cher** or **sep·ul·chre** \'sep-əl-kər\ n : burial vault : TOMB
**²sepulcher** or **sepulchre** vb **-chered** or **-chred**, **-cher·ing** or **-chring** \-k(ə-)riŋ\ : BURY, ENTOMB
**se·pul·chral** \sə-'pəl-krəl\ adj 1 : relating to burial or the grave 2 : GLOOMY
**sep·ul·ture** \'sep-əl-,chùr\ n 1 : BURIAL, INTERMENT 2 : SEPULCHER
**seq** abbr [L sequens, sequentes, sequentia] the following
**seqq** abbr [L sequentes, sequentia] the following
**se·quel** \'sē-kwəl\ n 1 : logical consequence 2 : EFFECT, RESULT 3 : a literary work continuing a story begun in a preceding issue
**se·quence** \'sē-kwəns\ n 1 : the condition or fact of following something else 2 : SERIES 3 : RESULT, SEQUEL 4 : chronological order of events syn succession, set — **se·quen·tial** \si-'kwen-chəl\ adj
**se·quent** \'sē-kwənt\ adj 1 : SUCCEEDING, CONSECUTIVE 2 : RESULTANT
**se·ques·ter** \si-'kwes-tər\ vb : to set apart : SEGREGATE
**se·ques·trate** \'sek-wəs-,trāt, si-'kwes-\ vb **-trat·ed**; **-trat·ing** : SEQUESTER — **se·ques·tra·tion** \,sek-wəs-'trā-shən, (,)sē-,kwes-\ n
**se·quin** \'sē-kwən\ n 1 : an obsolete gold coin of Turkey and Italy 2 : SPANGLE
**se·quoia** \si-'kwòi-ə\ n : either of two huge California coniferous trees
**ser** abbr 1 serial 2 series

**sera** pl of SERUM

**se·ra·glio** \sə-'ral-yō\ n, pl **-glios** : HAREM

**se·ra·pe** \sə-'räp-ē\ n : a colorful woolen shawl worn over the shoulders esp. by Mexican men

**ser·aph** \'ser-əf\ also **ser·a·phim** \-ə-,fim\ n, pl **sera·phim** or **seraphs** : an angel of a high order of celestial beings — **se·raph·ic** \sə-'raf-ik\ adj

**Serb** \'sərb\ n 1 : a native or inhabitant of Serbia 2 : a Slavic language of Serbia

**sere** \'sir\ adj : DRY, WITHERED

¹**ser·e·nade** \,ser-ə-'nād\ n : music sung or played as a compliment esp. outdoors at night for a lady

²**serenade** vb **-nad·ed; -nad·ing** : to entertain with or perform a serenade

**ser·en·dip·i·ty** \,ser-ən-'dip-ət-ē\ n : the gift of finding valuable or agreeable things not sought for — **ser·en·dip·i·tous** \-əs\ adj

**se·rene** \sə-'rēn\ adj 1 : CLEAR ⟨~ skies⟩ 2 : QUIET, CALM **syn** tranquil, peaceful, placid — **se·rene·ly** adv — **se·ren·i·ty** \sə-'ren-ət-ē\ n

**serf** \'sərf\ n : a peasant bound to the land and subject in some degree to the owner — **serf·dom** \-dəm\ n

**serg** or **sergt** abbr sergeant

**serge** \'sərj\ n : a twilled woolen cloth

**ser·geant** \'sär-jənt\ n [ME, servant, attendant, officer who keeps order, fr. OF *sergent, serjant*, fr. L *servient-, serviens,* prp. of *servire* to serve] 1 : a noncommissioned officer (as in the army) ranking next below a staff sergeant 2 : an officer in a police force

**sergeant first class** n : a noncommissioned officer in the army ranking next below a master sergeant

**sergeant major** n, pl **sergeants major** or **sergeant majors** 1 : a noncommissioned officer in the army, air force, or marine corps serving as chief administrative assistant in a headquarters 2 : a noncommissioned officer in the marine corps ranking above a first sergeant

¹**se·ri·al** \'sir-ē-əl\ adj : appearing in parts that follow regularly ⟨a ~ story⟩ — **se·ri·al·ly** adv

²**serial** n : a serial story or other writing — **se·ri·al·ist** \-ləst\ n

**se·ries** \'si(ə)r-ēz\ n, pl **series** : a number of things or events arranged in order and connected by being alike in some way **syn** succession, progression, sequence, set, suit, chain, train, string

**seri·graph** \'ser-ə-,graf\ n : an original silk-screen print — **se·rig·ra·pher** \sə-'rig-rə-fər\ n — **se·rig·ra·phy** \-fē\ n

**se·ri·ous** \'sir-ē-əs\ adj 1 : thoughtful or subdued in appearance or manner : SOBER 2 : requiring much thought or work 3 : EARNEST, DEVOTED 4 : DANGEROUS, HARMFUL **syn** grave, sedate, sober — **se·ri·ous·ly** adv — **se·ri·ous·ness** n

**ser·mon** \'sər-mən\ n [ME, fr. OF, fr. ML *sermon , sermo,* fr. L, speech, conversation, fr. *serere* to link together]

1 : a religious discourse esp. as part of a worship service 2 : a lecture on conduct or duty

**se·rol·o·gy** \sə-'räl-ə-jē, sir-'äl-\ n : a science dealing with serums and esp. their reactions and properties — **se·ro·log·i·cal** \,sir-ə-'läj-i-kəl\ or **se·ro·log·ic** \-ik\ adj

**ser·pent** \'sər-pənt\ n : SNAKE

¹**ser·pen·tine** \'sər-pən-,tēn, -,tīn\ ad 1 : SLY, CRAFTY 2 : WINDING, TURNING

²**ser·pen·tine** \-,tēn\ n : a dull-green mineral having a mottled appearance

**ser·rate** \'ser-,āt\ adj : having a saw-toothed edge

**ser·ried** \'ser-ēd\ adj : DENSE

**se·rum** \'sir-əm\ n, pl **serums** or **se·ra** \-ə\ : the watery part of an animal fluid (as blood) remaining after coagulation; esp : blood serum that contains specific immune bodies (as antitoxins) — **se·rous** \-əs\ adj

**serv** abbr service

**ser·vant** \'sər-vənt\ n : a person employed esp. for domestic work

¹**serve** \'sərv\ vb **served; serv·ing** 1 : to work as a servant 2 : to render obedience and worship to (God) 3 : to comply with the commands or demands of 4 : to work through or perform a term of service (as in the army) 5 : to put in ⟨served five years in jail⟩ 6 : to be of use : ANSWER ⟨pine boughs served for a bed⟩ 7 : BENEFIT 8 : to prove adequate or satisfactory for ⟨a pie that ~s eight people⟩ 9 : to make ready and pass out ⟨~ drinks⟩ 10 : to wait on ⟨~ a customer⟩ 11 : to furnish or supply with something ⟨one power company serving the whole state⟩ 12 : to put the ball in play (as in tennis) 13 : to treat or act toward in a specified way — **serv·er** n

²**serve** n : the act of serving a ball (as in tennis)

¹**ser·vice** \'sər vəs\ n 1 : the occupation of a servant 2 : the act, fact, or means of serving 3 : required duty 4 : a meeting for worship; also : a form followed in worship or in a ceremony ⟨burial ~⟩ 5 : performance of official or professional duties 6 : a branch of public employment; also : the persons in it ⟨civil ~⟩ 7 : military or naval duty 8 : a set of dishes or silverware 9 : HELP, BENEFIT 10 : a serving of the ball (as in tennis) **syn** use, advantage, profit, account, avail

²**service** vb **ser·viced; ser·vic·ing** : to do maintenance or repair work on or for

**ser·vice·able** \'sər-və-sə-bəl\ adj : prepared for service : USEFUL, USABLE

**ser·vice·man** \'sər-vəs-,man, mən\ n 1 : a male member of the armed forces 2 : a man employed to repair or maintain equipment

**service module** n : a space vehicle module that contains propellant tanks, fuel cells, and the main rocket engine

**service station** n : a retail station for servicing motor vehicles

**ser·vile** \'sər-vəl, -,vīl\ adj 1 : befitting a slave or servant 2 : behaving like a slave **:** SUBMISSIVE — **ser·vil·i·ty** \,sər-'vil-ət-ē\ n

**serv·ing** \'sər-viŋ\ n **:** HELPING

**ser·vi·tor** \'sər-vət-ər\ n **:** a male servant

**ser·vi·tude** \'sər-və-,t(y)üd\ n **:** SLAVERY, BONDAGE

**ser·vo** \'sər-vō\ n, pl **servos** **1 :** SERVOMOTOR **2 :** SERVOMECHANISM

**ser·vo·mech·a·nism** \'sər-vō-,mek-ə-,niz-əm\ n **:** an automatic device for controlling large amounts of power by means of very small amounts of power and automatically correcting performance of a mechanism

**ser·vo·mo·tor** \'sər-vō-,mōt-ər\ n **:** a power-driven mechanism that supplements a primary control operated by a comparatively feeble force (as in a servomechanism)

**ses·a·me** \'ses-ə-mē\ n **:** an East Indian annual herb; also **:** its seeds that yield an edible oil (**sesame oil**) and are used in flavoring

**ses·qui·cen·ten·ni·al** \,ses-kwi-sen-'ten-ē-əl\ n **:** a 150th anniversary or its celebration — **sesquicentennial** adj

**ses·qui·pe·da·lian** \,ses-kwə-pə-'dāl-yən\ adj **1 :** having many syllables **:** LONG **2 :** using long words

**ses·sile** \'ses-īl, -əl\ adj **:** attached by the base ⟨a ~ leaf⟩

**ses·sion** \'sesh-ən\ n **1 :** a meeting or series of meetings of a body (as a court or legislature) for the transaction of business **2 :** a meeting or period devoted to a particular activity

**¹set** \'set\ vb **set; set·ting 1 :** to cause to sit **2 :** PLACE **3 :** SETTLE, DECREE **4 :** to cause to be or do **5 :** ARRANGE, ADJUST **6 :** to fix in a frame **7 :** ESTIMATE **8 :** WAGER, STAKE **9 :** to make fast or rigid **10 :** to adapt (as words) to something (as music) **11 :** BROOD **12 :** to be suitable **:** FIT **13 :** to pass below the horizon **14 :** to have a certain direction **15 :** to become fixed or firm or solid **16 :** to defeat in bridge — **set forth :** to begin a trip — **set off :** to set forth — **set out :** to begin a trip or undertaking — **set sail :** to begin a voyage

**²set** adj **1 :** fixed by authority or custom **2 :** DELIBERATE **3 :** RIGID **4 :** PERSISTENT **5 :** FORMED, MADE

**³set** n **1 :** a setting or a being set **2 :** FORM, BUILD **3 :** DIRECTION, COURSE; also **:** TENDENCY **4 :** the fit of something (as a coat) **5 :** a group of persons or things of the same kind or having a common characteristic usu. classed together **6 :** an artificial setting for the scene of a play or motion picture **7 :** an electronic apparatus ⟨a television ~⟩ **8 :** a group of tennis games in which one side wins at least six to an opponent's four or less **9 :** a collection of mathematical elements (as numbers or points)

**set·back** \'set-,bak\ n **:** REVERSE

**set back** \(')set-'bak\ vb **:** HINDER, DELAY; also **:** REVERSE

**set·screw** \'set-,skrü\ n **:** a screw screwed through one part tightly upon

or into another part to prevent relative movement

**set·tee** \se-'tē\ n **:** a bench or sofa with a back and arms

**set·ter** \'set-ər\ n **:** a large long-coated hunting dog

**set·ting** \'set-iŋ\ n **1 :** the act of setting ⟨the ~ of type⟩ **2 :** that in which something is mounted **3 :** BACKGROUND, ENVIRONMENT; also **:** SCENERY **4 :** music written for a text (as of a poem) **5 :** the eggs that a fowl sits on for hatching at one time

**set·tle** \'set-°l\ vb **set·tled; set·tling** \'set-(°-)liŋ\ [ME settlen to seat, bring to rest, come to rest, fr. OE setlan, fr. setl seat] **1 :** to put in place **2 :** to locate permanently **3 :** to make compact **4 :** to sink gradually to a lower level **5 :** to establish in life, business, or a home **6 :** to direct one's efforts **7 :** to fix by agreement **8 :** to give legally **9 :** ADJUST, ARRANGE **10 :** QUIET, CALM **11 :** DECIDE, DETERMINE **12 :** to make a final disposition of ⟨~ an account⟩ **13 :** to reach an agreement on **14 :** to become clear by depositing sediment **syn** set, fix — **set·tler** \-(°-)lər\ n

**set·tle·ment** \'set-°l-mənt\ n **1 :** the act or process of settling **2 :** establishment in life, business, or a home **3 :** something that settles or is settled **4 :** BESTOWAL ⟨a marriage ~⟩ **5 :** payment of an account **6 :** adjustment of doubts and differences **7 :** COLONIZATION; also **:** COLONY **8 :** a small village **9 :** an institution in a poor district of a city to give aid to the community

**set·to** \'set-,tü\ n, pl **set·tos :** FIGHT

**set·up** \'set-,əp\ n **1 :** the manner or act of arranging **2 :** glass, ice, and nonalcoholic beverage for mixing served to patrons who supply their own liquor

**set up** \(')set-'əp\ vb **:** ERECT, ASSEMBLE; also **:** CAUSE

**sev·en** \'sev-ən\ n **1 :** one more than six **2 :** the seventh in a set or series **3 :** something having seven units — **seven** adj or pron — **sev·enth** \-ənth\ adj or adv or n

**sev·en·teen** \,sev-ən-'tēn\ n **:** one more than 16 — **seventeen** adj or pron — **sev·en·teenth** \-'tēnth\ adj or n

**seventeen-year locust** n **:** a cicada of the U.S. that has in the North a life of 17 years and in the South of 13 years of which most is spent underground as a nymph and only a few weeks as a winged adult

**sev·en·ty** \'sev-ən-tē\ n, pl **-ties :** seven times 10 — **sev·en·ti·eth** \-tē-əth\ adj or n — **seventy** adj or pron

**sev·en·ty-eight** \,sev-ən-tē-'āt\ n **:** a phonograph record designed to be played at 78 revolutions per minute

**sev·er** \'sev-ər\ vb **sev·ered; sev·er·ing** \-(ə-)riŋ\ **:** DIVIDE; esp **:** to separate by force (as by cutting or tearing) — **sev·er·ance** \-(ə-)rəns\ n

**sev·er·al** \'sev-(ə-)rəl\ adj [ME, fr.

ML *separalis,* fr. L *separ* separate, fr. *separare* to separate] **1** : INDIVIDUAL, DISTINCT ⟨federal union of the ~ states⟩ **2** : consisting of an indefinite number but yet not very many — **sev·er·al·ly** \-ē\ *adv*

**severance pay** *n* : extra pay given an employee upon his leaving a job permanently

**se·vere** \sə-'viər\ *adj* **se·ver·er; -est** **1** : marked by strictness or sternness : AUSTERE **2** : strict in discipline **3** : causing distress and esp. physical discomfort or pain ⟨~ weather⟩ ⟨a ~ wound⟩ **4** : hard to endure ⟨~ trials⟩ **syn** stern — **se·vere·ly** *adv* — **se·ver·i·ty** \-'ver-ət-ē\ *n*

**sew** \'sō\ *vb* **sewed; sewn** \'sōn\ *or* **sewed; sew·ing** **1** : to fasten by stitches made with thread and needle **2** : to practice sewing esp. as an occupation

**sew·age** \'sü-ij\ *n* : matter (as refuse liquids) carried off by sewers

¹**sew·er** \'sō-(ə)r\ *n* : one that sews

²**sew·er** \'sü-ər\ *n* : an artificial pipe or channel to carry off waste matter

**sew·er·age** \'sü-ə-rij\ *n* **1** : SEWAGE **2** : a system of sewers

**sew·ing** \'sō-iŋ\ *n* **1** : the occupation of one who sews **2** : material that has been or is to be sewed

**sex** \'seks\ *n* **1** : either of two divisions of organisms distinguished respectively as male and female; *also* : the qualities by which these sexes are differentiated and which directly or indirectly function in biparental reproduction **2** : sexual activity or intercourse — **sexed** \'sekst\ *adj* — **sex·less** *adj*

**sex·a·ge·nar·i·an** \,sek-sə-jə-'ner-ē-ən\ *n* : a person who is 60 or more but less than 70 years old — **sexagenarian** *adj*

**sex chromosome** *n* : one of usu. a pair of chromosomes that are usu. similar in one sex but different in the other sex and are concerned with the inheritance of sex

**sex hormone** *n* : a hormone (as from the gonads) that affects the growth or function of the reproductive organs or the development of secondary sex characteristics

**sex·ism** \'sek-,siz-əm\ *n* : prejudice or discrimination against women — **sex·ist** \'sek-səst\ *adj or n*

**sex·pot** \'seks-,pät\ *n* : a sexually stimulating woman

**sex·tant** \'sek-stənt\ *n* [NL *sextant-, sextans* sixth part of a circle, fr. L, sixth part, fr. *sextus* sixth] : an instrument for measuring angular distances of celestial bodies which is used esp. at sea to ascertain latitude and longitude

**sex·tet** \sek-'stet\ *n* **1** : a musical composition for six voices or six instruments; *also* : the six performers of such a composition **2** : a group or set of six

**sex·ton** \'sek-stən\ *n* : one who takes care of church property

**sex·u·al** \'sek-sh(ə-w)əl\ *adj* : of, relating to, or involving sex or the sexes ⟨a ~ spore⟩ ⟨~ relations⟩ — **sex·u·al·**

**i·ty** \,sek-shə-'wal-ət-ē\ *n* — **sex·u·al·ly** \'sek-shə-(wə-)lē\ *adv*

**sexual intercourse** *n* : sexual connection esp. between human beings : COITUS, COPULATION

**sexy** \'sek-sē\ *adj* **sex·i·er; -est** : sexually suggestive or stimulating : EROTIC

**SF** *abbr, often not cap* **1** sacrifice fly **2** science fiction

**SFC** *abbr* sergeant first class

**SG** *abbr* **1** senior grade **2** sergeant **3** solicitor general **4** surgeon general

**sgd** *abbr* signed

**Sgt** *abbr* sergeant

**Sgt Maj** *abbr* sergeant major

**sh** *abbr* share

**shab·by** \'shab-ē\ *adj* **shab·bi·er; -est** **1** : threadbare and faded from wear **2** : dressed in worn clothes **3** : MEAN ⟨~ treatment⟩ — **shab·bi·ly** \'shab-ə-lē\ *adv* — **shab·bi·ness** \-ē-nəs\ *n*

**shack** \'shak\ *n* : HUT, SHANTY

¹**shack·le** \'shak-əl\ *n* **1** : something (as a manacle or fetter) that confines the legs or arms **2** : a check on free action made as if by fetters **3** : a device for making something fast or secure

²**shackle** *vb* **shack·led; shack·ling** \-(ə-)liŋ\ : to fasten with shackles

**shad** \'shad\ *n* : a No. American food fish of the Atlantic coast that ascends rivers to spawn

¹**shade** \'shād\ *n* **1** : partial obscurity **2** : space sheltered from the light esp. of the sun **3** : a dark color or a variety of a color **4** : a small difference **5** : PHANTOM **6** : something that shelters from or intercepts light or heat; *also, pl* : SUNGLASSES — **shady** *adj*

²**shade** *vb* **shad·ed; shad·ing** **1** : to shelter from light and heat **2** : DARKEN, OBSCURE **3** : to mark with degrees of light or color **4** : to show slight differences esp. in color or meaning

**shad·ing** \'shād-iŋ\ *n* : the color and lines representing darkness or shadow in a drawing or painting

¹**shad·ow** \'shad-ō\ *n* **1** : partial darkness in a space from which light rays are cut off **2** : SHELTER **3** : a small portion or degree : TRACE ⟨a ~ of doubt⟩ **4** : influence that casts a gloom **5** : shade cast upon a surface by something intercepting rays from a light ⟨the ~ of a tree⟩ **6** : PHANTOM **7** : a shaded portion of a picture — **shad·owy** *adj*

²**shadow** *vb* **1** : to cast a shadow on **2** : to represent faintly or vaguely **3** : to follow and watch closely : TRAIL

**shad·ow·box** \'shad-ō-,bäks\ *vb* : to box with an imaginary opponent esp. for training — **shad·ow·box·ing** *n*

¹**shaft** \'shaft\ *n, pl* **shafts 1** : the long handle of a spear or lance **2** *or pl* **shaves** \'shavz\ : POLE; *esp* : one of two poles between which a horse is hitched to pull a vehicle **3** : SPEAR, LANCE **4** : something (as a column) long and slender **5** : a bar to support a rotating piece or to transmit power by rotation **6** : a vertical opening (as for an elevator) through the floors of a building **7** : an inclined opening in the

ground (as for finding or mining ore)
²**shaft** \vb\ : to fit with a shaft

**shag** \'shag\ n **1** : a shaggy tangled mat (as of wool) **2** : a strong finely shredded tobacco

**shag·gy** \'shag-ē\ adj **shag·gi·er**; **-est 1** : rough with or as if with long hair or wool **2** : tangled or rough in surface

**shah** \'shä, 'shò\ n, often cap : the sovereign of Iran — **shah·dom** \'shäd-əm, 'shòd-\ n

**Shak** abbr Shakespeare

¹**shake** \'shāk\ vb **shook** \'shùk\; **shak·en** \'shā-kən\; **shak·ing 1** : to move or cause to move jerkily or irregularly **2** : BRANDISH, WAVE ⟨shaking his fist⟩ **3** : to disturb emotionally ⟨shaken by her death⟩ **4** : WEAKEN ⟨shook his faith⟩ **5** : to bring or come into a certain position, condition, or arrangement by or as if by moving jerkily **6** : to clasp (hands) in greeting or as a sign of goodwill or agreement **syn** tremble, quake, totter, shiver, rock, convulse — **shak·able** \'shā-kə-bəl\ adj

²**shake** n **1** : the act or a result of shaking **2** : DEAL, TREATMENT ⟨a fair ∼⟩

**shake·down** \'shāk-,daùn\ n **1** : an improvised bed **2** : EXTORTION **3** : a process or period of adjustment **4** : a test (as of a new ship or airplane) under operating conditions

**shake down** \(')shāk-'daùn\ vb **1** : to take up temporary quarters **2** : to occupy a makeshift bed **3** : to become accustomed esp. to new surroundings or duties **4** : to settle down **5** : to give a shakedown test to **6** : to obtain money from in a dishonest or illegal manner **7** : to bring about a reduction of

**shak·er** \'shā-kər\ n **1** : one that shakes (pepper ∼) **2** cap : a member of a religious sect founded in England in 1747

**shake-up** \'shāk-,əp\ n : an extensive often drastic reorganization

**shaky** \'shā-kē\ adj **shak·i·er**; **-est** : UNSOUND, WEAK — **shak·i·ly** \'shā-kə-lē\ adv — **shak·i·ness** \-kē-nəs\ n

**shale** \'shāl\ n : a rock formed of densely packed clay, mud, or silt that splits easily into layers

**shall** \shəl, (')shal\ vb, past **should** \shəd, (')shùd\; pres sing & pl **shall** — used as an auxiliary to express a command, what seems inevitable or likely in the future, simple futurity, or determination

**shal·lop** \'shal-əp\ n : a light open boat

¹**shal·low** \'shal-ō\ adj **1** : not deep **2** : not intellectually profound **syn** superficial

²**shallow** n : a shallow place in a body of water — usu. used in pl.

¹**sham** \'sham\ n **1** : COUNTERFEIT, IMITATION **2** : something resembling an article of household linen and used in its place as a decoration ⟨a pillow ∼⟩

²**sham** vb **shammed**; **sham·ming** : FEIGN, PRETEND — **sham·mer** n

³**sham** adj : FALSE

**sha·man** \'shäm-ən, 'shā-mən\ n : a priest who uses magic to cure the sick, to divine the hidden, and to control events

**sham·ble** \'sham-bəl\ vb **sham·bled**; **sham·bling** \-b(ə-)liŋ\ : to shuffle along — **shamble** n

**sham·bles** \'sham-bəlz\ n [shamble (meat market) & obs. E shamble (table for exhibition of meat for sale)] **1** : a scene of great slaughter **2** : a scene or state of great destruction or disorder

¹**shame** \'shām\ n **1** : a painful sense of having done something wrong, improper, or immodest **2** : DISGRACE, DISHONOR — **shame·ful** \-fəl\ adj — **shame·ful·ly** \-ē\ adv — **shame·less** adj — **shame·less·ly** adv

²**shame** vb **shamed**; **sham·ing 1** : to make ashamed **2** : DISGRACE

**shame·faced** \'shām-'fāst\ adj : ASHAMED, ABASHED — **shame·faced·ly** \-'fā-səd-lē, -'fāst-lē\ adv

¹**sham·poo** \sham-'pü\ vb [Hindi cāpo, imper. of cāpnā to press, shampoo] : to wash (as the hair) with soap and water or with a special preparation; also : to clean (as a rug) similarly

²**shampoo** n, pl **shampoos 1** : the act or process of shampooing **2** : a preparation for use in shampooing

**sham·rock** \'sham-,räk\ n [IrGael seamrōg, dim. of seamar clover, honeysuckle] : a plant with three leaflets used as an Irish floral emblem

**shang·hai** \shaŋ-'hī\ vb **shang·haied**; **shang·hai·ing** : to force aboard a ship for service as a sailor; also : to trick or force into something

**Shan·gri·la** \,shaŋ-gri-'lä\ n [Shangri-La, imaginary land depicted in the novel Lost Horizon (1933) by James Hilton] : a remote idyllic hideaway

**shank** \'shaŋk\ n **1** : the part of the leg between the knee and ankle in man or a corresponding part of a quadruped **2** : a cut of meat from the leg **3** : the part of a tool or instrument (as a key or anchor) connecting the functioning part with the handle

**shan·tung** \'shan-'təŋ\ n : a fabric in plain weave having a slightly irregular surface

**shan·ty** \'shant-ē\ n, pl **shanties** : a small roughly built shelter or dwelling

¹**shape** \'shāp\ vb **shaped**; **shap·ing 1** : to form esp. in a particular shape **2** : DESIGN **3** : ADAPT, ADJUST **4** : REGULATE **syn** make, fashion, fabricate, manufacture

²**shape** n **1** : APPEARANCE **2** : surface configuration : FORM **3** : bodily contour apart from the head and face : FIGURE **4** : PHANTOM **5** : CONDITION

**shape·less** \'shāp-ləs\ adj **1** : having no definite shape **2** : not shapely — **shape·less·ly** adv — **shape·less·ness** n

**shape·ly** \'shāp-lē\ adj **shape·li·er**; **-est** : having a pleasing shape — **shape·li·ness** n

**shard** \'shärd\ also **sherd** \'shərd\ n : a broken piece : FRAGMENT

¹**share** \'sheər\ n **1** : a portion belong-

ing to one person **2** : any of the equal interests, each represented by a certificate, into which the capital stock of a corporation is divided

²**share** vb **shared; shar·ing 1** : APPORTION **2** : to use or enjoy with others **3** : PARTICIPATE — **shar·er** n

³**share** n : PLOWSHARE

**share·crop·per** \-ˌkräp-ər\ n : a farmer who works another's land in return for a share of the crop — **share·crop** vb

**share·hold·er** \-ˌhōl-dər\ n : STOCKHOLDER

**shark** \'shärk\ n **1** : any of various active, predaceous, and mostly large sea fishes with skeletons of cartilage **2** : a greedy crafty person

**shark·skin** \-ˌskin\ n **1** : the hide of a shark or leather made from it **2** : a fabric (as of cotton or rayon) woven from strands of many fine threads and having a sleek appearance and silky feel

¹**sharp** \'shärp\ adj **1** : having a thin cutting edge or fine point : not dull or blunt **2** : COLD, NIPPING ⟨a ∼ wind⟩ **3** : keen in intellect, perception, or attention **4** : BRISK, ENERGETIC **5** : IRRITABLE ⟨a ∼ temper⟩ **6** : causing intense distress ⟨a ∼ pain⟩ **7** : HARSH, CUTTING ⟨∼ words⟩ **8** : affecting the senses as if cutting or piercing ⟨a ∼ sound⟩ ⟨a ∼ smell⟩ **9** : not smooth or rounded ⟨∼ features⟩ **10** : involving an abrupt or extreme change ⟨a ∼ turn⟩ **11** : CLEAR, DISTINCT ⟨mountains in ∼ relief⟩; also : easy to perceive ⟨a ∼ contrast⟩ **12** : higher than the true pitch; also : raised by a half step **syn** keen, acute **13** : STYLISH ⟨a ∼ dresser⟩ — **sharp·ly** adv — **sharp·ness** n

²**sharp** vb : to raise in pitch by a half step

³**sharp** adv **1** : in a sharp manner **2** : EXACTLY, PRECISELY ⟨left at 8 ∼⟩

⁴**sharp** n **1** : a sharp edge or point **2** : a character ♯ indicating a note a half step higher than the note named **3** : SHARPER

**sharp·en** \'shär-pən\ vb **sharp·ened; sharp·en·ing** \'shärp-(ə-)niŋ\ : to make or become sharp — **sharp·en·er** \'shärp-(ə-)nər\ n

**sharp·er** \'shär-pər\ n : SWINDLER; esp : a cheating gambler

**sharp·ie** or **sharpy** \'shär-pē\ n, pl **sharp·ies 1** : SHARPER **2** : a person who is exceptionally keen or alert

**sharp·shoot·er** \'shärp-ˌshüt-ər\ n : MARKSMAN — **sharp·shoot·ing** \-iŋ\ n

**shat·ter** \'shat-ər\ vb : to dash or burst into fragments — **shat·ter·proof** \ˌshat-ər-'prüf\ adj

¹**shave** \'shāv\ vb **shaved; shaved** or **shav·en** \'shā-vən\; **shav·ing 1** : to cut or pare off by the sliding movement of a razor **2** : to make bare or smooth by cutting the hair from **3** : to slice in thin pieces **4** : to skim along or near the surface of

²**shave** n **1** : any of various tools for cutting thin slices **2** : an act or process of shaving **3** : an act of passing very near so as to almost graze

**shav·er** \'shā-vər\ n : an electric-powered razor

**shaves** pl of SHAFT

**shav·ing** \'shā-viŋ\ n **1** : the act of one that shaves **2** : a thin slice pared off

**shawl** \'shȯl\ n : a square or oblong piece of fabric used esp. by women as a loose covering for the head or shoulders

**Shaw·nee** \shȯ-'nē, shä-\ n, pl **Shawnee** or **Shawnees** : a member of an Indian people orig. of the central Ohio valley; also : their language

**she** \(')shē\ pron : that female one (who is ∼); also : that one regarded as feminine ⟨∼'s a fine ship⟩

**sheaf** \'shēf\ n, pl **sheaves** \'shēvz\ **1** : a bundle of stalks and ears of grain **2** : a group of things bound together ⟨a ∼ of arrows⟩

¹**shear** \'shir\ vb **sheared; sheared** or **shorn** \'shȯrn\; **shear·ing 1** : to cut the hair or wool from : CLIP, TRIM **2** : to cut or break sharply **3** : to deprive by or as if by cutting

²**shear** n **1** : the act, an instance, or the result of shearing **2** : any of various cutting tools that consist of two blades fastened together so that the edges slide one by the other — usu. used in pl. **3** : an action across two forces caused by applied forces that causes two parts of a body to slide on each other

**sheath** \'shēth\ n, pl **sheaths** \'shēthz, 'shēths\ **1** : a case for a blade (as of a knife); also : an anatomical covering suggesting such a case **2** : a close-fitting dress usu. worn without a belt

**sheathe** \'shēth\ also **sheath** \'shēth\ vb **sheathed; sheath·ing 1** : to put into a sheath **2** : to cover with something that guards or protects

**sheath·ing** \'shē-thiŋ, -thiŋ\ n : material used to sheathe something; esp : the first covering of boards or of waterproof material on the outside wall of a frame house or on a timber roof

**sheave** \'shiv, 'shēv\ n : a grooved wheel or pulley (as on a pulley block)

**she·bang** \shi-'baŋ\ n : CONTRIVANCE, AFFAIR, CONCERN ⟨blew up the whole ∼⟩

¹**shed** \'shed\ vb **shed; shed·ding 1** : to pour down in drops ⟨∼ tears⟩ **2** : to cause to flow from a cut or wound ⟨∼ blood⟩ **3** : to give out (as light) : DIFFUSE **4** : to throw off (as a natural covering) : DISCARD

²**shed** n : a slight structure built for shelter or storage

**sheen** \'shēn\ n : a subdued luster

**sheep** \'shēp\ n, pl **sheep 1** : a domesticated mammal related to the goat and raised for meat, wool, and hide **2** : a timid or defenseless person **3** : SHEEPSKIN

**sheep dog** n : a dog used to tend, drive, or guard sheep

**sheep·fold** \'shēp-ˌfōld\ n : a pen or shelter for sheep

**sheep·ish** \'shē-pish\ adj : BASHFUL, TIMID; esp : embarrassed by consciousness of a fault — **sheep·ish·ly** adv

**sheep·skin** \'shēp-ˌskin\ n **1** : the

hide of a sheep or leather prepared from it; *also* : PARCHMENT **2** : DIPLOMA

¹**sheer** \'shiər\ *adj* **1** : UNQUALIFIED ⟨~ folly⟩ **2** : very steep **3** : of very thin or transparent texture **syn** pure, simple, absolute, precipitous, abrupt — **sheer** *adv*

²**sheer** *vb* : to turn from a course

¹**sheet** \'shēt\ *n* **1** : a broad piece of plain cloth (as for a bed) **2** : a single piece of paper **3** : a broad flat surface ⟨a ~ of water⟩ **4** : something broad and long and relatively thin

²**sheet** *n* **1** : a rope that regulates the angle at which a sail is set to catch the wind **2** *pl* : spaces at either end of an open boat

**sheet·ing** \'shēt-iŋ\ *n* : material in the form of sheets or suitable for forming into sheets

**sheikh** *or* **sheik** \'shēk, 'shāk\ *n* : an Arab chief — **sheikh·dom** *or* **sheik·dom** \-dəm\ *n*

**shelf** \'shelf\ *n, pl* **shelves** \'shelvz\ **1** : a thin flat usu. long and narrow structure fastened against a wall above the floor to hold things **2** : a sandbank or ledge of rocks usu. partially submerged

**shelf life** *n* : the period of storage time during which a material will remain useful

¹**shell** \'shel\ *n* **1** : a hard or tough outer covering of an animal (as a beetle, turtle, or mollusk) or of an egg or a seed or fruit (as a nut); *also* : something that resembles a shell (a pastry ~) **2** : a case holding an explosive and designed to be fired from a cannon; *also* : a case holding the charge of powder and shot or bullet for small arms **3** : a light narrow racing boat propelled by oarsmen **4** : a plain usu. sleeveless blouse or sweater — **shelled** \'sheld\ *adj* — **shelly** \'shel-ē\ *adj*

²**shell** *vb* **1** : to remove from a shell or husk **2** : BOMBARD — **shell·er** *n*

¹**shel·lac** \shə-'lak\ *n* **1** : a purified lac used esp. in varnishes **2** : lac dissolved in alcohol and used as a varnish

²**shellac** *vb* **shel·lacked; shel·lack·ing** **1** : to coat or treat with shellac **2** : to defeat decisively

**shel·lack·ing** \shə-'lak-iŋ\ *n* : a sound drubbing

**shell bean** *n* : a bean grown esp. for its edible seeds; *also* : its edible seed

**shell·fire** \'shel-,fī(ə)r\ *n* : firing or shooting of shells

**shell·fish** \-,fish\ *n* : a water animal (as an oyster or lobster) with a shell

**shell out** *vb* : PAY

**shell shock** *n* : a nervous disorder appearing in soldiers exposed to modern warfare — **shell–shock** *vb*

¹**shel·ter** \'shel-tər\ *n* : something that gives protection : REFUGE

²**shelter** *vb* **shel·tered; shel·ter·ing** \-t(ə-)riŋ\ : to give protection or refuge to **syn** harbor, lodge, house

**shelve** \'shelv\ *vb* **shelved; shelv·ing** **1** : to slope gradually **2** : to store on shelves **3** : to dismiss from service or use

**shelv·ing** \'shel-viŋ\ *n* : material for shelves

**she·nan·i·gan** \shə-'nan-i-gən\ *n* **1** : an underhand trick **2** : questionable conduct **3** : high-spirited or mischievous activity — usu. used in pl.

¹**shep·herd** \'shep-ərd\ *n* : one that tends sheep — **shep·herd·ess** \-əs\ *n*

²**shepherd** *vb* : to tend as or in the manner of a shepherd

**sher·bet** \'shər-bət\ *or* **sher·bert** \-bərt\ *n* [Turk *serbet*, fr. Per *sharbat*, fr. Ar *sharbah* drink] **1** : a drink of sweetened diluted fruit juice **2** : a frozen dessert of fruit juices, sugar, milk or water, and egg whites or gelatin

**sher·iff** \'sher-əf\ *n* : a county officer charged with the execution of the law and the preservation of peace

**sher·ry** \'sher-ē\ *n, pl* **sherries** [alter. of earlier *sherris* (taken as pl.), fr. *Xeres* (now *Jerez*), Spain] : a fortified wine with a nutty flavor

**Shet·land pony** \,shet-lən(d)-\ *n* : any of a breed of small stocky shaggy hardy ponies

**shew** \'shō\ *Brit var of* SHOW

**shib·bo·leth** \'shib-ə-ləth\ *n* [Heb *shibbōleth* stream; fr. the use of this word as a test to distinguish the men of Gilead from members of the tribe of Ephraim, who pronounced it *sibbōleth* (Judges 12:5, 6)] **1** : a pet phrase **2** : language that is a criterion for distinguishing members of a group

¹**shield** \'shēld\ *n* **1** : a broad piece of defensive armor carried on the arm **2** : something that protects or hides

²**shield** *vb* : to protect or hide with a shield **syn** protect, guard, safeguard

**shier** *comparative of* SHY

**shiest** *superlative of* SHY

¹**shift** \'shift\ *vb* **1** : EXCHANGE, REPLACE **2** : to change place, position, or direction : MOVE; *also* : to change the arrangement of gears transmitting power in an automobile **3** : to get along : MANAGE **syn** remove

²**shift** *n* **1** : TRANSFER **2** : SCHEME, TRICK **3** : a group working together alternating with other groups **4** : GEARSHIFT **5** : a woman's slip or loose-fitting dress

**shift·less** \'shif(t)-ləs\ *adj* : LAZY, INEFFICIENT — **shift·less·ness** *n*

**shifty** \'shif-tē\ *adj* **shift·i·er; -est** **1** : TRICKY; *also* : ELUSIVE **2** : indicative of a tricky nature (~ eyes)

**shi·lingi** \shil-'iŋ-ē\ *n, pl* **shi·lingi** — see MONEY table

**shill** \'shil\ *n* : one who acts as a decoy (as for a cheater) — **shill** *vb*

**shil·le·lagh** *also* **shil·la·lah** \shə-'lā-lē\ *n* : CUDGEL, CLUB

**shil·ling** \'shil-iŋ\ *n* **1** — see *pound* at MONEY table **2** — see MONEY table **3** : SHILLINGI

**shilly–shally** \'shil-ē-,shal-ē\ *vb* **shilly–shal·lied; shilly–shal·ly·ing** **1** : to show hesitation or lack of decisiveness **2** : to waste time

**shim** \'shim\ *n* : a thin often tapered piece of wood, metal, or stone used (as in leveling something) to fill in

**shim·mer** \'shim-ər\ *vb* **shim-mered; shim·mer·ing** \-(ə-)riŋ\ **:** to shine waveringly or tremulously **:** GLIMMER **syn** flash, gleam, glint, sparkle, glitter — **shimmer** *n* — **shim·mery** *adj*

**shim·my** \'shim-ē\ *n, pl* **shimmies :** an abnormal vibration esp. in the front wheels of a motor vehicle — **shimmy** *vb*

¹**shin** \'shin\ *n* **:** the front part of the leg below the knee

²**shin** *vb* **shinned; shin·ning :** to climb (as a pole) by gripping alternately with arms or hands and legs

**shin·bone** \'shin-'bōn, -ˌbōn\ *n* **:** TIBIA

¹**shine** \'shīn\ *vb* **shone** \'shōn\ *or* **shined; shin·ing** **1 :** to give light **2 :** GLEAM, GLITTER **3 :** to be eminent **4 :** to cause to shed light **5 :** POLISH

²**shine** *n* **1 :** BRIGHTNESS, RADIANCE **2 :** LUSTER, BRILLIANCE **3 :** SUNSHINE

**shin·er** \'shī-nər\ *n* **1 :** a small silvery fish **:** MINNOW **2 :** a bruised eye

¹**shin·gle** \'shiŋ-gəl\ *n* **1 :** a small thin piece of building material (as wood or an asbestos composition) used in overlapping rows for covering a roof or outside wall **2 :** a small sign

²**shingle** *vb* **shin·gled; shin·gling** \-g(ə-)liŋ\ **:** to cover with shingles

³**shingle** *n* **:** a beach strewn with gravel; *also* **:** coarse gravel (as on a beach)

**shin·gles** \'shiŋ-gəlz\ *n pl* **:** acute inflammation of the spinal and cranial nerves caused by a virus and associated with eruptions and pain along the course of the affected nerves

**shin·ny** \'shin-ē\ *vb* **shin·nied; shin·ny·ing :** SHIN

**Shin·to** \'shin-ˌtō\ *n* **:** the indigenous religion of Japan consisting esp. in reverence of the spirits of natural forces and imperial ancestors — **Shin·to·ism** *n* — **Shin·to·ist** *n or adj* — **Shin·to·is·tic** \ˌshin-tō-'is-tik\ *adj*

**shiny** \'shī-nē\ *adj* **shin·i·er; -est :** BRIGHT, RADIANT; *also* **:** POLISHED

¹**ship** \'ship\ *n* **1 :** a large oceangoing boat **2 :** AIRSHIP, AIRCRAFT, SPACECRAFT **3 :** a ship's officers and crew

²**ship** *vb* **shipped; ship·ping 1 :** to put or receive on board a ship for transportation **2 :** to have transported by a carrier **3 :** to take or draw into a boat (⟨~ oars⟩ ⟨~ water⟩ **4 :** to engage to serve on a ship — **ship·per** *n*

**-ship** \ˌship\ *n suffix* **1 :** state **:** condition **:** quality ⟨friendship⟩ **2 :** office **:** dignity **:** profession ⟨lordship⟩ ⟨clerkship⟩ **3 :** art **:** skill ⟨horsemanship⟩ **4 :** something showing, exhibiting, or embodying a quality or state ⟨township⟩ **5 :** one entitled to a (specified) rank, title, or appellation ⟨his Lordship⟩

**ship·board** \'ship-ˌbōrd\ *n* **:** SHIP

**ship·build·er** \'ship-ˌbil-dər\ *n* **:** one who designs or builds ships

**ship·fit·ter** \'ship-ˌfit-ər\ *n* **1 :** one who constructs ships **2 :** a naval enlisted man who works as a plumber aboard ship

**ship·mate** \-ˌmāt\ *n* **:** a fellow sailor

**ship·ment** \-mənt\ *n* **:** the process of shipping; *also* **:** the goods shipped

**ship·ping** \'ship-iŋ\ *n* **1 :** SHIPS; *esp* **:** ships in one port or belonging to one country **2 :** transportation of goods

**ship·shape** \'ship-'shāp\ *adj* **:** TRIM, TIDY

**ship's service** *n* **:** a ship or navy post exchange

**shipt** *abbr* shipment

**ship·worm** \-ˌwərm\ *n* **:** a wormlike sea clam that burrows in wood and damages wooden ships and wharves

¹**ship·wreck** \-ˌrek\ *n* **1 :** a wrecked ship **2 :** destruction or loss of a ship **3 :** total loss or failure **:** RUIN

²**shipwreck** *vb* **:** to cause or meet disaster at sea through destruction or foundering

**ship·wright** \'ship-ˌrīt\ *n* **:** a carpenter skilled in ship construction and repair

**ship·yard** \-ˌyärd\ *n* **:** a place where ships are built or repaired

**shire** \'shī(ə)r, *in place-name compounds* ˌshiər, shər\ *n* **:** a county in Great Britain

**shirk** \'shərk\ *vb* **:** to avoid performing (duty or work) — **shirk·er** *n*

**shirr** \'shər\ *vb* **1 :** to make shirring in **2 :** to bake (eggs) in a dish with cream or bread crumbs

**shirr·ing** \'shər-iŋ\ *n* **:** a decorative gathering in cloth made by drawing up parallel lines of stitches

**shirt** \'shərt\ *n* **1 :** a loose cloth garment usu. having a collar, sleeves, a front opening, and a tail long enough to be tucked inside trousers or a skirt **2 :** UNDERSHIRT — **shirt·less** *adj*

**shirt·ing** \-iŋ\ *n* **:** cloth suitable for making shirts

**shish ke·bab** \'shish-kə-ˌbäb\ *n* **:** kabob cooked on skewers

**shiv** \'shiv\ *n, slang* **:** KNIFE

¹**shiv·er** \'shiv-ər\ *vb* **shiv·ered; shiv·er·ing** \-(ə-)riŋ\ **:** TREMBLE, QUIVER **syn** shudder, quaver, shake, quake

²**shiver** *n* **:** an instance of shivering — **shiv·er·er** *n* — **shiv·ery** *adj*

¹**shoal** \'shōl\ *n* **1 :** a shallow place in a sea, lake, or river **2 :** a sandbank or bar creating a shallow

²**shoal** *n* **:** a large group (as of fish)

**shoat** \'shōt\ *n* **:** a weaned young pig

¹**shock** \'shäk\ *n* **:** a pile of sheaves of grain set up in the field

²**shock** *n* [MF *choc,* fr. *choquer* to strike against, fr. OF *choquier*] **1 :** a sharp impact or violent shake or jar **2 :** a sudden violent mental or emotional disturbance **3 :** the effect of a charge of electricity passing through the body **4 :** a depressed bodily condition caused esp. by crushing wounds, blood loss, or burns **5 :** an attack of apoplexy or heart disease — **shock·proof** \-'prüf\ *adj*

³**shock** *vb* **1 :** to strike with surprise, horror, or disgust **2 :** to subject to the action of an electrical discharge

⁴**shock** *n* **:** a thick bushy mass (as of hair)

⁵**shock** *n* **:** SHOCK ABSORBER

**shock absorber** *n* **:** any of several

devices for absorbing the energy of sudden impulses in machinery

**shock·er** \'shäk-ər\ *n* **:** one that shocks; *esp* **:** a sensational work of fiction or drama

**shock·ing** \-iŋ\ *adj* **:** extremely startling and offensive — **shock·ing·ly** *adv*

**shock therapy** *n* **:** the treatment of mental disorder by induction of convulsion through the use of drugs or electricity

¹**shod·dy** \'shäd-ē\ *n* **1 :** wool reclaimed from old rags; *also* **:** a fabric made from it **2 :** inferior or imitation material **3 :** pretentious vulgarity

²**shoddy** *adj* **shod·di·er; -est 1 :** made of shoddy **2 :** cheaply imitative **:** INFERIOR, SHAM — **shod·di·ly** \'shäd-ᵊl-ē\ *adv* — **shod·di·ness** \-ē-nəs\ *n*

¹**shoe** \'shü\ *n* **1 :** a covering for the human foot **2 :** HORSESHOE **3 :** the part of a brake that presses on the wheel **4 :** the casing of an automobile tire

²**shoe** *vb* **shod** \'shäd\ *also* **shoed** \'shüd\; **shoe·ing** \'shü-iŋ\ **:** to put a shoe or shoes on

**shoe·lace** \-ˌlās\ *n* **:** a lace or string for fastening a shoe

**shoe·mak·er** \-ˌmā-kər\ *n* **:** one who makes or repairs shoes

**shoe·string** \'shü-ˌstriŋ\ *n* **1 :** SHOELACE **2 :** a small sum of money

**shone** *past of* SHINE

**shook** *past of* SHAKE

**shook–up** \(ˈ)shu̇k-ˈəp\ *adj* **:** nervously upset **:** AGITATED

¹**shoot** \'shüt\ *vb* **shot** \'shät\; **shooting 1 :** to drive (as an arrow or bullet) forward quickly or forcibly **2 :** to hit, kill, or wound with a missile **3 :** to cause a missile to be driven forth or forth from ⟨~ a gun⟩ ⟨~ an arrow⟩ **4 :** to send forth (as a ray of light) **5 :** to thrust forward or out **6 :** to pass rapidly along ⟨~ the rapids⟩ **7 :** PHOTOGRAPH, FILM **8 :** to drive or rush swiftly **:** DART **9 :** to grow by or as if by sending out shoots; *also* **:** MATURE, DEVELOP — **shoot·er** *n*

²**shoot** *n* **1 :** a shooting match; *also* **:** SHOT **2 :** the aerial part of a plant; *also* **:** a plant part (as a branch) developed from one bud

**shooting iron** *n* **:** FIREARM

**shooting star** *n* **:** METEOR 2

**shoot up** *vb* **:** to inject a narcotic into a vein

¹**shop** \'shäp\ *n* [ME *shoppe,* fr. OE *sceoppa* booth] **1 :** a place where things are made or worked on **:** FACTORY, MILL **2 :** a retail store ⟨dress ~⟩

²**shop** *vb* **shopped; shop·ping :** to visit stores for purchasing or examining goods — **shop·per** *n*

**shop·keep·er** \'shäp-ˌkē-pər\ *n* **:** a retail merchant

**shop·lift** \-ˌlift\ *vb* **:** to steal goods on display from a store — **shop·lift·er** \-ˌlif-tər\ *n*

**shop·worn** \-ˌwȯrn\ *adj* **:** soiled or frayed from much handling in a store

¹**shore** \'shōr\ *n* **:** land along the edge of a body of water — **shore·less** *adj*

²**shore** *vb* **shored; shor·ing :** to give support to **:** BRACE, PROP

³**shore** *n* **:** ¹PROP

**shore·bird** \-ˌbərd\ *n* **:** any of a large group of birds (as the plovers and sandpipers) mostly found along the seashore

**shore patrol** *n* **:** a branch of a navy that exercises guard and police functions

**shor·ing** \'shōr-iŋ\ *n* **:** the act of supporting with or as if with a prop

**shorn** *past part of* SHEAR

¹**short** \'shȯrt\ *adj* **1 :** not long or tall **2 :** not great in distance **3 :** brief in time **4 :** CURT, ABRUPT **5 :** not coming up to standard or to an expected amount **6 :** insufficiently supplied **7 :** made with shortening **:** FLAKY **8 :** not having goods or property that one has sold in anticipation of a fall in prices; *also* **:** consisting of or relating to a sale of securities or commodities that the seller does not possess or has not contracted for at the time of the sale ⟨~ sale⟩ — **short·ness** *n*

²**short** *adv* **1 :** ABRUPTLY, CURTLY **2 :** at some point before a goal aimed at

³**short** *n* **1 :** something shorter than normal or standard **2** *pl* **:** drawers or trousers of less than knee length **3 :** SHORT CIRCUIT

⁴**short** *vb* **:** SHORT-CIRCUIT

**short·age** \'shȯrt-ij\ *n* **:** a deficiency in the amount required **:** DEFICIT

**short·cake** \'shȯrt-ˌkāk\ *n* **:** a dessert consisting of short biscuit spread with sweetened fruit

**short·change** \-'chānj\ *vb* **:** to cheat esp. by giving less than the correct amount of change

**short circuit** *n* **:** a connection of comparatively low resistance accidentally or intentionally made between points in an electric circuit — **short–circuit** *vb*

**short·com·ing** \'shȯrt-ˌkəm-iŋ\ *n* **:** FAILING, DEFECT

**short·cut** \-ˌkət\ *n* **1 :** a route more direct than that usu. taken **2 :** a quicker way of doing something

**short·en** \'shȯrt-ᵊn\ *vb* **short·ened; short·en·ing** \'shȯrt-(ᵊ-)niŋ\ **:** to make or become short **syn** curtail, abbreviate, abridge, retrench

**short·en·ing** \'shȯrt-(ᵊ-)niŋ\ *n* **:** a substance (as lard or butter) that makes pastry tender and flaky

**short·hand** \'shȯrt-ˌhand\ *n* **:** a method of writing rapidly by using symbols and abbreviations for letters, words, or phrases **:** STENOGRAPHY

**short·hand·ed** \-'han-dəd\ *adj* **:** short of the needed number of workers

**short·horn** \-ˌhȯrn\ *n, often cap* **:** any of a breed of mostly red cattle of English origin

**short hundredweight** *n* — see WEIGHT table

**short–lived** \'shȯrt-'līvd, -'livd\ *adj* **:** of short life or duration

**short·ly** \'shȯrt-lē\ *adv* **1 :** in a few words **2 :** in a short time **:** SOON

**short order** *n* **:** an order for food that can be quickly cooked

**short shrift** *n* **1 :** a brief respite from death **2 :** little consideration

**short·sight·ed** \'shòrt-'sīt-əd\ *adj* 1 : NEARSIGHTED 2 : lacking foresight — **short·sight·ed·ness** *n*

**short·stop** \-,stäp\ *n* : a baseball player defending the area between second and third base

**short story** *n* : a short invented prose narrative usu. dealing with a few characters and aiming at unity of effect

**short-tem·pered** \'shòrt-'tem-pərd\ *adj* : having a quick temper

**short-term** \-'tərm\ *adj* 1 : occurring over or involving a relatively short period of time 2 : of or relating to a financial transaction based on a term usu. of less than a year

**short ton** *n*　see WEIGHT table

**short·wave** \'shòrt-'wāv\ *n* : a radio wave of 60-meter wavelength or less used esp. in long-distance broadcasting

**Sho·sho·ne** *or* **Sho·sho·ni** \shə-'shō-nē\ *n, pl* **Shoshones** *or* **Shoshoni** : a member of an Indian people orig. ranging through California, Colorado, Idaho, Nevada, Utah, and Wyoming

**shot** \'shät\ *n* 1 : an act of shooting 2 : a stroke in some games 3 : something that is shot : MISSILE, PROJECTILE; *esp* : small pellets forming a charge for a shotgun 4 : a metal sphere that is thrown for distance in the shot put 5 : RANGE, REACH 6 : MARKSMAN 7 : a single photographic exposure 8 : a single sequence of a motion picture or a television program made by one camera 9 : an injection (as of medicine) into the body 10 : a portion (as of liquor or medicine) taken at one time

**shot·gun** \'shät-'gən\ *n* : a gun with a smooth bore used to fire small shot at short range

**shot put** *n* : a field event consisting in putting the shot for distance

**should** \shəd, (')shùd\ *past of* SHALL — used as an auxiliary to express condition, obligation or propriety, probability, or futurity from a point of view in the past

¹**shoul·der** \'shōl-dər\ *n* 1 : the part of the human body formed by the bones and muscles where the arm joins the trunk; *also* : a corresponding part of a lower animal 2 : a projecting part resembling a human shoulder

²**shoulder** *vb* **shoul·dered; shoul·der·ing** \-d(ə-)riŋ\ 1 : to push or thrust with the shoulder 2 : to take upon the shoulder 3 : to take the responsibility of

**shoulder belt** *n* : an anchored belt worn across the upper torso and over the shoulders to hold a person steady in a seat esp. in an automobile

**shoulder blade** *n* : the flat triangular bone at the back of the shoulder

**shout** \'shaùt\ *vb* : to utter a sudden loud cry — **shout** *n*

**shove** \'shəv\ *vb* **shoved; shov·ing** : to push along, aside, or away — **shove** *n*

¹**shov·el** \'shəv-əl\ *n* 1 : a broad long-handled scoop used to lift and throw loose material 2 : the amount of something held by a shovel

²**shovel** *vb* **-eled** *or* **-elled; -el·ing** *or* **-el·ling** \-(ə-)liŋ\ 1 : to take up and throw with a shovel 2 : to dig or clean out with a shovel

¹**show** \'shō\ *vb* **showed** \'shōd\; **shown** \'shōn\ *or* **showed; show·ing** [ME *shewen, showen,* fr. OE *scēawian* to look, look at, see] 1 : to cause or permit to be seen : EXHIBIT ⟨~ anger⟩ 2 : CONFER, BESTOW ⟨~ mercy⟩ 3 : REVEAL, DISCLOSE ⟨~ed courage in battle⟩ 4 : INSTRUCT ⟨~ed me how to do it⟩ 5 : PROVE ⟨~s he was guilty⟩ 6 : APPEAR 7 : to be noticeable 8 : to be third in a horse race

²**show** *n* 1 : a demonstrative display 2 : outward appearance ⟨a ~ of resistance⟩ 3 : SPECTACLE 4 : a theatrical presentation 5 : a radio or television program 6 : third place in a horse race

¹**show·case** \'shō-,kās\ *n* : a cabinet for displaying items (as in a store or museum)

²**showcase** *vb* **show·cased; show·cas·ing** : EXHIBIT

**show·down** \'shō-,daùn\ *n* : the final settlement of a contested issue; *also* : the test of strength by which a contested issue is resolved

¹**show·er** \'shaù(-ə)r\ *n* 1 : a brief fall of rain 2 : a bath in which water is showered on the person 3 : a party given by friends who bring gifts — **show·ery** *adj*

²**shower** *vb* 1 : to fall in a shower 2 : to bathe in a shower

**show·man** \'shō-mən\ *n* : one having a gift for dramatization and visual effectiveness — **show·man·ship** *n*

**show-off** \'shō-,òf\ *n* : one that seeks to attract attention by conspicuous behavior

**show off** \(')shō-'òf\ *vb* 1 : to display proudly 2 : to act as a show-off

**show·piece** \'shō-,pēs\ *n* : an outstanding example used for exhibition

**show·place** \-,plās\ *n* : an estate or building that is a showpiece

**show up** *n* : ARRIVE

**showy** \'shō-ē\ *adj* **show·i·er; -est** : superficially impressive or striking — **show·i·ly** \'shō-ə-lē\ *adv* — **show·i·ness** \-ē-nəs\ *n*

**shpt** *abbr* shipment

**shrap·nel** \'shrap-nəl\ *n, pl* **shrapnel** [Henry *Shrapnel* d1842 E artillery officer] 1 : a case filled with shot and having a bursting charge which explodes it in flight 2 : bomb, mine, or shell fragments

¹**shred** \'shred\ *n* : a narrow strip cut or torn off : a small fragment

²**shred** *vb* **shred·ded; shred·ding** : to cut or tear into shreds

**shrew** \'shrü\ *n* 1 : a scolding woman 2 : a very small mouselike mammal

**shrewd** \'shrüd\ *adj* : KEEN, ASTUTE — **shrewd·ly** *adv* — **shrewd·ness** *n*

**shrew·ish** \'shrü-ish\ *adj* : having an irritable disposition : ILL-TEMPERED

**shriek** \'shrēk\ *n* : a shrill cry : SCREAM, YELL — **shriek** *vb*

**shrift** \'shrift\ *n, archaic* : the act of shriving

**shrike** \'shrīk\ *n* **:** a grayish or brownish bird that often impales its usu. insect prey upon thorns before devouring it

¹**shrill** \'shril\ *vb* **:** to make a high-pitched piercing sound

²**shrill** *adj* **:** high-pitched **:** PIERCING ⟨~ whistle⟩ — **shril·ly** \'shril-lē\ *adv*

**shrimp** \'shrimp\ *n, pl* **shrimps** *also* **shrimp** **1 :** any of various small sea crustaceans related to the lobsters **2 :** a small or puny person

**shrine** \'shrīn\ *n* [ME, receptacle for the relics of a saint, fr. OE *scrīn*, fr. L *scrinium* case, chest] **1 :** the tomb of a saint; *also* **:** a place where devotion is paid to a saint or deity **2 :** a place or object hallowed by its associations

¹**shrink** \'shriŋk\ *vb* **shrank** \'shraŋk\ *also* **shrunk** \'shrəŋk\; **shrunk** *or* **shrunk·en** \'shrəŋ-kən\ **1 :** to draw back or away **2 :** to become smaller in width or length or both **3 :** to lessen in value **syn** recoil, flinch, quail, contract, constrict, compress, condense, deflate — **shrink·able** *adj*

²**shrink** *n* **:** PSYCHIATRIST

**shrink·age** \'shriŋ-kij\ *n* **1 :** the act of shrinking **2 :** a decrease in value **3 :** the amount by which something contracts or lessens in extent

**shrive** \'shrīv\ *vb* **shrived** *or* **shrove** \'shrōv\; **shriv·en** \'shriv-ən\ *or* **shrived** **:** to minister the sacrament of penance to

**shriv·el** \'shriv-əl\ *vb* **shriv·eled** *or* **shriv·elled; shriv·el·ing** *or* **shriv·el·ling** \-(ə-)liŋ\ **:** to shrink and draw together into wrinkles **:** wither up

¹**shroud** \'shraud\ *n* **1 :** a cloth placed over a dead body **2 :** something that covers or screens **3 :** one of the ropes leading usu. in pairs from the masthead of a ship to the side to support the mast

²**shroud** *vb* **:** to veil or screen from view

**shrub** \'shrəb\ *n* **:** a low usu. several-stemmed woody plant — **shrub·by** *adj*

**shrub·bery** \'shrəb-(ə-)rē\ *n, pl* **-ber·ies :** a planting or growth of shrubs

**shrug** \'shrəg\ *vb* **shrugged; shrug·ging :** to hunch (the shoulders) up to express doubt, indifference, or dislike — **shrug** *n*

**shrug off** *vb* **1 :** to brush aside **:** MINIMIZE **2 :** to shake off **3 :** to remove (a garment) by wriggling out

**sht** *abbr* sheet

**shtg** *abbr* shortage

¹**shuck** \'shək\ *n* **:** SHELL, HUSK

²**shuck** *vb* **:** to strip of shucks

**shud·der** \'shəd-ər\ *vb* **shud·dered; shud·der·ing** \-(ə-)riŋ\ **:** TREMBLE, QUAKE — **shudder** *n*

**shuf·fle** \'shəf-əl\ *vb* **shuf·fled; shuf·fling** \-(ə-)liŋ\ **1 :** to mix in a disorderly mass **2 :** to rearrange the order of (cards in a pack) by mixing two parts of the pack together **3 :** to move with a sliding or dragging gait **4 :** to shift from place to place **5 :** to dance in a slow lagging manner — **shuffle** *n*

**shuf·fle·board** \'shəf-əl-,bōrd\ *n* **:** a game in which players use long-handled cues to shove wooden disks into scoring areas marked on a smooth surface

**shun** \'shən\ *vb* **shunned; shun·ning :** to avoid deliberately or habitually **syn** evade, elude, escape

**shun·pik·ing** \-,pī-kiŋ\ *n* **:** the practice of avoiding superhighways esp. for the pleasure of driving on back roads — **shun·pik·er** \-kər\ *n*

¹**shunt** \'shənt\ *vb* [ME *shunten* to flinch] **:** to turn off to one side; *esp* **:** to switch (a train) from one track to another

²**shunt** *n* **1 :** a means for turning or thrusting aside **2** *chiefly Brit* **:** a railroad switch

**shut** \'shət\ *vb* **shut; shut·ting 1 :** CLOSE **2 :** to forbid entrance into **3 :** to lock up **4 :** to fold together ⟨~ a penknife⟩ **5 :** to cease or suspend activity ⟨~ down an assembly line⟩

**shut-down** \-,daun\ *n* **:** a temporary cessation of activity (as in a factory)

**shut-in** \'shət-,in\ *n* **:** an invalid confined to his home, room, or bed

**shut-out** \'shət-,aut\ *n* **:** a game or contest in which one side fails to score

**shut out** \,shət-'aut\ *vb* **1 :** EXCLUDE **2 :** to prevent (an opponent) from scoring in a game or contest

**shut·ter** \'shət-ər\ *n* **1 :** a movable cover for a door or window for privacy or to keep out light or air **:** BLIND **2 :** the part of a camera that opens or closes to expose the film

**shut·ter·bug** \'shət-ər-,bəg\ *n* **:** a photography enthusiast

¹**shut·tle** \'shət-ᵊl\ *n* **1 :** an instrument used in weaving for passing the horizontal threads between the vertical threads **2 :** a vehicle traveling back and forth over a short route ⟨a ~ bus⟩

²**shuttle** *vb* **shut·tled; shut·tling** \'shət-(ᵊ-)liŋ\ **:** to move back and forth rapidly or frequently

**shut·tle·cock** \'shət-ᵊl-,käk\ *n* **:** a light feathered object (as of cork or plastic) used in badminton

**shut up** *vb* **:** to cease or cause to cease to talk

¹**shy** \'shī\ *adj* **shi·er** *or* **shy·er** \'shī(-ə)r\; **shi·est** *or* **shy·est** \'shī-əst\ **1 :** easily frightened **:** TIMID **2 :** WARY **3 :** BASHFUL **4 :** DEFICIENT, LACKING — **shy·ly** *adv* — **shy·ness** *n*

²**shy** *vb* **shied; shy·ing 1 :** to shrink back **:** RECOIL **2 :** to start suddenly aside through fright ⟨the horse *shied*⟩

**Shy·lock** \'shī-,läk\ *n* [after Shylock, moneylender in Shakespeare's *Merchant of Venice*] **:** a hardhearted greedy person; *esp* **:** an extortionate moneylender

**shy·ster** \'shī-stər\ *n* **:** an unscrupulous lawyer or politician

**Si** *symbol* silicon

**SI** *abbr* Staten Island

**Si·a·mese** \,sī-ə-'mēz, -'mēs\ *n, pl* **Siamese :** THAI — **Siamese** *adj*

**Siamese twin** *n* [fr. Chang d1874 and Eng d1874 twins born in Siam with bodies united] **:** one of a pair of twins with bodies united at birth

**sib·i·lant** \'sib-ə-lənt\ *adj* **:** having, containing, or producing the sound of or a sound resembling that of the *s* or the *sh* in *sash*

²**sibilant** n : a sibilant speech sound (as English \s\, \z\, \sh\, \zh\, \ch (=tsh)\, or \j (=dzh)\)

**sib·ling** \'sib-liŋ\ n : one of the offspring of a pair of parents

**sib·yl** \'sib-əl\ n, often cap : PROPHETESS — **sib·yl·line** \-ə-,līn, -,lēn\ adj

**sic** \'sik, 'sēk\ adv : intentionally so written — used after a printed word or passage to indicate that it exactly reproduces an original ⟨said he seed [sic] it all⟩

**sick** \'sik\ adj 1 : not in good health : ILL; also : of, relating to, or intended for the sick ⟨~ pay⟩ 2 : NAUSEATED 3 : LANGUISHING, PINING 4 : DISGUSTED — **sick·ly** adv

**sick·bed** \'sik-,bed\ n : a bed upon which one lies sick

**sick·en** \'sik-ən\ vb **sick·ened; sick·en·ing** \-(ə-)niŋ\ : to make or become sick — **sick·en·ing·ly** adv

**sick·le** \'sik-əl\ n : a curved metal blade with a short handle used esp. for cutting grass

**sickle-cell anemia** n : an inherited anemia in which red blood cells tend to become crescent-shaped and which occurs esp. in individuals of Negro ancestry

**sick·ness** \'sik-nəs\ n 1 : ill health; also : a specific disease 2 : NAUSEA

**side** \'sīd\ n 1 : a border of an object; esp : one of the longer borders as contrasted with an end 2 : an outer surface of an object 3 : the right or left part of the trunk of a body 4 : a place away from a central point or line 5 : a position regarded as opposite to another 6 : a body of contestants — **side** adj

**side·arm** \-,ärm\ adj : made with a sideways sweep of the arm — **sidearm** adv

**side arm** n : a weapon worn at the side or in the belt

**side·board** \-,bōrd\ n : a piece of dining-room furniture for holding articles of table service

**side·burns** \-,bərnz\ n pl : whiskers on the side of the face in front of the ears

**side·car** \'sīd-,kär\ n : a one-wheeled passenger car attached to the side of a motorcycle

**side effect** n : a secondary and usu. adverse effect (as of a drug)

**side·kick** \'sīd-,kik\ n : PAL, PARTNER

¹**side·long** \'sīd-,loŋ\ adv : in the direction of or along the side : OBLIQUELY

²**side·long** \,sīd-,loŋ\ adj : directed to one side : SLANTING ⟨~ look⟩

**side·man** \'sīd-,man\ n : a member of a jazz or swing orchestra

**side·piece** \-,pēs\ n : a piece forming or contained in the side of something

**si·de·re·al** \sī-'dir-ē-əl, sə-\ adj 1 : of or relating to the stars 2 : measured by the apparent motion of the fixed stars

**sid·er·ite** \'sid-ə-,rīt\ n : a native carbonate of iron that is a valuable iron ore

**side·show** \'sīd-,shō\ n 1 : a minor show offered in addition to a main exhibition (as of a circus) 2 : an incidental diversion

**side·step** \'sīd-,step\ vb 1 : to step aside 2 : AVOID, EVADE

**side·stroke** \'sīd-,strōk\ n : a swimming stroke which is executed on the side and in which the arms are swept backward and downward and the legs do a scissors kick

**side·swipe** \-,swīp\ vb : to strike with a glancing blow along the side — **sideswipe** n

¹**side·track** \'sīd-,trak\ n : SIDING 1

²**sidetrack** vb 1 : to switch from a main railroad line to a siding 2 : to turn aside from a purpose

**side·walk** \'sīd-,wȯk\ n : a paved walk at the side of a road or street

**side·wall** \'sīd-,wȯl\ n 1 : a wall forming the side of something 2 : the side of an automobile tire

**side·ways** \-,wāz\ adv or adj 1 : from the side 2 : with one side to the front 3 : to, toward, or at one side

**side·wind·er** \'sīd-,wīn-dər\ n : a small pale-colored desert rattlesnake of the southwestern U.S.

**sid·ing** \'sīd-iŋ\ n 1 : a short railroad track connected with the main track 2 : material (as boards) covering the outside of frame buildings

**si·dle** \'sīd-ʲl\ vb **si·dled; si·dling** \'sīd-(ʲ-)liŋ\ : to move sideways or side foremost

**siege** \'sēj\ n [ME sege, fr. OF, seat, blockade, fr. (assumed) VL sedicum, fr. sedicare, to settle, fr. L sedēre to sit] 1 : the placing of an army around or before a fortified place to force its surrender 2 : a persistent attack (as of illness)

**si·er·ra** \sē-'er-ə\ n [Sp, lit., saw, fr. L serra] : a range of mountains whose peaks make a jagged outline

**si·es·ta** \sē-'es-tə\ n [Sp, fr. L sexta (hora) noon, lit., sixth hour] : a midday rest or nap

**sieve** \'siv\ n : a utensil with meshes or holes to separate finer particles from coarser or solids from liquids

**sift** \'sift\ vb 1 : to pass through a sieve 2 : to separate with or as if with a sieve 3 : to examine carefully 4 : to scatter by or as if by passing through a sieve — **sift·er** n

**sig** abbr 1 signal 2 signature

**sigh** \'sī\ vb 1 : to make a long audible respiration (as to express weariness or sorrow) 2 : GRIEVE, YEARN — **sigh** n

¹**sight** \'sīt\ n 1 : something seen or worth seeing 2 : the process, function, or power of seeing; esp : the special sense of which the eye is the receptor and by which qualities of appearance (as position, shape, and color) are perceived 3 : INSPECTION 4 : a device (as a small bead on a gun barrel) that aids the eye in aiming 5 : VIEW, GLIMPSE 6 : the range of vision — **sight·less** adj

²**sight** vb 1 : to get sight of 2 : to aim by means of a sight

**sight·ed** \'sīt-əd\ adj : having sight

**sight·ly** \-lē\ adjⁱ : pleasing to the sight

**sight-see·ing** \'sīt-,sē-iŋ\ *adj* : engaged in or used for seeing sights of interest — **sight-seer** \-,sē-ər\ *n*

**sigill** *abbr* [L *sigillum*] seal

¹**sign** \'sīn\ *n* 1 : SYMBOL 2 : a gesture expressing a command, wish, or thought 3 : a notice publicly displayed for advertising purposes or for giving direction or warning 4 : OMEN, PORTENT 5 : TRACE, VESTIGE

²**sign** *vb* 1 : to mark with a sign 2 : to represent by a sign 3 : to make a sign or signal 4 : to write one's name on in token of assent or obligation 5 : to assign legally — **sign·er** *n*

¹**sig·nal** \'sig-nᵊl\ *n* 1 : a sign agreed on as the start of some joint action 2 : a sign giving warning or notice of something 3 : the message, sound, or image transmitted in electronic communication (as radio)

²**signal** *vb* **sig·naled** *or* **sig·nalled**; **sig·nal·ing** *or* **sig·nal·ling** \-nə-liŋ\ 1 : to communicate by signals 2 : to notify by a signal

³**signal** *adj* : DISTINGUISHED, OUTSTANDING \a ~ honor\ 2 : used in signaling — **sig·nal·ly** \-ē\ *adv*

**sig·nal·ize** \'sig-nə-,līz\ *vb* **-ized**; **-iz·ing** : to point out or make conspicuous — **sig·nal·i·za·tion** \,sig-nə-lə-'zā-shən\ *n*

**sig·nal·man** \'sig-nᵊl-mən, -,man\ *n* : one who signals or works with signals

**sig·na·to·ry** \'sig-nə-,tōr-ē\ *n*, *pl* **-ries** : a person or government that signs jointly with others — **signatory** *adj*

**sig·na·ture** \'sig-nə-,chùr\ *n* 1 : the name of a person written by himself 2 : the sign placed after the clef to indicate the key or the meter of a piece of music 3 : a tune or sound effect or in television a visual effect to identify a program, entertainer, or orchestra

**sign·board** \'sīn-,bōrd\ *n* : a board bearing a sign or notice

**sig·net** \'sig-nət\ *n* : a small intaglio seal (as in a ring)

**sig·nif·i·cance** \sig-'nif-i-kəns\ *n* 1 : something signified : MEANING 2 : SUGGESTIVENESS 3 : CONSEQUENCE, IMPORTANCE

**sig·nif·i·cant** \-kənt\ *adj* 1 : having meaning; *esp* : having a hidden or special meaning 2 : having or likely to have considerable influence or effect : IMPORTANT — **sig·nif·i·cant·ly** *adv*

**sig·ni·fy** \'sig-nə-,fī\ *vb* **-fied**; **-fy·ing** 1 : to show by a sign 2 : MEAN, IMPORT 3 : to have significance — **sig·ni·fi·ca·tion** \,sig-nə-fə-'kā-shən\ *n*

**sign in** *vb* : to make a record of arrival (as by signing a register)

**sign off** \('\)sīn-'óf\ *vb* : to announce the end of a message, program, or broadcast and discontinue transmitting

**sign on** \('\)sīn-'ón, -'än\ *vb* 1 : ENLIST 2 : to announce the start of broadcasting for the day

**sign out** *vb* : to indicate departure by signing a register

**sign·post** \'sīn-,pōst\ *n* : a post bearing a sign

**Sikh** \'sēk\ *n* : an adherent of a religion of India marked by rejection of caste — **Sikh·ism** *n*

**si·lage** \'sī-lij\ *n* : chopped fodder stored in a silo to ferment for use as animal feed

¹**si·lence** \'sī-ləns\ *n* 1 : the state of being silent 2 : SECRECY 3 : STILLNESS

²**silence** *vb* **si·lenced**; **si·lenc·ing** 1 : to reduce to silence : STILL 2 : to cause to cease hostile firing by one's own fire or by bombing

**si·lenc·er** \'sī-lən-sər\ *n* : a device for muffling the noise of a gunshot

**si·lent** \'sī-lənt\ *adj* 1 : not speaking : MUTE; *also* : TACITURN 2 : STILL, QUIET 3 : performed or borne without utterance **syn** reticent, reserved, secretive, close — **si·lent·ly** *adv*

¹**sil·hou·ette** \,sil-ə-'wet\ *n* [F, fr. Étienne de *Silhouette* d1767 F controller general of finances; fr. his petty economies] 1 : a representation of the outlines of an object filled in with black or some other uniform color 2 : OUTLINE \~ of a ship\

²**silhouette** *vb* **-ett·ed**; **-ett·ing** : to represent by a silhouette; *also* : to show against a light background

**sil·i·ca** \'sil-i-kə\ *n* : a mineral that consists of silicon and oxygen and is found as quartz and opal

**sil·i·cate** \'sil-ə-,kāt, 'sil-i-kət\ *n* : a compound formed from silica and any of various oxides of metals

**si·li·ceous** *or* **si·li·cious** \sə-'lish-əs\ *adj* : of, relating to, or containing silica or a silicate

**si·lic·i·fy** \sə-'lis-ə-,fī\ *vb* **-fied**; **-fy·ing** : to convert into or impregnate with silica — **si·lic·i·fi·ca·tion** \-,lis-ə-fə-'kā-shən\ *n*

**sil·i·con** \'sil-i-kən, 'sil-ə-,kän\ *n* : a nonmetallic chemical element that is found in nature always combined with some other substance and that is the most abundant element next to oxygen in the earth's crust

**sil·i·cone** \'sil-ə-,kōn\ *n* : an organic silicon compound obtained as oil, grease, or plastic

**sil·i·co·sis** \,sil-ə-'kō-səs\ *n* : a lung disease caused by prolonged inhaling of silica dusts

**silk** \'silk\ *n* 1 : a fine strong lustrous protein fiber produced by insect larvae for their cocoons; *esp* : one from moth larvae (**silk·worms** \-,wərmz\) used for cloth 2 : thread or cloth made from silk — **silk·en** \'sil-kən\ *adj* — **silky** *adj*

**silk screen** *n* : a stencil process in which coloring matter is forced through the meshes of a prepared silk or organdy screen — **silk-screen** *vb*

**sill** \'sil\ *n* 1 : a heavy crosspiece (as of wood or stone) that forms the bottom member of a window frame or a doorway; *also* : a horizontal supporting piece at the base of a structure 2 : a tabular body of intrusive igneous rock

**sil·ly** \'sil-ē\ *adj* **sil·li·er**; **-est** [ME *sely*, *silly* happy, innocent, pitiable, feeble, fr. (assumed) OE *sǣlig*, fr. OE *sæl* happiness] **:** FOOLISH, ABSURD, STUPID — **sil·li·ness** *n*

**si·lo** \'sī-lō\ *n, pl* **silos : a** trench, pit, or tall cylinder in which silage is stored

**¹silt** \'silt\ *n* **1 :** fine earth; *esp* **:** particles of such soil floating in rivers, ponds, or lakes **2 :** a deposit (as by a river) of silt — **silty** *adj*

**²silt** *vb* **:** to obstruct or cover with silt — **silt·ation** \sil-'tā-shən\ *n*

**silt·stone** \'silt-,stōn\ *n* **:** a rock composed chiefly of compacted silt

**¹sil·ver** \'sil-vər\ *n* **1 :** a white ductile metallic chemical element that takes a high polish and is used for money, jewelry, and table utensils **2 :** coin made of silver **3 :** SILVERWARE **4 :** a grayish white color — **sil·very** *adj*

**²silver** *adj* **1 :** relating to, made of, or coated with silver **2 :** SILVERY

**³silver** *vb* **sil·vered; sil·ver·ing** \'silv-(ə-)riŋ\ **:** to coat with or as if with silver — **sil·ver·er** *n*

**silver bromide** *n* **:** a light-sensitive compound used in the making of photographic emulsions

**silver chloride** *n* **:** a light-sensitive compound used for photographic materials

**sil·ver·fish** \'sil-vər-,fish\ *n* **:** a small wingless insect found in houses and sometimes injurious to sized paper and starched clothes

**silver iodide** *n* **:** a light-sensitive compound used in photography, rainmaking, and medicine

**silver maple** *n* **:** a No. American maple with deeply cut leaves that are green above and silvery white below

**silver nitrate** *n* **:** a soluble salt of silver used in photography and as an antiseptic

**sil·ver·ware** \'sil-vər-,waər\ *n* **:** articles (as knives, forks, and spoons) made of silver, silver-plated metal, or stainless steel

**sim·i·an** \'sim-ē-ən\ *n* **:** MONKEY, APE — **simian** *adj*

**sim·i·lar** \'sim-ə-lər\ *adj* **:** marked by correspondence or resemblance **syn** alike, akin, comparable, parallel — **sim·i·lar·i·ty** \,sim-ə-'lar-ət-ē\ *n* — **sim·i·lar·ly** \'sim-ə-lər-lē\ *adv*

**sim·i·le** \'sim-ə-(,)lē\ *n* [L, likeness, comparison, fr. neut. of *similis* like, similar] **:** a figure of speech in which two dissimilar things are compared by the use of *like* or *as* (as in "cheeks like roses")

**si·mil·i·tude** \sə-'mil-ə-,t(y)üd\ *n* **:** LIKENESS, RESEMBLANCE **syn** similarity

**sim·mer** \'sim-ər\ *vb* **sim·mered; sim·mer·ing** \-(ə-)riŋ\ **:** to stew at or just below the boiling point **2 :** to be on the point of bursting out with violence or emotional disturbance

**si·mo·nize** \'sī-mə-,nīz\ *vb* **-nized; -niz·ing :** to polish with or as if with wax

**si·mo·ny** \'sī-mə-nē, 'sim-ə-\ *n* [LL *simonia,* fr. *Simon* Magus 1st cent. A.D. sorcerer of Samaria (Acts 8:9–24)] **:** the buying or selling of a church office

**sim·pa·ti·co** \sim-'pät-i-,kō, -'pat-\ *adj* **:** CONGENIAL, LIKABLE

**sim·per** \'sim-pər\ *vb* **sim·pered; sim·per·ing** \-p(ə-)riŋ\ **:** to smile in a silly manner — **simper** *n*

**¹sim·ple** \'sim-pəl\ *adj* **sim·pler** \-p(ə-)lər\; **sim·plest** \-p(ə-)ləst\ [ME, fr. OF, plain, uncomplicated, artless, fr. L *simplus, simplex,* lit., single; L *simplus* fr. *sim-* one + *-plus* multiplied by; L *simplex* fr. *sim-* + *-plex* -fold] **1 :** not combined with anything else **2 :** not other than **:** MERE **3 :** not complex **:** PLAIN **4 :** ABSOLUTE 〈land held in fee ∼〉 **5 :** STRAIGHTFORWARD; *also* **:** ARTLESS **6 :** UNADORNED **7 :** lacking education, experience, or intelligence **8 :** developing from a single ovary 〈a ∼ fruit〉 **syn** pure, sheer, easy, facile, light, effortless, natural, ingenuous, naive, unsophisticated, foolish, silly — **sim·ple·ness** *n* — **sim·ply** \-plē\ *adv*

**²simple** *n* **1 :** a person of humble birth **2 :** a medicinal plant

**sim·ple·ton** \'sim-pəl-tən\ *n* **:** FOOL

**sim·plic·i·ty** \sim-'plis-ət-ē\ *n* **1 :** lack of complication **:** CLEARNESS **2 :** CANDOR, ARTLESSNESS **3 :** plainness in manners or way of life **4 :** IGNORANCE, FOOLISHNESS

**sim·pli·fy** \'sim-plə-,fī\ *vb* **-fied; -fy·ing :** to make simple **:** make less complex **:** CLARIFY — **sim·pli·fi·ca·tion** \,sim-plə-fə-'kā-shən\ *n*

**sim·plis·tic** \sim-'plis-tik\ *adj* **:** excessively simple **:** tending to overlook complexities 〈a ∼ solution〉

**sim·u·late** \'sim-yə-,lāt\ *vb* **-lat·ed; -lat·ing :** to create the effect or appearance of **:** FEIGN — **sim·u·la·tion** \,sim-yə-'lā-shən\ *n* — **sim·u·la·tor** \'sim-yə-,lāt-ər\ *n*

**si·mul·ta·ne·ous** \,sī-məl-'tā-nē-əs, ,sim-əl-\ *adj* **:** occurring or operating at the same time — **si·mul·ta·ne·ous·ly** *adv* — **si·mul·ta·ne·ous·ness** *n*

**¹sin** \'sin\ *n* **1 :** an offense esp. against God **2 :** FAULT **3 :** a weakened state of human nature in which the self is estranged from God — **sin·less** *adj*

**²sin** *vb* **sinned; sin·ning :** to commit a sin — **sin·ner** *n*

**¹since** \(')sins\ *adv* **1 :** from a past time until now **2 :** backward in time **:** AGO

**²since** *prep* **1 :** in the period after 〈changes made ∼ the war〉 **2 :** continuously from 〈has been here ∼ 1970〉

**³since** *conj* **1 :** from the time when **2 :** seeing that **:** BECAUSE

**sin·cere** \sin-'siər\ *adj* **1 :** free from hypocrisy **:** HONEST **2 :** GENUINE, REAL — **sin·cere·ly** *adv* — **sin·cer·i·ty** \-'ser-ət-ē\ *n*

**si·ne·cure** \'sī-ni-,kyuər, 'sin-i-\ *n* **:** a well-paid job that requires little work

**si·ne die** \,sī-ni-'dī-,ē, ,sin-ā-'dē-,ā\ *adv* [L, without day] **:** INDEFINITELY

**si·ne qua non** \,sin-i-,kwä-'nän, -'nōn\ *n* [LL, without which not] **:** an indispensable or essential thing

**sin·ew** \'sin-yü\ *n* **1 :** TENDON **2 :** physical strength — **sin·ewy** *adj*

**sin·ful** \'sin-fəl\ *adj* **:** marked by or full

of sin ⟨ WICKED — **sin·ful·ly** \-ē\ *adv* — **sin·ful·ness** *n*

¹**sing** \'siŋ\ *vb* **sang** \'saŋ\ *or* **sung** \'səŋ\; **sung**; **sing·ing** \'siŋ-iŋ\ **1** : to produce musical tones with the voice; *also* : to utter with musical tones **2** : to produce harmonious sustained sounds ⟨birds ~*ing*⟩ **3** : CHANT, INTONE **4** : to make a prolonged shrill sound ⟨locusts ~*ing*⟩ **5** : to write poetry; *also* : to celebrate in song or verse **6** : to give information or evidence — **sing·er** *n*

²**sing** *abbr* singular

**singe** \'sinj\ *vb* **singed**; **singe·ing** \'sin-jiŋ\ : to scorch lightly the outside of; *esp* : to remove the hair or down from (a plucked fowl) with flame

¹**sin·gle** \'siŋ-gəl\ *adj* **1** : one only **2** : ALONE **3** : UNMARRIED **4** : having only one feature or part **5** : made for one person or family **syn** sole, unique, lone, solitary, separate, particular — **sin·gle·ness** *n* — **sin·gly** \-glē\ *adv*

²**single** *n* **1** : a separate person or thing **2** : a hit in baseball that enables the batter to reach first base **3** *pl* : a tennis match with one player on each side

³**single** *vb* **sin·gled**; **sin·gling** \-g(ə-)liŋ\ **1** : to select (one) from a group **2** : to hit a single

**sin·gle·ton** \'siŋ-gəl-tən\ *n* : a card that is the only one of its suit orig. held in a hand

**sin·gle·tree** \-(')trē\ *n* : WHIFFLETREE

**sin·gu·lar** \'siŋ-gyə-lər\ *adj* **1** : of, relating to, or constituting a word form denoting one person, thing, or instance **2** : of unusual quality **3** : OUTSTANDING, EXCEPTIONAL **4** : ODD, STRANGE — **singular** *n* — **sin·gu·lar·i·ty** \,siŋ-gyə-'lar-ət-ē\ *n* — **sin·gu·lar·ly** \'siŋ-gyə-lər-lē\ *adv*

**sin·is·ter** \'sin-əs-tər\ *adj* **1** : threatening or foreboding evil or disaster **2** : indicative of lurking evil **syn** baleful, malign

¹**sink** \'siŋk\ *vb* **sank** \'saŋk\ *or* **sunk** \'səŋk\; **sunk**; **sink·ing 1** : SUBMERGE **2** : to descend lower and lower **3** : to grow less in volume or height **4** : to slope downward **5** : to penetrate downward **6** : to fail in health or strength **7** : LAPSE, DEGENERATE **8** : to cause (a ship) to plunge to the bottom **9** : to make (a hole or shaft) by digging, boring, or cutting **10** : INVEST — **sink·able** *adj*

²**sink** *n* **1** : DRAIN, SEWER **2** : a basin connected with a drain **3** : an extensive depression in the land surface

**sink·er** \'siŋ-kər\ *n* : a weight for sinking a fishing line or net

**sink·hole** \'siŋk-,hōl\ *n* **1** : a hollow place in which drainage collects **2** : a hollow in a limestone region that connects with a cave

**sin·u·ous** \'sin-yə-wəs\ *adj* : bending in and out ⟨ WINDING — **sin·u·os·i·ty** \,sin-yə-'wäs-ət-ē\ *n*

**si·nus** \'sī-nəs\ *n* **1** : any of several cavities of the skull mostly connecting with the nostrils **2** : a space forming a channel (as for the passage of blood)

**si·nus·itis** \,sī-nə-'sīt-əs\ *n* : inflammation of a sinus esp. of the skull

**Sioux** \'sü\ *n, pl* **Sioux** \'sü(z)\ : DAKOTA

**sip** \'sip\ *vb* **sipped**; **sip·ping** : to drink in small quantities — **sip** *n*

¹**si·phon** \'sī-fən\ *n* **1** : a bent tube through which a liquid can be transferred by means of air pressure up and over the edge of one container and into another container placed at a lower level **2** *usu* **sy·phon** : a bottle that ejects soda water through a tube when a valve is opened

²**siphon** *vb* **si·phoned**; **si·phon·ing** \'sīf-(ə)niŋ\ : to draw off by means of a siphon

**sir** \(')sər\ *n* [ME *sire* sire, fr. OF, fr. L *senior*, compar. of *senex* old, old man] **1** : a man of rank or position — used as a title before the given name of a knight or baronet **2** — used in addressing a man without using his name

¹**sire** \'sī(ə)r\ *n* **1** : FATHER; *also*, *archaic* : FOREFATHER **2** : the male parent of an animal (as a horse or dog) **3** *archaic* : LORD — used as a title of respect esp. in addressing a sovereign

²**sire** *vb* **sired**; **sir·ing** : BEGET, PROCREATE

**si·ren** \'sī-rən\ *n* **1** : a seductive or alluring woman **2** : a loud wailing often electrically operated whistle used to sound warning signals — **siren** *adj*

**sir·loin** \'sər-,lȯin\ *n* [alter. of earlier *surloin*, modif. of MF *surlonge*, fr. *sur* over (fr. L *super*) + *loigne, longe* loin] : a cut of beef taken from the part in front of the round

**si·roc·co** \sə-'räk-ō\ *n, pl* **-cos 1** : a hot wind blowing north from the Libyan deserts **2** : a hot southerly wind

**sirup** *var of* SYRUP

**si·sal** \'sī-səl, -zəl\ *n* : a strong cordage fiber from an agave

**sis·sy** \'sis-ē\ *n, pl* **sissies** : an effeminate boy or man; *also* : a timid or cowardly person

**sis·ter** \'sis-tər\ *n* **1** : a female having one or both parents in common with another individual **2** : a member of a religious order of women : NUN **3** *chiefly Brit* : NURSE — **sis·ter·ly** *adj*

**sis·ter·hood** \-,hud\ *n* **1** : the state of being sisters or a sister **2** : a community or society of sisters

**sis·ter-in-law** \'sis-t(ə-)rən-,lȯ\ *n, pl* **sis·ters-in-law** \-tər-zən-\ : the sister of one's husband or wife; *also* : the wife of one's brother

**sit** \'sit\ *vb* **sat** \'sat\; **sit·ting 1** : to rest upon the buttocks or haunches **2** : ROOST, PERCH **3** : to occupy a seat **4** : to hold a session **5** : to cover eggs for hatching : BROOD **6** : to pose for a portrait **7** : to remain quiet or inactive **8** : FIT **9** : to cause (oneself) to be seated **10** : to place in position **11** : to keep one's seat upon ⟨~ a horse⟩ **12** : BABY-SIT — **sit·ter** *n*

**si·tar** \si-'tär\ *n* : an Indian lute with a long neck and a varying number of strings

**site** \'sīt\ *n* **:** LOCATION

**sit–in** \'sit-,in\ *n* **:** an act of sitting in the seats or on the floor of an establishment as a means of organized protest

**sit·u·at·ed** \'sich-ə-,wāt-əd\ *adj* **1 :** LOCATED, PLACED **2 :** placed in a particular place or environment or in certain circumstances

**sit·u·a·tion** \,sich-ə-'wā-shən\ *n* **1 :** LOCATION, SITE **2 :** CONDITION, CIRCUMSTANCES **3 :** place of employment

**sit–up** \'sit-,əp\ *n* **:** an exercise performed from a supine position by raising the trunk to a sitting position usu. while keeping the legs straight and returning to the original position

**six** \'siks\ *n* **1 :** one more than five **2 :** the sixth in a set or series **3 :** something having six units; *esp* **:** a 6-cylinder engine or automobile — **six** *adj or pron* — **sixth** \'siksth\ *adj or adv or n*

**six–gun** \'siks-,gən\ *n* **:** a 6-chambered revolver

**six–pack** \'siks-,pak\ *n* **:** a container for six bottles or cans purchased together; *also* **:** the contents of a six-pack

**six·pence** \-pəns, *US also* -,pens\ *n* **:** the sum of six pence; *also* **:** an English silver coin of this value — **six·pen·ny** \-pən-ē, *US also* -,pen-ē\ *adj*

**six–shoot·er** \'sik(s)-'shüt-ər\ *n* **:** SIX-GUN

**six·teen** \'siks-'tēn\ *n* **:** one more than 15 — **sixteen** *adj or pron* — **six·teenth** \-'tēnth\ *adj or n*

**six·ty** \'siks-tē\ *n, pl* **sixties :** six times 10 — **six·ti·eth** \'siks-tē-əth\ *adj or n* — **sixty** *adj or pron*

**siz·able** *or* **size·able** \'sī-zə-bəl\ *adj* **:** quite large — **siz·ably** \-blē\ *adv*

¹**size** \'sīz\ *n* **:** physical extent or bulk **:** DIMENSIONS; *also* **:** MAGNITUDE

²**size** *vb* **sized; siz·ing :** to grade or classify according to size

³**size** *n* **:** a gluey material used for filling the pores in paper, plaster, or textiles — **siz·ing** \'sī-ziŋ\ *n*

⁴**size** *vb* **sized; siz·ing :** to cover, stiffen, or glaze with size

**siz·zle** \'siz-əl\ *vb* **siz·zled; siz·zling** \-(ə-)liŋ\ **:** to fry or shrivel up with a hissing sound — **sizzle** *n*

**SJ** *abbr* Society of Jesus

**SJD** *abbr* doctor of juridicial science

**skag** \'skag\ *n, slang* **:** HEROIN

¹**skate** \'skāt\ *n, pl* **skates** *also* **skate :** any of numerous rays with thick broad fins

²**skate** *n* **1 :** a metal runner with a frame fitting on a shoe used for gliding over ice **2 :** ROLLER SKATE — **skate** *vb* — **skat·er** *n*

**skate·board** \'skāt-,bōrd\ *n* **:** a somewhat short and narrow board mounted on roller-skate wheels — **skate·board·er** \-ər\ *n* — **skate·board·ing** \-iŋ\ *n*

**skeet** \'skēt\ *n* **:** trapshooting in which clay targets are thrown in such a way as to simulate the angle of flight of a flushed game bird

**skein** \'skān\ *n* **:** a loosely twisted quantity (as of yarn) as it is taken from the reel

**skel·e·ton** \'skel-ət-ə'n\ *n* **1 :** the usu. bony supporting framework of an animal body **2 :** FRAMEWORK **3 :** a bare minimum — **skel·e·tal** \-ət-ə'l\ *adj*

**skep·tic** \'skep-tik\ *n* **1 :** one who believes in skepticism **2 :** one having a critical or doubting attitude **3 :** one who doubts or disbelieves in religious tenets — **skep·ti·cal** \-ti-kəl\ *adj*

**skep·ti·cism** \'skep-tə-,siz-əm\ *n* **1 :** a doctrine that certainty of knowledge cannot be attained **2 :** a doubting state of mind **3 :** unbelief in religion

**sketch** \'skech\ *n* **1 :** a rough drawing or outline **2 :** a short or slight literary composition (as a story or essay); *also* **:** a vaudeville act — **sketch** *vb* — **sketchy** *adj*

¹**skew** \'skyü\ *vb* **:** SWERVE

²**skew** *n* **:** SLANT

**skew·er** \'skyü-ər\ *n* **:** a pin for holding meat in form while roasting — **skewer** *vb*

¹**ski** \'skē\ *n, pl* **skis** [Norw. fr. ON *skīth* stick of wood, ski] **:** one of a pair of long strips (as of wood) bound one on each foot for gliding over snow

²**ski** *vb* **skied** \'skēd\; **ski·ing :** to glide on skis — **ski·er** *n*

¹**skid** \'skid\ *n* **1 :** a plank for supporting something above the ground **2 :** a device placed under a wheel to prevent turning **3 :** a timber or rail over or on which something is slid or rolled **4 :** a runner on the landing gear of an airplane **5 :** ²PALLET **6 :** the action of skidding

²**skid** *vb* **skid·ded; skid·ding 1 :** to slide without rotating ⟨a *skidding* wheel⟩ **2 :** to slide sideways on the road ⟨the car *skidded* on ice⟩

**skid row** *n* **:** a district of cheap saloons frequented by vagrants and alcoholics

**skiff** \'skif\ *n* **:** a small open boat

**skif·fle** \'skif-əl\ *n* **:** jazz or folk music played by a group all or some of whose members play nonstandard instruments or noisemakers (as jugs or washboards)

**ski lift** *n* **:** a motor-driven conveyor for transporting esp. skiers up a slope

**skill** \'skil\ *n* **1 :** ability to use one's knowledge effectively in doing something **2 :** developed or acquired ability *syn* art, craft — **skilled** \'skild\ *adj*

**skil·let** \'skil-ət\ *n* **:** a frying pan

**skill·ful** *or* **skil·ful** \'skil-fəl\ *adj* **1 :** having or displaying skill **:** EXPERT **2 :** accomplished with skill — **skill·ful·ly** \-ē\ *adv* — **skill·ful·ness** *n*

¹**skim** \'skim\ *vb* **skimmed; skim·ming 1 :** to take off from the top of a liquid; *also* **:** to remove (scum or cream) from ⟨~ milk⟩ **2 :** to read rapidly and superficially **3 :** to pass swiftly over — **skim·mer** *n*

²**skim** *adj* **1 :** having the cream removed **2 :** made of skim milk

**skim·ming** \'skim-iŋ\ *n* **:** the practice of concealing gambling profits so as to avoid tax payments

**ski·mo·bile** \'skē-mō-,bēl\ *n* **:** SNOWMOBILE

**skimp** \'skimp\ *vb* **:** to give insufficient

attention, effort, or funds; *also* : to save by skimping

**skimpy** \'skim-pē\ *adj* **skimp·i·er; -est** : deficient in supply or execution

¹**skin** \'skin\ *n* **1** : the outer limiting layer of an animal body; *also* : the usu. thin tough tissue of which this is made **2** : an outer or surface layer (as a rind or peel) — **skin·less** *adj*

²**skin** *vb* **skinned; skin·ning** : to free from skin : remove the skin of

**skin–dive** \'skin-,dīv\ *vb* : to swim below the surface of water with a face mask and portable breathing device — **skin diver** *n*

**skin flick** *n* : a motion picture characterized by nudity and sex

**skin·flint** \'skin-,flint\ *n* : a very stingy person

**skin graft** *n* : a piece of skin that is taken from one area to replace skin in another area — **skin grafting** *n*

**skin·ny** \'skin-ē\ *adj* **skin·ni·er; -est 1** : resembling skin **2** : very thin

**skin·ny–dip·ping** \-,dip-iŋ\ *n* : swimming in the nude

**skin·tight** \'skin-'tīt\ *adj* : closely fitted to the figure

¹**skip** \'skip\ *vb* **skipped; skip·ping 1** : to move with leaps and bounds **2** : to pass from point to point (as in reading) disregarding what is in between **3** : to leap lightly over **4** : to pass over without notice or mention

²**skip** *n* : a light bound; *also* : a gait of alternate hops and steps

**skip·per** \'skip-ər\ *n* [ME, fr. Middle Dutch *schipper*, fr. *schip* ship] : the master of a ship — **skipper** *vb*

**skir·mish** \'skər-mish\ *n* : a minor engagement in war — **skirmish** *vb*

¹**skirt** \'skərt\ *n* : a garment or part of a garment that hangs below the waist

²**skirt** *vb* **1** : BORDER **2** : to pass around the outer edge of

**skit** \'skit\ *n* : a brief dramatic sketch

**ski tow** *n* : SKI LIFT

**skit·ter** \'skit-ər\ *vb* : to glide or skip lightly or quickly : skim along a surface

**skit·tish** \'skit-ish\ *adj* **1** : CAPRICIOUS, IRRESPONSIBLE **2** : easily frightened ⟨a ~ horse⟩

**ski·wear** \'skē-,waər\ *n* : clothing suitable for wear while skiing

**Skt** *abbr* Sanskrit

**skulk** \'skəlk\ *vb* : to move furtively : SNEAK, LURK — **skulk·er** *n*

**skull** \'skəl\ *n* : the bony or cartilaginous case that protects the brain and supports the jaws

**skull·cap** \'skəl-,kap\ *n* : a close-fitting brimless cap

¹**skunk** \'skəŋk\ *n, pl* **skunks** *also* **skunk 1** : a No. American mammal related to the weasels that can forcibly eject an ill-smelling fluid when startled **2** : a contemptible person

²**skunk** *vb* : to defeat decisively; *esp* : to shut out in a game

**skunk cabbage** *n* : a perennial herb of eastern No. America with an unpleasant smelling early spring flower

¹**sky** \'skī\ *n, pl* **skies 1** : the upper air **2** : HEAVEN — **sky·ey** \'skī-ē\ *adj*

**sky·cap** \-,kap\ *n* : a person employed to carry luggage at an airport

**sky·div·ing** \-,dī-viŋ\ *n* : the sport of jumping from an airplane and executing various body maneuvers before pulling the cord to open the parachute — **sky diver** *n*

**sky·jack·er** \-,jak-ər\ *n* : one who commandeers a flying airplane — **sky·jack·ing** \-iŋ\ *n*

¹**sky·lark** \'skī-,lärk\ *n* : a European lark noted for its song and its steep upward flight

²**skylark** *vb* : to frolic boisterously or recklessly

**sky·light** \'skī-,līt\ *n* : a window in a roof or ceiling

**sky·line** \-,līn\ *n* **1** : HORIZON **2** : an outline against the sky

**sky·lounge** \-,laúnj\ *n* : a passenger vehicle carried by helicopter from a downtown terminal to an airport

**sky marshal** *n* : an armed federal plainclothesman assigned to prevent skyjackings

¹**sky·rock·et** \'skī-,räk-ət\ *n* : ¹ROCKET 1

²**skyrocket** *vb* : ²ROCKET 2

**sky·scrap·er** \-,skrā-pər\ *n* : a very tall building

**sky·ward** \-wərd\ *adv or adj* : toward the sky

**sky·writ·ing** \-,rīt-iŋ\ *n* : writing in the sky formed by smoke emitted from an airplane — **sky·writ·er** \-ər\ *n*

**SL** *abbr* salvage loss

**slab** \'slab\ *n* **1** : a thick plate or slice **2** : the outside piece taken from a log in sawing it

¹**slack** \'slak\ *adj* **1** : CARELESS, NEGLIGENT **2** : SLUGGISH, LISTLESS **3** : not taut : LOOSE **4** : not busy or active **syn** lax, remiss, neglectful — **slack·ly** *adv* — **slack·ness** *n*

²**slack** *vb* **1** : to make or become slack : LOOSEN, RELAX **2** : SLAKE 2

³**slack** *n* **1** : cessation of movement or flow : LETUP **2** : a part that hangs loose without strain ⟨~ of a rope⟩ **3** *pl* : trousers for casual wear

**slack·en** \'slak-ən\ *vb* **slack·ened; slack·en·ing** \-(ə-)niŋ\ : to make or become slack

**slack·er** \'slak-ər\ *n* : one that shirks work or evades military duty

**slag** \'slag\ *n* : the waste left after the melting of ores and the separation of metal from them

**slain** *past part of* SLAY

**slake** \'slāk, *for 2 also* 'slak\ *vb* **slaked; slak·ing 1** : to cause to subside with or as if with refreshing drink ⟨~ thirst⟩ **2** : to cause (lime) to crumble by mixture with water

**sla·lom** \'släl-əm\ *n* [Norw, lit., sloping track] : skiing in a zigzag course between obstacles

¹**slam** \'slam\ *n* : the winning of every trick or of all tricks but one in bridge

²**slam** *n* : a heavy jarring impact : BANG

³**slam** *vb* **slammed; slam·ming 1** : to shut violently and noisily **2** : to throw or strike with a loud impact

**SLAN** *abbr* [L *sine loco, anno, (vel) nomine*] without place, year, or name

¹**slan·der** \'slan-dər\ n [ME *sclaundre*, *slaundre*, fr. OF *esclandre*, fr. LL *scandalum* stumbling block, offense] **:** a false report maliciously uttered and tending to injure the reputation of a person — **slan·der·ous** adj

²**slander** vb **slan·dered; slan·der·ing** \-d(ə-)riŋ\ **:** to utter slander against **:** DEFAME — **slan·der·er** n

**slang** \'slaŋ\ n **:** an informal nonstandard vocabulary composed typically of coinages, arbitrarily changed words, and extravagant figures of speech — **slangy** adj

¹**slant** \'slant\ vb **: SLOPE 2 :** to interpret or present in accordance with a special viewpoint **syn** incline, lean — **slant·ing** adj — **slant·ing·ly** adv

²**slant** n **1 :** a sloping direction, line, or plane **2 :** a particular or personal viewpoint — **slant** adj — **slant·wise** \-,wīz\ adv or adj

**slap** \'slap\ vb **slapped; slap·ping 1 :** to strike sharply with the open hand **2 :** REBUFF, INSULT — **slap** n

¹**slash** \'slash\ vb **1 :** to cut with sweeping strokes **2 :** to cut slits in (a garment) **3 :** to reduce sharply

²**slash** n **1 :** GASH **2 :** an ornamental slit in a garment **3 :** a clearing in a forest littered with debris; *also* **:** the debris present

**slat** \'slat\ n **:** a thin narrow flat strip

¹**slate** \'slāt\ n **1 :** a dense fine-grained rock that splits into thin layers **2 :** a roofing tile or a writing tablet made from this rock **3 :** a list of candidates for election

²**slate** vb **slat·ed; slat·ing 1 :** to cover with slate **2 :** to designate for action or appointment

**slath·er** \'slath-ər\ vb **slath·ered; slath·er·ing** \-(ə-)riŋ\ **:** to spread with or on thickly or lavishly

**slat·tern** \'slat-ərn\ n **:** a slovenly woman — **slat·tern·ly** adv or adj

¹**slaugh·ter** \'slȯt-ər\ n **1 :** the butchering of livestock for market **2 :** great destruction of lives esp. in battle

²**slaughter** vb **1 :** to kill (animals) for food **:** BUTCHER **2 :** to kill in large numbers or in a bloody way **:** MASSACRE

**slaugh·ter·house** \-,haŭs\ n **:** an establishment where animals are butchered

**Slav** \'släv, 'slav\ n **:** a person speaking a Slavic language

¹**slave** \'slāv\ n [ME *sclave*, fr. OF or ML; OF *esclave*, fr. ML *sclavus*, fr. *Sclavus* Slav; fr. the reduction to slavery of many Slavic peoples of central Europe] **1 :** a person held in servitude as property **2 :** a mechanical device (as the typewriter unit of a computer) that is directly responsive to another — **slave** adj

²**slave** vb **slaved; slav·ing :** to work like a slave **:** DRUDGE

¹**sla·ver** \'slav-ər, 'släv-\ n **:** SLOBBER — **slaver** vb

²**slav·er** \'slā-vər\ n **:** a ship or a person engaged in transporting slaves

**slav·ery** \'slāv-(ə-)rē\ n **1 :** wearisome drudgery **2 :** the condition of being a slave **3 :** the custom or practice of owning slaves **syn** servitude, bondage

¹**Slav·ic** \'slav-ik, 'släv-\ adj **:** of or relating to the Slavs or their languages

²**Slavic** n **:** a branch of the Indo-European language family including various languages (as Russian or Polish) of eastern Europe

**slav·ish** \'slā-vish\ adj **1 :** SERVILE **2 :** obeying or imitating with no freedom of judgment or choice — **slav·ish·ly** adv

**slaw** \'slȯ\ n **:** COLESLAW

**slay** \'slā\ vb **slew** \'slü\; **slain** \'slān\; **slay·ing; slay·ing :** KILL — **slay·er** n

**sld** abbr **1** sailed **2** sealed

**slea·zy** \'slē-zē, 'slā-\ adj **slea·zi·er; -est :** FLIMSY, SHODDY

¹**sled** \'sled\ n **:** a vehicle on runners adapted esp. for sliding on snow

²**sled** vb **sled·ded, sled·ding :** to ride or carry on a sled

¹**sledge** \'slej\ n **:** SLEDGEHAMMER

²**sledge** n **:** a strong heavy vehicle with low runners for carrying heavy loads over snow or ice

**sledge·ham·mer** \'slej-,ham-ər\ n **:** a large heavy hammer usu. wielded with both hands — **sledgehammer** adj or vb

¹**sleek** \'slēk\ vb **1 :** to make smooth or glossy **2 :** to gloss over

²**sleek** adj **:** having a smooth well-groomed look

¹**sleep** \'slēp\ n **1 :** a natural periodic suspension of consciousness **2 :** a state (as death or coma) suggesting sleep — **sleep·less** adj — **sleep·less·ness** n

²**sleep** vb **slept** \'slept\; **sleep·ing 1 :** to rest or be in a state of sleep; *also* **:** to spend in sleep **2 :** to lie in a state of inactivity or stillness

**sleep·er** \'slē-pər\ n **1 :** one that sleeps **2 :** a horizontal beam to support something on or near the ground level **3 :** a railroad car with berths for sleeping **4 :** someone or something unpromising or unnoticed that suddenly attains prominence or value

**sleeping bag** n **:** a warmly lined bag for sleeping esp. outdoors

**sleeping car** n **:** SLEEPER 3

**sleeping pill** n **:** a drug in tablet or capsule form taken to induce sleep

**sleeping sickness** n **:** a serious disease that is prevalent in tropical Africa, is marked by fever, lethargy, tremors, and loss of weight, and is caused by protozoans transmitted by the tsetse fly

**sleep·walk·er** \'slēp-,wȯ-kər\ n **:** one who walks in his sleep

**sleepy** \'slē-pē\ adj **sleep·i·er; -est 1 :** ready for sleep **2 :** quietly inactive — **sleep·i·ly** \'slē-pə-lē\ adv — **sleep·i·ness** \-pē-nəs\ n

**sleet** \'slēt\ n **1 :** partly frozen rain **2 :** GLAZE 1 — **sleet** vb — **sleety** adj

**sleeve** \'slēv\ n **1 :** the part of a garment covering the arm **2 :** a tubular part fitting over another part — **sleeve·less** adj

¹**sleigh** \'slā\ n **:** a vehicle on runners for use on snow or ice

²**sleigh** vb **:** to drive or travel in a sleigh

**sleight** \'slīt\ *n* 1 : TRICK 2 : DEXTERITY

**sleight of hand** : a trick requiring skillful manual manipulation

**slen·der** \'slen-dər\ *adj* 1 : SLIM, THIN 2 : WEAK, SLIGHT 3 : MEAGER, INADEQUATE

**slen·der·ize** \-də-,rīz\ *vb* -ized; -iz·ing : to make slender

**sleuth** \'slüth\ *n* [short for *sleuthhound* bloodhound, fr. ME, fr. *sleuth* track of an animal or person, fr. ON *sloth*] : DETECTIVE

¹**slew** \'slü\ *past of* SLAY

²**slew** *var of* SLUE

¹**slice** \'slīs\ *n* 1 : a thin flat piece cut from something 2 : a wedge-shaped blade (as for serving fish) 3 : a flight of a ball (as in golf) that curves in the direction of the dominant hand of the player propelling it

²**slice** *vb* sliced; slic·ing 1 : to cut a slice from; *also* : to cut into slices 2 : to hit (a ball) so that a slice results

¹**slick** \'slik\ *vb* : to make smooth or sleek

²**slick** *adj* 1 : very smooth : SLIPPERY 2 : CLEVER, SMART

³**slick** *n* 1 : a smooth patch of water covered with a film of oil 2 : a popular magazine printed on coated stock

**slick·er** \'slik-ər\ *n* 1 : a long loose raincoat 2 : a clever crook

¹**slide** \'slīd\ *vb* slid \'slid\; slid·ing \'slīd-iŋ\ 1 : to move smoothly along a surface 2 : to fall by a loss of support 3 : to slip along quietly

²**slide** *n* 1 : an act or instance of sliding 2 : a fall of a mass of earth or snow down a hillside 3 : something (as a cover or fastener) that operates by sliding 4 : a surface on which something slides 5 : a plate from which a picture may be projected 6 : a glass plate on which a specimen can be placed for examination under a microscope

**slid·er** \'slīd-ər\ *n* 1 : one that slides 2 : a baseball pitch that looks like a fast ball but curves slightly

**slide rule** *n* : an instrument for rapid calculation consisting of a ruler and a medial slide graduated with logarithmic scales

**slier** *comparative of* SLY

**sliest** *superlative of* SLY

¹**slight** \'slīt\ *adj* 1 : SLENDER; *also* : FRAIL 2 : SCANTY, MEAGER 3 : UNIMPORTANT — **slight·ly** *adv*

²**slight** *vb* 1 : to treat as unimportant 2 : to ignore discourteously 3 : to perform or attend to carelessly **syn** neglect, overlook, disregard

³**slight** *n* : a humiliating discourtesy

¹**slim** \'slim\ *adj* slim·mer; slim·mest [Dutch, bad, inferior, fr. Middle Dutch *slimp* crooked, bad] 1 : SLENDER, SLIGHT, THIN 2 : SCANTY, MEAGER

²**slim** *vb* slimmed; slim·ming : to make or become slender

**slime** \'slīm\ *n* 1 : sticky mud 2 : a slippery substance (as on the skin of a slug or catfish) — **slimy** *adj*

**slim–jim** \'slim-,jim, -,jim\ *n* : one that is notably slender

¹**sling** \'sliŋ\ *vb* slung \'sləŋ\; sling·ing \'sliŋ-iŋ\ 1 : to hurl with a sling 2 : to throw forcibly : FLING 3 : to place in a sling for hoisting or carrying

²**sling** *n* 1 : a short strap with strings attached for hurling stones or shot 2 : a strap, rope, or chain for holding securely something being lifted, lowered, or carried

**sling·shot** \'sliŋ-,shät\ *n* : a forked stick with elastic bands for shooting small stones or shot

**slink** \'sliŋk\ *vb* slunk \'sləŋk\ *also* slinked \'sliŋkt\; slink·ing 1 : to move stealthily or furtively 2 : to move sinuously — **slinky** *adj*

¹**slip** \'slip\ *vb* slipped; slip·ping 1 : to escape quietly or secretly 2 : to slide along or cause to slide along smoothly 3 : to make a mistake 4 : to pass unnoticed or undone 5 : to fall off from a standard or level

²**slip** *n* 1 : a ramp for repairing ships 2 : a ship's berth between two piers 3 : secret or hurried departure, escape, or evasion 4 : a sudden mishap 5 : BLUNDER 6 : PILLOWCASE 7 : a woman's one-piece garment worn under a dress

³**slip** *n* 1 : a shoot or twig from a plant for planting or grafting 2 : a long narrow strip; *esp* : one of paper used for a record ⟨deposit ~⟩

⁴**slip** *vb* slipped; slip·ping : to take slips from (a plant)

**slip·knot** \'slip-,nät\ *n* : a knot that slips along the rope around which it is made

**slipped disk** *n* : a protrusion of one of the cartilage disks between vertebrae with pressure on spinal nerves resulting esp. in low back pain

**slip·per** \'slip-ər\ *n* : a light low shoe that may be easily slipped on and off

**slip·pery** \'slip-(ə-)rē\ *adj* slip·peri·er; -est 1 : icy, wet, smooth, or greasy enough to cause one to fall or lose one's hold 2 : TRICKY, UNRELIABLE — **slip·peri·ness** *n*

**slip·shod** \'slip-'shäd\ *adj* : SLOVENLY, CARELESS ⟨~ work⟩

**slip·stream** \'slip-,strēm\ *n* : the stream of air driven aft by the propeller of an aircraft

**slip–up** \'slip-,əp\ *n* 1 : MISTAKE 2 : ACCIDENT

¹**slit** \'slit\ *vb* slit; slit·ting 1 : SLASH 2 : to cut off or away

²**slit** *n* : a long narrow cut or opening

**slith·er** \'slith-ər\ *vb* : to slip or glide along like a snake — **slith·ery** *adj*

**sliv·er** \'sliv-ər\ *n* : SPLINTER

**slob** \'släb\ *n* : a slovenly or boorish person

**slob·ber** \'släb-ər\ *vb* : to dribble saliva — **slobber** *n*

**sloe** \'slō\ *n* : the fruit of the blackthorn

**slo·gan** \'slō-gən\ *n* [alter. of earlier *slogorn*, fr. ScGael *sluagh-ghairm* army cry] : a word or phrase expressing the spirit or aim of a party, group, or cause

**sloop** \'slüp\ *n* : a sailing boat with one mast, a fore-and-aft rig, and a single jib

**¹slop** \'släp\ *n* **1** : thin tasteless drink or liquid food — usu. used in pl. **2** : food waste or gruel for animal feed **3** : body and toilet waste — usu. used in pl.

**²slop** *vb* **slopped; slop·ping 1** : SPILL **2** : to feed with slop ⟨~ hogs⟩

**¹slope** \'slōp\ *vb* **sloped; slop·ing** : SLANT, INCLINE

**²slope** *n* **1** : ground that forms an incline **2** : upward or downward slant or degree of slant **3** : the part of a landmass draining into a particular ocean

**slop·py** \'släp-ē\ *adj* **slop·pi·er; -est 1** : MUDDY, SLUSHY **2** : SLOVENLY, MESSY

**slosh** \'släsh\ *vb* **1** : to flounder through or splash about in or with water, mud, or slush **2** : to move with a splashing motion

**slot** \'slät\ *n* **1** : a long narrow opening or groove **2** : a position in a sequence

**slot car** *n* : an electric toy racing automobile that runs on a track

**sloth** \'slòth, 'slōth\ *n, pl* **sloths** \with ths *or* thz\ **1** : LAZINESS, INDOLENCE **2** : a slow-moving So. and Central American mammal related to the armadillos — **sloth·ful** *adj*

**slot machine** *n* **1** : a machine whose operation is begun by dropping a coin into a slot **2** : a coin-operated gambling machine that pays off according to the matching of symbols on wheels spun by a handle

**¹slouch** \'slauch\ *n* **1** : a loose or drooping gait or posture **2** : a lazy or incompetent person

**²slouch** *vb* : to walk, stand, or sit with a slouch : SLUMP

**¹slough** \'slau, *3 usu* 'slü\ *n* **1** : SWAMP **2** : a muddy place **3** : a discouraged state of mind

**²slough** \'sləf\ *or* **sluff** *n* : something (as a snake's skin) that may be shed

**³slough** \'sləf\ *or* **sluff** *vb* : to cast off

**slov·en** \'sləv-ən\ *n* [ME *sloveyn* rascal, perh. fr. Flem *sloovin* woman of low character] : an untidy person

**slov·en·ly** \'sləv-ən-lē\ *adj* **1** : untidy in dress or person **2** : lazily or carelessly done : SLIPSHOD

**¹slow** \'slō\ *adj* **1** : SLUGGISH; *also* : dull in mind : STUPID **2** : moving, flowing, or proceeding at less than the usual speed **3** : taking more than the usual time **4** : registering behind the correct time **5** : not lively : BORING **syn** dilatory, laggard, deliberate, leisurely — **slow** *adv* — **slow·ly** *adv* — **slow·ness** *n*

**²slow** *vb* **1** : to make slow : hold back **2** : to go slower

**slow motion** *n* : motion-picture action photographed so as to appear much slower than normal

**sludge** \'sləj\ *n* : a slushy mass : OOZE; *esp* : solid matter produced by sewage treatment processes

**slue** \'slü\ *vb* **slued; slu·ing** : TURN, VEER, SKID — **slue** *n*

**¹slug** \'sləg\ *n* : a slimy wormlike mollusk related to the snails

**²slug** *n* **1** : a small mass of metal; *esp* : BULLET **2** : a metal disk for use (as in a slot machine) in place of a coin **3** : a single drink of liquor

**³slug** *vb* **slugged; slug·ging** : to strike forcibly and heavily — **slug·ger** *n*

**slug·gard** \'sləg-ərd\ *n* : a lazy person

**slug·gish** \'sləg-ish\ *adj* **1** : SLOTHFUL, LAZY **2** : slow in movement or flow **3** : STAGNANT, DULL — **slug·gish·ly** *adv* — **slug·gish·ness** *n*

**¹sluice** \'slüs\ *n* **1** : an artificial passage for water with a gate for controlling the flow; *also* : the gate so used **2** : a channel that carries off surplus water **3** : an inclined trough or flume for washing ore or floating logs

**²sluice** *vb* **sluiced; sluic·ing 1** : to draw off through a sluice **2** : to wash with running water : FLUSH **3** : to transport (as logs) in a sluice

**sluice·way** \'slüs-,wā\ *n* : an artificial channel into which water is let by a sluice

**¹slum** \'sləm\ *n* : a thickly populated area marked by poverty and dirty or deteriorated houses

**²slum** *vb* **slummed; slum·ming** : to visit slums esp. out of curiosity

**¹slum·ber** \'sləm-bər\ *vb* **slumbered; slum·ber·ing** \-b(ə-)riŋ\ **1** : DOZE; *also* : SLEEP **2** : to be in a sluggish or torpid state

**²slumber** *n* : SLEEP

**slum·ber·ous** *or* **slum·brous** \'sləmb(ə-)rəs\ *adj* **1** : SLUMBERING, SLEEPY **2** : PEACEFUL, INACTIVE

**slum·lord** \'sləm-,lòrd\ *n* : a landlord who receives unusually large profits from substandard properties

**slump** \'sləmp\ *vb* **1** : to sink down suddenly : COLLAPSE **2** : SLOUCH **3** : to decline sharply — **slump** *n*

**slung** *past of* SLING

**slunk** *past of* SLINK

**¹slur** \'slər\ *vb* **slurred; slur·ring 1** : to slide or slip over without due mention or emphasis **2** : to perform two or more successive notes of different pitch in a smooth or connected way

**²slur** *n* : a curved line ⌣ or ⌢ connecting notes to be slurred; *also* : a group of slurred notes

**³slur** *n* : a slighting remark : ASPERSION

**slurp** \'slərp\ *vb* : to eat or drink noisily — **slurp** *n*

**slur·ry** \'slər-ē\ *n, pl* **slur·ries** : a watery mixture of insoluble matter

**slush** \'sləsh\ *n* **1** : partly melted or watery snow **2** : soft mud — **slushy** *adj*

**slut** \'slət\ *n* **1** : a slovenly woman **2** : PROSTITUTE — **slut·tish** \'slət-ish\ *adj*

**sly** \'slī\ *adj* **sli·er** *also* **sly·er** \'slī(-ə)r\; **sli·est** *also* **sly·est** \'slī-əst\ **1** : CRAFTY, CUNNING **2** : SECRETIVE, FURTIVE **3** : ROGUISH **syn** tricky, wily, artful — **sly·ly** *adv* — **sly·ness** *n*

**sm** *abbr* small

**Sm** *symbol* samarium

**SM** *abbr* **1** master of science **2** sergeant major **3** Society of Mary

**SMA** *abbr* sergeant major of the army

¹**smack** \'smak\ *n* **:** characteristic flavor; *also* **:** a slight trace

²**smack** *vb* **1 :** to have a taste **2 :** to have a trace or suggestion

³**smack** *vb* **1 :** to move (the lips) so as to make a sharp noise **2 :** to kiss or slap with a loud noise

⁴**smack** *n* **1 :** a sharp noise made by the lips **2 :** a noisy slap •

⁵**smack** *adv* **:** squarely and sharply

⁶**smack** *n* **:** a sailing ship used in fishing

⁷**smack** *n, slang* **:** HEROIN

**SMaj** *abbr* sergeant major

¹**small** \'smȯl\ *adj* **1 :** little in size or amount **2 :** few in number **3 :** TRIFLING, UNIMPORTANT **4 :** operating on a limited scale **5 :** MEAN, PETTY **6 :** made up of little things **syn** diminutive, petite, wee, tiny, minute — **small·ish** *adj* — **small·ness** *n*

²**small** *n* **:** a small part or product ⟨the ~ of the back⟩

**small·pox** \'smȯl-,päks\ *n* **:** a contagious virus disease marked by fever and eruption

**small-time** \'smȯl-'tīm\ *adj* **:** insignificant in performance and standing **:** MINOR — **small-tim·er** \-'tī-mər\ *n*

¹**smart** \'smärt\ *vb* **1 :** to cause or feel a stinging pain **2 :** to feel or endure distress — **smart** *n*

²**smart** *adj* **1 :** making one smart ⟨a ~ blow⟩ **2 :** mentally quick **:** BRIGHT **3 :** WITTY, CLEVER **4 :** STYLISH **syn** knowing, quick-witted, intelligent — **smart·ly** *adv* — **smart·ness** *n*

**smart al·eck** \'smärt-,al-ik\ *n* **:** a person given to obnoxious cleverness

¹**smash** \'smash\ *vb* **1 :** to break or be broken into pieces **2 :** to move forward with force and shattering effect **3 :** to destroy utterly **:** WRECK

²**smash** *n* **1 :** a smashing blow; *esp* **:** a hard overhand stroke in tennis **2 :** the act or sound of smashing **3 :** collision of vehicles **:** CRASH **4 :** COLLAPSE, RUIN; *esp* **:** BANKRUPTCY **5 :** a striking success **:** HIT — **smash** *adj*

**smat·ter·ing** \'smat-ə-riŋ\ *n* **1 :** superficial knowledge **2 :** a small scattered number or amount

¹**smear** \'smiər\ *n* **:** a spot left by an oily or sticky substance

²**smear** *vb* **1 :** to overspread with something oily or sticky **2 :** SMUDGE, SOIL **3 :** to injure by slander or insults

¹**smell** \'smel\ *vb* **smelled** \'smeld\ *or* **smelt** \'smelt\; **smell·ing 1 :** to perceive the odor of by sense organs of the nose; *also* **:** to detect or seek with or as if with these organs **2 :** to have or give off an odor

²**smell** *n* **1 :** the process or power of perceiving odor; *also* **:** the special sense by which one perceives odor **2 :** ODOR, SCENT **3 :** an act of smelling — **smelly** *adj*

**smelling salts** *n pl* **:** an aromatic preparation used as a stimulant and restorative (as to relieve faintness)

¹**smelt** \'smelt\ *n, pl* **smelts** *or* **smelt** **:** any of several small food fishes of coastal or fresh waters

²**smelt** *vb* **:** to melt or fuse (ore) in order to separate the metal; *also* **:** REFINE

**smelt·er** \'smel-tər\ *n* **1 :** one that smelts **2 :** an establishment for smelting

**smid·gen** *or* **smid·geon** *or* **smid·gin** \'smij-ən\ *n* **:** a small amount **:** BIT

**smi·lax** \'smī-,laks\ *n* **1 :** any of various mostly climbing and prickly plants related to the lilies **2 :** an ornamental asparagus

¹**smile** \'smīl\ *vb* **smiled; smil·ing 1 :** to look with a smile **2 :** to be favorable **3 :** to express by a smile

²**smile** *n* **:** a change of facial expression to express amusement, pleasure, or affection

**smirch** \'smərch\ *vb* **1 :** to make dirty or stained **2 :** to bring disgrace on — **smirch** *n*

**smirk** \'smərk\ *vb* **:** to wear a self-conscious or conceited smile **:** SIMPER — **smirk** *n*

**smite** \'smīt\ *vb* **smote** \'smōt\; **smit·ten** \'smit-ᵊn\ *or* **smote; smit·ing** \'smīt-iŋ\ **1 :** to strike heavily; *also* **:** to kill by striking **2 :** to affect as if by a heavy blow

**smith** \'smith\ *n* **:** a worker in metals; *esp* **:** BLACKSMITH

**smith·er·eens** \,smith-ə-'rēnz\ *n pl* [IrGael *smidirín*] **:** FRAGMENTS, BITS

**smithy** \'smith-ē\ *n, pl* **smith·ies :** a smith's workshop

¹**smock** \'smäk\ *n* **:** a loose garment worn over other clothes as a protection

²**smock** *vb* **:** to gather (cloth) in regularly spaced tucks — **smock·ing** *n*

**smog** \'smäg, 'smȯg\ *n* [blend of *smoke* and *fog*] **:** a fog made heavier and darker by smoke and chemical fumes — **smog·gy** *adj*

¹**smoke** \'smōk\ *n* **1 :** the gas from burning material (as coal, wood, or tobacco) in which are suspended particles of soot **2 :** a suspension of solid or liquid particles in a gas **3 :** vapor resulting from action of heat on moisture — **smoke·less** *adj* — **smoky** *adj*

²**smoke** *vb* **smoked; smok·ing 1 :** to emit smoke **2 :** to inhale and exhale the fumes of burning tobacco; *also* **:** to use in smoking ⟨~ a pipe⟩ **3 :** to stupefy or drive away by smoke **4 :** to discolor with smoke **5 :** to cure (as meat) with smoke — **smok·er** *n*

**smoke jumper** *n* **:** a forest-fire fighter who parachutes to locations otherwise difficult to reach

**smoke·stack** \'smōk-,stak\ *n* **:** a chimney or funnel through which smoke and gases are discharged

**smol·der** *or* **smoul·der** \'smōl-dər\ *vb* **smol·dered** *or* **smoul·dered; smol·der·ing** *or* **smoul·der·ing** \-d(ə-)riŋ\ **1 :** to burn and smoke without flame **2 :** to burn inwardly — **smolder** *n*

**smooch** \'smüch\ *vb* **:** KISS, PET — **smooch** *n*

¹**smooth** \'smüth\ *adj* **1 :** not rough or uneven **2 :** not jarring or jolting **3 :** BLAND, MILD **4 :** fluent in speech and agreeable in manner **syn** even,

flat, level, diplomatic, suave, urbane — **smooth·ly** *adv* — **smooth·ness** *n*

²**smooth** *vb* **1 :** to make smooth **2 :** to free from trouble or difficulty

**smooth muscle** *n* **:** muscle with no cross striations that is typical of visceral organs and is not under voluntary control

**smor·gas·bord** \'smȯr-gǝs-ˌbȯrd\ *n* [Sw *smörgasbord*, fr. *smörgas* open sandwich + *bord* table] **:** a luncheon or supper buffet consisting of many foods

**smote** *past of* SMITE

¹**smoth·er** \'smǝth-ǝr\ *n* **1 :** thick stifling smoke **2 :** dense fog, spray, foam, or dust **3 :** a confused multitude of things **:** WELTER

²**smother** *vb* **1 :** to kill by depriving of air **2 :** SUPPRESS **3 :** to cover thickly

**SMSgt** *abbr* senior master sergeant

¹**smudge** \'smǝj\ *vb* **smudged; smudg·ing :** to soil or blur by rubbing or smearing

²**smudge** *n* **1 :** thick smoke **2 :** a dirty or blurred spot — **smudgy** *adj*

**smug** \'smǝg\ *adj* **smug·ger; smug·gest :** conscious of one's virtue and importance **:** SELF-SATISFIED — **smug·ly** *adv* — **smug·ness** *n*

**smug·gle** \'smǝg-ǝl\ *vb* **smug·gled; smug·gling** \-(ǝ-)liŋ\ **1 :** to import or export secretly, illegally, or without paying the duties required by law **2 :** to convey secretly — **smug·gler** \'smǝg-lǝr\ *n*

**smut** \'smǝt\ *n* **1 :** something (as soot) that smudges; *also* **:** SMUDGE, SPOT **2 :** indecent language or matter **3 :** any of various destructive fungous diseases of plants — **smut·ty** *adj*

**smutch** \'smǝch\ *n* **:** SMUDGE

**Sn** *symbol* [LL *stannum*] tin

**snack** \'snak\ *n* **:** a light meal **:** BITE

**snaf·fle** \'snaf-ǝl\ *n* **:** a simple jointed bit for a horse's bridle

**snag** \'snag\ *n* **1 :** a stump or piece of a tree esp. when under water **2 :** an unexpected difficulty **syn** obstacle, obstruction, impediment, bar

²**snag** *vb* **snagged; snag·ging 1 :** to become caught on or as if on a snag **2 :** to seize quickly **:** SNATCH

**snail** \'snāl\ *n* **:** a small mollusk with a spiral shell into which it can withdraw

**snake** \'snāk\ *n* **1 :** a long-bodied limbless crawling reptile **:** SERPENT **2 :** a treacherous person — **snaky** *adj*

**snake·bird** \'snāk-ˌbǝrd\ *n* **:** any of several fish-eating birds related to the cormorants but having a long slender neck and sharp-pointed bill

**snake·bite** \-ˌbīt\ *n* **:** the bite of a snake and esp. a venomous snake

¹**snap** \'snap\ *vb* **snapped; snap·ping 1 :** to grasp or slash at something with the teeth **2 :** to utter sharp or angry words **3 :** to get or buy quickly **4 :** to break suddenly with a sharp sound **5 :** to give a sharp cracking noise **6 :** to throw with a quick motion **7 :** FLASH ⟨her eyes *snapped*⟩ **8 :** to put a football into play — **snap·per** *n* — **snap·pish** *adj* — **snap·py** *adj*

²**snap** *n* **1 :** the act or sound of snapping **2 :** a short period of cold weather **3 :** a catch or fastening that closes with a click **4 :** a thin brittle cookie **5 :** ENERGY, VIM; *also* **:** smartness of movement **6 :** the putting of the ball into play in football **7 :** something very easy to do **:** CINCH

**snap bean** *n* **:** a bean grown primarily for its young tender pods that are usu. broken in pieces and cooked as a vegetable

**snap·drag·on** \'snap-ˌdrag-ǝn\ *n* **:** a garden plant with long spikes of showy 2-lipped flowers

**snapping turtle** *n* **:** either of two large edible American turtles with powerful jaws and a strong musky odor

**snap·shot** \'snap-ˌshät\ *n* **:** a photograph made by rapid exposure with a hand-held camera

**snare** \'snaǝr\ *n* **:** a trap often consisting of a noose for catching birds or mammals — **snare** *vb*

¹**snarl** \'snärl\ *n* **:** TANGLE

²**snarl** *vb* **:** to cause to become knotted and intertwined

³**snarl** *vb* **:** to growl angrily or threateningly

⁴**snarl** *n* **:** an angry ill-tempered growl

¹**snatch** \'snach\ *vb* **1 :** to try to grasp something suddenly **2 :** to seize or take away suddenly **syn** clutch, seize

²**snatch** *n* **1 :** an act of snatching **2 :** a short period **3 :** something brief or fragmentary ⟨~es of song⟩

¹**sneak** \'snēk\ *vb* **sneaked** \'snēkt\ *also* **snuck** \'snǝk\; **sneak·ing :** to move, act, or take in a furtive manner — **sneak·ing·ly** *adv*

²**sneak** *n* **1 :** one who acts in a furtive or shifty manner **2 :** a stealthy or furtive move or escape — **sneaky** *adj*

**sneak·er** \'snē-kǝr\ *n* **:** a canvas sports shoe with pliable rubber sole

**sneer** \'sniǝr\ *vb* **:** to show scorn or contempt by curling the lip or by a jeering tone — **sneer** *n*

**sneeze** \'snēz\ *vb* **sneezed; sneez·ing :** to force the breath out with sudden and involuntary violence — **sneeze** *n*

**snick·er** \'snik-ǝr\ *n* **:** a partly suppressed laugh — **snicker** *vb*

**snide** \'snīd\ *adj* **1 :** MEAN, LOW ⟨a ~ trick⟩ **2 :** slyly disparaging ⟨a ~ remark⟩

**sniff** \'snif\ *vb* **1 :** to draw air audibly up the nose **2 :** to show disdain or scorn **3 :** to detect by or as if by smelling — **sniff** *n*

**snif·fle** \'snif-ǝl\ *n* **1 :** SNUFFLE **2** *pl* **:** a head cold marked by nasal discharge — **sniffle** *vb*

¹**snip** \'snip\ *n* **1 :** a fragment snipped off **2 :** a simple stroke of the scissors or shears

²**snip** *vb* **snipped; snip·ping :** to cut off by bits **:** CLIP; *also* **:** to remove by cutting off

**snipe** \'snīp\ *n, pl* **snipes** *or* **snipe :** any of several game birds that occur esp. in marshy areas and resemble the related woodcocks

²**snipe** \vb **sniped; snip·ing :** to shoot at an exposed enemy from a concealed position usu. at long range

**snip·py** \'snip-ē\ adj **snip·pi·er; -est : CURT, SNAPPISH**

**snips** \'snips\ n pl : hand shears used esp. for cutting sheet metal ⟨tin ~⟩

**snitch** \'snich\ vb : PILFER, SNATCH

**sniv·el** \'sniv-əl\ vb **sniv·eled** or **sniv·elled; sniv·el·ing** or **sniv·el·ling** \-(ə-)liŋ\ **1 :** to have a running nose, also : SNUFFLE **2 :** to whine in a snuffling manner – **snivel** n

**snob** \'snäb\ n [obs. snob member of the lower classes, fr. E dial., shoemaker] **:** one who seeks association with persons of higher social position than himself and looks down on those he considers inferior – **snob·bish** adj – **snob·bish·ly** adv – **snob·bish·ness** n

**snob·bery** \'snäb-(ə-)rē\ n, pl **-ber·ies :** snobbish conduct

¹**snoop** \'snüp\ vb [D snoepen to buy or eat on the sly] **:** to pry in a furtive or meddlesome way

²**snoop** n : a prying meddlesome person

**snooty** \'snüt-ē\ adj **snoot·i·er; -est : DISDAINFUL, SNOBBISH**

**snooze** \'snüz\ vb **snoozed snooz·ing :** to take a nap : DOZE – **snooze** n

**snore** \'snōr\ vb **snored; snor·ing :** to breathe with a rough hoarse noise while sleeping – **snore** n

**snor·kel** \'snor-kəl\ n : a tube projecting above the water used by swimmers for breathing with the head under water – **snorkel** vb

**snort** \'snort\ vb : to force air violently and noisily through the nose ⟨his horse ~ed⟩ – **snort** n

**snout** \'snaut\ n **1 :** a long projecting muzzle (as of a swine) **2 :** a usu. large or grotesque nose

¹**snow** \'snō\ n **1 :** crystals of ice formed from the vapor of water in the air **2 :** a descent or shower of snow crystals – **snowy** adj

²**snow** vb **1 :** to fall or cause to fall in or as snow **2 :** to cover or shut in with or as if with snow

**snow·ball** \'snō-,bol\ vb : to increase or expand at a rapidly accelerating rate

**snow·bank** \'snō-,baŋk\ n : a mound or slope of snow

**snow·drift** \'snō-,drift\ n : a bank of drifted snow

**snow·drop** \-,dräp\ n : a plant with narrow leaves and a nodding white flower that blooms early in the spring

**snow·fall** \-,fol\ n : a fall of snow

**snow fence** n : a barrier across the path of prevailing winds to deflect drifting snow

**snow·field** \'snō-,fēld\ n : a mass of perennial snow at the head of a glacier

**snow·mo·bile** \'snō-mō-,bēl\ n : any of various automotive vehicles for travel on snow – **snow·mo·bil·er** \-,bē-lər\ n – **snow·mo·bil·ing** \-liŋ\ n

**snow·plow** \'snō-,plaù\ n : a device for clearing away snow

¹**snow·shoe** \-,shü\ n : a light frame of wood strung with thongs that is worn under the shoe to prevent sinking down into soft snow

²**snowshoe** vb **snow·shoed; snow·shoe·ing :** to travel on snowshoes

**snow·storm** \-,storm\ n : a storm of falling snow

**snowy** \'snō-ē\ adj **snow·i·er; -est 1 :** marked by snow **2 :** white as snow

**snub** \'snəb\ vb **snubbed; snub·bing 1 :** to treat with disdain : SLIGHT **2 :** to slow up or check the motion of – **snub** n

**snub-nosed** \'snəb-'nōzd\ adj **:** having a nose slightly turned up at the end

**snuck** past of SNEAK

¹**snuff** \'snəf\ vb **1 :** to pinch off the charred end of (a candle) **2 :** to put out (a candle) – **snuff·er** n

²**snuff** vb **1 :** to draw forcibly into or through the nose **2 :** SMELL

³**snuff** n **1 :** SNIFF **2 :** pulverized tobacco

**snuf·fle** \'snəf-əl\ vb **snuf·fled; snuf·fling** \-(ə-)liŋ\ **1 :** to snuff or sniff audibly and repeatedly **2 :** to breathe with a sniffing sound – **snuffle** n

**snug** \'snəg\ adj **snug·ger; snug·gest 1 :** COMFORTABLE, COZY **2 :** CONCEALED **3 :** fitting closely : TIGHT – **snug·ly** adv – **snug·ness** n

**snug·gle** \'snəg-əl\ vb **snug·gled; snug·gling** \-(ə-)liŋ\ **:** to curl up or draw close comfortably : NESTLE

¹**so** \(')sō\ adv **1 :** in the manner indicated **2 :** in the same way **3 :** to the extent indicated **4 :** THEREFORE **5 :** FINALLY **6 :** THUS

²**so** conj : for that reason ⟨he wanted it, ~ he took it⟩

³**so** \,sō, 'sō\ pron **1 :** the same ⟨became chairman and remained ~⟩ **2 :** approximately that ⟨I'd like a dozen or ~⟩

⁴**so** abbr south; southern

**SO** abbr **1** seller's option **2** strikeout

¹**soak** \'sōk\ vb **1 :** to remain in a liquid **2 :** WET, SATURATE **3 :** to draw in by or as if by absorption **syn** drench, steep, impregnate

²**soak** n **1 :** the act of soaking **2 :** the liquid in which something is soaked **3 :** DRUNKARD

**soap** \'sōp\ n : a cleansing substance made usu. by action of alkali on fat – **soap** vb – **soapy** adj

**soap opera** n [fr. its frequently being sponsored by soap manufacturers] **:** a radio or television daytime serial drama

**soap·stone** \'sōp-,stōn\ n : a soft stone having a soapy feel and containing talc

**soar** \'sōr\ vb : to fly upward or at a height on or as if on wings

**sob** \'säb\ vb **sobbed; sob·bing :** to weep with convulsive heavings of the chest or contractions of the throat – **sob** n

**so·ber** \'sō-bər\ adj **so·ber·er** \-bər-ər\; **so·ber·est** \-b(ə-)rəst\ **1 :** temperate in the use of liquor **2 :** not drunk **3 :** serious or grave in mood or disposition **4 :** not affected by passion or prejudice **syn** solemn, earnest –

**so·ber·ly** adv — **so·ber·ness** n

**so·bri·ety** \sə-'brī-ət-ē, sō-\ n : the quality or state of being sober

**so·bri·quet** \'sō-bri-ˌkā, -ˌket\ n : NICKNAME

**soc** abbr social; society

**so-called** \'sō-'kȯld\ adj : commonly or popularly but often inaccurately so termed

**soc·cer** \'säk-ər\ n [by shortening & alter. fr. association football] : a football game played on a field by two teams with a round inflated ball

¹**so·cia·ble** \'sō-shə-bəl\ adj 1 : liking companionship : FRIENDLY 2 : characterized by pleasant social relations **syn** gracious, cordial, affable, genial — **so·cia·bil·i·ty** \ˌsō-shə-'bil-ət-ē\ n — **so·cia·bly** \'sō-shə-blē\ adv

²**sociable** n : an informal social gathering

¹**so·cial** \'sō-shəl\ adj 1 : marked by pleasant companionship with one's friends 2 : naturally living or growing in groups or communities ⟨~ insects⟩ 3 : of or relating to human society, the interaction of the group and its members, and the welfare of these members ⟨~ behavior⟩ 4 : of, relating to, or based on rank in a particular society ⟨~ circles⟩; also : of or relating to fashionable society 5 : SOCIALIST — **so·cial·ly** \-ē\ adv

²**social** n : a social gathering

**social disease** n 1 : VENEREAL DISEASE 2 : a disease (as tuberculosis) whose occurrence is directly related to social and economic factors

**so·cial·ism** \'sō-shə-ˌliz-əm\ n : a theory of social organization based on government ownership, management, or control of the means of production and the distribution and exchange of goods — **so·cial·ist** \'sōsh-(ə-)ləst\ n or adj — **so·cial·is·tic** \ˌsō-shə-'lis-tik\ adj

**so·cial·ite** \'sō-shə-ˌlīt\ n : a person prominent in fashionable society

**so·cial·ize** \'sō-shə-ˌlīz\ vb **-ized**; **-iz·ing** 1 : to regulate according to the theory and practice of socialism 2 : to adapt to social needs or uses 3 : to participate actively in a social gathering — **so·cial·iza·tion** \ˌsōsh-(ə-)lə-'zā-shən\ n

**socialized medicine** n : medical and hospital services administered by an organized group and paid for by funds obtained usu. by assessments, taxation, or philanthropy

**social work** n : services, activities, or methods concerned with aiding the economically underprivileged and socially maladjusted — **social worker** n

**so·ci·ety** \sə-'sī-ət-ē\ n, pl **-et·ies** [MF societé fr. L societat-, societas, fr. socius companion] 1 : COMPANIONSHIP 2 : community life 3 : a part of a community bound together by common interests and standards; esp : a leisure class indulging in social affairs 4 : a voluntary association of persons for common ends

**sociol** abbr sociology

**so·ci·ol·o·gy** \ˌsō-s(h)ē-'äl-ə-jē\ n : the study of the development and structure of society and social relationships — **so·ci·o·log·i·cal** \-ə-'läj-i-kəl\ adj — **so·ci·ol·o·gist** \-'äl-ə-jəst\ n

**so·cio·re·li·gious** \ˌsō-s(h)ē-ō-ri-'lij-əs\ adj : of, relating to, or involving both social and religious factors

¹**sock** \'säk\ n, pl **socks** 1 or pl **sox** : a stocking with a short leg 2 : comic drama

²**sock** vb : to hit, strike, or apply forcefully

³**sock** n : a vigorous blow : PUNCH

**sock·et** \'säk-ət\ n : an opening or hollow that receives and holds something

**sock in** vb : to close to takeoffs or landings by aircraft

¹**sod** \'säd\ n : the surface layer of the soil filled with roots (as of grass)

²**sod** vb **sod·ded**; **sod·ding** : to cover with sod or turfs

**so·da** \'sōd-ə\ n 1 : SODIUM CARBONATE 2 : SODIUM BICARBONATE 3 : SODIUM HYDROXIDE 4 : SODIUM 5 : SODA WATER 6 : a sweet drink of soda water, flavoring, and often ice cream

**soda pop** n : a carbonated, sweetened, and flavored soft drink

**soda water** n 1 : a beverage of water charged with carbon dioxide 2 : SODA POP

**sod·den** \'säd-ᵊn\ adj 1 : lacking spirit : DULLED 2 : SOAKED, DRENCHED 3 : heavy or doughy from being improperly cooked ⟨~ biscuits⟩

**so·di·um** \'sōd-ē-əm\ n : a soft waxy silver white metallic chemical element occurring in nature in combined form (as in salt)

**sodium bicarbonate** n : a white crystalline salt used in cooking and in medicine

**sodium carbonate** n : a carbonate of sodium used esp. in washing and bleaching textiles

**sodium chloride** n : SALT 1

**sodium hydroxide** n : a white brittle caustic substance used in making soap and rayon and in bleaching

**sodium nitrate** n : a crystalline salt found in rock in Chile and used as a fertilizer and in curing meat

**sodium thiosulfate** n : a hygroscopic crystalline salt used as a photographic fixing agent

**sod·omy** \'säd-ə-mē\ n [ME, fr. OF sodomie, fr. LL Sodoma Sodom; fr the homosexual proclivities of the men of the city (Gen 19:1–11)] 1 : copulation with a member of the same sex or with an animal 2 : noncoital and esp. anal or oral copulation with a member of the opposite sex

**so·ev·er** \sō-'ev-ər\ adv 1 • in any degree or manner ⟨how bad ~⟩ 2 : at all : of any kind ⟨any help ~⟩

**so·fa** \'sō-fə\ n [Ar ṣuffah long bench] : a couch usu. with upholstered back and arms

**soft** \'sȯft\ adj 1 : not hard or rough : NONVIOLENT 2 : RESTFUL, GENTLE, SOOTHING 3 : emotionally susceptible

**4** : not prepared to endure hardship **5** : not containing certain salts that prevent lathering ⟨~ water⟩ **6** : not alcoholic; *also* : less detrimental than a hard narcotic **7** : occurring at such a speed as to avoid destructive impact ⟨~ landing of a spacecraft on the moon⟩ **8** : BIODEGRADABLE ⟨a ~ detergent⟩ **syn** bland, mild — **soft·ly** \'sȯft-lē\ *adv* — **soft·ness** \'sȯf(t)-nəs\ *n*

**soft·ball** \'sȯf(t)-,bȯl\ *n* : a game similar to baseball played with a ball larger and softer than a baseball; *also* : the ball used in this game

**soft·bound** \-,baůnd\ *adj* : not bound in hard covers ⟨~ books⟩

**soft coal** *n* : bituminous coal

**soft·en** \'sȯ-fən\ *vb* **soft·ened; soft·en·ing** \'sȯf-(ə-)niŋ\ : to make or become soft — **soft·en·er** \-(ə-)nər\ *n*

**soft palate** *n* : the fold at the back of the hard palate that partially separates the mouth and the pharynx

**soft·ware** \'sȯft-,waȯr\ *n* : the entire set of programs, procedures, and related documentation associated with a system; *esp* : computer programs

¹**soft·wood** \-,wůd\ *n* **1** : the wood of a coniferous tree including both soft and hard woods **2** : a tree that yields softwood

²**softwood** *adj* **1** : having or made of softwood **2** : consisting of immature still pliable tissue ⟨~ cuttings⟩

**sog·gy** \'säg-ē\ *adj* **sog·gier; -est** : heavy with moisture ⟨SOAKED, SODDEN — **sog·gi·ly** \'säg-ə-lē\ *adv* — **sog·gi·ness** \-ē-nəs\ *n*

**soi·gné** *or* **soi·gnée** \swän-'yā\ *adj* : elegantly maintained; *esp* : WELL-GROOMED

¹**soil** \'sȯil\ *vb* **1** : CORRUPT, POLLUTE **2** : to make or become dirty **3** : STAIN, DISGRACE

²**soil** *n* **1** : STAIN, DEFILEMENT **2** : EXCREMENT, WASTE

³**soil** *n* **1** : firm land : EARTH **2** : the loose surface material of the earth in which plants grow **3** : COUNTRY, REGION

**soi·ree** *or* **soi·rée** \swä-'rā\ *n* [F *soirée* evening period, evening party, fr. MF, fr *soir* evening, fr. L *sero* at a late hour, fr. *serus* late] : an evening party

**so·journ** \'sō-,jərn, sō-'jərn\ *vb* : to dwell in a place temporarily — **sojourn** *n* — **so·journ·er** *n*

¹**sol** \'säl, 'sōl\ *n* — see MONEY table

²**sol** *n* : a fluid colloidal system

³**sol** *abbr* **1** solicitor **2** soluble **3** solution

¹**Sol** \'säl\ *n* : SUN

²**Sol** *abbr* Solomon

¹**so·lace** \'säl-əs\ *n* : COMFORT

²**solace** *vb* **so·laced; so·lac·ing** : to give solace to : CONSOLE

**so·lar** \'sō-lər\ *adj* **1** : of, derived from, or relating to the sun **2** : measured by the earth's course in relation to the sun ⟨the ~ year⟩ **3** : operated by or utilizing the sun's heat ⟨~ house⟩

**solar battery** *n* : a device for converting the energy of sunlight into electrical energy

¹**solar flare** *n* : a sudden temporary outburst of energy from a small area of the sun's surface

**so·lar·i·um** \sō-'lar-ē-əm, sə-\ *n, pl* **-ia** \-ē-ə\ *also* **-ums** : a room exposed to the sun; *esp* : a room in a hospital for exposure of the body to sunshine

**solar plexus** \'sō-lər-'plek-səs\ *n* **1** : a network of nerves situated behind the stomach **2** : the hollow below the lower end of the breastbone

**solar system** *n* : the sun with the group of celestial bodies that revolve about it

**solar wind** *n* : the continuous ejection of plasma from the sun's surface into and through interplanetary space

**sold** *past of* SELL

¹**sol·der** \'säd-ər, 'sȯd-\ *n* : a metallic alloy used when melted to mend or join metallic surfaces

²**solder** *vb* **soldered; sol·der·ing** \-(ə-)riŋ\ **1** : to unite or repair with solder **2** : to join securely : CEMENT

**soldering iron** *n* : a metal device for applying heat in soldering

¹**sol·dier** \'sōl-jər\ *n* [ME *soudier*, fr. OF, fr. *soulde* pay, fr. LL *solidus* a Roman coin, fr. L, solid] : a person in military service; *esp* : an enlisted man — **sol·dier·ly** *adj or adv*

²**soldier** *vb* **sol·diered; sol·dier·ing** \,sōlj-(ə-)riŋ\ **1** : to serve as a soldier **2** : to pretend to work while actually doing nothing

**soldier of fortune** : ADVENTURER

**sol·diery** \'sōlj-(ə-)rē\ *n* **1** : a body of soldiers **2** : the profession of soldiering

¹**sole** \'sōl\ *n* **1** : the undersurface of the foot **2** : the bottom of a shoe

²**sole** *vb* **soled; sol·ing** : to furnish (a shoe) with a sole

³**sole** *n* : any of various mostly small-mouthed flatfishes valued as food

⁴**sole** *adj* : ONLY, SINGLE — **sole·ly** \'sō(l)-lē\ *adv*

**so·le·cism** \'säl-ə-,siz-əm, 'sō-lə-\ *n* **1** : a mistake in grammar **2** : a breach of etiquette

**sol·emn** \'säl-əm\ *adj* **1** : marked by or observed with full religious ceremony **2** : FORMAL, CEREMONIOUS **3** : highly serious : GRAVE **4** : SOMBER, GLOOMY **syn** ceremonial, conventional, sober — **so·lem·ni·ty** \sə-'lem-nət-ē\ *n* — **sol·emn·ly** \'säl-əm-lē\ *adv* — **sol·emn·ness** *n*

**sol·em·nize** \'säl-əm-,nīz\ *vb* **-nized; -niz·ing** **1** : to observe or honor with solemnity **2** : to celebrate (a marriage) with religious rites — **sol·em·ni·za·tion** \,säl-əm-nə-'zā-shən\ *n*

**so·le·noid** \'sō-lə-,nȯid\ *n* : a coil of wire usu. in cylindrical form that when carrying a current acts like a magnet

**so·lic·it** \sə-'lis-ət\ *vb* **1** : ENTREAT, BEG **2** : to approach with a request or plea **3** : TEMPT, LURE **syn** ask, request — **so·lic·i·ta·tion** \-,lis-ə-'tā-shən\ *n*

**so·lic·i·tor** \sə-'lis-ət-ər\ *n* **1** : one that solicits **2** : LAWYER; *esp* : a legal official of a city or state

**so·lic·i·tous** \sə-'lis-ət-əs\ *adj* **1** : WORRIED, CONCERNED **2** : EAGER, WILLING **syn** careful, anxious — **so·lic·i·tous·ly** *adv*

**so·lic·i·tude** \sə-'lis-ə-,t(y)üd\ *n* : CONCERN, ANXIETY

**¹sol·id** \'säl-əd\ *adj* **1** : not hollow; *also* : written as one word without a hyphen ⟨a ~ compound⟩ **2** : having, involving, or dealing with three dimensions or with solids **3** : not loose or spongy : COMPACT ⟨a ~ mass of rock⟩; *also* : neither gaseous nor liquid : HARD, RIGID ⟨~ ice⟩ **4** : of good substantial quality or kind ⟨~ comfort⟩ **5** : UNANIMOUS, UNITED ⟨~ for pay increases⟩ **6** : thoroughly dependable : RELIABLE ⟨a ~ citizen⟩; *also* : serious in purpose or character ⟨~ reading⟩ **7** : of one substance or character — **solid** *adv* — **so·lid·i·ty** \sə-'lid-ət-ē\ *n* — **sol·id·ly** \'säl-əd-lē\ *adv* — **sol·id·ness** *n*

**²solid** *n* **1** : a geometrical figure (as a cube or sphere) having three dimensions **2** : a solid substance

**sol·i·dar·i·ty** \,säl-ə-'dar-ət-ē\ *n* : a unity of interest or purpose among a group

**solid geometry** *n* : a branch of geometry that deals with figures of three-dimensional space

**so·lid·i·fy** \sə-'lid-ə-,fī\ *vb* **-fied; -fy·ing** : to make or become solid — **so·lid·i·fi·ca·tion** \-,lid-ə-fə-'kā-shən\ *n*

**solid-state** *adj* : utilizing the electric, magnetic, or light-sensitive properties of solid materials : not utilizing electron tubes

**so·lil·o·quize** \sə-'lil-ə-,kwīz\ *vb* **-quized; -quiz·ing** : to talk to oneself : utter a soliloquy

**so·lil·o·quy** \sə-'lil-ə-kwē\ *n*, *pl* **-quies 1** : the act of talking to oneself **2** : a dramatic monologue that gives the illusion of being a series of unspoken reflections

**sol·i·taire** \'säl-ə-,taər\ *n* **1** : a single gem (as a diamond) set alone **2** : a card game played by one person alone

**sol·i·tary** \'säl'ə-,ter-ē\ *adj* **1** : being or living apart from others **2** : LONELY, SECLUDED **3** : SOLE, ONLY

**sol·i·tude** \'säl-ə-,t(y)üd\ *n* **1** : the state of being alone : SECLUSION **2** : a lonely place **syn** isolation

**soln** *abbr* solution

**¹so·lo** \'sō-lō\ *n*, *pl* **solos** [It, fr. *solo* alone, fr. L *solus*] **1** : a piece of music for a single voice or instrument with or without accompaniment **2** : an action in which there is only one performer — **solo** *adj or vb* — **so·lo·ist** *n*

**²solo** *adv* : without a companion : ALONE

**so·lon** \'sō-lən\ *n* **1** : a wise and skillful lawgiver **2** : a member of a legislative body

**sol·stice** \'säl-stəs\ *n* [ME, fr. OF, fr. L *solstitium*, fr. *sol* sun + *status*, pp. of *sistere* to come to a stop, cause to stand] : the time of the year when the sun is farthest north of the equator (**summer solstice**) about June 22 or farthest south (**winter solstice**) about Dec. 22 — **sol·sti·tial** \säl-'stish-əl\ *adj*

**sol·u·ble** \'säl-yə-bəl\ *adj* **1** : capable of being dissolved in or as if in a fluid **2** : capable of being solved or explained — **sol·u·bil·i·ty** \,säl-yə-'bil-ət-ē\ *n*

**so·lu·tion** \sə-'lü-shən\ *n* **1** : an action or process of solving a problem; *also* : an answer to a problem **2** : an act or the process by which one substance is homogeneously mixed with another usu. liquid substance; *also* : a mixture thus formed

**solve** \'sälv\ *vb* **solved; solv·ing** : to find the answer to or a solution for — **solv·able** *adj*

**sol·ven·cy** \'säl-vən-sē\ *n* : the condition of being solvent

**¹sol·vent** \-vənt\ *adj* **1** : able or sufficient to pay all legal debts **2** : dissolving or able to dissolve

**²solvent** *n* : a usu. liquid substance capable of dissolving or dispersing one or more other substances

**So·ma·li shilling** \sō-,mäl-ē-\ *n* : the shilling of Somalia

**som·ber** *or* **som·bre** \'säm-bər\ *adj* **1** : DARK, GLOOMY **2** : GRAVE, MELANCHOLY — **som·ber·ly** *adv*

**som·bre·ro** \səm-'bre(ə)r-ō\ *n*, *pl* **-ros** : a broad-brimmed felt hat worn esp. in the Southwest and in Mexico

**¹some** \(')səm\ *adj* **1** : one unspecified ⟨~ man called⟩ **2** : an unspecified or indefinite number of ⟨~ berries are ripe⟩ **3** : at least a few or a little ⟨~ years ago⟩

**²some** \'səm\ *pron* : a certain number or amount ⟨~ of them are here⟩ ⟨~ of it is missing⟩

**¹-some** \səm\ *adj suffix* : characterized by a (specified) thing, quality, state, or action ⟨awesome⟩

**²-some** *n suffix* : a group of (so many) members and esp. persons ⟨foursome⟩

**¹some·body** \'səm-,bäd-ē, -bəd-\ *pron* : some person

**²somebody** *n* : a person of importance

**some·day** \'səm-,dā\ *adv* : at some future time

**some·how** \-,haů\ *adv* : by some means

**some·one** \-(,)wən\ *pron* : some person

**som·er·sault** \'səm-ər-,sȯlt\ *n* [MF *sombresaut* leap, deriv. of L *super* over + *saltus* leap, fr. *salire* to jump] : a leap or roll in which a person turns his heels over his head — **somersault** *vb*

**som·er·set** \-,set\ *n or vb* : SOMERSAULT

**some·thing** \'səm-thiŋ\ *pron* : some undetermined or unspecified thing

**some·time** \'səm-,tīm\ *adv* **1** : at a future time **2** : at an unknown or unnamed time

**some·times** \'səm-,tīmz\ *adv* : OCCASIONALLY

**¹some·what** \-,hwät, -,hwət\ *pron* : SOMETHING

**²somewhat** *adv* : in some degree

**some·where** \-,hwear\ *adv* : in, at, or to an unknown or unnamed place

**som·nam·bu·lism** \säm-'nam-byə-,liz-əm\ *n* : activity (as walking about) during sleep — **som·nam·bu·list** \-ləst\ *n*

**som·no·lent** \'säm-nə-lənt\ *adj* : SLEEPY, DROWSY — **som·no·lence** \-ləns\ *n*

**son** \'sən\ *n* **1 :** a male offspring or descendant **2** *cap* **:** Jesus Christ **3 :** a person deriving from a particular source (as a country, race, or school)

**so·nar** \'sō-,när\ *n* [*sound navigation ranging*] **:** an apparatus that detects the presence and location of submerged objects (as submarines) by reflected vibrations

**so·na·ta** \sə-'nät-ə\ *n* **:** an instrumental composition with three or four movements differing in rhythm and mood but related in key

**son·a·ti·na** \,sän-ə-'tē-nə\ *n* **:** a short usu. simplified sonata

**song** \'sȯŋ\ *n* **1 :** vocal music; *also* **:** a short composition of words and music **2 :** poetic composition **3 :** a small amount ⟨sold for a ∼⟩

**song·bird** \'sȯŋ-,bərd\ *n* **:** a bird with musical tones

**song·ster** \-stər\ *n* **:** one that sings — **song·stress** \-stris\ *n*

**son·ic** \'sän-ik\ *adj* **:** of or relating to sound waves or the speed of sound

**sonic boom** *n* **:** an explosive sound produced by an aircraft traveling at supersonic speed

**son-in-law** \'sən-ən-,lȯ\ *n, pl* **sons-in-law :** the husband of one's daughter

**son·net** \'sän-ət\ *n* **:** a poem of 14 lines usu. in iambic pentameter with a definite rhyme scheme

**so·no·rous** \sə-'nōr-əs, 'sän-ə-rəs\ *adj* **1 :** giving out sound when struck **2 :** loud, deep, or rich in sound **:** RESONANT **3 :** high-sounding **:** IMPRESSIVE — **so·nor·i·ty** \sə-'nȯr-ət-ē\ *n*

**soon** \'sün\ *adv* **1 :** before long **2 :** PROMPTLY, QUICKLY **3 :** EARLY **4 :** WILLINGLY, READILY

**soot** \'sùt, 'sət, 'süt\ *n* **:** a black substance that is formed when something burns, that colors smoke, and that sticks to the sides of the chimney carrying the smoke — **sooty** *adj*

**sooth** \'süth\ *n, archaic* **:** TRUTH

**soothe** \'süth\ *vb* **soothed; sooth·ing 1 :** to please by flattery or attention **2 :** to calm down **:** COMFORT — **sooth·er** *n* — **sooth·ing·ly** *adv*

**sooth·say·er** \'süth-,sā-ər\ *n* **:** one that foretells events — **sooth·say·ing** \-iŋ\ *n*

¹**sop** \'säp\ *n* **:** a conciliatory bribe, gift, or concession

²**sop** *vb* **sopped; sop·ping 1 :** to steep or dip in or as if in a liquid **2 :** to wet thoroughly **:** SOAK; *also* **:** to mop up (a liquid)

**SOP** *abbr* standard operating procedure; standing operating procedure

**soph** *abbr* sophomore

**soph·ism** \'säf-,iz-əm\ *n* **1 :** an argument correct in form but embodying *a* subtle fallacy **2 :** SOPHISTRY

**soph·ist** \'säf-əst\ *n* **:** PHILOSOPHER; *esp* **:** a captious or fallacious reasoner

**so·phis·tic** \sə-'fis-tik, sə-\ *or* **so·phis·ti·cal** \-ti-kəl\ *adj* **:** of or characteristic of sophists or sophistry syn fallacious

**so·phis·ti·cat·ed** \-tə-,kāt-əd\ *adj* **1 :** made wise or worldly-wise by experience or disillusionment **2 :** intellectually appealing ⟨∼ novel⟩ **3 :** COMPLEX ⟨∼ instruments⟩ — **so·phis·ti·ca·tion** \-,fis-tə-'kā-shən\ *n*

**soph·ist·ry** \'säf-ə-strē\ *n* **:** subtly fallacious reasoning or argument

**soph·o·more** \'säf-(ə-),mōr\ *n* **:** a student in his second year of college or secondary school

**soph·o·mor·ic** \,säf-ə-'mōr-ik\ *adj* **1 :** of, relating to, or characteristic of a sophomore **2 :** being conceited and overconfident of knowledge but poorly informed and immature

**so·po·rif·ic** \,säp-ə-'rif-ik, ,sōp-\ *adj* **1 :** causing sleep or drowsiness **2 :** LETHARGIC

**so·pra·no** \sə-'pran-ō\ *n, pl* **-nos** [It, fr. *sopra* above, fr. L *supra*] **1 :** the highest singing voice; *also* **:** a part for this voice **2 :** a singer with a soprano voice — **soprano** *adj*

**sorb** \'sȯrb\ *vb* **:** to take up and hold by adsorption or absorption

**sor·cery** \'sȯrs-(ə-)rē\ *n* [ME *sorcerie*, fr. OF, fr. *sorcier* sorcerer, fr. (assumed) VL *sortiarius*, fr. L *sort-, sors* chance, lot] **:** the use of magic **:** WITCHCRAFT — **sor·cer·er** \-rər\ *n* — **sor·cer·ess** \-rəs\ *n*

**sor·did** \'sȯrd-əd\ *adj* **1 :** FILTHY, DIRTY **2 :** marked by baseness or grossness **:** VILE — **sor·did·ly** *adv* — **sor·did·ness** *n*

¹**sore** \'sōr\ *adj* **sor·er; sor·est 1 :** causing pain or distress ⟨a ∼ bruise⟩ **2 :** painfully sensitive ⟨∼ eyes⟩ **3 :** SEVERE, INTENSE **4 :** IRRITATED, ANGRY — **sore·ly** *adv* — **sore·ness** *n*

²**sore** *n* **1 :** a sore spot on the body; *esp* **:** one (as an ulcer) with the tissues broken and usu. infected **2 :** a source of pain or vexation

**sore throat** *n* **:** painful throat due to inflammation

**sor·ghum** \'sȯr-gəm\ *n* **:** a tall variable Old World tropical grass grown widely for its edible seed, for forage, or for its sweet juice which yields a syrup

**so·ror·i·ty** \sə-'rȯr-ət-ē\ *n, pl* **-ties** [ML *sororitas* sisterhood, fr. L *soror* sister] **:** a club of girls or women esp. at a college

**sorp·tion** \'sȯrp-shən\ *n* **:** the process of sorbing **:** the state of being sorbed — **sorp·tive** \'sȯrp-tiv\ *adj*

**sor·rel** \'sȯr-əl\ *n* **:** any of several sour-juiced herbs

**sor·row** \'sär-ō\ *n* **1 :** deep distress and regret **2 :** a cause of grief or sadness **3 :** a display of grief or sadness — **sor·row·ful** \-fəl\ *adj* — **sor·row·ful·ly** \-f(ə-)lē\ *adv*

**sor·ry** \'sär-ē\ *adj* **sor·ri·er; -est 1 :** feeling sorrow, regret, or penitence **2 :** WORTHLESS **3 :** DISMAL, GLOOMY

¹**sort** \'sȯrt\ *n* **1 :** a group of persons or things that have similar characteristics **:** CLASS **2 :** WAY, MANNER **3 :** QUALITY, NATURE — **out of sorts 1 :** somewhat ill **2 :** GROUCHY, IRRITABLE

²**sort** *vb* **1 :** to put in a certain place according to kind, class, or nature **2** *archaic* **:** to be in accord **:** AGREE

**sor·tie** \'sȯrt-ē, sȯr-'tē\ *n* **1** : an assault by troops from a besieged place against the besiegers **2** : one mission or attack by one airplane

**SOS** \,es-(,)ō-'es\ *n* : a call or request for help or rescue

**so-so** \'sō-'sō\ *adv or adj* : PASSABLY

**sot** \'sät\ *n* : an habitual drunkard — **sot·tish** *adj*

**sou·brette** \sü-'bret\ *n* : a coquettish maidservant or a frivolous young woman in a comedy; *also* : an actress playing such a part

**souf·flé** \sü-'flā\ *n* [F, fr. *soufflé*, pp. of *souffler* to blow, puff up, fr. L *suf-flare*, fr. *sub-* up + *flare* to blow] : a spongy hot dish made light in baking by stiffly beaten egg whites

**sough** \'saù, 'səf\ *vb* : to make a moaning or sighing sound — **sough** *n*

**sought** *past of* SEEK

**¹soul** \'sōl\ *n* **1** : the immaterial essence of an individual life **2** : the spiritual principle embodied in human beings or the universe **3** : an active or essential part **4** : man's moral and emotional nature **5** : spiritual or moral force **6** : PERSON ⟨a kindly ~⟩ **7** : a strong, positive feeling (as of intense sensitivity and emotional fervor) conveyed esp. by American Negro performers; *also* : NEGRITUDE — **souled** \'sōld\ *adj* — **soul·less** \'sōl-ləs\ *adj*

**²soul** *adj* **1** : of, relating to, or characteristic of American Negroes or their culture ⟨~ food⟩ ⟨~ music⟩ **2** : designed for or controlled by Negroes ⟨~ radio stations⟩

**soul brother** *n* : a male Negro —used esp. by other Negroes

**soul·ful** \'sōl-fəl\ *adj* : full of or expressing deep feeling — **soul·ful·ly** \-ē\ *adv*

**¹sound** \'saùnd\ *adj* **1** : free from flaw or defect **2** : not diseased or sickly **3** : FIRM, STRONG **4** : SOLID **5** : free from error **6** : RIGHT **6** : showing good judgment **7** : THOROUGH **8** : UNDISTURBED ⟨~ sleep⟩ **9** : LEGAL, VALID — **sound·ly** *adv* — **sound·ness** *n*

**²sound** *n* **1** : the sensation experienced through the sense of hearing; *also* : mechanical energy transmitted by longitudinal pressure waves (as in air) that is the stimulus to hearing **2** : something heard : NOISE, TONE; *also* : hearing distance : EARSHOT **3** : a musical style — **sound·less** *adj* — **sound·proof** \-'prüf\ *adj or vb*

**³sound** *vb* **1** : to make or cause to make a noise **2** : to order or proclaim by a sound ⟨~ the alarm⟩ **3** : to convey a certain impression : SEEM **4** : to examine the condition of by causing to give out sounds

**⁴sound** *n* **1** : a long passage of water wider than a strait often connecting two larger bodies of water ⟨Long Island ~⟩ **2** : a gas-containing sac functioning as an accessory respiratory organ in most fishes

**⁵sound** *vb* **1** : to measure the depth of (water) esp. by a weighted line dropped from the surface : FATHOM **2** : PROBE

**3** : to dive down suddenly ⟨the hooked fish ~ed⟩ — **sound·ing** *n*

**sound·er** \'saùn-dər\ *n* : one that sounds; *esp* : a device for making soundings

**¹soup** \'süp\ *n* **1** : a liquid food with a meat, fish, or vegetable stock as a base and often containing pieces of solid food **2** : something having the consistency of soup **3** : an unfortunate predicament ⟨in the ~⟩

**²soup** *vb* : to increase the power of ⟨~ up an engine⟩ — **souped–up** \'süpt-'əp\ *adj*

**soup·çon** \süp-'sōⁿ\ *n* : ▨a little bit : TRACE

**soupy** \'sü-pē\ *adj* **soup·i·er; -est 1** : having the consistency of soup **2** : densely foggy or cloudy

**¹sour** \'saù(ə)r\ *adj* **1** : having an acid or tart taste ⟨~ as vinegar⟩ **2** : SPOILED, PUTRID ⟨a ~ odor⟩ **3** : UNPLEASANT, DISAGREEABLE ⟨~ disposition⟩ — **sour·ish** *adj* — **sour·ly** *adv* — **sour·ness** *n*

**²sour** *vb* : to become or make sour

**source** \'sōrs\ *n* **1** : the beginning of a stream of water **2** : ORIGIN, BEGINNING **3** : a supplier of information

**¹souse** \'saùs\ *vb* **soused; sous·ing 1** : PICKLE **2** : to plunge into a liquid **3** : DRENCH **4** : to make drunk

**²souse** *n* **1** : something (as pigs' feet) steeped in pickle **2** : BRINE **3** : a soaking in liquid **4** : DRUNKARD

**¹south** \'saùth\ *adv* : to or toward the south

**²south** *adj* **1** : situated toward or at the south **2** : coming from the south

**³south** *n* **1** : the direction to the right of one facing east **2** : the compass point directly opposite to north **3** *cap* : regions or countries south of a specified or implied point; *esp* : the part of the U.S. that lies south of the Mason-Dixon line, the Ohio river, and the southern boundaries of Missouri and Kansas — **south·er·ly** \'səth-ər-lē\ *adj or adv* — **south·ern** \'səth-ərn\ *adj* — **South·ern·er** *n* — **south·ern·most** \-,mōst\ *adj* — **south·ward** \'saùth-wərd\ *adv or adj* — **south·wards** \-wərdz\ *adv*

**south·east** \saùth-'ēst, *naut* saù-'ēst\ *n* **1** : the general direction between south and east **2** : the compass point midway between south and east **3** *cap* : regions or countries southeast of a specified or implied point — **southeast** *adj or adv* — **south·east·er·ly** *adv or adj* — **south·east·ern** \-ərn\ *adj*

**south·paw** \'saùth-,pȯ\ *n* : a left-handed baseball pitcher — **southpaw** *adj*

**south pole** *n, often cap S&P* : the southernmost point of the earth

**south·west** \saùth-'west, *naut* saù-'west\ *n* **1** : the general direction between south and west **2** : the compass point midway between south and west **3** *cap* : regions or countries southwest of a specified or implied point — **southwest** *adj or adv* — **south·west·er·ly** *adv or adj* — **south·west·ern** \-ərn\ *adj*

**sou·ve·nir** \sü-və-ˌniər\ *n* : something serving as a reminder

**sou'·west·er** \saů-'wes-tər\ *n* : a waterproof hat worn at sea in stormy weather; *also* : a long waterproof coat

¹**sov·er·eign** \'säv-(ə-)rən\ *n* 1 : one possessing the supreme power and authority in a state  2 : a gold coin of Great Britain worth one pound

²**sovereign** *adj* 1 : CHIEF, HIGHEST  2 : supreme in power or authority  3 : having independent authority  4 : EXCELLENT, FINE syn dominant, predominant, paramount, free

**sov·er·eign·ty** \-tē\ *n*, *pl* **-ties** 1 : supremacy in rule or power  2 : power to govern without external control  3 : the supreme political power in a state

**so·vi·et** \'sōv-ē-ˌet, 'säv-, -ē-ət\ *n* 1 : an elected governmental council in a Communist country  2 *pl, cap* : the people and esp. the leaders of the U.S.S.R. — **so·vi·et·ism** *n, often cap* — **so·vi·et·ize** *vb, often cap*

¹**sow** \'saů\ *n* : a female swine

²**sow** \'sō\ *vb* **sowed**; **sown** \'sōn\ *or* **sowed**; **sow·ing** 1 : to plant seed for growing esp. by scattering  2 : to strew with or as if with seed  3 : to scatter abroad — **sow·er** \'sō(-ə)r\ *n*

**sow bug** \'saů-\ *n* : WOOD LOUSE

**sox** *pl of* SOCK

**soy** \'sói\ *n* : a sauce made from soybeans fermented in brine

**soy·bean** \'sói-ˌbēn, -ˌbēn\ *n* : an Asiatic legume widely grown for forage and for its edible seeds that yield a valuable oil (**soybean oil**); *also* : its seed

**sp** *abbr* 1 special 2 species 3 specimen 4 spelling, 5 spirit

**Sp** *abbr* Spain; Spanish

**SP** *abbr* 1 shore patrol 2 [L *sine prole*] without issue 3 specialist

**spa** \'spä\ *n* [*Spa*, watering place in Belgium] : a mineral spring; *also* : a resort with mineral springs

¹**space** \'spās\ *n* 1 : the limitless area in which all things exist and move  2 : some small measurable part of space  3 : the region beyond the earth's atmosphere  4 : a definite place (as a seat or stateroom on a train or ship)  5 : a period of time  6 : an empty place

²**space** *vb* **spaced**; **spac·ing** : to place at intervals

**space·craft** \-ˌkraft\ *n* : a manned or unmanned device designed to orbit the earth or to travel beyond the earth's atmosphere

**space·flight** \-ˌflīt\ *n* : flight beyond the earth's atmosphere

**space heater** *n* : a device for heating an enclosed space

**space·man** \'spās-ˌman, -mən\ *n* : one concerned with traveling beyond the earth's atmosphere

**space·ship** \'spās(h)-ˌship\ *n* : a vehicle for travel beyond the earth's atmosphere

**space station** *n* : a manned artificial satellite in a fixed orbit serving as a base (as for refueling spaceships)

**space suit** *n* : a suit with provisions to make life beyond the earth's atmosphere possible for its wearer

**space walk** *n* : a moving about in open space outside a spacecraft by an astronaut protected by a space suit — **space walk** *vb* — **space·walk·er** \'spās-ˌwȯ-kər\ *n* — **space·walk·ing** \-kiŋ\ *n*

**spa·cious** \'spā-shəs\ *adj* : very large in extent : ROOMY syn commodious, capacious, ample — **spa·cious·ly** *adv* — **spa·cious·ness** *n*

¹**spade** \'spād\ *n* : a shovel with a flat blade — **spade·ful** *n*

²**spade** *vb* **spad·ed**; **spad·ing** : to dig with a spade

³**spade** *n* : any of a suit of playing cards marked with a black figure resembling an inverted heart with a short stem at the bottom

**spa·dix** \'spād-iks\ *n*, *pl* **spa·di·ces** \'spād-ə-ˌsēz\ : a floral spike with a fleshy or succulent axis usu. enclosed in a spathe

**spa·ghet·ti** \spə-'get-ē\ *n* [It, fr. pl. of *spaghetto*, dim. of *spago* cord, string] : a dough made chiefly from wheat flour and formed in thin solid strings

¹**span** \'span\ *n* 1 : an English unit of length equal to nine inches  2 : a limited portion of time  3 : the spread of an arch, beam, truss, or girder from one support to another  4 : a pair of animals (as mules) driven together

²**span** *vb* **spanned**; **span·ning** 1 : MEASURE  2 : to extend across

**Span** *abbr* Spanish

**span·gle** \'span-gəl\ *n* : a small disk of shining metal used esp. on a dress for ornament — **spangle** *vb*

**Span·iard** \'span-yərd\ *n* : a native or inhabitant of Spain

**span·iel** \'span-yəl\ *n* [ME *spaniell*, fr. MF *espaignol*, lit., Spaniard, fr. L *Hispania* Spain] : any of several mostly small and short-legged dogs with long silky hair and drooping ears

**Span·ish** \'span-ish\ *n* 1 Spanish *pl* : the people of Spain  2 : the chief language of Spain and of many countries colonized by the Spanish — **Spanish** *adj*

**Spanish American** *n* : a native or inhabitant of a country colonized by Spain in South or Central America; *also* : a resident of the U.S. whose native language is Spanish — **Spanish–American** *adj*

**Spanish fly** *n* : a green European beetle containing a substance irritating to the skin; *also* : a dried preparation of these beetles with diuretic and aphrodisiac effects produced by irritating the urinary tract

**Spanish moss** *n* : a plant related to the pineapple that grows in pendent tufts of grayish green filaments on trees in the southern U.S. and the West Indies

**spank** \'spank\ *vb* : to strike the buttocks with the open hand — **spank** *n*

**spank·ing** \'span-kiŋ\ *adj* : BRISK, LIVELY 〈~ breeze〉

¹**spar** \'spär\ *n* : a rounded wood or

metal piece (as a mast, yard, boom, or gaff) for supporting sail rigging

²spar *vb* sparred; spar·ring : to box scientifically without serious hitting; *also* : SKIRMISH, WRANGLE

Spar \'spär\ *n* : a member of the women's reserve of the U.S. Coast Guard

¹spare \'spaər\ *vb* spared; spar·ing 1 : to use frugally or rarely 2 : to exempt from something 3 : to get along without 4 : to refrain from punishing or injuring : show mercy to

²spare *adj* spar·er; spar·est 1 : held in reserve 2 : SUPERFLUOUS 3 : not liberal or profuse 4 : LEAN, THIN 5 : SCANTY syn extra, lanky, scrawny, meager, sparse, skimpy

³spare *n* 1 : a duplicate kept in reserve; *esp* : a spare tire 2 : the knocking down of all the bowling pins with the first two balls

spar·ing \'spa(ə)r-iŋ\ *adj* : SAVING, FRUGAL syn thrifty, economical — spar·ing·ly *adv*

¹spark \'spärk\ *n* 1 : a small particle of a burning substance or a hot glowing particle struck from a mass (as by steel on flint) 2 : SPARKLE 3 : a particle capable of being kindled or developed : GERM 4 : a luminous electrical discharge of short duration between two conductors

²spark *vb* 1 : to emit or produce sparks 2 : to stir to activity : INCITE

³spark *n* : DANDY, GALLANT

¹spar·kle \'spär-kəl\ *vb* spar·kled; spar·kling \-k(ə-)liŋ\ 1 : FLASH, GLEAM 2 : EFFERVESCE 3 : to perform brilliantly — spark·ler \-k(ə-)lər\ *n*

²sparkle *n* 1 : GLEAM 2 : ANIMATION

spark plug *n* : a device that produces a spark for combustion in an engine cylinder

spar·row \'spar-ō\ *n* : any of several small dull singing birds

sparrow hawk *n* : any of various small hawks or falcons

sparse \'spärs\ *adj* spars·er; spars·est : thinly scattered : SCANTY syn meager, spare, skimpy — sparse·ly *adv*

spasm \'spaz-əm\ *n* 1 : an involuntary and abnormal muscular contraction 2 : a sudden, violent, and temporary effort or feeling — spas·mod·ic \spaz-'mäd-ik\ *adj* — spas·mod·i·cal·ly \-i-k(ə-)lē\ *adv*

spas·tic \'spas-tik\ *adj* : of, relating to, or marked by muscular spasm ⟨~ paralysis⟩ — spastic *n*

¹spat \'spat\ *past of* SPIT

²spat *n, pl* spat *or* spats : the young of a bivalve mollusk (as the oyster)

³spat *n* : a gaiter covering instep and ankle

⁴spat *n* : a brief petty quarrel : DISPUTE

⁵spat *vb* spat·ted; spat·ting : to quarrel briefly

spate \'spāt\ *n* : a sudden outburst

spathe \'spāth\ *n* : a sheathing bract or pair of bracts enclosing an inflorescence (as of the calla) and esp. a spadix on the same axis

spa·tial \'spā-shəl\ *adj* : of or relating to space — spa·tial·ly \-ē\ *adv*

spat·ter \'spat-ər\ *vb* 1 : to splash with drops of liquid 2 : to sprinkle around — spatter *n*

spat·u·la \'spach-ə-lə\ *n* : a flexible knifelike implement for scooping, spreading, or mixing soft substances (as paints or drugs)

spav·in \'spav-ən\ *n* : a bony enlargement of the hock of a horse — spav·ined \-ənd\ *adj*

¹spawn \'spȯn\ *vb* [ME *spawnen*, fr. OF *espandre* to spread out, expand; fr. L *expandere*, fr. *ex-* out + *pandere* to spread] 1 : to produce eggs or offspring esp. in large numbers 2 : to bring forth : GENERATE

²spawn *n* 1 : the eggs of water animals (as fishes or oysters) that lay many small eggs 2 : offspring esp. when produced in great quantities

spay \'spā\ *vb* : to remove the ovaries from (an animal)

SPCA *abbr* Society for the Prevention of Cruelty to Animals

SPCC *abbr* Society for the Prevention of Cruelty to Children

speak \'spēk\ *vb* spoke \'spōk\; spo·ken \'spō-kən\; speak·ing 1 : to utter words 2 : to express orally : make known one's thoughts, feelings, or opinions in words 3 : to address an audience 4 : to use or be able to use (a language) in speech

speak·easy \'spē-kē-zē\ *n, pl* -eas·ies : an illicit drinking place

speak·er \'spē-kər\ *n* 1 : one that speaks 2 : the presiding officer of a deliberative assembly 3 : LOUD-SPEAKER

¹spear \'spiər\ *n* 1 : a long-shafted weapon with a sharp point for thrusting or throwing 2 : a sharp-pointed instrument with barbs (as for spearing fish) 3 : a young shoot (as of grass) — spear·man \-mən\ *n*

²spear *vb* : to strike or pierce with or as if with a spear

spear·head \-,hed\ *n* : a leading force, element, or influence — spearhead *vb*

spear·mint \-,mint\ *n* : a common highly aromatic garden mint

spec *abbr* 1 special 2 specifically

spe·cial \'spesh-əl\ *adj* 1 : UNCOMMON, NOTEWORTHY 2 : INDIVIDUAL, UNIQUE 3 : particularly favored 4 : EXTRA, ADDITIONAL 5 : confined to or designed for a definite field of action, purpose, or occasion — special *n* — spe·cial·ly \-ē\ *adv*

Special Forces *n pl* : a branch of the army composed of men specially trained in guerrilla warfare

spe·cial·ist \'spesh-(ə-)ləst\ *n* 1 : one who devotes himself to some special branch of learning or activity 2 : any of four enlisted ranks in the army corresponding to the grades of corporal through sergeant first class

spe·cial·ize \'spesh-ə-,līz\ *vb* -ized; -iz·ing : to concentrate one's efforts in a special activity or field; *also* : to change in an adaptive manner — spe-

cial·iza·tion \,spesh-ə-lə-'zā-shən\ n
spe·cial·ty \'spesh-əl-tē\ n, pl -ties
1 : a particular quality or detail  2 : a
product of a special kind or of special
excellence  3 : a branch of knowledge,
business, or professional work in which
one specializes
spe·cie \'spē-shē, -sē\ n : money in
coin
spe·cies \'spē-shēz, -sēz\ n, pl species [L, appearance, kind, species, fr.
specere to look]  1 : SORT, KIND  2 : a
taxonomic group comprising closely
related organisms potentially able to
breed with one another
specif abbr specific; specifically
¹spe·cif·ic \spi-'sif-ik\ adj  1 : of, relating to, or constituting a species  2
: DEFINITE, EXACT  3 : having a unique
relation to something (~ antibodies);
esp : exerting a distinctive and usu.
curative or causative influence — spe-
cif·i·cal·ly \-i-k(ə-)lē\ adv
²specific n : a specific remedy
spec·i·fi·ca·tion \,spes-ə-fə-'kā-
shən\ n  1 : something specified : ITEM
2 : a description of work to be done
and materials to be used (as in building) — usu. used in pl.
specific gravity n : the ratio of the
weight of any volume of a substance to
the weight of an equal volume of another substance (as water for solids and
liquids or air or hydrogen for gases)
taken as the standard
spec·i·fy \'spes-ə-,fī\ vb -fied; -fy-
ing : to mention or name explicitly
spec·i·men \'spes-ə-mən\ n : an item
or part typical of a group or whole
spe·cious \'spē-shəs\ adj : seeming to
be genuine, correct, or beautiful but
not really so (~ reasoning)
speck \'spek\ n  1 : a small spot or
blemish  2 : a small particle : BIT —
speck vb
speck·le \'spek-əl\ n : a little speck —
speck·le vb
spec·ta·cle \'spek-ti-kəl\ n  1 : something exhibited to view; esp : an impressive public display  2 pl : EYE-
GLASSES — spec·ta·cled \-kəld\ adj
¹spec·tac·u·lar \spek-'tak-yə-lər\ adj
: SENSATIONAL, STRIKING, SHOWY
²spectacular n : an elaborate spectacle
spec·ta·tor \'spek-,tāt-ər\ n : one
who looks on (as at a sports event) syn
observer, witness
spec·ter or spec·tre \'spek-tər\ n : a
visible disembodied spirit : GHOST
spec·tral \'spek-trəl\ adj  1 : of, relating to, or resembling a specter  2 : of,
relating to, or made by a spectrum
spec·tro·gram \'spek-trə-,gram\ n : a
photograph or diagram of a spectrum
spec·tro·graph \-,graf\ n : an instrument for dispersing radiation into a
spectrum and photographing or map-
ping the spectrum — spec·tro-
graph·ic \,spek-trə-'graf-ik\ adj —
spec·tro·graph·i·cal·ly \-i-k(ə-)lē\
adv
spec·trom·e·ter \spek-'träm-ət-ər\ n
1 : an instrument for determining the
index of refraction  2 : a spectroscope

fitted for measuring spectra — spec-
tro·met·ric \,spek-trə-'met-rik\ adj
spec·tro·scope \'spek-trə-,skōp\ n
: an optical instrument for forming and
examining spectra — spec·tro·scop-
ic \,spek-trə-'skäp-ik\ or spec·tro-
scop·i·cal \-i-kəl\ adj — spec·tro-
scop·i·cal·ly \-i-k(ə-)lē\ adv —
spec·tros·co·pist \spek-'träs-kə-
pəst\ n — spec·tros·co·py \-pē\ n
spec·trum \'spek-trəm\ n, pl spectra \-trə\ or spec·trums [NL, fr. L,
appearance, specter, fr. specere to look]
1 : a series of colors formed when a
beam of white light is dispersed (as by a
prism) so that its parts are arranged in
the order of their wavelengths  2 : a
series of radiations arranged in regular
order  3 : a continuous sequence or
range (a wide ~ of political opinions)
spec·u·late \'spek-yə-,lāt\ vb -lat-
ed; -lat·ing [L speculari to spy out,
examine, fr. specula watchtower, fr.
specere to look, look at]  1 : REFLECT,
MEDITATE  2 : to engage in a business
deal where a good profit may be made
at considerable risk syn reason, think,
deliberate — spec·u·la·tion \,spek-
yə-'lā-shən\ n — spec·u·la·tive
\'spek-yə-,lāt-iv\ adj — spec·u·la-
tive·ly adv — spec·u·la·tor \-,lāt-
ər\ n
speech \'spēch\ n  1 : the power of
speaking  2 : act or manner of speaking  3 : TALK, CONVERSATION  4 : a
public discourse  5 : LANGUAGE, DIA-
LECT — speech·less adj
¹speed \'spēd\ n  1 archaic : SUCCESS
2 : SWIFTNESS, RAPIDITY  3 : rate of
motion or performance  4 : a transmission gear in an automotive vehicle  5
: METHAMPHETAMINE; also : a related
drug syn haste, hurry, dispatch, momentum, pace — speed·i·ly \'spēd-
²l-ē\ adv — speedy adj
²speed vb speed \'spēd\ or speed·ed;
speed·ing  1 : to get along : FARE,
PROSPER  2 : to go fast; esp : to go at an
excessive or illegal speed  3 : to cause
to go faster — speed·er n
speed·boat \-,bōt\ n : a fast launch or
motorboat
speed·om·e·ter \spi-'däm-ət-ər\ n
: an instrument for indicating speed or
speed and distance traveled
speed·up \'spēd-,əp\ n  1 : ACCELERA-
TION  2 : an employer's demand for accelerated output without increased pay
speed·way \'spēd-,wā\ n : a road on
which fast driving is allowed; also : a
racecourse for motor vehicles
speed·well \'spēd-,wel\ n : a low
creeping plant with spikes of small usu.
bluish flowers
¹spell \'spel\ n [ME, talk, tale, fr. OE]
1 : a magic formula : INCANTATION  2
: a controlling influence
²spell vb spelled \'speld, 'spelt\;
spel·ling  1 : to name, write, or print
in order the letters of a word  2 : MEAN
³spell vb spelled \'speld\; spell·ing
: to take the place of for a time in work
or duty : RELIEVE
⁴spell n  1 : the relief of one person by

another in any work or duty **2** : one's turn at work or duty **3** : a period of rest from work or duty **4** : a stretch of a specified kind of weather **5** : a period of bodily or mental distress or disorder — ATTACK

**spell·bind·er** \-,bīn-dər\ n : a speaker of compelling eloquence

**spell·bound** \-'baůnd\ adj : held by or as if by a spell — FASCINATED

**spell·er** \'spel-ər\ n **1** : one who spells **2** : a book with exercises for teaching spelling

**spe·lunk·er** \spi-'lən̩-kər, 'spē-,lən̩-kər\ n : one who makes a hobby of exploring caves — **spe·lunk·ing** \-kin̩\ n

**spend** \'spend\ vb spent \'spent\; **spend·ing 1** : to use up or pay out **2** : to wear out : EXHAUST; also : to consume wastefully **3** : to cause or permit to elapse : PASS **4** : to make use of — **spend·er** n

**spend·thrift** \'spen(d)-,thrift\ n : one who spends wastefully or recklessly

**spent** \'spent\ adj : drained of energy

**sperm** \'spərm\ n, pl **sperm** or **sperms** : SEMEN; also : SPERMATOZOON

**sper·ma·to·zo·on** \(,)spər-,mat-ə-'zō-,än, -'zō-ən\ n, pl **-zoa** \-'zō-ə\ : a male germ cell

**sperm whale** \'spərm-\ n : a whale with conical teeth and no whalebone

**spew** \'spyü\ vb : VOMIT

**sp gr** abbr specific gravity

**sphag·num** \'sfag-nəm\ n : any of a large genus of atypical mosses that grow only in wet acid areas where their remains become compacted with other plant debris to form peat

**sphere** \'sfiər\ n [ME spere globe, celestial sphere, fr. MF espere, fr. L sphaera, fr. Gk sphaira, lit., ball] **1** : a figure so shaped that every point on its surface is an equal distance from the center : BALL **2** : a globular body : GLOBE; esp : a celestial body **3** : range of action or influence : FIELD — **spher·i·cal** \'sfir-i-kəl, 'sfer-\ adj — **spher·i·cal·ly** \-i-k(ə-)lē\ adv

**spher·oid** \'sfi(ə)r-,ȯid, 'sfe(ə)r-\ n : a figure similar to a sphere but not perfectly round — **sphe·roi·dal** \sfir-'ȯid-ᵊl\ adj

**sphinc·ter** \'sfin̩k-tər\ n : a muscular ring that closes a bodily opening

**sphinx** \'sfin̩ks\ n, pl **sphinx·es** or **sphin·ges** \'sfin-,jēz\ **1** : a monster in Greek mythology with the head and bust of a woman, the body of a lion, and wings; esp : one who asks a riddle of persons who pass and destroys those who cannot answer it **2** : an enigmatic or mysterious person

**spice** \'spīs\ n **1** : any of various aromatic plant products (as pepper or nutmeg) used to season or flavor foods **2** : something that adds interest and relish — **spice** vb — **spicy** adj

**spice·bush** \'spīs-,bůsh\ n : an aromatic shrub related to the laurels that bears dense clusters of small yellow flowers followed by scarlet or yellow berries

**spick-and-span** or **spic-and-span** \,spik-ən-'span\ adj : quite new; also : spotlessly clean

**spic·ule** \'spik-yül\ n : a slender pointed body esp. of bony material ⟨sponge ~s⟩

**spi·der** \'spīd-ər\ n **1** : any of numerous small wingless animals that resemble insects but have eight legs and a body divided into two parts **2** : a cast-iron frying pan — **spi·dery** adj

**spiel** \'spēl\ vb : to talk volubly or extravagantly — **spiel** n

**spig·ot** \'spig-ət, 'spik-ət\ n : FAUCET

**¹spike** \'spīk\ n **1** : a very large nail **2** : any of various pointed projections (as on the sole of a shoe to prevent slipping) — **spiky** adj

**²spike** vb **spiked**; **spik·ing 1** : to fasten with spikes **2** : to put an end to : QUASH ⟨~ a rumor⟩ **3** : to pierce with or impale on a spike **4** : to add alcoholic liquor to (a drink)

**³spike** n **1** : an ear of grain **2** : a long cluster of usu. stemless flowers

**¹spill** \'spil\ vb **spilled** \'spild, 'spilt\ also **spilt** \'spilt\; **spill·ing 1** : to cause or allow unintentionally to fall, flow, or run out **2** : to lose or allow to be scattered **3** : to cause (blood) to flow **4** : to run out or over with resulting loss or waste — **spill·able** adj

**²spill** n **1** : an act of spilling; also : a fall from a horse or vehicle or in running **2** : something spilled **3** : SPILLWAY

**spill·way** \-,wā\ n : a passage for surplus water to run over or around an obstruction (as a dam)

**¹spin** \'spin\ vb **spun** \'spən\; **spin·ning 1** : to draw out (fiber) and twist into thread; also : to form (thread) by such means **2** : to form thread by extruding a sticky quickly hardening fluid; also : to construct from such thread ⟨spiders ~ their webs⟩ **3** : to produce slowly and by degrees ⟨~ a story⟩ **4** : TWIRL **5** : WHIRL, REEL ⟨my head is spinning⟩ **6** : to move rapidly along — **spin·ner** n

**²spin** n **1** : a rapid rotating motion **2** : an excursion in a wheeled vehicle

**spin·ach** \'spin-ich\ n : a garden herb grown for its edible leaves

**spi·nal** \'spīn-ᵊl\ adj : of or relating to the backbone or spinal cord — **spi·nal·ly** \-ē\ adv

**spinal column** n : BACKBONE

**spinal cord** n : the thick strand of nervous tissue that extends from the brain along the back in the cavity of the backbone

**spinal nerve** n : any of the paired nerves which leave the spinal cord of a vertebrate with a cranium, supply muscles of the trunk and limbs, and connect with nerves of the sympathetic nervous system

**spin·dle** \'spin-dᵊl\ n **1** : a round tapering stick or rod by which fibers are twisted in spinning **2** : a turned part of a piece of furniture ⟨the ~s of a chair⟩ **3** : a slender pin or rod which turns or on which something else turns

**spin·dling** \'spin-(d)lin̩\ adj : being

long or tall and thin and usu. weak

**spin·dly** \'spin-(d)lē\ *adj* : SPINDLING

**spin·drift** \'spin-‚drift\ *n* : spray blown from waves

**spine** \'spīn\ *n* 1 : BACKBONE 2 : a stiff sharp process on a plant or animal; *esp* : one that is a modified leaf — **spine·less** *adj* — **spiny** *adj*

**spi·nel** \spə-'nel\ *n* : a hard crystalline mineral of variable color used as a gem

**spin·et** \'spin-ət\ *n* 1 : an early harpsichord having a single keyboard and only one string for each note 2 : a small upright piano

**spin·na·ker** \'spin-i-kər\ *n* : a large triangular sail set on a long light pole

**spinning jen·ny** \-‚jen-ē\ *n* : an early multiple-spindle machine for spinning wool or cotton

**spinning wheel** *n* : a small domestic machine for spinning thread or yarn in which a large wheel drives a single spindle

**spin-off** \'spin-‚òf\ *n* 1 : the distribution by a business to its stockholders of particular assets and esp. of stock of another company 2 : a usu. useful by-product ⟨~s from missile research⟩

**spin·ster** \'spin-stər\ *n* : an unmarried woman past the common age for marrying — **spin·ster·hood** \-‚hùd\ *n*

**spiny lobster** *n* : an edible crustacean differing from the related lobster in lacking the large front claws and in having a very spiny carapace

**¹spi·ral** \'spī-rəl\ *adj* 1 : circling around a center like the thread of a screw 2 : winding or coiling around a center or pole in gradually enlarging circles — **spi·ral·ly** \-ē\ *adv*

**²spiral** *n* 1 : something that has a spiral form; *also* : a single turn in a spiral object 2 : a continuously spreading and accelerating increase or decrease

**³spiral** *vb* **-raled** *or* **-ralled; -ral·ing** *or* **-ral·ling** 1 : to move in a spiral course 2 : to rise or fall in a spiral

**spi·rant** \'spī-rənt\ *n* : a consonant (as \f\, \s\, \sh\) uttered with decided friction of the breath against some part of the oral passage — **spirant** *adj*

**spire** \'spī(ə)r\ *n* 1 : a slender tapering stalk (as of grass) 2 : a pointed tip (as of a tree or antler) 3 : STEEPLE — **spiry** *adj*

**spi·rea** *or* **spi·raea** \spī-'rē-ə\ *n* : any of a genus of shrubs related to the roses with dense clusters of small white or pink flowers

**¹spir·it** \'spir-ət\ *n* [ME, fr. OF or L; OF, fr. L *spiritus,* lit., breath] 1 : a life-giving force; *also* : the animating principle : SOUL 2 *cap* : the active presence of God in human life : the third person of the Trinity 3 : SPECTER, GHOST 4 : PERSON 5 : DISPOSITION, MOOD 6 : VIVACITY, ARDOR 7 : LOYALTY ⟨school ~⟩ 8 : essential or real meaning : INTENT 9 : distilled alcoholic liquor — **spir·it·less** *adj*

**²spirit** *vb* : to carry off secretly or mysteriously

**spir·it·ed** \'spir-ət-əd\ *adj* 1 : ANIMATED, LIVELY 2 : COURAGEOUS

**¹spir·i·tu·al** \'spir-ich-(ə-w)əl\ *adj* 1 : of, relating to, or consisting of spirit : INCORPOREAL 2 : of or relating to sacred matters 3 : ecclesiastical rather than lay or temporal — **spir·i·tu·al·i·ty** \‚spir-i-chə-'wal-ət-ē\ *n* — **spir·i·tu·al·ize** \'spir-ich-(ə-w)ə-‚līz\ *vb* — **spir·i·tu·al·ly** \-lē\ *adv*

**²spiritual** *n* : a religious song originating among Negroes of the southern U.S.

**spir·i·tu·al·ism** \'spir-ich-(ə-w)ə-‚liz-əm\ *n* : a belief that spirits of the dead communicate with the living usu. through a medium — **spir·i·tu·al·ist** \-ləst\ *n, often cap* — **spir·i·tu·al·is·tic** \‚spir-ich-(ə-w)ə-'lis-tik\ *adj*

**spir·i·tu·ous** \'spir-ich-(ə-w)əs, 'spir-ət-əs\ *adj* : containing alcohol ⟨~ liquors⟩

**spi·ro·chete** *or* **spi·ro·chaete** \'spī-rə-‚kēt\ *n* : any of various spiral bacteria including one that causes syphilis

**spirt** *var of* SPURT

**¹spit** \'spit\ *n* 1 : a thin pointed rod for holding meat over a fire 2 : a point of land that runs out into the water

**²spit** *vb* **spit·ed; spit·ting** : to pierce with or as if with a spit

**³spit** *vb* **spit** *or* **spat** \'spat\; **spit·ting** 1 : to eject (saliva) from the mouth 2 : to send forth forcefully, defiantly, or disgustedly 3 : to rain or snow slightly

**⁴spit** *n* 1 : SALIVA 2 : perfect likeness ⟨~ and image of his father⟩ 3 : a sprinkle of rain or flurry of snow

**spit·ball** \'spit-‚bòl\ *n* 1 : paper chewed and rolled into a ball to be thrown as a missile 2 : a baseball pitch delivered after the ball has been moistened with saliva or sweat

**¹spite** \'spīt\ *n* : ill will with a wish to annoy, anger, or defeat : petty malice **syn** malignity, spleen, grudge, malevolence — **spite·ful** \-fəl\ *adj* — **spite·ful·ly** \-ē\ *adv* — **spite·ful·ness** *n* — **in spite of** : in defiance or contempt of : NOTWITHSTANDING

**²spite** *vb* **spit·ed; spit·ing** : to treat maliciously (as by insulting or thwarting)

**spit·tle** \'spit-ᵊl\ *n* : SALIVA

**spit·tle·bug** \-‚bəg\ *n* : any of numerous leaping insects with froth-secreting larvae that are related to the aphids

**spit·toon** \spi-'tün\ *n* : a receptacle for spit

**splash** \'splash\ *vb* 1 : to dash a liquid about 2 : to scatter a liquid upon : SPATTER 3 : to fall or strike with a splashing noise **syn** sprinkle, bespatter — **splash** *n*

**splash·down** \'splash-‚daún\ *n* : the landing of a manned spacecraft in the ocean — **splash down** \(‚)splash-'daún\ *vb*

**splat·ter** \'splat-ər\ *vb* : SPATTER — **splatter** *n*

**¹splay** \'splā\ *vb* 1 : to spread out 2 : to slope or slant outward ⟨~ed doorway⟩ — **splay** *n*

**²splay** *adj* 1 : spread out : turned outward 2 : AWKWARD, CLUMSY

**spleen** \'splēn\ *n* 1 : a vascular organ located near the stomach in most vertebrates that is concerned esp. with the storage, formation, and destruction of blood cells **2 :** SPITE, MALICE **syn** malignity, grudge, malevolence

**splen·did** \'splen-dəd\ *adj* [L *splendidus,* fr. *splendēre* to shine] **1 :** SHINING, BRILLIANT **2 :** SHOWY, GORGEOUS **3 :** ILLUSTRIOUS **4 :** EXCELLENT **syn** resplendent, glorious, sublime, superb — **splen·did·ly** *adv*

**splen·dor** \'splen-dər\ *n* **1 :** BRILLIANCE **2 :** POMP, MAGNIFICENCE

**sple·net·ic** \spli-'net-ik\ *adj* **1 :** SPLENIC **2 :** SPITEFUL **3 :** IRRITABLE

**splen·ic** \'splen-ik\ *adj* **:** of, relating to, or located in the spleen

**splice** \'splīs\ *vb* **spliced; splic·ing 1 :** to unite (as two ropes) by weaving the strands together **2 :** to unite (as two timbers) by lapping the ends and making them fast — **splice** *n*

**splint** \'splint\ *or* **splent** \'splent\ *n* **1 :** a thin strip of wood interwoven with others to make something (as a basket) **2 :** material or a device used to protect and keep in place an injured body part (as a broken arm)

**¹splin·ter** \'splint-ər\ *n* **:** a thin piece of something split off lengthwise **:** SLIVER

**²splinter** *vb* **:** to split into splinters

**split** \'split\ *vb* **split; split·ting 1 :** to divide lengthwise or along a grain or seam **2 :** to burst or break in pieces **3 :** to divide into parts or sections **:** LEAVE **syn** rend, cleave, rip, tear — **split** *n*

**split-lev·el** \'split-'lev-əl\ *adj* **:** divided vertically so that the floor level of rooms in one part is approximately midway between the levels of two successive stories in an adjoining part (∼ house) — **split-lev·el** \-,lev-əl\ *n*

**split personality** *n* **:** a personality composed of two or more internally consistent groups of behavior tendencies and attitudes each acting independently of and apparently dissociated from the other

**split·ting** \'split-iŋ\ *adj* **:** causing a piercing sensation (∼ headache)

**splotch** \'spläch\ *n* **:** BLOTCH

**splurge** \'splərj\ *n* **:** a showy display or expense — **splurge** *vb*

**splut·ter** \'splət-ər\ *n* **:** SPUTTER — **splutter** *vb*

**¹spoil** \'spȯil\ *n* **:** PLUNDER, BOOTY

**²spoil** *vb* **spoiled** \'spȯild, 'spȯilt\ *or* **spoilt** \'spȯilt\; **spoil·ing 1 :** ROB, PILLAGE **2 :** to damage seriously **:** RUIN **3 :** to impair the quality or effect of **4 :** to damage the disposition of by pampering; *also* **:** INDULGE, CODDLE **5 :** DECAY, ROT **6 :** to have an eager desire (∼ing for a fight) **syn** injure, harm, hurt, mar — **spoil·age** \'spȯi-lij\ *n*

**spoil·er** \'spȯi-lər\ *n* **1 :** one that spoils **2 :** a metallic device used on the front or on the rear of an automobile to divert the flow of air and thus reduce the tendency to lift off the road at high speeds

**spoil·sport** \'spȯil-,spȯrt\ *n* **:** one who spoils the sport or pleasure of others

**¹spoke** \'spōk\ *past & archaic past part of* SPEAK

**²spoke** *n* **1 :** any of the rods extending from the hub of a wheel to the rim **2 :** a rung of a ladder

**spo·ken** \'spō-kən\ *past part of* SPEAK

**spokes·man** \'spōks-mən\ *n* **:** one who speaks as the representative of another or others — **spokes·wom·an** \-,wùm-ən\ *n*

**spo·li·a·tion** \,spō-lē-'ā-shən\ *n* **:** the act of plundering **:** the state of being plundered

**¹sponge** \'spənj\ *n* **1 :** the elastic porous mass of fibers that forms the skeleton of any of a group of lowly sea animals; *also* **:** one of the animals **2 :** the act of washing or wiping with a sponge **3 :** a spongelike or porous mass or material (as used for sponging) — **spongy** \'spən-jē\ *adj*

**²sponge** *vb* **sponged; spong·ing 1 :** to gather sponges **2 :** to bathe or wipe with a sponge **3 :** to live at another's expense — **spong·er** *n*

**sponge cake** *n* **:** a cake made without shortening

**sponge rubber** *n* **:** a cellular rubber resembling natural sponge

**spon·sor** \'spän-sər\ *n* [LL, fr. L, guarantor, surety, fr. *sponsus,* pp. of *spondēre* to promise] **1 :** one who takes the responsibility for some other person or thing **:** SURETY **2 :** GODPARENT **3 :** a business firm that pays a broadcaster or performer for a radio or television program that allots some time to advertising its product **syn** patron, guarantor — **sponsor** *vb* — **spon·sor·ship** *n*

**spon·ta·ne·ous** \spän-'tā-nē-əs\ *adj* [LL *spontaneus,* fr. L *sponte* of one's free will, voluntarily] **1 :** done or produced freely, naturally, and without constraint **2 :** acting or taking place without external force or cause **syn** impulsive, instinctive, automatic, mechanical — **spon·ta·ne·i·ty** \,spänt-ən-'ē-ət-ē\ *n* — **spon·ta·ne·ous·ly** \spän-'tā-nē-əs-lē\ *adv*

**spontaneous combustion** *n* **:** a bursting into flame of combustible material through heat produced within itself by chemical action (as oxidation)

**spoof** \'spüf\ *vb* **1 :** DECEIVE, HOAX **2 :** to make good-natured fun of — **spoof** *n*

**¹spook** \'spük\ *n* **:** GHOST, APPARITION — **spooky** *adj*

**²spook** *vb* **:** FRIGHTEN

**spool** \'spül\ *n* **:** a cylinder on which flexible material (as thread) is wound

**spoon** \'spün\ *n* [ME, fr. OE *spōn* splinter, chip] **1 :** an eating or cooking implement consisting of a shallow bowl with a handle **2 :** a metal piece used on a fishing line as a lure — **spoon** *vb* — **spoon·ful** *n*

**spoon·bill** \'spün-,bil\ *n* **:** any of several wading birds related to the herons that have the bill greatly expanded and flattened at the tip

**spoon-feed** \'spün-,fēd\ *vb* **-fed** \-,fed\; **-feed·ing 1 :** to feed by means of a spoon　**2** : to present (information) so completely as to preclude independent thought

**spoor** \'spu̇r, 'spȯr\ *n* : a track or trail esp. of a wild animal

**spo·rad·ic** \spə-'rad-ik\ *adj* : occurring in scattered single instances **syn** occasional, rare, scarce, infrequent, uncommon — **spo·rad·i·cal·ly** \-i-k(ə-)lē\ *adv*

**spore** \'spȯr\ *n* : a primitive usu. one-celled resistant or reproductive body produced by plants and some lower animals

¹**sport** \'spȯrt\ *vb* [ME *sporten* to divert, disport, short for *disporten*, fr. MF *desporter*, fr. *des-* (fr. L *dis-* apart) + *porter* to carry, fr. L *portare*] **1** : to amuse oneself : FROLIC　**2** : to wear or display ostentatiously — **sport·ive** *adj*

²**sport** *n* **1** : a source of diversion : PASTIME　**2** : physical activity engaged in for pleasure　**3** : JEST　**4** : MOCKERY ⟨make ~ of his efforts⟩　**5** : BUTT, LAUGHINGSTOCK　**6** : one who accepts results cheerfully whether favoring his interests or not　**7** : a person devoted to a luxurious easy life　**8** : an individual distinguished by a mutation　**syn** play, frolic, fun — **sporty** *adj*

³**sport** *or* **sports** *adj* : of, relating to, or suitable for sport ⟨~ coats⟩

**sport fish** *n* : a fish important for the sport it affords anglers

**sports·cast** \'spȯrts-,kast\ *n* : a broadcast dealing with sports events — **sports·cast·er** \-,kas-tər\ *n*

**sports·man** \'spȯrts-mən\ *n* **1** : one who engages in field sports　**2** : one who plays fairly and wins or loses gracefully — **sports·man·ship** *n* — **sports·wom·an** \-,wu̇m-ən\ *n*

**sports·writ·er** \-,rīt-ər\ *n* : one who writes about sports esp. for a newspaper — **sports·writ·ing** \-iŋ\ *n*

¹**spot** \'spät\ *n* **1** : STAIN, BLEMISH　**2** : a small part different (as in color) from the main part　**3** : LOCATION, SITE — **spot·less** *adj* — **spot·less·ly** *adv* — **on the spot** : in difficulty or danger

²**spot** *vb* **spot·ted; spot·ting 1** : to mark or disfigure with spots　**2** : to pick out : RECOGNIZE, IDENTIFY

³**spot** *adj* **1** : being, done, or originating on the spot ⟨a ~ broadcast⟩　**2** : paid upon delivery　**3** : made at random or at a few key points ⟨a ~ check⟩

**spot-check** \'spät-,chek\ *vb* : to make a spot check of

**spot·light** \-,līt\ *n* **1** : a circle of brilliant light projected upon a particular area, person, or object (as on a stage); *also* : the device that produces this light　**2** : public notice — **spotlight** *vb*

**spot·ter** \'spät-ər\ *n* **1** : one that watches for approaching airplanes　**2** : one that locates enemy targets

**spot·ty** \'spät-ē\ *adj* **spot·ti·er; -est** : uneven in quality

**spou·sal** \'spau̇-zəl, -səl\ *n* : NUPTIALS — usu. used in pl.

**spouse** \'spau̇s\ *n* : one's husband or wife

¹**spout** \'spau̇t\ *vb* **1** : to eject or issue forth forcibly and freely ⟨wells ~ing oil⟩　**2** : to declaim pompously

²**spout** *n* **1** : a pipe or hole through which liquid spouts　**2** : a jet of liquid; *esp* : WATERSPOUT

**spp** *abbr* species

¹**sprain** \'sprān\ *n* : a sudden or severe twisting of a joint with stretching and tearing of ligaments; *also* : a sprained condition

²**sprain** *vb* : to subject to sprain

**sprat** \'sprat\ *n* : a small European herring; *also* : a young herring

**sprawl** \'sprȯl\ *vb* **1** : to lie or sit with limbs spread out awkwardly　**2** : to spread out irregularly — **sprawl** *n*

¹**spray** \'sprā\ *n* : a usu. flowering branch or a decorative arrangement of flowers and foliage

²**spray** *n* **1** : liquid flying in small drops like water blown from a wave　**2** : a jet of fine vapor (as from an atomizer)　**3** : an instrument (as an atomizer) for scattering fine liquid

³**spray** *vb* **1** : to scatter or let fall in a spray　**2** : to discharge spray on or into — **spray·er** *n*

**spray gun** *n* : a device for spraying paints and insecticides

¹**spread** \'spred\ *vb* **spread; spread·ing 1** : to scatter over a surface　**2** : to flatten out : open out　**3** : to stretch, force, or push apart　**4** : to distribute over a period of time or among many persons　**5** : to pass on from person to person　**6** : to cover with something ⟨~ a floor with rugs⟩　**7** : to prepare for a meal ⟨~ a table⟩ — **spread·er** *n*

²**spread** *n* **1** : the act or process of spreading　**2** : EXPANSE, EXTENT　**3** : distance between two points : GAP　**4** : a cloth cover for a bed　**5** : a food to be spread on bread or crackers　**6** : a prominent display in a magazine or newspaper

**spree** \'sprē\ *n* : an unrestrained outburst ⟨buying ~⟩; *esp* : a drinking bout

**sprig** \'sprig\ *n* : a small shoot or twig

**spright·ly** \'sprīt-lē\ *adj* **spright·li·er; -est** : LIVELY, SPIRITED **syn** animated, vivacious, gay — **spright·li·ness** *n*

¹**spring** \'spriŋ\ *vb* **sprang** \'spraŋ\ *or* **sprung** \'sprəŋ\; **sprung; spring·ing** \'spriŋ-iŋ\ **1** : to move suddenly upward or forward　**2** : to shoot up ⟨weeds ~ up overnight⟩　**3** : to move quickly by elastic force　**4** : to make lame : STRAIN　**5** : WARP　**6** : to develop (a leak) through the seams　**7** : to make known suddenly ⟨~ a surprise⟩　**8** : to cause to close suddenly ⟨~ a trap⟩

²**spring** *n* **1** : a source of supply; *esp* : an issuing of water from the ground　**2** : SOURCE, ORIGIN; *also* : MOTIVE　**3** : the season between winter and summer　**4** : an elastic body or device that recovers its original shape when it is released after being distorted　**5** : the act or an instance of leaping up or forward　**6** : elastic power — **springy** *adj*

**spring·board** \'spriŋ-,bȯrd\ *n* : a springy board used in jumping or vaulting or for diving

**spring fever** *n* : a lazy or restless feeling often associated with the onset of spring

**spring tide** *n* : either of two tides in the lunar month at new moon or full moon when the range is the greatest

**spring·time** \'spriŋ-,tīm\ *n* : the season of spring

**¹sprin·kle** \'spriŋ-kəl\ *vb* **sprin·kled; sprin·kling** \-k(ə-)liŋ\ : to scatter in small drops or particles — **sprin·kler** \-k(ə-)lər\ *n*

**²sprinkle** *n* : a light rainfall

**sprin·kling** \'spriŋ-kliŋ\ *n* : SMATTERING

**¹sprint** \'sprint\ *vb* : to run at top speed esp. for a short distance — **sprint·er** *n*

**²sprint** *n* **1** : a short run at top speed **2** : a short distance race

**sprite** \'sprīt\ *n* **1** : GHOST, SPIRIT **2** : ELF, FAIRY

**sprock·et** \'spräk-ət\ *n* : a tooth on a wheel (**sprocket wheel**) shaped so as to interlock with a chain

**¹sprout** \'spraùt\ *vb* : to send out new growth esp. rapidly ⟨~ing seeds⟩

**²sprout** *n* : a usu. young and growing plant shoot

**¹spruce** \'sprüs\ *n* : any of various conical evergreen trees related to the pines

**²spruce** *adj* **spruc·er; spruc·est** : neat and smart in appearance **syn** stylish, fashionable, modish

**³spruce** *vb* **spruced; spruc·ing** : to make or become spruce

**sprung** *past of* SPRING

**spry** \'sprī\ *adj* **spri·er** *or* **spry·er** \'sprī(-ə)r\; **spri·est** *or* **spry·est** \'sprī-əst\ : NIMBLE, ACTIVE **syn** agile, brisk

**spud** \'spəd\ *n* **1** : a sharp narrow spade **2** : POTATO

**spume** \'spyüm\ *n* : frothy matter on liquids : FOAM

**spu·mo·ni** *or* **spu·mo·ne** \spù-'mō-nē\ *n* : ice cream in layers of different colors, flavors, and textures often with candied fruits and nuts

**spun** *past of* SPIN

**spun glass** *n* : FIBERGLASS

**spunk** \'spəŋk\ *n* [fr. *spunk* tinder, fr. ScGael *spong* sponge, tinder, fr. L *spongia* sponge] : PLUCK, COURAGE — **spunky** *adj*

**¹spur** \'spər\ *n* **1** : a pointed device fastened to a rider's boot and used to urge on a horse **2** : something that urges to action **3** : a stiffly projecting part or process (as on the leg of a cock or on some flowers) **4** : a ridge extending sideways from a mountain **5** : a branch of railroad track extending from the main line **syn** goad, motive, impulse, incentive, inducement — **spurred** \'spərd\ *adj* — **on the spur of the moment** : on hasty impulse

**²spur** *vb* **spurred; spur·ring 1** : to urge a horse on with spurs **2** : INCITE

**spurge** \'spərj\ *n* : any of various herbs and woody plants with milky often poisonous juice

**spu·ri·ous** \'spyùr-ē-əs\ *adj* [LL *spurius* false, fr. L, of illegitimate birth,

fr. *spurius*, n., bastard] : not genuine : FALSE

**spurn** \'spərn\ *vb* **1** : to kick away or trample on **2** : to reject with disdain **syn** repudiate, refuse, decline

**¹spurt** \'spərt\ *n* **1** : a sudden brief burst of effort or speed **2** : a sharp increase of activity ⟨~ in sales⟩

**²spurt** *vb* : to make a spurt

**³spurt** *vb* : to gush out : spout forth

**⁴spurt** *n* : a sudden gushing or spouting

**sput·nik** \'spùt-nik, 'spət-\ *n* : a man-made satellite

**sput·ter** \'spət-ər\ *vb* **1** : to spit small scattered particles : SPLUTTER **2** : to utter words hastily or explosively in excitement or confusion **3** : to make small popping sounds — **sputter** *n*

**spu·tum** \'spyüt-əm\ *n, pl* **spu·ta** \-ə\ : expectorated material consisting of saliva and mucus

**¹spy** \'spī\ *vb* **spied; spy·ing 1** : to watch secretly usu. for hostile purposes : SCOUT **2** : to get a momentary or quick glimpse of : SEE **3** : to search for information secretly

**²spy** *n, pl* **spies 1** : one who secretly watches others **2** : one who secretly tries to obtain information for his own country in the territory of an enemy country

**spy·glass** \'spī-,glas\ *n* : a small telescope

**sq** *abbr* **1** squadron **2** square

**squab** \'skwäb\ *n, pl* **squabs** *or* **squab** : a young pigeon

**squab·ble** \'skwäb-əl\ *n* : a noisy altercation : WRANGLE **syn** quarrel, spat — **squabble** *vb*

**squad** \'skwäd\ *n* **1** : a small organized group of military personnel **2** : a small group engaged in some common effort

**squad car** *n* : a police automobile connected by radiotelephone with headquarters

**squad·ron** \'skwäd-rən\ *n* **1** : a body of men in regular formation **2** : any of several units of military organization

**squal·id** \'skwäl-əd\ *adj* **1** : filthy or degraded through neglect or poverty **2** : SORDID, DEBASED **syn** nasty, foul

**squall** \'skwòl\ *n* : a sudden violent gust of wind often with rain or snow — **squally** *adj*

**squa·lor** \'skwäl-ər\ *n* : the quality or state of being squalid

**squan·der** \'skwän-dər\ *vb* **squandered; squan·der·ing** \-d(ə-)riŋ\ : to spend wastefully or foolishly

**¹square** \'skwaər\ *n* **1** : an instrument used to lay out or test right angles **2** : a flat figure that has four equal sides and four right angles **3** : something square **4** : an area bounded by four streets **5** : an open area in a city where streets meet **6** : the product of a number multiplied by itself **7** : a highly conventional person

**²square** *adj* **squar·er; squar·est 1** : having four equal sides and four right angles **2** : forming a right angle ⟨cut a ~ corner⟩ **3** : multiplied by itself : SQUARED ⟨$X^2$ is the symbol for $X \sim$⟩

**4** : converted from a linear unit into a square unit of area having the same length of side ⟨a ~ foot is the area of a square each side of which is a foot⟩ **5** : being of a specified length in each of two dimensions ⟨an area 10 feet ~⟩ **6** : exactly adjusted **7** : JUST, FAIR ⟨a ~ deal⟩ **8** : leaving no balance ⟨make accounts ~⟩ **9** : SUBSTANTIAL ⟨a ~ meal⟩ **10** : highly conservative or conventional — **square·ly** *adv*

³**square** *vb* **squared; squar·ing 1** : to form with four equal sides and right angles or with flat surfaces ⟨~ a timber⟩ **2** : to multiply a number by itself **3** : CONFORM, AGREE **4** : BALANCE, SETTLE ⟨~ an account⟩

**square dance** *n* : a dance for four couples arranged to form a square

**square measure** *n* : a unit or system of units for measuring area — see METRIC SYSTEM table, WEIGHT table

**square-rigged** \'skwaor-'rigd\ *adj* : having the chief sails extended on yards that are fastened to the masts horizontally and at their center

**square-rig·ger** \-'rig-ər\ *n* : a square-rigged craft

**square root** *n* : a factor of a number that when multiplied by itself gives the number ⟨the *square root* of 9 is ± 3⟩

¹**squash** \'skwäsh, 'skwȯsh\ *vb* **1** : to beat or press into a pulp or flat mass **2** : QUASH, SUPPRESS

²**squash** *n* **1** : the impact of something soft and heavy; *also* : the sound of such impact **2** : a crushed mass **3** : SQUASH RACQUETS

³**squash** *n*, *pl* **squash·es** *or* **squash** : a fruit of any of various plants related to the gourds that is used esp. as a vegetable; *also* : a plant bearing squashes

**squash racquets** *n* : a game played on a 4-wall court with a racket and rubber ball

¹**squat** \'skwät\ *vb* **squat·ted; squat·ting 1** : to sit down upon the hams or heels **2** : to settle on land without right or title; *also* : to settle on public land with a view to acquiring title — **squat·ter** *n*

²**squat** *n* : the act or posture of squatting

³**squat** *adj* **squat·ter; squat·test** : low to the ground; *also* : short and thick in stature **syn** thickset, stocky

**squaw** \'skwȯ\ *n* : an American Indian woman

**squawk** \'skwȯk\ *n* : a harsh loud cry;* *also* : a noisy protest — **squawk** *vb*

**squeak** \'skwēk\ *vb* **1** : to utter or speak in a weak shrill tone **2** : to make a thin high-pitched sound — **squeak** *n* — **squeaky** *adj*

¹**squeal** \'skwēl\ *vb* **1** : to make a shrill sound or cry **2** : COMPLAIN, PROTEST **3** : to betray a secret or turn informer

²**squeal** *n* : a shrill sharp somewhat prolonged cry

**squea·mish** \'skwē-mish\ *adj* **1** : easily nauseated; *also* : NAUSEATED **2** : easily disgusted **syn** fussy, nice, dainty — **squea·mish·ness** *n*

**squee·gee** \'skwē-jē\ *n* : a blade

crosswise on a handle used for spreading or wiping liquid on, across, or off a surface — **squeegee** *vb*

¹**squeeze** \'skwēz\ *vb* **squeezed; squeez·ing 1** : to exert pressure on the opposite sides or parts of **2** : to obtain by pressure ⟨~ juice from a lemon⟩ **3** : to force, thrust, or cause to pass by pressure — **squeez·er** *n*

²**squeeze** *n* **1** : an act of squeezing **2** : a quantity squeezed out

**squeeze bottle** *n* : a flexible plastic bottle that dispenses its contents by being pressed

**squelch** \'skwelch\ *vb* **1** : to suppress completely; CRUSH **2** : to move in soft mud — **squelch** *n*

**squib** \'skwib\ *n* **1** a small firecracker; *esp* : one that fizzes instead of exploding **2** : a brief witty writing or speech

**squid** \'skwid\ *n*, *pl* **squid** *or* **squids** : a 10-armed long-bodied sea mollusk with no shell

**squint** \'skwint\ *vb* **1** : to look or aim obliquely **2** : to close the eyes partly ⟨the glare made him ~⟩ **3** : to be cross-eyed — **squint** *n or adj*

¹**squire** \'skwī(ə)r\ *n* [ME *squier*, fr. OF *esquier*, fr. LL *scutarius*, fr. L *scutum* shield] **1** : an armor-bearer of a knight **2** : a member of the British gentry ranking below a knight and above a gentleman; *also* : a prominent landowner **3** : a local magistrate **4** : a man gallantly devoted to a lady

²**squire** *vb* **squired; squir·ing** : to attend as a squire or escort

**squirm** \'skwərm\ *vb* : to twist about like a worm — WRIGGLE

**squir·rel** \'skwər(-ə)l\ *n*, *pl* **squirrels** *also* **squirrel** [ME *squirel*, fr. MF *esquireul*, fr. VL *scurius*, alter. of L *sciurus*, fr. Gk *skiouros*, fr. *skia* shadow + *oura* tail] : any of various rodents usu. with a long bushy tail and strong hind legs; *also* : the fur of a squirrel

¹**squirt** \'skwərt\ *vb* : to eject liquid in a thin spurt

²**squirt** *n* **1** : an instrument (as a syringe) for squirting **2** : a small forcible jet of liquid

¹**Sr** *abbr* **1** senior **2** sister

²**Sr** *symbol* strontium

**SR** *abbr* **1** seaman recruit **2** shipping receipt

**SRO** *abbr* standing room only

**SS** *abbr* **1** saints **2** steamship **3** Sunday school **4** sworn statement

**SSA** *abbr* Social Security Administration

**SSE** *abbr* south-southeast

**SSG** *or* **SSgt** *abbr* staff sergeant

**ssp** *abbr* subspecies

**SSR** *abbr* Soviet Socialist Republic

**SSS** *abbr* Selective Service System

**SST** *abbr* supersonic transport

**SSW** *abbr* south-southwest

**st** *abbr* **1** stanza **2** state **3** stitch **4** stone **5** street

**St** *abbr* saint

**ST** *abbr* short ton

**-st** — see -EST

**sta** *abbr* station; stationary

¹**stab** \'stab\ *n* **1** : a wound given by a

pointed weapon **2 :** a quick thrust; *also* **:** a brief attempt

²**stab** *vb* **stabbed; stab·bing :** to pierce or wound with or as if with a pointed weapon; *also* **:** THRUST, DRIVE

**sta·bile** \'stā-,bēl\ *n* **:** a stable abstract sculpture or construction typically made of sheet metal, wire, and wood

**sta·bi·lize** \'stā-bə-,līz\ *vb* **-lized; -liz·ing 1 :** to make stable **2 :** to hold steady ⟨~ prices⟩ **syn** balance — **sta·bi·li·za·tion** \,stā-bə-lə-'zā-shən\ *n* — **sta·bi·liz·er** \'stā-bə-,lī-zər\ *n*

¹**sta·ble** \'stā-bəl\ *n* **:** a building in which livestock is sheltered and fed — **sta·ble·man** \-mən, -,man\ *n*

²**stable** *vb* **sta·bled; sta·bling** \-b(ə-)liŋ\ **:** to put or keep in a stable

³**stable** *adj* **sta·bler** \-b(ə-)lər\; **sta·blest** \-b(ə-)ləst\ **1 :** firmly established; *also* **:** mentally healthy and well-balanced **2 :** steady in purpose **:** CONSTANT **3 :** DURABLE, ENDURING **4 :** resistant to chemical or physical change **syn** lasting, permanent, perpetual — **sta·bil·i·ty** \stə-'bil-ət-ē\ *n*

**stac·ca·to** \stə-'kät-ō\ *adj* **:** cut short or apart in performing ⟨~ notes⟩

¹**stack** \'stak\ *n* **1 :** a large pile (as of hay) **2 :** a large quantity **3 :** a vertical pipe **:** SMOKESTACK **4 :** an orderly pile (as of poker chips) **5 :** a rack with shelves for storing books

²**stack** *vb* **1 :** to pile up **2 :** to arrange (cards) secretly for cheating **3 :** to assign (an airplane) by radio to a particular altitude and position within a group circling before landing

**stack up** *vb* **:** to measure up

**sta·di·um** \'stād-ē-əm\ *n, pl* **-dia** \-ē-ə\ *or* **di·ums :** a structure with tiers of seats for spectators built around a field for sports events

¹**staff** \'staf\ *n, pl* **staffs** \'stafs, 'stavz\ *or* **staves** \'stavz, 'stāvz\ **1 :** a pole, stick, rod, or bar used for supporting, for measuring, or as a symbol of authority; *also* **:** CLUB, CUDGEL **2 :** something that sustains ⟨bread is the ~ of life⟩ **3 :** a body of assistants to an executive **4 :** a group of officers holding no command but having duties concerned with planning and managing **5 :** the five horizontal lines on which music is written

²**staff** *vb* **:** to supply with a staff or with workers

**staff·er** \'staf-ər\ *n* **:** a member of a staff (as of a newspaper)

**staff sergeant** *n* **:** a noncommissioned officer ranking in the army next below a sergeant first class, in the air force next below a technical sergeant, and in the marine corps next below a gunnery sergeant

¹**stag** \'stag\ *n, pl* **stags** *or* **stag :** an adult male of various large deer

²**stag** *adj* **:** restricted to or intended for men ⟨a ~ party⟩ ⟨~ movies⟩

³**stag** *adv* **:** unaccompanied by a date

¹**stage** \'stāj\ *n* **1 :** a raised platform on which an orator may speak or a play may be presented **2 :** the acting pro-

fession **:** THEATER **3 :** the scene of a notable action or event **4 :** a station or resting place on a traveled road **5 :** STAGECOACH **6 :** a degree of advance in an undertaking, process, or development **7 :** a propulsion unit in a rocket — **stagy** \'stā-jē\ *adj*

²**stage** *vb* **staged; stag·ing :** to produce or perform on or as if on a stage

**stage·coach** \'stāj-,kōch\ *n* **:** a coach that runs regularly between stations

¹**stag·ger** \'stag-ər\ *vb* **stag·gered; stag·ger·ing** \-(ə-)riŋ\ **1 :** to reel from side to side **:** TOTTER **2 :** to begin to doubt **:** WAVER **3 :** to cause to reel or waver **4 :** to arrange in overlapping or alternating positions or times ⟨~ working hours⟩ **5 :** ASTONISH — **stag·ger·ing·ly** *adv*

²**stagger** *n* **1** *pl* **:** an abnormal condition of domestic mammals and birds associated with damage to the central nervous system and marked by lack of coordination and a reeling unsteady gait **2 :** a reeling or unsteady gait or stance

**stag·ing** \'stā-jiŋ\ *n* **1 :** SCAFFOLDING **2 :** the assembling of troops and matériel in transit in a particular place

**stag·nant** \'stag-nənt\ *adj* **1 :** not flowing **:** MOTIONLESS ⟨~ water in a pond⟩ **2 :** DULL, INACTIVE ⟨~ business⟩

**stag·nate** \'stag-,nāt\ *vb* **stag·nat·ed; stag·nat·ing :** to be or become stagnant — **stag·na·tion** \stag-'nā-shən\ *n*

**staid** \'stād\ *adj* **:** SOBER, SEDATE **syn** grave, serious, earnest

¹**stain** \'stān\ *vb* **1 :** DISCOLOR, SOIL **2 :** to color (as wood, paper, or cloth) by processes affecting the material itself **3 :** TAINT, CORRUPT **4 :** DISGRACE

²**stain** *n* **1 :** SPOT, DISCOLORATION **2 :** a taint of guilt **:** STIGMA **3 :** a preparation (as a dye or pigment) used in staining — **stain·less** *adj*

**stainless steel** *n* **:** steel alloyed with chromium that is highly resistant to stain, rust, and corrosion

**stair** \'staər\ *n* **1 :** any one step of a series for ascending or descending from one level to another **2** *pl* **:** a flight of steps

**stair·case** \-,kās\ *n* **:** a flight of steps with their supporting framework, casing, and balusters

**stair·way** \-,wā\ *n* **:** one or more flights of stairs with connecting landings

**stair·well** \-,wel\ *n* **:** a vertical shaft in which stairs are located

¹**stake** \'stāk\ *n* **1 :** a pointed piece of material (as of wood) driven into the ground as a marker or a support **2 :** a post to which a person who is to be burned is bound; *also* **:** death by such burning **3 :** something that is staked for gain or loss **4 :** the prize in a contest

²**stake** *vb* **staked; stak·ing 1 :** to mark the limits of with stakes **2 :** to tether to a stake **3 :** to support or secure with stakes **4 :** to place as a bet

**stake·out** \'stāk-,aůt\ *n* **:** a surveillance by police (as of an area)

**sta·lac·tite** \stə-'lak-,tīt\ *n* [NL *stalactites,* fr. Gk *stalaktos* dripping, fr. *stalassein* to let drip] **:** an icicle‑shaped deposit hanging from the roof or sides of a cavern

**sta·lag·mite** \stə-'lag-ˌmīt\ *n* [NL *stalagmites*, fr. Gk *stalagma* drop or *stalagmos* dripping] **:** a deposit resembling an inverted stalactite rising from the floor of a cavern

**stale** \'stāl\ *adj* **stal·er; stal·est 1 :** flat and tasteless from age ⟨~ beer⟩ **2 :** not freshly made ⟨~ bread⟩ **3 :** COMMONPLACE, TRITE — **stale** *vb*

**stale·mate** \'stāl-ˌmāt\ *n* **:** a drawn contest **:** DEADLOCK — **stalemate** *vb*

**¹stalk** \'stȯk\ *vb* **1 :** to walk stiffly or haughtily **2 :** to approach (game) stealthily

**²stalk** *n* **:** a plant stem; *also* **:** any slender usu. upright supporting or connecting part — **stalked** \'stȯkt\ *adj*

**¹stall** \'stȯl\ *n* **1 :** a compartment in a stable for one animal **2 :** a booth or counter where articles may be displayed for sale **3 :** a seat in a church choir; *also* **:** a church pew **4** *Brit* **:** a front orchestra seat in a theater

**²stall** *vb* **:** to bring or come to a standstill unintentionally ⟨~ an engine⟩

**³stall** *n* **:** the condition of an airfoil or airplane operating so that there is a flow breakdown and loss of lift

**stal·lion** \'stal-yən\ *n* **:** a male horse

**stal·wart** \'stȯl-wərt\ *adj* **:** STOUT, STRONG; *also* **:** BRAVE, VALIANT

**sta·men** \'stā-mən\ *n, pl* **stamens** *also* **sta·mi·na** \'stā-mə-nə, 'stam-ə-\ **:** an organ of a flower that produces pollen

**stam·i·na** \'stam-ə-nə\ *n* [L, pl. of *stamen* warp, thread of life spun by the Fates] **:** VIGOR, ENDURANCE

**sta·mi·nate** \'stā-mə-nət, 'stam-ə-, -ˌnāt\ *adj* **1 :** having or producing stamens **2 :** having stamens but no pistils

**stam·mer** \'stam-ər\ *vb* **stammered; stam·mer·ing** \-(ə-)riŋ\ **:** to hesitate or stumble in speaking — **stammer** *n* — **stam·mer·er** *n*

**¹stamp** \'stamp; *for 2 also* 'stämp *or* 'stȯmp\ *vb* **1 :** to pound or crush with a heavy instrument **2 :** to strike or beat with the bottom of the foot **3 :** to impress or imprint with a mark **4 :** to cut out or indent with a stamp or die **5 :** to attach a postage stamp to

**²stamp** *n* **1 :** a device or instrument for stamping **2 :** the mark made by stamping; *also* **:** a distinctive mark or quality **3 :** a paper or a mark put on a thing to show that a required charge has been paid **4 :** the act of stamping

**¹stam·pede** \stam-'pēd\ *n* **:** a wild headlong rush or flight esp. of frightened animals

**²stampede** *vb* **stam·ped·ed; stamped·ing 1 :** to flee or cause to flee in panic **2 :** to act or cause to act together suddenly and heedlessly

**stance** \'stans\ *n* **:** a way of standing

**¹stanch** \'stȯnch, 'stänch\ *vb* **:** to check the flowing of (as blood); *also* **:** to cease flowing or bleeding

**²stanch** *var of* STAUNCH

**stan·chion** \'stan-chən\ *n* **:** an upright bar, post, or support

**¹stand** \'stand\ *vb* **stood** \'stu̇d\; **stand·ing 1 :** to take or be at rest in an upright or firm position **2 :** to assume a specified position **3 :** to remain stationary or unchanged **4 :** to be steadfast **5 :** to act in resistance ⟨~ against a foe⟩ **6 :** to maintain a relative position or rank **7 :** to gather slowly and remain briefly ⟨tears *stood* in her eyes⟩ **8 :** to set upright **9 :** ENDURE, TOLERATE ⟨I won't ~ for that⟩ **10 :** to submit to ⟨~ trial⟩ — **stand pat :** to oppose or resist change

**²stand** *n* **1 :** an act of standing, staying, or resisting **2 :** a place taken by a witness to testify in court **3 :** a structure for a small retail business **4 :** a raised platform (as for speakers) **5 :** a structure for supporting or holding something upright ⟨music ~⟩ **6 :** a group of plants growing in a continuous area **7** *pl* **:** tiered seats for spectators **8 :** a stop made to give a performance **9 :** POSITION, VIEWPOINT

**stan·dard** \'stan-dərd\ *n* **1 :** a figure adopted as an emblem by a people **2 :** the personal flag of a ruler; *also* **:** FLAG **3 :** something set up as a rule for measuring or as a model to be followed **4 :** an upright support ⟨lamp ~⟩ — **standard** *adj*

**stan·dard–bear·er** \-ˌbar-ər\ *n* **:** the leader of a cause

**stan·dard·ize** \'stan-dərd-ˌīz\ *vb* **-ized; -iz·ing :** to make standard or uniform — **stan·dard·iza·tion** \ˌstan-dərd-ə-'zā-shən\ *n*

**standard of living :** the necessities, comforts, and luxuries that a person or group is accustomed to

**standard time** *n* **:** the time established by law or by general usage over a region or country

**stand·by** \'stan(d)-ˌbī\ *n, pl* **stand·bys** \-ˌbīz\ **1 :** one that can be relied on **2 :** a substitute in reserve — **on standby :** ready or available for immediate action or use

**stand–in** \'stan-ˌdin\ *n* **1 :** someone employed to occupy an actor's place while lights and camera are readied **2 :** SUBSTITUTE

**¹stand·ing** \'stan-diŋ\ *adj* **1 :** ERECT **2 :** not flowing **:** STAGNANT **3 :** remaining at the same level or amount for an indefinite period ⟨~ offer⟩ **4 :** PERMANENT **5 :** done from a standing position ⟨a ~ jump⟩

**²standing** *n* **1 :** length of service; *also* **:** relative position in society or in a profession **:** RANK **2 :** DURATION

**stand·off** \'stand-ˌȯf\ *n* **:** TIE, DRAW

**stand·out** \'stand-ˌau̇t\ *n* **:** something conspicuously excellent

**stand·pipe** \'stan(d)-ˌpīp\ *n* **:** a high vertical pipe or reservoir for water used to produce a uniform pressure

**stand·point** \-ˌpȯint\ *n* **:** a position from which objects or principles are judged

**stand·still** \-ˌstil\ *n* **:** a state of rest

**stank** \'staŋk\ *past of* STINK

**stan·za** \'stan-zə\ *n* : a group of lines forming a division of a poem

**sta·pes** \'stā-,pēz\ *n, pl* **stapes** *or* **sta·pe·des** \'stā-pə-,dēz\ : the small innermost bone of the ear of mammals

**staph·y·lo·coc·cus** \,staf-ə-lō-'käk-əs\ *n, pl* **-coc·ci** \-'käk-,(s)ī, -(,)(s)ē\ : any of various spherical bacteria including some that cause purulent infections — **staph·y·lo·coc·cal** \-'käk-əl\ *adj* — **staph·y·lo·coc·cic** \-'käk-(s)ik\ *adj*

¹**sta·ple** \'stā-pəl\ *n* : a U-shaped piece of metal with sharp points to be driven into a surface to hold something (as a hook or wire); *also* : a similarly shaped piece of wire driven through papers and bent over at the ends to fasten them together or through thin material to fasten it to a surface — **staple** *vb* — **sta·pler** \-p(ə-)lər\ *n*

²**staple** *n* **1** : a chief commodity or product **2** : the main part of a thing : chief item **3** : unmanufactured or raw material **4** : a textile fiber suitable for spinning into yarn

³**staple** *adj* **1** : regularly produced in large quantities **2** : PRINCIPAL, MAIN

¹**star** \'stär\ *n* **1** : a natural celestial body that is visible as an apparently fixed point of light; *esp* : such a body that is gaseous, self-luminous, and of great mass **2** : a planet or configuration of planets that is held in astrology to influence one's fortune — usu. used in pl. **3** : DESTINY, FORTUNE **4** : a conventional figure representing a star **5** : ASTERISK **6** : a brilliant performer **7** : an actor or actress playing the leading role — **star·dom** \'stärd-əm\ *n* — **star·less** *adj* — **star·like** *adj* — **star·ry** *adj*

²**star** *vb* **starred; star·ring 1** : to adorn with stars **2** : to mark with an asterisk **3** : to play the leading role

**star·board** \'stär-bərd\ *n* [ME *sterbord*, fr. OE *stēorbord*, fr. *stēor-* steering oar + *bord* ship's side] : the right side of a ship or airplane looking forward — **starboard** *adj*

¹**starch** \'stärch\ *vb* : to stiffen with starch

²**starch** *n* : a complex carbohydrate that is stored in plants, is an important foodstuff, and is used in adhesives and sizes, in laundering, and in pharmacy — **starchy** *adj*

**stare** \'staər\ *vb* **stared; star·ing** : to look fixedly with wide-open eyes — **stare** *n* — **star·er** *n*

**star·fish** \'stär-,fish\ *n* : a star-shaped sea animal that feeds on mollusks

**stark** \'stärk\ *adj* **1** : STRONG, ROBUST **2** : rigid as if in death; *also* : STRICT **3** : SHEER, UTTER **4** : BARREN, DESOLATE ⟨~ landscape⟩; *also* : UNADORNED ⟨~ realism⟩ **5** : sharply delineated — **stark** *adv* — **stark·ly** *adv*

**star·light** \'stär-,līt\ *n* : the light given by the stars

**star·ling** \'stär-liŋ\ *n* : a dark brown or greenish black European bird related to the crows that is naturalized and often a pest in the U.S.

¹**start** \'stärt\ *vb* **1** : to give an involuntary twitch or jerk (as from surprise) **2** : BEGIN, COMMENCE **3** : to set going **4** : to enter (as a horse) in a contest **5** : TAP ⟨~ a cask⟩ — **start·er** *n*

²**start** *n* **1** : a sudden involuntary motion : LEAP **2** : a spasmodic and brief effort or action **3** : BEGINNING; *also* : the place of beginning

**star·tle** \'stärt-ᵊl\ *vb* **star·tled; star·tling** \'stärt-(ᵊ-)liŋ\ : to frighten or surprise suddenly : cause to start

**star·tling** *adj* : causing sudden fear, surprise, or anxiety

**starve** \'stärv\ *vb* **starved; starv·ing** [ME *sterven* to die, fr. OE *steorfan*] **1** : to perish from hunger **2** : to suffer extreme hunger **3** : to kill with hunger; *also* : to distress or subdue by famine — **star·va·tion** \stär-'vā-shən\ *n*

**starve·ling** \'stärv-liŋ\ *n* : one that is thin from lack of nourishment

**stash** \'stash\ *vb* : to store in a secret place — **stash** *n*

**stat** *abbr* statute

¹**state** \'stāt\ *n* [ME *stat*, fr. OF & L; OF *estat*, fr. L *status*, fr. *stare* to stand] **1** : mode or condition of being ⟨gaseous ~ of water⟩ **2** : condition of mind **3** : social position; *esp* : high rank **4** : a body of people occupying a definite territory and politically organized under one government; *also* : the government of such a body of people **5** : one of the constituent units of a nation having a federal government — **state·hood** \-,hůd\ *n*

²**state** *vb* **stat·ed; stat·ing 1** : to express in words **2** : FIX ⟨*stated* intervals⟩

**state·craft** \'stāt-,kraft\ *n* : state management : STATESMANSHIP

**state·house** \-,haůs\ *n* : the building in which a state legislature meets

**state·ly** \'stāt-lē\ *adj* **state·li·er; -est 1** : having lofty dignity : HAUGHTY **2** : IMPRESSIVE, MAJESTIC **syn** magnificent, imposing, august — **state·li·ness** *n*

**state·ment** \'stāt-mənt\ *n* **1** : the act or result of presenting in words **2** : a summary of a financial account

**state·room** \'stāt-,rüm, -,rům\ *n* : a private room on a ship or on a railroad car

**state·side** \'stāt-,sīd\ *adj* : of or relating to the U.S. as regarded from outside its continental limits ⟨~ mail⟩ — **stateside** *adv*

**states·man** \'stāts-mən\ *n* : one skilled in government and wise in handling public affairs; *also* : one influential in shaping public policy — **states·man·like** *adj* — **states·man·ship** *n*

¹**stat·ic** \'stat-ik\ *adj* **1** : acting by mere weight without motion ⟨~ pressure⟩ **2** : relating to bodies or forces at rest or in equilibrium **3** : not moving : not active **4** : of or relating to stationary charges of electricity **5** : of, relating to, or caused by radio static

²**static** *n* : noise produced in a radio or television receiver by atmospheric or other electrical disturbances

¹**sta·tion** \'stā-shən\ n 1 : the place where a person or thing stands or is appointed to remain 2 : a regular stopping place on a transportation route ⟨a railroad ∼⟩ ⟨a bus ∼⟩; also : DEPOT 3 : a stock farm or ranch in Australia or New Zealand 4 : a place where a fleet is assigned for duty 5 : a military post 6 : social standing 7 : a complete assemblage of radio or television equipment for sending or receiving

²**station** vb **sta·tioned; sta·tion·ing** \'stā-sh(ə-)niŋ\ : to assign to a station

**sta·tion·ary** \'stā-shə-,ner-ē\ adj 1 : fixed in a certain place or position 2 : not changing condition : neither improving nor getting worse

**station break** n : a pause in a radio or television broadcast for announcement of the identity of the network or station

**sta·tio·ner** \'stā-sh(ə-)nər\ n : one that sells stationery

**sta·tio·nery** \'stā-shə-,ner-ē\ n : materials (as paper, pens, or ink) for writing; esp : letter paper with envelopes

**station wagon** n : an automobile having an interior longer than a sedan's, one or more folding or removable seats to facilitate trucking, and no separate luggage compartment

**sta·tis·tic** \stə-'tis-tik\ n 1 : a single term or datum in a collection of statistics 2 : a quantity (as the mean) that is computed from a sample

**sta·tis·tics** \stə-'tis-tiks\ n pl [G statistik study of political facts and figures, fr. NL statisticus of politics, fr. L status state] 1 : a branch of mathematics dealing with the analysis and interpretation of masses of numerical data 2 : facts collected and arranged in an orderly way for study — **sta·tis·ti·cal** \-ti-kəl\ adj — **sta·tis·ti·cal·ly** \-ti-k(ə-)lē\ adv — **stat·is·ti·cian** \,stat-ə-'stish-ən\ n

**stat·u·ary** \'stach-ə-,wer-ē\ n, pl -ar·ies 1 : a branch of sculpture dealing with figures in the round 2 : a collection of statues

**stat·ue** \'stach-ü\ n : a likeness of a living being sculptured in a solid substance

**stat·u·esque** \,stach-ə-'wesk\ adj : resembling a statue esp. in well-proportioned or massive dignity

**stat·u·ette** \,stach-ə-'wet\ n : a small statue

**stat·ure** \'stach-ər\ n 1 : natural height (as of a person) 2 : quality or status gained (as by growth or achievement)

**sta·tus** \'stāt-əs, 'stat-\ n 1 : the state or condition of a person in the eyes of the law or of others 2 : condition of affairs

**sta·tus quo** \-'kwō\ n [L, state in which] : the existing state of affairs

**stat·ute** \'stach-üt\ n : a law enacted by a legislative body

**stat·u·to·ry** \'stach-ə-,tōr-ē\ adj : imposed by statute : LAWFUL

¹**staunch** \'stónch\ var of STANCH

²**staunch** adj 1 : WATERTIGHT ⟨a ∼ ship⟩ 2 : FIRM, STRONG; also : STEAD-

FAST, LOYAL **syn** resolute, constant, true, faithful — **staunch·ly** adv

¹**stave** \'stāv\ n 1 : CUDGEL, STAFF 2 : any of several narrow strips of wood placed edge to edge to make something (as a barrel or bucket) 3 : STANZA

²**stave** vb **staved** or **stove** \'stōv\; **stav·ing** 1 : to break in the staves of; also : to break a hole in 2 : to drive or thrust away ⟨∼ off trouble⟩

**staves** pl of STAFF

¹**stay** \'stā\ n 1 : a strong rope or wire used to support or steady something (as a ship's mast) 2 : a holding or stiffening part in a structure (as a bridge) 3 : PROP, SUPPORT 4 pl : CORSET

²**stay** vb **stayed** \'stād\ or **staid** \'stād\; **stay·ing** 1 : PAUSE, WAIT 2 : LIVE, DWELL 3 : to stand firm 4 : STOP, CHECK 5 : DELAY, POSTPONE 6 : to last out ⟨∼ a race⟩ **syn** remain, abide, linger, sojourn, lodge, reside

³**stay** n 1 : STOP, HALT 2 : a residence or sojourn in a place

⁴**stay** vb 1 : to hold up : PROP 2 : to satisfy (as hunger) for a time

**staying power** n : STAMINA

**stbd** abbr starboard

**std** abbr standard

**STD** abbr [L sacrae theologiae doctor] doctor of sacred theology

**Ste** abbr saint (female)

**stead** \'sted\ n 1 : the place or function that another person has ⟨his brother served in his ∼⟩ 2 : ADVANTAGE, AVAIL ⟨stood him in good ∼⟩

**stead·fast** \'sted-,fast\ adj 1 : firmly fixed in place 2 : not subject to change 3 : firm in belief, determination, or adherence : LOYAL **syn** resolute, true, faithful, staunch — **stead·fast·ly** adv — **stead·fast·ness** n

¹**steady** \'sted-ē\ adj **steadi·er; -est** 1 : STABLE, FIRM 2 : not faltering or swerving; also : CALM 3 : CONSTANT, RESOLUTE 4 : REGULAR 5 : RELIABLE, SOBER **syn** uniform, even — **steadi·ly** \'sted-ᵊl-ē\ adv — **steadi·ness** \-ē-nəs\ n — **steady** adv

²**steady** vb **stead·ied; steady·ing** : to make or become steady

**steak** \'stāk\ n : a slice of meat cut from a fleshy part esp. of a beef carcass

¹**steal** \'stēl\ vb **stole** \'stōl\; **sto·len** \'stō-lən\; **steal·ing** 1 : to take and carry away without right or permission 2 : to get for oneself slyly or secretly 3 : to come or go secretly or gradually 4 : to gain a base in baseball by running without the aid of a hit or an error **syn** pilfer, filch, purloin

²**steal** n 1 : an act of stealing 2 : BARGAIN

**stealth** \'stelth\ n 1 : secret or underhand procedure : FURTIVENESS

**stealthy** \'stel-thē\ adj **stealth·i·er; -est** : done by stealth : FURTIVE, SLY **syn** secret, covert, clandestine, surreptitious, underhanded — **stealth·i·ly** \'stel-thə-lē\ adv

¹**steam** \'stēm\ n 1 : the vapor into which water is changed when heated to the boiling point 2 : water vapor when compressed so that it supplies heat and

power  **3** : POWER, FORCE, ENERGY — **steamy** adj

**¹steam** vb  **1** : to emit vapor  **2** : to pass off as vapor  **3** : to move by or as if by the agency of steam — **steam·er** n

**steam·boat** \'stēm-ˌbōt\ n : a boat propelled by steam power

**steam engine** n : an engine driven by steam; esp : a reciprocating engine having a piston driven in a closed cylinder by steam

**steam fitter** n : a workman who puts in or repairs equipment (as steam pipes) for heating, ventilating, or refrigerating systems — **steam fitting** n

**steam·roll·er** \'stēm-ˈrō-lər\ n : a machine for compacting roads or pavements — **steam·roll·er** also **steam·roll** \-ˌrōl\ vb

**steam·ship** \'stēm-ˌship\ n : a ship propelled by steam

**steed** \'stēd\ n : HORSE

**steel** \'stēl\ n  **1** : iron treated with intense heat and mixed with carbon to make it hard and tough  **2** : an instrument or implement made of steel  **3** : a quality (as of mind) that suggests steel — **steel** adj — **steely** adj

**²steel** vb  **1** : to sheathe, point, or edge with steel  **2** : to make able to resist

**steel wool** n : long fine steel shavings used esp. for scouring and smoothing

**steel·yard** \'stēl-ˌyärd\ n : a balance in which the object to be weighed is hung from the shorter arm of a lever and is balanced by a weight that slides along the longer arm

**steep** \'stēp\ adj  **1** : having a very sharp slope : PRECIPITOUS  **2** : too great or too high ⟨~ prices⟩ — **steep·ly** adv — **steep·ness** n

**²steep** n : a steep slope

**³steep** vb  **1** : to soak in a liquid; esp : to extract the essence of by soaking ⟨~ tea⟩  **2** : SATURATE ⟨~ed in learning⟩

**stee·ple** \'stē-pəl\ n : a tall tapering structure built on top of a church tower; also : a church tower

**stee·ple·chase** \-ˌchās\ n [fr. the use of church steeples as landmarks to guide the riders] : a race across country by horsemen; also : a race over a course obstructed by hurdles

**steer** \'stiər\ n : an ox castrated before sexual maturity and usu. raised for beef

**²steer** vb  **1** : to direct the course of (as by a rudder or wheel)  **2** : GUIDE, CONTROL  **3** : to be subject to guidance or direction  **4** : to pursue a course of action — **steers·man** \'stiərz-mən\ n

**steer·age** \'sti(ə)r-ij\ n  **1** : DIRECTION, GUIDANCE  **2** : a section in a passenger ship for passengers paying the lowest fares

**stein** \'stīn\ n : an earthenware mug

**stel·lar** \'stel-ər\ adj : of or relating to stars : resembling a star

**stem** \'stem\ n  **1** : the main shaft of a plant; also : a plant part that supports another part (as a leaf or fruit)  **2** : a line of ancestry : STOCK  **3** : something resembling the stem of a plant  **4** : the prow of a ship  **5** : that part of an inflected word which remains unchanged throughout a given inflection — **stem·less** adj

**²stem** vb  **stemmed; stem·ming** : to have a specified source : DERIVE

**³stem** vb  **stemmed; stem·ming** : to make headway against ⟨~ the tide⟩

**⁴stem** vb  **stemmed; stem·ming** : to stop or check by or as if by damming

**stench** \'stench\ n : STINK

**sten·cil** \'sten-səl\ n [ME stanselen to ornament with sparkling colors, fr. MF estanceler, fr. estancele spark, fr. (assumed) VL stincilla, fr. L scintilla] : a piece of thin impervious material (as metal or paper) that is perforated with lettering or a design through which a substance (as ink or paint) is applied to a surface to be printed — **stencil** vb

**ste·nog·ra·phy** \stə-ˈnäg-rə-fē\ n : the art or process of writing in shorthand — **ste·nog·ra·pher** \-fər\ n — **steno·graph·ic** \ˌsten-ə-ˈgraf-ik\ adj

**sten·to·ri·an** \sten-ˈtōr-ē-ən\ adj : extremely loud

**¹step** \'step\ n  **1** : an advance made by raising one foot and putting it down in a different spot  **2** : a rest for the foot in ascending or descending : STAIR  **3** : a degree, rank, or plane in a series  **4** : a small space or distance  **5** : manner of walking  **6** : a sequential measure leading to a result

**²step** vb  **stepped; step·ping  1** : to advance or recede by steps  **2** : to go on foot : WALK  **3** : to move along briskly  **4** : to measure by steps  **5** : to press down with the foot  **6** : to construct or arrange in or as if in steps

**step·broth·er** \'step-ˌbrəth-ər\ n : the son of one's stepparent by a former marriage

**step·child** \-ˌchīld\ n : a child of one's husband or wife by a former marriage

**step·daugh·ter** \-ˌdȯt-ər\ n : a daughter of one's wife or husband by a former marriage

**step down** vb : to lower voltage by means of a transformer

**step·fa·ther** \-ˌfäth-ər\ n : the husband of one's mother by a subsequent marriage

**step·lad·der** \'step-ˌlad-ər\ n : a light portable set of steps in a hinged frame

**step·moth·er** \-ˌməth-ər\ n : the wife of one's father by a subsequent marriage

**step·par·ent** \-ˌpar-ənt\ n : the husband or wife of one's mother or father by a subsequent marriage

**steppe** \'step\ n : dry grass-covered land in regions of wide temperature range esp. in southeastern Europe and Asia

**step·sis·ter** \'step-ˌsis-tər\ n : the daughter of one's stepparent by a former marriage

**step·son** \-ˌsən\ n : a son of one's wife or husband by a former marriage

**step up** \(')step-'əp\ vb  **1** : to increase voltage by means of a transformer  **2** : INCREASE, ACCELERATE — **step-up** \'step-ˌəp\ n

**ster** abbr sterling

**stere** \'sti(ə)r, 'ste(ə)r\ *n* — see METRIC SYSTEM table

**ste·reo** \'ster-ē-,ō, 'stir-\ *n, pl* **ste·re·os** **1 :** a stereoscopic method or effect **2 :** a stereoscopic photograph **3 :** stereophonic reproduction **4 :** a stereophonic sound system — **stereo** *adj*

**ste·reo·phon·ic** \,ster-ē-ə-'fän-ik, ,stir-\ *adj* **:** giving, relating to, or being a three-dimensional effect of reproduced sound — **ste·reo·phon·i·cal·ly** \-i-k(ə-)lē\ *adv*

**ster·e·o·scope** \'ster-ē-ə-,skōp, 'stir-\ *n* [Gk *stereos* solid + *skopein* to look at] **:** an optical instrument with two eyeglasses through which a person looks at two photographs of the same scene taken a little way apart so that the two pictures blend into one and give the effect of solidity and depth

**ste·reo·scop·ic** \,ster-ē-ə-'skäp-ik, ,stir-\ *adj* **1 :** of or relating to the stereoscope **2 :** characterized by stereoscopy ⟨~ vision⟩ — **ste·reo·scop·i·cal·ly** \-i-k(ə-)lē\ *adv*

**ste·re·os·co·py** \,ster-ē-'äs-kə-pē, ,stir-\ *n* **:** the seeing of objects in three dimensions

**ste·reo·tape** \'ster-ē-ō-,tāp, 'stir-\ *n* **:** a stereophonic magnetic tape

**ste·reo·type** \'ster-ē-ə-,tīp, 'stir-\ *n* **:** a metal printing plate cast from a mold made from set type

**ste·reo·typed** \-,tīpt\ *adj* **:** repeated without variation **:** lacking originality or individuality **syn** trite

**ster·ile** \'ster-əl\ *adj* **1 :** unable to bear fruit, crops, or offspring **2 :** free from infectious matter — **ste·ril·i·ty** \stə-'ril-ət-ē\ *n*

**ster·il·ize** \'ster-ə-,līz\ *vb* **-ized; -iz·ing :** to make sterile; *esp* **:** to free from germs — **ster·il·iza·tion** \,ster-ə-lə-'zā-shən\ *n* — **ster·il·iz·er** \'ster-ə-,lī-zər\ *n*

**¹ster·ling** \'stər-liŋ\ *n* **1 :** British money **2 :** sterling silver

**²sterling** *adj* **1 :** of, relating to, or calculated in terms of British sterling **2 :** having a fixed standard of purity represented by an alloy of 925 parts of silver with 75 parts of copper **3 :** made of sterling silver **4 :** EXCELLENT

**¹stern** \'stərn\ *adj* **1 :** SEVERE, AUSTERE **2 :** STOUT, STURDY ⟨~ resolve⟩ — **stern·ly** *adv* — **stern·ness** *n*

**²stern** *n* **:** the rear end of a boat

**ster·num** \'stər-nəm\ *n, pl* **sternums** *or* **ster·na** \-nə\ **:** a long flat bone or cartilage at the center front of the chest connecting the ribs of the two sides — **ster·nal** \'stərn-ᵊl\ *adj*

**stetho·scope** \'steth-ə-,skōp\ *n* **:** an instrument used for listening to sounds produced in the body and esp. in the chest

**ste·ve·dore** \'stē-və-,dōr\ *n* [Sp *estibador,* fr. *estibar* to pack, fr. L *stipare* to press together] **:** one who works at loading and unloading ships

**¹stew** \'st(y)ü\ *n* **:** a dish of stewed meat and vegetables served in gravy

**stew** *vb* **:** to boil slowly **:** SIMMER

**stew·ard** \'st(y)ü-ərd\ *n* [ME, fr. OE *stīweard,* fr. *stī* hall, sty + *weard* ward] **1 :** one employed on a large estate to manage domestic concerns (as collecting rents, keeping accounts, and directing servants) **2 :** one actively concerned with the direction of the affairs of an organization **3 :** one who supervises the provision and distribution of food (as on a ship); *also* **:** an employee on a ship or airplane who serves passengers generally — **stew·ard·ess** \-əs\ *n* — **stew·ard·ship** *n*

**stg** *abbr* sterling

**¹stick** \'stik\ *n* **1 :** a cut or broken branch or twig; *also* **:** a long slender piece of wood **2 :** ROD, STAFF **3 :** something resembling a stick **4 :** a dull uninteresting person

**²stick** *vb* **stuck** \'stək\; **stick·ing** **1 :** STAB, PRICK **2 :** to thrust or project in some direction or manner **3 :** IMPALE **4 :** to hold fast by or as if by gluing **:** ADHERE **5 :** ATTACH, FASTEN **6 :** to hold to something firmly or closely **:** CLING **7 :** to become jammed or blocked **8 :** to be unable to proceed or move freely

**stick·er** \'stik-ər\ *n* **:** one that sticks (as a bur) or causes sticking (as glue); *esp* **:** a gummed label

**stick insect** *n* **:** any of various usu. wingless insects with a long round body resembling a stick

**stick·ler** \'stik-(ə-)lər\ *n* **:** one who insists on exactness or completeness

**stick shift** *n* **:** a manually operated gearshift mounted on the steering-wheel column or floor of an automobile

**stick-to-it·ive·ness** \stik-'tü-ət-iv-nəs\ *n* **:** dogged perseverance **:** TENACITY

**stick up** \(')stik-'əp\ *vb* **:** to rob at gunpoint — **stick·up** \'stik-,əp\ *n*

**sticky** \'stik-ē\ *adj* **stick·i·er; -est** **1 :** ADHESIVE **2 :** VISCOUS, GLUEY **3 :** tending to stick ⟨~ valve⟩

**stiff** \'stif\ *adj* **1 :** not pliant **:** RIGID **2 :** not limber ⟨~ joints⟩ **3 :** TENSE, TAUT **4 :** not flowing or working easily ⟨~ paste⟩ **5 :** not natural and easy **:** FORMAL **6 :** STRONG, FORCEFUL ⟨~ breeze⟩ **7 :** HARSH, SEVERE **8 :** DIFFICULT **syn** inflexible — **stiff·ly** *adv* — **stiff·ness** *n*

**stiff·en** \'stif-ən\ *vb* **stiff·ened; stiff·en·ing** \-(ə-)niŋ\ **:** to make or become stiff — **stiff·en·er** \-(ə-)nər\ *n*

**stiff-necked** \-'nekt\ *adj* **:** STUBBORN, HAUGHTY

**sti·fle** \'stī-fəl\ *vb* **sti·fled; sti·fling** \-f(ə-)liŋ\ **1 :** SUFFOCATE **2 :** QUENCH, SUPPRESS **3 :** SMOTHER, MUFFLE **4 :** to die because of obstruction of the breath

**stig·ma** \'stig-mə\ *n, pl* **stig·ma·ta** \stig-'mät-ə, 'stig-mət-ə\ *or* **stigmas** **1 :** a mark of disgrace or discredit **2** *pl* **:** bodily marks resembling the wounds of the crucified Christ **3 :** the part of the pistil of a flower that receives the pollen in fertilization — **stig·mat·ic** \stig-'mat-ik\ *adj*

**stig·ma·tize** \'stig-mə-,tīz\ *vb* **-tized;**

-tiz·ing **1** : to mark with a stigma **2** : to set a mark of disgrace upon

stile \'stīl\ n : steps used for crossing a fence or wall

sti·let·to \stə-'let-ō\ n, pl -tos or -toes : a slender dagger

¹still \'stil\ adj **1** : MOTIONLESS **2** : making no sound : QUIET, SILENT — still·ness n

²still vb : to make or become still : QUIET

³still adv **1** : without motion ⟨sit ~⟩ **2** : up to and during this or that time **3** : in spite of that : NEVERTHELESS **4** : EVEN, YET ⟨ran ~ faster⟩

⁴still n **1** : STILLNESS, SILENCE **2** : a static photograph esp. of an instant in a motion picture

⁵still n **1** : DISTILLERY **2** : apparatus used in distillation

still·born \'stil-,bȯrn\ n : the birth of a dead fetus

still·born \-'bȯrn\ adj : born dead

still life n, pl still lifes : a picture of inanimate objects

stilt \'stilt\ n : one of a pair of poles for walking with each having a step or loop for the foot; also : a polelike support of a structure above ground or water level

stilt·ed \'stil-təd\ adj : FORMAL, POMPOUS ⟨~ writing⟩

Stil·ton \'stilt-ᵊn\ n : a blue-veined cheese with wrinkled rind

stim·u·lant \'stim-yə-lənt\ n **1** : an agent (as a drug) that temporarily increases the activity of an organism or any of its parts **2** : STIMULUS **3** : an alcoholic beverage — stimulant adj

stim·u·late \-,lāt\ vb -lat·ed; -lat·ing : to make active or more active : ANIMATE, AROUSE **syn** excite, provoke — stim·u·la·tion \,stim-yə-'lā-shən\ n — stim·u·la·tive \'stim-yə-,lāt-iv\ adj

stim·u·lus \'stim-yə-ləs\ n, pl -li \-,lī\ : something that stimulates : SPUR

¹sting \'stiŋ\ vb stung \'stəŋ\; sting·ing \'stiŋ-iŋ\ **1** : to prick painfully esp. with a sharp or poisonous process **2** : to cause to suffer acutely — sting·er n

²sting n **1** : an act of stinging; also : a resultant sore, pain, or mark **2** : a pointed often venom-bearing organ (as of a bee) used esp. in defense

stin·gy \'stin-jē\ adj stin·gi·er; -est : not generous : SPARING, NIGGARDLY — stin·gi·ness n

stink \'stiŋk\ vb stank \'staŋk\ or stunk \'stəŋk\; stunk; stink·ing : to give forth a strong and offensive smell; also : to be extremely bad in quality or repute — stink n — stink·er n

stink·bug \'stiŋk-,bəg\ n : any of various bugs that emit a disagreeable odor

¹stint \'stint\ vb **1** : to restrict to a scant allowance : cut short in amount **2** : to be sparing or frugal

²stint n **1** : RESTRAINT, LIMITATION **2** : an assigned amount of work

sti·pend \'stī-,pend, -pənd\ n [alter. of ME stipendy, fr. L stipendium, fr. stips gift + pendere to weigh, pay] : a

fixed sum of money paid periodically for services or to defray expenses

stip·ple \'stip-əl\ vb stip·pled; stip·pling \-(ə-)liŋ\ **1** : to engrave by means of dots and light strokes instead of by lines **2** : to apply (as paint or ink) with small short touches that together produce an even and softly graded shadow — stipple n

stip·u·late \'stip-yə-,lāt\ vb -lat·ed; -lat·ing : to make an agreement; esp : to make a special demand for something as a condition in an agreement — stip·u·la·tion \,stip-yə-'lāsh-ən\ n

¹stir \'stər\ vb stirred; stir·ring **1** : to move slightly **2** : to move to activity (as by pushing, beating, or prodding) **3** : to mix, dissolve, or make by continued circular movement ⟨~ eggs into cake batter⟩ **4** : AROUSE, EXCITE

²stir n **1** : a state of agitation or activity **2** : an act of stirring

³stir n, slang : PRISON

stir·ring \'stər-iŋ\ adj **1** : ACTIVE, BUSTLING **2** : ROUSING, INSPIRING

stir·rup \'stər-əp\ n [OE stigrāp, lit., mounting rope] : a light frame hung from a saddle to support the foot of a horseback rider

¹stitch \'stich\ n **1** : one of the series of loops formed by or over a needle in sewing **2** : a particular method of stitching **3** : a sudden sharp pain esp. in the side **syn** twinge

²stitch vb **1** : to fasten or join with stitches **2** : to decorate with stitches **3** : SEW

stk abbr stock

stoat \'stōt\ n, pl stoats also stoat : the European ermine esp. in its brown summer coat

¹stock \'stäk\ n **1** : a block of wood **2** : a stupid person **3** : a wooden part of a thing serving as its support, frame, or handle **4** : the original from which others derive; also : a group having a common origin : FAMILY **5** : farm animals **6** : the supply of goods kept by a merchant **7** : the sum of money invested in a large business **8** pl : PILLORY **9** : a company of actors playing at a particular theater and presenting a series of plays **10** : raw material

²stock vb : to provide with stock

³stock adj : kept regularly for sale or use; also : used regularly : STANDARD

stock·ade \stä-'kād\ n [Sp estacada, fr. estaca stake, pale, of Gmc origin] : an enclosure of posts and stakes for defense or confinement

stock·bro·ker \-,brō-kər\ n : one who executes orders to buy and sell securities

stock car n **1** : an automotive vehicle of a model and type kept in stock for regular sales **2** : a racing car having the basic chassis of a commercially produced regular model

stock exchange n **1** : an association of stockbrokers **2** : a place where trading in securities is accomplished under an organized system

stock·hold·er \'stäk-,hōl-dər\ n : one who owns stock

**stock·i·nette** or **stock·i·net** \,stäk-ə-'net\ n : an elastic knitted textile fabric used esp. for infants' wear and bandages

**stock·ing** \'stäk-iŋ\ n : a close-fitting knitted covering for the foot and leg

**stock market** n 1 : STOCK EXCHANGE 2 2 : a market for stocks

**stock·pile** \'stäk-,pīl\ n : a reserve supply esp. of something essential — **stockpile** vb

**stocky** \'stäk-ē\ adj **stock·i·er; -est** : being short and relatively thick : STURDY **syn** thickset, squat

**stock·yard** \'stäk-,yärd\ n : a yard for stock; esp : one for livestock about to be slaughtered or shipped

**stodgy** \'stäj-ē\ adj **stodg·i·er; -est** : HEAVY, DULL, UNINSPIRED

¹**sto·ic** \'stō-ik\ n [ME, fr. L stoicus, fr. Gk stōïkos, lit., of the portico, fr. Stoa (Poikilē) the Painted Portico, portico at Athens where Zeno taught] : one who suffers silently and without complaining

²**stoic** or **sto·i·cal** \-i-kəl\ adj : not affected by passion or feeling; esp : showing indifference to pain **syn** impassive, phlegmatic, apathetic, stolid — **stoical·ly** \-i-k(ə-)lē\ adv — **sto·icism** \'stō-ə-,siz-əm\ n

**stoke** \'stōk\ vb **stoked; stok·ing** 1 : to stir up a fire 2 : to tend and supply fuel to a furnace — **stok·er** n

**STOL** abbr short takeoff and landing

¹**stole** \'stōl\ past of STEAL

²**stole** n 1 : a long narrow band worn round the neck by some clergymen 2 : a long wide scarf or similar covering worn by women

**stolen** past part of STEAL

**stol·id** \'stäl-əd\ adj : not easily aroused or excited : showing little or no emotion **syn** phlegmatic, apathetic — **sto·lid·i·ty** \stä-'lid-ət-ē\ n — **stolid·ly** \'stäl-əd-lē\ adv

**sto·lon** \'stō-lən, -,län\ n : RUNNER 7

¹**stom·ach** \'stəm-ək, -ik\ n 1 : a sac-like digestive organ into which food goes from the mouth by way of the throat and which opens below into the intestine 2 : ABDOMEN 3 : desire for food caused by hunger : APPETITE 4 : INCLINATION, DESIRE

²**stomach** vb : to bear without overt resentment : BROOK

**stom·ach·ache** \-,āk\ n : pain in or in the region of the stomach

**stom·ach·er** \'stəm-i-kər, -i-chər\ n : the front of a bodice often appearing between the laces of an outer garment (as in 16th century costume)

**sto·mach·ic** \stə-'mak-ik\ adj : stimulating the function of the stomach — **stomachic** n

¹**stomp** \'stämp, 'stȯmp\ vb : STAMP

²**stomp** n 1 : STAMP 4 2 : a jazz dance marked by heavy stamping

¹**stone** \'stōn\ n 1 : hardened earth or mineral matter : ROCK 2 : a small piece of rock 3 : a precious stone : GEM 4 pl usu **stone** : a British unit of weight equal to 14 pounds 5 : a hard stony seed or one (as of a plum) with a stony covering 6 : a hard abnormal mass in a bodily cavity or duct — **stony** adj

²**stone** vb **stoned; ston·ing** 1 : to pelt or kill with stones 2 : to remove the stones of (a fruit)

**Stone Age** n : the first known period of prehistoric human culture characterized by the use of stone tools

**stoned** \'stōnd\ adj 1 : DRUNK 2 : being under the influence of a drug

**stood** past of STAND

**stooge** \'stüj\ n 1 : an actor whose function is to feed lines to the chief comedian 2 : a person who plays a subordinate or compliant role to a principal

**stool** \'stül\ n 1 : a seat usu. without back or arms 2 : FOOTSTOOL 3 : a discharge of fecal matter

**stool pigeon** n : DECOY, INFORMER

¹**stoop** \'stüp\ vb 1 : to bend over 2 : CONDESCEND 3 : to humiliate or lower oneself socially or morally

²**stoop** n 1 : an act of bending over 2 : a bent position of head and shoulders

³**stoop** n : a small porch or platform at a house door

¹**stop** \'stäp\ vb **stopped; stop·ping** 1 : to close (an opening or hole) by filling or covering closely 2 : BLOCK, HALT 3 : to cease to go on 4 : to cease activity or operation 5 : STAY, TARRY **syn** quit, discontinue, desist, lodge, sojourn

²**stop** n 1 : CHECK, OBSTRUCTION 2 : END, CESSATION 3 : a set of organ pipes of one tone quality; also : a control knob for such a set 4 : PLUG, STOPPER 5 : an act of stopping 6 : a delay in a journey : STAY 7 : a place for stopping 8 chiefly Brit : any of several punctuation marks

**stop·gap** \'stäp-,gap\ n : something that serves as a temporary expedient

**stop·light** \-,līt\ n : a system of colored lights to control traffic

**stop·page** \'stäp-ij\ n : the act of stopping : the state of being stopped

**stop·per** \'stäp-ər\ n : something (as a cork or plug) for sealing an opening

**stop·watch** \'stäp-,wäch\ n : a watch having a hand that can be started or stopped at will for exact timing

**stor·age** \'stōr-ij\ n 1 : the act of storing; esp : the safekeeping of goods (as in a warehouse) 2 : space for storing; also : cost of storing

**storage battery** n : a group of connected cells that converts chemical energy into electrical energy by reversible chemical reactions and that may be recharged by electrical means

¹**store** \'stōr\ vb **stored; stor·ing** 1 : to provide esp. for a future need 2 : to place or leave in a safe location for preservation or future use

²**store** n 1 : something accumulated and kept for future use 2 : a large or ample quantity 3 : STOREHOUSE 4 : a retail business establishment

**store·house** \-,haús\ n : a building for storing goods or supplies; also : an abundant source or supply

**store·keep·er** \-,kē-pər\ n : one who operates a retail store

**store·room** \-,rüm, -,rùm\ n : a room for storing goods or supplies

**sto·ried** \'stōr-ēd\ adj : celebrated in story or history

**stork** \'stòrk\ n : a large stout-billed Old World wading bird related to the herons

¹**storm** \'stòrm\ n 1 : a heavy fall of rain, snow, or hail with high wind 2 : a violent outbreak or disturbance 3 : a mass attack on a defended position — **storm·i·ly** \'stòr-mə-lē\ adv — **storm·i·ness** \-mē-nəs\ n — **stormy** adj

²**storm** vb 1 : to blow with violence; also : to rain, snow, or hail heavily 2 : to be violently angry : RAGE 3 : to rush along furiously 4 : to make a mass attack against

¹**sto·ry** \'stōr-ē\ n, pl **stories** 1 : NARRATIVE, ACCOUNT 2 : REPORT, STATEMENT 3 : ANECDOTE 4 : FIB syn chronicle, lie, falsehood, untruth

²**story** also **sto·rey** \'stōr-ē\ n, pl **stories** also **storeys** : a floor of a building or the habitable space between two floors

**sto·ry·tell·er** \-,tel-ər\ n : a teller of stories — **sto·ry·tell·ing** \-,iŋ\ adj or n

**sto·tin·ka** \stō-'tiŋ-kə, stə-\ n, pl **-tin·ki** \-kē\ — see lev at MONEY table

¹**stout** \'staút\ adj 1 : BRAVE 2 : STURDY, STAUNCH 3 : FIRM, SOLID 4 : FORCEFUL 5 : BULKY, THICKSET syn strong, stalwart, tough, tenacious, fleshy, fat, portly, corpulent, obese, plump — **stout·ly** adv — **stout·ness** n

²**stout** n : a dark heavy alcoholic beverage brewed from roasted malt and hops

¹**stove** \'stōv\ n : an apparatus that burns fuel or uses electricity to provide heat (as for cooking or room heating)

²**stove** past of STAVE

**stow** \'stō\ vb 1 : to pack in a compact mass 2 : HIDE, STORE

**stow·away** \'stō-ə-,wā\ n : one who conceals himself on a vehicle to obtain transportation

¹**STP** \,es-,tē-'pē\ n : a psychedelic drug chemically related to amphetamine

²**STP** abbr standard temperature and pressure

**strad·dle** \'strad-ºl\ vb **strad·dled**; **strad·dling** \'strad-(ª-)liŋ\ 1 : to stand, sit, or walk with legs spread apart 2 : to favor or seem to favor two apparently opposite sides — **straddle** n

**strafe** \'strāf\ vb **strafed**; **straf·ing** : to fire upon with machine guns from a low-flying airplane

**strag·gle** \'strag-əl\ vb **strag·gled**; **strag·gling** \-(ə-)liŋ\ 1 : to wander from the direct course : ROVE 2 : to become separated from others of the same kind : STRAY — **strag·gler** \-(ə-)lər\ n — **strag·gly** \-(ə-)lē\ adj

¹**straight** \'strāt\ adj 1 : free from curves, bends, angles, or irregularities : DIRECT 2 : not wandering from the main point or proper course (~ thinking) 3 : HONEST, UPRIGHT 4 : not marked by confusion : correctly ar-ranged or ordered 5 : UNMIXED, UNDILUTED (~ whiskey) 6 : CONVENTIONAL, SQUARE; also : HETEROSEXUAL

²**straight** adv : in a straight manner

³**straight** n 1 : a straight line, course, or arrangement 2 : the part of a racetrack between the last turn and the finish 3 : a sequence of five cards in a poker hand

**straight–arm** \'strāt-,ärm\ vb : to ward off an opponent with the arm held straight — **straight–arm** n

**straight·away** \'strāt-ə-,wā\ n : a straight stretch (as at a racetrack)

**straight·edge** \'strāt-,ej\ n : a piece of material with a straight edge for testing straight lines and surfaces or drawing straight lines

**straight·en** \'strāt-ºn\ vb **straight·ened**; **straight·en·ing** \'strāt-(ª-)niŋ\ : to make or become straight

**straight·for·ward** \strāt-'fòr-wərd\ adj 1 : proceeding in a straight course or manner 2 : CANDID, HONEST

**straight man** n : an entertainer who feeds lines to a comedian

**straight·way** \'strāt-'wā, -,wā\ adv : IMMEDIATELY

¹**strain** \'strān\ n [ME streen progeny, lineage, fr. OE strēon gain, acquisition] 1 : LINEAGE, ANCESTRY 2 : a group (as of people or plants) of presumed common ancestry; also : a distinctive quality shared by its members 3 : STREAK, TRACE 4 : the general style or tone 5 : MELODY

²**strain** vb [ME strainen, fr. MF estraindre, fr. L stringere to bind or draw tight, press together] 1 : to draw taut 2 : to exert to the utmost 3 : to filter or remove by filtering 4 : to stretch beyond a proper limit 5 : to injure by improper or excessive use (a ~ed back) 6 : to strive violently — **strain·er** n

³**strain** n 1 : excessive tension or exertion (as of body or mind) 2 : bodily injury from excessive tension, effort, or use; esp : one in which muscles or ligaments are unduly stretched usu. from a wrench or twist 3 : deformation of a material body under the action of applied forces

¹**strait** \'strāt\ adj 1 archaic : NARROW, CONSTRICTED 2 archaic : STRICT 3 : DIFFICULT, STRAITENED

²**strait** n 1 : a narrow channel connecting two bodies of water 2 pl : DISTRESS

**strait·en** \'strāt-ºn\ vb **strait·ened**; **strait·en·ing** \'strāt-(ª-)niŋ\ 1 : to hem in : CONFINE 2 : to make distressing or difficult

**strait·jack·et** or **straight·jack·et** \'strāt-,jak-ət\ n : a cover or garment of strong material (as canvas) used to bind the body and esp. the arms closely in restraining a violent prisoner or patient — **straitjacket** or **straightjacket** vb

**strait·laced** or **straight·laced** \'strāt-'lāst\ adj : strict in observing moral or religious laws

¹**strand** \'strand\ n : SHORE; esp : a shore of a sea or ocean

²**strand** vb 1 : to run, drift, or drive

upon the shore ⟨a ~ed ship⟩ **2** : to place or leave in a helpless position

**³strand** n **1** : one of the fibers twisted or plaited together into a cord, rope, or cable; *also* : a cord, rope, or cable made up of such fibers **2** : a twisted or plaited ropelike mass ⟨a ~ of pearls⟩ — **strand·ed** \'stran-dəd\ *adj*

**strange** \'strānj\ *adj* **strang·er; strang·est** [ME, fr. OF *estrange*, fr. L *extraneus*, lit., external, fr. *extra* outside] **1** : of external origin, kind, or character **2** : UNUSUAL; *also* : UNNATURAL **3** : NEW, UNFAMILIAR **4** : SHY **5** : UNACCUSTOMED, INEXPERIENCED **syn** singular, unique, peculiar, eccentric, erratic, odd, queer, quaint, curious — **strange·ly** *adv* — **strange·ness** n

**strang·er** \'strān-jər\ n **1** : FOREIGNER **2** : INTRUDER **3** : a person with whom one is unacquainted

**stran·gle** \'straŋ-gəl\ *vb* **stran·gled; stran·gling** \-g(ə-)liŋ\ **1** : to choke to death : THROTTLE **2** : STIFLE, SUFFOCATE — **stran·gler** \-g(ə-)lər\ n

**stran·gu·late** \'straŋ-gyə-,lāt\ *vb* **-lat·ed; -lat·ing** : to become so constricted as to stop circulation

**stran·gu·la·tion** \,straŋ-gyə-'lā-shən\ n : the act or process of strangling or strangulating : the state of being strangled or strangulated

**¹strap** \'strap\ n : a narrow strip of flexible material used esp. for fastening, holding together, or wrapping

**²strap** *vb* **strapped; strap·ping 1** : to secure with a strap **2** : BIND, CONSTRICT **3** : to flog with a strap **4** : STROP

**strap·less** \-ləs\ *adj* : having no straps; *esp* : having no shoulder straps

**strap·ping** \'strap-iŋ\ *adj* : LARGE, STRONG, HUSKY

**strat·a·gem** \'strat-ə-jəm, -,jem\ n **1** : a trick in war to deceive or outwit the enemy; *also* : a deceptive scheme **2** : skill in deception

**strat·e·gy** \'strat-ə-jē\ n, *pl* **-gies** [Gk *stratēgia* generalship, fr. *stratēgos* general, fr. *stratos* army + *agein* to lead] **1** : the science and art of military command employed with the object of meeting the enemy under conditions advantageous to one's own force **2** : a careful plan or method esp. for achieving an end — **stra·te·gic** \strə-'tē-jik\ *adj* — **strat·e·gist** \'strat-ə-jəst\ n

**strat·i·fy** \'strat-ə-,fī\ *vb* **-fied; -fy·ing** : to form or arrange in layers — **strat·i·fi·ca·tion** \,strat-ə-fə-'kā-shən\ n

**stra·tig·ra·phy** \strə-'tig-rə-fē\ n : geology that deals with strata — **strati·graph·ic** \,strat-ə-'graf-ik\ *adj*

**strato·sphere** \'strat-ə-,sfiər\ n : a portion of the earth's atmosphere from about 7 to 37 miles above the earth's surface — **strato·spher·ic** \,strat-ə-'sfi(ə)r-ik, -'sfer-\ *adj*

**stra·tum** \'strāt-əm, 'strat-\ n, *pl* **stra·ta** \'strāt-ə, 'strat-\ [NL, fr. L, spread, bed, fr. neut. of *stratus*, pp. of *sternere* to spread out] **1** : a bed, layer, or sheetlike mass (as of one kind of

rock lying between layers of other kinds of rock) **2** : a level of culture; *also* : a group of people representing one stage in cultural development

**¹straw** \'strȯ\ n **1** : stalks of grain after threshing; *also* : a single coarse dry stem (as of a grass) **2** : a thing of small worth : TRIFLE **3** : a prepared tube for sucking up a beverage

**²straw** *adj* **1** : made of straw **2** : having no real force or validity ⟨a ~ vote⟩

**straw·ber·ry** \'strȯ-,ber-ē, -b(ə-)rē\ n : an edible juicy red pulpy fruit borne by a low herb related to the roses; *also* : this plant

**straw boss** n : a foreman of a small gang of workers

**straw·flow·er** \'strȯ-,flau̇(-ə)r\ n : any of several plants whose flowers can be dried with little loss of form or color

**¹stray** \'strā\ *vb* **1** : to wander from a course : DEVIATE **2** : ROVE, ROAM

**²stray** n **1** : a domestic animal wandering at large or lost **2** : WAIF

**³stray** *adj* **1** : having strayed : separated from the group or the main body **2** : occurring at random ⟨~ remarks⟩

**¹streak** \'strēk\ n **1** : a line or mark of a different color or texture from its background **2** : a narrow band of light; *also* : a lightning bolt **3** : a slight admixture : TRACE **4** : a brief run (as of luck); *also* : an unbroken series

**²streak** *vb* **1** : to form streaks in or on **2** : to move very swiftly

**¹stream** \'strēm\ n **1** : a body of water (as a river) flowing on the earth **2** : a course of running liquid **3** : a steady flow (as of water or air) **4** : a continuous procession ⟨the ~ of history⟩

**²stream** *vb* **1** : to flow in or as if in a stream **2** : to pour out streams of liquid **3** : to stretch or trail out in length **4** : to move forward in a steady stream

**stream·bed** \'strēm-,bed\ n : the channel occupied or formerly occupied by a stream

**stream·er** \'strē-mər\ n **1** : a long narrow ribbonlike flag **2** : a long ribbon on a dress or hat **3** : a column of light (as from the aurora borealis) **4** : a newspaper headline that runs across the entire sheet

**stream·let** \'strēm-lət\ n : a small stream

**stream·lined** \-,līnd, -'līnd\ *adj* **1** : made with contours to reduce resistance to motion through water or air **2** : SIMPLIFIED **3** : MODERNIZED — **streamline** *vb*

**stream·lin·er** \'strēm-'lī-nər\ n : a streamlined train

**street** \'strēt\ n [ME *strete*, fr. OE *strǣt*, fr. LL *strata* paved road, fr. L, fem. of *stratus*, pp. of *sternere* to spread out] **1** : a thoroughfare esp. in a city, town, or village **2** : the occupants of the houses on a street

**street·car** \-,kär\ n : a passenger vehicle running on rails on the public streets

**street railway** n : a line operating streetcars or buses

**street theater** *n* : GUERRILLA THEATER
**street·walk·er** \'strēt-ˌwȯ-kər\ *n* : PROSTITUTE
**strength** \'streŋth\ *n* **1** : the quality of being strong : ability to do or endure **2** : POWER **2** : TOUGHNESS, SOLIDITY **3** : power to resist attack **4** : INTENSITY **5** : force as measured in numbers ⟨the ~ of an army⟩
**strength·en** \'streŋ-thən\ *vb* **strength·ened; strength·en·ing** \'streŋth-(ə-)niŋ\ : to make, grow, or become stronger — **strength·en·er** \'streŋth-(ə-)nər\ *n*
**stren·u·ous** \'stren-yə-wəs\ *adj* **1** : VIGOROUS, ENERGETIC **2** : requiring energetic effort or stamina — **stren·u·ous·ly** *adv*
**strep throat** \'strep-\ *n* : an inflammatory sore throat caused by streptococci and marked by fever, prostration, and toxemia
**strep·to·coc·cus** \ˌstrep-tə-'käk-əs\ *n*, *pl* **-coc·ci** \-'käk-ˌ(s)ī, -'käk-ˌ(ˌ)(s)ē\ : any of various spherical bacteria that usu. grow in chains and include causers of serious diseases — **strep·to·coc·cal** \-əl\ *adj*
**strep·to·my·cin** \-'mīs-ᵊn\ *n* : an antibiotic produced by soil bacteria and used esp. in treating tuberculosis
**¹stress** \'stres\ *n* **1** : PRESSURE, STRAIN; *esp* : a force that tends to distort a body **2** : URGENCY, EMPHASIS **3** : intense effort **4** : prominence of sound : ACCENT; *also* : any syllable carrying the accent **5** : a factor that induces bodily or mental tension; *also* : a state induced by such a stress
**²stress** *vb* **1** : to put pressure or strain on **2** : to put emphasis on : ACCENT
**¹stretch** \'strech\ *vb* **1** : to spread or reach out : EXTEND **2** : to draw out in length or breadth : EXPAND **3** : to make tense : STRAIN **4** : EXAGGERATE **5** : to become extended without breaking ⟨rubber ~es easily⟩
**²stretch** *n* **1** : an act of extending or drawing out beyond ordinary or normal limits **2** : a continuous extent in length, area, or time **3** : the extent to which something may be stretched **4** : either of the straight sides of a racecourse
**³stretch** *adj* : easily stretched ⟨~ pants⟩
**stretch·er** \'strech-ər\ *n* **1** : one that stretches **2** : a litter (as of canvas) esp. for carrying a disabled person
**stretch·er-bear·er** \-ˌbar-ər\ *n* : one who carries one end of a stretcher
**strew** \'strü\ *vb* **strewed; strewed** *or* **strewn** \'strün\; **strew·ing 1** : to spread by scattering **2** : to cover by or as if by scattering something over or on **3** : DISSEMINATE
**stria** \'strī-ə\ *n*, *pl* **stri·ae** \'strī-ˌē\ **1** : a minute groove or channel **2** : a threadlike line or narrow band (as of color) esp. when one of a series of parallel lines — **stri·at·ed** \-ˌāt-əd\ *adj* — **stri·a·tion** \strī-'ā-shən\ *n*
**strick·en** \'strik-ən\ *adj* **1** : WOUNDED **2** : afflicted with disease, misfortune, or sorrow
**strict** \'strikt\ *adj* **1** : allowing no

evasion or escape : RIGOROUS ⟨~ discipline⟩ **2** : ACCURATE, PRECISE **syn** stringent, rigid — **strict·ly** \'strik-(t)lē\ *adv* — **strict·ness** \'strik(t)-nəs\ *n*
**stric·ture** \'strik-chər\ *n* **1** : hostile criticism : a critical remark **2** : an abnormal narrowing of a bodily passage; *also* : the narrowed part
**¹stride** \'strīd\ *vb* **strode** \'strōd\; **strid·den** \'strid-ᵊn\; **strid·ing** \'strīd-iŋ\ : to walk or run with long regular steps — **strid·er** *n*
**²stride** *n* **1** : a long step; *also* : the distance covered by such a step **2** : manner of striding : GAIT
**stri·dent** \'strīd-ᵊnt\ *adj* : of loud harsh sound : SHRILL
**strife** \'strīf\ *n* : CONFLICT, FIGHT, STRUGGLE **syn** discord, contention, dissension
**¹strike** \'strīk\ *vb* **struck** \'strək\; **struck** *also* **strick·en** \'strik-ən\; **strik·ing** \'strī-kiŋ\ **1** : to take a course : GO ⟨~ out for home⟩ **2** : to touch or hit sharply; *also* : to deliver a blow **3** : to produce by or as if by a blow ⟨struck terror in the foe⟩ **4** : to lower (as a flag or sail) usu. in salute or surrender **5** : to collide with; *also* : to injure or destroy by collision **6** : DELETE, CANCEL **7** : to produce by impressing ⟨struck a medal⟩; *also* : COIN ⟨~ a new cent⟩ **8** : to cause to sound ⟨~ a bell⟩ **9** : to afflict suddenly : lay low ⟨stricken with a high fever⟩ **10** : to appear to; *also* : to appear to as remarkable : IMPRESS **11** : to reach by reckoning ⟨~ an average⟩ **12** : to stop work in order to obtain a change in conditions of employment **13** : to cause (a match) to ignite by rubbing **14** : to come upon ⟨~ a detour from the main road⟩ **15** : to take on ⟨~ a pose⟩ — **strik·er** *n*
**²strike** *n* **1** : an act or instance of striking **2** : a sudden discovery of rich ore or oil deposits **3** : a pitched baseball recorded against a batter **4** : the knocking down of all the bowling pins with the first ball **5** : a military attack
**strike·break·er** \-ˌbrā-kər\ *n* : one hired to replace a striking worker
**strike·out** \'strīk-ˌaůt\ *n* : an out in baseball as a result of a batter's being charged with three strikes
**strike out** \(')strīk-'aůt\ *vb* **1** : to enter upon a course of action **2** : to start out vigorously **3** : to make an out in baseball by a strikeout
**strike up 1** : to begin or cause to begin to sing or play **2** : BEGIN
**strike zone** *n* : the area over home plate through which a pitched baseball must pass to be called a strike
**strik·ing** \'strī-kiŋ\ *adj* : attracting attention : very noticeable **syn** arresting, salient, conspicuous, outstanding, remarkable, prominent — **strik·ing·ly** *adv*
**¹string** \'striŋ\ *n* **1** : a line usu. composed of twisted threads **2** : a series of things arranged as if strung on a cord **3** : a plant fiber (ar a leaf vein) **4** *pl*

: the stringed instruments of an orchestra **syn** succession, progression, sequence, set

²**string** vb **strung** \'strəŋ\; **string·ing** \'striŋ-iŋ\ 1 : to provide with strings ⟨~ a racket⟩ 2 : to thread on or as if on a string ⟨~ pearls⟩ 3 : to take the strings out of ⟨~ beans⟩ 4 : to hang, tie, or fasten by a string 5 : to make taut 6 : to extend like a string

**stringed** \'striŋd\ adj 1 : having strings 2 : produced by strings

**string bean** n : a bean of one of the older varieties of kidney bean that have stringy fibers on the lines of separation of the pods; also : SNAP BEAN

**strin·gen·cy** \'strin-jən-sē\ n 1 : STRICTNESS, SEVERITY 2 : SCARCITY ⟨~ of money⟩ — **strin·gent** \-jənt\ adj

**string·er** \'striŋ-ər\ n 1 : a long horizontal member in a framed structure or a bridge 2 : a usu. part-time news correspondent

**stringy** \'striŋ-ē\ adj **string·i·er; -est** 1 : resembling string esp. in tough, fibrous, or disordered quality ⟨~ meat⟩ ⟨~ hair⟩ 2 : lean and sinewy in build

¹**strip** \'strip\ vb **stripped** \'stript\ also **stript; strip·ping** 1 : to take the covering or clothing from 2 : to take off one's clothes 3 : to pull or tear off 4 : to make bare or clear (as by cutting or grazing) 5 : PLUNDER, PILLAGE **syn** divest, denude — **strip·per** n

²**strip** n 1 : a long narrow flat piece 2 : AIRSTRIP

¹**stripe** \'strīp\ n 1 : a line or long narrow division having a different color from the background 2 : a strip of braid (as on a sleeve) indicating military rank or length of service 3 : TYPE, CHARACTER **syn** description, nature, kind, sort

²**stripe** vb **striped** \'strīpt\; **strip·ing** : to make stripes on

**striped bass** \'strīpt-, 'strī-pəd-\ n : a large food and sport fish that occurs along the Atlantic coast of the U.S.

**strip·ling** \'strip-liŋ\ n : YOUTH, LAD

**strip mine** n : a mine that is worked from the earth's surface by the stripping of the topsoil — **strip-mine** vb — **strip miner** n

**strip·tease** \'strip-,tēz\ n : a burlesque act in which a female performer removes her clothing piece by piece in view of the audience — **strip·teas·er** n

**strive** \'strīv\ vb **strove** \'strōv\ also **strived** \'strīvd\; **striv·en** \'striv-ən\ or **strived; striv·ing** \'strī-viŋ\ 1 : to struggle in opposition : CONTEND 2 : to make effort : labor hard **syn** endeavor, attempt, try

**strobe** \'strōb\ n 1 : STROBOSCOPE 2 : a device for high-speed intermittent illumination

**stro·bo·scope** \'strō-bə-,skōp\ n : an instrument for studying rapid motion by means of a rapidly flashing light — **stro·bo·scop·ic** \,strō-bə-'skäp-ik\ adj

**strode** past of STRIDE

³**stroke** \'strōk\ vb **stroked; strok-**

**ing** 1 : to rub gently 2 : to set the stroke for (a racing crew)

²**stroke** n 1 : the act of striking : BLOW, KNOCK 2 : a sudden action or process producing an impact ⟨~ of lightning⟩; also : APOPLEXY 3 : a vigorous effort 4 : the sound of striking (as of a clock) 5 : one of a series of movements against air or water to get through or over it ⟨the ~ of a bird's wing⟩ 6 : a single movement with or as if with a tool or implement (as a pen) 7 : an oarsman who sets the tempo for a crew

**stroll** \'strōl\ vb : to walk in a leisurely or idle manner **syn** saunter, amble — **stroll** n — **stroll·er** n

**strong** \'strȯŋ\ adj **stron·ger** \'strȯŋ-gər\; **stron·gest** \'strȯŋ-gəst\ 1 : POWERFUL, VIGOROUS 2 : HEALTHY, ROBUST 3 : of a specified number ⟨an army 10 thousand ~⟩ 4 : not mild or weak 5 : VIOLENT ⟨~ wind⟩ 6 : ZEALOUS 7 : not easily broken 8 : FIRM, SOLID **syn** stout, sturdy, stalwart, tough — **strong·ly** adv

**strong-arm** \'strȯŋ-'ärm\ adj : having or using undue force ⟨~ methods⟩

**strong·hold** \'strȯŋ-,hōld\ n : a fortified place : FORTRESS

**stron·tium** \'strän-ch(ē-)əm, 'stränt-ē-əm\ n : a soft malleable metallic chemical element

¹**strop** \'sträp\ n : STRAP; esp : one for sharpening a razor

²**strop** vb **stropped; strop·ping** : to sharpen a razor on a strop

**stro·phe** \'strō-fē\ n [Gk strophē, lit., act of turning, fr. strephein to turn, twist] : a division of a poem — **stroph·ic** \'sträf-ik\ adj

**strove** past of STRIVE

**struck** \'strək\ adj : closed or affected by a labor strike

**struc·ture** \'strək-chər\ n [ME, fr. L structura, fr. structus, pp. of struere to heap up, build] 1 : the manner of building : CONSTRUCTION 2 : something built (as a house or a dam); also : something made up of interdependent parts in a definite pattern of organization 3 : arrangement or relationship of elements in a substance, body, or system — **struc·tur·al** adj

**stru·del** \'s(h)trüd-ᵊl\ n : a pastry made of a thin sheet of dough rolled up with filling and baked (apple ~)

¹**strug·gle** \'strəg-əl\ vb **strug·gled; strug·gling** \-(ə-)liŋ\ 1 : to make strenuous efforts against opposition : STRIVE 2 : to proceed with difficulty or with great effort **syn** endeavor, attempt, try

²**struggle** n 1 : a violent effort or exertion 2 : CONTEST, STRIFE

**strum** \'strəm\ vb **strummed; strum·ming** : to play on a stringed instrument by brushing the strings with the fingers ⟨~ a guitar⟩

**strum·pet** \'strəm-pət\ n : PROSTITUTE

**strung** \'strəŋ\ past of STRING

¹**strut** \'strət\ vb **strut·ted; strut·ting** : to walk with an affectedly proud gait **syn** swagger

²**strut** n 1 : a haughty or pompous gait

**2** : a bar or rod for resisting length-wise pressure

**strych·nine** \'strik-,nīn, -nən, -,nēn\ *n* : a bitter poisonous alkaloid from some plants used to kill vermin and in small doses as a stimulant

¹**stub** \'stəb\ *n* **1** : STUMP 1 **2** : a short blunt end **3** : a small part of each leaf (as of a checkbook) kept as a memorandum of the items on the detached part

²**stub** *vb* **stubbed; stub·bing** : to strike (as one's toe) against something

**stub·ble** \'stəb-əl\ *n* : the stumps of herbs and esp. grasses left in the soil after harvest — **stub·bly** \-(ə-)lē\ *adj*

**stub·born** \'stəb-ərn\ *adj* **1** : FIRM, DETERMINED **2** : not easily controlled or remedied ⟨a ~ fever⟩ **3** : done or continued in a willful, unreasonable, or persistent manner — **stub·born·ly** *adv* — **stub·born·ness** *n*

**stub·by** \'stəb-ē\ *adj* : short, blunt, and thick like a stub

¹**stuc·co** \'stək-ō\ *n, pl* **stuccos** *or* **stuccoes** : plaster for coating exterior walls

²**stucco** *vb* : to coat with stucco

**stuck** *past of* STICK

**stuck-up** \'stək-'əp\ *adj* : CONCEITED

¹**stud** \'stəd\ *n* : a male animal and esp. a horse (**stud·horse** \-,hórs\) kept for breeding

²**stud** *n* **1** : one of the smaller uprights in a building to which sheathing, paneling, or laths are fastened **2** : a removable device like a button used as a fastener or ornament ⟨shirt ~s⟩ **3** : a projecting nail, pin, or rod

³**stud** *vb* **stud·ded; stud·ding 1** : to supply with or adorn with studs **2** : DOT

⁴**stud** *abbr* student

**stud·book** \'stəd-,búk\ *n* : an official record of the pedigree of purebred animals

**stud·ding** \'stəd-iŋ\ *n* **1** : material for studs **2** : STUDS

**stu·dent** \'st(y)üd-°nt\ *n* : SCHOLAR, PUPIL; *esp* : one who attends a school

**stud·ied** \'stəd-ēd\ *adj* : INTENTIONAL ⟨a ~ insult⟩ **syn** deliberate, considered, premeditated

**stu·dio** \'st(y)üd-ē-,ō\ *n, pl* **-dios 1** : a place where an artist works; *also* : a place for the study of an art **2** : a place where motion pictures are made **3** : a place equipped for the transmission of radio or television programs

**stu·di·ous** \'st(y)üd-ē-əs\ *adj* : devoted to study — **stu·di·ous·ly** *adv*

¹**study** \'stəd-ē\ *n, pl* **stud·ies 1** : the use of the mind to gain knowledge **2** : the act or process of learning about something **3** : a branch of learning **4** : INTENT, PURPOSE **5** : careful examination **6** : a room esp. for reading and writing

²**study** *vb* **stud·ied; study·ing 1** : to apply the attention and mind to a subject **2** : MEDITATE, PONDER **syn** consider, contemplate, weigh

¹**stuff** \'stəf\ *n* **1** : personal property **2** : raw material **3** : a finished textile fabric; *esp* : a worsted fabric **4** : writing, talk, or ideas of little or transitory

worth **5** : an aggregate of matter; *also* : matter of a particular often unspecified kind **6** : fundamental material **7** : special knowledge or capability

²**stuff** *vb* **1** : to fill by packing something into : CRAM **2** : to stop up : PLUG **3** : to prepare (as meat) by filling with seasoned bread crumbs and spices **4** : to eat greedily : GORGE

**stuffed shirt** \'stəft-\ *n* : a smug, conceited, and usu. pompous and inflexibly conservative person

**stuff·ing** \'stəf-iŋ\ *n* : material used to fill tightly; *esp* : a mixture of bread crumbs and spices used to stuff meat and poultry

**stuffy** \'stəf-ē\ *adj* **stuff·i·er, -est 1** : lacking fresh air : CLOSE; *also* : blocked up ⟨a ~ nose⟩ **2** : STODGY

**stul·ti·fy** \'stəl-tə-,fī\ *vb* **-fied; -fy·ing 1** : to cause to appear foolish or stupid **2** : make untrustworthy; *also* : DISGRACE, DISHONOR — **stul·ti·fi·ca·tion** \,stəl-tə-fə-'kā-shən\ *n*

**stum·ble** \'stəm-bəl\ *vb* **stum·bled; stum·bling** \-b(ə-)liŋ\ **1** : to trip in walking or running **2** : to walk unsteadily; *also* : to speak or act in a blundering or clumsy manner **3** : to blunder morally; *also* : to come or happen by chance — **stumble** *n*

¹**stump** \'stəmp\ *n* **1** : the part of a plant and esp. a tree remaining with the root after the top is cut off **2** : the base of a bodily part (as a leg or tooth) left after the rest is removed **3** : a place or occasion for political public speaking — **stumpy** *adj*

²**stump** *vb* **1** : to clear (land) of stumps **2** : to tour (a region) making political speeches **3** : BAFFLE, PERPLEX **4** : to walk clumsily and heavily

**stun** \'stən\ *vb* **stunned; stun·ning 1** : to make senseless or dizzy by or as if by a blow **2** : BEWILDER, STUPEFY

**stung** *past of* STING

**stunk** *past of* STINK

**stun·ning** \'stən-iŋ\ *adj* : strikingly beautiful — **stun·ning·ly** *adv*

¹**stunt** \'stənt\ *vb* : to hinder the normal growth of : DWARF

²**stunt** *n* : an unusual or spectacular feat

**stu·pe·fy** \'st(y)ü-pə-,fī\ *vb* **-fied; -fy·ing** : to make dull, torpid, or numb by or as if by drugs; *also* : AMAZE, BEWILDER — **stu·pe·fac·tion** \,st(y)ü-pə-'fak-shən\ *n*

**stu·pen·dous** \st(y)ù-'pen-dəs\ *adj* : causing astonishment esp. because of great size or height **syn** tremendous, prodigious, monumental, monstrous — **stu·pen·dous·ly** *adv*

**stu·pid** \'st(y)ü-pəd\ *adj* [MF stupide, fr. L stupidus, fr. stupēre to be benumbed, be astonished] **1** : very dull in mind **2** : showing or resulting from dullness of mind — **stu·pid·i·ty** \st(y)ù-'pid-ət-ē\ *n* — **stu·pid·ly** \'st(y)ü-pəd-lē\ *adv*

**stu·por** \'st(y)ü-pər\ *n* **1** : a condition marked by great dulling or suspension of sense or feeling **2** : a torpid state often following stress or shock — **stu·por·ous** *adj*

**stur·dy** \'stərd-ē\ *adj* **stur·di·er; -est** [ME, reckless, brave, fr. OF *estourdi* stunned, fr. pp. of *estourdir* to stun, fr. (assumed) VL *exturdire* to be dizzy like a thrush drunk from eating grapes, fr. L *ex-*, intensive prefix + *turdus* thrush] **1** : RESOLUTE, UN-YIELDING **2** : STRONG, ROBUST syn stout, stalwart, tough, tenacious — **stur·di·ly** \'stərd-ᵊl-ē\ *adv* — **stur·di·ness** \-ē-nəs\ *n*

**stur·geon** \'stər-jən\ *n* : any of various large food fishes whose roe is made into caviar

**stut·ter** \'stət-ər\ *vb* : to speak with involuntary disruption or blocking of sounds — **stutter** *n*

**¹sty** \'stī\ *n*, *pl* **sties** : a pen or housing for swine

**²sty** *or* **stye** \'stī\ *n*, *pl* **sties** *or* **styes** : an inflamed swelling on the edge of an eyelid

**¹style** \'stīl\ *n* **1** : a slender pointed instrument or process; *esp* : STYLUS **2** : a way of speaking or writing; *esp* : one characteristic of an individual, period, school, or nation ⟨ornate ~⟩ **3** : the custom or plan followed in spelling, capitalization, punctuation, and typographic arrangement and display **4** : mode of address : TITLE **5** : manner or method of acting or performing esp. as sanctioned by some standard; *also* : a distinctive or characteristic manner **6** : a fashionable manner or mode **7** : overall excellence, skill, or grace in performance, manner, or appearance —**sty·lis·tic** \stī-'lis-tik\ *adj*

**²style** *vb* **styled; styl·ing 1** : NAME, DESIGNATE **2** : to make or design in accord with a prevailing mode

**styl·ing** \'stī-liŋ\ *n* : the way in which something is styled

**styl·ish** \'stī-lish\ *adj* : conforming to an accepted standard of style : FASH-IONABLE syn modish, smart, chic — **styl·ish·ly** *adv* — **styl·ish·ness** *n*

**styl·ist** \'stī-ləst\ *n* **1** : a master of style esp. in writing **2** : a developer or designer of styles

**styl·ize** \'stīl-ˌīz\ *vb* **styl·ized; styl·iz·ing** : to conform to a style : CON-VENTIONALIZE; *esp* : to represent or design according to a pattern or style rather than according to nature

**sty·lus** \'stī-ləs\ *n*, *pl* **sty·li** \'stī(ə)l-ˌī\ *also* **sty·lus·es** \'stī-lə-səz\ **1** : a pointed implement used by the ancients for writing on wax **2** : a phonograph needle

**¹sty·mie** \'stī-mē\ *n* : a position in golf when the ball nearer the hole lies in the line of play of another ball

**²stymie** *vb* **sty·mied; sty·mie·ing** : BLOCK, FRUSTRATE

**styp·tic** \'stip-tik\ *adj* : tending to check bleeding

**suave** \'swäv\ *adj* [MF, pleasant, sweet, fr. L *suavis*] : persuasively pleasing : smoothly agreeable syn urbane, diplomatic, bland — **suave·ly** *adv* — **sua·vi·ty** \'swäv-ət-ē\ *n*

**¹sub** \'səb\ *n* : SUBSTITUTE — **sub** *vb*

**²sub** *n* : SUBMARINE

**sub-** \ˌsəb, 'səb\ *prefix* **1** : under : beneath **2** : subordinate : secondary **3** : subordinate portion of : subdivision of **4** : with repetition of a process described in a simple verb so as to form, stress, or deal with subordinate parts or relations **5** : somewhat **6** : falling nearly in the category of : bordering on

subacute
subagency
subagent
subaqueous
subarctic
subarea
subatmospheric
subaverage
subbasement
subclass
subclassify
subclinical
subcontract
subcontractor
subculture
subdeacon
subdean
subdepot
subentry
subequal
subequatorial
subessential
subfamily
subfreezing
subgenus
subgroup
subhead
subheading
subhuman
subindex
subinterval
subkingdom
sublease
sublethal

subliterate
submaximal
subminimal
subopaque
suboptimal
suborder
subparagraph
subparallel
subpermanent
subphylum
subplot
subpolar
subprincipal
subproblem
subprofessional
subprogram
subregion
subroutine
subsaturated
subsection
subsense
subspecies
substage
subsystem
subteen
subtemperate
subthreshold
subtopic
subtotal
subtreasury
subtype
subunit
subvisible
subvocal

**sub·al·pine** \ˌsəb-'al-ˌpīn, 'səb-\ *adj* **1** : of or relating to the region about the foot and lower slopes of the Alps **2** *cap* : of, relating to, or growing on high upland slopes

**sub·al·tern** \sə-'bȯl-tərn\ *n* : SUB-ORDINATE; *also* : a commissioned officer in the British army below the rank of captain

**sub·as·sem·bly** \ˌsəb-ə-'sem-blē\ *n* : an assembled unit to be incorporated with other units in a finished product

**sub·atom·ic** \ˌsəb-ə-'täm-ik\ *adj* : of or relating to the inside of the atom or to particles smaller than atoms

**sub·com·mit·tee** \'səb-kə-ˌmit-ē, ˌsəb-kə-'mit-ē\ *n* : a subordinate division of a committee

**sub·com·pact** \'səb-'käm-ˌpakt\ *n* : an automobile smaller than a compact

**¹sub·con·scious** \ˌsəb-'kän-chəs, 'səb-\ *adj* : existing in the mind and affecting thought and behavior without entering conscious awareness — **sub·con·scious·ly** *adv* — **sub·con·scious·ness** *n*

**²subconscious** *n* : mental activities just below the threshold of conscious-ness

**sub·con·ti·nent** \'səb-'känt-(ᵊ-)nənt\ *n* : a vast subdivision of a continent —

**sub·con·ti·nen·tal** \,səb-,känt-ᵊn-'ent-ᵊl\ adj

**sub·cu·ta·ne·ous** \,səb-kyù-'tā-nē-əs\ adj : located, made, or used under the skin ⟨~ fat⟩ ⟨a ~ needle⟩

**sub·dis·ci·pline** \-'dis-ə-plən\ n : a subdivision of a branch of learning

**sub·di·vide** \,səb-də-'vīd, 'səb-də-,vīd\ vb : to divide into several parts; esp : to divide (a tract of land) into building lots — **sub·di·vi·sion** \-'vizh-ən, -,vizh-\ n

**sub·due** \səb-'d(y)ü\ vb sub·dued; sub·du·ing 1 : to bring into subjection : VANQUISH 2 : to bring under control : CURB 3 : to reduce the intensity of

**subj** abbr 1 subject 2 subjunctive

¹**sub·ject** \'səb-jikt\ n [ME, fr. MF, fr. L subjectus one under authority & subjectum subject of a proposition, fr. subicere to subject, lit., to throw under, fr. sub- under + jacere to throw] 1 : a person under the authority of another 2 : a person subject to a sovereign 3 : an individual subjected to an operation or process 4 : the person or thing discussed or treated : TOPIC, THEME 5 : a word or word group denoting that of which something is predicated

²**subject** adj 1 : being under the power or rule of another 2 : LIABLE, EXPOSED ⟨~ to floods⟩ 3 : dependent on some act or condition ⟨appointment ~ to senate approval⟩ syn subordinate, secondary, tributary, open, prone, susceptible

³**sub·ject** \səb-'jekt\ vb 1 : to bring under control : CONQUER 2 : to make liable 3 : to cause to undergo or submit to — **sub·jec·tion** \-'jek-shən\ n

**sub·jec·tive** \(,)səb-'jek-tiv\ adj 1 : of, relating to, or constituting a subject 2 : of, relating to, or arising within one's self or mind in contrast to what is outside : PERSONAL — **sub·jec·tive·ly** adv — **sub·jec·tiv·i·ty** \-,jek-'tiv-ət-ē\ n

**subject matter** n : matter presented for consideration, discussion, or study

**sub·join** \(,)səb-'jóin\ vb : APPEND

**sub ju·di·ce** \(')süb-'yüd-i-,kā, 'səb-'jüd-ə-(,)sē\ adv : before a judge or court : not yet legally decided

**sub·ju·gate** \'səb-ji-,gāt\ vb -gat·ed; -gat·ing 1 : CONQUER, SUBDUE; also : ENSLAVE syn reduce, overcome, overthrow, rout, vanquish, defeat, beat — **sub·ju·ga·tion** \,səb-ji-'gā-shən\ n

**sub·junc·tive** \səb-'jəŋk-tiv\ adj : of, relating to, or constituting a verb form that represents a denoted act or state as contingent or possible or viewed emotionally (as with desire) ⟨~ mood⟩ — **subjunctive** n

**sub·let** \'səb-'let\ vb -let; -let·ting : to let all or a part of (a leased property) to another; also : to rent (a property) from a lessee

**sub·li·mate** \'səb-lə-,māt\ vb -mat·ed; -mat·ing 1 : to cause to pass from a solid to a vapor state by the action of heat and then condense to

solid form 2 : to direct the expression of (as desires) toward more socially or culturally acceptable ends — **sub·li·ma·tion** \,səb-lə-'mā-shən\ n

¹**sub·lime** \sə-'blīm\ vb sub·limed; sub·lim·ing : SUBLIMATE

²**sublime** adj 1 : EXALTED, NOBLE 2 : having awe-inspiring beauty or grandeur syn glorious, splendid, superb, resplendent, gorgeous — **sub·lim·i·ty** \-'blim-ət-ē\ n

**sub·lim·i·nal** \(,)səb-'lim-ən-ᵊl, 'səb-\ adj 1 : inadequate to produce a sensation or a perception ⟨~ stimuli⟩ 2 : existing or functioning outside the area of conscious awareness ⟨the ~ mind⟩ ⟨~ techniques in advertising⟩

**sub·lu·na·ry** \,səb-'lü-nə-rē, 'səb-\ also **sub·lu·nar** \,səb-'lü-nər, 'səb-\ adj : situated beneath the moon

**sub·ma·chine gun** \,səb-mə-'shēn-,gən\ n : an automatic or partly automatic firearm fired from the shoulder or hip

¹**sub·ma·rine** \'səb-mə-,rēn, ,səb-mə-'rēn\ adj : existing, acting, or growing under the sea

²**submarine** n 1 : a naval boat capable of operation either on or below the surface of the water 2 : a large sandwich made from a long roll split and generously filled

**sub·merge** \səb-'mərj\ vb sub·merged; sub·merg·ing 1 : to put or plunge under the surface of water 2 : INUNDATE syn immerse, duck, dip — **sub·mer·gence** \-'mər-jəns\ n

**sub·merse** \səb-'mərs\ vb sub·mersed; sub·mers·ing : SUBMERGE — **sub·mer·sion** \-'mər-zhən\ n

**sub·mers·ible** \səb-'mər-sə-bəl\ adj : capable of being submerged

**sub·mi·cro·scop·ic** \,səb-,mī-krə-'skäp-ik\ adj : too small to be seen in an ordinary microscope

**sub·min·ia·ture** \,səb-'min-ē-ə-,chùr, 'səb-, -'min-i-,chùr, -chər\ adj : very small

**sub·mit** \səb-'mit\ vb sub·mit·ted; sub·mit·ting 1 : to commit to the discretion or decision of another or of others 2 : YIELD, SURRENDER 3 : to put forward as an opinion — **sub·mis·sion** \-'mish-ən\ n — **sub·mis·sive** \-'mis-iv\ adj

**sub·nor·mal** \,səb-'nór-məl\ adj : falling below what is normal — **sub·nor·mal·i·ty** \,səb-nór-'mal-ət-ē\ n

**sub·or·bit·al** \,səb-'ór-bət-ᵊl, 'səb-\ adj : being or involving less than one orbit

¹**sub·or·di·nate** \sə-'bórd-(ᵊ)nət\ adj 1 : of lower class or rank 2 : INFERIOR 3 : submissive to authority 4 : subordinated to other elements in a sentence : DEPENDENT ⟨~ clause⟩ syn secondary, subject, tributary

²**subordinate** n : one that is subordinate

³**sub·or·di·nate** \sə-'bórd-ᵊn-,āt\ vb -nat·ed; -nat·ing 1 : to place in a lower rank or class 2 : SUBDUE — **sub·or·di·na·tion** \-,bórd-ᵊn-'ā-shən\ n

**sub·orn** \sə-'bȯrn\ *vb* **1** : to incite secretly : INSTIGATE **2** : to induce to commit perjury — **sub·or·na·tion** \,səb-,ȯr-'nā-shən\ *n*

¹**sub·poe·na** \sə-'pē-nə\ *n* [ME *suppena*, fr. L *sub poena* under penalty] : a writ commanding the person named in it to attend court under penalty for failure to do so

²**subpoena** *vb* **-naed; -na·ing** : to summon with a subpoena

**sub·scribe** \səb-'skrīb\ *vb* **subscribed; sub·scrib·ing 1** : to sign one's name to a document **2** : to give consent by or as if by signing one's name **3** : to promise to contribute by signing one's name with the amount promised **4** : to place an order by signing **5** : FAVOR, APPROVE **syn** agree, acquiesce — **sub·scrib·er** *n*

**sub·scrip·tion** \səb-'skrip-shən\ *n* **1** : the act of subscribing : SIGNATURE **2** : a purchase by signed order

**sub·se·quent** \'səb-si-kwənt, -sə-'kwent\ *adj* : following after : SUCCEEDING — **sub·se·quent·ly** \-,kwent-lē,-kwənt-\ *adv*

**sub·ser·vi·ence** \səb-'sər-vē-əns\ *n* **1** : a subordinate place or condition; *also* : willingness to serve in a subordinate capacity **2** : SERVILITY — **sub·ser·vi·en·cy** \-ən-sē\ *n* — **sub·ser·vi·ent** \-ənt\ *adj*

**sub·set** \'səb-,set\ *n* : a set each of whose elements is an element of an inclusive set

**sub·side** \səb-'sīd\ *vb* **sub·sid·ed; sub·sid·ing** [L *subsidere*, fr. *sub-* under + *sidere* to sit down, sink] **1** : to settle to the bottom of a liquid **2** : to tend downward : DESCEND **3** : SINK, SUBMERGE **4** : to become quiet and tranquil **syn** abate, wane — **sub·sid·ence** \səb-'sīd-ᵊns, 'səb-səd-əns\ *n*

¹**sub·sid·iary** \səb-'sid-ē-,er-ē\ *adj* **1** : furnishing aid or support; *also* : owned or controlled by some main company **2** : of or relating to a subsidy **syn** auxiliary, contributory, subservient

²**subsidiary** *n, pl* **-iar·ies** : one that is subsidiary; *esp* : a company controlled by another

**sub·si·dize** \'səb-sə-,dīz\ *vb* **-dized; -diz·ing** : to aid or furnish with a subsidy

**sub·si·dy** \'səb-səd-ē\ *n, pl* **-dies** [ME, fr. L *subsidium* reserve troops, support, assistance, fr. *sub-* near + *sedēre* to sit] : a gift of public money to another country or to a private enterprise **syn** grant, appropriation

**sub·sist** \səb-'sist\ *vb* **1** : EXIST, PERSIST **2** : to receive the means (as food and clothing) of maintaining life

**sub·sis·tence** \səb-'sis-təns\ *n* **1** : EXISTENCE **2** : means of subsisting : the minimum (as of food and clothing) necessary to support life

**sub·soil** \'səb-,sȯil\ *n* : a layer of weathered material just under the surface soil

**sub·son·ic** \,səb-'sän-ik, 'səb-\ *adj* **1** : being or relating to a speed less than

that of sound; *also* : moving at such a speed **2** : INFRASONIC

**sub·stance** \'səb-stəns\ *n* **1** : essential nature : ESSENCE ⟨divine ~⟩; *also* : the fundamental or essential part or quality ⟨the ~ of his speech⟩ **2** : physical material from which something is made or which has discrete existence; *also* : matter of particular or definite chemical constitution **3** : material possessions : PROPERTY, WEALTH

**sub·stan·dard** \,səb-'stan-dərd, 'səb-\ *adj* : falling short of a standard or norm

**sub·stan·tial** \səb-'stan-chəl\ *adj* **1** : existing as or in substance : MATERIAL; *also* : not illusory : REAL **2** : IMPORTANT, ESSENTIAL **3** : NOURISHING, SATISFYING ⟨~ meal⟩ **4** : having means : WELL-TO-DO **5** : CONSIDERABLE ⟨~ profit⟩ **6** : STRONG, FIRM — **sub·stan·tial·ly** \-ē\ *adv*

**sub·stan·ti·ate** \səb-'stan-chē-,āt\ *vb* **-at·ed; -at·ing 1** : VERIFY, PROVE **2** : to give substance or body to — **sub·stan·ti·a·tion** \-,stan-chē-'ā-shən\ *n*

**sub·stan·tive** \'səb-stən-tiv\ *n* : NOUN; *also* : a word or phrase used as a noun

**sub·sta·tion** \'səb-,stā-shən\ *n* : a station (as a post-office branch) subordinate to another station

¹**sub·sti·tute** \'səb-stə-,t(y)üt\ *n* : a person or thing replacing another — **substitute** *adj*

²**substitute** *vb* **-tut·ed; -tut·ing 1** : to put in the place of another **2** : to serve as a substitute — **sub·sti·tu·tion** \,səb-stə-'t(y)ü-shən\ *n*

**sub·stra·tum** \'səb-,strāt-əm, -,strat-\ *n, pl* **-stra·ta** \-ə\ : the layer or structure lying underneath

**sub·struc·ture** \'səb-,strək-chər\ *n* : FOUNDATION, GROUNDWORK

**sub·sur·face** \'səb-,sər-fəs\ *n* : earth material near the surface of the ground — **subsurface** *adj*

**sub·ter·fuge** \'səb-tər-,fyüj\ *n* : a trick or device used in order to conceal, escape, or evade **syn** fraud, deception, trickery

**sub·ter·ra·nean** \,səb-tə-'rā-nē-ən\ *or* **sub·ter·ra·neous** \-nē-əs\ *adj* **1** : lying or being underground **2** : SECRET, HIDDEN

**sub·tile** \'sət-ᵊl, 'səb-tᵊl\ *adj* **sub·til·er** \'sət-lər, -ᵊl-ər; 'səb-tə-lər\; **sub·til·est** \'sət-ləst, -ᵊl-əst; 'səb-tə-ləst\ : SUBTLE

**sub·ti·tle** \'səb-,tīt-ᵊl\ *n* **1** : a secondary or explanatory title (as of a book) **2** : printed matter projected on a motion-picture screen during or between the scenes

**sub·tle** \'sət-ᵊl\ *adj* **sub·tler** \'sət-(ᵊ-)lər\; **sub·tlest** \'sət-(ᵊ-)ləst\ [ME *sutil, sotil*, fr. OF *soutil*, fr. L *subtilis*, lit., finely woven, fr. *sub-* under, near + *tela* web] **1** : hardly noticeable : DELICATE, REFINED **2** : SHREWD, KEEN **3** : CLEVER, SLY — **sub·tle·ty** \-tē\ *n* — **sub·tly** \'sət-(ᵊ-)lē\ *adv*

**sub·tract** \səb-'trakt\ *vb* : to take away (as one number from another) — **sub·trac·tion** \-'trak-shən\ *n*

**sub·tra·hend** \'səb-trə-ˌhend\ n : the quantity to be subtracted in mathematics

**sub·trop·i·cal** \ˌsəb-'träp-i-kəl, 'səb-\ also **sub·trop·ic** \-ik\ adj : of, relating to, or being regions bordering on the tropical zone

**sub·urb** \'səb-ˌərb\ n 1 : an outlying part of a city; also : a small community adjacent to a city 2 pl : a residential area adjacent to a city — **sub·ur·ban** \sə-'bər-bən\ adj or n

**sub·ur·ban·ite** \sə-'bər-bə-ˌnīt\ n : one living in a suburb

**sub·ur·bia** \sə-'bər-bē-ə\ n 1 : SUBURBS 2 : suburban people or customs

**sub·ven·tion** \səb-'ven-chən\ n : SUBSIDY, ENDOWMENT

**sub·vert** \səb-'vərt\ vb 1 : OVERTHROW, RUIN 2 : CORRUPT syn overturn, upset — **sub·ver·sion** \-'vər-zhən\ n — **sub·ver·sive** \-'vər-siv\ adj

**sub·way** \'səb-ˌwā\ n : an underground way; esp : an underground electric railway

**suc·ceed** \sək-'sēd\ vb 1 : to follow next in order or next after another; esp : to inherit sovereignty 2 : to attain a desired object or end : be successful

**suc·cess** \sək-'ses\ n 1 : satisfactory completion of something 2 : the gaining of wealth and fame 3 : one that succeeds — **suc·cess·ful** \-fəl\ adj — **suc·cess·ful·ly** \-ē\ adv

**suc·ces·sion** \sək-'sesh-ən\ n 1 : the order, act, or right of succeeding to a property, title, or throne 2 : the act or process of following in order 3 : a series of persons or things that follow one after another syn progression, sequence, set, chain, train, string

**suc·ces·sive** \sək-'ses-iv\ adj : following in order : CONSECUTIVE — **suc·ces·sive·ly** adv

**suc·ces·sor** \sək-'ses-ər\ n : one that succeeds (as to a throne, title, estate, or office)

**suc·cinct** \(ˌ)sək-'siŋkt, sə-'siŋkt\ adj : BRIEF, CONCISE syn terse, laconic, summary — **suc·cinct·ly** adv — **suc·cinct·ness** n

**suc·cor** \'sək-ər\ n [ME succur, fr. earlier sucurs, taken as pl., fr. OF sucors, fr. ML succursus, fr. L succursus, pp. of succurrere to run up, run to help, fr. sub- up + currere to run] : AID, HELP, RELIEF — **succor** vb

**suc·co·tash** \'sək-ə-ˌtash\ n : beans and kernels of sweet corn cooked together

¹**suc·cu·lent** \'sək-yə-lənt\ adj : full of juice : JUICY; also : having fleshy tissues that conserve moisture — **suc·cu·lence** \-ləns\ n

²**succulent** n : a succulent plant (as a cactus)

**suc·cumb** \sə-'kəm\ vb 1 : to give up 2 : DIE syn submit, capitulate, relent

¹**such** \('ˌ)səch, (ˌ)sich\ adj 1 : of this or that kind 2 : having a quality just specified or to be specified

²**such** pron 1 : such a one or ones ⟨he's the boss, and had the right to act as ∼⟩

2 : that or those similar or related thereto ⟨boards and nails and ∼⟩

³**such** adv : to that degree : so

**such·like** \'səch-ˌlīk\ adj : SIMILAR

¹**suck** \'sək\ vb 1 : to draw in liquid and esp. mother's milk from the mouth 2 : to draw liquid from by action of the mouth ⟨∼ an orange⟩ 3 : to take in or up or remove by or as if by suction

²**suck** n : the act of sucking : SUCTION

**suck·er** \'sək-ər\ n 1 : one that sucks 2 : a part of an animal's body used for sucking or for clinging 3 : a fish with thick soft lips for sucking in food 4 : a shoot from the roots or lower part of a plant 5 : a person easily deceived

**suck·le** \'sək-əl\ vb **suck·led**; **suck·ling** \-(ə-)liŋ\ : to give or draw milk from the breast or udder; also : NURTURE, REAR

**suck·ling** \'sək-liŋ\ n : a young unweaned mammal

**su·cre** \'sü-(ˌ)krā\ n — see MONEY table

**su·crose** \'sü-ˌkrōs, -ˌkrōz\ n : cane or beet sugar

**suc·tion** \'sək-shən\ n 1 : the act of sucking 2 : the act or process of drawing something (as liquid or dust) into a space (as in a vacuum cleaner or a pump) by partially exhausting the air in the space — **suc·tion·al** \-sh(ə-)nəl\ adj

**sud·den** \'səd-ᵊn\ adj [ME sodain, fr. MF, fr. L subitaneus, fr. subitus sudden, fr. pp. of subire to come up, fr. sub- up + ire to go] 1 : happening or coming quickly or unexpectedly ⟨∼ shower⟩; also : come upon unexpectedly ⟨∼ turn in the road⟩ 2 : ABRUPT, STEEP ⟨∼ descent to the sea⟩ 3 : HASTY, RASH ⟨∼ decision⟩ 4 : made or brought about in a short time : PROMPT ⟨∼ cure⟩ syn precipitate, headlong, impetuous — **sud·den·ly** adv — **sud·den·ness** n

**suds** \'sədz\ n pl : soapy water esp. when frothy — **sudsy** \'səd-zē\ adj

**sue** \'sü\ vb **sued**; **su·ing** 1 : PETITION, SOLICIT 2 : to seek justice or right by bringing legal action syn pray, plead

**suede** or **suède** \'swād\ n [F gants de Suède Swedish gloves] 1 : leather with a napped surface 2 : a fabric with a suedelike nap

**su·et** \'sü-ət\ n : the hard fat from beef and mutton that yields tallow

**suff** abbr 1 sufficient 2 suffix

**suf·fer** \'səf-ər\ vb **suf·fered**; **suf·fer·ing** \-(ə-)riŋ\ 1 : to feel or endure pain 2 : EXPERIENCE, UNDERGO 3 : to bear loss, damage, or injury 4 : ALLOW, PERMIT syn endure, abide, tolerate, stand, brook, let, leave — **suf·fer·er** n

**suf·fer·ance** \'səf-(ə-)rəns\ n 1 : consent or approval implied by lack of interference or resistance 2 : ENDURANCE, PATIENCE

**suf·fer·ing** \-(ə-)riŋ\ n : PAIN, MISERY, HARDSHIP

**suf·fice** \sə-'fīs\ vb **suf·ficed**; **suf·fic·ing** 1 : to satisfy a need : be sufficient **2 :** to be capable or competent

**suf·fi·cien·cy** \sə-'fish-ən-sē\ *n* **1 :** a sufficient quantity to meet one's needs **2 :** ADEQUACY **3 :** SELF-CONFIDENCE

**suf·fi·cient** \sə-'fish-ənt\ *adj* **:** adequate to accomplish a purpose or meet a need — **suf·fi·cient·ly** *adv*

**¹suf·fix** \'səf-,iks\ *n* **:** an affix occurring at the end of a word

**²suf·fix** \'səf-,iks, (,)sə-'fiks\ *vb* **:** to attach as a suffix — **suf·fix·a·tion** \,səf-,ik-'sā-shən\

**suf·fo·cate** \'səf-ə-,kāt\ *vb* **-cat·ed; -cat·ing :** STIFLE, SMOTHER, CHOKE — **suf·fo·cat·ing·ly** *adv* — **suf·fo·ca·tion** \,səf-ə-'kā-shən\ *n*

**suf·fra·gan** \'səf-rə-gən\ *n* **:** an assistant bishop; *esp* **:** one not having the right of succession — **suffragan** *adj*

**suf·frage** \'səf-rij\ *n* **1 :** VOTE **2 :** the right to vote **:** FRANCHISE

**suf·frag·ette** \,səf-ri-'jet\ *n* **:** a woman who advocates suffrage for her sex

**suf·frag·ist** \'səf-ri-jəst\ *n* **:** one who advocates extension of the suffrage esp. to women

**suf·fuse** \sə-'fyüz\ *vb* **suf·fused; suf·fus·ing :** to spread over or through in the manner of a fluid or light **syn** infuse, imbue, ingrain — **suf·fu·sion** \-'fyü-zhən\ *n*

**¹sug·ar** \'shùg-ər\ *n* **1 :** a sweet substance that is colorless or white when pure and is chiefly derived from sugarcane or sugar beets **2 :** a water-soluble compound (as glucose) that varies widely in sweetness — **sug·ary** *adj*

**²sugar** *vb* **sug·ared; sug·ar·ing** \'shùg-(ə-)riŋ\ **1 :** to mix, cover, or sprinkle with sugar **2 :** SWEETEN ⟨~ advice with flattery⟩ **3 :** to form sugar ⟨a syrup that ~s⟩ **4 :** GRANULATE

**sugar beet** *n* **:** a large beet with a white root from which sugar is made

**sug·ar·cane** \'shùg-ər-,kān\ *n* **:** a tall grass widely grown in warm regions for the sugar in its stalks

**sugar maple** *n* **:** a maple with a sweet sap; *esp* **:** one of eastern No. America with sap that is the chief source of maple syrup and maple sugar

**sug·ar·plum** \'shùg-ər-,pləm\ *n* **:** a small ball of candy

**sug·gest** \sə(g)-'jest\ *vb* **1 :** to put (as a thought, plan, or desire) into a person's mind **2 :** to remind or evoke by association of ideas **syn** imply, hint, intimate, insinuate — **sug·gest·ible** \-'jes-tə-bəl\ *adj*

**sug·ges·tion** \-'jes-chən\ *n* **1 :** an act or instance of suggesting; *also* **:** something suggested **2 :** a slight indication

**sug·ges·tive** \-'jes-tiv\ *adj* **:** tending to suggest something; *esp* **:** suggesting something improper or indecent — **sug·ges·tive·ly** *adv* — **sug·ges·tive·ness** *n*

**sui·cide** \'sü-ə-,sīd\ *n* **1 :** the act of killing oneself purposely **2 :** a person who kills himself purposely — **sui·cid·al** \,sü-ə-'sīd-ᵊl\ *adj*

**sui ge·ner·is** \,sü-,ī-'jen-ə-rəs; ,sü-ē-'jen-\ *adj* [L, of its own kind] **:** being in a class by itself **:** UNIQUE

**¹suit** \'süt\ *n* **1 :** an action in court to recover a right or claim **2 :** an act of suing or entreating; *esp* **:** COURTSHIP **3 :** a number of things used together ⟨~ of clothes⟩ **4 :** one of the four sets of playing cards in a pack **syn** prayer, plea, petition, appeal

**²suit** *vb* **1 :** to be appropriate or fitting **2 :** to be becoming to **3 :** to meet the needs or desires of **:** PLEASE

**suit·able** \'süt-ə-bəl\ *adj* **:** FITTING, PROPER, APPROPRIATE **syn** fit, meet, apt — **suit·abil·i·ty** \,süt-ə-'bil-ət-ē\ *n* — **suit·able·ness** \'süt-ə-bəl-nəs\ *n* — **suit·ably** \-ə-blē\ *adv*

**suit·case** \'süt-,kās\ *n* **:** a flat rectangular traveling bag

**suite** \'swēt, *for 4 also* 'süt\ *n* **1 :** a personal staff attending a dignitary or ruler **:** RETINUE **2 :** a group of rooms occupied as a unit **:** APARTMENT **3 :** a modern instrumental composition free in its character and number of movements; *also* **:** a long orchestral concert arrangement in suite form of material drawn from a longer work **4 :** a set of matched furniture for a room

**suit·ing** \'süt-iŋ\ *n* **:** fabric for suits of clothes

**suit·or** \'süt-ər\ *n* **1 :** one who sues or petitions **2 :** one who seeks to marry a woman

**su·ki·ya·ki** \skē-'(y)äk-ē; ,sùk-ē-'(y)äk-ē, ,sük-\ *n* **:** thin slices of meat, bean curd, and vegetables cooked in soy sauce, sake, and sugar

**sul·fa** \'səl-fə\ *adj* **1 :** related chemically to sulfanilamide **2 :** of, relating to, or using sulfa drugs ⟨~ therapy⟩

**sulfa drug** *n* **:** any of various synthetic organic bacteria-inhibiting drugs that are closely related chemically to sulfanilamide

**sul·fa·nil·amide** \,səl-fə-'nil-ə-,mīd\ *n* **:** a sulfur-containing organic compound used in the treatment of various infections

**sul·fate** \'səl-,fāt\ *n* **:** a salt or ester of sulfuric acid

**sul·fide** \'səl-'fīd\ *n* **:** a compound of sulfur with an element or radical

**sul·fur** *or* **sul·phur** \'səl-fər\ *n* **:** a nonmetallic element that occurs in nature combined or free in the form of yellow crystals and in masses, crusts, and powder and is used in making gunpowder and matches, in vulcanizing rubber, and in medicine — **sul·fu·re·ous** \,səl-'fyùr-ē-əs\ *adj*

**sulfur dioxide** *n* **:** a heavy pungent toxic gas that is used esp. in bleaching, as a preservative, and as a refrigerant, and is a major air pollutant

**sul·fu·ric** \,səl-'fyùr-ik\ *adj* **:** of, relating to, or containing sulfur

**sulfuric acid** *n* **:** a heavy corrosive oily acid used esp. in making fertilizers, chemicals, and petroleum products

**sul·fu·rous** \'səl-f(y)ə-rəs, *also esp for 1* ,səl-'fyùr-əs\ *adj* **1 :** of, relating to, or containing sulfur **2 :** of or relating to brimstone or the fire of hell **:** INFERNAL **3 :** FIERY, SCORCHING

¹**sulk** \'səlk\ *vb* : to be or become moodily silent

²**sulk** *n* : a sulky mood or spell

¹**sulky** \'səl-kē\ *adj* : inclined to sulk : MOROSE, MOODY **syn** surly, glum, sullen, gloomy — **sulk·i·ly** \'səl-kə-lē\ *adv* — **sulk·i·ness** \-kē-nəs\ *n*

²**sulky** *n, pl* **sulkies** : a light 2-wheeled vehicle with a seat for the driver and usu. no body

**sul·len** \'səl-ən\ *adj* **1** : gloomily silent : MOROSE **2** : DISMAL, GLOOMY ⟨a ~ sky⟩ **syn** glum, surly — **sul·len·ly** *adv* — **sul·len·ness** \'səl-ən-(n)əs\ *n*

**sul·ly** \'səl-ē\ *vb* **sul·lied; sul·ly·ing** : SOIL, SMIRCH, DEFILE

**sul·tan** \'səlt-ᵊn\ *n* : a sovereign esp. of a Muslim state — **sul·tan·ate** \-ˌāt\ *n*

**sul·ta·na** \ˌsəl-'tan-ə\ *n* **1** : a female member of a sultan's family **2** : a pale seedless grape; *also* : a raisin of this grape

**sul·try** \'səl-trē\ *adj* **sul·tri·er; -est** [obs. E *sulter* to swelter, alter. of E *swelter*] : very hot and moist : SWELTERING; *also* : burning hot : TORRID

¹**sum** \'səm\ *n* [ME *summe*, fr. OF, fr. L *summa*, fr. fem. of *summus* highest] **1** : a quantity of money **2** : the whole amount **3** : GIST **4** : the result obtained by adding numbers **5** : a problem in arithmetic **syn** aggregate, total, whole

²**sum** *vb* **summed; sum·ming** : to find the sum of by adding or counting

**su·mac** *or* **su·mach** \'s(h)ü-ˌmak\ *n* : any of various shrubs or small trees with pinnate compound leaves and spikes of red or whitish berries

**sum·ma·rize** \'səm-ə-ˌrīz\ *vb* **-rized; -riz·ing** : to tell in a summary

¹**sum·ma·ry** \'səm-ə-rē\ *adj* **1** : covering the main points briefly : CONCISE **2** : done without delay or formality ⟨~ punishment⟩ **syn** terse, succinct, laconic — **sum·mar·i·ly** \(ˌ)sə-'mer-ə-lē, 'səm-ə-rə-lē\ *adv*

²**sum·ma·ry** *n, pl* **-ries** : a concise statement of the main points

**sum·ma·tion** \(ˌ)sə-'mā-shən\ *n* : a summing up; *esp* : a speech in court summing up the arguments in a case

**sum·mer** \'səm-ər\ *n* : the season of the year in a region in which the sun shines most directly : the warmest period of the year — **sum·mery** *adj*

**sum·mer·house** \'səm-ər-ˌhaus\ *n* : a rustic covered structure in a garden to provide a shady retreat

**summer squash** *n* : any of various garden squashes (as zucchini) used as a vegetable while immature

**sum·mit** \'səm-ət\ *n* : the highest point

**sum·mon** \'səm-ən\ *vb* **sum·moned; sum·mon·ing** \-(ə-)niŋ\ [ME *somonen*, fr. OF *somondre*, fr. (assumed) VL *summonere*, alter. of L *summonēre* to remind secretly, fr. *sub-* secretly + *monēre* to warn] **1** : to call to a meeting : CONVOKE **2** : to send for; *also* : to order to appear in court **3** : to evoke esp. by an act of the will ⟨~ up courage⟩ — **sum·mon·er** *n*

**sum·mons** \'səm-ənz\ *n, pl* **sum-** mons·es **1** : an authoritative call to appear at a designated place or to attend to a duty **2** : a warning or citation to appear in court at a specified time to answer charges

**sump·tu·ous** \'səmp-chə(-wə)s\ *adj* : LAVISH, LUXURIOUS

**sum up** *vb* : SUMMARIZE

¹**sun** \'sən\ *n* **1** : the shining celestial body around which the earth and other planets revolve and from which they receive light and heat **2** : a celestial body that like the sun is the center of a system of planets **3** : SUNSHINE — **sun·less** *adj* — **sun·ny** *adj*

²**sun** *vb* **sunned; sun·ning 1** : to expose to or as if to the rays of the sun **2** : to sun oneself

**Sun** *abbr* Sunday

**sun·bath** \'sən-ˌbath, -ˌbàth\ *n* : an exposure to sunlight or a sunlamp — **sun·bathe** \-ˌbàth\ *vb*

**sun·beam** \-ˌbēm\ *n* : a ray of sunlight

**sun·bon·net** \-ˌbän-ət\ *n* : a bonnet with a wide brim to shield the face and neck from the sun

¹**sun·burn** \-ˌbərn\ *vb* **-burned** \-ˌbərnd\ *or* **-burnt** \-ˌbərnt\; **-burn·ing** : to burn or discolor by the sun

²**sunburn** *n* : a skin inflammation caused by overexposure to sunlight

**sun·dae** \'sən-dē\ *n* : ice cream served with topping

**Sun·day** \'sən-dē\ *n* : the first day of the week : the Christian Sabbath

**sun·der** \'sən-dər\ *vb* **sun·dered; sun·der·ing** \-d(ə-)riŋ\ : to force apart **syn** sever, part

**sun·di·al** \-ˌdī(-ə)l\ *n* : a device for showing the time of day from the shadow cast by an upright pin on a plate

**sun·down** \'sən-ˌdaun\ *n* : the time of the setting of the sun

**sun·dries** \'sən-drēz\ *n pl* : various small articles or items

**sun·dry** \'sən-drē\ *adj* : SEVERAL, DIVERS, VARIOUS **syn** many, numerous

**sun·fish** \-ˌfish\ *n* **1** : a huge sea fish with a deep flattened body **2** : any of various American freshwater fishes resembling the perches

**sun·flow·er** \-ˌflau̇(-ə)r\ *n* : a tall plant related to the daisies and often grown for the oil-rich seeds of its yellow-petaled dark-centered flower heads

**sung** *past of* SING

**sun·glasses** \'sən-ˌglas-əz\ *n pl* : glasses to protect the eyes from the sun

**sunk** *past of* SINK

**sunk·en** \'səŋ-kən\ *adj* **1** : SUBMERGED **2** : fallen in : HOLLOW ⟨~ cheeks⟩ **3** : lying in a depression ⟨~ garden⟩; *also* : constructed below the general floor level ⟨~ living room⟩

**sun·lamp** \'sən-ˌlamp\ *n* : an electric lamp that emits a wide band of wavelengths and that is used esp. for therapeutic purposes

**sun·light** \-ˌlīt\ *n* : SUNSHINE

**sun·lit** \-ˌlit\ *adj* : lighted by direct sunshine

**sun·rise** \ˈsən-ˌrīz\ *n* : the apparent rising of the sun above the horizon; *also* : the time of this rising

**sun·roof** \-ˌrüf, -ˌrúf\ *n* : an automobile roof having a panel that can be opened

**sun·seek·er** \-ˌsē-kər\ *n* : a person who travels to an area of warmth and sun esp. in winter

**sun·set** \-ˌset\ *n* : the apparent descent of the sun below the horizon; *also* : the time of this descent

**sun·shade** \ˈsən-ˌshād\ *n* : something (as a parasol or awning) used as a protection from the sun's rays

**sun·shine** \-ˌshīn\ *n* : the direct light of the sun — **sun·shiny** *adj*

**sun·spot** \-ˌspät\ *n* : one of the dark spots that appear from time to time on the sun's surface

**sun·stroke** \-ˌstrōk\ *n* : heatstroke caused by exposure to the sun

**sun·tan** \-ˌtan\ *n* : a browning of the skin from exposure to the sun's rays

**sun·up** \-ˌəp\ *n* : the time of the rising of the sun

**¹sup** \ˈsəp\ *vb* **supped; sup·ping** : to take or drink in swallows or gulps

**²sup** *n* : a mouthful esp. of liquor or broth; *also* : a small quantity of liquid

**³sup** *vb* **supped; sup·ping 1** : to eat the evening meal **2** : to make one's supper ⟨*supped* on roast beef⟩

**⁴sup** *abbr* **1** superior **2** supplement; supplementary **3** supply **4** supra

**¹su·per** \ˈsü-pər\ *n* : SUPERINTENDENT

**²super** *adj* **1** : very fine : EXCELLENT **2** : EXTREME, EXCESSIVE

**super-** \ˌsü-pər, ˈsü-\ *prefix* **1** : over and above : higher in quantity, quality, or degree than : more than **2** : in addition **3** : exceeding a norm **4** : in excessive degree or intensity **5** : surpassing all or most others of its kind **6** : situated above, on, or at the top of **7** : next above or higher **8** : more inclusive than **9** : superior in status or position

| | |
|---|---|
| superacid | superphysical |
| superagency | superpower |
| superalkaline | supersalesman |
| superblock | supersales- |
| superbomb | manship |
| supercity | supersecret |
| supereminent | supersize |
| superendur- | supersized |
| ance | superspectacle |
| superfine | superspeed |
| supergalaxy | superstar |
| superglacial | superstate |
| supergovern- | superstratum |
| ment | superstrength |
| superheat | supersubtle |
| superhuman | supersubtlety |
| superhumanly | supersystem |
| superindividual | supertanker |
| superliner | supertax |
| superman | supertemporal |
| supernormal | supertower |
| superpatriot | supervoltage |
| superpatriotic | superwoman |
| superpatriotism | superzealot |

**su·per·abun·dant** \ˌsü-pər-ə-ˈbən-dənt\ *adj* : more than ample — **su·per·abun·dance** \-dəns\ *n*

**su·per·an·nu·ate** \ˌsü-pər-ˈan-yə-ˌwāt\ *vb* **-at·ed; -at·ing** : to retire and pension because of age or infirmity — **su·per·an·nu·at·ed** *adj*

**su·perb** \sù-ˈpərb\ *adj* [L *superbus* excellent, proud, fr. *super* above + *-bus* (akin to OE *bēon* to be)] **1** : LORDLY, MAJESTIC **2** : RICH, SPLENDID **3** : of highest quality **syn** resplendent, glorious, gorgeous, sublime — **su·perb·ly** *adv*

**su·per·car·go** \ˌsü-pər-ˈkär-gō, ˈsü-pər-ˈkär-gō\ *n* : an officer on a merchant ship who manages the business part of the voyage

**su·per·charg·er** \ˈsü-pər-ˌchär-jər\ *n* : a device for increasing the amount of air supplied to an internal-combustion engine

**su·per·cil·ious** \ˌsü-pər-ˈsil-ē-əs\ *adj* [L *superciliosus*, fr. *supercilium* eyebrow, haughtiness] : haughtily contemptuous **syn** disdainful, overbearing, arrogant

**su·per·con·duc·tiv·i·ty** \ˈsü-pər-ˌkän-ˌdək-ˈtiv-ət-ē\ *n* : a complete disappearance of electrical resistance in various metals at temperatures near absolute zero — **su·per·con·duc·tive** \ˌsü-pər-kən-ˈdək-tiv\ *adj* — **su·per·con·duc·tor** \-ˈdək-tər\ *n*

**su·per·ego** \ˌsü-pər-ˈē-gō\ *n* : the one of the three divisions of the psyche in psychoanalytic theory that functions to reward and punish through a system of moral attitudes, conscience, and a sense of guilt

**su·per·fi·cial** \ˌsü-pər-ˈfish-əl\ *adj* **1** : of or relating to the surface or appearance only **2** : not thorough : SHALLOW **syn** cursory — **su·per·fi·ci·al·i·ty** \-ˌfish-ē-ˈal-ət-ē\ *n* — **su·per·fi·cial·ly** \-ˈfish-(ə-)lē\ *adv*

**su·per·flu·ous** \sù-ˈpər-flə-wəs\ *adj* : exceeding what is sufficient or necessary : SURPLUS **syn** extra, spare — **su·per·flu·i·ty** \ˌsü-pər-ˈflü-ət-ē\ *n*

**su·per·high·way** \ˌsü-pər-ˈhī-ˌwā\ *n* : a broad highway designed for high-speed traffic

**su·per·im·pose** \-im-ˈpōz\ *vb* : to lay (one thing) over and above something else **syn** superpose

**su·per·in·tend** \ˌsü-p(ə-)rin-ˈtend\ *vb* : to have or exercise the charge and oversight of : DIRECT — **su·per·in·ten·dence** \-ˈten-dəns\ *n* — **su·per·in·ten·den·cy** \-dən-sē\ *n* — **su·per·in·ten·dent** \-dənt\ *n*

**¹su·pe·ri·or** \sù-ˈpir-ē-ər\ *adj* **1** : situated higher up; *also* : higher in rank or numbers **2** : better than most others of its kind **3** : of greater value or importance **4** : courageously indifferent (as to pain or misfortune) **5** : ARROGANT, HAUGHTY — **su·pe·ri·or·i·ty** \-ˌpir-ē-ˈôr-ət-ē\ *n*

**²superior** *n* **1** : one who is above another in rank, office, or station; *esp* : the head of a religious house or order **2** : one higher in quality or merit

**su·per·jet** \'sü-pər-,jet\ *n* : a supersonic jet airplane

**¹su·per·la·tive** \sù-'pər-lət-iv\ *adj* **1** : of, relating to, or constituting the degree of grammatical comparison that denotes an extreme or unsurpassed level or extent **2** : surpassing others : SUPREME **syn** peerless, incomparable — **su·per·la·tive·ly** *adv*

**²superlative** *n* **1** : the superlative degree or a superlative form in a language **2** : the utmost degree : ACME

**su·per·mar·ket** \'sü-pər-,mär-kət\ *n* : a self-service retail market selling foods and household merchandise

**su·per·nal** \sù-'pərn-əl\ *adj* **1** : of or from on high : TOWERING **2** : of heavenly or spiritual character : ETHEREAL

**su·per·nat·u·ral** \,sü-pər-'nach-(ə-)rəl\ *adj* : of or relating to phenomena beyond or outside of nature; *esp* : relating to or attributed to a divinity, ghost, or infernal spirit — **su·per·nat·u·ral·ly** \-ē\ *adv*

**su·per·no·va** \,sü-pər-'nō-və\ *n* : a rare exceedingly bright nova

**¹su·per·nu·mer·ary** \-'n(y)ü-mə-,rer-ē\ *adj* : exceeding the usual or required number : EXTRA **syn** surplus, superfluous

**²supernumerary** *n*, *pl* **-ar·ies** : an extra person or thing; *esp* : an actor hired for a nonspeaking part

**su·per·pose** \,sü-pər-'pōz\ *vb* **-posed; -pos·ing** : SUPERIMPOSE — **su·per·po·si·tion** \-pə-'zish-ən\ *n*

**su·per·scribe** \'sü-pər-,skrīb\ ,sü-pər-'skrīb\ *vb* **-scribed; -scrib·ing** : to write on the top or outside : ADDRESS — **su·per·scrip·tion** \,sü-pər-'skrip-shən\ *n*

**su·per·sede** \,sü-pər-'sēd\ *vb* **-sed·ed; -sed·ing** [MF *superseder* to refrain from, fr. L *supersedēre* to be superior to, refrain from, fr. *super-* above + *sedēre* to sit] : to take the place of : REPLACE **syn** displace, supplant

**su·per·son·ic** \-'sän-ik\ *adj* **1** : having a frequency above the human ear's audibility limit ⟨∼ vibrations⟩ **2** : relating to supersonic waves or vibrations **3** : being or relating to speeds from five to six times the speed of sound; *also* : capable of moving at such a speed ⟨a ∼ airplane⟩

**su·per·son·ics** \-'sän-iks\ *n* : the science of supersonic phenomena

**su·per·sti·tion** \,sü-pər-'stish-ən\ *n* **1** : beliefs or practices resulting from ignorance, fear of the unknown, or trust in magic or chance **2** : an irrationally abject attitude of mind toward nature, the unknown, or God resulting from superstition — **su·per·sti·tious** \-əs\ *adj*

**su·per·struc·ture** \'sü-pər-,strək-chər\ *n* : something built on a base or as a vertical extension

**su·per·vene** \,sü-pər-'vēn\ *vb* **-vened; -ven·ing** : to occur as something additional or unexpected **syn** follow, succeed, ensue — **su·per·ve·nient** \-'vē-nyənt\ *adj*

**su·per·vise** \'sü-pər-,vīz\ *vb* **-vised;**
**-vis·ing** : OVERSEE, SUPERINTEND — **su·per·vi·sion** \,sü-pər-'vizh-ən\ *n* — **su·per·vi·sor** \'sü-pər-,vī-zər\ *n* — **su·per·vi·so·ry** \,sü-pər-'vīz-(ə-)rē\ *adj*

**su·pine** \sù-'pīn\ *adj* **1** : lying on the back with face upward **2** : LETHARGIC, SLUGGISH; *also* : ABJECT **syn** inactive, inert, passive, idle

**supp** *or* **suppl** *abbr* supplement; supplementary

**sup·per** \'sep-ər\ *n* : the evening meal when dinner is taken at midday — **sup·per·less** *adj* — **sup·per·time** \-,tīm\ *n*

**sup·plant** \sə-'plant\ *vb* **1** : to take the place of (another) esp. by force or trickery **2** : REPLACE **syn** displace, supersede

**sup·ple** \'səp-əl\ *adj* **sup·pler** \-(ə-)lər\; **sup·plest** \-(ə-)ləst\ **1** : capable of bending without breaking or creasing : LIMBER **2** : COMPLIANT, ADAPTABLE **syn** resilient, elastic

**¹sup·ple·ment** \'səp-lə-mənt\ *n* **1** : something that supplies a want or makes an addition **2** : a continuation (as of a book) containing corrections or additional material — **sup·ple·men·tal** \,səp-lə-'ment-ə̇l\ *adj* — **sup·ple·men·ta·ry** \-'men-t(ə-)rē\ *adj*

**²sup·ple·ment** \'səp-lə-,ment\ *vb* : to fill up the deficiencies of : add to

**sup·pli·ant** \'səp-lē-ənt\ *n* : one who supplicates : PETITIONER, PLEADER

**sup·pli·cant** \'səp-li-kənt\ *n* : SUPPLIANT

**sup·pli·cate** \'səp-lə-,kāt\ *vb* **-cat·ed; -cat·ing 1** : to make a humble entreaty; *esp* : to pray to God **2** : to ask earnestly and humbly : BESEECH **syn** implore, beg — **sup·pli·ca·tion** \,səp-lə-'kā-shən\ *n*

**¹sup·ply** \sə-'plī\ *vb* **sup·plied; sup·ply·ing** [ME *supplien*, fr. MF *soupleier*, fr. L *supplēre* to fill up, supplement, supply, fr. *sub-* up + *plēre* to fill] **1** : to add as a supplement **2** : to satisfy the needs of **3** : FURNISH, PROVIDE — **sup·pli·er** \-'plī(-ə)r\ *n*

**²supply** *n*, *pl* **supplies 1** : the quantity or amount (as of a commodity) needed or available; *also* : PROVISIONS, STORES — usu. used in pl. **2** : the act or process of filling a want or need : PROVISION **3** : the quantities of goods or services offered for sale at a particular time or at one price

**¹sup·port** \sə-'pōrt\ *vb* **1** : BEAR, TOLERATE **2** : to take sides with : BACK, ASSIST **3** : to provide with food, clothing, and shelter **4** : to hold up or serve as a foundation for **syn** uphold, advocate, champion — **sup·port·able** *adj* — **sup·port·er** *n*

**²support** *n* **1** : the act of supporting : the state of being supported **2** : one that supports : PROP, BASE

**sup·pose** \sə-'pōz\ *vb* **sup·posed; sup·pos·ing 1** : to assume to be true (as for the sake of argument) **2** : EXPECT ⟨I am *supposed* to go⟩ **3** : to think probable — **sup·pos·al** *n*

**sup·posed** \sə-'pōz(-ə)d\ *adj* : BE-

LIEVED; *also* **:** mistakenly believed —
**sup·pos·ed·ly** \-'pō-zəd-lē, -'pōz-dlē\ *adv*

**sup·pos·ing** \sə-'pō-ziŋ\ *conj* **:** if by way of hypothesis **:** on the assumption that

**sup·po·si·tion** \,səp-ə-'zish-ən\ *n* **1** **:** something that is supposed **:** HYPOTHESIS **2 :** the act of supposing

**sup·pos·i·to·ry** \sə-'päz-ə-,tōr-ē\ *n*, *pl* **-ries :** a small easily melted mass of usu. medicated material for insertion (as into the rectum)

**sup·press** \sə-'pres\ *vb* **1 :** to put down by authority or force **:** SUBDUE ⟨~ a revolt⟩ **2 :** to keep from being known; *also* **:** to stop the publication or circulation of **3 :** to exclude from consciousness **:** REPRESS — **sup·press·ible** \-'pres-ə-bəl\ *adj* — **sup·pres·sion** \-'presh-ən\ *n*

**sup·pres·sant** \sə-'pres-°nt\ *n* **:** an agent (as a drug) that tends to suppress rather than eliminate something undesirable

**sup·pu·rate** \'səp-yə-,rāt\ *vb* **-rat·ed; -rat·ing :** to form or give off pus — **sup·pu·ra·tion** \,səp-yə-'rā-shən\ *n*

**su·pra** \'sü-prə, -,prä\ *adv* **:** earlier in this writing **:** ABOVE

**su·pra·na·tion·al** \,sü-prə-'nash-(ə-)nəl, -,prä\ *adj* **:** transcending national boundaries, authority, or interests ⟨~ organizations⟩

**su·prem·a·cist** \su̇-'prem-ə-səst\ *n* **:** an advocate of group supremacy

**su·prem·a·cy** \su̇-'prem-ə-sē\ *n*, *pl* **-cies :** supreme rank, power, or authority

**su·preme** \su̇-'prēm\ *adj* [L *supremus*, superl of *superus* upper, fr. *super* over, above] **1 :** highest in rank or authority **2 :** UTMOST **3 :** most excellent ⟨he is ~ among poets⟩ **4 :** ULTIMATE ⟨the ~ sacrifice⟩ *syn* superlative, surpassing, peerless, incomparable — **su·preme·ly** *adv* — **su·preme·ness** *n*

**Supreme Being** *n* **:** GOD 1

**supt** *abbr* superintendent

**supvr** *abbr* supervisor

**sur·cease** \'sər-,sēs\ *n* **:** CESSATION, RESPITE

**¹sur·charge** \'sər-,chärj\ *vb* **1 :** to fill to excess **:** OVERLOAD **2 :** to print or write a surcharge on (postage stamps)

**²surcharge** *n* **1 :** an excessive load or burden **2 :** an extra fee or cost **3 :** something officially printed on a postage stamp to give it a new value or use

**sur·cin·gle** \'sər-,siŋ-gəl\ *n* **:** a band passing around a horse's body to make something (as a saddle or pack) fast

**¹sure** \'shu̇r\ *adj* **sur·er; sur·est** [ME, fr. MF *sur*, fr. L *securus* secure] **1 :** firmly established **2 :** CONFIDENT, CERTAIN **3 :** TRUSTWORTHY, RELIABLE **4 :** not to be disputed **:** UNDOUBTED **5 :** bound to happen *syn* assured, positive — **sure·ly** *adv* — **sure·ness** *n*

**²sure** *adv* **:** SURELY

**sure-fire** \,shu̇r-,fī(ə)r\ *adj* **:** certain to get results **:** DEPENDABLE

**sure·ty** \'shu̇r-ət-ē\ *n*, *pl* **-ties 1**

**:** SURENESS, CERTAINTY **2 :** something that makes sure **:** GUARANTEE **3 :** one who becomes a guarantor for another person *syn* security, bond, bail, sponsor, backer

**¹surf** \'sərf\ *n* **:** the swell of the sea as it breaks on the shore; *also* **:** the sound or foam caused by breaking waves

**²surf** *vb* **:** to ride the surf (as on a surfboard) — **surf·er** *n* — **surf·ing** *n*

**¹sur·face** \'sər-fəs\ *n* **1 :** the outside of an object or body **2 :** outward aspect or appearance

**²surface** *vb* **sur·faced; sur·fac·ing 1 :** to give a surface to **:** make smooth **2 :** to rise to the surface

**surf·board** \'sərf-,bōrd\ *n* **:** a buoyant board used in riding the crests of waves

**¹sur·feit** \'sər-fət\ *n* **1 :** EXCESS, SUPERABUNDANCE **2 :** excessive indulgence (as in food or drink) **3 :** disgust caused by excess (as in eating and drinking)

**²surfeit** *vb* **:** to feed, supply, or indulge to the point of surfeit **:** CLOY

**surg** *abbr* **1** surgeon **2** surgery; surgical

**¹surge** \'sərj\ *vb* **surged; surg·ing 1 :** to rise and fall actively **:** TOSS **2 :** to move in waves **3 :** to rise suddenly to a high value *syn* arise, mount, soar

**²surge** *n* **1 :** a large billow **2 :** a sweeping onward like a wave of the sea ⟨a ~ of emotion⟩ **3 :** a transient sudden increase of current in an electrical circuit

**sur·geon** \'sər-jən\ *n* **:** a physician who specializes in surgery

**sur·gery** \'sərj-(ə-)rē\ *n*, *pl* **-ger·ies** [ME *surgerie*, fr. OF *cirurgie*, *surgerie*, fr. L *chirurgia*, fr. Gk *cheirourgia*, fr. *cheirourgos* surgeon, fr. *cheirourgos* working with the hand, fr. *cheir* hand + *ergon* work] **1 :** a branch of medicine concerned with the correction of physical defects, the repair of injuries, and the treatment of disease esp. by operation **2 :** a surgeon's operating room or laboratory **3 :** work done by a surgeon

**sur·gi·cal** \'sər-ji-kəl\ *adj* **:** of, relating to, or associated with surgeons or surgery — **sur·gi·cal·ly** \-k-(ə-)lē\ *adv*

**sur·ly** \'sər-lē\ *adj* **sur·li·er; -est** [alter. of ME *sirly* lordly, imperious, fr. *sir*] **:** ILL-NATURED, CRABBED *syn* morose, glum, sullen, sulky, gloomy — **sur·li·ness** *n*

**sur·mise** \sər-'mīz\ *vb* **sur·mised; sur·mis·ing :** GUESS *syn* conjecture — **surmise** *n*

**sur·mount** \sər-'maunt\ *vb* **1 :** to rise superior to **:** OVERCOME **2 :** to get to or lie at the top of *syn* overthrow, rout, vanquish, defeat, subdue

**sur·name** \'sər-,nām\ *n* **1 :** NICKNAME **2 :** the name borne in common by members of a family

**sur·pass** \sər-'pas\ *vb* **1 :** to be superior to in quality, degree, or performance **:** EXCEL **2 :** to be beyond the reach or powers of *syn* transcend, outdo, outstrip, exceed — **sur·pass·ing·ly** *adv*

**sur·plice** \'sər-pləs\ *n* **:** a loose white outer ecclesiastical vestment usu. of knee length with large open sleeves

**sur·plus** \'sər-(,)pləs\ *n* **1** : quantity left over : EXCESS **2** : the excess of assets over liabilities **syn** superfluity

¹**sur·prise** \sə(r)-'prīz\ *n* **1** : an attack made without warning **2** : a taking unawares **3** : something that surprises **4** : AMAZEMENT, ASTONISHMENT

²**surprise** *also* **sur·prize** *vb* **sur·prised; sur·pris·ing 1** : to come upon and attack unexpectedly **2** : to take unawares **3** : AMAZE **4** : to effect or accomplish by means of a surprise **syn** waylay, ambush, astonish, astound — **sur·pris·ing** *adj* — **sur·pris·ing·ly** *adv*

**sur·re·al·ism** \sə-'rē-ə-,liz-əm\ *n* : art, literature, or theater characterized by fantastic or incongruous imagery or effects produced by unnatural juxtapositions and combinations — **sur·re·al·ist** \-ləst\ *n or adj* — **sur·re·al·is·tic** \sə-,rē-ə-'lis-tik\ *adj* — **sur·re·al·is·ti·cal·ly** \-ti-k(ə-)lē\ *adv*

¹**sur·ren·der** \sə-'ren-dər\ *vb* **sur·ren·dered; sur·ren·der·ing** \-d(ə-)riŋ\ **1** : to yield to the power of another : give up under compulsion **2** : RELINQUISH

²**surrender** *n* : the act of giving up or yielding oneself or the possession of something to another **syn** submission, capitulation

**sur·rep·ti·tious** \,sər-əp-'tish-əs\ *adj* : done, made, or acquired by stealth : CLANDESTINE **syn** underhand, covert, furtive — **sur·rep·ti·tious·ly** *adv*

**sur·rey** \'sər-ē\ *n, pl* **surreys** : a 4-wheeled 2-seated horse-drawn carriage

**sur·ro·gate** \'sər-ə-,gāt, -gət\ *n* **1** : DEPUTY, SUBSTITUTE **2** : a law officer in some states with authority in the probate of wills, the settlement of estates, and the appointment of guardians

**sur·round** \sə-'raùnd\ *vb* **1** : to enclose on all sides : ENCIRCLE **2** : to enclose so as to cut off retreat or escape

**sur·round·ings** \sə-'raùn-diŋz\ *n pl* : conditions by which one is surrounded

**sur·tax** \'sər-,taks\ *n* : an additional tax over and above a normal tax

**sur·tout** \(,)sər-'tü\ *n* [F, fr. *sur* over (fr. L *super*) + *tout* all, fr. L *totus* whole] : a man's long close-fitting overcoat

**surv** *abbr* survey; surveying; surveyor

**sur·veil·lance** \sər-'vā-ləns, -'vāl-yəns, -'vā-əns\ *n* : close watch; *also* : SUPERVISION

¹**sur·vey** \sər-'vā\ *vb* **sur·veyed; sur·vey·ing 1** : to look over and examine closely **2** : to make a survey of (as a tract of land) **3** : to view or study something as a whole **syn** behold, see, observe, remark — **sur·vey·or** \-ər\ *n*

²**sur·vey** \'sər-,vā\ *n, pl* **surveys 1** : INSPECTION, EXAMINATION **2** : a wide general view (a ~ of English literature) **3** : the process of finding and representing the contours, measurements, and position of a part of the earth's surface; *also* : a measured plan and description of a region

**sur·vey·ing** \sər-'vā-iŋ\ *n* : the branch of mathematics that teaches the art of making surveys

**sur·vive** \sər-'vīv\ *vb* **sur·vived; sur·viv·ing 1** : to remain alive or existent **2** : OUTLIVE, OUTLAST — **sur·viv·al** *n* — **sur·vi·vor** \-'vī-vər\ *n*

**sus·cep·ti·ble** \sə-'sep-tə-bəl\ *adj* **1** : of such a nature as to permit (words ~ of being misunderstood) **2** : having little resistance to a stimulus or agency (~ to colds) **3** : easily affected or emotionally moved : RESPONSIVE **syn** sensitive, subject, exposed, prone, liable, open — **sus·cep·ti·bil·i·ty** \-,sep-tə-'bil-ət-ē\ *n*

¹**sus·pect** \'səs-,pekt, sə-'spekt\ *adj* : regarded with suspicion

²**sus·pect** \'səs-,pekt\ *n* : one who is suspected (as of a crime)

³**sus·pect** \sə-'spekt\ *vb* **1** : to have doubts of : MISTRUST **2** : to imagine to be guilty without proof **3** : SURMISE

**sus·pend** \sə-'spend\ *vb* **1** : to bar temporarily from a privilege, office, or function **2** : to stop temporarily : make inactive for a time **3** : to withhold (judgment) for a time **4** : HANG; *esp* : to hang so as to be free except at one point **5** : to fail to meet obligations **syn** exclude, eliminate, stay, postpone, defer

**sus·pend·er** \sə-'spen-dər\ *n* **1** : one of two supporting straps which pass over the shoulders and to which the trousers are fastened **2** *Brit* : GARTER

**sus·pense** \sə-'spens\ *n* **1** : SUSPENSION **2** : mental uncertainty : ANXIETY **3** : excitement as to an outcome — **sus·pense·ful** *adj*

**sus·pen·sion** \sə-'spen-chən\ *n* **1** : the act of suspending : the state or period of being suspended **2** : the state of a substance when its particles are mixed with but undissolved in a fluid or solid; *also* : a substance in this state **3** : something suspended **4** : a device by which something is suspended

**sus·pen·so·ry** \sə-'spens-(ə-)rē\ *adj* **1** : SUSPENDED **2** : fitted or serving to suspend something **3** : temporarily leaving undetermined

**sus·pi·cion** \sə-'spish-ən\ *n* **1** : the act or an instance of suspecting something wrong without proof **2** : a slight trace **syn** mistrust, uncertainty

**sus·pi·cious** \sə-'spish-əs\ *adj* **1** : open to or arousing suspicion **2** : inclined to suspect **3** : showing suspicion — **sus·pi·cious·ly** *adv*

**sus·tain** \sə-'stān\ *vb* **1** : to provide with nourishment **2** : to keep going : PROLONG (~ed effort) **3** : to hold up : PROP **4** : to hold up under : ENDURE **5** : SUFFER (~ a broken arm) **6** : to support as true, legal, or valid **7** : PROVE, CORROBORATE

**sus·te·nance** \'səs-tə-nəns\ *n* **1** : FOOD, NOURISHMENT **2** : a supplying with the necessities of life **3** : something that sustains or supports

**su·ture** \'sü-chər\ *n* **1** : a seam or line along which two things or parts are joined by or as if by sewing (the ~s of the skull) **2 :** material or a stitch for sewing a wound together

**su·zer·ain** \'süz-(ə-)rən, -ə-,rān\ n **1 :** a feudal lord **2 :** a nation that has political control over another nation — **su·zer·ain·ty** \-tē\ n

**sv** abbr [L sub verbo or sub voce] under the word

**svc** or **svce** abbr service

**svelte** \'sfelt\ adj [F, fr. It svelto, fr. svellere to pluck out, modif. of L evellere, fr. e- out + vellere to pluck] **:** SLENDER, LITHE

**svgs** abbr savings

**Sw** abbr Sweden; Swedish

**SW** abbr **1** shipper's weight **2** shortwave **3** southwest

**SWA** abbr South-West Africa

**¹swab** \'swäb\ n **1 :** MOP **2 :** a wad of absorbent material esp. for applying medicine or for cleaning **3 :** SAILOR

**²swab** vb **swabbed; swab·bing :** to use a swab on **:** MOP

**swad·dle** \'swäd-ªl\ vb **swad·dled; swad·dling** \'swäd-(ª-)liŋ\ **1 :** to bind (an infant) in bands of cloth **2 :** to wrap up **:** SWATHE

**swaddling clothes** n pl **1 :** bands of cloth wrapped around an infant **2 :** period of infancy; also **:** restrictions placed on the young

**swag** \'swag\ n **:** stolen goods **:** LOOT

**swage** \'swāj, 'swej\ n **:** a tool used by metal workers for shaping their work — **swage** vb

**swag·ger** \'swag-ər\ vb **swag·gered; swag·ger·ing** \-(ə-)riŋ\ **1 :** to walk with a conceited swing or strut **2 :** BOAST, BRAG — **swagger** n

**Swa·hi·li** \swä-'hē-lē\ n, pl **Swahili** or **Swahilis :** a language that is a trade and governmental language over much of East Africa and the Congo region

**swain** \'swān\ n [ME swein boy, servant, fr. ON sveinn] **1 :** RUSTIC; esp **:** SHEPHERD **2 :** ADMIRER, SUITOR

**¹swal·low** \'swäl-ō\ n **:** any of various small long-winged fork-tailed migratory birds

**²swallow** vb **1 :** to take into the stomach through the throat **2 :** to envelop or take in as if by swallowing **3 :** to accept or believe too easily **4 :** ENDURE

**³swallow** n **1 :** an act of swallowing **2 :** as much as can be swallowed at one time

**swal·low·tail** \'swäl-ō-,tāl\ n **1 :** a deeply forked and tapering tail like that of a swallow **2 :** TAILCOAT **3 :** any of various large butterflies with the border of the hind wing drawn out into a process resembling a tail — **swal·low-tailed** \,swäl-ō-'tāld\ adj

**swam** past of SWIM

**swa·mi** \'swäm-ē\ n **:** a Hindu ascetic or religious teacher

**¹swamp** \'swämp\ n **1 :** wet spongy land **2 :** a tract of swamp — **swamp** adj — **swampy** adj

**²swamp** vb **1 :** to plunge or sink in or as if in a swamp **2 :** to deluge with or as if with water; also **:** to sink by filling with water

**swamp·land** \-,land\ n **:** a swamp 1

**swan** \'swän\ n, pl **swans** also **swan :** any of several heavy-bodied long-necked mostly pure white swimming birds related to the geese

**¹swank** \'swaŋk\ n **1 :** PRETENTIOUS-NESS **2 :** ELEGANCE

**²swank** or **swanky** \'swaŋ-kē\ adj **swank·er** or **swank·i·er; -est :** showily smart and dashing; also **:** fashionably elegant

**swans·down** \'swänz-,daùn\ n **1 :** the very soft down of a swan used esp. for trimming or powder puffs **2 :** a soft thick cotton flannel

**swan song** n **:** a farewell appearance, act, or pronouncement

**swap** \'swäp\ vb **swapped; swapping :** TRADE, EXCHANGE — **swap** n

**sward** \'sword\ n **:** the grassy surface of land

**¹swarm** \'sworm\ n **1 :** a great number of honeybees including a queen and leaving a hive to start a new colony; also **:** a hive of bees **2 :** a large crowd

**²swarm** vb **1 :** to form in a swarm and depart from a hive **2 :** to throng together **:** gather in great numbers

**swart** \'swort\ adj **:** SWARTHY

**swar·thy** \'swor-thē, -thē\ adj **swar·thi·er; -est :** dark in color or complexion **:** dark-skinned

**swash** \'swäsh\ vb **:** to move about with a splashing sound — **swash** n

**swash·buck·ler** \-,bək-lər\ n **:** a boasting blustering soldier or daredevil — **swash·buck·ling** \-,bək-(ə-)liŋ\ adj

**swas·ti·ka** \'swäs-ti-kə, swä-'stē-\ n [Skt svastika, fr. svasti welfare, fr. su-well + asti he is] **:** a symbol or ornament in the form of a Greek cross with the arms bent at right angles

**swat** \'swät\ vb **swat·ted; swat·ting :** to hit sharply (⁓ a fly) (⁓ a ball) — **swat** n — **swat·ter** n

**swatch** \'swäch\ n **:** a sample piece (as of fabric) or a collection of samples

**swath** \'swäth, 'swoth\ or **swathe** \'swäth, 'swoth, 'swäth\ n [ME, fr. OE swæth footstep, trace] **1 :** the sweep of a scythe or mowing machine or the path cut in mowing **2 :** a row of cut grass or grain

**swathe** \'swäth, 'swoth, 'swäth\ vb **swathed; swath·ing :** to bind or wrap with or as if with a bandage

**¹sway** \'swā\ vb **1 :** to swing gently from side to side **2 :** RULE, GOVERN **3 :** to cause to swing from side to side **4 :** BEND, SWERVE; also **:** INFLUENCE syn oscillate, fluctuate, vibrate, waver

**²sway** n **1 :** a gentle swinging from side to side **2 :** sovereign power **:** DOMINION; also **:** a controlling influence

**sway·back** \'swā-'bak, -,bak\ n **:** a sagging of the back found esp. in horses — **sway·backed** \-'bakt\ adj

**swear** \'swaər\ vb **swore** \'swōr\; **sworn** \'swōrn\; **swear·ing 1 :** to make a solemn statement or promise under oath **:** VOW **2 :** to use profane or obscene language **3 :** to assert emphatically as true with an appeal to God or one's honor **4 :** to charge or confirm under oath; *also* **:** to bind by or as if by an oath **5 :** to administer an oath to — **swear·er** *n* — **swear·ing** *n*

**swear in** *vb* **:** to induct into office by administration of an oath

¹**sweat** \'swet\ *vb* **sweat** *or* **sweat·ed; sweat·ing 1 :** to excrete salty moisture from glands of the skin **:** PERSPIRE **2 :** to form drops of moisture on the surface **3 :** to work so that one sweats **:** TOIL **4 :** to cause to sweat **5 :** to draw out or get rid of by perspiring **6 :** to make a person overwork

²**sweat** *n* **1 :** perceptible liquid exuded through pores from glands (**sweat glands**) of the skin **:** PERSPIRATION **2 :** moisture issuing from or gathering on a surface in drops — **sweaty** *adj*

**sweat·er** \'swet-ər\ *n* **1 :** one that sweats **2 :** a knitted or crocheted jacket or pullover

**sweat·shop** \'swet-,shäp\ *n* **:** a shop or factory in which workers are employed for long hours at low wages and under unhealthy conditions

**Swed** *abbr* Sweden; Swedish

**Swede** \'swēd\ *n* **:** a native or inhabitant of Sweden

**Swed·ish** \'swēd-ish\ *n* **1 Swedish** *pl* **:** the people of Sweden **2 :** the language of Sweden — **Swedish** *adj*

¹**sweep** \'swēp\ *vb* **swept** \'swept\; **sweep·ing 1 :** to remove or clean by brushing **2 :** to remove or destroy by vigorous continuous action **3 :** to strip or clear by gusts of wind or rain **4 :** to move over with speed and force ⟨the tide *swept* over the shore⟩ **5 :** to gather in with a single swift movement **6 :** to move or extend in a wide curve — **sweep·er** *n* — **sweep·ing** *adj*

²**sweep** *n* **1 :** a clearing off or away **2 :** a sweeping movement ⟨~ of a scythe⟩ **3 :** RANGE, SCOPE **4 :** CURVE, BEND **5 :** something (as a long oar) that operates with a sweeping motion **6 :** a winning of all the contests or prizes in a competition

**sweep·ing** *n* **1 :** the act or action of one that sweeps **2** *pl* **:** things collected by sweeping **:** REFUSE

**sweep·sec·ond** \'swēp-,sek-ənd\ *n* **:** a hand marking seconds on a timepiece

**sweep·stakes** \'swēp-,stāks\ *also* **sweep·stake** \-,stāk\ *n, pl* **sweep·stakes 1 :** a race or contest in which the entire prize may go to the winner; *esp* **:** a horse race in which the stakes are contributed at least in part by the owners of the horses **2 :** any of various lotteries

¹**sweet** \'swēt\ *adj* **1 :** being or causing the primary taste sensation that is typical of sugars; *also* **:** pleasing to the taste **2 :** not stale or spoiled **:** WHOLESOME ⟨~ milk⟩ **3 :** not salted ⟨~ butter⟩ **4 :** pleasing to a sense other than taste ⟨a ~ smell⟩ ⟨~ music⟩ **5 :** KINDLY, MILD — **sweet·ish** *adj* — **sweet·ly** *adv* — **sweet·ness** *n*

²**sweet** *n* **1 :** something sweet **:** CANDY **2 :** DARLING

**sweet·bread** \'swēt-,bred\ *n* **:** the pancreas or thymus of an animal (as a calf or lamb) used for food

**sweet·bri·er** \-,brī-(-ə)r\ *n* **:** a thorny European rose with fragrant white to deep pink flowers

**sweet clover** *n* **:** any of a genus of erect legumes widely grown for soil improvement or hay

**sweet corn** *n* **:** an Indian corn with kernels rich in sugar and suitable for table use when young

**sweet·en** \'swēt-ᵊn\ *vb* **sweet·ened; sweet·en·ing** \-(ᵊ-)niŋ\ **:** to make sweet — **sweet·en·er** \'swēt-(ᵊ-)nər\ *n* — **sweet·en·ing** *n*

**sweet fern** *n* **:** a small No. American shrub with sweet-scented or aromatic leaves

**sweet·heart** \'swēt-,härt\ *n* **:** a loved person **:** LOVER

**sweet·meat** \'swēt-,mēt\ *n* **:** CANDY

**sweet pea** *n* **:** a garden plant with climbing stems and fragrant flowers of many colors; *also* **:** its flower

**sweet pepper** *n* **:** a large mild thick-walled fruit of a pepper related to the nightshades; *also* **:** a plant bearing sweet peppers

**sweet potato** *n* **:** a tropical vine related to the morning glory; *also* **:** its sweet yellow edible root

**sweet-talk** \'swēt-,tók\ *vb* **:** FLATTER, COAX — **sweet talk** *n*

**sweet tooth** *n* **:** a craving or fondness for sweet food

**sweet wil·liam** \swēt-'wil-yəm\ *n, often cap W* **:** a widely cultivated Eurasian pink with small white to deep red or purple flowers often showily spotted, banded, or mottled

¹**swell** \'swel\ *vb* **swelled; swelled** *or* **swol·len** \'swō-lən\; **swell·ing 1 :** to grow big or make bigger **2 :** to expand or distend abnormally or excessively ⟨a *swollen* joint⟩; *also* **:** BULGE **3 :** to fill or be filled with emotion (as pride) **syn** expand, amplify, distend, inflate, dilate — **swell·ing** *n*

²**swell** *n* **1 :** sudden or gradual increase in size or value **2 :** a long crestless wave or series of waves in the open sea **3 :** a person dressed in the height of fashion; *also* **:** a person of high social position or outstanding competence

³**swell** *adj* **1 :** FASHIONABLE, STYLISH; *also* **:** socially prominent **2 :** EXCELLENT, FIRST-RATE

**swelled head** *n* **:** an exaggerated opinion of oneself **:** SELF-CONCEIT

**swell·head** \'swel-,hed\ *n* **:** one who has a swelled head — **swell·head·ed** \-'hed-əd\ *adj*

**swell·ing** \'swel-iŋ\ *n* **:** something that is swollen; *also* **:** the condition of being swollen

**swel·ter** \'swel-tər\ *vb* **swel·tered; swel·ter·ing** \-t(ə-)riŋ\ [ME *sweltren,* fr. *swelten* to die, be overcome by heat, fr. OE *sweltan* to die] **:** to be faint or oppressed with the heat

**swept** *past of* SWEEP

**swerve** \'swərv\ *vb* **swerved; swerv·ing :** to move abruptly aside from a straight line or course **syn** veer, deviate, diverge — **swerve** n

¹**swift** \'swift\ adj **1** : moving or capable of moving with great speed **2** : occurring suddenly **3** : READY, ALERT — **swift·ly** adv — **swift·ness** \'swif(t)-nəs\ n

²**swift** n : a small insect-eating bird with long narrow wings

**swig** \'swig\ vb **swigged**; **swig·ging** : to drink in long drafts — **swig** n

¹**swill** \'swil\ vb **1** : to swallow greedily : GUZZLE **2** : to feed (as hogs) on swill

²**swill** n **1** : food for animals composed of edible refuse mixed with liquid **2** : GARBAGE

¹**swim** \'swim\ vb **swam** \'swam\; **swum** \'swəm\; **swim·ming 1** : to propel oneself along in water by natural means (as by hands and legs, by tail, or by fins) **2** : to glide smoothly along **3** : FLOAT **4** : to be covered with or as if with a liquid **5** : to cross or go over by swimming **6** : to be dizzy ⟨his head swam⟩ — **swim·mer** n — **swim·suit** \-,süt\ n

²**swim** n **1** : an act of swimming **2** : the main current of activity or fashion ⟨in the social ∼⟩

**swim·ming** \'swim-iŋ\ n : the action, art, or sport of swimming and diving

**swin·dle** \'swin-dᵊl\ vb **swin·dled**; **swin·dling** \-(d)liŋ, -dᵊl-iŋ\ [fr. swindler, fr. G schwindler giddy person, fr. schwindeln to be dizzy, fr. Old High German swintilōn, fr. swintan to diminish, vanish] : CHEAT, DEFRAUD — **swindle** n — **swin·dler** \-d(ᵊ-)lər\ n

**swine** \'swīn\ n, pl **swine 1** : any of various stout short-legged hoofed mammals with bristly skin and flexible snout; esp : one widely raised as a meat animal **2** : a contemptible person — **swin·ish** \'swī-nish\ adj

¹**swing** \'swiŋ\ vb **swung** \'swəŋ\; **swing·ing** \'swiŋ-iŋ\ **1** : to move rapidly in an arc **2** : to sway or cause to sway back and forth **3** : to hang so as to move freely back and forth or in a curve **4** : to be executed by hanging **5** : to move or turn on a hinge or pivot **6** : to march or walk with free swaying movements **7** : to manage or handle successfully **8** : to have a steady pulsing rhythm **9** : to be lively and up-to-date; also : to engage freely in sex **syn** wave, flourish, brandish, thrash, oscillate, vibrate, fluctuate, wield, manipulate, ply — **swing·er** n — **swing·ing** adj

²**swing** n **1** : the act of swinging **2** : a swinging blow, movement, or rhythm **3** : the distance through which something swings : FLUCTUATION **4** : a seat suspended by a rope or chain for swinging back and forth for pleasure **5** : jazz music played esp. by a large band and marked by a steady lively rhythm, simple harmony, and a basic melody often submerged in improvisation — **swing** adj

¹**swipe** \'swīp\ n : a strong sweeping blow

²**swipe** vb **swiped**; **swip·ing 1** : to

strike or wipe with a sweeping motion **2** : PILFER, SNATCH

**swirl** \'swərl\ vb : EDDY — **swirl** n

**swish** \'swish\ n **1** : a prolonged hissing sound **2** : a light sweeping or brushing sound — **swish** vb

**Swiss** \'swis\ n, pl **Swiss 1** : a native or inhabitant of Switzerland **2** : a hard cheese with large holes

**Swiss chard** n : CHARD

¹**switch** \'swich\ n **1** : a slender flexible whip, rod, or twig **2** : a blow with a switch **3** : a shift from one thing to another **4** : a device for adjusting the rails of a track so that a locomotive or train may be turned from one track to another; also : a railroad siding **5** : a device for making, breaking or changing the connections in an electrical circuit **6** : a heavy strand of hair often used in addition to a person's own hair for some coiffures

²**switch** vb **1** : to punish or urge on with a switch **2** : WHISK ⟨a cow ∼ing her tail⟩ **3** : to shift or turn by operating a switch **4** : CHANGE, EXCHANGE

**switch·back** \'swich-,bak\ n : a zigzag road or arrangement of railroad tracks for climbing a steep grade

**switch·blade** \-,blād\ n : a pocketknife with a spring-operated blade

**switch·board** \-,bōrd\ n : a panel on which is mounted a group of electric switches so arranged that a number of circuits may be connected, combined, and controlled

**switch-hit·ter** \-'hit-ər\ n : a baseball player who bats either right-handed or left-handed — **switch-hit** \-'hit\ vb

**switch·man** \'swich-mən\ n : one who attends a railroad switch

**Switz** abbr Switzerland

¹**swiv·el** \'swiv-əl\ n : a part that turns on or as if on a headed bolt or pin; also : a system of links joined by such a part so as to permit rotation

²**swivel** vb **-eled** or **-elled**; **-el·ing** or **-el·ling** \-(ə-)liŋ\ : to swing or turn on or as if on a swivel

**swizzle stick** \'swiz-əl-\ n : a stick used to stir mixed drinks

**swollen** past part of SWELL

**swoon** \'swün\ n : FAINT — **swoon** vb

**swoop** \'swüp\ vb : to descend or pounce swiftly like a hawk on its prey — **swoop** n

**sword** \'sōrd\ n **1** : a weapon with a long pointed blade and sharp cutting edges **2** : a symbol of authority or military power **3** : the use of force

**sword·fish** \-,fish\ n : a very large ocean food fish with the bones of the upper jaw prolonged in a long swordlike beak

**sword·play** \-,plā\ n : the art or skill of wielding a sword

**swords·man** \'sōrdz-mən\ n : one skilled in wielding a sword; esp : FENCER

**sword·tail** \'sōrd-,tāl\ n : a small brightly marked Central American fish

**swore** past of SWEAR

**sworn** past part of SWEAR

**swum** past part of SWIM

**swung** past of SWING

**syb·a·rite** \'sib-ə-ˌrīt\ *n* : a lover of luxury : VOLUPTUARY

**syc·a·more** \'sik-ə-ˌmōr\ *n* : any of several shade trees (as an Old World maple or an American plane tree)

**sy·co·phant** \'sik-ə-fənt\ *n* : a servile flatterer — **syc·o·phan·tic** \ˌsik-ə-'fant-ik\ *adj*

**syl** *or* **syll** *abbr* syllable

**syl·lab·i·ca·tion** \sə-ˌlab-ə-'kā-shən\ *n* : the dividing of words into syllables

**syl·lab·i·fy** \sə-'lab-ə-ˌfī\ *vb* **-fied; -fy·ing** : to form or divide into syllables — **syl·lab·i·fi·ca·tion** \-ˌlab-ə-fə-'kā-shən\ *n*

**syl·la·ble** \'sil-ə-bəl\ *n* [ME, fr. MF *sillabe*, fr. L *syllaba*, fr. Gk *syllabē*, fr. *syllambanein* to gather together, fr. *syn* with + *lambanein* to take] : a unit of spoken language consisting of an uninterrupted utterance and forming either a whole word (as *man*) or a commonly recognized division of a word (as *syl* in *syl-la-ble*); *also* : one or more letters representing such a unit — **syl·lab·ic** \sə-'lab-ik\ *adj*

**syl·la·bus** \'sil-ə-bəs\ *n, pl* **-bi** \-ˌbī\ *or* **-bus·es** : a summary containing the heads or main topics of a speech, book, or course of study

**syl·lo·gism** \'sil-ə-ˌjiz-əm\ *n* : a logical scheme of a formal argument consisting of a major and a minor premise and a conclusion which must logically be true if the premises are true — **syl·lo·gis·tic** \ˌsil-ə-'jis-tik\ *adj*

**sylph** \'silf\ *n* 1 : an imaginary being inhabiting the air 2 : a slender graceful woman

**syl·van** \'sil-vən\ *adj* 1 : living or located in a wooded area; *also* : of, relating to, or characteristic of forest 2 : abounding in woods or trees : WOODED

**sym** *abbr* 1 symbol 2 symmetrical

**sym·bi·o·sis** \ˌsim-ˌbī-'ō-səs, -bē-\ *n, pl* **-bi·o·ses** \-ˌsēz\ : the living together in intimate association or close union of two dissimilar organisms esp. when mutually beneficial — **sym·bi·ot·ic** \-'ät-ik\ *adj*

**sym·bol** \'sim-bəl\ *n* 1 : something that stands for something else; *esp* : something concrete that represents or suggests another thing that cannot in itself be represented or visualized 2 : a letter, character, or sign used in writing or printing relating to a particular field (as mathematics, physics, or music) to represent operations, quantities, elements, sounds, or other ideas — **sym·bol·ic** \sim-'bäl-ik\ *or* **sym·bol·i·cal** \-i-kəl\ *adj* — **sym·bol·i·cal·ly** \-k(ə-)lē\ *adv*

**sym·bol·ism** \'sim-bə-ˌliz-əm\ *n* : representation of abstract or intangible things by means of symbols or emblems

**sym·bol·ize** \'sim-bə-ˌlīz\ *vb* **-ized; -iz·ing** 1 : to serve as a symbol of 2 : to represent by symbols — **sym·bol·iza·tion** \ˌsim-bə-lə-'zā-shən\ *n*

**sym·me·try** \'sim-ə-trē\ *n, pl* **-tries** 1 : correspondence in size, shape, and position of parts that are on opposite sides of a dividing line or center 2 : an arrangement marked by regularity and balanced proportions **syn** proportion, balance, harmony — **sym·met·ri·cal** \sə-'met-ri-kəl\ *adj* — **sym·met·ri·cal·ly** \-k(ə-)lē\ *adv*

**sympathetic nervous system** *n* : the part of the autonomic nervous system that tends to depress secretion, decrease the tone and contractility of muscle not under direct voluntary control, and cause the contraction of blood vessels

**sym·pa·thize** \'sim-pə-ˌthīz\ *vb* **-thized; -thiz·ing** : to feel or show sympathy — **sym·pa·thiz·er** *n*

**sym·pa·thy** \'sim-pə-thē\ *n, pl* **-thies** 1 : a relationship between persons or things wherein whatever affects one similarly affects the others 2 : harmony of interests and aims 3 : the ability of entering into and sharing the feelings or interests of another; *also* : COMPASSION, PITY 4 : FAVOR, SUPPORT 5 : an expression of sorrow for another's loss, grief, or misfortune — **sym·pa·thet·ic** \ˌsim-pə-'thet-ik\ *adj* — **sym·pa·thet·i·cal·ly** \-i-k(ə-)lē\ *adv*

**sym·pho·ny** \'sim-fə-nē\ *n, pl* **-nies** 1 : harmony of sounds 2 : a large and complex composition for a full orchestra 3 : a large orchestra of a kind that plays symphonies — **sym·phon·ic** \sim-'fän-ik\ *adj*

**sym·po·sium** \sim-'pō-zē-əm\ *n, pl* **-sia** \-zē-ə\ *or* **-siums** [L, fr. Gk *symposion*, fr. *sympinein* to drink together, fr. *syn-* together + *pinein* to drink] : a conference at which a particular topic is discussed by various speakers; *also* : a collection of opinions about a subject

**symp·tom** \'simp-təm\ *n* 1 : a change in an organism indicative of disease or abnormality; *esp* : one (as headache) directly perceptible only to the victim 2 : SIGN, INDICATION — **symp·tom·at·ic** \ˌsimp-tə-'mat-ik\ *adj*

**syn** *abbr* synonym; synonymous; synonymy

**syn·a·gogue** *or* **syn·a·gog** \'sin-ə-ˌgäg\ *n* [ME *synagoge*, fr. OF, fr. LL *synagoga*, fr. Gk *synagōgē* assembly, synagogue, fr. *synagein* to bring together, fr. *syn-* together + *agein* to lead] 1 : a Jewish congregation 2 : the house of worship of a Jewish congregation

**syn·apse** \'sin-ˌaps, sə-'naps\ *n* : the point at which a nervous impulse passes from one neuron to another

¹**sync** *also* **synch** \'siŋk\ *n* : SYNCHRONIZATION, SYNCHRONISM — **sync** *adj*

²**sync** *also* **synch** *vb* **synced** *also* **synched** \'siŋkt\; **sync·ing** *also* **synch·ing** \'siŋ-kiŋ\ : SYNCHRONIZE

**syn·chro·mesh** \'siŋ-krō-ˌmesh, 'sin-\ *adj* : designed for effecting synchronized shifting of gears — **syn·chromesh** *n*

**syn·chro·nize** \'siŋ-krə-ˌnīz, 'sin-\ *vb* **-nized; -niz·ing** 1 : to occur or cause to occur at the same instant 2 : to represent, arrange, or tabulate according to dates or time 3 : to cause to agree in time **4** : to make synchronous in operation — **syn·chro·nism** \-,niz-əm\ n — **syn·chro·ni·za·tion** \,siŋ-krə-nə-'zā-shən, ,sin-\ n — **syn·chro·niz·er** \'siŋ-krə-,nī-zər, 'sin-\ n

**syn·chro·nous** \'siŋ-krə-nəs, 'sin-\ adj **1** : happening at the same time : CONCURRENT **2** : working, moving, or occurring together at the same rate and at the proper time

**syn·co·pa·tion** \,siŋ-kə-'pā-shən, ,sin-\ n : a shifting of the regular musical accent : occurrence of accented notes on the weak beat — **syn·co·pate** \'siŋ-kə-,pāt, 'sin-\ vb

**syn·co·pe** \'siŋ-kə-(,)pē, 'sin-\ n : the loss of one or more sounds or letters in the interior of a word (as in fo'c'sle from forecastle)

¹**syn·di·cate** \'sin-di-kət\ n **1** : a group of persons who combine to carry out a financial or industrial undertaking **2** : a business concern that sells materials for publication in many newspapers and periodicals at the same time

²**syn·di·cate** \-də-,kāt\ vb **-cat·ed; -cat·ing 1** : to combine into or manage as a syndicate **2** : to publish through a syndicate — **syn·di·ca·tion** \,sin-də-'kā-shən\ n

**syn·drome** \'sin-,drōm\ n : a group of signs and symptoms that occur together and characterize a particular abnormality

**syn·er·gism** \'sin-ər-,jiz-əm\ n : joint action of discrete agencies (as drugs) in which the total effect is greater than the sum of their effects when acting independently — **syn·er·gist** \-jəst\ n — **syn·er·gis·tic** \-'jis-tik\ adj — **syn·er·gis·ti·cal·ly** \-ti-k(ə-)lē\ adv

**syn·od** \'sin-əd\ n **1** : COUNCIL, ASSEMBLY; esp : a religious governing body — **syn·od·al** \-əd-ºl, -,äd-ºl\ adj — **syn·od·i·cal** \sə-'näd-i-kəl\ or **syn·od·ic** \-ik\ adj

**syn·onym** \'sin-ə-,nim\ n : one of two or more words in the same language which have the same or very nearly the same meaning — **syn·on·y·mous** \sə-'nän-ə-məs\ adj — **syn·on·y·my** \-mē\ n

**syn·op·sis** \sə-'näp-səs\ n, pl **-op·ses** \-,sēz\ : a condensed statement or outline (as of a treatise) : ABSTRACT

**syn·op·tic** \sə-'näp-tik\ also **syn·op·ti·cal** \-ti-kəl\ adj : characterized by or affording a comprehensive view

**syn·tax** \'sin-,taks\ n : the way in which words are put together to form phrases, clauses, or sentences — **syn-**

**tac·tic** \sin-'tak-tik\ adj — **syn·tac·ti·cal** \-ti-kəl\ adj

**syn·the·sis** \'sin-thə-səs\ n, pl **-the·ses** \-,sēz\ : the combination of parts or elements into a whole — **syn·the·size** \-,sīz\ vb — **syn·the·siz·er** n

**syn·thet·ic** \sin-'thet-ik\ also **syn·thet·i·cal** \-i-kəl\ adj : produced artificially esp. by chemical means; also : not genuine — **synthetic** n — **syn·thet·i·cal·ly** \-i-k(ə-)lē\ adv

**syph·i·lis** \'sif-(ə-)ləs\ n : a destructive contagious usu. venereal disease caused by a bacterium — **syph·i·lit·ic** \,sif-ə-'lit-ik\ adj or n

**sy·phon** var of SIPHON

¹**sy·ringe** \sə-'rinj, 'sir-inj\ n : a device used esp. for injecting liquids into or withdrawing them from the body

²**syringe** vb **sy·ringed; sy·ring·ing** : to inject or cleanse with or as if with a syringe

**syr·up** \'sər-əp, 'sir-əp\ n **1** : a thick sticky solution of sugar and water often flavored or medicated **2** : the concentrated juice of a fruit or plant — **syr·upy** adj

**syst** abbr system

**sys·tem** \'sis-təm\ n **1** : a group of units so combined as to form a whole and to operate in unison **2** : the body as a functioning whole; also : a group of bodily organs that together carry on some vital function (the nervous ~) **3** : a definite scheme or method of procedure or classification **4** : regular method or order — **sys·tem·at·ic** \,sis-tə-'mat-ik\ adj — **sys·tem·at·i·cal** \-i-kəl\ adj — **sys·tem·at·i·cal·ly** \-k(ə-)lē\ adv

**sys·tem·atize** \'sis-tə-mə-,tīz\ vb **-atized; -atiz·ing** : to make into a system : arrange methodically

¹**sys·tem·ic** \sis-'tem-ik\ adj : of, relating to, or affecting the whole body (~ disease)

²**systemic** n : a systemic pesticide

**sys·tem·ize** \'sis-tə-,mīz\ vb **-ized; -iz·ing** : SYSTEMATIZE

**systems analysis** n : the act, process, or profession of studying an activity (as a procedure, a business, or a physiological function) typically by mathematical means in order to determine its desired or essential end and how this may most efficiently be attained — **systems analyst** n

**sys·to·le** \'sis-tə-(,)lē\ n : a rhythmically recurrent contraction esp. of the heart — **sys·tol·ic** \sis-'täl-ik\ adj

---

¹**t** \'tē\ n, pl **t's** or **ts** \'tēz\ often cap : the 20th letter of the English alphabet

²**t** abbr, often cap **1** table-spoon **2** teaspoon **3** temperature **4** ton **5** troy **6** true **7** Tuesday

**Ta** symbol tantalum

¹**tab** \'tab\ n **1** : a short projecting flap, loop, or tag; also : a small insert or addition **2** : close surveillance : WATCH

(keep ~s on him) **3** : BILL, CHECK

²**tab** vb **tabbed; tabbing** : DESIGNATE

**tab·by** \'tab-ē\ n, pl **tabbies** : a usu. striped or mottled domestic cat; also : a female cat

**tab·er·na·cle** \'tab-ər-,nak-əl\ n often cap : a tent sanctuary used by the Israelites during the Exodus **2** : a receptacle for the consecrated elements of the Eucharist **3** : a house of worship

¹**ta·ble** \'tā-bəl\ n **1** : a flat slab or

plaque : TABLET **2** : a piece of furniture consisting of a smooth flat slab fixed on legs **3** : a supply of food : BOARD, FARE **4** : a group of people assembled at or as if at a table **5** : a systematic arrangement of data for ready reference **6** : a condensed enumeration — **ta·ble·top** \-,täp\ *n*

²**table** *vb* **ta·bled; ta·bling** \-b(ə-)liŋ\ **1** *Brit* : to place on the agenda **2** : to remove (a parliamentary motion) from consideration indefinitely

**tab·leau** \'tab-,lō\ *n, pl* **tab·leaux** \-,lōz\ *also* **tableaus 1** : a graphic description : PICTURE **2** : a striking or artistic grouping **3** : a static depiction of a scene usu. presented on a stage by costumed participants

**ta·ble·cloth** \'tā-bəl-,klóth\ *n* : a covering spread over a dining table before the table is set

**ta·ble d'hôte** \,täb-əl-'dōt\ *n* [F, lit., host's table] : a complete meal of several courses offered at a fixed price

**ta·ble·land** \'tā-bəl-,(l)and\ *n* : PLATEAU

**ta·ble·spoon** \'tā-bəl-,spün\ *n* **1** : a large spoon used esp. for serving **2** : TABLESPOONFUL

**ta·ble·spoon·ful** \,tā-bəl-'spün-,fúl, 'tā-bəl-,spün-\ *n* : a unit of measure equal to one half fluid ounce

**tab·let** \'tab-lət\ *n* **1** : a flat slab suited for or bearing an inscription **2** : a collection of sheets of paper glued together at one edge **3** : a compressed or molded block of material; *esp* : a usu. disk-shaped medicated mass

**table tennis** *n* : a game resembling tennis played on a tabletop with wooden paddles and a small hollow plastic ball

**ta·ble·ware** \'tā-bəl-,waər\ *n* : utensils (as of china, glass, or silver) for table use

¹**tab·loid** \'tab-,lóid\ *adj* : condensed into small scope

²**tabloid** *n* : a newspaper of small page size marked by condensation of the news and usu. much photographic matter; *esp* : one characterized by sensationalism

¹**ta·boo** *also* **ta·bu** \tə-'bü, ta-\ *adj* **1** : set apart as charged with a dangerous supernatural power : INVIOLABLE **2** : banned esp. as immoral or dangerous

²**taboo** *also* **tabu** *n, pl* **taboos** *also* **tabus 1** : an act or object avoided as taboo **2** : a prohibition imposed by social usage or as a protection

**ta·bor** *also* **ta·bour** \'tā-bər\ *n* : a small drum used to accompany a pipe or fife played by the same person

**tab·u·lar** \'tab-yə-lər\ *adj* **1** : having a flat surface **2** : arranged in a table; *esp* : set up in rows and columns **3** : computed by means of a table

**tab·u·late** \-,lāt\ *vb* **-lat·ed; -lat·ing** : to put into tabular form — **tab·u·la·tion** \,tab-yə-'lā-shən\ *n* — **tab·u·la·tor** \'tab-yə-,lāt-ər\ *n*

**TAC** \'tak\ *abbr* Tactical Air Command

**tach** \'tak\ *n* : TACHOMETER

**ta·chom·e·ter** \ta-'käm-ət-ər, tə-\ *n* : a device to indicate speed of rotation

**tachy·car·dia** \,tak-i-'kärd-ē-ə\ *n* : rapid heart action

**tac·it** \'tas-ət\ *adj* [F or L; F *tacite*, fr. L *tacitus* silent, fr. *tacēre* to be silent] **1** : expressed without words or speech **2** : implied or indicated but not actually expressed ⟨~ consent⟩ — **tac·it·ly** *adv* — **tac·it·ness** *n*

**tac·i·turn** \'tas-ə-,tərn\ *adj* : disinclined to talk : habitually silent **syn** uncommunicative, reserved, reticent, secretive — **tac·i·tur·ni·ty** \,tas-ə-'tər-nət-ē\ *n*

¹**tack** \'tak\ *n* **1** : a small sharp nail with a broad flat head **2** : the direction a ship is sailing as shown by the way the sails are trimmed; *also* : the run of a ship on one tack **3** : a change of course from one tack to another **4** : a zigzag course **5** : a course of action **6** : gear for harnessing a horse

²**tack** *vb* **1** : to fasten with tacks; *also* : to add on **2** : to change the direction of (a sailing ship) from one tack to another **3** : to follow a zigzag course

¹**tack·le** \'tak-əl, *naut often* 'tāk-\ *n* **1** : GEAR, APPARATUS, EQUIPMENT **2** : the rigging of a ship **3** : an arrangement of ropes and pulleys for hoisting or pulling heavy objects **4** : the act or an instance of tackling; *also* : a football lineman playing between guard and end

²**tackle** *vb* **tack·led; tack·ling** \-(ə-)liŋ\ **1** : to attach and secure with or as if with tackle **2** : to seize, grapple with, or throw down with the intention of subduing or stopping **3** : to set about dealing with ⟨~ a problem⟩

¹**tacky** \'tak-ē\ *adj* **tack·i·er; -est** : sticky to the touch

²**tacky** *adj* **tack·i·er; -est 1** : SHABBY, SEEDY **2** : cheaply showy : GAUDY

**ta·co** \'täk-ō\ *n, pl* **tacos** \-ōz, -ōs\ : a sandwich made of a tortilla rolled up with or folded over a filling

**tact** \'takt\ *n* [F, sense of touch, fr. L *tactus*, fr. *tactus*, pp. of *tangere* to touch] : a keen sense of what to do or say to keep good relations with others or avoid offense — **tact·ful** \-fəl\ *adj* — **tact·ful·ly** \-ē\ *adv* — **tact·less** *adj* — **tact·less·ly** *adv*

**tac·tic** \'tak-tik\ *n* : a device for accomplishing an end

**tac·tics** \'tak-tiks\ *n sing or pl* **1** : the science and art of disposing and maneuvering forces in combat **2** : the art or skill of using available means to reach an end — **tac·ti·cal** \-ti-kəl\ *adj* — **tac·ti·cian** \tak-'tish-ən\ *n*

**tac·tile** \'tak-tᵊl, -,tīl\ *adj* : of, relating to, or perceptible through the sense of touch

**tad·pole** \'tad-,pōl\ *n* [ME *taddepol*, fr. *tode* toad + *polle* head] : a larval frog or toad with tail and gills

**taf·fe·ta** \'taf-ət-ə\ *n* : a crisp lustrous fabric (as of silk or rayon)

**taff·rail** \'taf-,rāl, -rəl\ *n* : the rail around a ship's stern

**taf·fy** \'taf-ē\ *n, pl* **taffies** : a candy usu. of molasses or brown sugar stretched until porous and light-colored

¹**tag** \'tag\ *n* **1** : a metal or plastic

binding on an end of a shoelace **2** : a piece of hanging or attached material **3** : a hackneyed quotation or saying **4** : a descriptive or identifying epithet

²**tag** vb **tagged; tag·ging 1** : to provide or mark with or as if with a tag; esp : IDENTIFY **2** : to attach as an addition **3** : to follow closely and persistently 〈~s along everywhere we go〉 **4** : to hold responsible for something

³**tag** n : a game in which one player chases others and tries to touch one of them

⁴**tag** vb **tagged; tag·ging 1** : to touch in or as if in a game of tag **2** : SELECT

**TAG** abbr the adjutant general

**tag sale** n : GARAGE SALE

**Ta·hi·tian** \tə-'hē-shən\ n **1** : a native or inhabitant of Tahiti **2** : the Polynesian language of the Tahitians — **Tahitian** adj

**tai·ga** \'tī-gä\ n : swampy coniferous northern forest (as of parts of Canada) beginning where the tundra ends

¹**tail** \'tāl\ n **1** : the rear end or a process extending from the rear end of an animal **2** : something resembling an animal's tail **3** pl : full evening dress for men **4** : the back, last, lower, or inferior part of something; esp : the reverse of a coin **5** : one who follows or keeps watch on someone — **tailed** \'tāld\ adj — **tail·less** \'tāl-ləs\ adj

²**tail** vb : FOLLOW; esp : to follow for the purpose of surveillance **syn** pursue, chase, trail, tag

**tail·coat** \-'kōt\ n : a coat with tails; esp : a man's full-dress coat with two long tapering skirts at the back

¹**tail·gate** \'tāl-,gāt\ n : a board or gate at the back end of a vehicle that can be let down (as for loading)

²**tailgate** vb **tail·gat·ed; tail·gat·ing** : to drive dangerously close behind another vehicle

**tail·light** \-,līt\ n : a usu. red warning light mounted at the rear of a vehicle

¹**tai·lor** \'tā-lər\ n [ME taillour, fr. OF tailleur, fr. taillier to cut, fr. LL taliare, fr. L talea twig, cutting] : one whose occupation is making or altering outer garments

²**tailor** vb **1** : to make or fashion as the work of a tailor **2** : to make or adapt to suit a special purpose

**tail pipe** n : the pipe discharging exhaust gases from the muffler of an automotive engine

**tail·spin** \'tāl-,spin\ n : a spiral dive by an airplane

**tail wind** n : a wind blowing in the same general direction as the course of a moving airplane or ship

¹**taint** \'tānt\ vb **1** : to affect or become affected with something bad and esp. putrefaction **2** : CORRUPT, CONTAMINATE **syn** pollute, defile

²**taint** n **1** : a trace of decay : BLEMISH, FLAW **2** : a contaminating influence

**ta·ka** \'täk-ə\ n — see MONEY table

¹**take** \'tāk\ vb **took** \'tůk\; **tak·en** \'tā-kən\; **tak·ing 1** : to get into one's hands or possession : GRASP, SEIZE **2** : CAPTURE; also : DEFEAT **3** : to catch

or attack through the effect of a sudden force or attraction 〈taken ill〉 **4** : CAPTIVATE, DELIGHT **5** : to receive into one's body (as by eating) 〈~ a pill〉 **6** : to bring into a relation 〈~ a wife〉 **7** : RECEIVE, ACCEPT **8** : to obtain or secure for use **9** : ASSUME, UNDERTAKE **10** : to pick out : CHOOSE **11** : to use for transportation 〈~ a bus〉 **12** : NEED, REQUIRE **13** : to obtain as the result of a special procedure 〈~ a snapshot〉 **14** : ENDURE, UNDERGO **15** : to become impregnated with : ABSORB 〈~s a dye〉 **16** : to lead, carry, or cause to go along to another place **17** : REMOVE, SUBTRACT **18** : to undertake and do, make, or perform 〈~ a walk〉 **19** : to take effect : ACT, OPERATE **syn** grab, clutch, snatch, enchant, fascinate, allure, attract — **tak·er** n — **take advantage of** : to profit by : EXPLOIT — **take after 1** : FOLLOW, CHASE **2** : RESEMBLE — **take care** : to be careful — **take care of** : to care for : attend to — **take effect** : to become operative — **take exception** : OBJECT — **take for** : to suppose to be; esp : to mistake for — **take place** : HAPPEN — **take to 1** : to go to **2** : to apply or devote oneself to **3** : to conceive a liking for

²**take** n **1** : an act or the action of taking **2** : the number or quantity taken; also : PROCEEDS, RECEIPTS **3** : a television or movie scene filmed or taped at one time; also : a sound recording made at one time **4** : mental response

**take·off** \-,óf\ n : an act or instance of taking off

**take off** \'tāk-'óf\ vb **1** : REMOVE **2** : to set out : go away : WITHDRAW **3** : COPY, REPRODUCE; esp : MIMIC **4** : to leave the surface; esp : to begin flight

**take over** \'tāk-'ō-vər\ vb : to assume control or possession of or responsibility for — **take·over** \-,ō-vər\ n

¹**tak·ing** \'tā-kiŋ\ n **1** : SEIZURE **2** pl : receipts esp. of money

²**taking** adj : ATTRACTIVE, CAPTIVATING **syn** charming, enchanting, fascinating, bewitching, alluring

**ta·la** \'täl-ə, -(,)ä\ n — see MONEY table

**talc** \'talk\ n : a soft mineral of a soapy feel used esp. in making toilet powder **(tal·cum powder** \'tal-kəm-\)

**tale** \'tāl\ n **1** : a relation of a series of events **2** : a report of a confidential matter **3** : idle talk; esp : harmful gossip **4** : a usu. imaginative narrative **5** : FALSEHOOD **6** : COUNT, TALLY

**tal·ent** \'tal-ənt\ n **1** : an ancient unit of weight and value **2** : the natural endowments of a person **3** : a special often creative or artistic aptitude **4** : mental power : ABILITY **5** : a person of talent **syn** genius, gift, faculty, aptitude, knack — **tal·ent·ed** \-əd\ adj

**ta·ler** \'täl-ər\ n : any of numerous silver coins issued by German states from the 15th to the 19th centuries

**tales·man** \'tālz-mən\ n [ME tales talesmen, fr. ML tales de circumstantibus such (persons) of the bystanders; fr. the wording of the writ summoning them] **:** a person summoned for jury duty

**tal·is·man** \'tal-əs-mən, -əz-\ *n, pl* **-mans** [F *talisman* or Sp *talismán* or It *talismano,* fr. Ar *tilsam,* fr. MGk *telesma,* fr. Gk, consecration, fr. *telein* to initiate into the mysteries, complete, fr. *telos* end] **:** an object thought to act as a charm

¹**talk** \'tȯk\ *vb* **1 :** to express in speech **:** utter words **:** SPEAK **2 :** DISCUSS ⟨~ business⟩ **3 :** to influence or cause by talking ⟨~ed him into agreeing⟩ **4 :** to use (a language) for communicating **5 :** CONVERSE **6 :** to reveal confidential information; *also* **:** GOSSIP **7 :** to give a talk **:** LECTURE — **talk·er** *n* — **talk back :** to answer impertinently

²**take** *n* **1 :** the act of talking **2 :** a way of speaking **3 :** a formal discussion **4 :** REPORT, RUMOR **5 :** the topic of comment or gossip ⟨the ~ of the town⟩ **6 :** an informal address or lecture

**talk·ative** \'tȯ-kət-iv\ *adj* **:** given to talking **syn** loquacious, voluble, garrulous — **talk·ative·ly** *adv* — **talk·ative·ness** *n*

**talk·ing-to** \'tȯ-kiŋ-,tü\ *n* **:** REPRIMAND, LECTURE

**tall** \'tȯl\ *adj* **1 :** high in stature; *also* **:** of a specified height ⟨six feet ~⟩ **2 :** LARGE, FORMIDABLE ⟨a ~ order⟩ **3 :** UNBELIEVABLE, IMPROBABLE ⟨a ~ story⟩ **syn** lofty — **tall·ness** *n*

**tal·low** \'tal-ō\ *n* **1 :** animal fat; *esp* **:** SUET **2 :** a hard white fat rendered usu. from cattle or sheep tissues and used esp. in soap and lubricants

¹**tal·ly** \'tal-ē\ *n, pl* **tallies** [ME *talye,* fr. ML *talea, tallia* fr. L *talea* twig, cutting] **1 :** a device for visibly recording or accounting esp. business transactions **2 :** a recorded account **3 :** a corresponding part; *also* **:** CORRESPONDENCE

²**tally** *vb* **tal·lied; tal·ly·ing 1 :** to mark on or as if on a tally **2 :** to make a count of **:** RECKON; *also* **:** SCORE **3 :** CORRESPOND, MATCH **syn** square, accord, harmonize, conform, jibe

**tal·ly·ho** \,tal-ē-'hō\ *n, pl* **-hos 1 :** a call of a huntsman at sight of the fox **2 :** a four-in-hand coach

**Tal·mud** \'täl-,mùd, 'tal-məd\ *n* [Heb *talmūdh,* lit., instruction] **:** the authoritative body of Jewish tradition — **tal·mu·dic** \tal-'m(y)üd-ik, -'məd-; täl-'mùd-\ *adj, often cap* — **Tal·mud·ist** \'täl-,mùd-əst, 'tal-məd-\ *n, cap*

**tal·on** \'tal-ən\ *n* **:** the claw of an animal and esp. of a bird of prey

**ta·lus** \'tā-ləs, 'tal-əs\ *n* **:** rock debris at the base of a cliff

**tam** \'tam\ *n* **:** TAM-O'-SHANTER

**ta·ma·le** \tə-'mäl-ē\ *n* **:** ground meat seasoned with chili, rolled in cornmeal dough, wrapped in corn husks, and steamed

**tam·a·rack** \'tam-ə-,rak\ *n* **:** an American larch; *also* **:** its hard resinous wood

**tam·a·rind** \'tam-ə-rənd, -,rind\ *n* [Sp & Port *tamarindo,* fr. Ar *tamr hindī,* lit., Indian date] **:** a tropical tree with hard yellowish wood and feathery leaves; *also* **:** its acid brown fruit

**tam·ba·la** \täm-'bäl-ə\ *n, pl* **-la** *or* **-las** — see *kwacha* at MONEY table

**tam·bou·rine** \,tam-bə-'rēn\ *n* **:** a small shallow drum with loose disks at the sides played by shaking or striking with the hand

¹**tame** \'tām\ *adj* **tam·er; tam·est 1 :** reduced from a state of native wildness esp. so as to be useful to man **:** DOMESTICATED **2 :** made docile **:** SUBDUED **3 :** lacking spirit or interest **:** INSIPID **syn** submissive — **tame·ly** *adv* — **tame·ness** *n*

²**tame** *vb* **tamed; tam·ing 1 :** to make or become tame; *also* **:** to subject (land) to cultivation **2 :** HUMBLE, SUBDUE — **tam·able** *or* **tame·able** \'tā-mə-bəl\ *adj* — **tame·less** *adj* — **tam·er** *n*

**tam-o'-shan·ter** \'tam-ə-,shant-ər\ *n* **:** a Scottish woolen cap with a wide flat circular crown and usu. a pompon in the center

**tamp** \'tamp\ *vb* **:** to drive down or in by a series of light blows

**tam·per** \'tam-pər\ *vb* **tam·pered; tam·per·ing** \-p(ə-)riŋ\ **1 :** to carry on underhand negotiations (as by bribery) ⟨~ with a witness⟩ **2 :** to interfere so as to weaken or change for the worse ⟨~ with a document⟩ **3 :** to try foolish or dangerous experiments

**tam·pon** \'tam-,pän\ *n* **:** a plug (as of cotton) introduced into a cavity usu. to check bleeding or absorb secretions

¹**tan** \'tan\ *vb* **tanned; tan·ning 1 :** to change (hide) into leather esp. by soaking in a liquid containing tannin **2 :** to make or become brown (as by exposure to the sun) **3 :** WHIP, THRASH

²**tan** *n* **1 :** TANBARK; *also* **:** a tanning material **2 :** a brown skin color induced by sun or weather **3 :** a light yellowish brown color

³**tan** *symbol* tangent

**tan·a·ger** \'tan-i-jər\ *n* **:** any of numerous American passerine birds with brightly colored males

**tan·bark** \'tan-,bärk\ *n* **:** bark (as of oak or sumac) that is rich in tannin and used in tanning

¹**tan·dem** \'tan-dəm\ *n* [L, at last, at length (taken to mean "lengthwise"), fr. *tam* so] **1 :** a 2-seated carriage with horses hitched tandem; *also* **:** its team **2 :** a bicycle for two persons sitting one behind the other

²**tandem** *adv* **:** one behind another

³**tandem** *adj* **1 :** consisting of things arranged one behind the other **2 :** working in conjunction with each other

**tang** \'taŋ\ *n* **1 :** a part in a tool that connects the blade with the handle **2 :** a sharp distinctive flavor; *also* **:** a pungent odor — **tangy** *adj*

¹**tan·gent** \'tan-jənt\ *adj* [L *tangent-, tangens,* prp. of *tangere* to touch] **:** TOUCHING; *esp* **:** meeting a curve or surface and not cutting it if extended

²**tangent** *n* **1 :** a tangent line, curve, or surface **2 :** an abrupt change of course — **tan·gen·tial** \tan-'jen-chəl\ *adj*

**tan·ger·ine** \'tan-jə-,rēn, ,tan-jə-'rēn\ *n* **:** a deep orange loose-skinned citrus fruit

¹tan·gi·ble \'tan-jə-bəl\ adj 1 : perceptible esp. by the sense of touch : PALPABLE 2 : substantially real : MATERIAL ⟨~ rewards⟩ 3 : capable of being appraised syn appreciable — tan·gi·bil·i·ty \,tan-jə-'bil-ət-ē\ n

²tangible n : something tangible; esp : a tangible asset

¹tan·gle \'tan-gəl\ vb tan·gled; tangling \-g(ə-)liŋ\ 1 : to involve so as to hamper or embarrass; also : ENTRAP 2 : unite or knit together in intricate confusion : ENTANGLE

²tangle n 1 : a tangled twisted mass (as of vines) 2 : a confusedly complicated state : MUDDLE

tan·go \'tan-gō\ n, pl -gos : a dance of Spanish-American origin — tango vb

tank \'taŋk\ n 1 : a large artificial receptacle for liquids 2 : an armored and armed tractor for military use — tank·ful n

tan·kard \'tan-kərd\ n : a tall one-handled drinking vessel

tank·er \'taŋ-kər\ n : a vehicle equipped with one or more tanks for transporting a liquid (as fuel)

tank town n 1 : a town at which trains stop for water 2 : a small town

tan·ner \'tan-ər\ n : one that tans hides

tan·nery \'tan-(ə-)rē\ n, pl -ner·ies : a place where tanning is carried on

tannic acid \,tan-ik-\ n : TANNIN

tan·nin \'tan-ən\ n : any of various substances of plant origin used in tanning and dyeing, in inks, and as astringents

tan·sy \'tan-zē\ n, pl tansies [ME tanesey, fr. OF tanesie, fr. ML athanasia, fr. Gk. immortality, fr. athanatos immortal, fr. a- not + thanatos death] : a common weedy herb related to the daisies with an aromatic odor and very bitter taste

tan·ta·lize \'tant-ᵊl-,īz\ vb -lized; -liz·ing [fr. Tantalus, mythical Greek king punished in Hades by having to stand up to his chin in water that receded as he bent to drink] : to tease or torment by presenting something desirable to the view but continually keeping it out of reach — tan·ta·liz·er n — tan·ta·liz·ing·ly adv

tan·ta·lum \'tant-ᵊl-əm\ n : a hard ductile acid-resisting chemical element

tan·ta·mount \'tant-ə-,maunt\ adj : equivalent in value or meaning syn same, selfsame, identical

tan·trum \'tan-trəm\ n : a fit of bad temper

Tan·za·ni·an \,tan-zə-'nē-ən\ n : a native or inhabitant of Tanzania — Tanzanian adj

Tao·ism \'tau̇-,iz-əm, 'dau̇-\ n : a religion developed from a Chinese mystic philosophy and Buddhist religion — Tao·ist \-əst\ adj or n

¹tap \'tap\ n 1 : FAUCET, COCK 2 : liquor drawn through a tap 3 : the removing of fluid from a container or cavity by tapping 4 : a tool for forming an internal screw thread 5 : a point in an electric circuit where a connection may be made

²tap vb tapped; tap·ping 1 : to release or cause to flow by piercing or by drawing a plug from a container or cavity 2 : to pierce so as to let out or draw off a fluid 3 : to draw from ⟨~ resources⟩ 4 : to connect into (a telephone wire) to get information or to connect into (an electrical circuit) 5 : to form an internal screw thread in by means of a tap 6 : to connect (as a gas or water main) with a local supply — tap·per n

³tap vb tapped; tap·ping 1 : to rap lightly 2 : to make (as a hole) by repeated light blows 3 : to repair by putting a half sole on 4 : SELECT; esp : to elect to membership

⁴tap n 1 : a light blow or stroke; also : its sound 2 : a small metal plate for the sole or heel of a shoe

¹tape \'tāp\ n 1 : a narrow band of woven fabric 2 : a narrow flexible strip (as of paper, plastic, or metal) 3 : MAGNETIC TAPE 4 : TAPE MEASURE

²tape vb taped; tap·ing 1 : to fasten or support with tape 2 : to measure with a tape measure 3 : to record on magnetic tape

tape deck n 1 : a device used for the recording and playback of magnetic tapes that usu. has to be connected to a separate audio system 2 : TAPE PLAYER

tape measure n : a long flexible measuring instrument made of tape

tape player n : a self-contained device for the playback of recorded magnetic tapes

¹ta·per \'tā-pər\ n 1 : a slender wax candle or a long waxed wick 2 : a gradual lessening of thickness or width in a long object ⟨the ~ of a steeple⟩

²taper vb ta·pered; ta·per·ing \'tā-p(ə-)riŋ\ 1 : to make or become gradually smaller toward one end 2 : to diminish gradually

tape-re·cord \,tāp-ri-'kȯrd\ vb : to make a recording of on magnetic tape — tape recorder n — tape record·ing n

tap·es·try \'tap-ə-strē\ n, pl -tries : a heavy handwoven reversible textile characterized by complicated pictorial designs and used esp. as a wall hanging

tape·worm \'tāp-,wərm\ n : a long flat segmented worm that lives in the intestines

tap·i·o·ca \,tap-ē-'ō-kə\ n : a usu. granular preparation of cassava starch used esp. in puddings

ta·pir \'tā-pər\ n, pl tapir or tapirs : any of several large harmless hoofed mammals of tropical America and southeast Asia

tap·pet \'tap-ət\ n : a lever or projection moved by some other piece (as a cam) or intended to tap or touch something else to cause a particular motion

tap·room \'tap-,rüm, -,rüm\ n : BARROOM

tap·root \-,rüt, -,rut\ n : a large main root growing vertically downward and giving off small lateral roots

taps \'taps\ n sing or pl : the last bugle call at night blown as a signal that lights are to be put out; *also* : a similar call blown at military funerals and memorial services

**tap·ster** \'tap-stər\ *n* : one employed to dispense liquors in a barroom

**tar** \'tär\ *n* **1** : a thick dark sticky liquid distilled from organic material (as wood or coal) **2** : SAILOR, SEAMAN

**¹tar** *vb* **tarred; tar·ring** : to treat or smear with tar

**tar·an·tel·la** \,tar-ən-'tel-ə\ *n* : a vivacious folk dance of southern Italy in 6/8 time

**ta·ran·tu·la** \tə-'ranch-(ə-)lə, -'rant-ᵊl-ə\ *n, pl* **ta·ran·tu·las** *also* **ta·ran·tu·lae** \-'ranch-ə,lē, -'rant-ᵊl-,ē\ **1** : a large European spider once thought very dangerous **2** : any of various large hairy American spiders essentially harmless to man

**tar·dy** \'tärd-ē\ *adj* **tar·di·er; -est 1** : moving slowly : SLUGGISH **2** : LATE; *also* : DILATORY **syn** behindhand, overdue — **tar·di·ly** \'tärd-ᵊl-ē\ *adv* — **tar·di·ness** \-ē-nəs\ *n*

**tare** \'taər\ *n* : a weed of fields where grain is grown

**tare** *n* : a deduction from the gross weight of a substance and its container made in allowance for the weight of the container — **tare** *vb*

**tar·get** \'tär-gət\ *n* [ME, fr. MF *targette,* dim. of *targe* light shield, of Gmc origin] **1** : a mark to shoot at **2** : an object of ridicule or criticism **3** : a goal to be achieved

**target** *vb* : to make a target of

**tar·iff** \'tar-əf\ *n* [It *tariffa,* fr. Ar *ta'rīf* notification] **1** : a schedule of duties imposed by a government esp. on imported goods; *also* : a duty or rate of duty imposed in such a schedule **2** : a schedule of rates or charges **syn** customs, toll, tax, levy, assessment

**tarn** \'tärn\ *n* : a small mountain lake or pool

**tar·nish** \'tär-nish\ *vb* : to make or become dull or discolored — **tarnish** *n*

**ta·ro** \'tär-ō, 'tar-\ *n, pl* **taros** : a tropical plant grown for its edible fleshy root; *also* : this root

**tar·ot** \'tar-ō\ *n* : one of a set of 22 pictorial playing cards used esp. for fortune-telling

**tar·pau·lin** \tär-'pȯ-lən, 'tär-pə-\ *n* : waterproof material and esp. canvas used in sheets for protecting exposed objects (as goods)

**tar·pon** \'tär-pən\ *n, pl* **tarpon** *or* **tarpons** : a large silvery sport fish common off the Florida coast

**tar·ra·gon** \'tar-ə-gən\ *n* : a small European perennial wormwood with pungent aromatic foliage used as a flavoring

**tar·ry** \'tar-ē\ *vb* **tar·ried; tar·ry·ing 1** : to be tardy : DELAY; *esp* : to be slow in leaving **2** : to stay in or at a place : SOJOURN **syn** remain, wait

**tar·ry** \'tär-ē\ *adj* : of, resembling, or smeared with tar

**tar·sus** \'tär-səs\ *n, pl* **tar·si** \-,sī, -,sē\ : the part of the foot of a vertebrate between the metatarsus and the leg; *also* : the small bones that support this part of the limb — **tar·sal** \-səl\ *adj or n*

**¹tart** \'tärt\ *adj* **1** : agreeably sharp to the taste : PUNGENT **2** : BITING, CAUSTIC **syn** sour, acid — **tart·ly** *adv* — **tart·ness** *n*

**²tart** *n* **1** : a small pie or pastry shell containing jelly, custard, or fruit **2** : PROSTITUTE

**tar·tan** \'tärt-ᵊn\ *n* : a twilled woolen fabric with a plaid design of Scottish origin consisting of stripes of varying width and color against a solid ground

**tar·tar** \'tärt-ər\ *n* **1** : a substance in the juice of grapes deposited (as in wine casks) as a reddish crust or sediment **2** : a hard crust of saliva, debris, and calcium salts on the teeth — **tar·tar·ic** \tär-'tar-ik\ *adj*

**tar·tar sauce** *or* **tar·tare sauce** \,tärt-ər-\ *n* : mayonnaise with chopped pickles, olives, or capers

**¹task** \'task\ *n* [ME *taske,* fr. OF *tasque,* fr. ML *tasca* tax or service imposed by a feudal superior, fr. *taxare* to tax] : a usu. assigned piece of work often to be finished within a certain time **syn** job duty, chore, stint, assignment

**²task** *vb* : to oppress with great labor

**task force** *n* : a temporary grouping to accomplish a particular objective

**task·mas·ter** \'task-,mas-tər\ *n* : one that imposes a task or burdens another with labor

**¹tas·sel** \'tas-əl, 'täs-\ *n* **1** : a pendent ornament made by laying parallel a bunch of cords of even length and fastening them at one end **2** : something suggesting a tassel; *esp* : a male flower cluster of Indian corn

**²tassel** *vb* **-seled** *or* **-selled; -sel·ing** *or* **-sel·ling** \-(ə-)liŋ\ : to adorn with or put forth tassels

**¹taste** \'tāst\ *vb* **tast·ed; tast·ing 1** : to try or determine the flavor of by taking a bit into the mouth **2** : to eat or drink esp. in small quantities : SAMPLE **3** : EXPERIENCE, UNDERGO **4** : to have a specific flavor

**²taste** *n* **1** : a small amount tasted **2** : BIT; *esp* : a sample of experience **3** : the special sense that identifies sweet, sour, bitter, or salty qualities and is mediated by receptors in the tongue **4** : a quality perceptible to the sense of taste; *also* : a complex sensation involving true taste, smell, and touch **5** : individual preference **6** : critical judgment, discernment, or appreciation; *also* : aesthetic quality **syn** tang, relish — **taste·ful** \-fəl\ *adj* — **taste·ful·ly** \-ē\ *adv* — **taste·less** *adj* — **taste·less·ly** *adv* — **tast·er** *n*

**taste bud** *n* : a sense organ mediating the sensation of taste

**tasty** \'tā-stē\ *adj* **tast·i·er; -est** : pleasing to the taste : SAVORY **syn** palatable, appetizing, toothsome, flavorsome — **tast·i·ness** \'tā-stē-nəs\ *n*

**tat** \'tat\ *vb* **tat·ted; tat·ting** : to work at or make by tatting

**¹tat·ter** \'tat-ər\ *n* **1** : a part torn and left hanging **2** *pl* : tattered clothing

²**tat·ter** vb : to make or become ragged

**tat·ter·de·ma·lion** \,tat-ərd-i-'māl-yən\ n : one that is ragged or disreputable

**tat·ter·sall** \'tat-ər-,sȯl, -səl\ n : a pattern of colored lines forming squares on solid background; also : a fabric in a tattersall pattern

**tat·ting** \'tat-iŋ\ n : a delicate handmade lace formed usu. by looping and knotting with a single thread and a small shuttle; also : the act or process of making such lace

**tat·tle** \'tat-ᵊl\ vb **tat·tled; tat·tling** \'tat-(ᵊ-)liŋ\ 1 : CHATTER, PRATE 2 : to tell secrets; also : to inform against another — **tat·tler** \'tat-(ᵊ-)lər\ n

**tat·tle·tale** \'tat-ᵊl-,tāl\ n : one that tattles : INFORMER

¹**tat·too** \ta-'tü\ n, pl **tattoos** [alter. of earlier taptoo, fr. D taptoe, fr. the phrase tap toe! taps shut!] 1 : a call sounded before taps as notice to go to quarters 2 : a rapid rhythmic rapping

²**tattoo** n, pl **tattoos** [Tahitian tatau] : an indelible figure fixed upon the body esp. by insertion of pigment under the skin

³**tattoo** vb : to mark (the skin) with tattoos

**taught** past of TEACH

¹**taunt** \'tȯnt\ vb : to reproach or challenge in a mocking manner : jeer at syn mock, deride, ridicule, twit — **taunt·er** n

²**taunt** n : a sarcastic challenge or insult

**taupe** \'tōp\ n : a brownish gray

**taut** \'tȯt\ adj 1 : tightly drawn : not slack 2 : extremely nervous : TENSE 3 : TRIM, TIDY ⟨a ~ ship⟩ — **taut·ly** adv — **taut·ness** n

**tau·tol·o·gy** \tȯ-'täl-ə-jē\ n, pl **-gies** : a needless repetition of an idea, statement, or word; also : an instance of such repetition — **tau·to·log·i·cal** \,tȯt-ᵊl-'äj-i-kəl\ adj — **tau·to·log·i·cal·ly** \-i-k(ə-)lē\ adv — **tau·tol·o·gous** \tȯ-'täl-ə-gəs\ adj — **tau·tol·o·gous·ly** adv

**tav·ern** \'tav-ərn\ n [ME taverne, fr. OF, fr. L taberna, lit., shed, hut, shop, fr. trabs beam] 1 : an establishment where alcoholic liquors are sold to be drunk on the premises 2 : INN

**taw** \'tȯ\ n 1 : a marble used as a shooter 2 : the line from which players shoot at marbles

**tawdry** \'tȯ-drē\ adj **taw·dri·er; -est** [fr. tawdry lace (a tie of lace for the neck), fr. St. Audrey (St. Etheldreda) d679 queen of Northumbria] : cheap and gaudy in appearance and quality syn garish, flashy — **taw·dri·ly** adv

**taw·ny** \'tȯ-nē\ adj **taw·ni·er; -est** : of a brownish orange color

¹**tax** \'taks\ vb 1 : to levy a tax on 2 : CHARGE, ACCUSE 3 : to put under pressure — **tax·able** \'tak-sə-bəl\ adj — **tax·a·tion** \tak-'sā-shən\ n

²**tax** n 1 : a charge usu. of money imposed by authority upon persons or property for public purposes 2 : a heavy charge : STRAIN syn assessment, customs, duty, tariff

¹**taxi** \'tak-sē\ n, pl **tax·is** \-sēz\ also **tax·ies** : TAXICAB; also : a similarly operated boat or airplane

²**taxi** vb **tax·ied; taxi·ing** or **taxy·ing; tax·is** or **tax·ies** 1 : to go by taxicab 2 : to run along the ground or on the water under an airplane's own power when starting or after a landing

**taxi·cab** \'tak-sē-,kab\ n : an automobile that carries passengers for a fare usu. determined by the distance traveled

**taxi·der·my** \'tak-sə-,dər-mē\ n : the art of preparing, stuffing, and mounting skins of animals — **taxi·der·mist** \-məst\ n

**tax·on·o·my** \tak-'sän-ə-mē\ n : classification esp. of animals or plants according to natural relationships — **tax·o·nom·ic** \,tak-sə-'näm-ik\ adj — **tax·on·o·mist** \tak-'sän-ə-məst\ n

**tax·pay·er** \'taks-,pā-ər\ n : one who pays or is liable for a tax — **tax·pay·ing** \-iŋ\ adj

**tb** abbr tablespoon

**Tb** symbol terbium

¹**TB** \(')tē-'bē\ n : TUBERCULOSIS

²**TB** abbr trial balance

**TBA** abbr, often not cap to be announced

**T–bar lift** \'tē-,bär-\ n : a ski lift with a series of T-shaped bars

**tbs** or **tbsp** abbr tablespoon

**TC** abbr teachers college

**TD** abbr 1 touchdown 2 treasury department

**TDY** abbr temporary duty

**Te** symbol tellurium

**tea** \'tē\ n 1 : the cured leaves and leaf buds of a shrub grown chiefly in China, Japan, India, and Ceylon; also : this shrub 2 : a drink made by steeping tea in boiling water 3 : refreshments usu. including tea served in late afternoon; also : a reception at which tea is served

**teach** \'tēch\ vb **taught** \'tȯt\; **teach·ing** 1 : to cause to know a subject : act as a teacher 2 : to show how ⟨~ a child to swim⟩ 3 : to guide the studies of 4 : to make to know the disagreeable consequences of an action 5 : to impart the knowledge of ⟨~ algebra⟩ — **teach·able** adj — **teach·er** n

**teach·ing** \-iŋ\ n 1 : the act, practice, or profession of a teacher 2 : something taught; esp : DOCTRINE

**teaching machine** n : any of various mechanical devices for presenting a program of educational material

**tea·cup** \'tē-,kəp\ n : a small cup used with a saucer for hot beverages

**teak** \'tēk\ n : a tall East Indian timber tree; also : its hard durable yellowish brown wood

**tea·ket·tle** \'tē-,ket-ᵊl, -,kit-\ n : a covered kettle with a handle and spout for boiling water

**teal** \'tēl\ n, pl **teal** or **teals** : any of several small short-necked wild ducks

¹**team** \'tēm\ n [ME teme, fr. OE tēam offspring, lineage, group of draft animals] 1 : two or more draft animals harnessed to the same vehicle or implement 2 : a number of persons associated in work or activity; esp : a group

on one side in a match — **team·mate** \'tēm-ˌmāt\ n

²**team** vb **1** : to haul with or drive a team **2** : to form a team : join forces

³**team** adj : of or performed by a team

**team·ster** \'tēm-stər\ n : one that drives a team or motortruck esp. as an occupation

**team·work** \-ˌwərk\ n : the work or activity of a number of persons acting in close association as members of a unit

**tea·pot** \'tē-ˌpät\ n : a vessel with a spout for brewing and serving tea

¹**tear** \'tiər\ n : a drop of the salty liquid that moistens the eye and inner side of the eyelids — **tear·ful** \-fəl\ adj — **tear·ful·ly** \-ē\ adv

²**tear** \'taər\ vb **tore** \'tōr\; **torn** \'tōrn\; **tear·ing 1** : to separate parts of or pull apart by force : REND **2** : LACERATE **3** : to disrupt by the pull of contrary forces **4** : to remove by force : WRENCH **5** : to move or act with violence, haste, or force **syn** rip, split, cleave

³**tear** \'taər\ n **1** : the act of tearing **2** : a hole or flaw made by tearing : RENT

**tear gas** \'tiər-\ n : a substance that on dispersion in the atmosphere blinds the eyes with tears — **tear gas** vb

**tear·jerk·er** \'tiər-ˌjər-kər\ n : an extravagantly pathetic story, play, or movie

¹**tease** \'tēz\ vb **teased; teas·ing 1** : to disentangle and lay parallel by combing or carding ⟨∼ wool⟩ **2** : to scratch the surface of (cloth) so as to raise a nap **3** : to annoy persistently esp. in fun by goading, coaxing, or tantalizing **4** : to comb (hair) by taking a strand and pushing the short hairs toward the scalp with the comb **syn** harass, worry, pester

²**tease** n **1** : the act of teasing or state of being teased **2** : one that teases

**tea·sel** or **tea·zel** or **tea·zle** \'tē-zəl\ n : a prickly herb or its flower head covered with stiff bracts and used to raise the nap on cloth; also : an artificial device used for this purpose

**tea·spoon** \'tē-ˌspün\ n **1** : a small spoon suitable for stirring and sipping tea or coffee and holding one third of a tablespoon **2** : TEASPOONFUL

**tea·spoon·ful** \-ˌfül\ n : a unit of measure equal to one-sixth fluidounce

**teat** \'tit, 'tēt\ n : the protuberance through which milk is drawn from an udder or breast

**tech** abbr **1** technical; technically; technician **2** technological; technology

**tech·ne·tium** \tek-'nē-sh(ē-)əm\ n : a radioactive metallic chemical element obtained artificially

**tech·nic** \'tek-nik, tek-'nēk\ n : TECHNIQUE 1

**tech·ni·cal** \'tek-ni-kəl\ adj [Gk technikos of art, skillful, fr. technē art, craft, skill] **1** : having special knowledge esp. of a mechanical or scientific subject ⟨∼ experts⟩ **2** : of or relating to a particular or esp. a practical or scientific subject ⟨∼ training⟩ **3** : according to a strict interpretation of the rules **4** : of or relating to technique — **tech·ni·cal·ly** \-k(ə-)lē\ adv

**tech·ni·cal·i·ty** \ˌtek-nə-'kal-ət-ē\ n, pl **-ties 1** : the quality or state of being technical **2** : a detail meaningful only to a specialist

**technical sergeant** n : a noncommissioned officer in the air force ranking next below a master sergeant

**tech·ni·cian** \tek-'nish-ən\ n : a person who has acquired the technique of a specialized skill or subject

**tech·nique** \tek-'nēk\ n **1** : the manner in which technical details are treated or basic physical movements are used **2** : technical methods

**tech·noc·ra·cy** \tek-'näk-rə-sē\ n : management of society by technical experts — **tech·no·crat** \'tek-nə-ˌkrat\ n — **tech·no·crat·ic** \ˌtek-nə-'krat-ik\ adj

**tech·nol·o·gy** \tek-'näl-ə-jē\ n, pl **-gies** : applied science; also : a technical method of achieving a practical purpose — **tech·no·log·i·cal** \ˌtek-nə-'läj-i-kəl\ adj

**tec·ton·ics** \tek-'tän-iks\ n sing or pl **1** : geological structural features **2** : geology dealing with faulting and folding **3** : DIASTROPHISM — **tec·ton·ic** \-ik\ adj

**tec·to·nism** \'tek-tə-ˌniz-əm\ n : DIASTROPHISM

**ted·dy bear** \'ted-ē-ˌbaər\ n : a stuffed toy bear

**te·dious** \'tēd-ē-əs, 'tē-jəs\ adj : tiresome because of length or dullness **syn** boring, wearisome, irksome — **te·dious·ly** adv — **te·dious·ness** n

**te·di·um** \'tēd-ē-əm\ n : TEDIOUSNESS; also : BOREDOM

¹**tee** \'tē\ n : a small mound or peg on which a golf ball is placed before beginning play on a hole; also : the area from which the ball is hit to begin play

²**tee** vb **teed; tee·ing** : to place (a ball) on a tee

**teem** \'tēm\ vb : to become filled to overflowing : ABOUND **syn** swarm

**teen** adj : TEENAGE

**teen·age** \'tēn-ˌāj\ or **teen-aged** \-ˌājd\ adj : of, being, or relating to people in their teens — **teen·ag·er** \-ˌā-jər\ n

**teens** \'tēnz\ n pl : the numbers 13 to 19 inclusive; esp : the years 13 to 19 in a person's life

**tee·ny** \'tē-nē\ adj **tee·ni·er; -est** : TINY

**tee·pee** var of TEPEE

**tee shirt** var of T-SHIRT

**tee·ter** \'tēt-ər\ vb **1** : to move un steadily **2** : SEESAW — **teeter** n

**teeth** pl of TOOTH

**teethe** \'tēth\ vb **teethed; teeth·ing** : to grow teeth : cut one's teeth

**teeth·ing** \'tē-thin\ n : the first growth of teeth; also : the phenomena accompanying growth of teeth through the gums

**teeth·ridge** \'tēth-ˌrij\ n : the inner surface of the gums of the upper front teeth

**tee·to·tal** \'tē-'tōt-ᵊl, -ˌtōt-\ adj : of or

relating to the practice of complete abstinence from alcoholic drinks — **tee·to·tal·er** or **tee·to·tal·ier** \-'tōt-²l-ər\ n — **tee·to·tal·ism** \-'l-,iz-əm\ n

**tek·tite** \'tek-,tīt\ n : a glassy body of probably meteoric origin — **tek·tit·ic** \tek-'tit-ik\ adj

**tel** abbr 1 telegram 2 telegraph 3 telephone

**tele·cast** \'tel-i-,kast\ vb **-cast** also **-cast·ed; -cast·ing** : to broadcast by television — **telecast** n — **tele·cast·er** n

**tele·com·mu·ni·ca·tion** \,tel-i-kə-,myü-nə-'kā-shən\ n : communication at a distance (as by telephone or radio)

**tele·film** \'tel-i-,film\ n : a motion picture produced for televising

**teleg** abbr telegraphy

**tele·ge·nic** \,tel-ə-'jen-ik, -'jēn-\ adj : having an appearance and manner that are markedly attractive to television viewers

**tele·gram** \'tel-ə-,gram\ n : a message sent by telegraph

¹**tele·graph** \-,graf\ n : an apparatus or system for communication at a distance by electrical transmission of coded signals

²**telegraph** vb : to send or communicate by telegraph — **te·leg·ra·pher** \tə-'leg-rə-fər\ n — **te·leg·ra·phist** \-fəst\ n

**te·leg·ra·phy** \tə-'leg-rə-fē\ n : the use or operation of a telegraph apparatus or system — **tel·e·graph·ic** \,tel-ə-'graf-ik\ adj

**tele·me·ter** \'tel-ə-,mēt-ər\ n : an electrical apparatus for measuring something (as temperature) and transmitting the result by radio to a distant station — **telemeter** vb — **tele·met·ric** \,tel-ə-'met-rik\ adj — **te·lem·e·try** \tə-'lem-ə-trē\ n

**te·lep·a·thy** \tə-'lep-ə-thē\ n : apparent communication from one mind to another otherwise than through known sensory channels — **tele·path·ic** \,tel-ə-'path-ik\ adj — **tele·path·i·cal·ly** \-i-k(ə-)lē\ adv

¹**tele·phone** \'tel-ə-,fōn\ n : an instrument for reproducing sounds and esp. spoken words transmitted from a distance by electrical means over wires

²**telephone** vb **-phoned; -phon·ing** 1 : to send or communicate by telephone 2 : to speak to (a person) by telephone — **tele·phon·er** n

**te·le·pho·ny** \tə-'lef-ə-nē, 'tel-ə-,fō-\ n : use or operation of apparatus for electrical transmission of sounds between distant points with or without connecting wires — **tel·e·phon·ic** \,tel-ə-'fän-ik\ adj

**tele·pho·to** \,tel-ə-'fōt-ō\ adj : being a camera lens giving a large image of a distant object — **tele·pho·to·graph** \-'fōt-ə-,graf\ n or vb — **tele·pho·to·graph·ic** \-,fōt-ə-'graf-ik\ adj — **tele·pho·tog·ra·phy** \-fə-'täg-rə-fē\ n

**tele·play** \'tel-i-,plā\ n : a play written for television

**tele·print·er** \'tel-ə-,print-ər\ n : TELETYPEWRITER

¹**tele·scope** \'tel-ə-,skōp\ n : a long tube-shaped instrument equipped with lenses for viewing objects at a distance and esp. for observing celestial bodies

²**telescope** vb **-scoped; -scop·ing** : to slide, pass, or force or cause to slide, pass, or force one within another like the sections of a hand telescope

**tele·scop·ic** \,tel-ə-'skäp-ik\ adj 1 : of or relating to a telescope 2 : seen only by a telescope 3 : able to discern objects at a distance 4 : having parts that telescope — **tele·scop·i·cal·ly** \-i-k(ə-)lē\ adv

**tele·thon** \'tel-ə-,thän\ n : a long television program usu. to solicit funds for a charity

**tele·type·writ·er** \,tel-ə-'tīp-,rīt-ər\ n : a printing telegraph recording like a typewriter — **tele·typ·ist** \'tel-ə-,tī-pəst\ n

**tele·view** \'tel-i-,vyü\ vb : to watch by means of a television receiver — **tele·view·er** n

**tele·vise** \'tel-ə-,vīz\ vb **-vised; -vis·ing** : to pick up and broadcast by television

**tele·vi·sion** \'tel-ə-,vizh-ən\ n [F *télévision*, fr. Gk *tēle* far, at a distance + F *vision* vision] : transmission and reproduction of a rapid series of images by a device that converts light waves into radio waves and then converts these back into visible light rays

**tell** \'tel\ vb **told** \'tōld\; **tell·ing** 1 : COUNT, ENUMERATE 2 : to relate in detail : NARRATE 3 : SAY, UTTER 4 : to make known : REVEAL 5 : to report to : INFORM 6 : ORDER, DIRECT 7 : to ascertain by observing 8 : to have a marked effect 9 : to serve as evidence **syn** reveal, disclose, discover, betray

**tell·er** \'tel-ər\ n 1 : one that relates : NARRATOR 2 : one that counts 3 : a bank employee handling money received or paid out

**tell·ing** \'tel-iŋ\ adj : producing a marked effect : EFFECTIVE **syn** cogent, convincing, sound

**tell off** vb : REPRIMAND, SCOLD

**tell·tale** \'tel-,tāl\ n 1 : INFORMER, TATTLETALE 2 : something that serves to disclose : INDICATION — **telltale** adj

**tel·lu·ri·um** \tə-'lür-ē-əm, te-\ n : a chemical element that resembles sulfur in properties

**te·mer·i·ty** \tə-'mer-ət-ē\ n, pl **-ties** : rash or presumptuous daring : BOLDNESS **syn** audacity, effrontery, gall, nerve, cheek

**temp** abbr 1 temperature 2 temporary 3 [L *tempore*] in the time of

¹**tem·per** \'tem-pər\ vb **tem·pered; tem·per·ing** \-p(ə-)riŋ\ 1 : to dilute or soften by the addition of something else (⟨~ justice with mercy⟩) 2 : to bring to a desired consistency or texture (as clay by moistening and kneading, steel by gradual heating and cooling) 3 : TOUGHEN 4 : TUNE

²**temper** n 1 : characteristic tone : TENDENCY 2 : the state of a metal or other substance with respect to various qualities (as hardness) ⟨~ of a knife blade⟩

**3 :** a characteristic frame of mind **:** DISPOSITION **4 :** calmness of mind **:** COMPOSURE **5 :** state of feeling or frame of mind at a particular time **6 :** heat of mind or emotion **syn** temperament, character, personality

**tem·pera** \'tem-pə-rə\ *n* **:** a painting process using an albuminous or colloidal medium as a vehicle; *also* **:** a painting done in tempera

**tem·per·a·ment** \'tem-p(ə-)rə-mənt\ *n* **1 :** characteristic or habitual inclination or mode of emotional response **:** DISPOSITION ⟨nervous ~⟩ **2 :** excessive sensitiveness or irritability **syn** character, personality — **tem·per·a·men·tal** \,tem-p(ə-)rə-'ment-ʲl\ *adj*

**tem·per·ance** \'tem-p(ə-)rəns\ *n* **:** habitual moderation in the indulgence of the appetites or passions; *esp* **:** moderation in or abstinence from the use of intoxicating drink

**tem·per·ate** \'tem-p(ə-)rət\ *adj* **1 :** not extreme or excessive **:** MILD **2 :** moderate in indulgence of appetite or desire **3 :** moderate in the use of intoxicating liquors **4 :** having a moderate climate **syn** sober, continent

**temperate zone** *n, often cap T&Z* **:** the region between the tropic of Cancer and the arctic circle or between the tropic of Capricorn and the antarctic circle

**tem·per·a·ture** \'tem-pər-,chùr, -p(ə-)rə-,chùr, -chər\ *n* **1 :** degree of hotness or coldness of something (as air, water, or the body) as shown by a thermometer **2 :** FEVER

**tem·pest** \'tem-pəst\ *n* [ME, fr. OF *tempeste*, fr. L *tempestas* season, weather, storm, fr. *tempus* time] **:** a violent wind esp. with rain, hail, or snow

**tem·pes·tu·ous** \tem-'pes-chə-wəs\ *adj* **:** of, involving, or resembling a tempest **:** STORMY — **tem·pes·tu·ous·ly** *adv* — **tem·pes·tu·ous·ness** *n*

**tem·plate** *or* **tem·plet** \'tem-plət\ *n* **:** a gauge, mold, or pattern used as a guide to the form of a piece being made

**tem·ple** \'tem-pəl\ *n* **1 :** an edifice for the worship of a deity **2 :** a place devoted to a special or exalted purpose

**temple** *n* **:** the flattened space on each side of the forehead esp. of man

**tem·po** \'tem-pō\ *n, pl* **tem·pi** \-(,)pē\ *or* **tempos** **1 :** the rate of speed of a musical piece or passage **2 :** rate of motion or activity **:** PACE

**tem·po·ral** \'tem-p(ə-)rəl\ *adj* **1 :** of, relating to, or limited by time ⟨~ and spatial bounds⟩ **2 :** of or relating to earthly life or secular concerns ⟨~ power⟩ **syn** temporary, secular, lay

**temporal** *adj* **:** of or relating to the temples or to the sides of the skull

**tem·po·rary** \'tem-pə-,rer-ē\ *adj* **:** lasting for a time only **:** TRANSITORY **syn** provisional, impermanent — **tem·po·rar·i·ly** \,tem-pə-'rer-ə-lē\ *adv*

**temporary** *n, pl* **-rar·ies :** one serving for a limited time

**tem·po·rize** \'tem-pə-,rīz\ *vb* **-rized; -riz·ing 1 :** to adapt one's actions to the time or the dominant opinion **:** COM-

PROMISE **2 :** to draw out matters so as to gain time — **tem·po·riz·er** *n*

**tempt** \'tempt\ *vb* **1 :** to entice to do wrong by promise of pleasure or gain **2 :** PROVOKE **3 :** to risk the dangers of **4 :** to induce to do something **:** INCITE **syn** inveigle, decoy, seduce — **tempt·er** *n* — **tempt·ing·ly** *adv* — **tempt·ress** \'temp-trəs\ *n*

**temp·ta·tion** \temp-'tā-shən\ *n* **1 :** the act of tempting **:** the state of being tempted **2 :** something that tempts

**ten** \'ten\ *n* **1 :** one more than nine **2 :** the 10th in a set or series **3 :** something having 10 units — **ten** *adj or pron* — **tenth** \'tenth\ *adj or adv or n*

**ten·a·ble** \'ten-ə-bəl\ *adj* **:** capable of being held, maintained, or defended — **ten·a·bil·i·ty** \,ten-ə-'bil-ət-ē\ *n*

**te·na·cious** \tə-'nā-shəs\ *adj* **1 :** not easily pulled apart **:** COHESIVE, TOUGH ⟨steel is a ~ metal⟩ **2 :** holding fast ⟨~ of his rights⟩ **3 :** RETENTIVE ⟨~ memory⟩ — **te·na·cious·ly** *adv* — **te·nac·i·ty** \tə-'nas-ət-ē\ *n*

**ten·an·cy** \'ten-ən-sē\ *n, pl* **-cies :** the temporary possession or occupancy of something (as a house) that belongs to another; *also* **:** the period of a tenant's occupancy

**ten·ant** \'ten-ənt\ *n* **1 :** one who rents or leases (as a house) from a landlord **2 :** DWELLER, OCCUPANT — **tenant** *vb* — **ten·ant·less** *adj*

**tenant farmer** *n* **:** a farmer who works land owned by another and pays rent either in cash or in shares of produce

**ten·ant·ry** \'ten-ən-trē\ *n, pl* **-ries :** the body of tenants esp. on a great estate

**¹tend** \'tend\ *vb* **1 :** to apply oneself ⟨~ to your affairs⟩ **2 :** to take care of ⟨~ a plant⟩ **3 :** to manage the operations of ⟨~ a machine⟩ **syn** mind, watch

**²tend** *vb* **1 :** to move or develop one's course in a particular direction **2 :** to show an inclination or tendency

**ten·den·cy** \'ten-dən-sē\ *n, pl* **-cies 1 :** DRIFT, TREND **2 :** a proneness to or readiness for a particular kind of thought or action **:** PROPENSITY **syn** tenor, current, bent, leaning

**ten·den·tious** *also* **ten·den·cious** \ten-'den-chəs\ *adj* **:** marked by a tendency in favor of a particular point of view **:** BIASED — **ten·den·tious·ly** *adv* — **ten·den·tious·ness** *n*

**¹ten·der** \'ten-dər\ *adj* **1 :** having a soft texture **:** easily broken, chewed, or cut **2 :** physically weak **:** DELICATE; *also* **:** IMMATURE **3 :** expressing or responsive to love or sympathy **:** LOVING, COMPASSIONATE **4 :** SENSITIVE, TOUCHY **syn** sympathetic, warm, warmhearted — **ten·der·ly** *adv* — **ten·der·ness** *n*

**²tend·er** \'ten-dər\ *n* **1 :** one that tends or takes care **2 :** a vehicle attached to a locomotive to carry fuel and water **3 :** a boat carrying passengers and freight to a larger ship

**³ten·der** *n* **1 :** an offer or proposal made for acceptance; *esp* **:** an offer of a bid for a contract **2 :** something (as money) that may be offered in payment

**ten·der** *vb* **:** to present for acceptance

**ten·der·foot** \'ten-dər-ˌfu̇t\ *n, pl* **tender·feet** \-ˌfēt\ *also* **ten·der·foots** \-ˌfu̇ts\ **1 :** one not hardened to frontier or rough outdoor life **2 :** an inexperienced beginner **:** NEOPHYTE

**ten·der·heart·ed** \ˌten-dər-'härt-əd\ *adj* **:** easily moved to love, pity, or sorrow **:** COMPASSIONATE

**ten·der·ize** \'ten-də-ˌrīz\ *vb* **-ized; -iz·ing :** to make (meat) tender — **ten·der·iz·er** \'ten-də-ˌrī-zər\ *n*

**ten·der·loin** \'ten-dər-ˌlȯin\ *n* **1 :** a strip of very tender meat on each side of the backbone for beef or pork **2 :** a district of a city marked by extensive vice, crime, and corruption

**ten·der·om·e·ter** \ˌten-də-'räm-ət-ər\ *n* **:** a device for determining the maturity and tenderness of samples of fruits and vegetables

**ten·don** \'ten-dən\ *n* **:** a tough cord of dense tissue uniting a muscle with another part (as a bone) — **ten·di·nous** \-də-nəs\ *adj*

**ten·dril** \'ten-drəl\ *n* **:** a slender coiling organ by which some climbing plants attach themselves to a support

**te·neb·ri·ous** \tə-'neb-rē-əs\ *adj* **:** TENEBROUS

**ten·e·brous** \'ten-ə-brəs\ *adj* **:** shut off from the light **:** GLOOMY, OBSCURE

**ten·e·ment** \'ten-ə-mənt\ *n* **1 :** a house used as a dwelling **2 :** a dwelling house divided into separate apartments for rent to families; *esp* **:** one meeting only minimum standards of safety and comfort **3 :** APARTMENT, FLAT

**te·net** \'ten-ət\ *n* [L, he holds, fr. *tenēre* to hold] **:** one of the principles or doctrines held in common by members of an organized group (as a church or profession) **syn** doctrine, dogma, belief

**ten·fold** \'ten-ˌfōld, -'fōld\ *adj* **:** being 10 times as great or as many — **tenfold** \-'fōld\ *adv*

**ten-gallon hat** *n* **:** a wide-brimmed hat with a large soft crown

**Tenn** *abbr* Tennessee

**ten·nis** \'ten-əs\ *n* **:** a game played with a ball and racket on a court divided by a net

**ten·on** \'ten-ən\ *n* **:** the shaped end of one piece of wood that fits into the hole in another piece and thus joins the two pieces together

**ten·or** \'ten-ər\ *n* **1 :** the general drift of something spoken or written **:** PURPORT **2 :** the highest natural adult male voice **3 :** TREND, TENDENCY

**ten·pen·ny** \ˌten-ˌpen-ē\ *adj* **:** amounting to, worth, or costing 10 pennies

**tenpenny nail** *n* **:** a nail three inches long

**ten·pin** \'ten-ˌpin\ *n* **:** a bottle-shaped bowling pin set in groups of 10 and bowled at in a game (**tenpins**)

**¹tense** \'tens\ *n* [ME *tens* time, tense, fr. MF, fr. L *tempus*] **:** distinction of form of a verb to indicate the time of the action or state

**²tense** *adj* **tens·er; tens·est** [L *tensus*,

fr. pp. of *tendere* to stretch] **1 :** stretched tight **:** TAUT **2 :** feeling or marked by nervous tension **syn** stiff, rigid, inflexible — **tense·ly** *adv* — **tense·ness** *n* — **ten·si·ty** \'ten-sət-ē\ *n*

**³tense** *vb* **tensed; tens·ing :** to make or become tense

**ten·sile** \'ten-səl, -ˌsīl\ *adj* **:** of or relating to tension ⟨~ strength⟩

**ten·sion** \'ten-chən\ *n* **1 :** the act of straining or stretching; *also* **:** the condition of being strained or stretched **2 :** a state of mental unrest often with signs of bodily stress **3 :** a state of latent hostility or opposition **4 :** VOLTAGE ⟨a high-*tension* wire⟩

**¹tent** \'tent\ *n* **1 :** a collapsible shelter of canvas or other material stretched and supported by poles **2 :** a canopy placed over the head and shoulders to retain vapors or oxygen being medically administered

**²tent** *vb* **1 :** to lodge in tents **2 :** to cover with or as if with a tent

**ten·ta·cle** \'tent-i-kəl\ *n* **:** a long flexible projection about the head or mouth (as of an insect, mollusk, or fish) — **ten·ta·cled** \-kəld\ *adj* — **ten·tac·u·lar** \ten-'tak-yə-lər\ *adj*

**ten·ta·tive** \'tent-ət-iv\ *adj* **:** of the nature of an experiment or hypothesis **:** not final — **ten·ta·tive·ly** *adv*

**ten·u·ous** \'ten-yə-wəs\ *adj* **1 :** not dense **:** RARE ⟨a ~ fluid⟩ **2 :** not thick **:** SLENDER ⟨a ~ rope⟩ **3 :** having little substance **:** FLIMSY, WEAK ⟨~ influences⟩ **syn** thin, slim, slight — **te·nu·i·ty** \te-'n(y)ü-ət-ē, tə-\ *n* — **ten·u·ous·ly** \'ten-yə-wəs-lē\ *adv* — **ten·u·ous·ness** *n*

**ten·ure** \'ten-yər\ *n* **:** the act, right, manner, or period of holding something (as a landed property or a position)

**ten·ured** \'ten-yərd\ *adj* **:** having tenure ⟨~ faculty members⟩

**te·o·sin·te** \ˌtā-ō-'sint-ē\ *n* **:** a large annual fodder grass of Mexico and Central America closely related to and possibly ancestral to maize

**te·pee** \'tē-(ˌ)pē\ *n* [Dakota *tipi*, fr. *ti* to dwell + *pi* to use for] **:** an American Indian conical tent usu. of skins

**tep·id** \'tep-əd\ *adj* **1 :** moderately warm **:** LUKEWARM **2 :** HALFHEARTED

**te·qui·la** \tə-'kē-lə, tā-\ *n* **:** a Mexican liquor made from mescal

**ter** *abbr* **1** terrace **2** territory

**ter·bi·um** \'tər-bē-əm\ *n* **:** a metallic chemical element

**ter·cen·te·na·ry** \ˌtər-ˌsen-'ten-ə-rē, tər-'sent-ᵊn-ˌer-ē\ *n, pl* **-ries :** a 300th anniversary; *also* **:** its celebration — **tercentenary** *adj*

**ter·cen·ten·ni·al** \ˌtər-ˌsen-'ten-ē-əl\ *adj or n* **:** TERCENTENARY

**te·re·do** \tə-'rēd-ō, -'rād-\ *n, pl* **teredos** *or* **te·red·i·nes** \-'red-ᵊn-ˌēz\ **:** SHIPWORM

**¹term** \'tərm\ *n* **1 :** END, TERMINATION **2 :** DURATION; *esp* **:** a period of time fixed esp. by law or custom **3 :** a mathematical expression connected with another by a plus or minus sign; *also* **:** any of the members of a ratio or of a series **4** : a word or expression that has a precise meaning in some uses or is peculiar to a subject or field **5** *pl* : PROVISIONS, CONDITIONS ⟨~s of a contract⟩ **6** *pl* : mutual relationship ⟨are on good ~s⟩ **7** : AGREEMENT, CONCORD

²**term** *vb* : to apply a term to : CALL

**ter·ma·gant** \'tər-mə-gənt\ *n* : an overbearing or nagging woman : SHREW **syn** virago, vixen

¹**ter·mi·nal** \'tər-mən-ᵊl\ *adj* : of, relating to, or forming an end, limit, or terminus **syn** final, concluding, last, latest, extreme

²**terminal** *n* **1** : EXTREMITY, END **2** : a device at the end of a wire or on an apparatus for making an electrical connection **3** : either end of a carrier line (as a railroad) with its handling and storage facilities and stations; *also* : a freight or passenger station

**ter·mi·nate** \'tər-mə-ˌnāt\ *vb* -nated; -nat·ing : to bring or come to an end **syn** conclude, finish, complete — **ter·mi·na·ble** \-nə-bəl\ *adj* — **ter·mi·na·tion** \ˌtər-mə-'nā-shən\ *n*

**ter·mi·na·tor** \'tər-mə-ˌnāt-ər\ *n* : one that terminates

**ter·mi·nol·o·gy** \ˌtər-mə-'näl-ə-jē\ *n* : the technical or special terms used in a business, art, science, or special subject

**ter·mi·nus** \'tər-mə-nəs\ *n, pl* -ni \-ˌnī\ *or* -nus·es **1** : final goal : END **2** : either end of a transportation line, travel route, pipeline, or canal; *also* : the station or city at such a place

**ter·mite** \'tər-ˌmīt\ *n* : any of a large group of pale soft-bodied social insects that feed on wood

**tern** \'tərn\ *n* : any of various small sea gulls with narrow wings and a black cap and light body

**ter·na·ry** \'tər-nə-rē\ *adj* **1** : of, relating to, or proceeding by threes **2** : having three elements or parts **3** : third in order or rank

**terr** *abbr* territory

¹**ter·race** \'ter-əs\ *n* **1** : a flat roof or open platform **2** : a level paved or planted area next to a building **3** : an embankment with level top **4** : a bank or ridge on a slope to conserve moisture and soil **5** : a row of houses on raised land; *also* : a street with such a row of houses **6** : a strip of park in the middle of a street

²**terrace** *vb* **ter·raced; ter·rac·ing** : to form into a terrace or supply with terraces

**ter·ra-cot·ta** \ˌter-ə-'kät-ə\ *n* [It *terra cotta*, lit., baked earth] : a reddish brown earthenware used for vases and small statues

**terra fir·ma** \-'fər-mə\ *n* : solid ground

**ter·rain** \tə-'rān\ *n* : a tract of ground considered with reference to its surface features ⟨a rough ~⟩

**ter·ra in·cog·ni·ta** \ˌter-ə-ˌin-ˌkäg-'nēt-ə\ *n, pl* **ter·rae in·cog·ni·tae** \'ter-ˌī-ˌin-ˌkäg-nē-tī\ : an unexplored area or field of knowledge

**ter·ra·pin** \'ter-ə-pən\ *n* : any of various No. American edible turtles of fresh or brackish water

**ter·rar·i·um** \tə-'rar-ē-əm\ *n, pl* -ia \-ē-ə\ *or* -i·ums : a vivarium without standing water

**ter·res·tri·al** \tə-'res-t(r)ē-əl\ *adj* **1** : of or relating to the earth or its inhabitants **2** : living or growing on land ⟨~ plants⟩ **syn** mundane, mortal

**ter·ri·ble** \'ter-ə-bəl\ *adj* **1** : exciting terror : FEARFUL, DREADFUL ⟨~ weapons⟩ **2** : hard to bear : DISTRESSING ⟨a ~ situation⟩ **3** : extreme in degree : INTENSE ⟨~ heat⟩ **4** : of very poor quality : AWFUL ⟨a ~ play⟩ **syn** frightful, horrible, shocking, appalling — **ter·ri·bly** \-blē\ *adv*

**ter·ri·er** \'ter-ē-ər\ *n* [F (chien) terrier, lit., earth dog, fr. terrier of earth, fr. ML terrarius, fr. L terra earth] : any of various usu. small dogs orig. used by hunters to drive small game from holes

**ter·rif·ic** \tə-'rif-ik\ *adj* **1** : exciting terror : AWESOME **2** : EXTRAORDINARY, ASTOUNDING ⟨~ speed⟩ **3** : unusually fine : MAGNIFICENT **syn** terrible, frightful, dreadful, fearful, horrible, awful

**ter·ri·fy** \'ter-ə-ˌfī\ *vb* -fied; -fy·ing : to fill with terror : FRIGHTEN **syn** scare, terrorize, startle, intimidate — **ter·ri·fy·ing·ly** *adv*

¹**ter·ri·to·ri·al** \ˌter-ə-'tōr-ē-əl\ *adj* **1** : of or relating to a territory ⟨~ government⟩ **2** : of or relating to an assigned area ⟨~ commanders⟩

²**territorial** *n* : a member of a territorial military unit

**ter·ri·to·ry** \'ter-ə-ˌtōr-ē\ *n, pl* -ries **1** : a geographical area belonging to or under the jurisdiction of a governmental authority **2** : a part of the U.S. not included within any state but organized with a separate legislature **3** : REGION, DISTRICT; *also* : a region in which one feels at home **4** : a field of knowledge or interest **5** : an assigned area

**ter·ror** \'ter-ər\ *n* **1** : a state of intense fear : FRIGHT **2** : one that inspires fear **syn** panic, consternation, dread, alarm, dismay, horror, trepidation

**ter·ror·ism** \'ter-ər-ˌiz-əm\ *n* : the systematic use of terror esp. as a means of coercion — **ter·ror·ist** \-əst\ *adj or n*

**ter·ror·ize** \'ter-ər-ˌīz\ *vb* -ized; -iz·ing **1** : to fill with terror : SCARE **2** : to coerce by threat or violence **syn** terrify, frighten, alarm, startle

**ter·ry** \'ter-ē\ *n, pl* **terries** : an absorbent fabric with a loose pile of uncut loops

**terry cloth** *n* : TERRY

**terse** \'tərs\ *adj* **ters·er; ters·est** [L *tersus* clean, neat, fr. pp. of *tergēre* to wipe off] : effectively brief : CONCISE — **terse·ly** *adv* — **terse·ness** *n*

**ter·tia·ry** \'tər-shē-ˌer-ē\ *adj* **1** : of third rank, importance, or value **2** : occurring or being in the third stage

**tes·sel·late** \'tes-ə-ˌlāt\ *vb* -lat·ed; -lat·ing : to form into or adorn with mosaic

¹**test** \'test\ *n* [ME, vessel in which metals were assayed, fr. MF, fr. L

*testum* earthen vessel] **1 :** a critical examination or evaluation **:** TRIAL **2 :** a means or result of testing

²**test** *vb* **1 :** to put to test **:** TRY, EXAMINE **2 :** to undergo or score on tests ⟨an ore that ∼s high in gold⟩

**tes·ta·ment** \'tes-tə-mənt\ *n* **1** *cap* **:** either of two main divisions (**Old Testament, New Testament**) of the Bible **2 :** EVIDENCE, WITNESS **3 :** CREDO **4 :** an act by which a person determines the disposition of his property after his death **:** WILL — **tes·ta·men·ta·ry** \,tes-tə-'ment-(ə-)rē\ *adj*

**tes·tate** \'tes-,tāt, -tət\ *adj* **:** having made a valid will

**tes·ta·tor** \'tes-,tāt-ər, tes-'tāt-\ *n* **:** a person who leaves a will in force at his death — **tes·ta·trix** \tes-'tā-triks\ *n*

¹**tes·ter** \'tēs-tər, 'tes-\ *n* **:** a canopy over a bed, pulpit, or altar

²**test·er** \'tes-tər\ *n* **:** one that tests

**tes·ti·cle** \'tes-ti-kəl\ *n* **:** TESTIS

**tes·ti·fy** \'tes-tə-ˌfī\ *vb* **-fied; -fy·ing 1 :** to make a statement based on personal knowledge or belief **:** bear witness **2 :** to serve as evidence or proof *syn* swear, affirm

**tes·ti·mo·ni·al** \,tes-tə-'mō-nē-əl\ *n* **1 :** a statement testifying to a person's good character or to the worth of something **2 :** an expression of appreciation **:** TRIBUTE — **testimonial** *adj*

**tes·ti·mo·ny** \'tes-tə-,mō-nē\ *n, pl* **-nies 1 :** a solemn declaration made by a witness under oath esp. in a court **2 :** evidence based on observation or knowledge **3 :** an outward sign **:** SYMBOL *syn* evidence, affidavit

**tes·tis** \'tes-təs\ *n, pl* **tes·tes** \'tes-,tēz\ **:** a male reproductive gland

**tes·tos·ter·one** \te-'stäs-tə-,rōn\ *n* **:** a male sex hormone responsible for maintaining secondary sex characters

**test tube** *n* **:** a thin glass tube closed at one end and used esp. in chemistry and biology

**tes·ty** \'tes-tē\ *adj* **tes·ti·er; -est** [ME *testif*, fr. Anglo-French (the French of medieval England), headstrong, fr. OF *teste* head, fr. LL *testa* skull, fr. L, shell] **:** marked by ill humor **:** easily annoyed

**tet·a·nus** \'tet-ᵊn-əs\ *n* **:** a disease caused by bacterial poisons and marked by violent muscular spasm esp. of the jaw — **tet·a·nal** \-əl\ *adj*

**tetchy** \'tech-ē\ *adj* **tetchi·er; -est :** irritably or peevishly sensitive

**tête-à-tête** \,tāt-ə-'tāt\ *adv* [F, lit., head to head] **:** PRIVATELY, FAMILIARLY

**tête-à-tête** \'tāt-ə-,tāt\ *n* **:** a private conversation between two persons

**tête-à-tête** \,tāt-ə-,tāt\ *adj* **:** being face-to-face **:** PRIVATE

¹**teth·er** \'teth-ər\ *n* **1 :** a line (as of rope or chain) by which an animal is fastened so as to restrict its range **2 :** the limit of one's strength or resources

²**tether** *vb* **:** to fasten or restrain by or as if by a tether

**tet·ra·eth·yl·lead** \-,eth-əl-'led\ *n* **:** a heavy oily poisonous liquid used as an antiknock agent

**tet·ra·hy·dro·can·nab·i·nol** \-,hī-drə-kə-'nab-ə-,nól, -,nōl\ *n* **:** THC

**te·tram·e·ter** \te-'tram-ət-ər\ *n* **:** a line consisting of four metrical feet

**Teu·ton·ic** \t(y)ü-'tän-ik\ *adj* **:** GERMANIC

**Tex** *abbr* Texas

**text** \'tekst\ *n* **1 :** the actual words of an author's work **2 :** the main body of printed or written matter on a page **3 :** a scriptural passage chosen as the subject esp. of a sermon **4 :** TEXTBOOK **5 :** THEME, TOPIC — **tex·tu·al** \'teks-chə-(-wə)l\ *adj*

**text·book** \'teks(t)-,bük\ *n* **:** a book used in the study of a subject

**tex·tile** \'tek-,stīl, 'teks-tᵊl\ *n* **:** CLOTH; *esp* **:** a woven or knit cloth

**tex·ture** \'teks-chər\ *n* **1 :** the visual or tactile surface characteristics and appearance of something ⟨a coarse ∼⟩ **2 :** essential part **3 :** basic scheme or structure **:** FABRIC **4 :** overall structure

**T-group** \'tē-,grüp\ *n* [*training group*] **:** a group of people under a trainer who seek to develop self-awareness and sensitivity to others by verbalizing feelings uninhibitedly

¹**Th** *abbr* Thursday

²**Th** *symbol* thorium

¹**-th** — see ¹-ETH

²**-th** *or* **-eth** *adj suffix* — used in forming ordinal numbers ⟨hundred*th*⟩

³**-th** *n suffix* **1 :** act or process **2 :** state or condition ⟨dear*th*⟩

**Thai** \'tī\ *n* **:** a native or inhabitant of Thailand — **Thai** *adj*

**thal·a·mus** \'thal-ə-məs\ *n, pl* **-mi** \-,mī\ **:** a subdivision of the brain that forms a coordinating center through which afferent nerve impulses are directed to appropriate parts of the brain cortex

**tha·lid·o·mide** \thə-'lid-ə-,mīd\ *n* **:** a sedative and hypnotic drug found to cause malformation of infants born to mothers using it during pregnancy

**thal·li·um** \'thal-ē-əm\ *n* **:** a poisonous metallic chemical element

¹**than** \than, (')than\ *conj* **1** — used after a comparative adjective or adverb to introduce the second part of a comparison expressing inequality ⟨older ∼ I am⟩ **2** — used after *other* or a word of similar meaning to express a difference of kind, manner, or identity ⟨adults other ∼ parents⟩

²**than** *prep* **:** in comparison with ⟨older ∼ me⟩

**thane** \'thān\ *n* **1 :** a free retainer of an Anglo-Saxon lord **2 :** a Scottish feudal lord

**thank** \'thaŋk\ *vb* **:** to express gratitude to ⟨∼ed him for the present⟩

**thank·ful** \'thaŋk-fəl\ *adj* **1 :** conscious of benefit received **2 :** expressive of thanks **3 :** GLAD — **thank·ful·ly** \-ē\ *adv* — **thank·ful·ness** *n*

**thank·less** \'thaŋ-kləs\ *adj* **1 :** UNGRATEFUL **2 :** UNAPPRECIATED

**thanks** \'thaŋks\ *n pl* **:** an expression of gratitude

**thanks·giv·ing** \thaŋks-'giv-iŋ\ *n* **1 :** the act of giving thanks **2 :** prayer expressing gratitude **3** *cap* **:** the fourth Thursday in November observed as a legal holiday for giving thanks for divine goodness

**¹that** \(')that\ *pron, pl* **those** \(')thōz\ **1 :** the one indicated, mentioned, or understood ⟨~'s my wife⟩ **2 :** the one farther away or first mentioned ⟨this is an elm, ~'s a maple⟩ **3 :** what has been indicated or mentioned ⟨after ~, we left⟩ **4 :** the one or ones **:** IT, THEY ⟨*those* who wish to leave may do so⟩

**²that** *adj, pl* **those 1 :** being the one mentioned, indicated, or understood ⟨~ boy⟩ ⟨*those* people⟩ **2 :** being the one farther away or first mentioned ⟨this chair or ~ one⟩

**³that** \that, (,)that\ *conj* **1 :** the following, namely ⟨he said ~ he would⟩; *also* **:** which is, namely ⟨there's a chance ~ it may fail⟩ **2 :** to this end or purpose ⟨shouted ~ all might hear⟩ **3 :** as to result in the following, namely ⟨so heavy ~ it can't be moved⟩ **4 :** for this reason, namely **:** BECAUSE ⟨we're glad ~ you came⟩ **5 :** I wish this, or I am surprised or indignant at this, namely ⟨~ it should come to this⟩

**⁴that** \that, (,)that\ *pron* **1 :** WHO, WHOM, WHICH ⟨the man ~ saw you⟩ ⟨the man ~ you saw⟩ ⟨the money ~ was spent⟩ **2 :** in, on, or at which ⟨the way ~ he drives⟩ ⟨the day ~ it rained⟩

**⁵that** \'that\ *adv* **:** to such an extent or degree ⟨I like it, but not ~ much⟩

**¹thatch** \'thach\ *vb* **:** to cover with thatch

**²thatch** *n* **1 :** plant material (as straw) for use as roofing **2 :** a covering of or as if of thatch ⟨a ~ of white hair⟩

**thaw** \'thȯ\ *vb* **1 :** to melt or cause to melt **2 :** to become so warm as to melt ice or snow **3 :** to abandon aloofness or hostility **syn** liquefy — **thaw** *n*

**THC** \,tē-,āch-'sē\ *n* [*tetra*hydro*c*annabinol] **:** a physiologically active liquid from hemp plant resin that is the chief intoxicant in marijuana

**ThD** *abbr* [NL *theologiae doctor*] doctor of theology

**¹the** \the, before vowel sounds usu thē\ *definite article* **1 :** that in particular **2** — used before adjectives functioning as nouns ⟨a word to ~ wise⟩

**²the** *adv* **1 :** to what extent ⟨~ sooner, the better⟩ **2 :** to that extent ⟨the sooner, ~ better⟩

**theat** *abbr* theatrical

**the·ater** *or* **the·atre** \'thē-ət-ər\ *n* **1 :** a building for dramatic performances; *also* **:** a building or area for showing motion pictures **2 :** a place (as a lecture room) similar to such a building **3 :** a place of enactment of significant events **4 :** dramatic literature or performance

**theater–in–the–round** *n* **:** ARENA THEATER

**the·at·ri·cal** \thē-'a-tri-kəl\ *adj* **1 :** of or relating to the theater **2 :** marked by artificiality of emotion **:** HISTRIONIC **3 :** marked by extravagant display **:** SHOWY **syn** dramatic, melodramatic

**the·at·ri·cals** \-kəlz\ *n pl* **:** the performance of plays

**the·at·rics** \thē-'a-triks\ *n pl* **1 :** THEATRICALS **2 :** staged or contrived effects

**thee** \(')thē\ *pron, objective case of* THOU

**theft** \'theft\ *n* **:** the act of stealing

**thegn** \'thān\ *n* **:** THANE 1

**their** \thər, (,)theər\ *adj* **:** of or relating to them or themselves

**theirs** \'theərz\ *pron* **:** their one **:** their ones

**the·ism** \'thē-,iz-əm\ *n* **:** belief in the existence of a god or gods — **the·ist** \-əst\ *n or adj* — **the·is·tic** \thē-'is-tik\ *adj*

**them** \(th)əm, (')them\ *pron, objective case of* THEY

**theme** \'thēm\ *n* **1 :** a subject or topic of discourse or of artistic representation **2 :** a written exercise **:** COMPOSITION **3 :** a melodic subject of a musical composition or movement — **the·mat·ic** \thi-'mat-ik\ *adj*

**them·selves** \thəm-'selvz, them-\ *pron pl* **:** THEY, THEM — used reflexively, for emphasis, or in absolute constructions ⟨they govern ~⟩ ⟨they ~ couldn't come⟩ ⟨~ busy, they sent me⟩

**¹then** \(')then\ *adv* **1 :** at that time **2 :** soon after that **:** NEXT **3 :** in addition **:** BESIDES **4 :** in that case **5 :** CONSEQUENTLY

**²then** \'then\ *n* **:** that time ⟨since ~⟩

**³then** \'then\ *adj* **:** existing or acting at that time ⟨the ~ king⟩

**thence** \'thens, 'thens\ *adv* **1 :** from that place **2** *archaic* **:** THENCEFORTH **3 :** from that fact **:** THEREFROM

**thence·forth** \-,fōrth\ *adv* **:** from that time forward **:** THEREAFTER

**thence·for·ward** \thens-'fȯr-wərd, thens-\ *also* **thence·for·wards** \-wərdz\ *adv* **:** onward from that place or time **:** THENCEFORTH

**the·oc·ra·cy** \thē-'äk-rə-sē\ *n, pl* **-cies 1 :** government by officials regarded as divinely inspired **2 :** a state governed by a theocracy — **the·o·crat·ic** \,thē-ə-'krat-ik\ *adj*

**theol** *abbr* theological; theology

**the·ol·o·gy** \thē-'äl-ə-jē\ *n, pl* **-gies 1 :** the study of religion and of religious ideas and beliefs; *esp* **:** a branch of theology treating of God and his relation to the world **2 :** a theory or system of theology — **the·o·lo·gian** \,thē-ə-'lō-jən\ *n* — **the·o·log·i·cal** \-'läj-i-kəl\ *adj*

**the·o·rem** \'thē-ə-rəm, 'thir-əm\ *n* **1 :** a statement in mathematics that has been or is to be proved **2 :** an idea accepted or proposed as a demonstrable truth **:** PROPOSITION

**the·o·ret·i·cal** \,thē-ə-'ret-i-kəl\ *also* **the·o·ret·ic** \-ik\ *adj* **1 :** relating to or having the character of theory **2 :** existing only in theory — **the·o·ret·i·cal·ly** \-i-k(ə-)lē\ *adv*

**the·o·rize** \'thē-ə-,rīz\ *vb* **-rized; -riz·ing :** to form a theory **:** SPECULATE — **the·o·rist** *n*

**the·o·ry** \'thē-ə-rē, 'thir-ē\ *n, pl* **-ries**

**1 :** the general principles drawn from any body of facts (as in science) **2 :** a plausible or scientifically acceptable general principle offered to explain observed facts **3 :** HYPOTHESIS, GUESS **4 :** abstract thought

**theory of games :** the analysis of a situation involving conflicting interests (as in business) in terms of gains and losses among opposing players

**the·os·o·phy** \thē-'äs-ə-fē\ *n* **:** belief about God and the world held to be based on mystical insight — **theo·soph·i·cal** \,thē-ə-'säf-i-kəl\ *adj* — **the·os·o·phist** \thē-'äs-ə-fəst\ *n*

**ther·a·peu·tic** \,ther-ə-'pyüt-ik\ *adj* [Gk *therapeutikos,* fr. *therapeuein* to attend, treat, fr. *theraps* attendant] **:** of, relating to, or dealing with healing and esp. with remedies for diseases — **ther·a·peu·ti·cal·ly** \-i-k(ə-)lē\ *adv*

**ther·a·peu·tics** \,ther-ə-'pyüt-iks\ *n* **:** a branch of medical science dealing with the use of remedies

**ther·a·py** \'ther-ə-pē\ *n, pl* **-pies :** remedial treatment of bodily, mental, or social disorders or maladjustment — **ther·a·pist** \-pəst\ *n*

**¹there** \thaər, 'theər\ *adv* **1 :** in or at that place — often used interjectionally **2 :** to or into that place **:** THITHER **3 :** in that matter or respect

**²there** \(,)thā(ə)r, (,)the(ə)r, thər\ *pron* — used as a function word to introduce a sentence or clause ⟨~'s a man here⟩ ⟨~'s trouble brewing⟩

**³there** \'thaər, 'theər\ *n* **1 :** that place ⟨get away from ~⟩ **2 :** that point ⟨you take it from ~⟩

**there·abouts** *or* **there·about** \,thar-ə-baùt(s), 'thar-ə-,baùt(s), ,ther-ə-'baùt(s), 'ther-ə-,\ *adv* **1 :** near that place or time **2 :** near that number, degree, or quantity

**there·af·ter** \thar-'af-tər, ther-\ *adv* **:** after that **:** AFTERWARD

**there·at** \-'at\ *adv* **1 :** at that place **2 :** at that occurrence **:** on that account

**there·by** \tha(ə)r-'bī, the(ə)r-, 'tha(ə)r-,bī, 'the(ə)r-,bī\ *adv* **1 :** by that **:** by that means **2 :** connected with or with reference to that

**there·for** \tha(ə)r-'fòr, the(ə)r-\ *adv* **:** for or in return for that

**there·fore** \'tha(ə)r-,fòr, 'the(ə)r-\ *adv* **:** for that reason **:** CONSEQUENTLY

**there·from** \tha(ə)r-'frəm, the(ə)r-\ *adv* **:** from that or it

**there·in** \thar-'in, ther-\ *adv* **1 :** in or into that place, time, or thing **2 :** in that respect

**there·of** \-'əv, -'äv\ *adv* **1 :** of that or it **2 :** from that **:** THEREFROM

**there·on** \'òn, -'än\ *adv* **1 :** on that **2** *archaic* **:** THEREUPON 3

**there·to** \tha(ə)r-'tü, the(ə)r-\ *adv* **:** to that

**there·un·to** \thar-'ən-(,)tü; ,thar-ən-'tü, ,ther-\ *adv, archaic* **:** THERETO

**there·upon** \'thar-ə-,pón, 'ther-,-,pän; ,thar-ə-'pón, -'pän, ,ther-\ *adv* **1 :** on that matter **:** THEREON **2 :** THEREFORE **3 :** immediately after that **:** at once

**there·with** \tha(ə)r-'with, the(ə)r-,

-'with\ *adv* **1 :** with that **2** *archaic* **:** THEREUPON, FORTHWITH

**there·with·al** \'tha(ə)r-with-,ól, 'the(ə)r-, -with-\ *adv* **1** *archaic* **:** BESIDES **2 :** THEREWITH

**therm** *abbr* thermometer

**ther·mal** \'thər-məl\ *adj* **1 :** of, relating to, or caused by heat **2 :** designed to prevent the loss of body heat ⟨~ underwear⟩ — **ther·mal·ly** \-ē\ *adv*

**thermal pollution** *n* **:** the discharge of liquid (as waste water from a factory) into a natural body of water at such a high temperature that harm to plant and animal life may result

**therm·is·tor** \'thər-,mis-tər\ *n* **:** an electrical resistor whose resistance varies sharply with temperature

**ther·mo·cline** \'thər-mə-,klīn\ *n* **:** a layer in a thermally stratified body of water that separates zones of different temperature

**ther·mo·dy·nam·ics** \,thər-mə-dī-'nam-iks\ *n* **:** physics that deals with the mechanical action or relations of heat — **ther·mo·dy·nam·ic** \-ik\ *adj* — **ther·mo·dy·nam·i·cal·ly** \-i-k(ə-)lē\ *adv*

**ther·mom·e·ter** \thə(r)-'mäm-ət-ər\ *n* [F *thermomètre,* fr. Gk *thermē* heat + *metron* measure] **:** an instrument for measuring temperature commonly by means of the expansion or contraction of mercury or alcohol as indicated by its rise or fall in a thin glass tube — **ther·mo·met·ric** \,thər-mə-'met-rik\ *adj* — **ther·mo·met·ri·cal·ly** \-ri-k(ə-)lē\ *adv*

**ther·mo·nu·cle·ar** \,thər-mō-'n(y)ü-klē-ər\ *adj* **1 :** of or relating to changes in the nucleus of atoms of low atomic weight (as hydrogen) that require a very high temperature (as in the hydrogen bomb) **2 :** utilizing or relating to a thermonuclear bomb ⟨~ war⟩

**ther·mo·plas·tic** \,thər-mə-'plas-tik\ *adj* **:** having the property of softening when heated and of hardening when cooled ⟨~ resins⟩ — **thermoplastic** *n* — **ther·mo·plas·tic·i·ty** \-,plas-'tis-ət-ē\ *n*

**ther·mo·reg·u·la·tor** \,thər-mō-'reg-yə-,lāt-ər\ *n* **:** a device for the regulation of temperature

**ther·mos** \'thər-məs\ *n* **:** VACUUM BOTTLE

**ther·mo·sphere** \'thər-mə-,sfiər\ *n* **:** the part of the earth's atmosphere that begins at about 50 miles above the earth's surface, extends to outer space, and is characterized by steadily increasing temperature with height — **ther·mo·spher·ic** \,thər-mə-'sfiər-ik, -'sfer-\ *adj*

**ther·mo·stat** \'thər-mə-,stat\ *n* **:** a device that automatically controls temperature (as by regulating a flow of oil or electricity) — **ther·mo·stat·ic** \,thər-mə-'stat-ik\ *adj* — **ther·mo·stat·i·cal·ly** \-i-k(ə-)lē\ *adv*

**the·sau·rus** \thi-'sór-əs\ *n, pl* **-sau·ri** \-'sór-,ī\ *or* **-sau·rus·es** \-'sór-ə-səz\ [NL, fr. L, treasure, collection, fr. Gk *thēsauros*] **:** a book of words or of information about a particular field; *esp* : a dictionary of synonyms — **the·sau·ral** \-'sȯr-əl\ *adj*

**these** *pl of* THIS

**the·sis** \'thē-səs\ *n, pl* **the·ses** \'thē-ˌsēz\ **1** : a proposition that a person advances and offers to maintain by argument **2** : an essay embodying results of original research; *esp* : one written by a candidate for an academic degree

**¹thes·pi·an** \'thes-pē-ən\ *adj, often cap* [fr. *Thespis*, 6th cent. B.C. Greek poet and reputed originator of tragedy] : relating to the drama : DRAMATIC

**²thespian** *n* : ACTOR

**Thess** *abbr* Thessalonians

**thew** \'th(y)ü\ *n* : MUSCLE, SINEW — usu. used in pl.

**they** \(')thā\ *pron* **1** : those individuals under discussion : the ones previously mentioned or referred to **2** : unspecified persons : PEOPLE

**thi·a·mine** \'thī-ə-mən, -ˌmēn\ *also* **thi·a·min** \-mən\ *n* : a vitamin essential to normal metabolism and nerve function

**¹thick** \'thik\ *adj* **1** : having relatively great depth or extent from one surface to its opposite ⟨a ~ plank⟩; *also* : heavily built : THICKSET **2** : densely massed : CROWDED; *also* : FREQUENT, NUMEROUS **3** : dense or viscous in consistency ⟨~ syrup⟩ **4** : marked by haze, fog, or mist ⟨~ weather⟩ **5** : measuring in thickness (12 inches ~) **6** : imperfectly articulated : INDISTINCT ⟨~ speech⟩ **7** : STUPID, OBTUSE **8** : associated on close terms : INTIMATE **9** : EXCESSIVE **syn** stocky, compact, close, confidential — **thick·ly** *adv*

**²thick** *n* **1** : the most crowded or active part **2** : the part of greatest thickness

**thick·en** \'thik-ən\ *vb* **thick·ened; thick·en·ing** \-(ə-)niŋ\ : to make or become thick — **thick·en·er** \-(ə-)nər\ *n*

**thick·et** \'thik-ət\ *n* : a dense growth of bushes or small trees

**thick·ness** \-nəs\ *n* **1** : the quality or state of being thick **2** : the smallest of three dimensions ⟨length, width, and ~⟩ **3** : LAYER, SHEET ⟨a single ~ of canvas⟩

**thick·set** \'thik-'set\ *adj* **1** : closely placed or planted **2** : having a thick body : BURLY

**thick-skinned** \-'skind\ *adj* **1** : having a thick skin **2** : INSENSITIVE

**thief** \'thēf\ *n, pl* **thieves** \'thēvz\ : one that steals esp. secretly

**thieve** \'thēv\ *vb* **thieved; thiev·ing** : STEAL, ROB **syn** plunder, rifle, loot, burglarize

**thiev·ery** \'thēv-(ə-)rē\ *n, pl* **-er·ies** : the act of stealing : THEFT

**thigh** \'thī\ *n* : the part of the vertebrate hind limb between the knee and the hip

**thigh·bone** \'thī-'bōn, -ˌbōn\ *n* : FEMUR

**thim·ble** \'thim-bəl\ *n* : a cap or guard used in sewing to protect the finger when pushing the needle — **thim·ble·ful** *n*

**¹thin** \'thin\ *adj* **thin·ner; thin·nest** **1** : having little extent from one surface through to its opposite : not thick : SLENDER **2** : not closely set or placed : SPARSE ⟨~ hair⟩ **3** : not dense or not dense enough : more fluid or rarefied than normal ⟨~ air⟩ ⟨~ syrup⟩ **4** : lacking substance, fullness, or strength ⟨~ broth⟩ **5** : FLIMSY **syn** slim, slight, tenuous — **thin·ly** *adv* — **thin·ness** \'thin-nəs\ *n*

**²thin** *vb* **thinned; thin·ning** : to make or become thin

**thine** \'thīn\ *pron, archaic* : one or the ones belonging to thee

**thing** \'thiŋ\ *n* **1** : a matter of concern : AFFAIR ⟨~s to do⟩ **2** *pl* : state of affairs ⟨~s are improving⟩ **3** : EVENT, CIRCUMSTANCE ⟨the crime was a terrible ~⟩ **4** : DEED, ACT ⟨expected great ~s of him⟩ **5** : a distinct entity : OBJECT **6** : an inanimate object distinguished from a living being **7** *pl* : POSSESSIONS, EFFECTS ⟨packed his ~s⟩ **8** : an article of clothing **9** : DETAIL, POINT **10** : IDEA, NOTION **11** : something one likes to do : SPECIALTY ⟨doing his ~⟩

**think** \'thiŋk\ *vb* **thought** \'thȯt\; **think·ing** **1** : to form or have in the mind **2** : to have as an opinion : BELIEVE **3** : to reflect on : PONDER **4** : to call to mind : REMEMBER **5** : to devise by thinking ⟨*thought* up a plan to escape⟩ **6** : to form a mental picture of : IMAGINE **7** : REASON **syn** conceive, fancy, realize, cogitate, reflect, speculate, deliberate — **think·er** *n*

**think tank** *n* : an institute, corporation, or group organized for interdisciplinary research (as in technological or social problems)

**thin·ner** \'thin-ər\ *n* : a volatile liquid (as turpentine) used to thin paint

**thin-skinned** \'thin-'skind\ *adj* **1** : having a thin skin **2** : extremely sensitive to criticism

**¹third** \'thərd\ *adj* **1** : being number three in a countable series **2** : next after the second — **third** *or* **third·ly** *adv*

**²third** *n* **1** : one that is third **2** : one of three equal parts of something **3** : the third forward gear in an automotive vehicle

**third degree** *n* : the subjection of a prisoner to mental or physical torture to force a confession

**third dimension** *n* **1** : thickness, depth, or apparent thickness or depth that confers solidity on an object **2** : a quality that confers reality — **third-dimensional** *adj*

**third world** *n, often cap T&W* **1** : a group of nations esp. in Africa and Asia that are not aligned with either the Communist or the non-Communist blocs **2** : an aggregate of minority groups within a larger predominant culture **3** : the aggregate of the underdeveloped nations of the world

**¹thirst** \'thərst\ *n* **1** : a feeling of dryness in the mouth and throat associated with a wish to drink; *also* : a bodily condition producing this **2** : an ardent desire **:** CRAVING ⟨a ~ for knowledge⟩ — **thirsty** adj

²**thirst** vb **1 :** to need drink **:** suffer thirst **2 :** to have a strong desire **:** CRAVE

**thir·teen** \,thər-'tēn, 'thər-\ n **:** one more than 12 — **thirteen** adj or pron — **thir·teenth** \-'tēnth\ adj or n

**thir·ty** \'thərt-ē\ n, pl **thirties : 1 :** three times 10 — **thir·ti·eth** \-ē-əth\ adj or n — **thirty** adj or pron

¹**this** \(')this\ pron, pl **these** \(')thēz\ **1 :** the one close or closest in time or space ⟨~ is your book⟩ **2 :** what is in the present or under immediate observation or discussion ⟨~ is a mess⟩; also **:** what is happening or being done now ⟨after ~ we'll leave⟩

²**this** adj, pl **these 1 :** being the one near, present, just mentioned, or more immediately under observation ⟨~ book⟩ **2 :** constituting the immediate past or future ⟨friends all these years⟩

³**this** \'this\ adv **:** to such an extent or degree ⟨we need a book about ~ big⟩

**this·tle** \'this-əl\ n **:** any of several tall prickly herbs

**this·tle·down** \-,daun\ n **:** the down from the ripe flower head of a thistle

¹**thith·er** \'thith-ər\ adv **:** to that place

²**thither** adj **:** being on the farther side

ˌ**thith·er·ward** \-wərd\ adv **:** toward that place **:** THITHER

**thole** \'thōl\ n **:** a pin set in the gunwale of a boat against which an oar pivots in rowing

**thong** \'thòŋ\ n **1 :** a strip esp. of leather or hide **2 :** a sandal held on the foot by a thong fitting between the toes

**tho·rax** \'thōr-,aks\ n, pl **tho·rax·es** or **tho·ra·ces** \'thōr-ə-,sēz\ **1 :** the part of the body of a mammal between the neck and the abdomen; also **:** its cavity **2 :** the middle of the three divisions of the body of an insect — **tho·rac·ic** \thə-'ras-ik\ adj

**tho·ri·um** \'thōr-ē-əm\ n **:** a radioactive metallic chemical element

**thorn** \'thòrn\ n **1 :** a woody plant bearing sharp processes **2 :** a sharp rigid plant process that is usu. a modified leafless branch **3 :** something that causes distress — **thorny** adj

**thor·ough** \'thər-ō\ adj **1 :** COMPLETE, EXHAUSTIVE ⟨a ~ search⟩ **2 :** very careful **:** PAINSTAKING ⟨a ~ scholar⟩ **3 :** having full mastery — **thor·ough·ly** adv — **thor·ough·ness** n

¹**thor·ough·bred** \'thər-ə-,bred\ adj **1 :** bred from the best blood through a long line **2** cap **:** of or relating to the Thoroughbred breed of horses **3 :** marked by high-spirited grace

²**thoroughbred** n **1** cap **:** any of an English breed of light speedy horses kept chiefly for racing **2 :** one (as a pedigreed animal) of excellent quality

**thor·ough·fare** \-,faər\ n **:** a public road or street

**thor·ough·go·ing** \,thər-ə-'gō-iŋ,,thə-rə-,gō-iŋ\ adj **:** marked by thoroughness or zeal

**thorp** \'thòrp\ n, archaic **:** VILLAGE

ˌ**hose** pl of THAT

¹**thou** \(')thau\ pron, **:** archaic the person addressed

²**thou** \'thau\ n, pl **thou** or **thous** \'thauz\ **:** a thousand of something

¹**though** \'thō\ adv **:** HOWEVER, NEVERTHELESS ⟨not for long, ~⟩

²**though** \(,)thō\ conj **1 :** despite the fact that ⟨~ the odds are hopeless, they fight on⟩ **2 :** granting that ⟨~ it may look bad, still, all is not lost⟩

¹**thought** \'thòt\ past of THINK

²**thought** n **1 :** the process of thinking **2 :** serious consideration **:** REGARD **3 :** reasoning power **4 :** the power to imagine **:** CONCEPTION **5 :** IDEA, NOTION **6 :** OPINION, BELIEF **7 :** a slight amount

**thought·ful** \'thòt-fəl\ adj **1 :** absorbed in thought **2 :** marked by careful thinking ⟨a ~ essay⟩ **3 :** considerate of others ⟨a ~ host⟩ — **thought·ful·ly** \-ē\ adv — **thought·ful·ness** n

**thought·less** \-ləs\ adj **1 :** insufficiently alert **:** CARELESS ⟨a ~ worker⟩ **2 :** RECKLESS ⟨a ~ act⟩ **3 :** lacking concern for others **:** INCONSIDERATE ⟨~ remarks⟩ — **thought·less·ly** adv — **thought·less·ness** n

**thou·sand** \'thauz-'nd\ n, pl **thousands** or **thousand :** 10 times 100 — **thousand** adj — **thou·sandth** \-'nth\ adj or n

**thrall** \'thròl\ n **1 :** SLAVE, BONDMAN **2 :** THRALLDOM

**thrall·dom** or **thral·dom** \'thròl-dəm\ n **:** the condition of a thrall

**thrash** \'thrash\ vb **1 :** THRESH **1 2 :** BEAT, WHIP; also **:** DEFEAT **3 :** to move about violently **4 :** to go over again and again ⟨~ over the matter⟩; also **:** to hammer out ⟨~ out a plan⟩

¹**thrash·er** \'thrash-ər\ n **:** one that thrashes or threshes

²**thrasher** n **:** a long-tailed bird resembling a thrush

¹**thread** \'thred\ n **1 :** a thin fine cord formed by spinning and twisting short textile fibers into a continuous strand **2 :** something resembling a textile thread **3 :** a train of thought **4 :** a continuing element **5 :** the ridge or groove that winds around a screw

²**thread** vb **1 :** to pass a thread through the eye of (a needle) **2 :** to pass through in the manner of a thread **3 :** to put together on a thread **4 :** to make one's way through or between **5 :** to form a screw thread on or in

**thread·bare** \-,baər\ adj **1 :** worn so that the thread shows **:** SHABBY **2 :** TRITE

**thready** \-ē\ adj **1 :** consisting of or bearing fibers or filaments ⟨a ~ bark⟩ **2 :** lacking in fullness, body, or vigor

**threat** \'thret\ n **1 :** an expression of intention to do harm **2 :** something that threatens

**threat·en** \'thret-ᵊn\ vb **threatened; threat·en·ing** \'thret-(ᵊ-)niŋ\ **1 :** to utter threats against **2 :** to give signs or warning of **:** PORTEND **3 :** to hang over as a threat **:** MENACE — **threat·en·ing·ly** adv

**three** \'thrē\ n **1 :** one more than two **2 :** the third in a set or series **3 :** something having three units — **three** *adj or pron*

**3–D** \'thrē-'dē\ *n* **:** three-dimensional form

**three–dimensional** *adj* **1 :** relating to or having three dimensions **2 :** giving the illusion of varying distances ⟨a ~ picture⟩

**three·fold** \'thrē-,fōld, -'fōld\ *adj* **1 :** having three parts **:** TRIPLE **2 :** being three times as great or as many — **three·fold** \-'fōld\ *adv*

**three·pence** \'threp-əns, 'thrip-, 'thrəp-, *US also* 'thrē-pens\ *n* **1 :** the sum of three usu. British pennies **2 :** a coin worth three pennies

**three·score** \'thrē-'skōr\ *adj* **:** being three times twenty **:** SIXTY

**three·some** \'thrē-səm\ *n* **:** a group of three persons or things

**thren·o·dy** \'thren-əd-ē\ *n, pl* **-dies** **:** a song of lamentation **:** ELEGY

**thresh** \'thrash, 'thresh\ *vb* **1 :** to separate (as grain from straw) by beating **2 :** THRASH — **thresh·er** *n*

**thresh·old** \'thresh-,ōld\ *n* **1 :** the sill of a door **2 :** a point or place of beginning or entering **:** OUTSET **3 :** a point at which a physiological or psychological effect begins to be produced

**threw** *past of* THROW

**thrice** \'thrīs\ *adv* **1 :** three times **2 :** in a threefold manner or degree

**thrift** \'thrift\ *n* [ME, fr. ON, prosperity, fr. *thrīfask* to thrive] **:** careful management esp. of money **:** FRUGALITY — **thrift·i·ly** \'thrif-tə-lē\ *adv* — **thrift·less** *adj* — **thrifty** *adj*

**thrill** \'thril\ *vb* [ME *thirlen, thrillen* to pierce, fr. OE *thyrlian,* fr. *thyrel* hole, fr. *thurh* through] **1 :** to have or cause to have a sudden sharp feeling of excitement; *also* **:** TINGLE, SHIVER **2 :** TREMBLE, VIBRATE — **thrill** *n* — **thrill·er** *n* — **thrill·ing·ly** \-iŋ-lē\ *adv*

**thrive** \'thrīv\ *vb* **throve** \'thrōv\ *or* **thrived; thriv·en** \'thriv-ən\ *also* **thrived; thriv·ing** \'thrī-viŋ\ **1 :** to grow luxuriantly **:** FLOURISH **2 :** to gain in wealth or possessions **:** PROSPER

**throat** \'thrōt\ *n* **:** the part of the neck in front of the spinal column; *also* **:** the passage through it to the stomach and lungs — **throat·ed** \-əd\ *adj*

**throaty** \'thrōt-ē\ *adj* **throat·i·er; -est 1 :** uttered or produced from low in the throat ⟨a ~ voice⟩ **2 :** heavy, thick, or deep as if from the throat ⟨~ notes of a horn⟩ — **throat·i·ly** \'thrōt-ʼl-ē\ *adv* — **throat·i·ness** \-ē-nəs\ *n*

**¹throb** \'thräb\ *vb* **throbbed; throbbing :** to pulsate or pound esp. with abnormal force or rapidity **:** BEAT, VIBRATE

**²throb** *n* **:** BEAT, PULSE

**throe** \'thrō\ *n* **1 :** PANG, SPASM **2** *pl* **:** a hard or painful struggle

**throm·bo·sis** \thräm-'bō-səs\ *n, pl* **-bo·ses** \-,sēz\ **:** the formation or presence of a clot in a blood vessel during life — **throm·bot·ic** \-'bät-ik\ *adj*

**throm·bus** \'thräm-bəs\ *n, pl* **thrombi** \-,bī\ **:** a clot of blood formed within a blood vessel and remaining attached to its place of origin

**throne** \'thrōn\ *n* **1 :** the chair of state esp. of a king or bishop **2 :** royal power **:** SOVEREIGNTY

**¹throng** \'thröŋ\ *n* **1 :** a crowding together of many persons **2 :** MULTITUDE

**²throng** *vb* **thronged; throng·ing** \'thröŋ-iŋ\ **:** CROWD

**throt·tle** \'thrät-ʼl\ *vb* **throt·tled; throt·tling** \'thrät-(ʼ-)liŋ\ [ME *throtlen,* fr. *throte* throat] **1 :** CHOKE, STRANGLE **2 :** SUPPRESS **3 :** to obstruct the flow of (fuel) to an engine; *also* **:** to reduce the speed of (an engine) by such means — **throt·tler** \-(ʼ-)lər\ *n*

**²throttle** *n* **1 :** THROAT, TRACHEA **2 :** a valve regulating the volume of steam or fuel charge delivered to the cylinders of an engine; *also* **:** the lever controlling this valve

**¹through** \(')thrü\ *prep* **1 :** into at one side and out at the other side of ⟨go ~ the door⟩ **2 :** by way of ⟨entered ~ a skylight⟩ **3 :** AMONG ⟨a path ~ the trees⟩ **4 :** by means of ⟨succeeded ~ hard work⟩ **5 :** over the whole of ⟨rumors swept ~ the office⟩ **6 :** during the whole of ⟨~ the night⟩ **7 :** DURING ⟨~ the summer⟩ **8 :** to and including ⟨Monday ~ Friday⟩

**²through** \'thrü\ *adv* **1 :** from one end or side to the other **2 :** from beginning to end **:** to completion (see it ~) **3 :** to the core **:** THOROUGHLY ⟨he was wet ~⟩ **4 :** into the open **:** OUT ⟨break ~⟩

**³through** \'thrü\ *adj* **1 :** permitting free or continuous passage **:** DIRECT ⟨a ~ road⟩ **2 :** going from point of origin to destination without change or reshipment ⟨~ train⟩ **3 :** initiated at and destined for points outside a local zone ⟨~ traffic⟩ **4 :** FINISHED ⟨~ with the job⟩

**¹through·out** \thrü-'aùt\ *adv* **1 :** EVERYWHERE **2 :** from beginning to end

**²throughout** *prep* **1 :** in or to every part of **2 :** during the whole period of

**through·put** \'thrü-,pùt\ *n* **:** OUTPUT, PRODUCTION ⟨the ~ of a computer⟩

**through street** *n* **:** a street on which the through movement of traffic is given preference

**through·way** *var of* THRUWAY

**throve** *past of* THRIVE

**¹throw** \'thrō\ *vb* **threw** \'thrü\; **thrown** \'thrōn\; **throw·ing 1 :** to propel through the air esp. with a forward motion of the hand and arm ⟨~ a ball⟩ **2 :** to cause to fall or fall off **3 :** to put suddenly in a certain position or condition ⟨~ into panic⟩ **4 :** to lose intentionally ⟨~ a game⟩ **5 :** to move (a lever) so as to connect or disconnect parts of something (as a clutch) **6 :** to put on or take off hastily ⟨~ on a coat⟩ **7 :** to act as host for ⟨~ a party⟩ **syn** toss, fling, pitch, sling — **throw·er** \'thrō-(ə)r\ *n*

**²throw** *n* **1 :** an act of throwing, hurling, or flinging; *also* **:** CAST **2 :** the distance a missile may be thrown **3 :** a light coverlet 4 : a woman's scarf or light wrap

throw·away \'thrō-ə-,wā\ n : a hand-bill or circular distributed free

throw·back \'thrō-,bak\ n : reversion to an earlier type or phase; also : an instance or product of this

throw up vb 1 : to build hurriedly 2 : VOMIT

thrum \'thrəm\ vb thrummed; thrum·ming : to play or pluck a stringed instrument idly : STRUM

thrush \'thrəsh\ n : any of numerous songbirds usu. of a plain color but sometimes with spotted underparts

¹thrust \'thrəst\ vb thrust; thrust·ing 1 : to push or drive with force : SHOVE 2 : STAB, PIERCE 3 : INTERJECT 4 : to press the acceptance of upon someone

²thrust n 1 : a lunge with a pointed weapon 2 : a violent push : SHOVE 3 : ATTACK 4 : force exerted endwise through a propeller shaft (as of a ship or airplane); also : forward force produced (as in a rocket) by a high-speed jet of fluid discharged rearward 5 : the pressure of one part of a construction against another (as of an arch against an abutment)

thrust·er also thrust·or \'thrəs-tər\ n : one that thrusts; esp : a rocket engine

thru·way \'thrü-,wā\ n : EXPRESSWAY

¹thud \'thəd\ vb thud·ded; thud·ding : to move or strike so as to make a thud

²thud n 1 : BLOW 2 : a dull sound

thug \'thəg\ n [Hindi thag, lit., thief, fr. Skt sthaga rogue fr. sthagati he covers, conceals] : a brutal ruffian; also : ASSASSIN

thu·li·um \'th(y)ü-lē-əm\ n : a rare metallic chemical element

¹thumb \'thəm\ n 1 : the short thick first digit of the human hand or a corresponding digit of a lower animal 2 : the part of a glove that covers the thumb

²thumb vb 1 : to leaf through (pages) with the thumb 2 : to wear or soil with the thumb by frequent handling 3 : to request or obtain (a ride) in a passing automobile by signaling with the thumb

thumb index n : a series of notches cut in the fore edge of a book to facilitate reference

¹thumb·nail \'thəm-,nāl, -'nāl\ n : the nail of the thumb

²thumb·nail \,thəm-,nāl\ adj : BRIEF, CONCISE ⟨a ~ sketch⟩

thumb·screw \-,skrü\ n 1 : a screw with a head that may be turned by the thumb and forefinger 2 : a device of torture for squeezing the thumb

thumb·tack \-,tak\ n : a tack with a broad flat head for pressing with one's thumb into a board or wall

¹thump \'thəmp\ vb 1 : to strike with or as if with something thick or heavy so as to cause a dull heavy sound 2 : POUND

²thump n : a blow with or as if with something blunt or heavy; also : the sound made by such a blow

¹thun·der \'thən-dər\ n 1 : the sound following a flash of lightning; also : a noise like such a sound 2 : a loud utterance or threat

²thunder vb thun·dered; thun·der·ing \-d(ə-)riŋ\ 1 : to produce thunder 2 : ROAR, SHOUT

thun·der·bolt \-,bōlt\ n : a single discharge of lightning with its accompanying thunder

thun·der·clap \-,klap\ n : a crash of thunder

thun·der·cloud \-,klau̇d\ n : a cloud producing lightning and thunder

thun·der·head \-,hed\ n : a rounded mass of cloud often appearing before a thunderstorm

thun·der·ous \'thən-d(ə-)rəs\ adj : producing thunder; also : making a noise like thunder — thun·der·ous·ly adv

thun·der·show·er \'thən-dər-,shau̇(-ə)r\ n : a shower accompanied by thunder and lightning

thun·der·storm \-,stȯrm\ n : a storm accompanied by thunder and lightning

thun·der·struck \-,strək\ adj : struck dumb : ASTONISHED

Thurs or Thu abbr Thursday

Thurs·day \'thərz-dē\ n : the fifth day of the week

thus \'thəs\ adv 1 : in this or that manner 2 : to this degree or extent : so 3 : because of this or that : HENCE

¹thwack \'thwak\ vb : to strike with something flat or heavy

²thwack n : a heavy blow : WHACK

¹thwart \'thwȯrt\ adv, naut often \'thȯrt\ adv : ATHWART

²thwart adj : situated or placed across something else

³thwart vb 1 : BAFFLE 2 : BLOCK, DE-FEAT syn balk, foil, outwit, frustrate

⁴thwart \'th(w)ȯrt\ n : a rower's seat extending across a boat

thy \(,)thī\ adj, archaic : of, relating to, or done by or to thee or thyself

thyme \'tīm, 'thīm\ n [ME, fr. MF thym, fr. L thymum, fr. Gk thymon, fr. thyein to make a burnt offering, sacrifice] : any of several mints with aromatic leaves used esp. in seasoning

thy·mine \'thī-,mēn\ n : a pyrimidine base that is one of the four bases coding genetic information in the molecular chain of DNA

thy·mus \'thī-məs\ n : a glandular organ of the neck that in lambs and calves is a sweetbread

thy·roid \'thī-,rȯid\ or thy·roi·dal \thī-'rȯid-ᵊl\ adj [NL thyroides, fr. Gk thyreoeidēs shield-shaped, thyroid, fr. thyreos shield shaped like a door, fr. thyra door] : of, relating to, or being a large endocrine gland (thyroid gland) that lies at the base of the neck and produces a hormone with a profound influence on growth and metabolism — thyroid n

thy·rox·ine or thy·rox·in \thī-'räk-,sēn, -sən\ n : an iron-containing amino acid that is the active principle of the thyroid gland and is used to treat thyroid disorders

**thy·self** \thī-'self\ *pron. archaic* : YOURSELF

**Ti** *symbol* titanium

**ti·ara** \tē-'ar-ə, -'er-, -'är-\ *n* **1** : the pope's triple crown **2** : a decorative headband or semicircle for formal wear by women

**Ti·bet·an** \tə-'bet-ᵊn\ *n* : a native or inhabitant of Tibet — **Tibetan** *adj*

**tib·ia** \'tib-ē-ə\ *n, pl* **-i·ae** \-ē-,ē\ *also* **-i·as** : the inner of the two bones of the vertebrate hind limb between the knee and the ankle

**tic** \'tik\ *n* : a local and habitual twitching of muscles esp. of the face

**ti·cal** \ti-'käl, 'tik-əl\ *n pl* **ticals** *or* **tical** : BAHT

**¹tick** \'tik\ *n* : any of numerous small eight-legged blood-sucking animals

**²tick** *n* **1** : a light rhythmic audible tap or beat **2** : a small mark used to draw attention to or check something

**³tick** *vb* **1** : to make a tick or series of ticks **2** : to mark or check with a tick **3** : to mark, count, or announce by or as if by ticking beats **4** : to function as an operating mechanism : RUN

**⁴tick** *n* : the fabric case of a mattress or pillow; *also* : a mattress consisting of a tick and its filling

**⁵tick** *n* : CREDIT; *also* : a credit account

**tick·er** \'tik-ər\ *n* **1** : something (as a watch) that ticks **2** : a telegraph instrument that prints off news on paper tape **3** *slang* : HEART

**ticker tape** *n* : the paper ribbon on which a telegraphic ticker prints off its information(as stock quotations)

**¹tick·et** \'tik-ət\ *n* **1** : CERTIFICATE, LICENSE, PERMIT; *esp* : a certificate or token showing that a fare or admission fee has been paid **2** : TAG, LABEL **3** : a summons issued to a traffic offender **4** : SLATE 3

**²ticket** *vb* **1** : to attach a ticket to **2** : to furnish or serve with a ticket

**tick·ing** \'tik-iŋ\ *n* : a strong fabric used in upholstering and as a mattress covering

**tick·le** \'tik-əl\ *vb* **tick·led**; **tick·ling** \-(ə-)liŋ\ **1** : to have a tingling sensation **2** : to excite or stir up agreeably : PLEASE, AMUSE **3** : to touch (as a body part) lightly so as to cause uneasiness, laughter, or spasmodic movements **syn** gratify, delight, regale — **tickle** *n*

**tick·lish** \'tik-(ə-)lish\ *adj* **1** : sensitive to tickling **2** : OVERSENSITIVE, TOUCHY **3** : UNSTABLE ⟨a ~ foothold⟩ **4** : requiring delicate handling ⟨~ subject⟩ — **tick·lish·ly** *adv* — **tick·lish·ness** *n*

**TID** *abbr* [L *ter in die*] three times a day

**tid·al wave** \,tīd-ᵊl-\ *n* **1** : a high sea wave that sometimes follows an earthquake **2** : the great rise of water alongshore due to exceptionally strong winds

**tid·bit** \'tid-,bit\ *n* : a choice morsel

**⁸tide** \'tīd\ *n* [ME, time, fr. OE *tīd*] **1** : the alternate rising and falling of the surface of the ocean **2** : something that fluctuates like the tides of the sea — **tid·al** \'tīd-ᵊl\ *adj*

**²tide** *vb* **tid·ed**; **tid·ing** : to carry through or help along as if by the tide ⟨a loan to ~ him over⟩

**tide·land** \'tīd-,land, -lənd\ *n* **1** : land overflowed during flood tide **2** : land under the ocean within a nation's territorial waters — often used in pl.

**tide·wa·ter** \-,wȯt-ər, -,wät-\ *n* **1** : water overflowing land at flood tide **2** : low-lying coastal land

**tid·ings** \'tīd-iŋz\ *n pl* : NEWS, MESSAGE

**ti·dy** \'tīd-ē\ *adj* **ti·di·er**; **-est** **1** : well ordered and cared for : NEAT **2** : LARGE, SUBSTANTIAL ⟨a ~ sum⟩ — **ti·di·ness** \'tīd-ē-nəs\ *n*

**²tidy** *vb* **ti·died**; **ti·dy·ing** **1** : to put in order **2** : to make things tidy

**³tidy** *n, pl* **tidies** : a piece of decorated cloth or needlework used to protect the back or arms of a chair from wear or soil

**¹tie** \'tī\ *n* **1** : a line, ribbon, or cord used for fastening, uniting, or closing **2** : a structural element (as a beam or rod) holding two pieces together **3** : one of the cross supports to which railroad rails are fastened **4** : a connecting link : BOND ⟨family ~s⟩ **5** : an equality in number (as of votes or scores); *also* : an undecided or deadlocked contest **6** : NECKTIE

**²tie** *vb* **tied**; **ty·ing** \'tī-iŋ\ *or* **tie·ing** **1** : to fasten, attach, or close by means of a tie **2** : to bring together firmly : UNITE **3** : to form a knot or bow in ⟨~ a scarf⟩ **4** : to restrain from freedom of action : CONSTRAIN **5** : to make or have an equal score with

**tie·back** \'tī-,bak\ *n* : a decorative strip for draping a curtain to the side of a window

**tie–dye·ing** \'tī-,dī-iŋ\ *n* : a method of producing patterns in textiles by tying parts of the fabric so that they will not absorb the die — **tie–dyed** \-,dīd\ *adj*

**tie–in** \'tī-,in\ *n* : CONNECTION

**tier** \'tiər\ *n* : ROW, LAYER; *esp* : one of two or more rows arranged one above another

**tie–rod** \'tī-,räd\ *n* : a rod used as a connecting member or brace

**tie–up** \'tī-,əp\ *n* **1** : a suspension of traffic or business **2** : CONNECTION

**tiff** \'tif\ *n* : a petty quarrel — **tiff** *vb*

**tif·fin** \'tif-ən\ *n, chiefly Brit* : LUNCHEON

**ti·ger** \'tī-gər\ *n, pl* **tigers** : a large tawny black-striped Asiatic flesh-eating mammal related to the cat — **ti·ger·ish** \-g(ə-)rish\ *adj* — **ti·gress** \-grəs\ *n*

**¹tight** \'tīt\ *adj* **1** : so close in structure as not to permit passage of a liquid or gas **2** : fixed or held very firmly in place **3** : TAUT **4** : fitting usu. too closely ⟨~ shoes⟩ **5** : set close together : COMPACT ⟨a ~ formation⟩ **6** : DIFFICULT, TRYING ⟨get in a ~ spot⟩ **7** : STINGY, MISERLY **8** : evenly contested : CLOSE **9** : INTOXICATED **10** : low in supply : hard to get ⟨money is ~⟩ — **tight·ly** *adv* — **tight·ness** *n*

**²tight** *adv* **1** : TIGHTLY, FIRMLY **2** : SOUNDLY ⟨sleep ~⟩

**tight·en** \'tīt-²n\ *vb* **tight·ened; tight·en·ing** \'tīt-(²-)niŋ\ : to make or become tight

**tight-fist·ed** \'tīt-'fis-təd\ *adj* : STINGY

**tight-rope** \'tīt-,rōp\ *n* : a taut rope or wire for acrobats to perform on

**tights** \'tīts\ *n pl* : skintight garments covering the body esp. from the waist down

**tight·wad** \'tīt-,wäd\ *n* : a stingy person

**til·de** \'til-də\ *n* : a mark ~ placed esp. over the letter *n* (as in Spanish *señor* sir) to denote the sound \nʸ\ or over vowels (as in Portuguese *irmã* sister) to indicate nasal quality

**¹tile** \'tīl\ *n* **1** : a thin piece of fired clay, stone, or concrete used for roofs, floors, or walls; *also* : a hollow or concave earthenware or concrete piece used for a drain **2** : a thin piece (as of a rubber composition) used for covering walls or floors — **til·ing** \-iŋ\ *n*

**²tile** *vb* **tiled; til·ing 1** : to cover with tiles **2** : to install drainage tile in — **til·er** *n*

**¹till** \(,)til\ *prep or conj* : UNTIL

**²till** \'til\ *vb* : to work by plowing, sowing, and raising crops : CULTIVATE — **till·able** *adj*

**³till** \'til\ *n* : DRAWER; *esp* : a money drawer in a store or bank

**till·age** \'til-ij\ *n* **1** : the work of tilling land **2** : cultivated land

**¹till·er** \'til-ər\ *n* : one that tills

**²til·ler** \'til-ər\ *n* [ME *tiler* stock of a crossbow, fr. MF *telier*, lit., beam of a loom, fr. ML *telarium*, fr. L *tela* web] : a lever used for turning a boat's rudder from side to side

**³til·ler** *n* [OE *telgor, telgra* twig, shoot] : a sprout or stalk esp. from the base or lower part of a plant

**¹tilt** \'tilt\ *vb* **1** : to move or shift so as to incline : TIP **2** : to engage in or as if in a combat with lances : JOUST

**²tilt** *n* **1** : a military exercise in which two combatants charging usu. with lances try to unhorse each other : JOUST; *also* : a tournament of tilts **2** : a verbal contest **3** : SLANT, TIP

**tilth** \'tilth\ *n* **1** : TILLAGE **2** : the state of being tilled ⟨land in good ~⟩

**Tim** *abbr* Timothy

**¹tim·ber** \'tim-bər\ *n* [ME, fr. OE, building, wood] **1** : wood for use in making something **2** : a usu. large squared or dressed piece of wood **3** : wooded land or growing trees from which timber may be obtained — **tim·ber·land** \-bər-,land\ *n*

**²timber** *vb* **tim·bered; tim·ber·ing** \-b(ə-)riŋ\ : to cover, frame, or support with timbers

**tim·bered** \'tim-bərd\ *adj* **1** : having walls framed by exposed timbers **2** : covered with growing timber

**tim·ber·ing** \'tim-b(ə-)riŋ\ *n* : a set or arrangement of timbers

**tim·ber·line** \'tim-bər-,līn\ *n* : the upper limit of tree growth on mountains or in high latitudes

**timber rattlesnake** *n* : a moderate-sized rattlesnake widely distributed

through the eastern half of the U.S.

**timber wolf** *n* : a large usu. gray No. American wolf

**tim·bre** *also* **tim·ber** \'tam-bər, 'tim-\ *n* [F, fr. MF, bell struck by a hammer, fr. OF, drum, fr. MGk *tymbanon* kettle-drum, fr. Gk *tympanon*] : the distinctive quality given to a sound by its overtones

**tim·brel** \'tim-brəl\ *n* : a small hand drum or tambourine

**¹time** \'tīm\ *n* **1** : a period during which an action, process, or condition exists or continues ⟨gone a long ~⟩ **2** : LEISURE ⟨found ~ to read⟩ **3** : a point or period when something occurs : OCCASION ⟨the last ~ we met⟩ **4** : a set or customary moment or hour for something to occur ⟨arrived on ~⟩ **5** : AGE, ERA **6** *pl* : state of affairs : CONDITIONS ⟨hard ~s⟩ **7** : a rate of speed : TEMPO **8** : a moment, hour, day, or year as indicated by a clock or calendar ⟨what ~ is it⟩ **9** : a system of reckoning time ⟨solar ~⟩ **10** : one of a series of recurring instances; *also, pl* : multiplied instances ⟨five ~s greater⟩ **11** : a person's experience during a particular period ⟨had a good ~ at the beach⟩

**²time** *vb* **timed; tim·ing 1** : to arrange or set the time of : SCHEDULE ⟨~s his calls conveniently⟩ **2** : to set the tempo or duration of ⟨~ a performance⟩ **3** : to cause to keep time with ⟨~s her steps to the music⟩ **4** : to determine or record the time, duration, or rate of ⟨~ a sprinter⟩ — **tim·er** *n*

**time clock** *n* : a clock that records the times of arrival and departure of workers

**time-hon·ored** \'tīm-,än-ərd\ *adj* : honored because of age or long usage

**time·keep·er** \'tīm-,kē-pər\ *n* **1** : a clerk who keeps records of the time worked by employees **2** : one appointed to mark and announce the time in an athletic game or contest

**time·less** \'tīm-ləs\ *adj* **1** : UNENDING **2** : not limited or affected by time ⟨~ works of art⟩ — **time·less·ly** *adv* — **time·less·ness** *n*

**time·ly** \'tīm-lē\ *adj* **time·li·er; -est 1** : coming early or at the right time : OPPORTUNE ⟨a ~ arrival⟩ **2** : appropriate to the time ⟨a ~ book⟩ — **time·li·ness** *n*

**time-out** \'tīm-'aùt\ *n* : a brief suspension of activity esp. in an athletic game

**time·piece** \'tīm-,pēs\ *n* : a device (as a clock) to show the passage of time

**times** \,tīmz\ *prep* : multiplied by ⟨2 ~ 2 is 4⟩

**time-shar·ing** \'tīm-,sheər-iŋ\ *n* : simultaneous access to a computer by many users with programs being interspersed

**times sign** *n* : the symbol × used to indicate multiplication

**time·ta·ble** \'tīm-,tā-bəl\ *n* **1** : a table of the departure and arrival times (as of trains) **2** : a schedule showing a planned order or sequence

**time·worn** \-,wōrn\ adj 1 : worn by time 2 : HACKNEYED, STALE

**tim·id** \'tim-əd\ adj : lacking in courage or self-confidence : FEARFUL — **ti·mid·i·ty** \tə-'mid-ət-ē\ n — **tim·id·ly** \'tim-əd-lē\ adv

**tim·o·rous** \'tim-(ə-)rəs\ adj : of a timid disposition : AFRAID — **tim·o·rous·ly** adv — **tim·o·rous·ness** n

**tim·o·thy** \'tim-ə-thē\ n : a grass with long cylindrical spikes widely grown for hay

**tim·pa·ni** \'tim-pə-nē\ n pl : a set of kettledrums played by one performer in an orchestra — **tim·pa·nist** \-nəst\ n

¹**tin** \'tin\ n 1 : a soft white crystalline metallic element malleable at ordinary temperatures but brittle when heated that is used in solders and alloys 2 : a container (as a can) made of tinplate

²**tin** vb **tinned; tin·ning** 1 : to cover or plate with tin 2 chiefly Brit : to pack in tins : CAN

**tinct** \'tinkt\ n : TINCTURE, TINGE

¹**tinc·ture** \'tink-chər\ n 1 : a substance that colors or dyes 2 : a slight admixture : TRACE 3 : an alcoholic solution of a medicinal substance syn touch, suggestion, suspicion

²**tincture** vb **tinc·tured; tinc·tur·ing** : COLOR, TINGE

**tin·der** \'tin-dər\ n : something that catches fire easily; esp : a substance used to kindle a fire from a slight spark

**tin·der·box** \'tin-dər-,bäks\ n : a metal box for holding tinder and usu. flint and steel for striking a spark

**tine** \'tīn\ n : a slender pointed part (as of a fork or an antler) : PRONG

**tin·foil** \'tin-,fȯil\ n : a thin metal sheeting usu. of aluminum or tin-lead alloy

¹**tinge** \'tinj\ vb **tinged; tinge·ing** or **ting·ing** \'tin-jin\ 1 : to color slightly : TINT 2 : to affect or modify esp. with a slight color or taste

²**tinge** n : a slight coloring, flavor, or quality syn touch, suggestion

**tin·gle** \'tin-gəl\ vb **tin·gled; tin·gling** \-g(ə-)lin\ 1 : to feel a pricking or thrilling sensation 2 : TINKLE — **tingle** n

¹**tin·ker** \'tin-kər\ n 1 : a usu. itinerant mender of household utensils 2 : an unskillful mender : BUNGLER

²**tinker** vb **tin·kered; tin·ker·ing** \-k(ə-)rin\ : to repair or adjust something in an unskillful or experimental manner — **tin·ker·er** n

¹**tin·kle** \'tin-kəl\ vb **tin·kled; tin·kling** \-k(ə-)lin\ : to make or cause to make a tinkle

²**tinkle** n : a series of short high ringing or clinking sounds

**tin·ny** \'tin-ē\ adj **tin·ni·er; -est** 1 : of, abounding in, or yielding tin 2 : resembling tin; also : LIGHT, CHEAP 3 : thin in tone ⟨a ~ voice⟩ — **tin·ni·ly** \'tin-ᵊl-ē\ adv — **tin·ni·ness** \-ē-nəs\ n

**tin·plate** \'tin-'plāt\ n : thin sheet iron or steel coated with tin — **tin-plate** vb

**tin·sel** \'tin-səl\ n 1 : a thread, strip, or sheet of metal, paper, or plastic used

to produce a glittering appearance (as in fabrics) 2 : something superficially attractive but of little worth

**tin·smith** \'tin-,smith\ n : one that works with sheet metal (as tinplate)

¹**tint** \'tint\ n 1 : a slight or pale coloration : HUE 2 : any of various shades of a color

²**tint** vb : to impart a tint to : COLOR

**tin·tin·nab·u·la·tion** \,tin-tə-,nab-yə-'lā-shən\ n 1 : the ringing of bells 2 : a tingling sound as if of bells

**tin·ware** \'tin-,waər\ n : articles made of tinplate

**ti·ny** \'tī-nē\ adj **ti·ni·er; -est** : very small : MINUTE syn miniature, diminutive, wee, little

¹**tip** \'tip\ n 1 : the usu. pointed end of something 2 : a small piece or part serving as an end, cap, or point

²**tip** vb **tipped; tip·ping** 1 : to furnish with a tip 2 : to cover or adorn the tip of

³**tip** vb **tipped; tip·ping** 1 : OVERTURN, UPSET 2 : LEAN, SLANT; also : TILT

⁴**tip** n : the act or an instance of tipping

⁵**tip** n : a light touch or blow

⁶**tip** vb **tipped; tip·ping** : to strike lightly : TAP

⁷**tip** vb **tipped; tip·ping** : to give a gratuity to

⁸**tip** n : a gift or small sum given for a service performed or anticipated

⁹**tip** n : a piece of expert or confidential information : HINT

¹⁰**tip** vb **tipped; tip·ping** : to impart a piece of information about or to

**tip-off** \'tip-,ȯf\ n : WARNING, TIP

**tip·pet** \'tip-ət\ n : a long scarf or shoulder cape

**tip·ple** \'tip-əl\ vb **tip·pled; tip·pling** \-(ə-)lin\ : to drink intoxicating liquor esp. habitually or excessively — **tip·pler** \-(ə-)lər\ n

**tip·ster** \'tip-stər\ n : one who gives or sells tips esp. for gambling

**tip·sy** \'tip-sē\ adj **tip·si·er; -est** : unsteady or foolish from the effects of alcohol

¹**tip·toe** \'tip-,tō\ n : the tip of a toe; also : the ends of the toes

²**tiptoe** adv or adj : on or as if on tiptoe

³**tiptoe** vb **tip·toed; tip·toe·ing** : to walk or proceed on or as if on tiptoe

¹**tip-top** \'tip-'täp\ n : the highest point

²**tip-top** adj : EXCELLENT, FIRST-RATE

**ti·rade** \'tī-,rād, 'tī-,rād\ n [F, shot, tirade, fr. MF, fr. It tirata, fr. tirare to draw, shoot] : a prolonged speech of abuse or condemnation

¹**tire** \'tī(ə)r\ vb **tired; tir·ing** 1 : to make or become weary : FATIGUE 2 : to wear out the patience of : BORE

²**tire** n 1 : a wheel band that forms the tread of a wheel 2 : a rubber cushion usu. containing compressed air that encircles a wheel (as of an automobile)

**tired** \'tī(ə)rd\ adj 1 : WEARY, FATIGUED 2 : HACKNEYED

**tire·less** \'tī(ə)r-ləs\ adj : not tiring : UNTIRING, INDEFATIGABLE — **tire·less·ly** adv — **tire·less·ness** n

**tire·some** \'tī(ə)r-səm\ adj : tending to bore : WEARISOME, TEDIOUS — **tire-**

some·ly adv — tire·some·ness n

tis·sue \'tish-ü\ n [ME tissu, a rich fabric, fr. OF, fr. tistre to weave, fr. L texere] 1 : a fine lightweight often sheer fabric 2 : NETWORK, WEB 3 : a soft absorbent paper 4 : a mass or layer of cells forming a basic structural element of an animal or plant body

¹tit \'tit\ n : TEAT

²tit n : TITMOUSE

Tit abbr Titus

ti·tan \'tīt-ᵊn\ n : one gigantic in size or power

ti·tan·ic \tī-'tan-ik, tə-\ adj : enormous in size, force, or power syn immense, huge, vast, gigantic, giant, colossal, mammoth

ti·ta·ni·um \tī-'tān-ē-əm, tə-\ n : a gray light strong metallic chemical element used in alloys

tit·bit \'tit-,bit\ var of TIDBIT

tithe \'tīth\ n : a tenth part paid or given esp. for the support of a church — tithe vb — tith·er n

tit·il·late \'tit-ᵊl-,āt\ vb -lat·ed; -lat·ing 1 : TICKLE 2 : to excite pleasurably — tit·il·la·tion \,tit-ᵊl-'ā-shən\ n

tit·i·vate or tit·ti·vate \'tit-ə-,vāt\ vb : to dress up : spruce up

ti·tle \'tīt-ᵊl\ n 1 : CLAIM, RIGHT; esp : a legal right to the ownership of property 2 : the distinguishing name esp. of an artistic production (as a book) 3 : an appellation of honor, rank, or office 4 : CHAMPIONSHIP syn designation, denomination

ti·tled \'tīt-ᵊld\ adj : having a title esp. of nobility

title page n : a page of a book bearing the title and usu. the names of the author and publisher

tit·mouse \'tit-,maûs\ n, pl tit·mice \-,mīs\ : any of numerous small long‑tailed songbirds

tit·ter \'tit-ər\ vb : to laugh in an affected or in a nervous or half-suppressed manner — titter n

tit·tle \'tit-ᵊl\ n : a tiny piece : JOT

tit·tle-tat·tle \'tit-ᵊl-,tat-ᵊl\ n : idle talk : GOSSIP

tit·u·lar \'tich-(ə-)lər\ adj 1 : existing in title only : NOMINAL ⟨~ ruler⟩ 2 : of, relating to, or bearing a title ⟨~ role⟩

tiz·zy \'tiz-ē\ n, pl tizzies : a highly excited and distracted state of mind

tk abbr 1 tank 2 truck

tkt abbr ticket

Tl symbol thallium

TL abbr total loss

TLC abbr tender loving care

Tm symbol thulium

TM abbr trademark

T-man \'tē-,man\ n : a special agent of the U.S. Treasury Department

TMO abbr telegraph money order

tn abbr 1 ton 2 town

TN abbr Tennessee

tng abbr training

tnpk abbr turnpike

TNT \,tē-,en-'tē\ n : a high explosive used in artillery shells and bombs and in blasting

¹to \tə, (')tü\ prep 1 : in the direction of and reaching ⟨drove ~ town⟩ 2 : in the direction of : TOWARD ⟨walking ~ school⟩ 3 : ON, AGAINST ⟨apply salve ~ a burn⟩ 4 : as far as ⟨can pay up ~ a dollar⟩ 5 : so as to become or bring about ⟨beaten ~ death⟩ ⟨broken ~ pieces⟩ 6 : BEFORE ⟨it's five minutes ~ six⟩ 7 : UNTIL ⟨from May ~ December⟩ 8 : fitting or being a part of : FOR ⟨key ~ the lock⟩ 9 : with the accompaniment of ⟨sing ~ the music⟩ 10 : in relation or comparison with ⟨similar ~ that one⟩ ⟨won 10 ~ 6⟩ 11 : in accordance with ⟨add salt ~ taste⟩ 12 : within the range of ⟨~ my knowledge⟩ 13 : contained, occurring, or included in ⟨two pints ~ a quart⟩ 14 : as regards ⟨attitude ~ our friends⟩ 15 : affecting as the receiver or beneficiary ⟨whispered ~ her⟩ ⟨gave it ~ me⟩ 16 : for no one except ⟨a room ~ myself⟩ 17 : into the action of ⟨we got ~ talking⟩ 18 — used for marking the following verb as an infinitive ⟨wants ~ go⟩ ⟨easy ~ like⟩ ⟨the man ~ beat⟩ and often used by itself at the end of a clause in place of an infinitive suggested by the preceding context ⟨goes to town whenever he wants ~⟩ ⟨can leave if you'd like ~⟩

²to \'tü\ adv 1 : in a direction toward ⟨run ~ and fro⟩ ⟨wrong side ~⟩ 2 : into contact esp. with the frame of a door ⟨the door slammed ~⟩ 3 : to the matter in hand ⟨fell ~ and ate heartily⟩ 4 : to a state of consciousness or awareness ⟨came ~ hours after the accident⟩

TO abbr 1 telegraph office 2 turn over

toad \'tōd\ n : a tailless leaping amphibian differing typically from the related frogs in shorter stockier build, rough dry warty skin, and less aquatic habits

toad·stool \-,stül\ n : MUSHROOM; esp : one that is poisonous or inedible

toady \'tōd-ē\ n, pl toad·ies : one who flatters in the hope of gaining favors : SYCOPHANT — toady vb

¹toast \'tōst\ vb 1 : to make (as bread) crisp, hot, and brown by heat 2 : to warm thoroughly

²toast n 1 : sliced toasted bread 2 : someone or something in whose honor persons drink 3 : an act of drinking in honor of a toast

³toast vb : to propose or drink to as a toast

toast·er \'tō-stər\ n : one that toasts; esp : an electrical appliance for toasting

toast·mas·ter \'tōst-,mas-tər\ n : one that presides at a banquet and introduces the after-dinner speakers — toast·mis·tress \-,mis-trəs\ n

to·bac·co \tə-'bak-ō\ n, pl -cos 1 : a tall broad-leaved herb related to the potato; also : its leaves prepared for smoking or chewing or as snuff 2 : manufactured tobacco products

to·bac·co·nist \tə-'bak-ə-nəst\ n : a dealer in tobacco

¹to·bog·gan \tə-'bäg-ən\ n : a long flat-bottomed light sled made of thin boards curved up at one end

²toboggan vb 1 : to coast on a tobog‑

gan **2** : to decline suddenly (as in value)

**toc·sin** \'täk-sən\ *n* **1** : an alarm bell **2** : a warning signal

**¹to·day** \tə-'dā\ *adv* **1** : on or for this day **2** : at the present time

**²today** *n* : the present day, time, or age

**tod·dle** \'täd-²l\ *vb* **tod·dled; tod·dling** \'täd-(²-)liŋ\ : to walk with short tottering steps in the manner of a young child — **toddle** *n* — **tod·dler** \-(²-)lər\ *n*

**tod·dy** \'täd-ē\ *n*, *pl* **toddies** [Hindi *tārī* juice of a palm, fr. *tār* a palm, fr. Skt *tāla*] : a drink made of liquor, sugar, spices, and hot water

**to-do** \tə-'dü\ *n*, *pl* **to-dos** \-'düz\ : BUSTLE, STIR

**¹toe** \'tō\ *n* **1** : one of the terminal jointed members of the foot **2** : the front part of a foot or hoof

**²toe** *vb* **toed; toe·ing** : to touch, reach, or drive with the toes

**toe·hold** \'tō-,hōld\ *n* **1** : a place of support for the toes **2** : a slight footing

**toe·nail** \'tō-,nāl\ *n* : a nail of a toe

**tof·fee** *or* **tof·fy** \'tó-fē, 'täf-ē\ *n*, *pl* **toffees** *or* **toffies** : candy of brittle but tender texture made by boiling sugar and butter together

**tog** \'täg, 'tóg\ *vb* **togged; tog·ging** : to put togs on : DRESS

**to·ga** \'tō-gə\ *n* : the loose outer garment worn in public by citizens of ancient Rome — **to·gaed** \-gəd\ *adj*

**to·geth·er** \tə-'geth-ər\ *adv* **1** : in or into one place or group **2** : in or into contact or association ⟨mix ∼⟩ **3** : at one time : SIMULTANEOUSLY ⟨talk and work ∼⟩ **4** : in succession ⟨for days ∼⟩ **5** : in or into harmony or coherence ⟨get ∼ on a plan⟩ **6** : as a group : JOINTLY — **to·geth·er·ness** *n*

**tog·gery** \'täg-(ə-)rē, 'tóg-\ *n* : CLOTHING

**tog·gle switch** \,täg-əl-\ *n* : an electric switch with a spring to open or close the circuit when a projecting lever is pushed through a small arc

**togs** \'tägz, 'tógz\ *n pl* : CLOTHING; *esp* : clothes for a specified use ⟨riding ∼⟩

**¹toil** \'tóil\ *n* **1** : laborious effort **2** : long fatiguing labor : DRUDGERY — **toil·some** *adj*

**²toil** *vb* [ME *toilen* to argue, struggle, fr. OF *toeillier* to stir, disturb, dispute, fr. L *tudiculare* to crush, grind, fr. *tudicula* machine for crushing olives, dim. of *tudes* hammer] **1** : to work hard and long **2** : to proceed with laborious effort : PLOD — **toil·er** *n*

**³toil** *n* [MF *toile* cloth, net, fr. L *tela* web, fr. *texere* to weave, construct] : NET, TRAP — usu. used in pl.

**toi·let** \'tói-lət\ *n* **1** : the act or process of dressing and grooming oneself **2** : BATHROOM **2** : a fixture for use in urinating and defecating; *esp* : one consisting essentially of a hopper that can be flushed with water

**toi·let·ry** \'tói-lə-trē\ *n*, *pl* **-ries** : an article or preparation used in making one's toilet — usu. used in pl.

**toi·lette** \twä-'let\ *n* **2** : TOILET 1

**2** : formal attire; *also* : a particular costume

**toilet training** *n* : the process of training a child to control bladder and bowel movements and to use the toilet — **toilet train** *vb*

**toil·worn** \'tóil-,wórn\ *adj* : showing the effects of toil

**To·kay** \tō-'kā\ *n* : a sweet usu. dark gold dessert wine

**toke** \'tōk\ *n*, *slang* : a puff on a marijuana cigarette

**¹to·ken** \'tō-kən\ *n* **1** : an outward sign **2** : SYMBOL, EMBLEM **3** : SOUVENIR, KEEPSAKE **4** : a small part representing the whole **5** : a piece resembling a coin issued as money or for use by a particular group on specified terms

**²token** *adj* **1** : done or given as a token esp. in partial fulfillment of an obligation **2** : MINIMAL, PERFUNCTORY

**to·ken·ism** \'tō-kə-,niz-əm\ *n* : the policy or practice of making only a token effort (as to end racial segregation)

**told** *past of* TELL

**tole** \'tōl\ *n* : sheet metal and esp. tinplate for use in domestic and ornamental wares

**tol·er·a·ble** \'täl-(ə-)rə-bəl\ *adj* **1** : capable of being borne or endured **2** : moderately good : PASSABLE — **tol·er·a·bly** \-blē\ *adv*

**tol·er·ance** \'täl-(ə)-rəns\ *n* **1** : the act or practice of tolerating; *esp* : sympathy or indulgence for beliefs or practices differing from one's own **2** : capacity for enduring or adapting (as to a poor environment) **3** : the allowable deviation from a standard (as of size) **syn** forbearance, leniency, clemency — **tol·er·ant** *adj* — **tol·er·ant·ly** *adv*

**tol·er·ate** \'täl-ə-,rāt\ *vb* **-at·ed; -at·ing** **1** : to allow to be or to be done without hindrance **2** : to endure or resist the action of (as a drug) **syn** abide, bear, suffer, stand — **tol·er·a·tion** \,täl-ə-'rā-shən\ *n*

**¹toll** \'tōl\ *n* **1** : a tax paid for a privilege (as for passing over a bridge) **2** : a charge for a service (as for a long-distance telephone call) **3** : the cost in loss or suffering at which something is achieved **syn** levy, assessment

**²toll** *vb* **1** : to give signal of : SOUND **2** : to cause the slow regular sounding of (a bell) esp. by pulling a rope **3** : to sound with slow measured strokes **4** : to announce by tolling

**³toll** *n* : the sound of a tolling bell

**toll·booth** \'tōl-,büth\ *n* : a booth where tolls are paid

**toll·gate** \'tōl-,gāt\ *n* : a point where vehicles stop to pay toll

**toll·house** \-,haus\ *n* : a house or booth where tolls are paid

**tol·u·ene** \'täl-yə-,wēn\ *n* : a liquid hydrocarbon used as a solvent and as an antiknock agent

**tom** \'täm\ *n* : the male of various animals; *esp* : TOMCAT

**¹tom·a·hawk** \'täm-i-,hók\ *n* : a light ax used as a missile and as a hand weapon by No. American Indians

²**tomahawk** vb **:** to strike or kill with a tomahawk

**to·ma·to** \tə-'māt-ō, -'mät-\ n, pl **-toes :** a tropical American herb related to the potato and widely grown for its usu. large, rounded, and red or yellow pulpy edible berry; also **:** this fruit

**tomb** \'tüm\ n **1 :** a place of burial **:** GRAVE **2 :** a house, chamber, or vault for the dead

**tom·boy** \'täm-,bȯi\ n **:** a girl of boyish behavior

**tomb·stone** \'tüm-,stōn\ n **:** a stone marking a grave

**tom·cat** \'täm-,kat\ n **:** a male cat

**Tom Collins** \'täm-'käl-ənz\ n **:** a tall iced drink with a base of gin

**tome** \'tōm\ n **:** BOOK; esp **:** a large or weighty one

**tom·fool·ery** \täm-'fül-(ə-)rē\ n **:** foolish trifling **:** NONSENSE

**tom·my gun** \'täm-ē-,gən\ n **:** SUBMACHINE GUN

**to·mor·row** \tə-'mär-ō\ adv **:** on or for the day after today — **tomorrow** n

**tom·tit** \'täm-,tit, täm-'tit\ n **:** any of several small active birds

**tom–tom** \'täm-,täm\ n **:** a smallheaded drum beaten with the hands

**ton** \'tən\ n, pl **tons** also **ton 1** — see WEIGHT table **2 :** a unit of internal capacity for ships equal to 100 cubic feet **3 :** a unit equal to the volume of a long-ton weight of seawater or 35 cubic feet used in reckoning the displacement of ships **4 :** a unit of volume for a ship's cargo freight usu. reckoned at 40 cubic feet

**to·nal·i·ty** \tō-'nal-ət-ē\ n **:** tonal quality

¹**tone** \'tōn\ n [ME, fr. L tonus tension, tone, fr. Gk tonos, lit., act of stretching; fr. the dependence of the pitch of a musical string on its tension] **1 :** vocal or musical sound; esp **:** sound quality **2 :** a sound of definite pitch **3 :** WHOLE STEP **4 :** accent or inflection expressive of an emotion **5 :** the pitch of a word often used to express differences of meaning **6 :** style or manner of expression **7 :** color quality; also **:** SHADE, TINT **8 :** the effect in painting of light and shade together with color **9 :** the healthy and vigorous condition of a living body or bodily part **10 :** general character, quality, or trend syn atmosphere, feeling, savor — **ton·al** \'tōn-ᵊl\ adj

²**tone** vb **toned; ton·ing 1 :** to give a particular intonation or inflection to **2 :** to impart tone to **3 :** SOFTEN, MELLOW **4 :** to harmonize in color **:** BLEND

**tone arm** n **:** the movable part of a record player that carries the pickup and permits the needle to follow the record groove

**tong** \'täŋ, 'tȯŋ\ n **:** a Chinese secret society in the U.S.

**tongs** \'täŋz, 'tȯŋz\ n pl **:** any of numerous grasping devices consisting commonly of two pieces joined at one end by a pivot or hinged like scissors

¹**tongue** \'təŋ\ n **1 :** a fleshy movable process of the floor of the mouth used in tasting and in taking and swallowing food and in man as a speech organ **2 :** the flesh of a tongue (as of the ox) used as food **3 :** the power of communication **4 :** LANGUAGE 1 **5 :** ecstatic usu. unintelligible utterance accompanying religious excitation **6 :** manner or quality of utterance; also **:** intended meaning **7 :** something resembling an animal's tongue in being elongated and fastened at one end only — **tongued** \'təŋd\ adj — **tongue·less** adj

²**tongue** vb **tongued; tongu·ing** \'təŋ-iŋ\ **1 :** to touch or lick with the tongue **2 :** to articulate notes on a wind instrument

**tongue–in–cheek** adv or adj **:** with insincerity, irony, or whimsical exaggeration

**tongue–lash** \'təŋ-,lash\ vb **:** CHIDE, REPROVE — **tongue–lash·ing** \-iŋ\ n

**tongue–tied** \'təŋ-,tīd\ adj **:** unable to speak clearly or freely usu. from shortness of the membrane under the tongue or from shyness

**tongue twister** n **:** an utterance that is difficult to articulate because of a succession of similar consonants

¹**ton·ic** \'tän-ik\ adj **1 :** of, relating to, or producing a healthy physical or mental condition **:** INVIGORATING **2 :** of or relating to tones **3 :** relating to or based on the first tone of a scale

²**tonic** n **1 :** something (as a drug) that invigorates, restores, or refreshes **2 :** the first degree of a musical scale

¹**to·night** \tə-'nīt\ adv **:** on this present night or the night following this present day

²**tonight** n **:** the present or the coming night

**ton·nage** \'tən-ij\ n **1 :** a duty on ships based on tons carried **2 :** ships in terms of the number of tons registered or carried **3 :** the cubical content of a ship in units of 100 cubic feet **4 :** total weight in tons shipped, carried, or mined

**ton·neau** \'tän-,ō, tə-'nō\ n, pl **ton·neaus :** the rear seating compartment of an automobile body

**ton·sil** \'tän-səl\ n **:** either of a pair of oval masses of spongy tissue in the throat at the back of the mouth

**ton·sil·lec·to·my** \,tän-sə-'lek-tə-mē\ n, pl **-mies :** the surgical removal of the tonsils

**ton·sil·li·tis** \-'līt-əs\ n **:** inflammation of the tonsils

**ton·so·ri·al** \tän-'sōr-ē-əl\ adj **:** of or relating to a barber or his work

**ton·sure** \'tän-chər\ n [ME, fr. ML tonsura, fr. L, act of shearing, fr. tonsus, pp. of tondēre to shear] **1 :** the rite of admission to the clerical state by the clipping or shaving of the head **2 :** the shaven crown or patch worn by clerics (as monks)

**too** \(')tü\ adv **1 :** in addition **:** ALSO **2 :** EXCESSIVELY **3 :** to such a degree as to be regrettable **4 :** VERY syn besides, moreover, furthermore

**took** past of TAKE

**¹tool** \'tül\ n  1 : a hand instrument used to aid in mechanical operations  2 : the cutting or shaping part in a machine; also : a machine for shaping metal in any way  3 : an instrument or apparatus used in performing an operation or needed in the practice of a vocation or profession ⟨a scholar's books are his ∼s⟩; also : a means to an end  4 : a person used by another : DUPE

**²tool** vb  1 : to shape, form, or finish with a tool; esp : to letter or decorate (as a book cover) by means of hand tools  2 : to equip a plant or industry with machines and tools for production  3 : DRIVE, RIDE ⟨∼ing along at 60⟩

**¹toot** \'tüt\ vb  1 : to sound or cause to sound esp. in short blasts  2 : to blow a wind instrument (as a horn)

**²toot** n : a short blast (as on a horn)

**tooth** \'tüth\ n, pl **teeth** \'tēth\  1 : one of the hard bony structures borne esp. on the jaws of vertebrates and used for seizing and chewing food and as weapons  2 : something resembling an animal's tooth  3 : one of the projections on the edge of a wheel that fits into corresponding projections on another wheel — **toothed** \'tütht\ adj — **tooth·less** adj

**tooth·ache** \'tüth-,āk\ n : pain in or about a tooth

**tooth·brush** \-,brəsh\ n : a brush for cleaning the teeth

**tooth·paste** \-,pāst\ n : a paste for cleaning the teeth

**tooth·pick** \-,pik\ n : a pointed instrument for removing substances lodged between the teeth

**tooth powder** n : a powder for cleaning the teeth

**tooth·some** \'tüth-səm\ adj  1 : pleasing to the taste : DELICIOUS  2 : ATTRACTIVE ⟨a ∼ blond⟩ syn palatable, appetizing, savory, tasty

**toothy** \'tü-thē\ adj **tooth·i·er; -est** : having or showing prominent teeth

**¹top** \'täp\ n  1 : the highest part, point, or level of something  2 : the stalks and leaves of a plant with edible roots ⟨beet ∼s⟩  3 : the upper end, edge, or surface ⟨the ∼ of a page⟩  4 : an upper piece, lid, or covering  5 : a platform around the head of the lower mast  6 : the highest degree, pitch, or rank

**²top** vb **topped; top·ping**  1 : to remove or trim the top of : PRUNE ⟨∼ a tree⟩  2 : to cover with a top or on the top : CROWN, CAP  3 : to be superior to : EXCEL, SURPASS  4 : to go over the top of  5 : to strike (a golf ball) above the center  6 : to make an end or conclusion ⟨∼ off a meal with coffee⟩

**³top** adj : of, relating to, or being at the top : HIGHEST

**⁴top** n : a child's toy that has a tapering point on which it is made to spin

**to·paz** \'tō-,paz\ n : a hard silicate mineral that when occurring as perfect yellow crystals is valued as a gem

**top·coat** \'täp-,kōt\ n : a lightweight overcoat

**top–dress** \'täp-,dres\ vb : to apply material to (as land) without working it in; esp : to scatter fertilizer over

**top–dress·ing** \-,iŋ\ n : a material used to top-dress soil

**tope** \'tōp\ vb **toped; top·ing** : to drink intoxicating liquor to excess

**top·er** \'tō-pər\ n : one that topes; esp : DRUNKARD

**top flight** n : the highest level of excellence or rank — **top–flight** adj

**top hat** n : a man's tall-crowned hat of beaver or silk

**top–heavy** \'täp-,hev-ē\ adj : having the top part too heavy for the lower part

**top·ic** \'täp-ik\ n  1 : a heading in an outlined argument  2 : the subject of a discourse or a section of it : THEME

**top·i·cal** \-i-kəl\ adj  1 : of, relating to, or arranged by topics ⟨a ∼ outline⟩  2 : relating to current or local events — **top·i·cal·ly** \-k(ə-)lē\ adv

**top·knot** \'täp-,nät\ n  1 : an ornament (as a knot of ribbons) forming a headdress  2 : a crest of feathers or hair on the top of the head

**top·less** \-ləs\ adj  1 : wearing no clothing on the upper body  2 : featuring topless waitresses or entertainers — **top·less·ness** n

**top·mast** \'täp-,mast, -məst\ n : the second mast above a ship's deck

**top·most** \'täp-,mōst\ adj : highest of all : UPPERMOST

**top–notch** \-'näch\ adj : of the highest quality : FIRST-RATE

**topog** abbr topography

**to·pog·ra·phy** \tə-'päg-rə-fē\ n  1 : the art of showing in detail on a map or chart the physical features of a place or region  2 : the outline of the form of a place showing its relief and the position of features (as rivers, roads, or cities) — **to·pog·ra·pher** \-fər\ n — **top·o·graph·ic** \,täp-ə-'graf-ik\ adj — **top·o·graph·i·cal** \-i-kəl\ adj

**top·ping** \'täp-iŋ\ n : something (as a garnish or sauce) that forms a top

**top·ple** \'täp-əl\ vb **top·pled; top·pling** \-(ə-)liŋ\  1 : to fall from or as if from being top-heavy  2 : to push over : OVERTURN; also : OVERTHROW

**tops** \'täps\ adj : topmost in quality or eminence ⟨is considered ∼ in his field⟩

**top·sail** \'täp-,sāl, -səl\ also **top·s'l** \-səl\ n : the sail next above the lowest sail on a mast in a square-rigged ship

**top secret** adj : demanding inviolate secrecy among those concerned

**top·side** \'täp-'sīd\ adv or adj  1 : on deck  2 : to or on the top or surface

**top·sides** \-'sīds\ n pl : the top portion of the outer surface of a ship on each side above the waterline

**top·sy–tur·vy** \,täp-sē-'tər-vē\ adv or adj  1 : upside down  2 : in utter confusion

**toque** \'tōk\ n : a woman's small hat without a brim

**tor** \'tȯr\ n : a high craggy hill

**To·rah** \'tōr-ə\ n  1 : a scroll of the

first five books of the Old Testament used in a synagogue; *also* **:** these five books **2 :** the body of divine knowledge and law found in the Jewish scriptures and tradition

**torch** \'tórch\ *n* **1 :** a flaming light made of something that burns brightly and usu. carried in the hand **2 :** something that resembles a torch in giving light, heat, or guidance **3** *chiefly Brit* **:** FLASHLIGHT — **torch·bear·er** \-,bar-ər\ *n* — **torch·light** \-,līt\ *n*

**torch song** *n* **:** a popular sentimental song of unrequited love

**tore** *past of* TEAR

**to·re·ador** \'tór-ē-ə-,dór\ *n* **:** BULLFIGHTER

**to·re·ro** \tə-'re(ə)r-ō\ *n, pl* **-ros :** BULLFIGHTER

**¹tor·ment** \'tór-,ment\ *n* **1 :** extreme pain or anguish of body or mind **2 :** a source of vexation or pain

**²tor·ment** \tór-'ment\ *vb* **1 :** to cause severe suffering of body or mind to **2 :** VEX, HARASS **syn** rack, afflict, try, torture — **tor·men·tor** \-ər\ *n*

**torn** *past part of* TEAR

**tor·na·do** \tór-'nād-ō\ *n, pl* **-does** *or* **-dos** [modif. of Sp *tronada* thunderstorm, fr. *tronar* to thunder; fr. L *tonare*] **:** a violent destructive whirling wind accompanied by a funnel-shaped cloud that moves over a narrow path

**¹tor·pe·do** \tór-'pēd-ō\ *n, pl* **-does :** a self-propelling cigar-shaped submarine missile filled with an explosive charge

**²torpedo** *vb* **tor·pe·doed; tor·pe·do·ing** \-'pēd-ə-wiŋ\ **:** to hit with or destroy by a torpedo

**torpedo boat** *n* **:** a small very fast thinly plated boat for discharging torpedoes

**tor·pid** \'tór-pəd\ *adj* **1 :** having lost motion or the power of exertion **:** SLUGGISH **2 :** lacking vigor **:** DULL — **tor·pid·i·ty** \tór-'pid-ət-ē\ *n*

**tor·por** \'tór-pər\ *n* **1 :** extreme sluggishness **:** STAGNATION **2 :** DULLNESS, APATHY **syn** stupor, lethargy, languor, lassitude

**¹torque** \'tórk\ *n* **:** a force that produces or tends to produce rotation or torsion

**²torque** *vb* **torqued; torqu·ing :** to impart torque to **:** cause to twist (as about an axis)

**torr** \'tór\ *n, pl* **torr :** a unit of pressure equal to $1/760$ of an atmosphere

**tor·rent** \'tór-ənt\ *n* [F, fr. L *torrent-, torrens,* fr. *torrent-, torrens* burning, seething, rushing, fr. prp. of *torrēre* to parch, burn] **1 :** a rushing stream (as of water) **2 :** a tumultuous outburst

**tor·ren·tial** \tó-'ren-chəl, tə-\ *adj* **1 :** relating to or having the character of a torrent (~ rains) **2 :** resembling a torrent in violence or rapidity of flow

**tor·rid** \'tór-əd\ *adj* **1 :** parched with heat esp. of the sun **:** HOT **2 :** ARDENT

**torrid zone** *n* **:** the region of the earth between the tropics over which the sun is vertical at some time of the year

**tor·sion** \'tór-shən\ *n* **:** a twisting or being twisted **:** a wrenching by which one part of a body is under pressure to turn about a longitudinal axis while the other part is held fast or is under pressure to turn in the opposite direction — **tor·sion·al** \'tór-sh(ə-)nəl\ *adj* — **tor·sion·al·ly** \-ē\ *adv*

**tor·so** \'tór-sō\ *n, pl* **torsos** *or* **tor·si** \'tór-,sē\ **:** the trunk of the human body

**tort** \'tórt\ *n* **:** a wrongful act except one involving a breach of contract for which the injured party can recover damages in a civil action

**tor·ti·lla** \tór-'tē-(y)ə\ *n* **:** a round thin cake of unleavened cornmeal bread usu. eaten hot with a topping of ground meat or cheese

**tor·toise** \'tórt-əs\ *n* **:** TURTLE; *esp* **:** a sea turtle whose shell yields tortoiseshell

**¹tor·toise·shell** \'tórt-ə-,shel, -əs(h)-,shel\ *n* **:** the mottled horny substance of the shell of some turtles used in inlaying and in making various ornamental articles

**²tortoiseshell** *adj* **:** made of or resembling tortoiseshell esp. in spotted brown and yellow coloring

**tor·to·ni** \tór-'tō-nē\ *n* **:** ice cream made of heavy cream often with minced almonds and chopped cherries and flavored with rum

**tor·tu·ous** \'tórch-(ə-)wəs\ *adj* **1 :** marked by twists or turns **:** WINDING **2 :** DEVIOUS, TRICKY

**¹tor·ture** \'tór-chər\ *n* **1 :** the infliction of severe pain esp. to punish or coerce **2 :** anguish of body or mind **:** AGONY

**²torture** *vb* **tor·tured; tor·tur·ing** \'tórch-(ə-)riŋ\ **1 :** to punish or coerce by inflicting severe pain **2 :** to cause intense suffering to **:** TORMENT **3 :** TWIST, DISTORT **syn** rack, grill, afflict, try — **tor·tur·er** *n*

**To·ry** \'tōr-ē\ *n, pl* **Tories** [Ir Gael *tōraidhe* pursued man, robber, fr. Middle Irish *tóir* pursuit] **1 :** a member of a chiefly 18th century British party upholding the established church and the traditional political structure **2 :** an American supporter of the British during the American Revolution **3 :** a member of the Conservative party in the United Kingdom **4** *often not cap* **:** an extreme conservative — **Tory** *adj*

**¹toss** \'tós, 'täs\ *vb* **1 :** to fling to and fro or up and down **2 :** to throw with a quick light motion; *also* **:** BANDY **3 :** to fling or lift with a sudden motion (~ed her head angrily) **4 :** to move restlessly or turbulently (~es on the waves) **5 :** to twist and turn repeatedly **6 :** FLOUNCE **7 :** to accomplish readily (~ off an article) **8 :** to decide an issue by flipping a coin

**²toss** *n* **:** an act or instance of tossing; *esp* **:** TOSS-UP **1**

**toss-up** \-,əp\ *n* **1 :** a deciding by flipping a coin **2 :** an even chance

**¹tot** \'tät\ *n* **1 :** a small child **2 :** a small drink of alcoholic liquor **:** SHOT

**²tot** *vb* **tot·ted; tot·ting :** to add up

**³tot** *abbr* total

¹**to·tal** \'tōt-ᵊl\ *adj* **1 :** making up a whole **:** ENTIRE ⟨∼ amount⟩ **2 :** COMPLETE, UTTER ⟨a ∼ failure⟩ **3 :** concentrating all personnel and resources on an objective — **to·tal·ly** \-ē\ *adv*

²**total** *n* **:** the entire amount **:** SUM **syn** aggregate, whole, quantity

³**total** *vb* **to·taled** *or* **to·talled; to·tal·ing** *or* **to·tal·ling 1 :** to add up **:** COMPUTE **2 :** to amount to **:** NUMBER **3 :** to make a total wreck of (a car)

**to·tal·i·tar·i·an** \tō-ˌtal-ə-'ter-ē-ən\ *adj* **:** of or relating to a political regime based on subordination of the individual to the state and strict control of all aspects of life esp. by coercive measures; *also* **:** advocating, constituting, or characteristic of such a regime — **totalitarian** *n* — **to·tal·i·tar·i·an·ism** \-ē-ə-ˌniz-əm\ *n*

**to·tal·i·ty** \tō-'tal-ət-ē\ *n, pl* **-ties 1 :** an aggregate amount **:** SUM, WHOLE **2 :** ENTIRETY, WHOLENESS

**to·tal·iza·tor** *or* **to·tal·isa·tor** \'tōt-ᵊl-ə-ˌzāt-ər\ *n* **:** a machine for registering and indicating the nature and number of bets made on a horse or dog race

¹**tote** \'tōt\ *vb* **toted; tot·ing :** CARRY

²**tote** *vb* **toted; tot·ing :** ADD, TOTAL — usu. used with *up*

**to·tem** \'tōt-əm\ *n* **:** an object (as an animal or plant) serving as the emblem of a family or clan and often as a reminder of its ancestry; *also* **:** a usu. carved or painted representation of such an object

**totem pole** *n* **:** a pole that is carved with a series of totems and is erected before the houses of some northwest American Indians

**tot·ter** \'tät-ər\ *vb* **1 :** to tremble or rock as if about to fall **:** SWAY **2 :** to move unsteadily **:** STAGGER

**tou·can** \'tü-ˌkan\ *n* **:** a brilliantly colored fruit-eating tropical American bird with a very large bill

¹**touch** \'təch\ *vb* **1 :** to bring a bodily part (as the hand) into contact with so as to feel **2 :** to be or cause to be in contact **3 :** to strike or push lightly esp. with the hand or foot **4 :** to make use of ⟨never ∼es alcohol⟩ **5 :** DISTURB, HARM **6 :** to induce to give or lend **7 :** to get to **:** REACH **8 :** to refer to in passing **:** MENTION **9 :** to affect the interest of **:** CONCERN **10 :** to leave a mark on; *also* **:** BLEMISH **11 :** to move to sympathetic feeling **12 :** to come close **:** VERGE **13 :** to have a bearing **:** RELATE **14 :** to make a usu. brief or incidental stop in port **syn** affect, influence, impress, strike, sway

²**touch** *n* **1 :** a light stroke or tap **2 :** the act or fact of touching or being touched **3 :** the sense by which pressure or traction is felt; *also* **:** a particular sensation conveyed by this sense **4 :** mental or moral sensitiveness **:** TACT **5 :** a small quantity **:** TRACE **6 :** a manner of striking or touching esp. the keys of a keyboard instrument **7 :** an improving detail ⟨add a few ∼es to the painting⟩ **8 :** distinctive manner or

skill ⟨∼ of a master⟩ **9 :** the state of being in contact ⟨keep in ∼⟩ **syn** suggestion, suspicion, tincture, tinge

**touch·down** \'təch-ˌdaùn\ *n* **:** the act of scoring six points in American football by being lawfully in possession of the ball on, above, or behind an opponent's goal line

**tou·ché** \tü-'shā\ *interj* — used to acknowledge a hit in fencing or the success of an argument, an accusation, or a witty point

**touch football** *n* **:** football played informally and chiefly characterized by the substitution of touching for tackling

**touch·ing** \'təch-iŋ\ *adj* **:** capable of stirring emotions **:** PATHETIC **syn** moving, impressive, poignant

**touch off** *vb* **1 :** to describe with precision **2 :** to cause to explode **3 :** to release or initiate with sudden intensity

**touch·stone** \'təch-ˌstōn\ *n* **:** a test or criterion of genuineness or quality **syn** standard, gauge

**touch up** \(')təch-'əp\ *vb* **:** to improve or perfect by small additional strokes or alterations

**touchy** \'təch-ē\ *adj* **touch·i·er; -est 1 :** easily offended **:** PEEVISH **2 :** calling for tact in treatment ⟨a ∼ subject⟩ **syn** irascible, cranky, cross

¹**tough** \'təf\ *adj* **1 :** strong or firm in texture but flexible and not brittle **2 :** not easily chewed **3 :** characterized by severity and determination ⟨a ∼ policy⟩ **4 :** capable of enduring strain or hardship **:** ROBUST **5 :** hard to influence **:** STUBBORN **6 :** difficult to cope with ⟨a ∼ problem⟩ **7 :** ROWDYISH, RUFFIANLY **syn** tenacious, stout, sturdy, stalwart — **tough·ly** *adv* — **tough·ness** *n*

²**tough** *n* **:** a tough person; *esp* **:** a rowdy person

**tough·en** \'təf-ən\ *vb* **tough·ened; tough·en·ing** \-(ə-)niŋ\ **:** to make or become tough

**tou·pee** \tü-'pā\ *n* **:** a small wig for a bald spot

¹**tour** \'tùr, *1 is also* 'taù(ə)r\ *n* **1 :** one's turn **:** SHIFT **2 :** a journey in which one returns to the starting point

²**tour** *vb* **:** to travel over as a tourist

**tour de force** \ˌtùrd-ə-'fōrs\ *n, pl* **tours de force** \*same*\ **:** a feat of strength, skill, or ingenuity

**tour·ist** \'tùr-əst\ *n* **:** one that makes a tour for pleasure or culture

**tourist class** *n* **:** economy accommodation on a ship, airplane, or train

**tour·ma·line** \'tùr-mə-lən, -ˌlēn\ *n* **:** a mineral that when transparent is valued as a gem

**tour·na·ment** \'tùr-nə-mənt, 'tər-\ *n* **1 :** a medieval sport in which mounted armored knights contended with blunted lances or swords; *also* **:** the whole series of knightly sports, jousts, and tilts occurring at one time and place. **2 :** a championship series of games or athletic contests

**tour·ney** \-nē\ *n, pl* **tourneys :** TOURNAMENT

**tour·ni·quet** \'tùr-ni-kət, 'tər-\ *n* **:** a

device (as a bandage twisted tight with a stick) for stopping bleeding or blood flow

**tou·sle** \'taù-zəl\ vb **tou·sled; tou·sling** \'taùz-(ə-)liŋ\ : to disorder by rough handling : DISHEVEL, MUSS

¹**tout** \'taùt\ vb : to give a tip or solicit bets on a racehorse — **tout** n

²**tout** \'taùt, 'tüt\ vb : to praise or publicize loudly

¹**tow** \'tō\ vb : to draw or pull along behind syn tug, haul, drag

²**tow** n 1 : an act of towing or condition of being towed 2 : something (as a barge) that is towed

³**tow** n : short or broken fiber (as of flax or hemp) used esp. for yarn, twine, or stuffing

**to·ward** or **to·wards** \(')tō-(-ə)rd(z), tə-'wòrd(z)\ prep 1 : in the direction of ⟨heading ∼ the river⟩ 2 : along a course leading to ⟨efforts ∼ reconciliation⟩ 3 : in regard to ⟨tolerance ∼ minorities⟩ 4 : FACING ⟨the gun's muzzle was ∼ him⟩ 5 : close upon ⟨it was getting along ∼ sundown⟩ 6 : for part payment of ⟨paid $100 ∼ his tuition⟩

**tow·boat** \'tō-,bōt\ n : TUGBOAT

**tow·el** \'taù(-ə)l\ n : an absorbent cloth or paper for wiping or drying

**tow·el·ing** or **tow·el·ling** \'taù-(ə-)liŋ\ n : a cotton or linen fabric often used for making towels

¹**tow·er** \'taù(-ə)r\ n 1 : a tall structure either isolated or built upon a larger structure ⟨an observation ∼⟩ ⟨a bell ∼ of a church⟩ 2 : a towering citadel — **tow·ered** \'taù(-ə)rd\ adj

²**tower** vb : to reach or rise to a great height syn soar, mount, ascend, surge

**tow·er·ing** \-iŋ\ adj 1 : LOFTY ⟨∼ pines⟩ 2 : reaching high intensity ⟨a ∼ rage⟩ 3 : EXCESSIVE ⟨∼ ambition⟩

**tow·head** \'tō-,hed\ n : a person having flaxen hair — **tow·head·ed** \-,hed-əd\ adj

**to·whee** \'tō-,hē, 'tō-(,)ē, tō-'hē\ n : a common finch of eastern No. America having the male black, white, and reddish; also : any of several related finches

**to wit** \tə-'wit\ adv : NAMELY

**town** \'taùn\ n 1 : a compactly settled area usu. larger than a village but smaller than a city 2 : CITY 3 : a New England territorial and political unit usu. containing both rural and urban areas; also : a New England community in which matters of local government are decided by a general assembly ⟨**town meeting**⟩ of qualified voters

**town house** n 1 : the city residence of a person having a country home 2 : a single-family house of two or sometimes three stories connected to another house by a common wall

**towns·folk** \'taùnz-,fōk\ n pl : TOWNSPEOPLE

**town·ship** \'taùn-,ship\ n 1 : TOWN 3 2 : a unit of local government in some states 3 : an unorganized subdivision of a county; also : an administrative division 4 : a division of territory in surveys of U.S. public land containing 36 square miles

**towns·man** \'taùnz-mən\ n 1 : a native or resident of a town or city 2 : a fellow citizen of a town

**towns·peo·ple** \-,pē-pəl\ n pl 1 : the inhabitants of a town or city 2 : town-bred persons

**tow·path** \'tō-,path, -,pȧth\ n : a path (as along a canal) traveled by men or animals towing boats

**tow truck** n : WRECKER 3

**tox·emia** \täk-'sē-mē-ə\ n : abnormality associated with the presence of toxic matter in the blood

**tox·ic** \'täk-sik\ adj [LL toxicus, fr. L toxicum poison, fr. Gk toxikon arrow poison, fr. neut. of toxikos of a bow, fr. toxon bow, arrow] : of, relating to, or caused by poison or a toxin : POISONOUS — **tox·ic·i·ty** \täk-'sis-ət-ē\ n

**tox·i·col·o·gy** \,täk-sə-'käl-ə-jē\ n : a science that deals with poisons and esp. with problems of their use and control — **tox·i·co·log·ic** \,täk-si-kə-'läj-ik\ adj — **tox·i·col·o·gist** \-'käl-ə-jəst\ n

**tox·in** \'täk-sən\ n : a substance produced by a living organism that is very poisonous when introduced into the tissues but is usu. destroyed by digestive processes when taken by mouth

¹**toy** \'tòi\ n 1 : something trifling 2 : a small ornament : BAUBLE 3 : something for a child to play with

²**toy** vb 1 : FLIRT 2 : to deal with something lightly : TRIFLE 3 : to amuse oneself as if with a plaything

³**toy** adj 1 : designed for use as a toy 2 : DIMINUTIVE

**tp** abbr 1 title page 2 township

**tpk** or **tpke** abbr turnpike

**tr** abbr 1 translated; translation; translator 2 transpose 3 troop

¹**trace** \'trās\ n 1 : a mark (as a footprint or track) left by something that has passed : VESTIGE 2 : a minute or barely detectable amount

²**trace** vb **traced; trac·ing** 1 : to mark out : SKETCH 2 : to form (as letters) carefully 3 : to copy (a drawing) by marking lines on transparent paper laid over the drawing to be copied 4 : to follow the trail of : track down 5 : to study out and follow the development of — **trace·able** adj — **trac·er** n

³**trace** n : either of two lines of a harness for fastening a draft animal to a vehicle

**trac·ery** \'trās-(ə-)rē\ n, pl **-er·ies** : ornamental work having a design with branching or interlacing lines

**tra·chea** \'trā-kē-ə\ n, pl **-che·ae** \-kē-,ē\ also **-che·as** : the main tube by which air enters the lungs : WINDPIPE — **tra·che·al** \-kē-əl\ adj

**trac·ing** \'trā-siŋ\ n 1 : the act of one that traces 2 : something that is traced 3 : a graphic record made by an instrument for measuring vibrations or pulsations

¹**track** \'trak\ n 1 : a mark left in passing 2 : PATH, ROUTE, TRAIL 3 : a course laid out for racing; also : track-and-field sports 4 : a way for various wheeled vehicles; esp : a way made by two parallel lines of metal rails 5 : awareness of a fact or progression

⟨lost ~ of his movements⟩  **6 :** either of two endless metal belts on which a vehicle (as a tractor) travels  **7 :** one of a series of paths along which material (as music) is recorded (as on magnetic tape)

²**track** *vb*  **1 :** to follow the tracks or traces of **:** TRAIL  **2 :** to make tracks on  **3 :** to carry on the feet and deposit ⟨~ed mud on the floor⟩ — **track·er** *n*

**track·age** \'trak-ij\ *n* **:** lines of railway track

**track–and–field** \,trak-ən-'fēld\ *adj* **:** of or relating to athletic contests held on a running track or on the adjacent field

¹**tract** \'trakt\ *n* **:** a pamphlet of political or religious propaganda

²**tract** *n*  **1 :** a stretch of land without precise boundaries ⟨broad ~s of prairie⟩  **2 :** a defined area of land ⟨a garden ~⟩  **3 :** a system of body parts or organs together serving some special purpose ⟨the digestive ~⟩

**trac·ta·ble** \'trak-tə-bəl\ *adj*  **1 :** easily controlled **:** DOCILE  **2 :** easily wrought **:** MALLEABLE  **syn** amenable, obedient

**trac·tate** \'trak-,tāt\ *n* **:** TREATISE

**trac·tion** \'trak-shən\ *n*  **1 :** the act of drawing **:** the state of being drawn  **2 :** the drawing of a vehicle by motive power; *also* **:** the particular form of motive power used  **3 :** the adhesive friction of a body on a surface on which it moves — **trac·tion·al** \-sh(ə-)nəl\ *adj* — **trac·tive** \'trak-tiv\ *adj*

**trac·tor** \'trak-tər\ *n*  **1 :** an automotive vehicle that is borne on four wheels or beltlike metal tracks and used for drawing, pushing, or bearing implements or vehicles  **2 :** a motortruck with short chassis for hauling a trailer

¹**trade** \'trād\ *n*  **1 :** one's regular business or work **:** OCCUPATION  **2 :** an occupation requiring manual or mechanical skill  **3 :** the persons engaged in a business or industry  **4 :** the business of buying and selling or bartering commodities  **5 :** an act of trading **:** TRANSACTION  **syn** craft, profession, commerce, industry

²**trade** *vb* **trad·ed; trad·ing**  **1 :** to give in exchange for another commodity **:** BARTER  **2 :** to engage in the exchange, purchase, or sale of goods  **3 :** to deal regularly as a customer — **trade on :** EXPLOIT ⟨*trades on* his family name⟩

**trade–in** \'trād-,in\ *n* **:** an item of merchandise taken as part payment of a purchase

**trade in** \(')trād-'in\ *vb* **:** to turn in as part payment for a purchase

¹**trade·mark** \'trād-,märk\ *n* **:** a device (as a word or mark) that points distinctly to the origin or ownership of merchandise to which it is applied and that is legally reserved for the exclusive use of the owner

²**trademark** *vb* **1 :** to label with a trademark  **2 :** to secure the trademark rights for

**trade name** *n*  **1 :** the name by which an article is called in its own trade  **2 :** a name that is given by a manufacturer or merchant to a product to distinguish it as made or sold by him and that may be used and protected as a trademark  **3 :** the name under which a firm does business

**trad·er** \'trād-ər\ *n*  **1 :** a person whose business is buying or selling  **2 :** a ship engaged in trade

**trades·man** \'trādz-mən\ *n*  **1 :** one who runs a retail store **:** SHOPKEEPER  **2 :** CRAFTSMAN

**trades·peo·ple** \-,pē-pəl\ *n pl* **:** people engaged in trade

**trade wind** *n* **:** a wind blowing regularly from northeast to southwest north of the equator and from southeast to northwest south of the equator

**trading stamp** *n* **:** a printed stamp of value given as a premium to a retail customer and when accumulated in numbers redeemed in merchandise

**tra·di·tion** \trə-'dish-ən\ *n*  **1 :** the handing down of beliefs and customs by word of mouth or by example without written instruction; *also* **:** a belief or custom thus handed down  **2 :** an inherited pattern of thought or action — **tra·di·tion·al** \-,dish(ə-)nəl\ *adj* — **tra·di·tion·al·ly** \-ē\ *adv* — **tra·di·tion·ary** \-ə-,ner-ē\ *adj*

**tra·duce** \trə-'d(y)üs\ *vb* **tra·duced; tra·duc·ing :** to lower the reputation of **:** DEFAME, SLANDER  **syn** malign, libel — **tra·duc·er** *n*

¹**traf·fic** \'traf-ik\ *n*  **1 :** the business of bartering or buying and selling  **2 :** communication or dealings between individuals or groups  **3 :** the movement (as of vehicles) along a route  **4 :** the passengers or cargo carried by a transportation system

²**traffic** *vb* **traf·ficked; traf·fick·ing :** to carry on traffic — **traf·fick·er** *n*

**traffic circle** *n* **:** ROTARY 2

**traffic light** *n* **:** an electrically operated visual signal for controlling traffic

**tra·ge·di·an** \trə-'jēd-ē-ən\ *n*  **1 :** a writer of tragedies  **2 :** an actor who plays tragic roles

**tra·ge·di·enne** \trə-,jēd-ē-'en\ *n* **:** an actress who plays tragic roles

**trag·e·dy** \'traj-əd-ē\ *n*, *pl* **-dies** [ME *tragedie*, fr. MF, fr. L *tragoedia*, fr. Gk *tragōidia*, fr. *tragos* goat + *aeidein* to sing; prob. fr. the satyrs represented by the original chorus]  **1 :** a serious drama describing a conflict between the protagonist and a superior force (as destiny) and having a sad end that excites pity or terror  **2 :** a disastrous event **:** CALAMITY; *also* **:** MISFORTUNE  **3 :** tragic quality or element

**trag·ic** \'traj-ik\ *also* **trag·i·cal** \-i-kəl\ *adj*  **1 :** of, relating to, or expressive of tragedy  **2 :** appropriate to tragedy  **3 :** LAMENTABLE, UNFORTUNATE — **trag·i·cal·ly** \-i-k(ə)lē\ *adv*

¹**trail** \'trāl\ *vb*  **1 :** to hang down so as to drag along or sweep the ground  **2 :** to draw or drag along behind  **3 :** to extend over a surface in a straggling

manner 4 : to follow slowly : lag behind 5 : to follow upon the track of : PURSUE 6 : DWINDLE ⟨her voice ~ed off⟩ syn chase, tag, tail

²**trail** n 1 : something that trails or is trailed ⟨a ~ of smoke⟩ 2 : a trace or mark left by something that has passed or been drawn along : TRACK ⟨a ~ of blood⟩ 3 : a beaten path; also : a marked path through woods 4 : SCENT

**trail bike** n : a small motorcycle for use other than on highways

**trail·blaz·er** \-,blā-zər\ n : PATH-FINDER, PIONEER — **trail·blaz·ing** \-,ziŋ\ adj or n

**trail·er** \'trā-lər\ n 1 : one that trails; esp : a creeping plant (as an ivy) 2 : a vehicle that is hauled by another (as a tractor) 3 : a vehicle equipped to serve wherever parked as a dwelling or as a place of business

**trailing arbutus** n : a trailing spring-flowering plant with fragrant pink or white flowers; also : its flower

¹**train** \'trān\ n 1 : a part of a gown that trails behind the wearer 2 : RETINUE 3 : a moving file of persons, vehicles, or animals 4 : a connected series ⟨a ~ of thought⟩ 5 : a connected line of railroad cars usu. hauled by a locomotive 6 : AFTERMATH syn succession, sequence, procession, chain

²**train** vb 1 : to cause to grow as desired ⟨~ a vine on a trellis⟩ 2 : to form by instruction, discipline, or drill 3 : to make or become prepared (as by exercise) for a test of skill 4 : to aim or point at an object ⟨~ guns on a fort⟩ syn discipline, school, educate, direct, level — **train·er** n

**train·ee** \trā-'nē\ n : one who is being trained for a job

**train·ing** \'trā-niŋ\ n 1 : the act, process, or method of one who trains 2 : the state of being trained

**train·load** \'trān-'lōd\ n : the full freight or passenger capacity of a railroad train

**train·man** \-mən\ n : a member of a train crew

**traipse** \'trāps\ vb **traipsed; traips·ing** : TRAMP, WALK

**trait** \'trāt\ n : a distinguishing quality (as of personality) : CHARACTERISTIC

**trai·tor** \'trāt-ər\ n [ME traitre, fr. OF, fr. L traditor, fr. traditus, pp. of tradere to hand over, deliver, betray, fr. trans- across + dare to give] 1 : one who betrays another's trust or is false to an obligation 2 : one who commits treason — **trai·tor·ous** adj — **trai·tress** \'trā-trəs\ n

**tra·jec·to·ry** \trə-'jek-t(ə-)rē\ n, pl -ries : the curve that a body (as a planet in its orbit) describes in space

**tram** \'tram\ n 1 chiefly Brit : STREET-CAR 2 : a boxlike car running on a railway (**tram·way** \-,wā\) in a mine or a logging camp

¹**tram·mel** \'tram-əl\ n [ME tramayle, a kind of net, fr. MF tremail, fr. LL tremaculum, fr. L tres three + macula mesh, spot] : something impeding activity, progress, or freedom

²**trammel** vb **-meled** or **-melled; -mel·ing** or **-mel·ling** \-(ə-)liŋ\ 1 : to catch and hold in or as if in a net 2 : HAMPER syn clog, fetter, shackle

¹**tramp** \'tramp, 1 & 3 are also 'trämp, 'trȯmp\ vb 1 : to walk, tread, or step heavily 2 : to walk about or through; also : HIKE 3 : to tread on forcibly and repeatedly

²**tramp** \'tramp, 5 is also 'trämp, 'trȯmp\ n 1 : a foot traveler 2 : a begging or thieving vagrant 3 : an immoral woman; esp : PROSTITUTE 4 : a walking trip : HIKE 5 : the succession of sounds made by the beating of feet on a road 6 : a ship that does not follow a regular course but takes cargo to any port

**tram·ple** \'tram-pəl\ vb **tram·pled; tram·pling** \-p(ə-)liŋ\ 1 : to tread heavily so as to bruise, crush, or injure 2 : to inflict injury or destruction 3 : to press down or crush by or as if by treading : STAMP — **trample** n — **tram·pler** \-p(ə-)lər\ n

**tram·po·line** \,tram-pə-'lēn, 'tram-pə-,lēn\ n : a resilient canvas sheet or web supported by springs in a metal frame used as a springboard in tumbling — **tram·po·lin·er** \-'lē-nər, -,lē-\ n — **tram·po·lin·ist** \-nəst\ n

**trance** \'trans\ n [ME, fr. MF transe, fr. transir to pass away, swoon, fr. L transire to pass, pass away, fr. trans-across + ire go] 1 : DAZE, STUPOR 2 : a prolonged and profound sleeplike condition (as of deep hypnosis) 3 : a state of mystical absorption

**tran·quil** \'traŋ-kwəl, 'tran-\ adj : free from agitation or disturbance : QUIET syn serene, placid, peaceful — **tran·quil·li·ty** or **tran·quil·i·ty** \tran-'kwil-ət-ē, traŋ-\ n — **tran·quil·ly** \'traŋ-kwə-lē, 'tran-\ adv

**tran·quil·ize** or **tran·quil·lize** \'traŋ-kwə-,līz, 'tran-\ vb **-ized** or **-lized; -iz·ing** or **-liz·ing** : to make or become tranquil; esp : to relieve of mental tension and anxiety

**tran·quil·iz·er** also **tran·quil·liz·er** \-,lī-zər\ n : a drug used to relieve tension and anxiety

**trans** abbr 1 transaction 2 transitive 3 translated; translation; translator 4 transportation 5 transverse

**trans·act** \trans-'akt, tranz-\ vb : to carry out : PERFORM; also : CONDUCT

**trans·ac·tion** \-'ak-shən\ n 1 : an act or process of transacting 2 : something transacted; esp : a business deal 3 pl : the records of the proceedings of a society or organization

**trans·at·lan·tic** \,trans-ət-'lant-ik, ,tranz-\ adj : crossing or extending across or situated beyond the Atlantic ocean

**trans·ceiv·er** \trans-'ē-vər, tranz-\ n : a radio transmitter-receiver that uses some of the same components for transmission and reception

**tran·scend** \trans-'end\ vb 1 : to rise above the limits of 2 : SURPASS syn exceed, outdo

**tran·scen·dent** \-'en-dənt\ adj 1

: exceeding usual limits : SURPASSING 2 : transcending material existence **syn** superlative, supreme, peerless, incomparable

**tran·scen·den·tal** \,trans-,en-'dent-°l, -ən-\ *adj* 1 : TRANSCENDENT 2 : of, relating to, or characteristic of transcendentalism; *also* : ABSTRUSE

**tran·scen·den·tal·ism** \-'°l-,iz-əm\ *n* : a philosophy holding that ultimate reality is unknowable or asserting the primacy of the spiritual over the material and empirical — **tran·scen·den·tal·ist** \-'°l-əst\ *adj or n*

**trans·con·ti·nen·tal** \,trans-,känt-°n-'ent-°l\ *adj* 1 : extending or going across a continent 2 : situated on the farther side of a continent

**tran·scribe** \trans-'krīb\ *vb* **tran·scribed; tran·scrib·ing** 1 : to write a copy of 2 : to make a copy of in longhand or on a typewriter 3 : to represent (speech sounds) by means of phonetic symbols; *also* : to make a musical transcription of 4 : to record on a phonograph record or magnetic tape for later radio broadcast; *also* : to broadcast recorded matter

**tran·script** \'trans-,kript\ *n* 1 : a written, printed, or typed copy 2 : an official copy esp. of a student's educational record

**tran·scrip·tion** \trans-'krip-shən\ *n* 1 : an act or process of transcribing 2 : COPY, TRANSCRIPT 3 : an arrangement of a musical composition for some instrument or voice other than the original 4 : radio broadcasting from a phonograph record; *also* : the record itself

**trans·duce** \trans-'d(y)üs, tranz-\ *vb* **trans·duced; trans·duc·ing** 1 : to convert (as energy) into another form 2 : to produce by transducing

**trans·duc·er** \-'d(y)ü-sər\ *n* : a device that is actuated by power from one system and supplies power usu. in another form to a second system

**tran·sept** \'trans-,ept\ *n* : the part of a cruciform church that crosses at right angles to the greatest length; *also* : either of the projecting ends

¹**trans·fer** \trans-'fər, 'trans-,fər\ *vb* **trans·ferred; trans·fer·ring** 1 : to pass or cause to pass from one person, place, or situation to another : TRANSPORT, TRANSMIT 2 : to make over the possession of : CONVEY 3 : to print or copy from one surface to another by contact 4 : to change from one vehicle or transportation line to another — **trans·fer·able** \trans-'fər-ə-bəl\ *adj* — **trans·fer·al** \-əl\ *n*

²**trans·fer** \'trans-,fər\ *n* 1 : conveyance of right, title, or interest in property from one person to another 2 : an act or process of transferring 3 : one that transfers or is transferred 4 : a ticket entitling a passenger on a public conveyance to continue his journey on another route

**trans·fer·ence** \trans-'fər-əns\ *n* : an act, process, or instance of transferring

**trans·fig·ure** \trans-'fig-yər\ *vb*

-ured; -uring 1 : to change the form or appearance of 2 : EXALT, GLORIFY **trans·fig·u·ra·tion** \,trans-,fig-(y)ə-'rā-shən\ *n*

**trans·fix** \trans-'fiks\ *vb* 1 : to pierce through with or as if with a pointed weapon 2 : to hold motionless by or as if by piercing

**trans·form** \trans-'fòrm\ *vb* 1 : to change in structure, appearance, or character 2 : to change (an electric current) in potential or type **syn** transmute, transfigure — **trans·for·ma·tion** \,trans-fər-'mā-shən\ *n* — **trans·form·er** \trans-'fòr-mər\ *n*

**trans·fuse** \trans-'fyüz\ *vb* **trans·fused; trans·fus·ing** 1 : to cause to pass from one to another 2 : to diffuse into or through 3 : to transfer (as blood) into a vein of a man or animal — **trans·fu·sion** \-'fyü-zhən\ *n*

**trans·gress** \trans-'gres, tranz-\ *vb* [F *transgresser*, fr. L *transgressus*, pp. of *transgredi* to step beyond or across, fr. *trans*- across + *gradi* to step] 1 : to go beyond the limits set by ⟨~ the divine law⟩ 2 : to go beyond : EXCEED 3 : SIN — **trans·gres·sion** \-'gresh-ən\ *n* — **trans·gres·sor** \-'gres-ər\ *n*

¹**tran·sient** \'tranch-ənt\ *adj* 1 : not lasting long : SHORT-LIVED 2 : passing through a place with only a brief stay **syn** transitory, passing, momentary, fleeting — **tran·sient·ly** *adv*

²**transient** *n* : one that is transient; *esp* : a transient guest

**tran·sis·tor** \tranz-'is-tər, trans-\ *n* [*transfer* + *resistor*: fr. its transferring an electrical signal across a resistor] 1 : a small electronic semiconductor device similar in use to an electron tube 2 : a radio having transistors

**tran·sis·tor·ize** \-tə-,rīz\ *vb* **-ized; -iz·ing** : to equip (a device) with transistors

**tran·sit** \'trans-ət, 'tranz-\ *n* 1 : a passing through, across, or over : PASSAGE 2 : conveyance of persons or things from one place to another 3 : usu. local transportation esp. of people by public conveyance 4 : a surveyor's instrument for measuring angles

**tran·si·tion** \trans-'ish-ən, tranz-\ *n* : passage from one state, place, stage, or subject to another : CHANGE — **tran·si·tion·al** \-'ish-(ə-)nəl\ *adj*

**tran·si·tive** \'trans-ət-iv, 'tranz-\ *adj* 1 : having or containing an object required to complete the meaning 2 : TRANSITIONAL — **tran·si·tive·ly** *adv* — **tran·si·tive·ness** *n* — **tran·si·tiv·i·ty** \,trans-ə-'tiv-ət-ē, ,tranz-\ *n*

**tran·si·to·ry** \'trans-ə-,tòr-ē, 'tranz-\ *adj* : of brief duration : SHORT-LIVED, TEMPORARY **syn** transient *n*: passing, momentary, fleeting

**transl** *abbr* translated; translation

**trans·late** \trans-'lāt, tranz-\ *vb* **trans·lat·ed; trans·lat·ing** 1 : to bear or change from one place, state, or form to another 2 : to convey to heaven without death **3 :** to transfer (a bishop) from one see to another **4 :** to turn into one's own or another language — **trans·lat·able** *adj* — **trans·la·tion** \-'lā-shən\ *n* — **trans·la·tor** \-'lāt-ər\ *n*

**trans·lu·cent** \trans-'lüs-ᵊnt, tranz-\ *adj* **:** admitting and diffusing light so that objects beyond cannot be clearly distinguished **:** partly transparent — **trans·lu·cence** \-ᵊns\ *n* — **trans·lu·cen·cy** \-ᵊn-sē\ *n* — **trans·lu·cent·ly** *adv*

**trans·mi·grate** \-'mī-,grāt\ *vb* **:** to pass at death from one body or being to another — **trans·mi·gra·tion** \,trans-mī-'grā-shen, ,tranz-\ *n* — **trans·mi·gra·tor** \trans-'mī-,grāt-ər, tranz-\ *n* — **trans·mi·gra·to·ry** \-'mī-grə-,tōr-ē\ *adj*

**trans·mis·sion** \-'mish-ən\ *n* **1 :** an act or process of transmitting **2 :** the passage of radio waves between transmitting stations and receiving stations **3 :** the gears by which power is transmitted from the engine of an automobile to the axle that propels the vehicle **4 :** something transmitted

**trans·mit** \-'mit\ *vb* **trans·mit·ted; trans·mit·ting 1 :** to transfer from one person or place to another **:** FORWARD **2 :** to pass on by or as if by inheritance **3 :** to cause (as light, electricity, or force) to pass through space or a medium **4 :** to send out (radio or television signals) **syn** carry, bear, convey, transport — **trans·mis·si·ble** \-'mis-ə-bəl\ *adj* — **trans·mit·ta·ble** \-'mit-ə-bəl\ *adj* — **trans·mit·tal** \-'mit-ᵊl\ *n*

**trans·mit·ter** \-'mit-ər\ *n* **1 :** one that transmits **2 :** the part of a telephone into which one speaks **3 :** a set of apparatus for transmitting telegraph, radio, or television signals

**trans·mog·ri·fy** \trans-'mäg-rə-,fī, tranz-\ *vb* **-fied; -fy·ing 1 :** to change or alter often with grotesque or humorous effect — **trans·mog·ri·fi·ca·tion** \-,mäg-rə-fə-'kā-shən\ *n*

**trans·mute** \-'myüt\ *vb* **trans·muted; trans·mut·ing 1 :** to change or alter in form, appearance, or nature **syn** transform, convert — **trans·mu·ta·tion** \,trans-myü-'tā-shən, ,tranz-\ *n*

**trans·na·tion·al** \-'nash-(ə-)nəl\ *adj* **:** extending beyond national boundaries

**trans·oce·an·ic** \,trans-,ō-shē-'an-ik, ,tranz-\ *adj* **1 :** lying or dwelling beyond the ocean **2 :** crossing or extending across the ocean

**tran·som** \'tran-səm\ *n* **1 :** a piece (as a crossbar in the frame of a window or door) that lies crosswise in a structure **2 :** a window above an opening (as a door) built on and often hinged to a horizontal crossbar

**tran·son·ic** *also* **trans·son·ic** \tran(s)-'sän-ik\ *adj* **:** being, relating to, or moving at a speed that is about that of sound in air or about 738 miles per hour

**transp** *abbr* transportation

**trans·pa·cif·ic** \,trans-pə-'sif-ik\ *adj* **:** crossing, extending across, or situated beyond the Pacific ocean

**trans·par·ent** \trans-'par-ənt\ *adj* **1 :** transmitting light **:** clear enough to be seen through **2 :** SHEER, DIAPHANOUS ⟨a ~ fabric⟩ **3 :** readily understood **:** CLEAR; *also* **:** easily detected ⟨a ~ lie⟩ **syn** lucid — **trans·par·en·cy** \-ən-sē\ *n* — **trans·par·ent·ly** *adv*

**tran·spire** \trans-'pī(ə)r\ *vb* **transpired; tran·spir·ing** [MF *transpirer*, fr. L *trans-* across + *spirare* to breathe] **1 :** to pass off (as watery vapor) through pores or a membrane **2 :** to become known **:** come to light **3 :** to take place **:** OCCUR — **tran·spi·ra·tion** \,trans-pə-'rā-shən\ *n*

**¹trans·plant** \trans-'plant\ *vb* **1 :** to take up and set again in another soil or location **2 :** to remove from one place and settle or introduce elsewhere **:** TRANSPORT **3 :** to transfer (an organ or tissue) from one part or individual to another **4 :** to admit of being transplanted — **trans·plan·ta·tion** \,trans-,plan-'tā-shən\ *n*

**²trans·plant** \'trans-,plant\ *n* **1 :** the act or process of transplanting **2 :** something transplanted

**trans·po·lar** \trans-'pō-lər\ *adj* **:** going or extending across either of the polar regions

**¹trans·port** \trans-'pōrt\ *vb* **1 :** to convey from one place to another **:** CARRY **2 :** to carry away by strong emotion **:** ENRAPTURE **3 :** to send to a penal colony overseas **syn** bear, transmit, deport, exile — **trans·por·ta·tion** \,trans-pər-'tā-shən\ *n* — **trans·port·er** \trans-'pōrt-ər\ *n*

**²trans·port** \'trans-,pōrt\ *n* **1 :** an act of transporting **:** TRANSPORTATION **2 :** strong or intensely pleasurable emotion **:** RAPTURE **3 :** a ship used in transporting troops or supplies; *also* **:** a vehicle (as a truck or plane) used to transport persons or goods

**trans·pose** \trans-'pōz\ *vb* **transposed; trans·pos·ing 1 :** to change the position or sequence of ⟨~ the letters in a word⟩ **2 :** to write or perform (a musical composition) in a different key **syn** reverse, invert — **trans·po·si·tion** \,trans-pə-'zish-ən\ *n*

**trans·ship** \tran(ch)-'ship, trans-\ *vb* **:** to transfer for further transportation from one ship or conveyance to another — **trans·ship·ment** *n*

**tran·sub·stan·ti·a·tion** \,trans-əb-,stan-chē-'ā-shən\ *n* **:** the change in the eucharistic elements from the substance of bread and wine to the substance of the body of Christ with only the accidents (as taste and color) remaining

**trans·verse** \trans-'vərs, tranz-\ *adj* **:** lying across **:** set crosswise — **transverse** \'trans-,vərs, 'tranz-\ *n* — **trans·verse·ly** *adv*

**trans·ves·tism** \trans-'ves-,tiz-əm, tranz-\ *n* **:** adoption of the dress and often the behavior of the opposite sex — **trans·ves·tite** \-,tīt\ *adj or n*

**¹trap** \'trap\ *n* **1 :** a device for catching

animals **2 :** something by which one is caught unawares **3 :** a machine for throwing objects into the air to be targets for shooters; *also* **:** a hazard on a golf course consisting of a depression containing sand **4 :** a light 2-wheeled or 4-wheeled one-horse carriage on springs **5 :** a device to allow some one thing to pass through while keeping other things out ⟨a ∼ in a drainpipe⟩ **6** *pl* **:** a group of percussion instruments used in a jazz or dance orchestra

²**trap** *vb* **trapped; trap·ping 1 :** to catch in or if in a trap; *also* **:** CONFINE **2 :** to provide or set (a place) with traps **3 :** to set traps for animals esp. as a business syn snare, entrap, ensnare, bag, lure, decoy — **trap·per** *n*

³**trap** *n* **:** any of various dark fine-grained igneous rocks used esp. in road making

**trap·door** \'trap-'dōr\ *n* **:** a lifting or sliding door covering an opening in a floor or roof

**tra·peze** \tra-'pēz\ *n* **:** a gymnastic apparatus consisting of a horizontal bar suspended by two parallel ropes

**trap·e·zoid** \'trap-ə-,zȯid\ *n* [NL *trapezoides*, fr. Gk *trapezoeidēs* trapezoid-shaped, fr. *trapeza* table, fr. *tra-* four + *peza* foot] **:** a plane 4-sided figure with two parallel sides — **trap·e·zoi·dal** \,trap-ə-'zȯi-d-²l\ *adj*

**trap·pings** \'trap-iŋz\ *n pl* **1 :** ornamental covering esp. for a horse **2 :** outward decoration or dress

**trap·rock** \'trap-'räk\ *n* **:** ³TRAP

**traps** \'traps\ *n pl* **:** personal belongings **:** luggage

**trap·shoot·ing** \'trap-,shüt-iŋ\ *n* **:** shooting at clay pigeons sprung into the air from a trap

**trash** \'trash\ *n* **1 :** something of little worth **:** RUBBISH **2 :** a worthless person; *also* **:** such persons as a group **:** RIFFRAFF — **trashy** *adj*

**trau·ma** \'traú-mə, 'trȯ-\ *n, pl* **trau·ma·ta** \-mət-ə\ *or* **traumas :** a bodily or mental injury usu. caused by an external agent; *also* **:** a cause of trauma — **trau·mat·ic** \trə-'mat-ik, trȯ-, traú-\ *adj*

¹**tra·vail** \trə-'vāl, 'trav-,āl\ *n* **1 :** painful work or exertion **:** TOIL **2 :** AGONY, TORMENT **3 :** CHILDBIRTH, LABOR syn work, drudgery

²**travail** *vb* **:** to labor hard **:** TOIL

¹**trav·el** \'trav-əl\ *vb* **-eled** *or* **-elled; -el·ing** *or* **-el·ling** \-(ə-)liŋ\ **1 :** to go on or as if on a trip or tour **:** JOURNEY **2 :** to move as if by traveling **:** PASS ⟨news ∼s fast⟩ **3 :** ASSOCIATE **4 :** to go from place to place as a salesman **5 :** to move from point to point ⟨light waves ∼ very fast⟩ **6 :** to journey over or through ⟨∼*ing* the highways⟩ — **trav·el·er** *or* **trav·el·ler** *n*

²**travel** *n* **1 :** the act of traveling **:** PASSAGE **2 :** JOURNEY, TRIP — often used in pl. **3 :** the number traveling **:** TRAFFIC **4 :** the motion of a piece of machinery and esp. when to and fro; *also* **:** length of motion (as of a piston)

**traveling bag** *n* **:** a bag carried by hand and designed to hold a traveler's clothing and personal articles

**trav·el·ogue** *or* **trav·el·og** \'trav-ə-,lȯg, -,läg\ *n* **:** a usu. illustrated lecture on travel

¹**tra·verse** \'trav-ərs\ *n* **:** something (as a crosswise beam) that crosses or lies across

²**tra·verse** \trə-'vərs, tra-'vərs *or* 'tra-vərs\ *vb* **tra·versed; tra·vers·ing 1 :** to pass through **:** PENETRATE **2 :** to go or travel across or over **3 :** to extend over **4 :** SWIVEL

³**tra·verse** \'tra-,vərs\ *adj* **:** TRANSVERSE

**trav·er·tine** \'trav-ər-,tēn, -tən\ *n* **:** a crystalline mineral formed by deposition from spring waters

¹**trav·es·ty** \'trav-ə-stē\ *n, pl* **-ties** [obs. E *travesty*, disguised, parodied, fr. F *travesti*, pp. of *travestir* to disguise, fr. It *travestire*, fr. *tra-* across (fr. L *trans-*) + *vestire* to dress, fr. L, fr. *vestis* garment] **:** a burlesque and usu. grotesque translation or imitation

²**travesty** *vb* **-tied; -ty·ing :** to make a travesty of

¹**trawl** \'trȯl\ *vb* **:** to fish or catch with a trawl — **trawl·er** *n*

²**trawl** *n* **1 :** a large conical net dragged along the sea bottom in fishing **2 :** a long fishing line anchored at both ends and equipped with many hooks

**tray** \'trā\ *n* **:** an open receptacle with flat bottom and low rim for holding, carrying, or exhibiting articles

**treach·er·ous** \'trech-(ə-)rəs\ *adj* **1 :** characterized by treachery **2 :** UNTRUSTWORTHY, UNRELIABLE **3 :** providing insecure footing or support syn traitorous, faithless, false, disloyal — **treach·er·ous·ly** *adv*

**treach·ery** \'trech-(ə-)rē\ *n, pl* **-er·ies :** violation of allegiance or trust

**trea·cle** \'trē-kəl\ *n* [ME *triacle* a medicinal compound, fr. MF, fr. L *theriaca*, fr. Gk *thēriakē* antidote against a poisonous bite, fr. *thērion* wild animal, dim. of *thēr* wild animal] **1** *chiefly Brit* **:** MOLASSES **2 :** something heavily sweet and cloying

¹**tread** \'tred\ *vb* **trod** \'träd\; **trod·den** \'träd-²n\ *or* **trod; tread·ing 1 :** to step or walk on or over **2 :** to move on foot **:** WALK; *also* **:** DANCE **3 :** to beat or press with the feet

²**tread** *n* **1 :** a mark made by or as if by treading **2 :** manner of stepping **3 :** the sound of treading **4 :** the part of something that is trodden upon ⟨the ∼ of a step in a flight of stairs⟩ **5 :** the part of a thing on which it runs ⟨the ∼ of a tire⟩

**trea·dle** \'tred-²l\ *n* **:** a lever device pressed by the foot to drive a machine

**tread·mill** \'tred-,mil\ *n* **1 :** a mill worked by persons who tread steps around the edge of a wheel or by animals that walk on an endless belt **2 :** a wearisome routine

**treas** *abbr* treasurer; treasury

**trea·son** \'trēz-²n\ *n* **:** the offense of attempting by overt acts to overthrow the government of the state to which one owes allegiance or to kill or injure the sovereign or his family — **trea-son·able** \-(°-)nə-bəl\ adj — **trea-son·ous** \-(°-)nəs\ adj

¹**trea·sure** \'trezh-ər, 'trāzh-\ n 1 : wealth stored up or held in reserve 2 : something of great value

²**treasure** vb **trea·sured; trea·sur·ing** \-(ə-)riŋ\ 1 : HOARD 2 : to keep as precious : CHERISH syn prize, value, appreciate

**trea·sur·er** \'trezh-rər, 'trezh-ər-ər, 'trāzh-\ n : an officer entrusted with the receipt, care, and disbursement of funds

**treasure trove** \-,trōv\ n 1 : treasure (as money in gold) which is found hidden and whose ownership is unknown 2 : a valuable discovery

**trea·sury** \'trezh-(ə-)rē, 'trāzh-\ n, pl -sur·ies 1 : a place in which stores of wealth are kept 2 : the place of deposit and disbursement of collected funds; esp : one where public revenues are deposited, kept, and disbursed 3 cap : a governmental department in charge of finances

¹**treat** \'trēt\ vb 1 : NEGOTIATE 2 : to deal with esp. in writing; also : HANDLE 3 : to pay for the food or entertainment of 4 : to behave or act toward ⟨~ them well⟩ 5 : to regard in a specified manner ⟨~ as inferiors⟩ 6 : to care for medically or surgically 7 : to subject to some action (as of a chemical) ⟨~ soil with lime⟩

²**treat** n 1 : food or entertainment paid for by another 2 : a source of joy or amusement

**trea·tise** \'trēt-əs\ n : a systematic written exposition or argument

**treat·ment** \'trēt-mənt\ n : the act or manner or an instance of treating someone or something; also : a substance or method used in treating

**trea·ty** \'trēt-ē\ n, pl **treaties** : an agreement made by negotiation or diplomacy esp. between two or more states or governments syn contract, bargain, pact

¹**tre·ble** \'treb-əl\ n 1 : the highest of the four voice parts in vocal music : SOPRANO 2 : a high-pitched or shrill voice or sound 3 : the upper half of the musical pitch range

²**treble** adj 1 : triple in number or amount 2 : relating to or having the range of a musical treble 3 : high-pitched : SHRILL — **tre·bly** \'treb-(ə-)lē\ adv

³**treble** vb **tre·bled; tre·bling** \'treb-(ə-)liŋ\ : to make or become three times the size, amount, or number

¹**tree** \'trē\ n 1 : a woody perennial plant usu. with a single main stem and a head of branches and leaves at the top 2 : a piece of wood adapted to a particular use ⟨a shoe ~⟩ 3 : something resembling a tree ⟨a genealogical ~⟩ — **tree·less** adj

²**tree** vb **treed; tree·ing** : to drive to or up a tree ⟨~ a raccoon⟩

**tree farm** n : an area of forest land managed to ensure continuous commercial production

**tree line** n : TIMBERLINE

**tree of heaven** : an ailanthus that is widely grown as a shade and ornamental tree

**tree surgery** n : operative treatment of diseased trees esp. for control of decay — **tree surgeon** n

**tre·foil** \'trē-,foil, 'tref-,oil\ n 1 : a clover or related herb with leaves with three leaflets 2 : a decorative design with three leaflike parts

¹**trek** \'trek\ n 1 : a migration esp. of settlers by ox wagon 2 : TRIP; esp : one involving difficulties or complex organization

²**trek** vb **trekked; trek·king** 1 : to travel or migrate by ox wagon 2 : to make one's way arduously

¹**trel·lis** \'trel-əs\ n [ME trelis, fr. MF treliz fabric of coarse weave, trellis, fr. (assumed) VL trilicius woven with triple thread, fr. L tres three + liceum thread] : a structure of latticework

²**trellis** vb : to train (as a vine) on a trellis

**trem·a·tode** \'trem-ə-,tōd\ n : any of a class of parasitic worms

¹**trem·ble** \'trem-bəl\ vb **trem·bled; trem·bling** \-b(ə-)liŋ\ 1 : to shake involuntarily (as with fear or cold) : SHIVER 2 : to move, sound, pass, or come to pass as if shaken or tremulous 3 : to be affected with fear or doubt

²**tremble** n : a spell of shaking or quivering : TREMOR

**tre·men·dous** \tri-'men-dəs\ adj 1 : such as may excite trembling : TERRIFYING 2 : astonishingly large, powerful, great, or excellent syn stupendous, monumental, monstrous — **tre·men·dous·ly** adv

**trem·o·lo** \'trem-ə-,lō\ n, pl -los : a rapid fluttering of a tone or alternating tones to produce a tremulous effect

**trem·or** \'trem-ər\ n 1 : a trembling or shaking esp. from weakness or disease 2 : a quivering motion of the earth (as during an earthquake)

**trem·u·lous** \'trem-yə-ləs\ adj 1 : marked by trembling or tremors : QUIVERING 2 : TIMOROUS, TIMID — **trem·u·lous·ly** adv

¹**trench** \'trench\ n [ME trenche track cut through a wood, fr. MF, act of cutting, fr. trenchier to cut] 1 : a long narrow cut in land : DITCH; also : a similar depression in an ocean floor 2 : a ditch protected by banks of earth and used to shelter soldiers

²**trench** vb 1 : to cut or dig trenches in; also : to drain by trenches 2 : to protect (troops) with trenches 3 : to come close : VERGE

**tren·chant** \'tren-chənt\ adj 1 : vigorously effective; esp : CAUSTIC 2 : sharply perceptive : KEEN 3 : CLEARCUT, DISTINCT syn incisive, biting, crisp

**tren·cher** \'tren-chər\ n : a wooden platter for serving food

**tren·cher·man** \'tren-chər-mən\ n : a hearty eater

**trench foot** n : a painful foot disorder resembling frostbite and resulting from exposure to cold or wet

**trench mouth** n : a contagious infection of the mouth and adjacent parts that is marked by ulceration and caused by a bacterium in association with a spirochete

¹**trend** \'trend\ vb 1 : to have or take a general direction : TEND 2 : to show a tendency : INCLINE

²**trend** n 1 : a general direction taken (as by a stream or mountain range) 2 : a prevailing tendency : DRIFT 3 : a current style or preference : VOGUE

**tre·pan** \tri-'pan\ vb **tre·panned**; **tre·pan·ning** : to remove surgically a disk of bone from (the skull) — **trep·a·na·tion** \,trep-ə-'nā-shən\ n

**trep·i·da·tion** \,trep-ə-'dā-shən\ n : nervous agitation : APPREHENSION syn horror, terror, panic, consternation, dread, fright, dismay

¹**tres·pass** \'tres-pəs, -,pas\ n 1 : SIN, OFFENSE 2 : wrongful entry on real property syn transgression, violation, infraction, infringement

²**trespass** vb 1 : to commit an offense : ERR, SIN 2 : INTRUDE, ENCROACH; esp : to enter unlawfully upon the land of another — **tres·pass·er** n

**tress** \'tres\ n : a long lock of hair — usu. used in pl.

**tres·tle** also **tres·sel** \'tres-əl\ n 1 : a supporting framework consisting usu. of a horizontal piece with spreading legs at each end 2 : a braced framework of timbers, piles, or steel for carrying a road or railroad over a depression

**trey** \'trā\ n, pl **treys** : a card or the side of a die with three spots

**tri·ad** \'trī-,ad, -əd\ n : a union of three esp. closely related persons or things : TRINITY

**tri·age** \trē-'äzh, 'trē-,äzh\ n : the sorting of and allocation of treatment to patients and esp. battle and disaster victims designed to maximize the number of survivors

¹**tri·al** \'trī-(ə)l\ n 1 : the action or process of trying or putting to the proof : TEST 2 : the hearing and judgment of a matter in issue before a competent tribunal 3 : a source of vexation or annoyance 4 : a temporary use or experiment to test quality or usefulness 5 : EFFORT, ATTEMPT syn proof, demonstration, tribulation, affliction

²**trial** adj 1 : of, relating to, or used in a trial 2 : made or done as a test

**tri·an·gle** \'trī-,aŋ-gəl\ n : a plane figure that is bounded by three straight lines and has three angles; also : something shaped like such a figure — **tri·an·gu·lar** \trī-'aŋ-gyə-lər\ adj — **tri·an·gu·lar·ly** adv

**tri·an·gu·late** \trī-'aŋ-gyə-,lāt\ vb **-lat·ed**; **-lat·ing** : to divide into triangles (as in surveying an area) — **tri·an·gu·la·tion** \-,aŋ-gyə-'lā-shən\ n

**trib** abbr tributary

**tribe** \'trīb\ n 1 : a social group comprising numerous families, clans, or generations 2 : a group of persons having a common character, occupation, or interest 3 : a group of related plants or animals ⟨the cat ∼⟩ — **trib·al** \'trī-bəl\ adj

**tribes·man** \'trībz-mən\ n : a member of a tribe

**trib·u·la·tion** \,trib-yə-'lā-shən\ n [ME tribulacion, fr. OF, fr. L tribulatio, fr. tribulare to press, oppress, fr. tribulum drag used in threshing, fr. terere to rub] : distress or suffering resulting from oppression or persecution; also : a trying experience syn trial, affliction

**tri·bu·nal** \trī-'byün-ᵊl, trib-'yün-\ n 1 : the seat of a judge 2 : a court of justice 3 : something that decides or determines ⟨the ∼ of public opinion⟩

**tri·bune** \'trib-,yün, trib-'yün\ n 1 : an official in ancient Rome with the function of protecting the interests of plebeian citizens from the patricians 2 : a defender of the people

¹**trib·u·tary** \'trib-yə-,ter-ē\ adj 1 : paying tribute : SUBJECT 2 : flowing into a larger stream or a lake syn subordinate, secondary, dependent

²**tributary** n, pl **-tar·ies** 1 : a ruler or state that pays tribute 2 : a tributary stream

**trib·ute** \'trib-(,)yüt, -yət\ n 1 : a payment by one ruler or nation to another as acknowledgment of submission or price of protection 2 : a usu. excessive tax, rental, or levy exacted by a sovereign or superior 3 : a gift or service showing respect, gratitude, or affection; also : PRAISE syn assessment, rate, eulogy, citation

**trice** \'trīs\ n : INSTANT, MOMENT

**tri·ceps** \'trī-,seps\ n, pl **tri·ceps·es** also **triceps** : a 3-headed muscle along the back of the upper arm

**tri·chi·na** \trik-'ī-nə\ n, pl **-nae** \-(,)nē\ also **-nas** : a small slender worm that in the larval state is parasitic in the voluntary muscles of flesh-eating mammals

**trich·i·no·sis** \,trik-ə-,nō-səs\ n : a disease caused by infestation of muscle tissue by trichinae and marked by pain, fever, and swelling

¹**trick** \'trik\ n 1 : a crafty procedure meant to deceive 2 : a mischievous action : PRANK 3 : a childish action 4 : a deceptive or ingenious feat designed to puzzle or amuse 5 : PECULIARITY, MANNERISM 6 : a quick or artful way of getting a result : KNACK 7 : the cards played in one round of a card game 8 : a tour of duty : SHIFT syn ruse, maneuver, artifice, wile, feint

²**trick** vb 1 : to deceive by cunning or artifice : CHEAT 2 : to dress ornately

**trick·ery** \'trik-(ə-)rē\ n : deception by tricks and stratagems

**trick·le** \'trik-əl\ vb **trick·led**; **trick·ling** \-(ə-)liŋ\ 1 : to run or fall in drops 2 : to flow in a thin gentle stream — **trickle** n

**trick·ster** \'trik-stər\ n : one who tricks or cheats

**tricky** \'trik-ē\ adj **trick·i·er**; **-est** 1 : inclined to trickery ⟨a ∼ person⟩ 2 : requiring skill or caution ⟨a ∼ situation to handle⟩ 3 : UNRELIABLE

**tri·col·or** \'trī-,kəl-ər\ *n* **:** a flag of three colors ⟨the French ∼⟩

**tri·cy·cle** \'trī-,sik-əl\ *n* **:** a 3-wheeled vehicle propelled by pedals, hand levers, or motor

**tri·dent** \'trīd-ᵊnt\ *n* [L *trident-*, *tridens*, fr. *tres* three + *dent-*, *dens* tooth] **:** a 3-pronged spear

**tried** \'trīd\ *adj* **1 :** found trustworthy through testing **2 :** subjected to trials **syn** reliable, dependable, trusty

**tri·en·ni·al** \trī-'en-ē-əl\ *adj* **1 :** lasting for three years **2 :** occurring or being done every three years — **tri·en·ni·al** *n*

**¹tri·fle** \'trī-fəl\ *n* **:** something of little value or importance; *esp* **:** an insignificant amount (as of money)

**²trifle** *vb* **tri·fled; tri·fling** \-f(ə-)liŋ\ **1 :** to talk in a jesting or mocking manner **2 :** to act frivolously or playfully **3 :** DALLY, FLIRT **4 :** to handle idly **:** TOY — **tri·fler** \-f(ə-)lər\ *n*

**tri·fling** \'trī-fliŋ\ *adj* **1 :** FRIVOLOUS **2 :** TRIVIAL, INSIGNIFICANT **syn** petty, paltry

**tri·fo·cals** \trī-'fō-kəlz\ *n pl* **:** eyeglasses with lenses having one part for close focus, one for intermediate focus, and one for distant focus

**tri·fo·li·ate** \trī-'fō-lē-ət\ *adj* **:** having three leaves or leaflets

**¹trig** \'trig\ *adj* **:** stylishly trim **:** SMART **syn** tidy, spruce

**²trig** *n* **:** TRIGONOMETRY

**¹trig·ger** \'trig-ər\ *n* [alter. of earlier *tricker*, fr. Dutch *trekker*, fr. Middle Dutch *trecker* one that pulls, fr. *trecken* to pull] **:** the part of a firearm lock moved by the finger to release the hammer in firing — **trigger** *adj* — **trig·gered** \-ərd\ *adj*

**²trigger** *vb* **1 :** to fire by pulling a trigger **2 :** to initiate, actuate, or set off as if by a trigger

**trig·o·nom·e·try** \,trig-ə-'näm-ə-trē\ *n* **:** the branch of mathematics dealing with the relations of the sides and angles of triangles and of methods of deducing from given parts other required parts — **trig·o·no·met·ric** \-nə-'met-rik\ *or* **trig·o·no·met·ri·cal** \-rik-əl\ *adj*

**¹trill** \'tril\ *n* **1 :** the alternation of two musical tones a scale degree apart **2 :** WARBLE **3 :** the rapid vibration of one speech organ against another (as of the tip of the tongue against the ridge of the teeth)

**²trill** *vb* **:** to utter as or with a trill

**tril·lion** \'tril-yən\ *n* **1 :** a thousand billions **2** *Brit* **:** a million billions — **trillion** *adj* — **tril·lionth** \-yənth\ *adj or n*

**tril·li·um** \'tril-ē-əm\ *n* **:** any of a genus of herbs of the lily family with an erect stem bearing a whorl of three leaves and a large solitary flower

**tril·o·gy** \'tril-ə-jē\ *n, pl* **-gies :** a series of three dramas or literary or musical compositions that are closely related and develop one theme

**¹trim** \'trim\ *vb* **trimmed; trim·ming** [OE *trymian*, *trymman* to strengthen,

arrange, fr. *trum* strong, firm] **1 :** to put ornaments on **:** ADORN **2 :** to defeat esp. resoundingly **3 :** CHEAT **4 :** to make trim, neat, regular, or less bulky by or as if by cutting ⟨∼ a beard⟩ ⟨∼ a budget⟩ **5 :** to cause (a boat) to assume a desired position in the water by arrangement of ballast, cargo, or passengers; *also* **:** to adjust (as a submarine or airplane) for motion and esp. for horizontal motion **6 :** to adjust (a sail) to a desired position **7 :** to change one's views for safety or expediency **syn** stabilize, steady, poise, balance, ballast — **trim·ly** *adv* — **trim·mer** *n* — **trim·ness** *n*

**²trim** *adj* **trim·mer; trim·mest** **:** showing neatness, good order, or compactness ⟨∼ figure⟩ **syn** tidy, trig

**³trim** *n* **1 :** the readiness of a ship for sailing; *also* **:** the position of a ship in the water **2 :** good condition **:** FITNESS **3 :** material used for ornament or trimming; *esp* **:** the woodwork in the finish of a house esp. around doors and windows **4 :** something that is trimmed off

**tri·ma·ran** \'trī-mə-,ran, ,trī-mə-'ran\ *n* **:** a fast pleasure sailboat with three hulls side by side

**tri·mes·ter** \trī-'mes-tər, 'trī-,mes-tər\ *n* **1 :** a period of three or about three months **2 :** one of three terms into which an academic year is sometimes divided

**trim·e·ter** \'trim-ət-ər\ *n* **:** a line consisting of three metrical feet

**trim·ming** \'trim-iŋ\ *n* **1 :** the action of one that trims **2 :** DEFEAT **3 :** something that trims, ornaments, or completes **4** *pl* **:** parts removed by trimming

**tri·month·ly** \trī-'mənth-lē\ *adj* **:** occurring every three months

**trine** \'trīn\ *adj* **:** THREEFOLD, TRIPLE

**Trin·i·da·di·an** \,trin-ə-'dād-ē-ən, -'dad-\ *n* **:** a native or inhabitant of the island of Trinidad — **Trinidadian** *adj*

**Trin·i·tar·i·an** \,trin-ə-'ter-ē-ən\ *n* **:** a believer in the doctrine of the Trinity — **Trin·i·tar·i·an·ism** \-ē-ə-,niz-əm\ *n*

**Trin·i·ty** \'trin-ət-ē\ *n* **:** the unity of Father, Son, and Holy Spirit as three persons in one Godhead

**trin·ket** \'triŋ-kət\ *n* **1 :** a small ornament (as a jewel or ring) **2 :** TRIFLE

**trio** \'trē-ō\ *n, pl* **tri·os 1 :** a musical composition for three voices or three instruments **2 :** the performers of a musical or dance trio **3 :** a group or set of three

**tri·ode** \'trī-,ōd\ *n* **:** an electron tube with three electrodes

**¹trip** \'trip\ *vb* **tripped; trip·ping 1 :** to move with light quick steps **2 :** to catch the foot against something so as to stumble or cause to stumble **3 :** to make a mistake **:** SLIP; *also* **:** to detect in a mistake **:** EXPOSE **4 :** to release (as a spring or switch) by moving a catch; *also* **:** ACTIVATE **5 :** to get high on a psychedelic drug

²**trip** *n* 1 : JOURNEY, VOYAGE 2 : a quick light step 3 : a false step : STUMBLE; *also* : ERROR 4 : the action of tripping mechanically: *also* : a device for tripping 5 : an intense visionary experience undergone by a person who has taken a psychedelic drug (as LSD)

**tri·par·tite** \trī-'pär-,tīt\ *adj* 1 : divided into three parts 2 : having three corresponding parts or copies 3 : made between three parties ⟨a ∼ treaty⟩

**tripe** \'trīp\ *n* 1 : stomach tissue of a ruminant and esp. an ox for use as food 2 : something poor, worthless, or offensive : TRASH

¹**tri·ple** \'trip-əl\ *vb* **tri·pled; tri·pling** \-(ə-)liŋ\ 1 : to make or become three times as great or as many 2 : to hit a triple

²**triple** *n* 1 : a triple quantity 2 : a group of three 3 : a hit in baseball that enables the batter to reach third base

³**triple** *adj* 1 : having three units or members 2 : being three times as great or as many 3 : repeated three times

**trip·let** \'trip-lət\ *n* 1 : a unit of three lines of verse 2 : a group of three of a kind 3 : one of three offspring born at one birth

**tri·plex** \'trip-,leks, 'trī-,pleks\ *adj* : THREEFOLD, TRIPLE

¹**trip·li·cate** \'trip-li-kət\ *adj* : made in three identical copies

²**trip·li·cate** \-lə-,kāt\ *vb* **-cat·ed; -cat·ing** 1 : TRIPLE 2 : to provide three copies of ⟨∼ a document⟩

³**trip·li·cate** \-li-kət\ *n* : one of three identical copies

**tri·ply** \'trip-(ə-)lē\ *adv* : in a triple degree, amount, or manner

**tri·pod** \'trī-,päd\ *n* : something (as a caldron, stool, or camera stand) that rests on three legs — **tripod** *or* **tri·po·dal** \'trip-əd-əl, 'trī-,päd-\ *adj*

**trip·tych** \'trip-tik\ *n* : a picture or carving (as an altarpiece) in three panels side by side

**tri·reme** \'trī-,rēm\ *n* : an ancient galley having three banks of oars

**tri·sect** \'trī-,sekt, trī-'sekt\ *vb* : to divide into three usu. equal parts — **tri·sec·tion** \trī-'sek-shən\ *n*

**trite** \'trīt\ *adj* **trit·er; trit·est** [L *tritus,* fr. pp. of *terere* to rub, wear away] : used so commonly that the novelty is worn off : STALE **syn** hackneyed, stereotyped, commonplace

**tri·ti·um** \'trit-ē-əm, 'trish-ē-\ *n* : a radioactive form of hydrogen with atoms of three times the mass of ordinary hydrogen atoms

**tri·ton** \'trīt-ʰn\ *n* : any of various large marine mollusks with a heavy elongated conical shell

**trit·u·rate** \'trich-ə-,rāt\ *vb* **-rat·ed; -rat·ing** : to rub or grind to a fine powder — **trit·u·ra·ble** \'trich-ə-rə-bəl\ *adj* — **trit·u·ra·tor** \-,rāt-ər\ *n*

¹**tri·umph** \'trī-əmf\ *n, pl* **tri·umphs** \-əmfs, -əm(p)s\ 1 : the joy or exultation of victory or success 2 : VICTORY, CONQUEST — **tri·um·phal** \trī-'əm-fəl\ *adj*

²**triumph** *vb* 1 : to celebrate victory or success exultantly 2 : to obtain victory : PREVAIL — **tri·um·phant** \trī-'əm-fənt\ *adj* — **tri·um·phant·ly** *adv*

**tri·um·vir** \trī-'əm-vər\ *n, pl* **-virs** *also* **-vi·ri** \-və-,rī\ : a member of a triumvirate

**tri·um·vi·rate** \-və-rət\ *n* : a ruling body of three persons

**tri·une** \'trī-,(y)ün\ *adj, often cap* : being three in one ⟨the ∼ God⟩

**triv·et** \'triv-ət\ *n* 1 : a 3-legged stand : TRIPOD 2 : a metal stand with short feet for use under a hot dish

**triv·ia** \'triv-ē-ə\ *n sing or pl* : unimportant matters: TRIFLES

**triv·i·al** \'triv-ē-əl\ *adj* [L *trivialis* found everywhere, commonplace, trivial, fr. *trivium* crossroads, fr. *tres* three + *via* way] : of little importance — **triv·i·al·i·ty** \,triv-ē-'al-ət-ē\ *n*

**triv·i·um** \'triv-ē-əm\ *n, pl* **triv·ia** \-ē-ə\ : the three liberal arts of grammar, rhetoric, and logic in a medieval university

**tri·week·ly** \trī-'wē-klē\ *adj* 1 : occurring or appearing three times a week 2 : occurring or appearing every three weeks — **triweekly** *adv*

**tro·che** \'trō-kē\ *n* : a medicinal lozenge

**tro·chee** \'trō-(,)kē\ *n* : a metrical foot of one accented syllable followed by one unaccented syllable — **tro·cha·ic** \trō-'kā-ik\ *adj*

**trod** *past of* TREAD

**trod·den** *past part of* TREAD

**troi·ka** \'trói-kə\ *n* [Russ *troĭka* a vehicle drawn by three horses, fr. *troe* three] : a group of three; *esp* : an administrative or ruling body of three

¹**troll** \'trōl\ *vb* 1 : to sing the parts of (a song) in succession 2 : to angle for with a hook and line drawn through the water 3 : to sing or play jovially

²**troll** *n* : a lure used in trolling; *also* : the line with its lure

³**troll** *n* : a dwarf or giant of Teutonic folklore inhabiting caves or hills

**trol·ley** *or* **trol·ly** \'träl-ē\ *n, pl* **trolleys** *or* **trollies** 1 : a device (as a grooved wheel on the end of a pole) to carry current from a wire to an electrically driven vehicle 2 : TROLLEY CAR 3 : a wheeled carriage running on an overhead rail or track (as on a parcel railway in a store)

**trol·ley·bus** \'träl-ē-,bəs\ *n* : a bus powered by electric power from two overhead wires

**trolley car** *n* : a public conveyance that runs on tracks and gets its electric power through a trolley

**trol·lop** \'träl-əp\ *n* 1 : a slovenly woman 2 : a loose woman : WANTON

**trom·bone** \träm-'bōn, 'träm-,bōn\ *n* [It, lit., big trumpet, fr. *tromba* trumpet] : a brass wind instrument that consists of a long metal tube with two turns and a flaring end and that has a movable slide to vary the pitch — **trom·bon·ist** \-'bō-nəst, -,bō-\ *n*

**tromp** \'trämp, 'trȯmp\ vb **1** : TRAMP, MARCH **2** : to stamp with the foot **3** : DEFEAT

¹**troop** \'trüp\ n **1** : a cavalry unit corresponding to an infantry company **2** : an armed force : SOLDIERS — usu. used in pl. **3** : a collection of people or things **4** : a unit of boy or girl scouts under a leader **syn** band, troupe, party

²**troop** vb : to move or gather in crowds

**troop·er** \'trü-pər\ n **1** : an enlisted cavalryman; also : a cavalry horse **2** : a mounted or state policeman

**troop·ship** \'trüp-,ship\ n : a ship for carrying troops

**trope** \'trōp\ n : the use of a word or expression in a figurative sense

**tro·phy** \'trō-fē\ n, pl **trophies** : something gained or given in conquest or victory esp. when preserved or mounted as a memorial

**trop·ic** \'träp-ik\ n [ME tropik, fr. L tropicus of the solstice, fr. Gk tropikos, fr tropē turn] **1** : either of the two parallels of latitude one 23½ degrees north of the equator (**tropic of Cancer** \-'kan-sər\) and one 23½ degrees south of the equator (**tropic of Capri·corn** \-'kap-rə-,kȯrn\) where the sun is directly overhead when apparently at its greatest distance north or south of the equator **2** pl, often cap : the region lying between the tropics of Cancer and Capricorn — **tropic** or **trop·i·cal** \-i-kəl\ adj

**tro·pism** \'trō-,piz-əm\ n : involuntary orientation of an organism in response to a source of stimulation; also : a reflex reaction involving this

**tro·po·sphere** \'trōp-ə-,sfiər, 'träp-\ n : the portion of the atmosphere that is below the stratosphere and extends outward about 10 miles from the earth's surface — **tro·po·spher·ic** \,trōp-ə-'sfi(ə)r-ik, ,träp-, -'sfer-\ adj

¹**trot** \'trät\ n **1** : a moderately fast gait of a 4-footed animal (as a horse) in which the legs move in diagonal pairs **2** : a jogging gait of a man between a walk and a run

²**trot** vb **trot·ted; trot·ting 1** : to ride, drive, or go at a trot **2** : to proceed briskly : HURRY — **trot·ter** n

**troth** \'träth, 'troth, 'trōth\ n **1** : pledged faithfulness : FIDELITY **2** : one's pledged word; also : BETROTHAL

**trou·ba·dour** \'trü-bə-,dȯr\ n : one of a class of poet-musicians flourishing esp. in southern France and northern Italy during the 11th, 12th, and 13th centuries

¹**trou·ble** \'trəb-əl\ vb **trou·bled; trou·bling** \'trəb-(ə-)liŋ\ **1** : to agitate mentally or spiritually : DISTURB, WORRY **2** : to produce physical disorder in : AFFLICT **3** : to put to inconvenience **4** : to make an effort **5** : RUFFLE ⟨~ the waters⟩ **syn** distress, discommode, molest — **trou·ble·some** adj — **trou·ble·some·ly** adv — **trou·blous**\-(ə-)ləs\ adj

²**trouble** n **1** : the quality or state of being troubled : MISFORTUNE **2** : an instance of distress or annoyance **3** : a cause of disturbance or distress **4** : EXERTION, PAINS ⟨took the ~ to phone⟩ **5** : DISEASE, AILMENT ⟨heart ~⟩

**trou·ble·mak·er** \-,mā-kər\ n : a person who causes trouble

**trou·ble·shoot·er** \-,shüt-ər\ n **1** : a skilled workman employed to locate trouble and make repairs in machinery and technical equipment **2** : a man expert in resolving disputes or problems — **trou·ble·shoot** vb

**trough** \'trȯf, 'trȯth, by bakers often 'trō\ n, pl **troughs** \'trȯfs, 'trȯvz; 'trȯths, 'trȯ(th)z; 'trōz\ **1** : a long shallow open boxlike container esp. for water or feed for livestock **2** : a gutter along the eaves of a house **3** : a long channel or depression (as between waves or hills)

**trounce** \'traùns\ vb **trounced; trounc·ing 1** : to thrash or punish severely **2** : to defeat decisively

**troupe** \'trüp\ n : COMPANY; esp : a group of performers on the stage — **troup·er** n

**trou·sers** \'traù-zərz\ n pl [alter. of earlier trouse, fr. ScGael triubhas] : an outer garment extending from the waist to the ankle or sometimes only to the knee, covering each leg separately, and worn esp. by males — **trouser** adj

**trous·seau** \'trü-sō, trü-'sō\ n, pl **trous·seaux** \-,sōz, -'sōz\ or **trous·seaus** : the personal outfit of a bride

**trout** \'traùt\ n, pl **trout** also **trouts** [ME, fr. OE trūht, fr. LL trocta, tructa, a fish with sharp teeth, fr. Gk trōktēs, lit., gnawer, fr. trōgein to gnaw] : any of various mostly freshwater food and game fishes usu. smaller than the related salmons

**trout lily** n : DOGTOOTH VIOLET

**trow** \'trō\ vb, archaic : THINK, SUPPOSE

**trow·el** \'traù-(-ə)l\ n **1** : any of various hand implements used for spreading, shaping, or smoothing loose or plastic material (as mortar or plaster) **2** : a small flat or scooplike implement used in gardening — **trowel** vb

**troy** \'trȯi\ adj : of or relating to a system of weights (**troy weights**) based on a pound of 12 ounces and an ounce of 480 grains

**tru·ant** \'trü-ənt\ n [ME, vagabond, idler, fr. OF, vagrant] : one who shirks duty; esp : one who stays out of school without permission — **tru·an·cy** \-ən-sē\ n — **truant** adj

**truce** \'trüs\ n **1** : ARMISTICE **2** : a respite esp. from a disagreeable state or action

¹**truck** \'trək\ vb **1** : EXCHANGE, BARTER **2** : to have dealings : TRAFFIC

²**truck** n **1** : BARTER **2** : small goods or merchandise; esp : vegetables grown for market **3** : DEALINGS

³**truck** n **1** : a vehicle (as a strong heavy automobile) designed for carrying heavy articles **2** : a swiveling frame with springs and one or more pairs of wheels used to carry and guide one end of a locomotive or of a railroad or electric car

⁴**truck** *vb* **1** : to transport on a truck **2** : to be employed in driving a truck — **truck·er** *n*

**truck·age** \'trək-ij\ *n* : transportation by truck; *also* : the cost of such transportation

**truck farm** *n* : a farm growing vegetables for market — **truck farmer** *n*

**truck·le** \'trək-əl\ *vb* **truck·led; truck·ling** \-(ə-)liŋ\ : to yield slavishly to the will of another : SUBMIT **syn** fawn, toady, cringe, cower

**truckle bed** *n* : TRUNDLE BED

**truck·load** \'trək-'lōd, -,lōd\ *n* **1** : a load that fills a truck **2** : the minimum weight required for shipping at truckload rates

**tru·cu·lent** \'trək-yə-lənt\ *adj* **1** : feeling or showing ferocity : SAVAGE **2** : aggressively self-assertive : PUGNACIOUS — **truc·u·lence** \-ləns\ *n* — **truc·u·len·cy** \-lən-sē\ *n* — **tru·cu·lent·ly** *adv*

**trudge** \'trəj\ *vb* **trudged; trudg·ing** : to walk or march steadily and usu. laboriously

¹**true** \'trü\ *adj* **tru·er; tru·est** **1** : STEADFAST, LOYAL **2** : conformable to fact or reality ⟨a ~ description⟩ **3** : conformable to a standard or pattern; *also* : placed or formed accurately **4** : GENUINE, REAL; *also* : properly so called ⟨the ~ stomach⟩ **5** : CONSISTENT ⟨~ to expectations⟩ **6** : RIGHTFUL ⟨~ and lawful king⟩ **syn** constant, staunch, resolute, actual — **tru·ly** *adv*

²**true** *n* **1** : TRUTH, REALITY — usu. used with *the* **2** : the state of being accurate (as in alignment) ⟨out of ~⟩

³**true** *vb* **trued; tru·ing** *also* **tru·ing** : to make level, square, balanced, or concentric

⁴**true** *adv* **1** : TRUTHFULLY **2** : ACCURATELY ⟨the bullet flew straight and ~⟩; *also* : without variation from type ⟨breed ~⟩

**true–blue** *adj* : marked by unswerving loyalty

**true·heart·ed** \'trü-'härt-əd\ *adj* : FAITHFUL, LOYAL

**truf·fle** \'trəf-əl, 'trüf-\ *n* : a European underground fungus; *also* : its dark wrinkled edible fruit

**tru·ism** \'trü-,iz-əm\ *n* : an undoubted or self-evident truth **syn** commonplace, platitude, bromide, cliché

¹**trump** \'trəmp\ *n* : TRUMPET

²**trump** *n* : a card of a designated suit any of whose cards will win over a card that is not of this suit; *also* : the suit itself — often used in pl.

³**trump** *vb* : to take with a trump

**trumped–up** \'trəm(p)t-'əp\ *adj* : fraudulently concocted : SPURIOUS

**trum·pery** \'trəm-p(ə-)rē\ *n* **1** : trivial articles : JUNK **2** : NONSENSE

¹**trum·pet** \'trəm-pət\ *n* **1** : a wind instrument consisting of a long curved metal tube flaring at one end and with a cup-shaped mouthpiece at the other **2** : a funnel-shaped instrument for collecting, directing, or intensifying sound **3** : something that resembles a trumpet or its tonal quality

²**trumpet** *vb* **1** : to blow a trumpet **2** : to proclaim on or as if on a trumpet — **trum·pet·er** *n*

¹**trun·cate** \'trəŋ-,kāt, 'trən-\ *vb* **trun·cat·ed; trun·cat·ing** : to shorten by or as if by cutting : LOP — **trun·ca·tion** \,trəŋ-'kā-shən\ *n*

²**truncate** *adj* : having the end square or blunt

**trun·cheon** \'trən-chən\ *n* : a policeman's club

**trun·dle** \'trən-dᵊl\ *vb* **trun·dled; trun·dling** : to roll along : WHEEL

**trundle bed** *n* : a low bed that can be slid under a higher bed

**trunk** \'trəŋk\ *n* **1** : the main stem of a tree **2** : the body of a man or animal apart from the head and limbs **3** : the main or basal part of something **4** : the long muscular nose of an elephant **5** : a box or chest used to hold usu. clothes or personal effects (as of a traveler); *also* : the enclosed luggage space in the rear of an automobile **6** *pl* : men's shorts worn chiefly for sports **7** : a passage or duct serving as a conduit or conveyor **8** : a circuit between telephone exchanges for making connections between subscribers

**trunk line** *n* : a system handling long-distance through traffic

**truss** \'trəs\ *vb* **1** : to secure tightly : BIND **2** : to arrange for cooking by binding close the wings or legs of (a fowl) **3** : to support, strengthen, or stiffen by a truss

²**truss** *n* **1** : a collection of structural parts (as beams, bars, or rods) so put together as to form a rigid framework (as in bridge or building construction) **2** : an appliance worn to hold a hernia in place

¹**trust** \'trəst\ *n* **1** : assured reliance on the character, strength, or truth of someone or something **2** : a basis of reliance, faith, or hope **3** : confident hope **4** : financial credit **5** : a property interest held by one person for the benefit of another **6** : a combination of firms formed by a legal agreement; *esp* : one that reduces competition **7** : something entrusted to one to be cared for in the interest of another **8** : CARE, CUSTODY **syn** confidence, dependence, faith, monopoly, corner, pool

²**trust** *vb* **1** : to place confidence : DEPEND **2** : to be confident : HOPE **3** : ENTRUST **4** : to permit to stay or go or to do something without fear or misgiving **5** : to rely on or on the truth of : BELIEVE **6** : to extend credit to

**trust·ee** \,trəs-'tē\ *n* **1** : a person to whom property is legally committed in trust **2** : a country charged with the supervision of a trust territory

**trust·ee·ship** \,trəs-'tē-,ship\ *n* **1** : the office or function of a trustee **2** : supervisory control by one or more nations over a trust territory

**trust·ful** \'trəst-fəl\ *adj* : full of trust : CONFIDING — **trust·ful·ly** \-ē\ *adv* — **trust·ful·ness** *n*

**trust territory** *n* : a non-self-governing

territory placed under a supervisory authority by the Trusteeship Council of the United Nations

**trust·wor·thy** \-,wər-_thē_\ *adj* : worthy of confidence : DEPENDABLE **syn** trusty, tried, reliable — **trust·wor·thi·ness** *n*

¹**trusty** \'trəs-tē\ *adj* **trust·i·er; -est** : TRUSTWORTHY, DEPENDABLE

²**trusty** \'trəs-tē, ,trəs-'tē\ *n, pl* **trust·ies** : a trusted person; *esp* : a convict considered trustworthy and allowed special privileges

**truth** \'trüth\ *n, pl* **truths** \'trüthz, 'trüths\ **1** : TRUTHFULNESS, HONESTY **2** : the real state of things : FACT **3** : the body of real events or facts : ACTUALITY **4** : a true or accepted statement or proposition ⟨the ~s of science⟩ **5** : agreement with fact or reality : CORRECTNESS **syn** veracity, verity, verisimilitude

**truth·ful** \'trüth-fəl\ *adj* : telling or disposed to tell the truth — **truth·ful·ly** \-ē\ *adv* — **truth·ful·ness** *n*

**truth serum** *n* : a drug held to induce a subject under questioning to talk freely

¹**try** \'trī\ *vb* **tried; try·ing 1** : to examine or investigate judicially **2** : to conduct the trial of **3** : to put to test or trial **4** : to subject to strain, affliction, or annoyance **5** : to extract or clarify (as lard) by melting **6** : to make an effort to do something : ATTEMPT, ENDEAVOR **syn** essay, assay, strive, struggle

²**try** *n, pl* **tries** : an experimental trial

**try·ing** \'trī-iŋ\ *adj* : severely straining the powers of endurance

**try on** *vb* : to put on (a garment) to test the fit and looks

**try out** \(')trī-'aút\ *vb* : to participate in competition esp. for a position on an athletic team or a part in a play — **try·out** \'trī-,aút\ *n*

**tryst** \'trist, ,trīst\ *n* : an agreement (as between lovers) to meet; *also* : an appointed place of meeting **syn** rendezvous, engagement

**tsar** \'zär, '(t)sär\ *var of* CZAR

**tset·se** \'(t)set-sē, 'tet-, '(t)sēt-, 'tēt-\ *n, pl* **tsetse** *or* **tsetses** : any of several flies that occur in Africa south of the Sahara desert and include the vector of sleeping sickness

**TSgt** *abbr* technical sergeant

**T-shirt** \'tē-,shərt\ *n* : a collarless short-sleeved or sleeveless cotton undershirt for men; *also* : an outer shirt of similar design

**tsp** *abbr* teaspoon

**T square** *n* : a ruler with a crosspiece or head at one end for making parallel lines

**tsu·na·mi** \(t)sù-'näm-ē\ *n* : a tidal wave caused by an earthquake or volcanic eruption — **tsu·na·mic** \-ik\ *adj*

**tub** \'təb\ *n* **1** : a wide low bucketlike vessel **2** : BATHTUB; *also* : BATH **3** : the amount that a tub will hold

**tu·ba** \'t(y)ü-bə\ *n* : a large low-pitched brass wind instrument

**tube** \'t(y)üb\ *n* **1** : a hollow cylinder

to convey fluids : CHANNEL, DUCT **2** : any of various usu. cylindrical structures or devices **3** : a round metal container from which a paste is squeezed **4** : a tunnel for vehicular or rail travel **5** : an airtight tube of rubber inside a tire to hold air under pressure **6** : ELECTRON TUBE **7** : TELEVISION — **tubed** \'t(y)übd\ *adj* — **tube·less** *adj*

**tu·ber** \'t(y)ü-bər\ *n* : a short fleshy usu. underground stem (as of a potato plant) bearing minute scalelike leaves each with a bud at its base

**tu·ber·cle** \'t(y)ü-bər-kəl\ *n* **1** : a small knobby prominence or outgrowth esp. on an animal or plant **2** : a small abnormal lump in an organ or the skin; *esp* : one caused by tuberculosis

**tubercle bacillus** *n* : a bacterium that is the cause of tuberculosis

**tu·ber·cu·lar** \t(y)ù-'bər-kyə-lər\ *adj* **1** : of, resembling, or being a tubercle **2** : TUBERCULATE 1 **3** : TUBERCULOUS

**tu·ber·cu·late** \t(y)ü-'bər-kyə-lət\ *or* **tu·ber·cu·lat·ed** \-,lāt-əd\ *adj* **1** : having or covered with tubercles **2** : TUBERCULAR 1

**tu·ber·cu·lin** \t(y)ù-'bər-kyə-lən\ *n* : a sterile liquid extracted from the tubercle bacillus and used in the diagnosis of tuberculosis esp. in children and cattle

**tu·ber·cu·lo·sis** \t(y)ù-,bər-kyə-'lō-səs\ *n, pl* **-lo·ses** \-,sēz\ : a communicable bacterial disease typically marked by wasting, fever, and formation of cheesy tubercles often in the lungs — **tu·ber·cu·lous** \-'bər-kyə-ləs\ *adj*

**tube·rose** \'t(y)üb-,rōz\ *n* : a bulbous herb related to the amaryllis and often grown for its spike of fragrant waxy-white flowers

**tu·ber·ous** \'t(y)ü-b(ə-)rəs\ *adj* : of, resembling, or being a plant tuber

**tub·ing** \'t(y)ü-biŋ\ *n* **1** : material in the form of a tube; *also* : a length of tube **2** : a series of tubes

**tu·bu·lar** \'t(y)ü-byə-lər\ *adj* : having the form of or consisting of a tube; *also* : made with tubes

**tu·bule** \'t(y)ü-byül\ *n* : a small tube

¹**tuck** \'tək\ *vb* [ME *tuken* to pull up sharply, scold, fr. OE *tūcian* to ill-treat] **1** : to pull up into a fold ⟨~ed up her skirt⟩ **2** : to make tucks in **3** : to put into a snug often concealing place ⟨~ a book under the arm⟩ **4** : to secure in place by pushing the edges under ⟨~ in a blanket⟩ **5** : to cover by tucking in bedclothes

²**tuck** *n* : a fold stitched into cloth to shorten, decorate, or control fullness

**tuck·er** \'tək-ər\ *vb* **tuck·ered; tuck·er·ing** \'tək-(ə-)riŋ\ : EXHAUST, FATIGUE

**Tues** *or* **Tue** *abbr* Tuesday

**Tues·day** \'t(y)üz-dē\ *n* : the third day of the week

**tu·fa** \'t(y)ü-fə\ *n* : a porous rock formed as a deposit from springs or streams — **tu·fa·ceous** \t(y)ü-'fā-shəs\ *adj*

**tuff** \'təf\ *n* : a rock composed of volcanic detritus — **tuff·a·ceous** \,tə-ˈfā-shəs\ *adj*

¹**tuft** \ˈtəft\ *n* **1 :** a small cluster of long flexible outgrowths (as hairs); *also* **:** a bunch of soft fluffy threads cut off short and used as ornament **2 :** CLUMP, CLUSTER — **tuft·ed** \ˈtəf-təd\ *adj*

²**tuft** *vb* **1 :** to provide or adorn with a tuft **2 :** to make (as a mattress) firm by stitching at intervals and sewing on tufts

¹**tug** \ˈtəg\ *vb* **tugged; tug·ging 1 :** to pull hard **2 :** to struggle in opposition **:** CONTEND **3 :** to move by pulling hard **:** HAUL **4 :** to tow with a tugboat

²**tug** *n* **1 :** a harness trace **2 :** an act of tugging **:** PULL **3 :** a straining effort **4 :** a struggle between opposing people or forces **5 :** TUGBOAT

**tug·boat** \-,bōt\ *n* **:** a strongly built boat used for towing or pushing

**tug–of–war** \,təg-ə-(v)-ˈwòr\ *n, pl* **tugs–of–war 1 :** a struggle for supremacy **2 :** an athletic contest in which two teams pull against each other at opposite ends of a rope

**tu·grik** \ˈtü-grik\ *n* — see MONEY table

**tu·ition** \t(y)ù-ˈish-ən\ *n* **1 :** INSTRUCTION **2 :** the price of or payment for instruction

**tu·la·re·mia** \,t(y)ü-lə-ˈrē-mē-ə\ *n* **:** an infectious bacterial disease of rodents, man, and some domestic animals that in man is marked by symptoms (as fever) of toxemia

**tu·lip** \ˈt(y)ü-ləp\ *n* [NL *tulipa*, fr. Turk *tülbend* turban] **:** any of various Old World bulbous herbs related to the lilies and grown for their large showy erect cup-shaped flowers; *also* **:** a flower or bulb of a tulip

**tulip tree** *n* **:** a tall American timber tree with greenish tuliplike flowers and soft white wood

**tulle** \ˈtül\ *n* **:** a sheer silk, rayon, or nylon net ⟨a bridal veil of ∼⟩

¹**tum·ble** \ˈtəm-bəl\ *vb* **tum·bled; tum·bling** \-b(ə-)liŋ\ [ME *tumblen*, fr. *tumben* to dance, fr. OE *tumbian*] **1 :** to perform gymnastic feats of rolling and turning **2 :** to fall or cause to fall suddenly and helplessly **3 :** to fall into ruin **4 :** to roll over and over **:** TOSS **5 :** to issue forth hurriedly and confusedly **6 :** to come to understand **7 :** to throw together in a confused mass

²**tumble** *n* **1 :** a disorderly state **2 :** an act or instance of tumbling

**tum·ble·down** \,təm-bəl-,daùn\ *adj* **:** DILAPIDATED, RAMSHACKLE

**tum·bler** \ˈtəm-blər\ *n* **1 :** one that tumbles; *esp* **:** ACROBAT **2 :** a drinking glass without foot or stem **3 :** a domestic pigeon having the habit of somersaulting backward **4 :** a movable obstruction in a lock that must be adjusted to a particular position (as by a key) before the bolt can be thrown

**tum·ble·weed** \ˈtəm-bəl-,wēd\ *n* **:** a plant that breaks away from its roots in autumn and is driven about by the wind

**tum·brel** *or* **tum·bril** \ˈtəm-brəl\ *n* **1 :** CART **2 :** a vehicle carrying condemned persons (as political prisoners during the French Revolution) to a place of execution

**tu·mid** \ˈt(y)ü-məd\ *adj* **1 :** SWOLLEN, DISTENDED **2 :** BOMBASTIC, TURGID — **tu·mid·i·ty** \t(y)ü-ˈmid-ət-ē\ *n*

**tum·my** \ˈtəm-ē\ *n, pl* **tummies :** BELLY, ABDOMEN, STOMACH

**tu·mor** \ˈt(y)ü-mər\ *n* **:** an abnormal and functionless mass of tissue that is not inflammatory and arises without obvious cause from preexistent tissue — **tu·mor·ous** *adj*

**tu·mult** \ˈt(y)ü-,məlt\ *n* **1 :** disorderly agitation of a crowd usu. with uproar and confusion of voices **2 :** DISTURBANCE, RIOT **3 :** a confusion of loud noise and usu. turbulent movement **4 :** violent agitation of mind or feelings

**tu·mul·tu·ous** \t(y)ü-ˈməlch-(ə-)wəs, -ˈməl-chəs\ *adj* **1 :** marked by tumult **2 :** tending to incite a tumult **3 :** marked by violent upheaval

**tun** \ˈtən\ *n* **1 :** a large cask **2 :** the capacity of a tun; *esp* **:** a unit of 252 gallons

**tu·na** \ˈt(y)ü-nə\ *n, pl* **tuna** *or* **tunas :** any of several mostly large sea fishes related to the mackerels and important for food and sport

**tun·able** *also* **tune·able** \ˈt(y)ü-nə-bəl\ *adj* **:** capable of being tuned — **tun·abil·i·ty** \,t(y)ü-nə-ˈbil-ət-ē\ *n* — **tun·ably** \-ˈt(y)ü-nə-blē\ *adv*

**tun·dra** \ˈtən-drə\ *n* **:** a treeless plain of northern arctic regions

¹**tune** \ˈt(y)ün\ *n* **1 :** an easily remembered melody **2 :** correct musical pitch **3 :** harmonious relationship **:** AGREEMENT ⟨in ∼ with the times⟩ **4 :** general attitude ⟨changed his ∼⟩ **5 :** AMOUNT, EXTENT ⟨in debt to the ∼ of millions⟩

²**tune** *vb* **tuned; tun·ing 1 :** to bring or come into harmony **:** ATTUNE **2 :** to adjust in musical pitch **3 :** to adjust a radio or television receiver so as to receive a broadcast **4 :** to put in first-class working order — **tun·er** *n*

**tune·ful** \-fəl\ *adj* **:** MELODIOUS, MUSICAL — **tune·ful·ly** \-ē\ *adv* — **tune·ful·ness** *n*

**tune·less** \-ləs\ *adj* **1 :** UNMELODIOUS **2 :** not producing music — **tune·less·ly** *adv*

**tune–up** \ˈt(y)ün-,əp\ *n* **:** an adjustment to ensure efficient functioning ⟨a motor ∼⟩

**tung·sten** \ˈtəŋ-stən\ *n* **:** a white hard heavy ductile metallic element used for electrical purposes and in an alloy (**tungsten steel**) noted for its strength and hardness

**tu·nic** \ˈt(y)ü-nik\ *n* **1 :** a usu. knee-length belted under or outer garment worn by ancient Greeks and Romans **2 :** a hip-length or longer blouse or jacket

**tuning fork** *n* **:** a 2-pronged metal implement that gives a fixed tone when struck and is useful for tuning musical instruments

**Tu·ni·sian** \t(y)ü-ˈnēzh-ən, - nizh-\ *n* **:** a native or inhabitant of Tunisia — **Tunisian** *adj*

¹**tun·nel** \ˈtən-ᵊl\ *n* **:** an underground

passageway excavated esp. for a road, railroad, water system, or sewer; *also* **:** a horizontal passage in a mine

²**tunnel** *vb* **tun·neled** *or* **tun·nelled; tun·nel·ing** *or* **tun·nel·ling** \'tən-(²-)liŋ\ **:** to make a tunnel through or under

**tun·ny** \'tən-ē\ *n, pl* **tunnies** *also* **tunny :** TUNA

**-tu·ple** \,təp-əl, ,tüp-\ *n comb form* **:** set of (so many) elements

**tuque** \'t(y)ük\ *n* **:** a warm knitted cone-shaped cap with a tassel or pom-pom worn esp. for winter sports or play

**tur·ban** \'tər-bən\ *n* **1 :** a headdress worn esp. by Muslims and made of a cap around which is wound a long cloth **2 :** a headdress resembling a Muslim turban; *esp* **:** a woman's close-fitting hat without a brim

**tur·bid** \'tər-bəd\ *adj* [L *turbidus* confused, turbid, fr. *turba* confusion, crowd] **1 :** thick with roiled sediment ⟨a ∼ stream⟩ **2 :** heavy with smoke or mist **:** DENSE **3 :** CONFUSED, MUDDLED — **tur·bid·i·ty** \,tər-'bid-ət-ē\ *n* — **tur·bid·ly** \'tər-bəd-lē\ *adv* — **tur·bid·ness** *n*

**tur·bine** \'tər-bən, -,bīn\ *n* [F, fr. L *turbin-, turbo* top, whirlwind, whirl] **:** an engine whose central drive shaft is fitted with curved vanes whirled by the pressure of water, steam, or gas

**tur·bo·elec·tric** \'tər-bō-i-'lek-trik\ *adj* **:** involving or depending as a power source on electricity produced by turbine generators

**tur·bo·fan** \-,fan\ *n* **1 :** a fan that is directly connected to and driven by a turbine and is used to supply air for cooling, ventilation, or combustion **2 :** a jet engine having a turbofan

**tur·bo·jet** \-,jet\ *n* **:** an airplane powered by a jet engine (**turbojet engine**) having a turbine-driven air compressor supplying compressed air to the combustion chamber

**tur·bo·prop** \'tər-bō-,präp\ *n* **:** an airplane powered by a jet engine (**turbo-propeller engine**) having a turbine-driven propeller but usu. obtaining additional thrust from the discharge of a jet of hot gases

**tur·bot** \'tər-bət\ *n, pl* **turbot** *also* **turbots :** a European flatfish that is a popular food fish; *also* **:** any of several similar flatfishes

**tur·bu·lence** \'tər-byə-ləns\ *n* **:** the quality or state of being turbulent

**tur·bu·lent** \-lənt\ *adj* **1 :** causing violence or disturbance **2 :** marked by agitation or tumult **:** TEMPESTUOUS — **tur·bu·lent·ly** *adv*

**tu·reen** \tə-'rēn, tyů-\ *n* [F *terrine*, fr. MF, fr. fem. of *terrin* of earth, fr. L *terra* earth] **:** a deep bowl from which foods (as soup) are served at table

¹**turf** \'tərf\ *n, pl* **turfs** \'tərfs\ *or* **turves** \'tərvz\ **1 :** the upper layer of soil bound by grass and roots into a close mat; *also* **:** a piece of this **:** SOD **2 :** an artificial substitute for turf (as on a playing field) **3 :** a piece of peat dried for fuel **4 :** a track or course for

horse racing; *also* **:** horse racing as a sport or business

²**turf** *vb* **:** to cover with turf

**tur·gid** \'tər-jəd\ *adj* **1 :** marked by distension **:** SWOLLEN **2 :** excessively embellished in style or language **:** BOMBASTIC — **tur·gid·i·ty** \,tər-'jid-ət-ē\ *n*

¹**Turk** \'tərk\ *n* **:** a native or inhabitant of Turkey

²**Turk** *abbr* Turkey; Turkish

**tur·key** \'tər-kē\ *n, pl* **turkeys** [*Turkey*, country in western Asia and southeastern Europe; fr. confusion with the guinea fowl, supposed to be imported from Turkish territory] **:** a large American bird related to the common fowl and widely raised for food; *also* **:** its flesh

**turkey buzzard** *n* **:** BUZZARD 2

**Turk·ish** \'tər-kish\ *n* **:** the language of Turkey — **Turkish** *adj*

**tur·mer·ic** \'tər-mə-rik, 't(y)ü-mə-\ *n* **:** an East Indian perennial herb with a large aromatic deep-yellow rhizome; *also* **:** a spice or dyestuff obtained from turmeric

**tur·moil** \'tər-,mȯil\ *n* **:** an extremely confused or agitated condition

¹**turn** \'tərn\ *vb* **1 :** to move or cause to move around an axis or center **:** ROTATE, REVOLVE ⟨∼ a wheel⟩ **2 :** to twist so as to effect a desired end ⟨∼ a key⟩ **3 :** WRENCH ⟨∼ an ankle⟩ **4 :** to change or cause to change position by moving through an arc of a circle ⟨∼ed his chair to the fire⟩ **5 :** to cause to move around a center so as to show another side of ⟨∼ a page⟩ **6 :** to revolve mentally **:** PONDER **7 :** to become dizzy **:** REEL **8 :** to reverse the sides or surfaces of ⟨∼ a pancake⟩ **9 :** UPSET, DISORDER ⟨things ∼ed topsy-turvy⟩ ⟨∼ed his stomach⟩ **10 :** to set in another esp. contrary direction **11 :** to change one's course or direction **12 :** TRANSFER ⟨∼ the task over to him⟩ **13 :** to go around ⟨∼ a corner⟩ **14 :** to reach or pass beyond ⟨∼ed twenty-one⟩ **15 :** to direct toward or away from something; *also* **:** DEVOTE, APPLY **16 :** to have recourse **17 :** to become or make hostile **18 :** to make or become spoiled **:** SOUR **19 :** to cause to become of a specified nature or appearance ⟨∼s the leaves yellow⟩ **20 :** to pass from one state to another ⟨water ∼s to ice⟩ **21 :** CONVERT, TRANSFORM **22 :** TRANSLATE, PARAPHRASE **23 :** to give a rounded form to; *esp* **:** to shape by means of a lathe **24 :** to gain by passing in trade ⟨∼ a quick profit⟩ — **turn color 1 :** BLUSH **2 :** to become pale — **turn loose :** to set free

²**turn** *n* **1 :** a turning about a center or axis **:** REVOLUTION, ROTATION **2 :** the action or an act of giving or taking a different direction ⟨make a left ∼⟩ **3 :** a change of course or tendency ⟨a ∼ for the better⟩ **4 :** a place at which something turns **:** BEND, CURVE **5 :** a short walk or trip round about ⟨take a ∼ around the deck⟩ **6 :** an act affecting another ⟨did him a good ∼⟩ **7 :** a place, time, or opportunity accorded in a scheduled order ⟨waited his

~ to be served⟩ **8 :** a period of duty **: SHIFT 9 :** a short act esp. in a variety show **10 :** a special purpose or requirement ⟨the job serves his ~⟩ **11 :** a skillful fashioning ⟨neat ~ of phrase⟩ **12 :** a single round (as of rope passed around an object) **13 :** natural or special aptitude **14 :** a usu. sudden and brief disorder of body or spirits; *esp* **:** a spell of nervous shock or faintness

**turn-about** \'tər-nə-,baut\ *n* **1 :** a reversal of direction, trend, or policy **: RETALIATION**

**turn-buck-le** \'tərn-,bək-əl\ *n* **:** a link with a screw thread at one or both ends for tightening a rod or stay

**turn-coat** \-,kōt\ *n* **:** one who forsakes his party or principles **: RENEGADE**

**turn down** \,tərn-'daun, 'tərn-\ *vb* **:** to decline to accept **: REJECT — turn-down** \'tərn-,daun\ *n*

**turn-er** \'tər-nər\ *n* **1 :** one that turns or is used for turning **2 :** one that forms articles with a lathe

**turn-ery** \'tər-nə-rē\ *n, pl* **-er-ies :** the work, products, or shop of a turner

**turn in** *vb* **1 :** to deliver up **2 :** to inform on **3 :** to acquit oneself of ⟨*turn in* a good job⟩ **4 :** to go to bed

**turn-ing** \'tər-niŋ\ *n* **1 :** the act or course of one that turns **2 :** a place of a change of direction

**tur-nip** \'tər-nəp\ *n* **:** the thick edible root of either of two herbs related to the mustards; *also* **:** either of these plants

**turn-key** \'tərn-,kē\ *n, pl* **turnkeys :** one who has charge of a prison's keys

**turn-off** \'tərn-,óf\ *n* **:** a place for turning off esp. from an expressway

**turn off** \,tərn-'óf, 'tərn-\ *vb* **1 :** to stop the functioning or flow of **2 :** to cause to lose interest; *also* **:** to evoke a negative feeling in **3 :** to deviate from a straight course or a main road

**turn on** *vb* **1 :** to get high or cause to get high as a result of using a drug (as marijuana **2 :** EXCITE, STIMULATE

**turn-out** \'tərn-,aut\ *n* **1 :** an act of turning out **2 :** a gathering of people for a special purpose **3 :** a widened place in a highway for vehicles to pass or park **4 :** manner of dress **5 :** net yield **:** OUTPUT

**turn out** \,tərn-'aut, 'tərn-\ *vb* **1 :** EXPEL, EVICT **2 :** PRODUCE **3 :** to come forth and assemble **4 :** to get out of bed **5 :** to prove to be in the end

¹**turn-over** \'tərn-,ō-vər\ *n* **1 :** UPSET **2 :** SHIFT, REVERSAL **3 :** a filled pastry made by turning half of the crust over the other half **4 :** the volume of business done **5 :** movement (as of goods or people) into, through, and out of a place; *esp* **:** a cycle of purchase, sale, and replacement of a stock of goods **6 :** the number of persons hired within a period to replace those leaving or dropped; *also* **:** the ratio of this number to that of the average force maintained

²**turn-over** \,tərn-,ō-vər\ *adj* **:** capable of being turned over

**turn-pike** \'tərn-,pīk\ *n* [ME *turnepike*

revolving frame bearing spikes and serving as a barrier, fr. *turnen* to turn + *pike*] **1 :** TOLLGATE; *also* **:** an expressway on which tolls are charged **2 :** a main road

**turn-spit** \-,spit\ *n* **:** a device for turning a spit

**turn-stile** \-,stīl\ *n* **:** a post with arms pivoted on the top set in a passageway so that persons can pass through only on foot one by one

**turn-ta-ble** \-,tā-bəl\ *n* **:** a circular platform that revolves (as for turning a locomotive or a phonograph record)

**turn to** *vb* **:** to apply oneself to work

**turn up** *vb* **1 :** to come to light or bring to light **: DISCOVER, APPEAR 2 :** to arrive at an appointed time or place **3 :** to happen unexpectedly

**tur-pen-tine** \'tər-pən-,tīn\ *n* **1 :** a mixture of oil and resin obtained from various cone-bearing trees (as pines) as a substance that oozes from cuts in the trunk **2 :** a colorless or yellowish oil obtained from various turpentines by distillation and used as a solvent and thinner (as in paint); *also* **:** a similar oil obtained from distillation of pine wood

**tur-pi-tude** \'tər-pə-,t(y)üd\ *n* **:** inherent baseness **: DEPRAVITY**

**turps** \'tərps\ *n* **: TURPENTINE**

**tur-quoise** *also* **tur-quois** \'tər-,k(w)öiz\ *n* [ME *turkeis, turcas,* fr. MF *turquoyse,* fr. fem. of *turquoys* Turkish, fr. OF, fr. *Turc* Turk] **1 :** a blue, bluish green, or greenish gray mineral that contains a little copper and is valued as a gem **2 :** a light greenish blue color

**tur-ret** \'tər-ət\ *n* **1 :** a little tower often at an angle of a larger structure and merely ornamental **2 :** a revolvable holder in a machine tool **3 :** a towerlike armored and usu. revolving structure within which guns are mounted in a warship or tank; *also* **:** a similar structure in an airplane

¹**tur-tle** \'tərt-²l\ *n, archaic* **: TURTLE-DOVE**

²**turtle** *n, pl* **turtles** *also* **turtle :** any of a group of horny-beaked land, freshwater, or sea reptiles with the trunk enclosed in a bony shell

**tur-tle-dove** \'tərt-²l-,dəv\ *n* **:** any of several small wild pigeons; *esp* **:** an Old World bird noted for plaintive cooing

**tur-tle-neck** \-,nek\ *n* **:** a high close-fitting turnover collar used esp. for sweaters; *also* **:** a sweater with a turtleneck

**turves** *pl of* TURF

**Tus-ca-ro-ra** \,təs-kə-'rōr-ə\ *n, pl* **Tuscarora** *or* **Tuscaroras :** a member of an Indian people of No. Carolina and later of New York and Ontario

**tusk** \'təsk\ *n* **1 :** a long enlarged protruding tooth (as of an elephant, walrus, or boar) used to dig up food or as a weapon **2 :** a long projecting tooth — **tusked** \'təskt\ *adj*

**tusk-er** \'təs-kər\ *n* **:** an animal with tusks; *esp* **:** a male elephant with two normally developed tusks

**¹tus·sle** \'təs-əl\ vb **tus·sled; tus·sling** \-(ə-)liŋ\ **:** to struggle roughly

**²tussle** n **1 :** a physical struggle **:** SCUFFLE **2 :** a rough controversy or struggle against difficult odds

**tus·sock** \'təs-ək\ n **:** a dense tuft esp. of grass or sedge; also **:** a hummock in marsh bound together by roots — **tus·socky** adj

**tussock moth** n **:** any of numerous dull-colored moths that usu. have wingless females and larvae with long tufts or brushes of hair

**tu·te·lage** \'t(y)üt-ᵊl-ij\ n **1 :** an act of guarding or protecting **2 :** the state of being under a guardian or tutor **:** instruction esp. of an individual

**tu·te·lar** \'t(y)üt-ᵊl-ər, -ᵊl-,är\ adj **:** TUTELARY

**tu·te·lary** \'t(y)üt-ᵊl-,er-ē\ adj **:** acting as a guardian ⟨∼ deity⟩ ⟨a ∼ power⟩

**¹tu·tor** \'t(y)üt-ər\ n **1 :** a person charged with the instruction and guidance of another **2 :** a private teacher **3 :** a college or university teacher ranking below an instructor

**²tutor** vb **1 :** to have the guardianship of **2 :** to teach or guide individually **:** COACH ⟨∼ed the boy in Latin⟩ **3 :** to receive instruction esp. privately

**tu·to·ri·al** \t(y)ü-'tōr-ē-əl\ n **:** a class conducted by a tutor for one student or a small number of students

**tut·ti-frut·ti** \,tüt-i-'früt-ē, ,tüt-\ n **:** a confection or ice cream containing chopped usu. candied fruits

**tux·e·do** \,tək-'sēd-ō\ n, pl **-dos** or **-does** [Tuxedo Park, N.Y.] **1 :** a usu. black or blackish blue jacket **2 :** semiformal evening clothes for men

**tv** \'tē-'vē\ n, often cap T&V **:** TELEVISION

**TVA** abbr Tennessee Valley Authority

**TV dinner** \,tē-,vē-\ n **:** a frozen packaged dinner that needs only heating before serving

**twad·dle** \'twäd-ᵊl\ n **:** silly idle talk **:** DRIVEL — **twaddle** vb — **twad·dler** \-(ᵊ-)lər\ n

**twain** \'twān\ n **1 :** TWO **2 :** PAIR

**¹twang** \'twaŋ\ n **1 :** a harsh quick ringing sound like that of a plucked bowstring **2 :** nasal speech or resonance **3 :** the characteristic speech of a region

**²twang** vb **twanged; twang·ing** \'twaŋ-iŋ\ **1 :** to sound or cause to sound with a twang **2 :** to speak with a nasal twang

**tweak** \'twēk\ vb **:** to pinch and pull with a sudden jerk and twitch — **tweak** n

**tweed** \'twēd\ n [alter. of Sc tweel twill, fr. ME twyll] **1 :** a rough woolen fabric made usu. in twill weaves **2** pl **:** tweed clothing; esp **:** a tweed suit

**tweedy** \'twēd-ē\ adj **tweed·i·er; -est 1 :** of or resembling tweed **2 :** given to wearing tweeds **3 :** suggestive of the outdoors in taste or habits

**tween** \(')twēn\ prep **:** BETWEEN

**tweet** \'twēt\ n **:** a chirping note — **tweet** vb

**‖tweet·er** \'twēt-ər\ n **:** a small loudspeaker that reproduces sounds of high pitch

**twee·zers** \'twē-zərz\ n pl [obs. E tweeze, n. (case for small implements) short for obs. E etweese, fr. pl. of obs. E etwee, fr. F étui] **:** a small pincerlike implement held between the thumb and forefinger for grasping or extracting something

**twelve** \'twelv\ n **1 :** one more than 11 **2 :** the 12th in a set or series **3 :** something having 12 units — **twelfth** \'twelfth\ adj or n — **twelve** adj or pron

**twelve-month** \-,mənth\ n **:** YEAR

**twen·ty** \'twent-ē\ n, pl **twenties :** two times 10 — **twen·ti·eth** \-ē-əth\ adj or n — **twenty** adj or pron

**twenty-twenty** or **20/20** \,twent-ē-'twent-ē\ adj **:** having a visual capacity to see detail that is normal for the human eye

**twice** \'twīs\ adv **1 :** on two occasions **2 :** two times ⟨∼ two is four⟩

**¹twid·dle** \'twid-ᵊl\ vb **twid·dled; twid·dling** \'twid-(ᵊ-)liŋ\ **1 :** to be busy with trifles; also **:** to play idly with something **2 :** to rotate lightly or idly

**²twiddle** n **:** TURN, TWIST

**twig** \'twig\ n **:** a small branch — **twig·gy** adj

**twi·light** \'twī-,līt\ n **1 :** the light from the sky between full night and sunrise or between sunset and full night **2 :** a state of imperfect clarity; also **:** a period of decline — **twilight** adj

**twill** \'twil\ n [ME twyll, fr. OE twilic having a double thread, modif. of L bilic-, bilix, fr. bi- two + licium thread] **1 :** a fabric with a twill weave **2 :** a textile weave that gives an appearance of diagonal lines in the fabric

**twilled** \'twild\ adj **:** made with a twill weave

**¹twin** \'twin\ adj **1 :** born with one another or as a pair at one birth ⟨∼ brother⟩ ⟨∼ girls⟩ **2 :** made up of two similar or related members or parts **3 :** being one of a pair ⟨∼ city⟩

**²twin** n **1 :** either of two offspring produced at a birth **2 :** one of two persons or things closely related to or resembling each other

**³twin** vb **twinned; twin·ning 1 :** to bring forth twins **2 :** to be coupled with another

**¹twine** \'twīn\ n **1 :** a strong thread of two or three strands twisted together **2 :** an act of entwining or interlacing — **twiny** adj

**²twine** vb **twined; twin·ing 1 :** to twist together; also **:** to form by twisting **2 :** INTERLACE, WEAVE **3 :** to coil about a support **4 :** to stretch or move in a sinuous manner — **twin·er** n

**¹twinge** \'twinj\ vb **twinged; twing·ing** \'twin-jiŋ\ or **twinge·ing :** to affect with or feel a sharp sudden pain

**²twinge** n **:** a sudden sharp stab (as of pain or distress)

**¹twin·kle** \'twiŋ-kəl\ vb **twin·kled; twin·kling** \-k(ə-)liŋ\ **1 :** to shine or cause to shine with a flickering or sparkling light **2 :** to flutter or flit rapidly **3** : to appear bright with merriment — **twin·kler** \-k(ə-)lər\ *n*

²**twinkle** *n* **1** : a wink of the eyelids; *also* : the duration of a wink **2** : an intermittent radiance **3** : a rapid flashing motion

**twin·kling** \'twiŋ-kliŋ\ *n* **1** : a wink of the eyelids **2** : the time occupied by a single wink **syn** instant, moment, minute, second, flash

¹**twirl** \'twərl\ *vb* **1** : to whirl round **2** : to pitch in a baseball game **syn** turn, revolve, rotate, circle, spin, swirl, pirouette — **twirl·er** \'twər-lər\ *n*

²**twirl** *n* **1** : an act of twirling **2** : COIL, WHORL

¹**twist** \'twist\ *vb* **1** : to unite by winding one thread or strand round another **2** : WREATHE, TWINE **3** : to turn so as to hurt ⟨*~ed* her ankle⟩ **4** : to twirl into spiral shape **5** : to subject (as a shaft) to torsion **6** : to pull off or break by torsion **7** : to turn from the true form or meaning **8** : to follow a winding course **9** : to turn around

²**twist** *n* **1** : something formed by twisting or winding **2** : an act of twisting : the state of being twisted **3** : a spiral turn or curve; *also* : SPIN **4** : a turning aside **5** : ECCENTRICITY **6** : a distortion of meaning **7** : an unexpected turn or development **8** : a variant approach or method **9** : DEVICE, TRICK

**twist·er** \'twis-tər\ *n* **1** : one that twists; *esp* : a ball with a forward and spinning motion **2** : a tornado or waterspout in which the rotary ascending column of air is apparent

**twit** \'twit\ *vb* **twit·ted; twit·ting** : to reproach, taunt, or tease esp. by reminding of a fault or defect **syn** ridicule, deride, mock

¹**twitch** \'twich\ *vb* **1** : to move or pull with a sudden motion : JERK **2** : to move jerkily : QUIVER

²**twitch** *n* **1** : an act or movement of twitching **2** : a short sharp contraction of muscle fibers

¹**twit·ter** \'twit-ər\ *vb* **1** : to make a succession of chirping noises **2** : to talk in a chattering fashion; *also* : TITTER **3** : to have a slight trembling of the nerves : FLUTTER

²**twitter** *n* **1** : a small tremulous intermittent noise (as made by a swallow) **2** : a light chattering; *also* : TITTER **3** : a slight agitation of the nerves

**twixt** \(')twikst\ *prep* : BETWEEN

**two** \'tü\ *n, pl* **twos 1** : one more than one **2** : the second in a set or series **3** : something having two units — **two** *adj or pron*

**two-faced** \'tü-'fāst\ *adj* **1** : having two faces **2** : DOUBLE-DEALING, FALSE — **two-fac·ed·ly** \-'fā-səd-lē\ *adv*

**two-fold** \'tü-,fōld, -'fōld\ *adj* **1** : having two units or members **2** : being twice as much or as many — **two·fold** \-'fōld\ *adv*

**2,4-D** \,tü-,fōr-'dē\ *n* : a white crystalline compound used as a weed killer

**2,4,5-T** \-,fiv-'tē\ *n* : an irritant compound used in brush and weed control

**two·pence** \'təp-əns, *US also* 'tü-,pens\ *n* : the sum of two pence

**two·pen·ny** \'təp-(ə-)nē, *US also* 'tü-,pen-ē\ *adj* : of the value of or costing twopence

**two-ply** \'tü-'plī\ *adj* **1** : woven as a double cloth **2** : consisting of two strands or thicknesses

**two·some** \'tü-səm\ *n* **1** : a group of two persons or things : COUPLE **2** : a golf match between two players

**two-step** \'tü-,step\ *n* : a ballroom dance performed with a sliding step in march or polka time; *also* : a piece of music for this dance — **two-step** *vb*

**two-time** \'tü-,tīm\ *vb* : to betray (a spouse or lover) by secret lovemaking with another — **two-tim·er** *n*

**two-way** *adj* : involving two elements or allowing movement or use in two directions or manners

**two-winged fly** \,tü-,wiŋd-\ *n* : any of a large group of insects mostly with one pair of functional wings and another pair that if present are reduced to balancing organs

**twp** *abbr* township

**TWX** *abbr* teletypewriter exchange

**TX** *abbr* Texas

**-ty** *n suffix* : quality : condition : degree ⟨real*ty*⟩

**ty·coon** \tī-'kün\ *n* [Jap *taikun*, fr. Chin *ta⁴* great + *chün¹* ruler] **1** : a powerful businessman or industrialist **2** : a masterful leader (as in politics)

**tying** *pres part of* TIE

**tyke** \'tīk\ *n* **1** : DOG, CUR **2** : a small child

**tym·pan·ic membrane** \tim-'pan-ik-\ *n* : EARDRUM

**tym·pa·num** \'tim-pə-nəm\ *n, pl* **-na** \-nə\ *also* **-nums** : the cavity of the middle part of the ear closed externally by the eardrum; *also* : EARDRUM — **tym·pan·ic** \tim-'pan-ik\ *adj*

¹**type** \'tīp\ *n* [LL *typus*, fr. L & Gk; L *typus* image, fr. Gk *typos* blow, impression, model, fr. *typtein* to strike, beat] **1** : a distinctive stamp, mark, or sign : EMBLEM **2** : a person, thing, or event that foreshadows another to come : TOKEN, SYMBOL **3** : general character or form common to a number or individuals and setting them off as a distinguishable class ⟨horses of draft *~*⟩ **4** : a class, kind, or group set apart by common characteristics ⟨a seedless *~* of orange⟩; *also* : something distinguishable as a variety ⟨reactions of this *~*⟩ **5** : MODEL, EXAMPLE **6** : rectangular blocks usu. of metal each having a face so shaped as to produce a character when printed **7** : the letters or characters printed from or as if from type **syn** sort, nature, character, description

²**type** *vb* **typed; typ·ing 1** : to represent beforehand as a type **2** : to produce a copy of; *also* : REPRESENT, TYPIFY **3** : TYPEWRITE **4** : to identify as belonging to a type **5** : TYPECAST

**type·cast** \-,kast\ *vb* **-cast; -casting 1** : to cast (an actor) in a part calling for characteristics possessed by the actor himself 2 : to cast repeatedly in the same type of role

**type·face** \-,fās\ n : all type of a single design

**type·found·er** \-,faùn-dər\ n : one engaged in the design and production of metal printing type for hand composition — **type·found·ing** \-,diŋ\ n — **type·found·ry** \-,drē\ n

**type·script** \'tīp-,skript\ n : typewritten matter

**type·set·ter** \-,set-ər\ n : one that sets type — **type·set·ting** \-,set-iŋ\ adj or n

**type·write** \-,rīt\ vb -**wrote** \-,rōt\; -**writ·ten** \-,rit-ᵊn\ : to write with a typewriter

**type·writ·er** \-,rīt-ər\ n 1 : a machine for writing in characters similar to those produced by printers' types by means of types striking through an inked ribbon 2 : TYPIST

**type·writ·ing** \-,rīt-iŋ\ n : the use of a typewriter ⟨teach ∼⟩; also : the printing done with a typewriter

¹**ty·phoid** \'tī-,fóid, tī-'fóid\ adj : of, relating to, or being a communicable bacterial disease (**typhoid fever**) marked by fever, diarrhea, prostration, and intestinal inflammation

²**typhoid** n : TYPHOID FEVER

**ty·phoon** \tī-'fün\ n : a tropical cyclone in the region of the Philippines or the China sea

**ty·phus** \'tī-fəs\ n : a severe disease transmitted esp. by body lice and marked by high fever, stupor and delirium, intense headache, and a dark red rash

**typ·i·cal** \'tip-i-kəl\ adj 1 : being or having the nature of a type 2 : exhibiting the essential characteristics of a group 3 : conforming to a type — **typ-**

**i·cal·ly** \-ē\ adv — **typ·i·cal·ness** n

**typ·i·fy** \'tip-ə-,fī\ vb -**fied**; -**fy·ing** 1 : to represent by an image, form, model, or resemblance 2 : to embody the essential or common characteristics of

**typ·ist** \'tī-pəst\ n : one who operates a typewriter

**ty·po** \'tī-pō\ n, pl **typos** : an error in typing or in setting type

**ty·pog·ra·pher** \tī-'päg-rə-fər\ n 1 : PRINTER 2 : one who designs or arranges printing

**ty·pog·ra·phy** \tī-'päg-rə-fē\ n : the art of printing with type; also : the style, arrangement, or appearance of matter printed from type — **ty·po·graph·ic** \,tī-pə-'graf-ik\ or **ty·po·graph·i·cal** \-i-kəl\ adj — **ty·po·graph·i·cal·ly** \-ē\ adv

**ty·ran·ni·cal** \tə-'ran-i-kəl, tī-\ also **ty·ran·nic** \-ik\ adj : of or relating to a tyrant : DESPOTIC **syn** arbitrary, absolute, autocratic — **ty·ran·ni·cal·ly** \-i-k(ə-)lē\ adv

**tyr·an·nize** \'tir-ə-,nīz\ vb -**nized**; -**niz·ing** : to act as a tyrant : rule with unjust severity — **tyr·an·niz·er** n

**tyr·an·nous** \'tir-ə-nəs\ adj : TYRANNICAL — **tyr·an·nous·ly** adv

**tyr·an·ny** \'tir-ə-nē\ n, pl -**nies** 1 : the rule or authority of a tyrant : government in which absolute power is vested in a single ruler 2 : despotic use of power 3 : a tyrannical act

**ty·rant** \'tī-rənt\ n 1 : an absolute ruler : DESPOT 2 : a ruler who governs oppressively or brutally 3 : one who uses authority or power harshly

**ty·ro** \'tī-rō\ n, pl **tyros** [ML, fr. L *tiro* young soldier, tyro] : a beginner in learning : NOVICE

**tzar** \'zär, '(t)sär\ var of CZAR

---

**U**

¹**u** \'yü\ n, pl **u's** or **us** \'yüz\ often cap : the 21st letter of the English alphabet

²**u** abbr, often cap unit

¹**U** \'yü\ adj : characteristic of the upper classes

²**U** abbr university

³**U** symbol uranium

**UAR** abbr United Arab Republic

**ubiq·ui·tous** \yü-'bik-wət-əs\ adj : existing or being everywhere at the same time : OMNIPRESENT — **ubiq·ui·tous·ly** adv — **ubiq·ui·ty** \-wət-ē\ n

**U-boat** \'yü-,bōt, -,bōt\ n [trans. of G *u-boot*, short for *unterseeboot*, lit., undersea boat] : a German submarine

**ud·der** \'əd-ər\ n : an organ (as of a cow) consisting of two or more milk glands enclosed in a large hanging sac and each provided with a nipple

**UFO** \,yü-(,)ef-'ō\ n, pl **UFO's** or **UFOs** \-'ōz\ : an unidentified flying object; esp : FLYING SAUCER

**ug·ly** \'əg-lē\ adj **ug·li·er**; -**est** [ME, fr. ON *uggligr*, fr. *uggr* fear] 1 : FRIGHTFUL, DIRE 2 : offensive to the sight : HIDEOUS 3 : offensive or unpleasing to any sense 4 : morally

objectionable : REPULSIVE 5 : likely to cause inconvenience or discomfort 6 : SURLY, QUARRELSOME ⟨an ∼ disposition⟩ — **ug·li·ness** \-lē-nəs\ n

**UH** abbr upper half

**UHF** abbr ultrahigh frequency

**UK** abbr United Kingdom

**ukase** \yü-'kās, -'kāz\ n [F & Russ; F, fr. Russ *ukaz*, fr. *ukazat'* to show, order] : an edict esp. of a Russian emperor or government

**Ukrai·ni·an** \yü-'krā-nē-ən\ n : a native or inhabitant of the Ukraine — **Ukrainian** adj

**uku·le·le** \,yü-kə-'lā-lē\ n [Hawaiian *'ukulele*, fr. *'uku* flea + *lele* jumping] : a small usu. 4-stringed guitar popularized in Hawaii

**ul·cer** \'əl-sər\ n 1 : an eroded sore often discharging pus 2 : something that festers and corrupts like an open sore — **ul·cer·ous** adj

**ul·cer·ate** \'əl-sə-,rāt\ vb -**at·ed**; -**at·ing** : to cause or become affected with an ulcer — **ul·cer·a·tion** \,əl-sə-'rā-shən\ n — **ul·cer·a·tive** \'əl-sə-,rāt-iv\ adj

**ul·lage** \'əl-ij\ n [ME *ulage*, fr. MF *eullage* act of filling a cask, fr. *euillier* to fill a cask, fr. OF *ouil* eye, bunghole, fr. L *oculus* eye] **:** the amount that a container (as a cask) lacks of being full

**ul·na** \'əl-nə\ *n* **:** the inner of the two bones of the forearm or corresponding part of the forelimb of vertebrates above fishes

**ul·ster** \'əl-stər\ *n* **:** a long loose overcoat

**ult** *abbr* **1** ultimate **2** ultimo

**ul·te·ri·or** \,əl-'tir-ē-ər\ *adj* **1 :** situated beyond or on the farther side **2 :** lying farther away **:** more remote **3 :** going beyond what is openly said or shown **:** HIDDEN 〈~ motives〉

¹**ul·ti·mate** \'əl-tə-mət\ *adj* **1 :** most remote in space or time **:** FARTHEST **2 :** last in a progression **:** FINAL **3 :** EXTREME, UTMOST **4 :** finally reckoned **5 :** FUNDAMENTAL, ABSOLUTE, SUPREME 〈~ reality〉 **6 :** incapable of further analysis or division **:** ELEMENTAL **7 :** MAXIMUM — **ul·ti·mate·ly** *adv*

²**ultimate** *n* **:** something ultimate

**ul·ti·ma·tum** \,əl-tə-'māt-əm, -'mät-\ *n, pl* **-tums** *or* **-ta** \-ə\ **:** a final proposition, condition, or demand; *esp* **:** one whose rejection will bring about an end of negotiations

**ul·ti·mo** \'əl-tə-,mō\ *adj* [L *ultimo mense* in the last month] **:** of or occurring the month preceding the present

¹**ul·tra** \'əl-trə\ *adj* **:** going beyond others or beyond due limits **:** EXTREME

²**ultra** *n* **:** EXTREMIST

**ul·tra·cen·tri·fuge** \,əl-trə-'sen-trə-,fyüj\ *n* **:** a high-speed centrifuge able to cause sedimentation of small (as colloidal) particles — **ul·tra·cen·trif·u·gal** \-sen-'trif-yə-gəl\ *adj* — **ul·tra·cen·trif·u·ga·tion** \-sen-,trif-yə-'gā-shən\ *n*

**ul·tra·con·ser·va·tive** \,əl-trə-kən-'sər-vət-iv\ *adj* **:** extremely conservative

**ul·tra·fash·ion·able** \-'fash-(ə-)nə-bəl\ *adj* **:** extremely fashionable

**ul·tra·high** \-'hī\ *adj* **:** very high **:** exceedingly high 〈~ vacuum〉

**ultrahigh frequency** *n* **:** a frequency of a radio wave between 300 and 3000 megacycles

¹**ul·tra·ma·rine** \,əl-trə-mə-'rēn\ *n* **1 :** a deep blue pigment **2 :** a very bright deep blue color

²**ultramarine** *adj* **:** situated beyond the sea

**ul·tra·mi·cro·scope** \,əl-trə-'mī-krə-,skōp\ *n* **:** an apparatus that uses scattered light to view particles too small to be perceived with an ordinary microscope

**ul·tra·mi·cro·scop·ic** \-,mī-krə-'skäp-ik\ *adj* **1 :** too small to be seen with an ordinary microscope **2 :** of or relating to an ultramicroscope — **ul·tra·mi·cro·scop·i·cal·ly** \-i-k(ə-)lē\ *adv*

**ul·tra·min·ia·ture** \-'min-ē-ə-,chùr, -'min-i-,chùr, -chər\ *adj* **:** SUBMINIATURE — **ul·tra·min·ia·tur·iza·tion** \-,min-ē-ə-,chùr-ə-'zā-shən, ,min-i-,chùr-, -chər-\ *n*

**ul·tra·mod·ern** \,əl-trə-'mäd-ərn\ *adj*

**:** extremely or excessively modern in idea, style, or tendency

**ul·tra·mon·tane** \-'män-,tān, -,män-'tān\ *adj* **1 :** of or relating to countries or peoples beyond the mountains (as the Alps) **2 :** favoring greater or absolute supremacy of papal over national or diocesan authority in the Roman Catholic Church — **ultramontane** *n, often cap* — **ul·tra·mon·tan·ism** \-'mänt-ᵊn-,iz-əm\ *n*

**ul·tra·pure** \-'pyùr\ *adj* **:** of the utmost purity — **ul·tra·pure·ly** *adv*

**ul·tra·short** \-'shòrt\ *adj* **1 :** very short **2 :** having a wavelength below 10 meters

**ul·tra·son·ic** \,əl-trə-'sän-ik\ *adj* **:** SUPERSONIC — **ultrasonic** *n* — **ul·tra·son·i·cal·ly** \-i-k(ə-)lē\ *adv*

**ul·tra·son·ics** \-'sän-iks\ *n* **:** the science of ultrasonic phenomena

**ul·tra·sound** \-,saùnd\ *n* **:** sound vibrations with frequencies above the range of human hearing

**ul·tra·vi·o·let** \,əl-trə-'vī-ə-lət\ *adj* **:** having a wavelength shorter than those of visible light and longer than those of X rays 〈~ radiation〉; *also* **:** producing or employing ultraviolet radiation — **ultraviolet** *n*

**ul·tra vi·res** \,əl-trə-'vī-rēz\ *adv or adj* [NL, lit., beyond power] **:** beyond the scope of legal power or authority

**ul·u·late** \'əl-yə-,lāt\ *vb* **-lat·ed; -lat·ing :** HOWL, WAIL

**um·bel** \'əm-bəl\ *n* **:** a flat or rounded flower cluster in which the individual flower stalks all arise at one point on the main stem — **um·bel·late** \-bə-,lāt\ *adj*

**um·ber** \'əm-bər\ *n* **:** a brown earthy substance valued as a pigment either in its raw state or burnt — **umber** *adj*

**um·bi·li·cus** \,əm-bə-'lī-kəs, ,əm-'bil-i-\ *n, pl* **um·bi·li·ci** \,əm-bə-'lī-,kī, -,sī; ,əm-'bil-ə-,kī, -,kē\ *or* **um·bi·li·cus·es :** a small depression on the abdominal wall marking the site of the cord (**umbilical cord**) that joins the unborn fetus to its mother — **um·bil·i·cal** \,əm-'bil-i-kəl\ *adj*

**um·bra** \'əm-brə\ *n, pl* **umbras** *or* **um·brae** \-(,)brē, -,brī\ **1 :** SHADE, SHADOW **2 :** the shadow which is thrown by a planet or satellite on the side away from the sun and within which a spectator could see no part of the sun's disk — **um·bral** \-brəl\ *adj*

**um·brage** \'əm-brij\ *n* **1 :** SHADE; *also* **:** FOLIAGE **2 :** RESENTMENT, OFFENSE 〈take ~ at a remark〉

**um·brel·la** \,əm-'brel-ə\ *n* **1 :** a collapsible shade for protection against weather consisting of fabric stretched over hinged ribs radiating from a center pole **2 :** the saucer-shaped transparent body of a jellyfish

**umi·ak** \'ü-mē-,ak\ *n* **:** an open Eskimo boat made of a wooden frame covered with skins

**um·pire** \'əm-,pī(ə)r\ *n* [ME *oumpere*, alter. of *noumpere* (the phrase *a noumpere* being understood as *an oumpere*), fr. MF *nomper* not equal, not paired, fr. *non* not + *per* equal, fr. L *par*] **1** : one having authority to decide finally a controversy or question between parties **2** : an official in a sport who rules on plays — **umpire** *vb*

**ump·teen** \'əmp-'tēn\ *adj* : very many : indefinitely numerous — **ump·teenth** \-'tēnth\ *adj*

**UMT** *abbr* universal military training

**UN** *abbr* United Nations

**un-** \ˌən, 'ən\ *prefix* **1** : not : IN-, NON- **2** : opposite of : contrary to

| | |
|---|---|
| unabashed | unauthentic |
| unabated | unauthenti- |
| unabbreviated | cated |
| unabsolved | unauthorized |
| unabsorbed | unavailable |
| unacademic | unavenged |
| unaccented | unavowed |
| unacceptable | unawakened |
| unacclimatized | unbaked |
| unaccommo- | unbaptized |
| dating | unbefitting |
| unaccomplished | unblamed |
| unaccredited | unbleached |
| unacknowledged | unblemished |
| unacquainted | unblinking |
| unadapted | unbound |
| unadjusted | unbranched |
| unadorned | unbranded |
| unadvertised | unbreakable |
| unaffiliated | unbridgeable |
| unafraid | unbrotherly |
| unaged | unbruised |
| unaided | unbrushed |
| unaimed | unbudging |
| unaired | unburied |
| unalarmed | unburned |
| unalike | unburnished |
| unallied | uncanceled |
| unallowable | uncanonical |
| unalterable | uncapitalized |
| unalterably | uncared-for |
| unaltered | uncataloged |
| unambiguous | uncaught |
| unambiguously | uncensored |
| unambitious | uncensured |
| unanchored | unchallenged |
| unanimated | unchangeable |
| unannounced | unchanged |
| unanswerable | unchanging |
| unanswered | unchaperoned |
| unanticipated | uncharacteris- |
| unapologetic | tic |
| unappalled | uncharged |
| unapparent | unchastened |
| unappealing | unchecked |
| unappeased | unchivalrous |
| unappetizing | unchristened |
| unappreciated | unclaimed |
| unappreciative | unclassified |
| unapproachable | uncleaned |
| unappropriated | unclear |
| unapproved | uncleared |
| unartistic | unclogged |
| unashamed | unclosed |
| unasked | unclothed |
| unassertive | unclouded |
| unassisted | uncluttered |
| unattainable | uncoated |
| unattempted | uncollected |
| unattended | uncolored |
| unattested | uncombed |
| unattractive | uncombined |

| | |
|---|---|
| uncomely | undeterred |
| uncomforted | undeveloped |
| uncommercial | undifferen- |
| uncompensated | tiated |
| uncomplaining | undigested |
| uncompleted | undignified |
| uncomplicated | undiluted |
| uncomplimen- | undiminished |
| tary | undimmed |
| uncompounded | undiplomatic |
| uncomprehend- | undirected |
| ing | undiscerning |
| unconcealed | undisciplined |
| unconfined | undisclosed |
| unconfirmed | undiscovered |
| unconformable | undiscrimi- |
| uncongealed | nating |
| uncongenial | undisguised |
| unconnected | undismayed |
| unconquered | undisputed |
| unconscientious | undissolved |
| unconsecrated | undistinguished |
| unconsidered | undistributed |
| unconsolidated | undisturbed |
| unconstrained | undivided |
| unconsumed | undivulged |
| uncontaminated | undogmatic |
| uncontested | undomesticated |
| uncontradicted | undone |
| uncontrolled | undoubled |
| unconverted | undramatic |
| unconvincing | undraped |
| uncooked | undrawn |
| uncooperative | undreamed |
| uncoordinated | undressed |
| uncordial | undrinkable |
| uncorrected | undulled |
| uncorroborated | undutiful |
| uncorrupted | undyed |
| uncountable | uneatable |
| uncovered | uneaten |
| uncredited | uneconomic |
| uncropped | uneconomical |
| uncrowded | unedifying |
| uncrowned | uneducated |
| uncrystallized | unembarrassed |
| uncultivated | unemotional |
| uncultured | unemphatic |
| uncurbed | unenclosed |
| uncured | unencumbered |
| uncurtained | unendorsed |
| undamaged | unendurable |
| undamped | unenforceable |
| undated | unenforced |
| undazzled | unengaged |
| undecipherable | unenjoyable |
| undecked | unenlightened |
| undeclared | unenterprising |
| undecorated | unentertaining |
| undefeated | unenthusiastic |
| undefended | unenviable |
| undefiled | unequipped |
| undefinable | unessential |
| undefined | unethical |
| undemanding | unexaggerated |
| undemocratic | unexcelled |
| undenomina- | unexceptional |
| tional | unexchange- |
| undependable | able |
| undeserved | unexcited |
| undeserving | unexciting |
| undetachable | unexecuted |
| undetected | unexperienced |
| undetermined | unexpired |

| | | | |
|---|---|---|---|
| unexplained | unimpaired | unnameable | unprovoked |
| unexploded | unimpassioned | unnamed | unpublished |
| unexplored | unimpeded | unnaturalized | unpunished |
| unexposed | unimportant | unnavigable | unquenchable |
| unexpressed | unimposing | unnecessary | unquestioned |
| unexpurgated | unimpressive | unneighborly | unraised |
| unextended | unimproved | unnoticeable | unratified |
| unextinguished | unincorporated | unnoticed | unreadable |
| unfading | uninflammable | unobjectionable | unready |
| unfaltering | uninfluenced | unobliging | unrealistic |
| unfashionable | uninformative | unobscured | unrealized |
| unfashionably | uninformed | unobservant | unrecognizable |
| unfathomable | uninhabitable | unobserved | unrecompensed |
| unfavored | uninhabited | unobserving | unrecorded |
| unfeasible | uninitiated | unobstructed | unredeemable |
| unfed | uninjured | unobtainable | unrefined |
| unfeminine | uninspired | unoffending | unreflecting |
| unfenced | uninstructed | unofficial | unreflective |
| unfermented | uninsured | unofficially | unregarded |
| unfertilized | unintended | unopened | unregistered |
| unfettered | uninteresting | unopposed | unregulated |
| unfilled | uninvested | unordained | unrehearsed |
| unfiltered | uninvited | unoriginal | unrelated |
| unfinished | uninviting | unorthodox | unreliable |
| unfitted | unjointed | unostentatious | unrelieved |
| unflagging | unjustifiable | unowned | unremembered |
| unflattering | unjustified | unpaid | unremunerative |
| unflavored | unkept | unpainted | unrented |
| unfocused | unknowable | unpaired | unrepentant |
| unfolded | unknowledge- | unpalatable | unreported |
| unforced | able | unpardonable | unrepresenta- |
| unforeseeable | unlabeled | unpasteurized | tive |
| unforeseen | unlabored | unpatriotic | unrepressed |
| unforgivable | unlamented | unpaved | unreproved |
| unforgiving | unleaded | unpedigreed | unrequited |
| unformulated | unleavened | unpeopled | unresisting |
| unfortified | unlicensed | unperceived | unresolved |
| unframed | unlighted | unperceptive | unresponsive |
| unfulfilled | unlikable | unperformed | unrestful |
| unfunded | unlimited | unperturbed | unrestricted |
| unfurnished | unlined | unpitied | unreturned |
| ungentle | unlisted | unplanned | unrewarding |
| ungentlemanly | unlit | unplanted | unrhymed |
| ungerminated | unlivable | unpleasing | unripened |
| unglazed | unlobed | unplowed | unromantic |
| unglue | unloved | unpoetic | unsafe |
| ungoverned | unmade | unpolished | unsaid |
| ungraded | unmanageable | unpolitical | unsalable |
| ungrammatical | unmanned | unpolluted | unsalted |
| ungrudging | unmanufac- | unposed | unsanitary |
| unguided | tured | unpractical | unsatisfactory |
| unhackneyed | unmapped | unpracticed | unsatisfied |
| unhampered | unmarked | unprejudiced | unscented |
| unhardened | unmarketable | unpremeditated | unscheduled |
| unharmed | unmarred | unprepared | unscholarly |
| unharvested | unmarried | unprepossess- | unsealed |
| unhatched | unmastered | ing | unseasoned |
| unhealed | unmatched | unpresentable | unseen |
| unhealthful | unmeant | unpressed | unsentimental |
| unheeded | unmeasured | unpretending | unserviceable |
| unhelpful | unmeditated | unpreventable | unshaded |
| unheralded | unmelodious | unprivileged | unshakable |
| unheroic | unmelted | unprocessed | unshaken |
| unhesitating | unmentioned | unproductive | unshapely |
| unhindered | unmerited | unprofessed | unshaven |
| unhonored | unmethodical | unprogressive | unshed |
| unhoused | unmilitary | unpromising | unshorn |
| unhurried | unmilled | unprompted | unsifted |
| unhurt | unmixed | unpronounce- | unsigned |
| unhygienic | unmolested | able | unsinkable |
| unidentified | unmounted | unpropitious | unsmiling |
| unidiomatic | unmovable | unprotected | unsociable |
| unimaginable | unmusical | unproven | unsoiled |
| unimaginative | | unprovided | unsold |

unsoldierly
unsolicited
unsolvable
unsolved
unsorted
unspecified
unspoiled
unspoken
unsportsman-
like
unstained
unstated
unsterile
unstinting
unstoppable
unstressed
unstructured
unsubdued
unsubstantiated
unsuccessful
unsuccessfully
unsuited
unsullied
unsupervised
unsupported
unsuppressed
unsure
unsurpassed
unsuspected
unsuspecting
unsuspicious
unswayed
unsweetened
unswept
unswerving
unsymmetrical
unsympathetic
unsystematic
untactful
untainted
untalented
untamed
untanned
untapped
untarnished
untaxed
unteachable
untenable
untenanted
unterrified
untested

unthankful
unthoughtful
untidy
untilled
untiring
untitled
untouched
untraceable
untrained
untrammeled
untranslatable
untraveled
untraversed
untrimmed
untrod
untroubled
untrustworthy
untruthful
unusable
unvaried
unvarying
unventilated
unverifiable
unverified
unversed
unvexed
unvisited
unwanted
unwarranted
unwary
unwashed
unwatched
unwavering
unweaned
unwearable
unwearied
unweathered
unwed
unwelcome
unwifely
unwished
unwitnessed
unwomanly
unworkable
unworn
unworried
unwounded
unwoven
unwrinkled
unwrought

**un·a·ble** \,ən-'ā-bəl, 'ən-\ *adj* **1** : not able **2** : UNQUALIFIED, INCOMPETENT

**un·abridged** \,ən-ə-'brijd\ *adj* **1** : not abridged ⟨an ~ edition of Shakespeare⟩ **2** : complete of its class : not based on one larger ⟨an ~ dictionary⟩

**un·ac·com·pa·nied** \,ən-ə-'kəmp-(ə-)nēd\ *adj* : not accompanied; *esp* : being without instrumental accompaniment

**un·ac·count·able** \,ən-ə-'kaůnt-ə-bəl\ *adj* **1** : not to be accounted for : INEXPLICABLE **2** : not responsible — **un·ac·count·ably** \-blē\ *adv*

**un·ac·count·ed** \-əd\ *adj* : not accounted ⟨the loss was ~ for⟩

**un·ac·cus·tomed** \,ən-ə-'kəs-təmd\ *adj* **1** : not customary : not usual or common **2** : not accustomed or habituated ⟨~ to noise⟩

**un·adul·ter·at·ed** \,ən-ə-'dəl-tə-,rāt-əd\ *adj* : PURE, UNMIXED

**un·ad·vised** \,ən-əd-'vīzd\ *adj* **1**

: done without due consideration : RASH **2** : not prudent — **un·ad·vis·ed·ly** \-'vī-zəd-lē\ *adv*

**un·af·fect·ed** \,ən-ə-'fek-təd\ *adj* **1** : not influenced or changed mentally, physically, or chemically **2** : free from affectation : NATURAL, GENUINE — **un·af·fect·ed·ly** *adv*

**un·alien·able** \-'āl-yə-nə-bəl, -'ā-lē-ə-\ *adj* : INALIENABLE

**un·aligned** \,ən-ə-'līnd\ *adj* : not associated with any one of competing international blocs ⟨~ nations⟩

**un·al·loyed** \,ən-ə-l-'ȯid\ *adj* : UNMIXED, UNQUALIFIED, PURE ⟨~ metals⟩

**un–Amer·i·can** \,ən-ə-'mer-ə-kən\ *adj* : not characteristic of or consistent with American customs, principles, or traditions

**unan·i·mous** \yů-'nan-ə-məs\ *adj* [L *unanimus*, fr. *unus* one + *animus* mind] **1** : being of one mind : AGREEING **2** : formed with or indicating the agreement of all — **una·nim·i·ty** \,yü-nə-'nim-ət-ē\ *n* — **unan·i·mous·ly** \yů-'nan-ə-məs-lē\ *adv*

**un·arm** \,ən-'ärm, 'ən-\ *vb* : DISARM

**un·armed** \-'ärmd\ *adj* : not armed or armored

**un·as·sail·able** \,ən-ə-'sā-lə-bəl\ *adj* : not assailable : not liable to doubt, attack, or question

**un·as·sum·ing** \,ən-ə-'sü-miŋ\ *adj* : MODEST, RETIRING

**un·at·tached** \,ən-ə-'tacht\ *adj* **1** : not attached **2** : not married or engaged

**un·avail·ing** \,ən-ə-'vā-liŋ\ *adj* : being of no avail — **un·avail·ing·ly** *adv*

**un·avoid·able** \,ən-ə-'vȯid-ə-bəl\ *adj* : not avoidable : INEVITABLE — **un·avoid·ably** \-blē\ *adv*

**¹un·aware** \,ən-ə-'waȯr\ *adv* : UNAWARES

**²unaware** *adj* : not aware : IGNORANT — **un·aware·ness** *n*

**un·awares** \-'waȯrz\ *adv* **1** : without warning : by surprise ⟨taken ~⟩ **2** : without knowing : UNINTENTIONALLY

**un·bal·anced** \,ən-'bal-ənst\ *adj* **1** : not equally poised or balanced **2** : mentally disordered **3** : not adjusted so as to make credits equal to debits

**un·bar** \-'bär\ *vb* : UNBOLT, OPEN

**un·bear·able** \,ən-'bar-ə-bəl\ *adj* : greater than can be borne ⟨~ pain⟩ — **un·bear·ably** \-blē\ *adv*

**un·beat·able** \-'bēt-ə-bəl\ *adj* : not capable of being defeated

**un·beat·en** \-'bēt-ᵊn\ *adj* **1** : not pounded, beaten, or whipped **2** : UNTROD **3** : UNDEFEATED

**un·be·com·ing** \,ən-bi-'kəm-iŋ\ *adj* : ot becoming : UNSUITABLE, IMPROPER — **un·be·com·ing·ly** *adv*

**un·be·known** \,ən-bi-'nōn\ *or* **un·be·knownst** \-'nōnst\ *adj* : happening without one's knowledge

**un·be·lief** \,ən-bə-'lēf\ *n* : the withholding or absence of belief : DOUBT — **un·be·liev·ing** \-'lē-viŋ\ *adj*

**un·be·liev·able** \-'lē-və-bəl\ *adj* : too improbable for belief : INCREDIBLE — **un·be·liev·ably** \-blē\ *adv*

**un·be·liev·er** \-'lē-vər\ *n* **1** : DOUBTER **2** : INFIDEL

**un·bend** \-'bend\ *vb* -bent \-'bent\; -bend·ing **1** : to free from being bent : make or become straight **2** : UNTIE **3** : to make or become less stiff or more affable : RELAX

**un·bend·ing** \-'ben-diŋ\ *adj* : formal and distant in manner : INFLEXIBLE

**un·bi·ased** \,ən-'bī-əst, 'ən-\ *adj* : free from bias; *esp* : UNPREJUDICED

**un·bid·den** \-'bid-ᵊn\ *also* **un·bid** \-'bid\ *adj* : not bidden : UNASKED

**un·bind** \-'bīnd\ *vb* -bound \-'baûnd\; -bind·ing **1** : to remove bindings from : UNTIE **2** : RELEASE

**un·blessed** *also* **un·blest** \,ən-'blest, 'ən-\ *adj* **1** : not blessed **2** : EVIL

**un·block** \-'bläk\ *vb* : to free from being blocked

**un·blush·ing** \-'bləsh-iŋ\ *adj* **1** : not blushing **2** : SHAMELESS — **un·blush·ing·ly** *adv*

**un·bod·ied** \-'bäd-ēd\ *adj* **1** : having no body; *also* : DISEMBODIED **2** : FORMLESS

**un·bolt** \,ən-'bōlt, 'ən-\ *vb* : to open or unfasten by withdrawing a bolt

**un·bolt·ed** \-'bōl-təd\ *adj* : not fastened by bolts

**un·born** \-'bôrn\ *adj* : not yet born

**un·bo·som** \-'bûz-əm, -'büz-\ *vb* **1** : DISCLOSE, REVEAL (*~ed* his secrets) **2** : to disclose the thoughts or feelings of oneself

**un·bound·ed** \-'baûn-dəd\ *adj* : having no bounds or limits (*~* enthusiasm)

**un·bowed** \,ən-'baûd, 'ən-\ *adj* **1** : not bowed down **2** : UNSUBDUED

**un·bri·dled** \-'brīd-ᵊld\ *adj* **1** : not confined by a bridle **2** : UNRESTRAINED

**un·bro·ken** \-'brō-kən\ *adj* **1** : not damaged **2** : not subdued or tamed **3** : not interrupted : CONTINUOUS

**un·buck·le** \-'bək-əl\ *vb* : to loose the buckle of : UNFASTEN (*~* a belt)

**un·bur·den** \-'bərd-ᵊn\ *vb* **1** : to free or relieve from a burden **2** : to relieve oneself of (as cares or worries) : cast off

**un·but·ton** \-'bət-ᵊn\ *vb* : to unfasten the buttons of (*~* your coat)

**un·called-for** \,ən-'kóld-,fór\ *adj* : not called for, needed, or wanted

**un·can·ny** \-'kan-ē\ *adj* **1** : GHOSTLY, MYSTERIOUS, EERIE **2** : suggesting superhuman or supernatural powers — **un·can·ni·ly** \-'kan-ᵊl-ē\ *adv*

**un·cap** \-'kap\ *vb* : to remove a cap or covering from

**un·ceas·ing** \-'sē-siŋ\ *adj* : never ceasing — **un·ceas·ing·ly** *adv*

**un·cer·e·mo·ni·ous** \,ən-,ser-ə-'mō-nē-əs\ *adj* : acting without or lacking ordinary courtesy : ABRUPT — **un·cer·e·mo·ni·ous·ly** *adv*

**un·cer·tain** \,ən-'sərt-ᵊn, 'ən-\ *adj* **1** : not determined or fixed (an *~* quantity) **2** : subject to chance or change : not dependable **3** : not sure (*~* of the truth) **4** : not definitely known — **un·cer·tain·ly** *adv*

**un·cer·tain·ty** \-ᵊn-tē\ *n* **1** : lack of certainty : DOUBT **2** : something that is uncertain

**un·chain** \,ən-'chān, 'ən-\ *vb* : to free by or as if by removing a chain

**un·char·i·ta·ble** \-'char-ət-ə-bəl\ *adj* : not charitable; *esp* : severe in judging others — **un·char·i·ta·ble·ness** *n* — **un·char·i·ta·bly** \-blē\ *adv*

**un·chart·ed** \-'chärt-əd\ *adj* **1** : not recorded on a map, chart, or plan **2** : UNKNOWN

**un·chaste** \-'chāst\ *adj* : not chaste — **un·chaste·ly** *adv* — **un·chaste·ness** \-'chās(t)-nəs\ *n* — **un·chas·ti·ty** \-'chas-tət-ē\ *n*

**un·chris·tian** \-'kris-chən\ *adj* **1** : not of the Christian faith **2** : contrary to the Christmas spirit

**un·church** \-'chərch\ *vb* **1** : EXCOMMUNICATE **2** : to deprive of a church or of status as a church

**un·cial** \'ən-shəl, -chəl; 'ən-sē-əl\ *adj* [L *uncialis* inch-high, fr. *uncia* twelfth part, ounce, inch] : relating to or written in a form of script with rounded letters used esp. in early Greek and Latin manuscripts — **uncial** *n*

**un·cir·cum·cised** \,ən-'sər-kəm-,sīzd, 'ən-\ *adj* : not circumcised; *also* : HEATHEN

**un·civ·il** \,ən-'siv-əl, 'ən-\ *adj* **1** : not civilized : BARBAROUS **2** : DISCOURTEOUS, ILL-MANNERED, IMPOLITE

**un·civ·i·lized** \-'siv-ə-,līzd\ *adj* **1** : not civilized : BARBAROUS **2** : remote from civilization : WILD

**un·clad** \-'klad\ *adj* : not clothed : UNDRESSED, NAKED

**un·clasp** \-'klasp\ *vb* : to open by or as if by loosing the clasp

**un·cle** \'əŋ-kəl\ *n* [ME, fr. OF, fr. L *avunculus* mother's brother] : the brother of one's father or mother; *also* : the husband of one's aunt

**un·clean** \,ən-'klēn, 'ən-\ *adj* **1** : morally or spiritually impure **2** : prohibited by ritual law for use or contact **3** : DIRTY, FILTHY — **un·clean·ness** \-'klēn-nəs\ *n*

**un·clean·ly** \-'klen-lē\ *adj* : morally or physically unclean — **un·clean·li·ness** \-lē-nəs\ *n*

**un·clench** \-'klench\ *vb* : to open from a clenched position : RELAX

**Uncle Tom** \,ən-kəl-'täm\ *n* [fr. *Uncle Tom,* faithful Negro slave in Harriet Beecher Stowe's novel *Uncle Tom's Cabin* (1851-52)] : a black eager to win the approval of whites and willing to cooperate with them

**un·cloak** \,ən-'klōk, 'ən-\ *vb* **1** : to remove a cloak or cover from **2** : UNMASK, REVEAL

**un·clog** \-'kläg\ *vb* : to remove an obstruction from

**un·close** \-'klōz\ *vb* : OPEN

**un·clothe** \-'klōth\ *vb* : to strip of clothes or a covering

**un·coil** \,ən-'kóil, 'ən-\ *vb* : to release or become released from a coiled state

**un·com·fort·able** \,ən-'kəm(p)f-tə-bəl, 'ən-, -'kəm(p)-fərt-ə-\ *adj* **1** : causing discomfort **2** : feeling discomfort : UNEASY — **un·com·fort·ably** \-blē\ *adv*

**un·com·mit·ted** \,ən-kə-'mit-əd\ *adj*

: not committed; *esp* : not pledged to a particular belief, allegiance, or program

**un·com·mon** \,ən-'käm-ən, 'ən-\ *adj* **1** : not ordinarily encountered : UN·USUAL, RARE **2** : REMARKABLE, EXCEPTIONAL — **un·com·mon·ly** *adv*

**un·com·mu·ni·ca·tive** \,ən-kə-'myü-nə-,kāt-iv, -ni-kət-\ *adj* : not inclined to talk or impart information : RESERVED

**un·com·pro·mis·ing** \'ən-'käm-prə-,mī-ziŋ\ *adj* : not making or accepting a compromise : UNYIELDING

**un·con·cern** \,ən-kən-'sərn\ *n* **1** : lack of care or interest : INDIFFERENCE **2** : freedom from excessive concern or anxiety

**un·con·cerned** \-'sərnd\ *adj* **1** : not having any part or interest **2** : not anxious or upset : free of worry — **un·con·cern·ed·ly** \-'sər-nəd-lē\ *adv*

**un·con·di·tion·al** \,ən-kən-'dish-(ə-)nəl\ *adj* : not limited in any way — **un·con·di·tion·al·ly** \-ē\ *adv*

**un·con·di·tioned** \-'dish-ənd\ *adj* **1** : not subject to conditions **2** : not acquired or learned : INHERENT, NATURAL **3** : producing an unconditioned response ⟨~ stimuli⟩

**un·con·quer·able** \,ən-'käŋ-k(ə-)rə-bəl, 'ən-\ *adj* : incapable of being conquered or overcome : INDOMITABLE

**un·con·scio·na·ble** \-'känch-(ə-)nə-bəl\ *adj* **1** : not in accordance with what is right or just **2** : not guided or controlled by conscience — **un·con·scio·na·bly** \-blē\ *adv*

**¹un·con·scious** \,ən-'kän-chəs, 'ən-\ *adj* **1** : deprived of consciousness or awareness **2** : not realized by oneself : not consciously done — **un·con·scious·ly** *adv* — **un·con·scious·ness** *n*

**²unconscious** *n* : the part of one's mental life not ordinarily available to consciousness but revealed esp. in spontaneous behavior (as slips of the tongue) or in dreams

**un·con·sti·tu·tion·al** \,ən-,kän-stə-'t(y)üsh-(ə-)nəl\ *adj* : not according to or consistent with the constitution of a state or society — **un·con·sti·tu·tion·al·i·ty** \-t(y)ü-shə-'nal-ət-ē\ *n* — **un·con·sti·tu·tion·al·ly** \-'t(y)üsh-(ə-)nə-lē\ *adv*

**un·con·trol·la·ble** \,ən-kən-'trō-lə-bəl\ *adj* : incapable of being controlled : UNGOVERNABLE — **un·con·trol·la·bly** \-blē\ *adv*

**un·con·ven·tion·al** \-'vench-(ə-)nəl\ *adj* : not conventional : being out of the ordinary — **un·con·ven·tion·al·i·ty** \-,ven-chə-'nal-ət-ē\ *n* — **un·con·ven·tion·al·ly** \-'vench-(ə-)nə-lē\ *adv*

**un·cork** \,ən-'kork, 'ən-\ *vb* **1** : to draw a cork from **2** : to release from a sealed or pent-up state; *also* : to let go

**un·count·ed** \-'kaunt-əd\ *adj* : not counted; *also* : INNUMERABLE

**un·cou·ple** \-'kəp-əl\ *vb* : DISCONNECT

**un·couth** \-'küth\ *adj* [OB *uncūth* unknown, unfamiliar, fr. *un-* + *cūth* known] **1** : strange, awkward, and clumsy in shape or appearance **2** : vulgar in conduct or speech : RUDE

**un·cov·er** \-'kəv-ər\ *vb* **1** : to make known : DISCLOSE, REVEAL **2** : to expose to view by removing some covering **3** : to take the cover from **4** : to remove the hat from; *also* : to take off the hat as a token of respect

**un·crit·i·cal** \,ən-'krit-i-kəl, 'ən-\ *adj* **1** : not critical : lacking in discrimination **2** : showing lack or improper use of critical standards or procedures — **un·crit·i·cal·ly** \-ē\ *adv*

**un·cross** \-'kros\ *vb* : to change from a crossed position ⟨~ed his legs⟩

**unc·tion** \'əŋk-shən\ *n* **1** : the act of anointing as a rite of consecration or healing **2** : exaggerated, assumed, or superficial earnestness of language or manner

**unc·tu·ous** \'əŋk-chə-(wə)s\ *adj* [ME, fr. MF or ML; MF *unctueux*, fr. ML *unctuosus*, fr. L *unctum* ointment, fr. *unguere* to anoint] **1** : FATTY, OILY **2** : full of unction in speech and manner; *esp* : insincerely smooth — **unc·tu·ous·ly** *adv*

**un·curl** \,ən-'kərl, 'ən-\ *vb* : to make or become straightened out from a curled or coiled position

**un·cut** \,ən-'kət, 'ən-\ *adj* **1** : not cut down or into **2** : not shaped by cutting ⟨an ~ diamond⟩ **3** : not having the folds of the leaves slit **4** : not abridged or curtailed

**un·daunt·ed** \-'dont-əd\ *adj* : not daunted : not discouraged or dismayed — **un·daunt·ed·ly** *adv*

**un·de·ceive** \,ən-di-'sēv\ *vb* : to free from deception, illusion, or error

**un·de·cid·ed** \-'sīd-əd\ *adj* **1** : not yet determined : UNSETTLED **2** : uncertain what to do : WAVERING

**un·de·mon·stra·tive** \,ən-di-'män-strət-iv\ *adj* : restrained in expression of feeling : RESERVED

**un·de·ni·able** \,ən-di-'nī-ə-bəl\ *adj* **1** : plainly true : INCONTESTABLE **2** : unquestionably excellent or genuine — **un·de·ni·ably** \-blē\ *adv*

**¹un·der** \'ən-dər\ *adv* **1** : in or into a position below or beneath something **2** : below some quantity, level, or norm ⟨$10 or ~⟩ **3** : in or into a condition of subjection, subordination, or unconsciousness ⟨the ether put him ~⟩

**²under** \,ən-dər, 'ən-\ *prep* **1** : lower than and overhung, surmounted, or sheltered by ⟨~ a tree⟩ **2** : below the surface of ⟨~ the sea⟩ **3** : in or into such a position as to be covered or concealed by ⟨a vest ~ his jacket⟩ ⟨the moon went ~ a cloud⟩ **4** : subject to the authority of guidance of ⟨served ~ him⟩ ⟨had the man ~ contract⟩ **5** : with the guarantee of ⟨~ the royal seal⟩ **6** : controlled, limited, or oppressed by ⟨~ lock and key⟩ **7** : subject to the action or effect of ⟨~ an anesthetic⟩ **8** : within the division or grouping of ⟨items ~ this head⟩ **9** : less or lower than ⟨as in size, amount, or rank⟩ ⟨makes ~ $5000⟩

**³under** \'ən-dər\ *adj* **1** : lying below, beneath, or on the ventral side **2** : facing or protruding downward **3** : SUB-

**or·di·nate** 4 : lower than usual, proper, or desired in amount, quality, or degree

**un·der·achiev·er** \,ən-dər-ə-'chē-vər\ n : a student who fails to achieve his scholastic potential

**un·der·act** \-'akt\ vb : to perform feebly or with restraint

**un·der·age** \-'āj\ adj : of less than mature or legal age

**un·der·arm** \-'ärm\ adj 1 : placed under or on the underside of the arm ⟨~ seams⟩ 2 : performed with the hand kept below the level of the shoulder : UNDERHAND ⟨an ~ throw⟩ — **under·arm** adv or n

**un·der·bel·ly** \'ən-dər-,bel-ē\ n : the under surface of a body or mass; also : a vulnerable area

**un·der·bid** \,ən-dər-'bid\ vb -bid; -bid·ding 1 : to bid less than another 2 : to bid too low

**un·der·body** \'ən-dər-,bäd-ē\ n : the lower parts of the body of a vehicle

**un·der·bred** \,ən-dər-'bred\ adj : marked by lack of good breeding

**un·der·brush** \'ən-dər-,brəsh\ n : shrubs and small trees growing beneath large trees

**un·der·car·riage** \-,kar-ij\ n 1 : a supporting framework (as of an automobile) 2 : the landing structure of an airplane

**un·der·charge** \,ən-dər-'chärj\ vb : to charge (as a person) too little — **undercharge** \'ən-dər-,chärj\ n

**un·der·class·man** \,ən-dər-'klas-mən\ n : a member of the freshman or sophomore class

**un·der·clothes** \'ən-dər-,klō(th)z\ n pl : UNDERWEAR

**un·der·cloth·ing** \-,klō-thiŋ\ n : UNDERWEAR

**un·der·coat** \-,kōt\ n 1 : a coat worn under another 2 : a growth of short hair or fur partly concealed by a longer growth ⟨a dog's ~⟩ 3 : a coat of paint under another

**un·der·coat·ing** \-,kōt-iŋ\ n : a special waterproof coating applied to the undersurfaces of a vehicle

**un·der·cov·er** \,ən-dər-'kəv-ər\ adj : acting or executed in secret; esp : employed or engaged in secret investigation ⟨~ agent⟩

**un·der·croft** \'ən-dər-,krȯft\ n [ME, fr. under + crofte crypt, fr. Middle Dutch, fr. ML crupta, fr. L crypta] : a vaulted chamber under a church

**un·der·cur·rent** \-,kər-ənt\ n 1 : a current below the surface 2 : a hidden tendency of feeling or opinion

**un·der·cut** \,ən-dər-'kət\ vb -cut; -cut·ting 1 : to cut away the underpart of 2 : to offer to sell or to work at a lower rate than 3 : to strike (the ball) in golf, tennis, or hockey obliquely downward so as to give a backward spin or elevation to the shot — **un·der·cut** \'ən-dər-,kət\ n

**un·der·de·vel·oped** \,ən-dər-di-'vel-əpt\ adj 1 : not normally or adequately developed ⟨~ muscles⟩ 2 : failing to reach a potential level of economic development ⟨the ~ nations⟩

**un·der·dog** \'ən-dər-,dȯg\ n 1 : the loser or predicted loser in a struggle 2 : a victim of injustice or persecution

**un·der·done** \,ən-dər-'dən\ adj : not thoroughly done or cooked : RARE

**un·der·draw·ers** \'ən-dər-,drȯ(-ə)rz\ n pl : UNDERPANTS

**un·der·em·pha·size** \,ən-dər-'em-fə-sīz\ vb : to emphasize inadequately — **un·der·em·pha·sis** \-səs\ n

**un·der·em·ployed** \-im-'plȯid\ adj : having less than full-time or adequate employment

**un·der·es·ti·mate** \-'es-tə-,māt\ vb : to set too low a value on

**un·der·ex·pose** \-ik-'spōz\ vb : to expose (a photographic plate or film) for less time than is needed — **un·der·ex·po·sure** \-'spō-zhər\ n

**un·der·feed** \,ən-dər-'fēd\ vb -fed \-'fed\; -feed·ing 1 : to feed inadequately 2 : to feed (as a furnace) with fuel admitted from below

**un·der·foot** \-'fùt\ adv 1 : under the feet ⟨flowers trampled ~⟩ 2 : close about one's feet : in the way

**un·der·fur** \'ən-dər-,fər\ n : the thick soft undercoat of fur lying beneath the longer and coarser hair of a mammal

**un·der·gar·ment** \-,gär-mənt\ n : a garment to be worn under another

**un·der·gird** \,ən-dər-'gərd\ vb 1 : to make secure underneath 2 : to brace up : STRENGTHEN

**un·der·go** \,ən-dər-'gō\ vb -went \-'went\; -gone \-'gȯn, -'gän\; -go·ing \-'gō-iŋ, -'gȯ(-)iŋ\ 1 : to be subjected to : ENDURE 2 : to pass through : EXPERIENCE

**un·der·grad·u·ate** \,ən-dər-'graj-(ə-)wət, -ə-,wāt\ n : a student at a university or college who has not taken a first degree

**¹un·der·ground** \,ən-dər-'graùnd\ adv 1 : beneath the surface of the earth 2 : in secret

**²un·der·ground** \'ən-dər-,graùnd\ adj 1 : being or growing under the surface of the ground ⟨~ stems⟩ 2 : conducted by secret means 3 : produced or published outside the establishment esp. by the avant-garde ⟨~ movies⟩; also : of or relating to the avant-garde underground

**³underground** \'ən-dər-,graùnd\ n 1 : a space under the surface of the ground; esp : an underground railway 2 : a secret political movement or group; esp : an organized body working in secret to overthrow a government or an occupying power 3 : an avant-garde group or movement that operates outside the establishment

**un·der·growth** \'ən-dər-,grōth\ n : low growth (as of herbs and shrubs) on the floor of a forest

**¹un·der·hand** \'ən-dər-,hand\ adv 1 : in an underhand or secret manner 2 : with an underhand motion

**²underhand** adj 1 : marked by secrecy and deception 2 : made with the hand kept below the level of the shoulder

**un·der·hand·ed** \,ən-dər-'han-dəd\ adj or adv : UNDERHAND — **un·der·**

**hand·ed·ly** *adv* — **un·der·hand·ed·ness** *n*

**un·der·lie** \-'lī\ *vb* **-lay** \-'lā\; **-lain** \-'lān\; **-ly·ing** \-'lī-iŋ\ **1** : to lie or be situated under **2** : to be at the basis of : form the foundation of : SUPPORT

**un·der·line** \'ən-dər-,līn\ *vb* **1** : to draw a line under **2** : EMPHASIZE, STRESS — **underline** *n*

**un·der·ling** \'ən-dər-liŋ\ *n* : SUBORDINATE, INFERIOR

**un·der·lip** \,ən-dər-'lip\ *n* : the lower lip

**un·der·ly·ing** \,ən-dər-,lī-iŋ\ *adj* **1** : lying under or below **2** : FUNDAMENTAL, BASIC ⟨~ principles⟩

**un·der·mine** \-'mīn\ *vb* **1** : to excavate beneath **2** : to weaken or wear away secretly or gradually

**un·der·most** \'ən-dər-,mōst\ *adj* : lowest in relative position — **undermost** *adv*

¹**un·der·neath** \,ən-dər-'nēth\ *prep* **1** : directly under **2** : under subjection to

²**underneath** *adv* **1** : below a surface or object : BENEATH **2** : on the lower side

**un·der·nour·ished** \,ən-dər-'nər-isht\ *adj* : supplied with insufficient nourishment — **un·der·nour·ish·ment** \-'nər-ish-mənt\ *n*

**un·der·pants** \'ən-dər-,pants\ *n pl* : short or long pants worn under an outer garment : DRAWERS

**un·der·part** \-,pärt\ *n* **1** : a part lying on the lower side esp. of a bird or mammal **2** : a subordinate or auxiliary part or role

**un·der·pass** \-,pas\ *n* : a passage underneath ⟨a railroad ~⟩

**un·der·pay** \,ən-dər-'pā\ *vb* : to pay too little

**un·der·pin·ning** \'ən-dər-,pin-iŋ\ *n* : the material and construction (as a foundation) used for support of a structure — **un·der·pin** \,ən-dər-'pin\ *vb*

**un·der·play** \,ən-dər-'plā\ *vb* : to treat or handle with restraint; *esp* : to play a role with subdued force

**un·der·priv·i·leged** \-'priv-(ə-)lijd\ *adj* : having fewer esp. economic and social privileges than others : POOR

**un·der·pro·duc·tion** \,ən-dər-prə-'dək-shən\ *n* : the production of less than enough to satisfy the demand or of less than the usual supply

**un·der·rate** \,ən-də(r)-'rāt\ *vb* : to rate or value too low

**un·der·rep·re·sent·ed** \-,rep-ri-'zent-əd\ *adj* : inadequately represented

**un·der·score** \'ən-dər-,skōr\ *vb* **1** : to draw a line under : UNDERLINE **2** : EMPHASIZE — **underscore** *n*

¹**un·der·sea** \,ən-dər-,sē\ *adj* : being, carried on, or used beneath the surface of the sea

²**un·der·sea** \,ən-dər-'sē\ *or* **un·der·seas** \-'sēz\ *adv* : beneath the surface of the sea

**un·der·sec·re·tary** \-'sek-rə-,ter-ē\ *n* : a secretary immediately subordinate to a principal secretary ⟨~ of state⟩

**un·der·sell** \-'sel\ *vb* **-sold** \-'sōld\; **-sell·ing** : to sell articles cheaper than

**un·der·sexed** \-'sekst\ *adj* : deficient in sexual desire

**un·der·shirt** \'ən-dər-,shərt\ *n* : a collarless undergarment with or without sleeves

**un·der·shoot** \,ən-dər-'shüt\ *vb* **-shot** \-'shät\; **-shoot·ing 1** : to shoot short of or below (a target) **2** : to fall short of (a runway) in landing an airplane

**un·der·shorts** \,ən-dər-,shôrts\ *n pl* : SHORT 2

**un·der·shot** \,ən-dər-,shät\ *adj* **1** : having the lower front teeth projecting beyond the upper when the mouth is closed ⟨an ~ jaw⟩ **2** : moved by water passing beneath ⟨an ~ waterwheel⟩

**un·der·side** \'ən-dər-,sīd, ,ən-dər-'sīd\ *n* : the side or surface lying underneath

**un·der·signed** \'ən-dər-,sīnd\ *n, pt* **undersigned** : one who signs his name at the end of a document

**un·der·sized** \,ən-dər-'sīzd\ *also* **un·der·size** \-'sīz\ *adj* : of a size less than is common, proper, or normal

**un·der·skirt** \'ən-dər-,skərt\ *n* : a skirt worn under an outer skirt; *esp* : PETTICOAT

**un·der·slung** \,ən-dər-'sləŋ\ *adj* : suspended so as to extend below the axles ⟨an ~ automobile frame⟩

**un·der·stand** \,ən-dər-'stand\ *vb* **-stood** \-'stůd\; **-stand·ing 1** : to grasp the meaning of : COMPREHEND **2** : to have thorough or technical acquaintance with or expertness in ⟨~ finance⟩ **3** : GATHER, INFER ⟨I ~ that you spread this rumor⟩ **4** : INTERPRET ⟨we ~ this to be a refusal⟩ **5** : to have a sympathetic attitude **6** : to accept as settled ⟨it is *understood* that he will pay the expenses⟩ — **un·der·stand·able** \-'stan-də-bəl\ *adj* — **un·der·stand·ably** \-blē\ *adv*

¹**un·der·stand·ing** \,ən-dər-'stan-diŋ\ *n* **1** : knowledge and ability to apply judgment : INTELLIGENCE **2** : ability to comprehend and judge ⟨a man of ~⟩ **3** : agreement of opinion or feeling **4** : a mutual agreement informally or tacitly entered into

²**understanding** *adj* : endowed with understanding : TOLERANT, SYMPATHETIC

**un·der·state** \,ən-dər-'stāt\ *vb* **1** : to represent as less than is the case **2** : to state with restraint esp. for greater effect — **un·der·state·ment** *n*

**un·der·stood** \,ən-dər-'stůd\ *adj* **1** : agreed upon **2** : IMPLICIT

**un·der·sto·ry** \'ən-dər-,stōr-ē, -,stôr-\ *n* : the plants of a forest undergrowth

**un·der·study** \'ən-dər-,stəd-ē, ,ən-dər-'stəd-ē\ *vb* : to study another actor's part in order to be his substitute in an emergency — **understudy** \'ən-dər-,stəd-ē\ *n*

**un·der·sur·face** \'ən-dər-,sər-fəs\ *n* : UNDERSIDE

**un·der·take** \,ən-dər-'tāk\ *vb* **-took** \-'tůk\; **-tak·en** \-'tā-kən\; **-tak·ing 1** : to take upon oneself as a task : set about **2** : to put oneself under obligation **3** : GUARANTEE, PROMISE

**un·der·tak·er** \'ən-dər-,tā-kər\ *n*

**:** one whose business is to prepare the dead for burial and to take charge of funerals

**un·der·tak·ing** \'ən-dər-ˌtā-kiŋ, ˌən-dər-'tā-kiŋ; *2 is* 'ən-dər-ˌtā-kiŋ *only*\ *n* **1 :** the act of one who undertakes or engages in any project **2 :** the business of an undertaker **3 :** something undertaken **4 :** PROMISE, GUARANTEE

**under-the-counter** *adj* **:** UNLAWFUL, ILLICIT 〈~ sale of drugs〉

**un·der·tone** \'ən-dər-ˌtōn\ *n* **1 :** a low or subdued tone or utterance **2 :** a subdued color (as seen through and modifying another color)

**un·der·tow** \-ˌtō\ *n* **:** the current beneath the surface that sets seaward when waves are breaking upon the shore

**un·der·trick** \-ˌtrik\ *n* **:** a trick by which a declarer in bridge falls short of making his contract

**un·der·val·ue** \ˌən-dər-'val-yü\ *vb* **1 :** to value or estimate below the real worth **2 :** to esteem lightly

**un·der·waist** \'ən-dər-ˌwāst\ *n* **:** a waist for wear under another garment

**un·der·wa·ter** \ˌən-dər-'wȯt-ər,-ˌwät-\ *adj* **:** lying, growing, worn, or operating below the surface of the water — **un·der·wa·ter** \-'wȯt-, -'wät-\ *adv*

**under way** \-ˈwā\ *adv* **1 :** into motion from a standstill **2 :** in progress

**un·der·wear** \'ən-dər-ˌwa(ə)r\ *n* **:** a garment worn next to the skin and under other clothing

**un·der·weight** \ˌən-dər-'wāt\ *n* **:** weight below what is normal, average, or necessary — **underweight** *adj*

**un·der·wood** \'ən-dər-ˌwůd\ *n* **:** UNDERBRUSH, UNDERGROWTH

**un·der·world** \-ˌwərld\ *n* **1 :** the place of departed souls **:** HADES **2 :** a social sphere below the level of ordinary life, *esp* **:** the world of organized crime

**un·der·write** \'ən-də(r)-ˌrīt, ˌən-də(r)-'rīt\ *vb* **-wrote** \-ˌrōt, -'rōt\; **-writ·ten** \-ˌrit-ᵊn, -'rit-ᵊn\; **-writ·ing** \-ˌrīt-iŋ, -'rīt-\ **1 :** to write under or at the end of something else **2 :** to set one's name to an insurance policy and thereby become answerable for a designated loss or damage **3 :** to subscribe to **:** agree to **4 :** to agree to purchase (as bonds) usu. on a fixed date at a fixed price; *also* **:** to guarantee financial support of — **un·der·writ·er** *n*

**un·de·sign·ing** \ˌən-di-'zī-niŋ\ *adj* **:** having no artful, ulterior, or fraudulent purpose **:** SINCERE

**un·de·sir·able** \-'zī-rə-bəl\ *adj* **:** not desirable — **undesirable** *n*

**un·de·vi·at·ing** \ˌən-'dē-vē-ˌāt-iŋ, 'ən-\ *adj* **:** keeping a true course

**un·dies** \'ən-dēz\ *n pl* **:** UNDERWEAR; *esp* **:** women's underwear

**un·do** \ˌən-'dü, 'ən-\ *vb* **-did** \-'did\; **-done** \-'dən\; **-do·ing** \-'dü-iŋ\ **1 :** to make or become unfastened or loosened **:** OPEN **2 :** to make null or as if not done **:** REVERSE **3 :** to bring to ruin; *also* **:** UPSET

**un·do·ing** \-'dü-iŋ\ *n* **1 :** LOOSING, UNFASTENING **2 :** RUIN; *also* **:** a cause of ruin **3 :** REVERSAL

**un·doubt·ed** \-'daůt-əd\ *adj* **:** not doubted or called into question **:** CERTAIN — **un·doubt·ed·ly** *adv*

**¹un·dress** \ˌən-'dres, 'ən-\ *vb* **:** to remove the clothes or covering of **:** STRIP, DISROBE

**²undress** *n* **1 :** informal dress; *esp* **:** a loose robe or dressing gown **2 :** ordinary dress **3 :** NUDITY

**un·due** \-'d(y)ü\ *adj* **1 :** not due **2 :** INAPPROPRIATE, UNSUITABLE **3 :** EXCESSIVE, IMMODERATE 〈~ severity〉

**un·du·lant** \'ən-jə-lənt, 'ən-d(y)ə-\ *adj* **:** UNDULATING

**undulant fever** *n* **:** a persistent human disease caused by bacteria and marked by remittant fever, pain and swelling in the joints, and great weakness

**un·du·late** \-ˌlāt\ *vb* **-lated; -lating** [LL *undula* small wave, fr. L *unda* wave] **1 :** to have a wavelike motion or appearance **2 :** to rise and fall in pitch or volume **syn** waver, swing, sway, oscillate, vibrate, fluctuate

**un·du·la·tion** \ˌən-jə-'lā-shən, ˌən-d(y)ə-\ *n* **1 :** wavy or wavelike motion **2 :** pulsation of sound **3 :** a wavy appearance or outline — **un·du·la·to·ry** \'ən-jə-lə-ˌtōr-ē, 'ən-d(y)ə-\ *adj*

**un·du·ly** \ˌən-'d(y)ü-lē, 'ən-\ *adv* **:** in an undue manner; *esp* **:** EXCESSIVELY

**un·dy·ing** \-'dī-iŋ\ *adj* **:** not dying **:** IMMORTAL, PERPETUAL

**un·earned** \-'ərnd\ *adj* **:** not earned by labor, service, or skill 〈~ income〉

**un·earth** \ˌən-'ərth, 'ən-\ *vb* **1 :** to draw from the earth **:** dig up 〈~ buried treasure〉 **2 :** to bring to light **:** DISCOVER 〈~ a secret〉

**un·earth·ly** \-'ē\ *adj* **1 :** not of or belonging to the earth **2 :** SUPERNATURAL, WEIRD, TERRIFYING

**un·easy** \'ən-'ē-zē\ *adj* **1 :** AWKWARD, EMBARRASSED 〈~ among strangers〉 **2 :** disturbed by pain or worry; *also* **:** RESTLESS — **un·eas·i·ly** \-'ē-zə-lē\ *adv* — **un·eas·i·ness** \-'ē-zē-nəs\ *n*

**un·em·ployed** \ˌən-im-'plȯid\ *adj* **:** not employed; *esp* **:** not engaged in a gainful occupation

**un·em·ploy·ment** \-'plȯi-mənt\ *n* **:** lack of employment

**un·end·ing** \ˌən-'en-diŋ, 'ən-\ *adj* **:** having no ending **:** ENDLESS

**un·equal** \ˌən-'ē-kwəl, 'ən-\ *adj* **1 :** not alike (as in size, amount, number, or value) **2 :** not uniform **:** VARIABLE **3 :** badly balanced or matched **4 :** INADEQUATE, INSUFFICIENT — **un·equal·ly** \-'ē\ *adv*

**un·equaled** \-kwəld\ *adj* **:** not equaled **:** UNPARALLELED

**un·equiv·o·cal** \ˌən-i-'kwiv-ə-kəl\ *adj* **:** leaving no doubt **:** CLEAR — **un·equiv·o·cal·ly** \-ē\ *adv*

**un·err·ing** \ˌən-'e(ə)r-iŋ, ˌən-'ər-, 'ən-\ *adj* **:** making no errors **:** CERTAIN, UNFAILING — **un·err·ing·ly** *adv*

**UNES·CO** \yü-'nes-kō\ *abbr* United Nations Educational, Scientific, and Cultural Organization

**un·even** \ˌən-'ē-vən, 'ən-\ *adj* **1 :** ODD **2 :** not even **:** not level or smooth **:** RUGGED, RAGGED **3 :** IRREGULAR;

*also* : varying in quality — **un·even·ly** *adv* — **un·even·ness** \-vən-nəs\ *n*

**un·event·ful** \ˌən-i-'vent-fəl\ *adj* : not eventful **:** lacking interesting or noteworthy incidents

**un·ex·am·pled** \ˌən-ig-'zam-pəld\ *adj* : UNPRECEDENTED, UNPARALLELED

**un·ex·cep·tion·able** \ˌən-ik-'sep-sh(ə-)nə-bəl\ *adj* : not open to exception or objection : beyond reproach

**un·ex·pect·ed** \ˌən-ik-'spek-təd\ *adj* : not expected : UNFORESEEN — **un·ex·pect·ed·ly** *adv*

**un·fail·ing** \ˌən-'fā-liŋ, 'ən-\ *adj* **1** : not failing, flagging, or waning : CONSTANT **2** : INEXHAUSTIBLE **3** : INFALLIBLE — **un·fail·ing·ly** *adv*

**un·fair** \-'faər\ *adj* **1** : marked by injustice, partiality, or deception : UNJUST, DISHONEST **2** : not equitable in business dealings — **un·fair·ly** *adv* — **un·fair·ness** *n*

**un·faith·ful** \ˌən-'fāth-fəl, 'ən-\ *adj* **1** : not observant of vows, allegiance, or duty : DISLOYAL **2** : INACCURATE, UNTRUSTWORTHY — **un·faith·ful·ly** \-ē\ *adv* — **un·faith·ful·ness** *n*

**un·fa·mil·iar** \ˌən-fə-'mil-yər\ *adj* **1** : not well known : STRANGE ⟨an ∼ place⟩ **2** : not well acquainted ⟨∼ with the subject⟩ — **un·fa·mil·iar·i·ty** \-ˌmil-'yar-ət-ē, -ˌmil-ē-'(y)ar-\ *n*

**un·fas·ten** \ˌən-'fas-ᵊn, 'ən-\ *vb* : to make or become loose : UNDO, DETACH

**un·fa·vor·able** \ˌən-'fāv-(ə-)rə-bəl, 'ən-\ *adj* : not favorable — **un·fa·vor·ably** \-blē\ *adv*

**un·feel·ing** \-'fē-liŋ\ *adj* **1** : lacking feeling : INSENSATE **2** : HARDHEARTED, CRUEL — **un·feel·ing·ly** *adv*

**un·feigned** \-'fānd\ *adj* : not feigned : not hypocritical : GENUINE

**un·fet·ter** \-'fet-ər\ *vb* **1** : to free from fetters : LIBERATE

**un·fil·ial** \ˌən-'fil-ē-əl, 'ən-, -'fil-yəl\ *adj* : not observing the obligations of a child to a parent : UNDUTIFUL

**¹un·fit** \-'fit\ *adj* : not fit or suitable; *esp* : physically or mentally unsound — **un·fit·ness** *n*

**²unfit** *vb* : DISABLE, DISQUALIFY

**un·fix** \-'fiks\ *vb* **1** : to loosen from a fastening : DETACH **2** : UNSETTLE

**un·flap·pa·ble** \-'flap-ə-bəl\ *adj* : not easily upset or panicked

**un·fledged** \ˌən-'flejd, 'ən-\ *adj* : not feathered or ready for flight; *also* : IMMATURE, CALLOW

**un·flinch·ing** \-'flin-chiŋ\ *adj* : not flinching or shrinking : STEADFAST

**un·fold** \-'fōld\ *vb* **1** : to open the folds of : open up **2** : to lay open to view : DISCLOSE **3** : BLOSSOM, DEVELOP

**un·for·get·ta·ble** \ˌən-fər-'get-ə-bəl\ *adj* : not to be forgotten — **un·for·get·ta·bly** \-blē\ *adv*

**un·formed** \-'fórmd\ *adj* : not regularly formed : SHAPELESS

**un·for·tu·nate** \-'fórch-(ə-)nət\ *adj* **1** : not fortunate : UNLUCKY **2** : attended with misfortune **3** : UNSUITABLE — **unfortunate** *n* — **un·for·tu·nate·ly** *adv*

**un·found·ed** \ˌən-'faùn-dəd, 'ən-\

: lacking a sound basis : GROUNDLESS

**un·freeze** \-'frēz\ *vb* **-froze** \-'frōz\; **-fro·zen** \-'frōz-ᵊn\; **-freez·ing** : to cause to thaw

**un·fre·quent·ed** \ˌən-frē-'kwent-əd; ˌən-'frē-kwənt-, 'ən-\ *adj* : seldom visited or traveled over

**un·friend·ly** \ˌən-'fren-(d)lē, 'ən-\ *adj* **1** : not friendly or kind **:** HOSTILE **2** : UNFAVORABLE — **un·friend·li·ness** \-'fren-(d)lē-nəs\ *n*

**un·frock** \-'fräk\ *vb* : to divest of a frock; *esp* : to deprive (as a priest) of the right to exercise the functions of his office

**un·fruit·ful** \-'früt-fəl\ *adj* **1** : not producing fruit or offspring : UNPRODUCTIVE **2** : yielding no desired or valuable result ⟨∼ efforts⟩ — **un·fruit·ful·ness** *n*

**un·furl** \-'fərl\ *vb* : to loose from a furled state : UNFOLD

**un·gain·ly** \-'gān-lē\ *adj* [*un*- + *gainly* graceful, fr. *gain* direct, handy, fr. ME *geyn*, fr. OE *gēn*, fr. ON*gegn*] : CLUMSY, AWKWARD — **un·gain·li·ness** \-lē-nəs\ *n*

**un·gen·er·ous** \ˌən-'jen-(ə-)rəs, 'ən-\ *adj* : not generous or liberal : STINGY

**un·gird** \-'gərd\ *vb* : to divest of a restraining band or girdle : UNBIND

**un·god·ly** \ˌən-'gäd-lē, -'gód-; 'ən-\ *adj* **1** : IMPIOUS, IRRELIGIOUS **2** : SINFUL, WICKED **3** : OUTRAGEOUS — **un·god·li·ness** \-lē-nəs\ *n*

**un·gov·ern·able** \-'gəv-ər-nə-bəl\ *adj* : not capable of being governed, guided, or restrained : UNRULY

**un·grace·ful** \-'grās-fəl\ *adj* : not graceful : AWKWARD — **un·grace·ful·ly** \-ē\ *adv*

**un·gra·cious** \-'grā-shəs\ *adj* **1** : not courteous : RUDE **2** : not pleasing : DISAGREEABLE

**un·grate·ful** \ˌən-'grāt-fəl, 'ən-\ *adj* **1** : not thankful for favors **2** : not pleasing — **un·grate·ful·ly** \-ē\ *adv* — **un·grate·ful·ness** *n*

**un·ground·ed** \-'graùn-dəd\ *adj* **1** : UNFOUNDED, BASELESS **2** : not instructed or informed

**un·guard·ed** \-'gärd-əd\ *adj* **1** : UNPROTECTED **2** : DIRECT, INCAUTIOUS

**un·guent** \'əŋ-gwənt, 'ən-\ *n* : a soothing or healing salve : OINTMENT

**¹un·gu·late** \'əŋ-gyə-lət, 'ən-, -ˌlāt\ *adj* [LL *ungulatus*, fr. L *ungula* hoof, fr. *unguis* nail, hoof] : having hoofs

**²ungulate** *n* : a hoofed mammal (as a cow, horse, or rhinoceros)

**un·hal·lowed** \ˌən-'hal-ōd, 'ən-\ *adj* **1** : not consecrated : UNHOLY **2** : IMPIOUS, PROFANE

**un·hand** \ˌən-'hand, 'ən-\ *vb* : to remove the hand from : let go

**un·hand·some** \-'han-səm\ *adj* **1** : not beautiful or handsome : HOMELY **2** : UNBECOMING **3** : DISCOURTEOUS, RUDE

**un·handy** \-'han-dē\ *adj* : INCONVENIENT; *also* : AWKWARD

**un·hap·py** \-'hap-ē\ *adj* **1** : UNLUCKY, UNFORTUNATE **2** : SAD, MISERABLE **3** : INAPPROPRIATE — **un·hap-**

pi·ly \\'hap-ə-lē\\ *adv* — un·hap·pi·ness \\-ē-nəs\\ *n*

un·har·ness \\-'här-nəs\\ *vb* : to remove the harness from (as a horse)

un·healthy \\-'hel-thē\\ *adj* 1 : not conducive to health : UNWHOLESOME 2 : SICKLY, DISEASED

un·heard \\-'hərd\\ *adj* 1 : not heard 2 : not granted a hearing

un·heard–of \\-,əv, -,äv\\ *adj* : previously unknown : UNPRECEDENTED

un·hinge \\,ən-'hinj, 'ən-\\ *vb* 1 : to take from the hinges 2 : to make unstable (as one's mind)

un·hitch \\-'hich\\ *vb* : UNFASTEN, LOOSE

un·ho·ly \\-'hō-lē\\ *adj* : not holy : PROFANE, WICKED — un·ho·li·ness \\-lē-nəs\\ *n*

un·hook \\-'hùk\\ *vb* : to loose from a hook

un·horse \\-'hòrs\\ *vb* : to dislodge from or as if from a horse : UNSEAT

uni·ax·i·al \\,yü-nē-'ak-sē-əl\\ *adj* : having only one axis — uni·ax·i·al·ly \\-ē\\ *adv*

uni·cam·er·al \\,yü-ni-kam-(ə-)rəl\\ *adj* : having a single legislative house or chamber

UNI·CEF \\'yü-nə-,sef\\ *abbr* [*United Nations Children's Emergency Fund,* its former name] United Nations Children's Fund

uni·cel·lu·lar \\,yü-ni-'sel-yə-lər\\ *adj* : of or having a single cell

uni·corn \\'yü-nə-,kòrn\\ *n* [ME *unicorne,* fr. OF, fr. LL *unicornis,* fr. L, having one horn, fr. *unus* one + *cornu* horn] : a legendary animal with one horn in the middle of the forehead

uni·cy·cle \\'yü-ni-,sī-kəl\\ *n* : a vehicle that has a single wheel and is usu. propelled by pedals

uni·di·rec·tion·al \\,yü-ni-də-'reksh(ə-)nəl, -dī-\\ *adj* : having, moving in, or responsive in a single direction ⟨a ~ current⟩ ⟨a ~ microphone⟩

uni·fi·ca·tion \\,yü-nə-fə-'kā-shən\\ *n* : the act, process, or result of unifying : the state of being unified

¹uni·form \\'yü-nə-,fòrm\\ *adj* 1 : having always the same form, manner, or degree : not varying 2 : of the same form with others : conforming to one rule — uni·for·mi·ly *adv*

²uniform *vb* : to clothe with a uniform

³uniform *n* : distinctive dress worn by members of a particular group (as an army or a police force)

uni·for·mi·ty \\,yü-nə-'fòr-mət-ē\\ *n,* *pl* -ties : the state of being uniform

uni·fy \\'yü-nə-,fī\\ *vb* -fied; -fy·ing : to make into a unit or a coherent whole : UNITE

uni·lat·er·al \\,yü-nə-'lat-(ə-)rəl\\ *adj* : of, having, affecting, or done by one side only — uni·lat·er·al·ly \\-ē\\ *adv*

un·im·peach·able \\,ən-im-'pē-chə-bəl\\ *adj* : exempt from liability to accusation : BLAMELESS; *also* : not doubtable ⟨an ~ authority⟩

un·in·hib·it·ed \\,ən-in-'hib-ət-əd\\ *adj* : free from inhibition; *esp* : boisterously informal — un·in·hib·it·ed·ly *adv*

un·in·tel·li·gent \\-'tel-ə-jənt\\ *adj* : lacking intelligence

un·in·tel·li·gi·ble \\-jə-bəl\\ *adj* : not intelligible : OBSCURE — un·in·tel·li·gi·bly \\-blē\\ *adv*

un·in·ten·tion·al \\,ən-in-'tench-(ə-)nəl\\ *adj* : not intentional — un·in·ten·tion·al·ly \\-ē\\ *adv*

un·in·ter·est·ed \\,ən-'in·t-(ə-)rəs-təd, -tə-,res-; 'ən-\\ *adj* 1 : having no interest and esp. no property interest in 2 : not having the mind or feelings engaged or aroused

un·in·ter·rupt·ed \\,ən-,int-ə-'rəp-təd\\ *adj* : not interrupted : CONTINUOUS

union \\'yü-nyən\\ *n* 1 : an act or instance of uniting two or more things into one : the state of being so united : COMBINATION, JUNCTION 2 : a uniting in marriage 3 : something formed by a combining of parts or members; *esp* : a confederation of independent individuals (as nations or persons) for some common purpose 4 : an organization of workers (**labor union,** **trade union**) formed to advance its members' interests esp. in respect to wages and working conditions 5 : a device emblematic of union used on or as a national flag; *also* : the upper inner corner of a flag 6 : any of various devices for connecting parts; *esp* : a coupling for pipes

union·ism \\'yü-nyə-,niz-əm\\ *n* 1 : the principle or policy of forming or adhering to a union; *esp, cap* : adherence to the policy of a firm federal union prior to or during the U.S. Civil War 2 : the principles or system of trade unions — union·ist *n, often cap*

union·ize \\'yü-nyə-,nīz\\ *vb* -ized; -iz·ing : to form into or cause to join a labor union — union·iza·tion \\,yü-nyən-ə-'zā-shən\\ *n*

union jack *n* 1 : a flag consisting of the part of a national flag that signifies union 2 *cap U&J* : the national flag of the United Kingdom

unique \\yù-'nēk\\ *adj* 1 : being the only one of its kind : SINGLE, SOLE 2 : very unusual : NOTABLE — unique·ly *adv* — unique·ness *n*

uni·sex \\'yü-nə-,seks\\ *n* : the state of not being distinguishable (as by hair or clothing) as to sex — unisex *adj*

uni·sex·u·al \\,yü-nə-'sek-sh(ə-w)əl\\ *adj* : of, relating to, or restricted to one sex

uni·son \\'yü-nə-sən, -nə-zən\\ *n* [MF, fr. ML *unisonus* having the same sound, fr. L *unus* one + *sonus* sound] 1 : sameness or identity in pitch 2 : the condition of being tuned or sounded at the same pitch or at an octave ⟨sing in ~ rather than in harmony⟩ 3 : exact agreement : ACCORD

unit \\'yü-nət\\ *n* 1 : the least whole number : ONE 2 : a definite amount or quantity used as a standard of measurement 3 : a single thing or person or group that is a constituent of a whole; *also* : a part of a military establishment that has a prescribed organization — **unit** adj

**Uni·tar·i·an** \,yü-nə-'ter-ē-ən\ n : a member of a religious denomination stressing individual freedom of belief — **Uni·tar·i·an·ism** n

**uni·tary** \'yü-nə-,ter-ē\ adj 1 : of or relating to a unit : characterized by unity 2 : not divided — **uni·tar·i·ly** \,yü-nə-'ter-ə-lē\ adv

**unite** \yù-'nīt\ vb **unit·ed; unit·ing** 1 : to put or join together so as to make one : COMBINE, COALESCE 2 : to join by a legal or moral bond (as nations by treaty); also : to join in interest or fellowship 3 : AMALGAMATE, CONSOLIDATE 4 : to join in an act

**unit·ed** \yù-'nīt-əd\ adj 1 : made one : COMBINED 2 : relating to or produced by joint action 3 : being in agreement : HARMONIOUS

**unit·ize** \'yü-nət-,īz\ vb **-ized; -iz·ing** 1 : to form or convert into a unit 2 : to divide into units

**unit train** n : a train that transports a single commodity ⟨a unit train of coal⟩

**uni·ty** \'yü-nət-ē\ n, pl **-ties** 1 : the quality or state of being one : ONENESS, SINGLENESS 2 : a definite quantity or combination of quantities taken as one or for which 1 is made to stand in calculation 3 : CONCORD, ACCORD, HARMONY 4 : continuity without change ⟨~ of purpose⟩ 5 : reference of all the parts of a literary or artistic composition to a single main idea 6 : totality of related parts **syn** solidarity, union

**univ** abbr 1 universal 2 university

**uni·va·lent** \,yü-ni-'vā-lənt\ adj : having a valence of one

**uni·valve** \'yü-ni-,valv\ n : a mollusk (as a snail or whelk) having a shell with one valve

**uni·ver·sal** \,yü-nə-'vər-səl\ adj 1 : including, covering, or affecting the whole without limit or exception : UNLIMITED, GENERAL ⟨a ~ rule⟩ 2 : present or occurring everywhere 3 : used or for use among all ⟨a ~ language⟩ 4 : affirming or denying something of all members of a class ⟨"No man knows everything" is a ~ negative⟩ — **uni·ver·sal·ly** \-ē\ adv

**Uni·ver·sal·ist** \,yü-nə-'vər-s(ə-)ləst\ n : a member of a religious denomination now united with Unitarians that upholds the belief that all men will be saved

**uni·ver·sal·i·ty** \-vər-'sal-ət-ē\ n : the quality or state of being universal

**uni·ver·sal·ize** \-'vər-sə-,līz\ vb **-ized; -iz·ing** : to make universal : GENERALIZE — **uni·ver·sal·iza·tion** \-,vər-sə-lə-'zā-shən\ n

**universal joint** n : a shaft coupling for transmitting rotation from one shaft to another not in a straight line with it

**uni·verse** \'yü-nə-,vərs\ n [L universum, fr. neut. of universus entire, whole, fr. unus one + versus turned toward, fr. pp. of vertere to turn] : all created things and phenomena viewed as constituting one system or whole

**uni·ver·si·ty** \,yü-nə-'vər-s(ə-)tē\ n, pl **-ties** : an institution of higher learning authorized to confer degrees in various special fields (as theology, law, and medicine) as well as in the arts and sciences generally

**un·just** \,ən-'jəst, 'ən-\ adj : characterized by injustice — **un·just·ly** adv

**un·kempt** \-'kempt\ adj 1 : not combed : DISHEVELED 2 : ROUGH, UNPOLISHED

**un·kind** \-'kīnd\ adj : wanting in kindness or sympathy : CRUEL, HARSH — **un·kind·ly** \-'kīn-(d)lē\ adv — **un·kind·ness** \-'kīn(d)-nəs\ n

**un·kind·ly** \-'kīn-(d)lē\ adj : UNKIND

**un·know·ing** \,ən-'nō-iŋ, 'ən-\ adj : not knowing : IGNORANT — **un·know·ing·ly** adv

**un·known** \-'nōn\ adj : not known : UNFAMILIAR; also : not ascertained — **unknown** n

**un·lace** \,ən-'lās, 'ən-\ vb : to loose by undoing a lacing

**un·lade** \-'lād\ vb **lad·ed; -laded** or **-lad·en** \-'lād-ᵊn\; **-lad·ing** : to take the load or cargo from : UNLOAD

**un·latch** \-'lach\ vb 1 : to open or loose by lifting the latch 2 : to become loosed or opened

**un·law·ful** \,ən-'lȯ-fəl, 'ən-\ adj 1 : not lawful : ILLEGAL 2 : ILLEGITIMATE — **un·law·ful·ly** \-ē\ adv

**un·lead·ed** \-'led-əd\ adj : not treated or mixed with lead or lead compounds

**un·learn** \-'lərn\ vb : to put out of one's knowledge or memory

**un·learned** \-'lər-nəd for 1, 2; -'lərnd for 3\ adj 1 : UNEDUCATED, ILLITERATE 2 : not learned by study : not known 3 : not learned by previous experience

**un·leash** \-'lēsh\ vb : to free from or as if from a leash

**un·less** \ən-,les, ən-\ conj : except on condition that ⟨won't go ~ you do⟩

**un·let·tered** \,ən-'let-ərd, 'ən-\ adj : not educated : ILLITERATE

**¹un·like** \,ən-'līk\ prep 1 : different from ⟨he's quite ~ his brother⟩ 2 : unusual for ⟨it's ~ him to be late⟩ 3 : differently from ⟨behaves ~ his brother⟩

**²unlike** adj 1 : not like : DISSIMILAR, DIFFERENT 2 : UNEQUAL — **un·like·ness** n

**un·like·li·hood** \,ən-'lī-klē-,hùd, 'ən-\ n : IMPROBABILITY

**un·like·ly** \-'lī-klē\ adj 1 : not likely : IMPROBABLE 2 : likely to fail

**un·lim·ber** \,ən-'lim-bər, 'ən-\ vb : to get ready for action

**un·load** \-'lōd\ vb 1 : to take away or off : REMOVE ⟨~ cargo from a hold⟩; also : to get rid of 2 : to take a load from; also : to relieve or set free : UNBURDEN ⟨~ one's mind of worries⟩ 3 : to get rid of or be relieved of a burden 4 : to sell in volume

**un·lock** \-'läk\ vb 1 : to unfasten through release of a lock 2 : RELEASE ⟨~ed her emotions⟩ 3 : DISCLOSE, REVEAL

**un·looked–for** \-'lùkt-,fȯr\ adj : UNEXPECTED

**un·loose** \,ən-'lüs, 'ən-\ *vb* **:** to relax the strain of **:** set free; *also* **:** UNTIE

**un·loos·en** \-'lüs-ᵊn\ *vb* **:** UNLOOSE

**un·love·ly** \-'ləv-lē\ *adj* **:** having no charm or appeal **:** not amiable

**un·lucky** \-'lək-ē\ *adj* **1 :** UNFORTUNATE, ILL-FATED **2 :** likely to bring misfortune **:** INAUSPICIOUS **3 :** REGRETTABLE — **un·luck·i·ly** \-'lək-ə-lē\ *adv*

**un·man** \,ən-'man, 'ən-\ *vb* **1 :** to deprive of manly courage **2 :** to deprive of men

**un·man·ly** \-'man-lē\ *adj* **:** not manly **:** COWARDLY; *also* **:** EFFEMINATE

**un·man·ner·ly** \-'man-ər-lē\ *adj* **:** RUDE, IMPOLITE — **unmannerly** *adv*

**un·mask** \,ən-'mask, 'ən-\ *vb* **1 :** to strip of a mask or a disguise **:** EXPOSE **2 :** to remove one's own disguise (as at a masquerade)

**un·mean·ing** \-'mē-niŋ\ *adj* **:** having no meaning **:** SENSELESS

**un·meet** \-'mēt\ *adj* **:** not meet or fit **:** UNSUITABLE, IMPROPER

**un·men·tion·able** \-'mench-(ə-)nə-bəl\ *adj* **:** not fit or proper to be talked about

**un·mer·ci·ful** \-'mər-si-fəl\ *adj* **:** not merciful **:** CRUEL, MERCILESS — **un·mer·ci·ful·ly** \-ē\ *adv*

**un·mind·ful** \-'mīnd-fəl\ *adj* **:** not mindful **:** CARELESS, UNAWARE

**un·mis·tak·able** \,ən-mə-'stā-kə-bəl\ *adj* **:** not capable of being mistaken or misunderstood **:** CLEAR, OBVIOUS — **un·mis·tak·ably** \-blē\ *adv*

**un·mit·i·gat·ed** \,ən-'mit-ə-,gāt-əd, '-ən-\ *adj* **1 :** not softened or lessened **2 :** ABSOLUTE, DOWNRIGHT (an ~ liar)

**un·moor** \-'mur\ *vb* **1 :** to loose from or as if from moorings **2 :** to cast off moorings

**un·mor·al** \-'mȯr-əl\ *adj* **:** having no moral perception or quality **:** being neither moral nor immoral — **un·mo·ral·i·ty** \,ən-mə-'ral-ət-ē\ *n*

**un·moved** \,ən-'müvd, 'ən-\ *adj* **1 :** not moved **2 :** FIRM, RESOLUTE, UNSHAKEN; *also* **:** CALM, UNDISTURBED

**un·muz·zle** \-'məz-əl\ *vb* **:** to remove a muzzle from

**un·nat·u·ral** \,ən-'nach-(ə-)rəl, 'ən-\ *adj* **:** contrary to or acting contrary to nature or natural instincts **:** ARTIFICIAL, IRREGULAR; *also* **:** ABNORMAL — **un·nat·u·ral·ly** \-ē\ *adv* — **un·nat·u·ral·ness** *n*

**un·nec·es·sar·i·ly** \,ən-,nes-ə-'ser-ə-lē\ *adv* **1 :** not by necessity (spent more money ~) **2 :** to an unnecessary degree (~ cautious)

**un·nerve** \,ən-'nərv, 'ən-\ *vb* **:** to deprive of nerve, courage, or self-control

**un·num·bered** \-'nəm-bərd\ *adj* **:** not numbered or counted **:** INNUMERABLE

**un·ob·tru·sive** \,ən-əb-'trü-siv\ *adj* **:** not obtrusive or forward **:** not bold **:** INCONSPICUOUS — **un·ob·tru·sive·ly** *adv*

**un·oc·cu·pied** \,ən-'äk-yə-,pīd, 'ən-\ *adj* **1 :** not busy **:** UNEMPLOYED **2 :** not occupied **:** EMPTY, VACANT

**un·or·ga·nized** \-'ȯr-gə-,nīzd\ *adj* **1 :** not formed or brought into an inte-

grated or ordered whole **2 :** not organized into unions (~ labor)

**un·pack** \,ən-'pak, 'ən-\ *vb* **1 :** to separate and remove things packed **2 :** to open and remove the contents of

**un·par·al·leled** \,ən-'par-ə-,leld, 'ən-, -ˌleld\ *adj* **:** having no parallel; *esp* **:** having no equal or match

**un·par·lia·men·ta·ry** \,ən-,pär-lə-'ment-ə-rē, -,pärl-yə-, -'men-trē\ *adj* **:** contrary to parliamentary practice

**un·peg** \,ən-'peg, 'ən-\ *vb* **:** to remove a peg from **:** UNFASTEN

**un·per·son** \'ən-,pərs-ᵊn, -,pərs-\ *n* **:** an individual who usu. for political or ideological reasons is removed completely from recognition, cognizance, consideration, or memory

**un·pile** \,ən-'pīl, 'ən-\ *vb* **:** to take or disentangle from a pile; *also* **:** to become disentangled from a pile

**un·pin** \-'pin\ *vb* **:** to remove a pin from **:** UNFASTEN

**un·pleas·ant** \-'plez-ᵊnt\ *adj* **:** not pleasant **:** DISAGREEABLE — **un·pleas·ant·ly** *adv* — **un·pleas·ant·ness** *n*

**un·plug** \,ən-'pləg, 'ən-\ *vb* **1 :** UNCLOG **2 :** to remove (a plug) from a receptacle; *also* **:** to disconnect from an electric circuit by removing a plug

**un·plumbed** \-'pləmd\ *adj* **1 :** not tested with a plumb line **2 :** not measured with a plumb **3 :** not explored in depth, intensity, or significance

**un·pop·u·lar** \,ən-'päp-yə-lər, 'ən-\ *adj* **:** not popular **:** looked upon or received unfavorably — **un·pop·u·lar·i·ty** \,ən-,päp-yə-'lar-ət-ē\ *n*

**un·prec·e·dent·ed** \,ən-'pres-ə-,dent-əd, 'ən-\ *adj* **:** having no precedent **:** NOVEL, NEW

**un·pre·dict·able** \,ən-pri-'dik-tə-bəl\ *adj* **:** not predictable — **un·pre·dict·abil·i·ty** \-,dik-tə-'bil-ət-ē\ *n* — **un·pre·dict·ably** \-'dik-tə-blē\ *adv*

**un·pre·ten·tious** \,ən-pri-'ten-chəs\ *adj* **:** not pretentious or pompous

**un·prin·ci·pled** \,ən-'prin-sə-pəld, 'ən-\ *adj* **:** lacking sound or honorable principles **:** UNSCRUPULOUS

**un·print·able** \-'print-ə-bəl\ *adj* **:** unfit to be printed

**un·pro·fes·sion·al** \,ən-prə-'fesh-(ə-)nəl\ *adj* **:** not conforming to the technical or ethical standards of a profession

**un·prof·it·able** \,ən-'präf-ət-ə-bəl, 'ən-, -'präf-tə-bəl\ *adj* **:** not profitable

**un·qual·i·fied** \,ən-'kwäl-ə-,fīd, 'ən-\ *adj* **1 :** not having requisite qualifications **2 :** not modified or restricted by reservations — **un·qual·i·fied·ly** \-,fī(-ə)d-lē\ *adv*

**un·ques·tion·able** \-'kwes-chə-nə-bəl\ *adj* **1 :** acknowledged as beyond doubt **2 :** INDISPUTABLE — **un·ques·tion·ably** \-blē\ *adv*

**un·ques·tion·ing** \-chə-niŋ\ *adj* **:** not questioning **:** accepting without examination or hesitation — **un·ques·tion·ing·ly** *adv*

**un·qui·et** \-'kwī-ət\ *adj* **:** AGITATED, DISTURBED, RESTLESS, UNEASY

**un·quote** \'ən-,kwōt\ *n* — used orally

to indicate the end of a direct quotation

**un·rav·el** \ˌən-'rav-əl, 'ən-\ vb **1** : to separate the threads of **2** : SOLVE ⟨∼ a mystery⟩ **3** : to become unraveled

**un·read** \-'red\ adj **1** : not read **2** : not well informed through reading **3** : UNEDUCATED

**un·re·al** \-'rē(-ə)l\ adj : lacking in reality, substance, or genuineness — **un·re·al·i·ty** \ˌən-rē-'al-ət-ē\ n

**un·rea·son·able** \-'rēz-(ə-)nə-bəl\ adj **1** : not governed by or acting according to reason; also : not conformable to reason : ABSURD **2** : exceeding the bounds of reason or moderation — **un·rea·son·able·ness** n — **un·rea·son·ably** adv

**un·rea·soned** \-'rēz-ᵊnd\ adj : not based on reason or reasoning

**un·rea·son·ing** \-'rēz-(ᵊ-)niŋ\ adj : not using or showing the use of reason as a guide or control

**un·re·con·struct·ed** \ˌən-ˌrē-kən-'strək-təd\ adj : not reconciled to some political, economic, or social change; esp : holding stubbornly to principles, beliefs, or views that are or are held to be outmoded

**un·reel** \ˌən-'rēl, 'ən-\ vb : to unwind from or as if from a reel

**un·re·gen·er·ate** \ˌən-ri-'jen-(ə-)rət\ adj : not regenerated or reformed

**un·re·lent·ing** \-'lent-iŋ\ adj **1** : not yielding in determination **2** : not letting up or weakening in vigor or pace — **un·re·lent·ing·ly** adv

**un·re·mit·ting** \-'mit-iŋ\ adj : CONTINUOUS, INCESSANT, PERSEVERING — **un·re·mit·ting·ly** adv

**un·re·served** \-'zərvd\ adj **1** : not limited or partial : ENTIRE, UNQUALIFIED ⟨∼ enthusiasm⟩ **2** : not cautious or reticent : FRANK, OPEN **3** : not set aside for special use — **un·re·serv·ed·ly** \-'zər-vəd-lē\ adv

**un·rest** \ˌən-'rest, 'ən-\ n : a disturbed or uneasy state : TURMOIL

**un·re·strained** \ˌən-ri-'strānd\ adj **1** : IMMODERATE, UNCONTROLLED **2** : SPONTANEOUS

**un·rid·dle** \ˌən-'rid-ᵊl, 'ən-\ vb : to read the riddle of : SOLVE

**un·righ·teous** \-'rī-chəs\ adj **1** : SINFUL, WICKED **2** : UNJUST — **un·righ·teous·ness** n

**un·ripe** \-'rīp\ adj : not ripe : IMMATURE

**un·ri·valed** or **un·ri·valled** \ˌən-'rī-vəld, 'ən-\ adj : having no rival

**un·robe** \-'rōb\ vb : DISROBE, UNDRESS

**un·roll** \-'rōl\ vb **1** : to unwind a roll of : open out **2** : DISPLAY, DISCLOSE **3** : to become unrolled or spread out

**un·roof** \-'rüf, -'rùf\ vb : to strip off the roof or covering of

**un·ruf·fled** \ˌən-'rəf-əld, 'ən-\ adj **1** : not agitated or upset **2** : not ruffled : SMOOTH ⟨∼ water⟩

**un·ru·ly** \-'rü-lē\ adj [ME unreuly, fr. un- + reuly disciplined, fr. reule rule, fr. OF, fr. L regula straightedge, rule, fr. regere to lead straight] : not submissive to rule or restraint : TURBULENT — **un·rul·i·ness** \-'rü-lē-nəs\ n

**UNRWA** abbr United Nations Relief and Works Agency

**un·sad·dle** \ˌən-'sad-ᵊl, 'ən-\ vb **1** : to remove the saddle from a horse **2** : UNHORSE

**un·sat·u·rat·ed** \-'sach-ə-ˌrāt-əd\ adj **1** : capable of absorbing or dissolving more of something **2** : containing double or triple linkages between carbon atoms ⟨∼ fats or oils⟩ — **un·sat·u·rate** \-rət\ n

**un·saved** \ˌən-'sāvd, 'ən-\ adj : not saved; esp : not rescued from eternal punishment

**un·sa·vory** \-'sāv-(ə-)rē\ adj **1** : TASTELESS **2** : unpleasant to taste or smell **3** : morally offensive

**un·say** \-'sā\ vb -**said** \-'sed\; -**say·ing** \-'sā-iŋ\ : to take back (something said) : RETRACT, WITHDRAW

**un·scathed** \-'skāthd\ adj : wholly unharmed : not injured

**un·schooled** \-'sküld\ adj : not schooled : UNTAUGHT, UNTRAINED

**un·sci·en·tif·ic** \ˌən-ˌsī-ən-'tif-ik\ adj : not scientific : not in accord with the principles and methods of science

**un·scram·ble** \ˌən-'skram-bəl, 'ən-\ vb **1** : RESOLVE, CLARIFY **2** : to restore (as a radio message) to intelligible form

**un·screw** \-'skrü\ vb **1** : to draw the screws from **2** : to loosen by turning

**un·scru·pu·lous** \-'skrü-pyə-ləs\ adj : not scrupulous : UNPRINCIPLED — **un·scru·pu·lous·ly** adv — **un·scru·pu·lous·ness** n

**un·seal** \-'sēl\ vb : to break and remove the seal of : OPEN

**un·search·able** \-'sər-chə-bəl\ adj : not to be searched or explored

**un·sea·son·able** \-'sēz-(ᵊ-)nə-bəl\ adj : not seasonable : happening or coming at the wrong time : UNTIMELY — **un·sea·son·ably** \-blē\ adv

**un·seat** \-'sēt\ vb **1** : to throw from one's seat esp. on horseback **2** : to remove from political office

**un·seem·ly** \-'sēm-lē\ adj : not according with established standards of good form or taste; also : not suitable

**un·seg·re·gat·ed** \-'seg-ri-ˌgāt-əd\ adj : not segregated; esp : free from racial segregation

**un·self·ish** \-'sel-fish\ adj : not selfish : GENEROUS — **un·self·ish·ly** adv — **un·self·ish·ness** n

**un·set·tle** \ˌən-'set-ᵊl, 'ən-\ vb : to move or loosen from a settled position : DISPLACE, DISTURB

**un·set·tled** \-'set-ᵊld\ adj **1** : not settled : not fixed (as in position or character) **2** : not calm : DISTURBED **3** : not decided in mind : UNDETERMINED **4** : not paid ⟨∼ accounts⟩ **5** : not occupied by settlers

**un·shack·le** \-'shak-əl\ vb : to free from shackles

**un·shaped** \-'shāpt\ adj : not shaped : RUDE ⟨∼ ideas⟩ ⟨∼ timber⟩

**un·sheathe** \ˌən-'shēth, 'ən-\ vb : to draw from or as if from a sheath

**un·ship** \-'ship\ vb **1** : to remove from a ship **2** : to remove or become removed from position ⟨∼ an oar⟩

**un·shod** \,ən-'shäd, 'ən-\ *adj* **:** not shod **:** not wearing shoes

**un·sight·ly** \,ən-'sīt-lē, 'ən-\ *adj* **:** unpleasant to the sight **:** UGLY

**un·skilled** \-'skild\ *adj* **1 :** not skilled **:** *esp* **:** not skilled in a specified branch of work **2 :** not requiring skill

**un·skill·ful** \-'skil-fəl\ *adj* **:** lacking in skill or proficiency — **un·skill·ful·ly** \-ē\ *adv*

**un·sling** \-'slin\ *vb* **-slung** \-'sləŋ\; **-sling·ing** \-'sliŋ-iŋ\ **1 :** to remove from being slung **2 :** to take off the slings of esp. aboard ship

**un·snap** \-'snap\ *vb* **:** to loosen or free by or as if by undoing a snap

**un·snarl** \-'snärl\ *vb* **:** to remove snarls from **:** UNTANGLE

**un·so·phis·ti·cat·ed** \,ən-sə-'fis-tə-,kāt-əd\ *adj* **1 :** not worldly-wise **:** lacking sophistication **2 :** SIMPLE

**un·sought** \,ən-'sȯt, 'ən-\ *adj* **:** not sought or searched for or asked for **:** not obtained by effort

**un·sound** \-'saund\ *adj* **1 :** not healthy or whole; *also* **:** not mentally normal **2 :** not valid **3 :** not firmly made or fixed — **un·sound·ly** *adv* — **un·sound·ness** *n*

**un·spar·ing** \-'spa(ə)r-iŋ\ *adj* **1 :** HARD, RUTHLESS **2 :** LIBERAL, PROFUSE

**un·speak·able** \-'spē-kə-bəl\ *adj* **1 :** impossible to express in words **2 :** extremely bad — **un·speak·ably** \-blē\ *adv*

**un·spot·ted** \-'spät-əd\ *adj* **:** free from spot or stain; *esp* **:** free from moral stain

**un·sprung** \-'sprəŋ\ *adj* **:** not sprung; *esp* **:** not equipped with springs

**un·sta·ble** \-'stā-bəl\ *adj* **1 :** not stable **2 :** FICKLE, VACILLATING; *also* **:** having defective emotional control **3 :** readily changing chemically or physically; *esp* **:** tending to decompose spontaneously ⟨an ∼ atomic nucleus⟩

**un·steady** \,ən-'sted-ē, 'ən-\ *adj* **:** not steady **:** UNSTABLE — **un·steadi·ly** \-'sted-ᵊl-ē\ *adv* — **un·steadi·ness** \-'sted-ē-nəs\ *n*

**un·stop** \-'stäp\ *vb* **1 :** UNCLOG **2 :** to remove a stopper from

**un·strap** \-'strap\ *vb* **:** to remove or loose a strap from

**un·strung** \-'strəŋ\ *adj* **1 :** having the strings loose or detached **2 :** nervously tired or anxious

**un·stud·ied** \-'stəd-ēd\ *adj* **1 :** not acquired by study **2 :** NATURAL, UNFORCED

**un·sub·stan·tial** \,ən-səb-'stan-chəl\ *adj* **:** INSUBSTANTIAL

**un·suit·able** \,ən-'süt-ə-bəl, 'ən-\ *adj* **:** not suitable or fitting **:** INAPPROPRIATE — **un·suit·ably** \-blē\ *adv*

**un·sung** \,ən-'səŋ, 'ən-\ *adj* **1 :** not sung **2 :** not celebrated in song or verse ⟨∼ heroes⟩

**un·tan·gle** \-'taŋ-gəl\ *vb* **1 :** DISENTANGLE **2 :** to straighten out **:** RESOLVE ⟨∼ a problem⟩

**un·taught** \-'tȯt\ *adj* **1 :** not instructed or taught **:** IGNORANT **2 :** NATURAL, SPONTANEOUS

**un·think·able** \-'thiŋ-kə-bəl\ *adj* **:** not to be thought of or considered as possible **:** INCREDIBLE

**un·think·ing** \,ən-'thiŋ-kiŋ, 'ən-\ *adj* **:** not thinking; *esp* **:** THOUGHTLESS, HEEDLESS — **un·think·ing·ly** *adv*

**un·thought–of** \'ən-'thȯt-,əv, -,äv\ *adj* **:** not thought of **:** not considered

**un·tie** \-'tī\ *vb* **-tied; -ty·ing** *or* **-tie·ing** **1 :** to free from something that ties, fastens, or restrains **:** UNBIND **2 :** DISENTANGLE, RESOLVE **3 :** to become loosened or unbound

**¹un·til** \(,)ən-,til\ *prep* **:** up to the time of ⟨worked ∼ 5 o'clock⟩

**²until** *conj* **1 :** up to the time that ⟨wait ∼ he calls⟩ **2 :** to the point or degree that ⟨ran ∼ he was breathless⟩

**¹un·time·ly** \,ən-'tīm-lē, 'ən-\ *adv* **:** at an inopportune time **:** UNSEASONABLY; *also* **:** PREMATURELY

**²untimely** *adj* **:** PREMATURE ⟨∼ death⟩; *also* **:** INOPPORTUNE, UNSEASONABLE

**un·to** \,ən-tə, 'ən-(,)tü\ *prep* **:** TO

**un·told** \,ən-'tōld, 'ən-\ *adj* **1 :** not told **:** not revealed **2 :** not counted **:** VAST, NUMBERLESS

**¹un·touch·able** \,ən-'təch-ə-bəl, 'ən-\ *adj* **:** forbidden to the touch

**²untouchable** *n* **:** a member of the lowest social class in India having in traditional Hindu belief the quality of defiling by contact a member of a higher caste

**un·to·ward** \,ən-'tō(-ə)rd\ *adj* **1 :** difficult to manage **:** STUBBORN, WILLFUL ⟨an ∼ child⟩ **2 :** INCONVENIENT, TROUBLESOME ⟨an ∼ encounter⟩

**un·tried** \,ən-'trīd, 'ən-\ *adj* **:** not tested or proved by experience or trial; *also* **:** not tried in court

**un·true** \-'trü\ *adj* **1 :** not faithful **:** DISLOYAL **2 :** not according with a standard of correctness **3 :** FALSE

**un·truth** \,ən-'trüth, 'ən-\ *n* **1 :** lack of truthfulness **2 :** FALSEHOOD

**un·tune** \-'t(y)ün\ *vb* **1 :** to put out of tune **2 :** DISARRANGE, DISCOMPOSE

**un·tu·tored** \-'t(y)üt-ərd\ *adj* **:** UNTAUGHT, UNLEARNED, IGNORANT

**un·twine** \-'twīn\ *vb* **:** UNWIND, DISENTANGLE

**un·twist** \,ən-'twist, 'ən-\ *vb* **1 :** to separate the twisted parts of **:** UNTWINE **2 :** to become untwined

**un·used** \-'yüst, -'yüzd *for 1;* -'yüzd *for 2*\ *adj* **1 :** UNACCUSTOMED **2 :** not used

**un·usu·al** \-'yü-zhə(-wə)l\ *adj* **:** not usual **:** UNCOMMON, RARE — **un·usu·al·ly** \-ē\ *adv*

**un·ut·ter·able** \,ən-'ət-ə-rə-bəl, 'ən-\ *adj* **1 :** not pronounceable **2 :** INEXPRESSIBLE — **un·ut·ter·ably** \-blē\ *adv*

**un·var·nished** \-'vär-nisht\ *adj* **1 :** not varnished **2 :** not embellished **:** PLAIN ⟨the ∼ truth⟩

**un·veil** \,ən-'vāl, 'ən-\ *vb* **1 :** to remove a veil or covering from **:** DISCLOSE **2 :** to reveal in public **:** reveal oneself

**un·voiced** \-'vȯist\ *adj* **1 :** not verbally expressed **:** UNSPOKEN **2 :** VOICELESS 2

**un·war·rant·able** \-'wȯr-ənt-ə-bel\ *adj* : not justifiable : INEXCUSABLE

**un·weave** \-'wēv\ *vb* **-wove** \-'wōv\; **-wo·ven** \-'wō-vən\; **-weav·ing** : DISENTANGLE, RAVEL

**un·well** \,ən-'wel, 'ən-\ *adj* **1** : SICK, AILING **2** : MENSTRUATING

**un·wept** \-'wept\ *adj* : not mourned : UNLAMENTED ⟨died ~ and unsung⟩

**un·whole·some** \-'hōl-səm\ *adj* : harmful to physical, mental, or moral well-being

**un·wieldy** \-'wēl-dē\ *adj* : not easily managed or handled because of size or weight : AWKWARD ⟨an ~ tool⟩

**un·will·ing** \-'wil-iŋ\ *adj* : not willing — **un·will·ing·ly** *adv* — **un·will·ing·ness** *n*

**un·wind** \-'wīnd\ *vb* **-wound** \-'waȯnd\; **-wind·ing 1** : to undo something that is wound : loose from coils **2** : to become unwound : be capable of being unwound **3** : RELAX

**un·wise** \,ən-'wīz, 'ən-\ *adj* : not wise : FOOLISH — **un·wise·ly** *adv*

**un·wit·ting** \-'wit-iŋ\ *adj* **1** : not intended : INADVERTENT **2** : not knowing : UNAWARE — **un·wit·ting·ly** *adv*

**un·wont·ed** \-'wȯnt-əd, -'wōnt-, -'wənt-\ *adj* **1** : RARE, UNUSUAL **2** : not accustomed by experience — **un·wont·ed·ly** *adv*

**un·world·ly** \-'wərl-(d)lē\ *adj* **1** : not of this world; *esp* : SPIRITUAL **2** : NAIVE **3** : not swayed by worldly considerations — **un·world·li·ness** \-'(d)lē-nəs\ *n*

**un·wor·thy** \,ən-'wər-thē, 'ən-\ *adj* **1** : BASE, DISHONORABLE **2** : not meritorious : not worthy : UNDESERVING — **un·wor·thi·ly** \-thə-lē\ *adv* — **un·wor·thi·ness** \-thē-nəs\ *n*

**un·wrap** \-'rap\ *vb* : to free from wrappings : DISCLOSE

**un·writ·ten** \-'rit-ᵊn\ *adj* **1** : not in writing : ORAL, TRADITIONAL ⟨an ~ law⟩ **2** : containing no writing : BLANK

**un·yield·ing** \,ən-'yēl-diŋ, 'ən-\ *adj* **1** : characterized by lack of softness or flexibility **2** : characterized by firmness or obduracy

**un·yoke** \-'yōk\ *vb* : to free from a yoke; *also* : SEPARATE, DISCONNECT

**un·zip** \-'zip\ *vb* : to zip open : open by means of a zipper

**un·zipped** \-'zipt\ *adj* : having no zip code indicated ⟨~ mail⟩

**¹up** \'əp\ *adv* **1** : in or to a higher position or level **2** : away from the center of the earth **3** : from beneath a surface (as ground or water) **4** : in or into an upright position **5** : out of bed **6** : with greater intensity ⟨speak ~⟩ **7** : in or into a better or more advanced state or a state of greater intensity or activity ⟨stir ~ a fire⟩ **8** : into existence, evidence, or knowledge ⟨the missing book turned ~⟩ **9** : into consideration ⟨brought the matter ~⟩ **10** : to or at bat **11** : into possession or custody ⟨gave himself ~⟩ **12** : ENTIRELY, COMPLETELY ⟨eat it ~⟩ **13** — used for emphasis ⟨clean ~ a room⟩ **14** : ASIDE,

BY ⟨lay ~ supplies⟩ **15** : into a state of tightness or confinement ⟨wrap ~ the bread⟩ **16** : so as to arrive or approach ⟨ran ~ the path⟩ **17** : in a direction opposite to down **18** : so as to be even with, overtake, or arrive at ⟨catch ~⟩ **19** : in or into parts ⟨tear ~ paper⟩ **20** : to a stop ⟨pull ~ at the curb⟩ **21** : in advance ⟨one ~ on his opponent⟩ **22** : for each side ⟨the score was 15 ~⟩

**²up** *adj* **1** : risen above the horizon **2** : being out of bed **3** : relatively high ⟨prices are ~⟩ **4** : RAISED, LIFTED **5** : BUILT ⟨the house is ~⟩ **6** : grown above a surface **7** : moving, inclining, or directed upward **8** : marked by agitation, excitement, or activity **9** : READY; *esp* : highly prepared **10** : going on : taking place ⟨find out what is ~⟩ **11** : EXPIRED, ENDED ⟨the time is ~⟩ **12** : well informed ⟨~ on the news⟩ **13** : being ahead or in advance of an opponent ⟨one hole ~ in a match⟩ **14** : presented for or being under consideration **15** : charged before a court ⟨~ for robbery⟩

**³up** *vb* **upped** *or in 1* **up**; **upped**; **up·ping**; **ups** *or in 1* **up 1** : to act abruptly or surprisingly ⟨she *upped* and left home⟩ **2** : to rise from a lying or sitting position **3** : to move or cause to move upward : ASCEND ⟨*upped* prices⟩

**⁴up** *prep* **1** : to, toward, or at a higher point of ⟨~ a ladder⟩ **2** : to or toward the source of ⟨~ the river⟩ **3** : to or toward the northern part of ⟨~ the coast⟩ **4** : to or toward the interior of ⟨traveling ~ the country⟩ **5** : ALONG ⟨walk ~ the street⟩

**⁵up** *n* **1** : an upward course or slope **2** : a period or state of prosperity or success ⟨he had his ~s and downs⟩

**Upa·ni·shad** \ü-'pän-i-,shäd\ *n* : one of a set of Vedic philosophical treatises

**¹up·beat** \'əp-,bēt\ *n* : an unaccented beat in a musical measure; *esp* : the last beat of the measure

**²upbeat** *adj* : OPTIMISTIC, CHEERFUL

**up·braid** \,əp-'brād\ *vb* : to criticize, reproach, or scold severely

**up·bring·ing** \'əp-,briŋ-iŋ\ *n* : the process of bringing up and training

**up·chuck** \'əp-,chək\ *vb* : VOMIT

**up·com·ing** \,əp-,kəm-iŋ\ *adj* : FORTHCOMING, APPROACHING

**up·coun·try** \,əp-,kən-trē\ *adj* : of or relating to the interior of a country or a region — **up-country** \'əp-'kən-\ *adv*

**up·date** \,əp-'dāt\ *vb* : to bring up to date — **update** \'əp-,dāt\ *n*

**up·draft** \'əp-,draft, -,dräft\ *n* : an upward movement of gas (as air)

**up·end** \,əp-'end\ *vb* : to set, stand, or rise on end

**¹up·grade** \'əp-,grād\ *n* **1** : an upward grade or slope **2** : INCREASE, RISE **3** : a rise toward a better state or position

**²up·grade** \'əp-,grād, ,əp-'grād\ *vb* : to raise to a higher grade or position

**up·growth** \'əp-,grōth\ *n* : the process or result of growing up : upward growth : DEVELOPMENT

**up·heav·al** \,əp-'hē-vəl\ n 1 : the action or an instance of uplifting esp. of part of the earth's crust 2 : a violent agitation or change

¹**up·hill** \'əp-'hil\ adv : upward on a hill or incline; also : against difficulties

²**up·hill** \-,hil\ adj 1 : situated on elevated ground 2 : ASCENDING 3 : DIFFICULT, LABORIOUS

**up·hold** \,əp-'hōld\ vb -held \-'held\; -hold·ing 1 : to give support to 2 : to support against an opponent 3 : to keep elevated — **up·hold·er** n

**up·hol·ster** \,əp-'hōl-stər\ vb up·hol·stered; up·hol·ster·ing \-st(ə-)riŋ\ : to furnish with or as if with upholstery;¦esp : to cover with padding and fabric that is fastened over the padding — **up·hol·ster·er** n

**up·hol·stery** \-st(ə-)rē\ n, pl -ster·ies [ME upholdester upholsterer, fr. upholden to uphold, fr. up + holden to hold] : materials (as fabrics, padding, and springs) used to make a soft covering esp. for a seat

**UPI** abbr United Press International

**up·keep** \'əp-,kēp\ n : the act or cost of keeping up or maintaining; also : the state of being maintained

**up·land** \'əp-lənd, -,land\ n : high land esp. at some distance from the sea — **upland** adj

¹**up·lift** \,əp-'lift\ vb 1 : to lift or raise up : ELEVATE 2 : to improve the condition of esp. morally, socially, or intellectually (~ the drama)

²**up·lift** \'əp-,lift\ n 1 : a lifting up; esp : an upheaval of the earth's surface 2 : moral or social improvement; also : a movement to make such improvement

**up·most** \'əp-,mōst\ adj : UPPERMOST

**up·on** \ə-'pȯn, -'pän\ prep : ON

¹**up·per** \'əp-ər\ adj 1 : higher in physical position, rank, or order 2 : constituting the smaller and more restricted branch of a bicameral legislature 3 cap : being a later part or formation of a specific geological period 4 : being toward the interior (the ~ Amazon) 5 : NORTHERN (~ New York State)

²**upper** n : one that is upper; esp : the parts of a shoe or boot above the sole

**up·per·case** \,əp-ər-'kās\ adj : CAPITAL 4 — **uppercase** n

**upper class** n : a social class occupying a position above the middle class and having the highest status in a society — **upper–class** adj

**up·per·class·man** \,əp-ər-'klas-mən\ n : a junior or senior in a college or high school

**upper crust** n : the highest social class or group

**up·per·cut** \'əp-ər-,kət\ n : a short swinging punch delivered in an upward direction

**upper hand** n : MASTERY, ADVANTAGE

**up·per·most** \'əp-ər-,mōst\ adv : in or into the highest or most prominent position — **uppermost** adj

**up·pish** \'əp-ish\ adj : UPPITY

**up·pi·ty** \'əp-ət-ē\ adj : ARROGANT, PRESUMPTUOUS

**up·raise** \,əp-'rāz\ vb : to lift up : ELEVATE

**up·rear** \,əp-'riər\ vb 1 : to lift up : RAISE, ERECT 2 : RISE

¹**up·right** \'əp-,rīt\ adj 1 : PERPENDICULAR, VERTICAL 2 : erect in carriage or posture 3 : morally correct : JUST — **upright** adv — **up·right·ly** adv — **up·right·ness** n

²**upright** n 1 : the state of being upright : a vertical position 2 : something upright

**upright piano** n : a piano whose strings run vertically

**up·ris·ing** \'əp-,rī-ziŋ\ n : INSURRECTION, REVOLT, REBELLION

**up·riv·er** \'əp-'riv-ər\ adv or adj : toward or at a point nearer the source of a river

**up·roar** \'əp-,rōr\ n [Dutch oproer, fr. Middle Dutch, fr. op up + roer motion] : a state of commotion, excitement, or violent disturbance

**up·roar·i·ous** \,əp-'rōr-ē-əs\ adj 1 : marked by uproar 2 : extremely funny — **up·roar·i·ous·ly** adv

**up·root** \,əp-'rüt, -'rut\ vb : to remove by or as if by pulling up by the roots

**up·rush** \'əp-,rəsh\ n : an upward rush (as of liquid)

¹**up·set** \,əp-'set\ vb -set; -set·ting 1 : to force or be forced out of the usual upright, level, or proper position 2 : to disturb emotionally : WORRY; also : to make somewhat ill 3 : UNSETTLE, DISARRANGE 4 : to defeat unexpectedly

²**up·set** \'əp-,set\ n 1 : an upsetting or being upset; esp : a minor physical disorder 2 : a derangement of plans or ideas

**up·shift** \'əp-,shift\ vb : to shift an automotive vehicle into a higher gear — **upshift** n

**up·shot** \'əp-,shät\ n : final result

**up·side** \'əp-,sīd\ n : the upper side

**up·side down** \,əp-,sīd-'daun\ adv 1 : with the upper and the lower parts reversed in position 2 : in or into confusion or disorder — **upside–down** adj

¹**up·stage** \'əp-'stāj\ adv or adj : toward or at the rear of a theatrical stage

²**up·stage** \,əp-'stāj\ vb 1 : to force (as an actor) to face away from the audience by staying upstage 2 : to treat snobbishly

¹**up·stairs** \'əp-'staərz\ adv 1 : up the stairs : to or on a higher floor 2 : to or at a higher position

²**up·stairs** \,əp-,staərz\ adj : situated above the stairs; also : of or relating to the upper floors (~ maid)

³**up·stairs** \'əp-'staərz, 'əp-,staərs\ n sing or pl : the part of a building above the ground floor

**up·stand·ing** \,əp-'stan-diŋ, 'əp-,standiŋ\ adj 1 : ERECT 2 : STRAIGHTFORWARD, HONEST

¹**up·start** \,əp-'stärt\ vb : to jump up suddenly

²**up·start** \'əp-,stärt\ n : one that has risen suddenly; esp : one that claims

more personal importance than he warrants — **up-start** \,əp-\ *adj*

**¹up-state** \'əp-'stāt\ *adj* **:** of, relating to, or characteristic of a part of a state away from a large city and esp. to the north — **upstate** *adv*

**²upstate** \'əp-,stāt\ *n* **:** an upstate region

**up-stream** \'əp-'strēm\ *adv* **:** at or toward the source of a stream — **up-stream** *adj*

**up-stroke** \'əp-,strōk\ *n* **:** an upward stroke (as of a pen)

**up-surge** \-,sərj\ *n* **:** a rapid or sudden rise

**up-swept** \'əp-,swept\ *adj* **:** swept upward ⟨~ hairdo⟩

**up-swing** \'əp-,swiŋ\ *n* **:** an upward swing; *esp* **:** a marked increase or rise (as in activity)

**up-take** \'əp-,tāk\ *n* **1 :** UNDERSTANDING, COMPREHENSION ⟨quick on the ~⟩ **2 :** the process of absorbing and incorporating esp. into a living organism ⟨~ of iodine by the thyroid gland⟩

**up-thrust** \'əp-,thrəst\ *n* **:** an upward thrust; *esp* **:** an uplift of part of the earth's crust — **upthrust** *vb*

**up-tight** \'əp-'tīt\ *adj* **1 :** TENSE, NERVOUS, UNEASY; *also* **:** ANGRY, INDIGNANT **2 :** rigidly conventional

**up-to-date** *adj* **1 :** extending up to the present time **2 :** abreast of the times **:** MODERN — **up-to-date-ness** *n*

**¹up-town** \'əp-'taůn\ *adv* **:** toward, to, or in the upper part of a town or city — **up-town** \,əp-,taůn\ *adj*

**²up-town** \'əp-,taůn\ *n* **:** the section of a town or city located uptown

**¹up-turn** \'əp-,tərn, ,əp-'tərn\ *vb* **1 :** to turn (as earth) up or over **2 :** to turn or direct upward

**²up-turn** \'əp-,tərn\ *n* **:** an upward turn esp. toward better conditions or higher prices

**¹up-ward** \'əp-wərd\ *or* **up-wards** \-wərdz\ *adv* **1 :** in a direction from lower to higher **2 :** toward a higher or better condition **3 :** toward a greater amount or higher number, degree, or rate

**²upward** *adj* **:** directed or moving toward or situated in a higher place or level **:** ASCENDING

**upwards of** *also* **upward of** *adv* **:** more than **:** in excess of

**up-well** \,əp-'wel\ *vb* **:** to move or flow upward

**up-wind** \'əp-'wind\ *adv or adj* **:** in the direction from which the wind is blowing

**ura-cil** \'yůr-ə-,sil\ *n* **:** a pyrimidine base that is one of the four bases coding genetic information in the molecular chain of RNA

**ura-nic** \yů-'ran-ik, -'rā-nik\ *adj* **:** of, relating to, or containing uranium

▌**ura-ni-um** \yů-'rā-nē-əm\ *n* **:** a heavy white metallic radioactive chemical element used as a source of atomic energy

**ura-nous** \yů-'rā-nəs, 'yůr-ə-\ *adj* **:** of, relating to, or containing uranium

**Ura-nus** \'yůr-ə-nəs, yů-'rā-\ *n* [LL,

heaven personified as a god, fr. Gk *Ouranos,* fr. *ouranos* sky, heaven] **:** the third largest planet and the one seventh in order of distance from the sun

**ur-ban** \'ər-bən\ *adj* **:** of, relating to, characteristic of, or constituting a city

**ur-bane** \,ər-'bān\ *adj* [L *urbanus* urban, urbane, fr. *urbs* city] **:** COURTEOUS, POLITE, POLISHED, SUAVE

**ur-ban-ite** \'ər-bə-,nīt\ *n* **:** one living in a city

**ur-ban-i-ty** \,ər-'ban-ət-ē\ *n, pl* **-ties :** the quality or state of being urbane

**ur-ban-ize** \'ər-bə-,nīz\ *vb* **-ized; -iz-ing :** to cause to take on urban characteristics — **ur-ban-iza-tion** \,ər-bə-nə-'zā-shən\ *n*

**ur-chin** \'ər-chən\ *n* [ME, hedgehog, fr. MF *herichon,* fr. L *ericius,* fr. *er*] **:** a pert or mischievous youngster

**Ur-du** \'ůr-dü, 'ər-\ *n* [Hindi *urdū-zabān,* lit., camp language] **:** a language that is an official literary language of Pakistan and is widely used in India

**urea** \yů-'rē-ə\ *n* **:** a soluble nitrogenous compound that is the chief solid constituent of mammalian urine

**ure-mia** \yů-'rē-mē-ə\ *n* **:** accumulation in the blood of materials normally passed off in the urine resulting in a poisoned condition — **ure-mic** \-mik\ *adj*

**ure-ter** \'yůr-ət-ər\ *n* **:** a duct that carries the urine from a kidney to the bladder

**ure-thra** \yů-'rē-thrə\ *n, pl* **-thras** *or* **-thrae** \-,(,)thrē\ **:** the canal that in most mammals carries off the urine from the bladder and in the male also serves as a genital duct — **ure-thral** \-thrəl\ *adj*

**ure-thri-tis** \,yůr-i-'thrīt-əs\ *n* **:** inflammation of the urethra

**¹urge** \'ərj\ *vb* **urged; urg-ing 1 :** to present, advocate, or demand earnestly **2 :** to try to persuade or sway ⟨~ a guest to stay⟩ **3 :** to serve as a motive or reason for **4 :** to impress or impel to some course or activity ⟨the dog urged the sheep onward⟩

**²urge** *n* **1 :** the act or process of urging **2 :** a force or impulse that urges or drives

**ur-gent** \'ər-jənt\ *adj* **1 :** calling for immediate attention **:** PRESSING **2 :** urging insistently — **ur-gen-cy** \-jən-sē\ *n* — **ur-gent-ly** *adv*

**uric** \'yůr-ik\ *adj* **:** of, relating to, or found in urine

**uric acid** *n* **:** a nearly insoluble acid that is the chief nitrogenous excretion of birds and present in small amounts in mammalian urine

**uri-nal** \'yůr-ən-ᵊl\ *n* **1 :** a receptacle for urine **2 :** a place for urinating

**uri-nal-y-sis** \,yůr-ə-'nal-ə-səs\ *n* **:** analysis of urine usu. for medical purposes

**uri-nary** \'yůr-ə-,ner-ē\ *adj* **1 :** relating to, occurring in, or being organs for the formation and discharge of urine **2 :** of, relating to, or found in urine

**urinary bladder** *n* **:** a membranous sac in many vertebrates that serves for the

temporary retention of urine and discharges by the urethra

**uri·nate** \'yūr-ə-,nāt\ *vb* **-nat·ed;
-nat·ing :** to discharge urine — **uri-
na·tion** \,yūr-ə-'nā-shən\ *n*

**urine** \'yūr-ən\ *n* **:** a usu. yellowish and
liquid waste material from the kidneys

**urn** \'ərn\ *n* **1 :** a vessel that typically
has the form of a vase on a pedestal and
often is used to hold the ashes of the
dead **2 :** a closed vessel usu. with a
spout for serving a hot beverage

**uro·gen·i·tal** \,yūr-ō-'jen-ə-t²l\ *adj*
**:** of, relating to, or being the organs or
functions of excretion and reproduction

**urol·o·gy** \yū-'räl-ə-jē\ *n* **:** a branch of
medical science dealing with the urinary
or urogenital tract and its disorders —
**uro·log·ic** \,yūr-ə-'läj-ik\ *or* **uro-
log·i·cal** \-i-kəl\ *adj* — **urol·o·gist**
\yū-'räl-ə-jəst\ *n*

**Ur·sa Ma·jor** \,ər-sə-'mā-jər\ *n* [L,
lit., greater bear] **:** the most conspicuous of the northern constellations
that contains the stars which form the
Big Dipper

**Ursa Mi·nor** \-'mī-nər\ *n* [L, lit., lesser
bear] **:** the constellation including the
north pole of the heavens and the stars
that form the Little Dipper with the
North Star at the tip of the handle

**ur·sine** \'ər-,sīn\ *adj* **:** of, relating to,
or resembling a bear

**ur·ti·car·ia** \,ərt-ə-'kar-ē-ə\ *n* [NL, fr.
L *urtica* nettle] **:** HIVES

**us** \('ˌ)əs\ *pron, objective case of* WE

**US** *abbr* **1** [L *ubi supra*] where above
mentioned **2** United States **3** [L *ut
supra*] as above

**USA** *abbr* **1** United States Army
**2** United States of America

**us·able** *also* **use·able** \'yū-zə-bəl\
*adj* **:** suitable or fit for use — **us·abil-
i·ty** \,yū-zə-'bil-ət-ē\ *n*

**USAF** *abbr* United States Air Force

**us·age** \'yū-sij, -zij\ *n* **1 :** habitual or
customary practice or procedure **2
:** the way in which words and phrases
are actually used **3 :** the action or
mode of using **4 :** manner of treating

**USCG** *abbr* United States Coast Guard

**USDA** *abbr* United States Department
of Agriculture

¹**use** \'yüs\ *n* **1 :** the act or practice of
using or employing something **:** EM-
PLOYMENT, APPLICATION **2 :** the fact or
state of being used **3 :** the way of
using **4 :** USAGE, CUSTOM **5 :** the privilege or benefit of using something **6
:** the ability or power to use something
(as a limb) **7 :** the legal enjoyment of
property that consists in its employment, occupation, or exercise; *also :* the
benefit or profit esp. from property held
in trust **8 :** USEFULNESS, UTILITY; *also*
**:** the end served **:** OBJECT, FUNCTION **9
:** the occasion or need to employ (he had
no more ~ for it) **10 :** ESTEEM, LIKING
(had no ~ for modern art)

²**use** \'yüz\ *vb* **used** \'yüzd; *"used to"*
*usu* 'yüs-tə\; **us·ing** \'yü-ziŋ\ **1
:** ACCUSTOM, HABITUATE (he was *used*
to the heat) **2 :** to put into action or
service **:** EMPLOY **3 :** to consume or

take (as drugs) regularly **4 :** UTILIZE
(~ tact) **5 :** to expend or consume by
putting to use **6 :** to behave toward
**:** TREAT (*used* the horse cruelly) **7 —**
used in the past with *to* to indicate a
former practice, fact, or state (we *used*
to work harder) — **us·er** *n*

**used** \'yüzd\ *adj* **:** having been used by
another **:** SECOND-HAND (~ cars)

**use·ful** \'yüs-fəl\ *adj* **:** capable of being
put to use **:** ADVANTAGEOUS; *esp :* ser-
viceable for a beneficial end — **use-
ful·ly** \-ē\ *adv* — **use·ful·ness** *n*

**use·less** \'yüs-ləs\ *adj* **:** having or
being of no use **:** WORTHLESS —
**use·less·ly** *adv* — **use·less·ness** *n*

**USES** *abbr* United States Employment
Service

**use up** *vb* **:** to consume completely

¹**ush·er** \'əsh-ər\ *n* [ME *ussher*, fr. MF
*ussier*, fr. (assumed) VL *ustiarius* door-
keeper, fr. L *ostium, ustium* door, mouth
of a river] **1 :** an officer who walks before a person of rank **2 :** one who escorts people to their seats (as in a
church or theater) — **ush·er·ette**
\,əsh-ə-'ret\ *n*

²**usher** *vb* **1 :** to conduct to a place **2
:** to precede as an usher, forerunner, or
harbinger **3 :** INAUGURATE, INTRODUCE
(~ in a new era)

**USIA** *abbr* United States Information
Agency

**USM** *abbr* United States mail

**USMC** *abbr* United States Marine Corps

**USN** *abbr* United States Navy

**USO** *abbr* United Service Organizations

**USP** *abbr* United States Pharmacopeia

**USS** *abbr* United States Ship

**USSR** *abbr* Union of Soviet Socialist
Republics

**usu** *abbr* usual; usually

**usu·al** \'yü-zhə(-wə)l\ *adj* **1 :** ac-
cordant with usage, custom, or habit
**:** NORMAL **2 :** commonly or ordinarily
used **3 :** ORDINARY **syn** customary,
habitual, accustomed — **usu·al·ly**
\'yüzh-(ə-)wə-lē, 'yüzh-(ə-)lē\ *adv*

**usu·fruct** \'yü-zə-,frəkt\ *n* [L *ususfruc-
tus,* fr. *usus et fructus* use and enjoy-
ment] **:** the legal right to use and enjoy the benefits and profits of something belonging to another

**usu·rer** \'yü-zhər-ər\ *n* **:** one that lends
money esp. at an exorbitant rate

**usu·ri·ous** \yù-'zhùr-ē-əs\ *adj* **:** practicing, involving, or constituting usury
(a ~ rate of interest)

**usurp** \yù-'sərp, -'zərp\ *vb* [ME
*usurpen,* fr. MF *usurper,* fr. L *usurpare,*
lit., to take possession of by use, fr. *usu*
(abl. of *usus* use) + *rapere* to seize] **:** to
seize and hold by force or without
right (~ a throne) — **usur·pa·tion**
\,yü-sər-'pā-shən, -zər-\ *n* — **usurper** \yù-'sər-pər, -'zər-\ *n*

**usu·ry** \'yüzh-(ə-)rē\ *n, pl* **-ries** [ME,
fr. ML *usuria,* alter. of L *usura,* fr. *usus,*
pp. of *uti* to use] **1 :** the lending of
money with an interest charge for its
use **2 :** an excessive rate or amount of
interest charged; *esp :* interest above
an established legal rate

**UT** *abbr* Utah

**Ute** \'yüt\ *n, pl* **Ute** *or* **Utes** : a member of an Indian people orig. ranging through Utah, Colorado, Arizona, and New Mexico

**uten·sil** \yủ-'ten-səl\ *n* [ME, vessels for domestic use, fr. MF *utensile*, fr. L *utensilia*, fr. neut. pl. of *utensilis* useful, fr. *uti* to use] **1** : an instrument or vessel used in a household and esp. a kitchen **2** : an article serving a useful purpose

**uter·us** \'yüt-ə-rəs\ *n, pl* **uteri** \'yüt-ə-,rī\ *also* **uter·us·es** : an organ of a female mammal for containing and usu. for nourishing the young during the development previous to birth — **uter·ine** \-,rīn, -rən\ *adj*

**utile** \'yüt-ªl, 'yü-,tīl\ *adj* : USEFUL

¹**util·i·tar·i·an** \yủ-,til-ə-'ter-ē-ən\ *n* : a person who believes in utilitarianism

²**utilitarian** *adj* **1** : of or relating to utilitarianism **2** : of or relating to utility : aiming at usefulness rather than beauty; *also* : serving a useful purpose

**util·i·tar·i·an·ism** \-ē-ə-,niz-əm\ *n* : a doctrine that one's conduct should be determined by the usefulness of its results; *esp* : a theory that the greatest good of the greatest number should be the main consideration in making a choice of actions

¹**util·i·ty** \yü-'til-ət-ē\ *n, pl* **-ties 1** : USEFULNESS **2** : something useful or designed for use **3** : a business organization performing a public service and subject to special governmental regulation **4** : a public service or a commodity provided by a public utility; *also* : equipment (as plumbing) to provide such or a similar service

²**utility** *adj* **1** : capable of serving esp. as a substitute in various uses or positions ⟨a ~ outfielder⟩ ⟨a ~ knife⟩ **2** : being of a usable but inferior grade ⟨~ beef⟩

**uti·lize** \'yüt-ªl-,īz\ *vb* **-lized; -liz·ing** : to make use of : turn to profitable account or use — **uti·li·za·tion** \,yüt-ªl-ə-'zā-shən\ *n*

**ut·most** \'ət-,mōst\ *adj* **1** : situated at the farthest or most distant point : EXTREME **2** : of the greatest or highest degree, quantity, number, or amount — **utmost** *n*

**uto·pia** \yủ-'tō-pē-ə\ *n* [fr. *Utopia*, imaginary island described in Sir Thomas More's *Utopia*, fr. Gk *ou* not, no + *topos* place] **1** *often cap* : a place of ideal perfection esp. in laws, government, and social conditions **2** : an impractical scheme for social improvement

¹**uto·pi·an** \-pē-ən\ *adj, often cap* **1** : of, relating to, or resembling a utopia **2** : proposing ideal social and political schemes that are impractical : VISIONARY

²**utopian** *n* **1** : a believer in the perfectibility of human society **2** : one that proposes or advocates utopian schemes

¹**ut·ter** \'ət-ər\ *adj* [ME, remote, fr. OE *ūtera* outer, compar. adj. fr. *ūt* out, adv.] : ABSOLUTE, TOTAL ⟨~ ruin⟩ — **ut·ter·ly** *adv*

²**utter** *vb* [ME *uttren*, fr. *utter* outside, adv., fr. OE *ūtor*, compar. of *ūt* out] **1** : to send forth usu. as a sound : express in usu. spoken words : PRONOUNCE, SPEAK **2** : to put (as currency) into circulation

**ut·ter·ance** \'ət-ə-rəns, 'ə-trəns\ *n* **1** : something uttered; *esp* : an oral or written statement **2** : the action of uttering with the voice : SPEECH **3** : power, style, or manner of speaking

**ut·ter·most** \'ət-ər-,mōst\ *adj* : EXTREME, UTMOST ⟨the ~ parts of the earth⟩ — **uttermost** *n*

**UV** *abbr* ultraviolet

**uvu·la** \'yü-vyə-lə\ *n, pl* **-las** *or* **-lae** \-,lē, -,lī\ : the fleshy lobe hanging at the back of the palate — **uvu·lar** \-lər\ *adj*

**UW** *abbr* underwriter

**ux** *abbr* [L *uxor*] wife

**ux·o·ri·ous** \,ək-'sōr-ē-əs, ,əg-'zōr-\ *adj* : excessively devoted or submissive to a wife

---

**V**

¹**v** \'vē\ *n, pl* **v's** *or* **vs** \'vēz\ *often cap* : the 22d letter of the English alphabet

²**v** *abbr, often cap* **1** vector **2** velocity **3** verb **4** verse **5** versus **6** victory **7** vide **8** voice **9** volt; voltage **10** volume **11** vowel

**V** *symbol* vanadium

**Va** *abbr* Virginia

**VA** *abbr* **1** Veterans Administration **2** vice admiral **3** Virginia

**va·can·cy** \'vā-kən-sē\ *n, pl* **-cies 1** : a vacating esp. of an office, position, or piece of property **2** : the state of being vacant **3** : a vacant office, position, or tenancy; *also* : the period during which it stands vacant **4** : empty space : VOID

**va·cant** \'vā-kənt\ *adj* **1** : not occupied ⟨~ seat⟩ ⟨~ room⟩ **2** : EMPTY ⟨~ space⟩ **3** : free from business or care

: LEISURE **4** : FOOLISH, STUPID ⟨~ laugh⟩; *also* : EXPRESSIONLESS ⟨~ stare⟩ — **va·cant·ly** *adv*

**va·cate** \'vā-,kāt\ *vb* **va·cat·ed; va·cat·ing 1** : to make void : ANNUL **2** : to make vacant (as an office or house); *also* : to give up the occupancy of

¹**va·ca·tion** \vā-'kā-shən, və-\ *n* : a period of rest from work : HOLIDAY

²**vacation** *vb* **va·ca·tioned; va·ca·tion·ing** \-sh(ə-)niŋ\ : to take or spend a vacation — **va·ca·tion·er** \-sh(ə-)nər\ *n*

**va·ca·tion·ist** \-sh(ə-)nəst\ *n* : a person taking a vacation

**va·ca·tion·land** \-shən-,land\ *n* : an area with recreational attractions and facilities for vacationists

**vac·ci·nate** \'vak-sə-,nāt\ *vb* **-nat·ed; -nat·ing** : to inoculate with a related harmless virus to produce immunity to smallpox; *also* : to administer a vaccine to usu. by injection

**vac·ci·na·tion** \,vak-sə-'nā-shən\ *n* : the act of or the scar left by vaccinating

**vac·cine** \vak-'sēn, 'vak-,sēn\ *n* [L *vaccinus* of or from cows, fr. *vacca* cow; so called from the derivation of smallpox vaccine from cows] : material (as a preparation of killed or weakened virus or bacteria) used in vaccinating to induce immunity to a disease — **vaccine** *adj*

**vac·cin·ia** \vak-'sin-ē-ə\ *n* : COWPOX

**vac·il·late** \'vas-ə-,lāt\ *vb* -lat·ed; -lat·ing **1** : SWAY, TOTTER; *also* : FLUCTUATE **2** : to incline first to one course or opinion and then to another : WAVER — **vac·il·la·tion** \,vas-ə-'lā-shən\ *n*

**va·cu·i·ty** \va-'kyü-ət-ē, və-\ *n, pl* -ities **1** : an empty space **2** : EMPTINESS, HOLLOWNESS **3** : vacancy of mind **4** : a foolish remark

**vac·u·ole** \'vak-yə-,wōl\ *n* : a usu. fluid-filled cavity in tissues or in the protoplasm of an individual cell — **vac·u·o·lar** \,vak-yə-'wō-lər, -,lär\ *adj*

**vac·u·ous** \'vak-yə-wəs\ *adj* **1** : EMPTY, VACANT, BLANK **2** : DULL, STUPID, INANE — **vac·u·ous·ly** *adv* — **vac·u·ous·ness** *n*

**¹vac·u·um** \'vak-yü-əm, -,(,)yüm, -yəm\ *n, pl* **vac·u·ums** *or* **vac·ua** \-yə-wə\ [L, fr. neut. of *vacuus* empty] **1** : a space entirely empty of matter **2** : a space almost exhausted of air (as by a special pump) **3** : VOID, GAP — **vacuum** *adj*

**²vacuum** *vb* : to use a vacuum device (as a cleaner) on

**vacuum bottle** *n* : a double-walled bottle with a vacuum between inner and outer walls used to keep liquids hot or cold

**vacuum cleaner** *n* : an electrical appliance for cleaning (as floors or rugs) by suction

**vac·u·um–packed** \,vak-yü-əm-'pakt, -(,)yüm-, -yəm-\ *adj* : having much of the air removed before being hermetically sealed

**vacuum tube** *n* : an electron tube having a high degree of vacuum

**va·de me·cum** \,vād-ē-'mē-kəm\ *n, pl* **vade mecums** [L, go with me] : something (as a handbook or manual) carried as a constant companion

**VADM** *abbr* vice admiral

**¹vag·a·bond** \'vag-ə-,bänd\ *adj* **1** : WANDERING, HOMELESS **2** : of, characteristic of, or leading the life of a vagrant or tramp **3** : leading an unsettled or irresponsible life

**²vagabond** *n* : one leading a vagabond life; *esp* : TRAMP

**va·gar·i·ous** \vā-'ger-ē-əs, və-\ *adj* : marked by vagaries : CAPRICIOUS — **va·gar·i·ous·ly** *adv*

**va·ga·ry** \'vā-gə-rē, və-'ge(ə)r-ē\ *n, pl* -ries : an odd or eccentric idea or action : WHIM, CAPRICE

**va·gi·na** \və-'jī-nə\ *n, pl* -nae \-(,)nē\ *or* -nas : a canal that leads out from the uterus — **vag·i·nal** \'vaj-ən-²l\ *adj*

**vag·i·ni·tis** \,vaj-ə-'nīt-əs\ *n* : inflammation of the vagina

**va·gran·cy** \'vā-grən-sē\ *n, pl* -cies **1** : the quality or state of being vagrant; *also* : a vagrant act or notion **2** : the offense of being a vagrant

**¹va·grant** \'vā-grənt\ *n* : one who wanders idly with no residence and no visible means of support

**²vagrant** *adj* **1** : of, relating to, or characteristic of a vagrant **2** : following no fixed course : RANDOM, CAPRICIOUS (~ thoughts) — **va·grant·ly** *adv*

**va·grom** \'vā-grəm\ *adj* : VAGRANT

**vague** \'vāg\ *adj* **vagu·er; vagu·est** [MF, fr. L *vagus*, lit., wandering] **1** : not clear : not definite or exact : not distinct **2** : not clearly felt or analyzed (a ~ unrest) **syn** obscure, dark, enigmatic, ambiguous, equivocal — **vague·ly** *adv* — **vague·ness** *n*

**vain** \'vān\ *adj* [ME, fr. OF, fr. L *vanus* empty, vain] **1** : of no real value : IDLE, WORTHLESS **2** : FUTILE, UNSUCCESSFUL **3** : CONCEITED **syn** empty, hollow, fruitless, proud, vainglorious — **vain·ly** *adv*

**vain·glo·ri·ous** \(')vān-'glōr-ē-əs\ *adj* : marked by vainglory : BOASTFUL

**vain·glo·ry** \'vān-,glōr-ē\ *n* **1** : excessive or ostentatious pride esp. in one's own achievements **2** : vain display : VANITY

**val** *abbr* value; valued

**va·lance** \'val-əns, 'vāl-\ *n* **1** : drapery hanging from an edge (as of an altar table, bed, or shelf) **2** : a drapery or a decorative frame across the top of a window

**vale** \'vāl\ *n* : VALLEY, DALE

**vale·dic·tion** \,val-ə-'dik-shən\ *n* [L *valedictus*, pp. of *valedicere* to say farewell, fr. *vale* farewell + *dicere* to say] : an act or utterance of leave-taking : FAREWELL

**vale·dic·to·ri·an** \-,dik-'tōr-ē-ən\ *n* : the student of the graduating class who pronounces the valedictory oration at commencement

**vale·dic·to·ry** \-'dik-t(ə-)rē\ *adj* : bidding farewell :,delivered as a valediction (a ~ address) — **valedictory** *n*

**va·lence** \'vā-ləns\ *n* [LL *valentia* power, capacity, fr. L *valēre* to be strong] : the degree of combining power of a chemical element or radical as shown by the number of atomic weights of hydrogen, chlorine, or sodium with which the atomic weight of the element will combine or for which it can be substituted

**Va·len·ci·ennes** \və-,len-sē-'en(z), ,val-ən-sē-\ *n* : a fine handmade lace

**val·en·tine** \'val-ən-,tīn\ *n* : a sweetheart chosen or complimented on St. Valentine's Day; *also* : a greeting card sent on this day

**¹va·let** \'val-ət, 'val-(,)ā, va-'lā\ *n* **1** : a male servant who takes care of a man's clothes and performs personal services **2** : an attendant in a hotel who performs for patrons the services of a man-servant

²**valet** *vb* : to serve as a valet

**val·e·tu·di·nar·i·an** \,val-ə-,t(y)üd-ⁿ-'er-ē-ən\ *n* : a person of a weak or sickly constitution; *esp* : one whose chief concern is his invalidism — **val·e·tu·di·nar·i·an·ism** \-ē-ə-,niz-əm\ *n*

**val·iant** \'val-yənt\ *adj* : having or showing valor : BRAVE, HEROIC **syn** valorous, doughty, courageous, bold, audacious, dauntless, undaunted, intrepid — **val·iant·ly** *adv*

**val·id** \'val-əd\ *adj* **1** : having legal force ⟨a ~ contract⟩ **2** : founded on truth or fact : capable of being justified or defended : SOUND ⟨a ~ argument⟩ ⟨~ reasons⟩ — **va·lid·i·ty** \və-'lid-ət-ē, va-\ *n* — **val·id·ly** \'val-əd-lē\ *adv* — **val·id·ness** *n*

**val·i·date** \'val-ə-,dāt\ *vb* -**dat·ed;** -**dat·ing 1** : to make legally valid **2** : to confirm the validity of **3** : VERIFY — **val·i·da·tion** \,val-ə-'dā-shən\ *n*

**va·lise** \və-'lēs\ *n* : TRAVELING BAG

**val·ley** \'val-ē\ *n, pl* **valleys 1** : a long depression between ranges of hills or mountains **2** : a channel at the meeting place of two slopes of a roof

**val·or** \'val-ər\ *n* [ME, fr. MF *valour*, fr. ML *valor* value, valor, fr. L *valēre* to be strong] : personal bravery **syn** heroism, prowess, gallantry — **val·or·ous** \'val-ə-rəs\ *adj*

**val·o·ri·za·tion** \,val-ə-rə-'zā-shən\ *n* : the support of commodity prices by any of various forms of government subsidy — **val·o·rize** \'val-ə-,rīz\ *vb*

**valse** \väls\ *n* : WALTZ; *esp* : a concert waltz

¹**valu·able** \'val-yə-(wə-)bəl\ *adj* **1** : having money value **2** : having great money value **3** : of great use or service **syn** invaluable, priceless, costly, expensive, dear, precious

²**valuable** *n* : a usu. personal possession of considerable value

**val·u·ate** \'val-yə-,wāt\ *vb* -**at·ed;** -**at·ing** : to place a value on : APPRAISE — **val·u·a·tor** \-,wāt-ər\ *n*

**val·u·a·tion** \,val-yə-'wā-shən\ *n* **1** : the act or process of valuing; *esp* : appraisal of property **2** : the estimated or determined market value of a thing

¹**val·ue** \'val-yü\ *n* **1** : a fair return or equivalent in money, goods, or services for something exchanged **2** : the worth of a thing : market price, purchasing power, or estimated worth **3** : an assigned or computed numerical quantity ⟨the ~ of *x* in an equation⟩ **4** : precise meaning ⟨~ of a word⟩ **5** : distinctive quality of sound in speech **6** : luminosity of a color : BRILLIANCE; *also* : the relation of one detail in a picture to another with respect to lightness or darkness **7** : the relative length of a tone or note **8** : something (as a principle or ideal) intrinsically valuable or desirable ⟨human rather than material ~s⟩ — **val·ue·less** *adj*

²**value** *vb* **val·ued; valu·ing 1** : to

estimate the monetary worth of : APPRAISE **2** : to rate in usefulness, importance, or general worth **3** : to consider or rate highly : PRIZE, ESTEEM — **val·u·er** *n*

**val·ue-add·ed tax** *n* : an incremental excise tax that is levied on the value added at each stage of the processing of a raw material or the production and distribution of a commodity

**val·ued** \'val-yüd\ *adj* : highly esteemed : PRIZED

**valve** \'valv\ *n* **1** : a structure (as in a vein) that temporarily closes a passage or that permits movement in one direction only **2** : one of the pieces into which a ripe seed capsule or pod separates **3** : a device by which the flow of liquid or gas may be regulated by a movable part that either opens or obstructs passage; *also* : the movable part of such a device **4** : a device in a brass wind instrument for quickly varying the tube length in order to change the fundamental tone by some definite interval **5** : one of the separable usu. hinged pieces of which the shell of some animals and esp. bivalve mollusks consists — **valved** \'valvd\ *adj* — **valve·less** *adj*

**val·vu·lar** \'val-vyə-lər\ *adj* **1** : resembling or functioning as a valve; *also* : opening by valves **2** : of or relating to a valve esp. of the heart

**va·moose** \va-'müs, va-\ *vb* **va·moosed; va·moos·ing** [Sp *vamos* let us go] *slang* : to leave or go away quickly

¹**vamp** \'vamp\ *n* **1** : the part of a boot or shoe upper covering esp. the front part of the foot **2** : a short introductory musical passage often repeated

²**vamp** *vb* **1** : to provide with a new vamp **2** : to patch up with a new part **3** : INVENT, IMPROVISE

³**vamp** *n* : a woman who uses her charm and allurements to seduce and exploit men

⁴**vamp** *vb* : to practice seductive wiles on

**vam·pire** \'vam-,pī(ə)r\ *n* **1** : a night-wandering bloodsucking ghost **2** : a person who preys on other people; *esp* : a woman who exploits and ruins her lover **3** : a So. American bat that feeds on the blood of animals including man; *also* : any of several bats believed to suck blood

¹**van** \'van\ *n* : VANGUARD

²**van** *n* : a usu. enclosed wagon or motor-truck for moving goods or animals; *also* : a closed railroad freight or baggage car

**va·na·di·um** \və-'nād-ē-əm\ *n* : a soft ductile metallic chemical element used to form alloys

**Van Al·len belt** \van-'al-ən-\ *n* : a belt of intense ionizing radiation that surrounds the earth in the outer atmosphere

**van·dal** \'van-dᵊl\ *n* **1** *cap* : a member of a Germanic people charged with sacking Rome in A.D. 455 **2** : one who willfully or ignorantly mars or destroys property belonging to another or to the public

**van·dal·ism** \-ˌiz-əm\ n : willful or malicious destruction or defacement of public or private property

**van·dal·ize** \-ˌīz\ vb -ized; -iz·ing : to subject to vandalism : DAMAGE

**Van·dyke** \van-'dīk\ n : a trim pointed beard

**vane** \'vān\ n [ME, fr. OE *fana* banner] **1** : a movable device attached to a high object to show the way the wind blows **2** : a flat extended surface attached to an axis and moved by air or wind ⟨the ~s of a wind mill⟩; *also* : a fixture revolving in a manner resembling this and moving in or by water or air ⟨the ~s of a propeller⟩

**van·guard** \'van-ˌgärd\ n **1** : the troops moving at the front of an army : VAN **2** : the forefront of an action or movement

**va·nil·la** \və-'nil-ə\ n [NL, genus name, fr. Sp *vainilla* vanilla (plant and fruit), dim. of *vaina* sheath, fr. L *vagina* sheath, vagina] : a tropical American climbing orchid with bean-like pods; *also* : its pods or a flavoring extract made from these

**van·ish** \'van-ish\ vb : to pass from sight or existence : disappear completely — **van·ish·er** n

**van·i·ty** \'van-ət-ē\ n, pl -ties **1** : something that is vain, empty, or useless **2** : the quality or fact of being useless or futile : FUTILITY **3** : undue pride in oneself or one's appearance : CONCEIT **4** : a small box for cosmetics : COMPACT

**vanity plate** n : an automobile license plate bearing distinctive letters or numbers or a combination of these and usu. available at extra cost

**van·quish** \'vaŋ-kwish, 'van-\ vb **1** : to overcome in battle or in a contest **2** : to gain mastery over (as an emotion)

**van·tage** \'vant-ij\ n **1** : superiority in a contest **2** : a position or condition of affairs giving a strategic advantage or a commanding perspective

**van·ward** \'van-wərd\ adj : being in or toward the vanguard : ADVANCED — **vanward** adv

**va·pid** \'vap-əd, 'vā-pəd\ adj : lacking spirit, liveliness, or zest : FLAT, INSIPID — **va·pid·i·ty** \va-'pid-ət-ē\ n — **vap·id·ly** \'vap-əd-lē\ adv — **vap·id·ness** n

**¹va·por** \'vā-pər\ n **1** : fine separated particles (as fog or smoke) floating in the air and clouding it **2** : a substance in the gaseous state; *esp* : one that is liquid under ordinary conditions **3** : something unsubstantial or fleeting **4** pl, *archaic* : a depressed or hysterical nervous condition

**²vapor** vb **1** : to rise or pass off in vapor **2** : to emit vapor

**va·por·ing** \'vā-p(ə-)riŋ\ n : an idle, boastful, or high-flown expression or speech — usu. used in pl.

**va·por·ish** \'vā-p(ə-)rish\ adj **1** : resembling or suggestive of vapor **2** : given to fits of depression or hysteria — **va·por·ish·ness** n

**va·por·ize** \'vā-pə-ˌrīz\ vb -ized; -iz·ing : to convert into vapor either naturally or artificially — **va·por·iza·tion** \ˌvā-pə-rə-'zā-shən\ n

**va·por·iz·er** \-ˌrī-zər\ n : a device that vaporizes something (as a fuel oil or a medicated liquid)

**vapor lock** n : a partial or complete interruption of flow of a fluid (as fuel in an internal-combustion engine) caused by the formation of bubbles of vapor in the feeding system

**va·por·ous** \'vā-p(ə-)rəs\ adj **1** : consisting of or characteristic of vapor **2** : producing vapors : VOLATILE **3** : full of vapors : FOGGY, MISTY — **va·por·ous·ly** adv — **va·por·ous·ness** n

**vapor pressure** n : the pressure exerted by a vapor that is in equilibrium with its solid or liquid form

**va·pory** \'vā-p(ə-)rē\ adj : VAPOROUS, VAGUE

**va·que·ro** \vä-'ke(ə)r-ō\ n, pl -ros [Sp, fr. *vaca* cow, fr. L *vacca*] : a ranch hand : COWBOY

**var** abbr **1** variable **2** variant **3** variation **4** variety **5** various

**var·ia** \'ver-ē-ə\ n pl : MISCELLANY; *esp* : a literary miscellany

**¹vari·able** \'ver-ē-ə-bəl\ adj **1** : able or apt to vary : CHANGEABLE **2** : FICKLE **3** : not true to type : not breeding true ⟨a ~ wheat⟩ — **vari·abil·i·ty** \ˌver-ē-ə-'bil-ət-ē\ n — **vari·able·ness** \'ver-ē-ə-bəl-nəs\ n — **vari·ably** \-blē\ adv

**²variable** n **1** : something that is variable **2** : a quantity that may assume a succession of values; *also* : a symbol standing for any one of a class of things

**vari·ance** \'ver-ē-əns\ n **1** : variation or a degree of variation : DEVIATION **2** : DISAGREEMENT, DISPUTE **3** : a license to do something contrary to the usual rule ⟨a zoning ~⟩ **syn** discord, contention, dissension, strife, conflict

**¹vari·ant** \'ver-ē-ənt\ adj **1** : differing from others of its kind or class **2** : varying usu. slightly from the standard or type **3** : VARYING, DISCREPANT

**²variant** n **1** : one that exhibits variation from a type or norm **2** : one of two or more different spellings or pronunciations of a word

**vari·a·tion** \ˌver-ē-'ā-shən\ n : an act or instance of varying : a change in form, position, or condition : MODIFICATION, ALTERATION **2** : extent of change or difference **3** : divergence in qualities from those typical or usual to a group; *also* : one exhibiting such variation **4** : repetition of a musical theme with modifications in rhythm, tune, harmony, or key

**vari·col·ored** \'ver-i-ˌkəl-ərd\ adj : having various colors : VARIEGATED

**var·i·cose** \'ver-ə-ˌkōs\ adj : abnormally and irregularly swollen ⟨~veins⟩

**var·i·cos·i·ty** \ˌvar-ə-'käs-ət-ē\ n, pl -ties **1** : the quality or state of being varicose **2** : a varicose part or lesion (as of a vein)

**var·ied** \'ver-ēd\ adj **1** : CHANGED, ALTERED **2** : of different kinds : VARIOUS **3** : VARIEGATED — **var·ied·ly** adv

**var·ie·gate** \'ver-ē-ə-ˌgāt, 'ver-i-ˌgāt\ vb **-gat·ed; -gat·ing** 1 : to diversify in external appearance esp. with different colors 2 : to introduce variety into : DIVERSIFY — **var·ie·gat·ed** adj — **var·ie·ga·tion** \ˌver-ē-ə-'gā-shən, ˌver-i-'gā-\ n

**va·ri·etal** \və-'rī-ət-ᵊl\ adj : of or relating to a variety; also : being a variety rather than an individual or species — **va·ri·etal·ly** \-ē\ adv

**va·ri·ety** \və-'rī-ət-ē\ n, pl **-et·ies** 1 : the state of being varied or various : DIVERSITY 2 : VARIATION, DIFFERENCE 3 : a collection of different things 4 : something varying from other things of the same general kind 5 : entertainment such as is given in a stage presentation comprising a series of performances (as songs, dances, or acrobatic acts) 6 : any of various groups of animals or plants ranking lower than the species

**var·i·o·rum** \ˌver-ē-'ōr-əm\ n : an edition or text of a work containing notes by various persons or variant readings of the text

**var·i·ous** \'ver-ē-əs\ adj 1 : VARICOLORED 2 : of differing kinds : MULTIFARIOUS 3 : UNLIKE ⟨animals as ~ as the jaguar and the sloth⟩ 4 : having a number of different aspects 5 : NUMEROUS, MANY 6 : INDIVIDUAL, SEPARATE syn divergent, disparate, sundry, divers, manifold, multifold — **var·i·ous·ly** adv

**va·ris·tor** \va-'ris-tər\ n : a voltage-dependent electrical resistor

**var·let** \'vär-lət\ n [ME, fr. MF vaslet, varlet young nobleman, page, domestic servant, fr. ML vassus servant] 1 archaic : ATTENDANT 2 : SCOUNDREL, KNAVE

**var·mint** \'vär-mənt\ n [alter. of vermin] 1 : an animal or bird considered a pest; specif : an animal classed as vermin and unprotected by game law 2 : a contemptible person : RASCAL

**¹var·nish** \'vär-nish\ n 1 : a liquid preparation that is spread on a surface and dries into a hard glossy coating; also : the glaze of this coating 2 : something suggesting varnish by its gloss 3 : outside show : GLOSS

**²varnish** vb 1 : to cover with varnish 2 : to cover or conceal with something that gives a fair appearance : gloss over

**var·si·ty** \'vär-sət-ē, -stē\ n, pl **-ties** [by shortening & alter. fr. university] 1 chiefly Brit : UNIVERSITY 2 : a first team representing a college, school, or club

**vary** \'ver-ē\ vb **var·ied; vary·ing** 1 : ALTER, CHANGE 2 : to make or be of different kinds : introduce or have variety : DIVERSIFY, DIFFER 3 : DEVIATE, SWERVE 4 : to diverge structurally or physiologically from typical members of a group

**vas·cu·lar** \'vas-kyə-lər\ adj [NL vascularis, fr. L vasculum small vessel, dim. of vas vase, vessel] : of or relating to a channel for the conveyance of a body fluid (as blood or sap) to a system of such channels; also : supplied with or containing such vessels and esp. blood vessels

**vascular plant** n : a plant having a specialized conducting system that includes xylem and phloem

**vase** \'vās, 'vāz\ n : a usu. round vessel of greater depth than width used chiefly for ornament or for flowers

**va·sec·to·my** \və-'sek-tə-mē, vā-'zek-\ n, pl **-mies** : surgical excision or cutting of the sperm-carrying ducts of the testis usu. to induce permanent sterility

**va·so·con·stric·tion** \ˌvas-ō-kən-'strik-shən, ˌvāz-\ n : narrowing of the interior diameter of blood vessels

**va·so·con·stric·tor** \-tər\ n : an agent (as a nerve fiber or a drug) that initiates or induces vasoconstriction

**vas·sal** \'vas-əl\ n 1 : a person acknowledging another as his feudal lord and protector to whom he owes homage and loyalty : a feudal tenant 2 : one occupying a dependent or subordinate position — **vassal** adj

**vas·sal·age** \-ə-lij\ n 1 : the state of being a vassal 2 : the homage and loyalty due from a vassal to his lord 3 : SERVITUDE, SUBJECTION 4 : a politically dependent territory

**¹vast** \'vast\ adj : very great in size, amount, degree, intensity, or esp. extent syn enormous, huge, gigantic, colossal, mammoth — **vast·ly** adv — **vast·ness** n

**²vast** n : a great expanse : IMMENSITY

**vasty** \'vas-tē\ adj : VAST, IMMENSE

**vat** \'vat\ n : a large vessel (as a tub or barrel) esp. for holding liquids in manufacturing processes

**VAT** abbr value-added tax

**vat·ic** \'vat-ik\ adj : PROPHETIC, ORACULAR

**Vat·i·can** \'vat-i-kən\ n 1 : the papal headquarters in Rome 2 : the papal government

**vaude·ville** \'vȯd-(ə-)vəl, 'väd-, 'vōd-, -(ə-)ˌvil\ n [F, fr. MF, popular satirical song, alter. of vaudevire, fr. vau-de-Vire valley of Vire, fr. Vire, town in northwest France where such songs were composed] : a stage entertainment consisting of unrelated acts (as of acrobats, comedians, dancers, or singers)

**¹vault** \'vȯlt\ n **1a** : an arched masonry structure usu. forming a ceiling or roof **b** : something (as the sky) resembling a vault 2 : a room or space covered by a vault esp. when underground and used for a special purpose (as for storage of valuables or wine supplies) 3 : a burial chamber; also : a usu. metal or concrete case in which a casket is enclosed at burial — **vaulty** adj

**²vault** vb : to form or cover with a vault

**³vault** vb : to leap vigorously esp. by aid of the hands or a pole — **vault·er** n

**⁴vault** n : an act of vaulting : LEAP

**vault·ed** \'vȯl-təd\ adj 1 : built in the form of a vault : ARCHED 2 : covered with a vault

**vault·ing** \-tiŋ\ adj : leaping upward : reaching for the heights ⟨~ ambition⟩

**vaunt** \'vȯnt\ vb [ME vaunten, fr. MF vanter, fr. LL vanitare, fr. L vanitas vanity] : BRAG, BOAST — **vaunt** n

**vb** abbr verb

**VC** abbr Vietcong

**VD** abbr venereal disease

**V-day** \'vē-,dā\ n : a day of victory

**veal** \'vēl\ n : the flesh of a young calf

**vec·tor** \'vek-tər\ n **1** : a quantity that has magnitude and direction **2** : an organism (as a fly) that transmits disease germs

**Ve·da** \'vād-ə\ n [Skt, lit., knowledge] : any of a class of Hindu sacred writings — **Ve·dic** \'vād-ik\ adj

**Ve·dan·ta** \vā-'dänt-ə, və-, -'dant-\ n : an orthodox Hindu philosophy based on the Upanishads

**veep** \'vēp\ n : VICE-PRESIDENT

**veer** \'viər\ vb : to shift from one direction or course to another syn swerve. deviate, depart, digress, diverge — **veer** n

**vee·ry** \'vi(ə)r-ē\ n, pl **veer·ies** : a tawny brown thrush of the woods of the eastern U.S.

**veg·an·ism** \'vej-ə-,niz-əm\ n : extreme vegetarianism — **veg·an** \-ən, -,an\ n

¹**veg·e·ta·ble** \'vej-(ə-)tə-bəl\ adj [ME fr. ML vegetabilis vegetative, fr. vegetare to grow, fr. L, to animate, fr. vegetus lively, fr. vegēre to rouse, excite] **1** : of, relating to, or made up of plants **2** : obtained from plants ⟨~ oils⟩ ⟨the ~ kingdom⟩ **3** : suggesting that of a plant ⟨a ~ existence⟩

²**vegetable** n **1** : PLANT **2** : a usu. herbaceous plant grown for an edible part that is usu. eaten with the principal course of a meal; also : such an edible part

**veg·e·tal** \'vej-ət-ᵊl\ adj **1** : VEGETABLE **2** : VEGETATIVE

**veg·e·tar·i·an** \,vej-ə-'ter-ē-ən\ n : one that believes in or practices living solely on plant products — **vegetarian** adj — **veg·e·tar·i·an·ism** \-ē-ə-,niz-əm\ n

**veg·e·tate** \'vej-ə-,tāt\ vb **-tat·ed; -tat·ing** : to grow in the manner of a plant; esp : to lead a dull inert life

**veg·e·ta·tion** \,vej-ə-'tā-shən\ n **1** : the act or process of vegetating; also : a dull inert existence **2** : plant life or cover (as of an area) **3** : an abnormal bodily outgrowth — **veg·e·ta·tion·al** \-sh(ə-)nəl\ adj

**veg·e·ta·tive** \'vej-ə-,tāt-iv\ adj **1** : of or relating to nutrition and growth esp. as contrasted with reproduction **2** : leading or marked by a passive, stupid, and dull existence **3** : VEGETATIONAL

**ve·he·mence** \'vē-ə-məns\ n : the quality or state of being vehement : INTENSITY, VIOLENCE

**ve·he·ment** \-mənt\ adj **1** : marked by great force or energy **2** : marked by strong feeling or expression : PASSIONATE **3** : strong in effect : INTENSE — **ve·he·ment·ly** adv

**ve·hi·cle** \'vē-,(h)ik-əl, 'vē-ə-kəl\ n **1** : a medium through or by means of

which something is conveyed or expressed **2** : a medium by which a thing is applied or administered ⟨linseed oil is a ~ for pigments⟩ **3** : a means of carrying or transporting something : CONVEYANCE syn means, instrument, agent, agency, organ, channel — **ve·hic·u·lar** \vē-'hik-yə-lər\ adj

¹**veil** \'vāl\ n **1** : a piece of often sheer or diaphanous material used to screen or curtain something or to cover the head or face **2** : the state accepted or the vows made when a woman becomes a nun (take the ~) **3** : something that hides or obscures like a veil

²**veil** vb : to cover with or as if with a veil : wear a veil

**veil·ing** \'vā-liŋ\ n **1** : VEIL **2** : any of various sheer fabrics (as net or chiffon)

¹**vein** \'vān\ n **1** : a fissure in rock filled with mineral matter; also : a bed of useful mineral matter **2** : one of the tubular branching vessels that carry blood from the capillaries toward the heart **3** : one of the vascular bundles forming the framework of a leaf **4** : one of the thickened ribs that stiffen the wings of an insect **5** : something (as a wavy variegation in marble) suggesting veins **6** : something of distinctive character considered as running through something else : STRAIN **7** : a distinctive mode of expression : STYLE **8** : MOOD, HUMOR — **veined** \'vānd\ adj

²**vein** vb : to form or mark with or as if with veins — **vein·ing** n

**vel** abbr **1** vellum **2** velocity

**ve·lar** \'vē-lər\ adj : of or relating to a velum and esp. that of the soft palate

**veld** or **veldt** \'velt, 'felt\ n [Afrikaans veld, fr. Middle Dutch, field] : open grassland esp. in Africa usu. with scattered shrubs or trees

**vel·le·ity** \ve-'lē-ət-ē, və-\ n, pl **-ities** **1** : the lowest degree of volition **2** : a slight wish or tendency

**vel·lum** \'vel-əm\ n [ME velim, fr. MF veelin, fr. veelin, adj., of a calf, fr. veel calf] **1** : a fine-grained lambskin, kidskin, or calfskin prepared for writing on or for binding books **2** : a paper manufactured to resemble vellum — **vellum** adj

**ve·loc·i·pede** \və-'läs-ə-,pēd\ n : a light vehicle propelled by the rider; esp : a child's tricycle

**ve·loc·i·ty** \və-'läs-(ə-)tē\ n, pl **-ties** : quickness of motion : SPEED ⟨the ~ of light⟩ syn momentum, impetus, pace

**ve·lour** or **ve·lours** \və-'lùr\ n, pl **velours** \-'lùrz\ : any of various textile fabrics with pile like that of velvet

**ve·lum** \'vē-ləm\ n, pl **ve·la** \-lə\ : a membranous partition (as the soft back part of the palate) resembling a veil

¹**vel·vet** \'vel-vət\ n [ME veluet, velvet, fr. MF velu shaggy, fr. L villus shaggy hair] **1** : a fabric characterized by a short soft dense pile **2** : something resembling or suggesting velvet (as in softness or luster) **3** : soft skin covering the growing antlers of deer **4** : the

amount a player is ahead in a gambling game : WINNING — **velvety** adj

²**velvet** adj 1 : made of or covered with velvet 2 : resembling or suggesting velvet : SMOOTH, SOFT, SLEEK

**vel·ve·teen** \,vel-və-'tēn\ n 1 : a fabric woven usu. of cotton in imitation of velvet 2 pl : clothes made of velveteen

**Ven** abbr venerable

**ve·nal** \'vēn-ᵊl\ adj : capable of being bought esp. by underhand means : MERCENARY, CORRUPT — **ve·nal·i·ty** \vi-'nal-ət-ē\ n — **ve·nal·ly** \'vēn-ᵊl-ē\ adv

**ve·na·tion** \ve-'nā-shən, vē-\ n : an arrangement or system of veins ⟨the ~ of the hand⟩ ⟨leaf ~⟩

**vend** \'vend\ vb : SELL; esp : to sell as a hawker or peddler — **vend·ible** adj

**vend·ee** \ven-'dē\ n : one to whom a thing is sold : BUYER

**vend·er** \'ven-dər\ n : VENDOR

**ven·det·ta** \ven-'det-ə\ n : a feud between clans or families

**vending machine** n : a coin-operated machine for vending merchandise

**ven·dor** \'ven-dər, for 1 also ven-'dȯr\ n 1 : one that vends : SELLER 2 : a vending machine

¹**ve·neer** \və-'niər\ n [G furnier, fr. furnieren to veneer, fr. F fournir to furnish] 1 : a thin usu. superficial layer of material ⟨brick ~⟩; esp : a thin layer of fine wood glued over a cheaper wood 2 : superficial display : GLOSS

²**veneer** vb : to overlay with a veneer

**ven·er·a·ble** \'ven-ər-(ə-)bəl, 'ven-rə-bəl\ adj 1 : deserving to be venerated — often used as a religious title 2 : made sacred by association

**ven·er·ate** \'ven-ə-,rāt\ vb -at·ed; -at·ing : to regard with reverential respect **syn** adore, revere, reverence, worship — **ven·er·a·tion** \,ven-ə-'rā-shən\ n

**ve·ne·re·al** \və-'nir-ē-əl\ adj : of or relating to sexual intercourse or to diseases transmitted by it ⟨a ~ infection⟩

**venereal disease** n : a contagious disease (as gonorrhea or syphilis) that is typically acquired in sexual intercourse

**ve·ne·tian blind** \və-,nē-shən-\ n : a blind having thin horizontal parallel slats that can be set to overlap to keep out light or tipped to let light come in between them

**ven·geance** \'ven-jəns\ n : punishment inflicted in retaliation for an injury or offense : RETRIBUTION

**venge·ful** \'venj-fəl\ adj : filled with a desire for revenge : VINDICTIVE — **venge·ful·ly** \-ē\ adv

**V-en·gine** \'vē-\ n : an internal-combustion engine with two banks of cylinders arranged at an angle

**ve·nial** \'vē-nē-əl, -nyəl\ adj : capable of being forgiven : EXCUSABLE ⟨~ sin⟩

**ven·i·punc·ture** \'vēn-ə-,pəŋk-chər, 'ven-ə-\ n : surgical puncture of a vein esp. for withdrawal of blood or for intravenous medication

**ve·ni·re** \və-'nī-rē\ n 1 : a writ summoning persons to appear in court to serve as jurors 2 : a panel from which a jury is drawn

**ve·ni·re·man** \və-'nī-rē-mən, -'nir-ē-\ n : a juror summoned by a venire

**ven·i·son** \'ven-ə-sən, -ə-zən\ n, pl **venisons** also **venison** [ME, fr. OF veneison hunting, game, fr. L venatio, fr. venari to hunt, pursue] : the edible flesh of a deer

**ven·om** \'ven-əm\ n [ME venim, venom, fr. OF venim, fr. (assumed) VL venimen, alter. of L venenum magic charm, drug, poison] 1 : poisonous material secreted by some animals (as snakes, spiders, or bees) and transmitted usu. by biting or stinging 2 : something that poisons or embitters the mind or spirit : MALIGNITY, MALICE

**ven·om·ous** \'ven-ə-məs\ adj 1 : full of venom : POISONOUS 2 : MALIGNANT, SPITEFUL, MALICIOUS 3 : secreting and using venom ⟨~ snakes⟩ — **ven·om·ous·ly** adv

**ve·nous** \'vē-nəs\ adj 1 : of, relating to, or full of veins 2 : being purplish red oxygen-deficient blood present in most veins

¹**vent** \'vent\ vb 1 : to provide with a vent 2 : to serve as a vent for 3 : to let out at a vent : EXPEL, DISCHARGE 4 : to give expression to

²**vent** n 1 : an opportunity or way of escape or passage : OUTLET 2 : an opening for passage or escape (as of a fluid, gas, or smoke) or for relieving pressure 3 : ANUS

³**vent** n : a slit in a garment esp. in the lower part of a seam (as of a jacket or skirt)

**ven·ti·late** \'vent-ᵊl-,āt\ vb -lat·ed; -lat·ing 1 : to cause fresh air to circulate through (as a room or mine) so as to replace foul air 2 : to give vent to ⟨~ one's grievances⟩ 3 : to discuss freely and openly ⟨~ a question⟩ 4 : to provide with a vent or outlet **syn** aerate, express, vent, air, utter, voice, broach — **ven·ti·la·tor** \-ᵊl-,āt-ər\ n

**ven·ti·la·tion** \,vent-ᵊl-'ā-shən\ n 1 : the act or process of ventilating 2 : circulation of air (as in a room) 3 : a system or means of providing fresh air

**ven·tral** \'ven-trəl\ adj 1 : of or relating to the belly : ABDOMINAL 2 : of, relating to, or located on or near the surface of the body that in man is the front but in most other animals is the lower surface — **ven·tral·ly** \-ē\ adv

**ven·tri·cle** \'ven-tri-kəl\ n 1 : a chamber of the heart that receives blood from the atrium of the same side and pumps it into the arteries 2 : one of the communicating cavities of the brain that are continuous with the central canal of the spinal cord

**ven·tril·o·quism** \ven-'tril-ə-,kwiz-əm\ n [LL ventriloquus ventriloquist, fr. L venter belly + loqui to speak; fr. the belief that the voice is produced from the ventriloquist's stomach] : the production of the voice in such a manner that the sound appears to come from a source other than the speaker — **ven·tril·o·quist** \-kwəst\ n

**ven·tril·o·quy** \-kwē\ *n* : VENTRILO-
QUISM

**¹ven·ture** \'ven-chər\ *vb* **ven·tured**;
**ven·tur·ing** \'ven-ch-(ə-)riŋ\ **1** : to
expose to hazard : RISK **2** : to undertake the risks of : BRAVE **3** : to advance
or put forward or expose to criticism or
argument (~ an opinion) **4** : to make
a venture : run a risk : proceed despite
danger : DARE

**²venture** *n* **1** : an undertaking involving
chance or risk; *esp* : a speculative business enterprise **2** : something risked in
a speculative venture : STAKE

**ven·ture·some** \'ven-chər-səm\ *adj*
**1** : inclined to venture : BOLD, DARING
**2** : involving risk : DANGEROUS, HAZ-
ARDOUS **syn** adventurous, venturous,
rash, reckless, foolhardy — **ven·ture-
some·ly** *adv* — **ven·ture·some-
ness** *n*

**ven·tur·ous** \'ven-ch-(ə-)rəs\ *adj*
: VENTURESOME — **ven·tur·ous·ly** *adv*
— **ven·tur·ous·ness** *n*

**ven·ue** \'ven-yü\ *n* : the place in which
the alleged events from which a legal action arises took place; *also* : the place
from which the jury is taken and where
the trial is held

**Ve·nus** \'vē-nəs\ *n* : the brightest
planet and the one second in order of
distance from the sun

**Ve·nu·sian** \vi-'n(y)ü-zhən\ *adj* : of
or relating to the planet Venus —
**Venusian** *n*

**Ve·nus's-fly·trap** \,vē-nəs(-əz)-'flī-
,trap\ *n* : an insectivorous plant of the
Carolina coast with the leaf apex modified into an insect trap

**ve·ra·cious** \və-'rā-shəs\ *adj* **1**
: TRUTHFUL, HONEST **2** : TRUE, ACCU-
RATE — **ve·ra·cious·ly** *adv*

**ve·rac·i·ty** \və-'ras-ət-ē\ *n, pl* **-ties**
**1** : devotion to truth : TRUTHFULNESS
**2** : conformity with fact : ACCURACY
**3** : something true

**ve·ran·da** *or* **ve·ran·dah** \və-'ran-
də\ *n* : a usu. roofed open gallery or
portico attached to the exterior of a
building : PORCH

**verb** \'vərb\ *n* : a word that is the
grammatical center of a predicate and
expresses an act, occurrence, or mode
of being

**¹ver·bal** \'vər-bəl\ *adj* **1** : of, relating
to, or consisting of words; *esp* : having
to do with words rather than with the
ideas to be conveyed **2** : expressed in
usu. spoken words : not written : ORAL
(a ~ contract) **3** : LITERAL, VERBATIM
**4** : of, relating to, or formed from a
verb — **ver·bal·ly** \-ē\ *adv*

**²verbal** *n* : a word that combines characteristics of a verb with those of a
noun or adjective

**verbal auxiliary** *n* : an auxiliary verb

**ver·bal·ize** \'vər-bə-,līz\ *vb* **-ized**;
**-iz·ing 1** : to speak or write in wordy
or empty fashion **2** : to express something in words : describe verbally **3**
: to convert into a verb — **ver·bal-
iza·tion** \,vər-bə-lə-'zā-shən\ *n*

**verbal noun** *n* : a noun derived directly
from a verb or verb stem and in some

uses having the sense and constructions
of a verb

**ver·ba·tim** \(,)vər-'bāt-əm\ *adv or adj*
: in the same words : word for word

**ver·be·na** \(,)vər-'bē-nə\ *n* : VERVAIN;
*esp* : any of several garden plants grown
for their showy spikes of bright, long-
lasting, and often fragrant flowers

**ver·biage** \'vər-bē-ij\ *n* **1** : superfluity of words or words with little
meaning : WORDINESS **2** : DICTION,
WORDING

**ver·bose** \(,)vər-'bōs\ *adj* : using more
words than are needed to convey a
meaning : WORDY **syn** prolix, diffuse,
redundant — **ver·bos·i·ty** \-'bäs-ət-
ē\ *n*

**ver·bo·ten** \vər-'bōt-ᵊn\ *adj* : forbidden usu. by authority and often un-
reasonably

**ver·dant** \'vərd-ᵊnt\ *adj* **1** : green with
growing plants **2** : unripe in experience
: GREEN — **ver·dant·ly** *adv*

**ver·dict** \'vər-(,)dikt\ *n* [alter. of ME
*verdit*, fr. Anglo-French (the French of
medieval England), fr. OF *ver* true (fr.
L *verus*) + *dit* saying, dictum, fr. L
*dictum*, fr. *dicere* to say] **1** : the finding
or decision of a jury on the matter submitted to them in trial **2** : DECISION,
JUDGMENT

**ver·di·gris** \'vərd-ə-,grēs, -,gris\ *n* : a
green or bluish deposit that forms on
copper, brass, or bronze surfaces when
exposed to the weather

**ver·dure** \'vər-jər\ *n* : the greenness of
growing vegetation; *also* : green vegetation

**¹verge** \'vərj\ *n* **1** : a staff carried as an
emblem of authority or office **2**
: something that borders or bounds
: EDGE, MARGIN **3** : BRINK, THRESHOLD

**²verge** *vb* **verged**; **verg·ing 1** : to be
contiguous **2** : to be on the verge or
border

**³verge** *vb* **verged**; **verg·ing 1** : to incline toward the horizon : SINK **2** : to
move or incline in a particular direction
**3** : to be in transition or change

**verg·er** \'vər-jər\ *n* **1** *Brit* : an attendant who carries a verge (as before a
bishop) **2** : SEXTON

**ve·rid·i·cal** \və-'rid-i-kəl\ *adj* **1**
: TRUTHFUL **2** : not illusory : GENUINE

**ver·i·fy** \'ver-ə-,fī\ *vb* **-fied**; **-fy·ing**
**1** : to confirm in law by oath **2** : to
establish the truth, accuracy, or reality
of **syn** authenticate, confirm, corroborate, substantiate, validate — **ver-
i·fi·able** *adj* — **ver·i·fi·ca·tion**
\,ver-ə-fə-'kā-shən\ *n*

**ver·i·ly** \'ver-ə-lē\ *adv* **1** : in very
truth : CERTAINLY **2** : TRULY, CONFI-
DENTLY

**veri·si·mil·i·tude** \,ver-ə-sə-'mil-ə-
,t(y)üd\ *n* : the quality or state of appearing to be true : PROBABILITY; *also*
: a statement that is apparently true
**syn** truth, veracity, verity

**ver·i·ta·ble** \'ver-ət-ə-bəl\ *adj* : AC-
TUAL, GENUINE, TRUE — **ver·i·ta·bly**
*adv*

**ver·i·ty** \'ver-ət-ē\ *n, pl* **-ties 1** : the
quality or state of being true or real

: TRUTH, REALITY **2** : a true fact or statement **3** : HONESTY, VERACITY

**ver·meil** *n* **1** \'vər-məl, -,māl\ : VERMILION **2** \ver-'mā\ : gilded silver, bronze, or copper

**ver·mi·cel·li** \,vər-mə-'chel-ē, -'sel-\ *n* : a dough made in long solid strings smaller in diameter than spaghetti

**ver·mic·u·lite** \vər-'mik-yə-,līt\ *n* : any of numerous minerals that are usu. altered micas whose granules expand greatly at high temperatures to give a lightweight absorbent heat-resistant material

**ver·mi·form** \'vər-mə-,form\ *adj* : long and slender like a worm

**vermiform appendix** *n* : APPENDIX 2

**ver·mi·fuge** \'vər-mə-,fyüj\ *n* : a medicine for destroying or expelling intestinal worms

**ver·mil·ion** *or* **ver·mil·lion** \vər-'mil-yən\ *n* : any of a number of very bright red colors not quite as bright as scarlet; *also* : a pigment yielding one of these colors

**ver·min** \'vər-mən\ *n, pl* **vermin** [ME, fr. MF, fr. (assumed) L *vermin-, vermen* worm; akin to L *vermis* worm] : small common harmful or disgusting animals (as lice or mice) that are difficult to get rid of — **ver·min·ous** *adj*

**ver·mouth** \vər-'müth\ *n* [F *vermout*, fr. G *wermut* wormwood] : a white wine flavored with herbs

**1ver·nac·u·lar** \və(r)-'nak-yə-lər\ *adj* [L *vernaculus* native, fr. *verna* slave born in his master's house, native] **1** : of, relating to, or being a language or dialect native to a region or country rather than a literary, cultured, or foreign language **2** : of, relating to, or being the normal spoken form of a language

**2vernacular** *n* **1** : a vernacular language **2** : the mode of expression of a group or class **3** : a vernacular name of a plant or animal

**ver·nal** \'vərn-ᵊl\ *adj* : of, relating to, or occurring in the spring of the year

**ver·nal·ize** \'vərn-ᵊl-,īz\ *vb* **-ized; -iz·ing** : to hasten the flowering and fruiting of plants by treating seeds, bulbs, or seedlings so as to shorten the vegetative period — **ver·nal·iza·tion** \,vern-ᵊl-ə-'zā-shən\ *n*

**ver·ni·er** \'vər-nē-ər\ *n* : a short scale made to slide along the divisions of a graduated instrument to indicate parts of divisions

**ve·ron·i·ca** \və-'rän-i-kə\ *n* : SPEEDWELL

**ver·sa·tile** \'vər-sət-ᵊl\ *adj* : turning with ease from one thing or position to another; *esp* : having many aptitudes (a ~ genius) — **ver·sa·til·i·ty** \,vər-sə-'til-ət-ē\ *n*

**verse** \'vərs\ *n* **1** : a line of poetry; *also* : STANZA **2** : metrical writing distinguished from poetry esp. by its lower level of intensity **3** : POETRY; *also* : POEM **4** : one of the short divisions of a chapter in the Bible

**versed** \'vərst\ *adj* : familiar from experience, study, or practice : SKILLED

**ver·si·cle** \'vər-si-kəl\ *n* : a verse or sentence said or sung by a clergyman and followed by a response from the people

**ver·si·fi·ca·tion** \,vər-sə-fə-'kā-shən\ *n* **1** : the making of verses **2** : metrical structure

**ver·si·fy** \'vər-sə-,fī\ *vb* **-fied; -fy·ing 1** : to write verse **2** : to turn into verse — **ver·si·fi·er** \-,fī-(-ə)r\ *n*

**ver·sion** \'vər-zhən\ *n* **1** : TRANSLATION; *esp* : a translation of the Bible **2** : an account or description from a particular point of view esp. as contrasted with another **3** : a form or variant of a type or original

**vers li·bre** \ve(ə)r-'lēbr⁼\ *n, pl* **vers li·bres** \*same*\ : FREE VERSE

**ver·so** \'vər-sō\ *n* : a left-hand page

**verst** \'vərst\ *n* : a Russian measure of length equal to 0.6629 mile

**ver·sus** \'vər-səs\ *prep* **1** : AGAINST ⟨John Doe ~ Richard Roe⟩ **2** : in contrast or as an alternative to ⟨free trade ~ protection⟩

**vert** *abbr* vertical

**ver·te·bra** \'vərt-ə-brə\ *n, pl* **-brae** \-,brā, -,(,)brē\ *or* **-bras** : one of the segments making up the backbone

**ver·te·bral** \(,)vər-'tē-brəl, 'vərt-ə-\ *adj* : of, relating to, or made up of vertebrae : SPINAL

**vertebral column** *n* : BACKBONE

**1ver·te·brate** \'vərt-ə-brət, -,brāt\ *adj* **1** : having a backbone **2** : of or relating to the vertebrates

**2vertebrate** *n* : any of a large group of animals (as mammals, birds, reptiles, amphibians, or fishes) distinguished by possession of a backbone

**ver·tex** \'vər-,teks\ *n, pl* **ver·tex·es** *or* **ver·ti·ces** \'vərt-ə-,sēz\ [L *vertex, vortex* whirl, whirlpool, top of the head, summit, fr. *vertere* to turn] **1** : the point opposite to and farthest from the base of a geometrical figure **2** : the termination or intersection of lines or curves ⟨the ~ of an angle⟩ **3** : ZENITH **4** : the highest point : TOP, SUMMIT

**ver·ti·cal** \'vərt-i-kəl\ *adj* **1** : of, relating to, or located at the vertex : directly overhead **2** : rising perpendicularly from a level surface : UPRIGHT — **vertical** *n* — **ver·ti·cal·ly** \-k(ə-)lē\ *adv* — **ver·ti·cal·ness** \-kəl-nəs\ *n*

**ver·ti·cil·late** \,vərt-ə-'sil-ət\ *adj* : arranged in whorls about a stem ⟨~ leaves⟩

**ver·tig·i·nous** \(,)vər-'tij-ə-nəs\ *adj* **1** : marked by, suffering from, or tending to cause dizziness **2** : marked by turning : WHIRLING, ROTARY

**ver·ti·go** \'vərt-i-,gō\ *n, pl* **vertigoes** *or* **ver·tig·i·nes** \(,)vər-'tij-ə-,nēz\ : DIZZINESS, GIDDINESS

**ver·vain** \'vər-,vān\ *n* : any of a group of herbs or low woody plants with often showy heads or spikes of five-parted regular flowers

**verve** \'vərv\ *n* : liveliness of imagination; *also* : VIVACITY

**1very** \'ver-ē\ *adj* **veri·er; -est** [ME *verray, verry*, fr. OF *verai*, fr. L *verax* truthful, fr. *verus* true] **1** : EXACT, PRE-

CISE ⟨the ∼ heart of the city⟩ **2** : exactly suitable ⟨the ∼ tool for the job⟩ **3** : ABSOLUTE, UTTER ⟨the *veriest* nonsense⟩ **4** : MERE, BARE ⟨the ∼ idea scared him⟩ **5** : SELFSAME, IDENTICAL ⟨the ∼ man I saw⟩ **6** : even the : EVEN ⟨made the ∼ walls shake⟩

**²very** *adv* **1** : to a high degree : EXTREMELY **2** : in actual fact : TRULY

**very high frequency** *n* : a frequency of a radio wave between 30 and 300 megacycles

**ves·i·cant** \'ves-i-kənt\ *n* : an agent that causes blistering — **vesicant** *adj*

**ves·i·cle** \'ves-i-kəl\ *n* : a membranous and usu. fluid-filled cavity in a plant or animal; also : BLISTER — **ve·sic·u·lar** \və-'sik-yə-lər\ *adj*

**¹ves·per** \'ves-pər\ *n* **1** *cap* : EVENING STAR **2** : a vesper bell **3** *archaic* : EVENING, EVENTIDE

**²vesper** *adj* : of or relating to vespers or to the evening

**ves·pers** \-pərz\ *n pl, often cap* : a late afternoon or evening worship service

**ves·per·tine** \'ves-pər-ˌtīn\ *adj* **1** : of, relating to, or taking place in the evening **2** : active or flourishing in the evening

**ves·sel** \'ves-əl\ *n* **1** : a hollow or concave utensil (as a barrel, bottle, bowl, or cup) for holding something **2** : a craft bigger than a rowboat for navigation of the water **3** : a person regarded as one into whom some quality is infused **4** : a tube in which a body fluid (as blood) is contained and circulated

**¹vest** \'vest\ *vb* **1** : to place or give into the possession or discretion of some person or authority **2** : to clothe with a particular authority, right, or property **3** : to become legally vested **4** : to clothe with or as if with a garment; *esp* : to garb in ecclesiastical vestments

**²vest** *n* **1** : a man's sleeveless garment worn under a suit coat; *also* : a similar garment for women **2** *chiefly Brit* : UNDERSHIRT **3** : a front piece of a dress resembling the front of a vest

**¹ves·tal** \'ves-tᵊl\ *adj* : CHASTE — **vestal·ly** \-ē\ *adv*

**²vestal** *n* : a chaste woman

**vestal virgin** *n* : a virgin consecrated to the Roman goddess Vesta and to the service of watching the sacred fire perpetually kept burning on her altar

**vested interest** *n* : an interest (as in an existing political, economic, or social arrangement) to which the holder has a strong commitment; *also* : one (as a corporation) having a vested interest

**vest·ee** \ve-'stē\ *n* : an ornamental piece showing between the open edges on the front of a woman's jacket or blouse

**ves·ti·bule** \'ves-tə-ˌbyül\ *n* **1** : a passage or room between the outer door and the interior of a building **2** : the enclosed entrance to a railroad passenger car **3** : a bodily cavity forming or suggesting an entrance to some other part — **ves·tib·u·lar** \ve-'stib-yə-lər\ *adj*

**ves·tige** \'ves-tij\ *n* [F, fr. L *vestigium*

footstep, footprint, track, vestige] : a trace or visible sign left by something lost or vanished; *also* : a minute remaining amount — **ves·ti·gial** \ve-'stij-(ē-)əl\ *adj* — **ves·ti·gial·ly** \-ē\ *adv*

**vest·ing** \'ves-tiŋ\ *n* : the conveying to an employee of inalienable rights to share in a pension fund; *also* : the right so conveyed

**vest·ment** \'ves(t)-mənt\ *n* **1** : an outer garment; *esp* : a ceremonial or official robe **2** *pl* : CLOTHING, GARB **3** : a garment or insignia worn by a clergyman when officiating or assisting at a religious service

**vest-pocket** *adj* : very small ⟨a ∼ park⟩

**ves·try** \'ves-trē\ *n, pl* **vestries 1** : a room in a church for vestments, altar linens, and sacred vessels **2** : a room used for church meetings and classes **3** : a body administering the temporal affairs of an Episcopal parish

**ves·try·man** \-mən\ *n* : a member of a vestry

**ves·ture** \'ves-chər\ *n* **1** : a covering garment (as a robe) **2** : CLOTHING, APPAREL

**¹vet** \'vet\ *n* : VETERINARIAN, VETERINARY

**²vet** *adj or n* : VETERAN

**vetch** \'vech\ *n* : any of several herbs related to the pea including some valued for fodder

**vet·er·an** \'vet-(ə-)rən\ *n* [L *veteranus*, fr. *veteranus* old, of long experience, fr. *veter-, vetus* old] **1** : an old soldier of long service **2** : a former member of the armed forces **3** : a person of long experience in an occupation or skill — **veteran** *adj*

**Veterans Day** *n* : the 4th Monday in October or formerly November 11 observed as a legal holiday in commemoration of the end of hostilities in 1918 and 1945

**vet·er·i·nar·i·an** \ˌvet-(ə-)rən-'er-ē-ən, ˌvet-ᵊn-\ *n* : one qualified and authorized to treat injuries and diseases of animals

**¹vet·er·i·nary** \'vet-(ə-)rən-ˌer-ē, 'vet-ᵊn-\ *adj* : of, relating to, or being the medical care of animals and esp. domestic animals

**²veterinary** *n, pl* **-nar·ies** : VETERINARIAN

**¹ve·to** \'vēt-ō\ *n, pl* **vetoes** [L, I forbid, fr. *vetare* to forbid] **1** : an authoritative prohibition **2** : a power of one part of a government to forbid the carrying out of projects attempted by another part; *esp* : a power vested in a chief executive to prevent the carrying out of measures adopted by a legislature **3** : the exercise of the power of veto; *also* : a document or message stating the reasons for a specific use of this power

**²veto** *vb* **1** : FORBID, PROHIBIT **2** : to refuse assent to (a legislative bill) so as to prevent enactment or cause reconsideration — **ve·to·er** *n*

**vex** \'veks\ *vb* **vexed** *also* **vext**; **vex·ing 1** : to bring trouble, distress, or agitation to **2** : to irritate or annoy by petty provocations **3** : to debate or discuss at length : DISPUTE ⟨a ~ed question⟩ **4** : to shake or toss about

**vex·a·tion** \vek-'sā-shən\ n **1** : the quality or state of being vexed : IRRITATION **2** : the act of vexing **3** : a cause of trouble or annoyance

**vex·a·tious** \-shəs\ adj **1** : causing vexation : ANNOYING, DISTRESSING **2** : full of distress or annoyance : TROUBLED — **vex·a·tious·ly** adv — **vex·a·tious·ness** n

**VF** abbr **1** video frequency **2** visual field

**VFD** abbr volunteer fire department

**VFW** abbr Veterans of Foreign Wars

**VG** abbr **1** very good **2** vicar-general

**VHF** abbr very high frequency

**vi** abbr **1** verb intransitive **2** ⌊L *vide infra*⌋ see below

**VI** abbr Virgin Islands

**via** \'vī-ə, 'vē-ə\ prep : by way of ⟨goods shipped ~ the Panama Canal⟩

**vi·a·ble** \'vī-ə-bəl\ adj **1** : capable of living or growing; esp : born alive and sufficiently developed physically as to be normally capable of living ⟨a ~ infant⟩ **2** : capable of being put into practice : WORKABLE — **vi·a·bil·i·ty** \,vī-ə-'bil-ət-ē\ n — **vi·a·bly** \'vī-ə-blē\ adv

**via·duct** \'vī-ə-,dəkt\ n : a bridge with high supporting towers or piers for carrying a road or railroad over something (as a valley, river, or road)

**vi·al** \'vī(-ə)l\ n : a small vessel for liquids

**vi·and** \'vī-ənd\ n : an article of food — usu. used in pl.

**vi·at·i·cum** \vī-'at-i-kəm, vē-\ n, pl **-cums** or **-ca** \-kə\ **1** : an allowance esp. in money for traveling needs and expenses **2** : the Christian Eucharist given to a person in danger of death

**vibes** \'vībz\ n pl **1** : VIBRAPHONE **2** : VIBRATIONS

**vi·brant** \'vī-brənt\ adj **1** : VIBRATING, PULSING **2** : pulsing with vigor or activity **3** : readily set in vibration : RESPONSIVE, SENSITIVE **4** : sounding from vibration — **vi·bran·cy** \-brən-sē\ n

**vi·bra·phone** \'vī-brə-,fōn\ n : a percussion instrument like the xylophone but with metal bars and motor-driven resonators

**vi·brate** \'vī-,brāt\ vb **vi·brat·ed; vi·brat·ing 1** : OSCILLATE **2** : to set in vibration **3** : to be in vibration **4** : to respond sympathetically : THRILL **5** : WAVER, FLUCTUATE — **vi·bra·tor** \-,brāt-ər\ n

**vi·bra·tion** \vī-'brā-shən\ n **1** : an act of vibrating : a state of being vibrated : OSCILLATION **2** : a rapid to-and-fro motion of the particles of an elastic body or medium (as a stretched cord) that produces sound **3** : a trembling motion **4** : VACILLATION **5** pl : a distinctive usu. emotional emanation or atmosphere that can be instinctively sensed — **vi·bra·tion·al** \-sh(ə-)nəl\ adj

**vi·bra·to** \vē-'brät-ō\ n pl **-tos** : a

slightly tremulous effect imparted to vocal or instrumental music

**vi·bra·to·ry** \'vī-brə-,tōr-ē\ adj : consisting in, capable of, or causing vibration

**vi·bur·num** \vī-'bər-nəm\ n : any of several shrubs or trees related to the honeysuckle with small usu. white flowers in broad clusters

**vic** abbr vicinity

**Vic** abbr Victoria

**vic·ar** \'vik-ər\ n **1** : an administrative deputy **2** : an Anglican clergyman in charge of a dependent parish — **vi·car·i·al** \vī-'kar-ē-əl\ adj — **vi·car·i·ate** \-ē-ət\ n

**vic·ar·age** \'vik-ə-rij\ n : the benefice or house of a vicar

**vicar–general** n, pl **vicars-general** : an administrative deputy (as of a Roman Catholic bishop)

**vi·car·i·ous** \vī-'ker-ē-əs, -'kar-\ adj **1** : acting for another **2** : done or suffered by one person on behalf of another or others ⟨a ~ sacrifice⟩ **3** : realized or experienced by one person through sympathetic sharing in the experience of another — **vi·car·i·ous·ly** adv — **vi·car·i·ous·ness** n

**¹vice** \'vīs\ n **1** : a moral fault; esp : an immoral habit **2** : DEPRAVITY, WICKEDNESS **3** : a physical imperfection : BLEMISH **4** : an undesirable behavior pattern in a domestic animal

**²vice** n, chiefly Brit : VISE

**³vi·ce** \'vī-sē\ prep : in the place of : SUCCEEDING ⟨appointed chairman ~ J.W.Doe, resigned⟩

**vice admiral** n : a commissioned officer in the navy or coast guard ranking above a rear admiral

**vice·ge·rent** \'vīs-'jir-ənt\ n : an administrative deputy of a king or magistrate — **vice·ge·ren·cy** \-ən-sē\ n

**vi·cen·ni·al** \vī-'sen-ē-əl\ adj : occurring once every 20 years

**vice–pres·i·den·cy** \'vīs-'prez-əd-ən-sē\ n : the office of vice-president

**vice–pres·i·dent** \-'prez-əd-ənt\ n **1** : an officer ranking next to a president and usu. empowered to act for him during an absence or disability **2** : a president's deputy in charge of a particular location or function

**vice–re·gal** \'vīs-'rē-gəl\ adj : of or relating to a viceroy

**vice·roy** \'vīs-,rȯi\ n : the governor of a country or province who rules as representative of his sovereign — **vice·roy·al·ty** \-əl-tē\ n

**vice ver·sa** \,vī-si-'vər-sə, (')vīs-'vər-\ adv : with the order reversed : CONVERSELY

**vi·chys·soise** \,vish-ē-'swäz, ,vē-shē-\ n : a thick soup made esp. from leeks or onions and potatoes, cream, and chicken stock and usu. served cold

**Vi·chy water** \'vish-ē-\ n : water impregnated with carbon dioxide

**vic·i·nage** \'vis-ᵊn-ij\ n : a neighboring or surrounding district : VICINITY

**vic·i·nal** \'vis-ᵊn-əl\ adj : of or relating to a limited district : LOCAL

**vi·cin·i·ty** \və-'sin-ət-ē\ n, pl **-ties**

[MF *vicinité*, fr. L *vicinitas*, fr. *vicinus* neighboring, fr. *vicus* row of houses, village] **1 :** NEARNESS, PROXIMITY **2 :** a surrounding area **:** NEIGHBORHOOD

**vi·cious** \'vish-əs\ *adj* **1 :** addicted to vice **:** WICKED, DEPRAVED **2 :** DEFECTIVE, FAULTY; *also* **:** INVALID **3 :** IMPURE, FOUL **4 :** having a savage disposition **5 :** MALICIOUS, SPITEFUL **6 :** worsened by internal causes that augment each other ⟨~ wage-price spiral⟩ **— vi·cious·ly** *adv* **— vi·cious·ness** *n*

**vi·cis·si·tude** \və-'sis-ə-ˌt(y)üd, vī-\ *n* **1 :** the quality or state of being changeable **2 :** a change or succession from one thing to another; *esp* **:** an irregular, unexpected, or surprising change — usu. used in pl.

**vic·tim** \'vik-təm\ *n* **1 :** a living being offered as a sacrifice in a religious rite **2 :** an individual injured or killed (as by disease or accident) **3 :** a person cheated, fooled, or injured ⟨a ~ of circumstances⟩

**vic·tim·ize** \'vik-tə-ˌmīz\ *vb* **-ized; -iz·ing :** to make a victim of **— vic·tim·iza·tion** \ˌvik-tə-mə-'zā-shən\ *n* **— vic·tim·iz·er** \'vik-tə-ˌmī-zər\ *n*

**vic·tor** \'vik-tər\ *n* **:** WINNER, CONQUEROR

**vic·to·ria** \vik-'tōr-ē-ə\ *n* **:** a low 4-wheeled carriage with a folding top and a raised seat in front for the driver

**¹Vic·to·ri·an** \vik-'tōr-ē-ən\ *adj* **1 :** of or relating to the reign of Queen Victoria of England or the art, letters, or taste of her time **2 :** typical of the standards or conduct of the age of Victoria esp. when considered prudish or narrow

**²Victorian** *n* **:** a person and esp. an author of the Victorian period

**vic·to·ri·ous** \vik-'tōr-ē-əs\ *adj* **1 :** having won a victory **:** CONQUERING **2 :** of, relating to, or characteristic of victory **— vic·to·ri·ous·ly** *adv*

**vic·to·ry** \'vik-t(ə-)rē\ *n, pl* **-ries 1 :** the overcoming of an enemy or an antagonist **2 :** achievement of mastery or success in a struggle or endeavor against odds

**¹vict·ual** \'vit-ᵊl\ *n* **1 :** food usable by man **2** *pl* **:** food supplies **:** PROVISIONS

**²victual** *vb* **-ualed** *or* **-ualled; -ual·ing** *or* **-ual·ling 1 :** to supply with food **2 :** to lay in provisions

**vict·ual·ler** *or* **vict·ual·er** \'vit-ᵊl-ər\ *n* **1 :** the keeper of a restaurant or tavern **2 :** one that supplies an army, a navy, or a ship with food

**vi·cu·ña** *or* **vi·cu·na** \vī-'kün-yə, vī-; vī-'k(y)ü-nə\ *n* **1 :** a So. American wild mammal related to the llama and alpaca; *also* **:** its wool **2 :** a soft fabric woven from the wool of the vicuña; *also* **:** a sheep's wool imitation of this

**vi·de** \'vīd-ē, 'vē-ˌdā\ *vb imper* **:** SEE — used to direct a reader to another item

**vi·de·li·cet** \və-'del-ə-ˌset, vī-; vi-'dā-li-ˌket\ *adv* [ME, fr. L, fr. *videre* to see + *licet* it is permitted, fr. *licere* to be permitted] **:** that is to say **:** NAMELY

**¹vid·eo** \'vid-ē-ˌō\ *adj* **:** relating to or

used in transmission or reception of the television image

**²video** *n* **:** TELEVISION

**vid·eo·phone** \'vid-ē-ə-ˌfōn\ *n* **:** a telephone for transmitting both audio and video signals

**vid·eo·tape** \'vid-ē-ō-ˌtāp\ *vb* **:** to make a recording of (a television production) on magnetic tape **— videotape** *n*

**vie** \'vī\ *vb* **vied; vy·ing** \'vī-iŋ\ **:** to strive for superiority **:** CONTEND **— vi·er** \'vī(-ə)r\ *n*

**Viet·cong** \vē-'et-'käŋ, ˌvē-ət-, -'kóŋ\ *n, pl* **Vietcong :** an adherent of the Vietnamese communist movement supported by North Vietnam

**Viet·nam·ese** \vē-ˌet-nə-'mēz, ˌvē-ət-, -'mēs\ *n, pl* **Vietnamese :** a native or inhabitant of Vietnam **— Vietnamese** *adj*

**Viet·nam·iza·tion** \-nə-mə-'zā-shən\ *n* **:** the act or process of transferring responsibility to the Vietnamese

**¹view** \'vyü\ *n* **1 :** the act of seeing or examining **:** INSPECTION; *also* **:** SURVEY **2 :** ESTIMATE, JUDGMENT ⟨stated his ~s⟩ **3 :** a sight (as of a landscape) regarded for its pictorial quality **4 :** extent or range of vision ⟨within ~⟩ **5 :** a picture of a scene **6 :** OBJECT, PURPOSE ⟨done with a ~ to promotion⟩

**²view** *vb* **1 :** SEE, BEHOLD **2 :** to look at attentively **:** EXAMINE **3 :** to examine mentally **:** CONSIDER **— view·er** *n*

**view·point** \-ˌpóint\ *n* **:** a position from which something is considered **:** point of view **:** STANDPOINT

**vi·ges·i·mal** \vī-'jes-ə-məl\ *adj* **:** based on the number 20

**vig·il** \'vij-əl\ *n* **1 :** a religious observance formerly held on the night before a religious feast **2 :** the day before a religious feast observed as a day of spiritual preparation **3 :** evening or nocturnal devotions or prayers — usu. used in pl. **4 :** an act or a time of keeping awake when sleep is customary; *esp* **:** WATCH **1**

**vig·i·lance** \'vij-ə-ləns\ *n* **:** the quality or state of being vigilant

**vigilance committee** *n* **:** a volunteer committee of citizens organized to suppress and punish crime summarily (as when the processes of law appear inadequate)

**vig·i·lant** \'vij-ə-lənt\ *adj* **:** alertly watchful esp. to avoid danger **— vig·i·lant·ly** *adv*

**vig·i·lan·te** \ˌvij-ə-'lant-ē\ *n* **:** a member of a vigilance committee

**¹vi·gnette** \vin-'yet\ *n* [F, fr. MF *vignete*, fr. dim. of *vigne* vine] **1 :** a small decorative design on or just before the title page of a book or at the beginning or end of a chapter **2 :** a picture (as an engraving or a photograph) that shades off gradually into the surrounding ground **3 :** a short descriptive literary sketch

**²vignette** *vb* **vi·gnett·ed; vi·gnett·ing :** to finish (as a photograph) in the manner of a vignette

**vig·or** \'vig-ər\ *n* **1 :** active strength or

energy of body or mind　**2 :** INTENSITY, FORCE

**vig·or·ous** \'vig-(ə-)rəs\ *adj* **1 :** having vigor **:** ROBUST　**2 :** done with vigor **:** carried out forcefully and energetically — **vig·or·ous·ly** *adv* — **vig·or·ous·ness** *n*

**Vi·king** \'vī-kiŋ\ *n* **:** one of the pirate Norsemen plundering the coasts of Europe in the 8th to 10th centuries

**vil** *abbr* village

**vile** \'vīl\ *adj* **vil·er; vil·est** **1 :** of little worth　**2 :** morally despicable　**3 :** physically repulsive **:** FOUL **4 :** DEGRADING, IGNOMINIOUS **5 :** utterly bad or inferior ⟨~ weather⟩ — **vile·ly** \'vīl-lē\ *adv* — **vile·ness** *n*

**vil·i·fy** \'vil-ə-ˌfī\ *vb* **-fied; -fy·ing** **:** to blacken the character of with abusive language **:** DEFAME　**syn** malign, calumniate, slander, libel, traduce — **vil·i·fi·ca·tion** \ˌvil-ə-fə-'kā-shən\ *n* — **vil·i·fi·er** \'vil-ə-ˌfī-(-ə)r\ *n*

**vil·la** \'vil-ə\ *n* **1 :** a country estate **2 :** a usu. somewhat pretentious rural or suburban residence

**vil·lage** \'vil-ij\ *n* **1 :** a settlement usu. larger than a hamlet and smaller than a town　**2 :** an incorporated minor municipality　**3 :** the people of a village

**vil·lag·er** \'vil-ij-ər\ *n* **:** an inhabitant of a village

**vil·lain** \'vil-ən\ *n* **1 :** VILLEIN　**2 :** a deliberate scoundrel or criminal — **vil·lain·ess** \-ə-nəs\ *n*

**vil·lain·ous** \-ə-nəs\ *adj* **1 :** befitting a villain **:** WICKED, EVIL　**2 :** highly objectionable **:** DETESTABLE　**syn** vicious, iniquitous, nefarious, infamous, corrupt, degenerate — **vil·lain·ous·ly** *adv* — **vil·lain·ous·ness** *n*

**vil·lainy** \-ə-nē\ *n, pl* **-lain·ies** **1 :** villainous conduct; *also* **:** a villainous act　**2 :** villainous character or nature **:** DEPRAVITY

**vil·lein** \'vil-ən, 'vil-ˌān\ *n* **1 :** a free villager of Anglo-Saxon times　**2 :** a serf of a class gradually changing its status to that of free peasants

**vil·len·age** \'vil-ə-nij\ *n* **1 :** the holding of land at the will of a feudal lord **2 :** the status of a villein

**vil·lous** \'vil-əs\ *adj* **:** covered with fine hairs or villi

**vil·lus** \'vil-əs\ *n, pl* **vil·li** \'vil-ˌī, -(ˌ)ē\ **:** a slender usu. vascular process; *esp* **:** one of the tiny projections of the mucous membrane of the small intestine that function in the absorption of food

**vim** \'vim\ *n* **:** robust energy and enthusiasm **:** VITALITY

**vin·ai·grette** \ˌvin-i-'gret\ *n* **:** a small box or bottle for holding aromatic preparations (as smelling salts)

**vin·ci·ble** \'vin-sə-bəl\ *adj* **:** capable of being overcome or subdued

**vin·di·cate** \'vin-də-ˌkāt\ *vb* **-cat·ed; -cat·ing** **1 :** AVENGE　**2 :** EXONERATE, ABSOLVE　**3 :** CONFIRM, SUBSTANTIATE **4 :** to provide defense for **:** JUSTIFY **5 :** to maintain a right to **:** ASSERT — **vin·di·ca·tor** \-ˌkāt-ər\ *n*

**vin·di·ca·tion** \ˌvin-də-'kā-shən\ *n* **:** a vindicating or being vindicated; *esp* **:** justification against denial or censure

**vin·dic·tive** \vin-'dik-tiv\ *adj* **1 :** disposed to revenge　**2 :** intended for or involving revenge　**3 :** VICIOUS, SPITEFUL — **vin·dic·tive·ly** *adv* — **vin·dic·tive·ness** *n*

**vine** \'vīn\ *n* [ME, fr. OF *vigne*, fr. L *vinea* vine, vineyard, fr. fem. of *vineus* of wine, fr. *vinum* wine] **1 :** GRAPE　**2 :** a plant whose stem requires support and which climbs (as by tendrils) or trails along the ground; *also* **:** the stem of such a plant

**vin·e·gar** \'vin-i-gər\ *n* [ME *vinegre*, fr. OF *vinaigre*, fr. *vin* wine + *aigre* keen, sour] **:** a sour liquid obtained by fermentation (as of cider, wine, or malt) and used in cookery and pickling

**vin·e·gary** \'vin-i-g(ə-)rē\ *adj* **1 :** resembling vinegar **:** SOUR　**2 :** disagreeable in manner or disposition **:** CRABBED

**vine·yard** \'vin-yərd\ *n* **1 :** a plantation of grapevines　**2 :** an area of physical or mental occupation

**vi·nous** \'vī-nəs\ *adj* **1 :** of, relating to, or made with wine ⟨~ medications⟩ **2 :** showing the effects of the use of wine

**¹vin·tage** \'vint-ij\ *n* **1 :** a season's yield of grapes or wine　**2 :** the act or period of gathering grapes or making wine　**3 :** WINE; *esp* **:** a wine of a particular type, region, and year and usu. of superior quality　**4 :** a period of origin ⟨clothes of the ~ of 1890⟩

**²vintage** *adj* **1 :** of or relating to a vintage　**2 :** of old, recognized, and enduring interest, importance, or quality **:** CLASSIC ⟨~ cars⟩　**3 :** of the best and most characteristic — used with a proper noun

**vint·ner** \'vint-nər\ *n* **:** a dealer in wines

**vi·nyl** \'vīn-ᵊl\ *n* **:** any of various tough plastics used esp. for coatings, sheeting, tile, flooring, and molded objects

**vi·ol** \'vī(-ə)l\ *n* **:** a bowed stringed instrument chiefly of the 16th and 17th centuries having a fretted neck and usu. six strings

**vi·o·la** \vē-'ō-lə\ *n* **:** an instrument of the violin family slightly larger and tuned lower than a violin — **vi·o·list** \-ləst\ *n*

**vi·o·la·ble** \'vī-ə-lə-bəl\ *adj* **:** capable of being violated

**vi·o·late** \'vī-ə-ˌlāt\ *vb* **-lat·ed; -lat·ing** **1 :** BREAK, DISREGARD ⟨~ a law⟩ ⟨~ a frontier⟩　**2 :** RAPE　**3 :** PROFANE, DESECRATE　**4 :** INTERRUPT, DISTURB ⟨*violated* his privacy⟩ — **vi·o·la·tor** \-ˌlāt-ər\ *n*

**vi·o·la·tion** \ˌvī-ə-'lā-shən\ *n* **:** an act or instance of violating **:** the state of being violated　**syn** breach, infraction, trespass, infringement

**vi·o·lence** \'vī-ə-ləns\ *n* **1 :** exertion of physical force so as to injure or abuse　**2 :** injury by or as if by infringement or profanation　**3 :** intense or furious often destructive action or force **4 :** vehement feeling or expression **:** INTENSITY　**5 :** jarring quality **:** DISCORD-

ANCE **syn** compulsion, coercion, duress, constraint, restraint

**vi·o·lent** \-lənt\ *adj* **1 :** marked by extreme force or sudden intense activity; *esp* **:** marked by improper use of such force **2 :** EXTREME, INTENSE **3 :** caused by force **:** not natural ⟨~ death⟩ **4 :** caused by or showing strong feeling ⟨~ words⟩ — **vi·o·lent·ly** *adv*

**vi·o·let** \'vī-ə-lət\ *n* **1 :** any of numerous low plants usu. with heart-shaped leaves and both aerial and underground flowers; *esp* **:** one with small solid-colored flowers **2 :** a variable color averaging a reddish blue — **violet** *adj*

**vi·o·lin** \,vī-ə-'lin\ *n* **:** a bowed stringed instrument with four strings that has a shallower body and a more curved bridge than a viol — **vi·o·lin·ist** \-əst\ *n*

**vi·o·lon·cel·lo** \,vī-ə-lən-'chel-ō\ *n* **:** CELLO — **vi·o·lon·cel·list** \-əst\ *n*

**VIP** \,vē-,ī-'pē\ *n*, *pl* **VIPs** \-'pēz\ [*very important person*] **:** a person of great influence or prestige; *esp* **:** a high official with special privileges

**vi·per** \'vī-pər\ *n* **1 :** any of a group of sluggish heavy-bodied Old World venomous snakes **2 :** PIT VIPER **3 :** a venomouf or reputedly venomous snake **4 :** a treacherous or malignant person — **vi·per·ine** \-pə-,rīn\ *adj*

**vi·ra·go** \və-'räg-ō, -'rāg-; 'vir-ə-,gō\ *n*, *pl* **-goes** *or* **-gos** [L, manlike heroic woman, fr. *vir* man] **:** a scolding, quarrelsome, or loud overbearing woman **syn** amazon, termagant, scold, shrew, vixen

**vi·ral** \'vī-rəl\ *adj* **:** of, relating to, or caused by a virus

**vir·eo** \'vir-ē-,ō\ *n*, *pl* **-e·os** [L, a small bird, fr. *virēre* to be green] **:** any of various small insect-eating American songbirds mostly olive green and grayish in color

¹**vir·gin** \'vər-jən\ *n* **1 :** an unmarried woman devoted to religion **2** *cap* **:** the mother of Jesus **3 :** an unmarried woman **4 :** a person who has not had sexual intercourse

²**virgin** *adj* **1 :** free from stain **:** PURE, SPOTLESS **2 :** CHASTE **3 :** befitting a virgin **:** MODEST **4 :** FRESH, UNSPOILED; *esp* **:** not altered by human activity ⟨~ forest⟩ **5 :** INITIAL, FIRST

¹**vir·gin·al** \'vər-jən-ᵊl\ *adj* **:** of, relating to, or characteristic of a virgin or virginity — **vir·gin·al·ly** \-ē\ *adv*

²**virginal** *n* **:** a small rectangular spinet without legs popular in the 16th and 17th centuries

**Vir·gin·ia creeper** \vər-,jin-yə-\ *n* **:** a No. American vine having leaves with five leaflets and bluish black berries

**Virginia reel** *n* **:** an American country-dance

**vir·gin·i·ty** \vər-'jin-ət-ē\ *n*, *pl* **-ties 1 :** the quality or state of being virgin; *esp* **:** MAIDENHOOD **2 :** the unmarried life **:** CELIBACY

**vir·gule** \'vər-gyül\ *n* **:** a mark / used typically to denote "or" (as in *and/or*) or "per" (as in *feet/second*)

**vir·i·des·cent** \,vir-ə-'des-ᵊnt\ *adj* **:** slightly green **:** GREENISH

**vir·ile** \'vir-əl\ *adj* **1 :** having the nature, powers, or qualities of a man **2 :** MASTERFUL, FORCEFUL **3 :** MASCULINE, MALE — **vi·ril·i·ty** \və-'ril-ət-ē\ *n*

**vi·ri·on** \'vī-rē-,än, 'vir-ē-\ *n* **:** a complete virus particle with membrane intact

**vi·rol·o·gy** \vī-'räl-ə-jē\ *n* **:** a branch of science that deals with viruses — **vi·rol·o·gist** \-jəst\ *n*

**vir·tu** \,vər-'tü, viər-\ *n* **1 :** a love of or taste for objects of art **2 :** objects of art (as curios and antiques)

**vir·tu·al** \'vər-chə(-wə)l\ *adj* **:** being in essence or in effect though not formally recognized or admitted ⟨a ~ dictator⟩ — **vir·tu·al·ly** \-ē\ *adv*

**vir·tue** \'vər-chü\ *n* [ME *virtu*, fr. OF, fr. L *virtus* strength, manliness, virtue, fr. *vir* man] **1 :** conformity to a standard of right **:** MORALITY **2 :** a particular moral excellence **3 :** active power to accomplish a given effect **:** POTENCY, EFFICACY **4 :** manly strength or courage **:** VALOR **5 :** a commendable quality **:** MERIT **6 :** chastity esp. in a woman

**vir·tu·os·i·ty** \,vər-chə-'wäs-ət-ē\ *n*, *pl* **-ties :** great technical skill in the practice of a fine art

**vir·tu·o·so** \,vər-chə-'wō-sō, -zō\ *n*, *pl* **-sos** *or* **-si** \-,sē, -,zē\ **1 :** one skilled in or having a taste for the fine arts **2 :** one who excels in the technique of an art; *esp* **:** a highly skilled musical performer **syn** connoisseur, aesthete, dilettante, expert, adept, artist — **virtuoso** *adj*

**vir·tu·ous** \'vər·ch(-ə-)wəs\ *adj* **1 :** having or showing virtue and esp. moral virtue **2 :** CHASTE — **vir·tu·ous·ly** *adv*

**vir·u·lent** \'vir-(y)ə-lənt\ *adj* **1 :** extremely poisonous or venomous **:** NOXIOUS **2 :** bitterly hostile **:** MALIGNANT **3 :** highly infectious ⟨a ~ germ⟩; *also* **:** marked by a rapid and very severe course ⟨a ~ disease⟩ — **vir·u·lence** \-ləns\ *n* — **vir·u·len·cy** \-lən-sē\ *n* — **vir·u·lent·ly** *adv*

**vi·rus** \'vī-rəs\ *n* [L, slimy liquid, poison, stench] **1 :** an infective agent too small to be seen with a light microscope and active after passage through a filter too fine for a bacterium to pass; *also* **:** a disease caused by a virus **2 :** something (as a corrupting influence) that poisons the mind or spirit

**vis** *abbr* **1** visibility **2** visual

¹**vi·sa** \'vē-zə, -sə\ *n* **1 :** an endorsement by the proper authorities on a passport to show that it has been examined and the bearer may proceed **2 :** a signature by a superior official signifying approval of a document

²**visa** *vb* **vi·saed** \-zəd, -səd\; **vi·sa·ing** \-zə-iŋ, -sə-\ **:** to give a visa to (a passport)

**vis·age** \'viz-ij\ *n* **:** the face or countenance of a person or sometimes an animal; *also* **:** LOOK, APPEARANCE

¹**vis-à-vis** \,vēz-ə-'vē, ,vēs-\ *n*, *pl* **vis-à-vis** \-ə-'vē(z)\ [F, lit., face to

face] **1 :** one that is face to face with another **2 :** ESCORT **3 :** COUNTERPART **4 :** TÊTE-À-TÊTE

²**vis-à-vis** *prep* **1 :** face to face with **:** OPPOSITE **2 :** in relation to **:** as compared with

³**vis-à-vis** *adv* **:** in company **:** TOGETHER

**viscera** *pl of* VISCUS

**vis·cer·al** \'vis-ə-rəl\ *adj* **1 :** felt in or as if in the viscera **2 :** of or relating to the viscera — **vis·cer·al·ly** \-ē\ *adv*

**vis·cid** \'vis-əd\ *adj* **:** VISCOUS — **vis·cid·i·ty** \vis-'id-ət-ē\ *n* — **vis·cid·ly** \'vis-əd-lē\ *adv*

**vis·cose** \'vis-,kōs\ *n* **:** a syruplike solution made by chemically treating cellulose and used in making rayon and transparent films

**vis·cos·i·ty** \vis-'käs-ət-ē\ *n, pl* **-ties** **:** the quality of being viscous; *esp* **:** the property of fluids that causes them not to flow easily because of the friction of their molecules ⟨the ∼ of oil⟩

**vis·count** \'vī-,kaunt\ *n* **:** a member of the British peerage ranking below an earl and above a baron — **vis·count·ess** \-əs\ *n*

**vis·cous** \'vis-kəs\ *adj* [ME *viscouse*, fr. LL *viscosus* full of birdlime, viscous, fr. L *viscum* mistletoe, birdlime] **1 :** having the sticky consistency of glue **2 :** having or characterized by viscosity **:** THICK

**vis·cus** \'vis-kəs\ *n, pl* **vis·cera** \'vis-ə-rə\ **:** an internal organ of the body; *esp* **:** one (as the heart or liver) located in the cavity of the trunk

**vise** \'vīs\ *n* [MF *vis* something winding, fr. L *vitis* vine] **:** a device for holding or clamping work typically having two jaws closed by a screw or lever

**vi·sé** \'vē-,zā\ *n* **:** VISA — **visé** *vb*

**vis·i·bil·i·ty** \,viz-ə-'bil-ət-ē\ *n, pl* **-ties 1 :** the quality, condition, or degree of being visible **2 :** the degree of clearness of the atmosphere

**vis·i·ble** \'viz-ə-bəl\ *adj* **:** capable of being seen ⟨∼ stars⟩; *also* **:** MANIFEST, APPARENT ⟨has no ∼ means of support⟩ — **vis·i·bly** \-blē\ *adv*

¹**vi·sion** \'vizh-ən\ *n* **1 :** something seen otherwise than by ordinary sight (as in a dream or trance) **2 :** a vivid picture created by the imagination **3 :** the act or power of imagination **4 :** unusual wisdom in foreseeing what is going to happen **5 :** the act or power of seeing **:** SIGHT **6 :** something seen; *esp* **:** a lovely sight

²**vision** *vb* **vi·sioned; vi·sion·ing** \'vizh-(ə-)niŋ\ **:** to see in or as if in a vision **:** IMAGINE, ENVISION

¹**vi·sion·ary** \'vizh-ə-,ner-ē\ *adj* **1 :** seeing or likely to see visions : given to dreaming or imagining **2 :** of the nature of a vision : ILLUSORY, UNREAL **3 :** not practical : UTOPIAN **syn** imaginary, fantastic, chimerical, quixotic

²**visionary** *n, pl* **-ar·ies 1 :** one who sees visions **2 :** one whose ideas or projects are impractical : DREAMER

¹**vis·it** \'viz-ət\ *vb* **1 :** to go to see in order to comfort or help **2 :** to call upon either as an act of courtesy or in a professional capacity **3 :** to dwell with for a time as a guest **4 :** to come to or upon as a reward, affliction, or punishment **5 :** INFLICT **6 :** to make a visit or regular or frequent visits **7 :** CHAT, CONVERSE — **vis·it·able** *adj*

²**visit** *n* **1 :** a short stay : CALL **2 :** a brief residence as a guest **3 :** a journey to and stay at a place **4 :** a formal or professional call (as by a doctor)

**vis·i·tant** \'viz-ət-ənt\ *n* **:** VISITOR

**vis·i·ta·tion** \,viz-ə-'tā-shən\ *n* **1 :** VISIT; *esp* **:** an official visit **2 :** a special dispensation of divine favor or wrath; *also* **:** a severe trial

**visiting nurse** *n* **:** a nurse employed to visit sick persons or perform public-health services in a community

**vis·i·tor** \'viz-ət-ər\ *n* **:** one that visits

**vi·sor** \'vī-zər\ *n* **1 :** the front piece of a helmet; *esp* **:** a movable upper piece **2 :** VIZARD **3 :** a projecting part (as on a cap or an automobile windshield) to shade the eyes — **vi·sored** \-zərd\ *adj*

**vis·ta** \'vis-tə\ *n* **1 :** a distant view through or along an avenue or opening **2 :** an extensive mental view over a series of years or events

**VISTA** *abbr* Volunteers in Service to America

**vi·su·al** \'vizh-(ə-w)əl\ *adj* **1 :** of, relating to, or used in sight ⟨∼ organs⟩ **2 :** perceived by vision ⟨a ∼ impression⟩ **3 :** attained or performed by sight ⟨∼ tests⟩ **4 :** done by sight only ⟨∼ navigation⟩ **5 :** VISIBLE **6 :** of or relating to instruction by means of sight ⟨∼ aids⟩ — **vi·su·al·ly** \-ē\ *adv*

**vi·su·al·ize** \'vizh-(ə-)wə-,līz\ *vb* **-ized; -iz·ing :** to make visible; *esp* **:** to form a mental image of — **vi·su·al·iza·tion** \,vizh-ə-(wə-)lə-'zā-shən\ *n* — **vi·su·al·iz·er** \'vizh-ə-(wə-),līzər\ *n*

**vi·ta** \'wē-,tä, 'vīt-ə\ *n, pl* **vi·tae** \'wē-,tī, 'vīt-ē\ [L, lit., life] **:** a brief autobiographical sketch

**vi·tal** \'vīt-ᵊl\ *adj* **1 :** of, relating to, or characteristic of life **2 :** concerned with or necessary to the maintenance of life **3 :** full of life and vigor **:** ANIMATED **4 :** FATAL, MORTAL ⟨∼ wound⟩ **5 :** FUNDAMENTAL, BASIC, INDISPENSABLE **6 :** dealing with births, deaths, marriages, health, and disease ⟨∼ statistics⟩ — **vi·tal·ly** \-ē\ *adv*

**vi·tal·i·ty** \vī-'tal-ət-ē\ *n, pl* **-ties 1 :** the peculiarity distinguishing the living from the nonliving; *also* **:** capacity to live **:** mental and physical vigor **2 :** enduring quality **3 :** ANIMATION, LIVELINESS

**vi·tal·ize** \'vīt-ᵊl-,īz\ *vb* **-ized; -iz·ing :** to impart life or vigor to **:** ANIMATE, ENERGIZE — **vi·tal·iza·tion** \,vīt-ᵊl-ə-'zā-shən\ *n* — **vi·tal·iz·er** \'vīt-ᵊl-,ī-zər\ *n*

**vi·tals** \'vīt-ᵊlz\ *n pl* **1 :** vital organs **2 :** essential parts

**vital signs** *n pl* **:** the pulse rate, respiratory rate, body temperature, and sometimes blood pressure of a person

**vi·ta·min** \'vīt-ə-mən\ *n* **:** any of various organic substances that are essential in tiny amounts to most animals and some plants and are mostly obtained from foods

**vitamin A** n **:** a vitamin (as from egg yolk or fish-liver oils) required for healthy epithelium and sight

**vitamin B** n **:** any of various vitamins important in metabolic reactions and as growth factors; esp **:** THIAMINE

**vitamin B₆** \-'bē-,siks\ n **:** a compound that is considered essential to vertebrate nutrition

**vitamin B₁₂** \-'bē-'twelv\ n **:** a complex cobalt-containing compound that occurs esp. in liver and is essential to normal blood formation, neural function, and growth; also **:** any of several compounds of similar action

**vitamin B₂** \-'bē-'tü\ n **:** RIBOFLAVIN

**vitamin C** n **:** a vitamin esp. from fruits and leafy vegetables that functions chiefly as a cellular enzyme and is used to prevent scurvy

**vitamin D** n **:** a vitamin esp. from fish-liver oils that is essential to normal bone formation

**vitamin E** n **:** any of several fat soluble vitamins that are essential in the nutrition of various vertebrates and are found esp. in leaves and in seed germ oils

**vitamin K** n [Dan koagulation coagulation] **:** either of two naturally occurring fat-soluble vitamins essential for the clotting of blood

**vi·ti·ate** \'vish-ē-,āt\ vb **-at·ed; -at·ing 1 :** CONTAMINATE, POLLUTE; also **:** DEBASE, PERVERT **2 :** to make legally without force **:** INVALIDATE — **vi·ti·a·tion** \,vish-ē-'ā-shən\ n — **vi·ti·a·tor** \'vish-ē-,āt-ər\ n

**vi·ti·cul·ture** \'vit-ə-,kəl-chər\ n **:** the growing of grapes — **vi·ti·cul·tur·al** \,vit-ə-'kəlch-(ə)-rəl\ adj — **vi·ti·cul·tur·ist** \-rəst\ n

**vit·re·ous** \'vi-trē-əs\ adj **1 :** of, relating to, or resembling glass **2 :** GLASSY ⟨~ rocks⟩ **3 :** of, relating to, or being the clear colorless transparent jelly (**vitreous humor**) behind the lens in the eyeball

**vit·ri·fy** \'vi-trə-,fī\ vb **-fied; -fy·ing :** to change into glass or a glassy substance by heat and fusion — **vit·ri·fi·ca·tion** \,vi-trə-fə-'kā-shən\ n

**vit·ri·ol** \'vi-trē-əl\ n **1 :** a sulfate of any of various metals (as copper, iron, or zinc) **2 :** SULFURIC ACID **3 :** something resembling vitriol in being caustic, corrosive, or biting — **vit·ri·ol·ic** \,vi-trē-'äl-ik\ adj

**vit·tles** \'vit-ᵊlz\ n pl **:** VICTUALS

**vi·tu·per·ate** \vī-'t(y)ü-pə-,rāt, və-\ vb **-at·ed; -at·ing :** to abuse in words **:** SCOLD **syn** revile, berate, rate, upbraid, rail — **vi·tu·per·a·tion** \-,t(y)ü-pə-'rā-shən\ n — **vi·tu·per·a·tive** \-'t(y)ü-p(ə-)rət-iv, -pə-,rāt-\ adj — **vi·tu·per·a·tive·ly** adv

**vi·va** \'vē-və, -,vä\ interj [It, long live, fr. vivere to live, fr. L] — used to express goodwill or approval

**vi·va·ce** \vē-'väch-ā\ adv or adj **:** in

a brisk spirited manner — used as a direction in music

**vi·va·cious** \və-'vā-shəs, vī-\ adj **:** lively in temper or conduct **:** ANIMATED, SPRIGHTLY — **vi·va·cious·ly** adv — **vi·va·cious·ness** n

**vi·vac·i·ty** \-'vas-ət-ē\ n **:** the quality or state of being vivacious

**vi·var·i·um** \vī-'var-ē-əm, -'ver-\ n, pl **-ia** \-ē-ə\ or **-i·ums :** an enclosure for keeping or raising and observing animals or plants indoors; esp **:** one for terrestrial animals

**vi·va vo·ce** \,vī-və-'vō-sē\ adj [ML, with the living voice] **:** expressed or conducted by word of mouth **:** ORAL ⟨viva voce examination⟩ ⟨viva voce voting⟩ — **viva voce** adv

**viv·id** \'viv-əd\ adj **1 :** having the appearance of vigorous life or freshness **:** LIVELY **2 :** BRILLIANT, INTENSE ⟨a ~ red⟩ **3 :** producing a strong impression on the senses **:** SHARP **4 :** calling forth lifelike mental images — **viv·id·ly** adv — **viv·id·ness** n

**viv·i·fy** \'viv-ə-,fī\ vb **-fied; -fy·ing 1 :** to endue with life **:** ANIMATE **2 :** to make vivid — **viv·i·fi·ca·tion** \,viv-ə-fə-'kā-shən\ n — **viv·i·fi·er** \'viv-ə-,fī(-ə)r\ n

**vi·vip·a·rous** \vī-'vip-(ə-)rəs, və-\ adj **:** producing living young from within the body rather than from eggs — **vi·vi·par·i·ty** \,vī-və-'par-ət-ē, ,viv-ə-\ n

**vivi·sec·tion** \,viv-ə-'sek-shən, 'viv-ə-,sek-shən\ n **:** the cutting of or operation on a living animal; also **:** animal experimentation

**vix·en** \'vik-sən\ n **1 :** a female fox **2 :** an ill-tempered scolding woman **syn** shrew, scold, termagant, virago

**viz** \'näm-lē, 'viz, və-'del-ə-,set\ abbr videlicet

**viz·ard** \'viz-ərd\ n **:** a mask for disguise or protection

**vi·zier** \və-'ziər\ n **:** a high executive officer of many Muslim countries and esp. of the former Turkish empire

**vi·zor** var of VISOR

**VL** Vulgar Latin

**VOA** Voice of America

**voc** abbr vocative

**vocab** abbr vocabulary

**vo·ca·ble** \'vō-kə-bəl\ n **:** TERM, NAME; esp **:** a word composed of various sounds or letters without regard to its meaning

**vo·cab·u·lary** \vō-'kab-yə-,ler-ē\ n, pl **-lar·ies 1 :** a list or collection of words usu. alphabetically arranged and defined or explained **:** LEXICON **2 :** a stock of words used in a language by a class or individual or in relation to a subject

**vocabulary entry** n **:** a word (as the noun **book**), hyphened or open compound (as the verb **cross-refer** or the noun **boric acid**), word element (as the affix **-an**), abbreviation (as **agt**), verbalized symbol (as **Na**), or term (as **master of ceremonies**) entered alphabetically in a dictionary for the purpose of definition or identification or expressly included as an inflected form (as the noun *mice* or the verb *saw*) or as a derived form (as the noun *godlessness* or the adverb *globally*) or related phrase (as *in spite of*) run on at its base word and usu. set in a type (as boldface) readily distinguishable from that of the lightface running text which defines, explains, or identifies the entry

¹**vo·cal** \'vō-kəl\ *adj* **1 :** uttered by the voice **:** ORAL  **2 :** relating to, composed or arranged for, or sung by the human voice ⟨~ music⟩  **3 :** of, relating to, or having the power of producing voice  **4 :** full of voices **:** RESOUNDING  **5 :** given to expressing one's feelings or opinions in speech **:** TALKATIVE; *also* **:** OUTSPOKEN  **syn** articulate, fluent, eloquent, voluble, glib

²**vocal** *n* **1 :** a vocal sound  **2 :** a vocal solo (as in a dance number)

**vocal cords** *n pl* **:** either of two pairs of elastic folds of mucous membrane that project into the cavity of the larynx and have free edges and that play a major role in the production of vocal sounds

**vo·cal·ic** \vō-'kal-ik\ *adj* **:** of, relating to, or functioning as a vowel

**vo·cal·ist** \'vō-kə-ləst\ *n* **:** SINGER

**vo·cal·ize** \-ˌlīz\ *vb* **-ized; -iz·ing** **1 :** to give vocal expression to **:** UTTER; *esp* **:** SING  **2 :** to make voiced rather than voiceless — **vo·cal·iz·er** *n*

**vo·ca·tion** \vō-'kā-shən\ *n* **1 :** a summons or strong inclination to a particular state or course of action ⟨religious ~⟩  **2 :** the work to which one feels he is called or specially fitted  **3 :** regular employment **:** OCCUPATION, PROFESSION — **vo·ca·tion·al** \-sh(ə-)nəl\ *adj*

**vo·ca·tion·al·ism** \-sh(ə-)nəl-ˌiz-əm\ *n* **:** emphasis on vocational training in education

**voc·a·tive** \'väk-ət-iv\ *adj* **:** of, relating to, or constituting a grammatical case marking the one addressed — **vocative** *n*

**vo·cif·er·ate** \vō-'sif-ə-ˌrāt\ *vb* **-at·ed; -at·ing** [L *vociferari*, fr. *voc-, vox* voice + *ferre* to bear] **:** to cry out loudly **:** CLAMOR, SHOUT — **vo·cif·er·a·tion** \-ˌsif-ə-'rā-shən\ *n*

**vo·cif·er·ous** \vō-'sif-(ə-)rəs\ *adj* **:** making or given to loud outcry **:** CLAMOROUS — **vo·cif·er·ous·ly** *adv* — **vo·cif·er·ous·ness** *n*

**vod·ka** \'väd-kə\ *n* [Russ, fr. *voda* water] **:** a colorless and unaged liquor of neutral spirits distilled from a mash (as of rye or wheat)

**vogue** \'vōg\ *n* [MF, action of rowing, course, fashion, fr. It *voga*, fr. *vogare* to row] **1 :** popular acceptance or favor **:** POPULARITY  **2 :** a period of popularity  **3 :** something or someone in fashion at a particular time  **syn** mode, fad, rage

**vogu·ish** \'vō-gish\ *adj* **1 :** FASHIONABLE, SMART  **2 :** suddenly or temporarily popular

¹**voice** \'vȯis\ *n* **1 :** sound produced through the mouth by vertebrates and esp. by human beings in speaking or shouting  **2 :** musical sound produced by the vocal cords **:** the power to produce such sound; *also* **:** one of the melodic parts in a vocal or instrumental composition  **3 :** the vocal organs as a means of tone production ⟨train the ~⟩  **4 :** sound produced by vibration of the vocal cords as heard in vowels and some consonants  **5 :** the faculty of speech  **6 :** a sound suggesting vocal utterance ⟨the ~ of the sea⟩  **7 :** an instrument or medium of expression  **8 :** a choice, opinion, or wish openly expressed; *also* **:** right of expression  **9 :** distinction of form of a verb to indicate the relation of the subject to the action expressed by the verb

²**voice** *vb* **voiced; voic·ing** **1 :** to give voice or expression to **:** UTTER; *also* **:** ANNOUNCE  **2 :** to regulate the tone of ⟨~ the pipes of an organ⟩  **syn** express, vent, air, ventilate

**voice box** *n* **:** LARYNX

**voiced** \'vȯist\ *adj* **1 :** furnished with a voice ⟨soft-*voiced*⟩  **2 :** expressed by the voice  **3 :** uttered with voice — **voiced·ness** \'vȯis(t)-nəs, 'vȯi-səd-nəs\ *n*

**voice·less** \'vȯis-ləs\ *adj* **1 :** having no voice  **2 :** not pronounced with voice — **voice·less·ly** *adv* — **voice·less·ness** *n*

**voice·print** \'vȯis-ˌprint\ *n* **:** an individually distinctive pattern of voice characteristics that is spectrographically produced

¹**void** \'vȯid\ *adj* **1 :** containing nothing **:** EMPTY  **2 :** UNOCCUPIED, VACANT  **3 :** LACKING, DEVOID ⟨proposals ~ of sense⟩  **4 :** VAIN, USELESS  **5 :** of no legal force or effect **:** NULL

²**void** *n* **1 :** empty space **:** EMPTINESS, VACUUM  **2 :** a feeling of want or hollowness

³**void** *vb* **1 :** to make or leave empty; *also* **:** VACATE, LEAVE  **2 :** DISCHARGE, EMIT ⟨~ urine⟩  **3 :** to render void **:** ANNUL, NULLIFY — **void·able** *adj* — **void·er** *n*

**voile** \'vȯil\ *n* **:** a sheer fabric from various fibers used for women's clothing and curtains

**vol** *abbr* **1** volume  **2** volunteer

**vol·a·tile** \'väl-ət-ºl\ *adj* **1 :** readily becoming a vapor at a relatively low temperature ⟨a ~ liquid⟩  **2 :** LIGHTHEARTED  **3 :** easily erupting into violent action  **4 :** CHANGEABLE — **vol·a·til·i·ty** \ˌväl-ə-'til-ət-ē\ *n* — **vol·a·til·ize** \'väl-ət-ºl-ˌīz\ *vb*

¹**vol·can·ic** \väl-'kan-ik\ *adj* **1 :** of or relating to a volcano  **2 :** explosively violent **:** VOLATILE ⟨~ emotions⟩

²**volcanic** *n* **:** a volcanic rock

**volcanic glass** *n* **:** natural glass produced by cooling of molten lava

**vol·ca·nism** \'väl-kə-ˌniz-əm\ *n* **:** volcanic power or action

**vol·ca·no** \väl-'kā-nō\ *n, pl* **-noes** *or* **-nos** [It *vulcano*, fr. L *Volcanus, Vulcanus* Roman god of fire and metalworking] **:** an opening in the earth's crust from which molten rock and steam issue; *also* **:** a hill or mountain composed of the ejected material

**vol·ca·nol·o·gy** \,väl-kə-'näl-ə-jē\ n
;· a branch of science that deals with
volcanic phenomena — **vol·ca·no·
log·i·cal** \-kən-ºl-'äj-i-kəl\ adj —
**vol·ca·nol·o·gist** \-kə-'näl-ə-jəst\ n

**vole** \'vōl\ n : any of various mouselike or ratlike rodents

**vo·li·tion** \vō-'lish-ən\ n 1 : the act
or the power of making a choice or decision : WILL 2 : a choice or decision
made — **vo·li·tion·al** \-'lish-(ə-)nəl\
adj

**¹vol·ley** \'väl-ē\ n, pl **volleys** 1 : a
flight of missiles (as arrows or bullets)
2 : simultaneous discharge of a number of missile weapons 3 : a pouring
forth of many things at the same instant ⟨a ~ of oaths⟩ 4 : the act of
volleying

**²volley** vb **vol·leyed; vol·ley·ing**
1 : to discharge or become discharged
in or as if in a volley 2 : to hit an
object of play in the air before it
touches the ground

**vol·ley·ball** \-,bȯl\ n : a game played
by volleying an inflated ball over a net

**vol·plane** \'väl-,plān\ vb **vol·planed;
vol·plan·ing** [F vol plané gliding
flight] : to glide in an airplane

**volt** \'vōlt\ n : the unit of electromotive
force equal to a force that when steadily
applied to a conductor whose resistance
is one ohm will produce a current of
one ampere

**volt·age** \'vōl-tij\ n : electromotive
force measured in volts

**vol·ta·ic** \väl-'tā-ik, vōl-\ adj : of, relating to, or producing direct electric
current by chemical action ⟨~ current⟩

**volte-face** \,vȯlt-(ə-)'fäs\ n : a facing about esp. in policy

**volt·me·ter** \'vōlt-,mēt-ər\ n : an instrument for measuring in volts the differences of potential between different
points of an electrical circuit

**vol·u·ble** \'väl-yə-bəl\ adj : fluent and
smooth in speech : GLIB **syn** eloquent,
vocal, articulate, garrulous, loquacious,
talkative — **vol·u·bil·i·ty** \,väl-yə-
'bil-ət-ē\ n — **vol·u·bly** \'väl-yə-
blē\ adv

**vol·ume** \'väl-yəm\ n [ME, fr. MF, fr.
L volumen roll, scroll, fr. volvere to
roll] 1 : a series of printed sheets
bound typically in book form; also : an
arbitrary number of issues of a periodical 2 : sufficient matter to fill a
book ⟨his glance spoke ~s⟩ 3 : space
occupied as measured by cubic units
⟨the ~ of a cylinder⟩ 4 : AMOUNT
⟨increasing ~ of business⟩; also : MASS,
BULK 5 : the degree of loudness or the
intensity of a sound **syn** magnitude,
size, extent, dimensions, area

**vol·u·met·ric** \,väl-yu-'met-rik\ adj
: of or relating to the measurement of
volume — **vol·u·met·ri·cal·ly** \-ri-
k(ə-)lē\ adv

**vo·lu·mi·nous** \və-'lü-mə-nəs\ adj
1 : consisting of many folds or windings 2 : BULKY, LARGE, SWELLING
3 : filling or sufficient to fill a large
volume or several volumes — **vo·lu·
mi·nos·i·ty** \-,lü-mə-'näs-ət-ē\ n —

**vo·lu·mi·nous·ly** \-'lü-mə-nəs-lē\
adv — **vo·lu·mi·nous·ness** n

**¹vol·un·tary** \'väl-ən-,ter-ē\ adj 1
: done, made, or given freely and without compulsion ⟨a ~ sacrifice⟩ 2 : not
accidental : INTENTIONAL ⟨a ~ slight⟩
3 : of, relating to, or controlled by the
will ⟨~ muscles⟩ 4 : having power of
free choice ⟨man is a ~ agent⟩ 5 : supported by gifts rather than by the state
⟨~ churches⟩ **syn** deliberate, willful,
willing — **vol·un·tari·ly** \,väl-ən-
'ter-ə-lē\ adv

**²voluntary** n, pl **-tar·ies** : an organ solo
played in a religious service

**¹vol·un·teer** \,väl-ən-'tiər\ n 1 : a
person who of his own free will offers
himself for a service or duty 2 : a
plant growing spontaneously esp. from
seeds lost from a previous crop

**²volunteer** vb 1 : to offer or give
voluntarily 2 : to offer oneself as a
volunteer

**vo·lup·tu·ary** \və-'ləp-chə-,wer-ē\ n,
pl **-ar·ies** : one whose chief interest in
life is the indulgence of sensual appetites

**vo·lup·tu·ous** \-chə-(w)əs\ adj 1 : giving sensual gratification ⟨~ furnish-
ings⟩ 2 : given to or spent in enjoyment of luxury or pleasure **syn**
luxurious, epicurean, sensuous, sensual
— **vo·lup·tu·ous·ly** adv — **vo·lup·
tu·ous·ness** n

**vo·lute** \və-'lüt\ n : a spiral or scroll-
shaped decoration

**¹vom·it** \'väm-ət\ n : an act or instance
of discharging the stomach contents
through the mouth; also : the matter
discharged

**²vomit** vb 1 : to discharge the stomach
contents as vomit 2 : to belch forth
: GUSH

**voo·doo** \'vüd-ü\ n, pl **voodoos**
1 : VOODOOISM 2 : one who practices
voodooism 3 : a charm or a fetish
used in voodooism — **voodoo** adj

**voo·doo·ism** \-,iz-əm\ n 1 : a religion
derived from African ancestor worship
and consisting largely of sorcery 2
: the practice of sorcery

**vo·ra·cious** \vȯ-'rā-shəs, və-\ adj
1 : greedy in eating : RAVENOUS 2 : excessively eager : INSATIABLE ⟨a ~ reader⟩
**syn** gluttonous, ravening, rapacious —
**vo·ra·cious·ly** adv — **vo·ra·cious·
ness** n — **vo·rac·i·ty** \-'ras-ət-ē\ n

**vor·tex** \'vȯr-,teks\ n, pl **vor·ti·ces**
\'vȯrt-ə-,sēz\ also **vor·tex·es** \'vȯr-
,tek-səz\ : a mass of liquid in whirling
motion forming in the center of the
mass a depression or cavity toward
which things are drawn : WHIRLPOOL —
**vor·ti·cal** \'vȯrt-i-kəl\ adj

**vo·ta·ry** \'vōt-ə-rē\ n, pl **-ries** 1 : EN-
THUSIAST, DEVOTEE; also : a devoted
adherent or admirer 2 : a devout or
zealous worshiper

**¹vote** \'vōt\ n [ME, fr. L votum vow,
wish, fr. vovēre to vow] 1 : a choice or
opinion of a person or body of persons
expressed usu. by a ballot, spoken word,
or raised hand; also : the ballot, word,
or gesture used to express a choice or
opinion 2 : the decision reached by

voting **3 :** the right of suffrage **4 :** a group of voters with some common characteristics ⟨the big city ~⟩ — **vote·less** adj

²vote vb vot·ed; vot·ing **1 :** to cast a vote **2 :** to choose, endorse, authorize, or defeat by vote **3 :** to express an opinion **4 :** to adjudge by general agreement **:** DECLARE **5 :** to offer as a suggestion **:** PROPOSE **6 :** to cause to vote esp. in a given way — **vot·er** n

vo·tive \'vōt-iv\ adj **:** offered or performed in fulfillment of a vow or in petition, gratitude, or devotion

vou abbr voucher

vouch \'vaûch\ vb **1 :** PROVE, SUBSTANTIATE **2 :** to verify by examining documentary evidence **3 :** to give a guarantee **4 :** to supply supporting evidence or testimony; also **:** to give personal assurance

vouch·er \'vaû-chər\ n **1 :** an act of vouching **2 :** one that vouches for another **3 :** a documentary record of a business transaction **4 :** a written affidavit or authorization

vouch·safe \vaûch-'sāf\ vb vouch·safed; vouch·saf·ing **1 :** to grant or give often in a condescending manner **2 :** to grant as a privilege or as a special favor — **vouch·safe·ment** n

¹vow \'vaû\ n **:** a solemn promise or assertion; esp **:** one by which a person binds himself to an act, service, or condition

²vow vb **1 :** to make a vow or as a vow **2 :** to bind or commit by a vow — **vow·er** \'vaû(-ə)r\ n

vow·el \'vaû(-ə)l\ n **1 :** a speech sound produced without obstruction or friction in the mouth **2 :** a letter representing such a sound

vox po·pu·li \'väks-'päp-yə-ˌlī\ n [L, voice of the people] **:** popular sentiment

¹voy·age \'vói-ij\ n [ME, fr. OF voiage, fr. LL viaticum, fr. L, traveling money, fr. neut. of viaticus of a journey, fr. via way] **1 :** JOURNEY **2 :** a journey by water from one place or country to another **3 :** a journey through air or space

²voyage vb voy·aged; voy·ag·ing **:** to take or make a voyage — **voy·ag·er** n

voya·geur \ˌvói-ə-'zhər, ˌvwä-yä-\ n **:** a boatman and trapper in the Northwest; esp **:** one employed by a fur company

voy·eur \vwä-'yər, vói-'ər\ n **:** one who habitually seeks sexual stimulation by visual means — **voy·eur·ism** \-ˌiz-əm\ n

VP abbr **1** verb phrase **2** vice-president

VS abbr **1** verse **2** versus **3** [L vide supra] see above

vss abbr **1** verses **2** versions

---

V/STOL abbr vertical short takeoff and landing

vt abbr verb transitive

Vt or VT abbr Vermont

VTOL abbr vertical takeoff and landing

vul·ca·nism \'vəl-kə-ˌniz-əm\ n **:** VOLCANISM

vul·ca·nize \'vəl-kə-ˌnīz\ vb -nized; -niz·ing **:** to subject to or undergo a process of treating rubber or rubberlike material chemically to give useful properties (as elasticity and strength) — **vul·ca·ni·za·tion** \ˌvəl-kə-nə-'zā-shən\ n — **vul·ca·niz·er** \'vəl-kə-ˌnī-zər\ n

Vulg abbr Vulgate

vul·gar \'vəl-gər\ adj [ME, fr. L vulgaris of the mob, vulgar, fr. vulgus mob, common people] **1 :** of or relating to the common people **:** GENERAL, COMMON **2 :** VERNACULAR ⟨the ~ tongue⟩ **3 :** lacking cultivation or refinement **:** BOORISH; also **:** offensive to good taste or refined feelings syn common, ordinary, familiar, popular, gross, obscene, ribald — **vul·gar·ly** adv

vul·gar·i·an \ˌvəl-'gar-ē-ən\ n **:** a vulgar person

vul·gar·ism \'vəl-gə-ˌriz-əm\ n **1 :** a word or expression originated or used chiefly by illiterate persons **2 :** a coarse expression **:** OBSCENITY **3 :** VULGARITY

vul·gar·i·ty \ˌvəl-'gar-ət-ē\ n, pl -ties **1 :** the quality or state of being vulgar **2 :** an instance of coarseness of manners or language

vul·gar·ize \'vəl-gə-ˌrīz\ vb -ized; -iz·ing **:** to make vulgar — **vul·gar·iza·tion** \ˌvəl-gə-rə-'zā-shən\ n — **vul·gar·iz·er** \'vəl-gə-ˌrī-zər\ n

Vul·gate \'vəl-ˌgāt\ n [ML vulgata, fr. LL vulgata editio edition in general circulation] **:** a Latin version of the Bible used by the Roman Catholic Church

vul·ner·a·ble \'vəln-(ə-)rə-bəl\ adj **1 :** capable of being wounded **:** susceptible to wounds **2 :** open to attack **3 :** liable to increased penalties in contract bridge — **vul·ner·a·bil·i·ty** \ˌvəln-(ə-)rə-'bil-ət-ē\ n — **vul·ner·a·bly** \'vəln-(ə-)rə-blē\ adv

vul·pine \'vəl-ˌpīn\ adj **:** of, relating to, or resembling a fox esp. in cunning

vul·ture \'vəl-chər\ n **1 :** any of various large birds related to hawks and eagles but having weaker claws and the head usu. naked and living chiefly on carrion **2 :** a rapacious person

vul·va \'vəl-və\ n, pl vul·vae \-ˌvē, -ˌvī\ **:** the external genital parts of the female or their opening — **vul·val** \'vəl-vəl\ or **vul·var** \-vər, -ˌvär\ adj

vv abbr **1** verses **2** vice versa

vying pres part of VIE

---

¹w \'dəb-əl-(ˌ)yü\ n, often cap **:** the 23d letter of the English alphabet

²w abbr, often cap **1** water **2** watt **3** week **4** weight **5** Welsh **6** west **7** western **8** wide **9** width **10** wife **11** with

W symbol tungsten

WA abbr **1** Washington **2** Western Australia

wab·ble \'wäb-əl\ var of WOBBLE

Wac \'wak\ n [Women's Army Corps] **:** a member of the Women's Army Corps

**wacky** \'wak-ē\ *adj* **wacki·er; -est**
: ECCENTRIC, CRAZY

**¹wad** \'wäd\ *n* **1** : a little mass, bundle, or tuft ⟨~*s* of clay⟩ **2** : a soft mass of usu. light fibrous material **3** : a pliable plug (as of felt) used to retain a powder charge (as in a cartridge) **4** : a roll of paper money **5** : a considerable amount (as of money)

**²wad** *vb* **wad·ded; wad·ding 1** : to form into a wad **2** : to push a wad into ⟨~ a gun⟩ **3** : to hold in by a wad ⟨~ a bullet in a gun⟩ **4** : to stuff or line with a wad : PAD

**wad·able** *or* **wade·able** \'wād-ə-bəl\ *adj* : capable of being waded ⟨a ~ stream⟩

**wad·ding** \'wäd-iŋ\ *n* **1** : WADS; *also* : material for making wads **2** : a soft mass or sheet of short loose fibers used for stuffing or padding

**wad·dle** \'wäd-²l\ *vb* **wad·dled; wad·dling** \'wäd-(²-)liŋ\ : to walk with short steps swaying from side to side like a duck — **waddle** *n*

**wade** \'wād\ *vb* **wad·ed; wad·ing 1** : to step in or through a medium (as water) more resistant than air **2** : to move or go with difficulty or effort and often with determined vigor ⟨~ through a dull book⟩ — **wade** *n*

**wad·er** \'wād-ər\ *n* **1** : one that wades **2** : WADING BIRD **3** *pl* : high waterproof rubber boots or trousers for wading

**wa·di** \'wäd-ē\ *n* : a watercourse dry except in the rainy season esp. in the Near East and northern Africa

**wading bird** *n* : a long-legged bird (as a sandpiper or heron) that wades in water in search of food

**Waf** \'waf\ *n* [Women in the Air Force] : a member of the women's component of the Air Force

**wa·fer** \'wā-fər\ *n* **1** : a thin crisp cake or cracker **2** : a thin round piece of unleavened bread used in the Eucharist **3** : something (as a piece of candy or an adhesive seal) that resembles a wafer

**waf·fle** \'wäf-əl\ *n* : a soft but crisped cake of pancake batter cooked in a special hinged metal utensil (**waffle iron**)

**¹waft** \'wäft, 'waft\ *vb* : to cause to move or go lightly by or as if by the impulse of wind or waves

**²waft** *n* **1** : a slight breeze : PUFF **2** : the act of waving

**¹wag** \'wag\ *vb* **wagged; wag·ging 1** : to sway or swing shortly from side to side or to and fro ⟨the dog *wagged* his tail⟩ **2** : to move in chatter or gossip ⟨scandal caused tongues to ~⟩

**²wag** *n* **1** : WIT, JOKER **2** : an act of wagging : a wagging movement

**¹wage** \'wāj\ *vb* **waged; wag·ing 1** : to engage in : carry on ⟨~ a war⟩ **2** : to be in process of being waged

**²wage** *n* **1** : payment for labor or services usu. according to contract **2** *pl* : RECOMPENSE, REWARD

**¹wa·ger** \'wā-jər\ *n* **1** : BET, STAKE **2** : an act of betting : GAMBLE

**²wager** *vb* : BET — **wa·ger·er** *n*

**wag·ery** \'wag-ə-rē\ *n, pl* **-ger·ies**

**1** : mischievous merriment : PLEASANTRY **2** : JEST, TRICK

**wag·gish** \'wag-ish\ *adj* **1** : resembling or characteristic of a wag : MISCHIEVOUS, ROGUISH, FROLICSOME **2** : SPORTIVE, HUMOROUS

**wag·gle** \'wag-əl\ *vb* **wag·gled; wag·gling** \-(ə-)liŋ\ : to move backward and forward or from side to side : WAG — **waggle** *n*

**wag·on** \'wag-ən\ *n* **1** : a 4-wheeled vehicle; *esp* : one drawn by animals and used for freight or merchandise **2** : a child's 4-wheeled cart **3** : STATION WAGON **4** : PATROL WAGON

**wag·on·er** \'wag-ə-nər\ *n* : the driver of a wagon

**wag·on·ette** \,wag-ə-'net\ *n* : a light wagon with two facing seats along the sides behind a cross seat in front

**wa·gon-lit** \vä-gōⁿ-lē\ *n, pl* **wagons-lits** *or* **wagon-lits** \-gōⁿ-lē(z)\ [F, fr. *wagon* railroad car + *lit* bed] : a railroad sleeping car

**wagon train** *n* : a group of wagons traveling overland

**wag·tail** \'wag-,tāl\ *n* : any of various slender-bodied mostly Old World birds with a long tail that jerks up and down

**wa·hi·ne** \wä-'hē-nä\ *n* **1** : a Polynesian woman **2** : a girl surfer

**wa·hoo** \'wä-,hü\ *n, pl* **wahoos** : any of several American trees or shrubs

**waif** \'wāf\ *n* **1** : something found without an owner and esp. by chance **2** : a stray person or animal; *esp* : a homeless child

**wail** \'wāl\ *vb* **1** : LAMENT, WEEP **2** : to make a sound suggestive of a mournful cry **3** : COMPLAIN — **wail** *n*

**wail·ful** \-fəl\ *adj* : SORROWFUL, MOURNFUL — **wail·ful·ly** \-ē\ *adv*

**wain** \'wān\ *n* : a usu. large heavy farm wagon

**wain·scot** \'wān-skət, -,skōt, -,skät\ *n* **1** : a usu. paneled wooden lining of an interior wall of a room **2** : the lower part of an interior wall when finished differently from the rest — **wainscot** *vb*

**wain·scot·ing** *or* **wain·scot·ting** \-,skōt-iŋ, -,skät-, -skət-\ *n* : material for a wainscot; *also* : WAINSCOT

**wain·wright** \'wān-,rīt\ *n* : a builder and repairer of wagons

**waist** \'wāst\ *n* **1** : the narrowed part of the body between the chest and hips **2** : a part resembling the human waist esp. in narrowness or central position ⟨the ~ of a ship⟩ **3** : a garment (as a blouse or bodice) for the upper part of the body **4** : a child's undergarment to which other garments may be buttoned

**waist·band** \'wās(t)-,band\ *n* : a band (as on trousers or a skirt) that fits around the waist

**waist·coat** \'wes-kət, 'wās(t)-,kōt\ *n, chiefly Brit* : VEST

**waist·line** \'wāst-,līn\ *n* **1** : a line thought of as surrounding the waist at its narrowest part; *also* : the length of this **2** : the line at which the waist and skirt of a dress meet

**¹wait** \'wāt\ *vb* **1** : to remain inactive

in readiness or expectation : AWAIT ⟨~ for orders⟩ **2** : POSTPONE, DELAY ⟨~ dinner for late guests⟩ **3** : to act as attendant or servant ⟨~ on customers⟩ **4** : to attend as a waiter : SERVE ⟨~ tables⟩ ⟨~ at a banquet⟩ **5** : to be ready

²**wait** n **1** : a position of concealment usu. with intent to attack or surprise ⟨lie in ~⟩ **2** : an act or period of waiting

**wait·er** \'wāt-ər\ n **1** : one that waits upon another; esp : a man who waits on table **2** : TRAY

**waiting game** n : a strategy in which one or more participants withhold action temporarily in the hope of having a favorable opportunity for more effective action later

**waiting room** n : a room (as at a railroad station or in the office suite of a doctor) for the use of persons waiting

**wait·ress** \'wā-trəs\ n : a girl or woman who waits on table

**waive** \'wāv\ vb **waived; waiv·ing** [ME weiven, fr. OF weyver, fr. waif lost, unclaimed] **1** : to give up claim to ⟨waived his right to a trial⟩ **2** : POSTPONE

**waiv·er** \'wā-vər\ n : the act of waiving right, claim, or privilege; also : a document containing a declaration of such an act

¹**wake** \'wāk\ vb **waked** \'wākt\ or **woke** \'wōk\; **waked** or **wo·ken** \'wō-kən\ or **woke; wak·ing 1** : to be or remain awake; esp : to keep watch (as over a corpse) **2** : AWAKE, AWAKEN ⟨the baby waked up early⟩ ⟨the thunder waked him up⟩

²**wake** n **1** : the state of being awake **2** : a watch held over the body of a dead person prior to burial

³**wake** n : the track left by a ship in the water; also : a track left behind

**wake·ful** \'wāk-fəl\ adj : not sleeping or able to sleep : SLEEPLESS, ALERT — **wake·ful·ness** n

**wak·en** \'wā-kən\ vb **wak·ened; wak·en·ing** \'wāk-(ə-)niŋ\ : WAKE

**wake-rob·in** \'wāk-ˌräb-ən\ n : TRILLIUM

¹**wale** \'wāl\ n **1** : a streak or ridge made on the skin usu. by a rod or whip : WHEAL **2** : a ridge esp. on cloth; also : TEXTURE

²**wale** vb **waled; wal·ing** : to mark with wales or stripes

¹**walk** \'wok\ vb [partly fr. ME walken, fr. OE wealcan to roll, toss and partly fr. ME walkien, fr. OE wealcian to roll up, muffle up] **1** : to move or cause to move along on foot usu. at a natural unhurried gait ⟨~ to town⟩ ⟨~ a horse⟩ **2** : to pass over, through, or along by walking ⟨~ the streets⟩ **3** : to perform or accomplish by walking ⟨~ guard⟩ **4** : to follow a course of action or way of life ⟨~ humbly in the sight of God⟩ **5** : to receive a base on balls; also : to give a base on balls to — **walk·er** n

²**walk** n **1** : a going on foot ⟨go for a ~⟩ **2** : a place, path, or course for walking **3** : distance to be walked ⟨a 10-minute

~ from here⟩ **4** : manner of living : CONDUCT, BEHAVIOR; also : social or economic status ⟨various ~s of life⟩ **5** : manner of walking : GAIT; esp : a slow 4-beat gait of a horse **6** : BASE ON BALLS

**walk·away** \'wok-ə-ˌwā\ n : an easily won contest

**walk·ie-talk·ie** \'wo-kē-'to-kē\ n : a small portable radio transmitting and receiving set

¹**walk-in** \'wok-ˌin\ adj : large enough to be walked into ⟨a ~ refrigerator⟩

²**walk-in** \'wok-ˌin\ n **1** : an easy election victory **2** : one that walks in

**walking papers** n pl : DISMISSAL, DISCHARGE

**walking stick** n **1** : a stick used in walking **2** : a stick insect common in parts of the U.S.

**walk-on** \'wok-ˌon, -ˌän\ n : a small usu. nonspeaking part in a dramatic production

**walk·out** \-ˌaut\ n **1** : a labor strike **2** : the action of leaving a meeting or organization as an expression of disapproval

**walk·over** \-ˌō-vər\ n : a one-sided contest : an easy victory

¹**walk-up** \'wok-ˌəp\ adj **1** : located above the ground floor in a building with no elevator ⟨a ~ apartment⟩ **2** : consisting of several stories and having no elevator ⟨~ tenement⟩ **3** : designed to allow pedestrians to be served without entering a building ⟨the ~ window of a bank⟩

²**walk-up** \'wok-ˌəp\ n : a building or apartment house without an elevator

**walk·way** \-ˌwā\ n : a passage for walking

¹**wall** \'wol\ n [ME, fr. OE weall, fr. L vallum rampart, fr. vallus stake, palisade] **1** : a structure (as of stone or brick) intended for defense or security or for enclosing something **2** : one of the upright enclosing parts of a building or room **3** : something like a wall in appearance or function ⟨a tariff ~⟩ **4** : the inside surface of a cavity or vessel ⟨the ~ of a boiler⟩ — **walled** \'wold\ adj

²**wall** vb **1** : to provide, separate, or surround with or as if with a wall ⟨~ in a garden⟩ **2** : to close (an opening) with or as if with a wall ⟨~ up a door⟩

**wal·la·by** \'wäl-ə-bē\ n, pl **wallabies** also **wallaby** : any of various small or medium-sized kangaroos

**wall·board** \'wol-ˌbōrd\ n : a structural material (as of wood pulp or plaster) made in large sheets and used for sheathing interior walls and ceilings

**wal·let** \'wäl-ət\ n **1** : a bag or sack for carrying things on a journey **2** : a pocketbook with compartments (as for cards and photographs) : BILLFOLD

**wall·eye** \'wol-ˌī\ n **1** : an eye with whitish iris or an opaque white cornea **2** : an eye that turns outward **3** : a large No. American food and sport fish related to the perches — **wall·eyed** \-ˌīd\ adj

**wall·flow·er** \'wol-ˌflaù-(-ə)r\ n **1** : any

of several Old World plants related to the mustards; *esp* : one widely grown for its showy fragrant flowers  **2** : a person who usu. from shyness or unpopularity remains on the sidelines of a social activity

**Wal·loon** \wä-'lün\ *n* : a member of a chiefly Celtic people of southern and southeastern Belgium and adjacent parts of France — **Walloon** *adj*

¹**wal·lop** \'wäl-əp\ *n* [ME, gallop, fr. OF *walop*, fr. *waloper* to gallop] **1** : a powerful blow or impact  **2** : the ability to hit hard  **3** : emotional or psychological force : IMPACT

²**wallop** *vb* **1** : to beat soundly : TROUNCE  **2** : to hit hard : SOCK

**wal·lop·ing** \'wäl-ə-piŋ\ *adj* **1** : LARGE, WHOPPING  **2** : exceptionally fine or impressive

¹**wal·low** \'wäl-ō\ *vb* **1** : to roll oneself about in or as if in deep mud : FLOUNDER ⟨hogs ~*ing* in the mire⟩  **2** : to live or be filled with excessive pleasure in some condition ⟨~ in luxury⟩

²**wallow** *n* : a muddy or dust-filled area where animals wallow

**wall·pa·per** \'wȯl-,pā-pər\ *n* : decorative paper for the walls of a room — **wallpaper** *vb*

**wal·nut** \'wȯl-(,)nət\ *n* [ME *walnot*, fr. OE *wealhhnutu*, lit., foreign nut, fr. *Wealh* Welshman, foreigner + *hnutu* nut] **1** : an edible nut with a furrowed usu. rough shell and an adherent husk; *also* : any of several trees related to the hickories that produce such nuts  **2** : the usu. reddish to dark brown wood of a walnut used esp. in cabinetwork and veneers  **3** : a hickory nut or tree

**wal·rus** \'wȯl-rəs, 'wäl-\ *n, pl* **walrus** *or* **wal·rus·es** : either of two large mammals of northern seas related to the seals and hunted esp. for hides, the ivory tusks of the male, and oil

¹**waltz** \'wȯlts\ *n* [G *walzer*, fr. *walzen* to roll, dance, fr. Old High German *walzan* to turn, roll] **1** : a gliding dance done to music having three beats to the measure  **2** : music for or suitable for waltzing

²**waltz** *vb* **1** : to dance a waltz  **2** : to move or advance easily, successfully, or conspicuously ⟨he ~*ed* through customs⟩

**wam·ble** \'wäm-bəl\ *vb* **wam·bled**; **wam·bling** \-b(ə-)liŋ\ **1** : to feel or become nauseated  **2** : to progress unsteadily or with a lurching shambling gait

**wam·pum** \'wäm-pəm\ *n* [short for *wampumpeag*, fr. Narraganset (a North American Indian language) *wampompeag*, fr. *wampan* white + *api* string + *-ag* pl. suffix] **1** : beads made of shells strung in strands, belts, or sashes used by No. American Indians as money and ornaments  **2** *slang* : MONEY

**wan** \'wän\ *adj* **wan·ner**; **wan·nest** **1** : SICKLY, PALLID; *also* : FEEBLE  **2** : DIM, FAINT  **3** : LANGUID ⟨a ~ smile⟩ — **wan·ly** *adv* — **wan·ness** \'wän-nəs\ *n*

**wand** \'wänd\ *n* **1** : a slender staff carried in a procession  **2** : the staff of a fairy, diviner, or magician

**wan·der** \'wän-dər\ *vb* **wan·dered**; **wan·der·ing** \-d(ə-)riŋ\ **1** : to move about aimlessly or without a fixed course or goal : RAMBLE  **2** : STRAY  **3** : to go astray in conduct or thought; *esp* : to become delirious — **wan·der·er** *n*

**wan·der·ing Jew** *n* : any of several trailing or creeping plants some of which are often planted in hanging baskets

**wan·der·lust** \'wän-dər-,ləst\ *n* : strong longing for or impulse toward wandering

¹**wane** \'wān\ *vb* **waned**; **wan·ing** **1** : to grow gradually smaller or less after being at the full ⟨the moon ~*s*⟩ ⟨his strength *waned*⟩  **2** : to lose power, prosperity, or influence  **3** : to draw near an end ⟨summer ~*s* away⟩

²**wane** *n* : a waning (as in size or power); *also* : a period in which something is waning

**wan·gle** \'waŋ-gəl\ *vb* **wan·gled**; **wan·gling** \-g(ə-)liŋ\ **1** : to obtain by sly or roundabout means; *also* : to use trickery or questionable means to achieve an end  **2** : MANIPULATE; *also* : FINAGLE

¹**want** \'wȯnt\ *vb* **1** : to fail to possess : LACK ⟨they ~ the necessities of life⟩  **2** : to fall short by ⟨it ~*s* three minutes to six⟩  **3** : to feel or suffer the need of  **4** : NEED, REQUIRE ⟨the house ~*s* painting⟩  **5** : to desire earnestly : WISH

²**want** *n* **1** : a lack of a required or usual amount : SHORTAGE  **2** : dire need : DESTITUTION  **3** : something wanted : DESIRE  **4** : FAULT

¹**want·ing** \-iŋ\ *adj* **1** : not present or in evidence : ABSENT  **2** : falling below standards or expectations  **3** : lacking in ability or capacity : DEFICIENT ⟨~ in common sense⟩

²**wanting** *prep* **1** : WITHOUT ⟨a book ~ a cover⟩  **2** : LESS, MINUS ⟨a month ~ two days⟩

¹**wan·ton** \'wȯnt-ᵊn\ *adj* [ME, undisciplined, fr. *wan-* deficient, wrong, (fr. OE, fr. *wan* deficient) + *towen*, pp. of *teen* to draw, train, discipline, fr. OE *tēon*] **1** : excessively merry : FROLICSOME ⟨~ holidays⟩ ⟨a ~ breeze⟩  **2** : UNCHASTE, LEWD, LUSTFUL; *also* : SENSUAL  **3** : having no regard for justice or for other persons' feelings, rights, or safety : MERCILESS, INHUMANE ⟨~ cruelty⟩  **4** : having no just cause ⟨a ~ attack⟩ — **wan·ton·ly** *adv* — **wan·ton·ness** *n*

²**wanton** *n* : a wanton individual; *esp* : a lewd or immoral person

³**wanton** *vb* **1** : to be wanton : act wantonly  **2** : to pass or waste wantonly

**wa·pi·ti** \'wäp-ət-ē\ *n, pl* **wapiti** *or* **wapitis** : the American elk

¹**war** \'wȯr\ *n* **1** : a state or period of usu. open and declared armed fighting between states or nations  **2** : the art

or science of warfare **3 :** a state of hostility, conflict, or antagonism **4 :** a struggle between opposing forces or for a particular end ⟨~ against disease⟩

**²war** *vb* **warred; war·ring :** to engage in warfare **:** be in conflict

**war³** *abbr* warrant

**¹war·ble** \'wȯr-bəl\ *n* **1 :** a melodious succession of low pleasing sounds **2 :** a musical trill

**²warble** *vb* **war·bled; war·bling** \-b(ə-)liŋ\ **1 :** to sing or utter in a trilling manner or with variations **2 :** to express by or as if by warbling

**³warble** *n* **:** a swelling under the hide esp. of the back of cattle, horses, and wild mammals caused by the maggot of a fly (**warble fly**); *also* **:** the maggot

**war·bler** \'wȯr-blər\ *n* **1 :** SONGSTER **2 :** any of various small slender-billed Old World singing birds related to the thrushes and noted for their song **3 :** any of various small bright-colored American insect-eating birds with a usu. weak and unmusical song

**war·bon·net** \'wȯr-ˌbän-ət\ *n* **:** an Indian ceremonial headdress with a feathered extension down the back

**war crime** *n* **:** a crime (as genocide or maltreatment of prisoners) committed during or in connection with war — usu. used in pl. — **war criminal** *n*

**war cry** *n* **1 :** a cry used by fighters in war **2 :** a slogan used esp. to rally people to a cause

**¹ward** \'wȯrd\ *n* **1 :** a guarding or being under guard or guardianship; *esp* **:** CUSTODY **2 :** a body of guards **3 :** a division of a prison **4 :** a division in a hospital **5 :** a division of a city for electoral or administrative purposes **6 :** a person (as a child) under the protection of a guardian or a law court **7 :** a person or body of persons under the protection or tutelage of a government **8 :** means of defense **:** PROTECTION

**²ward** *vb* **:** to turn aside **:** DEFLECT — usu. used with *off* ⟨~ off a blow⟩

**¹-ward** \wərd\ *also* **-wards** \wərdz\ *adj suffix* **1 :** that moves, tends, faces, or is directed toward ⟨wind*ward*⟩ **2 :** that occurs or is situated in the direction of ⟨left*ward*⟩

**²-ward** *or* **-wards** *adv suffix* **1 :** in a (specified) direction ⟨up*wards*⟩ **2 :** toward a (specified) point, position, or area ⟨earth*ward*⟩

**war dance** *n* **:** a dance performed by primitive peoples before going to war or in celebration of victory

**war·den** \'wȯrd-ᵊn\ *n* **1 :** GUARDIAN, KEEPER **2 :** the governor of a town, district, or fortress **3 :** an official charged with special supervisory duties or with the enforcement of specified laws or regulations ⟨game ~⟩ ⟨air raid ~⟩ **4 :** an official in charge of the operation of a prison **5 :** one of two ranking lay officers of an Episcopal parish **6 :** any of various British college officials

**ward·er** \'wȯrd-ər\ *n* **:** WATCHMAN, WARDEN

**ward heeler** \-ˌhē-lər\ *n* **:** a local worker for a political boss

**ward·robe** \'wȯrd-ˌrōb\ *n* [ME *warderobe*, fr. OF, fr. *warder* to guard + *robe* robe] **1 :** a room or closet where clothes are kept; *also* **:** CLOTHESPRESS **2 :** a collection of wearing apparel ⟨his summer ~⟩

**ward·room** \-ˌrüm, -ˌrùm\ *n* **:** the quarters in a warship allotted to the commissioned officers except the captain; *esp* **:** the room allotted to these officers for meals

**ward·ship** \'wȯrd-ˌship\ *n* **1 :** GUARDIANSHIP **2 :** the state of being under care of a guardian

**ware** \'waər\ *n* **1 :** manufactured articles or products of art or craft **:** GOODS **2 :** an article of merchandise ⟨a peddler hawking his ~s⟩ **3 :** items (as dishes) of fired clay **:** POTTERY

**ware·house** \-ˌhaus\ *n* **:** place for the storage of merchandise or commodities **:** STOREHOUSE — **warehouse** *vb* — **ware·house·man** \-mən\ *n* — **ware·hous·er** \-haù-zər, -sər\ *n*

**ware·room** \'waər-ˌrüm, -ˌrùm\ *n* **:** a room in which goods are exhibited for sale

**war·fare** \'wȯr-ˌfaər\ *n* **1 :** military operations between enemies **:** WAR; *also* **:** an activity undertaken by one country to weaken or destroy another ⟨economic ~⟩ **2 :** STRUGGLE, CONFLICT

**war·fa·rin** \'wȯr-fə-rən\ *n* **:** an anticoagulant used as a rodent poison and in medicine

**war·head** \-ˌhed\ *n* **:** the section of a missile (as a bomb) that breaks faith, the charge

**war·horse** \-ˌhȯrs\ *n* **1 :** a horse for use in war **2 :** a veteran soldier or public person (as a politician)

**war·less** \'wȯr-ləs\ *adj* **:** free from war

**war·like** \-ˌlīk\ *adj* **1 :** fond of war ⟨~ peoples⟩ **2 :** of, relating to, or having to do with war **:** MILITARY, MARTIAL ⟨~ supplies⟩ **3 :** threatening war **:** HOSTILE ⟨~ attitudes⟩

**war·lock** \-ˌläk\ *n* [ME *warloghe*, fr. OE *wǣrloga* one that breaks faith, the Devil, fr. *wǣr* faith, troth + *-loga* (fr. *lēogan* to lie)] **:** SORCERER, WIZARD

**war·lord** \-ˌlȯrd\ *n* **1 :** a high military leader **2 :** a military commander exercising local civil power by force ⟨former Chinese ~s⟩

**¹warm** \'wȯrm\ *adj* **1 :** having or giving out heat to a moderate or adequate degree ⟨~ milk⟩ ⟨a ~ stove⟩ **2 :** serving to retain heat ⟨~ clothes⟩ **3 :** feeling or inducing sensations of heat ⟨~ from exercise⟩ ⟨a ~ climb⟩ **4 :** showing or marked by strong feeling **:** ARDENT ⟨~ support⟩ **5 :** marked by tense excitement or hot anger ⟨a ~ campaign⟩ **6 :** marked by or tending toward injury, distress, or pain ⟨made things ~ for the enemy⟩ **7 :** newly made **:** FRESH ⟨a ~ scent⟩ **8 :** near to a goal ⟨getting ~ in a search⟩ **9 :** giving a pleasant impression of warmth, cheerfulness, or friendliness ⟨~ colors⟩ ⟨a ~ tone of voice⟩ — **warm·ly** *adv*

-**warm** *vb* **1** : to make or become warm **2** : to give a feeling of warmth or vitality to **3** : to experience feelings of affection or pleasure ⟨she ~ed to her guest⟩ **4** : to reheat for eating ⟨~ed over the roast⟩ **5** : to make ready for operation or performance by preliminary exercise or operation ⟨~ up the motor⟩ **6** : to become increasingly ardent, interested, or competent ⟨the speaker ~ed to his topic⟩ — **warm·er** *n*

**warm-blood·ed** \-'bləd-əd\ *adj* : able to maintain a relatively high and constant body temperature essentially independent of that of the surroundings

**warmed-over** \'wȯrmd-'ō-vər\ *adj* **1** : REHEATED ⟨~ cabbage⟩ **2** : not fresh or new ⟨~ ideas⟩

**warm·heart·ed** \'wȯrm-'härt-əd\ *adj* : marked by warmth of feeling : CORDIAL — **warm·heart·ed·ness** *n*

**warming pan** *n* : a long-handled covered pan filled with live coals and formerly used to warm a bed

**war·mon·ger** \'wȯr-,məŋ-gər, -,mäŋ-\ *n* : one who urges or attempts to stir up war

**warmth** \'wȯrmth\ *n* **1** : the quality or state of being warm **2** : ZEAL, ARDOR, FERVOR

**warm up** \(')wȯrm-'əp\ *vb* : to engage in exercise or practice esp. before entering a game or contest — **warm-up** \'wȯrm-,əp\ *n*

**warn** \'wȯrn\ *vb* **1** : to put on guard : CAUTION; *also* : ADMONISH, COUNSEL **2** : to notify esp. in advance : INFORM **3** : to order to go or keep away

¹**warn·ing** \-iŋ\ *n* **1** : the act of warning : the state of being warned **2** : something that warns or serves to warn

²**warning** *adj* : serving as an alarm, signal, summons, or admonition ⟨~ bell⟩ — **warn·ing·ly** *adv*

¹**warp** \'wȯrp\ *n* **1** : the lengthwise threads on a loom or in a woven fabric **2** : a warping or being warped : a twist out of a true plane or straight line ⟨a ~ in a board⟩

²**warp** *vb* [ME *warpen*, fr. OE *weorpan* to throw] **1** : to turn or twist out of shape; *also* : to become so twisted **2** : to lead astray : PERVERT; *also* : FALSIFY, DISTORT **3** : to move (a ship) by hauling on a line attached to some fixed object (as a buoy, anchor, or dock)

**war paint** *n* : paint put on the face and body by savages as a sign of going to war

**war·path** \'wȯr-,path, -,pȧth\ *n* **1** : the course taken by a party of American Indians going on a hostile expedition **2** : a hostile course of action or frame of mind

**war·plane** \-,plān\ *n* : a military airplane; *esp* : one armed for combat

¹**war·rant** \'wȯr-ənt, 'wär-\ *n* **1** : AUTHORIZATION; *also* : JUSTIFICATION, GROUND **2** : evidence (as a document) of authorization; *esp* : a legal writ authorizing an officer to take action (as in making an arrest, seizure, or search) **3** : a certificate of appointment issued to an officer of lower rank than a commissioned officer

²**warrant** *vb* **1** : to declare or maintain positively ⟨I ~ this is so⟩ **2** : to assure (a person) of the truth of what is said **3** : to guarantee to be as it appears or as it is represented ⟨~ goods as of the first quality⟩ **4** : to guarantee security or immunity to : SECURE **5** : SANCTION, AUTHORIZE **6** : to give proof of : ATTEST; *also* : GUARANTEE **7** : JUSTIFY ⟨his need ~s the expenditure⟩

**warrant officer** *n* **1** : an officer in the armed forces ranking next below a commissioned officer **2** : a commissioned officer in the navy or coast guard ranking below an ensign

**war·ran·ty** \'wȯr-ənt-ē, 'wär-\ *n, p -ties* : an expressed or implied statement that some situation or thing is as it appears to be or is represented to be; *esp* : a usu. written guarantee of the integrity of a product and of the maker's responsibility for the repair or replacement of defective parts

**war·ren** \'wȯr-ən, 'wär-\ *n* **1** : an area for the keeping and rearing of small game and esp. rabbits; *also* : an area where rabbits breed **2** : a crowded tenement or district

**war·rior** \'wȯr-yər, 'wȯr-ē-ər; 'wär-ē-, 'wär-yər\ *n* : a man engaged or experienced in warfare

**war·ship** \'wȯr-,ship\ *n* : a military ship armed for combat

**wart** \'wȯrt\ *n* **1** : a small usu. horny projection on the skin; *esp* : one caused by a virus **2** : a protuberance resembling a wart (as on a plant) — **warty** *adj*

**wart·hog** \'wȯrt-,hȯg, -,häg\ *n* : an African wild hog with large tusks and two pairs of rough warty protuberances below the eyes

**war·time** \'wȯr-,tīm\ *n* : a period during which a war is in progress

**wary** \'wa(ə)r-ē\ *adj* **wari·er; -est** : very cautious; *esp* : careful in guarding against danger or deception

**was** *past 1st & 3d sing of* BE

¹**wash** \'wȯsh, 'wäsh\ *vb* **1** : to cleanse with or as if with a liquid (as water) **2** : to wet thoroughly with water or other liquid **3** : to flow along the border of ⟨waves ~ the shore⟩ **4** : to pass (a gas or gaseous mixture) through or over a liquid for purifying **5** : to pour or flow in a stream or current **6** : to move or remove by or as if by the action of water **7** : to cover or daub lightly with a liquid (as whitewash) **8** : to run water over (as gravel or ore) in order to separate valuable matter from refuse ⟨~ sand for gold⟩ **9** : to undergo laundering ⟨a dress that doesn't ~ well⟩ **10** : to stand a test ⟨that story will not ~⟩ **11** : to be worn away by water

²**wash** *n* **1** : the act or process or an instance of washing or being washed **2** : articles to be washed or being washed **3** : the flow, sound, or action of a mass of water (as a wave) **4** : water or waves thrown back (as by oars or

paddles) **5** : erosion by waves (as of the sea) **6** West : the dry bed of a stream **7** : worthless esp. liquid waste : REFUSE, SWILL **8** : the liquid with which something is washed or tinted **9** : a disturbance in the air caused by the passage of an airplane wing or propeller

**³wash** adj : WASHABLE

**Wash** abbr Washington

**wash·able** \-ə-bəl\ adj : capable of being washed without damage

**wash and wear** adj : of, relating to, or constituting a fabric or garment that needs little or no ironing after washing

**wash·ba·sin** \'wȯsh-,bās-ᵊn, 'wäsh-\ n : WASHBOWL

**wash·board** \-,bȯrd\ n : a grooved board to scrub clothes on

**wash·bowl** \-,bōl\ n : a large bowl for water for washing hands and face

**wash·cloth** \-,klȯth\ n : a cloth used for washing one's face and body

**wash drawing** n : watercolor painting in or chiefly in washes

**washed-out** \'wȯsht-'aȯt, 'wäsht-\ adj **1** : faded in color **2** : EXHAUSTED ⟨felt ~ after working all night⟩

**wash·er** \'wȯsh-ər, 'wäsh-\ n **1** : one that washes; esp : a machine for washing **2** : a ring or perforated plate used around a bolt or screw to ensure tightness or relieve friction

**wash·er·wom·an** \-,wu̇m-ən\ n : a woman who works at washing clothes

**wash·house** \'wȯsh-,hau̇s, 'wäsh-\ n : a house or building used or equipped for washing and esp. for washing clothes

**wash·ing** \'wȯsh-iŋ, 'wäsh-\ n **1** : material obtained by washing **2** : a thin covering or coat ⟨a ~ of silver⟩ **3** : articles washed or to be washed

**washing soda** n : a form of sodium carbonate used in washing and bleaching textiles

**Wash·ing·ton pie** \,wȯsh-iŋ-tən-, ,wäsh-\ n : layer cake with a filling of jam or jelly

**Washington's Birthday** n : February 22 observed as a legal holiday

**wash·out** \'wȯsh-,au̇t, 'wäsh-\ n **1** : the washing out or away of earth esp. in a roadbed by a freshet; also : a place where earth is washed away **2** : FAILURE; esp : one who fails in a course of training or study

**wash·room** \-,rüm, -,ru̇m\ n : a room equipped with washing and toilet facilities : LAVATORY

**wash·stand** \-,stand\ n **1** : a stand holding articles needed for washing face and hands **2** : a washbowl permanently set in place

**wash·tub** \-,təb\ n : a tub for washing clothes or for soaking them before washing

**wash·wom·an** \'wȯsh-,wu̇m-ən, 'wäsh-\ n : WASHERWOMAN

**washy** \'wȯsh-ē, 'wäsh-\ adj **wash·i·er; -est 1** : WEAK, WATERY **2** : PALLID **3** : lacking in vigor, individuality, or definiteness

**wasp** \'wäsp, 'wȯsp\ n : a slender-bodied winged insect related to the bees and ants with biting mouthparts and in females and workers a formidable sting

**WASP** or **Wasp** \'wäsp, 'wȯsp\ n [white Anglo-Saxon Protestant] : an American of northern European and esp. British stock and of Protestant background : one often considered to be a member of the dominating and most privileged class in the U.S. — **Wasp·ish** \'wäs-pish, 'wȯs-\ adj

**wasp·ish** \'wäs-pish, 'wȯs-\ adj **1** : SNAPPISH, IRRITABLE **2** : resembling a wasp in form; esp : slightly built

**wasp waist** n : a very slender waist

**was·sail** \'wäs-əl, wä-'sāl\ n [ME wæs hæil, fr. ON ves heill be well] **1** : an early English toast to someone's health **2** : a liquor formerly drunk in England on festive occasions **3** : riotous drinking : REVELRY

**²wassail** vb **1** : CAROUSE **2** : to drink to the health or thriving of — **was·sail·er** n

**Was·ser·mann test** \,wäs-ər-mən-, ,väs-\ n : a blood test for infection with syphilis

**wast·age** \'wā-stij\ n : loss by use, decay, erosion, or leakage or through wastefulness

**¹waste** \'wāst\ n **1** : a sparsely settled or barren region : DESERT; also : uncultivated land **2** : the act or an instance of wasting : the state of being wasted **3** : gradual loss or decrease by use, wear, or decay **4** : damaged, defective, or superfluous material; esp : refuse matter of cotton or wool used for wiping machinery or absorbing oil **5** : refuse (as garbage or rubbish) that accumulates about habitations; also : material (as feces) produced but not used by a living body — **waste·ful** \-fəl\ adj — **waste·ful·ly** \-ē\ adv — **waste·ful·ness** n

**²waste** vb **wast·ed; wast·ing 1** : DEVASTATE **2** : to wear away or diminish gradually : CONSUME **3** : to spend money or use property carelessly or uselessly : SQUANDER; also : to allow to be used inefficiently or become dissipated **4** : to lose or cause to lose weight, strength, or vitality ⟨wasting away from fever⟩ **5** : to become diminished in bulk or substance : DWINDLE — **wast·er** n

**³waste** adj **1** : being wild and uninhabited : BARREN, DESOLATE; also : UNCULTIVATED **2** : RUINED, DEVASTATED ⟨bombs laid ~ the city⟩ **3** : discarded as worthless after being used ⟨~ water⟩ **4** : of no further use to a person, animal, or plant ⟨~ matter thrown off by the body⟩ **5** : serving to conduct or hold refuse material; esp : carrying off superfluous water

**waste·bas·ket** \'wās(t)-,bas-kət\ n : a receptacle for refuse

**waste·land** \'wāst-,land, -lənd\ n : barren or uncultivated land

**waste·pa·per** \'wās(t)-'pā-pər\ n : paper discarded as used, superfluous, or not fit for use

**waste product** n : material resulting

from a process (as of metabolism or manufacture) that is of no futher use to the system producing it

**wast·rel** \'wā-strəl, 'wäs-trəl\ *n* : one that wastes : SPENDTHRIFT

**¹watch** \'wäch, 'wòch\ *vb* **1** : to be or stay awake intentionally : keep vigil ⟨~ed by the patient's bedside⟩ ⟨~ and pray⟩ **2** : to be on 'he lookout for danger : be on one's guard **3** : to keep guard ⟨~ outside the door⟩ **4** : OBSERVE ⟨~ a game⟩ **5** : to keep in view so as to prevent harm or warn of danger ⟨~ a brush fire carefully⟩ **6** : to keep oneself informed about ⟨~ his progress⟩ **7** : to lie in wait for esp. so as to take advantage of ⟨~ed his opportunity⟩ — **watch·er** *n*

**²watch** *n* **1** : the act of keeping awake to guard, protect, or attend; *also* : a state of alert and continuous attention **2** : close observation **3** : one that watches : LOOKOUT, WATCHMAN, GUARD **4** : an allotted period of usu. 4 hours for being on nautical duty; *also* : the members of a ship's company operating the vessel during such a period **5** : a portable timepiece carried on the person

**watch·band** \'wäch-,band, 'wòch-\ *n* : the bracelet or strap of a wristwatch

**watch·case** \-,kās\ *n* : the outside metal covering of a watch

**watch·dog** \-,dòg\ *n* **1** : a dog kept to guard property **2** : one that guards or protects

**watch·ful** \'wäch-fəl, 'wòch-\ *adj* : steadily attentive and alert esp. to danger : VIGILANT — **watch·ful·ly** \-ē\ *adv* — **watch·ful·ness** *n*

**watch·mak·er** \-,mā-kər\ *n* : one that makes or repairs watches — **watch·mak·ing** \-,mā-kiŋ\ *n*

**watch·man** \-mən\ *n* : a person assigned to watch : GUARD

**watch night** *n* : a devotional service lasting until after midnight esp. on New Year's Eve

**watch·tow·er** \'wäch-,taù(-ə)r, 'wòch-\ *n* : a tower for a lookout

**watch·word** \-,wòrd\ *n* **1** : a secret word used as a signal or sign of recognition **2** : a motto used as a slogan or rallying cry

**¹wa·ter** \'wòt-ər, 'wät-\ *n* **1** : the liquid that descends as rain and forms rivers, lakes, and seas **2** : a natural mineral water — usu. used in pl. **3** *pl* : the water occupying or flowing in a particular bed; *also* : a band of seawater bordering on and under the control of a country ⟨sailing Canadian ~s⟩ **4** : any of various liquids containing or resembling water; *esp* : a watery fluid (as tears, urine, or sap) formed in a living body **5** : the clearness and luster of a precious stone ⟨a diamond of the purest ~⟩ **6** : a specified degree of thoroughness or completeness ⟨a scoundrel of the first ~⟩ **7** : a wavy lustrous pattern (as of a textile)

**²water** *vb* **1** : to supply with or get or take water ⟨~ horses⟩ ⟨the ship ~ed at each port⟩ **2** : to treat (as cloth) so as to give a lustrous appearance in wavy lines **3** : to dilute by or as if by adding water to **4** : to form or secrete water or watery matter ⟨his eyes ~ed⟩ ⟨my mouth ~ed⟩

**water ballet** *n* : a synchronized sequence of evolutions performed by a group of swimmers

**water bed** *n* : a bed whose mattress is a plastic bag filled with water

**wa·ter·borne** \-,bōrn\ *adj* : supported or carried by water

**water buffalo** *n* : a common oxlike often domesticated Asiatic buffalo

**water chestnut** *n* : a Chinese sedge; *also* : its edible tuber

**water closet** *n* : a compartment or room containing a device for flushing a toilet bowl with water : BATHROOM; *also* : such a toilet with its accessories

**wa·ter·col·or** \'wòt-ər-,kəl-ər, 'wät-\ *n* **1** : a paint whose liquid part is water **2** : the art of painting with watercolors **3** : a picture made with watercolors

**wa·ter·course** \-,kōrs\ *n* : a stream of water; *also* : the bed of a stream

**wa·ter·craft** \-,kraft\ *n* : a craft for water transport : SHIP, BOAT

**wa·ter·cress** \-,kres\ *n* : a perennial cress with white flowers found chiefly in clear running water and used esp. in salads

**wa·ter·fall** \-,fòl\ *n* : a very steep descent of the water of a stream

**water flea** *n* : any of various tiny active freshwater crustaceans

**wa·ter·fowl** \'wòt-ər-,faùl, 'wät-\ *n* **1** : a bird that frequents the water **2** *pl* : swimming game birds

**wa·ter·front** \-,frənt\ *n* : land or a section of a town fronting or abutting on a body of water

**water gap** *n* : a pass in a mountain ridge through which a stream runs

**water gas** *n* : a gas made by forcing air and steam over glowing hot coke or coal to give a mixture of hydrogen and carbon monoxide used as a fuel

**water glass** *n* **1** : a drinking glass **2** : a whitish powdery substance that is usu. a silicate of sodium and forms a syrupy liquid when dissolved in water that is used as a cement and a protective coating and in preserving eggs

**watering place** *n* : a resort that features mineral springs or bathing

**water lily** *n* : an aquatic plant with floating roundish leaves and showy solitary flowers

**wa·ter·line** \'wòt-ər-,līn, 'wät-\ *n* : any of several lines that are marked on the outside of a ship and correspond with the surface of the water when it is afloat on an even keel

**wa·ter·logged** \-,lògd, -,lägd\ *adj* : so filled or soaked with water as to be heavy or unmanageable ⟨a ~ boat⟩ ⟨~ timbers⟩

**wa·ter·loo** \,wòt-ər-'lü, ,wät-\ *n, pl* **-loos** [*Waterloo*, Belgium, scene of Napoleon's defeat in 1815] : a decisive defeat

**¹wa·ter·mark** \'wòt-ər-,märk, 'wät-\ *n* **1** : a mark indicating height to which water has risen **2** : a marking in paper visible when the paper is held up to the light

²**watermark** vb : to mark (paper) with a watermark

**wa·ter·mel·on** \-,mel-ən\ n : a large roundish or oblong fruit with sweet juicy usu. red pulp; also : an African vine related to the gourds that produces watermelons

**water moccasin** n : a venomous snake of the southern U.S. related to the copperhead

**water ouzel** n : any of several birds that are related to the thrushes but dive into swift mountain streams and walk on the bottom in search of food

**water pipe** n : a tobacco-smoking device so arranged that the smoke is drawn through water

**water polo** n : a team game played in a swimming pool with a ball resembling a soccer ball

**wa·ter·pow·er** \'wȯt-ər-,paù-(-ə)r, 'wät-\ n : the power of moving water used to run machinery

¹**wa·ter·proof** \,wȯt-ər-'prüf, ,wät-\ adj : not letting water through; esp : covered or treated with a material to prevent permeation by water — **wa·ter·proof·ing** \-iŋ\ n

²**waterproof** \'wȯt-ər-,prüf, 'wät-\ n 1 : a waterproof fabric 2 chiefly Brit : RAINCOAT

³**waterproof** \,wȯt-ər-'prüf, ,wät-\ vb : to make waterproof

**wa·ter·re·pel·lent** \,wȯt-ə(r)-ri-'pel-ənt, ,wät-\ adj : treated with a finish that is resistant to penetration by water

**wa·ter·re·sis·tant** \-ri-'zis-tənt\ adj : WATER-REPELLENT

**wa·ter·shed** \'wȯt-ər-,shed, 'wät-\ n 1 : a dividing ridge between two drainage areas 2 : the region or area drained by a particular body of water

**wa·ter·side** \-,sīd\ n : the land bordering a body of water

**water ski** n : a ski used on water when the wearer is towed — **wa·ter·ski** vb — **wa·ter·ski·er** \-,skē-ər\ n

**wa·ter·spout** \'wȯt-ər-,spaùt, 'wät-\ n 1 : a pipe from which water is spouted 2 : a funnel-shaped column of rotating cloud-filled wind extending from a cumulus cloud down to a cloud of spray torn up by whirling winds from an ocean or lake

**water strider** n : any of various long-legged bugs that move about on the surface of the water

**water table** n : the upper limit of the ground wholly saturated with water

**wa·ter·tight** \,wȯt-ər-'tīt, ,wät-\ adj 1 : so tight as not to let water in 2 : so worded that its meaning cannot be misunderstood or its purpose defeated ⟨a ~ contract⟩

**wa·ter·way** \'wȯt-ər-,wā, 'wät-\ n : a navigable body of water

**wa·ter·wheel** \-,hwēl\ n : a wheel rotated by direct action of water flowing against it

**water wings** n pl : an air-filled device to give support to a person's body when he is swimming or learning to swim

**wa·ter·works** \'wȯt-ər-,wərks, 'wät-\ n pl : a system including reservoirs, pipes, and machinery by which water is supplied (as to a city)

**wa·tery** \'wȯt-ə-rē, 'wät-\ adj 1 : of or relating to water 2 : containing, full of, or giving out water ⟨~ clouds⟩ 3 : being like water : THIN, WEAK ⟨~ lemonade⟩ 4 : being soft and soggy ⟨~ turnips⟩

**WATS** \'wäts\ abbr Wide Area Telephone Service

**watt** \'wät\ n [after James Watt d1819 Scottish engineer and inventor] : a unit of electric power equal to the power produced in a circuit when a pressure of one volt causes a current of one ampere to flow

**watt·age** \'wät-ij\ n : amount of electric power expressed in watts

**wat·tle** \'wät-ᵊl\ n 1 : a framework of rods with flexible branches or reeds interlaced used for fencing and esp. formerly in building; also : material for this framework 2 : a naked fleshy process hanging usu. about the head or neck (as of a bird) — **wat·tled** \-ᵊld\ adj

**W Aust** abbr Western Australia

¹**wave** \'wāv\ vb **waved**; **wav·ing** 1 : FLUTTER ⟨flags waving in the breeze⟩ 2 : to motion with the hands or with something held in them in signal or salute 3 : to become moved or brandished to and fro; also : BRANDISH, FLOURISH ⟨~ a sword⟩ 4 : to move before the wind with a wavelike motion ⟨fields of waving grain⟩ 5 : to curve up and down like a wave : UNDULATE

²**wave** n 1 : a moving ridge or swell on the surface of water 2 : a wavelike formation or shape ⟨a ~ in the hair⟩ 3 : the action or process of making wavy or curly 4 : a waving motion; esp : a signal made by waving something 5 : FLOW, GUSH ⟨a ~ of color swept her face⟩ 6 : a rapid increase : SURGE ⟨a ~ of buying⟩ ⟨a heat ~⟩ 7 : a disturbance somewhat similar to a wave in water that transfers energy progressively from point to point ⟨a light ~⟩ ⟨a sound ~⟩ ⟨a radio ~⟩ — **wave·like** adj

**Wave** \'wāv\ n [Women Accepted for Volunteer Emergency Service] : a woman serving in the navy

**wave band** n : a band of radio-wave frequencies

**wave·length** \'wāv-,leŋth\ n : the distance in the line of advance of a wave from any one point (as a crest) to the next corresponding point

**wave·let** \-lət\ n : a little wave : RIPPLE

**wa·ver** \'wā-vər\ vb **wa·vered**; **wa·ver·ing** \'wāv-(ə-)riŋ\ 1 : to vacillate between choices : fluctuate in opinion, allegiance, or direction 2 : REEL, TOTTER; also : QUIVER, FLICKER ⟨~ing flames⟩ 3 : FALTER 4 : to give an unsteady sound : QUAVER — **waver** n — **wa·ver·er** n — **wa·ver·ing·ly** adv

**wavy** \'wā-vē\ adj **wav·i·er**; **-est** : having waves : moving in waves

¹wax \'waks\ n 1 : a yellowish plastic substance secreted by bees for constructing the honeycomb : BEESWAX 2 : any of various substances resembling beeswax; esp : a solid mixture of higher hydrocarbons

²wax vb : to treat or rub with wax

³wax vb 1 : to increase in size, numbers, strength, volume, or duration 2 : to increase in apparent size ⟨the moon ~es toward the full⟩ 3 : to pass from one state to another : BECOME ⟨~ed indignant⟩ ⟨the party ~ed merry⟩

wax bean n : a kidney bean with pods that turn creamy yellow to bright yellow when mature enough to use as a snap bean

wax·en \'wak-sən\ adj 1 : made of or covered with wax 2 : resembling wax (as in color or consistency)

wax myrtle n : any of various shrubs or trees with aromatic leaves; esp : BAYBERRY 2

wax·wing \'waks-,wiŋ\ n : any of several singing birds that are mostly brown with a showy crest and velvety plumage

wax·work \-,wərk\ n 1 : an effigy usu. of a person in wax 2 pl : an exhibition of wax figures

waxy \'wak-sē\ adj wax·i·er; -est 1 : made of or full of wax 2 : resembling wax 3 : PLASTIC, IMPRESSIONABLE

way \'wā\ n 1 : a thoroughfare for travel or passage : ROAD, PATH, STREET 2 : ROUTE 3 : a course of action ⟨chose the easy ~⟩; also : opportunity, capability, or fact of doing as one pleases ⟨always had his own ~⟩ 4 : a possible course : POSSIBILITY ⟨no two ~s about it⟩ 5 : METHOD, MODE ⟨this ~ of thinking⟩ ⟨a new ~ of painting⟩ 6 : FEATURE, RESPECT ⟨a good worker in many ~s⟩ 7 : the usual or characteristic state of affairs ⟨as is the ~ with old people⟩ 8 : STATE, CONDITION ⟨that is the ~ things are⟩ 9 : individual characteristic or peculiarity ⟨used to his ~s⟩ 10 : a regular continuous course (as of life or action) ⟨the American ~⟩ 11 : DISTANCE ⟨a short ~ from here⟩ ⟨a long ~ from success⟩ 12 : progress along a course ⟨working his ~ through college⟩ 13 : something having direction : LOCALITY ⟨out our ~⟩ 14 pl : an inclined structure upon which a ship is built or is supported in launching 15 : CATEGORY, KIND ⟨get what you need in the ~ of supplies⟩ 16 : motion or speed of a boat through the water — by way of 1 : for the purpose of ⟨by way of illustration⟩ 2 : by the route through : VIA — out of the way 1 : WRONG, IMPROPER 2 : SECLUDED, REMOTE — under way 1 : in motion through the water 2 : in progress

way·bill \'wā-,bil\ n : a paper that accompanies a freight shipment and gives details of goods, route, and charges

way·far·er \'wā-,far-ər\ n : a traveler esp. on foot — way·far·ing \-,far-iŋ\ adj

way·lay \'wā-,lā\ vb -laid \-,lād\; -lay·ing 1 : to lie in wait for often in order to seize, rob, or kill 2 : to stop or attempt to stop so as to speak with

way–out \'wā-'aůt\ adj : FAR-OUT

-ways \,wāz\ adv suffix : in (such) a way, course, direction, or manner ⟨sideways⟩ ⟨flatways⟩

ways and means n pl : methods and resources for accomplishing something and esp. for raising revenues needed by a state; also : a legislative committee concerned with this function

way·side \'wā-,sīd\ n : the side of or land adjacent to a road or path

way station n : an intermediate station on a line of travel (as a railroad)

way·ward \'wā-wərd\ adj [ME, short for awayward turned away, fr. away, adv. + -ward directed toward] 1 : taking one's own and usu. irregular or improper way : DISOBEDIENT ⟨~ children⟩ 2 : UNPREDICTABLE, IRREGULAR 3 : opposite to what is desired or expected ⟨~ fate⟩

WB abbr 1 water ballast 2 waybill

WBC abbr white blood cells

WC abbr 1 water closet 2 without charge

WCTU abbr Women's Christian Temperance Union

we \(')wē\ pron 1 — used of a group that includes the speaker or writer 2 — used for the singular I by sovereigns and by writers (as of editorials)

weak \'wēk\ adj 1 : lacking strength or vigor : FEEBLE 2 : not able to sustain or resist much weight, pressure, or strain 3 : deficient in vigor of mind or character; also : resulting from or indicative of such deficiency ⟨a ~ policy⟩ ⟨a ~ will⟩ ⟨weak-minded⟩ 4 : deficient in the usual or required ingredients : of less than usual strength ⟨~ tea⟩ 5 : not supported by truth or logic ⟨a ~ argument⟩ 6 : not able to function properly 7 : lacking skill or proficiency; also : indicative of a lack of skill or aptitude 8 : wanting in vigor of expression or effect 9 : not having or exerting authority ⟨~ government⟩; also : INEFFECTIVE, IMPOTENT 10 : of, relating to, or constituting a verb or verb conjugation that forms the past tense and past participle by adding -ed or -d or -t — weak·ly adv

weak·en \'wē-kən\ vb weak·ened; weak·en·ing \'wēk-(ə-)niŋ\ : to make or become weak syn enfeeble, debilitate, undermine, sap, cripple, disable

weak·fish \'wēk-,fish\ n [obs. D weekvis, fr. D week soft + vis fish; fr. its tender flesh] : any of several food fishes related to the perches; esp : a common sport and market fish of the Atlantic coast of the U.S.

weak-kneed \'wēk-'nēd\ adj : lacking willpower or resolution

weak·ling \-liŋ\ n : a person who is physically, mentally, or morally weak

weak·ly \'wēk-lē\ adj : FEEBLE, WEAK

**weak·ness** \-nəs\ *n* **1** : the quality or state of being weak; *also* : an instance or period of being weak 〈in a moment of ~ he agreed to go〉 **2** : FAULT, DEFECT **3** : an object of special desire or fondness 〈coffee is her ~〉

¹**weal** \'wēl\ *n* : WELL-BEING, PROSPERITY

²**weal** *n* : WHEAL, WELT

**weald** \'wēld\ *n* [the *Weald*, wooded district in England, fr. ME *Weelde* the Weald, fr. OE *weald* wood, forest] **1** : FOREST **2** : a wild or uncultivated usu. upland region : WOLD

**wealth** \'welth\ *n* [ME *welthe*, welfare, prosperity, fr. *wele* weal] **1** : large possessions or resources : AFFLUENCE, RICHES **2** : abundant supply : PROFUSION 〈a ~ of detail〉 **3** : all property that has a money or an exchange value; *also* : all objects or resources that have usefulness for man

**wealthy** \'wel-thē\ *adj* **wealth·i·er**; **-est** : having wealth : RICH, AFFLUENT, OPULENT

**wean** \'wēn\ *vb* **1** : to accustom (a young mammal) to take food otherwise than by nursing **2** : to free from a cause of dependence or preoccupation

**weap·on** \'wep-ən\ *n* **1** : something (as a gun, knife, or club) that may be used to fight with **2** : a means by which one contends against another

**weap·on·less** \'wep-ən-ləs\ *adj* : lacking weapons : UNARMED

**weap·on·ry** \-rē\ *n* **1** : the science of designing and making weapons **2** : WEAPONS

¹**wear** \'waər\ *vb* **wore** \'wōr\; **worn** \'wōrn\; **wear·ing** **1** : to bear on the person or use habitually for clothing or adornment 〈~ a coat〉 〈~ a wig〉; *also* : to carry on the person 〈~ a gun〉 **2** : to have or show an appearance of 〈~ a smile〉 **3** : to impair, diminish, or decay by use or by scraping or rubbing 〈clothes *worn* to shreds〉 〈letters on the stone *worn* away by weathering〉; *also* : to produce gradually by friction, rubbing, or wasting away 〈~ a hole in the rug〉 **4** : to exhaust or lessen the strength of : WEARY, FATIGUE 〈*worn* by care and toil〉 **5** : to endure use : last under use or the passage of time 〈this cloth ~*s* well〉 **6** : to diminish or fail with the passage of time 〈the day ~*s* on〉 〈the effect of the drug *wore* off〉 **7** : to grow or become by attrition, use, or age 〈the coin was *worn* thin〉 — **wear·able** \'war-ə-bəl\ *adj* — **wear·er** *n*

²**wear** *n* **1** : the act of wearing : the state of being worn 〈clothes for everyday ~〉 **2** : clothing usu. of a particular kind or for a special occasion or use 〈men's ~〉 **3** : wearing or lasting quality 〈the coat still has lots of ~ in it〉 **4** : the result of wearing or use : impairment resulting from use 〈her suit shows ~〉

**wear and tear** \,war-ən-'taər\ *n* : the loss or injury to which something is subjected in the course of use; *esp* : normal depreciation

**wear down** *vb* : to weary and overcome by persistent resistance or pressure

**wea·ri·some** \'wir-ē-səm\ *adj* : causing weariness : TIRESOME — **wea·ri·some·ly** *adv* — **wea·ri·some·ness** *n*

**wear out** *vb* **1** : to make or become useless by wear **2** : TIRE

¹**wea·ry** \'wi(ə)r-ē\ *adj* **wea·ri·er**; **-est** **1** : worn out in strength, endurance, vigor, or freshness **2** : expressing or characteristic of weariness 〈a ~ sigh〉 **3** : having one's patience, tolerance, or pleasure exhausted 〈~ of war〉 — **wea·ri·ly** \'wir-ə-lē\ *adv* — **wea·ri·ness** \-ē-nəs\ *n*

²**weary** *vb* **wea·ried**; **wea·ry·ing** : to become or make weary : TIRE

**wea·sand** \'wēz-ʰnd\ *n* : WINDPIPE; *also* : THROAT

**wea·sel** \'wē-zəl\ *n*, *pl* **weasels** : any of various small slender flesh-eating mammals related to the minks

**weasel word** *n* [fr. the weasel's reputed habit of sucking the contents out of an egg while leaving the shell superficially intact] : a word used in order to evade or retreat from a direct or forthright statement or position

¹**weath·er** \'weth-ər\ *n* **1** : condition of the atmosphere with respect to heat or cold, wetness or dryness. calm or storm, clearness or cloudiness **2** : a particular and esp. a disagreeable atmospheric state : RAIN, STORM

²**weather** *adj* : WINDWARD

³**weather** *vb* **1** : to expose to or endure the action of weather; *also* : to alter (as in color or texture) by such exposure **2** : to sail or pass to the windward of **3** : to bear up against successfully 〈~ a storm〉 〈~ troubles〉

**weath·er·abil·i·ty** \,weth-(ə-)rə-'bil-ət-ē\ *n* : capability of withstanding weather 〈~ of a plastic〉

**weath·er·beat·en** \'weth-ər-,bēt-ʰn\ *adj* : altered by exposure to the weather; *also* : toughened or tanned by the weather 〈~ face〉

**weath·er·board** \-,bōrd\ *n* : CLAPBOARD

**weath·er·board·ing** \-,bōrd-iŋ\ *n* : CLAPBOARDS, SIDING

**weath·er·bound** \-,baúnd\ *adj* : kept in port or at anchor or from travel or sport by bad weather

**weath·er·cock** \-,käk\ *n* **1** : a vane often in the figure of a cock that turns with the wind to show the wind's direction **2** : a fickle person

**weath·er·glass** \'weth-ər-,glas\ *n* : an instrument (as a barometer) that shows atmospheric conditions

**weath·er·ing** \'weth-(ə-)riŋ\ *n* : the action of the weather in altering the color, texture, composition, or form of exposed objects; *also* : alteration thus effected

**weath·er·man** \-,man\ *n* : one who reports and forecasts the weather : METEOROLOGIST

**weath·er·proof** \,weth-ər-'prüf\ *adj* : able to withstand exposure to weather without appreciable harm — **weatherproof** *vb*

**weather strip** *n* : a strip of material to make a seal where a door or window joins the sill or casing — **weath·er·strip** *vb*

**weather vane** *n* : VANE 1

**weath·er·wise** \'weth-ər-,wīz\ *adj* : skillful in forecasting changes in the weather

**weath·er·worn** \'weth-ər-,wôrn\ *adj* : worn by exposure to the weather

¹**weave** \'wēv\ *vb* **wove** \'wōv\ *or* **weaved; wo·ven** \'wō-vən\ *or* **weaved; weav·ing 1** : to form by interlacing strands of material; *esp* : to make on a loom by interlacing warp and filling threads ⟨~ cloth⟩ **2** : to interlace (as threads) into a fabric and esp. cloth **3** : SPIN **2  4** : CONTRIVE **5** : to unite in a coherent whole **6** : to work in ⟨*wove* the episodes into a story⟩ **7** : to direct or move in a winding or zigzag course esp. to avoid obstacles ⟨we *wove* our way through the crowd⟩ — **weav·er** *n*

²**weave** *n* : a pattern or method of weaving ⟨a course loose ~⟩

¹**web** \'web\ *n* **1** : a fabric on a loom or coming from a loom **2** : COBWEB; *also* : SNARE, ENTANGLEMENT ⟨caught as in a ~ of deceit⟩ **3** : an animal or plant membrane; *esp* : one uniting the toes (as in many birds) **4** : a thin metal sheet or strip **5** : NETWORK ⟨a ~ of highways⟩ **6** : the series of barbs on each side of the shaft of a feather

²**web** *vb* **webbed; web·bing 1** : to cover or provide with webs or a network **2** : ENTANGLE, ENSNARE **3** : to make a web

**webbed** \'webd\ *adj* : having or being toes or fingers united by a web ⟨a ~ foot⟩

**web·bing** \'web-iŋ\ *n* : a strong closely woven tape designed for bearing weight and used esp. for straps, harness, or upholstery

**web-foot·ed** \'web-'fut-əd\ *adj* : having webbed feet

**wed** \'wed\ *vb* **wed·ded** *also* **wed; wed·ding 1** : to take, give, or join in marriage : enter into matrimony : MARRY **2** : to unite firmly

**Wed** *abbr* Wednesday

**wed·ding** \'wed-iŋ\ *n* **1** : a marriage ceremony usu. with accompanying festivities : NUPTIALS **2** : a joining in close association **3** : a wedding anniversary or its celebration

¹**wedge** \'wej\ *n* **1** : a solid triangular piece of wood or metal that tapers to a thin edge and is used to split logs or rocks or to raise heavy weights **2** : a wedge-shaped object or part ⟨a ~ of pie⟩ **3** : something (as an action or policy) that serves to open up a way for a breach, change, or intrusion

²**wedge** *vb* **wedged; wedg·ing 1** : to hold firm by or as if by driving in a wedge **2** : to force (something) into a narrow space **3** : to split apart with or as if with a wedge

**wed·lock** \'wed-,läk\ *n* [ME *wedlok*, fr. OE *wedlāc* marriage bond, fr *wedd* pledge + *-lāc*, suffix denoting activity] : the state of being married : MARRIAGE, MATRIMONY

**Wednes·day** \'wenz-dē\ *n* : the fourth day of the week

**wee** \'wē\ *adj* [ME *we*, fr. *we*, n., little bit, fr. OE *wǣge* weight] **1** : very small : TINY **2** : very early ⟨~ hours of the morning⟩

¹**weed** \'wēd\ *n* : a plant of no value and usu. of rank growth; *esp* : one growing in cultivated ground to the damage of the crop

²**weed** *vb* **1** : to clear of or remove weeds or something harmful, inferior, or superfluous ⟨~ a garden⟩ **2** : to get rid of (unwanted items) ⟨~ out the loafers from the crew⟩ — **weed·er** *n*

³**weed** *n* : GARMENT; *esp* : dress worn (as by a widow) as a sign of mourning — usu. used in pl.

**weedy** \'wēd-ē\ *adj* **1** : full of weeds **2** : resembling a weed esp. in vigor of growth or spread **3** : noticeably lean and scrawny : LANK

**week** \'wēk\ *n* **1** : seven successive days; *esp* : a calendar period of seven days beginning with Sunday and ending with Saturday **2** : the working or school days of the calendar week

**week·day** \'wēk-,dā\ *n* : a day of the week except Sunday or sometimes except Saturday and Sunday

¹**week·end** \-,end\ *n* : the period between the close of one working or business or school week and the beginning of the next

²**weekend** *vb* : to spend the weekend

¹**week·ly** \'wēk-lē\ *adj* **1** : occurring, done, produced, or issued every week **2** : computed in terms of one week — **weekly** *adv*

²**weekly** *n, pl* **weeklies** : a weekly publication

**ween** \'wēn\ *vb, archaic* : IMAGINE, SUPPOSE

**wee·ny** \'wē-nē\ *also* **ween·sy** \'wēn(t)-sē\ *adj* : exceptionally small

**weep** \'wēp\ *vb* **wept** \'wept\; **weep·ing 1** : to express emotion and esp. sorrow by shedding tears : BEWAIL, CRY **2** : to drip or exude (liquid) — **weep·er** *n*

**weep·ing** \'wē-piŋ\ *adj* **1** : TEARFUL; *also* : RAINY **2** : having slender drooping branches ⟨a ~ willow⟩

**weepy** \'wē-pē\ *adj* : inclined to weep : TEARFUL

**wee·vil** \'wē-vəl\ *n* : any of numerous mostly small beetles with a long head usu. curved into a snout and larvae that feed esp. in fruits or seeds — **wee·vily** *or* **wee·vil·ly** \'wēv-(ə-)lē\ *adj*

**weft** \'weft\ *n* **1** : WOOF **2** : WEB; *also* : something woven

¹**weigh** \'wā\ *vb* [ME *weyen*, fr. OE *wegan* to move, carry, weigh] **1** : to ascertain the heaviness of by a balance **2** : to have weight or a specified weight **3** : to consider carefully : PONDER **4** : to merit consideration as important : COUNT ⟨evidence ~*ing* against him⟩ **5** : to heave up (an anchor) **6** : to press down with or as if with a heavy weight

²**weigh** *n* [alter. of *way*] : WAY — used in the phrase *under weigh*

**weigh in** *vb* **:** to have something weighed; *esp* **:** to have oneself weighed preliminary to participation in a sports event

**¹weight** \\'wāt\ *n* **1 :** quantity as determined by weighing **2 :** the property of a body measurable by weighing **3 :** the amount that something weighs **4 :** relative heaviness (as of a textile) **5 :** a unit (as a pound or kilogram) of weight or mass; *also* **:** a system of such units **6 :** a heavy object for holding or pressing something down; *also* **:** a heavy object for throwing or lifting in an athletic contest **7 :** BURDEN ⟨a ~ of grief⟩ **8 :** PRESSURE ⟨~ of an attack⟩ **9 :** IMPORTANCE; *also* **:** INFLUENCE ⟨threw his ~ around⟩ **syn** significance, moment, consequence, import, authority, prestige, credit

## Weights and Measures[1]

| unit | equivalents in other units of same system | metric equivalent |
|---|---|---|
| | **WEIGHT** | |
| | *avoirdupois* | |
| **ton** | | |
| short ton | 20 short hundredweight, 2000 pounds | 0.907 metric tons |
| long ton | 20 long hundredweight, 2240 pounds | 1.016 metric tons |
| **hundredweight** | | |
| short hundredweight | 100 pounds, 0.05 short tons | 45.359 kilograms |
| long hundredweight | 112 pounds, 0.05 long tons | 50.802 kilograms |
| pound | 16 ounces, 7000 grains | 0.453 kilograms |
| ounce | 16 drams, 437.5 grains | 28.349 grams |
| dram | 27.343 grains, 0.0625 ounces | 1.771 grams |
| grain | 0.036 drams, 0.002285 ounces | 0.0648 grams |
| | *apothecaries'* | |
| pound | 12 ounces, 5760 grains | 0.373 kilograms |
| ounce | 8 drams, 480 grains | 31.103 grams |
| dram | 3 scruples, 60 grains | 3.887 grams |
| scruple | 20 grains, 0.333 drams | 1.295 grams |
| grain | 0.05 scruples, 0.002083 ounces, 0.0166 drams | 0.0648 grams |
| | **CAPACITY** | |
| | *U.S. liquid measure* | |
| gallon | 4 quarts (231 cubic inches) | 3.785 liters |
| quart | 2 pints (57.75 cubic inches) | 0.946 liters |
| pint | 4 gills (28.875 cubic inches) | 0.473 liters |
| gill | 4 fluidounces (7.218 cubic inches) | 118.291 milliliters |
| fluidounce | 8 fluidrams (1.804 cubic inches) | 29.573 milliliters |
| fluidram | 60 minims (0.225 cubic inches) | 3.696 milliliters |
| minim | ¹⁄₆₀ fluidram (0.003759 cubic inches) | 0.061610 milliliters |
| | *U.S. dry measure* | |
| bushel | 4 pecks (2150.42 cubic inches) | 35.238 liters |
| peck | 8 quarts (537.605 cubic inches) | 8.809 liters |
| quart | 2 pints (67.200 cubic inches) | 1.101 liters |
| pint | ½ quart (33.600 cubic inches) | 0.550 liters |
| | **LENGTH** | |
| mile | 5280 feet, 320 rods, 1760 yards | 1.609 kilometers |
| rod | 5.50 yards, 16.5 feet | 5.029 meters |
| yard | 3 feet, 36 inches | 0.9144 meters |
| foot | 12 inches, 0.333 yards | 30.480 centimeters |
| inch | 0.083 feet, 0.027 yards | 2.540 centimeters |
| | **AREA** | |
| square mile | 640 acres, 102,400 square rods | 2.590 square kilometers |
| acre | 4840 square yards, 43,560 square feet | 4047 square meters |
| square rod | 30.25 square yards, 0.006 acres | 25.293 square meters |
| square yard | 1296 square inches, 9 square feet | 0.836 square meters |
| square foot | 144 square inches, 0.111 square yards | 0.093 square meters |
| square inch | 0.007 square feet, 0.00077 square yards | 6.451 square centimeters |

## Weights and Measures¹, Continued

| unit | equivalents in other units of same system | metric equivalent |
|------|--------------------------------------------|-------------------|
| | **VOLUME** | |
| cubic yard | 27 cubic feet, 46,656 cubic inches | 0.765 cubic meters |
| cubic foot | 1728 cubic inches, 0.0370 cubic yards | 0.028 cubic meters |
| cubic inch | 0.00058 cubic feet, 0.000021 cubic yards | 16.387 cubic centimeters |

¹For U.S. equivalents of metric units see Metric System table

**²weight** vb **1 :** to load with or as if with a weight **2 :** to oppress with a burden ⟨~ed down with cares⟩

**weight·less** \'wāt-ləs\ adj **1 :** having little weight **2 :** lacking apparent gravitational pull — **weight·less·ly** adv — **weight·less·ness** n

**weighty** \'wāt-ē\ adj **weight·i·er; -est 1 :** of much importance or consequence **:** MOMENTOUS, SERIOUS ⟨~ problems⟩ **2 :** SOLEMN ⟨a ~ manner⟩ **3 :** HEAVY **:** BURDENSOME, GRIEVOUS **5 :** exerting force, influence, or authority ⟨~ arguments⟩

**weir** \'waər, 'wiər\ n **1 :** a dam in a river for the purpose of directing water to a mill or making a pond **2 :** a fence (as of brush) set in a stream or waterway for catching fish

**weird** \'wiərd\ adj [ME wird, werd fate, destiny, fr. OE wyrd] **1 :** MAGICAL **2 :** UNEARTHLY, MYSTERIOUS **3 :** ODD, UNUSUAL, FANTASTIC **syn** eerie, uncanny — **weird·ly** adv — **weird·ness** n

**Welch** \'welch\ var of WELSH

**¹wel·come** \'wel-kəm\ vb **wel·comed; wel·com·ing 1 :** to greet cordially or courteously **2 :** to accept, meet, or face with pleasure ⟨he ~s criticism⟩

**²welcome** adj **1 :** received gladly into one's presence ⟨a ~ visitor⟩ **2 :** giving pleasure **:** PLEASING ⟨~ news⟩ **3 :** willingly permitted or admitted ⟨all are ~ to use the books⟩

**³welcome** n **:** a cordial greeting or reception

**¹weld** \'weld\ vb **1 :** to unite (metal or plastic parts) either by heating and allowing the parts to flow together or by hammering or pressing together **2 :** to unite closely or intimately ⟨~ed together in friendship⟩ — **weld·er** n

**²weld** n **1 :** a welded joint **2 :** union by welding

**weld·ment** \'weld-mənt\ n **:** a unit formed by welding together an assembly of pieces

**wel·fare** \'wel-,faər\ n **1 :** the state of doing well esp. in respect to happiness, well-being, or prosperity ⟨the ~ of mankind⟩ **2 :** organized efforts for the social betterment of a group in society **3 :** RELIEF 2

**welfare state** n **:** a nation or state that assumes primary responsibility for the individual and social welfare of its citizens

**wel·kin** \'wel-kən\ n [ME, lit., cloud, fr. OE wolcen] **:** SKY; also **:** AIR

**¹well** \'wel\ n **1 :** a spring with its pool **:** FOUNTAIN **2 :** a hole sunk in the earth to obtain a natural deposit (as of water, oil, or gas) **3 :** a source of supply ⟨a ~ of information⟩ **4 :** something (as a container or space) suggesting a well **5 :** the reservoir of a fountain pen **6 :** an open space (as for a staircase or elevator) extending vertically through floors **7 :** an enclosure in the middle of a ship's hold around the pumps

**²well** vb **:** to rise up and flow forth **:** RUN ⟨tears ~ed from her eyes⟩

**³well** adv **bet·ter** \'bet-ər\; **best** \'best\ **1 :** in a good or proper manner **:** RIGHTLY, also **:** EXCELLENTLY, SKILLFULLY **2 :** SATISFACTORILY, FORTUNATELY ⟨the party turned out ~⟩ **3 :** ABUNDANTLY ⟨eat ~⟩ **4 :** with reason or courtesy **:** PROPERLY ⟨I cannot ~ refuse⟩ **5 :** COMPLETELY, FULLY, QUITE ⟨~ worth the price⟩ ⟨well-hidden⟩ **6 :** INTIMATELY, CLOSELY ⟨I know him ~⟩ **7 :** CONSIDERABLY, FAR ⟨~ over a million⟩ ⟨~ ahead⟩ **8 :** without trouble or difficulty ⟨he could ~ have gone⟩ **9 :** EXACTLY, DEFINITELY ⟨remember it ~⟩

**⁴well** adj **1 :** SATISFACTORY, PLEASING ⟨all is ~⟩ **2 :** PROSPEROUS; also **:** being in satisfactory condition or circumstances **3 :** ADVISABLE, DESIRABLE ⟨it is not ~ to anger him⟩ **4 :** free or recovered from infirmity or disease **:** HEALTHY **5 :** FORTUNATE ⟨it is ~ that this has happened⟩

**well-ad·vised** \,wel-əd-'vīzd\ adj **1 :** PRUDENT **2 :** resulting from, based on, or showing careful deliberation or wise counsel ⟨~ plans⟩

**well-ap·point·ed** \-ə-'point-əd\ adj **:** having good and complete equipment

**well-be·ing** \'wel-'bē-iŋ\ n **:** the state of being happy, healthy, or prosperous

**well-born** \-'born\ adj **:** born of good stock either socially or physically

**well-bred** \-'bred\ adj **:** having or indicating good breeding **:** REFINED

**well-con·di·tioned** \,wel-kən-'dish-ənd\ adj **1 :** characterized by proper disposition, morals, or behavior **2 :** having a good physical condition **:** SOUND ⟨a ~ animal⟩

**well-de·fined** \,wel-di-'fīnd\ adj **:** having clearly distinguishable limits or boundaries ⟨a ~ scar⟩

**well-dis-posed** \-dis-'pōzd\ *adj* : disposed to be friendly, favorable, or sympathetic

**well-done** \'wel-'dən\ *adj* **1** : rightly or properly performed **2** : cooked thoroughly

**well-fa-vored** \'wel-'fā-vərd\ *adj* : GOOD-LOOKING, HANDSOME

**well-fixed** \-'fikst\ *adj* : financially well-off

**well-found-ed** \-'faùn-dəd\ *adj* : based on sound information, reasoning, judgment, or grounds (~ rumors)

**well-groomed** \-'grümd, -'grúmd\ *adj* : well and neatly dressed or cared for (~ men) (a ~ lawn)

**well-ground-ed** \-'graùnd-dəd\ *adj* : having a firm foundation

**well-head** \'wel-,hed\ *n* **1** : the source of a spring or a stream **2** : principal source **3** : the top of or a structure built over a well

**well-heeled** \-'hēld\ *adj* : financially well-off

**well-knit** \'wel-'nit\ *adj* : well and firmly formed or framed (a ~ argument)

**well-mean-ing** \-'mē-niŋ\ *adj* : having or based on excellent intentions

**well-nigh** \-'nī\ *adv* : ALMOST, NEARLY

**well-off** \-'òf\ *adj* : being in good condition or circumstances; *esp* : WELL-TO-DO

**well-or-dered** \'wel-'òrd-ərd\ *adj* : having an orderly procedure or arrangement

**well-read** \-'red\ *adj* : well informed through reading

**well-round-ed** \-'raùn-dəd\ *adj* **1** : broadly trained, educated, and experienced **2** : COMPREHENSIVE (a ~ program of activities)

**well-spo-ken** \'wel-'spō-kən\ *adj* **1** : having a good command of language : speaking well and esp. courteously **2** : spoken with propriety (~ words)

**well-spring** \-,spriŋ\ *n* : FOUNTAINHEAD, SPRING

**well-timed** \'wel-'tīmd\ *adj* : coming or happening at an opportune moment : TIMELY

**well-to-do** \,wel-tə-'dü\ *adj* : having more than adequate material resources : PROSPEROUS

**well-turned** \'wel-'tərnd\ *adj* **1** : pleasingly rounded : SHAPELY (a ~ ankle) **2** : pleasingly and appropriately (a ~ phrase)

**well-wish-er** \'wel-,wish-ər, -'wish-\ *n* : one that wishes well to another — **well-wish-ing** \-,iŋ\ *adj or n*

**well-worn** \-'wörn\ *adj* **1** : worn by much use (~ shoes) **2** : TRITE **3** : worn well or properly (~ honors)

**welsh** \'welsh, 'welch\ *vb* **1** : to cheat by avoiding payment of bets **2** : to avoid dishonorably the fulfillment of an obligation (~ed on his promises)

**Welsh** \'welsh\ *n* **1 Welsh** *pl* : the people of Wales **2** : the Celtic language of Wales — **Welsh** *adj* — **Welsh-man** \-mən\ *n*

**Welsh cor-gi** \-'kòr-gē\ *n* [W *corgi*, fr. *cor* dwarf + *ci* dog] : a short-legged long-backed dog with foxy head that occurs in two varieties of Welsh origin

**Welsh rabbit** *n* : melted often seasoned cheese poured over toast or crackers

**Welsh rare-bit** \-'raər-bət\ *n* : WELSH RABBIT

**welt** \'welt\ *n* **1** : the narrow strip of leather between a shoe upper and sole to which other parts are stitched **2** : a doubled edge, strip, insert, or seam for ornament or reinforcement **3** : a ridge or lump raised on the skin usu. by a blow; *also* : a heavy blow

**²welt** *vb* **1** : to furnish with a welt **2** : to hit hard

**¹wel-ter** \'wel-tər\ *vb* **1** : WRITHE, TOSS; *also* : WALLOW **2** : to rise and fall or toss about in or with waves **3** : to lie soaked or drenched (~ing in his gore) **4** : to become deeply sunk or involved (~ed in misery) **5** : to be in turmoil

**²welter** *n* **1** : TURMOIL **2** : a chaotic mass or jumble

**wel-ter-weight** \'wel-tər-,wāt\ *n* : a boxer weighing more than 135 but not over 147 pounds

**wen** \'wen\ *n* : a cyst formed by blocking of a skin gland and filled with fatty material

**wench** \'wench\ *n* [ME *wenche*, short for *wenchel* child, fr. OE *wencel*] **1** : a young woman : GIRL **2** : a female servant

**wend** \'wend\ *vb* : to direct one's course : proceed on (one's way)

**went** *past of* GO

**wept** *past of* WEEP

**were** *past 2d sing, past pl, or past subjunctive of* BE

**were-wolf** \'wiər-,wúlf, 'wər-, 'weər-\ *n, pl* **were-wolves** \-,wúlvz\ [ME, fr. OE *werwulf*, fr. *wer* man + *wulf* wolf] : a person held to be transformed into or able to transform into a wolf

**wes-kit** \'wes-kət\ *n* : VEST 1

**¹west** \'west\ *adv* : to or toward the west

**²west** *adj* **1** : situated toward or at the west **2** : coming from the west

**³west** *n* **1** : the general direction of sunset **2** : the compass point directly opposite to east **3** *cap* : regions or countries west of a specified or implied point **4** *cap* : Europe and the Americas — **west-er-ly** \'wes-tər-lē\ *adv or adj* — **west-ward** *adv or adj* — **west-wards** *adv*

**¹west-ern** \'wes-tərn\ *adj* **1** *cap* : of, relating to, or characteristic of a region conventionally designated West **2** : lying toward or coming from the west **3** *cap* : of or relating to the Roman Catholic or Protestant segment of Christianity — **West-ern-er** *n*

**²western** *n* **1** : one that is produced in or is characteristic of a western region and esp. the western U.S. **2** *often cap* : a novel, story, motion picture, or broadcast dealing with life in the western U.S. during the latter half of the 19th century

**west-ern-ize** \'wes-tər-,nīz\ *vb* **-ized; -iz-ing** : to give western characteristics to

**¹wet** \'wet\ *adj* **wet-ter; wet-test 1**

**:** consisting of or covered or soaked with liquid (as water) **2 :** RAINY **3 :** not dry ⟨~ paint⟩ **4 :** permitting or advocating the manufacture and sale of intoxicating liquor ⟨a ~ town⟩ ⟨a ~ candidate⟩ **syn** damp, dank, moist, humid — **wet·ly** adv — **wet·ness** n

**²wet** n **1 :** WATER; also **:** WETNESS, MOISTURE **2 :** rainy weather **:** RAIN **3 :** an advocate of a wet liquor policy

**³wet** vb **wet** or **wet·ted; wet·ting :** to make or become wet

**wet·back** \'wet-,bak\ n **:** a Mexican who enters the U.S. illegally (as by wading the Rio Grande)

**wet blanket** n **:** one that quenches or dampens enthusiasm or pleasure

**weth·er** \'weth-ər\ n **:** a male sheep castrated while immature

**wet·land** \'wet-,land, -lənd\ n **:** land containing much soil moisture **:** swampy or boggy land

**wet nurse** n **:** one who cares for and suckles young not her own

**wet suit** n **:** a heat-retaining suit of permeable material (as sponge rubber) worn (as by a skin diver) in cold water

**wetting agent** n **:** a substance that when adsorbed on a surface reduces its tendency to repel a liquid

**wh** abbr which

**¹whack** \'hwak\ vb **1 :** to strike with a smart or resounding blow **2 :** to cut with or as if with a whack

**²whack** n **1 :** a smart or resounding blow; also **:** the sound of such a blow **2 :** PORTION, SHARE **3 :** CONDITION; esp **:** proper working order ⟨the machine is out of ~⟩ **4 :** an opportunity or attempt to do something **:** CHANCE **5 :** a single action or occasion **:** TIME ⟨made three pies at a ~⟩

**¹whale** \'hwāl\ n, pl **whales** 1 or pl **whale :** a large sea mammal that superficially resembles a fish but breathes air and suckles its young **2 :** a person or thing impressive in size or quality ⟨a ~ of a story⟩

**²whale** vb **whaled; whal·ing :** to fish or hunt for whales

**³whale** vb **whaled; whal·ing 1 :** THRASH **2 :** to strike or hit vigorously

**whale·boat** \-,bōt\ n **:** a long narrow rowboat made with both ends sharp and sloping and used by whalers

**whale·bone** \-,bōn\ n **:** a horny substance attached in plates to the upper jaw of some large whales (**whalebone whales**) and used esp. for ribs in corsets or fans

**whal·er** \'hwā-lər\ n **1 :** a person or ship employed in the whale fishery **2 :** WHALEBOAT

**wham·my** \'hwam-ē\ n, pl **whammies :** JINX, HEX

**wharf** \'hworf\ n, pl **wharves** \'hworvz\ also **wharfs :** a structure alongside which ships lie to load and unload

**wharf·age** \'hwor-fij\ n **:** the provision or use of a wharf; also **:** the charge for using a wharf

**wharf·in·ger** \'hwor-fən-jər\ n **:** the operator or manager of a wharf

**¹what** \(')hwät\ pron **1 —** used to inquire the identity or nature of a being, an object, or some matter or situation ⟨~ is he, a salesman⟩ ⟨~'s that⟩ ⟨~ happened⟩ **2 :** that which ⟨I know ~ you want⟩ **3 :** WHATEVER 1 ⟨take ~ you want⟩

**²what** adv **1 :** in what respect **:** HOW ⟨~ does he care⟩ **2 —** used with with to introduce a prepositional phrase that expresses cause ⟨kept busy ~ with school and work⟩

**³what** adj **1 —** used to inquire about the identity or nature of a person, object, or matter ⟨~ books does he read⟩ **2 :** how remarkable or surprising ⟨~ an idea⟩ **3 :** WHATEVER

**¹what·ev·er** \hwät-'ev-ər\ pron **1 :** anything or everything that ⟨does ~ he wants to⟩ **2 :** no matter what ⟨~ you do, don't cheat⟩ **3 :** WHAT 1 — used as an intensive ⟨~ happened⟩

**²whatever** adj **:** of any kind at all ⟨no food ~⟩

**what·not** \'hwät-,nät\ n **:** a light open set of shelves for small ornaments

**what·so·ev·er** \,hwät-sə-'wev-ər\ pron or adj **:** WHATEVER

**wheal** \'hwēl\ n **:** a wale or welt on the skin; also **:** a suddenly-appearing itching or burning raised patch of skin

**wheat** \'hwēt\ n **:** a cereal grain that yields a fine white flour and is the chief breadstuff of temperate regions; also **:** any of several grasses whose white to dark red grains are wheat — **wheat·en** adj

**wheat germ** n **:** the vitamin-rich wheat embryo separated in milling

**whee·dle** \'hwēd-ºl\ vb **whee·dled; whee·dling** \'hwēd-( º-)liŋ\ **1 :** to coax or entice by flattery **2 :** to gain or get by wheedling

**¹wheel** \'hwēl\ n **1 :** a disk or circular frame capable of turning on a central axis **2 :** something resembling a wheel in shape, use, or method of turning; esp **:** a circular frame with handles for controlling a ship's rudder **3 :** a device the chief part of which is a wheel or wheels; esp **:** BICYCLE **4 :** a former wheellike instrument of torture to which a victim was bound **5 :** a revolution or rotation **:** a turn around an axis; esp **:** a turning movement of troops or ships in line in which units preserve alignment and relative position as they change direction **6 :** machinery that imparts motion **:** moving power ⟨the ~s of government⟩ **7 :** a directing or controlling person; esp **:** a political leader **8** pl, slang **:** AUTOMOBILE — **wheeled** \'hwēld\ adj — **wheel·less** \'hwēl-ləs\ adj

**²wheel** vb **1 :** to convey or move on wheels or in a vehicle having wheels **2 :** ROTATE, REVOLVE **3 :** to turn so as to change direction

**wheel·bar·row** \-,bar-ō\ n **:** a vehicle with handles and usu. one wheel for conveying small loads

**wheel·base** \-,bās\ n **:** the distance in inches between the front and rear axles of an automotive vehicle

**wheel·chair** \-,cheər\ *n* : a chair mounted on wheels esp. for the use of invalids

**wheel·er** \'hwē-lər\ *n* **1** : one that wheels **2** : something that has wheels — used in combination ⟨a 4-*wheeler* carriage⟩ **3** : WHEELHORSE

**wheel·er-dealer** \,hwē-lər-'dē-lər\ *n* : a shrewd operator esp. in business or politics

**wheel·horse** \'hwēl-,hòrs\ *n* **1** : a horse in a position nearest the wheels in a tandem or similar arrangement **2** : a steady and effective worker esp. in a political body

**wheel·house** \,haus\ *n* : a small house on or above the deck of a ship and containing the steering wheel

**wheel·wright** \-,rīt\ *n* : a man whose occupation is to make or repair wheels and wheeled vehicles

**¹wheeze** \'hwēz\ *vb* **wheezed**; **wheezing** : to breathe with difficulty usu. with a whistling sound

**²wheeze** *n* **1** : a sound of wheezing **2** : GAG, JOKE **3** : a trite saying

**wheezy** \'hwē-zē\ *adj* **wheez·i·er**; **-est 1** : inclined to wheeze **2** : having a wheezing sound

**whelk** \'hwelk\ *n* : a large sea snail; *esp* : one much used as food in Europe

**whelm** \'hwelm\ *vb* : to overcome or engulf completely : OVERWHELM

**¹whelp** \'hwelp\ *n* **1** : one of the young of various carnivorous mammals (as a dog) **2** : a low contemptible fellow

**²whelp** *vb* : to give birth to (whelps) : bring forth whelps

**¹when** \(')hwen, hwən\ *adv* **1** : at what time ⟨~ will he return⟩ **2** : at or during which time ⟨a time ~ things were upset⟩

**²when** *conj* **1** : at or during the time that ⟨leave ~ I do⟩ **2** : every time that ⟨they all laughed ~ he sang⟩ **3** : in the event that : IF ⟨the batter is out ~ he bunts foul with two strikes⟩ **4** : ALTHOUGH ⟨gave up politics ~ he might have made a great career of it⟩

**³when** \,hwen\ *pron* : what or which time since ⟨~ have you been the boss⟩

**⁴when** \'hwen\ *n* : the time of a happening

**whence** \(')hwens\ *adv* **1** : from what place, source, or cause ⟨asked ~ the gifts came⟩ **2** : from or out of which ⟨the land ~ he came⟩

**when·ev·er** \hwen-'ev-ər, hwən-\ *conj or adv* : at whatever time

**when·so·ev·er** \'hwen-sə-,wev-ər\ *conj* : at whatever time

**¹where** \(')hwear\ *adv* **1** : at, in, or to what place ⟨~ is he⟩ ⟨~ did he go⟩ **2** : at, in, or to what situation, position, direction, circumstances, or respect ⟨~ does this road lead⟩

**²where** *conj* **1** : at, in, or to what place ⟨knows ~ the house is⟩ **2** : at, in, or to what situation, position, direction, circumstances, or respect shows ~ the road leads⟩ **3** : WHEREVER ⟨goes ~ he likes⟩ **4** : at, in, or to which place ⟨the town ~ she lives⟩ **5** : at, in, or to the place at, in, or to which ⟨stay ~ you

are⟩ **6** : in a case, situation, or respect in which ⟨outstanding ~ endurance is called for⟩

**³where** \'hwear\ *n* **1** : PLACE, LOCATION ⟨the ~ and how of the accident⟩ **2** : what place ⟨~ is he from⟩

**¹where·abouts** \-ə-,bauts\ *also* **whereabout** \-,baut\ *adv* : about where ⟨~ does he live⟩

**²whereabouts** *n sing or pl* : the place where a person or thing is ⟨his present ~ are unknown⟩

**where·as** \hwer-'az\ *conj* **1** : in view of the fact that : SINCE **2** : when in fact : while on the contrary

**where·at** \-'at\ *conj* **1** : at or toward which **2** : in consequence of which : WHEREUPON

**where·by** \-'bī\ *conj* : by, through, or in accordance with ⟨the means ~ he achieved his goal⟩

**¹where·fore** \'hwear-,fōr\ *adv* **1** : for what reason or purpose : WHY **2** : THEREFORE

**²wherefore** *n* : CAUSE, REASON

**where·in** \hwer-'in\ *adv* : in what : in what respect ⟨~ was he wrong⟩

**²wherein** *conj* **1** : in which : WHERE ⟨the city ~ he lives⟩ **2** : during which **3** : in what way : HOW ⟨showed him ~ he was wrong⟩

**where·of** \-'əv, 'äv\ *conj* **1** : of what ⟨knows ~ he speaks⟩ **2** : of which or whom books ~ the best are lost⟩

**where·on** \-'òn, 'än\ *conj* : on which ⟨the base ~ it rests⟩

**where·so·ev·er** \'hwer-sə-,wev-ər\ *conj, archaic* : WHEREVER

**where·to** \'hwear-,tü\ *conj* : to which

**where·up·on** \'hwer-ə-,pòn, -,pän\ *conj* **1** : on which **2** : closely following and in consequence of which

**¹wher·ev·er** \hwer-'ev-ər\ *adv* : where in the world ⟨~ did she get that hat⟩

**²wherever** *conj* **1** : at, in, or to whatever place **2** : in any circumstance in which

**where·with** \'hwear-,with, -,with\ *conj* : with or by means of which

**where·with·al** \'hwer-with-,òl, -with-\ *n* : MEANS, RESOURCES, *esp* : MONEY

**wher·ry** \'hwer-ē\ *n, pl* **wherries** : a light boat; *esp* : a long light rowboat sharp at both ends

**whet** \'hwet\ *vb* **whet·ted**; **whet·ting 1** : to sharpen by rubbing against or with a hard substance (as a whetstone) **2** : to make keen : STIMULATE ⟨~ the appetite⟩

**whether** \'hweth-ər\ *conj* **1** : if it is or was true that ⟨ask ~ he is going⟩ **2** : if it is or was better uncertain ~ to go or stay⟩ **3** : whichever is or was the case, namely that ⟨~ we succeed or fail, we must try⟩ **4** : EITHER ⟨seated him next to her ~ by accident or design⟩

**whet·stone** \'hwet-,stōn\ *n* : a stone for whetting sharp-edged tools

**whey** \'hwā\ *n* : the watery part of milk that separates after the milk sours and thickens

**whf** *abbr* wharf

**¹which** \(')hwich\ *adj* **1** : being what

one or ones out of a group ⟨~ tie should I wear⟩ **2** : WHICHEVER

**²which** *pron* **1** : which one or ones ⟨~ is yours⟩ ⟨~ are his⟩ ⟨he's a Swede or a Dane, I don't remember ~⟩ **2** : WHICHEVER ⟨we have all kinds of them; take ~ you like⟩ **3** — used to introduce a relative clause and to serve as a substitute therein for the substantive modified by the clause ⟨give me the money ~ is coming to me⟩

**¹which·ev·er** \hwich-'ev-ər\ *pron* : whatever one or ones

**²whichever** *adj* : no matter which ⟨~ way you go⟩

**which·so·ev·er** \,hwich-sə-'wev-ər\ *pron or adj* : WHICHEVER

**whick·er** \'hwik-ər\ *vb* : NEIGH, WHINNY — **whicker** *n*

**¹whiff** \'hwif\ *n* **1** : a quick puff or slight gust esp. of air, gas, smoke, or spray **2** : an inhalation of odor, gas, or smoke **3** : a slight trace : HINT

**²whiff** *vb* **1** : to expel, puff out, or blow away in or as if in whiffs **2** : to inhale an odor

**whif·fle·tree** \'hwif-əl-(,)trē\ *n* : the pivoted swinging bar to which the traces of a harness are fastened

**Whig** \'hwig\ *n* [short for *Whiggamore* (member of a Scottish group that marched to⟨⟩Edinburgh in 1648 to oppose the court party)] **1** : a member or supporter of a British political group of the 18th and early 19th centuries seeking to limit royal authority and increase parliamentary power **2** : an American favoring independence from Great Britain during the American Revolution **3** : a member or supporter of an American political party formed about 1834 to oppose the Democrats

**¹while** \'hwīl\ *n* **1** : a period of time ⟨stay a ~⟩ **2** : the time and effort used : TROUBLE ⟨worth your ~⟩

**²while** \(,)hwīl\ *conj* **1** : during the time that ⟨she called ~ you were out⟩ **2** : as long as ⟨~ there's life there's hope⟩ **3** : ALTHOUGH ⟨~ he's respected, he's not liked⟩

**³while** \'hwīl\ *vb* whiled; whil·ing : to cause to pass esp. pleasantly ⟨~ away an hour⟩

**¹whi·lom** \'hwī-ləm\ *adv* [ME, lit., at times, fr. OE *hwīlum*, dat. pl. of *hwīl* time, while] *archaic* : FORMERLY

**²whilom** *adj* : FORMER ⟨his ~ friends⟩

**whilst** \'hwīlst\ *conj, chiefly Brit* : WHILE

**whim** \'hwim\ *n* : a sudden wish, desire, or change of mind : NOTION, FANCY, CAPRICE

**whim·per** \'hwim-pər\ *vb* whim·pered; whim·per·ing \-p(ə-)riŋ\ : to make a low whining plaintive or broken sound — **whimper** *n*

**whim·si·cal** \'hwim-zi-kəl\ *adj* **1** : full of whims : CAPRICIOUS **2** : resulting from or characterized by whim or caprice : ERRATIC — **whim·si·cal·i·ty** \,hwim-zə-'kal-ət-ē\ *n* — **whim·si·cal·ly** \'hwim-zi-k(ə-)lē\ *adv*

**whim·sy** *or* **whim·sey** \'hwim-zē\ *n, pl* **whimsies** *or* **whimseys** **1**

: WHIM, CAPRICE **2** : a fanciful or fantastic device, object, or creation esp. in writing or art

**whine** \'hwīn\ *vb* whined; whin·ing [ME *whinen*, fr. OE *hwīnan* to whiz] **1** : to utter a usu. high-pitched plaintive or distressed cry; *also* : to make a sound similar to such a cry **2** : to utter a complaint with or as if with a whine — **whine** *n*

**¹whin·ny** \'hwin-ē\ *vb* whin·nied; whin·ny·ing : to neigh usu. in a low or gentle manner

**²whinny** *n, pl* **whinnies** : NEIGH

**¹whip** \'hwip\ *vb* whipped; whip·ping **1** : to move, snatch, or jerk quickly or forcefully ⟨~ out a gun⟩ **2** : to strike with a slender lithe implement (as a lash) esp. as a punishment; *also* : SPANK **3** : to drive or urge on by or as if by using a whip **4** : to bind or wrap (as a rope or rod) with cord in order to protect and strengthen; *also* : to wind or wrap around something **5** : DEFEAT **6** : to stir up : INCITE ⟨~ up enthusiasm⟩ **7** : to produce in a hurry ⟨~ up a meal⟩ **8** : to beat (as eggs or cream) into a froth **9** : to gather together or hold together for united action **10** : to move nimbly or briskly; *also* : to thrash about like a whiplash — **whip·per** *n* — **whip into shape** : to bring forcefully to a desired state or condition

**²whip** *n* **1** : a flexible instrument used for whipping **2** : a stroke or cut with or as if with a whip **3** : a dessert made by whipping a portion of the ingredients ⟨prune ~⟩ **4** : a person who handles a whip; *esp* : a driver of horses **5** : a member of a legislative body appointed to enforce party discipline and to secure the attendance of party members at important sessions **6** : a whipping or thrashing motion ⟨a ~ of his tail⟩

**whip·cord** \-,kȯrd\ *n* **1** : a thin tough cord made of braided or twisted hemp or catgut **2** : a cloth that is made of hard-twisted yarns and has fine diagonal cords or ribs

**whip hand** *n* : positive control : ADVANTAGE

**whip·lash** \'hwip-,lash\ *n* : the lash of a whip

**whiplash injury** *n* : injury resulting from a sudden sharp movement of the neck and head (as of a person in a vehicle that is struck from the front or rear)

**whip·per·snap·per** \'hwip-ər-,snap-ər\ *n* : a small, insignificant, or presumptuous person

**whip·pet** \'hwip-ət\ *n* : a small swift dog of greyhound type often used for racing

**whipping boy** *n* : SCAPEGOAT

**whip·ple·tree** \'hwip-əl-(,)trē\ *n* : WHIFFLETREE

**whip·poor·will** \'hwip-ər-,wil\ *n* : an American bird with dull variegated plumage whose call is heard at nightfall and just before dawn

**¹whip·saw** \'hwip-,sȯ\ *n* **1** : a narrow tapering saw that has hook teeth and is from 5 to 7½ feet long  **2 :** a 2-man crosscut saw

²**whipsaw** *vb*  **1 :** to saw with a whipsaw  **2 :** to worst in two opposite ways at once, by a two-phase operation, or by the collusive action of two opponents

¹**whir** *also* **whirr** \'hwər\ *vb* **whirred; whir·ring :** to move, fly, or revolve with a whizzing sound : WHIZ

²**whir** *also* **whirr** *n* **:** a continuous fluttering or vibratory sound made by something in rapid motion

¹**whirl** \'hwərl\ *vb*  **1 :** to move or drive in a circle or similar curve esp. with force or speed  **2 :** to turn or cause to turn on or around an axis : SPIN  **3 :** to turn abruptly : WHEEL  **4 :** to pass, move, or go quickly  **5 :** to become dizzy or giddy : REEL

²**whirl** *n*  **1 :** a rapid rotating or circling movement; *also* **:** something undergoing such a movement  **2 :** COMMOTION, BUSTLE  **3 :** a state of mental confusion

**whirl·i·gig** \'hwər-li-ˌgig\ *n* [ME *whirlegigg*, fr. *whirlen* to whirl + *gigg* top]  **1 :** a child's toy having a whirling motion  **2 :** MERRY-GO-ROUND  **3 :** something that continuously whirls or changes; *also* **:** a whirling course (as of events)

**whirl·pool** \'hwərl-ˌpül\ *n* **:** water moving rapidly in a circle so as to produce a depression in the center into which floating objects may be drawn

**whirl·wind** \-ˌwind\ *n*  **1 :** a small whirling windstorm  **2 :** a confused rush : WHIRL

**whirly·bird** \'hwər-lē-ˌbərd\ *n* **:** HELICOPTER

¹**whish** \'hwish\ *vb* **:** to move with a whizzing or swishing sound

²**whish** *n* **:** a rushing sound : SWISH

¹**whisk** \'hwisk\ *n*  **1 :** a quick light sweeping or brushing motion  **2 :** a small usu. wire kitchen implement for hand beating of food  **3 :** a flexible bunch (as of twigs, feathers, or straw) attached to a handle for use as a brush

²**whisk** *vb*  **1 :** to move nimbly and quickly  **2 :** to move or convey briskly ⟨~ out a knife⟩ ⟨~ed the children off to bed⟩  **3 :** to beat or whip lightly ⟨~ eggs⟩  **4 :** to brush or wipe off lightly ⟨~ a coat⟩

**whisk broom** *n* **:** a small broom with a short handle used esp. as a clothes brush

**whis·ker** \'hwis-kər\ *n*  **1** *pl* **:** the part of the beard that grows on the sides of the face or on the chin  **2 :** one hair of the beard  **3 :** one of the long bristles or hairs growing near the mouth of an animal (as a cat or bird)  **4 :** a thin hairlike crystal (as of sapphire or a metal) of exceptional mechanical strength — **whis·kered** \-kərd\ *adj*

**whis·key** *or* **whis·ky** \'hwis-kē\ *n, pl* **whiskeys** *or* **whiskies** [IrGael *uisce beathadh* & ScGael *uisge beatha*, lit., water of life] **:** a liquor distilled from a fermented mash of grain (as rye, corn, or barley)

¹**whis·per** \'hwis-pər\ *vb* **whis·pered;**

**whis·per·ing** \-p(ə-)riŋ\  **1 :** to speak very low or under the breath; *also* **:** to tell or utter by whispering ⟨~ a secret⟩  **2 :** to make a low rustling sound ⟨~*ing* leaves⟩

²**whisper** *n*  **1 :** an act or instance of whispering; *esp* **:** speech without vibration of the vocal cords  **2 :** something communicated by or as if by whispering : HINT, RUMOR

**whist** \'hwist\ *n* **:** a card game played by four players in two partnerships with a deck of 52 cards

¹**whis·tle** \'hwis-əl\ *n*  **1 :** a device by which a shrill sound is produced ⟨steam ~⟩ ⟨tin ~⟩  **2 :** a shrill clear sound made by forcing breath out or air in through the puckered lips  **3 :** the sound or signal produced by a whistle or as if by whistling  **4 :** the shrill clear note of an animal (as a bird)

²**whistle** *vb* **whis·tled; whis·tling** \-(ə-)liŋ\  **1 :** to utter a shrill clear sound by blowing or drawing air through the puckered lips  **2 :** to utter a shrill note or call resembling a whistle  **3 :** to make a shrill clear sound esp. by rapid movements ⟨bullets *whistled* by him⟩  **4 :** to blow or sound a whistle  **5 :** to signal or call by a whistle  **6 :** to produce, utter, or express by whistling ⟨~ a tune⟩ — **whis·tler** \-(ə-)lər\ *n*

**whis·tle-stop** \'hwis-əl-ˌstäp\ *n*  **1 :** a small station at which trains stop only on signal  **2 :** a small community  **3 :** a brief personal appearance by a political candidate orig. on the rear platform of a touring train

**whit** \'hwit\ *n* [alter. of ME *wiht, wight* creature, thing, bit, fr. OE *wiht*] **:** the smallest part or particle imaginable : BIT

¹**white** \'hwīt\ *adj* **whit·er; whit·est**  **1 :** free from color  **2 :** of the color of new snow or milk; *esp* **:** of the color white  **3 :** light or pallid in color ⟨lips ~ with fear⟩  **4 :** SILVERY; *also* **:** made of silver  **5 :** of, relating to, or being a member of a group or race characterized by light-colored skin  **6 :** free from spot or blemish : PURE, INNOCENT  **7 :** BLANK ⟨~ space in printed matter⟩  **8 :** not intended to cause harm ⟨a ~ lie⟩  **9 :** wearing white ⟨~ friars⟩  **10 :** SNOWY ⟨~ Christmas⟩  **11 :** ARDENT, PASSIONATE ⟨~ fury⟩  **12 :** conservative or reactionary in politics

²**white** *n*  **1 :** the color of maximal lightness that characterizes objects which both reflect and transmit light : the opposite of black  **2 :** a white or light-colored part or thing ⟨the ~ of an egg⟩; *also, pl* **:** white garments  **3 :** the light-colored pieces in a 2-handed board game; *also* **:** the person by whom these are played  **4 :** one that is or approaches the color white  **5 :** a member of a light-skinned race  **6 :** a member of a conservative or reactionary political group

**white ant** *n* **:** TERMITE

**white·bait** \'hwīt-ˌbāt\ *n* **:** the young of a herring or a similar small fish used for food

**white blood cell** *n* : a blood cell that does not contain hemoglobin : LEUKOCYTE

**white-cap** \'hwīt-ˌkap\ *n* : a wave crest breaking into foam

**white-col-lar** \'hwīt-'käl-ər\ *adj* : of, relating to, or constituting the class of salaried workers whose duties do not require the wearing of work clothes or protective clothing

**white dwarf** *n* : a small very dense whitish star of high surface temperature and low luminosity

**white elephant** *n* [so called because white elephants were venerated in parts of Asia and maintained without being required to work] **1** : an Indian elephant of a pale color that is sometimes venerated in India, Ceylon, Thailand, and Burma **2** : something requiring much care and expense and yielding little profit **3** : an object no longer wanted by its owner though not without value to others

**white-faced** \'hwīt-'fāst\ *adj* **1** : having a wan pale face **2** : having the face white in whole or in part (~ cattle)

**white feather** *n* [fr. the superstition that a white feather in the plumage of a gamecock is a mark of a poor fighter] : a mark or symbol of cowardice

**white-fish** \'hwīt-ˌfish\ *n* : any of various freshwater food fishes related to the salmons and trouts

**white flag** *n* : a flag of plain white used as a flag of truce or as a token of surrender

**white-fly** \'hwīt-ˌflī\ *n* : any of numerous small insects that are injurious plant pests related to the scale insects

**white gasoline** *n* : gasoline containing no tetraethyllead

**white gold** *n* : a pale alloy of gold resembling platinum in appearance and usu. containing nickel

**white goods** *n pl* : white fabrics or articles (as sheets or towels) typically made of cotton or linen

**White-hall** \'hwīt-ˌhȯl\ *n* : the British government

**white-head** \-ˌhed\ *n* : a small whitish lump in the skin due to retention of secretion in an oil gland duct

**white heat** *n* : a temperature higher than red heat at which a body becomes brightly incandescent so as to appear white — **white-hot** *adj*

**White House** \-ˌhaůs\ *n* **1** : the executive department of the U.S. government **2** : a residence of the president of the U.S.

**white lead** *n* : a heavy white powder that is a carbonate of lead and is used as a pigment

**white matter** *n* : the whitish part of nervous tissue consisting mostly of nerve-cell processes

**whit-en** \'hwīt-ᵊn\ *vb* **whit-ened**; **whit-en-ing** \'hwīt-(ᵊ-)niŋ\ : to make or become white **syn** blanch, bleach — **whit-en-er** \'hwīt-(ᵊ-)nər\ *n*

**white-ness** \'hwīt-nəs\ *n* : the quality or state of being white

**white pine** *n* : a tall-growing pine of

eastern No. America with leaves in clusters of five; *also* : its wood

**white-pine blister rust** *n* : a destructive disease of white pine caused by a rust fungus that passes part of its complex life cycle on currant or gooseberry bushes; *also* : this fungus

**white room** *n* : CLEAN ROOM

**white sale** *n* : a sale on white goods

**white slave** *n* : a woman or girl held unwillingly for purposes of prostitution — **white slavery** *n*

**white-tail** \'hwīt-ˌtāl\ *n* : a No. American deer with a rather long tail white on the underside and with forward-arching antlers

**white-tailed deer** \ˌhwīt-ˌtāl-'diər\ *n* : WHITETAIL

**white-wall** \'hwīt-ˌwȯl\ *n* : an automobile tire having white sides

¹**white-wash** \-ˌwȯsh, -ˌwäsh\ *vb* **1** : to whiten with whitewash **2** : to clear of a charge of wrongdoing by offering excuses, hiding facts, or conducting a perfunctory investigation **3** : to defeat (an opponent) so that he fails to score

²**whitewash** *n* **1** : a liquid preparation (as of lime and water or of whiting, size, and water) for whitening structural surfaces **2** : WHITEWASHING

**white-wood** \-ˌwůd\ *n* : any of various trees (as a tulip tree) having light-colored wood; *also* : the wood of such a tree

**whith-er** \'hwith-ər\ *adv* **1** : to what place **2** : to what situation, position, degree, or end (~ will this drive him) **3** : to the place at, in, or to which; *also* : to which place **4** : to whatever place

**whith-er-so-ev-er** \ˌhwith-ər-sə-'wev-ər\ *conj* : to whatever place

¹**whit-ing** \'hwīt-iŋ\ *n* : any of several usu. light or silvery food fishes (as a hake) found mostly near seacoasts

²**whiting** *n* : pulverized chalk or limestone used as a pigment and in putty

**whit-ish** \'hwīt-ish\ *adj* : somewhat white

**whit-low** \'hwit-ˌlō\ *n* : FELON 2

**Whit-sun-day** \'hwit-'sən-dē,-sən-ˌdā\ *n* [ME *Whitsonday*, fr. OE *hwīta sunnandæg*, lit., white Sunday; prob. fr. the custom of wearing white robes by the newly baptized, who were numerous at this season] : PENTECOST

**whit-tle** \'hwit-ᵊl\ *vb* **whit-tled**; **whit-tling** \'hwit-(ᵊ-)liŋ\ **1** : to pare or cut off chips from the surface of (wood) with a knife; *also* : to cut or shape by such paring **2** : to reduce, remove, or destroy gradually as if by paring down : PARE (~ down expenses)

¹**whiz** *or* **whizz** \'hwiz\ *vb* **whizzed**; **whiz-zing** : to hum, whir, or hiss like a speeding object (as an arrow or ball) passing through air

²**whiz** *or* **whizz** *n, pl* **whiz-zes** : a hissing, buzzing, or whirring sound

³**whiz** *n, pl* **whiz-zes** : WIZARD 2

**who** \(')hü\ *pron* **1** — used to inquire the identity of an indicated person or group (~ did it) (~ is he) (~ are they) **2** : the person or persons that (knows ~ did it) **3** \(ˌ)hü, ü\ — used to introduce a relative clause and to serve as a substitute therein for the substantive modified by the clause ⟨the man ~ lives there is rich⟩ ⟨the people ~ did it were caught⟩

**WHO** abbr World Health Organization

**who·dun·it** also **who·dun·nit** \hü-'dən-ət\ n : a detective story or mystery story presented as a novel, play, or motion picture

**who·ev·er** \hü-'ev-ər\ pron : whatever person : no matter who

¹**whole** \'hōl\ adj [ME hool healthy, unhurt, entire, fr. OE hāl] 1 : being in healthy or sound condition : free from defect or damage : WELL, INTACT 2 : having all its proper parts or elements ⟨~ milk⟩ 3 : constituting the total sum of : INTEGRAL ⟨~ continental landmasses⟩ 4 : each or all of the (the ~ family) 5 : not scattered or divided : CONCENTRATED ⟨gave me his ~ attention⟩ 6 : seemingly complete or total ⟨the ~ idea is to help, not hinder⟩ syn entire, perfect — **whole·ness** n

²**whole** n 1 : a complete amount or sum : a number, aggregate, or totality lacking no part, member, or element 2 : something constituting a complex unity : a coherent system or organization of parts fitting or working together as one — **on the whole** 1 : in view of all the circumstances or conditions 2 : in general

**whole·heart·ed** \'hōl-'härt-əd\ adj : undivided in purpose, enthusiasm, or will : HEARTY, ZESTFUL, SINCERE

**whole number** n : INTEGER

¹**whole·sale** \'hōl-ˌsāl\ n : the sale of goods in quantity usu. for resale by a retail merchant

²**wholesale** adj 1 : of, relating to, or engaged in wholesaling 2 : performed on a large scale without discrimination ⟨~ slaughter⟩ — **wholesale** adv

³**wholesale** vb **wholesaled; wholesal·ing** : to sell at wholesale — **whole·sal·er** n

**whole·some** \'hōl-səm\ adj 1 : promoting mental, spiritual, or bodily health or well-being ⟨~ advice⟩ ⟨a ~ environment⟩ 2 : not detrimental to health or well-being; esp : fit for food 3 : sound in body, mind, or morals : HEALTHY 4 : PRUDENT ⟨~ respect for the law⟩ — **whole·some·ness** n

**whole step** n : a musical interval comprising two half steps (as C–D or F♯–G♯)

**whole wheat** adj : made of ground entire wheat kernels

**whol·ly** \'hōl-(l)ē\ adv 1 : COMPLETELY, TOTALLY 2 : SOLELY, EXCLUSIVELY

**whom** \(')hüm\ pron, objective case of WHO

**whom·ev·er** \hüm-'ev-ər\ pron, objective case of WHOEVER

**whom·so·ev·er** \ˌhüm-sə-'wev-ər\ pron, objective case of WHOSOEVER

¹**whoop** \'h(w)üp, 'h(w)ùp\ vb 1 : to shout or call loudly and vigorously 2 : to make the sound that follows a fit of coughing in whooping cough 3 : to

go or pass with a loud noise 4 : to utter or express with a whoop; also : to urge, drive, or cheer with a whoop

²**whoop** n 1 : a whooping sound or utterance : SHOUT, HOOT 2 : a crowing sound accompanying the intake of breath after a fit of coughing in whooping cough

**whooping cough** n : an infectious disease esp. of children marked by convulsive coughing fits sometimes followed by a whoop

**whooping crane** n : a large white nearly extinct No. American crane noted for its loud whooping note

**whoop·la** \'h(w)üp-ˌlä, 'h(w)ùp-\ n 1 : a noisy commotion 2 : boisterous merrymaking

**whop·per** \'hwäp-ər\ n : something unusually large or extreme of its kind; esp : a monstrous lie

**whop·ping** \'hwäp-iŋ\ adj : extremely large

**whore** \'hōr\ n : PROSTITUTE

**whorl** \'hwórl, 'hwərl\ n 1 : a row of parts (as leaves or petals) encircling an axis and esp. a plant stem 2 : something that whirls or coils or whose form suggests such movement : COIL, SPIRAL 3 : one of the turns of a snail shell

**whorled** \'hwórld, 'hwərld\ adj : having or arranged in whorls

¹**whose** \(')hüz\ adj : of or relating to whom or which esp. as possessor or possessors, agent or agents, or object or objects of an action ⟨asked ~ bag it was⟩

²**whose** pron : whose one or ones ⟨~ is this car⟩ ⟨~ are those books⟩

**who·so** \'hü-ˌsō\ pron : WHOEVER

**who·so·ev·er** \ˌhü-sə-'wev-ər\ pron : WHOEVER

**whs** or **whse** warehouse

**whsle** abbr wholesale

¹**why** \(')hwī\ adv : for what reason, cause, or purpose ⟨~ did you do it⟩

²**why** conj 1 : the cause, reason, or purpose for which ⟨that is ~ you did it⟩ 2 : for which : on account of which ⟨knows the reason ~ you did it⟩

³**why** \'hwī\ n, pl **whys** : REASON, CAUSE ⟨the ~ of race prejudice⟩

⁴**why** \(ˌ)wī, (ˌ)hwī\ interj — used to express surprise, hesitation, approval, disapproval, or impatience ⟨~, here's what I was looking for⟩

**WI** abbr 1 West Indies 2 Wisconsin

**wick** \'wik\ n : a loosely bound bundle of soft fibers that draws up oil, tallow, or wax to be burned in a candle, oil lamp, or stove

**wick·ed** \'wik-əd\ adj 1 : morally bad : EVIL, SINFUL 2 : FIERCE, VICIOUS 3 : HARMFUL, DANGEROUS ⟨a ~ attack⟩ 4 : REPUGNANT, VILE ⟨a ~ odor⟩ 5 : ROGUISH ⟨a ~ glance⟩ — **wick·ed·ly** adv — **wick·ed·ness** n

**wick·er** \'wik-ər\ n 1 : a small pliant branch (as an osier or a withe) 2 : WICKERWORK — **wicker** adj

**wick·er·work** \-ˌwərk\ n : work made of osiers, twigs, or rods : BASKETRY

**wick·et** \'wik-ət\ n 1 : a small gate or door; esp : one forming a part of or placed near a larger one **2** : a window-like opening usu. with a grille or grate (as at a ticket office) **3** : a small gate for regulating the amount of water in a canal lock **4** : a set of three upright rods topped by two crosspieces bowled at in cricket **5** : an arch through which the ball is driven in croquet

**wick·i·up** \'wik-ē-,əp\ *n* : a hut used by nomadic Indians of the western and southwestern U.S. with a usu. oval base and a rough frame covered with reed mats, grass, or brushwood

**wid** *abbr* widow, widower

**¹wide** \'wīd\ *adj* **wid·er; wid·est 1** : covering a vast area **2** : measured across or at right angles to the length **3** : not narrow : BROAD; *also* : ROOMY **4** : opened to full width ⟨eyes ~ with wonder⟩ **5** : not limited : EXTENSIVE ⟨~ experience⟩ **6** : far from the goal, mark, or truth ⟨a ~ guess⟩ — **wide·ly** *adv*

**²wide** *adv* **wid·er; wid·est 1** : over a great distance or extent : WIDELY ⟨searched far and ~⟩ **2** : over a specified distance, area, or extent **3** : so as to leave a wide space between ⟨~ apart⟩ **4** : so as to clear by a considerable distance ⟨ran ~ around left end⟩ **5** : COMPLETELY, FULLY ⟨opened her eyes ~⟩ **6** : ASTRAY, AFIELD ⟨the bullet went ~⟩

**wide-awake** \,wīd-ə-'wāk\ *adj* : fully awake; *also* : KNOWING, ALERT ⟨a group of ~ young men⟩

**wide-eyed** \'wīd-'īd\ *adj* **1** : having the eyes wide open **2** : AMAZED **3** : NAIVE

**wide-mouthed** \'wīd-'maủthd, -'maủtht\ *adj* **1** : having a wide mouth ⟨~ jars⟩ **2** : having one's mouth opened wide (as in awe)

**wid·en** \'wīd-ᵊn\ *vb* **wid·ened; wid·en·ing** \'wīd-(ᵊ-)niŋ\ : to make or become wide : BROADEN

**wide·spread** \'wīd-'spred\ *adj* **1** : widely extended or spread out ⟨~ wings⟩ **2** : widely scattered or prevalent ⟨~ fear⟩

**wid·geon** *also* **wi·geon** \'wij-ən\ *n* : any of several freshwater ducks between the teal and the mallard in size

**¹wid·ow** \'wid-ō\ *n* : a woman who has lost her husband by death and has not married again — **wid·ow·hood** *n*

**²widow** *vb* : to cause to become a widow

**wid·ow·er** \'wid-ə-wər\ *n* : a man who has lost his wife by death and has not married again

**width** \'width\ *n* **1** : a distance from side to side : the measurement taken at right angles to the length : BREADTH **2** : largeness of extent or scope; *also* : FULLNESS **3** : a measured and cut piece of material ⟨a ~ of calico⟩ ⟨a ~ of lumber⟩

**wield** \'wēld\ *vb* **1** : to use or handle esp. effectively ⟨~ a broom⟩ ⟨~ a pen⟩ **2** : to exert authority by means of : EMPLOY ⟨~ influence⟩ — **wield·er** *n*

**wie·ner** \'wē-nər\ *n* [short for *wiener-wurst*, fr. G, lit., Vienna sausage] : FRANKFURTER

**wife** \'wīf\ *n, pl* **wives** \'wīvz\ **1** *dial* : WOMAN **2** : a woman acting in a specified capacity — used in combination **3** : a married woman — **wife-hood** *n* — **wife·less** *adj* — **wife·ly** *adj*

**wig** \'wig\ *n* [short for *periwig*, fr. MF *perruque*, fr. It *perrucca* hair, wig] : a manufactured covering of natural or synthetic hair for the head; *also* : TOUPEE

**wig·gle** \'wig-əl\ *vb* **wig·gled; wig·gling** \-(ə-)liŋ\ **1** : to move to and fro with quick jerky or shaking movements : JIGGLE **2** : WRIGGLE — **wiggle** *n*

**wig·gler** \'wig-(ə-)lər\ *n* **1** : one that wiggles **2** : a larva or pupa of a mosquito

**wig·gly** \-(ə-)lē\ *adj* **1** : tending to wiggle ⟨a ~ worm⟩ **2** : WAVY ⟨~ lines⟩

**wight** \'wīt\ *n* : a living being : CREATURE

**wig·let** \'wig-lət\ *n* : a small wig used esp. to enhance a hairstyle

**¹wig·wag** \'wig-,wag\ *vb* **1** : to signal by or as if by a flag or light waved according to a code **2** : to make or cause to make a signal (as with the hand or arm)

**²wigwag** *n* **1** : the art or practice of wigwagging **2** : a wigwagged message

**wig·wam** \'wig-,wäm\ *n* : a hut of the Indians of the eastern U.S. having typically an arched framework of poles overlaid with bark, rush mats, or hides

**¹wild** \'wīld\ *adj* **1** : living in a state of nature and not ordinarily tamed ⟨~ ducks⟩ **2** : growing or produced without human aid or care ⟨~ honey⟩ ⟨~ plants⟩ **3** : WASTE, DESOLATE ⟨~ country⟩ **4** : UNCONTROLLED, UNRESTRAINED, UNRULY ⟨~ passions⟩ ⟨a ~ young stallion⟩ **5** : TURBULENT, STORMY ⟨a ~ night⟩ **6** : EXTRAVAGANT, FANTASTIC, CRAZY ⟨~ ideas⟩ **7** : indicative of strong passion, desire, or emotion ⟨a ~ stare⟩ **8** : UNCIVILIZED, SAVAGE **9** : deviating from the natural or expected course : ERRATIC ⟨a ~ throw⟩ **10** : having a denomination determined by the holder ⟨deuces ~⟩ — **wild·ly** *adv* — **wild·ness** \'wīl(d)-nəs\ *n*

**²wild** *n* **1** : WILDERNESS **2** : a natural or undomesticated state or existence

**³wild** *adv* **1** : WILDLY **2** : without regulation or control ⟨running ~⟩

**wild carrot** *n* : a widely naturalized Eurasian weed that is prob. the original of the cultivated carrot

**¹wild·cat** \'wīl(d)-,kat\ *n, pl* **wildcats 1** : any of various small or medium-sized cats (as a lynx or ocelot) **2** : a quick-tempered hard-fighting person **3** : a well drilled for oil or gas in a region not known to be productive

**²wildcat** *adj* **1** : not sound or safe ⟨~ schemes⟩ **2** : initiated by a group of workers without formal union approval ⟨~ strike⟩

**³wildcat** *vb* **wild·cat·ted; wild·cat·ting** : to drill an oil or gas well in a region not known to be productive

**wil·de·beest** \'wil-də-,bēst\ *n, pl* **wildebeests** *also* **wildebeest** [Afrikaans *wildebees,* fr. *wilde* wild + *bees* ox] : GNU

**wil·der·ness** \'wil-dər-nəs\ *n* [ME, fr. *wildern* wild, fr. OE *wilddēoren* of wild beasts] : an uncultivated and uninhabited region

**wild·fire** \'wīl(d)-,fī(ə)r\ *n* : a sweeping and destructive fire ⟨the news spread like ∼⟩

**wild·fowl** \-,faul\ *n* : a game bird; *esp* : a game waterfowl (as a wild duck or goose)

**wild-goose chase** *n* : the pursuit of something unattainable

**wild·life** \'wīl(d)-,līf\ *n* : creatures that are neither human nor domesticated; *esp* : mammals, birds, and fishes hunted by man

**wild oat** *n* 1 : any of several wild grasses 2 *pl* : offenses and indiscretions attributed to youthful exuberance ⟨was just sowing his *wild oats*⟩

**wild rice** *n* : a No. American aquatic grass; *also* : its edible seed

**wild·wood** \'wīld-,wud\ *n* : a wild or unfrequented wood

¹**wile** \'wīl\ *n* 1 : a trick or stratagem intended to ensnare or deceive; *also* : a playful trick 2 : TRICKERY, GUILE

²**wile** *vb* **wiled; wil·ing** : LURE, ENTICE

¹**will** \wəl, (ə)l, (')wil\ *vb, past* **would** \wəd, (ə)d, (')wud\; *pres sing & pl* **will** 1 : WISH, DESIRE ⟨call it what you ∼⟩ 2 — used as an auxiliary verb to express (1) desire, willingness, or in negative constructions refusal ⟨∼ you have another⟩ ⟨he *won't* do it⟩, (2) customary or habitual action ⟨∼ get angry over nothing⟩, (3) simple futurity ⟨tomorrow we ∼ go shopping⟩, (4) capability or sufficiency ⟨the back seat ∼ hold three⟩, (5) determination or willfulness ⟨I ∼ go despite them⟩, (6) probability ⟨that ∼ be the mailman⟩, (7) inevitability ⟨accidents ∼ happen⟩, or (8) a command ⟨you ∼ do as I say⟩

²**will** \'wil\ *n* 1 : wish or desire often combined with determination ⟨the ∼ to win⟩ 2 : something desired; *esp* : a choice or determination of one having authority or power 3 : the act, process, or experience of willing : VOLITION 4 : the mental powers manifested as wishing, choosing, desiring, or intending 5 : a disposition to act according to principles or ends 6 : power of controlling one's own actions or emotions ⟨a man of iron ∼⟩ 7 : a legal document in which a person declares to whom his possessions are to go after his death

³**will** \'wil\ *vb* 1 : to dispose of by or as if by a will : BEQUEATH 2 : to determine by an act of choice; *also* : DECREE, ORDAIN 3 : INTEND, PURPOSE; *also* : CHOOSE

**will·ful** *or* **wil·ful** \'wil-fəl\ *adj* 1 : governed by will without regard to reason : OBSTINATE, STUBBORN 2 : INTENTIONAL ⟨∼ murder⟩ — **will·ful·ly** \-lē\ *adv*

**wil·lies** \'wil-ēz\ *n pl* : a fit of nervousness : JITTERS

**will·ing** \'wil-iŋ\ *adj* 1 : inclined or

favorably disposed in mind : READY ⟨∼ to go⟩ 2 : prompt to act or respond ⟨∼ workers⟩ 3 : done, borne, or accepted voluntarily or without reluctance : VOLUNTARY 4 : of or relating to the will : VOLITIONAL — **will·ing·ly** *adv* — **will·ing·ness** *n*

**wil·li·waw** \'wil-ē-,wò\ *n* : a sudden violent gust of cold land air common along mountainous coasts of high latitudes

**will-o'-the-wisp** \,wil-ə-thə-'wisp\ *n* 1 : a light that appears at night over marshy grounds 2 : a misleading or elusive goal or hope

**wil·low** \'wil-ō\ *n* 1 : any of numerous quick-growing shrubs and trees with tough pliable shoots used in basketry 2 : the wood of a willow 3 : an object made of willow wood

**wil·low·ware** \-,waər\ *n* : dinnerware that is usu. blue and white and that is decorated with a story-telling design featuring a large willow tree by a little bridge

**wil·lowy** \'wil-ə-wē\ *adj* : PLIANT; *also* : gracefully tall and slender ⟨a ∼ young woman⟩

**will·pow·er** \'wil-,pau(ə)r\ *n* : energetic determination : RESOLUTENESS

**wil·ly-nil·ly** \,wil-ē-'nil-ē\ *adv or adj* [alter. of *will I nill I* or *will ye nill ye* or *will he nill he*; *nill* fr. archaic *nill* to be unwilling, fr. ME *nilen*, fr. OE *nyllan*, fr. *ne* not + *wyllan* to wish] : without regard for one's choice : by compulsion ⟨they rushed us along ∼⟩

¹**wilt** \'wilt\ *vb* 1 : to lose or cause to lose freshness and become limp : DROOP 2 : to grow weak or faint: LANGUISH 3 : to lose courage or spirit 4 : to lower the spirit, force, or vigor of

²**wilt** *n* : any of various plant disorders marked by wilting and often shriveling

**wily** \'wī-lē\ *adj* **wil·i·er; -est** : full of guile : TRICKY — **wil·i·ness** \'wī-lē-nəs\ *n*

**wim·ble** \'wim-bəl\ *n* : an instrument for boring holes

¹**wim·ple** \'wim-pəl\ *n* : a cloth covering worn outdoors over the head and around the neck and chin by women esp. in the late medieval period and by some nuns

²**wimple** *vb* **wim·pled; wim·pling** \-p(ə-)liŋ\ 1 : to cover with or as if with a wimple 2 : to ripple or cause to ripple 3 : to fall or lie in folds

¹**win** \'win\ *vb* **won** \'wən\; **win·ning** [ME *winnen,* fr. OE *winnan* to struggle] 1 : to gain the victory in or as if in a contest : SUCCEED 2 : to get possession of esp. by effort : GAIN 3 : to gain in or as if in battle or contest; *also* : to be the victor in ⟨*won* the war⟩ 4 : to obtain by work : EARN 5 : to solicit and gain the favor of; *esp* : to induce to accept oneself in marriage

²**win** *n* : VICTORY; *esp* : first place at the finish of a horse race

**wince** \'wins\ *vb* **winced; winc·ing** : to shrink back involuntarily (as from pain) : FLINCH — **wince** *n*

**winch** \'winch\ *n* 1 : a machine to

hoist, haul, turn, or strain something forcibly **2** : a crank with a handle for giving motion to a machine (as a grindstone) — **winch** vb

**¹wind** \'wind\ n **1** : a movement of the air of any velocity **2** : a force or agency that carries along or influences : TENDENCY, TREND **3** : BREATH ⟨he had the ~ knocked out of him⟩ **4** : gas generated in the stomach or intestines **5** : something insubstantial; esp : idle words **6** : air carrying a scent (as of game) **7** : INTIMATION ⟨they got ~ of our plans⟩ **8** : WIND INSTRUMENTS; also, pl : players of wind instruments

**²wind** vb **1** : to get a scent of ⟨the dogs ~ed the game⟩ **2** : to cause to be out of breath ⟨he was ~ed from the climb⟩ **3** : to allow (as a horse) to rest so as to recover breath

**³wind** \'wind, 'wind\ vb **wind·ed** \'win-dəd, 'win-\ or **wound** \'wau̇nd\; **wind·ing** : to sound by blowing ⟨~ a horn⟩

**⁴wind** \'wind\ vb **wound** \'wau̇nd\ also **wind·ed; wind·ing 1** : to have a curving course or shape ⟨a river ~ing through the valley⟩ **2** : to move or lie so as to encircle **3** : ENTANGLE, INVOLVE **4** : to introduce stealthily : INSINUATE **5** : to encircle or cover with something pliable : WRAP, COIL TWINE, TWIST ⟨~ a bobbin⟩ **6** : to hoist or haul by a rope or chain ⟨~ a ship to the wharf⟩ **7** : to tighten the spring of; also : CRANK **8** : to raise to a high level (as of excitement) **9** : to cause to move in a curving line or path **10** : TURN **11** : to traverse on a curving course

**⁵wind** \'wind\ n : COIL, TURN

**wind·age** \'win-dij\ n : the influence of the wind in deflecting the course of a projectile through the air; also : the amount of such deflection

**wind·bag** \'win(d)-ˌbag\ n : an idly talkative person

**wind-blown** \-ˌblōn\ adj : blown by the wind; also : having the appearance of being blown by the wind

**wind-break** \-ˌbrāk\ n : something serving to break the force of the wind; esp : a growth of trees and shrubs

**wind–bro·ken** \-ˌbrō-kən\ adj, of a horse : having the power of breathing impaired by disease

**wind-burn** \-ˌbərn\ n : skin irritation caused by wind

**wind-chill** \'win(d)-ˌchil\ n : a still-air temperature that would have the same cooling effect on exposed human flesh as a given combination of temperature and wind speed

**wind·er** \'wīn-dər\ n : one that winds

**wind-fall** \'win(d)-ˌfȯl\ n **1** : something (as a tree or fruit) blown down by the wind **2** : an unexpected or sudden gift, gain, or advantage

**wind-flow·er** \-ˌflau̇-(ə)r\ n **1** : ANEMONE **2** : RUE ANEMONE

**wind gap** n : a notch in the crest of a mountain ridge

**¹wind·ing** \'wīn-diŋ\ n : material (as wire) wound or coiled about an object

**²winding** adj **1** : having a pronounced curve; esp : SPIRAL ⟨~ stairs⟩ **2** : having a course that winds ⟨a ~ road⟩

**wind·ing-sheet** \-ˌshēt\ n : SHROUD

**wind instrument** n : a musical instrument (as a flute or horn) sounded by wind and esp. by the breath

**wind-jam·mer** \'win(d)-ˌjam-ər\ n : a sailing ship; also : one of its crew

**wind-lass** \'win-dləs\ n [ME wyndlas, alter. of wyndas, fr. ON vindāss, fr. vinda to wind + āss pole] : a machine for hoisting or hauling that consists in its simple form of a horizontal barrel wound with the hoisting rope and supported in vertical frames and that has a crank with a handle for turning it

**wind-mill** \'win(d)-ˌmil\ n : a mill or machine worked by the wind turning sails or vanes that radiate from a central shaft

**win·dow** \'win-dō\ n [ME windowe, fr. ON vindauga, fr. vindr wind + auga eye] **1** : an opening in the wall of a building to let in light and air; also : the framework with fittings that closes such an opening **2** : WINDOWPANE **3** : an opening resembling or suggesting that of a window in a building — **win·dow-less** adj

**window dressing** n **1** : display of merchandise in a store window **2** : a showing made to create a good but sometimes false impression

**win·dow·pane** \'win-dō-ˌpān\ n : a pane in a window

**win·dow–shop** \-ˌshäp\ vb : to look at the displays in store windows without going inside the stores to make purchases — **win·dow-shop·per** n

**win·dow-sill** \-ˌsil\ n : the horizontal member at the bottom of a window opening

**wind·pipe** \'win(d)-ˌpīp\ n : the passage for the breath from the larynx to the lungs

**wind-proof** \-ˈprüf\ adj : proof against the wind ⟨a ~ jacket⟩

**wind-row** \'win-ˌ(d)rō\ n **1** : hay raked up into a row to dry **2** : a row of something (as dry leaves) swept up by or as if by the wind

**wind-shield** \'win(d)-ˌshēld\ n : a transparent screen in front of the occupants of a vehicle

**wind sock** n : an open-ended truncated cloth cone mounted in an elevated position to indicate the direction of the wind

**wind-storm** \-ˌstȯrm\ n : a storm with high wind and little or no precipitation

**wind-swept** \'win(d)-ˌswept\ adj : swept by or as if by wind ⟨~ plains⟩

**wind tunnel** n : an enclosed passage through which air is blown to determine the effects of wind pressure on an object

**wind–up** \'wīn-ˌdəp\ n **1** : CONCLUSION, FINISH **2** : a pitcher's motion preliminary to delivering a pitch

**wind up** \(')wīn-'dəp\ vb **1** : to bring or come to a conclusion : END **2** : SETTLE **3** : to arrive in a place, situation, or condition at the end or as a result of a course of action ⟨**wound up** as paupers⟩ **4** : to give a preliminary swing to the arm

¹**wind·ward** \'win-(d)wərd\ *adj* : moving toward or situated on the side toward the direction from which the wind is blowing

²**windward** *n* : the point or side from which the wind is blowing

**windy** \'win-dē\ *adj* **wind·i·er; -est 1** : having wind : exposed to winds ⟨a ~ day⟩ ⟨a ~ prairie⟩ **2** : STORMY **3** : FLATULENT **4** : indulging in or characterized by useless talk : VERBOSE

¹**wine** \'wīn\ *n* **1** : fermented grape juice **2** : the usu. fermented juice of a plant product (as fruit) used as a beverage ⟨rice ~⟩ ⟨cherry ~⟩

²**wine** *vb* **wined; win·ing** : to treat to or drink wine

**wine cellar** *n* : a room for storing wines; *also* : a stock of wines

**wine·grow·er** \-,grō-(ə)r\ *n* : one that cultivates a vineyard and makes wine

**wine·press** \'wīn-,pres\ *n* : a vat in which juice is expressed from grapes by treading or by means of a plunger

**wine·shop** \'wīn-,shäp\ *n* : a tavern that specializes in serving wine

¹**wing** \'wiŋ\ *n* **1** : one of the movable feathered or membranous paired appendages by means of which a bird, bat, or insect is able to fly **2** : something suggesting a wing in shape, position, or appearance **3** : a plant or animal appendage or part likened to a wing; *esp* : one that is flat or broadly extended **4** : a turned-back or extended edge on an article of clothing **5** : a unit in military aviation consisting of a varying number of airplanes **6** : a means of flight or rapid progress **7** : the act or manner of flying : FLIGHT **8** : ARM; *esp* : a throwing or pitching arm **9** : a part of a building projecting from the main part **10** *pl* : the area at the side of the stage out of sight **11** : the right or left division of an army, fleet, or command as it faces an enemy **12** : a position or player on each side of the center (as in hockey) **13** : either of two opposing groups within an organization : FACTION — **wing·less** *adj* — **on the wing** : in flight : FLYING — **under one's wing** : in one's charge or care

²**wing** *vb* **1** : to fit with wings; *also* : to enable to fly easily **2** : to pass through in flight : FLY ⟨~ the air⟩ ⟨swallows ~ing southward⟩ **3** : to achieve or accomplish by flying **4** : to let fly : DISPATCH ⟨~ an arrow through the air⟩ **5** : to wound in the wing ⟨~ a bird⟩; *also* : to wound without killing

**wing-ding** \'wiŋ-,diŋ\ *n* : a wild, lively, or lavish party

**winged** \'wiŋd, *also except for "esp."* sense of 1 'wiŋ-əd\ *adj* **1** : having wings esp. of a specified character **2** : soaring with or as if with wings : ELEVATED **3** : SWIFT, RAPID

**wing·span** \'wiŋ-,span\ *n* : WING-SPREAD; *esp* : the distance between the tips of an airplane's wings

**wing·spread** \-,spred\ *n* : the spread of the wings; *esp* : the distance between the tips of the fully extended wings of a winged animal

¹**wink** \'wiŋk\ *vb* **1** : to close and open the eyes quickly : BLINK **2** : to avoid seeing or noticing something ⟨~ at a violation of the law⟩ **3** : TWINKLE, FLICKER **4** : to close and open one eye quickly as a signal or hint **5** : to affect or influence by or as if by blinking the eyes ⟨he ~ed back his tears⟩

²**wink** *n* **1** : a brief period of sleep : NAP **2** : an act of winking; *esp* : a hint or sign given by winking **3** : INSTANT ⟨dries in a ~⟩

**wink·er** \'wiŋ-kər\ *n* **1** : one that winks **2** : EYELASH

**win·kle** \'wiŋ-kəl\ *n* **1** : ²PERIWINKLE **2** : any of various whelks

**win·ner** \'win-ər\ *n* : one that wins

¹**win·ning** \'win-iŋ\ *n* **1** : VICTORY **2** : something won; *esp* : money won at gambling ⟨large ~s⟩

²**winning** *adj* **1** : successful in competition **2** : ATTRACTIVE, CHARMING

**win·now** \'win-ō\ *vb* **1** : to remove (as chaff from grain) by a current of air; *also* : to free (as grain) from waste in this manner **2** : to get rid of (something unwanted) or to separate, sift, or sort (something) as if by winnowing

**wino** \'wī-nō\ *n, pl* **win·os** : one who is chronically addicted to drinking wine

**win·some** \'win-səm\ *adj* [ME winsum, fr. OE wynsum, fr. wynn joy] **1** : causing joy or pleasure : PLEASANT, WINNING ⟨a ~ lass⟩ **2** : CHEERFUL, GAY — **win·some·ly** *adv* — **win·some·ness** *n*

¹**win·ter** \'wint-ər\ *n* **1** : the season of the year in any region in which the noonday sun shines most obliquely : the coldest period of the year **2** : YEAR ⟨a man of 70 ~s⟩ **3** : a time or season of inactivity or decay

²**winter** *adj* : occurring in or surviving winter; *esp* : sown in autumn for harvesting in the following spring or summer ⟨~ wheat⟩

³**winter** *vb* **win·tered; win·ter·ing** \'win-t(ə-)riŋ\ **1** : to pass or survive the winter **2** : to keep, feed, or manage through the winter ⟨~ cattle on silage⟩

**win·ter·green** \'wint-ər-,grēn\ *n* **1** : any of several low evergreen plants related to the heaths; *esp* : one with spicy red berries **2** : an aromatic oil from the common wintergreen or its flavor or something flavored with it

**win·ter·ize** \'wint-ə-,rīz\ *vb* **-ized; -iz·ing** : to make ready or safe for use in winter conditions

**win·ter·kill** \'wint-ər-,kil\ *vb* **1** : to kill or die by exposure to winter weather

**win·ter·tide** \'wint-ər-,tīd\ *n* : the season of winter : WINTERTIME

**win·ter·time** \-,tīm\ *n* : WINTER

**win·try** \'win-trē\ *or* **win·tery** \'win-t(ə-)rē\ *adj* **win·tri·er; -est 1** : of or characteristic of winter : coming in winter ⟨~ weather⟩ **2** : CHILLING, COLD, CHEERLESS ⟨a ~ welcome⟩

¹**wipe** \'wīp\ *vb* **wiped; wip·ing 1** : to clean or dry by rubbing ⟨~ dishes⟩

**2** : to remove by or as if by rubbing or cleaning ⟨~ away tears⟩ **3** : to erase completely : OBLITERATE **4** : DESTROY, ANNIHILATE ⟨the platoon was *wiped* out⟩ **5** : to pass or draw over a surface ⟨*wiped* his hand across his face⟩ — **wip·er** *n*

²**wipe** *n* **1** : an act or instance of wiping; *also* : BLOW, STRIKE, SWIPE **2** : something used for wiping

¹**wire** \'wī(ə)r\ *n* **1** : metal in the form of a thread or slender rod; *also* : a thread or rod of metal **2** : work made of wire threads or rods and esp. of wire netting **3** : a telegraph or telephone wire or system **4** : TELEGRAM, CABLEGRAM **5** *usu pl* : hidden or secret influences controlling the action of a person or body of persons ⟨pull ~s to get a nomination⟩ **6** : the finish line of a race

²**wire** *vb* **wired; wir·ing 1** : to provide or equip with wire ⟨~ a house for electricity⟩ **2** : to bind, string, or mount with wire **3** : to telegraph or telegraph to

**wire·draw** \'wī(ə)r-,drȯ\ *vb* **1** : to draw or spin out to great length, tenuity, or overrefinement **2** : to draw (metal) into wire

**wire·hair** \-,haər\ *n* : a wirehaired fox terrier

**wire·haired** \-'haərd\ *adj* : having a stiff wiry outer coat of hair

¹**wire·less** \-ləs\ *adj* **1** : having or using no wire or wires **2** *chiefly Brit* : RADIO

²**wireless** *n* **1** : a system for communicating by code signals and radio waves and without connecting wires **2** *chiefly Brit* : RADIO — **wireless** *vb*

**wire-puller** \'wī(ə)r-,pu̇l-ər\ *n* : one who uses secret or underhand means to influence the acts of a person or organization — **wire-pull·ing** \-,pu̇l-iŋ\ *n*

**wire recorder** *n* : a magnetic recorder using magnetic wire

**wire service** *n* : a news agency that sends out syndicated news copy by wire to subscribers

**wire·tap** \-,tap\ *vb* : to tap a telephone or telegraph wire to get information — **wiretap** *n* — **wire·tap·per** \-,tap-ər\ *n*

**wire·worm** \-,wərm\ *n* : the slender hard-coated larva of certain beetles often destructive to plant roots

**wir·ing** \'wī(ə)r-iŋ\ *n* : a system of wires; *esp* : one for distributing electricity through a building

**wiry** \'wī(ə)r-ē\ *adj* **wir·i·er** \'wī-rē-ər\; **-est 1** : of, relating to, or resembling wire **2** : slender yet strong and sinewy — **wir·i·ness** \'wī-rē-nəs\ *n*

**Wis** *or* **Wisc** *abbr* Wisconsin

**Wisd** *abbr* Wisdom

**wis·dom** \'wiz-dəm\ *n* **1** : accumulated philosophic or scientific learning : KNOWLEDGE; *also* : INSIGHT **2** : good sense : JUDGMENT **3** : a wise attitude or course of action

**wisdom tooth** *n* : the last tooth of the full set on each half of each jaw in man

¹**wise** \'wīz\ *n* : WAY, MANNER, FASHION ⟨in no ~⟩ ⟨in this ~⟩

²**wise** *adj* **wis·er; wis·est 1** : having wisdom : SAGE **2** : having or showing good sense or good judgment : SENSIBLE, SOUND, PRUDENT **3** : aware of what is going on : KNOWING; *also* : CRAFTY, SHREWD — **wise·ly** *adv*

**wise·acre** \'wī-,zā-kər\ *n* [Middle Dutch *wijssegger* soothsayer, fr. Old High German *wizzago*] : one who pretends to knowledge or cleverness

¹**wise·crack** \'wīz-,krak\ *n* : a clever, smart, or flippant remark

²**wisecrack** *vb* : to make a wisecrack

¹**wish** \'wish\ *vb* **1** : to have a desire : long for : CRAVE, WANT ⟨~ you were here⟩ ⟨~ for a puppy⟩ **2** : to form or express a wish concerning ⟨~ed him a happy birthday⟩ **3** : BID ⟨he ~ed me good morning⟩ **4** : to request by expressing a desire ⟨I ~ you to go now⟩

²**wish** *n* **1** : an act or instance of wishing or desire : WANT; *also* : GOAL **2** : an expressed will or desire : MANDATE

**wish·bone** \-,bōn\ *n* : a forked bone in front of the breastbone in most birds

**wish·ful** \'wish-fəl\ *adj* **1** : expressive of a wish : HOPEFUL, LONGING; *also* : DESIROUS **2** : according with wishes rather than fact ⟨~ thinking⟩

**wishy-washy** \'wish-ē-,wȯsh-ē, -,wȧsh-\ *adj* : WEAK, INSIPID; *also* : morally feeble

**wisp** \'wisp\ *n* **1** : a small bunch of hay or straw **2** : a thin strand, strip, or fragment ⟨a ~ of hair⟩; *also* : a thready streak ⟨a ~ of smoke⟩ **3** : something frail, slight, or fleeting ⟨a ~ of a girl⟩ ⟨a ~ of a smile⟩ — **wispy** *adj*

**wis·tar·ia** \wis-'tir-ē-ə, -'ter-\ *n* : WISTERIA

**wis·te·ria** \-'tir-ē-ə\ *n* : any of various Asiatic woody vines related to the peas and widely grown for their long showy clusters of blue, white, purple, or rose flowers

**wist·ful** \'wist-fəl\ *adj* : full of longing and unfulfilled desire : YEARNING ⟨a ~ expression⟩ — **wist·ful·ly** \-ē\ *adv* — **wist·ful·ness** *n*

**wit** \'wit\ *n* **1** : reasoning power : INTELLIGENCE **2** : mental soundness : SANITY — usu. used in pl. **3** : RESOURCEFULNESS, INGENUITY; *esp* : quickness and cleverness in handling words and ideas **4** : a talent for making clever remarks; *also* : one noted for making witty remarks — **at one's wit's end** : at a loss for a means of solving a problem

¹**witch** \'wich\ *n* **1** : a person believed to have magic power; *esp* : SORCERESS **2** : an ugly old woman : HAG **3** : a charming or alluring girl or woman

²**witch** *vb* : BEWITCH

**witch·craft** \'wich-,kraft\ *n* : the power or practices of a witch : SORCERY

**witch doctor** *n* : a practitioner of magic in a primitive society

**witch·ery** \'wich-(ə-)rē\ *n, pl* **-er·ies 1** : SORCERY **2** : FASCINATION, CHARM

**witch·grass** \'wich-,gras\ *n* : any of

several grasses that are weeds in cultivated areas

**witch ha·zel** \'wich-ˌhā-zəl\ *n* **1** : a No. American shrub having small yellow flowers after the leaves have fallen **2** : an alcoholic solution of material from witch hazel bark used as a soothing astringent lotion

**witch-hunt** \'wich-ˌhənt\ *n* **1** : a searching out and persecution of persons accused of witchcraft **2** : the searching out and deliberate harassment of those (as political opponents) with unpopular views

**witch·ing** \'wich-iŋ\ *adj* **1** : of, relating to, or suitable for sorcery or supernatural occurrences **2** : BEWITCHING, FASCINATING

**wi·te·na·ge·mot** *or* **wi·te·na·ge·mote** \'wit-ᵊn-ə-gə-ˌmōt\ *n* [OE *witena gemōt*, fr. *witena* (gen. pl. of *wita* sage, adviser) + *gemōt* assembly] : an Anglo-Saxon council of nobles, prelates, and officials to advise the king on administrative and judicial matters

**with** \(ʰ)with, (ʰ)with\ *prep* **1** : AGAINST ⟨a fight ~ his wife⟩ **2** : in mutual relation to ⟨talk ~ a friend⟩ **3** : as regards ⟨is patient ~ the children⟩ **4** : compared to ⟨on equal terms ~ another⟩ **5** : in support of ⟨I'm ~ you all the way⟩ **6** : in the opinion of : as judged by ⟨their arguments had weight ~ him⟩ **7** : because of : THROUGH ⟨pale ~ anger⟩ **8** : in a manner indicating ⟨work ~ a will⟩ **9** : GIVEN, GRANTED ⟨~ your permission I'll leave⟩ **10** : in the company of ⟨a professor ~ his students⟩ **11** : HAVING ⟨came ~ good news⟩ ⟨stood there ~ his mouth open⟩ **12** : DESPITE ⟨~ all his cleverness, he failed⟩ **13** : at the time of : right after ⟨~ that he left⟩ **14** : CONTAINING ⟨tea ~ sugar⟩ **15** : FROM ⟨parting ~ friends⟩ **16** : by means of ⟨hit him ~ a club⟩ **17** : so as not to cross or oppose ⟨swim ~ the tide⟩

**with·al** \with-'ȯl, with-\ *adv* **1** : together with this : BESIDES **2** *archaic* : THEREWITH **3** : on the other hand : NEVERTHELESS

**with·draw** \with-'drȯ, with-\ *vb* -**drew** \-'drü\; -**drawn** \-'drȯn\; -**draw·ing** \-'drȯ(-)iŋ\ **1** : to take back or away : draw away : REMOVE **2** : to call back (as from consideration) : RECALL, RESCIND; *also* : RETRACT ⟨~ an accusation⟩ **3** : to go away : RETREAT, LEAVE **4** : to terminate one's participation in or use of something

**with·draw·al** \-'drȯ(-ə-)l\ *n* **1** : an act or instance of withdrawing **2** : a pathological retreat from objective reality (as in some schizophrenic states)

**with·drawn** \with-'drȯn\ *adj* **1** : ISOLATED, SECLUDED **2** : socially detached and unresponsive

**withe** \'with\ *n* : a slender flexible twig or branch; *esp* : one used as a band or rope

**with·er** \'with-ər\ *vb* **with·ered**; **with·er·ing** \-(ə-)riŋ\ **1** : to shrivel from dry and shrunken; *esp* : to shrivel from or as if from loss of bodily moisture **2** : to lose or cause to lose vitality, force, or freshness **3** : to cause to feel shriveled or blighted : STUN ⟨~ed him with a glance⟩

**with·ers** \'with-ərz\ *n pl* : the ridge between the shoulder bones of a horse

**with·hold** \with-'hōld, with-\ *vb* -**held** \-'held\; -**hold·ing** **1** : to hold back : RESTRAIN; *also* : RETAIN **2** : to refrain from granting, giving, or allowing ⟨~ permission⟩ ⟨~ names⟩

**withholding tax** *n* : a tax on income withheld at the source

**¹with·in** \with-'in, with-\ *adv* **1** : in or into the interior : INSIDE **2** : inside oneself : INWARDLY ⟨calm without but furious ~⟩

**²within** *prep* **1** : in or to the inner part of ⟨~ the room⟩ **2** : in the limits or compass of ⟨~ a mile⟩ **3** : inside the limits or influence of ⟨~ call⟩

**³within** *n* : an inner place or area ⟨revolt from ~⟩

**with-it** \'with-ət\ *adj* : socially or culturally up-to-date

**¹with·out** \with-'aut, with-\ *prep* **1** : at, to, or on the outside of ⟨~ the gate⟩ **2** : out of the limits of **3** : LACKING ⟨he's ~ hope⟩; *also* : unaccompanied or unmarked by ⟨spoke ~ thinking⟩ ⟨took his punishment ~ flinching⟩

**²without** *adv* **1** : on the outside : EXTERNALLY **2** : with something lacking or absent ⟨has learned to do ~⟩

**with·stand** \with-'stand, with-\ *vb* -**stood** \-'stud\; -**stand·ing** : to stand against : RESIST; *esp* : to oppose (as an attack) successfully

**withy** \'with-ē\ *n, pl* **with·ies** : WITHE

**wit·less** \'wit-ləs\ *adj* : lacking wit or understanding : mentally defective : FOOLISH — **wit·less·ly** *adv* — **wit·less·ness** *n*

**¹wit·ness** \'wit-nəs\ *n* [ME *witnesse*, fr. OE *witnes* knowledge, testimony, witness, fr. *wit* mind, intelligence] **1** : TESTIMONY ⟨bear ~ to the fact⟩ **2** : one that gives evidence; *esp* : one who testifies in a cause or before a court **3** : one present at a transaction so as to be able to testify that it has taken place **4** : one who has personal knowledge or experience of something **5** : something serving as evidence or proof : SIGN

**²witness** *vb* **1** : to bear witness : TESTIFY **2** : to act as legal witness of **3** : to furnish proof of : BETOKEN **4** : to be a witness of **5** : to be the scene of ⟨this region has ~ed many wars⟩

**wit·ted** \'wit-əd\ *adj* : having wit or understanding ⟨dull-*witted*⟩

**wit·ti·cism** \'wit-ə-ˌsiz-əm\ *n* : a witty saying or phrase

**wit·ting** \'wit-iŋ\ *adj* : done knowingly : INTENTIONAL — **wit·ting·ly** *adv*

**wit·ty** \'wit-ē\ *adj* **wit·ti·er**; -**est** : marked by or full of wit : AMUSING ⟨a ~ writer⟩ ⟨a ~ remark⟩ **syn** humorous, facetious, jocular, jocose — **wit·ti·ly** \'wit-ᵊl-ē\ *adv* — **wit·ti·ness** \-ē-nəs\ *n*

**wive** \'wīv\ *vb* **wived**; **wiv·ing** **1** : to marry a woman **2** : to take for a wife

**wives** *pl of* WIFE

**wiz·ard** \'wiz-ərd\ n [ME *wysard* wise man, fr. *wys* wise] 1 : MAGICIAN, SORCERER 2 : a very clever or skillful person ⟨a ~ at chess⟩

**wiz·ard·ry** \'wiz-ə(r)-drē\ n, pl **-ries** 1 : magic skill : SORCERY, WITCHCRAFT 2 : great skill or cleverness in an activity

**wiz·ened** \'wiz-ᵊnd\ adj : dried up : SHRIVELED, WITHERED

**wk** abbr 1 week 2 work

**WL** abbr wavelength

**wmk** abbr watermark

**WNW** west-northwest

**WO** abbr warrant officer

**w/o** abbr without

**woad** \'wōd\ n : a European herb related to the mustards; also : a blue dyestuff made from its leaves

**wob·ble** \'wäb-əl\ vb **wob·bled**; **wob·bling** \-(ə-)liŋ\ 1 : to move or cause to move with an irregular rocking or side-to-side motion 2 : TREMBLE, QUAVER 3 : WAVER, VACILLATE — **wobble** n — **wob·bly** \'wäb-(ə-)lē\ adj

**woe** \'wō\ n 1 : a condition of deep suffering from misfortune, affliction, or grief 2 : CALAMITY, MISFORTUNE ⟨economic ~s⟩

**woe·be·gone** \'wō-bi-,gòn\ adj : exhibiting woe, sorrow, or misery; also : DISMAL, DESOLATE

**woe·ful** also **wo·ful** \'wō-fəl\ adj 1 : full of woe : AFFLICTED 2 : involving, bringing, or relating to woe 3 : PALTRY, DEPLORABLE — **woe·ful·ly** \-ē\ adv

**wok** \'wäk\ n : a bowl-shaped cooking utensil used esp. in the preparation of Chinese food

**woke** past of WAKE

**woken** past part of WAKE

**wold** \'wōld\ n : an upland plain or stretch of rolling land without woods

**¹wolf** \'wùlf\ n, pl **wolves** \'wùlvz\ often attrib 1 : any of several large erect-eared bushy-tailed doglike predatory mammals that are destructive to game and livestock and may rarely attack man esp. when in a pack 2 : a fierce or destructive person 3 : a man forward, direct, and zealous in amatory attentions to women — **wolf·ish** adj

**²wolf** vb : to eat greedily : DEVOUR

**wolf·hound** \-,haùnd\ n : any of several large dogs orig. used in hunting wolves

**wol·fram** \'wùl-frəm\ n : TUNGSTEN

**wolfs·bane** \'wùlfs-,bān\ n : ACONITE 1; esp : a poisonous yellow-flowered Eurasian herb

**wol·ver·ine** \,wùl-və-'rēn\ n, pl **wolverines** also **wolverine** : a dark shaggy-coated American flesh-eating mammal related to the sables and noted for its strength and cunning

**wom·an** \'wùm-ən\ n, pl **wom·en** \'wim-ən\ [ME, fr. OE *wīfman*, fr. *wīf* woman, wife + *man* human being, man] 1 : an adult female person 2 : WOMANKIND 3 : feminine nature : WOMANLINESS 4 : a female servant or attendant

**wom·an·hood** \'wùm-ən-,hùd\ n 1 : the state of being a woman : the distinguishing qualities of a woman or of womankind 2 : WOMEN, WOMANKIND

**wom·an·ish** \'wùm-ə-nish\ adj 1 : of, relating to, or characteristic of a woman 2 : suitable to a woman rather than to a man : EFFEMINATE

**wom·an·kind** \'wùm-ən-,kīnd\ n : the females of the human race : WOMEN

**wom·an·like** \-,līk\ adj : WOMANLY

**wom·an·ly** \-lē\ adj : having qualities characteristic of a woman — **wom·an·li·ness** \-lē-nəs\ n

**woman suffrage** n : possession and exercise of suffrage by women

**womb** \'wüm\ n 1 : UTERUS 2 : a place where something is generated or developed

**wom·bat** \'wäm-,bat\ n : an Australian burrowing marsupial mammal resembling a small bear

**wom·en·folk** \'wim-ən-,fōk\ also **wom·en·folks** \-,fōks\ n pl : WOMEN

**¹won** \'wən\ past of WIN

**²won** \'wòn\ n, pl **won** — see MONEY table

**¹won·der** \'wən-dər\ n 1 : a cause of astonishment or surprise : MARVEL; also : MIRACLE 2 : a feeling (as of awed astonishment or uncertainty) aroused by something extraordinary or affecting 3 : the quality of exciting wonder ⟨the charm and ~ of the scene⟩

**²wonder** vb **won·dered**; **won·der·ing** \-d(ə-)riŋ\ 1 : to feel surprise or amazement 2 : to feel curiosity or doubt

**wonder drug** n : a medicinal substance of outstanding effectiveness

**won·der·ful** \'wən-dər-fəl\ adj 1 : exciting wonder : MARVELOUS, ASTONISHING 2 : unusually good : ADMIRABLE — **won·der·ful·ly** \-f(ə-)lē\ adv — **won·der·ful·ness** \-fəl-nəs\ n

**won·der·land** \-,land, -lənd\ n 1 : a fairylike imaginary realm 2 : a place that excites admiration or wonder

**won·der·ment** \-mənt\ n 1 : ASTONISHMENT, SURPRISE 2 : a cause of or occasion for wonder 3 : curiosity about something

**won·drous** \'wən-drəs\ adj : WONDERFUL, MARVELOUS — **wondrous** adv, archaic — **won·drous·ly** adv — **wondrous·ness** n

**¹wont** \'wònt, 'wōnt\ adj [ME *woned*, *wont*, fr. pp. of *wonen* to dwell, be used to, fr. OE *wunian*] 1 : ACCUSTOMED, USED ⟨as he was ~ to do⟩ 2 : INCLINED, APT

**²wont** n : CUSTOM, USAGE, HABIT ⟨according to her ~⟩

**wont·ed** \'wònt-əd, 'wōnt-\ adj : ACCUSTOMED, CUSTOMARY ⟨his ~ courtesy⟩

**woo** \'wü\ vb 1 : to try to gain the love of and usu. marriage with : COURT 2 : SOLICIT, ENTREAT 3 : to try to gain or bring about ⟨~ public favor⟩ — **woo·er** n

**¹wood** \'wùd\ n 1 : a dense growth of trees usu. larger than a grove and smaller than a forest — often used in pl.

**2** : a hard fibrous substance that forms the bulk of trees and shrubs beneath the bark; *also* : this material fit or prepared for some use (as burning or building) **3** : something made of wood

²**wood** *adj* **1** : WOODEN **2** : suitable for holding, cutting, or working with wood **3** *or* **woods** \'wu̇dz\ : living or growing in woods

³**wood** *vb* **1** : to supply or load with wood esp. for fuel **2** : to cover with a growth of trees

**wood alcohol** *n* : a flammable liquid that resembles ordinary alcohol but is very poisonous and is used as a solvent and an antifreeze

**wood·bine** \'wu̇d-ˌbīn\ *n* : any of several climbing vines (as a honeysuckle or Virginia creeper)

**wood·block** \-ˌbläk\ *n* **1** : a block of wood **2** : WOODCUT

**wood·chop·per** \-ˌchäp-ər\ *n* : one engaged esp. in chopping down trees

**wood·chuck** \-ˌchək\ *n* : a thickset grizzled marmot of the northeastern U.S. and Canada

**wood coal** *n* **1** : CHARCOAL **2** : LIGNITE

**wood·cock** \'wu̇d-ˌkäk\ *n, pl* **woodcocks** : either of two long-billed mottled birds related to the snipe; *esp* : an American upland game bird

**wood·craft** \-ˌkraft\ *n* **1** : skill and practice in matters relating to the woods esp. in maintaining oneself and making one's way or in hunting or trapping **2** : skill in shaping or constructing articles from wood

**wood·cut** \-ˌkət\ *n* **1** : a relief printing surface engraved on wood **2** : a print from a woodcut

**wood·cut·ter** \-ˌkət-ər\ *n* : a person who cuts wood esp. as an occupation

**wood·ed** \'wu̇d-əd\ *adj* : covered with woods or trees ⟨~ slopes⟩

**wood·en** \'wu̇d-ᵊn\ *adj* **1** : made of wood **2** : lacking resilience : STIFF **3** : AWKWARD, CLUMSY — **wood·en·ly** *adv* — **wood·en·ness** \-ᵊn-(n)əs\ *n*

**wood·en·ware** \'wu̇d-ᵊn-ˌwaər\ *n* : articles made of wood for domestic use

**wood·land** \'wu̇d-lənd -ˌland\ *n* : land covered with trees : FOREST

**wood·lot** \'wu̇d-ˌlät\ *n* : a relatively small area of trees kept usu. to meet fuel and timber needs ⟨a farm ~⟩

**wood louse** *n* : a small flat grayish crustacean that lives esp. under stones and bark

**wood·man** \'wu̇d-mən\ *n* : WOODSMAN

**wood·note** \-ˌnōt\ *n* : a sound or call (as of a bird) natural in a wood

**wood nymph** *n* : a nymph living in the woods

**wood·peck·er** \'wu̇d-ˌpek-ər\ *n* : any of various usu. brightly marked climbing birds with stiff spiny tail feathers and a chisellike bill used to drill into trees for insects

**wood·pile** \-ˌpīl\ *n* : a pile of wood and esp. firewood

**wood·ruff** \'wu̇d-(ˌ)rəf\ *n* : a small European sweet-scented herb used in perfumery and in flavoring wine

**wood·shed** \-ˌshed\ *n* : a shed for storing wood and esp. firewood

**woods·man** \'wu̇dz-mən\ *n* : one who frequents or works in the woods; *esp* : one skilled in woodcraft

**woodsy** \'wu̇d-zē\ *adj* : relating to or suggestive of woods

**wood·wind** \'wu̇d-ˌwind\ *n* : one of a group of wind instruments including flutes, clarinets, oboes, bassoons, and sometimes saxophones

**wood·work** \-ˌwərk\ *n* : work made of wood; *esp* : interior fittings (as moldings or stairways) of wood

**woody** \'wu̇d-ē\ *adj* **wood·i·er; -est 1** : abounding or overgrown with woods **2** : of or containing wood or wood fibers **3** : resembling or characteristic of wood — **wood·i·ness** \'wu̇d-ē-nəs\ *n*

**woof** \'wu̇f\ *n* [alter. of ME *oof*, fr. OE *ōwef*, fr. *ō*- (fr. *on* on) + *wefan* to weave] **1** : the threads in a woven fabric that cross the warp **2** : a woven fabric; *also* : its texture

**woof·er** \'wu̇f-ər\ *n* : a loudspeaker that reproduces sounds of low pitch

**wool** \'wu̇l\ *n* **1** : the soft wavy or curly hair of some mammals and esp. the sheep; *also* : something (as a textile or garment) made of wool **2** : short thick often crisply curled human hair **3** : a light and fleecy woollike substance — **wooled** \'wu̇ld\ *adj*

¹**wool·en** *or* **wool·len** \'wu̇l-ən\ *adj* **1** : made of wool **2** : of or relating to the manufacture or sale of woolen products ⟨~ mills⟩

²**woolen** *or* **woollen** *n* **1** : a fabric made of wool **2** : garments of woolen fabric — usu. used in pl.

**wool·gath·er·ing** \-ˌgath-(ə-)riŋ\ *n* : the act of indulging in idle daydreaming

¹**wool·ly** *also* **wooly** \'wu̇l-ē\ *adj* **wool·li·er; -est 1** : of, relating to, or bearing wool **2** : consisting of or resembling wool **3** : CONFUSED, BLURRY ⟨~ thinking⟩ **4** : marked by a lack of order or restraint ⟨the wild and ~ West of frontier times⟩

²**wool·ly** *also* **wool·ie** *or* **wooly** \'wu̇l-ē\ *n, pl* **wool·lies** : a garment made from wool; *esp* : underclothing of knitted wool

**woolly aphid** *n* : a plant louse covered with a dense coat of white filaments

**woolly bear** *n* : any of numerous very hairy caterpillars

**wool·sack** \'wu̇l-ˌsak\ *n* **1** : a sack of or for wool **2** : the seat of the Lord Chancellor in the House of Lords

**woo·zy** \'wü-zē\ *adj* **woo·zi·er; -est 1** : BEFUDDLED **2** : somewhat dizzy, nauseated, or weak — **woo·zi·ness** \'wü-zē-nəs\ *n*

¹**word** \'wərd\ *n* **1** : something that is said; *esp* : a brief remark **2** : a speech sound or series of speech sounds that communicates a meaning; *also* : a graphic representation of such a sound or series of sounds **3** : ORDER, COMMAND **4** *often cap* : the second person of the Trinity; *also* : GOSPEL **5** : NEWS,

INFORMATION 6 **:** PROMISE 7 *pl* **:** QUARREL, DISPUTE 8 **:** a verbal signal **:** PASSWORD — **word·less** *adj*

²**word** *vb* **:** to express in words **:** PHRASE

**word·age** \'wərd-ij\ *n* 1 **:** WORDS 2 **:** number of words 3 **:** WORDING

**word·book** \'wərd-,buk\ *n* **:** VOCABULARY, DICTIONARY

**word·ing** \'wərd-iŋ\ *n* **:** verbal expression **:** PHRASEOLOGY

**word of mouth** **:** oral communication

**word·play** \'wərd-,plā\ *n* **:** verbal wit

**wordy** \'wərd-ē\ *adj* **word·i·er; -est** **:** using many words **:** VERBOSE **syn** prolix, diffuse, redundant — **word·i·ness** \'wərd-ē-nəs\ *n*

**wore** *past of* WEAR

¹**work** \'wərk\ *n* 1 **:** TOIL, LABOR; *also* **:** EMPLOYMENT (out of ~) 2 **:** TASK, JOB (have ~ to do) 3 **:** DEED, ACHIEVEMENT 4 **:** material in the process of manufacture 5 **:** something produced by mental effort or physical labor, *esp* **:** an artistic production (as a book or needlework) 6 *pl* engineering structures 7 *pl* **:** the buildings, grounds, and machinery of a factory 8 *pl* **:** the moving parts of a mechanism 9 **:** WORKMANSHIP (careless ~) 10 **:** a fortified structure of any kind 11 **:** the transference of energy when a force produces movement of a body 12 *pl* **:** everything possessed, available, or belonging (the whole ~s went overboard); *also* **:** subjection to drastic treatment (gave him the ~s) **syn** occupation, employment, business, pursuit, calling, travail, grind, drudgery — **in the works** **:** in process of preparation

²**work** *adj* 1 **:** suitable or styled for wear while working (~ clothes) 2 **:** used for work (~ elephants)

³**work** *vb* **worked** \'wərkt\ *or* **wrought** \'rȯt\, **work·ing** 1 **:** to bring to pass **:** EFFECT 2 **:** to fashion or create by expending labor or exertion upon 3 **:** to prepare for use *esp.* by stirring or kneading 4 **:** to bring into a desired form by a gradual process of cutting, hammering, scraping, pressing, or stretching (~ cold steel) 5 **:** to set or keep in operation **:** OPERATE (a pump ~ed by hand) 6 **:** to solve by reasoning or calculation (~ a problem) 7 **:** to cause to toil or labor (~ed his men hard); *also* **:** EXPLOIT 8 **:** to pay for with labor or service (~ off a debt) 9 **:** to bring into some (specified) position or condition by stages (the stream ~ed itself clear) 10 **:** CONTRIVE, ARRANGE (we'll go if we can ~ it) 11 **:** to practice trickery or cajolery on for some end (~ed the management for a free ticket) 12 **:** EXCITE, PROVOKE (~ed himself into a rage) 13 **:** to exert oneself physically or mentally; *esp* **:** to perform work regularly for wages 14 **:** to function according to plan or design 15 **:** to produce a desired effect **:** SUCCEED 16 **:** to make way slowly and with difficulty (he ~ed forward through the crowd) 17 **:** to permit of being worked (this wood ~s

easily) 18 **:** to be in restless motion; *also* **:** FERMENT 1 19 **:** to move slightly in relation to another part; *also* **:** to get into a specified condition slowly or imperceptibly (the knot ~ed loose) — **work on** 1 **:** AFFECT 2 **:** to try to influence or persuade — **work upon** **:** to have effect upon **:** operate on **:** PERSUADE, INFLUENCE

**work·able** \'wər-kə-bəl\ *adj* 1 **:** capable of being worked 2 **:** PRACTICABLE, FEASIBLE **work·able·ness** *n*

**work·a·day** \'wər-kə-,dā\ *adj* 1 **:** relating to or suited for working days 2 **:** PROSAIC, ORDINARY

**work·bag** \'wərk-,bag\ *n* **:** a bag for holding implements or materials for work, *esp* **:** a bag for needlework

**work·bas·ket** \-,bas-kət\ *n* **:** a basket for needlework

**work·bench** \-,bench\ *n* **:** a bench on which work *esp.* of mechanics, machinists, and carpenters is performed

**work·book** \-,buk\ *n* 1 **:** a booklet outlining a course of study 2 **:** a workman's manual 3 **:** a record book of work one 4 **:** a student's individual book of problems to be solved directly on the pages

**work·box** \-,bäks\ *n* **:** a box for work instruments and materials

**work·day** \-,dā\ *n* 1 **:** a day on which work is done as distinguished from sunday or a holiday 2 **:** the period of time in a day when work is performed

**work·er** \'wər-kər\ *n* 1 **:** one that works, *esp* **:** a person who works for wages 2 **:** one of the sexually undeveloped individuals of a colony of social insects as bees, ants, or termites) that perform the work of the community

**work arm** *n* **:** a farm on which persons guilty of minor law violations are confined

**work·horse** \'wərk-,hȯrs\ *n* 1 **:** a horse used chiefly for labor 2 **:** a person who undertakes arduous labor

**work·house** \-,haus\ *n* 1 *Brit* **:** POORHOUSE 2 **:** a house of correction where persons who have committed minor offenses are confined

¹**work·ing** \'wər-kiŋ\ *adj* 1 **:** adequate to allow work to be done (a ~ majority) (a ~ knowledge of French) 2 **:** adopted or assumed to help further work or activity (a draft of a peace treaty)

²**working** *n* 1 **:** manner of functioning **:** OPERATION 2 *pl* **:** an excavation made in mining or tunneling

**work·ing·man** \'wər-kiŋ-,man\ *n* **:** one who works for wages usu. at manual labor

**work·load** *n* **:** the amount of work performed or capable of being performed (as by a mechanical device) usu. within a specific period

**work·man** \'wərk-mən\ *n* 1 **:** WORKINGMAN 2 **:** ARTISAN, CRAFTSMAN

**work·man·like** \-,līk\ *adj* **:** worthy of a good workman **:** SKILLFUL

**work·man·ship** \-,ship\ *n* **:** the art or skill of a workman **:** CRAFTSMANSHIP; *also* **:** the quality imparted to something in the process of making it ⟨a vase of exquisite ~⟩

**work·out** \'wərk-ˌaùt\ n 1 : a practice or exercise to test or improve one's fitness esp. for athletic competition, ability, or performance 2 : a test or trial to determine ability or capacity or suitability

**work out** \ˌwərk-'aút, 'wərk-\ vb 1 : to bring about esp. by resolving difficulties 2 : DEVELOP, ELABORATE 3 : to prove effective, practicable, or suitable 4 : to amount to a total or calculated figure — used with at 5 : to engage in a workout

**work·room** \'wərk-ˌrüm, -ˌrùm\ n : a room used esp. for manual work

**work·shop** \-ˌshäp\ n 1 : a small establishment where manufacturing or handicrafts are carried on 2 : a seminar emphasizing exchange of ideas and practical methods and given mainly for adults already employed in the field

**work·ta·ble** \-ˌtā-bəl\ n : a table for holding working materials and implements (as for needlework)

**world** \'wərld\ n [ME, fr. OE woruld human existence, this world, age, fr. a prehistoric compound whose first constituent is represented by OE wer man and whose second constituent is akin to OE eald old] 1 : UNIVERSE, CREATION 2 : the earth with its inhabitants and all things upon it 3 : people in general : MANKIND 4 : a state of existence : scene of life and action ⟨the ~ of the future⟩ 5 : a great number or quantity ⟨a ~ of troubles⟩ 6 : a part or section of the earth or its inhabitants by itself 7 : the affairs of men ⟨withdraw from the ~⟩ 8 : a celestial body esp. if inhabited 9 : a distinctive class of persons or their sphere of interest ⟨the musical ~⟩

**world-beat·er** \-ˌbēt-ər\ n : one that excels all others of its kind

**world·ling** \-liŋ\ n : a person absorbed in the affairs and pleasures of the present world

**world·ly** \'wərld-lē\ adj 1 : of, relating to, or devoted to this world and its pursuits rather than to religion or spiritual affairs 2 : WORLDLY-WISE, SOPHISTICATED — **world·li·ness** \-lē-nəs\ n

**world·ly-wise** \-ˌwīz\ adj : possessing a practical and often shrewd understanding of human affairs

**world-wide** \'world-'wīd\ adj : extended throughout the entire world ⟨~ fame⟩

**¹worm** \'wərm\ n 1 : an earthworm or a closely related and similar animal; also : any of various small long usu. naked and soft-bodied creeping animals (as a maggot) 2 : a human being who is an object of contempt, loathing, or pity : WRETCH 3 : something that inwardly torments or devours 4 : a spiral or wormlike thing (as the thread of a screw) 5 pl : infestation with or disease caused by parasitic worms — **wormy** adj

**²worm** vb 1 : to move or cause to move

or proceed slowly and deviously 2 : to insinuate or introduce (oneself) by devious or subtle means 3 : to free from worms ⟨~ a dog⟩ 4 : to obtain or extract by artful or insidious pleading, asking, or persuading ⟨~ed the truth out of him⟩

**worm-eat·en** \'wərm-ˌēt-ᵊn\ adj 1 : eaten or burrowed by worms 2 : PITTED 3 : WORN-OUT, ANTIQUATED ⟨tried to update the ~ regulations⟩

**worm gear** n 1 : WORM WHEEL 2 : a gear consisting of a short threaded revolving screw and a worm wheel meshing and working together

**worm·hole** \'wərm-ˌhōl\ n : a hole or passage burrowed by a worm

**worm wheel** n : a toothed wheel gearing with the threads of a revolving threaded screw

**worm·wood** \'wərm-ˌwùd\ n 1 : any of several aromatic woody herbs related to the daisies; esp : a European plant used in making absinthe 2 : something bitter or grievous : BITTERNESS

**worn** past part of WEAR

**worn-out** \'wōrn-'aút\ adj : exhausted or used up by or as if by wear ⟨an old ~ suit⟩ ⟨a ~ automobile⟩

**wor·ri·some** \'wər-ē-səm\ adj 1 : causing distress or worry 2 : inclined to worry or fret

**¹wor·ry** \'wər-ē\ vb **wor·ried**; **wor·ry·ing** 1 : to shake and mangle with the teeth ⟨a terrier ~ing a rat⟩ 2 : TROUBLE, PLAGUE ⟨his poor health worries his parents⟩ 3 : to feel or express great care or anxiety : FRET — **wor·ri·er** n

**²worry** n, pl **worries** 1 : ANXIETY 2 : a cause of anxiety : TROUBLE

**wor·ry·wart** \'wər-ē-ˌwòrt\ n : one who is inclined to worry unduly

**¹worse** \'wərs\ adj, comparative of BAD or of ILL 1 : bad or evil in a greater degree : less good; esp : more unwell 2 : more unfavorable, unpleasant, or painful

**²worse** n 1 : one that is worse 2 : a greater degree of ill or badness

**³worse** adv, comparative of BAD or of ILL : in a worse manner : to a worse extent or degree

**wors·en** \'wərs-ᵊn\ vb **wors·ened**; **wors·en·ing** \'wərs-(ᵊ-)niŋ\ : to make or become worse

**¹wor·ship** \'wər-shəp\ n [ME worshipe worthiness, repute, respect, reverence paid to a divine being, fr. OE weorthscipe worthiness, repute, respect, fr. weorth worthy, worth + -scipe -ship, suffix denoting quality or condition] 1 chiefly Brit : a person of importance — used as a title for officials (as magistrates and some mayors) 2 : reverence toward a divine being or supernatural power; also : the expression of such reverence 3 : extravagant respect or admiration for or devotion to an object of esteem ⟨~ of the dollar⟩

**²worship** vb **-shiped** or **-shipped**; **-ship·ing** or **-ship·ping** 1 : to honor or reverence as a divine being or supernatural power **2** : IDOLIZE **3** : to perform or take part in worship — **wor-ship-er** or **wor-ship-per** n

**wor-ship-ful** \'wər-shəp-fəl\ adj **1** archaic : NOTABLE, DISTINGUISHED **2** chiefly Brit — used as a title for various persons or groups of rank or distinction **3** : VENERATING, WORSHIPING

¹**worst** \'wərst\ adj, superlative of BAD or of ILL **1** : most bad, evil, ill, or corrupt **2** : most unfavorable, unpleasant, or painful; also : most unsuitable, faulty, or unattractive **3** : least skillful or efficient **4** : most wanting in quality, value, or condition

²**worst** n **1** : one that is worst **2** : the greatest degree of ill or badness

³**worst** adv, superlative of ILL or of BAD or BADLY : to the extreme degree of badness or inferiority : in the worst manner

⁴**worst** vb : DEFEAT

**wor-sted** \'wus-təd, 'wər-stəd\ n [ME, fr. Worsted (now Worstead), England] : a smooth compact yarn from long wool fibers used esp. for firm napless fabrics, carpeting, or knitting; also : a fabric made from such yarn

¹**wort** \'wərt, 'wort\ n : PLANT; esp : an herbaceous plant

²**wort** n : a solution obtained by infusion from malt and fermented to form beer

¹**worth** \'wərth\ prep **1** : equal in value to; also : having possessions or income equal to **2** : deserving of ⟨well ~ the effort⟩ **3** : capable of ⟨ran for all he was ~⟩

²**worth** n **1** : monetary value : the equivalent of a specified amount or figure **2** : the value of something measured by its qualities or by the esteem in which it is held **3** : moral or personal value : MERIT, EXCELLENCE **4** : WEALTH, RICHES

**worth-less** \'wərth-ləs\ adj **1** : lacking worth : VALUELESS; also : USELESS **2** : LOW, DESPICABLE — **worth-less-ness** n

**worth-while** \'wərth-'hwīl\ adj : being worth the time or effort spent

¹**wor-thy** \'wər-thē\ adj **wor-thi-er**; **-est** **1** : having worth or value : ESTIMABLE **2** : HONORABLE, MERITORIOUS **3** : having sufficient worth ⟨a man ~ of the honor⟩ — **wor-thi-ly** \'wər-thə-lē\ adv — **wor-thi-ness** \-thē-nəs\ n

²**worthy** n, pl **worthies** : a worthy person

**would** \wəd, əd, d, (')wud\ past of WILL **1** archaic : wish for : WANT **2** : strongly desire : WISH ⟨I ~ I were young again⟩ **3** — used as an auxiliary to express (1) preference ⟨~ rather run than fight⟩, (2) wish, desire, or intent ⟨those who ~ forbid gambling⟩, (3) habitual action ⟨we ~ meet often for lunch⟩, (4) a contingency or possibility ⟨if he were coming, he ~ be here by now⟩, (5) probability ⟨~ have won if he hadn't tripped⟩, or (6) a request ⟨~ you help us⟩ **4** : COULD **5** : SHOULD

**would-be** \,wud-,bē\ adj : desiring or professing to be ⟨a ~ artist⟩

¹**wound** \'wünd\ n **1** : an injury in which the skin is broken (as by violence or by surgery) **2** : an injury or hurt to feelings or reputation

²**wound** vb : to inflict a wound to or in

³**wound** \'waund\ past of WIND

**wove** past of WEAVE

**woven** past part of WEAVE

¹**wow** \'wau\ n : a striking success : HIT

²**wow** vb : to arouse enthusiastic approval

³**wow** n : a distortion in reproduced sound consisting of a slow rise and fall of pitch caused by speed variation in the reproducing system

**WPM** abbr words per minute

**wpn** abbr weapon

¹**wrack** \'rak\ n [ME, fr. OE wræc misery, punishment, something driven by the sea] **1** : RUIN, DESTRUCTION **2** : a remnant of something destroyed

²**wrack** n **1** : a wrecked ship; also : WRECKAGE, WRECK **2** : sea vegetation (as kelp) esp. when cast up on the shore

**wraith** \'rāth\ n, pl **wraiths** \'rāths, 'rāthz\ **1** : APPARITION; also : GHOST, SPECTER **2** : an insubstantial appearance : SHADOW

¹**wran-gle** \'raŋ-gəl\ vb **wran-gled**; **wran-gling** \-g(ə-)liŋ\ **1** : to quarrel angrily or peevishly : BICKER **2** : ARGUE **3** : to obtain by persistent arguing **4** : to herd and care for (livestock) on the range — **wran-gler** n

²**wrangle** n : an angry, noisy, or prolonged dispute or quarrel; also : CONTROVERSY

¹**wrap** \'rap\ vb **wrapped**; **wrap-ping** **1** : to cover esp. by winding or folding **2** : to envelop and secure for transportation or storage : BUNDLE **3** : to enclose wholly : ENFOLD **4** : to coil, fold, draw, or twine about something **5** : SURROUND, ENVELOP; also : SUFFUSE **6** : INVOLVE, ENGROSS ⟨wrapped up in a hobby⟩ **7** : to conceal as if by enveloping or enfolding : HIDE **8** : to put on clothing : DRESS **9** : to be subject to covering or enclosing ⟨~s up into a small package⟩

²**wrap** n **1** : WRAPPER, WRAPPING **2** : an article of clothing that may be wrapped around a person; esp : an outer garment (as a coat or shawl) **3** pl : SECRECY ⟨kept under ~s⟩

**wrap-around** \'rap-ə-,raund\ n : a garment (as a dress) made with a full-length opening and adjusted to the figure by wrapping around

**wrap-per** \'rap-ər\ n **1** : that in which something is wrapped **2** : one that wraps **3** : an article of clothing worn wrapped around the body; also : a loose outer garment

**wrap-ping** \'rap-iŋ\ n : something used to wrap an object : WRAPPER

**wrap-up** \'rap-,əp\ n : a summarizing news report

**wrap up** \(')rap-'əp\ vb **1** : END, CONCLUDE **2** : to make a single comprehensive report of

**wrasse** \'ras\ n : any of various usu. brightly colored spiny-finned sea fishes including many food fishes

**wrath** \'rath\ n 1 : violent anger : RAGE 2 : retributory punishment for an offense or a crime : divine chastisement **syn** indignation, ire, fury

**wrath·ful** \-fəl\ adj 1 : filled with wrath : very angry 2 : showing, marked by, or arising from anger — **wrath·ful·ly** \-ē\ adv — **wrath·ful·ness** n

**wreak** \'rēk\ vb 1 : to exact as a punishment : INFLICT ⟨~ vengeance on an enemy⟩ 2 : to give free scope or rein to ⟨~ed his wrath⟩

**wreath** \'rēth\ n, pl **wreaths** \'rēthz, 'rēths\ : something (as boughs or flowers) intertwined into a circular shape

**wreathe** \'rēth\ vb **wreathed**; **wreath·ing** 1 : to twist or become twisted esp. so as to show folds or creases ⟨a face *wreathed* in smiles⟩ 2 : to shape or take on the shape of a wreath : move or extend in circles or spirals 3 : to fold or coil around : ENTWINE

¹**wreck** \'rek\ n 1 : something (as goods) cast up on the land by the sea after a shipwreck 2 : broken remains (as of a ship or vehicle after heavy damage) 3 : something disabled or in a state of ruin; also : an individual broken in health or strength 4 : SHIPWRECK 5 : the action of breaking up or destroying something : WRECKING

²**wreck** vb 1 : SHIPWRECK 2 : to ruin or damage by breaking up : involve in disaster or ruin

**wreck·age** \'rek-ij\ n 1 : the act of wrecking : the state of being wrecked : RUIN 2 : the remains of a wreck

**wreck·er** \'rek-ər\ n 1 : one that wrecks; esp : one occupied with tearing down and removing buildings 2 : one who searches for or works upon the wrecks of ships 3 : an automotive vehicle equipped to remove disabled cars 4 : one that salvages junked automobile parts

**wren** \'ren\ n : any of various small mostly brown singing birds with short wings and tail

¹**wrench** \'rench\ vb 1 : to move with a violent twist 2 : to pull, strain, or tighten with violent twisting or force 3 : to injure or disable by a violent twisting or straining 4 : to change (as the meaning of a word) violently : DISTORT 5 : to snatch forcibly : WREST 6 : to cause to suffer anguish

²**wrench** n 1 : a forcible twisting; also : an injury (as to one's ankle) by twisting 2 : a tool for exerting a twisting force (as on a nut or bolt)

¹**wrest** \'rest\ vb 1 : to pull or move by a forcible twisting movement 2 : to gain with difficulty or as if by force or violence ⟨~ a living⟩ ⟨~ the power from the usurper⟩ 3 : to wrench (a word or passage) from its proper meaning or use

²**wrest** n : a forcible twist : WRENCH

¹**wres·tle** \'res-əl, 'ras-\ vb **wres·tled**; **wres·tling** \-(ə-)liŋ\ 1 : to scuffle with an opponent in an attempt to trip

him or throw him down 2 : to contend against in wrestling 3 : to struggle for mastery (as with something difficult) ⟨~ with a problem⟩ — **wres·tler** \'res-lər, 'ras-\ n

²**wrestle** n : the action or an instance of wrestling : STRUGGLE

**wres·tling** \'res-liŋ\ n : the sport of hand-to-hand combat between two opponents who seek to throw and pin each other

**wretch** \'rech\ n [ME *wrecche*, fr. OE *wrecca* outcast, exile] 1 : a miserable unhappy person 2 : a base, despicable, or vile person

**wretch·ed** \'rech-əd\ adj 1 : deeply afflicted, dejected, or distressed : MISERABLE 2 : WOEFUL, GRIEVOUS ⟨a ~ accident⟩ 3 : DESPICABLE ⟨a ~ trick⟩ 4 : poor in quality or ability : INFERIOR ⟨~ workmanship⟩ — **wretch·ed·ness** n

**wrig·gle** \'rig-əl\ vb **wrig·gled**; **wrig·gling** \-(ə-)liŋ\ 1 : to twist and turn restlessly : SQUIRM ⟨*wriggled* in his chair⟩; also : to move or advance by twisting and turning ⟨a snake *wriggled* along the path⟩ 2 : to extricate oneself or bring into a state or place by maneuvering, twisting, or dodging ⟨~ out of a difficulty⟩ — **wriggle** n

**wrig·gler** \'rig-(ə-)lər\ n 1 : one that wriggles 2 : WIGGLER 2

**wring** \'riŋ\ vb **wrung** \'rəŋ\; **wring·ing** \'riŋ-iŋ\ 1 : to squeeze or twist esp. so as to make dry or to extract moisture or liquid ⟨~ clothes⟩ 2 : to get by or as if by forcible exertion or pressure : EXTORT ⟨~ the truth out of him⟩ 3 : to twist so as to strain or sprain : CONTORT ⟨~ his neck⟩ 4 : to twist together as a sign of anguish ⟨*wrung* her hands⟩ 5 : to affect painfully as if by wringing : TORMENT ⟨her plight *wrung* my heart⟩ 6 : to shake (a hand) vigorously in greeting

**wring·er** \'riŋ-ər\ n : one that wrings; esp : a device for squeezing out liquid or moisture ⟨clothes ~⟩

¹**wrin·kle** \'riŋ-kəl\ n 1 : a crease or small fold on a surface (as in the skin or in cloth) 2 : METHOD, TECHNIQUE; also : information about a method 3 : an innovation in method, technique, or equipment : NOVELTY ⟨the latest ~ in hairdos⟩ — **wrin·kly** \-k(ə-)lē\ adj

²**wrinkle** vb **wrin·kled**; **wrin·kling** \-k(ə-)liŋ\ : to develop or cause to develop wrinkles

**wrist** \'rist\ n : the joint or region between the hand and the arm; also : a corresponding part in a lower animal

**wrist·band** \'ris(t)-,band\ n 1 : the part of a sleeve covering the wrist 2 : a band encircling the wrist

**wrist·let** \'ris(t)-lət\ n : a band encircling the wrist; esp : a close-fitting knitted band worn for warmth

**wrist·watch** \-,wäch\ n : a small watch attached to a bracelet or strap to fasten about the wrist

**writ** \'rit\ n 1 : something written 2 : a legal order in writing issued in the name of the sovereign power or in the name of a court or judicial authority commanding the performance or non-performance of a specified act  3 : a written order constituting a symbol of the power and authority of the issuer

**write** \'rīt\ *vb* **wrote** \'rōt\; **writ·ten** \'rit-ᵊn\ *also* **writ** \'rit\; **writ·ing** \'rīt-iŋ\ [ME *writen*, fr. OE *wrītan* to scratch, draw, inscribe]  **1** : to form characters, letters, or words on a surface (as with a pen) ⟨learn to read and ~⟩  **2** : to form the letters or the words of (as on paper) : INSCRIBE ⟨*wrote* his name⟩  **3** : to put down on paper : give expression to in writing  **4** : to make up and set down for others to read : COMPOSE ⟨~ music⟩  **5** : to pen, typewrite, or dictate a letter to  **6** : to communicate by letter : CORRESPOND  **7** : to be fitted for writing ⟨this pen ~s easily⟩

**write-in** \'rīt-ˌin\ *n* : a vote cast by writing in the name of a candidate; *also* : a candidate whose name is written in

**write in** \(')rīt-'in\ *vb* : to insert (a name not listed on a ballot) in an appropriate space; *also* : to cast (a vote) in this manner

**write off** *vb*  **1** : to reduce the estimated value of : DEPRECIATE  **2** : CANCEL ⟨*write off* a bad debt⟩

**writ·er** \ rīt-ər\ *n* : one that writes esp. as a business or occupation : AUTHOR

**writer's cramp** *n* : a painful spasmodic cramp of muscles of the hand or fingers brought on by excessive writing

**write-up** \'rīt-ˌəp\ *n* : a written account (as in a newspaper); *esp* : a flattering article

**writhe** \'rīth\ *vb* **writhed**; **writh·ing**  **1** : to move or proceed with twists and turns ⟨~ in pain⟩  **2** : to suffer with shame or confusion : SQUIRM

**writ·ing** \'rīt-iŋ\ *n*  **1** : the act of one that writes; *also* : HANDWRITING  **2** : something (as a letter, book, or document) that is written or printed  **3** : INSCRIPTION  **4** : a style or form of composition  **5** : the occupation of a writer

**wrnt** *abbr* warrant

**¹wrong** \'ròŋ\ *n*  **1** : an injurious, unfair, or unjust act  **2** : something that is contrary to justice, goodness, equity, or law ⟨know right from ~⟩  **3** : the state, position, or fact of being or doing wrong; *also* : the state of being guilty ⟨in the ~⟩  **4** : a violation of the legal rights of another person

**²wrong** *adj* **wrong·er** \'ròŋ-ər\; **wrong·est** \'ròŋ-əst\  **1** : SINFUL, IMMORAL  **2** : not right according to a standard or code : IMPROPER  **3** : UNSUITABLE, INAPPROPRIATE  **4** : INCORRECT ⟨a ~ solution⟩  **5** : UNSATISFACTORY  **6** : constituting a surface that is considered the back, bottom, inside, or reverse of something ⟨iron only on the ~ side of the fabric⟩ **syn** false, bad, poor

**³wrong** *adv*  **1** : in a wrong direction, manner, position, or relation  **2** : INCORRECTLY

**⁴wrong** *vb* **wronged**; **wrong·ing** \'ròŋ-iŋ\  **1** : to do wrong to : INJURE, HARM  **2** : to treat unjustly : DISHONOR, MALIGN **syn** oppress, persecute, aggrieve

**wrong-do·er** \'ròŋ-'dü-ər\ *n* : a person who does wrong and esp. moral wrong — **wrong-do·ing** \-'dü-iŋ\ *n*

**wrong·ful** \'ròŋ-fəl\ *adj*  **1** : WRONG, UNJUST  **2** : UNLAWFUL — **wrong·ful·ly** \-ē\ *adv* — **wrong·ful·ness** *n*

**wrong·head·ed** \'ròŋ-'hed-əd\ *adj* : obstinately wrong : PERVERSE — **wrong·head·ed·ly** *adv* — **wrong·head·ed·ness** *n*

**wrong·ly** \'ròŋ-lē\ *adv*  **1** : in an improper or inappropriate way  **2** : UNFAIRLY, UNJUSTLY  **3** : INCORRECTLY  **4** : in error : by mistake ⟨rightly or ~⟩

**wrote** *past of* WRITE

**wroth** \'ròth, 'rōth\ *adj* : filled with wrath : ANGRY

**wrought** \'ròt\ *adj* [ME, fr. pp. of *worken* to work]  **1** : FASHIONED, FORMED  **2** : ORNAMENTED  **3** : beaten into shape : HAMMERED ⟨~ silver dishes⟩  **4** : deeply stirred : EXCITED ⟨gets easily ~ up over nothing⟩

**wrought iron** *n* : a commercial form of iron that contains less than 0.3 percent carbon and is tough, malleable, and relatively soft — **wrought-iron** *adj*

**wrung** *past of* WRING

**wry** \'rī\ *adj* **wri·er** \'rī(-ə)r\; **wri·est** \'rī-əst\  **1** : turned abnormally to one side : CONTORTED; *also* : made by twisting the facial muscles ⟨a ~ smile⟩  **2** : cleverly and often ironically humorous — **wry·ly** *adv* — **wry·ness** *n*

**wry·neck** \'rī-ˌnek\ *n*  **1** : a disorder marked by a twisting of the neck and head  **2** : any of several birds related to the woodpeckers that have a peculiar manner of twisting the head and neck

**WSW** *abbr* west-southwest

**wt** *abbr* weight

**wurst** \'wərst, 'wùrst\ *n* : SAUSAGE

**WV** *or* **W Va** *abbr* West Virginia

**WW** *abbr* World War

**WY** *or* **Wyo** *abbr* Wyoming

---

**¹x** \'eks\ *n, pl* **x's** *or* **xs** \'ek-səz\ *often cap*  **1** : the 24th letter of the English alphabet  **2** : an unknown quantity

**²x** *vb* **x-ed** *also* **x'd** *or* **xed**; **x-ing** *or* **x'ing** : to cancel or obliterate with a series of x's — usu. used with *out*

**³x** *abbr, often cap* experimental

**⁴x** *symbol*  **1** times ⟨3 x 2 is 6⟩  **2** by ⟨a 3 x 5 index card⟩  **3** *often cap* power of magnification

**Xan·thip·pe** \zan-'t(h)ip-ē\ *or* **Xan·tip·pe** \-'tip-ē\ *n* [Gk *Xanthippē*, shrewish wife of Socrates] : an ill-tempered woman

**x-ax·is** \'eks-ˌak-səs\ *n* : the axis in a plane coordinate system parallel to which abscissas are measured

**X chromosome** *n* : a sex chromosome that usu. occurs paired in each female zygote and cell and single in each male zygote and cell in species in which the male typically has two unlike sex chromosomes

**XD** or **x** div abbr without dividend

**Xe** symbol xenon

**xe·bec** \'zē-,bek\ n : a usu. three-masted Mediterranean sailing ship with long overhanging bow and stern

**xe·no·lith** \'zen-ᵊl-,ith, 'zēn-\ n : a fragment of a rock included in another rock — **xe·no·lith·ic** \,zen-ᵊl-'ith-ik, ,zēn-\ adj

**xe·non** \'zē-,nän, 'zen-,än\ n [Gk, neut. of xenos strange] : a heavy gaseous chemical element occurring in minute quantities in air

**xe·no·pho·bia** \,zen-ə-'fō-bē-ə, ,zēn-\ n : fear and hatred of strangers or foreigners or of what is strange or foreign — **xe·no·phobe** \'zen-ə-,fōb, 'zēn-\ n

**xe·ric** \'zir-ik, 'zer-\ adj : low or deficient in moisture for the support of life

**xe·rog·ra·phy** \zə-'räg-rə-fē, zir-'äg-\ n : the formation of pictures or copies of graphic matter by the action of light on an electrically charged surface in which the latent image usu. is developed with powders — **xe·ro·graph·ic** \,zir-ə-'graf-ik\ adj

**xe·ro·phyte** \'zir-ə-,fīt\ n : a plant adapted for growth with a limited water supply — **xe·ro·phyt·ic** \,zir-ə-'fit-ik\ adj

**XI** or **x in** or **x int** abbr without interest

**x-ir·ra·di·ate** \,ek-sir-'ād-ē-,āt\ vb, often cap : to irradiate with X rays — **x-ir·ra·di·a·tion** \-,ād-ē-'ā-shən\ n

**XL** abbr extra large

**Xmas** \'kris-məs also 'eks-məs\ n [X

(symbol for Christ, fr. the Gk letter chi (X), initial of Christos Christ) + -mas (in Christmas)] : CHRISTMAS

**Xn** abbr Christian

**Xnty** abbr Christianity

**x-ra·di·a·tion** \,eks-,rād-ē-'ā-shən\ n, often cap **1** : exposure to X rays **2** : radiation consisting of X rays

**x-ray** \'eks-,rā\ vb, often cap : to examine, treat, or photograph with X rays

**X ray** \'eks-,rā\ n **1** : a radiation of the same nature as light rays but of extremely short wavelength that is generated by the striking of a stream of electrons against a metal surface in a vacuum and that is able to penetrate through various thicknesses of solids **2** : a photograph taken with X rays

**X-ray astronomy** n : astronomy dealing with investigations of celestial bodies by means of the X rays they emit

**X-ray star** n : a luminous starlike celestial object emitting a major portion of its radiation in the form of X rays

**xu** \'sü\ n, pl **xu** **1** — see dong at MONEY table **2** : a coin of South Vietnam equivalent to the cent

**xy·lem** \'zī-ləm, -,lem\ n : woody tissue of higher plants that transports water and dissolved materials upward, functions also in support and storage, and lies central to the phloem

**xy·lo·phone** \'zī-lə-,fōn\ n [Gk xylon wood + phōnē voice, sound] : a musical instrument consisting of a series of wooden bars graduated in length to sound the musical scale, supported on belts of straw or felt, and sounded by striking with two small wooden hammers — **xy·lo·phon·ist** \-,fō-nəst\ n

---

**¹y** \'wī\ n, pl **y's** or **ys** \'wīz\ often cap : the 25th letter of the English alphabet

**²y 1** abbr yard **2** year

**¹Y** \'wī\ n : YMCA

**²Y** symbol yttrium

**¹-y** also **-ey** \ē\ adj suffix **1** : characterized by : full of ⟨dirty⟩ ⟨clayey⟩ **2** : having the character of : composed of ⟨icy⟩ **3** : like : like that of ⟨homey⟩ ⟨wintry⟩ ⟨stagy⟩ **4** : devoted to : addicted to : enthusiastic over ⟨horsy⟩ **5** : tending or inclined to ⟨sleepy⟩ ⟨chatty⟩ **6** : giving occasion for (specified) action ⟨teary⟩ **7** : performing (specified) action ⟨curly⟩ **8** : somewhat : rather : -ISH ⟨chilly⟩ **9** : having (such) characteristics to a marked degree or in an affected or superficial way ⟨Frenchy⟩

**²-y** \ē\ n suffix, pl **-ies 1** : state : condition : quality ⟨beggary⟩ **2** : activity, place of business, or goods dealt with ⟨laundry⟩ **3** : whole body or group ⟨soldiery⟩

**³-y** n suffix, pl **-ies** : instance of a (specified) action ⟨entreaty⟩ ⟨inquiry⟩

**¹yacht** \'yät\ n [obs. D jaght, D jacht, fr. Middle Low German jacht, short for jachtschiff, lit., hunting ship] : any of various

relatively small sailing or mechanically driven ships that usu. have a sharp prow and graceful lines and are ordinarily used for pleasure cruising and racing

**²yacht** vb : to race or cruise in a yacht

**yacht·ing** \-iŋ\ n : the action, fact, or pastime of racing or cruising in a yacht

**yachts·man** \'yäts-mən\ n : one who owns or sails a yacht

**ya·hoo** \'yä-hü, 'yā-\ n, pl **yahoos** [fr. Yahoo one of a race of brutes having the form of men in Jonathan Swift's Gulliver's Travels] : an uncouth or rowdy person

**Yah·weh** \'yä-,wā\ also **Yah·veh** \-,vā\ n : the God of the Hebrews

**¹yak** \'yak\ n, pl **yaks** also **yak** : a large long-haired blackish brown ox of Tibet and adjacent Asiatic uplands

**²yak** also **yack** \'yak\ n : persistent or voluble talk — **yak** also **yack** vb

**yam** \'yam\ n **1** : the edible starchy root of a twining vine that largely replaces the potato as food in the tropics **2** : a usu. deep orange sweet potato

**yam·mer** \'yam-ər\ vb **yam·mered**; **yam·mer·ing** \-(ə-)riŋ\ [alter. of ME yomeren to murmur, be sad, fr. OE gēomrian] **1** : WHIMPER **2** : CHATTER — **yammer** n

¹yank \'yaŋk\ *n* **:** a strong sudden pull **:** JERK

²yank *vb* **:** to pull with a quick vigorous movement

Yank \'yaŋk\ *n* **:** YANKEE

Yan·kee \'yaŋ-kē\ *n* **1 :** a native or inhabitant of New England; *also* **:** a native or inhabitant of the northern U.S. **2 :** AMERICAN **2** — Yankee *adj*

yan·qui \'yäŋ-kē\ *n, often cap* **:** a citizen of the U.S. as distinguished from a Latin American

¹yap \'yap\ *vb* yapped; yap·ping **1 :** BARK, YELP **2 :** GAB

²yap *n* **1 :** a quick sharp bark **2 :** CHATTER

¹yard \'yärd\ *n* [ME *yarde*, fr. OE *gierd* twig, measure, yard] **1** — see WEIGHT table **2 :** a long spar tapered toward the ends that supports and spreads the head of a sail

²yard *n* [ME, fr. OE *geard* enclosure, yard] **1 :** a small enclosed area open to the sky and adjacent to a building **2 :** the grounds of a building **3 :** an enclosure for livestock **4 :** an area set aside for a particular business or activity **5 :** a system of railroad tracks for storing cars and making up trains

yard·age \-ij\ *n* **:** an aggregate number of yards; *also* **:** the length, extent, or volume of something as measured in yards

yard·arm \'yärd-ˌ ärm\ *n* **:** either end of the yard of a square-rigged ship

yard·man \'yärd-mən, -ˌman\ *n* **:** a man employed in or about a yard

yard·mas·ter \-ˌmas-tər\ *n* **:** the man in charge of operations in a railroad yard

yard·stick \'yärd-ˌstik\ *n* **1 :** a graduated measuring stick three feet long **2 :** a standard for making a critical judgment **:** CRITERION   syn gauge, touchstone

yarn \'yärn\ *n* **1 :** a continuous often plied strand composed of fibers or filaments and used in weaving and knitting to form cloth **2 :** STORY; *esp* **:** a tall tale

yar·row \'yar-ō\ *n* **:** a strong-scented herb related to the daisies that has white or pink flowers in flat clusters

yaw \'yo̊\ *vb* **:** to deviate erratically from side to side of a course ⟨the ship *∼ed* in the heavy seas⟩ — yaw *n*

yawl \'yo̊l\ *n* **1 :** a ship's small boat **2 :** a fore-and-aft-rigged sailboat carrying a mainsail and one or more jibs

¹yawn \'yo̊n\ *vb* **:** to open wide; *esp* **:** to open the mouth wide usu. as an involuntary reaction to fatigue or boredom — yawn·er *n*

²yawn *n* **:** a deep usu. involuntary intake of breath through the wide-open mouth

yawp *or* yaup \'yo̊p\ *vb* **1 :** to make a raucous noise **:** SQUAWK **2 :** CLAMOR, COMPLAIN — yawp·er *n*

yaws \'yo̊z\ *n pl* **:** a tropical disease related to syphilis but not venereal

y-ax·is \'wī-ˌak-səs\ *n* **:** the axis in a plane coordinate system parallel to which ordinates are measured

Yb *symbol* ytterbium

YB *abbr* yearbook

Y chromosome *n* **:** a sex chromosome that is characteristic of male zygotes and cells in species in which the male typically has two unlike sex chromosomes

yd *abbr* yard

¹ye \(')yē\ *pron* **:** YOU 1

²ye \yē, yə, *or like* THE\ *definite article, archaic* **:** THE — used by early printers to represent the manuscript word *þe* (the)

¹yea \'yā\ *adv* **1 :** YES — used in oral voting **2 :** INDEED, TRULY

²yea *n* **:** an affirmative vote; *also* **:** a person casting such a vote

year \'yir\ *n* **1 :** the period of about 365¼ solar days required for one revolution of the earth around the sun **2 :** a cycle in the Gregorian calendar of 365 or 366 days beginning with January 1; *also* **:** a calendar year specified usu. by a number **3** *pl* **:** a time of special significance ⟨*∼s* of plenty⟩ **4** *pl* **:** AGE ⟨advanced in *∼s*⟩ **5 :** a period of time other than a calendar year ⟨the school *∼*⟩

year·book \-ˌbu̇k\ *n* **1 :** a book published annually esp. as a report **2 :** a school publication recording the history and activities of a graduating class

year·ling \'yir-liŋ, 'yər-lən\ *n* **:** one that is or is rated as a year old

year·long \'yir-'lȯŋ\ *adj* **:** lasting through a year

¹year·ly \'yir-lē\ *adj* **:** ANNUAL

²yearly *adv* **:** every year

yearn \'yərn\ *vb* **1 :** to feel a longing or craving **2 :** to feel tenderness or compassion syn long, pine, hanker, hunger, thirst

yearn·ing \-iŋ\ *n* **:** a tender or urgent longing

year-round \'yir-'raund\ *adj* **:** effective, employed, or operating for the full year **:** not seasonal ⟨a *∼* resort⟩

yeast \'yēst\ *n* **1 :** a surface froth or a sediment in sugary liquids (as fruit juices) that consists largely of cells of a tiny fungus and is used in making alcoholic liquors and as a leaven in baking **2 :** any of various usu. one-celled fungi that reproduce by budding and promote alcoholic fermentation **3 :** a commercial product containing yeast plants in a moist or dry medium **4 :** the foam of waves **:** SPUME **5 :** something that causes ferment or activity

yeasty \'yē-stē\ *adj* yeast·i·er; -est **1 :** of, relating to, or resembling yeast **2 :** UNSETTLED **3 :** EXUBERANT; *also* **:** FRIVOLOUS

yegg \'yeg\ *n* **:** one that breaks open safes to steal **:** ROBBER

¹yell \'yel\ *vb* **:** to utter a loud cry or scream **:** SHOUT

²yell *n* **1 :** SHOUT **2 :** a cheer used esp. to encourage an athletic team (as at a college)

¹yel·low \'yel-ō\ *adj* **1 :** of the color yellow **2 :** having a yellow complexion or skin **3 :** SENSATIONAL ⟨*∼* journalism⟩ **4 :** COWARDLY — yel·low·ish \'yel-ə-wish\ *adj*

²yellow *vb* **:** to make or turn yellow

³**yellow** *n* **1** : a color between green and orange in the spectrum : the color of ripe lemons or sunflowers **2** : something yellow; *esp* : the yolk of an egg **3** *pl* : JAUNDICE **4** *pl* : any of several plant virus diseases marked by stunted growth and yellowing of foliage

**yellow birch** *n* : a No. American birch with thin lustrous gray or yellow bark; *also* : its strong hard pale wood

**yellow fever** *n* : an acute destructive virus disease marked by prostration, jaundice, fever, and often hemorrhage and transmitted by a mosquito

**yellow jack** *n* **1** : YELLOW FEVER **2** : a flag raised on ships in quarantine

**yellow jacket** *n* : an American social wasp having the body barred with bright yellow

**yelp** \'yelp\ *vb* [ME *yelpen* to boast, cry out, fr. OE *gielpan* to boast, exult] : to utter a sharp quick shrill cry — **yelp** *n*

¹**yen** \'yen\ *n, pl* **yen** — see MONEY table

²**yen** *n* [obs. E slang *yen-yen* craving for opium, fr. Chin *in-yan*, fr. *in* opium + *yan* craving] : a strong desire : LONGING

**yeo·man** \'yō-mən\ *n* **1** : an attendant or officer in a royal or noble household **2** : a small farmer who cultivates his own land; *esp* : one of a class of English freeholders below the gentry **3** : a naval petty officer who performs clerical duties

**yeo·man·ry** \'yō-mən-rē\ *n* : the body of yeomen and esp. of small landed proprietors

**-yer** — see -ER

**yer·ba ma·té** \,yer-bə-'mä-,tā\ *n* : MATÉ

¹**yes** \'yes\ *adv* — used as a function word esp. to express assent or agreement or to introduce a more emphatic or explicit phrase

²**yes** *n* : an affirmative reply

**ye·shi·va** *or* **ye·shi·vah** \yə-'shē-və\ *n, pl* **yeshivas** *or* **ye·shi·voth** \-,shē-'vōt(h)\ **1** : a school for talmudic study **2** : an orthodox Jewish rabbinical seminary **3** : a Jewish day school providing secular and religious instruction

**yes–man** \'yes-,man\ *n* : a person who endorses uncritically every opinion or proposal of a superior

¹**yes·ter·day** \'yes-tərd-ē\ *adv* **1** : on the day preceding today **2** : only a short time ago

²**yesterday** *n* **1** : the day last past **2** : time not long past

**yes·ter·year** \'yes-tər-,yiər\ *n* **1** : last year **2** : the recent past

¹**yet** \(')yet\ *adv* **1** : in addition : BESIDES; *also* : EVEN **2** : up to now; *also* : STILL **3** : so soon as now ⟨not time to go ∼⟩ **4** : EVENTUALLY **5** : NEVERTHELESS, HOWEVER

²**yet** *conj* : despite the fact that : BUT

**ye·ti** \'yet-ē, 'yāt-\ *n* : ABOMINABLE SNOWMAN

**yew** \'yü\ *n* **1** : any of various evergreen trees or shrubs with dark stiff poisonous needles and fleshy fruits **2** : the fine-grained wood of a yew; *esp* : that of an Old World yew valued for bows, hoops, and cabinetwork

**Yid·dish** \'yid-ish\ *n* [Yiddish *yidish*, short for *yidish daytsh*, lit., Jewish German] : a language derived from German and spoken by Jews esp. of eastern Europe — **Yiddish** *adj*

¹**yield** \'yēld\ *vb* **1** : to give as fitting, owed, or required **2** : to give up; *esp* : to give up possession of on claim or demand **3** : to bear as a natural product **4** : PRODUCE, SUPPLY **5** : to bring in : RETURN **6** : to give way (as to force or influence) **7** : to give place **syn** relinquish, cede, waive, submit, capitulate, defer

²**yield** *n* : something yielded; *esp* : the amount or quantity produced or returned

**yield·ing** \'yēl-diŋ\ *adj* **1** : not rigid or stiff : FLEXIBLE **2** : SUBMISSIVE, COMPLIANT

**YMCA** \,wī-,em-(,)sē-'ā\ *n* : Young Men's Christian Association

**YMHA** \,wī-,em-,ā-'chā\ *n* : Young Men's Hebrew Association

**YOB** *abbr* year of birth

**yo·del** \'yōd-ᵊl\ *vb* **yo·deled** *or* **yo·delled**; **yo·del·ing** *or* **yo·del·ling** \'yōd-(ᵊ-)liŋ\ : to sing by suddenly changing from chest voice to falsetto and the reverse; *also* : to shout or call in this manner — **yodel** *n* — **yo·del·er** \'yōd-(ᵊ-)lər\ *n*

**yo·ga** \'yō-gə\ *n* [Skt, lit., yoking, fr. *yunakti* he yokes] **1** *cap* : a Hindu theistic philosophy teaching the suppression of all activity of body, mind, and will in order that the self may realize its distinction from them and attain liberation **2** : a system of exercises for attaining bodily or mental control and well-being

**yo·gi** \'yō-gē\ *or* **yo·gin** \-gən, -,gin\ *n* **1** : a person who practices yoga **2** *cap* : an adherent of Yoga philosophy

**yo·gurt** *or* **yo·ghurt** \'yō-gərt\ *n* : a fermented slightly acid semifluid milk food made of skimmed cow's milk and milk solids to which cultures of bacteria have been added

¹**yoke** \'yōk\ *n, pl* **yokes** **1** : a wooden bar or frame by which two draft animals (as oxen) are coupled at the heads or necks for working together; *also* : a frame fitted to a person's shoulders to carry a load in two equal portions **2** : a clamp that embraces two parts to hold or unite them in position **3** *pl* **yoke** : two animals yoked together **4** : SERVITUDE, BONDAGE **5** : TIE, LINK ⟨the ∼ of matrimony⟩ **6** : a fitted or shaped piece esp. at the shoulder of a garment **syn** couple, pair, brace

²**yoke** *vb* **yoked**; **yok·ing** **1** : to put a yoke on : couple with a yoke **2** : to attach a draft animal to ⟨∼ a plow⟩ **3** : JOIN; *esp* : MARRY

**yo·kel** \'yō-kəl\ *n* : BUMPKIN

**yolk** \'yō(l)k\ *n* **1** : the yellow rounded inner mass of the egg of a bird or reptile : the stored food material of an egg **2** : oily matter in sheep's wool — **yolked** \'yō(l)kt\ *adj*

**Yom Kip·pur** \,yŏm-'kĭp-ər, -kĭ-'pŭr\ *n* [Heb *yōm kippūr*, fr. *yōm* day + *kippūr* atonement] **:** a Jewish holiday observed in September or October with fasting and prayer as a day of atonement

¹**yon** \'yän\ *adj* **:** YONDER

²**yon** *adv* **1 :** YONDER **2 :** THITHER ⟨ran hither and ∼⟩

¹**yon·der** \'yän-dər\ *adv* **:** at or to that place

²**yonder** *adj* **1 :** more distant ⟨the ∼ side of the river⟩ **2 :** being at a distance within view ⟨∼ hills⟩

**yore** \'yŏr\ *n* [ME, fr. *yore*, adv., long ago, fr. OE *geāra*, fr. *gēar* year] **:** time long past ⟨in days of ∼⟩

**you** \(')yü, yə\ *pron* **1 :** the person or persons addressed ⟨∼ are a nice person⟩ ⟨∼ are nice people⟩ **2 :** ONE **2** ⟨∼ turn this knob to open it⟩

¹**young** \'yəŋ\ *adj* **youn·ger** \'yəŋ-gər\; **young·est** \'yəŋ-gəst\ **1 :** being in the first or an early stage of life, growth, or development **2 :** having little experience **3 :** recently come into being **4 :** YOUTHFUL **5** *cap* **:** belonging to or representing a new or revived usu. political group or movement

²**young** *n, pl* **young : young** persons or lower animals

**young·ish** \'yəŋ-ish\ *adj* **:** somewhat young

**young·ling** \'yəŋ-liŋ\ *n* **:** one that is young — **youngling** *adj*

**young·ster** \-stər\ *n* **1 :** a young person **2 :** CHILD

**youn·ker** \'yəŋ-kər\ *n* [D *jonker* young nobleman] **1 :** a young man **2 :** YOUNGSTER

**your** \yər, (')yur, (')yor\ *adj* **:** of or relating to you or yourself

**yours** \'yurz, 'yorz\ *pron* **:** one or the ones belonging to you

**your·self** \yər-'self\ *pron, pl* **your·selves** \-'selvz\ **:** YOU — used reflexively, for emphasis, or in absolute constructions ⟨you'll hurt ∼⟩ ⟨do it ∼⟩ ⟨∼ a man, you should understand⟩

**youth** \'yüth\ *n, pl* **youths** \'yüthz,

**'yüths\ 1 :** the period of life between childhood and maturity **2 :** a young man; *also* **:** young persons **3 :** YOUTHFULNESS

**youth·ful** \'yüth-fəl\ *adj* **1 :** of, relating to, or appropriate to youth **2 :** being young and not yet mature **3 :** FRESH, VIGOROUS — **youth·ful·ly** \-ē\ *adv* — **youth·ful·ness** *n*

**youth hostel** *n* **:** HOSTEL **2**

**yowl** \'yaúl\ *vb* **:** to utter a loud long mournful cry **:** WAIL — **yowl** *n*

**yo-yo** \'yō-(,)yō\ *n, pl* **yo-yos :** a thick grooved double disk with a string attached to its center which is made to fall and rise to the hand by unwinding and rewinding on the string

**yr** *abbr* **1** year **2** your

**yrbk** *abbr* yearbook

**YT** *abbr* Yukon Territory

**yt·ter·bi·um** \i-'tər-bē-əm\ *n* **:** a rare metallic chemical element

**yt·tri·um** \'i-trē-əm\ *n* **:** a rare metallic chemical element

**yu·an** \'yü-ən, yü-'än\ *n, pl* **yuan —** see MONEY table

**yuc·ca** \'yək-ə\ *n* **:** any of several plants related to the lilies that grow in dry regions and have white cup-shaped flowers in erect clusters; *also* **:** the flower of this plant

**Yu·go·slav** \,yü-gō-'släv, -'slav\ *n* **:** a native or inhabitant of Yugoslavia — **Yugoslav** *adj* — **Yu·go·sla·vi·an** \-'släv-ē-ən\ *adj or n*

**yule** \'yül\ *n, often cap* **:** CHRISTMAS

**Yule log** *n* **:** a large log formerly put on the hearth on Christmas Eve as the foundation of the fire

**yule·tide** \'yül-,tīd\ *n, often cap* **:** CHRISTMASTIDE

**yum·my** \'yəm-ē\ *adj* **yum·mi·er; -est :** highly attractive or pleasing

**yurt** \'yurt\ *n* **:** a light round tent of skins or felt stretched over a lattice framework used by various nomadic tribes in Siberia

**YWCA** \,wī-,dəb-əl-yü-(,)sē-'ā\ *n* **:** Young Women's Christian Association

**YWHA** \-,ā-'chā\ *n* **:** Young Women's Hebrew Association

---

Z

¹**z** \'zē\ *n, pl* **z's** *or* **zs** *often cap* **:** the 26th letter of the English alphabet

²**z** *abbr* **1** zero **2** zone

**Z** *symbol* atomic number

**zaire** \'zī(ə)r\ *n, pl* **zaire —** see MONEY table

**Zam·bi·an** \'zam-bē-ən\ *n* **:** a native or inhabitant of Zambia — **Zambian** *adj*

¹**za·ny** \'zā-nē\ *n, pl* **zanies** [It *zanni*, a traditional masked clown, fr. It (dial.) *Zanni*, nickname for *Giovanni* John] **1 :** CLOWN, BUFFOON **2 :** a silly or foolish person

²**zany** *adj* **za·ni·er; -est 1 :** characteristic of a zany **2 :** CRAZY, FOOLISH — **za·ni·ly** \'zā-nə-lē, 'zān-ᵊl-ē\ *adv* — **za·ni·ness** \'zā-nē-nəs\ *n*

**zap** \'zap\ *vb* **zapped; zap·ping :** DESTROY, KILL

**zeal** \'zēl\ *n* **:** eager and ardent interest in the pursuit of something **:** FERVOR **syn** enthusiasm, passion

**zeal·ot** \'zel-ət\ *n* **:** a zealous person; *esp* **:** a fanatical partisan **syn** enthusiast, bigot

**zeal·ous** \'zel-əs\ *adj* **:** filled with, characterized by, or due to zeal — **zeal·ous·ly** *adv* — **zeal·ous·ness** *n*

**ze·bra** \'zē-brə\ *n, pl* **zebras** *also* **zebra :** any of several African mammals related to the horse and ass but conspicuously striped with black or brown and white or buff

**ze·bu** \'zē-b(y)ü\ *n* **:** an Asiatic ox occurring in many domestic breeds and differing from European cattle esp in the presence of a fleshy hump on the shoulders and a loose folded skin

**Zech** *abbr* Zechariah

**zed** \'zed\ *n, chiefly Brit* **:** the letter z

**zeit·geist** \'tsīt-,gīst, 'zīt-\ *n* [G, fr. *zeit* time + *geist* spirit] : the general intellectual, moral, and cultural state of an era

**Zen** \'zen\ *n* : a Japanese Buddhist sect that teaches self-discipline, meditation, and attainment of enlightenment through direct intuitive insight

**ze·na·na** \zə-'nän-ə\ *n* : HAREM, SERAGLIO

**ze·nith** \'zē-nəth\ *n* **1** : the point in the heavens directly overhead **2** : the highest point : ACME **syn** culmination, pinnacle, apex — **ze·nith·al** \-əl\ *adj*

**ze·o·lite** \'zē-ə-,līt\ *n* : any of various feldsparlike silicates used as water softeners — **ze·o·lit·ic** \,zē-ə-'lit-ik\ *adj*

**Zeph** *abbr* Zephaniah

**zeph·yr** \'zef-ər\ *n* **1** : a breeze from the west; *also* : a gentle breeze **2** : any of various lightweight fabrics and articles of clothing

**zep·pe·lin** \'zep-(ə-)lən\ *n* [after Count Ferdinand von *Zeppelin* d 1917 G airship manufacturer] : a rigid airship consisting of a cylindrical trussed and covered frame supported by internal gas cells

**¹ze·ro** \'zē-rō\ *n, pl* **zeros** *also* **zeroes** **1** : the numerical symbol 0 **2** : the number represented by the symbol 0 **3** : the point at which the graduated degrees or measurements on a scale (as of a thermometer) begin **4** : the lowest point

**²zero** *adj* **1** : having no magnitude or quantity **2** : ABSENT, LACKING; *esp* : having no modified inflectional form

**³zero** *vb* : TRAIN ⟨~ in artillery on the crossroads⟩

**zero hour** *n* **1** : the hour at which a previously planned military operation is started **2** : the scheduled time for an action or operation to begin

**zero-zero** *adj* : characterized by or being atmospheric conditions that reduce ceiling and visibility to zero ⟨~ weather⟩

**zest** \'zest\ *n* **1** : a quality of enhancing enjoyment : PIQUANCY **2** : keen enjoyment : RELISH, GUSTO — **zest·ful** \-fəl\ *adj* — **zest·ful·ly** \-ē\ *adv* — **zest·ful·ness** *n*

**¹zig·zag** \'zig-,zag\ *n* : one of a series of short sharp turns, angles, or alterations in a course; *also* : something marked by such a series

**²zigzag** *adv* : in or by a zigzag path

**³zigzag** *adj* : having short sharp turns or angles

**⁴zigzag** *vb* **zig·zagged; zig·zag·ging** : to form into or proceed along a zigzag

**zil·lion** \'zil-yən\ *n* : a large indeterminate number

**¹zinc** \'ziŋk\ *n* : a bluish white crystalline metallic chemical element that tarnishes only slightly in moist air at ordinary temperatures and is used to make alloys and as a protective coating for iron

**²zinc** *vb* **zinced** *or* **zincked** \'ziŋkt\;

**zinc·ing** *or* **zinck·ing** \'ziŋ-kiŋ\ : GALVANIZE 2

**zinc ointment** *n* : an ointment containing 20 percent of zinc oxide and used for skin disorders

**zinc oxide** *n* : an infusible white solid used as a pigment, in compounding rubber, and in ointments

**zing** \'ziŋ\ *n* **1** : a shrill humming noise **2** : VITALITY — **zing** *vb*

**zin·nia** \'zin-ē-ə, 'zēn-yə\ *n* : an American herb related to the daisies and widely grown for its showy long-lasting flower heads

**Zi·on** \'zī-ən\ *n* **1** : the Jewish people **2** : the Jewish homeland as a symbol of Judaism or of Jewish national aspiration **3** : HEAVEN **4** : UTOPIA

**Zi·on·ism** \'zī-ə-,niz-əm\ *n* : a theory, plan, or movement for setting up a Jewish national or religious community in Palestine — **Zi·on·ist** \-nəst\ *adj or n*

**¹zip** \'zip\ *vb* **zipped; zip·ping** : to move or act with speed or vigor

**²zip** *n* **1** : a sudden sharp hissing sound **2** : ENERGY, VIM

**³zip** *vb* **zipped; zip·ping** : to close or open with a zipper

**zip code** *n, often cap Z&I&P* [*zone* improvement *plan*] : a 5-digit number that identifies each postal delivery area in the U.S.

**zip·per** \'zip-ər\ *n* : a fastener consisting of two rows of metal or plastic teeth or spirals on strips of tape and a sliding piece that closes an opening by drawing the teeth together

**zip·py** \'zip-ē\ *adj* **zip·pi·er; -est** : BRISK, SNAPPY

**zir·con** \'zər-,kän\ *n* : a zirconium-containing mineral several transparent varieties of which are used as gems

**zir·co·ni·um** \,zər-'kō-nē-əm\ *n* : a heat-resistant and corrosion-resistant metallic element used in alloys and ceramics

**zith·er** \'zith-ər, 'zith-\ *n* : a musical instrument having 30 to 40 strings played with plectrum and fingers

**zlo·ty** \'zlȯt-ē\ *n, pl* **zlo·tys** \-ēz\ *also* **zloty** — see MONEY table

**Zn** *symbol* zinc

**zo·di·ac** \'zōd-ē-,ak\ *n* [ME, fr. MF *zodiaque*, fr. L *zodiacus*, fr. Gk *zōidiakos*, fr. *zōidion* carved figure, sign of the zodiac, fr. dim. of *zōion* living being, figure] **1** : an imaginary elongated region in the heavens that encompasses the paths of all the principal planets except Pluto, that has the ecliptic as its central line, and that is divided into 12 signs with each taken for astrological purposes to extend 30 degrees of longitude **2** : a figure representing the signs of the zodiac and their symbols — **zo·di·a·cal** \zō-'dī-ə-kəl\ *adj*

**zom·bie** *also* **zom·bi** \'zäm-bē\ *n* **1** : the voodoo snake deity **2** : the supernatural power held in voodoo belief to enter into and reanimate a dead body

**zon·al** \'zōn-²l\ *adj* : of, relating to, or

having the form of a zone — **zon·al·ly** \-ē\ *adv*

**¹zone** \'zōn\ *n* [L *zona* belt, zone, fr. Gk *zōnē*] **1** : any of five great divisions of the earth's surface that is made according to latitude and temperature and includes the torrid zone extending 23°27′ on each side of the equator, the two temperate zones lying between the torrid zone and the polar circles which are 23°27′ from the poles, and the two frigid zones lying between the polar circles and the poles **2** *archaic* : GIRDLE, BELT **3** : an encircling band or girdle ⟨a ∼ of trees⟩ **4** : an area or region set off or distinguished in some way from adjoining parts

**²zone** *vb* **zoned; zon·ing 1** : ENCIRCLE **2** : to arrange in or mark off into zones; *esp* : to divide (as a city) into sections reserved for different purposes — **zo·na·tion** \zō-'nā-shən\ *n* — **zoned** \'zōnd\ *adj*

**zonked** \'zäŋkt\ *adj* : being under the influence of alcohol or a drug (as LSD) : HIGH

**zoo** \'zü\ *n, pl* **zoos** : a zoological garden or collection of living animals usu. for public display

**zoo·ge·og·ra·phy** \,zō-ə-jē-'äg-rə-fē\ *n* : a branch of biogeography concerned with the geographical distribution of animals — **zoo·ge·og·ra·pher** \-fər\ *n* — **zoo·geo·graph·ic** \-,jē-ə-'graf-ik\ *also* **zoo·geo·graph·i·cal** \-i-kəl\ *adj*

**zool** *abbr* zoological; zoology

**zoological garden** *n* : a garden or park where wild animals are kept for exhibition

**zo·ol·o·gy** \zō-'äl-ə-jē\ *n* : a science that deals with animals and the animal kingdom — **zo·o·log·i·cal** \,zō-ə-'läj-i-kəl\ *adj* — **zo·ol·o·gist** \zō-'äl-ə-jəst\ *n*

**zoom** \'züm\ *vb* **1** : to move with a loud hum or buzz **2** : to climb sharply and briefly by means of momentum ⟨the airplane ∼ed⟩ **3** : to focus a camera or microscope using a special lens that permits the apparent distance of the object to be varied — **zoom** *n*

**zoom lens** *n* : a camera lens in which the image size can be varied continuously so that the image remains in focus at all times

**zoo·mor·phism** \,zō-ə-'mȯr-,fiz-əm\ *n* **1** : the representation of a deity in the form or with the attributes of an animal **2** : the use of animal forms in art — **zoo·mor·phic** \-fik\ *adj*

**zoo·phyte** \'zō-ə-,fīt\ *n* [Gk *zōophyton*, fr. *zōion* animal + *phyton* plant] : any of numerous invertebrate animals (as a coral or sponge) suggesting plants esp. in growth

**zoo·plank·ton** \,zō-ə-'plaŋk-tən, -,tän\ *n* : animal life of the plankton

**zoo·spore** \'zō-ə-,spōr\ *n* : a motile spore

**zoot suit** \'züt-\ *n* : a flashy suit of extreme cut typically consisting of a thigh-length jacket with wide padded shoulders and trousers that are wide at the top and narrow at the bottom — **zoot-suit·er** \-,süt-ər\ *n*

**Zo·ro·as·tri·an·ism** \,zōr-ə-'was-trē-ə-,niz-əm\ *n* : a religion founded by the Persian prophet Zoroaster — **Zo·ro·as·tri·an** *adj or n*

**Zou·ave** \zü-'äv\ *n* : a member of a French infantry unit orig. composed of Algerians wearing a brilliant uniform and conducting a quick spirited drill; *also* : a member of a military unit modeled on the Zouaves

**zounds** \'zaün(d)z\ *interj* [euphemism for *God's wounds*] — used as a mild oath

**zoy·sia** \'zȯi-shə, -zhə, -sē-ə, -zē-ə\ *n* : any of a genus of creeping perennial grasses having fine wiry leaves and including some used as lawn grasses

**ZPG** *abbr* zero population growth

**Zr** *symbol* zirconium

**zuc·chet·to** \zü-'ket-ō, tsü-\ *n, pl* **-tos** : a small round skullcap worn by Roman Catholic ecclesiastics

**zuc·chi·ni** \zü-'kē-nē\ *n, pl* **-ni** or **-nis** : a summer squash of bushy growth with smooth cylindrical dark green fruits; *also* : its fruit

**Zu·ni** \'zü-nē\ *or* **Zu·ñi** \-nyē\ *n, pl* **Zuni** *or* **Zunis** *or* **Zuñi** *or* **Zuñis** : a member of an Indian people of northeastern Arizona; *also* : the language of the Zuni people

**zwie·back** \'swē-bak, 'swī-, 'zwē-, 'zwī-\ *n* [G, lit., twice baked, fr. *zwie-* twice + *backen* to bake] : a usu. sweetened bread that is baked and then sliced and toasted until dry and crisp

**Zwing·li·an** \'zwiŋ-(g)lē-ən, 'swiŋ\ *n* : a follower or adherent of the Swiss religious reformer Ulrich Zwingli or his teachings — **Zwinglian** *adj*

**zy·gote** \'zī-,gōt\ *n* : a cell formed by the union of two sexual cells — **zy·got·ic** \zī-'gät-ik\ *adj*

**zy·mur·gy** \'zī-(,)mər-jē\ *n* : chemistry dealing with fermentation processes

**ab·eunt stu·dia in mo·res** \ˈäb-e-ˌu̇nt-ˈstüd-ē-ˌä-ˌin-ˈmō-ˌrās\ [L] : practices zealously pursued pass into habits

**à bien·tôt** \à-byaⁿ-tō\ [F] : so long : farewell

**ab in·cu·na·bu·lis** \ˌäb-ˌiŋ-kə-ˈnäb-ə-ˌlēs\ [L] : from the cradle : from infancy

**à bon chat, bon rat** \à-bōⁿ-ˈshà-bōⁿ-ˈrà\ [F] : to a good cat, a good rat : retaliation in kind

**à bouche ou·verte** \à-bü-shü-vert\ [F] : with open mouth : eagerly : uncritically

**ab ovo us·que ad ma·la** \ˌäb-ˈō-vō-ˌu̇s-kwe-ˌäd-ˈmäl-ä\ [L] : from egg to apples : from soup to nuts : from beginning to end

**à bras ou·verts** \à-brà-zü-ver\ [F] : with open arms : cordially

**ab·sit in·vi·dia** \ˈäb-ˌsit-in-ˈwid-ē-ˌä\ [L] : let there be no envy or ill will

**ab uno dis·ce om·nes** \ä-ˈü-nō-ˌdis-ke-ˈôm-ˌnās\ [L] : from one learn to know all

**ab ur·be con·di·ta** \äb-ˈu̇r-be-ˈkȯn-də-ˌtä\ [L] : from the founding of the city (Rome, founded 753 B.C.) — used by the Romans in reckoning dates

**ab·usus non tol·lit usum** \ˈäb-ˌü-səs-ˌnōn-ˌtō-lət-ˈü-səm\ [L] : abuse does not take away use, i.e., is not an argument against proper use

**à compte** \à-kōⁿt\ [F] : on account

**à coup sûr** \à-kü-sūr\ [F] : with sure stroke : surely

**ad ar·bi·tri·um** \ˌad-är-ˈbit-rē-əm\ [L] : at will : arbitrarily

**ad as·tra per as·pera** \ˌad-ˈas-trə-ˌpər-ˈas-pə-rə\ [L] : to the stars by hard ways — motto of Kansas

**ad ex·tre·mum** \ˌad-ik-ˈstrē-məm\ [L] : to the extreme : at last

**ad ka·len·das Grae·cas** \ˌäd-kə-ˈlen-dəs-ˈgrī-ˌkäs\ [L] : at the Greek calends : never (since the Greeks had no calends)

**ad ma·jo·rem Dei glo·ri·am** \ˌäd-mä-ˈyȯr-ˌem-ˈde-ˌē-ˈglȯr-ē-ˌäm, -ˈyȯr-, -ˈglȯr\ [L] : to the greater glory of God — motto of the Society of Jesus

**ad pa·tres** \ˌäd-ˈpä-ˌträs\ [L] : (gathered) to his fathers : deceased

**à droite** \à-drwàt\ [F] : to or on the right hand

**ad un·guem** \ˌäd-ˈu̇ŋ-ˌgwem\ [L] : to the fingernail : to a nicety : exactly (from the use of the fingernail to test the smoothness of marble)

**ad utrum·que pa·ra·tus** \ˌäd-ü-ˈtru̇m-kwe-pə-ˈrät-əs\ [L] : prepared for either (event)

**ad vi·vum** \ˌäd-ˈwē-ˌwu̇m\ [L] : to the life

**ae·gri som·nia** \ˌī-grē-ˈsȯm-nē-ˌä\ [L] : a sick man's dreams

**ae·quam ser·va·re men·tem** \ˈī-ˌkwäm-sər-ˌwä-rē-ˈmen-ˌtem\ [L] : to preserve a calm mind

**ae·quo ani·mo** \ˌī-ˌkwō-ˈän-ə-ˌmō\ [L] : with even mind : calmly

**ae·re per·en·ni·us** \ˈī-rā-pə-ˈren-ē-ˌu̇s\ [L] : more lasting than bronze

**à gauche** \à-gōsh\ [F] : to or on the left hand

**age quod agis** \ˈäg-e-ˌkwȯd-ˈäg-ˌis\ [L] : do what you are doing : to the business at hand

**à grands frais** \à-gräⁿ-fre\ [F] : at great expense

**à huis clos** \à-wᵉē-klō\ [F] : with closed doors

**aide-toi, le ciel t'aidera** \ed-twà-lə-ˈsyel-te-drà\ [F] : help yourself (and) heaven will help you

**ai·né** \e-nā\ [F] : elder : senior (masc.)

**ai·née** \e-nā\ [F] : elder : senior (fem.)

**à l'aban·don** \à-là-bäⁿ-dōⁿ\ [F] : carelessly : in disorder

**à la belle étoile** \à-là-bel-ā-twàl\ [F] : under the beautiful star : in the open air at night

**à la bonne heure** \à-là-bò-nœr\ [F] : at a good time : well and good : all right

**à la fran·çaise** \à-là-fräⁿ-sez\ [F] : in the French style

**à l'an·glaise** \à-läⁿ-glez\ [F] : in the English style

**alea jac·ta est** \ˈäl-ē-ˌä-ˌyäk-tə-ˈest\ [L] : the die is cast

**à l'im·pro·viste** \à-laⁿ-prȯ-vēst\ [F] : unexpectedly

**ali·quan·do bo·nus dor·mi·tat Ho·me·rus** \ˌäl-ə-ˌkwän-dō-ˈbò-nəs-dȯr-ˈmē-ˌtät-hō-ˈmer-əs\ [L] : sometimes (even) good Homer nods

**alis vo·lat pro·pri·is** \ˈäl-ˌēs-ˈwò-ˌlät-ˈprō-prē-ˌēs\ [L] : she flies with her own wings — motto of Oregon

**al·ki** \ˈal-ˌkī, -kē\ [Chinook Jargon] : by and by — motto of Washington

**alo·ha oe** \à-ˌlō-hä-ˈȯi, -ˈō-ē\ [Hawaiian] : love to you ; greetings : farewell

**al·ter idem** \ˌȯl-tər-ˈī-dem, ˌäl-tər-ˈī-\ [L] : second self

**a max·i·mis ad mi·ni·ma** \ä-ˈmäk-sə-ˌmēs-ˌäd-ˈmin-ə-ˌmä\ [L] : from the greatest to the least

**ami·cus hu·ma·ni ge·ner·is** \ä-ˈmē-kəs-hü-ˌmän-ē-ˈgen-ə-rəs\ [L] : friend of the human race

**amicus us·que ad aras** \-ˌu̇s-kwe-ˌäd-ˈär-ˌäs\ [L] : a friend as far as to the altars, i.e., except in what is contrary to one's religion; *also* : a friend to the last extremity

**ami de cour** \à-ˌmēd-ə-ˈku̇r\ [F] : court friend : insincere friend

**amor pa·tri·ae** \ˌäm-ˌȯr-ˈpä-trē-ˌī\ [L] : love of one's country

**amor vin·cit om·nia** \ˈä-ˌmȯr-ˌwiŋ-kət-ˈȯm-nē-ˌä\ [L] : love conquers all things

**an·cienne no·blesse** \äⁿ-syen-nò-bles\ [F] : old-time nobility : the French nobility before the Revolution of 1789

818

**an·guis in her·ba** \ˌäŋ-gwəs-in-'her-ˌbä\ [L] : snake in the grass

**ani·mal bi·pes im·plu·me** \'än-i-ˌmäl-ˌbip-ˌäs-im-'plü-me\ [L] : two-legged animal without feathers (i.e., man)

**ani·mis opi·bus·que pa·ra·ti** \'än-ə-ˌmēs-ˌó-pə-'bús-kwe-pə-'rät-ē\ [L] : prepared in spirits and resources — one of the mottoes of South Carolina

**an·no ae·ta·tis su·ae** \'än-ō-ī-ˌtät-əs-'sü-ˌī\ [L] : in the (specified) year of his (or her) age

**an·no mun·di** \ˌän-ō-'mún-dē\ [L] : in the year of the world — used in reckoning dates from the supposed period of the creation of the world, esp. as fixed by James Ussher at 4004 B.C. or by the Jews at 3761 B.C.

**an·no ur·bis con·di·tae** \ˌän-ō-ˌûr-bəs-'kón-də-ˌtī\ [L] : in the year of the founded city (Rome, founded 753 B.C.)

**an·nu·it coep·tis** \ˌän-ə-ˌwit-'kóip-ˌtēs\ [L] : He (God) has smiled on our undertakings — motto on the reverse of the Great Seal of the United States

**à peu près** \ˌä-pœ-pre'\ [F] : nearly : approximately

**à pied** \ä-pyä\ [F] : on foot

**après moi le dé·luge** \ä-pre-mwä-lə-dä-lüzh\ [F] : after me the deluge (attributed to Louis XV)

**à pro·pos de bottes** \ˌä-prə-pōd-ə-bót\ [F] : apropos of boots — used to change the subject

**à propos de rien** \-ryaⁿ\ [F] : apropos of nothing

**aqua et ig·ni in·ter·dic·tus** \ˌäk-wä-et-'ig-nē-ˌint-ər-'dik-təs\ [L] : forbidden to be furnished with water and fire : outlawed

**Ar·ca·des am·bo** \ˌär-kə-ˌdes-'äm-bō\ [L] : both Arcadians : two persons of like occupations or tastes; *also* : two rascals

**a ri·ve·der·ci** \ˌär-ē-vä-'der-chē\ [It] : till we meet again : farewell

**ar·rec·tis au·ri·bus** \ä-'rek-ˌtēs-'aú-ri-ˌbús\ [L] : with ears pricked up : attentively

**ars est ce·la·re ar·tem** \ˌärs-ˌest-kä-ˌlär-ē-'är-ˌtem\ [L] : it is (true) art to conceal art

**ars lon·ga, vi·ta bre·vis** \ärs-'lóŋ-gä-ˌwē-tä-'bre-wəs\ [L] : art is long, life is short

**à tort et à tra·vers** \ä-tòr-tä-ä-trä-ver'\ [F] : wrong and crosswise : at random : without rhyme or reason

**au bout de son la·tin** \ō-büd-(ə-)sōⁿ-lä-taⁿ\ [F] : at the end of one's Latin : at the end of one's mental resources

**au con·traire** \ō-kōⁿ-trer\ [F] : on the contrary

**au·de·mus ju·ra no·stra de·fen·dere** \aú-'dä-məs-ˌyúr-ə-'nó-strə-dä-

**'fen-də-rē\** [L] : we dare defend our rights — motto of Alabama

**au·den·tes for·tu·na ju·vat** \aú-'den-ˌtäs-fór-ˌtü-nə-'yù-ˌwät\ [L] : fortune favors the bold

**au·di al·teram partem** \'aú-ˌdē-ˌäl-tə-ˌräm-'pär-ˌtem\ [L] : hear the other side

**au grand sé·rieux** \ō-grän-sā-ryœ\ [F] : in all seriousness

**au pays des aveugles les borgnes sont rois** \ō-pā-ē-dā-zà-vœgl' lā-bórnᵛ-ə-sōⁿ-rwä\ [F] : in the country of the blind the one-eyed men are kings

**au·rea me·di·o·cri·tas** \'aú-rē-ə-ˌmed-ē-'ó-krə-ˌtäs\ [L] : the golden mean

**au reste** \ō-rest\ [F] : for the rest : besides

**au·spi·ci·um me·li·o·ris ae·vi** \aú-'spik-ē-ˌùm-ˌmel-ē-ˌōr-əs-'ī-ˌwē\ [L] : an omen of a better age — motto of the Order of St. Michael and St. George

**aus·si·tôt dit, aus·si·tôt fait** \ō-sē-tō-dē ō-sē-tō-fe\ [F] : no sooner said than done

**aut Cae·sar aut ni·hil** \aút-'kī-sär-ˌaút-'ni-ˌhil\ [L] : either a Caesar or nothing

**aut Caesar aut nul·lus** \-'nùl-əs\ [L] : either a Caesar or a nobody

**au·tres temps, au·tres mœurs** \ō-trə-täⁿ ō-trə-mœrs\ [F] : other times; other customs

**aut vin·ce·re aut mo·ri** \aút-'wiŋ-kə-rē-ˌaút-'mó-ˌrē\ [L] : either to conquer or to die

**aux armes** \ō-zärm\ [F] : to arms

**ave at·que va·le** \'ä-ˌwä-ˌät-kwe-'wä-ˌlā\ [L] : hail and farewell

**à vo·tre san·té** \ä-vót-sä°-tā, -vó-trə-\ [F] : to your health — used as a toast

**beaux yeux** \bō-zyœ\ [F] : beautiful eyes : beauty of face

**bien en·ten·du** \byaⁿ-näⁿ-täⁿ-dœ\ [F] : well understood : of course

**bien sé·ance** \byaⁿ-sā-äⁿs\ [F] : propriety

**bis dat qui ci·to dat** \ˌbis-ˌdät-kwē-'ki-tō-ˌdät\ [L] : he gives twice who gives promptly

**bon gré, mal gré** \'bōⁿ-ˌgrä-'màl-ˌgrä\ [F] : whether with good grace or bad : willy-nilly

**bo·nis avi·bus** \ˌbó-ˌnēs-'ä-wi-ˌbús\ [L] : under good auspices

**bon jour** \bōⁿ-zhür\ [F] : good day : good morning

**bonne foi** \bón-fwä\ [F] : good faith

**bon soir** \bōⁿ-swär\ [F] : good evening

**bru·tum ful·men** \ˌbrüt-əm-'fúl-mən\ [L] : insensible thunderbolt : a futile threat or display of force

**buon gior·no** \bwón-'jōr-nō\ [It] : good day

**ca·dit quae·stio** \ˌkäd-ət-'kwī-stē-ˌō\

---

**[L]** : the question drops : the argument collapses

**cau·sa si·ne qua non** \ˈkau̇-sä-ˌsin-ē-kwä-ˈnōn\ **[L]** : an indispensable cause or condition

**ca·ve ca·nem** \ˌkä-wā-ˈkän-ˌem\ **[L]** : beware the dog

**ce·dant ar·ma to·gae** \ˈkā-ˌdänt-ˌär-mə-ˈtō-ˌgī\ **[L]** : let arms yield to the toga : let military power give way to civil power — motto of Wyoming

**ce n'est que le pre·mier pas qui coûte** \snek-lə-prə-myā-kē-küt\ **[F]** : it is only the first step that costs

**c'est à dire** \se-tà-dēr\ **[F]** : that is to say : namely

**c'est au·tre chose** \se-tōt-shōz, -tō-trə-\ **[F]** : that's a different thing

**c'est ma·gni·fique, mais ce n'est pas la guerre** \se-mà-nyē-fēk-mes-ne-pä-là-ger\ **[F]** : it's magnificent, but it isn't war

**c'est plus qu'un crime, c'est une faute** \se-plǖ-kœⁿ-krēm se-tēⁿ-fōt\ **[F]** : it is worse than a crime, it is a blunder

**ce·tera de·sunt** \ˌkāt-ə-ˌrä-ˈdā-ˌsùnt\ **[L]** : the rest is missing

**cha·cun à son gout** \shà-kœ̄ⁿ-nà-sōⁿ-gü\ **[F]** : everyone to his taste

**châ·teau en Es·pagne** \shä-tō-ä-ⁿnes-pányⁱ\ **[F]** : castle in Spain : a visionary project

**cher·chez la femme** \sher-shä-làfàm\ **[F]** : look for the woman

**che sa·rà, sa·rà** \ˌkā-sä-ˌrä-sä-ˈrä\ **[It]** : what will be, will be

**che·val de ba·taille** \shə-vàl-də-bàtäⁱ\ **[F]** : war-horse : argument constantly relied on : favorite subject

**co·gi·to, er·go sum** \ˈkō-gə-ˌtō-ˌergō-ˈsùm\ **[L]** : I think, therefore I exist

**com·ment vous por·tez-vous?** \kōmä-vü-pȯr-tā-vü\ **[F]** : how are you?

**com·pa·gnon de voy·age** \kōⁿ-pà-nʸōⁿ-də-vwà-yàzh\ **[F]** : traveling companion

**compte rendu** \kōⁿt-rän-dǖ\ **[F]** : report (as of proceedings in an investigation)

**cor·rup·tio op·ti·mi pes·si·ma** \kə-ˈrùp-tē-ˌō-ˈäp-tə-ˌmē-ˈpes-ə-ˌmä\ **[L]** : the corruption of the best is the worst of all

**coup de maî·tre** \küd-(ə-)metrⁿ\ **[F]** : masterstroke

**coup d'es·sai** \kü-dā-se\ **[F]** : experiment : trial

**coûte que coûte** \küt-kə-küt\ **[F]** : cost what it may

**cre·do quia ab·sur·dum est** \ˌkrādō-ˈkwē-ä-äp-ˌsùrd-əm-ˈest\ **[L]** : I believe it because it is absurd

**cres·cit eun·do** \ˌkres-kət-ˈeùn-dō\ **[L]** : it grows as it goes — motto of New Mexico

**crux cri·ti·co·rum** \ˈkrùks-ˌkrit-ə-ˈkȯr-əm\ **[L]** : crux of critics

**cum gra·no sa·lis** \ˌkùm-ˌgrän-ō-ˈsäl-əs\ **[L]** : with a grain of salt

**cus·tos mo·rum** \ˌkùs-tōs-ˈmȯr-əm\ **[L]** : guardian of manners or morals : censor

**d'ac·cord** \dà-kȯr\ **[F]** : in accord : agreed

**dame d'hon·neur** \dàm-dȯ-nœr\ **[F]** : lady-in-waiting

**dam·nant quod non in·tel·li·gunt** \ˈdäm-ˌnänt-ˌkwȯd-ˌnōn-in-ˈtel-ə-ˌgùnt\ **[L]** : they condemn what they do not understand

**de bonne grâce** \də-bȯn-gräs\ **[F]** : with good grace : willingly

**de gus·ti·bus non est dis·pu·tan·dum** \dä-ˈgùs-tə-ˌbùs-ˌnōn-ˌest-ˌdis-pù-ˈtän-ˌdùm\ **[L]** : there is no disputing about tastes

**Dei gra·tia** \ˌde-ˌē-ˈgrät-ē-ˌä\ **[L]** : by the grace of God

**de in·te·gro** \dā-ˈint-ə-ˌgrō\ **[L]** : anew : afresh

**de l'au·dace, en·core de l'au·dace, et tou·jours de l'au·dace** \də-lō-ˈdàs-ä-ⁿkȯr-də-lō-dàs, -ā-tü-ˈzhür-də-lō-dàs\ **[F]** : audacity, more audacity, and ever more audacity

**de·len·da est Car·tha·go** \dā-ˈlen-dä-ˌest-kär-ˈtäg-ō\ **[L]** : Carthage must be destroyed

**de·li·ne·a·vit** \dā-ˌlē-nä-ˈä-wit\ **[L]** : he (or she) drew it

**de mal en pis** \də-mȧ-lä-ⁿpē\ **[F]** : from bad to worse

**de mi·ni·mis non cu·rat lex** \dā-ˈmin-ə-ˌmēs-ˌnōn-ˌkü-ˌrät-ˈleks\ **[L]** : the law takes no account of trifles

**de mor·tu·is nil ni·si bo·num** \dā-ˈmȯrt-ə-ˌwēs-ˌnēl-ˌnis-ē-ˈbȯ-ˌnùm\ **[L]** : of the dead (say) nothing but good

**Deo fa·ven·te** \ˌdā-ō-fə-ˈvent-ē\ **[L]** : with God's favor

**Deo gra·ti·as** \ˌdā-ō-ˈgrät-ē-ˌäs\ **[L]** : thanks (be) to God

**de pro·fun·dis** \ˌdā-prō-ˈfùn-dēs, -ˈfən-\ **[L]** : out of the depths

**der Geist der stets ver·neint** \dər-ˈgīst-dər-ˌshtäts-fer-ˈnīnt\ **[G]** : the spirit that ever denies — applied originally to Mephistopheles

**de·si·pere in lo·co** \dā-ˈsip-ə-rē-in-ˈlō-kō\ **[L]** : to indulge in trifling at the proper time

**Deus vult** \ˌdā-əs-ˈwùlt\ **[L]** : God wills it — rallying cry of the First Crusade

**di·es fau·stus** \ˌdē-ˌäs-ˈfau̇-stəs\ **[L]** : lucky day

**dies in·fau·stus** \-ˌin-ˈfau̇-stəs\ **[L]** : unlucky day

**dies irae** \-ˈē-ˌrī, -ˌrä\ **[L]** : day of wrath — used of the Judgment Day

**Dieu et mon droit** \dyœ̄-ā-mōⁿ-ˈdrwä\ **[F]** : God and my right — motto on the British royal arms

**Dieu vous garde** \dyœ̄-vü-gàrd\ **[F]** : God keep you

**di·ri·go** \ˈdē-ri-ˌgō\ **[L]** : I direct — motto of Maine

**dis ali·ter vi·sum** \ˌdēs-ˌal-ə-ˌter-ˈwē-ˌsùm\ **[L]** : the Gods decreed otherwise

**di·tat De·us** \ˌdē-ˌtät-ˈdā-əs\ **[L]** : God enriches — motto of Arizona

**di·vi·de et im·pe·ra** \ˈdē-wi-ˌde-ˌet-ˈim-pə-ˌrä\ **[L]** : divide and rule

**do·cen·do dis·ci·mus** \dȯ-ˌken-dō-ˈdis-ki-ˌmùs\ **[L]** : we learn by teaching

**Domine, dirige nos** \ˈdȯ-mi-ˌne-ˌdē-ri-ˌge-ˈnōs\ **[L]** : Lord, direct us — motto of the City of London

**Do·mi·nus vo·bis·cum** \ˌdȯ-mi-ˌnùswō-'bēs-,kùm\ [L] : the Lord be with you

**dul·ce et de·co·rum est pro pa·tria mo·ri** \,dùl-,ket-de-'kōr-,est-prō-,pä-trē-,ä-'mō-,rē\ [L] : it is sweet and seemly to die for one's country

**dum spi·ro, spe·ro** \dùm-'spē-rō-'spä-rō\ [L] : while I breathe I hope — one of the mottoes of South Carolina

**dum vi·vi·mus vi·va·mus** \dùm-'wē-wē-,mús-wē-'wäm-ùs\ [L] : while we live, let us live

**dux fe·mi·na fac·ti** \,dúks-,fā-mi-nä-'fäk-,tē\ [L] : a woman was leader of the exploit

**ec·ce sig·num** \,ek-e-'sig-,nùm\ [L] : behold the sign : look at the proof

**e con·tra·rio** \,ā-kòn-'trär-ē-,ō\ [L] : on the contrary

**écra·sez l'in·fâme** \ā-krä-zā-laⁿ-fäm\ [F] : crush the infamous thing

**eheu fu·ga·ces la·bun·tur an·ni** \,ā-,heù-fù-'gä-,käs-lä-,bùn-,túr-'än-,ē\ [L] : alas! the fleeting years glide on

**ein' fes·te Burg ist un·ser Gott** \īn-,fes-tə-'bùrk-ist-,ùn-zər-'gòt\ [G] : a mighty fortress is our God

**em·bar·ras de ri·chesses** \äⁿ-bä-räd-(ə-)rē-shes\ [F] : embarrassing surplus of riches : confusing abundance

**em·bar·ras du choix** \äⁿ-bä-rä-dü-shwä\ [F] : embarrassing variety of choice

**en ami** \äⁿ-nä-mē\ [F] : as a friend

**en ef·fet** \äⁿ-nä-fe\ [F] : in fact : indeed

**en fa·mille** \äⁿ-fä-mēy\ [F] : in one's family : at home : informally

**en·fant gâ·té** \äⁿ-fäⁿ-gä-tā\ [F] : spoiled child

**en·fants per·dus** \äⁿ-fäⁿ-per-dᵫ\ [F] : lost children : soldiers sent to a dangerous post

**en·fin** \äⁿ-faⁿ\ [F] : in conclusion : in a word

**en gar·çon** \äⁿ-gàr-sōⁿ\ [F] : as or like a bachelor

**en pan·tou·fles** \äⁿ-päⁿ-tüflᵊ\ [F] : in slippers : at ease : informally

**en plein air** \äⁿ-plen-er\ [F] : in the open air

**en plein jour** \äⁿ-plaⁿ-zhür\ [F] : in broad day

**en règle** \äⁿ-reglᵊ\ [F] : in order : in due form

**en re·tard** \äⁿr-(ə-)tàr\ [F] : behind time : late

**en re·traite** \äⁿ-rə-tret\ [F] : in retreat : in retirement

**en re·vanche** \äⁿr-(ə-)väⁿsh\ [F] : in return : in compensation

**en se·condes noces** \äⁿs-(ə-)gōⁿd-nòs\ [F] : in a second marriage

**en·se·pe·tit pla·ci·dam sub li·ber·ta·te qui·e·tem** \,en-se-,pet-ət-'pläki-,däm-sùb-,lē-ber-,tä-te-kwē-'ā-,tem\ [L] : with the sword she seeks calm re-

pose under liberty — motto of Massachusetts

**épa·ter les bour·geois** \ā-pà-tā-lā-bür-zhwà\ [F] : to shock the middle classes

**e plu·ri·bus unum** \,e-,plùr-ə-bəs-'(y)ü-nəm, ,ā-,plür-\ [L] : one out of many — motto of the United States

**e pur si muo·ve** \ā-,pùr-sē-'mwò-vā\ [It] : and yet it does move — attributed to Galileo after recanting his assertion of the earth's motion

**er·ra·re hu·ma·num est** \e-'rär-e-hü-,män-əm-'est\ [L] : to err is human

**es·prit de l'es·ca·lier** \es-prēd-les-kà-lyā\ or **es·prit d'es·ca·lier** \-prē-des-\ [F] : spirit of the staircase : repartee thought of only too late, on the way home

**es·se quam vi·de·ri** \'es-ē-,kwäm-wi-'dā-rē\ [L] : to be rather than to seem — motto of North Carolina

**est mo·dus in re·bus** \est-'mò-,dùs-in-'rā-,bùs\ [L] : there is a proper measure in things, i.e., the golden mean should always be observed

**es·to per·pe·tua** \'es-,to-pər-'pet-e-,wä\ [L] : may she endure forever — motto of Idaho

**et hoc ge·nus om·ne** \et-,hōk-,genəs-'ōm-ne\ or **et id genus om·ne** \et-,id-\ [L] : and everything of this kind

**et in Ar·ca·dia ego** \,et-in-är-,käd-ē-ə-'eg-ō\ [L] : I too (lived) in Arcadia

**et sic de si·mi·li·bus** \et-,sēk-dā-sə-'mil-ə-,bùs\ [L] : and so of like things

**et tu Bru·te** \et-'tü-'brü-te\ [L] : thou too, Brutus — exclamation attributed to Julius Caesar on seeing his friend Brutus among his assassins

**eu·re·ka** \yù-'rē-kə\ [Gk] : I have found it — motto of California

**Ewig-Weib·li·che** \,ā-vik-'vīp-li-kə\ [G] : eternal feminine

**ex ani·mo** \ek-'sän-ə-,mō\ [L] : from the heart : sincerely

**ex·cel·si·or** \ik-'sel-sē-ər, eks-'kel-sē-,òr\ [L] : still higher — motto of New York

**ex·cep·tio pro·bat re·gu·lam de re·bus non ex·cep·tis** \eks-'kep-tē-,ō-,prō-bät-'rā-gə-,läm-dā-'rā-,bùs-,nōn-eks-'kep-,tēs\ [L] : an exception establishes the rule as to things not excepted

**ex·cep·tis ex·ci·pi·en·dis** \eks-'kep-,tēs-eks-,kip-ē-'en-,dēs\ [L] : with the proper or necessary exceptions

**ex·i·tus ac·ta pro·bat** \'ek-sə-,tùs-,äk-tə-'prō-,bät\ [L] : the event justifies the deed

**ex li·bris** \eks-'lē-brəs\ [L] : from the books of — used on bookplates

**ex me·ro mo·tu** \,eks-,mer-ō-'mō-tü\ [L] : out of mere impulse of one's own accord

**ex ne·ces·si·ta·te rei** \,eks-nə-,kes-ə-

| ə abut | ᵊ kitten, F table | ər further | a back | ā bake | ä cot, cart |
|---|---|---|---|---|---|
| â F bac | aú out | ch chin | e less | ē easy | g gift |
| k G ich | ⁿ F vin | ŋ sing | ō flow | ò flaw | œ F bœuf |
| oi coin | th thing | t͟h this | ü loot | ù foot | ᵫ G Füllen |
| y yet | ʸ F digne \dēnʸ\, nuit \nwᵊē\ | | yü few | yù furious | zh vision |

i trip   ī life   j joke   œ F feu   œ F rue

'tä-te-'rä(-,ē)\ [L] : from the necessity of the case

**ex ni·hi·lo ni·hil fit** \eks-'ni-hi-,lō-,ni-,hil-'fit\ [L] : from nothing nothing is produced

**ex pe·de Her·cu·lem** \eks-,ped-e-'her-kə-,lem\ [L] : from the foot (we may judge of the size of) Hercules : from a part we may judge of the whole

**ex·per·to cre·di·te** \eks-,pert-ō-'krād-ə-,te\ [L] : believe one who has had experience

**ex un·gue le·o·nem** \eks-'ûn̄-gwe-le-'ō-,nem\ [L] : from the claw (we may judge of) the lion : from a part we may judge of the whole

**ex vi ter·mi·ni** \eks-,wē-'ter-mə-,nē\ [L] : from the force of the term

**fa·ci·le prin·ceps** \,fäk-i-le-'prin-,keps\ [L] : easily first

**fa·ci·lis de·scen·sus Aver·no** \'fäk-i-,lis-dā-,skän-,sûs-ä-'wer-nō\ *or* facilis descensus Aver·ni \-(,)nē\ [L] : the descent to Avernus is easy : the road to evil is easy

**faire suivre** \fer-sw'ēvr³\ [F] : have forwarded : please forward

**fas est et ab ho·ste do·ce·ri** \fäs-'est-et-äb-'hȯ-ste-dȯ-'kä-(,)rē\ [L] : it is right to learn even from an enemy

**Fa·ta vi·am in·ve·ni·ent** \,fä-tä-'wē-,äm-in-'wen-ē-,ent\ [L] : the Fates will find a way

**fat·ti mas·chii, pa·ro·le fe·mi·ne** \,fät-tē-'mäs-,kē pä-,rȯ-lā-fā-mē-,nā\ [It] : deeds are males, words are females : deeds are more effective than words — motto of Maryland, where it is generally interpreted as meaning "manly deeds, womanly words"

**faux bon·homme** \fō-bȯ-nȯm\ [F] : pretended good fellow

**faux-naïf** \fō-nȧ-ēf\ [F] : pretending to be childlike

**femme de cham·bre** \fäm-də-shäⁿbr³\ [F] : chambermaid : lady's maid

**fes·ti·na len·te** \fe-,stē-nə-'len-,tā\ [L] : make haste slowly

**feux d'ar·ti·fice** \fœ-dȧr-tē-fēs\ [F] : fireworks : display of wit

**fi·at ex·pe·ri·men·tum in cor·po·re vi·li** \'fē-,ät-ek-,sper-ē-'men-,tûm-in-,kȯr-pə-re-'wē-,lē\ [L] : let experiment be made on a worthless body

**fi·at ju·sti·tia, ru·at cae·lum** \,fē-ät-yûs-'tit-ē-ä ,rü-,ät-'kī-,lûm\ [L] : let justice be done though the heavens fall

**fi·at lux** \,fē-,ät-'lûks\ [L] : let there be light

**Fi·dei De·fen·sor** \,fid-e-,ē-dā-'fän-,sȯr\ [L] : Defender of the Faith — a title of the sovereigns of England

**fi·dus Acha·tes** \,fēd-əs-ä-'kä-,tās\ [L] : faithful Achates : trusty friend

**fille de cham·bre** \fēy-də-shäⁿbr³\ [F] : lady's maid

**fille d'hon·neur** \fēy-dȯ-nœr\ [F] : maid of honor

**fils** \fēs\ [F] : son — used after French proper names to distinguish a son from his father

**fi·nem re·spi·ce** \,fē-,nem-'rä-spi-,ke\ [L] : consider the end

**fi·nis co·ro·nat opus** \,fē-nəs-kə-,rō-,nät-'ō-,pùs\ [L] : the end crowns the work

**fluc·tu·at nec mer·gi·tur** \'flûk-tə-,wät-,nek-'mer-gə-,tùr\ [L] : it is tossed by the waves but does not sink — motto of Paris

**fors·an et haec olim me·mi·nis·se ju·va·bit** \,fȯr-,sän-,et-'hīk-,ō-lim-,mem-ə-'nis-e-yü-'wä-bit\ [L] : perhaps this too will be a pleasure to look back on one day

**for·tes for·tu·na ju·vat** \'fȯr-,tās-fȯr-,tü-nə-'yü-,wät\ [L] : fortune favors the brave

**fron·ti nul·la fi·des** \'frȯn-,tē-,nùl-ə-'fid-,ās\ [L] : no reliance can be placed on appearance

**fu·it Ili·um** \'fü-ət-'il-ē-əm\ [L] : Troy has been (i.e., is no more)

**fu·ror lo·quen·di** \,fùr-,ȯr-lȯ-'kwen-(,)dē\ [L] : rage for speaking

**furor po·e·ti·cus** \-pȯ-'āt-i-kùs\ [L] : poetic frenzy

**furor scri·ben·di** \-skrē-'ben-(,)dē\ [L] : rage for writing

**Gal·li·ce** \'gäl-ə-,ke\ [L] : in French : after the French manner

**gar·çon d'hon·neur** \gȧr-sōⁿ-dȯ-nœr\ [F] : bridegroom's attendant

**garde du corps** \gȧrd-dǖ-kȯr\ [F] : bodyguard

**gar·dez la foi** \gȧr-dā-lȧ-fwȧ\ [F] : keep faith

**gau·de·a·mus igi·tur** \,gaùd-ē-'äm-əs-'ig-ə-,tùr\ [L] : let us then be merry

**gens d'é·glise** \zhäⁿ-dā-glēz\ [F] : church people : clergy

**gens de guerre** \zhäⁿ-də-ger\ [F] : military people : soldiery

**gens du monde** \zhäⁿ-dǖ-mōⁿd\ [F] : people of the world : fashionable people

**gno·thi se·au·ton** \gə-'nō-thē-,se-aù-'tȯn\ [Gk] : know thyself

**grand monde** \gräⁿ-mōⁿd\ [F] : great world : high society

**guerre à ou·trance** \ger-ȧ-ü-träⁿs\ [F] : war to the uttermost

**gu·ten Tag** \,gǖt-²n-'täk\ [G] : good day

**has·ta la vis·ta** \,äs-tä-lä-'vēs-tä\ [Sp] : good-bye

**haut goût** \ō-gǖ\ [F] : high flavor : slight taint of decay

**hic et ubi·que** \,hēk-et-ǖ-'bē-kwe\ [L] : here and everywhere

**hic ja·cet** \hik-'jä-sət, hēk-'yäk-ət\ [L] : here lies — used preceding a name on a tombstone

**hinc il·lae la·cri·mae** \,hiŋk-,il-,ī-'läk-ri-,mī\ [L] : hence those tears

**hoc age** \hōk-'äg-e\ [L] : do this : apply yourself to what you are about

**hoc opus, hic labor est** \hōk-'ȯ-,pùs, ,hēk-,lä-,bȯr-'est\ [L] : this is the hard work, this is the toil

**homme d'af·faires** \ȯm-dȧ-fer\ [F] : man of business : business agent

**homme d'es·prit** \-des-prē\ [F] : man of wit

**homme moyen sen·suel** \ȯm-mwȧ-yaⁿ-säⁿ-sw³el\ [F] : the average non-intellectual man

**ho·mo sum: hu·ma·ni nil a me ali·e·num pu·to** \ˈhō-mō-ˌsum-hü-ˌmän-ē-ˈnēl-ä-ˌmā-ˌäl-ē-ˈä-nəm-ˈpü-tō\ [L] : I am a man; I regard nothing that concerns man as foreign to my interests

**ho·ni soit qui mal y pense** \ȯ-nē-swä-kē-mȧl-ē-päⁿs\ [F] : shamed be he who thinks evil of it — motto of the Order of the Garter

**hô·tel–Dieu** \ȯ-tel-dyœ̄\ [F] : hospital

**hu·ma·num est er·ra·re** \hü-ˌmän-əm-ˌest-e-ˈrär-e\ [L] : to err is human

**Ich dien** \ik-ˈdēn\ [G] : I serve — motto of the Prince of Wales

**ici on parle français** \ē-sē-ōⁿ-pȧrl-(-ə)-fräⁿ-se\ [F] : French is spoken here

**id est** \id-ˈest\ [L] : that is

**ig·no·ran·tia ju·ris ne·mi·nem ex·cu·sat** \ˌig-nō-ˌränt-ē-ä-ˈyu̇r-əs-ˈnā-mə-ˌnem-eks-ˈkü-ˌsät\ [L] : ignorance of the law excuses no one

**ig·no·tum per ig·no·ti·us** \ig-ˈnōt-əm-ˌper-ig-ˈnōt-ē-ˌu̇s\ [L] : (explaining) the unknown by means of the more unknown

**il faut cul·ti·ver no·tre jar·din** \ēl-fō-kūēl-tē-vā-nȯt-zhȧr-daⁿ, -nȯ-trə-zhȧr-\ [F] : we must cultivate our garden : we must tend to our own affairs

**in ae·ter·num** \ˌin-ī-ˈter-ˌnu̇m\ [L] : forever

**in du·bio** \in-ˈdu̇b-ē-ˌō\ [L] : in doubt : undetermined

**in fu·tu·ro** \ˌin-fə-ˈtu̇r-ō\ [L] : in the future

**in hoc sig·no vin·ces** \in-hōk-ˈsig-nō-ˈvin-ˌkās\ [L] : by this sign (the Cross) you will conquer

**in li·mi·ne** \in-ˈlē-mə-ˌne\ [L] : on the threshold : at the beginning

**in om·nia pa·ra·tus** \in-ˈōm-nē-ə-pə-ˈrä-ˌtu̇s\ [L] : ready for all things

**in par·ti·bus in·fi·de·li·um** \in-ˈpärt-ə-ˌbu̇s-ˌin-fə-ˈdā-lē-ˌu̇m\ [L] : in the regions of the infidels  _used of a titular bishop having no diocesan jurisdiction, usu. in non-Christian countries_

**in prae·sen·ti** \ˌin-prī-ˈsen-ˌtē\ [L] : at the present time

**in sae·cu·la sae·cu·lo·rum** \in-ˈsī-kü-ˌlä-ˌsī-kə-ˈlōr-əm, -ˈsä-kü-ˌlä-ˌsä-\ [L] : for ages of ages : forever and ever

**in sta·tu quo an·te bel·lum** \in-ˈstä-ˌtü-kwō-ˌänt-ē-ˈbel-əm\ [L] : in the same state as before the war

**in·te·ger vi·tae sce·le·ris·que pu·rus** \ˌin-tə-ˌger-ˈwē-ˌtī-ˌskel-ə-ˈris-kwe-ˈpü-rəs\ [L] : upright of life and free from wickedness

**in·ter nos** \ˌint-ər-ˈnōs\ [L] : between ourselves

**in·tra mu·ros** \ˌin-trä-ˈmü-ˌrōs\ [L] : within the walls

**in usum Del·phi·ni** \in-ˈü-səm-del-ˈfē-nē\ [L] : for the use of the Dauphin : expurgated

**in utrum·que pa·ra·tus** \ˌin-ü-ˈtru̇m-kwe-pə-ˈrä-ˌtu̇s\ [L] : prepared for either (event)

**in·ve·nit** \in-ˈwā-nit\ [L] : he (or she) devised it

**in vi·no ve·ri·tas** \in-wē-nō-ˈwā-rə-ˌtäs\ [L] : there is truth in wine

**in·vi·ta Mi·ner·va** \in-ˈwē-ˌtä-mi-ˈner-ˌwä\ [L] : Minerva being unwilling : without natural talent or inspiration

**ip·sis·si·ma ver·ba** \ip-ˌsis-ə-ˌmä-ˈwer-ˌbä\ [L] : the very words

**ira fu·ror bre·vis est** \ˌē-rä-ˈfu̇r-ˌȯr-ˈbre-wəs-ˌest\ [L] : anger is a brief madness

**jacta alea est** \ˈyäk-ˌtä-ˌä-lē-ˌä-ˈest\ [L] : the die is cast

**j'adoube** \zhä-düb\ [F] : I adjust — used in chess when touching a piece without intending to move it

**ja·nu·is clau·sis** \ˌyän-ə-ˌwēs-ˈklau̇-ˌsēs\ [L] : with closed doors

**je main·tien·drai** \zhə-maⁿ-tyaⁿ-drā\ [F] : I will maintain — motto of the Netherlands

**jeu de mots** \zhœ̄d-(ə-)mō\ [F] : play on words : pun

**Jo·an·nes est no·men eius** \yō-ˈän-äs-est-ˌnō-men-ˈā-yu̇s\ [L] : John is his name — motto of Puerto Rico

**jour·nal in·time** \zhür-nȧl-aⁿ-tēm\ [F] : intimate journal : private diary

**jus di·vi·num** \ˌyüs-di-ˈwē-ˌnu̇m\ [L] : divine law

**jus·ti·tia om·ni·bus** \ˌyu̇s-ˌtit-ē-ˌä-ˈōm-ni-ˌbu̇s\ [L] : justice for all — motto of the District of Columbia

**j'y suis, j'y reste** \zhē-swˈē-zhē-rest\ [F] : here I am, here I remain

**kte·ma es aei** \(kə-)ˈtä-ˌmä-es-ä-ˈā\ [Gk] : a possession forever — applied to a work of art or literature of enduring significance

**la belle dame sans mer·ci** \lä-bel-däm-säⁿ-mer-sē\ [F] : the beautiful lady without mercy

**la·bo·ra·re est ora·re** \ˈläb-ō-ˌrär-e-ˌest-ō-ˌrär-e\ [L] : to work is to pray

**la·bor om·nia vin·cit** \ˈlä-ˌbȯr-ˌōm-nē-ˌä-ˈwiŋ-kit\ [L] : labor conquers all things — motto of Oklahoma

**la·cri·mae re·rum** \ˌläk-ri-ˌmī-ˈrä-ˌru̇m\ [L] : tears for things : pity for misfortune; _also_ : tears in things : tragedy of life

**lais·ser-al·ler** \le-sä-ä-lā\ [F] : letting go : lack of restraint

**lap·sus ca·la·mi** \ˌläp-sùs-ˈkäl-ə-ˌmē, ˌlap-səs-ˈkal-ə-ˌmī\ [L] : slip of the pen

**lap·sus lin·guae** \ˌlap-səs-ˈliŋ-ˌgwī, ˌläp-ˌsu̇s-\ [L] : slip of the tongue

**la reine le veut** \lä-ren-lə-vœ̄\ [F] : the queen wills it

**la·scia·te ogni spe·ran·za, voi ch'en·tra·te** \läsh-ˈshä-tä ˌō-n⁓yē-spä-ˈrän-tsä-ˌvō-ē-kän-ˈträ-tä\ [It] : abandon all hope, ye who enter

---

| ə abut | ᵊ kitten, F table | ər further | a back | ā bake | ä cot, cart |
|---|---|---|---|---|---|
| à F bac | au̇ out | ch chin | e less | ē easy | g gift | i trip | ī life | j joke |
| k G ich | ⁱ F vin | ŋ sing | ō flow | ȯ flaw | œ F bœuf | œ̄ F feu |
| oi coin | th thing | th this | ü loot | u̇ foot | ᵫ G Füllen | œ̄ F rue |
| y yet | ʸ F digne \dēnʸ\, nuit \nwʸē\ | yü few | yu̇ furious | zh vision |

**lau·da·tor tem·po·ris ac·ti** \laủ-'dä̇-
,tȯr-,tem-pə-'ris-'äk-,tē\ [L] : one who
praises past times

**laus Deo** \laùs-'dā-ō\ [L] : praise (be)
to God

**le cœur a ses rai·sons que la rai·
son ne con·nait point** \lə-kœr-ȧ-
sā-re-zōⁿk-la-re-zōⁿn-(ə-)kȯ-ne-pwäⁿ\
[F] : the heart has its reasons that
reason knows nothing of

**le roi est mort, vive le roi** \lə-rwä-e-
mȯr vēv-lə-rwä\ [F] : the king is dead,
long live the king

**le roi le veut** \-lə-vœ̄\ [F] : the king
wills it

**le roi s'avi·se·ra** \-sȧ-vēz-rȧ\ [F]
: the king will consider

**le style, c'est l'homme** \lə-stēl-se-
lȯm\ [F] : the style is the man

**l'état, c'est moi** \lā-tȧ-se-mwȧ\ [F]
: the state, it is I

**l'étoile du nord** \lā-twȧl-dǖ-nȯr\
[F] : the star of the north — motto of
Minnesota

**li·cen·tia va·tum** \li-'ken-tē-ä-'vä-
,tùm\ [L] : poetic license

**Lie·der·kranz** \'lēd-ər-,kräns\ [G]
: wreath of songs : German singing
society

**lit·tera scrip·ta ma·net** \,lit-ə-,rä-
,skrip-tə-'män-et\ [L] : the written
letter abides

**lo·cus in quo** \,lȯ-kəs-in-'kwō\ [L]
: place in which

**l'union fait la force** \lū̄-nyōⁿ-fe-lȧ-
fȯrs\ [F] : union makes strength —
motto of Belgium

**lu·sus na·tu·rae** \,lü-səs-nə-'tùr-ē,
-'tùr-,ī\ [L] : freak of nature

**ma foi** \mȧ-fwä\ [F] : my faith! : indeed

**mag·na est ve·ri·tas et prae·va·le·
bit** \,mäg-nä-,est-'wä-ri-,täs-et-,prī-wä-
'lā-bit\ [L] : truth is mighty and will
prevail

**mag·ni no·mi·nis um·bra** \,mäg-
nē-,nō-mə-nis-'ùm-brä\ [L] : the
shadow of a great name

**mai·son de san·té** \mā-zōⁿd-(ə-)säⁿ-
tā\ [F] : private hospital : asylum

**ma·lade ima·gi·naire** \mȧ-lȧd-ē-mȧ-
zhē-ner\ [F] : imaginary invalid
: hypochondriac

**ma·lis avi·bus** \,mäl-,ēs-'ä-wi-,bùs\
[L] : under evil auspices

**man spricht Deutsch** \män-shprik̇t-
'dȯich\ [G] : German spoken

**ma·riage de con·ve·nance** \mȧ-
ryȧzh-də-kōⁿv-näⁿs\ [F] : marriage of
convenience

**mau·vaise honte** \mȯ-vez-ōⁿt\ [F]
: bad shame : bashfulness

**mau·vais quart d'heure** \mȯ-ve-
kȧr-dœr\ [F] : bad quarter hour : an
uncomfortable though brief experience

**me·den agan** \(,)mā-,den-'äg-,än\
[Gk] : nothing in excess

**me·dio tu·tis·si·mus ibis** \'med-ē-
,ō-tü-,tis-ə-mùs-'ē-bəs\ [L] : you will
go most safely by the middle course

**me ju·di·ce** \mā-'yüd-ə-ke\ [L] : I
being judge : in my judgment

**mens sa·na in cor·po·re sa·no**
\mäns-'sän-ə-in-,kȯr-pə-re-'sän-ō\ [L]
: a sound mind in a sound body

**me·um et tu·um** \,mē-əm-,et-'tü-əm,
,me-əm-\ [L] : mine and thine : distinction of private property

**mi·ra·bi·le vi·su** \mə-,räb-ə-lē-'wē-
sü\ [L] : wonderful to behold

**mi·ra·bi·lia** \,mir-ə-'bil-ē-ə\ [L] : wonders : miracles

**mo·le ru·it sua** \'mō-le-,rü-it-,sù-ä\
[L] : it collapses from its own bigness

**monde** \mōⁿd\ [F] : world : fashionable world : society

**mon·ta·ni sem·per li·be·ri** \mōn-
'tän-ē-,sem-pər-'lē-bə-,rē\ [L] : moun-
taineers are always free men — motto of
West Virginia

**mo·nu·men·tum ae·re per·en·ni·
us** \,mȯ-nə-'men-tùm-,ī-re-pə-'ren-ē-ùs\
[L] : a monument more lasting than
bronze — used of an immortal work of
art or literature

**mo·ri·tu·ri te sa·lu·ta·mus** \,mȯr-ə-
'tür-ē-,tā-,säl-ə-'täm-ùs\ [L] : we who
are about to die salute thee

**mul·tum in par·vo** \,mùl-təm-in-
'pär-vō\ [L] : much in little

**mu·ta·to no·mi·ne de te fa·bu·la
nar·ra·tur** \mü-,tät-ō-'nō-mə-ne-dā-
'tā-,fäb-ə-lä-nä-'rä-,tùr\ [L] : with
the name changed the story applies to
you

**na·tu·ram ex·pel·las fur·ca, ta·
men us·que re·cur·ret** \nä-'tü-
,räm-ek-,spel-äs-'fùr-,kä ,tä-mən-'ùs-
kwe-re-'kùr-et\ [L] : you may drive
nature out with a pitchfork, but she will
keep coming back

**na·tu·ra non fa·cit sal·tum** \nä-
'tü-rä-,nōn-,fäk-ət-'säl-,tùm\ [L] : nature makes no leap

**ne ce·de ma·lis** \,nā-,kä-de-'mäl-,ēs\
[L] : yield not to misfortunes

**ne·mo me im·pu·ne la·ces·sit** \'nā-
mō-'mā-im-,pü-nā-lä-'kes-ət\ [L] : no
one attacks me with impunity — motto
of Scotland and of the Order of the
Thistle

**ne quid ni·mis** \,nā-,kwid-'nim-əs\
[L] : not anything in excess

**n'est-ce pas?** \nes-pä\ [F] : isn't it
so?

**nil ad·mi·ra·ri** \'nēl-,äd-mə-'rär-ē\
[L] : to be excited by nothing : equanim-
ity

**nil de·spe·ran·dum** \'nēl-,dā-spā-
'rän-dùm\ [L] : never despair

**nil si·ne nu·mi·ne** \'nēl-,sin-e-'nü-
mə-ne\ [L] : nothing without the
divine will — motto of Colorado

**n'im·porte** \naⁿ-pȯrt\ [F] : it's no
matter

**no·lens vo·lens** \,nō-,lenz-'vō-,lenz\
[L] : unwilling (or) willing : willy-
nilly

**non om·nia pos·su·mus om·nes**
\nōn-'ȯm-nē-ä-,pȯ-sə-mùs-'ȯm-,näs\
[L] : we can't all (do) all things

**non om·nis mo·ri·ar** \nōn-'ȯm-nəs-
,mȯr-ē-,är\ [L] : I shall not wholly die

**non sans droict** \nōⁿ-säⁿ-drwä\ [OF]
: not without right — motto on Shakespeare's coat of arms

**non sum qua·lis eram** \nōn-,sùm-
,kwäl-əs-'er-,äm\ [L] : I am not what I
used to be

**nos·ce te ip·sum** \,nòs-ke-,tā-'ip-,sùm\ [L] : know thyself

**nos·tal·gie de la boue** \nòs-tál-zhēd-(ə-)là-bü\ [F] : nostalgia for the mud ; homesickness for the gutter

**nous avons chan·gé tout ce·la** \nü-zȧ-vōⁿ-shǟ-zhä-tü-s(l)à\ [F] : we have changed all that

**nous ver·rons ce que nous ver·rons** \nü-ve-rōⁿs-(ə-)kə-nü-ve-rōⁿ\ [F] : we shall see what we shall see

**no·vus ho·mo** \,nò-wəs-'hò-mō\ [L] : new man ; man newly ennobled : upstart

**no·vus or·do se·clo·rum** \-'òr-,dō-sā-'klòr-əm\ [L] : a new cycle of the ages — motto on the reverse of the Great Seal of the United States

**nu·gae** \'nü-,gī\ [L] : trifles

**nuit blanche** \nwē-blän̈sh\ [F] : white night : a sleepless night

**nyet** \'nyet\ [Russ] : no

**ob·iit** \'ò-bē-,it\ [L] : he (or she) died

**ob·scu·rum per ob·scu·ri·us** \ab-'skyür-əm-,per-əb-'skyür-ē-əs\ [L] : (explaining) the obscure by means of the more obscure

**ode·rint dum me·tu·ant** \'ōd-ə-,rint-,dúm-met-ə-,wänt\ [L] : let them hate, so long as they fear

**odi et amo** \'ō-,dē-et-'äm-(,)ō\ [L] : I hate and I love

**om·ne ig·no·tum pro mag·ni·fi·co** \,òm-ne-ig-'nō-,tüm-prō-mäg-'nif-i-,kō\ [L] : everything unknown (is taken) as grand : the unknown tends to be exaggerated in importance or difficulty

**om·nia mu·tan·tur, nos et mu·ta·mur in il·lis** \,òm-nē-ä-mü-'tän-,tür ,nōs-,et-mü-,täm-ər-in-'il-,ēs\ [L] : all things are changing, and we are changing with them

**om·nia vin·cit amor** \'òm-nē-ä-'wiŋ-kət-'äm-,òr\ [L] : love conquers all

**onus pro·ban·di** \,ō-nəs-prō-'ban-,dī, -dē\ [L] : burden of proof

**ora pro no·bis** \,ō-rä-prō-'nō-,bēs\ [L] : pray for us

**ore ro·tun·do** \,òr-ē-rō-'tən-dō\ [L] : with round mouth : eloquently

**oro y pla·ta** \, òr-ō-ē-'plät-ə\ [Sp] : gold and silver — motto of Montana

**o tem·po·ra! o mo·res!** \ō-'tem-pə-rä-ō-'mō-,räs\ [L] : oh the times! oh the manners!

**oti·um cum dig·ni·ta·te** \'ōt-ē-,úm-kúm-,dig-nə-'tä-te\ [L] : leisure with dignity

**où sont les neiges d'an·tan?** \ü-sōⁿ-lā-nezh-dǟⁿ-'tǟⁿ\ [F] : where are the snows of yesteryear?

**pal·li·da Mors** \,pal-əd-ə-'mórz\ [L] : pale Death

**pal·mam qui me·ru·it fe·rat** \'päl-mäm-kwē-'mer-ə-wit-'fe-rät\ [L] : let him who has earned the palm of victory bear it

**pa·nem et cir·cen·ses** \'pän-,em-et-kir-'kän-,sēs\ [L] : bread and circuses : provision of the means of life and recreation by government to appease discontent

**pan·ta rhei** \,pän-,tä-'(h)rä, ,pant-ə-'rā\ [Gk] : all things are in flux

**par avance** \pȧr-ȧ-vä̈ⁿs\ [F] : in advance : by anticipation

**par avion** \pȧr-ȧ-vyōⁿ\ [F] : by airplane — used on airmail

**par ex·em·ple** \pȧr-ȧg-zä̈ⁿpl'\ [F] : for example

**par·tu·ri·unt mon·tes, nas·ce·tur ri·dic·u·lus mus** \pȧr-,tür-ē-,únt-'mòn-,täs-nȧs-'kä-,tür-ri-,dik-ə-lùs-'miis\ [L] : the mountains are in labor, and a ridiculous mouse will be brought forth

**pa·ter pa·tri·ae** \'pä-,ter-'pä-trē-,ī\ [L] : father of his country

**pau·cis ver·bis** \,paù-,kēs-'wer-,bēs\ [L] : in a few words

**pax vo·bis·cum** \,päks-vō-'bēs-,kùm\ [L] : peace (be) with you

**peine forte et dure** \pen-fòr-tä-dēr\ [F] : strong and hard punishment : torture

**per an·gus·ta ad au·gus·ta** \per-'än-,gùs-tə-äd-'aù-,gùs-tə, per-'äṅ-\ [L] : through difficulties to honors

**père** \per\ [F] : father — used after French proper names to distinguish a father from his son

**per·eant qui an·te nos nos·tra dix·e·runt** \'per-e-,änt-kwē-,än-te-'nōs-'nòs-trä-dēk-'sä-,rùnt\ [L] : may they perish who have expressed our bright ideas before us

**per·eunt et im·pu·tan·tur** \'per-e-,ùnt-et-,im-pə-'tän-,tür\ [L] : they (the hours) pass away and are reckoned on (our) account

**per·fide Al·bion** \per-fēd-ȧl-byōⁿ\ [F] : perfidious Albion (England)

**peu a peu** \pœ̄-ȧ-pœ̄\ [F] : little by little

**peu de chose** \pœ̄d-(ə-)shōz\ [F] : a trifle

**pièce d'oc·ca·sion** \pyes-dò-kä-zyōⁿ\ [F] : piece for a special occasion

**pinx·it** \'piṅk-sət\ [L] : he (or she) painted it

**place aux dames** \plȧs-ō-dȧm\ [F] : (make) room for the ladies

**ple·no ju·re** \,plā-nō-'yür-e\ [L] : with full right

**plus ça change, plus c'est la même chose** \plǖ-sä-shä̈ⁿzh plǖ-se-lä-mem-shōz\ [F] : the more that changes, the more it's the same thing

**plus roy·a·liste que le roi** \plǖ-rwȧ-yȧ-lēst-kəl-rwȧ\ [F] : more royalist than the king

**po·cas pa·la·bras** \,pō-käs-pä-'läv-räs\ [Sp] : few words

**po·eta nas·ci·tur, non fit** \pò-,ä-tä-'näs-kə-,tùr nōn-'fit\ [L] : a poet is born, not made

pol·li·ce ver·so \,pó-li-ke-'ver-sō\ [L] : with thumb turned : with a gesture or expression of condemnation

post hoc, er·go prop·ter hoc \'pòst-,hōk ,er-gō-'pròp-ter-,hōk\ [L] : after this, therefore on account of it (a fallacy of argument)

post ob·itum \pòst-'ó-bə-,túm\ [L] : after death

pour ac·quit \pür-à-kē\ [F] : received payment

pour le mé·rite \pür-lə-mā-rēt\ [F] : for merit

pro aris et fo·cis \prō-,ä-,rēs-et-'fó-,kēs\ [L] : for altars and firesides

pro bo·no pu·bli·co \prō-,bó-nō-'pü-bli-,kō\ [L] : for the public good

pro hac vi·ce \prō-,häk-'wik-e\ [L] : for this occasion

pro pa·tria \prō-'pä-trē-,ä\ [L] : for one's country

pro re·ge, le·ge, et gre·ge \prō-'rā-ge-'lā-,ge-et-'greg-,e\ [L] : for the king, the law, and the people

pro re na·ta \,prō-,rā-'nät-ə\ [L] : for an occasion that has arisen : as needed — used in medical prescriptions

quand même \käⁿ-mem\ [F] : even though : whatever may happen

quan·tum mu·ta·tus ab il·lo \,kwänt-əm-mü-'tät-əs-äb-'il-ō\ [L] : how changed from what he once was

quan·tum suf·fi·cit \,kwänt-əm-'səf-ə-,kit\ [L] : as much as suffices : a sufficient quantity — used in medical prescriptions

¿quién sa·be? \kyän-'sä-vä\ [Sp] : who knows?

qui fa·cit per ali·um fa·cit per se \kwē-,fäk-it-,per-'äl-ē-,ùm-,fäk-it-,per-'sā\ [L] : he who does (anything) through another does it through himself

quis cus·to·di·et ip·sos cus·to·des? \,kwis-kús-'tōd-ē-,et-ip-,sōs-kús-'tō-,dās\ [L] : who will keep the keepers themselves?

qui s'ex·cuse s'ac·cuse \kē-'sek-,skūēz-'sä-,kūēz\ [F] : he who excuses himself accuses himself

quis se·pa·ra·bit? \,kwis-,sā-pə-'räb-it\ [L] : who shall separate (us)? — motto of the Order of St. Patrick

qui trans·tu·lit sus·ti·net \kwē-'träns-tə-,lit-'sus-tə-,net\ [L] : He who transplanted sustains (us) — motto of Connecticut

qui va là? \kē-vä-là\ [F] : who goes there?

quo·ad hoc \,kwò-,äd-'hōk\ [L] : as far as this : to this extent

quod erat de·mon·stran·dum \,kwòd-'er-,ät-,dem-ən-'stran-dəm, -,dä-,món-'strän-,dúm\ [L] : which was to be proved

quod erat fa·ci·en·dum \-,fäk-ē-'en-,dùm\ [L] : which was to be done

quod sem·per, quod ubi·que, quod ab om·ni·bus \kwòd-'sem-,per kwòd-üb-i-,kwä ,kwòd-äb-'òm-ni-,bùs, -,kwòd-ù-'bē-(,)kwä-\ [L] : what (has been held) always, everywhere, by everybody

quod vi·de \kwòd-'wid-,e\ [L] : which see

quo·rum pars mag·na fui \'kwòr-om-,pärs-,mäg-nə-'fü-ē\ [L] : in which I played a great part

quos de·us vult per·de·re pri·us de·men·tat \kwōs-'de-ùs-,wùlt-'perd-ə-,re-,pri-ùs-dā-'men-,tät\ [L] : those whom a god wishes to destroy he first drives mad

quot ho·mi·nes, tot sen·ten·i·ae \kwòt-'hò-mə-,näs-,tòt-sen-'ten-tē-,ī\ [L] : there are as many opinions as there are men

quo va·dis? \kwō-'väd-əs, -wäd-\ [L] : whither are you going?

rai·son d'état \re-zōⁿ-dä-tä\ [F] : reason of state

re·cu·ler pour mieux sau·ter \rə-kū-lā-pür-myœ-sō-tā\ [F] : to draw back in order to make a better jump

reg·nat po·pu·lus \,reg-,nät-'pò-pə-,lùs\ [L] : the people rule — motto of Arkansas

re in·fec·ta \,rā-in-'fek-,tä\ [L] : the business being unfinished : without accomplishing one's purpose

re·li·gio lo·ci \re-,lig-ē-,ō-'lò-,kē\ [L] : religious sanctity of a place

rem acu te·ti·gis·ti \rem-'ä-,kü-,tet-ə-'gis-tē\ [L] : you have touched the point with a needle : you have hit the nail on the head

ré·pon·dez s'il vous plait \rā-pōⁿ-dā-sēl-vü-ple\ [F] : reply, if you please

re·qui·es·cat in pa·ce \,rek-wē-'es-,kät-in-'päk-,e, ,rā-kwē-'es-,kät-in-'päch-,ä\ [L] : may he (or she) rest in peace — used on tombstones

re·spi·ce fi·nem \,rā-spi-,ke-'fē-,nem\ [L] : look to the end : consider the outcome

re·sur·gam \re-'sùr-,gäm\ [L] : I shall rise again

re·te·nue \rət-nē\ [F] : self-restraint : reserve

re·ve·nons à nos mou·tons \rəv-nōⁿ-à-nō-mü-tōⁿ\ [F] : let us return to our sheep : let us get back to the subject

ruse de guerre \rēz-də-ger\ [L] : war stratagem

rus in ur·be \,rüs-in-'ùr-,be\ [L] : country in the city

sal At·ti·cum \sal-'at-i-kəm\ [L] : Attic salt : wit

salle à man·ger \sàl-à-mäⁿ-zhā\ [F] : dining room

sa·lus po·pu·li su·pre·ma lex es·to \,säl-,üs-'pò-pə-,lē-sù-,prā-mə-,leks-'es-tō\ [L] : let the welfare of the people be the supreme law — motto of Missouri

sans doute \säⁿ-düt\ [F] : without doubt

sans gêne \säⁿ-zhen\ [F] : without embarrassment or constraint

sans peur et sans re·proche \säⁿ-pœr-ā-säⁿ-rə-'prósh\ [F] : without fear and without reproach

sans sou·ci \säⁿ-sü-sē\ [F] : without worry

sa·yo·na·ra \,sä-yə-'när-ə\ [Jap] : good-bye

**sculp·sit** \'skəlp-sət, 'skŭlp-\ [L] : he (or she) carved it

**scu·to bo·nae vo·lun·ta·tis tu·ae co·ro·nas·ti nos** \'skü-,tō-'bō-,nī-,vō-lün-,tät-əs-'tü-,ī-,kȯr-ə-,näs-tē-'nōs\ [L] : Thou hast crowned us with the shield of Thy good will — a motto on the Great Seal of Maryland

**se·cun·dum ar·tem** \se-,kŭn-dəm-'är-,tem\ [L] : according to the art : according to the accepted practice of a profession or trade

**secundum na·tu·ram** \-nä- tü-,räm\ [L] : according to nature : naturally

**se de·fen·den·do** \'sā-,dā-,fen-'den-dō\ [L] : in self-defense

**se ha·bla es·pa·ñol** \sā-,äv-lä-,äs-pä-'n'ol\ [Sp] : Spanish spoken

**sem·per ea·dem** \,sem-,per-'e-ä-,dem\ [L] : always the same (fem.) — motto of Queen Elizabeth I

**sem·per fi·de·lis** \,sem-pər-fə-'dā-ləs\ [L] : always faithful — motto of the U.S. Marine Corps

**sem·per idem** \,sem-,per-'ē-,dem\ [L] : always the same (masc.)

**sem·per pa·ra·tus** \,sem-pər-pə-'rät-əs\ [L] : always prepared — motto of the U.S. Coast Guard

**se non è ve·ro, è ben tro·va·to** \sā-,nōn-e-'vā-rō-e-,ben-trō'vä-tō\ [It] : even if it is not true, it is well conceived

**sic itur ad as·tra** \sēk-'ĭ-,tür-,äd-'äs-trə\ [L] : thus one goes to the stars : such is the way to immortality

**sic sem·per ty·ran·nis** \,sik-,sem-pər-tə-'ran-əs\ [L] : thus ever to tyrants — motto of Virginia

**sic trans·it glo·ria mun·di** \sēk-'trän-sət-,glōr-ē-ä-'mùn-dē\ [L] : so passes away the glory of the world

**sic·ut pa·tri·bus sit De·us no·bis** \,sē-,kŭt-'pä-tri-,bùs-sit-,de-ùs-'nō-,bēs\ [L] : as to our fathers may God be to us — motto of Boston

**si jeu·nesse sa·vait, si vieil·lesse pou·vait** \sē-'zhœ-nes-'sá-ve ,sē-'vye-yes-'pü-ve\ [F] : if youth only knew, if age only could!

**si·lent le·ges in·ter ar·ma** \,sil-ent-'lä-,gās-,int-ər-'är-mä\ [L] : the laws are silent in the midst of arms

**s'il vous plait** \sēl-vü-ple\ [F] : if you please

**si·mi·lia si·mi·li·bus cu·ran·tur** \sim-'il-ē-ä-sim-'il-ə-bùs-kü-'rän-,tür\ [L] : like is cured by like

**si·mi·lis si·mi·li gau·det** \'sim-ə-ləs-'sim-ə-lē-'gaù-,det\ [L] : like takes pleasure in like

**si mo·nu·men·tum re·qui·ris, cir·cum·spi·ce** \,sē-,mò-nə-,ment-əm-re-'kwē-rəs kir-'kùm-spi-ke\ [L] : if you seek his monument, look around — epitaph of Sir Christopher Wren in St. Paul's, London, of which he was architect

**si quae·ris pen·in·su·lam amoe·nam, cir·cum·spi·ce** \sē-,kwī-rəs-pā-,nin-sə-,läm-ə-'mòi-,näm kir-'kùm-spi-ke\ [L] : if you seek a beautiful peninsula, look around — motto of Michigan

**sis·te vi·a·tor** \,sis-te-wē-'ä-,tòr\ [L] : stop, traveler — used on Roman roadside tombs

**si vis pa·cem, pa·ra bel·lum** \sē-,wēs-'pä-,kem ,pä-rä-'bel-,ùm\ [L] : if you wish peace, prepare for war

**sol·vi·tur am·bu·lan·do** \'sòl-wə-,tür-,äm-bə-'län-dō\ [L] : it is solved by walking : the problem is solved by a practical experiment

**splen·di·de men·dax** \,splen-də-,dā-'men-,däks\ [L] : nobly untruthful

**spo·lia opi·ma** \,spó-lē-ä-ō-'pē-mə\ [L] : rich spoils : the arms taken by the victorious from the vanquished general

**sta·tus in quo** \,stät-əs-,in-'kwō\ [L] : state in which : the existing state

**sta·tus quo an·te bel·lum** \'stät-əs-kwō-,änt-ə-'bel-ùm\ [L] : the state existing before the war

**sua·vi·ter in mo·do, for·ti·ter in re** \swä-wə-,ter-in-'mòd-ō 'fòrt-ə-,ter-in-'rā\ [L] : gently in manner, strongly in deed

**sub ver·bo** \sùb-'wer-bō\ or sub **vo·ce** \sùb-'wō-ke\ [L] : under the word — introducing a cross-reference in a dictionary or index

**sunt la·cri·mae re·rum** \sùnt-,läk-ri-,mī-'rā-rùm\ [L] : there are tears for things

**suo ju·re** \,sù-ō-'yùr-e\ [L] : in his (or her) own right

**suo lo·co** \-'lō-kō\ [L] : in its proper place

**suo Mar·te** \-'mär-te\ [L] : by one's own exertions

**su·um cui·que** \,sù-əm-'kwik-we\ [L] : to each his own

**tant mieux** \tä⁸-myœ\ [F] : so much the better

**tant pis** \-pē\ [F] : so much the worse

**tem·po·ra mu·tan·tur, nos et mu·ta·mur in il·lis** \,tem-pə-rä-mü-'tän-,tür ,nōs-et-mü-,täm-ər-in-'il-,ēs\ [L] : the times are changing, and we are changing with them

**tem·pus edax re·rum** \'tem-pùs-,ed-,äks-'rā-rùm\ [L] : time, that devours all things

**tem·pus fu·git** \,tem-pəs-'fyü-jət, -'fü-git\ [L] : time flies

**ti·meo Da·na·os et do·na fe·ren·tes** \,tim-ē-,ō-'dän-ä-,ōs-,et-,dō-nä-fe-'ren-,tās\ [L] : I fear the Greeks even when they bring gifts

**to·ti·dem ver·bis** \,tòt-ə-,dem-'wer-,bēs\ [L] : in so many words

**to·tis vi·ri·bus** \,tō-,tēs-'wē-ri-,bùs\ [L] : with all one's might

**to·to cae·lo** \,tō-tō-'kī-lō\ or toto

| ə abut | ᵊ kitten, F table | ər further | a back | ā bake | ä cot, cart |
|---|---|---|---|---|---|
| ᵊ F bac | aủ out | ch chin | e less | ē easy | g gift | i trip | ī life | j joke |
| g G ich | ⁿ F vin | ŋ sing | ō flow | ȯ flaw | œ F bœuf | œ̄ F feu |
| ȯi coin | th thing | th this | ü loot | ủ foot | ᵫ G Füllen | ᴕ F rue |
| y yet | ᵞ F digne \dēnʸ\, nuit \nwᵫ̄\ | yü few | yủ furious | zh vision |

**coe·lo** \-'kȯi-lō\ [L] : by the whole extent of the heavens : diametrically

**tou·jours per·drix** \tü-zhür-per-drē\ [F] : always partridge : too much of a good thing

**tous frais faits** \tü-fre-fe\ [F] : all expenses defrayed

**tout à fait** \tü-tà-fe\ [F] : altogether : quite

**tout au con·traire** \tü-tō-kōⁿ-trer\ [F] : quite the contrary

**tout à vous** \tü-tà-vü\ [F] : wholly yours : at your service

**tout bien ou rien** \tü-'byaⁿ-nü-'ryaⁿ\ [F] : everything well (done) or nothing (attempted)

**tout com·pren·dre c'est tout par·don·ner** \'tü-kōⁿ-präⁿ-drə se-'tü-pàr-dò-nā\ [F] : to understand all is to forgive all

**tout court** \tü-kür\ [F] : quite short : simply; *also* : brusquely

**tout de même** \tüt-mem\ [F] : all the same : nevertheless

**tout de suite** \tüt-swʸēt\ [F] : immediately; *also* : all at once : consecutively

**tout en·sem·ble** \tü-täⁿ-säⁿblᵉ\ [F] : all together : general effect

**tout est per·du fors l'hon·neur** \tü-te-per-dǖ-fȯr-lȯ-nœr\ *or* **tout est perdu hors l'honneur** \-dǖ-ȯr-\ [F] : all is lost save honor

**tout le monde** \tül-mōⁿd\ [F] : all the world : everybody

**tranche de vie** \träⁿsh-də-'vē\ [F] : slice of life

**tria junc·ta in uno** \,tri-à-'yuŋk-tä-in-'ü-nō\ [L] : three joined in one — motto of the Order of the Bath

**tru·di·tur di·es die** \'trüd-ə-,tùr-,dī-,ās-'dī-,ä\ [L] : day is pushed forth by day : one day hurries on another

**tu·e·bor** \tü-'ā-,bȯr\ [L] : I will defend — a motto on the Great Seal of Michigan

**ua mau ke ea o ka ai·na i ka po·no** \,ü-à-'mä-ü-ke-'e-ä-ō-kä-'ä-ē-nä-,ē-kä-'pō-nō\ [Hawaiian] : the life of the land is established in righteousness — motto of Hawaii

**ue·ber·mensch** \'ē-bər-,mench\ [G] : superman

**ul·ti·ma ra·tio re·gum** \'ùl-ti-mä-,rät-ē-ō-'rā-gùm\ [L] : the final argument of kings, i.e., war

**und so wei·ter** \ùnt-zō-'vī-tər\ [G] : and so on

**uno an·i·mo** \,ü-nō-'än-ə-,mō\ [L] : with one mind : unanimously

**ur·bi et or·bi** \,ùr-bē-,et-'ȯr-bē\ [L] : to the city (Rome) and the world

**uti·le dul·ci** \,üt-ʰl-e-'dùl-,kē\ [L] : the useful with the agreeable

**ut in·fra** \ùt-'in-frä\ [L] : as below

**ut su·pra** \üt-'sü-prä\ [L] : as above

**va·de re·tro me, Sa·ta·na** \,wä-de-'rä-trō-,mä-'sä-tə-,nä\ [L] : get thee behind me, Satan

**vae vic·tis** \wī-'wik-,tēs\ [L] : woe to the vanquished

**va·ria lec·tio** \,wär-ē-ä-'lek-tē-,ō\ *pl* **va·ri·ae lec·ti·o·nes** \'wär-ē-,ī-,lek-tē-'ō-,näs\ [L] : variant reading

**va·ri·um et mu·ta·bi·le sem·per fe·mi·na** \,wär-ē-,et-,mü-'tä-bə-le-,sem-,per-'fä-mə-nä\ [L] : woman is ever a fickle and changeable thing

**ve·di Na·po·li e poi mo·ri** \,vä-dē-'nä-pō-lē-ä-,pȯ-ē-'mȯ-rē\ [It] : see Naples, and then die

**ve·ni, vi·di, vi·ci** \,wā-nē-,wēd-ē-'wē-kē\ [L] : I came, I saw, I conquered

**ven·tre à terre** \väⁿ-trà-ter\ [F] : belly to the ground : at very great speed

**ver·ba·tim ac lit·te·ra·tim** \wer-'bä-tim-,äk-,lit-ə-'rä-tim\ [L] : word for word and letter for letter

**ver·bum sat sa·pi·en·ti est** \,wer-bùm-'sät-,säp-ē-'ent-ē-,est\ [L] : a word to the wise is sufficient

**vin·cit om·nia ve·ri·tas** \,win-ket-'ōm-nē-ä-'wä-rə-,täs\ [L] : truth conquers all things

**vin·cu·lum ma·tri·mo·nii** \,win-kə-lùm-,mä-trə-'mō-nē-,ē\ [L] : bond of marriage

**vir·gin·i·bus pu·er·is·que** \wir-'gin-ə-bùs-,pú-ə-'rēs-kwe\ [L] : for girls and boys

**vir·tu·te et ar·mis** \wir-'tü-te-,et-'är-mēs\ [L] : by valor and arms — motto of Mississippi

**vis me·di·ca·trix na·tu·rae** \'wēs-,med-i-'kä-triks-nä-'tü-,rī\ [L] : the healing power of nature

**vive la reine** \vēv-là-ren\ [F] : long live the queen

**vive le roi** \vēv-lə-rwä\ [F] : long live the king

**vix·e·re for·tes an·te Aga·mem·no·na** \wik-,sä-re-'fȯr-,täs-,änt-,äg-ə-'mem-nə-,nä\ [L] : brave men lived before Agamemnon

**vogue la ga·lère** \vȯg-là-gà-ler\ [F] : let the galley be kept rowing : keep on, whatever may happen

**voi·là** \vwà-là\ [F] : there you are : there you see (it)

**voi·la tout** \vwà-là-tü\ [F] : that's all

**vox et prae·te·rea ni·hil** \'wōks-et-prī-,ter-e-ä-'nī-,hil\ [L] : voice and nothing more

**vox po·pu·li vox Dei** \wōks-'pȯ-pə-,lē-,wōks-'de-ē\ [L] : the voice of the people is the voice of God

**Wan·der·jahr** \'vän-dər-,yär\ [G] : year of wandering

**wie geht's?** \vē-'gāts\ [G] : how goes it?

# Nations of The World

| name and pronunciation | population |
|---|---|
| Afghanistan \af-'gan-ə-,stan\ | 17,480,000 |
| Albania \al-'bā-nē-ə\ | 2,230,000 |
| Algeria \al-'jir-ē-ə\ | 14,770,000 |
| Andorra \an-'dór-ə\ | 20,550 |
| Argentina \,är-jen-'tē-nə\ | 23,550,000 |
| Australia \ó-'strāl-yə\ | 12,730,000 |
| Austria \'ós-trē-ə\ | 7,460,000 |
| Bahrain \bä-'rān\ | 220,000 |
| Bangladesh \,bäŋ-glə-'desh, -'däsh\ | 75,000,000 |
| Barbados \bär-'bād-(,)üs, -əs\ | 240,000 |
| Belgium \'bel-jəm\ | 9,730,000 |
| Bhutan \bü-'tan, -'tän\ | 800,000 |
| Bolivia \bə-'liv-ē-ə\ | 5,060,000 |
| Botswana \bät-'swän-ə\ | 670,000 |
| Brazil \brə-'zil\ | 95,410,000 |
| Bulgaria \,bəl-'gar-ē-ə, bùl-\ | 8,540,000 |
| Burma \'bər-mə\ | 26,980,000 |
| Burundi \bú-'rün-dē\ | 3,620,000 |
| Cambodia — see KHMER REPUBLIC | |
| Cameroon \,kam-ə-'rün\ | 5,840,000 |
| Canada \'kan-əd-ə\ | 21,681,000 |
| Central African Republic \-'af-ri-kən-\ | 1,640,000 |
| Ceylon — see SRI LANKA | |
| Chad \'chad\ | 3,800,000 |
| Chile \'chil-ē\ | 8,990,000 |
| China \'chī-nə\ | 787,180,000 |
| Colombia \kə-'ləm-bē-ə\ | 21,770,000 |
| Congo Republic \'käŋ-go-\ | 960,000 |
| Costa Rica \käs-tə-'rē-kə\ | 1,790,000 |
| Cuba \'kyü-bə\ | 8,660,000 |
| Cyprus \'sī-prəs\ | 640,000 |
| Czechoslovakia \,chek-ə-slō-'väk-ē-ə\ | 14,500,000 |
| Dahomey \də-'hō-mē\ | 2,760,000 |
| Denmark \'den-,märk\ | 4,970,000 |
| Dominican Republic \də-,min-i-kən-\ | 4,190,000 |
| East Germany \-'jər-mən-ē\ | 15,950,000 |
| Ecuador \'ek-wə-,dór\ | 6,300,000 |
| Egypt, Arab Republic of \-'ē-jəpt\ | 34,130,000 |
| El Salvador \el-'sal-və-,dór\ | 3,534,000 |
| Equatorial Guinea \-'gin-ē\ | 290,000 |
| Ethiopia (Abyssinia) \,ē-thē-'ō-pē-ə (,ab-ə-'sin-ē-ə, -'sin-yə)\ | 25,250,000 |
| Fiji \'fē-(,)jē\ | 530,000 |
| Finland \'fin-lənd\ | 4,680,000 |
| France \'frans\ | 51,260,000 |
| Gabon \ga-,bōn\ | 500,000 |
| Gambia \'gam-bē-ə\ | 370,000 |
| Ghana \'gän-ə\ | 8,860,000 |
| Greece \'grēs\ | 8,850,000 |
| Grenada \grə-'nād-ə\ | 87,300 |
| Guatemala \,gwät-ə-'mäl-ə\ | 5,350,000 |
| Guinea \'gin-ē\ | 4,010,000 |
| Guyana \gī-'an-ə\ | 740,000 |
| Haiti \'hāt-ē\ | 4,970,000 |
| Honduras \hän-'d(y)ùr-əs\ | 2,580,000 |
| Hungary \'həŋ-g(ə)rē\ | 10,360,000 |
| Iceland \'īs-lənd, -,land\ | 210,000 |
| India \'in-dē-ə\ | 550,370,000 |
| Indonesia \,in-də-'nē-zhə\ | 124,890,000 |
| Iran (Persia) \i-'ran, -'rän ('pər-zhə)\ | 29,780,000 |
| Iraq \i-'räk, -'rak\ | 9,750,000 |
| Ireland, Republic of \-'ī(ə)r-lənd\ | 2,970,000 |
| Israel \'iz-rē-əl\ | 3,010,000 |
| Italy \'it-ə-lē\ | 54,080,000 |
| Ivory Coast \'īv-(ə)rē-\ | 4,420,000 |
| Jamaica \jə-'mā-kə\ | 1,900,000 |
| Japan \jə-'pan\ | 104,660,000 |
| Jordan \'jórd-ən\ | 2,380,000 |
| Kenya \'ken-yə, 'kēn-\ | 11,690,000 |
| Khmer Republic (Cambodia) \kə-'mer-(kam-'bōd-ē-ə)\ | 6,818,000 |
| Kuwait \kə-'wāt\ | 830,000 |
| Laos \'laús, 'lȧös\ | 3,030,000 |
| Lebanon \'leb-ə-nən\ | 2,870,000 |
| Lesotho \lə-'sō-tō\ | 930,000 |
| Liberia \lī-'bir-ē-ə\ | 1,570,000 |
| Libya \'lib-ē-ə\ | 2,010,000 |
| Liechtenstein \'lik-tən-,s(h)tīn\ | 20,000 |
| Luxembourg \'lək-səm-,bərg, 'lúk-səm-,bùrg\ | 339,000 |
| Malagasy Republic \,mal-ə-,gas-ē-\ | 6,750,000 |
| Malawi \mə-'lä-wē\ | 4,550,000 |
| Malaysia \mə-'lā-zh(ē-)ə\ | 10,650,000 |
| Maldive Islands \'mól-,dēv, ,dīv; 'mal-\ | 114,500 |
| Mali \'mäl-ē\ | 5,140,000 |
| Malta \'mól-tə\ | 330,000 |
| Mauritania \,mór-ə-'tā-nē-ə, ,mär-\ | 1,200,000 |
| Mauritius \mó-'rish-(ē-)əs\ | 820,000 |
| Mexico \'mek-si-,kō\ | 50,830,000 |
| Monaco \'män-ə-,kō\ | 20,000 |
| Mongolian People's Republic \män-'gōl-yən, mäŋ-, -'gō-lē-ən\ | 1,280,000 |
| Morocco \mə-'räk-ō\ | 15,230,000 |
| Nauru \nä-'ü-(,)rü\ | 6,600 |
| Nepal \nə-'pól\ | 11,290,000 |
| Netherlands \'neth-ər-lən(d)z\ | 13,190,000 |
| New Zealand \-'zē-lənd\ | 2,850,000 |
| Nicaragua \,nik-ə-'räg-wə\ | 1,980,000 |
| Niger \'nī-jər\ | 4,130,000 |
| Nigeria \nī-'jir-ē-ə\ | 56,510,000 |
| North Korea \-kə-'rē-ə\ | 14,280,000 |
| North Vietnam \-vē-'et-'näm, -'nam\ | 21,600,000 |
| Norway \'nór-,wā\ | 3,910,000 |
| Oman \ō-'män\ | 680,000 |
| Pakistan \,pak-i-'stan, ,päk-i-'stän\ | 53,990,000 |
| Panama \'pan-ə-,mä, -,mó\ | 1,480,000 |

| name and pronunciation | population | name and pronunciation | population |
|---|---|---|---|
| Paraguay \'par-ə-ˌgwī, -ˌgwä\ | 2,390,000 | Togo \'tō-gō\ | 1,440,000 |
| Peru \pə-'rü\ | 14,010,000 | Trinidad and Tobago \'trin-ə-ˌdad-ən-tə-'bā-gō\ | 1,030,000 |
| Philippines \ˌfil-ə-'pēnz, 'fil-ə-ˌpēnz\ | 37,960,000 | Tunisia \t(y)ü-'nē-zh(ē-)ə, -'nizh-(ē-)ə\ | 5,140,000 |
| Poland \'pō-lənd\ | 32,750,000 | Turkey \'tər-kē\ | 36,160,000 |
| Portugal \'pōr-chi-gəl\ | 8,950,000 | Uganda \yü-'gan-də\ | 10,130,000 |
| Qatar \'kät-ər\ | 80,000 | Union of Soviet Socialist Republics (U.S.S.R.) \-'sō-vē-,et-, -ət-, 'säv-ē-(,yü-,es-,es-'är)\ | 245,070,000 |
| Rumania \rü-'mā-nē-ə, -nyə\ | 20,470,000 | | |
| Rwanda \rü-'än-də\ | 3,830,000 | | |
| San Marino \ˌsan-mə-'rē-nō\ | 18,300 | United Arab Emirates \i-'mir-əts, ā-, -'mi(ə)r-ˌäts\ | 179,000 |
| Saudi Arabia \ˌsaüd-ē-ə-'rā-bē-ə, sü-,üd-ē-\ | 7,200,000 | United Kingdom of Great Britain and Northern Ireland \-'brit-ən ... 'ī(ə)r-lənd\ | 55,346,551 |
| Senegal \ˌsen-i-'gól\ | 4,020,000 | | |
| Seychelles \sā-'shel(z)\ | 54,000 | England \'iŋ-glənd\ | |
| Sierra Leone \sē-,er-ə-lē-'ōn\ | 2,600,000 | Northern Ireland | |
| Singapore \'siŋ-(g)ə-,pōr\ | 2,110,000 | Scotland \'skät-lənd\ | |
| Somalia \sō-'mäl-ē-ə\ | 2,860,000 | Wales \'wālz\ | |
| South Africa, Republic of | 22,090,000 | United States of America \-ə-'mer-ə-kə\ | 203,184,772 |
| Southern Yemen (People's Democratic Republic of Yemen) \-'yem-ən\ | 1,470,000 | Upper Volta \-'vül-tə, 'vōl-\ | 5,490,000 |
| South Korea \-kə-'rē-ə\ | 31,920,000 | Uruguay \'(y)ùr-ə-,gwī, 'yùr-ə-,gwä\ | 2,290,000 |
| South Vietnam \-vē-'et-'näm, -'nam\ | 18,330,000 | Vatican City State \,vat-i-kən-\ | 600 |
| Spain \'spān\ | 34,130,000 | Venezuela \,ven-əz(-ə)-'wā-lə, -'wē-\ | 10,400,000 |
| Sri Lanka (Ceylon) \(')srē-'läŋ-kə (si-'län, sā-)\ | 9,172,000 | Western Samoa \-sə-'mō-ə\ | 140,000 |
| Sudan \sü-'dan\ | 16,090,000 | West Germany \-'jər-mə-nē\ | 59,180,000 |
| Swaziland \'swäz-ē-,land\ | 420,000 | Yemen Arab Republic \'yem-ən-\ | 5,900,000 |
| Sweden \'swēd-ən\ | 8,110,000 | | |
| Switzerland \'swit-sər-lənd\ | 6,310,000 | Yugoslavia \,yü-gō-'släv-ē-ə\ | 20,550,000 |
| Syria \'sir-ē-ə\ | 6,450,000 | Zaire \'zī(ə)r\ | 22,480,000 |
| Tanzania \,tan-zə-'nē-ə\ | 13,630,000 | Zambia \'zam-bē-ə\ | 4,280,000 |
| Thailand (Siam) \'tī-,land, -lənd (sī-'am)\ | 35,340,000 | | |

# Population of Places in the United States

*Having 12,000 or More Inhabitants in 1970*

## A

| | |
|---|---|
| Aberdeen, Md. | 12,375 |
| Aberdeen, S. Dak. | 26,476 |
| Aberdeen, Wash. | 18,489 |
| Abilene, Tex. | 89,653 |
| Abington, Mass. | 12,334 |
| Acton, Mass. | 14,770 |
| Ada, Okla. | 14,859 |
| Addison, Ill. | 24,482 |
| Adrian, Mich. | 20,382 |
| Agawam, Mass. | 21,717 |
| Aiea, Hawaii | 12,560 |
| Aiken, S.C. | 13,436 |
| Akron, Ohio | 275,425 |
| Alameda, Calif. | 70,968 |
| Alamogordo, N. Mex. | 23,035 |
| Albany, Calif. | 14,674 |
| Albany, Ga. | 72,623 |
| Albany, N.Y. | 114,873 |
| Albany, Oreg. | 18,181 |
| Albert Lea, Minn. | 19,418 |
| Albion, Mich. | 12,112 |
| Albuquerque, N. Mex. | 243,751 |
| Alexander City, Ala. | 12,358 |
| Alexandria, La. | 41,557 |
| Alexandria, Va. | 110,938 |
| Alhambra, Calif. | 62,125 |
| Alice, Tex. | 20,121 |
| Aliquippa, Pa. | 22,277 |
| Allen Park, Mich. | 40,747 |
| Allentown, Pa. | 109,527 |
| Alliance, Ohio | 26,547 |
| Alpena, Mich. | 13,805 |
| Alton, Ill. | 39,700 |
| Altoona, Pa. | 62,900 |
| Altus, Okla. | 23,302 |
| Amarillo, Tex. | 127,010 |
| Americus, Ga. | 16,091 |
| Ames, Iowa | 39,505 |
| Amherst, Mass. | 26,331 |
| Amsterdam, N.Y. | 25,524 |
| Anaheim, Calif. | 166,701 |
| Anchorage, Alaska | 48,029 |
| Anderson, Ind. | 70,787 |
| Anderson, S.C. | 27,556 |
| Andover, Mass. | 23,695 |
| Annapolis, Md. | 29,592 |
| Ann Arbor, Mich. | 99,797 |
| Anniston, Ala. | 31,533 |
| Anoka, Minn. | 13,489 |
| Ansonia, Conn. | 21,160 |
| Antioch, Calif. | 28,060 |
| Appleton, Wis. | 57,143 |
| Arcadia, Calif. | 42,868 |
| Ardmore, Okla. | 20,881 |
| Arkansas City, Kans. | 13,216 |
| Arlington, Mass. | 53,524 |
| Arlington, Tex. | 90,643 |
| Arlington Heights, Ill. | 64,884 |
| Artesia, Calif. | 14,757 |
| Arvada, Colo. | 46,814 |
| Asbury Park, N.J. | 16,533 |
| Asheville, N.C. | 57,681 |
| Ashland, Ky. | 29,245 |
| Ashland, Ohio | 19,872 |
| Ashland, Oreg. | 12,342 |
| Ashtabula, Ohio | 24,313 |
| Atchison, Kans. | 12,565 |
| Athens, Ala. | 14,360 |
| Athens, Ga. | 44,342 |
| Athens, Ohio | 23,310 |
| Atlanta, Ga. | 496,973 |

| | |
|---|---|
| Atlantic City, N.J. | 47,859 |
| Attleboro, Mass. | 32,907 |
| Auburn, Ala. | 22,767 |
| Auburn, Mass. | 15,347 |
| Auburn, Me. | 24,151 |
| Auburn, N.Y. | 34,599 |
| Auburn, Wash. | 21,817 |
| Augusta, Ga. | 59,864 |
| Augusta, Me. | 21,945 |
| Aurora, Colo. | 74,974 |
| Aurora, Ill. | 74,182 |
| Austin, Minn. | 25,074 |
| Austin, Tex. | 251,808 |
| Avon Lake, Ohio | 12,261 |
| Azusa, Calif. | 25,217 |

## B

| | |
|---|---|
| Babylon, N.Y. | 12,588 |
| Bakersfield, Calif. | 69,515 |
| Baldwin, Pa. | 26,729 |
| Baldwin Park, Calif. | 47,285 |
| Baltimore, Md. | 905,759 |
| Bangor, Me. | 33,168 |
| Banning, Calif. | 12,034 |
| Barberton, Ohio | 33,052 |
| Barnstable, Mass. | 19,842 |
| Barrington, R.I. | 17,554 |
| Barstow, Calif. | 17,442 |
| Bartlesville, Okla. | 29,683 |
| Bartow, Fla. | 12,891 |
| Bastrop, La. | 14,713 |
| Batavia, N.Y. | 17,338 |
| Baton Rouge, La. | 165,963 |
| Battle Creek, Mich. | 38,931 |
| Bay City, Mich. | 49,449 |
| Bayonne, N.J. | 72,743 |
| Baytown, Tex. | 43,980 |
| Bay Village, Ohio | 18,163 |
| Beacon, N.Y. | 13,255 |
| Beatrice, Nebr. | 12,389 |
| Beaumont, Tex. | 115,919 |
| Beaver Dam, Wis. | 14,265 |
| Beaver Falls, Pa. | 14,375 |
| Beaverton, Oreg. | 18,577 |
| Beckley, W. Va. | 19,884 |
| Bedford, Ind. | 13,087 |
| Bedford, Mass. | 13,513 |
| Bedford, Ohio | 17,552 |
| Bedford Heights, Ohio | 13,063 |
| Beech Grove, Ind. | 13,468 |
| Beeville, Tex. | 13,506 |
| Bell, Calif. | 21,836 |
| Bellaire, Tex. | 19,009 |
| Bellefontaine Neighbors, Mo. | 13,987 |
| Belle Glade, Fla. | 15,949 |
| Belleville, Ill. | 41,699 |
| Belleville, N.J. | 34,643 |
| Bellevue, Nebr. | 19,449 |
| Bellevue, Wash. | 61,102 |
| Bellflower, Calif. | 51,454 |
| Bell Gardens, Calif. | 29,308 |
| Bellingham, Mass. | 13,967 |
| Bellingham, Wash. | 39,375 |
| Bellmawr, N.J. | 15,618 |
| Bellwood, Ill. | 22,096 |
| Belmont, Calif. | 23,667 |
| Belmont, Mass. | 28,285 |
| Beloit, Wis. | 35,729 |
| Belvidere, Ill. | 14,061 |
| Bend, Oreg. | 13,710 |
| Bennington, Vt. | 14,586 |
| Bensenville, Ill. | 12,833 |
| Benton, Ark. | 16,499 |

| | | | |
|---|---|---|---|
| Benton Harbor, Mich. | 16,481 | Brown Deer, Wis. | 12,622 |
| Berea, Ohio | 22,396 | Brownsville, Tex. | 52,522 |
| Bergenfield, N.J. | 33,131 | Brownwood, Tex. | 17,368 |
| Berkeley, Calif. | 116,716 | Brunswick, Ga. | 19,585 |
| Berkeley, Mo. | 19,743 | Brunswick, Me. | 16,195 |
| Berkley, Mich. | 22,618 | Brunswick, Ohio | 15,852 |
| Berlin, Conn. | 14,149 | Bryan, Tex. | 33,719 |
| Berlin, N.H. | 15,256 | Bucyrus, Ohio | 13,111 |
| Berwick, Pa. | 12,274 | Buena Park, Calif. | 63,646 |
| Berwyn, Ill. | 52,502 | Buffalo, N.Y. | 462,768 |
| Bessemer, Ala. | 33,428 | Burbank, Calif. | 88,871 |
| Bethany, Okla. | 21,785 | Burlingame, Calif. | 27,320 |
| Bethel Park, Pa. | 34,791 | Burlington, Iowa | 32,366 |
| Bethlehem, Pa. | 72,686 | Burlington, Mass. | 21,980 |
| Bettendorf, Iowa | 22,126 | Burlington, N.C. | 35,930 |
| Beverly, Mass. | 38,348 | Burlington, Vt. | 38,633 |
| Beverly Hills, Calif. | 33,416 | Burnsville, Minn. | 19,940 |
| Beverly Hills, Mich. | 13,598 | Butler, Pa. | 18,691 |
| Bexley, Ohio | 14,888 | Butte, Mont. | 23,368 |
| Biddeford, Me. | 19,983 | | |
| Big Spring, Tex. | 28,735 | **C** | |
| Billerica, Mass. | 31,648 | Cahokia, Ill. | 20,649 |
| Billings, Mont. | 61,581 | Caldwell, Idaho | 14,219 |
| Biloxi, Miss. | 48,486 | Calumet City, Ill. | 32,956 |
| Binghamton, N.Y. | 64,123 | Camarillo, Calif. | 19,219 |
| Birmingham, Ala. | 300,910 | Cambridge, Mass. | 100,361 |
| Birmingham, Mich. | 26,170 | Cambridge, Ohio | 13,656 |
| Bismarck, N. Dak. | 34,703 | Camden, Ark. | 15,147 |
| Blaine, Minn. | 20,640 | Camden, N.J. | 102,551 |
| Bloomfield, Conn. | 18,301 | Campbell, Calif. | 24,770 |
| Bloomfield, N.J. | 52,029 | Campbell, Ohio | 12,577 |
| Bloomington, Ill. | 39,992 | Canton, Ill. | 14,217 |
| Bloomington, Ind. | 42,890 | Canton, Mass. | 17,100 |
| Bloomington, Minn. | 81,970 | Canton, Ohio | 110,053 |
| Bluefield, W. Va. | 15,921 | Cape Girardeau, Mo. | 31,282 |
| Blue Island, Ill. | 22,958 | Carbondale, Ill. | 22,816 |
| Blytheville, Ark. | 24,752 | Carbondale, Pa. | 12,808 |
| Boca Raton, Fla. | 28,506 | Carlisle, Pa. | 18,079 |
| Bogalusa, La. | 18,412 | Carlsbad, Calif. | 14,944 |
| Boise, Idaho | 74,990 | Carlsbad, N. Mex. | 21,297 |
| Boone, Iowa | 12,468 | Carpentersville, Ill. | 24,059 |
| Borger, Tex. | 14,195 | Carrollton, Ga. | 13,520 |
| Bossier City, La. | 41,595 | Carrollton, Tex. | 13,855 |
| Boston, Mass. | 641,071 | Carson, Calif. | 71,150 |
| Boulder, Colo. | 66,870 | Carson City, Nev. | 15,468 |
| Bountiful, Utah | 27,853 | Carteret, N.J. | 23,137 |
| Bourne, Mass. | 12,636 | Casper, Wyo. | 39,361 |
| Bowie, Md. | 35,028 | Cedar Falls, Iowa | 29,597 |
| Bowling Green, Ky. | 36,253 | Cedar Rapids, Iowa | 110,642 |
| Bowling Green, Ohio | 21,760 | Central Falls, R.I. | 18,716 |
| Boynton Beach, Fla. | 18,115 | Centralia, Ill. | 15,217 |
| Bozeman, Mont. | 18,670 | Cerritos, Calif. | 15,856 |
| Bradenton, Fla. | 21,040 | Chambersburg, Pa. | 17,315 |
| Bradford, Pa. | 12,672 | Champaign, Ill. | 56,532 |
| Braintree, Mass. | 35,050 | Chandler, Ariz. | 13,763 |
| Branford, Conn. | 20,444 | Chapel Hill, N.C. | 25,537 |
| Brattleboro, Vt. | 12,239 | Charleston, Ill. | 16,421 |
| Brawley, Calif. | 13,746 | Charleston, S.C. | 66,945 |
| Brea, Calif. | 18,447 | Charleston, W. Va. | 71,505 |
| Bremerton, Wash. | 35,307 | Charlotte, N.C. | 241,178 |
| Brentwood, Pa. | 13,732 | Charlottesville, Va. | 38,880 |
| Bridgeport, Conn. | 156,542 | Chattanooga, Tenn. | 119,082 |
| Bridgeton, Mo. | 19,992 | Chelmsford, Mass. | 31,432 |
| Bridgeton, N.J. | 20,435 | Chelsea, Mass. | 30,625 |
| Bridge View, Ill. | 12,522 | Chesapeake, Va. | 89,580 |
| Brigham City, Utah | 14,007 | Cheshire, Conn. | 19,051 |
| Bristol, Conn. | 55,487 | Chester, Pa. | 56,331 |
| Bristol, Pa. | 12,085 | Cheyenne, Wyo. | 40,914 |
| Bristol, R.I. | 17,860 | Chicago, Ill. | 3,366,957 |
| Bristol, Tenn. | 20,064 | Chicago Heights, Ill. | 40,900 |
| Bristol, Va. | 14,857 | Chickasha, Okla. | 14,194 |
| Brockton, Mass. | 89,040 | Chico, Calif. | 19,580 |
| Brookfield, Ill. | 20,284 | Chicopee, Mass. | 66,676 |
| Brookfield, Wis. | 32,140 | Chillicothe, Ohio | 24,842 |
| Brookings, S. Dak. | 13,717 | Chino, Calif. | 20,411 |
| Brookline, Mass. | 58,886 | Chippewa Falls, Wis. | 12,351 |
| Brooklyn, Ohio | 13,142 | Chula Vista, Calif. | 67,901 |
| Brooklyn Center, Minn. | 35,173 | Cicero, Ill. | 67,058 |
| Brooklyn Park, Minn. | 26,230 | Cincinnati, Ohio | 452,524 |
| Brook Park, Ohio | 30,774 | Clairton, Pa. | 15,051 |

| | | | |
|---|---:|---|---:|
| Claremont, Calif. | 23,464 | Cumberland, Md. | 29,724 |
| Claremont, N.H. | 14,221 | Cumberland, R.I. | 26,605 |
| Clarksburg, W. Va. | 24,864 | Cupertino, Calif. | 18,216 |
| Clarksdale, Miss. | 21,673 | Cuyahoga Falls, Ohio | 49,678 |
| Clarksville, Ind. | 13,806 | Cypress, Calif. | 31,026 |
| Clarksville, Tenn. | 31,719 | | |
| Clawson, Mich. | 17,617 | **D** | |
| Clayton, Mo. | 16,222 | Dallas, Tex. | 844,401 |
| Clearfield, Utah | 13,316 | Dalton, Ga. | 18,872 |
| Clearwater, Fla. | 52,074 | Daly City, Calif. | 66,922 |
| Cleburne, Tex. | 16,015 | Danbury, Conn. | 50,781 |
| Cleveland, Miss. | 13,327 | Danvers, Mass. | 26,151 |
| Cleveland, Ohio | 750,903 | Danville, Ill. | 42,570 |
| Cleveland, Tenn. | 20,651 | Danville, Va. | 46,391 |
| Cleveland Heights, Ohio | 60,767 | Darby, Pa. | 13,729 |
| Cliffside Park, N.J. | 14,387 | Darien, Conn. | 20,411 |
| Clifton, N.J. | 82,437 | Dartmouth, Mass. | 18,800 |
| Clinton, Iowa | 34,719 | Davenport, Iowa | 98,469 |
| Clinton, Mass. | 13,383 | Davis, Calif. | 23,488 |
| Clovis, Calif. | 13,856 | Dayton, Ohio | 243,601 |
| Clovis, N. Mex. | 28,495 | Daytona Beach, Fla. | 45,327 |
| Coatesville, Pa. | 12,331 | Dearborn, Mich. | 104,199 |
| Cocoa, Fla. | 16,110 | Dearborn Heights, Mich. | 80,069 |
| Coeur d'Alene, Idaho | 16,228 | Decatur, Ala. | 38,044 |
| Coffeyville, Kans. | 15,116 | Decatur, Ga. | 21,943 |
| Cohoes, N.Y. | 18,613 | Decatur, Ill. | 90,397 |
| College Park, Ga. | 18,203 | Dedham, Mass. | 26,938 |
| College Park, Md. | 26,156 | Deerfield, Ill. | 18,949 |
| College Station, Tex. | 17,676 | Deerfield Beach, Fla. | 17,130 |
| Collingswood, N.J. | 17,422 | Deer Park, Tex. | 12,773 |
| Collinsville, Ill. | 17,773 | Defiance, Ohio | 16,281 |
| Colonial Heights, Va. | 15,097 | De Kalb, Ill. | 32,949 |
| Colorado Springs, Colo. | 135,060 | Delano, Calif. | 14,559 |
| Colton, Calif. | 19,974 | Delaware, Ohio | 15,008 |
| Columbia, Mo. | 58,804 | Del City, Okla. | 27,133 |
| Columbia, S.C. | 113,542 | Delray Beach, Fla. | 19,366 |
| Columbia, Tenn. | 21,471 | Del Rio, Tex. | 21,330 |
| Columbia Heights, Minn. | 23,997 | Denison, Tex. | 24,923 |
| Columbus, Ga. | 154,168 | Denton, Tex. | 39,874 |
| Columbus, Ind. | 27,141 | Denver, Colo. | 514,678 |
| Columbus, Miss. | 25,795 | De Pere, Wis. | 13,309 |
| Columbus, Nebr. | 15,471 | Depew, N.Y. | 22,158 |
| Columbus, Ohio | 539,677 | Derby, Conn. | 12,599 |
| Commerce City, Colo. | 17,407 | Des Moines, Iowa | 200,587 |
| Compton, Calif. | 78,611 | Des Plaines, Ill. | 57,239 |
| Concord, Calif. | 85,164 | Detroit, Mich. | 1,511,482 |
| Concord, Mass. | 16,148 | Dickinson, N. Dak. | 12,405 |
| Concord, N.H. | 30,022 | Dixon, Ill. | 18,147 |
| Concord, N.C. | 18,464 | Dodge City, Kans. | 14,127 |
| Conneaut, Ohio | 14,552 | Dolton, Ill. | 25,937 |
| Connersville, Ind. | 17,604 | Dormont, Pa. | 12,856 |
| Conway, Ark. | 15,510 | Dothan, Ala. | 36,733 |
| Cookeville, Tenn. | 14,270 | Douglas, Ariz. | 12,462 |
| Coon Rapids, Minn. | 30,505 | Dover, Del. | 17,488 |
| Coos Bay, Oreg. | 13,466 | Dover, N.H. | 20,850 |
| Coral Gables, Fla. | 42,494 | Dover, N.J. | 15,039 |
| Corning, N.Y. | 15,792 | Downers Grove, Ill. | 32,751 |
| Corona, Calif. | 27,519 | Downey, Calif. | 88,445 |
| Coronado, Calif. | 20,910 | Dracut, Mass. | 18,214 |
| Corpus Christi, Tex. | 204,525 | Duarte, Calif. | 14,981 |
| Corsicana, Tex. | 19,972 | Dublin, Ga. | 15,143 |
| Cortland, N.Y. | 19,621 | Dubuque, Iowa | 62,309 |
| Corvallis, Oreg. | 35,153 | Duluth, Minn. | 100,578 |
| Coshocton, Ohio | 13,747 | Dumont, N.J. | 17,534 |
| Costa Mesa, Calif. | 72,660 | Duncan, Okla. | 19,718 |
| Cottage Grove, Minn. | 13,419 | Duncanville, Tex. | 14,105 |
| Council Bluffs, Iowa | 60,348 | Dunedin, Fla. | 17,639 |
| Coventry, R.I. | 22,947 | Dunkirk, N.Y. | 16,855 |
| Covina, Calif. | 30,380 | Dunmore, Pa. | 17,300 |
| Covington, Ky. | 52,535 | Durham, N.C. | 95,438 |
| Cranston, R.I. | 73,037 | Dyersburg, Tenn. | 14,523 |
| Crawfordsville, Ind. | 13,842 | | |
| Crestwood, Mo. | 15,398 | **E** | |
| Crowley, La. | 16,104 | Eagle Pass, Tex. | 15,364 |
| Crystal, Minn. | 30,925 | East Chicago, Ind. | 46,982 |
| Crystal Lake, Ill. | 14,541 | East Cleveland, Ohio | 39,600 |
| Cudahy, Calif. | 16,998 | East Detroit, Mich. | 45,920 |
| Cudahy, Wis. | 22,078 | East Grand Rapids, Mich. | 12,565 |
| Cullman, Ala. | 12,601 | Easthampton, Mass. | 13,012 |
| Culver City, Calif. | 31,035 | East Hartford, Conn. | 57,583 |

| | | | |
|---|---:|---|---:|
| East Haven, Conn. | 25,120 | Farmers Branch, Tex. | 27,492 |
| Eastlake, Ohio | 19,690 | Farmington, Conn. | 14,390 |
| East Lansing, Mich. | 47,540 | Farmington, Mich. | 13,337 |
| East Liverpool, Ohio | 20,020 | Farmington, N. Mex. | 21,979 |
| East Longmeadow, Mass. | 13,029 | Fayetteville, Ark. | 30,729 |
| East Moline, Ill. | 20,832 | Fayetteville, N.C. | 53,510 |
| Easton, Mass. | 12,157 | Fergus Falls, Minn. | 12,443 |
| Easton, Pa. | 30,256 | Ferguson, Mo. | 28,915 |
| East Orange, N.J. | 75,471 | Ferndale, Mich. | 30,850 |
| East Paterson, N.J. | 22,749 | Findlay, Ohio | 35,800 |
| East Peoria, Ill. | 18,455 | Fitchburg, Mass. | 43,343 |
| East Point, Ga. | 39,315 | Flagstaff, Ariz. | 26,117 |
| East Providence, R.I. | 48,151 | Flint, Mich. | 193,317 |
| East Ridge, Tenn. | 21,799 | Floral Park, N.Y. | 18,422 |
| East St. Louis, Ill. | 69,996 | Florence, Ala. | 34,031 |
| Eatontown, N.J. | 14,619 | Florence, S.C. | 25,997 |
| Eau Claire, Wis. | 44,619 | Florissant, Mo. | 65,908 |
| Ecorse, Mich. | 17,515 | Fond du Lac, Wis. | 35,515 |
| Eden, N.C. | 15,871 | Fontana, Calif. | 20,673 |
| Edina, Minn. | 44,046 | Forest Park, Ga. | 19,994 |
| Edinburg, Tex. | 17,163 | Forest Park, Ill. | 15,472 |
| Edmond, Okla. | 16,633 | Forest Park, Ohio | 15,139 |
| Edmonds, Wash. | 23,998 | Forrest City, Ark. | 12,521 |
| El Cajon, Calif. | 52,273 | Fort Collins, Colo. | 43,337 |
| El Centro, Calif. | 19,272 | Fort Dodge, Iowa | 31,263 |
| El Cerrito, Calif. | 25,190 | Fort Lauderdale, Fla. | 139,590 |
| El Dorado, Ark. | 25,283 | Fort Lee, N.J. | 30,631 |
| El Dorado, Kans. | 12,308 | Fort Madison, Iowa | 13,996 |
| Elgin, Ill. | 55,691 | Fort Myers, Fla. | 27,351 |
| Elizabeth, N.J. | 112,654 | Fort Pierce, Fla. | 29,721 |
| Elizabeth City, N.C. | 14,069 | Fort Smith, Ark. | 62,802 |
| Elizabethton, Tenn. | 12,269 | Fort Thomas, Ky. | 16,338 |
| Elk Grove Village, Ill. | 24,516 | Fort Walton Beach, Fla. | 19,994 |
| Elkhart, Ind. | 43,152 | Fort Wayne, Ind. | 177,671 |
| Ellensburg, Wash. | 13,568 | Fort Worth, Tex. | 393,476 |
| Elmhurst, Ill. | 50,547 | Fostoria, Ohio | 16,037 |
| Elmira, N.Y. | 39,945 | Fountain Valley, Calif. | 31,826 |
| El Monte, Calif. | 69,837 | Foxboro, Mass. | 14,218 |
| Elmwood Park, Ill. | 26,160 | Framingham, Mass. | 64,048 |
| El Paso, Tex. | 322,261 | Frankfort, Ind. | 14,956 |
| El Reno, Okla. | 14,510 | Frankfort, Ky. | 21,356 |
| El Segundo, Calif. | 15,620 | Franklin, Mass. | 17,830 |
| Elyria, Ohio | 53,427 | Franklin, Wis. | 12,247 |
| Emporia, Kans. | 23,327 | Franklin Park, Ill. | 20,497 |
| Endicott, N.Y. | 16,556 | Frederick, Md. | 23,641 |
| Enfield, Conn. | 46,189 | Fredericksburg, Va. | 14,450 |
| Englewood, Colo. | 33,695 | Freeport, Ill. | 27,736 |
| Englewood, N.J. | 24,985 | Freeport, N.Y. | 40,374 |
| Enid, Okla. | 44,008 | Fremont, Calif. | 100,869 |
| Enterprise, Ala. | 15,591 | Fremont, Nebr. | 22,962 |
| Erie, Pa. | 129,231 | Fremont, Ohio | 18,490 |
| Erlanger, Ky. | 12,676 | Fresno, Calif. | 165,972 |
| Escanaba, Mich. | 15,368 | Fridley, Minn. | 29,233 |
| Escondido, Calif. | 36,792 | Fullerton, Calif. | 85,826 |
| Euclid, Ohio | 71,552 | Fulton, Mo. | 12,148 |
| Eugene, Oreg. | 76,346 | Fulton, N.Y. | 14,003 |
| Euless, Tex. | 19,316 | | |
| Eureka, Calif. | 24,337 | **G** | |
| Evanston, Ill. | 79,808 | Gadsden, Ala. | 53,928 |
| Evansville, Ind. | 138,764 | Gaffney, S.C. | 13,253 |
| Everett, Mass. | 42,485 | Gahanna, Ohio | 12,400 |
| Everett, Wash. | 53,622 | Gainesville, Fla. | 64,510 |
| Evergreen Park, Ill. | 25,487 | Gainesville, Ga. | 15,459 |
| | | Gainesville, Tex. | 13,830 |
| **F** | | Galesburg, Ill. | 36,290 |
| Fairbanks, Alaska | 14,771 | Galion, Ohio | 13,123 |
| Fairborn, Ohio | 32,267 | Gallatin, Tenn. | 13,093 |
| Fairfax, Va. | 21,970 | Gallup, N. Mex. | 14,596 |
| Fairfield, Ala. | 14,369 | Galveston, Tex. | 61,809 |
| Fairfield, Calif. | 44,146 | Gardena, Calif. | 41,021 |
| Fairfield, Conn. | 56,487 | Garden City, Kans. | 14,708 |
| Fairfield, Ohio | 14,680 | Garden City, Mich. | 41,864 |
| Fairhaven, Mass. | 16,332 | Garden City, N.Y. | 25,373 |
| Fair Lawn, N.J. | 37,975 | Garden Grove, Calif. | 122,524 |
| Fairmont, W. Va. | 26,093 | Gardner, Mass. | 19,748 |
| Fairview Park, Ohio | 21,681 | Garfield, N.J. | 30,722 |
| Fall River, Mass. | 96,898 | Garfield Heights, Ohio | 41,417 |
| Falmouth, Mass. | 15,942 | Garland, Tex. | 81,437 |
| Fargo, N. Dak. | 53,365 | Gary, Ind. | 175,415 |
| Faribault, Minn. | 16,595 | Gastonia, N.C. | 47,142 |

| | | | |
|---|---|---|---|
| Irving, Tex. | 97,260 | Lakeland, Fla. | 41,550 |
| Irvington, N.J. | 59,743 | Lake Oswego, Oreg. | 14,573 |
| Ithaca, N.Y. | 26,226 | Lakewood, Calif. | 82,973 |
| | | Lakewood, Colo. | 92,787 |
| **J** | | Lakewood, Ohio | 70,173 |
| Jackson, Mich. | 45,484 | Lake Worth, Fla. | 23,714 |
| Jackson, Miss. | 153,968 | La Marque, Tex. | 16,131 |
| Jackson, Tenn. | 39,996 | La Mesa, Calif. | 39,178 |
| Jacksonville, Ark. | 19,832 | La Mirada, Calif. | 30,808 |
| Jacksonville, Fla. | 528,865 | Lancaster, N.Y. | 13,365 |
| Jacksonville, Ill. | 20,553 | Lancaster, Ohio | 32,911 |
| Jacksonville, N.C. | 16,021 | Lancaster, Pa. | 57,690 |
| Jamestown, N.Y. | 39,795 | Lansdale, Pa. | 18,451 |
| Jamestown, N. Dak. | 15,385 | Lansdowne, Pa. | 14,090 |
| Janesville, Wis. | 46,426 | Lansing, Ill. | 25,805 |
| Jeannette, Pa. | 15,209 | Lansing, Mich. | 131,546 |
| Jefferson City, Mo. | 32,407 | La Porte, Ind. | 22,140 |
| Jeffersonville, Ind. | 20,008 | La Puente, Calif. | 31,092 |
| Jennings, Mo. | 19,379 | Laramie, Wyo. | 23,143 |
| Jersey City, N.J. | 260,545 | Laredo, Tex. | 69,024 |
| Johnson City, N.Y. | 18,025 | Largo, Fla. | 22,031 |
| Johnson City, Tenn. | 33,770 | Las Cruces, N. Mex. | 37,857 |
| Johnston, R.I. | 22,037 | Las Vegas, Nev. | 125,787 |
| Johnstown, Pa. | 42,476 | Laurel, Miss. | 24,145 |
| Joliet, Ill. | 80,378 | La Verne, Calif. | 12,965 |
| Jonesboro, Ark. | 27,050 | Lawndale, Calif. | 24,825 |
| Joplin, Mo. | 39,256 | Lawrence, Ind. | 16,646 |
| Junction City, Kans. | 19,018 | Lawrence, Kans. | 45,698 |
| | | Lawrence, Mass. | 66,915 |
| **K** | | Lawton, Okla. | 74,470 |
| Kailua, Hawaii | 33,783 | Layton, Utah | 13,603 |
| Kalamazoo, Mich. | 85,555 | Leavenworth, Kans. | 25,147 |
| Kaneohe, Hawaii | 29,903 | Lebanon, Pa. | 28,572 |
| Kankakee, Ill. | 30,944 | Lebanon, Tenn. | 12,492 |
| Kansas City, Kans. | 168,213 | Ledyard, Conn. | 14,558 |
| Kansas City, Mo. | 507,087 | Lee's Summit, Mo. | 16,230 |
| Kearney, Nebr. | 19,181 | Lenoir, N.C. | 14,705 |
| Kearny, N.J. | 37,585 | Leominster, Mass. | 32,939 |
| Keene, N.H. | 20,467 | Lewiston, Idaho | 26,068 |
| Kenmore, N.Y. | 20,980 | Lewiston, Me. | 41,779 |
| Kenner, La. | 29,858 | Lexington, Ky. | 108,137 |
| Kennewick, Wash. | 15,212 | Lexington, Mass. | 31,886 |
| Kenosha, Wis. | 78,805 | Lexington, N.C. | 17,205 |
| Kent, Ohio | 28,183 | Liberal, Kans. | 13,471 |
| Kent, Wash. | 21,510 | Liberty, Mo. | 13,679 |
| Kentwood, Mich. | 20,310 | Lima, Ohio | 53,734 |
| Keokuk, Iowa | 14,631 | Lincoln, Ill. | 17,582 |
| Kerrville, Tex. | 12,672 | Lincoln, Nebr. | 149,518 |
| Kettering, Ohio | 69,599 | Lincoln, R.I. | 16,182 |
| Kewanee, Ill. | 15,762 | Lincoln Park, Mich. | 52,984 |
| Key West, Fla. | 27,563 | Lincolnwood, Ill. | 12,929 |
| Killeen, Tex. | 35,507 | Linden, N.J. | 41,409 |
| Killingly, Conn. | 13,573 | Lindenhurst, N.Y. | 28,338 |
| Kingsport, Tenn. | 31,938 | Lindenwold, N.J. | 12,199 |
| Kingston, N.Y. | 25,544 | Little Rock, Ark. | 132,483 |
| Kingston, Pa. | 18,325 | Littleton, Colo. | 26,466 |
| Kingsville, Tex. | 28,711 | Livermore, Calif. | 37,703 |
| Kinston, N.C. | 22,309 | Livonia, Mich. | 110,109 |
| Kirkland, Wash. | 15,249 | Lockport, N.Y. | 25,399 |
| Kirksville, Mo. | 15,560 | Lodi, Calif. | 28,691 |
| Kirkwood, Mo. | 31,890 | Lodi, N.J. | 25,213 |
| Klamath Falls, Oreg. | 15,775 | Logan, Utah | 22,333 |
| Knoxville, Tenn. | 174,587 | Logansport, Ind. | 19,255 |
| Kokomo, Ind. | 44,042 | Lombard, Ill. | 35,977 |
| | | Lomita, Calif. | 19,784 |
| **L** | | Lompoc, Calif. | 25,284 |
| Lackawanna, N.Y. | 28,657 | Long Beach, Calif. | 358,633 |
| Laconia, N.H. | 14,888 | Long Beach, N.Y. | 33,127 |
| La Crosse, Wis. | 51,153 | Long Branch, N.J. | 31,744 |
| Lafayette, Calif. | 20,484 | Longmeadow, Mass. | 15,630 |
| Lafayette, Ind. | 44,955 | Longmont, Colo. | 23,209 |
| Lafayette, La. | 68,908 | Longview, Tex. | 45,547 |
| La Grange, Ga. | 23,301 | Longview, Wash. | 28,373 |
| La Grange, Ill. | 16,773 | Lorain, Ohio | 78,185 |
| La Grange Park, Ill. | 15,626 | Los Altos, Calif. | 24,956 |
| Laguna Beach, Calif. | 14,550 | Los Angeles, Calif. | 2,816,061 |
| La Habra, Calif. | 41,350 | Los Gatos, Calif. | 23,735 |
| Lake Charles, La. | 77,998 | Louisville, Ky. | 361,472 |
| Lake Forest, Ill. | 15,642 | Loveland, Colo. | 16,220 |
| Lake Jackson, Tex. | 13,376 | Loves Park, Ill. | 12,390 |

| | | | |
|---|---:|---|---:|
| Lowell, Mass. | 94,239 | Mequon, Wis. | 12,110 |
| Lower Burrell, Pa. | 13,654 | Merced, Calif. | 22,670 |
| Lubbock, Tex. | 149,101 | Mercer Island, Wash. | 19,047 |
| Ludlow, Mass. | 17,580 | Meriden, Conn. | 55,959 |
| Lufkin, Tex. | 23,049 | Meridian, Miss. | 45,083 |
| Lumberton, N.C. | 16,961 | Mesa, Ariz. | 62,853 |
| Lynbrook, N.Y. | 23,776 | Mesquite, Tex. | 55,131 |
| Lynchburg, Va. | 54,083 | Methuen, Mass. | 35,456 |
| Lyndhurst, Ohio | 19,749 | Metuchen, N.J. | 16,031 |
| Lynn, Mass. | 90,294 | Miami, Fla. | 334,859 |
| Lynnwood, Wash. | 16,919 | Miami, Okla. | 13,880 |
| Lynwood, Calif. | 43,353 | Miami Beach, Fla. | 87,072 |
| | | Miamisburg, Ohio | 14,797 |
| **M** | | Miami Springs, Fla. | 13,279 |
| | | Michigan City, Ind. | 39,369 |
| McAlester, Okla. | 18,802 | Middleboro, Mass. | 13,607 |
| McAllen, Tex. | 37,636 | Middleburg Heights, Ohio | 12,367 |
| McKeesport, Pa. | 37,977 | Middlesex, N.J. | 15,038 |
| McKinney, Tex. | 15,193 | Middletown, Conn. | 36,924 |
| Macomb, Ill. | 19,643 | Middletown, N.Y. | 22,607 |
| Macon, Ga. | 122,423 | Middletown, Ohio | 48,767 |
| Madera, Calif. | 16,044 | Middletown, R.I. | 29,621 |
| Madison, Ind. | 13,081 | Midland, Mich. | 35,176 |
| Madison, N.J. | 16,710 | Midland, Tex. | 59,463 |
| Madison, Wis. | 173,258 | Midlothian, Ill. | 15,939 |
| Madison Heights, Mich. | 38,599 | Midwest City, Okla. | 48,114 |
| Madisonville, Ky. | 15,332 | Milford, Conn. | 50,858 |
| Malden, Mass. | 56,127 | Milford, Mass. | 19,352 |
| Mamaroneck, N.Y. | 18,909 | Millbrae, Calif. | 20,781 |
| Manchester, Conn. | 47,994 | Millington, Tenn. | 21,106 |
| Manchester, N.H. | 87,754 | Mill Valley, Calif. | 12,942 |
| Manhattan, Kans. | 27,575 | Millville, N.J. | 21,366 |
| Manhattan Beach, Calif. | 35,352 | Milpitas, Calif. | 27,149 |
| Manitowoc, Wis. | 33,430 | Milton, Mass. | 27,190 |
| Mankato, Minn. | 30,895 | Milwaukee, Wis. | 717,099 |
| Mansfield, Conn. | 19,994 | Milwaukie, Oreg. | 16,379 |
| Mansfield, Ohio | 55,047 | Minden, La. | 13,996 |
| Manteca, Calif. | 13,845 | Mineola, N.Y. | 21,845 |
| Manville, N.J. | 13,029 | Mineral Wells, Tex. | 18,411 |
| Maple Heights, Ohio | 34,093 | Minneapolis, Minn. | 434,400 |
| Maplewood, Minn. | 25,222 | Minnetonka, Minn. | 35,776 |
| Maplewood, Mo. | 12,785 | Minot, N. Dak. | 32,290 |
| Marblehead, Mass. | 21,295 | Miramar, Fla. | 23,973 |
| Marietta, Ga. | 27,216 | Mishawaka, Ind. | 35,517 |
| Marietta, Ohio | 16,861 | Mission, Tex. | 13,043 |
| Marinette, Wis. | 12,696 | Missoula, Mont. | 29,497 |
| Marion, Ind. | 39,607 | Mitchell, S. Dak. | 13,425 |
| Marion, Iowa | 18,028 | Moberly, Mo. | 12,988 |
| Marion, Ohio | 38,646 | Mobile, Ala. | 190,026 |
| Markham, Ill. | 15,987 | Modesto, Calif. | 61,712 |
| Marlboro, Mass. | 27,936 | Moline, Ill. | 46,237 |
| Marquette, Mich. | 21,967 | Monessen, Pa. | 15,216 |
| Marshall, Tex. | 22,937 | Monroe, Conn. | 12,047 |
| Marshalltown, Iowa | 26,219 | Monroe, La. | 56,374 |
| Marshfield, Mass. | 15,223 | Monroe, Mich. | 23,894 |
| Marshfield, Wis. | 15,619 | Monroeville, Pa. | 29,011 |
| Martinez, Calif. | 16,506 | Monrovia, Calif. | 30,015 |
| Martinsburg, W. Va. | 14,626 | Montclair, Calif. | 22,546 |
| Martinsville, Va. | 19,653 | Montclair, N.J. | 44,043 |
| Maryville, Tenn. | 13,808 | Montebello, Calif. | 42,807 |
| Mason City, Iowa | 30,491 | Monterey, Calif. | 26,302 |
| Massapequa Park, N.Y. | 22,112 | Monterey Park, Calif. | 49,166 |
| Massena, N.Y. | 14,042 | Montgomery, Ala. | 133,386 |
| Massillon, Ohio | 32,539 | Montville, Conn. | 15,662 |
| Mattoon, Ill. | 19,681 | Moore, Okla. | 18,761 |
| Maumee, Ohio | 15,937 | Moorhead, Minn. | 29,687 |
| Mayfield Heights, Ohio | 22,139 | Morgan City, La. | 16,586 |
| Maywood, Calif. | 16,996 | Morganton, N.C. | 13,625 |
| Maywood, Ill. | 30,036 | Morgantown, W. Va. | 29,431 |
| Meadville, Pa. | 16,573 | Morristown, N.J. | 17,662 |
| Medford, Mass. | 64,397 | Morristown, Tenn. | 20,318 |
| Medford, Oreg. | 28,454 | Morton Grove, Ill. | 26,369 |
| Melbourne, Fla. | 40,236 | Moscow, Idaho | 14,146 |
| Melrose, Mass. | 33,180 | Moss Point, Miss. | 19,321 |
| Melrose Park, Ill. | 22,706 | Moultrie, Ga. | 14,302 |
| Melvindale, Mich. | 13,862 | Moundsville, W. Va. | 13,560 |
| Memphis, Tenn. | 623,530 | Mountain Brook, Ala. | 19,474 |
| Menasha, Wis. | 14,905 | Mountain View, Calif. | 51,092 |
| Menlo Park, Calif. | 26,734 | Mount Clemens, Mich. | 20,476 |
| Menomonee Falls, Wis. | 31,697 | Mountlake Terrace, Wash. | 16,600 |
| Mentor, Ohio | 36,912 | | |

| | | | |
|---|---|---|---|
| Mount Pleasant, Mich. | 20,504 | Niles, Ill. | 31,432 |
| Mount Prospect, Ill. | 34,995 | Niles, Mich. | 12,988 |
| Mount Vernon, Ill. | 15,980 | Niles, Ohio | 21,581 |
| Mount Vernon, N.Y. | 72,778 | Norco, Calif. | 14,511 |
| Mount Vernon, Ohio | 13,373 | Norfolk, Nebr. | 16,607 |
| Muncie, Ind. | 69,080 | Norfolk, Va. | 307,951 |
| Mundelein, Ill. | 16,128 | Normal, Ill. | 26,396 |
| Munhall, Pa. | 16,674 | Norman, Okla. | 52,117 |
| Munster, Ind. | 16,514 | Norridge, Ill. | 16,880 |
| Murfreesboro, Tenn. | 26,360 | Norristown, Pa. | 38,169 |
| Murray, Ky. | 13,537 | North Adams, Mass. | 19,195 |
| Murray, Utah | 21,206 | Northampton, Mass. | 29,664 |
| Muscatine, Iowa | 22,405 | North Andover, Mass. | 16,284 |
| Muskegon, Mich. | 44,631 | North Arlington, N.J. | 18,096 |
| Muskegon Heights, Mich. | 17,304 | North Attleboro, Mass. | 18,665 |
| Muskogee, Okla. | 37,331 | North Augusta, S.C. | 12,883 |
| | | Northbrook, Ill. | 27,297 |
| **N** | | North Canton, Ohio | 15,228 |
| Nacogdoches, Tex. | 22,544 | North Chicago, Ill. | 47,275 |
| Nampa, Idaho | 20,768 | North College Hill, Ohio | 12,363 |
| Nanticoke, Pa. | 14,632 | North Glenn, Colo. | 27,937 |
| Napa, Calif. | 35,978 | North Haven, Conn. | 22,194 |
| Naperville, Ill. | 23,885 | North Kingstown, R.I. | 27,673 |
| Naples, Fla. | 12,042 | Northlake, Ill. | 14,212 |
| Nashua, N.H. | 55,820 | North Las Vegas, Nev. | 36,216 |
| Nashville, Tenn. | 447,877 | North Little Rock, Ark. | 60,040 |
| Natchez, Miss. | 19,704 | North Miami, Fla. | 34,767 |
| Natchitoches, La. | 15,974 | North Miami Beach, Fla. | 30,723 |
| Natick, Mass. | 31,057 | North Olmsted, Ohio | 34,861 |
| National City, Calif. | 43,184 | North Plainfield, N.J. | 21,796 |
| Naugatuck, Conn. | 23,034 | North Platte, Nebr. | 19,447 |
| Nederland, Tex. | 16,810 | North Providence, R.I. | 24,337 |
| Needham, Mass. | 29,748 | North Richland Hills, Tex. | 16,514 |
| Neenah, Wis. | 22,892 | North Ridgeville, Ohio | 13,152 |
| New Albany, Ind. | 38,402 | North Royalton, Ohio | 12,807 |
| Newark, Calif. | 27,153 | North Tonawanda, N.Y. | 36,012 |
| Newark, Del. | 20,757 | Norton, Ohio | 12,308 |
| Newark, N.J. | 382,417 | Norton Shores, Mich. | 22,271 |
| Newark, Ohio | 41,836 | Norwalk, Calif. | 91,827 |
| New Bedford, Mass. | 101,777 | Norwalk, Conn. | 79,113 |
| New Berlin, Wis. | 26,937 | Norwalk, Ohio | 13,386 |
| New Bern, N.C. | 14,660 | Norwich, Conn. | 41,433 |
| New Braunfels, Tex. | 17,859 | Norwood, Mass. | 30,815 |
| New Brighton, Minn. | 19,507 | Norwood, Ohio | 30,420 |
| New Britain, Conn. | 83,441 | Novato, Calif. | 31,006 |
| New Brunswick, N.J. | 41,885 | Nutley, N.J. | 32,099 |
| Newburgh, N.Y. | 26,219 | | |
| Newburyport, Mass. | 15,807 | **O** | |
| New Canaan, Conn. | 17,455 | Oak Creek, Wis. | 13,901 |
| New Carrollton, Md. | 13,395 | Oak Forest, Ill. | 17,870 |
| New Castle, Ind. | 21,215 | Oakland, Calif. | 361,561 |
| New Castle, Pa. | 38,559 | Oakland, N.J. | 14,420 |
| New Haven, Conn. | 137,707 | Oakland Park, Fla. | 16,261 |
| New Hope, Minn. | 23,180 | Oak Lawn, Ill. | 60,305 |
| New Iberia, La. | 30,147 | Oak Park, Ill. | 62,511 |
| Newington, Conn. | 26,037 | Oak Park, Mich. | 36,762 |
| New Kensington, Pa. | 20,312 | Oak Ridge, Tenn. | 28,319 |
| New London, Conn. | 31,630 | Ocala, Fla. | 22,583 |
| New Milford, Conn. | 14,601 | Oceanside, Calif. | 40,494 |
| New Milford, N.J. | 20,201 | Odessa, Tex. | 78,380 |
| New Orleans, La. | 593,471 | Ogden, Utah | 69,478 |
| New Philadelphia, Ohio | 15,184 | Ogdensburg, N.Y. | 14,554 |
| Newport, Ky. | 25,998 | Oil City, Pa. | 15,033 |
| Newport, R.I. | 34,562 | Oklahoma City, Okla. | 366,481 |
| Newport Beach, Calif. | 49,422 | Okmulgee, Okla. | 15,180 |
| Newport News, Va. | 138,177 | Olathe, Kans. | 17,917 |
| New Providence, N.J. | 13,796 | Olean, N.Y. | 19,169 |
| New Rochelle, N.Y. | 75,385 | Olympia, Wash. | 23,111 |
| Newton, Iowa | 15,619 | Omaha, Nebr. | 347,328 |
| Newton, Kans. | 15,439 | Oneonta, N.Y. | 16,030 |
| Newton, Mass. | 91,066 | Ontario, Calif. | 64,118 |
| Newton, Conn. | 16,942 | Opelika, Ala. | 19,027 |
| New Ulm, Minn. | 13,051 | Opelousas, La. | 20,121 |
| New York City, N.Y. | 7,867,760 | Orange, Calif. | 77,374 |
| Bronx | 1,472,216 | Orange, Conn. | 13,524 |
| Brooklyn | 2,601,852 | Orange, N.J. | 32,566 |
| Manhattan | 1,524,541 | Orange, Tex. | 24,457 |
| Queens | 1,973,708 | Orangeburg, S.C. | 13,252 |
| Richmond | 295,443 | Oregon, Ohio | 16,563 |
| Niagara Falls, N.Y. | 85,615 | Orem, Utah | 25,729 |

| | |
|---|---|
| Ridgefield Park, N.J. | 14,453 |
| Ridgewood, N.J. | 27,547 |
| Riverdale, Ill. | 15,806 |
| River Edge, N.J. | 12,850 |
| River Forest, Ill. | 13,402 |
| River Rouge, Mich. | 15,947 |
| Riverside, Calif. | 140,089 |
| Riviera Beach, Fla. | 21,401 |
| Roanoke, Va. | 92,115 |
| Roanoke Rapids, N.C. | 13,508 |
| Robbinsdale, Minn. | 16,845 |
| Rochester, Minn. | 53,766 |
| Rochester, N.H. | 17,938 |
| Rochester, N.Y. | 296,233 |
| Rockford, Ill. | 147,370 |
| Rock Hill, S.C. | 33,846 |
| Rock Island, Ill. | 50,166 |
| Rockland, Mass. | 15,674 |
| Rockville, Md. | 41,564 |
| Rockville Centre, N.Y. | 27,444 |
| Rocky Mount, N.C. | 34,284 |
| Rocky River, Ohio | 22,958 |
| Rolla, Mo. | 13,245 |
| Rolling Meadows, Ill. | 19,178 |
| Rome, Ga. | 30,759 |
| Rome, N.Y. | 50,148 |
| Romeoville, Ill. | 12,674 |
| Roseburg, Oreg. | 14,461 |
| Roselle, N.J. | 22,585 |
| Roselle Park, N.J. | 14,277 |
| Rosemead, Calif. | 40,972 |
| Rosenberg, Tex. | 12,098 |
| Roseville, Calif. | 17,895 |
| Roseville, Mich. | 60,529 |
| Roseville, Minn. | 34,518 |
| Roswell, N. Mex. | 33,908 |
| Roy, Utah | 14,356 |
| Royal Oak, Mich. | 85,499 |
| Ruston, La. | 17,365 |
| Rutherford, N.J. | 20,802 |
| Rutland, Vt. | 19,293 |
| Rye, N.Y. | 15,869 |

**S**

| | |
|---|---|
| Sacramento, Calif. | 254,413 |
| Saginaw, Mich. | 91,849 |
| St. Albans, W. Va. | 14,356 |
| St. Ann, Mo. | 18,215 |
| St. Augustine, Fla. | 12,352 |
| St. Charles, Ill. | 12,928 |
| St. Charles, Mo. | 31,834 |
| St. Clair Shores, Mich. | 88,093 |
| St. Cloud, Minn. | 39,691 |
| St. Joseph, Mo. | 72,691 |
| St. Louis, Mo. | 622,236 |
| St. Louis Park, Minn. | 48,883 |
| St. Matthews, Ky. | 13,152 |
| St. Paul, Minn. | 309,980 |
| St. Petersburg, Fla. | 216,232 |
| Salem, Mass. | 40,556 |
| Salem, N.H. | 20,142 |
| Salem, Ohio | 14,186 |
| Salem, Oreg. | 68,296 |
| Salem, Va. | 21,982 |
| Salina, Kans. | 37,714 |
| Salinas, Calif. | 58,896 |
| Salisbury, Md. | 15,252 |
| Salisbury, N.C. | 22,515 |
| Salt Lake City, Utah | 175,885 |
| San Angelo, Tex. | 63,884 |
| San Anselmo, Calif. | 13,031 |
| San Antonio, Tex. | 654,153 |
| San Benito, Tex. | 15,176 |
| San Bernardino, Calif. | 104,251 |
| San Bruno, Calif. | 36,254 |
| San Carlos, Calif. | 25,924 |
| San Clemente, Calif. | 17,063 |
| San Diego, Calif. | 696,769 |
| San Dimas, Calif. | 15,692 |
| Sandusky, Ohio | 32,674 |

| | |
|---|---|
| San Fernando, Calif. | 16,571 |
| Sanford, Fla. | 17,393 |
| Sanford, Me. | 15,812 |
| San Francisco, Calif. | 715,674 |
| San Gabriel, Calif. | 29,176 |
| San Jose, Calif. | 445,779 |
| San Leandro, Calif. | 68,698 |
| San Luis Obispo, Calif. | 28,036 |
| San Marcos, Tex. | 18,860 |
| San Marino, Calif. | 14,177 |
| San Mateo, Calif. | 78,991 |
| San Pablo, Calif. | 21,461 |
| San Rafael, Calif. | 38,977 |
| Santa Ana, Calif. | 156,601 |
| Santa Barbara, Calif. | 70,215 |
| Santa Clara, Calif. | 87,717 |
| Santa Cruz, Calif. | 32,076 |
| Santa Fe, N. Mex. | 41,167 |
| Santa Fe Springs, Calif. | 14,750 |
| Santa Maria, Calif. | 32,749 |
| Santa Monica, Calif. | 88,289 |
| Santa Paula, Calif. | 18,001 |
| Santa Rosa, Calif. | 50,006 |
| Sapulpa, Okla. | 15,159 |
| Sarasota, Fla. | 40,237 |
| Saratoga, Calif. | 27,110 |
| Saratoga Springs, N.Y. | 18,845 |
| Saugus, Mass. | 25,110 |
| Sault Ste. Marie, Mich. | 15,136 |
| Savannah, Ga. | 118,349 |
| Sayreville, N.J. | 32,508 |
| Scarsdale, N.Y. | 19,229 |
| Schaumburg, Ill. | 18,730 |
| Schenectady, N.Y. | 77,859 |
| Schiller Park, Ill. | 12,712 |
| Schofield Barracks, Hawaii | 13,516 |
| Scituate, Mass. | 16,973 |
| Scottsbluff, Nebr. | 14,507 |
| Scottsdale, Ariz. | 67,823 |
| Scranton, Pa. | 103,564 |
| Seal Beach, Calif. | 24,441 |
| Seaside, Calif. | 35,935 |
| Seattle, Wash. | 530,831 |
| Secaucus, N.J. | 13,228 |
| Sedalia, Mo. | 22,847 |
| Seguin, Tex. | 15,934 |
| Selma, Ala. | 27,379 |
| Seven Hills, Ohio | 12,700 |
| Seymour, Conn. | 12,776 |
| Seymour, Ind. | 13,352 |
| Shaker Heights, Ohio | 36,306 |
| Sharon, Mass. | 12,367 |
| Sharon, Pa. | 22,653 |
| Shawnee, Kans. | 20,482 |
| Shawnee, Okla. | 25,075 |
| Sheboygan, Wis. | 48,484 |
| Sheffield, Ala. | 13,115 |
| Shelby, N.C. | 16,328 |
| Shelbyville, Ind. | 15,094 |
| Shelbyville, Tenn. | 12,262 |
| Shelton, Conn. | 27,165 |
| Sherman, Tex. | 29,061 |
| Shively, Ky. | 19,223 |
| Shorewood, Wis. | 15,576 |
| Shreveport, La. | 182,064 |
| Shrewsbury, Mass. | 19,196 |
| Sidney, Ohio | 16,332 |
| Sierra Madre, Calif. | 12,140 |
| Sikeston, Mo. | 14,699 |
| Simi Valley, Calif. | 56,464 |
| Simsbury, Conn. | 17,475 |
| Sioux City, Iowa | 85,925 |
| Sioux Falls, S. Dak. | 72,488 |
| Skokie, Ill. | 68,627 |
| Slidell, La. | 16,101 |
| Smithfield, R.I. | 13,468 |
| Smyrna, Ga. | 19,157 |
| Somerset, Mass. | 18,088 |
| Somerville, Mass. | 88,779 |
| Somerville, N.J. | 13,652 |

| | |
|---|---|
| South Bend, Ind. | 125,580 |
| Southbridge, Mass. | 17,057 |
| South Charleston, W. Va. | 16,333 |
| South El Monte, Calif. | 13,443 |
| South Euclid, Ohio. | 29,579 |
| Southfield, Mich. | 69,285 |
| South Gate, Calif. | 56,909 |
| Southgate, Mich. | 33,909 |
| South Hadley, Mass. | 17,033 |
| South Holland, Ill. | 23,931 |
| Southington, Conn. | 30,946 |
| South Kingstown, R.I. | 16,913 |
| South Lake Tahoe, Calif. | 12,921 |
| South Miami, Fla. | 19,571 |
| South Milwaukee, Wis. | 23,297 |
| South Orange, N.J. | 16,971 |
| South Pasadena, Calif. | 22,979 |
| South Plainfield, N.J. | 21,142 |
| South Portland, Me. | 23,267 |
| South River, N.J. | 15,428 |
| South St. Paul, Minn. | 25,016 |
| South San Francisco, Calif. | 46,646 |
| South Windsor, Conn. | 15,553 |
| Sparks, Nev. | 24,187 |
| Spartanburg, S.C. | 44,546 |
| Speedway, Ind. | 15,056 |
| Spokane, Wash. | 170,516 |
| Springdale, Ark. | 16,783 |
| Springfield, Ill. | 91,753 |
| Springfield, Mass. | 163,905 |
| Springfield, Mo. | 120,096 |
| Springfield, Ohio. | 81,926 |
| Springfield, Oreg. | 27,047 |
| Spring Valley, N.Y. | 18,112 |
| Stamford, Conn. | 108,798 |
| Stanton, Calif. | 17,947 |
| State College, Pa. | 33,778 |
| Statesboro, Ga. | 14,616 |
| Statesville, N.C. | 19,996 |
| Staunton, Va. | 24,504 |
| Sterling, Ill. | 16,113 |
| Sterling Heights, Mich. | 61,365 |
| Steubenville, Ohio. | 30,771 |
| Stevens Point, Wis. | 23,479 |
| Stillwater, Okla. | 31,126 |
| Stockton, Calif. | 107,644 |
| Stoneham, Mass. | 20,725 |
| Stonington, Conn. | 15,940 |
| Stoughton, Mass. | 23,459 |
| Stow, Ohio. | 19,847 |
| Stratford, Conn. | 49,775 |
| Streamwood, Ill. | 18,176 |
| Streator, Ill. | 15,600 |
| Strongsville, Ohio. | 15,182 |
| Struthers, Ohio. | 15,343 |
| Sudbury, Mass. | 13,506 |
| Sulphur, La. | 13,551 |
| Summit, N.J. | 23,620 |
| Sumter, S.C. | 24,435 |
| Sunbury, Pa. | 13,025 |
| Sunnyvale, Calif. | 95,408 |
| Superior, Wis. | 32,237 |
| Swampscott, Mass. | 13,578 |
| Swansea, Mass. | 12,640 |
| Sweetwater, Tex. | 12,020 |
| Swissvale, Pa. | 13,821 |
| Sylacauga, Ala. | 12,255 |
| Sylvania, Ohio. | 12,031 |
| Syracuse, N.Y. | 197,208 |

## T

| | |
|---|---|
| Tacoma, Wash. | 154,581 |
| Takoma Park, Md. | 18,455 |
| Talladega, Ala. | 17,662 |
| Tallahassee, Fla. | 71,897 |
| Tallmadge, Ohio. | 15,274 |
| Tampa, Fla. | 277,767 |
| Taunton, Mass. | 43,756 |

| | |
|---|---|
| Taylor, Mich. | 70,020 |
| Tempe, Ariz. | 62,907 |
| Temple, Tex. | 33,431 |
| Temple City, Calif. | 29,673 |
| Tenafly, N.J. | 14,827 |
| Terre Haute, Ind. | 70,286 |
| Terrell, Tex. | 14,182 |
| Tewksbury, Mass. | 22,755 |
| Texarkana, Ark. | 21,682 |
| Texarkana, Tex. | 30,497 |
| Texas City, Tex. | 38,908 |
| The Village, Okla. | 13,695 |
| Thibodaux, La. | 14,925 |
| Thomasville, Ga. | 18,155 |
| Thomasville, N.C. | 15,230 |
| Thornton, Colo. | 13,326 |
| Thousand Oaks, Calif. | 36,334 |
| Tiffin, Ohio. | 21,596 |
| Tifton, Ga. | 12,179 |
| Tinley Park, Ill. | 12,382 |
| Titusville, Fla. | 30,515 |
| Tiverton, R.I. | 12,559 |
| Toledo, Ohio. | 383,818 |
| Tonawanda, N.Y. | 21,898 |
| Tooele, Utah. | 12,539 |
| Topeka, Kans. | 125,011 |
| Torrance, Calif. | 134,584 |
| Torrington, Conn. | 31,952 |
| Tracy, Calif. | 14,724 |
| Traverse City, Mich. | 18,048 |
| Trenton, Mich. | 24,127 |
| Trenton, N.J. | 104,638 |
| Troy, Mich. | 39,419 |
| Troy, N.Y. | 62,918 |
| Troy, Ohio. | 17,186 |
| Trumbull, Conn. | 31,394 |
| Tucson, Ariz. | 262,933 |
| Tulare, Calif. | 16,235 |
| Tullahoma, Tenn. | 15,311 |
| Tulsa, Okla. | 331,638 |
| Tupelo, Miss. | 20,471 |
| Turlock, Calif. | 13,992 |
| Tuscaloosa, Ala. | 65,773 |
| Tustin, Calif. | 21,178 |
| Twin Falls, Idaho. | 21,914 |
| Two Rivers, Wis. | 13,553 |
| Tyler, Tex. | 57,770 |

## U

| | |
|---|---|
| Union City, Calif. | 14,724 |
| Union City, N.J. | 58,537 |
| Uniontown, Pa. | 16,282 |
| University City, Mo. | 46,309 |
| University Heights, Ohio. | 17,055 |
| University Park, Tex. | 23,498 |
| Upland, Calif. | 32,551 |
| Upper Arlington, Ohio. | 38,630 |
| Urbana, Ill. | 32,800 |
| Urbandale, Iowa. | 14,434 |
| Utica, N.Y. | 91,611 |

## V

| | |
|---|---|
| Vacaville, Calif. | 21,690 |
| Valdosta, Ga. | 32,303 |
| Vallejo, Calif. | 66,733 |
| Valley Stream, N.Y. | 40,413 |
| Valparaiso, Ind. | 20,020 |
| Vancouver, Wash. | 42,493 |
| Ventura (San Buenaventura), Calif. | 55,797 |
| Vernon, Conn. | 27,237 |
| Verona, N.J. | 15,067 |
| Vicksburg, Miss. | 25,478 |
| Victoria, Tex. | 41,349 |
| Vienna, Va. | 17,152 |
| Villa Park, Ill. | 25,891 |
| Vincennes, Ind. | 19,867 |
| Vineland, N.J. | 47,399 |
| Virginia, Minn. | 12,450 |
| Virginia Beach, Va. | 172,106 |

# Population of the United States in 1970

## SUMMARY BY STATES AND DEPENDENCIES
(Figures in parentheses give rank of states in population)

**THE STATES AND THE DISTRICT OF COLUMBIA**

| State | Rank | Population |
|---|---|---|
| Alabama | (21) | 3,444,165 |
| Alaska | (50) | 302,173 |
| Arizona | (33) | 1,772,482 |
| Arkansas | (32) | 1,923,295 |
| California | (1) | 19,953,134 |
| Colorado | (30) | 2,207,259 |
| Connecticut | (24) | 3,032,217 |
| Delaware | (46) | 548,104 |
| District of Columbia | | 756,510 |
| Florida | (9) | 6,789,443 |
| Georgia | (15) | 4,589,575 |
| Hawaii | (40) | 768,561 |
| Idaho | (42) | 712,567 |
| Illinois | (5) | 11,113,976 |
| Indiana | (11) | 5,193,669 |
| Iowa | (25) | 2,825,041 |
| Kansas | (28) | 2,249,071 |
| Kentucky | (23) | 3,219,311 |
| Louisiana | (20) | 3,643,180 |
| Maine | (38) | 992,048 |
| Maryland | (18) | 3,922,399 |
| Massachusetts | (10) | 5,689,170 |
| Michigan | (7) | 8,875,083 |
| Minnesota | (19) | 3,805,069 |
| Mississippi | (29) | 2,216,912 |
| Missouri | (13) | 4,677,399 |
| Montana | (43) | 694,409 |
| Nebraska | (35) | 1,483,791 |
| Nevada | (47) | 488,738 |
| New Hampshire | (41) | 737,681 |
| New Jersey | (8) | 7,168,164 |
| New Mexico | (37) | 1,016,000 |
| New York | (2) | 18,190,740 |
| North Carolina | (12) | 5,082,059 |
| North Dakota | (45) | 617,761 |
| Ohio | (6) | 10,652,017 |
| Oklahoma | (27) | 2,559,253 |
| Oregon | (31) | 2,091,385 |
| Pennsylvania | (3) | 11,793,909 |
| Rhode Island | (39) | 949,723 |
| South Carolina | (26) | 2,590,516 |
| South Dakota | (44) | 665,507 |
| Tennessee | (17) | 3,924,164 |
| Texas | (4) | 11,196,730 |
| Utah | (36) | 1,059,273 |
| Vermont | (48) | 444,330 |
| Virginia | (14) | 4,648,494 |
| Washington | (22) | 3,409,169 |
| West Virginia | (34) | 1,744,237 |
| Wisconsin | (16) | 4,417,933 |
| Wyoming | (49) | 332,416 |
| **TOTAL** | | **203,184,772** |

**DEPENDENCIES**

| | |
|---|---|
| American Samoa | 27,159 |
| Canal Zone | 44,198 |
| Guam | 84,996 |
| Puerto Rico | 2,712,033 |
| Trust Territory of the Pacific Islands | 90,940 |
| Virgin Islands of the U.S. | 62,468 |
| **TOTAL** | **3,021,794** |
| TOTAL U.S. & Dependencies | 206,206,566 |

# Population of Places in Canada

*Having 12,000 or More Inhabitants in 1971*

|  |  |
|---|---|
| Ajax, Ont. | 12,515 |
| Alma, Que. | 22,622 |
| Anjou, Que. | 33,886 |
| Arvida, Que. | 18,448 |
| Aurora, Ont. | 13,614 |
| Baie-Comeau, Que. | 12,109 |
| Barrie, Ont. | 27,676 |
| Bathurst, N.B. | 16,674 |
| Beaconsfield, Que. | 19,389 |
| Beauport, Que. | 14,681 |
| Belleville, Ont. | 35,128 |
| Beloeil, Que. | 12,274 |
| Boucherville, Que. | 19,997 |
| Brampton, Ont. | 41,211 |
| Brandon, Man. | 31,150 |
| Brantford, Ont. | 64,421 |
| Brockville, Ont. | 19,765 |
| Brossard, Que. | 23,452 |
| Burlington, Ont. | 87,023 |
| Calgary, Alta. | 403,319 |
| Cap-de-la-Madeleine, Que. | 31,463 |
| Charlesbourg, Que. | 33,443 |
| Charlottetown, P.E.I. | 19,133 |
| Châteauguay, Que. | 15,797 |
| Châteauguay-Centre, Que. | 17,942 |
| Chatham, Ont. | 35,317 |
| Chicoutimi, Que. | 33,893 |
| Chicoutimi-Nord, Que. | 14,086 |
| Corner Brook, Nfld. | 26,309 |
| Cornwall, Ont. | 47,116 |
| Côte-St-Luc, Que. | 24,375 |
| Cranbrook, B.C. | 12,000 |
| Dartmouth, N.S. | 64,770 |
| Dollard-des-Ormeaux, Que. | 25,217 |
| Dorval, Que. | 20,469 |
| Drummondville, Que. | 31,813 |
| Dundas, Ont. | 17,208 |
| East Kildonan, Man. | 30,152 |
| Edmonton, Alta. | 438,152 |
| Edmundston, N.B. | 12,365 |
| Fort Erie, Ont. | 23,113 |
| Fredericton, N.B. | 24,254 |
| Galt, Ont. | 38,897 |
| Gaspé, Que. | 17,211 |
| Gatineau, Que. | 22,321 |
| Georgetown, Ont. | 17,053 |
| Giffard, Que. | 13,135 |
| Glace Bay, N.S. | 22,440 |
| Granby, Que. | 34,385 |
| Grande Prairie, Alta. | 13,079 |
| Grand'Mère, Que. | 17,137 |
| Greenfield Park, Que. | 15,348 |
| Grimsby, Ont. | 15,770 |
| Guelph, Ont. | 60,087 |
| Halifax, N.S. | 122,035 |
| Hamilton, Ont. | 309,173 |
| Hauterive, Que. | 13,181 |
| Hull, Que. | 63,580 |
| Joliette, Que. | 20,127 |
| Jonquière, Que. | 28,430 |

|  |  |  |  |
|---|---|---|---|
| Kamloops, B.C. | 26,168 | Richmond Hill, Ont. | 32,384 |
| Kapuskasing, Ont. | 12,834 | Rimouski, Que. | 26,887 |
| Kelowna, B.C. | 19,412 | Rivière-du-Loup, Que. | 12,760 |
| Kingston, Ont. | 59,047 | Rouyn, Que. | 17,821 |
| Kitchener, Ont. | 111,804 | St. Boniface, Man. | 46,714 |
| Lachine, Que. | 44,423 | St-Bruno-de-Montarville, Que. | 15,780 |
| Laflèche, Que. | 15,113 | St. Catharines, Ont. | 109,722 |
| LaSalle, Que. | 72,912 | Ste-Foy, Que. | 68,385 |
| La Tuque, Que. | 13,099 | Ste-Scholastique, Que. | 14,787 |
| Lauzon, Que. | 12,809 | Ste-Thérèse, Que. | 17,175 |
| Laval, Que. | 228,010 | St-Hubert, Que. | 21,741 |
| Lethbridge, Alta. | 41,217 | St-Hyacinthe, Que. | 24,562 |
| Lévis, Que. | 15,597 | St. James, Man. | 71,431 |
| Lincoln, Ont. | 14,247 | St-Jean, Que. | 32,863 |
| Lindsay, Ont. | 12,746 | St-Jerôme, Que. | 26,524 |
| London, Ont. | 223,222 | Saint John, N.B. | 89,039 |
| Longueuil, Que. | 97,590 | St. John's, Nfld. | 88,102 |
| Magog, Que. | 13,281 | St-Lambert, Que. | 18,616 |
| Markham, Ont. | 36,684 | St-Laurent, Que. | 62,955 |
| Medicine Hat, Alta. | 26,518 | St-Léonard, Que. | 52,040 |
| Mississauga, Ont. | 156,070 | St. Thomas, Ont. | 25,545 |
| Moncton, N.B. | 47,891 | St. Vital, Man. | 32,963 |
| Montmagny, Que. | 12,432 | Sarnia, Ont. | 57,644 |
| Montreal, Que. | 1,214,352 | Saskatoon, Sask. | 126,449 |
| Montreal-Nord, Que. | 89,139 | Sault Ste. Marie, Ont. | 80,332 |
| Mont-Royal, Que. | 21,561 | Sept-Iles, Que. | 24,320 |
| Moose Jaw, Sask. | 31,854 | Shawinigan, Que. | 27,792 |
| Nanaimo, B.C. | 14,948 | Sherbrooke, Que. | 80,711 |
| Newmarket, Ont. | 18,941 | Sillery, Que. | 13,932 |
| New Westminster, B.C. | 42,835 | Sorel, Que. | 19,347 |
| Niagara Falls, Ont. | 67,163 | Stratford, Ont. | 24,508 |
| Niagara-on-the-Lake, Ont. | 12,552 | Sudbury, Ont. | 90,535 |
| North Battleford, Sask. | 12,698 | Swift Current, Sask. | 15,415 |
| North Bay, Ont. | 49,187 | Sydney, N.S. | 33,230 |
| North Vancouver, B.C. | 31,847 | Thetford Mines, Que. | 22,003 |
| Oakville, Ont. | 61,483 | Thompson, Man. | 19,001 |
| Orillia, Ont. | 24,040 | Thorold, Ont. | 15,065 |
| Orsainville, Que. | 12,520 | Thunder Bay, Ont. | 108,411 |
| Oshawa, Ont. | 91,587 | Timmins, Ont. | 28,542 |
| Ottawa, Ont. | 302,341 | Toronto, Ont. | 712,786 |
| Outremont, Que. | 28,552 | Transcona, Man. | 22,490 |
| Owen Sound, Ont. | 18,469 | Trenton, Ont. | 14,589 |
| Pembroke, Ont. | 16,544 | Trois-Rivières, Que. | 55,869 |
| Penticton, B.C. | 18,146 | Truro, N.S. | 13,047 |
| Peterborough, Ont. | 58,111 | Val-d'Or, Que. | 17,421 |
| Pierrefonds, Que. | 33,010 | Valleyfield, Que. | 30,173 |
| Pointe-aux-Trembles, Que. | 35,567 | Vancouver, B.C. | 426,256 |
| Pointe-Claire, Que. | 27,303 | Vanier, Ont. | 22,477 |
| Pointe-Gatineau, Que. | 15,640 | Vaughan, Ont. | 15,873 |
| Portage la Prairie, Man. | 12,950 | Verdun, Que. | 74,718 |
| Port Alberni, B.C. | 20,063 | Vernon, B.C. | 13,283 |
| Port Colborne, Ont. | 21,420 | Victoria, B.C. | 61,761 |
| Port Coquitlam, B.C. | 19,560 | Victoriaville, Que. | 22,047 |
| Preston, Ont. | 16,723 | Waterloo, Ont. | 36,677 |
| Prince Albert, Sask. | 28,464 | Welland, Ont. | 44,397 |
| Prince George, B.C. | 33,101 | West Kildonan, Man. | 23,959 |
| Prince Rupert, B.C. | 15,747 | Westmount, Que. | 23,606 |
| Quebec, Que. | 186,088 | Whitby, Ont. | 25,324 |
| Red Deer, Alta. | 27,674 | Windsor, Ont. | 203,300 |
| Regina, Sask. | 139,469 | Winnipeg, Man. | 246,246 |
| Repentigny, Que. | 19,520 | Woodstock, Ont. | 26,173 |
|  |  | Yorkton, Sask. | 13,430 |

# Population of Canada

*Estimated June 1, 1971*

## SUMMARY BY PROVINCES AND TERRITORIES

| Province | Population | Province | Population |
|---|---|---|---|
| Alberta | 1,634,000 | Prince Edward Island | 111,000 |
| British Columbia | 2,196,000 | Quebec | 6,030,000 |
| Manitoba | 988,000 | Saskatchewan | 928,000 |
| New Brunswick | 632,000 | Yukon Territory | 17,000 |
| Newfoundland | 524,000 | Northwest Territories | 36,000 |
| Nova Scotia | 770,000 |  |  |
| Ontario | 7,815,000 | TOTAL | 21,681,000 |

# Signs and Symbols

## Astronomy

| | | | |
|---|---|---|---|
| ☉ | the sun; Sunday | ⊕, ⊖, or ♁ | the earth |
| ☽, ☾, or ☽ | the moon; Monday | ♂ | Mars; Tuesday |
| ● | new moon | ♃ | Jupiter; Thursday |
| ☽, ◐, ☽, ) | first quarter | ♄ or ♄ | Saturn; Saturday |
| ○ or 🌕 | full moon | ♅, ⛢, or ♅ | Uranus |
| ☾, ◑, ☾, ☾ | last quarter | ♆, ♆, or ♆ | Neptune |
| ☿ | Mercury; Wednesday | ♇ | Pluto |
| ♀ | Venus; Friday | ☄ | comet |
| | | * or ✳ | fixed star |

## Business

| | | | |
|---|---|---|---|
| a/c | account ⟨in a/c with⟩ | % | percent |
| @ | at; each ⟨4 apples @ 5¢ = 20¢⟩ | ‰ | per thousand |
| ℔ | per | $ | dollars |
| c/o | care of | ¢ | cents |
| # | number if it precedes a numeral ⟨track #3⟩; pounds if it follows ⟨a 5# sack of sugar⟩ | £ | pounds |
| | | / | shillings |
| | | © | copyrighted |
| ℔ | pound; pounds | ® | registered trademark |

## Mathematics

| | |
|---|---|
| + | plus; positive ⟨$a+b=c$⟩—used also to indicate omitted figures or an approximation |
| − | minus; negative |
| ± | plus or minus ⟨the square root of $4a^2$ is $\pm\ 2a$⟩ |
| × | multiplied by; times ⟨$6 \times 4 = 24$⟩—also indicated by placing a dot between the factors ⟨$6 \cdot 4 = 24$⟩ or by writing factors other than numerals without signs |
| ÷ or : | divided by ⟨$24 \div 6 = 4$⟩—also indicated by writing the divisor under the dividend with a line between ⟨$\frac{24}{6} = 4$⟩ or by writing the divisor after the dividend with an oblique line between ⟨3/8⟩ |
| = | equals ⟨$6 + 2 = 8$⟩ |
| ≠ or ≠ | is not equal to |

| | |
|---|---|
| > | is greater than ⟨6>5⟩ |
| ≫ | is much greater than |
| < | is less than ⟨3<4⟩ |
| ≪ | is much less than |
| ≧ *or* ≥ | is greater than or equal to |
| ≦ *or* ≤ | is less than or equal to |
| ⊁ | is not greater than |
| ⊀ | is not less than |
| ≈ | is approximately equal to |
| ≡ | is identical to |
| ∽ | equivalent; similar |
| ≅ | is congruent to |
| ∝ | varies directly as; is proportional to |
| : | is to; the ratio of |
| ∴ | therefore |
| ∞ | infinity |
| ∠ | angle; the angle ⟨∠ABC⟩ |
| ∟ | right angle ⟨∟ABC⟩ |
| ⊥ | the perpendicular; is perpendicular to ⟨AB⊥CD⟩ |
| ∥ | parallel; is parallel to ⟨AB∥CD⟩ |
| ⊙ *or* ○ | circle |
| ⌒ | arc of a circle |
| △ | triangle |
| □ | square |
| ▭ | rectangle |
| √ *or* √ | radical—used without a figure to indicate a square root (as in √4=2) or with an index above the sign to indicate the root to be taken (as $\sqrt[3]{x}$ ) if the root is not a square root |
| ( ) | parentheses ⎫ indicate that the quantities enclosed by them |
| [ ] | brackets ⎬ are to be taken together |
| {} | braces ⎭ |
| δ | variation ⟨δx; the variation of x⟩ |
| ∪ | union of two sets |
| ∩ | intersection of two sets |
| ⊂ | is included in, is a subset of |
| ⊃ | contains as a subset |
| ∈ *or* ε | is an element of |
| ∉ | is not an element of |
| Λ *or* 0 *or* φ *or* {} | empty set, null set |

## Medicine

| | |
|---|---|
| ĀA, Ā, *or* āā | of each |
| ℞ | take—used on prescriptions; prescription; treatment |
| ☠ | poison |

## APOTHECARIES' MEASURES

|         |            |
|---------|------------|
| ℥       | ounce      |
| f℥      | fluidounce |
| f℥      | fluidram   |
| ℳ, ℳ, ℳ, *or* min | minim |

## APOTHECARIES' WEIGHTS

| | |
|---|---|
| ℔ | pound |
| ℥ | ounce (as ℥ i or ℥ j, one ounce; ℥ ss, half an ounce; ℥ iss *or* ℥ jss, one ounce and a half; ℥ ij, two ounces) |
| ℨ | dram |
| ℈ | scruple |

# Miscellaneous

| | |
|---|---|
| & | and |
| &c | et cetera; and so forth |
| " *or* " | ditto marks |
| / | virgule; used to mean "or" (as in *and/or*), "and/or" (as in *dead/wounded*), "per" (as in *feet/second*), indicates end of a line of verse; separates the figures of a date (4/8/74) |
| ☞ | index *or* fist |
| < | derived from |
| > | whence derived |
| + | and |
| * | assumed |

used in etymologies

| | |
|---|---|
| † | died—used esp. in genealogies |
| ✝ | cross |
| ✶ | monogram from Greek XP signifying Christ |
| 卐 | swastika |
| ✡ | Judaism |
| ☦ | ankh |
| ℣ | versicle |
| ℟ | response |
| * | —used in Roman Catholic and Anglican service books to divide each verse of a psalm, indicating where the response begins |
| ✠ *or* + | —used in some service books to indicate where the sign of the cross is to be made; also used by certain Roman Catholic and Anglican prelates as a sign of the cross preceding their signatures |
| LXX | Septuagint |
| f/ *or* f: | relative aperture of a photographic lens |
| ⊕ | civil defense |
| ☮ | peace |

# Reference marks

| | |
|---|---|
| * | asterisk *or* star |
| † | dagger |
| ‡ | double dagger |
| § | section *or* numbered clause |
| ‖ | parallels |
| ¶ *or* ℙ | paragraph |

These marks are placed in written or printed text to direct attention to a footnote.

# Stamps and stamp collecting

| | |
|---|---|
| ★ | unused |
| ○ | used |
| ⊞ | block of four or more |
| ⊠ | entire cover or card |
| △ | on a piece of cover |

# Weather

| | |
|---|---|
| | barometer, changes of |
| ∧ | Rising, then falling |
| ⁄ | Rising, then steady; or rising, then rising more slowly |
| / | Rising steadily, or unsteadily |
| √ | Falling or steady, then rising; or rising, then rising more quickly |
| — | Steady, same as 3 hours ago |
| ∨ | Falling, then rising, same or lower than 3 hours ago |
| ＼ | Falling, then steady; or falling, then falling more slowly |
| ＼ | Falling steadily, or unsteadily |
| ∧ | Steady or rising, then falling; or falling, then falling more quickly |
| ◎ | calm |
| ○ | clear |
| ◑ | cloudy (partly) |
| ● | cloudy (completely overcast) |
| ⊹ | drifting or blowing snow |
| ῾ | drizzle |

| | |
|---|---|
| ≡ | fog |
| ⊚ | freezing rain |
| ▲▲▲▲ | cold front |
| ⌒⌒⌒ | warm front |
| ▼⌒▼⌒ | stationary front |
| )( | funnel clouds |
| ∞ | haze |
| ◉ | hurricane |
| ♀ | tropical storm |
| ● | rain |
| ✳ | rain and snow |
| ⋈ | rime |
| ⚡ | sandstorm or dust storm |
| ▽ | shower(s) |
| ▽̇ | shower of rain |
| ▵̇ | shower of hail |
| △ | sleet |
| * | snow |
| ↙ | thunderstorm |
| ⌒ | visibility reduced by smoke |